WEBSTER'S NEW WORLD™

D0596614

Spanish Dictionary

WILEY

Wiley Publishing, Inc.

Webster's New World™ Spanish Dictionary
Copyright © 2003 by Chambers Harrap Publishers Ltd. All rights reserved.

Published by Wiley Publishing, Inc., Indianapolis, Indiana
Published simultaneously in Canada

For general information on our other products and services or to obtain technical support
please contact our Customer Care Department within the U.S. at 800-762-2974, outside
the U.S. at 317-572-3993 or fax 317-572-4002.

Wiley also publishes its books in a variety of electronic formats. Some content that appears
in print may not be available in electronic books.

ISBN: 0-7645-4161-7

*Library of Congress Cataloging-in-Publication Data available from the
publisher.*

Designed and typeset by Chambers Harrap Publishers Ltd, Edinburgh.

Manufactured in the United States of America.
10 9 8 7 6 5 4 3 2 1

Contents/Índice

Preface

This new pocket-sized dictionary is aimed at students at beginner and intermediate level. It covers all the essential words and phrases needed and packs a wealth of vocabulary into its pages.

Content is fully up to date with the latest changes in language and in the world. In particular, there is excellent coverage of computing terms (including e-mail and the Internet), as well as Latin American Spanish.

A number of extra features add to the effectiveness of the dictionary as a learning tool. We have included false friend boxes to help the user avoid common translation pitfalls, and grammar notes to indicate correct usage. In the pronunciation guides, special attention has been given to the problems Spanish speakers encounter in pronouncing English.

As regards presentation, adverbs and phrasal verbs have separate entries, and each part of speech within an entry starts on a new line. This makes for a clear layout of the text, so the book is easy to consult.

Prefacio

Este nuevo diccionario de bolsillo, dirigido a estudiantes de nivel elemental e intermedio, recoge todas las palabras y expresiones básicas, incluyéndose en sus páginas una gran cantidad de vocabulario.

El contenido refleja los cambios en el lenguaje y en el mundo. En particular, contiene una excelente selección de términos de informática (además del correo electrónico e Internet) y del español de América.

La utilidad del diccionario como herramienta de aprendizaje ha sido potenciada con varios elementos adicionales. Hemos incluido cuadros sobre falsos amigos para evitar trampas en las traducciones y notas gramaticales que indican el uso correcto de las palabras. Las guías sobre la pronunciación prestan especial atención a los problemas que tienen los hablantes nativos de español al pronunciar el inglés.

En lo que respecta a la presentación, los adverbios y los "phrasal verbs" tienen entradas individuales, y cada categoría gramatical comienza en una nueva línea. Esto hace que la presentación del texto sea más clara y que el libro sea fácil de consultar.

Structure of Entries

---

ceviche *nm* = raw fish marinated in lemon and garlic

- The equals sign = introduces an explanation when there is no direct translation.

---

inocentada *nf Fam* ≃ April Fool's joke; **hacer una i. a algn** to play an April Fool's joke on sb

---

- The sign ≃ introduces a word that has a roughly equivalent status but is not identical.

---

aflojar 1 *vt* to loosen
2 *vi (viento etc)* to weaken, to grow weak
3 aflojarse *upr* to come *o* work loose; *(rueda)* to go down

---

- The different grammatical categories are cleary indicated, introduced by a bold Arabic numeral.

---

abrir² *(pp* **abierto)** **1** *vi* to open
2 *vt* **(a)** to open; *(cremallera)* to undo **(b)** *(gas, grifo)* to turn on **(c)** *Jur* **a. (un) expediente** to start proceedings
3 abrirse *upr* **(a)** to open; *Fig* **a. paso** to make one's way **(b)** *Fam* **¡me abro!** I'm off!

- Usage and field labels are clearly shown.

---

reconocer [34] *vt* **(a)** to recognize **(b)** *(admitir)* to recognize, to admit **(c)** *Med (paciente)* to examine

---

- A number before an irregular Spanish verb refers the user to the verb tables in the middle of the book for information on how to conjugate it.

---

bland [blænd] *adj (food)* soso(a)

> ✎ Note that the Spanish word **blando** is a false friend and is never a translation for the English word **bland**. In Spanish, **blando** means "soft".

- Usage notes warn the user when a word is a false friend.

---

acodarse *upr* to lean **(en on)**

- The most common prepositions used are given after the translation.

---

acústica *nf* acoustics *sing*

- The number of a translation is indicated where this is ambiguous.

Estructura de las entradas

> **ceviche** *nm* **=** raw fish marinated in lemon and garlic

- Cuando no es posible dar una traducción se ofrece una explicación precedida por el signo igual (=).

> **inocentada** *nf Fam* ≃ April Fool's joke; **hacer una i. a algn** to play an April Fool's joke on sb

- El signo ≃ precede a una traducción que tiene un significado aproximado pero no idéntico.

> **aflojar 1** *vt* to loosen
> **2** *vi (viento etc)* to weaken, to grow weak
> **3 aflojarse** *vpr* to come *o* work loose; *(rueda)* to go down

- Las diferentes categorías gramaticales están separadas por un número en negrita.

> **abrir²** (*pp* **abierto**) **1** *vi* to open
> **2** *vt* (**a**) to open; *(cremallera)* to undo (**b**) *(gas, grifo)* to turn on (**c**) *Jur* **a. (un) expediente** to start proceedings
> **3 abrirse** *vpr* (**a**) to open; *Fig* **a. paso** to make one's way (**b**) *Fam* **¡me abro!** I'm off!

- Las marcas de uso y de campo semántico están claramente indicadas.

> **reconocer** [34] *vt o* (**a**) to recognize (**b**) *(admitir)* to recognize, to admit (**c**) *Med (paciente)* to examine

- Los números que aparecen detrás de los verbos irregulares remiten a las tablas verbales que se encuentran en el medio del diccionario.

> **blando,-a** *adj* soft
>
> *Observa que la palabra inglesa* **bland** *es un falso amigo y no es la traducción de la palabra española* **blando**. *En inglés,* **bland** *significa "soso".*

- Las notas de uso informan sobre los falsos amigos.

> **acodarse** *vpr* to lean (**en** on)

- Las preposiciones más comunes aparecen después de las traducciones.

> **acústica** *nf* acoustics *sing*

- El número de la traducción aparece en los casos en los que éste es ambiguo.

Abbreviations used in this dictionary
Abreviaturas usadas en este diccionario

abbreviation	*abbr, abr*	abreviatura
adjective	*adj*	adjetivo
adverb	*adv*	adverbio
agriculture	*Agr*	agricultura
somebody, someone	*algn*	alguien
Latin American Spanish	*Am*	español de América
anatomy	*Anat*	anatomía
Andean Spanish (Bolivia, Chile Colombia, Ecuador, Peru)	*Andes*	español andino (Bolivia, Chile, Colombia, Ecuador, Perú)
approximately	*aprox*	aproximadamente
architecture	*Archit*	arquitectura
Argentinian Spanish	*Arg*	español de Argentina
architecture	*Arquit*	arquitectura
article	*art*	artículo
astronomy	*Astron*	astronomía
Australian	*Austral*	australiano
motoring	*Aut*	automóviles
auxiliary	*aux*	auxiliar
aviation	*Av*	aviación
biology	*Biol*	biología
Bolivian Spanish	*Bol*	español de Bolivia
botany	*Bot*	botánica
British English	*Br*	inglés británico
Central American Spanish	*CAm*	español centroamericano
Canary Islands Spanish	*Can*	español de Canarias
Caribbean Spanish (Cuba, Puerto Rico, Dominican Republic, Venezuela)	*Carib*	español caribeño (Cuba, Puerto Rico, República Dominicana, Venezuela)
chemistry	*Chem*	química
Chilean Spanish	*Chile*	español de Chile
cinema	*Cin*	cine
Colombian Spanish	*Col*	español de Colombia
commerce	*Com*	comercio
comparative	*comp*	comparativo
computers	*Comput*	informática
conditional	*cond*	condicional
conjunction	*conj*	conjunción
building industry	*Constr*	construcción
sewing	*Cost*	costura
Costa Rican Spanish	*CRica*	español de Costa Rica
Spanish from the Southern Cone region (Argentina, Uruguay, Paraguay, Chile)	*CSur*	español del Cono Sur (Argentina, Uruguay, Paraguay, Chile)
Cuban Spanish	*Cuba*	español de Cuba
cookery	*Culin*	cocina
definite	*def*	definido
defective	*defect*	defectivo
demonstrative	*dem*	demostrativo
sport	*Dep*	deporte
economics	*Econ*	economía
Ecuadorian Spanish	*Ecuad*	español de Ecuador
education	*Educ*	educación
electricity	*Elec*	electricidad
especially	*esp*	especialmente
Peninsular Spanish	*Esp*	español de España
etcetera	*etc*	etcétera
euphemism	*Euph, Euf*	eufemismo
feminine	*f*	femenino

familiar	*Fam*	familiar
pharmacy	*Farm*	farmacia
railways	*Ferroc*	ferrocarriles
figurative use	*Fig*	uso figurado
finance	*Fin*	finanzas
physics	*Fís*	física
formal use	*Fml*	uso formal
photography	*Fot*	fotografía
feminine plural	*fpl*	plural femenino
football	*Ftb*	fútbol
future	*fut*	futuro
geography	*Geog*	geografía
geology	*Geol*	geología
geometry	*Geom*	geometría
present participle	*ger*	gerundio
Guatemalan Spanish	*Guat*	español de Guatemala
history	*Hist*	historia
humorous	*Hum*	humorístico
imperative	*imperat*	imperativo
imperfect	*imperf*	imperfecto
impersonal	*impers*	impersonal
printing	*Impr*	imprenta
industry	*Ind*	industria
indefinite	*indef*	indefinido
indeterminate	*indet*	indeterminado
indicative	*indic*	indicativo
infinitive	*infin*	infinitivo
computers	*Informát*	informática
insurance	*Ins*	seguros
interjection	*interj*	interjección
interrogative	*interr*	interrogativo
invariable	*inv*	invariable
ironic	*Irón*	irónico
law	*Jur*	derecho
linguistics	*Ling*	lingüística
literature	*Lit*	literatura
phrase	*loc*	locución
masculine	*m*	masculino
mathematics	*Math, Mat*	matemáticas
medicine	*Med*	medicina
meteorology	*Met*	meteorología
Mexican Spanish	*Méx*	español de México
military	*Mil*	militar
mining	*Min*	minas
masculine plural	*mpl*	plural masculino
music	*Mus, Mús*	música
noun	*n*	nombre
nautical	*Naut, Náut*	náutica
neuter	*neut*	neutro
feminine noun	*nf*	nombre femenino
plural feminine noun	*nfpl*	nombre femenino plural
masculine noun	*nm*	nombre masculino
masculine and feminine noun	*nmf/nm,f*	nombre masculino y femenino
plural masculine noun	*nmpl*	nombre masculino plural
plural noun	*npl*	nombre plural
optics	*Opt*	óptica
ornithology	*Orn*	ornitología
Panamanian Spanish	*Pan*	español de Panamá
Paraguayan Spanish	*Par*	español de Paraguay
pejorative	*Pej*	peyorativo
personal	*pers*	personal
Peruvian Spanish	*Perú*	español de Perú
pejorative	*Pey*	peyorativo
pharmacy	*Pharm*	farmacia

Abbreviations/Abreviaturas

photography	*Phot*	fotografía
physics	*Phys*	física
plural	*pl*	plural
politics	*Pol*	política
possessive	*pos, poss*	posesivo
past participle	*pp*	participio pasado
prefix	*pref*	prefijo
preposition	*prep*	preposición
present	*pres*	presente
present participle	*pres p*	gerundio
Puerto Rican Spanish	*PRico*	español de Puerto Rico
pronoun	*pron*	pronombre
psychology	*Psi, Psy*	psicología
past tense	*pt*	pretérito
chemistry	*Quím*	química
radio	*Rad*	radio
railways	*Rail*	ferrocarriles
relative	*rel*	relativo
religion	*Rel*	religión
Spanish from the River Plate region (Argentina, Uruguay, Paraguay)	*RP*	español de los países ribereños del Río de la Plata
somebody, someone	*sb*	alguien
Scottish	*Scot*	escocés
insurance	*Seg*	seguros
singular	*sing*	singular
something	*sth*	algo
subjunctive	*subj*	subjuntivo
superlative	*superl*	superlativo
bullfighting	*Taurom*	tauromaquia
technical	*Tech, Téc*	técnica
telephones	*Tel*	teléfonos
textiles	*Tex*	textiles
theatre	*Th*	teatro
television	*TV*	televisión
typography	*Typ*	tipografía
university	*Univ*	universidad
Uruguayan Spanish	*Urug*	español de Uruguay
American English	*US*	inglés norteamericano
usually	*usu*	usualmente
verb	*v*	verbo
auxiliary verb	*v aux*	verbo auxiliar
Venezuelan Spanish	*Ven*	español de Venezuela
intransitive verb	*vi*	verbo intransitivo
impersonal verb	*v impers*	verbo impersonal
reflexive verb	*vpr*	verbo pronominal
transitive verb	*vt*	verbo transitivo
vulgar	*Vulg*	vulgar
zoology	*Zool*	zoología
cultural equivalent	$\simeq$	equivalente cultural
registered trademark	®	marca registrada

Spanish Pronunciation Guide

The pronunciation of most Spanish words is predictable as there is a close match between spelling and pronunciation. The table below gives an explanation of that pronunciation. In the dictionary text therefore, pronunciation is only given when the word does not follow these rules, usually because it is a word of foreign origin. In these cases, the IPA (International Phonetic Alphabet) is used (see column 2 of the table below).

Letter in Spanish	IPA Symbol	Example in Spanish	Pronunciation (example in English)
Vowels			
Note that all vowel sounds in Spanish are shorter than in English			
a	a	a**la**	Similar to the sound in "father" but more central
e	e	e**có**	Similar to the sound in "met"
i	i	**iris**	Like the vowel sound in "meat" but much shorter
o	o	**oso**	off, on
u	u	**uva**	Like the vowel sound in "soon" but much shorter
Semiconsonants			
"i" in the diphthongs: ia, ie, io, iu	j	h**i**ato, h**i**elo, av**i**ón, v**i**uda	**y**es
"u" in the diphthongs: ua, ue, ui, uo	w	s**u**ave, f**u**ego, h**u**ida	**w**in
Consonants			
b	b	**b**omba (at beginning of word or after m)	**b**oom
	β	a**b**ajo (all other contexts)	A "**b**" pronounced without quite closing the lips completely

Letter in Spanish	IPA Symbol	Example in Spanish	Pronunciation (example in English)
c	θ (in Spain)	ceño (before e) cinco (before i)	thanks (in Spain)
	s (in Latin America and southern Spain)		sun (in Latin America and southern Spain)
	k	casa (all other contexts)	cat
ch	tʃ	caucho	arch
d	d	donde (at beginning of word or after n) aldea (after l)	day
	ð	adorno (all other contexts)	Similar to the sound in "mother" but less strong
f	f	furia	fire
g	χ	gema (before e) girasol (before i)	Like an "h" but pronounced at the back of the throat (similar to Scottish "loch")
	g	gato (at beginning of word) lengua (after n)	goose
	ɣ	agua (all other contexts)	Like a "w" pronounced while trying to say "g"
j	χ	jabalí	Like an "h" but pronounced at the back of the throat (similar to Scottish "loch")
l	l	lado	lake
ll	j	lluvia	million
	ʒ		In some regions (eg the Rio de la Plata area of South America) it is pronounced like the "s" in "pleasure"
m	m	mano	man
n	n	nulo	no
	ŋ	manco, fango (before c and g)	parking
ñ	ɲ	año	onion
p	p	papa	pool

Letter in Spanish	IPA Symbol	Example in Spanish	Pronunciation (example in English)
r	r	dorado (in between vowels) hablar (at end of syllable or word)	A rolled "r" sound (similar to Scottish "r")
	rr	rosa (at beginning of word) alrededor (after l) enredo (after n)	A much longer rolled "r" sound (similar to Scottish "r")
rr	rr	arroyo	A much longer rolled "r" sound (similar to Scottish "r")
s	s	saco	sound
sh	ʃ	show	show
t	t	tela	tea
v	b	invierno (after "n")	boom
	β	ave (all other contexts)	A "b" pronounced without quite closing the lips completely
x	ks	examen	extra
y	j	ayer	yellow
	ʒ		In some regions (eg the Rio de la Plata area of South America) it is pronounced like the "s" in "pleasure"
z	θ (in Spain)	zapato	thanks (in Spain)
	s (in Latin America and southern Spain)		sun (in Latin America and southern Spain)

Pronunciación del inglés

Para ilustrar la pronunciación inglesa, en este diccionario utilizamos los símbolos del AFI (Alfabeto Fonético Internacional). En el siguiente cuadro, para cada sonido del inglés hay ejemplos de palabras en inglés y palabras en español donde aparece un sonido similar. En los casos en los que no hay sonido similar en español, ofrecemos una explicación de cómo pronuncialos.

Carácter AFI	Ejemplo en inglés	Ejemplo en español
Consonantes		
[b]	ba**bb**le	be**b**é
[d]	**d**ig	**d**e**d**o
[dʒ]	**g**iant, **j**ig	se pronuncia como [ʒ] en "plea**s**ure" pero con una "**d**" adelante, o como "**gi**" en italiano: **Gi**ovanna
[f]	**f**it, **ph**ysics	**f**aro
[g]	**g**rey, bi**g**	**g**ris
[h]	**h**appy	"**h**" aspirada
[j]	**y**ellow	se pronuncia como "**y**" o "**ll**" en España: **y**o, **ll**uvia
[k]	**c**lay, **k**i**ck**	**c**asa
[l]	**l**ip	**l**abio
	pi**ll**	pape**l**
[m]	**mu**mmy	**m**a**m**á
[n]	**n**ip, pi**n**	**n**ada
[ŋ]	si**ng**	se pronuncia como "**n**" antes de "**c**": ba**n**co
[p]	**p**i**p**	**p**a**p**á
[r]	**r**ig, w**r**ite	sonido entre "**r**" y "**rr**"
[s]	**s**ick, **sc**ience	**s**apo
[ʃ]	**sh**ip, na**ti**on	**sh**ow
[t]	**t**ip, bu**tt**	**t**ela
[tʃ]	**ch**ip, ba**tch**	cau**ch**o
[θ]	**th**ick	**z**apato (como se pronuncia en España)

Carácter AFI	Ejemplo en inglés	Ejemplo en español
[ð]	**th**is	se pronuncia como la "**d**" de "ha**d**a" pero más fuerte
[v]	**v**ague, gi**v**e	se pronuncia como "**v**" de **v**ida, con los dientes apoyados sobre el labio inferior
[w]	**w**it, **wh**y	**wh**isky
[z]	**z**ip, phy**s**ics	"**s**" con sonido zumbante
[ʒ]	plea**s**ure	se pronuncia como "**y**" o "**ll**" en el Río de la Plata: **y**o, **ll**uvia
[χ]	lo**ch**	**j**ota

Vocales

En inglés, las vocales marcadas con dos puntos son mucho más alargadas

[æ]	r**a**g	se pronuncia "**a**" con posición bucal para "**e**"
[ɑ:]	l**ar**ge, b**a**th	"**a**" muy alargada
[ʌ]	c**u**p	"**a**" breve y cerrada
[e]	s**e**t	se pronuncia como "**e**" de **e**lefante pero más corta
[ɜ:]	c**ur**tain, w**e**re	se pronuncia como una "**e**" larga con posición bucal entre "**o**" y "**e**"
[ə]	utt**er**	se pronuncia como "**e**" con posición bucal para "**o**"
[ɪ]	b**i**g, w**o**men	"**i**" breve, a medio camino entre "**e**" e "**i**"
[i:]	l**ea**k, w**ee**	"**i**" muy alargada
[ɒ]	l**o**ck	"**o**" abierta
[ɔ:]	w**a**ll, c**o**rk	"**o**" cerrada y alargada
[ʊ]	p**u**t, l**oo**k	"**u**" breve
[u:]	m**oo**n	"**u**" muy alargada

Pronunciación del inglés

Carácter AFI	Ejemplo en inglés	Ejemplo en español
Diptongos		
[aɪ]	why, high, lie	aire
[aʊ]	how	aura
[eə]	bear	"ea" pronunciado muy brevemente y con sonido de "e" más marcado que el de "a"
[eɪ]	day, make, main	reina
[əʊ]	show, go	"ou" como en COU
[ɪə]	here, gear	hielo pronunciado con el sonido de "i" más marcado y alargado que el de "e"
[ɔɪ]	boy, soil	voy
[ʊə]	poor	cuerno pronunciado con el sonido de "u" más marcado y alargado que el de "e"

Spanish – English
Español – Inglés

A, a [a] *nf (la letra)* A, a
a (*abr* **área**) area
a *prep*

> **a** combines with the article **el** to form the contraction **al** (e.g. **al centro** to the centre).

(**a**) *(dirección)* to; **ir a Colombia** to go to Colombia; **llegar a Valencia** to arrive in Valencia; **subir al tren** to get on the train; **ir al cine** to go to the cinema; **vete a casa** go home

(**b**) *(lugar)* at, on; **a la derecha** on the right; **a la entrada** at the entrance; **a lo lejos** in the distance; **a mi lado** at o by my side, next to me; **al sol** in the sun; **a la mesa** at (the) table

(**c**) *(tiempo)* at; **a las doce** at twelve o'clock; **a los sesenta años** at the age of sixty; **a los tres meses/la media hora** three months/half an hour later; **al final** in the end; **al principio** at first

(**d**) *(distancia)* away; **a 100 km de aquí** 100 km from here

(**e**) *(manera)* **a la inglesa** (in the) English fashion o manner o style; **escrito a máquina** typed, typewritten; **a mano** by hand

(**f**) *(proporción)* **a 90 km por hora** at 90 km an hour; **a 300 pesetas el kilo** 300 pesetas a kilo; **tres veces a la semana** three times a week

(**g**) *Dep* **ganar cuatro a dos** to win four (to) two

(**h**) *(complemento indirecto)* to; *(procedencia)* from; **díselo a Javier** tell Javier; **te lo di a ti** I gave it to you; **comprarle algo a algn** to buy sth from sb; *(para algn)* to buy sth for sb; *(complemento directo de persona)* **saludé a tu tía** I said hello to your aunt

(**i**) *Fam* **ir a por algn/algo** to go and fetch sb/sth

(**j**) *(verbo + a + infin)* to; **aprender a nadar** to learn (how) to swim; **fueron a ayudarle** they went to help him

(**k**) *(nombre + a + infin)* **distancia a recorrer** distance to be covered

(**l**) **a decir verdad** to tell (you) the truth; **a no ser por …** if it were not for …; **a no ser**

que unless; **a ver** let's see; **¡a comer!** lunch/dinner/*etc* is ready!; **¡a dormir!** bedtime!; **¿a que no lo haces?** *(desafío)* I bet you don't do it!

abad *nm* abbot
abadía *nf* abbey
abajeño,-a *nm,f Am* lowlander
abajo 1 *adv* (**a**) *(en una casa)* downstairs; **el piso de a.** the downstairs flat (**b**) *(dirección)* down, downwards; **ahí/aquí a.** down there/here; **la parte de a.** the bottom (part); **más a.** further down; **hacia a.** down, downwards; **calle a.** down the street; **echar algo a.** to knock sth down; **venirse a.** *(edificio)* to fall down; *Fig (proyecto)* to fall through

2 *interj* **¡a. la censura!** down with censorship!

abalanzarse [40] *vpr* **a. sobre/contra** to rush towards

abalear *vt Andes, CAm, Ven* to shoot at

abalorio *nm* (**a**) *(cuenta)* glass bead (**b**) *(baratija)* trinket

abanderado,-a *nm,f* standard bearer

abandonado,-a *adj* (**a**) abandoned; **tiene a su familia muy abandonada** he takes absolutely no interest in his family (**b**) *(desaseado)* untidy, unkempt

abandonar 1 *vt* (**a**) *(lugar)* to leave, to quit; *(persona, cosa)* to abandon; *(proyecto, plan)* to give up (**b**) *Dep (carrera)* to drop out of

2 abandonarse *vpr* to let oneself go

abandono *nm* (**a**) *(acción)* abandoning, desertion (**b**) *(de proyecto, idea)* giving up (**c**) *(descuido)* neglect

abanicarse *vpr* to fan oneself

abanico *nm* (**a**) fan (**b**) *(gama)* range; **un amplio a. de posibilidades** a wide range of possibilities

abaratar 1 *vt* to cut o reduce the price of

2 abaratarse *vpr (artículos)* to become cheaper, to come down in price; *(precios)* to come down

abarcar [44] *vt (incluir)* to cover

abarrotado,-a *adj* packed, crammed (**de** with)

abarrotar *vt* to pack, to cram (**de** with); **el público abarrotaba la sala** the room was packed (with people)

abarrote *nm* *Andes, CAm, Méx* grocer's (shop), grocery store; **abarrotes** groceries; **tienda de abarrotes** grocer's (shop), grocery store

abarrotería *nf* *Andes, CAm, Méx* grocer's (shop), grocery store

abarrotero,-a *nm,f* *Andes, CAm, Méx* grocer

abastecedor,-a *nm,f* supplier

abastecer [33] 1 *vt* to supply
2 abastecerse *upr* **a. de** to be supplied with

abastecimiento *nm* supplying; **a. de agua** water supply

abasto *nm* (a) *Fam* **no doy a.** I can't cope, I can't keep up (b) **mercado de abastos** wholesale food market

abatible *adj* folding, collapsible; **asiento a.** reclining seat

abatido,-a *adj* downcast

abatir 1 *vt* (a) *(derribar)* to knock down, to pull down (b) *(matar)* to kill; **a. a tiros** to shoot down (c) *(desanimar)* to depress, to dishearten
2 abatirse *upr* *(desanimarse)* to lose heart, to become depressed

abdicación *nf* abdication

abdicar [44] *vt & vi* to abdicate

abdomen *nm* abdomen

abdominales *nmpl* sit-ups

abecedario *nm* alphabet

abedul *nm* birch

abeja *nf* bee; **a. reina** queen bee

abejorro *nm* bumblebee

aberración *nf* aberration

aberrante *adj* deviant

abertura *nf* *(hueco)* opening, gap; *(grieta)* crack, slit

abertzale *adj & nmf* Basque nationalist

abeto *nm* *Bot* fir (tree); **a. rojo** spruce

abierto,-a *adj* (a) open; *(grifo)* (turned) on; **a. de par en par** wide open (b) *(persona)* open-minded

abigarrado,-a *adj* *(mezclado)* jumbled, mixed up

abismal *adj* abysmal; *Fig* **una diferencia a.** a world of a difference

abismo *nm* abyss; *Fig* **al borde del a.** on the brink of ruin; *Fig* **entre ellos media un a.** they are worlds apart

ablandar 1 *vt* to soften
2 ablandarse *upr* (a) to soften, to go soft (b) *Fig (persona)* to mellow

abnegación *nf* abnegation, self-denial

abnegado,-a *adj* selfless, self-sacrificing

abocado,-a *adj* (a) **está a. al fracaso** it is

doomed to failure (b) *(vino)* medium dry

abochornar *vt* to shame, to embarrass

abofetear *vt* to slap

abogacía *nf* legal profession

abogado,-a *nm,f* lawyer, solicitor; *(en tribunal supremo)* lawyer, *Br* barrister; **a. de oficio** legal aid lawyer; **a. defensor** counsel for the defense; **a. del diablo** devil's advocate; **a. laboralista** union lawyer

abogar [42] *vt* to plead; **a. a favor de** to plead for, to defend; **a. por algo** to advocate *o* champion sth

abolengo *nm* ancestry, lineage

abolición *nf* abolition

abolir *vt defect* to abolish

abolladura *nf* dent

abollar *vt* to dent

abominable *adj* abominable

abominar *vt & vi* **a. (de)** to abominate, to loathe

abonado,-a 1 *nm,f* subscriber
2 *adj* *Fin (pagado)* paid; **a. en cuenta** credited

abonar 1 *vt* (a) *Agr* to fertilize (b) *(pagar)* to pay (for) (c) *(subscribir)* to subscribe
2 abonarse *upr* to subscribe (**a** to)

abonero,-a *nm,f* *Méx* hawker, street trader

abono *nm* (a) *Agr (producto)* fertilizer; *(estiércol)* manure (b) *(pago)* payment (c) *(a revista etc)* subscription; *(billete)* season ticket (d) *Méx (plazo)* instalment; **pagar en abonos** to pay by instalments

abordar *vt (persona)* to approach; *(barco)* to board; **a. un asunto** to tackle a subject

aborigen *(pl* **aborígenes)** **1** *adj* native, indigenous; *esp Austral* aboriginal
2 *nmf* native; *esp Austral* aborigine

aborrecer [33] *vt* to detest, to loathe

abortar 1 *vi (involuntariamente)* to miscarry, to have a miscarriage; *(intencionadamente)* to abort, to have an abortion
2 *vt* to abort

abortista *nmf* abortionist

aborto *nm* miscarriage; *(provocado)* abortion

abotargado,-a *adj* swollen

abotonar *vt (ropa)* to button (up)

abovedado,-a *adj* vaulted, arched

abracadabra *nm* abracadabra

abrasador,-a *adj* scorching

abrasar 1 *vt & vi* to scorch
2 abrasarse *upr* to burn

abrazadera *nf* clamp

abrazar [40] 1 *vt* to embrace, to hug; *Fig (doctrina)* to embrace

2 abrazarse *vpr* **a. a algn** to embrace sb; **se abrazaron** they embraced each other

abrazo *nm* embrace, hug; **un a., abrazos** *(en carta)* best wishes

abrecartas *nm inv* letter-opener, paperknife

abrefácil *nm Com* **caja con a.** easy-open carton

abrelatas *nm inv* tin-opener, *US* can opener

abreviar **[43]** **1** (a) *vt* to shorten; *(texto)* to abridge; *(palabra)* to abbreviate

2 *vi* to be quick o brief; **para a.** to cut a long story short

abreviatura *nf* abbreviation

abridor *nm (de latas, botellas)* opener

abrigado,-a *adj* wrapped-up; **ir muy a.** to be well wrapped-up

abrigar **[42]** *vt* (a) to keep warm; **esta chaqueta abriga mucho** this cardigan is very warm (b) *(proteger)* to protect, to shelter (c) *(esperanza)* to cherish; *(duda)* to have, to harbour

abrigo *nm* (a) *(prenda)* coat, overcoat; **ropa de a.** warm clothes (b) **al a. de** protected o sheltered from

abril *nm* April

abrillantador *nm* polish

abrillantar *vt* to polish

abrir [1] *nm* **en un a. y cerrar de ojos** in the twinkling of an eye

abrir [2] *(pp* **abierto)** **1** *vi* to open

2 *vt* (a) to open; *(cremallera)* to undo (b) *(gas, grifo)* to turn on (c) *Jur* **a. (un) expediente** to start proceedings

3 abrirse *vpr* (a) to open; *Fig* **a. paso** to make one's way (b) *Fam* **¡me abro!** I'm off!

abrochar *vt,* **abrocharse** *vpr (botones)* to do up; *(camisa)* to button (up); *(cinturón)* to fasten; *(zapatos)* to tie up; *(cremallera)* to do up

abrumado,-a *adj* overwhelmed

abrumador,-a *adj* overwhelming

abrumar *vt* to overwhelm, to crush; **tantos problemas me abruman** all these problems are getting on top of me

abrupto,-a *adj* (a) *(terreno)* steep, abrupt (b) *Fig* abrupt, sudden

absceso *nm* abscess

absentismo *nm* absenteeism; **a. laboral** absenteeism from work

absolución *nf* (a) *Rel* absolution (b) *Jur* acquittal

absolutamente *adv* absolutely, completely; **a. nada** nothing at all

absoluto,-a *adj* absolute; **en a.** not at all, by no means

absolutorio,-a *adj Jur* **sentencia absolutoria** verdict of not guilty

absolver **[4]** *(pp* **absuelto)** *vt* (a) *Rel* to absolve (b) *Jur* to acquit

absorbente *adj* (a) *(papel)* absorbent (b) *Fig* absorbing, engrossing

absorber *vt* to absorb

absorción *nf* absorption

absorto,-a *adj* absorbed, engrossed (**en** in)

abstemio,-a **1** *adj* teetotal, abstemious

2 *nm,f* teetotaller

abstención *nf* abstention

abstenerse **[24]** *vpr* to abstain (**de** from); *(privarse)* to refrain (**de** from)

abstinencia *nf* abstinence; **síndrome de a.** withdrawal symptoms

abstracción *nf* abstraction

abstracto,-a *adj* abstract

abstraer **[25]** **1** *vt* to abstract

2 abstraerse *vpr* to become lost in thought

abstraído,-a *adj (ensimismado)* absorbed, engrossed (**en** in); *(distraído)* absent-minded

absuelto,-a *pp de* absolver

absurdo,-a **1** *adj* absurd

2 *nm* absurdity, absurd thing

abuchear *vt* to boo, to jeer at

abucheo *nm* booing, jeering

abuela *nf* grandmother; *Fam* grandma, granny; *Fig* old woman

abuelo *nm* (a) *(prenda)* grandfather; *Fam* grandad, grandpa; *Fig* old man (b) **abuelos** grandparents

abulense **1** *adj* of/from Avila

2 *nmf* person from Avila

abulia *nf* apathy, lack of willpower

abultado,-a *adj* bulky, big

abultar **1** *vi* to be bulky; **abulta mucho** it takes up a lot of space

2 *vt* to exaggerate

abundancia *nf* abundance, plenty; *Fig* **nadar en la a.** to be rolling in money

abundante *adj* abundant, plentiful

abundar *vi* to abound, to be plentiful

abur *interj Fam* cheerio!, see you!

aburrido,-a *adj* (a) **ser a.** to be boring (b) **estar a.** to be bored; **estar a. de** *(harto)* to be tired of

aburrimiento *nm* boredom; **¡qué a.!** how boring!, what a bore!

aburrir **1** *vt* to bore

2 aburrirse *vpr* to get bored; **a. como una ostra** to be bored stiff

abusado,-a *adj Méx* astute, shrewd

abusar *vi* (a) *(propasarse)* to go too far (b) **a. de** *(situación, persona)* to take (unfair) advantage of; *(poder, amabilidad)* to abuse; **a. de la bebida/del tabaco** to drink/smoke too much *o* to excess; *Jur* **a. de un niño/una mujer** to abuse a child/woman

abusivo,-a *adj (precio)* exorbitant

abuso *nm* abuse

abyecto,-a *adj* abject

a. C. (*abr antes de Cristo*) BC

a/c *Com* (*abr* **a cuenta**) on account

acá *adv* (**a**) *(lugar)* here, over here; **más a.** nearer; **¡ven a.!** come here! (**b**) **de entonces a.** since then

acabado,-a 1 *adj* (**a**) *(terminado)* finished (**b**) *Fig (persona)* worn-out, spent
  2 *nm* finish

acabar 1 *vt* to finish (off); *(completar)* to complete
  2 *vi* (**a**) to finish, to end; **a. bien** to have a happy ending; **a. con algo** *(terminarlo)* to finish sth; *(romperlo)* to break sth (**b**) **a. de ...** to have just ...; **acaba de entrar** he has just come in; **no acaba de convencerme** I'm not quite convinced (**c**) **acabaron casándose** *o* **por casarse** they ended up getting married; **acabó en la cárcel** he ended up in jail
  3 acabarse *upr* to finish, to come to an end; **se nos acabó la gasolina** we ran out of *Br* petrol *o US* gas; *Fam* **¡se acabó!** that's that!

acabóse *nm Fam* **esto es el a.** this is the end

acacia *nf* acacia

academia *nf* academy; **a. de idiomas** language school

académico,-a *adj & nm,f* academic

acaecer [33] *v impers* to happen, to occur

acallar *vt* to silence

acalorado,-a *adj* (**a**) hot (**b**) *Fig (excitado)* worked up, excited; *(debate etc)* heated, angry

acalorarse *upr* (**a**) to get warm *o* hot (**b**) *Fig* to get excited *o* worked up

acampada *nf* camping; **ir de a.** to go camping; **zona de a.** camp site, *US* campground

acampanado,-a *adj* bell-shaped; *(prendas)* flared

acampar *vi* to camp

acantilado *nm* cliff

acantonar *vt (tropas)* to billet, to quarter (**en** in)

acaparar *vt* (**a**) *(productos)* to hoard; *(el mercado)* to corner (**b**) *Fig* to monopolize

acápite *nm Am (párrafo)* paragraph

acaramelado,-a *adj* (**a**) *(color)* caramel-coloured (**b**) *(pareja)* lovey-dovey, starry-eyed

acariciar [43] *vt* to caress; *(pelo, animal)* to stroke; *(esperanza)* to cherish

acarrear *vt* (**a**) *(transportar)* to carry, to transport (**b**) *Fig (conllevar)* to entail

acaso *adv* perhaps, maybe; **¿a. no te lo dije?** did I not tell you, by any chance?; **por si a.** just in case; **si a. viene ...** if he should come ...

acatamiento *nm* respect; *(de la ley)* observance

acatar *vt* to observe, to comply with

acatarrado,-a *adj* **estar a.** to have a cold

acatarrarse *upr* to catch a cold

acaudalado,-a *adj* rich, wealthy

acaudalar *vt* to accumulate, to amass

acaudillar *vt* to lead

acceder *vi* **a.** *(consentir)* to accede to, to consent to; *(tener acceso)* to gain admittance to; *Informát* to access

accesible *adj* accessible; *(persona)* approachable

acceso *nm* (**a**) *(entrada)* access, entry; *Informát* **a. al azar, a. directo** random access; *Univ* **prueba de a.** entrance examination; **a. a Internet** Internet access (**b**) *(carretera)* approach, access (**c**) *Med & Fig* fit

accesorio,-a *adj & nm* accessory

accidentado,-a 1 *adj (terreno)* uneven, hilly; *(viaje, vida)* eventful
  2 *nm,f* casualty, accident victim

accidental *adj* accidental; **un encuentro a.** a chance meeting

accidente *nm* (**a**) accident; **por a.** by chance; **a. laboral** industrial accident (**b**) *Geog* **accidentes geográficos** geographical features

acción *nf* (**a**) action; *(acto)* act; **poner en a.** to put into action; **ponerse en a.** to go into action; **campo de a.** field of action; **película de a.** adventure film (**b**) *Fin* share

accionar *vt* to drive

accionista *nmf* shareholder

acebo *nm (hoja)* holly; *(árbol)* holly tree

acechar *vt* to lie in wait for; **un grave peligro nos acecha** great danger awaits us

acecho *nm* **estar al a. de** *(esperar)* to lie in wait for

acedía *nf (pez)* dab

aceite *nm* oil; **a. de girasol/maíz/oliva** sunflower/corn/olive oil

aceitera *nf* (**a**) *Culin* oil bottle; **aceiteras** oil and vinegar set (**b**) *Aut* oil can

aceitero,-a 1 *adj* oil
  2 *nm,f* oil merchant
aceitoso,-a *adj* oily
aceituna *nf* olive; **a. rellena** stuffed olive
aceitunado,-a *adj* olive, olive-coloured
aceitunero,-a *nm,f* (**a**) *(recolector)* olive picker *o* harvester (**b**) *(vendedor)* olive seller
acelerado,-a *adj* accelerated, fast
acelerador *nm Aut* accelerator
acelerar *vt* to accelerate
acento *nm* (**a**) accent; *(de palabra)* stress (**b**) *(énfasis)* stress, emphasis
acentuar [30] 1 *vt* (**a**) to stress (**b**) *Fig* to emphasize, to stress
  2 acentuarse *vpr Fig* to become more pronounced *o* noticeable
aceña *nf* watermill
acepción *nf* meaning, sense
aceptable *adj* acceptable
aceptación *nf* (**a**) acceptance (**b**) **tener poca a.** to have little success, not to be popular
aceptar *vt* to accept
acequia *nf* irrigation ditch *o* channel
acera *nf Br* pavement, *US* sidewalk; *Fam Pey* **ser de la a. de enfrente** to be gay *o* queer
acerado *nm* pavement
acerbo,-a *adj* harsh, bitter
acerca *adv* **a. de** about
acercamiento *nm* bringing together, coming together; *Pol* rapprochement
acercar [44] 1 *vt* to bring near *o* nearer, to bring (over); *Fig* to bring together; **¿te acerco a casa?** can I give you a lift home?
  2 acercarse *vpr* (**a**) **acercarse (a)** to approach (**b**) *(ir)* to go; *(venir)* to come
acerico *nm* pincushion
acero *nm* steel; **a. inoxidable** stainless steel
acérrimo,-a *adj (partidario)* staunch; *(enemigo)* bitter
acertado,-a *adj* (**a**) *(solución)* right, correct; *(decisión)* wise (**b**) **no estuviste muy a. al decir eso** it wasn't very wise of you to say that
acertante 1 *nmf* winner
  2 *adj* winning
acertar [1] 1 *vt (pregunta)* to get right; *(adivinar)* to guess correctly; **a. las quinielas** to win the pools
  2 *vi* to be right; **acertó con la calle que buscaba** she found the street she was looking for
acertijo *nm* riddle
acervo *nm* **a. cultural** cultural tradition *o* heritage

achacar [44] *vt (atribuir)* to attribute
achacoso,-a *adj* ailing, unwell
achaque *nm* ailment, complaint
achicar [44] 1 *vt* (**a**) *(amilanar)* to intimidate (**b**) *(encoger)* to reduce, to make smaller (**c**) *(barco)* to bale out
  2 achicarse *vpr* (**a**) *(amilanarse)* to lose heart (**b**) *(encogerse)* to get smaller
achicharrar *vt* to burn to a crisp
achicoria *nf* chicory
achinado,-a *adj* (**a**) *(ojos)* slanting (**b**) *Am* Indian-looking
acholado,-a *adj Andes Pey* half-caste
achuchar *vt (empujar)* to shove
achuchón *nm (empujón)* push, shove
aciago,-a *adj* ill-fated, fateful
acicalado,-a *adj* well-dressed, smart
acicalarse *vpr* to dress up, to smarten up
acicate *nm Fig (aliciente)* spur, incentive
acidez *nf (de sabor)* sharpness, sourness; *Quím* acidity; *Med* **a. de estómago** heartburn
ácido,-a 1 *adj (sabor)* sharp, tart; *Quím* acidic; *Fig (tono)* harsh
  2 *nm Quím* acid
acierto *nm (buena decisión)* good choice *o* idea; **con gran a.** very wisely
aclamación *nf* acclamation, acclaim
aclamar *vt* to acclaim
aclaración *nf* explanation
aclarado *nm* rinsing, rinse
aclarar 1 *vt* (**a**) *(explicar)* to clarify, to explain; *(color)* to lighten, to make lighter (**b**) *(enjuagar)* to rinse
  2 *v impers Met* to clear (up)
  3 aclararse *vpr* (**a**) *(decidirse)* to make up one's mind; *(entender)* to understand (**b**) *Met* to clear (up)
aclaratorio,-a *adj* explanatory
aclimatación *nf Br* acclimatization, *US* acclimation
aclimatar 1 *vt Br* to acclimatize, *US* to acclimate (**a** to)
  2 aclimatarse *vpr Fig* **a. a algo** to get used to sth
acné *nf* acne
acobardar 1 *vt* to frighten
  2 acobardarse *vpr* to get frightened, to lose one's nerve
acodarse *vpr* to lean (**en** on)
acogedor,-a *adj* cosy, warm
acoger [53] 1 *vt* (**a**) *(recibir)* to receive; *(a invitado)* to welcome (**b**) *(persona desvalida)* to take in
  2 acogerse *vpr Fig* **a. a** to take refuge in; *(amnistía)* to avail oneself of; **a. a la ley** to have recourse to the law
acogida *nf* reception, welcome

acojonado,-a *adj muy Fam* shit-scared

acojonante *adj muy Fam* damn o *Br* bloody great o terrific

acojonarse *vpr muy Fam (acobardarse)* to shit oneself, to be shit-scared

acolchar *vt (rellenar)* to pad; *(prenda)* to quilt

acometer *vt* (a) *(emprender)* to undertake (b) *(atacar)* to attack

acometida *nf (ataque)* attack; *(de gas etc)* connection

acomodado,-a *adj* well-off, well-to-do

acomodador,-a *nm,f (hombre)* usher; *(mujer)* usherette

acomodar 1 *vt* (a) *(alojar)* to lodge, to accommodate (b) *(en cine etc)* to find a place for
   2 **acomodarse** *vpr* (a) to make oneself comfortable (b) *(adaptarse)* to adapt

acomodaticio,-a *adj* (a) accommodating, easy-going (b) *Pey* pliable

acompañante 1 *nmf* companion
   2 *adj* accompanying

acompañar *vt* (a) to accompany; **le acompañó hasta la puerta** she saw him to the door; **me acompañó al médico** he came with me to see the doctor; **¿te acompaño a casa?** can I walk you home?; *Fml* **le acompaño en el sentimiento** my condolences (b) *(adjuntar)* to enclose

acompasado,-a *adj (rítmico)* rhythmic

acomplejado,-a *adj* **estar a.** to have a complex (**por** about)

acomplejar 1 *vt* **a. alguien** to give sb a complex
   2 **acomplejarse** *vpr* **a. por** to develop a complex about

acondicionado,-a *adj* **aire a.** air conditioning

acondicionador *nm* conditioner

acondicionar *vt* to prepare, to set up; *(mejorar)* to improve; *(cabello)* to condition

acongojar *vt* to distress

aconsejable *adj* advisable

aconsejar *vt* to advise

acontecer [33] *v impers* to happen, to take place

acontecimiento *nm* event

acopio *nm* store, stock; **hacer a. de** to store

acoplar 1 *vt* (a) to fit (together), to join (b) *Téc* to couple, to connect
   2 **acoplarse** *vpr (nave espacial)* to dock

acorazado,-a 1 *adj* armoured, armourplated
   2 *nm* battleship

acordado,-a *adj* agreed; **según lo a.** as agreed

acordar [2] 1 *vt* to agree; *(decidir)* to decide
   2 **acordarse** *vpr* to remember; **no me acuerdo (de Silvia)** I can't remember (Silvia)

acorde 1 *adj* in agreement
   2 *nm Mús* chord

acordeón *nm* (a) *(instrument)* accordion (b) *Col, Méx Fam (en examen)* crib

acordonado,-a *adj* cordoned off, sealed off

acordonar *vt* (a) *(zona)* to cordon off, to seal off (b) *(atar)* to lace up

acorralar *vt* to corner

acortar *vt* to shorten; **a. distancias** to cut down the distance

acosar *vt* to harass; *Fig* **a. a algn a preguntas** to bombard sb with questions

acoso *nm* harassment; **a. sexual** sexual harassment

acostar [2] 1 *vt* to put to bed
   2 **acostarse** *vpr* (a) to go to bed (b) *Fam* **a. con algn** to sleep with sb, to go to bed with sb

acostumbrado,-a *adj* (a) usual, customary; **es lo a.** it is the custom (b) **a. al frío/calor** used to the cold/heat

acostumbrar 1 *vi* **a. a** *(soler)* to be in the habit of
   2 *vt* **a. a algn a algo** *(habituar)* to get sb used to sth
   3 **acostumbrarse** *vpr (habituarse)* **a. a algo** to get used to sth

acotación *nf* (a) *(en escrito)* (marginal) note; *Teatro* stage direction (b) *(en mapa)* elevation mark

acotamiento *nm Méx (arcén)* verge; *(de autopista) Br* hard shoulder, *US* shoulder

acotar *vt* (a) *(área)* to enclose; *Fig (tema)* to delimit (b) *(texto)* to annotate (c) *(mapa)* to mark with elevations

ácrata *adj & nmf* anarchist

acre¹ *adj* (a) *(sabor)* sour, bitter; *(olor)* acrid (b) *Fig (palabras)* bitter, harsh; *(crítica)* biting

acre² *nm (medida)* acre

acrecentar [1] *vt* to increase

acreditación *nf* badge

acreditar *vt* (a) to be a credit to (b) *(probar)* to prove (c) *(embajador)* to accredit (d) *Fin* to credit

acreditativo,-a *adj* which proves, which gives proof

acreedor,-a *nm,f Com* creditor

acribillar *vt* to riddle, to pepper; **a. a algn a balazos** to riddle sb with bullets

acrílico,-a *adj* acrylic

acriollarse *vpr Am* to adopt native ways

acritud nf (mordacidad) acrimony

acrobacia nf acrobatics sing

acróbata nmf acrobat

acta nf (a) (de reunión) minutes, record (b) (certificado) certificate, official document; **a. notarial** affidavit; **A. Única (Europea)** Single European Act

> Takes the masculine articles **el** and **un**.

actitud nf attitude

activar vt (a) to activate (b) (avivar) to liven up

actividad nf activity

activista nmf activist

activo,-a 1 adj active; **en a.** on active service

   2 nm Fin assets

acto nm (a) act, action; **a. sexual** sexual intercourse; **en el a.** at once; **a. seguido** immediately afterwards; Mil **en a. de servicio** in action; **hacer a. de presencia** to put in an appearance (b) (ceremonia) ceremony (c) Teatro act

actor nm actor

actriz nf actress

actuación nf (a) performance (b) (intervención) intervention, action

actual adj current, present; (al día) up-to-date; **un tema muy a.** a very topical subject

actualidad nf (a) present time; **en la a.** at present; **estar de a.** to be fashionable; **temas de a.** topical subjects (b) (hechos) current affairs

actualizar [40] vt to update, to bring up to date; Informát (software, hardware) to upgrade

actualmente adv (hoy en día) nowadays, these days; (ahora) at the moment, at present

> 🖉 Observa que las palabras inglesas **actual** y **actually** son falsos amigos y no son la traducción de las palabras españolas **actual** y **actualmente**. En inglés, **actual** significa "real, verdadero", y **actually** significa "en realidad".

actuar [30] vi (a) to act; **a. como** o **de** to act as (b) Cin & Teatro to perform, to act

acuarela nf watercolour

Acuario nm Aquarius

acuario nm aquarium

acuartelar vt to confine to barracks

acuático,-a adj aquatic; **esquí a.** waterskiing

acuchillar vt to knife, to stab

acuciante adj urgent, pressing

acuciar [43] vt to urge on

acudir vi (ir) to go; (venir) to come, to arrive; **nadie acudió en su ayuda** nobody came to help him; **no sé dónde a.** I don't know where to turn

acueducto nm aqueduct

acuerdo nm agreement; **¡de a.!** all right!, O.K.!; **de a. con** in accordance with; **de común a.** by common consent; **estar de a. en algo** to agree on sth; **ponerse de a.** to agree; **a. marco** framework agreement

acumular 1 vt to accumulate

   2 acumularse vpr (a) to accumulate, to build up (b) (gente) to crowd

acunar vt to rock

acuñar vt (moneda) to mint; (frase) to coin

acuoso,-a adj watery; (jugoso) juicy

acupuntura nf acupuncture

acurrucarse [44] vpr to curl up, to snuggle up

acusación nf (a) accusation (b) Jur charge

acusado,-a 1 nm,f accused, defendant

   2 adj (marcado) marked, noticeable

acusar 1 vt (a) to accuse (de of); Jur to charge (de with) (b) (golpe etc) to feel; Fig **su cara acusaba el cansancio** his face showed his exhaustion (c) Com **a. recibo** to acknowledge receipt

   2 acusarse vpr (a) (acentuarse) to become more pronounced (b) Fig (notarse) to show

acuse nm **a. de recibo** acknowledgment of receipt

acusica adj & nmf Fam telltale

acústica nf acoustics sing

acústico,-a adj acoustic

adán nm Fam untidy o slovenly person

adaptable adj adaptable

adaptación nf adaptation

adaptador nm adapter

adaptar 1 vt (a) to adapt (b) (ajustar) to adjust

   2 adaptarse vpr to adapt oneself (a to)

adecentar vt to tidy (up), to clean (up)

adecuado,-a adj appropriate, suitable

adecuar [47] vt to adapt

adefesio nm (persona) freak; (cosa) monstrosity

a. de J.C. (abr antes de Jesucristo) BC

adelantado,-a adj (a) advanced; (desarrollado) developed; (precoz) precocious (b) (reloj) fast (c) **pagar por a.** to pay in advance

adelantamiento nm overtaking; **hacer un a.** to overtake

adelantar 1 vt (a) to move o bring forward; (reloj) to put forward; Fig to advance (**b**) *Aut* to overtake (**c**) *(fecha)* to bring forward; *Fig* a. (los) acontecimientos to get ahead of oneself

2 *vi* (**a**) to advance (**b**) *(progresar)* to make progress (**c**) *(reloj)* to be fast

3 adelantarse *vpr* (**a**) *(ir delante)* to go ahead (**b**) *(reloj)* to gain, to be fast (**c**) **el verano se ha adelantado** we are having an early summer

adelante **1** *adv* forward; **más a.** *(lugar)* further on; *(tiempo)* later; **seguir a.** to keep going, to carry on; **llevar a. un plan** to carry out a plan

2 *interj* ¡a! come in!

adelanto *nm* (**a**) advance; *(progreso)* progress (**b**) **el reloj lleva diez minutos de a.** the watch is ten minutes fast (**c**) *(de dinero)* advance payment

adelfa *nf* oleander, rosebay

adelgazamiento *nm* slimming

adelgazar [40] *vi* to slim, to lose weight

ademán *nm* (**a**) gesture (**b**) **ademanes** manners

además *adv* moreover, furthermore; **a., no lo he visto nunca** what's more, I've never seen him; **a. de él** besides him

adentrarse *vpr* **a. en** *(bosque)* to go deep into; *(asunto)* to study thoroughly

adentro **1** *adv* *(dentro)* inside; **mar a.** out to sea; **tierra a.** inland

2 *nmpl* **decir algo para sus adentros** to say sth to oneself

adepto,-a *nm,f* follower, supporter

> ⚠ Observa que la palabra inglesa **adept** es un falso amigo y no es la traducción de la palabra española **adepto**. En inglés, **adept** significa "experto".

aderezar [40] *vt* *(comida)* to season; *(ensalada)* to dress

aderezo *nm* *(de comida)* seasoning; *(de ensalada)* dressing

adeudar **1** *vt* to owe

2 adeudarse *vpr* to get into debt

adherencia *nf* adherence; *Aut* roadholding

adherir [5] **1** *vt* to stick on

2 adherirse *vpr* **a. a** to adhere to; *(partido)* to join

adhesión *nf* adhesion; *(a partido)* joining; *(a teoría)* adherence

adhesivo,-a *adj & nm* adhesive

adicción *nf* addiction; **crear a.** to be addictive

adición *nf* addition

adicional *adj* additional

adicto,-a **1** *nm,f* addict

2 *adj* addicted (**a** to)

adiestrar *vt* to train

adinerado,-a **1** *adj* wealthy, rich

2 *nm,f* rich person

adiós *(pl* adioses*)* **1** *interj* goodbye; *Fam* bye-bye; *(al cruzarse)* hello

2 *nm* goodbye

aditivo,-a *adj & nm* additive

adivinanza *nf* riddle, puzzle

adivinar *vt* to guess; **a. el pensamiento de algn** to read sb's mind

adivino,-a *nm,f* fortune-teller

adjetivo,-a **1** *nm* adjective

2 *adj* adjectival

adjudicación *nf* award; *(en subasta)* sale

adjudicar [44] **1** *vt* (**a**) *(premio, contrato)* to award (**b**) *(en subasta)* to sell

2 adjudicarse *vpr* to appropriate, to take over

adjuntar *vt* to enclose

adjunto,-a **1** *adj* (**a**) enclosed, attached (**b**) *Educ* assistant

2 *nm,f* *Educ* assistant teacher

adm., admón. *(abr* **administración**) admin.

administración *nf* (**a**) *(gobierno)* administration, authorities; *Pol* **a. central** central government; **a. pública** civil service (**b**) *(de empresa)* administration, management (**c**) *(oficina)* (branch) office

administrador,-a **1** *nm,f* administrator

2 *adj* administrating

administrar **1** *vt* (**a**) to administer (**b**) *(dirigir)* to run, to manage

2 administrarse *vpr* to manage one's own money

administrativo,-a **1** *adj* administrative

2 *nm,f* *(funcionario)* official

admirable *adj* admirable

admiración *nf* (**a**) admiration; **causar a.** to impress (**b**) *Ling* exclamation mark

admirador,-a *nm,f* admirer

admirar **1** *vt* (**a**) to admire (**b**) *(sorprender)* to amaze, to astonish

2 admirarse *vpr* to be amazed, to be astonished

admisible *adj* admissible, acceptable

admisión *nf* admission; **reservado el derecho de a.** *(en letrero)* the management reserves the right to refuse admission

admitir *vt* (**a**) to admit, to let in (**b**) *(aceptar)* to accept; **no se admiten cheques** *(en letrero)* no cheques accepted (**c**) *(tolerar)* to allow (**d**) *(reconocer)* to admit, to acknowledge; **admito que mentí** I admit that I lied

admonición *nf* warning

ADN *nm* *(abr* **ácido desoxirribonucleico**) DNA

adobar *vt Culin* to marinate
adobe *nm* adobe
adobo *nm* marinade
adoctrinar *vt* to indoctrinate
adolecer [33] *vi* a. de *(carecer de)* to lack; *Fig Fml* to suffer from
adolescencia *nf* adolescence
adolescente *adj & nmf* adolescent
adonde *adv* where
adónde *adv interr* where (to)?
adondequiera *adv* wherever
adopción *nf* adoption
adoptar *vt* to adopt
adoptivo,-a *adj (hijo)* adopted; *(padres)* adoptive; *Fig* país a. country of adoption
adoquín *nm* cobble, paving stone
adorable *adj* adorable
adorar *vt* (a) *Rel* to worship (b) *Fig* to adore
adormecer [33] 1 *vt* to send to sleep, to make sleepy
  2 adormecerse *vpr* (a) *(dormirse)* to doze off (b) *(brazo etc)* to go to sleep, to go numb
adormecido,-a *adj* sleepy, drowsy
adormilarse *vpr* to doze, to drowse
adornar *vt* to adorn, to decorate
adorno *nm* decoration, adornment; de a. decorative
adosado,-a *adj* adjacent; *(casa)* semidetached
adquirir [31] *vt* to acquire; *(comprar)* to purchase
adquisición *nf* acquisition; *(compra)* buy, purchase
adquisitivo,-a *adj* poder a. purchasing power
adrede *adv* deliberately, on purpose
adrenalina *nf* adrenalin
adriático,-a *nm* el (Mar) A. the Adriatic (Sea)
adscribir *(pp adscrito)* **1** *vt* (a) *(atribuir)* to ascribe to (b) *(a un trabajo)* to appoint to
  2 adscribirse *vpr* to affiliate (a to)
adscrito,-a *pp de* adscribir
aduana *nf* customs
aduanero,-a 1 *adj* customs
  2 *nm,f* customs officer
aducir [10] *vt (motivo, pretexto)* to give
adueñarse *vpr* a. de to take over; *(pánico etc)* to take hold of
aduje *pt indef de* aducir
adulación *nf* adulation
adular *vt* to adulate
adulterar *vt* to adulterate
adulterio *nm* adultery
adúltero,-a 1 *adj* adulterous

2 *nm,f (hombre)* adulterer; *(mujer)* adulteress
adulto,-a *adj & nm,f* adult
adusto,-a *adj* harsh, severe
aduzco *indic pres de* aducir
advenedizo,-a *adj & nm,f* upstart
advenimiento *nm* advent, coming
adverbio *nm* adverb
adversario,-a 1 *nm,f* adversary, opponent
  2 *adj* opposing
adversidad *nf* adversity; *(revés)* setback
adverso,-a *adj* adverse
advertencia *nf* warning
advertido,-a *adj* warned; *(informado)* informed; estás o quedas a. you've been warned
advertir [5] *vt* (a) to warn; *(informar)* to inform, to advise; *Fam* te advierto que yo tampoco lo vi mind you, I didn't see it either (b) *(notar)* to realize, to notice
adviento *nm* Advent
adyacente *adj* adjacent
aéreo,-a *adj* (a) aerial (b) *Av* air; tráfico a. air traffic; *Com* por vía aerea by air
aero- *pref* aero-
aeróbic *nm* aerobics *sing*
aerodinámico,-a *adj* aerodynamic; de línea aerodinámica streamlined
aeródromo *nm* aerodrome
aeromodelismo *nm* aeroplane modelling
aeromoza *nf Am* air hostess
aeronáutica *nf* aeronautics *sing*
aeronáutico,-a *adj* la industria aeronáutica the aeronautics industry
aeronave *nf* airship
aeroplano *nm* light aeroplane
aeropuerto *nm* airport
aerosol *nm* aerosol
aerostático,-a *adj* globo a. hot-air balloon
a/f *(abr a favor)* in favour
afable *adj* affable
afamado,-a *adj* famous, well-known
afán *nm* *(pl* afanes*)* (a) *(esfuerzo)* effort (b) *(celo)* zeal
afanador,-a *nm,f Méx* cleaner
afanar 1 *vt Fam (robar)* to pinch
  2 afanarse *vpr* a. por conseguir algo to do one's best to achieve sth
afanoso,-a *adj* (a) *(persona)* keen, eager (b) *(tarea)* hard, tough
afección *nf* disease
afectación *nf* affectation
afectado,-a *adj* affected
afectar *vt* a. to affect; le afectó mucho she was deeply affected; nos afecta a

todos it concerns all of us
afecto *nm* affection; **tomarle a. a algn** to become fond of sb
afectuoso,-a *adj* affectionate
afeitado *nm* shave
afeitar *vt*, **afeitarse** *vpr* to shave
afeminado,-a *adj* effeminate
aferrado,-a *adj*. **a.** clinging to
aferrar 1 *vt Náut* to anchor, to moor
　2 aferrarse *vpr* to clutch, to cling; *Fig* **a. a una creencia** to cling to a belief
Afganistán *n* Afghanistan
afgano,-a *adj & nm,f* Afghan
afianzamiento *nm* strengthening, reinforcement
afianzar [40] 1 *vt* to strengthen, to reinforce
　2 afianzarse *vpr (persona)* to become established
afiche *nm Am* poster
afición *nf* (a) liking; **tiene a. por la música** he is fond of music (b) *Dep* **la a.** the fans
aficionado,-a 1 *nm,f* (a) enthusiast; **un a. a la música** a music lover (b) *(no profesional)* amateur
　2 *adj* (a) keen, fond; **ser a. a algo** to be fond of sth (b) *(no profesional)* amateur
aficionarse *vpr* to become fond (**a** of), to take a liking (**a** to)
afilado,-a *adj* sharp
afilar *vt* to sharpen
afiliación *nf* affiliation
afiliado,-a *nm,f* member
afiliarse [43] *vpr* to become a member
afín *adj (semejante)* kindred, similar; *(relacionado)* related
afinar *vt* (a) *(puntería)* to sharpen (b) *(instrumento)* to tune
afincarse [44] *vpr* to settle down
afinidad *nf* affinity
afirmación *nf* affirmation; **afirmaciones** *(declaración)* statement
afirmar (a) *vt (aseverar)* to state, to declare (b) *(afianzar)* to strengthen, to reinforce
afirmativo,-a *adj* affirmative; **en caso a. ...** if the answer is yes ...
aflicción *nf* affliction
afligir [57] 1 *vt* to afflict
　2 afligirse *vpr* to grieve, to be distressed
aflojar 1 *vt* to loosen
　2 *vi (viento etc)* to weaken, to grow weak
　3 aflojarse *vpr* to come o work loose; *(rueda)* to go down
aflorar *vi (río)* to come to the surface; *(sentimiento)* to surface, to show
afluencia *nf* inflow, influx; **gran a. de**

público great numbers of people
afluente *nm* tributary
afluir [37] *vi* to flow (**a** into)
afónico,-a *adj* **estar a.** to have lost one's voice
aforismo *nm* aphorism
aforo *nm (capacidad)* seating capacity
afortunado,-a *adj* fortunate; **las Islas Afortunadas** the Canaries
afrenta *nf Fml* affront
África *n* Africa
africano,-a *adj & nm,f* African
afrodisíaco,-a *adj & nm* aphrodisiac
afrontar *vt* to confront, to face; **a. las consecuencias** to face the consequences
afuera 1 *adv* outside; **la parte de a.** the outside; **más a.** further out; **salir a.** to come o go out
　2 *nfpl* **afueras** outskirts
agachar 1 *vt* to lower
　2 agacharse *vpr* to duck
agalla *nf* (a) *(de pez)* gill (b) **tiene agallas** she's got guts
agarraderas *nfpl Fam* **tener buenas a.** to be well-connected
agarrado,-a *adj* (a) *Fam* stingy, tight (b) **baile a.** cheek-to-cheek dancing
agarrar 1 *vt* (a) to grasp, to seize; **agárralo fuerte** hold it tight (b) *Am (tomar)* to take; **a. un taxi** to take a taxi (c) *Fam (pillar)* to catch; **a. una borrachera** to get drunk o pissed
　2 agarrarse *vpr* to hold on; **agarraos bien** hold tight
agarrotarse *vpr* (a) *(músculo)* to stiffen (b) *(máquina)* to seize up
agasajar *vt* to smother with attentions
ágata *nf* agate

> Takes the masculine articles **el** and **un**.

agazaparse *vpr* to crouch (down)
agencia *nf* agency; *(sucursal)* branch; **a. de viajes** travel agency; **a. de seguros** insurance agency; **a. inmobiliaria** estate agency
agenciarse [43] *vpr* (a) to get oneself; **se agenció una moto** he got himself a motorbike (b) **agenciárselas** to manage
agenda *nf* diary
agente *nmf* agent; **a. de policía** *(hombre)* policeman; *(mujer)* policewoman; **a. de bolsa** stockbroker; **a. de seguros** insurance broker
agigantado,-a *adj* **a pasos agigantados** by leaps and bounds
ágil *adj* agile
agilidad *nf* agility
agilización *nf* speeding up

agilizar [40] *vt (trámites)* to speed up

agitación *nf (intranquilidad)* restlessness; *(social, político)* unrest

agitado,-a *adj* agitated; *(persona)* anxious; *(mar)* rough; **una vida muy agitada** a very hectic life

agitar 1 *vt (botella)* to shake; *(multitud)* to agitate

   2 **agitarse** *vpr (persona)* to become agitated; *(mar)* to become rough

aglomeración *nf* agglomeration; *(de gente)* crowd

aglomerar 1 *vt* to bring together

   2 **aglomerarse** *vpr* to mass o gather together

agnóstico,-a *adj & nm,f* agnostic

agobiado,-a *adj Fig* **a. de problemas** snowed under with problems; *Fig* **a. de trabajo** up to one's eyes in work

agobiante *adj (trabajo)* overwhelming; *(lugar)* claustrophobic; *(calor)* oppressive; *(persona)* tiresome, tiring

agobiar [43] 1 *vt* to overwhelm

   2 **agobiarse** *vpr (con problemas)* to be over-anxious; *(por el calor)* to suffocate

agobio *nm* (a) *(angustia)* anxiety (b) *(sofoco)* suffocation

agolpamiento *nm* crowd, crush

agolparse *vpr* to crowd, to throng

agonía *nf* dying breath, last gasp

agonizante *adj* dying

agonizar [40] *vi* to be dying

agosto *nm* August; *Fam* **hacer su a.** to make a packet

agotado,-a *adj* (a) *(cansado)* exhausted, worn out (b) *Com* sold out; *(existencias)* exhausted; *(libro)* out of print

agotador,-a *adj* exhausting

agotamiento *nm* exhaustion

agotar 1 *vt* (a) *(cansar)* to exhaust, to wear out (b) *(acabar)* to exhaust, to use up (completely)

   2 **agotarse** *vpr* (a) *(acabarse)* to run out, to be used up; *Com* to be sold out (b) *(persona)* to become exhausted o tired out

agraciado,-a *adj* (a) *(hermoso)* pretty (b) *(ganador)* winning; **ser a. con** to win

agradable *adj* pleasant

agradar *vi* to please; **no me agrada** I don't like it

agradecer [33] *vt* (a) *(dar las gracias)* to thank for; **les agradezco su atención** (I) thank you for your attention; **te lo agradezco mucho** thank you very much (b) *(estar agradecido)* to be grateful to; **te agradecería que vinieras** I'd be grateful if you'd come (c) *(uso impers)* **siempre se**

agradece un descanso a rest is always welcome

agradecido,-a *adj* grateful; **le estoy muy a.** I am very grateful to you

agradecimiento *nm* gratitude

agrado *nm* pleasure; **no es de su a.** it isn't to his liking

agrandar 1 *vt* to enlarge, to make larger

   2 **agrandarse** *vpr* to enlarge, to become larger

agrario,-a *adj* agrarian; **política agraria** agricultural policy

agravamiento *nm* aggravation

agravante 1 *adj Jur* aggravating

   2 *nm Jur* aggravating circumstance

agravar 1 *vt* to aggravate

   2 **agravarse** *vpr* to worsen, to get worse

agraviar [43] *vt* to offend, to insult

agravio *nm* offense, insult

agredir *vt defect* to assault

agregación *nf* aggregation

agregado,-a 1 *adj Educ* **profesor a.** *(escuela)* secondary school teacher; *Univ* assistant teacher

   2 *nm,f Pol* attaché

agregar [42] 1 *vt* (a) *(añadir)* to add (b) *(destinar)* to appoint

   2 **agregarse** *vpr* **a.** a to join

agresión *nf* aggression

agresividad *nf* aggressiveness

agresivo,-a *adj* aggressive

agresor,-a 1 *nm,f* aggressor, attacker

   2 *adj* attacking

agriarse *vpr* to turn sour

agrícola *adj* agricultural

agricultor,-a *nm,f* farmer

agricultura *nf* agriculture; **a. biológica** o **ecológica** organic farming

agridulce *adj* bittersweet

agrietar 1 *vt* to crack; *(piel, labios)* to chap

   2 **agrietarse** *vpr* to crack; *(piel)* to get chapped

agringarse [42] *vpr Am Pey* to behave like a gringo

agrio,-a 1 *adj* sour

   2 *nmpl* **agrios** citrus fruits

agrónomo,-a *nm,f* **(ingeniero) a.** agronomist

agropecuario,-a *adj* farming, agricultural

agrupación *nf* association

agrupar 1 *vt* to group

   2 **agruparse** *vpr* (a) *(congregarse)* to group together, to form a group (b) *(asociarse)* to associate

agua *nf* water; **a. potable** drinking water; **a. corriente/del grifo** running/tap water;

a. dulce/salada fresh/salt water; **a. mineral sin/con gas** still/fizzy o sparkling mineral water; **a. de colonia** (eau de) cologne; *Fig* **estar con el a. al cuello** to be up to one's neck in it; **aguas jurisdiccionales** territorial waters; **aguas residuales** sewage

Takes the masculine articles **el** and **un**.

aguacate *nm* (*árbol*) avocado; (*fruto*) avocado (pear)
aguacero *nm* shower, downpour
aguado,-a *adj* watered down
aguafiestas *nmf inv* spoilsport, wet blanket
aguafuerte *nm* (a) *Arte* etching (b) *Quím* nitric acid
aguamala *nf Carib, Col, Ecuad, Méx* jellyfish
aguamarina *nf* aquamarine
aguamiel *nm o nf* (a) *Am (bebida)* = water mixed with honey or cane syrup (b) *Carib, Méx (jugo)* maguey juice
aguanieve *nf* sleet
aguantar 1 *vt* (a) (*soportar*) to tolerate; **no lo aguanto más** I can't stand it any longer (b) (*sostener*) to support, to hold; **aguanta esto** hold this (c) **aguanta la respiración** hold your breath
2 aguantarse *vpr* (a) (*contenerse*) to keep back; (*lágrimas*) to hold back; **no pude aguantarme la risa** I couldn't help laughing (b) (*resignarse*) to resign oneself
aguante *nm* endurance; **tener mucho a.** (*ser paciente*) to be very patient; (*tener resistencia*) to be strong, to have a lot of stamina
aguar [45] *vt* to water down; *Fig* **a. la fiesta a algn** to spoil sb's fun
aguardar 1 *vt* to await
2 *vi* to wait
aguardiente *nm* liquor, brandy
aguarrás *nm* turpentine
aguatero,-a *nm,f Am* water seller
aguaviva *nf RP* jellyfish
agudeza *nf* (a) sharpness; (*del dolor*) acuteness (b) *Fig* (*ingenio*) witticism, witty saying
agudización *nf* (a) sharpening (b) (*empeoramiento*) worsening
agudizar [40] 1 *vt* to intensify, to make more acute
2 agudizarse *vpr* to intensify, to become more acute
agudo,-a *adj* (*dolor*) acute; (*voz*) high-pitched; (*sonido*) treble, high; *Fig* (*ingenioso*) witty; *Fig* (*sentido*) sharp, keen

agüero *nm* omen
aguijón *nm* sting; *Fig* (*estímulo*) spur
águila *nf* eagle; **á. real** golden eagle; *Méx* **¿á. o sol?** heads or tails?

Takes the masculine articles **el** and **un**.

aguileño,-a *adj* aquiline; **nariz aguileña** aquiline nose
aguinaldo *nm* Christmas box; **pedir el a.** to go carol singing
agüita *nf Chile* (herbal) tea
aguja *nf* (a) needle; (*de reloj*) hand; (*de tocadiscos*) stylus (b) *Arquit* spire (c) *Ferroc* point, *US* switch
agujerear *vt* to make holes in
agujero *nm* (a) hole; **a. negro** black hole (b) *Econ* deficit, shortfall
agujetas *nfpl* stiffness; **tener a.** to be stiff
agur *interj Fam* bye!, see you!
aguzar [40] *vt* (a) (*afilar*) to sharpen (b) *Fig* **a. el oído** to prick up one's ears; **a. la vista** to look attentively; **aguzar el ingenio** to sharpen one's wits
ahí *adv* there; **a. está** there he/she/it is; **ve por a.** go that way; **está por a.** it's over there; **setenta o por a.** seventy or thereabouts; **de a.** hence
ahijado,-a *nm,f* godchild; (*niño*) godson; (*niña*) goddaughter; **ahijados** godchildren
ahínco *nm* eagerness; **con a.** eagerly
ahíto,-a *adj* (*de comida*) full, stuffed; (*harto*) fed up
ahogado,-a 1 *adj* (a) (*en líquido*) drowned; **morir a.** to drown (b) (*asfixiado*) suffocated
2 *nm,f* drowned person
ahogar [42] 1 *vt* (a) (*en líquido*) to drown (b) (*asfixiar*) to suffocate
2 ahogarse *vpr* (a) (*en líquido*) to drown, to be drowned; *Fig* **a. en un vaso de agua** to make a mountain out of a molehill (b) (*asfixiarse*) to suffocate (c) (*motor*) to be flooded
ahondar 1 *vt* to deepen
2 *vi* to go deep; *Fig* **a. en un problema** to go into a problem in depth
ahora 1 *adv* (a) (*en este momento*) now; **a. mismo** right now; **de a. en adelante** from now on; **por a.** for the time being (b) **a. voy** I'm coming; **a. vuelvo** I'll be back in a minute (c) **hasta a.** (*hasta el momento*) until now, so far; (*hasta luego*) see you later
2 conj a. bien (*sin embargo*) however; (*y bueno*) well then
ahorcado,-a 1 *nm,f* hanged person
2 *adj* hanged

ahorcar [44] 1 vt to hang
2 ahorcarse vpr to hang oneself
ahorita, ahoritica adv Andes, CAm, Carib, Méx Fam (**a**) (en el presente) (right) now; **a. voy** I'm just coming (**b**) (pronto) in a second (**c**) (hace poco) just now, a few minutes ago
ahorrador,-a adj thrifty
ahorrar 1 vt to save
2 ahorrarse vpr **ahórrate los comentarios** keep your comments to yourself
ahorrativo,-a adj thrifty
ahorro nm (**a**) saving; **a. energético** energy saving (**b**) **ahorros** savings; Fin **caja de ahorros** savings bank
ahuecar [44] vt (**a**) to hollow out; Fam **a. el ala** to clear off, to beat it (**b**) (voz) to deepen
ahuevado,-a adj Andes, CAm Fam (tonto) **estar a. con algo** to be bowled over by sth
ahumado,-a adj (cristal, jamón) smoked; (bacon) smoky; **salmón a.** smoked salmon
ahumar 1 vt to smoke
2 vi (echar humo) to smoke, to give off smoke
ahuyentar vt to scare away
aindiado,-a adj Am Indian-like
airado,-a adj angry
airar 1 vt to anger
2 airarse vpr to get angry
airbag ['era, air'a] nm (pl **airbags**) airbag
aire nm (**a**) air; **a. acondicionado** air conditioning; **al a.** (hacia arriba) into the air; (al descubierto) uncovered; **al a. libre** in the open air; **en el a.** (pendiente) in the air; Rad on the air; **hacerse a.** to fan oneself; **saltar por los aires** to blow up; **tomar el a.** to get some fresh air; **necesito un cambio de aires** I need a change of scene (**b**) Aut choke (**c**) (viento) wind; **hace a.** it's windy (**d**) (aspecto) air, appearance (**e**) **él va a su a.** he goes his own sweet way (**f**) **darse aires** to put on airs
airear vt (ropa, lugar) to air; Fig (asunto) to publicize
airoso,-a adj graceful, elegant; Fig **salir a. de una situación** to come out of a situation with flying colours
aislacionismo nm isolationism
aislado,-a adj (**a**) isolated (**b**) Téc insulated
aislamiento nm (**a**) isolation (**b**) Téc insulation
aislante 1 adj **cinta a.** insulating tape
2 nm insulator
aislar vt (**a**) to isolate (**b**) Téc to insulate
ajar vt to wear out

ajedrez nm (**a**) (juego) chess (**b**) (piezas y tablero) chess set
ajeno,-a adj belonging to other people; **los bienes ajenos** other peoples' goods; **por causas ajenas a nuestra voluntad** for reasons beyond our control
ajetreado,-a adj (very) busy, hectic
ajetreo nm activity, hard work, bustle
ají nm (**a**) Andes, RP (pimiento) chilli (pepper) (**b**) Andes, RP (salsa) = sauce made from oil, vinegar, garlic and chilli
ajiaco nm (**a**) Andes, Carib (estofado) = chilli-based stew (**b**) Méx (estofado con ajo) = tripe stew flavoured with garlic
ajillo nm Culin **al a.** fried with garlic
ajo nm garlic; **cabeza/diente de a.** head/clove of garlic; Fam **estar en el a.** to be in on it
ajonjolí nm sesame
ajorca nf bracelet; (en el tobillo) anklet
ajuar nm (de novia) trousseau
ajustado,-a adj tight
ajustador,-a nm,f fitter
ajustar vt (**a**) to adjust (**b**) (apretar) to tighten (**c**) Fin (cuenta) to settle; Fig **ajustarle las cuentas a algn** to settle a score with sb
ajuste nm (**a**) adjustment; Téc assembly; TV **carta de a.** test card (**b**) (de precio) fixing; (de cuenta) settlement; Fig **a. de cuentas** settling of scores
ajusticiar [43] vt to execute
al (contracción de **a + el**) (**a**) ver **a** (**b**) (**al + infin**) **al salir** on leaving; **está al caer** it's about to happen; **al parecer** apparently
ala 1 nf (**a**) wing; Fig **cortarle las alas a algn** to clip sb's wings (**b**) (de sombrero) brim
2 nmf Dep winger

Takes the masculine articles **el** and **un**.

alabanza nf praise
alabar vt to praise
alabastro nm alabaster
alacena nf (food) cupboard
alacrán nm scorpion
alambicado,-a adj intricate
alambique nm still
alambrada nf, **alambrado** nm wire fence
alambrar vt to fence with wire
alambre nm wire; **a. de púas** barbed wire
alambrista nmf tightrope walker
alameda nf (**a**) poplar grove (**b**) (paseo) avenue, boulevard
álamo nm poplar
alano,-a nm,f (**perro**) **a.** mastiff
alarde nm (ostentación) bragging,

boasting; **hacer a. de** to show off

alardear *vi* to brag, to boast; **a. de rico** *o* **de riqueza** to flaunt one's wealth

alargadera *nf Elec* extension

alargado,-a *adj* elongated

alargar [42] **1** *vt* (a) to lengthen; *(estirar)* to stretch; **ella alargó la mano para cogerlo** she stretched out her hand to get it (b) *(prolongar)* to prolong, to extend (c) *(dar)* to pass, to hand over; **alárgame ese jersey** can you pass me that sweater?

2 alargarse *upr* (a) to get longer (b) *(prolongarse)* to go on (c) **¿puedes a. a casa?** can you give me a lift home?

alarido *nm* screech, shriek; **dar un a.** to howl

alarma *nf* alarm; **la a. saltó** the alarm went off; **falsa a.** false alarm; **señal de a.** alarm (signal)

alarmado,-a *adj* alarmed

alarmante *adj* alarming

alarmar 1 *vt* to alarm

2 alarmarse *upr* to be alarmed

alazán,-ana *adj & nm,f* **(caballo) a.** chestnut

alba *nf* dawn, daybreak

Takes the masculine articles **el** and **un**.

albacea *nmf (hombre)* executor; *(mujer)* executrix

albahaca *nf* basil

albanés,-esa *adj & nm,f* Albanian

Albania *n* Albania

albañal *nm* sewer, drain

albañil *nm* bricklayer

albañilería *nf* bricklaying; **pared de a.** *(obra)* brick wall

albarán *nm Com* delivery note, despatch note

albaricoque *nm* apricot

albaricoquero *nm* apricot tree

albatros *nm inv* albatross

albedrío *nm* will; **libre a.** free will

alberca *nf* (a) *(depósito)* water tank (b) *Méx (piscina)* swimming pool

albergar [42] **1** *vt (alojar)* to house, to accommodate; *Fig (sentimientos)* to cherish, to harbour

2 albergarse *upr* to stay

albergue *nm* hostel; **a. juvenil** youth hostel

albino,-a *adj & nm,f* albino

albóndiga *nf* meatball

albores *nmpl* beginning; **en los a. de ...** at the beginning of ...

albornoz *nm* bathrobe

alborotado,-a *adj* (a) worked up, agitated (b) *(desordenado)* untidy, messy (c)

(mar) rough; *(tiempo)* stormy

alborotar 1 *vt* (a) *(agitar)* to agitate, to work up (b) *(desordenar)* to make untidy, to turn upside down

2 *vi* to kick up a racket

3 alborotarse *upr* (a) to get excited *o* worked up (b) *(mar)* to get rough; *(tiempo)* to get stormy

alboroto *nm* (a) *(jaleo)* din, racket (b) *(desorden)* disturbance, uproar

alborozo *nm* merriment, gaiety

albufera *nf* lagoon

álbum *nm* album

alcachofa *nf* (a) *Bot* artichoke (b) *(de tubo, regadera)* rose, sprinkler

alcalde *nm* mayor

alcaldesa *nf* mayoress

alcaldía *nf* (a) *(cargo)* mayorship (b) *(oficina)* mayor's office

alcalino,-a *adj* alkaline

alcance *nm* (a) reach; **al a. de cualquiera** within everybody's reach; **dar a. a** to catch up with; **fuera del a. de los niños** out of the reach of children (b) *Fig* scope; *(de noticia)* importance

alcancía *nf* money box; *(cerdito)* piggy bank

alcanfor *nm* camphor

alcantarilla *nf* sewer; *(boca)* drain

alcantarillado *nm* sewer system

alcanzar [40] **1** *vt* (a) to reach; *(persona)* to catch up with; **la producción alcanza dos mil unidades** production is up to two thousand units (b) **alcánzame la sal** *(pasar)* pass me the salt (c) *(conseguir)* to attain, to achieve

2 *vi (ser suficiente)* to be sufficient; **con un kilo no alcanza para todos** one kilo won't be enough for all of us

alcaparra *nf (fruto)* caper; *(planta)* caper bush

alcatraz *nm Orn* gannet

alcaucil *nm RP* artichoke

alcayata *nf* hook

alcazaba *nf* fortress, citadel

alcázar *nm* (a) *(fortaleza)* fortress, citadel (b) *(castillo)* castle, palace

alcista 1 *adj (bolsa)* rising, bullish; **tendencia a.** upward tendency

2 *nmf (bolsa)* bull

alcoba *nf* bedroom

ℓ Observa que la palabra inglesa **alcove** es un falso amigo y no es la traducción de la palabra española **alcoba**. En inglés, **alcove** significa "hueco".

alcohol *nm* alcohol

alcoholemia *nf* blood alcohol level;

prueba de a. Breathalyser® test
alcohólico,-a *adj & nm,f* alcoholic
alcoholímetro *nm* Breathalyser®
alcoholismo *nm* alcoholism
alcoholizado,-a *adj & nm,f* alcoholic
alcornoque *nm* cork oak
alcurnia *nf* lineage, ancestry; **de alta a.** of noble lineage
alcuzcuz *nm* couscous
aldaba *nf (llamador)* door knocker
aldabonazo *nm* (a) loud knock (b) *(advertencia)* warning
aldea *nf* village
aldeano,-a 1 *adj* village
  2 *nm,f* villager
aleación *nf* alloy
aleatorio,-a *adj* random
alebrestarse *vpr Col (ponerse nervioso)* to get nervous o excited
aleccionador,-a *adj (instructivo)* instructive; *(ejemplar)* exemplary
aleccionar *vt (instruir)* to teach, to instruct; *(adiestrar)* to train
aledaño,-a 1 *adj* adjoining, adjacent
  2 *nmpl* aledaños outskirts
alegar [42] *vt* (a) *(aducir)* to claim; *Jur* to allege (b) *(presentar)* to put forward
alegato *nm* argument
alegoría *nf* allegory
alegrar 1 *vt* (a) *(complacer)* to make happy o glad; **me alegra que se lo hayas dicho** I am glad you told her (b) *Fig (avivar)* to enliven, to brighten up
  2 **alegrarse** *vpr* to be glad, to be happy; **me alegro de verte** I am pleased to see you; **me alegro por ti** I am happy for you
alegre *adj* (a) *(contento)* happy, glad (b) *(color)* bright; *(música)* lively; *(lugar)* pleasant, cheerful (c) *Fig (borracho)* tipsy, merry
alegría *nf* joy, happiness
alejado,-a *adj* far away, remote
alejar 1 *vt* to move further away
  2 **alejarse** *vpr* to go away, to move away; **no te alejes de mí** keep close to me
aleluya *nm o nf* hallelujah, alleluia
alemán,-ana 1 *adj & nm,f* German
  2 *nm (idioma)* German
Alemania *n* Germany; **A. del Este/Oeste** East/West Germany; **A. Occidental/Oriental** West/East Germany
alentador,-a *adj* encouraging; **un panorama poco a.** a rather bleak outlook
alentar [1] *vt Fig* to encourage
alergia *nf* allergy
alérgico,-a *adj* allergic
alero *nm* eaves
alerón *nm Av* aileron

alerta *nf & adj* alert; **estar en estado de a.** to be (on the) alert
alertar *vt* to alert (**de** to); **nos alertó del peligro** he alerted us to the danger
aleta *nf (de pez)* fin; *(de foca, de nadador)* flipper
aletargado,-a *adj* lethargic
aletargar [42] *vt* to make lethargic
  2 aletargarse *vpr* to become lethargic
aletear *vi* to flutter o flap its wings
alevín *nm (pescado)* young fish; *Fig (principiante)* beginner
alevosía *nf (traición)* treachery; *(premeditación)* premeditation
alevoso,-a *adj (persona)* treacherous; *(acto)* premeditated
alfabético,-a *adj* alphabetic
alfabetización *nf* teaching to read and write; **campaña de a.** literacy campaign
alfabeto *nm* alphabet
alfajor *nm CSur* = large biscuit filled with toffee and coated with coconut
alfalfa *nf* lucerne, alfalfa
alfarería *nf* (a) *(arte)* pottery (b) *(taller)* potter's workshop; *(tienda)* pottery shop
alfarero,-a *nm,f* potter
alféizar *nm* sill, windowsill
alférez *nm* second lieutenant
alfil *nm* bishop
alfiler *nm* pin; *(broche)* pin, brooch; *(de corbata)* tiepin; *(para tender)* peg; *Andes, RP, Ven* **a. de gancho** *(imperdible)* safety pin
alfiletero *nm* pin box, pin case
alfombra *nf (moqueta)* carpet
alfombrar *vt* to carpet
alfombrilla *nf* rug, mat
alforja *nf (para caballos)* saddlebag; *(para hombro)* knapsack
alga *nf* alga; *(marina)* seaweed

> Takes the masculine articles **el** and **un**.

algarabía *nf* hubbub, hullabaloo
algarrobo *nm* carob tree
algazara *nf* din, row
álgebra *nf* algebra

> Takes the masculine articles **el** and **un**.

álgido,-a *adj* culminating, critical; **el punto a.** the climax
algo 1 *pron indef* (a) *(afirmativo)* something; *(interrogativo)* anything; **a. así** something like that; **¿a. más?** anything else?; **por a. será** there must be a reason for it; *Fam* **a. es a.** it's better than nothing (b) *(cantidad indeterminada)* some; **¿queda a. de pastel?** is there any cake left?

2 *adv (un poco)* quite, somewhat; **se siente a. mejor** she's feeling a bit better

algodón *nm* cotton; **a. (hidrófilo)** *Br* cotton wool, *US* absorbent cotton; **a. de azúcar** *Br* candy floss, *US* cotton candy

algodonero,-a 1 *nm,f* cotton grower
2 *adj* cotton

alguacil *nm* bailiff

alguien *pron indef (afirmativo)* somebody, someone; *(interrogativo)* anybody, anyone

alguno,-a 1 *adj* (**a**) *(delante de nombre)* *(afirmativo)* some; *(interrogativo)* any; **algunos días** some days; **algunas veces** some times; **alguna que otra vez** now and then; **¿has tomado alguna medicina?** have you taken any medicine?; **¿le has visto alguna vez?** have you ever seen him? (**b**) *(después de nombre)* not at all; **no vino persona alguna** nobody came

---

algún is used instead of **alguno** before masculine singular nouns (e.g. **algún día** some day).

---

2 *pron indef* (**a**) someone, somebody; **a. dirá que ...** someone might say that ...; **a. que otro** some (**b**) **algunos,-as** some (people)

alhaja *nf* jewel

alhelí *nm (pl alhelíes)* wallflower, stock

aliado,-a 1 *adj* allied
2 *nm,f* **los Aliados** the Allies

alianza *nf* (**a**) *(pacto)* alliance (**b**) *(anillo)* wedding ring

aliarse [29] *vpr* to become allies, to form an alliance

alias *adv & nm inv* alias

alicaído,-a *adj* (**a**) *Fig (débil)* weak, feeble (**b**) *Fig (deprimido)* down, depressed

alicatar *vt* to tile

alicates *nmpl* pliers

aliciente *nm* (**a**) *(atractivo)* lure, charm (**b**) *(incentivo)* incentive

alienación *nf* alienation

alienado,-a *adj* insane, deranged

alienar *vt* to alienate

alienígena *adj & nmf* alien

aliento *nm* (**a**) breath; **sin a.** breathless (**b**) *(ánimo)* encouragement

aligerar 1 *vt (acelerar)* to speed up; **a. el paso** to quicken one's pace
2 *vi Fam* **¡aligera!** hurry up!

alijo *nm* haul; **un a. de drogas** a consignment of drugs

alimaña *nf* vermin

alimentación *nf (comida)* food; *(acción)* feeding; *Téc* supply

alimentar 1 *vt* (**a**) *(dar alimento)* to feed; *(ser nutritivo)* to be nutritious (**b**) *Fig* *(sentimientos)* to nourish (**c**) *Informát* to feed; *Téc* to supply
2 alimentarse *vpr* **a. con** o **de** to live on

alimentario,-a *adj* food

alimenticio,-a *adj* nutritious; **productos alimenticios** food products, foodstuffs; **valor a.** nutritional value

alimento *nm* (**a**) *(comida)* food (**b**) *Fig* **tiene poco a.** it is not very nourishing

alimón *adv* **al a.** together

alineación *nf* (**a**) alignment (**b**) *Dep (equipo)* line-up

alineado,-a *adj* aligned, lined-up; **países no alineados** non-aligned countries

alineamiento *nm* alignment

alinear 1 *vt* to align, to line up
2 alinearse *vpr* to line up

aliñar *vt* to season, to flavour; *(ensalada)* to dress

aliño *nm* seasoning, dressing

alioli *nm* garlic mayonnaise

alisar *vt*, **alisarse** *vpr* to smooth

aliscafo, alíscafo *nm RP* hydrofoil

alistar 1 *vt Mil* to recruit, to enlist
2 alistarse *vpr* (**a**) *Mil* to enlist, to enrol (**b**) *Am (prepararse)* to get ready

aliviar [43] 1 *vt (dolor)* to soothe, to relieve; *(carga)* to lighten, to make lighter
2 aliviarse *vpr (dolor)* to diminish, to get better

alivio *nm* relief

aljibe *nm* cistern, tank

allá *adv* (**a**) *(lugar alejado)* there, over there; **a. abajo/arriba** down/up there; **¡a. voy!** here I go!; **más a.** further on; **más a. de** beyond; **el más a.** the beyond (**b**) *(tiempo)* **a. por los años veinte** back in the twenties (**c**) **a. tú** that your problem

allanamiento *nm Jur* **a. de morada** breaking and entering

allanar *vt* (**a**) *(terreno)* to level, to flatten; *Fig (camino)* to smooth (**b**) *Jur* to break into

allegado,-a 1 *adj* close
2 *nm,f* close friend

allende *adv Fml* beyond; **a. los mares** overseas

allí *adv* there, over there; **a. abajo/arriba** down/up there; **de a. para acá** back and forth; **por a.** *(movimiento)* that way; *(posición)* over there

alma *nf* soul; **no había ni un a.** there was not a soul

Takes the masculine articles **el** and **un**.

---

almacén *nm* (**a**) *(local)* warehouse; *(habitación)* storeroom (**b**) *Com* **(grandes) almacenes** department store (**c**) *Andes,*

RP (de alimentos) grocer's (shop), grocery store

almacenaje *nm* storage, warehousing

almacenamiento *nm* storage, warehousing; *Informát* storage

almacenar *vt* to store

almacenista *nmf (vendedor)* wholesaler; *(propietario)* warehouse owner

almanaque *nm* calendar

almeja *nf* clam; *muy Fam* pussy

almena *nf* merlon

almendra *nf* almond; **a. garapiñada** sugared almond

almendro *nm* almond tree

almiar *nm* haystack

almíbar *nm* syrup

almidón *nm* starch

almidonar *vt* to starch

alminar *nm* minaret

almirante *nm* admiral

almizcle *nm* musk

almohada *nf* pillow; *Fam* **consultarlo con la a.** to sleep on it

almohadilla *nf* (small) cushion

almohadón *nm* large pillow, cushion

almorrana *nf Fam* pile

almorzar [2] 1 *vi* to have lunch

  2 *vt* to have for lunch

almuerzo *nm* lunch

aló *interj Andes, Carib (al teléfono)* hello!

alocado,-a *adj* thoughtless, rash

alocución *nf* speech, address

alojamiento *nm* accommodation; **dar a.** to accommodate

alojar 1 *vt* to accommodate

  2 alojarse *vpr* to stay

alondra *nf* lark; **a. común** skylark

alpaca *nf* alpaca

alpargata *nf* canvas sandal, espadrille

Alpes *npl* **los A.** the Alps

alpinismo *nm* mountaineering, climbing

alpinista *nmf* mountaineer, climber

alpino,-a *adj* Alpine; **esquí a.** downhill skiing

alquilar *vt* to hire; *(pisos, casas)* to rent; **se alquila** *(en letrero)* to let

alquiler *nm* (**a**) *(de pisos, casas)* renting, letting; **a. de coches** car hire; **de a.** *(pisos, casas)* to let, rented; *(coche)* for hire; *(televisión)* for rent (**b**) *(precio)* hire, rental; *(de pisos, casas)* rent

alquimia *nf* alchemy

alquitrán *nm* tar

alrededor 1 *adv (lugar)* round, around; **mira a.** look around; **a. de la mesa** round the table; **a. de las dos** around two o'clock; **a. de quince** about fifteen;

  2 *nmpl* **alrededores** surrounding area;

en los alrededores de Murcia in the area round Murcia

alta *nf* **dar de** o **el a.** *(a un enfermo)* to discharge from hospital

> Takes the masculine articles **el** and **un**.

altamente *adv* highly, extremely

altanería *nf* arrogance

altanero,-a *adj* arrogant

altar *nm* altar

altavoz *nm* loudspeaker

alterable *adj* changeable

alteración *nf* (**a**) *(cambio)* alteration (**b**) *(alboroto)* quarrel, row; **a. del orden público** disturbance of the peace (**c**) *(excitación)* agitation

alterar 1 *vt* to alter, to change; **a. el orden público** to disturb the peace

  2 alterarse *vpr* (**a**) *(cambiar)* to change (**b**) *(inquietarse)* to be upset (**c**) *(alimentos)* to go off

altercado *nm* quarrel, argument

alternar 1 *vt* to alternate

  2 *vi (relacionarse)* to meet people, to socialize

  3 alternarse *vpr* to alternate

alternativa *nf* alternative

alternativo,-a *adj* alternative

alterno,-a *adj* alternate; **días alternos** alternate days

alteza *nf* Highness; **Su A. Real** His/Her Royal Highness

altibajos *nmpl Fig* ups and downs

altiplano *nm* high plateau

altísimo *nm* **el A.** the Almighty

altisonante *adj* grandiloquent

altitud *nf* altitude

altivez *nf* arrogance, haughtiness

altivo,-a *adj* arrogant, haughty

alto¹ *nm* (**a**) *(interrupción)* stop, break (**b**) *Mil* halt; **dar el a.** to order to halt; **un a. el fuego** a cease-fire

alto²,-a 1 *adj (persona, árbol, edificio)* tall; *(montaña, techo, presión)* high; *(sonido)* loud; *Fig (precio, tecnología)* high; *(tono)* high-pitched; **los pisos altos** the top floors; **en lo a.** at the top; **alta sociedad** high society; **clase alta** upper class; **en voz alta** aloud, in a loud voice; **a altas horas de la noche** late at night

  2 *adv* (**a**) high, high up (**b**) *(sonar, hablar etc)* loud, loudly; **pon la radio más alta** turn the radio up; **¡habla más a.!** speak up!

  3 *nm* (**a**) *(altura)* height; **¿cuánto tiene de a.?** how tall/high is it?; *Fig* **por todo lo a.** in a grand way (**b**) *(elevación)* hill

altoparlante *nm Am* loudspeaker

altozano *nm* hillock, hill

altramuz *nm* lupin

altruista 1 *adj* altruistic

2 *nmf* altruist

altura *nf* (a) height; **de 10 m de a.** 10 m high (b) *(nivel)* level; **a la misma a.** on the same level; *Geog* on the same latitude; **a la a. del cine** by the cinema; *Fig* **estar a la a. de las circunstancias** to meet the challenge; *Fig* **no está a su a.** he does not measure up to him; *Fig* **a estas alturas** at this stage (c) *Rel* **alturas** heaven

alubia *nf* bean

alucinación *nf* hallucination

alucinado,-a *adj Fam* amazed

alucinante *adj Fam* brilliant, mind-blowing

alucinar 1 *vt* to hallucinate; *Fig (encantar)* to fascinate

2 *vi Fam* to be amazed, to be spaced out

alucinógeno,-a 1 *adj* hallucinogenic

2 *nm* hallucinogen

alud *nm* avalanche

aludido,-a *adj Fig* **darse por a.** to take it personally

aludir *vi* to allude to, to mention

alumbrado,-a 1 *adj* lit

2 *nm Elec* lighting; **a. público** street lighting

alumbrar 1 *vt (iluminar)* to light, to illuminate

2 *vi (parir)* to give birth

aluminio *nm* aluminium

alumnado *nm (de colegio)* pupils; *Univ* student body

alumno,-a *nm,f* (a) *(de colegio)* pupil; **a. externo** day pupil; **a. interno** boarder (b) *Univ* student

alusión *nf* allusion, mention

aluvión *nm* downpour; *Fig* **un a. de preguntas** a barrage of questions

alverja, alverjana *nf Am* pea

alza *nf* (a) rise; **en a.** rising; **jugar al a.** *(bolsa)* to bull the market (b) *Mil* sight

Takes the masculine articles **el** and **un**.

alzado,-a 1 *adj* raised, lifted; **votación a mano alzada** vote by a show of hands

2 *nm Arquit* elevation

alzamiento *nm (rebelión)* uprising

alzar [40] 1 *vt* to raise, to lift; **a. el vuelo** to take off; **a. los ojos/la vista** to look up; **álzate el cuello** turn your collar up

2 alzarse *vpr* (a) *(levantarse)* to get up, to rise (b) *(rebelarse)* to rise, to rebel (c) **a. con la victoria** to win, to be victorious

AM *nf (abr* amplitude modulation) AM

a.m. *adv* a.m.

ama *nf (señora)* lady of the house; *(dueña)* owner; **a. de casa** housewife; **a. de llaves** housekeeper

Takes the masculine articles **el** and **un**.

amabilidad *nf* kindness; *Fml* **tenga la a. de esperar** would you be so kind as to wait?

amable *adj* kind, nice; *Fml* **¿sería usted tan a. de ayudarme?** would you be so kind as to help me?

amado,-a 1 *adj* loved, beloved

2 *nm,f* sweetheart

amaestrar *vt* to train; *(domar)* to tame

amagar [42] *vt (amenazar)* to threaten; **amaga tormenta** a storm is threatening

amago *nm* (a) *(indicio)* first sign; **a. de infarto** onset of a heart attack (b) *(intento)* attempt (c) *Fig (amenaza)* threat

amainar *vi (viento etc)* to drop, to die down

amalgama *nf* amalgam

amalgamar *vt* to amalgamate

amamantar *vt* to breast-feed; *Zool* to suckle

amancay *nm Andes* amaryllis

amancebarse *vpr* to cohabit

amanecer [33] 1 *v impers* to dawn; **¿a qué hora amanece?** when does it get light?; **amaneció lluvioso** it was rainy at daybreak

2 *vi* **amanecimos en Finlandia** we were in Finland at daybreak; **amaneció muy enfermo** he woke up feeling very ill

3 *nm* dawn, daybreak; **al a.** at dawn

amanerado,-a *adj* mannered, affected

amansar *vt* (a) to tame (b) *Fig (apaciguar)* to tame, to calm

amante *nmf* lover; **a. del arte** art lover

amañar *vt* to fix, to fiddle; *(elecciones)* to rig

amapola *nf* poppy

amar 1 *vt* to love

2 amarse *vpr* to love each other

amaraje *nm Av* landing at sea

amargado,-a 1 *adj (rencoroso)* embittered, bitter; *Fam (agobiado)* pissed off; **estoy a. con los exámenes** I'm pissed off with the exams

2 *nm,f* bitter person

amargar [42] 1 *vt* to make bitter; *Fig* to embitter, to sour

2 amargarse *vpr Fig* to become embittered *o* bitter; **no te amargues por eso** don't let that make you bitter

amargo,-a *adj* bitter

amargor *nm*, **amargura** *nf* bitterness

amarillento,-a *adj* yellowish

amarillo,-a *adj & nm* yellow; **prensa amarilla** gutter press

amarilloso,-a *adj Ven* yellowish

amarra *nf* mooring rope; **soltar amarras** to cast off, to let go

amarradero *nm* mooring

amarrar *vt Náut* to moor, to tie up; *(atar)* to tie (up), to bind

amarrete,-a *adj Andes, RP Fam* mean, tight

amasar *vt* (a) *Culin* to knead (b) *Fig (fortuna)* to amass

amasiato *nm CAm, Méx* cohabitation, common-law marriage

amasijo *nm Fam* hotchpotch, jumble

amasio,-a *nm,f CAm, Méx* live-in lover, common-law partner

amateur *adj & nmf* amateur

amatista *nf* amethyst

amazona *nf* (a) *(jinete)* horsewoman (b) *(en mitología)* Amazon

Amazonas *n* **el A.** the Amazon

amazónico,-a *adj* Amazonian

ambages *nmpl* **hablar sin a.** to go straight to the point

ámbar *nm* amber

Amberes *n* Antwerp

ambición *nf* ambition

ambicionar *vt* to have as an ambition; **ambiciona ser presidente** his ambition is to become president

ambicioso,-a 1 *adj* ambitious
  2 *nm,f* ambitious person

ambidextro,-a *nm,f* ambidextrous person

ambientación *nf Cin & Teatro* setting

ambientado,-a *adj (bar etc)* lively

ambientador *nm* air freshener

ambiental *adj* environmental

ambientar 1 *vt* (a) *(bar etc)* to liven up (b) *Cin & Teatro* to set
  2 ambientarse *vpr (adaptarse)* to get used to

ambiente 1 *nm* (a) *(gen)* environment; *Fig (medio)* environment, milieu (b) *Andes, RP (habitación)* room
  2 *adj* environmental; **temperatura a.** room temperature

ambigüedad *nf* ambiguity

ambiguo,-a *adj* ambiguous

ámbito *nm* field, sphere; **empresa de a. nacional** nationwide company

ambos,-as *adj pl Fml* both; **por a. lados** on both sides

ambulancia *nf* ambulance

ambulante *adj* travelling, mobile; **biblioteca a.** mobile library

ambulatorio *nm* surgery, clinic

amedrentar *vt* to frighten, to scare

amén¹ *nm* amen

amén² *adv* **a. de** in addition to

amenaza *nf* threat

amenazador,-a, amenazante *adj* threatening, menacing

amenazar [40] *vt* to threaten; **a. de muerte a algn** to threaten to kill sb

amenizar [40] *vt* to liven up

ameno,-a *adj* entertaining

América *n* America; **A. Central/del Norte/ del Sur** Central/North/South America

americana *nf (prenda)* jacket

americano,-a *adj & nm,f* American

amerindio,-a *adj & nm,f* Amerindian, American Indian

ameritar *vt Am* to deserve

amerizar [40] *vi* to land at sea

ametralladora *nf* machine gun

ametrallar *vt* to machine-gun

amianto *nm* asbestos

amigable *adj* friendly

amígdala *nf* tonsil

amigdalitis *nf* tonsillitis

amigo,-a 1 *nm,f* friend; **hacerse a. de** to make friends with; **hacerse amigos** to become friends; **son muy amigos** they are very good friends
  2 *adj (aficionado)* fond (**de** of)

amilanar 1 *vt* to frighten, to scare
  2 amilanarse *vpr* to be frightened *o* daunted

aminorar *vt* to reduce; **a. el paso** to slow down

amistad *nf* (a) friendship (b) **amistades** friends

amistoso,-a *adj* friendly

amnesia *nf* amnesia

amnistía *nf* amnesty

amo *nm* (a) *(dueño)* owner (b) *(señor)* master

amodorrarse *vpr* to become sleepy *o* drowsy

amoldar 1 *vt* to adapt, to adjust
  2 amoldarse *vpr* to adapt oneself

amonestación *nf* (a) rebuke, reprimand; *Dep* warning (b) *Rel* **amonestaciones** banns

amonestar *vt* (a) *(advertir)* to rebuke, to reprimand; *Dep* to warn (b) *Rel* to publish the banns of

amoniaco, amoníaco *nm* ammonia

amontonar 1 *vt* to pile up, to heap up
  2 amontonarse *vpr* to pile up, to heap up; *(gente)* to crowd together

amor *nm* love; **hacer el a.** to make love; **a. propio** self-esteem; **¡por el a. de Dios!** for God's sake!

amoral *adj* amoral

amoratado,-a *adj (de frío)* blue with cold; *(de un golpe)* black and blue

amordazar [40] *vt (perro)* to muzzle; *(persona)* to gag

amorfo,-a *adj* amorphous

amorío *nm* love affair, flirtation

amoroso,-a *adj* loving, affectionate

amortajar *vt* to shroud, to wrap in a shroud

amortiguador *nm Aut* shock absorber

amortiguar [45] *vt (golpe)* to cushion; *(ruido)* to muffle; *(luz)* to subdue

amortización *nf* repayment

amortizar [40] *vt* to pay off

amotinado,-a *nm,f* rioter; *Mil* mutineer

amotinamiento *nm* riot, rioting; *Mil* mutiny

amotinar 1 *vt* to incite to riot; *Mil* to incite to mutiny
2 amotinarse *vpr* to rise up; *Mil* to mutiny

amparar 1 *vt* to protect
2 ampararse *vpr* to seek refuge

amparo *nm* protection, shelter; **al a. de la ley** under the protection of the law

amperio *nm* ampère, amp

ampliación *nf* enlargement; *(de plazo, casa)* extension

ampliar [29] *vt* to enlarge; *(casa, plazo)* to extend

amplificador *nm* amplifier

amplificar [44] *vt* to amplify

amplio,-a *adj* large, roomy; *(ancho)* wide, broad; **en el sentido más a. de la palabra** in the broadest sense of the word

amplitud *nf* (a) spaciousness; **a. de miras** broad-mindedness (b) *(de espacio)* room, space (c) *Fís* amplitude

ampolla *nf* (a) *Med* blister; *Fig* **levantar ampollas** to raise people's hackles (b) *(de medicina)* ampoule

ampuloso,-a *adj* pompous, bombastic

amputar *vt Med* to amputate; *Fig* to cut out

amueblar *vt* to furnish

amuermar *vt Fam* (a) *(atontar)* to make feel dopey o groggy (b) *(aburrir)* to bore

amuleto *nm* amulet; **a. de la suerte** lucky charm

amurallar *vt* to wall, to fortify

anacronismo *nm* anachronism

ánade *nm* duck; **á. real** mallard

anales *nmpl* annals

analfabetismo *nm* illiteracy

analfabeto,-a *nm,f* illiterate

analgésico,-a *adj & nm* analgesic

análisis *nm inv* analysis; **a. de sangre** blood test

analista *nmf* analyst

analizar [40] *vt* to analyse

analogía *nf* analogy

analógico,-a *adj* analogue

análogo,-a *adj* analogous, similar

ananá *nm (pl ananaes)*, **ananás** *nm (pl ananases)* pineapple

anaquel *nm* shelf

anaranjado,-a *adj & nm* orange

anarquía *nf* anarchy

anarquismo *nm* anarchism

anarquista *adj & nmf* anarchist

anatomía *nf* anatomy

anatómico,-a *adj* anatomical

anca *nf* haunch; **ancas de rana** frogs' legs

Takes the masculine articles **el** and **un**.

---

ancestral *adj* ancestral

ancho,-a 1 *adj* wide, broad; **a lo a.** breadthwise; **te está muy a.** it's too big for you
2 *nm* (a) *(anchura)* width, breadth; **2 m de a.** 2 m wide; **¿qué a. tiene?** how wide is it? (b) *Cost* width
3 *nfpl Fam* **a mis** o **tus anchas** at ease, comfortable

anchoa *nf* anchovy

anchura *nf* width, breadth

anciano,-a 1 *adj* very old
2 *nm,f* old person; **los ancianos** old people

ancla *nf* anchor

Takes the masculine articles **el** and **un**.

---

anclar *vt & vi* to anchor

andadas *nfpl* **volver a las a.** to go back to one's old tricks

andaderas *nfpl* baby-walker

andadura *nf* walking

ándale *interj CAm, Méx Fam* come on!

Andalucía *n* Andalusia

andaluz,-a *adj & nm,f* Andalusian

andamiaje, andamio *nm* scaffolding

andanza *nf* adventure, happening

andar¹ *nm* **a.** o **andares** *nmpl* walk, gait

andar² [8] **1** *vi* (a) to walk (b) *(coche etc)* to move; **este coche anda despacio** this car goes very slowly (c) *(funcionar)* to work; **esto no anda** this doesn't work (d) *Fam* **anda por los cuarenta** he's about forty; **anda siempre diciendo que ...** he's always saying that ...; **¿cómo andamos de tiempo?** how are we off for time?; **tu bolso debe a. por ahí** your bag must be over there somewhere
2 *vt (recorrer)* to walk

andariego,-a *adj* fond of walking

andén *nm* (a) *(en estación)* platform (b)

Andes, CAm (acera) Br pavement, *US* sidewalk (**c**) *Andes (bancal de tierra)* terrace

Andes *nmpl* Andes

andinismo *nm Am* mountaineering

andinista *nmf Am* mountaineer

andino,-a *adj & nm,f* Andean

andrajo *nm* rag, tatter

andrajoso,-a *adj* ragged, tattered

android *nm* android

andurriales *nmpl Fam* out-of-the-way place

anécdota *nf* anecdote

anecdótico,-a *adj* anecdotal

anegar [42] *vt*, **anegarse** *vpr* to flood

anejo,-a 1 *adj* attached, joined (**a** to)
  2 *nm* appendix

anemia *nf* anaemia

anestesia *nf* anaesthesia

anestésico,-a *adj & nm* anaesthetic

anexar *vt* to annex

anexión *nf* annexation

anexionar *vt* to annex

anexo,-a 1 *adj* attached, joined (**a** to)
  2 *nm* appendix

anfetamina *nf* amphetamine

anfibio,-a 1 *adj* amphibious
  2 *nm* amphibian

anfiteatro *nm* (**a**) amphitheatre (**b**) *Cin & Teatro* gallery

anfitrión,-ona *nm,f* host, *f* hostess

ángel *nm* (**a**) angel; **á. de la guarda** guardian angel (**b**) *Am (micrófono)* hand-held microphone

angelical, angélico,-a *adj* angelic

angina *nf* angina; **tener anginas** to have tonsillitis; *Med* **a. de pecho** angina pectoris

anglófono,-a 1 *adj* English-speaking
  2 *nm,f* English speaker

anglosajón,-ona *adj & nm,f* Anglo-Saxon

Angola *n* Angola

angosto,-a *adj Fml* narrow

anguila *nf* eel; **a. de mar** conger eel

angula *nf* elver

angular *adj* angular; *Fot* (**objetivo**) **gran a.** wide-angle lens; **piedra a.** cornerstone

ángulo *nm* angle; *(rincón)* corner

angustia *nf* anguish

angustiar [43] *vt* to distress

angustioso,-a *adj* distressing

anhelar *vt* to long for, to yearn for

anhelo *nm* longing, yearning

anhídrido *nm* **a. carbónico** carbon dioxide

anidar *vi* to nest

anilla *nf* ring; **carpeta de anillas** ringbinder

anillo *nm* ring; **a. de boda** wedding ring

ánima *nf* soul

Takes the masculine articles **el** and **un**.

animación *nf (diversión)* entertainment

animado,-a *adj (fiesta etc)* lively

animador,-a *nm,f* (**a**) entertainer; *TV* presenter; **a. cultural** cultural organizer (**b**) *Dep* cheerleader

animadversión *nf* ill feeling, animosity

animal 1 *nm* animal; *Fig (basto)* brute; *(necio)* dunce
  2 *adj* animal

animar 1 *vt* (**a**) *(alentar)* to encourage (**b**) *(alegrar) (persona)* to cheer up; *(fiesta, bar)* to liven up, to brighten up
  2 animarse *vpr* (**a**) *(persona)* to cheer up; *(fiesta, reunión)* to brighten up (**b**) **¿te animas a venir?** do you fancy coming along?

anímico,-a *adj* **estado a.** frame *o* state of mind

ánimo *nm* (**a**) *(espíritu)* spirit; **estado de á.** frame *o* state of mind (**b**) **con á. de** *(intención)* with the intention of (**c**) *(valor, coraje)* courage; **dar ánimos a** to encourage; **¡á.!** cheer up!

animosidad *nf* animosity

animoso,-a *adj* cheerful

aniñado,-a *adj* childlike; *Pey* childish

aniquilación *nf* annihilation

aniquilar *vt* to annihilate

anís *nm* (**a**) *(bebida)* anisette (**b**) *(grano)* aniseed

anisete *nm* anisette

aniversario *nm* anniversary

ano *nm* anus

anoche *adv* last night; *(por la tarde)* yesterday evening; **antes de a.** the night before last

anochecer [33] 1 *v impers* to get dark; **cuando anochece** at nightfall, at dusk
  2 *vi* to be somewhere at dusk; **anochecimos en Cuenca** we were in Cuenca at dusk
  3 *nm* nightfall, dusk

anodino,-a *adj (insustancial)* insubstantial; *(soso)* insipid, dull

anomalía *nf* anomaly

anómalo,-a *adj* anomalous

anonadado,-a *adj* **me quedé/dejó a.** I was astonished

anonimato *nm* anonymity; **permanecer en el a.** to remain anonymous *o* nameless

anónimo,-a 1 *adj* (**a**) *(desconocido)*

anonymous (**b**) *Com* **sociedad anónima** public liability company, *US* incorporated company

2 *nm* (*carta*) anonymous letter

anorak *nm* (*pl* **anoraks**) anorak

anorexia *nf* anorexia

anormal 1 *adj* (**a**) abnormal (**b**) (*inhabitual*) unusual; **una situación a.** an irregular situation (**c**) *Med* subnormal

2 *nmf Med* subnormal person

anotación *nf* (**a**) annotation (**b**) (*apunte*) note

anotar 1 *vt* (**a**) to annotate (**b**) (*apuntar*) to take down, to make a note of

2 anotarse *upr RP* (*en curso*) to enrol

anquilosado,-a *adj Fig* fossilized; **a. en el pasado** locked in the past

anquilosarse *upr Fig* to stagnate

ansia *nf* (**a**) (*deseo*) longing, yearning (**b**) (*ansiedad*) anxiety (**c**) *Med* sick feeling

Takes the masculine articles **el** and **un**.

ansiar [29] *vt* to long for, to yearn for

ansiedad *nf* anxiety; **con a.** anxiously

ansioso,-a *adj* (**a**) (*deseoso*) eager (**por** for) (**b**) (*avaricioso*) greedy

antagónico,-a *adj* antagonistic

antagonismo *nm* antagonism

antagonista 1 *adj* antagonistic

2 *nmf* antagonist

antaño *adv* in the past, formerly

antártico,-a 1 *adj* Antarctic

2 *nm* **el A.** the Antarctic

Antártida *nf* Antarctica

ante¹ *nm* (**a**) *Zool* elk, moose (**b**) (*piel*) suede

ante² *prep* (**a**) before, in the presence of; *Jur* **a. notario** in the presence of a notary; **a. todo** most of all (**b**) (*en vista de*) faced with, in view of; **a. la crisis energética** faced with the energy crisis

anteanoche *adv* the night before last

anteayer *adv* the day before yesterday

antecedente 1 *adj* previous

2 *nm* antecedent

3 *nmpl* (**a**) **antecedentes** (*historial*) record; *Jur* **antecedentes penales** criminal record (**b**) *Fig* **poner en antecedentes** to put in the picture

anteceder *vt* to precede, to go before

antecesor,-a *nm,f* (**a**) (*en un cargo*) predecessor (**b**) (*antepasado*) ancestor

antedicho,-a *adj* above-mentioned

antelación *nf* notice; **con poca a.** at short notice; **con un mes de a.** a month beforehand, with a month's notice

antemano *adv* **de a.** beforehand, in advance

antena *nf* (**a**) *Rad & TV* aerial; **a. parabólica** satellite dish; **en a.** on the air (**b**) *Zool* antenna, feeler

anteojo *nm* (**a**) telescope (**b**) **anteojos** (*binoculares*) binoculars; *Am* (*gafas*) glasses, spectacles

antepasado,-a *nm,f* ancestor

antepecho *nm* (*de ventana*) sill; (*pretil*) parapet, guardrail

antepenúltimo,-a *adj* antepenultimate; **el capítulo a.** the last chapter but two

anteponer [19] (*pp* **antepuesto**) *vt Fig* to give preference to

anteproyecto *nm* preliminary plan, draft; *Pol* **a. de ley** draft bill

antepuesto,-a *pp de* **anteponer**

antepuse *pt indef de* **anteponer**

anterior *adj* (**a**) previous; **el día a.** the day before (**b**) (*delantero*) front; **parte a.** front part

anterioridad *nf* **con a.** before; **con a. a** prior to, before

anteriormente *adv* previously, before

antes *adv* (**a**) (*tiempo*) before; **a. de las tres** before three o'clock; **mucho a.** long before; **la noche a.** the night before; **cuanto a.** as soon as possible (**b**) (*antaño*) in the past; **a. llovía más** it used to rain more in the past (**c**) (*lugar*) before; **a. del semáforo** before the traffic lights (**d**) **a. prefiero hacerlo yo** I'd rather do it myself; **a. (bien)** on the contrary

antesala *nf* antechamber, anteroom; *Fig* **en la a. de** on the eve of

anti- *pref* anti-

antiadherente *adj* nonstick

antiaéreo,-a *adj* anti-aircraft

antibiótico,-a *adj & nm* antibiotic

anticaspa *adj* anti-dandruff

anticiclón *nm* anticyclone, high pressure area

anticipación *nf* bringing forward; **con a.** in advance

anticipadamente *adv* in advance

anticipado,-a *adj* brought forward; **elecciones anticipadas** early elections; **gracias anticipadas** thanks in advance; *Com* **por a.** in advance

anticipar 1 *vt* (*acontecimiento*) to bring forward; (*dinero*) to pay in advance; **no anticipemos acontecimientos** we'll cross that bridge when we come to it

2 anticiparse *upr* (**a**) (*adelantarse*) to beat to it; **iba a decírtelo, pero él se me anticipó** I was going to tell you, but he beat me to it (**b**) (*llegar pronto*) to arrive early; *Fig* **a. a su tiempo** to be ahead of one's time

anticipo *nm (adelanto)* advance; **pedir un a.** to ask for an advance (on one's wages)

anticonceptivo,-a *adj & nm* contraceptive

anticongelante *adj & nm (de radiador)* antifreeze; *(de parabrisas)* de-icer

anticonstitucional *adj* unconstitutional

anticuado,-a *adj* antiquated

anticuario,-a *nm,f* antique dealer

anticucho *nm Andes (brocheta)* kebab

anticuerpo *nm* antibody

antídoto *nm* antidote

antier *adv Am Fam* the day before yesterday

antiestético,-a *adj* ugly, unsightly

antifaz *nm* mask

antigás *adj* **careta/mascarilla a.** gas mask

antigualla *nf Pey* museum piece

antigüedad *nf* (**a**) *(período histórico)* antiquity; **en la a.** in olden days, in former times (**b**) *(en cargo)* seniority (**c**) **tienda de antigüedades** antique shop

antiguo,-a *adj* (**a**) old, ancient (**b**) *(pasado de moda)* old-fashioned (**c**) *(en cargo)* senior (**d**) *(anterior)* former

antihigiénico,-a *adj* unhygienic, unhealthy

antihistamínico,-a *adj & nm* antihistamine

Antillas *nfpl* **las A.** the West Indies, the Antilles

antinatural *adj* unnatural, contrary to nature

antiniebla *adj inv* **luces a.** foglights

antipatía *nf* antipathy, dislike; **tener a.** to dislike

antipático,-a *adj* unpleasant; **Pedro me es a.** I don't like Pedro

antípodas *nfpl* **las A.** the Antipodes

antiquísimo,-a *adj (superl de antiguo) adj* very old, ancient

antirrobo 1 *adj inv* antitheft; **alarma a.** burglar alarm; *(para coche)* car alarm

    2 *nm (para coche)* car alarm; *(para casa)* burglar alarm

antisemita 1 *adj* anti-Semitic

    2 *nmf* anti-Semite

antiséptico,-a *adj & nm* antiseptic

antítesis *nf inv* antithesis

antivirus *nm inv Informát* antivirus system

antojadizo,-a *adj* capricious, unpredictable

antojarse *vpr* (**a**) **cuando se me antoja** when I feel like it; **se le antojó un helado** he fancied an ice-cream (**b**) *(suponer)* **se me antoja que no lo sabe** I have the feeling that he doesn't know

antojitos *nmpl Méx* snacks, appetizers

antojo *nm* (**a**) *(capricho)* whim, caprice; *(de embarazada)* craving; **a su a.** in one's own way, as one pleases (**b**) *(en la piel)* birthmark

antología *nf* anthology

antonomasia *nf* **por a.** par excellence

antorcha *nf* torch

antro *nm* dump, hole; *Fig* **a. de perdición** den of vice

antropología *nf* anthropology

antropólogo,-a *nm,f* anthropologist

anual *adj* annual; **ingresos anuales** yearly income

anualidad *nf* annual payment, annuity

anuario *nm* yearbook

anudar *vt* (**a**) *(atar)* to knot, to tie (**b**) *Fig (unir)* to join, to bring together

anulación *nf* cancellation; *(de matrimonio)* annulment; *(de ley)* repeal

anular¹ *nm* ring finger

anular² *vt* (**a**) *Com (pedido)* to cancel; *Dep (gol)* to disallow; *(matrimonio)* to annul; *Jur (ley)* to repeal (**b**) *Informát* to delete

anunciador,-a *adj* **empresa anunciadora** advertising company

anunciante *nm* advertiser

anunciar [43] **1** *vt* (**a**) *(producto etc)* to advertise (**b**) *(avisar)* to announce

    2 anunciarse *vpr* to advertise oneself; **a. en un periódico** to put an advert in a newspaper

anuncio *nm* (**a**) *(comercial)* advertisement, advert, ad (**b**) *(aviso)* announcement (**c**) *(cartel)* notice, poster

anzuelo *nm (fish)* hook

añadidura *nf* addition; **por a.** besides, on top of everything else

añadir *vt* to add (**a** to)

añejo,-a *adj* (**a**) *(vino, queso)* mature (**b**) *(estropeado)* stale

añicos *nmpl* smithereens; **hacer a.** to smash to smithereens

añil 1 *adj* indigo, blue

    2 *nm* (**a**) *Bot* indigo plant (**b**) *(color)* indigo

año *nm* (**a**) year; **el a. pasado** last year; **el a. que viene** next year; **hace años** a long time ago, years ago; **los años noventa** the nineties; **todo el a.** all the year (round); **a. luz** light year (**b**) **¿cuántos años tienes?** how old are you?; **tiene seis años** he's six years old; **entrado en años** getting on

añoranza *nf* longing, yearning

añorar *vt* (*pasado*) to long for, to yearn for; (*país*) to feel homesick for, to miss

APA *nf* (*abr* **Asociación de Padres de Alumnos**) = Spanish association for parents of schoolchildren, ≃ PTA

Takes the masculine articles **el** and **un**.

apabullar *vt* to bewilder

apacentar [1] *vt* to put out to pasture, to graze

apacible *adj* mild, calm

apaciguar [45] 1 *vt* (*calmar*) to pacify, to appease
2 apaciguarse *vpr* (*persona*) to calm down; (*tormenta*) to abate

apadrinar *vt* (a) (*en bautizo*) to act as godfather to; (*en boda*) to be best man for (b) (*artista*) to sponsor

apagado,-a *adj* (a) (*luz, cigarro*) out (b) (*color*) dull; (*voz*) sad; (*mirada*) expressionless, lifeless; (*carácter, persona*) spiritless

apagar [42] *vt* (*fuego*) to put out; (*luz, tele etc*) to turn off, to switch off; (*color*) to soften; (*sed*) to quench

apagón *nm* power cut, blackout

apaisado,-a *adj* (a) oblong (b) (*papel*) landscape

apalabrar *vt* (*concertar*) to make a verbal agreement on

apalancar [44] 1 *vt* to lever up
2 apalancarse *vpr Fam* to ensconce oneself, to settle down

apalear¹ *vt* to beat, to thrash

apalear² *vt Agr* (*grano*) to winnow

apañar 1 *vt* to mend, to fix
2 apañarse *vpr Fam* **apañárselas** to manage

apaño *nm* mend, repair

apapachar *vt Méx Fam* (*mimar*) to cuddle; (*consentir*) to spoil

apapacho *nm Méx Fam* (*mimo*) cuddle

aparador *nm* (*mueble*) sideboard; (*de tienda*) shop window

aparato *nm* (a) (piece of) apparatus; (*dispositivo*) device; (*instrumento*) instrument; **a. de radio/televisión** radio/television set; **a. digestivo** digestive system; **a. eléctrico** thunder and lightning (b) *Tel* **¿quién está al a.?** who's speaking? (c) (*ostentación*) display

aparatoso,-a *adj* (a) (*pomposo*) ostentatious, showy (b) (*espectacular*) spectacular (c) (*grande*) bulky

aparcamiento *nm* (*en la calle*) parking place; (*parking*) *Br* car park, *US* parking lot

aparcar [44] *vt* to park

aparcería *nf Agr* sharecropping

apareamiento *nm* (a) (*de cosas*) pairing off (b) (*de animales*) mating

aparear *vt*, **aparearse** *vpr* to mate

aparecer [33] 1 *vi* (a) to appear; **no aparece en mi lista** he is not on my list (b) to turn up, to show up; **¿apareció el dinero?** did the money turn up?; **no apareció nadie** nobody turned up
2 aparecerse *vpr* to appear

aparejado,-a *adj* **llevar** o **traer a.** to entail

aparejador,-a *nm,f* quantity surveyor

aparejar *vt* (a) (*caballo*) to harness (b) (*emparejar*) to pair off

aparejo *nm* (a) (*equipo*) equipment (b) (*de caballo*) harness

aparentar 1 *vt* (a) (*fingir*) to affect (b) (*tener aspecto*) to look; **no aparenta esa edad** she doesn't look that age
2 *vi* to show off

aparente *adj* (a) apparent; **sin motivo a.** for no apparent reason (b) *Fam* (*conveniente*) suitable

aparición *nf* (a) appearance (b) (*visión*) apparition

apariencia *nf* appearance; **en a.** apparently; *Fig* **guardar las apariencias** to keep up appearances

apartado,-a 1 *adj* (*lugar*) remote, isolated; **mantente a. de él** keep away from him
2 *nm* (a) (*párrafo*) section, paragraph (b) **a. de correos** Post Office Box

apartamento *nm* (small) flat, apartment

apartar 1 *vt* (a) (*alejar*) to move away, to remove; **a. la mirada** to look away (b) (*guardar*) to put aside
2 *vi* **¡aparta!** move out of the way!
3 apartarse *vpr* (*alejarse*) to move over, to move away; **apártate de en medio** move out of the way

aparte 1 *adv* (a) aside; **ponlo a.** put it aside; **modestia/bromas a.** modesty/joking apart (b) **eso hay que pagarlo a.** (*separadamente*) you have to pay for that separately (c) **a. de eso** (*además*) besides that; (*excepto*) apart from that (d) **eso es caso a.** that's completely different
2 *nm* (a) *Teatro* aside (b) *Ling* **punto y a.** full stop, new paragraph

apasionado,-a 1 *adj* passionate; **a. de la música** very fond of music
2 *nm,f* enthusiast

apasionante *adj* exciting

apasionar *vt* to excite, to thrill; **le apasiona el jazz** he is mad about jazz

apatía *nf* apathy

apático,-a 1 adj apathetic
2 nm,f apathetic person
apátrida 1 adj stateless
2 nmf stateless person
apdo. (abr **apartado**) P.O. Box
apeadero nm halt
apearse vpr (de un autobús, tren) to get off, to alight; (de un coche) to get out; **se apeó en Jerez** he got off in Jerez
apechugar [42] vi **a. con** to shoulder
apedrear vt to throw stones at
apegado,-a adj devoted, attached (**a** to)
apegarse [42] vpr to become devoted o attached (**a** to)
apego nm love, affection; **tener a. a** to be attached to
apelación nf appeal; **interponer a.** to lodge an appeal
apelar vi (**a**) Jur to appeal (**b**) (recurrir) to resort (**a** to)
apellidarse vpr to have as a surname, to be called
apellido nm surname; **a. de soltera** maiden name
apelmazado,-a adj stodgy
apelotonar 1 vt to pile up, to put into a pile
2 apelotonarse vpr (gente) to crowd together
apenado,-a adj (**a**) (entristecido) sad (**b**) Andes, CAm, Carib, Méx (avergonzado) ashamed, embarrassed
apenar 1 vt to sadden
2 apenarse vpr (**a**) (entristecerse) to be saddened (**b**) Andes, CAm, Carib, Méx (avergonzarse) to be ashamed, to be embarrassed
apenas adv (**a**) (casi no) hardly, scarcely; **a. come** he hardly eats anything; **a. (si) hay nieve** there is hardly any snow (**b**) (tan pronto como) scarcely; **a. llegó, sonó el teléfono** no sooner had he arrived than the phone rang
apéndice nm appendix
apendicitis nf appendicitis
apercibir 1 vt to warn
2 apercibirse vpr **apercibirse (de)** to notice
aperitivo nm (bebida) apéritif; (comida) appetizer
apero nm (usu pl) equipment, tools; **aperos de labranza** farming implements
apertura nf (**a**) (comienzo) opening (**b**) Pol liberalization
apestar 1 vi to stink (**a** of)
2 vt to infect with the plague
apetecer [33] vi **¿qué te apetece para cenar?** what would you like for supper?;

¿te apetece ir al cine? do you fancy going to the cinema?
apetecible adj tempting, inviting
apetito nm appetite; **tengo mucho a.** I'm really hungry
apetitoso,-a adj appetizing, tempting; (comida) delicious, tasty
apiadarse vpr to take pity (**de** on)
ápice nm (**a**) (punta) apex (**b**) Fig **ni un á.** not a bit
apicultura nf beekeeping, apiculture
apilar vt, **apilarse** vpr to pile up, to heap up
apiñarse vpr to crowd together
apio nm celery
apisonadora nf roadroller, steamroller
apisonar vt to roll
aplacar [44] 1 vt to placate, to calm
2 aplacarse vpr to calm down
aplanar vt to level
aplastante adj crushing; Pol **victoria a.** landslide victory
aplastar vt (**a**) to flatten, to squash (**b**) Fig (vencer) to crush
aplatanarse vpr Fam to become lethargic
aplaudir vt (**a**) to clap, to applaud (**b**) Fig to applaud
aplauso nm applause
aplazamiento nm postponement, adjournment; (de un pago) deferment
aplazar [40] vt to postpone, to adjourn; Fin (pago) to defer
aplicación nf application
aplicado,-a adj hard-working
aplicar [44] 1 vt to apply
2 aplicarse vpr (**a**) (esforzarse) to apply oneself, to work hard (**b**) (norma, ley) to apply, to be applicable
aplique nm wall light, wall lamp
aplomo nm aplomb
apocado,-a adj shy, timid
apocamiento nm timidity, lack of self-confidence
apocarse [44] vpr to become frightened
apodar vt to nickname
apoderado,-a nm,f (**a**) agent, representative (**b**) (de torero, deportista) manager
apoderarse vpr to take possession (**de** of), to seize; Fig **el miedo se apoderó de ella** she was seized by fear
apodo nm nickname
apogeo nm height; **estar en pleno a.** (fama etc) to be at its height
apolillarse vpr to get moth-eaten
apolítico,-a adj apolitical
apología nf apology, defence
apoltronarse vpr Fam to vegetate

apoplejía nf apoplexy

apoquinar vt Fam to cough up, to fork out

aporrear vt to beat, to hit, to thrash; (puerta) to bang; Fam **a. el piano** to bang (away) on the piano

aportación nf contribution

aportar 1 vt to contribute

2 vi Náut to reach port

aposentarse vpr to stay, to lodge

aposento nm room

aposta adv on purpose, intentionally

apostar¹ [2] **1** vt to bet; **te apuesto una cena a que no viene** I bet you a dinner that he won't come

2 vi to bet (por on); **a. a los caballos** to bet on horses; **apuesto a que sí viene** I bet she will come

3 apostarse vpr to bet; **me apuesto lo que quieras** I bet you anything

apostar² vt (situar) to post, to station

apostilla nf note

apóstol nm apostle

apóstrofo nm apostrophe

apostura nf good bearing

apoteósico,-a adj enormous, tremendous

apoyacabezas nm Aut headrest

apoyar 1 vt (a) to lean (b) (causa) to support

2 apoyarse vpr (a) **a. en** to lean on; **apóyate en mi brazo** take my arm (b) **a. en** (opinión) to be based on, to rest on

apoyo nm support

apreciable adj appreciable, noticeable

apreciación nf appreciation

apreciar [43] **1** vt (a) to appreciate (b) (percibir) to notice, to see

2 apreciarse vpr to be noticeable

aprecio nm regard, esteem; **tener a. a algn** to be fond of sb

aprehender vt (alijo, botín) to apprehend, to seize

aprehensión nf seizure

apremiante adj urgent, pressing

apremiar [43] vi to be urgent; **el tiempo apremia** time is at a premium

aprender vt to learn; **así aprenderás** that'll teach you

aprendiz,-a nm,f apprentice, trainee

aprendizaje nm (a) learning (b) (instrucción) apprenticeship, traineeship

aprensión nf apprehension

aprensivo,-a adj apprehensive

apresar vt to seize, to capture

aprestar 1 vt to prepare, to get ready

2 aprestarse vpr to get ready

apresurado,-a adj (persona) in a hurry; (cosa) hurried

apresuramiento nm haste, hurry

apresurar 1 vt (paso etc) to speed up

2 apresurarse vpr to hurry up

apretado,-a adj (a) (ropa, cordón) tight; **íbamos todos apretados en el coche** we were all squashed together in the car (b) (día, agenda) busy

apretar [1] **1** vt (botón) to press; (nudo, tornillo) to tighten; **a. el gatillo** to pull the trigger; **me aprietan las botas** these boots are too tight for me

2 vi **apretaba el calor** it was really hot

3 apretarse vpr to squeeze together, to cram together; Fig **a. el cinturón** to tighten one's belt

apretón nm squeeze; **a. de manos** handshake

apretujar 1 vt to squeeze, to crush

2 apretujarse vpr to squeeze together, to cram together

aprieto nm tight spot, fix, jam; **poner a algn en un a.** to put sb in an awkward position

aprisa adv quickly

aprisionar vt (atrapar) to trap

aprobación nf approval

aprobado nm Educ pass

aprobar [2] vt (a) (autorizar) to approve (b) (estar de acuerdo con) to approve of (c) Educ to pass (d) Pol (ley) to pass

aprontar 1 vt (preparar) to quickly prepare o get ready

2 aprontarse vpr RP (prepararse) to get ready; **aprontate para cuando llegue tu papá!** just wait till your father gets back!

apropiado,-a adj suitable, appropriate

apropiarse [43] vpr to appropriate

aprovechado,-a adj (a) **mal a.** (recurso, tiempo) wasted; **bien a.** put to good use (b) (espacio) well-planned (c) (egoísta) self-seeking

aprovechamiento nm use

aprovechar 1 vt (a) to make good use of, to make the most of; **aprovechamos bien la tarde** we've done lots of things this afternoon (b) (recursos etc) to take advantage of; **a. la ocasión** to seize the opportunity

2 vi **¡que aproveche!** enjoy your meal!, bon appétit!

3 aprovecharse vpr to use to one's advantage, to take advantage; **a. de algn** to take advantage of sb; **a. de algo** to make the most of sth

aprovisionar vt to supply, to provide; **a. las tropas** to give supplies to the troops

aproximación nf (a) approximation (b) (en lotería) consolation prize

aproximadamente *adv* approximately, roughly

aproximado,-a *adj* approximate; **un cálculo a.** a rough estimate

aproximar 1 *vt* to bring o put nearer

2 aproximarse *vpr* **aproximarse (a)** to approach

aproximativo,-a *adj* approximate, rough

aptitud *nf* aptitude; **prueba de a.** aptitude test

apto,-a *adj* (a) *(apropiado)* suitable, appropriate; *Cin* **a. para todos los públicos** *Br* U, *US* G (b) *(capacitado)* capable, able (c) *Educ* passed

apuesta *nf* bet, wager

apuesto,-a *adj* good-looking; *(hombre)* handsome

apunado,-a *adj Andes* **estar a.** to have altitude sickness

apunarse *vpr Andes* to get altitude sickness

apuntador,-a *nm,f Teatro* prompter

apuntalar *vt* to prop up, to shore up, to underpin

apuntar 1 *vt* (a) *(con arma)* to aim (b) *(señalar)* to point out (c) *(anotar)* to note down, to make a note of (d) *(indicar)* to indicate, to suggest; **todo parece a. a ...** everything seems to point to ...

2 *vi* **cuando apunta el día** when day breaks

3 apuntarse *vpr* (a) *(en una lista)* to put one's name down (b) *Fam* **¿te apuntas?** are you game?; **me apunto** count me in

apunte *nm (usu pl)* note; **tomar apuntes** to take notes

apuñalar *vt* to stab

apurado,-a 1 *adj* (a) *(necesitado)* in need; **a. de dinero** hard up for money; **a. de tiempo** in a hurry (b) *(preocupado)* worried; *(avergonzado)* embarrassed (c) *(situación)* awkward, difficult (d) *(afeitado)* close

2 *nm (afeitado)* close shave

apurar 1 *vt* (a) *(terminar)* to finish off, to end (b) *(preocupar)* to worry

2 apurarse *vpr* (a) *(preocuparse)* to worry, to get worried; **no te apures** don't worry (b) *(darse prisa)* to rush, to hurry, to pester; **apúrate** get a move on

apuro *nm* (a) *(situación difícil)* tight spot, fix, jam; **estar en un a.** to be in a tight spot (b) *(escasez de dinero)* hardship; **pasar apuros** to be hard up (c) *(vergüenza)* embarrassment; **¡qué a.!** how embarrassing!

aquejado,-a *adj* suffering (**de** from)

aquel,-ella *adj dem* (a) that; **a. niño** that boy (b) **aquellos,-as** those; **aquellas niñas** those girls

aquél,-élla *pron dem m,f* (a) that one; *(el anterior)* the former; **aquél/aquélla ... éste/ésta** the former ... the latter (b) **todo a. que** anyone who, whoever (c) **aquéllos,-as** those; *(los anteriores)* the former

> Note that **aquél** and its various forms can be written without an accent when there is no risk of confusion with the adjective.

aquella *adj dem f ver* **aquel**

aquélla *pron dem f ver* **aquél**

aquello *pron neut* that, it

aquellos,-as *adj dem pl ver* **aquel,-ella**

aquéllos,-as *pron dem m,fpl ver* **aquél, -élla**

aquí *adv* (a) *(lugar)* here; **a. arriba/fuera** up/out here; **a. está** here it is; **a. mismo** right here; **de a. para allá** up and down, to and fro; **hasta a.** this far; **por a., por favor** this way please; **está por a.** it's around here somewhere (b) *(tiempo)* **de a. en adelante** from now on; **de aquí a junio** between now and June; **hasta a.** up till now

aquietar *vt* to pacify, to calm down

ara *nf Fml* **en aras de** for the sake of

> Takes the masculine articles **el** and **un**.

árabe 1 *adj (de Arabia)* Arab

2 *nmf (persona)* Arab

3 *nm (idioma)* Arabic

Arabia *n* Arabia; **A. Saudita** Saudi Arabia

arado *nm* plough

Aragón *n* Aragon

aragonés,-esa *adj & nm,f* Aragonese

arancel *nm* tariff, customs duty

arancelario,-a *adj* tariff, duty; **derechos arancelarios** duties; **barreras arancelarias** customs barriers

arandela *nf Téc* washer; *(anilla)* ring

araña *nf* (a) *(animal)* spider (b) *(lámpara)* chandelier

arañar *vt* to scratch

arañazo *nm* scratch

arar *vt* to plough

araucaria *nf* araucaria, monkey puzzle tree

arbitraje *nm* (a) arbitration (b) *Dep* refereeing; *Ten* umpiring

arbitrar *vt* (a) to arbitrate (b) *Dep* to referee; *Ten* to umpire

arbitrariedad *nf* (a) arbitrariness (b) *(acto)* arbitrary action

arbitrario,-a *adj* arbitrary

arbitrio *nm (voluntad)* will; *(juicio)* judgement

árbitro,-a nm,f (a) Dep referee; (de tenis) umpire (b) (mediador) arbitrator

árbol nm (a) Bot tree (b) Téc shaft (c) Náut mast (d) (gráfico) tree (diagram); **á. genealógico** family o genealogical tree

arbolado,-a 1 adj wooded
2 nm woodland

arboleda nf grove

arbusto nm bush, shrub

arca nf (a) chest (b) (para caudales) strongbox, safe; **arcas públicas** Treasury

Takes the masculine articles **el** and **un**.

arcada nf (a) arcade; (de puente) arch (b) (náusea) retching

arcaico,-a adj archaic

arcén nm verge; (de autopista) Br hard shoulder, US shoulder

archi- pref super-

archiconocido,-a adj extremely well-known

archipiélago nm archipelago

archivador nm filing cabinet

archivar vt (a) (documento etc) to file (away) (b) (caso, asunto) to shelve (c) Informát to save

archivo nm (a) file (b) (archivador) filing cabinet (c) **archivos** archives (d) Informát file; **a. adjunto** attachment

arcilla nf clay

arco nm (a) Arquit arch (b) Mat & Elec arc (c) (de violín) bow (d) (para flechas) bow; **tiro con a.** archery (e) **a. iris** rainbow (f) Am Dep (portería) goal, goalmouth

arder vi to burn; Fam **la conversación está que arde** the conversation is really heating up; **Juan está que arde** Juan is really fuming

ardid nm scheme, plot

ardiente adj (a) (encendido) burning; **capilla a.** chapel of rest (b) Fig (fervoroso) eager

ardilla nf squirrel

ardor nm (a) heat; Med **a. de estómago** heartburn (b) Fig ardour, fervour

ardoroso,-a adj Fig ardent, passionate

arduo,-a adj arduous

área nf (a) area; Dep penalty area (b) (medida) are (100 square metres)

Takes the masculine articles **el** and **un**.

arena nf (a) sand; **playa de a.** sandy beach (b) Taurom bullring

arengar [42] vt to harangue

arenisca nf sandstone

arenoso,-a adj sandy

arenque nm herring; Culin **a. ahumado** kipper

arepa nf Carib, Col = pancake made of maize flour

arete nm Andes, Méx earring

argamasa nf mortar

Argel n Algiers

Argelia n Algeria

argelino,-a adj & nm,f Algerian

Argentina n Argentina

argentino,-a adj & nm,f Argentinian, Argentine

argolla nf (a) (aro) (large) ring (b) Col, Méx (alianza) wedding ring

argot nm (popular) slang; (técnico) jargon

argucia nf ruse

argüende nm Méx Fam (a) (alboroto) rumpus, shindy; **armar (un) a.** to kick up a rumpus (b) (enredo, confusión) mess, trouble; **meterse en un a.** to get into a mess

argüir [62] vt (a) (deducir) to deduce, to conclude (b) (argumentar) to argue

argumentación nf argument

argumentar vt = argüir

argumento nm (a) Lit & Teatro (trama) plot (b) (razonamiento) argument

arguyo indic pres de argüir

aridez nf aridity; Fig dryness

árido,-a adj arid; Fig dry

Aries nm Aries

ariete nm Mil battering ram

ario,-a adj & nm,f Aryan

arisco,-a adj (persona) unfriendly, standoffish; (animal) unfriendly

arista nf edge

aristocracia nf aristocracy

aristócrata nmf aristocrat

aristocrático,-a adj aristocratic

aritmética nf arithmetic

arma nf weapon; **a. blanca** knife; **a. de fuego** firearm; **a. homicida** murder weapon; **a. nuclear** nuclear weapon; Fig **a. de doble filo** double-edged sword

Takes the masculine articles **el** and **un**.

armada nf navy

armado,-a adj armed; **ir a.** to be armed; **lucha armada** armed struggle

armador,-a nm,f shipowner

armadura nf (a) (armazón) frame (b) Hist suit of armour

armamentista adj arms; **la carrera a.** the arms race

armamento nm armaments; **a. nuclear** nuclear weapons

armar 1 vt (a) (tropa, soldado) to arm (b) (piezas) to fit o put together, to assemble (c) Fam **armaron un escándalo** they created a scandal

2 armarse *vpr* to arm oneself; *Fig* **a. de paciencia** to summon up one's patience; *Fig* **a. de valor** to pluck up courage; *Fam* **se armó la gorda** all hell broke loose

armario *nm* *(para ropa)* wardrobe; *(de cocina)* cupboard; **a. empotrado** built-in wardrobe o cupboard

armatoste *nm* *(cosa)* monstrosity

armazón *nm* frame; *(de madera)* timberwork; *Arquit* shell

Armenia *n* Armenia

armería *nf* gunsmith's (shop)

armiño *nm* ermine

armisticio *nm* armistice

armonía *nf* harmony

armonioso,-a *adj* harmonious

armonizar [40] *vt & vi* to harmonize

aro *nm* (a) *(gen)* hoop; *Fam* **pasar por el a.** to knuckle under (b) *Am (pendiente)* earring

aroma *nm* aroma; *(de vino)* bouquet

aromático,-a *adj* aromatic

arpa *nf* harp

Takes the masculine articles **el** and **un**.

arpía *nf* *(en mitología)* harpy; *Fig* harpy, old witch

arpón *nm* harpoon

arquear *vt*, **arquearse** *vpr* to bend, to curve

arqueología *nf* archaeology

arqueólogo,-a *nm,f* archaeologist

arquero,-a *nm,f* (a) *(tirador)* archer (b) *Am (portero de fútbol)* goalkeeper

arquetipo *nm* archetype

arquitecto,-a *nm,f* architect

arquitectónico,-a *adj* architectural

arquitectura *nf* architecture

arrabalero,-a *adj Pey* coarse

arrabales *nmpl* slums

arraigado,-a *adj* deeply rooted

arraigar [42] *vi* to take root

arraigo *nm Fig* roots; **una tradición con mucho a.** a deeply-rooted tradition

arrancar [44] **1** *vt* (a) *(planta)* to uproot, to pull up; **a. de raíz** to uproot (b) *(extraer)* to pull o tear off o out; *(diente, pelo)* to pull out; *Fig (confesión etc)* to extract; **arranca una hoja del cuaderno** tear a page out of the notebook (c) *(coche, motor)* to start; *Informát* to boot

2 *vi* (a) *Aut & Téc* to start; *Informát* to boot (up) (b) *(empezar)* to begin; **a. a llorar** to burst out crying

arranque *nm* (a) *Aut & Téc* starting (b) *(comienzo)* start (c) *Fam (arrebato)* outburst, fit

arrasar 1 *vt* to devastate, to destroy

2 *vi (en elecciones etc)* to win by a landslide

arrastrado,-a *Fam* **1** *adj* wretched

2 *nm,f* bad egg

arrastrar 1 *vt* to pull (along), to drag (along); **vas arrastrando el vestido** your dress is trailing on the ground; **lo arrastró la corriente** he was swept away by the current

2 arrastrarse *vpr* to drag oneself; *Fig (humillarse)* to crawl

arrastre *nm* (a) pulling, dragging; *Fam* **para el a.** *(persona)* on one's last legs; *(cosa)* done for (b) **(pesca de) a.** trawling (c) *Am Fam* **tener a.** to have a lot of influence

arrayán *nm* myrtle

arre *interj* gee up!, giddy up!

arrear *vt* (a) to spur on; *(caballos)* to urge on (b) *Fam (bofetada)* to give

arrebatador,-a *adj Fig* captivating, fascinating

arrebatar 1 *vt (coger)* to snatch, to seize; *Fig (cautivar)* to captivate, to fascinate

2 arrebatarse *vpr (enfurecerse)* to become furious; *(exaltarse)* to get carried away

arrebato *nm* outburst, fit

arreciar [43] *vi (viento, tormenta)* to get worse

arrecife *nm* reef

arreglado,-a *adj* (a) *(reparado)* repaired, fixed (b) *(solucionado)* settled (c) *(habitación)* tidy, neat (d) *(persona)* well-dressed, smart

arreglar 1 *vt* (a) *(arreglar)* to arrange; *(problema)* to sort out; *(habitación)* to tidy; *(papeles)* to put in order (b) *(reparar)* to repair, to fix (c) *(vestir)* to get ready

2 arreglarse *vpr* (a) *(vestirse)* to get ready (b) *Fam* **arreglárselas** to manage (c) *(reconciliarse)* to make up

arreglo *nm* (a) arrangement; *(acuerdo)* compromise (b) *(reparación)* repair; **no tiene a.** it is beyond repair; *Fam* **¡no tienes a.!** you're hopeless! (c) *Fml* **con a. a** in accordance with

arrellanarse *vpr* to sit back

arremangarse [42] *vpr* to roll one's sleeves o trousers up

arremeter *vi* to attack

arremolinarse *vpr* to whirl about; *Fig (gente)* to crowd together, to cram together

arrendamiento *nm* (a) *(alquiler)* renting (b) *(precio)* rent

arrendar [1] *vt (piso)* to rent; *(dar en arriendo)* to let on lease; *(tomar en* *arriendo)* to take on lease

arrendatario,-a *nm,f* leaseholder, lessee; *(inquilino)* tenant

arreos *nmpl* (a) *(de caballería)* harness, trappings (b) *(adornos)* adornments

arrepentido,-a *adj* regretful

arrepentimiento *nm* regret

arrepentirse [5] *vpr* a. de to regret; *Rel* to repent

arrestar *vt* to arrest, to detain; *(encarcelar)* to put in prison

arresto *nm* arrest; *Jur* a. **domiciliario** house arrest

arriar [29] *vt (bandera)* to strike; *(velas)* to lower

arriba 1 *adv* up; *(encima)* on the top; **ahí a.** up there; **de a. abajo** from top to bottom; *Fam* **mirar a algn de a. abajo** to look sb up and down; **desde a.** from above; **hacia a.** upwards; **de un millón para a.** from one million upwards; **más a.** higher up, further up; **a. del todo** right on *o* at the top; **la parte de a.** the top (part); **vive a.** he lives upstairs; **véase más a.** see above

2 *interj* get up!, up you get!; **¡a. la República!** long live the Republic!; **¡a. las manos!** hands up!

3 *prep Am* **a. (de)** on top of

arribar *vi* to reach port, to arrive

arribeño,-a *Am* **1** *adj* highland

2 *nm,f* highlander

arribista *nmf* parvenu, social climber

arriendo *nm* lease; *(de un piso)* renting; **dar en a.** to let out on lease; **tomar en a.** to take on lease

arriesgado,-a *adj* (a) *(peligroso)* risky (b) *(temerario)* fearless, daring

arriesgar [42] **1** *vt* to risk

2 arriesgarse *vpr* to risk; **se arriesga demasiado** he's taking too many risks

arrimar 1 *vt* to move closer, to bring near *o* nearer; *Fam* **a. el hombro** to lend a hand

2 arrimarse *vpr* to move *o* get close, to come near *o* nearer

arrinconar *vt* (a) *(poner en un rincón)* to put in a corner (b) *(abandonar)* to put away, to lay aside (c) *(acorralar)* to corner

arrobo *nm* rapture, enthralment

arrocero,-a *adj* **la industria arrocera** the rice industry

arrodillarse *vpr* to kneel down

arrogancia *nf* arrogance

arrogante *adj* arrogant

arrojadizo,-a *adj* **arma arrojadiza** missile

arrojado,-a *adj (osado)* bold, daring

arrojar 1 *vt* (a) *(tirar)* to throw, to fling (b) *Com (saldo)* to show

2 arrojarse *vpr* to throw oneself, to fling oneself

arrojo *nm* daring, courage

arrollador,-a *adj Fig* overwhelming; *(éxito)* resounding; *(personalidad)* captivating

arrollar *vt* **1** *(atropellar)* to run over, to knock down

2 *vi Dep & Pol* to win easily

arropar 1 *vt* to wrap up; *(en la cama)* to tuck in

2 arroparse *vpr* to wrap oneself up

arrostrar *vt* to face

arroyo *nm* brook, stream

arroz *nm* rice; **a. con leche** rice pudding

arruga *nf (en la piel)* wrinkle; *(en la ropa)* crease

arrugar [42] **1** *vt (piel)* to wrinkle; *(ropa)* to crease; *(papel)* to crumple (up)

2 arrugarse *vpr (piel)* to wrinkle; *(ropa)* to crease

arruinado,-a *adj* bankrupt, ruined

arruinar 1 *vt* to ruin

2 arruinarse *vpr* to be ruined

arrullar 1 *vt (bebé)* to lull

2 *vi (paloma)* to coo

arrullo *nm* (a) *(de paloma)* cooing (b) *(nana)* lullaby

arrumaco *nm Fam* kissing and hugging; *(halago)* flattery

arsenal *nm* arsenal

arsénico *nm* arsenic

arte *nm o nf* (a) art; **bellas artes** fine arts; *Fam* **por amor al a.** for the love of it (b) *(habilidad)* skill

| Takes the masculine articles **el** and **un**. |

artefacto *nm* device; **a. explosivo** explosive device

arteria *nf* artery; *(carretera)* highway

artesanal *adj* handmade

artesanía *nf* (a) *(cualidad)* craftsmanship (b) *(objetos)* crafts, handicrafts

artesano,-a **1** *nm,f* craftsman, *f* craftswoman

2 *adj* handmade

ártico,-a **1** *adj* arctic; **el océano Á.** the Arctic Ocean

2 *nm* **el Á.** the Arctic

articulación *nf* (a) *Anat* joint, articulation (b) *Téc* joint

articulado,-a *adj (tren etc)* articulated

articular *vt* to articulate

artículo *nm* article; **a. de fondo** leader (article)

artífice *nmf* author; *Fig* **el a. del acuerdo** the architect of the agreement

artificial *adj* artificial; *Tex* man-made *o* synthetic

artificio *nm* (a) artifice; **fuego de a.** firework (b) *(artimaña)* ruse

artillería *nf* artillery; **a. antiaérea** anti-aircraft guns

artillero *nm* artilleryman

artilugio *nm* gadget, device

artimaña *nf* trick, ruse

artista *nmf* artist; **a. de cine** film star

artístico,-a *adj* artistic

artritis *nf* arthritis

arveja *nf Andes, Carib, RP* pea

arzobispo *nm* archbishop

as *nm* ace

asa *nf* handle

Takes the masculine articles **el** and **un**.

asado,-a 1 *adj Culin* roast; **pollo a.** roast chicken; *Fig* **a. de calor** roasting, boiling hot

2 *nm Culin* roast; *Col, CSur (barbacoa)* barbecue

asaduras *nfpl* offal; *(de ave)* giblets

asalariado,-a 1 *adj* salaried

2 *nm,f* wage earner, salaried worker

asaltador,-a *nm,f,* **asaltante** *nmf* attacker; *(en un robo)* robber

asaltar *vt* to assault, to attack; *(banco)* to rob; *Fig* to assail

asalto *nm* (a) assault, attack; **a. a un banco** bank robbery (b) *(en boxeo)* round

asamblea *nf* meeting; **a. general** general meeting

asar 1 *vt* to roast

2 asarse *upr Fig* to be roasting, to be boiling hot

ascendencia *nf* ancestry, ancestors; **de a. escocesa** of Scottish descent

ascender [3] 1 *vt (en un cargo)* to promote

2 *vi* (a) to move upward; *(temperatura)* to rise; **la factura asciende a ...** the bill adds up to ... (b) *(al trono)* to ascend (c) *(de categoría)* to be promoted

ascendiente *nmf* ancestor

ascensión *nf* (a) climb (b) *(al trono)* accession

ascenso *nm* promotion; *(subida)* rise

ascensor *nm Br* lift, *US* elevator

asco *nm* disgust, repugnance; **me da a.** it makes me (feel) sick; **¡qué a.!** how disgusting *o* revolting!

ascua *nf* ember; *Fig* **en ascuas** on tenterhooks

Takes the masculine articles **el** and **un**.

aseado,-a *adj* tidy, neat

asear 1 *vt* to clean, to tidy up

2 asearse *upr* to wash, to get washed

asediar [43] *vt* to besiege

asedio *nm* siege

asegurado,-a *adj* (a) insured (b) *(indudable)* secure

asegurador,-a 1 *adj* insurance

2 *nm,f* insurer

asegurar 1 *vt* (a) to insure (b) *(garantizar)* **me aseguró que ...** he assured me that ...; **a. el éxito de un proyecto** to ensure the success of a project (c) *(cuerda)* to fasten

2 asegurarse *upr* (a) to make sure; **a. de que ...** to make sure that ... (b) *Seg* to insure oneself

asemejarse *upr* **a. a** to look like

asentado,-a *adj (establecido)* established, settled

asentamiento *nm* settlement

asentar [1] 1 *vt* **a. la cabeza** to settle down

2 asentarse *upr* (a) *(establecerse)* to settle down, to establish oneself (b) *(té, polvo)* to settle

asentimiento *nm* assent, consent

asentir [5] *vi* to assent, to agree; **a. con la cabeza** to nod

aseo *nm* (a) cleanliness, tidiness (b) **aseos** *o* **(cuarto de) a.** bathroom; *(retrete)* toilet

asequible *adj* affordable; *(comprensible)* easy to understand; *(alcanzable)* attainable

aserrín *nm* sawdust

asesinar *vt* to murder; *(rey, ministro)* to assassinate

asesinato *nm* murder; *(de rey, ministro)* assassination

asesino,-a 1 *adj* murderous

2 *nm,f* killer; *(hombre)* murderer; *(mujer)* murderess; *Pol* assassin

asesor,-a 1 *nm,f* adviser; **a. fiscal** tax adviser

2 *adj* advisory

asesoramiento *nm* (a) *(acción)* advising (b) *(consejo)* advice

asesorar 1 *vt* (a) to advise, to give (professional) advice to (b) *Com* to act as consultant to

2 asesorarse *upr* to consult

asesoría *nf* consultant's office

asestar *vt* to deal; **a. un golpe a algn** to deal sb a blow

aseverar *vt* to assert

asfalto *nm* asphalt

asfixia *nf* asphyxiation, suffocation

asfixiante *adj* asphyxiating, suffocating; *Fam* **hace un calor a.** it's stifling

asfixiar [43] *vt,* **asfixiarse** *upr* to asphyxiate, to suffocate

así *adv* (**a**) *(de esta manera)* like this *o* that, this way, thus; **ponlo a.** put it this way; **a. de grande/alto** this big/tall; **algo a.** something like this *o* that; **¿no es a.?** isn't that so *o* right?; **a. es la vida** such is life; **a. a. so-so; a. sin más,** *Am* **a. no más** *o* **nomás** just like that (**b**) **a las seis o a.** around six o'clock; **diez años o a.** ten years more or less (**c**) **a. como** as well as (**d**) **a. tenga que ...** *(aunque)* even if I have to ... (**e**) **aun a.** and despite that (**f**) **a. pues** so; **a. que ... so ...** (**g**) **a. que llegues** as soon as

Asia *n* Asia; **A. Menor** Asia Minor

asiático,-a *adj & nm,f* Asian

asidero *nm (asa)* handle; *Fig* pretext, excuse

asiduidad *nf* assiduity; **con a.** frequently, regularly

asiduo,-a 1 *adj* assiduous

  2 *nm,f* regular customer

asiento *nm* (**a**) seat; **a. trasero/delantero** front/back seat; **tome a.** take a seat (**b**) *(poso)* sediment (**c**) *Fin* entry

asignación *nf* (**a**) *(de dinero)* assignment, allocation (**b**) *(de puesto)* appointment (**c**) *(paga)* allowance

asignar *vt* (**a**) to assign, to allocate (**b**) *(nombrar)* to appoint

asignatura *nf* subject; **a. pendiente** failed subject

asilado,-a *nm,f* refugee

asilar *vt* to grant *o* give political asylum to

asilo *nm* asylum; **a. de ancianos** old people's home; *Pol* **a. político** political asylum

asimilación *nf* assimilation

asimilar *vt* to assimilate

asimismo *adv* also, as well

asir [46] *vt* to grasp, to seize

asistencia *nf* (**a**) *(presencia)* attendance; **falta de a.** absence (**b**) **a. médica/técnica** medical/technical assistance (**c**) *(público)* audience, public

asistenta *nf* charlady, cleaning lady

asistente 1 *adj* attending; **el público a.** the audience

  2 *nmf* (**a**) *(ayudante)* assistant; **a. social** social worker (**b**) **los asistentes** the public

asistido,-a *adj* assisted; **a. por ordenador** computer-assisted; *Aut* **dirección asistida** power steering

asistir 1 *vt* to assist, to help

  2 *vi* **a.** (**a**) to attend, to be present (at)

asma *nf* asthma

asno *nm* donkey, ass

asociación *nf* association

asociado,-a 1 *adj* associated

  2 *nm,f* associate, partner

asociar [43] 1 *vt* to associate

  2 asociarse *vpr* (**a**) to be associated (**b**) *Com* to become partners

asolar [2] *vt* to devastate, to destroy

asomar 1 *vt* to appear, to stick out; **asomó la cabeza por la ventana** he put his head out of the window

  2 *vi* to appear

  3 asomarse *vpr* (**a**) to lean out; **a. a la ventana** to lean out of the window (**b**) *(entrar)* to pop in; *(salir)* to pop out

asombrar 1 *vt* to amaze, to astonish

  2 asombrarse *vpr* to be astonished; **a. de algo** to be amazed at sth

asombro *nm* amazement, astonishment

asombroso,-a *adj* amazing, astonishing

asomo *nm* trace, hint

asonada *nf* putsch, uprising

asorocharse *vpr Andes* to get altitude sickness

aspa *nf* (**a**) *(de molino)* arm; *(de ventilador)* blade (**b**) *(cruz)* cross

aspaviento *nm* **hacer aspavientos** to wave one's arms about

aspecto *nm* (**a**) look, appearance (**b**) *(de un asunto)* aspect

aspereza *nf* roughness; *Fig* **limar asperezas** to smooth things over

áspero,-a *adj* rough; *Fig (carácter)* surly

aspersión *nf* sprinkling

aspersor *nm* sprinkler

aspiración *nf* (**a**) inhalation, breathing in (**b**) *(pretensión)* aspiration

aspiradora *nf* vacuum cleaner

aspirante *nmf* candidate, applicant

aspirar 1 *vt* (**a**) *(respirar)* to inhale, to breathe in (**b**) *Téc (absorber)* to suck in, to draw in

  2 *vi Fig* **a. a algo** to aspire after sth

aspirina *nf* aspirin

asquear *vt* to disgust

asquerosidad *nf* filthy *o* revolting thing; **¡que a.!** how revolting!

asqueroso,-a 1 *adj (sucio)* filthy; *(desagradable)* revolting, disgusting

  2 *nm,f* filthy *o* revolting person

asta *nf* (**a**) *(de bandera)* staff, pole; **a media a.** at half-mast (**b**) *Zool (cuerno)* horn

asterisco *nm* asterisk

astilla *nf* splinter

astillero *nm* shipyard

astral *adj* astral; **carta a.** birth chart

astringente *adj & nm* astringent

astro *nm* star

astrología *nf* astrology

astrólogo,-a *nm,f* astrologer

astronauta *nmf* astronaut

astronave *nf* spaceship

astronomía *nf* astronomy

astronómico,-a *adj* astronomical

astrónomo,-a *nm,f* astronomer

astucia *nf* shrewdness; *(artimaña)* ruse

asturiano,-a *adj & nm,f* Asturian

Asturias *n* Asturias

astuto,-a *adj* astute, shrewd

asumir *vt* to assume

asunción *nf* assumption

asunto *nm* (a) subject; **no es a. tuyo** it's none of your business (b) **Asuntos Exteriores** Foreign Affairs

asustar 1 *vt* to frighten, to scare

   2 asustarse *vpr* to be frightened, to be scared

atacante *nmf* attacker, assailant

atacar [44] *vt* to attack, to assault; *Fig* **me ataca los nervios** he gets on my nerves

atado,-a *adj* tied; *(ocupado)* tied up

atadura *nf Fig* hindrance

atajar *vi* to take a shortcut (**por** across *o* through)

atajo *nm* (a) shortcut (b) *(grupo)* bunch

atalaya *nf* watchtower

atañer *v impers* to concern, to have to do with; **eso no te atañe** that has nothing to do with you

ataque *nm* (a) attack, assault; **a. aéreo** air raid (b) *Med* fit; **a. cardíaco** *o* **al corazón** heart attack; **a. de nervios/tos** fit of hysterics/coughing

atar 1 *vt* (a) to tie; *Fig* **a. cabos** to put two and two together; *Fam* **loco de a.** as mad as a hatter (b) *Fig* to tie down

   2 atarse *vpr Fig* to get tied up; **átate los zapatos** do your shoes up

atardecer [33] 1 *v impers* to get *o* grow dark

   2 *nm* evening, dusk

atareado,-a *adj* busy

atascado,-a *adj* stuck

atascar [44] 1 *vt (bloquear)* to block, to obstruct

   2 atascarse *vpr* (a) *(bloquearse)* to become obstructed, to become blocked (b) *Fig (estancarse)* to get bogged down

atasco *nm* traffic jam

ataúd *nm* coffin

ataviarse [29] *vpr* to dress oneself up

atavío *nm* dress, attire

ate *nm Méx* quince jelly

atemorizar [40] *vt* to frighten, to scare

atemperar *vt* to moderate, to temper

Atenas *n* Athens

atención 1 *nf* attention; **llamar la a.** to attract attention; **prestar/poner a.** to pay attention (**a** to)

   2 *interj* attention!

atender [3] 1 *vt* to attend to; *(petición)* to agree to

   2 *vi (alumno)* to pay attention (**a** to)

atenerse [24] *vpr* (a) *(a reglas etc)* to abide (**a** by); **a. a las consecuencias** to bear the consequences (b) *(remitirse)* to go by; **me atengo a sus palabras** I'm going by what he said; **no saber a qué a.** not to know what to expect

atentado *nm* attack; **a. terrorista** terrorist attack

atentamente *adv* **le saluda a.** *(en carta)* yours sincerely *o* faithfully

atentar *vi* **a. o contra** to commit a crime against; **a. contra la vida de algn** to make an attempt on sb's life

atento,-a *adj* (a) attentive; **estar a. a** to be mindful *o* aware of (b) *(amable)* thoughtful, considerate; **atentos saludos de** *(en carta)* yours faithfully

atenuante 1 *adj* attenuating

   2 *nm Jur* extenuating circumstance

atenuar [30] *vt* (a) to attenuate; *Jur* to extenuate (b) *(importancia)* to lessen, to diminish

ateo,-a 1 *adj* atheistic

   2 *nm,f* atheist

aterciopelado,-a *adj* velvety; *(vino)* smooth

aterido,-a *adj* **a. de frío** stiff with cold, numb

aterrador,-a *adj* terrifying

aterrar 1 *vt* to terrify

   2 aterrarse *vpr* to be terrified

aterrizaje *nm Av* landing; **a. forzoso** forced landing

aterrizar [40] *vi* to land

aterrorizar [40] 1 *vt* to terrify; *Mil & Pol* to terrorize

   2 aterrorizarse *vpr* to be terrified

atesorar *vt* to accumulate; *(dinero)* to hoard

atestado¹ *nm Jur* affidavit, statement; **atestados** testimonials

atestado²,-a *adj* packed, crammed; **estaba a. de gente** it was full of people

atestar¹ *vt Jur* to testify

atestar² *vt (abarrotar)* to pack, to cram (**de** with)

atestiguar [45] *vt* (**a**)*Jur* to testify to (**b**) *Fig* to vouch for

atiborrar 1 *vt* to pack, to stuff (**de** with)

2 atiborrarse *vpr Fam* to stuff oneself (**de** with)

ático *nm* attic

atinado,-a *adj (juicioso)* sensible; *(pertinente)* pertinent

atinar *vi* to get it right; **a. a hacer algo** to succeed in doing sth; **a. al blanco** to hit the target; **atinó con la solución** he found the solution

atingencia *nf Am* connection; *(observación)* comment

atípico,-a *adj* atypical

atisbar *vt* to make out

atisbo *nm Fig* slight sign, inkling

atizar [40] *vt* (**a**) *(fuego)* to poke, to stoke (**b**) *Fig (rebelión)* to stir up; *(pasión)* to rouse, to excite

atlántico,-a 1 *adj* Atlantic

2 *nm* **el (océano) A.** the Atlantic (Ocean)

atlas *nm inv* atlas

atleta *nmf* athlete

atlético,-a *adj* athletic

atletismo *nm* athletics *sing*

atmósfera *nf* atmosphere

atmosférico,-a *adj* atmospheric

atole, atol *nm CAm, Méx* = drink made of corn meal

atolladero *nm* fix, jam; **estar en un a.** to be in a jam

atolondrado,-a *adj* stunned, bewildered; *(atontado)* stupid

atolondrar 1 *vt* to confuse, to bewilder

2 atolondrarse *vpr* to be confused, to bewildered

atómico,-a *adj* atomic

átomo *nm* atom

atónito,-a *adj* amazed, astonished

atontado,-a *adj* (**a**) *(tonto)* silly, foolish (**b**) *(aturdido)* bewildered, amazed

atontar 1 *vt* to confuse, to bewilder

2 atontarse *vpr* to be o get confused, to be bewildered

atorarse *vpr* (**a**) *(atragantarse)* to choke (**con** on) (**b**) *Am (atascarse)* to get stuck

atormentar 1 *vt* to torment

2 atormentarse *vpr* to torment oneself, to suffer agonies

atornillar *vt* to screw on

atorón *nm Méx* traffic jam

atorrante *adj CSur (holgazán)* lazy

atosigar [42] *vt* to harass

atracador,-a *nm,f (de banco)* (bank) robber; *(en la calle)* attacker, mugger

atracar [44] 1 *vt* to hold up; *(persona)* to rob

2 *vi Náut* to come alongside, to tie up

3 atracarse *vpr (de comida)* to stuff oneself (**de** with), to gorge oneself (**de** on)

atracción *nf* attraction; **parque de atracciones** funfair

atraco *nm* hold-up, robbery; **a. a mano armada** armed robbery

atracón *nm Fam* binge, blowout; **darse un a. de comer** to make a pig of oneself

atractivo,-a 1 *adj* attractive, appealing

2 *nm* attraction, appeal

atraer [25] *vt* to attract

atragantarse *vpr* to choke (**con** on), to swallow the wrong way; *Fig* **esa chica se me ha atragantado** I can't stand that girl

atraigo *indic pres de* atraer

atraje *pt indef de* atraer

atrancar [44] 1 *vt (puerta)* to bolt

2 atrancarse *vpr* to get stuck; *(al hablar, leer)* to get bogged down

atrapar *vt* to catch

atrás *adv* (**a**) *(lugar)* at the back, behind; **hacia/para a.** backwards; **puerta de a.** back o rear door; *Fig* **echarse a.** to back out (**b**) *(tiempo)* previously, in the past, ago; **un año a.** a year ago; **venir de muy a.** to go o date back a long time

atrasado,-a *adj* late, slow; *(pago)* overdue; *(reloj)* slow; *(país)* backward; *Prensa* **número a.** back number

atrasar 1 *vt* to put back

2 *vi (reloj)* to be slow

3 atrasarse *vpr* (**a**) to remain o stay behind, to lag behind (**b**) *(tren)* to be late

atraso *nm* (**a**) delay (**b**) *(de país)* backwardness (**c**) *Fin* **atrasos** arrears

atravesado,-a *adj (cruzado)* lying crosswise; *(persona)* difficult; **lo tengo a.** I can't stand him

atravesar [1] 1 *vt* (**a**) *(calle)* to cross (**b**) *(muro)* to pierce, to go through (**c**) *(poner a través)* to lay across, to put across, to put crosswise

2 atravesarse *vpr* to get in the way; *Fig* **se me ha atravesado Luis** I can't stand Luis

atrayente *adj* attractive

atreverse *vpr* to dare; **a. a hacer algo** to dare to do sth

atrevido,-a *adj* (**a**) *(osado)* daring, bold (**b**) *(insolente)* insolent, impudent (**c**) *(ropa etc)* daring, risqué

atrevimiento *nm* (**a**) *(osadía)* daring, audacity (**b**) *(insolencia)* insolence, impudence

atribuir [37] 1 *vt* to attribute, to ascribe

2 atribuirse *vpr* to assume

atribular vt to afflict
atributo nm attribute
atril nm music stand
atrochar vi to take a short cut
atrocidad nf atrocity
atrofiar [43] vt, **atrofiarse** vpr to atrophy
atropellado,-a adj hasty, impetuous
atropellar vt to knock down, to run over
atropello nm (**a**) Aut knocking down, running over (**b**) (abuso) abuse
atroz adj (**a**) (bárbaro) atrocious (**b**) Fam (hambre, frío) enormous, tremendous
ATS nmf (abr **ayudante técnico sanitario**) = qualified Spanish nurse
atuendo nm dress, attire
atún nm tuna, tunny
aturdido,-a adj stunned, dazed
aturdimiento nm confusion, bewilderment
aturdir vt (**a**) (con un golpe) to stun, to daze (**b**) (confundir) to bewilder, to confuse
aturrullar vt to confuse, to bewilder
atuve pt indef de **atenerse**
audacia nf audacity
audaz adj audacious, bold
audible adj audible
audición nf (**a**) hearing (**b**) Teatro audition
audiencia nf (**a**) (público) audience; TV & Rad **horas de máxima a.** prime time; **índice de a.** viewing figures, ratings (**b**) (entrevista) audience (**c**) Jur court hearing
audiovisual adj audio-visual
auditivo,-a 1 adj auditory; **comprensión auditiva** listening comprehension
2 nm receiver
auditor nm Fin auditor
auditorio nm (**a**) (público) audience (**b**) (sala) auditorium, hall
auge nm peak; Econ boom; Fig **estar en a.** to be thriving o booming
augurar vt to augur
augurio nm omen
aula nf (en colegio) classroom; Univ lecture room; **a. magna** amphitheatre

Takes the masculine articles **el** and **un**.

aulaga nf gorse
aullar vt to howl, to yell
aullido nm howl, yell
aumentar 1 vt to increase; (precios) to put up; (producción) to step up; Fot to enlarge; Opt to magnify
2 vi (precios) to go up, to rise; (valor) to appreciate

3 aumentarse vpr to increase, to be on the increase
aumento nm increase; Opt magnification; **a. de precios** rise in prices; **ir en a.** to be on the increase
aun adv even; **a. así** even so, even then; **a. más** even more
aún adv still; (en negativas) yet; **a. está aquí** he's still here; **ella no ha venido a.** she hasn't come yet
aunar vt to unite, to join
aunque conj although, though; (enfático) even if, even though; **a. no vengas** even if you don't come
aúpa interj up!, get up!
aura nf aura

Takes the masculine articles **el** and **un**.

aureola nf halo
auricular nm (**a**) Tel receiver (**b**) **auriculares** earphones, headphones
aurora nf daybreak, dawn
auscultar vt to sound (with a stethoscope)
ausencia nf absence
ausentarse vpr to leave
ausente 1 adj absent
2 nmf absentee
ausentismo nm Am absenteeism
austeridad nf austerity
austero,-a adj austere
austral 1 adj southern
2 nm Fin = former standard monetary unit of Argentina
Australia n Australia
australiano,-a adj & nm,f Australian
Austria n Austria
austríaco,-a adj & nm,f Austrian
autenticidad nf authenticity
auténtico,-a adj authentic
autentificar [44] vt to authenticate
autismo nm autism
autista adj autistic
auto¹ nm RP (coche) car
auto² nm Jur decree, writ; **autos** (pleito) papers, documents
autoadhesivo,-a adj self-adhesive
autobiografía nf autobiography
autobiográfico,-a adj autobiographical
autobombo nm Fam self-praise, blowing one's own trumpet
autobús nm bus
autocar nm coach
autocrítica nf self-criticism
autóctono,-a adj indigenous
autodefensa nf self-defence
autodisciplina nf self-discipline
autoedición nf Informát desktop publishing

autoescuela *nf* driving school, school of motoring

autogobierno *nm* self-government

autógrafo *nm* autograph

autómata *nm* automaton

automático,-a *adj* automatic

automatización *nf* automation

automatizar [40] *vt* to automate

automotor,-a 1 *adj* self-propelled
2 *nm Ferroc* diesel train

automóvil *nm* car

automovilismo *nm* motoring

automovilista *nmf* motorist

automovilístico,-a *adj* car; **accidente a.** car accident

autonomía *nf* (a) autonomy (b) *(región)* autonomous region

autonómico,-a *adj* autonomous, self-governing; **elecciones autonómicas** elections for the autonomous parliament; **televisión autonómica** regional television

autónomo,-a *adj* autonomous

autopista *nf* motorway; *Informát* **autopista de la información** information superhighway

autopsia *nf* autopsy, postmortem

autor,-a *nm,f (hombre)* author; *(mujer)* authoress; *(de crimen)* perpetrator

autoridad *nf* authority

autoritario,-a *adj* authoritarian

autorizado,-a *adj* authoritative, official

autorizar [40] *vt* to authorize

autorretrato *nm* self-portrait

autoservicio *nm* self-service; *(supermercado)* supermarket

autostop *nm* hitch-hiking; **hacer a.** to hitch-hike

autostopista *nmf* hitch-hiker

autosuficiencia *nf* self-sufficiency

autosuficiente *adj* self-sufficient

auxiliar [43] **1** *adj & nmf* auxiliary, assistant
2 *vt* to help, to assist

auxilio *nm* help, assistance; **primeros auxilios** first aid

auyama *nf Carib, Col* pumpkin

Av. *(abr Avenida)* Ave

aval *nm Com & Fin* endorsement

avalancha *nf* avalanche

avalar *vt* to guarantee, to endorse

avance *nm* (a) advance (b) *Fin* advance payment (c) *TV* **a. informativo** news summary, *US* news in brief

avanzado,-a *adj* advanced; **de avanzada edad** advanced in years

avanzar [40] *vt* to advance

avaricia *nf* avarice

avaricioso,-a *adj* greedy

avaro,-a 1 *adj* avaricious, miserly
2 *nm,f* miser

avasallar *vt* to subdue

avatares *nmpl* quirks

Avda. = **Av.**

AVE *nf (abr Alta Velocidad Española)* High Speed Train

ave *nf* bird; **aves de corral** poultry; **a. de rapiña** bird of prey

> Takes the masculine articles **el** and **un**.

avecinarse *vpr* to approach, to come near

avellana *nf* hazelnut

avellano *nm* hazelnut tree

avena *nf* oats

avendré *indic fut de* avenir

avenencia *nf* compromise

avengo *indic pres de* avenir

avenida *nf* avenue

avenido,-a *adj* **bien/mal avenidos** on good/bad terms

avenir [27] **1** *vt* to reconcile
2 **avenirse** *vpr* to be on good terms; *(consentir)* to agree (**en** to)

aventajado,-a *adj (destacado)* outstanding, exceptional; *(en cabeza)* in the lead

aventajar *vt* (a) to be ahead o in front of (**a** of) (b) *(superar)* to surpass, to outdo

aventar [1] **1** *vt* (a) *Agr* to winnow (b) *(el fuego)* to fan (c) *Andes, CAm, Méx (tirar)* to throw (d) *CAm, Méx, Perú (empujar)* to push, to shove
2 **aventarse** *vpr Méx* (a) *(tirarse)* to throw oneself (b) *(atreverse)* **a. a hacer algo** to dare to do sth

aventón *nm Méx* **dar a. a algn** to give sb a ride; **pedir a.** to hitch a ride

aventura *nf* (a) adventure (b) *(amorosa)* (love) affair

aventurado,-a *adj* risky

aventurarse *vpr* to venture

aventurero,-a *adj* adventurous

avergonzado,-a *adj* ashamed

avergonzar [63] **1** *vt* to shame
2 **avergonzarse** *vpr* to be ashamed (**de** of)

avería *nf* breakdown

averiado,-a *adj* out of order; *(coche)* broken down

averiar [29] **1** *vt* to break
2 **averiarse** *vpr (estropearse)* to malfunction, to go wrong; *(coche)* to break down

averiguación *nf* enquiry

averiguar [45] *vt* to ascertain

aversión *nf* aversion

avestruz *nm* ostrich

aviación *nf* (**a**) aviation; **accidente de a.** plane crash; **a. civil** civil aviation (**b**) *Mil* air force

aviador,-a *nm,f* aviator, flier; *Mil (piloto)* air force pilot

aviar [29] *vt (preparar)* to prepare, to get ready

avícola *adj* poultry

avicultura *nf* aviculture; *(de aves de corral)* poultry keeping

avidez *nf* avidity, eagerness

ávido,-a *adj* avid; **a. de** eager for

avinagrado,-a *adj* vinegary, sour; *Fig* sour

avinagrarse *vpr* to turn sour; *Fig* to become sour o bitter

avión¹ *nm* aircraft, *Br* aeroplane, *US* airplane; **viajar en a.** to fly, to go by plane; **por a.** *(en carta)* airmail

avión² *nm Orn* martin

avioneta *nf* light aircraft o plane

avíos *nmpl Culin* ingredients

avisar *vt* (**a**) *(informar)* to inform; **avísame cuando hayas acabado** let me know when you finish (**b**) *(advertir)* to warn; **ya te avisé** I warned you (**c**) *(llamar)* to call for; **a. a la policía** to notify the police; **a. al médico** to send for the doctor

aviso *nm* (**a**) notice; *(advertencia)* warning; *(nota)* note; **hasta nuevo a.** until further notice; **sin previo a.** without notice (**b**) **estar sobre a.** to know what's going on, to be in on it (**c**) *Am (anuncio)* advertisement; **a. clasificado** classified advertisement

avispa *nf* wasp

avispado,-a *adj Fam* quick-witted

avispero *nm (nido)* wasps' nest

avistar *vt* to see, to sight

avituallamiento *nm* provisioning

avivar *vt (fuego)* to stoke (up); *(pasión)* to intensify; *(paso)* to quicken

avizor,-a *adj* **estar ojo a.** to be on the alert o on the lookout

axila *nf* armpit, axilla

axioma *nm* axiom

ay *interj (dolor)* ouch!

aya *nf (niñera)* nanny

Takes the masculine articles **el** and **un**.

ayer 1 *adv* yesterday; **a. por la mañana/por la tarde** yesterday morning/afternoon; **a. por la noche** last night; **antes de a.** the day before yesterday

2 *nm* **el a.** yesteryear

ayuda *nf* help, assistance; **ir en a. de algn** to come to sb's assistance; **a. al desarrollo** development aid

ayudante *nmf* assistant; *Med* **a. técnico-sanitario** nurse

ayudar 1 *vt* to help; **¿en qué puedo ayudarle?** (how) can I help you?

2 ayudarse *vpr* (**a**) *(unos a otros)* to help (**b**) **a. de** to use, to make use of

ayunar *vi* to fast

ayunas *nfpl* **en a.** without having eaten breakfast

ayuno *nm* fasting; **guardar/hacer a.** to fast

ayuntamiento *nm (institución)* town council; *(edificio)* town hall

azabache *nm* jet; **negro a.** jet black

azada *nf* hoe

azafata *nf* (**a**) *Av* air hostess (**b**) *(de congresos)* stewardess; *(de concurso)* hostess

azafate *nm Andes (bandeja)* tray

azafrán *nm* saffron

azahar *nm (del naranjo)* orange blossom; *(del limonero)* lemon blossom

azar *nm* chance; **por a.** by chance; **al a.** at random; **juegos de a.** games of chance; **los azares de la vida** the ups and downs of life

azaroso,-a *adj* hazardous, dangerous

azogue *nm* mercury, quicksilver

azorado,-a *adj* embarrassed

azorar 1 *vt* to embarrass

2 azorarse *vpr* to be embarrassed

Azores *nfpl* **las (Islas) A.** the Azores

azotar *vt* to beat; *(con látigo)* to whip, to flog; *Fig* to scourge

azote *nm* (**a**) *(golpe)* smacking; *(latigazo)* lash, stroke (of the whip) (**b**) *Fig* scourge

azotea *nf* flat roof

azteca *adj & nmf* Aztec

azúcar *nm o nf* sugar; **a. blanco** refined sugar; **a. moreno** brown sugar

azucarado,-a *adj* sweetened

azucarero,-a 1 *nm o nf* sugar bowl

2 *adj* sugar

azucena *nf* white lily

azufre *nm* sulphur

azul *adj & nm* blue; **a. celeste** sky blue; **a. marino** navy blue; **a. turquesa** turquoise; **sangre a.** blue blood

azulado,-a *adj* bluish

azulejo *nm (glazed)* tile

azuzar [40] *vt* **a. los perros a algn** to set the dogs on sb

B

B, b [be] *nf (la letra)* B, b

baba *nf* dribble; *Fig* **se le caía la b.** he was delighted

babear *vi (niño)* to dribble; *(adulto, animal)* to slobber

babel *nm o nf* bedlam

babero *nm* bib

Babia *n Fig* **estar en B.** to be daydreaming

babor *nm Náut* port, port side

babosa *nf* slug

babosada *nf CAm, Méx Fam (disparate)* daft thing

baboso,-a 1 *adj* **(a)** *Fam (despreciable)* slimy **(b)** *Am Fam (tonto)* daft, stupid
2 *nm,f Fam* **(a)** *(persona despreciable)* creep **(b)** *Am (tonto)* twit, idiot

babucha *nf* slipper

baca *nf Aut* roof rack

bacalao *nm (pez)* cod

bache *nm* **(a)** *(en carretera)* pot hole **(b)** *Av* air pocket **(c)** *Fig* bad patch; **pasar un b.** to go through a bad patch

bachillerato *nm* = academically orientated Spanish secondary school course for pupils aged 14-17

bacilo *nm* bacillus

bacon *nm* bacon

bacteria *nf* bacterium; **bacterias** bacteria

bacteriológico,-a *adj* bacteriological; **guerra bacteriológica** germ warfare

báculo *nm* walking stick; *(de obispo)* crosier

badén *nm Aut* bump

bádminton *nm* badminton

bafle *nm* loudspeaker

bagaje *nm* baggage

bagatela *nf (baratija)* knick-knack; *Fig* trifle

Bagdad *n* Baghdad

Bahamas *npl* **las (Islas) B.** the Bahamas

bahía *nf* bay

baila(d)or,-a *nm,f* flamenco dancer

bailar *vt & vi* to dance; *Fig* **b. al son que le tocan** to toe the line; *Fam* **¡que me quiten lo baila(d)o!** but at least I had a good time!

bailarín,-ina *nm,f* dancer; *(clásico)* ballet dancer

baile *nm* **(a)** *(danza)* dance **(b)** *(fiesta popular)* dance; *(formal)* ball; **b. de disfraces** fancy dress ball

baja *nf* **(a)** *(descenso)* drop, fall; *Fin* **jugar a la b.** to bear **(b)** *Mil* loss, casualty **(c)** **dar de b. a algn** *(despedir)* to lay sb off; **darse de b.** *(por enfermedad)* to take sick leave; *(de un club)* to resign **(de** from), to drop out **(de** of)

bajada *nf* **(a)** *(descenso)* descent **(b)** *(cuesta)* slope **(c)** **b. de bandera** *(de taxi)* minimum fare

bajamar *nf* low tide

bajar 1 *vt* **(a)** *(a)* to come/go down; **b. la escalera** to come/go downstairs **(b)** *(descender)* to bring/get/take down; *(volumen)* to turn down; *(voz, telón)* to lower; *(precios etc)* to reduce, to cut; *(persiana)* to let down; *(cabeza)* to bow o lower
2 *vi* **(a)** to go/come down **(b)** *(apearse)* to get off; *(de un coche)* to get out **(de** of) **(c)** *(disminuir)* to fall, to drop
3 bajarse *vpr* **(a)** to come/go down **(b)** *(apearse)* to get off; *(de un coche)* to get out **(de** of)

bajativo *nm Andes, RP (licor)* digestive liqueur; *(tisana)* herbal tea

bajeza *nf* despicable action

bajial *nm Perú* lowland

bajinis: • **por lo bajinis** *loc adv Fam* on the sly

bajío *nm* **(a)** sandbank **(b)** *(terreno bajo)* lowland

bajista 1 *adj Fin* bearish; **tendencia b.** downward trend
2 *nmf* **(a)** *Fin* bear **(b)** *Mús* bass guitarist

bajo,-a 1 *adj* **(a)** low; *(persona)* short; *(sonido)* faint, soft; **en voz baja** in a low voice; **planta baja** ground floor; **de baja calidad** of poor quality; **la clase baja** the lower class **(b)** *Fig (vil)* base, contemptible
2 *nm* **(a)** *Mús* bass **(b)** *(planta baja)* ground floor
3 *adv* low; **hablar b.** to speak quietly; *Fig* **por lo b.** on the sly
4 *prep* **(a)** *(lugar)* under, underneath; **b. tierra** underground; **b. la lluvia** in the rain **(b)** *Pol & Hist* under; **b. la República** under the Republic **(c)** **b. cero** *(temperatura)*

below zero (**d**) *Jur* under; **b. juramento** under oath; **b. pena de muerte** on pain of death; **b. fianza** on bail

bajón *nm* (**a**) *(bajada)* sharp fall, decline (**b**) *Com* slump (**c**) *(de salud)* relapse, deterioration

bajorrelieve *nm* bas-relief

bajura *nf* **pesca de b.** coastal fishing

bala *nf* bullet; *Fig* **como una b.** like a shot

balacear *vt Am (tirotear)* to shoot

balacera *nf Am* shootout

balada *nf* ballad

baladí *adj* (*pl* **baladíes**) trivial

balance *nm* (**a**) *Fin* balance; *(declaración)* balance sheet; *Fig* **hacer b. de una situación** to take stock of a situation (**b**) *(resultado)* outcome

balancear 1 *vt* to rock

2 balancearse *vpr (en mecedora)* to rock; *(en columpio)* to swing

balanceo *nm* rocking, swinging; *(de barco, avión)* rolling; *Am Aut* wheel balance

balanza *nf* scales; *Fig* **estar en la b.** to be in the balance *o* in danger; **b. comercial** balance of trade; **b. de pagos** balance of payments

balar *vi* to bleat

balaustrada *nf* balustrade, railing

balazo *nm* (**a**) *(disparo)* shot; **matar a algn de un b.** to shoot sb dead (**b**) *(herida)* bullet wound

balboa *nm Fin* = standard monetary unit of Panama

balbucear *vi (adulto)* to stutter, stammer; *(niño)* to babble

balbuceo *nm (de adulto)* stuttering, stammering; *(de niño)* babbling

balbucir *vi defect* = **balbucear**

Balcanes *nmpl* **los B.** the Balkans

balcón *nm* balcony

baldado,-a *adj Fam* shattered

baldar *vt* to cripple, to maim

balde¹ *nm* pail, bucket

balde² *loc adv* (**a**) **de b.** *(gratis)* free (**b**) **en b.** *(en vano)* in vain

baldío,-a *adj (terreno)* uncultivated, waste; *(esfuerzo)* vain, useless

baldosa *nf* (ceramic) floor tile; *(para pavimentar)* flagstone, paving stone

balear¹ 1 *adj* Balearic

2 *nmf* person from the Balearic Islands

balear² *vt Am (disparar)* to shoot

Baleares *npl* **las (Islas) B.** the Balearic Islands

baleo *nm Am* shootout

balido *nm* bleating, bleat

balística *nf* ballistics *sing*

balístico,-a *adj* ballistic

baliza *nf* (**a**) *Náut* buoy (**b**) *Av* beacon

ballena *nf* whale

ballet *nm* ballet

balneario *nm* spa, health resort

balompié *nm* football

balón *nm* (**a**) ball, football; *Fig* **b. de oxígeno** boost (**b**) *(bombona)* gas cylinder

baloncesto *nm* basketball

balonmano *nm* handball

balonvolea *nm* volleyball

balsa *nf* (**a**) *Náut* raft (**b**) *Fig* **como una b. de aceite** very quiet

bálsamo *nm* balsam, balm

balsero,-a *nm,f (de Cuba)* = refugee fleeing Cuba on a raft

Báltico *nm* **el (Mar) B.** the Baltic (Sea)

baluarte *nm Fig* stronghold

bambas® *nfpl* trainers

bambolear *vi*, **bambolearse** *vpr* to swing; *(persona, árbol)* to sway; *(mesa, silla)* to wobble

bambú *nm* (*pl* **bambúes**) bamboo

banal *adj* banal, trivial

banalidad *nf* triviality, banality

banana *nf* banana

banano *nm (árbol)* banana tree; *Col (fruto)* banana

banca *nf* (**a**) *(asiento)* bench (**b**) *Com & Fin* (the) banks; *(actividad)* banking; **b. electrónica** electronic banking (**c**) *(en juegos)* bank

bancario,-a *adj* banking

bancarrota *nf Fin* bankruptcy; **estar en b.** to be bankrupt

banco *nm* (**a**) bench (**b**) *Com & Fin* bank (**c**) **b. de arena** sandbank (**d**) *(de peces)* shoal, school (**e**) *Geol* layer

banda *nf* (**a**) *Mús* band (**b**) *Cin* **b. sonora** sound track (**c**) *(de pájaros)* flock (**d**) *(cinta)* sash (**e**) *(lado)* side; *Ftb* **línea de b.** touchline; **saque de b.** throw-in

bandada *nf* flock

bandazo *nm* **dar bandazos** to lurch

bandeja *nf* tray; *Fig* **servir algo a algn en b.** to hand sth to sb on a plate

bandera *nf* flag; **b. azul** *(en playa)* blue flag

banderín *nf* pennant, small flag

bandido *nm* bandit, outlaw

bando¹ *nm* (**a**) *Jur (edicto)* edict, proclamation (**b**) **bandos** banns

bando² *nm* faction, side; **pasarse al otro b.** to go over to the other side, to change allegiances

bandolero *nm* bandit, outlaw

banquero,-a *nm,f* banker

banqueta *nf* (**a**) *(asiento)* stool (**b**) *(para*

los pies) footstool (**c**) *CAm, Méx (acera) Br*
pavement, *US* sidewalk

banquete *nm* banquet, feast; **b. de bo-das** wedding reception

banquillo *nm* (**a**) *Jur* dock (**b**) *Dep*
bench

banquina *nf RP (arcén)* verge; *(de auto-pista) Br* hard shoulder, *US* shoulder

bañadera *nf* (**a**) *Arg (bañera)* bath (**b**) *RP
(vehículo)* minibus

bañado *nm Bol, RP (terreno)* marshy area

bañador *nm (de mujer)* bathing *o*
swimming costume; *(de hombre)* swim-ming trunks

bañar 1 *vt* (**a**) to bath (**b**) *(cubrir)* to coat,
to cover; **b. en oro** to goldplate
2 bañarse *vpr (en baño)* to have *o* take a
bath; *(en mar, piscina)* to go for a swim;
Am (ducharse) to have a shower

bañera *nf* bath, bathtub

bañista *nmf* bather, swimmer

baño *nm* (**a**) bath; **tomar un b.** to have *o*
take a bath; *Fig* **darse un b. de sol** to
sunbathe; **b. de sangre** bloodbath (**b**)
(de oro etc) coat; *(de chocolate etc)* coat-ing, covering (**c**) *(cuarto de baño)* bath-room; *(lavabo)* toilet

bar *nm* bar, pub

barahúnda *nf* din, uproar

baraja *nf* pack, deck

barajar *vt (cartas)* to shuffle; *Fig (nom-bres, cifras)* to juggle with

baranda, barandilla *nf (de escalera)*
handrail, banister; *(de balcón)* handrail

baratija *nf* trinket, knick-knack

baratillo *nm* flea market

barato,-a 1 *adj* cheap
2 *adv* cheaply

baraúnda *nf* din, uproar

barba *nf* (**a**) *Anat* chin (**b**) *(pelo)* beard;
Fig **100 pesetas por b.** 100 pesetas a head

barbacoa *nf* barbecue

barbaridad *nf* (**a**) atrocity (**b**) *(dispa-rate)* piece of nonsense; **no digas barba-ridades** don't talk nonsense (**c**) **una b.** a
lot; **costar una b.** to cost a fortune

barbarie *nf* savagery, cruelty

bárbaro,-a 1 *adj* (**a**) *Hist* barbarian (**b**)
(cruel) barbaric, barbarous (**c**) *Fam
(enorme)* massive (**d**) *RP Fam (estupen-do)* tremendous, terrific
2 *nm,f Hist* barbarian

barbecho *nm* fallow land; **dejar en b.** to
leave fallow

barbería *nf* barber's (shop)

barbero *nm* barber

barbilla *nf* chin

barbitúrico *nm* barbiturate

barbudo,-a *adj* with a heavy beard

barca *nf* small boat

barcaza *nf* lighter

barcelonés,-esa 1 *adj* of/from Barcelona
2 *nm,f* person from Barcelona

barco *nm* boat, ship; **b. de pasajeros** liner;
b. de vapor steamer

baremo *nm* scale

barítono *nm* baritone

barlovento *nm* windward

barman *nm* barman

barniz *nm* (**a**) *(en madera)* varnish; *(en
cerámica)* glaze (**b**) *Fig* veneer

barnizar [40] *vt (madera)* to varnish;
(cerámica) to glaze

barómetro *nm* barometer

barón *nm* baron

baronesa *nf* baroness

barquero,-a *nm,f (hombre)* boatman;
(mujer) boatwoman

barquillo *nm* wafer

barra *nf* (**a**) bar; **b. de pan** French loaf,
baguette; **b. de labios** lipstick (**b**) *(mos-trador)* bar; **b. americana** = bar where
hostesses chat with clients (**c**) *Dep* **b. fija**
horizontal bar; **barras paralelas** parallel
bars (**d**) *Andes, RP Fam (grupo de amigos)*
gang, group of friends; **b. brava** = group
of violent soccer supporters

barraca *nf* (**a**) *(caseta)* shack, hut (**b**) *(en
Valencia y Murcia)* thatched farmhouse

barracón *nm Mil* prefabricated hut

barranco *nm (despeñadero)* cliff, preci-pice; *(torrentera)* gully, ravine

barranquismo *nm Dep* canyoning

barrena *nf* twist drill

barrenar *vt Téc* to drill

barrendero,-a *nm,f* sweeper, street
sweeper

barreno *nm* (**a**) *(taladro)* large drill (**b**)
Min charge

barreño *nm* tub

barrer 1 *vt* to sweep
2 *vi (en elecciones)* to win by a landslide

barrera *nf* barrier

barriada *nf* (**a**) *(barrio popular)* neigh-bourhood, area (**b**) *Am (barrio de chabo-las)* shanty town

barricada *nf* barricade

barrida *nf* landslide victory

barriga *nf* belly; *Fam* tummy

barrigón,-ona, barrigudo,-a *adj* pot-bellied

barril *nm* barrel; **cerveza de b.** draught
beer

barrillo *nm* pimple, spot

barrio *nm* area, district; **del b.** local; **el
B. Gótico** the Gothic Quarter; **b. chino**

red-light district; **barrios bajos** slums

barrizal *nm* mire, quagmire

barro *nm* (a) *(lodo)* mud (b) *(arcilla)* clay; **objetos de b.** earthenware

barroco,-a *adj* baroque

barruntar *vt (sospechar)* to suspect; *(presentir)* to have a feeling

barrunto *nm (presentimiento)* feeling, presentiment; *(sospecha)* suspicion

bartola: • **a la bartola** *loc adv Fam* **tenderse** o **tumbarse a la b.** to laze around, to idle away one's time

bártulos *nmpl Fam* things, bits and pieces

barullo *nm (alboroto)* row, din; *(confusión)* confusion

basar **1** *vt* to base (**en** on)

　2 basarse *vpr (teoría, película)* **b. en** to be based on; **¿en qué te basas para decir eso?** what grounds do you have for saying that?

basca *nf Fam* people, crowd

báscula *nf* scales; *(para camiones)* weighbridge

bascular *vi* to tilt

base *nf* (a) base; **sueldo b.** minimum wage; *Informát* **b. de datos** database (b) *(de argumento, teoría)* basis; **en b. a** on the basis of; **a b. de estudiar** by studying; **a b. de productos naturales** using natural products (c) *(de partido)* grass roots; **miembro de b.** rank and file member (d) *(nociones)* grounding

básico,-a *adj* basic

basílica *nf* basilica

básquet *nm* basketball

bastante **1** *adj* (a) *(suficiente)* enough; **b. tiempo/comida** enough time/food; **bastantes platos** enough plates (b) *(abundante)* quite a lot of; **hace b. calor/frío** it's quite hot/cold; **bastantes amigos** quite a lot of friends

　2 *adv* (a) *(suficiente)* enough; **con eso hay b.** that is enough; **no soy lo b. rico (como) para …** I am not rich enough to … (b) *(considerablemente)* fairly, quite; **me gusta b.** I quite like it; **vamos b. al cine** we go to the cinema quite o fairly often

bastar **1** *vi* to be sufficient o enough, to suffice; **basta con tres** three will be enough; **¡basta de tonterías!** enough of this nonsense!; **basta con tocarlo para que se abra** you only have to touch it and it opens; **¡basta (ya)!** that's enough!, that will do!

　2 bastarse *vpr* **b. a sí mismo** to be self-sufficient, to rely only on oneself

bastardilla *nf Impr* italics

bastardo,-a *adj & nm,f* bastard

bastidor *nm* (a) frame (b) *Teatro* **bastidores** wings; *Fig* **entre bastidores** behind the scenes

bastión *nm* bastion

basto,-a *adj (cosa)* rough, coarse; *(persona)* coarse, uncouth

bastón *nm* stick, walking stick

bastos *nmpl Naipes* ≃ clubs

basura *nf Br* rubbish, *US* garbage, *US* trash

basurero *nm* (a) *(persona) Br* dustman, *US* garbage man (b) *(lugar) Br* rubbish tip o dump, *US* garbage dump

bata *nf (para casa)* dressing gown; *(de médico etc)* white coat; *(de científico)* lab coat

batacazo *nm* (a) crash, bang (b) *CSur Fam (triunfo inesperado)* surprise victory;

batalla *nf* battle; **librar b.** to do o join battle; **b. campal** pitched battle

batallar *vi* to fight, quarrel

batallón *nm* battalion

batata *nf* sweet potato

batatazo *nm Am* = batacazo

bate *nm Dep* bat; **b. de béisbol** baseball bat

batear **1** *vi* to bat

　2 *vt* to hit

batería **1** *nf* (a) battery (b) *Mús* drums (c) **b. de cocina** pots and pans, set of pans

　2 *nmf* drummer

batiburrillo *nm* jumble, mess

batida *nf* (a) *(de la policía)* raid (b) *(en caza)* beat

batido,-a **1** *adj* (a) *Culin* whipped (b) *Dep* **tierra batida** clay

　2 *nm* milk shake

batidora *nf (eléctrica)* mixer

batiente *adj* **reírse a mandíbula b.** to laugh one's head off

batín *nm* short dressing gown

batir **1** *vt* (a) to beat (b) *(huevo)* to beat; *(nata)* to whip, to whisk (c) *(récord)* to break (d) *(en caza)* to beat

　2 batirse *vpr* to fight

batuta *nf Mús* baton; *Fig* **llevar la b.** to be in charge

baúl *nm* (a) *(cofre)* trunk (b) *RP (maletero) Br* boot, *US* trunk

bautismo *nm* baptism, christening

bautizar [40] *vt* to baptize, to christen; *(vino)* to water down

bautizo *nm* baptism, christening

Baviera *n* Bavaria

baya *nf* berry

bayeta *nf* floorcloth

bayo,-a *adj* whitish yellow

bayoneta *nf* bayonet

baza *nf* trick; *Fig* **meter b.** to butt in

bazar *nm* bazaar

bazo *nm* spleen

bazofia *nf* rubbish

be *nf (letra)* b; *Am* **be baja** *o* **corta** v *(to distinguish from "b")*; *Am* **be alta** *o* **grande** *o* **larga** b *(to distinguish from "v")*

beatería *nf* sanctimoniousness

beato,-a *adj (piadoso)* devout; *Pey* prudish, sanctimonious

bebe,-a *nm,f Andes, RP* baby

bebé *nm* baby; **b. probeta** test-tube baby

bebedero *nm* drinking trough, water trough

bebedor,-a *nm,f* (hard o heavy) drinker

beber *vt & vi* to drink

bebible *adj* drinkable

bebida *nf* drink; **darse a la b.** to take to drink

bebido,-a *adj* drunk

beca *nf* grant

becar [44] *vt* to award a grant to

becario,-a *nm,f* grant holder

becerro *nm* calf

bechamel *nf* bechamel; **salsa b.** bechamel sauce, white sauce

becuadro *nm Mús* natural sign

bedel *nm* beadle

begonia *nf* begonia

beige *adj & nm inv* beige

béisbol *n* baseball

bejuco *nm (en América)* liana; *(en Asia)* rattan

Belén *n* Bethlehem

belén *nm* nativity scene, crib

belga *adj & nmf* Belgian

Bélgica *n* Belgium

Belgrado *n* Belgrade

Belice *n* Belize

bélico,-a *adj* warlike, bellicose; *(preparativos etc)* war; **material b.** armaments

belicoso,-a *adj* warlike, bellicose; *(agresivo)* aggressive

beligerancia *nf* belligerence

beligerante *adj* belligerent; **los países beligerantes** the countries at war

bellaco,-a 1 *adj* wicked, roguish

   2 *nm,f* scoundrel, rogue

belleza *nf* beauty

bello,-a *adj* beautiful

bellota *nf Bot* acorn; *Fig* **animal de b.** blockhead

bemol 1 *adj Mús* flat

   2 *nm* **esto tiene bemoles** this is a tough one

bencina *nf Chile (gasolina) Br* petrol, *US* gas

bencinera *nf Chile Br* petrol station, *US* gas station

bendecir [12] *vt* to bless; **b. la mesa** to say grace; **¡Dios te bendiga!** God bless you!

bendición *nf* blessing

bendito,-a 1 *adj* blessed; *(maldito)* damned

   2 *nm,f (bonachón)* good sort, kind soul; *(tontorrón)* simple soul

beneficencia *nf* beneficence, charity

beneficiado,-a *adj* favoured; **salir b. de algo** to do well out of sth

beneficiar [43] 1 *vt* to benefit

   2 beneficiarse *vpr* **b. de** *o* **con algo** to profit from *o* by sth

beneficiario,-a *nm,f* beneficiary; **margen b.** profit margin

beneficio *nm* (a) *Com & Fin* profit (**b**) *(bien)* benefit; **en b. propio** in one's own interest; **un concierto a b. de ...** a concert in aid of ...

beneficioso,-a *adj* beneficial

benéfico,-a *adj* charitable

benemérita *nf* **la B.** the Spanish Civil Guard

beneplácito *nm Fml* approval, consent

benevolencia *nf* benevolence

benevolente, benévolo,-a *adj* benevolent

bengala *nf* flare

benigno,-a *adj (persona)* gentle, benign; *(clima)* mild; *(tumor)* benign

benjamín,-ina *nm,f* youngest child

beodo,-a *adj* drunk

berberecho *nm* (common) cockle

berbiquí *nm Téc* drill

berenjena *nf Br* aubergine, *US* eggplant

Berlín *n* Berlin

berlina *nf (coche)* saloon; *(carruaje)* sedan

berlinés,-esa 1 *adj* of/from Berlin

   2 *nm,f* Berliner

berma *nf Andes (arcén)* verge; *(de autopista) Br* hard shoulder, *US* shoulder

bermejo,-a *adj* reddish

bermellón *nm* vermilion

Bermudas 1 *nfpl* **las (Islas) B.** Bermuda

   2 *nmpl* **bermudas** *(prenda)* Bermuda shorts

Berna *n* Bern

berrear *vi* to bellow, low

berrido *nm* bellowing, lowing

berrinche *nm Fam* rage, tantrum

berro *nm* cress, watercress

berza *nf* cabbage

besar 1 *vt* to kiss

   2 besarse *vpr* to kiss

beso *nm* kiss

bestia 1 *nf* beast, animal; **b. de carga** beast of burden
  2 *nmf Fam Fig* brute, beast
  3 *adj Fig* brutish, boorish; **a lo b.** rudely

bestial *adj* bestial; *Fam (enorme)* huge, tremendous; *(extraordinario)* fantastic, terrific

bestialidad *nf* (a) *Fam (estupidez)* stupidity (b) *(crueldad)* act of cruelty (c) *Fam* **una b. de** tons of, stacks of

best-seller *nm* best-seller

besugo *nm* (a) *(pez)* sea bream (b) *(persona)* idiot, half-wit

besuquear *Fam* **1** *vt* to kiss, to cover with kisses
  2 besuquearse *vpr* to smooch

betabel *nf Méx Br* beetroot, *US* beet

betarraga *nf Andes Br* beetroot, *US* beet

betún *nm (para el calzado)* shoe polish; *Quím* bitumen

biberón *nm* baby's bottle, feeding bottle

Biblia *nf* Bible

bíblico,-a *adj* biblical

bibliografía *nf* bibliography

bibliorato *nm RP* file

biblioteca *nf* (a) *(institución)* library; **b. ambulante** mobile library (b) *RP (mueble)* bookcase

bibliotecario,-a *nm,f* librarian

bicameral *adj Pol* bicameral, two-chamber

bicarbonato *nm* bicarbonate; **b. sódico** bicarbonate of soda

bicentenario *nm Br* bicentenary, *US* bicentennial

bíceps *nm inv* biceps

bicha *nf* snake

bicho *nm* (a) bug, insect; **¿qué b. te ha picado?** what's bugging you? (b) *Taurom* bull (c) *Fam* **todo b. viviente** every living soul; **un b. raro** a weirdo, an oddball

bici *nf Fam* bike

bicicleta *nf* bicycle; **montar en b.** to ride a bicycle

bicolor *adj* two-coloured; *Pol* **gobierno b.** two-party government

bidé *nm* bidet

bidón *nm* drum

biela *nf Aut* connecting rod

Bielorrusia *n* Belarus

bien¹ 1 *adv* (a) *(correctamente)* well; **habla b. (el) inglés** she speaks English well; **responder b.** to answer correctly; **hiciste b. en decírmelo** you were right to tell me; **las cosas le van b.** things are going well for him; **¡b.!** good!, great!; **¡muy b.!** excellent, first class!; **¡qué b.!** great!, fantastic!

(b) *(de salud)* well; **sentirse/encontrarse/estar b.** to feel well

(c) **vivir b.** to be comfortably off; **¡está b.!** *(¡de acuerdo!)* fine!, all right!; **¡ya está b.!** that's (quite) enough!; **aquí se está muy b.** it's really nice here; **esta falda te sienta b.** this skirt suits you; *Fam* **ese libro está muy b.** that book is very good; *Fam* **su novia está muy b.** his girlfriend is very nice

(d) *(intensificador)* very, quite; **b. temprano** very early, nice and early; **b. caliente** pretty hot; **b. es verdad que ...** it's quite clear that ...

(e) **más b.** rather, a little

(f) **b. podía haberme avisado** she might have let me know

(g) *(de buena gana)* willingly, gladly; **b. me tomaría una cerveza** I'd really love a beer

2 *conj* **ahora b.** now, now then; **o b.** or, or else; **b. ... o b. ...** either ... or ...; **no b.** as soon as; **no b. llegó ...** no sooner had she arrived than ...; **si b.** although, even if

3 *adj* **la gente b.** the wealthy, the upper classes

bien² **nm* (a) *(bondad)* good; **el b. y el mal good and evil; **un hombre/familia de b.** a good man/family (b) *(bienestar)* **por el b. de** for the good of; **lo hace por tu b.** he does it for your sake (c) *Econ* **bienes** goods; **bienes de equipo** capital goods; **bienes gananciales** communal property; **bienes inmuebles** real estate; **bienes de consumo** consumer goods

bienal *nf* biennial exhibition

bienestar *nm (personal)* well-being, contentment; *(comodidad)* ease, comfort; **la sociedad del b.** the affluent society

bienhechor,-a *nm,f (hombre)* benefactor; *(mujer)* benefactress

bienintencionado,-a *adj* well-meaning, well-intentioned

bienio *nm* biennium, two-year period

bienvenida *nf* welcome; **dar la b. a algn** to welcome sb

bienvenido,-a *adj* welcome

bife *nm Andes, RP (bistec)* steak

bifocal *adj* bifocal; **gafas bifocales** bifocals

bifurcación *nf* bifurcation; *(de la carretera)* fork

bifurcarse **[44]** *vpr* to fork, to branch off

bigamia *nf* bigamy

bígamo,-a 1 *adj* bigamous
  2 *nm,f* bigamist

bigote *nm (de persona)* moustache; *(de animal) (usu pl)* whiskers *ℓ* Observa que la palabra inglesa **bigot** es un falso amigo y no es la traducción de la palabra española **bigote**. En inglés, **bigot** significa "intolerante".

bilateral *adj* bilateral; **acuerdo b.** bilateral agreement

bilbaíno,-a 1 *adj* of/from Bilbao
2 *nm,f* person from Bilbao

bilingüe *adj* bilingual

bilis *nf* bile

billar *nm* (**a**) *(juego)* billiards *sing*; **b. americano** pool; **b. ruso** snooker (**b**) *(mesa)* billiard table

billete *nm* (**a**) ticket; **b. de ida** *Br* single (ticket), *US* one-way ticket; **b. de ida y vuelta** *Br* return (ticket), *US* round-trip (ticket); (**b**) *(de banco) Br* note, *US* bill; **un b. de mil pesetas** a thousand peseta note

billetera *nf*, **billetero** *nm* wallet, *US* billfold

billón *nm* trillion

bimensual *adj* twice-monthly, bi-monthly

bimotor 1 *adj* twin-engined
2 *nm* twin-engined plane

binario,-a *adj* binary

bingo *nm* (**a**) *(juego)* bingo (**b**) *(sala)* bingo hall

binomio *nm* binomial

biodegradable *adj* biodegradable

biofísica *nf* biophysics *sing*

biografía *nf* biography

biográfico,-a *adj* biographical

biógrafo,-a *nm,f* biographer

biología *nf* biology

biológico,-a *adj* biological; *(agricultura, productos)* organic

biólogo,-a *nm,f* biologist

biomasa *nf* bio-mass

biombo *nm* (folding) screen

biopsia *nf* biopsy

bioquímica *nf* biochemistry

bioquímico,-a 1 *adj* biochemical
2 *nm,f* biochemist

bióxido *nm* dioxide; **b. de carbono** carbon dioxide

bipartidismo *nm* two-party system

biquini *nm* bikini

birlar *vt Fam* to pinch, to nick

Birmania *n* Burma

birmano,-a *adj & nm,f* Burmese

birome *nf RP* ballpoint pen, *Br* Biro®

birrete *nm* cap, beret; *Rel* biretta; *Univ* mortar-board

birria *nf Fam* rubbish

bis 1 *nm* encore
2 *adv* twice

bisabuela *nf* great-grandmother

bisabuelo *nm* great-grandfather; **bisabuelos** great-grandparents

bisagra *nf* hinge; **partido b.** party holding the balance of power

bisbisar, bisbisear *vt* to whisper

bisexual *adj & nmf* bisexual

bisiesto *adj* **año b.** leap year

bisnieto,-a *nm,f (niño)* great-grandson; *(niña)* great-granddaughter; **mis bisnietos** my great-grandchildren

bisonte *nm* bison, American buffalo

bisoño,-a *adj* inexperienced

bisté, bistec *nm* steak

bisturí *nm* scalpel

bisutería *nf* imitation jewellery

bit *nm Informát* bit

bíter *nm* bitters

bizantino,-a *adj Fig* **discusiones bizantinas** hair-splitting arguments

bizco,-a 1 *adj* cross-eyed
2 *nm,f* cross-eyed person

bizcocho *nm* sponge cake

biznieto,-a *nm,f* = bisnieto,-a

blanca *nf Fam* **estar sin b.** to be flat broke

blanco¹,-a 1 *adj* white; *(tez)* fair
2 *nm,f (hombre)* white man; *(mujer)* white woman; **los blancos** whites

blanco² *nm* (**a**) *(color)* white (**b**) *(hueco)* blank; **dejó la hoja en b.** he left the page blank; **votos en b.** blank votes; *Fig* **pasar la noche en b.** to have a sleepless night; **me quedé en b.** my mind went blank (**c**) *(diana)* target; **dar en el b.** to hit the target; *Fig* **ser el b. de todas las miradas** to be the centre of attention

blancura *nf* whiteness

blandengue *adj Pey* weak, soft

blandir *vt* to brandish

blando,-a *adj* soft

ℓ Observa que la palabra inglesa **bland** es un falso amigo y no es la traducción de la palabra española **blando**. En inglés, **bland** significa "soso".

blanquear *vt* (**a**) to whiten (**b**) *(encalar)* to whitewash (**c**) *(dinero)* to launder

blanquecino,-a *adj* whitish

blanqueo *nm* (**a**) whitening (**b**) *(encalado)* whitewashing (**c**) *(de dinero)* laundering

blanquillo *nm CAm, Méx (huevo)* egg

blasfemar *vi* to blaspheme (**contra** against)

blasfemia *nf* blasphemy

blasón *nm* coat of arms

bledo *nm Fam* **me importa un b.** I couldn't give a damn

blindado,-a *adj Mil* armoured, armour-plated; *(antibalas)* bullet-proof; **coche b.** bullet-proof car; **puerta blindada** reinforced door, security door

blindaje *nm* armour; *(vehículo)* armour plating

bloc *nm* pad; **b. de notas** notepad

bloomer ['blumer], **blúmer** *nm CAm, Carib* panties, *Br* knickers

bloque *nm* (a) block; **en b.** en bloc; **b. de pisos** *BR* (block of) flats, *US* apartment block (b) *Pol* bloc; **el b. comunista** the Communist Bloc

bloquear *vt* (a) to block (b) *Mil* to blockade

bloqueo *nm* blockade; *Dep* block

blues *nm* blues

blusa *nf* blouse

blusón *nm* loose blouse, smock

bluyín *nm*, **bluyines** *nmpl Andes, Ven* jeans

boato *nm* show, ostentation

bobada *nf* nonsense; **decir bobadas** to talk nonsense

bobalicón,-ona *Fam* **1** *adj* simple, stupid **2** *nm,f* simplet. .n, idiot

bobería *nf* = bobada

bobina *nf* (a) reel (b) *Elec* coil

bobo,-a 1 *adj (tonto)* stupid, silly; *(ingenuo)* naïve **2** *nm,f* fool

boca *nf* (a) mouth; **b. abajo** face downward; **b. arriba** face upward; *Fig* **a pedir de b.** in accordance with one's wishes; *Fig* **andar de b. en b.** to be the talk of the town; *Fam* **¡cierra la b!** shut up!; *Fam* **con la b. abierta** open-mouthed; *Fam* **se le hizo la b. agua** his mouth watered; **el b. a b.** kiss of life, mouth-to-mouth resuscitation (b) **la b. del metro** the entrance to the *Br* underground *o US* subway station; **b. de riego** hydrant

bocacalle *nf* entrance to a street

bocadillo *nm* (a) *(con pan)* sandwich; **un b. de jamón/tortilla** a ham/an omelette sandwich (b) *(de cómic)* balloon

bocado *nm* (a) *(mordedura)* bite (b) *(de caballo)* bit

bocajarro: • **a bocajarro** *loc adv* point-blank

bocanada *nf* (a) *(de vino)* mouthful (b) *(de humo)* puff; **una b. de viento** a gust of wind

bocata *nm* sandwich

bocazas *nmf inv Fam* bigmouth, blabbermouth

boceto *nm Arte* sketch, outline; *(esquema)* outline, plan

bochinche *nm Fam* uproar; **armar un b.** to kick up a row

bochorno *nm* (a) *(tiempo)* sultry *o* close weather; *(calor sofocante)* stifling heat (b) *Fig (vergüenza)* shame, embarrassment

bochornoso,-a *adj* (a) *(tiempo)* sultry, close, muggy; *(calor)* stifling (b) *Fig (vergonzoso)* shameful, embarrassing

bocina *nf* horn; **tocar la b.** to blow *o* sound one's horn

bocinazo *nm* hoot, toot

bocón,-ona *nm,f Am Fam* bigmouth

boda *nf* wedding, marriage; **bodas de plata** silver wedding

bodega *nf* (a) wine cellar; *(tienda)* wine shop (b) *Náut* hold (c) *(almacén)* warehouse (d) *Am* grocery store, grocer's (shop)

bodegón *nm* still-life

bodrio *nm Fam* rubbish, trash

body *nm* bodystocking, leotard

BOE *nm* (*abr* **Boletín Oficial del Estado**) Official Gazette

bofetada *nf*, **bofetón** *nm* slap on the face; **dar una b./un b. a algn** to slap sb's face

boga *nf Fig* **estar en b.** to be in vogue

bogar [42] *vi* (a) *(remar)* to row (b) *(navegar)* to sail

bogavante *nm* lobster

bogotano,-a 1 *adj* of/from Bogotá **2** *nm,f* person from Bogotá

bohío *nm Am* hut, cabin

boicot *nm* (*pl* **boicots**) boycott

boicotear *vt* to boycott

boicoteo *nm* boycott

bóiler *nm Méx* boiler

boina *nf* beret

bol *nm* bowl

bola *nf* (a) ball; *(canica)* marble; **b. de nieve** snowball; **no dar pie con b.** to be unable to do anything right (b) *Fam (mentira)* fib, lie; **meter bolas** to tell fibs (c) *(rumor)* rumour; **corre la b. por ahí de que te has echado novio** they say you've got yourself a boyfriend

bolchevique *adj & nmf* Bolshevik

bolear *vt Méx (sacar brillo)* to shine, to polish

bolera *nf* bowling alley

bolería *nf Méx* shoeshine store

boleta *nf* (a) *Méx, RP (para votar)* ballot, voting slip (b) *CSur (comprobante)* receipt (c) *CAm, CSur (multa)* parking ticket (d) *Méx (boletín)* (school) report card

boletería *nf Am (de cine, teatro)* box office; *(de estación)* ticket office

boletero,-a *nm,f Am* box office attendant

boletín *nm* bulletin; **B. Oficial del Estado** Official Gazette

boleto *nm* (a) *(de rifa)* ticket (b) *Am (de tren, metro)* ticket (c) *Méx (para espectáculo)* ticket

boli *nm Fam* pen, *Br* Biro®

boliche *nm* (a) *(juego)* bowling (b) *(bola)* jack (c) *(lugar)* bowling alley (d) *CSur Fam (bar)* small bar

bólido *nm Aut* racing car

bolígrafo *nm* ballpoint (pen), *Br* Biro®

bolita *nf CSur (bola)* marble; **jugar a las bolitas** to play marbles

bolívar *nm Fin* = standard monetary unit of Venezuela

Bolivia *n* Bolivia

boliviano,-a *adj & nm,f* Bolivian

bollar *vt* to dent

bollo *nm* (a) *Culin* bun, bread roll (b) *(abolladura)* dent

bolo¹ *nm (pieza)* skittle, pin; **bolos** *(juego)* (ten-pin) bowling

bolo²,-a *nm,f CAm Fam (borracho)* drunk

bolsa¹ *nf* bag; *Méx (de mano) Br* handbag, *US* purse; *Av* **b. de aire** air pocket; **b. de deportes** sports bag; **b. de la compra** shopping bag; **b. de viaje** travel bag

bolsa² *nf Fin* Stock Exchange; **jugar a la b.** to play the market

bolsillo *nm (en prenda)* pocket; **de b.** pocket, pocket-size; **libro de b.** paperback; **lo pagó de su b.** he paid for it out of his own pocket

bolso *nm Br* handbag, *US* purse

boludear *vi RP Fam* (a) *(hacer tonterías)* to mess about (b) *(decir tonterías)* to talk rubbish (c) *(perder el tiempo)* to waste one's time

boludo,-a *nm,f RP Fam (estúpido)* idiot, twit

bomba¹ *nf* pump; *Andes, Ven (gasolinera) Br* petrol station, *US* gas station; **b. de aire** air pump; **b. de incendios** fire engine; *Andes, Ven* **b. (de gasolina)** *(surtidor) Br* petrol pump, *US* gas pump

bomba² *nf* bomb; **b. atómica/de hidrógeno/de neutrones** atomic/hydrogen/neutron bomb; **b. de relojería** time bomb; **b. fétida** stink bomb; *Fam* **noticia b.** shattering piece of news; *Fam* **pasarlo b.** to have a whale of a time

bombacha *nf RP (braga)* panties, *Br* knickers; **bombachas** *(pantalones)* = loose-fitting trousers worn by cowboys

bombardear *vt* to bomb, to shell; **b. a algn a preguntas** to bombard sb with questions

bombardeo *nm* bombing, bombardment

bombardero *nm Av* bomber

bombazo *nm* bomb blast

bombear *vt* (a) *(agua etc)* to pump (b) *(pelota)* to blow up

bombeo *nm (de líquido)* pumping; **estación de b.** pumping station

bombero,-a *nm,f* (a) *(de incendios)* firefighter; *(hombre)* fireman; *(mujer)* firewoman; **cuerpo de bomberos** *Br* fire brigade, *US* fire department; **parque de bomberos** fire station (b) *Ven (de gasolinera) Br* petrol-pump *o US* gas-pump attendant

bombilla *nf* (light) bulb

bombillo *nm CAm, Carib, Col, Méx* light bulb

bombín *nm* bowler hat

bombita *nf RP* light bulb

bombo *nm* (a) *Mús* bass drum; *Fig* **a b. y platillo(s)** with a great song and dance; *Fam* **darse b.** to blow one's own trumpet (b) *(de sorteo)* lottery drum

bombón *nm* chocolate

bombona *nf* cylinder; **b. de butano** butane gas cylinder

bombonera *nf* chocolate box

bonachón,-ona *adj* good-natured, easy-going

bonaerense 1 *adj* of/from Buenos Aires **2** *nmf* person from Buenos Aires

bonanza *nf* (a) *Náut (tiempo)* fair weather; *(mar)* calm at sea (b) *Fig (prosperidad)* prosperity

bondad *nf* goodness; *Fml* **tenga la b. de esperar** please be so kind as to wait

bondadoso,-a *adj* kind, good-natured

bonete *nm Rel* cap, biretta; *Univ* mortarboard

boniato *nm* sweet potato

bonificación *nf* bonus

bonificar [44] *vt Com* to give a bonus to

bonito¹,-a *adj (de valor)* pretty, nice

bonito² *nm* tuna

bono *nm* (a) *(vale)* voucher (b) *Fin* bond, debenture; **bonos del tesoro** *o* **del Estado** Treasury bonds

bono-bus *nm* bus pass

boom *nm* boom

boomerang *nm* boomerang

boquerón *nm* anchovy

boquete *nm* hole

boquiabierto,-a *adj* open-mouthed; **se quedó b.** he was flabbergasted

boquilla *nf* (a) *(de cigarro)* tip; *(de pipa)* mouthpiece; **decir algo de b.** to pay lip service to sth (b) *Mús* mouthpiece (c) *(orificio)* opening

borbotar, borbotear *vi* to bubble

borbotón *nm* bubbling; *Fig* **salir a borbotones** to gush forth

borda *nf Náut* gunwale; **arrojar** *o* **echar por la b.** to throw overboard; **fuera b.** *(motor)* outboard motor

bordado,-a 1 *adj* embroidered; **el examen me salió b.** I made a good job of that exam

  2 *nm* embroidery

bordar *vt* (a) to embroider (b) *Fig* to do excellently

borde¹ *nm (de mesa, camino)* edge; *Cost* hem, edge; *(de vasija)* rim, brim; **al b. de** on the brink of, on the verge of; **al b. del mar** at the seaside

borde² *Fam* **1** *adj* stroppy

  2 *nmf* stroppy person

bordear *vt* to go round the edge of, to skirt

bordillo *nm Br* kerb, *US* curb

bordo *nm* **a b.** on board; **subir a b.** to go on board

bordó *adj inv RP* maroon, burgundy

borla *nf* tassel

borne *nm Elec* terminal

borra *nf* (a) *(pelusa)* fluff (b) *(poso)* sediment, dregs

borrachera *nf (embriaguez)* drunkenness; **agarrarse** *o* **cogerse una b.** to get drunk;

borracho,-a 1 *adj* (a) *(bebido)* drunk; **estar b.** to be drunk (b) *(bizcocho)* with rum

  2 *nm,f* drunkard, drunk

borrador *nm* (a) *(escrito)* rough copy, first draft (b) *(croquis)* rough *o* preliminary sketch (c) *(de pizarra)* duster

borraja *nf* **quedar en agua de borrajas** to come to nothing, to fizzle *o* peter out

borrar **1** *vt* (a) *(con goma)* to erase, to rub out; *(pizarra)* to clean (b) *Informát* to delete

  2 borrarse *vpr (de un club etc)* to drop out, to withdraw

borrasca *nf* area of low pressure

borrascoso,-a *adj* stormy

borrego,-a *nm,f* (a) *(yearling)* yearling lamb (b) *Fam (persona)* sheep

borrico *nm* ass, donkey; *Fam Fig* ass, dimwit

borrón *nm* blot, smudge

borroso,-a *adj* blurred; **veo b.** I can't see clearly, everything's blurred

Bosnia *n* Bosnia; **B. y Herzegóvina** Bosnia-Herzegovina

bosnio,-a *adj & nm,f* Bosnian

bosque *nm* wood

bosquejar *vt (dibujo)* to sketch, outline; *(plan)* to draft, to outline

bosquejo *nm (de dibujo)* sketch, study; *(de plan)* draft, outline

bostezar [40] *vi* to yawn

bostezo *nm* yawn

bota *nf* (a) boot; *Fig* **ponerse las botas** to make a killing (b) *(de vino)* wineskin

botana *nf Méx* snack, appetizer

botánica *nf* botany

botánico,-a 1 *adj* botanic; **jardín b.** botanic gardens

  2 *nm,f* botanist

botar **1** *vi* (a) *(saltar)* to jump (b) *(pelota)* to bounce

  2 *vt* (a) *(barco)* to launch (b) *(pelota)* to bounce (c) *Am (arrojar)* to throw out

botarate *nmf* madcap, fool

bote¹ *nm* (a) jump, bound; **dar botes** to jump up and down; **de un b.** with one leap (b) *(de pelota)* bounce, rebound

bote² *nm (lata)* can, tin; *(para propinas)* jar *o* box for tips; *(en lotería)* jackpot; *Fam* **chupar del b.** to scrounge

bote³ *nm (lancha)* boat; **b. salvavidas** lifeboat

bote⁴ *nm* **de b. en b.** packed, full to bursting

botella *nf* (a) bottle (b) *Cuba (autostop)* **dar b. a algn** to give sb a lift; **hacer b.** to hitchhike

botellín *nm* small bottle

botepronto *nm Fam* **a b.** all of a sudden

botica *nf* pharmacy, *Br* chemist's (shop), *US* drugstore; *Fam* **hay de todo como en b.** there's everything under the sun

boticario,-a *nm,f* pharmacist, *Br* chemist, *US* druggist

botijo *nm* earthenware pitcher *(with spout and handle)*

botín¹ *nm (de un robo)* loot, booty

botín² *nm (calzado)* ankle boot

botiquín *nm* (a) medicine chest *o* cabinet; *(portátil)* first-aid kit (b) *(enfermería)* first-aid post

botón *nm* button; **pulsar el b.** to press the button; **b. de muestra** sample

botones *nm inv (en hotel)* bellboy, *US* bellhop; *(recadero)* messenger, errand boy

boutique *nf* boutique

bóveda *nf* vault

bovino,-a *adj* bovine; **ganado b.** cattle

box *nm (pl* **boxes***)* (a) *(de caballo)* stall (b) *(de coches)* pit (c) *Am (boxeo)* boxing

boxeador *nm* boxer

boxear *vi* to box

boxeo *nm* boxing

boya nf (a) Náut buoy (b) (corcho) float

boyante adj buoyant

boy-scout nm boy scout

bozal nm (a) (para perro) muzzle (b) Am (cabestro) halter

bracero nm (day) labourer

bragas nfpl panties, Br knickers

bragueta nf (de pantalón etc) fly, flies

braguetazo nm Fam **dar el b.** to marry for money

braille nm braille

bramar vi to low, to bellow

bramido nm lowing, bellowing

brandy nm brandy

branquia nf gill

brasa nf ember, red-hot coal; **chuletas a la b.** barbecued chops

brasero nm brazier

brasier nm Carib, Col, Méx bra

Brasil n Brazil

brasileño,-a, RP **brasilero,-a** adj & nm,f Brazilian

bravata nf piece o act of bravado

bravo,-a 1 adj (a) (valiente) brave, courageous (b) (feroz) fierce, ferocious; **un toro b.** a fighting bull (c) (mar) rough, stormy

2 interj **¡b.!** well done!, bravo!

bravucón,-ona nm,f boaster, braggart

bravura nf (a) (de animal) ferocity, fierceness (b) (de persona) courage, bravery (c) (de toro) fighting spirit

braza nf (a) Náut fathom (b) (en natación) breaststroke; **nadar a b.** to do the breaststroke

brazada nf (en natación) stroke

brazalete nm (a) (insignia) armband (b) (pulsera) bracelet

brazo nm arm; (de animal) foreleg; (de sillón, tocadiscos) arm; **en brazos** in one's arms; **ir del b.** to walk arm in arm; Fig **con los brazos abiertos** with open arms; Fig **no dar su b. a torcer** not to give in, stand firm; **b. de gitano** = type of Swiss roll containing cream

brea nf tar, pitch

brebaje nm concoction, brew

brecha nf (en muro) opening, gap; Mil & Fig breach; Fig **estar siempre en la b.** to be always in the thick of things

brécol nm broccoli

bregar [42] vi to fight

Bretaña nf (a) Brittany (b) **Gran B.** Great Britain

brete nm Fig **poner a algn en un b.** to put sb in a tight spot

bretel nm CSur strap; **un vestido sin breteles** a strapless dress

breva nf early fig; Fam **de higos a brevas** once in a blue moon; Fam **¡no caerá esa b.!** no such luck!

breve adj brief; **en b., en breves momentos** shortly, soon; **en breves palabras** in short

brevedad nf briefness; (concisión) brevity; **con la mayor b. posible** as soon as possible

brevet nm Chile (de avión) pilot's licence; Ecuad, Perú (de automóvil) Br driving licence, US driver's license; RP (de velero) sailor's licence

brezo nm heather

bribón,-ona 1 adj roguish, dishonest

2 nm,f rogue, rascal

bricolaje nm do-it-yourself, DIY

brida nf (a) (rienda) rein, bridle (b) Téc flange

bridge nm Naipes bridge

brigada 1 nf (a) Mil brigade (b) (de policías) squad; **b. antiterrorista** anti-terrorist squad

2 nm Mil sergeant major

brigadier nm brigadier

brillante 1 adj brilliant

2 nm diamond

brillantez nf brilliance

brillantina nf brilliantine

brillar vi (resplandecer) to shine; (ojos, joyas) to sparkle; (lentejuelas etc) to glitter; **b. por su ausencia** to be conspicuous by one's absence

brillo nm (resplandor) shine; (del sol, de la luna) brightness; (de lentejuelas etc) glittering; (del cabello, tela) sheen; (de color) brilliance; (de pantalla) brightness; (de zapatos) shine; **sacar b. a** to shine, to polish

brilloso,-a adj Am shining

brincar [44] vi to skip

brinco nm skip

brindar 1 vi to drink a toast; **b. por algn/algo** to drink to sb/sth

2 vt (a) (oportunidad) to offer, to provide (b) Taurom to dedicate (a to)

3 brindarse vpr to offer (a to), to volunteer (a to)

brindis nm (a) toast (b) Taurom dedication (of the bull)

brío nm energy

brioso,-a adj energetic, vigorous

brisa nf breeze; **b. marina** sea breeze

británico,-a 1 adj British; **las Islas Británicas** the British Isles

2 nm,f Briton; **los británicos** the British

brizna nf (de hierba) blade; (de carne) string

broca *nf Téc* bit

brocha *nf (para pintar)* paintbrush; **b. de afeitar** shaving brush

broche *nm* (**a**) *(joya)* brooch; *Fig* **poner el b. de oro** to finish with a flourish (**b**) *(de vestido)* fastener

bróculi *nm* broccoli

broma *nf (chiste)* joke; **bromas aparte** joking apart; **en b.** as a joke; **¡ni en b.!** not on your life!; **b. pesada** practical joke; **gastar una b.** to play a joke

bromear *vi* to joke

bromista 1 *adj* fond of joking *o* playing jokes

2 *nmf* joker, prankster

bronca *nf* (**a**) *(riña)* quarrel, row (**b**) **echar una b. a algn** to bawl sb out (**c**) *RP Fam (rabia)* **me da b.** it hacks me off; **el jefe le tiene b.** the boss can't stand him

bronce *nm* bronze

bronceado,-a 1 *adj* suntanned, tanned

2 *nm* suntan, tan

bronceador,-a 1 *adj* **leche bronceadora** suntan cream

2 *nm* suntan cream *o* lotion

broncearse *vpr* to get a tan *o* a suntan

bronco,-a *adj* rough, coarse

bronquitis *nf inv* bronchitis

brotar *vi (planta)* to sprout; *(agua)* to spring, to gush; *(lágrimas)* to well up; *(epidemia)* to break out

brote *nm* (**a**) *Bot (renuevo)* bud, shoot; *(de agua)* gushing (**b**) *(de epidemia, violencia)* outbreak

bruces: • **bruces** *loc adv* face downwards; **se cayó de b.** he fell flat on his face

bruja *nf* witch, sorceress

brujería *nf* witchcraft, sorcery

brujo,-a 1 *nm* wizard, sorcerer

2 *adj Méx Fam* **estar b.** to be broke

brújula *nf* compass

bruma *nf* mist

brumoso,-a *adj* misty

bruñir *vt* to polish

brusco,-a *adj* (**a**) *(persona)* brusque, abrupt (**b**) *(repentino)* sudden, sharp

Bruselas *n* Brussels; **coles de B.** Brussels sprouts

brusquedad *nf* brusqueness, abruptness

brutal *adj* brutal

brutalidad *nf* brutality

bruto,-a 1 *adj* (**a**) *(necio)* stupid, thick; *(grosero)* coarse, uncouth (**b**) *Fin* gross; **peso b.** gross weight (**c**) **un diamante en b.** an uncut diamond

2 *nm,f* blockhead, brute

búcaro *nm* earthenware jug

bucear *vi* to swim under water

buche *nm* maw; *(de ave)* craw; *Fam (estómago)* belly, stomach

bucle *nm* curl, ringlet

budín *nm* pudding

budismo *nm* Buddhism

budista *adj & nmf* Buddhist

buen *adj (delante de un nombre masculino singular)* good; **¡b. viaje!** have a good trip!; *ver* **bueno,-a**

buenamente *adv* **haz lo que b. puedas** just do what you can; **si b. puedes** if you possibly can

buenaventura *nf* good fortune, good luck; **echar la b. a algn** to tell sb's fortune

bueno,-a 1 *adj* (**a**) good; **un alumno muy b.** a very good pupil; **una buena película** a good film; **lo b.** the good thing

(**b**) *(amable)* (con ser) good, kind; **el b. de Carlos** good old Carlos; **es muy buena persona** he's a very kind soul

(**c**) *(sano)* (con estar) well, in good health

(**d**) *(tiempo)* good; **hoy hace buen tiempo** it's fine today; **mañana hará b.** it will be fine *o* a nice day tomorrow

(**e**) *(conveniente)* good; **no es b. comer tanto** it's not good for you to eat so much; **sería b. que vinieras** it would be a good idea if you came

(**f**) *(considerable)* considerable; **un buen número de** a good number of; **una buena cantidad** a considerable amount

(**g**) *(grande)* good, big; **un buen trozo de pastel** a nice *o* good big piece of cake

(**h**) *Fam (atractivo)* gorgeous, sexy; **¡Rosa está muy buena!** Rosa's a bit of all right!; **una tía buena** a good-looking girl

(**i**) *Irón* fine, real, proper; **¡en buen lío te has metido!** that's a fine mess you've got yourself into!

(**j**) **¡buenas!** *(saludos)* hello!; **buenas tardes** *(desde mediodía hasta las cinco)* good afternoon; *(desde las cinco)* good evening; **buenas noches** *(al llegar)* good evening; *(al irse)* good night; **buenos días** good morning

(**k**) *(locuciones)* **de buenas a primeras** suddenly, all at once; **estar de buenas** to be in a good mood; **los buenos tiempos** the good old days; **por las buenas** willingly; **por las buenas o por las malas** willy-nilly; *Irón* **¡buena la has hecho!** that's done it!; **un susto de los buenos** a real fright; *Irón* **¡estaría b.!** I should jolly well hope not!; *Irón* **librarse de una buena** to get off scot free

buen is used instead of **bueno** before masculine singular nouns (e.g. **buen hombre** good man). The comparative form of **bueno** is **mejor** (better), and the superlative form is **el mejor** (masculine) or **la mejor** (feminine) (the best).

2 *interj* (**a**) *(vale)* all right, OK (**b**) *(expresa sorpresa)* hey! (**c**) *Col, Méx (al teléfono)* hello
buey *nm* ox, bullock
búfalo,-a *nm,f* buffalo
bufanda *nf* scarf
bufar *vi* (**a**) *(toro)* to snort; *(caballo)* to neigh (**b**) *(persona)* to be fuming
bufé *nm* buffet; **b. libre** self-service buffet meal
bufete *nm (despacho de abogado)* lawyer's office
buffet *nm (pl* **buffets**) = **bufé**
bufido *nm (de toro)* snort; *(de caballo)* neigh
bufón,-ona *nm,f* clown, buffoon
buhardilla *nf* attic, garret
búho *nm* owl; **b. real** eagle owl
buhonero,-a *nm,f* pedlar, hawker
buitre *nm* vulture
bujía *nf* (**a**) *Aut* spark plug (**b**) *Fís* candlepower
bulbo *nm* bulb
buldog *nm* bulldog
bulevar *nm* boulevard
Bulgaria *n* Bulgaria
búlgaro,-a *adj & nm,f* Bulgarian
bulín *nm RP Fam* bachelor pad
bulla *nf* (**a**) *(muchedumbre)* crowd, mob (**b**) *(ruido)* din; **armar b.** to kick up a din
bullicio *nm* din, hubbub
bullir *vi* (**a**) *(hervir)* to boil, to bubble (up) (**b**) **b. de gente** to be teeming with people
bulto *nm* (**a**) *(cosa indistinta)* shape, form (**b**) *(maleta, caja)* piece of luggage (**c**) *Med* lump (**d**) **hacer mucho b.** to be very bulky; *Fam* **escurrir el b.** to pass the buck
bumerán, bumerang *nm* boomerang
bungalow *nm* bungalow
búnker *nm* bunker
buñuelo *nm* doughnut
BUP *nm (abr* **Bachillerato Unificado Polivalente**) = academically orientated Spanish secondary school course for pupils aged 14-17
buque *nm* ship; **b. de guerra** warship; **b. de pasajeros** liner, passenger ship; **b. insignia** flagship
burbuja *nf* bubble; **hacer burbujas** to bubble, make bubbles
burbujear *vi* to bubble
burdel *nm* brothel

Burdeos *n* Bordeaux
burdo,-a *adj* coarse, rough
burgalés,-esa 1 *adj* of/from Burgos
2 *nm,f* person from Burgos
burgués,-esa *adj & nm,f* bourgeois
burguesía *nf* bourgeoisie
burla *nf* gibe, jeer; **hacer b. de algo/algn** to make fun of sth/sb; **hacer b. a algn** to stick one's tongue out at sb
burladero *nm Taurom* refuge in bullring
burlar 1 *vt* (**a**) *(engañar)* to deceive (**b**) *(eludir)* to dodge, to evade
2 burlarse *vpr* to make fun (**de** of), to laugh (**de** at)
burlón,-ona *adj* mocking
buró *nm* (**a**) *Pol* executive committee (**b**) *(escritorio)* bureau, desk (**c**) *Méx (mesa de noche)* bedside table
burocracia *nf* bureaucracy
burócrata *nmf* bureaucrat
burocrático,-a *adj* bureaucratic
buromática *nf* office automation
burrada *nf (comentario)* stupid o foolish remark; *(hecho)* stupid o foolish act
burro,-a 1 *nm,f* (**a**) *(donkey, ass; Fam Fig* **bajarse del b.** to climb o back down (**b**) *Fam (estúpido)* dimwit, blockhead (**c**) **b. de carga** dogsbody, drudge
2 *adj Fam* (**a**) *(necio)* stupid, dumb (**b**) *(obstinado)* stubborn
bursátil *adj* stock-market
bus *nm* bus
busca *nf* search; **ir en b. de** to go in search of
buscapersonas *nm* pager
buscapleitos *nmf inv* troublemaker
buscar [44] 1 *vt* (**a**) to look o search for; **b. una palabra en el diccionario** to look up a word in the dictionary (**b**) **ir a b. algo** to go and get sth, to fetch sth; **fue a buscarme a la estación** she picked me up at the station
2 buscarse *vpr Fam* **b. la vida** to try and earn one's living; *Fam* **te la estás buscando** you're asking for it; **se busca** *(en anuncios)* wanted
buseta *nf Col, CRica, Ecuad, Ven* minibus
búsqueda *nf* search, quest; *Informát* search
busto *nm* bust
butaca *nf* (**a**) *(sillón)* armchair, easy chair (**b**) *Cin & Teatro* seat; **b. de platea** o **patio** seat in the stalls
butano *nm* butane; **(gas) b.** butane gas
butifarra *nf* sausage
buzo *nm* (**a**) *(persona)* diver (**b**) *Arg, Col (sudadera)* sweatshirt (**c**) *Col, Urug (jersey)* sweater, *Br* jumper

buzón *nm Br* letter box, *US* mailbox; *Informát (de correo electrónico)* (electronic) mailbox; **echar una carta al b.** to *Br* post *o US* mail a letter; **b. de voz** voice mail

byte *nm Informát* byte

C

C, c [θe] *nf (la letra)* C, c

C (a) *(abr* **Celsius)** C **(b)** *(abr* **centígrado)** C

c/ (a) *(abr* **calle)** St; Rd **(b)** *(abr* **cargo)** cargo, freight **(c)** *(abr* **cuenta)** a/c

C., Ca *(abr* **compañía)** Co

cabal 1 *adj* **(a)** *(exacto)* exact, precise **(b)** *(honesto)* honest, upright

2 *nmpl Fam* **no está en sus cabales** he's not in his right mind

cábala *nf Fig* **hacer cábalas sobre algo** to speculate about sth

cabalgadura *nf* mount

cabalgar [42] *vt & vi* to ride

cabalgata *nf* cavalcade; **la c. de los Reyes Magos** the procession of the Three Wise Men

caballa *nf* mackerel

caballar *adj* **ganado c.** horses

caballería *nf* **(a)** *(cabalgadura)* mount, steed **(b)** *Mil* cavalry

caballeriza *nf* stable

caballero *nm* **(a)** gentleman; **¿qué desea, c.?** can I help you, sir?; **ropa de c.** menswear **(b)** *Hist* knight **(c)** **caballeros** *(en letrero)* gents

caballeroso,-a *adj* gentlemanly, chivalrous

caballete *nm* **(a)** *(de pintor)* easel **(b)** *Téc* trestle **(c)** *(de nariz)* bridge

caballito *nm* **(a)** **c. de mar** seahorse **(b)** **caballitos** merry-go-round, *US* carousel

caballo *nm* **(a)** horse; **a c.** on horseback; **montar a c.** to ride; *Fig* **a c. entre ...** halfway between ... **(b)** *Téc* **c. de vapor** horse power **(c)** *(pieza de ajedrez)* knight **(d)** *Naipes* queen **(e)** *Fam (heroína)* horse, smack

cabaña *nf* cabin

cabaret *nm (pl* **cabarets)** cabaret

cabecear 1 *vi* to nod

2 *vt Dep* to head

cabecera *nf* **(a)** top, head **(b)** *Impr* headline

cabecilla *nmf* leader

cabellera *nf* head of hair

cabello *nm* **(a)** hair **(b)** *Culin* **c. de ángel** = sweet made of gourd and syrup

cabelludo,-a *adj* **cuero c.** scalp

caber [9] *vi* **(a)** to fit, to be (able to be) contained; **cabe en el maletero** it fits in the boot; **¿cabemos todos?** is there room for all of us?; **en este coche/jarro caben ...** this car/jug holds ...; **no cabe por la puerta** it won't go through the door; **no c. en sí de gozo** to be beside oneself with joy; **no me cabe en la cabeza** I can't understand it; **no cabe duda** there is no doubt; **cabe la posibilidad de que ...** there is a possibility o chance that ...; **no está mal dentro de lo que cabe** it isn't bad, under the circumstances

(b) **cabe señalar que ...** we should point out that ...

(c) *Mat* **doce entre cuatro caben a tres** four into twelve goes three (times)

cabestrillo *nm* sling

cabeza 1 *nf* head; **en c.** in the lead; **por c.** a head, per person; *Fig* **a la c. de** at the front o top of; *Fig* **estar mal de la c.** to be a mental case; **c. de turco** scapegoat; **el o la c. de familia** the head of the family

2 *nm* **c. rapada** skinhead

cabezada *nf* **(a)** *(golpe)* butt, blow on the head **(b)** *Fam* **echar una c.** to have a snooze; **dar cabezadas** to nod

cabezal *nm Téc* head; *(de tocadiscos)* pick-up

cabezota *Fam* **1** *adj* pigheaded

2 *nmf* pigheaded person

cabezudo *nm* = carnival figure with a huge head

cabida *nf* capacity; **dar c. a** to leave room for

cabildo *nm Rel* chapter

cabina *nf* cabin; **c. telefónica** telephone box, telephone booth

cabinera *nf Col* air hostess

cabizbajo,-a *adj* crestfallen

cable *nm* cable; *Fam* **echarle un c. a algn** to give sb a hand

cableoperador *nm* cable company, cable operator

cabo *nm* **(a)** *(extremo)* end; **al c. de** after; **de c. a rabo** from start to finish **(b)** *Mil* corporal; *(policía)* sergeant **(c)** *Náut* rope, cable; *Fig* **atar cabos** to put two and two together; *Fig* **no dejar ningún c.**

suelto to leave no loose ends (**d**) *Geog* cape; **Ciudad del C.** Cape Town; **C. Verde** Cape Verde

cabra *nf* goat; *Fam* **estar como una c.** to be off one's head

cabré *indic fut de* **caber**

cabreado,-a *adj muy Fam* pissed off

cabrear *muy Fam* **1** *vt* to make angry, *Br* to piss off
　2 cabrearse *vpr* to get *Br* pissed off *o US* pissed

cabreo *nm muy Fam* anger

cabrío,-a *adj* **macho c.** billy goat; **ganado c.** goats

cabriola *nf* skip

cabrito *nm Zool* kid

cabro,-a *nm,f Chile Fam* kid

cabrón,-ona *nm,f Vulg (hombre) Br* bastard, *US* asshole; *(woman)* bitch

cabronada *nf muy Fam* dirty trick

cabuya *nf* (**a**) *(planta)* agave (**b**) *(fibra)* fibre hemp (**c**) *CAm, Col, Ven (cuerda)* rope

caca *nf Fam* poopoo

cacahuete, *CAm, Méx* **cacahuate** *nm* peanut

cacao *nm* (**a**) *Bot* cacao (**b**) *(polvo, bebida)* cocoa (**c**) *Fam (lío)* mess

cacarear **1** *vi (gallina)* to cluck
　2 *vt Fig* to boast about

cacareo *nm* (**a**) *(de gallina)* clucking (**b**) *Fig* boasting, bragging

catatúa *nf* cockatoo

cacereño,-a 1 *adj* of/from Cáceres
　2 *nm,f* person from Cáceres

cacería *nf* (**a**) *(actividad)* hunting, shooting (**b**) *(partida)* hunt, shoot

cacerola *nf* saucepan

cacha *nf Fam (muslo)* thigh; **estar cachas** to be really muscular

cachalote *nm* sperm whale

cacharro *nm* (**a**) *(earthenware pot o jar* (**b**) *Fam (cosa)* thing, piece of junk (**c**) **cacharros** *(de cocina)* pots and pans

caché *nm Informát* **(memoria) c.** cache memory

cachear *vt* to frisk, to search

cachemir *nm,* **cachemira** *nf* cashmere

cacheo *nm* frisk, frisking

cachetada *nf Am* slap

cachete *nm* (**a**) *(bofetada)* slap (**b**) *Am (mejilla)* cheek

cachila *nf RP (automóvil)* vintage car

cachimba *nf* (**a**) *(pipa)* pipe (**b**) *RP (pozo)* well

cachiporra *nf* club, truncheon

cachivache *nm Fam* thing, knick-knack

cacho¹ *nm Fam (pedazo)* bit, piece; *Fig* ¡**qué c. de animal!** what a nasty piece of work!

cacho² *nm Andes, Ven (cuerno)* horn

cachondearse *vpr Fam* **c. de** to take the mickey out of

cachondeo *nm Fam* laugh; **tomar algo a c.** to take sth as a joke

cachondo,-a *adj Fam* (**a**) *(sexualmente)* randy (**b**) *(divertido)* funny

cachorro,-a *nm,f (de perro)* pup, puppy; *(de gato)* kitten; *(de otros animales)* cub, baby

cacique *nm (jefe)* local boss

caco *nm Fam* thief

cacofonía *nf* cacophony

cacto *nm,* **cactus** *nm inv Bot* cactus

cada *adj (de dos)* each; *(de varios)* each, every; **c. día** every day; **c. dos días** every second day; **c. vez más** more and more; ¿**c. cuánto?** how often?; **c. dos por tres** every other minute; **cuatro de c. diez** four out of (every) ten; ¡**tienes c. cosa!** you come up with some fine ideas!

cadalso *nm* scaffold

cadáver *nm (de persona)* corpse, (dead) body; *(de animal)* body, carcass; **ingresar c.** to be dead on arrival

cadena *nf* (**a**) chain; *(correa de perro)* lead, leash (**b**) *TV* channel (**c**) *Ind* line; **c. de montaje** assembly line; **trabajo en c.** assembly line work (**d**) *Geog* **c. montañosa** mountain range (**e**) *Jur* **c. perpetua** life imprisonment (**f**) *Aut* **cadenas** tyre chains

cadencia *nf* rhythm; *Mús* cadenza

cadera *nf* hip

cadete *nm* cadet; *RP (chico de los recados)* errand boy, office junior

caducar [44] *vi* to expire

caducidad *nf* expiry; **fecha de c.** *(en alimentos)* ≃ sell-by date; *(en medicinas)* to be used before

caduco,-a *adj* (**a**) *Bot* deciduous (**b**) *(anticuado)* out-of-date

caer [39] 1 *vi* (**a**) to fall; **dejar c.** to drop; *Fig* **está al c.** *(llegar)* he'll arrive any minute now; *(ocurrir)* it's on the way
　(**b**) *(fecha)* to be; **su cumpleaños cae en sábado** his birthday falls on a Saturday
　(**c**) *(entender)* to understand, to see; **ya caigo** I get it; **no caí** I didn't twig
　(**d**) *(hallarse)* to be; **cae por Granada** it is somewhere near Granada
　(**e**) **me cae bien/mal** I like/don't like her
　(**f**) **al c. el día** in the evening; **al c. la noche** at nightfall
　2 caerse *vpr* to fall (down); **me caí de la moto** I fell off the motorbike; **se le ha cayó**

el pañuelo she dropped her handkerchief

café *nm* (a) coffee; **c. solo/con leche** black/white coffee (b) *(cafetería)* café

cafeína *nf* caffeine

cafetal *nm* coffee plantation

cafetera *nf* coffee-maker

cafetería *nf* snack bar, coffee bar; *Ferroc* buffet car

cafetero,-a *adj* (a) coffee (b) *Fam* **es muy c.** *(persona)* he loves coffee

cafiche *nm Andes Fam (proxeneta)* pimp

cafre *nmf* savage, beast

cagado,-a *adj muy Fam (cobarde)* coward; **estar c. de miedo** to be shit-scared

cagar [42] *muy Fam* **1** *vi* (a) (to have a) shit (b) *(estropear)* to ruin, to spoil; **cagarla** to cock it up ·

2 cagarse *vpr* to shit oneself; **c. de miedo** to be shit-scared; **¡me cago en diez!** *Br* bloody hell!, *US* goddamn it!

caída *nf* (a) fall; *(de pelo, diente)* loss (b) *(de precios)* drop (c) *Pol* downfall, collapse

caído,-a 1 *adj* fallen

2 *nmpl* **los caídos** the fallen

caigo *indic pres de* **caer**

caimán *nm* alligator

Cairo *n* **El C.** Cairo

caja *nf* (a) box; **c. fuerte** safe; *FamTV* **la c. tonta** the idiot box (b) *(de leche etc)* carton (c) *(de embalaje)* crate, case; **una c. de cerveza** a crate of beer (d) *Fin (en tienda)* cash desk; *(en banco)* cashier's desk (e) *Aut* **c. de cambios** gearbox (f) *Com* **c. de ahorros** o **de pensiones** savings bank (g) *(féretro)* coffin

cajero,-a *nm,f* cashier; **c. automático** cash point, cash dispenser

cajetilla *nf* packet, pack

cajón *nm* (a) *(en un mueble)* drawer; *Fig* **c. de sastre** jumble; *Fam* **de c.** obvious, self-evident (b) *(caja grande)* crate, chest

cajuela *nf CAm, Méx (maletero) Br* boot, *US* trunk

cal¹ *nf* lime; *Fig* **a c. y canto** hermetically; *Fam* **una de c. y otra de arena** six of one and half a dozen of the other

cal² *(abr* **caloría(s))** cal

cala *nf* (a) *Geog* creek, cove (b) *Náut* hold

calabacín *nm Bot* (a) *(pequeño) Br* courgette, *US* zucchini (b) *(grande) Br* marrow, *US* squash

calabaza *nf* pumpkin, gourd

calabobos *nm inv Fam* drizzle

calabozo *nm* (a) *(prisión)* jail, prison (b) *(celda)* cell

calada *nf Fam (de cigarrillo)* drag, puff

calado,-a 1 *adj* soaked

2 *nm Náut* draught

calamar *nm* squid *inv*; *Culin* **calamares a la romana** squid fried in batter

calambre *nm* (a) *Elec (descarga)* electric shock; **ese cable da c.** that wire is live (b) *(en músculo)* cramp

calamidad *nf* calamity

calaña *nf* kind, sort; **una persona de mala c.** a bad sort

calar 1 *vt* (a) *(mojar)* to soak, to drench (b) *(agujerear)* to pierce, to penetrate (c) *Fam (a alguien)* to rumble; **¡te hemos calado!** we've got your number!

2 *vi* (a) *(prenda)* to let in water (b) *Náut* to draw

3 calarse *vpr* (a) *(prenda, techo)* to let in water; *(mojarse)* to get soaked (b) *(el sombrero)* to pull down (c) *Aut* to stall

calavera 1 *nf* (a) *(cráneo)* skull (b) *Méx Aut* **calaveras** tail lights

2 *nm* tearaway

calcar [44] *vt* (a) *(un dibujo)* to trace (b) *Fig (imitar)* to copy, to imitate

calceta *nf* (a) *(prenda)* stocking (b) **hacer c.** to knit

calcetín *nm* sock

calcinar *vt* to burn

calcio *nm* calcium

calco *nm* tracing; **papel de c.** carbon paper

calcomanía *nf* transfer

calculadora *nf* calculator

calcular *vt* (a) *Mat* to calculate (b) *(evaluar)* to (make an) estimate (c) *(suponer)* to figure, to guess

cálculo *nm* (a) calculation; **según mis cálculos** by my reckoning (b) *Med* gallstone (c) *Mat* calculus

caldear *vt* to heat up

caldera *nf* (a) *(industrial)* boiler; *(olla)* cauldron (b) *Urug (hervidor)* kettle

caldereta *nf* stew

calderilla *nf* small change

caldo *nm* stock, broth; **c. de cultivo** culture medium; *Fig* breeding ground

calé *adj & nm* gypsy

calefacción *nf* heating; **c. central** central heating

calefaccionar *vt CSur (calentar)* to heat (up), to warm (up)

calefactor *nm* heater

calefón *nm CSur (calentador)* water heater

caleidoscopio *nm* kaleidoscope

calendario *nm* calendar

calentador *nm* heater

calentamiento *nm Dep* warm-up

calentar [1] 1 *vt* (**a**) *(agua, horno)* to heat; *(comida, habitación)* to warm up; *Fig* **no me calientes la cabeza** don't bug me (**b**) *Fam (pegar)* to smack (**c**) *Fam (excitar)* to arouse (sexually), to turn on
2 calentarse *vpr* (**a**) to get hot *o* warm, to heat up (**b**) *Fig* **se calentaron los ánimos** people became very excited

calentón,-ona, calentorro,-a *adj Fam* randy

calentura *nf* fever, temperature

calesita *nf RP* merry-go-round, carousel

calibrar *vt* to gauge, to bore

calibre *nm* (**a**) *(de arma)* calibre (**b**) *Fig (importancia)* importance

calidad *nf* (**a**) quality; **de primera c.** first-class; **un vino de c.** good-quality wine (**b**) **en c. de as**

cálido,-a *adj* warm; **una cálida acogida** a warm welcome

calidoscopio *nm* = caleidoscopio

caliente *adj* (**a**) hot (**b**) *Fig (debate)* heated; **en c.** in the heat of the moment (**c**) *Fam (cachondo)* hot, randy

calificación *nf* (**a**) qualification (**b**) *Educ* mark

calificar [44] *vt* (**a**) to describe (**de** as); **le calificó de inmoral** he called him immoral (**b**) *(examen)* to mark, to grade

calificativo *nm* epithet

caligrafía *nf* calligraphy; *(modo de escribir)* handwriting

calima *nf* haze, mist

calimocho *nm* = drink made with wine and Coca-Cola®

calina *nf* = calima

cáliz *nm* chalice

caliza *nf* limestone

calizo,-a *adj* lime

callado,-a *adj* quiet; **te lo tenías muy c.** you were keeping that quiet

callar 1 *vi* (**a**) *(dejar de hablar)* to stop talking; **¡calla!** be quiet!, *Fam* shut up! (**b**) *(no hablar)* to keep quiet, to say nothing
2 *vt (noticia)* not to mention, to keep to oneself
3 • callarse *vpr* to stop talking, to be quiet; **¡cállate!** shut up!

calle *nf* (**a**) street, road; **c. de dirección única** one-way street; **c. mayor** *Br* high street, *US* main street; **el hombre de la c.** the man in the street (**b**) *Dep* lane

calleja *nf* narrow street

callejero,-a 1 *nm (mapa)* street directory
2 *adj* street; **gato c.** alley cat

callejón *nm* back alley *o* street; **c. sin salida** cul-de-sac, dead end

callejuela *nf* narrow street, lane

callista *nmf* chiropodist

callo *nm* (**a**) *Med* callus, corn; *Fam* **dar el c.** to slog (**b**) *Culin* **callos** tripe

calma *nf* (**a**) calm; **¡c.!** calm down!; **en c.** calm; **tómatelo con c.** take it easy (**b**) *Met* calm weather; **c. chicha** dead calm

calmante *nm* painkiller

calmar 1 *vt (persona)* to calm (down); *(dolor)* to soothe, to relieve
2 calmarse *vpr* (**a**) *(persona)* to calm down (**b**) *(dolor, viento)* to ease off

caló *nm* gypsy dialect

calor *nm* (**a**) heat; **hace c.** it's hot; **tengo c.** I'm hot; **entrar en c.** to warm up (**b**) *Fig (afecto)* warmth

caloría *nf* calorie

calote *nm RP Fam* swindle

calumnia *nf* (**a**) calumny (**b**) *Jur* slander

calumniar [43] *vt* (**a**) to calumniate (**b**) *Jur* to slander

caluroso,-a *adj* hot; *(acogida etc)* warm

calva *nf* bald patch

calvicie *nf* baldness

calvinismo *nm* Calvinism

calvo,-a 1 *adj* bald; **ni tanto ni tan c.** neither one extreme nor the other
2 *nm* bald man

calza *nf* wedge

calzada *nf* road, carriageway

calzado *nm* shoes, footwear

calzador *nm* shoehorn

calzar [40] 1 *vt* (**a**) *(poner calzado)* to put shoes on; **¿qué número calzas?** what size do you take? (**b**) *(mueble)* to wedge
2 calzarse *vpr* **c. los zapatos** to put on one's shoes

calzón *nm* (**a**) *Dep* shorts (**b**) *Andes, RP* **calzones** *(bragas)* panties, *Br* knickers (**c**) *Méx* **calzones** *(calzoncillos)* underpants

calzonazos *nm inv Fam* henpecked husband

calzoncillos *nmpl* underpants, pants

calzoneta *nf CAm* swimming trunks

cama *nf* bed; **estar en** *o* **guardar c.** to be confined to bed; **hacer la c.** to make the bed; **irse a la c.** to go to bed; **c. doble/ sencilla** double/single bed; **c. turca** couch

camada *nf* litter; *(de pájaros)* brood

camafeo *nm* cameo

camaleón *nm* chameleon

cámara 1 *nf* (**a**) *(aparato)* camera; **a c. lenta** in slow motion (**b**) *Pol* Chamber, House; **C. Alta/Baja** Upper/Lower House (**c**) *Aut* inner tube (**d**) *(habitación)* room, chamber; **c. de gas** gas chamber; **c. frigorífica** cold-storage room; **música de c.** chamber music

2 *nmf (hombre)* cameraman; *(mujer)* camerawoman

camarada *nmf* comrade

camaradería *nf* camaraderie

camarera *nf (de hotel)* chambermaid

camarero,-a *nm,f* (**a**) *(de restaurante)* *(hombre)* waiter; *(mujer)* waitress; *(trás la barra) (hombre)* barman; *(mujer)* barmaid (**b**) *(de avión) (hombre)* steward; *(mujer)* stewardess

camarilla *nf* clique

camarón *nm* (common) prawn

camarote *nm* cabin

camba *Bol Fam* **1** *adj* of/from the forested lowland region of Bolivia
2 *nmf* person from the forested lowland region of Bolivia

cambalache *nm RP (tienda)* junk shop

cambiante *adj* changing; *(carácter)* changeable

cambiar [43] **1** *vt* (**a**) to change; **c. algo de sitio** to move sth (**b**) *(intercambiar)* to swap, to exchange (**c**) *(dinero)* to change
2 *vi* to change; **c. de casa** to move (house); **c. de idea** to change one's mind; **c. de trabajo** to get another job; **c. de velocidad** to change gear
3 cambiarse *upr* (**a**) *(de ropa)* to change (clothes) (**b**) *(de casa)* to move (house)

cambiazo *nm Fam* switch

cambio *nm* (**a**) change; *(de impresiones)* exchange; **c. de planes** change of plans; **un c. en la opinión pública** a shift in public opinion; *Fig* **a c. de** in exchange for; **en c.** on the other hand (**b**) *(dinero)* change; **¿tienes c. de mil pesetas?** have you got change for a thousand pesetas? (**c**) *Fin (de divisas)* exchange; *(de acciones)* price (**d**) *Aut* gear change; **c. automático** automatic transmission

cambista *nmf* moneychanger

Camboya *n* Cambodia

cambur *nm Ven (plátano)* banana

camelar *vt*, **camelarse** *upr Fam* (**a**) to cajole (**b**) *(galantear)* to win over

camelia *nf* camellia

camello,-a **1** *nm,f* camel
2 *nm Fam (traficante de drogas)* (drug) pusher

camellón *nm Col, Méx (en avenida)* Br central reservation, *US* median (strip)

camelo *nm Fam* (**a**) *(engaño)* hoax (**b**) *(trola)* cock-and-bull story

camerino *nm* dressing room

Camerún *n* Cameroon

camilla *nf* (**a**) stretcher (**b**) **mesa c.** = small round table under which a heater is placed

caminante *nmf* walker

caminar **1** *vi* to walk
2 *vt* to cover, to travel; **caminaron 10 km** they walked for 10 km

caminata *nf* long walk

camino *nm* (**a**) *(ruta)* route, way; **ir c.** **de** to be going to; **ponerse en c.** to set off; *Fig* **ir por buen/mal c.** to be on the right/wrong track; **abrirse c.** to break through; **a medio c.** half-way; **en el c. a o de c.** a on the way to; **estar en c.** to be on the way; **nos coge** o **pilla de c.** it is on the way (**b**) *(vía)* path, track (**c**) *(modo)* way

camión *nm* (**a**) truck, *Br* lorry; **c. cisterna** tanker; **c. de la basura** *Br* dustcart, *US* garbage truck; **c. frigorífico** refrigerated truck (**b**) *CAm, Méx (autobús)* bus

camionero,-a *nm,f* truck o *Br* lorry driver

camioneta *nf* van

camisa *nf* shirt; **en mangas de c.** in one's shirtsleeves; *Fig* **cambiar de c.** to change sides; **c. de fuerza** straightjacket

camiseta *nf* (**a**) *(de uso interior)* *Br* vest, *US* undershirt (**b**) *(de uso exterior)* T-shirt (**c**) *Dep* shirt; **sudar la c.** to run oneself into the ground

camisón *nm* nightdress, *Fam* nightie

camomila *nf* camomile

camorra *nf Fam* trouble

camorrista **1** *adj* quarrelsome, rowdy
2 *nmf* troublemaker

camote *nm Andes, CAm, Méx (batata)* sweet potato

campal *adj* **batalla c.** pitched battle

campamento *nm* camp

campana *nf* bell; **pantalones de campana** bell-bottom trousers

campanada *nf* peal o ring of a bell

campanario *nm* belfry, bell tower

campanilla *nf* (**a**) small bell (**b**) *Anat* uvula (**c**) *Bot* bell flower

campante *adj Fam* **se quedó tan c.** he didn't bat an eyelid

campaña *nf* (**a**) campaign; **c. electoral** election campaign; **c. publicitaria** advertising campaign (**b**) *Mil* campaign; **hospital/ambulancia de c.** field hospital/ambulance (**c**) *RP (campo)* countryside

campar *vi Fam* **c. por sus respetos** to do as one pleases

campechano,-a *adj* unpretentious

campeón,-ona *nm,f* champion; **c. mundial** world champion

campeonato *nm* championship; **un tonto de c.** an utter idiot

campera *nf* (**a**) **camperas** *(botas)* cowboy boots (**b**) *RP (chaqueta)* jacket

campero,-a *adj* country, rural; **(botas) camperas** leather boots

campesino,-a *nm,f (hombre)* country-man; *(mujer)* countrywoman

campestre *adj* rural

camping *nm* campsite; **hacer** *o* **ir de c.** to go camping

campiña *nf* open country

campista *nmf* camper

campo *nm* (a) country, countryside; **a c. traviesa** *o* **través** cross-country; **trabaja (en) el c.** he works (on) the land; **trabajo de c.** fieldwork (b) *(parcela)* field (c) *Fís & Fot* field (d) *(ámbito)* field; **c. de acción** field of action; *Mil* **c. de batalla** battlefield; **c. de concentración** concentration camp; **c. de trabajo** work camp (e) *Dep* field; *(de fútbol)* pitch; *(de golf)* course (f) *RP (hacienda)* farm (g) *Andes (sitio)* room, space

camposanto *nm* cemetery

camuflaje *nm* camouflage

camuflar *vt* to camouflage

cana *nf (gris)* grey hair; *(blanco)* white hair; **tener canas** to have grey hair; *Fam* **echar una c. al aire** to let one's hair down

Canadá *n* Canada

canadiense *adj & nmf* Canadian

canal *nf* (a) *(artificial)* canal; *(natural)* channel; **C. de la Mancha** English Channel (b) *TV, Elec & Informát* channel

canalizar [40] *vt* to channel

canalla 1 *nm* swine, rotter
  2 *nf* riffraff, mob

canallesco,-a *adj* rotten, despicable

canalón *nm* gutter

canapé *nm* (a) *Culin* canapé (b) *(sofá)* couch, sofa

canario,-a 1 *adj & nm,f* Canarian; **Islas Canarias** Canary Islands, Canaries
  2 *nm Orn* canary

canasta *nf* basket

canastilla *nf* small basket; *(de un bebé)* layette

canasto *nm* big basket, hamper

cancán *nm* frilly petticoat; *RP* **cancanes** *(leotardos) Br* tights, *US* pantyhose

cancela *nf* wrought-iron gate

cancelación *nf* cancellation

cancelar *vt* (a) *(acto etc)* to cancel (b) *(deuda)* to pay off (c) *Chile, Ven (compra)* to pay for

cáncer *nm* cancer; **c. de pulmón/mama** lung/breast cancer

cancerbero,-a *nm,f Ftb* goalkeeper

cancerígeno,-a *adj* carcinogenic

canceroso,-a *adj* cancerous

cancha *nf* ground; *Ten* court

canchero,-a *adj RP Fam (desenvuelto)* streetwise, savvy

canciller *nm* chancellor

cancillería *nf Am* foreign ministry

canción *nf* song

candado *nm* padlock

candela *nf* fire

candelabro *nm* candelabrum

candelero *nm* candlestick; *Fig* **en el c.** at the top

candente *adj* red-hot; *Fig* **tema c.** topical issue

candidato,-a *nm,f* candidate; *(a un puesto)* applicant

candidatura *nf* (a) *(lista)* list of candidates (b) **presentar su c.** to submit one's application

candidez *nf* candour

cándido,-a *adj* ingenuous, naive

> 🔔 Observa que la palabra inglesa **candid** es un falso amigo y no es la traducción de la palabra española **cándido**. En inglés, **candid** significa "franco, sincero".

candil *nm* oil lamp; *Méx (candelabro)* chandelier

candilejas *nfpl Teatro* footlights

candor *nm* innocence, naivety

> 🔔 Observa que la palabra inglesa **candour** es un falso amigo y no es la traducción de la palabra española **candor**. En inglés, **candour** significa "sinceridad, franqueza".

candoroso,-a *adj* innocent, pure

canela *nf* cinnamon

canelones *nmpl* cannelloni

cangrejo *nm (de mar)* crab; *(de río)* fresh-water crayfish

canguro 1 *nm* kangaroo
  2 *nmf Fam* baby-sitter

caní bal *adj & nmf* cannibal

canica *nf* marble

caniche *nm* poodle

canícula *nf* dog days, midsummer heat

canijo,-a *adj Fam* puny, weak

canilla *nf* (a) *Fam (espinilla)* shinbone (b) *RP (grifo) Br* tap, *US* faucet

canillera *nf Am (cobardía)* cowardice; *(miedo)* fear

canillita *nm Andes, RP* newspaper vendor

canino,-a 1 *adj* canine; *Fam* **tener un hambre canina** to be starving
  2 *nm (colmillo)* canine

canjear *vt* to exchange

cano,-a *adj (blanco)* white; *(gris)* grey

canoa *nf* canoe

canódromo *nm* dog *o* greyhound track

canon *nm* (a) canon, norm (b) *Mús & Rel* canon (c) *Com* royalty

canónigo *nm* canon

canonizar [40] *vt* to canonize

canoso,-a *adj* (de pelo blanco) white-haired; (de pelo gris) grey-haired; (pelo) white, grey

cansado,-a *adj* (a) (agotado) tired, weary; **estar c.** to be tired (b) **ser c.** (pesado) to be boring o tiresome

cansador,-a *adj Andes, RP* (que cansa) tiring; (que aburre) boring

cansancio *nm* tiredness, weariness; *Fam* **estoy muerto de c.** I'm on my last legs

cansar 1 *vt* to tire

2 *vi* to be tiring

3 cansarse *upr* to get tired; **se cansó de esperar** he got fed up (with) waiting

Cantabria *n* Cantabria

cantábrico,-a *adj* Cantabrian; **Mar C.** Bay of Biscay

cántabro,-a *adj & nm,f* Cantabrian

cantaleta *nf Am* **la misma c.** the same old story

cantante 1 *nmf* singer

2 *adj* singing; **llevar la voz c.** to rule the roost

cantaor,-a *nm,f* flamenco singer

cantar¹ *vt & vi* (a) *Mús* to sing; *Fig* **en menos que canta un gallo** in a flash (b) *Fam* (confesar) to sing, to spill the beans (c) *Fam* (oler mal) to hum

cantar² *nm Literario* song; *Fam* **¡eso es otro c.!** that's a totally different thing!

cantarín,-ina *adj* (voz) singsong

cántaro *nm* pitcher; *Fig* **llover a cántaros** to rain cats and dogs

cante *nm* (a) (canto) singing; **c. hondo, c. jondo** flamenco (b) *Fam* **dar el c.** to attract attention

cantegril *nm Urug* shanty town

cantera *nf* (a) (de piedra) quarry (b) *Fig Ftb* young players

cantero *nm* (a) (masón) stonemason (b) *Cuba, RP* (parterre) flowerbed

cantidad 1 *nf* quantity; (de dinero) amount, sum; **en c.** a lot; *Fam* **c. de gente** thousands of people

2 *adv Fam* a lot; **me gusta c.** I love it

cantimplora *nf* water bottle

cantina *nf* canteen

cantinero,-a *nm,f* bar attendant

canto¹ *nm* (a) (arte) singing (b) (canción) song

canto² *nm* (borde) edge; **de c.** on its side

canto³ *nm* (guijarro) pebble, stone; **c. rodado** (grande) boulder; (pequeño) pebble

cantor,-a 1 *adj* singing; **pájaro c.** songbird

2 *nm,f* singer

canturrear *vi* to hum, to croon

canutas *nfpl Fam* **pasarlas c.** to have a hard time

canuto *nm* (a) (tubo) tube (b) *Fam* (porro) joint

caña *nf* (a) (vaso) glass; (de cerveza) glass of beer (b) *Bot* reed; (tallo) cane, stem; **c. de azúcar** sugar cane (c) (de pescar) rod (d) *Fam* **darle c. al coche** to go at full speed (e) *Andes, Cuba, RP* (aguardiente) cane spirit, cheap rum

cañada *nf* gully, ravine

cáñamo *nm* hemp

cañería *nf* (piece of) piping; **cañerías** plumbing

cañero,-a *nm,f Am* (trabajador) = worker on sugar plantation

cañí *adj & nmf* (pl **cañís**) *Fam* gypsy

caño *nm* (tubo) tube; (tubería) pipe

cañón *nm* (a) cannon; *Fig* **estar siempre al pie del c.** to be always ready for a fight (b) (de fusil) barrel (c) *Geog* canyon

cañonazo *nm* gunshot

caoba *nf* mahogany

caos *nm* chaos

caótico,-a *adj* chaotic

cap. (abr **capítulo**) ch

capa *nf* (a) (prenda) cloak, cape; **de c. caída** low-spirited (b) (de pintura) layer, coat; *Culin* coating (c) *Geol* stratum, layer

capacidad *nf* (a) (cabida) capacity (b) (aptitud) capacity, ability

capacitación *nf* qualification

capacitar *vt* (autorizar) to authorize

capar *vt* to castrate

caparazón *nm* shell

capataz,-a *nm,f* (hombre) foreman; (mujer) forewoman

capaz *adj* (a) capable, able; **ser c. de hacer algo** (tener la habilidad de) to be able to do sth; (atreverse a) to dare to do sth; **si se entera es c. de despedirle** if he finds out, he could quite easily sack him (b) *Am* **es c. que** it is likely that

capcioso,-a *adj* captious; **pregunta capciosa** catch question

capea *nf* amateur bullfight

capear *vt* (dificultad etc) to dodge, to shirk; *Fig* **c. el temporal** to weather the storm

capellán *nm* chaplain

caperuza *nf* hood

capicúa *adj* **número c.** reversible number; **palabra c.** palindrome

capilar *adj* hair; **loción c.** hair lotion

capilla *nf* chapel; **c. ardiente** chapel of rest

capirote *nm Fam* **tonto de c.** silly idiot

capital 1 *nf* capital

  2 *nm Fin* capital; **c. activo** *o* **social** working *o* share capital

  3 *adj* capital, main; **de importancia c.** of capital importance; **pena c.** capital punishment

capitalismo *nm* capitalism

capitalista *adj & nmf* capitalist

capitalizar [40] *vt* to capitalize

capitán,-ana *nm,f* captain; **c. general** *Br* field marshal, *US* general of the army

capitanear *vt* (**a**) *Mil & Náut* to captain, to command (**b**) *(dirigir)* to lead; *Dep* to captain

capitulación *nf* agreement; *Mil* capitulation; **capitulaciones matrimoniales** marriage settlement

capitular *vi* (**a**) *Mil* to capitulate, to surrender (**b**) *(convenir)* to reach an agreement

capítulo *nm* (**a**) *(de libro)* chapter (**b**) *Fig* **dentro del c. de ...** *(tema)* under the heading of ...

capó *nm Aut Br* bonnet, *US* hood

capón *nm* rap on the head with the knuckles

capota *nf Aut* folding hood *o* top

capote *nm* (**a**) *Taurom* cape (**b**) *Mil* greatcoat

capricho *nm* (**a**) *(antojo)* whim, caprice (**b**) *Mús* caprice, capriccio

caprichoso,-a *adj* whimsical

Capricornio *nm* Capricorn

cápsula *nf* capsule

captar *vt* (**a**) *(ondas)* to receive, to pick up (**b**) *(comprender)* to understand, to grasp (**c**) *(interés etc)* to attract

captura *nf* capture

capturar *vt (criminal)* to capture; *(cazar, pescar)* to catch; *Mil* to seize

capucha *nf* hood

capuchino *nm (café)* cappuccino

capullo *nm* (**a**) *(de insecto)* cocoon (**b**) *Bot* bud (**c**) *Vulg (prepucio)* foreskin (**d**) *muy Fam (persona despreciable) Br* dickhead, *US* jerk

caqui 1 *adj (color)* khaki

  2 *nm (fruto)* persimmon

cara 1 *nf* (**a**) face; **c. a c.** face to face; **c. a la pared** facing the wall; **poner mala c.** to pull a long face; **tener buena/mala c.** to look good/bad; *Fig* **dar la c.** to face the consequences (of one's acts); *Fig* **dar la**

c. por algn to stand up for sb; *Fig* **(de) c. a** with a view to; *Fig* **echarle a algn algo en c.** to reproach sb for sth; *Fig* **plantar c. a algn** to face up to sb

  (**b**) *(lado)* side; *(de moneda)* right side; **¿c. o cruz?** heads or tails?; **echar algo a c. o cruz** to toss (a coin) for sth

  (**c**) *Fam (desfachatez)* cheek, nerve; **¡qué c. (más dura) tienes!** what a cheek you've got!

  2 *nm Fam (desvergonzado)* cheeky person

carabela *nf* caravel

carabina *nf* (**a**) *(arma)* carbine, rifle (**b**) *(persona)* chaperon

carabinero *nm* (**a**) *(marisco)* scarlet shrimp, = type of large red prawn (**b**) *Chile (policía)* military policeman

caracense 1 *adj* of/from Guadalajara

  2 *nmf* person from Guadalajara

caracol 1 *nm* (**a**) *(de tierra)* snail; *Am* shell (**b**) *(rizo)* kiss-curl

  2 *interj* **¡caracoles!** good heavens!

caracola *nf* conch

carácter *nm* (*pl* **caracteres**) (**a**) *(temperamento)* character; **de mucho c.** with a strong character; **tener buen/mal c.** to be good-natured/bad-tempered (**b**) *Fig (índole)* nature; **con c. de invitado** as a guest (**c**) *Impr* character

característica *nf* characteristic

característico,-a *adj* characteristic

caracterizar [40] *vt* to characterize

caradura *nmf Fam* cheeky devil; **¡qué c. eres!** you're so cheeky!

carajillo *nm Fam* = coffee with a dash of brandy

carajo *interj Vulg* shit!; **¡vete al c.!** go to hell!

caramba *interj Fam (sorpresa)* good grief!; *(enfado)* damn it!

carámbano *nm* icicle

carambola *nf Br* cannon, *US* carom

caramelo *nm* (**a**) *(dulce) Br* (boiled) sweet, *US* candy (**b**) *(azúcar quemado)* caramel; *Culin* **a punto de c.** syrupy

carantoña *nf* caress

caraota *nf Ven* bean

caraqueño,-a 1 *adj* of/from Caracas

  2 *nm,f* person from Caracas

carátula *nf* (**a**) *(cubierta)* cover (**b**) *(máscara)* mask

caravana *nf* (**a**) *(vehículo)* caravan (**b**) *(de tráfico) Br* tailback, *US* backup (**c**) *Urug (aro, pendiente)* earring

caray *interj* God!, good heavens!

carbón *nm* coal; **c. vegetal** charcoal; **c. mineral** coal

carboncillo nm charcoal

carbonero nm coal merchant

carbónico,-a adj carbonic; **agua carbónica** mineral water

carbonilla nf coal dust

carbonizar [40] 1 vt to carbonize, to char; **morir carbonizado** to be burnt to death

2 carbonizarse vpr to carbonize, to char

carbono nm carbon

carburador nm carburettor

carburante nm fuel

carburar vi Fam (funcionar) to work properly

carca adj & nmf Fam old fogey; Pol reactionary

carcaj nm quiver

carcajada nf guffaw

carcamal nm Fam old fogey

cárcel nf prison, jail

carcelario,-a adj prison, jail

carcelero,-a nm,f jailer, warder

carcoma nf woodworm

carcomer 1 vt to eat away

2 carcomerse vpr to be consumed (de with)

cardar vt (a) (lana, algodón) to card (b) (pelo) to backcomb

cardenal nm (a) Rel cardinal (b) Med bruise

cárdeno,-a adj purple

cardiaco,-a, cardíaco,-a 1 adj cardiac, heart; **ataque c.** heart attack

2 nm,f person with a heart condition

cardinal adj cardinal; **punto/número c.** cardinal point/number

cardiólogo,-a nm,f cardiologist

cardo nm (con espinas) thistle

carear vt (a) Jur to bring two people face to face (b) (cotejar) to compare

carecer [33] vi **c. de** to lack

carencia nf lack (**de** of)

carente adj lacking; **c. de interés** lacking interest

careo nm Jur confrontation

carestía nf (a) (falta) lack, shortage (b) Fin high price o cost

careta nf mask; **c. antigás** gas mask

carey nm tortoiseshell

carezco indic pres de **carecer**

carga nf (a) (acción) loading (b) (cosa cargada) load; (de avión, barco) cargo, freight; Fig **c. afectiva** emotional content (**c**) Fin (gasto) debit; **c. fiscal** tax charge (**d**) Fig (obligación) burden (**e**) Mil & Elec charge

cargado,-a adj (**a**) loaded (**b**) (bebida) strong; **un café c.** a strong coffee (**c**) (ambiente) heavy; **atmósfera cargada** stuffy atmosphere (**d**) Fig burdened; **c. de deudas** up to one's eyes in debt (**e**) Elec charged

cargamento nm (**a**) (carga) load (**b**) (mercancías) cargo, freight

cargante adj Fam annoying

cargar [42] 1 vt (**a**) to load; (mechero, pluma) to fill; (batería) to charge; Fig **c. las culpas a algn** to put the blame on sb (**b**) Com to charge; **cárguelo a mi cuenta** charge it to my account; Fam Educ **me han cargado las matemáticas** I failed maths

2 vi (**a**) **c. con** (llevar) to carry; Fig **c. con la responsabilidad** to take the responsibility; Fig **c. con las consecuencias** to suffer the consequences (**b**) Mil **c. contra** to charge

3 cargarse vpr (**a**) Fam **te la vas a c.** you're asking for trouble and you're going to get it (**b**) Fam (estropear) to smash, to ruin (**c**) Fam (matar) to kill, to bump off

cargo nm (**a**) (puesto) post, position; **alto c.** (puesto) top job, high ranking position; (persona) top person (**b**) **estar al c. de** to be in charge of; **correr a c. de** (gastos) to be met by; **hacerse c. de** to take charge of; **hazte c. de mi situación** please try to understand my situation; **c. de conciencia** weight on one's conscience (**c**) Fin charge, debit; **con c. a mi cuenta** charged to my account (**d**) Jur charge, accusation

cargosear vt CSur to annoy, to pester

cargoso,-a adj CSur annoying

carguero nm (**a**) (avión) transport plane (**b**) (barco) freighter

cariarse vpr to decay

caribe nm (idioma) Carib; **el (mar) C.** the Caribbean Sea

caricatura nf caricature

caricaturizar [40] vt to caricature

caricia nf caress, stroke

caridad nf charity

caries nf inv decay, caries

carilla nf page, side of a piece of paper

cariño nm (**a**) (amor) affection; **coger/tener c. a algo/algn** to grow/to be fond of sth/sb; **con c.** (en carta) love (**b**) (querido) darling (**c**) (abrazo) cuddle

cariñoso,-a adj loving, affectionate

carisma nm charisma

carismático,-a adj charismatic

caritativo,-a adj charitable

cariz nm look

carmesí adj & nm crimson

carmín nm (**de color**) **c.** carmine; **c. (de labios)** lipstick

carnal *adj* (**a**) *(de carne)* carnal (**b**) *(pariente)* first; **primo c.** first cousin

carnaval *nm* carnival

carne *nf* (**a**) flesh; *Fam* **ser de c. y hueso** to be only human; *Fig* **c. de cañón** cannon fodder; **c. de gallina** goosepimples; **c. viva** raw flesh (**b**) *(alimento)* meat; **c. de cerdo/cordero/ternera/vaca** pork/lamb/veal/beef (**c**) *(de fruta)* pulp

carné *nm* card; **c. de conducir** *Br* driving licence, *US* driver's license; **c. de identidad** identity card

carnear *vt Andes, RP (sacrificar)* to slaughter, to butcher

carnero *nm* ram; *Culin* mutton

carnet *nm* = **carné**

carnicería *nf* (**a**) butcher's (shop) (**b**) *Fig (masacre)* slaughter

carnicero,-a *nm,f* butcher

cárnico,-a *adj* **productos cárnicos** meat products

carnitas *nfpl Méx* = small pieces of fried or grilled pork

carnívoro,-a 1 *adj* carnivorous
2 *nm,f* carnivore

carnoso,-a *adj* fleshy

caro,-a 1 *adj* expensive, dear
2 *adv* **salir c.** to cost a lot; **te costará c.** *(amenaza)* you'll pay dearly for this

carozo *nm RP (de fruta, aceituna)* stone, *US* pit

carpa *nf* (**a**) *(pez)* carp (**b**) *(de circo)* big top; *(en parque, la calle)* marquee (**c**) *Am (de camping)* tent

Cárpatos *nmpl* Carpathians

carpeta *nf* file, folder

*✏ Observa que la palabra inglesa **carpet** es un falso amigo y no es la traducción de la palabra española **carpeta**. En inglés, **carpet** significa "alfombra".*

carpetazo *nm* **dar c. a un asunto** to shelve a matter

carpintería *nf* (**a**) *(oficio)* carpentry; **c. metálica** metalwork (**b**) *(taller)* carpenter's (shop)

carpintero,-a *nm,f* carpenter

carraca *nf* rattle

carraspear *vi* to clear one's throat

carraspeo *nm* clearing of the throat

carraspera *nf* hoarseness

carrera *nf* (**a**) run; *(de media)* run, ladder; **a la c.** in a hurry (**b**) *(competición)* race; **c. contra reloj** race against the clock; **c. de coches** rally, meeting; **echar una c. a algn** to race sb; **c. de armamentos** arms race (**c**) *(estudios)* university course; **hacer la c. de derecho/físicas** to study law/

physics (at university) (**d**) *(profesión)* career, profession

carreta *nf* run; **tomar c.** to take a run; **de c.** parrot fashion

carreta *nf* cart

carrete *nm* *(de hilo)* reel; *(de película)* spool; *(de cable)* coil

carretera *nf* road; **c. de acceso** access road; *(en autopista)* slip road; **c. de circunvalación** *Br* ring road, *US* beltway; **c. comarcal** minor road; *Méx* **c. de cuota** toll road; **c. nacional** *Br* ≃ A road, *US* ≃ state highway

carretero,-a *adj Am* road; **un accidente c.** a road accident

carretilla *nf* wheelbarrow

carricoche *nm* caravan

carril *nm* (**a**) *Ferroc* rail (**b**) *Aut* lane

carrillo *nm* cheek; *Fam* **comer a dos carrillos** to devour, to gobble up

carriola *nf* (**a**) *(cama)* truckle bed (**b**) *Méx (coche de bebé)* *Br* pram, *US* baby carriage

carro *nm* (**a**) *(carreta)* cart; *RP Fam* **¡pará el c.!** hold your horses! (**b**) *Mil* **c. de combate** tank (**c**) *(de máquina de escribir)* carriage (**d**) *Andes, CAm, Carib, Méx* car (**e**) *Méx (vagón)* car; **c. comedor** dining car

carrocería *nf Aut* bodywork

carroña *nf* carrion

carroza 1 *nf* (**a**) *(coche de caballos)* coach, carriage (**b**) *(de carnaval)* float
2 *nmf Fam* old fogey

carruaje *nm* carriage, coach

carrusel *nm Andes* roundabout, merry-go-round

carta *nf* (**a**) letter; **c. certificada/urgente** registered/express letter (**b**) *(menú)* menu; **a la c.** à la carte; **c. de vinos** wine list (**c**) *Naipes* card; **echar las cartas a algn** to tell sb's fortune; *Fig* **poner las cartas sobre la mesa** to put o lay one's cards on the table, to come clean (**d**) *Geog (mapa)* chart (**e**) *Fig* **adquirir c. de naturaleza** to become widely accepted; **tomar cartas en un asunto** to take part in an affair

cartabón *nm* set square

cartearse *vpr* to correspond (**con** with), to exchange letters (**con** with)

cartel *nm* poster; **pegar/fijar carteles** to put o stick up bills

cartél *nm Com* cartel

cartelera *nf* billboard, *Br* hoarding; *Prensa* **c. de espectáculos** entertainments section o page

cartera *nf* (**a**) *(de bolsillo)* wallet, *US*

billfold (**b**) *(de mano)* handbag; *(para documentos etc)* briefcase; *(de colegial)* satchel, schoolbag (**c**) *Pol (ministerio)* portfolio (**d**) *Com* portfolio; **c. de pedidos** order book

carterista *nm* pickpocket

cartero,-a *nm,f (hombre) Br* postman, *US* mailman; *(mujer) Br* postwoman, *US* mailwoman

cartilla *nf* (**a**) *(libreta)* book; **c. de ahorros** savings book (**b**) *(libro)* first reader; *Fam* **leerle la c. a algn** to tell sb off

cartografía *nf* cartography

cartón *nm* (**a**) *(material)* card, cardboard; **c. piedra** papier mâché (**b**) *(de cigarrillos)* carton

cartucho *nm* (**a**) *(de balas)* cartridge (**b**) *(de papel)* cone

cartulina *nf* card

casa *nf* (**a**) *(edificio)* house; **c. de huéspedes** boarding house; **c. de socorro** first-aid post (**b**) *(hogar)* home; **vete a c.** go home; **en c. de Daniel** at Daniel's; **andar por c.** everyday (**c**) *(empresa)* company, firm; **c. matriz/principal** head/central office

casación *nf Jur* annulment

casadero,-a *adj* of marrying age

casado,-a **1** *adj* married
2 *nm,f* married person; **los recién casados** the newlyweds

casamiento *nm* marriage; *(boda)* wedding

casar¹ **1** *vt* to marry
2 *vi* to match, to go *o* fit together
3 **casarse** *vpr* to marry, to get married; **c. por la iglesia/por lo civil** to get married in church/in a registry office

casar² *vt Jur* to annul, to quash

cascabel *nm* bell

cascada *nf* waterfall, cascade

cascanueces *nm inv* nutcracker

cascar **[44]** **1** *vt* (**a**) to crack (**b**) *Fam* **cascarla** to kick the bucket, to snuff it
2 *vi Fam (charlar)* to chat away
3 **cascarse** *vpr* to crack

cáscara *nf* shell; *(de fruta)* skin, peel; *(de grano)* husk

cascarón *nm* eggshell

cascarrabias *nmf inv Fam* short-tempered person

casco *nm* (**a**) *(para la cabeza)* helmet (**b**) *(de caballo)* hoof (**c**) *(envase)* empty bottle (**d**) **c. urbano** city centre (**e**) *(de barco)* hull (**f**) **cascos** *(auriculares)* headphones

cascote *nm* piece of rubble *o* debris

caserío *nm* country house

casero,-a **1** *adj* (**a**) *(hecho en casa)* homemade (**b**) *(persona)* home-loving
2 *nm,f (dueño) (hombre)* landlord; *(mujer)* landlady

caseta *nf* hut, booth; *(de feria, exposición)* stand, stall; *Méx* **c. de cobro** tollbooth; *Méx* **c. telefónica** phone box, phone booth

casete **1** *nm (magnetófono)* cassette player *o* recorder
2 *nf (cinta)* cassette (tape)

casi *adv* almost, nearly; **c. mil personas** almost one thousand people; **c. ni me acuerdo** I can hardly remember it; **c. nunca** hardly ever; **c. nadie** hardly anyone; **c. me caigo** I almost fell

casilla *nf* (**a**) *(de casillero)* pigeonhole; *Andes, RP* **c. de correos** PO Box; *CAm, Carib, Méx* **c. postal** PO Box (**b**) *(recuadro)* box (**c**) *Fig* **sacar a algn de sus casillas** to drive sb mad

casillero *nm* pigeonholes

casino *nm* casino

caso *nm* case; **el c. es que ...** the fact *o* thing is that ...; **el c. Mattei** the Mattei affair; **(en) c. contrario** otherwise; **en c. de necesidad** if need be; **en cualquier c.** in any case; **en el mejor/peor de los casos** at best/worst; **en ese c.** in such a case; **en todo c.** in any case; **en un c. extremo, en último c.** as a last resort; **hacer c. a** *o* **de algn** to pay attention to sb; **hacer c. omiso de** to take no notice of; **no venir al c.** to be beside the point; **pongamos por c.** let's say

caspa *nf* dandruff

casquete *nm* (**a**) *(de bala)* case, shell (**b**) *Geog* **c. polar** polar cap

> *⚡* Observa que la palabra inglesa **casket** es un falso amigo y no es la traducción de la palabra española **casquete**. En inglés, **casket** significa "cofre, ataúd".

casquillo *nm (de bala)* case

cassette *nm & nf* = **casete**

casta *nf* (**a**) *(linaje)* lineage, descent (**b**) *(animales)* breed; **de c.** thoroughbred, purebred (**c**) *(división social)* caste

castaña *nf* chestnut; *Fig* **sacarle a algn las castañas del fuego** to save sb's bacon

castañetear *vi (dientes)* to chatter

castaño,-a **1** *adj* chestnut-brown; *(pelo, ojos)* brown, dark
2 *nm Bot* chestnut

castañuela *nf* castanet

castellano,-a **1** *adj* Castilian
2 *nm,f (persona)* Castilian
3 *nm (idioma)* Spanish, Castilian

castidad *nf* chastity

castigar [42] *vt* (**a**) to punish (**b**) *(dañar)* to harm, to ruin (**c**) *Jur & Dep* to penalize

castigo *nm* punishment; *Jur* penalty; *Dep* **área de c.** penalty area

Castilla *n* Castile

castillo *nm* castle

castizo,-a *adj* pure, authentic

casto,-a *adj* chaste

castor *nm* beaver

castrar *vt* to castrate

castrense *adj* military

casual 1 *adj* accidental, chance
2 *nm Fam* chance

casualidad *nf* chance, coincidence; **de o por c.** by chance; **dio la c. que ...** it so happened that ...; **¿tienes un lápiz, por c.?** do you happen to have a pencil?; **¡que c.!** what a coincidence!

> 🖉 Observa que la palabra inglesa **casualty** es un falso amigo y no es la traducción de la palabra española **casualidad**. En inglés, **casualty** significa "víctima".

casualmente *adv* by chance

cata *nf* tasting

cataclismo *nm* cataclysm

catador,-a *nm,f* taster

catalán,-ana 1 *adj & nm,f* Catalan
2 *nm (idioma)* Catalan

catalejo *nm* telescope

catalepsia *nf* catalepsy

catalizador *nm* catalyst; *Aut* catalytic converter

catalizar [40] *vt Fig* to act as a catalyst for

catalogar [42] *vt* (**a**) to catalogue (**b**) *(clasificar)* to classify

catálogo *nm* catalogue

Cataluña *n* Catalonia

cataplasma *nf* (**a**) *Farm* cataplasm, poultice (**b**) *Fam (pelmazo)* bore

catapulta *nf* catapult; *Fig* springboard

catapultar *vt* to catapult

catar *vt* to taste

catarata *nf* (**a**) waterfall (**b**) *Med* cataract

catarro *nm* (common) cold

catastral *adj* **valor c.** rateable value

catastro *nm* land registry

catástrofe *nf* catastrophe

catastrófico,-a *adj* catastrophic

catear *vt* (**a**) *Fam (suspender)* to fail, *US* to flunk (**b**) *Am (casa)* to search

catecismo *nm* catechism

cátedra *nf* (professorial) chair; **le han dado la c.** they have appointed him professor

catedral *nf* cathedral

catedrático,-a *nm,f Educ* (**a**) *Univ* professor (**b**) *(de instituto)* head of department

categoría *nf* category; *Fig* class; **de c.** *(persona)* important; *(vino etc)* quality

categórico,-a *adj* categoric; **un no c.** a flat refusal

cateto,-a *nm,f Pey* yokel, bumpkin

catire,-a *adj Carib (rubio)* blond, blonde

catolicismo *nm* Catholicism

católico,-a *adj & nm,f* Catholic

catorce *adj & num inv* fourteen

catre *nm Fam* bed

Cáucaso *n* Caucasus

cauce *nm* (**a**) *(de un río)* bed (**b**) *Fig (canal)* channel; **cauces oficiales** official channels

caucho *nm* (**a**) rubber (**b**) *Am (cubierta)* tyre

caudal *nm* (**a**) *(de un río)* flow (**b**) *(riqueza)* wealth, riches

caudaloso,-a *adj (río)* plentiful

caudillo *nm* leader, head

causa *nf* (**a**) cause; **a o por c. de** because of (**b**) *(ideal)* cause (**c**) *Jur (caso)* case; *(juicio)* trial

causante 1 *adj* causal, causing
2 *nmf* **el c. del incendio** the person who caused the fire

causar *vt* to cause, to bring about; **me causa un gran placer** it gives me great pleasure; **c. buena/mala impresión** to make a good/bad impression

cáustico,-a *adj* caustic

cautela *nf* caution

cautivar *vt* (**a**) to capture, to take prisoner (**b**) *Fig (fascinar)* to captivate

cautiverio *nm*, **cautividad** *nf* captivity

cautivo,-a *adj & nm,f* captive

cauto,-a *adj* cautious, wary

cava 1 *nf (bodega)* wine cellar
2 *nm (vino espumoso)* cava, champagne

cavar *vt* to dig

caverna *nf* cave; **hombre de las cavernas** caveman

cavernícola *nmf* cave dweller

caviar *nm* caviar

cavidad *nf* cavity

cavilar *vt* to ponder

cayado *nm* (**a**) *(de pastor)* crook (**b**) *(de obispo)* crosier, crozier

cayuco *nm Am* small flat-bottomed canoe

caza 1 *nf* (**a**) hunting; **ir de c.** to go hunting; **c. furtiva** poaching (**b**) *(animales)* game; **c. mayor/menor** big/small game (**c**) *Fig (persecución)* hunt; **c. de brujas** witch hunt

2 *nm Av* fighter, fighter plane

cazabe *nm Am* cassava bread

cazabombardero *nm Av* fighter bomber

cazador,-a *nm,f* hunter; **c. furtivo** poacher

cazadora *nf* (waist-length) jacket

cazar [40] *vt* to hunt; *Fam* **cazarlas al vuelo** to be quick on the uptake

cazatalentos *nmf inv* head-hunter

cazo *nm* (a) *(cacerola)* saucepan (b) *(cucharón)* ladle

cazuela *nf* saucepan; *(guiso)* casserole, stew; **a la c.** stewed

c/c *(abr* **cuenta corriente**) c/a

CC. OO. *nfpl (abr* **Comisiones Obreras**) = Spanish left-wing trade union

CD-ROM *nm* CD-ROM

cebada *nf* barley

cebar 1 *vt* (a) *(animal)* to fatten; *(persona)* to feed up (b) *(anzuelo)* to bait (c) *(fuego, caldera)* to stoke, to fuel; *(máquina, arma)* to prime (d) *RP (mate)* to prepare, to brew

2 cebarse *vpr* **c. con** *(ensañarse)* to delight in tormenting

cebo *nm* bait

cebolla *nf* onion

cebolleta *nf* (a) *(especie)* chives (b) *(cebolla tierna)* spring onion

cebra *nf* zebra; **paso de c.** *Br* zebra crossing, *US* crosswalk

cecear *vi* to lisp

ceceo *nm* lisp

cedazo *nm* sieve

ceder 1 *vt* to give, to hand over; *Aut* **c. el paso** to give way

2 *vi* (a) *(cuerda, cable)* to give way (b) *(lluvia, calor)* to diminish, to slacken (c) *(consentir)* to give in

cederrón *nm* CD-ROM

cedro *nm* cedar

cédula *nf* (a) document, certificate; *Am* **c. de identidad** identity card (b) *Com & Fin* bond, certificate, warrant

C(E)E *nf (abr* **Comunidad (Económica) Europea**) E(E)C

cegador,-a *adj* blinding

cegar [1] *vt* (a) to blind (b) *(puerta, ventana)* to wall up

ceguera *nf* blindness

CEI *(abr* **Comunidad de Estados Independientes**) CIS

Ceilán *n* Ceylon

ceja *nf* eyebrow

cejar *vi* **c. en el empeño** to give up

celada *nf* trap, ambush

celador,-a *nm,f* attendant; *(de una cárcel)* warder

celda *nf* cell; **c. de castigo** punishment cell

celebración *nf* (a) *(festejo)* celebration (b) *(de juicio etc)* holding

celebrar 1 *vt* (a) to celebrate; **celebro que todo saliera bien** I'm glad everything went well (b) *(reunión, juicio, elecciones)* to hold (c) *(triunfo)* to laud

2 celebrarse *vpr* to take place, to be held

célebre *adj* famous, well-known

celebridad *nf* (a) celebrity, fame (b) *(persona)* celebrity

celeste 1 *adj* (a) *(de cielo)* celestial (b) *(color)* sky-blue

2 *nm* sky blue

celestial *adj* celestial, heavenly

celibato *nm* celibacy

célibe *adj & nmf* celibate

celo *nm* (a) zeal (b) **en c.** *(macho)* in rut; *(hembra)* on o in heat (c) **celos** jealousy; **tener celos (de algn)** to be jealous (of sb)

celo® *nm Fam Br* Sellotape®, *US* Scotch tape®

celofán *nm* cellophane®

celosía *nf* lattice

celoso,-a *adj* (a) jealous (b) *(cumplidor)* conscientious

celta 1 *adj* Celtic

2 *nmf* Celt

3 *nm (idioma)* Celtic

célula *nf* cell

celular 1 *adj* (a) cellular (b) **coche c.** police van (c) *Am* **teléfono c.** mobile phone, cellphone

2 *nm Am* mobile, cellphone

celulitis *nf inv* cellulitis

celuloide *nm* celluloid

celulosa *nf* cellulose

cementerio *nm* cemetery, graveyard; **c. de coches** scrapyard

cemento *nm* cement; **c. armado** reinforced cement

cena *nf* evening meal; *(antes de acostarse)* supper; **la Ultima C.** the Last Supper

cenagal *nm* marsh, swamp

cenar 1 *vi* to have supper o dinner

2 *vt* to have for supper o dinner

cencerro *nm* cowbell

cenefa *nf* *(de ropa)* edging, trimming; *(de suelo, techo)* ornamental border, frieze

cenetista 1 *adj* = of or related to the CNT (Confederación Nacional del Trabajo)

2 *nmf* member of the CNT

cenicero *nm* ashtray

cenit *nm* zenith

ceniza *nf* ash

cenizo *nm Fam (gafe)* jinx

censo *nm* census; **c. electoral** electoral roll

censor *nm* censor

censura *nf* (a) censorship (b) *Pol* **moción de c.** vote of no confidence

censurar *vt* (a) *(libro, película)* to censor (b) *(criticar)* to censure, to criticize

centavo *nm Am Fin* cent, centavo

centella *nf* spark

centellear *vi* to flash, to sparkle

centelleo *nm* flashing, sparkling

centena *nf*, **centenar** *nm* hundred; **a centenares** in hundreds

centenario *nm* centenary, hundredth anniversary

centeno *nm* rye

centésimo,-a *adj & nm,f* hundredth

centígrado,-a *adj* centigrade

centilitro *nm* centilitre

centímetro *nm* centimetre

céntimo *nm* cent

centinela *nm* sentry

centollo *nm* spider crab

centrado,-a *adj* (a) centred (b) *(equilibrado)* balanced

central 1 *adj* central

   2 *nf* (a) *Elec* **c. nuclear/térmica** nuclear/coal-fired power station (b) *(oficina principal)* head office

centralismo *nm* centralism

centralita *nf Tel* switchboard

centralizar [40] *vt* to centralize

centrar 1 *vt* (a) to centre (b) *(esfuerzos, atención)* to concentrate, to centre (**en** on)

   2 centrarse *vpr* (a) to be centred o based (b) **c. en** *(concentrarse)* to concentrate on

céntrico,-a *adj* centrally situated; **zona céntrica** centrally situated area

centrifugar [42] *vt* to centrifuge; *(ropa)* to spin-dry

centrista *Pol* **1** *adj* centre; **partido c.** centre party

   2 *nmf* centrist

centro *nm* (a) middle, centre; **c. de la ciudad** town o city centre (b) *(establecimiento)* institution, centre; **c. comercial** shopping centre

Centroamérica *n* Central America

centroamericano,-a *adj & nm,f* Central American

centrocampista *nmf Ftb* midfielder

centuria *nf* century

ceñido,-a *adj* tight-fitting, clinging

ceñirse [6] *vpr* (a) *(atenerse, limitarse)* to limit oneself, to stick (**a** to); **c. al tema** to keep to the subject; **ciñéndonos a este caso en concreto** coming down to this particular case (b) **c. a** *(prenda)* to cling to

ceño *nm* scowl, frown; **con el c. fruncido** frowning

CEOE *nf* (*abr* **Confederación Española de Organizaciones Empresariales**) = Spanish employers' organization, ≃ CBI

cepa *nf* (a) *(de vid)* vine (b) *Fig* **vasco de pura c.** *(origen)* Basque through and through

cepillar 1 *vt* (a) to brush (b) *(en carpintería)* to plane (down) (c) *Fam (robar)* to pinch

   2 cepillarse *vpr* (a) *(con cepillo)* to brush (b) *Fam (matar)* to do in (c) *muy Fam* to lay

cepillo *nm* brush; *(en carpintería)* plane; **c. de dientes** toothbrush; **c. del pelo** hairbrush

cepo *nm* (a) *(para cazar)* trap (b) *Aut* clamp

CEPYME *nf* (*abr* **Confederación Española de la Pequeña y Mediana Empresa**) = Spanish confederation of small and medium-sized businesses

cera *nf* wax; *(de abeja)* beeswax

cerámica *nf* ceramics *sing*

cerca¹ *adv* (a) near, close; **ven más c.** come closer; **ya estamos c.** we are almost there (b) **c. de** *(al lado de)* near, close to; **el colegio está c. de mi casa** the school is near my house (c) **c. de** *(casi)* nearly, around; **c. de cien personas** about one hundred people (d) **de c.** closely; **lo vi muy de c.** I saw it close up

cerca² *nf* fence, wall

cercado *nm* (a) *(lugar cerrado)* enclosure (b) *(valla)* fence, wall

cercanía *nf* (a) proximity, nearness (b) **cercanías** outskirts, suburbs; **(tren de) cercanías** suburban train

cercano,-a *adj* nearby; **el C. Oriente** the Near East

cercar [44] *vt* (a) *(tapiar)* to fence, to enclose (b) *(rodear)* to surround

cercenar *vt* to cut off, to amputate

cerciorar 1 *vt* to assure

   2 cerciorarse *vpr* to make sure

cerco *nm* (a) circle, ring (b) *Mil (sitio)* siege; **poner c. (a una ciudad)** to besiege (a town)

cerda *nf* (a) *Zool* sow (b) *(pelo)* bristle; **cepillo de c.** bristle brush

Cerdeña *n* Sardinia

cerdo *nm* (a) pig (b) *(carne)* pork (c) *Fam* pig, arsehole

cereal *nm* cereal

cerebral *adj* (a) cerebral (b) *(frío)* calculating

cerebro *nm* brain; *Fig (inteligencia)* brains

ceremonia *nf* ceremony

ceremonioso,-a *adj* ceremonious, formal; *Pey* pompous, stiff

cereza *nf* cherry

cerezo *nm* cherry tree

cerilla *nf* match

cerillo *nm CAm, Méx* match

cernerse [3] *vpr Fig* to loom (**sobre** above)

cernícalo *nm* kestrel

cernirse [54] *vpr* = cernerse

cero *nm* zero; *Dep* nil; *Fig* **partir de c.** to start from scratch; *Fig* **ser un c. a la izquierda** to be useless *o* a good-for-nothing

cerquillo *nm Am Br* fringe, *US* bangs

cerrado,-a *adj* (**a**) closed, shut; **a puerta cerrada** behind closed doors (**b**) *(reservado)* reserved; *(intransigente)* uncompromising, unyielding; *Fam (torpe)* thick; *(acento)* broad; *(curva)* tight, sharp (**c**) *(barba)* bushy

cerradura *nf* lock

cerrajero,-a *nm,f* locksmith

cerrar [1] **1** *vt* to shut, to close; *(grifo, gas)* to turn off; *(luz)* to turn off, to switch off; *(cremallera)* to do up; *(negocio)* to close down; *(cuenta)* to close; *(carta)* to seal; *(puños)* to clench; **c. con llave** to lock; **c. el paso a algn** to block sb's way; *Fam* **c. el pico** to shut one's trap
2 *vi* to close, to shut
3 cerrarse *vpr* to close, to shut; *Fam* **c. en banda** to stick to one's guns

cerro *nm* hill; *Fig* **irse por los cerros de Ubeda** to beat around the bush

cerrojo *nm* bolt; **echar el c. (de una puerta)** to bolt (a door)

certamen *nm* competition, contest

certero,-a *adj* accurate

certeza, certidumbre *nf* certainty; **saber (algo) con c.** to be certain (of sth); **tener la c. de que ...** to be sure *o* certain that ...

certificado,-a 1 *adj* (**a**) certified (**b**) *(correo)* registered
2 *nm* certificate

certificar [44] *vt* (**a**) to certify (**b**) *(carta)* to register

cervatillo *nm* fawn

cervecería *nf* (**a**) *(bar)* pub, bar (**b**) *(fábrica)* brewery

cerveza *nf* beer; **c. de barril** draught beer; **c. dorada** *o* **ligera** lager; **c. negra** stout

cervical *adj* cervical

cesante *adj (destituido)* dismissed, *Br* sacked; *CSur, Méx (parado)* unemployed

cesantear *vt CSur* to make redundant

cesar 1 *vi* **c. (de)** to stop, to cease; **sin c.** incessantly
2 *vt (empleado)* to dismiss, *Br* to sack

cesárea *nf* Caesarean (section)

cese *nm* (**a**) cessation, suspension (**b**) *(despido)* dismissal

Cesid *nm* (*abr* **Centro Superior de Investigación de la Defensa**) = Spanish military intelligence and espionage service

césped *nm* lawn, grass

cesta *nf* basket; **c. de Navidad** Christmas hamper

cesto *nm* basket

cetáceo *nm* cetacean, whale

cetrino,-a *adj* sallow

cetro *nm* sceptre

Ceuta *n* Ceuta

ceutí 1 *adj* of/from Ceuta
2 *nmf* person from Ceuta

ceviche *nm* = raw fish marinated in lemon and garlic

chabacano,-a 1 *adj* cheap
2 *nm Méx (fruto)* apricot; *(árbol)* apricot tree

chabola *nf* shack; **barrio de chabolas** shanty town

chacal *nm* jackal

chacarero,-a *nm,f Andes, RP* farmer

chacha *nf* maid

cháchara *nf Fam* small talk, chinwag; **estar de c.** to have a yap

chachi *adj* smashing

chacinados *nmpl RP* pork products

chacinería *nf* pork butcher's (shop)

chacra *nf Andes, RP* farm

chafar *vt* (**a**) *Fam (plan etc)* to ruin, to spoil (**b**) *(aplastar)* to squash, to flatten

chal *nm* shawl

chalado,-a *adj Fam* crazy, nuts (**por** about)

chalé *nm (pl* **chalés***)* = chalet

chaleco *nm Br* waistcoat, *US* vest; *(de punto)* sleeveless pullover; **c. antibalas** bullet-proof vest; **c. salvavidas** life jacket

chalet *nm* villa

chalupa *nf* (**a**) *(embarcación)* boat, launch (**b**) *Méx (torta)* = small tortilla with a raised rim to contain a filling

chamaco,-a *nm,f Méx Fam* kid

chamarra *nf* sheepskin jacket

chamba *nf CAm, Méx, Perú, Ven Fam (trabajo)* job

chambelán *nm* chamberlain

chambergo *nm* heavy coat

chambón,-ona *nm,f Am Fam* sloppy *o* shoddy worker

chamizo *nm* thatched hut

champa *nf CAm (tienda de campaña)* tent

champán, champaña *nm o nf* champagne

champiñón *nm* mushroom

champú *nm* shampoo

chamuscar [44] *vt* to singe, to scorch

chamusquina *nf* singeing, scorching; *Fam* **esto me huele a c.** there's something fishy going on here

chancaca *nf CAm (torta)* syrup cake

chance 1 *nm Am* opportunity
  2 *adv Méx* maybe

chancear *vi Am* to joke, to horse around

chanchada *nf Am* (a) *(porquería)* **no hagas chanchadas** stop that, don't be disgusting! (b) *Fam (jugarreta)* dirty trick

chancho,-a *nm,f Am* pig, hog, *f* sow

chanchullo *nm Fam* fiddle, wangle

chancla *nf Br* flip-flop, *US* thong

chanclo *nm (zueco)* clog; *(de goma)* overshoe, galosh

chándal *nm* track *o* jogging suit

changa *nf Bol, RP (trabajo temporal)* odd job

changador *nm RP (cargador)* porter

changarro *nm Méx* small shop

chantaje *nm* blackmail; **hacer c. a algn** to blackmail sb

chantajear *vt* to blackmail

chantajista *nmf* blackmailer

chanza *nf* joke

chapa *nf* (a) *(de metal)* sheet (b) *(de madera)* panel-board (c) *(tapón)* bottle top, cap (d) *(de adorno)* badge (e) *RP Br* number plate, *US* license plate (f) *Col (cerradura)* lock

chapado,-a *adj (metal)* plated; **c. en oro** gold-plated; *Fig* **c. a la antigua** old-fashioned

chaparro *nm Bot* holm oak

chaparrón *nm* downpour, heavy shower

chapopote *nm Carib, Méx* bitumen, pitch

chapotear *vi* to splash about, to paddle

chapucero,-a *adj (trabajo)* slapdash, shoddy; *(persona)* bungling

chapulín *nm CAm, Méx (saltamontes)* grasshopper

chapurrear *vt* to speak badly *o* with difficulty; **sólo chapurreaba el francés** he spoke only a few words of French

chapuza *nf* (a) *(trabajo mal hecho)* shoddy piece of work (b) *(trabajo ocasional)* odd job

chapuzón *nm (baño corto)* dip; **darse un c.** to have a dip

chaqué *nm* morning coat

chaqueta *nf* jacket; *Pol* **cambiar de c.** to change sides

chaquetero,-a *nm,f Fam Pol* turncoat

chaquetilla *nf* short jacket

charanga *nf Mús* brass band

charca *nf* pond, pool

charco *nm* puddle

charcutería *nf* delicatessen

charla *nf (conversación)* talk, chat; *(conferencia)* informal lecture *o* address; *Informát* chat

charlar *vi* to talk, to chat; *Informát* to chat

charlatán,-ana 1 *adj (parlanchín)* talkative; *(chismoso)* gossipy
  2 *nm,f* (a) *(parlanchín)* chatterbox; *(chismoso)* gossip; *(bocazas)* bigmouth (b) *(embaucador)* trickster, charmer

charol *nm* (a) *(piel)* patent leather; **zapatos de c.** patent leather shoes (b) *Andes (bandeja)* tray

charola *nf CAm, Méx* tray

charqui *nm Andes, RP (carne)* jerked *o* salted beef

chárter *adj inv* **(vuelo) c.** charter (flight)

chasca *nf Andes (greña)* mop of hair

chascar [44] *vt (lengua)* to click; *(dedos)* to snap; *(látigo)* to crack

chascarrillo *nm* shaggy dog story

chasco *nm Fam* disappointment; **llevarse un c.** to be disappointed

chasis *nm inv* chassis

chasquear *vt (lengua)* to click; *(dedos)* to snap; *(látigo)* to crack

chasqui *nm* = Inca messenger or courier

chasquido *nm (de la lengua)* click; *(de los dedos)* snap; *(de látigo, madera)* crack

chatarra *nf* scrap (metal), scrap iron; *Fam* junk

chato,-a 1 *adj* (a) *(nariz)* snub; *(persona)* snub-nosed (b) *(objeto)* flat, flattened (c) *PRico, RP Fam (sin ambiciones)* commonplace; **una vida chata** a humdrum existence
  2 *nm* (small) glass of wine

chau *interj Andes, RP Fam* bye!, see you!

chaucha 1 *adj RP Fam* dull, boring
  2 *nf Bol, RP* green bean

chauvinista *adj & nmf* chauvinist

chaval,-a *nm,f Fam (chico)* boy, lad; *(chica)* girl

chaveta *nf* (a) *(clavija)* cotter pin (b) *Fam (cabeza)* nut, head; **perder la c.** *(volverse loco)* to go off one's rocker (c) *Andes (navaja)* penknife

chavo,-a *Fam* **1** *nm,f Méx (chico)* guy; *(chica)* girl
  2 *nm (dinero)* **no tener un c.** to be broke

che *interj RP Fam* **¿qué hacés, c.?, ¿cómo andás, c.?** how are things *o* how's it going, then?; **c., ¡vení para acá!** over here, you!

checo,-a *adj* Czech

checoslovaco,-a 1 *adj* Czechoslovakian, Czech

2 *nm,f (persona)* Czechoslovakian, Czechoslovak, Czech

Checoslovaquia *n* Czechoslovakia

chele,-a *CAm* **1** *adj (rubio)* blond, blonde; *(de piel blanca)* fair-skinned

2 *nm,f (rubio)* blond(e) person; *(de piel blanca)* fair-skinned person

chelín *nm* shilling

chepa *nf Fam* hump

cheque *nm* cheque; **c. al portador** cheque payable to bearer; **c. de viaje** *o* **(de) viajero** traveller's cheque

chequeo *nm Med* checkup; *Aut* service

chévere *adj Andes, CAm, Carib, Méx Fam* great, fantastic

chic *adj inv* chic, elegant

chicano,-a *adj & nm,f* chicano

chicha¹ *nf Andes* = alcoholic drink made from fermented maize

chicha² *adj inv Náut* **calma c.** dead calm

chícharo *nm CAm, Méx* pea

chicharra *nf (persona) (insecto)* cicada (b) *Méx, RP (timbre)* electric buzzer

chiche *nm* (a) *Andes, RP Fam (juguete)* toy (b) *Andes, RP (adorno)* delicate ornament (c) *CAm, Méx muy Fam (pecho)* tit

chichón *nm* bump, lump

chichonera *nf* helmet

chicle *nm* chewing gum

chico,-a 1 *nm,f (muchacho)* boy, lad; *(muchacha)* girl

2 *adj* small, little

chicoria *nf* chicory

chicote *nm Am (látigo)* whip

chiflado,-a *adj Fam* mad, crazy (**por** about)

chiflar *vt* (a) *(silbar)* to hiss (at), to boo (at) (b) *Fam* **le chiflan las motos** he's really into motorbikes

chiflido *nm Am* whistle, whistling

chigüín,-ina *nm,f CAm Fam* kid

chiita *adj & nmf* Shiite

chilango,-a *Méx Fam* **1** *adj* of/from Mexico City

2 *nm,f* person from Mexico City

Chile *n* Chile

chile *nm* chilli (pepper)

chileno,-a *adj & nm,f* Chilean

chillar *vi (persona)* to scream, to shriek; *(ratón)* to squeak; *(frenos)* to screech, to squeal; *(puerta)* to creak, to squeak

chillido *nm (de persona)* scream, shriek; *(de ratón)* squeak; *(de frenos)* screech, squeal; *(de puerta)* creaking, squeaking

chillón,-ona *adj* (a) *(voz)* shrill, high-pitched; *(sonido)* harsh, strident (b) *(color)* loud, gaudy

chilpotle *nm Méx* = smoked or pickled jalapeño chilli

chimbo,-a *adj Col, Ven Fam* (a) *(de mala calidad)* crap, useless (b) *(complicado)* screwed-up

chimenea *nf* (a) *(hogar abierto)* fireplace, hearth (b) *(conducto)* chimney; *(de barco)* funnel, stack

chimichurri *nm RP* = barbecue sauce made from garlic, parsley, herbs and vinegar

China *n* China

china *nf* (a) *(piedra, small stone; Fam* **tocarle a uno la c.** to get the short straw (b) *Fam (droga)* deal

---

📕 Observa que la palabra inglesa **china** es un falso amigo y no es la traducción de la palabra española **china**. En inglés, **china** significa "loza, porcelana".

---

chinampa *nf Méx* = man-made island for growing flowers, fruit and vegetables, found in Xochimilco near Mexico City

chinche 1 *nf* bug, bedbug; *Fam* **caer como chinches** to fall like flies

2 *nmf Fam* nuisance, pest

chincheta *nf Br* drawing pin, *US* thumbtack

chinchín *interj* **¡c.!** cheers!, (to) your (good) health!

chinchulín *nm*, **chinchulines** *nmpl Andes, RP (plato)* = piece of sheep or cow intestine, plaited and then roasted

chinesco,-a *adj* **sombras chinescas** shadow theatre

chingado,-a *adj muy Fam (estropeado)* bust, *Br* knackered

chingana *nf Perú Fam* bar

chingar [42] *vt* (a) *(fastidiar)* to annoy (b) *muy Fam (estropear)* to bust, *Br* to knacker (c) *Vulg (joder)* to fuck, to screw

chino¹ *nm (piedrecita)* pebble, stone

chino²,-a *adj* (a) *(de la China)* Chinese; *Fam* **eso me suena a c.** it's all Greek to me (b) *Am (mestizo)* of mixed ancestry

chip *nm (pl* **chips)** *Informát* chip

chipirón *nm* baby squid

Chipre *n* Cyprus

chipriota *adj & nmf* Cypriot

chiqueo *nm Méx* cuddle

chiquilín,-ina *nm,f RP* small boy, *f* small girl

chiquillo,-a *nm,f* kid

chiquito,-a *adj* tiny

chirimiri *nm* drizzle, fine misty rain

chirimoya *nf* custard apple

chiringuito *nm* (*en playa etc*) refreshment stall; (*en carretera*) roadside snack bar

chiripa *nf* fluke, lucky stroke; *Fam Fig* **de o por c.** by a fluke, by chance; **cogió el tren por c.** it was sheer luck that he caught the train

chiripá *nm* (*pl* **chiripaes**) *Bol, CSur* = garment worn by gauchos as trousers

chirla *nf* small clam

chirona *nf Fam* clink, nick

chirriar [29] *vi* (*puerta etc*) to creak; (*frenos*) to screech, to squeal

chirrido *nm* (*de puerta etc*) crack, cracking; (*de frenos*) screech, squeal

chisme *nm* (a) (*habladuría*) piece of gossip (b) *Fam* (*trasto*) knick-knack; (*cosa*) thing

chismorrear *vi Fam* to gossip

chismorreo *nm Fam* gossip, gossiping

chismoso,-a **1** *adj* gossipy
　　2 *nm,f* gossip

chispa *nf* (a) spark; **echar chispas** to fume (b) *Fam* (*un poco*) bit, tiny amount (c) *Fam* (*agudeza*) wit, sparkle; (*viveza*) liveliness

chispear *vi* (a) to spark, to throw out sparks (b) (*lloviznar*) to spit

chiste *nm* joke; **contar un c.** to tell a joke; **c. verde** blue joke, dirty joke

chistera *nf* top hat

chistoso,-a *adj* (*persona*) funny, witty; (*anécdota*) funny, amusing

chivarse *vpr Fam* to tell tales

chivatazo *nm Fam* tip-off; **dar el c.** to squeal

chivato,-a **1** *nm,f Fam* (*delator*) *Br* grass, *US* rat; (*acusica*) telltale
　　2 *nm* (a) (*luz*) warning light (b) (*alarma*) alarm bell (c) *Ven Fam* (*pez gordo*) big cheese

chivito *nm Urug* = steak sandwich (*containing cheese and salad*)

chivo,-a *nm,f Zool* kid, young goat; *Fig* **c. expiatorio** scapegoat

chocante *adj* (a) (*persona*) off-putting (b) (*sorprendente*) surprising, startling; (*raro*) strange

chocar [44] **1** *vi* (a) (*topar*) to crash, to collide; **c. con o contra** to run into, to collide with (b) (*en discusión*) to clash
　　2 *vt* (a) to knock; (*la mano*) to shake; *Fam* **¡chócala!, ¡choca esos cinco!** shake (on it)!, put it there! (b) (*sorprender*) to surprise

chochear *vi* (a) to be senile *o* in one's dotage (b) **c. con algn** to dote on sb

chocho,-a **1** *adj* (*senil*) senile; **viejo c.** old dodderer
　　2 *nm* (a) (*altramuz*) lupin (b) *muy Fam Br* fanny, *US* beaver

choclo *nm Andes, RP* (*mazorca*) corncob, ear of maize *o US* corn; (*granos*) sweetcorn; (*cultivo*) maize, *US* corn

chocolate *nm* (a) chocolate; **c. con leche** milk chocolate (b) *Fam* (*droga*) dope

chocolatina *nf* bar of chocolate, chocolate bar

chófer *nm* (*pl* **chóferes**), *Am* **chofer** *nm* (*pl* **choferes**) driver; (*particular*) chauffeur

chollo *nm Fam* (*ganga*) bargain, snip

chomba *nf Arg* polo shirt

chompa *nf Andes* sweater, *Br* jumper

chompipe *nm CAm, Méx* turkey

chongo *nm Méx* (a) (*moño*) bun (b) **chongos zamoranos** (*dulce*) = Mexican dessert made from milk curds, served in syrup

chonta *nf Am* palm tree

chop *nm CSur* (a) (*jarra*) beer mug/glass (b) (*cerveza*) (glass of) beer

chopo *nm* poplar

chopp *nm CSur* = **chop**

choque *nm* (a) impact; (*de coches etc*) crash, collision; **c. frontal** head-on collision; **c. múltiple** pile-up (b) *Fig* (*contienda*) clash

choricear, chorizar *vt Fam* to pinch

chorizo *nm* (a) chorizo, highly-seasoned pork sausage (b) *Fam* (*ratero*) thief, pickpocket

chorlito *nm Orn* plover; *Fam Fig* **cabeza de c.** scatterbrain

choro *nm Andes* mussel

chorra *Fam* **1** *nmf* (*tonto*) idiot, fool
　　2 *nf* (*suerte*) luck

chorrada *nf Fam* piece of nonsense

chorrear *vi* to drip, to trickle; *Fam* **c. de sudor** to pour with sweat; *Fam* **tengo el abrigo chorreando** my coat is dripping wet

chorro *nm* (a) (*de agua etc*) spurt; (*muy fino*) trickle; **salir a chorros** to gush forth (b) *Téc* jet (c) *Fig* stream, flood

chovinismo *nm* chauvinism

chovinista **1** *adj* chauvinistic
　　2 *nmf* chauvinist

choza *nf* hut, shack

christmas *nm* Christmas card

chubasco *nm* heavy shower, downpour

chubasquero *nm* raincoat

chúcaro,-a *adj Andes, CAm, RP* (a) (*animal*) wild (b) (*persona*) unsociable

chuchería *nf Fam Br* sweet, *US* candy

chueco,-a **1** *adj Am* (*torcido*) twisted;

(patizambo) bowlegged; *Méx, Ven Fam (cojo)* lame

  2 *nm,f Am (patizambo)* bowlegged person; *Méx, Ven (cojo)* lame person

chufa *nf* groundnut

chulear *vi Fam* to strut around; **c. de** to go on about

chuleta *nf* **(a)** chop, cutlet; **c. de cerdo** pork chop **(b)** *Educ Fam* crib

chullo *nm Andes* woollen cap

chulo,-a *Fam* **1** *nm,f* show-off

  2 *nm (proxeneta)* pimp

  3 *adj (bonito)* smashing

chungo,-a *adj Fam* dodgy

chuño *nm Andes, RP* potato starch

chupa *nf Arg* short jacket

chupachups® *nm* lollipop

chupacirios *nmf inv Fam Pey* holy Joe

chupado,-a *adj* **(a)** *(flaco)* skinny, thin **(b)** *Fam* **está c.** it's dead easy

chupamedias *nmf Andes, RP, Ven Fam* toady, sycophant

chupar 1 *vt* **(a)** to suck **(b)** *(lamer)* to lick **(c)** *(absorber)* to soak up, to absorb

  2 *vi* to suck

  3 chuparse *vpr* **(a) está para c. los dedos** it's really mouthwatering **(b)** *Fam* to put up with; **nos chupamos toda la película** we sat through the whole film

chupatintas *nm inv Pey* penpusher

chupe *nm Andes, Arg* stew

chupete *nm Br* dummy, *US* pacifier

chupi *adj Fam* great, terrific, fantastic

chupón *nm* **(a)** lollipop **(b)** *(desatrancador)* plunger

churrasco *nm* barbecued meat

churrería *nf* fritter shop

churrete *nm* dirty mark, grease spot

churro *nm* **(a)** = dough formed into sticks or rings, fried in oil and covered in sugar **(b)** *Fam (chapuza)* mess

chusco *nm* chunk of stale bread; *Mil Fam* ration bread

chusma *nf* rabble, mob

chutar 1 *vi* **(a)** *Dep (a gol)* to shoot **(b)** *Fam* **¡y vas que chutas!** and then you're well away!

  2 chutarse *vpr Fam (drogas)* to shoot up

chute *nm* **(a)** *Dep* shot **(b)** *Fam (drogas)* fix

CI *nm (abr coeficiente intelectual)* IQ

Cía., cía *(abr compañía)* Co

cianuro *nm* cyanide

cibercafé *nm Informát* Internet cafe, cybercafe

ciberespacio *nm Informát* cyberspace

cibernética *nf* cybernetics *sing*

cicatero,-a 1 *adj* stingy, mean

  2 *nm,f* miser

cicatriz *nf* scar

cicatrizar [40] *vt & vi Med* to heal

cíclico,-a *adj* cyclical

ciclismo *nm* cycling

ciclista 1 *adj* cycling

  2 *nmf* cyclist

ciclo *nm* cycle; *(de conferencias etc)* course, series

ciclocróss *nm* cyclo-cross

ciclomotor *nm* moped

ciclón *nm* cyclone

ciego,-a 1 *adj (persona)* blind; *Fam (borracho)* blind drunk; *(de droga)* stoned; **a ciegas** blindly

  2 *nm,f* blind person; **los ciegos** the blind

cielo *nm* **(a)** sky **(b)** *Rel* heaven; *Fig* **caído del c.** *(oportuno)* heaven-sent; *(inesperado)* out of the blue; **¡c. santo!** good heavens! **(c)** *Arquit* **c. raso** ceiling **(d) c. de la boca** roof of the mouth

ciempiés *nm inv* centipede

ciénaga *nf* marsh, bog

ciencia *nf* **(a)** science; *Fig* **saber algo a c. cierta** to know sth for certain; **c. ficción** science fiction; **c. infusa** intuition; **ciencias ocultas** the occult **(b)** *(conocimiento)* knowledge

cieno *nm* mud, mire

científico,-a 1 *adj* scientific

  2 *nm,f* scientist

cientista *nmf CSur* **c. social** social scientist

ciento *adj* hundred; **c. tres** one hundred and three; **por c.** percent

cierne *nm Fig* **en ciernes** budding

cierre *nm* **(a)** *(acción)* closing, shutting; *(de fábrica)* shutdown; *TV* close-down; **c. patronal** lockout **(b)** *(de bolso)* clasp; *(de puerta)* catch; *(prenda)* fastener; **c. de seguridad** safety lock; **c. centralizado** central locking; *Am* **c. relámpago** *Br* zip, *US* zipper

cierto,-a 1 *adj* **(a)** *(verdadero)* true; *(seguro)* certain; **estar en lo c.** to be right; **lo c. es que ...** the fact is that ...; **por c.** by the way **(b)** *(algún)* certain; **ciertas personas** certain *o* some people

  2 *adv* certainly

ciervo,-a *nm,f* deer; *(macho)* stag; *(hembra)* doe, hind

cifra *nf* **(a)** *(número)* figure, number **(b)** *(código)* cipher, code

cifrar *vt* to express in figures

cigala nf Norway lobster, scampi

cigarra nf cicada

cigarrillo nm cigarette

cigarro nm (**a**) (puro) cigar (**b**) (cigarrillo) cigarette

cigüeña nf (**a**) Orn stork (**b**) Téc crank

cigüeñal nm crankshaft

cilindrada nf Aut cylinder capacity

cilíndrico,-a adj cylindrical

cilindro nm cylinder

cima nf summit

cimbrearse vpr to sway

cimentar vt to lay the foundations of; Fig (amistad) to strengthen

cimientos nmpl foundations; **echar** o **poner los c.** to lay the foundations

cinc nm zinc

cincel nm chisel

cincelar vt to chisel

cinco adj & nm inv five

cincuenta adj & nm inv fifty

cine nm (**a**) (local), US movie theater (**b**) (arte) cinema; **c. mudo/sonoro** silent/talking films

cineasta nmf movie director, movie maker

cinéfilo,-a nm,f (que va al cine) (keen) moviegoer o Br filmgoer; (que entiende de cine) movie o Br film buff

cinematográfico,-a adj cinematographic; **la industria cinematográfica** the movie o Br film industry

cíngaro,-a adj & nm,f gypsy

cínico,-a 1 adj shameless

2 nm,f shameless person; **es un c.** he's shameless, he has no shame

> *Observa que la palabra inglesa* **cynic** *es un falso amigo y no es la traducción de la palabra española* **cínico**. *En inglés,* **cynic** *significa tanto "descreído, suspicaz" como "desaprensivo".*

cinismo nm shamelessness

> *Observa que la palabra inglesa* **cynicism** *es un falso amigo y no es la traducción de la palabra española* **cinismo**. *En inglés,* **cynicism** *significa "descreimiento, suspicacia".*

cinta nf (**a**) (tira) band, strip; (para adornar) ribbon; Cost braid, edging (**b**) Téc & Mús tape; **c. adhesiva/aislante** adhesive/insulating tape; **c. de vídeo** video tape; **c. transportadora** conveyor belt (**c**) Cin film

cinto nm belt

cintura nf waist

cinturón nm belt; Fig **apretarse el c.** to tighten one's belt; **c. de seguridad** safety belt; Am **c. de miseria** = slum or shanty

town area round a large city

ciprés nm cypress

circense adj circus

circo nm circus

circuito nm circuit

circulación nf (**a**) circulation (**b**) Aut (tráfico) traffic

circular 1 adj & nf circular

2 vi (moverse) to circulate; (líquido) to flow; (tren, autobús) to run; Fig (rumor) to go round; **circule por la izquierda** (en letrero) keep to the left

circulatorio,-a adj circulatory; Aut **un caos c.** traffic chaos

círculo nm circle; Fig **c. vicioso** vicious circle

circuncisión nf circumcision

circundante adj surrounding

circundar vt to surround, to encircle

circunferencia nf circumference

circunloquio nm circumlocution

circunscribirse (pp circunscrito) vpr **c. a** to confine o limit oneself to

circunscripción nf district; **c. electoral** constituency

circunscrito,-a adj circumscribed

circunspecto,-a adj circumspect

circunstancia nf circumstance; **en estas circunstancias ...** under the circumstances ...

circunstancial adj circumstantial

cirio nm wax candle

cirrosis nf cirrhosis

ciruela nf plum; **c. claudia** greengage; **c. pasa** prune

ciruelo nm plum tree

cirugía nf surgery; **c. estética** o **plástica** plastic surgery

cirujano,-a nm,f surgeon

cisma nm (**a**) Rel schism (**b**) Pol split

cisne nm swan

cisterna nf cistern, tank

cistitis nf inv cystitis

cita nf (**a**) appointment; **darse c.** to come together (**b**) (amorosa) date (**c**) (mención) quotation

citación nf Jur citation, summons sing

citado,-a adj aforementioned

citar 1 vt (**a**) (dar cita) to arrange to meet, to make an appointment with (**b**) (mencionar) to quote (**c**) Jur to summons

2 **citarse** vpr to arrange to meet, to make a date (**con** with)

cítrico,-a 1 adj citric, citrus

2 nmpl **cítricos** citrus fruits

ciudad nf town; (capital) city; Méx **c. perdida** shanty town

ciudadanía nf citizenship

ciudadano,-a 1 *nm,f* citizen; **el c. de a pie** the man in the street
  2 *adj* civic

cívico,-a *adj* civic

civil 1 *adj* (**a**) civil; **matrimonio c.** civil marriage (**b**) *Mil* civilian
  2 *nm* member of the Guardia Civil

civilización *nf* civilization

civilizado,-a *adj* civilized

civilizar [40] *vt* to civilize

civismo *nm* (**a**) *(urbanidad)* public-spiritedness (**b**) *(cortesía)* civility

cizaña *nf Bot* bearded darnel; *Fig* **sembrar c.** to sow discord

cl *(abr* **centilitro(s))** cl

clamar *vt* to cry out for, to clamour for

clamor *nm* clamour

clamoroso,-a *adj* resounding

clan *nm* clan

clandestinidad *nf* **en la c.** underground

clandestino,-a *adj* clandestine, underground; **aborto c.** backstreet abortion

clara *nf (de huevo)* white

claraboya *nf* skylight

clarear *vi* (**a**) *(amanecer)* to dawn (**b**) *(despejar)* to clear up (**c**) *(transparentar)* to wear thin, to become transparent

clarete *adj & nm* claret

claridad *nf* (**a**) *(luz)* light, brightness (**b**) *(inteligibilidad)* clarity; **con c.** clearly

clarificador,-a *adj* clarifying

clarificar [44] *vt* to clarify

clarín *nm* bugle

clarinete *nm* clarinet

clarividente 1 *adj* (**a**) far-sighted (**b**) *(lúcido)* lucid
  2 *nmf (persona)* clairvoyant

claro,-a 1 *adj* (**a**) clear; **dejar algo c.** to make sth clear (**b**) *(líquido, salsa)* thin (**c**) *(color)* light
  2 *interj* of course!; **¡c. que no!** of course not!; **¡c. que sí!** certainly!
  3 *nm* (**a**) *(espacio)* gap, space; *(en un bosque)* clearing (**b**) *Met* bright spell
  4 *adv* clearly

clase *nf* (**a**) *(grupo)* class; **c. alta/media** upper/middle class; **clases pasivas** pensioners; **primera/segunda c.** first/second class (**b**) *(tipo)* kind, sort; **toda c. de ...** all kinds of ... (**c**) *Educ (curso)* class; *(aula)* classroom; **c. particular** private class *o* lesson (**d**) *(estilo)* class; **tener c.** to have class

clásico,-a 1 *adj* classical; *(típico)* classic; *(en el vestir)* classic
  2 *nm* classic

clasificación *nf* (**a**) classification; *Dep* league table (**b**) *(para campeonato,* *concurso)* qualification

clasificar [44] 1 *vt* to classify, to class
  2 clasificarse *vpr Dep* to qualify

claudicar [44] *vi* to give in

claustro *nm* (**a**) *Arquit* cloister (**b**) *(reunión)* staff meeting

claustrofobia *nf* claustrophobia

cláusula *nf* clause

clausura *nf* (**a**) *(cierre)* closure; **ceremonia de c.** closing ceremony (**b**) *Rel* enclosure

clausurar *vt* to close

clavadista *nmf CAm, Méx* diver

clavar 1 *vt* (**a**) to nail; *(clavo)* to bang *o* hammer in; *(estaca)* to drive in (**b**) *Fam (timar)* to sting *o* fleece
  2 clavarse *vpr* **c. una astilla** to get a splinter

clave 1 *nf* key; **la palabra c.** the key word
  2 *nm* harpsichord

clavel *nm* carnation

clavícula *nf* collarbone

clavija *nf Téc* jack

clavo *nm* (**a**) nail; *Fig* **dar en el c.** to hit the nail on the head (**b**) *Bot* clove

claxon *nm (pl* **cláxones)** horn; **tocar el c.** to sound the horn

clemencia *nf* mercy, clemency

clementina *nf* clementine

cleptómano,-a *adj & nm,f* kleptomaniac

clerical *adj* clerical

clericó *nm RP* = drink made of white wine and fruit

clérigo *nm* priest

clero *nm* clergy

cliché *nm* (**a**) *Fig (tópico)* cliché (**b**) *Fot* negative (**c**) *Impr* plate

cliente *nmf* customer, client

clientela *nf* clientele

clima *nm* climate

climatizado,-a *adj* air-conditioned

climatizar [40] *vt* to air-condition

clímax *nm inv* climax

clínica *nf* clinic

clínico,-a *adj* clinical

clip *nm* clip

clítoris *nm inv* clitoris

cloaca *nf* sewer, drain

clorhídrico,-a *adj* hydrochloric

cloro *nm* chlorine

cloroformo *nm* chloroform

cloruro *nm* chloride; **c. sódico** sodium chloride

clóset *nm (pl* **clósets)** *Am* fitted cupboard

club *nm (pl* **clubs** *o* **clubes)** club; **c. náutico** yacht club

cm *(abr* **centímetro(s))** cm

CNT *nf (abr* **Confederación Nacional del**

Trabajo) = Spanish anarchist trade union federation

coacción *nf* coercion

coaccionar *vt* to coerce

coactivo,-a *adj* coercive

coadyuvar *vt* to assist

coagular *vt & vi*, **coagularse** *vpr* to coagulate; *(sangre)* to clot; *(leche)* to curdle

coágulo *nm* coagulum, clot

coalición *nf* coalition

coartada *nf* alibi

coartar *vt* to restrict

coba *nf Fam* **dar c. a algn** to soft-soap sb

cobalto *nm* cobalt

cobarde 1 *adj* cowardly
   2 *nmf* coward

cobardía *nf* cowardice

cobaya *nf* guinea pig

cobertizo *nm* shed, shack

cobertor *nm* bedspread

cobertura *nf* cover; *(de noticia)* coverage

cobija *nf Am* blanket

cobijar 1 *vt* to shelter
   2 cobijarse *vpr* to take shelter

cobijo *nm* shelter; *Fig (protección)* protection

cobra *nf* cobra

cobrador,-a *nm,f* (**a**) *(de autobús)* *(hombre)* conductor; *(mujer)* conductress (**b**) *(de luz, agua etc)* collector

cobrar 1 *vt* (**a**) *(dinero)* to charge; *(cheque)* to cash; *(salario)* to earn (**b**) *Fig (fuerza)* to gain, to get; **c. ánimos** to take courage o heart; **c. importancia** to become important
   2 *vi Fam* to catch it
   3 cobrarse *vpr* **¿se cobra?** *(al pagar)* take it out of this, please

cobre *nm* (**a**) copper (**b**) *Am (moneda)* copper cent

cobrizo,-a *adj* copper, copper-coloured

cobro *nm (pago)* collecting; *(de cheque)* cashing; *Tel* **llamada a c. revertido** *Br* reverse-charge call, *US* collect call

coca *nf* (**a**) *Bot* coca (**b**) *Fam (droga)* cocaine, coke

cocaína *nf* cocaine

cocainómano,-a *nm,f* cocaine addict

cocalero,-a *Bol, Perú* **1** *adj* **región cocalera** coca-producing area; **productor c.** coca farmer o producer
   2 *nm,f* coca farmer o producer

cocción *nf* cooking; *(en agua)* boiling; *(en horno)* baking

cocer [41] 1 *vt* to cook; *(hervir)* to boil; *(hornear)* to bake
   2 *vi (hervir)* to boil

3 cocerse *vpr* (**a**) *(comida)* to cook; *(hervir)* to boil; *(hornear)* to bake (**b**) *(tramarse)* to be going on

cochambroso,-a *adj* squalid

coche *nm* (**a**) car; **en c.** by car; **c. de carreras** racing car; **c. de bomberos** fire engine; **c. fúnebre** hearse (**b**) *Ferroc* carriage, coach; **c. cama** sleeping car, sleeper (**c**) *(de caballos)* carriage, coach

cochecito *nm (de niño) Br* pram, *US* baby carriage

cochera *nf* (**a**) garage (**b**) *(de autobuses)* depot

cochinillo *nm* suckling pig

cochino,-a 1 *nm,f* (**a**) *(macho)* pig; *(hembra)* sow (**b**) *Fam (persona)* filthy person, pig
   2 *adj (sucio)* filthy, disgusting

cocido *nm* stew

cociente *nm* quotient

cocina *nf* (**a**) kitchen (**b**) *(aparato)* cooker, stove; **c. eléctrica/de gas** electric/gas cooker (**c**) *(arte)* cooking; **c. casera** home cooking; **c. española** Spanish cooking o cuisine

cocinar *vt & vi* to cook

cocinero,-a *nm,f* cook

cocktail *nm* = **cóctel**

coco[1] *nm* coconut; *Fam (cabeza)* nut; **comerle el c. a algn** to brainwash sb; **comerse el c.** to get obsessed

coco[2] *nm Fam (fantasma)* bogeyman

cocodrilo *nm* crocodile

cocoliche *nm RP Fam* = pidgin Spanish spoken by Italian immigrants

cocotero *nm* coconut palm

cóctel *nm* cocktail; **c. Molotov** Molotov cocktail

coctelera *nf* cocktail shaker

codazo *nm* (**a**) *(señal)* nudge with one's elbow (**b**) *(golpe)* blow with one's elbow

codearse *vpr* to rub shoulders (**con** with), to hobnob (**con** with)

codeína *nf* codeine

codicia *nf* greed

codiciar [43] *vt* to covet

codicioso,-a *adj* covetous, greedy

codificar [44] *vt (ley)* to codify; *(mensajes)* to encode

código *nm* code; **c. de circulación** highway code; **c. postal** *Br* postcode, postal code, *US* zip code

codo *nm* elbow; *Fig* **c. con c.** side by side; *Fam* **hablar por los codos** to talk nonstop

codorniz *nf* quail

coeficiente *nm* (**a**) coefficient (**b**) *(grado)* rate; **c. intelectual** intelligence quotient

coercitivo,-a *adj* coercive

coetáneo,-a *adj & nm,f* contemporary

coexistencia *nf* coexistence

coexistir *vi* to coexist

cofia *nf* bonnet

cofradía *nf (hermandad)* brotherhood; *(asociación)* association

cofre *nm (arca)* trunk, chest; *(para joyas)* box, casket

coger [53] **1** *vt* (a) to take; *(del suelo)* to pick (up); *(fruta, flores)* to pick; *(asir)* to seize, to take hold of; *(bus, tren)* to take, to catch; *(pelota, ladrón, resfriado)* to catch; *(entender)* to grasp; *(costumbre)* to pick up; *(velocidad, fuerza)* to gather; *(atropellar)* to run over, to knock down (b) *Am Vulg* to fuck

2 *vi Fam* **cogió y se fue** he upped and left

3 cogerse *vpr (agarrarse)* to hold on

cogida *nf* goring

cogollo *nm (de lechuga)* heart

cogotazo *nm Fam* blow on the back of the neck

cogote *nm* nape o back of the neck

cohabitación *nf* cohabitation

cohabitar *vi* to live together, to cohabit

cohecho *nm Jur* bribery

coherencia *nf* coherence

coherente *adj* coherent

cohesión *nf* cohesion

cohete *nm* rocket; **c. espacial** space rocket

cohibido,-a *adj* inhibited

cohibir **1** *vt* to inhibit

2 cohibirse *vpr* to feel inhibited

COI *nm Dep (abr* **Comité Olímpico Internacional***)* IOC

coima *nf Andes, RP Fam* bribe, *Br* backhander

coincidencia *nf* coincidence

coincidir *vi* (a) to coincide (b) *(concordar)* to agree; **todos coincidieron en señalar que** everyone agreed that (c) *(encontrarse)* to meet by chance

coito *nm* coitus, intercourse

cojear *vi (persona)* to limp, to hobble; *(mueble)* to wobble

cojera *nf* limp

cojín *nm* cushion

cojinete *nm Téc* bearing; **c. de agujas/bolas** needle/ball bearing

cojo,-a 1 *adj (persona)* lame; *(mueble)* rickety

2 *nm,f* lame person

cojón *nm Vulg* ball; **de cojones** *(estupendo)* fucking brilliant o good; *(pésimo)* fucking awful o bad

cojonudo,-a *adj muy Fam Br* bloody

o *US* goddamn brilliant

cojudez *nf Andes muy Fam* **¡qué c.!** *(acto)* what a *Br* bloody o *US* goddamn stupid thing to do!; *(dicho)* what a *Br* bloody o *US* goddamn stupid thing to say!

cojudo,-a *adj Andes muy Fam Br* bloody o *US* goddamn stupid

col *nf* cabbage; **c. de Bruselas** Brussels sprout

cola¹ *nf* (a) *(de animal)* tail; *(de vestido)* train; *(de pelo)* ponytail; *Am (de persona) Br* bum, *US* fanny; **a la c.** at the back o rear; *Fam* **traer c.** to have consequences (b) *(fila) Br* queue, *US* line; **hacer c.** *Br* to queue (up), *US* to stand in line

cola² *nf (pegamento)* glue

colaboración *nf* (a) collaboration (b) *Prensa* contribution

colaboracionismo *nm Pol* collaboration

colaborador,-a 1 *nm,f* (a) collaborator (b) *Prensa* contributor

2 *adj* collaborating

colaborar *vi* to collaborate, to cooperate

colación *nf* **sacar** o **traer (algo) a c.** to bring (sth) up

colada *nf* wash, laundry; **hacer la c.** to do the washing o laundry

colador *nm* colander, sieve; *(de té, café)* strainer

colapsar 1 *vt* to bring to a standstill

2 colapsarse *vpr* to come to a standstill

colapso *nm* (a) *Med* collapse (b) *Aut* **c. circulatorio** traffic jam, hold-up

colar [2] 1 *vt* (a) *(líquido)* to strain, to filter (b) *(por agujero)* to slip

2 *vi Fam* **esa mentira no cuela** that lie won't wash

3 colarse *vpr* (a) to slip in; *(a fiesta)* to gatecrash; *(en una cola)* to jump the queue (b) *Fam (pasarse)* to go too far

colateral *adj* collateral

colcha *nf* bedspread

colchón *nm* mattress

colchoneta *nf* air bed

colear *vi* (a) to wag its tail; *Fam* **vivito y coleando** alive and kicking (b) *Fam* **el asunto aún colea** we haven't heard the last of it yet

colección *nf* collection

coleccionable *adj & nm* collectable

coleccionar *vt* to collect

coleccionista *nmf* collector

colecta *nf* collection

colectividad *nf* community

colectivo,-a 1 *adj* collective

2 *nm* (a) *(asociación)* association (b) *Andes (taxi)* (collective) taxi (c) *Arg (autobús)* bus

colega nmf (**a**) colleague (**b**) Fam (amigo) pal, Br mate, US buddy

colegiado,-a nm,f Dep referee

colegial,-ala 1 adj (escolar) school

2 nm,f (alumno) schoolboy; (alumna) schoolgirl; **los colegiales** the schoolchildren

colegio nm (**a**) (escuela) school; **c. privado** private school, Br public o independent school (**b**) (profesional) association, college; **c. de abogados** the Bar; Pol **c. electoral** electoral college (**c**) Univ **c. mayor** o **universitario** hall of residence

colegir [58] vt to infer, to deduce

cólera[1] nf anger, rage

cólera[2] nm Med cholera

colérico,-a adj furious

colesterol nm cholesterol

coleta nf pigtail, ponytail; Fig **cortarse la c.** to retire

coletazo nm **dar los últimos coletazos** to be on one's last legs

coletilla nf postcript

colgado,-a adj (**a**) Fam **dejar (a algn) c.** to leave (sb) in the lurch (**b**) Fam weird; (drogado) high

colgante 1 nm (joya) pendant

2 adj hanging

colgar [2] **1** vt (**a**) to hang (up); (colada) to hang (out) (**b**) (ahorcar) to hang

2 vi to hang (**a**) to hang (from); Fig **c. de un hilo** to hang by a thread (**b**) Tel to hang up

3 colgarse vpr (ahorcarse) to hang oneself

colibrí nm hummingbird

cólico nm colic

coliflor nf cauliflower

colijo indic pres de **colegir**

colilla nf (cigarette) end o butt

colimba nf Arg Fam military service

colina nf hill

colindante adj adjoining, adjacent

colindar vi to be adjacent (**con** to)

colirio nm eye-drops

colisión nf collision, crash; (de ideas) clash

colisionar vi to collide, to crash

colitis nf colitis

colla Bol **1** adj of/from the altiplano

2 nmf = indigenous person from the altiplano

collage nm collage

collar nm (**a**) (adorno) necklace (**b**) (de perro) collar

colmado,-a adj full, filled; (cucharada) heaped

colmar vt (**a**) to fill (right up); (vaso, copa) to fill to the brim; Fig to shower (**de** with) (**b**) (ambiciones) to fulfil, to satisfy

colmena nf beehive

colmillo nm eye o canine tooth; Zool (de carnívoro) fang; (de jabalí, elefante) tusk

colmo nm height; **el c. de** the height of; **¡eso es el c.!** that's the last straw!; **para c.** to top it all

colocación nf (**a**) (acto) positioning (**b**) (disposición) lay-out (**c**) (empleo) job, employment

colocado,-a adj (**a**) (empleado) employed (**b**) Fam (drogado) high

colocar [44] **1** vt (**a**) to place, to put (**b**) Fin (invertir) to invest (**c**) (emplear) to give work to (**d**) Fam (drogar) to stone

2 colocarse vpr (**a**) (situarse) to put oneself (**b**) (emplearse) to take a job (**de** as) (**c**) Fam (drogarse) to get high

colofón nm (**a**) (apéndice) colophon (**b**) Fig climax

Colombia n Colombia

colombiano,-a adj & nm,f Colombian

Colón n Columbus

colón nm Fin = standard monetary unit of Costa Rica and El Salvador

colonia[1] nf (**a**) colony; (campamento) summer camp; Méx (barrio) district

colonia[2] nf (perfume) cologne

colonial adj colonial

colonialismo nm colonialism

colonización nf colonization

colonizar [40] vt to colonize

coloquial adj colloquial

coloquio nm discussion, colloquium

color nm colour; Cin & Fot **en c.** in colour; **de colores** multicoloured; **persona de c.** coloured person

colorado,-a 1 adj red; **ponerse c.** to blush

2 nm red

> 📖 Observa que la palabra inglesa **coloured** es un falso amigo y no es la traducción de la palabra española **colorado**. En inglés, **coloured** significa "coloreado".

---

colorante nm colouring

colorear vt to colour

colorete nm rouge

colorido nm colour

colorín nm goldfinch

colosal adj colossal

columna nf column; Anat **c. vertebral** vertebral column, spinal column

columpiar [43] **1** vt to swing

2 columpiarse vpr to swing

columpio nm swing

coma[1] nf (**a**) Ling & Mús comma (**b**) Mat

point; **tres c. cinco** three point five
coma² *nm Med* coma
comadre *nf* (**a**) *(madrina)* = godmother
of one's child, or mother of one's godchild
(**b**) *Am Fam (amiga)* friend
comadreja *nf* weasel
comadreo *nm* gossip, gossiping
comadrona *nf* midwife
comal *nm CAm, Méx* = flat clay or metal
dish used for baking "tortillas"
comandancia *nf* command
comandante *nm* (**a**) *Mil* commander,
commanding officer (**b**) *Av* captain
comandar *vt* to command
comando *nm* (**a**) *Mil* commando (**b**)
Informát command
comarca *nf* region
comarcal *adj* regional
comba *nf* (**a**) *(curvatura)* curve, bend (**b**)
(cuerda) skipping rope; **saltar a la c.** to
skip, *US* to jump rope
combar *vt* to bend
combate *nm* combat; *(en boxeo)* fight;
Mil battle; **fuera de c.** out for the count;
(eliminado) out of action
combatiente 1 *adj* fighting
  2 *nmf* combatant
combatir 1 *vt* to combat
  2 *vi* **c. contra** to fight against
combativo,-a *adj* spirited, aggressive
combinación *nf* (**a**) combination (**b**)
(prenda) slip
combinado,-a 1 *adj* combined
  2 *nm* (**a**) *(cóctel)* cocktail (**b**) *Dep* line-
up
combinar *vt*, **combinarse** *vpr* to
combine
combustible 1 *nm* fuel
  2 *adj* combustible
combustión *nf* combustion
comedia *nf* comedy
comediante,-a *nm,f (hombre)* actor;
(mujer) actress
comedido,-a *adj* self-restrained, reserved
comedor *nm* dining room
comensal *nmf* companion at table
comentar *vt* **c. algo con algn** to talk sth
over with sb; **me han comentado que** I've
been told that
comentario *nm* (**a**) comment, remark;
(crítica) commentary; **sin c.** no comment
(**b**) **comentarios** *(cotilleos)* gossip
comentarista *nmf* commentator
comenzar [51] *vt & vi* to begin, to start;
comenzó a llover it started raining *o* to
rain; **comenzó diciendo que ...** he started
by saying that ...

comer 1 *vt* (**a**) to eat (**b**) *(en juegos)* to
take, to capture
  2 *vi* to eat; **dar de c. a algn** to feed sb
  3 comerse *vpr* (**a**) to eat (**b**) *Fig (saltarse)*
to skip
comercial *adj* commercial
comercialización *nf* marketing
comercializar [40] *vt* to market
comerciante *nmf* merchant
comerciar [43] *vi* to trade; **comercia con
oro** he trades in gold
comercio *nm* (**a**) commerce, trade; **c.
exterior** foreign trade; *Informát* **c. electrónico** e-commerce; **c. justo** fair trade
(**b**) *(tienda)* shop
comestible 1 *adj* edible
  2 *nmpl* **comestibles** food, foodstuff(s);
tienda de comestibles grocer's shop, *US*
grocery store
cometa 1 *nm Astron* comet
  2 *nf (juguete)* kite
cometer *vt (error, falta)* to make; *(delito,
crimen)* to commit
cometido *nm* (**a**) *(tarea)* task, assignment (**b**) *(deber)* duty; **cumplir su c.** to do
one's duty
comezón *nm* itch
cómic *nm* comic
comicios *nmpl* elections
cómico,-a 1 *adj* (**a**) comical, funny (**b**)
Teatro **actor c.** comedian
  2 *nm,f* comic; *(hombre)* comedian; *(mujer)* comedienne
comida *nf* (**a**) *(alimento)* food (**b**) *(almuerzo, cena)* meal
comidilla *nf Fam* **la c. del pueblo** the talk
of the town
comienzo *nm* beginning, start; **a comien-
zos de** at the beginning of; **dar c. (a algo)**
to begin *o* start (sth)
comillas *nfpl* inverted commas; **entre c.**
in inverted commas
comilón,-ona 1 *adj* greedy, gluttonous
  2 *nm,f* big eater, glutton
comilona *nf Fam* big meal, feast
comino *nm* cumin, cummin; *Fam* **me
importa un c.** I don't give a damn (about
it)
comisaría *nf* police station
comisario *nm* (**a**) *(de policía)* police inspector (**b**) *(delegado)* commissioner; **c.
europeo** European Commissioner
comisión *nf* (**a**) *Com (retribución)*
commission; **a o con c.** on a commission
basis (**b**) *(comité)* committee; **la C. Europea** the European Commission
comité *nm* committee
comitiva *nf* suite, retinue

como 1 *adv* (**a**) *(manera)* how; **me gusta c. cantas** I like the way you sing; **dilo c. quieras** say it however you like

(**b**) *(comparación)* as; **blanco c. la nieve** as white as snow; **habla c. su padre** he talks like his father

(**c**) *(según)* as; **c. decíamos ayer** as we were saying yesterday

(**d**) *(en calidad de)* as; **c. presidente** as president; **lo compré c. recuerdo** I bought it as a souvenir

(**e**) *(aproximadamente)* about; **c. a la mitad de camino** halfway; **c. unos diez** about ten

2 *conj* (**a**) *(+ subjunctive) (si)* if; **c. no estudies vas a suspender** if you don't study hard, you'll fail

(**b**) *(porque)* as, since; **c. no venías me marché** as you didn't come, I left

(**c**) **c. si** as if; **c. si nada** *o* **tal cosa** as if nothing had happened; *Fam* **c. si lo viera** I can imagine perfectly well

cómo 1 *adv* (**a**) **¿c.?** *(¿perdón?)* what?

(**b**) *(interrogativo)* how; **¿c. estás?** how are you?; **¿c. lo sabes?** how do you know?; **¿c. es de grande/ancho?** how big/wide is it?; **¿a c. están los tomates?** how much are the tomatoes?; **¿c. es que no viniste a la fiesta?** *(por qué)* how come you didn't come to the party?; *Fam* **¿c. es eso?** how come?

(**c**) *(exclamativo)* how; **¡c. has crecido!** you've really grown a lot!; **¡c. no!** but of course!

2 un el c. y el porqué the whys and wherefores

cómoda *nf* chest of drawers

comodidad *nf* (**a**) comfort (**b**) *(conveniencia)* convenience

> *Observa que la palabra inglesa* **commodity** *es un falso amigo y no es la traducción de la palabra española* **comodidad**. *En inglés,* **commodity** *significa "producto básico".*

comodín *nm Naipes* joker

cómodo,-a *adj* (**a**) comfortable; **ponerse c.** to make oneself comfortable (**b**) *(útil)* handy, convenient

comoquiera *adv* (**a**) however, whatever way; **c. que sea** one way or another (**b**) **c. que no estaba enterado** *(puesto que)* as he didn't know

compa *nmf Fam* pal, *Br* mate, *US* buddy

compacto,-a *adj* compact; **disco c.** compact disc

compadecer [33] **1** *vt* to feel sorry for, to pity

2 compadecerse *vpr* to have *o* take pity (**de** on)

compadre *nm* (**a**) *(padrino)* = godfather of one's child, or father of one's godchild (**b**) *Am Fam (amigo)* friend, mate

compadrear *vi RP* to brag, to boast

compaginar *vt* to combine

compañerismo *nm* companionship, comradeship

compañero,-a *nm,f* companion; **c. de colegio** school friend; **c. de piso** flat-mate

compañía *nf* company; **hacer c. (a algn)** to keep (sb) company; **c. de seguros/de teatro** insurance/theatre company

comparable *adj* comparable

comparación *nf* comparison; **en c.** comparatively; **en c. con** compared to; **sin c.** beyond compare

comparar *vt* to compare (**con** with)

comparativo,-a *adj & nm* comparative

comparecencia *nf* appearance

comparecer [33] *vi Jur* to appear (**ante** before)

comparsa *nf* band of revellers

compartimento, compartimiento *nm* compartment; **c. de primera/segunda clase** first-/second-class compartment

compartir *vt* to share

compás *nm* (**a**) *Téc* (pair of) compasses (**b**) *Náut* compass (**c**) *Mús (división)* time; *(intervalo)* beat; *(ritmo)* rhythm; **c. de espera** *Mús* bar rest; *Fig (pausa)* delay; **al c. de** in time to

compasión *nf* compassion, pity; **tener c. (de algn)** to feel sorry (for sb)

compasivo,-a *adj* compassionate

compatible *adj* compatible

compatriota *nmf* compatriot; *(hombre)* fellow countryman; *(mujer)* fellow countrywoman

compendiar [43] *vt* to abridge, to summarize

compendio *nm* compendium

compenetrarse *vpr* to understand each other *o* one another

compensación *nf* compensation

compensar 1 *vt (pérdida, error)* to make up for; *(indemnizar)* to compensate (for)

2 *vi* to be worthwhile; **este trabajo no compensa** this job's not worth my time

competencia *nf* (**a**) *(rivalidad, empresas rivales)* competition (**b**) *(capacidad)* competence (**c**) *(incumbencia)* field, province; **no es de mi c.** it's not up to me

competente *adj* competent

competición *nf* competition, contest

competido,-a *adj* hard-fought

competidor,-a 1 *nm,f* (**a**) *Com & Dep*

competitor (**b**) *(participante)* contestant
2 *adj* competing
competir [6] *vi* to compete (**con** with *o* against; **en** in; **por** for)
competitividad *nf* competitivity
competitivo,-a *adj* competitive
compilar *vt* to compile
compinche *nmf* (**a**) *(compañero)* chum, pal (**b**) *(cómplice)* accomplice
complacencia *nf* (**a**) *(satisfacción)* satisfaction (**b**) *(indulgencia)* indulgence

> ⚠ Observa que la palabra inglesa **complacency** es un falso amigo y no es la traducción de la palabra española **complacencia**. En inglés, **complacency** significa "autocomplacencia".

complacer [60] 1 *vt* to please; *Fml* **me complace presentarles a ...** it gives me great pleasure to introduce to you ...
2 **complacerse** *vpr* to delight (**en** in), to take pleasure (**en** in)
complaciente *adj* obliging
complejidad *nf* complexity
complejo,-a *adj & nm* complex
complementar *vt* to complement
2 **complementarse** *vpr* to complement (each other), to be complementary to (each other)
complementario,-a *adj* complementary
complemento *nm* complement; *Ling* object
completamente *adv* completely
completar *vt* to complete
completo,-a *adj* (**a**) *(terminado)* complete; **por c.** completely (**b**) *(lleno)* full; **al c.** full up to capacity
complexión *nf* build; **de c. fuerte** well-built

> ⚠ Observa que la palabra inglesa **complexion** es un falso amigo y no es la traducción de la palabra española **complexión**. En inglés, **complexion** significa "tez".

complicación *nf* complication
complicado,-a *adj* (**a**) *(complejo)* complicated (**b**) *(implicado)* involved
complicar [44] 1 *vt* (**a**) to complicate (**b**) **c. en** *(involucrar)* to involve in
2 **complicarse** *vpr* to get complicated; **c. la vida** to make life difficult for oneself
cómplice *nmf* accomplice
complot *nm* (*pl* **complots**) conspiracy, plot
componente 1 *adj* component
2 *nm* (**a**) *(pieza)* component; *(ingrediente)* ingredient (**b**) *(persona)* member

componer [19] (*pp* **compuesto**) 1 *vt* (**a**) *(formar)* to compose, to make up (**b**) *Mús & Lit* to compose (**c**) *(reparar)* to mend, to repair
2 **componerse** *vpr* (**a**) **c. de** *(consistir)* to be made up of, to consist of (**b**) *(arreglarse)* to dress up (**c**) *Fam* **componérselas** to manage
comportamiento *nm* behaviour
comportar 1 *vt* to entail, to involve
2 **comportarse** *vpr* to behave; **c. mal** to misbehave
composición *nf* composition
compositor,-a *nm,f* composer
compostelano,-a *adj* from Santiago de Compostela
compostura *nf* composure
compota *nf* compote
compra *nf* *(acción)* buying; *(cosa comprada)* purchase, buy; **ir de c.** to go shopping
comprador,-a *nm,f* purchaser, buyer
comprar *vt* (**a**) to buy (**b**) *Fig (sobornar)* to bribe, to buy off
compraventa *nf* buying and selling; **contrato de c.** contract of sale
comprender *vt* (**a**) *(entender)* to understand; **se comprende** it's understandable (**b**) *(contener)* to comprise, to include
comprensible *adj* understandable
comprensión *nf* understanding
comprensivo,-a *adj* understanding

> ⚠ Observa que la palabra inglesa **comprehensive** es un falso amigo y no es la traducción de la palabra española **comprensivo**. En inglés, **comprehensive** significa "amplio, detallado".

compresa *nf* (**a**) *(para mujer)* sanitary towel (**b**) *Med* compress
comprimido,-a 1 *nm Farm* tablet
2 *adj* compressed; **escopeta de aire c.** air rifle
comprimir *vt* to compress
comprobante *nm* *(de compra etc)* voucher, receipt
comprobar [2] *vt* to check
comprometer 1 *vt* (**a**) *(arriesgar)* to compromise, to jeopardize (**b**) *(obligar)* to compel, to force
2 **comprometerse** *vpr* (**a**) **c. a hacer algo** to undertake to do sth (**b**) *(novios)* to become engaged
comprometido,-a *adj* (**a**) *(situación)* difficult (**b**) *(para casarse)* engaged
compromiso *nm* (**a**) *(obligación)* obligation, commitment; **sin c.** without obligation; **por c.** out of a sense of duty (**b**) **poner (a algn) en un c.** to put (sb) in a

difficult o embarrassing situation (c) *(acuerdo)* agreement; *Fml* **c. matrimonial** engagement; **soltero y sin c.** single and unattached

📖 Observa que la palabra inglesa **compromise** es un falso amigo y no es la traducción de la palabra española **compromiso**. En inglés, **compromise** significa "solución negociada".

compuesto,-a 1 *adj* (a) compound (b) **c. de** composed of
2 *nm* compound
compulsar *vt* to make a certified true copy of
compungido,-a *adj (arrepentido)* remorseful; *(triste)* sorrowful, sad
compuse *pt indef de* **componer**
computadora *nf* computer
cómputo *nm* calculation
comulgar [42] *vi* (a) to receive Holy Communion (b) *Fig* **no comulgo con sus ideas** I don't share his ideas
común 1 *adj* (a) common; **de c. acuerdo** by common consent; **hacer algo en c.** to do sth jointly; **poco c.** unusual; **por lo c.** generally (b) *(compartido)* shared, communal; **amigos comunes** mutual friends
2 *nm Br Pol* **los Comunes** the Commons
comuna *nf Am (municipalidad)* municipality
comunal *adj* communal
comunero,-a *nm,f Perú, Méx (indígena)* = member of an indigenous village community
comunicación *nf* (a) communication; **ponerse en c. (con algn)** to get in touch (with sb) (b) *(comunicado)* communication; **c. oficial** communiqué (c) *Tel* connection; **se nos cortó la c.** we were cut off (d) *(unión)* link, connection
comunicado,-a 1 *adj* **una zona bien comunicada** a well-served zone; **dos ciudades bien comunicadas** two towns with good connections (between them)
2 *nm* communiqué; **c. de prensa** press release
comunicar [44] 1 *vt* to communicate; **comuníquenoslo lo antes posible** let us know as soon as possible
2 *vi* (a) to communicate (b) *Tel* to be engaged; **está comunicando** it's engaged
3 comunicarse *upr* to communicate
comunicativo,-a *adj* communicative
comunidad *nf* community; **C. Europea** European Community; **C. de Estados**

Independientes Commonwealth of Independent States
comunión *nf* communion
comunismo *nm* communism
comunista *adj & nmf* communist
comunitario,-a *adj* (a) of o relating to the community (b) *(de UE)* of o relating to the EU; **la política agraria comunitaria** the common agricultural policy
con *prep* (a) with; **córtalo c. las tijeras** cut it with the scissors; **voy cómodo c. este jersey** I'm comfortable in this sweater
(b) *(compañía)* with; **vine c. mi hermana** I came with my sister
(c) **c. ese frío/niebla** in that cold/fog; **estar c. (la) gripe** to have the flu
(d) *(contenido)* with; **una bolsa c. dinero** a bag (full) of money
(e) *(a)* to; **habló c. todos** he spoke to everybody; **sé amable c. ella** be nice to her
(f) *(con infinitivo)* **c. llamar será suficiente** it will be enough just to phone
(g) *(+ que + subjuntivo)* **bastará c. que lo esboces** a general idea will do
(h) **c. tal (de) que ...** provided that ...; **c. todo (y eso)** even so
conato *nm* attempt; **c. de asesinato** attempted murder
concebible *adj* conceivable, imaginable
concebir [6] 1 *vt* (a) *(plan, hijo)* to conceive (b) *(entender)* to understand
2 *vi (mujer)* to become pregnant, to conceive
conceder *vt* to grant; *(premio)* to award
concejal,-a *nm,f* town councillor
concejo *nm* council
concentración *nf* concentration; *(de manifestantes)* gathering; *(de coches, motos)* rally; *(de equipo)* base
concentrado *nm* concentrate
concentrar 1 *vt* to concentrate
2 concentrarse *upr* (a) to concentrate (**en** on) (b) *(reunirse)* to gather
concepción *nf* conception
concepto *nm* (a) *(idea)* concept; **tener buen/mal c. de** to have a good/a bad opinion of; **bajo/por ningún c.** under no circumstances (b) **en c. de** under the heading of (c) *(en factura)* item
concerniente *adj* **c. (a)** concerning, regarding; *Fml* **en lo c. a** with regard to
concernir [54] *v impers* (a) *(afectar)* to concern; **en lo que a mí concierne** as far as I am concerned; **en lo que concierne a** with regard/respect to (b) *(corresponder)* to be up to
concertación *nf* compromise, agreement

concertar [1] 1 vt (a) (cita) to arrange; (precio) to agree on; (acuerdo) to reach (b) (una acción etc) to plan, to co-ordinate
2 vi to agree, to tally

concesión nf (a) concession (b) (de un premio, contrato) awarding

concesionario,-a nm,f dealer

concha nf (a) Zool (caparazón) shell; (carey) tortoiseshell (b) Andes, RP Vulg Br fanny, US beaver (c) Ven (de árbol) bark; (de fruta) peel, rind; (del pan) crust; (de huevo) shell

conchabarse vpr to gang up

concheto,-a RP Fam **1** adj posh
2 nm,f rich kid

conchudo,-a nm,f Perú, RP Vulg prick, Br dickhead

conciencia nf (a) conscience; **tener la c. tranquila** with a clear conscience (b) (conocimiento) consciousness, aware-ness; **a c.** conscientiously; **tener/tomar c. (de algo)** to be/to become aware (of sth)

concienciar [43], Am **concientizar [40] 1** vt **c. de** to make aware of
2 concienciarse vpr to become aware (**de** of)

concienzudo,-a adj conscientious

concierto nm (a) Mús concert; (compo-sición) concerto (b) (acuerdo) agreement

conciliar [43] vt to reconcile; **c. el sueño** to get to sleep

concilio nm council

conciso,-a adj concise

conciudadano,-a nm,f fellow citizen

concluir [37] vt to conclude

conclusión nf conclusion; **sacar una c.** to draw a conclusion

concluyente adj conclusive

concomerse vpr to be consumed; **c. de envidia** to be green with envy

concordar [2] 1 vi to agree; **esto no concuerda con lo que dijo ayer** this doesn't fit in with what he said yesterday
2 vt to bring into agreement

concordia nf concord

concretamente adv specifically

concretar vt (precisar) to specify, to state explicitly; (fecha, hora) to fix

concreto,-a 1 adj (a) (preciso, real) concrete (b) (particular) specific; **en c.** specifically; **en el caso c. de ...** in the specific case of ...
2 nm Am concrete

concurrencia nf (a) (de dos cosas) concurrence (b) (público) audience

concurrido,-a adj crowded, busy

concurrir vi (a) (gente) to converge (**en** on), to meet (**en** in) (b) (coincidir) to concur, to coincide (c) (participar) to compete; (en elecciones) to be a candid-ate

concursante nmf (a) contestant, competitor (b) (para un empleo) candid-ate

concursar vi to compete, to take part

concurso nm (a) (competición) competi-tion; (de belleza etc) contest; TV quiz show; **presentar (una obra) a c.** to invite tenders (for a piece of work) (b) Fml (ayuda) help

> ✎ Observa que la palabra inglesa **con-course** es un falso amigo y no es la traduc-ción de la palabra española **concurso**. En inglés, **concourse** significa "vestíbulo".

condal adj of o relating to a count; **la Ciudad C.** Barcelona

conde nm count

condecoración nf decoration

condecorar vt to decorate

condena nf (a) Jur sentence (b) (des-aprobación) condemnation, disapproval

condenado,-a 1 adj (a) Jur convicted; **c. a muerte** condemned to death (b) Rel & Fam damned; **c. al fracaso** doomed to failure
2 nm,f (a) Jur convicted person; (a muerte) condemned person (b) Rel damned person

condenar 1 vt (a) Jur to convict, to find guilty; **c. a algn a muerte** to condemn sb to death (b) (desaprobar) to condemn
2 condenarse vpr Rel to be damned

condensado,-a adj condensed; **leche condensada** condensed m.ik

condensador nm condenser

condensar vt, **condensarse** vpr to condense

condesa nf countess

condescender [3] vi (a) to condescend (b) (ceder) to comply (with), to consent (to)

condescendiente adj (a) (displicente) condescending (b) (complaciente) complacent

condición nf (a) condition; **en buenas/ malas condiciones** in good/bad condi-tion; **condiciones de trabajo** working conditions; **con la c. de que ...** on the condition that ... (b) (manera de ser) nature, character (c) **en su c. de director** (calidad) in his capacity as director

condicional adj conditional

condicionar vt (a) to condition (b) una

cosa condiciona la otra one thing determines the other

condimentar *vt* to season, to flavour

condimento *nm* seasoning, flavouring

condolerse [4] *vpr* **c. de** to sympathize with

condominio *nm Am (edificio) Br* block of flats, *US* condominium

condón *nm* condom

condonar *vt (ofensa)* to condone; *(deuda)* to cancel

cóndor *nm* condor

conducir [10] 1 *vt (coche)* to drive; *(electricidad)* to conduct

2 *vi* (a) *Aut* to drive; **permiso de c.** *Br* driving licence, *US* driver's license (b) *(camino, actitud)* to lead; **eso no conduce a nada** this leads nowhere

conducta *nf* behaviour, conduct; **mala c.** misbehaviour, misconduct

conducto *nm* (a) *(tubería)* pipe; *Fig* **por conductos oficiales** through official channels (b) *Anat* duct, canal

conductor,-a 1 *nm,f Aut* driver

2 *nm Elec* conductor

conectar *vt* (a) to connect up (b) *Elec* to plug in, to switch on

coneja *nf* doe rabbit

conejillo *nm* **c. de Indias** guinea pig

conejo *nm* rabbit

conexión *nf* connection

confabularse *vpr* to conspire, to plot

confección *nf* (a) *Cost* dressmaking, tailoring; **la industria de la c.** the rag trade (b) *(de un plan etc)* making, making up

confeccionar *vt* to make (up)

confederación *nf* confederation

conferencia *nf* (a) lecture; **dar una c. (sobre algo)** to give a lecture (on sth) (b) **c. de prensa** press conference (c) *Tel* long-distance call

conferenciante *nmf* lecturer

conferir [5] *vt Fml (honor, privilegio)* to confer

confesar [1] 1 *vt* to confess, to admit; *(crimen)* to own up to; *Rel (pecados)* to confess

2 *vi* to own up

3 ● **confesarse** *vpr* to confess; **c. culpable** to admit one's guilt; *Rel* to go to confession

confesión *nf* confession, admission; *Rel* confession

confesionario *nm Rel* confessional

confeti *nm (pl* confetis) confetti

confiado,-a *adj* (a) *(seguro)* self-confident (b) *(crédulo)* gullible, unsuspecting

confianza *nf* (a) *(seguridad)* confidence; **tener c. en uno mismo** to be self-confident (b) **de c.** reliable (c) **tener c. con algn** to be on intimate terms with sb; **con toda c.** in all confidence; **tomarse (demasiadas) confianzas** to take liberties

confiar [29] 1 *vt (entregar)* to entrust; *(información, secreto)* to confide

2 *vi* **c. en** to trust; **confío en ella** I trust her; **no confíes en su ayuda** don't count on his help

3 **confiarse** *vpr* to confide (**en** *o* **a** in); **c. demasiado** to be over-confident

confidencia *nf* confidence

confidencial *adj* confidential

confidente,-a *nm,f* (a) *(hombre)* confidant; *(mujer)* confidante (b) *(de la policía)* informer

configuración *nf* configuration; *Informát* configuration

configurar *vt* to shape, to form

confín *nm* limit, boundary

confinar *vt Jur* to confine

confirmación *nf* confirmation

confirmar *vt* to confirm; *Prov* **la excepción confirma la regla** the exception proves the rule

confiscar [44] *vt* to confiscate

confite *nm Br* sweet, *US* candy

confitería *nf* (a) confectioner's (shop), *US* candy store (b) *CSur* café

confitura *nf* preserve, jam

conflagración *nf Fig* **c. mundial** world war

conflictividad *nf* **c. laboral** industrial unrest

conflictivo,-a *adj (asunto)* controversial; *(época)* unsettled; **niño c.** problem child

conflicto *nm* conflict; **c. laboral** industrial dispute

confluencia *nf* confluence

confluir [37] *vi* to converge; *(caminos, ríos)* to meet, to come together

conformar 1 *vt* to shape

2 **conformarse** *vpr* to resign oneself, to be content

conforme 1 *adj* (a) *(satisfecho)* satisfied; **c.** agreed, all right; **no estoy c.** I don't agree (b) **c. a** in accordance *o* keeping with

2 *conj* (a) *(según, como)* as; **c. lo vi/lo oí** as I saw/heard it (b) *(a medida que)* as; **la policía los detenía** *o* **iban saliendo** the police were arresting them as they came out

conformidad *nf* (a) approval, consent (b) **en c. con** in conformity with

conformismo *nm* conformity

conformista *adj & nmf* conformist

confort nm (pl **conforts**) comfort; **todo c. (en anuncio)** all mod cons

confortable adj comfortable

confortar vt to comfort

confraternizar [40] vi to fraternize

confrontación nf (a) (enfrentamiento) confrontation (b) (comparación) contrast

confrontar vt (a) to confront (b) (cotejar) to compare, to collate

confundir 1 vt (a) to confuse (con with); **c. a una persona con otra** to mistake somebody for somebody else (b) (persona) to mislead (c) (turbar) to confound

2 confundirse vpr (a) (equivocarse) to be mistaken; **Tel se ha confundido** you've got the wrong number (b) (mezclarse) to mingle; **se confundió entre el gentío** he disappeared into the crowd

confusión nf confusion

confuso,-a adj (a) confused; (formas, recuerdo) blurred, vague (b) (mezclado) mixed up

congelación nf (a) freezing (b) Fin freeze; **c. salarial** wage freeze (c) Med frostbite

congelado,-a 1 adj frozen; Med frostbitten

2 nmpl **congelados** frozen food

congelador nm freezer

congelar 1 vt to freeze

2 congelarse vpr (a) to freeze; Fam **me estoy congelando** I'm freezing (b) Med to get o become frostbitten

congeniar [43] vi to get on (con with)

congénito,-a adj congenital

congestión nf congestion; Med **c. cerebral** stroke

congestionar vt to congest

conglomerado nm conglomerate

conglomerar vt, **conglomerarse** vpr to conglomerate

congoja nf sorrow, grief

congraciarse [43] vpr to ingratiate oneself (con with)

congratular vt Fml to congratulate (por on)

congregación nf congregation

congregar [42] vt, **congregarse** vpr to congregate, to assemble

congresista nmf member of a congress

congreso nm congress, conference; Pol **c. de los Diputados** Br ≃ Parliament, US ≃ Congress

congrio nm conger (eel)

congruente adj coherent, suitable

conjetura nf conjecture; **por c.** by guesswork

conjeturar vt to conjecture

conjugación nf conjugation

conjugar [42] vt to conjugate; Fig (planes, opiniones) to combine

conjunción nf conjunction

conjuntar vt to co-ordinate

conjuntivitis nf conjunctivitis

conjunto,-a 1 nm (a) (grupo) collection, group (b) (todo) whole; **de c.** overall; **en c.** on the whole (c) Mús (pop) group, band (d) (prenda) outfit, ensemble (e) Mat set (f) Dep team

2 adj joint

conjurar 1 vt to exorcise; (peligro) to ward off

2 conjurarse vpr to conspire, to plot

conjuro nm (a) (exorcismo) exorcism (b) (encantamiento) spell, incantation

conllevar vt to entail

conmemoración nf commemoration

conmemorar vt to commemorate

conmigo pron pers with me; **vino c.** he came with me; **él habló c.** he talked to me

conminar vt to threaten, to menace

conmoción nf commotion, shock; **c. cerebral** concussion

conmocionar vt to shock; Med to concuss

conmovedor,-a adj touching; **una película conmovedora** a moving film

conmover [4] vt to touch, to move

conmutador nm (a) Elec switch (b) Am Tel switchboard

conmutar vt to exchange; Jur to commute; Elec to commutate

connivencia nf connivance, collusion

connotación nf connotation

cono nm cone; **C. Sur** South America

conocedor,-a adj & nm,f expert; (de vino, arte etc) connoisseur

conocer [34] **1** vt (a) to know; **dar (algo/algn) a c.** to make (sth/sb) known (b) (a una persona) to meet (c) (reconocer) to recognize; **te conocí por la voz** I recognized you by your voice

2 conocerse (dos personas) to know each other; (por primera vez) to meet

conocido,-a 1 adj known; (famoso) well-known

2 nm,f acquaintance

conocimiento nm (a) knowledge; **con c. de causa** with full knowledge of the facts (b) (conciencia) consciousness; **perder/recobrar el c.** to lose/regain consciousness (c) **conocimientos** knowledge

conque conj so

conquense 1 adj of/from Cuenca

2 nmf person from Cuenca

conquista *nf* conquest

conquistador,-a *nm,f* conqueror

conquistar *vt (país, ciudad)* to conquer; *Fig (puesto, título)* to win; *(a una persona)* to win over

consabido,-a *adj* (a) *(bien conocido)* well-known (b) *(usual)* familiar, usual

consagración *nf* (a) *Rel* consecration (b) *(de un artista)* recognition

consagrar 1 *vt* (a) *Rel* to consecrate (b) *(artista)* to confirm (c) *(tiempo, vida)* to devote

   2 consagrarse *vpr* (a) **c. a** *(dedicarse)* to devote oneself to, to dedicate oneself to (b) *(lograr fama)* to establish oneself

consciente *adj* (a) conscious, aware; **ser c. de algo** to be aware of sth (b) *Med* conscious

conscripto *nm Andes, Arg* conscript

consecución *nf* (a) *(de un objetivo)* achievement (b) *(obtención)* obtaining

consecuencia *nf* (a) *(de un objetivo)* consequence; **a o como c. de** as a consequence *o* result of; **en c.** therefore; **tener** *o* **traer (malas) consecuencias** to have (ill) effects; **sacar como** *o* **en c.** to come to a conclusion (b) *(coherencia)* consistency; **actuar en c.** to be consistent

consecuente *adj* consistent

consecutivo,-a *adj* consecutive; **tres días consecutivos** three days in a row

conseguir [6] *vt* (a) to get, to obtain; *(objetivo)* to achieve (b) **conseguí terminar** I managed to finish

consejero,-a *nm,f* (a) *(asesor)* adviser (b) *Pol* councillor (c) *Com* **c. delegado** managing director

consejo *nm* (a) *(recomendación)* advice; **un c.** a piece of advice (b) *(junta)* council; **c. de ministros** cabinet; *(reunión)* cabinet meeting; **c. de administración** board of directors; **c. de guerra** court martial

consenso *nm* consensus

consensuar *vt* to approve by consensus

consentido,-a *adj* spoiled

consentimiento *nm* consent

consentir [5] 1 *vt* (a) *(tolerar)* to allow, to permit; **no consientas que haga eso** don't allow him to do that (b) *(mimar)* to spoil

   2 *vi* to consent; **c. en** to agree to

conserje *nm* commissionaire; *(en escuela etc)* janitor

conserva *nf* tinned *o* canned food

conservación *nf* (a) preservation (b) *(mantenimiento)* maintenance, upkeep

conservador,-a 1 *adj & nm,f* conservative; *Pol* Conservative

   2 *nm (de museo)* curator

conservadurismo *nm* conservatism

conservante *nm* preservative

conservar 1 *vt* to conserve, to preserve; *(mantener)* to keep up, to maintain; *(alimentos)* to preserve

   2 conservarse *vpr* (a) *(tradición etc)* to survive (b) **c. bien** *(persona)* to age well

conservatorio *nm* conservatory

considerable *adj* considerable

consideración *nf* (a) consideration; **tomar algo en c.** to take sth into account (b) *(respeto)* regard (c) **de c.** important, considerable; **herido de c.** seriously injured

considerado,-a *adj* (a) *(atento)* considerate, thoughtful (b) **estar bien/mal c.** to be well/badly thought of

considerar *vt* to consider; **lo considero imposible** I think it's impossible

consigna *nf* (a) *(para maletas) Br* left-luggage office, *US* checkroom (b) *Mil* orders, instructions

consignar *vt* (a) *(puesto)* to allocate; *(cantidad)* to assign (b) *(mercancía)* to ship, to dispatch

consigo¹ *pron pers* (a) *(tercera persona) (hombre)* with him; *(mujer)* with her; *(cosa, animal)* with it; *(plural)* with them; *(usted)* with you (b) **hablar c. mismo** to speak to oneself

consigo² *indic pres de* **conseguir**

consiguiente *adj* resulting, consequent; **por c.** therefore, consequently

consistencia *nf* (a) consistency (b) *(de argumento)* soundness

consistente *adj* (a) *(firme)* firm, solid (b) *(teoría)* sound (c) **c. en** consisting of

---

   📖 Observa que la palabra inglesa **consistent** es un falso amigo y no es la traducción de la palabra española **consistente**. En inglés, **consistent** significa "consecuente".

---

consistir *vi* to consist (**en** of); **el secreto consiste en tener paciencia** the secret lies in being patient

consistorial *adj* **casa c.** town hall

consola *nf* console table; *Informát* console

consolación *nf* consolation; **premio de c.** consolation prize

consolador,-a 1 *adj* consoling, comforting

   2 *nm* dildo

consolar [2] 1 *vt* to console, to comfort

   2 consolarse *vpr* to console oneself, to take comfort (**con** from)

consolidar *vt*, **consolidarse** *vpr* to consolidate

consomé *nm* clear soup, consommé

consonancia *nf* **en c. con** in keeping with

consonante *adj & nf* consonant

consorcio *nm* consortium

consorte 1 *adj* **príncipe c.** prince consort
2 *nmf (cónyuge)* partner, spouse

conspicuo,-a *adj* prominent, outstanding

conspiración *nf* conspiracy, plot

conspirar *vi* to conspire, to plot

constancia *nf* (a) constancy, perseverance (b) *(testimonio)* proof, evidence; **dejar c. de algo** to put sth on record

constante 1 *adj* constant; *(persona)* steadfast
2 *nf* constant feature; *Mat* constant

constantemente *adv* constantly

constar *vi* (a) *(figurar)* to figure, to be included (**en** in); **c. en acta** to be on record (b) **me consta que ...** I am absolutely certain that ... (c) **c. de** to be made up of, to consist of

constatar *vt* to state; *(comprobar)* to check

constelación *nf* constellation

consternación *nf* consternation

consternar *vt* to dismay

constipado,-a 1 *adj* **estar c.** to have a cold *o* a chill
2 *nm* cold, chill

> *Observa que la palabra inglesa* **constipated** *es un falso amigo y no es la traducción de la palabra española* **constipado**. *En inglés,* **constipated** *significa "estreñido".*

constiparse *vpr* to catch a cold *o* a chill

constitución *nf* constitution

constitucional *adj* constitutional

constituir [37] 1 *vt* (a) *(formar)* to constitute; **estar constituido por** to consist of (b) *(suponer)* to represent (c) *(fundar)* to constitute, to set up
2 **constituirse** *vpr* **c. en** to set oneself up as

constituyente *adj & nmf* constituent

constreñir [6] *vt* (a) *(forzar)* to compel, to force (b) *(oprimir)* to restrict (c) *Med* to constrict

construcción *nf* (a) construction; *(sector)* the building industry; **en c.** under construction (b) *(edificio)* building

constructivo,-a *adj* constructive

constructor,-a 1 *nm,f* builder
2 *adj* **empresa constructora** builders, construction company

construir [37] *vt* to build, to manufacture

> *Observa que el verbo inglés* **to construe** *es un falso amigo y no es la traducción del verbo español* **construir**. *En inglés,* **to construe** *significa "interpretar".*

consuelo *nm* consolation

cónsul *nmf* consul

consulado *nm* consulate

consulta *nf* (a) consultation; **obra de c.** reference book (b) *Med* surgery; *(despacho)* consulting room; **horas de c.** surgery hours

consultar *vt* to consult, to seek advice (**con** from); *(libro)* to look up

consultivo,-a *adj* consultative, advisory

consultorio *nm* (a) *Med* medical centre (b) *Prensa* problem page, advice column

consumado,-a *adj* (a) consummated; **hecho c.** fait accompli, accomplished fact (b) *Fig (artista)* consummate

consumar *vt* to complete, to carry out; *(crimen)* to commit

consumición *nf* (a) consumption (b) *(bebida)* drink

consumidor,-a 1 *nm,f* consumer
2 *adj* consuming

consumir 1 *vt* to consume
2 **consumirse** *vpr (al hervir)* to boil away; *Fig (persona)* to waste away

consumismo *nm* consumerism

consumo *nm* consumption; **bienes de c.** consumer goods; **sociedad de c.** consumer society

contabilidad *nf Com* (a) *(profesión)* accountancy (b) *(de empresa, sociedad)* accounting, book-keeping

contabilizar [40] *vt Com* to enter in the books; *Dep* to score

contable *nmf* accountant

contactar *vi* **c. con** to contact, to get in touch with

contacto *nm* contact; *Aut* ignition; **perder el c.** to lose touch; **ponerse en c.** to get in touch

contado,-a 1 *adj* few and far between; **contadas veces** very seldom; **tiene los días contados** his days are numbered
2 *nm* **pagar al c.** to pay cash

contador,-ora 1 *nm,f Am (persona)* accountant; **c. público** *Br* chartered accountant, *US* certified public accountant
2 *nm (aparato)* meter; **c. de agua** water meter

contagiar [43] 1 *vt Med* to pass on
2 **contagiarse** *vpr* (a) *(persona)* to get infected (b) *(enfermedad)* to be contagious

contagio *nm* contagion

contagioso,-a *adj* contagious; *Fam (risa)* infectious

contaminación *nf* contamination; *(del aire)* pollution

contaminar *vt* to contaminate; *(aire, agua)* to pollute

contante *adj* dinero c. **(y sonante)** hard *o* ready cash

contar [2] 1 *vt* (**a**) *(sumar)* to count (**b**) *(narrar)* to tell

2 *vi* (**a**) to count (**b**) c. con *(confiar en)* to count on; *(tener)* to have

3 contarse *vpr Fam* ¿qué te cuentas? how's it going?

contemplación *nf* contemplation; *Fam* no andarse con contemplaciones to make no bones about it

contemplar *vt* to contemplate; *(considerar)* to consider; *(estipular)* to stipulate

contemporáneo,-a *adj & nm,f* contemporary

contención *nf* muro de c. retaining wall; c. salarial wage restraint

contencioso,-a 1 *adj* contentious; *Jur* litigious

2 *nm Jur* legal dispute

contendiente *nmf* contender, contestant

contenedor *nm* container

contener [24] 1 *vt* (**a**) to contain (**b**) *(pasiones etc)* to restrain, to hold back

2 contenerse *vpr* to control oneself, to hold (oneself) back

contenido *nm* content, contents

contentar 1 *vt* (**a**) *(satisfacer)* to please (**b**) *(alegrar)* to cheer up

2 contentarse *vpr* (**a**) *(conformarse)* to make do (**con** with), to be satisfied (**con** with) (**b**) *(alegrarse)* to cheer up

contento,-a *adj* happy, pleased (**con** with)

contestación *nf* answer; dar c. to answer

contestador *nm* c. automático answering machine

contestar *vt* (**a**) to answer (**b**) *Fam (replicar)* to answer back

contestatario,-a *adj* anti-establishment

contexto *nm* context

contienda *nf* struggle

contigo *pron* pers with you

contiguo,-a *adj* contiguous (**a** to), adjoining

continente *nm* (**a**) *Geog* continent (**b**) *(compostura)* countenance

contingencia *nf* contingency

contingente *nm* contingent

continuación *nf* continuation; a c. next

continuamente *adv* continuously

continuar [30] *vt & vi* to continue, to carry on (with); continúa en Francia he's still in France; continuará to be continued

continuidad *nf* continuity

continuo,-a 1 *adj* (**a**) continuous; *Aut* línea continua solid white line (**b**) *(reiterado)* continual, constant

2 *nm* continuum

contonearse *vpr* to swing one's hips

contorno *nm* (**a**) outline (**b**) contornos surroundings, environment

contorsión *nf* contortion

contorsionarse *vpr* to contort *o* twist oneself

contra 1 *prep* against; **en c. de** against

2 *nm* los pros y los contras the pros and cons

contraataque *nm* counterattack

contrabajo *nm* double bass

contrabandista *nmf* smuggler; c. de armas gunrunner

contrabando *nm* smuggling; c. de armas gunrunning; pasar algo de c. to smuggle sth in

contracción *nf* contraction

contracepción *nf* contraception

contrachapado *nm* plywood

contracorriente 1 *nf* crosscurrent

2 *adv* ir (**a**) c. to go against the tide

contradecir [12] *(pp* contradicho*)* *vt* to contradict

contradicción *nf* contradiction

contradictorio,-a *adj* contradictory

contraer [25] 1 *vt* to contract; c. matrimonio con algn to marry sb

2 contraerse *vpr* to contract

contraigo *indic pres de* contraer

contraindicación *nf* contraindication

contraje *pt indef de* contraer

contralor *nm Am* = inspector of public spending

contraloría *nf Am* = office controlling public spending

contraluz *nm* view against the light; a c. against the light

contramaestre *nm* (**a**) *(en buque)* boatswain (**b**) *(capataz)* foreman

contramano: • a contramano *loc adv* the wrong way *o* direction

contrapartida *nf* en c. in return

contrapelo: • a contrapelo *loc adv* the wrong way; *Fig* against the grain

contrapesar *vt* (**a**) to counterbalance, to counterpoise (**b**) *Fig (compensar)* to offset, to balance

contrapeso *nm* counterweight

contraportada *nf* back page

contraposición *nf* contrast
contraproducente *adj* counterproductive
contraprogramación *nf TV* competitive scheduling
contrapunto *nm* counterpoint
contrariamente *adv* **c. a ...** contrary to ...
contrariar [29] *vt* (a) *(oponerse a)* to oppose, to go against (b) *(disgustar)* to upset
contrariedad *nf* (a) *(contratiempo)* obstacle, setback (b) *(disgusto)* annoyance
contrario,-a 1 *adj* (a) opposite; **lo c. de** the opposite of; **en el lado/sentido c.** on the other side/in the other direction; **al c., por el c.** on the contrary; **de lo c.** otherwise; **todo lo c.** quite the opposite (b) *(perjudicial)* contrary (a to)
2 *nm,f* opponent, rival
3 *nf* **llevar la contraria** to be contrary
contrarrestar *vt* to offset, to counteract
contrasentido *nm* contradiction
contraseña *nf* password
contrastar *vt* to contrast (con with)
contraste *nm* (a) contrast (b) *(en oro, plata)* hallmark
contrata *nf* contract
contratar *vt* to hire, to engage
contratiempo *nm* setback, hitch
contratista *nmf* contractor
contrato *nm* contract; **c. de trabajo** work contract; **c. de alquiler** lease, leasing agreement; **c. basura** short-term contract with poor conditions
contravenir [27] *vt* to contravene, to infringe
contraventana *nf* shutter
contribución *nf* (a) contribution (b) *(impuesto)* tax
contribuir [37] **1** *vt* to contribute (a to)
2 *vi* (a) to contribute (b) *(pagar impuestos)* to pay taxes
contribuyente *nmf* taxpayer
contrincante *nmf* rival, opponent
control *nm* (a) control; **c. a distancia** remote control (b) *(inspección)* check; *(de policía etc)* checkpoint
controlador,-a *nm,f* **c. (aéreo)** air traffic controller
controlar 1 *vt* (a) to control (b) *(comprobar)* to check
2 controlarse *vpr* to control oneself
controversia *nf* controversy
controvertido,-a *adj* controversial
contumaz *adj* obstinate
contundente *adj* (a) *(arma)* blunt (b) *(argumento)* forceful, convincing
contusión *nf* contusion, bruise

conuco *nm Carib, Col* small farm, *Br* smallholding
convalecencia *nf* convalescence
convaleciente *adj & nmf* convalescent
convalidar *vt* to validate; *(documento)* to ratify
convencer [49] *vt* to convince; **c. a algn de algo** to convince sb about sth
convencimiento *nm* conviction; **tener el c. de que ...** to be convinced that ...
convención *nf* convention
convencional *adj* conventional
convenido,-a *adj* agreed; **según lo c.** as agreed
conveniencia *nf* (a) *(provecho)* convenience (b) **conveniencias sociales** social proprieties
conveniente *adj* (a) *(oportuno)* convenient; *(aconsejable)* advisable (b) *(precio)* good, fair
convenio *nm* agreement; **c. laboral** agreement on salary and conditions
convenir [27] *vt & vi* (a) *(acordar)* to agree; **c. una fecha** to agree on a date; **sueldo a c.** salary negotiable; **c. en** to agree on (b) *(ser oportuno)* to suit, to be good for; **conviene recordar que ...** it's as well to remember that ...
convento *nm (de monjas)* convent; *(de monjes)* monastery
convergente *adj* convergent
converger [53] *vi* to converge
conversación *nf* conversation
conversada *nf Am Fam* chat
conversar *vi* to converse, to talk
conversión *nf* conversion
converso,-a *nm,f* convert
convertible *adj* convertible
convertir [54] **1** *vt* to change, to convert
2 convertirse *vpr* (a) **c. en** to turn into, to become (b) *Rel* to be converted (a to)
convexo,-a *adj* convex
convicción *nf* conviction; **tengo la c. de que ...** I am convinced that ..
convicto,-a *adj* convicted
convidado,-a *adj & nm,f* guest
convidar *vt* to invite
convincente *adj* convincing
convite *nm* reception
convivencia *nf* life together; *Fig* coexistence
convivir *vi* to live together; *Fig* to coexist (con with)
convocar [44] *vt* to summon; *(reunión, elecciones)* to call
convocatoria *nf* (a) *(a huelga etc)* call (b) *Educ* diet

convulsión *nf Med* convulsion; *(agitación social)* upheaval

convulsivo,-a *adj* convulsive

conyugal *adj* conjugal; **vida c.** married life

cónyuge *nmf* spouse; **cónyuges** married couple, husband and wife

coña *nf muy Fam* **estar de c.** to be joking

coñac *nm* brandy, cognac

coñazo *nm muy Fam* pain, drag; **dar el c.** to be a real pain

coño 1 *nm Vulg* cunt
   2 *interj Vulg* for fuck's sake!

cooperación *nf* co-operation

cooperador,-a *nm,f* collaborator, co-operator

cooperante *nmf* aid worker

cooperar *vi* to co-operate (**con** with)

cooperativa *nf* co-operative

coordenada *nf* co-ordinate

coordinación *nf* co-ordination

coordinador,-a *nm,f* co-ordinator

coordinadora *nf* co-ordinating committee; **c. general** joint committee

coordinar *vt* to co-ordinate

copa *nf* (a) glass; **tomar una c.** to have a drink (b) *(de árbol)* top (c) *Dep* cup (d) *Naipes* **copas** hearts

copar *vt* to take up

copartícipe *adj & nmf (socio)* partner; *(colaborador)* collaborator; *(copropietario)* joint owner, co-owner

Copenhague *n* Copenhagen

copetín *nm RP* pre-lunch/pre-dinner drinks

copia *nf* copy; *Informát* **c. de seguridad** backup; *Informát* **hacer una c. de seguridad de algo** to back up sth

copiar [43] *vt* to copy

copiloto *nm Av* copilot; *Aut* co-driver

copioso,-a *adj* abundant, copious

copistería *nf* photocopying service

copla *nf* verse, couplet

copo *nm* flake; *(de nieve)* snowflake; **copos de maíz** cornflakes

coproducción *nf* co-production, joint production

cópula *nf* (a) *(coito)* copulation, intercourse (b) *Ling* conjunction

copular *vi* to copulate (**con** with)

coqueta *nf* dressing table

coquetear *vi* to flirt (**con** with)

coqueto,-a 1 *adj* coquettish
   2 *nm,f* flirt

coraje *nm* (a) *(valor)* courage (b) *(ira)* anger, annoyance; *Fig* **dar c. a algn** to infuriate sb; **¡qué c.!** how maddening!

coral¹ *nm Zool* coral

coral² *nf Mús* choral, chorale

Corán *nm* Koran

coraza *nf* armour; *Fig* protection

corazón *nm* (a) heart; *Fig* **de (todo) c.** in all sincerity; *Fig* **tener buen c.** to be kindhearted (b) *(parte central)* heart; *(de fruta)* core (c) *Naipes* **corazones** hearts

corazonada *nf* hunch, feeling

corbata *nf* tie, *US* necktie; **con c.** wearing a tie

Córcega *n* Corsica

corchete *nm* (a) *Impr* square bracket (b) *Cost* hook and eye, snap fastener

corcho *nm* cork; *(de pesca)* float

cordel *nm* rope, cord

cordero,-a *nm,f* lamb

cordial *adj* cordial, warm

cordialidad *nf* cordiality, warmth

cordillera *nf* mountain chain *o* range

córdoba *nm Fin* = monetary unit of Nicaragua

cordón *nm* string; *(de zapatos)* shoelace; *Anat* **c. umbilical** umbilical cord; **c. policial** police cordon; *CSur, Cuba (de la vereda)* *Br* kerb, *US* curb

cordura *nf* common sense

Corea *n* Korea; **C. del Norte/Sur** North/South Korea

coreano,-a *adj & nm,f* Korean

corear *vt* (a) *(cantar a coro)* to sing in chorus (b) *(aclamar)* to applaud

coreografía *nf* choreography

cornada *nf Taurom* goring

corneja *nf* crow

córner *nm Ftb* corner (kick); **sacar un c.** to take a corner

corneta *nf* bugle; **c. de llaves** cornet

cornisa *nf* cornice

cornudo *nm Fam (marido)* cuckold

coro *nm Mús* choir; *Teatro* chorus; *Fig* **a c.** all together

corona *nf* (a) crown (b) *(de flores etc)* wreath, garland; **c. funeraria** funeral wreath

coronación *nf* (a) coronation (b) *Fig (culminación)* crowning point

coronar *vt* to crown

coronel *nm* colonel

coronilla *nf* crown of the head; *Fam* **estar hasta la c. (de)** to be fed up (with)

corpiño *nm (vestido)* bodice; *Arg (sostén)* bra

corporación *nf* corporation

corporal *adj* corporal; **castigo c.** corporal punishment; **olor c.** body odour, BO

corporativo,-a *adj* corporative

corpulento,-a *adj* corpulent, stout

corpus *nm* corpus

corral *nm* farmyard, *US* corral; *(de casa)* courtyard

correa *nf* (a) *(tira)* strap; *(de reloj)* watchstrap; *(de pantalón)* belt; *(de perro)* lead, leash (b)*Téc* belt

corrección *nf* (a) *(rectificación)* correction (b) *(urbanidad)* courtesy, politeness

correcto,-a *adj* (a) *(sin errores)* correct (b) *(educado)* polite, courteous (**con** to); *(conducta)* proper

corredera *nf* **puerta/ventana de c.** sliding door/window

corredizo,-a *adj* sliding; **nudo c.** slipknot; **techo c.** sunroof

corredor,-a *nm,f* (a) *Dep* runner (b) *Fin* **c. de bolsa** stockbroker

corregir [58] *vt* to correct

2 corregirse *vpr* to mend one's ways

correo *nm* (a) post, mail; **echar al c.** to post; **por c.** by post; **c. aéreo** airmail; **c. certificado** registered post; *Informát* **c. electrónico** electronic mail, e-mail; *Informát* **me envió un c. (electrónico)** *(un mensaje)* she e-mailed me, she sent me an e-mail; **(tren) c.** mail train (b) **correos** *(edificio)* post office

correr 1 *vi* (a) to run; *(coche)* to go fast; *(conductor)* to drive fast; *(viento)* to blow; *Fig* **no corras, habla más despacio** don't rush, speak slower; **c. prisa** to be urgent (b) **c. con los gastos** to foot the bill; **corre a mi cargo** I'll take care of it

2 *vt* (a) *(cortina)* to draw; *(cerrojo)* to close; *(aventura etc)* to have; **c. el riesgo** *o* **peligro** to run the risk (b) *(mover)* to pull up, to draw up

3 correrse *vpr* (a) *(moverse)* to move over (b) *Fam* **c. una juerga** to go on a spree (c) *muy Fam (tener orgasmo)* to come

correspondencia *nf* (a) correspondence (b) *Ferroc* connection

corresponder 1 *vi* (a) to correspond (**a** to; **con** with) (b) *(incumbir)* to concern, to be incumbent upon; **esta tarea te corresponde a ti** it's your job to do this (c) *(pertenecer)* to belong; **me dieron lo que me correspondía** they gave me my share

2 corresponderse *vpr* (a) *(ajustarse)* to correspond (b) *(dos cosas)* to tally; **no se corresponde con la descripción** it does not match the description (c) *(dos personas)* to love each other

correspondiente *adj* corresponding (**a** to)

corresponsal *nmf* correspondent

corrida *nf* **c. (de toros)** bullfight

corrido,-a *adj* (a) *(avergonzado)* abashed (b) **de c.** without stopping; **se lo sabe de c.** she knows it by heart

corriente 1 *adj* (a) *(común)* common (b) *(agua)* running (c) *(mes, año)* current, present; **el diez del c.** the tenth of this month (d) *Fin (cuenta)* current (e) **estar al c.** to be up to date

2 *nf* (a) *(corriente, stream; Fig* **ir** *o* **navegar contra c.** to go against the tide; *Fam* **seguirle** *o* **llevarle la c. a algn** to humour sb; *Elec* **c. eléctrica** (electric) current (b) *(de aire)* draught (c) *(tendencia)* trend, current

corrijo *indic pres de* **corregir**

corrillo *nm* small group of people talking; *Fig* clique

corro *nm* (a) circle, ring (b) *(juego)* ring-a-ring-a-roses

corroborar *vt* to corroborate

corroer [38] *vt* to corrode; *Fig* **la envidia le corroe** envy eats away at him

corromper 1 *vt* (a) *(pudrir)* to turn bad, to rot (b) *(pervertir)* to corrupt, to pervert

2 corromperse *vpr* (a) *(pudrirse)* to go bad, to rot (b) *(pervertirse)* to become corrupted

corrosivo,-a *adj* corrosive; *Fig (mordaz)* caustic

corrupción *nf* (a) *(putrefacción)* rot, decay (b) *Fig* corruption; *Jur* **c. de menores** corruption of minors

corrupto,-a *adj* corrupt

corsé *nm* corset

cortacésped *nm o nf* lawnmower

cortado,-a 1 *adj* (a) cut (up) (b) *(leche)* sour (c) *(labios)* chapped (d) *Fam (tímido)* shy

2 *nm* small coffee with a dash of milk

cortafuego *nm* firebreak

cortapisa *nf Fig* restriction, limitation

cortar 1 *vt* (a) to cut; *(carne)* to carve; *(árbol)* to cut down; *Fam* **c. por lo sano** to take drastic measures; *Fam* **cortó con su novio** she split up with her boyfriend (b) *(piel)* to chap, to crack (c) *(luz, teléfono)* to cut off (d) *(paso, carretera)* to block

2 cortarse *vpr* (a) *(herirse)* to cut oneself (b) **c. el pelo** to have one's hair cut (c) *(leche etc)* to curdle (d) *Tel* **se cortó la comunicación** we were cut off (e) *Fam (aturdirse)* to become all shy

cortaúñas *nm inv* nail clippers

corte¹ *nm* (a) cut; **c. de pelo** haircut; *TV* **c. publicitario** commercial break; **c. de mangas** ≃ V-sign (b) *(sección)* section; **c. transversal** cross section (c) *Fam* rebuff; **dar un c. a algn** to cut sb dead

corte² *nf* (**a**) *(real)* court (**b**) **Las Cortes** (Spanish) Parliament

cortejar *vt* to court

cortejo *nm* (**a**) *(galanteo)* courting (**b**) *(comitiva)* entourage, retinue; **c. fúnebre** funeral cortège

cortés *adj* courteous, polite

cortesía *nf* courtesy, politeness

corteza *nf (de árbol)* bark; *(de queso)* rind; *(de pan)* crust

cortijo *nm* Andalusian farm *o* farmhouse

cortina *nf* curtain; **c. de humo** smoke screen

corto,-a 1 *adj* (**a**) *(distancia, tiempo)* short; *Fam* **c. de luces** dim-witted; **c. de vista** short-sighted; *Aut* **luz corta** dipped headlights (**b**) *Fam* **quedarse c.** *(calcular mal)* to underestimate (**c**) *(apocado)* timid, shy

   2 *nm Cin* short (film)

cortocircuito *nm* short circuit

cortometraje *nm* short (film)

corvo,-a *adj* curved, bent

cosa *nf* (**a**) thing; **no he visto c. igual** I've never seen anything like it; **no ser gran c.** not to be up to much (**b**) *(asunto)* matter, business; **eso es c. tuya** that's your business *o* affair; **eso es otra c.** that's different (**c**) **hace c. de una hora** about an hour ago

coscorrón *nm* knock *o* blow on the head

cosecha *nf* (**a**) *Agr* harvest, crop (**b**) *(año del vino)* vintage

cosechadora *nf* combine harvester

cosechar *vt* to harvest, to gather (in)

coser *vt* (**a**) to sew; *Fam* **es c. y cantar** it's a piece of cake (**b**) *Med* to stitch up

cosmético,-a *adj & nm* cosmetic

cósmico,-a *adj* cosmic

cosmonauta *nmf* cosmonaut

cosmopolita *adj & nmf* cosmopolitan

cosmos *nm inv* cosmos

coso *nm* (**a**) *Taurom* bullring (**b**) *CSur Fam (objeto)* whatnot, thing

cosquillas *nfpl* tickling; **hacer c. a algn** to tickle sb; **tener c.** to be ticklish

cosquilleo *nm* tickling

costa¹ *nf* coast; *(litoral)* coastline; *(playa)* beach, seaside

costa² *nf* **a c. de** at the expense of; **a toda c.** at all costs, at any price; **vive a c. mía** he lives off me

costado *nm* side; **de c.** sideways; **es catalana por los cuatro costados** she's Catalan through and through

costal *nm* sack

costanera *nf CSur* seaside promenade

costar [2] *vi* (**a**) to cost; **¿cuánto cuesta?** how much is it?; **c. barato/caro** to be

cheap/expensive (**b**) *Fig* **te va a c. caro** you'll pay dearly for this; **c. trabajo** *o* **mucho** to be hard; **me cuesta hablar francés** I find it difficult to speak French; **cueste lo que cueste** at any cost

costarricense *adj & nmf*, **costarriqueño,-a** *adj & nm,f* Costa Rican

coste *nm* cost; **a precio de c.** (at) cost price; **c. de la vida** cost of living

costear 1 *vt* to afford, to pay for; **c. los gastos** to foot the bill

   2 costearse *vpr* to pay for

costero,-a 1 *adj* coastal; **ciudad costera** seaside town

   2 *nf Méx* **costera** seaside promenade

costilla *nf* (**a**) *Anat* rib (**b**) *Culin* cutlet

costo¹ *nm* cost

costo² *nm Fam (hachís)* dope, shit, stuff

costoso,-a *adj* costly, expensive

costra *nf* crust; *Med* scab

costumbre *nf* (**a**) *(hábito)* habit; **como de c.** as usual; **tengo la c. de levantarme temprano** I usually get up early; **tenía la c. de ...** he used to ... (**b**) *(tradición)* custom

costura *nf* (**a**) sewing (**b**) *(confección)* dressmaking; **alta c.** haute couture (**c**) *(línea de puntadas)* seam

costurera *nf* seamstress

costurero *nm* sewing basket

cota *nf Geog* height above sea level; *Fig* rating

cotejar *vt* to compare

cotidiano,-a *adj* daily; **vida cotidiana** everyday life

cotilla *nmf Fam* busybody, gossip

cotillear *vi Fam* to gossip (**de** about)

cotilleo *nm Fam* gossip

cotización *nf* (**a**) *Fin* (market) price, quotation (**b**) *(cuota)* membership fees, subscription

cotizar [40] 1 *vt Fin* to quote

   2 *vi* to pay national insurance

   3 cotizarse *vpr Fin* **c. a** to sell at

coto *nm* (**a**) enclosure, reserve; **c. de caza** game reserve (**b**) **poner c. a** to put a stop to

cotorra *nf* parrot; *Fig (persona)* chatterbox

COU *nm Educ (abr* **Curso de Orientación Universitaria***)* = one-year course which prepares students aged 17-18 for Spanish university entrance examinations

country ['kaʊntrɪ] *nm Arg* = luxury suburban housing development

coyote *nm* coyote, prairie wolf

coyuntura *nf* (**a**) *Anat* articulation, joint (**b**) *Fig (circunstancia)* juncture; **la c.**

económica the economic situation
coz *nf* kick; **dar una c.** to kick
C.P. (*abr* **código postal**) *Br* postcode, *US* zip code
crac(k) *nm* (**a**) *Fin* crash (**b**) (*droga*) crack
cráneo *nm* cranium, skull
cráter *nm* crater
creación *nf* creation
creador,-a *nm,f* creator
crear *vt* to create
creatividad *nf* creativity
creativo,-a *adj* creative
crecer [33] *vi* (**a**) to grow; **c. en importancia** to become more important (**b**) (*al tricotar*) to increase
creces *nfpl* **con c.** fully, in full; **devolver con c.** to return with interest
crecido,-a *adj* (*persona*) grown-up
creciente *adj* growing, increasing; **cuarto c.** crescent
crecimiento *nm* growth
credencial *nf* credential; (**cartas**) **credenciales** credentials
credibilidad *nf* credibility
crédito *nm* (**a**) *Com & Fin* credit (**b**) (*confianza*) belief; **dar c. a** to believe
credo *nm* creed
crédulo,-a *adj* credulous, gullible
creencia *nf* belief
creer [36] **1** *vt* (**a**) to believe (**b**) (*pensar*) to think; **creo que no** I don't think so; **creo que sí** I think so; **ya lo creo** I should think so
2 *vi* to believe; **c. en** to believe in
3 creerse *vpr* (**a**) to consider oneself to be; **¿qué te has creído?** what *o* who do you think you are? (**b**) **no me lo creo** I can't believe it
creíble *adj* credible, believable
creído,-a 1 *adj* arrogant, vain
2 *nm,f* big head
crema *nf* cream
cremallera *nf Br* zip (fastener), *US* zipper
crematorio *nm* (**horno**) **c.** crematorium
cremoso,-a *adj* creamy
crepe *nm* crêpe, pancake
crepería *nf* creperie
crepitar *vi* to crackle
crepúsculo *nm* twilight
crespo,-a *adj* frizzy
crespón *nm* crepe
cresta *nf* (**a**) crest; (*de gallo*) comb (**b**) (*de punk*) mohican
Creta *n* Crete
cretino,-a 1 *adj* stupid, cretinous
2 *nm,f* cretin
creyente *nmf* believer
crezco *indic pres de* **crecer**

cría *nf* (**a**) (*cachorro*) young (**b**) (*crianza*) breeding, raising
criada *nf* maid
criadero *nm* nursery
criadilla *nf Culin* bull's testicle
criado,-a 1 *adj* **mal c.** spoilt
2 *nm,f* servant
crianza *nf* (*de animales*) breeding; *Fig* **vinos de c.** vintage wines
criar [29] *vt* (**a**) (*animales*) to breed, to raise; (*niños*) to bring up, to rear (**b**) (*producir*) to have, to grow
criatura *nf* (**a**) (living) creature (**b**) (*crío*) baby, child
criba *nf* sieve
cribar *vt* to sieve, to sift
crimen *nm* (*pl* **crímenes**) murder; **c. de guerra** war crime
criminal *nmf & adj* criminal
crin *nf*, **crines** *nfpl* mane
crío,-a 1 *nm Fam* kid
2 *adj* babyish
criollo,-a *adj & nm,f* Creole
críquet *nm* cricket
crisantemo *nm* chrysanthemum
crisis *nf inv* (**a**) crisis (**b**) (*ataque*) fit, attack; **c. nerviosa** nervous breakdown
crispación *nf* tension
crispar *vt* to make tense; *Fig* **eso me crispa los nervios** that sets my nerves on edge
cristal *nm* (**a**) crystal; **c. de roca** rock crystal (**b**) (*vidrio*) glass; (*de gafas*) lense; (*de ventana*) (window) pane
cristalera *nf* window
cristalería *nf* (*conjunto*) glassware; (*vasos*) glasses
cristalino,-a *adj* crystal clear
cristalizar [40] *vi* to crystallize
cristiandad *nf* Christendom
cristianismo *nm* Christianity
cristiano,-a *adj & nm,f* Christian
Cristo *nm* Christ
criterio *nm* (**a**) (*pauta*) criterion (**b**) (*opinión*) opinion (**c**) (*discernimiento*) discretion; **lo dejo a tu c.** I'll leave it up to you
crítica *nf* (**a**) criticism (**b**) *Prensa* review; **tener buena c.** to get good reviews (**c**) (*conjunto de críticos*) critics
criticar [44] **1** *vt* to criticize
2 *vi* (*murmurar*) to gossip
crítico,-a 1 *adj* critical
2 *nm,f* critic
criticón,-ona *nm,f Fam* fault-finder
Croacia *n* Croatia
croar *vi* to croak
croata 1 *adj* Croatian
2 *nmf* Croat, Croatian

croché *nm* crochet

croissant *nm* croissant

crol *nm* crawl

cromo *nm* (**a**) *(metal)* chromium, chrome (**b**) *(estampa)* picture card

cromosoma *nm* chromosome

crónica *nf* (**a**) account, chronicle (**b**) *Prensa* feature, article

crónico,-a *adj* chronic

cronista *nmf Prensa* feature writer

cronología *nf* chronology

cronológico,-a *adj* chronological

cronometrar *vt* to time

cronómetro *nm* stopwatch

croqueta *nf* croquette

croquis *nm inv* sketch

cruce *nm* (**a**) crossing; *(de carreteras)* crossroads; *(de razas)* crossbreeding (**b**) *Tel* crossed line

crucero *nm Náut* cruise; *(barco)* cruiser

crucial *adj* crucial

crucificar [44] *vt* to crucify

crucifijo *nm* crucifix

crucigrama *nm* crossword (puzzle)

crudeza *nf* crudeness, coarseness

crudo,-a **1** *adj* (**a**) raw; *(comida)* underdone; *Fam Fig* **lo veo muy c.** it doesn't look too good (**b**) *(clima)* harsh (**c**) *(color)* cream
   2 *nm (petróleo)* crude

cruel *adj* cruel

crueldad *nf* cruelty; *Fig (del clima)* severity

cruento,-a *adj* bloody

crujido *nm (de puerta)* creak, creaking; *(de dientes)* grinding

crujiente *adj* crunchy

crujir *vi (madera)* to creak; *(comida)* to crunch; *(dientes)* to grind

cruz *nf* (**a**) cross; **C. Roja** Red Cross; **c. gamada** swastika (**b**) **¿cara o c.?** ≃ heads or tails?

cruza *nf Am* cross, crossbreed

cruzada *nf* crusade

cruzado,-a **1** *adj* (**a**) crossed; **con los brazos cruzados** arms folded (**b**) *Cost* double-breasted (**c**) *(atravesado)* lying across (**d**) *(animal)* crossbred
   2 *nm Hist* crusader

cruzar [40] **1** *vt* (**a**) to cross (**b**) *(palabras, miradas)* to exchange (**c**) *(animal, planta)* to cross, to crossbreed
   2 *vi (atravesar)* to cross
   3 cruzarse *vpr* to cross; **c. con algn** to pass sb

cta. *Com (abr* **cuenta***)* a/c

cta. cte. *Com (abr* **cuenta corriente***)* c/a

c/u *(abr* **cada uno***)* ea

cuaderno *nm* notebook

cuadra *nf* (**a**) *(establo)* stable (**b**) *Am* block (of houses)

cuadrado,-a **1** *adj* (**a**) *Geom* square (**b**) *(complexión física)* broad, stocky (**c**) *Fig (mente)* rigid
   2 *nm* (**a**) *Geom* square (**b**) *Mat* square; **elevar (un número) al c.** to square (a number)

cuadrar **1** *vt* (**a**) *Mat* to square (**b**) *Andes (aparcar)* to park
   2 *vi (coincidir)* to square, to agree (**con** with); *(sumas, cifras)* to tally
   3 cuadrarse *vpr (soldado)* to stand to attention

cuadriculado,-a *adj* **papel c.** square paper

cuadrilátero,-a **1** *adj* quadrilateral
   2 *nm (en boxeo)* ring

cuadrilla *nf (equipo)* gang, team; *Mil* squad; *Taurom* bullfighter's team

cuadro *nm* (**a**) *(dibujo)* square; **tela a cuadros** checked cloth (**b**) *Arte* painting, picture (**c**) *Teatro* scene (**d**) *Elec & Téc* panel; **c. de mandos** control panel (**e**) *(gráfico)* chart, graph

cuádruple *adj* quadruple, fourfold

cuajada *nf* curd

cuajar **1** *vt (leche)* to curdle; *(sangre)* to clot
   2 *vi* (**a**) *(nieve)* to lie (**b**) *(moda)* to catch on; *(plan, esfuerzo)* to get off the ground

cual **1** *pron rel (precedido de artículo)* (**a**) *(persona) (sujeto)* who; *(objeto)* whom (**b**) *(cosa)* which
   2 *pron* (**a**) **tal c.** exactly as (**b**) *Literario (comparativo)* such as, like

cuál **1** *pron interr* which (one)?, what?; **¿c. quieres?** which one do you want?
   2 *adj interr* which
   3 *loc adv* **a c. más tonto** each more stupid than the other

cualidad *nf* quality

cualificado,-a *adj* qualified

cualquier *adj indef* any; **c. cosa** anything; **en c. momento** at any moment *o* time

cualquiera *(pl* **cualesquiera***)* **1** *adj indef* (**a**) *(indefinido)* any; **un profesor c.** any teacher (**b**) *(corriente)* ordinary

> Note that **cualquier** is used before singular nouns (e.g. **cualquier hombre** any man).

   2 *pron indef* (**a**) *(persona)* anybody; **c. te lo puede decir** anybody can tell you (**b**) *(cosa, animal)* anyone (**c**) **c. que sea** whatever it is
   3 *nmf Fig* **ser un c.** to be a nobody; **es una c.** she's a tart

cuando 1 *adv (de tiempo)* when; **c. más** at the most; **c. menos** at least; **de c. en c., de vez en c.** from time to time

2 *conj* (**a**) *(temporal)* when; **c. quieras** whenever you want; **c. vengas** when you come (**b**) *(condicional) (si)* if (**c**) *(concesiva) (aunque)* (**aun**) **c.** even if

3 *prep* during, at the time of; **c. la guerra** during the war; **c. niño** as a child

cuándo *adv interr* when?; **¿desde c.?** since when?; **¿para c. lo quieres?** when do you want it for?

cuantía *nf* quantity, amount

cuantioso,-a *adj* substantial, considerable

cuanto,-a 1 *adj* all; **gasta c. dinero gana** he spends all the money *o* as much as he earns; **unas cuantas niñas** a few girls

2 *pron rel* as much as; **coma c. quiera** eat as much as you want; **regala todo c. tiene** he gives away everything he's got

3 *pron indef pl* **unos cuantos** a few

4 *adv* (**a**) *(tiempo)* **c. antes** as soon as possible; **en c.** as soon as

(**b**) *(cantidad)* **c. más ... más** the more ... the more; **c. más lo miro, más me gusta** the more I look at it, the more I like it; **cuantas más personas (haya) mejor** the more the merrier

(**c**) **en c. a** with respect to, regarding; **en c. a Juan** as for Juan, as far as Juan is concerned

cuánto,-a 1 *adj & pron interr (sing)* how much?; *(pl)* how many?; **¿cuántas veces?** how many times?; **¿c. es?** how much is it?

2 *adv* how, how much; **¡cuánta gente hay!** what a lot of people there are!

cuarenta *adj & nm inv* forty; *Fam* **cantarle a algn las c.** to give sb a piece of one's mind

cuarentena *nf Med* quarantine

cuarentón,-ona *nm,f* forty-year-old

cuaresma *nf* Lent

cuartear *vt* to quarter

cuartel *nm Mil* barracks; **c. general** headquarters; *Fig* **no dar c.** to give no quarter

cuartelada *nf,* **cuartelazo** *nm* putsch, military uprising

cuartelillo *nm Mil* post, station

cuarteto *nm* quartet

cuartilla *nf* sheet of paper

cuarto,-a 1 *nm* (**a**) *(habitación)* room; **c. de baño** bathroom; **c. de estar** living room (**b**) *(cuarta parte)* quarter; **c. de hora** quarter of an hour; *Dep* **cuartos de final** quarter finals (**c**) *Fam* **cuartos** *(dinero)* dough, money

2 *adj & nm,f* fourth

cuarzo *nm* quartz

cuate *nmf Méx Fam* pal, *Br* mate, *US* buddy

cuatro 1 *adj & nm inv* four

2 *nm Fam* a few; **cayeron c. gotas** it rained a little bit

cuatrocientos,-as *adj & nm* four hundred

Cuba *n* Cuba

cuba *nf* cask, barrel; *Fam* **como una c.** (as) drunk as a lord

cubalibre *nm* rum/gin and coke

cubano,-a *adj & nm,f* Cuban

cubata *nm Fam* = cubalibre

cubertería *nf* cutlery

cúbico,-a *adj* cubic; *Mat* **raíz cúbica** cube root

cubierta *nf* (**a**) cover (**b**) *(de rueda)* tyre (**c**) *Náut* deck (**d**) *(techo)* roof

cubierto,-a 1 *adj* (**a**) covered; *(piscina)* indoors; *(cielo)* overcast (**b**) *(trabajo, plaza)* filled

2 *nm* (**a**) *(en la mesa)* place setting (**b**) **cubiertos** cutlery

cubil *nm* lair

cubismo *nm* cubism

cubito *nm* little cube; **c. de hielo** ice cube

cubo *nm* (**a**) bucket; **c. de la basura** rubbish bin (**b**) *Mat* cube (**c**) *(de rueda)* hub

cubrecama *nm* bedspread

cubrir *(pp* **cubierto)** **1** *vt* to cover

2 cubrirse *vpr (cielo)* to become overcast

cucaracha *nf* cockroach

cuchara *nf* spoon

cucharada *nf* spoonful; **c. rasa/colmada** level/heaped spoonful

cucharilla *nf* teaspoon; **c. de café** coffee spoon

cucharón *nm* ladle

cuchichear *vi* to whisper

cuchicheo *nm* whispering

cuchilla *nf* blade; **c. de afeitar** razor blade

cuchillada *nf,* **cuchillazo** *nm* stab

cuchillo *nm* knife

cuchitril *nm Fam* hovel, hole

cuclillas: • **en cuclillas** *loc adv* **en c.** crouching; **ponerse en c.** to crouch down

cuco,-a 1 *nm* cuckoo

2 *adj Fam (astuto)* shrewd, crafty

cucurucho *nm* (**a**) *(para helado)* cornet (**b**) *(de papel)* paper cone

cuello *nm* (**a**) neck (**b**) *(de camisa etc)* collar

cuenca *nf* (**a**) *Geog* basin (**b**) *(de los ojos)* socket

cuenco *nm* earthenware bowl

cuenta *nf* (**a**) *(factura)* bill (**b**) *Fin (de*

banco) account; **c. corriente** current account (**c**) (*cálculo*) count; **hacer cuentas** to do sums; **c. atrás** countdown (**d**) (*de collar*) bead (**e**) (*locuciones*) **caer en la c., darse c.** to realize; **dar c.** to report; **tener en c.** to take into account; **traer c.** to be worthwhile; **más sillas de la c.** too many chairs; **en resumidas cuentas** in short; **pedir cuentas** to ask for an explanation; **trabajar por c. propia** to be self-employed

cuentagotas *nm inv* dropper

cuentakilómetros *nm inv* (*distancia*) mileometer; (*velocidad*) speedometer

cuento *nm* story; *Lit* short story; **contar un c.** to tell a story; **Fig eso no viene a c.** that's beside the point; **c. chino** tall story; **c. de hadas** fairy story

cuerda *nf* (**a**) (*cordel*) rope; *Fig* **bajo c.** dishonestly; **c. floja** tightrope; **cuerdas vocales** vocal chords (**b**) (*de instrumento*) string (**c**) (*del reloj*) spring; **dar c. al reloj** to wind up a watch

cuerdo,-a *adj* sane

cueriza *nf Andes Fam* beating, leathering

cuerno *nm* horn; (*de ciervo*) antler; *Fam* **¡vete al c.!** get lost!; *Fam* **ponerle cuernos a algn** to be unfaithful to sb

cuero *nm* (**a**) leather; **chaqueta de c.** leather jacket (**b**) **c. cabelludo** scalp; *Fam* **en cueros (vivos)** (stark) naked

cuerpo *nm* (**a**) body; **de c. entero** full-length; *Fig* **tomar c.** to take shape (**b**) (*cadáver*) corpse; **de c. presente** lying in state (**c**) (*parte*) section, part (**d**) (*grupo*) corps, force; **c. de bomberos** fire brigade; **c. diplomático** diplomatic corps

cuervo *nm* raven

cuesta 1 *nf* slope; **c. abajo** downhill; **c. arriba** uphill
2 *loc adv* **a cuestas** on one's back *o* shoulders

cuestión *nf* (**a**) (*asunto*) matter, question; **es c. de vida o muerte** it's a matter of life or death; **en c. de unas horas** in just a few hours (**b**) (*pregunta*) question

cuestionario *nm* questionnaire

cueva *nf* cave

cuezo *indic pres de* **cocer**

cuico,-a *nm,f Méx Fam* cop

cuidado 1 *nm* (**a**) care; **con c.** carefully; **tener c.** to be careful; **estar al c. de** (*cosa*) to be in charge of; (*persona*) to look after; **me trae sin c.** I couldn't care less (**b**) *Med* **cuidados intensivos** intensive care
2 *interj* **¡c.!** look out!, watch out!; **¡c. lo que dices!** watch what you say!; **¡c. con el escalón!** mind the step!

cuidadoso,-a *adj* careful

cuidar 1 *vt* to care for, to look after; **c. de que todo salga bien** to make sure that everything goes all right; **c. los detalles** to pay attention to details
2 cuidarse *vpr* **cuídate** look after yourself

cuitlacoche *nm CAm, Méx* corn smut, = edible fungus which grows on maize

culata *nf* (**a**) (*de arma*) butt (**b**) *Aut* cylinder head

culebra *nf* snake

culebrilla *nf Med* ringworm

culebrón *nm* soap opera

culinario,-a *adj* culinary

culminación *nf* culmination

culminante *adj* (*punto*) highest; (*momento*) culminating

culminar *vi* to culminate

culo *nm* (**a**) *Fam* (*trasero*) backside; *Vulg* **¡vete a tomar por c.!** fuck off! (**b**) (*de recipiente*) bottom

culpa *nf* (**a**) blame; **echar la c. a algn** to put the blame on sb; **fue c. mía** it was my fault; **por tu c.** because of you (**b**) (*culpabilidad*) guilt

culpabilidad *nf* guilt, culpability

culpable 1 *nmf* offender, culprit
2 *adj* guilty; *Jur* **declararse c.** to plead guilty

culpar *vt* to blame; **c. a algn de un delito** to accuse sb of an offence

cultivado,-a *adj* (**a**) *Agr* cultivated (**b**) (*con cultura*) cultured, refined

cultivar *vt* (**a**) to cultivate (**b**) *Biol* to culture

cultivo *nm* (**a**) cultivation; (*planta*) crop (**b**) *Biol* culture

culto,-a 1 *adj* educated; (*palabra*) learned
2 *nm* cult; *Rel* worship

cultura *nf* culture

cultural *adj* cultural

culturismo *nm* body building

culturista *nmf* body builder

cumbre *nf* (**a**) (*de montaña*) summit, top; (*conferencia*) **c.** summit conference (**b**) *Fig* (*culminación*) pinnacle

cumple *nm Fam* birthday

cumpleaños *nm inv* birthday; **¡feliz c.!** happy birthday!

cumplido,-a 1 *adj* (**a**) completed; (*plazo*) expired; **misión cumplida** mission accomplished (**b**) (*cortés*) polite
2 *nm* compliment

cumplidor,-a *adj* reliable, dependable

cumplimiento *nm* fulfilment; **c. de la ley** observance of the law

cumplir 1 *vt* (**a**) to carry out, to fulfil; (*deseo*) to fulfil; (*promesa*) to keep;

(sentencia) to serve (**b**) **ayer cumplí veinte años** I was twenty (years old) yesterday

2 *vi* (**a**) *(plazo)* to expire, to end (**b**) **c. con el deber** to do one's duty

3 cumplirse *upr* (**a**) *(deseo, sueño)* to be fulfilled, to come true (**b**) *(plazo)* to expire

cúmulo *nm* pile, load

cuna *nf* (**a**) cot (**b**) *Fig (origen)* cradle

cundir *vi* (**a**) **me cunde mucho el trabajo** *o* **el tiempo** I seem to get a lot done (**b**) *(extenderse)* to spread; **cundió el pánico** panic spread; **cundió la voz de que ...** rumour had it that ...

cuneta *nf (de la carretera)* gutter; **quedarse en la c.** to be left behind

cuña *nf* (**a**) *(pieza)* wedge; **c. publicitaria** commercial break (**b**) *Andes, RP Fam (enchufe)* **tener c.** to have friends in high places

cuñado,-a *nm,f (hombre)* brother-in-law; *(mujer)* sister-in-law

cuño *nm* **de nuevo c.** newly-coined

cuota *nf* (**a**) *(de club etc)* membership fees, dues (**b**) *(porción)* quota, share (**c**) *Méx* **carretera de c.** toll road

cupe *pt indef de* **caber**

cupiera *subj imperf de* **caber**

cupo *nm* ceiling; *Mil* **excedente de c.** exempt from military service

cupón *nm* coupon, voucher

cúpula *nf* dome, cupola; *(líderes)* leadership

cura 1 *nm Rel* priest

2 *nf Med* cure; *Fig* **no tiene c.** there's no remedy

curación *nf* cure, treatment

curandero,-a *nm,f* quack

curar 1 *vt* (**a**) *(sanar)* to cure; *(herida)* to dress; *(enfermedad)* to treat (**b**) *(carne, pescado)* to cure

2 *vi (sanar)* to recover, to get well; *(herida)* to heal up

3 •**curarse** *upr* to recover, to get well; *(herida)* to heal up; **c. en salud** to make sure

curcuncho,-a *adj Andes Fam* hunchbacked

curiosear *vi* to pry

curiosidad *nf* curiosity; **tener c. de** to be curious about

curioso,-a 1 *adj* (**a**) *(indiscreto)* curious, inquisitive (**b**) *(extraño)* strange, odd; **lo c. es que ...** the strange thing is that ... (**c**) *(limpio)* neat, tidy

2 *nm,f* (**a**) *(mirón)* onlooker (**b**) *(chismoso)* nosey-parker, busybody

curita *nf Am Br* sticking-plaster, *US* Band-aid®

currante *nmf Fam* worker

currar, currelar *vi Fam* to graft, to grind

currículum *nm* (*pl* **curricula**) **c. vitae** curriculum vitae

curro *nm Fam* job

cursar *vt (estudiar)* to study; *(enviar)* to send

cursi *adj* vulgar

cursillo *nm* short course; **c. de reciclaje** refresher course

cursivo,-a *adj* **letra cursiva** italics

curso *nm* (**a**) *(año académico)* year; *(clase)* class (**b**) *Fig* **año/mes en c.** current year/month; **en el c. de** during (**c**) *(de acontecimientos, río)* course (**d**) *Fin* **moneda de c. legal** legal tender

cursor *nm* cursor

curtido,-a *adj* (**a**) *(piel)* weatherbeaten; *(cuero)* tanned (**b**) *Fig (persona)* hardened

curtiembre *nf Andes, RP* tannery

curtir *vt* (**a**) *(cuero)* to tan (**b**) *Fig (avezar)* to harden, to toughen

curva *nf* (**a**) curve (**b**) *(en carretera)* bend; **c. cerrada** sharp bend

curvilíneo,-a *adj* curvaceous

curvo,-a *adj* curved

cuscús *nm* couscous

cúspide *nf* summit, peak; *Fig* peak

custodia *nf* custody

custodiar [43] *vt* to watch over

cutáneo,-a *adj* cutaneous, skin; *Med* **erupción cutánea** rash

cutícula *nf* cuticle

cutis *nm* complexion

cuyo,-a *pron rel & pos (de persona)* whose; *(de cosa)* of which; **en c. caso** in which case

cv *(abr* **caballos de vapor**) hp

D

D, d [de] *nf (la letra)* D, d
D. (*abr* **don**) Mr
Da. (*abr* **doña**) Mrs/Miss
dactilar *adj* **huellas dactilares** finger-prints
dádiva *nf (regalo)* gift, present; *(donativo)* donation
dadivoso,-a *adj* generous
dado¹,-a *adj* (a) given; **en un momento d.** at a certain point (b) **ser d. a** to be given to (c) **d. que** since, given that
dado² *nm* die, dice
daga *nf* dagger
dalia *nf* dahlia
dálmata *nm* Dalmatian (dog)
daltónico,-a *adj* colour-blind
dama *nf* (a) *(señora)* lady (b) *(en damas)* king (c) **damas** *(juego) Br* draughts, *US* checkers
damasco *nm* (a) *(tela)* damask (b) *Andes, CAm, Carib, RP (albaricoque)* apricot
damnificado,-a *nm,f* victim, injured person
danés,-esa 1 *adj* Danish
2 *nm,f (persona)* Dane
3 *nm* (a) *(idioma)* Danish (b) **gran d.** *(perro)* Great Dane
Danubio *nm* **el D.** the Danube
danza *nf* dancing; *(baile)* dance
danzar [40] *vt & vi* to dance
dañar *vt (cosa)* to damage; *(persona)* to hurt, to harm
dañino,-a *adj* harmful, damaging (**para** to)
daño *nm (a cosa)* damage; *(a persona) (físico)* hurt; *(perjuicio)* harm; **se hizo d. en la pierna** he hurt his leg; *Jur* **daños y perjuicios** (legal) damages
dar [11] **1** *vt* (a) to give; *(recado, recuerdos)* to pass on, to give; *(noticia)* to tell
(b) *(mano de pintura, cera)* to apply, to put on
(c) *(película)* to show, to screen; *(fiesta)* to throw, to give
(d) *(cosecha)* to produce, to yield; *(fruto, flores)* to bear; *(beneficio, interés)* to give, to yield
(e) *(bofetada etc)* to deal; **d. a algn en la cabeza** to hit sb on the head

(f) **dale a la luz** switch the light on; **d. la mano a algn** to shake hands with sb; **d. los buenos días/las buenas noches a algn** to say good morning/good evening to sb; **me da lo mismo, me da igual** it's all the same to me; **¿qué más da?** what difference does it make?
(g) *(hora)* to strike; **ya han dado las nueve** it's gone nine (o'clock)
(h) **d. de comer a** to feed
(i) **d. a conocer** *(noticia)* to release; **d. a entender a algn que ...** to give sb to understand that ...
(j) **d. por** *(considerar)* to assume, to consider; **lo dieron por muerto** he was assumed dead, he was given up for dead; **d. por descontado/sabido** to take for granted, to assume
2 *vi* (a) **me dio un ataque de tos/risa** I had a coughing fit/an attack of the giggles
(b) **d. a** *(ventana, habitación)* to look out onto, to overlook; *(puerta)* to open onto, to lead to
(c) **d. con** *(persona)* to come across; **d. con la solución** to hit upon the solution
(d) **d. de sí** *(ropa)* to stretch, to give
(e) **d. en** to hit; **el sol me daba en los ojos** the sun was (shining) in my eyes
(f) **d. para** to be enough *o* sufficient for; **el presupuesto no da para más** the budget will not stretch any further
(g) **le dio por nadar** he took it into his head to go swimming
(h) **d. que hablar** to set people talking; **el suceso dio que pensar** the incident gave people food for thought
3 darse *vpr* (a) **se dio un caso extraño** something strange happened
(b) *(hallarse)* to be found, to exist
(c) **d. a** to take to; **se dio a la bebida** he took to drink
(d) **d. con** *o* **contra** to bump *o* crash into
(e) **dárselas de** to consider oneself
(f) **d. por satisfecho** to feel satisfied; **d. por vencido** to give in
(g) **se le da bien/mal el francés** she's good/bad at French
dardo *nm* dart

dársena *nf* dock

datar 1 *vt* to date

2 *vi* **d. de** to date back to *o* from

dátil *nm* date

dato *nm* (**a**) piece of information; **datos personales** personal details (**b**) *Informát* **datos** data

d.C. (*abr* **después de Cristo**) AD

dcha. (*abr* **derecha**) rt.

de *prep*

> **de** combines with the article **el** to form the contraction **del** (e.g. **del hombre** of the man).

(**a**) *(pertenencia)* of; **el título de la novela** the title of the novel; **el coche/hermano de Sofía** Sofía's car/brother; **las bicicletas de los niños** the boys' bicycles

(**b**) *(procedencia)* from; **de Madrid a Valencia** from Madrid to Valencia; **soy de Palencia** I'm from *o* I come from Palencia

(**c**) *(descripción)* **el niño de ojos azules** the boy with blue eyes; **el señor de la chaqueta** the man in the jacket; **el bobo del niño** the silly boy; **un reloj de oro** a gold watch; **un joven de veinte años** a young man of twenty

(**d**) *(contenido)* of; **un saco de patatas** a sack of potatoes

(**e**) **gafas de sol** sunglasses; **goma de borrar** eraser, *Br* rubber

(**f**) *(oficio)* by, as; **es arquitecto de profesión** he's an architect by profession; **trabaja de secretaria** she's working as a secretary

(**g**) *(acerca de)* about; **curso de informática** computer course

(**h**) *(tiempo)* **a las tres de la tarde** at three in the afternoon; **de día** by day; **de noche** at night; **de lunes a jueves** from Monday to Thursday; **de pequeño** as a child; **de año en año** year in year out

(**i**) *(precio)* at; **patatas de 30 pesetas el kilo** potatoes at 30 pesetas a kilo

(**j**) **una avenida de 15 km** an avenue 15 km long; **una botella de litro** a litre bottle

(**k**) *(con superlativo)* in; **el más largo de España** the longest in Spain

(**l**) *(causa)* with, because of; **llorar de alegría** to cry with joy; **morir de hambre** to die of hunger

(**m**) *(condicional)* **de haber llegado antes** if he had arrived before; **de no ser así** if that wasn't *o* weren't the case; **de ser cierto** if it was *o* were true

(**n**) **lo mismo de siempre** the usual thing

(**o**) **de cuatro en cuatro** in fours, four at a time

deambular *vi* to saunter, to stroll

debajo *adv* underneath, below; **el mío es el de la d.** mine is the one below; **está d. de la mesa** it's under the table; **por d. de lo normal** below normal; **salió por d. del coche** he came out from under the car

debate *nm* debate

debatir 1 *vt* to debate

2 **debatirse** *vpr* to struggle; **d. entre la vida y la muerte** to fight for one's life

debe *nm* *Com* debit, debit side

deber[1] *nm* (**a**) duty; **cumplir con su d.** to do one's duty (**b**) *Educ* **deberes** homework

deber[2] 1 *vt* *(dinero, explicación)* to owe

2 *vi* (**a**) must, to have to; **debe (de) comer** he must eat; **debe (de) irse ahora** she has to leave now; **la factura debe pagarse mañana** the bill must be paid tomorrow; **el tren debe llegar a las dos** the train is expected to arrive at two

(**b**) *(consejo)* **deberías visitar a tus padres** you ought to visit your parents; **debería haber ido ayer** I should have gone yesterday; **no debiste hacerlo** you shouldn't have done it

(**c**) *(suposición)* **deben de estar fuera** they must be out

3 **deberse** *vpr* **d. a** to be due to; **esto se debe a la falta de agua** this is due to lack of water

debidamente *adv* duly, properly

debido,-a *adj* (**a**) due; **a su d. tiempo** in due course; **con el d. respeto** with due respect (**b**) *(adecuado)* proper; **más de lo d.** too much; **tomaron las debidas precauciones** they took the proper precautions; **como es d.** properly (**c**) **d. a** because of, due to; **d. a que** because of the fact that

débil *adj* weak; *(luz)* dim; **punto d.** weak spot

debilidad *nf* weakness; *Fig* **tener d. por** *(persona)* to have a soft spot for; *(cosa)* to have a weakness for

debilitamiento *nm* weakening

debilitar 1 *vt* to weaken, to debilitate

2 **debilitarse** *vpr* to weaken, to grow weak

débito *nm* (**a**) *(deuda)* debt (**b**) *(debe)* debit

debut *nm* début, debut

debutar *vi* to make one's début *o* debut

década *nf* decade; **en la d. de los noventa** during the nineties

decadencia *nf* decadence

decadente *adj* & *nmf* decadent

decaer [39] *vi* to deteriorate

decaído,-a *adj* down
decaimiento *nm* (**a**) *(debilidad)* weakness (**b**) *(desaliento)* low spirits
decano,-a *nm,f Univ* dean
decantarse *vpr* to lean towards; **d. por** to come down on the side of
decapitar *vt* to behead, to decapitate
decena *nf* (about) ten; **una d. de veces** (about) ten times; **por decenas** in tens
decencia *nf* (**a**) *(decoro)* decency (**b**) *(honradez)* honesty
decenio *nm* decade
decente *adj* decent; *(decoroso)* modest
decepción *nf* disappointment

📖 Observa que la palabra inglesa **deception** es un falso amigo y no es la traducción de la palabra española **decepción**. En inglés, **deception** significa "engaño".

decepcionante *adj* disappointing
decepcionar *vt* to disappoint
decididamente *adv* (**a**) *(resueltamente)* resolutely (**b**) *(definitivamente)* definitely
decidido,-a *adj* determined, resolute
decidir 1 *vt & vi* to decide
2 decidirse *vpr* to make up one's mind; **d. a hacer algo** to make up one's mind to do sth; **d. por algo** to decide on sth
décima *nf* tenth
decimal *adj & nm* decimal; **el sistema métrico d.** the decimal system
décimo,-a 1 *adj & nm,f* tenth
2 *nm* (**a**) *(parte)* tenth (**b**) *(billete de lotería)* tenth part of a lottery ticket
decir [1] *nm* saying
decir [2] **[12]** *(pp dicho)* **1** *vt* (**a**) to say; **dice que no quiere venir** he says he doesn't want to come
(**b**) **d. una mentira/la verdad** to tell a lie/the truth
(**c**) *Tel* **dígame** hello
(**d**) **¿qué me dices del nuevo jefe?** what do you think of the new boss?
(**e**) *(mostrar)* to tell, to show; **su cara dice que está mintiendo** you can tell from his face that he's lying
(**f**) *(sugerir)* to mean; **esta película no me dice nada** this film doesn't appeal to me; **¿qué te dice el cuadro?** what does the picture mean to you?
(**g**) **querer d.** to mean
(**h**) *(locuciones)* **es d.** that is (to say); **por así decirlo** as it were, so to speak; **digamos** let's say; **digo yo** in my opinion; **el qué dirán** what people say; **ni que d. tiene** needless to say; **¡no me digas!** really!; **¡y que lo digas!** you bet!
2 decirse *vpr* **¿cómo se dice "mesa" en inglés?** how do you say "mesa" in English?; **se dice que ...** they say that ...; **sé lo que me digo** I know what I am saying
decisión *nf* (**a**) decision; **tomar una d.** to take *o* make a decision (**b**) *(resolución)* determination; **con d.** decisively
decisivo,-a *adj* decisive
decisorio,-a *adj* decision-making
declamar *vt & vi* to declaim, to recite
declaración *nf* (**a**) declaration; **d. de (la) renta** tax declaration *o* return (**b**) *(afirmación)* statement; **hacer declaraciones** to comment (**c**) *Jur* **prestar d.** to give evidence
declarante *nmf Jur* witness
declarar 1 *vt* (**a**) to declare; **d. la guerra a** to declare war on (**b**) *(afirmar)* to state (**c**) *Jur* **d. culpable/inocente a algn** to find sb guilty/not guilty
2 *vi* (**a**) to declare (**b**) *Jur* to testify
3 declararse *vpr* (**a**) **d. a favor/en contra de** to declare oneself in favour of/against; **d. en huelga** to go on strike; **d. a algn** to declare one's love for sb (**b**) *(guerra, incendio)* to start, to break out (**c**) *Jur* **d. culpable** to plead guilty
declinar *vt & vi* to decline
declive *nm* (**a**) *(del terreno)* incline, slope (**b**) *(de imperio etc)* decline
decolaje *nm Am* take-off
decolar *vi Am* to take off
decolorante *nm* bleaching agent
decolorar 1 *vt* to fade; *(pelo)* to bleach
2 decolorarse *vpr* to fade
decomisar *vt* to confiscate, to seize
decoración *nf* decoration
decorado *nm* scenery, set
decorador,-a *nm,f* (**a**) decorator (**b**) *Teatro* set designer
decorar *vt* to decorate
decorativo,-a *adj* decorative
decoro *nm* (**a**) *(respeto)* dignity, decorum (**b**) *(pudor)* modesty, decency
decoroso,-a *adj* (**a**) *(correcto)* seemly, decorous (**b**) *(decente)* decent, modest
decrecer **[33]** *vi* to decrease, to diminish
decrépito,-a *adj* decrepit
decretar *vt* to decree
decreto *nm* decree; **d.-ley** decree
dedal *nm* thimble
dedicación *nf* dedication
dedicar **[44] 1** *vt* to dedicate; *(tiempo, esfuerzos)* to devote (**a** to)
2 dedicarse *vpr* **¿a qué se dedica Vd.?** what do you do for a living?; **los fines de semana ella se dedica a pescar** at weekends she spends her time fishing
dedicatoria *nf* dedication

dedillo *nm* **saber algo al d.** to have sth at one's fingertips, to know sth very well

dedo *nm (de la mano)* finger; *(del pie)* toe; **d. anular/corazón/índice/meñique** ring/middle/index/little finger; **d. pulgar, d. gordo** thumb; *RP* **hacer d.** to hitchhike; *Fig* **elegir a algn a d.** to hand-pick sb

deducción *nf* deduction

deducible *adj Com* deductible

deducir [10] 1 *vt* (a) to deduce, to infer (b) *Com* to deduct

2 deducirse *vpr* **de aquí se deduce que ...** from this it follows that ...

deductivo,-a *adj* deductive

defecar [44] *vi* to defecate

defecto *nm* defect, fault; **d. físico** physical defect

defectuoso,-a *adj* defective, faulty

defender [3] 1 *vt* to defend (**de** from); **d. del frío/viento** to shelter from the cold/wind

2 defenderse *vpr* (a) to defend oneself (b) *Fam* **se defiende en francés** he can get by in French

defendido,-a *adj Jur* defendant

defensa 1 *nf* defence; **en d. propia, en legítima d.** in self-defence; **salir en d. de algn** to come out in defence of sb

2 *nm Dep* defender, back

defensiva *nf* defensive; **estar/ponerse a la d.** to be/go on the defensive

defensivo,-a *adj* defensive

defensor,-a *nm,f* defender; **abogado d.** counsel for the defence; **el defensor del pueblo** the ombudsman

deferencia *nf* deference; **en** *o* **por d. a** out of deference for

deficiencia *nf* deficiency, shortcoming; **d. mental** mental deficiency; **d. renal** kidney failure

deficiente 1 *adj* deficient

2 *nmf* **d. mental** mentally retarded person

3 *nm Educ* fail

déficit *nm (pl* **déficits**) deficit; *(carencia)* shortage

deficitario,-a *adj* showing a deficit

definición *nf* definition; **por d.** by definition

definido,-a *adj* clear; *Ling* definite

definir *vt* to define

definitivamente *adv* (a) *(para siempre)* for good, once and for all (b) *(con toda seguridad)* definitely

definitivo,-a *adj* definitive; **en definitiva** in short

deflación *nf Econ* deflation

deflacionista *adj Econ* deflationary

deformación *nf* deformation

deformar 1 *vt* to deform, to put out of shape; *(cara)* to disfigure; *Fig (la verdad, una imagen)* to distort

2 deformarse *vpr* to go out of shape, to become distorted

deforme *adj* deformed; *(objeto)* misshapen

defraudación *nf* fraud; **d. fiscal** tax evasion

defraudar *vt* (a) *(decepcionar)* to disappoint (b) *(al fisco)* to defraud, to cheat; **d. a Hacienda** to evade taxes

defunción *nf Fml* decease, demise

degeneración *nf* degeneration

degenerado,-a *adj & nm,f* degenerate

degenerar *vi* to degenerate

degollar [2] *vt* to behead

degradación *nf* degradation

degradante *adj* degrading

degradar *vt* to degrade

degustación *nf* tasting

degustar *vt* to taste, to sample

dehesa *nf* pasture, meadow

deificar [44] *vt* to deify

dejadez *nf* slovenliness

dejado,-a *adj* (a) *(descuidado)* untidy, slovenly (b) *(negligente)* negligent, careless (c) *Fam* **d. de la mano de Dios** godforsaken

dejar 1 *vt* (a) to leave; **déjame en paz** leave me alone; **d. dicho** to leave word *o* a message

(b) *(prestar)* to lend

(c) *(abandonar)* to give up; **d. algo por imposible** to give sth up; **dejé el tabaco y la bebida** I gave up smoking and drinking

(d) *(permitir)* to let, to allow; **d. caer** to drop; **d. entrar/salir** to let in/out

(e) *(omitir)* to leave out, to omit

(f) *(ganancias)* to produce

(g) *(+ adj)* to make; **d. triste** to make sad; **d. preocupado/sorprendido** to worry/surprise

(h) *(posponer)* **dejaron el viaje para el verano** they put the trip off until the summer

2 *v aux* **d. de** + *inf* to stop, to give up; **dejó de fumar el año pasado** he gave up smoking last year; **no deja de llamarme** she's always phoning me up

3 dejarse *vpr* (a) **me he dejado las llaves dentro** I've left the keys inside (b) *(locuciones)* **d. barba** to grow a beard; **d. caer** to flop down; **d. llevar por** to be influenced by

del *(contracción de* **de** + **el**) *ver* **de**

delantal *nm* apron

delante *adv* (**a**) in front; **la entrada de d.** the front entrance (**b**) **d. de** in front of; *(en serie)* ahead of (**c**) **por d.** in front; **se lo lleva todo por d.** he destroys everything in his path; **tiene toda la vida por d.** he has his whole life ahead of him

delantera *nf* (**a**) *(ventaja)* lead; **tomar la d.** take the lead (**b**) *Ftb* forward line, forwards

delantero,-a 1 *adj* front

2 *nm Ftb* forward; **d. centro** centre forward

delatar *vt* (**a**) to inform against (**b**) *Fig* to give away

delator,-a *nm,f* informer

delegación *nf* (**a**) *(acto, delegados)* delegation (**b**) *(oficina)* local office, branch; **D. de Hacienda** Tax Office (**c**) *Méx (distrito municipal)* district; *(comisaría)* police station

delegado,-a *nm,f* (**a**) delegate; **d. de Hacienda** chief tax inspector (**b**) *Com* representative

delegar [42] *vt* to delegate (**en** to)

deleitar 1 *vt* to delight

2 deleitarse *vpr* to delight in, to take delight in

deleite *nm* delight

deletrear *vt* to spell (out)

deleznable *adj* brittle

delfín *nm* dolphin

delgadez *nf* slimness

delgado,-a *adj* slim; *(capa)* fine

deliberación *nf* deliberation

deliberado,-a *adj* deliberate

deliberar *vi* to deliberate (on), to consider

delicadeza *nf* (**a**) *(finura)* delicacy, daintiness (**b**) *(tacto)* tactfulness; **falta de d.** tactlessness

delicado,-a *adj* (**a**) delicate (**b**) *(exigente)* fussy, hard to please (**c**) *(sensible)* hypersensitive

delicia *nf* delight; **hacer las delicias de algn** to delight sb

delicioso,-a *adj (comida)* delicious; *(agradable)* delightful

delictivo,-a *adj* criminal, punishable

delimitar *vt* to delimit

delincuencia *nf* delinquency

delincuente *adj & nmf* delinquent; **d. juvenil** juvenile delinquent

delineante *nmf (hombre)* draughtsman; *(mujer)* draughtswoman

delinear *vt* to delineate, to outline

delinquir [48] *vi* to break the law, to commit an offence

delirante *adj* delirious

delirar *vi* to be delirious

delirio *nm* delirium; **delirios de grandeza** delusions of grandeur

delito *nm* crime, offence

delta *nm* delta; **ala d.** hang-glider

demacrado,-a *adj* emaciated

demagogia *nf* demagogy

demagogo,-a *nm,f* demagogue

demanda *nf* (**a**) *Jur* lawsuit (**b**) *Com* demand

demandado,-a 1 *nm,f* defendant

2 *adj* in demand

demandante *nmf* claimant

demandar *vt* to sue

demarcar [44] *vt* to demarcate

demás 1 *adj* **los/las d.** the rest of; **la d. gente** the rest of the people

2 *pron* **lo/los/las d.** the rest; **por lo d.** otherwise, apart from that; **y d.** etcetera

demasía *nf* **en d.** excessively

demasiado,-a 1 *adj (singular)* too much; *(plural)* too many; **hay demasiada comida** there is too much food; **quieres demasiadas cosas** you want too many things

2 *adv* too (much); **es d. grande/caro** it is too big/dear; **fumas/trabajas d.** you smoke/work too much

demencia *nf* dementia, insanity

demente 1 *adj* insane, mad

2 *nmf* mental patient

democracia *nf* democracy

demócrata 1 *adj* democratic

2 *nmf* democrat

democrático,-a *adj* democratic

democratizar [40] *vt* to democratize

demografía *nf* demography

demográfico,-a *adj* demographic; **crecimiento d.** population growth

demoledor,-a *adj Fig* devastating

demoler [4] *vt* to demolish

demonio *nm* devil, demon; *Fam* **¿cómo/dónde demonios ...?** how/where the hell ...?; *Fam* **¡demonio(s)!** hell!, damn!; *Fam* **¡d. de niño!** you little devil!

demora *nf* delay

demorar 1 *vt* (**a**) *(retrasar)* to delay, to hold up (**b**) *(tardar)* **demoraron tres días en pintar la casa** it took them three days to paint the house

2 *vi Am (tardar)* **¡no demores!** don't be late!; **demorar en hacer algo** *(llevar tiempo)* to take one's time doing sth; *(retrasarse)* to take too long doing sth; **no demoraron en venir** they came immediately

3 demorarse *vpr* (**a**) *(retrasarse)* to be delayed, to be held up (**b**) *(detenerse)* to dally

demostrable *adj* demonstrable

demostración *nf* demonstration; **una d. de fuerza/afecto** a show of strength

demostrar [2] *vt* (a) *(mostrar)* to show, to demonstrate (b) *(evidenciar)* to prove

demudado,-a *adj* pale

denegar [1] *vt* to refuse; *Jur* **d. una demanda** to dismiss a claim

denigrante *adj* humiliating

denigrar *vt* to humiliate

denominación *nf* denomination; **d. de origen** *(vinos)* = guarantee of region of origin

denominado,-a *adj* so-called

denominador *nm* denominator

denominar *vt* to name, to designate

denotar *vt* to denote

densidad *nf* density; **d. de población** population density

denso,-a *adj* dense

dentadura *nf* teeth, set of teeth; **d. postiza** false teeth, dentures

dental *adj* dental

dentera *nf* **me da d.** it sets my teeth on edge

dentífrico,-a 1 *adj* **pasta/crema dentífrica** toothpaste
2 *nm* toothpaste

dentista *nmf* dentist

dentro *adv* (a) *(en el interior)* inside; **aquí d.** in here; **por d.** (on the) inside; **por d. está triste** deep down (inside) he feels sad (b) **d. de** *(lugar)* inside (c) **d. de poco** shortly, soon; **d. de un mes** in a month's time; **d. de lo que cabe** all things considered

denuncia *nf* (a) *Jur* report (b) *(crítica)* denunciation

denunciar [43] *vt* (a) *(delito)* to report (a to) (b) *(criticar)* to denounce

deparar *vt* to give; **no sabemos qué nos depara el destino** we don't know what fate has in store for us

departamento *nm* (a) department (b) *Ferroc* compartment (c) *(territorial)* province, district (d) *Arg (piso) Br* flat, *US* apartment

dependencia *nf* (a) dependence (**de** on) (b) **dependencias** premises

depender *vi* to depend (**de** on); *(económicamente)* to be dependent (**de** on)

dependienta *nf* shop assistant

dependiente 1 *adj* dependent (**de** on)
2 *nm* shop assistant

depilación *nf* depilation; **d. a la cera** waxing

depilar *vt* to remove the hair from; *(cejas)* to pluck

depilatorio,-a *adj & nm* depilatory; **crema depilatoria** hair-remover, hair-removing cream

deplorable *adj* deplorable

deplorar *vt* to deplore

deponer [19] *(pp* depuesto*) vt* (a) *(destituir)* to remove from office; *(líder)* to depose (b) *(actitud)* to abandon

deportado,-a *nm,f* deportee, deported person

deportar *vt* to deport

deporte *nm* sport; **hacer d.** to practise sports; **d. de aventura** adventure sport

deportista 1 *nmf (hombre)* sportsman; *(mujer)* sportswoman
2 *adj* sporty

deportividad *nf* sportsmanship

deportivo,-a 1 *adj* sports; **club/chaqueta d.** sports club/jacket
2 *nm Aut* sports car

deposición *nf* removal from office; *(de un líder)* deposition

depositar 1 *vt* (a) *Fin* to deposit (b) *(colocar)* to place, to put
2 depositarse *vpr* to settle

depósito *nm* (a) *Fin* deposit; **en d.** on deposit (b) *(de agua, gasolina)* tank (c) **d. de basuras** rubbish tip *o* dump; **d. de cadáveres** mortuary, morgue

depravación *nf* depravity

depravar *vt* to deprave

depre *nf Fam* downer, depression

depreciación *nf* depreciation

depreciar [43] **1** *vt* to reduce the value of
2 depreciarse *vpr* to depreciate, to lose value

depredador,-a 1 *adj* predatory
2 *nm,f* predator

depresión *nf* depression; **d. nerviosa** nervous breakdown

depresivo,-a *adj* depressive

deprimente *adj* depressing

deprimido,-a *adj* depressed

deprimir 1 *vt* to depress
2 deprimirse *vpr* to get depressed

deprisa *adv* quickly

depuesto,-a *pp de* deponer

depuración *nf* (a) *(del agua)* purification (b) *(purga)* purge

depurador,-a *adj* **planta depuradora** purification plant

depuradora *nf* purifier

depurar *vt* (a) *(agua)* to purify (b) *(partido)* to purge (c) *(estilo)* to refine

derecha *nf* (a) *(mano)* right hand (b) *(lugar)* right, right-hand side; **a la d.** to *o* on the right, on the right-hand side (c) *Pol* **la d.** the right; **de derechas** right-wing

derechista *nmf* right-winger

derecho,-a 1 *adj* (a) *(de la derecha)* right (b) *(recto)* upright, straight

2 *nm* (a) *(privilegio)* right; **derechos civiles/humanos** civil/human rights; **tener d. a** to be entitled to, to have the right to; **estar en su d.** to be within one's rights; **no hay d.** it's not fair; **d. de admisión** right to refuse admission (b) *Jur* law; **d. penal/político** criminal/constitutional law (c) *Com* **derechos** duties; **derechos de autor** royalties; **derechos de matrícula** enrolment fees

3 *adv* **siga todo d.** go straight ahead

deriva *nf* drift; **ir a la d.** to drift

derivado *nm* *(producto)* derivative, by-product

derivar 1 *vt* to divert; *(conversación)* to steer

2 *vi* (a) to drift (b) **d. de** to derive from

3 derivarse *upr* (a) **d. de** *(proceder)* to result o stem from (b) **d. de** *Ling* to be derived from

dermatitis *nf inv* dermatitis

dermatólogo,-a *nm,f* dermatologist

derogar [42] *vt* to repeal

derramamiento *nm* spilling; **d. de sangre** bloodshed

derramar 1 *vt* to spill; *(lágrimas)* to shed

2 derramarse *upr* to spill

derrame *nm* *Med* discharge; **d. cerebral** brain haemorrhage

derrapar *vi* to skid

derredor *nm* **en d. de** round, around

derretir [6] *vt*, **derretirse** *upr* to melt; *(hielo, nieve)* to thaw

derribar *vt* (a) *(edificio)* to pull down, to knock down (b) *(avión)* to shoot down (c) *(gobierno)* to bring down

derrocar [44] *vt* to bring down; *(violentamente)* to overthrow

derrochador,-a 1 *adj* wasteful

2 *nm,f* wasteful person, squanderer

derrochar *vt* to waste, to squander

derroche *nm* (a) *(de dinero, energía)* waste, squandering (b) *(abundancia)* profusion, abundance

derrota *nf* (a) defeat (b) *Náut* (ship's) course

derrotar *vt* to defeat, to beat

derrotero *nm* (a) *Fig* path, course o plan of action (b) *Náut* sailing directions

derrotista *adj & nmf* defeatist

derruido,-a *adj* in ruins

derruir [37] *vt* to demolish

derrumbar 1 *vt* *(edificio)* to knock down, to pull down

2 derrumbarse *upr* to collapse, to fall

down; *(techo)* to fall in, to cave in

desabastecido,-a *adj* **d. de** out of

desaborido,-a 1 *adj* (a) *(comida)* tasteless (b) *Fig (persona)* dull

2 *nm,f Fig* dull person

desabrido,-a *adj* (a) *(comida)* tasteless (b) *(tiempo)* unpleasant (c) *Fig (tono)* harsh; *(persona)* moody, irritable

desabrigado,-a *adj* **ir/estar d.** to be lightly dressed

desabrochar 1 *vt* to undo

2 desabrocharse *upr* (a) **desabróchate la camisa** undo your shirt (b) *(prenda)* to come undone

desacatar *vt* to disobey

desacato *nm* lack of respect, disrespect (a for); *Jur* **d. al tribunal** contempt of court

desacertado,-a *adj* unwise

desacierto *nm* mistake, error

desaconsejar *vt* to advise against

desacorde *adj* **estar d. con** to be in disagreement with

desacreditar *vt* (a) *(desprestigiar)* to discredit, to bring into discredit (b) *(criticar)* to disparage

desactivador,-a *nm,f* bomb disposal expert

desactivar *vt* *(bomba)* to defuse

desacuerdo *nm* disagreement

desafiante *adj* defiant

desafiar [29] *vt* to challenge

desafinado,-a *adj* out of tune

desafinar 1 *vi* to sing out of tune; *(instrumento)* to play out of tune

2 *vt* to put out of tune

3 desafinarse *upr* to go out of tune

desafío *nm* challenge

desaforado,-a *adj* wild

desafortunado,-a *adj* unlucky, unfortunate

desagradable *adj* unpleasant, disagreeable

desagradar *vi* to displease

desagradecido,-a 1 *adj* ungrateful

2 *nm,f* ungrateful person

desagrado *nm* displeasure

desagraviar [43] *vt* to make amends for

desaguar [45] *vt* to drain

desagüe *nm* *(vaciado)* drain; *(cañería)* waste pipe, drainpipe

desaguisado *nm* mess

desahogado,-a *adj* (a) *(acomodado)* well-off, well-to-do (b) *(espacioso)* spacious, roomy

desahogarse [42] *upr* to let off steam; **se desahogó de su depresión** he got his depression out of his system

desahogo nm (a) (alivio) relief (b) **vivir con d.** to live comfortably

desahuciado,-a adj (a) (enfermo) hopeless (b) (inquilino) evicted

desahuciar [43] vt (a) (desalojar) to evict (b) (enfermo) to deprive of all hope

desahucio nm eviction

desairado,-a adj (a) (humillado) spurned (b) (sin gracia) awkward

desairar vt to slight, to snub

desaire nm slight, rebuff

desajustar 1 vt to upset
  2 desajustarse vpr (piezas) to come apart

desajuste nm upset; **d. económico** economic imbalance; **un d. de horarios** clashing timetables

desalentador,-a adj discouraging, disheartening

desalentar [1] **1** vt to discourage, to dishearten
  2 desalentarse vpr to get discouraged, to lose heart

desaliento nm discouragement

desaliñado,-a adj scruffy, untidy

desaliño nm scruffiness, untidiness

desalmado,-a adj cruel, heartless

desalojamiento nm (de inquilino) eviction; (de público) removal; (de lugar) evacuation

desalojar vt (a) (inquilino) to evict; (público) to move on; (lugar) to evacuate (b) (abandonar) to move out of, to abandon

desalojo nm = desalojamiento

desamor nm lack of affection

desamortizar [40] vt to alienate, to disentail

desamparado,-a 1 adj (persona) helpless, unprotected; (lugar) abandoned, forsaken
  2 nm,f helpless o abandoned person

desamparar vt (a) to abandon, to desert (b) Jur to renounce, to relinquish

desamparo nm helplessness

desamueblado,-a adj unfurnished

desandar [8] vt **d. lo andado** to retrace one's steps

desangrarse vpr to lose (a lot of) blood

desanimado,-a adj (a) (persona) downhearted, dejected (b) (fiesta etc) dull, lifeless

desanimar 1 vt to discourage, to dishearten
  2 desanimarse vpr to lose heart, to get discouraged

desánimo nm discouragement, dejection

desapacible adj unpleasant

desaparecer [33] vi to disappear

desaparecido,-a 1 adj missing
  2 nm,f missing person

desaparición nf disappearance

desapego nm indifference, lack of affection

desapercibido,-a adj (a) (inadvertido) unnoticed; **pasar d.** to go unnoticed (b) (desprevenido) unprepared

desaprensivo,-a 1 adj unscrupulous
  2 nm,f unscrupulous person

desaprobar [2] vt (a) (no aprobar) to disapprove of (b) (rechazar) to reject

desaprovechar vt (dinero, tiempo) to waste; **d. una ocasión** to fail to make the most of an opportunity

desarmable adj that can be taken to pieces

desarmador nm Méx screwdriver

desarmar vt (a) (desmontar) to dismantle, to take to pieces (b) Mil to disarm

desarme nm disarmament; **d. nuclear** nuclear disarmament

desarraigado,-a adj rootless, without roots

desarraigar [42] vt to uproot

desarraigo nm rootlessness

desarreglado,-a adj (a) (lugar) untidy (b) (persona) untidy, slovenly

desarreglar vt (a) (desordenar) to make untidy, to mess up (b) (planes etc) to spoil, to upset

desarreglo nm difference of opinion

desarrollado,-a adj developed; **país d.** developed country

desarrollar 1 vt to develop
  2 desarrollarse vpr (a) (persona, enfermedad) to develop (b) (tener lugar) to take place

desarrollo nm development; **países en vías de d.** developing countries

desarticular vt to dismantle; **d. un complot** to foil a plot

desaseado,-a adj unkempt

desasir [46] **1** vt to release
  2 desasirse vpr to get loose; **d. de** to free o rid oneself of

desasosegar [1] vt to make restless o uneasy

desasosiego nm restlessness, uneasiness

desastrado,-a 1 adj untidy, scruffy
  2 nm,f scruffy person

desastre nm disaster; **eres un d.** you're just hopeless

desastroso,-a adj disastrous

desatar 1 vt to untie, to undo; (provocar) to unleash

2 desatarse *vpr* (**a**) *(zapato, cordón)* to come undone (**b**) *(tormenta)* to break; *(pasión)* to run wild

desatascar [44] *vt* to unblock, to clear

desatender [3] *vt* to neglect, not to pay attention to

desatento,-a *adj* inattentive; *(descortés)* impolite, discourteous

desatinado,-a *adj* unwise

desatino *nm* blunder

desatornillar *vt* to unscrew

desatrancar [44] *vt* to unblock; *(puerta)* to unbolt

desautorizar [40] *vt* (**a**) to disallow (**b**) *(huelga etc)* to ban, to forbid (**c**) *(desmentir)* to deny

desavenencia *nf* disagreement

desaventajado,-a *adj* at a disadvantage

desayunar 1 *vi* to have breakfast; *Fml* to breakfast
   2 *vt* to have for breakfast

desayuno *nm* breakfast

desazón *nf* unease

desazonar *vt* to cause unease to, to worry

desbancar [44] *vt* to oust

desbandada *nf* scattering; **hubo una d. general** everyone scattered

desbandarse *vpr* to scatter, to disperse

desbarajuste *nm* confusion, disorder

desbaratar *vt* to ruin, to wreck; *(jersey)* to unravel

desbloquear *vt* (**a**) *(negociaciones)* to get going again (**b**) *(créditos, precios)* to unfreeze

desbocado,-a *adj (caballo)* runaway

desbocarse *vpr (caballo)* to bolt, to run away

desbolado,-a *RP Fam* **1** *adj* messy, untidy
   2 *nm,f* untidy person

desbolarse *vpr RP Fam* to undress, to strip

desbole *nm RP Fam* mess, chaos

desbordante *adj* overflowing, bursting

desbordar 1 *vt* to overflow; *Fig* to overwhelm
   2 *vi* to overflow (**de** with)
   2 desbordarse *vpr* to overflow, to flood

descabalgar [42] *vi* to dismount

descabellado,-a *adj* crazy, wild

descafeinado,-a *adj* (**a**) *(café)* decaffeinated (**b**) *Fig* watered-down, diluted

descalabrar *vt* (**a**) to wound in the head (**b**) *Fig* to damage, to harm

descalabro *nm* setback, misfortune

descalificar [44] *vt* to disqualify

descalzarse [40] *vpr* to take one's shoes off

descalzo,-a *adj* barefoot

descambiar [43] *vt* to exchange

descaminado,-a *adj Fig* **ir d.** to be on the wrong track

descampado *nm* waste ground

descansado,-a *adj* (**a**) *(persona)* rested (**b**) *(vida, trabajo)* restful

descansar *vi* (**a**) to rest, to have a rest; *(corto tiempo)* to take a break (**b**) *Euf* **que en paz descanse** may he/she rest in peace

descansillo *nm* landing

descanso *nm* (**a**) rest, break; **un día de d.** a day off (**b**) *Cin & Teatro* interval; *Dep* half-time, interval (**c**) *(alivio)* relief (**d**) *(rellano)* landing

descapotable *adj & nm* convertible

descarado,-a 1 *adj* (**a**) *(insolente)* cheeky, insolent; *(desvergonzado)* shameless (**b**) *Fam* **d. que sí/no** *(por supuesto)* of course/course not
   2 *nm,f* cheeky person

descarga *nf* (**a**) unloading (**b**) *Elec & Mil* discharge

descargar [42] 1 *vt* (**a**) to unload (**b**) *Elec* to discharge (**c**) *(disparar)* to fire; *(golpe)* to deal
   2 *vi (tormenta)* to burst
   3 descargarse *vpr (batería)* to go flat

descargo *nm Jur* discharge; **testigo de d.** witness for the defence

descarnado,-a *adj* crude

descaro *nm* cheek, nerve; **¡qué d.!** what a cheek!

descarriar [29] 1 *vt* to lead astray, to put on the wrong road
   2 descarriarse *vpr* to go astray, to lose one's way

descarrilar *vi* to go off the rails, to be derailed

descartar 1 *vt* to rule out
   2 descartarse *vpr Naipes* to discard cards; **me descarté de un cinco** I got rid of a five

descascarillarse *vpr* to chip, to peel

descendencia *nf* descendants; **morir sin d.** to die without issue

descendente *adj* descending, downward

descender [3] 1 *vi* (**a**) *(temperatura, nivel)* to fall, to drop (**b**) **d. de** to descend from
   2 *vt* to lower

descendiente *nmf* descendant

descenso *nm* (**a**) descent; *(de temperatura)* fall, drop (**b**) *Dep* relegation

descentrado,-a *adj* off-centre

descentralizar [40] *vt* to decentralize

descifrar *vt* to decipher; *(mensaje)* to decode; *(misterio)* to solve; *(motivos, causas)* to figure out

descojonarse *upr muy Fam (reírse)* to piss oneself laughing

descolgar [2] 1 *vt (el teléfono)* to pick up; *(cuadro, cortinas)* to take down
2 descolgarse *upr* to let oneself down, to slide down

descolorido,-a *adj* faded

descombros *nmpl* rubble, debris

descompasado,-a *adj* inconsistent

descomponer [19] *(pp* **descompuesto)**
1 *vt (a)* to break down **(b)** *(corromper)* to rot, to decompose
2 descomponerse *upr (a) (corromperse)* to rot, to decompose **(b)** *(ponerse nervioso)* to lose one's cool **(c)** *Am (el tiempo)* to turn nasty

descomposición *nf (a) (de carne)* decomposition, rotting; *(de país)* disintegration **(b)** *Quím* breakdown

descompostura *nf (a) Am (malestar)* unpleasant turn **(b)** *Méx, RP (avería)* breakdown

descompuesto,-a *adj (a) (podrido)* rotten, decomposed **(b)** *(furioso)* furious

descompuse *pt indef de* **descomponer**

descomunal *adj* huge, massive

desconcertante *adj* disconcerting

desconcertar [1] 1 *vt* to disconcert
2 desconcertarse *upr* to be bewildered, to be puzzled

desconchón *nm* bare patch

desconcierto *nm* chaos, confusion

desconectar *vt* to disconnect

desconexión *nf* disconnection

desconfiado,-a *adj* distrustful, wary

desconfianza *nf* distrust, mistrust

desconfiar [29] *vi* d. (de) to distrust, to mistrust

descongelar *vt (nevera)* to defrost; *(créditos)* to unfreeze

descongestionar *vt* to clear

desconocer [34] *vt* not to know, to be unaware of

desconocido,-a 1 *adj* unknown; *(irreconocible)* unrecognizable
2 *nm* lo d. the unknown
3 *nm,f* stranger

desconsiderado,-a 1 *adj* inconsiderate, thoughtless
2 *nm,f* inconsiderate o thoughtless person

desconsolado,-a *adj* disconsolate, grief-stricken

desconsuelo *nm* grief, sorrow

descontado,-a *adj Fam* dar por d. to take

for granted; **por d.** needless to say, of course

descontar [2] *vt (a)* to deduct **(b)** *Dep (tiempo)* to add on

descontento,-a 1 *adj* unhappy
2 *nm* dissatisfaction

descontrol *nm Fam* lack of control; **había un d. total** it was absolute chaos

descontrolarse *upr* to lose control

desconvocar *vt* to call off

descorchar *vt* to uncork

descornarse [2] *upr Fam (trabajar)* to slave (away)

descorrer *vt* to draw back

descortés *adj* impolite, discourteous

descortesía *nf* discourtesy, impoliteness

descoser *vt* to unstitch, to unpick

descosido *nm (en camisa etc)* open seam; *Fam* **como un d.** like mad, wildly

descoyuntar *vt* to dislocate

descrédito *nm* disrepute, discredit

descremado,-a *adj* skimmed

describir *(pp* **descrito)** *vt* to describe

descripción *nf* description

descriptivo,-a *adj* descriptive

descrito,-a *pp de* **describir**

descuajaringar [42] *vt Fam* to pull o take to pieces

descuartizar [40] *vt* to cut up, to cut into pieces

descubierto,-a 1 *adj* open, uncovered; **a cielo d.** in the open
2 *nm (a) Fin* overdraft **(b)** *al d.* in the open; **poner al d.** to uncover, to bring out into the open

descubridor,-a *nm,f* discoverer

descubrimiento *nm* discovery

descubrir *(pp* **descubierto)** *vt* to discover; *(conspiración)* to uncover; *(placa)* to unveil

descuento *nm* discount

descuidado,-a *adj (a) (desaseado)* untidy, neglected **(b)** *(negligente)* careless, negligent **(c)** *(desprevenido)* off one's guard

descuidar 1 *vt* to neglect, to overlook
2 *vi* **descuida, voy yo** don't worry, I'll go
3 descuidarse *upr (despistarse)* to be careless; **como te descuides, llegarás tarde** if you don't watch out, you'll be late

descuido *nm (a)* oversight, mistake; **por d.** inadvertently, by mistake **(b)** *(negligencia)* negligence, carelessness

desde *adv (a) (tiempo)* since; **d. ahora** from now on; **d. el lunes/entonces** since Monday/then; **espero d. hace media hora** I've been waiting for half an hour; **no lo he visto d. hace un año** I haven't seen him for a year; **¿d. cuándo?** since when?; **d. siempre** always

(**b**) *(lugar)* from; **d. aquí** from here; **d. arriba/abajo** from above/below

(**c**) **d. luego** of course

(**d**) **d. que** ever since; **d. que lo conozco** ever since I've known him

desdecir [12] *(pp* **desdicho**) **1** *vi* **d. de** not to live up to

2 desdecirse *upr* to go back on one's word

desdén *nm* disdain

desdentado,-a *adj* toothless

desdeñar *vt* to disdain

desdeñoso,-a *adj* disdainful

desdibujarse *upr* to become blurred *o* faint

desdicha *nf* misfortune; **por d.** unfortunately

desdichado,-a 1 *adj* unfortunate

2 *nm,f* poor devil, wretch

desdigo *indic pres de* **desdecir**

desdiré *indic fut de* **desdecir**

desdoblar *vt* to unfold

deseable *adj* desirable

desear *vt* (**a**) to desire; **deja mucho que d.** it leaves a lot to be desired (**b**) *(querer)* to want; **¿qué desea?** can I help you?; **estoy deseando que vengas** I'm looking forward to your coming (**c**) **te deseo buena suerte/feliz Navidad** I wish you good luck/a merry Christmas

desecar [44] *vt* to dry up

desechable *adj* disposable, throw-away

desechar *vt* (**a**) *(tirar)* to discard, to throw out *o* away (**b**) *(oferta)* to turn down, to refuse; *(idea, proyecto)* to drop, to discard

desechos *nmpl* waste

desembalar *vt* to unpack

desembarcar [44] **1** *vt (mercancías)* to unload; *(personas)* to disembark

2 *vi* to disembark

desembarco, desembarque *nm (de mercancías)* unloading; *(de personas)* disembarkation

desembocadura *nf* mouth

desembocar [44] *vi* **d. en** *(río)* to flow into; *(calle, situación)* to lead to

desembolsar *vt* to pay out

desembolso *nm* expenditure

desembragar [42] *vt Aut* to declutch

desembrollar *vt Fam* (**a**) *(aclarar)* to clarify, to clear up (**b**) *(desenredar)* to disentangle

desembuchar *vt Fig* to blurt out; *Fam* **¡desembucha!** out with it!

desempañar *vt* to wipe the condensation from; *Aut* to demist

desempaquetar *vt* to unpack, to unwrap

desempatar *vi Dep* to break the deadlock

desempate *nm* play-off; **partido de d.** play-off, deciding match

desempeñar *vt* (**a**) *(cargo)* to hold, to occupy; *(función)* to fulfil; *(papel)* to play (**b**) *(recuperar)* to redeem

desempleado,-a 1 *adj* unemployed, out of work

2 *nm,f* unemployed person; **los desempleados** the unemployed

desempleo *nm* unemployment; **cobrar el d.** to be on the dole

desempolvar *vt* (**a**) to dust (**b**) *Fig (pasado)* to revive

desencadenar 1 *vt* (**a**) to unchain (**b**) *(provocar)* to unleash

2 desencadenarse *upr* (**a**) *(prisionero)* to break loose; *(viento, pasión)* to rage (**b**) *(conflicto)* to start, to break out

desencajar 1 *vt* (**a**) *(pieza)* to knock out; *(hueso)* to dislocate

2 desencajarse *upr* (**a**) *(pieza)* to come out; *(hueso)* to become dislocated (**b**) *(cara)* to become distorted

desencaminado,-a *adj* = **descaminado, -a**

desencanto *nm* disenchantment

desenchufar *vt* to unplug

desenfadado,-a *adj* carefree, free and easy

desenfado *nm* ease

desenfocado,-a *adj* out of focus

desenfoque *nm* incorrect focusing; *Fig (de asunto)* wrong approach

desenfrenado,-a *adj* frantic, uncontrolled; *(vicio, pasión)* unbridled

desenfreno *nm* debauchery

desenganchar *vt* to unhook; *(vagón)* to uncouple

desengañar 1 *vt* **d. a algn** to open sb's eyes

2 desengañarse *upr* (**a**) to be disappointed (**b**) *Fam* **¡desengáñate!** get real!

desengaño *nm* disappointment; **llevarse** *o* **sufrir un d. con algo** to be disappointed in sth

desengrasar *vt* to degrease, to remove the grease from

desenlace *nm* (**a**) result, outcome; **un feliz d.** a happy end (**b**) *Cin & Teatro* ending, dénouement

desenmarañar *vt (pelo)* to untangle; *(problema)* to unravel; *(asunto)* to sort out

desenmascarar *vt* to unmask

desenredar vt to untangle, to disentangle

desenrollar vt to unroll; (cable) to unwind

desenroscar [44] vt to unscrew

desentenderse [3] vpr se desentendió de mi problema he didn't want to have anything to do with my problem

desenterrar [1] vt (a) (cadáver) to exhume, to disinter; (tesoro etc) to dig up (b) (recuerdo) to revive

desentonar vi (a) Mús to sing out of tune, to be out of tune (b) (colores etc) not to match (c) (persona, comentario) to be out of place

desentrañar vt (misterio) to unravel, to get to the bottom of

desentrenado,-a adj out of training o shape

desentumecer [33] vt to put the feeling back into

desenvoltura nf ease

desenvolver [4] (pp desenvuelto) 1 vt to unwrap

2 **desenvolverse** vpr (a) (persona) to manage, to cope (b) (hecho) to develop

desenvuelto,-a adj relaxed

deseo nm wish; (sexual) desire; **formular un d.** to make a wish

deseoso,-a adj eager; **estar d. de** to be eager to

desequilibrado,-a 1 adj unbalanced

2 nm,f unbalanced person

desequilibrar 1 vt to unbalance, to throw off balance

2 **desequilibrarse** vpr to become mentally disturbed

desequilibrio nm imbalance; **d. mental** mental disorder

deserción nf desertion

desertar vi to desert

desértico,-a adj desert

desertización nf desertification

desertor,-a nm,f deserter

desesperación nf (desesperanza) despair; (exasperación) desperation

desesperado,-a adj (a) (sin esperanza) desperate, hopeless (b) (exasperado) exasperated, infuriated

desesperante adj exasperating

desesperar 1 vt to drive to despair; (exasperar) to exasperate

2 **desesperarse** vpr to despair

desestabilizar [40] vt to destabilize

desestatización nf Am privatization

desestatizar vt Am to privatize

desestimar vt to reject

desfachatez nf cheek, nerve

desfalco nm embezzlement, misappropriation

desfallecer [33] vi (a) (debilitarse) to feel faint; (desmayarse) to faint (b) (desanimarse) to lose heart

desfasado,-a adj (a) outdated (b) (persona) old-fashioned, behind the times (c) Téc out of phase

desfase nm gap; **d. horario** time lag

desfavorable adj unfavourable

desfigurar vt (cara) to disfigure; (verdad) to distort

desfiladero nm narrow pass

desfilar vi (a) to march in single file (b) Mil to march past, to parade

desfile nm Mil parade, march past; **d. de modas** fashion show

desfogar [42] 1 vt to give vent to

2 **desfogarse** vpr to let off steam

desgajar 1 vt (arrancar) to rip o tear out; (rama) to tear off

2 **desgajarse** vpr to come off

desgana nf (a) (inapetencia) lack of appetite (b) (apatía) apathy, indifference; **con d.** reluctantly, unwillingly

desganado,-a adj (a) **estar d.** (inapetente) to have no appetite (b) (apático) apathetic

desgañitarse vpr Fam to shout oneself hoarse

desgarbado,-a adj ungraceful, ungainly

desgarrador,-a adj harrowing

desgarrar vt to tear

desgarrón nm big tear, rip

desgastar 1 vt to wear out

2 **desgastarse** vpr (consumirse) to wear out; (persona) to wear oneself out

desgaste nm wear; **d. del poder** wear and tear of power

desgracia nf (a) misfortune; **por d.** unfortunately (b) (deshonor) disgrace (c) **desgracias personales** loss of life

desgraciadamente adv unfortunately

desgraciado,-a 1 adj unfortunate; (infeliz) unhappy

2 nm,f unfortunate person; **un pobre d.** a poor devil

desgravable adj tax-deductible

desgravación nf deduction; **d. fiscal** tax deduction

desgravar vt to deduct

desguazar [40] vt (un barco) to break up; Aut to scrap

deshabitado,-a adj uninhabited, unoccupied

deshabitar vt to abandon, to vacate

deshacer [15] (pp deshecho) 1 vt (a) (paquete) to undo; (maleta) to unpack (**b**) *(plan)* to destroy, to ruin (**c**) *(acuerdo)* to break off (**d**) *(disolver)* to dissolve; *(derretir)* to melt

  2 deshacerse *vpr* (**a**) to come undone o untied (**b**) **d. de algn/algo** to get rid of sb/ sth (**c**) *(afligirse)* to go to pieces; **d. en lágrimas** to cry one's eyes out (**d**) *(disolverse)* to dissolve; *(derretirse)* to melt (**e**) *(niebla)* to fade away, to disappear

deshecho,-a *adj* (**a**) *(cama)* unmade; *(maleta)* unpacked; *(paquete)* unwrapped (**b**) *(roto)* broken, smashed (**c**) *(disuelto)* dissolved; *(derretido)* melted (**d**) *(abatido)* devastated, shattered (**e**) *(cansado)* exhausted, tired out

desheredar *vt* to disinherit

deshidratar *vt* to dehydrate

deshielo *nm* thaw

deshilachar *vt* to fray

deshilvanado,-a *adj Fig (inconexo)* disjointed

deshonesto,-a *adj* (**a**) dishonest (**b**) *(indecente)* indecent, improper

deshonor *nm*, **deshonra** *nf* dishonour

deshonrar *vt* (**a**) to dishonour (**b**) *(a la familia etc)* to bring disgrace on

deshora: • **a deshora** *loc adv* at an inconvenient time; **comer a d.** to eat at odd times

deshuesar *vt (carne)* to bone; *(fruta)* to stone

deshumanizar [40] *vt* to dehumanize

desidia *nf* apathy

desierto,-a 1 *nm* desert

  2 *adj* (**a**) *(deshabitado)* uninhabited (**b**) *(vacío)* empty, deserted (**c**) *(premio)* void

designación *nf* designation

designar *vt* (**a**) to designate (**b**) *(fecha, lugar)* to fix

designio *nm* intention, plan

desigual *adj* (**a**) uneven (**b**) *(lucha)* unequal (**c**) *(carácter)* changeable

desigualdad *nf* (**a**) inequality (**b**) *(del terreno)* unevenness

desilusión *nf* disappointment, disillusionment

desilusionar *vt* to disappoint, to disillusion

desinfectante *adj & nm* disinfectant

desinfectar *vt* to disinfect

desinflar 1 *vt* to deflate; *(rueda)* to let down

  2 desinflarse *vpr* to go flat

desintegración *nf* disintegration

desintegrar *vt*, **desintegrarse** *vpr* to disintegrate

desinterés *nm* (**a**) *(indiferencia)* lack of interest, apathy (**b**) *(generosidad)* unselfishness

desinteresado,-a *adj* selfless, unselfish

desintoxicar [44] 1 *vt* to detoxicate; *(de alcohol)* to dry out

  2 desintoxicarse *vpr Med* to detoxicate oneself; *(de alcohol)* to dry out

desistir *vi* to desist

deslavazado,-a *adj* disjointed

deslave *nm Am* landslide *(caused by flooding or rain)*

desleal *adj* disloyal; *(competencia)* unfair

deslealtad *nf* disloyalty

deslenguado,-a *adj (insolente)* insolent, cheeky; *(grosero)* coarse, foul-mouthed

desliar [29] *vt* to unwrap

desligar [42] 1 *vt* (**a**) *(separar)* to separate (**b**) *(desatar)* to untie, to unfasten

  2 desligarse *vpr* **d. de** to disassociate oneself from

desliz *nm* mistake, slip; **cometer** o **tener un d.** to slip up

deslizar [40] 1 *vi* to slide

  2 deslizarse *vpr* (**a**) *(patinar)* to slide (**b**) *(fluir)* to flow

deslucir [35] *vt* (**a**) *(espectáculo)* to spoil (**b**) *(metal)* to make dull

deslumbrador,-a, deslumbrante *adj* dazzling; *Fig* stunning

deslumbrar *vt* to dazzle

desmadrarse *vpr Fam* to go wild

desmadre *nm Fam* hullabaloo

desmandarse *vpr* to get out of hand, to run wild; *(caballo)* to bolt

desmano: • **a desmano** *loc adv* out of the way; **me coge a d.** it is out of my way

desmantelar *vt* (**a**) to dismantle (**b**) *Náut* to dismast, to unrig

desmaquillador,-a 1 *nm* make-up remover

  2 *adj* **leche desmaquilladora** cleansing cream

desmaquillarse *vpr* to remove one's make-up

desmarcarse [44] *vpr Dep* to lose one's marker

desmayado,-a *adj* unconscious; **caer d.** to faint

desmayarse *vpr* to faint

desmayo *nm* faint, fainting fit; **tener un d.** to faint

desmedido,-a *adj* disproportionate, out of all proportion; *(ambición)* unbounded

desmejorar *vi*, **desmejorarse** *vpr* to deteriorate, to go downhill

desmelenarse *vpr Fam* to let one's hair down

desmembración *nf*, **desmembramiento** *nm* dismemberment

desmemoriado,-a *adj* forgetful, absent-minded

desmentir [5] *vt* to deny

desmenuzar [40] *vt* (**a**) *(deshacer)* to break into little pieces, to crumble; *(carne)* to cut into little pieces (**b**) *(asunto)* to examine in detail

desmerecer [33] *vi* to lose value

desmesura *nf* excess

desmesurado,-a *adj* excessive

desmilitarizar [40] *vt* to demilitarize

desmontable *adj* that can be taken to pieces

desmontar 1 *vt* (**a**) *(desarmar)* to take to pieces, to dismantle (**b**) *(allanar)* to level
2 *vi* **d. (de)** to dismount, to get off

desmoralizar [40] *vt* to demoralize

desmoronarse *upr* to crumble, to fall to pieces

desnatado,-a *adj (leche)* skimmed

desnivel *nm (en el terreno)* drop, difference in height

desnivelar *vt* to throw out of balance

desnucarse [44] *upr* to break one's neck

desnuclearizar *vt* to denuclearize

desnudar 1 *vt* to undress
2 desnudarse *upr* to get undressed

desnudismo *nm* nudism

desnudista *adj & nmf* nudist

desnudo,-a 1 *adj* naked, nude
2 *nm Arte* nude

desnutrición *nf* malnutrition

desnutrido,-a *adj* undernourished

desobedecer [33] *vt* to disobey

desobediencia *nf* disobedience

desobediente 1 *adj* disobedient
2 *nmf* disobedient person

desocupado,-a *adj* (**a**) *(vacío)* empty, vacant (**b**) *(ocioso)* free, not busy (**c**) *(sin empleo)* unemployed

desocupar *vt* to empty, to vacate

desodorante *adj & nm* deodorant

desolación *nf* desolation

desolar *vt* to devastate

desollar [2] 1 *vt* to skin
2 • desollarse *upr* to scrape; **me desollé el brazo** I scraped my arm

desorbitado,-a *adj (precio)* exorbitant

desorden *nm* untidiness, mess; **¡qué d.!** what a mess!; **d. público** civil disorder

desordenado,-a *adj* messy, untidy

desordenar *vt* to make untidy, to mess up

desorganizar [40] *vt* to disorganize, to disrupt

desorientación *nf* disorientation

desorientar 1 *vt* to disorientate
2 desorientarse *upr* to lose one's sense

of direction, to lose one's bearings; *Fig* to become disorientated

despabilado,-a *adj* (**a**) *(sin sueño)* wide awake (**b**) *(listo)* quick, smart

despachar *vt* (**a**) *(asunto)* to get through (**b**) *(correo)* to send, to dispatch (**c**) *(en tienda)* to serve (**d**) *Fam (despedir)* to send packing, to sack (**e**) *Am (facturar)* to check in

despacho *nm* (**a**) *(oficina)* office; *(en casa)* study (**b**) *(venta)* sale (**c**) *(comunicación)* dispatch

despachurrar *vt Fam* to squash, to flatten

despacio *adv* (**a**) *(lentamente)* slowly (**b**) *(en voz baja)* quietly

despampanante *adj Fam* stunning

desparpajo *nm* self-assurance; **con d.** in a carefree manner

desparramar *vt*, **desparramarse** *upr* to spread, to scatter; *(líquido)* to spill

despavorido,-a *adj* terrified

despecho *nm* spite; **por d.** out of spite

despectivo,-a *adj* derogatory, disparaging

despedazar [40] *vt* to cut *o* tear to pieces

despedida *nf* farewell, goodbye; **d. de soltera/soltero** hen/stag party

despedido,-a *adj* **salir d.** to be off like a shot

despedir [6] 1 *vt* (**a**) *(empleado)* to fire, *Br* to sack (**b**) *(decir adiós)* to see off, to say goodbye to (**c**) *(olor, humo etc)* to give off
2 despedirse *upr* (**a**) *(decir adiós)* to say goodbye (**de** to) (**b**) *Fig* to forget, to give up; **ya puedes despedirte del coche** you can say goodbye to the car

despegado,-a *adj* (**a**) *(unstuck* (**b**) *(persona)* couldn't-care-less

despegar [42] 1 *vt* to take off, to detach
2 *vi Av* to take off
3 despegarse *upr* to come unstuck

despego *nm* detachment

despegue *nm* take-off

despeinado,-a *adj* dishevelled, with untidy hair

despejado,-a *adj* clear; *(cielo)* cloudless

despejar 1 *vt* to clear; *(misterio, dudas)* to clear up
2 despejarse *upr* (**a**) *(cielo)* to clear (**b**) *(persona)* to clear one's head

despeje *nm Dep* clearance

despellejar *vt* to skin

despelotarse *upr Fam* (**a**) *(desnudarse)* to strip (**b**) **d. de risa** to laugh one's head off

despensa *nf* pantry, larder

despeñadero *nm* cliff, precipice

despeñarse *vpr* to go over a cliff

desperdiciar [43] *vt* to waste; *(oportunidad)* to throw away

desperdicio *nm* (a) *(acto)* waste (b) **desperdicios** *(basura)* rubbish; *(desechos)* scraps, leftovers

desperdigar [42] *vt,* **desperdigarse** *vpr* to scatter, to separate

desperezarse [40] *vpr* to stretch (oneself)

desperfecto *nm* (a) *(defecto)* flaw, imperfection (b) *(daño)* damage

despertador *nm* alarm clock

despertar [1] **1** *vt* to wake (up), to awaken; *Fig (sentimiento etc)* to arouse
2 despertarse *vpr* to wake (up)

despiadado,-a *adj* merciless

despido *nm* dismissal, sacking

despierto,-a *adj* (a) *(desvelado)* awake (b) *(vivo)* quick, sharp

despilfarrar *vt* to waste, to squander

despilfarro *nm* wasting, squandering

despintar *vi,* **despintarse** *vpr (ropa)* to fade

despiole *nm RP Fam* rumpus, shindy

despistado,-a 1 *adj* (a) *(olvidadizo)* scatterbrained (b) *(confuso)* confused
2 *nm,f* scatterbrain

despistar 1 *vt* (a) *(hacer perder la pista a)* to lose, to throw off one's scent (b) *Fig* to mislead
2 despistarse *vpr* (a) *(perderse)* to get lost (b) *(distraerse)* to switch off

despiste *nm* (a) *(cualidad)* absent-mindedness (b) *(error)* slip-up

desplazamiento *nm (viaje)* trip, journey; **dietas de d.** travelling expenses

desplazar [40] **1** *vt* to displace
2 desplazarse *vpr* to travel

desplegar [1] **1** *vt* (a) to open (out), to spread (out) (b) *(energías etc)* to use, to deploy
2 desplegarse *vpr* (a) *(abrirse)* to open (out), to spread (out) (b) *Mil* to deploy

despliegue *nm* (a) *Mil* deployment (b) *(de medios etc)* display

desplomarse *vpr* to collapse; *(precios)* to slump, to fall sharply

desplumar *vt* to pluck

despoblar [2] *vt* to depopulate

despojar *vt* (a) to strip (**de** of) (b) *Fig* to divest, to deprive (**de** of)

despojo *nm* (a) stripping (b) **despojos** leftovers, scraps

desposado,-a *adj Fml* newly-wed

desposar *vt Fml* to marry

desposeer [36] *vt* **d. de** to dispossess of; *(autoridad)* to strip of

desposeído *nm* **los desposeídos** the have-nots

déspota *nmf* despot

despótico,-a *adj* despotic

despotismo *nm* despotism

despotricar [44] *vi* to rant and rave (**contra** about)

despreciable *adj* despicable, contemptible; *(cantidad)* negligible

despreciar [43] *vt* (a) *(desdeñar)* to scorn, to despise (b) *(rechazar)* to reject, to spurn

desprecio *nm* (a) *(desdén)* scorn, disdain (b) *(desaire)* slight, snub

desprender 1 *vt* (a) *(separar)* to remove, to detach (b) *(olor, humo etc)* to give off
2 desprenderse *vpr* (a) *(soltarse)* to come off o away (b) **d. de** to rid oneself of, to free oneself from (c) **de aquí se desprende que ...** it can be deduced from this that ...

desprendido,-a *adj Fig* generous, unselfish

desprendimiento *nm* (a) loosening, detachment; **d. de tierras** landslide (b) *Fig (generosidad)* generosity, unselfishness

despreocupado,-a *adj* (a) *(tranquilo)* unconcerned (b) *(descuidado)* careless; *(estilo)* casual

despreocuparse *vpr* (a) *(tranquilizarse)* to stop worrying (b) *(desentenderse)* to be unconcerned, to be indifferent (**de** to)

desprestigiar [43] *vt* to discredit, to run down

desprestigio *nm* discredit, loss of reputation; **campaña de d.** smear campaign

desprevenido,-a *adj* unprepared; **coger** o **pillar a algn d.** to catch sb unawares

desprolijo,-a *adj Am (casa)* messy, untidy; *(cuaderno)* untidy; *(persona)* unkempt, dishevelled

desproporción *nf* disproportion, lack of proportion

desproporcionado,-a *adj* disproportionate

desprovisto,-a *adj* **d. (de)** lacking, without, devoid (of)

después *adv* (a) *(afterwards)* afterwards, later; *(entonces)* then; *(seguidamente)* next; **una semana d.** a week later; **poco d.** soon after (b) *(lugar)* next (c) **d. de** after; **d. de la guerra** after the war; **mi calle está d. de la tuya** my street is the one after yours; **d. de cenar** after eating; **d. de todo** after all (**d**) **d. de que** after; **d. de que vi-niera** after he came

despuntar 1 *vt* to blunt, to make blunt

2 *vi* (**a**) (*día*) to dawn (**b**) (*destacar*) to excel, to stand out

desquiciar [43] 1 *vt* (*persona*) to unhinge

2 desquiciarse *upr* (*persona*) to go crazy

desquitarse *upr* to take revenge (**de** for)

desquite *nm* revenge

destacado,-a *adj* outstanding

destacamento *nm* detachment

destacar [44] 1 *vt* *Fig* to emphasize, to stress

2 *vi* to stand out

3 destacarse *upr* to stand out

destajo *nm* piecework; **trabajar a d.** to do piecework

destapador *nm* *Am* bottle opener

destapar 1 *vt* to take the lid off; (*botella*) to open; *Fig* (*asunto*) to uncover; *RP* (*caño*) to unblock

2 destaparse *upr* to get uncovered

destartalado,-a *adj* rambling; (*desvencijado*) ramshackle

destello *nm* flash, sparkle

destemplado,-a *adj* (**a**) (*voz, gesto*) sharp, snappy; **con cajas destempladas** rudely, brusquely (**b**) (*tiempo*) unpleasant (**c**) (*enfermo*) indisposed, out of sorts (**d**) *Mús* out of tune, discordant

desteñir [6] 1 *vt & vi* to discolour

2 desteñirse *upr* to lose colour, to fade

desternillarse *upr* **d. (de risa)** to split one's sides laughing

desterrar [1] *vt* to exile

destiempo *nm* • **a destiempo** *loc adv* at the wrong time *o* moment

destierro *nm* exile

destilado,-a *adj* distilled; **agua destilada** distilled water

destilar *vt* to distil

destilería *nf* distillery

destinado,-a *adj* destined, bound, *Fig* **d. al fracaso** doomed to failure

destinar *vt* (**a**) (*dinero etc*) to set aside, to assign (**b**) (*empleado*) to appoint

destinatario,-a *nm,f* (**a**) (*de carta*) addressee (**b**) (*de mercancías*) consignee

destino *nm* (**a**) (*rumbo*) destination; **el avión con d. a Bilbao** the plane to Bilbao (**b**) (*sino*) fate, fortune (**c**) (*de empleo*) post

destitución *nf* dismissal from office

destituir [37] *vt* to dismiss *o* remove from office

destornillador *nm* screwdriver

destornillar *vt* to unscrew

destreza *nf* skill

destrozado,-a *adj* (**a**) (*roto*) torn-up, smashed (**b**) (*cansado*) worn-out, exhausted (**c**) (*abatido*) shattered

destrozar [40] *vt* (**a**) (*destruir*) to destroy; (*rasgar*) to tear to shreds *o* pieces (**b**) (*afligir*) to shatter; (*vida, reputación*) to ruin

destrozo *nm* (**a**) destruction (**b**) **destrozos** damage

destrucción *nf* destruction

destructivo,-a *adj* destructive

destructor,-a 1 *adj* destructive

2 *nm* *Náut* destroyer

destruir [37] *vt* to destroy

desubicado,-a *nm,f* *Andes, RP* **ser un d.** to have no idea how to behave, to be clueless

desusado,-a *adj* old-fashioned, outdated

desuso *nm* disuse; **caer en d.** to fall into disuse; **en d.** obsolete, outdated

desvalido,-a *adj* defenceless

desvalijar *vt* (*robar*) to clean out, to rob; (*casa, tienda*) to burgle

desvalorizar [40] *vt* to devalue

desván *nm* attic, loft

desvanecerse [33] *upr* (**a**) (*disiparse*) to vanish, to fade away (**b**) (*desmayarse*) to faint

desvariar [29] *vi* to talk nonsense

desvarío *nm* (**a**) (*delirio*) raving, delirium (**b**) (*disparate*) nonsense

desvelado,-a *adj* awake, wide awake

desvelar 1 *vt* to keep awake

2 desvelarse *upr* (**a**) (*despabilarse*) to stay awake (**b**) (*desvivirse*) to devote oneself (**por** to) (**c**) *CAm, Méx* (*quedarse despierto*) to stay up *o* awake

desvencijar 1 *vt* to take apart

2 desvencijarse *upr* to fall apart

desventaja *nf* (**a**) disadvantage; **estar en d.** to be at a disadvantage (**b**) (*inconveniente*) drawback

desventura *nf* misfortune, bad luck

desvergonzado,-a 1 *adj* (**a**) (*indecente*) shameless (**b**) (*descarado*) insolent

2 *nm,f* (**a**) (*sinvergüenza*) shameless person (**b**) (*fresco*) insolent *o* cheeky person

desvergüenza *nf* (**a**) (*indecencia*) shamelessness (**b**) (*atrevimiento*) insolence; **tuvo la d. de negarlo** he had the cheek to deny it (**c**) (*impertinencia*) insolent *o* rude remark

desvestir [6] 1 *vt* to undress

2 desvestirse *upr* to undress, to get undressed

desviación *nf* (**a**) deviation; (*de carretera*)

diversion, detour; *Med* **d. de columna** slipped disc

desviar [29] 1 *vt (río, carretera)* to divert; *(golpe, conversación)* to deflect; **d. la mirada** to look away

  2 desviarse *upr* to go off course; *(coche)* to turn off; *Fig* **d. del tema** to digress

desvincular 1 *vt* to separate

  2 desvincularse *upr* to separate, to cut oneself off

desvío *nm* diversion, detour

desvirgar [42] *vt* to deflower

desvirtuar [30] *vt* to distort

desvivirse *upr* to bend over backwards

detalladamente *adv* in (great) detail

detallado,-a *adj* detailed, thorough

detallar *vt* to give the details of

detalle *nm* (a) detail; **entrar en detalles** to go into details (b) *(delicadeza)* nice thought, nicety; **¡qué d.!** how nice!, how sweet! (c) *(toque decorativo)* touch, ornament

detallista 1 *adj* perfectionist

  2 *nmf Com* retailer

detectar *vt* to detect

detective *nmf* detective; **d. privado** private detective *o* eye

detector,-a *nm,f* detector; **d. de incendios** fire detector

detención *nf* (a) *Jur* detention, arrest (b) **con d.** carefully, thoroughly

detener [24] 1 *vt* (a) to stop, to halt (b) *Jur (arrestar)* to arrest, to detain

  2 detenerse *upr* to stop

detenidamente *adv* carefully, thoroughly

detenido,-a 1 *adj* (a) *(parado)* standing still, stopped (b) *(arrestado)* detained (c) *(minucioso)* detailed, thorough

  2 *nm,f* detainee, person under arrest

detenimiento *nm* **con d.** carefully, thoroughly

detentar *vt* to hold

detergente *adj & nm* detergent

deteriorar 1 *vt* to spoil, to damage

  2 deteriorarse *upr* (a) *(estropearse)* to get damaged (b) *(empeorar)* to get worse

deterioro *nm* (a) *(empeoramiento)* deterioration, worsening (b) *(daño)* damage; **ir en d. de** to be to the detriment of

determinación *nf* (a) determination; **con d.** determinedly (b) *(decisión)* decision

determinado,-a *adj* (a) *(preciso)* definite, precise (b) *(resuelto)* decisive, resolute (c) *Ling* definite

determinante *adj* decisive

determinar 1 *vt* (a) *(fecha etc)* to fix, to set (b) *(decidir)* to decide on (c) *(condicionar)* to determine (d) *(ocasionar)* to bring about

  2 determinarse *upr* to make up one's mind to

detestable *adj* detestable, repulsive

detestar *vt* to detest, to hate

detonante *nm* detonator; *Fig* trigger

detonar *vt* to detonate

detractor,-a *nm,f* detractor

detrás *adv* (a) behind, on *o* at the back (**de** of) (b) **d. de** behind

detrimento *nm* detriment; **en d. de** to the detriment of

detuve *pt indef de* detener

deuda *nf* debt; **estoy en d. contigo** *(monetaria)* I am in debt to you; *(moral)* I am indebted to you; **d. del Estado** public debt; **d. pública** national debt

deudor,-a 1 *adj* indebted

  2 *nm,f* debtor

devaluación *nf* devaluation

devaluar [30] *vt* to devalue

devanar 1 *vt (hilo)* to wind; *(alambre)* to coil

  2 devanarse *upr Fam* **d. los sesos** to rack one's brains

devaneo *nm* dabbling

devastador,-a *adj* devastating

devastar *vt* to devastate, to ravage

devengar [42] *vt Com* to earn, to accrue

devenir [27] *vi* to become

devoción *nf* (a) *Rel* devoutness (b) *(al trabajo etc)* devotion; *Fam* **Juan no es santo de mi d.** Juan isn't really my cup of tea

devolución *nf* (a) giving back, return; *Com* refund, repayment (b) *Jur* devolution

devolver [4] *(pp* **devuelto) 1** *vt* to give back, to return; *(dinero)* to refund

  2 *vi (vomitar)* to vomit, to throw *o* bring up

  3 devolverse *upr Am* to go *o* come back, to return

devorar *vt* to devour

devoto,-a 1 *adj* pious, devout

  2 *nm,f* (a) *Rel* pious person (b) *(seguidor)* devotee

devuelto,-a *pp de* devolver

DF *nm (abr* **Distrito Federal)** *(en México)* Mexico City

DGI *nf RP (abr* **Dirección General Impositiva)** *Br* ≃ Inland Revenue, *US* ≃ IRS

DGT *nf (abr* **Dirección General de Tráfico)** = government department responsible for road transport

di (a) *pt indef de* **dar** (b) *imperat de* **decir**

día *nm* day; **¿qué d. es hoy?** what's the date today?; **d. a d.** day by day; **de d.** by day; **durante el d.** during the daytime; **de un d. para otro** overnight; **un d. sí y otro no** every other day; **pan del d.** fresh bread; **hoy (en) d.** nowadays; **el d. de mañana** in the future; *Fig* **estar al d.** to be up to date; *Fig* **poner al d.** to bring up to date; **d. festivo** holiday; **d. laborable** working day; **d. libre** free day, day off; **es de d.** it is daylight; **hace buen/mal d.** it's a nice/bad day, the weather is nice/bad today

diabetes *nf* diabetes

diabético,-a *adj & nm,f* diabetic

diablo *nm* devil; *Fam* **¡al d. con ...!** to hell with ...!; *Fam* **vete al d.** get lost; *Fam* **¿qué/ cómo diablos ...?** what/how the hell ...?

diablura *nf* mischief

diácono *nm* deacon

diadema *nf* tiara

diáfano,-a *adj* clear

diafragma *nm* diaphragm; *Fot* aperture; *Med* cap

diagnosis *nf inv* diagnosis

diagnosticar [44] *vt* to diagnose

diagnóstico *nm* diagnosis

diagonal *adj & nf* diagonal; **en d.** diagonally

diagrama *nm* diagram; *Informát* **d. de flujo** flowchart

dial *nm* dial

dialecto *nm* dialect

dialogar [42] *vi* to have a conversation; *(para negociar)* to talk

diálogo *nm* dialogue

diamante *nm* diamond

diámetro *nm* diameter

diana *nf* (a) *Mil* reveille (b) *(blanco)* bull's eye

diapositiva *nf* slide

diariamente *adv* daily, every day

diariero,-a *nm,f Andes, RP* newspaper seller

diario,-a 1 *nm* (a) *Prensa* (daily) newspaper (b) *(memorias)* diary; *Náut* **d. de a bordo, d. de navegación** logbook

2 *adj* daily; **a d.** daily, every day

diarrea *nf* diarrhoea

diatriba *nf* diatribe

dibujante *nmf* (a) drawer (b) *(de cómic)* cartoonist (c) *Téc (hombre)* draughtsman; *(mujer)* draughtswoman

dibujar *vt* to draw

dibujo *nm* (a) drawing; **dibujos animados** cartoons (b) *(arte)* drawing; **d. artístico** artistic drawing; **d. lineal** draughtsmanship

diccionario *nm* dictionary; **buscar/mirar una palabra en el d.** to look up a word in the dictionary

dicha *nf* happiness

dicharachero,-a *adj* talkative and witty

dicho,-a *adj* (a) said; **mejor d.** or rather; **d. de otro modo** to put it another way; **d. sea de paso** let it be said in passing; **d. y hecho** no sooner said than done (b) **dicha persona** *(mencionado)* the above-mentioned person

dichoso,-a *adj* (a) *(feliz)* happy (b) *Fam* damned; **¡este d. trabajo!** this damned job!

diciembre *nm* December

dictado *nm* dictation; *Fig* **dictados** dictates

dictador,-a *nm,f* dictator

dictadura *nf* dictatorship

dictáfono® *nm* Dictaphone®

dictamen *nm* *(juicio)* ruling; *(informe)* report

dictaminar *vi* to rule (**sobre** on)

dictar *vt* (a) to dictate (b) *(ley)* to enact; *(sentencia)* to pass

dictatorial *adj* dictatorial

didáctico,-a *adj* didactic

diecinueve *adj & nm inv* nineteen

dieciocho *adj & nm inv* eighteen

dieciséis *adj & nm inv* sixteen

diecisiete *adj & nm inv* seventeen

diente *nm* tooth; *Téc* cog; *(de ajo)* clove; **d. de leche** milk tooth; **dientes postizos** false teeth; *Fig* **hablar entre dientes** to mumble; *Fig* **poner los dientes largos a algn** to make sb green with envy

diera *subj imperf de* dar

diéresis *nf inv* diaeresis

diesel *adj & nm* diesel

diestra *nf* right hand

diestro,-a 1 *adj* (a) *(hábil)* skilful, clever (b) **a d. y siniestro** right, left and centre **2** *nm Taurom* bullfighter, matador

dieta *nf* (a) diet; **estar a d.** to be on a diet (b) **dietas** expenses o subsistence allowance

dietética *nf* dietetics *sing*

dietista *nmf* dietician

diez *adj & nm inv* ten

difamación *nf* defamation, slander; *(escrita)* libel

difamar *vt* to defame, to slander; *(por escrito)* to libel

diferencia *nf* difference; **a d. de** unlike

diferencial 1 *adj* distinguishing **2** *nm* differential

diferenciar [43] **1** *vt* to differentiate, to distinguish (**entre** between)

2 diferenciarse *vpr* to differ (**de** from), to be different (**de** from)
diferente 1 *adj* different (**de** from *o US* than)
  2 *adv* differently
diferido,-a *adj* TV **en d.** recorded
difícil *adj* difficult, hard; **d. de creer/hacer** difficult to believe/do; **es d. que venga** it is unlikely that she'll come
dificultad *nf* difficulty; *(aprieto)* trouble, problem
dificultar *vt* to make difficult
dificultoso,-a *adj* difficult, hard
difuminar *vt* to blur
difundir *vt*, **difundirse** *vpr* to spread
difunto,-a 1 *adj* late, deceased
  2 *nm,f* deceased
difusión *nf* (a) *(de noticia)* spreading; **tener gran d.** to be widely broadcast (b) *Rad & TV* broadcasting
difuso,-a *adj* diffuse
digerir [5] *vt* to digest; *Fig* to assimilate
digestión *nf* digestion; **corte de d.** sudden indigestion
digestivo,-a *adj* easy to digest
digitador,-a *nm,f Am* keyboarder
digital *adj* digital; **huellas digitales** fingerprints; **tocadiscos d.** CD player
digitalizar *vt* digitize
digitar *vt Am* to key
dígito *nm* digit
dignarse *vpr* **d. (a)** to deign to, to condescend to
dignidad *nf* dignity
digno,-a *adj* (a) *(merecedor)* worthy; **d. de admiración** worthy of admiration; **d. de mención/verse** worth mentioning/seeing (b) *(decoroso)* decent, good
digo *indic pres de* **decir**
dije *pt indef de* **decir**
dilación *nf* delay, hold-up; **sin d.** without delay
dilatado,-a *adj* (a) *(agrandado)* dilated (b) *(vasto)* vast, extensive
dilatar 1 *vt* (a) *(agrandar)* to expand (b) *(pupila)* to dilate
  2 dilatarse *vpr* (a) *(agrandarse)* to expand (b) *(pupila)* to dilate
dilema *nm* dilemma
diligencia *nf* (a) diligence; **con d.** diligently (b) **diligencias** formalities
diligente *adj* diligent
dilucidar *vt* to elucidate, to clarify
diluir [37] 1 *vt* to dilute
  2 diluirse *vpr* to dilute
diluviar [43] *v impers* to pour with rain
diluvio *nm* flood; **el D. (Universal)** the Flood

diluyo *indic pres de* **diluir**
dimensión *nf* (a) dimension, size; **de gran d.** very large (b) *Fig (importancia)* importance
diminutivo,-a *adj & nm* diminutive
diminuto,-a *adj* minute, tiny
dimisión *nf* resignation; **presentar la d.** to hand in one's resignation
dimitir *vi* to resign (**de** from); **d. de un cargo** to give in *o* tender one's resignation
Dinamarca *n* Denmark
dinámica *nf* dynamics *sing*
dinámico,-a *adj* dynamic
dinamita *nf* dynamite
dinamitar *vt* to dynamite
dinamo, dínamo *nf* dynamo
dinar *nm Fin* dinar
dinastía *nf* dynasty
dineral *nm Fam* fortune
dinero *nm* money; **d. contante (y sonante)** cash; **d. efectivo** *o* **en metálico** cash; **gente de d.** wealthy people
dinosaurio *nm* dinosaur
diócesis *nf inv* diocese
dios *nm* god; **¡D. mío!** my God!; **¡por D.!** for goodness sake!; **a la buena de D.** any old how; **hacer algo como D. manda** to do sth properly; *Fam* **ni d.** nobody; *Fam* **todo d.** everybody
diosa *nf* goddess
diploma *nm* diploma
diplomacia *nf* diplomacy
diplomarse *vpr* to graduate
diplomático,-a 1 *adj* diplomatic; **cuerpo d.** diplomatic corps
  2 *nm,f* diplomat
diptongo *nm* diphthong
diputación *nf* **d. provincial** ≃ county council
diputado,-a *nm,f Br* ≃ Member of Parliament, MP; *US (hombre)* Congressman; *(mujer)* Congresswoman; **Congreso de Diputados** *Br* ≃ House of Commons, *US* ≃ Congress; **d. provincial** ≃ county councillor
dique *nm* dike
diré *fut de* **decir**
dirección *nf* (a) direction; *Aut (en letrero)* **d. prohibida** no entry; **calle de d. única** one-way street (b) *(señas)* address; *Informát* **d. de correo electrónico** e-mail address (c) *Cin & Teatro* direction (d) *(destino)* destination (e) *Aut & Téc* steering (f) *(dirigentes)* management; *(cargo)* directorship; *(de un partido)* leadership; *(de un colegio)* headship
direccional *nm Col, Méx Aut Br* indicator, *US* turn signal

directa *nf Aut* top gear

directamente *adv* directly, straight away

directiva *nf* board of directors, management

directivo,-a *adj* directive; **junta directiva** board of directors

directo,-a *adj* direct; *TV & Rad* **en d.** live

director,-a *nm,f* director; *(de colegio)* *(hombre)* headmaster; *(mujer)* headmistress; *(de periódico)* editor; **d. de cine** (film) director; **d. de orquesta** conductor; **d. gerente** managing director

directorio *nm Informát* directory; *Andes, Méx* **d. telefónico** telephone directory

directriz *nf* directive; *Mat* directrix

dirigente 1 *adj* leading; **clase d.** ruling class

   2 *nmf* leader

dirigir [57] 1 *vt* to direct; *(empresa)* to manage; *(negocio, colegio)* to run; *(orquesta)* to conduct; *(partido)* to lead; *(periódico)* to edit; *(coche, barco)* to steer; **d. la palabra a algn** to speak to sb

   2 dirigirse *vpr* **(a) d. a** o **hacia** to go to, to make one's way towards **(b)** *(escribir)* to write; **diríjase al apartado de correos 42** write to PO Box 42 **(c)** *(hablar)* to speak

discapacidad *nf* disability

discar *vt Andes, RP* to dial

discernir [54] *vt* to discern

disciplina *nf* discipline

disciplinado,-a *adj* disciplined

discípulo,-a *nm,f* disciple

disco *nm* **(a)** disc; **d. de freno** brake disc **(b)** *Mús* record; **d. compacto** compact disc **(c)** *Informát* disk; **d. duro** o **fijo/flexible** hard/floppy disk **(d)** *Dep* discus **(e)** *Tel* dial

discográfico,-a *adj* **casa/compañía discográfica** record company

disconforme *adj* **estar d. con** to disagree with

discontinuo,-a *adj* discontinuous; *Aut* **línea discontinua** broken line

discordante *adj* discordant; **ser la nota d.** to be the odd man out

discordia *nf* discord; **la manzana de la d.** the bone of contention; **sembrar d.** to sow discord

discoteca *nf* **(a)** *(lugar)* discotheque **(b)** *(colección)* record collection

discreción *nf* **(a)** discretion **(b)** **a d.** at will

discrecional *adj* optional; **servicio d.** special service

discrepancia *nf* *(desacuerdo)* disagreement; *(diferencia)* discrepancy

discrepar *vi* *(disentir)* to disagree **(de**

with; **en** on); *(diferenciarse)* to be different **(de** from)

discreto,-a *adj* **(a)** discreet **(b)** *(mediocre)* average

discriminación *nf* discrimination

discriminar *vt* **(a)** to discriminate against **(b)** *Fml (diferenciar)* to discriminate between, to distinguish

disculpa *nf* excuse; **dar disculpas** to make excuses; **pedir disculpas a algn** to apologize to sb

disculpar 1 *vt* to excuse

   2 disculparse *vpr* to apologize **(por** for)

discurrir *vi* **(a)** *(reflexionar)* to think **(b)** *Fig (transcurrir)* to pass, to go by **(c)** *Fml (río)* to wander

discurso *nm* speech; **dar** o **pronunciar un d.** to make a speech

discusión *nf* argument

discutir 1 *vi* to argue **(de** about)

   2 *vt* to discuss, to talk about

disecar [44] *vt* **(a)** *(animal)* to stuff **(b)** *(planta)* to dry

diseminar *vt* to disseminate, to spread

disentir [54] *vi* to dissent, to disagree **(de** with)

diseñar *vt* to design

diseño *nm* design; **d. de interiores** interior design

disertar *vi* to expound **(sobre** on o upon)

disfraz *nm* disguise; *(para fiesta)* fancy dress; **fiesta de disfraces** fancy dress party

disfrazar [40] 1 *vt* to disguise

   2 disfrazarse *vpr* to disguise oneself; **d. de pirata** to dress up as a pirate

disfrutar 1 *vi* **(a)** *(gozar)* to enjoy oneself **(b)** *(poseer)* **d. (de)** to enjoy

   2 *vt* to enjoy

disgregar [42] *vt* **(a)** to disintegrate, to break up **(b)** *(dispersar)* to disperse

disgustado,-a *adj* upset, displeased

disgustar 1 *vt* to upset

   2 disgustarse *vpr* **(a)** *(molestarse)* to get upset, to be annoyed **(b)** *(dos amigos)* to quarrel

> 🔊 Observa que el verbo inglés **to disgust** es un falso amigo y no es la traducción del verbo español **disgustar**. En inglés, **to disgust** significa "repugnar, indignar".

disgusto *nm* **(a)** *(preocupación)* annoyance; **llevarse un d.** to get upset; **dar un d. a algn** to upset sb **(b)** *(desgracia)* trouble; **a d.** unwillingly; **sentirse** o **estar a d.** to feel ill at ease **(c)** *(desavenencia)* fall-out, disagreement

📖 Observa que la palabra inglesa **disgust** es un falso amigo y no es la traducción de la palabra española **disgusto**. En inglés, **disgust** significa "repugnancia, asco".

disidente *adj & nmf* dissident
disimuladamente *adv* surreptitiously
disimulado,-a *adj* (a) *(persona)* sly, crafty (b) *(oculto)* hidden, concealed
disimular *vt* to conceal, to hide
disimulo *nm* pretence
disipar 1 *vt (niebla)* to drive away; *(temor, duda)* to dispel
    2 **disiparse** *vpr (gaseosa)* to go flat; *(niebla, temor etc)* to disappear
disketera *nf Informát* disk drive
dislexia *nf* dyslexia
dislocar [44] *vt* to dislocate
disminución *nf* decrease
disminuir [37] 1 *vt* to reduce
    2 *vi* to diminish
disolución *nf* dissolution
disolvente *adj & nm* solvent
disolver [4] *(pp disuelto)* *vt* to dissolve
disparar 1 *vt (pistola etc)* to fire; *(flecha, balón)* to shoot; **d. a algn** to shoot at sb
    2 **dispararse** *vpr* (a) *(arma)* to go off, to fire (b) *(precios)* to rocket
disparatado,-a *adj* absurd
disparate *nm* (a) *(dicho)* nonsense; **decir disparates** to talk nonsense (b) *(acto)* foolish act
disparidad *nf* disparity
disparo *nm* shot; *Dep* **d. a puerta** shot
dispensar *vt* (a) *(disculpar)* to pardon, to forgive (b) *(eximir)* to exempt
dispersar 1 *vt* to disperse; *(esparcir)* to scatter
    2 **dispersarse** *vpr* to disperse
disperso,-a *adj (separado)* dispersed; *(esparcido)* scattered
displicencia *nf* condescension, disdain
displicente *adj* condescending, disdainful
disponer [19] *(pp dispuesto)* 1 *vt* (a) *(arreglar)* to arrange, to set out (b) *(ordenar)* to order
    2 *vi* **d. de** to have at one's disposal
    3 **disponerse** *vpr* to prepare, to get ready
disponible *adj* available
disposición *nf* (a) *(uso)* disposal; **a su d.** at your disposal o service (b) *(colocación)* arrangement, layout (c) **no estar en d. de** not to be prepared to (d) *(orden)* order, law
dispositivo *nm* device
dispuesto,-a *adj* (a) *(ordenado)* arranged (b) *(a punto)* ready (c) *(decidido)*

determined; **no estar d. a** not to be prepared to (d) **según lo d. por la ley** in accordance with what the law stipulates
disputa *nf* *(discusión)* argument; *(contienda)* contest
disputar 1 *vt* (a) *(premio)* to compete for (b) *Dep (partido)* to play
    2 **disputarse** *vpr (premio)* to compete for
disquete *nm Informát* diskette, floppy disk
disquetera *nf Informát* disk drive
distancia *nf* distance; **a d.** from a distance
distanciamiento *nm* distancing
distanciar [43] 1 *vt* to separate
    2 **distanciarse** *vpr* to become separated; *(de otra persona)* to distance oneself
distante *adj* distant, far-off
distar *vi* to be distant o away; *Fig* to be far from; **dista mucho de ser perfecto** it's far from (being) perfect
distender [3] *vt Fig* to ease, to relax
distensión *nf Pol* détente
distinción *nf* distinction; **a d. de** unlike; **sin d. de** irrespective of
distinguido,-a *adj* distinguished
distinguir [59] 1 *vt* (a) *(diferenciar)* to distinguish (b) *(reconocer)* to recognize (c) *(honrar)* to honour
    2 *vi (diferenciar)* to discriminate
    3 **distinguirse** *vpr* to distinguish oneself
distintivo,-a 1 *adj* distinctive, distinguishing
    2 *nm* distinctive sign o mark
distinto,-a *adj* different
distorsión *nf* (a) *(distortion)* (b) *Med* sprain
distracción *nf* (a) entertainment; *(pasatiempo)* pastime, hobby (b) *(descuido)* distraction, absent-mindedness
distraer [25] 1 *vt* (a) *(atención)* to distract (b) *(divertir)* to entertain, to amuse
    2 **distraerse** *vpr* (a) *(divertirse)* to amuse oneself (b) *(abstraerse)* to let one's mind wander
distraído,-a *adj* (a) *(divertido)* entertaining (b) *(abstraído)* absent-minded
distribución *nf* (a) distribution (b) *(disposición)* layout
distribuidor,-a 1 *adj* distributing
    2 *nm,f* (a) distributor (b) *Com* wholesaler
distribuir [37] *vt* to distribute; *(trabajo)* to share out
distrito *nm* district; **d. postal** postal district
disturbio *nm* riot, disturbance
disuadir *vt* to dissuade

disuasión *nf* dissuasion

disuelto,-a *pp de* disolver

DIU *nm* (*abr* dispositivo intrauterino) IUD

diurético,-a *adj & nm* diuretic

diurno,-a *adj* daytime

divagar [42] *vi* to digress, to wander

diván *nm* divan, couch

divergencia *nf* divergence

divergente *adj* diverging

diversidad *nf* diversity

diversificar [44] 1 *vt* to diversify

2 **diversificarse** *vpr* to be diversified *o* varied; (*empresa*) to diversify

diversión *nf* fun

diverso,-a *adj* different; **diversos** several, various

divertido,-a *adj* amusing, funny

divertir [5] 1 *vt* to amuse, to entertain

2 **divertirse** *vpr* to enjoy oneself, to have a good time; **¡que te diviertas!** enjoy yourself!, have fun!

dividendo *nm* dividend

dividir 1 *vt* to divide (**en** into); *Mat* **15 dividido entre 3** 15 divided by 3

2 **dividirse** *vpr* to divide, to split up

divinidad *nf* divinity

divino,-a *adj* divine

divisa *nf* (**a**) (*emblema*) symbol, emblem (**b**) *Com* **divisas** foreign currency

divisar *vt* to make out, to discern

división *nf* division

divisorio,-a *adj* dividing

divorciado,-a 1 *adj* divorced

2 *nm,f* (*hombre*) divorcé; (*mujer*) divorcée

divorciar [43] 1 *vt* to divorce

2 **divorciarse** *vpr* to get divorced; **se divorció de él** she divorced him, she got a divorce from him

divorcio *nm* divorce

divulgación *nf* disclosure

divulgar [42] *vt* to disclose; *Rad & TV* to broadcast

dizque *adv Andes, Carib, Méx* apparently

DNI *nm* (*abr* Documento Nacional de Identidad) Identity Card, ID card

do *nm Mús* (*de solfa*) doh, do; (*de escala diatónica*) C; **do de pecho** high C

doberman *nm* Doberman (pinscher)

dobladillo *nm* hem

doblaje *nm Cin* dubbing

doblar 1 *vt* (**a**) to double; **me dobla la edad** he is twice as old as I am (**b**) (*plegar*) to fold *o* turn up (**c**) (*torcer*) to bend (**d**) (*la esquina*) to go round (**e**) (*película*) to dub

2 *vi* (**a**) (*girar*) to turn; **d. a la derecha/izquierda** to turn right/left (**b**) (*campanas*) to toll

3 **doblarse** *vpr* (**a**) (*plegarse*) to fold (**b**) (*torcerse*) to bend

doble 1 *adj* double; **arma de d. filo** double-edged weapon

2 *nm* (**a**) double; **gana el d. que tú** she earns twice as much as you do (**b**) *Dep* **dobles** doubles

doblegar [42] 1 *vt* to bend

2 **doblegarse** *vpr* to give in

doblez 1 *nm* (*pliegue*) fold

2 *nm o nf Fig* two-facedness, hypocrisy

doce *adj & nm inv* twelve

docena *nf* dozen

docencia *nf* teaching

docente *adj* teaching; **centro d.** educational centre

dócil *adj* docile

doctor,-a *nm,f* doctor

doctorado *nm Univ* doctorate, PhD

doctrina *nf* doctrine

documentación *nf* documentation; (*DNI, de conducir etc*) papers

documental *adj & nm* documentary

documentar 1 *vt* to document

2 **documentarse** *vpr* **d. (sobre)** to research, to get information (about *o* on)

documento *nm* document; **d. nacional de identidad** identity card

dogma *nm* dogma

dogmático,-a *adj & nm,f* dogmatic

dogo *nm* bulldog

dólar *nm* dollar

dolarización *nf* dollarization

dolencia *nf* ailment

doler [4] 1 *vi* to hurt, to ache; **me duele la cabeza** I've got a headache; **me duele la mano** my hand is sore

2 **dolerse** *vpr* to be sorry *o* sad

dolido,-a *adj* **estar d.** to be hurt

dolor *nm* (**a**) *Med* pain; **d. de cabeza** headache; **d. de muelas** toothache (**b**) (*pena*) grief, sorrow

dolorido,-a *adj* (**a**) (*dañado*) sore, aching (**b**) (*apenado*) hurt

doloroso,-a *adj* painful

domar *vt* to tame; (*caballo*) to break in

domesticar [44] *vt* to domesticate; (*animal*) to tame

doméstico,-a *adj* domestic; **animal d.** pet

domiciliación *nf* payment by standing order

domiciliar [43] *vt* (**a**) to house (**b**) *Fin* to pay by standing order

domiciliario,-a *adj* **arresto d.** house arrest

domicilio *nm* home, residence; *(señas)* address; **sin d. fijo** of no fixed abode; **d. fiscal** registered office

dominación *nf* domination

dominante *adj* (**a**) dominant (**b**) *(déspota)* domineering

dominar 1 *vt* (**a**) to dominate, to rule (**b**) *(situación)* to control; *(idioma)* to speak very well; *(asunto)* to master; *(paisaje etc)* to overlook

   2 *vi* (**a**) to dominate (**b**) *(resaltar)* to stand out

   3 dominarse *vpr* to control oneself

domingo *nm inv* Sunday; **D. de Resurrección** *o* **Pascua** Easter Sunday

dominguero,-a *nm,f Fam (excursionista)* weekend tripper; *(conductor)* weekend driver

dominical 1 *adj* Sunday

   2 *nm (suplemento)* Sunday supplement

dominicano,-a *adj & nm,f* Dominican; **República Dominicana** Dominican Republic

dominio *nm* (**a**) *(poder)* control; *(de un idioma)* command; **d. de sí mismo** self-control (**b**) *(ámbito)* scope, sphere; **ser del d. público** to be public knowledge (**c**) *(territorio)* dominion (**d**) *Informát* domain

dominó, dómino *nm* dominoes

don¹ *nm* (**a**) *(habilidad)* gift, talent; **tener el d. de** to have a knack for; **tener d. de gentes** to get on well with people (**b**) *(regalo)* present, gift

don² *nm* **Señor D. José García** Mr José García; **D. Fulano de Tal** Mr So-and-So; **un d. nadie** a nobody

donaire *nm* grace, elegance

donante *nmf* donor; *Med* **d. de sangre** blood donor

donar *vt Fml* to donate; *(sangre)* to give

donativo *nm* donation

doncella *nf Literario* (**a**) *(joven)* maid, maiden (**b**) *(criada)* maid, housemaid

donde *adv rel* where; **a** *o* **en d.** where; **de** *o* **desde d.** from where; **está d. lo dejaste** it is where you left it; *Fam* **está d. su tía** he's at his aunt's

> **donde** combines with the preposition **a** to form **adonde** when following a noun, a pronoun or an adverb expressing location (e.g. **el sitio adonde vamos** the place where we're going; **es allí adonde iban** that's where they were going).

dónde *adv interr* where?; **¿de d. eres?** where are you from?; **¿por d. se va a la playa?** which way is it to the beach?

> **dónde** can combine with the preposition **a** to form **adónde** (e.g. **¿adónde vamos?** where are we going?).

dondequiera *adv* everywhere; **d. que vaya** wherever I go

donostiarra 1 *adj* of/from San Sebastián

   2 *nmf* person from San Sebastián

doña *nf* **(Señora) D. Leonor Benítez** Mrs Leonor Benítez

dopaje *nm Dep* drug-taking

dopar 1 *vt (caballo etc)* to dope

   2 doparse *vpr* to take drugs

doping *nm Dep* drug-taking

doquier, doquiera *adv Literario* **por d.** everywhere

dorada *nf (pez)* gilthead bream

dorado,-a 1 *adj* golden

   2 *nm Téc* gilding

dorar *vt* (**a**) to gild (**b**) *Culin* to brown

dormido,-a *adj* (**a**) asleep; **quedarse d.** to fall asleep; *(no despertarse)* to oversleep, to sleep in (**b**) *(pierna, brazo)* numb

dormilón,-ona 1 *adj Fam* sleepyheaded

   2 *nm,f* sleepyhead

   3 *nf Ven* **dormilona** nightdress

dormir [7] 1 *vi* to sleep; **tener ganas de d.** to feel sleepy;

   2 *vt* **d. la siesta** to have an afternoon nap

   3 dormirse *vpr* to fall asleep; **se me ha dormido el brazo** my arm has gone to sleep

dormitar *vi* to doze, to snooze

dormitorio *nm* (**a**) *(de una casa)* bedroom (**b**) *(de colegio, residencia)* dormitory; **ciudad d.** dormitory town

dorsal 1 *adj* **espina d.** spine

   2 *nm Dep* number

dorso *nm* back; **instrucciones al d.** instructions over; **véase al d.** see overleaf

dos *adj & nm inv* two; **los d.** both; **nosotros/vosotros d.** both of us/you; *Fam* **cada d. por tres** every other minute; *Fam* **en un d. por tres** in a flash

doscientos,-as *adj & nm* two hundred

dosel *nm* canopy

dosificación *nf* dosage

dosificar [44] *vt* (**a**) to dose (**b**) *(esfuerzos, energías)* to measure

dosis *nf inv* dose

dossier *nm* dossier

dotación *nf (dinero)* grant; *(personal)* personnel, staff; *(de barco)* crew

dotado,-a *adj* (**a**) *(persona)* gifted (**b**) *(equipado)* equipped; **d. de** provided with

dotar *vt* **d. de** to provide with

dote *nf* (**a**) *(de novia)* dowry (**b**) **dotes** *(talento)* gift, talent

doy *indic pres de* **dar**
dpto. (*abr* **departamento**) Dept
Dr. (*abr* **doctor**) Dr
Dra. (*abr* **doctora**) Dr
dragar [42] *vt* to dredge
dragón *nm* dragon
drama *nm* drama
dramático,-a *adj* dramatic
dramatismo *nm* drama, dramatic quality
dramaturgo,-a *nm,f* playwright, dramatist
drástico,-a *adj* drastic
drenar *vt* to drain
driblar *vi* to dribble
droga *nf* drug; **d. blanda/dura** soft/hard drug
drogadicto,-a *nm,f* drug addict
drogar [42] **1** *vt* to drug
  2 drogarse *vpr* to drug oneself, to take drugs
droguería *nf* hardware and household goods shop
dto. (*abr* **descuento**) discount
dual *adj* dual
dualidad *nf* duality
dubitativo,-a *adj* doubtful
Dublín *n* Dublin
dublinés,-esa 1 *adj* of/from Dublin
  2 *nm,f* Dubliner
ducha *nf* shower; **darse/tomar una d.** to take/have a shower
ducharse *vpr* to shower, to have o take a shower
ducho,-a *adj* expert; **ser d. en** to be well versed in
duda *nf* doubt; **sin d.** without a doubt; **no cabe d.** (there is) no doubt; **poner algo en d.** to question sth; **sacar a algn de dudas** to dispel sb's doubts
dudar 1 *vi* (**a**) to doubt (**b**) (*vacilar*) to hesitate (**en** to); **dudaba entre ir o quedarme** I hesitated whether to go o to stay (**c**) **d. de algn** (*desconfiar*) to suspect sb
  2 *vt* to doubt
dudoso,-a *adj* (**a**) **ser d.** (*incierto*) to be uncertain o doubtful (**b**) **estar d.** (*indeciso*) to be undecided (**c**) (*poco honrado*) dubious
duelo¹ *nm* (*combate*) duel
duelo² *nm* (*luto*) mourning
duende *nm* (**a**) (*espíritu*) goblin, elf (**b**) (*encanto*) magic, charm

dueña *nf* owner; (*de pensión*) landlady
dueño *nm* owner; (*de casa etc*) landlord; *Fig* **ser d. de sí mismo** to be self-possessed
Duero *n* **el D.** the Douro
dulce 1 *adj* (**a**) (*sabor*) sweet (**b**) (*carácter, voz*) gentle (**c**) (*metal*) soft (**d**) **agua d.** fresh water
  2 *nm* (**a**) *Culin* (*pastel*) cake (**b**) (*caramelo*) *Br* sweet, *US* candy
dulzura *nf* (**a**) sweetness (**b**) *Fig* gentleness, softness
duna *nf* dune
dúo *nm* duet
duodécimo,-a *adj & nm,f* twelfth
dúplex *nm* (**a**) (*piso*) duplex, duplex apartment (**b**) *Tel* link-up
duplicado,-a 1 *adj* **por d.** in duplicate
  2 *nm* duplicate, copy
duplicar [44] **1** *vt* to duplicate; (*cifras*) to double
  2 duplicarse *vpr* to double
duplo,-a *adj & nm,f* double
duque *nm* duke
duquesa *nf* duchess
duración *nf* duration, length; **disco de larga d.** long-playing record
duradero,-a *adj* durable, lasting
durante *prep* during; **d. el día** during the day; **d. todo el día** all day long; **viví en La Coruña d. un año** I lived in La Coruña for a year
durar *vi* (**a**) to last (**b**) (*ropa, calzado*) to wear well, to last
durazno *nm* (*fruto*) peach; (*árbol*) peach tree
dúrex *nm Méx Br* Sellotape®, *US* Scotch tape®
dureza *nf* (**a**) hardness; (*severidad*) harshness, severity (**b**) (*callosidad*) corn

┌─────────────────────────────────────┐
│ 🖋 Observa que la palabra inglesa **duress** es │
│ un falso amigo y no es la traducción de la │
│ palabra española **dureza**. En inglés, **duress** │
│ significa "coacción". │
└─────────────────────────────────────┘

duro,-a 1 *adj* (**a**) hard; *Dep* **juego d.** rough play (**b**) (*resistente*) tough; (*severo*) hard (**c**) (*clima*) harsh
  2 *nm* (*moneda*) 5-peseta coin
  3 *adv* hard; **trabajar d.** to work hard
DVD *nm Informát* (*abr* **Disco Versátil Digital**) DVD

E, e [e] *nf (la letra)* E, e
E *(abr* **Este**) E
e *conj* and

> **e** is used instead of **y** in front of words beginning with "i" or "hi" (e.g. **apoyo e interés** support and interest; **corazón e hígado** heart and liver).

ebanista *nm* cabinet-maker
ébano *nm* ebony
ebrio,-a *adj* inebriated; **e. de dicha** drunk with joy
ebullición *nf* boiling; **punto de e.** boiling point
eccema *nm* eczema
echar 1 *vt* (a) *(lanzar)* to throw; *Fig* **e. una mano** to give a hand; *Fig* **e. una mirada/una ojeada** to have a look/a quick look *o* glance
  (b) *(carta)* to post; *(vino, agua)* to pour; **e. sal al estofado** to put salt in the stew; **e. gasolina al coche** to put *Br* petrol *o US* gas in the car
  (c) *(expulsar)* to throw out; *(despedir)* to fire, *Br* to sack
  (d) *(humo, olor etc)* to give off
  (e) *Fam (película)* to show
  (f) **le echó 37 años** he reckoned she was about 37
  (g) **e. de menos** *o* **en falta** to miss
  (h) **e. abajo** *(edificio)* to demolish
2 *vi* (+ **a** + *infin*) *(empezar)* to begin to; **echó a correr** he ran off
3 echarse *vpr* (a) *(tumbarse)* to lie down; *(lanzarse)* to throw oneself; *Fig* **la noche se nos echó encima** it was night before we knew it
  (b) **échate a un lado** stand aside; *Fig* **e. atrás** to get cold feet
  (c) *Fam* **e. novio/novia** to get a boyfriend/girlfriend
  (d) (+ **a** + *infin*) *(empezar)* to begin to; **e. a llorar** to burst into tears; **e. a reír** to burst out laughing; **e. a perder** *(comida)* to go bad
ecléctico,-a *adj & nm,f* eclectic
eclesiástico,-a 1 *adj* ecclesiastical
2 *nm* clergyman
eclipsar *vt* to eclipse

eclipse *nm* eclipse
eco *nm* echo; *Fig* **hacerse e. de una noticia** to publish an item of news; **tener e.** to arouse interest
ecografía *nf* scan
ecología *nf* ecology
ecológico,-a *adj* ecological; *(alimentos)* organic; *(detergente)* environmentally-friendly
ecologista 1 *adj* ecological; *Pol* **partido e.** ecology party
  2 *nmf* ecologist
economía *nf* (a) economy; **con e.** economically (b) *(ciencia)* economics *sing*
económico,-a *adj* (a) economic (b) *(barato)* economical, inexpensive (c) *(persona)* thrifty
economista *nmf* economist
economizar [40] *vt & vi* to economize
ecosistema *nm* ecosystem
ecotasa *nf* ecotax
ecoturismo *nm* ecotourism
ecuación *nf* equation
Ecuador *n* Ecuador
ecuador *nm Geog* equator
ecualizador *nm* **e. (gráfico)** graphic equalizer
ecuánime *adj* (a) *(temperamento)* equable, even-tempered (b) *(juicio)* impartial
ecuatorial *adj* equatorial; **Guinea E.** Equatorial Guinea
ecuatoriano,-a *adj & nm,f* Ecuadorian
ecuestre *adj* equestrian
ecuménico,-a *adj* ecumenical
eczema *nm* eczema
edad *nf* age; **¿qué e. tienes?** how old are you?; **la tercera e.** senior citizens; **E. Media** Middle Ages
edición *nf* (a) *(publicación)* publication; *(de sellos)* issue (b) *(conjunto de ejemplares)* edition
edicto *nm* edict, proclamation
edificante *adj* edifying
edificar [44] *vt* to build
edificio *nm* building
edil,-a *nm,f* town councillor
Edimburgo *n* Edinburgh
editar *vt* (a) *(libro, periódico)* to publish;

(disco) to release (**b**) *Informát* to edit

editor,-a 1 *adj* publishing

  2 *nm,f* publisher

editorial 1 *adj* publishing

  2 *nf* publishers, publishing house

  3 *nm Prensa* editorial, leader article

edredón *nm Br* duvet, *US* comforter

educación *nf* (**a**) education; **e. física** physical education (**b**) *(formación)* upbringing (**c**) **buena/mala e.** *(modales)* good/bad manners; **falta de e.** bad manners

educado,-a *adj* polite

educador,-a 1 *adj* educating

  2 *nm,f* educationalist

educar [**44**] *vt (hijos)* to raise; *(alumnos)* to educate; *(la voz)* to train

educativo,-a *adj* educational; **sistema e.** education system

edulcorante *nm* sweetener

EE.UU. *(abr* **Estados Unidos***)* USA

efectista *adj* spectacular

efectivamente *adv* quite!, yes indeed!

efectividad *nf* effectiveness

efectivo,-a 1 *adj* effective; **hacer algo e.** to carry sth out; *Fin* **hacer e. un cheque** to cash a cheque

  2 *nm* (**a**) *Fin* **en e.** in cash (**b**) *Mil* **efectivos** forces

efecto *nm* (**a**) *(resultado)* effect; **efectos especiales/sonoros** special/sound effects; **efectos personales** personal belongings o effects; **a efectos de ...** for the purposes of ...; **en e.** quite!, yes indeed! (**b**) *(impresión)* impression; **causar** o **hacer e.** to make an impression (**c**) *Dep* spin

efectuar [**30**] *vt* to carry out; *(viaje)* to make; *Com (pedido)* to place

efeméride *nf* event

efervescente *adj* effervescent; **aspirina e.** soluble aspirin

eficacia *nf (de persona)* efficiency; *(de remedio etc)* effectiveness

eficaz *adj (persona)* efficient; *(remedio, medida etc)* effective

eficiencia *nf* efficiency

eficiente *adj* efficient

efigie *nf* effigy

efímero,-a *adj* ephemeral

efusivo,-a *adj* effusive

EGB *nf Educ (abr* **Enseñanza General Básica***)* = formerly, stage of Spanish education system for pupils aged 6-14

Egeo *n* **el (Mar) E.** the Aegean Sea

egipcio,-a *adj & nm,f* Egyptian

Egipto *n* Egypt

egocéntrico,-a *adj* egocentric, self-centred

egoísmo *nm* egoism, selfishness

egoísta 1 *adj* ego(t)istic, selfish

  2 *nmf* ego(t)ist, selfish person

egregio,-a *adj* eminent, illustrious

egresar *vi Am* to leave school, *US* to graduate

Eire *n* Eire, Republic of Ireland

ej. *(abr* **ejemplo***)* example

eje *nm* (**a**) *Téc (de rueda)* axle; *(de máquina)* shaft (**b**) *Mat* axis (**c**) *Hist* **El E.** the Axis

ejecución *nf* (**a**) *(de orden)* carrying out (**b**) *(ajusticiamiento)* execution (**c**) *Mús* performance

ejecutar *vt* (**a**) *(orden)* to carry out (**b**) *(ajusticiar)* to execute (**c**) *Mús* to perform, to play (**d**) *Informát* to run

ejecutiva *nf Pol* executive

ejecutivo,-a 1 *adj* executive; *Pol* **el poder e.** the government

  2 *nm* executive

ejecutor,-a *nm,f* (**a**) *Jur* executor (**b**) *(verdugo)* executioner

ejemplar 1 *nm* (**a**) *(de libro)* copy; *(de revista, periódico)* number, issue (**b**) *(espécimen)* specimen

  2 *adj* exemplary, model

ejemplificar [**44**] *vt* to exemplify

ejemplo *nm* example; **por e.** for example; **dar e.** to set an example

ejercer [**49**] **1** *vt* (**a**) *(profesión etc)* to practise (**b**) *(influencia)* to exert (**c**) **e. el derecho de/a ...** to exercise one's right to ...

  2 *vi* to practise (**de** as)

ejercicio *nm* (**a**) exercise; *(de profesión)* practice; **hacer e.** to take o do exercise (**b**) *Fin* tax year; **e. económico** financial o fiscal year

ejercitar *vt* to practise

ejército *nm* army

ejote *nm CAm, Méx* green bean

el 1 *art def m* (**a**) the (**b**) *(no se traduce)* **el Sr. García** Mr. García; **el hambre/destino** hunger/fate (**c**) *(con partes del cuerpo, prendas de vestir)* **me he cortado el dedo** I've cut my finger; **métetelo en el bolsillo** put it in your pocket (**d**) *(con días de la semana)* **el lunes** on Monday

---

el is used instead of **la** before feminine nouns which are stressed on the first syllable and begin with "a" or "ha" (e.g. **el agua, el hacha**). Note that **el** combines with the prepositions **a** and **de** to produce the contracted forms **al** and **del**.

---

2 *pron* (**a**) the one; **el de las once** the eleven o'clock one; **el que tienes en la mano** the one you've got in your hand; **el**

que quieras whichever one you want (**b**) *(no se traduce)* **el de tu amigo** your friend's

él *pron pers* (**a**) *(sujeto) (persona)* he; *(animal, cosa)* it (**b**) *(complemento) (persona)* him; *(animal, cosa)* it

> Usually omitted in Spanish as a subject except for emphasis or contrast.

elaboración *nf* (**a**) *(de un producto)* manufacture, production (**b**) *(de una idea)* working out, development

elaborar *vt* (**a**) *(producto)* to manufacture, to produce (**b**) *(teoría)* to develop

elasticidad *nf* elasticity; *Fig* flexibility

elástico,-a *adj & nm* elastic

elección *nf* choice; *Pol* election

elector,-a *nm,f* elector

electorado *nm* electorate

electoral *adj* electoral; **campaña e.** election campaign; **colegio e.** polling station

electoralismo *nm* electioneering

electricidad *nf* electricity

electricista *nmf* electrician

eléctrico,-a *adj* electric

electrificar [44] *vt* to electrify

electrizar [40] *vt* to electrify

electrochoque *nm* electric shock therapy

electrocutar *vt* to electrocute

electrodo *nm* electrode

electrodoméstico *nm* (domestic) electrical appliance

electroimán *nm* electromagnet

electromagnético,-a *adj* electromagnetic

electrón *nm* electron

electrónica *nf* electronics *sing*

electrónico,-a *adj* electronic

elefante *nm* elephant

elegancia *nf* elegance

elegante *adj* elegant

elegía *nf* elegy

elegir [58] *vt* (**a**) to choose (**b**) *Pol* to elect

elemental *adj* (**a**) *(fundamental)* basic, fundamental (**b**) *(simple)* elementary

elemento *nm* (**a**) element (**b**) *(componente)* component, part (**c**) *(individuo)* type, individual (**d**) **elementos** elements; *(fundamentos)* rudiments

elepé *nm* LP (record)

elevación *nf* elevation; **e. de precios** rise in prices; **e. del terreno** rise in the ground

elevado,-a *adj* (**a**) high; *(edificio)* tall (**b**) *(pensamiento etc)* lofty, noble

elevalunas *nm inv* *Aut* **e. eléctrico** electric windows

elevar 1 *vt* to raise

2 **elevarse** *vpr* (**a**) *(subir)* to rise; *(edificio)* to stand (**b**) **e. a** *(cantidad)* to amount o come to

elijo *indic pres de* elegir

eliminación *nf* elimination

eliminar *vt* to eliminate

eliminatoria *nf Dep* heat, qualifying round

eliminatorio,-a *adj* qualifying, eliminatory

élite *nf* elite, élite

elitista *adj* elitist

elixir *nm (enjuague bucal)* mouthwash; *Literario* elixir

ella *pron pers f* (**a**) *(sujeto)* she; *(animal, cosa)* it, she (**b**) *(complemento)* her; *(animal, cosa)* it, her

> Usually omitted in Spanish as a subject except for emphasis or contrast.

ellas *pron pers fpl ver* ellos

ello *pron pers neut* it; **por e.** for that reason

ellos *pron pers mpl* (**a**) *(sujeto)* they (**b**) *(complemento)* them

> Usually omitted in Spanish as a subject except for emphasis or contrast.

elocuencia *nf* eloquence

elocuente *adj* eloquent; **los hechos son elocuentes** the facts speak for themselves

elogiar [43] *vt* to praise

elogio *nm* praise

elote *nm CAm, Méx* corncob, ear of maize

El Salvador *n* El Salvador

elucidar *vt* to elucidate

eludir *vt* to avoid

emanar *vi* to emanate; *Fig* **e. de** *(derivar)* to derive o come from

emancipar 1 *vt* to emancipate

2 **emanciparse** *vpr* to become emancipated

embadurnar *vt* to daub, to smear (**de** with)

embajada *nf* embassy

embajador,-a *nm,f* ambassador

embalaje *nm* packing, packaging

embalar *vt* to pack

embalarse *vpr* to speed up; *Fig* **no te embales** hold your horses

embalsamar *vt* to embalm

embalsar 1 *vt* to dam; *(problema)* to contain

2 **embalsarse** *vpr* to form a pool

embalse *nm* dam, reservoir

embarazada 1 *adj* pregnant; **dejar e. to** get pregnant

2 *nf* pregnant woman, expectant mother

> *𝒬* Observa que la palabra inglesa **embarrassed** es un falso amigo y no es la traducción de la palabra española **embarazada**. En inglés **embarrassed** significa "avergonzado".

embarazar [40] *vt Fig* to hinder
embarazo *nm* (**a**) *(preñez)* pregnancy (**b**) *(obstáculo)* obstacle (**c**) *(turbación)* embarrassment
embarazoso,-a *adj* awkward, embarrassing
embarcación *nf* (**a**) *(nave)* boat, craft (**b**) *(embarco)* embarkation
embarcadero *nm* quay
embarcar [44] 1 *vt* to ship
  2 *vi* to embark, to go on board
  3 embarcarse *vpr* (**a**) *Náut* **e. (en)** to go on board; *Av* to board (**b**) **e. en un proyecto** to embark on a project
embarco *nm* embarkation
embargar [42] *vt* (**a**) *Jur* to seize, to impound (**b**) *Fig* **le embarga la emoción** he's overwhelmed with joy
embargo *nm* (**a**) *Jur* seizure of property (**b**) *Com & Pol* embargo (**c**) **sin e.** however, nevertheless
embarque *nm* *(de persona)* boarding; *(de mercancías)* loading; **tarjeta de e.** boarding card
embarrancar [44] *vi,* **embarrancarse** *vpr Náut* to run aground
embaucador,-a 1 *adj* deceitful
  2 *nm,f* swindler, cheat
embaucar [44] *vt* to swindle, to cheat
embeber 1 *vt* to soak up
  2 embeberse *vpr* to become absorbed *o* engrossed
embelesar *vt* to fascinate
embellecer [33] *vt* to embellish
embestida *nf* (**a**) onslaught (**b**) *Taurom* charge
embestir [6] *vt* (**a**) *Taurom* to charge (**b**) *(atacar)* to attack
emblandecer [33] 1 *vt* to soften
  2 emblandecerse *vpr Fig* to relent
emblema *nm* emblem
embobado,-a *adj* fascinated
embobarse *vpr* to be fascinated *o* besotted (**con** by)
embolia *nf* embolism
émbolo *nm* piston
embolsar *vt,* **embolsarse** *vpr* to pocket
emborrachar *vt,* **emborracharse** *vpr* to get drunk
emboscada *nf* ambush; **tender una e.** to lay an ambush

embotar *vt* to blunt; *Fig (sentidos)* to dull; *(mente)* to befuddle
embotellado *nm* bottling
embotellamiento *nm* *Aut* traffic jam
embotellar *vt* (**a**) to bottle (**b**) *(tráfico)* to block
embragar [42] *vi Aut* to engage the clutch
embrague *nm* clutch
embravecerse [33] *vpr* (**a**) *(enfadarse)* to become enraged (**b**) *(mar)* to become rough
embriagador,-a *adj* intoxicating
embriagar [42] 1 *vt* to intoxicate; *Fig* to enrapture
  2 embriagarse *vpr* to get drunk; *Fig* to be enraptured
embriaguez *nf* intoxication
embridar *vt* to bridle
embrión *nm* embryo
embrollar 1 *vt* to confuse, to muddle
  2 embrollarse *vpr* to get muddled *o* confused
embrollo *nm* (**a**) *(lío)* muddle, confusion (**b**) *(aprieto)* fix, jam
embrujado,-a *adj* *(persona)* bewitched; *(sitio)* haunted
embrujo *nm* spell, charm; *Fig* attraction, fascination
embrutecer [33] *vt* to stultify
embuchar *vt* to stuff
embudo *nm* funnel
embuste *nm* lie, trick
embustero,-a *nm,f* cheater, liar
embutido *nm* sausage
embutir *vt* (**a**) *(carne)* to stuff (**b**) *(meter)* to stuff *o* cram *o* squeeze (**en** into) (**c**) *(incrustar)* to inlay
emergencia *nf* emergency; **salida de e.** emergency exit; **en caso de e.** in an emergency
emerger [53] *vi* to emerge
emigración *nf* emigration; *(de pájaros)* migration
emigrado,-a *nm,f* emigrant; *Pol* émigré
emigrante *adj & nmf* emigrant
emigrar *vi* to emigrate; *(pájaros)* to migrate
emilio *nm* *Fam Informát* e-mail (message)
eminencia *nf* eminence; *(genio)* genius
eminente *adj* eminent
emirato *nm* emirate
emisario,-a *nm,f* emissary
emisión *nf* (**a**) emission (**b**) *(de bonos, sellos)* issue (**c**) *Rad & TV* broadcasting
emisora *nf* radio *o* television station
emitir *vt* (**a**) to emit; *(luz, calor)* to give off

(**b**) *(opinión, juicio)* to express (**c**) *Rad & TV* to transmit (**d**) *(bonos, sellos)* to issue

emoción *nf* (**a**) emotion (**b**) *(excitación)* excitement; **¡qué e.!** how exciting!

emocionado,-a *adj* deeply moved *o* touched

emocionante *adj* (**a**) *(conmovedor)* moving, touching (**b**) *(excitante)* exciting, thrilling

emocionar 1 *vt* (**a**) *(conmover)* to move, to touch (**b**) *(excitar)* to thrill

2 emocionarse *vpr* (**a**) *(conmoverse)* to be moved (**b**) *(excitarse)* to get excited

emotivo,-a *adj* emotional

empacar [44] *vt* (**a**) *(mercancías)* to pack (**b**) *Am* to annoy

empachar *vt* to give indigestion to

empacho *nm* *(de comida)* indigestion, upset stomach; *Fig* surfeit

empadronar *vt*, **empadronarse** *vpr* to register

empalagar [42] *vi* to pall

empalagoso,-a *adj* (**a**) *(dulce)* sickly sweet (**b**) *Fig (persona)* smarmy

empalizada *nf* fence

empalmar 1 *vt* (**a**) *(unir)* to join; *(cuerdas, cables)* to splice (**b**) *Ftb* to volley

2 *vi* to converge; *Ferroc* to connect

3 empalmarse *vpr Vulg* to get a hard-on

empalme *nm* (**a**) connection (**b**) *Ferroc* junction; *(en carretera)* intersection, T-junction

empanada *nf* pie

empanadilla *nf* pasty

empanado,-a *adj (filete etc)* breaded, in breadcrumbs

empantanarse *vpr* (**a**) *(inundarse)* to become flooded (**b**) *Fig* to be bogged down

empañar *vt*, **empañarse** *vpr (cristales)* to steam up

empapado,-a *adj* soaked

empapar 1 *vt* (**a**) *(mojar)* to soak (**b**) *(absorber)* to soak up

2 empaparse *vpr* (**a**) *(persona)* to get soaked (**b**) *Fam Fig* **empaparse (de)** to take in

empapelar *vt* to wallpaper

empaque *nm* bearing, presence

empaquetar *vt* to pack

emparedado *nm* sandwich

emparejar *vt (cosas)* to match; *(personas)* to pair off

empastar *vt (diente)* to fill

empaste *nm (de diente)* filling

empatado,-a *adj* drawn; **estar/ir empatados** to be drawing

empatar 1 *vi Dep* to tie, to draw

2 *vt* (**a**) *Dep* **e. el partido** to equalize (**b**) *Am (unir)* to join

empate *nm Dep* draw, tie

empecinarse *vpr* to dig one's heels in

empedernido,-a *adj (fumador, bebedor)* hardened

empedrado,-a 1 *adj* cobbled

2 *nm* (**a**) *(adoquines)* cobblestones (**b**) *(acción)* paving

empeine *nm* instep

empellón *nm* push, shove

empeñar 1 *vt* to pawn

2 empeñarse *vpr* (**a**) *(insistir)* to insist (**en** on), to be determined (**en** to) (**b**) *(endeudarse)* to get into debt

empeño *nm* (**a**) *(insistencia)* insistence; **poner e. en algo** to put a lot of effort into sth (**b**) *(deuda)* pledge; **casa de empeños** pawnshop

empeoramiento *nm* deterioration, worsening

empeorar 1 *vi* to deteriorate, to worsen

2 *vt* to make worse

3 empeorarse *vpr* to deteriorate, to worsen

empequeñecer [33] *vt Fig* to belittle

emperador *nm* emperor

emperatriz *nf* empress

emperifollarse *vpr Fam* to get dolled up

emperrarse *vpr* to dig one's heels in, to become stubborn

empezar [51] *vt & vi (a hacer algo)* to begin; *(algo)* to start, to commence

empinado,-a *adj (cuesta)* steep

empinar 1 *vt* to raise; *Fam* **e. el codo** to drink

2 empinarse *vpr (persona)* to stand on tiptoe

empírico,-a *adj* empirical

emplasto *nm* poultice

emplazamiento *nm* (**a**) *(colocación)* site, location (**b**) *Jur* summons *sing*

emplazar¹ [40] *vt* to locate, to situate

emplazar² [40] *vt* (**a**) *Jur* to summons (**b**) *(a una reunión etc)* to call

empleado,-a *nm,f* employee; *(de oficina, banco)* clerk; **empleada del hogar** servant, maid

emplear *vt* (**a**) *(usar)* to use; *(contratar)* to employ (**b**) *(dinero, tiempo)* to spend

empleo *nm* (**a**) *(oficio)* job; *Pol* employment (**b**) *(uso)* use; **modo de e.** instructions for use

emplomar *vt Am (diente)* to fill

empobrecer [33] **1** *vt* to impoverish

2 empobrecerse *vpr* to become impoverished *o* poor

empobrecimiento *nm* impoverishment

empollar vt (a) (huevos) to sit on (b) Fam (estudiar) to bone up on, Br to swot up

empollón,-ona nm,f Br Fam swot, US grind

empolvar 1 vt to cover in dust

2 empolvarse vpr (la cara) to powder

emponzoñar vt to poison

emporcar [44] vt to foul, to dirty

emporio nm (a) Com emporium, trading o commercial centre (b) Am department store

emporrarse vpr Fam to get high

empotrado,-a adj fitted

emprendedor,-a adj enterprising

emprender vt to undertake; Fam emprenderla con algn to pick on sb

empresa nf (a) Com & Ind firm, company; **e. punto com** dot com (company); **e. de trabajo temporal** temping agency (b) Pol **la libre e.** free enterprise (c) (tarea) undertaking

empresariado nm employers

empresarial adj (a) (de empresa) business; **(ciencias) empresariales** business studies (b) (espíritu) entrepreneurial; **organización e.** employers' organization

empresario,-a nm,f (a) (hombre) businessman; (mujer) businesswoman (b) (patrón) employer

empréstito nm Fin debenture loan

empujar vt to push, to shove

empuje nm push; Fig (brío) verve, get-up-and-go

empujón nm push, shove; **dar empujones** to push and shove

empuñadura nf (de espada) hilt

empuñar vt to grasp, to seize

emular vt to emulate

emulsión nf emulsion

en prep (a) (posición) in, on, at; **en Madrid/Bolivia** in Madrid/Bolivia; **en la mesa** on the table; **en el bolso** in the bag; **en casa/el trabajo** at home/work

(b) (movimiento) into; **entró en el cuarto** he went into the room

(c) (tiempo) in, on, at; **en 1940** in 1940; **en verano** in summer; Am **en la mañana** in the morning; **cae en martes** it falls on a Tuesday; **en ese momento** at that moment

(d) (transporte) by, in; **en coche/tren** by car/train; **en avión** by air

(e) (modo) **en español** in Spanish; **en broma** jokingly; **en serio** seriously

(f) (reducción, aumento) by; **los precios aumentaron en un diez por ciento** the prices went up by ten percent

(g) (tema, materia) at, in; **bueno en deportes** good at sports; **experto en política** expert in politics

(h) (división, separación) in; **lo dividió en tres partes** he divided it in three

(i) (con infinitivo) **fue rápido en responder** he was quick to answer; **la conocí en el andar** I recognized her by her walk; **ser sobrio en el vestir** to dress simply

enaguas nfpl underskirt, petticoat

enajenación nf, **enajenamiento** nm alienation; **e. mental** mental derangement, insanity

enajenar 1 vt (a) Jur to alienate (b) (turbar) to drive insane

2 enajenarse vpr (enloquecer) to go insane

enaltecer [33] vt (a) (alabar) to praise, to extol (b) (ennoblecer) to do credit to

enamorado,-a 1 adj in love

2 nm,f person in love

enamorar 1 vt to win the heart of

2 enamorarse vpr to fall in love (**de** with)

enano,-a adj & nm,f dwarf

enardecer [33] **1** vt (sentimientos) to rouse, to stir up; (persona) to fill with enthusiasm

2 enardecerse vpr Fig to become excited

encabezamiento nm (de carta) heading; (de periódico) headline; (préambulo) foreword, preamble

encabezar [40] vt (a) (carta, lista) to head; (periódico) to lead (b) (rebelión, carrera, movimiento) to lead

encabritarse vpr (a) (caballo) to rear (up) (b) Fig (persona) to get cross

encadenar vt to chain

encajar 1 vt (a) (ajustar) to insert; **e. la puerta** to push the door to (b) Fam (asimilar) to take (c) (comentario) to get in; **e. un golpe a algn** to land sb a blow

2 vi (a) (ajustarse) to fit (b) Fig **e. con** to fit (in) with, to square with

encaje nm lace

encalar vt to whitewash

encallar vi (a) Náut to run aground (b) Fig to flounder, to fail

encaminado,-a adj **estar bien/mal e.** to be on the right/wrong track

encaminar 1 vt to direct

2 encaminarse vpr to head (**a** for; **hacia** towards)

encandilar vt to dazzle

encantado,-a adj (a) (contento) delighted; **e. de conocerle** pleased to meet you (b) (embrujado) enchanted

encantador,-a 1 adj charming, delightful

2 nm,f magician

encantamiento nm spell

encantar *vt (hechizar)* to bewitch, to cast a spell on; *Fig* **me encanta nadar** I love swimming

encanto *nm* (a) *(atractivo)* charm; **ser un e.** to be charming (b) *(hechizo)* spell

encapricharse *vpr* **e. con** to set one's mind on; *(encariñarse)* to take a fancy to; *(enamorarse)* to get a crush on

encapuchado,-a *adj* hooded

encaramarse *vpr* to climb up

encarar 1 *vt* to face, to confront

2 encararse *vpr* **e. con** to face up to

encarcelar *vt* to imprison, to jail

encarecer [33] **1** *vt* to put up the price of

2 encarecerse *vpr* to go up (in price)

encarecidamente *adv* earnestly, insistently; **le rogamos e. que ...** we would earnestly request you to ...

encarecimiento *nm* increase *o* rise in price

encargado,-a 1 *nm,f Com (hombre)* manager; *(mujer)* manager, manageress; *(responsable)* person in charge

2 *adj* in charge

encargar [42] **1** *vt* (a) to put in charge of, to entrust with (b) *Com (mercancías)* to order, to place an order for; *(encuesta)* to commission

2 encargarse *vpr* **e. de** to see to, to deal with

encargo *nm* (a) *Com* order; **hecho de e.** *(a petición)* made to order (b) *(recado)* errand (c) *(tarea)* job, assignment

encariñarse *vpr* **e. con** to become fond of, to get attached to

encarnación *nf* incarnation, embodiment

encarnado,-a *adj (rojo)* red

encarnar *vt* to personify, to embody

encarnizado,-a *adj* fierce

encarrilar *vt (coche, tren)* to put on the road *o* rails; *Fig* to put on the right track

encasillar *vt* to pigeonhole

encausar *vt* to prosecute

encauzar [40] *vt* to channel

encenagarse [42] *vpr* to get covered in mud

encendedor *nm* lighter

encender [3] **1** *vt* (a) *(luz, radio, tele)* to switch on, to put on; *(cigarro, vela, fuego)* to light; *(cerilla)* to strike, to light (b) *Fig* to inflame, to stir up

2 encenderse *vpr* (a) *(fuego)* to catch; *(luz)* to go *o* come on (b) *(cara)* to blush, to go red

encendido *nm* ignition

encerado *nm (pizarra)* blackboard

encerar *vt* to wax, polish

encerrar [1] **1** *vt* (a) to shut in; *(con llave)* to lock in (b) *Fig (contener)* to contain, to include

2 encerrarse *vpr* to shut oneself up *o* in; *(con llave)* to lock oneself in

encestar *vi Dep* to score (a basket)

enchaquetado,-a *adj* smartly dressed

encharcar [44] **1** *vt* to flood, to swamp

2 encharcarse *vpr* to get flooded

enchilada *nf Culin* = stuffed corn tortilla seasoned with chilli

enchironar *vt Fam* to put away

enchufado,-a 1 *adj Fam* **estar e.** to have good connections *o* contacts

2 *nm,f Fam (favorito)* pet

enchufar *vt* (a) *Elec* to plug in (b) *(unir)* to join, to connect (c) *Fam (para un trabajo)* to pull strings for

enchufe *nm* (a) *Elec (hembra)* socket; *(macho)* plug (b) *Fam* contact

enchufismo *nm Fam* string-pulling

encía *nf* gum

enciclopedia *nf* encyclopedia

encierro *nm Pol (protesta)* sit-in

encima *adv* (a) on top; *(arriba)* above; *(en el aire)* overhead; **déjalo e.** put it on top; **¿llevas cambio e.?** do you have any change on you?; *Fig* **quitarse algo de e.** to get rid of sth; **ahí e.** up there (b) *(además)* besides (c) **e. de** *(sobre)* on; *(en el aire)* above; *Fig (además)* besides; **e. de la mesa** on the table (d) **por e.** above; *Fig* **por e. de sus posibilidades** beyond his abilities; **leer un libro por e.** to skip through a book

encimera *nf (de cocina)* worktop

encina *nf* holm oak

encinta *adj* pregnant

enclaustrarse *vpr* to shut oneself up

enclave *nm* enclave

enclenque *adj (débil)* puny; *(enfermizo)* sickly

encoger [53] **1** *vi (contraerse)* to contract; *(prenda)* to shrink

2 *vt* to contract; *(prenda)* to shrink

3 encogerse *vpr (contraerse)* to contract; *(prenda)* to shrink; **e. de hombros** to shrug (one's shoulders)

encolar *vt (papel)* to paste; *(madera)* to glue

encolerizar [40] **1** *vt* to infuriate, to anger

2 encolerizarse *vpr* to become furious

encomendar [1] **1** *vt* to entrust with, to put in charge of

2 encomendarse *vpr* **e. a** to entrust oneself to

encomienda nf (a) assignment, mission (b) (paquete postal) parcel

encomio nm praise

enconado,-a adj (a) (discusión) bitter, fierce (b) Med inflamed, sore

enconarse vpr (a) (exasperarse) to get angry o irritated (b) Med (herida) to become inflamed o sore

encono nm spitefulness, ill feeling

encontrado,-a adj (contrario) conflicting

encontrar [2] 1 vt (a) (hallar) to find; **no lo encuentro** I can't find it; **lo encuentro muy agradable** I find it very pleasant (b) (dar con) to meet; (problema) to run into, to come up against
2 encontrarse vpr (a) (persona) to meet (b) (sentirse) to feel, to be; **e. a gusto** to feel comfortable (c) (estar) to be

encontronazo nm (a) (choque) collision, crash (b) Fig (de ideas etc) clash

encorvar 1 vt to bend
2 encorvarse vpr to stoop o bend (over)

encrespar 1 vt (a) (pelo) to curl (b) (mar) to make choppy o rough (c) Fig (enfurecer) to infuriate
2 encresparse vpr (a) (mar) to get rough (b) Fig (enfurecerse) to get cross o irritated

encrucijada nf crossroads

encrudecer [33] vi, **encrudecerse** vpr to get worse

encuadernación nf (a) (oficio) bookbinding (b) (cubierta) binding

encuadernador,-a nm,f bookbinder

encuadernar vt to bind

encuadrar vt (a) (imagen etc) to frame (b) Fig (encajar) to fit, to insert

encuadre nm Cin & TV framing

encubierto,-a adj (secreto) hidden; (operación) covert

encubridor,-a nm,f Jur accessory (after the fact), abettor

encubrir vt to conceal

encuentro nm (a) encounter, meeting (b) Dep meeting, match; **e. amistoso** friendly (match)

encuesta nf (a) (sondeo) (opinion) poll, survey (b) (investigación) investigation, inquiry

encuestador,-a nm,f pollster

encuestar vt to poll

encumbrar 1 vt to exalt
2 encumbrarse vpr to rise to a high (social) position

ende: • **por ende** loc adv therefore

endeble adj weak, feeble

endeblez nf weakness, feebleness

endémico,-a adj Med endemic; Fig chronic

endemoniado,-a adj (a) (poseso) possessed (b) Fig (travieso) mischievous

enderezar [40] 1 vt (poner derecho) to straighten out; (poner vertical) to set upright
2 enderezarse vpr to straighten up

endeudarse vpr to get o fall into debt

endiablado,-a adj (a) (poseso) possessed (b) (travieso) mischievous, devilish

endibia nf endive

endiosar vt to deify

endomingarse [42] vpr Fam to put on one's Sunday best

endosar vt (a) (cheque) to endorse (b) Fam **e. algo a algn** (tarea) to lumber sb with sthg

endrina nf Bot sloe

endrogarse [42] vpr Am to take drugs, to use drugs

endulzar [40] vt to sweeten

endurecer [33] 1 vt to harden
2 endurecerse vpr to harden, to become hard

enebro nm juniper

enema nm enema

enemigo,-a 1 adj enemy; **soy e. de la bebida** I'm against drink
2 nm,f enemy

enemistad nf hostility, enmity

enemistar 1 vt to set at odds, to cause a rift between
2 enemistarse vpr to become enemies; **e. con algn** to fall out with sb

energético,-a adj energy

energía nf energy; **e. hidráulica/nuclear** hydro-electric/nuclear power; Fig **e. vital** vitality

enérgico,-a adj energetic; (decisión) firm; (tono) emphatic

energúmeno,-a nm,f Fam (hombre) madman; (mujer) mad woman; **ponerse como un e.** to go up the wall

enero nm January

enervante adj enervating

enervar vt to enervate

enésimo,-a adj (a) Mat nth (b) Fam umpteenth; **por enésima vez** for the umpteenth time

enfadado,-a adj (enojado) angry; (molesto) annoyed; **estamos enfadados** we've fallen out with each other

enfadar 1 vt to make angry o annoyed
2 enfadarse vpr (a) to get angry (con with) (b) (dos personas) to fall out

enfado nm anger; (desavenencia) fall-out

enfangarse [42] vpr to get muddy; Fig to

get involved (in dirty business)

énfasis nm inv emphasis, stress; **poner e. en algo** to lay stress on sth

enfático,-a adj emphatic

enfatizar [40] vt to emphasize, to stress

enfermar vi, **enfermarse** vpr to become o fall ill, to be taken ill

enfermedad nf illness; (contagiosa) disease

enfermería nf infirmary

enfermero,-a nm,f (mujer) nurse; (hombre) male nurse

enfermizo,-a adj unhealthy, sickly

enfermo,-a 1 adj ill; **caer e.** to be taken ill; Fam **esa gente me pone e.** those people make me sick
   2 nm,f ill person; (paciente) patient

enfervorizar [40] vt to enthuse

enfilar vi e. **hacia** to make for

enflaquecer [33] vt (adelgazar) to make thin; (debilitar) to weaken

enfocado,-a adj Fot **bien/mal enfocado** in/out of focus

enfocar [44] vt (a) (imagen) to focus; (persona) to focus on (b) (tema) to approach (c) (con linterna) to shine a light on

enfoque nm (a) focus; (acción) focusing (b) (de un tema) approach

enfrentamiento nm clash

enfrentar 1 vt (a) (situación, peligro) to confront (b) (enemistar) to set at odds
   2 enfrentarse vpr **a. e. con** o **a** to face up to, to confront (b) Dep **enfrentarse (a)** (rival) to meet

enfrente adv (a) opposite, facing; **la casa de e.** the house opposite o across the road (b) **e. de.** opposite (to), facing; **e. del colegio** opposite the school

enfriamiento nm (a) (proceso) cooling (b) Med (catarro) cold, chill

enfriar [29] 1 vt to cool (down), to chill
   2 vi to cool down
   3 enfriarse vpr (a) to get o go cold (b) (resfriarse) to get o catch a cold (c) Fig (pasión) to cool down

enfurecer [33] 1 vt to enrage, to infuriate
   2 enfurecerse vpr to get furious, to lose one's temper

enfurruñarse vpr Fam to sulk

engalanar 1 vt to deck out, to adorn
   2 engalanarse vpr to dress up, to get dressed up

enganchado,-a adj Fam **estar e.** (a la droga) to be hooked (on drugs)

enganchar 1 vt (a) to hook; Ferroc to couple (b) Fam (pillar) to nab
   2 engancharse vpr to get caught o

hooked; Fam (a la droga) to get hooked

enganche nm (gancho) hook; Ferroc coupling

engañabobos nm inv (persona) con man, confidence trickster; (truco) con trick

engañar 1 vt to deceive, to mislead; (estafar) to cheat, to trick; (mentir a) to lie to; (al marido, mujer) to be unfaithful to
   2 engañarse vpr to deceive oneself

engañifa nf Fam swindle

engaño nm (a) deceit; (estafa) fraud, swindle; (mentira) lie (b) (error) mistake, misunderstanding

engañoso,-a adj (palabras) deceitful; (apariencias) deceptive; (consejo) misleading

engarzar [40] vt (a) (unir) to link (b) (engastar) to mount, to set

engastar vt to set, to mount

engatusar vt Fam to coax; **e. a algn para que haga algo** to coax sb into doing sth

engendrar vt (a) Biol to engender (b) Fig to give rise to, to cause

engendro nm freak

englobar vt to include

engomar vt to gum, to glue

engordar 1 vt to fatten (up), to make fat
   2 vi (a) to put on weight, to get fat; **he engordado 3 kilos** I've put on 3 kilos (b) (comida, bebida) to be fattening

engorro nm Fam bother, nuisance

engorroso,-a adj Fam bothersome, tiresome

engranaje nm (a) Téc gearing (b) Fig machinery

engranar vt Téc to engage

engrandecer [33] vt to exalt

engrasar vt (a) (lubricar) to lubricate, to oil (b) (manchar) to make greasy, to stain with grease

engrase nm lubrication

engreído,-a adj vain, conceited

engreírse [56] vpr to become vain o conceited

engrosar [2] vt (incrementar) to enlarge; (cantidad) to increase, to swell

engrudo nm paste

enguatar vt to pad

engullir vt to gobble up

enharinar vt to cover with flour

enhebrar vt to thread

enhorabuena nf congratulations; **dar la e. a algn** to congratulate sb

enigma nm enigma

enigmático,-a adj enigmatic

enjabonar vt to soap

enjalbegar [42] vt to whitewash

enjambre *nm* swarm

enjaular *vt* (**a**) *(animal)* to cage (**b**) *Fam* to put inside, to put in jail

enjuagar [42] *vt* to rinse

enjuague *nm* rinse; **e. bucal** mouthwash

enjugar [42] *vt*, **enjugarse** *vpr* (**a**) *(secar)* to mop up; *(lágrimas)* to wipe away (**b**) *(deuda, déficit)* to clear, to wipe out

enjuiciamiento *nm* (**a**) *(opinión)* judgement (**b**) *Jur (civil)* lawsuit; *(criminal)* trial, prosecution

enjuiciar [43] *vt* (**a**) *(juzgar)* to judge, to examine (**b**) *Jur (criminal)* to indict, to prosecute

enjundia *nf Fig (sustancia)* substance; *(importancia)* importance

enjuto,-a *adj* lean, skinny

enlace *nm* (**a**) *(unión)* link, connection; **e. químico** chemical bond (**b**) *Ferroc* connection (**c**) *(casamiento)* marriage (**d**) *(persona)* liaison officer; **e. sindical** shop steward

enlatado,-a *adj* canned, tinned

enlatar *vt* to can, to tin

enlazar [40] *vt & vi* to link, to connect (**con** with)

enlodar *vt* (**a**) *(enfangar)* to muddy, to cover with mud (**b**) *Fig (reputación)* to stain, to besmirch

enloquecedor,-a *adj* maddening

enloquecer [33] **1** *vi* to go mad
  2 *vt* (**a**) *(volver loco)* to drive mad (**b**) *Fam* **me enloquecen las motos** I'm mad about motorbikes
  3 **enloquecerse** *vpr* to go mad, to go out of one's mind

enlosar *vt* to tile

enlucir [35] *vt (pared)* to plaster; *(plata, oro)* to polish

enlutado,-a *adj* in mourning

enmadrado,-a *adj* **estar e.** to be tied to one's mother's apron strings

enmarañar **1** *vt* (**a**) *(pelo)* to tangle (**b**) *Fig (complicar)* to complicate, confuse
  2 **enmarañarse** *vpr* (**a**) *(pelo)* to get tangled (**b**) *Fig (situación)* to get confused, to get into a mess *o* a muddle

enmarcar [44] *vt* to frame

enmascarar **1** *vt* (**a**) to mask (**b**) *(problema, la verdad)* to mask, to disguise
  2 **enmascararse** *vpr* to put on a mask

enmendar [1] **1** *vt (corregir)* to correct, to put right; *Jur* to amend
  2 **enmendarse** *vpr (persona)* to reform, to mend one's ways

enmienda *nf* correction; *Jur & Pol* amendment

enmohecerse [33] *vpr (metal)* to rust, to

get rusty; *Bot* to go mouldy

enmoquetar *vt* to carpet

enmudecer [33] *vi (callar)* to fall silent; *Fig* to be dumbstruck

ennegrecer [33] *vt*, **ennegrecerse** *vpr* to blacken, to turn black

ennoblecer *vt* to ennoble

enojadizo,-a *adj* irritable, touchy

enojado,-a *adj (enojado)* angry; *(molesto)* annoyed;

enojar **1** *vt* to anger, to annoy
  2 **enojarse** *vpr* to get angry, to lose one's temper

enojo *nm* anger, annoyance

enorgullecer [33] **1** *vt* to fill with pride
  2 **enorgullecerse** *vpr* to be *o* feel proud (**de** of)

enorme *adj* enormous

enormidad *nf* enormity; *Fam* **una e.** loads

enraizado,-a *adj* rooted

enraizar [40] *vi*, **enraizarse** *vpr (persona)* to put down roots; *(planta, costumbre)* to take root

enrarecerse [33] *vpr (aire)* to become rarefied

enredadera *nf* climbing plant, creeper

enredar **1** *vt* (**a**) *(pelo)* to entangle, to tangle up (**b**) *Fig (asunto)* to confuse, to complicate (**c**) *Fig (implicar)* to involve (**en** in) (**d**) *(confundir)* to mix up
  2 **enredarse** *vpr* (**a**) *(pelo)* to get entangled, to get tangled (up) *o* in a tangle (**b**) *Fig (asunto)* to get complicated *o* confused (**c**) *Fig* **e. con** *(involucrarse)* to get involved with (**d**) *(confundirse)* to get mixed up

enredo *nm* (**a**) *(maraña)* tangle (**b**) *Fig (lío)* muddle, mess

enrejado *nm (de ventana)* lattice

enrevesado,-a *adj* complicated, difficult

enriquecer [33] **1** *vt* to make rich; *Fig* to enrich
  2 **enriquecerse** *vpr* to get *o* become rich, to prosper; *Fig* to become enriched

enrocar [44] *vi (en ajedrez)* to castle

enrojecer [33] **1** *vt* to redden, to turn red
  2 *vi (ruborizarse)* to blush
  3 **enrojecerse** *vpr* to blush

enrolarse *vpr* to enrol, to sign on; *Mil* to enlist, to join up

enrollado,-a *adj* (**a**) rolled up (**b**) *(persona)* great (**c**) *Fam* **estar e. con algn** *(estar saliendo con)* to go out with sb

enrollar **1** *vt* to roll up; *(cable)* to coil; *(hilo)* to wind up
  2 **enrollarse** *vpr* (**a**) *Fam (hablar)* to chatter, to go on and on (**b**) *Fam* **e. con**

algn *(tener relaciones)* to have an affair with sb

> 🖉 Observa que el verbo inglés **to enrol** es un falso amigo y no es la traducción del verbo español **enrollar**. En inglés, **to enrol** significa "matricular, inscribir".

enroque *nm (en ajedrez)* castling

enroscar [44] 1 *vt* (a) to coil (round), to wind (b) *(tornillo, tapón)* to screw in o on
  2 enroscarse *vpr* to coil, to wind

ensaimada *nf* = kind of spiral pastry from Majorca

ensalada *nf* salad

ensaladera *nf* salad bowl

ensaladilla *nf* **e. rusa** Russian salad

ensalzar [40] *vt (enaltecer)* to exalt; *(elogiar)* to praise, to extol

ensamblador *nm Informát* assembler

ensamblaje *nm Téc* assembly

ensamblar *vt* to assemble

ensanchar 1 *vt* to enlarge, to widen; *Cost* to let out
  2 ensancharse *vpr* to get wider

ensanche *nm* enlargement, widening; *(de ciudad)* urban development

ensangrentado,-a *adj* bloodstained, covered in blood

ensangrentar [1] *vt* to stain with blood, to cover in blood

ensañarse *vpr* **e. con** to be brutal with; *(cebarse)* to delight in tormenting

ensartar *vt* (a) *(perlas etc)* to string together (b) *(mentiras etc)* to reel off, to rattle off

ensayar *vt* to test, to try out; *Teatro* to rehearse; *Mús* to practise

ensayista *nmf* essayist

ensayo *nm* (a) *(prueba)* test, trial (b) *Teatro* rehearsal; **e. general** dress rehearsal (c) *(escrito)* essay

enseguida, en seguida *adv (inmediatamente)* at once, straight away; *(poco después)* in a minute, soon; **e. voy** I'll be right there

ensenada *nf* inlet, cove

enseña *nf* ensign, standard

enseñanza *nf* (a) *(educación)* education (b) *(de idioma etc)* teaching (c) **enseñanzas** teachings

enseñar *vt* (a) to teach; **e. a algn a hacer algo** to teach sb how to do sth (b) *(mostrar)* to show; *(señalar)* to point out

enseres *nmpl (bártulos)* belongings, goods; *(de trabajo)* tools

ensillar *vt* to saddle (up)

ensimismado,-a *adj (en la lectura etc)* engrossed; *(abstraído)* lost in thought

ensimismarse *vpr (en la lectura etc)* to become engrossed; *(abstraerse)* to be lost in thought

ensombrecer [33] 1 *vt* to cast a shadow over
  2 ensombrecerse *vpr* to darken

ensopar *vt Am* to soak

ensordecedor,-a *adj* deafening

ensordecer [33] 1 *vt* to deafen
  2 *vi* to go deaf

ensortijado,-a *adj* curly

ensuciar [43] 1 *vt* (a) to get dirty (b) *Fig (reputación)* to harm, to damage
  2 ensuciarse *vpr* to get dirty

ensueño *nm* dream; **una casa de e.** a dream house

entablado *nm* (a) *(entarimado)* planking, planks (b) *(suelo)* wooden floor

entablar *vt* (a) *(conversación)* to open, to begin; *(amistad)* to strike up; *(negocios)* to start (b) *(en juegos de tablero)* to set up (c) *(pleito)* to initiate

entablillar *vt Med* to splint

entallado,-a *adj (vestido)* close-fitting; *(camisa)* fitted

entallar 1 *vt* to take in at the waist
  2 *vi* to fit at the waist

entarimado *nm* parquet floor

entarimar *vt* to cover with parquet

ente *nm* (a) *(institución)* organization, body; **e. público** public service organization (b) *(ser)* being

entendederas *nfpl Fam* brains; **ser duro de e.** to be slow on the uptake

entender [3] 1 *vt (comprender)* to understand; **a mi e.** to my way of thinking; **dar a algn a e. que ...** to give sb to understand that ...
  2 *vi* (a) *(comprender)* to understand (b) **e. de** *(saber)* to know about
  3 entenderse *vpr* (a) *(comprenderse)* to be understood, to be meant (b) *Fam* **e. (bien) con** to get on (well) with

entendido,-a 1 *nm,f* expert
  2 *adj* **tengo e. que ...** I understand that ...

entendimiento *nm* understanding

enterado,-a 1 *adj* knowledgeable, well-informed; **estar e.** to be in the know; **estar e. de ...** to be aware of ...
  2 *nm,f (listillo)* know-all

enteramente *adv* entirely, completely

enterar 1 *vt* to inform (**b** *about* o of)
  2 enterarse *vpr* to find out; **me he enterado de que ...** I understand ...; **ni me enteré** I didn't even realize it

entereza *nf* strength of character

enternecedor,-a *adj* moving, touching

enternecer [33] 1 *vt* to move, to touch

2 enternecerse *vpr* to be moved *o* touched

entero,-a 1 *adj* (**a**) *(completo)* entire, whole; **por e.** completely (**b**) *Fig (íntegro)* honest, upright (**c**) *Fig (firme)* strong

2 *nm* (**a**) *Mat* whole number (**b**) *Fin* point

enterrador *nm* gravedigger

enterramiento *nm* burial

enterrar [1] *vt* to bury

entidad *nf* organization; **e. comercial** company, firm

entierro *nm* (**a**) burial (**b**) *(ceremonia)* funeral

entomología *nf* entomology

entonación *nf* intonation

entonar 1 *vt* (**a**) *(canto)* to sing (**b**) *Med* to tone up

2 *vi* to be in harmony, to be in tune (**con** with)

entonces *adv* then; **por aquel e.** at that time; **el e. ministro** the then minister

entornar *vt (ojos etc)* to half-close; *(puerta)* to leave ajar

entorno *nm* environment

entorpecer [33] *vt (obstaculizar)* to hinder, to impede

entrada *nf* (**a**) entrance (**b**) *(billete)* ticket; *(recaudación)* takings (**c**) **de e.** for a start (**d**) *Culin* entrée (**e**) *Com* entry; *(pago inicial)* down payment, deposit; **e. de capital** capital inflow (**f**) *Com* **entradas** *(ingresos)* receipts, takings (**g**) *(en la frente)* receding hairline

entrado,-a *adj* **e. en años** advanced in years; **hasta bien entrada la noche** well into the night

entramado *nm* framework; *(de sistema etc)* network

entramparse *vpr Fam* to get into debt

entrante 1 *adj* coming; **el mes e.** next month; **el ministro e.** the incoming minister

2 *Culin* starter

entrañable *adj* (**a**) *(lugar)* intimate, close (**b**) *(persona)* affectionate, warmhearted

entrañar *vt* to entail

entrañas *nfpl* bowels

entrar 1 *vi* (**a**) to come in, to go in, to enter; *Fig* **no me entran las matemáticas** I can't get the hang of maths (**b**) *(encajar)* to fit (**c**) **el año que entra** next year, the coming year (**d**) *(venir)* to come over; **me entró dolor de cabeza** I got a headache; **me entraron ganas de reír** I felt like laughing

2 *vt* (**a**) to introduce (**b**) *Informát* to enter

entre *prep* (**a**) *(dos)* between (**b**) *(más de dos)* among(st)

entreabierto,-a *adj (ojos etc)* half-open; *(puerta)* ajar

entreacto *nm* interval, intermission

entrecejo *nm* space between the eyebrows; **fruncir el e.** to frown, to knit one's brow

entrecortado,-a *adj (voz)* faltering, hesitant

entrecot *nm* fillet steak

entrecruzar [40] *vt*, **entrecruzarse** *vpr* to entwine

entredicho *nm* (**a**) *Jur* injunction (**b**) **estar en e.** to be suspect; **poner algo en e.** to bring sth into question

entrega *nf* (**a**) *(de productos)* delivery; *(de premios)* presentation (**b**) *(fascículo)* part, instalment (**c**) *(devoción)* selflessness

entregar [42] **1** *vt* to hand over; *(deberes etc)* to give in, to hand in; *Com* to deliver

2 entregarse *vpr* (**a**) *(rendirse)* to give in, to surrender (**b**) **e. a** to devote oneself to; *Pey* to indulge in

entreguismo *nm Pol* appeasement

entrelazar [40] *vt*, **entrelazarse** *vpr* to entwine

entremedias *adv* in between; *(mientras tanto)* meanwhile, in the meantime

entremés *nm Culin* hors d'oeuvres

entremeterse *vpr* = entrometerse

entremezclarse *vpr* to mix, to mingle

entrenador,-a *nm,f* trainer, coach

entrenamiento *nm* training

entrenar *vi*, **entrenarse** *vpr* to train

entrepierna *nf* crotch, crutch

entresacar [44] *vt* to pick out, to select

entresijos *nmpl* nooks and crannies

entresuelo *nm* mezzanine

entretanto 1 *adv* meanwhile

2 *nm* **en el e.** in the meantime

entretejer *vt* to interweave

entretención *nf Am* amusement, entertainment

entretener [24] **1** *vt* (**a**) *(divertir)* to entertain, to amuse (**b**) *(retrasar)* to delay; *(detener)* to hold up, to detain

2 entretenerse *vpr* (**a**) *(distraerse)* to amuse oneself, to while away the time (**b**) *(retrasarse)* to be delayed, to be held up

entretenido,-a *adj* enjoyable, entertaining

entretenimiento *nm* entertainment, amusement

entretiempo: •de entretiempo *loc adj* **ropa de e.** lightweight clothing

entrever [28] *vt* to glimpse, to catch sight of; *Fig* **dejó e. que ...** she hinted that ...

entrevista *nf* interview

entrevistador,-a *nm,f* interviewer

entrevistar 1 *vt* to interview

2 entrevistarse *upr* **e. con algn** to have an interview with sb

entristecer [33] 1 *vt* to sadden, to make sad

2 entristecerse *upr* to be sad (**por** about)

entrometerse *upr* to meddle, to interfere (**en** in)

entrometido,-a 1 *nm,f* meddler, busybody

2 *adj* interfering

entroncar *vi* to connect

entumecer [33] 1 *vt* to numb

2 entumecerse *upr* to go numb

entumecido,-a *adj* numb

enturbiar [43] 1 *vt* (**a**) *(agua)* to make cloudy (**b**) *Fig (asunto)* to cloud, to obscure

2 enturbiarse *upr* to become cloudy

entusiasmar 1 *vt* to fill with enthusiasm

2 entusiasmarse *upr* to get excited *o* enthusiastic (**con** about)

entusiasmo *nm* enthusiasm; **con e.** enthusiastically

entusiasta 1 *adj* enthusiastic, keen (**de** on)

2 *nmf* enthusiast

enumerar *vt* to enumerate

enunciado *nm* *(de teoría, problema)* wording

envainar *vt* to sheathe

envanecer [33] 1 *vt* to make proud *o* vain

2 envanecerse *upr* to become conceited *o* proud, to give oneself airs

envasado,-a 1 *nm* *(en botella)* bottling; *(en paquete)* packing; *(en lata)* canning

2 *adj* **e. al vacío** vacuum-packed

envasar *vt* *(embotellar)* to bottle; *(empaquetar)* to pack; *(enlatar)* to can, to tin

envase *nm* (**a**) *(acto)* packing; *(de botella)* bottling; *(de lata)* canning (**b**) *(recipiente)* container (**c**) *(botella vacía)* empty

envejecer [33] 1 *vi* to grow old

2 *vt* to age

envejecimiento *nm* ageing

envenenar *vt* to poison

envergadura *nf* (**a**) *(importancia)* importance, scope; **de gran e.** large-scale (**b**) *(de pájaro, avión)* span, wingspan; *Náut* breadth (of sail)

envés *nm* other side

envestidura *nf* investiture

enviado,-a *nm,f* envoy; *Prensa* **e.** especial special correspondent

enviar [29] *vt* to send

enviciarse [43] *upr* to become addicted (**con** to)

envidia *nf* envy; **tener e. de algn** to envy sb

envidiable *adj* enviable

envidiar [43] *vt* to envy; **no tener nada que e.** to be in no way inferior (**a** to)

envidioso,-a *adj* envious

> 🖉 Observa que la palabra inglesa **invidious** es un falso amigo y no es la traducción de la palabra española **envidioso**. En inglés, **invidious** significa "ingrato" o "injusto".

envilecer [33] *vt* to degrade, to debase

envío *nm* sending; *(remesa)* consignment; *(paquete)* parcel; **gastos de e.** postage and packing; **e. contra reembolso** cash on delivery

enviudar *vi (hombre)* to become a widower, to lose one's wife; *(mujer)* to become a widow, to lose one's husband

envoltorio *nm*, **envoltura** *nf* wrapper, wrapping

envolver [4] *(pp* **envuelto)** **1** *vt* (**a**) *(con papel)* to wrap (**b**) *(cubrir)* to envelop (**c**) *(en complot etc)* to involve (**en** in)

2 envolverse *upr* (**a**) to wrap oneself up (**en** in) (**b**) *(implicarse)* to become involved (**en** in)

enyesar *vt* to plaster; *Med* to put in plaster

enzima *nf* enzyme

épica *nf* epic poetry

epicentro *nm* epicentre

épico,-a *adj* epic

epidemia *nf* epidemic

epilepsia *nf* epilepsy

epílogo *nm* epilogue

episcopal *adj* episcopal

episodio *nm* episode

epístola *nf* epistle

epitafio *nm* epitaph

epíteto *nm* epithet

época *nf* time; *Hist* period, epoch; *Agr* season; **en esta é. del año** at this time of the year; **hacer é.** to be a landmark; **mueble de é.** period furniture

equidad *nf* equity

equilátero *nm* equilateral

equilibrar *vt* to balance

equilibrio *nm* balance

equilibrismo *nm* balancing act

equilibrista *nmf* (**a**) tightrope walker (**b**) *Am Pol* opportunist

equipaje *nm* luggage; **hacer el e.** to pack, do the packing

equipar *vt* to equip, to furnish (**con** *o* **de** with)

equiparable *adj* comparable (**a** to; **con** with)

equiparar *vt* to compare (**con** with), to liken (**con** to)

equipo *nm* (**a**) *(de expertos, jugadores)* team (**b**) *(aparatos)* equipment; **e. de alta fidelidad** hi-fi stereo system (**c**) *(ropas)* outfit

equis *nf* = name of the letter X in Spanish

equitación *nf* horse *o* US horseback riding

equitativo,-a *adj* equitable, fair

equivalente *adj* equivalent

equivaler [26] *vi* to be equivalent (**a** to)

equivocación *nf* error, mistake

equivocado,-a *adj* mistaken, wrong

equivocar [44] **1** *vt* to mix up

2 equivocarse *vpr* to make a mistake; *Tel* **se equivocó de número** he dialled the wrong number; **se equivocó de fecha** he got the wrong date

equívoco,-a 1 *adj* equivocal, misleading

2 *nm* misunderstanding

era¹ *nf (época)* era, age

era² *nf Agr* threshing floor

era³ *pt indef de* **ser**

erario *nm* exchequer, treasury

eras *pt indef de* **ser**

erección *nf* erection

erecto,-a *adj* upright; *(pene)* erect

eres *indic pres de* **ser**

erguir [55] **1** *vt* to erect

2 erguirse *vpr* to straighten up, to stand/ sit up straight

erial *nm* uncultivated land

erigir [57] **1** *vt* to erect

2 erigirse *vpr* **e. en algo** to set oneself up in sth

erizado,-a *adj* bristly, prickly

erizarse [40] *vpr* to bristle, to stand on end

erizo *nm* hedgehog; **e. de mar** *o* **marino** sea urchin

ermita *nf* hermitage

📙 Observa que la palabra inglesa **hermit** es un falso amigo y no es la traducción de la palabra española **ermita**. En inglés, **hermit** significa "ermitaño".

ermitaño,-a *nm,f* hermit

erosión *nf* erosion

erosionar *vt* to erode

erótico,-a *adj* erotic

erotismo *nm* eroticism

erradicar [44] *vt* to eradicate

errante *adj* wandering

errar [50] **1** *vt* to miss, to get wrong

2 *vi* (**a**) *(vagar)* to wander, to roam (**b**) *(fallar)* to err

errata *nf* erratum, misprint

erre *nf* **e. que e.** stubbornly, pigheadedly

erróneo,-a *adj* erroneous, wrong

error *nm* error, mistake; *Informát* bug; **por e.** by mistake, in error; *Impr* **e. de imprenta** misprint; **caer en un e.** to make a mistake

Ertzaintza *nf* = Basque police force

eructar *vi* to belch, to burp

eructo *nm* belch, burp

erudición *nf* erudition

erudito,-a 1 *adj* erudite, learned

2 *nm,f* scholar

erupción *nf* (**a**) *(de volcán)* eruption (**b**) *(en la piel)* rash

es *indic pres de* **ser**

esa *adj dem ver* **ese**

ésa *pron dem ver* **ése**

esbelto,-a *adj* slender

esbirro *nm* henchman

esbozar [40] *vt* to sketch, to outline

esbozo *nm* sketch, outline, rough draft

escabeche *nm* brine

escabechina *nf* massacre

escabroso,-a *adj* (**a**) *(espinoso)* tricky (**b**) *(indecente)* crude

escabullirse *vpr* to slip away, to scuttle *o* scurry off

escacharrar *vt Fam* to break

escafandra *nf* diving suit; **e. espacial** spacesuit

escala *nf* (**a**) scale; *(de colores)* range; **e. musical** scale; **en gran e.** on a large scale (**b**) *(parada) Náut* port of call; *Av* stopover; **hacer e. en** to call in at, to stop over in (**c**) *(escalera)* ladder, stepladder

escalada *nf* (**a**) climb (**b**) *Fig (de violencia)* escalation; *(de precios)* rise

escalador,-a *nm,f* climber, mountaineer

📙 Observa que la palabra inglesa **escalator** es un falso amigo y no es la traducción de la palabra española **escalador**. En inglés, **escalator** significa "escalera mecánica".

escalafón *nm (graduación)* rank; *(de salarios)* salary *o* wage scale

escalar *vt* to climb, to scale

escaldar *vt* to scald

escalera *nf* (**a**) stair; **e. de incendios** fire escape; **e. mecánica** escalator; **e. de caracol** spiral staircase (**b**) *(escala)* ladder (**c**) *Naipes* run

escalerilla *nf (de piscina)* steps; *Náut* gangway; *Av* (boarding) ramp

escalfar *vt* to poach

escalinata *nf* stoop

escalofriante *adj* hair-raising, blood-curdling

escalofrío *nm* shiver; **me dio un e.** it gave me the shivers

escalón *nm* step; **e. lateral** *(en letrero)* ramp

escalonar *vt* to place at intervals, to space out

escalope *nm* escalope

escalpelo *nm* scalpel

escama *nf Zool* scale; *(de jabón)* flake

escamarse *upr* to smell a rat, to become suspicious

escamotear *vt Fam* to diddle out of, to do out of

escampar *vi* to stop raining, to clear up

escanciar [43] *vt (vino)* to pour out, to serve

escandalizar [40] **1** *vt* to scandalize, to shock

2 escandalizarse *upr* to be shocked (**de** at *o* by)

escándalo *nm* (**a**) *(alboroto)* racket, din; **armar un e.** to kick up a fuss (**b**) *(desvergüenza)* scandal

escandaloso,-a *adj* (**a**) *(ruidoso)* noisy, rowdy (**b**) *(ofensivo)* scandalous

Escandinavia *n* Scandinavia

escandinavo,-a *adj & nm,f* Scandinavian

escáner *nm Med & Informát* scanner

escaño *nm Parl* seat

escapada *nf* (**a**) *(de prisión)* escape; *(en ciclismo)* breakaway (**b**) *(viaje rápido)* flying visit, quick trip

> 🔈 Observa que la palabra inglesa **escapade** es un falso amigo y no es la traducción de la palabra española **escapada**. En inglés, **escapade** significa "aventura".

escapar 1 *vi* to escape, to run away

2 escaparse *upr* (**a**) to escape, to run away; **se me escapó de las manos** it slipped out of my hands; **se me escapó el tren** I missed the train (**b**) *(gas etc)* to leak, to escape

escaparate *nm* shop window

escapatoria *nf* escape; **no tener e.** to have no way out

escape *nm* (**a**) *(de gas etc)* leak, escape (**b**) *Téc* exhaust; **tubo de e.** exhaust (pipe) (**c**) *(huida)* escape; *(escapatoria)* way out

escaquearse *upr Fam* to duck out; **e. de hacer algo** to worm one's way out of doing sth

escarabajo *nm* beetle

escaramuza *nf Mil* skirmish; *Fig (riña)* squabble, brush

escarbar *vt* (**a**) *(suelo)* to scratch; *(fuego)* to poke (**b**) *Fig* to inquire into, to investigate

escarceo *nm* attempt

escarcha *nf* hoarfrost, frost

escarchado,-a *adj (fruta)* crystallized, candied

escardar *vt* to hoe

escardillo *nm* weeding hoe

escarlata *adj* scarlet

escarlatina *nf* scarlet fever

escarmentar [1] *vi* to learn one's lesson

escarmiento *nm* punishment, lesson

escarnio *nm* derision, mockery

escarola *nf* curly endive

escarpado,-a *adj (paisaje)* craggy; *(pendiente)* steep

escasear *vi* to be scarce

escasez *nf* scarcity

escaso,-a *adj* scarce; *(dinero)* tight; *(conocimientos)* scant; **e. de dinero** short of money

escatimar *vt* to skimp on; **no escatimó esfuerzos para ...** he spared no efforts to ...

escayola *nf* (**a**) plaster of Paris, stucco (**b**) *Med* plaster

escayolar *vt Med* to put in plaster

escena *nf* (**a**) scene (**b**) *(escenario)* stage; **poner en e.** to stage

escenario *nm* (**a**) *Teatro* stage (**b**) *(entorno)* scenario; *(de crimen)* scene; *(de película)* setting

escénico,-a *adj* scenic

escenografía *nf Cin* set design; *Teatro* stage design

escepticismo *nm* scepticism

escéptico,-a *adj & nm,f* sceptic

escindirse *upr* to split (off) (**en** into)

escisión *nf* split

esclarecer [33] *vt* to shed light on

esclava *nf* bangle

esclavitud *nf* slavery

esclavizar [40] *vt* to enslave

esclavo,-a *adj & nm,f* slave

esclusa *nf* lock, sluicegate

escoba *nf* brush, broom

escocer [41] **1** *vi* to sting, to smart

2 escocerse *upr (piel)* to chafe

escocés,-esa 1 *adj* Scottish, Scots; **falda escocesa** kilt

2 *nm,f (hombre)* Scotsman; *(mujer)* Scotswoman

Escocia *n* Scotland

escoger [53] *vt* to choose

escogido,-a *adj* chosen, selected;

(producto) choice, select; *Lit* **obras esco- gidas** selected works

escolar 1 *adj (curso, año)* school

2 *nmf (niño)* schoolboy; *(niña)* school- girl

escolaridad *nf* schooling

escollo *nm* reef; *Fig* pitfall

escolta *nf* escort

escoltar *vt* to escort

escombros *nmpl* rubbish, debris

esconder 1 *vt* to hide (**de** from), to conceal (**de** from)

2 esconderse *vpr* to hide (**de** from)

escondidas *adv* **a e.** secretly

escondite *nm* (**a**) *(lugar)* hiding place, hide-out (**b**) *(juego)* hide-and-seek

escondrijo *nm* hiding place, hide-out

escopeta *nf* shotgun; **e. de aire compri- mido** air gun; **e. de cañones recortados** sawn-off shotgun

escopetazo *nm* gunshot

escorbuto *nm* scurvy

escoria *nf* (**a**) *(de metal)* slag (**b**) *Fig* scum, dregs

Escorpio *nm* Scorpio

escorpión *nm* scorpion

escotado,-a *adj* low-cut

escote *nm* low neckline

escotilla *nf* hatch, hatchway

escozor *nm* stinging, smarting

escribiente *nmf* clerk

escribir *(pp escrito)* **1** *vt* to write; **e. a mano** to write in longhand; **e. a máquina** to type

2 escribirse *vpr* (**a**) *(dos personas)* to write to each other, to correspond (**b**) **se escribe con h** it is spelt with an h

escrito,-a 1 *adj* written; **e. a mano** hand- written, in longhand; **por e.** in writing

2 *nm* writing

escritor,-a *nm,f* writer

escritorio *nm* (**a**) *(mueble)* writing desk, bureau; *(oficina)* office (**b**) *Informát* desktop

escritura *nf* (**a**) *Jur* deed, document; **e. de propiedad** title deed (**b**) *Rel* **Sagradas Escrituras** Holy Scriptures

escrúpulo *nm* (**a**) scruple; **una persona sin escrúpulos** an unscrupulous person (**b**) *(esmero)* care (**c**) **me da e.** *(asco)* it makes me feel squeamish

escrupuloso,-a *adj* (**a**) *(honesto)* scru- pulous (**b**) *(meticuloso)* painstaking (**c**) *(delicado)* squeamish

escrutar *vt* (**a**) to scrutinize (**b**) *(votos)* to count

escrutinio *nm* (**a**) scrutiny (**b**) *(de votos)* count

escuadra *nf* (**a**) *(instrumento)* square (**b**) *Mil* squad; *Náut* squadron; *Dep* team; *(de coches)* fleet

escuadrilla *nf Náut* squadron

escuadrón *nm Av* squadron

escuálido,-a *adj* emaciated

escucha *nf* listening; **escuchas telefóni- cas** phone tapping; **estar a la e. de** to be listening out for

escuchar 1 *vt* to listen to; *(oír)* to hear

2 *vi* to listen; *(oír)* to hear

escudarse *vpr Fig* **e. en algo** to hide behind sth

escudería *nf* motor racing team

escudilla *nf* bowl

escudo *nm* (**a**) *(arma defensiva)* shield (**b**) *(blasón)* coat of arms

escudriñar *vt* to scrutinize

escuela *nf* school; **e. de Bellas Artes** Art School; **e. de conducir/de idiomas** driv- ing/language school

escueto,-a *adj* plain, unadorned

escuezo *indic pres de* **escocer**

esculcar [44] *vt Am* to search

esculpir *vt* to sculpt; *(madera)* to carve; *(metal)* to engrave

escultor,-a *nm,f (hombre)* sculptor; *(mu- jer)* sculptress; *(de madera)* woodcarver; *(de metales)* engraver

escultura *nf* sculpture

escultural *adj* sculptural; *(persona)* sta- tuesque

escupidera *nf* (**a**) *(recipiente)* spittoon (**b**) *(orinal)* chamberpot

escupir 1 *vi* to spit

2 *vt* to spit out

escupitajo *nm Fam* spit

escurreplatos *nm inv* dish rack

escurridizo,-a *adj* (**a**) *(resbaladizo)* slip- pery (**b**) *Fig (huidizo)* elusive, slippery

escurridor *nm* colander; *(escurreplatos)* dish rack

escurrir 1 *vt (plato, vaso)* to drain; *(ropa)* to wring out; **e. el bulto** to wriggle out

2 escurrirse *vpr* (**a**) *(platos etc)* to drip (**b**) *(escaparse)* to run *o* slip away (**c**) *(resbalarse)* to slip

escúter *nm* (motor) scooter

ese,-a *adj dem* (**a**) that (**b**) **esos,-as** those

ése,-a *pron dem m,f* (**a**) that one (**b**) **ésos, -as** those (ones); *Fam* **¡ni por ésas!** no way!; *Fam* **¡no me vengas con ésas!** come off it!

Note that **ése** and its various forms can be written without an accent when there is no risk of confusion with the adjective.

esencia *nf* essence

esencial *adj* essential; **lo e.** the main thing

esencialmente *adv* essentially

esfera *nf* (a) sphere; *Fig* sphere, field (b) *(de reloj de pulsera)* dial; *(de reloj de pared)* face

esférico,-a 1 *adj* spherical
  2 *nm (balón)* ball

esfinge *nf* sphinx

esforzarse [2] *upr* to make an effort (**por** to)

esfuerzo *nm* effort

esfumarse *upr Fam* to beat it

esgrima *nf Dep* fencing

esgrimir *vt* to wield

esguince *nm* sprain

eslabón *nm* link

eslavo,-a 1 *adj* Slav, Slavonic
  2 *nm,f (persona)* Slav
  3 *nm (idioma)* Slavonic

eslip *nm* (*pl* **eslips**) men's briefs, underpants

eslogan *nm* (*pl* **eslóganes**) slogan; **e. publicitario** advertising slogan

eslora *nf Náut* length

eslovaco,-a 1 *adj & nm,f* Slovak, Slovakian
  2 *nm (idioma)* Slovak

Eslovaquia *n* Slovakia

Eslovenia *n* Slovenia

esloveno,-a 1 *adj & nm,f* Slovene
  2 *nm (idioma)* Slovene

esmaltar *vt* to enamel

esmalte *nm* enamel; *(de uñas)* nail polish *o* varnish

esmerado,-a *adj* painstaking, careful

esmeralda *nf* emerald

esmerarse *upr* to be careful; *(esforzarse)* to go to great lengths

esmero *nm* great care

esmoquin *nm* (*pl* **esmóquines**) dinner jacket, *US* tuxedo

esnifar *vt Fam (drogas)* to sniff

esnob (*pl* **esnobs**) **1** *adj (persona)* snobbish; *(restaurante etc)* posh
  2 *nmf* snob

esnobismo *nm* snobbery, snobbishness

ESO *nf* (*abr* **Enseñanza Secundaria Obligatoria**) = mainstream secondary education in Spain for pupils aged 12-16

eso *pron neut* that; **¡e. es!** that's it!; **por e.** that's why; *Fam* **a e. de las diez** around ten; *Fam* **e. de las Navidades sale muy caro** this whole Christmas thing costs a fortune

esófago *nm* oesophagus

esos,-as *adj dem pl ver* **ese,-a**

ésos,-as *pron dem m,fpl ver* **ése,-a**

esotérico,-a *adj* esoteric

espabilado,-a *adj* (a) *(despierto)* wide awake (b) *(niño)* bright

espabilar 1 *vt* to wake up
  2 espabilarse *upr* to wake up, to waken up

espachurrar *vt* to squash

espacial *adj* spatial, spacial; **nave e.** space ship

espaciar [43] *vt* to space out

espacio *nm* (a) space; *(de tiempo)* length; **a doble e.** double-spaced (b) *Rad & TV* programme

espacioso,-a *adj* spacious, roomy

espada 1 *nf* (a) sword; **estar entre la e. y la pared** to be between the devil and the deep blue sea; **pez e.** swordfish (b) *Naipes* spade
  2 *nm Taurom* matador

> ♪ Observa que la palabra inglesa **spade** es un falso amigo y no es la traducción de la palabra española **espada**. En inglés, **spade** significa "pala".

espadaña *nf* belfry

espaguetis *nmpl* spaghetti

espalda *nf* (a) *Anat* back; **espaldas** back; **a espaldas de algn** behind sb's back; **por la e.** from behind; **volver la e. a algn** to turn one's back on sb; *Fam* **e. mojada** wetback (b) *(en natación)* backstroke

espaldar *nm (de silla)* back

espaldilla *nf* shoulder blade

espantapájaros *nm inv* scarecrow

espantar 1 *vt* (a) *(asustar)* to frighten, to scare (b) *(ahuyentar)* to frighten away
  2 espantarse *upr* to get *o* feel frightened (**de** of), to get *o* feel scared (**de** of)

espanto *nm* fright; *Fam* **de e.** dreadful, shocking

espantoso,-a *adj* dreadful

España *n* Spain

español,-a 1 *adj* Spanish
  2 *nm,f* Spaniard; **los españoles** the Spanish
  3 *nm (idioma)* Spanish

esparadrapo *nm* sticking plaster

esparcimiento *nm (relajación)* relaxation

esparcir [52] 1 *vt (papeles, semillas)* to scatter; *Fig (rumor)* to spread
  2 esparcirse *upr* (a) to be scattered (b) *(relajarse)* to relax

espárrago *nm* asparagus

espartano,-a *adj Fig* spartan

espasmo *nm* spasm

espástico,-a *adj* spastic

espátula *nf Culin* spatula; *Arte* palette

knife; *Téc* stripping knife; *(de albañil)* trowel

especia *nf* spice

especial *adj* special; **en e.** especially; **e. para ...** suitable for ...

especialidad *nf* speciality, *US* specialty; *Educ* main subject

especialista *nmf* specialist

especializarse [40] *vpr* to specialize (en in)

especialmente *adv (exclusivamente)* specially; *(muy)* especially

especie *nf* (a) *Biol* species *inv* (b) *(clase)* kind; **una e. de salsa** a kind of sauce (c) *Com* **en e.** in kind

específicamente *adv* specifically

especificar [44] *vt* to specify

específico,-a *adj* specific; **peso e.** specific gravity

espécimen *nm (pl* **especímenes**) specimen

espectacular *adj* spectacular

espectacularidad *nf* **de gran e.** really spectacular

espectáculo *nm* (a) *(escena)* spectacle, sight; *Fam* **dar un e.** to make a spectacle of oneself (b) *Teatro, Cin & TV* show; **montar un e.** to put on a show

espectador,-a *nm,f Dep* spectator; *(de accidente)* onlooker; *Teatro & Cin* member of the audience; **los espectadores** the audience; *TV* the viewers

espectro *nm* (a) *Fís* spectrum (b) *(fantasma)* spectre (c) *(gama)* range

especulación *nf* speculation; **e. del suelo** land speculation

especulador,-a *nm,f Fin* speculator

especular *vi* to speculate

especulativo,-a *adj* speculative

espejismo *nm* mirage

espejo *nm* mirror; *Aut* **e. retrovisor** rearview mirror

espeleología *nf* potholing, speleology

espeluznante *adj* hair-raising, horrifying

espera *nf* wait; **en e. de ...** waiting for ...; **a la e. de** expecting; **sala de e.** waiting room

esperanza *nf* hope; **tener la e. puesta en algo** to have one's hopes pinned on sth; **e. de vida** life expectancy; **en estado de buena e.** expecting, pregnant

esperanzador,-a *adj* encouraging

esperanzar *vt* to give hope to

esperar 1 *vi* (a) *(aguardar)* to wait (b) *(tener esperanza de)* to hope

2 *vt* (a) *(aguardar)* to wait for; **espero a mi hermano** I'm waiting for my brother

(b) *(tener esperanza de)* to hope for; **espero que sí** I hope so; **espero que vengas** I hope you'll come (c) *(estar a la espera de)* to expect; **te esperábamos ayer** we were expecting you yesterday (d) *Fig (bebé)* to expect

esperma (a) *nm Biol* sperm (b) *Am (vela)* candle

espermaticida *nm* spermicide

espermatozoide *nm* spermatozoid

esperpéntico,-a *adj Fam* grotesque

espesar 1 *vt* to thicken

2 espesarse *vpr* to thicken, to get thicker

espeso,-a *adj (bosque, niebla)* dense; *(líquido)* thick; *(masa)* stiff

espesor *nm* thickness; **3 m de e.** 3 m thick

espesura *nf* denseness

espetar *vt Fig* to spit out

espía *nmf* spy

espiar [29] **1** *vi* to spy

2 *vt* to spy on

espichar *vi Fam* **espichar(la)** *(morir)* to kick the bucket

espiga *nf* (a) *(de trigo)* ear (b) *Téc* pin

espigado,-a *adj* slender

espina *nf* (a) *Bot* thorn (b) *(de pescado)* bone (c) *Anat* **e. dorsal** spinal column, spine (d) *Fig* **ése me da mala e.** there's something fishy about that one

espinaca *nf* spinach

espinal *adj* spinal; **médula e.** spinal marrow

espinazo *nm* spine, backbone

espinilla *nf* (a) *Anat* shin (b) *(en la piel)* spot

espinillera *nf Dep* shin pad

espino *nm* hawthorn; **alambre de e.** barbed wire

espionaje *nm* spying, espionage; **novela de e.** spy story

espiral *adj & nf* spiral

espirar *vi* to breathe out, to exhale

espiritismo *nm* spiritualism

espíritu *nm* (a) *(alma)* spirit; **e. deportivo** sportsmanship (b) *Rel (alma)* soul; **el E. Santo** the Holy Ghost

espiritual *adj* spiritual

espléndido,-a *adj* (a) *(magnífico)* splendid (b) *(generoso)* lavish, generous

esplendor *nm* splendour

esplendoroso,-a *adj* magnificent

espliego *nm* lavender

espolear *vt* to spur on

espolio *nm* = expolio

espolvorear *vt* to sprinkle (de with)

esponja *nf* sponge

esponjoso,-a *adj* spongy; *(bizcocho)* light

esponsales *nmpl* betrothal, engagement

espontaneidad *nf* spontaneity; **con e.** naturally

espontáneo,-a 1 *adj* spontaneous

  2 *nm Taurom* = spectator who spontaneously joins in the bullfight

esporádico,-a *adj* sporadic

esposo,-a *adj* (a) *(recién casado)* newly married (b) *(con esposas)* handcuffed

esposar *vt* to handcuff

esposas *nfpl* handcuffs

esposo,-a *nm,f* spouse; *(hombre)* husband; *(mujer)* wife

esprint *nm* sprint

esprintar *vi* to sprint

espuela *nf* spur

espuerta *nf* hod

espuma *nf* foam; *(de olas)* surf; *(de cerveza)* froth, head; *(de jabón)* lather; **e. de afeitar** shaving foam

espumoso,-a *adj* frothy; *(vino)* sparkling

esputo *nm* spit

esquela *nf* notice, announcement; **e. mortuoria** announcement of a death

esquelético,-a *adj* (a) *Anat* skeletal (b) *(flaco)* skinny

esqueleto *nm* (a) skeleton (b) *Constr* framework

esquema *nm* diagram

esquemático,-a *adj (escueto)* schematic; *(con diagramas)* diagrammatic

esquí *nm* (a) *(objeto)* ski (b) *(deporte)* skiing; **e. acuático** waterskiing

esquiador,-a *nm,f* skier

esquiar [29] *vi* to ski

esquilar *vt* to shear

esquimal *adj & nmf* Eskimo

esquina *nf* corner; *Dep* **saque de e.** corner (kick)

esquinazo *nm* **dar e. a algn** to give sb the slip

esquirla *nf* splinter

esquirol *nm Ind* blackleg, scab

esquivar *vt (a una persona)* to avoid; *(un golpe)* to dodge

esquivo,-a *adj* cold, aloof

esquizofrenia *nf* schizophrenia

esquizofrénico,-a *adj & nm,f* schizophrenic

esta *adj dem ver* **este,-a**

ésta *pron dem f ver* **éste,-a**

está *indic pres de* **estar**

estabilidad *nf* stability

estabilizar [40] *vt* to stabilize

estable *adj* stable

establecer [33] 1 *vt* to establish; *(fundar)* to set up, to found; *(récord)* to set

  2 establecerse *vpr* to settle

establecimiento *nm* establishment

establo *nm* cow shed

estaca *nf* stake, post; *(de tienda de campaña)* peg

estacada *nf* fence; *Fig* **dejar a algn en la e.** to leave sb in the lurch

estacazo *nm* blow with a stick

estación *nf* (a) station; **e. de servicio** service station; **e. de esquí** ski resort (b) *(del año)* season

estacional *adj* seasonal

estacionamiento *nm Aut (acción)* parking; *(lugar) Br* car park, *US* parking lot

estacionar *vt,* **estacionarse** *vpr Aut* to park

estacionario,-a *adj* stationary

estada *nf,* **estadía** *nf Am* stay

estadio *nm* (a) *Dep* stadium (b) *(fase)* stage, phase

estadista *nmf Pol (hombre)* statesman; *(mujer)* stateswoman

estadística *nf* statistics *sing*; **una e.** a statistic

estado *nm* (a) *Pol* state (b) *(situación)* state, condition; **en buen e.** in good condition; **e. de salud** condition, state of health; **e. de excepción** state of emergency; **estar en e.** to be pregnant; **e. civil** marital status; *Com* **e. de cuentas** statement of accounts (c) *Mil* **e. mayor** general staff

Estados Unidos *npl* the United States

estadounidense 1 *adj* United States, American

  2 *nmf* American

estafa *nf* swindle

estafador,-a *nm,f* swindler

estafar *vt* to swindle

estafeta *nf* **e. de Correos** sub-post office

estalactita *nf* stalactite

estalagmita *nf* stalagmite

estallar *vi* (a) to burst; *(bomba)* to explode, to go off; *(guerra)* to break out (b) *Fig (de cólera etc)* to explode; **e. en sollozos** to burst into tears

estallido *nm* explosion; *(de guerra)* outbreak

estambre *nm Bot* stamen

Estambul *n* Istanbul

estamento *nm Hist* estate; *Fig (grupo)* group

estampa *nf* print, image

  🔎 Observa que la palabra inglesa **stamp** es un falso amigo y no es la traducción de la palabra española **estampa**. En inglés, **stamp** significa "sello, tampón".

---

estampado,-a 1 *adj (tela)* printed

2 nm (a) (tela) print (b) (proceso) printing

estampar vt (a) (tela) to print (b) (dejar impreso) to imprint (c) Fig (bofetada, beso) to plant, to place

estampida nf (a) (estampido) bang (b) (carrera rápida) stampede; **de e.** suddenly

estampido nm bang

estampilla nf Am (postage) stamp

estancado,-a adj (agua) stagnant; Fig static, at a standstill; **quedarse e.** to get stuck o bogged down

estancar [44] 1 vt (a) (agua) to hold back (b) Fig (asunto) to block; (negociaciones) to bring to a standstill

2 estancarse vpr to stagnate; Fig to get bogged down

estancia nf (a) (permanencia) stay (b) (habitación) room (c) Am (hacienda) ranch, farm

estanco,-a 1 nm tobacconist's

2 adj watertight

estándar (pl estándares) adj & nm standard

estandarizar [40] vt to standardize

estandarte nm standard, banner

estanque nm pool, pond

estanquero,-a nm,f tobacconist

estante nm shelf; (para libros) bookcase

estantería nf shelves, shelving

estaño nm tin

estar [13] vi (a) to be; **está en la playa** he is at the beach; **e. en casa** to be in, to be at home; **estamos en Caracas** we are in Caracas; **¿está tu madre?** is your mother in?; **¿cómo estás?** how are you?; **los precios están bajos** prices are low; **el problema está en el dinero** the problem is money; **e. en lo cierto** to be right; **e. en todo** not to miss a trick

(b) (+ adj) to be; **está cansado/enfermo** he's tired/ill; **está vacío** it's empty

(c) (+ adv) to be; **está bien/mal** it's all right/wrong; **e. mal de dinero** he's short of money; **estará enseguida** it'll be ready in a minute

(d) (+ ger) to be; **está escribiendo** she is writing; **estaba comiendo** he was eating

(e) (+ a + fecha) to be; **¿a cuántos estamos?** what's the date (today)?; **estamos a 2 de Noviembre** it is the 2nd of November

(f) (+ precio) to be at; **están a 100 pesetas el kilo** they're at 100 pesetas a kilo

(g) (locuciones) **e. al caer** to be just round the corner; **¿estamos?** OK?

(h) (+ de) **e. de más** not to be needed; **e. de paseo** to be out for a walk; **e. de vacaciones/viaje** to be (away) on holiday/a trip; **estoy de jefe hoy** I'm the boss today

(i) (+ para) **estará para las seis** it will be finished by six; **hoy no estoy para bromas** I'm in no mood for jokes today; **el tren está para salir** the train is just about to leave

(j) (+ por) **está por hacer** it has still to be done; **eso está por ver** it remains to be seen; **estoy por esperar** (a favor de) I'm for waiting

(k) (+ con) to have; **e. con la gripe** to have the flu, to be down with flu; **estoy con Jaime** (de acuerdo con) I agree with Jaime

(l) (+ sin) to have no; **e. sin luz/agua** to have no light/water

(m) (+ que) **está que se duerme** he is nearly asleep; Fam **está que rabia** he's hopping mad

2 estarse vpr **¡estáte quieto!** keep still!, stop fidgeting!

estatal adj state; **enseñanza e.** state education

estático,-a adj static

estatua nf statue

estatura nf (a) height; **¿cuál es tu e.?** how tall are you? (b) (renombre) stature

estatus nm status; **e. quo** status quo

estatutario,-a adj statutory

estatuto nm Jur statute; (de ciudad) by-law; (de empresa etc) rules

este¹ 1 adj eastern; (dirección) easterly

2 nm east; **al e. de** to the east of

este²,-a adj dem (a) this (b) **estos,-as** these

éste,-a pron dem m,f (a) this one; **aquél ... é.** the former ... the latter (b) **éstos,-as** these (ones); **aquéllos ... é.** the former ... the latter

Note that **éste** and its various forms can be written without an accent when there is no risk of confusion with the adjective.

esté subj pres de **estar**

estela nf (de barco) wake; (de avión) vapour trail; (de cometa) tail

estelar adj (a) Astron stellar (b) Fig Cin & Teatro star

estentóreo,-a adj stentorian, thundering

estepa nf steppe

estera nf rush mat

estercolero nm dunghill; Fig pigsty

estéreo nm & adj stereo

estereofónico,-a *adj* stereophonic, stereo

estereotipar *vt* to stereotype

estereotipo *nm* stereotype

estéril *adj* (a) sterile (b) *Fig (esfuerzo)* futile

esterilidad *nf* (a) sterility (b) *Fig* futility, uselessness

esterilizar [40] *vt* to sterilize

esterilla *nf* small mat

esterlina *adj & nf* sterling; **libra e.** pound (sterling)

esternón *nm* sternum, breastbone

estero *nm Am* marsh, swamp

estertor *nm* death rattle

estética *nf* aesthetics *sing*

esteticienne, esteticista *nf* beautician

estético,-a *adj* aesthetic; **cirugía estética** plastic surgery

estibador *nm* docker, stevedore

estiércol *nm* manure, dung

estigma *nm* stigma; *Rel* stigmata

estilarse *vpr* to be in vogue, to be fashionable

estilete *nm (punzón)* stylus; *(puñal)* stiletto

estilístico,-a *adj* stylistic

estilizar [40] *vt* to stylize

estilo *nm* (a) style; *(modo)* manner, fashion; **algo por el e.** something like that; **e. de vida** way of life (b) *(en natación)* stroke (c) *Ling* **e. directo/indirecto** direct/indirect speech

estilográfica *nf* (pluma) **e.** fountain pen

estima *nf* esteem, respect

estimación *nf* (a) *(estima)* esteem, respect (b) *(valoración)* evaluation; *(cálculo aproximado)* estimate

estimado,-a *adj* esteemed, respected; **E. Señor** *(en carta)* Dear Sir

estimar *vt* (a) *(apreciar)* to esteem (b) *(considerar)* to consider, to think; **lo estimo conveniente** I think it appropriate (c) *(valorar)* to value

estimativo,-a *adj* approximate, estimated

estimulante 1 *adj* stimulating

    2 *nm* stimulant

estimular *vt* (a) to stimulate (b) *Fig* to encourage

estímulo *nm Biol & Fís* stimulus; *Fig* encouragement

estío *nm* summer

estipendio *nm* stipend, fee

estipular *vt* to stipulate

estirado,-a *adj Fig* stiff

estirar 1 *vt* to stretch; *Fig (dinero)* to spin out; *Fig* **e. la pata** to kick the bucket

    2 estirarse *vpr* to stretch

estirón *nm* pull, jerk, tug; *Fam* **dar o pegar un e.** to shoot up *o* grow quickly

estirpe *nf* stock, pedigree

estival *adj* summer; **época e.** summertime

esto *pron neut* this, this thing, this matter; *Fam* **e. de la fiesta** this business about the party

estocada *nf Taurom* stab

Estocolmo *n* Stockholm

estofado *nm* stew

estoico,-a 1 *adj* stoical

    2 *nm,f* stoic

estómago *nm* stomach; **dolor de e.** stomach ache

Estonia *n* Estonia

estonio,-a 1 *adj & nm,f* Estonian

    2 *nm (lengua)* Estonian

estoque *nm Taurom* sword

estorbar 1 *vt* (a) *(dificultar)* to hinder, to get in the way of (b) *(molestar)* to disturb

    2 *vi* to be in the way

estorbo *nm* (a) *(obstáculo)* obstruction, obstacle (b) *(molestia)* nuisance

estornino *nm* starling

estornudar *vi* to sneeze

estornudo *nm* sneeze

estos,-as *adj dem pl ver* **este,-a**

éstos,-as *pron dem m,fpl ver* **éste,-a**

estoy *indic pres de* **estar**

estrabismo *nm* squint

estrado *nm* platform; *Mús* bandstand; *Jur* stand

estrafalario,-a *adj Fam* outlandish

estragos *nmpl* **hacer e. en** to wreak havoc with *o* on

estrambótico,-a *adj Fam* outlandish, eccentric

estrangulador,-a *nm,f* strangler

estrangular *vt* to strangle; *Med* to strangulate

estraperlo *nm* black market; **tabaco de e.** black market cigarettes

Estrasburgo *n* Strasbourg

estratagema *nf Mil* stratagem; *Fam* trick, ruse

estratega *nmf* strategist

estrategia *nf* strategy

estratégico,-a *adj* strategic

estratificar [44] *vt* to stratify

estrato *nm* stratum

estraza *nf* papel de e. brown paper

estrechamente *adv* *(íntimamente)* closely, intimately; **e. relacionados** closely related

estrechamiento *nm* (a) narrowing; **e. de calzada** *(en letrero)* road narrows (b) *(de amistad etc)* tightening

estrechar 1 *vt* (**a**) to make narrow (**b**) *(mano)* to shake; *(lazos de amistad)* to tighten; **me estrechó entre sus brazos** he hugged me

2 estrecharse *vpr* to narrow, to become narrower

📖 Observa que el verbo inglés **to stretch** es un falso amigo y no es la traducción del verbo español **estrechar**. En inglés, **to stretch** significa "estirar, desplegar".

estrechez *nf* (**a**) narrowness; *Fig* **e. de miras** narrow-mindedness (**b**) *Fig (dificultad económica)* want, need; **pasar estrecheces** to be hard up

estrecho,-a 1 *adj* (**a**) narrow; *(ropa, zapato)* tight; *(amistad, relación)* close, intimate (**b**) *Fig* **e. de miras** narrow-minded

2 *nm Geog* strait, straits

estregar *vt* to scrub

estrella *nf* star; **e. de cine** film star; *Zool* **e. de mar** starfish; **e. fugaz** shooting star

estrellado,-a *adj* (**a**) *(en forma de estrella)* star-shaped (**b**) *(cielo)* starry (**c**) *(huevos)* scrambled

estrellar 1 *vt Fam* to smash

2 estrellarse *vpr (morir)* to die in a car crash; *Aut & Av* **e. contra** *(chocar)* to crash into

estrellato *nm* stardom

estremecedor,-a *adj* bloodcurdling

estremecer [33] *vt*, **estremecerse** *vpr* to shake

estrenar *vt* (**a**) to use for the first time; *(ropa)* to wear for the first time (**b**) *Teatro & Cin* to premiere

estreno *nm Teatro* first performance; *Cin* premiere

estreñido,-a *adj* constipated

estreñimiento *nm* constipation

estrépito *nm* din, racket

estrepitoso,-a *adj* deafening; *Fig (fracaso)* spectacular

estrés *nm* stress

estresante *adj* stressful

estría *nf* (**a**) *(en la piel)* stretch mark (**b**) *Arquit* flute, fluting

estribar *vi* **e. en** to lie in, to be based on

estribillo *nm (en canción)* chorus; *(en poema)* refrain

estribo *nm* (**a**) stirrup; *Fig* **perder los estribos** to lose one's temper, to lose one's head (**b**) *Arquit* buttress; *(de puente)* pier, support

estribor *nm* starboard

estricto,-a *adj* strict

estridente *adj* strident

estrofa *nf* verse

estropajo *nm* scourer

estropear 1 *vt (máquina, cosecha)* to damage; *(fiesta, plan)* to spoil, to ruin; *(pelo, manos)* to ruin

2 estropearse *vpr* to be ruined; *(máquina)* to break down

estropicio *nm Fam (destrozo)* damage; *(ruido)* crash, clatter

estructura *nf* structure; *(armazón)* frame, framework

estructurar *vt* to structure

estruendo *nm* roar

estrujar 1 *vt (limón etc)* to squeeze; *(ropa)* to wring; *(apretar)* to crush

2 estrujarse *vpr Fam* **e. los sesos** *o* **el cerebro** to rack one's brains

estrujón *nm* tight squeeze, big hug

estuche *nm* case; *(para lápices)* pencil case

estuco *nm* stucco

estudiante *nmf* student

estudiantil *adj* student

estudiar [43] *vt & vi* to study

estudio *nm* (**a**) study; *(encuesta)* survey; *Com* **e. de mercado** market research (**b**) *(sala)* studio; **e. cinematográfico/de grabación** film/recording studio (**c**) *(apartamento)* studio (flat) (**d**) **estudios** studies

estudioso,-a 1 *adj* studious

2 *nm,f* specialist

estufa *nf (calentador)* heater; *(de leña)* stove

estupefaciente *nm* drug, narcotic

estupefacto,-a *adj* astounded, flabbergasted

estupendamente *adv* marvellously, wonderfully

estupendo,-a *adj* super, marvellous; **¡e.!** great!

estupidez *nf* stupidity

estúpido,-a 1 *adj* stupid

2 *nm,f* idiot

estupor *nm* amazement, astonishment

estuve *pt indef de* estar

esvástica *nf* swastika

ETA *nf (abr* **Euzkadi Ta Askatasuna** *(Patria Vasca y Libertad))* ETA

etapa *nf* stage; **por etapas** in stages

etarra *nmf* = member of ETA

etc. *(abr* **etcétera)** etc

etcétera *adv* etcetera

éter *nm* ether

etéreo,-a *adj* ethereal

eternidad *nf* eternity; *Fam* **una e.** ages

eterno,-a *adj* eternal

ética *nf* ethic; *(ciencia)* ethics *sing*

ético,-a *adj* ethical
etílico,-a *adj* ethylic; **alcohol e.** ethyl
alcohol; **en estado e.** intoxicated; **intoxicación etílica** alcohol poisoning
etimología *nf* etymology
etimológico,-a *adj* etymological
etiope, etíope *adj & nmf* Ethiopian
Etiopía *nf* Ethiopia
etiqueta *nf* (**a**) *(de producto)* label (**b**)
(ceremonia) etiquette; **de e.** formal
etiquetar *vt* to label
etnia *nf* ethnic group
étnico,-a *adj* ethnic
ETT *nf* (*abr* **Empresa de Trabajo Temporal**)
temping agency
eucalipto *nm* eucalyptus
eucaristía *nf* eucharist
eufemismo *nm* euphemism
euforia *nf* euphoria
eufórico,-a *adj* euphoric
eureka *interj* eureka!
euro *nm (moneda)* euro
eurocomunismo *nm* Eurocommunism
eurodiputado,-a *nm,f* Euro MP
euromisil *nm* Euromissile
Europa *n* Europe
europeísmo *nm* Europeanism
europeizar [40] *vt* to europeanize
europeo,-a *adj & nm,f* European
euscalduna 1 *adj* Basque; *(que habla
vasco)* Basque-speaking
 2 *nmf* Basque speaker
euskera *adj & nm* Basque
eutanasia *nf* euthanasia
evacuación *nf* evacuation
evacuar [47] *vt* to evacuate
evadir 1 *vt (respuesta, peligro, impuestos)*
to avoid; *(responsabilidad)* to shirk
 2 evadirse *vpr* to escape
evaluación *nf* evaluation; *Educ* assessment; **e. continua** continuous assessment
evaluar [30] *vt* to evaluate, to assess
evangélico,-a *adj* evangelical
evangelio *nm* gospel
evangelista *nm* evangelist
evaporación *nf* evaporation
evaporar 1 *vt* to evaporate
 2 evaporarse *vpr* to evaporate; *Fig* to
vanish
evasión *nf (fuga)* escape; *Fig* evasion; **e.
fiscal** *o* **de impuestos** tax evasion
evasiva *nf* evasive answer
evasivo,-a *adj* evasive
evento *nm* (**a**) *(acontecimiento)* event (**b**)
(incidente) contingency, unforeseen
event
eventual *adj* (**a**) *(posible)* possible;

(gastos) incidental (**b**) *(trabajo, obrero)*
casual, temporary
eventualidad *nf* contingency
eventualmente *adv* by chance; **los problemas que e. surjan** such problems as
may arise

> 🖉 Observa que las palabras inglesas **even-
> tual** y **eventually** son falsos amigos y no
> son la traducción de las palabras españolas
> **eventual** y **eventualmente**. En inglés,
> **eventual** significa "final" o "consiguiente" y
> **eventually** "finalmente".

evidencia *nf* obviousness; **poner a algn
en e.** to show sb up
evidenciar [43] *vt* to show, to demonstrate
evidente *adj* obvious
evidentemente *adv* obviously
evitar *vt* to avoid; *(prevenir)* to prevent;
(desastre) to avert
evocador,-a *adj* evocative
evocar [44] *vt (traer a la memoria)* to
evoke; *(acordarse de)* to recall
evolución *nf* evolution; *(desarrollo)* development
evolucionar *vi* to develop; *Biol* to evolve;
el enfermo evoluciona favorablemente
the patient is improving
ex 1 *pref* former, ex-; **ex alumno** former
pupil, ex-student; **ex combatiente** *Br* ex-
serviceman, *f* ex-servicewoman, *US*
(war) veteran; **ex marido** ex-husband
 2 *nmf Fam* **mi ex** my ex
exabrupto *nm* sharp comment
exacerbar 1 *vt* (**a**) *(agravar)* to exacerbate, to aggravate (**b**) *(irritar)* to exasperate, to irritate
 2 exacerbarse *vpr* (**a**) *(agravarse)* to get
worse (**b**) *(irritarse)* to feel exasperated
exactamente *adv* exactly, precisely
exactitud *nf* accuracy; **con e.** precisely
exacto,-a *adj* exact; **¡e.!** precisely!; **para
ser e.** to be precise
exageración *nf* exaggeration
exagerado,-a *adj* exaggerated; *(excesivo)* excessive
exagerar 1 *vt* to exaggerate
 2 *vi* to overdo it
exaltado,-a 1 *adj (persona)* excitable,
hot-headed
 2 *nm,f Fam* fanatic
exaltar 1 *vt (ensalzar)* to praise, to extol
 2 exaltarse *vpr (acalorarse)* to get over-
excited, to get carried away
examen *nm* examination, exam; **e. de
conducir** driving test; *Med* **e. médico**
checkup

examinador,-a *nm,f* examiner
examinar 1 *vt* to examine
  2 examinarse *upr* to take *o* sit an examination
exasperante *adj* exasperating
exasperar 1 *vt* to exasperate
  2 exasperarse *upr* to become exasperated
Exc., Exca., Exc.a (*abr* **Excelencia**) Excellency
excavación *nf* excavation; (*en arqueología*) dig
excavadora *nf* digger
excavar *vt* to excavate, to dig
excedencia *nf* leave (of absence)
excedente *adj & nm* excess, surplus
exceder 1 *vt* to exceed, to surpass
  2 excederse *upr* to go too far
excelencia *nf* (**a**) excellence; **por e. par** excellence (**b**) (*título*) **Su E.** His/Her Excellency
excelente *adj* excellent
excelso,-a *adj* sublime, lofty
excentricidad *nf* eccentricity
excéntrico,-a *adj* eccentric
excepción *nf* exception; **a e. de** with the exception of, except for; **de e.** exceptional; *Pol* **estado de e.** state of emergency
excepcional *adj* exceptional
excepto *adv* except (for), apart from
exceptuar [30] *vt* to except, to exclude
excesivo,-a *adj* excessive
exceso *nm* excess; **en e.** in excess, excessively; **e. de equipaje** excess baggage; **e. de velocidad** speeding
excitable *adj* excitable
excitación *nf* (*sentimiento*) excitement
excitante 1 *adj* exciting; *Med* stimulating
  2 nm stimulant
excitar 1 *vt* to excite
  2 excitarse *upr* to get excited
exclamación *nf* exclamation
exclamar *vt & vi* to exclaim, to cry out
excluir [37] *vt* to exclude; (*rechazar*) to reject
exclusión *nf* exclusion
exclusiva *nf* *Prensa* exclusive; *Com* sole right
exclusive *adv* (*en fechas*) exclusive
exclusivo,-a *adj* exclusive
Excma. (*abr* **Excelentísima**) Most Excellent
Excmo. (*abr* **Excelentísimo**) Most Excellent
excomulgar [42] *vt* *Rel* to excommunicate
excomunión *nf* excommunication
excremento *nm* excrement

exculpar *vt* to exonerate
excursión *nf* excursion
excursionista *nmf* tripper; (*a pie*) hiker
excusa *nf* (*pretexto*) excuse; (*disculpa*) apology
excusado *nm* (*retrete*) toilet
excusar 1 *vt* (**a**) (*justificar*) to excuse (**b**) (*eximir*) to exempt (**de** from)
  2 excusarse *upr* (*disculparse*) to apologize
execrar *vt* to execrate, to abhor
exención *nf* exemption; **e. de impuestos** tax exemption
exento,-a *adj* exempt, free (**de** from)
exequias *nfpl* funeral rites
exhalar *vt* to exhale, to breathe out; (*gas*) to give off, to emit; (*suspiro*) to heave
exhaustivo,-a *adj* exhaustive
exhausto,-a *adj* exhausted
exhibición *nf* exhibition
exhibicionista *nmf* exhibitionist
exhibir 1 *vt* (**a**) (*mostrar*) to exhibit, to display (**b**) (*lucir*) to show off
  2 exhibirse *upr* to show off, to make an exhibition of oneself
exhortar *vt* to exhort
exhumar *vt* to exhume
exigencia *nf* (**a**) demand (**b**) (*requisito*) requirement
exigente *adj* demanding, exacting
exigir [57] *vt* to demand
exiguo,-a *adj* minute
exilado,-a 1 *adj* exiled, in exile
  2 nm,f exile
exilar 1 *vt* to exile, to send into exile
  2 exilarse *upr* to go into exile
exiliado,-a *adj & nm,f* = **exilado,-a**
exiliar [43] *vt*, **exiliarse** *upr* = **exilar**
exilio *nm* exile
eximio,-a *adj* distinguished, eminent
eximir *vt* to exempt (**de** from)
existencia *nf* (**a**) (*vida*) existence (**b**) *Com* **existencias** stock, stocks
existente *adj* existing; *Com* in stock
existir *vi* to exist, to be (in existence)
éxito *nm* success; **con é.** successfully; **tener é.** to be successful

> ♪ Observa que la palabra inglesa **exit** es un falso amigo y no es la traducción de la palabra española **éxito**. En inglés, **exit** significa "salida".

exitoso,-a *adj* successful
éxodo *nm* exodus
exonerar *vt* to exonerate
exorbitante *adj* exorbitant, excessive
exorcista *nmf* exorcist
exorcizar [40] *vt* to exorcize

exótico,-a *adj* exotic

expandir 1 *vt* to expand

  2 expandirse *vpr (gas etc)* to expand; *(noticia)* to spread

expansión *nf* (**a**) expansion; *(de noticia)* spreading (**b**) *(diversión)* relaxation, recreation

expansionarse *vpr Fig (divertirse)* to relax, to let one's hair down

expatriado,-a *adj & nm,f* expatriate

expatriar [29] 1 *vt* to exile, to banish

  2 expatriarse *vpr* to leave one's country

expectación *nf* excitement

expectativa *nf* expectancy; **estar a la e. de** to be on the lookout for

expectorante *nm* expectorant

expedición *nf* expedition

expedientar *vt* to place under enquiry

expediente *nm* (**a**) *(informe)* dossier, record; *(ficha)* file; *Educ* **e. académico** student's record; **abrirle e. a algn** to place sb under enquiry (**b**) *Jur* proceedings, action

expedir [6] *vt* (**a**) *(carta)* to send, to dispatch (**b**) *(pasaporte etc)* to issue

expedito,-a *adj* free, clear

expendedor,-a 1 *nm,f* seller

  2 nm **e. automático** vending machine

expendeduría *nf* tobacconist's

expensas *nfpl* **a e. de** at the expense of

experiencia *nf* (**a**) experience; **por e.** from experience (**b**) *(experimento)* experiment

experimentado,-a *adj* experienced

experimental *adj* experimental

experimentar 1 *vi* to experiment

  2 vt to undergo; *(aumento)* to show; *(pérdida)* to suffer; *(sensación)* to experience, to feel; *Med* **e. una mejoría** to improve, to make progress

experimento *nm* experiment

experto,-a *nm,f* expert

expiar [29] *vt* to expiate, to atone for

expirar *vi* to expire

explanada *nf* esplanade

explayarse *vpr* to talk at length (about)

explicación *nf* explanation

explicar [44] 1 *vt* to explain

  2 explicarse *vpr (persona)* to explain (oneself); **no me lo explico** I can't understand it

explicativo,-a *adj* explanatory

explícito,-a *adj* explicit

exploración *nf* exploration; *Téc* scanning; *Med (interna)* exploration; *(externa)* examination; *Mil* reconnaissance

explorador,-a *nm,f* (**a**) *(persona)* explorer (**b**) *Med* probe; *Téc* scanner

explorar *vt* to explore; *Med (internamente)* to explore; *(externamente)* to examine; *Téc* to scan; *Mil* to reconnoitre

explosión *nf* explosion, blast; **hacer e.** to explode; **motor de e.** internal combustion engine; **e. demográfica** population explosion

explosionar *vt & vi* to explode, to blow up

explosivo,-a *adj & nm* explosive

explotación *nf* (**a**) *(abuso)* exploitation (**b**) *(uso)* exploitation, working; *Agr* cultivation (of land); *(granja)* farm

explotador,-a *nm,f* exploiter

explotar 1 *vi (bomba)* to explode, to go off

  2 vt (**a**) *(aprovechar)* to exploit; *(recursos)* to tap; *(tierra)* to cultivate (**b**) *(abusar de)* to exploit

expoliar [43] *vt* to plunder, to pillage

exponente *nmf* exponent

exponer [19] *(pp* **expuesto**) 1 *vt* (**a**) *(mostrar)* to exhibit, to display (**b**) *(explicar)* to expound, to put forward (**c**) *(arriesgar)* to expose

  2 exponerse *vpr* to expose oneself (**a** to); **te expones a perder el trabajo** you run the risk of losing your job

exportación *nf* export

exportador,-a 1 *adj* exporting

  2 nm,f exporter

exportar *vt* to export

exposición *nf* (**a**) *Arte* exhibition; **e. universal** world fair; **sala de exposiciones** gallery (**b**) *(de hechos, ideas)* exposé (**c**) *Fot* exposure

exprés *adj* express; **(olla) e.** pressure cooker; **(café) e.** espresso (coffee)

expresamente *adv* specifically, expressly

expresar 1 *vt* to express; *(manifestar)* to state

  2 expresarse *vpr* to express oneself

expresión *nf* expression; **la mínima e.** the bare minimum

expresivo,-a *adj* expressive

expreso,-a 1 *adj* express; **con el fin e. de** with the express purpose of

  2 nm *Ferroc* express (train)

  3 adv on purpose, deliberately

exprimidor *nm* squeezer, juicer

exprimir *vt (limón)* to squeeze; *(zumo)* to squeeze out; *Fig (persona)* to exploit, to bleed dry

expropiar [43] *vt* to expropriate

expuesto,-a *adj* (**a**) *(sin protección)* exposed; **estar e. a** to be exposed to (**b**) *(peligroso)* risky, dangerous (**c**) *(exhibido)* on display, on show

expulsar *vt* (**a**) to expel, to throw out; *Dep* (*jugador*) to send off (**b**) (*gas etc*) to belch out

expulsión *nf* expulsion; *Dep* sending off

expurgar [42] *vt* to expurgate; *Fig* to purge

expuse *pt indef de* **exponer**

exquisito,-a *adj* exquisite; (*comida*) delicious; (*gusto*) refined

extasiado,-a *adj* ecstatic; **quedarse e.** to go into ecstasies *o* raptures

extasiarse [29] *upr* to go into ecstasies *o* raptures

éxtasis *nm inv* ecstasy

extender [3] **1** *vt* (**a**) to extend; (*agrandar*) to enlarge (**b**) (*mantel, mapa*) to spread (out), to open (out); (*mano, brazo*) to stretch (out) (**c**) (*crema, mantequilla*) to spread (**d**) (*cheque*) to make out; (*documento*) to draw up; (*certificado*) to issue

2 extenderse *upr* (**a**) (*en el tiempo*) to extend, to last (**b**) (*en el espacio*) to spread out, to stretch (**c**) (*rumor, noticia*) to spread, to extend (**d**) *Fig* (*hablar demasiado*) to go on

extendido,-a *adj* (**a**) extended; (*mapa, plano*) spread out, open; (*mano, brazo*) outstretched (**b**) (*costumbre, rumor*) widespread

extensible *adj* extending

extensión *nf* (*de libro etc*) length; (*de cuerpo*) size; (*de terreno*) area, expanse; (*edificio anexo*) extension; **en toda la e. de la palabra** in every sense of the word; **por e.** by extension

extensivo,-a *adj* **hacer e.** to extend; **ser e. a** to cover

extenso,-a *adj* (*terreno*) extensive; (*libro, película*) long

extenuar [30] **1** *vt* to exhaust

2 extenuarse *upr* to exhaust oneself

exterior **1** *adj* (**a**) (*de fuera*) outer; (*puerta*) outside (**b**) (*política, deuda*) foreign; *Pol* **Ministerio de Asuntos Exteriores** Ministry of Foreign Affairs, *Br* ≃ Foreign Office, *US* ≃ State Department

2 *nm* (**a**) (*parte de fuera*) exterior, outside (**b**) (*extranjero*) abroad (**c**) **exteriores** *Cin* location

exteriorizar [40] *vt* to show

exteriormente *adv* outwardly

exterminar *vt* to exterminate

exterminio *nm* extermination

externalización *nf Com* outsourcing

externo,-a 1 *adj* external; *Farm* **de uso e.** for external use only

2 *nm,f Educ* day pupil

extinción *nf* extinction

extinguir [59] **1** *vt* (*fuego*) to extinguish, to put out; (*raza*) to wipe out

2 extinguirse *upr* (*fuego*) to go out; (*especie*) to become extinct, to die out

extinto,-a *adj* extinct

extintor *nm* fire extinguisher

extirpar *vt* (**a**) *Med* to remove (**b**) *Fig* to eradicate, to stamp out

extorsión *nf* extortion

extorsionar *vt* to extort

extra 1 *adj* (**a**) (*suplementario*) extra; **horas e.** overtime; **paga e.** bonus (**b**) (*superior*) top-quality

2 *nmf* extra

3 *nmf Cin & Teatro* extra

extra- *pref* extra-; **extramatrimonial** extramarital

extracción *nf* (**a**) extraction (**b**) (*en lotería*) draw

extracto *nm* (**a**) extract; **e. de fresa** strawberry extract; **e. de regaliz** liquorice; *Fin* **e. de cuenta** statement of account (**b**) (*resumen*) summary

extractor *nm* extractor

extradición *nf* extradition

extraer [25] *vt* to extract, to take out

extraescolar *adj* (*actividad etc*) extracurricular

extrafino,-a *adj* superfine

extralimitarse *upr* to overstep the mark

extranjería *nf* **ley de e.** law on aliens

extranjero,-a 1 *adj* foreign

2 *nm,f* foreigner

3 *nm* abroad; **en el e.** abroad

extrañar 1 *vt* (**a**) (*sorprender*) to surprise; **no es de e.** it's hardly surprising (**b**) *Am* (*echar de menos*) to miss

2 extrañarse *upr* **e. de** to be surprised at

extrañeza *nf* (**a**) (*sorpresa*) surprise, astonishment (**b**) (*singularidad*) strangeness

extraño,-a 1 *adj* strange; *Med* **cuerpo e.** foreign body

2 *nm,f* stranger

extraoficial *adj* unofficial

extraordinaria *nf* (*paga*) bonus

extraordinario,-a *adj* extraordinary; *Prensa* **edición extraordinaria** special edition

extrarradio *nm* outskirts, suburbs

extraterrestre *nmf* alien

extravagancia *nf* extravagance

extravagante *adj* odd, outlandish

extravertido,-a *adj* = **extrovertido,-a**

extraviado,-a *adj* lost, missing

extraviar [29] **1** *vt* to mislay, to lose

2 extraviarse *upr* to be missing, to get mislaid

extremadamente *adv* extremely

extremado,-a *adj* extreme

Extremadura *n* Estremadura

extremar 1 *vt* **e. la prudencia** to be extremely careful

  2 extremarse *upr* to take great pains, to do one's utmost

extremaunción *nf* extreme unction

extremeño,-a 1 *adj* of/from Estremadura

  2 *nm,f* person from Estremadura

extremidad *nf* (**a**) *(extremo)* end, tip (**b**) *Anat (miembro)* limb, extremity

extremista *adj & nmf* extremist

extremo,-a 1 *nm (de calle, cable)* end; *(máximo)* extreme; **en e.** very much; **en último e.** as a last resort

  2 *nm,f (en fútbol)* winger; **e. derecha/izquierda** outside right/left

  3 *adj* extreme; **E. Oriente** Far East

extrovertido,-a *adj & nm,f* extrovert

exuberante *adj* exuberant; *(vegetación)* lush, abundant

eyaculación *nf* ejaculation; **e. precoz** premature ejaculation

eyacular *vi* to ejaculate

eyectable *adj* **asiento e.** ejector seat

F, f ['efe] *nf (la letra)* F, f
fa *nm Mús* F
fabada *nf* stew of beans, pork sausage and bacon
fábrica *nf* factory; **marca de f.** trademark; **precio de f.** factory *o* ex-works price

⚠ Observa que la palabra inglesa **fabric** es un falso amigo y no es la traducción de la palabra española **fábrica**. En inglés, **fabric** significa "tejido".

fabricación *nf* manufacture; **de f. casera** home-made; **de f. propia** our own make; **f. en cadena** mass production
fabricante *nmf* manufacturer
fabricar [44] *vt* (**a**) *Ind* to manufacture (**b**) *Fig (mentiras etc)* to fabricate
fabril *adj* manufacturing
fábula *nf* fable
fabuloso,-a *adj* fabulous
faca *nf* large curved knife
facción *nf* (**a**) *Pol* faction (**b**) **facciones** *(rasgos)* features
faccioso,-a 1 *adj* seditious
  2 *nm,f* rebel
faceta *nf* facet
facha[1] *nf Fam* appearance, look
facha[2] *nmf Pey* fascist
fachada *nf* façade
facial *adj* facial
fácil *adj* (**a**) *(sencillez)* easy; **f. de comprender** easy to understand (**b**) *(probable)* likely, probable; **es f. que ...** it's (quite) likely that ...
facilidad *nf* (**a**) *(sencillez)* easiness (**b**) *(soltura)* ease (**c**) *(servicio)* facility; **dar facilidades** to make things easy; *Com* **facilidades de pago** easy terms (**d**) **f. para los idiomas** gift for languages
facilitar *vt (proporcionar)* to provide, to supply (**a** with)
fácilmente *adv* easily
facineroso,-a *adj* criminal
facsímil, facsímile *nm* facsimile
factible *adj* feasible
fáctico,-a *adj* **poderes fácticos** vested interests
factor *nm* (**a**) factor (**b**) *Ferroc* luggage clerk

factoría *nf (fábrica)* factory
factura *nf* (**a**) *Com* invoice (**b**) *Arg (bollo)* = rolls and pastries
facturación *nf* (**a**) *Com* invoicing (**b**) *(de equipajes) (en aeropuerto)* check-in; *(en estación)* registration
facturar *vt* (**a**) *Com* to invoice (**b**) *(en aeropuerto)* to check in; *(en estación)* to register
facultad *nf* faculty; **facultades mentales** faculties
facultativo,-a 1 *adj* optional
  2 *nm,f* doctor
faena *nf* (**a**) *(tarea)* task (**b**) *Fam (mala pasada)* dirty trick (**c**) *Taurom* performance
faenar *vi* to fish
fagot *nm Mús* bassoon
fainá *nf Urug (plato)* = baked dough made with chickpea flour and olive oil, served with pizza
faisán *nm* pheasant
faja *nf* (**a**) *(corsé)* girdle, corset (**b**) *(banda)* sash (**c**) *(de terreno)* strip
fajo *nm (de ropa etc)* bundle; *(de billetes)* wad
falacia *nf* fallacy
falaz *adj* (**a**) *(erróneo)* fallacious (**b**) *(engañoso)* deceitful
falda *nf* (**a**) *(prenda)* skirt; **f. pantalón** culottes (**b**) *(de montaña)* slope, hillside (**c**) *(de mesa)* cover (**d**) *(regazo)* lap
faldero,-a *adj* **perro f.** lapdog
falencia *nf* (**a**) *Am Com (bancarrota)* bankruptcy (**b**) *CSur (error)* fault
falla[1] *nf Am (defecto)* defect, fault
falla[2] *nf Geol* fault
fallar[1] **1** *vi Jur* to rule
  2 *vt (premio)* to award
fallar[2] **1** *vi* to fail; **le falló la puntería** he missed his aim; *Fig* **no me falles** don't let me down
  2 *vt* to miss
fallecer [33] *vi Fml* to pass away, to die
fallecido,-a *adj* deceased
fallecimiento *nm* demise
fallido,-a *adj* unsuccessful, vain
fallo[1] *nm* (**a**) *(error)* mistake; **f. humano** human error (**b**) *(del corazón, de los frenos)* failure

fallo² nm (**a**) Jur judgement, sentence (**b**) (en concurso) awarding

falluto,-a RP Fam **1** adj phoney, hypocritical

2 nm,f hypocrite

falo nm phallus

falsear vt (**a**) (informe etc) to falsify; (hechos, la verdad) to distort (**b**) (moneda) to forge

falsedad nf (**a**) falseness, (doblez) hypocrisy (**b**) (mentira) falsehood

falsificar [44] vt to falsify; (cuadro, firma, moneda) to forge

falso,-a adj (**a**) false; **dar un paso en f.** (tropezar) to trip, to stumble; Fig to make a blunder; **jurar en f.** to commit perjury (**b**) (persona) insincere

falta nf (**a**) (carencia) lack; **por f. de** for want o lack of; **sin f.** without fail; **f. de educación** bad manners

(**b**) (escasez) shortage

(**c**) (ausencia) absence; **echar algo/a algn en f.** to miss sth/sb

(**d**) (error) mistake; (defecto) fault, defect; **f. de ortografía** spelling mistake; **sacar faltas a algo/a algn** to find fault with sth/sb

(**e**) Jur misdemeanour

(**f**) (en fútbol) foul; (en tenis) fault

(**g**) **hacer f.** to be necessary; **(nos) hace f. una escalera** we need a ladder; **harán f. dos personas para mover el piano** it'll take two people to move the piano; **no hace f. que ...** there is no need for ...

faltante nm Am deficit

faltar vi (**a**) (no estar) to be missing; **¿quién falta?** who is missing?

(**b**) (escasear) to be lacking o needed; **le falta confianza en sí mismo** he lacks confidence in himself; **¡lo que me faltaba!** that's all I needed!; **¡no faltaría o faltaba más!** (por supuesto) (but) of course!

(**c**) (quedar) to be left; **¿cuántos kilómetros faltan para Managua?** how many kilometres is it to Managua?; **ya falta poco para las vacaciones** it won't be long now till the holidays; **faltó poco para que me cayera** I very nearly fell

(**d**) **f. a la verdad** not to tell the truth; **f. al deber** to fail in one's duty; **f. a su palabra/promesa** to break one's word/promise; **f. al respeto a algn** to treat sb with disrespect

falto,-a adj **f. de** lacking in

fama nf (**a**) fame, renown; **de f. mundial** world-famous (**b**) (reputación) reputation

famélico,-a adj starving, famished

familia nf family; **estar en f.** to be among friends; **f. numerosa** large family

familiar 1 adj (**a**) (de la familia) family; **empresa f.** family business (**b**) (conocido) familiar

2 nmf relation, relative

familiaridad nf familiarity

familiarizarse [40] vpr **f. con** to familiarize oneself with

famoso,-a 1 adj famous

2 nm famous person

fan nmf fan

fanático,-a 1 adj fanatical

2 nm,f fanatic

fanatismo nm fanaticism

fanfarrón,-ona Fam **1** adj boastful

2 nm,f show-off

fanfarronear vi Fam (chulear) to show off; (bravear) to brag, to boast

fango nm (**a**) (barro) mud (**b**) Fig degradation

fantasear vi to daydream, to dream

fantasía nf fantasy; **joya de f.** imitation jewellery

fantasioso,-a adj imaginative

fantasma nm (**a**) (espectro) ghost (**b**) Fam (fanfarrón) braggart, show-off

fantasmal adj ghostly

fantástico,-a adj fantastic

fantoche nm Pey nincompoop, ninny

faraón nm Pharaoh

fardar vi Fam to show off

fardo nm bundle

farfullar vt to jabber

faringe nf pharynx

faringitis nf pharyngitis

fariseo,-a nm,f (falso) hypocrite

farmacéutico,-a 1 adj pharmaceutical

2 nm,f pharmacist, Br chemist, US druggist

farmacia nf (**a**) (tienda) Br chemist's (shop), US drugstore (**b**) (ciencia) pharmacology

fármaco nm medicine, medication

faro nm (**a**) (torre) lighthouse (**b**) (de coche) headlight, headlamp

farol nm (**a**) lantern; (en la calle) streetlight, streetlamp (**b**) Fam (fanfarronada) bragging; **tirarse un f.** to brag (**c**) (en naipes) bluff

farola nf streetlight, streetlamp

farolear vi Fam to brag

farolillo nm Fig **ser el f. rojo** to bring up the rear

farragoso,-a adj confused, rambling

farruco,-a adj Fam cocky

farsa nf farce

farsante *nmf* fake, impostor

fascículo *nm Impr* instalment

fascinador,-a, fascinante *adj* fascinating

fascinar *vt* to fascinate

fascismo *nm* fascism

fascista *adj & nmf* fascist

fase *nf* (a) *(etapa)* phase, stage (b) *Elec & Fís* phase

fastidiado,-a *adj Fam* (a) *(roto)* broken (b) *(enfermo)* sick; **tiene el estómago f.** he's got a bad stomach

fastidiar [43] **1** *vt* (a) *(molestar)* to annoy, to bother; *(dañar)* to hurt; *Fam* **¡no fastidies!** you're kidding! (b) *Fam (estropear)* to damage, to ruin; *(planes)* to spoil

2 fastidiarse *vpr* (a) *(aguantarse)* to put up with it, to resign oneself; **que se fastidie** that's his tough luck (b) *Fam (estropearse)* to get damaged, to break down (c) **me he fastidiado el tobillo** I've hurt my ankle

fastidio *nm* nuisance

fastuoso,-a *adj* (a) *(acto)* splendid, lavish (b) *(persona)* lavish, ostentatious

fatal 1 *adj* (a) *Fam (muy malo)* awful, dreadful (b) *(mortal)* deadly, fatal (c) *(inexorable)* fateful, inevitable

2 *adv Fam* awfully, terribly; **lo pasó f.** he had a rotten time

fatalidad *nf* (a) *(destino)* fate (b) *(desgracia)* misfortune

> *Observa que la palabra inglesa **fatality** es un falso amigo y no es la traducción de la palabra española **fatalidad**. En inglés, **fatality** significa "víctima mortal".*

fatalista 1 *adj* fatalistic
 2 *nmf* fatalist

fatiga *nf* (a) *(cansancio)* fatigue (b) **fatigas** *(dificultades)* troubles, difficulties

fatigar [42] **1** *vt* to tire, to weary
 2 fatigarse *vpr* to tire, to become tired

fatigoso,-a *adj* tiring, exhausting

fatuo,-a *adj* (a) *(envanecido)* vain, conceited (b) *(necio)* fatuous, foolish

fauces *nfpl Fig* jaws

fauna *nf* fauna

favor *nm* favour; **por f.** please; **¿puedes hacerme un f.?** can you do me a favour?; **estar a f. de** to be in favour of; **haga el f. de sentarse** please sit down

favorable *adj* favourable; **f. a** in favour of

favorecedor,-a *adj* flattering

favorecer [33] *vt* (a) to favour (b) *(sentar bien)* to flatter

favoritismo *nm* favouritism

favorito,-a *adj & nm,f* favourite

faz *nf* (*pl* **faces**) *Literario (cara)* face

fe *nf* (a) faith; **de buena/mala fe** with good/dishonest intentions (b) *(certificado)* certificate; **fe de bautismo/matrimonio** baptism/marriage certificate (c) *Impr* **fe de erratas** errata

fealdad *nf* ugliness

febrero *nm* February

febril *adj* (a) *Med* feverish (b) *(actividad)* hectic

fecha *nf* (a) date; **f. límite** *o* **tope** deadline; **f. de caducidad** sell-by date; **hasta la f.** so far; **en f. próxima** at an early date (b) **fechas** *(época)* time; **el año pasado por estas fechas** this time last year

fechar *vt* to date

fechoría *nf* *(de niños)* mischief; *Literario* misdeed

fécula *nf* starch

fecundación *nf* fertilization; **f. in vitro** in vitro fertilization

fecundar *vt* to fertilize

fecundo,-a *adj* fertile

federación *nf* federation

federal *adj & nmf* federal

fehaciente *adj* (a) *Fml* authentic, reliable (b) *Jur* irrefutable; **documento** *o* **prueba f.** irrefutable proof

felicidad *nf* happiness; **(muchas) felicidades** *(en cumpleaños)* many happy returns

felicitación *nf* **tarjeta de f.** greetings card

felicitar *vt* to congratulate (**por** on); **¡te felicito!** congratulations!

feligrés,-esa *nm,f* parishioner

felino,-a *adj & nm* feline

feliz *adj* (a) *(contento)* happy; **¡felices Navidades!** Happy *o* Merry Christmas! (b) *(decisión etc)* fortunate

felonía *nf* treachery

felpa *nf* (a) *Tex* plush; **oso** *o* **osito de f.** teddy bear (b) *(para el pelo)* hairband

felpudo *nm* mat, doormat

femenino,-a *adj* feminine; *(equipo, ropa)* women's; **el sexo f.** the female sex, women

feminismo *nm* feminism

feminista *adj & nmf* feminist

fémur *nm* femur

fenecer [33] *vi Euf* to pass away, to die

fenomenal 1 *adj* (a) phenomenal (b) *Fam (fantástico)* great, terrific

2 *adv Fam* wonderfully, marvellously; **lo pasamos f.** we had a fantastic time

fenómeno,-a 1 *nm* (a) phenomenon (b) *(prodigio)* genius (c) *(monstruo)* freak

2 *adj Fam* fantastic, terrific

3 *interj* fantastic!, terrific!

feo,-a 1 *adj* ugly; *(asunto etc)* nasty

2 *nm Fam* **hacerle un f. a algn** to offend sb

féretro *nm* coffin

feria *nf* fair; **f. de muestras/del libro** trade/book fair

feriado,-a *Am* **1** *adj* **día f.** (public) holiday

2 *nm* (public) holiday

ferial *adj* **recinto f.** *(de exposiciones)* exhibition centre; *(de fiestas)* fairground

ferina *adj* **tos f.** whooping cough

fermentar *vi* to ferment

fermento *nm* ferment

ferocidad *nf* ferocity, fierceness

feroz *adj* fierce, ferocious; **el lobo f.** the big bad wolf

férreo,-a *adj* ferreous; *Fig* iron

ferretería *nf* ironmonger's (shop), hardware store

ferrocarril *nm Br* railway, *US* railroad

ferroviario,-a *adj* rail, *Br* railway

ferry *nm* ferry

fértil *adj* fertile

fertilidad *nf* fertility

fertilizante 1 *adj* fertilizing

2 *nm* fertilizer

fertilizar [40] *vt* to fertilize

ferviente *adj* fervent

fervor *nm* fervour

fervoroso,-a *adj* fervent

festejar *vt* to celebrate

festejos *nmpl* festivities

festín *nm* feast, banquet

festival *nm* festival

festividad *nf* festivity

festivo,-a 1 *adj* (**a**) *(ambiente etc)* festive (**b**) **día f.** holiday

2 *nm* holiday

feta *nf RP* slice

fetal *adj* foetal

fetiche *nm* fetish

fétido,-a *adj* stinking, fetid

feto *nm* foetus

feudalismo *nm* feudalism

feudo *nm* fief; *Pol* stronghold

FEVE *nm* (*abr* **Ferrocarriles de Vía Estrecha**) = Spanish narrow-gauge railways

FF.AA. *nfpl* (*abr* **Fuerzas Armadas**) Armed Forces

FF.CC. *nmpl* (*abr* **ferrocarriles**) railways

fiabilidad *nf* reliability, trustworthiness

fiable *adj* reliable, trustworthy

fiaca *nf Méx, CSur Fam (pereza)* laziness

fiador,-a *nm,f* guarantor; **salir o ser f. de algn** *(pagar fianza)* to stand bail for sb; *(avalar)* to vouch for sb

fiambre *nm* (**a**) *Culin* cold meat (**b**) *Fam (cadáver)* stiff, corpse

fiambrera *nf* lunch box

fianza *nf (depósito)* deposit; *Jur* bail; **en libertad bajo f.** on bail

fiar [29] 1 *vt* (**a**) *(avalar)* to guarantee (**b**) *(vender sin cobrar)* to sell on credit

2 fiarse *upr* **fiarse (de)** to trust

fiasco *nm* fiasco

fibra *nf* fibre; *(de madera)* grain; **f. de vidrio** fibreglass

ficción *nf* fiction

ficha *nf* (**a**) *(tarjeta)* filing card; **f. técnica** specifications, technical data; *Cin* credits (**b**) *(en juegos)* counter; *(de ajedrez)* piece, man; *(de dominó)* domino

fichado,-a *adj* **está f. por la policía** he has a police record

fichaje *nm Dep* signing

fichar 1 *vt* (**a**) to put on file (**b**) *Dep* to sign up

2 *vi* (**a**) *(en el trabajo) (al entrar)* to clock in; *(al salir)* to clock out (**b**) *Dep* to sign

fichero *nm* card index

ficticio,-a *adj* fictitious

fidedigno,-a *adj* reliable, trustworthy; **fuentes fidedignas** reliable sources

fidelidad *nf* faithfulness; **alta f.** high fidelity, hi-fi

fideo *nm* noodle

fiebre *nf* fever; **tener f.** to have a temperature

fiel 1 *adj* (**a**) *(leal)* faithful, loyal (**b**) *(exacto)* accurate, exact

2 *nm* (**a**) *(de balanza)* needle, pointer (**b**) *Rel* **los fieles** the congregation

fieltro *nm* felt

fiera *nf* (**a**) wild animal; *Fam* **estaba hecho una f.** he was hopping mad (**b**) *Taurom* bull

fiero,-a *adj (salvaje)* wild; *(feroz)* fierce, ferocious

fierro *nm Am (hierro)* iron

fiesta *nf* (**a**) *(entre amigos)* party (**b**) **día de f.** holiday (**c**) *Rel* feast; **f. de guardar** holy day of obligation (**d**) *(festividad)* celebration, festivity

figura *nf* figure

figurado,-a *adj* figurative; **en sentido f.** figuratively

figurar 1 *vi (en lista)* to figure

2 figurarse *upr* (**a**) to imagine, to suppose; **ya me lo figuraba** I thought as much (**b**) **¡figúrate!, ¡figúrese!** just imagine!

figurinista *nmf Teatro & Cin* costume designer

fijador *nm* (**a**) *(gomina)* gel (**b**) *Fot* fixative

fijamente *adv* mirar f. to stare

fijar 1 *vt* to fix; **prohibido f. carteles** *(en letrero)* post no bills

2 fijarse *vpr* **(a)** *(darse cuenta)* to notice **(b)** *(poner atención)* to pay attention, to watch

fijo,-a *adj* **(a)** fixed; **sin domicilio f.** of no fixed abode **(b)** *(trabajo)* steady

fila *nf* **(a)** file; **en f. india** in single file; **poner en f.** to line up **(b)** *(de cine, teatro)* row **(c)** *Mil* **filas** ranks; **llamar a algn a filas** to call sb up; **¡rompan filas!** fall out!, dismiss!

filamento *nm* filament

filantropía *nf* philanthropy

filántropo,-a *nm,f* philanthropist

filarmónico,-a *adj* philharmonic

filatelia *nf* philately, stamp collecting

filete *nm (de carne, pescado)* fillet

filiación *nf Pol* affiliation

filial 1 *adj* **(a)** *(de hijos)* filial **(b)** *Com* subsidiary

2 *nf Com* subsidiary

filigrana *nf* **(a)** filigree **(b)** *Fig* **filigranas** intricacy, intricate work

Filipinas *npl* **(las) F.** (the) Philippines

filipino,-a *adj & nm,f* Philippine, Filipino

film *nm* film

filmar *vt* to film, to shoot

filme *nm* film

fílmico,-a *adj* film

filmoteca *nf (archivo)* film library

filo *nm* (cutting) edge; **al f. de la medianoche** on the stroke of midnight; *Fig* **de doble f.** double-edged

filón *nm* **(a)** *Min* seam, vein **(b)** *Fig (buen negocio)* gold mine

filoso,-a *adj Am* sharp

filosofal *adj* **piedra f.** philosopher's stone

filosofía *nf* philosophy; *Fig* **con f.** philosophically

filosófico,-a *adj* philosophical

filósofo,-a *nm,f* philosopher

filtración *nf* filtration; *(de información)* leak

filtrar 1 *vt* **(a)** to filter **(b)** *(información)* to leak

2 • filtrarse *vpr* **(a)** *(líquido)* to seep **(b)** *(información)* to leak out

filtro *nm* filter

fin *nm* **(a)** *(final)* end; **dar** *o* **poner f. a** to put an end to; **llegar** *o* **tocar a su f.** to come to an end; **en f.** anyway; **¡por** *o* **al f.!** at last!; **f. de semana** weekend; **al f. y al cabo** when all's said and done; **noche de F. de Año** New Year's Eve **(b)** *(objetivo)* purpose, aim; **a f. de** in order to, so as to;

a f. de que in order that, so that; **con el f. de** with the intention of

final 1 *adj* final

2 *nm* end; **al f.** in the end; **f. de línea** terminal; **f. feliz** happy ending; **a finales de octubre** at the end of October

3 *nf Dep* final

finalidad *nf* purpose, aim

finalista 1 *nmf* finalist

2 *adj* in the final

finalizar [40] *vt & vi* to end, to finish

finalmente *adv* finally

financiación *nf* financing

financiar [43] *vt* to finance

financiero,-a 1 *adj* financial

2 *nm,f* financier

financista *nmf Am* financier, financial expert

finanzas *nfpl* finances

finca *nf (inmueble)* property; *(de campo)* country house

finés,-esa *adj & nm,f* = **finlandés,-esa**

fingido,-a *adj* feigned, false; **nombre f.** assumed name

fingir [57] 1 *vt* to feign

2 fingirse *vpr* to pretend to be

finlandés,-esa 1 *adj* Finnish

2 *nm,f (persona)* Finn

3 *nm (idioma)* Finnish

Finlandia *n* Finland

fino,-a 1 *adj* **(a)** *(hilo, capa)* fine **(b)** *(flaco)* thin **(c)** *(educado)* refined, polite **(d)** *(oído)* sharp, acute; *(olfato)* keen **(e)** *(humor, ironía)* subtle

2 *nm (vino)* = type of dry sherry

finta *nf (en boxeo)* feint; *(en fútbol)* dummy

finura *nf* **(a)** *(refinamiento)* refinement, politeness **(b)** *(sutileza)* subtlety

firma *nf* **(a)** signature **(b)** *(empresa)* firm, company

firmamento *nm* firmament

firmante *adj & nmf* signatory; **el** *o* **la abajo f.** the undersigned

firmar *vt* to sign

firme 1 *adj* **(a)** firm; *Fig* **mantenerse f.** to hold one's ground; **tierra f.** terra firma **(b)** *Mil* **¡firmes!** attention!

2 *nm (de carretera)* road surface

3 *adv* hard

firmemente *adv* firmly

firmeza *nf* firmness

fiscal 1 *adj* fiscal, tax

2 *nmf Jur* public prosecutor, *US* district attorney

fisco *nm* treasury, exchequer

fisgar [42] *vi Fam* to snoop, to pry

fisgón,-ona *nm,f* snooper

fisgonear *vi* to snoop, to pry
física *nf* physics *sing*
físico,-a 1 *adj* physical
  2 *nm,f (profesión)* physicist
  3 *nm* physique
fisión *nf* fission
fisioterapeuta *nmf* physiotherapist
fisioterapia *nf Med* physiotherapy
fisonomía *nf* physiognomy
fisonomista *nmf Fam* **ser buen/mal f.** to be good/no good at remembering faces
fisura *nf* fissure
flácido,-a *adj* flaccid, flabby
flaco,-a 1 *adj* (a) *(delgado)* skinny (b) *Fig* **punto f.** weak spot
  2 *nm,f Am Fam (como apelativo)* **¿cómo estás, flaca?** hey, how are you doing?
flagelar *vt* to flagellate
flagelo *nm (látigo)* whip; *Fig* scourge
flagrante *adj* flagrant; **en f. delito** red-handed
flamante *adj* (a) **nuevecito f.** *(nuevo)* brand-new (b) *(vistoso)* splendid, brilliant
flamenco,-a 1 *adj* (a) *Mús* flamenco (b) *(de Flandes)* Flemish
  2 *nm* (a) *Mús* flamenco (b) *Orn* flamingo (c) *(idioma)* Flemish
flan *nm* crème caramel

> 🔎 Observa que la palabra inglesa **flan** es un falso amigo y no es la traducción de la palabra española **flan**. En inglés, **flan** significa "tarta".

flanco *nm* flank, side
flanquear *vt* to flank
flaquear *vi (fuerzas, piernas)* to weaken, to give way
flaqueza *nf* weakness
flash *nm Fot* flash
flato *nm* wind, flatulence
flatulencia *nf* flatulence
flauta *nf* flute; **f. dulce** recorder
flautín *nm (instrumento)* piccolo
flautista *nmf Mús* flute player, flautist, *US* flutist
flecha *nf* arrow
flechazo *nm Fig (enamoramiento)* love at first sight
fleco *nm* fringe
flema *nf* phlegm
flemático,-a *adj* phlegmatic
flemón *nm* gumboil, abscess
flequillo *nm Br* fringe, *US* bangs
fletar *vt* to charter
flete *nm* (a) *(alquiler)* charter (b) *(carga)* freight
flexibilidad *nf* flexibility
flexible *adj* flexible

flexión *nf* (a) *Gram* inflection (b) **flexiones** push-ups, *Br* press-ups
flexionar *vt* to bend; *(músculo)* to flex
flexo *nm* reading lamp
flipante *adj Fam* great, cool
flipar *vt Fam* **le flipan las motos** he's crazy about motorbikes
flirtear *vi* to flirt
flirteo *nm* flirting
flojear *vi (ventas etc)* to fall off, to go down; *(piernas)* to weaken, to grow weak; *(memoria)* to fail; *Andes Fam (holgazanear)* to laze around o about
flojedad *nf* weakness
flojera *nf Fam* weakness, faintness
flojo,-a *adj* (a) *(tornillo, cuerda etc)* loose, slack (b) *(perezoso)* lazy, idle; *(exámen, trabajo, resultado)* poor
flor *nf* (a) flower; **en f.** in blossom; *Fig* **en la f. de la vida** in the prime of life; *Fig* **la f. y nata** the cream (of society) (b) **a f. de piel** skin-deep
flora *nf* flora
floreado,-a *adj* flowery
florecer [33] *vi* (a) *(plantas)* to flower (b) *Fig (negocio)* to flourish, to thrive
floreciente *adj Fig* flourishing, prosperous
Florencia *n* Florence
florero *nm* vase
floricultura *nf* flower growing, floriculture
florido,-a *adj* (a) *(con flores)* flowery (b) *(estilo)* florid
floripondio *nm Pey (adorno)* heavy ornamentation
florista *nmf* florist
floristería *nf* florist's (shop)
flota *nf* fleet
flotador *nm* (a) *(de pesca)* float (b) *(para nadar)* rubber ring
flotar *vi* to float
flote *nm* floating; **a f.** afloat; **sacar a f. un negocio** to put a business on a sound footing
flotilla *nf* flotilla
fluctuación *nf* fluctuation
fluctuar [30] *vi* to fluctuate
fluidez *nf* fluency
fluido,-a 1 *adj* fluid; *(estilo etc)* fluent
  2 *nm* fluid; **f. eléctrico** current
fluir [37] *vi* to flow
flujo *nm* (a) flow (b) rising tide; **f. y reflujo** ebb and flow (c) *Fís* flux (d) *Med* discharge (e) *Informát* stream
flúor *nm* fluorine
fluorescente *adj* fluorescent
fluvial *adj* river

FM *nf* (*abr* **Frecuencia Modulada**) FM

FMI *nm* (*abr* **Fondo Monetario Internacional**) IMF

fobia *nf* phobia (**a** about)

foca *nf* seal

foco *nm* (**a**) *Elec* spotlight, floodlight (**b**) (*de ideas, revolución etc*) centre, focal point (**c**) *Am* (*de coche*) (car) headlight; (*farola*) street light (**d**) *Col, Méx* (*bombilla*) light bulb

fofo,-a *adj* soft; (*persona*) flabby

fogata *nf* bonfire

fogón *nm* (*de cocina*) ring

fogonazo *nm* flash

fogosidad *nf* ardour, fire

fogoso,-a *adj* fiery, spirited

fogueo *nm* **cartucho de f.** blank cartridge

fólder *nm Andes, CAm, Méx* (*carpeta*) folder

folio *nm* sheet of paper

folklore *nm* folklore

folklórico,-a *adj* **música folklórica** folk music

follaje *nm* foliage

follar *muy Fam* **1** *vi* to screw, to shag

2 *vt* (*suspender*) to fail

3 follarse *vpr* **f. a algn** to screw sb, to shag sb

folletín *nm* (**a**) (*relato*) newspaper serial (**b**) *Fig* melodrama

folleto *nm* leaflet; (*turístico*) brochure

follón *nm Fam* (**a**) (*alboroto*) rumpus, shindy; **armar (un) f.** to kick up a rumpus (**b**) (*enredo, confusión*) mess, trouble; **meterse en un f.** to get into a mess (**c**) **un f. de** (*montón*) a load of

follonero,-a *nm,f* troublemaker

fomentar *vt* to promote

fomento *nm* promotion

fonda *nf* inn

fondear *vi* to anchor

fondista *nmf Dep* long-distance runner

fondo¹ *nm* (**a**) (*parte más baja*) bottom; **a f.** thoroughly; **al f. de la calle** at the bottom of the street; **tocar f.** *Náut* to touch bottom; *Fig* to reach rock bottom; *Fig* **en el f. es bueno** deep down he's kind; **bajos fondos** dregs of society; **doble f.** false bottom

(**b**) (*de habitación*) back; (*de pasillo*) end

(**c**) (*segundo término*) background; **música de f.** background music

(**d**) *Prensa* **artículo de f.** leading article

(**e**) *Dep* **corredor de f.** long-distance runner; **esquí de f.** cross-country skiing

(**f**) *RP* (*patio*) back patio

(**g**) *Carib, Méx* (*prenda*) petticoat

fondo² *nm Fin* fund; **cheque sin fondos** bad cheque; *Fam* **f. común** kitty

fonendoscopio *nm* stethoscope

fonética *nf* phonetics *sing*

fonético,-a *adj* phonetic

fono *nm Am Fam* phone

fontanería *nf* plumbing

fontanero,-a *nm,f* plumber

footing *nm* jogging; **hacer f.** to go jogging

forajido,-a *nm,f* outlaw

foráneo,-a *adj* foreign

forastero,-a *nm,f* outsider, stranger

forcejear *vi* to wrestle, to struggle

forcejeo *nm* struggle

fórceps *nm inv* forceps

forense 1 *adj* forensic

2 *nmf* (**médico**) **f.** forensic surgeon

forestal *adj* forest; **repoblación f.** reafforestation

forjado,-a *adj* wrought

forjar *vt* (*metal*) to forge; *Fig* to create, to make

forma *nf* (**a**) form, shape; **en f. de L** L-shaped; **¿qué f. tiene?** what shape is it? (**b**) (*manera*) way; **de esta f.** in this way; **de f. que** so that; **de todas formas** anyway, in any case; **no hubo f. de convencerla** there was no way we could convince her; **f. de pago** method of payment (**c**) *Dep* form; **estar en f.** to be on form; **estar en baja f.** to be off form (**d**) *Rel* **Sagrada F.** Host (**e**) **formas** (*modales*) manners

formación *nf* (**a**) formation (**b**) (*educación*) upbringing (**c**) (*enseñanza*) training; **f. profesional** vocational training

formal *adj* (**a**) formal (**b**) (*serio*) serious, serious-minded (**c**) (*fiable*) reliable, dependable

formalidad *nf* (**a**) formality (**b**) (*seriedad*) seriousness (**c**) (*fiabilidad*) reliability (**d**) **formalidades** (*trámites*) formalities

formalizar [40] **1** *vt* to formalize

2 formalizarse *vpr* to settle down

formar 1 *vt* (**a**) to form; **f. parte de algo** to be a part of sth (**b**) (*educar*) to bring up; (*enseñar*) to educate, to train

2 formarse *vpr* (**a**) to be formed, to form; **se formó un charco** a puddle formed; **f. una impresión de algo** to get an impression of sth (**b**) (*educarse*) to be educated o trained

formatear *vt Informát* to format

formato *nm* format; (*del papel*) size

formica® *nf* Formica®

formidable *adj* (**a**) (*estupendo*) wonderful, terrific (**b**) (*espantoso*) formidable

fórmula *nf* formula; *Aut* **f. uno** formula one

formular *vt (quejas, peticiones)* to make; *(deseo)* to express; *(pregunta)* to ask; *(una teoría)* to formulate

formulario *nm* form

fornicación *nf* fornication

fornicar [44] *vi* to fornicate

fornido,-a *adj* strapping, hefty

foro *nm* (a) forum (b) *(mesa redonda)* round table (c) *Teatro* back (of the stage) (d) *Jur* law court, court of justice

forofo,-a *nm,f Fam* fan, supporter

forrado,-a *adj* lined; *Fam* **estar f.** to be well-heeled, to be well-off

forraje *nm* fodder

forrar 1 *vt (por dentro)* to line; *(por fuera)* to cover
  2 **forrarse** *vpr Fam (de dinero)* to make a packet

forro *nm* (a) *(por dentro)* lining; *(por fuera)* cover, case (b) *RP Fam (preservativo)* rubber, condom

fortalecer [33] *vt* to fortify, to strengthen

fortaleza *nf* (a) strength; *(de espíritu)* fortitude (b) *Mil* fortress, stronghold

fortificante 1 *adj* fortifying
  2 *nm* tonic

fortificar [44] *vt* to fortify

fortísimo,-a *adj* very strong

fortuito,-a *adj* fortuitous

fortuna *nf* (a) *(destino)* fortune, fate (b) *(suerte)* luck; **por f.** fortunately (c) *(capital)* fortune

forzado,-a *adj* forced; **a marchas forzadas** at a brisk pace; **trabajos forzados** hard labour

forzar [2] *vt* (a) *(obligar)* to force; **f. a algn a hacer algo** to force sb to do sth (b) *(puerta, candado)* to force, to break open

forzosamente *adv* necessarily

forzoso,-a *adj* obligatory, compulsory; *Av* **aterrizaje f.** forced landing

fosa *nf* (a) *(sepultura)* grave (b) *(hoyo)* pit (c) *Anat* **fosas nasales** nostrils

fosforescente *adj* phosphorescent

fósforo *nm (cerilla)* match

fósil *adj & nm* fossil

fosilizarse [40] *vpr* to fossilize, to become fossilized

foso *nm* (a) *(hoyo)* pit (b) *(de fortificación)* moat (c) *(en garage)* inspection pit

foto *nf Fam* photo; **sacar/echar una f.** to take a photo

fotocopia *nf* photocopy

fotocopiadora *nf* photocopier

fotocopiar [43] *vt* to photocopy

fotogénico,-a *adj* photogenic

fotografía *nf* (a) photograph; **echar** *o* **hacer** *o* **sacar fotografías** to take photographs (b) *(arte)* photography

fotografiar [29] *vt* to photograph, to take a photograph of

fotográfico,-a *adj* photographic

fotógrafo,-a *nm,f* photographer

fotograma *nm* still, shot

fotomatón *nm* passport photo machine

fotómetro *nm* light meter, exposure meter

FP *nf Educ (abr* **Formación Profesional***)* vocational training

frac *nm (pl* **fracs** *o* **fraques***)* dress coat, tails

fracasado,-a 1 *adj* unsuccessful
  2 *nm,f (persona)* failure

fracasar *vi* to fail

fracaso *nm* failure

> 🖉 Observa que la palabra inglesa **fracas** es un falso amigo y no es la traducción de la palabra española **fracaso**. En inglés, **fracas** significa "gresca, refriega".

---

fracción *nf* (a) fraction (b) *Pol* faction

fraccionamiento *nm Méx (urbanización)* housing estate

fraccionar *vt,* **fraccionarse** *vpr* to break up, to split up

fraccionario,-a *adj* fractional; **moneda fraccionaria** small change

fractura *nf* fracture

fracturar *vt,* **fracturarse** *vpr* to fracture, to break

fragancia *nf* fragrance

fragata *nf* frigate

frágil *adj* (a) *(quebradizo)* fragile (b) *(débil)* frail

fragmentar 1 *vt* to fragment
  2 **fragmentarse** *vpr* to break up

fragmento *nm* fragment; *(de novela etc)* passage

fragor *nm* din

fragua *nf* forge

fraguar [45] *vt* (a) *(metal)* to forge (b) *(plan)* to think up, to fabricate; *(conspiración)* to hatch

fraile *nm* friar, monk

frailecillo *nm* puffin

frambuesa *nf* raspberry

francamente *adv* frankly

francés,-esa 1 *adj* French; *Culin* **tortilla francesa** plain omelette
  2 *nm,f (hombre)* Frenchman; *(mujer)* Frenchwoman
  3 *nm (idioma)* French

Francfort, Francfurt *n* Frankfurt; *Culin* **salchicha estilo f.** frankfurter

Francia *n* France

francmasón,-ona *nm,f* freemason

franco¹,-a *adj* (a) *(persona)* frank (b) *Com* **f. a bordo** free on board; **f. fábrica** ex-works; **puerto f.** free port (c) *CSur (día)* **me dieron el día f.** they gave me the day off

franco² *nm Fin (moneda)* franc

francotirador,-a *nm,f* sniper

franela *nf* (a) *(paño)* flannel (b) *Bol, Col, Ven (camiseta)* T-shirt

franja *nf (de terreno)* strip; *(de bandera)* stripe; *Cost* fringe, border

franquear *vt* (a) *(atravesar)* to cross; *Fig (dificultad, obstáculo)* to overcome (b) *(carta)* to frank (c) *(camino, paso)* to free, to clear

franqueo *nm* postage

franqueza *nf* frankness

franquicia *nf* exemption; *Com* franchise

franquismo *nm Hist* (a) *(ideología)* Francoism (b) **el f.** *(régimen)* the Franco regime

franquista *adj & nmf* Francoist

frasco *nm* small bottle, flask

frase *nf (oración)* sentence; *(expresión)* phrase; **f. hecha** set phrase o expression

fraternidad *nf* brotherhood, fraternity

fraternizar [40] *vi* to fraternize

fraterno,-a *adj* fraternal, brotherly

fraude *nm* fraud; **f. fiscal** tax evasion

fraudulento,-a *adj* fraudulent

fray *nm Rel* brother

frazada *nf Am* blanket

frecuencia *nf* frequency; **con f.** frequently, often

frecuentar *vt* to frequent

frecuente *adj* frequent

frecuentemente *adv* frequently, often

fregadero *nm* (kitchen) sink

fregado¹ *nm* (a) *(lavado)* washing (b) *Fam (follón)* racket

fregado²,-a *adj Am Fam* (a) *(persona) (difícil)* tiresome, annoying (b) *(objeto) (roto)* broken

fregar [1] *vt* (a) *(lavar)* to wash; *(suelo)* to mop (b) *Am Fam (molestar)* to annoy, to irritate (c) *Am Fam (romper)* to bust, to break

fregón,-ona *adj Am* annoying

fregona *nf* mop

freidora *nf* (deep fat) fryer

freír [56] *(pp frito)* **1** *vt* to fry
  2 freírse *vpr* to fry; *Fig* **f. de calor** to be roasting

frenar *vt* to brake; *Fig (inflación etc)* to slow down; *(impulsos)* to restrain

frenazo *nm* sudden braking; **dar un f.** to jam on the brakes

frenesí *nm* frenzy

frenético,-a *adj* frantic

freno *nm* (a) *(de vehículo)* brake; **pisar/soltar el f.** to press/release the brake; **f. de disco/tambor** disc/drum brake; **f. de mano** handbrake (b) *(de caballería)* bit (c) *Fig* curb, check; **poner f. a algo** to curb sth

frente 1 *nm* front; **al f. de** at the head of; **chocar de f.** to crash head on; **hacer f. a algo** to face sth, to stand up to sth
  2 *nf Anat* forehead; **f. a f.** face to face
  3 *adv* **f. a** in front of, opposite

fresa *nf* (a) strawberry (b) *Téc* milling cutter

fresca *nf Fam* cheeky remark

fresco,-a 1 *adj* (a) *(frío)* cool (b) *(comida, fruta)* fresh (c) *(reciente)* fresh, new (d) *(descarado)* cheeky, shameless; **se quedó tan f.** he didn't bat an eyelid; **¡qué f.!** what a nerve!
  2 *nm* (a) *(frescor)* fresh air, cool air; **al f.** in the cool; **hace f.** it's chilly (b) *Arte* fresco

frescor *nm* freshness

frescura *nf* (a) freshness (b) *(desvergüenza)* cheek, nerve

fresno *nm* ash tree

fresón *nm* (large) strawberry

frialdad *nf* coldness

fríamente *adv* coolly

fricción *nf* (a) friction (b) *(masaje)* massage

friega *nf* rub

friegaplatos *nmf inv (persona)* dishwasher

frigider *nm Andes* refrigerator, fridge

frígido,-a *adj* frigid

frigorífico,-a 1 *nm* refrigerator, fridge
  2 *adj* **cámara frigorífica** cold store

frijol, fríjol *nm Andes, CAm, Carib, Méx* bean

frío,-a 1 *adj* (a) cold (b) *(indiferente)* cold, cool, indifferent; **su comentario me dejó f.** her remark left me cold
  2 *nm* cold; **hace f.** it's cold

friolento,-a *adj Am* sensitive to the cold

friolera *nf Fam* **la f. de diez mil pesetas/dos horas** a mere ten thousand pesetas/two hours

friolero,-a *adj* sensitive to the cold

fritanga *nf* fried food; *Am* greasy food

frito,-a 1 *adj* (a) *Culin* fried (b) *Fam* exasperated, fed up; **me tienes f.** I'm sick to death of you
  2 nm fritos fried food

frívolo,-a *adj* frivolous

frondoso,-a *adj* leafy, luxuriant

frontera *nf* frontier

fronterizo,-a *adj* frontier, border; **países fronterizos** neighbouring countries

frontón *nm Dep* pelota

frotar 1 *vt* to rub

  2 frotarse *vpr* to rub; **f. las manos** to rub one's hands together

fructífero,-a *adj* (*árbol*) fruit-bearing; (*esfuerzo*) fruitful

frugal *adj* frugal

fruncir [52] *vt* (**a**) *Cost* to gather (**b**) (*labios*) to purse, to pucker; **f. el ceño** to frown, to knit one's brow

frustración *nf* frustration

frustrado,-a *adj* frustrated; **intento f.** unsuccessful attempt

frustrante *adj* frustrating

frustrar 1 *vt* to frustrate; (*defraudar*) to disappoint

  2 frustrarse *vpr* (**a**) (*esperanza*) to fail, to go awry (**b**) (*persona*) to be frustrated *o* disappointed

fruta *nf* fruit; **f. del tiempo** fresh fruit

frutería *nf* fruit shop

frutero,-a 1 *nm,f* fruiterer

  2 *nm* fruit dish *o* bowl

frutilla *nf Bol, CSur, Ecuad* strawberry

fruto *nm* fruit; **frutos secos** nuts; **dar f.** to bear fruit; *Fig* (*dar buen resultado*) to be fruitful; **sacar f. de algo** to profit from sth

fu *interj* **ni fu ni fa** so-so

fucsia *nf* fuchsia

fuego *nm* (**a**) fire; **fuegos artificiales** fireworks (**b**) (*lumbre*) light; **¿me da f., por favor?** have you got a light, please? (**c**) *Culin* **a f. lento** on a low flame; (*al horno*) in a slow oven

fuel, fuel-oil *nm* diesel

fuente *nf* (**a**) fountain; *Chile, Col, Méx, Ven* **f. de soda** (*cafetería*) cafe (*serving soft drinks and alcohol*) (**b**) (*recipiente*) dish, serving dish (**c**) (*de información*) source

fuera¹ *adv* (**a**) outside, out; **quédate f.** stay outside; **sal f.** go out; **desde f.** from (the) outside; **por f.** on the outside; **la puerta de f.** the outer door (**b**) **f. de** out of; **f. de serie** extraordinary; *Fig* **estar f. de sí** to be beside oneself (**c**) *Dep* **el equipo de f.** the away team; **jugar f.** to play away; **f. de juego** offside

fuera² **1** *subj imperf de* **ir**

  2 *subj imperf de* **ser**

fuero *nm* (**a**) *Hist* code of laws (**b**) *Fig* **en tu f. interno** deep down, in your heart of hearts

fuerte 1 *adj* strong; (*dolor*) severe; (*sonido*) loud; (*comida*) heavy; **el plato f.** the main course; *Fig* the most important event

  2 *nm* (**a**) (*fortaleza*) fort (**b**) (*punto fuerte*) forte, strong point

  3 *adv* **¡abrázame f.!** hold me tight!; **comer f.** to eat a lot; **¡habla más f.!** speak up!; **¡pégale f.!** hit him hard!

fuerza *nf* (**a**) (*fortaleza*) strength; *Fig* **a f. de** by dint of (**b**) (*violencia*) force; **a la f.** (*por obligación*) of necessity; (*con violencia*) by force; **por f.** of necessity; **f. mayor** force majeure (**c**) *Fís* force (**d**) (*cuerpo*) force; **las fuerzas del orden** the forces of law and order; **f. aérea** air force; **fuerzas armadas** armed forces

fuese 1 *subj imperf de* **ir**

  2 *subj imperf de* **ser**

fuete *nm Am* whip

fuga *nf* (**a**) (*huida*) escape; **darse a la f.** to take flight (**b**) (*de gas etc*) leak

fugarse [42] *vpr* to escape; **f. de casa** to run away from home

fugaz *adj* fleeting, brief

fugitivo,-a *nm,f* fugitive

fui 1 *pt indef de* **ir**

  2 *pt indef de* **ser**

fulana *nf* whore, tart

fulano,-a *nm,f* so-and-so; (*hombre*) what's-his-name; (*mujer*) what's-her-name; **Doña Fulana de tal** Mrs So-and-so

fular *nm* headscarf

fulgor *nm Literario* brilliance, glow

fullería *nf* cheating; **hacer fullerías** to cheat

fullero,-a 1 *adj* cheating

  2 *nm,f* cheat

fulminante *adj* (*cese*) summary; (*muerte, enfermedad*) sudden; (*mirada*) withering

fulminar *vt Fig* to strike dead; **f. a algn con la mirada** to look daggers at sb

fumada *nf Am* (*calada*) pull, drag

fumado,-a *adj Fam* (*colocado*) stoned

fumador,-a *nm,f* smoker; **los no fumadores** nonsmokers

fumar 1 *vt & vi* to smoke; **no f.** (*en letrero*) no smoking

  2 fumarse *vpr* to smoke; **f. un cigarro** to smoke a cigarette

> 🎵 Observa que el verbo inglés **to fume** es un falso amigo y no es la traducción del verbo español **fumar**. En inglés, **to fume** significa "despedir humo".

fumigar [42] *vt* to fumigate

funambulista *nmf*, **funámbulo,-a** *nm,f* tightrope walker

función *nf* (**a**) function; **en f. de** according to (**b**) (*cargo*) duties; **entrar en funciones** to take up one's duties; **presidente**

en funciones acting president (**c**) *Cin &
Teatro* performance
funcionamiento *nm* operation; **poner/
entrar en f.** to put/come into operation
funcionar *vi* to work; **no funciona** *(en
letrero)* out of order
funcionario,-a *nm,f* civil servant; **f. público** public official
funda *nf* cover; *(de gafas etc)* case; *(de
espada)* sheath; **f. de almohada** pillowcase
fundación *nf* foundation
fundador,-a *nm,f* founder
fundamental *adj* fundamental
fundamentar *vt* to base (**en** on)
fundamento *nm* basis, grounds; **sin f.**
unfounded
fundar 1 *vt* (**a**) *(empresa)* to found (**b**)
(teoría) to base, to found
  2 fundarse *vpr* (**a**) *(empresa)* to be founded (**b**) *(teoría)* to be based (**en** on)

> 🖉 Observa que el verbo inglés **to fund** es
> un falso amigo y no es la traducción del ver-
> bo español **fundar**. En inglés, **to fund** sig-
> nifica "financiar".

fundición *nf* (**a**) *(de metales)* smelting
(**b**) *(fábrica)* foundry
fundir 1 *vt* (**a**) to melt; *(bombilla, plomos)*
to blow (**b**) *(unir)* to unite, to join
  2 fundirse *vpr* (**a**) *(derretirse)* to melt (**b**)
(bombilla, plomos) to blow (**c**) *(unirse)* to
merge (**d**) *RP Fam (arruinarse)* to go bust,
to be ruined
fúnebre *adj* (**a**) *(mortuorio)* funeral; **coche f.** hearse (**b**) *(lúgubre)* mournful,
lugubrious
funeral *nm* funeral
funeraria *nf* undertaker's, *US* funeral
home

funesto,-a *adj* ill-fated, fatal; *(consecuencias)* disastrous
fungir [57] *vi Méx* to act (**de** o **como** as)
funicular *nm* funicular (railway)
furcia *nf Pey* whore, tart
furgón *nm Aut* van
furgoneta *nf* van
furia *nf* fury; **ponerse hecho una f.** to
become furious, to fly into a rage
furibundo,-a *adj* furious, enraged
furioso,-a *adj* furious; **ponerse f.** to get
furious
furor *nm* fury, rage; *Fig* **hacer f.** to be all
the rage
furtivo,-a *adj* furtive, stealthy; **caza/pes-
ca furtiva** poaching; **cazador/pescador f.**
poacher
furúnculo *nm Med* boil
fuselaje *nm* fuselage
fusible *nm* fuse
fusil *nm* gun, rifle
fusilamiento *nm* shooting, execution
fusilar *vt* to shoot, to execute
fusión *nf* (**a**) *(de metales)* fusion; *(del
hielo)* thawing, melting; **punto de f.** melting point (**b**) *Com* merger
fusionar *vt,* **fusionarse** *vpr* (**a**) *Fís* to
fuse (**b**) *Com* to merge
fustán *nm Am* petticoat
fútbol *nm* soccer, *Br* football
futbolín *nm Br* table football, *US* foosball
futbolista *nmf* soccer player, *Br* footballer
fútil *adj* futile, trivial
futilidad *nf* futility, triviality
futurista *adj* futuristic
futuro,-a 1 *adj* future
  2 *nm* future; **en un f. próximo** in the near
future; *CSur, Méx* **a f.** in the future

G

G, g [xe] *nf (la letra)* G, g
gabán *nm* overcoat
gabardina *nf (prenda)* raincoat
gabinete *nm* (a) *(despacho)* study; **g. de abogados** lawyers' office (b) *Pol* cabinet
gaceta *nf* gazette
gachas *nfpl* porridge
gacho,-a *adj* **con la cabeza gacha** hanging one's head
gaditano,-a 1 *adj* of/from Cadiz
  2 *nm,f* person from Cadiz
gafar *vt Fam* to put a jinx on, to bring bad luck to
gafas *nfpl* glasses, spectacles; **g. de sol** sunglasses
gafe *adj & nm Fam* **ser g.** to be a jinx

> *Observa que la palabra inglesa* **gaffe** *es un falso amigo y no es la traducción de la palabra española* **gafe**. *En inglés,* **gaffe** *significa "metedura de pata, desliz".*

gafete *nm Méx* badge
gaita *nf* bagpipes
gajes *nmpl Fam Irón* **g. del oficio** occupational hazards
gajo *nm* (a) *(de naranja, pomelo etc)* segment (b) *(rama desprendida)* torn-off branch
gala *nf* (a) *(vestido)* full dress; **de g.** dressed up; *(ciudad)* decked out (b) *(espectáculo)* gala; **hacer g. de** to glory in (c) **galas** finery
galán *nm* (a) handsome young man; *Hum* ladies' man (b) *Teatro* leading man
galante *adj* gallant
galantear *vt* to court
galanteo *nm* courtship
galantería *nf* gallantry
galápago *nm* turtle
galardón *nm* prize
galardonado,-a *nm,f* prizewinner
galardonar *vt* to award a prize to
galaxia *nf* galaxy
galeón *nm* galleon
galeote *nm* galley slave
galera *nf* (a) *Náut* galley (b) *(carro)* covered wagon (c) *Impr* galley proof
galería *nf* (a) *Arquit* covered balcony (b)

(museo) art gallery (c) *Teatro* gallery, gods
Gales *n* **(el país de) G.** Wales
galés,-esa 1 *adj* Welsh
  2 *nm,f (hombre)* Welshman; *(mujer)* Welshwoman; **los galeses** the Welsh
  3 *nm (idioma)* Welsh
galgo *nm* greyhound
Galicia *n* Galicia
galimatías *nm inv Fam* gibberish
gallardo *adj* (a) *(apuesto)* smart (b) *(valeroso)* brave
gallego,-a 1 *adj* (a) Galician (b) *CSur, Cuba Pey* Spanish
  2 *nm,f* (a) Galician, person from Galicia (b) *CSur, Cuba Pey* Spaniard
  3 *nm (idioma)* Galician
galleta *nf* (a) *Culin Br* biscuit, *US* cookie (b) *Fam (cachete)* slap
gallina 1 *nf* hen
  2 *nmf Fam* coward, chicken
gallinero *nm* (a) hen run (b) *Teatro* **el g.** the gods
gallito *nm Fam (peleón)* bully
gallo *nm* (a) cock, rooster; *Fam Fig* **en menos que un canto de g.** before you could say Jack Robinson (b) *Fam Mús* off-key note
galón¹ *nm Mil* stripe
galón² *nm (medida)* gallon, *Br* = 4.55 l, *US* = 3.79 l
galopante *adj Fig (inflación etc)* galloping
galopar *vi* to gallop
galope *nm* gallop; **a g. tendido** flat out
galpón *nm Am* shed
gama *nf* range; *Mús* scale
gamba *nf* prawn
gamberrismo *nm* hooliganism
gamberro,-a 1 *nm,f* hooligan
  2 *adj* uncouth
gamo *nm* fallow deer
gamonal *nm Andes, CAm, Ven* local boss
gamuza *nf* (a) *Zool* chamois (b) *(trapo)* chamois o shammy leather
gana *nf* (a) *(deseo)* wish (**de** for); **de buena g.** willingly; **de mala g.** reluctantly; *Fam* **no me da la g.** I don't feel like it (b) **tener ganas de (hacer) algo** to feel like

(doing) sth; **quedarse con las ganas** not to manage (**c**) *(apetito)* appetite; **comer con ganas** to eat heartily

ganadería *nf* (**a**) *(crianza)* livestock farming (**b**) *(conjunto de ganado)* livestock

ganadero,-a *nm,f* livestock farmer

ganado *nm* (**a**) livestock (**b**) *Fam Fig (gente)* crowd

ganador,-a 1 *adj* winning
2 *nm,f* winner

ganancia *nf* profit

ganar 1 *vt* (**a**) *(sueldo)* to earn (**b**) *(victoria)* to win (**c**) *(aventajar)* to beat (**d**) *(alcanzar)* to reach
2 ganarse *vpr* (**a**) to earn; **g. el pan** to earn one's daily bread (**b**) *(merecer)* to deserve; **se lo ha ganado** he deserves it

ganchillo *nm* crochet work

gancho *nm* (**a**) hook (**b**) *Fam Fig (gracia, atractivo)* charm (**c**) *Andes, CAm, Méx (horquilla)* hairpin (**d**) *Andes, CAm, Méx, Ven (percha)* hanger

gandul,-a *nm,f* loafer

ganga *nf* bargain

gangoso,-a *adj* nasal

gangrena *nf* gangrene

gansada *nf Fam* silly thing to say/do

ganso,-a 1 *nm,f* (**a**) goose; *(macho)* gander (**b**) *Fam* dolt
2 *adj Fam* ginormous; **pasta gansa** bread, dough

ganzúa *nf* picklock

gañán *nm (obrero)* farmhand; *Fam (bribón)* cheat

garabatear *vt & vi* to scribble

garabato *nm* scrawl

garaje *nm* garage

garante *nmf Fin* guarantor

garantía *nf* (**a**) guarantee (**b**) *Jur (fianza)* bond, security

garantizar [40] *vt* to guarantee

garbanzo *nm* chickpea

garbeo *nm Fam (paseo)* stroll; **darse un g.** to go for a stroll

garbo *nm* grace

garfio *nm* hook, grappling iron

gargajo *nm* spit

garganta *nf* (**a**) throat (**b**) *(desfiladero)* narrow pass

gargantilla *nf* short necklace

gárgaras *nfpl* (**a**) gargling; *Fam* **¡vete a hacer g.!** get lost! (**b**) *Am (licor)* gargling solution

gárgola *nf* gargoyle

garita *nf (caseta)* hut; *Mil* sentry box

garito *nm Fam* joint

garra *nf* (**a**) *Zool* claw; *(de ave)* talon (**b**)

Fig (fuerza) force; **tener g.** to be compelling

garrafa *nf* carafe

garrafal *adj* monumental

garrapata *nf* tick

garrote *nm* (**a**) *(porra)* club (**b**) *Jur* garrotte

garrucha *nf* pulley

gárrulo,-a *adj Fig* garrulous

garúa *nf Andes, RP, Ven* drizzle

garza *nf* heron

gas *nm* (**a**) gas; **g. ciudad** town gas; **gases (nocivos)** fumes; **g. de escape** exhaust fumes (**b**) *(en bebida)* fizz; **agua con g.** fizzy water (**c**) *Med* **gases** flatulence

gasa *nf* gauze

gaseosa *nf* lemonade

gasfitería *nf Chile, Ecuad, Perú* plumber's (shop)

gasfitero,-a *nm,f Chile, Ecuad, Perú* plumber

gasoducto *nm* gas pipeline

gasoil, gasóleo *nm* diesel oil

gasolina *nf Br* petrol, *US* gasoline

gasolinera, *Méx* **gasolinería** *nf Br* petrol *o US* gas station

gastado,-a *adj (zapatos etc)* worn-out; *Fig (frase)* hackneyed

gastar 1 *vt* (**a**) *(consumir) (dinero, tiempo)* to spend; *(gasolina, electricidad)* to consume (**b**) *Fig (malgastar)* to waste (**c**) *(ropa)* to wear; **¿qué número gastas?** what size do you take? (**d**) **g. una broma a** algn to play a practical joke on sb
2 gastarse *vpr* (**a**) *(zapatos etc)* to wear out (**b**) *(gasolina etc)* to run out

gasto *nm* expenditure; **gastos** expenses; **gastos de viaje** travelling expenses

gatas: • **a gatas** *loc adv* on all fours

gatear *vi* (**a**) to crawl (**b**) *(trepar)* to climb

gatillo *nm (de armas)* trigger; **apretar el g.** to pull the trigger

gato *nm* (**a**) cat (**b**) *Aut & Téc* jack

gauchada *nf CSur* favour

gaucho,-a 1 *adj RP Fam (servicial)* helpful, obliging
2 *nm,f* gaucho

gaveta *nf* (**a**) *(cajón)* drawer (**b**) *Am Aut (guantera)* glove compartment

gavilán *nm Orn* sparrowhawk

gavilla *nf (de ramillas etc)* sheaf

gaviota *nf* seagull

gay *adj inv & nm (pl* **gays***)* homosexual, gay

gazapo *nm* (**a**) *(error)* misprint (**b**) *Zool* young rabbit

gaznate *nm* gullet

gazpacho *nm Culin* gazpacho

gel nm gel; **g. (de ducha)** shower gel

gelatina nf (ingrediente) gelatin; Culin jelly

gema nf gem

gemelo,-a 1 adj & nm,f (identical) twin
  2 nmpl **gemelos** (a) (de camisa) cufflinks (b) (anteojos) binoculars

gemido nm groan

Géminis nm Gemini

gemir [6] vi to groan

generación nf generation

general 1 adj general; **por lo** o **en g.** in general, generally;
  2 nm Mil & Rel general

Generalitat nf Catalan/Valencian/Balearic parliament

generalización nf (a) generalization (b) (extensión) spread

generalizar [40] 1 vt (a) to generalize (b) (extender) to spread
  2 generalizarse vpr to become widespread o common

generalmente adv generally

generar vt to generate

género nm (a) (clase) kind, sort (b) Arte & Lit genre (c) (mercancía) article (d) Ling gender (e) Biol genus; **el g. humano** mankind

generosidad nf generosity

generoso,-a adj (a) generous (con to) (b) (vino) full-bodied

Génesis nm Rel Genesis

genética nf genetics sing

genético,-a adj genetic

genial adj brilliant; Fam terrific

📖 Observa que la palabra inglesa **genial** es un falso amigo y no es la traducción de la palabra española **genial**. En inglés, **genial** significa "cordial, amable".

genio nm (a) (carácter) temperament; (mal carácter) temper; **estar de mal g.** to be in a bad mood (b) (facultad) genius

genocidio nm genocide

Génova n Genoa

gente nf (a) people (b) (familia) folks (c) Am respectable people

gentil adj (a) (amable) kind (b) (pagano) pagan

📖 Observa que la palabra inglesa **genteel** es un falso amigo y no es la traducción de la palabra española **gentil**. En inglés, **genteel** significa "fino, distinguido".

gentileza nf kindness; Fml **por g. de** by courtesy of

gentío nm crowd

gentuza nf Pey riffraff

genuino,-a adj (puro) genuine; (verdadero) authentic

geografía nf geography

geología nf geology

geometría nf geometry

geranio nm geranium

gerencia nf management

gerente nmf manager

germano,-a 1 adj German, Germanic
  2 nm,f German

gérmen nm (a) Biol germ (b) Fig (inicio) germ; (fuente) origin

germinar vi to germinate

gerundio nm gerund

gesta nf heroic exploit

gestación nf gestation

gestar vt to gestate

gesticular vi to gesticulate

gestión nf (a) (administración) management (b) **gestiones** (negociaciones) negotiations; (trámites) formalities

gestionar vt to take steps to acquire o obtain; (negociar) to negotiate

gesto nm (a) (mueca) face (b) (con las manos) gesture

gestor,-a nm,f ≃ solicitor

giba nf hump

gibar vt Fam to annoy

Gibraltar n Gibraltar; **el peñón de G.** the Rock of Gibraltar

gibraltareño,-a 1 adj of/from Gibraltar
  2 nm,f Gibraltarian

gigante,-a 1 nm,f giant
  2 adj giant, enormous

gigantesco,-a adj gigantic

gigoló nm gigolo

gil, gila nm,f CSur Fam twit, idiot

gili, gilí nm muy Fam = **gilipollas**

gilipollas nmf muy Fam Br prat, US dork

gimnasia nf gymnastics

gimnasio nm gymnasium

gimotear vi to whine

Ginebra n Geneva

ginebra nf (bebida) gin

ginecología nf gynaecology

ginecólogo,-a nm,f gynaecologist

gira nf Teatro & Mús tour

girar 1 vi (a) (dar vueltas) to spin (b) **g. a la derecha/izquierda** to turn right/left
  2 vt Fin (a) (expedir) to draw (b) (dinero) to transfer

girasol nm sunflower

giratorio,-a adj revolving

giro nm (a) (vuelta) turn (b) (de acontecimientos) direction (c) (frase) turn of phrase (d) Fin draft; **g. telegráfico** money order; **g. postal** postal o money order

gis *nm Andes, Méx* chalk

gitano,-a *adj & nm,f* gypsy, gipsy

glacial *adj* icy

glaciar *nm* glacier

glándula *nf* gland

glasear *vt Culin* to glaze

global *adj* comprehensive; **precio g.** all-inclusive price

globalmente *adv* as a whole

globo *nm* (a) balloon (b) *(esfera)* globe (c) *(lámpara)* globe, glass lampshade

glóbulo *nm* globule

gloria *nf* (a) *(fama)* glory (b) *Rel* heaven; *Fam Fig* **estar en la g.** to be in seventh heaven (c) *Fam (delicia)* delight

glorieta *nf* (a) *(plazoleta)* small square (b) *(encrucijada de calles) Br* roundabout, *US* traffic circle (c) *(en un jardín)* arbour

glorificar [44] *vt* to glorify

glorioso,-a *adj* glorious

glosa *nf* (a) gloss (b) *Lit (comentario)* notes, commentary

glosar *vt* (a) *(explicar)* to gloss; *(texto)* to interpret (b) *(comentar)* to comment on

glosario *nm* glossary

glotón,-ona 1 *adj* greedy
2 *nm,f* glutton

glotonería *nf* gluttony

glucosa *nf Quím* glucose

gobernación *nf* government; *Pol & Hist* **Ministerio de la G.** *Br* ≃ Home Office, *US* ≃ Department of the Interior

gobernador,-a *nm,f* governor

gobernante *adj* ruling

gobernar [1] 1 *vt* to govern; *(un país)* to rule
2 *vi Náut* to steer

gobiernista *Am* **1** *adj* government
2 *nmf* government supporter

gobierno *nm* (a) *Pol* government (b) *(mando)* running (c) *Náut* steering (d) *Náut (timón)* rudder

goce *nm* enjoyment

gofio *nm Am Can* roasted maize meal

gol *nm* goal

goleada *nf* lots of goals; **ganar por g.** to win by a barrowload

golear *vt* to hammer

golf *nm* golf; **palo de g.** golf club

golfista *nmf* golfer

golfo¹,-a 1 *nm,f* good-for-nothing
2 *nf* **golfa** *Fam Pey* tart

golfo² *nm Geog* gulf; **el g. Pérsico** the Persian Gulf

golondrina *nf* swallow

golosina *nf Br* sweet, *US* candy

goloso,-a *adj* sweet-toothed

golpe *nm* (a) blow; *(llamada)* knock; *(puñetazo)* punch; **de g.** all of a sudden; **g. de estado** coup d'état; **g. de suerte** stroke of luck; **no dar ni g.** not to lift a finger (b) *Aut* bump (c) *(desgracia)* blow; **un duro g.** a great blow (d) *(de humor)* witticism

golpear *vt* to hit; *(con el puño)* to punch; *(puerta, cabeza)* to bang

golpiza *nf Am* beating

goma *nf* (a) rubber; **g. de pegar** glue; **g. de borrar** eraser, *Br* rubber (b) *(elástica)* rubber band (c) *Cuba, CSur (neumático)* tyre (d) *Fam (preservativo)* rubber

gomaespuma *nf* foam rubber

gomal *nm Agr* rubber plantation

gomería *nf CSur* tyre centre

gomero *nm Am* (a) *Bot* gum tree (b) *(recolector)* rubber collector

gomina *nf* hair cream

góndola *nf* (a) *(embarcación)* gondola (b) *Bol, Chile (autobús)* (long distance) bus

gordo,-a 1 *adj* (a) *(carnoso)* fat (b) *(grueso)* thick (c) *(importante)* big; **me cae g.** I can't stand him; **de g.** in a big way
2 *nm,f* (a) fat person; *Fam* fatty (b) *Am Fam (como apelativo)* **¿cómo estás, gorda?** hey, how are you doing?
3 *nm* **el g.** *(de lotería)* the jackpot

gordura *nf* fatness

gorgorito *nm* trill

gorila *nm* (a) gorilla (b) *Fig (en discoteca etc)* bouncer

gorjear 1 *vi* to chirp
2 • gorjearse *vpr Am* **g. de algn** to laugh at sb's expense

gorjeo *nm* chirping

gorra *nf* cap; *(con visera)* peaked cap; *Fam* **de g.** free

gorrión *nm* sparrow

gorro *nm* (a) cap (b) *Fam* **estar hasta el g. (de)** to be up to here (with)

gorrón,-ona *nm,f* sponger

gota *nf* (a) drop; *(de sudor)* bead; **g. a g.** drop by drop; **ni g.** not a bit (b) *Med* gout

gotear *v impers* to drip; **el techo gotea** there's a leak in the ceiling

gotera *nf* leak

gótico,-a *adj* Gothic

gozar [40] 1 *vt* to enjoy
2 *vi (disfrutar)* **g. (de)** to enjoy

gozne *nm* hinge

gozo *nm* pleasure

grabación *nf* recording

grabado *nm* (a) *(arte)* engraving (b) *(dibujo)* drawing

grabadora *nf* tape recorder

grabar *vt* (**a**) *(sonidos, imágenes)* to record (**b**) *Informát* to save (**c**) *Arte* to engrave

gracia *nf* (**a**) *(atractivo)* grace (**b**) *(chiste)* joke; **hacer** *o* **tener g.** to be funny (**c**) *(indulto)* pardon

gracias *nfpl (agradecimiento)* thanks; **g. a Dios** thank God, thank goodness; **g. a** thanks to; **muchas** *o* **muchísimas g.** thank you very much

gracioso,-a 1 *adj* (**a**) *(divertido)* funny (**b**) *(garboso)* graceful
2 *nm,f Teatro* comic character

grada *nf* (**a**) *(peldaño)* step (**b**) **gradas** *(en estadio)* terraces

gradación *nf* (**a**) gradation (**b**) *Mús* scale

graderío *nm* tiers of seats; *Dep* terraces, *US* bleachers

gradiente 1 *nm* gradient
2 *nf Am* slope

grado *nm* (**a**) degree (**b**) *Mil* rank (**c**) **de buen g.** willingly, gladly

graduable *adj* adjustable

graduación *nf* (**a**) gradation (**b**) *Mil* rank

graduado,-a *nm,f* graduate

gradual *adj* gradual

gradualmente *adv* gradually

graduar [30] 1 *vt* (**a**) *Educ & Mil* to confer degree *o* a rank on (**b**) *(regular)* to regulate
2 graduarse *vpr* (**a**) *Educ & Mil* to graduate (**b**) **g. la vista** to have one's eyes tested

gráfico,-a 1 *adj* graphic; **diseño g.** graphic design
2 *nm* graph

grafista *nmf* graphic designer

gragea *nf Med* pill

grajo,-a 1 *nm,f Orn* rook
2 *nm Am* body odour

gral. *(abr* **General***)* gen

gramática *nf* grammar

gramo *nm* gram, gramme

gran *adj* = **grande**

grana *adj* scarlet

granada *nf* (**a**) *(fruto)* pomegranate (**b**) *Mil* grenade

granate 1 *adj inv (color)* maroon
2 *nm (color)* maroon

Gran Bretaña *n* Great Britain

grande *adj* (**a**) *(tamaño)* big, large; *Fig (persona)* great (**b**) *(cantidad)* large; **vivir a lo g.** to live in style; *Fig* **pasarlo en g.** to have a great time

---

gran is used instead of **grande** before masculine singular nouns (e.g. **gran hombre** great man).

---

grandeza *nf* (**a**) *(importancia)* greatness (**b**) *(grandiosidad)* grandeur; **delirios de g.** delusions of grandeur

grandioso,-a *adj* grandiose

granel: •**a granel** *loc adv (sin medir exactamente)* loose

granero *nm Agr* granary

granito *nm* granite

granizada *nf,* **granizado** *nm* iced drink

granizar [40] *v impers* to hail

granizo *nm* hail

granja *nf* farm

granjear *vt,* **granjearse** *vpr* to gain

granjero,-a *nm,f* farmer

grano *nm* (**a**) *(de café)* bean; **ir al g.** to get to the point (**b**) *(espinilla)* spot

granuja *nm* (**a**) *(pilluelo)* ragamuffin (**b**) *(estafador)* con-man

grapa *nf* (**a**) staple (**b**) *Constr* cramp (**c**) *CSur (bebida)* grappa

grapadora *nf* stapler

grapar *vt* to staple

grasa *nf* grease

grasiento,-a *adj* greasy

graso,-a *adj (pelo)* greasy; *(materia)* fatty

gratificar [44] *vt* (**a**) *(satisfacer)* to gratify (**b**) *(recompensar)* to reward

gratinar *vt Culin* to cook in a sauce until golden brown

gratis *adj inv & adv* free

gratitud *nf* gratitude

grato,-a *adj* pleasant

gratuito,-a *adj* (**a**) *(de balde)* free (of charge) (**b**) *(arbitrario)* gratuitous

grava *nf (guijas)* gravel; *(en carretera)* chippings

gravamen *nm Jur* (**a**) *(carga)* burden (**b**) *(impuesto)* tax

gravar *vt Jur* (**a**) *(cargar)* to burden (**b**) *(impuestos)* to tax

grave *adj* (**a**) *(importante)* serious (**b**) *(muy enfermo)* seriously ill (**c**) *(voz, nota)* low

gravedad *nf* (**a**) *(seriedad, importancia)* seriousness (**b**) *Fís* gravity

gravilla *nf* chippings

gravitar *vi* (**a**) *Fís* to gravitate (**b**) **g. sobre** to rest on

gravoso,-a *adj* (**a**) *(costoso)* costly (**b**) *(molesto)* burdensome

graznar *vi* to squawk; *(de pato)* to quack; *(de cuervo)* to caw

graznido *nm (un sonido)* squawk; *(varios)* squawking; *(de pato)* quack; *(de cuervo)* caw

Grecia *n* Greece

gregario,-a *adj* gregarious; **instinto g.** herd instinct

gremio *nm* (**a**) *Hist* guild (**b**) *(profesión)* profession

greña *nf* lock of entangled hair; *Fam* **andar a la g.** to squabble

gres *nm* **artículos de g.** stoneware

gresca *nf* (**a**) *(bulla)* racket (**b**) *(riña)* row

griego,-a *adj & nm,f* Greek

grieta *nf* crack; *(en la piel)* chap

grifo *nm* (**a**) *(llave) Br* tap, *US* faucet (**b**) *Perú (gasolinera) Br* petrol station, *US* gas station

grillete *nm* shackle

grillo *nm* cricket

gringo,-a *Fam* **1** *adj* (**a**) *(estadounidense)* gringo, American (**b**) *Am (extranjero)* foreign

2 *nm,f* (**a**) *(estadounidense)* gringo, American (**b**) *Am (extranjero)* = non-Spanish-speaking foreigner

gripa *nf Col, Méx* flu

gripe *nf* flu

gris *adj & nm* grey

grisáceo,-a *adj* greyish

gritar *vt & vi* to shout

grito *nm* shout; **a voz en g.** at the top of one's voice

Groenlandia *n* Greenland

grosella *nf (fruto)* redcurrant; **g. negra** blackcurrant; **g. silvestre** gooseberry

grosería *nf* (**a**) *(ordinariez)* rude word o expression (**b**) *(rusticidad)* rudeness

grosero,-a *adj (tosco)* coarse; *(maleducado)* rude

grosor *nm* thickness

grotesco,-a *adj* grotesque

grúa *nf* (**a**) *Constr* crane (**b**) *Aut Br* breakdown van o truck, *US* tow truck

grueso,-a 1 *adj* thick; *(persona)* stout

2 *nm (parte principal)* bulk

grulla *nf Orn* crane

grumo *nm* lump; *(de leche)* curd

gruñido *nm* grunt

gruñir *vi* to grunt

gruñón,-ona *adj* grumpy

grupa *nf* hindquarters

grupo *nm* (**a**) group; *Informát* **g. de noticias** newsgroup (**b**) *Téc* unit, set

gruta *nf* cave

guaca *nf Am (sepultura)* = pre-Columbian Indian tomb

guacal *nm* (**a**) *CAm, Méx (calabaza)* calabash (**b**) *Carib, Col, Méx (jaula)* cage

guacamayo,-a *nm,f Orn* macaw

guacamol, guacamole *nm Culin* guacamole

guachafita *nf Am* uproar

guachimán *nm Am* night watchman

guacho,-a *adj & nm,f Andes, RP* (**a**) *muy Fam (persona huérfana)* orphan (**b**) *Fam (sinvergüenza)* bastard, swine

guaco *nm Am (cerámica)* = pottery object found in pre-Columbian Indian tomb

guadaña *nf* scythe

guagua¹ *nf Can, Cuba* bus

guagua² *nf Andes* baby

guajiro,-a *nm,f Cuba Fam (campesino)* peasant

guajolote *nm CAm, Méx* (**a**) *(pavo)* turkey (**b**) *(tonto)* fool, idiot

guampa *nf Bol, CSur* horn

guanajo *nm Carib* turkey

guantazo *nm* slap

guante *nm* glove

guantera *nf Aut* glove compartment

guapo,-a *adj* (**a**) *(hombre)* handsome, good-looking; *(mujer)* pretty, good-looking (**b**) *Am (matón)* bully

guaraca *nf Am* sling

guarache *nm Méx (sandalia)* sandal

guarangada *nf Bol, CSur* rude remark

guarango,-a *adj Bol, CSur* rude

guarda *nmf* guard; **g. jurado** security guard

guardabarros *nm inv Aut Br* mudguard, *US* fender

guardabosque *nmf* gamekeeper

guardacoches *nmf inv* parking attendant

guardacostas *nm inv (persona)* coastguard; *(embarcación)* coastguard vessel

guardaespaldas *nmf inv* bodyguard

guardafangos *nm inv Andes, CAm, Carib Aut Br* mudguard, *US* fender

guardameta *nmf Dep* goalkeeper

guardapolvo *nm* overalls

guardar 1 *vt* (**a**) *(conservar)* to keep (**b**) *(un secreto)* to keep; **g. silencio** to remain silent; **g. cama** to stay in bed (**c**) *(poner en un sitio)* to put away (**d**) *(reservar)* to keep (**e**) *Informát* to save

2 guardarse *vpr* **g. de hacer algo** *(abstenerse)* to be careful not to do sth; **guardársela a algn** to have it in for sb

guardarropa *nm* (**a**) *(cuarto)* cloakroom (**b**) *(armario)* wardrobe

guardería *nf* **g. infantil** nursery (school)

guardia 1 *nf* (**a**) *(vigilancia)* watch (**b**) **la G. Civil** the civil guard (**c**) *(turno de servicio)* duty; *Mil* guard duty; **de g.** on duty; **farmacia de g.** duty chemist

2 *nmf* policeman; *(mujer)* policewoman

guardián,-ana *nm,f* watchman

guarecer [33] **1** *vt* to shelter

2 guarecerse *vpr* to take shelter o refuge (**de** from)

guarida *nf (de animal)* lair; *(refugio)* hideout

guarismo *nm* digit

guarnecer [33] *vt* (**a**) *Culin* to garnish (**b**) (*dotar*) to provide (**de** with) (**c**) *Mil* to garrison

guarnición *nf* (**a**) *Culin* garnish (**b**) *Mil* garrison

guarro,-a 1 *adj* filthy
 2 *nm,f* pig

guarura *nm Méx Fam* bodyguard

guasa *nf* mockery

guasearse *upr Fam* **g. de** to make fun of

guaso,-a *adj Am* peasant

guasón,-ona 1 *adj* humorous
 2 *nm,f* joker

guata *nf* (**a**) (*relleno*) padding (**b**) *Am* (*barriga*) paunch

Guatemala *n* (**a**) (*país*) Guatemala (**b**) (*ciudad*) Guatemala City

guatemalteco,-a *adj & nm,f* Guatemalan

guay *adj inv Fam* brilliant, terrific

guayabera *nf* short jacket

guayabo,-a *nm,f Am Fig* (*chica bonita*) pretty young girl; (*chico guapo*) good-looking boy

guepardo *nm* cheetah

güero,-a *adj Méx Fam* blond, blonde

guerra *nf* war; **en g.** at war; **g. bacteriológica** germ warfare; **g. civil/fría/mundial/ nuclear** civil/cold/world/nuclear war; *Fam* **dar g.** to be a real nuisance

guerrero,-a 1 *nm,f* warrior
 2 *adj* warlike

guerrilla *nf* (**a**) (*partida armada*) guerrilla force *o* band (**b**) (*lucha*) guerrilla warfare

güevón,-ona *nm,f Andes, Arg, Ven muy Fam* (*estúpido*) *Br* prat, *US* dork

guía 1 *nmf* (*persona*) guide
 2 *nf* (**a**) (*norma*) guideline (**b**) (*libro*) guide; (*lista*) directory; **g. de teléfonos** telephone directory

guiar [29] **1** *vt* (**a**) (*indicar el camino*) to guide (**b**) *Aut* to drive; *Náut* to steer; (*caballo, bici*) to ride
 2 guiarse *upr* **g. por** to be guided by, to go by

guija *nf* pebble

guijarro *nm* pebble

guinda *nf* (*fruto*) morello (cherry)

guindilla *nf* chilli

guineo *nm Andes, CAm* banana

guiñapo *nm* (**a**) (*andrajo*) rag (**b**) *Fig* (*persona*) wreck; **poner a algn como un g.** to tear sb to pieces

guiñar *vt* to wink

guiño *nm* wink

guión *nm* (**a**) *Cin & TV* script (**b**) *Ling* hyphen, dash (**c**) (*esquema*) sketch

guionista *nmf* scriptwriter

guiri *nmf Fam* foreigner

guirigay *nm* hubbub

guirnalda *nf* garland

guisa *nf* way, manner; **a g. de** as, by way of

guisado *nm Culin* stew

guisante *nm* pea

guisar *vt* to cook

guiso *nm* dish; (*guisado*) stew

guita *nf* (**a**) (*cuerda*) rope (**b**) *Fam* dough

guitarra 1 *nf* guitar
 2 *nmf* guitarist

guitarreada *nf CSur* singalong (*to guitars*)

guitarrista *nmf* guitarist

gula *nf* gluttony

gurí,-isa *nm,f RP Fam* (*niño*) kid, child; (*joven*) (*hombre*) lad; (*mujer*) lass

gusano *nm* worm; (*oruga*) caterpillar; *Fam Pey* (*exiliado cubano*) = anti-Castro Cuban living in exile; **g. de seda** silkworm

gustar 1 *vt* (**a**) **me gusta el vino** I like wine; **me gustaban los caramelos** I used to like sweets; **me gusta nadar** I like swimming; **me gustaría ir** I would like to go (**b**) *Fml* **¿gustas?** would you like some?; **cuando gustes** whenever you like
 2 *vi* **g. de** to enjoy

gusto *nm* (**a**) (*sentido*) taste (**b**) (*en fórmulas de cortesía*) pleasure; **con (mucho) g.** with (great) pleasure; **tanto g.** pleased to meet you (**c**) **estar a g.** to feel comfortable *o* at ease; **por g.** for the sake of it; **ser de buen/mal g.** to be in good/bad taste; **tener buen/mal g.** to have good/bad taste; **tenemos el gusto de comunicarle que ...** we are pleased to inform you that ...

gutural *adj* guttural

H

H, h [atʃe] *nf (la letra)* H,h; **bomba H** H-bomb

ha *indic pres de* **haber**

haba *nf* broad bean

> Takes the masculine articles **el** and **un**.

Habana *nf* **La H.** Havana

habano *nm* Havana cigar

haber [14] 1 *v aux* (**a**) *(en tiempos compuestos)* to have; **lo he visto** I have seen it; **ya lo había hecho** he had already done it
(**b**) **h. de** + *infin (obligación)* to have to; **has de ser bueno** you must be good
2 *v impers (special form of present tense:* **hay**) (**a**) *(existir, estar) (singular used also with plural nouns)* **hay** there is/are; **había** there was/were; **había un gato en el tejado** there was a cat on the roof; **había muchos libros** there were a lot of books; **hay 500 km entre Madrid y Granada** it's 500 km from Madrid to Granada
(**b**) **h. que** + *infin* it is necessary to; **hay que trabajar** you've got to *o* you must work; **habrá que comprobarlo** I/you/we/*etc* will have to check it
(**c**) *(tener lugar)* **habrá una fiesta** there will be a party; **hoy hay partido** there's a match today; **los accidentes habidos en esta carretera** the accidents which have happened on this road
(**d**) **había una vez ...** once upon a time ...; **no hay de qué** you're welcome, don't mention it; **¿qué hay?** how are things?
3 *nm* (**a**) *Fin* credit; **haberes** assets
(**b**) **en su h.** in his possession

habichuela *nf (judía)* kidney bean; *Carib, Col (judía verde)* green bean

hábil *adj* (**a**) *(diestro)* skilful (**b**) *(astuto)* smart (**c**) **días hábiles** working days

habilidad *nf* (**a**) *(destreza)* skill (**b**) *(astucia)* cleverness

habilitar *vt* (**a**) *(espacio)* to fit out (**b**) *(persona)* to entitle (**c**) *Fin (financiar)* to finance

habiloso,-a *adj Chile* shrewd, astute

habitación *nf (cuarto)* room; *(dormitorio)* bedroom; **h. individual/doble** single/double room

habitante *nmf* inhabitant

habitar 1 *vt* to live in, to inhabit
2 *vi* to live

hábitat *nm (pl* **hábitats**) habitat

hábito *nm* (**a**) *(costumbre)* habit (**b**) *Rel* habit

habitual *adj* usual, habitual; *(cliente, lector)* regular

habituar [30] 1 *vt* to accustom (**a** to)
2 **habituarse** *vpr* **habituarse a** to get used to, to become accustomed to

habla *nf* (**a**) *(idioma)* language; **países de h. española** Spanish-speaking countries (**b**) *(facultad de hablar)* speech; **quedarse sin h.** to be left speechless (**c**) *Tel* **¡al h.!** speaking!

> Takes the masculine articles **el** and **un**.

hablado,-a *adj* spoken; **el inglés h.** spoken English; **mal h.** coarse, foul-mouthed

hablador,-a *adj (parlanchín)* talkative; *(chismoso)* gossipy

habladuría *nf (rumor)* rumour; *(chisme)* piece of gossip

hablante *nmf* speaker

hablar 1 *vi* (**a**) to speak, to talk; **h. con algn** to speak to sb (**b**) **¡ni h.!** certainly not!; *Fam* **¡quién fue a h.!** look who's talking!
2 *vt* (**a**) *(idioma)* to speak; **habla alemán** he speaks German (**b**) *(tratar un asunto)* to talk over, to discuss
3 **hablarse** *vpr* (**a**) to speak *o* talk to one another (**b**) **se habla español** *(en letrero)* Spanish spoken

habré *indic fut de* **haber**

hacendado,-a *nm,f Am* farmer

hacendoso,-a *adj* hardworking

hacer [15] 1 *vt* (**a**) *(crear, producir, fabricar)* to make; **h. una casa** to build a house
(**b**) *(obrar, ejecutar)* to do; **eso no se hace** it isn't done; **hazme un favor** do me a favour; **¿qué haces?** *(en este momento)* what are you doing?; *(para vivir)* what do you do (for a living)?; **tengo mucho que h.** I have a lot to do; **h. deporte** to do sports; **h. una carrera/medicina** to do a degree/medicine
(**c**) *(conseguir) (amigos, dinero)* to make
(**d**) *(obligar)* to make; **hazle callar/**

trabajar make him shut up/work
 (**e**) *(arreglar)* to make; **h. la cama** to make the bed
 (**f**) *Mat (sumar)* to make; **y con éste hacen cien** and that makes a hundred
 (**g**) *(dar aspecto)* to make look; **el negro le hace más delgado** black makes him look slimmer
 (**h**) *(sustituyendo a otro verbo)* to do; **ya no puedo leer como solía hacerlo** I can't read as well as I used to
 (**i**) *(representar)* to play; **h. el bueno** to play the (part of the) goody
 (**j**) **¡bien hecho!** well done!
 2 *vi* (**a**) *(actuar)* to play; **hizo de Desdémona** she played Desdemona
 (**b**) **h. por** *o* **para** + *infin* to try to; **hice por venir** I tried to come
 (**c**) *(fingir)* to pretend; **h. como si** to act as if
 (**d**) *(convenir)* to be suitable; **a las ocho si te hace** will eight o'clock be all right for you?
 3 *v impers* (**a**) **hace calor/frío** it's hot/cold
 (**b**) *(tiempo transcurrido)* ago; **hace mucho (tiempo)** a long time ago; **hace dos días que no le veo** I haven't seen him for two days; **hace dos años que vivo en Glasgow** I've been living in Glasgow for two years
 4 hacerse *upr* (**a**) *(volverse)* to become, to grow; **h. viejo** to grow old
 (**b**) *(simular)* to pretend; **h. el dormido** to pretend to be sleeping
 (**c**) **h. con** *(apropiarse)* to get hold of
 (**d**) **h. a** *(habituarse)* to get used to; **enseguida me hago a todo** I soon get used to anything

hacha *nf* (**a**) *(herramienta)* axe (**b**) *Fam* **ser un h. en algo** to be an ace *o* a wizard at sth

Takes the masculine articles **el** and **un**.

hachís *nm* hashish

hacia *prep* (**a**) *(dirección)* towards; to; **h. abajo** down, downwards; **h. adelante** forwards; **h. arriba** up, upwards; **h. atrás** back, backwards (**b**) *(tiempo)* at about, at around; **h. las tres** at about three o'clock

hacienda *nf* (**a**) *Am (finca agrícola)* estate, *US* ranch (**b**) *Fin* Treasury; **h. pública** public funds *o* finances; **Ministerio de H.** = Exchequer, Treasury

hacinamiento *nm* (**a**) *Agr* stacking; *Fig (montón)* piling (**b**) *(de gente)* overcrowding

hacinar 1 *vt Agr* to stack; *Fig (amontonar)* to pile up, to heap up
 2 hacinarse *upr* **h. en** *(gente)* to be packed into

hada *nf* fairy; **cuento de hadas** fairy tale; **h. madrina** fairy godmother

Takes the masculine articles **el** and **un**.

hado *nm* destiny

hago *indic pres de* **hacer**

halagar [42] *vt* to flatter

halago *nm* flattery

halagüeño,-a *adj (noticia, impresión)* promising

halcón *nm* falcon; **h. peregrino** peregrine (falcon)

hálito *nm* (**a**) *(aliento)* breath (**b**) *(vapor)* vapour

hallar 1 *vt (encontrar)* to find; *(averiguar)* to find out; *(descubrir)* to discover
 2 hallarse *upr (estar)* to be, to find oneself; *(estar situado)* to be situated

hallazgo *nm* (**a**) *(descubrimiento)* discovery (**b**) *(cosa encontrada)* find

hamaca *nf (hammock; (mecedora)* rocking chair

hambre *nf (apetito)* hunger; *(inanición)* starvation; *(catástrofe)* famine; **tener h.** to be hungry

Takes the masculine articles **el** and **un**.

hambriento,-a *adj* starving

hamburguesa *nf* hamburger

hampa *nf* underworld

Takes the masculine articles **el** and **un**.

han *indic pres de* **haber**

harapo *nm* rag; **hecho un h.** in tatters

haré *indic fut de* **hacer**

harén *nm (pl* **harenes**) harem

harina *nf* flour

hartar 1 *vt* (**a**) *(cansar, fastidiar)* to annoy (**b**) *(atiborrar)* to satiate; **el dulce harta enseguida** sweet things soon fill you up
 2 hartarse *upr* (**a**) *(saciar el apetito)* to eat one's fill (**b**) *(cansarse)* to get fed up (**de** with), to grow tired (**de** of)

harto,-a 1 *adj* (**a**) *(de comida)* full (**b**) *(cansado)* fed up; **¡me tienes h.!** I'm fed up with you!; **estoy h. de trabajar** I'm fed up working (**c**) *Andes, CAm, Carib, Méx (mucho)* lots of; **tiene h. dinero** he's got lots of money
 2 *adv* (**a**) *Fml (muy)* very (**b**) *Andes, CAm, Carib, Méx (muy, mucho)* really

hartura *nf* bellyful; **¡qué h.!** what a drag!

has *indic pres de* **haber**

hasta 1 *prep* (**a**) *(lugar)* up to, as far as,

down to (**b**) *(tiempo)* until, till, up to; **h. el domingo** until Sunday; **h. el final** right to the end; **h. la fecha** up to now; **h. luego** see you later (**c**) *(con cantidad)* up to, as many as (**d**) *(incluso)* even (**e**) *CAm, Col, Méx (no antes de)* **pintaremos la casa h. fin de mes** we won't paint the house till the end of the month

2 *conj* **h. que** until

hastiado,-a *adj* sick, tired (**de** of)
hastiar [29] *vt* to sicken
hastío *nm* weariness
hato *nm* bundle
hay *indic pres de* **haber**
Haya *nf* **La H.** The Hague
haya¹ *nf* (**a**) *Bot (árbol)* beech (**b**) *(madera)* beech (wood)

Takes the masculine articles **el** and **un**.

haya² *subj pres de* **haber**
haz¹ *nm* (**a**) *Agr* sheaf (**b**) *(de luz)* shaft
haz² *nf (de hoja)* top side
haz³ *imperat de* **hacer**
hazaña *nf* deed, exploit
hazmerreír *nm* laughing stock
he¹ *adv* **he ahí/aquí** ... there/here you have ...
he² *indic pres de* **haber**
hebilla *nf* buckle
hebra *nf* thread; *(de carne)* sinew; *(de madera)* grain; **pegar la h.** to chat
hebreo,-a 1 *adj* Hebrew

2 *nm,f* Hebrew
hecatombe *nf* disaster
hechicería *nf* witchcraft
hechicero,-a 1 *adj* bewitching

2 *nm,f (hombre)* wizard, sorcerer; *(mujer)* witch, sorceress
hechizar [40] *vt* (**a**) *(embrujar)* to cast a spell on (**b**) *Fig (fascinar)* to bewitch, to charm
hechizo *nm* (**a**) *(embrujo)* spell (**b**) *Fig (fascinación)* fascination, charm
hecho,-a 1 *adj* (**a**) made; done; **¡bien h.!** well done! (**b**) *(carne)* done (**c**) *(persona)* mature (**d**) *(frase)* set; *(ropa)* ready-made

2 *nm* (**a**) *(realidad)* fact; **de h.** in fact; **el h. es que ...** the fact is that ... (**b**) *(acto)* act, deed (**c**) *(suceso)* event, incident
hechura *nf (forma)* shape; *Cost* cut
hectárea *nf* hectare
hectolitro *nm* hectolitre
heder [3] *vi* to stink, to smell foul
hediondo,-a *adj* foul-smelling
hedor *nm* stink, stench
hegemonía *nf* hegemony
helada *nf* frost

heladera *nf RP (nevera)* refrigerator, fridge
heladería *nf* ice-cream parlour
helado,-a 1 *nm* ice cream

2 *adj* (**a**) *(muy frío)* frozen, freezing cold; **estoy h. (de frío)** I'm frozen (**b**) *Fig* **quedarse h.** *(atónito)* to be flabbergasted
helar [1] 1 *vt (congelar)* to freeze

2 *v impers (congelarse)* **anoche heló** there was a frost last night

3 **helarse** *vpr (congelarse)* to freeze
helecho *nm Bot* fern
hélice *nf* (**a**) *Av & Náut* propeller (**b**) *Anat, Arquit & Mat* helix
helicóptero *nm Av* helicopter
helipuerto *nm Av* heliport
hematoma *nm Med* haematoma
hembra *nf* (**a**) *Bot & Zool* female (**b**) *(mujer)* woman (**c**) *Téc* female; *(de tornillo)* nut; *(de enchufe)* socket
hemiciclo *nm Fam* (Spanish) parliament
hemisferio *nm* hemisphere
hemorragia *nf Med* haemorrhage
hemos *indic pres de* **haber**
henchir [6] *vt* to stuff
hender [3] *vt* (**a**) *(resquebrajar)* to crack, to split; *Fig (olas)* to cut
hendidura *nf* crack
hendir [5] *vt* = **hender**
heno *nm* hay
heráldica *nf* heraldry
herbicida *nm* weedkiller, herbicide
herbívoro,-a 1 *adj* herbivorous, grass-eating

2 *nm,f Zool* herbivore
herbolario *nm* herbalist's (shop)
herboso,-a *adj* grassy
hercio *nm* Herz
heredad *nf* (**a**) *(finca)* country estate (**b**) *(conjunto de bienes)* private estate
heredar *vt* (**a**) *Jur* to inherit (**b**) **ha heredado la sonrisa de su madre** she's got her mother's smile
heredero,-a *nm,f (hombre)* heir; *(mujer)* heiress; **príncipe h.** crown prince
hereditario,-a *adj* hereditary
hereje *nmf Rel* heretic
herejía *nf Rel* heresy
herencia *nf* (**a**) *Jur* inheritance, legacy (**b**) *Biol* heredity
herida *nf (lesión)* injury; *(corte)* wound
herido,-a *nm,f* injured person; **no hubo heridos** there were no casualties
herir [5] 1 *vt* (**a**) *(físicamente) (lesionar)* to injure; *(cortar)* to wound (**b**) *(emocionalmente)* to hurt, to wound (**c**) *(vista)* to offend

2 **herirse** *vpr* to injure o hurt oneself

hermana nf (a) sister (b) Rel (monja) sister

hermanado,-a adj twinned; **ciudad hermanada** twin town

hermanar 1 vt (a) (personas) to unite spiritually (b) (ciudades) to twin (c) (unir) to unite, to combine

2 hermanarse vpr (a) (ciudades) to twin (b) (combinar) to combine

hermanastro,-a nm,f (hombre) stepbrother; (mujer) stepsister

hermandad nf (a) (grupo) fraternity, brotherhood, sisterhood (b) (relación) brotherhood, sisterhood

hermano nm (a) brother; **h. político** brother-in-law; **primo h.** first cousin (b) Rel (fraile) brother (c) **hermanos** brothers and sisters

herméticamente adv **h. cerrado** hermetically sealed

hermético,-a adj (a) (cierre) hermetic, airtight (b) Fig (abstruso) secretive

hermetismo nm airtightness; Fig impenetrability

hermoso,-a adj beautiful, lovely; (grande) fine

hermosura nf beauty

héroe nm hero

heroico,-a adj heroic

heroína nf (a) (mujer) heroine (b) (droga) heroin

heroinómano,-a nm,f heroin addict

heroísmo nm heroism

herrador nm blacksmith

herradura nf horseshoe

herramienta nf Téc tool; **caja de herramientas** toolbox

herrar [1] vt (a) (caballo) to shoe (b) (ganado) to brand

herrería nf forge, smithy

herrero nm blacksmith, smith

herrumbre nf rust

hervidero nm Fig (lugar) hotbed

hervir [5] **1** vt (hacer bullir) to boil

2 vi (a) Culin to boil; **romper a h.** to come to the boil (b) (abundar) to swarm, to seethe (**de** with)

heterodoxo,-a adj unorthodox

heterogéneo,-a adj heterogeneous

hez nf (a) (usu pl) (poso) sediment, dregs (b) **heces** faeces

hiato nm Ling hiatus

híbrido,-a adj & nm,f hybrid

hice pt indef de **hacer**

hiciste pt indef de **hacer**

hidalgo nm Hist nobleman, gentleman

hidalguía nf nobility; Fig chivalry, gentlemanliness

hidratación nf (a) Quím hydration (b) (de la piel) moisturizing

hidratante adj moisturizing; **crema/leche h.** moisturizing cream/lotion

hidráulico,-a adj hydraulic; **energía hidráulica** hydro-electric energy

hidroavión nm seaplane, US hydroplane

hidrocarburo nm hydrocarbon

hidrófilo,-a adj absorbent; **algodón h.** Br cotton wool, Am absorbent cotton

hidrógeno nm Quím hydrogen

hidroterapia nf Med hydrotherapy

hiedra nf ivy

hiel nf (a) Anat bile (b) Fig bitterness, gall

hielo nm ice; Fig **romper el h.** to break the ice

hiena nf hyena

hierba nf (a) grass; **mala h.** Bot weed; Fig (persona) bad lot; Fam Hum **y otras hierbas** among others (b) Culin herb; **h. luisa** lemon verbena (c) Fam (marihuana) grass

hierbabuena nf mint

hierro nm (a) (metal) iron; **h. forjado** wrought iron (b) (punta de arma) head, point (c) (marca en el ganado) brand

hígado nm (a) Anat liver (b) Euf guts

higiene nf hygiene

higiénico,-a adj hygienic; **papel h.** toilet paper

higo nm Fam Fig **hecho un h.** wizened, crumpled

higuera nf Bot fig tree

hija nf daughter

hijastro,-a nm,f (hombre) stepson; (mujer) stepdaughter

hijo nm (a) son, child; Pey **h. de papá** rich kid; Vulg **h. de puta** o Méx **de la chingada** bastard, US asshole (b) **hijos** children

hijoputa nm Vulg bastard, US asshole

hilacha nf, **hilacho** nm loose o hanging thread

hilandería nf mill; (de algodón) cotton mill

hilandero,-a nm,f spinner

hilar vt & vi (a) to spin (b) Fig (idea, plan) to work out; **h. muy fino** to split hairs

hilaridad nf hilarity, mirth

hilera nf line, row

hilo nm (a) Cost thread; (grueso) yarn (b) Fig (de historia, discurso) thread; (de pensamiento) train; **perder el h.** to lose the thread; **h. musical** background music (c) Tex linen

hilvanar vt (a) Cost to tack, to baste (b) Fig (ideas etc) to outline

himno nm hymn; **h. nacional** national anthem

hincapié *nm* **hacer h. en** *(insistir)* to insist on; *(subrayar)* to emphasize, to stress

hincar [44] 1 *vt (clavar)* to drive (in); **h. el diente a** to sink one's teeth into

2 hincarse *vpr* **h. de rodillas** to kneel (down)

hincha *Fam* **1** *nmf Ftb* fan, supporter

2 *nf (antipatía)* grudge, dislike; **me tiene h.** he's got it in for me

hinchada *nf Ftb Fam* fans, supporters

hinchado,-a *adj* (a) inflated, blown up (b) *Med (cara etc)* swollen, puffed up; *(estómago)* bloated (c) *Fig (estilo)* bombastic, pompous

hinchar 1 *vt* (a) *(inflar)* to inflate, to blow up (b) *Fig (exagerar)* to inflate, to exaggerate

2 hincharse *vpr* (a) *Med* to swell (up) (b) *Fam* **me hinché de comida** I stuffed myself; **me hinché de llorar** I cried for all I was worth

hinchazón *nf Med* swelling

hindú *adj & nmf* Hindu

hipermercado *nm* hypermarket

hipertensión *nf* high blood pressure

hípica *nf* (horse) riding

hípico,-a *adj* horse; **club h.** riding club

hipnotizar [40] *vt* to hypnotize

hipo *nm* hiccups, hiccough; **me ha dado h.** it's given me the hiccups

hipocondríaco,-a *adj & nm,f* hypochondriac

hipocresía *nf* hypocrisy

hipócrita 1 *adj* hypocritical

2 *nmf* hypocrite

hipódromo *nm* racetrack, racecourse

hipopótamo *nm* hippopotamus

hipoteca *nf Fin* mortgage

hipotecar [44] *vt* (a) *Fin* to mortgage (b) *Fig* to jeopardize

hipótesis *nf inv* hypothesis

hipotético,-a *adj* hypothetical

hiriente *adj* offensive, wounding; *(palabras)* cutting

hirsuto,-a *adj* hirsute, hairy; *(cerdoso)* bristly

hispánico,-a *adj* Hispanic, Spanish

hispanidad *nf* **el Día de la H.** Columbus Day *(12 October)*

hispano,-a 1 *adj (español)* Spanish; *(español y sudamericano)* Hispanic; *(sudamericano)* Spanish American

2 *nm,f (hispanoamericano)* Spanish American; *(estadounidense)* Hispanic

Hispanoamérica *nf* Latin America

hispanoamericano,-a *adj & nm,f* Latin American

hispanohablante 1 *adj* Spanish-speaking

2 *nmf* Spanish speaker

histeria *nf* hysteria; **un ataque de h.** hysterics

histérico,-a *adj* hysterical; *Fam Fig* **me pones h.** you're driving me mad

historia *nf* (a) history; **esto pasará a la h.** this will go down in history (b) *(narración)* story, tale; *Fam* **¡déjate de historias!** don't give me that!

historiador,-a *nm,f* historian

historial *nm* (a) *Med* medical record, case history (b) *(antecedentes)* background

historiar [29] *vt* to recount

histórico,-a *adj* (a) historical (b) *(auténtico)* factual, true; **hechos históricos** true facts (c) *(de gran importancia)* historic, memorable

historieta *nf* (a) *(cuento)* short story, tale (b) *(tira cómica)* comic strip

hito *nm* milestone; **mirar de h. en h.** to stare at

hizo *pt indef de* hacer

hnos. *(abr* Hermanos*)* Bros

hocico *nm* (a) *(de animal)* snout (b) *(de persona)* mug, snout; *Fam* **meter los hocicos en algo** to stick *o* poke one's nose into sth

hogar *nm* (a) *(casa)* home (b) *(de la chimenea)* hearth, fireplace (c) *Fig* **formar *o* crear un h.** *(familia)* to start a family

hogareño,-a *adj (vida)* home, family; *(persona)* home-loving, stay-at-home

hoguera *nf* bonfire

hoja *nf* (a) *Bot* leaf (b) *(pétalo)* petal (c) *(de papel)* sheet, leaf; **h. de cálculo** spreadsheet (d) *(de libro)* leaf, page (e) *(de metal)* sheet (f) *(de cuchillo, espada)* blade (g) *(impreso)* hand-out, printed sheet (h) *(de puerta o ventana)* leaf

hojalata *nf* tin, tin plate

hojaldre *nm Culin* puff pastry

hojarasca *nf* fallen *o* dead leaves

hojear *vt* to leaf through, to flick through

hola *interj* hello!, hullo!, hi!

Holanda *n* Holland

holandés,-esa 1 *adj* Dutch

2 *nm,f (hombre)* Dutchman; *(mujer)* Dutchwoman

3 *nm (idioma)* Dutch

holding *nm Fin* holding company

holgado,-a *adj* (a) *(ropa)* loose, baggy (b) *(económicamente)* comfortable (c) *(espacio)* roomy; **andar h. de tiempo** to have plenty of time

holgar [2] *vi* (a) *(no trabajar)* to be idle

(**b**) *(sobrar)* **huelga decir que ...** it goes without saying that ...

holgazán,-ana 1 *adj* lazy, idle

  2 *nm,f* lazybones, layabout

holgura *nf* (**a**) *(ropa)* looseness (**b**) *(espacio)* space, roominess; *Téc* play, give (**c**) *(bienestar económico)* affluence, comfort; **vivir con h.** to be comfortably off, to be well-off

hollar [2] *vt Fig* to walk on; **terrenos jamás hollados** uncharted territory

hollín *nm* soot

hombre 1 *nm* (**a**) man; **de h. a h.** man-to-man; **¡pobre h.!** poor chap!; **ser muy h.** to be every inch a man; **h. de estado** statesman; **h. de negocios** businessman (**b**) *(especie)* mankind, man

  2 *interj* (**a**) *(saludo)* hey!, hey there!; **¡h., Juan!** hey, Juan! (**b**) **¡sí h.!, ¡h. claro!** *(enfático)* sure!, you bet!; **¡anda, h.!** *(incredulidad)* oh come on!

hombrera *nf* shoulder pad

hombría *nf* manliness, virility

hombrillo *nm Ven (arcén)* verge; *(de autopista) Br* hard shoulder, *US* shoulder

hombro *nm* shoulder; **a hombros** on one's shoulders; **encogerse de hombros** to shrug one's shoulders; **mirar a algn por encima del h.** to look down one's nose at sb

hombruno,-a *adj* mannish, butch

homenaje *nm* homage, tribute; **rendir h. a algn** to pay homage o tribute to sb

homenajear *vt* to pay tribute to

homicida 1 *nmf (hombre)* murderer; *(mujer)* murderess

  2 *adj* homicidal; **el arma h.** the murder weapon

homicidio *nm* homicide

homogéneo,-a *adj* homogeneous, uniform

homologable *adj* comparable (**con** with)

homologar [42] *vt* to give official approval o recognition to

homólogo,-a 1 *adj (equiparable)* comparable

  2 *nm,f (persona con mismas condiciones)* counterpart

homosexual *adj & nmf* homosexual

homosexualidad *nf* homosexuality

honda *nf (arma)* sling

hondo,-a *adj* (**a**) *(profundo)* deep; **plato h.** soup dish (**b**) *Fig (pesar)* profound, deep

hondonada *nf Geog* hollow, depression

hondura *nf* depth; *Fig* **meterse en honduras** *(profundizar)* to go into too much detail

Honduras *n* Honduras

hondureño,-a *adj & nm,f* Honduran

honestidad *nf* (**a**) *(honradez)* honesty, uprightness (**b**) *(decencia)* modesty

honesto,-a *adj* (**a**) *(honrado)* honest, upright (**b**) *(decente)* modest

hongo *nm* (**a**) *Bot* fungus; **h. venenoso** toadstool (**b**) *(sombrero) Br* bowler (hat), *US* derby

honor *nm* (**a**) *(virtud)* honour; **palabra de h.** word of honour (**b**) **en h. a la verdad ...** to be fair ...; **es un h. para mí** it's an honour for me (**c**) **hacer h. a** to live up to

honorable *adj* honourable; *Pol* **el h.** = head of the Catalan government

honorario,-a 1 *adj* honorary

  2 *nmpl* **honorarios** fees, fee

honorífico,-a *adj* honorary

honra *nf* (**a**) *(dignidad)* dignity, self-esteem (**b**) *(fama)* reputation, good name (**c**) *(honor)* honour; **me cabe la h. de ...** I have the honour of ...; **¡a mucha h.!** and proud of it!

honradez *nf* honesty, integrity

honrado,-a *adj* (**a**) *(de fiar)* honest (**b**) *(decente)* upright, respectable

honrar *vt* (**a**) *(respetar)* to honour (**b**) *(enaltecer)* to be a credit to

honrilla *nf* self-respect, pride

honroso,-a *adj (loable)* honourable

hora *nf* (**a**) hour; **media h.** half an hour; **a altas horas de la madrugada** in the small hours; **dar la h.** to strike the hour; **(trabajo) por horas** (work) paid by the hour; **h. punta,** *Am* **h. pico** *(de mucho tráfico)* rush hour; *(de agua, electricidad)* peak times; **horas extra** overtime (hours) (**b**) *Fig* time; **¿qué h. es?** what time is it?; **a su h.** at the proper time; **a última h.** at the last moment; **la h. de la verdad** the moment of truth (**c**) *(cita)* appointment; **pedir h.** *(al médico etc)* to ask for an appointment

horadar *vt (perforar)* to drill o bore a hole in

horario,-a 1 *nm* timetable, *US* schedule

  2 *adj* time; *Rad* **señal horaria** pips

horca *nf* gallows *sing*

horcajada: • **a horcajadas** *loc adv* astride

horchata *nf Culin* = sweet, milky drink made from chufa nuts o almonds

horda *nf* horde, mob

horizonte *nm* horizon

horma *nf (de zapato)* last

hormiga *nf* ant

hormigón *nm Constr* concrete; **h. armado** reinforced concrete

hormiguear *vi* to itch, to tingle; **me hormigueaba la pierna** I had pins and needles in my leg

hormigueo *nm* (**a**) pins and needles, tingling o itching sensation (**b**) *Fig* anxiety

hormiguero *nm* (**a**) anthill (**b**) *Fig* **ser un h.** *(lugar)* to be swarming (with people)

hormona *nf* hormone

hornada *nf* (**a**) *(pan)* batch (**b**) *Fig* set, batch

hornillo *nm* *(de cocinar)* stove; *(placa)* hotplate

horno *nm* *(cocina)* oven; *Téc* furnace; *(para cerámica, ladrillos)* kiln; *Culin* **pescado al h.** baked fish; *Fam Fig* **esta habitación es un h.** this room is boiling hot

Hornos *n* **Cabo de H.** Cape Horn

horóscopo *nm* horoscope

horquilla *nf* (**a**) *(del pelo)* hairpin, *Br* hair-grip, *US* bobby-pin (**b**) *(estadística)* chart (**c**) **h. de precios** price range

horrendo,-a *adj* horrifying, horrible

hórreo *nm Agr* granary

horrible *adj* horrible, dreadful, awful

horripilante *adj* hair-raising, scary

horror *nm* (**a**) horror, terror; **¡qué h.!** how awful!; *Fam* **tengo h. a las motos** I hate motorbikes (**b**) *Fam Fig* **me gusta horrores** *(muchísimo)* I like it an awful lot

horrorizar [40] *vt* to horrify, to terrify

horroroso,-a *adj* (**a**) *(que da miedo)* horrifying, terrifying (**b**) *Fam (muy feo)* hideous, ghastly (**c**) *Fam (malísimo)* awful, dreadful

hortaliza *nf* vegetable

hortelano,-a *nm,f Br* market gardener, *US* truck farmer

hortensia *nf Bot* hydrangea

hortera *adj Fam (persona)* flashy; *(cosa)* tacky, kitsch

horterada *nf Fam* tacky thing o act

hosco,-a *adj* (**a**) *(poco sociable)* surly, sullen (**b**) *(tenebroso)* dark, gloomy (**c**) *(difícil)* tough

hospedaje *nm* lodgings, *Br* accommodation, *US* accommodations

hospedar 1 *vt* to put up, to lodge

2 hospedarse *vpr* to stay (**en** at)

hospicio *nm* orphanage

hospital *nm* hospital

hospitalario,-a *adj* (**a**) *(acogedor)* hospitable (**b**) *Med* hospital; **instalaciones hospitalarias** hospital facilities

hospitalidad *nf* hospitality

hospitalizar [40] *vt* to take o send into hospital, to hospitalize

hostal *nm* guest house

hostelería *nf (negocio)* catering business; *(estudios)* hotel management

hostelero,-a *nm,f (hombre)* landlord; *(mujer)* landlady

hostería *nf CSur* inn, lodging house

hostia 1 *nf* (**a**) *Rel* host (**b**) *Vulg (tortazo)* bash (**c**) *Vulg* **estar de mala h.** to be in a foul mood; **ser la h.** *(fantástico)* to be *Br* bloody o *US* goddamn amazing; *(penoso)* to be *Br* bloody o *US* goddamn awful

2 *interj Vulg* damn! *Br* bloody hell!

hostiar [29] *vt Vulg* to bash, to sock

hostigar [42] *vt* (**a**) to harass (**b**) *(caballerías)* to whip

hostil *adj* hostile

hostilidad *nf* hostility

hotel *nm* hotel

hotelero,-a 1 *adj* hotel; **el sector h.** the hotel sector

2 *nm,f* hotel-keeper, hotelier

hoy *adv* (**a**) *(día)* today (**b**) *Fig (presente)* now; **h. (en) día** nowadays; **h. por h.** at the present time

hoya *nf Geog* dale, valley

hoyo *nm* (**a**) *(agujero)* hole, pit (**b**) *(sepultura)* grave (**c**) *(de golf)* hole

hoyuelo *nm* dimple

hoz *nf Agr* sickle; **la h. y el martillo** the hammer and sickle

HR *nm* (*abr* **Hostal Residencia**) boarding house

huachafo,-a *adj Perú Fam* tacky

huasipungo *nm Andes* = plot of land given to Indian for his own use in exchange for work on the landowner's farm

huaso,-a *nm,f Chile Fam* farmer, peasant

hube *pt indef de* **haber**

hubiera *subj imperf de* **haber**

hucha *nf* piggy bank

hueco,-a 1 *adj* (**a**) *(vacío)* empty, hollow (**b**) *(sonido)* resonant

2 *nm* (**a**) *(cavidad)* hollow, hole (**b**) *(sitio no ocupado)* empty space (**c**) *(rato libre)* free time

huele *indic pres de* **oler**

huelga *nf* strike; **estar en** o **de h.** to be on strike; **h. de brazos caídos** go-slow; **h. de celo** work-to-rule

huelguista *nmf* striker

huella *nf* (**a**) *(del pie)* footprint; *(coche)* track; **h. dactilar** fingerprint (**b**) *Fig (vestigio)* trace, sign; **dejar h.** to leave one's mark

huérfano,-a *nm,f* orphan

huero,-a *adj Fig* empty

huerta *nf Agr* (**a**) *(parcela) Br* market garden, *US* truck farm (**b**) *(región)* = irrigated area used for cultivation

huerto *nm (de verduras)* vegetable garden, kitchen garden; *(de frutales)* orchard

hueso *nm* (**a**) *Anat* bone; **estar en los**

huesos to be all skin and bone (**b**) *(de fruto)* stone, *US* pit (**c**) *Fig (difícil)* hard work; *(profesor)* hard nut (**d**) *Méx (enchufe)* contact

huésped,-a *nm,f (invitado)* guest; *(en hotel etc)* lodger, boarder; **casa de huéspedes** guesthouse

hueste *nf Mil* army, host

huesudo,-a *adj* bony

huevada *nf Andes, RP muy Fam (dicho)* garbage, bullshit, *Br* bollocks

huevera *nf (caja)* egg box

huevo *nm* (**a**) egg; **h. duro** hard-boiled egg; **h. escalfado** poached egg; **h. frito** fried egg; **h. pasado por agua,** *Am* **h. tibio** *o* **a la copa** soft-boiled egg; **huevos revueltos** scrambled eggs (**b**) *muy Fam (usu pl)* balls; **hacer algo por huevos** to do sth even if it kills you; **tener huevos** to have guts

huida *nf* flight, escape

huidizo,-a *adj* elusive

huipil *nm CAm, Méx* = traditional Indian woman's dress or blouse

huir [37] *vi* to run away (**de** from), to flee; **h. de la cárcel** to escape from prison; **h. de algn** to avoid sb

hule *nm* (**a**) *(tela impermeable)* oilcloth, oilskin (**b**) *(de mesa)* tablecloth (**c**) *Am* rubber

hulla *nf* soft coal

humanidad *nf* (**a**) *(género humano)* humanity, mankind (**b**) *(cualidad)* humanity, humaneness (**c**) *(bondad)* compassion, kindness

humanitario,-a *adj* humanitarian

humano,-a *adj* (**a**) *(relativo al hombre)* human (**b**) *(compasivo)* humane
  2 *nm* human (being); **ser h.** human being

humear *vi (echar humo)* to smoke; *(arrojar vapor)* to steam, to be steaming hot

humedad *nf (atmosférica)* humidity; *(de lugar)* dampness; **a prueba de h.** dampproof

humedecer [33] **1** *vt* to moisten, to dampen
  2 humedecerse *vpr* to become damp *o* wet *o* moist

húmedo,-a *adj (casa, ropa)* damp; *(clima)* humid, damp, moist

humildad *nf* humility; *(pobreza)* humbleness

humilde *adj* humble, modest; *(pobre)* poor

humillación *nf* humiliation

humillante *adj* humiliating, humbling

humillar **1** *vt (rebajar)* to humiliate, to humble
  2 humillarse *vpr* **humillarse ante algn** to humble oneself before sb

humita *nf Andes, Arg (pasta de maíz)* = paste made of mashed maize *o US* corn, used to make steamed dumplings

humo *nm* (**a**) smoke; *(gas)* fumes; *(vapor)* vapour, steam (**b**) **¡qué humos tiene!** she thinks a lot of herself!

humor *nm* (**a**) *(genio)* mood; **estar de buen/mal h.** to be in a good/bad mood (**b**) *(carácter)* temper; **es persona de mal h.** he's bad-tempered (**c**) *(gracia)* humour; **sentido del h.** sense of humour

humorismo *nm* humour

humorista *nmf* humorist; **h. gráfico** cartoonist

humorístico,-a *adj* humorous, funny

hundido,-a *adj* (**a**) *(barco)* sunken; *(ojos)* deep-set (**b**) *Fig (abatido)* down, demoralized

hundimiento *nm* (**a**) *(de edificio)* collapse (**b**) *(de barco)* sinking (**c**) *(de tierra)* subsidence (**d**) *Fig Fin* crash, slump; *(ruina)* downfall

hundir **1** *vt* (**a**) *(barco)* to sink (**b**) *(edificio)* to bring *o* knock down (**c**) *Fig (desmoralizar)* to demoralize
  2 hundirse *vpr* (**a**) *(barco)* to sink (**b**) *(edificio)* to collapse (**c**) *Fig (empresa)* to collapse, to crash

húngaro,-a **1** *adj* Hungarian
  2 *nm,f (persona)* Hungarian
  3 *nm (idioma)* Hungarian

Hungría *n* Hungary

huracán *nm* hurricane

huraño,-a *adj Pey* unsociable

hurgar [42] **1** *vi (fisgar)* to poke one's nose in
  2 *vt (fuego etc)* to poke, to rake
  3 hurgarse *vpr* **h. las narices** to pick one's nose

hurón,-ona **1** *nm Zool* ferret
  2 *nm,f Fam Fig (fisgón)* busybody, nosey-parker

hurraca *nf Orn* = **urraca**

hurtadillas *adv* **a h.** stealthily, on the sly

hurtar *vt* to steal, to pilfer

hurto *nm* petty theft, pilfering

husmear **1** *vt (olfatear)* to sniff out, to scent
  2 *vi Fig (curiosear)* to snoop, to pry

huyo *indic pres de* **huir**

I

I, i [i] *nf (la letra)* I, i; **i griega** Y, y
IB *nm Educ (abr* **Instituto de Bachillerato**)
≃ state secondary school
ib. *(abr* **ibídem**) ibid.
ibérico,-a *adj* Iberian
Iberoamérica *n* Latin America
iberoamericano,-a *adj & nm,f* Latin
American
iceberg *nm (pl* **icebergs**) iceberg
ICONA *nm Antes (abr* **Instituto Nacional
para la Conservación de la Naturaleza**) =
Spanish national institute for conservation
icono *nm* icon; *Informát* icon
iconoclasta 1 *adj* iconoclastic
2 *nmf* iconoclast
iconografía *nf* iconography
ictericia *nf Med* jaundice
íd. *(abr* **ídem**) id
I+D *(abr* **Investigación más Desarrollo**)
R&D
ida *nf* billete de i. y vuelta *Br* return ticket,
US round-trip ticket; **idas y venidas** comings and goings
idea *nf* (a) idea; **i. fija** fixed idea (b)
(noción) idea; **hacerse a la i. de** to get
used to the idea of; *Fam* **ni i.** no idea, not a
clue (c) *(opinión)* opinion; **cambiar de i.**
to change one's mind (d) *(intención)* intention; **a mala i.** on purpose
ideal *adj & nm* ideal
idealismo *nm* idealism
idealista 1 *adj* idealistic
2 *nmf* idealist
idealizar [40] *vt* to idealize, to glorify
idear *vt* (a) *(inventar)* to devise, to invent
(b) *(concebir)* to think up, to conceive
ídem *adv* idem, ditto; *Fam* **í. de í.** exactly
the same
idéntico,-a *adj* identical
identidad *nf* (a) identity; **carnet de i.**
identity card (b) *(semejanza)* identity,
sameness
identificación *nf* identification
identificar [44] *vt* to identify
2 identificarse *vpr* to identify oneself;
Fig **i. con** to identify with
ideología *nf* ideology
ideológico,-a *adj* ideological

idílico,-a *adj* idyllic
idilio *nm* (a) *Lit* idyll (b) *Fig (romance)*
romance, love affair
idioma *nm* language
idiomático,-a *adj* idiomatic
idiosincrasia *nf* idiosyncrasy
idiota 1 *adj* idiotic, stupid
2 *nmf* idiot, fool
idiotez *nf* idiocy, stupidity
ido,-a *adj* (a) *(distraído)* absent-minded
(b) *Fam (chiflado)* crazy, nuts
idólatra 1 *adj* idolatrous
2 *nmf (hombre)* idolater; *(mujer)* idol-
atress
idolatrar *vt* to worship; *Fig* to idolize
idolatría *nf* idolatry
ídolo *nm* idol
idóneo,-a *adj* suitable, fit
iglesia *nf* (a) *(edificio)* church (b) **la I.**
(institución) the Church
ignominia *nf* ignominy
ignominioso,-a *adj* ignominious, shameful
ignorancia *nf* ignorance
ignorante 1 *adj* (a) *(sin instrucción)* ignorant (b) *(no informado)* ignorant, unaware *(de* of)
2 *nmf* ignoramus
ignorar 1 *vt* (a) *(algo)* not to know (b) *(a
algn)* to ignore
2 ignorarse *vpr* to be unknown
ignoto,-a *adj* unknown
igual 1 *adj* (a) *(idéntico)* the same, alike;
son todos iguales they're all the same;
es i. it doesn't matter; **i. que** the same as (b)
(equivalente) equal; **a partes iguales** fifty-
fifty (c) *Dep (empatados)* even; **treinta
iguales** thirty all (d) *Mat* equal; **tres más
tres i. a seis** three plus three equals six
(e) **al i. que** just like (f) **por i.** equally
2 *nm* equal; **de i. a i.** on an equal footing;
sin i. unique, unrivalled
3 *adv* (a) **lo haces i. que yo** you do it
the same way I do (b) *(probablemente)*
probably; **i. vengo** I'll probably come (c)
Andes, RP (aún así) anyway, still; **estaba
nublado pero i. fuimos a la playa** it was
cloudy but we still went to the beach *o* we
went to the beach anyway

igualar 1 *vt* (**a**) to make equal (**b**) *(nivelar)* to level (**c**) *Dep* **i. el partido** to equalize, to square the match

2 igualarse *vpr* (**a**) to be equal (**b**) **igualarse con algn** to place oneself on an equal footing with sb

igualdad *nf* (**a**) equality; **i. ante la ley** equality before the law (**b**) *(identidad)* sameness; **en i. de condiciones** on equal terms

igualitario,-a *adj* egalitarian

igualmente *adv* equally; *(también)* also, likewise; *Fam* **encantado de conocerlo – ¡i.!** pleased to meet you – likewise!

ijada *nf*, **ijar** *nr*₃ *Anat* flank

ikastola *nf* = primary school in the Basque Country where classes are given entirely in Basque

ikurriña *nf* = Basque national flag

ilegal *adj* illegal

ilegalidad *nf* illegality

ilegalmente *adv* illegally

ilegible *adj* illegible, unreadable

ilegítimo,-a *adj* illegitimate

ileso,-a *adj* unhurt, unharmed

ilícito,-a *adj* illicit, unlawful

ilimitado,-a *adj* unlimited, limitless

Ilmo. *(abr* **Ilustrísimo)** His Excellence *o* Excellency

ilógico,-a *adj* illogical

iluminación *nf* *(alumbrado)* illumination, lighting

iluminar *vt* (**a**) to illuminate, to light (up) (**b**) *Fig (a persona)* to enlighten; *(tema)* to throw light upon

ilusión *nf* (**a**) *(esperanza)* hope; *(esperanza vana)* illusion, delusion; **hacerse ilusiones** to build up one's hopes (**b**) *(sueño)* dream (**c**) *(emoción)* excitement, thrill; **me hace i. verla** I'm looking forward to seeing her; **¡qué i.!** how exciting!

ilusionar 1 *vt* (**a**) *(esperanzar)* to build up sb's hopes (**b**) *(entusiasmar)* to excite, to thrill

2 ilusionarse *vpr* (**a**) *(esperanzarse)* to build up one's hopes (**b**) *(entusiasmarse)* to be excited *o* thrilled (**con** about)

iluso,-a *adj* easily deceived, gullible

ilusorio,-a *adj* illusory, unreal

ilustración *nf* (**a**) *(grabado)* illustration, picture; *(ejemplo)* illustration (**b**) *(erudición)* learning, erudition; *Hist* **la I.** the Enlightenment

ilustrado,-a *adj* (**a**) *(con dibujos, ejemplos)* illustrated (**b**) *(erudito)* learned, erudite

ilustrar 1 *vt* (**a**) to illustrate (**b**) *(aclarar)* to explain, to make clear

2 ilustrarse *vpr* to acquire knowledge (**sobre** of), to learn (**sobre** about)

ilustrativo,-a *adj* illustrative

ilustre *adj* illustrious, distinguished

imagen *nf* (**a**) image; **ser la viva i. de algn** to be the spitting image of sb; **tener buena i.** to have a good image (**b**) *Rel* image, statue (**c**) *TV* picture

imaginación *nf* imagination; **eso son imaginaciones tuyas** you're imagining things

imaginar 1 *vt* to imagine

2 imaginarse *vpr* to imagine; **me imagino que sí** I suppose so

imaginario,-a *adj* imaginary

imaginativo,-a *adj* imaginative

imán *nm* magnet

imbatible *adj* unbeatable

imbatido,-a *adj* unbeaten, undefeated

imbécil 1 *adj* stupid, silly

2 *nmf* idiot, imbecile

imbecilidad *nf* stupidity, imbecility

imborrable *adj* indelible

imbuir [37] *vt Fml* to imbue

imitación *nf* imitation

imitar *vt* to imitate; *(gestos)* to mimic; **este collar imita al oro** this necklace is imitation gold

impaciencia *nf* impatience

impacientar 1 *vt* **i. a algn** to make sb lose patience, to exasperate sb

2 impacientarse *vpr* to get *o* grow impatient (**por** at)

impaciente *adj* *(deseoso)* impatient; *(intranquilo)* anxious

impactante *adj* **una noticia i.** a sensational piece of news

impactar *vt* to shock, to stun

impacto *nm* impact; *Mil* hit

impar *adj Mat* odd; **número i.** odd number

imparable *adj Dep* unstoppable

imparcial *adj* impartial, unbiased

imparcialidad *nf* impartiality

impartir *vt (clases)* to give

impasible *adj* impassive

impávido,-a *adj* fearless

impecable *adj* impeccable

impedido,-a 1 *adj* disabled, handicapped

2 *nm,f* disabled *o* handicapped person

impedimento *nm* impediment; *(obstáculo)* hindrance, obstacle

impedir [6] *vt (obstaculizar)* to impede, to hinder; *(imposibilitar)* to prevent, to stop; **i. el paso** to block the way

impeler *vt Téc* to drive, to propel; *Fig* to drive, to impel

impenetrable *adj* impenetrable

impenitente *adj* Rel impenitent, unrepentant

impensable *adj* unthinkable

impepinable *adj* Fam dead sure, certain

imperante *adj (gobernante)* ruling; *(predominante)* prevailing

imperar *vi (gobernar)* to rule; *(predominar)* to prevail

imperativo,-a 1 *adj* imperative
2 *nm* Ling imperative

imperceptible *adj* imperceptible

imperdible *nm* safety pin

imperdonable *adj* unforgivable, inexcusable

imperecedero,-a *adj* imperishable; Fig enduring

imperfección *nf* (a) imperfection (b) *(defecto)* defect, fault

imperfecto,-a *adj* (a) imperfect, fallible (b) *(defectuoso)* defective, faulty (c) Ling imperfect

imperial *adj* imperial

imperialismo *nm* imperialism

impericia *nf* incompetence

imperio *nm* empire; **el i. de la ley** the rule of law

imperioso,-a *adj* (a) *(autoritario)* imperious (b) *(ineludible)* urgent, imperative; **una necesidad imperiosa** a pressing need

impermeable 1 *adj* impermeable, impervious; *(ropa)* waterproof
2 *nm* raincoat, mac

impersonal *adj* impersonal

impertérrito,-a *adj* undaunted, fearless

impertinencia *nf* impertinence

impertinente 1 *adj (insolente)* impertinent; *(inoportuno)* irrelevant
2 *nmpl* **impertinentes** lorgnette

imperturbable *adj* imperturbable, unruffled

ímpetu *nm* (a) *(impulso)* impetus, momentum (b) *(violencia)* violence (c) *(energía)* energy

impetuosidad *nf* (a) *(violencia)* violence (b) *(fogosidad)* impetuosity, impulsiveness

impetuoso,-a *adj* (a) *(violento)* violent (b) *(fogoso)* impetuous, impulsive

impío,-a *adj* ungodly, irreligious

implacable *adj* relentless, implacable

implantar *vt (costumbres)* to implant, to instil; *(reformas)* to introduce; Med to implant

implicación *nf (participación)* involvement; *(significado)* implication

implicancia *nf* CSur implication

implicar [44] *vt* (a) *(involucrar)* to involve, to implicate (**en** in) (b) *(conllevar)* to imply

implícito,-a *adj* implicit, implied

implorar *vt* to implore, to beg

impoluto,-a *adj* pure, spotless

imponente *adj* (a) *(impresionante)* imposing, impressive (b) *(sobrecogedor)* stunning (c) Fam *(atractivo)* terrific, tremendous, smashing

imponer [19] *(pp* impuesto*)* **1** *vt* (a) to impose (b) *(respeto)* to inspire (c) Fin to deposit
2 *vi (impresionar)* to be impressive;
3 **imponerse** *vpr* (a) *(infundir respeto)* to command respect (b) *(prevalecer)* to prevail (c) *(ser necesario)* to be necessary

imponible *adj* Fin taxable

impopular *adj* unpopular, disliked

importación *nf (mercancía)* import; *(acción)* importing; **artículos de i.** imported goods

importancia *nf* importance, significance; **dar i. a** to attach importance to; **sin i.** unimportant

importante *adj* important, significant; **una suma i.** a considerable sum

importar¹ 1 *vi* (a) *(atañer)* **eso no te importa a tí** that doesn't concern you, that's none of your business (b) *(tener importancia)* to be important; **no importa** it doesn't matter; Fam **me importa un bledo** *o* **un pito** I couldn't care less (c) *(molestar)* **¿te importaría repetirlo?** would you mind repeating it?; **¿te importa si fumo?** do you mind if I smoke?
2 *vt (valer)* to amount to; **los libros importan 2.000 pesetas** the books come to 2,000 pesetas

importar² *vt* to import

importe *nm* Com & Fin amount, total

importunar *vt* to bother, to pester

imposibilidad *nf* impossibility

imposibilitar *vt* (a) *(impedir)* to make impossible, to prevent (b) *(incapacitar)* to disable, to cripple

imposible *adj* impossible; **me es i. hacerlo** I can't (possibly) do it

imposición *nf* (a) *(disciplina, condiciones)* imposing (b) Fin deposit; *(impuesto)* taxation

impostor,-a *nm,f (farsante)* impostor

impotencia *nf* powerlessness, helplessness; Med impotence

impotente *adj* powerless, helpless; Med impotent

impracticable *adj* (a) *(inviable)* impracticable, unviable (b) *(camino)* impassable

imprecar [44] *vt* to imprecate, to curse

imprecisión *nf* imprecision, vagueness

impreciso,-a *adj* imprecise, vague

impregnar 1 *vt* to impregnate (**de** with)
2 **impregnarse** *upr* to become impregnated

imprenta *nf* (**a**) *(taller)* printer's, print works (**b**) *(aparato)* printing press (**c**) **libertad de i.** freedom of the press

imprescindible *adj* essential, indispensable

impresentable *adj* unpresentable

impresión *nf* (**a**) *Fig (efecto)* impression; **causar i.** to make an impression (**b**) *Fig (opinión)* impression; **cambiar impresiones** to exchange impressions (**c**) *Impr (acto)* printing; *(edición)* edition (**d**) *(huella)* impression, imprint

impresionable *adj* impressionable

impresionante *adj* impressive, striking; *Fam* **un error i.** *(tremendo)* a terrible mistake

impresionar *vt* (**a**) *(causar admiración)* to impress; *(sorprender)* to stun, to shock (**b**) *Fot* to expose

impresionismo *nm Arte* impressionism

impresionista *adj & nmf* impressionist

impreso,-a 1 *adj* printed
2 *nm* (**a**) *(papel, folleto)* printed matter (**b**) *(formulario)* form; **i. de solicitud** application form (**c**) **impresos** *(de correos)* printed matter

impresora *nf Informát* printer; **i. láser** laser printer; **i. de chorro de tinta** inkjet printer

imprevisible *adj* unforeseeable, unpredictable

imprevisión *nf* lack of foresight

imprevisto,-a 1 *adj* unforeseen, unexpected
2 *nm (incidente)* unforeseen event

imprimir (*pp* **impreso**) *vt* (**a**) *Impr & Informát* to print (**b**) *(marcar)* to stamp

improbable *adj* improbable, unlikely

ímprobo,-a *adj (inmoral)* dishonest, corrupt

improcedente *adj* (**a**) inappropriate, unsuitable (**b**)*Jur* inadmissible

improductivo,-a *adj* unproductive

improperio *nm* insult, offensive remark

impropio,-a *adj (inadecuado)* inappropriate, unsuitable; **i. de** uncharacteristic of

improvisación *nf* improvisation; *Mús* extemporization

improvisado,-a *adj (espontáneo)* improvised, impromptu, ad lib; *(provisional)* makeshift; **discurso i.** impromptu speech

improvisar *vt* to improvise; *Mús* to extemporize

improviso *adj* **de i.** unexpectedly, suddenly; *Fam* **coger** *o* **pillar a algn de i.** to catch sb unawares

imprudencia *nf* imprudence, rashness; *(indiscreción)* indiscretion

imprudente *adj* imprudent, unwise; *(indiscreto)* indiscreet

impudicia *nf (falta de pudor)* immodesty; *(desvergüenza)* shamelessness

impudor *nm* immodesty; *(desvergüenza)* shamelessness

impuesto,-a 1 *nm Fin* tax; **i. sobre la renta** income tax; **libre de impuestos** tax-free; **i. sobre el valor añadido** value-added tax
2 *adj* imposed

impugnar *vt (teoría)* to refute, to disprove; *(decisión)* to challenge, to contest

impulsar *vt* to impel, to drive

impulsivo,-a *adj* impulsive

impulso *nm* impulse, thrust; *Dep* **tomar i.** to take a run-up

impune *adj* unpunished

impunemente *adv* with impunity

impunidad *nf* impunity

impureza *nf* impurity

impuro,-a *adj* impure

impuse *pt indef de* **imponer**

imputar *vt* to impute, to attribute

inabarcable *adj* unfathomable

inabordable *adj* unapproachable, inaccessible

inacabable *adj* interminable, endless

inaccesible *adj* inaccessible

inaceptable *adj* unacceptable

inactividad *nf* inactivity; *Fin* lull, stagnation

inactivo,-a *adj* inactive

inadaptación *nf* maladjustment

inadaptado,-a 1 *adj* maladjusted
2 *nm,f* misfit

inadecuado,-a *adj* unsuitable, inappropriate

inadmisible *adj* inadmissible

inadvertido,-a *adj (desapercibido)* unnoticed, unseen; **pasar i.** to escape notice, to pass unnoticed

inagotable *adj* (**a**) *(recursos etc)* inexhaustible (**b**) *(persona)* tireless, indefatigable

inaguantable *adj* unbearable, intolerable

inalámbrico,-a 1 *adj* cordless
2 *nm* cordless telephone

inalcanzable *adj* unattainable, unachievable

inalterable *adj* (**a**) unalterable (**b**) (*persona*) impassive, imperturbable

inamovible *adj* immovable, fixed

inanición *nf* starvation; *Med* inanition

inanimado,-a *adj* inanimate

inapreciable *adj* (**a**) (*valioso*) invaluable, inestimable (**b**) (*insignificante*) insignificant, trivial

inasequible *adj* (**a**) (*producto*) unaffordable (**b**) (*meta*) unattainable, unachievable (**c**) (*persona*) unapproachable, inaccessible (**d**) (*cuestión*) incomprehensible

inaudito,-a *adj* (**a**) (*sin precedente*) unprecedented (**b**) *Fig* (*escandaloso*) outrageous

inauguración *nf* inauguration, opening

inaugural *adj* inaugural, opening; **ceremonia i.** inaugural ceremony

inaugurar *vt* to inaugurate, to open

inca *adj & nmf* Inca

incalculable *adj* incalculable, indeterminate

incandescente *adj* white-hot, incandescent

incansable *adj* tireless, indefatigable

incapacidad *nf* (**a**) incapacity, inability; **i. física** physical disability (**b**) (*incompetencia*) incompetence, inefficiency

incapacitado,-a *adj* (*imposibilitado*) incapacitated, disabled; (*desautorizado*) incapacitated

incapacitar *vt* (**a**) to incapacitate, to disable (**b**) (*inhabilitar*) to disqualify, to make unfit (**para** for)

incapaz *adj* (**a**) unable (**de** to), incapable (**de** of); **soy i. de continuar** I can't go on (**b**) *Jur* unfit

incario *nm* = period of the Inca empire

incautación *nf Jur* seizure, confiscation

incautarse *vpr Jur* **i. de** to seize, to confiscate

incauto,-a *adj* (**a**) (*imprudente*) incautious, unwary (**b**) (*crédulo*) gullible

incendiar [43] **1** *vt* to set fire to, to set alight

2 incendiarse *vpr* to catch fire

incendiario,-a 1 *adj* incendiary; *Fig* (*discurso etc*) inflammatory

2 *nm,f* (*persona*) arsonist, fire-raiser

incendio *nm* fire; **i. forestal** forest fire

incentivar *vt* to give an incentive to

incentivo *nm* incentive

incertidumbre *nf* uncertainty, doubt

incesante *adj* incessant, never-ending

incesto *nm* incest

incestuoso,-a *adj* incestuous

incidencia *nf* (**a**) (*repercusión*) impact, effect; **la huelga tuvo escasa i.** the strike had little effect (**b**) (*hecho*) incident (**c**) *Fís* incidence

incidente *nm* incident

incidir *vi* (**a**) (*incurrir*) to fall (**en** into) (**b**) **i. en** (*afectar*) to affect, to influence

incienso *nm* incense

incierto,-a *adj* (*inseguro*) uncertain

incineración *nf* (*de basuras*) incineration; (*de cadáveres*) cremation

incinerar *vt* (*basura*) to incinerate; (*cadáveres*) to cremate

incipiente *adj* incipient, budding

incisión *nf* incision, cut

incisivo,-a 1 *adj* (*mordaz*) incisive, cutting; (*cortante*) sharp

2 *nm Anat* incisor

inciso *nm* (*paréntesis*) digression; **a modo de i.** in passing, incidentally

incitación *nf* incitement

incitante *adj* (**a**) (*instigador*) inciting (**b**) (*provocativo*) provocative

incitar *vt* to incite, to urge

incivil *adj* uncivil, rude

inclemencia *nf* inclemency, harshness

inclemente *adj* inclement, harsh

inclinación *nf* (**a**) (*de terreno*) slope, incline; (*del cuerpo*) stoop (**b**) (*reverencia*) bow (**c**) *Fig* (*tendencia*) tendency, inclination, penchant

inclinado,-a *adj* inclined, slanting; *Fig* **me siento i. a creerle** I feel inclined to believe him

inclinar 1 *vt* (**a**) to incline, to bend; (*cabeza*) to nod (**b**) *Fig* (*persuadir*) to persuade, to induce

2 inclinarse *vpr* (**a**) to lean, to slope, to incline (**b**) (*al saludar*) to bow; **i. ante** to bow down to (**c**) *Fig* (*optar*) **a.** to be o feel inclined to; **me inclino por éste** I'd rather have this one, I prefer this one

incluido,-a *adj* (**a**) (*después del sustantivo*) included; (*antes del sustantivo*) including; **servicio no i.** service not included; **i. I.V.A.** including VAT; **todos pagan, incluidos los niños** everyone has to pay, including children (**b**) (*adjunto*) enclosed

incluir [37] *vt* (**a**) to include (**b**) (*contener*) to contain, to comprise (**c**) (*adjuntar*) to enclose

inclusión *nf* inclusion

inclusive *adv* (**a**) (*incluido*) inclusive; **de martes a viernes i.** from Tuesday to Friday inclusive; **hasta la lección ocho i.** up to and including lesson eight (**b**) (*incluso*) even

incluso *adv* even; **i. mi madre** even my mother

incoar *vt defect Jur* to initiate
incógnita *nf* (**a**) *Mat* unknown quantity, unknown (**b**) *(misterio)* mystery
incógnito *nm* **de i.** incognito
incoherencia *nf* incoherence
incoherente *adj* incoherent
incoloro,-a *adj* colourless
incólume *adj Fml* unharmed; **salir i.** to escape unharmed
incombustible *adj* incombustible, fireproof
incomodar **1** *vt* (**a**) *(causar molestia)* to inconvenience, to put out (**b**) *(fastidiar)* to bother, to annoy
  2 incomodarse *vpr* (**a**) *(tomarse molestias)* to put oneself out, to go out of one's way (**b**) *(disgustarse)* to get annoyed *o* angry
incomodidad *nf (falta de comodidad)* discomfort; *(molestia)* inconvenience
incómodo,-a *adj* uncomfortable; **sentirse i.** to feel uncomfortable *o* awkward
incompatibilidad *nf* incompatibility; *Jur* **i. de caracteres** mutual incompatibility
incompatible *adj* incompatible
incompetencia *nf* incompetence
incompetente *adj & nmf* incompetent
incompleto,-a *adj* incomplete; *(inacabado)* unfinished
incomprensible *adj* incomprehensible
incomprensión *nf* lack of understanding, failure to understand; *(indiferencia)* lack of sympathy
incomunicado,-a *adj* (**a**) *(aislado)* isolated; **el pueblo se quedó i.** the town was cut off (**b**) *(en la cárcel)* in solitary confinement
incomunicar [44] *vt* (**a**) *(ciudad)* to isolate, to cut off (**b**) *(recluso)* to place in solitary confinement
inconcebible *adj* inconceivable, unthinkable
inconcluso,-a *adj* unfinished
incondicional **1** *adj* unconditional; *(apoyo)* wholehearted; *(amigo)* faithful; *(partidario)* staunch
  2 *nm* die-hard
inconexo,-a *adj (incoherente)* incoherent, confused
inconformismo *nm* nonconformity
inconformista *adj & nmf* nonconformist
inconfundible *adj* unmistakable, obvious
incongruencia *nf* incongruity
incongruente *adj* incongruous
inconmensurable *adj* immeasurable, vast

inconsciencia *nf Med* unconsciousness; *Fig (irreflexión)* thoughtlessness; *(irresponsabilidad)* irresponsibility
inconsciente *adj* (**a**) *(con estar) (desmayado)* unconscious (**b**) *(con ser) (despreocupado)* unaware (**de** of); *Fig (irreflexivo)* thoughtless, irresponsible
inconsecuente *adj* inconsistent
inconsistente *adj* flimsy; *(argumento)* weak
inconstancia *nf* inconstancy, fickleness
inconstante *adj* inconstant, fickle
incontable *adj* countless, innumerable
incontenible *adj* uncontrollable, irrepressible
incontestable *adj* indisputable, unquestionable
incontinencia *nf* incontinence
incontrolable *adj* uncontrollable
incontrolado,-a **1** *adj* uncontrolled
  2 *nm,f* troublemaker
inconveniencia *nf* (**a**) inconvenience (**b**) *(impropiedad)* unsuitability
inconveniente **1** *adj* (**a**) inconvenient (**b**) *(inapropiado)* unsuitable
  2 *nm* (**a**) *(objeción)* objection; **poner inconvenientes** to raise objections (**b**) *(desventaja)* disadvantage, drawback; *(problema)* difficulty; **¿tienes i. en acompañarme?** would you mind coming with me?
incordiar [43] *vt Fam* to bother, to pester
incordio *nm Fam* nuisance, pain
incorporación *nf* incorporation
incorporar **1** *vt* (**a**) to incorporate (**en** into) (**b**) *(levantar)* to help to sit up
  2 incorporarse *vpr* (**a**) **i. a** *(sociedad)* to join; *(trabajo)* to start; *Mil* **i. a filas** to join up (**b**) *(en la cama)* to sit up
incorrección *nf* (**a**) *(falta)* incorrectness, inaccuracy; *(gramatical)* mistake (**b**) *(descortesía)* discourtesy, impropriety
incorrecto,-a *adj* (**a**) *(equivocado)* incorrect, inaccurate (**b**) *(grosero)* impolite, discourteous
incorregible *adj* incorrigible
incrédulo,-a **1** *adj* (**a**) incredulous, disbelieving (**b**) *Rel* unbelieving
  2 *nm,f* (**a**) disbeliever (**b**) *Rel* unbeliever
increíble *adj* incredible, unbelievable
incrementar **1** *vt* to increase
  2 incrementarse *vpr* to increase
incremento *nm (aumento)* increase; *(crecimiento)* growth; **i. de la temperatura** rise in temperature
increpar *vt Fml* to rebuke, to reprimand
incruento,-a *adj* bloodless
incrustar *vt* (**a**) *(insertar)* to encrust *o*

incrust (**b**) *(embutir)* to inlay; **incrustado con perlas** inlaid with pearls

incubadora *nf* incubator

incubar *vt* to incubate

incuestionable *adj* unquestionable, indisputable

inculcar [**44**] *vt (principios, ideas)* to instil (**en** into)

inculpado,-a *nm,f* **el i.** the accused

inculpar *vt* to accuse (**de** of), to blame (**de** for); *Jur* to charge (**de** with)

inculto,-a 1 *adj (ignorante)* uneducated, uncouth
2 *nm,f* ignoramus

incultura *nf (ignorancia)* ignorance, lack of culture

incumbencia *nf* **no es de mi i.** it doesn't come within my province, it isn't my concern

incumbir *vi* to be incumbent (**a** upon); **esto no te incumbe** this is none of your business

incumplimiento *nm (de un deber)* non-fulfilment; *(de una orden)* failure to execute; **i. de contrato** breach of contract

incumplir *vt* not to fulfil; *(deber)* to fail to fulfil; *(promesa, contrato)* to break; *(orden)* to fail to carry out

incurrir *vi (cometer)* to fall (**en** into); **i. en delito** to commit a crime; **i. en (un) error** to fall into error

incursión *nf* raid, incursion

incursionar *vi Am* (**a**) *(en ciudad, territorio)* to make an incursion (**b**) **i. en algo** *(tema, asunto)* to dabble in sth

indagar [**42**] *vt* to investigate, to inquire into

indebido,-a *adj* (**a**) *(desconsiderado)* improper, undue (**b**) *(ilegal)* unlawful, illegal

indecencia *nf* indecency, obscenity

indecente *adj* (**a**) *(impúdico)* indecent (**b**) *(impresentable)* dreadful

indecible *adj* unspeakable; *(inefable)* indescribable; **sufrir lo i.** to suffer agonies

indecisión *nf* indecision, hesitation

indeciso,-a *adj* (**a**) *(vacilante)* hesitant, irresolute (**b**) *(resultados etc)* inconclusive

indefenso,-a *adj* defenceless, helpless

indefinidamente *adv* indefinitely

indefinido,-a *adj* (**a**) *(indeterminado)* indefinite; *(impreciso)* undefined, vague (**b**) *Ling* indefinite

indeleble *adj* indelible

indemne *adj (persona)* unharmed, unhurt; *(cosa)* undamaged

indemnización *nf* (**a**) *(acto)* indemnification (**b**) *Fin (compensación)* indemnity,

compensation; **i. por despido** redundancy payment

indemnizar [**40**] *vt* to indemnify, to compensate (**por** for)

independencia *nf* independence

independiente *adj (libre)* independent; *(individualista)* self-reliant

independientemente *adv* (**a**) independently (**de** of) (**b**) *(aparte de)* regardless, irrespective (**de** of)

independizar [**40**] **1** *vt* to make independent, to grant independence to
2 independizarse *vpr* to become independent

indescifrable *adj* indecipherable

indescriptible *adj* indescribable

indeseable *adj & nmf* undesirable

indeterminación *nf* indecision, irresolution

indeterminado,-a *adj* (**a**) indefinite; *(impreciso)* vague (**b**) *(persona)* irresolute (**c**) *Ling* indefinite

India *nf* (**la**) **I.** India

Indias *nfpl* (**las**) **l.** the Indies; **las l. Orientales/Occidentales** the East/West Indies

indicación *nf* (**a**) *(señal)* indication, sign (**b**) *(instrucción)* instruction, direction; **por i. de algn** at sb's suggestion

indicado,-a *adj* right, suitable; **a la hora indicada** at the specified time; **en el momento menos i.** at the worst possible moment

indicador *nm* (**a**) indicator (**b**) *Téc* gauge, dial, meter; *Aut* **i. del nivel de aceite** (oil) dipstick; *Aut* **i. de velocidad** speedometer

indicar [**44**] *vt (señalar)* to indicate, to show, to point out; **¿me podría i. el camino?** could you show me the way?

indicativo,-a *adj* (**a**) indicative (**de** of) (**b**) *Ling (modo)* **i.** indicative (mood)

índice *nm* (**a**) *(de libro)* index, table of contents (**b**) *(relación)* rate; **í. de natalidad/mortalidad** birth/death rate; *Fin* **í. de precios** price index (**c**) *Anat (dedo)* **í.** index finger, forefinger

indicio *nm* (**a**) *(señal)* indication, sign, token (**de** of) (**b**) *Jur* **indicios** *(prueba)* evidence

índico,-a *adj* Indian; **Océano Í.** Indian Ocean

indiferencia *nf* indifference, apathy

indiferente *adj* (**a**) *(no importante)* unimportant; **me es i.** it makes no difference to me (**b**) *(apático)* indifferent

indígena 1 *adj* indigenous, native (**de** to)
2 *nmf* native (**de** of)

indigencia *nf Fml* poverty, indigence

indigente *adj Fml* needy, poverty-stricken

indigestarse *vpr* (**a**) **se le indigestó la comida** the meal gave her indigestion (**b**) *(sufrir indigestión)* to get indigestion

indigestión *nf* indigestion

indigesto,-a *adj (comida)* indigestible, difficult to digest; **me siento i.** I've got indigestion

indignación *nf* indignation

indignado,-a *adj* indignant (**por** at *o* about)

indignante *adj* outrageous, infuriating

indignar 1 *vt* to infuriate, to make angry
  2 indignarse *vpr* to be *o* feel indignant (**por** at *o* about)

indigno,-a *adj* (**a**) unworthy (**de** of) (**b**) *(despreciable)* wretched, dreadful

indio,-a *adj & nm,f* Indian; **en fila india** in single file; *Fam* **hacer el i.** to act the fool

indirecta *nf Fam (insinuación)* hint, insinuation; **tirar** *o* **lanzar una i.** to drop a hint; **coger la i.** to get the message

indirecto,-a *adj* indirect; *Ling* **estilo i.** indirect *o* reported speech

indisciplinado,-a *adj* undisciplined, unruly

indiscreción *nf* indiscretion; *(comentario)* tactless remark

indiscreto,-a *adj* indiscreet, tactless

indiscutible *adj* indisputable, unquestionable

indispensable *adj* indispensable, essential

indisponer [19] *(pp* **indispuesto) 1** *vt* to upset, to make unwell
  2 indisponerse *vpr* (**a**) to fall ill, to become unwell (**b**) *Fig* **i. con algn** to fall out with sb

indispuesto,-a *adj* indisposed, unwell

indispuse *pt indef de* **indisponer**

indistintamente *adv* **pueden escribir en inglés o en español, i.** you can write in English or Spanish, it doesn't matter which

indistinto,-a *adj (indiferente)* immaterial, inconsequential

individual 1 *adj* individual; **habitación i.** single room
  2 *nmpl Dep* **individuales** singles

individualismo *nm* individualism

individualista 1 *adj* individualistic
  2 *nmf* individualist

individuo *nm* (**a**) individual (**b**) *(tío)* bloke, guy

índole *nf* (**a**) *(carácter)* character, nature (**b**) *(clase, tipo)* kind, sort

indolencia *nf* indolence, laziness

indolente 1 *adj* indolent, lazy
  2 *nmf* idler

indomable *adj* (**a**) *(animal)* untamable (**b**) *(pueblo)* ungovernable, unruly; *(niño)* uncontrollable; *(pasión)* indomitable

indómito,-a *adj* (**a**) *(no domado)* untamed; *(indomable)* untamable (**b**) *(pueblo)* unruly; *(persona)* uncontrollable

Indonesia *n* Indonesia

inducir [10] *vt* (**a**) *(incitar, mover)* to lead, to induce; **i. a error** to lead into error, to mislead (**b**) *Elec (corriente)* to induce

inductivo,-a *adj* inductive

indudable *adj* indubitable, unquestionable; **es i. que** there is no doubt that

induje *pt indef de* **inducir**

indulgencia *nf* indulgence, leniency

indulgente *adj* indulgent (**con** towards), lenient (**con** with)

indultar *vt Jur* to pardon

indulto *nm Jur* pardon, amnesty

indumentaria *nf* clothing, clothes

industria *nf* industry

industrial 1 *adj* industrial
  2 *nmf* industrialist

industrialización *nf* industrialization

industrializar [40] *vt* to industrialize

induzco *indic pres de* **inducir**

INE *nm (abr* **Instituto Nacional de Estadística)** = organization that publishes official statistics about Spain

inédito,-a *adj* (**a**) *(libro, texto)* unpublished (**b**) *(nuevo)* completely new; *(desconocido)* unknown

inefable *adj* ineffable, indescribable

ineficacia *nf (ineptitud)* inefficiency; *(inutilidad)* ineffectiveness

ineficaz *adj (inepto)* inefficient; *(inefectivo)* ineffective

ineludible *adj* inescapable, unavoidable

INEM *nm (abr* **Instituto Nacional de Empleo)** = Spanish department of employment

ineptitud *nf* ineptitude, incompetence

inepto,-a 1 *adj* inept, incompetent
  2 *nm,f* incompetent person

inequívoco,-a *adj* unmistakable, unequivocal

inercia *nf* (**a**) *Fís* inertia (**b**) *Fig (pasividad)* inertia, passivity; **hacer algo por i.** to do sth out of habit

inerte *adj (inanimado)* inert; *(inmóvil)* motionless

inesperado,-a *adj (fortuito)* unexpected, unforeseen; *(imprevisto)* sudden

inestabilidad *nf* instability

inestable *adj* unstable, unsteady

inestimable *adj* inestimable, invaluable
inevitable *adj* inevitable, unavoidable
inexistente *adj* non-existent
inexorable *adj* inexorable
inexperiencia *nf* lack of experience
inexperto,-a *adj (inexperto)* inexpert; *(sin experiencia)* inexperienced
inexplicable *adj* inexplicable
inexpugnable *adj Mil* impregnable
infalible *adj* infallible
infamar *vt* to defame, to slander
infame *adj (vil)* infamous, vile; *(despreciable)* dreadful, awful
infamia *nf* disgrace, infamy
infancia *nf* childhood, infancy
infanta *nf* infanta, princess
infante *nm* (a) infante, prince (b) *Mil* infantryman
infantería *nf Mil* infantry; **la i. de marina** the marines
infantil *adj* (a) **literatura i.** *(para niños)* children's literature (b) *(aniñado)* childlike; *Pey* childish, infantile
infarto *nm Med* infarction, infarct; **i. (de miocardio)** heart attack, coronary thrombosis; *Fam* **de i.** thrilling, stunning
infatigable *adj* indefatigable, tireless
infección *nf* infection
infeccioso,-a *adj* infectious
infectar 1 *vt* to infect
  2 **infectarse** *vpr* to become infected (**de** with)
infeliz 1 *adj* unhappy; *(desdichado)* unfortunate
  2 *nmf Fam* simpleton; **es un pobre i.** he is a poor devil
inferior 1 *adj* (a) *(más bajo)* lower (b) *(calidad)* inferior; **de calidad i.** of inferior quality (c) *(cantidad)* lower, less; **i. a la media** below average
  2 *nmf (persona)* subordinate, inferior
inferioridad *nf* inferiority; **estar en i. de condiciones** to be at a disadvantage; **complejo de i.** inferiority complex
inferir [5] *vt Literario (deducir)* to infer, to deduce (**de** from)
infernal *adj* infernal, hellish; *Fig* **había un ruido i.** there was a hell of a noise
infestar *vt* (a) *infestado de (parásitos)* infested with; *(plantas)* overgrown with (b) *Fig (llenar)* to overrun, to invade; **infestado de turistas** swarming with tourists (c) *(infectar)* to infect
infición *nf Méx* pollution
infidelidad *nf* infidelity, unfaithfulness
infiel 1 *adj (desleal)* unfaithful
  2 *nmf Rel* infidel
infierno *nm* (a) *Rel* hell (b) *Fig (tormento)*

hell; **su vida es un i.** his life is sheer hell (c) *(horno)* inferno; **en verano esto es un i.** in summer it's like an inferno here; *Fam* **¡vete al i.!** go to hell!, get lost!
infiltración *nf (de agua)* infiltration; *(de noticia)* leak
infiltrado,-a *nm,f* infiltrator
infiltrar 1 *vt* to infiltrate; *(noticia)* to leak
  2 **infiltrarse** *vpr* to infiltrate (**en** into)
ínfimo,-a *adj Fml (mínimo)* extremely low; **detalle í.** smallest detail; **ínfima calidad** very poor quality
infinidad *nf* (a) infinity (b) *(sinfín)* great number; **en i. de ocasiones** on countless occasions
infinitivo,-a *adj & nm Ling* infinitive
infinito,-a 1 *adj* infinite, endless
  2 *nm* infinity
  3 *adv Fam (muchísimo)* infinitely, immensely
inflación *nf Econ* inflation
inflacionario,-a, inflacionista *adj Econ* inflationary
inflamable *adj* flammable
inflamación *nf Med* inflammation
inflamar 1 *vt* (a) *Med* to inflame (b) *(encender)* to set on fire, to ignite
  2 **inflamarse** *vpr* (a) *Med* to become inflamed (b) *(incendiarse)* to catch fire
inflar 1 *vt* (a) *(hinchar)* to inflate, to blow up; *Náut (vela)* to swell (b) *Fig (exagerar)* to exaggerate
  2 **inflarse** *vpr* (a) to inflate; *Náut (vela)* to swell (b) *Fam* **i. de** to overdo; **se inflaron de macarrones** they stuffed themselves with macaroni
inflexible *adj* inflexible
infligir [57] *vt* to inflict
influencia *nf* influence; **ejercer** *o* **tener i. sobre algn** to have an influence on *o* upon sb; **tener influencias** to be influential; **tráfico de influencias** Old-Boy network
influenciar [43] *vt* to influence
influir [37] 1 *vt* to influence
  2 *vi* (a) to have influence (b) **i. en** *o* **sobre** to influence, to have an influence on
influjo *nm* influence
influyente *adj* influential
información *nf* (a) information; **oficina de i.** information bureau (b) *(noticia)* a piece of news, news *sing* (c) *Tel Br* directory enquiries, *US* information (d) *(referencias)* references
informado,-a *adj* informed; **de fuentes bien informadas** from well-informed sources

informal *adj* (**a**) *(reunión, cena)* informal (**b**) *(comportamiento)* casual (**c**) *(persona)* unreliable, untrustworthy

informalidad *nf* *(incumplimiento)* unreliability; *(desenfado)* informality

informar 1 *vt* to inform (**de** of); *(dar informes)* to report
  2 informarse *vpr* *(procurarse noticias)* to find out (**de** about); *(enterarse)* to inquire (**de** about)

informática *nf* computing, information technology

informático,-a 1 *adj* computer, computing
  2 *nm,f* (computer) technician

informativo,-a 1 *adj* (**a**) *Rad & TV* news; **boletín i.** news (broadcast) (**b**) *(explicativo)* informative, explanatory
  2 *nm Rad & TV* news bulletin

informe *nm* (**a**) report (**b**) **informes** references; **pedir informes sobre algn** to make inquiries about sb

infracción *nf* *(de ley)* infringement, breach (**de** of)

infractor,-a *nm,f* offender

infraestructura *nf* infrastructure

in fraganti *loc adv* in the act; **coger** *o* **pillar a algn i.** to catch sb redhanded

infrahumano,-a *adj* subhuman

infranqueable *adj* impassable; *Fig* insurmountable

infrarrojo,-a *adj* infrared

infrautilizar *vt* to underutilize

infringir [57] *vt* to infringe, to contravene; **i. una ley** to break a law

infructuoso,-a *adj* fruitless, unsuccessful

infundado,-a *adj* unfounded, groundless

infundir *vt* to infuse; *Fig* to instil; **i. dudas** to give rise to doubt; **i. respeto** to command respect

infusión *nf* infusion

infuso,-a *adj Fam Irón* **ciencia infusa** sheer genius

ingeniar [43] 1 *vt* to invent, to devise
  2 ingeniarse *vpr* **ingeniárselas para hacer algo** to manage to do sth

ingeniería *nf* engineering

ingeniero,-a *nm,f* engineer; **i. agrónomo** agricultural engineer; **i. de caminos** civil engineer; **i. de minas/montes** mining/forestry engineer; **i. de telecomunicaciones** telecommunications engineer; **i. técnico** technician

ingenio *nm* (**a**) *(talento)* talent; *(inventiva)* inventiveness, creativeness; *(agudeza)* wit (**b**) *(aparato)* device

ingenioso,-a *adj* ingenious, clever; *(vivaz)* witty

ingente *adj* huge, enormous

ingenuidad *nf* ingenuousness, naïveté

ingenuo,-a 1 *adj* ingenuous, naïve
  2 *nm,f* naïve person

ingerir [5] *vt* *(comida)* to ingest, to consume; *(líquidos, alcohol)* to drink, to consume

Inglaterra *n* England

ingle *nf Anat* groin

inglés,-esa 1 *adj* English
  2 *nm,f* *(hombre)* Englishman; *(mujer)* Englishwoman; **los ingleses** the English
  3 *nm (idioma)* English

ingratitud *nf* ingratitude, ungratefulness

ingrato,-a 1 *adj* (**a**) *(persona)* ungrateful (**b**) *(noticia)* unpleasant (**c**) *(trabajo)* thankless, unrewarding (**d**) *(tierra)* unproductive
  2 *nm,f* ungrateful person

ingrediente *nm* ingredient

ingresar 1 *vt* (**a**) *Fin* to deposit, to pay in (**b**) *Med* to admit; **la ingresaron en el hospital** she was admitted to hospital
  2 *vi* (**a**) to enter; **i. en el ejército** to enlist in the army, to join the army; **i. en un club** to join a club (**b**) **i. cadáver** to be dead on arrival

ingreso *nm* (**a**) *Fin* deposit; **hacer un i. en una cuenta** to pay money into an account (**b**) *(entrada)* entry (**en** into); *(admisión)* admission (**en** to) (**c**) **ingresos** *(sueldo, renta)* income; *(beneficios)* revenue

inhábil *adj* (**a**) *(incapaz)* unfit; **i. para el trabajo** unfit for work (**b**) **día i.** non-working day

inhabilitación *nf* (**a**) *Fml (incapacidad)* disablement (**b**) *Jur* disqualification

inhabilitar *vt* (**a**) *Fml (incapacitar)* to disable; **inhabilitado para el trabajo** unfit for work (**b**) *Jur* to disqualify

inhabitable *adj* uninhabitable

> 🔎 Observa que la palabra inglesa **inhabitable** es un falso amigo y no es la traducción de la palabra española **inhabitable**. En inglés, **inhabitable** significa "habitable".

inhalación *nf* inhalation

inhalador *nm Med* inhaler

inhalar *vt* to inhale

inherente *adj* inherent (**a** in)

inhibición *nf* inhibition

inhibir 1 *vt* to inhibit
  2 inhibirse *vpr* (**a**) *(cohibirse)* to be *o* feel inhibited (**b**) *(abstenerse)* to refrain (**de** from)

inhóspito,-a *adj* inhospitable
inhumación *nf* burial
inhumano,-a *adj* inhumane; *(cruel)* inhuman
inhumar *vt* to bury
INI *nm Antes* (*abr* **Instituto Nacional de Industria**) = Spanish governmental organization that promotes industry
inicial *adj & nf* initial; **punto i.** starting point
iniciar [43] 1 *vt* (a) *(empezar)* to begin, to start; *(discusión)* to initiate; *(una cosa nueva)* to pioneer (b) *(introducir)* to initiate
2 iniciarse *vpr* (a) **i. en algo** *(aprender)* to start to study sth (b) *(empezar)* to begin, to start
iniciativa *nf* initiative; **i. privada** private enterprise; **por i. propia** on one's own initiative
inicio *nm* beginning, start; **a inicios de** at the beginning of
inimitable *adj* inimitable
ininterrumpido,-a *adj* uninterrupted, continuous
iniquidad *nf* iniquity
injerencia *nf* interference, meddling (**en** in)
injerirse *vpr* to interfere, to meddle (**en** in)
injertar *vt Agr & Med* to graft
injerto *nm* graft
injuria *nf* *(insulto)* insult, affront; *(agravio)* outrage
injuriar [43] *vt* *(insultar)* to insult; *(ultrajar)* to outrage
injusticia *nf* injustice, unfairness
injustificado,-a *adj* unjustified
injusto,-a *adj* unjust, unfair
inmaculado,-a *adj* immaculate
inmadurez *nf* immaturity
inmaduro,-a *adj* immature
inmediaciones *nfpl* neighbourhood
inmediatamente *adv* immediately, at once
inmediato,-a *adj* (a) *(en el tiempo)* immediate; **de i.** at once (b) *(en el espacio)* next (**a** to), adjoining
inmejorable *adj* *(trabajo)* excellent; *(precio)* unbeatable
inmemorial *adj* immemorial; **desde tiempos inmemoriales** since time immemorial
inmensidad *nf* immensity, enormity
inmenso,-a *adj* immense, vast
inmerecido,-a *adj* undeserved, unmerited
inmersión *nf* immersion; *(de submarino)* dive

inmerso,-a *adj* immersed (**en** in)
inmigración *nf* immigration
inmigrante *adj & nmf* immigrant
inmigrar *vi* to immigrate
inminente *adj* imminent, impending
inmiscuirse [37] *vpr* to interfere, to meddle (**en** in)
inmobiliaria *nf Br* estate agent's, *US* real estate company
inmobiliario,-a *adj* property, *US* real-estate; **agente i.** *Br* estate agent, *US* realtor
inmolar *vt Fml* to immolate, to sacrifice
inmoral *adj* immoral
inmoralidad *nf* immorality
inmortal *adj & nmf* immortal
inmortalidad *nf* immortality
inmortalizar [40] *vt* to immortalize
inmóvil *adj* motionless, immobile
inmovilista *adj* ultra-conservative
inmovilizar [40] *vt* (a) *(persona, cosa)* to immobilize (b) *Fin (capital)* to immobilize, to tie up
inmueble 1 *adj* **bienes inmuebles** real estate
2 *nm* building
inmundicia *nf* (a) *(suciedad)* dirt, filth; *Fig* dirtiness (b) *(basura)* rubbish, refuse
inmundo,-a *adj* dirty, filthy; *Fig* nasty
inmune *adj* immune (**a** to), exempt (**de** from)
inmunidad *nf* immunity (**contra** against); **i. diplomática/parlamentaria** diplomatic/parliamentary immunity
inmunizar [40] *vt* to immunize (**contra** against)
inmutarse *vpr* to change countenance; **ni se inmutó** he didn't turn a hair
innato,-a *adj* innate, inborn
innecesario,-a *adj* unnecessary
innegable *adj* undeniable
innovación *nf* innovation
innovar *vt & vi* to innovate
innumerable *adj* innumerable, countless
inocencia *nf* (a) innocence (b) *(ingenuidad)* naïveté
inocentada *nf Fam* ≃ April Fool's joke; **hacer una i. a algn** to play an April Fool's joke on sb
inocente 1 *adj* innocent
2 *nmf* innocent; **día de los Inocentes** Holy Innocents' Day, 28 December, ≃ April Fools' Day
inocuo,-a *adj* innocuous
inodoro,-a 1 *adj* odourless
2 *nm* toilet, lavatory
inofensivo,-a *adj* harmless

inolvidable *adj* unforgettable

inoperante *adj* ineffective

inopia *nf Fig* **estar en la i.** to be in the clouds, to be miles away

inopinado,-a *adj* unexpected

inoportuno,-a *adj* inappropriate; **llegó en un momento muy i.** he turned up at a very awkward moment

inorgánico,-a *adj* inorganic

inoxidable *adj* **acero i.** stainless steel

inquebrantable *adj Fig* unshakable; *(persona)* unyielding

inquietante *adj* worrying

inquietar 1 *vt* to worry

2 inquietarse *vpr* to worry (**por** about)

inquieto,-a *adj* (**a**) *(preocupado)* worried (**por** about) (**b**) *(intranquilo)* restless (**c**) *(emprendedor)* eager

inquietud *nf* (**a**) *(preocupación)* worry (**b**) *(agitación)* restlessness (**c**) *(anhelo)* eagerness

inquilino,-a *nm,f* tenant

inquirir [31] *vt* to investigate

inquisitivo,-a *adj* inquisitive

inri *nm Fam* insult; **para más o mayor i.** to make matters worse

insaciable *adj* insatiable

insalubre *adj* unhealthy

INSALUD *nm* (*abr* **Instituto Nacional de la Salud**) = Spanish national health service, *Br* ≃ NHS, *US* ≃ Medicaid

insano,-a *adj* (**a**) *(loco)* insane, mad (**b**) *(insalubre)* unhealthy

insatisfecho,-a *adj* dissatisfied

inscribir (*pp* **inscrito**) **1** *vt* (**a**) *(registrar)* to register; **i. a un niño en el registro civil** to register a child's birth (**b**) *(matricular)* to enrol (**c**) *(grabar)* to inscribe

2 inscribirse *vpr* (**a**) *(registrarse)* to register; *(hacerse miembro)* to join (**b**) *(matricularse)* to enrol

inscripción *nf* (**a**) *(matriculación)* enrolment, registration (**b**) *(escrito etc)* inscription

insecticida *nm* insecticide

insecto *nm* insect

inseguridad *nf* (**a**) *(falta de confianza)* insecurity (**b**) *(duda)* uncertainty (**c**) *(peligro)* lack of safety; **la i. ciudadana** the breakdown of law and order

inseguro,-a *adj* (**a**) *(poco confiado)* insecure (**b**) *(dubitativo)* uncertain (**c**) *(peligroso)* unsafe

inseminar *vt* to inseminate

insensatez *nf* foolishness

insensato,-a 1 *adj* foolish

2 *nm,f* fool

insensibilidad *nf* insensitivity

insensible *adj* (**a**) *(indiferente)* insensitive (**a** to), unfeeling (**b**) *(imperceptible)* imperceptible (**c**) *Med* numb

inseparable *adj* inseparable

insertar *vt* to insert

inservible *adj* useless

insidia *nf* (**a**) *(trampa)* malicious ploy (**b**) *(malicia)* maliciousness

insidioso,-a *adj* insidious

insigne *adj* distinguished

insignia *nf* (**a**) *(emblema)* badge (**b**) *(bandera)* flag

insignificancia *nf* (**a**) *(intrascendencia)* insignificance (**b**) *(nadería)* trifle

insignificante *adj* insignificant

insinuación *nf* insinuation

insinuante *adj* insinuating; *(atrevido)* forward

insinuar [30] 1 *vt* to insinuate

2 insinuarse *vpr* **i. a algn** to make advances to sb

insípido,-a *adj* insipid; *Fig* dull, flat

insistencia *nf* insistence; **con i.** insistently

insistente *adj* insistent

insistir *vi* to insist (**en** on); **insistió en ese punto** he stressed that point

insociable *adj* unsociable

insolación *nf Med* sunstroke; **coger una i.** to get sunstroke

insolencia *nf* insolence

insolente *adj* insolent

insolidaridad *nf* unsupportive stance

insólito,-a *adj* *(poco usual)* unusual; *(extraño)* strange, odd

insoluble *adj* insoluble

insolvencia *nf Fin* insolvency

insolvente *adj Fin* insolvent

insomnio *nm* insomnia; **noche de i.** sleepless night

insondable *adj* unfathomable

insonorizado,-a *adj* soundproof

insonorizar [40] *vt* to soundproof

insoportable *adj* unbearable

insospechado,-a *adj* unsuspected

insostenible *adj* untenable

inspección *nf* inspection

inspeccionar *vt* to inspect

inspector,-a *nm,f* inspector; **i. de Hacienda** tax inspector

inspiración *nf* (**a**) inspiration (**b**) *(inhalación)* inhalation

inspirado,-a *adj* inspired

inspirar 1 *vt* (**a**) to inspire (**b**) *(inhalar)* to inhale, to breathe in

2 inspirarse *vpr* **i. en** to be inspired by

instalación *nf* installation; **instalaciones deportivas** sports facilities

instalar 1 *vt* (**a**) to install (**b**) *(puesto, tienda)* to set up
 2 instalarse *vpr (persona)* to settle (down)
instancia *nf* (**a**) *(solicitud)* request; **a instancia(s) de** at the request of (**b**) *(escrito)* application form (**c**) *Jur* **tribunal de primera i.** court of first instance (**d**) **en primera i.** first of all; **en última i.** as a last resort

> 🖉 Observa que la palabra inglesa **instance** es un falso amigo y no es la traducción de la palabra española **instancia**. En inglés, **instance** significa "caso, ejemplo".

instantánea *nf* snapshot
instantáneamente *adv* instantly
instantáneo,-a *adj* instantaneous; **café i.** instant coffee
instante *nm* instant, moment; **a cada i.** constantly; **al i.** immediately, right away; **por instantes** with every second; **¡un i.!** just a moment!
instar *vt* to urge
instauración *nf* founding
instaurar *vt* to found
instigador,-a *nm,f* instigator
instigar [42] *vt* to instigate; **i. a la rebelión** to incite a rebellion
instintivo,-a *adj* instinctive
instinto *nm* instinct; **por i.** instinctively; **i. de conservación** survival instinct
institución *nf* institution
instituir [37] *vt* to institute
instituto *nm* (**a**) institute (**b**) *Educ Br* state secondary school, *US* high school
institutriz *nf* governess
instituyo *indic pres de* **instituir**
instrucción *nf* (**a**) *(educación)* education (**b**) *(usu pl)* *(indicación)* instruction; **instrucciones para el** *o* **de uso** directions for use (**c**) *Jur* preliminary investigation; **i. del sumario** proceedings; **juez de i.** examining magistrate (**d**) *Mil* drill
instructivo,-a *adj* instructive
instruido,-a *adj* educated, well-educated
instruir [37] *vt* (**a**) to instruct (**b**) *(enseñar)* to educate (**c**) *Mil* to drill (**d**) *Jur* to investigate
instrumental *adj* instrumental
instrumento *nm* instrument
insubordinación *nf* insubordination
insubordinado,-a *adj* insubordinate
insubordinarse *vpr (sublevarse)* to rebel (**contra** against)
insuficiencia *nf* insufficiency
insuficiente 1 *adj* insufficient

 2 *nm Educ (nota)* fail
insufrible *adj* insufferable
insular 1 *adj* insular, island
 2 *nmf* islander
insulso,-a *adj* insipid
insultante *adj* insulting
insultar *vt* to insult
insulto *nm* insult
insumisión *nf* = refusal to do military service
insumiso,-a 1 *adj* unsubmissive
 2 *nm* = person who refuses to do military service
insuperable *adj* (**a**) *(inmejorable)* unsurpassable (**b**) *(problema)* insurmountable
insurgente *adj & nmf* insurgent
insurrección *nf* insurrection
intachable *adj* irreproachable; **conducta i.** impeccable behaviour
intacto,-a *adj* intact
integral 1 *adj* integral; *Culin* **pan i.** wholemeal bread; **arroz i.** brown rice
 2 *nf Mat* integral
integrante 1 *adj* integral; **ser parte i. de** to be an integral part of
 2 *nmf* member
integrar 1 *vt (formar)* to compose, to make up; **el equipo lo integran once jugadores** there are eleven players in the team
 2 integrarse *vpr* to integrate (**en** with)
integridad *nf* integrity
íntegro,-a *adj* (**a**) *(entero)* whole, entire; *Cin & Lit* **versión íntegra** unabridged version (**b**) *(honrado)* upright
intelecto *nm* intellect
intelectual *adj & nmf* intellectual
inteligencia *nf (intelecto)* intelligence; **cociente de i.** intelligence quotient, IQ
inteligente *adj* intelligent
inteligible *adj* intelligible
intemperie *nf* bad weather; **a la i.** in the open (air)
intempestivo,-a *adj* untimely
intención *nf* intention; **con i.** deliberately, on purpose; **con segunda** *o* **doble i.** with an ulterior motive; **tener la i. de hacer algo** to intend to do sth
intencionadamente *adv* on purpose
intencionado,-a *adj* deliberate
intencional *adj* intentional
intendencia *nf* (**a**) *RP (corporación municipal)* town council, *US* city council (**b**) *RP (edificio)* town hall, *US* city hall (**c**) *Chile (gobernación)* administrative region
intendente *nm* (**a**) *RP (alcalde)* mayor (**b**) *Chile (gobernador)* governor

intensidad *nf* intensity; *(del viento)* force

intensificar [44] *vt*, **intensificarse** *vpr* to intensify; *(amistad)* to strengthen

intensivo,-a *adj* intensive; *Agr* **cultivo i.** intensive farming; *Educ* **curso i.** crash course

intenso,-a *adj* intense

intentar *vt* to try, to attempt; *Fam* **¡inténtalo!** give it a go!

intento *nm* attempt; **i. de suicidio** attempted suicide

intentona *nf* putsch

inter- *pref* inter-

intercalar *vt* to insert

intercambiar [43] *vt* to exchange

intercambio *nm* exchange; **i. comercial** trade

interceder *vi* to intercede

interceptar *vt* (**a**) *(detener)* to intercept (**b**) *(carretera)* to block; *(tráfico)* to hold up

intercesión *nf* intercession

intercontinental *adj* intercontinental

interdicto *nm* prohibition

interés *nm* (**a**) interest; **poner i. en** to take an interest in; **tener i. en** *o* **por** to be interested in (**b**) *(provecho personal)* self-interest; **hacer algo (sólo) por i.** to do sth out of self-interest; **intereses creados** vested interests (**c**) *Fin* interest; **con un i. del 11 por ciento** at an interest of 11 percent; **tipos de i.** interest rates

interesado,-a **1** *adj* (**a**) interested (**en** in); **las partes interesadas** the interested parties (**b**) *(egoísta)* selfish

  2 *nm,f* interested person; **los interesados** those interested *o* concerned

interesante *adj* interesting

interesar **1** *vt* (**a**) *(tener interés)* to interest; **la poesía no me interesa nada** poetry doesn't interest me at all (**b**) *(concernir)* to concern

  2 *vi* *(ser importante)* to be of interest, to be important; **interesaría llegar pronto** it is important to get there early

  3 interesarse *vpr* **i. por** *o* **en** to be interested in; **se interesó por ti** he asked about *o* after you

interferencia *nf* interference; *Rad & TV* jamming

interferir [5] *vt* (**a**) to interfere with; *(plan)* to upset (**b**) *Rad & TV* to jam

interfono *nm Tel* intercom

interinidad *nf* (**a**) *(temporalidad)* temporariness (**b**) *(empleo)* temporary employment

interino,-a **1** *adj (persona)* acting

  2 *nm,f (trabajador temporal)* temporary worker

interior **1** *adj* (**a**) inner, inside, interior; **habitación i.** inner room; **ropa i.** underwear (**b**) *Pol* domestic, internal (**c**) *Geog* inland

  2 *nm* (**a**) inside, interior; *Fig* **en su i. no estaba de acuerdo** deep down she disagreed (**b**) *Geog* interior; *Pol* **Ministerio del I.** *Br* ≃ Home Office, *US* ≃ Department of the Interior

interiorizar [40] *vt* to internalize

interjección *nf Ling* interjection

interlocutor,-a *nm,f* speaker; *(negociador)* negotiator

intermediario *nm Com* middleman

intermedio,-a **1** *adj* intermediate

  2 *nm TV (intervalo)* break

interminable *adj* endless

intermitente **1** *adj* intermittent

  2 *nm Aut Br* indicator, *US* turn signal

internacional *adj* international

internado,-a **1** *nm,f* inmate

  2 *nm (colegio)* boarding-school

internar **1** *vt (en hospital)* to confine

  2 internarse *vpr* (**a**) *(penetrar)* to advance (**en** into) (**b**) *Dep* to break through

internauta *nmf Informát* Net user

Internet *nf Informát* Internet; **está en I.** it's on the Internet

interno,-a **1** *adj* (**a**) internal; **por vía interna** internally (**b**) *Pol* domestic

  2 *nm,f (alumno)* boarder; *Med (enfermo)* patient; *(preso)* inmate

  3 *nm RP (extensión)* (telephone) extension; **i. 28, por favor** extension 28, please

interponer [19] *(pp* **interpuesto)** **1** *vt* to insert; *Jur* **i. un recurso** to give notice of appeal

  2 interponerse *vpr* to intervene

interpretación *nf* (**a**) interpretation (**b**) *Mús & Teatro* performance

interpretar *vt* (**a**) to interpret (**b**) *Teatro (papel)* to play; *(obra)* to perform; *Mús (concierto)* to play, to perform; *(canción)* to sing

intérprete *nmf* (**a**) *(traductor)* interpreter (**b**) *Teatro* performer; *Mús (cantante)* singer; *(músico)* performer

interpuse *pt indef de* interponer

interrogación *nf* interrogation; *Ling* **(signo de) i.** question *o* interrogation mark

interrogante *nf Fig* question mark

interrogar [42] *vt* to question; *(testigo etc)* to interrogate

interrogatorio *nm* interrogation

interrumpir *vt* to interrupt; *(tráfico)* to block

interrupción *nf* interruption; **i. del embarazo** termination of pregnancy

interruptor *nm Elec* switch

intersección *nf* intersection

interurbano,-a *adj* intercity; *Tel* **conferencia interurbana** long-distance call

intervalo *nm* interval; **habrá intervalos de lluvia** there will be periods of rain

intervención *nf* (**a**) *(participación)* intervention, participation (**en** in); *(aportación)* contribution (**en** to) (**b**) *Med* intervention

intervenir [27] **1** *vi (mediar)* to intervene (**en** in); *(participar)* to take part (**en** in); *(contribuir)* to contribute (**en** to)

2 *vt* (**a**) *(confiscar)* to confiscate, to seize (**b**) *Tel (teléfono)* to tap (**c**) *Med* to operate on

interventor,-a *nm,f (supervisor)* inspector; *Fin* **i. (de cuentas)** auditor

interviú *nf* (*pl* **interviús**) interview

intestino,-a 1 *adj (luchas)* internal

2 *nm Anat* intestine

intimar *vi* to become close (**con** to)

intimidad *nf (amistad)* intimacy; *(vida privada)* private life; *(privacidad)* privacy; **en la i.** privately, in private

intimidar *vt* to intimidate

íntimo,-a 1 *adj* (**a**) intimate (**b**) *(vida)* private; **una boda íntima** a quiet wedding (**c**) *(amistad)* close

2 *nm,f* close friend, intimate

intolerable *adj* intolerable

intolerancia *nf* intolerance

intolerante 1 *adj* intolerant

2 *nmf* intolerant person

intoxicación *nf* poisoning; **i. alimentaria** food poisoning

> 🖉 Observa que la palabra inglesa **intoxication** es un falso amigo y no es la traducción de la palabra española **intoxicación**. En inglés, **intoxication** significa "embriaguez".

intoxicar [44] *vt* to poison

> 🖉 Observa que el verbo inglés **to intoxicate** es un falso amigo y no es la traducción del verbo español **intoxicar**. En inglés, **to intoxicate** significa "embriagar, emborrachar".

intra- *pref* intra-

intranet *nf Informát* intranet

intranquilidad *nf* worry

intranquilizarse *upr* to get worried

intranquilo,-a *adj (preocupado)* worried; *(agitado)* restless

intransigente *adj* intransigent

intransitable *adj* impassable

intransitivo,-a *adj Ling* intransitive

intratable *adj* (**a**) *(problema)* intractable

(**b**) *(persona)* unsociable

intrépido,-a *adj* intrepid

intriga *nf* intrigue; *Cin & Teatro* plot

intrigante 1 *adj* (**a**) *(interesante)* intriguing, interesting (**b**) *(maquinador)* scheming

2 *nmf (persona)* schemer

intrigar [42] **1** *vt (interesar)* to intrigue, to interest

2 *vi (maquinar)* to plot

intrincado,-a *adj* (**a**) *(cuestión, problema)* intricate (**b**) *(bosque)* dense

intrínseco,-a *adj* intrinsic

introducción *nf* introduction

introducir [10] *vt* (**a**) to introduce (**b**) *(meter)* to insert, to put in

intromisión *nf (injerencia)* meddling; **perdón por la i.** forgive the intrusion

introspectivo,-a *adj* introspective

introvertido,-a 1 *adj* introverted

2 *nm,f* introvert

intruso,-a 1 *adj* intrusive

2 *nm,f* intruder; *Jur* trespasser

intuición *nf* intuition

intuir [37] *vt* to know by intuition

intuitivo,-a *adj* intuitive

inundación *nf* flood

inundar *vt* to flood; *Fig (de trabajo etc)* to swamp

inusitado,-a *adj* unusual

inútil 1 *adj* (**a**) useless; *(esfuerzo, intento)* vain, pointless (**b**) *Mil* unfit (for service)

2 *nmf Fam* good-for-nothing

inutilidad *nf* uselessness

inutilizar [40] *vt* to make *o* render useless; *(máquina etc)* to put out of action

invadir *vt* to invade; *Fig* **los estudiantes invadieron la calle** students poured out onto the street

invalidar *vt* to invalidate

invalidez *nf* (**a**) *Jur (nulidad)* invalidity (**b**) *Med (minusvalía)* disability

inválido,-a 1 *adj* (**a**) *Jur (nulo)* invalid (**b**) *Med (minusválido)* disabled, handicapped

2 *nm,f Med* disabled *o* handicapped person

invariable *adj* invariable

invasión *nf* invasion

invasor,-a 1 *adj* invading

2 *nm,f* invader

invencible *adj* (**a**) *(enemigo)* invincible (**b**) *(obstáculo)* insurmountable

invención *nf (invento)* invention; *(mentira)* fabrication

inventar *vt* to invent; *(excusa, mentira)* to make up, to concoct

inventario *nm* inventory

inventiva nf inventiveness; *(imaginación)* imagination

invento nm invention

inventor,-a nm,f inventor

invernadero nm greenhouse; **efecto i.** greenhouse effect

invernal adj winter, wintry

invernar [1] vi to hibernate

inverosímil adj unlikely, improbable

inversión nf (a) inversion (b) *Fin* investment

inverso,-a adj opposite; **en sentido i.** in the opposite direction; **en orden i.** in reverse order

inversor,-a nm,f *Fin* investor

invertebrado,-a adj & nm *Zool* invertebrate

invertido,-a 1 adj inverted, reversed
2 nm,f homosexual

invertir [5] vt (a) *(orden)* to invert, to reverse (b) *(dinero)* to invest (**en** in); *(tiempo)* to spend (**en** on)

investidura nf investiture; *Pol* vote of confidence

investigación nf (a) *(policial etc)* investigation (b) *(científica)* research

investigador,-a nm,f (a) *(detective)* investigator (b) *(científico)* researcher, research worker

investigar [42] vt to research; *(indagar)* to investigate

investir [6] vt to invest

invidente 1 adj unsighted
2 nmf unsighted person

invierno nm winter

invisible adj invisible

invitación nf invitation

invitado,-a 1 adj invited; **artista i.** guest artist
2 nm,f guest

invitar vt to invite; **hoy invito yo** it's on me today; **me invitó a una copa** he treated me to a drink

invocar [44] vt to invoke

involucrar 1 vt to involve (**en** in)
2 involucrarse vpr to get involved (**en** in)

involuntario,-a adj involuntary; *(impremeditado)* unintentional

invulnerable adj invulnerable

inyección nf injection; **poner una i.** to give an injection

inyectar vt to inject (**en** into); **i. algo a algn** to inject sb with sth

IPC nm *(abr* **Índice de Precios al Consumo)** RPI

ir [16] **1** vi (a) to go; **¡vamos!** let's go!; **voy a Lima** I'm going to Lima; **¡ya voy!** (I'm) coming!

(b) *(río, camino)* to lead; **esta carretera va a la frontera** this road leads to the border

(c) *(funcionar)* to work (properly); **el ascensor no va** the lift is out of order

(d) *(desenvolverse)* **¿cómo le va el nuevo trabajo?** how is he getting on in his new job?; **¿cómo te va?** how are things?, how are you doing?

(e) *(sentar bien)* to suit; **el verde te va mucho** green really suits you

(f) *(combinar)* to match; **el rojo no va con el verde** red doesn't go with green

(g) *(vestir)* to wear; **ir con falda** to wear a skirt; **ir de blanco/de uniforme** to be dressed in white/in uniform

(h) *Fam (importar, concernir)* to concern; **eso va por ti también** and the same goes for you; **ni me va ni me viene** I don't care one way or the other

(i) *Fam (comportarse)* to act; **ir de guapo por la vida** to be a flash Harry

(j) **va para abogado** he's studying to be a lawyer

(k) *(ir + por)* **ir por la derecha** to keep (to the) right; *(ir a buscar)* **ve (a) por agua** go and fetch some water; *(haber llegado)* **voy por la página 90** I've got as far as page 90

(l) *(locuciones)* **a eso iba** I was coming to that; **¡ahí va!** catch!; **en lo que va de año** so far this year; **ir a parar** to end up; **¡qué va!** of course not!, nothing of the sort!; **va a lo suyo** he looks after his own interests; **¡vamos a ver!** let's see!; **¡vaya!** fancy that!; **¡vaya moto!** what a bike!

2 v aux (a) *(ir + gerundio)* **ir andando** to go on foot; **va mejorando** she's improving

(b) *(ir + pp)* **ya van rotos tres** three (of them) have already been broken

(c) *(ir a + inf)* **iba a decir que** I was going to say that; **va a llover** it's going to rain; **vas a caerte** you'll fall

3 irse vpr (a) *(marcharse)* to go away, to leave; **me voy** I'm off; **¡vámonos!** let's go!; **¡vete!** go away!; **vete a casa** go home

(b) *(líquido, gas) (escaparse)* to leak

(c) *(direcciones)* **¿por dónde se va a ...?** which is the way to ...? **por aquí se va al río** this is the way to the river

ira nf wrath, rage, anger

iracundo,-a adj (a) *(irascible)* irascible (b) *(enfadado)* irate, angry

Irak n Iraq

Irán n Iran

iraní adj & nmf *(pl* **iraníes**) Iranian

Iraq n = **Irak**

iraquí adj & nmf *(pl* **iraquíes**) Iraqi

irascible *adj* irascible, irritable

iris *nm inv Anat* iris; **arco i.** rainbow

Irlanda *n* Ireland; **I. del Norte** Northern Ireland

irlandés,-esa 1 *adj* Irish
2 *nm,f (hombre)* Irishman; *(mujer)* Irishwoman; **los irlandeses** the Irish
3 *nm (idioma)* Irish

ironía *nf* irony

irónico,-a *adj* ironic

IRPF *nm Econ (abr* **impuesto sobre la renta de las personas físicas**) income tax

irracional *adj* irrational

irradiar [43] *vt* (**a**) *(emitir)* to radiate (**b**) *Am Fig (expulsar)* to expel

irreal *adj* unreal

irrealizable *adj* unattainable, unfeasible; *Fig* unreachable

irreconocible *adj* unrecognizable

irregular *adj* irregular

irregularidad *nf* irregularity

irremediable *adj* irremediable, incurable

irremplazable *adj* irreplaceable

irreparable *adj* irreparable

irreprochable *adj* irreproachable, blameless

irresistible *adj* (**a**) *(impulso, persona)* irresistible (**b**) *(insoportable)* unbearable

irresoluto,-a *adj* irresolute

irresponsable *adj* irresponsible

irrestricto,-a *adj Am* unconditional, complete

irreverente *adj* irreverent

irrigación *nf* irrigation

irrigar [42] *vt* to irrigate, to water

irrisorio,-a *adj* derisory, ridiculous

irritación *nf* irritation

irritante *adj* irritating

irritar 1 *vt* (**a**) *(enfadar)* to irritate, to exasperate (**b**) *Med* to irritate

2 irritarse *vpr* (**a**) *(enfadarse)* to lose one's temper, to get angry (**b**) *Med* to become irritated

irrompible *adj* unbreakable

irrumpir *vi* to burst (**en** into)

isla *nf* island, isle

islam *nm Rel* Islam

islámico,-a *adj* Islamic

islandés,-esa 1 *adj* Icelandic
2 *nm,f (persona)* Icelander
3 *nm (idioma)* Icelandic

Islandia *n* Iceland

isleño,-a 1 *adj* island
2 *nm,f* islander

islote *nm* small island

ismo *nm Fam* ism

Israel *n* Israel

israelí *adj & nmf (pl* israelíes) Israeli

istmo *nm Geog* isthmus

itacate *nm Méx* packed lunch

Italia *n* Italy

italiano,-a 1 *adj* Italian
2 *nm,f (persona)* Italian
3 *nm (idioma)* Italian

itinerante *adj* itinerant, itinerating

itinerario *nm* itinerary, route

IVA *nm Econ (abr* **impuesto sobre el valor añadido**)VAT

izar [40] *vt* to hoist, to raise

izqda., izqda *(abr* izquierda) left

izqdo., izqdo *(abr* izquierdo) left

izquierda *nf* (**a**) left; **a la i.** on the left; **girar a la i.** to turn left (**b**) *(mano)* left hand (**c**) *Pol* **la i.** the left; **de izquierdas** left-wing

izquierdista *Pol* **1** *adj* leftist, left-wing
2 *nmf* leftist, left-winger

izquierdo,-a *adj* (**a**) left; **brazo i.** left arm (**b**) *(zurdo)* left-handed

izquierdoso,-a *adj Fam* leftish

J

J, j ['xota] *nf (la letra)* J, j
jabalí *nm (pl jabalíes)* wild boar
jabalina *nf Dep* javelin
jabón *nm* soap; **j. de afeitar/tocador** shaving/toilet soap
jabonera *nf* soap dish
jaca *nf* gelding
jacal *nm Méx* hut
jacinto *nm Bot* hyacinth
jactancia *nf* boastfulness
jactancioso,-a 1 *adj* boastful
   2 *nm,f* braggart
jactarse *upr* to boast, to brag (**de** about)
jadeante *adj* panting, breathless
jadear *vi* to pant, to gasp
jadeo *nm* panting, gasping
jaez *nm Pey (ralea)* kind, sort
jaiba *nf Andes, CAm, Carib, Méx (cangrejo)* crayfish
jalar 1 *vt* (**a**) *Fam (comer)* to wolf down (**b**) *Andes, CAm, Carib, Méx (tirar)* to pull
   2 jalarse *upr Fam (comerse)* to wolf down, to scoff
jalbegar [42] *vt* to whitewash
jalea *nf* jelly; **j. real** royal jelly
jalear *vt (animar)* to cheer (on)
jaleo *nm (alboroto)* din, racket; *(riña)* row; *(confusión)* muddle; **armar j.** to make a racket
jalón¹ *nm (estaca)* stake; *Fig (hito)* milestone
jalón² *nm* (**a**) *(tirón)* pull, tug (**b**) *Am Aut* lift
jamaicano,-a *adj & nm,f* Jamaican
jamar *vt Fam* to scoff, to eat
jamás *adv* (**a**) never; **j. he estado allí** I have never been there (**b**) ever; **el mejor libro que j. se ha escrito** the best book ever written (**c**) **nunca j.** never again; **por siempre j.** for ever (and ever)
jamba *nf Arquit* jamb
jamón *nm* ham; **j. de York/serrano** boiled/cured ham
jamona *adj Fam* buxom
Japón *n* **(el) J.** Japan
japonés,-esa 1 *adj* Japanese
   2 *nm,f (persona)* Japanese; **los japoneses** the Japanese
   3 *nm (idioma)* Japanese

japuta *nf (pez)* Ray's bream
jaque *nm (en ajedrez)* check; **dar j. a** to check; **j. mate** checkmate; **j. al rey** check; *Fig* **estar en j.** to be stymied
jaqueca *nf* migraine
jara *nf Bot* rock rose
jarabe *nm* syrup; **j. para la tos** cough mixture
jarana *nf Fam* (**a**) *(juerga)* wild party, spree; **ir de j.** to go on a spree *o* a binge (**b**) *(jaleo)* racket, din
jaranero,-a 1 *adj* fun-loving, party-loving
   2 *nm,f* pleasure seeker, party-lover
jardín *nm* garden; **j. botánico** botanical garden; **j. de infancia** nursery school, kindergarten
jardinería *nf* gardening
jardinero *nm* gardener
jarra *nf* pitcher; **j. de cerveza** beer mug; *Fig* **de** *o* **en jarras** (with) arms akimbo, hands on hips
jarro *nm (recipiente)* jug; *(contenido)* jugful; *Fig* **echar un j. de agua fría a** to pour cold water on
jarrón *nm* vase; *(en arqueología)* urn
jaspe *nm* jasper; **como el j.** spotless, like a new pin
Jauja *nf Fig* promised land; **¡esto es J.!** this is the life!
jaula *nf (para animales)* cage
jauría *nf* pack of hounds
jazmín *nm Bot* jasmine
J.C. *(abr Jesucristo)* J.C.
jeba = **jeva**
jebo,-a = **jevo,-a**
jeep [jip] *nm Aut* jeep
jefa *nf* female boss, manageress
jefatura *nf* (**a**) *(cargo, dirección)* leadership (**b**) *(sede)* central office; **j. de policía** police headquarters
jefe *nm* (**a**) head, chief, boss; *Com* manager; **j. de estación** stationmaster; **j. de redacción** editor-in-chief; **j. de ventas** sales manager (**b**) *Pol* leader; **J. de Estado** Head of State (**c**) *Mil* officer in command; **comandante en j.** commander-in-chief
Jehová *nm* Jehovah; **testigos de J.** Jehovah's Witnesses

jején *nm Am* gnat

jengibre *nm Bot* ginger

jeque *nm* sheik, sheikh

jerarquía *nf* (**a**) hierarchy (**b**) *(categoría)* rank

jerárquico,-a *adj* hierarchical

jeremías *nmf inv* whiner, whinger

jerez *nm* sherry

jerga *nf* *(argot)* *(técnica)* jargon; *(vulgar)* slang; **la j. legal** legal jargon

jerigonza *nf* (**a**) *(extravagancia)* oddness (**b**) *(galimatías)* gibberish

jeringa *nf Med* syringe; *Aut* **j. de engrase** grease gun

jeringar [42] *vt Fam* (**a**) *(molestar)* to pester, to annoy (**b**) *(romper)* to break

jeringuilla *nf* (hypodermic) syringe

jeroglífico,-a 1 *adj* hieroglyphic

   2 *nm* (**a**) *Ling* hieroglyph, hieroglyphic (**b**) *(juego)* rebus

jersey *nm* (*pl* **jerseis**) sweater, *Br* jumper

Jerusalén *n* Jerusalem

Jesucristo *nm* Jesus Christ

jesuita *adj & nmf* Jesuit

Jesús 1 *nm* Jesus

   2 *interj* (**a**) *(expresa sorpresa)* good heavens! (**b**) *(al estornudar)* bless you!

jet *nf* jet set

jeta *nf Fam* (**a**) *(descaro)* cheek; **tener j.** to be cheeky, to have a nerve (**b**) *(cara)* mug, face (**c**) *(hocico)* snout

jet-set *nf* jet set

jeva *nf Carib Fam (mujer)* chick, *Br* bird

jevo,-a *nm,f Ven Fam (novio)* guy, boy-friend; *(novia)* girl, girlfriend

jíbaro,-a *nm,f Am* peasant

jícama *nf* yam bean, jicama

jícara *nf CAm, Méx, Ven (bol)* small cup; *(calabaza)* gourd

jilguero *nm Orn* goldfinch

jilipollas *nmf inv muy Fam* = **gilipollas**

jinete *nm* rider, horseman

jinetera *nf Cuba Fam* prostitute

jiñar *vi muy Fam* to shit

jirafa *nf* (**a**) giraffe (**b**) *(de micrófono)* boom

jirón *nm* (**a**) *(trozo desgarrado)* shred, strip; *(pedazo suelto)* bit, scrap; **hecho jirones** in shreds *o* tatters (**b**) *Perú (calle)* street

jitomate *nm Méx* tomato

JJOO *nmpl (abr* **Juegos Olímpicos**) Olympic Games

jocoso,-a *adj* funny, humorous

joda *nf RP muy Fam* (**a**) *(fastidio)* pain, drag (**b**) *(broma)* joke; **decir/hacer algo en j.** to say/do sth as a joke (**c**) *(juerga)* wild party

joder *Vulg* **1** *interj* shit!, *Br* bloody hell!

   2 *vt* (**a**) *(fastidiar)* to piss off; **¡no me jodas!** come on, don't give me that! (**b**) *(copular)* to fuck (**c**) *(echar a perder)* to screw up; **¡la jodiste!** you screwed it up! (**d**) *(romper)* to bugger

   3 joderse *vpr* (**a**) *(aguantarse)* to put up with it; **¡hay que j.!** you'll just have to grin and bear it! (**b**) *(echarse a perder)* to get screwed up; **¡se jodió el invento!** that's really screwed things up!; **¡que se joda!** to hell with him! (**c**) *(romperse)* to go bust

jodido,-a *adj Vulg* (**a**) *(maldito)* damned, *Br* bloody (**b**) *(molesto)* annoying (**c**) *(enfermo)* in a bad way; *(cansado)* knackered, exhausted (**d**) *(estropeado, roto)* bust, kaput, buggered (**e**) *(difícil)* shitty

jodienda *nf Vulg* (**a**) *(coito)* fuck (**b**) *(molestia)* pain in the arse

jofaina *nf* washbasin

jogging ['joɡin] *nm Urug (ropa)* track *o* jogging suit

jolgorio *nm Fam (juerga)* binge; *(algaza-ra)* fun

jolín, jolines *interj Fam (sorpresa)* gosh!, good grief!; *(enfado)* blast!, damn!

Jordania *n* Jordan

jornada *nf* (**a**) **j. (laboral)** *(día de trabajo)* working day; **j. intensiva** continuous working day; **j. partida** working day with a lunch break; **trabajo de media j./j. completa** part-time/full-time work (**b**) **jornadas** conference

jornal *nm (paga)* day's wage; **trabajar a j.** to be paid by the day

---

> 🖉 Observa que la palabra inglesa **journal** es un falso amigo y no es la traducción de la palabra española **jornal**. En inglés, **journal** significa "revista, diario".

---

jornalero,-a *nm,f* day labourer

joroba 1 *nf (jiba)* hump

   2 *interj* drat!

jorobado,-a 1 *adj* hunchbacked

   2 *nm,f* hunchback

jorobar *Fam* **1** *vt* (**a**) *(fastidiar)* to annoy, to bother; **me joroba** it really gets up my nose; **¡no jorobes!** *(incredulidad)* pull the other one! (**b**) *(estropear)* to ruin, to wreck

   2 jorobarse *vpr* (**a**) *(fastidiarse)* to grin and bear it (**b**) *(estropearse)* to break

jorongo *nm Méx* (**a**) *(manta)* blanket (**b**) *(poncho)* poncho

jota¹ *nf* (**a**) = name of the letter J in Spanish (**b**) *(cantidad mínima)* jot, scrap; **ni j.** not an iota; **no entiendo ni j.** I don't understand a thing

jota² *nf Mús* = Spanish dance and music

joven 1 *adj* young; **de aspecto j.** young-looking
   2 *nmf (hombre)* youth, young man; *(mujer)* girl, young woman; **de j.** as a young man/woman; **los jóvenes** young people, youth

jovial *adj* jovial, good-humoured

joya *nf* (a) jewel, piece of jewellery; **joyas de imitación** imitation jewellery (b) *Fig* **ser una j.** *(persona)* to be a real treasure *o* gem

joyería *nf (tienda)* jewellery shop, jeweller's (shop)

joyero,-a 1 *nm,f* jeweller
   2 *nm* jewel case *o* box

juanete *nm (en el pie)* bunion

jubilación *nf* (a) *(acción)* retirement; **j. anticipada** early retirement (b) *(pensión)* pension

jubilado,-a 1 *adj* retired
   2 *nm,f* retired person, pensioner; **los jubilados** retired people

jubilar 1 *vt (retirar)* to retire, to pension off; *Fam Fig* to get rid of, to ditch
   2 jubilarse *vpr (retirarse)* to retire, to go into retirement

júbilo *nm* jubilation, joy

jubón *nm* doublet, jerkin

judería *nf (barrio)* Jewish quarter

judía *nf* bean; **j. verde** French bean, green bean

judicial *adj* judicial; **vía j.** legal channels

judío,-a 1 *adj* Jewish
   2 *nm,f* Jew

judo *nm Dep* judo

juego *nm* (a) game; **j. de azar** game of chance; **j. de cartas** card game; *Fig* **j. de manos** sleight of hand; *Fig* **j. de palabras** play on words, pun; **j. de rol** fantasy role-playing game; *Fig* **j. limpio/sucio** fair/foul play (b) *Dep* game; **Juegos Olímpicos** Olympic Games; **terreno de j.** *Ten* court; *Ftb* field; **fuera de j.** offside (c) *(apuestas)* gambling; *Fig* **poner algo en j.** to put sth at stake (d) *(conjunto de piezas)* set; **j. de café/té** coffee/tea service; *Fig* **ir a j. con** to match

juerga *nf Fam* binge, rave-up; **ir de j.** to go on a binge

juerguista 1 *adj* fun-loving
   2 *nmf* fun-loving person, raver

jueves *nm inv* Thursday; **J. Santo** Maundy Thursday

juez *nmf* judge; **j. de instrucción** examining magistrate; **j. de paz** justice of the peace; *Dep* **j. de salida** starter; **j. de línea** linesman

jugada *nf* (a) move; *(en billar)* shot (b) *Fam* dirty trick

jugador,-a *nm,f* player; *(apostador)* gambler

jugar [32] 1 *vi* (a) to play; **j. a(l) fútbol/tenis** to play football/tennis; *Fig* **j. sucio** to play dirty (b) **j. con** *(no tomar en serio)* to toy with
   2 *vt* (a) to play (b) *(apostar)* to bet, to stake
   3 jugarse *vpr* (a) *(arriesgar)* to risk; *Fam* **j. el pellejo** to risk one's neck (b) *(apostar)* to bet, to stake

jugarreta *nf Fam* dirty trick

jugo *nm* juice; *Fig* **sacar el j.** a *(aprovechar)* to make the most of; *(explotar)* to squeeze dry

jugoso,-a *adj* (a) juicy; **un filete j.** a juicy steak (b) *Fig (sustancioso)* substantial, meaty; **un tema j.** a meaty topic

juguete *nm* toy; **pistola de j.** toy gun; *Fig* **ser el j. de algn** to be sb's plaything

juguetear *vi* to play

juguetón,-ona *adj* playful

juicio *nm* (a) *(facultad mental)* judgement, discernment; *(opinión)* opinion, judgement; **a j. de** in the opinion of; **a mi j.** in my opinion (b) *(sensatez)* reason, common sense; **en su sano j.** in one's right mind; **perder el j.** to go mad *o* insane (c) *Jur* trial, lawsuit; **llevar a algn a j.** to take legal action against sb, to sue sb

juicioso,-a *adj* judicious, wise

julepe *nm PRico, RP Fam (susto)* scare, fright; **dar un j. a algn** to give sb a scare

julio *nm* July

junco *nm Bot* rush

jungla *nf* jungle

junio *nm* June

júnior *adj Dep* junior; **campeonato j. de golf** junior golf championship

junta *nf* (a) *(reunión)* meeting, assembly; *Pol* **j. de gobierno** cabinet meeting (b) *(dirección)* board, committee; **j. directiva** board of directors (c) *Mil* junta; **j. militar** military junta (d) *(parlamento regional)* regional parliament (e) *Téc* joint

juntar 1 *vt* (a) *(unir)* to join, to put together; *(piezas)* to assemble (b) *(reunir) (sellos)* to collect; *(dinero)* to raise
   2 juntarse *vpr* (a) *(unirse)* to join; *(ríos, caminos)* to meet; *(personas)* to gather (b) *(amancebarse)* to live together

junto,-a 1 *adj* together; **dos mesas juntas** two tables side by side; **todos juntos** all together
   2 *adv* **j. con** together with; **j. a** next to

juntura *nf* (**a**) *Téc* joint, seam (**b**) *Anat* joint

jura *nf* (*acción*) oath; (*ceremonia*) swearing in; **j. de bandera** oath of allegiance to the flag

jurado *nm* (**a**) (*tribunal*) jury; (*en un concurso*) panel of judges, jury (**b**) (*miembro del tribunal*) juror, member of the jury

juramento *nm* (**a**) *Jur* oath; **bajo j.** under oath (**b**) (*blasfemia*) swearword, curse

jurar 1 *vi Jur & Rel* to swear, to take an oath

2 *vt* to swear; **j. el cargo** to take the oath of office; **j. por Dios** to swear to God

3 **jurarse** *vpr Fam* **jurársela(s) a algn** to have it in for sb

jurel *nm* (*pez*) scad, horse mackerel

jurídico,-a *adj* legal

jurisdicción *nf* jurisdiction

jurisdiccional *adj* jurisdictional; **aguas jurisdiccionales** territorial waters

jurista *nmf* jurist, lawyer

justamente *adv* **¡j.!** precisely!; **j. detrás de** right behind

justicia *nf* justice; **tomarse la j. por su mano** to take the law into one's own hands

justicialismo *nm Pol* = Argentinian nationalistic political movement founded by Juan Domingo Perón

justicialista *adj Pol* = belonging or related to "justicialismo"

justiciero,-a *adj* severe

justificable *adj* justifiable

justificación *nf* justification

justificado,-a *adj* justified, well-grounded

justificante *nm* written proof; **j. de pago** proof of payment

justificar [**44**] *vt* to justify

2 **justificarse** *vpr* to clear oneself, to justify oneself

justo,-a 1 *adj* (**a**) just, fair, right; **un trato j.** a fair deal (**b**) (*apretado*) (*ropa*) tight; **estamos justos de tiempo** we're pressed for time (**c**) (*exacto*) right, accurate; **la palabra justa** the right word (**d**) (*preciso*) **llegamos en el momento j. en que salían** we arrived just as they were leaving (**e**) **lo j.** just enough

2 *nm,f* just o righteous person; **los justos** the just, the righteous

3 *adv* (*exactamente*) exactly, precisely; **j. al lado** right beside

juvenil 1 *adj* (*aspecto*) youthful, young; **ropa j.** young people's clothes; **delincuencia j.** juvenile delinquency

2 *nmf* **los juveniles** the juveniles

juventud *nf* (**a**) (*edad*) youth (**b**) (*jóvenes*) young people

juzgado *nm* court, tribunal; **j. de guardia** police court

juzgar [**42**] *vt* to judge; **a j. por ...** judging by...

K

K, k [ka] *nf (la letra)* K, k
ka *nf* = name of the letter K in Spanish
kárate *nm Dep* karate
karateka *nmf Dep* person who does karate
Kenia *n* Kenya
kermés [ker'mes] (*pl* **kermeses**), **kermesse** [ker'mes] (*pl* **kermesses**) *nf* fair, kermesse
Kg, kg (*abr* **kilogramo(s)**) kg
kilo *nm* (**a**) *(medida)* kilo; *Fam* **pesa un k.** it weighs a ton (**b**) *Fam (millón)* a million pesetas
kilogramo *nm* kilogram, kilogramme
kilolitro *nm* kilolitre

kilometraje *nm* ≃ mileage
kilométrico,-a *adj* kilometric, kilometrical; **billete k.** multiple-journey ticket
kilómetro *nm* kilometre
kilovatio *nm* kilowatt; **k. hora** kilowatt-hour
kínder *nm Andes, Méx* kindergarten, nursery school
kiosco *nm* = **quiosco**
kiwi *nm* (**a**) *Orn* kiwi (**b**) *(fruto)* kiwi (fruit), Chinese gooseberry
Kleenex® *nm* Kleenex®, tissue
Km, km (*abr* **kilómetro(s)**) km
Kw, kw (*abr* **kilovatio(s)**) kW

L, l ['ele] *nf (la letra)* L, l

l (*abr* **litro(s)**) l

la¹ 1 *art def f* the; **la mesa** the table

2 *pron dem* the one; **la del vestido azul** the one in the blue dress; **la que vino ayer** the one who came yesterday; *ver* **el**

la² *pron pers f (persona)* her; *(usted)* you; *(cosa)* it; **la invitaré** I'll invite her along; **no la dejes abierta** don't leave it open; **ya la avisaremos, señora** we'll let you know, madam; *ver* **le**

la³ *nm Mús* la, A

laberinto *nm* labyrinth

labia *nf Fam* loquacity; *Pey* glibness; **tener mucha l.** to have the gift of the gab

labio *nm* lip

labor *nf* (a) job, task; **l. de equipo** teamwork; **(de profesión) sus labores** housewife (b) *Agr* farmwork (c) *(de costura)* needlework, sewing

laborable *adj* (a) **día l.** *(no festivo)* working day (b) *Agr* arable

laboral *adj* industrial; **accidente l.** industrial accident; **conflictividad l.** industrial unrest; **jornada l.** working day; **Universidad L.** technical training college

laboratorio *nm* laboratory

laborioso,-a *adj* (a) *(persona)* hardworking (b) *(tarea)* laborious

laborista *Pol* **1** *adj* Labour; **partido l.** Labour Party

2 *nmf* Labour (Party) member/supporter

labrado,-a *adj Arte* carved

labrador,-a *nm,f (granjero)* farmer; *(trabajador)* farm worker

labranza *nf* farming

labrar 1 *vt* (a) *Agr* to till (b) *(madera)* to carve; *(piedra)* to cut; *(metal)* to work

2 labrarse *vpr Fig* **l. un porvenir** to build a future for oneself

laburar *vi RP Fam* to work

laburo *nm RP Fam* job

laca *nf* (a) hair lacquer, hairspray; **l. de uñas** nail polish *o* varnish (b) *Arte* lacquer

lacio,-a *adj* (a) *(pelo)* lank, limp (b) **qué l.!** *(soso)* what a weed!

lacónico,-a *adj* laconic; *(conciso)* terse

lacra *nf* evil, curse; **una l. social** a scourge of society

lacrar *vt* to seal with wax

lacre *nm* sealing wax

lacrimógeno,-a *adj* (a) **gas l.** tear gas (b) *Fig* **una película lacrimógena** a tearjerker

lactar *vi* to breast-feed

lácteo,-a *adj* **productos lácteos** milk *o* dairy products; *Astron* **Vía Láctea** Milky Way

ladear 1 *vt (inclinar)* to tilt; *(cabeza)* to lean

2 ladearse *vpr* (a) *(inclinarse)* to lean, to tilt (b) *(desviarse)* to go off to one side

ladera *nf* slope

ladino,-a 1 *adj (astuto)* cunning, crafty

2 *nm,f CAm, Méx, Ven (no blanco)* = Spanish-speaking person of mixed race

lado *nm* (a) side; **a un l.** aside; **al l.** close by, nearby; **al l. de** next to, beside; **ponte de l.** stand sideways (b) *(en direcciones)* direction; **por todos lados** on/from all sides (c) *Fig* **dar de l. a algn** to coldshoulder sb; **por otro l.** *(además)* moreover; **por un l. ..., por otro l. ...** on the one hand ..., on the other hand ...

ladrar *vi* to bark

ladrillo *nm* (a) *Constr* brick (b) *Fam (pesado)* bore, drag

ladrón,-ona 1 *nm,f* thief, robber; **¡al l.!** stop thief!

2 *nm Elec* multiple socket

lagartija *nf* small lizard

lagarto *nm* lizard

lago *nm* lake

lágrima *nf* (a) tear; **llorar a l. viva** to cry one's eyes out (b) *(en lámpara)* teardrop

lagrimoso,-a *adj* tearful

laguna *nf* (a) small lake (b) *Fig (hueco)* gap

La Haya *n* The Hague

laico,-a 1 *adj* lay

2 *nm,f* lay person; *(hombre)* layman; *(mujer)* laywoman

lameculos *nmf inv muy Fam* bootlicker, arselicker

lamentable *adj* regrettable; *(infame)* lamentable

lamentar 1 *vt* to regret; **lo lamento** I'm sorry
　2 lamentarse *vpr* to complain
lamento *nm* moan, wail
lamer *vt* to lick
lámina *nf* (a) sheet, plate; **l. de acero** steel sheet (b) *Impr* plate
laminado,-a 1 *adj* (a) laminated (b) *(metales)* rolled; **acero l.** rolled steel
　2 *nm* lamination
laminar *vt* *(metal)* to roll
lámpara *nf* (a) lamp; **l. de pie** standard lamp (b) *Elec (bombilla)* bulb (c) *Rad* valve
lamparón *nm Fam* oil *o* grease stain
lana *nf* (a) *(de oveja)* wool; **pura l. virgen** pure new wool (b) *Andes, Méx Fam (dinero)* dough, cash
lanar *adj* **ganado l.** sheep
lance *nm Literario (episodio)* event, incident

> ℓ Observa que la palabra inglesa **lance** es un falso amigo y no es la traducción de la palabra española **lance**. En inglés, **lance** significa "lanza".

lanceta *nf Andes, Méx* sting
lancha *nf* motorboat, launch; **l. motora** speedboat; **l. neumática** rubber dinghy; **l. salvavidas** lifeboat
langosta *nf* (a) lobster (b) *(insecto)* locust
langostino *nm* king prawn
languidecer [33] *vi* to languish
lánguido,-a *adj* languid; *(sin vigor)* listless
lanudo,-a *adj* woolly, fleecy; *(peludo)* furry
lanza *nf* spear, lance; **punta de l.** spearhead; *Fig* **romper una l. en favor de algn/de algo** to defend sb/sth
lanzadera *nf* shuttle; **l. espacial** space shuttle
lanzado,-a *adj Fam* reckless; **ir l.** to tear along
lanzagranadas *nm inv Mil* grenade launcher
lanzamiento *nm* (a) throwing, hurling (b) *Dep (de disco, jabalina)* throw; *(de peso)* put (c) *Mil (de cohete etc)* launching (d) *Com* launch; **precio de l.** launch price (e) *Náut* launch
lanzar [40] 1 *vt* (a) *(arrojar)* to throw, to fling (b) *Fig (grito)* to let out (c) *Náut, Com & Mil* to launch
　2 lanzarse *vpr* (a) *(arrojarse)* to throw *o* hurl oneself; **l. al suelo** to throw oneself to the ground (b) *(emprender)* **l. a** to embark

on; **l. a los negocios** to go into business (c) *Fam (irse, largarse)* to scram
lapa *nf* (a) *Zool* limpet (b) **es una verdadera l.** he/she sticks to you like glue
lapicera *nf CSur* ballpoint (pen), *Br* Biro®; **l. fuente** fountain pen
lapicero *nm* (a) *(lápiz)* pencil (b) *CAm, Perú (bolígrafo)* ballpoint (pen), *Br* Biro®
lápida *nf* headstone
lapidario,-a *adj* lapidary
lápiz *nm* pencil; **l. labial** *o* **de labios** lipstick; **l. de ojos** eyeliner
lapso *nm* (a) *(periodo de tiempo)* period (b) *(error)* lapse, slip
lapsus *nm* slip; **l. linguae** slip of the tongue
largar [42] 1 *vt* (a) *Fam (golpe, discurso, dinero)* to give (b) *Náut* **l. amarras** to cast off
　2 largarse *vpr Fam* to clear off, to split; **¡lárgate!** beat it!
largas *nfpl* **dar l. a algo** to put sth off
largavistas *nm inv Bol, CSur* binoculars
largo,-a 1 *adj* (a) *(espacio)* long; *(tiempo)* long, lengthy; **pasamos un mes l. allí** we spent a good month there; **a lo l. de** *(espacio)* along; *(tiempo)* through; **a la larga** in the long run (b) *(excesivo)* too long; **se hizo l. el día** the day dragged on (c) **largos años** many years
　2 *nm* (a) *(longitud)* length; **¿cuánto tiene de l.?** how long is it? (b) *Mús* largo
　3 *adv* **l. y tendido** at length; *Fam* **¡l. (de aquí)!** clear off!; **esto va para l.** this is going to last a long time

> ℓ Observa que la palabra inglesa **large** es un falso amigo y no es la traducción de la palabra española **largo**. En inglés, **large** significa "grande".

largometraje *nm* feature film, full-length film
laringe *nf* larynx
laringitis *nf* laryngitis
las¹ 1 *art def fpl* the; **l. sillas** the chairs; **lávate l. manos** wash your hands; *(no se traduce)* **me gustan l. flores** I like flowers
　2 *pron* **l. que** *(personas)* the ones who, those who; *(objetos)* the ones that, those that; **toma l. que quieras** take whichever ones you want; *ver* **la** *y* **los**
las² *pron pers fpl (ellas)* them; *(ustedes)* you; **l. llamaré mañana (a ustedes)** I'll call you tomorrow; **no l. rompas** don't break them; **Pepa es de l. mías** Pepa thinks the way I do; *ver* **los**
lasaña *nf* lasagna, lasagne
lascivo,-a *adj* lewd, lecherous

láser *nm inv* laser; **impresora l.** laser printer

lástima *nf* pity; **¡qué l.!** what a pity!, what a shame!; **es una l. que ...** it's a pity (that) ...; **estar hecho una l.** to be a sorry sight; **tener l. a algn** to feel sorry for sb

lastimar *vt* to hurt, to injure

lastre *nm* (a) *(peso)* ballast (b) *Fig* dead weight

lata¹ *nf* (a) *(envase)* tin, can; **en l.** tinned, canned (b) *(hojalata)* tin(plate); **hecho de l.** made of tin

lata² *nf Fam* nuisance, drag; **dar la l.** to be a nuisance *o* a pest

latente *adj* latent

lateral 1 *adj* side, lateral; **salió por la puerta l.** he went out by the side door; **escalón l.** *(en letrero)* ramp

  2 *nm* side passage; *Aut* **(carril) l.** side lane

latido *nm (del corazón)* beat

latifundio *nm* large landed estate

latigazo *nm* (a) lash (b) *Fam (trago)* drink, swig

látigo *nm* whip

latín *nm* Latin

latino,-a 1 *adj* Latin; **América Latina** Latin America

  2 *nm,f* Latin American

Latinoamérica *nf* Latin America

latinomericano,-a *adj & nm,f* Latin American

latir *vi* to beat

latitud *nf* (a) *Geog* latitude (b) **latitudes** region, area

latón *nm* brass

latoso,-a *adj Fam* annoying

laucha *nf Am* mouse

laúd *nm* lute

laurel *nm Bot* laurel, (sweet) bay; *Culin* bay leaf; *Fig* **dormirse en los laureles** to rest on one's laurels

lava *nf* lava

lavable *adj* washable

lavabo *nm* (a) *(pila)* washbasin (b) *(cuarto de aseo)* washroom (c) *(retrete)* lavatory, toilet

lavadero *nm (de coches)* carwash

lavado *nm* wash, washing; *Fig* **l. de cerebro** brainwashing; **l. en seco** dry-cleaning

lavadora *nf* washing machine

lavanda *nf* lavender

lavandería *nf* (a) *(automática) Br* launderette, *US* Laundromat® (b) *(atendida por personal)* laundry

lavaplatos *nm inv* dishwasher

lavar *vt* to wash; **l. en seco** to dry-clean

lavativa *nf* enema

lavatorio *nm Andes, RP (lavabo) Br* washbasin, *US* washbowl

lavavajillas *nm inv* dishwasher

laxante *adj & nm* laxative

laxar *vt (vientre)* to loosen

laxitud *nf* laxity, laxness

lazada *nf (nudo)* bow

lazarillo *nm* **perro l.** guide dog, *US* seeing-eye dog

lazo *nm* (a) *(adorno)* bow (b) *(nudo)* knot; **l. corredizo** slipknot (c) *(para reses)* lasso (d) *Fig (usu pl) (vínculo)* tie, bond

le 1 *pron pers mf (objeto indirecto) (a él)* (to) him; *(a ella)* (to) her; *(a cosa)* (to) it; *(a usted)* (to) you; **le compraré uno** I'll buy one for her; **¿qué le pasa (a usted)?** what's the matter with you?

  2 *pron pers m (objeto directo) (él)* him; *(usted)* you; **no le oigo** I can't hear him; **no quiero molestarle** I don't wish to disturb you

leal 1 *adj* loyal, faithful

  2 *nmf* loyalist

lealtad *nf* loyalty, faithfulness

lebrel *nm* greyhound

lección *nf* lesson; *Fig* **dar una l. a algn** to teach sb a lesson; *Fig* **te servirá de l.** let that be a lesson to you

leche *nf* (a) milk; *Anat* **dientes de l.** milk teeth; **l. descremada** *o* **desnatada** skim *o* skimmed milk (b) *Fam* **mala l.** badness (c) **¡l.!** damn! (d) *muy Fam (golpe)* knock; **dar** *o* **pegar una l. a algn** to clobber sb (e) *Vulg* semen

lechera *nf* (a) *(vasija)* churn (b) *muy Fam* police car

lechería *nf* dairy, creamery

lechero,-a 1 *adj* milk, dairy; **central lechera** dairy co-operative; **vaca lechera** milk cow

  2 *nm* milkman

lecho *nm Lit* bed; **l. del río** river-bed; **l. mortuorio** death-bed

lechón *nm* sucking-pig

lechosa *nf Carib* papaya

lechoso,-a *adj* milky

lechuga *nf* lettuce

lechuza *nf* owl

lectivo,-a *adj* school; **horas lectivas** teaching hours

lector,-a 1 *nm,f* (a) *(persona)* reader (b) *Univ* lector, (language) assistant

  2 *nm* **l. de microfichas** *(aparato)* microfiche reader

lectura *nf* reading

leer [36] *vt* to read; **léenos el menú** read

out the menu for us; *Fig* **l. entre líneas** to read between the lines

legado *nm (herencia)* legacy

legajo *nm* bundle (of papers)

legal *adj* (a) *Jur* legal, lawful; **requisitos legales** legal formalities (b) *Fam (persona)* honest, trustworthy

legalidad *nf* legality, lawfulness

legalizar [40] *vt* to legalize; *(documento)* to authenticate

legaña *nf* sleep

legar [42] *vt (propiedad etc)* to bequeath; *Fig (tradiciones etc)* to hand down, to pass on

legendario,-a *adj* legendary

legión *nf* legion

legionella *nf* Legionnaire's Disease

legislación *nf* legislation

legislar *vi* to legislate

legislativo,-a *adj* legislative; **el poder l.** parliament

legislatura *nf* legislature

legitimar *vt* to legitimize; *(legalizar)* to legalize

legitimidad *nf Jur* legitimacy; *(licitud)* justice

legítimo,-a *adj* (a) *Jur* legitimate; **en legítima defensa** in self-defence (b) *(auténtico)* authentic, real; **oro l.** pure gold

lego,-a 1 *adj Rel* lay
    2 *nm* (a) layman; **ser l. en la materia** to be a layman in the subject (b) *Rel* lay brother

legua *nf (medida)* league; *Fig* **se nota a la l.** it stands out a mile

legumbres *nfpl* pulses

lejanía *nf* distance

lejano,-a *adj* distant, far-off; **parientes lejanos** distant relatives; **el L. Oriente** the Far East

lejía *nf* bleach

lejos *adv* far (away); **a lo l.** in the distance; **de l.** from a distance; *Fig* **ir demasiado l.** to go too far; *Fig* **llegar l.** to go a long way; *Fig* **sin ir más l.** to take an obvious example

lelo,-a *Fam* **1** *adj* stupid, silly
    2 *nm,f* ninny

lema *nm* (a) *(divisa)* motto, slogan (b) *(contraseña)* code name

lencería *nf* (a) *(prendas)* lingerie (b) *(ropa blanca)* linen (goods)

lendakari *nm* = head of the Basque government

lengua *nf* (a) tongue; *Fig* **malas lenguas** gossips; *Fam Fig* **irse de la l.** to spill the beans; *Fam Fig* **tirarle a algn de la l.** to draw sb out (b) *Ling* language; **l. materna**

native o mother tongue

lenguado *nm (pez)* sole

lenguaje *nm* language; *Informát* language; **l. corporal** body language

lengüeta *nf* (a) *(de zapato)* tongue (b) *Mús* reed

lente 1 *nf* lens; **l. de contacto** contact lens
    2 *nm Am* **lentes** *(gafas)* glasses, spectacles; **l. de contacto** contact lens

lenteja *nf* lentil

lentejuela *nf* sequin, spangle

lentilla *nf* contact lens

lentitud *nf* slowness; **con l.** slowly

lento,-a *adj* slow; **a fuego l.** on a low heat

leña *nf* (a) firewood; *Fig* **echar l. al fuego** to add fuel to the fire (b) *Fam (golpes)* knocks

leñazo *nm Fam (golpe)* blow, smash

leñe *interj Fam* damn it!

leño *nm* (a) log (b) *Fam (persona)* blockhead, halfwit

león *nm* lion

leona *nf* lioness

leonera *nf* lion's den; *Fig (habitación)* den

leopardo *nm* leopard

leotardos *nmpl* thick tights

lépero,-a *adj Fam* (a) *CAm, Méx (vulgar)* coarse, vulgar (b) *Cuba (ladino)* smart, crafty

lepra *nf* leprosy

leproso,-a 1 *adj* leprous
    2 *nm,f* leper

les 1 *pron pers mfpl (objeto indirecto) (a ellos,-as)* them; *(a ustedes)* you; **dales el dinero** give them the money; **l. he comprado un regalo** I've bought you a present
    2 *pron pers mpl (objeto directo) (ellos)* them; *(ustedes)* you; **l. esperaré** I shall wait for you; **no quiero molestarles** I don't wish to disturb you

lesbiana *nf* lesbian

leseras *nfpl Chile Fam (tonterías)* nonsense, *Br* rubbish

lesión *nf* (a) *(corporal)* injury (b) *Jur (perjuicio)* damage

lesionar *vt* to injure

leso,-a *adj Jur* **crimen de lesa humanidad** crime against humanity

letal *adj* lethal, deadly

letanía *nf* litany

letargo *nm* lethargy

letón,-ona 1 *adj* Latvian
    2 *nm,f* Latvian
    3 *nm (idioma)* Latvian, Lettish

Letonia *n* Latvia

letra *nf* (a) letter; **l. de imprenta** block capitals; **l. mayúscula** capital letter; **l.**

minúscula small letter; **l. pequeña** small print (**b**) *(escritura)* (hand)writing (**c**) *Mús (texto)* lyrics, words (**d**) *Fin* **l. (de cambio)** bill of exchange, draft (**e**) *Univ* **letras** arts

letrado,-a *nm,f* lawyer

letrero *nm (aviso)* notice, sign; *(cartel)* poster; **l. luminoso** neon sign

leucemia *nf* leukaemia

levadizo,-a *adj* **puente l.** drawbridge

levadura *nf* yeast; **l. en polvo** baking powder

levantamiento *nm* (**a**) raising, lifting; *Dep* **l. de pesos** weightlifting (**b**) *(insurrección)* uprising, insurrection

levantar 1 *vt* (**a**) to raise, to lift; *(mano, voz)* to raise; *(edificio)* to erect; *Fig (ánimos)* to raise; **l. los ojos** to look up (**b**) *(castigo)* to suspend

2 levantarse *vpr* (**a**) *(ponerse de pie)* to stand up, to rise (**b**) *(salir de la cama)* to get up (**c**) *(concluir)* to finish; **se levanta la sesión** the meeting is closed (**d**) *Pol* to rise, to revolt; **l. en armas** to rise up in arms (**e**) *(viento)* to come up; *(tormenta)* to gather

levante *nm* (**a**) **(el) L.** Levante, = the regions of Valencia and Murcia (**b**) *(viento)* east wind, Levanter

levar *vt* **l. ancla** to weigh anchor

leve *adj (ligero)* light; *Fig (de poca importancia)* slight

levedad *nf (ligereza)* lightness; *Fig* slightness; *Fig (de ánimo)* levity; **heridas de l.** minor injuries

levemente *adv* slightly

levitar *vi* to levitate

léxico,-a *Ling* **1** *nm (diccionario)* lexicon; *(vocabulario)* vocabulary, word list

2 *adj* lexical

ley *nf* (**a**) law; *Parl* bill, act; **aprobar una l.** to pass a bill (**b**) **oro de l.** pure gold; **plata de l.** sterling silver

leyenda *nf* (**a**) *(relato)* legend (**b**) *(en un mapa)* legend; *(en una moneda)* inscription; *(bajo ilustración)* caption

liar [29] **1** *vt* (**a**) *(envolver)* to wrap up; *(un cigarrillo)* to roll (**b**) *(enredar)* to muddle up; *(confundir)* to confuse

2 liarse *vpr* (**a**) *(embarullarse)* to get muddled up (**b**) *Fam (salir con)* to get involved; *(besarse)* to neck (**c**) **l. a bofetadas** to come to blows

libanés,-esa *adj & nm,f* Lebanese

Líbano *n* **el L.** the Lebanon

libelo *nm (difamación)* lampoon, satire

libélula *nf* dragonfly

liberación *nf (de país)* liberation; *(de rehén)* release, freeing

liberal 1 *adj* (**a**) liberal; *(carácter)* open-minded; *Pol* **Partido L.** Liberal Party; **profesión l.** profession (**b**) *(generoso)* generous, liberal

2 *nmf* liberal

liberalizar [40] *vt* to liberalize

liberar *vt (país)* to liberate; *(prisionero)* to free, to release

líbero *nm* *Ftb* sweeper

libertad *nf* freedom, liberty; **en l.** free; *Jur* **(en) l. bajo palabra/fianza** (on) parole/bail; *Jur* **(en) l. condicional** (on) parole; **l. de comercio** free trade; **l. de expresión** freedom of speech

libertador,-a *nm,f* liberator

libertar *vt* to set free, to release

libertinaje *nm* licentiousness

libertino,-a *adj & nm,f* libertine

Libia *n* Libya

libio,-a *adj & nm,f* Libyan

libra *nf (moneda, peso)* pound; **l. esterlina** pound sterling

librador,-a *nm,f* *Fin* drawer

librar 1 *vt* (**a**) to free; *Jur* to free, to release (**b**) *Com (una letra)* to draw (**c**) **l. batalla** to do *o* join battle

2 *vi* **libro los martes** *(no ir a trabajar)* I have Tuesdays off

3 librarse *vpr* to escape; **l. de algn** to get rid of sb

libre *adj* free; **entrada l.** *(gratis)* admission free; *(sin restricción)* open to the public; **l. cambio** free trade; **l. de impuestos** tax-free

librecambio, librecambismo *nm* free trade

librería *nf* (**a**) *(tienda)* bookshop, *US* bookstore (**b**) *(estante)* bookcase

📖 Observa que la palabra inglesa **library** es un falso amigo y no es la traducción de la palabra española **librería**. En inglés, **library** significa "biblioteca".

librero,-a **1** *nm,f* bookseller

2 *nm CAm, Col, Méx (mueble)* bookcase

📖 Observa que la palabra inglesa **librarian** es un falso amigo y no es la traducción de la palabra española **librero**. En inglés, **librarian** significa "bibliotecario".

libreta *nf* notebook; **l. (de ahorro)** savings book

libretista *nmf Am Cin* screenwriter, scriptwriter

libreto *nm Am Cin* script

libro *nm* book; **l. de texto** textbook; *Com* **l. de caja** cashbook; *Fin* **l. mayor** ledger

liceal *nmf Urug Br* secondary school *o US* high school pupil

liceano,-a *nm,f Chile Br* secondary school *o US* high school pupil

liceísta *nmf Ven Br* secondary school *o US* high school pupil

licencia *nf* (a) *(permiso)* permission; *(documentos)* permit, licence; **l. de armas/caza** gun/hunting licence (b) *(libertad abusiva)* licence, licentiousness (c) *Am Aut Br* driving licence, *US* driver's license

licenciado,-a *nm,f* (a) *Univ* graduate; **l. en Ciencias** Bachelor of Science (b) *Am* lawyer

licenciar [43] **1** *vt* (a) *Mil* to discharge (b) *Univ* to confer a degree on
  2 licenciarse *vpr Univ* to graduate

licenciatura *nf Univ (título)* (bachelor's) degree (course); *(carrera)* degree (course)

liceo *nm* (a) *(sociedad literaria)* literary society (b) *(escuela) Br* secondary school, *US* high school

licitar *vt Com (pujar)* to bid for

lícito,-a *adj (permisible)* allowed; *Jur* lawful

licor *nm* liquor, spirits

licuadora *nf* liquidizer

licuar [30] *vt* to liquidize

lid *nf (combate)* contest

líder *nmf* leader

liderar *vt* to lead, to head

liderato, liderazgo *nm* leadership; *Dep* top *o* first position

lidia *nf* bullfight, bullfighting

lidiador *nm* bullfighter

lidiar [43] **1** *vt Taurom* to fight
  2 *vi* to fight; **l. con** to contend with, to fight against

liebre *nf* (a) hare (b) *Dep* pacemaker

liendre *nf* nit

lienzo *nm* (a) *Tex* linen (b) *Arte* canvas

lifting *nm* face-lift

liga *nf* (a) *Dep & Pol* league; **hacer buena l.** to get on well together (b) *(prenda)* garter

ligamento *nm* ligament

ligar [42] **1** *vt* (a) to join; *Fig (dos personas)* to unite (b) *Fam (coger)* to get
  2 *vi Fam* **l. con algn** *(seducir)* to *Br* get off *o US* make out with sb
  3 ligarse *vpr (vincularse)* to become attached (**a** to)

ligazón *nf* bond, tie

ligeramente *adv* (a) *(levemente)* lightly (b) *(un poco)* slightly

ligereza *nf* (a) lightness; *(de tela, argumento)* flimsiness (b) *(frivolidad)* flippancy; *(acto)* indiscretion; *(dicho)* indiscreet remark (c) *(rapidez)* speed

ligero,-a 1 *adj* (a) *(peso)* light, lightweight; **l. de ropa** lightly clad (b) *(ágil)* light on one's feet; *(veloz)* swift, quick (c) *(leve)* slight; **brisa/comida ligera** light breeze/meal (d) **a la ligera** lightly
  2 *adv (rápido)* fast, swiftly

light *adj inv (tabaco)* mild; *Fig (persona)* lightweight

ligón,-ona *adj & nm,f Fam (hombre)* ladies' man; **es muy ligona** she's hot stuff

ligue *nm* pick-up

liguero,-a 1 *adj Dep* league; **partido l.** league match
  2 *nm Br* suspender belt, *US* garter belt

lija *nf* sandpaper; **papel de l.** sandpaper

lijar *vt* to sand *o* sandpaper (down)

lila¹ 1 *nm (color)* lilac
  2 *nf (flor)* lilac
  3 *adj inv* lilac

lila² Fam 1 *adj (tonto)* dumb, stupid
  2 *nmf (tonto)* twit

lima¹ *nf (fruto)* lime

lima² *nf (herramienta)* file; **l. de uñas** nail-file

limar *vt* to file; *Fig* **l. asperezas** to smooth things over

limbo *nm* limbo

limitación *nf* limitation; **l. de velocidad** speed limit

limitar 1 *vt* to limit, to restrict
  2 *vi* to border; **l. con** to border on

límite *nm* limit; *Geog & Pol* boundary, border; **caso l.** borderline case; **fecha l.** deadline; **velocidad l.** maximum speed

limítrofe *adj* neighbouring

limo *nm* slime

limón *nm* lemon

limonada *nf* lemon squash

limonero *nm* lemon tree

limosna *nf* alms; **pedir l.** to beg

limpiabotas *nm inv* bootblack, shoeshine

limpiacristales *nm inv* window cleaner

limpiador,-a 1 *adj* cleansing
  2 *nm,f (persona)* cleaner
  3 *nm (producto)* cleaner

limpiaparabrisas *nm inv Br* windscreen *o US* windshield wiper

limpiar [43] *vt* (a) to clean; *(con un trapo)* to wipe; *(zapatos)* to polish; *Fig* to cleanse (b) *Fam (hurtar)* to pinch, to nick

limpieza *nf (calidad)* cleanliness; *(acción)* cleaning; *Fig (integridad)* integrity; **con l.** cleanly

limpio,-a 1 *adj* (a) *(aseado)* clean (b) *Dep*

juego l. fair play (**c**) *Fin (neto)* net; **beneficios en l.** net profit (**d**) *Fam* **pasar algo a l.** to produce a fair copy of sth
2 *adv* fairly; **jugar l.** to play fair
linaje *nm* lineage
linaza *nf* **aceite de l.** linseed oil
lince *nm* lynx; **tiene ojos de l.** he's eagle-eyed
linchar *vt* to lynch; *Fam (pegar)* to beat up
lindante *adj* bordering
lindar *vi* **l. con** to border on
linde *nm o nf* boundary, limit
lindero,-a 1 *adj* bordering, adjoining
2 *nm* boundary, limit
lindo,-a 1 *adj (bonito)* pretty, lovely; **de lo l.** a great deal
2 *adv Am (bien)* nicely
línea *nf* (**a**) line; **l. aérea** airline; **en líneas generales** roughly speaking; *Informát* **fuera de l.** off-line; **en l.** on-line (**b**) **guardar la l.** to watch one's figure
lineal *adj* linear; **dibujo l.** line drawing
lingote *nm* ingot; *(de oro, plata)* bar
lingüista *nmf* linguist
lino *nm* (**a**) *Bot* flax (**b**) *Tex* linen
linterna *nf* torch
linyera *nmf CSur (vagabundo)* tramp, *US* bum
lío *nm* (**a**) *(paquete)* bundle (**b**) *Fam (embrollo)* mess, muddle; **hacerse un l.** to get mixed up; **meterse en líos** to get into trouble; **armar un l.** to kick up a fuss (**c**) *Fam (relación amorosa)* affair
lioso,-a *adj Fam (asunto)* confusing
lipotimia *nf* fainting fit
liquidación *nf* (**a**) *Com (saldo)* clearance sale (**b**) *Fin* liquidation
liquidar 1 *vt Com (deuda, cuenta)* to settle; *(mercancías)* to sell off
2 liquidarse *vpr Fam* (**a**) *(gastar)* to spend (**b**) **l. a algn** *(matar)* to bump sb off
liquidez *nf Fin* liquidity
líquido,-a 1 *adj* (**a**) liquid (**b**) *Fin* net
2 *nm* (**a**) *(fluido)* liquid (**b**) *Fin* liquid assets; **l. imponible** taxable income
lira *nf (moneda)* lira
lírico,-a *adj* lyrical
lirio *nm* iris
lirismo *nm* lyricism
lirón *nm* dormouse; *Fig* **dormir como un l.** to sleep like a log
Lisboa *n* Lisbon
lisiado,-a 1 *adj* crippled
2 *nm,f* cripple
lisiar [43] *vt* to maim, to cripple
liso,-a 1 *adj* (**a**) *(superficie)* smooth, even; *Dep* **los cien metros lisos** the one hundred metres sprint (**b**) *(pelo, falda)* straight (**c**)

(tela) self-coloured (**d**) *Am (desvergonzado)* rude (**e**) **lisa y llanamente** purely and simply
lisonjero,-a 1 *adj* flattering
2 *nm,f* flatterer
lista *nf* (**a**) *(relación)* list; **l. de espera** waiting list; *(en avión)* standby; **pasar l.** to call the register o the roll; *Informát* **l. de correo** mailing list (**b**) *(franja)* stripe; **a listas** striped
listado,-a 1 *adj* striped
2 *nm* list; *Informát* listing
listar *vt Am* to list
listín *nm* **l. telefónico** telephone directory
listo,-a *adj* (**a**) **ser l.** *(inteligente)* to be clever o smart (**b**) **estar l.** *(a punto)* to be ready
listón *nm Dep* bar; *Fig* **subir el l.** to raise the requirements level
litera *nf (cama)* bunk bed; *(en tren)* couchette
literal *adj* literal
literario,-a *adj* literary
literato,-a *nm,f* writer, author

Observa que la palabra inglesa **literate** *es un falso amigo y no es la traducción de la palabra española* **literato**. *En inglés,* **literate** *significa "alfabetizado".*

---

literatura *nf* literature
litigar [42] *vi Jur* to litigate
litigio *nm Jur* lawsuit; *Fig* dispute; **en l.** in dispute
litografía *nf* (**a**) *(técnica)* lithography (**b**) *(imagen)* lithograph
litoral 1 *nm* coast, seaboard
2 *adj* coastal
litro *nm* litre
Lituania *n* Lithuania
lituano,-a 1 *adj & nm,f* Lithuanian
2 *nm (idioma)* Lithuanian
liturgia *nf* liturgy
liviano,-a *adj (de poco peso)* lightweight
lívido,-a *adj* livid
living ['liin] *(pl livings) nm* living room
liza *nf* contest
llaga *nf* sore; *(herida)* wound
llama *nf* flame; **en llamas** in flames, ablaze
llamada *nf* call; *Tel* **l. interurbana** long-distance call; **señal de l.** ringing tone
llamado,-a 1 *adj* so-called
2 *nm Am* (**a**) *(en general)* call; *(a la puerta)* knock; *(con timbre)* ring (**b**) *(telefónico)* call; **hacer un l.** to make a phone call (**c**) *(apelación)* appeal, call; **hacer un l. a algn para que haga algo** to call upon sb to do sth; **hacer un l. a la huelga** to call a strike

llamamiento *nm* appeal

llamar 1 *vt* (**a**) to call; **l. (por teléfono)** to ring up, to call (**b**) *(atraer)* to draw, to attract; **l. la atención** to attract attention

2 *vi (a la puerta)* to knock

3 llamarse *vpr* to be called; **¿cómo te llamas?** what's your name?

llamarada *nf* blaze

llamativo,-a *adj* (**a**) *(color, ropa)* loud, flashy (**b**) *(persona)* striking

llanero,-a *nm,f (del llano)* plainsman, *f* plainswoman

llaneza *nf (sencillez)* simplicity

llano,-a 1 *adj* (**a**) *(superficie)* flat, level (**b**) *(claro)* clear (**c**) *(sencillo)* simple; **el pueblo l.** the common people

2 *nm* plain

llanta *nf* (**a**) *(de rueda)* wheel rim (**b**) *Am (neumático)* tyre

llanto *nm* crying, weeping

llanura *nf* plain

llave *nf* (**a**) key; **cerrar con l.** to lock; **llaves en mano** *(en anuncio)* available for immediate occupation; *Aut* **l. de contacto** ignition key (**b**) *Téc* spanner; **l. inglesa** adjustable spanner (**c**) *(interruptor)* switch; **l. de paso** stopcock (**d**) *(en lucha)* lock (**e**) *Impr* brace (**f**) *Chile, Méx (grifo)* tap, *US* faucet

llavero *nm* key-ring

llegada *nf* arrival; *Dep* finish

llegar [42] 1 *vi* (**a**) to arrive; **l. a Madrid** to arrive in Madrid (**b**) *(ser bastante)* to be enough (**c**) *(alcanzar)* **l. a** to reach; **¿llegas al techo?** can you reach the ceiling? (**d**) *Fig* **l. a las manos** to come to blows; **l. a presidente** to become president (**e**) **l. a** + *inf* to go so far as to (**f**) **l. a ser** to become

2 llegarse *vpr* to stop by

llenar 1 *vt* (**a**) to fill; *(cubrir)* to cover (**b**) *(satisfacer)* to satisfy

2 *vi (comida)* to be filling

3 llenarse *vpr* to fill (up), to become full

lleno,-a 1 *adj* full (up); *Fig* **de l.** fully

2 *nm Teatro* full house

llevadero,-a *adj* bearable, tolerable

llevar 1 *vt* (**a**) to take; *(hacia el oyente)* to bring; **¿adónde llevas eso?** where are you taking that?; **te llevaré un regalo** I'll bring you a present

(**b**) *(transportar)* to carry; **dejarse l.** to get carried away

(**c**) *(prenda)* to wear; **llevaba falda** she was wearing a skirt

(**d**) *(soportar)* to bear; **¿cómo lleva lo de su enfermedad?** how's he bearing up?

(**e**) *(tiempo)* **llevo dos años aquí** I've been here for two years; **esto lleva mucho tiempo** this takes a long time

(**f**) *(negocio)* to be in charge of

2 *v aux* (**a**) **l.** + *gerundio* to have been + *present participle*; **llevo dos años estudiando español** I've been studying Spanish for two years

(**b**) **l.** + *participio pasado* to have + *past participle*; **llevaba escritas seis cartas** I had written six letters

3 llevarse *vpr* (**a**) to take away; *(premio)* to win; *(recibir)* to get

(**b**) *(arrastrar)* to carry away

(**c**) *(estar de moda)* to be fashionable

(**d**) **l. bien con algn** to get on well with sb

llorar *vi* to cry; *Lit* to weep

llorica *nmf Fam* crybaby

lloriquear *vi* to whimper, to snivel

llorón,-ona *adj* **un bebé l.** a baby which cries a lot

lloroso,-a *adj* tearful

llover [4] *v impers* to rain

llovizna *nf* drizzle

lloviznar *v impers* to drizzle

lluvia *nf* rain; **una l. de** lots of; **l. radiactiva** fallout; **l. ácida** acid rain

lluvioso,-a *adj* rainy

lo¹ *art neut* the; **lo mejor** the best (part); **lo mismo** the same thing; **lo mío** mine; **lo tuyo** yours

lo² *pron pers m & neut* (**a**) *(cosa)* it; **debes hacerlo** you must do it; **no lo creo** I don't think so; *(no se traduce)* **no se lo dije** I didn't tell her; *ver* **le** (**b**) **lo que ...** what ...; **no sé lo que pasa** I don't know what's going on (**c**) **lo cual** ... which ... (**d**) **lo de ...** the business of ...; **cuéntame lo del juicio** tell me about the trial

loable *adj* praiseworthy, laudable

loar *vt* to praise

lobo *nm* wolf; **como boca de l.** pitch-dark; *Fam* **¡menos lobos!** pull the other one!

lóbrego,-a *adj* gloomy

lóbulo *nm* lobe

local 1 *adj* local

2 *nm (recinto)* premises, site

localidad *nf* (**a**) *(pueblo)* locality; *(en impreso)* place of residence (**b**) *Cin & Teatro (asiento)* seat; *(entrada)* ticket

localizar [40] *vt* (**a**) *(encontrar)* to find (**b**) *(fuego, dolor)* to localize

loción *nf* lotion

loco,-a 1 *adj* mad, crazy; **a lo l.** crazily; **l. por** crazy about; **volverse l.** to go mad; *Fam* **¡ni l.!** I'd sooner die!

2 *nm,f* madman, *f* madwoman; **hacerse el l.** to act the fool

3 *nm Chile (molusco)* = type of abalone

locomotora nf locomotive

locomotriz adj locomotive

locuaz adj loquacious, talkative

locución nf phrase

locura nf (enfermedad) madness, insanity; **con l.** madly; Fam **esto es una l.** this is crazy

locutor,-a nm,f TV & Rad presenter

locutorio nm telephone booth

lodo nm mud

logaritmo nm logarithm

lógica nf logic; **no tiene l.** there's no logic to it

lógico,-a adj logical; **era l. que ocurriera** it was bound to happen

logística nf logistics sing o pl

logotipo nm logo

lograr vt (a) to get, to obtain; (premio) to win; (ambición) to achieve (b) **l. hacer algo** to manage to do sth

logro nm achievement

loma nf hillock, rise

lombriz nf worm, earthworm

lomo nm (a) back; **a lomo(s)** on the back (b) Culin loin (c) (de libro) spine

lona nf canvas

loncha nf slice; **l. de bacon** rasher of bacon

lonche nm (a) Méx, Perú, Ven (merienda) (en escuela) mid-morning snack; (en casa) (afternoon) tea (b) Méx, Ven (comida rápida) (mid-morning) snack, Br elevenses

lonchería nf Méx snack-bar

londinense 1 adj of/from London

2 nmf Londoner

Londres n London

longaniza nf spicy (pork) sausage

longevo,-a adj long-lived

longitud nf (a) length; **2 m de l.** 2 m long; **l. de onda** wavelength; Dep **salto de l.** long jump (b) Geog longitude

lonja¹ nf (loncha) slice; **l. de bacon** rasher of bacon

lonja² nf **l. de pescado** fish market

loquería nf Am mental asylum, mental hospital

lord nm (pl **lores**) lord; Br Parl **Cámara de los Lores** House of Lords

loro nm parrot

los¹ 1 art def mpl the; **l. libros** the books; **cierra l. ojos** close your eyes; **l. García** the Garcías; ver **el, las y lo**

2 pron **l. que** (personas) those who; (cosas) the ones (that); **toma l. que quieras** take whichever ones you want; **esos son l. míos/tuyos** these are mine/yours; ver **les**

los² pron pers mpl them; **¿l. has visto?** have you seen them?

losa nf (stone) slab, flagstone

lote nm (a) set (b) Com lot (c) Informát batch (d) Fam **darse el l.** to pet (e) Am (solar) plot (of land)

loteamiento nm Bol, Urug parcelling out, division into plots

loteo nm Chile, Col = loteamiento

lotería nf lottery; **me tocó la l.** I won a prize in the lottery

lotización nf Ecuad, Perú = loteamiento

loto 1 nm Bot lotus

2 nf (lotería) lottery

loza nf (a) (material) earthenware (b) (de cocina) crockery

lozano,-a adj (a) (persona) healthy-looking (b) (plantas) lush, luxuriant

Ltda. (abr Limitada) Ltd

lubricante nm lubricant

lubricar [44] vt to lubricate

lucero nm (bright) star

lucha nf (a) fight, struggle; **l. de clases** class struggle (b) Dep wrestling; **l. libre** freestyle wrestling

luchador,-a nm,f (a) fighter (b) Dep wrestler

luchar vi (a) to fight, to struggle (b) Dep to wrestle

lucidez nf lucidity

lúcido,-a adj lucid, clear

luciérnaga nf glow-worm

lucir [35] 1 vi (a) (brillar) to shine (b) Am (parecer) to seem (c) Fam (compensar) **no le luce lo que estudia** his studies don't get him anywhere

2 vt (ropas) to sport; (talento) to display

3 lucirse vpr (a) (hacer buen papel) to do very well (b) (pavonearse) to show off

lucrativo,-a adj lucrative, profitable

lucro nm profit, gain; **afán de l.** greed for money

lúcuma nf Andes lucuma, = sweet, pear-shaped fruit

lúdico,-a adj relating to games, recreational

luego 1 adv (a) (después) then, next, afterwards (b) (más tarde) later (on); **¡hasta l.!** so long!; **l. de** after (c) **desde l.** of course (d) Chile, Ven (pronto) soon; Méx Fam **l. l. o l. lueguito** right o straight away

2 conj therefore

lugar nm (a) place; **en primer l.** in the first place; **en l. de** instead of; **sin l. a dudas** without a doubt; **tener l.** to take place (b) **dar l. a** to cause, to give rise to

lugareño,-a adj & nm,f local

lugarteniente *nmf* lieutenant

lúgubre *adj* gloomy, lugubrious

lujo *nm* luxury; **productos de l.** luxury products; **no puedo permitirme ese l.** I can't afford that

lujoso,-a *adj* luxurious

lujuria *nf* lust

> ⚠ Observa que la palabra inglesa **luxury** es un falso amigo y no es la traducción de la palabra española **lujuria**. En inglés, **luxury** significa "lujo".

lujurioso,-a *adj* lecherous, lustful

lumbre *nf* fire

lumbrera *nf* luminary

luminoso,-a *adj* luminous; *Fig* bright

luna *nf* (a) moon; *Fig* **estar en la l.** to have one's head in the clouds; **l. creciente/llena** crescent/full moon; *Fig* **l. de miel** honeymoon (b) (*de escaparate*) pane; (*espejo*) mirror

lunar 1 *adj* lunar

 2 *nm* (*redondel*) dot; (*en la piel*) mole, beauty spot; **vestido de lunares** spotted dress

lunático,-a *nm,f* lunatic

lunes *nm inv* Monday; **vendré el l.** I'll come on Monday

lupa *nf* magnifying glass

luso,-a *adj & nm,f* Portuguese

lustrabotas *nm inv*, **lustrador,-a** *nm,f* *Andes, RP* bootblack

lustradora *nf* *Andes, RP* floor polisher

lustrar *vt* to polish; (*zapatos*) to shine

lustre *nm* (*brillo*) shine, lustre; *Fig* (*esplendor*) splendour, glory; **dar** *o* **sacar l. a algo** to polish sth

lustro *nm* five-year period

lustroso,-a *adj* shiny, glossy

luto *nm* mourning

Luxemburgo *n* Luxembourg

luz *nf* (a) light; **apagar la l.** to put out the light; **a la l. de** in the light of; **a todas luces** obviously; *Fig* **dar a l.** (*parir*) to give birth to; *Fig* **dar l. verde a** to give the green light to (b) *Aut* light; **luces de cruce** dipped headlights; **luces de posición** sidelights; **l. larga** headlights (c) **luces** (*inteligencia*) intelligence; **corto de luces** dim-witted (d) **traje de luces** bullfighter's costume

luzco *indic pres de* **lucir**

M

M, m ['eme] *nf (la letra)* M, m

m (**a**) *(abr* **metro(s)**) m (**b**) *(abr* **minuto(s)**) min

macabro,-a *adj* macabre

macana *nf* (**a**) *Andes, Carib, Méx (palo)* club (**b**) *CSur, Perú, Ven Fam (fastidio)* pain, drag

macanear *vt CSur, Ven (hacer mal)* to botch, to do badly

macanudo,-a *adj Fam* great, terrific

macarra *nm Fam* yob

macarrón *nm* (**a**) macaroon (**b**) *Elec* sheath

macarrones *nmpl* macaroni

macedonia *nf* fruit salad

macerar *vt* to macerate

maceta *nf (tiesto)* plant-pot, flowerpot

machacar [44] **1** *vt* (**a**) to crush; *Dep* to smash (**b**) *Fam (estudiar con ahínco) Br* to swot up on, *US* to bone up on (**c**) *Fam (insistir en)* to harp on about, to go on about

   2 *vi* (**a**) *Fam (insistir mucho)* to harp on, to go on (**b**) *Fam (estudiar con ahínco) Br* to swot, *US* to grind (**c**) *(en baloncesto)* to smash

machacón,-ona *Fam* **1** *adj (repetitivo)* repetitious; *(pesado)* boring, tiresome

   2 *nm,f (muy estudioso) Br* swot, *US* grind

machamartillo: • **a machamartillo** *loc adv (con firmeza)* firmly; *(con obstinación)* obstinately

machete *nm* (**a**) *(arma)* machete (**b**) *Arg Fam (chuleta)* crib

machismo *nm* machismo, male chauvinism

machista *adj & nm* male chauvinist

macho **1** *adj* (**a**) *(animal, planta)* male (**b**) *Fam (viril)* manly, virile, macho

   2 *nm* (**a**) *(animal, planta)* male (**b**) *Téc (pieza)* male piece o part; *(de enchufe)* plug (**c**) *Fam (hombre viril)* macho, he-man, tough guy

machote *nm Am (borrador)* rough draft

maciento,-a *adj* gaunt

macizo,-a **1** *adj* (**a**) *(sólido)* solid; **de oro m.** of solid gold (**b**) *(robusto)* solid, robust; *Fam (atractivo)* well-built

   2 *nm (masa sólida)* mass

macramé *nm* macramé

macro *nf Informát* macro

macro- *pref* macro-

macroeconomía *nf* macroeconomics sing

macuto *nm (morral)* knapsack, haversack

madeja *nf (de lana etc)* hank, skein

madera *nf* (**a**) wood; *(de construcción)* timber, *US* lumber; **de m.** wood, wooden (**b**) *Fig* **tiene m. de líder** he has all the makings of a leader

madero *nm* (**a**) *(de construcción)* timber; *(leño)* log (**b**) *muy Fam (policía)* cop; **los maderos** the fuzz *pl*

madrastra *nf* stepmother

madre **1** *nf* (**a**) mother; **es m. de tres hijos** she is a mother of three (children); **m. adoptiva** adoptive mother; **m. alquilada** surrogate mother; **m. de familia** mother, housewife; **m. política** mother-in-law; **m. soltera** unmarried mother; *Fig* **la m. patria** one's motherland; *Méx muy Fam* **me vale m.** I couldn't give a damn o *Br* a toss (**b**) *(de río)* bed

   2 *interj* **¡m. de Dios!, ¡m. mía!** good heavens!

madreperla *nf (nácar)* mother-of-pearl

madreselva *nf* honeysuckle

Madrid *n* Madrid

madriguera *nf* burrow, hole

madrileño,-a **1** *adj* of/from Madrid

   2 *nm,f* person from Madrid

madrina *nf* (**a**) *(de bautizo)* godmother (**b**) *(de boda)* ≃ bridesmaid (**c**) *Fig (protectora)* protectress

madrugada *nf* (**a**) dawn; **de m.** in the wee small hours (**b**) early morning; **las tres de la m.** three o'clock in the morning

madrugador,-a **1** *adj* early-rising

   2 *nm,f* early riser

madrugar [42] *vi* to get up early

madurar **1** *vt Fig (un plan)* to think out

   2 *vi* (**a**) *(persona)* to mature (**b**) *(fruta)* to ripen

madurez *nf* (**a**) maturity (**b**) *(de la fruta)* ripeness

maduro,-a *adj* (**a**) mature; **de edad madura** middle-aged (**b**) *(fruta)* ripe

maestría *nf* mastery; **con m.** masterfully

maestro,-a 1 *nm,f* (**a**) *Educ* teacher; **m. de escuela** schoolteacher (**b**) *Méx* (*en universidad*) *Br* lecturer, *US* professor (**c**) (*especialista*) master; **m. de obras** foreman (**d**) *Mús* maestro

  2 *adj* **obra maestra** masterpiece; **llave maestra** master key

mafia *nf* mafia

mafioso,-a 1 *adj* of/relating to the mafia

  2 *nm,f* member of the mafia, mafioso

magdalena *nf* bun, cake

magia *nf* magic; **por arte de m.** as if by magic

mágico,-a *adj* (**a**) magic (**b**) *Fig* (*maravilloso*) magical, wonderful

magisterio *nm* teaching

magistrado,-a *nm,f* judge; *Am* **primer m.** prime minister

magistral *adj* (*excelente*) masterly; **una jugada m.** a master stroke

magistratura *nf* magistracy

magnánimo,-a *adj* magnanimous

magnate *nm* magnate, tycoon

magnesio *nm* magnesium

magnético,-a *adj* magnetic

magnetizar [40] *vt* (**a**) (*imantar*) to magnetize (**b**) *Fig* (*hipnotizar*) to hypnotize

magnetofón, magnetófono *nm* tape recorder

magnetofónico,-a *adj* magnetic

magnífico,-a *adj* magnificent, splendid

magnitud *nf* magnitude, dimension; **de primera m.** of the first order

magno,-a *adj Literario* great; **aula magna** main amphitheatre

mago,-a *nm,f* wizard, magician; **los tres Reyes Magos** the Three Wise Men, the Three Kings

magrear *vt muy Fam* to grope

magro,-a 1 *nm* (*de cerdo*) lean meat

  2 *adj* (*sin grasa*) lean

magullar 1 *vt* to bruise, to damage

  2 magullarse *vpr* to get bruised, to get damaged

mahometano,-a *adj & nm,f Rel* Mohammedan, Muslim

mahonesa *nf* mayonnaise

maillot *nm* (*malla*) leotard; *Dep* shirt

maíz *nm* maize, *US* corn

maizal *nm* field of maize o *US* corn

majadería *nf* silly thing, absurdity

majadero,-a *nm,f* fool, idiot

majara, majareta *adj Fam* loony, nutty

majestad *nf* majesty

majestuosidad *nf* majesty

majestuoso,-a *adj* majestic, stately

majo,-a *adj* (*bonito*) pretty, nice; *Fam* (*simpático*) nice; **tiene un hijo muy m.** she's got a lovely little boy; *Fam* **ven aquí, m.** come here, dear

mal 1 *nm* (**a**) evil, wrong (**b**) (*daño*) harm; **no le deseo ningún m.** I don't wish him any harm (**c**) (*enfermedad*) illness, disease; *Fam* **el m. de las vacas locas** mad cow disease

  2 *adj* bad; **un m. año** a bad year; *ver* **malo,-a**

  3 *adv* badly, wrong; **lo hizo muy m.** he did it very badly; **menos m. que ...** it's a good job (that) ...; **no está (nada) m.** it is not bad (at all); **te oigo/veo (muy) m.** I can hardly hear/see you; **tomar a m.** (*enfadarse*) to take badly

malabar *adj* (**juegos**) **malabares** juggling

malabarista *nmf* juggler

malapata *nf Fam* (*mala suerte*) bad luck

malaria *nf* malaria

malcriado,-a 1 *adj* ill-mannered, ill-bred

  2 *nm,f* ill-mannered o uncivil person

malcriar [29] *vt* to spoil

maldad *nf* (**a**) badness, evil (**b**) (*acción perversa*) evil o wicked thing

maldecir [12] 1 *vt* to curse

  2 *vi* (**a**) (*blasfemar*) to curse (**b**) (*criticar*) to speak ill (**de** of)

maldición 1 *nf* curse

  2 *interj* damnation!

maldito,-a *adj* (**a**) *Fam* (*molesto*) damned, *Br* bloody (**b**) (*endemoniado*) damned, cursed; **¡maldita sea!** damn it!

maleante *adj & nmf* criminal

malear 1 *vt Fig* to corrupt, to pervert

  2 malearse *vpr* to go bad

maleducado,-a 1 *adj* bad-mannered

  2 *nm,f* bad-mannered person

maleficio *nm* (*hechizo*) curse, spell

maléfico,-a *adj* evil, harmful

malentendido *nm* misunderstanding

malestar *nm* (**a**) (*molestia*) discomfort (**b**) *Fig* (*inquietud*) uneasiness; **tengo m.** I feel uneasy

maleta 1 *nf* suitcase, case; **hacer la m.** to pack one's things o case

  2 *nm Fam* (*persona*) bungler

maletero *nm Aut Br* boot, *US* trunk

maletín *nm* briefcase

malévolo,-a *adj* malevolent

maleza *nf* (**a**) (*arbustos*) thicket, undergrowth (**b**) (*malas hierbas*) weeds

malgastar *vt & vi* to waste, to squander

malhablado,-a 1 *adj* foul-mouthed

  2 *nm,f* foul-mouthed person

malhechor,-a *nm,f* wrongdoer, criminal

malhumor *nm* bad temper o mood; **de m.** in a bad temper o mood

malicia *nf* (**a**) *(mala intención)* malice, maliciousness (**b**) *(astucia)* cunning, slyness (**c**) *(maldad)* badness, evil

malicioso,-a 1 *adj* malicious, spiteful

2 *nm,f* malicious o spiteful person

maligno,-a *adj* malignant

malintencionado,-a 1 *adj* ill-intentioned

2 *nm,f* ill-intentioned person

malla *nf* (**a**) *(prenda)* leotard (**b**) *(red)* mesh (**c**) *Perú, RP (bañador)* swimsuit, swimming costume

Mallorca *n* Majorca

mallorquín,-ina *adj & nm,f* Majorcan

malo,-a 1 *adj* (**a**) bad; **un año m.** a bad year; **estar a malas** to be on bad terms; **por las malas** by force (**b**) *(persona) (malvado)* wicked, bad; *(travieso)* naughty (**c**) *(de poca calidad)* bad, poor; **una mala canción/comida** a poor song/meal (**d**) *(perjudicial)* harmful; **el tabaco es m.** tobacco is harmful (**e**) **lo m. es que ...** the problem is that ... (**f**) *(enfermo)* ill, sick

---

Mal is used instead of **malo** before masculine singular nouns (e.g. **un mal ejemplo** a bad example). The comparative form of **malo** (= worse) is **peor**, the superlative forms (= the worst) are **el peor** (masculine) and **la peor** (feminine).

---

2 *nm,f Fam* **el m.** the baddy o villain

malograr 1 *vt Andes (estropear)* to make a mess of, to ruin

2 malograrse *vpr* (**a**) *(fracasar)* to fail, to fall through (**b**) *Andes (estropearse) (el tiempo)* to turn nasty; *(máquina)* to break down; *(alimento)* to go off, to spoil

maloliente *adj* foul-smelling

malparado,-a *adj* **salir m.** to end up in a sorry state

malpensado,-a 1 *adj* nasty-minded

2 *nm,f* nasty-minded person

malsonante *adj (grosero)* rude, offensive; **palabras malsonantes** foul language

malta *nf (cebada)* malt

maltratado,-a *adj* battered

maltratar *vt* to ill-treat, to mistreat

maltrecho,-a *adj* in a sorry state, wrecked

malva 1 *adj inv* mauve

2 *nm (color)* mauve

3 *nf Bot* mallow

malvado,-a 1 *adj* evil, wicked

2 *nm,f* villain, evil person

malvender *vt* to sell at a loss

malversar *vt* to misappropriate, to embezzle

Malvinas *npl* **las (Islas) M.** the Falkland Islands

malviviente *nmf CSur* criminal

malvivir *vi* to live very badly

mama *nf* (**a**) *(de mujer)* breast; *(de animal)* teat (**b**) *Fam (mamá)* mum, mummy

mamá *nf Fam* mum, mummy; *Col, Méx Fam* **m. grande** grandma

mamada *nf* (**a**) *(bebé)* feed (**b**) *Vulg (felatio)* blowjob

mamadera *nf Am* feeding bottle

mamar *vt (leche)* to suck; *Fig (adquirir)* to absorb

mamarracho,-a *nm,f Fam (persona)* ridiculous-looking person, mess, sight; *(cosa)* mess

mameluco *nm Fig* (**a**) fool, idiot, dimwit (**b**) *Am* boiler suit

mamey *nm* (**a**) *(árbol)* mamey, mammee (**b**) *(fruto)* mamey, mammee (apple)

mamífero,-a *nm,f* mammal

mamón *nm muy Fam Br* prat, *US* jerk

mampara *nf* screen

mamporro *nm Fam* wallop

mampostería *nf* masonry

mamut *nm* mammoth

manada *nf* (**a**) *Zool (de vacas, elefantes)* herd; *(de ovejas)* flock; *(de lobos, perros)* pack; *(de leones)* pride (**b**) *Fam (multitud)* crowd, mob; **en manada(s)** in crowds

manager *nmf Dep & Mús* manager

manantial *nm* spring

manar 1 *vi* to flow, to run (**de** from)

2 *vt* to run with, to flow with; **la herida manaba sangre** blood flowed from his wound

manazas *nmf inv Fam* ham-fisted person

mancebo *nm* (**a**) *(de farmacia)* assistant (**b**) *Literario (muchacho)* young man

Mancha *n* **el Canal de la M.** the English Channel

mancha *nf* stain, spot; **m. solar** sunspot; **m. de tinta/vino** ink/wine stain

manchar 1 *vt* to stain, to dirty; *Fig* to stain, to blemish

2 mancharse *vpr* to get dirty

manchego,-a 1 *adj* of/from La Mancha

2 *nm,f* person from La Mancha

manco,-a 1 *adj* (**a**) *(de un brazo)* one-armed *(sin brazos)* armless (**b**) *(de una mano)* one-handed; *(sin manos)* handless

2 *nm,f* (**a**) *(de brazos)* one-armed/armless person (**b**) *(de manos)* one-handed/handless person

mancomunidad *nf* community, association

mancornas, mancuernas *nfpl CAm, Chile, Col, Méx, Ven* cufflinks

mandado *nm (recado)* order, errand; **hacer un m.** to run an errand

mandamás *nmf (pl* **mandamases***) Fam* bigwig, boss

mandamiento *nm* (a) *(orden)* order, command (b) **los Diez Mandamientos** the Ten Commandments

mandar *vt* (a) to order; *Fam* ¿**mande?** pardon? (b) *(grupo)* to lead, to be in charge o command of; *Mil* to command (c) *(enviar)* to send; **m. (a) por** to send for; **m. algo por correo** to post sth, to send sth by post; **m. recuerdos** to send regards

mandarina *nf* mandarin (orange), tangerine

mandatario,-a *nm,f Pol* president

mandato *nm* (a) *(orden)* order, command (b) *Jur* writ, warrant (c) *Pol (legislatura)* mandate, term of office

mandíbula *nf* jaw; *Fam* **reír a m. batiente** to laugh one's head off

mandil *nm* apron

Mandinga *nm Am* the Devil

mando *nm* (a) *(autoridad)* command, control (b) **los altos mandos del ejército** high-ranking army officers (c) *Téc (control)* controls; *Aut* **cuadro** o **tablero de mandos** dashboard; **m. a distancia** remote control; **palanca de m.** *Téc* control lever; *(de avión, videojuego)* joystick

mandón,-ona 1 *adj Fam* bossy, domineering

  2 *nm,f Fam* bossy o domineering person

  3 *nm Am* (mine) foreman

manecilla *nf (de reloj)* hand

manejable *adj* manageable; *(herramienta)* easy-to-use; *(coche)* manoeuvrable

manejar 1 *vt* (a) *(máquina)* to handle, to operate; *Fig (situación)* to handle (b) *(negocio)* to run, to manage (c) *Fig (a otra persona)* to domineer, to boss about (d) *Am (coche)* to drive

  2 *vi Am (conducir)* to drive

  3 manejarse *vpr* to manage

manejo *nm* (a) *(uso)* handling, use; **de fácil m.** easy-to-use (b) *Fig (de un negocio)* management; *(de un coche)* driving (c) *Fig* tricks

manera *nf* (a) way, manner; **a mi/tu m.** (in) my/your way; **de cualquier m.** *(mal)* carelessly, any old how; *(en cualquier caso)* in any case; **de esta m.** in this way; **de ninguna m.** in no way, certainly not; **de todas maneras** anyway, at any rate, in any case; **es mi m. de ser** that's the way I

am; **no hay m.** it's impossible (b) **de m. que** so; **de tal m. que** in such a way that (c) **maneras** manners; **de buenas maneras** politely

manga *nf* (a) sleeve; **de m. corta/larga** short-/long-sleeved; **sin mangas** sleeveless; *Fig* **hacer un corte de mangas a algn** ≃ to give sb the fingers; *Fig* **m. por hombro** messy and untidy; *Fig* **sacarse algo de la m.** to pull sth out of one's hat (b) *(de riego)* hose (c) *(del mar)* arm (d) *Dep* leg, round; *Ten* set

mangante *nmf Fam* thief

mangar [42] *vt Fam* to pinch, to nick, to swipe

mango *nm* (a) *(asa)* handle (b) *RP Fam (dinero)* **no tengo un m.** I haven't got a bean, I'm broke

mangonear *vi Fam* (a) *(entrometerse)* to meddle (b) *(dar órdenes)* to throw one's weight around

manguera *nf* hose

mangui *nmf Fam* thief

manguito *nm* (a) *(para las mangas)* oversleeve; *(para flotar)* armband (b) *Téc* sleeve

maní *nm (pl* **maníes***)* peanut

manía *nf* (a) dislike, ill will; **me tiene m.** he has it in for me (b) *(costumbre)* habit; **tiene la m. de llegar tarde** he's always arriving late (c) *(afición exagerada)* craze; **la m. de las motos** the motorbike craze (d) *Med* mania

maniaco,-a, maníaco,-a *adj & nm,f Psi* manic; *Fam (obseso)* maniac

maniatar *vt* to tie the hands of

maniático,-a 1 *adj* fussy

  2 *nm,f* fusspot

manicomio *nm* mental hospital

manicura *nf* manicure

manido,-a *adj* (a) *(comida)* off (b) *(asunto)* trite, hackneyed

manifestación *nf* (a) demonstration (b) *(expresión)* manifestation, expression

manifestante *nmf* demonstrator

manifestar [1] *vt* (a) *(declarar)* to state, to declare (b) *(mostrar)* to show, to display

  2 manifestarse *vpr* (a) *(por la calle)* to demonstrate (b) *(declararse)* to declare oneself; **se manifestó contrario a ...** he spoke out against ...

manifiesto,-a 1 *adj* clear, obvious; **poner de m.** *(revelar)* to reveal, to show; *(hacer patente)* to make clear

  2 *nm* manifesto

manigua *nf Am Geog* scrubland

manilla *nf* (a) *(de reloj)* hand (b) *Am (palanca)* lever

manillar *nm* handlebar

maniobra *nf* manoeuvre

maniobrar *vi* to manoeuvre

manipulación *nf* manipulation

manipular *vt* to manipulate; *(máquina)* to handle

maniquí *nm (muñeco)* dummy

manitas *nmf inv Fam* (a) **ser un m.** to be handy, to be very good with one's hands (b) **hacer m.** to hold hands

manito *nm Méx Fam* pal, *Br* mate, *US* buddy

manivela *nf Téc* crank

manjar *nm* dish, food

mano 1 *nf* (a) hand; **a m.** *(sin máquina)* by hand; *(asequible)* at hand; **escrito a m.** hand-written; **hecho a m.** hand-made; **a m. armada** armed; **estrechar la m. a algn** to shake hands with sb; **de segunda m.** second-hand; **echar una m. a algn** to give sb a hand; **¡manos a la obra!** shoulders to the wheel!; **meter m. a** *(un problema)* to tackle; *Fam* to touch up; **traerse algo entre manos** to be up to sth; **equipaje de m.** hand luggage (b) *(lado)* side; **a m. derecha/izquierda** on the right/left(-hand side) (c) **m. de pintura** coat of paint (d) **m. de obra** labour (force) (e) *RP (dirección)* direction *(of traffic)*; **calle de una/doble m.** one-/two-way street

2 *nm Andes, CAm, Carib, Méx Fam* pal, *Br* mate, *US* buddy

manojo *nm* bunch; **ser un m. de nervios** to be a bundle of nerves

manopla *nf* mitten

manoseado,-a *adj (objeto)* worn(-out); *(tema)* hackneyed

manosear *vt* to touch repeatedly, to finger; *Fam* to paw

manotazo *nm* cuff, slap

mansalva: • **a mansalva** *loc adv (en gran cantidad)* galore

mansedumbre *nf* (a) *(de persona)* meekness, gentleness (b) *(de animal)* tameness, docility

manso,-a *adj* (a) *(persona)* gentle, meek (b) *(animal)* tame, docile (c) *Chile (extraordinario)* great

manta 1 *nf* (a) blanket; **m. eléctrica** electric blanket (b) *(zurra)* beating, hiding (c) *Ven (vestido)* = traditional costume worn by women from Guajira

2 *nmf Fam* lazy person, idler

manteca *nf* (a) *(de animal)* fat; **m. de cacao/cacahuete** cocoa/peanut butter; **m. de cerdo** lard (b) *Am (mantequilla)* butter

mantecado *nm* shortcake

mantel *nm* tablecloth

📖 Observa que la palabra inglesa **mantle** es un falso amigo y no es la traducción de la palabra española **mantel**. En inglés, **mantle** significa "manto, capa".

mantener [24] 1 *vt* (a) *(conservar)* to keep; **mantén el fuego encendido** keep the fire burning; **m. la línea** to keep in trim (b) *(entrevista, reunión)* to have; **m. correspondencia con algn** to correspond with sb (c) *(ideas, opiniones)* to defend, to maintain (d) *(familia)* to support, to feed (e) *(peso)* to support, to hold up

2 mantenerse *vpr* (a) *(sostenerse)* to stand (b) **m. firme** *(perseverar)* to hold one's ground (c) *(sustentarse)* to live (**de on**)

mantenimiento *nm* (a) *Téc* maintenance, upkeep; **servicio de m.** maintenance service (b) *(alimento)* sustenance, support (c) **gimnasia y m.** keep fit

mantequilla *nf* butter

manto *nm* cloak

mantón *nm* shawl

mantuve *pt indef de* **mantener**

manual 1 *adj* manual; **trabajo m.** manual labour; *Educ* **trabajos manuales** handicrafts

2 *nm* manual, handbook

manubrio *nm Am (manillar)* handlebars

manufactura *nf* (a) *(fabricación)* manufacture (b) *(fábrica)* factory

manufacturar *vt* to manufacture

manuscrito *nm* manuscript

manutención *nf* maintenance

manzana *nf* (a) apple (b) *(de edificios)* block

manzanilla *nf* (a) *Bot* camomile (b) *(infusión)* camomile tea (c) *(vino)* manzanilla

maña *nf* (a) *(astucia)* cunning (b) *(habilidad)* skill

mañana 1 *nf* morning; **a las dos de la m.** at two in the morning; **de m.** early in the morning; **por la m.** in the morning

2 *nm* tomorrow, the future

3 *adv* tomorrow; **¡hasta m.!** see you tomorrow!; **m. por la m.** tomorrow morning; **pasado m.** the day after tomorrow

mañanitas *nfpl Méx* birthday song

mañoco *nm Ven* tapioca

mañoso,-a *adj* skilful

mapa *nm* map; **m. mudo** blank map; *Fam* **borrar del m.** to wipe out

maqueta *nf* (a) *(miniatura)* scale model, maquette (b) *Mús* demo (tape)

maquiavélico,-a *adj* Machiavellian

maquila nf Méx (of machines) assembly

maquiladora nf Méx assembly plant

maquillaje nm make-up

maquillar 1 vt to make up

  2 maquillarse vpr (a) (ponerse maquillaje) to put one's make-up on, to make (oneself) up (b) (usar maquillaje) to wear make-up

máquina nf (a) machine; **escrito a m.** typewritten; **hecho a m.** machine-made; Fam **a toda m.** at full speed **m. de afeitar (eléctrica)** (electric) razor o shaver; **m. de coser** sewing machine; **m. de escribir** typewriter; **m. fotográfica** o **de fotos** camera; **m. tragaperras** o Am **tragamonedas** slot machine, one-armed bandit (b) CAm, Cuba (coche) car

maquinar vt to machinate, to plot

maquinaria nf (a) machinery, machines (b) (de reloj etc) (mecanismo) mechanism, works

maquinilla nf **m. de afeitar** safety razor

maquinista nmf (de tren) engine driver

mar 1 nm o nf (a) sea; **en alta m.** on the high seas; **por m.** by sea; **m. gruesa** heavy sea; **m. picada** rough sea (b) Fam **está la m. de guapa** she's looking really beautiful; **llover a mares** to rain cats and dogs

> Note that the feminine is used in literary language, by people such as fishermen with a close connection with the sea, and in some idiomatic expressions.

2 nm sea; **M. del Norte** North Sea; **M. Muerto/Negro** Dead/Black Sea

maracuyá nf passion fruit

maraña nf tangle

maratón nm marathon

maratoniano,-a adj marathon

maravilla nf marvel, wonder; **de m.** wonderfully; **¡qué m. de película!** what a wonderful film!; Fam **a las mil maravillas** marvellously

maravillar 1 vt to amaze, to astonish

  2 maravillarse vpr to marvel (con at), to wonder (con at)

maravilloso,-a adj wonderful, marvellous

marca nf (a) mark, sign (b) Com brand, make; **ropa de m.** brand-name clothes; **m. de fábrica** trademark; **m. registrada** registered trademark (c) Dep (récord) record; **batir la m. mundial** to break the world record

marcador nm (a) marker (b) Dep (tablero) scoreboard; (persona) scorer (c) Am (rotulador) felt-tip pen; Méx (fluorescente) highlighter pen

marcaje nm Dep marking

marcapasos nm inv Med pacemaker

marcar [44] 1 vt (a) to mark (b) Tel to dial (c) (indicar) to indicate, to show; **el contador marca 1.327** the meter reads 1,327 (d) Dep (gol, puntos) to score; (a jugador) to mark (e) (cabello) to set

  2 marcarse vpr Fam **m. un farol** to show off, to boast

marcha nf (a) march; **hacer algo sobre la m.** to do sth as one goes along; **a marchas forzadas** against the clock (b) **estar en m.** (vehículo) to be in motion; (máquina) to be working; (proyecto etc) to be under way; **poner en m.** to start (c) Aut gear; **m. atrás** reverse (gear) (d) Mús march (e) Fam (juerga) **hay mucha m.** there's lots going on; **ella tiene mucha m.** she likes a good time

marchante,-a nm,f (a) (de arte) dealer (b) CAm, Méx, Ven Fam (cliente) customer, patron

marchar 1 vi (a) (ir) to go, to walk; Fam **¡marchando!** on your way!; **¡una cerveza! – ¡marchando!** a beer, please! – coming right up! (b) (aparato) to be on; **m. bien** (negocio) to be going well (c) Mil to march

  2 marcharse vpr (irse) to leave, to go away

marchitar vt, **marchitarse** vpr to shrivel, to wither

marchito,-a adj shrivelled, withered

marchoso,-a Fam **1** adj (persona) fun-loving, wild

  2 nm,f raver, fun-lover

marcial adj martial; **artes marciales** martial arts

marcianitos nmpl (juego) space invaders

marciano,-a adj & nm,f Martian

marco nm (a) (de cuadro etc) frame (b) Fig (ámbito) framework; **acuerdo m.** framework agreement (c) Fin (moneda) mark

marea nf (a) tide; **m. alta/baja** high/low tide; **m. negra** oil slick (b) Fig (multitud) crowd, mob

mareado,-a adj (a) sick; (en un avión) airsick; (en un coche) car-sick, travel-sick; (en el mar) seasick (b) Euf (bebido) tipsy (c) (aturdido) dizzy

marear 1 vt (a) to make sick; (en el mar) to make seasick; (en un avión) to make airsick; (en un coche) to make car-sick o travel-sick (b) (aturdir) to make dizzy (c) Fam (fastidiar) to annoy, to pester (d) Culin to stir

2 marearse *vpr* (**a**) to get sick/seasick/ airsick/car-sick *o* travel-sick (**b**) *(quedar aturdido)* to get dizzy (**c**) *Euf (emborra-charse)* to get tipsy

mareo *nm* (**a**) *(náusea)* sickness; *(en el mar)* seasickness; *(en un avión)* airsickness; *(en un coche)* car-sickness, travelsickness (**b**) *(aturdimiento)* dizziness, light-headedness

marfil *nm* ivory

margarina *nf* margarine

margarita *nf* daisy

margen 1 *nm* (**a**) border, edge; *Fig* **dejar algn/algo al m.** to leave sb/sth out; *Fig* **mantenerse al m.** not to get involved; **al m. de** leaving aside (**b**) *(del papel)* margin (**c**) *Com* **m. beneficiario** profit margin
2 *nf (de río)* bank

marginación *nf (exclusión)* exclusion

marginado,-a 1 *adj* excluded
2 *nm,f* dropout

marginal *adj* (**a**) marginal (**b**) *Pol* fringe

marginar *vt (de un grupo, sociedad)* to leave out, to exclude

maría *nf Fam* (**a**) *(droga)* marijuana, pot (**b**) *Educ (asignatura fácil)* easy subject (**c**) *(ama de casa)* housewife

marica *nm Fam* queer, *Br* poof, *US* fag

maricón *nm muy Fam* queer, *Br* poof, *US* fag

marido *nm* husband

mariguana, marihuana, marijuana *nf* marijuana

marimacho *nm Fam* mannish woman, butch woman

marimandón,-ona *nm,f Fam* domineering person

marimorena *nf Fam* row, fuss; *Fam* **armar(se) la m.** to kick up a racket

marina *nf* (**a**) *Náut* seamanship (**b**) *Mil* navy; **m. de guerra** navy; **m. mercante** merchant navy (**c**) *Geog (zona costera)* seacoast

marinero,-a 1 *nm* sailor, seaman
2 *adj* seafaring

marino,-a 1 *adj* marine; **brisa marina** sea breeze
2 *nm* sailor

marioneta *nf* marionette, puppet

mariposa *nf* (**a**) *(insecto)* butterfly (**b**) *(lamparilla)* oil lamp (**c**) *(en natación)* butterfly

mariposear *vi Fig* (**a**) *(flirtear)* to flirt (**b**) *(ser inconstante)* to be fickle

mariposón *nm* (**a**) *(galanteador)* flirt (**b**) *Fam (marica)* fairy, pansy

mariquita 1 *nf (insecto) Br* ladybird, *US* ladybug

2 *nm Fam (marica)* queer, *Br* poof, *US* fag

mariscal *nm Mil* marshal; **m. de campo** *Br* field marshal, *US* general of the army

marisco *nm* shellfish; **mariscos** seafood

marisma *nf* marsh

marisquería *nf* seafood restaurant, shellfish bar

marítimo,-a *adj* maritime, sea; **ciudad marítima** coastal town; **paseo m.** promenade

mármol *nm* marble

marmóreo,-a *adj* marble

maroma *nf* (**a**) *Náut* cable (**b**) *(cuerda)* thick rope

marqués *nm* marquis

marquesa *nf* marchioness

marquesina *nf* canopy; **m. (del autobús)** bus shelter

marquetería *nf* marquetry, inlaid work

marrano,-a 1 *adj (sucio)* filthy, dirty
2 *nm,f* (**a**) *Fam (persona)* dirty pig, slob (**b**) *(animal)* pig

marras: •de marras *loc adv* **el individuo de m.** the man in question

marrón 1 *adj (color)* brown
2 *nm* (**a**) *(color)* brown (**b**) *Fam (condena)* sentence

marroquí *adj & nmf* Moroccan

marroquinería *nf* leather goods

Marruecos *n* Morocco

marrullero,-a 1 *adj* cajoling, wheedling
2 *nm,f* cajoler, wheedler

Marte *n* Mars

martes *nm inv* Tuesday; **m. y trece** ≃ Friday the thirteenth

martillero *nm CSur* auctioneer

martillo *nm* hammer

mártir *nmf* martyr

martirio *nm* (**a**) martyrdom (**b**) *Fig (fastidio)* torment

martirizar [40] *vt* (**a**) to martyr (**b**) *Fig (fastidiar)* to torture, to torment

marxista *adj & nmf* Marxist

marzo *nm* March

mas *conj Literario* but

más 1 *adv* (**a**) *(adicional)* more; **no tengo m.** I haven't got any more

(**b**) *(comparativo)* more; **es m. alta/inteligente que yo** she's taller/more intelligent than me; **tengo m. dinero que tú** I've more money than you; **m. gente de la que esperas** more people than you're expecting; **m. de** *(con numerales, cantidad)* more than, over

(**c**) *(superlativo)* most; **es el m. bonito/ caro** it's the prettiest/most expensive

(**d**) *interj* so ..., what a ...; **¡qué casa m. bonita!** what a lovely house! **¡está m.**

guapa! she looks so beautiful!

(**e**) (después de pron interr e indef) else; **¿algo m.?** anything else?; **no, nada m.** no, nothing else; **¿quién m.?** who else?; **nadie/alguien m.** nobody/somebody else

(**f**) **cada día** o **vez m.** more and more; **estar de m.** to be unnecessary; **traje uno de m.** I brought a spare one; **es m.** what's more, furthermore; **lo m. posible** as much as possible; **m. bien** rather; **m. o menos** more or less; **m. aún** even more; **¿qué m. da?** what's the difference?; **todo lo m.** at the most

(**g**) **por m.** (+ adj/adv) + **que** (+ subjunctive) however (much), no matter how (much); **por m. fuerte que sea** however strong he may be; **por m. que grites no te oirá nadie** no matter how much you shout nobody will hear you

2 nm inv **los m.** the majority, most people; **sus m. y sus menos** its pros and cons

3 prep Mat plus; **dos m. dos** two plus o and two

masa nf (**a**) mass (**b**) (de cosas) bulk, volume; **m. salarial** total wage bill (**c**) (gente) mass; **en m.** en masse; **medios de comunicación de masas** mass media (**d**) Culin dough (**e**) Constr mortar (**f**) RP (pastelito) shortcake cookie

masacrar vt to massacre

masacre nf massacre

masaje nm massage; **dar masaje(s) (a)** to massage

masajista nmf (hombre) masseur; (mujer) masseuse

mascar [44] vt & vi to chew, to masticate

máscara nf mask; **m. de gas** gas mask; **traje de m.** fancy dress

> ℓ Observa que la palabra inglesa **mascara** es un falso amigo y no es la traducción de la palabra española **máscara**. En inglés, **mascara** significa "rímel".

mascarilla nf (**a**) mask; **m. de oxígeno** oxygen mask (**b**) Med face mask (**c**) (cosmética) face pack

mascota nf mascot

masculino,-a adj (**a**) Zool & Bot male (**b**) (de hombre) male, manly; **una voz masculina** a manly voice (**c**) (para hombre) men's; **ropa masculina** men's clothes, menswear (**d**) Ling masculine

mascullar vt to mumble

masificación nf overcrowding

masificado,-a adj overcrowded

masilla nf putty

masivo,-a adj massive

masón nm freemason, mason

masonería nf freemasonry, masonry

masoquista 1 adj masochistic

2 nmf masochist

máster nm master's degree

masticar [44] vt to chew

mástil nm (**a**) (asta) mast, pole (**b**) Náut mast (**c**) (de guitarra) neck

mastín nm mastiff

masturbación nf masturbation

masturbar vt, **masturbarse** vpr to masturbate

mata nf (**a**) (matorral) bush, shrub; **m. de pelo** head of hair (**b**) (ramita) sprig

matadero nm slaughterhouse, abattoir

matador nm matador, bullfighter

matadura nf sore

matambre nm Andes, RP = flank steak rolled with boiled egg, olives and red pepper, which is cooked, then sliced and served cold

matamoscas nm inv (pala) fly swat

matanza nf slaughter

matar vt (**a**) to kill; Fam **m. el hambre/el tiempo** to kill one's hunger/the time; Fam **que me maten si ...** I'll be damned if ... (**b**) (cigarro, bebida) to finish off (**c**) (sello) to frank

matasellos nm inv postmark

matasuegras nm inv party blower

mate¹ adj (sin brillo) matt

mate² nm (en ajedrez) mate; **jaque m.** checkmate

mate³ nm (infusión) maté

matemática nf, **matemáticas** nfpl mathematics sing

matemático,-a 1 adj mathematical

2 nm,f mathematician

materia nf (**a**) matter; **m. prima** raw material (**b**) (tema) matter, question; **índice de materias** table of contents (**c**) Educ (asignatura) subject

material 1 adj material, physical; **daños materiales** damage to property

2 nm (**a**) material; **m. escolar/de construcción** teaching/building material o materials (**b**) (equipo) equipment; **m. de oficina** office equipment

materialista adj & nmf materialist

materialmente adv physically

maternal adj maternal, motherly

maternidad nf maternity, motherhood

materno,-a adj maternal; **abuelo m.** maternal grandfather; **lengua materna** native o mother tongue

mates nfpl Fam Br maths sing, US math

matinal adj morning; **televisión m.** breakfast television

matiz nm (**a**) (de color) shade (**b**) (de

palabra) shade of meaning, nuance; **un m. irónico** a touch of irony

matización *nf* **hacer una m.** to add a rider

matizar [40] *vt* (**a**) *Fig (precisar)* to be more precise o explicit about (**b**) *Arte* to blend, to harmonize (**c**) *Fig (palabras, discurso)* to tinge; *(voz)* to vary, to modulate

matón,-ona *nm,f Fam* thug, bully

matorral *nm* brushwood, thicket

matraca *nf (ruido)* rattle; *Fam* **dar la m. a algn** to pester o bother sb

matrero,-a *nm,f Am (bandolero)* bandit, brigand

matriarcado *nm* matriarchy

matrícula *nf* (**a**) registration; **derechos de m.** registration fee; **m. de honor** distinction; **plazo de m.** registration period (**b**) *Aut (número) Br* registration number, *US* license number; *(placa) Br* number plate, *US* license plate

matriculación *nf* registration

matricular *vt*, **matricularse** *vpr* to register

matrimonial *adj* matrimonial; **agencia m.** marriage bureau; **enlace m.** wedding; **vida m.** married life

matrimonio *nm* (**a**) marriage; **m. civil/ religioso** registry office/church wedding; **contraer m.** to marry; **cama de m.** double bed (**b**) *(pareja casada)* married couple; **el m. y los niños** the couple and their children; **el m. Romero** Mr and Mrs Romero, the Romeros

matriz *nf* (**a**) *Anat* womb, uterus (**b**) *Mat* matrix (**c**) *(de documento) (original)* original, master copy (**d**) *Téc* mould (**e**) **casa m.** parent company

matrona *nf* midwife

matutino,-a *adj* morning; **prensa matutina** morning papers

maullar *vi* to miaow

maullido *nm* miaowing, miaow

maxilar *nm* jaw, jawbone

máxima *nf* (**a**) *Met* maximum temperature (**b**) *(aforismo)* maxim

máxime *adv* especially, all the more so

máximo,-a 1 *adj* maximum, highest; **la máxima puntuación** the highest score

2 *nm* maximum; **al m.** to the utmost; **como m.** *(como mucho)* at the most; *(lo más tarde)* at the latest

mayo *nm* May

mayonesa *nf* mayonnaise

mayor 1 *adj* (**a**) *(comparativo) (tamaño)* larger, bigger (**que** than); *(edad)* older, elder; **m. que yo** older than me (**b**) *(superlativo) (tamaño)* largest, biggest;

(edad) oldest, eldest; **la m. parte** the majority; **la m. parte de las veces** most often (**c**) *(adulto)* grown-up; **ser m. de edad** to be of age (**d**) *(maduro)* elderly, mature (**e**) *(principal)* major, main; *Educ* **colegio m.** hall of residence (**f**) *Mús* major (**g**) *Com* **al por m.** wholesale; *Fig (en abundancia)* by the score, galore

2 *nm* (**a**) *Mil* major (**b**) **mayores** *(adultos)* grown-ups, adults

mayordomo *nm* butler

mayoreo *nm Andes, Méx Com* wholesale

mayoría *nf* majority; **en su m.** in the main; **la m. de los niños** most children; **m. absoluta/relativa** absolute/relative majority; **m. de edad** majority

mayorista 1 *adj* wholesale

2 *nmf* wholesaler; **precios de m.** wholesale prices

mayoritario,-a *adj* majority; **un gobierno m.** a majority government

mayúscula *nf* capital letter

mayúsculo,-a *adj* (**a**) *Ling (letra)* capital (**b**) *(error)* very big, enormous

mazacote *nm* (**a**) *Culin* solid mass, stodge (**b**) *(mezcla confusa)* hotchpotch

mazapán *nm* marzipan

mazmorra *nf* dungeon

mazo *nm* mallet

mazorca *nf Agr* cob

me *pron pers* (**a**) *(objeto directo)* me; **no me mires** don't look at me (**b**) *(objeto indirecto)* me, to me, for me; **¿me das un caramelo?** will you give me a sweet?; **me lo dio** he gave it to me; **me es difícil hacerlo** it is difficult for me to do it (**c**) *(pron reflexivo)* myself; **me he cortado** I've cut myself; **me voy/muero** *(no se traduce)* I'm off/dying

meada *nf Fam* piss; **echar una m.** to have a piss

meadero *nm Fam Br* bog, *US* john

meandro *nm* meander

mear *Fam* **1** *vi* to (have a) piss

2 mearse *vpr* to wet oneself; *Fig* **m. de risa** to piss oneself (laughing)

MEC *nm* (*abr* **Ministerio de Educación y Ciencia**) = Spanish ministry of education and science

mecachis *interj Fam* darn it!, damn it!

mecánica *nf* (**a**) *(ciencia)* mechanics *sing* (**b**) *(mecanismo)* mechanism, works

mecánico,-a 1 *adj* mechanical

2 *nm,f* mechanic

mecanismo *nm* mechanism

mecanizar [40] *vt* to mechanize

mecanografía *nf* typewriting, typing

mecanografiar [29] *vt* to type

mecanógrafo,-a *nm,f* typist
mecapal *nm CAm, Méx* = porter's leather harness
mecedora *nf* rocking-chair
mecenas *nmf inv* patron
mecer [49] 1 *vt* to rock
  2 mecerse *vpr* to swing, to rock
mecha *nf* (a) *(de vela)* wick (b) *Mil & Min* fuse; *Fam* **aguantar m.** to grin and bear it (c) *(de pelo)* streak; **hacerse mechas** to have one's hair streaked
mechar *vt (carne)* to lard
mechero *nm* (cigarette) lighter
mechón *nm* (a) *(de pelo)* lock (b) *(de lana)* tuft
medalla 1 *nf* medal
  2 *nmf Dep (campeón)* medallist
medallón *nm* medallion
media *nf* (a) stocking; *Am (calcetín)* sock (b) *(promedio)* average; *Mat* mean; **m. aritmética/geométrica** arithmetic/geometric mean (c) **a medias** *(incompleto)* unfinished; *(entre dos)* half and half; **ir a medias** to go halves

> ✐ Observa que la palabra inglesa **media** es un falso amigo y no es la traducción de la palabra española **media**. En inglés, **media** significa "medios de comunicación".

mediación *nf* mediation, intervention; **por m. de un amigo** through a friend
mediado,-a *adj* half-full, half-empty; **a mediados de mes/semana** about the middle of the month/week
mediador,-a *nm,f* mediator
medialuna *nf* (a) *(símbolo musulmán)* crescent (b) *Am Culin (pasta)* croissant
mediano,-a *adj* (a) middling, average (b) *(tamaño)* medium-sized
medianoche *nf* midnight
mediante *prep* by means of, with the help of, using; **Dios m.** God willing
mediar [43] *vi* (a) *(intervenir)* to mediate, to intervene; **m. en favor de** o **por algn** to intercede on behalf of sb (b) *(tiempo)* to pass; **mediaron tres semanas** three weeks passed
mediático,-a *adj* media
medicación *nf* medication, medical treatment
medicamento *nm* medicine, medicament
medicina *nf* medicine; **estudiante de m.** medical student, medic
médico,-a 1 *nm,f* doctor; **m. de cabecera** family doctor, general practitioner, GP
  2 *adj* medical
medida *nf* (a) measure; **a (la) m.** *(ropa)*

made-to-measure; **a m. que avanzaba** as he advanced; **en gran m.** to a great extent (b) *(dimensión)* measurement (c) *(disposición)* measure; **adoptar** o **tomar medidas** to take steps; **m. represiva** deterrent
medidor *nm Am (contador)* meter
medieval *adj* medieval
medievo *nm* Middle Ages
medio,-a 1 *adj* (a) half; **a m. camino** halfway; **m. kilo** half a kilo; **una hora y media** one and a half hours, an hour and a half (b) *(intermedio)* middle; **a media mañana/tarde** in the middle of the morning/afternoon; **clase media** middle class; **punto m.** middle ground (c) *(normal)* average; **salario m.** average wage
  2 *adv* half; **está m. muerta** she is half dead
  3 *nm* (a) *(mitad)* half (b) *(centro)* middle; **en m. (de)** *(en el centro)* in the middle (of); *(entre dos)* in between (c) **medios de transporte** means of transport; **por m. de ...** by means of ...; **medios económicos** means; **medios de comunicación** (mass) media (d) **m. ambiente** environment (e) *Dep (jugador)* half back
medioambiental *adj* environmental
medioambientalista *nmf* environmentalist
mediocre *adj* mediocre
mediocridad *nf* mediocrity
mediodía *nm* (a) *(hora exacta)* midday, noon (b) *(período aproximado)* early afternoon, lunch-time (c) *(sur)* south
medir [6] 1 *vt* (a) *(distancia, superficie, temperatura)* to measure (b) *(moderar)* to weigh; **mide tus palabras** weigh your words
  2 *vi* to measure, to be; **¿cuánto mides?** how tall are you?; **mide 2 m** he is 2 m tall; **mide 2 m de alto/ancho/largo** it is 2 m high/wide/long
meditar *vt & vi* to meditate, to ponder; **m. sobre algo** to ponder over sth
mediterráneo,-a 1 *adj* Mediterranean
  2 *nm* **el M.** the Mediterranean
medrar *vi* to climb the social ladder
medroso,-a *adj* (a) *(temeroso)* fearful, faint-hearted (b) *(que causa miedo)* frightening
médula *nf* (a) marrow; **m. ósea** bone marrow (b) *Fig (lo más profundo)* marrow, pith; **hasta la m.** to the marrow
medusa *nf* jellyfish
megafonía *nf* public-address system, PA system
megáfono *nm* megaphone
megalito *nm* megalith

megalómano,-a *adj* megalomaniac

mejicano,-a *adj & nm,f* Mexican

Méjico *n* Mexico; **ciudad de M.** Mexico City; **Nuevo M.** New Mexico

mejilla *nf* cheek

mejillón *nm* mussel

mejor 1 *adj* (a) *(comparativo)* better (**que** than); **el m. de los dos** the better of the two; **es m. no decírselo** it's better not to tell her; **es m. que vayas** you'd better go (b) *(superlativo)* best; **el m. de los tres** the best of the three; **tu m. amiga** your best friend; **lo m.** the best thing

   2 *adv* (a) *(comparativo)* better (**que** than); **cada vez m.** better and better; **ella conduce m.** she drives better; **m. dicho** or rather; **¡mucho** *o* **tanto m.!** so much the better! (b) *(superlativo)* best; **es el que m. canta** he is the one who sings the best; **a lo m.** *(quizás)* perhaps; *(ojalá)* hopefully

mejora *nf* improvement

mejorar 1 *vt* to improve; **m. la red vial** to improve the road system; **m. una marca** *o* **un récord** to break a record

   2 *vi* to improve, to get better

   3 mejorarse *vpr* to get better; **¡que te mejores!** get well soon!

mejoría *nf* improvement

melancolía *nf* melancholy

melancólico,-a *adj* melancholic, melancholy

melé *nf Dep* scrum

melena *nf* (head of) hair; *(de león)* mane

Melilla *n* Melilla

melindroso,-a 1 *adj* affected, fussy, finicky

   2 *nm,f* affected *o* finicky person

mella *nf* (a) *(hendedura)* nick, notch; *(en plato, taza etc)* chip (b) *(en dentadura)* gap (c) *Fig* impression; **hacer m. en algn** to make an impression on sb

mellado,-a *adj (sin dientes)* gap-toothed

mellizo,-a *adj & nm,f* twin

melocotón *nm* peach

melodía *nf* melody, tune

melodrama *nm* melodrama

melón *nm* (a) *(fruto)* melon (b) *Fam (tonto)* ninny (c) *muy Fam* **melones** *(tetas)* boobs

melopea *nf Fam* **coger** *o* **agarrar/llevar una m.** to get/be drunk *o* pissed

meloso,-a *adj* sweet, honeyed

membrana *nf* membrane

membresía *nf Am* membership

membrete *nm* letterhead

membrillo *nm* (a) *Bot* quince; *(árbol)* quince tree; *(dulce)* quince preserve *o* jelly (b) *Fam (tonto)* dimwit

memela *nf Méx* = thick corn tortilla

memo,-a *Fam* **1** *adj* silly, stupid

   2 *nm,f* nincompoop, ninny

memorable *adj* memorable

memorándum *nm* (*pl* **memorándums**) memorandum

memoria *nf* (a) memory; **aprender/saber algo de m.** to learn/know sth by heart; **irse de la m.** to slip one's mind (b) *(informe)* report, statement; **m. anual** annual report (c) *(recuerdo)* memory, recollection (d) **memorias** *(biografía)* memoirs

memorístico,-a *adj* acquired by memory

memorizar [40] *vt* to memorize

menaje *nm* furniture and furnishing; **m. de cocina** kitchen equipment *o* utensils

mención *nf* mention; **m. honorífica** honourable mention

mencionar *vt* to mention

mendicidad *nf* begging

mendigar [42] *vt & vi* to beg

mendigo,-a *nm,f* beggar

mendrugo *nm* (a) crust *o* chunk (of stale bread) (b) *(tonto)* dimwit

mene *nm Ven* = deposit of oil at surface level

menear 1 *vt* to shake, to move; *(cola)* to wag, to waggle; *Fam (culo)* to wiggle

   2 menearse *vpr* to move, to shake; *Fam* **una tormenta de no te menees** a hell of a storm; *Vulg* **meneársela** to wank

meneo *nm* shake; *(de cola)* wag, waggle; *(de culo)* wiggle

menester *nm* (a) **es m.** it is necessary (b) **menesteres** *(deberes)* jobs

menestra *nf* vegetable stew

mengano,-a *nm,f Fam* so-and-so, what's-his- *o* her-name

menguante *adj* waning, on the wane; **cuarto m.** last quarter

menguar [45] 1 *vt* (a) to diminish, to reduce (b) *(en labor de punto)* to decrease

   2 *vi* (a) to diminish, to decrease (b) *(la luna)* to wane

menopausia *nf Med* menopause

menor 1 *adj* (a) *(comparativo)* *(de tamaño)* smaller (**que** than); *(de edad)* younger (**que** than); **mal m.** the lesser of two evils; **el m. de los dos** the smaller of the two; **ser m. de edad** to be a minor *o* under age (b) *(superlativo)* *(de tamaño)* smallest; *(de intensidad)* least, slightest; *(de edad)* youngest; **al m. ruido** at the slightest noise; **el m. de los tres** the youngest of the three; **es la m.** she's the youngest child (**c**) *Mús* minor (**d**) *Com* **al por m.** retail

2 *nmf* minor; *Jur* **tribunal de menores** juvenile court

menos 1 *adj* (**a**) *(comparativo)* (con singular) less; (con plural) fewer; **m. dinero/ leche/ tiempo que** less money/milk/time than; **m. libros/pisos que** fewer books/ flats than; *(con cláusula)* **tiene m. años de lo que parece** he's younger than he looks

(**b**) *(superlativo)* **fui el que perdí m. dinero** I lost the least money

2 *adv* (**a**) **m. de** (con singular) less than; (con plural) fewer than, less than; **m. de media hora** less than half an hour

(**b**) *(superlativo)* (con singular) least; (con plural) the fewest; (con cantidad) the least; **el m. inteligente de la clase** the least intelligent boy in the class; **ayer fue cuando vinieron m. personas** yesterday was when the fewest people came

3 *(locuciones)* **a m. que** (+ subjunctive) unless; **al** *o* **por lo m.** at least; **echar a algn de m.** to miss sb; **eso es lo de m.** that's the least of it; **¡m. mal!** just as well!; **nada m. que** no less *o* no fewer than; **ni mucho m.** far from it

4 *prep* (**a**) but, except; **todo m. eso** anything but that

(**b**) *Mat* minus; **tres m. uno** three minus one

menoscabar *vt* (**a**) *(perjudicar)* to damage (**b**) *Fig (desacreditar)* to discredit

menoscabo *nm* harm, damage; **ir en m. de algo** to be to the detriment of sth

menospreciar [43] *vt* to scorn, to disdain

menosprecio *nm* contempt, scorn, disdain

mensáfono *nm* pager

mensaje *nm* message

mensajero,-a *nm,f* messenger, courier

menso,-a *adj Méx Fam* foolish, stupid

menstruación *nf* menstruation

mensual *adj* monthly; **dos visitas mensuales** two visits a month

mensualidad *nf (pago)* monthly payment; *(sueldo)* monthly salary *o* wage

menta *nf* (**a**) *Bot* mint (**b**) *(licor)* crème de menthe

mental *adj* mental

mentalidad *nf* mentality; **de m. abierta/ cerrada** open-/narrow-minded

mentalizar [40] 1 *vt (concienciar)* to make aware

2 mentalizarse *upr* (**a**) *(concienciarse)* to become aware (**b**) *(hacerse a la idea)* to come to terms (**a** with)

mentar [1] *vt* to mention, to name

mente *nf* mind; **se me quedó la m. en blanco** my mind went blank; **m. abierta/ tolerante/cerrada** open/broad/closed mind

mentecato,-a *nm,f* fool, idiot

mentir [5] *vi* to lie, to tell lies

mentira *nf* lie; **aunque parezca m.** strange as it may seem; **parece m.** it is unbelievable

mentiroso,-a 1 *adj* lying

2 *nm,f* liar

mentís *nm* denial

mentón *nm Anat* chin

menú *nm* menu

menudeo *nm Andes, Méx Com* retailing

menudillos *nmpl* giblets

menudo,-a 1 *adj* minute, tiny; *(irónico)* tremendous; **la gente menuda** the little ones; **¡m. lío/susto!** what a mess/fright!

2 *adv* **a m.** often

meñique *adj & nm* (**dedo**) **m.** little finger

meollo *nm* (**a**) *Fig (quid)* essence (**b**) *(miga)* crumb

mercado *nm* market; **M. Común** Common Market; **m. negro** black market; **m. único** single market; **sacar algo al m.** to put sth on the market

mercadotecnia *nf* marketing

mercancía *nf* commodity, goods

mercante *adj* merchant; **barco/marina m.** merchant ship/navy

mercantil *adj* mercantile, commercial

merced *nf Fml* favour, grace; **a m. de** at the mercy of

mercenario,-a *adj & nm,f* mercenary

mercería *nf Br* haberdasher's (shop), *US* notions store

MERCOSUR *nm* (*abr* **Mercado Común del Sur**) = South American economic community consisting of Argentina, Brazil, Paraguay and Uruguay

mercurio *nm* (**a**) *Quím* mercury, quicksilver (**b**) **M.** Mercury

merecer [33] 1 *vt* (**a**) to deserve (**b**) *(uso impers)* **no merece la pena hacerlo** it's not worth while doing it

2 merecerse *upr* to deserve

merecido,-a 1 *adj* deserved; **ella lo tiene m.** *(recompensa)* she deserves it; *(castigo)* it serves her right

2 *nm* just deserts

merendar [1] 1 *vt* to have as an afternoon snack, to have for tea

2 *vi* to have an afternoon snack, to have tea

merendero *nm (establecimiento)* tea

room, snack-bar; *(en el campo)* picnic spot
merengue *nm* Culin meringue
merezco *indic pres de* **merecer**
meridiano *nm* meridian
meridional 1 *adj* southern
   2 *nmf* southerner
merienda *nf* afternoon snack, tea
mérito *nm* merit, worth; **hacer méritos para algo** to strive to deserve sth
merluza *nf (pez)* hake
merma *nf* decrease, reduction
mermar 1 *vt* to cause to decrease *o* diminish
   2 *vi* to decrease, to diminish
   3 *mermarse* *vpr* to decrease, to diminish
mermelada *nf* (a) jam; **m. de fresa** strawberry jam (b) *(de agrios)* marmalade; **m. de naranja** orange marmalade
mero,-a *adj* mere, pure; **por el m. hecho de** through the mere fact of
merodear *vi* to prowl
mes *nm* (a) monthly; **el m. pasado/que viene** last/next month (b) *(cobro)* monthly salary *o* wages; *(pago)* monthly payment (c) *Fam (menstruación)* period
mesa *nf* (a) table; **poner/recoger la m.** to set/clear the table; *(de despacho etc)* desk; **m. redonda** round table (b) *(junta directiva)* board, executive; **el presidente de la m.** the chairman; **m. electoral** electoral college
mesada *nf* (a) *Am (dinero)* monthly payment (b) *RP (para adolescentes)* (monthly) pocket money, *US* (monthly) allowance (c) *RP (encimera)* worktop
mesero,-a *nm,f* CAm, Col, Méx waiter, *f* waitress
meseta *nf* plateau, tableland, meseta; **la M.** the plateau of Castile
mesilla *nf* **m. de noche** bedside table
mesón *nm* = old-style tavern
mesonero,-a *nm,f* (a) *(en mesón)* innkeeper (b) *Chile, Ven (camarero)* waiter, *f* waitress
mestizo,-a *adj & nm,f* half-breed, half-caste, mestizo
mesura *nf* Fml moderation, restraint

♪ Observa que la palabra inglesa **measure** es un falso amigo y no es la traducción de la palabra española **mesura**. En inglés, **measure** significa "medida".

meta *nf* (a) *(objetivo)* goal, aim, objective (b) *(de carrera)* finish, finishing line (c) *Ftb (portería)* goal
metafísica *nf* metaphysics *sing*
metáfora *nf* metaphor

metal *nm* (a) metal; **metales preciosos** precious metals (b) *(timbre de la voz)* timbre (c) *Mús* brass
metálico,-a 1 *adj* metallic
   2 *nm* cash; **pagar en m.** to pay (in) cash
metalizado,-a *adj* metallic
metalúrgico,-a 1 *adj* metallurgical
   2 *nm,f* metallurgist
metate *nm* Guat, Méx grinding stone
metedura *nf* Fam **m. de pata** blunder
meteorito *nm* meteorite
meteorología *nf* meteorology
meteorológico,-a *adj* meteorological; **parte m.** weather report *o* forecast
meter 1 *vt* (a) *(poner)* to put (**en** in); *Fig* **m. las narices en algo** to poke one's nose into sth (b) *(comprometer)* to involve (**en** in), to get mixed up (**en** in) (c) *Fam Fig (dar)* to give; **m. un rollo** to go on and on; **m. prisa a algn** to hurry sb up (d) *(hacer)* to make; **m. ruido** to make a noise
   2 meterse *vpr* (a) *(entrar)* to go *o* come in, to get into (b) *(estar)* to be; **¿dónde te habías metido?** where have you been (all this time)? (c) *(entrometerse)* to meddle (d) **m. con algn** *(en broma)* to get at sb
meterete *nmf* RP Fam meddler
metete *nmf* Andes, CAm Fam meddler, busybody
metiche *nmf* Méx, Ven Fam meddler
meticuloso,-a *adj* meticulous
metido,-a *adj* Fam **estar muy m. en algo** to be deeply involved in sth; **m. en años** getting on (in years)
metódico,-a *adj* methodical
método *nm* (a) method (b) *Educ* course
metodología *nf* methodology
metomentodo *nmf inv* Fam busybody
metralleta *nf* submachine-gun
métrico,-a *adj* metric; **sistema m.** metric system
metro *nm* (a) *(medida)* metre (b) *(tren)* Br underground, Br tube, US subway
metrópoli *nf* metropolis
metropolitano,-a 1 *adj* metropolitan
   2 *nm Fml Br* underground, *Br* tube, *US* subway
mexicano,-a *adj & nm,f* Mexican
México *n* Mexico
mezcla *nf* (a) *(acción)* mixing, blending; *Rad & Cin* mixing (b) *(producto)* mixture, blend
mezclar 1 *vt* (a) *(dos o más cosas)* to mix, to blend (b) *(desordenar)* to mix up (c) *(involucrar)* to involve, to mix up
   2 mezclarse *vpr* (a) *(cosas)* to get mixed up; *(gente)* to mingle (b) *(relacionarse)* to get involved (**con** with)

mezcolanza *nf Fml* strange mixture, hotch-potch

mezquino,-a *adj* (a) *(persona)* mean, stingy (b) *(sueldo)* miserable

mezquita *nf* mosque

m/g *(abr* miligramo*)* mg

mi¹ *adj* my; **mi casa/trabajo** my house/ job; **mis cosas/libros** my things/books

mi² *nm Mús* E; **mi menor** E minor

mí *pron pers* me; **a mí me dio tres** he gave me three; **compra otro para mí** buy one for me too; **por mí mismo** just by myself

mía *adj & pron pos f ver* **mío**

miaja *nf* crumb; *Fig* bit

miche *nm Ven (aguardiente)* = cane spirit flavoured with herbs and spices

michelín *nm Fam* spare tyre

mico *nm* (a) *Zool* long-tailed monkey (b) *Fam (pequeñajo)* little kid

micra *nf (medida)* micron

micro 1 *nm Fam* mike, microphone
   2 *nm o nf Arg, Chile (microbús)* minibus

microbio *nm* microbe

microbús *nm* (a) *(autobús)* minibus (b) *Méx (taxi)* (collective) taxi

microchip *nm (pl* **microchips***) Informát* microchip

microficha *nf* microfiche

micrófono *nm* microphone

microonda *nf* **un (horno) microondas** a microwave (oven)

microscopio *nm* microscope

miedica *nmf Fam* scaredy-cat

miedo *nm (pavor)* fear; *(temor)* apprehension; **una película de m.** a horror film; **tener m. de algn/algo** to be afraid of sb/ sth; *Fam* **lo pasamos de m.** we had a fantastic time; **un calor de m.** sizzling heat

miedoso,-a *adj* fearful

miel *nf* honey; **luna de m.** honeymoon

miembro *nm* (a) *(socio)* member; **estado m.** member state (b) *Anat* limb; **m. viril** penis

mientras 1 *conj* (a) *(al mismo tiempo que)* while (b) *(durante el tiempo que)* when, while; **m. viví en Barcelona** when I lived in Barcelona (c) **m. que** *(por el contrario)* whereas (d) *Fam (cuanto más)* **m. más/ menos ...** the more/less ...
   2 *adv* **m. (tanto)** meanwhile, in the meantime

miércoles *nm inv* Wednesday; **M. de Ceniza** Ash Wednesday

mierda *nf Vulg* (a) shit; **ese libro es una m.** that book is crap; **¡vete a la m.!** piss off! (b) *Fig (porquería)* dirt, filth (c) *(borrachera)* bender

miga *nf (de pan etc)* crumb; *Fig* **hacer buenas migas con algn** to get on well with sb

migaja *nf* (a) *(de pan)* crumb (b) *Fig* bit, scrap (c) **migajas** *(del pan)* crumbs; *Fig* leftovers

migra *nf Méx Fam Pey* = US police border patrol

migraña *nf Med* migraine

mil *adj & nm* thousand; **m. pesetas** a *o* one thousand pesetas

milagro *nm* miracle

milagroso,-a *adj* miraculous

milanesa *nf (de ternera)* Wiener schnitzel, breaded veal escalope

milano *nm Orn* kite; **m. real** red kite

milenario,-a 1 *adj* millenarian, millennial
   2 *nm* millennium

milenio *nm* millennium

milésimo,-a *adj & nm,f* thousandth

mili *nf Fam* military *o* national service; **hacer la m.** to do one's military service

milicia *nf (ejército)* militia; *(servicio militar)* military service

milico *nm Andes, RP Fam Pey (militar)* soldier; **los milicos tomaron el poder** the military took power

milímetro *nm* millimetre

militar 1 *adj* military
   2 *nm* military man, soldier
   3 *vi Pol (en un partido)* to be a member

milla *nf* mile

millar *nm* thousand

millón *nm* million

millonario,-a *adj & nm,f* millionaire

milpa *nf CAm, Méx* cornfield

mimar *vt* to spoil, to pamper

> 🖉 Observa que el verbo inglés **to mime** es un falso amigo y no es la traducción del verbo español **mimar**. En inglés, **to mime** significa "representar con gestos".

---

mimbre *nm* wicker

mimetismo *nm* mimicry

mímica *nf* mimicry

mimo *nm* (a) *(delicadeza)* care (b) *Fig (zalamería)* pampering (c) *Teatro (actor)* mime

mina *nf* (a) mine; **ingeniero de minas** mining engineer (b) *(explosivo)* mine; **campo de minas** minefield (c) *(de lápiz)* lead; **lápiz de m.** propelling pencil (d) *Fig (ganga)* gold mine

minar *vt* (a) *Mil & Min* to mine (b) *Fig (desgastar)* to undermine

mineral 1 *adj* mineral
   2 *nm* ore

minería *nf* (a) *Min* mining (b) *Ind* mining industry

minero,-a 1 *nm,f* miner
  2 *adj* mining

miniatura *nf* miniature

minifalda *nf* miniskirt

minifundio *nm* smallholding

mínima *nf* minimum temperature

minimizar *vt* to minimize

mínimo,-a 1 *adj* (a) *(muy pequeño)* minute, tiny (b) *Mat & Téc* minimum, lowest; **m. común múltiplo** lowest common denominator
  2 *nm* minimum; **como m.** at least; **ni lo más m.** not in the least

minipimer® *nm o nf* liquidizer, blender

ministerio *nm* (a) *Pol Br* ministry, *US* department (b) *Rel* ministry

ministro,-a *nm,f* (a) *Pol* minister; **primer m.** Prime Minister (b) *Rel* minister

minoría *nf* minority; *Jur* **m. de edad** minority

minoritario,-a *adj* minority

minucioso,-a *adj* (a) *(persona)* meticulous (b) *(informe, trabajo etc)* minute, detailed

minúsculo,-a *adj* minuscule, minute; **letra minúscula** lower-case *o* small letter

minusválido,-a 1 *adj* handicapped, disabled
  2 *nm,f* handicapped person, disabled person

minuta *nf* (a) *(cuenta)* lawyer's bill (b) *(menú)* menu (c) *RP (comida)* one-plate meal

minutero *nm* minute hand

minuto *nm* minute

mío,-a 1 *adj pos* of mine; **un amigo m.** a friend of mine; **no es asunto m.** it is none of my business
  2 *pron pos* mine; **ese libro es m.** that book is mine; **lo m. es el tenis** tennis is my strong point; *Fam* **los míos** my people *o* folks

miope *nmf* myopic *o* short-sighted person

miopía *nf* myopia, short-sightedness

mira *nf* (a) *Téc* sight (b) *Fig (objetivo)* aim, target; **con miras a** with a view to; **amplitud de miras** broad-mindedness

mirada *nf* look; **lanzar** *o* **echar una m. a** to glance at; **levantar la m.** to raise one's eyes; **m. fija** stare

mirador *nm* (a) *(lugar con vista)* viewpoint (b) *(balcón)* bay window, windowed balcony

mirar 1 *vt* (a) to look at (b) *(observar)* to watch (c) **m. por algn/algo** *(cuidar)* to look after sb/sth (d) *(procurar)* to see;

mira que no le pase nada see that nothing happens to him
  2 *vi (dar a)* to look, to face; **la casa mira al sur** the house faces south

mirilla *nf* spyhole, peephole

mirlo *nm* blackbird

misa *nf* mass

misántropo,-a 1 *adj* misanthropic
  2 *nm,f* misanthrope, misanthropist

miscelánea *nf Méx (tienda)* = small general store

miserable 1 *adj* (a) *(mezquino) (persona)* despicable; *(sueldo etc)* miserable (b) *(pobre)* wretched, poor; **una vida m.** a wretched life
  2 *nmf* (a) *(mezquino)* miser (b) *(canalla)* wretch

miseria *nf* (a) *(pobreza extrema)* extreme poverty (b) *(insignificancia)* pittance; **ganar una m.** to earn next to nothing (c) *(tacañería)* miserliness, meanness

misericordia *nf* mercy, compassion

mísero,-a *adj* miserable, wretched

misil *nm* missile; **m. tierra-aire** surface-to-air missile

misión *nf* mission; **m. cumplida** mission accomplished

misionero,-a *nm,f* missionary

mismísimo,-a *adj superl Fam* (a) *(preciso)* very; **en el m. centro** right in the centre (b) *(en persona)* in person

mismo,-a 1 *adj* (a) same (b) *(uso enfático)* **yo m.** I myself; **aquí m.** right here
  2 *pron* same; **es el m. de ayer** it's the same one as yesterday; **estamos en las mismas** we're back to square one; **lo m.** the same (thing); **dar** *o* **ser lo m.** to make no difference; **por eso m.** that is why; **por uno** *o* **sí m.** by oneself
  3 *adv* (a) *(por ejemplo)* for instance; **que venga algn, Juan m.** ask one of them to come, Juan, for instance (b) **así m.** likewise

misógino,-a 1 *adj* misogynous
  2 *nm,f* misogynist

miss *nf* beauty queen

míster *nm Ftb* coach, trainer

misterio *nm* mystery

misterioso,-a *adj* mysterious

mitad *nf* (a) half; **a m. de camino** halfway there; **a m. de precio** half-price (b) *(centro)* middle; **en la m. del primer acto** halfway through the first act; *Fam* **me parte por la m.** that really screws things up for me

mítico,-a *adj* mythical

mitigar [42] *vt Fml* to mitigate, to palliate; *(luz)* to reduce

mitin *nm Pol* meeting, rally

mito *nm* myth

mitología *nf* mythology

mitote *nm Méx Fam (alboroto)* racket

mixto,-a *adj* mixed

moai *nm* = statue of giant head found on Easter Island

mobiliario *nm* furniture

moca *nm* mocha

mochila *nf* rucksack, backpack

mochuelo *nm Zool* little owl

moción *nf* motion; **m. de censura** vote of censure

moco *nm* snot; **sonarse los mocos** to blow one's nose

mocoso,-a *nm,f Fam* brat

moda *nf* (a) fashion; **a la m., de m.** in fashion; **pasado de m.** old-fashioned (b) *(furor pasajero)* craze

modales *nmpl* manners

modalidad *nf* form, category; *Com* **m. de pago** method of payment; *Dep* **m. deportiva** sport

modelar *vt* to model, to shape

modélico,-a *adj* model

modelo 1 *adj inv & nm* model

   2 *nmf* (fashion) model; **desfile de modelos** fashion show

módem *nm Informát* modem; **m. fax** fax modem

moderación *nf* moderation

moderado,-a *adj* moderate; **un m. aumento de temperatura** a mild increase in temperature

moderador,-a *nm,f* chairperson; *(hombre)* chairman; *(mujer)* chairwoman

moderar 1 *vt* (a) to moderate; *(velocidad)* to reduce (b) *(debate)* to chair

   2 moderarse *vpr* to be moderate

modernizar [40] *vt*, **modernizarse** *vpr* to modernize

moderno,-a *adj* modern

modestia *nf* modesty; **m. aparte** without wishing to be immodest

modesto,-a *adj* modest

módico,-a *adj* moderate; **una módica suma** a modest o small sum

modificar [44] *vt* to modify

modismo *nm* idiom

modisto,-a *nm,f* (a) *(diseñador)* fashion designer (b) *(sastre) (hombre)* couturier; *(mujer)* couturière

modo *nm* (a) *(manera)* way, manner; **m. de empleo** instructions for use; = **manera** (b) **modos** manners (c) *Ling* mood

modorra *nf (somnolencia)* drowsiness

modoso,-a *adj* (a) *(educado)* well-behaved (b) *(recatado)* modest

modulación *nf* modulation

modular *vt* to modulate

módulo *nm* module

mofa *nf* mockery; **en tono de m.** in a gibing tone

mofarse *vpr* to laugh (**de** at), to make fun (**de** of)

moflete *nm* chubby cheek

mogollón *nm Fam* (a) **m. de** loads of; **me gusta un m.** I like it loads (**b**) *(confusión)* commotion; *(ruido)* racket

moho *nm* (a) *Bot* mould (b) *(de metales)* rust

mohoso,-a *adj* (a) mouldy (b) *(oxidado)* rusty

mojado,-a *adj (empapado)* wet; *(húmedo)* damp

mojar 1 *vt* (a) to wet; *(humedecer)* to damp; **m. pan en la leche** to dip o dunk bread in one's milk (b) *muy Fam* **mojarla** to have it off

   2 mojarse *vpr* to get wet

mojón *nm* (a) **m. kilométrico** ≃ milestone (b) *muy Fam (mierda)* shit

moka *nm* mocha

molar 1 *vi Fam* **me mola cantidad** I really love it, it's brilliant

   2 *adj & nm Anat* molar

molcajete *nm Méx* mortar

molde *nm* mould; **letras de m.** printed letters; **pan de m.** ≃ sliced bread

moldeador *nm (del pelo)* wave

moldear *vt* to mould

mole 1 *nf* mass, bulk

   2 *nm Méx* (a) *(salsa)* = thick, cooked chilli sauce (b) *(guiso)* = dish served in "mole" sauce

molécula *nf* molecule

moler [4] *vt* (a) *(triturar)* to grind (**b**) **m. a algn a golpes** to beat sb up

molestar 1 *vt* (a) *(incomodar)* to disturb, to bother (b) *Fml* to bother; **¿le molestaría esperar fuera?** would you mind waiting outside? (**c**) *(causar malestar a)* to hurt

   2 molestarse *vpr* (a) *(tomarse la molestia)* to bother (b) *(ofenderse)* to take offence, to get upset

molestia *nf* (a) bother; **no es ninguna m.** it is no trouble at all; **perdone las molestias** forgive the inconvenience (b) *Med (dolor)* trouble, slight pain

molesto,-a *adj* (a) *(irritante)* annoying, upsetting (b) **estar m. con algn** *(enfadado)* to be annoyed o upset with sb

molinillo *nm* grinder

molino *nm* mill; **m. de agua** watermill; **m. de viento** windmill

mollera *nf Fam* brains; **duro de m.** *(tonto)* dense, thick; *(testarudo)* pigheaded

molón,-ona *adj Fam* flashy, showy

momentáneo,-a *adj* momentary

momento *nm* (a) *(instante)* moment; **al m.** at once; **por momentos** by the minute (b) *(periodo)* time; **de m.** for the time being; **en cualquier m.** at any time

momia *nf* mummy

mona *nf Fam* **coger una m.** to get drunk; **dormir la m.** to sleep it off

Mónaco *n* Monaco

monada *nf Fam* **¡qué m.!** how cute!

monaguillo *nm Rel* altar boy

monarca *nmf* monarch

monarquía *nf* monarchy

monasterio *nm Rel* monastery

monda *nf* (a) *(piel)* peel, skin (b) *Fam* **ser la m.** *(divertido)* to be a scream

mondadientes *nm inv* toothpick

mondar 1 *vt* to peel
2 mondarse *vpr Fam* **m. (de risa)** to laugh one's head off

moneda *nf* (a) *(pieza)* coin; **m. suelta** small change; **acuñar m.** to mint money (b) *Fin* currency; **m. única** single currency

monedero *nm* purse

monería *nf Fam* = **monada**

monetario,-a *adj* monetary

mongol 1 *adj* Mongolian
2 *nmf (persona)* Mongolian
3 *nm (idioma)* Mongolian

mongólico,-a *Med* **1** *adj* Down's syndrome
2 *nm,f* **ser m.** to have Down's syndrome

monigote *nm* (a) *Pey (persona)* wimp (b) *(dibujo)* rough drawing o sketch (of a person)

monitor,-a *nm,f* monitor; *(profesor)* instructor

monja *nf* nun

monje *nm* monk

mono,-a 1 *nm* (a) *(animal)* monkey (b) *(prenda) (de trabajo)* boiler suit, overalls; *(de vestir)* catsuit; *Ven (de deporte)* track o jogging suit (c) *Fam (droga)* cold turkey
2 *adj Fam (bonito)* pretty, cute

monobloque *nm Arg* tower block

monográfico,-a 1 *adj* monographic
2 *nm* monograph

monólogo *nm* monologue

monopolio *nm* monopoly

monopolizar [40] *vt* to monopolize

monótono,-a *adj* monotonous

monserga *nf Fam* drag

monstruo *nm* (a) monster (b) *(genio)* genius

monstruoso,-a *adj* (a) *(repugnante)* monstrous (b) *(enorme)* massive, huge

monta *nf Fig* **de poca m.** of little importance

montacargas *nm inv Br* service lift, *US* freight elevator

montado,-a 1 *adj (nata)* whipped
2 *nm* sandwich

montador,-a *nm,f* (a) *(operario)* fitter (b) *Cin & TV* film editor (c) *Teatro* producer

montaje *nm* (a) *Téc (instalación)* fitting; *(ensamblaje)* assembling; **cadena de m.** assembly line (b) *Cin* editing and mounting (c) *Teatro* staging (d) *Fot* montage (e) *Fam (farsa)* farce

montante *nm* (a) *Fin* amount (b) *(de puerta)* post

montaña *nf* mountain; **m. rusa** big dipper

montañismo *nm* mountaineering

montañoso,-a *adj* mountainous

montar 1 *vi* (a) *(subirse)* to get in; *(en bici, a caballo)* to ride (b) *Fin (ascender)* **m. a** to amount to, to come to
2 *vt* (a) *(colocar)* to put on (b) *(máquina etc)* to assemble, *(negocio)* to set up, to start (c) *Culin* to whip (d) *Cin & Fot (película)* to edit, to mount; *(fotografía)* to mount (e) *Teatro (obra)* to stage, to mount (f) *Zool (cubrir)* to mount
3 montarse *vpr* (a) *(subirse)* to get on; *(en coche)* to get in (en to) (b) *Fam (armarse)* to break out; *Fam* **montárselo bien** to have things (nicely) worked out o set up

monte *nm* (a) *(montaña)* mountain; *(con nombre propio)* mount; **de m.** wild (b) **el m.** *(zona)* the hills

montés *adj (animal)* wild

monto *nm* total

montón *nm* heap, pile; **un m. de** a load of; *Fam* **me gusta un m.** I really love it; *Fam* **del m.** run-of-the-mill, nothing special

montura *nf* (a) *(cabalgadura)* mount (b) *(de gafas)* frame

monumento *nm* monument

monzón *nm* monsoon

moño *nm* (a) *(de pelo)* bun (b) *Am (lazo)* bow

MOPU *nm (abr* **Ministerio de Obras Públicas y Urbanismo)** = Spanish ministry of public works and town planning

moquear *vi* to have a runny nose

moqueta *nf* fitted carpet

mora *nf (zarzamora)* blackberry

morado,-a 1 *adj* purple; *Fam* **pasarlas**

moradas to have a tough time; **ponerse m.** to stuff oneself

  2 *nm* purple

moral 1 *adj* moral

  2 *nf* (a) *(ética)* morals (b) *(ánimo)* morale, spirits; **levantar la m. a algn** to raise sb's spirits

moraleja *nf* moral

moralista 1 *adj* moralistic

  2 *nmf* moralist

moratoria *nf* moratorium

morbo *nm Fam (interés malsano)* morbid curiosity

morboso,-a *adj (malsano)* morbid

morcilla *nf Br* black pudding, *US* blood sausage; *Fam* **que le den m.** he can drop dead for all I care

mordaz *adj* biting

mordaza *nf* gag

mordedura *nf* bite

morder [4] *vt* to bite; **me ha mordido** it has bitten me; *Fig* **m. el anzuelo** to take the bait

mordida *nf CAm, Méx (soborno)* bribe

mordisco *nm* bite

mordisquear *vt* to nibble (at)

moreno,-a 1 *adj* (a) *(pelo)* dark-haired; *(piel)* dark-skinned (b) *(bronceado)* tanned; **ponerse m.** to get a suntan; **pan/ azúcar m.** brown bread/sugar

  2 *nm,f (persona) (de pelo)* dark-haired person; *(de piel)* dark-skinned person

morera *nf Bot* white mulberry

moretón *nm Fam* bruise

morfina *nf* morphine

morfinómano,-a 1 *nm,f* morphine addict

  2 *adj* addicted to morphine

morgue *nf Am* morgue

moribundo,-a *adj & nm,f* moribund

morir [7] **1** *vi* to die; **m. de frío/hambre/ cáncer** to die of cold/hunger/cancer; **m. de amor** *o* **pena** to die from a broken heart

  2 morirse *vpr* to die; **m. de hambre** to starve to death; *Fig* **m.** to be starving; **m. de aburrimiento** to be bored to death; **m. de ganas (de hacer algo)** to be dying (to do sth); **m. de risa** to die laughing

mormón,-ona *adj & nm,f* Mormon

moro,-a 1 *nm,f* (a) *Hist* Moor; *Fam* **no hay moros en la costa** the coast is clear (b) *Pey (musulmán)* Muslim; *(árabe)* Arab

morocho,-a 1 *adj* (a) *Andes, RP (moreno)* dark-haired (b) *Ven (gemelo)* twin

  2 *nm,f* (a) *Andes, RP (moreno)* dark-haired person (b) *Ven (gemelo)* twin

moronga *nf CAm, Méx Br* black pudding, *US* blood sausage

moroso,-a *nm,f* bad debtor

> 📙 Observa que la palabra inglesa **morose** es un falso amigo y no es la traducción de la palabra española **moroso**. En inglés, **morose** significa "hosco, huraño".

morral *nm* (a) *(para pienso)* nosebag (b) *Mil* haversack; *(de cazador)* game bag

moralla *nf* (a) *(cosas sin valor)* rubbish, junk (b) *(chusma)* scum

morrear *vt*, **morrearse** *vpr Fam* to snog

morreo *nm Fam* snog

morro *nm* (a) *(de animal) (hocico)* snout (b) *Fam (de persona)* mouth, (thick) lips; **caerse de m.** to fall flat on one's face; **por los morros** without so much as a by-your-leave; *Fam* **¡vaya m.!** what a cheek! (c) *(de coche)* nose

morrón *adj* **pimiento m.** (fleshy) red pepper

morsa *nf* walrus

morse *nm* Morse

mortadela *nf* mortadella

mortaja *nf* shroud

mortal 1 *adj* (a) mortal (b) *(mortífero)* fatal; **un accidente m.** a fatal accident

  2 *nmf* mortal

mortalidad *nf* mortality; **índice de m.** death rate

mortandad *nf* death toll

mortecino,-a *adj* colourless

mortero *nm Culin & Mil* mortar

mortífero,-a *adj* deadly, lethal

mortificar [44] *vt* to mortify

mortuorio,-a *adj* death; **lecho m.** death-bed

moruno,-a *adj* Moorish; *Culin* **pincho m.** ≃ kebab

mosaico *nm* mosaic

mosca *nf* fly; **peso m.** flyweight; *Fam* **estar m.** *(suspicaz)* to be suspicious; *(borracho)* to be pissed; *Fam* **por si las moscas** just in case; *Fam* **¿qué m. te ha picado?** what's biting you?

moscada *adj* **nuez m.** nutmeg

moscardón *nm* (a) *(insecto)* blowfly (b) *Fam (pesado)* pest

moscovita *adj & nmf* Muscovite

Moscú *n* Moscow

mosquearse *vpr Fam* (a) *(enfadarse)* to get cross (b) *(sospechar)* to smell a rat

mosquetero *nm Hist* musketeer

mosquitero *nm (red)* mosquito net

mosquito *nm* mosquito

mostaza *nf Bot & Culin* mustard

mosto *nm (bebida)* grape juice; *(del vino)* must

mostrador *nm* (a) *(de tienda)* counter (b) *(de bar)* bar

mostrar 1 *vt* to show; **muéstramelo** show it to me

2 mostrarse *vpr* to be; **se mostró muy comprensiva** she was very understanding

mostrenco,-a 1 *nm,f* (a) *(ignorante)* blockhead (b) *(gordo)* very fat person

2 *adj (sin dueño)* ownerless; **bienes mostrencos** ownerless property

mota *nf* speck

mote[1] *nm (apodo)* nickname; **poner m. a algn** to give sb a nickname

mote[2] *nm Andes* stewed maize o *US* corn

moteado,-a *adj* dotted

motín *nm (amotinamiento)* mutiny; *(disturbio)* riot

motivación *nf* motivation

motivar *vt* (a) *(causar)* to cause, to give rise to (b) *(inducir)* to motivate

motivo *nm* (a) *(causa)* reason; *(usu pl)* grounds; **con este** o **tal m.** for this reason; **con m. de** on the occasion of; **sin m.** for no reason at all; **bajo ningún m.** under no circumstances (b) *Arte & Mús* motif, leitmotiv

moto *nf Aut* motorbike; **m. náutica** o **acuática** jet ski

motocicleta *nf* motorbike

motociclismo *nm* motorcycling

motociclista *nmf* motorcyclist

motocross *nm* motocross

motoneta *nf Am* (motor) scooter

motonetista *nmf Am* scooter rider

motor,-a 1 *nm (grande)* engine; *(pequeño)* motor; **m. de reacción** jet engine; **m. de explosión** internal combustion engine; **m. eléctrico** electric motor; *Informát* **m. de busca** search engine

2 *adj Téc* motive

motora *nf* motorboat

motorista *nmf* motorcyclist

motorizar [40] 1 *vt* to motorize

2 motorizarse *vpr Fam* to get oneself a car o motorbike

motosierra *nf* power saw

motriz *adj* **fuerza m.** motive power

movedizo,-a *adj* **arenas movedizas** quicksand

mover [4] 1 *vt* (a) to move; **m. algo de su sitio** to move sth out of its place (b) *(hacer funcionar)* to drive; **el motor mueve el coche** the engine drives the car

2 moverse *vpr* (a) to move (b) *Fam (gestionar)* to do everything possible (c) *(darse prisa)* to hurry up; **¡muévete!** get a move on!

movida *nf Fam* **hay mucha m.** there's a lot going on

movido,-a *adj* (a) *Fot* blurred (b) *(ocupado)* busy

móvil 1 *adj* mobile; **teléfono m.** mobile phone; *TV & Rad* **unidad m.** outside broadcast unit

2 *nm* (a) *(de delito)* motive (b) *(teléfono)* mobile

movilización *nf* mobilization

movilizar [40] *vt* to mobilize

movimiento *nm* (a) *(gen)* movement; *Fís & Téc* motion; **(poner algo) en m.** (to set sth) in motion; **m. sísmico** earth tremor (b) *(actividad)* activity (c) *Com & Fin (entradas y salidas)* operations (d) *Hist* **el M.** the Falangist Movement

moviola *nf Cin & TV* (a) *(cámara)* editing projector (b) *(repetición)* action replay

moza *nf* lass, young girl

mozo,-a *nm,f* (a) *(niño)* young boy, young lad; *(niña)* young girl (b) *(de estación)* porter (c) *Mil* conscript (d) *Perú, RP (camarero)* waiter, *f* waitress

mucamo,-a *nm,f Andes, RP (en hotel)* chamberperson, *f* chambermaid

muchacha *nf* girl

muchachada *nf Am* group of youngsters

muchacho *nm* boy

muchedumbre *nf (de gente)* crowd

mucho,-a 1 *adj* (a) *sing (usu en frases afirmativas)* a lot of, lots of; *(usu en frases negativas)* much; **m. tiempo** a long time; **tengo m. sueño/mucha sed** I am very sleepy/thirsty; **hay m. tonto suelto** there are lots of idiots around; **¿bebes m. café? – no, no m.** do you drink a lot of coffee? – no, not much

(b) *(demasiado)* **es m. coche para mí** this car is a bit too much for me

(c) **muchos,-as** *(usu en frases afirmativas)* a lot of, lots of; *(usu en frases neg)* many; **tiene muchos años** he is very old

2 *pron* (a) a lot, a great deal; **¿cuánta leche queda? – mucha** how much milk is there left? – a lot

(b) **muchos,-as** a lot, lots, many; **¿cuántos libros tienes? – muchos** how many books have you got? – lots o a lot; **muchos creemos que ...** many of us believe that ...

3 *adv* (a) a lot, very much; **lo siento m.** I'm very sorry; **como m.** at the most; **con m.** by far; **m. antes/después** long before/after; **¡ni m. menos!** no way!; **por m. (que)** *(+ subjunctive)* however much

(b) *(tiempo)* **hace m. que no viene por aquí** he has not been to see us for a long time (**c**) *(a menudo)* often; **vamos m. al cine** we go to the cinema quite often

muda *nf (de ropa)* change of clothes

mudanza *nf* move; **estar de m.** to be moving; **camión de m.** removal van

mudar **1** *vt* (**a**) *(ropa)* to change (**b**) *(plumas, pelo)* to moult; *(piel)* to shed, to slough

2 mudarse *vpr* **m. de casa/ropa** to move house/to change one's clothes

mudo,-a **1** *adj* (**a**) *(que no habla)* dumb; **cine m.** silent films (**b**) *Fig (callado)* speechless

2 *nm,f* mute

mueble **1** *nm* piece of furniture; **muebles** furniture; **con/sin muebles** furnished/unfurnished; **m. bar** cocktail cabinet

2 *adj* movable

mueca *nf* (**a**) *(de burla)* mocking face; **hacer muecas** to pull faces (**b**) *(de dolor, asco)* grimace

muela *nf* (**a**) *Anat* molar; **dolor de muelas** toothache; **m. del juicio** wisdom tooth (**b**) *Téc (de molino)* millstone

muelle¹ *nm* spring

muelle² *nm Náut* dock

muermo *nm Fam (tedio)* boredom; *(rollo)* drag

muerte *nf* death; **m. natural** natural death; **dar m. a algn** to kill sb; **odiar a algn a m.** to loathe sb; *Fam* **de mala m.** lousy, rotten; *Fam* **un susto de m.** the fright of one's life

muerto,-a **1** *adj* dead; **caer m.** to drop dead; **m. de hambre** starving; **m. de frío** frozen to death; **m. de miedo** scared stiff; **m. de risa** laughing one's head off; **horas muertas** spare time; *Aut* **(en) punto m.** (in) neutral

2 *nm,f* (**a**) *(difunto)* dead person; **hacerse el m.** to pretend to be dead; *Fam* **cargar con el m.** to do the dirty work (**b**) *(víctima)* fatality; **hubo dos muertos** two (people) died

muesca *nf* notch

muestra *nf* (**a**) *(espécimen)* sample, specimen (**b**) *(modelo a copiar)* model (**c**) *(prueba, señal)* sign; **dar muestras de** to show signs of; **m. de cariño/respeto** token of affection/respect; **una m. más de ...** yet another example of ...

muestral *adj* **error m.** margin of error

muestreo *nm* sampling

mugido *nm (de vaca)* moo; *(de toro)* bellow

mugir [57] *vi (vaca)* to moo, to low; *(toro)* to bellow

mugre *nf* filth

mugriento,-a *adj* filthy

mujer *nf* (**a**) woman; **dos mujeres** two women; **m. de la limpieza** cleaner; **m. de su casa** houseproud woman (**b**) *(esposa)* wife; **su futura m.** his bride-to-be

mujeriego **1** *adj* woman-chasing

2 *nm* womanizer, woman chaser

muleta *nf* (**a**) *(prótesis)* crutch (**b**) *Taurom* muleta

muletilla *nf* pet word o phrase

mullido,-a *adj* soft

mulo *nm* mule

multa *nf* fine; *Aut* ticket

multar *vt* to fine

multi- *pref* multi-

multicolor *adj* multicoloured

multicopista *nf* duplicator

multilateral *adj* multilateral

multinacional *adj & nf* multinational

múltiple *adj* (**a**) multiple; **accidente m.** pile-up (**b**) **múltiples** *(muchos)* many

multiplicación *nf Mat* multiplication

multiplicar [44] **1** *vt & vi* to multiply (**por** by)

2 multiplicarse *vpr (reproducirse, aumentar)* to multiply

múltiplo,-a *adj & nm* multiple

multirriesgo *adj inv* **póliza m.** multiple risk policy

multitud *nf* (**a**) *(de personas)* crowd (**b**) *(de cosas)* multitude

mundano,-a *adj* worldly

🔊 Observa que la palabra inglesa **mundane** es un falso amigo y no es la traducción de la palabra española **mundano**. En inglés, **mundane** significa "prosaico".

---

mundial **1** *adj* worldwide; **campeón m.** world champion; **de fama m.** world-famous

2 *nm* world championship

mundialmente *adv* **m. famoso** world-famous, famous worldwide

mundo *nm* world; **todo el m.** everyone; **correr** o **ver m.** to travel widely; **nada del otro m.** nothing special; **el otro m.** the hereafter

munición *nf* ammunition

municipal **1** *adj* municipal

2 *nm (municipal)* policeman

municipio *nm* (**a**) *(territorio)* municipality (**b**) *(ayuntamiento)* town council

muñeca *nf* (**a**) wrist (**b**) *(juguete, muchacha)* doll (**c**) *Andes, RP Fam* **tener m.** *(enchufe)* to have friends in high places; *(habilidad)* to have the knack

muñeco *nm (juguete)* (little) boy doll; **m. de trapo** rag doll; **m. de nieve** snowman

muñequera *nf* wristband

muñón *nm Anat* stump
muralla *nf* wall
Murcia *n* Murcia
murciélago *nm Zool* bat
murmullo *nm* murmur
murmuración *nf* gossip
murmurar *vi* (**a**) *(criticar)* to gossip (**b**) *(susurrar)* to whisper; *(refunfuñar)* to grumble (**c**) *Fig (río)* to murmur
muro *nm* wall
murrio,-a *adj Fam* sad, blue
musa *nf* muse
musaraña *nf Fam* **estar mirando a** *o* **pensando en las musarañas** to be daydreaming *o* in the clouds
musculatura *nf* musculature; **desarrollar la m.** to develop one's muscles
músculo *nm* muscle
musculoso,-a *adj* muscular
museo *nm* museum; **m. de arte** *o* **pintura** art gallery
musgo *nm* moss
música *nf* music; **m. clásica** classical music; **m. de fondo** background music
musical 1 *adj* musical
2 *nm* musical

músico,-a 1 *adj* musical
2 *nm,f* musician
muslo *nm* thigh
mustio,-a *adj* (**a**) *(plantas)* wilted, withered (**b**) *(persona)* sad, gloomy
musulmán,-ana *adj & nm,f* Muslim, Moslem
mutación *nf Biol* mutation
mutilación *nf* mutilation
mutilado,-a *nm,f* disabled person; **m. de guerra** disabled serviceman
mutilar *vt* to mutilate
mutis *nm Teatro* exit
mutua *nf* mutual benefit society
mutual *nf Arg, Chile, Perú* mutual benefit society
mutualidad *nf* (**a**) *(reciprocidad)* mutuality (**b**) *(asociación)* mutual benefit society
mutuo,-a *adj* mutual
muy *adv* very; **m. bueno/malo** very good/bad; **¡m. bien!** very good!; *Fam* **m. mucho** very much; **M. señor mío** Dear Sir; **m. de los andaluces** typically Andalusian; **m. de mañana/noche** very early/late

N, n ['ene] *nf (la letra)* N, n

N (*abr* **Norte**) N

n/ (*abr* **nuestro,-a**) our

nabo *nm* (a) *Bot* turnip (b) *Vulg (pene)* prick

nácar *nm* mother-of-pearl

nacer [60] *vi* (a) to be born; **al n.** at birth; **nací en Montoro** I was born in Montoro; *Fam Fig* **n. de pie** to be born under a lucky star (b) *(pájaro)* to hatch (out) (c) *(pelo)* to begin to grow (d) *(río)* to rise

nacido,-a *adj* born; **n. de padre español** born of a Spanish father; **recién n.** newborn; *Fig* **mal n.** despicable, mean

naciente *adj (nuevo)* new, recent; *(sol)* rising

nacimiento *nm* (a) birth; **sordo de n.** deaf from birth; **lugar de n.** birthplace, place of birth (b) *Fig (principio)* origin, beginning; *(de río)* source (c) *(belén)* Nativity scene, crib

nación *nf* nation; **las Naciones Unidas** the United Nations

nacional 1 *adj* (a) national (b) *(producto, mercado)* domestic; **vuelos nacionales** domestic flights

2 *nmf* national; *Hist* **los nacionales** the Francoist forces

nacionalidad *nf* nationality

nacionalismo *nm* nationalism

nacionalista *adj & nmf* nationalist

nacionalizar [40] **1** *vt* (a) *Econ (banca, industria)* to nationalize (b) *(naturalizar)* to naturalize

2 nacionalizarse *vpr* to become naturalized; **n. español** to take up Spanish citizenship

nada 1 *pron* (a) *(como respuesta)* nothing; **¿qué quieres? – n.** what do you want? – nothing

(b) *(con verbo)* not ... anything; *(enfático)* nothing; **no sé n.** I don't know anything; **yo no digo n.** I'm saying nothing

(c) *(con otro negativo)* anything; **no hace nunca n.** he never does anything; **nadie sabía n.** nobody knew anything

(d) *(en ciertas construcciones)* anything; **más que n.** more than anything; **sin decir**

n. without saying anything; **casi n.** hardly anything

(e) **gracias – de n.** thanks – don't mention it; *Fam* **para n.** not at all; **casi n.** almost nothing; **como si n.** just like that; **un rasguño de n.** an insignificant little scratch; **n. de eso** nothing of the kind; **n. de n.** nothing at all; **n. más verla** as soon as he saw her

2 *adv* not at all; **no me gusta n.** I don't like it at all; **no lo encuentro n. interesante** I don't find it remotely interesting

3 *nf* nothingness; **salir de la n.** to come out of nowhere

nadador,-a *nm,f* swimmer

nadar *vi* (a) *Dep* to swim; **n. a braza** to do the breaststroke (b) *(flotar)* to float

nadie 1 *pron* (a) *(como respuesta)* no one, nobody; **¿quién vino? – n.** who came? – no one (b) *(con verbo)* not ... anyone, not ... anybody; *(enfático)* no one, nobody; **no conozco a n.** I don't know anyone *o* anybody; **no vi a n.** I saw no one (c) *(con otro negativo)* anyone, anybody; **nunca habla con n.** he never speaks to anybody (d) *(en ciertas construcciones)* anybody, anyone; **más que n.** more than anyone; **sin decírselo a n.** without telling anyone; **casi n.** hardly anyone

2 *nm* nobody; **ser un don n.** to be a nobody

nado: • **a nado** *loc adv* swimming; **cruzar** *o* **pasar a n.** to swim across

NAFTA *nm* (*abr* **North American Free Trade Agreement**) NAFTA

nafta *nf RP (gasolina)* Br petrol, US gas(oline)

nahua, náhuatl 1 *adj* Nahuatl

2 *nmf (individuo)* Nahuatl (Indian)

nailon *nm* nylon

naipe *nm* playing card

nalga *nf* buttock; **nalgas** bottom, buttocks

nana *nf* (a) *(canción)* lullaby (b) *Col, Méx (niñera)* nanny

napalm *nm* napalm

napias *nfpl Fam* snout

Nápoles *n* Naples

napolitano,-a *adj & nm,f* Neapolitan

naranja 1 *nf* orange; *Fig* **mi media n.** my better half
 2 *adj & nm (color)* orange
naranjada *nf* orangeade
naranjo *nm* orange tree
narciso *nm* (a) *(blanco)* narcissus; *(amarillo)* daffodil (b) *Fig (hombre)* narcissist
narcótico,-a *nm* narcotic; *(droga)* drug
narcotizar [40] *vt (drogar)* to drug
narcotraficante *nmf* drug trafficker
narcotráfico *nm* drug trafficking
nariz *nf* (a) nose; *Fam* **me da en la n. que ...** I've got this feeling that ... (b) *Fam* **narices** nose; *Fam* **en mis (propias) narices** right under my very nose; *Fam* **estar hasta las narices de** to be totally fed up with; *Fam* **meter las narices en algo** to poke one's nose into sth; *Fam* **por narices** because I say so; *Fam* **tocarle a algn las narices** to get on sb's wick
narración *nf* narration
narrar *vt* to narrate, to tell
narrativo,-a *adj & nf* narrative
nata *nf* (a) cream; **n. batida** *o* **montada** whipped cream (b) *(de leche hervida)* skin (c) *Fig* cream, best
natación *nf Dep* swimming
natal *adj* **mi país n.** my native country; **su pueblo n.** his home town
natalicio *nm Fml* birthday
natalidad *nf* birth rate; **control de n.** birth control
natillas *nfpl Culin* custard
natividad *nf* Nativity
nativo,-a *adj & nm,f* native
nato,-a *adj* born
natura *nf Literario* nature; **contra n.** against nature
natural 1 *adj* natural; *(fruta, flor)* fresh; **de tamaño n.** life-size; **en estado n.** in its natural state; *Jur* **hijo n.** illegitimate child
 2 *nmf* native
naturaleza *nf* (a) nature; **en plena n.** in the wild, in unspoilt countryside; *Arte* **n. muerta** still life (b) *(complexión)* physical constitution
naturalidad *nf (sencillez)* naturalness; **con n.** naturally, straightforwardly
naturalismo *nm* naturalism
naturalista 1 *adj* naturalistic
 2 *nmf* naturalist
naturalización *nf* naturalization
naturalizar [40] **1** *vt* to naturalize
 2 naturalizarse *vpr* to become naturalized
naturalmente *adv* naturally; **¡n.!** of course!
naturismo *nm* naturism

naturista *nmf* naturist
naufragar [42] *vi (barco)* to sink, to be wrecked; *(persona)* to be shipwrecked
naufragio *nm Náut* shipwreck
náufrago,-a *nm,f* shipwrecked person, castaway
náusea *nf (usu pl)* nausea, sickness; **me da n.** it makes me sick; **sentir náuseas** to feel sick
nauseabundo,-a *adj* nauseating, sickening
náutico,-a *adj* nautical
navaja *nf* (a) *(cuchillo)* penknife, pocketknife; **n. de afeitar** razor (b) *(molusco)* razor-shell
navajada *nf*, **navajazo** *nm* stab, gash
navajero *nm Fam* thug
naval *adj* naval
Navarra *n* Navarre
navarro,-a 1 *adj* Navarrese, of/from Navarre
 2 *nm,f* person from Navarre
nave *nf* (a) ship; **n. (espacial)** spaceship, spacecraft (b) *Ind* plant, building (c) *(de iglesia)* nave; **n. lateral** aisle
navegable *adj* navigable
navegación *nf* navigation; **n. costera** coastal shipping
navegador *nm Informát* browser
navegar [42] *vi* (a) to navigate, to sail (b) *Av* to navigate, to fly (c) **n. por Internet** to surf the Net
Navidad(es) *nf(pl)* Christmas; **árbol de Navidad** Christmas tree; **Feliz Navidad, Felices Navidades** Merry Christmas
navideño,-a *adj* Christmas
navío *nm* ship
nazi *adj & nmf* Nazi
nazismo *nm* Nazism
n/c., n/cta. *(abr* **nuestra cuenta)** our account, our acct
neblina *nf* mist, thin fog
nebulosa *nf Astron* nebula
nebuloso,-a *adj* (a) *Met* cloudy, hazy (b) *Fig* nebulous, vague
necedad *nf* (a) *(estupidez)* stupidity, foolishness (b) *(tontería)* stupid thing to say *o* to do
necesario,-a *adj* necessary; **es n. hacerlo** it has to be done; **es n. que vayas** you must go; **no es n. que vayas** there is no need for you to go; **si fuera n.** if need be
neceser *nm (de aseo)* toilet bag; *(de maquillaje)* make-up bag
necesidad *nf* (a) necessity, need; **artículos de primera n.** essentials; **por n.** of necessity; **tener n. de** to need (b) *(pobreza)* poverty, hardship (c) **hacer**

sus **necesidades** to relieve oneself

necesitado,-a 1 *adj (pobre)* needy, poor; **n. de** in need of

  2 *nmpl* **los necesitados** the needy

necesitar *vt* to need; **se necesita chico** *(en anuncios)* boy wanted

necio,-a 1 *adj* (**a**) *(tonto)* silly, stupid (**b**) *Méx (pesado)* boring

  2 *nm,f* (**a**) *(tonto)* fool, idiot (**b**) *Méx (pesado)* bore

necrología *nf* obituary

néctar *nm* nectar

nectarina *nf* nectarine

neerlandés,-esa 1 *adj* Dutch, of/from the Netherlands

  2 *nm,f (persona) (hombre)* Dutchman; *(mujer)* Dutchwoman; **los neerlandeses** the Dutch

  3 *nm (idioma)* Dutch

nefasto,-a *adj* (**a**) *(perjudicial)* harmful (**b**) *(funesto)* unlucky, ill-fated (**c**) *(inútil)* hopeless

negación *nf* (**a**) negation (**b**) *(negativa)* denial; *(rechazo)* refusal (**c**) *Ling* negative

negado,-a 1 *adj* **ser n. para algo** to be hopeless *o* useless at sth

  2 *nm,f* no-hoper

negar [1] *vt* (**a**) to deny; **negó haberlo robado** he denied stealing it (**b**) *(rechazar)* to refuse, to deny; **le negaron la beca** they refused him the grant

  2 negarse *vpr* to refuse (**a** to)

negativa *nf* denial

negativo,-a *adj & nm* negative

negligencia *nf* negligence

negociación *nf* negotiation

negociado *nm Andes, RP (chanchullo)* shady deal

negociador,-a *adj* negotiating; **comité n.** negotiating committee

negociante *nmf* dealer; *(hombre)* businessman; *(mujer)* businesswoman

negociar [43] 1 *vt Fin & Pol* to negotiate

  2 *vi (comerciar)* to do business, to deal

negocio *nm Com & Fin* business; *(transacción)* deal, transaction; *(asunto)* affair; **hombre de negocios** businessman; **mujer de negocios** businesswoman

negra *nf* (**a**) *Fig (mala suerte)* bad luck; **tener la n.** to be very unlucky (**b**) *Mús Br* crotchet, *US* quarter note

negrilla, negrita *adj & nf Impr* bold (face)

negro,-a 1 *adj* (**a**) black; **estar n.** *(bronceado)* to be suntanned (**b**) *Fig (suerte)* awful; *(desesperado)* desperate; *(furioso)* furious; **verlo todo n.** to be very pessimistic; **vérselas negras para hacer algo** to have a tough time doing sth

  2 *nm,f (hombre)* black; *(mujer)* black (woman)

  3 *nm (color)* black

nene,-a *nm,f (niño)* baby boy; *(niña)* baby girl

nenúfar *nm Bot* waterlily

neocelandés,-esa, neozelandés,-esa

  1 *adj* of/from New Zealand

  2 *nm,f* New Zealander

neoclásico,-a *adj Arte & Lit* neoclassic, neoclassical

neologismo *nm* neologism

neón *nm* neon

neoyorquino,-a 1 *adj* of/from New York

  2 *nm,f* New Yorker

neozelandés,-esa *adj & nm,f* = neocelandés,-esa

nepotismo *nm* nepotism

Neptuno *n* Neptune

nervio *nm* (**a**) *Anat & Bot* nerve; *(de la carne)* sinew (**b**) *Fig (fuerza, vigor)* nerve, courage (**c**) **nervios** nerves; **ataque de nervios** fit of hysterics; **ser un manojo de nervios** to be a bundle of nerves; **tener los nervios de acero** to have nerves of steel

nerviosismo *nm* nerves

nervioso,-a *adj* (**a**) nervous; **poner n. a algn** to get on sb's nerves (**b**) *(inquieto)* fidgety

neto,-a *adj* (**a**) *(peso, cantidad)* net (**b**) *(nítido)* neat, clear

neumático,-a 1 *adj* pneumatic

  2 *nm* tyre; **n. de recambio** spare tyre

neumonía *nf* pneumonia

neurálgico,-a *adj* neuralgic; *Fig* **punto n.** nerve centre

neurólogo,-a *nm,f* neurologist

neurosis *nf* neurosis

neurótico,-a *adj & nm,f* neurotic

neutral *adj* neutral

neutralidad *nf* neutrality

neutralizar [40] *vt* to neutralize

neutro,-a *adj* (**a**) *(imparcial)* neutral (**b**) *Ling* neuter

neutrón *nm Fís* neutron; **bomba de neutrones** neutron bomb

nevada *nf* snowfall

nevar [1] *v impers* to snow

nevera *nf* (**a**) *(frigorífico)* refrigerator, fridge (**b**) *(portátil)* cool box

nexo *nm* connection, link

ni *conj* (**a**) **no ... ni, ni ... ni** neither ... nor, not ... or; **no tengo tiempo ni dinero** I have got neither time nor money; **ni ha**

venido ni ha llamado he hasn't come or phoned; **no vengas ni hoy ni mañana** don't come today or tomorrow (**b**) *(ni siquiera)* not even; **ni por dinero** not even for money; **ni se te ocurra** don't even think about it; **¡ni hablar!** no way!

Nicaragua *n* Nicaragua

nicaragüense *adj & nmf* Nicaraguan

nicho *nm* niche

nicotina *nf* nicotine

nido *nm* nest

niebla *nf* fog; **hay mucha n.** it is very foggy

nieto,-a *nm,f (niño)* grandson; *(niña)* granddaughter; **mis nietos** my grandchildren

nieve *nf* (**a**) *Met* snow; *Culin* **a punto de n.** (beaten) stiff (**b**) *Fam (cocaína)* snow (**c**) *Carib, Méx (granizado)* = drink of flavoured crushed ice

nigeriano,-a *adj & nm,f* Nigerian

Nilo *n* el N. the Nile

nilón *nm Tex* nylon

nimio,-a *adj (insignificante)* insignificant, petty

ninfómana *nf* nymphomaniac

ninguno,-a 1 *adj* (**a**) *(con verbo)* not ... any; **no leí ninguna revista** I didn't read any magazines; **no tiene ninguna gracia** it is not funny at all (**b**) **en ninguna parte** nowhere; **de ningún modo** no way

> **Ningún** is used instead of **ninguno** before masculine singular nouns (e.g. **ningún hombre** no man).

2 *pron* (**a**) *(persona)* nobody, no one; **n. lo vio** no one saw it; **n. de los dos** neither of the two; **n. de ellos** none of them (**b**) *(cosa)* not ... any of them; *(enfático)* none of them; **me gusta n.** I don't like any of them; **no vi n.** I saw none of them

niña *nf* (**a**) girl; *ver* niño,-a (**b**) *Anat* pupil; *Fig* **es la n. de sus ojos** she's the apple of his eye

niñera *nf* nursemaid, nanny

niñez *nf* infancy; *(a partir de los cuatro años)* childhood

niño,-a *nm,f* (**a**) child; *(muchacho)* (small) boy; *(muchacha)* (little) girl; **de n.** as a child; **n. prodigio** child prodigy; *Pey* **n. bien** *o* **de papá** rich boy, rich kid; *Pey* **n. bonito** *o* **mimado** mummy's/daddy's boy (**b**) *(bebé)* baby (**c**) **niños** children; *Fig* **juego de niños** child's play (**d**) *Met* **el N.** el Niño

nipón,-ona *adj & nm,f* Japanese; **los nipones** the Japanese

níquel *nm* nickel

niqui *nm* T-shirt

níspero *nm (fruto)* medlar; *(árbol)* medlar tree

nítido,-a *adj (claro)* clear; *(imagen)* sharp

nitrógeno *nm* nitrogen

nitroglicerina *nf* nitroglycerine

nivel *nm* (**a**) *(altura)* level; **a. del mar** at sea level (**b**) *(categoría)* standard; **n. de vida** standard of living (**c**) *(instrumento)* level; **n. de aire** spirit level (**d**) *Ferroc* **paso a n.** *Br* level crossing, *US* grade crossing

nivelar *vt* (**a**) to level out *o* off (**b**) *(equilibrar)* to balance out

n *(abr* **número**) no

no 1 *adv* (**a**) *(como respuesta)* no; **¿te gusta? – no** do you like it? – no (**b**) *(en otros contextos)* not; **no vi a nadie** I didn't see anyone; **aún no** not yet; **ya no** no longer, not any more; **no sin antes ...** not without first ...; **¿por qué no?** why not? (**c**) **no fumar/aparcar** *(en letrero)* no smoking/parking (**d**) **no sea que** (*+ subjunctive*) in case (**e**) **es rubia, ¿no?** she's blonde, isn't she?; **llegaron anoche, ¿no?** they arrived yesterday, didn't they? (**f**) *(como prefijo negativo)* non; **la no violencia** non-violence

2 *nm* no; **un no rotundo** a definite no

noble 1 *adj* noble

2 *nmf (hombre)* nobleman; *(mujer)* noblewoman; **los nobles** the nobility

nobleza *nf* nobility

noche *nf* evening; *(después de las diez)* night, night-time; **de n., por la n.** at night; **esta n.** tonight; **mañana por la n.** tomorrow night *o* evening; **buenas noches** *(saludo)* good evening; *(despedida)* good night; **son las nueve de la n.** it's nine p.m.

nochebuena *nf* Christmas Eve

nochero *nm CSur (vigilante)* nightwatchman

nochevieja *nf* New Year's Eve

noción *nf* (**a**) notion, idea (**b**) **nociones** smattering, basic knowledge; **nociones de español** a smattering of Spanish

nocivo,-a *adj* noxious, harmful

noctámbulo,-a *nm,f* sleepwalker; *Fam* nightbird

nocturno,-a *adj* (**a**) night; **vida nocturna** night life; **clases nocturnas** evening classes (**b**) *Bot & Zool* nocturnal

nodriza *nf* (**a**) *(ama)* wet nurse (**b**) **buque n.** supply ship

nogal *nm Bot* walnut (tree)

nómada 1 *adj* nomadic

2 *nmf* nomad

nombrado,-a *adj (célebre)* famous, well-known

nombramiento *nm* appointment

nombrar *vt* (a) *(designar)* to name, to appoint; **n. a algn director** to appoint sb director (b) *(mencionar)* to name, to mention

nombre *nm* (a) name; **n. de pila** Christian name; **n. y apellidos** full name; *Informát* **n. de dominio** domain name; **a n. de** addressed to; **en n. de** on behalf of (b) *Ling* noun; **n. propio** proper noun

nómina *nf* (a) *(de sueldo)* pay slip (b) *(plantilla)* payroll

nominar *vt* to nominate

nominativo,-a *adj* **cheque n. a** cheque made out to

non *nm* (a) *Mat* odd number; **pares y nones** odds and evens (b) *Fam* **nones** *(negación)* no; **decir (que) nones** to refuse

nono,-a *adj* = **noveno,-a**

norcoreano,-a *adj & nm,f* North Korean

nordeste *nm* = **noreste**

nórdico,-a 1 *adj* (a) *(del norte)* northern (b) *(escandinavo)* Nordic
2 *nm,f* Nordic person

noreste *nm* northeast

noria *nf* (a) *(de feria)* big wheel (b) *(para agua)* water wheel

norirlandés,-esa 1 *adj* Northern Irish
2 *nm,f (persona) (hombre)* Northern Irishman; *(mujer)* Northern Irishwoman; **los norirlandeses** the Northern Irish

norma *nf* norm; **n. de seguridad** safety standard

normal *adj* normal, usual; **lo n.** the normal thing, what usually happens

normalidad *nf* normality; **volver a la n.** to return to normal

normalizar [40] 1 *vt* to normalize, to restore to normal
2 normalizarse *vpr* to return to normal

normativa *nf* rules

noroeste *nm* northwest

norte *nm* (a) north; **al n. de** to the north of (b) *Fig* aim, goal

norteafricano,-a *adj & nm,f* North African

Norteamérica *n* North America

norteamericano,-a *adj & nm,f* (North) American

norteño,-a 1 *adj* northern
2 *nm,f* Northerner

Noruega *n* Norway

noruego,-a 1 *adj* Norwegian
2 *nm,f* Norwegian
3 *nm (idioma)* Norwegian

nos 1 *pron pers (directo)* us; *(indirecto)* (to) us; **n. ha visto** he has seen us; **n. trajo un** regalo he brought us a present; **n. lo dio** he gave it to us
2 *pron (reflexivo)* ourselves; *(recíproco)* each other; **n. hemos divertido mucho** we enjoyed ourselves a lot; **n. queremos mucho** we love each other very much

nosotros,-as *pron pers pl* (a) *(sujeto)* we; **n. lo vimos** we saw it; **somos n.** it is us (b) *(complemento)* us; **con n.** with us

> Usually omitted in Spanish except for emphasis or contrast.

nostalgia *nf* nostalgia; *(morriña)* homesickness

nostálgico,-a *adj* nostalgic; *(con morriña)* homesick

nota *nf* (a) *(anotación)* note (b) *Educ* mark, grade; **sacar buenas notas** to get good marks (c) *Fig (detalle)* element, quality; **la n. dominante** the prevailing quality (d) *Mús* note; *Fam* **dar la n.** to make oneself noticed

notable 1 *adj (apreciable)* noticeable; *(destacado)* outstanding, remarkable
2 *nm (nota)* very good

notar 1 *vt (percibir)* to notice, to note
2 notarse *vpr* to be noticeable o evident, to show; **no se nota** it doesn't show; **se nota que ...** one can see that ...

notaría *nf (despacho)* notary's office

notarial *adj* notarial; **acta n.** affidavit

notario,-a *nm,f* notary (public), solicitor

noticia *nf* news *sing*; **una n.** a piece of news; **una buena n.** good news; **no tengo n. de esto** I don't know anything about it

> Observa que la palabra inglesa **notice** es un falso amigo y no es la traducción de la palabra española **noticia**. En inglés, **notice** significa "aviso, anuncio".

noticiario, *Am* **noticiero** *nm* (a) *Cin* newsreel (b) *Rad & TV* television news *sing*

notificación *nf* notification; **sin n. previa** without (previous) notice; *Jur* **n. judicial** summons *sing*

notificar [44] *vt* to notify

notorio,-a *adj* (a) *(evidente)* obvious, evident (b) *(famoso)* famous, well-known

> Observa que la palabra inglesa **notorious** es un falso amigo y no es la traducción de la palabra española **notorio**. En inglés, **notorious** significa "tristemente célebre".

novatada *nf* (a) *(broma)* rough joke, rag (b) **pagar la n.** to learn the hard way

novato,-a 1 *adj (persona)* inexperienced; *Fam* green

2 *nm,f* (**a**) *(principiante)* novice, beginner (**b**) *Univ* fresher

novecientos,-as *adj & nm* nine hundred

novedad *nf* (**a**) *(cosa nueva)* novelty; **últimas novedades** latest arrivals (**b**) *(cambio)* change, development (**c**) *(cualidad)* newness

novedoso,-a *adj* (**a**) *(nuevo)* new, full of novelties (**b**) *(innovador)* innovative

novel 1 *adj* new, inexperienced
2 *nmf* beginner, novice

novela *nf Lit* novel; **n. corta** short story; **n. policíaca** detective story

novelero,-a *adj* (**a**) *(amigo de novedades)* fond of new things (**b**) *(fantasioso)* highly imaginative

novelesco,-a *adj* (**a**) *(de novela)* novelistic, fictional (**b**) *(extraordinario)* bizarre, fantastic

novelista *nmf* novelist

noveno,-a *adj & nm* ninth; **novena parte** ninth

noventa *adj & nm inv* ninety

novia *nf* (**a**) *(amiga)* girlfriend (**b**) *(prometida)* fiancée (**c**) *(en boda)* bride

noviar *vi CSur, Méx* **n. con algn** to go out with sb; **novian hace tiempo** they've been going out together for a while

noviazgo *nm* engagement

noviembre *nm* November

novillada *nf Taurom* = bullfight with young bulls

novillero,-a *nm,f Taurom* apprentice matador

novillo,-a *nm,f* (**a**) *(toro)* young bull; *(vaca)* young cow (**b**) *Fam Educ* **hacer novillos** to play *Br* truant *o US* hooky

novio *nm* (**a**) *(amigo)* boyfriend (**b**) *(prometido)* fiancé (**c**) *(en boda)* bridegroom; **los novios** the bride and groom

nubarrón *nm Fam* storm cloud

nube *nf* cloud; *Fig* **vivir en las nubes** to have one's head in the clouds; *Fig* **poner a algn por las nubes** to praise sb to the skies

nublado,-a *adj* cloudy, overcast

nublarse *vpr* to become cloudy, to cloud over; *Fig* **se le nubló la vista** his eyes clouded over

nuboso,-a *adj* cloudy

nuca *nf* nape, back of the neck

nuclear *adj* nuclear; **central n.** nuclear power station

núcleo *nm* nucleus; *(parte central)* core; **n. urbano** city centre

nudillo *nm (usu pl)* knuckle

nudista *adj & nmf* nudist

nudo *nm* (**a**) knot; **hacer un n.** to tie a knot; *Fig* **se me hizo un n. en la garganta** I

got a lump in my throat (**b**) *(punto principal)* crux, core (**c**) *(de comunicaciones)* centre

nuera *nf* daughter-in-law

nuestro,-a 1 *adj pos* (**a**) our; **nuestra familia** our family (**b**) *(después del sustantivo)* of ours; **un amigo n.** a friend of ours
2 *pron pos* ours; **este libro es n.** this book is ours

nuevamente *adv* again

Nueva Zelanda *n* New Zealand

nueve *adj & nm inv* nine

nuevo,-a 1 *adj* (**a**) new; *Fam* **¿qué hay de n.?** what's new?; **de n.** again; **Nueva York** New York; **Nueva Zelanda** New Zealand (**b**) *(adicional)* further
2 *nm,f* newcomer; *(principiante)* beginner

nuez *nf* (**a**) walnut; **n. moscada** nutmeg (**b**) *Anat* **n. (de Adán)** Adam's apple

nulidad *nf* (**a**) *(ineptitud)* incompetence (**b**)*Jur* nullity

nulo,-a *adj* (**a**) *(inepto)* useless, totally incapable (**b**) *(sin valor)* null and void, invalid; **voto n.** invalid vote (**c**) **crecimiento n.** zero growth

núm. *(abr número)* no

numeral *adj & nm* numeral

numerar *vt* to number

numerario,-a 1 *adj* **profesor no n.** teacher on a temporary contract
2 *nm* (**a**) *(miembro)* full member (**b**) *(dinero)* cash

numérico,-a *adj* numerical

número *nm* (**a**) number; **n. de matrícula** *Br* registration number, *US* license number; **n. de serie** serial number; *Fig* **sin n.** countless (**b**) *Prensa* number, issue; **n. atrasado** back number (**c**) *(de zapatos)* size (**d**) *(en espectáculo)* sketch, act; *Fam* **montar un n.** to make a scene

numeroso,-a *adj* numerous

nunca *adv* (**a**) *(como respuesta)* never; **¿cuándo volverás? – n.** when will you come back? – never (**b**) *(con verbo)* never; *(enfático)* not ... ever; **no he estado n. en España** I've never been to Spain; **yo no haría n. eso** I wouldn't ever do that (**c**) *(en ciertas construcciones)* ever; **casi n.** hardly ever; **más que n.** more than ever (**d**) **n. jamás** never ever; *(futuro)* never again

nupcial *adj* wedding, nuptial; **marcha n.** wedding march

nupcias *nfpl Fml* wedding, nuptials; **casarse en segundas n.** to marry again

nutrición *nf* nutrition

nutricionista *nmf* nutritionist

nutrir 1 *vt* to nourish, to feed
  2 nutrirse *vpr* to feed (**de** o **con** on)

nutritivo,-a *adj* nutritious, nourishing;
  valor n. nutritional value

ñandutí *nm Par* fine lace
ñapa *nf Ven Fam* bonus, extra

ñato,-a *adj Andes, RP* snub-nosed

O

O, o [o] *nf (la letra)* O, o

o *conj* or; **jueves o viernes** Thursday or Friday; **o ... o** either ... or; **o sea** that is (to say), in other words

> **u** is used instead of **o** in front of words beginning with "o" or "ho" (e.g. **mujer u hombre** woman or man). Note that **ó** (with acute accent) is used between figures.

O. (*abr* **Oeste**) W

oasis *nm inv* oasis

obcecado,-a *adj Fig* stubborn

obcecar [44] **1** *vt Fig* to blind; **la ira lo obceca** he is blinded by anger

  2 obcecarse *vpr Fig* to refuse to budge; *(obsesionarse)* to become obsessed

obedecer [33] **1** *vt* to obey

  2 *vi* **o. a** *(provenir)* to be due to; **¿a qué obedece esa actitud?** what's the reason behind this attitude?

obediencia *nf* obedience

obediente *adj* obedient

obertura *nf* overture

obesidad *nf* obesity

obeso,-a *adj* obese

óbice *nm* obstacle; **eso no es ó. para que yo no lo haga** it won't prevent me from doing it

obispo *nm* bishop

objeción *nf* objection; **poner una o.** to raise an objection, to object

objetar 1 *vt* **no tengo nada que o.** I've got no objections

  2 *vi Mil* to be a conscientious objector

objetividad *nf* objectivity

objetivo,-a 1 *nm* (**a**) *(fin, meta)* objective, aim (**c**) *Mil* target (**c**) *Cin & Fot* lens; **o. zoom** zoom lens

  2 *adj* objective

objeto *nm* (**a**) object; **objetos perdidos** lost property; **mujer o.** sex object (**b**) *(fin)* aim, purpose; **con o. de ...** in order to ...; **tiene por o. ...** it is designed to ... (**c**) *Ling* object

objetor,-a 1 *nm,f* objector; **o. de conciencia** conscientious objector

  2 *adj* objecting, dissenting

obligación *nf* (**a**) *(deber)* obligation; **por o.** out of a sense of duty; **tengo o. de ...** I

have to ... (**b**) *Fin* bond, debenture

obligado,-a *adj* obliged; **verse o estar o. a** to be obliged to

obligar [42] *vt* to compel, to force

obligatorio,-a *adj* compulsory, obligatory

obra *nf* (**a**) *(trabajo)* (piece of) work; **por o. de** thanks to (**b**) *Arte* work; **o. maestra** masterpiece (**c**) *(acto)* deed (**d**) *Constr* building site (**e**) **obras** *(arreglos)* repairs; **carretera en obras** *(en letrero)* roadworks; **cerrado por obras** *(en letrero)* closed for repairs

obrar 1 *vi* (**a**) *(proceder)* to act, to behave; **o. bien/mal** to do the right/wrong thing (**b**) *Fml* **obra en nuestro poder ...** we are in receipt of ...

  2 *vt (milagro)* to work

obrero,-a 1 *nm,f* worker, labourer

  2 *adj* working; **clase obrera** working class; **movimiento o.** labour movement

obscenidad *nf* obscenity

obsceno,-a *adj* obscene

obscurecer [33] **1** *v impers* to get dark

  2 *vt* to darken

  3 obscurecerse *vpr (nublarse)* to become cloudy

obscuridad *nf* darkness; *Fig* obscurity

obscuro,-a *adj* (**a**) dark (**b**) *Fig (origen, idea)* obscure; *(futuro)* uncertain, gloomy; *(asunto)* shady; *(nublado)* overcast

obsequiar [43] *vt* to give away

obsequio *nm* gift, present

observación *nf* observation

observador,-a 1 *nm,f* observer

  2 *adj* observant

observancia *nf* observance

observar *vt* (**a**) *(mirar)* to observe, to watch (**b**) *(notar)* to notice (**c**) *(cumplir)* to observe

observatorio *nm* observatory

obsesión *nf* obsession

obsesionar 1 *vt* to obsess; **estoy obsesionado con eso** I can't get it out of my mind

  2 obsesionarse *vpr* to get obsessed

obsesivo,-a *adj* obsessive

obseso,-a *nm,f* obsessed person; **un o. sexual** a sex maniac

obsoleto,-a *adj* obsolete

obstaculizar [40] *vt* to obstruct, to get in the way of

obstáculo *nm* obstacle

obstante: •**no obstante 1** *loc adv* nevertheless

  2 *prep* notwithstanding

obstetricia *nf* obstetrics *sing*

obstinación *nf* obstinacy

obstinado,-a *adj* obstinate

obstinarse *vpr* to persist (**en** in)

obstrucción *nf* obstruction; *Med* blockage

obstruir [37] 1 *vt* (**a**) *(salida, paso)* to block, to obstruct (**b**) *(progreso)* to impede, to block

  2 obstruirse *vpr* to get blocked up

obtención *nf* obtaining

obtener [24] 1 *vt* *(alcanzar)* to obtain, to get

  2 obtenerse *vpr* **o. de** *(provenir)* to come from

obturador *nm Fot* shutter

obtuso,-a *adj* obtuse

obús *nm* shell

obviar [43] *vt* *(problema)* to get round

obvio,-a *adj* obvious

oca *nf* goose

ocasión *nf* (**a**) *(momento)* occasion; **con o. de ...** on the occasion of ...; **en cierta o.** once (**b**) *(oportunidad)* opportunity, chance; **aprovechar una o.** to make the most of an opportunity (**c**) *Com* bargain; **de o.** cheap; **precios de o.** bargain prices

ocasional *adj* (**a**) *(eventual)* occasional; **trabajo o.** casual work; **de forma o.** occasionally (**b**) *(fortuito)* accidental, chance

ocasionar *vt* to cause, to bring about

ocaso *nm* *(anochecer)* sunset; *Fig (declive)* fall, decline

occidental *adj* western, occidental

occidente *nm* west; **el O.** the West

OCDE *nf* (*abr* **Organización para la Cooperación y el Desarrollo Económico**) OECD

Oceanía *n* Oceania

oceánico,-a *adj* oceanic

océano *nm* ocean

ochenta *adj & nm inv* eighty

ocho *adj & nm inv* eight

ochocientos,-as *adj & nm* eight hundred

ocio *nm* leisure; **en mis ratos de o.** in my spare o leisure time

ocioso,-a *adj* (**a**) *(inactivo)* idle (**b**) *(inútil)* pointless

ocre *nm* ochre

octavilla *nf* *(panfleto)* handout, leaflet

octavo,-a *adj & nm,f* eighth

octogenario,-a *adj & nm,f* octogenarian

octogésimo,-a *adj & nm,f* eightieth

octubre *nm* October

ocular *adj* **testigo o.** eye witness

oculista *nmf* ophthalmologist

ocultar 1 *vt* to conceal, to hide; **o. algo a algn** to hide sth from sb

  2 ocultarse *vpr* to hide

oculto,-a *adj* concealed, hidden

ocupación *nf* occupation

ocupado,-a *adj* *(persona)* busy; *(asiento)* taken; *(aseos, teléfono)* engaged; *(puesto de trabajo)* filled

ocupante *nmf* *(de casa)* occupant, occupier; *(ilegal)* squatter; *(de vehículo)* occupant

ocupar 1 *vt* (**a**) to occupy (**b**) *(espacio, tiempo)* to take up; *(cargo)* to hold, to fill (**c**) *CAm, Méx (usar, emplear)* to use

  2 ocuparse *vpr* **o. de** *(cuidar)* to look after; *(encargarse)* to see to

ocurrencia *nf* *(agudeza)* witty remark, wisecrack; *(idea)* bright idea

> 🖉 Observa que la palabra inglesa **occurrence** es un falso amigo y no es la traducción de la palabra española **ocurrencia**. En inglés, **occurrence** significa "suceso, incidencia".

ocurrente *adj* witty

ocurrir 1 *v impers* to happen, to occur; **¿qué ocurre?** what's going on?; **¿qué te ocurre?** what's the matter with you?

  2 ocurrirse *vpr* **no se me ocurre nada** I can't think of anything; **se me ocurre que ...** it occurs to me that ...

odiar [43] *vt* to detest, to hate; **odio tener que ...** I hate having to ...

odio *nm* hatred, loathing; **mirada de o.** hateful look

odioso,-a *adj* hateful

odontología *nf* dentistry, odontology

odontólogo,-a *nm,f* dental surgeon, odontologist

odre *nm* wineskin

OEA *nf* (*abr* **Organización de Estados Americanos**) OAS

oeste *nm* west

ofender 1 *vt* to offend

  2 ofenderse *vpr* to get offended (**por** by), to take offence (**por** at)

ofensa *nf* offence

ofensiva *nf* offensive

ofensivo,-a *adj* offensive

oferta *nf* offer; *Fin & Ind* bid, tender, proposal; *Com* **de** o **en o.** on (special) offer; **o. y demanda** supply and demand

ofertar *vt* to offer

off *adj* voz en o. *Cin & TV* voice-over; *Teatro* voice offstage

offset *nm Impr* offset

oficial 1 *adj* official

2 *nmf* (**a**) *Mil & Náut* officer (**b**) *(empleado)* clerk (**c**) *(obrero)* skilled worker

oficialismo *nm Am* (**a**) **el o.** *(gobierno)* the Government (**b**) **el o.** *(partidarios del gobierno)* government supporters

oficialista *Am* **1** *adj* pro-government

2 *nmf* government supporter

oficina *nf* office; **o. de empleo** *Br* job centre, *US* job office; **o. de turismo** tourist office; **o. de correos** post office; **horas/horario de o.** business hours

oficinista *nmf* office worker, clerk

oficio *nm* (**a**) *(ocupación)* job, occupation; *(profesión)* trade; **ser del o.** to be in the trade (**b**) *(comunicación oficial)* official letter *o* note; **de o.** ex-officio; **abogado de o.** state-appointed lawyer (**c**) *Rel* service

oficioso,-a *adj (noticia, fuente)* unofficial

> *ℓ* Observa que la palabra inglesa **officious** es un falso amigo y no es la traducción de la palabra española **oficioso**. En inglés, **officious** significa "excesivamente celoso o diligente".

ofimática *nf* office automation

ofimático,-a *adj Informát* **paquete o.** business package

ofrecer [33] 1 *vt* (**a**) to offer (**b**) *(aspecto)* to present

2 ofrecerse *vpr* (**a**) *(prestarse)* to offer, to volunteer (**b**) *(situación)* to present itself (**c**) *Fml* **¿qué se le ofrece?** what can I do for you?

ofrecimiento *nm* offering

ofrendar *vt Rel* to offer up

ofrezco *indic pres de* **ofrecer**

oftalmología *nf* ophthalmology

oftalmólogo,-a *nm,f* ophthalmologist

ofuscación *nf,* **ofuscamiento** *nm* blinding, dazzling

ofuscar [44] *vt* (**a**) *Fig (confundir)* to blind (**b**) *(deslumbrar)* to dazzle

oídas: • de oídas *loc adv* by hearsay

oído *nm* (**a**) *(sentido)* hearing (**b**) *(órgano)* ear; **aprender de o.** to learn by ear; *Fig* **hacer oídos sordos** to turn a deaf ear

oír [17] *vt* to hear; **¡oye!** hey!; **¡oiga!** excuse me!; *Fam* **como lo oyes** believe it or not

OIT *nf* (*abr* **Organización Internacional del Trabajo**) ILO

ojal *nm* buttonhole

ojalá 1 *interj* let's hope so!, I hope so!

2 *conj* (+ *subjunctive*) **¡o. sea cierto!** I hope it's true!

ojeada *nf* **echar una o.** to have a quick look

ojeras *nfpl* rings *o* bags under the eyes

ojeriza *nf* dislike

ojo 1 *nm* (**a**) eye; **o. morado** black eye; **ojos saltones** bulging eyes; *Fig* **a ojos vista** clearly, openly; *Fig* **calcular a o.** to guess; *Fam* **no pegué o.** I didn't sleep a wink (**b**) *(de aguja)* eye; *(de cerradura)* keyhole (**c**) *(de un puente)* span

2 *interj* careful!, look out!

ojota *nf* (**a**) *Méx (sandalia)* sandal (**b**) *RP (chancletas) Br* flip-flop, *US* thong

okupa *nmf* squatter

ola *nf* wave; **o. de calor** heat wave

ole, olé *interj* bravo!

oleada *nf* wave; *Fig* **o. de turistas** influx of tourists

oleaje *nm* swell

óleo *nm Arte* oil; **pintura** *o* **cuadro al ó.** oil painting

oleoducto *nm* pipeline

oler [65] 1 *vt* (**a**) *(percibir olor)* to smell (**b**) *Fig (adivinar)* to smell, to feel

2 *vi* (**a**) *(exhalar)* to smell; **o. a** to smell of; **o. bien/mal** to smell good/bad (**b**) *Fig (parecer)* to smack (**a** of)

3 olerse *vpr Fig (adivinar)* to feel, to sense; **me lo olía** I thought as much

olfatear *vt* (**a**) *(oler)* to sniff (**b**) *Fig (indagar)* to pry into

olfato *nm* sense of smell; *Fig* good nose, instinct

oligarquía *nf* oligarchy

olimpiada *nf Dep* Olympiad, Olympic Games; **las olimpiadas** the Olympic Games

olímpicamente *adv* **paso o. de estudiar** I couldn't give a damn about studying

olímpico,-a *adj* Olympic; **Juegos Olímpicos** Olympic Games

oliva *nf* olive; **aceite de o.** olive oil

olivar *nm* olive grove

olivo *nm* olive (tree)

olla *nf* saucepan, pot; **o. exprés** *o* **a presión** pressure cooker

olmo *nm* smooth-leaved elm

olor *nm* smell; **o. corporal** body odour

oloroso,-a *adj* fragrant, sweet-smelling

OLP *nf* (*abr* **Organización para la Liberación de Palestina**) PLO

olvidadizo,-a *adj* forgetful

olvidar 1 *vt* (**a**) to forget; *Fam* **¡olvídame!** leave me alone! (**b**) **olvidé el paraguas allí** I left my umbrella there

2 olvidarse *vpr* to forget; **se me ha olvidado hacerlo** I forgot to do it

olvido nm (a) (desmemoria) oblivion (b) (lapsus) oversight
ombligo nm navel
ominoso,-a adj shameful
omisión nf omission
omiso,-a adj hacer caso o. de to take no notice of
omitir vt to omit, to leave out
ómnibus nm (pl ómnibus o omnibuses) Cuba, Urug bus
omnipotente adj omnipotent, almighty
omnipresente adj omnipresent
omnisciente adj omniscient, all-knowing
omnívoro,-a 1 adj omnivorous
  2 nm,f omnivore
omóplato, omoplato nm shoulder blade
OMS nf (abr **Organización Mundial de la Salud**) WHO
ONCE nf (abr **Organización Nacional de Ciegos Españoles**) ≃ RNIB
once 1 adj inv eleven
  2 nm inv eleven; Ftb eleven, team
onda nf (a) Fís wave; Fam Fig **estar en la o.** to be with it; **o. expansiva** shock wave; Rad **o. larga/media/corta** long/medium/short wave (b) (en el agua) ripple (c) (de pelo) wave (d) Méx, RP **¿qué o.?** (¿qué tal?) how's it going?, how are things?
ondear vi (a) (bandera) to flutter (b) (de agua) to ripple
ondulación nf undulation; (de agua) ripple
ondulado,-a adj (pelo) wavy; (paisaje) rolling
ondulante adj undulating
ondular 1 vt (el pelo) to wave
  2 vi (moverse) to undulate
oneroso,-a adj (impuesto) heavy
ONG nf inv (abr **Organización no Gubernamental**) NGO
onomástica nf saint's day
onomatopeya nf onomatopoeia
ONU nf (abr **Organización de las Naciones Unidas**) UN(O)
onubense 1 adj of/from Huelva
  2 nmf person from Huelva
onza nf (medida) ounce
OPA nf (abr **Oferta Pública de Adquisición**) takeover bid
opaco,-a adj opaque
ópalo nm opal
opción nf (a) (elección) option, choice; (alternativa) alternative (b) (posibilidad) opportunity, chance
opcional adj optional
open nm Dep open

OPEP nf (abr **Organización de los Países Exportadores de Petróleo**) OPEC
ópera nf Mús opera
operación nf (a) Med operation; **o. quirúrgica** surgical operation (b) Fin transaction, deal; **operaciones bursátiles** stock exchange transactions (c) Mat operation
operador,-a nm,f (a) (técnico) operator (b) Cin (de cámara) (hombre) cameraman; (mujer) camerawoman; (del proyector) projectionist (c) Tel operator
operante adj operative
operar 1 vt (a) Med **o. a algn (de algo)** to operate on sb (for sth) (b) (cambio etc) to bring about
  2 vi Fin to deal, to do business (con with)
  3 operarse vpr (a) Med to have an operation (de for) (b) (producirse) to occur, to come about
operario,-a nm,f operator; (obrero) worker
operativo,-a 1 adj operative
  2 nm Am operation
opereta nf operetta
opinar vi (a) (pensar) to think (b) (declarar) to give one's opinion, to be of the opinion
opinión nf (juicio) opinion; **cambiar de o.** to change one's mind
opio nm opium
oponente nmf opponent
oponer [19] (pp opuesto) **1** vt (resistencia) to offer
  2 oponerse vpr (estar en contra) to be opposed; **se opone a aceptarlo** he refuses to accept it
oporto nm (vino) port
oportunidad nf opportunity, chance
oportunista adj & nmf opportunist
oportuno,-a adj (a) (adecuado) timely; **¡qué o.!** what good timing! (b) (conveniente) appropriate; **si te parece o.** if you think it appropriate
oposición nf (a) opposition (b) (examen) competitive examination
opositar vi = to sit a competitive examination
opositor,-a nm,f (a) (candidato) = candidate for a competitive examination (b) Am Pol opponent
opresión nf oppression; **o. en el pecho** tightness of the chest
opresivo,-a adj oppressive
opresor,-a 1 nm,f oppressor
  2 adj oppressive, oppressing
oprimir vt (a) (pulsar) to press (b) (subyugar) to oppress

oprobio *nm* ignominy, opprobrium

optar *vi* (**a**) *(elegir)* to choose (**entre** between); **opté por ir yo mismo** I decided to go myself (**b**) *(aspirar)* to apply (**a** for); **puede o. a medalla** he's in with a chance of winning a medal

optativo,-a *adj* optional

óptica *nf* (**a**) *(tienda)* optician's (shop) (**b**) *(punto de vista)* angle

óptico,-a 1 *adj* optical
2 *nm,f* optician

optimismo *nm* optimism

optimista 1 *adj* optimistic
2 *nmf* optimist

óptimo,-a *adj* optimum, excellent

opuesto,-a *adj* (**a**) *(contrario)* contrary; **en direcciones opuestas** in opposite directions; **gustos opuestos** conflicting tastes (**b**) *(de enfrente)* opposite; **el extremo o.** the other end

opulencia *nf* opulence

opulento,-a *adj* opulent

opuse *pt indef de* **oponer**

oración *nf* (**a**) *Rel* prayer (**b**) *Ling* clause, sentence

oráculo *nm* oracle

orador,-a *nm,f* speaker, orator

oral *adj* oral; *Med* **por vía o.** to be taken orally

órale *interj Méx Fam* (**a**) *(venga)* come on! (**b**) *(de acuerdo)* right!, sure!

orangután *nm* orang-outang, orangutan

orar *vi Rel* to pray

oratoria *nf* oratory

órbita *nf* (**a**) orbit (**b**) *Anat* eye socket

orden 1 *nm* order; **o. público** law and order; **por o. alfabético** in alphabetical order; **de primer o.** first-rate; **o. del día** agenda; **del o. de** approximately
2 *nf* (**a**) *(mandato)* order; *Mil* **¡a la o.!** sir! (**b**) *Jur* warrant, order; **o. de registro** search warrant; **o. judicial** court order

ordenado,-a *adj* tidy

ordenador *nm* computer; **o. personal** personal computer

ordenamiento *nm* ordering

ordenanza 1 *nm* *(empleado)* office boy
2 *nf* regulations; **o. municipal** bylaw

ordenar 1 *vt* (**a**) *(organizar)* to put in order; *(habitación)* to tidy up (**b**) *(mandar)* to order (**c**) *Am (pedir)* to order
2 ordenarse *vpr Rel* to be ordained (**de** as), to take holy orders

ordeñar *vt* to milk

ordinario,-a *adj* (**a**) *(corriente)* ordinary, common (**b**) *(grosero)* vulgar, common

orégano *nm* oregano, marjoram

oreja *nf* ear; *(de sillón)* wing

orejero,-a *nm,f Am (soplón)* grass

orfanato *nm* orphanage

orfebre *nm* *(del oro)* goldsmith; *(de la plata)* silversmith

orfebrería *nf* gold/silver work

orfelinato *nm* orphanage

orgánico,-a *adj* organic

organigrama *nm* organization chart; *Informát* flow chart

organismo *nm* (**a**) *(ser vivo)* organism (**b**) *(institución)* organization, body

organista *nmf* organist

organización *nf* organization

organizado,-a *adj* organized; **viaje o.** package tour

organizador,-a 1 *adj* organizing
2 *nm,f* organizer

organizar [40] 1 *vt* to organize
2 organizarse *vpr Fig (armarse)* to happen

órgano *nm* organ

orgasmo *nm* orgasm

orgía *nf* orgy

orgullo *nm* (**a**) *(propia estima)* pride (**b**) *(arrogancia)* arrogance

orgulloso,-a *adj* (**a**) **estar o.** *(satisfecho)* to be proud (**b**) **ser o.** *(arrogante)* to be arrogant o haughty

orientación *nf* (**a**) *(dirección)* orientation, direction (**b**) *(guía)* guidance; **curso de o.** induction course

oriental 1 *adj* (**a**) *(del este)* eastern, oriental; *(del Lejano Oriente)* oriental (**b**) *Am (uruguayo)* Uruguayan
2 *nmf* (**a**) *(del Lejano Oriente)* oriental (**b**) *Am (uruguayo)* Uruguayan

orientar 1 *vt* (**a**) *(enfocar)* to aim (**a** at), to intend (**a** for); **orientado al consumo** intended for consumption (**b**) *(indicar camino)* to give directions to; *Fig (aconsejar)* to advise (**c**) **una casa orientada al sur** a house facing south (**d**) *(esfuerzo)* to direct
2 orientarse *vpr (encontrar el camino)* to get one's bearings, to find one's way about

oriente *nm* East, Orient; **el Extremo** o **Lejano/Medio/Próximo O.** the Far/Middle/Near East

orificio *nm* hole, opening; *Anat & Téc* orifice; **o. de entrada** inlet; **o. de salida** outlet

origen *nm* origin; **país de o.** country of origin; **dar o. a** to give rise to

original *adj & nm* original

originalidad *nf* originality

originar 1 *vt* to cause, to give rise to

2 originarse *vpr* to originate
originariamente *adv* originally
originario,-a *adj* native
orilla *nf (borde)* edge; *(del río)* bank; *(del mar)* shore
orillero,-a *adj Am (persona)* suburban
orín¹ *nm (herrumbre)* rust
orín² *nm (usu pl) (orina)* urine
orina *nf* urine
orinal *nm* chamberpot; *Fam* potty
orinar 1 *vi* to urinate
2 orinarse *vpr* to wet oneself
oriundo,-a *adj* ser o. de to come from
orla *nf Univ* graduation photograph
ornamentar *vt* to adorn, to embellish
ornamento *nm* ornament
ornar *vt* to adorn, to embellish
ornato *nm (atavío)* finery; *(adorno)* decoration
ornitología *nf* ornithology
ornitólogo,-a *nm,f* ornithologist
oro *nm* (**a**) gold; **de o.** gold, golden; **o. de ley** fine gold (**b**) *Naipes* **oros** *(baraja española)* ≃ diamonds
orquesta *nf* orchestra; *(de verbena)* dance band
orquestar *vt* to orchestrate
orquídea *nf* orchid
ortiga *nf (stinging)* nettle
ortodoxia *nf* orthodoxy
ortodoxo,-a *adj* orthodox
ortografía *nf* orthography, spelling; **faltas de o.** spelling mistakes
ortográfico,-a *adj* orthographic, orthographical; **signos ortográficos** punctuation
ortopédico,-a *adj* orthopaedic; **pierna ortopédica** artificial leg
oruga *nf* caterpillar
orzuelo *nm Med* sty, stye
os *pron pers pl* (**a**) *(complemento directo)* you; **os veo mañana** I'll see you tomorrow (**b**) *(complemento indirecto)* you, to you; **os daré el dinero** I'll give you the money; **os escribiré** I'll write to you (**c**) *(con verbo reflexivo)* yourselves (**d**) *(con verbo recíproco)* each other; **os queréis mucho** you love each other very much
osa *nf* **O. Mayor** *Br* Great Bear, *US* Big Dipper; **O. Menor** *Br* Little Bear, *US* Little Dipper
osadía *nf* (**a**) *(audacia)* daring (**b**) *(desvergüenza)* impudence
osado,-a *adj* (**a**) *(audaz)* daring (**b**) *(desvergonzado)* shameless
osar *vi* to dare
osario *nm* ossuary
Óscar *nm Cin* Oscar

oscilación *nf* (**a**) oscillation (**b**) *(de precios)* fluctuation
oscilante *adj* (**a**) oscillating (**b**) *(precios)* fluctuating
oscilar *vi* (**a**) *Fís* to oscillate (**b**) *(variar)* to vary, to fluctuate
oscuras: •a oscuras *loc adv* in the dark; **nos quedamos a o.** we were left in darkness
oscurecer [33] *v impers, vt & vpr* = obscurecer
oscuridad *nf* = obscuridad
oscuro,-a *adj* = obscuro,-a
óseo,-a *adj* osseous, bony; **tejido ó.** bone tissue
osito *nm Fam* **o. (de peluche)** teddy bear
ósmosis, osmosis *nf inv* osmosis
oso *nm* bear; **o. polar** polar bear; **o. hormiguero** anteater; **o. marino** fur seal; *Fam Fig* **hacer el o.** to play the fool
ostensible *adj* ostensible
ostentación *nf* ostentation; **hacer o. de algo** to show sth off
ostentar *vt* (**a**) *(lucir)* to flaunt (**b**) *(cargo)* to hold
ostentoso,-a *adj* ostentatious
osteópata *nmf* osteopath
osteopatía *nf* osteopathy
ostión *nm* (**a**) *Méx (ostra)* large oyster (**b**) *Chile (vieira)* scallop
ostra *nf* oyster; *Fig* **aburrirse como una o.** to be bored stiff; *Fam* **¡ostras!** *Br* crikey!, *US* gee!
ostracismo *nm* ostracism
OTAN *nf (abr* **Organización del Tratado del Atlántico Norte**) NATO
otear *vt (horizonte)* to scan, to search
OTI *nf (abr* **Organización de Televisiones Iberoamericanas**) = association of all Spanish-speaking television networks
otitis *nf inv* infection and inflammation of the ear, otitis
otoñal *adj* autumn, *US* fall
otoño *nm* autumn, *US* fall
otorgamiento *nm (concesión)* granting; *(de un premio)* award
otorgar [42] *vt* (**a**) *(premio)* to award (**a** to); **o. un indulto** to grant pardon (**b**) *(permiso)* to grant (**a** to)
otorrinolaringólogo,-a *nm,f* ear, nose and throat specialist
otro,-a 1 *adj indef* (**a**) *(sin artículo) (sing)* another; *(pl)* other; **o. coche** another car; **otras personas** other people (**b**) *(con artículo definido)* other; **el o. coche** the other car (**c**) **otra cosa** something else; **otra vez** again
2 *pron indef* (**a**) *(sin artículo) (sing)*

another (one); *(pl) (personas)* others; *(cosas)* other ones; **dame o.** give me another (one); **no es mío, es de o.** it's not mine, it's somebody else's (**b**) *(con artículo definido) (sing)* **el o./la otra** the other (one); *(pl) (personas)* **los otros/las otras** the others; *(cosas)* the other ones (**c**) **hacer o. tanto** to do likewise

ovación *nf* ovation

ovacionar *vt* to give an ovation to, to applaud

oval, ovalado,-a *adj* oval

óvalo *nm* oval

ovario *nm* ovary

oveja *nf* sheep; *(hembra)* ewe; *Fig* **la o. negra** the black sheep

overol *nm Am* overalls

ovillo *nm* ball (of wool); *Fig* **hacerse un o.** to curl up into a ball

ovino,-a *adj* ovine; **ganado o.** sheep *pl*

OVNI *nm* (*abr* **objeto volador no identificado**) UFO

ovular 1 *adj* ovular
  2 *vi* to ovulate

óvulo *nm* ovule

oxidación *nf (metal)* rusting

oxidado,-a *adj (metal)* rusty; *Fig* **su inglés está un poco o.** her English is a bit rusty

oxidar 1 *vt Quím* to oxidize; *(metales)* to rust
  2 oxidarse *vpr Quím* to oxidize; *(metales)* to rust, to go rusty

óxido *nm* (**a**) oxide; **ó. de carbono** carbon monoxide (**b**) *(orín)* rust

oxigenado,-a *adj* oxygenated; **agua oxigenada** (hydrogen) peroxide

oxígeno *nm* oxygen; **bomba de o.** oxygen cylinder *o* tank

oye *indic pres & imperat de* **oír**

oyente *nmf* (**a**) *Rad* listener (**b**) *Univ* occasional student -

ozono *nm* ozone; **capa de o.** ozone layer

P, p [pe] *nf (la letra)* P, p
pabellón *nm* (a) **p. de deportes** sports centre (b) *(en feria)* stand (c) *(bloque)* wing (d) *(bandera)* flag
pábulo *nm Fml Fig* fuel; **dar p. a** to encourage
pacer [60] *vt & vi* to graze, to pasture
pachá *nm Fam Fig* **vivir como un p.** to live like a king
Pachamama *n* Mother Earth
pachanguero,-a *adj Fam Pey (música)* catchy
pachón,-ona *nm,f (perro)* pointer
pachorra *nf Fam* sluggishness; **tener p.** to be phlegmatic
paciencia *nf* patience; **armarse de p.** to grin and bear it
paciente *adj & nmf* patient
pacificación *nf* pacification
pacificador,-a 1 *adj* pacifying
    2 *nm,f* peacemaker
pacificar [44] 1 *vt* to pacify; *Fig (apaciguar)* to appease, to calm
    2 **pacificarse** *vpr* to calm down
Pacífico *nm* **el (océano) P.** the Pacific (Ocean)
pacífico,-a *adj* peaceful
pacifismo *nm* pacifism
pacifista *adj & nmf* pacifist
paco *nm Andes, Pan Fam (policía)* cop
pacotilla *nf Fam* **de p.** second-rate
pactar *vt* to agree to
pacto *nm* pact; **el P. de Varsovia** the Warsaw Pact; **p. de caballeros** gentlemen's agreement
padecer [33] *vt & vi* to suffer; **padece del corazón** he suffers from heart trouble
padecimiento *nm* suffering
padrastro *nm* (a) stepfather (b) *(pellejo)* hangnail
padrazo *nm* easy-going o indulgent father
padre 1 *nm* (a) father; **p. de familia** family man (b) **padres** parents
    2 *adj inv Fam* (a) *(tremendo)* huge; **pegarse la vida p.** to live like a king (b) *Méx (genial)* great
padrenuestro *nm* Lord's Prayer
padrino *nm* (a) *(de bautizo)* godfather;

(de boda) best man; **padrinos** godparents (b) *(espónsor)* sponsor
padrísimo,-a *adj Méx Fam* fantastic, great
padrón *nm* census
padrote *nm Méx Fam (proxeneta)* pimp
paella *nf* paella, = rice dish made with vegetables, meat and/o seafood
paellera *nf* paella pan
pág *(abr página)* p
paga *nf (salario)* wage; *(de niños)* pocket money; **p. extra** bonus
pagadero,-a *adj* payable; *Fin* **cheque p. al portador** cheque payable to bearer
pagador,-a *nm,f* payer
pagano,-a *adj & nm,f* pagan, heathen
pagar [42] *vt* (a) to pay; **p. en metálico** o **al contado** to pay cash; **p. por** *(producto, mala acción)* to pay for; *Fig* **(ella) lo ha pagado caro** she's paid dearly for it (b) *(recompensar)* to repay
pagaré *nm Fin* promissory note, IOU; **p. del tesoro** treasury note
página *nf* page; **en la p. 3** on page 3; *Fig* **una p. importante de la historia** an important chapter in history; *Informát* **p. personal** home page; *Informát* **p. web** web page
pago *nm* payment; **p. adelantado** o **anticipado** advance payment; **p. contra reembolso** cash on delivery; **p. inicial** down payment; **p. por visión** pay-per-view
paila *nf Andes, CAm, Carib (frying)* pan
paipái, paipay *nm (pl paipáis)* = large palm fan
país *nm* country, land; **vino del p.** local wine; **P. Vasco** Basque Country; **P. Valenciano** Valencia
paisaje *nm* landscape, scenery
paisano,-a 1 *adj* of the same country
    2 *nm,f (compatriota)* fellow countryman/countrywoman, compatriot; **en traje de p.** in plain clothes
Países Bajos *npl* **(los) P.** the Netherlands, the Low Countries
paja *nf* (a) straw (b) *Fam Fig (bazofia)* padding, waffle (c)*Vulg* **hacerse una p.** to wank

pajar *nm* *(almacén)* straw loft; *(en el exterior)* straw rick

pajarita *nf* (a) bow tie (b) *(de papel)* paper bird

pájaro *nm* (a) bird; **Madrid a vista de p.** a bird's-eye view of Madrid; **p. carpintero** woodpecker (b) *Fam* **tener pájaros** to have daft ideas

pajita, pajilla *nf* (drinking) straw

Pakistán *n* Pakistan

pakistaní *adj & nmf* Pakistani

pala *nf* (a) shovel; *(de jardinero)* spade; *(de cocina)* slice (b) *Dep* *(de ping-pong, frontón)* bat, *US* paddle; *(de remo)* blade

palabra *nf* (a) word; **de p.** by word of mouth; **dirigir la p. a algn** to address sb; **juego de palabras** pun (b) *(promesa)* word; **p. de honor** word of honour (c) *(turno para hablar)* right to speak; **tener la p.** to have the floor

palabrería *nf* palaver

palabrota *nf* swearword

palacio *nm* *(grande)* palace; *(pequeño)* mansion; **P. de Justicia** Law Courts

paladar *nm* (a) palate (b) *(sabor)* taste

paladear *vt* to savour, to relish

palanca *nf* (a) lever (b) *(manecilla)* handle, stick; *Aut* **p. de cambio** *Br* gearstick, *US* gearshift; **p. de mando** control lever (c) *Dep* *(trampolín)* diving board

palangana *nf* washbasin

palco *nm* box

paleolítico,-a *adj* palaeolithic, paleolithic

paleontología *nf* palaeontology, paleontology

Palestina *n* Palestine

palestino,-a *adj & nm,f* Palestinian

palestra *nf* arena; *Fig* **salir** *o* **saltar a la p.** to enter the fray, to take the field

paleta *nf* (a) *(espátula)* slice (b) *(de pintor)* palette; *(de albañil)* trowel (c) *Dep* *(de pingpong)* bat (d) *CAm, Méx (pirulí)* lollipop; *(polo)* *Br* ice lolly, *US* Popsicle®

paletilla *nf* (a) shoulder blade (b) *Culin* shoulder

paleto,-a *Fam Pey* **1** *adj* unsophisticated, boorish

2 *nm,f* country bumpkin, yokel

paliar [43] *vt* to alleviate, to palliate

paliativo,-a *adj & nm* palliative

palidecer [33] *vi* (a) *(persona)* to turn pale (b) *Fig (disminuir)* to diminish, to be on the wane

palidez *nf* paleness, pallor

pálido,-a *adj* pale

palillero *nm* toothpick case

palillo *nm* (a) *(mondadientes)* toothpick;

palillos chinos chopsticks (b) *Mús* drumstick

palio *nm* (a) canopy (b) *Rel* pallium

palique *nm* *Fam* chat, small talk

paliza *nf* (a) *(zurra)* thrashing, beating; **darle a algn una p.** to beat sb up (b) *(derrota)* beating (c) *Fam (pesadez)* bore, pain (in the neck)

palma *nf* (a) *Anat* palm (b) *Bot* palm tree (c) **hacer palmas** to applaud

palmada *nf* (a) *(golpe)* slap (b) **palmadas** applause, clapping

palmar *vt* *Fam* **palmarla** to snuff it, to kick the bucket

palmarés *nm* (a) *(historial)* service record (b) *(vencedores)* list of winners

palmatoria *nf* candlestick

palmera *nf* palm tree

palmo *nm* *(medida)* span; *Fig* **p. a p.** inch by inch

palo *nm* (a) stick; *(vara)* rod; *(de escoba)* broomstick; *Fig* **a p. seco** on its own (b) *(golpe)* blow; *Fig* **dar un p. a algn** to let sb down (c) **de p.** wooden (d) *Dep (de portería)* woodwork (e) *(de golf)* club (f) *Naipes* suit

paloma *nf* pigeon; *Lit* dove; **p. mensajera** homing *o* carrier pigeon

palomar *nm* pigeon house, dovecot

palomilla *nf* (a) grain moth (b) *(tuerca)* wing *o* butterfly nut

palomitas (de maíz) *nfpl* popcorn

palpable *adj* palpable

palpar *vt* to touch, to feel; *Med* to palpate

palpitación *nf* palpitation, throbbing

palpitante *adj* palpitating, throbbing; *(asunto)* burning

palpitar *vi* to palpitate, to throb

palta *nf* *Andes, RP (fruto)* avocado

palúdico,-a *adj* malarial

paludismo *nm* malaria

palurdo,-a *adj* uncouth, boorish

pamela *nf* broad-brimmed hat

pampa *nf* pampa, pampas

pamplina *nf* *Fam* nonsense

pan *nm* bread; **p. de molde** loaf of bread; **p. integral** wholemeal *o* wholewheat bread; **p. rallado** breadcrumbs; **p. dulce** *Méx* cake; *RP* = type of fruitcake eaten at Christmas; *Arg* **p. lactal** sliced bread; *Fam Fig* **más bueno que el p.** as good as gold; *Fam Fig* **es p. comido** it's a piece of cake

pana *nf* corduroy

panacea *nf* panacea

panadería *nf* baker's (shop), bakery

panadero,-a *nm,f* baker

panal *nm* honeycomb

Panamá *n* Panama

panamá *nm (sombrero)* Panama hat

panameño,-a *adj & nm,f* Panamanian

pancarta *nf* placard; *(en manifestación)* banner

pancho *nm RP (perrito caliente)* hot dog

páncreas *nm inv* pancreas

panda¹ *nm* panda

panda² *nf* gang

pandereta *nf* tambourine

pandilla *nf Fam* gang

panecillo *nm* bread roll

panel *nm* panel

panera *nf* bread-basket

pánfilo,-a *adj Fam (bobo)* silly, stupid; *(crédulo)* gullible

panfleto *nm* lampoon, political pamphlet

pánico *nm* panic; **sembrar el p.** to cause panic

panocha *nf Bot* corn cob; *(de trigo etc)* ear

panoli *nmf Fam* idiot

panorama *nm (vista)* panorama, view; *Fig* panorama

panorámico,-a *adj* panoramic

panqueque *nm Am* pancake

pantaleta *nf*, **pantaletas** *nfpl Carib, Méx (bragas)* panties, *Br* knickers

pantalla *nf* (**a**) *Cin, TV & Informát* screen (**b**) *(de lámpara)* shade (**c**) *Fig* **servir de p.** to act as a decoy

pantalón *nm (usu pl)* trousers, *US* pants; **p. vaquero** jeans

pantano *nm Geog* (**a**) *(natural)* marsh, bog (**b**) *(artificial)* reservoir

panteón *nm* pantheon, mausoleum; **p. familiar** family vault

pantera *nf* panther

pantimedias *nfpl Méx Br* tights, *US* pantyhose

pantomima *nf Teatro* pantomime, mime; *Pey (farsa)* farce

pantorrilla *nf Anat* calf

pantry *nm Ven (comedor diario)* = family dining area off kitchen

pants *nmpl Méx* track *o* jogging suit

pantufla *nf* slipper

panty *nm* (pair of) *Br* tights, *US* pantyhose

> 🖉 Observa que la palabra inglesa **panties** es un falso amigo y no es la traducción de la palabra española **panty**. En inglés, **panties** significa "bragas".

panza *nf Fam* belly, paunch

panzada *nf Fam* bellyful

panzudo,-a, panzón,-ona *adj* potbellied, paunchy

pañal *nm Br* nappy, *US* diaper; *Fig* **estar en pañales** to be in one's infancy

paño *nm* (**a**) cloth material; *(de lana)* woollen cloth; *(para polvo)* duster, rag; *(de cocina)* dishcloth; *Fig* **paños calientes** half-measures (**b**) *(ropa)* clothes; **en paños menores** in one's underclothes

pañoleta *nf* (**a**) shawl (**b**) *Taurom* bullfighter's tie

pañuelo *nm* handkerchief; *(pañoleta)* shawl

Papa *nm* **el P.** the Pope

papa *nf* potato; *Fam* **no saber ni p. (de algo)** not to have the faintest idea (about sth); *Am* **papas fritas** *Br* chips, *US* (French) fries; *(de bolsa) Br* crisps, *US* (potato) chips

papá *nm Fam* dad, daddy

papada *nf* double chin

papagayo *nm* (**a**) *(animal)* parrot (**b**) *Carib, Méx (cometa)* kite

papalote *nm CAm, Méx* kite

papamoscas *nm inv* flycatcher

papanatas *nmf inv* sucker, twit

paparrucha(da) *nf* (piece of) nonsense

papaya *nf* papaya *o* pawpaw fruit

papear *vi Fam* to eat

papel *nm* (**a**) paper; *(hoja)* piece *o* sheet of paper; **papeles** *(documentos)* documents, identification papers; **p. higiénico** toilet paper; **p. carbón** carbon paper; **p. de carta** writing paper, stationery; *Chile* **p. confort** toilet paper; **p. de aluminio/de estraza** aluminium foil/brown paper; **p. de fumar** cigarette paper; **p. de lija** sandpaper; *Fin* **p. moneda** paper money, banknotes; **p. pintado** wallpaper; *Cuba* **p. sanitario** toilet paper; **p. secante** blotting paper; *Guat, Ven* **p. toilette** *o* **tualé** toilet paper (**b**) *Cin & Teatro* role, part

papeleo *nm Fam* paperwork

papelera *nf (en despacho)* wastepaper basket; *(en calle)* litter bin

papelería *nf (tienda)* stationer's (shop)

papeleta *nf* (**a**) *(de rifa)* ticket; *(de votación)* ballot paper; *(de resultados)* report (**b**) *Fam (dificultad)* tricky problem, difficult job

papeo *nm Fam* grub

paperas *nfpl Med* mumps *sing*

papilla *nf* pap, mush; *(de niños)* baby food

papista *nmf* papist

Papúa Nueva Guinea *n* Papua New Guinea

paquete *nm* (**a**) *(de cigarrillos etc)* packet; *(postal)* parcel, package (**b**) *(conjunto)* set, package; *Fin* **p. de acciones** share package (**c**) *Informát* software package (d) *Fam (castigo)* punishment (e) *muy Fam (genitales)* packet, bulge

Paquistán *n* Pakistan

paquistaní *adj & nmf* Pakistani

par 1 *adj Mat* even

  2 *nm* (a) *(pareja)* pair; *(dos)* couple (b) *Mat* even number; **pares y nones** odds and evens (c) *(noble)* peer (d) *(locuciones)* **a la p.** *(a la vez)* at the same time; **de p. en p.** wide open; *Fig* **sin p.** matchless

para *prep* (a) for; **bueno p. la salud** good for your health; **¿p. qué?** what for?; **p. ser inglés habla muy bien español** for an Englishman he speaks very good Spanish (b) *(finalidad)* to, in order to; **p. terminar antes** to o in order to finish earlier; **p. que lo disfrutes** for you to enjoy (c) *(tiempo)* by; **p. entonces** by then (d) *(a punto de)* **está p. salir** it's about to leave (e) *(locuciones)* **decir p. sí** to say to oneself; **ir p. viejo** to be getting old; **no es p. tanto** it's not as bad as all that; **p. mí** in my opinion

parábola *nf* (a) *Geom* parabola (b) *Rel* parable

parabólico,-a *adj* parabolic; *TV* **antena parabólica** satellite dish

parabrisas *nm inv Aut Br* windscreen, *US* windshield

paraca *nm Fam* para(chutist)

paracaídas *nm inv* parachute

paracaidista *nmf Dep* parachutist; *Mil* paratrooper

parachoques *nm inv Br* bumper, *US* fender

parada *nf* (a) stop; **p. de autobús** bus stop; **p. de taxis** taxi stand o rank (b) *Ftb* save, stop

paradero *nm* (a) *(lugar)* whereabouts *sing* (b) *Méx, Perú (apeadero)* stop

parado,-a 1 *adj* (a) stopped, stationary; *(quieto)* still; *(fábrica)* at a standstill; *Fig* **salir bien/mal p.** to come off well/badly (b) *(desempleado)* unemployed, out of work (c) *Fig (lento)* slow (d) *Am (de pie)* standing

  2 *nm,f* unemployed person

paradoja *nf* paradox

paradójico,-a *adj* paradoxical

parador *nm* roadside inn; **p. nacional** o **de turismo** state-run hotel

parafernalia *nf* paraphernalia *pl*

parafrasear *vt* to paraphrase

paráfrasis *nf inv* paraphrase

paragolpes *nm inv RP (de automóvil) Br* bumper, *US* fender

paraguas *nm inv* umbrella

Paraguay *n* Paraguay

paragüero *nm* umbrella stand

paraíso *nm* (a) paradise; **p. terrenal** heaven on earth; *Fin* **p. fiscal** tax haven (b) *Teatro* gods, gallery

paraje *nm* spot, place

paralelo,-a *adj & nm* parallel

parálisis *nf inv* paralysis; **p. infantil** poliomyelitis

paralítico,-a *adj & nm,f* paralytic

paralización *nf* (a) *Med* paralysis (b) *(detención)* halting, stopping

paralizar [40] 1 *vt* to paralyse; *(circulación)* to stop

  2 paralizarse *vpr Fig* to come to a standstill

parámetro *nm* parameter

paramilitar *adj* paramilitary

páramo *nm* bleak plain o plateau, moor

parangón *nm Fml* comparison; **sin p.** incomparable

paranoia *nf* paranoia

paranoico,-a *adj & nm,f* paranoiac, paranoid

parapente *nm (desde montaña)* paragliding, parapenting

parapeto *nm* (a) parapet (b) *(de defensa)* barricade

parapléjico,-a *adj & nm,f* paraplegic

parar 1 *vt* (a) to stop (b) *Dep* to save (c) *Am (levantar)* to raise

  2 *vi* (a) to stop; **p. de hacer algo** to stop doing sth; **sin p.** non-stop, without stopping; *Fam* **no p.** to be always on the go (b) *(alojarse)* to stay (c) *(acabar)* **fue a p. a la cárcel** he ended up in jail

  3 pararse *vpr* (a) to stop; **p. a pensar** to stop to think (b) *Am (ponerse en pie)* to stand up

pararrayos *nm inv* lightning rod o conductor

parásito,-a 1 *adj* parasitic

  2 *nm* parasite

parasol *nm* sunshade, parasol

parcela *nf* plot

parche *nm* (a) patch (b) *(emplasto)* plaster (c) *Pey (chapuza)* botched-up o slapdash job

parchís *nm Br* ludo, *US* Parcheesi®

parcial 1 *adj* (a) *(partidario)* biased (b) *(no completo)* partial; **a tiempo p.** part-time

  2 *nm* **(examen) p.** class examination

parcialmente *adv* partially, partly

parco,-a *adj (moderado)* sparing; *(frugal)* scant

pardillo,-a 1 *nm,f Pey* yokel, bumpkin

  2 *nm Orn* linnet

pardo,-a *adj (marrón)* brown; *(gris)* dark grey

parecer¹ *nm* (**a**) *(opinión)* opinion (**b**) *(aspecto)* appearance

parecer² [33] **1** *vi* to seem, to look (like); **parece difícil** it seems *o* looks difficult; **parecía (de) cera** it looked like wax; *(uso impers)* **parece que no arranca** it looks as if it won't start; **como te parezca** whatever you like; **¿te parece?** is that okay with you?; **parece que sí/no** I think/don't think so; **¿qué te parece?** what do you think of it?

2 parecerse (**a**) *vpr* to be alike; **no se parecen** they're not alike (**b**) **p. a** to look like, to resemble; **se parecen a su madre** they look like their mother

parecido,-a 1 *adj* (**a**) alike, similar (**b**) **bien p.** good-looking

2 *nm* likeness, resemblance; **tener p. con algn** to bear a resemblance to sb

pared *nf* wall

paredón *nm* (**a**) thick wall (**b**) *Fam* **le llevaron al p.** he was shot by firing squad

pareja *nf* (**a**) pair; **por parejas** in pairs (**b**) *(hombre y mujer)* couple; *(hijo e hija)* boy and girl; **hacen buena p.** they make a nice couple, they're well matched; **p. de hecho** = common-law heterosexual or homosexual relationship (**c**) *(en naipes)* pair; **doble p.** two pairs (**d**) *(de baile, juego)* partner

parejo,-a *adj* (**a**) *(parecido)* similar, alike (**b**) **ir parejos** to be neck and neck

parentela *nf Fam* relations, relatives

parentesco *nm* relationship, kinship

paréntesis *nm inv* (**a**) parenthesis, bracket; **entre p.** in parentheses *o* brackets (**b**) *(descanso)* break, interruption; *(digresión)* digression

parezco *indic pres de* **parecer**

paria *nmf* pariah

parida *nf Fam* silly thing

pariente *nmf* relative, relation

> *ℓ* Observa que la palabra inglesa **parent** es un falso amigo y no es la traducción de la palabra española **pariente**. En inglés, **parent** significa tanto "padre" como "madre".

parir *vt & vi* to give birth (to)

París *n* Paris

parking *nm Br* car park, *US* parking lot

parlamentario,-a 1 *adj* parliamentary

2 *nm,f Br* Member of Parliament, MP, *US* Congressman, *f* Congresswoman

parlamento *nm* parliament

parlanchín,-ina *adj Fam* talkative, chatty

parné *nm Fam* dough, cash

paro *nm* (**a**) *(huelga)* strike, stoppage (**b**) *(desempleo)* unemployment; **estar en p.** to be unemployed; **cobrar el p.** *Br* to be on the dole

parodia *nf* parody

parodiar [43] *vt* to parody

parpadear *vi (ojos)* to blink; *Fig (luz)* to flicker

parpadeo *nm (de ojos)* blinking; *Fig (de luz)* flickering

párpado *nm* eyelid

parque *nm* (**a**) park; **p. de atracciones** funfair; **p. zoológico** zoo; **p. nacional/natural** national park/nature reserve; **p. eólico** wind farm (**b**) *(de niños)* playpen (**c**) **p. móvil** total number of cars

parqué *nm* parquet

parqueadero *nm Carib, Col, Pan Br* car park, *US* parking lot

parquear *vt Carib, Col, Pan* to park

parquet *nm* = **parqué**

parquímetro *nm Aut* parking meter

parra *nf* grapevine

párrafo *nm* paragraph

parranda *nf Fam* spree

parricidio *nm* parricide

parrilla *nf* (**a**) *Culin* grill; **pescado a la p.** grilled fish (**b**) *Téc* grate (**c**) *Aut & Dep* starting grid

párroco *nm* parish priest

parronal *nm Chile* vineyard

parroquia *nf* parish; *(iglesia)* parish church

parroquiano,-a *nm,f* (regular) customer

parsimonia *nf* phlegm, calmness

parte 1 *nf* (**a**) *(sección)* part (**b**) *(en una repartición)* share (**c**) *(lugar)* place, spot; **en** *o* **por todas partes** everywhere; **se fue por otra p.** he went another way (**d**) *Jur* party (**e**) *(bando)* side; **estoy de tu p.** I'm on your side (**f**) *Euf* **partes** *(genitales)* private parts (**g**) *(locuciones)* **por mi p.** as far as I am concerned; **de p. de ...** on behalf of ...; *Tel* **¿de p. de quién?** who's calling?; **en gran p.** to a large extent; **en p.** partly; **la mayor p.** the majority; **por otra p.** on the other hand; **tomar p. en** to take part in

2 *nm (informe)* report

partición *nf (reparto)* division, sharing out; *(de herencia)* partition; *(de territorio)* partition

participación *nf* (**a**) participation (**b**) *Fin (acción)* share; **p. en los beneficios** profit-sharing (**c**) *(en lotería)* part of a lottery ticket (**d**) *(notificación)* notice, notification

participante 1 *adj* participating

2 *nmf* participant

participar 1 *vi* (a) to take part, to participate (**en** in) (b) *Fin* to have a share (**en** in)
(c) *Fig* **p. de** to share
  2 *vt* (*notificar*) to notify
partícipe *nmf* (a) participant; **hacer p. de**
algo (*notificar*) to inform about sth (b)
Com & Fin partner
participio *nm Ling* participle
partícula *nf* particle
particular 1 *adj* (a) (*concreto*) particular
  (b) (*privado*) private, personal (c) (*raro*)
peculiar
  2 *nmf* (*individuo*) private individual
  3 *nm* (*asunto*) subject, matter
particularidad *nf* special feature
partida *nf* (a) (*salida*) departure (b) *Com*
(*remesa*) batch, consignment (c) (*juego*)
game (d) *Fin* (*entrada*) item (e) *Jur* (*certificado*) certificate; **p. de nacimiento** birth
certificate
partidario,-a 1 *adj* **ser/no ser p. de algo**
to be for/against sth
  2 *nm,f* supporter, follower; **es p. del**
aborto he is in favour of abortion
partidista *adj* biased, partisan
partido *nm* (a) *Pol* party (b) *Dep* match,
game; **p. amistoso** friendly game; **p. de**
vuelta return match (c) (*provecho*) advantage; **sacar p. de** to profit from (d) *Jur*
(*distrito*) district (e) **tomar p. por** to side
with (f) **ser un buen p.** to be a good catch
partir 1 *vt* to break; (*dividir*) to split, to
divide; (*cortar*) to cut; **p. a algn por la**
mitad to mess things up for sb
  2 *vi* (a) (*marcharse*) to leave, to set out *o*
off (b) **a p. de** from
  3 partirse *upr* to split (up), to break (up);
Fam **p. de risa** to split one's sides laughing
partisano,-a *nm,f* partisan
partitura *nf Mús* score
parto *nm* childbirth, labour; **estar de p.** to
be in labour
parvulario *nm* nursery school, kindergarten
párvulo,-a *nm,f* infant
pasa *nf* raisin; **p. de Corinto** currant
pasable *adj* passable, tolerable
pasaboca *nm Col* snack, appetizer
pasacalle *nm Col, Urug* banner (*hung*
across street)
pasada *nf* (a) **de p.** in passing (b) (*jugarreta*) dirty trick (c) *Fam* **¡eso es una p.!**
it's too much!
pasadizo *nm* corridor, passage
pasado,-a 1 *adj* (a) (*último*) last; **el año/**
lunes p. last year/Monday (b) (*anticuado*) dated, old-fashioned; **p. (de moda)**
out of date *o* fashion (c) (*alimento*) bad

(d) *Culin* cooked; **lo quiero muy p.** I want
it well done (e) **p. mañana** the day after
tomorrow
  2 *nm* past
pasador *nm* (a) (*prenda*) pin, clasp; (*para el pelo*) (hair) slide (b) (*pestillo*) bolt,
fastener
pasaje *nm* (a) passage (b) (*calle*) alley
(c) (*pasajeros*) passengers (d) (*billete*)
ticket
pasajero,-a 1 *adj* passing, temporary;
aventura pasajera fling
  2 *nm,f* passenger
pasamanos *nm inv* (*barra*) handrail; (*de*
escalera) banister, bannister
pasamontañas *nm inv* balaclava
pasapalo *nm Ven* snack, appetizer
pasaporte *nm* passport
pasapurés *nm inv Culin* potato masher
pasar 1 *vt* (a) to pass; (*objeto*) to pass, to
give; (*mensaje*) to give; (*página*) to turn;
(*trasladar*) to move; **p. algo a limpio** to
make a clean copy of sth
  (b) (*tiempo*) to spend, to pass; **p. el rato**
to kill time
  (c) (*padecer*) to suffer, to endure; **p.**
hambre to go hungry
  (d) (*río, calle*) to cross; (*barrera*) to pass
through *o* over; (*límite*) to go beyond
  (e) (*perdonar*) to forgive, to tolerate; **p.**
algo (por alto) to overlook sth
  (f) (*introducir*) to insert, to put through
  (g) (*examen*) to pass
  (h) *Cin* to run, to show
  2 *vi* (a) to pass; **¿ha pasado el autobús?**
has the bus gone by?; **ha pasado un**
hombre a man has gone past; **p. de largo**
to go by (without stopping); **el tren pasa**
por Burgos the train goes via Burgos;
pasa por casa mañana come round to
my house tomorrow
  (b) **p. a** (*continuar*) to go on to; **p. a ser** to
become
  (c) (*entrar*) to come in
  (d) (*tiempo*) to pass, to go by
  (e) **p. sin** to do without; *Fam* **yo paso**
count me out
  3 *v impers* (*suceder*) to happen; **¿qué**
pasa aquí? what's going on here?; **¿qué**
te pasa? what's the matter?; *Fam* **¿qué**
pasa? (*saludo*) how are you?; **pase lo**
que pase whatever happens, come what
may
  4 pasarse *upr* (a) **se me pasó la ocasión** I
missed my chance; **se le pasó llamarme**
he forgot to phone me
  (b) (*gastar tiempo*) to spend *o* pass time;

pasárselo bien/mal to have a good/bad time
(**c**) *(comida)* to go off
(**d**) *Fam (excederse)* to go too far; **no te pases** don't overdo it
(**e**) **pásate por mi casa** call round at my place

pasarela *nf (puente)* footbridge; *(de barco)* gangway; *(de moda)* catwalk

pasatiempo *nm* pastime, hobby

pascua *nf* (**a**) Easter (**b**) **pascuas** *(Navidad)* Christmas; **¡felices Pascuas!** Merry Christmas!

pascualina *nf RP, Ven* = pie made with spinach and hard-boiled egg

pase *nm* (**a**) pass, permit (**b**) *Cin* showing

pasear 1 *vi* to go for a walk, to take a walk
2 *vt* (**a**) *(persona)* to take for a walk; *(perro)* to walk (**b**) *Fig (exhibir)* to show off
3 pasearse *vpr* to go for a walk

paseíllo *nm Taurom* opening parade

paseo *nm* (**a**) walk; *(en bicicleta, caballo)* ride; *(en coche)* drive; **dar un p.** to go for a walk/a ride (**b**) *(avenida)* avenue

pasillo *nm* corridor; *Av* **p. aéreo** air corridor

pasión *nf* passion

pasional *adj* passionate; **crimen p.** crime of passion

pasividad *nf* passivity, passiveness

pasivo,-a 1 *adj* passive; *(inactivo)* inactive
2 *nm Com* liabilities

pasmado,-a *adj (asombrado)* astounded, amazed; *(atontado)* flabbergasted; **dejar p.** to astonish; **quedarse p.** to be amazed

pasmo *nm* astonishment, amazement

paso¹,-a *adj* **ciruela pasa** prune; **uva pasa** raisin

paso² *nm* (**a**) step; *(modo de andar)* gait, walk; *(ruido al andar)* footstep; *Mil* **llevar el p.** to keep in step; *Fig* **a dos pasos** a short distance away; *Fig* **seguir los pasos de algn** to follow in sb's footsteps
(**b**) *(camino)* passage, way; **abrirse p.** to force one's way through; *Aut* **ceda el p.** *(en letrero)* give way; **prohibido el p.** *(en letrero)* no entry; **p. a nivel** *Br* level crossing, *US* grade crossing; **p. de cebra** zebra crossing; **p. de peatones** *Br* pedestrian crossing, *US* crosswalk; **p. elevado** *Br* flyover, *US* overpass; **p. subterráneo** *(para peatones)* subway; *(para coches)* underpass
(**c**) *(acción)* passage, passing; **a su p. por la ciudad** when he was in town; **el p.**

del tiempo the passage of time; **estar de p.** to be just passing through
(**d**) **p. de montaña** mountain pass

pasodoble *nm* paso doble

pasota *nmf Fam* waster

pasta *nf* (**a**) paste; **p. de dientes** *o* **dentífrica** toothpaste (**b**) *(de pan, pasteles)* dough; *(italiana)* pasta (**c**) *(galleta)* *Br* biscuit, *US* cookie (**d**) *Fam (dinero)* dough, bread

pastar *vt & vi* to graze, to pasture

pastel *nm* (**a**) cake; *(de carne, fruta)* pie (**b**) *Arte* pastel (**c**) *Fam* **descubrir el p.** to spill the beans

pastelería *nf* (**a**) *(tienda)* confectioner's (shop) (**b**) *(dulces)* confectionery

pastelero,-a *nm,f* pastry cook, confectioner

pastiche *nm* (**a**) pastiche (**b**) *Fam (chapuza)* botch(-up)

pastilla *nf* (**a**) tablet, pill; **pastillas para la tos** cough drops (**b**) *(de jabón)* bar (**c**) *Fam* **a toda p.** at full speed

pastizal *nm* grazing land, pasture

pasto *nm* (**a**) *(hierba)* grass (**b**) *(alimento)* fodder; **ser p. de** to fall prey to (**c**) *Am (césped)* lawn, grass

pastor,-a 1 *nm,f* shepherd; *(mujer)* shepherdess; **perro p.** sheepdog
2 *nm* (**a**) *Rel* pastor, minister (**b**) *(perro)* **p. alemán** Alsatian

pastoreo *nm* shepherding

pastoso,-a *adj* pasty; *(lengua)* furry

pata 1 *nf* leg; *Fig* **patas arriba** upside down; **estirar la p.** to kick the bucket; **mala p.** bad luck; **meter la p.** to put one's foot in it; **p. de gallo** crow's foot
2 *nm Perú Fam (amigo)* pal, *Br* mate, *US* buddy

patada *nf (puntapié)* kick, stamp

patalear *vi* to stamp one's feet (with rage)

pataleo *nm* kicking; *(de rabia)* stamping

patán *nm* bumpkin, yokel

patata *nf* potato; **patatas fritas** *Br* chips, *US* (French) fries; *(de bolsa)* *Br* crisps, *US* (potato) chips

patatús *nm inv Fam* dizzy spell, queer turn

paté *nm* pâté

patear 1 *vt (pelota)* to kick; *(pisotear)* to stamp on
2 *vi (patalear)* to stamp (one's foot with rage)

patentar *vt* to patent

patente 1 *nf* (**a**) *(autorización)* licence; *(de invención)* patent (**b**) *CSur (matrícula)* *Br* number plate, *US* license plate
2 *adj (evidente)* patent, obvious

pateo *nm* stamping; *(abucheo)* boo(ing), jeer(ing)

paternal *adj* paternal, fatherly

paternalista *adj* paternalistic

paternidad *nf* paternity, fatherhood

paterno,-a *adj* paternal

patético,-a *adj* moving

patíbulo *nm* scaffold, gallows *sing*

patidifuso,-a *adj Fam* dumbfounded, flabbergasted

patilla *nf* (a) *(de gafas)* leg (b) **patillas** *(pelo)* sideburns

patín *nm* (a) skate; *(patinete)* scooter; **p. de ruedas/de hielo** roller-/ice-skate; **p. en línea** rollerblade (b) *Náut* pedal boat

patinaje *nm* skating; **p. artístico** figure skating; **p. sobre hielo/ruedas** ice-/roller-skating

patinar *vi* (a) to skate; *(sobre ruedas)* to roller-skate; *(sobre hielo)* to ice-skate (b) *(deslizarse)* to slide; *(resbalar)* to slip; *(vehículo)* to skid (c) *Fam (equivocarse)* to put one's foot in it, to slip up

patinazo *nm* (a) skid (b) *Fam (equivocación)* blunder, boob

patinete *nm* scooter

patio *nm* (a) *(de una casa)* yard, patio; *(de recreo)* playground (b) *Teatro & Cin* **p. de butacas** stalls

pato *nm* duck; *Fam* **pagar el p.** to carry the can

patochada *nf* blunder, boob

patógeno,-a *adj* pathogenic

patología *nf* pathology

patológico,-a *adj* pathological

patoso,-a *adj* clumsy, awkward

patota *nf Perú, RP (de gamberros)* street gang

patraña *nf* nonsense

patria *nf* fatherland, native country; **madre p.** motherland; **p. chica** one's home town/region

patriarca *nm* patriarch

patrimonio *nm (bienes)* wealth; *(herencia)* inheritance

patriota *nmf* patriot

patriótico,-a *adj* patriotic

patriotismo *nm* patriotism

patrocinador,-a 1 *adj* sponsoring

2 *nm,f* sponsor

patrocinar *vt* to sponsor

patrocinio *nm* sponsorship, patronage

patrón,-ona 1 *nm,f* (a) *(jefe)* boss (b) *(de pensión) (hombre)* landlord; *(mujer)* landlady (c) *Rel* patron saint

2 *nm* (a) pattern (b) *(medida)* standard

patronal 1 *adj* employers'; **cierre p.** lockout; **clase p.** managerial class

2 *nf (dirección)* management

patronato, patronazgo *nm* (a) *(institución benéfica)* foundation (b) *(protección)* patronage

patrono,-a *nm,f* (a) boss; *(empresario)* employer (b) *Rel* patron saint

patrulla *nf* (a) patrol; **estar de p.** to be on patrol; **coche p.** patrol car (b) *(grupo)* group, band; **p. de rescate** rescue party; **p. ciudadana** vigilante group

patrullar 1 *vt* to patrol

2 *vi* to be on patrol

patrullero *nm CSur (auto)* police (patrol) car

paulatino,-a *adj* gradual

paupérrimo,-a *adj* extremely poor, poverty-stricken

pausa *nf* pause, break; *Mús* rest

pausado,-a *adj* unhurried, calm

pauta *nf* guidelines

pava *nf* (a) *Fam* **pelar la p.** to chat (b) *Arg (tetera)* kettle

pavada *nf RP (tontería)* stupid thing

pavesa *nf* ash

pavimentar *vt* to pave

pavimento *nm (de carretera)* road (surface), *US* pavement; *(de acera)* paving; *(de habitación)* flooring

pavo *nm* (a) turkey; *Fam* **no ser moco de p.** to be nothing to scoff at (b) *Fam (tonto)* twit; *Fam* **estar en la edad del p.** to be growing up

pavonearse *vpr Fam* to show off, to strut

pavoneo *nm Fam* showing off, strutting

pavor *nm* terror, dread

pay *nm Chile, Méx, Ven* pie

payaso *nm* clown; **hacer el p.** to act the clown

payés,-esa *nm,f* = Catalan or Balearic peasant

payo,-a *nm,f* non-gipsy person

paz *nf* peace; *(sosiego)* peacefulness; *Fam* **¡déjame en p.!** leave me alone!, **hacer las paces** to make (it) up

pazguato,-a *adj* (a) *(estúpido)* silly, stupid (b) *(mojigato)* prudish

PC *nm (abr* **personal computer** *)* PC

PCE *nm Pol (abr* **Partido Comunista de España** *)* = Spanish Communist party

pe *nf Fam* **de pe a pa** from A to Z

peaje *nm* toll; **autopista de p.** *Br* toll motorway, *US* turnpike

peatón *nm* pedestrian

peca *nf* freckle

pecado *nm Rel* sin; **p. capital** *o* **mortal** deadly sin

pecador,-a *nm,f* sinner

pecaminoso,-a *adj* sinful

pecar [44] *vi* to sin; *Fig* **p. por defecto** to fall short of the mark

pecera *nf* fish bowl, fish tank

pecho *nm* (**a**) chest; *(de mujer)* breast, bust; *(de animal)* breast; **dar el p. (a un bebé)** to breast-feed (a baby); *Fig* **tomar(se) (algo) a p.** to take (sth) to heart (**b**) *Am (en natación)* breaststroke; **nadar p.** to do the breaststroke

pechuga *nf* (**a**) *(de ave)* breast (**b**) *Fam (de mujer)* boob

pectoral *adj* pectoral, chest

peculiar *adj (raro)* peculiar; *(característico)* characteristic

peculiaridad *nf* peculiarity

pedagogía *nf* pedagogy

pedagógico,-a *adj* pedagogical

pedal *nm* pedal

pedalear *vi* to pedal

pedante 1 *adj* pedantic
2 *nmf* pedant

pedantería *nf* pedantry

pedazo *nm* piece, bit; **a pedazos** in pieces; **caerse a pedazos** to fall apart *o* to pieces; **hacer pedazos** to break *o* tear to pieces, to smash (up); *Fam* **¡qué p. de coche!** what a terrific car!

pederasta *nm* pederast

pedernal *nm* flint

pedestal *nm* pedestal

pediatra *nmf* paediatrician

pediatría *nf* paediatrics *sing*

pedicuro,-a *nm,f* chiropodist, *US* podiatrist

pedido *nm* (**a**) *Com* order; **hacer un p. a** to place an order with (**b**) *(petición)* request

pedigrí *nm* pedigree

pedir [6] *vt* (**a**) to ask (for); **p. algo a algn** to ask sb for sth; **te pido que te quedes** I'm asking you to stay; **p. prestado** to borrow; *Fig* **p. cuentas** to ask for an explanation (**b**) *Com & (en bar etc)* to order (**c**) *(mendigar)* to beg

pedo *nm* *Fam* (**a**) *(ventosidad)* fart; **tirarse un p.** to fart (**b**) *(borrachera)* bender

pedrada *nf* *(golpe)* blow from a stone; *(lanzamiento)* throw of a stone

pedrea *nf* *(en lotería)* small prizes

pedregoso,-a *adj* stony, rocky

pedrería *nf* precious stones, gems

pedrisco *nm* hailstorm

pega *nf* (**a**) *Fam (objeción)* objection; **poner pegas** to find fault (**b**) **de p.** *(falso)* sham

pegadizo,-a *adj* catchy

pegado,-a *adj* (**a**) *(adherido)* stuck (**b**) *(quemado)* burnt

pegajoso,-a *adj (pegadizo)* sticky; *Fig (persona)* tiresome, hard to get rid of

pegamento *nm* glue

pegar [42] 1 *vt* (**a**) *(adherir)* to stick; *(con pegamento)* to glue; *(coser)* to sew on; *Fam* **no pegó ojo** he didn't sleep a wink; **p. fuego a** to set fire to (**b**) *(golpear)* to hit (**c**) **p. un grito** to shout; **p. un salto** to jump (**d**) *Fam (contagiar)* to give; **me ha pegado sus manías** I've caught his bad habits (**e**) *(arrimar)* **p. algo a** *o* **contra algo** to put *o* place sth against sth
2 *vi* (**a**) *(adherirse)* to stick (**b**) *(armonizar)* to match, to go; **el azul no pega con el verde** blue and green don't go together *o* don't match; *Fig* **ella no pegaría aquí** she wouldn't fit in here (**c**) *(sol)* to beat down
3 pegarse *vpr* (**a**) *(adherirse)* to stick; *(pelarse)* to fight (**b**) *Fam (darse)* to have, to get; **p. un tiro** to shoot oneself (**c**) *(comida)* to get burnt; **se me ha pegado el sol** I've got a touch of the sun (**d**) *Fam* **pegársela a algn** to trick *o* deceive sb (**e**) *(arrimarse)* to get close (**f**) *Fam Fig* to stick (**g**) *Med (enfermedad)* to be catching *o* contagious; *Fig (melodía)* to be catchy

pegatina *nf* sticker

peinado *nm* hairstyle, *Fam* hairdo

peinar 1 *vt* (**a**) *(pelo)* to comb (**b**) *(registrar)* to comb
2 peinarse *vpr* to comb one's hair

peine *nm* comb

peineta *nf* = ornamental comb worn in hair

pela *nf* *Fam* peseta

pelado,-a 1 *adj* (**a**) *(cabeza)* shorn; *(piel, fruta)* peeled; *(terreno)* bare (**b**) *Fam* **saqué un cinco p.** *(en escuela)* I just scraped a pass; **a grito p.** shouting and bawling (**c**) *Fam (arruinado)* broke, penniless (**d**) *(desvergonzado)* impudent, insolent
2 *nm* *Fam* haircut
3 *nm,f* (**a**) *Andes Fam (niño, adolescente)* kid (**b**) *CAm, Méx Fam (pobre)* poor person

peladura *nf* peeling

pelagatos *nmf inv* *Fam* poor devil, nobody

pelaje *nm* (**a**) fur, hair (**b**) *Pey (apariencia)* looks, appearance

pelambrera *nf* *Fam* mop (of hair), long/thick hair

pelapatatas *nm inv* potato peeler

pelar 1 *vt (cortar el pelo a)* to cut the hair of; *(fruta, patata)* to peel; *Fam* **hace un frío que pela** it's brass monkey weather

2 *vi (despellejar)* to peel

3 pelarse *vpr* (a) *(cortarse el pelo)* to get one's hair cut (b) *Fam* **corre que se las pela** she runs like the wind

peldaño *nm* step; *(de escalera de mano)* rung

pelea *nf* fight; *(riña)* row, quarrel; **buscar p.** to look for trouble

peleado,-a *adj* **estar p. (con algn)** not to be on speaking terms (with sb)

pelear 1 *vi* to fight; *(reñir)* to quarrel

2 pelearse *vpr* (a) to fight; *(reñir)* to quarrel (b) *(enemistarse)* to fall out

pelele *nm (muñeco)* straw puppet; *Fig* puppet

peleón,-ona *adj* (a) quarrelsome, aggressive (b) *(vino)* cheap

peletería *nf* furrier's; *(tienda)* fur shop

peletero,-a *nm,f* furrier

peliagudo,-a *adj* difficult, tricky

pelícano *nm* pelican

película *nf* (a) *Cin* movie, *Br* film; **p. de miedo** *o* **terror** horror film; **p. del Oeste** Western; *Fam* **de p.** fabulous (b) *Fot* film

peligrar *vi* to be in danger, to be threatened; **hacer p.** to endanger, to jeopardize

peligro *nm* danger; *(riesgo)* risk; **con p. de ...** at the risk of ...; **correr (el) p. de ...** to run the risk of ...; **poner en p.** to endanger

peligroso,-a *adj* dangerous, risky

pelirrojo,-a 1 *adj* red-haired; *(anaranjado)* ginger-haired

2 *nm,f* redhead

pellejo *nm* (a) *(piel)* skin (b) *(odre)* wineskin (c) *Fam* **arriesgar** *o* **jugarse el p.** to risk one's neck

pelliza *nf* fur jacket

pellizcar [44] *vt* to pinch, to nip

pellizco *nm* pinch, nip

pelma *nmf*, **pelmazo,-a** *nm,f (persona)* bore, drag

pelo *nm* (a) hair; **cortarse el p.** *(uno mismo)* to cut one's hair; *(en la peluquería)* to have one's hair cut; *Fig* **no tiene ni un p. de tonto** he's no fool; *Fig* **no tener pelos en la lengua** to be very outspoken; *Fig* **tomar el p. a algn** to pull sb's leg, to take the mickey out of sb; *Fam* **con pelos y señales** in full detail; *Fam* **por los pelos** by the skin of one's teeth; *Fam* **me puso el p. de punta** it gave me the creeps (b) *(de animal)* fur, coat, hair (c) *Tex (de una tela)* nap, pile (d) *(cerda)* bristle

pelón,-ona *adj (sin pelo)* bald

pelota 1 *nf* (a) ball; *Fam* **devolver la p.** to give tit for tat (b) *Dep* pelota (c) *Fam (cabeza)* nut (d) **hacer la p. a algn** to toady to sb, to butter sb up (e) *muy Fam* **pelotas** *(testículos)* balls; **en pelotas** *Br* starkers, *US* butt-naked

2 *nmf Fam (pelotillero)* crawler

pelotari *nm* pelota player

pelotear *vi Dep* to kick a ball around; *Ten* to knock up

peloteo *nm Ten* knock-up

pelotilla *nf Fam* **hacer la p. (a algn)** to fawn (on sb)

pelotillero,-a *nm,f Fam* crawler

pelotón *nm* (a) *Mil* squad (b) *Fam (grupo)* small crowd, bunch; *(en ciclismo)* pack (c) *(amasijo)* bundle

pelotudo,-a *adj RP Fam* (a) *(estúpido)* stupid (b) *(grande)* great big, massive

peluca *nf* wig

peluche *nm* **osito de p.** teddy bear

peludo,-a *adj* hairy, furry

peluquería *nf* hairdresser's (shop)

peluquero,-a *nm,f* hairdresser

peluquín *nm* toupee

pelusa, pelusilla *nf* (a) fluff; *(de planta)* down (b) *Fam* jealousy

pelvis *nf inv* pelvis

pena *nf* (a) *(tristeza)* grief, sorrow; *Fig* **me da p. de ella** I feel sorry for her; **¡qué p.!** what a pity! (b) *(dificultad)* hardships, trouble; **no merece** *o* **vale la p. (ir)** it's not worth while (going); **a duras penas** with great difficulty (c) *(castigo)* punishment, penalty; **p. de muerte** *o* **capital** death penalty (d) *CAm, Carib, Col, Méx (vergüenza)* shame, embarrassment; **me da p.** I'm ashamed of it

penacho *nm* (a) *(de ave)* crest, tuft (b) *Mil (de plumas)* plume

penal 1 *adj* penal; *Jur* **código p.** penal code

2 *nm* prison, jail

penalidad *nf (usu pl)* hardships, troubles

penalización *nf* penalization; *Dep* penalty

penalizar [40] *vt* to penalize

penalti *nm Dep (pl* **penaltis)** penalty; *Fam* **casarse de p.** to have a shotgun wedding

penar 1 *vt* to punish

2 *vi* to be in torment, to suffer

pendejo,-a *nm,f muy Fam* (a) *Am (tonto)* jerk, idiot (b) *RP Pey (adolescente)* kid

pendenciero,-a *adj* quarrelsome, argumentative

pendiente 1 *adj* (a) *(por resolver)* pending; *Educ* **asignatura p.** failed subject;

Com **p. de pago** unpaid (**b**) **estar p. de** (*esperar*) to be waiting for; (*vigilar*) to be on the lookout for (**c**) (*colgante*) hanging (**de** from)

  2 *nm* (*joya*) earring

  3 *nf* slope; (*de tejado*) pitch

pendón *nm* (**a**) (*bandera*) banner (**b**) *Pey* (*mujer*) slut, whore; (*hombre*) playboy

péndulo *nm* pendulum

pene *nm* penis

penetración *nf* penetration; (*perspicacia*) insight, perception

penetrante *adj* penetrating; (*frío, voz, mirada*) piercing; *Fig* (*inteligencia*) sharp, acute

penetrar 1 *vt* to penetrate; **p. un misterio** to get to the bottom of a mystery

  2 *vi* (*entrar*) to go o get (**en** in)

penicilina *nf* penicillin

península *nf* peninsula

penique *nm* penny, *pl* pence

penitencia *nf* penance

penitenciaría *nf* prison

penitenciario,-a *adj* penitentiary, prison

penoso,-a *adj* (**a**) (*lamentable*) sorry, distressing (**b**) (*laborioso*) laborious, difficult (**c**) *CAm, Carib, Col, Méx* (*vergonzoso*) shy

pensado,-a *adj* (**a**) thought out; **bien p., ...** on reflection, ...; **en el momento menos p.** when least expected; **mal p.** twisted; **tener algo p.** to have sth planned, to have sth in mind; **tengo p. ir** I intend to go (**b**) (*concebido*) designed

pensamiento *nm* (**a**) thought (**b**) (*máxima*) saying, motto (**c**) *Bot* pansy

pensar [1] 1 *vi* to think (**en** o about; **sobre** about o over); *Fig* **sin p.** (*con precipitación*) without thinking; (*involuntariamente*) involuntarily

  2 *vt* (**a**) to think (**de** of); (*considerar*) to think over o about; **piénsalo bien** think it over; *Fam* **¡ni pensarlo!** not on your life! (**b**) (*proponerse*) to intend; **pienso quedarme** I plan to stay (**c**) (*concebir*) to make; **p. un plan** to make a plan; **p. una solución** to find a solution

pensativo,-a *adj* pensive, thoughtful

pensión *nf* (**a**) (*residencia*) boarding house; (*hotel*) guesthouse; **media p.** half board; **p. completa** full board (**b**) (*paga*) pension, allowance; **p. vitalicia** life annuity

pensionista *nmf* pensioner

pentágono *nm* pentagon

pentagrama *nm* staff, stave

penthouse [pent'χaus] *nm* *CSur, Ven* penthouse

penúltimo,-a *adj & nm,f* next to the last, penultimate

penumbra *nf* penumbra, half-light

penuria *nf* scarcity, shortage

peña *nf* (**a**) rock, crag (**b**) (*de amigos*) club (**c**) *Fam* (*gente*) people

peñasco *nm* rock, crag

peñón *nm* rock; **el P. de Gibraltar** the Rock of Gibraltar

peón *nm* (**a**) unskilled labourer; **p. agrícola** farmhand (**b**) (*en ajedrez*) pawn

peonada *nf* day's work

peonza *nf* (*spinning*) top

peor 1 *adj* (**a**) (*comparativo*) worse (**b**) (*superlativo*) worst; **en el p. de los casos** if the worst comes to the worst; **lo p. es que** the worst of it is that

  2 *adv* (**a**) (*comparativo*) worse; **¡p. para mí/ti/etc.!** too bad! (**b**) (*superlativo*) worst

pepa *nf* *Col, Ven* (*carozo*) stone, *US* pit (*of fruit*)

pepenador,-a *nm,f* *CAm, Méx* scavenger (*on rubbish tip*)

pepián *nm* *CAm, Méx* = sauce thickened with ground nuts or seeds

pepinillo *nm* gherkin

pepino *nm* cucumber; *Fam* **me importa un p.** I don't give a hoot

pepita *nf* (*de fruta*) pip, seed; (*de metal*) nugget

pepitoria *nf* fricassee; **pollo en p.** fricassee of chicken

peque *nm* *Fam* (*niño*) kid

pequeño,-a 1 *adj* small, little; (*bajo*) short

  2 *nm,f* child; **de p.** as a child

Pequín *n* Peking

pera *nf* (**a**) *Bot* pear; **p. de agua** juicy pear (**b**) *CSur Fam* (*mentón*) chin

peral *nm* pear tree

percance *nm* mishap, setback

percatarse *upr* **p. de** to realize

percepción *nf* perception

perceptible *adj* (**a**) perceptible (**b**) *Fin* receivable, payable

percha *nf* (*colgador*) (coat) hanger; (*de gallina*) perch

perchero *nm* clothes rack

percibir *vt* (**a**) (*notar*) to perceive, to notice (**b**) (*cobrar*) to receive

percusión *nf* percussion

perdedor,-a 1 *adj* losing

  2 *nm,f* loser

perder [3] 1 *vt* (**a**) to lose (**b**) (*tren, autobús*) to miss; (*tiempo*) to waste; (*oportunidad*) to miss (**c**) (*pervertir*) to be the ruin o downfall of

2 *vi* to lose; **echar (algo) a p.** to spoil (sth); **echarse a p.** to be spoilt; **salir perdiendo** to come off worst

3 perderse *vpr* (a) *(extraviarse) (persona)* to get lost; **se me ha perdido la llave** I've lost my key; **no te lo pierdas** don't miss it (b) *(pervertirse)* to go to rack and ruin

perdición *nf* undoing, downfall

pérdida *nf* (a) loss; **no tiene p.** you can't miss it (b) *(de tiempo, esfuerzos)* waste (c) *Mil* **pérdidas** losses

perdido,-a *adj* (a) *(extraviado)* lost (b) *Fam (sucio)* filthy (c) *Fam* **loco p.** mad as a hatter (d) **estar p. por algn** *(enamorado)* to be crazy about sb (e) *(acabado)* finished; **¡estoy p.!** I'm a goner!

perdigón *nm* pellet

perdiguero,-a *adj* partridge-hunting; **perro p.** setter

perdiz *nf* partridge

perdón *nm* pardon, forgiveness; **¡p.!** sorry!; **pedir p.** to apologize

perdonar *vt* (a) *(remitir)* to forgive (b) **¡perdone!** sorry!; **perdone que le moleste** sorry for bothering you (c) *(eximir)* to pardon; **perdonarle la vida a algn** to spare sb's life; **p. una deuda** to write off a debt

perdurable *adj* (a) *(eterno)* everlasting (b) *(duradero)* durable, long-lasting

perdurar *vi* (a) *(durar)* to endure, to last (b) *(persistir)* to persist, to continue to exist

perecedero,-a *adj* perishable; **artículos perecederos** perishables

perecer [33] *vi* to perish, to die

peregrinación *nf,* **peregrinaje** *nm* pilgrimage

peregrino,-a 1 *nm,f* pilgrim

2 *adj* **ideas peregrinas** crazy ideas

perejil *nm* parsley

perenne *adj* perennial, everlasting

perentorio,-a *adj* peremptory, urgent

pereza *nf* laziness, idleness

perezoso,-a *adj (vago)* lazy, idle

perfección *nf* perfection; **a la p.** to perfection

perfeccionamiento *nm* (a) *(acción)* perfecting (b) *(mejora)* improvement

perfeccionar *vt* to perfect; *(mejorar)* to improve, to make better

perfeccionista *adj & nmf* perfectionist

perfectamente *adv* perfectly; **¡p.!** *(de acuerdo)* agreed!, all right!

perfecto,-a *adj* perfect

perfidia *nf* perfidy, treachery

perfil *nm* (a) profile; *(contorno)* outline, contour; **de p.** in profile (b) *Geom* cross-section

perfilar 1 *vt (dar forma a)* to shape, to outline

2 perfilarse *vpr (tomar forma)* to take shape

perforación *nf,* **perforado** *nm* perforation; *Min* drilling, boring; *Informát (de tarjetas)* punching

perforadora *nf* punch; *Min* drill; *Informát* **p. de teclado** keypunch

perforar *vt* to perforate; *Min* to drill, to bore; *Informát* to punch

perfumar 1 *vt* to perfume

2 perfumarse *vpr* to put on perfume

perfume *nm* perfume, scent

pergamino *nm* parchment

pericia *nf* expertise, skill

periferia *nf* periphery; *(alrededores)* outskirts

periférico,-a 1 *adj* peripheral

2 *nm* (a) *Informát* peripheral (b) *CAm, Méx (carretera) Br* ring road, *US* beltway

perífrasis *nf inv* periphrasis, long-winded explanation

perilla *nf (barba)* goatee; *Fam* **de perilla(s)** *(oportuno)* at the right moment; *(útil)* very handy

perímetro *nm* perimeter

periódico,-a 1 *nm* newspaper

2 *adj* periodic(al); *Quím* **tabla periódica** periodic table

periodismo *nm* journalism

periodista *nmf* journalist, reporter

periodo, período *nm* period

peripecia *nf* sudden change, vicissitude

periplo *nm* voyage, tour

periquete *nm Fam* **en un p.** in a jiffy

periquito *nm* budgerigar, *Fam* budgie

periscopio *nm* periscope

peritaje *nm (estudios)* technical studies

perito,-a *nm,f* technician, expert; **p. industrial/agrónomo** ≃ industrial/agricultural expert

peritonitis *nf* peritonitis

perjudicar [44] *vt* to harm, to injure; *(intereses)* to prejudice

perjudicial *adj* prejudicial, harmful

perjuicio *nm* harm, damage; **en p. de** to the detriment of; **sin p. de** without prejudice to

perjurar *vi* to commit perjury

perjurio *nm* perjury

perla *nf* pearl; *Fig (persona)* gem, jewel; *Fam* **me viene de perlas** it's just the ticket

permanecer [33] *vi* to remain, to stay

permanencia *nf* (a) *(inmutabilidad)* permanence (b) *(estancia)* stay

permanente 1 *adj* permanent

  2 *nf (de pelo)* permanent wave, perm; **hacerse la p.** to have one's hair permed

permisivo,-a *adj* permissive

permiso *nm* (a) *(autorización)* permission (b) *(licencia)* licence, permit; **p. de conducir** *Br* driving licence, *US* driver's license; **p. de residencia/trabajo** residence/work permit; (c) *Mil* leave; **estar de p.** to be on leave

permitir 1 *vt* to permit, to allow; **¿me permite?** may I?

  2 permitirse *vpr* (a) to permit o allow oneself; **me permito recordarle que** let me remind you that (b) **no se permite fumar** *(en letrero)* no smoking

permutar *vt* to exchange

pernicioso,-a *adj* pernicious

pernil *nm (de pantalón)* leg; *(jamón)* leg of pork

pernocta *nf Mil* **(pase de) p.** overnight pass

pero 1 *conj* but; **p., ¿qué pasa aquí?** now, what's going on here?

  2 *nm* objection

perogrullada *nf* truism, platitude

perol *nm* large saucepan, pot

perorata *nf* boring speech

perpendicular *adj & nf* perpendicular

perpetrar *vt* to perpetrate, to commit

perpetuar [30] *vt* to perpetuate

perpetuo,-a *adj* perpetual, everlasting; *Jur* **cadena perpetua** life imprisonment

perplejidad *nf* perplexity, bewilderment

perplejo,-a *adj* perplexed, bewildered

perra *nf* (a) bitch (b) *Fam (moneda)* penny; **estar sin una p.** to be broke

perrera *nf* kennel, kennels

perrería *nf Fam* dirty trick

perro,-a 1 *nm* dog; *Fam* **un día de perros** a lousy day; *Fam* **vida de perros** dog's life; *Culin* **p. caliente** hot dog

  2 *adj Fam (vago)* lazy

persecución *nf* (a) pursuit (b) *Pol (represión)* persecution

perseguir [6] *vt* (a) to pursue, to chase; *(correr trás)* to run after, to follow (b) *(reprimir)* to persecute

perseverante *adj* persevering

perseverar *vi* (a) to persevere, to persist (b) *(durar)* to last

persiana *nf* blinds

pérsico,-a *adj* Persian; **golfo P.** Persian Gulf

persignarse *vpr* to cross oneself

persistencia *nf* persistence

persistente *adj* persistent

persistir *vi* to persist

persona *nf* person; **algunas personas** some people; *Fam* **p. mayor** grown-up

personaje *nm* (a) *Cin, Lit & Teatro* character (b) *(celebridad)* celebrity, important person

personal 1 *adj* personal, private

  2 *nm* (a) *(plantilla)* staff, personnel (b) *Fam (gente)* people

personalidad *nf* personality

personarse *vpr* to present oneself, to appear in person

personero,-a *nm,f Am* representative

personificar [44] *vt* to personify

perspectiva *nf* (a) perspective (b) *(futuro)* prospect

perspicacia *nf* insight, perspicacity

perspicaz *adj* sharp, perspicacious

persuadir *vt* to persuade; **estar persuadido de que** to be convinced that

persuasión *nf* persuasion

persuasivo,-a *adj* persuasive, convincing

pertenecer [33] *vi* to belong (a to)

perteneciente *adj* belonging

pertenencia *nf* (a) possessions, property (b) *(a un partido etc)* affiliation, membership

pértiga *nf* pole; *Dep* **salto con p.** pole vault

pertinaz *adj* (a) persistent (b) *(obstinado)* obstinate, stubborn

pertinente *adj* (a) pertinent, relevant (b) *(apropiado)* appropriate

perturbación *nf* disturbance; **p. del orden público** breach of the peace; *Med* **p. mental** mental disorder

perturbado,-a *adj* (mentally) deranged o unbalanced

perturbador,-a 1 *adj* disturbing

  2 *nm,f* unruly person

perturbar *vt (el orden)* to disturb

Perú *n* Peru

peruano,-a *adj & nm,f* Peruvian

perversión *nf* perversion

perverso,-a *adj* perverse, evil

pervertir [5] *vt* to pervert, to corrupt

pervivir *vi* to survive

pesa *nf* weight; **levantamiento de pesas** weightlifting

pesadez *nf* (a) heaviness; *(de estómago)* fullness (b) *Fam (fastidio)* drag, nuisance

pesadilla *nf* nightmare; **de p.** nightmarish

pesado,-a 1 *adj* (a) heavy (b) *(aburrido)* tedious, dull; **¡qué p.!** what a drag!

  2 *nm,f* bore

pesadumbre *nf* grief, affliction

pésame *nm* condolences, sympathy; **dar**

el p. to offer one's condolences; **mi más sentido p.** my deepest sympathy
pesar 1 *vt* to weigh; *Fig (entristecer)* to grieve
2 *vi* (**a**) to weigh; **¿cuánto pesas?** how much do you weigh? (**b**) *(ser pesado)* to be heavy (**c**) *Fig (tener importancia)* **este factor pesa mucho** this is a very important factor
3 *nm* (**a**) *(pena)* sorrow, grief (**b**) *(arrepentimiento)* regret; **a su p.** to his regret (**c**) **a p. de** in spite of
pesaroso,-a *adj* (**a**) *(triste)* sorrowful, sad (**b**) *(arrepentido)* regretful, sorry
pesca *nf* fishing; *Fam* **y toda la p.** and all that
pescadería *nf* fish shop, fishmonger's (shop)
pescadero,-a *nm,f* fishmonger
pescadilla *nf* young hake
pescado *nm* fish
pescador,-a 1 *adj* fishing
2 *nm,f (hombre)* fisherman; *(mujer)* fisherwoman
pescante *nm* (**a**) *(de carruaje)* coachman's seat (**b**) *Constr* jib, boom (**c**) *Náut* davit
pescar [44] 1 *vi* to fish
2 *vt* (**a**) to fish (**b**) *Fam (coger)* to catch
pescozada *nf,* **pescozón** *nm* slap on the neck/head
pescuezo *nm Fam* neck
pese a (que) *loc adv* in spite of (the fact that)
pesebre *nm* manger, stall
pesero *nm CAm, Méx* fixed-rate taxi service
peseta *nf* peseta
pesetero,-a *nm,f* skinflint
pesimismo *nm* pessimism
pesimista 1 *adj* pessimistic
2 *nmf* pessimist
pésimo,-a *adj* very bad, awful, terrible
peso *nm* (**a**) weight; **al p.** by weight; **p. bruto/neto** gross/net weight; *Fig* **me quité un p. de encima** it took a load off my mind; **p. mosca/pesado** *(en boxeo)* flyweight/heavyweight (**b**) *(importancia)* importance; **de p.** *(persona)* influential; *(razón)* convincing
pespunte *nm* backstitch
pesquero,-a 1 *adj* fishing
2 *nm* fishing boat
pesquisa *nf* inquiry
pestaña *nf* (**a**) eyelash, lash (**b**) *Téc* flange; *(de neumático)* rim
pestañear *vi* to blink; **sin p.** without batting an eyelid

peste *nf* (**a**) *(hedor)* stench, stink (**b**) *Med* plague; *Hist* **la p. negra** the Black Death (**c**) **decir** *o* **echar pestes** to curse
pesticida *nm* pesticide
pestilencia *nf* stench, stink
pestilente *adj* stinking, foul
pestillo *nm* bolt, latch
petaca *nf* (**a**) *(para cigarrillos)* cigarette case; *(para bebidas)* flask (**b**) *Méx (maleta)* suitcase (**c**) *Méx* **petacas** *(nalgas)* buttocks
petaco *nm (de juego)* flipper; **máquina de petacos** pinball machine
pétalo *nm* petal
petardo *nm* (**a**) firecracker, firework; *Mil* petard (**b**) *Fam (persona aburrida)* bore (**c**) *(droga)* joint
petate *nm Mil* luggage
petición *nf* request; *Jur* petition, plea
petiso,-a *adj Andes, RP Fam* short
peto *nm* **pantalón de p.** dungarees
petrificar [44] *vt,* **petrificarse** *vpr* to petrify
petróleo *nm* petroleum, oil

> _ℓ_ Observa que en el inglés británico **petrol** es un falso amigo y no es la traducción de la palabra española **petróleo**. En inglés británico, **petrol** significa "gasolina".

petrolero *nm* oil tanker
petulante *adj* arrogant, vain

> _ℓ_ Observa que la palabra inglesa **petulant** es un falso amigo y no es la traducción de la palabra española **petulante**. En inglés, **petulant** significa "caprichoso".

petunia *nf* petunia
peyorativo,-a *adj* pejorative, derogatory
pez¹ *nm* fish; **ella está como p. en el agua** she's in her element; **p. gordo** big shot
pez² *nf* pitch, tar
pezón *nm* nipple
pezuña *nf* hoof
piadoso,-a *adj* (**a**) *(devoto)* pious (**b**) *(compasivo)* compassionate; **mentira piadosa** white lie
pianista *nmf* pianist, piano player
piano *nm* piano
piar [29] *vi* to chirp, to tweet
piara *nf* herd of pigs
PIB *nm Fin (abr* **producto interior bruto***)* GDP
pibe,-a *nm,f Fam* (**a**) *(hombre)* guy; *(mujer)* girl (**b**) *RP (niño)* kid, boy; *(niña)* kid, girl
picada *nf RP (tapas)* appetizers, snacks
picadero *nm* riding school
picadillo *nm* (**a**) *(de carne)* Br minced o

US ground meat; *(de verduras)* vegetable salad (b) *Chile (tapas)* appetizers, snacks
picado,-a 1 *adj* (a) *(carne) Br* minced, *US* ground (b) *(fruta)* bad; *(diente)* decayed (c) *(mar)* choppy (d) *Fam (enfadado)* narked (e) **estar p. con** *(en competición)* to be at loggerheads with
2 *nm Av* dive; **caer en p.** to plummet
picador *nm Taurom* mounted bullfighter, picador
picadora *nf Br* mincer, *US* grinder
picadura *nf* (a) *(mordedura)* bite; *(de avispa, abeja)* sting (b) *(en fruta)* spot; *Med (de viruela)* pockmark; *(en diente)* decay, caries *sing*; *(en metalurgia)* pitting
picajoso,-a 1 *adj* touchy
2 *nm,f* touchy person
picante *adj* (a) *Culin* hot, spicy (b) *Fig (chiste etc)* risqué, spicy
picantería *nf Andes* cheap restaurant
picapica *nm* **(polvos de) p.** itching powder
picaporte *nm (aldaba)* door knocker; *(pomo)* door handle
picar [44] 1 *vt* (a) *(de insecto, serpiente)* to bite; *(de avispas, abejas)* to sting; *(barba)* to prick (b) *(comer) (aves)* to peck (at); *(persona)* to nibble, to pick at (c) *(de pez)* to bite (d) *(perforar)* to prick, to puncture (e) *Culin (carne) Br* to mince, *US* to grind (f) *(incitar)* to incite, to goad; **p. la curiosidad (de algn)** to arouse (sb's) curiosity
2 *vi* (a) *(escocer)* to itch; *(herida)* to smart; *(el sol)* to burn (b) *Culin* to be hot (c) *(pez)* to bite (d) *Fig (dejarse engañar)* to swallow it
3 picarse *vpr* (a) *(hacerse rivales)* to be at loggerheads (b) *(fruta)* to spot, to rot; *(ropa)* to become moth-eaten; *(dientes)* to decay (c) *(enfadarse)* to get cross (d) *(drogadicto)* to shoot up
picardía *nf* (a) *(astucia)* craftiness (b) *(palabrota)* swearword (c) *(prenda)* baby-doll pyjamas
pícaro,-a 1 *adj* (a) *(travieso)* naughty, mischievous; *(astuto)* sly, crafty (b) *(procaz)* risqué
2 *nm,f* rascal, rogue
picatoste *nm* crouton
pichi *nm Br* pinafore dress, *US* jumper
pichincha *nf RP Fam* snip, bargain
pichón *nm* young pigeon; **tiro al** o **p.** pigeon shooting
pickles ['pikles] *nmpl RP* pickles
pico *nm* (a) *(de ave)* beak, bill; *Fam (boca)* mouth; **tener un p. de oro** to have the gift of the gab (b) *(punta)* corner (c) *Geog* peak (d) *(herramienta)* pick, pickaxe (e)

(cantidad) odd amount; **cincuenta y p.** fifty odd; **las dos y p.** just after two (f) *(drogas)* fix
picoleto *nm Fam* civil guard
picor *nm* itch, tingling
picoso,-a *adj Méx* spicy, hot
picotazo *nm* peck
picotear *vt & vi* (a) *(pájaro)* to peck (b) *(comer)* to nibble
pictórico,-a *adj* pictorial
pídola *nf* leapfrog
pie *nm* (a) *(de persona)* foot; **pies** feet; **a p.** on foot; **de p.** standing up; **de pies a cabeza** from head to foot; **en p.** standing; **el acuerdo sigue en p.** the agreement still stands; **hacer p.** to touch the bottom; **perder p.** to get out of one's depth; *Fig* **a pies juntillas** blindly; *Fig* **al p. de la letra** to the letter, word for word; *Fig* **con buen/mal p.** on the right/wrong footing; *Fig* **con pies de plomo** gingerly, cautiously; *Fig* **dar p. a** to give cause for (b) *(de instrumento)* stand; *(de copa)* stem (c) *(de página)* foot; *(de una ilustración)* caption; **p. de página** foot of the page (d) *(medida)* foot (e) *Teatro* cue (f) *Lit* foot
piedad *nf* (a) *(devoutness, piety* (b) *(compasión)* compassion, pity
piedra *nf* stone; *(de mechero)* flint; **poner la primera p.** to lay the foundation stone; *Fam Fig* **me dejó** o **me quedé de p.** I was flabbergasted
piel *nf* (a) *(skin;* **p. de gallina** goose pimples (b) *(de fruta, de patata)* skin, peel (c) *(cuero)* leather; *(con pelo)* fur
pienso *nm* fodder, feed; **piensos compuestos** mixed feed
pierna *nf* leg
pieza *nf* (a) *(piece, part;* **p. de recambio** spare part; *Fig* **me dejó** o **me quedé de una p.** I was speechless o dumbfounded o flabbergasted (b) *(habitación)* room (c) *Teatro* play
pigmento *nm* pigment
pigmeo,-a 1 *adj* pigmy; *Fig* pygmean
2 *nm,f* Pygmy, Pigmy; *Fig* pygmy, pigmy
pijama *nm* pyjamas
pijo,-a *Fam* **1** *adj* posh; **un barrio p.** a posh area
2 *nm,f (chico)* poor little rich boy; *(chica)* poor little rich girl
3 *nm (pene)* willy
pila *nf* (a) *Elec* battery (b) *(montón)* pile, heap; *Fig* **una p. de** *(muchos)* piles o heaps o loads of (c) *(lavadero)* basin (d) *Fig* **nombre de p.** Christian name
pilar *nm* (a) *Arquit* pillar (b) *(fuente)* waterhole

píldora *nf* pill; **p. abortiva** morning-after pill; *Fig* **dorar la p. a algn** to butter sb up

pileta *nf* (a) *(pila)* sink (b) *Am (piscina)* swimming pool

pilila *nf Fam Br* willy, *US* peter

pillaje *nm* looting, pillage

pillar 1 *vt* (a) *(robar)* to plunder, to loot (b) *(coger)* to catch; *(alcanzar)* to catch up with; **lo pilló un coche** he was run over by a car (c) *Fam* to be; **me pilla un poco lejos** it's a bit far for o from me

2 pillarse *vpr* to catch; **p. un dedo/una mano** to catch one's finger/hand

pillo,-a 1 *adj* (a) *(travieso)* naughty (b) *(astuto)* sly, cunning

2 *nm,f* rogue

pilotar *vt Av* to pilot, to fly; *Aut* to drive; *Náut* to pilot, to steer

piloto *nm* (a) *Av & Náut* pilot; *Aut* driver; **piso p.** show flat; **programa p.** pilot programme (b) *(luz)* pilot lamp o light

piltrafa *nf* (a) *Fam* weakling; **estar hecho una p.** to be on one's last legs (b) *(desecho)* scraps

pimentón *nm* paprika, red pepper

pimienta *nf* pepper

pimiento *nm (fruto)* pepper; *(planta)* pimiento; **p. morrón** sweet pepper; *Fam* **me importa un p.** I don't give a damn, I couldn't care less

pimpollo *nm* (a) *Bot* shoot (b) *Fam (hombre)* handsome young man; *(mujer)* elegant young woman

pinacoteca *nf* art gallery

pináculo *nm* pinnacle

pinar *nm* pine grove, pine wood

pincel *nm* brush, paintbrush

pincelada *nf* brushstroke, stroke of a brush

pinchadiscos *nmf inv Fam* disc jockey, DJ

pinchar 1 *vt* (a) *(punzar)* to prick; *(balón, globo)* to burst; *(rueda)* to puncture (b) *Fam (incitar)* to prod; *(molestar)* to get at, to nag (c) *Med* to inject, to give an injection to (d) *Tel* to bug

2 *vi* (a) *Aut* to get a puncture (b) *Fam* **ni pincha ni corta** he cuts no ice

> 🖉 Observa que el verbo inglés **to pinch** es un falso amigo y no es la traducción del verbo español **pinchar**. En inglés, **to pinch** significa "pellizcar".

pinchazo *nm* (a) *(punzadura)* prick; *Aut* puncture, blowout (b) *(de dolor)* sudden o sharp pain

pinche *nm* (a) **p. de cocina** kitchen assistant (b) *Am (bribón)* rogue

pinchito *nm (de carne)* = type of kebab

pincho *nm* (a) *(púa)* barb (b) **p. moruno** ≃ shish kebab; **p. de tortilla** = small portion of omelette

ping-pong® *nm* table tennis, ping-pong

pingüe *adj* abundant, plentiful; **pingües beneficios** fat profits

pingüino *nm* penguin

pino *nm* pine; *Fig* **hacer el p.** to do a handstand; *Fam* **en el quinto p.** in the back of beyond

pinole *nm Am* maize o *US* corn drink

pinta 1 *nf* (a) *Fam (aspecto)* look; **tiene p. de ser interesante** it looks interesting (b) *(mota)* dot; *(lunar)* spot (c) *(medida)* pint

2 *nmf Fam* shameless person

pintada *nf* graffiti

pintado,-a *adj* **recién p.** *(en letrero)* wet paint; *Fam Fig* **nos viene que ni p.** it is just the ticket; *Fam Fig* **te está que ni p.** it suits you to a tee

pintar 1 *vt* (a) *(dar color)* to paint (b) *(dibujar)* to draw, to sketch

2 *vi (importar)* to count; *Fig* **yo aquí no pinto nada** I am out of place here

3 pintarse *vpr* (a) *(maquillarse)* to put make-up on (b) *Fam* **pintárselas** to manage

pintarraj(e)ar *vt* to daub

pintor,-a *nm,f* painter

pintoresco,-a *adj* (a) *(lugar)* picturesque (b) *(raro)* eccentric, bizarre

pintura *nf* (a) *(painting)* painting; **p. rupestre** cave painting; *Fam Fig* **no la puedo ver ni en p.** I can't stand the sight of her (b) *(materia)* paint

pinza *nf (para depilar)* tweezers; *(para tender)* *Br* clothes peg, *US* clothespin; *(de animal)* pincer, nipper; *Téc* tongs

piña *nf* (a) *(de pino)* pine cone; *(ananás)* pineapple (b) *Fig (grupo)* clan, clique (c) *Fam (golpe)* thump

piñón *nm* (a) pine seed o nut (b) *Téc* pinion

pío¹ *nm Fam* **no dijo ni p.** there wasn't a cheep out of him

pío²,-a *adj* pious

piojo *nm* louse

piola *adj RP Fam* (a) *(simpático)* fun (b) *Irón (listo)* smart, clever (c) *(lugar)* cosy

piolín *nm Am* cord

pionero,-a *nm,f* pioneer

pipa *nf* (a) *(de fumar)* pipe; **fumar en p.** to smoke a pipe (b) *(de fruta)* pip; *(de girasol)* sunflower seed

pipí *nm Fam* pee, *Br* wee-wee; **hacer p.** to pee, *Br* to wee-wee

pique *nm* (a) resentment (b) *(rivalidad)* needle (c) **a p. de** on the point of (d) **irse**

a p. *Náut* to sink; *(un plan)* to fall through; *(un negocio)* to go bust
piqueta *nf* pickaxe
piquete *nm* (a) *(de huelga)* picket (b) *Mil* p. de ejecución firing squad
pira *nf* pyre
pirado,-a *adj Fam* crazy
piragua *nf* canoe
piragüismo *nm* canoeing
piragüista *nmf* canoeist
pirámide *nf* pyramid
piraña *nf* piranha
pirarse, pirárselas *vpr Fam* to clear off, to hop it
pirata *adj & nmf* pirate
piratear *vt Fig* to pirate
Pirineo(s) *nm(pl)* Pyrenees
pirita *nf* pyrite
pirómano,-a *nm,f Med* pyromaniac; *Jur* arsonist
piropo *nm* echar un p. to pay a compliment
pirueta *nf* pirouette; *Fig Pol* hacer una p. to do a U-turn
pirulí *nm* lollipop; *TV* television tower
pis *nm Fam* pee, *Br* wee-wee; hacer p. to have a pee, *Br* to wee-wee
pisada *nf* step, footstep; *(huella)* footprint
pisapapeles *nm inv* paperweight
pisar *vt* to tread on, to step on
piscifactoría *nf* fish farm
piscina *nf* swimming pool
pisco *nm* pisco, = Andean grape brandy
piscolabis *nm inv Fam* snack
piso *nm* (a) apartment, *Br* flat; *Pol* p. franco safe house (b) *(planta)* floor; *(de carretera)* surface
pisotear *vt (aplastar)* to stamp on; *(pisar)* to trample on
pisotón *nm* me dio un p. he stood on my foot
pista *nf* (a) track; p. de baile dance floor; *Dep* p. de esquí ski run o slope; *Dep* p. de patinaje ice rink; *Dep* p. de tenis tennis court; p. de aterrizaje landing strip; p. de despegue runway (b) *(rastro)* trail, track (c) dame una p. give me a clue
pistacho *nm* pistachio nut
pisto *nm Culin* ≃ ratatouille
pistola *nf* (a) gun, pistol (b) *(para pintar)* spray gun
pistolero *nm* gunman, gangster
pistón *nm* (a) *Téc (émbolo)* piston (b) *(de arma)* cartridge cap (c) *Mús* key
pita *nf* agave
pitada *nf* (a) *(silbidos de protesta)* booing, whistling (b) *Am Fam (calada)* drag, puff

pitar 1 *vt* (a) *(silbato)* to blow (b) *Dep* el árbitro pitó un penalti the referee awarded a penalty
2 *vi* (a) to whistle (b) *Aut* to toot one's horn (c) *Dep* to referee (d) *Fam* salir pitando to fly off
pitido *nm* whistle
pitillera *nf* cigarette case
pitillo *nm* (a) *(cigarrillo)* cigarette (b) *Col (paja)* drinking straw
pito *nm* (a) whistle; *Aut* horn; *Fam* me importa un p. I don't give a hoot (b) *Fam (cigarrillo)* fag (c) *Fam (pene)* prick, willie
pitón *nm* (a) *(serpiente)* python (b) *(de toro)* horn
pitorreo *nm Fam* scoffing, teasing; hacer algo de p. to do sth for a laugh
pivot, pivote *nmf* pivot
pizarra *nf* (a) *(encerado)* blackboard (b) *(roca, material)* slate
pizarrón *nm Am (encerado)* blackboard
pizca *nf* little bit, tiny piece; ni p. not a bit; una p. de sal a pinch of salt
placa *nf* (a) plate (b) *(conmemorativa)* plaque
placaje *nm Dep* tackle
placentero,-a *adj* pleasant, agreeable
placer [33] 1 *vt* to please
2 *nm* pleasure; ha sido un p. (conocerle) it's been a pleasure (meeting you); *Fml* tengo el p. de it gives me great pleasure to; un viaje de p. a holiday trip
placidez *nf* placidity
plácido,-a *adj* placid, easy-going
plaga *nf* (a) plague (b) *Agr* pest, blight
plagar [42] *vt* to cover, to fill
plagiar [43] *vt* (a) *(copiar)* to plagiarize (b) *Andes, CAm, Méx (secuestrar)* to kidnap
plagiario,-a *nm,f Andes, CAm, Méx (secuestrador)* kidnapper
plagio *nm* plagiarism
plan *nm* (a) *(proyecto)* plan (b) *(programa)* scheme, programme; *Educ* p. de estudios syllabus; estar a p. to be on a diet (c) *Fam* en p. de broma for a laugh; si te pones en ese p. if you're going to be like that (about it); en p. barato cheaply (d) *Fam (cita)* date
plana *nf* (a) page; a toda p. full page; primera p. front page (b) *Mil* p. mayor staff
plancha *nf* (a) iron; *(de metal)* plate (b) *Culin* hotplate; sardinas a la p. grilled sardines (c) *Impr* plate
planchado *nm* ironing
planchar *vt* to iron

planchazo *nm Fam* blunder, boob

planeador *nm* glider

planear 1 *vt* to plan
2 *vi* to glide

planeta *nm* planet

planetario,-a 1 *adj* planetary
2 *nm* planetarium

planicie *nf* plain

planificación *nf* planning; **p. familiar** family planning

planificar [44] *vt* to plan

planilla *nf Am* application form

plano,-a 1 *nm* (**a**) (*de ciudad*) map; *Arquit* plan, draft (**b**) *Cin* shot; **un primer p.** a close-up; *Fig* **estar en primer/segundo p.** to be in the limelight/in the background (**c**) *Mat* plane
2 *adj* flat, even

planta *nf* (**a**) plant (**b**) (*del pie*) sole (**c**) (*piso*) floor, storey; **p. baja** *Br* ground floor, *US* first floor

plantación *nf* (**a**) plantation (**b**) (*acción*) planting

plantado,-a *adj Fam* **dejar a algn p.** to stand sb up

plantar 1 *vt* (**a**) (*árboles, campo*) to plant (**b**) (*poner*) to put, to place; **p. cara a algn** to stand up to sb (**c**) *Fam* **p. a algn en la calle** to throw sb out; **le ha plantado su novia** his girlfriend has ditched him
2 plantarse *vpr* (**a**) to stand (**b**) (*llegar*) to arrive; **en cinco minutos se plantó aquí** he got here in five minutes flat

planteamiento *nm* (*enfoque*) approach

plantear 1 *vt* (**a**) (*problema*) to pose, to raise (**b**) (*planear*) to plan (**c**) (*proponer*) to put forward (**d**) (*exponer*) to present
2 plantearse *vpr* (**a**) (*considerar*) to consider (**b**) (*problema*) to arise

plantel *nm Fig* cadre, clique

plantilla *nf* (**a**) (*personal*) staff, personnel (**b**) (*de zapato*) insole (**c**) (*patrón*) model, pattern

plantón *nm Fam* **dar un p. a algn** to stand sb up

plañir *vi* to mourn

plasmar 1 *vt* (**a**) (*reproducir*) to capture (**b**) (*expresar*) to express
2 plasmarse *vpr* **p. en** to take the shape of

plasta *nmf Fam* bore

plástico,-a 1 *adj* plastic
2 *nm* (**a**) plastic (**b**) (*disco*) record

plastificar [44] *vt* to coat *o* cover with plastic

plastilina® *nf* Plasticine®

plata *nf* (**a**) silver; (*objetos de plata*) silverware; *Fam* **hablar en p.** to lay (it) on

the line; **p. de ley** sterling silver (**b**) *Am* money

plataforma *nf* platform

plátano *nm* (**a**) (*fruta*) banana (**b**) (*árbol*) plane tree; **falso p.** sycamore

platea *nf Cin & Teatro Br* stalls, *US* orchestra

platear *vt* to silver-plate

platense 1 *adj* of/from the River Plate
2 *nmf* person from the River Plate

plática *nf CAm, Méx* chat, talk

platicar [44] *vi CAm, Méx* to chat, to talk

platillo *nm* (**a**) saucer; **p. volante** flying saucer (**b**) *Mús* cymbal

platina *nf* (*de tocadiscos*) deck; **doble p.** double deck

platino *nm* (**a**) platinum (**b**) *Aut* **platinos** contact breaker, points

plato *nm* (**a**) plate, dish (**b**) (*parte de una comida*) course; **de primer p.** for starters; **p. fuerte** main course; **p. combinado** one-course meal (**c**) (*guiso*) dish (**d**) (*de balanza*) pan, tray (**e**) (*de tocadiscos*) turntable

plató *nm Cin & TV* (film) set

platudo,-a *adj Am Fam* loaded, rolling in it

plausible *adj* (**a**) (*admisible*) plausible, acceptable (**b**) (*loable*) commendable

playa *nf* (**a**) beach; (*costa*) seaside (**b**) *Am* **p. de estacionamiento** *Br* car park, *US* parking lot

playera *nf* (**a**) (*zapatilla*) *Br* sandshoe, *US* sneaker (**b**) *Méx* (*camiseta*) teeshirt

plaza *nf* (**a**) square (**b**) (*mercado*) market, marketplace (**c**) *Aut* seat (**d**) (*laboral*) post, position (**e**) **p. de toros** bullring

plazo *nm* (**a**) (*periodo*) time, period; (*término*) deadline; **a corto/largo p.** in the short term/in the long run; **el p. termina el viernes** Friday is the deadline (**b**) *Fin* **comprar a plazos** to buy on *Br* hire purchase *o US* an installment plan; **en seis plazos** in six instalments

pleamar *nf* high tide

plebe *nf* masses, plebs

plebeyo,-a 1 *adj* plebeian
2 *nm,f* plebeian, pleb

plebiscito *nm* plebiscite

plegable *adj* folding, collapsible

plegar [1] 1 *vt* to fold
2 plegarse *vpr* to give way, to bow

plegaria *nf* prayer

pleitear *vi* to conduct a lawsuit, to plead

pleito *nm* (**a**) *Jur* lawsuit, litigation; **poner un p. (a algn)** to sue (sb) (**b**) *Am* (*discusión*) argument

plenilunio *nm* full moon

plenitud *nf* plenitude, fullness; **en la p. de la vida** in the prime of life

pleno,-a 1 *adj* full; **en plena noche** in the middle of the night; **los empleados en p.** the entire staff

  2 *nm* plenary meeting

pletórico,-a *adj* abundant

plexiglás® *nm* (*plástico*) Perspex®, *US* Plexiglass®

pliego *nm* (**a**) (*hoja*) sheet *o* piece of paper; **p. de condiciones** bidding specifications (**b**) (*carta*) sealed letter

pliegue *nm* (**a**) fold (**b**) (*de vestido*) pleat

plinto *nm Dep* horse

plisar *vt* to pleat

plomería *nf Méx, RP, Ven* plumber's

plomero *nm Méx, RP, Ven* plumber

plomizo,-a *adj* lead, leaden; (*color*) lead-coloured

plomo *nm* (**a**) (*en metalurgia*) lead (**b**) *Elec* (*fusible*) fuse (**c**) (*bala*) slug, pellet

pluma *nf* (**a**) feather (**b**) (*estilográfica*) fountain pen (**c**) *Carib, Méx* (*bolígrafo*) (ballpoint) pen

plumaje *nm* plumage

plumazo *nm* **de un p.** at a stroke

plumero *nm* (**a**) (*para el polvo*) feather duster (**b**) *Fam* **se te ve el p.** I can see through you

plumier *nm* pencil box

plural *adj & nm* plural

pluralismo *nm* pluralism

pluriempleo *nm* moonlighting

plus *nm* bonus, bonus payment

plusmarca *nf* record

plusmarquista *nmf* record breaker

plusvalía *nf* capital gain

Plza. (*abr* Plaza) Sq

población *nf* (**a**) (*ciudad*) town; (*pueblo*) village (**b**) (*habitantes*) population (**c**) *Chile* (*barrio*) **p. (callampa)** shanty town

poblado,-a *adj* (**a**) populated; *Fig* **p. de** full of (**b**) (*barba*) bushy, thick

poblador,-a *nm,f* settler

poblar [2] *vt* (**a**) (*con gente*) to settle, to people; (*con plantas*) to plant (**b**) (*vivir*) to inhabit

pobre 1 *adj* poor; **¡p.!** poor thing!; **un hombre p.** a poor man; **un p. hombre** a poor devil

  2 *nmf* poor person; **los pobres** the poor

pobreza *nf* poverty; *Fig* (*de medios, recursos*) lack

pocho,-a *adj* (**a**) (*fruta*) bad, overripe (**b**) *Fig* (*persona*) (*débil*) off-colour; (*triste*) depressed, down (**c**) *Méx Fam* (*americanizado*) Americanized

pochoclo *nm Arg* popcorn

pocilga *nf* pigsty

pocillo *nm RP* (**a**) (*pequeño*) small cup (**b**) *Méx, Ven* (*grande*) enamel mug

pócima, poción *nf* potion; *Pey* concoction, brew

poco,-a 1 *nm* (**a**) **un p.** (*con adj o adv*) a little; **un p. tarde/frío** a little late/cold

  (**b**) **un p.** (*con sustantivo*) a little; **un p. de azúcar** a little sugar

  2 *adj* (**a**) not much, little; **p. sitio/tiempo** not much *o* little space/time; **poca cosa** not much

  (**b**) **pocos,-as** not many, few; **pocas personas** not many *o* few people

  (**c**) **unos,-as pocos,-as** a few

  3 *pron* (**a**) (*escasa cantidad*) not much; **queda p.** there isn't much left

  (**b**) (*breve tiempo*) **p. antes/después** shortly *o* a little before/afterwards; **a p. de** shortly *o* a little after; **dentro de p.** soon

  (**c**) **pocos,-as** (*cosas*) few, not many; **tengo muy pocos** I have very few, I don't have very many

  (**d**) **pocos,-as** (*personas*) few people, not many people; **vinieron pocos** few people came, not many people came

  4 *adv* (**a**) (*con verbo*) not (very) much, little; **ella come p.** she doesn't eat much, she eats little

  (**b**) (*con adj*) not very; **es p. probable** it's not very likely

  (**c**) (*en frases*) **p. a p.** little by little, gradually; **por p.** almost

podadera, *Am* **podadora** *nf* garden shears

podar *vt* to prune

poder¹ *nm* power; *Econ* **p. adquisitivo** purchasing power

poder² **[18] 1** *vi* (**a**) (*capacidad*) to be able to; **no puede hablar** she can't speak; **no podré llamarte** I won't be able to phone; **no puedo más** I can't take any more; **guapa a más no p.** unbelievably pretty

  (**b**) (*permiso*) may, might; **¿puedo pasar?** can *o* may I come in?; **¿se puede (entrar)?** may I (come in)?; **aquí no se puede fumar** you can't smoke here

  (**c**) (*uso impers*) (*posibilidad*) may, might; **puede que no lo sepan** they may *o* might not know; **no puede ser** that's impossible; **puede (ser) (que sí)** maybe, perhaps

  (**d**) (*deber*) **podrías haberme advertido** you might have warned me

  (**e**) to cope (**con** with); **no puede con**

tanto trabajo he can't cope with so much work

2 *vt* (*batir*) to be stronger than; **les puede a todos** he can take on anybody

poderoso,-a *adj* powerful

podio, pódium *nm Dep* podium

podré *indic fut de* **poder**

podrido,-a *adj* (a) (*putrefacto*) rotten, putrid (b) (*corrupto*) corrupt; *Fam* **p. de dinero** *o Am* **en plata** stinking rich (c) *RP Fam* (*harto*) fed up, sick

podrir *vt defect =* **pudrir**

poema *nm* poem

poesía *nf* (a) (*género*) poetry (b) (*poema*) poem

poeta *nmf* poet

poético,-a *adj* poetic

póker *nm* poker

polaco,-a 1 *adj* Polish

2 *nm,f* Pole

3 *nm* (*idioma*) Polish

polaridad *nf* polarity

polarizar [40] *vt* (a) *Fís* to polarize (b) *Fig* (*ánimo, atención*) to concentrate

polea *nf* pulley

polémica *nf* controversy

polémico,-a *adj* controversial

polemizar [40] *vi* to argue, to debate

polen *nm* pollen

polera *nf RP* polo shirt

poli *Fam* **1** *nmf* cop

2 *nf* **la p.** the fuzz *pl*

poli- *pref* poly-

policía 1 *nf* police (force)

2 *nmf* (*hombre*) policeman; (*mujer*) policewoman

policíaco,-a, policiaco,-a, policial *adj* police; **novela/película policíaca** detective story/film

polideportivo *nm* sports centre

poliéster *nm* polyester

polietileno *nm Br* polythene, *US* polyethylene

polifacético,-a *adj* versatile, many-sided; **es un hombre muy p.** he's a man of many talents

poligamia *nf* polygamy

políglota *adj & nmf* polyglot

polígono *nm* polygon; **p. industrial** industrial estate

polilla *nf* moth

poliomielitis *nf* polio, poliomyelitis

politécnico,-a *adj & nm* polytechnic

política *nf* (a) politics *sing* (b) (*estrategia*) policy

políticamente *adv* **p. correcto** politically correct

político,-a 1 *adj* (a) political (b)

(*pariente*) in-law; **hermano p.** brother-in-law; **su familia política** her in-laws

2 *nm,f* politician

póliza *nf* (a) (*sello*) stamp (b) **p. de seguros** insurance policy

polizón *nm* stowaway

polla *nf* (a) *Vulg* (*pene*) prick (b) *Orn* **p. de agua** moorhen

pollera *nf* (a) *RP* (*occidental*) skirt (b) *Andes* (*indígena*) = long skirt worn by Indian women

pollo *nm* (a) chicken (b) *Fam* (*joven*) lad

polo *nm* (a) *Elec & Geog* pole; **P. Norte/Sur** North/South Pole (b) (*helado*) *Br* ice lolly, *US* Popsicle® (c) (*prenda*) sports shirt, polo neck (sweater) (d) *Dep* polo

pololear *vi Chile Fam* to go out (together)

pololo,-a *nm,f Chile Fam* boyfriend, *f* girlfriend

Polonia *n* Poland

poltrona *nf* easy chair

polución *nf* pollution

polvareda *nf* cloud of dust

polvera *nf* powder compact

polvo *nm* (a) dust; **limpiar** *o* **quitar el p.** to dust; **en p.** powdered; **polvo(s) de talco** talcum powder (b) *Fam* **estar hecho p.** (*cansado*) to be *Br* knackered *o US* bushed; (*deprimido*) to be depressed (c) *muy Fam* **echar un p.** to have a screw

pólvora *nf* gunpowder

polvoriento,-a *adj* dusty

polvorín *nm* gunpowder arsenal; *Fig* powder keg

polvorón *nm* sweet pastry

pomada *nf* ointment

pomelo *nm* (*fruto*) grapefruit; (*árbol*) grapefruit tree

pómez *adj inv* **piedra p.** pumice (stone)

pomo *nm* (*de puerta*) knob

pompa *nf* (a) bubble (b) (*ostentación*) pomp (c) *Méx Fam* **pompas** botty

pompis *nm inv Fam* botty

pomposo,-a *adj* pompous

pómulo *nm* cheekbone

ponchar 1 *vt* (a) *CAm, Carib, Méx* (*rueda*) to puncture (b) *Am* (*en béisbol*) to strike out

2 poncharse *vpr* (a) *CAm, Carib, Méx* (*rueda*) to get a puncture (b) *Am* (*en béisbol*) to strike out

ponche *nm* punch

poncho *nm* poncho

ponderar *vt* (a) (*asunto*) to weigh up *o* consider (b) (*alabar*) to praise

pondré *indic fut de* **poner**

ponencia *nf* paper

poner [19] (*pp* **puesto**) **1** *vt* (**a**) to put; (*mesa, huevo*) to lay; (*gesto*) to make; (*multa*) to impose; (*telegrama*) to send; (*negocio*) to set up

(**b**) (*tele, radio etc*) to turn *o* switch on

(**c**) (*+ adj*) to make; **p. triste a algn** to make sb sad; **p. colorado a algn** to make sb blush

(**d**) **¿qué llevaba puesto?** what was he wearing?

(**e**) (*decir*) **¿qué pone aquí?** what does it say here?

(**f**) (*suponer*) to suppose; **pongamos que Ana no viene** supposing Ana doesn't turn up

(**g**) *TV & Cin* to put on, to show; **¿qué ponen en la tele?** what's on the telly?

(**h**) *Tel* **ponme con Manuel** put me through to Manuel

(**i**) (*nombrar*) **le pondremos (de nombre) Pilar** we are going to call her Pilar

2 *v impers Am Fam* (*parecer*) **se me pone que ...** it seems to me that ...

3 ponerse *vpr* (**a**) to put oneself; **ponte en mi lugar** put yourself in my place; **ponte más cerca** come closer

(**b**) (*vestirse*) to put on; **ella se puso el jersey** she put her sweater on

(**c**) (*+ adj*) to become; **p. furioso/malo** to become furious/ill

(**d**) (*sol*) to set

(**e**) *Tel* **p. al teléfono** to answer the phone

(**f**) **p. a** to start to; **p. a trabajar** to get down to work

poney *nm* pony

pongo *indic pres de* **poner**

poniente *nm* (**a**) (*occidente*) West (**b**) (*viento*) westerly (wind)

ponqué *nm Col, Ven* = large sponge cake, filled with cream and/or fruit, and covered in icing or chocolate

pontífice *nm* Pontiff; **el Sumo P.** His Holiness the Pope

ponzoña *nf* (**a**) venom, poison (**b**) **tener p.** (*tristeza*) to be down in the dumps

ponzoñoso,-a *adj* (**a**) venomous, poisonous (**b**) (*triste*) down in the dumps

popa *nf* stern; *Fig* **ir viento en p.** to go full speed ahead

popote *nm Méx* drinking straw

populacho *nm Pey* plebs, masses

popular *adj* (**a**) folk; **arte/música p.** folk art/music (**b**) (*medida*) popular (**c**) (*actor*) well-known

popularidad *nf* popularity

popularizar [40] *vt* to popularize

populoso,-a *adj* densely populated

popurrí *nm Mús* medley

póquer *nm* poker

por *prep* (**a**) (*agente*) by; **pintado p. Picasso** painted by Picasso

(**b**) **p. qué** why

(**c**) (*causa*) because of; **p. sus ideas** because of her ideas; **p. necesidad/amor** out of need/love; **suspendió p. no estudiar** he failed because he didn't study

(**d**) (*tiempo*) **p. la mañana/noche** in the morning/at night; **p. ahora** for the time being; **p. entonces** at that time

(**e**) (*en favor de*) for; **lo hago p. mi hermano** I'm doing it for my brother('s sake)

(**f**) (*lugar*) **pasamos p. Córdoba** we went through Córdoba; **p. ahí** over there; **¿p. dónde vamos?** which way are we taking *o* going?; **p. la calle** in the street; **mirar p. la ventana** to look out the window; **entrar p. la ventana** to get in through the window

(**g**) (*medio*) by; **p. avión/correo** by plane/post

(**h**) (*a cambio de*) for; **cambiar algo p. otra cosa** to exchange sth for something else

(**i**) (*distributivo*) **p. cabeza** a head, per person; **p. hora/mes** per hour/month

(**j**) *Mat* **dos p. tres, seis** two times three is six; **un 10 p. ciento** 10 percent

(**k**) (*con infinitivo*) in order to, so as to; **hablar p. hablar** to talk for the sake of it

(**l**) (*locuciones*) **p. así decirlo** so to speak; **p. más o muy ... que sea** no matter how ... he/she is; **p. mí** as far as I'm concerned

porcelana *nf* porcelain

porcentaje *nm* percentage

porche *nm* porch

porcino,-a *adj* **ganado p.** pigs

porción *nf* portion, part

pordiosero,-a *nm,f* tramp, *US* bum

porfía *nf* (*obstinación*) obstinacy, stubbornness

porfolio *nm* portfolio

pormenor *nm* detail; **venta al p.** retail

porno *adj inv Fam* porn

pornografía *nf* pornography

pornográfico,-a *adj* pornographic

poro *nm* pore

poroso,-a *adj* porous

poroto *nm RP* (*judía*) kidney bean

porque *conj* (**a**) (*causal*) because; **¡p. no!** just because! (**b**) (*final*) (*+ subjunctive*) so that, in order that

porqué *nm* reason

porquería *nf* (**a**) (*suciedad*) dirt, filth (**b**) (*birria*) *Br* rubbish, *US* garbage (**c**) *Fam* *(chuchería)* junk food, *Br* rubbish

porra *nf* (a) *(de policía)* truncheon, baton (b) *Fam (locuciones)* **¡una p.!** *Br* rubbish!, *US* garbage!; **¡vete a la p.!** get lost!

porrazo *nm* thump

porro *nm* (a) *Fam (de droga)* joint (b) *Am (puerro)* leek

porrón *nm* = glass bottle with a spout coming out of its base, used for drinking wine

portaaviones *nm inv* aircraft carrier

portada *nf* (a) *(de libro etc)* cover; *(de periódico)* front page; *(de disco)* sleeve (b) *(fachada)* front, facade

portador,-a *nm,f Com* bearer; *Med* carrier

portaequipajes *nm inv* (a) *Aut (maletero) Br* boot, *US* trunk; *(baca)* roof rack (b) *(carrito)* luggage trolley

portafolios *nm inv* briefcase

portal *nm* (a) *(zaguán)* porch, entrance hall (b) *(puerta de la calle)* main door (c) **p. de Belén** Nativity scene (d) *Informát* portal

portamaletas *nm inv* = **portaequipajes**

portaminas *nm inv* propelling pencil

portamonedas *nm inv* purse

portarse *vpr* to behave; **p. mal** to misbehave

portátil *adj* portable

portaviones *nm inv* = **portaaviones**

portavoz *nmf* spokesperson; *(hombre)* spokesman; *(mujer)* spokeswoman

portazo *nm* **oímos un p.** we heard a slam o bang; **dar un p.** to slam the door

porte *nm* (a) *(aspecto)* bearing (b) *(transporte)* carriage

portento *nm* (a) *(cosa)* wonder, marvel (b) *(persona)* genius

portentoso,-a *adj* extraordinary, prodigious

porteño,-a 1 *adj* of/from Buenos Aires **2** *nm,f* person from Buenos Aires

portería *nf* (a) porter's lodge (b) *Dep* goal

portero,-a *nm,f* (a) *(de vivienda)* porter, caretaker; **p. automático** Entryphone® (b) *Dep* goalkeeper

pórtico *nm* (a) *(portal)* portico, porch (b) *(con arcadas)* arcade

portorriqueño,-a *adj & nm,f* Puerto Rican

portuario,-a *adj* harbour, port

Portugal *n* Portugal

portugués,-esa 1 *adj* Portuguese **2** *nm (idioma)* Portuguese

porvenir *nm* future; **sin p.** with no prospects

pos *adv* **en p. de** after

pos- *pref* post-

posada *nf* inn

posaderas *nfpl Fam* buttocks

posadero,-a *nm,f* innkeeper

posar 1 *vi (para retrato etc)* to pose **2** *vt* to put o lay down **3 posarse** *vpr* to settle, to alight

posdata *nf* postscript

pose *nf* (a) *(postura)* pose (b) *(afectación)* posing

poseedor,-a *nm,f* possessor

poseer [36] *vt* to possess, to own

poseído,-a *adj* possessed

posesión *nf* possession; **estar en p. de** to have; **tomar p. (de un cargo)** to take up (a post)

posesivo,-a *adj* possessive

poseso,-a *adj & nm,f* possessed

posguerra *nf* postwar period

posibilidad *nf* possibility; *(oportunidad)* chance

posibilitar *vt* to make possible

posible 1 *adj* possible; **de ser p.** if possible; **en (la medida de) lo p.** as far as possible; **haré todo lo p.** I'll do everything I can; **lo antes p.** as soon as possible; **es p. que venga** he might come **2** *nmpl* **posibles** means

posición *nf* position

positivo,-a *adj* positive

posmoderno,-a *adj* postmodern

poso *nm* dregs, sediment

posponer [19] *vt* (a) *(aplazar)* to postpone, to put off (b) *(relegar)* to put in second place o behind, to relegate

post- *pref* post-

posta *nf* **a p.** on purpose

postal 1 *adj* postal **2** *nf* postcard

poste *nm* pole; *Dep (de portería)* post

póster *nm* poster

postergar [42] *vt* (a) *(relegar)* to relegate (b) *(retrasar)* to delay; *(aplazar)* to postpone

posteridad *nf* posterity; **pasar a la p.** to go down in history

posterior *adj* (a) *(lugar)* posterior, rear (b) *(tiempo)* later (a than), subsequent (a to)

posterioridad *nf* posteriority; **con p.** later

posteriormente *adv* subsequently, later

postgraduado,-a *adj & nm,f* postgraduate

postigo *nm (de puerta)* wicket; *(de ventana)* shutter

postín *nm Fam* boasting, showing off;

261   **postizo ▶ precisamente**

darse p. to show off, to swank; **de p.** posh, swanky
postizo,-a 1 *adj* false, artificial; **dentadura postiza** false teeth, dentures
 2 *nm* hairpiece
postor *nm* bidder
postrarse *upr* to prostrate oneself, to kneel down
postre *nm* dessert, sweet
postrero,-a *adj* last

> **Postrer** is used instead of **postrero** before masculine singular nouns (e.g. **el postrer día** the last day).

postrimería *nf (usu pl)* last part o period
postular 1 *vt* (**a**) *(defender)* to call for (**b**) *Am (candidatar)* to propose, to nominate
 2 *vi (en colecta)* to collect
 3 postularse *vpr Am* (**a**) *Pol (para cargo)* to stand, to run (**b**) *(para trabajo)* to apply (**para** for)
póstumo,-a *adj* posthumous
postura *nf* (**a**) position, posture (**b**) *Fig (actitud)* attitude
pos(t)venta *adj* **servicio p.** after-sales service
potable *adj* drinkable; **agua p./no p.** drinking water/not drinking water
potaje *nm* hotpot, stew
pote *nm* pot; *(jarra)* jug
potencia *nf* power; **en p.** potential
potencial 1 *adj* potential
 2 *nm* (**a**) *(potential)*; **p. eléctrico** voltage; **p. humano** manpower (**b**) *Ling* conditional (tense)
potenciar [43] *vt* to promote, to strengthen
potente *adj* powerful, strong
potestad *nf* power, authority
potingue *nm Fam Pey* (**a**) *(bebida)* concoction (**b**) *(maquillaje)* make-up, face cream/lotion
potra *nf Fam* luck
potrero *nm Am* field, pasture
potro *nm Zool* colt; *(de gimnasia)* horse
poyo *nm* stone bench
pozo *nm* well; *Min* shaft, pit
pozole *nm CAm, Carib, Méx (guiso)* = stew made with maize kernels, pork or chicken and vegetables
PP *nm (abr* **Partido Popular**) = Spanish political party to the right of the political spectrum
práctica *nf* (**a**) practice; **en la p.** in practice (**b**) *(formación)* placement; **período de prácticas** practical training period
practicante 1 *adj Rel* practising
 2 *nmf Med* medical assistant

practicar [44] 1 *vt* to practise; *(operación)* to carry out
 2 *vi* to practise
práctico,-a *adj* practical; *(útil)* handy, useful
pradera *nf* meadow
prado *nm* meadow, field
Praga *n* Prague
pragmático,-a 1 *adj* pragmatic
 2 *nm,f* pragmatist
pre- *pref* pre-
preámbulo *nm* (**a**) *(introducción)* preamble (**b**) *(rodeo)* circumlocution
preaviso *nm* previous warning, notice
precalentamiento *nm* warm-up
precalentar [1] *vt* to preheat
precario,-a *adj* precarious
precaución *nf* (**a**) *(cautela)* caution; **con p.** cautiously (**b**) *(medida)* precaution
precaver 1 *vt* to guard against
 2 precaverse *vpr* to take precautions (**de** o **contra** against)
precavido,-a *adj* cautious, prudent
precedencia *nf* precedence, priority
precedente 1 *adj* preceding
 2 *nmf* predecessor
 3 *nm* precedent; **sin p.** unprecedented
preceder *vt* to precede
precepto *nm* precept
preciarse [43] *vpr* to fancy oneself (**de** as)
precintar *vt* to seal
precinto *nm* seal

> Observa que la palabra inglesa **precinct** es un falso amigo y no es la traducción de la palabra española **precinto**. En inglés, **precinct** significa "recinto" o "distrito".

precio *nm* price; **p. de coste** cost price; **a cualquier p.** at any price
preciosidad *nf* (**a**) *(hermosura) (cosa)* lovely thing; *(persona)* darling (**b**) *Fml (cualidad)* preciousness
precioso,-a *adj* (**a**) *(hermoso)* lovely, beautiful (**b**) *(valioso)* precious, valuable
precipicio *nm* precipice
precipitación *nf* (**a**) *(prisa)* haste (**b**) *(lluvia)* rainfall
precipitado,-a *adj* *(apresurado)* hasty, hurried; *(irreflexivo)* rash
precipitar 1 *vt* (**a**) *(acelerar)* to hurry, to rush (**b**) *(arrojar)* to throw, to hurl down
 2 precipitarse *vpr* (**a**) *(persona)* to hurl oneself; *(acontecimientos)* to gather speed (**b**) *(actuar irreflexivamente)* to hurry, to rush
precisamente *adv (con precisión)* precisely; *(exactamente)* exactly; **p. por**

eso for that very reason

precisar *vt* (**a**) *(determinar)* to determine, to give full details of; *(especificar)* to specify (**b**) *(necesitar)* to require, to need

precisión *nf* (**a**) *(exactitud)* precision, accuracy; **con p.** precisely, accurately (**b**) *(aclaración)* clarification

preciso,-a *adj* (**a**) *(necesario)* necessary, essential (**b**) *(exacto)* accurate, exact; **en este p. momento** at this very moment (**c**) *(claro)* concise, clear

preconizar [40] *vt* to advocate

precoz *adj* (**a**) *(persona)* precocious (**b**) *(fruta)* early

precursor,-a *nm,f* precursor

predecesor,-a *nm,f* predecessor

predecir [12] *(pp* **predicho**) *vt* to foretell, to predict

predestinado,-a *adj* predestined

predeterminar *vt* to predetermine

predicado *nm* predicate

predicador,-a *nm,f* preacher

predicar [44] *vt* to preach

predicción *nf* prediction, forecast

predice *indic pres de* **predecir**

predije *pt indef de* **predecir**

predilección *nf* predilection

predilecto,-a *adj* favourite, preferred

predisponer [19] *(pp* **predispuesto**) *vt* to predispose

predisposición *nf* predisposition

predominante *adj* predominant

predominar *vi* to predominate

predominio *nm* predominance

preescolar *adj* preschool; **en p.** in the nursery school

prefabricado,-a *adj* prefabricated

prefacio *nm* preface

preferencia *nf* preference

preferente *adj* preferable, preferential

preferible *adj* preferable; **es p. que no vengas** you'd better not come

preferido,-a *nm,f* favourite

preferir [5] *vt* to prefer

prefijo *nm* (**a**) *Tel Br* dialling code, *US* area code (**b**) *Ling* prefix

pregonar *vt (anunciar)* to announce publicly; *Fig (divulgar)* to reveal, to disclose

pregunta *nf* question; **hacer una p.** to ask a question

preguntar 1 *vt* to ask; **p. algo a algn** to ask sb sth; **p. por algn** to ask after *o* about sb

2 preguntarse *vpr* to wonder; **me pregunto si ...** I wonder whether ...

preguntón,-ona *nm,f Fam* busybody

prehistoria *nf* prehistory

prehistórico,-a *adj* prehistoric

prejuicio *nm* prejudice; **tener prejuicios** to be prejudiced, to be biased

preliminar *adj & nm* preliminary

preludio *nm* prelude

prematrimonial *adj* premarital

prematuro,-a *adj* premature

premeditación *nf* premeditation; **con p.** deliberately

premeditado,-a *adj* premeditated, deliberate

premiado,-a *adj* prize-winning

premiar [43] *vt* (**a**) to award a prize to (**b**) *(recompensar)* to reward

premio *nm* prize, award; *(recompensa)* reward

premisa *nf* premise

premonición *nf* premonition

premura *nf (urgencia)* urgency; **p. de tiempo** haste

prenatal *adj* antenatal, prenatal

prenda *nf* (**a**) *(prenda)* garment (**b**) *(garantía)* token, pledge

prendar 1 *vt* to captivate, to delight

2 prendarse *vpr (enamorarse)* to fall in love (**de** with)

prendedor *nm* brooch, pin

prender 1 *vt* (**a**) *(sujetar)* to fasten, to attach; *(con alfileres)* to pin (**b**) **p. fuego a** to set fire to (**c**) *(arrestar)* to arrest

2 *vi (fuego)* to catch; *(madera)* to catch fire; *(planta)* to take root

3 prenderse *vpr* to catch fire

prensa *nf* press; *Fig* **tener buena/mala p.** to have a good/bad press

prensar *vt* to press

preñado,-a *adj* (**a**) pregnant (**b**) *Fig (lleno)* pregnant (**de** with), full (**de** of)

preñar *vt (mujer)* to make pregnant; *(animal)* to impregnate

preocupación *nf* worry, concern

preocupado,-a *adj* worried, concerned

preocupar 1 *vt* to worry; **me preocupa que llegue tan tarde** I'm worried about him arriving so late

2 preocuparse *vpr* to worry, to get worried (**por** about); **no te preocupes** don't worry; **p. de algn** to look after sb; **p. de algo** to see to sth

preparación *nf* preparation; *(formación)* training

preparado,-a 1 *adj* (**a**) *(dispuesto)* ready, prepared; **comidas preparadas** readycooked meals (**b**) *(capacitado)* trained, qualified

2 *nm Farm* preparation

preparador,-a *nm,f* coach, trainer

preparar 1 *vt* (**a**) to prepare, to get ready;

p. un examen to prepare for an exam (**b**) *Dep (entrenar)* to train, to coach

2 prepararse *vpr* (**a**) to prepare oneself, to get ready (**b**) *Dep (entrenarse)* to train

preparativo *nm* preparation

preparatorio,-a *adj* preparatory

preponderante *adj* preponderant

preposición *nf Ling* preposition

prepotente *adj* domineering; *(arrogante)* overbearing

prerrogativa *nf* prerogative

presa *nf* (**a**) prey; *Fig* **ser p. de** to be a victim of; **p. del pánico** panic-stricken (**b**) *(embalse)* dam

presagiar [43] *vt* to predict, to foretell

presagio *nm* (**a**) *(señal)* omen; **buen/mal p.** good/bad omen (**b**) *(premonición)* premonition

presbiteriano,-a *adj & nm,f* Presbyterian

presbítero *nm* priest

prescindir *vi* **p. de** to do without

prescribir (*pp* **prescrito**) *vt* to prescribe

prescripción *nf* prescription; **p. facultativa** medical prescription

presencia *nf* presence; **hacer acto de p.** to put in an appearance; **p. de ánimo** presence of mind

presencial *adj* **testigo p.** eyewitness

presenciar [43] *vt (ver)* to witness

presentable *adj* presentable; **no estoy p.** I'm not dressed for the occasion

presentación *nf* presentation; *(aspecto)* appearance; *(de personas)* introduction

presentador,-a *nm,f Rad & TV* presenter, host, hostess

presentar 1 *vt* (**a**) to present; *(mostrar)* to show, to display; *(ofrecer)* to offer (**b**) *(una persona a otra)* to introduce; **le presento al doctor Ruiz** may I introduce you to Dr Ruiz

2 presentarse *vpr* (**a**) *(comparecer)* to present oneself; *(inesperadamente)* to turn o come up (**b**) *(ocasión, oportunidad)* to present itself, to arise (**c**) *(candidato)* to stand; **p. a unas elecciones** to stand for election, *US* to run for office; **p. a un examen** to sit an examination (**d**) *(darse a conocer)* to introduce oneself (**a** to)

presente 1 *adj* present; **la p. (carta)** this letter; **hacer p.** to declare, to state; **tener p.** *(tener en cuenta)* to bear in mind; *(recordar)* to remember

2 *nm* present

presentimiento *nm* presentiment, premonition; **tengo el p. de que ...** I have the feeling that ...

presentir [5] *vt* to have a presentiment o premonition of; **presiento que lloverá** I've got the feeling that it's going to rain

preservación *nf* preservation, protection

preservar *vt* to preserve, to protect (**de** from; **contra** against)

preservativo *nm* sheath, condom

presidencia *nf* (**a**) *Pol* presidency (**b**) *(de una reunión) (hombre)* chairmanship; *(mujer)* chairwomanship

presidenciable *nmf Am* potential president

presidencial *adj* presidential

presidente,-a *nm,f* (**a**) *Pol* president; **p. del gobierno** Prime Minister, Premier (**b**) *(de una reunión)* chairperson

presidiario,-a *nm,f* prisoner, convict

presidio *nm* prison, penitentiary

presidir *vt* (**a**) *Pol* to rule, to head (**b**) *(reunión)* to chair, to preside over

presión *nf* pressure; **a** o **bajo p.** under pressure; **grupo de p.** pressure group, lobby; **p. arterial** o **sanguínea** blood pressure; **p. atmosférica** atmospheric pressure

presionar *vt* to press; *Fig* to pressurize, to put pressure on

preso,-a 1 *adj* imprisoned

2 *nm,f* prisoner

prestación *nf* (**a**) service (**b**) **prestaciones** *(de coche etc)* performance

prestado,-a *adj* **dejar p.** to lend; **pedir p.** to borrow; **vivir de p.** to scrounge

prestamista *nmf* moneylender

préstamo *nm* loan

prestar 1 *vt* (**a**) to lend, to loan; **¿me prestas tu pluma?** can I borrow your pen? (**b**) *(atención)* to pay; *(ayuda)* to give; *(servicio)* to do

2 prestarse *vpr* (**a**) *(ofrecerse)* to offer oneself (**a** to) (**b**) **p. a** *(dar motivo)* to cause; **se presta a (crear) malentendidos** it makes for misunderstandings

presteza *nf* promptness; **con p.** promptly

prestidigitador,-a *nm,f* conjuror, magician

prestigiar [43] *vt* to give prestige to

prestigio *nm* prestige

prestigioso,-a *adj* prestigious

presto,-a *adj Fml* (**a**) *(dispuesto)* ready, prepared (**b**) *(rápido)* swift, prompt

presumible *adj* probable, likely

presumido,-a 1 *adj* vain, conceited

2 *nm,f* vain person

presumir 1 *vt (suponer)* to presume, to suppose

2 *vi* (**a**) *(ser vanidoso)* to show off (**b**)

presume de guapo he thinks he's good-looking

presunción *nf* (**a**) *(suposición)* presumption, supposition (**b**) *(vanidad)* vanity, conceit

presunto,-a *adj* supposed; *Jur* alleged

presuntuoso,-a *adj* (**a**) *(vanidoso)* vain, conceited (**b**) *(pretencioso)* pretentious, showy

---

ℓ Observa que la palabra inglesa **presumptuous** es un falso amigo y no es la traducción de la palabra española **presuntuoso**. En inglés, **presumptuous** significa "impertinente".

---

presuponer [19] (*pp* **presupuesto**) *vt* to presuppose

presupuestar *vt* to budget for; *(importe)* to estimate for

presupuestario,-a *adj* budgetary

presupuesto *nm* (**a**) *Fin* budget; *(cálculo)* estimate (**b**) *(supuesto)* supposition, assumption

presuroso,-a *adj* *(rápido)* quick; *(con prisa)* in a hurry

pretencioso,-a *adj* pretentious

pretender *vt* (**a**) *(intentar)* to try; **¿qué pretendes insinuar?** what are you getting at? (**b**) *(afirmar)* to claim (**c**) *(aspirar a)* to try for (**d**) *(cortejar)* to court, to woo

pretendiente,-a *nm,f* (**a**) *(al trono)* pretender (**b**) *(a un cargo)* applicant, candidate (**c**) *(amante)* suitor

pretensión *nf* (**a**) *(aspiración)* aim, aspiration (**b**) *(presunción)* pretentiousness

pretérito,-a 1 *adj* past, former
2 *nm* *Ling* preterite, simple past tense

pretextar *vt* to plead, to allege

pretexto *nm* pretext, excuse

pretil *nm* parapet

prevalecer [33] *vi* to prevail

prevaler [26] *vi* = **prevalecer**

prevención *nf* (**a**) *(precaución)* prevention; **en p. de** as a prevention against (**b**) *(medida)* precaution

prevenir [27] *vt* (**a**) *(preparar)* to prepare, to get ready (**b**) *(prever)* to prevent, to forestall; *(evitar)* to avoid; **para p. la gripe** to prevent flu; **más vale p. que curar** prevention is better than cure (**c**) *(advertir)* to warn

preventivo,-a *adj* preventive; *(medidas)* precautionary; *Jur* **detención** *o* **prisión preventiva** remand in custody

prever [28] (*pp* **previsto**) *vt* (**a**) *(prevenir)* to foresee, to forecast (**b**) *(preparar de antemano)* to cater for

previo,-a *adj* previous, prior; **p. pago de**

su importe only on payment; **sin p. aviso** without prior notice

previsible *adj* predictable

previsión *nf* (**a**) *(predicción)* forecast; **p. del tiempo** weather forecast (**b**) *(precaución)* precaution; **en p. de** as a precaution against (**c**) *Andes, RP* **p. social** social security

previsor,-a *adj* careful, far-sighted

previsto,-a *adj* foreseen, forecast; **según lo p.** as expected

prieto,-a *adj* (**a**) *(ceñido)* tight; **íbamos muy prietos en el coche** we were really squashed together in the car (**b**) *Méx Fam (moreno)* dark-skinned

prima *nf* (**a**) *(gratificación)* bonus; **p. de seguro** insurance premium (**b**) *(persona)* ver **primo,-a**

primacía *nf* primacy

primar 1 *vi* to have priority, to prevail
2 *vt* to give a bonus to

primario,-a *adj* primary

primavera *nf* spring

primer *adj (delante de nm)* ver **primero,-a**

primera *nf* (**a**) *(en tren)* first class (**b**) *Aut (marcha)* first gear (**c**) **a la p.** at the first attempt; *Fam* **de p.** great, first-class

primero,-a 1 *adj* first; **a primera hora de la mañana** first thing in the morning; **primera página** *o* **plana** front page; **de primera necesidad** basic

---

Primer is used instead of **primero** before masculine singular nouns (e.g. **el primer hombre** the first man).

---

2 *nm,f* first; **a primero(s) de mes** at the beginning of the month
3 *adv* (**a**) first (**b**) *(más bien)* rather, sooner; ver **primera**

primicia *nf* novelty; **p. informativa** scoop; **p. mundial** world premiere

primitivo,-a *adj* (**a**) primitive (**b**) *(tosco)* coarse, rough

primo,-a 1 *nm,f* (**a**) cousin; **p. hermano** first cousin (**b**) *Fam (tonto)* fool, drip, dunce
2 *adj* (**a**) **materia prima** raw material (**b**) *(número)* prime

primogénito,-a *adj & nm,f* first-born

primor *nm* (**a**) *(delicadeza)* delicacy (**b**) *(belleza)* beauty

primordial *adj* essential, fundamental

primoroso,-a *adj* delicate, exquisite

princesa *nf* princess

principado *nm* principality

principal *adj* main, principal; **lo p. es que** ... the main thing is that ...; **puerta p.** front door

príncipe *nm* prince

principiante 1 *adj* novice

  2 *nmf* beginner, novice

principio *nm* (**a**) beginning, start; **a principio(s) de** at the beginning of; **al p., en un p.** at first, in the beginning (**b**) *(fundamento)* principle; **en p.** in principle (**c**) **principios** rudiments, basics

pringar [42] **1** *vt (ensuciar)* to make greasy/dirty

  2 *vi Fam (trabajar)* to work hard

  3 pringarse *vpr* (**a**) *(ensuciarse)* to get greasy/dirty (**b**) *Fam (meterse de lleno)* to get involved

pringoso,-a *adj (grasiento)* greasy; *(sucio)* dirty

pringue *nm (grasa)* grease

prior,-a *nm,f (hombre)* prior; *(mujer)* prioress

priori: • **a priori** *loc adv* a priori

prioridad *nf* priority

prioritario,-a *adj* priority

prisa *nf* (**a**) *(rapidez)* hurry; **date p.** hurry up; **tener p.** to be in a hurry; **de/a p.** in a hurry (**b**) **correr p.** to be urgent; **me corre mucha p.** I need it right away

prisión *nf* prison, jail

prisionero,-a *nm,f* prisoner

prisma *nm* prism

prismáticos *nmpl* binoculars, field glasses

priva *nf Fam* booze

privación *nf* deprivation

privado,-a *adj* private

privar 1 *vt (despojar)* to deprive (**de** of)

  2 *vi* (**a**) *Fam (gustar)* to like; *(estar de moda)* to be fashionable *o* popular (**b**) *Fam (beber)* to booze

  3 privarse *vpr (abstenerse)* to deprive oneself (**de** of), to go without

privativo,-a *adj* exclusive (**de** of)

privilegiado,-a 1 *adj* privileged

  2 *nm,f* privileged person

privilegio *nm* privilege

pro 1 *nm* advantage; **los pros y los contras** the pros and cons; **en p. de** in favour of

  2 *prep* in favour of; **campaña p. desarme** campaign for disarmament, disarmament campaign

pro- *pref* pro-

proa *nf* prow, bows

probabilidad *nf* probability, likelihood; **tiene pocas probabilidades** he stands little chance

probable *adj* probable, likely; **es p. que llueva** it'll probably rain

probador *nm* fitting room

probar [2] **1** *vt* (**a**) *(comida, bebida)* to try

(**b**) *(comprobar)* to test, to check (**c**) *(intentar)* to try (**d**) *(demostrar)* to prove, to show

  2 *vi* to try; **p. a** to attempt *o* try to

  3 probarse *vpr (ropa)* to try on

probeta *nf* test tube; **niño p.** test-tube baby

problema *nm* problem

problemático,-a *adj* problematic

procedencia *nf* origin, source

procedente *adj* (**a**) *(originario)* coming (**de** from) (**b**) *(adecuado)* appropriate; *Jur* proper

proceder 1 *vi* (**a**) **p. de** *(provenir)* to come from (**b**) *(actuar)* to act (**c**) *(ser oportuno)* to be advisable *o* appropriate; *Jur* **la protesta no procede** objection overruled (**d**) **p. a** *(continuar)* to go on to

  2 *nm (comportamiento)* behaviour

procedimiento *nm* (**a**) *(método)* procedure (**b**) *Jur (trámites)* proceedings

procesado,-a 1 *nm,f* accused

  2 *nm Informát* processing

procesador *nm* processor; **p. de textos** word processor

procesamiento *nm* (**a**) *Jur* prosecution (**b**) *Informát* **p. de datos/textos** data/word processing

procesar *vt* (**a**) *Jur* to prosecute (**b**) *(elaborar, transformar)* to process; *Informát* to process

procesión *nf* procession

proceso *nm* (**a**) process; *Informát* **p. de datos** data processing (**b**) *Jur* trial

proclamación *nf* proclamation

proclamar *vt* to proclaim

proclive *adj* prone, inclined

procreación *nf* procreation

procrear *vt* to procreate

procurador,-a *nm,f Jur* attorney

procuraduría *nf Méx* **p. general** Ministry of Justice

procurar *vt* (**a**) *(intentar)* to try, to attempt; **procura que no te vean** make sure they don't see you (**b**) *(proporcionar)* (to manage) to get

prodigar [42] *Fml* **1** *vt (dar generosamente)* to lavish

  2 prodigarse *vpr* **p. en** to be lavish

prodigio *nm* prodigy, miracle; **hacer prodigios** to work wonders; **niño p.** child prodigy

prodigioso,-a *adj (sobrenatural)* prodigious; *(maravilloso)* wonderful, marvellous

pródigo,-a *adj* generous, lavish; **ella es pródiga en regalos** she's very generous with presents

producción *nf (acción)* production; *(producto)* product; *Cin* production; **p. en cadena/serie** assembly-line/mass production

producir [10] 1 *vt* (**a**) to produce; *(fruto, cosecha)* to yield, to bear; *(ganancias)* to yield (**b**) *Fig (originar)* to cause, to bring about

2 producirse *vpr* to take place, to happen

productividad *nf* productivity

productivo,-a *adj* productive; *(beneficioso)* profitable

producto *nm* product; *Agr (producción)* produce

productor,-a 1 *adj* producing
2 *nm,f* producer

proeza *nf* heroic deed, exploit

profanación *nf* desecration, profanation

profanar *vt* to desecrate, to profane

profano,-a 1 *adj* profane, secular
2 *nm,f (hombre)* layman; *(mujer)* laywoman

profecía *nf* prophecy

proferir [31] *vt* to utter; **p. insultos** to hurl insults

profesar *vt* to profess

profesión *nf* profession; **de p.** by profession

profesional *adj & nmf* professional

profesionista *adj & nmf Méx* professional

profeso *adv* **ex p.** intentionally

profesor,-a *nm,f* teacher; *Univ* lecturer

profesorado *nm (profesión)* teaching; *(grupo de profesores)* staff

profeta *nm* prophet

profetizar [40] *vt* to prophesy, to foretell

profiláctico,-a 1 *adj* prophylactic
2 *nm* condom

prófugo,-a 1 *adj & nm,f* fugitive
2 *nm Mil* deserter

profundidad *nf* depth; **un metro de p.** one metre deep *o* in depth; *Fig (de ideas etc)* profundity, depth

profundizar [40] *vt & vi (cavar)* to deepen; *Fig (examinar)* to study in depth

profundo,-a *adj* deep; *Fig (idea, sentimiento)* profound

profusión *nf* profusion

progenitor,-a *nm,f (antepasado)* ancestor, progenitor; **progenitores** *(padres)* parents

programa *nm* programme; *Informát* program; *Educ* syllabus

programación *nf Rad & TV* programme planning

programador,-a *nm,f Informát* programmer

programar *vt* to programme; *Informát* to program

progre *adj & nmf Fam* trendy, lefty

progresar *vi* to progress, to make progress

progresista *adj & nmf* progressive

progresivo,-a *adj* progressive

progreso *nm* progress; **hace grandes progresos** he's making great progress

prohibición *nf* prohibition, ban

prohibido,-a *adj* forbidden, prohibited; **prohibida la entrada** *(en letrero)* no admittance; **p. aparcar/fumar** *(en letrero)* no parking/smoking

prohibir *vt* to forbid, to prohibit; **se prohíbe pasar** *(en letrero)* no admittance *o* entry

prohibitivo,-a, prohibitorio,-a *adj* prohibitive

prójimo,-a *nm,f* one's fellow man, one's neighbour

proletariado *nm* proletariat

proletario,-a *adj & nm,f* proletarian

proliferar *vi* to proliferate

prolífico,-a *adj* prolific

prolijo,-a *adj* verbose, long-winded

prólogo *nm* prologue

prolongación *nf* prolonging, extension, prolongation

prolongado,-a *adj* long

prolongar [42] 1 *vt (alargar)* to prolong, to extend
2 prolongarse *vpr (continuar)* to carry on

promedio *nm* average; **como p.** on average

promesa *nf* promise; *Fig* **la joven p. de la música** the promising young musician

prometedor,-a *adj* promising

prometer 1 *vt* to promise; **te lo prometo** I promise
2 *vi* to be promising
3 prometerse *vpr (pareja)* to get engaged

prometido,-a 1 *adj* promised
2 *nm,f (hombre)* fiancé; *(mujer)* fiancée

prominente *adj (elevado)* protruding, projecting; *(importante)* prominent

promiscuo,-a *adj* promiscuous

promoción *nf* promotion; *Educ* **p. universitaria** class, year

promocionar *vt (cosas)* to promote; *(personas)* to give promotion to

promotor,-a 1 *adj* promoting
2 *nm,f* promoter

promover [4] *vt* (**a**) *(cosas, personas)* to promote; *(juicio, querella)* to initiate (**b**) *(causar)* to cause, to give rise to

promulgar [42] *vt* to promulgate

pronombre *nm* pronoun

pronosticar [44] *vt* to predict, to forecast; *Med* to make a prognosis of

pronóstico *nm* (*del tiempo*) forecast; *Med* prognosis

pronto,-a 1 *adj* quick, prompt; *Fml* (*dispuesto*) prepared

2 *nm* (*impulso*) sudden impulse

3 *adv* (**a**) (*deprisa*) quickly, rapidly; **al p.** at first; **de p.** suddenly; **por de** *o* **lo p.** (*para empezar*) to start with (**b**) (*temprano*) soon, early; **¡hasta p.!** see you soon!

pronunciación *nf* pronunciation

pronunciamiento *nm* (**a**) *Mil* uprising, insurrection (**b**) *Jur* pronouncement

pronunciar [43] **1** *vt* to pronounce; (*discurso*) to deliver

2 pronunciarse *vpr* (**a**) (*opinar*) to declare oneself (**b**) (*sublevarse*) to rise up

propagación *nf* propagation, spreading

propagador,-a *nm,f* propagator

propaganda *nf* (*política*) propaganda; (*comercial*) advertising, publicity

propagar [42] **1** *vt* to propagate, to spread

2 propagarse *vpr* to spread

propano *nm* propane

propasarse *vpr* to go too far

propensión *nf* tendency, inclination

propenso,-a *adj* (**a**) (*inclinado*) prone, inclined (**b**) *Med* susceptible

propiamente *adv* **p. dicho** strictly speaking

propiciar [43] *vt* (**a**) (*causar*) to cause (**b**) *Am* (*patrocinar*) to sponsor

propicio,-a *adj* propitious, suitable; **ser p. a** to be inclined to

propiedad *nf* (**a**) (*posesión*) ownership; (*cosa poseída*) property (**b**) (*cualidad*) property, quality; *Fig* **con p.** properly, appropriately

propietario,-a *nm,f* owner

propina *nf* tip; **dar p. (a algn)** to tip (sb)

propinar *vt* to give

propio,-a *adj* (**a**) (*de uno*) own; **en su propia casa** in his own house (**b**) (*correcto*) suitable, appropriate; **juegos propios para su edad** games suitable for their age (**c**) (*característico*) typical, peculiar (**d**) (*mismo*) (*hombre*) himself; (*mujer*) herself; (*animal, cosa*) itself; **el p. autor** the author himself (**e**) *propios,-as* themselves; **los propios inquilinos** the tenants themselves (**f**) *Ling* proper

proponer [19] (*pp* propuesto) **1** *vt* to propose, to suggest

2 proponerse *vpr* to intend

proporción *nf* (**a**) proportion; **en p. con** in proportion to (**b**) **proporciones** (*tamaño*) size

proporcionado,-a *adj* (*mesurado*) proportionate, in proportion

proporcional *adj* proportional

proporcionar *vt* (*dar*) to give, to supply, to provide

proposición *nf* (**a**) (*propuesta*) proposal (**b**) (*oración*) clause

propósito *nm* (**a**) (*intención*) intention (**b**) **a p.** (*por cierto*) by the way; (*adrede*) on purpose, intentionally; **a p. de viajes ...** speaking of travelling ...

propuesta *nf* suggestion, proposal

propuesto,-a *pp de* proponer

propugnar *vt* to advocate

propulsar *vt* (*vehículo*) to drive; *Fig* (*idea*) to promote

propulsión *nf* propulsion

propulsor,-a *nm,f Fig* (*persona*) promoter

propuse *pt indef de* proponer

prórroga *nf* (**a**) (*prolongación*) extension; *Dep Br* extra time, *US* overtime (**b**) (*aplazamiento*) postponement; *Mil* deferment

prorrogar [42] *vt* (**a**) (*prolongar*) to extend (**b**) (*aplazar*) to postpone; *Mil* to defer

prorrumpir *vi* to burst (**en** into)

prosa *nf* prose

proscrito,-a 1 *adj* (*persona*) exiled, banished; (*cosa*) banned

2 *nm,f* exile, outlaw

proseguir [6] *vt & vi* to carry on, to continue

prospección *nf* (**a**) *Min* prospect (**b**) *Com* survey

prospecto *nm* leaflet, prospectus

prosperar *vi* (*negocio, país*) to prosper, to thrive; (*propuesta*) to be accepted

prosperidad *nf* prosperity

próspero,-a *adj* prosperous, thriving; **¡p. año nuevo!** Happy New Year!

prostíbulo *nm* brothel

prostitución *nf* prostitution

prostituir [37] **1** *vt* to prostitute

2 prostituirse *vpr* to prostitute oneself

prostituta *nf* prostitute

protagonista *nmf* (**a**) main character, leading role; **¿quién es el p.?** who plays the lead? (**b**) *Fig* (*centro*) centre of attraction

protagonizar [40] *vt* to play the lead in, to star in

protección *nf* protection

proteccionismo *nm* protectionism

protector,-a 1 *adj* protecting, protective

2 *nm,f* protector

proteger [53] *vt* to protect, to defend
protegido,-a *nm,f (hombre)* protégé;
(mujer) protégée
proteína *nf* protein
prótesis *nf inv* prosthesis
protesta *nf* protest; *Jur* objection
protestante *adj & nmf Rel* Protestant
protestar *vi* (a) to protest; *Jur* to object
(b) *Fam (quejarse)* to complain
protestón,-ona *nm,f* moaner, grumbler
protocolo *nm* protocol
protón *nm* proton
prototipo *nm* prototype
protuberancia *nf* protuberance
protuberante *adj* protuberant, bulging
prov. *(abr* **provincia)** prov
provecho *nm* profit, benefit; ¡buen p.!
enjoy your meal!; sacar p. de algo to
benefit from sth
provechoso,-a *adj* beneficial
proveedor,-a *nm,f* supplier, purveyor;
Informát p. de acceso (a Internet) Internet access provider
proveer [36] *(pp* provisto) *vt* to supply,
to provide
proveniente *adj (procedente)* coming;
(resultante) arising, resulting
provenir [27] *vi* p. de to come from
proverbio *nm* proverb
providencia *nf* providence
provincia *nf* province
provincial *adj* provincial
provinciano,-a *adj & nm,f Pey* provincial
provisión *nf* provision
provisional, *Am* **provisorio,-a** *adj* provisional
provisto,-a *adj* p. de equipped with
provocación *nf* provocation
provocado,-a *adj* provoked, caused; incendio p. arson
provocador,-a 1 *nm,f* instigator, agent
provocateur
2 *adj* provocative
provocar [44] *vt* (a) *(causar)* to cause; p.
un incendio to start a fire (b) *(instigar)* to
provoke (c) *Carib, Col, Méx Fam (apetecer)* ¿te provoca ir al cine? would you like
to go to the movies?, *Br* do you fancy
going to the cinema?; ¿qué te provoca?
what would you like to do?, *Br* what do
you fancy doing?
provocativo,-a *adj* provocative
proxeneta *nmf* procurer, pimp
próximamente *adv (pronto)* soon; *Cin &
Teatro (en letrero)* coming soon
proximidad *nf* proximity, closeness; en
las proximidades de close to, in the vicinity of

próximo,-a *adj* (a) *(cercano)* near, close
(b) *(siguiente)* next
proyección *nf* (a) projection (b) *Cin*
showing
proyectar *vt* (a) *(luz)* to project (b) *(planear)* to plan (c) *Cin* to show
proyectil *nm* projectile
proyecto *nm (plan)* project, plan; tener
algo en p. to be planning sth; p. de ley bill
proyector *nm Cin* projector
prudencia *nf* prudence, discretion; *(moderación)* care
prudente *adj* prudent, sensible;
(conductor) careful; a una hora p. at a
reasonable time
prueba *nf* (a) proof; en p. de as a sign of
(b) *(examen etc)* test; a p. on trial; a p. de
agua/balas waterproof/bullet-proof; haz
la p. try it (c) *Dep* event
pseudo *adj* pseud, pseudo
psicoanálisis *nm inv* psychoanalysis
psicodélico,-a *adj* psychedelic
psicología *nf* psychology
psicológico,-a *adj* psychological
psicólogo,-a *nm,f* psychologist
psicópata *nmf* psychopath
psicosis *nf inv* psychosis
psicotécnico,-a *adj* psychometric
psicoterapeuta 1 *nmf* psychotherapist
2 *adj* psychotherapeutic
psicoterapia *nf* psychotherapy
psicótico,-a *adj & nm,f* psychotic
psique *nf* psyche
psiquiatra *nmf* psychiatrist
psiquiatría *nf* psychiatry
psiquiátrico,-a 1 *adj* psychiatric; hospital p. psychiatric hospital
2 *nm* psychiatric hospital
psíquico,-a *adj* psychic
PSOE *nm Pol (abr* **Partido Socialista
Obrero Español)** = Spanish political
party to the centre-left of the political
spectrum
pta(s). *(abr* **peseta(s))** peseta(s)
púa *nf* (a) *(de planta)* thorn; *(de animal)*
quill, spine; *(de peine)* tooth; alambre de
púas barbed wire (b) *Mús* plectrum
pub *nm (pl* pubs, pubes) pub
pubertad *nf* puberty
publicación *nf* publication
publicar [44] *vt* (a) *(libro etc)* to publish
(b) *(secreto)* to publicize
publicidad *nf* (a) *Com* advertising (b)
(conocimiento público) publicity
publicitario,-a *adj* advertising
público,-a 1 *adj* public
2 *nm* public; *Teatro* audience; *Dep* spectators

pucha *interj Andes, RP Fam Euf* (**a**) *(lamento) Br* sugar!, *US* shoot!; **¡p. digo, ya son las doce!** oh, *Br* sugar *o US* shoot! it's twelve o'clock already! (**b**) *(sorpresa)* wow!; **¿cincuenta años? ¡la p.!** fifty years old? get away! *o* never! (**c**) *(enojo) Br* sugar!, *US* shoot!; **¡la p.!, perdí las llaves** *Br* sugar *o US* shoot! I've lost my keys!

pucherazo *nm* rigging of an election

puchero *nm* (**a**) *(olla)* cooking pot; *(cocido)* stew (**b**) **hacer pucheros** to pout

pucho *nm CSur* dog-end

pude *pt indef de* **poder**

pudendo,-a *adj* **partes pudendas** private parts

púdico,-a *adj* modest

pudiente *adj* rich, wealthy

pudor *nm* modesty

pudoroso,-a *adj* modest

pudrir *vt* defect, **pudrirse** *vpr* to rot, to decay

pueblerino,-a *adj Pey (provinciano)* countrified, provincial

pueblo *nm* (**a**) *(población) (pequeña)* village; *(grande)* town (**b**) *(gente)* people; **el p. español** the Spanish people

puente *nm* (**a**) bridge; *Av* **p. aéreo** *(civil)* air shuttle service; *Mil* airlift; **p. colgante** suspension bridge; **p. levadizo** drawbridge (**b**) *(entre dos fiestas)* ≃ long weekend

puerco,-a 1 *adj* filthy
  2 *nm,f* pig
  3 *nm* **p. espín** porcupine

puericultura *nf* paediatrics *sing*

pueril *adj* childish, puerile

puerro *nm* leek

puerta *nf* door; *(verja, en aeropuerto)* gate; *Dep* goal; **p. corredera/giratoria** sliding/revolving door; *Fig* **a las puertas, en puertas** imminent; *Fig* **a p. cerrada** behind closed doors

puerto *nm* (**a**) *(de mar)* port, harbour; **p. deportivo** marina (**b**) *(de montaña)* (mountain) pass

Puerto Rico *n* Puerto Rico

puertorriqueño,-a *adj & nm,f* Puerto Rican

pues *conj* (**a**) *(puesto que)* as, since (**b**) *(por lo tanto)* therefore (**c**) *(entonces)* so (**d**) *(para reforzar)* **¡p. claro que sí!** but of course!; **p. como iba diciendo** well, as I was saying; **¡p. mejor!** so much the better!; **¡p. no!** certainly not! (**e**) *(como pregunta)* **¿p.?** why?

puesta *nf* (**a**) **p. de sol** sunset (**b**) *Fig* **p. a punto** tuning, adjusting; *Fig* **p. al día** updating; *Teatro* **p. en escena** staging;

p. en marcha starting-up, start-up; *ver* **puesto,-a**

puestero,-a *nm,f Am* stallholder

puesto,-a 1 *conj* **p. que** since, as
  2 *nm* (**a**) *(lugar)* place; *(asiento)* seat (**b**) *(empleo)* position, post, job; **p. de trabajo** job, post (**c**) *(tienda)* stall (**d**) *Mil* post
  3 *adj* (**a**) *(colocado)* set, put (**b**) **llevar p.** *(ropa)* to have on; *Fam* **ir muy p.** to be all dressed up (**c**) *Fam (borracho)* drunk (**d**) *Fam* **estar p. en una materia** to be well up in a subject

púgil *nm* boxer

pugilato *nm* boxing

pugna *nf* battle, fight

pugnar *vi* to fight, to struggle (**por** for)

puja *nf (acción)* bidding; *(cantidad)* bid

pujante *adj* thriving, prosperous

pujanza *nf* strength, vigour

pujar *vi* (**a**) *(pugnar)* to struggle (**b**) *(en una subasta)* to bid higher

pulcro,-a *adj* (extremely) neat

pulga *nf* flea; *Fam* **tener malas pulgas** to be nasty, to have a nasty streak

pulgada *nf* inch

pulgar *nm* thumb

pulimentar *vt* to polish

pulir *vt* (**a**) *(metal, madera)* to polish (**b**) *(mejorar)* to polish up

pulla *nf* dig

pulmón *nm* lung

pulmonía *nf* pneumonia

pulóver *nm* pullover

pulpa *nf* pulp

pulpería *nf Am* store

púlpito *nm* pulpit

pulpo *nm* octopus

pulque *nm CAm, Méx* pulque, = fermented maguey juice

pulquería *nf CAm, Méx* "pulque" bar

pulsación *nf* pulsation; *(en mecanografía)* stroke, tap; **pulsaciones por minuto** ≃ keystrokes per minute

pulsar *vt (timbre, botón)* to press; *(tecla)* to hit, to strike

pulsera *nf (aro)* bracelet; *(de reloj)* watchstrap; **reloj de p.** wristwatch

pulso *nm* (**a**) pulse; *Fig* **tomar el p. a la opinión pública** to sound out opinion (**b**) *(mano firme)* steady hand; **a p.** freehand; **ganarse algo a p.** to deserve sth (**c**) *Fig* trial of strength; **echarse un p.** to arm-wrestle

pulverizador *nm* spray, atomizer

pulverizar **[40]** *vt (sólidos)* to pulverize; *(líquidos)* to spray; *(un récord)* to smash

puma *nm* puma

puna *nf Andes* (**a**) high moor (**b**) *(mal)*

mountain o altitude sickness

pundonor nm self-respect, self-esteem

punta nf (a) *(extremo)* tip; *(extremo afilado)* point; *(de cabello)* end; **sacar p. a un lápiz** to sharpen a pencil; **tecnología p.** state-of-the-art technology; **me pone los nervios de p.** he makes me very nervous (b) *(periodo)* peak; **hora p.** rush hour (c) *(pequeña cantidad)* bit; **una p. de sal a** pinch of salt (d) *(clavo)* nail

puntada nf Am *(dolor)* stabbing pain

puntaje nm Am *(calificación)* Br mark, US grade; *(en concursos, competiciones)* score

puntal nm prop; *(travesaño)* beam; Fig *(soporte)* pillar, support

puntapié nm kick

puntear vt (a) *(dibujar)* to dot (b) Mús *(guitarra)* to pluck

punteo nm plucking

puntería nf aim; **tener buena/mala p.** to be a good/bad shot

puntero,-a 1 adj leading
   2 nm,f CSur Dep back

puntiagudo,-a adj pointed, sharp

puntilla nf (a) *(encaje)* lace (b) **dar la p.** Taurom to finish (the bull) off; Fig *(liquidar)* to finish off (c) **de puntillas** on tiptoe

puntilloso,-a adj touchy

punto nm (a) point; **a p.** ready; Culin **en su p.** just right; **a p. de** on the point of; **hasta cierto p.** to a certain o some extent; **p. muerto** Aut neutral; Fig *(impase)* deadlock; **p. de vista** point of view (b) *(marca)* dot; **línea de puntos** dotted line (c) *(lugar)* place, point (d) **p. y seguido** full stop; **p. y coma** semicolon; **dos puntos** colon; **p. y aparte** full stop, new paragraph (e) *(tiempo)* **en p.** sharp, on the dot (f) Dep *(tanto)* point (g) Cost & Med stitch; **hacer p.** to knit

puntuable adj Dep **una prueba p. para** a race counting towards

puntuación nf (a) Ling punctuation (b) Dep score (c) Educ mark

puntual 1 adj (a) punctual (b) *(exacto)* accurate, precise (c) *(caso)* specific
   2 adv punctually

puntualidad nf punctuality

puntualizar [40] vt to specify, to clarify

puntuar [30] 1 vt (a) *(al escribir)* to punctuate (b) Educ *(calificar)* to mark
   2 vi Dep (a) *(marcar)* to score (b) *(ser puntuable)* to count

punzada nf *(de dolor)* sudden sharp pain

punzante adj *(objeto)* sharp; *(dolor)* acute, piercing

punzar [40] vt Téc to punch

puñado nm handful; Fam **a puñados** by the score, galore

puñal nm dagger

puñalada nf stab; Fig **p. trapera** stab in the back

puñeta nf Fam **hacer la p. a algn** to pester sb, to annoy sb; **¡puñetas!** damn!; **¡vete a hacer puñetas!** go to hell!

puñetazo nm punch

puño nm (a) fist (b) *(de camisa etc)* cuff (c) *(de herramienta)* handle

pupa nf *(herida)* cold sore (b) Fam *(daño)* pain

pupila nf *(de ojo)* pupil

pupilo,-a nm,f pupil

pupitre nm desk

purasangre adj & nm thoroughbred

puré nm purée; **p. de patata** mashed potatoes; **p. de verduras** thick vegetable soup

pureta nmf old fogey

pureza nf (a) purity (b) *(castidad)* chastity

purga nf Med purgative; Fig purge

purgante adj & nm purgative

purgar [42] vt Med & Fig to purge

purgatorio nm purgatory

purificación nf purification

purificar [44] vt to purify

purista nmf purist

puritano,-a 1 adj puritanical
   2 nm,f puritan, Puritan

puro,-a 1 adj (a) *(sin mezclas)* pure; **aire p.** fresh air; **la pura verdad** the plain truth; Pol **p. y duro** hardline (b) *(mero)* sheer, mere; **por pura curiosidad** out of sheer curiosity (c) *(casto)* chaste, pure
   2 nm *(cigarro)* cigar

púrpura adj inv purple

purpúreo,-a adj purple

pus nm pus

puse pt indef de **poner**

pusilánime adj faint-hearted

pústula nf sore, pustule

puta nf Vulg whore; **de p. madre** great, terrific; **de p. pena** Br bloody o US goddamn awful; **no tengo ni p. idea** I haven't (got) a Br bloody o US goddamn clue; **pasarlas putas** to go through hell, to have a rotten time

putada nf Vulg dirty trick

puteada nf RP muy Fam *(insulto)* swearword

putear vt (a) Vulg *(fastidiar)* to fuck o piss around (b) RP muy Fam *(insultar)* **p. a algn** to call sb for everything, to call sb every name under the sun

puticlub *nm Fam* brothel

puto,-a 1 *adj Vulg* fucking
 2 *nm* male prostitute, stud

putrefacto,-a, pútrido,-a *adj* putre-
fied, rotten

puzzle *nm* jigsaw puzzle

PVC *nm* (*abr* **cloruro de polivinilo**) PVC

PVP *nm* (*abr* **precio de venta al público**)
 RRP

PYME *nf* (*abr* **Pequeña y Mediana Empresa**) SME

Pza. (*abr* **Plaza**) Sq

Q, q [ku] *nf (la letra)* Q, q

qué¹ *pron rel* (**a**) *(sujeto) (persona)* who; *(cosa)* that, which; **el hombre q. vino** the man who came; **la bomba q. estalló** the bomb that *o* which went off (**b**) *(complemento) (persona) no se traduce o* that *o* who *o Fml* whom; *(cosa) no se traduce o* that, which; **la chica q. conocí** the girl (that *o* who *o* whom) I met; **el coche q. compré** the car (that *o* which) I bought (**c**) **lo q.** what; **lo q. más me gusta** what I like best (**d**) *(con infinitivo) no se traduce*; **hay mucho q. hacer** there's a lot to do

que² *conj* (**a**) *no se traduce o* that; **dijo q. llamaría** he said (that) he would call; **quiero q. vengas** I want you to come (**b**) *(consecutivo) no se traduce o* that; *(en comparativas)* than; **habla tan bajo q. no se le oye** he speaks so quietly (that) he can't be heard; **más alto q. yo** taller than me (**c**) *(causal) no se traduce* **date deprisa q. no tenemos mucho tiempo** hurry up, we haven't got much time (**d**) *(enfático) no se traduce* **¡q. no!** no!; **¡q. te calles!** I said be quiet! (**e**) *(deseo, mandato)* (+ *subjunctive) no se traduce*; **¡q. te diviertas!** enjoy yourself! (**f**) *(final)* so that; **ven q. te dé un beso** come and let me give you a kiss (**g**) *(disyuntivo)* whether; **me da igual q. suba o no** it doesn't matter to me whether he comes up or not (**h**) *(locuciones)* **¿a q. no ...?** I bet you can't ...!; **q. yo sepa** as far as I know; **yo q. tú** if I were you

qué **1** *pron interr* (**a**) what; **¿q. quieres?** what do you want?; *Fam* **¿y q.?** so what? (**b**) *(exclamativo)* (+ *adj)* how; **¡q. bonito!** how pretty! (**c**) (+ *n)* what a; **¡q. lástima!** what a pity! (**d**) *Fam* **¡q. de ...!** what a lot of ...! **2** *adj interr* which; **¿q. libro quieres?** which book do you want?

quebrada *nf Am* stream

quebradero *nm Fig* **q. de cabeza** headache

quebradizo,-a *adj (débil)* fragile; *(cabello, hielo)* brittle

quebrado *nm Mat* fraction

quebradura *nf* (**a**) *(grieta)* crack (**b**) *Med* hernia, rupture

quebrantamiento *nm (de una ley)* violation, infringement

quebrantar **1** *vt (promesa, ley)* to break **2 quebrantarse** *upr* to break down

quebrar [1] **1** *vt (romper)* to break **2** *vi Fin* to go bankrupt **3 quebrarse** *upr* to break; *Med* to rupture oneself

queda *nf* **toque de q.** curfew

quedar **1** *vi* (**a**) *(restar)* to be left, to remain; **quedan dos** there are two left (**b**) *(en un lugar)* to arrange to meet; **quedamos en el bar** I'll meet you in the bar (**c**) **me queda corta** *(ropa)* it is too short for me; **quedaría muy bien allí** *(objeto)* it would look very nice there (**d**) *(acordar)* to agree (**en** to); **¿en qué quedamos?** so what's it to be? (**e**) *(estar situado)* to be; **¿dónde queda la estación?** where's the station? (**f**) *(terminar)* to end; **¿en qué quedó la película?** how did the film end? (**g**) *(locuciones)* **q. en ridículo** to make a fool of oneself; **q. bien/mal** to make a good/bad impression **2 quedarse** *upr* (**a**) *(permanecer)* to stay; **se quedó en casa** she stayed (at) home; **q. sin dinero/pan** to run out of money/bread; **q. con hambre** to still be hungry (**b**) **q. (con)** *(retener)* to keep; **quédese (con) el cambio** keep the change (**c**) *Fam* **q. con algn** to make a fool of sb

quedo *adv* softly, quietly

quehacer *nm* task, chore

queja *nf* complaint; *(de dolor)* groan, moan

quejarse *upr* to complain (**de** about)

quejica *Fam* **1** *adj* grumpy **2** *nmf* moaner

quejido *nm* groan, cry

quemado,-a *adj* (**a**) burnt, burned; *(del sol)* sunburnt (**b**) *Fig (agotado)* burnt-out

quemador *nm (de cocina etc)* burner

quemadura *nf* burn

quemar 1 *vt* to burn; *Fig (agotar)* to burn out

2 *vi* to be burning hot; **este café quema** this coffee's boiling hot

3 quemarse *vpr Fig* to burn oneself out

quemarropa: •**a quemarropa** *loc adv* point-blank

quemazón *nf* smarting

quena *nf* Andean flute

quepo *indic pres de* **caber**

queque *nm* *Andes, CAm, Méx* sponge (cake)

querella *nf* *Jur* lawsuit

querer [20] **1** *vt* (a) *(amar)* to love (b) *(desear)* to want; **¿cuánto quiere por la casa?** how much does he want for the house?; **sin q.** without meaning to; **queriendo** on purpose; **¡por lo que más quieras!** for heaven's sake!; **¿quiere pasarme el pan?** would you pass me the bread? (c) **q. decir** to mean (d) **no quiso darme permiso** he refused me permission

2 quererse *vpr* to love each other

3 *nm* love, affection

querido,-a 1 *adj* dear, beloved; **q. amigo** *(en carta)* dear friend

2 *nm,f (amante)* lover; *(mujer)* mistress

queroseno *nm* kerosene, kerosine

querré *indic fut de* **querer**

quesadilla *nf* *CAm, Méx* = filled fried tortilla

queso *nm* cheese; **q. rallado** grated cheese; **q. de cerdo** *Br* brawn, *US* head-cheese

quetzal *nm (moneda)* = standard monetary unit of Guatemala

quiché *adj & nm* Quiché

quicio *nm* (a) *(de puerta)* doorpost (b) *Fig* **fuera de q.** beside oneself; **sacar de q.** *(a algn)* to infuriate; *(algo)* to take too far

quid *nm* crux; **has dado en el q.** you've hit the nail on the head

quiebra *nf* *Fin (bancarrota)* bankruptcy; *(crack)* crash

quiebro *nm (con el cuerpo)* dodge; *Ftb* dribbling

quien *pron rel* (a) *(con prep)* no se traduce o *Fml* whom; **el hombre con q. vino** the man she came with; *Fml* the man with whom she came (b) *(indefinido)* whoever, anyone who; **q. quiera venir que venga** whoever wants to can come; **hay q. dice lo contrario** some people say the opposite; *Fig* **q. más q. menos** everybody

quién *pron interr* (a) *(sujeto)* who?; **¿q. es?** who is it? (b) *(complemento)* who, *Fml* whom; **¿para q. es?** who is it for?; **¿de q. es esa bici?** whose bike is that?

quienquiera *pron indef* (*pl* **quienes-quiera**) whoever

quieto,-a *adj* still; *(mar)* calm; **¡estáte q.!** keep still!, don't move!

quietud *nf* stillness; *(calma)* calm

quijada *nf* jawbone

quilate *nm* carat

quilla *nf* keel

quillango *nm* *Arg, Chile* hide blanket

quilo *nm* = **kilo**

quilombo *nm* *RP muy Fam* (a) *(burdel)* whorehouse (b) *(lío, desorden)* god-awful ruckus o rumpus

quimera *nf* *Fig* fantasy, pipe dream

química *nf* chemistry

químico,-a 1 *adj* chemical

2 *nm,f* chemist

quimioterapia *nf* chemotherapy

quimono *nm* kimono

quincalla *nf* metal pots and pans, tinware

quince *adj & nm inv* fifteen

quinceañero,-a *adj & nm,f* fifteen-year-old

quincena *nf* fortnight, two weeks

quincenal *adj* fortnightly

quincho *nm* *CSur* (a) *(techo)* thatched roof (b) *(refugio)* thatched shelter

quiniela *nf* football pools

quinientos,-as *adj & nm* five hundred

quinina *nf* quinine

quinqué *nm* oil lamp

quinquenal *adj* quinquennial, five-year

quinqui *nm* *Fam* delinquent, petty criminal

quinta *nf* (a) *(casa)* country house (b) *Mil* call-up year

quintaesencia *nf* quintessence

quintal *nm (medida)* = 46 kg; **q. métrico** ≃ 100 kg

quinteto *nm* quintet

quinto,-a 1 *adj & nm,f* fifth

2 *nm Mil* conscript, recruit

quiosco *nm* kiosk; **q. de periódicos** newspaper stand

quirófano *nm* operating theatre

quiromancia *nf* palmistry

quirúrgico,-a *adj* surgical

quise *indic fut de* **querer**

quisque, quisqui *pron Fam* **todo** o **cada q.** everyone, everybody

quisquilloso,-a 1 *adj* fussy, finicky

2 *nm,f* fusspot

quiste *nm* cyst

quitaesmalte(s) *nm inv* nail varnish o polish remover

quitamanchas *nm inv* stain remover

quitanieves *nm* (máquina) q. snow-plough

quitar 1 *vt* (**a**) to remove; *(ropa)* to take off; *(la mesa)* to clear; *(mancha)* to remove; *(dolor)* to relieve; *(hipo)* to stop; *(sed)* to quench; *(hambre)* to take away

(**b**) *(apartar)* to take away, to take off; *Fig* **q. importancia a algo** to play sth down; *Fig* **q. las ganas a algn** to put sb off

(**c**) *(robar)* to steal, to take; *Fig (tiempo)* to take up; *(sitio)* to take

(**d**) *(descontar)* to take off

(**e**) *Fam (apagar)* to turn off

(**f**) **eso no quita para que ...** that's no reason not to be ...

(**g**) **¡quita!** go away!

2 quitarse *vpr* (**a**) *(apartarse)* to move away

(**b**) *(mancha)* to come out; *(dolor)* to go away; **se me han quitado las ganas** I don't feel like it any more

(**c**) *(ropa, gafas)* to take off

(**d**) **q. de beber/fumar** to give up drinking/smoking

(**e**) **q. a algn de encima** to get rid of sb

> Observa que el verbo inglés **to quit** es un falso amigo y no es la traducción del verbo español **quitar**. En inglés, **to quit** significa "dejar, abandonar".

quizá(s) *adv* perhaps, maybe

R

R, r ['erre] *nf (la letra)* R, r

rábano *nm* radish; *Fam* **me importa un r.** I couldn't care less

rabia *nf* (**a**) *Fig (ira)* fury, rage; **¡qué r.!** how annoying!; **me da r.** it gets up my nose; **me tiene r.** he's got it in for me (**b**) *Med* rabies *sing*

rabiar [43] *vi* (**a**) *Fig (sufrir)* to be in great pain (**b**) *Fig (enfadar)* to rage; **hacer r. a algn** to make sb see red (**c**) *Med* to have rabies

rabieta *nf Fam* tantrum; **coger una r.** to throw a tantrum

rabillo *nm (del ojo)* corner

rabino *nm* rabbi

rabioso,-a *adj* (**a**) *Med* rabid; **perro r.** rabid dog (**b**) *Fig (enfadado)* furious (**c**) **de rabiosa actualidad** up-to-the-minute

rabo *nm* tail; *(de fruta etc)* stalk

racanear *vi Fam (ser tacaño)* to be stingy

rácano,-a *adj Fam (tacaño)* stingy, mean

racha *nf (de viento)* gust, squall; *Fam (período)* spell, patch; **a rachas** in fits and starts

racial *adj* **discriminación r.** racial discrimination; **disturbios raciales** race riots

racimo *nm* bunch, cluster

raciocinio *nm* reason

ración *nf* portion

racional *adj* rational

racionalizar [40] *vt* to rationalize

racionamiento *nm* rationing; **cartilla de r.** ration book

racionar *vt (limitar)* to ration; *(repartir)* to ration out

racismo *nm* racism

racista *adj & nmf* racist

radar *nm (pl* **radares***) Téc* radar

radiación *nf* radiation

radiactividad *nf* radioactivity

radiactivo,-a *adj* radioactive

radiador *nm* radiator

radial *adj* (**a**) *(en forma de estrella)* radial (**b**) *Am (de la radio)* radio

radiante *adj* radiant (**de** with)

radiar [43] *vt* to broadcast, to transmit

radical *adj* radical

radicalizar [40] *vt*, **radicalizarse** *vpr (conflicto)* to intensify; *(postura)* to harden

radicar [44] *vi (estar)* to be (situated) (**en** in), to be rooted (**en** in)

radio 1 *nf* radio; *(aparato)* radio (set)

2 *nm* (**a**) radius; **r. de acción** field of action, scope (**b**) *(de rueda)* spoke

radioactividad *nf* radioactivity

radioactivo,-a *adj* radioactive

radioaficionado,-a *nm,f* radio ham

radiocasete *nm (pl* **radiocasetes***)* radio cassette

radioescucha *nmf* listener

radiograbador *nm*, **radiograbadora** *nf CSur* radio cassette

radiografía *nf (imagen)* X-ray

radioyente *nmf* listener

ráfaga *nf (de viento)* gust, squall; *(de disparos)* burst

raído,-a *adj* (**a**) *(gastado)* worn (**b**) *Fam (desvergonzado)* insolent

raigambre *nf* roots

raíl *nm* rail

raíz *nf (pl* **raíces***)* root; **r. cuadrada** square root; *Fig* **a r. de** as a result of

raja *nf (corte)* cut, slit; *(hendidura)* crack, split

rajar 1 *vt (hender)* to crack, to split; *Fam (acuchillar)* to cut up

2 *vi Fam* to backbite

3 rajarse *vpr* (**a**) *(partirse)* to crack, to split (**b**) *Fam (echarse atrás)* to back out (**c**) *Am (acobardarse)* to chicken out

rajatabla: • a rajatabla *loc adv* strictly

ralea *nf Pey* type, sort

ralentí *nm* neutral; **estar al r.** to be ticking over

ralentizar *vt* to slow down

rallado,-a *adj* **queso r.** grated cheese; **pan r.** breadcrumbs

rallador *nm* grater

ralladura *nf* gratings

rallar *vt* to grate

ralo,-a *adj* sparse, thin

rama *nf* branch; *Fam* **andarse** *o* **irse por las ramas** to beat about the bush

ramaje *nm* branches

ramalazo *nm Fam (toque)* touch

rambla *nf (avenida)* boulevard, avenue

ramera *nf* prostitute, whore

ramificación *nf* ramification

ramificarse [44] *vpr* to ramify, to branch (out)

ramillete *nm (de flores)* posy

ramo *nm* (**a**) *(de flores)* bunch, bouquet (**b**) *(sector)* branch

rampa *nf* ramp; **r. de lanzamiento** launch pad

ramplón,-ona *adj* coarse, vulgar

rana *nf* frog; *Fam* **salir r.** to be a disappointment

ranchero,-a *nm,f (granjero)* rancher, farmer

rancho *nm* (**a**) *(granja)* ranch (**b**) *Mil (comida)* mess (**c**) *RP (en la playa)* = thatched beachside building (**d**) *CSur, Ven (en la ciudad)* shack, shanty

rancio,-a *adj* (**a**) *(comida)* stale (**b**) *(antiguo)* ancient

rango *nm* rank; *(jerarquía elevada)* high social standing

ranura *nf* slot

rapar *vt (afeitar)* to shave; *(pelo)* to crop

rapaz¹ *adj* predatory; **ave r.** bird of prey

rapaz²,-aza *nm,f* youngster; *(muchacho)* lad; *(muchacha)* lass

rape *nm* (**a**) *(pez)* angler fish (**b**) *Fam* **cortado al r.** close-cropped

rapidez *nf* speed, rapidity

rápido,-a 1 *adj* quick, fast, rapid

　2 *adv* quickly

　3 *nm* (**a**) *(tren)* fast train (**b**) **rápidos** *(de un río)* rapids

rapiña *nf* robbery, theft; **ave de r.** bird of prey

raptar *vt* to kidnap, to abduct

rapto *nm* (**a**) *(secuestro)* kidnapping, abduction (**b**) *Fig (arrebato)* outburst, fit

raqueta *nf* (**a**) *(de tenis)* racket; *(de pingpong) Br* bat, *US* paddle (**b**) *(de nieve)* snowshoe

raquítico,-a *adj Fam (escaso)* small, meagre; *(delgado)* emaciated

raquitismo *nm* rickets *sing*

rareza *nf* (**a**) rarity, rareness (**b**) *(extravagancia)* eccentricity

raro,-a *adj* (**a**) rare; **rara vez** seldom (**b**) *(extraño)* odd, strange

ras *nm* level; **a r. de** (on a) level with; **a r. de tierra** at ground level

rasante 1 *nf Aut* **cambio de r.** brow of a hill

　2 *adj (vuelo)* low

rasar *vt (nivelar)* to level

rasca *nf Fam (frío)* cold

rascacielos *nm inv* skyscraper

rascar [44] 1 *vt (con las uñas)* to scratch; *(guitarra)* to strum

　2 *vi* to chafe

rasero *nm Fig* **medir con el mismo r.** to treat impartially

rasgado,-a *adj (ojos)* slit, almond-shaped

rasgar [42] *vt* to tear, to rip

rasgo *nm (característica)* characteristic, feature; *(de la cara)* feature; *Fig* **a grandes rasgos** broadly speaking

rasgón *nm* tear, rip

rasguñar *vt* to scratch, to scrape

rasguño *nm* scratch, scrape

rasilla *nf (ladrillo)* tile

raso,-a 1 *adj (llano)* flat, level; *(vuelo)* low; *(cielo)* clear, cloudless; **soldado r.** private

　2 *nm* satin

raspa *nf (de pescado)* bone, backbone

raspador *nm* scraper

raspadura *nf (ralladura)* scraping, scrapings

raspar 1 *vt (limar)* to scrape (off)

　2 *vi (ropa etc)* to chafe

rasposo,-a *adj* rough, sharp

rastra *nf Agr* harrow; **a la r., a rastras** dragging; *Fig (de mal grado)* grudgingly

rastreador *nm* tracker

rastrear *vt (zona)* to comb

rastreo *nm* search

rastrero,-a *adj* creeping; *Fig (despreciable)* vile, base

rastrillo *nm* (**a**) rake (**b**) *Fam (mercadillo)* flea market

rastro *nm* (**a**) trace, sign; *(en el suelo)* track, trail (**b**) **el R.** = the Madrid flea market

rastrojo *nm* stubble

rasurar *vt*, **rasurarse** *vpr* to shave

rata 1 *nf* rat

　2 *nm Fam (tacaño)* mean o stingy person

ratero,-a *nm,f* pickpocket

raticida *nm* rat poison

ratificar [44] *vt* to ratify

rato *nm* (**a**) *(momento)* while, time; **a ratos** at times; **al poco r.** shortly after; **hay para r.** it'll take a while; **pasar un buen/mal r.** to have a good/bad time; **ratos libres** free time (**b**) *Fam* **un r.** *(mucho)* very, a lot

ratón *nm* mouse; *Informát* mouse

ratonera *nf* mousetrap

raudal *nm* torrent, flood; *Fig* **a raudales** in abundance

raya *nf* (**a**) *(línea)* line; *(del pantalón)* crease; *(del pelo)* parting; **camisa a rayas** striped shirt (**b**) *Fig* **tener a r.** to keep at bay; **pasarse de la r.** to go over the score (**c**) *(de droga)* fix, dose

rayano,-a *adj* bordering (**en** on)

rayar 1 *vt (arañar)* to scratch

2 *vi* **r. en** *o* **con** to border on

rayo *nm* (**a**) ray, beam; **rayos X** X-rays (**b**) *(relámpago)* (flash of) lightning; **¡mal r. la parta!** to hell with her!

rayón *nm* rayon

rayuela *nf* hopscotch

raza *nf* (**a**) *(humana)* race (**b**) *(de animal)* breed (**c**) *Perú (descaro)* cheek, nerve

razón *nf* (**a**) *(facultad)* reason; **uso de r.** power of reasoning (**b**) *(motivo)* reason; **r. de más para** all the more reason to (**c**) *(justicia)* rightness, justice; **dar la r. a algn** to say that sb is right; **tienes r.** you're right (**d**) *(proporción)* ratio, rate; **a r. de** at the rate of (**e**) **r. aquí** *(en letrero)* enquire within, apply within

razonable *adj* reasonable

razonado,-a *adj* reasoned, well-reasoned

razonamiento *nm* reasoning

razonar 1 *vt (argumentar)* to reason out

2 *vi (discurrir)* to reason

RDA *nf Hist (abr* **República Democrática Alemana** *o* **de Alemania**) GDR

re- *pref* re-

reacción *nf* reaction; **avión de r.** jet (plane); **r. en cadena** chain reaction

reaccionar *vi* to react

reaccionario,-a *adj & nm,f* reactionary

reacio,-a *adj* reluctant, unwilling

reactor *nm* reactor; *(avión)* jet (plane)

readaptación *nf* rehabilitation; **r. profesional** industrial retraining

reafirmar *vt* to reaffirm, to reassert

reagrupar *vt,* **reagruparse** *vpr* to regroup

reajuste *nm* readjustment; *Com* **r. de plantillas** downsizing; **r. ministerial** cabinet reshuffle

real¹ *adj (efectivo, verdadero)* real; **en la vida r.** in real life

real² *adj (regio)* royal

realce *nm (relieve)* relief; *Fig (esplendor)* splendour

realeza *nf* royalty

realidad *nf* reality; **en r.** in fact, actually; **la r. es que ...** the fact of the matter is that ...

realismo *nm* realism

realista 1 *adj* realistic

2 *nmf* realist

realizable *adj* feasible

realización *nf (ejecución)* carrying out; *Cin & TV* production

realizador,-a *nm,f Cin & TV* producer

realizar [40] 1 *vt* (**a**) *(hacer)* to carry out; *(ambición)* to achieve, to fulfil (**b**) *Cin & TV* to produce (**c**) *Fin* to realize

2 realizarse *vpr (persona)* to fulfil oneself; *(sueño)* to come true

realmente *adv* really; *(en realidad)* actually, in fact

realzar [40] *vt (recalcar)* to highlight; *Fig (belleza, importancia)* to enhance, to heighten

reanimación *nf* revival

reanimar *vt,* **reanimarse** *vpr* to revive

reanudación *nf* renewal, resumption, re-establishment; **r. de las clases** return to school

reanudar 1 *vt* to renew, to resume; **r. el paso** *o* **la marcha** to set off again; **r. las clases** to go back to school

2 reanudarse *vpr* to start again, to resume

reaparición *nf* reappearance, recurrence; *(de artista etc)* comeback

reapertura *nf* reopening

rearme *nm* rearmament

reaseguro *nm* reinsurance

reavivar *vt* to revive

rebaja *nf (descuento)* reduction, discount; **rebajas** sales; **precio de r.** sale price

rebajar 1 *vt* (**a**) *(precio)* to cut, to reduce; *(cantidad)* to take off (**b**) *(color)* to tone down, to soften; *(intensidad)* to diminish (**c**) *(trabajador)* to excuse, to exempt (**de** from) (**d**) *(humillar)* to humiliate

2 rebajarse *vpr (humillarse)* to humble oneself

rebanada *nf* slice

rebanar *vt* to slice, to cut into slices

rebañar *vt (plato etc)* to finish off

rebaño *nm (de ovejas)* flock; *(de otros animales)* herd

rebasar *vt* (**a**) *(exceder)* to exceed, to go beyond (**b**) *Aut* to overtake

rebatir *vt* to refute

> 🖉 Observa que la palabra inglesa **rebate** es un falso amigo y no es la traducción del verbo español **rebatir**. En inglés, **rebate** significa "devolución".

rebeca *nf* cardigan

rebelarse *vpr* to rebel, to revolt

rebelde 1 *nmf* rebel

2 *adj* rebellious; *Fig* **una tos r.** a persistent cough

rebeldía *nf* (**a**) rebelliousness (**b**) *Jur* default

rebelión *nf* rebellion, revolt

rebenque *nm RP* whip

reblandecer [33] *vt* to soften

rebobinar *vt* to rewind

rebosante *adj* overflowing (**de** with), brimming (**de** with)

rebosar 1 *vi* to overflow, to brim over; *Fig* **r. de** to be overflowing o brimming with **2** *vt (irradiar)* to radiate

rebotar *vi (pelota)* to bounce, to rebound; *(bala)* to ricochet

rebote *nm (de pelota)* bounce, rebound; *(de bala)* ricochet; **de r.** on the rebound

rebozar [40] *vt* to coat in breadcrumbs/batter

rebozo *nm Am* wrap, shawl

rebullir *vi*, **rebullirse** *vpr* to stir

rebuscado,-a *adj* recherché

rebuznar *vi* to bray

recabar *vt (información)* to obtain, to manage to get

recado *nm (mandado)* errand; *(mensaje)* message; **dejar un r.** to leave a message

recaer [39] *vi* (**a**) *Med* to relapse (**b**) *(culpa, responsabilidad)* to fall (**sobre** on)

recaída *nf* relapse

recalcar [44] *vt* to stress, to emphasize

recalcitrante *adj* recalcitrant

recalentar [1] *vt (comida)* to reheat, to warm up; *(calentar demasiado)* to overheat

recámara *nf* (**a**) *(de rueda)* tube (**b**) *(habitación)* dressing room (**c**) *CAm, Col, Méx (dormitorio)* bedroom

recamarera *nf CAm, Col, Méx* chambermaid

recambiar [43] *vt* to change (over)

recambio *nm* (**a**) *(repuesto)* spare (part); **rueda de r.** spare wheel (**b**) *(de pluma etc)* refill

recapacitar *vi* to reflect, to think

recargable *adj (pluma)* refillable; *(mechero)* rechargeable

recargado,-a *adj* overloaded; *Fig (estilo)* overelaborate, affected

recargar [42] 1 *vt* (**a**) *Elec* to recharge (**b**) *(sobrecargar)* to overload; *(adornar mucho)* to overelaborate (**c**) *Fin* to increase **2 recargarse** *vpr Méx (apoyarse)* to lean (**contra** against)

recargo *nm* extra charge, surcharge

recatado,-a *adj (prudente)* prudent, cautious; *(modesto)* modest, decent

recato *nm (cautela)* caution, prudence; *(pudor)* modesty

recaudación *nf (cobro)* collection; *(cantidad recaudada)* takings; *Dep* gate

recaudador,-a *nm,f* tax collector

recaudar *vt* to collect

recaudo *nm* **estar a buen r.** to be in safekeeping

recelar *vi* **r. de** to distrust

recelo *nm* suspicion, distrust

receloso,-a *adj* suspicious, distrustful

recepción *nf* reception; *(en hotel)* reception (desk)

recepcionista *nmf* receptionist

receptivo,-a *adj* receptive

receptor,-a 1 *nm,f (persona)* recipient **2** *nm Rad & TV* receiver

recesión *nf* recession

receta *nf* recipe; *Med* prescription

recetar *vt Med* to prescribe

rechace *nm Dep* clearance

rechazar [40] *vt* to reject, to turn down; *Mil* to repel, to drive back

rechazo *nm* rejection

rechiflar *vt* (**a**) *(silbar)* to hiss, to boo (**b**) *(mofarse)* to mock, to jeer at

rechinar *vi (madera)* to creak; *(metal)* to squeak, to screech; *(dientes)* to chatter

rechistar *vi* **sin r.** that's final

rechoncho,-a *adj Fam* chubby, tubby

rechupete: • de rechupete *loc Fam* **me sé el tema de r.** I know the subject inside out; **la comida estaba de r.** the food was mouthwateringly good

recibidor *nm* entrance hall

recibimiento *nm* reception, welcome

recibir 1 *vt* to receive; *(en casa)* to welcome; *(en la estación etc)* to meet **2 recibirse** *vpr Am (graduarse)* to graduate, to qualify (**de** as)

recibo *nm* (**a**) *(factura)* invoice, bill; *(resguardo)* receipt; **r. de la luz** electricity bill (**b**) **acusar r. de** to acknowledge receipt of

reciclado,-a 1 *adj* recycled **2** *nm (reciclaje)* recycling

reciclaje *nm (de residuos)* recycling; *Fig (renovación)* retraining; **curso de r.** refresher course

reciclar *vt (residuos)* to recycle; *Fig (profesores etc)* to retrain

recién *adv* (**a**) *(recientemente) (antes de pp)* recently, newly; **café r. hecho** freshly made coffee; **r. casados** newlyweds; **r. nacido** newborn baby (**b**) *Am (hace poco)* recently

reciente *adj* recent

recientemente *adv* recently, lately

recinto *nm (cercado)* enclosure; **r. comercial** shopping precinct

recio,-a 1 *adj (robusto)* strong, sturdy; *(grueso)* thick; *(voz)* loud **2** *adv* hard

recipiente *nm* receptacle, container

> 🔎 Observa que la palabra inglesa **recipient** es un falso amigo y no es la traducción de la palabra española **recipiente**. En inglés, **recipient** significa "receptor, destinatario".

recíproco,-a *adj* reciprocal

recital *nm Mús* recital; *Lit* reading

recitar *vt* to recite

reclamación *nf* (**a**) *(demanda)* claim, demand (**b**) *(queja)* complaint

reclamar 1 *vt* to claim, to demand

2 *vi* (**a**) to protest (**contra** against) (**b**) *Jur* to appeal

reclamo *nm* (**a**) *(publicitario)* appeal (**b**) *(en caza)* decoy bird, lure; *Fig* inducement (**c**) *Am (queja)* complaint (**d**) *Am (reivindicación)* claim

reclinar 1 *vt* to lean (**sobre** on)

2 reclinarse *vpr* to lean back, to recline

recluir [37] *vt* to shut away, to lock away; *(encarcelar)* to imprison, to intern

reclusión *nf* seclusion; *(encarcelamiento)* imprisonment, internment

recluso,-a *nm,f* prisoner

> 🖉 Observa que la palabra inglesa **recluse** es un falso amigo y no es la traducción de la palabra española **recluso**. En inglés, **recluse** significa "solitario".

recluta *nmf* recruit

reclutamiento *nm (voluntario)* recruitment; *(obligatorio)* conscription

recobrar 1 *vt* to recover, to retrieve; *(conocimiento)* to regain; **r. el aliento** to get one's breath back

2 recobrarse *vpr* to recover, to recuperate

recochineo *nm Fam* mockery

recodo *nm (de río)* twist, turn; *(de camino)* bend

recogedor *nm* dustpan

recoger [53] 1 *vt* (**a**) *(del suelo etc)* to pick up (**b**) *(datos etc)* to gather, to collect (**c**) *(ordenar, limpiar)* to clean; **r. la mesa** to clear the table (**d**) *(ir a buscar)* to pick up, to fetch (**e**) *(cosecha)* to gather, to pick

2 recogerse *vpr* (**a**) *(irse a casa)* to go home (**b**) *(pelo)* to lift up

recogida *nf* collection; *Agr (cosecha)* harvest, harvesting

recolección *nf Agr* harvest, harvesting; *(recogida)* collection, gathering

> 🖉 Observa que la palabra inglesa **recollection** es un falso amigo y no es la traducción de la palabra española **recolección**. En inglés, **recollection** significa "recuerdo".

recomendable *adj* recommendable

recomendación *nf* recommendation, reference

recomendado,-a *adj Am (carta, paquete)* registered

recomendar [1] *vt* to recommend

recompensa *nf* reward

recompensar *vt* to reward

recomponer [19] *(pp* **recompuesto**) *vt* to repair, to mend

reconciliación *nf* reconciliation

reconciliar [43] 1 *vt* to reconcile

2 reconciliarse *vpr* to be reconciled

recóndito,-a *adj* hidden, secret

reconfortante *adj* comforting

reconfortar *vt* to comfort

reconocer [34] *vt* (**a**) to recognize (**b**) *(admitir)* to recognize, to admit (**c**) *Med (paciente)* to examine

reconocimiento *nm* (**a**) recognition (**b**) *Med* examination, checkup

reconquista *nf* reconquest

reconstituyente *nm* tonic

reconstruir [37] *vt* to reconstruct

reconversión *nf* reconversion; **r. industrial** industrial redeployment

reconvertir [5] *vt* to reconvert; *Ind* to modernize

recopilación *nf* (**a**) *(resumen)* summary, résumé (**b**) *(compendio)* compilation, collection

recopilar *vt* to compile, to collect

récord *nm* record

recordar [2] 1 *vt* (**a**) *(rememorar)* to remember (**b**) **r. algo a algn** to remind sb of sth

2 *vi* to remember

recordatorio *nm (aviso)* reminder; *(de defunción)* notice of death

recordman *nm* record holder

recorrer *vt (distancia)* to cover, to travel; *(país)* to tour, to travel through *o* round; *(ciudad)* to visit, to walk round

recorrido *nm*, *Am* **recorrida** *nf (distancia)* distance travelled; *(trayecto)* trip, journey; *(itinerario)* itinerary, route

recortable *adj & nm* cutout

recortar *vt* to cut out

recorte *nm (acción, de periódico)* cutting; *(de pelo)* trim, cut; *Fig (de salarios etc)* cut

recostado,-a *adj* reclining, leaning

recostar [2] 1 *vt* to lean

2 recostarse *vpr (tumbarse)* to lie down

recoveco *nm (curva)* turn, bend; *(rincón)* nook, corner

recreación *nf* recreation

recrear 1 *vt* (**a**) *(divertir)* to amuse, to entertain (**b**) *(crear de nuevo)* to recreate

2 recrearse *vpr* to amuse oneself, to enjoy oneself; **r. con** to take pleasure *o* delight in

recreativo,-a *adj* recreational

recreo *nm* (**a**) *(diversión)* recreation (**b**) *(en el colegio)* break, recreation

recriminar *vt* to recriminate; *(reprochar)* to reproach

recrudecer [33] *vt*, **recrudecerse** *vpr* to worsen

recrudecimiento *nm* worsening

recta *nf Geom* straight line; *(de carretera)* straight stretch; *Dep* **la r. final** the home straight

rectangular *adj* rectangular

rectángulo *nm* rectangle

rectificación *nf* rectification; *(corrección)* correction

rectificar [44] *vt* to rectify; *(corregir)* to correct, to remedy

rectilíneo,-a *adj* straight

rectitud *nf* straightness; *Fig* uprightness, rectitude

recto,-a 1 *adj* (a) *(derecho)* straight (b) *(honesto)* upright, honest (c) *Geom* right
2 *nm Anat* rectum
3 *adv* straight (on)

rector,-a 1 *adj (principio)* guiding, ruling
2 *nm,f* rector

recua *nf Fig* string, series

recuadro *nm Prensa* box

recubrir *(pp recubierto) vt* to cover

recuento *nm* count; **hacer (el) r. de** to count

recuerdo *nm* (a) *(memoria)* memory (b) *(regalo etc)* souvenir (c) **recuerdos** regards

recuperación *nf* recovery; *(examen)* resit

recuperar 1 *vt (salud)* to recover; *(conocimiento)* to regain; *(tiempo, clases)* to make up
2 recuperarse *vpr* to recover

recurrir *vi* (a) *Jur* to appeal (b) **r. a** *(a algn)* to turn to; *(a algo)* to make use of, to resort to

> *Observa que el verbo inglés* **to recur** *es un falso amigo y no es la traducción del verbo español* **recurrir***. En inglés,* **to recur** *significa "repetirse".*

recurso *nm* (a) resource; **recursos naturales** natural resources; **como último r.** as a last resort (b) *Jur* appeal

recusar *vt* to challenge, to object to

red *nf* net; *(sistema)* network; *Com (cadena)* chain of supermarkets; *Fig (trampa)* trap; **la R.** *(Internet)* the Net

redacción *nf (escrito)* composition, essay; *(acción)* writing; *Prensa* editing; *(redactores)* editorial staff

redactar *vt* to draft; *Prensa* to edit

redactor,-a *nm,f Prensa* editor

redada *nf* **r. policial** *(en un solo sitio)* raid; *(en varios lugares a la vez)* round-up

redentor,-a *nm,f* redeemer

redicho,-a *adj Fam* affected, pretentious

redil *nm* fold, sheepfold

redimir *vt* to redeem

rédito *nm* yield, interest

redituable *adj* interest-yielding

redoblar 1 *vt* to redouble
2 *vi (tambor)* to roll

redoble *nm* roll; *(de campanas)* peal

redomado,-a *adj* utter, out-and-out

redonda *nf* **a la r.** around

redondear *vt (objeto)* to round, to make round; *(cantidad)* to round up

redondel *nm Fam (círculo)* circle, ring; *Taurom* ring, arena

redondo,-a *adj* (a) round; *Fig* **caer r.** to collapse (b) *(rotundo)* categorical; *(perfecto)* perfect

reducción *nf* reduction

reducido,-a *adj (disminuido)* reduced, decreased; *(pequeño)* limited, small

reducir [10] 1 *vt (disminuir)* to reduce
2 reducirse *vpr* (a) *(disminuirse)* to be reduced, to diminish (b) *(limitarse)* to confine oneself

redundancia *nf* redundancy, superfluousness; **valga la r.** if I might say so again

redundante *adj* redundant

redundar *vi* **r. en** *(resultar)* to result in, to lead to

reduplicar [44] *vt* to redouble

reembolsar *vt* to reimburse; *(deuda)* to repay; *(importe)* to refund

reembolso *nm* reimbursement; *(de deuda)* repayment; *(devolución)* refund; **contra r.** cash on delivery

reemplazar [40] *vt* to replace (**con** with)

reemplazo *nm* replacement; *Mil* call-up

reestructuración *nf* restructuring

reestructurar *vt* to restructure

ref. *(abr referencia)* ref

refacción *nf* (a) *Andes, CAm, RP, Ven (reparación)* repair (b) *Méx (recambio)* spare part

refaccionar *vt Am* to repair, to do up

refectorio *nm* refectory, canteen

referencia *nf* reference; **con r. a** with reference to

referéndum *nm (pl referéndums)* referendum

referente *adj* **r. a** concerning, regarding

referir [5] 1 *vt* to tell, to relate
2 referirse *vpr (aludir)* to refer (**a** to); **¿a qué te refieres?** what do you mean?

refilón: •**de refilón** *loc adv (de pasada)* briefly

refinado,-a *adj* refined
refinamiento *nm* refinement
refinar *vt* to refine
refinería *nf* refinery
reflector,-a 1 *adj* reflecting
  2 *nm Elec* spotlight, searchlight
reflejar 1 *vt* to reflect
  2 reflejarse *vpr* to be reflected (**en** in)
reflejo,-a 1 *nm* (**a**) *(imagen)* reflection
  (**b**) *(destello)* gleam, glint (**c**) *Anat* reflex
  (**d**) **reflejos** *(en el cabello)* streaks, high-
  lights
  2 *adj (movimiento)* reflex
reflexión *nf* reflection
reflexionar *vi* to reflect (**sobre** on), to
  think (**sobre** about)
reflexivo,-a *adj* (**a**) *(persona)* thoughtful
  (**b**) *Ling* reflexive
reflujo *nm* ebb (tide)
reforma *nf* (**a**) reform; **r. fiscal** tax reform
  (**b**) *(reparación)* repair
reformador,-a *nm,f* reformer
reformar 1 *vt* to reform; *(edificio)* to renovate
  2 reformarse *vpr* to reform
reformatorio *nm* reformatory, reform
  school
reforzar [2] *vt* to reinforce, to strengthen
refractario,-a *adj* (**a**) *Téc* heat-resistant
  (**b**) *(persona)* unwilling, reluctant
refrán *nm* proverb, saying
refregar [1] *vt* to rub vigorously; *Fig* **no
  me lo refriegues** don't rub it in
refrenar 1 *vt (contener)* to restrain, to
  curb
  2 refrenarse *vpr* to restrain oneself
refrendar *vt (firmar)* to endorse, to countersign; *(aprobar)* to approve
refrescante *adj* refreshing
refrescar [44] 1 *vt* to refresh
  2 *vi* (**a**) *(tiempo)* to turn cool (**b**) *(bebida)*
  to be refreshing
  3 refrescarse *vpr* to cool down
refresco *nm* soft drink, refreshments
refriega *nf (lucha)* scuffle, brawl; *(escaramuza)* skirmish
refrigeración *nf (enfriamiento)* refrigera-
  tion; *(aire acondicionado)* air conditioning
refrigerado,-a *adj* air-conditioned
refrigerador *nm* refrigerator, fridge
refrigerar *vt* to refrigerate; *(habitación)*
  to air-condition
refrigerio *nm* snack, refreshments
refuerzo *nm* reinforcement, strengthening
refugiado,-a *adj & nm,f* refugee

refugiarse [43] *vpr* to shelter, to take
  refuge
refugio *nm* refuge
refulgente *adj* radiant, brilliant
refulgir [57] *vi (brillar)* to shine; *(resplandecer)* to glitter, to sparkle
refunfuñar *vi* to grumble, to moan
refutar *vt* to refute
regadera *nf* (**a**) *(para regar)* watering
  can; *Fam* **estar como una r.** to be as mad
  as a hatter (**b**) *Col, Méx, Ven (ducha)*
  shower
regadío *nm (tierra)* irrigated land
regalado,-a *adj* (**a**) *(gratis)* free; *(muy
  barato)* dirt-cheap (**b**) **una vida regalada**
  an easy life
regalar *vt* (**a**) *(dar)* to give (as a present);
  (en ofertas etc) to give away (**b**) **r. el oído a
  algn** to flatter sb
regaliz *nm* liquorice
regalo *nm* (**a**) gift, present; **de r.** as a
  present (**b**) *(comodidad)* pleasure, comfort
regalón,-ona *adj CSur Fam (niño)* spoilt
regañadientes: •**a regañadientes** *loc
  adv* reluctantly, unwillingly
regañar 1 *vt Fam* to scold, to tell off
  2 *vi* to nag
regañina *nf* scolding, telling-off
regañón,-ona *nm,f Fam* nag
regar [1] *vt* to water
regata *nf* boat race
regatear 1 *vi* (**a**) to haggle, to bargain (**b**)
  Dep to dribble
  2 *vt* **no r. esfuerzos** to spare no effort
regateo *nm* (**a**) *(de precios)* haggling (**b**)
  Dep dribbling
regazo *nm* lap
regeneración *nf* regeneration
regenerar *vt* to regenerate
regentar *vt* to rule, to govern; *(cargo)* to
  hold
regente *nmf* (**a**) *Pol* regent (**b**) *(director)*
  manager (**c**) *Méx (alcalde)* mayor, *f*
  mayoress
régimen *nm* (*pl* **regímenes**) (**a**) *Pol* regime (**b**) *Med* diet; **estar a r.** to be on a diet
regimiento *nm* regiment
regio,-a *adj* (**a**) *(real)* royal, regal (**b**)
  (suntuoso) sumptuous, luxurious; *Am
  (magnífico)* splendid, majestic
región *nf* region
regional *adj* regional
regionalista *adj & nmf* regionalist
regir [58] 1 *vt* to govern
  2 *vi* to be in force
  3 regirse *vpr* to be guided, to go (**por** by)
registrado,-a *adj* (**a**) *(patentado, inscrito)*

registered; **marca registrada** registered trademark (**b**) *Am (certificado)* registered

registrador,-a *adj* **caja registradora** cash register

registradora *nf Am* cash register

registrar 1 *vt* (**a**) *(examinar)* to inspect; *(cachear)* to frisk (**b**) *(inscribir)* to register (**c**) *(grabar)* to record

2 registrarse *vpr* (**a**) *(inscribirse)* to register, to enrol (**b**) *(detectarse)* to be recorded

registro *nm* (**a**) inspection (**b**) *(inscripción)* registration, recording; *(oficina)* registry office (**c**) *Mús* register

regla *nf* (**a**) *(norma)* rule; **en r.** in order; **por r. general** as a (general) rule; **r. de oro** golden rule (**b**) *(instrumento)* ruler (**c**) *Mat* rule (**d**) *Med (periodo)* period

reglamentación *nf* (**a**) *(acción)* regulation (**b**) *(reglamento)* regulations, rules

reglamentar *vt* to regulate

reglamentario,-a *adj* statutory; *Mil* **arma reglamentaria** regulation gun

reglamento *nm* regulations, rules

reglar *vt* to regulate

regocijar 1 *vt* to delight, to amuse

2 regocijarse *vpr* to be delighted, to rejoice

regocijo *nm (placer)* delight, joy; *(alborozo)* rejoicing, merriment

regodearse *vpr Fam* to delight (**con** in)

regodeo *nm Fam* delight

regordete,-a *adj Fam* plump, chubby

regresar 1 *vi* to return

2 *vt Andes, CAm, Carib, Méx (devolver)* to give back

3 regresarse *vpr Andes, CAm, Carib, Méx (yendo)* to go back, to return; *(viniendo)* to come back, to return

regresión *nf* regression; *(decaimiento)* deterioration, decline

regreso *nm* return

reguero *nm (corriente)* trickle; *(de humo)* trail

regulable *adj* adjustable

regular 1 *vt* (**a**) to regulate, to control (**b**) *(ajustar)* to adjust

2 *adj* (**a**) regular; **por lo r.** as a rule; **vuelo r.** scheduled flight (**b**) *Fam (mediano)* average, so-so

3 *adv* so-so

regularidad *nf* regularity; **con r.** regularly

regularizar [40] *vt* to regularize

regusto *nm* aftertaste

rehabilitar *vt* to rehabilitate; *(edificio)* to convert

rehacer [15] *(pp* **rehecho**) **1** *vt* to redo

2 rehacerse *vpr (recuperarse)* to recover, to recuperate

rehén *nm* hostage

rehogar [42] *vt* to brown

rehuir [37] *vt* to shun, to avoid

rehusar *vt* to refuse

reina *nf* queen

reinado *nm* reign

reinante *adj (que reina)* reigning, ruling; *(prevaleciente)* prevailing

reinar *vi* to reign

reincidente *nmf Jur* recidivist

reincidir *vi* to relapse, to fall back (**en** into)

reincorporarse *vpr* **r. al trabajo** to return to work

reino *nm* kingdom; **el R. Unido** the United Kingdom

reinserción *nf* reintegration

reinsertar *vt*, **reinsertarse** *bpr* to reintegrate

reintegrar *vt* (**a**) *(trabajador)* to reinstate (**b**) *(dinero)* to reimburse, to refund

reintegro *nm (en lotería)* winning of one's stake

reír [56] 1 *vi* to laugh

2 reírse *vpr* (**a**) to laugh (**b**) *(mofarse)* to laugh (**de** at), to make fun (**de** of)

reiterar *vt* to reiterate, to repeat

reivindicación *nf* claim, demand

reivindicar [44] *vt* to claim, to demand; **el atentado fue reivindicado por los terroristas** the terrorists claimed responsibility for the attack

reivindicativo,-a *adj* protest

reja *nf* (**a**) *(de ventana)* grill, grating; *Fam* **estar entre rejas** to be behind bars (**b**) *Agr* ploughshare

rejilla *nf (de ventana, ventilador, radiador)* grill; *(de horno)* gridiron; *(para equipaje)* luggage rack

rejoneador,-a *nm,f Taurom* = bullfighter on horseback

rejonear *vt Taurom* to fight on horseback

rejuvenecer [33] *vt* to rejuvenate

relación *nf* (**a**) relationship; *(conexión)* connection, link; **con** *o* **en r.** with regard to; **relaciones públicas** public relations (**b**) *(lista)* list (**c**) *(relato)* account (**d**) *Mat & Téc* ratio

relacionado,-a *adj* related (**con** to), connected (**con** with)

relacionar 1 *vt* to relate (**con** to), to connect (**con** with)

2 • relacionarse *vpr* (**a**) to be related, to be connected (**con** with) (**b**) *(alternar)* to mix, to get acquainted

relajación *nf* relaxation

relajante *adj* relaxing

relajar 1 *vt* to relax

  2 relajarse *vpr* to relax; *(moral)* to deteriorate

relajo *nm Am Fam (alboroto)* racket, din

relamerse *vpr* to lick one's lips

relamido,-a *adj (afectado)* affected; *(pulcro)* prim and proper

relámpago *nm* flash of lightning; *Fig* **pasó como un r.** he flashed past; *Fig* **visita r.** flying visit

relampaguear *v impers* to flash

relanzar *vt* to relaunch

relatar *vt* to narrate, to relate

relatividad *nf* relativity

relativo,-a *adj* relative (**a** to); **en lo r. a** with regard to, concerning

relato *nm (cuento)* tale, story

relax *nm Fam* relaxation

relegar [42] *vt* to relegate

relente *nm* dew

relevancia *nf* importance

> *Observa que la palabra inglesa* **relevance** *es un falso amigo y no es la traducción de la palabra española* **relevancia**. *En inglés,* **relevance** *significa "pertinencia".*

relevante *adj* important

relevar 1 *vt* to relieve, to take over from; **fue relevado del cargo** he was relieved of his duties

  2 relevarse *vpr (turnarse)* to relieve one another

relevo *nm* relief; *Dep* relay

relieve *nm Arte* relief; *Fig* **poner de r.** to emphasize

religión *nf* religion

religioso,-a 1 *adj* religious

  2 *nm,f (hombre)* monk; *(mujer)* nun

relinchar *vi* to neigh, to whinny

relincho *nm* neigh, whinny

reliquia *nf* relic

rellamada *nf Tel* redial

rellano *nm* landing

rellenar *vt* (**a**) *(impreso etc)* to fill in (**b**) *(un ave)* to stuff; *(un pastel)* to fill

relleno,-a 1 *nm (de aves)* stuffing; *(de pasteles)* filling

  2 *adj* stuffed

reloj *nm* clock; *(de pulsera)* watch; **r. de arena** hourglass; **r. de sol** sundial; **r. despertador** alarm clock

relojería *nf (tienda)* watchmaker's, clockmaker's; **bomba de r.** time bomb

relojero,-a *nm,f* watchmaker, clockmaker

reluciente *adj* shining, gleaming

relucir [35] *vi (brillar)* to shine, to gleam; **sacar a r. un tema** to bring up a subject

relumbrar *vi* to shine, to gleam

reluzco *indic pres de* **relucir**

remachar *vt* to drive home, to hammer home

remache *nm* rivet

remanente *nm (restos)* remainder; *(extra)* surplus

remangar [42] *vt*, **remangarse** *vpr (mangas, pantalones)* to roll up; *(camisa)* to tuck up

remanso *nm* pool; *(lugar tranquilo)* quiet place

remar *vi* to row

remarcar [44] *vt* to stress, to underline

> *Observa que el verbo inglés* **to remark** *es un falso amigo y no es la traducción del verbo español* **remarcar**. *En inglés,* **to remark** *significa "comentar, observar".*

rematadamente *adv* **r. loco** as mad as a hatter

rematar *vt* (**a**) to finish off, to put the finishing touches to (**b**) *Com* to sell off cheaply (**c**) *Dep* to shoot

remate *nm* (**a**) *(final)* end, finish; **para r.** to crown it all (**b**) *Dep* shot at goal (**c**) **de r.** utter, utterly

rembolsar *vt* = **reembolsar**

rembolso *nm* = **reembolso**

remedar *vt* to imitate, to copy

remediar [43] *vt* (**a**) to remedy; *(enmendar)* to repair, to make good (**b**) *(evitar)* to avoid, to prevent; **no pude remediarlo** I couldn't help it

remedio *nm (cura)* remedy, cure; *(solución)* solution; **¡qué r.!** what else can I do?; **no hay más r.** there's no choice; **sin r.** without fail; *Fam* **¡no tienes r.!** you're hopeless!

remedo *nm (imitación)* imitation, copy; *(parodia)* parody

rememorar *vt* to remember, to recall

remendar [1] *vt (ropa)* to patch

remera *nf RP (prenda)* T-shirt

remero,-a *nm,f* rower

remesa *nf (de mercancías)* consignment, shipment; *(de dinero)* remittance

remiendo *nm (parche)* patch

remilgado,-a *adj (afectado)* affected; *(melindroso)* fussy, finicky; *(gazmoño)* prudish

remilgo *nm* affectation; *(gazmoñería)* prudishness

reminiscencia *nf* reminiscence

remise *nm RP* taxi *(in private car without meter)*

remisero,-a *nm,f RP* taxi driver *(of private car without meter)*

remiso,-a *adj* reluctant

remite *nm (en carta)* = sender's name and address

remitente *nmf* sender

remitir 1 *vt* (**a**) *(enviar)* to send (**b**) *(referir)* to refer

2 *vi (fiebre, temporal)* to subside

3 remitirse *upr* **si nos remitimos a los hechos** if we look at the facts; **remítase a la página 10** see page 10

remo *nm* oar; *(deporte)* rowing

remoción *nf Andes, RP (de objetos)* transport, removal; *(de heridos)* transport

remodelación *nf (modificación)* reshaping; *(reorganización)* reorganization; *Pol* **r. ministerial** *o* **del gobierno** cabinet reshuffle

remodelar *vt* to reshape; *(reorganizar)* to reorganize

remojar *vt* to soak (**en** in)

remojo *nm* **dejar** *o* **poner en r.** to soak, to leave to soak

remojón *nm Fam* **darse un r.** to go for a dip

remolacha *nf Br* beetroot, *US* beet

remolcador *nm* (**a**) *Náut* tug, tugboat (**b**) *Aut Br* breakdown van *o* truck, *US* tow truck

remolcar [44] *vt* to tow

remolino *nm (de agua)* whirlpool, eddy; *(de aire)* whirlwind

remolón,-ona 1 *adj* lazy

2 *nm,f* **hacerse el r.** to shirk, to slack

remolonear *vi* to shirk, to slack

remolque *nm (acción)* towing; *(vehículo)* trailer; *Fig* **ir a r. de algn** to trundle along behind sb

remontar 1 *vt* (**a**) *(subir)* to go up (**b**) *(superar)* to overcome

2 remontarse *upr* (**a**) *(pájaros, aviones)* to soar (**b**) *(datar)* to go back, to date back (**a** to)

remorder [4] *vt* to trouble; **me remuerde la conciencia por ...** I've got a bad conscience about ...

remordimiento *nm* remorse

remoto,-a *adj* remote, faraway; **no tengo la más remota idea** I haven't got the faintest idea

remover [4] *vt* (**a**) *(trasladar)* to move over (**b**) *(tierra)* to turn over; *(líquido)* to shake up; *(comida etc)* to stir; *(asunto)* to stir up

---

📖 Observa que el verbo inglés **to remove** es un falso amigo y no es la traducción del verbo español **remover**. En inglés, **to remove** significa "quitar, despedir".

---

remozar [40] *vt* to modernize

remplazar [40] *vt* = **reemplazar**

remplazo *nm* = **reemplazo**

remuneración *nf* remuneration

remunerar *vt* to remunerate

renacentista *adj* Renaissance

renacer [60] *vi* to be reborn; *Fig (revivir)* to revive, to come back to life

renacimiento *nm* **el R.** the Renaissance

renacuajo *nm* tadpole; *Fam (niño pequeño)* shrimp

renal *adj* kidney; **insuficiencia r.** kidney failure

rencilla *nf* quarrel

rencor *nm* rancour; *(resentimiento)* resentment; **guardar r. a algn** to have a grudge against sb

rencoroso,-a *adj (hostil)* rancorous; *(resentido)* resentful

rendición *nf* surrender

rendido,-a *adj (muy cansado)* exhausted, worn out

rendija *nf* crack, split

rendimiento *nm (producción)* yield, output; *(de máquina, motor)* efficiency, performance

rendir [6] 1 *vt* (**a**) *(fruto, beneficios)* to yield, to produce (**b**) *(cansar)* to exhaust, to wear out (**c**) **r. culto a** to worship; **r. homenaje a** to pay homage to

2 *vi (dar beneficios)* to pay, to be profitable

3 rendirse *upr* (**a**) to surrender, to give in; **¡me rindo!** I give up! (**b**) *(cansarse)* to wear oneself out

renegado,-a *adj & nm,f* renegade

renegar [1] *vt* **r. de** to renounce, to disown

renegrido,-a *adj* blackened

RENFE *nf (abr* **Red Nacional de los Ferrocarriles Españoles**) = Spanish state railway company

renglón *nm* line; **a r. seguido** immediately afterwards

rengo,-a *adj Andes, RP* lame

renguear *vi Andes, RP* to limp, to hobble

reno *nm* reindeer

renombrado,-a *adj* renowned, famous

renombre *nm* renown, fame

renovable *adj* renewable

renovación *nf (de contrato, pasaporte)* renewal; *(de una casa)* renovation

renovar [2] *vt* to renew; *(edificio)* to renovate

renta *nf* (**a**) *Fin (ingresos)* income; *(beneficio)* interest, return; **r. per cápita** per capita income; **r. fija** fixed-interest security (**b**) *(alquiler)* rent

rentable adj profitable

rentar 1 vt (rendir) to produce, to yield; Méx (alquilar) to rent

  2 vi to be profitable

renuncia nf (a) renunciation (b) (dimisión) resignation

renunciar [43] vi (a) r. a to renounce, to give up; (no aceptar) to decline (b) (dimitir) to resign

reñido,-a adj (disputado) tough, hard-fought

reñir [6] 1 vt (regañar) to scold, to tell off

  2 vi (discutir) to quarrel, to argue; (pelear) to fight; **r. con algn** to fall out with sb

reo nmf (acusado) defendant, accused; (culpable) culprit

reojo: • de reojo loc adv mirar algo de r. to look at sth out of the corner of one's eye

reparación nf repair; (compensación) reparation, amends

reparar 1 vt to repair; (ofensa, injuria) to make amends for; (daño) to make good

  2 vi r. en (darse cuenta de) to notice; (reflexionar sobre) to think about

reparo nm no tener reparos en not to hesitate to; **me da r.** I feel embarrassed

repartidor,-a nm,f distributor

repartir vt (a) (dividir) to distribute, to share out (b) (regalo, premio) to give out, to hand out; (correo) to deliver; Naipes to deal

reparto nm (a) distribution, sharing out (b) (distribución) handing out; (de mercancías) delivery (c) Cin & Teatro cast

repasador nm RP (trapo) tea towel

repasar vt (a) to revise, to go over (b) (ropa) to mend

repaso nm revision

repatear vt Fam to annoy, to turn off

repatriar [29] vt to repatriate

repecho nm short steep slope

repelente adj repulsive, repellent; Fam niño r. little know-all

repeler vt (rechazar) to repel, to repulse; (repugnar) to disgust

repente nm Fam (arrebato) fit, outburst; **de r.** suddenly, all of a sudden

repentino,-a adj sudden

repercusión nf repercussion

repercutir vi (a) (sonido) to resound, to reverberate; (objeto) to rebound (b) Fig r. en to have repercussions on, to affect

repertorio nm repertoire, repertory

repesca nf Fam second chance; (examen) resit

repetición nf repetition; **r. de la jugada** action replay

repetido,-a adj repetidas veces repeatedly

repetidor,-a 1 adj repeating

  2 nm,f Fam Educ = student who is repeating a year

repetir [6] 1 vt (a) to repeat (b) (plato) to have a second helping

  2 vi Educ to repeat a year

  3 repetirse vpr (a) (persona) to repeat oneself (b) (hecho) to recur (c) **el pepino se repite** cucumber repeats (on me/you/him/etc)

repicar [44] vt (las campanas) to peal, to ring out

repipi adj Fam niño r. little know-all

repique nm (de campanas) peal, ringing

repiquetear vt & vi (campanas) to ring; (tambor) to beat

repisa nf shelf, ledge

replantear vt, **replantearse** vpr to reconsider, to rethink

replegarse vpr to fall back, to retreat

repleto,-a adj full (up), jam-packed; **r. de** packed with, crammed with

réplica nf (a) answer, reply (b) (copia) replica

replicar [44] 1 vt to answer back

  2 vi (a) to reply, to retort (b) (objetar) to argue (c) Jur to answer

repliegue nm Mil withdrawal, retreat

repoblación nf repopulation; **r. forestal** reafforestation

repoblar [2] vt to repopulate; (bosque) to reafforest

repollo nm cabbage

reponer [19] 1 vt (a) to put back, to replace (b) Teatro (obra) to put on again; Cin (película) to rerun; TV (programa) to repeat

  2 reponerse vpr r. de to recover from, to get over

reportaje nm Prensa & Rad report; (noticias) article, news item

reportar 1 vt (beneficios etc) to bring; Am (informar) to report

  2 reportarse vpr Am (presentarse) to report (a to)

reporte nm Méx (informe) report; (noticia) news item o report; **recibí reportes de mi hermano** I was sent news by my brother; **el r. del tiempo** the weather report o forecast

reportero,-a nm,f reporter

reposar 1 vt to rest (en on)

  2 vi (descansar) to rest, to take a rest; (té) to infuse; (comida) to stand

reposera nf RP Br sun-lounger, US beach recliner

reposición *nf TV* repeat; *Cin* rerun, re-showing

reposo *nm* rest; **en r.** at rest

repostar *vt* *(provisiones)* to stock up with; *Aut (gasolina)* to fill up with

repostería *nf* confectionery; *(tienda)* confectioner's (shop)

repostero,-a *nm,f* confectioner

reprender *vt* to reprimand, to scold

represalia *nf* *(usu pl)* reprisals, retaliation

representación *nf* (a) representation (b) *Teatro* performance

representante *nmf* representative

representar *vt* (a) to represent (b) *(significar)* to mean, to represent (c) *Teatro (obra)* to perform

representativo,-a *adj* representative

represión *nf* repression

represivo,-a *adj* repressive

reprimenda *nf* reprimand

reprimir *vt* to repress

reprobar [2] *vt* *(cosa)* to condemn; *(a persona)* to reproach, to reprove; *Am (estudiante, examen)* to fail

réprobo,-a *adj & nm,f* reprobate

reprochable *adj* reproachable

reprochar *vt* to reproach; **r. algo a algn** to reproach sb for sth

reproche *nm* reproach

reproducción *nf* reproduction

reproducir [10] **1** *vt* to reproduce
2 reproducirse *vpr* (a) to reproduce, to breed (b) *(repetirse)* to recur, to happen again

reproductor,-a *adj* reproductive

reptar *vi* to slither

reptil *nm* reptile

república *nf* republic; **la R. Checa** the Czech Republic

republicano,-a *adj & nm,f* republican

repudiar [43] *vt* to repudiate

repuesto *nm* *(recambio)* spare part, spare; *Aut* **rueda de r.** spare wheel

repugnancia *nf* loathing, disgust

repugnante *adj* disgusting, revolting

repugnar *vt* to disgust, to revolt

repujar *vt* to emboss

repulsa *nf* rebuff

repulsión *nf* repulsion, repugnance

repulsivo,-a *adj* repulsive, revolting

repuntar *vi Am (mejorar)* to improve

repunte *nm Am (recuperación)* recovery; *(aumento)* rise, increase; **un r. en las ventas** an improvement *o* increase in sales

repuse *pt indef de* **reponer**

reputación *nf* reputation

reputar *vt* to consider, to deem

requemar *vt* to scorch

requerimiento *nm* (a) *(súplica)* request (b) *Jur (aviso)* summons *sing*

> Observa que la palabra inglesa **requirement** es un falso amigo y no es la traducción de la palabra española **requerimiento**. En inglés, **requirement** significa "requisito".

requerir [5] *vt* (a) to require (b) *(solicitar)* to request (c) *Jur (avisar)* to summon

requesón *nm* cottage cheese

requete- *pref Fam* really, very, incredibly; **requetebueno** brilliant

réquiem *nm* *(pl* **réquiems***)* requiem

requisa *nf* (a) *(inspección)* inspection (b) *Mil* requisition

requisar *vt* to requisition

requisito *nm* requirement, requisite

res *nf* animal

resabiado,-a *adj Pey* pedantic

resabio *nm* (a) *(mal sabor)* unpleasant *o* bad aftertaste (b) *(vicio)* bad habit

resaca *nf* (a) hangover (b) *Náut* undertow, undercurrent

resaltar *vi* (a) *(sobresalir)* to project, to jut out (b) *Fig* to stand out

resarcir [52] *vt* to compensate

resbalada *nf Am Fam* slip

resbaladizo,-a *adj* slippery

resbalar *vi*, **resbalarse** *vpr* to slip; *Aut* to skid

resbalón *nm* slip

rescatar *vt* *(persona)* to rescue; *(objeto)* to recover

rescate *nm* (a) *(salvamento)* rescue; *(recuperación)* recovery (b) *(suma)* ransom

rescindir *vt* to rescind, to annul; *(contrato)* to cancel

rescisión *nf* rescission, annulment

rescoldo *nm* (a) embers (b) *Fig (recelo)* lingering doubt

resecarse [44] *vpr* to dry up, to become parched

reseco,-a *adj* very dry, parched

resentido,-a *adj* resentful

resentimiento *nm* resentment

resentirse [5] *vpr* (a) **r. de** to suffer from, to feel the effects of (b) *(ofenderse)* to feel offended; **r. por algo** to take offence at sth, to feel bitter about sth

reseña *nf* review; *Prensa* write-up

reserva **1** *nf* (a) *(de entradas etc)* reservation, booking (b) *(provisión)* reserve, stock; **un vino de r.** a vintage wine (c) *Mil* reserve, reserves (d) *(duda)* reservation
2 *nmf Dep* reserve, substitute

reservado,-a 1 *adj (persona)* reserved, quiet
2 *nm* private room

reservar 1 *vt* (**a**) *(billetes etc)* to reserve, to book (**b**) *(dinero, tiempo etc)* to keep, to save
2 reservarse *upr* (**a**) to save oneself (**para** for) (**b**) *(sentimientos)* to keep to oneself (**c**) **r. el derecho de** to reserve the right to

resfriado,-a 1 *nm (catarro)* cold; **coger un r.** to catch (a) cold
2 *adj* **estar r.** to have a cold

resfriarse *upr* to catch (a) cold

resfrío *nm Andes, RP* cold

resguardar *vt (proteger)* to protect, to shelter (**de** from)

resguardo *nm* (**a**) *(recibo)* receipt (**b**) *(protección)* protection, shelter

residencia *nf* residence; **r. de ancianos** old people's home

residencial *adj* residential

residente *adj & nmf* resident

residir *vi* to reside, to live (**en** in); *Fig* to lie (**en** in)

residuo *nm* (**a**) *(residue)* residue (**b**) **residuos** waste

resignación *nf* resignation

resignado,-a *adj* resigned

resignarse *upr* to resign oneself (**a** to)

resina *nf* resin

resistencia *nf* (**a**) resistance (**b**) *(aguante)* endurance, stamina (**c**) *Elec* element

resistente *adj* (**a**) resistant (**a** to) (**b**) *(fuerte)* tough, hardy

resistir 1 *vi* (**a**) to resist (**b**) *(aguantar)* to hold (out)
2 *vt (situación, persona)* to put up with; *(tentación)* to resist
3 resistirse *upr* to resist; *(oponerse)* to offer resistance; *(negarse)* to refuse

resollar [2] *vi* to breathe heavily; *(con silbido)* to wheeze

resolución *nf* (**a**) *(solución)* solution (**b**) *(decisión)* resolution

resolver [4] (*pp* **resuelto**) **1** *vt (problema)* to solve; *(asunto)* to settle
2 *vi (decidir)* to resolve, to decide
3 resolverse *upr* (**a**) *(solucionarse)* to be solved (**b**) *(decidirse)* to resolve, to make up one's mind (**a** to)

resonancia *nf* (**a**) *(sonora)* resonance (**b**) *(repercusión)* repercussions

resonar [2] *vi* to resound; *(tener eco)* to echo

resoplar *vi (respirar)* to breathe heavily; *(de cansancio)* to puff and pant; *(de enfado)* to huff and puff

resoplido *nm (silbido)* wheezing; *(de cansancio)* panting; *(de enfado)* snort

resorte *nm* (**a**) *(muelle)* spring (**b**) *Fig* means

> 🔎 Observa que la palabra inglesa **resort** es un falso amigo y no es la traducción de la palabra española **resorte**. En inglés, **resort** significa "recurso" o "lugar de vacaciones".

respaldar *vt* to support, to back (up)

respaldo *nm (de silla etc)* back; *Fig (apoyo)* support, backing

respectar *vt* to concern, to regard; **por lo que a mí respecta** as far as I'm concerned

respectivo,-a *adj* respective; **en lo r. a** with regard to, regarding

respecto *nm*

al r., a este r. in this respect; **con r. a, r. a, r. de** with regard to; **r. a mí** as for me, as far as I am concerned

respetable 1 *adj* respectable
2 *nm Fam* **el r.** the audience

respetar *vt* to respect; **hacerse r. de todos** to command everyone's respect

respeto *nm* (**a**) respect; **por r.** out of consideration (**b**) *(recelo)* fear

respetuoso,-a *adj* respectful

respingar [42] *vi* to shy

respingo *nm* start, jump

respingón,-ona *adj (nariz)* snub, upturned

respiración *nf (acción)* breathing, respiration; *(aliento)* breath; **r. artificial** artificial resuscitation

respirar *vi* to breathe; **¡por fin respiro!** well, that's a relief!

respiratorio,-a *adj* respiratory

respiro *nm* (**a**) breathing (**b**) *(descanso)* breather, break

resplandecer [33] *vi* to shine

resplandeciente *adj (brillante)* shining; *(esplendoroso)* resplendent, radiant

resplandor *nm (brillo)* brightness; *(muy intenso)* brilliance; *(de fuego)* glow, blaze

responder 1 *vt* to answer
2 *vi* (**a**) *(una carta)* to reply (**b**) *(reaccionar)* to respond (**c**) *(protestar)* to answer back (**d**) **r. de algn** to be responsible for sb; **r. por algn** to vouch for sb

respondón,-ona *adj Fam* argumentative, cheeky

responsabilidad *nf* responsibility

responsabilizar [40] **1** *vt* to make o hold responsible (**de** for)
2 responsabilizarse *upr* to assume o claim responsibility (**de** for)

responsable 1 *adj* responsible
2 *nmf* **el/la r.** *(encargado)* the person in charge; *(de robo etc)* the perpetrator
respuesta *nf* answer, reply; *(reacción)* response
resquebrajarse *upr* to crack
resquemor *nm* resentment, ill feeling
resquicio *nm* crack, chink
resta *nf* subtraction
restablecer [33] 1 *vt* to re-establish; *(el orden)* to restore
2 restablecerse *upr Med* to recover
restablecimiento *nm* (a) re-establishment; *(del orden etc)* restoration (b) *Med* recovery
restante *adj* remaining; **lo r.** the rest, the remainder
restar 1 *vt* (a) *Mat* to subtract, to take away (b) **r. importancia a algo** to play sth down
2 *vi (quedar)* to be left, to remain
restauración *nf* restoration
restaurador,-a 1 *nm,f* restorer
2 *adj* restoring
restaurante *nm* restaurant
restaurar *vt* to restore
restitución *nf* restitution
restituir [37] *vt (restablecer)* to restore; *(devolver)* to return, to give back
resto *nm* (a) rest, remainder; *Mat* remainder (b) **restos** remains; *(de comida)* leftovers
restregar [1] *vt* to rub hard, to scrub
restricción *nf* restriction
restrictivo,-a *adj* restrictive
restringir [57] *vt* to restrict, to limit
resucitar *vt & vi* to resuscitate
resuello *nm* breath, gasp
resuelto,-a *adj (decidido)* resolute, determined
resultado *nm* result; *(consecuencia)* outcome; **dar buen r.** to work, to give results
resultante *adj* resulting
resultar *vi* (a) *(ser)* to turn o work out; **así resulta más barato** it works out cheaper this way; **me resultó fácil** it turned out to be easy for me (b) *(ocurrir)* **resulta que ...** the thing is ...; **y ahora resulta que no puede venir** and now it turns out that she can't come (c) *(tener éxito)* to be successful; **la fiesta no resultó** the party wasn't a success
resultas *nfpl* **a r. de** as a result of
resumen *nm* summary; **en r.** in short, to sum up
resumir 1 *vt* to sum up; *(recapitular)* to summarize
2 resumirse *upr* (a) *(abreviarse)* se

resume **en pocas palabras** it can be summed up in a few words (b) **r. en** *(saldarse con)* to result in

> 🔎 Observa que la palabra inglesa **resume** es un falso amigo y no es la traducción de la palabra española **resumir**. En inglés, **resume** significa "reanudar".

resurgir [57] *vi* to reappear
resurrección *nf* resurrection
retablo *nm* altarpiece
retaguardia *nf* rearguard
retahíla *nf* series *sing*, string
retal *nm (pedazo)* scrap
retar *vt* to challenge
retardarse *upr* to be delayed
retardo *nm* delay
retazo *nm (pedazo)* scrap; *(fragmento)* fragment, piece
rete- *pref Méx Fam* very
retén *nm* (a) **r. (de bomberos)** squad (of firefighters) (b) *Am (prisión)* reformatory, reform school
retención *nf* retention; *Fin* withholding; **r. de tráfico** (traffic) hold-up, traffic jam
retener [24] *vt* (a) *(conservar)* to retain (b) *Fin (descontar)* to deduct (c) *(detener)* to detain
reticencia *nf* reticence, reserve
reticente *adj* reticent, reserved
retina *nf* retina
retintín *nm (tono irónico)* innuendo, sarcastic tone
retirada *nf* retreat, withdrawal
retirado,-a 1 *adj* (a) *(alejado)* remote (b) *(jubilado)* retired
2 *nm,f* retired person, *US* retiree
retirar 1 *vt* to take away, to remove; *(dinero)* to withdraw; *(ofensa)* to take back
2 retirarse *upr* (a) *(apartarse)* to withdraw, to draw back; *(irse)* to retire (b) *(jubilarse)* to retire (c) *Mil* to retreat, to withdraw
retiro *nm* (a) *(jubilación)* retirement; *(pensión)* pension (b) *(lugar tranquilo)* retreat (c) *Rel* retreat
reto *nm* challenge
retocar [44] *vt* to touch up
retoño *nm (rebrote)* shoot, sprout; *Fig (niño)* kid
retoque *nm* retouching, touching up; **los últimos retoques** the finishing touches
retorcer [41] 1 *vt (cuerda, hilo)* to twist; *(ropa)* to wring (out)
2 retorcerse *upr* to twist, to become twisted; **r. de dolor** to writhe in pain
retorcido,-a *adj Fig* twisted

retórica *nf* rhetoric

retórico,-a *adj* rhetorical

retornable *adj* returnable; **envase no r.** non-deposit bottle

retornar 1 *vt* to return, to give back

  2 *vi* to return, to come back, to go back

retorno *nm* return

retortijón *nm (dolor)* stomach cramp

retozar [40] *vi* to frolic, to romp

retracción *nf* retraction

retractar 1 *vt* to retract

  2 retractarse *vpr* **r. (de)** to retract, to take back

retraerse *vpr (retirarse)* to withdraw; *(por miedo)* to shy away

retraído,-a *adj* shy, reserved

retraimiento *nm (timidez)* shyness

retransmisión *nf* broadcast, transmission

retransmitir *vt* to broadcast

retrasado,-a 1 *adj* (**a**) *(tren)* late; *(reloj)* slow; **voy r.** I'm behind schedule (**b**) *(país)* backward, underdeveloped (**c**) *(mental)* retarded, backward

  2 *nm,f* **r. (mental)** mentally retarded person

retrasar 1 *vt* (**a**) *(retardar)* to slow down (**b**) *(atrasar)* to delay, to postpone (**c**) *(reloj)* to put back

  2 retrasarse *vpr* to be late, to be delayed; *(reloj)* to be slow

retraso *nm* delay; **con r.** late; **una hora de r.** an hour behind schedule; **r. mental** mental deficiency

retratar 1 *vt (pintar)* to paint a portrait of; *Fot* to take a photograph of; *Fig (describir)* to describe, to depict

  2 retratarse *vpr Fot* to have one's photograph taken

retrato *nm (pintura)* portrait; *Fot* photograph; **r. robot** identikit picture, Photofit® picture; **ser el vivo r. de** to be the spitting image of

retreta *nf* retreat

retrete *nm* lavatory, toilet

retribución *nf (pago)* payment; *(recompensa)* reward

> 🔎 Observa que la palabra inglesa **retribution** es un falso amigo y no es la traducción de la palabra española **retribución**. En inglés, **retribution** significa "represalias".

retribuir *vt (pagar)* to pay; *(recompensar)* to reward

retro *adj inv Fam (retrógrado)* reactionary; *(antiguo)* old-fashioned

retroactivo,-a *adj* retroactive; **con efecto r.** retrospectively

retroceder *vi* to move back, to back away

retroceso *nm* (**a**) *(movimiento)* backward movement (**b**) *Med* deterioration, worsening (**c**) *Econ* recession

retrógrado,-a *adj & nm,f (reaccionario)* reactionary

retropropulsión *nf Av* jet propulsion

retrospectivo,-a *adj & nf* retrospective

retrovisor *nm Aut* rear-view mirror

retumbar *vi (resonar)* to resound, to echo; *(tronar)* to thunder, to boom

retuve *pt indef de* **retener**

reúma *nm* rheumatism

reumático,-a *adj & nm,f* rheumatic

reumatismo *nm* rheumatism

reunión *nf* meeting; *(reencuentro)* reunion

reunir 1 *vt* to gather together; *(dinero)* to raise; *(cualidades)* to have, to possess; *(requisitos)* to fulfil

  2 reunirse *vpr* to meet, to gather; **r. con algn** to meet sb

revalidar *vt* to ratify, to confirm; *Dep (título)* to retain

revalorizar [40] *vt*, **revalorizarse** *vpr (moneda)* to revalue

revancha *nf* revenge; *Dep* return match

revanchista *adj* vengeful, vindictive

revelación *nf* revelation

revelado *nm Fot* developing

revelar *vt* (**a**) *(mostrar)* to reveal, to disclose (**b**) *Fot (película)* to develop

revender *vt (entradas)* to tout

reventa *nf (de entradas)* touting

reventado,-a *adj Fam (cansado)* knackered

reventar [1] 1 *vt* (**a**) to burst (**b**) *(romper)* to break, to smash (**c**) *(fastidiar)* to annoy, to bother

  2 *vi (estallar)* to burst; **r. de ganas de hacer algo** to be dying to do sth; **está que revienta** he's bursting at the seams

  3 reventarse *vpr (estallar)* to burst, to explode

reventón *nm (de neumático)* blowout, puncture, flat tyre

reverberación *nf* reverberation

reverberar *vi* to reverberate

reverencia *nf* (**a**) *(respeto)* reverence (**b**) *(inclinación) (de hombre)* bow; *(de mujer)* curtsy

reverenciar [43] *vt* to revere, to venerate

reverendo,-a *adj & nm,f* reverend

reversa *nf Méx* reverse

reversible *adj* reversible

reverso *nm* reverse, back

revertido,-a *adj* **llamada a cobro r.** *Br*

reverse-charge call, *US* collect call

revertir [5] *vi* to result (**en** in)

revés *nm* (**a**) *(reverso)* reverse; **al** *o* **del r.** *(al contrario)* the other way round; *(la parte interior en el exterior)* inside out; *(boca abajo)* upside down; *(la parte de detrás delante)* back to front; **al r. de lo que dicen** contrary to what they say (**b**) *(bofetada)* slap; *Ten* backhand (stroke) (**c**) *Fig (contrariedad)* setback, reverse; **los reveses de la vida** life's misfortunes; **reveses de fortuna** setbacks, blows of fate

revestimiento *nm Téc* covering, coating

revestir [6] *vt* (**a**) *(recubrir)* to cover (**de** with), to coat (**de** with), to line (**de** with) (**b**) *Fig* **la herida no reviste importancia** the wound is not serious

revisar *vt* to check; *(coche)* to service

revisión *nf* checking; *(de coche)* service, overhaul; **r. médica** checkup

revisor,-a *nm,f* ticket inspector

revista *nf* (**a**) magazine (**b**) **pasar r. a** to inspect, to review (**c**) *Teatro* revue

revitalizar [40] *vt* to revitalize

revivido,-a *adj* revived

revivir *vt* & *vi* to revive

revocar [44] *vt* to revoke, to repeal

revolcar [2] **1** *vt Fam (oponente)* to floor, to crush

2 revolcarse *vpr* to roll about

revolcón *nm* fall, tumble; *Fam (sexual)* romp

revolotear *vi* to fly about, to flutter about

revoltijo, revoltillo *nm* mess, jumble

revoltoso,-a *adj (travieso)* mischievous, naughty

revolución *nf* revolution

revolucionar *vt* to revolutionize

revolucionario,-a *adj* & *nm,f* revolutionary

revolver [4] *(pp* **revuelto)** **1** *vt (mezclar)* to stir, to mix; *(desordenar)* to mess up; **me revuelve el estómago** it turns my stomach

2 revolverse *vpr* (**a**) *(agitarse)* to roll (**b**) *Fig* **r. contra algn** to turn against sb (**c**) *(el tiempo)* to turn stormy; *(el mar)* to become rough

> $\wp$ Observa que el verbo inglés **to revolve** es un falso amigo y no es la traducción del verbo español **revolver**. En inglés, **to revolve** significa "girar".

revólver *nm (pl* **revólveres)** revolver

revuelo *nm Fig* stir, commotion

revuelta *nf* (**a**) *(insurrección)* revolt (**b**) *(curva)* bend, turn

revuelto,-a *adj* (**a**) *(desordenado)* jumbled, in a mess (**b**) *(tiempo)* stormy, unsettled; *(mar)* rough (**c**) *(agitado)* excited

revulsivo,-a *adj* & *nm* revulsive

rey *nm* king; *Rel* **(el día de) Reyes** (the) Epiphany, 6 January

reyerta *nf* quarrel, dispute

rezagado,-a *nm,f* straggler, latecomer

rezagarse *vpr* to lag *o* fall behind

rezar [40] 1 *vi* (**a**) *(orar)* to pray (**b**) *(decir)* to say, to read

2 *vt (oración)* to say

rezo *nm* prayer

rezumar *vt* to ooze; *Fig* to exude

RFA *nf Hist (abr* **República Federal de Alemania)** FRG

ría *nf* estuary

riada *nf* flood

ribera *nf (de río)* bank; *(zona)* riverside, waterfront

ribete *nm* edging, border

ribetear *vt* to edge, to border

ricamente *adv Fam* **tan r.** very well

rico,-a 1 *adj* (**a**) **ser r.** *(adinerado)* to be rich *o* wealthy; *(abundante)* to be rich; *(bonito)* to be lovely *o* adorable; *(fértil)* to be rich *o* fertile (**b**) **estar r.** *(delicioso)* to be delicious

2 *nm,f* rich person

rictus *nm inv* grin

ridiculez *nf* ridiculous thing; *(cualidad)* ridiculousness

ridiculizar [40] *vt* to ridicule

ridículo,-a 1 *adj* ridiculous

2 *nm* ridicule; **hacer el r., quedar en r.** to make a fool of oneself; **poner a algn en r.** to make a fool of sb

riego *nm* watering, irrigation; **r. sanguíneo** blood circulation

riel *nm* rail

rienda *nf* rein; *Fig* **dar r. suelta a** to give free rein to; *Fig* **llevar las riendas** to hold the reins, to be in control

riesgo *nm* risk; **correr el r. de** to run the risk of; **seguro a todo r.** fully comprehensive insurance

riesgoso,-a *adj Am* risky

rifa *nf* raffle

rifar *vt* to raffle (off)

rifle *nm* rifle

rigidez *nf* rigidity, stiffness; *Fig (severidad)* strictness, inflexibility

rígido,-a *adj* rigid, stiff; *Fig (severo)* strict, inflexible

rigor *nm* rigour; *(severidad)* severity; **con r.** rigorously; **de r.** indispensable

rigurosamente *adv* rigorously; *(meticulosamente)* meticulously; *(severamente)* severely; **r. cierto** absolutely true

riguroso,-a *adj* rigorous; *(severo)* severe, strict

rijo *indic pres de* regir

rima *nf* rhyme

rimar *vt & vi* to rhyme (**con** with)

rimbombante *adj (lenguaje)* pompous, pretentious

rímel *nm* mascara

Rin *n* el R. the Rhine

rincón *nm* corner; *Fam (lugar remoto)* nook

rinoceronte *nm* rhinoceros

riña *nf (pelea)* fight; *(discusión)* row, quarrel

riñón *nm* kidney; *Fam* **costar un r.** to cost an arm and a leg; *Med* **r. artificial** kidney machine

río *nm* river; **r. abajo** downstream; **r. arriba** upstream

rioja *nm* Rioja (wine)

rioplatense *adj* of/from the River Plate region

ripio *nm (palabras de relleno)* waffle; *Fam* **no perder r.** not to miss a trick

riqueza *nf* (**a**) wealth (**b**) *(cualidad)* wealthiness

risa *nf* laugh; *(carcajadas)* laughter; **es (cosa) de r.** it's laughable; **me da r.** it makes me laugh; **tomarse algo a r.** to laugh sth off; *Fig* **morirse** *o* **mondarse de r.** to die *o* fall about laughing; *Fam* **mi hermano es una r.** my brother is a laugh; *Fam Fig* **tener algo muerto de r.** to leave sth lying around

risco *nm* crag, cliff

risible *adj* laughable

risilla, risita *nf* giggle, titter; *(risa falsa)* false laugh

risotada *nf* guffaw

ristra *nf* string

ristre *nm* **en r.** at the ready

risueño,-a *adj* smiling

rítmico,-a *adj* rhythmic; **gimnasia rítmica** eurhythmics *sing*

ritmo *nm* (**a**) rhythm (**b**) *(paso)* rate; **llevar un buen r. de trabajo** to work at a good pace

rito *nm* (**a**) rite (**b**) *(ritual)* ritual

ritual *adj & nm* ritual

rival *adj & nmf* rival

rivalidad *nf* rivalry

rivalizar [40] *vi* to rival (**en** in)

rizado,-a *adj* (**a**) *(pelo)* curly (**b**) *(mar)* choppy

rizar [40] 1 *vt (pelo)* to curl; *(tela, papel)* to crease; *Fig* **r. el rizo** to make things even more complicated

2 rizarse *upr (pelo)* to curl, to go curly

rizo *nm* (**a**) *(de pelo)* curl (**b**) *(en el agua)* ripple

RNE *nf (abr* **Radio Nacional de España**) = Spanish state radio station

robalo *nm (pez)* bass

robar *vt* (**a**) *(objeto)* to steal; *(banco, persona)* to rob; *(casa)* to burgle; *Fig* **en aquel supermercado te roban** they really rip you off in that supermarket (**b**) *Naipes* to draw

roble *nm* oak (tree)

robledal, robledo *nm* oak grove *o* wood

robo *nm* robbery, theft; *(en casa)* burglary; *Fam (timo)* rip-off

robot *nm (pl* **robots**) robot; **r. de cocina** food processor

robótica *nf* robotics *sing*

robustecer [33] *vt* to strengthen

robusto,-a *adj* robust, sturdy

roca *nf* rock

rocalla *nf* pebbles, stone chippings

rocambolesco,-a *adj* incredible, far-fetched

roce *nm* (**a**) *(fricción)* rubbing; *(en la piel)* chafing (**b**) *(marca) (en la pared etc)* scuff mark; *(en la piel)* chafing mark, graze (**c**) *(contacto ligero)* brush, light touch (**d**) *Fam (trato entre personas)* contact (**e**) *Fam (discusión)* brush

rociar [29] *vt (salpicar)* to spray, to sprinkle

rocín *nm* nag, hack

rocío *nm* dew

Rocosas *nfpl* las R. the Rockies

rocoso,-a *adj* rocky, stony

rodaballo *nm (pez)* turbot

rodado,-a *adj* (**a**) *(piedra)* smooth, rounded; **canto r.** boulder (**b**) **tráfico r.** road traffic, vehicular traffic

rodaja *nf* slice; **en rodajas** sliced

rodaje *nm* (**a**) *(filmación)* filming, shooting (**b**) *Aut* running in

Ródano *n* el R. the Rhone

rodante *adj* rolling

rodar [2] 1 *vt (película etc)* to film, to shoot

2 *vi* to roll, to turn

rodear 1 *vt* to surround, to encircle

2 rodearse *upr* to surround oneself (**de** with)

rodeo *nm* (**a**) *(desvío)* detour (**b**) *(al hablar)* evasiveness; **andarse con rodeos** to beat about the bush; **no andarse con rodeos** to get straight to the point (**c**) *Am* rodeo

rodilla *nf* knee; **de rodillas** *(arrodillado)* kneeling; **hincarse** *o* **ponerse de rodillas**

to kneel down, to go down on one's knees

rodillera *nf (de pantalón)* knee patch; *Dep* knee pad

rodillo *nm* roller; **r. de cocina** rolling pin

rododendro *nm* rhododendron

roedor *nm* rodent

roer [38] *vt (hueso)* to gnaw; *(galleta)* to nibble at; *Fig (conciencia)* to gnaw at, to nag at; *Fig* **un hueso duro de r.** a hard nut to crack

rogar [2] *vt (pedir)* to request, to ask; *(implorar)* to beg; **hacerse de r.** to play hard to get; **se ruega silencio** *(en letrero)* silence please; **rogamos disculpen la molestia** please forgive the inconvenience

roído,-a *adj* gnawed, eaten away

rojizo,-a *adj* reddish

rojo,-a 1 *adj (a)* red; *Fin* **estar en números rojos** to be in the red (**b**) *Pol (comunista)* red

2 *nm (color)* red; **al r. vivo** *(caliente)* red-hot; *Fig (tenso)* very tense

3 *nm,f Pol (comunista)* red

rol *nm* role; **juego de r.** role play

rollizo,-a *adj* chubby, plump

rollo *nm* (**a**) *(de papel etc)* roll (**b**) *Fam (pesadez)* drag, bore; **es el mismo r. de siempre** it's the same old story; **un r. de libro** a boring book (**c**) *Fam (amorío)* affair

Roma *n* Rome

romana *nf* **calamares a la r.** = squid in batter

romance *nm* (**a**) *(aventura amorosa)* romance (**b**) *(idioma)* Romance; *Fig* **hablar en r.** to speak plainly (**c**) *Lit* narrative poem, ballad

románico,-a *adj & nm* Romanesque

romanticismo *nm* romanticism

romántico,-a *adj & nm,f* romantic

rombo *nm* rhombus

romería *nf Rel* pilgrimage

romero *nm Bot* rosemary

romo,-a *adj* (**a**) blunt (**b**) *(nariz)* snub

rompecabezas *nm inv (juego)* (jigsaw) puzzle; *Fig (problema)* riddle, puzzle

rompeolas *nm inv* breakwater, jetty

romper (*pp* **roto**) **1** *vt* (**a**) to break; *(papel, tela)* to tear; *(vajilla, cristal)* to smash, to shatter (**b**) *(relaciones)* to break off

2 *vi* (**a**) *(olas, día)* to break (**b**) *(acabar)* to break (**con** with); **rompió con su novio** she broke it off with her boyfriend (**c**) **r. a llorar** to burst out crying; **r. en llanto** to burst into tears

3 romperse *vpr* to break; *(papel, tela)* to tear; **se rompió por la mitad** it broke o

split in half; *Fig* **r. la cabeza** to rack one's brains

rompevientos *nm RP (jersey)* polo neck jersey; *(anorak)* anorak

rompimiento *nm Am* breaking off

ron *nm* rum

roncar [44] *vi* to snore

roncha *nf (en la piel)* swelling, lump

ronco,-a *adj* hoarse; **quedarse r.** to lose one's voice

ronda *nf* (**a**) round; *(patrulla)* patrol (**b**) *(carretera)* ring road; *(paseo)* avenue (**c**) **pagar una r.** to pay for a round of drinks

rondar 1 *vt* (**a**) *(vigilar)* to patrol, to do the rounds of (**b**) *Pey (merodear)* to prowl around, to hang about (**c**) *(estar cerca de)* to be about o approximately; **ronda los cuarenta** she is about forty

2 *vi* (**a**) *(vigilar)* to patrol (**b**) *(merodear)* to prowl around, to roam around

ronquera *nf* hoarseness

ronquido *nm* snore

ronronear *vi* to purr

ronroneo *nm* purring

roña *nf* (**a**) *(mugre)* filth, dirt (**b**) *(sarna)* mange

roñica *Fam* **1** *adj* mean, stingy

2 *nmf* scrooge, miser

roñoso,-a *adj* (**a**) *(mugriento)* filthy, dirty (**b**) *(sarnoso)* mangy (**c**) *Fam (tacaño)* mean, stingy

ropa *nf* clothes, clothing; *Fig* **a quema r.** point-blank; **r. blanca** (household) linen; **r. interior** underwear

🖉 Observa que la palabra inglesa **rope** es un falso amigo y no es la traducción de la palabra española **ropa**. En inglés, **rope** significa "cuerda, soga".

ropaje *nm* clothes

ropero *nm (armario)* **r.** wardrobe

roque *nm* (**a**) *(en ajedrez)* rook (**b**) *Fam* **quedarse r.** to fall fast asleep

rosa 1 *adj inv (color)* pink; **novela r.** romantic novel

2 *nf Bot* rose; *(en la piel)* birthmark; **r. de los vientos** compass (rose)

3 *nm (color)* pink

rosáceo,-a *adj* rose-coloured, rosy

rosado,-a 1 *adj (color)* pink, rosy; *(vino)* rosé

2 *nm (vino)* rosé

rosal *nm* rosebush

rosaleda *nf* rose garden

rosario *nm Rel* rosary; *(sarta)* string, series *sing*

rosbif *nm* roast beef

rosca *nf* (**a**) *(de tornillo)* thread; **tapón de**

r. screw top; *Fig* **pasarse de r.** to go too far (**b**) *(espiral)* spiral, coil

rosco *nm (pastel)* = ring-shaped roll or pastry; *Fam* **no comerse un r.** not to get one's oats

rosetón *nm* rose window

rosquilla *nf* ring-shaped pastry; *Fam Fig* **venderse como rosquillas** to sell like hot cakes

rosticería *nf Chile, Méx* = shop selling roast chicken

rostro *nm* face; *Fam* **tener mucho r.** to have a lot of nerve; *Fam* **¡vaya r.!** what a cheek!

> 🖉 Observa que la palabra inglesa **rostrum** es un falso amigo y no es la traducción de la palabra española **rostro**. En inglés, **rostrum** significa "estrado".

rotación *nf* rotation

rotativo,-a 1 *adj* rotary, revolving
    2 *nm* newspaper

roto,-a 1 *adj* broken; *(papel)* torn; *(ropa)* in tatters, tattered
    2 *nm (agujero)* hole, tear
    3 *nm,f Chile Fam (trabajador)* worker

rotoso,-a *adj Andes, RP* ragged, in tatters

rótula *nf* (**a**) *Anat* kneecap (**b**) *Téc* ball-and-socket joint

rotulador *nm* felt-tip pen

rotular *vt* to letter, to label

rótulo *nm (letrero)* sign, notice; *(titular)* title, heading

rotundo,-a *adj* categorical; **éxito r.** resounding success; **un no r.** a flat refusal

rotura *nf (ruptura)* breaking; *Med* fracture

roturar *vt* to plough

roulotte *nf Br* caravan, *US* trailer

rozadura *nf* scratch, abrasion

rozamiento *nm* rubbing, friction

rozar [40] 1 *vt* to touch, to rub against, to brush against
    2 *vi* to rub
    3 **rozarse** *vpr* to rub, to brush (**con** against)

Rte. (*abr* **remite, remitente**) sender

RTVE *nf (abr* **Radiotelevisión Española**) = Spanish state broadcasting company

ruana *nf Andes* poncho

rubéola *nf* German measles *sing*, rubella

rubí *nm (pl* **rubíes**) ruby

rubicundo,-a *adj* rosy, reddish

rubio,-a 1 *adj (pelo, persona)* fair, blond, *f* blonde; **r. de bote** peroxide blonde; **tabaco r.** Virginia tobacco
    2 *nm,f* blond, *f* blonde

rublo *nm* rouble

rubor *nm* blush, flush

ruborizarse [40] *vpr* to blush, to go red

ruboroso,-a *adj* blushing, bashful

rúbrica *nf* (**a**) *(de firma)* = flourish added to a signature (**b**) *(título)* title, heading

rubricar [44] *vt* (**a**) *(firmar)* to sign with a flourish (**b**) *(respaldar)* to endorse, to ratify

rudeza *nf* roughness, coarseness

rudimentario,-a *adj* rudimentary

rudimento *nm* rudiment

rudo,-a *adj* rough, coarse

rueda *nf* (**a**) wheel; *Aut* **r. de recambio** spare wheel; *Aut* **r. delantera/trasera** front/rear wheel; *Pres* **r. de prensa** press conference; *Fam* **ir sobre ruedas** to go very smoothly (**b**) *(rodaja)* round slice

ruedo *nm* (**a**) *Taurom* bullring, arena (**b**) *(de falda)* hem

ruego *nm* request

rufián *nm* villain, scoundrel

rugby *nm* rugby

rugido *nm (de animal)* roar; *(del viento)* howl; *(de tripas)* rumbling

rugir [57] *vi* to roar; *(viento)* to howl

rugoso,-a *adj* rough

ruibarbo *nm* rhubarb

ruido *nm* noise; *(sonido)* sound; *(jaleo)* din, row; *Fig* stir, commotion; **hacer r.** to make a noise

ruidoso,-a *adj* noisy, loud

ruin *adj* (**a**) *(vil)* vile, despicable (**b**) *(tacaño)* mean, stingy

ruina *nf* ruin; *(derrumbamiento)* collapse; *(de persona)* downfall

ruindad *nf* vileness, meanness; *(acto)* mean act, low trick

ruinoso,-a *adj* dilapidated, tumbledown

ruiseñor *nm* nightingale

ruleta *nf* roulette

ruletear *vi CAm, Méx Fam (en taxi)* to drive a taxi

ruletero *nm CAm, Méx Fam (de taxi)* taxi driver

rulo *nm* (**a**) *(para el pelo)* curler, roller (**b**) *Culin* rolling pin

rulot(a) *nf (pl* **rulots**) *Br* caravan, *US* trailer

ruma *nf Andes, Ven* heap, pile

Rumanía, Rumania *n* Romania

rumba *nf* rhumba, rumba

rumbo *nm* direction, course; **(con) r. a** bound for, heading for

rumiante *nm* ruminant

rumiar [43] 1 *vt* (**a**) *(mascar)* to chew (**b**) *Fig (pensar)* to ruminate, to reflect on, to chew over
    2 *vi* to ruminate, to chew the cud

rumor *nm* (**a**) rumour (**b**) *(murmullo)* murmur

rumorearse *v impers* to be rumoured

runrún, runruneo *nm* buzz, noise

rupestre *adj* **pintura r.** cave painting

ruptura *nf* breaking; *(de relaciones)* breaking off

rural *adj* rural, country

Rusia *n* Russia

ruso,-a *adj & nm,f* Russian

rústico,-a *adj* rustic, rural

ruta *nf* route, road

rutilar *vi* to sparkle

rutina *nf* routine; **por r.** as a matter of course

rutinario,-a *adj* routine

S, s ['ese] *nf (la letra)* S, s

S (*abr* **Sur**) S

S. (*abr* **San, Santo**) St

s. (*abr* **siglo**) c

S.A. (*abr* **Sociedad Anónima**) *Br* ≃ PLC, *US* ≃ Inc

sábado *nm* Saturday

sabana *nf* savannah

sábana *nf* sheet; *Fam* **se me pegaron las sábanas** I overslept

sabandija *nf (insecto)* creepy-crawly; *(persona)* creep

sabañón *nm* chilblain

sabático,-a *adj* sabbatical

sabelotodo *nmf inv* know-all

saber[1] *nm* knowledge

saber[2] **[21] 1** *vt* (**a**) to know; **hacer s.** to inform; **para que lo sepas** for your information; **que yo sepa** as far as I know; **vete tú a s.** goodness knows; **¡y yo qué sé!** how should I know!; *Fig* **a s.** namely (**b**) *(tener habilidad)* to be able to; **¿sabes cocinar?** can you cook?; **¿sabes hablar inglés?** can you speak English? (**c**) *(enterarse)* to learn, to find out; **lo supe ayer** I found this out yesterday

2 *vi* (**a**) *(tener sabor)* to taste (**a** of); **sabe a fresa** it tastes of strawberries; *Fig* **me sabe mal** I feel guilty *o* bad about that (**b**) *Am (soler)* to be accustomed to

sabido,-a *adj* known; **como es s.** as everyone knows

sabiduría *nf* wisdom

sabiendas: • **a sabiendas** *loc adv* **lo hizo a s.** he did it in the full knowledge of what he was doing; **a s. de que ...** knowing full well that ...

sabihondo,-a *nm,f Fam (sabelotodo)* know-all; *(pedante)* pedant

sabio,-a 1 *adj (prudente)* wise
2 *nm,f* scholar

sabiondo,-a *nm,f Fam* = **sabihondo,-a**

sable *nm* sabre

sabor *nm (gusto)* taste, flavour; **con s. a limón** lemon-flavoured; **sin s.** tasteless; **me deja mal s. de boca** it leaves a bad taste in my mouth

saborear *vt (degustar)* to taste; *Fig (apreciar)* to savour

sabotaje *nm* sabotage

saboteador,-a *nm,f* saboteur

sabotear *vt* to sabotage

sabré *indic fut de* saber

sabroso,-a *adj* (**a**) tasty; *(delicioso)* delicious (**b**) *(agradable)* delightful

sabueso *nm* bloodhound

sacacorchos *nm inv* corkscrew

sacamuelas *nmf inv Fam* dentist

sacapuntas *nm inv* pencil sharpener

sacar [44] *vt* (**a**) to take out; *(con más fuerza)* to pull out; **s. dinero del banco** to withdraw money from the bank; **s. la lengua** to stick one's tongue out; *Fig* **s. faltas a algo** to find fault with sth; *Fig* **s. adelante** to help to get on; **s. provecho de algo** to benefit from sth; **s. algo en claro** *o* **en limpio** to make sense of sth (**b**) *(obtener)* to get; *(dinero)* to get, to make; *(conclusiones)* to draw, to reach; *(entrada)* to get, to buy (**c**) *(producto, libro, disco)* to bring out; *(nueva moda)* to bring in (**d**) *(fotografía)* to take; *(fotocopia)* to make (**e**) *Ten* to serve; *Ftb* to kick off

sacarina *nf* saccharin

sacerdotal *adj* priestly

sacerdote *nm* priest; **sumo s.** high priest

saciar [43] *vt* to satiate; *(sed)* to quench; *(deseos, hambre)* to satisfy; *(ambiciones)* to fulfil

saciedad *nf* satiety; **repetir algo hasta la s.** to repeat sth ad nauseam

saco *nm* (**a**) sack; **s. de dormir** sleeping bag (**b**) *Mil* **entrar a s. en una ciudad** to pillage a town (**c**) *Am (chaqueta)* jacket

sacralizar [40] *vt* to consecrate

sacramento *nm* sacrament

sacrificar [44] 1 *vt* to sacrifice
2 sacrificarse *vpr* to make a sacrifice *o* sacrifices

sacrificio *nm* sacrifice

sacrilegio *nm* sacrilege

sacrílego,-a *adj* sacrilegious

sacristán *nm* verger, sexton

sacristía *nf* vestry, sacristy

sacro,-a *adj* sacred

sacudida *nf* (**a**) shake; *(espasmo)* jolt, jerk; **s. eléctrica** electric shock (**b**) *(de terremoto)* tremor

sacudir *vt* (**a**) *(agitar)* to shake; *(alfombra, sábana)* to shake out; *(arena, polvo)* to shake off (**b**) *(golpear)* to beat (**c**) *(conmover)* to shock, to stun

sádico,-a 1 *adj* sadistic
2 *nm,f* sadist

sadismo *nm* sadism

sadomasoquista 1 *adj* sadomasochistic
2 *nmf* sadomasochist

saeta *nf* (**a**) *(dardo)* dart (**b**) *(canción)* = popular religious song

safari *nm* *(cacería)* safari; *(parque)* safari park

sagacidad *nf Fml (listeza)* cleverness; *(astucia)* astuteness, shrewdness

sagaz *adj (listo)* clever; *(astuto)* astute, shrewd

Sagitario *nm* Sagittarius

sagrado,-a *adj* sacred

sagrario *nm* tabernacle

Sáhara *n* Sahara

saharaui *adj & nmf* Saharan

sahariana *nf* safari jacket

sainete *nm Teatro* comic sketch, one-act farce

sajón,-ona *adj & nm,f* Saxon

sal¹ *nf* (**a**) salt; **s. fina** table salt; **s. gema** salt crystals; **s. gorda** cooking salt (**b**) *Fig (gracia)* wit

sal² *imperat de* **salir**

sala *nf* room; *(en un hospital)* ward; *Jur* courtroom; **s. de estar** lounge, living room; **s. de espera** waiting room; **s. de exposiciones** exhibition hall; **s. de fiestas** nightclub, discotheque; **s. de lectura** reading room

saladito *nm RP* savoury snack *o* appetizer

salado,-a *adj* (**a**) *(con sal)* salted; *(con exceso de sal)* salty; **agua salada** salt water (**b**) *Fig (encantador)* charming (**c**) *Am (infortunado)* unlucky

salamandra *nf* salamander

salamanquesa *nf* gecko

salame, salami *nm* salami

salar *vt* to salt, to add salt to

salarial *adj* salary, wage

salario *nm* salary, wages; **s. mínimo** minimum wage

salazones *nfpl* salted meat *o* fish

salchicha *nf* sausage

salchichón *nm* = salami-type sausage

salchichonería *nf Méx* delicatessen

saldar *vt* (**a**) *Fin (cuenta)* to settle; *(deuda)* to pay off (**b**) *Com (vender barato)* to sell off (**c**) *Fig (diferencias)* to settle, to resolve

saldo *nm* (**a**) **saldos** sales; **a precio de s.** at bargain prices (**b**) *Fin* balance (**c**) *(de una deuda)* liquidation, settlement (**d**) *(resto de mercancía)* remainder, leftover

saldré *indic fut de* **salir**

saledizo,-a *adj* projecting

salero *nm* (**a**) *(recipiente)* saltcellar (**b**) *Fig (gracia)* charm

salgo *indic pres de* **salir**

salida *nf* (**a**) *(partida)* departure; *(puerta etc)* exit, way out; **callejón sin s.** dead end; **s. de emergencia** emergency exit (**b**) *Dep* start; **línea de s.** starting line; **s. nula** false start (**c**) **te vi a la s. del cine** I saw you leaving the cinema (**d**) *(de un astro)* rising; **s. del sol** sunrise (**e**) *(profesional)* opening; *Com* outlet (**f**) *(recurso)* solution, way out; **no tengo otra s.** I have no other option (**g**) *Fam (ocurrencia)* witty remark, witticism (**h**) *Informát* output

salido,-a *adj* (**a**) prominent, projecting (**b**) *muy Fam (persona)* horny

saliente *adj* (**a**) projecting, prominent; *Fig* outstanding (**b**) *(cesante)* outgoing

salina *nf* salt mine

salino,-a *adj* saline

salir [22] **1** *vi* (**a**) *(de un sitio)* to go out, to leave; *(venir de dentro)* to come out; **salió de la habitación** she left the room; **s. de la carretera** to turn off the road
(**b**) *(tren etc)* to depart
(**c**) *(novios)* to go out (**con** with)
(**d**) *(aparecer)* to appear; *(revista, disco)* to come out; *(ley)* to come in; *(trabajo, vacante)* to come up
(**e**) *(resultar)* to turn out, to turn out to be; **el pequeño les ha salido muy listo** their son has turned out to be very clever; **¿cómo te salió el examen?** how did your exam go?; **s. ganando** to come out ahead *o* on top; **salió presidente** he was elected president
(**f**) **s. a** *(precio)* to come to, to work out at; **s. barato/caro** to work out cheap/expensive
(**g**) **ha salido al abuelo** she takes after her grandfather
(**h**) *(problema)* to work out; **esta cuenta no me sale** I can't work this sum out
(**i**) **¡con qué cosas sales!** the things you come out with!
2 salirse *vpr* (**a**) *(líquido, gas)* to leak (out); *Fig* **s. de lo normal** to be out of the ordinary; **se salió de la carretera** he went off the road
(**b**) *Fam* **s. con la suya** to get one's own way

saliva *nf* saliva

salivar *vi* to salivate

salivazo *nm* spit

salmantino,-a 1 *adj* of/from Salamanca
  2 *nm,f* person from Salamanca
salmo *nm* psalm
salmón 1 *nm (pescado)* salmon
  2 *adj inv (color)* salmon pink, salmon
salmonete *nm (pescado)* red mullet
salmorejo *nm (salsa)* = sauce made from vinegar, water, pepper and salt
salmuera *nf* brine
salobre *adj (agua)* brackish; *(gusto)* salty, briny
salón *nm* **(a)** *(en una casa)* lounge, sitting room **(b) s. de actos** assembly hall; **s. de baile** dance hall **(c) s. de belleza** beauty salon; **s. de té** tearoom, teashop **(d) s. del automóvil** motor show
salpicadera *nf Méx Br* mudguard, *US* fender
salpicadura *nf* splashing
salpicar **[44]** *vt* **(a)** *(rociar)* to splash; **me salpicó el abrigo de barro** he splashed mud on my coat **(b)** *Fig (esparcir)* to sprinkle
salpicón *nm* **(a)** splash **(b)** *Culin* cocktail
salpimentar **[1]** *vt* to season
salpullido *nm* rash
salsa *nf* sauce; *(de carne)* gravy; *Fig* **en su (propia) s.** in one's element
saltador,-a *nm,f Dep* jumper
saltamontes *nm inv* grasshopper
saltar 1 *vt (obstáculo, valla)* to leap (over)
  2 *vi* **(a)** to jump; *Fig* **s. a la vista** to be obvious **(b)** *(cristal etc)* to break, to shatter; *(plomos)* to go, to blow **(c)** *(desprenderse)* to come off **(d)** *(encolerizarse)* to explode, to blow up; **por menos de nada salta** the smallest thing makes him explode
  3 saltarse *vpr* **(a)** *(omitir)* to skip, to miss out; **s. el semáforo/turno** to jump the lights/the queue **(b)** *(botón)* to come off; **se me saltaron las lágrimas** tears came to my eyes
salteado,-a *adj* **(a)** *(espaciado)* spaced out **(b)** *Culin* sauté, sautéed
saltear *vt Culin* to sauté
saltimbanqui *nmf* acrobat, tumbler
salto *nm* **(a)** *(acción)* jump, leap; *Fig (paso adelante)* leap forward; **a saltos** in leaps and bounds; **dar** *o* **pegar un s.** to jump, to leap; **de un s.** in a flash; *Fig* **a s. de mata** every now and then; **s. de agua** waterfall; **s. de cama** negligée **(b)** *Dep* jump; **s. de altura** high jump; **s. de longitud** long jump; **s. mortal** somersault
saltón,-ona *adj* prominent; **ojos saltones** bulging eyes
salubre *adj* salubrious

salubridad *nf* healthiness; **por razones de s.** for health reasons
salud *nf* health; **beber a la s. de algn** to drink to sb's health; *Fam* **¡s.!** cheers!
saludable *adj* **(a)** *(sano)* healthy, wholesome **(b)** *Fig (beneficioso)* good, beneficial
saludar *vt* **(a)** *(decir hola a)* to say hello to, to greet; **saluda de mi parte a** give my regards to; **le saluda atentamente** *(en una carta)* yours faithfully **(b)** *Mil* to salute
saludo *nm* **(a)** greeting; **un s. de** best wishes from **(b)** *Mil* salute
salva *nf Mil* salvo, volley
salvación *nf* salvation
salvado *nm* bran
salvador,-a 1 *nm,f* saviour; *(rescatador)* rescuer
  2 *nm* **El S.** El Salvador
salvadoreño,-a *adj & nm,f* Salvadoran, Salvadorian
salvaguarda *nf (defensa)* protection
salvaguardar *vt* to safeguard **(de** from), to protect **(de** from)
salvaguardia *nf* = salvaguarda
salvajada *nf* brutal act
salvaje *adj* **(a)** *Bot* wild, uncultivated; *Zool* wild; *(pueblo, tribu)* savage, uncivilized **(b)** *Fam (violento)* savage, wild
salvajismo *nm* savagery
salvamento, salvamiento *nm* rescue
salvar 1 *vt* **(a)** to save, to rescue **(de** from) **(b)** *(obstáculo)* to clear; *(dificultad)* to get round, to overcome **(c)** *(exceptuar)* to exclude, to except; **salvando ciertos errores** except for a few mistakes
  2 salvarse *vpr* **(a)** *(sobrevivir)* to survive, to come out alive; *Fam (escaparse)* to escape **(de** from); **¡sálvese quien pueda!** every man for himself!; *Fam* **s. por los pelos** to have a narrow escape **(b)** *Rel* to be saved, to save one's soul
salvavidas *nm inv* life belt
salvedad *nf* **(a)** *(excepción)* exception **(b)** *(reserva)* proviso
salvia *nf Bot* sage
salvo,-a 1 *adj* unharmed, safe; **a s.** safe
  2 *adv (exceptuando)* except (for); **s. que** unless
salvoconducto *nm* safe-conduct
san *adj* saint
sanar 1 *vt (curar)* to cure, to heal
  2 *vi* **(a)** *(persona)* to recover, to get better **(b)** *(herida)* to heal
sanatorio *nm* sanatorium
sanción *nf* **(a)** sanction **(b)** *(aprobación)* sanction, approval **(c)** *Jur* penalty
sancionar *vt* **(a)** *(castigar)* to penalize

(**b**) *(aprobar)* to sanction

sancochar *vt* to parboil; *Am* = to boil in water and salt

sancocho *nm Andes, Ven (comida)* = stew of beef, chicken or fish, vegetables and green bananas

sandalia *nf* sandal

sándalo *nm* sandalwood

sandez *nf* piece of nonsense

sandía *nf* watermelon

sándwich *nm* sandwich

sandwichera *nf* toasted sandwich maker

saneamiento *nm (de terreno)* drainage, draining; *(de una empresa)* reorganization

sanear *vt (terrenos)* to drain; *(empresa)* to reorganize

sangrar 1 *vt* (**a**) to bleed (**b**) *Fam (sacar dinero)* to bleed dry

2 *vi* to bleed

sangre *nf* blood; **donar s.** to give blood; **s. fría** sangfroid; **a s. fría** in cold blood

sangría *nf* (**a**) *Med* bleeding, bloodletting; *Fig* drain (**b**) *(timo)* rip-off (**c**) *(bebida)* sangria

sangriento,-a *adj (guerra etc)* bloody

sanguijuela *nf* leech, bloodsucker

sanguinario,-a *adj* bloodthirsty

sanguíneo,-a *adj* blood; **grupo s.** blood group

sanidad *nf* health; **Ministerio de S.** Department of Health

> 🖉 Observa que la palabra inglesa **sanity** es un falso amigo y no es la traducción de la palabra española **sanidad**. En inglés, **sanity** significa "cordura, sensatez".

sanitario,-a 1 *adj* health

2 *nm* toilet

sano,-a *adj* (**a**) *(bien de salud)* healthy; **s. y salvo** safe and sound (**b**) *(comida)* healthy, wholesome (**c**) **en su s. juicio** in one's right mind

> 🖉 Observa que la palabra inglesa **sane** es un falso amigo y no es la traducción de la palabra española **sano**. En inglés, **sane** significa "cuerdo, sensato".

Santa Claus, *Méx, Ven* **Santa Clos** *n* Santa Claus

santería *nf* (**a**) *(religión)* santería, = form of religion common in the Caribbean, in which people allegedly have contact with the spirit world (**b**) *Am (tienda)* = shop selling religious mementos such as statues of saints

santero,-a *nm,f (curandero)* = faith healer who calls on the saints to assist with the healing process

santiamén *nm Fam* **en un s.** in a flash, in no time at all

santidad *nf* saintliness, holiness

santificar [**44**] *vt* to sanctify

santiguarse [**45**] *vpr* to cross oneself

santo,-a 1 *adj* (**a**) holy, sacred (**b**) *(bueno)* saintly; **un s. varón** a saint

2 *nm,f* (**a**) saint; *Fam* **¡por todos los santos!** for heaven's sake!; *Fig* **se me fue el s. al cielo** I clean forgot (**b**) *(día onomástico)* saint's day; *Fig* **¿a s. de qué?** why on earth?

santuario *nm* sanctuary, shrine

saña *nf* fury; **con s.** furiously

sapo *nm* toad; *Fam* **echar sapos y culebras** to rant and rave

saque *nm* (**a**) *Ftb* **s. inicial** kick-off; **s. de banda** throw-in; **s. de esquina** corner kick (**b**) *Ten* service

saquear *vt (ciudad)* to sack, to plunder; *(casas, tiendas)* to loot

saqueo *nm (de ciudades)* sacking, plundering; *(de casa, tienda)* looting

S.A.R. *(abr* **Su Alteza Real)** H.R.H.

sarampión *nm* measles *sing*

sarao *nm* knees-up

sarcasmo *nm* sarcasm

sarcástico,-a *adj* sarcastic

sarcófago *nm* sarcophagus

sardana *nf* sardana, = Catalan dance and music

sardina *nf* sardine

sardónico,-a *adj* sardonic

sargento *nm* sergeant

sarmiento *nm* vine shoot

sarna *nf Med* scabies *sing; Zool* mange

sarpullido *nm* rash

sarracina *nf* massacre

sarro *nm (sedimento)* deposit; *(en los dientes)* tartar; *(en la lengua)* fur

sarta *nf* string

sartén *nf* frying pan, *US* fry-pan; *Fig* **tener la s. por el mango** to have the upper hand

sastre *nm* tailor

Satanás *n* Satan

satánico,-a *adj* satanic

satélite *nm* satellite; *Fig* **país s.** satellite state; **televisión vía s.** satellite TV

satén *nm* satin

satinar *vt* to gloss, to make glossy

sátira *nf* satire

satírico,-a *adj* satirical

satirizar [**40**] *vt* to satirize

satisfacción *nf* satisfaction; **s. de un deseo** fulfilment of a desire

satisfacer [15] (*pp* **satisfecho**) *vt* (**a**) (*deseos, necesidades*) to satisfy (**b**) (*requisitos*) to meet, to satisfy (**c**) (*deuda*) to pay

satisfactorio,-a *adj* satisfactory

satisfecho,-a *adj* satisfied; **me doy por s.** that's good enough for me; **s. de sí mismo** self-satisfied, smug

saturar *vt* to saturate

Saturno *n* Saturn

sauce *nm* willow; **s. llorón** weeping willow

saudí, saudita *adj & nmf* Saudi; **Arabia Saudita** Saudi Arabia

sauna *nf* sauna

savia *nf* sap

saxo *nm Fam Mús* sax

saxofón *nm* saxophone

saxofonista *nmf* saxophonist

sayo *nm* cassock, smock

sazonar *vt* to season, to flavour

s/c. (*abr* **su cuenta**) your account

Sdad. (*abr* **sociedad**) Soc.

se¹ *pron* (**a**) (*reflexivo*) (*objeto directo*) (*a él mismo*) himself; (*animal*) itself; (*a ella misma*) herself; (*animal*) itself; (*a usted mismo*) yourself; (*a ellos mismos*) themselves; (*a ustedes mismos*) yourselves (**b**) (*objeto indirecto*) (*a él mismo*) (to/for) himself; (*animal*) (to/for) itself; (*a ella misma*) (to/for) herself; (*animal*) (to/for) itself; (*a usted mismo*) (to/for) yourself; (*a ellos mismos*) (to/for) themselves; (*a ustedes mismos*) (to/for) yourselves; **se compró un nuevo coche** he bought himself a new car; **todos los días se lava el pelo** she washes her hair every day (**c**) (*recíproco*) one another, each other (**d**) (*voz pasiva*) **el vino se guarda en cubas** wine is kept in casks (**e**) (*impersonal*) **nunca se sabe** you never know; **se habla inglés** (*en letrero*) English spoken here; **se dice que ...** it is said that ...

se² *pron pers* (*a él*) (to/for) him; (*a ella*) (to/for) her; (*a usted o ustedes*) (to/for) you; (*a ellos*) (to/for) them; **se lo diré en cuanto les vea** I'll tell them as soon as I see them; **¿se lo explico?** shall I explain it to you?; **¿se lo has dado ya?** have you given it to him yet?

sé¹ *indic pres de* **saber**

sé² *imperat de* **ser**

S.E. (*abr* **Su Excelencia**) HE

sea *subj pres de* **ser**

sebo *nm* (*grasa*) fat

secado *nm* drying

secador *nm* dryer; **s. de pelo** hairdryer

secadora *nf* tumble dryer

secano *nm* dry land

secante *adj* **papel s.** blotting paper

secar [44] **1** *vt* to dry **2 secarse** *vpr* (**a**) to dry; **sécate** dry yourself; **s. las manos** to dry one's hands (**b**) (*marchitarse*) to dry up, to wither

sección *nf* section

seco,-a *adj* (**a**) dry; **frutos secos** dried fruit; **limpieza en s.** dry-cleaning; *Fig* **a palo s.** on its own; *Fig* **a secas** just, only (**b**) (*tono*) curt, sharp; (*golpe, ruido*) sharp; *Fig* **frenar en s.** to pull up sharply; *Fig* **parar en s.** to stop dead (**c**) (*delgado*) skinny

secreción *nf* secretion

secretaría *nf* (*oficina*) secretary's office; **S. de Estado** (*en España*) = government department under the control of a *Br* junior minister *o US* under-secretary; (*en Latinoamérica*) department, *Br* ministry; (*en Estados Unidos*) State Department

secretariado *nm* (**a**) (*oficina*) secretariat (**b**) *Educ* secretarial course

secretario,-a *nm,f* secretary; **s. de dirección** secretary to the director; **s. de Estado** (*en España*) *Br* junior minister, *US* under-secretary; (*en Latinoamérica*) minister; (*en Estados Unidos*) Secretary of State

secreto,-a 1 *adj* secret; **en s.** in secret, secretly **2** *nm* secret; **guardar un s.** to keep a secret; **con mucho s.** in great secrecy

secta *nf* sect

sectario,-a *adj* sectarian

sector *nm* (**a**) sector (**b**) (*zona*) area; **un s. de la ciudad** an area of the city

sectorial *adj* sectoral

secuela *nf* consequence

secuencia *nf* sequence

secuestrador,-a *nm,f* (**a**) (*de persona*) kidnapper; (*de un avión*) hijacker (**b**) *Jur* sequestrator

secuestrar *vt* (**a**) (*persona*) to kidnap; (*aviones*) to hijack (**b**) *Jur* to confiscate

secuestro *nm* (**a**) (*de persona*) kidnapping; (*de un avión*) hijacking (**b**) *Jur* confiscation

secular *adj* (**a**) *Rel* secular, lay (**b**) (*antiquísimo*) ancient, age-old

secundar *vt* to back

secundario,-a *adj* secondary

secuoya *nf Bot* redwood, sequoia; **s. gigante** giant sequoia

sed *nf* thirst; **tener s.** to be thirsty

seda *nf* silk

sedal *nm* fishing line

sedante *adj & nm* sedative

sede *nf* (a) headquarters, head office; *(de gobierno)* seat (b) **la Santa S.** the Holy See

sedentario,-a *adj* sedentary

sedición *nf* sedition

sedicioso,-a 1 *adj* rebellious
 2 *nm,f* rebel

sediento,-a *adj* thirsty; *Fig* **s. de poder** hungry for power

sedimentario,-a *adj* sedimentary

sedimentarse *vpr* to settle

sedimento *nm* sediment, deposit

sedoso,-a *adj* silky, silken

seducción *nf* seduction

seducir [10] *vt* to seduce; *(persuadir)* to tempt

seductor,-a 1 *adj* seductive; *(persuasivo)* tempting
 2 *nm,f* seducer

segadora *nf (máquina)* reaper, harvester

segar [1] *vt* to reap, to cut

seglar 1 *adj* secular, lay
 2 *nmf* lay person; *(hombre)* layman; *(mujer)* laywoman

segmento *nm* segment

segregación *nf* (a) *(separación)* segregation (b) *(secreción)* secretion

segregar [42] *vt* (a) *(separar)* to segregate (b) *(secretar)* to secrete

seguida *nf* **en s.** immediately, straight away

seguido,-a 1 *adj* (a) *(continuo)* continuous (b) *(consecutivo)* consecutive, successive; **tres veces seguidas** on three consecutive occasions; **tres lunes seguidos** three Mondays in a row
 2 *adv* (a) *(en línea recta)* straight on; **todo s.** straight on *o* ahead (b) *Am (a menudo)* often

seguidor,-a *nm,f* follower

seguimiento *nm* (a) pursuit (b) *Prensa* in- depth coverage (c) **estación de s. (espacial)** tracking station

seguir [6] **1** *vt* (a) to follow (b) *(camino)* to continue (c) *(perseguir)* to chase
 2 *vi* (a) to follow (b) **s.** + *ger (continuar)* to continue, to go on, to keep on; **siguió hablando** he continued *o* went on *o* kept on speaking (c) **s.** + *adj/pp* to continue to be, to be still; **sigo resfriado** I've still got the cold; **sigue con vida** he's still alive
 3 seguirse *vpr* to follow, to ensue

según 1 *prep* (a) according to; **s. la Biblia** according to the Bible (b) *(en función de)* depending on; **varía s. el tiempo (que haga)** it varies depending on the weather
 2 *adv* (a) depending on; **s. estén las cosas** depending on how things stand;

¿vendrás mañana? – s. will you come tomorrow? – it depends (b) *(tal como)* just as; **estaba s. lo dejé** it was just as I had left it (c) *(a medida que)* as; **s. iba leyendo ...** as I read on ...

segundero *nm* second hand

segundo¹,-a 1 *adj* second; *Fig* **decir algo con segundas (intenciones)** to say sth with a double meaning
 2 *nm,f (de una serie)* second (one)

segundo² *nm (tiempo)* second; **sesenta segundos** sixty seconds

seguramente *adv* (a) *(seguro)* surely (b) *(probablemente)* most probably; **s. no lloverá** it isn't likely to rain

seguridad *nf* (a) security; **cerradura de s.** security lock (b) *(física)* safety; **s. en carretera** road safety; **para mayor s.** to be on the safe side (c) *(confianza)* confidence; **s. en sí mismo** self-confidence (d) *(certeza)* sureness; **con toda s.** most probably; **tener la s. de que ...** to be certain that ... (e) **S. Social** ≃ Social Security, *Br* ≃ National Health Service (f) *(fiabilidad)* reliability

seguro,-a 1 *adj* (a) *(cierto)* sure; **estoy s. de que ...** I am sure that ...; **dar algo por s.** to take sth for granted (b) *(libre de peligro)* safe; *Fig* **ir sobre s.** to play safe (c) *(protegido)* secure (d) *(fiable)* reliable (e) **está segura de ella misma** she has self-confidence (f) *(firme)* steady, firm
 2 *nm* (a) *Seg* insurance; **s. a todo riesgo** fully comprehensive insurance; **s. contra terceros** third-party insurance; **s. de vida** life insurance (b) *(dispositivo)* safety catch *o* device (c) *CAm, Méx (imperdible)* safety pin
 3 *adv* for sure, definitely

seis *adj & nm inv* six

seiscientos,-as *adj & nm* six hundred

seísmo *nm (terremoto)* earthquake; *(temblor de tierra)* earth tremor

selección *nf* (a) selection (b) *Dep* team

seleccionador,-a *nm,f* (a) selector (b) *Dep* manager

seleccionar *vt* to select

selectividad *nf* selectivity; *Univ* **(prueba de) s.** entrance examination

selectivo,-a *adj* selective

selecto,-a *adj* select; **ambiente s.** exclusive atmosphere

self-service *nm* self-service cafeteria

sellar *vt (documento)* to seal; *(carta)* to stamp

sello *nm* (a) *(de correos)* stamp; *(para documentos)* seal (b) *(precinto)* seal

selva *nf* jungle

semáforo *nm* traffic lights

semana *nf* week; **entre s.** during the week; **S. Santa** Holy Week

semanada *nf Am Br* (weekly) pocket money, *US* (weekly) allowance

semanal *adj & nm* weekly

semanario *nm* weekly magazine

semblante *nm Literario (cara)* face; *Fig (aspecto)* look

sembrado *nm* sown field

sembrar [1] *vt* (a) *Agr* to sow (b) *Fig* **s. el pánico** to spread panic

semejante 1 *adj* (a) *(parecido)* similar; **nunca he visto nada s.** I've never seen anything like it (b) *Pey (comparativo)* such; **s. desvergüenza** such insolence

   2 *nm (prójimo)* fellow being

semejanza *nf* similarity, likeness

semen *nm* semen

semental *nm* stud

semestral *adj* half-yearly

semestre *nm* six-month period, semester

semicírculo *nm* semicircle

semifinal *nf* semifinal

semifinalista *nmf* semifinalist

semilla *nf* seed

semillero *nm* seedbed

seminario *nm* (a) *Educ* seminar (b) *Rel* seminary

sémola *nf* semolina

Sena *n* **el S.** the Seine

senado *nm* senate

senador,-a *nm,f* senator

sencillez *nf* simplicity

sencillo,-a 1 *adj* (a) *(fácil)* simple, easy (b) *(natural)* natural, unaffected (c) *(billete)* single (d) *(sin adornos)* simple, plain

   2 *nm Andes, CAm, Méx Fam (cambio)* loose change

senda *nf*, **sendero** *nm* path

sendos,-as *adj pl* one each; **con sendas carteras** each carrying a briefcase

senil *adj* senile

seno *nm* (a) *(pecho)* breast (b) *Fig* bosom, heart; **en el s. de** within (c) *Mat* sine

sensación *nf* (a) *(sensation, feeling;* **tengo la s. de que ...** I have a feeling that ... (b) *(impresión)* sensation; **causar s.** to cause a sensation

sensacional *adj* sensational

sensacionalista *adj* sensationalist; **prensa s.** gutter press

sensato,-a *adj* sensible

sensibilizar [40] *vt* to make aware; **s. a la opinión pública** to increase public awareness

sensible *adj* (a) sensitive (b) *(perceptible)* perceptible

sensiblemente *adv* noticeably, considerably

> *ℐ* Observa que la palabra inglesa **sensible** es un falso amigo y no es la traducción de la palabra española **sensible**. En inglés, **sensible** significa tanto "sensato" como "práctico".

sensiblero,-a *adj* over-sentimental, mawkish

sensitivo,-a *adj* sense; **órgano s.** sense organ

sensorial, sensorio,-a *adj* sensory

sensual *adj* sensual

sensualidad *nf* sensuality

sentada *nf* (a) sitting (b) *Fam (protesta)* sit-in (demonstration)

sentado,-a *adj (establecido)* established, settled; **dar algo por s.** to take sth for granted; **dejar s. que ...** to make it clear that ...

sentar [1] **1** *vt* (a) to sit (b) *(establecer)* to establish; **s. las bases** to lay the foundations

   2 *vi* (a) *(color, ropa etc)* to suit; **el pelo corto te sienta mal** short hair doesn't suit you (b) **s. bien/mal a** *(comida)* to agree/disagree with; **la sopa te sentará bien** the soup will do you good (c) **le sentó mal la broma** she didn't like the joke

   3 sentarse *vpr* to sit, to sit down

sentencia *nf* (a) sentence; **visto para s.** ready for judgement (b) *(aforismo)* maxim, saying

sentenciar [43] *vt Jur* to sentence (**a** to)

sentido,-a 1 *nm* (a) sense; **los cinco sentidos** the five senses; **s. común** common sense; **s. del humor** sense of humour (b) *(significado)* meaning; **doble s.** double meaning; **no tiene s.** it doesn't make sense (c) *(dirección)* direction; **(de) s. único** one-way (d) *(conciencia)* consciousness; **perder el s.** to faint

   2 *adj* deeply felt; *Fml* **mi más s. pésame** my deepest sympathy

sentimental 1 *adj* sentimental; **vida s.** love life

   2 *nmf* sentimental person

sentimiento *nm* (a) feeling (b) *(pesar)* sorrow, grief; *Fml* **le acompaño en el s.** my deepest sympathy

sentir[1] *nm* (a) *(sentimiento)* feeling (b) *(opinión)* opinion, view

sentir[2] [5] **1** *vt* (a) to feel; **s. hambre/calor** to feel hungry/hot (b) *(lamentar)* to regret, to be sorry about; **lo siento**

(mucho) I'm (very) sorry; **siento moles-tarle** I'm sorry to bother you
2 sentirse *upr* to feel; **me siento mal** I feel ill; **s. con ánimos de hacer algo** to feel like doing sth

senyera *nf* Catalan flag

seña *nf* (a) (indicio) sign, indication; **en s. de** as a sign of, as a token of (b) (placa) sign; **s. de tráfico** road sign (c) (gesto etc) signal, sign (d) (marca) mark; (vestigio) trace (e) *Tel* tone; **s. de llamada** *Br* dialling tone, *US* dial tone (f) *Com* deposit

seña *nf* (a) mark (b) (gesto) sign; **hacer señas a algn** to signal to sb (c) (indicio) sign (d) **señas** (dirección) address

señalado,-a *adj* (importante) important; **un día s.** a red-letter day

señalar *vt* (a) (indicar) to mark, to indicate; **s. con el dedo** to point at (b) (resaltar) to point out (c) (precio, fecha) to fix, to arrange

señalero *nm* *Urug Br* indicator, *US* turn signal

señor *nm* (a) (hombre) man; (caballero) gentleman (b) *Rel* **El S.** the Lord (c) (con apellido) Mr; (tratamiento de respeto) sir; **el Sr. Gutiérrez** Mr Gutiérrez; **muy s. mío** (en carta) Dear Sir (d) (con título) (no se traduce) **el s. ministro** the Minister

señora *nf* (a) (mujer) woman, *Fml* lady; **¡señoras y señores!** ladies and gentlemen! (b) *Rel* **Nuestra S.** Our Lady (c) (con apellido) Mrs; (tratamiento de respeto) madam; **la Sra. Salinas** Mrs Salinas; **muy s. mía** (en carta) Dear Madam (d) (con título) (no se traduce) **la s. ministra** the Minister (e) (esposa) wife

señoría *nf* (a) *Jur* (hombre) lordship; (mujer) ladyship (b) *Pol* **sus señorías** the honourable gentlemen

señorita *nf* (a) (joven) young woman, *Fml* young lady (b) (tratamiento de respeto) Miss; **S. Padilla** Miss Padilla (c) *Educ* **la s.** the teacher, Miss

señuelo *nm* (en caza) decoy

sepa *subj pres de* **saber**

separación *nf* (a) separation; *Jur* **s. conyugal** legal separation (b) (espacio) space, gap

separado,-a *adj* (a) separate; **por s.** separately, individually (b) (divorciado) separated

separar 1 *vt* (a) to separate (b) (desunir) to detach, to remove (c) (dividir) to divide, to separate (d) (apartar) to move away

2 separarse *upr* (a) to separate, to part

company (b) (matrimonio) to separate (c) (apartarse) to move away (**de** from)

separata *nf* offprint

separatismo *nm* separatism

separatista *adj & nmf* separatist

separo *nm* *Méx* (prison) cell

sepia 1 *nf* (pez) cuttlefish
2 *adj & nm* (color) sepia

septentrional *adj* northern

septiembre *nm* September; **el 5 de s.** the 5th of September; **en s.** in September

séptimo,-a *adj & nm,f* seventh; **la** o **una séptima parte** a seventh

sepulcral *adj* (silencio) deathly

sepulcro *nm* tomb

sepultura *nf* grave

sepulturero,-a *nm,f* gravedigger

sequía *nf* drought

séquito *nm* entourage, retinue

ser ¹ *nm* being; **s. humano** human being; **s. vivo** living being

ser ² [23] *vi* (a) (+ adj) to be; **es alto y rubio** he is tall and fair; **el edificio es gris** the building is grey
(b) (+ profesión) to be a(n); **Rafael es músico** Rafael is a musician
(c) **s. de** (procedencia) to be o come from; **¿de dónde eres?** where are you from?, where do you come from?
(d) **s. de** (+ material) to be made of
(e) **s. de** (+ poseedor) to belong to; **el perro es de Miguel** the dog belongs to Miguel; **¿de quién es este abrigo?** whose coat is this?
(f) **s. para** (finalidad) to be for; **esta agua es para lavar** this water is for washing
(g) (+ día, hora) to be; **hoy es 2 de noviembre** today is the 2nd of November; **son las cinco de la tarde** it's five o'clock
(h) (+ cantidad) **¿cuántos estaremos en la fiesta?** how many of us will there be at the party?
(i) (costar) to be, to cost; **¿cuánto es?** how much is it?
(j) (tener lugar) to be; **el estreno será mañana** tomorrow is the opening night
(k) **¿qué es de Gonzalo?** what has become of Gonzalo?
(l) (auxiliar en pasiva) to be; **fue asesinado** he was murdered
(m) (locuciones) **¿cómo es eso?, ¿cómo puede s.?** how can that be?; **es más** furthermore; **es que ...** it's just that ...; **como sea** anyhow; **lo que sea** whatever; **o sea** that is (to say); **por si fuera poco** to top it all; **sea como sea** in any case, be that as it may; **a no s. que** unless; **de no s.**

por ... had it not been for ...; **eso era de esperar** it was to be expected

> The auxiliary verb **ser** is used with the past participle of a verb to form the passive (e.g. **la película fue criticada** the film was criticized).

serenarse *vpr* to calm down

serenidad *nf* serenity

sereno¹ *nm (vigilante)* nightwatchman

sereno²,-a *adj* (a) *(severo)* calm (b) *Fam* **estar s.** *(sobrio)* to be sober

serial *nm Rad & TV* serial

serie *nf* (a) series *sing*; **fabricación en s.** mass production; **lleva ABS de s.** it has ABS fitted as standard; **fuera de s.** out of the ordinary (b) *Rad & TV* series *sing*

seriedad *nf* (a) *(severo)* seriousness (b) *(formalidad)* reliability, dependability; **falta de s.** irresponsibility

serio,-a *adj* (a) *(severo)* serious; **en s.** seriously (b) *(formal)* reliable, responsible

sermón *nm* sermon

sermonear *vt & vi Fam* to lecture

seropositivo,-a *adj* HIV-positive

serpentear *vi (zigzaguear)* to wind one's way, to meander

serpentina *nf (de papel)* streamer

serpiente *nf* snake; **s. de cascabel** rattlesnake; **s. pitón** python

serranía *nf* mountainous area/country

serrar [1] *vt* to saw

serrín *nm* sawdust

serrucho *nm* handsaw

servicial *adj* helpful, obliging

servicio *nm* (a) service; **s. a domicilio** delivery service (b) *Mil* service; **s. militar** military service; **estar de s.** to be on duty (c) **servicios** *(retrete)* toilet, *US* rest room

servidor,-a *nm,f* servant; *Fam* **un s.** yours truly

servil *adj* servile

servilleta *nf* serviette, napkin

servilletero *nm* serviette ring, napkin ring

servio,-a *adj & nm,f* Serbian

servir [6] 1 *vt* to serve; **¿en qué puedo servirle?** what can I do for you?, may I help you?; **¿te sirvo una copa?** will I pour you a drink?

2 *vi* (a) to serve (b) *(valer)* to be useful, to be suitable; **no sirve de nada llorar** it's no use crying; **ya no sirve** it's no use; **¿para qué sirve esto?** what is this (used) for? (c) **s. de** to serve as, to act as

3 servirse *vpr* (a) *(comida etc)* to help oneself (b) *Fml* **sírvase comunicarnos su**

decisión please inform us of your decision

sésamo *nm* sesame

sesenta *adj & nm inv* sixty

sesgar [42] *vt* (a) *(cortar)* to cut diagonally (b) *(torcer)* to slant

sesgo *nm Fig* slant, turn; **tomar un s. favorable** to take a turn for the better

sesión *nf* (a) *(reunión)* meeting, session; *Jur* session, sitting (b) *Cin* showing

seso *nm* brain

set *nm Ten* set

seta *nf (comestible)* mushroom; **s. venenosa** toadstool

setecientos,-as *adj & nm* seven hundred

setenta *adj & nm inv* seventy

setiembre *nm* September

seto *nm* hedge

seudónimo *nm* pseudonym; *(de escritores)* pen name

severidad *nf* severity

severo,-a *adj* severe

Sevilla *n* Seville

sexismo *nm* sexism

sexista *adj* sexist

sexo *nm* (a) sex (b) *(órgano)* genitals

sexólogo,-a *nm,f* sexologist

sexto,-a *adj & nm,f* sixth

sexual *adj* sexual; **vida s.** sex life

sexualidad *nf* sexuality

sexy *adj* sexy

s/f. *(abr* su favor*)* your favour

shock *nm* shock

short *nm RP* swimming trunks

show *nm* show

si¹ *conj* (a) *(condicional)* if; **como si** as if; **si no** if not; **si quieres** if you like, if you wish (b) *(pregunta indirecta)* whether, if; **me preguntó si me gustaba** he asked me if I liked it; **no sé si ir o no** *(disyuntivo)* I don't know whether to go or not (c) *(sorpresa)* **¡si está llorando!** but she's crying!

si² *nm (pl* sis*) Mús* B; *(en solfeo)* ti

sí¹ *pron pers* (a) *(singular) (él)* himself; *(ella)* herself; *(cosa)* itself; *(plural)* themselves; **de por sí, en sí** in itself; **hablaban entre sí** they were talking among themselves *o* to each other; **por sí mismo** by himself *o* *(uno mismo)* oneself; **decir para sí** to say to oneself

sí² **1** *adv* (a) yes; **dije que sí** I said yes, I accepted, I agreed; **porque sí** just because; **¡que sí!** yes, I tell you!; **un día sí y otro no** every other day (b) *(uso enfático)* *(no se traduce)* **¡sí que me gusta** of course I like it; **¡eso sí que no!** certainly not!

2 *nm (pl* síes*)* yes; **los síes** *(en parlamento)* the ayes

siamés,-esa *nm,f* Siamese twin

sibarita *nmf* sybarite

sicario *nm* hired gunman; *Fam* hitman

Sicilia *n* Sicily

sico- = psico-

sicómoro *nm* sycamore

sida *nm* (*abr* síndrome de inmunodeficiencia adquirida) AIDS

sidecar *nm* sidecar

siderurgia *nf* iron and steel industry

siderúrgico,-a *adj* iron and steel; **la industria siderúrgica** the iron and steel industry

sidra *nf Br* cider, *US* hard cider

siempre *adv* (**a**) always; **s. pasa lo mismo** it's always the same; **como s.** as usual; **a la hora de s.** at the usual time; **eso es así desde s.** it has always been like that; **para s.** for ever; **s. que** (*cada vez que*) whenever; (*a condición de que*) provided, as long as; **s. y cuando** provided, as long as (**b**) *Am* (*todavía*) still; **s. viven allí** they still live there (**c**) *Méx Fam* (*enfático*) still; **s. sí quiero ir** I still want to go; **s. no me marcho** I'm still not leaving

sien *nf* temple

sierra *nf* (**a**) saw; **s. mecánica** power saw (**b**) *Geog* mountain range, sierra

siervo,-a *nm,f* slave

siesta *nf* siesta, nap; **dormir la s.** to have a siesta *o* an afternoon nap

siete 1 *adj* seven

  2 *nm inv* seven

  3 *nf RP Fam Euf* **¡la gran s.!** *Br* sugar!, *US* shoot!

sietemesino,-a *nm,f* seven-month baby, premature baby

sífilis *nf inv* syphilis

sifón *nm* siphon; **whisky con s.** whisky and soda

sig. (*abr* siguiente) following

sigilo *nm* secrecy; **entrar con mucho s.** to tiptoe in

sigilosamente *adv* (*secretamente*) secretly; **entró s. en la habitación** she crept *o* slipped into the room

sigiloso,-a *adj* secretive

sigla *nf* acronym

siglo *nm* century; **el s. veintiuno** the twenty-first century; *Fam* **hace siglos que no le veo** I haven't seen him for ages

signatario,-a *adj & nm,f* signatory

significación *nf* (**a**) (*sentido*) meaning (**b**) (*importancia*) significance

significado *nm* meaning

significar [44] *vt* to mean

significativo,-a *adj* significant; (*expresivo*) meaningful

signo *nm* (**a**) sign; **s. del zodiaco** zodiac sign (**b**) *Ling* mark; **s. de interrogación** question mark

sigo *indic pres de* seguir

siguiente *adj* following, next; **¡el s.!** next, please!; **al día s.** the following day

sílaba *nf* syllable

silbar *vi* to whistle; (*abuchear*) to hiss, to boo

silbato *nm* whistle

silbido *nm* whistle, whistling; (*agudo*) hiss

silenciador *nm* (*de arma*) silencer; (*de coche, moto*) *Br* silencer, *US* muffler

silenciar [43] *vt* (**a**) (*un sonido*) to muffle (**b**) (*noticia*) to hush up

silencio *nm* silence; **imponer s. a algn** to make sb be quiet

silencioso,-a *adj* (*persona*) quiet; (*motor etc*) silent

silicio *nm* silicon

silicona *nf* silicone

silla *nf* (**a**) chair; **s. de ruedas** wheelchair; **s. giratoria** swivel chair (**b**) (*de montura*) saddle

sillín *nm* saddle

sillón *nm* armchair

silo *nm* silo

silueta *nf* silhouette; (*de cuerpo*) figure

silvestre *adj* wild

simbólico,-a *adj* symbolic; **precio s.** token price

simbolizar [40] *vt* to symbolize

símbolo *nm* symbol

simetría *nf* symmetry

simétrico,-a *adj* symmetrical

simiente *nf* seed

similar *adj* similar

similitud *nf* similarity

simio *nm* monkey

simpatía *nf* liking, affection; **le tengo mucha s.** I am very fond of him

> *𝒫* Observa que la palabra inglesa **sympathy** es un falso amigo y no es la traducción de la palabra española **simpatía**. En inglés, **sympathy** significa tanto "compasión" como "comprensión".

simpático,-a *adj* (*amable*) nice, likeable; **me cae s.** I like him

> *𝒫* Observa que la palabra inglesa **sympathetic** es un falso amigo y no es la traducción de la palabra española **simpático**. En inglés, **sympathetic** significa tanto "comprensivo" como "compasivo".

simpatizante *nmf* sympathizer

simpatizar [40] *vi* (**a**) to sympathize

(**con** with) (**b**) *(llevarse bien)* to hit it off (**con** with)

simple 1 *adj* (**a**) simple (**b**) *(fácil)* simple, easy (**c**) *(mero)* mere (**d**) *(persona)* simple, simple-minded
  2 *nm (persona)* simpleton

simpleza *nf* simple-mindedness; *(tontería)* nonsense

simplificar [44] *vt* to simplify

simposio *nm* symposium

simulacro *nm* sham, pretence; **un s. de ataque** a mock attack

simular *vt* to simulate

simultanear *vt* to combine; **simultanea el trabajo y los estudios** he's working and studying at the same time

simultáneo,-a *adj* simultaneous

sin *prep* (**a**) without; **s. dinero/tí** without money/you; **estamos s. pan** we're out of bread; **s. hacer nada** without doing anything; **cerveza s.** alcohol-free beer; **s. más ni más** without further ado (**b**) (+ *inf*) **está s. secar** it hasn't been dried

sinagoga *nf* synagogue

sincerarse *vpr* to open one's heart (**con** to)

sinceridad *nf* sincerity; **con toda s.** in all sincerity

sincero,-a *adj* sincere

sincronizar [40] *vt* to synchronize

sindical *adj* (*Br* trade o *US* labor) union

sindicalista *nmf* union member, *Br* trade unionist

sindicar *vt Andes, RP, Ven* to accuse

sindicato *nm* union, trade union

síndrome *nm* syndrome

sinfín *nm* endless number; **un s. de** lots of

sinfonía *nf* symphony

singani *nm Bol* grape brandy

single *nm* (**a**) *(disco)* single, 7-inch (**b**) *CSur (habitación)* single room

singular 1 *adj* (**a**) singular (**b**) *(excepcional)* exceptional, unique (**c**) *(raro)* peculiar, odd
  2 *nm Ling* singular; **en s.** in the singular

siniestrado,-a *adj* stricken

siniestro,-a 1 *adj* sinister, ominous
  2 *nm* disaster, catastrophe

sino¹ *nm Fml* fate, destiny

sino² *conj* (**a**) but; **no fui a Madrid, s. a Barcelona** I didn't go to Madrid but to Barcelona (**b**) *(excepto)* **nadie s. él** no one but him; **no quiero s. que me oigan** I only want them to listen (to me)

sinónimo,-a 1 *adj* synonymous
  2 *nm* synonym

sinóptico,-a *adj* **cuadro s.** diagram, chart

sinsabor *nm (usu pl)* trouble, worry

sintético,-a *adj* synthetic

sintetizador *nm* synthesizer

sintetizar [40] *vt* to synthesize

síntoma *nm* symptom

sintonía *nf* (**a**) *Elec & Rad* tuning (**b**) *Mús & Rad (de programa)* signature tune (**c**) *Fig* harmony

sintonizador *nm Rad* tuning knob

sintonizar [40] *vt* (**a**) *Rad* to tune in to (**b**) *(simpatizar)* **sintonizaron muy bien** they clicked straight away

sinuoso,-a *adj (camino)* winding

sinvergüenza 1 *adj (desvergonzado)* shameless; *(descarado)* cheeky
  2 *nmf (desvergonzado)* rogue; *(caradura)* cheeky devil

sionismo *nm* Zionism

siquiera 1 *adv (por lo menos)* at least; **ni s.** not even
  2 *conj Fml (aunque)* although, even though

sirena *nf* (**a**) siren, mermaid (**b**) *(señal acústica)* siren

Siria *n* Syria

sirimiri *nm* fine drizzle

sirio,-a *adj & nm,f* Syrian

sirviente,-a *nm,f* servant

sisar *vt (hurtar)* to pilfer, to filch

sisear *vi* to hiss

sísmico,-a *adj* seismic

sismógrafo *nm* seismograph

sistema *nm* system; **por s.** as a rule; **s. nervioso** nervous system; **s. montañoso** mountain chain

sistemático,-a *adj* systematic

sitiar [43] *vt* to besiege

sitio¹ *nm* (**a**) *(lugar)* place; **en cualquier s.** anywhere; **en todos los sitios** everywhere; *Fig* **quedarse en el s.** to die (**b**) *(espacio)* room; **hacer s.** to make room (**c**) *Méx (parada de taxis)* taxi stand o *Br* rank

sitio² *nm* siege; **estado de s.** state of emergency

sito,-a *adj Fml* situated, located

situación *nf* (**a**) situation; **su s. económica es buena** his financial position is good (**b**) *(ubicación)* situation, location

situado,-a *adj* situated; *Fig* **estar bien s.** to have a good position

situar [30] 1 *vt* to locate
  2 situarse *vpr* to be situated o located

sketch *nm Cin & Teatro* sketch

S.L. *(abr* **Sociedad Limitada***) Br* ≃ Ltd, *US* ≃ Inc

slip *nm* underpants

slogan *nm* slogan

S.M. *(abr* **Su Majestad***) (rey)* His Majesty; *(reina)* Her Majesty

smoking *nm* dinner jacket, *US* tuxedo

s/n. (*abr* **sin número**) = abbreviation used in addresses after the street name, where the building has no number

snob *adj & nmf* = **esnob**

snobismo *nm* = **esnobismo**

so¹ *prep* (*bajo*) under; **so pena de** under penalty of

so² *nm Fam* **¡so imbécil!** you damned idiot!

sobaco *nm* armpit

sobar *Fam* **1** *vt* (*manosear*) to fondle, to paw
  2 *vi* (*dormir*) to sleep

soberanía *nf* sovereignty

soberano,-a 1 *adj* (**a**) sovereign (**b**) *Fam* huge, great
  2 *nm,f* (*monarca*) sovereign

soberbia *nf* pride

soberbio,-a *adj* (**a**) proud (**b**) (*magnífico*) splendid, magnificent

sobón,-ona *nm,f Fam* **ser un s.** to be fresh *o* all hands

sobornar *vt* to bribe

soborno *nm* (*acción*) bribery; (*dinero etc*) bribe

sobra *nf* (**a**) **de s.** (*no necesario*) superfluous; **tener de s.** to have plenty; **estar de s.** not to be needed; **saber algo de s.** to know sth only too well (**b**) **sobras** (*restos*) leftovers

sobradamente *adv* only too well

sobrado,-a *adj* (*que sobra*) abundant, more than enough; **sobradas veces** repeatedly; **andar s. de tiempo/dinero** to have plenty of time/money

sobrante 1 *adj* remaining, spare
  2 *nm* surplus, excess

sobrar *vi* (**a**) to be more than enough, (*sing*) to be too much, (*pl*) to be too many; **sobran tres sillas** there are three chairs too many; **sobran comentarios** I've nothing further to add; *Fam* **tú sobras aquí** you are not wanted here (**b**) (*quedar*) to be left over; **ha sobrado carne** there's still some meat left

sobrasada *nf* sausage spread

sobre¹ *nm* (**a**) (*para carta*) envelope (**b**) (*de sopa etc*) packet

sobre² *prep* (**a**) (*encima de*) on, upon, on top of (**b**) (*por encima*) over, above (**c**) (*acerca de*) about, on (**d**) (*aproximadamente*) about; **vendré s. las ocho** I'll come at about eight o'clock (**e**) **s. todo** especially, above all

sobre- *pref* super-, over-

sobrealimentado,-a *adj* overfed

sobrecarga *nf* overload

sobrecargar [42] *vt* to overload

sobrecogedor,-a *adj* dramatic, awesome

sobrecoger [53] *vt* (*conmover*) to shock

sobredosis *nf inv* overdose

sobreentenderse *upr* **se sobreentiende** that goes without saying

sobregiro *nm* overdraft

sobrehumano,-a *adj* superhuman

sobreimpresión *nf Fot & Cin* superimposing

sobrellevar *vt* to endure, to bear

sobremesa¹ *nf* afternoon

sobremesa² *nf* **ordenador de s.** desktop computer

sobrenatural *adj* supernatural

sobrenombre *nm* nickname

sobrepasar 1 *vt* to exceed, to surpass; (*rival*) to beat
  2 sobrepasarse *upr* to go too far

sobrepeso *nm* (*de carga*) overload, excess weight; (*de persona*) excess weight

sobreponerse *upr* (**a**) **s.** (*superar*) to overcome; **s. al dolor** to overcome pain (**b**) (*animarse*) to pull oneself together

sobreproducción *nf* overproduction

sobresaliente 1 *nm* (*nota*) ≃ A
  2 *adj* (*que destaca*) outstanding, excellent

sobresalir [22] *vi* to stick out, to protrude; *Fig* (*destacar*) to stand out, to excel

sobresaltar 1 *vt* to startle
  2 sobresaltarse *upr* to be startled, to start

sobresalto *nm* (*movimiento*) start; (*susto*) fright

sobreseer [36] *vt* *Jur* to stay; **s. una causa** to stay proceedings

sobretiempo *nm Andes* (**a**) (*en trabajo*) overtime (**b**) (*en deporte*) *Br* extra time, *US* overtime

sobretodo *nm* (*abrigo*) overcoat; (*guardapolvo*) overalls

sobrevalorar *vt* to overestimate

sobrevenir [27] *vi* to happen unexpectedly

sobreviviente 1 *adj* surviving
  2 *nmf* survivor

sobrevivir *vi* to survive

sobrevolar [2] *vt* to fly over

sobriedad *nf* sobriety; (*en la bebida*) soberness

sobrina *nf* niece

sobrino *nm* nephew

sobrio,-a *adj* sober

socarrón,-ona *adj* (**a**) (*sarcástico*) sarcastic (**b**) (*astuto*) sly, cunning

socavar *vt* *Fig* to undermine

socavón *nm (bache)* pothole

sociable *adj* sociable, friendly

social *adj* social

socialdemócrata 1 *adj* social democratic

  2 *nmf* social democrat

socialismo *nm* socialism

socialista *adj & nmf* socialist

socializar [40] *vt* to socialize

sociedad *nf* **(a)** society; **s. de consumo** consumer society **(b)** *(asociación)* association, society **(c)** *Com* company; **s. anónima** *Br* public (limited) company, *US* incorporated company; **s. limitada** private limited company

socio,-a *nm,f* **(a)** *(miembro)* member; **hacerse s. de un club** to become a member of a club, to join a club **(b)** *Com (asociado)* partner

sociología *nf* sociology

sociológico,-a *adj* sociological

sociólogo,-a *nm,f* sociologist

socorrer *vt* to help, to assist

socorrido,-a *adj* handy, useful

socorrista *nmf* life-saver, lifeguard

socorro *nm* help, assistance; **¡s.!** help!; **puesto de s.** first-aid post

soda *nf* soda water

soez *adj* vulgar, crude

sofá *nm (pl* **sofás)** sofa, settee; **s. cama** sofa bed, studio couch

Sofía *n* Sofia

sofisticado,-a *adj* sophisticated

sofocado,-a *adj* suffocated

sofocante *adj* suffocating, stifling; **hacía un calor s.** it was unbearably hot

sofocar [44] 1 *vt* **(a)** *(ahogar)* to suffocate, to smother **(b)** *(incendio)* to extinguish, to put out

  2 sofocarse *upr* **(a)** *(ahogarse)* to suffocate, to stifle **(b)** *Fam (irritarse)* to get upset

sofoco *nm Fig (vergüenza)* embarrassment; **le dio un s.** *(disgusto)* it gave her quite a turn

sofocón *nm Fam* shock; **llevarse un s.** to get upset

sofreír [56] *vt* to fry lightly, to brown

sofrito *nm* = fried tomato and onion sauce

software *nm* software

soga *nf* rope; *Fig* **estar con la s. al cuello** to be in dire straits

soja *nf* **(a)** *(planta, fruto) Br* soya bean, *US* soy bean **(b)** *(proteína)* soya

sojuzgar [42] *vt* to subjugate

sol¹ *nm* **(a)** sun **(b)** *(luz)* sunlight; *(luz y calor)* sunshine; **hace s.** it's sunny, the sun

is shining; **tomar el s.** to sunbathe; **al** *o* **bajo el s.** in the sun; **de s. a s.** from sunrise to sunset **(c)** *Fin* = standard monetary unit of Peru

sol² *nm Mús* G; *(solfeo)* so

solamente *adv* only; **no s.** not only; **s. con mirarte lo sé** I know just by looking at you; **s. que ...** except that ...

solapa *nf (de chaqueta)* lapel; *(de sobre, bolsillo, libro)* flap

solapadamente *adv* stealthily, in an underhand way

solapado,-a *adj (persona)* sly

solapamiento *nm* overlap

solapar 1 *vt Fig* to conceal, to cover up

  2 *vi* to overlap

solar¹ *adj* solar; **luz s.** sunlight

solar² *nm (terreno)* plot; *(en obras)* building site

solario, solárium *nm* sunbed

solaz *nm Fml (descanso)* rest, relaxation; *(esparcimiento)* recreation, entertainment

solazarse [40] *vpr (relajar)* to relax; *(divertir)* to entertain oneself, to amuse oneself

soldado *nm* soldier; **s. raso** private

soldador,-a 1 *nm,f* welder

  2 *nm* soldering iron

soldar [2] *vt (cable)* to solder; *(chapa)* to weld

soleado,-a *adj* sunny

soledad *nf (estado)* solitude; *(sentimiento)* loneliness

solemne *adj* **(a)** *(majestuoso)* solemn **(b)** *Pey* downright

solemnidad *nf* solemnity

soler [4] *vi defect* **(a)** *(en presente)* to be in the habit of; **solemos ir en coche** we usually go by car; **sueles equivocarte** you are usually wrong **(b)** *(en pasado)* **solía pasear por aquí** he used to walk round here

solera *nf Fig* tradition; **de s.** old-established; **vino de s.** vintage wine

solfa *nf* **(a)** *Mús* solfa; *Fam* **poner en s.** to ridicule **(b)** *Fam (paliza)* thrashing, beating

solicitar *vt (información etc)* to request, to ask for; *(trabajo)* to apply for

solícito,-a *adj* obliging, attentive

solicitud *nf (petición)* request; *(de trabajo)* application

solidaridad *nf* solidarity

solidario,-a *adj* **(a)** supportive; **una sociedad solidaria** a caring society **(b)** *Jur* jointly responsible

solidarizarse *vpr* to show one's solidarity **(con** with)

solidez *nf* solidity, strength

sólido,-a *adj* solid, strong

soliloquio *nm* soliloquy

solista *nmf* soloist

solitario,-a 1 *adj (que está solo)* solitary, lone; *(que se siente solo)* lonely

2 *nm* (a) *(diamante)* solitaire (b) *Naipes* solitaire, patience

soliviantar *vt (irritar)* to irritate

sollozar [40] *vi* to sob

sollozo *nm* sob

solo,-a 1 *adj* (a) only, single; **ni un s. día** not a single day; **una sola vez** only once, just once (b) *(solitario)* lonely (c) **hablar s.** to talk to oneself; **se enciende s.** it switches itself on automatically; **a solas** alone, by oneself

2 *nm Mús* solo

sólo *adv* only; **tan s.** only; **no s. ... sino (también)** not only ... but (also); **con s., (tan) s. con** just by

> Note that the adverb **sólo** can be written without an accent when there is no risk of confusion with the adjective.

solomillo *nm* sirloin

soltar [2] 1 *vt* (a) *(desasir)* to let go of; **¡suéltame!** let me go! (b) *(prisionero)* to release (c) *(humo, olor)* to give off (d) *(bofetada)* to deal; *(carcajada)* to let out; **me soltó un rollo** he bored me to tears

2 soltarse *vpr* (a) *(desatarse)* to come loose (b) *(perro etc)* to get loose, to break loose (c) *(desprenderse)* to come off

soltero,-a 1 *adj* single, unmarried

2 *nm (hombre)* bachelor, single man

3 *nf* **soltera** *(mujer)* single woman, spinster

solterón, -ona *nm,f* old bachelor, *f* old maid

soltura *nf (agilidad)* agility; *(seguridad)* confidence, assurance; **habla italiano con s.** he speaks Italian fluently

soluble *adj* soluble; **café s.** instant coffee

solución *nf* solution

solucionar *vt* to solve; *(arreglar)* to settle

solvencia *nf* (a) *Fin* solvency (b) *(fiabilidad)* reliability; **fuentes de toda s.** completely reliable sources

solventar *vt (problema)* to solve, to resolve; *(deuda, asunto)* to settle

solvente *adj* (a) *Fin* solvent (b) *(fiable)* reliable

sombra *nf* (a) shade (b) *(silueta proyectada)* shadow; **s. de ojos** eyeshadow; **sin s. de duda** beyond a shadow of doubt (c)

tener buena s. *(tener suerte)* to be lucky

sombrero *nm* hat; **s. de copa** top hat; **s. hongo** bowler hat

sombrilla *nf* parasol, sunshade

sombrío,-a *adj (oscuro)* dark; *(tenebroso)* sombre, gloomy; *Fig (persona)* gloomy, sullen

somero,-a *adj* superficial, shallow

someter 1 *vt* (a) to subject; **s. a prueba** to put to the test; **s. algo a votación** to put sth to the vote (b) *(rebeldes)* to subdue, to put down

2 someterse *vpr* (a) *(subordinarse)* to submit (b) *(rendirse)* to surrender, to yield (c) **s. a un tratamiento** to undergo treatment

somier *nm (pl* **somieres***)* spring mattress

somnífero *nm* sleeping pill

somnoliento,-a *adj* sleepy, drowsy

son *nm* sound; **al s. del tambor** to the sound of the drum; **venir en s. de paz** to come in peace

sonado,-a *adj* (a) much talked of (b) *(trastocado)* mad, crazy

sonajero *nm* baby's rattle

sonámbulo,-a *nm,f* somnambulist, sleepwalker

sonar [2] 1 *vi* (a) to sound; **s. a** to sound like; **suena bien** it sounds good (b) *(timbre, teléfono)* to ring; **sonaron las cinco** the clock struck five (c) **tu nombre/cara me suena** your name/face rings a bell

2 sonarse *vpr* **s. (la nariz)** to blow one's nose

sonda *nf* (a) *Med* sound, probe (b) **s. espacial** space probe

sondear *vt* (a) *(opinión)* to test, to sound out (b) *Med* to sound, to probe (c) *Náut* to sound

sondeo *nm* (a) *(encuesta)* poll (b) *Med* sounding, probing (c) *Náut* sounding

soneto *nm Lit* sonnet

sonido *nm* sound

sonoro,-a *adj* (a) *Cin* sound; **banda sonora** soundtrack (b) *(resonante)* loud, resounding (c) *Ling* voiced

sonreír [56] *vi*, **sonreírse** *vpr* to smile; **me sonrió** he smiled at me

sonriente *adj* smiling

sonrisa *nf* smile

sonrojarse *vpr* to blush

sonrojo *nm* blush

sonsacar [44] *vt* to wheedle; *(secreto)* to worm out

sonso,-a *adj Am* foolish, silly

soñador,-a *nm,f* dreamer

soñar [2] *vt & vi* (a) to dream; **s. con** to dream of o about; *Fig* **¡ni soñarlo!** not on your life! (b) *(fantasear)* to daydream, to dream

soñoliento,-a *adj* sleepy, drowsy

sopa *nf* soup; **s. juliana** spring vegetable soup; *Fig* **quedar hecho una s.** to get soaked to the skin

sope *nm Méx* = fried corn tortilla, with beans and cheese or other toppings

sopera *nf* soup tureen

sopero,-a *adj* **cucharada sopera** soup spoon

sopesar *vt* to try the weight of; *Fig* to weigh up

sopetón *nm Fam* slap; **de s.** all of a sudden

soplado *nm* glass-blowing

soplagaitas *nmf inv Fam (estúpido, pesado)* jerk, *Br* prat

soplar 1 *vi (viento)* to blow
2 *vt* (a) *(polvo etc)* to blow away; *(para enfriar)* to blow on (b) *(para apagar)* to blow out (c) *(para inflar)* to blow up (d) *(en examen etc)* **me sopló las respuestas** he whispered the answers to me

soplete *nm* blowlamp, blowtorch

soplido *nm* blow, puff

soplillo *nm* fan; *Fam* **orejas de s.** sticky-out ears

soplo *nm* (a) *(acción)* blow, puff; *(de viento)* gust (b) *Med* murmur

soplón,-ona *nm,f Fam (niño)* telltale, sneak; *(delator) Br* grass, *US* rat

soporífero,-a *adj* (a) *(que adormece)* soporific, sleep-inducing (b) *(aburrido)* boring, dull

soportable *adj* bearable

soportal *nm* porch; **soportales** arcade

soportar *vt* (a) *(peso)* to support, to bear (b) *Fig (calor, ruido)* to bear, to endure; *(situación)* to put up with, to bear; **no te soporto** I can't stand you

soporte *nm* support; **s. publicitario** advertising medium

soprano *nmf* soprano

sorber *vt* (a) *(beber)* to sip (b) *(absorber)* to soak up, to absorb

sorbete *nm* sorbet, sherbet

sorbo *nm* sip; *(trago)* gulp; **de un s.** in one gulp

sordera *nf* deafness

sórdido,-a *adj* squalid, sordid

sordo,-a 1 *adj* (a) *(persona)* deaf; **s. como una tapia** stone-deaf (b) *(golpe, ruido, dolor)* dull
2 *nm,f* deaf person; **los sordos** the deaf *pl; Fam Fig* **hacerse el s.** to turn a deaf ear

sordomudez *nf* deaf-muteness

sordomudo,-a 1 *adj* deaf and dumb, deaf-mute

2 *nm,f* deaf and dumb person, deaf-mute

soroche *nm Andes, Arg (mal de altura)* altitude sickness

sorprendente *adj* surprising

sorprender *vt* (a) *(extrañar)* to surprise (b) *(coger desprevenido)* to catch unawares, to take by surprise

sorpresa *nf* surprise; **coger de o por s.** to take by surprise

sorpresivo,-a *adj Am* unexpected, surprising

sortear *vt* (a) to draw o cast lots for; *(rifar)* to raffle (off) (b) *(evitar)* to avoid, to get round

sorteo *nm* draw; *(rifa)* raffle

sortija *nf* ring

sortilegio *nm* spell

S.O.S. *nm* SOS

sosa *nf* soda; **s. cáustica** caustic soda

sosegado,-a *adj (tranquilo)* calm, quiet; *(pacífico)* peaceful

sosegar [1] 1 *vt* to calm, to quieten
2 sosegarse *vpr* to calm down

sosiego *nm (calma)* calmness; *(paz)* peace, tranquillity

soslayo: • de soslayo *loc adv* **mirar de s.** to look sideways (at)

soso,-a *adj* lacking in salt; *Fig (persona)* insipid, dull

sospecha *nf* suspicion

sospechar 1 *vi (desconfiar)* to suspect; **s. de algn** to suspect sb
2 *vt (pensar)* to suspect

sospechoso,-a 1 *adj* suspicious; **s. de** suspected of
2 *nm,f* suspect

sostén *nm* (a) *(apoyo)* support (b) *(sustento)* sustenance (c) *(prenda)* bra, brassière

sostener [24] 1 *vt* (a) *(sujetar)* to support, to hold up (b) *(con la mano)* to hold (c) *Fig (teoría etc)* to defend, to uphold; **s. que ...** to maintain that ... (d) *(conversación)* to hold, to sustain (e) *(familia)* to support
2 sostenerse *vpr* (a) *(mantenerse)* to support oneself (b) *(permanecer)* to stay, to remain

sostenido,-a *adj* (a) *(continuado)* sustained (b) *Mús* sharp

sostuve *pt indef de* **sostener**

sota *nf Naipes* jack, knave

sotana *nf* cassock, soutane

sótano *nm* basement, cellar

soto *nm* grove

soviético,-a *adj & nm,f* Soviet; *Hist* **la Unión Soviética** the Soviet Union

soy *indic pres de* ser

soya *nf* = soja

SP (*abr* **servicio público**) = sign indicating public transport vehicle

sport: • **de sport** *loc adj* casual, sports; **chaqueta de s.** sports jacket

spot *nm* (*pl* **spots**) *TV* commercial, advert, ad

spray *nm* (*pl* **sprays**) spray

sprint *nm* sprint

Sr. (*abr* **Señor**) Mr

Sra. (*abr* **Señora**) Mrs

S.R.C., s.r.c. (*abr* **se ruega contestación**) please reply, R.S.V.P.

Srta. (*abr* **Señorita**) Miss

SS *nf* (*abr* **Seguridad Social**) Social Security

SS.AA. (*abr* **Sus Altezas**) Their Royal Highnesses

Sta., sta. (*abr* **Santa**) St

stand *nm Com* stand

standard *adj & nm* standard

status *nm inv* status

Sto., sto. (*abr* **Santo**) St

su *adj pos* (*de él*) his; (*de ella*) her; (*de usted, ustedes*) your; (*de animales o cosas*) its; (*impersonal*) one's; (*de ellos*) their; **su coche** his/her/your/their car; **su pata** its leg; **sus libros** his/her/your/their books; **sus patas** its legs

suave *adj* (**a**) smooth; (*luz, voz etc*) soft (**b**) *Met* (*templado*) mild

> *𝒮* Observa que la palabra inglesa **suave** es un falso amigo y no es la traducción de la palabra española **suave**. En inglés, **suave** significa "fino, cortés".

suavidad *nf* (**a**) smoothness; (*dulzura*) softness (**b**) *Met* mildness

suavizante *nm* (*para el pelo*) (hair) conditioner; (*para la ropa*) fabric softener

suavizar [40] **1** *vt* to smooth (out)

2 suavizarse *vpr* (*temperatura*) to get milder; (*persona*) to calm down

subacuático,-a *adj* underwater

subalimentado,-a *adj* undernourished, underfed

subalterno,-a *adj & nm,f* subordinate, subaltern

subarrendar [1] *vt Com* to sublet, to sublease

subasta *nf* auction

subastar *vt* to auction (off), to sell at auction

subcampeón *nm Dep* runner-up

subconsciente *adj & nm* subconscious

subcontratación *nf Com* outsourcing

subdesarrollado,-a *adj* underdeveloped

subdesarrollo *nm* underdevelopment

subdirector,-a *nm,f* assistant director/manager

súbdito,-a *nm,f* subject, citizen; **s. francés** French citizen

subdividir *vt* to subdivide

subestimar *vt* to underestimate

subida *nf* (**a**) (*de temperatura*) rise; (*de precios, salarios*) rise, increase (**b**) (*ascenso*) ascent, climb (**c**) (*pendiente*) slope, hill (**d**) *Fam* (*drogas*) high

subido,-a *adj* **s. de tono** daring, risqué

subir 1 *vt* (**a**) to go up (**b**) (*llevar arriba*) to take up, to bring up (**c**) (*cabeza, mano*) to lift, to raise (**d**) (*precio, salario*) to raise, to put up (**e**) (*volumen*) to turn up; (*voz*) to raise

2 *vi* (**a**) (*ir arriba*) to go up, to come up (**b**) **s. a** (*un coche*) to get into; (*un autobús*) to get on; (*un barco, avión, tren*) to board, to get on (**c**) (*aumentar*) to rise, to go up

3 subirse *vpr* (**a**) to climb up; *Fig* **el vino se le subió a la cabeza** the wine went to his head (**b**) **s. a** (*un coche*) to get into; (*un autobús, avión, tren*) to get on, to board; (*caballo, bici*) to get on (**c**) (*cremallera*) to do up; (*mangas*) to roll up

súbitamente *adv* suddenly

súbito,-a *adj* sudden

subjetivo,-a *adj* subjective

sublevación *nf* rising, rebellion

sublevar 1 *vt Fig* (*indignar*) to infuriate, to enrage

2 sublevarse *vpr* to rebel, to revolt

sublime *adj* sublime

submarinismo *nm* skin-diving

submarino,-a 1 *adj* submarine, underwater

2 *nm* submarine

subnormal 1 *adj* mentally handicapped

2 *nmf* mentally handicapped person

suboficial *nm* (**a**) *Mil* noncommissioned officer (**b**) *Náut* petty officer

subordinado,-a *adj & nm,f* subordinate

subordinar *vt* to subordinate

subproducto *nm* by-product

subrayar *vt* to underline; *Fig* (*recalcar*) to emphasize, to stress

subrepticio,-a *adj* surreptitious

subrutina *nf* subroutine

subsanar *vt* (*error*) to rectify, to put right; (*daño*) to make up for

subscribir (*pp* **subscrito**) *vt* = suscribir

subscripción *nf* subscription

subsecretario,-a *nm,f* undersecretary

subsidiario,-a *adj* subsidiary

subsidio *nm* allowance, benefit; **s. de desempleo** unemployment benefit

subsistencia *nf* subsistence

subsistir *vi* to subsist, to remain; *(vivir)* to live on, to survive

subsuelo *nm* subsoil

subte *nm RP Br* underground, *Br* tube, *US* subway

subterráneo,-a 1 *adj* underground

    2 *nm (túnel)* tunnel, underground passage

subtítulo *nm* subtitle

suburbano,-a *adj* suburban

suburbio *nm (barrio pobre)* slums; *(barrio periférico)* suburb

subvención *nf* subsidy

subvencionar *vt* to subsidize

subversión *nf* subversion

subversivo,-a *adj* subversive

subyacente *adj* underlying

subyugar [42] *vt* to subjugate

succionar *vt* to suck (in)

sucedáneo,-a *adj & nm* substitute

suceder 1 *vi* (a) *(ocurrir) (uso impers)* to happen, to occur; **¿qué sucede?** what's going on?, what's the matter? (b) *(seguir)* to follow, to succeed

    2 sucederse *vpr* to follow one another, to come one after the other

sucesión *nf* (a) *(serie)* series *sing*, succession (b) *(al trono)* succession (c) *(descendencia)* issue, heirs

sucesivamente *adv* **y así s.** and so on

sucesivo,-a *adj* following, successive; **en lo s.** from now on

suceso *nm (hecho)* event, occurrence; *(incidente)* incident; *Prensa* **sección de sucesos** accident and crime reports

---

      📖 Observa que la palabra inglesa **success** es un falso amigo y no es la traducción de la palabra española **suceso**. En inglés, **success** significa "éxito".

---

sucesor,-a *nm,f* successor

suciedad *nf* (a) *(dirt)* (b) *(calidad)* dirtiness

sucinto,-a *adj* concise, succinct

sucio,-a 1 *adj* dirty; **en s.** in rough; *Fig* **juego s.** foul play; *Fig* **negocio s.** shady business

    2 *adv* **jugar s.** to play dirty

sucre *nm Fin* = standard monetary unit of Ecuador

suculento,-a *adj* succulent, juicy

sucumbir *vi* to succumb, to yield

sucursal *nf Com & Fin* branch, branch office

sudaca *nmf Pey* South American

sudadera *nf* sweatshirt

Sudáfrica *n* South Africa

sudafricano,-a *adj & nm,f* South African

Sudamérica *n* South America

sudamericano,-a *adj & nm,f* South American

sudar *vt & vi* to sweat; *Fam Fig* **s. la gota gorda** to sweat blood

sudeste *nm* southeast

sudoeste *nm* southwest

sudor *nm* sweat; *Fig* **con el s. de mi frente** by the sweat of my brow

sudoroso,-a *adj* sweaty

Suecia *n* Sweden

sueco,-a 1 *adj* Swedish

    2 *nm,f (persona)* Swede

    3 *nm (idioma)* Swedish

suegra *nf* mother-in-law

suegro *nm* father-in-law; **mis suegros** my in-laws

suela *nf (de zapato)* sole

sueldo *nm* salary, wages

suelo *nm* (a) *(superficie)* ground; *(de interior)* floor; *Fig* **estar por los suelos** *(precios)* to be rock-bottom (b) *(territorio)* soil, land (c) *(campo, terreno)* land; **s. cultivable** arable land (d) *(de carretera)* surface

suelto,-a 1 *adj* (a) *(desatado)* undone (b) *Fig* **dinero s.** loose change; **hojas sueltas** loose sheets (of paper); **se venden sueltos** they are sold singly *o* separately *o* loose (c) *(en libertad)* free; *(huido)* at large (d) *(vestido, camisa)* loose, loose-fitting

    2 *nm (dinero)* (loose) change

sueño *nm* (a) *(sleep)* sleep; *(ganas de dormir)* sleepiness; **tener s.** to feel *o* be sleepy (b) *(cosa soñada)* dream

suero *nm Med* serum; *(de la leche)* whey

suerte *nf* (a) *(fortuna)* luck; **por s.** fortunately; **probar s.** to try one's luck; **tener s.** to be lucky; **¡que tengas s.!** good luck! (b) **echar algo a suertes** to draw lots for sth (c) *(destino)* fate, destiny (d) *Fml (género)* kind, sort, type

suéter *nm* sweater

suficiencia *nf* (a) *(engreimiento)* smugness, complacency (b) *Educ* **prueba de s.** final exam

suficiente 1 *adj (bastante)* sufficient, enough

    2 *nm Educ* pass

suficientemente *adv* sufficiently; **no es lo s. rico como para …** he isn't rich enough to …

sufijo *nm* suffix

sufragar [42] 1 *vt (gastos)* to pay, to defray

2 *vi Am* to vote (**por** for)

sufragio *nm Pol* suffrage; *(voto)* vote

sufrido,-a *adj (persona)* long-suffering

sufrimiento *nm* suffering

sufrir 1 *vi* to suffer; **s. del corazón** to have a heart condition

2 *vt* (**a**) *(accidente)* to have; *(operación)* to undergo; *(dificultades, cambios)* to experience; **s. dolores de cabeza** to suffer from headaches (**b**) *(aguantar)* to bear, to put up with

sugerencia *nf* suggestion

sugerente *adj* suggestive

sugerir [5] *vt* to suggest

sugestión *nf* suggestion

sugestionar *vt* to influence, to persuade

sugestivo,-a *adj* suggestive; *(atractivo)* alluring

suiche *nm Andes, Ven* switch

suicida 1 *nmf (persona)* suicide

2 *adj* suicidal

suicidarse *vpr* to commit suicide, to kill oneself

suicidio *nm* suicide

suite *nf* suite

Suiza *n* Switzerland

suizo,-a 1 *adj* Swiss

2 *nm,f (persona)* Swiss

3 *nm Culin* éclair

sujetador *nm (prenda)* bra, brassière

sujetar 1 *vt* (**a**) *(agarrar)* to hold (**b**) *(fijar)* to hold down, to hold in place (**c**) *Fig (someter)* to restrain

2 **sujetarse** *vpr (agarrarse)* to hold on

sujeto,-a 1 *nm* subject; *(individuo)* fellow, individual

2 *adj (atado)* fastened, secure; **s. a** *(sometido)* subject to, liable to

sulfato *nm* sulphate

sulfurar 1 *vt Fam (exasperar)* to exasperate, to infuriate

2 **sulfurarse** *vpr Fam* to lose one's temper, to blow one's top

sultán *nm* sultan

suma *nf* (**a**) *(cantidad)* sum, amount (**b**) *Mat* sum, addition; **s. total** sum total (**c**) **en s.** in short

sumamente *adv* extremely, highly

sumar 1 *vt Mat* to add, to add up

2 **sumarse** *vpr* **s. a** *(huelga)* to join; *(propuesta)* to support

sumario,-a 1 *adj* summary, brief; *Jur* **juicio s.** summary proceedings

2 *nm Jur* summary

sumarísimo,-a *adj Jur* swift, expeditious

sumergible *adj & nm* submersible

sumergir [57] 1 *vt* to submerge, to submerse; *(hundir)* to sink, to plunge

2 **sumergirse** *vpr* to submerge, to go underwater; *(hundirse)* to sink

sumidero *nm* drain, sewer

suministrar *vt* to supply, to provide; **s. algo a algn** to supply sb with sth

suministro *nm* supply

sumir *vt (hundir)* to sink, to plunge; *Fig* to plunge

sumiso,-a *adj* submissive, obedient

sumo,-a *adj (supremo)* supreme; **con s. cuidado** with extreme care; **a lo s.** at (the) most

suntuoso,-a *adj* sumptuous, magnificent

supe *pt indef de* **saber**

supeditar *vt* to subject (**a** to)

super- *pref* super-

súper *Fam* 1 *adj* super, great

2 *nm* (**a**) *(supermercado)* supermarket (**b**) *(gasolina)* 4-star

superado,-a *adj* outdated, obsolete

superar 1 *vt* (**a**) *(obstáculo etc)* to overcome, to surmount; *(prueba)* to pass (**b**) *(aventajar)* to surpass, to excel

2 **superarse** *vpr* to improve o better oneself

superávit *nm* surplus

superdotado,-a 1 *adj* exceptionally gifted

2 *nm,f* genius

superficial *adj* superficial

superficialidad *nf* superficiality

superficie *nf* surface; *(área)* area; *Com* **grandes superficies** hypermarkets

superfluo,-a *adj* superfluous

superhombre *nm* superman

superior 1 *adj* (**a**) *(posición)* top, upper (**b**) *(cantidad)* greater, higher, larger (**a** than) (**c**) *(calidad)* superior; **calidad s.** top quality (**d**) *Educ* higher

2 *nm (jefe)* superior

superioridad *nf* superiority

supermán *nm (pl* **supermanes**) superman

supermercado *nm* supermarket

superpoblación *nf* overpopulation

superponer [19] *vt* to superimpose

superpotencia *nf* superpower

superproducción *nf* (**a**) *Ind* overproduction (**b**) *Cin* mammoth production

supersónico,-a *adj* supersonic

superstición *nf* superstition

supersticioso,-a *adj* superstitious

supervisar *vt* to supervise

supervisor,-a *nm,f* supervisor

supervivencia *nf* survival

supino,-a adj (a) *(boca arriba)* supine, face up (b) *Fig (absoluto)* total absolute

súpito,-a adj Am sudden

suplantar vt to supplant, to take the place of

suplementario,-a adj supplementary, additional

suplemento nm supplement; **sin s.** without extra charge

suplente adj & nmf *(sustituto)* substitute, deputy; Dep substitute

supletorio,-a adj supplementary, additional; **cama supletoria** extra bed; **teléfono s.** extension

súplica nf entreaty, plea

suplicar [44] vt to beseech, to beg

suplicio nm *(tortura)* torture; Fig *(tormento)* torment

suplir vt (a) *(reemplazar)* to replace, to substitute (b) *(compensar)* to make up for

suponer [19] (pp supuesto) vt (a) *(significar)* to mean (b) *(implicar)* to entail (c) *(representar)* to account for (d) *(pensar)* to suppose; **supongo que sí** I suppose so; **supongamos que ...** let's assume that ... (e) *(adivinar)* to guess; **(me) lo suponía** I guessed as much

suposición nf supposition

supositorio nm suppository

supremacía nf supremacy

supremo,-a adj supreme

supresión nf *(de una ley etc)* abolition; *(de restricciones)* lifting; *(de una palabra)* deletion; *(de una rebelión)* suppression; *(omisión)* omission

suprimir vt (a) *(ley, impuesto)* to abolish; *(restricción)* to lift; *(palabra)* to delete, to take/leave out; *(rebelión)* to suppress (b) *(omitir)* to omit

supuesto,-a 1 adj (a) *(asumido)* supposed, assumed; **¡por s.!** of course!; **dar algo por s.** to take sth for granted (b) *(presunto)* alleged
    2 nm assumption; **en el s. de que** on the assumption that

supurar vi to suppurate, to fester

supuse pt indef de **suponer**

sur nm south

Suramérica n South America

suramericano,-a adj & nm,f South American

surcar [44] vt Agr to plough; Fig *(olas)* to cut through

surco nm Agr furrow; *(en un disco)* groove

sureño,-a 1 adj southern
    2 nm,f southerner

sureste nm = sudeste

surf(ing) nm Dep surfing

surfista nmf surfer

surgir [57] vi *(aparecer)* to arise, to emerge, to appear; *(problema, dificultad)* to crop up

suroeste nm = sudoeste

surrealista adj & nmf surrealist

surtido,-a 1 adj (a) *(variado)* assorted (b) **bien s.** well-stocked
    2 nm selection, assortment

surtidor nm spout; **s. de gasolina** Br petrol pump, US gas pump

surtir vt (a) to supply, to provide (b) **s. efecto** to have the desired effect

susceptible adj susceptible; *(quisquilloso)* oversensitive, touchy

suscitar vt *(provocar)* to cause, to provoke; *(rebelión)* to stir up, to arouse; *(interés etc)* to arouse

suscribir (pp suscrito) **1** vt (a) to subscribe to, to endorse (b) Fml *(firmar)* to sign
    2 suscribirse vpr to subscribe (**a** to)

suscripción nf subscription

susodicho,-a adj above-mentioned, aforesaid

suspender 1 vt (a) *(ley)* to suspend; *(reunión)* to adjourn (b) *(examen)* to fail; **me han suspendido** I've failed (the exam) (c) *(colgar)* to hang, to suspend
    2 vi Educ **he suspendido** I've failed

suspense nm suspense; **novela/película de s.** thriller

suspensión nf (a) hanging (up), suspension (b) Aut suspension (c) Fin & Jur **s. de pagos** suspension of payments

suspensivo,-a adj **puntos suspensivos** suspension points

suspenso nm (a) Educ fail (b) **en s.** *(asunto, trabajo)* pending; **estar en s.** to be pending

suspicacia nf suspiciousness

suspicaz adj suspicious; *(desconfiado)* distrustful

suspirar vi to sigh

suspiro nm sigh

sustancia nf substance

sustancial adj (a) substantial (b) *(fundamental)* essential, fundamental

sustantivo,-a 1 adj substantive
    2 nm Ling noun

sustentar vt (a) *(peso)* to support (b) *(familia)* to maintain, to support (c) *(teoría)* to support, to defend

sustento nm (a) *(alimento)* sustenance, food (b) *(apoyo)* support

sustitución nf substitution, replacement

sustituir [37] vt to substitute, to replace

sustituto,-a nm,f substitute, stand-in

susto *nm* fright, scare; **llevarse** *o* **darse un s.** to get a fright

sustraer [25] *vt* (**a**) *Mat* to subtract (**b**) *(robar)* to steal, to remove

sustrato *nm* substratum

susurrar *vt* to whisper

susurro *nm* whisper

sutil *adj* (**a**) *(diferencia, pregunta)* subtle (**b**) *(delgado)* thin, fine (**c**) *(aroma)* delicate

sutileza *nf* (**a**) *(dicho)* subtlety (**b**) *(finura)* fineness

suyo,-a *adj & pron pos (de él)* his; *(de ella)* hers; *(de usted, ustedes)* yours; *(de animal o cosa)* its; *(de ellos, ellas)* theirs; **los zapatos no son suyos** the shoes aren't hers; **varios amigos suyos** several friends of his/hers/yours/theirs; *Fam* **es muy s.** he's very aloof; *Fam* **hacer de las suyas** to be up to one's tricks; *Fam* **ir (cada uno) a lo s.** to mind one's own business; *Fam* **salirse con la suya** to get one's (own) way

svástica *nf* swastika

T, t [te] *nf (la letra)* T, t

t (*abr* **tonelada(s)**) t

tabacalero,-a 1 *nm,f (vendedor)* tobacco trader

2 *nf* La Tabacalera = Spanish state tobacco monopoly

tabaco *nm* (**a**) *(planta, hoja)* tobacco; **t. rubio** Virginia tobacco (**b**) *(cigarrillos)* cigarettes

tábano *nm* horsefly

tabaquismo *nm* nicotine poisoning

tabarra *nf Fam* nuisance, bore; **dar la t.** to go on and on

tabasco® *nm* Tabasco® sauce

taberna *nf* pub, bar; *(antiguamente)* tavern

tabernero,-a *nm,f* publican; *(hombre)* landlord; *(mujer)* landlady

tabique *nm* (**a**) *(pared)* partition (wall) (**b**) *Anat* **t. nasal** nasal wall

tabla *nf* (**a**) *(board)* board; *Dep* **t. de surf** surfboard; *Dep* **t. de windsurf** sailboard (**b**) *(de vestido)* pleat (**c**) *Mat* table (**d**) **tablas** *(en ajedrez)* stalemate, draw; **quedar en tablas** *(juego)* to end in a draw (**e**) *Taurom* **tablas** fence (**f**) *Teatro* **las tablas** the stage; *Fig* **tener (muchas) tablas** to be an old hand

tablado *nm* (**a**) *(plataforma)* wooden platform (**b**) *Teatro* stage

tablao *nm Fam* = flamenco bar or show

tablero *nm* (**a**) *(tablón)* panel, board; **t. de mandos** *(de coche)* dash(board) (**b**) *(en juegos)* board; **t. de ajedrez** chessboard

tableta *nf (de chocolate)* bar

tablón *nm* plank; *(en construcción)* beam; **t. de anuncios** *Br* noticeboard, *US* bulletin board

tabú *adj & nm (pl* **tabúes**) taboo

tabular *vt* to tabulate

taburete *nm* stool

tacaño,-a 1 *adj* mean, stingy

2 *nm,f* miser

tacatá, tacataca *nm* baby-walker

tacha *nf (defecto)* flaw, defect; **sin t.** flawless, without blemish

tachar *vt* (**a**) to cross out (**b**) *Fig* **t. de** to accuse of

tachero *nm RP Fam (de taxi)* taxi driver

tacho *nm Am* bucket

tachón *nm (borrón)* crossing out

tachuela *nf* tack, stud

tácito,-a *adj* tacit

taciturno,-a *adj* (**a**) *(callado)* taciturn (**b**) *(triste)* sullen

taco *nm* (**a**) plug; *(de billetes)* wad; *(de bota de fútbol)* stud; *(en billar)* cue (**b**) *(cubo) (de jamón, queso)* cube, piece (**c**) *Culin (tortilla de maíz)* taco, = rolled-up tortilla pancake (**d**) *Fam (palabrota)* swearword (**e**) *Fam (lío)* mess, muddle; **armarse** *o* **hacerse un t.** to get all mixed up (**f**) **me gusta un t.** I like it a lot (**g**) *Fam* **tacos** *(años)* years

tacón *nm* heel; **zapatos de t.** high-heeled shoes

taconeo *nm (pisada)* heel-tapping; *(golpe)* stamping with the heels

táctica *nf* tactics

táctico,-a *adj* tactical

táctil *adj* tactile; **pantalla t.** touch screen

tacto *nm* (**a**) *(sentido)* touch (**b**) *Fig (delicadeza)* tact; **tener t.** to be tactful

taekwondo *nm* tae kwon do

tafetán *nm* taffeta

tahúr *nm* cardsharp

tailandés,-esa 1 *adj* Thai

2 *nm,f (persona)* Thai; **los tailandeses** the Thai *o* Thais

3 *nm (idioma)* Thai

Tailandia *n* Thailand

taimado,-a *adj* sly, crafty

tajada *nf* (**a**) *(slice)* slice; *Fig* **sacar** *o* **llevarse t.** to take one's share (**b**) *Fam (borrachera)* drunkenness

tajante *adj* incisive

Tajo *n* **el T.** the Tagus

tal 1 *adj* (**a**) *(semejante)* such; *(más sustantivo singular contable)* such a; **en tales condiciones** in such conditions; **nunca dije t. cosa** I never said such a thing (**b**) *(indeterminado)* such and such; **t. día y a t. hora** such and such a day and at such and such a time (**c**) *(persona)* person called ...; **te llamó una t. Amelia** someone called Amelia phoned you (**d**) (*locuciones*) **t. vez** perhaps, maybe; **como si t. cosa** as if nothing had happened

2 *adv* (**a**) (*así*) just; **t. cual** just as it is; **t. (y) como** just as

(**b**) **¿qué t.?** how are things?; **¿qué t. ese vino?** how do you find this wine?

3 *conj* as; **con t. (de) que** (+ *subjunctive*) so long as, provided

4 *pron* (*cosa*) something; (*persona*) someone, somebody; **t. para cual** two of a kind; **y t. y cual** and so on

tala *nf* tree felling

taladradora *nf* drill

taladrar *vt* to drill; (*pared*) to bore through; (*papeles*) to punch

taladro *nm* (**a**) (*herramienta*) drill (**b**) (*agujero*) hole

talante *nm* (**a**) (*carácter*) disposition (**b**) (*voluntad*) **de buen t.** willingly; **de mal t.** unwillingly, reluctantly

talar *vt* (*árboles*) to fell, to cut down

talco *nm* talc; **polvos de t.** talcum powder

talega *nf* bag, sack

talego *nm* (**a**) long bag, long sack (**b**) *Fam* (*cárcel*) clink, hole (**c**) *Fam* (*mil pesetas*) = 1,000 peseta note

talento *nm* talent

Talgo *nm* = fast passenger train

talismán *nm* talisman, lucky charm

talla *nf* (**a**) (*de prenda*) size; **¿qué t. usas?** what size are you? (**b**) (*estatura*) height; *Fig* stature; *Fig* **dar la t.** to make the grade (**c**) (*escultura*) carving, sculpture (**d**) (*tallado*) cutting, carving

tallado *nm* (*de madera*) carving; (*de piedras preciosas*) cutting; (*de metales*) engraving

tallar *vt* (**a**) (*madera, piedra*) to carve, to shape; (*piedras preciosas*) to cut; (*metales*) to engrave (**b**) (*medir*) to measure the height of

tallarines *nmpl* tagliatelle

talle *nm* (**a**) (*cintura*) waist (**b**) (*cuerpo*) (*de hombre*) build, physique; (*de mujer*) figure, shape

taller *nm* (**a**) (*obrador*) workshop; *Aut* **t. de reparaciones** garage (**b**) *Ind* factory, mill

tallo *nm* stem, stalk

talón *nm* (**a**) (*del pie*) heel (**b**) (*cheque*) cheque

ℓ Observa que la palabra inglesa **talon** es un falso amigo y no es la traducción de la palabra española **talón**. En inglés, **talon** significa "garra".

talonario *nm* (*de cheques*) cheque book;

(*de billetes*) book of tickets

tamal *nm* (*comida*) tamale, = steamed maize dumpling with savoury or sweet filling, wrapped in maize husks or a banana leaf

tamaño,-a 1 *adj* such a big, so big a

2 *nm* size; **de gran t.** large; **del t. de** as large as, as big as

tamarindo *nm* tamarind

tambalearse *vpr* (*persona*) to stagger; (*mesa*) to wobble; *Fig* to teeter

tambero *nm* *Am* (*mesonero*) innkeeper, landlord

también *adv* (*igualmente*) too, also, as well; **tú t. puedes venir** you can come too; **¿lo harás? yo t.** are you going to do it? so am I

tambo *nm* *RP* (*granja*) dairy farm

tambor *nm* (**a**) (*Mús, de lavadora, de freno*) drum (**b**) *Anat* eardrum

Támesis *n* **el T.** the Thames

tamiz *nm* sieve

tamizar [40] *vt* to sieve

tampoco *adv* (**a**) (*en afirmativas*) nor, neither; **Juan no vendrá y María t.** Juan won't come and neither will Maria; **no lo sé – yo t.** I don't know – neither do I (**b**) (*en negativas*) either, not ... either; **la Bolsa no sube, pero t. baja** the stock market isn't going up, but it's not going down either

tampón *nm* tampon

tan *adv* (**a**) such; (*más sustantivo singular contable*) such a; **es t. listo** he's such a clever fellow; **no me gusta t. dulce** I don't like it so sweet; **¡qué gente t. agradable!** such nice people!; **¡qué vestido t. bonito!** what a beautiful dress! (**b**) (*comparativo*) **t. ... como as ... as**; **t. alto como tú** as tall as you (are) (**c**) (*consecutivo*) **so ... (that)**; **iba t. deprisa que no lo ví** he was going so fast that I couldn't see him (**d**) **t. siquiera** at least; **t. sólo** only

tanda *nf* (*conjunto*) batch, lot; (*serie*) series *sing*; **por tandas** in groups

tándem *nm* tandem

tanga *nm* tanga

tangente *nf* tangent; *Fig* **salirse** *o* **escaparse por la t.** to go off at a tangent

Tánger *n* Tangier

tangible *adj* tangible

tango *nm* tango

tanguería *nf* = nightclub for tango dancing

tanguero,-a *nm,f* (*aficionado*) tango enthusiast

tanque *nm* tank

tantear 1 *vt* (**a**) *Fig* **t. a algn** to sound sb

out; **t. el terreno** to see how the land lies
(**b**) *(calcular)* to estimate, to guess
2 *vi Dep* to (keep) score

tanteo *nm* (**a**) *(cálculo)* estimate, guess
(**b**) *Dep* score

tanto,-a 1 *nm* (**a**) *(punto)* point
(**b**) *(cantidad imprecisa)* so much, a certain amount; **t. por ciento** percentage
(**c**) **un t.** a bit; **la casa es un t. pequeña** the house is rather *o* somewhat small
(**d**) **estar al t.** *(informado)* to be informed; *(pendiente)* to be on the lookout
2 *adj* (**a**) (+ *singular*) so much; (+ *plural*) so many; **no le des t. dinero** don't give him so much money; **¡ha pasado t. tiempo!** it's been so long!; **no comas tantas manzanas** don't eat so many apples
(**b**) **cincuenta y tantas personas** fifty odd people; **en el año sesenta y tantos** in nineteen sixty something
(**c**) **t. como** as much as; **tantos,-as como** as many as
3 *pron* (**a**) (+ *singular*) so much; **otro t.** as much again, the same again; **no es** *o* **hay para t.** it's not that bad
(**b**) (+ *plural*) so many; **otros tantos** as many again; **uno de tantos** run-of-the-mill; *Fam* **a las tantas** very late, at an unearthly hour
4 *adv* (**a**) *(cantidad)* so much; **t. mejor/peor** so much the better/worse; **t. más cuanto que** all the more so because
(**b**) *(tiempo)* so long
(**c**) *(frecuencia)* so often
(**d**) **t. ... como** both ... and; **t. tú como yo** both you and I; **t. si vienes como si no** whether you come or not
(**e**) *(locuciones)* **por lo t.** therefore; **¡y t.!** oh yes!, and how!

tañer *vt* to play

tapa *nf* (**a**) *(cubierta)* lid; *Andes, RP (de botella)* top; *(de libro)* cover; *(de zapato)* heelplate; *Aut (de cilindro)* head (**b**) *(aperitivo)* appetizer, snack

tapadera *nf* *(tapa)* cover, lid; *Fig* cover, front

tapadillo *nm* **hacer algo de t.** to do sth secretly

tapado *nm CSur (abrigo)* overcoat

tapar 1 *vt* (**a**) to cover; *(botella etc)* to put the lid/top on; *(con ropas o mantas)* to wrap up (**b**) *(ocultar)* to hide; *(vista)* to block (**c**) *(encubrir)* to cover up
2 taparse *vpr (cubrirse)* to cover oneself; *(abrigarse)* to wrap up

taparrabos *nm inv* loincloth

tapete *nm* (table) cover; *Fig* **poner algo sobre el t.** to table sth

tapia *nf* garden wall

tapiar [43] *vt* (**a**) *(área)* to wall off (**b**) *(puerta, ventana etc)* to wall, to close up

tapicería *nf* (**a**) tapestry; *(de muebles, coche)* upholstery (**b**) *(tienda)* upholsterer's shop/workshop

tapioca *nf* tapioca

tapiz *nm* tapestry

tapizar [40] *vt* to upholster

tapón *nm* (**a**) *(de lavabo etc)* stopper, plug; *(de botella)* cap, cork; **t. de rosca** screw-on cap (**b**) *(de oídos)* earplug (**c**) *(en baloncesto)* block (**d**) *Aut* traffic jam (**e**) *Am (plomo)* fuse

taponar 1 *vt* (**a**) *(tubería, hueco)* to plug (**b**) *Med (herida)* to tampon
2 taponarse *vpr* **se me han taponado los oídos** my ears are blocked up

taquería *nf Méx (quiosco)* taco stall; *(restaurante)* taco restaurant

taquigrafía *nf* shorthand

taquígrafo,-a *nm,f* shorthand writer

taquilla *nf* (**a**) ticket office, booking office; *Cin & Teatro* box-office; **un éxito de t.** a box-office success (**b**) *(recaudación)* takings (**c**) *(armario)* locker

taquillero,-a 1 *adj* popular; **película taquillera** box-office hit
2 *nm,f* booking *o* ticket clerk

tara *nf* (**a**) *(peso)* tare (**b**) *(defecto)* defect, fault

tarántula *nf* tarantula

tararear *vt* to hum

tardanza *nf* delay

tardar 1 *vt (llevar tiempo)* to take; **¿cuánto va a t.?** how long will it take?; **tardé dos horas en venir** it took me two hours to get here
2 *vi (demorar)* to take long; **si tarda mucho, me voy** if it takes much longer, I'm going; **no tardes** don't be long; **a más t.** at the latest
3 tardarse *vpr* **¿cuánto se tarda en llegar?** how long does it take to get there?

tarde 1 *nf* (**a**) *(hasta las cinco)* afternoon (**b**) *(después de las cinco)* evening (**c**) **la t. noche** late evening
2 *adv* (**a**) late; **siento llegar t.** sorry I'm late (**b**) *(locuciones)* **de t. en t.** very rarely, not very often; **(más) t. o (más) temprano** sooner or later

tardío,-a *adj* late, belated

tardo,-a *adj* slow

tarea *nf* job, task; **tareas** *(de ama de casa)* housework; *(de estudiante)* homework

tarifa *nf* (**a**) *(precio)* tariff, rate; *(en transportes)* fare (**b**) *(lista de precios)* price list

tarima *nf* platform, dais

tarjeta *nf* card; **t. postal** postcard; **t. de crédito** credit card; **t. de visita** *Br* visiting card, *US* calling card; *Informát* **t. perforada** punch o punched card

tarraconense 1 *adj* of/from Tarragona

2 *nmf* person from Tarragona

tarro *nm* (**a**) *(vasija)* jar, pot, tub (**b**) *Fam (cabeza)* bonce (**c**) *Am (lata)* tin, can

tarta *nf* tart, pie

tartamudear *vi* to stutter, to stammer

tartamudo,-a 1 *adj* stuttering, stammering

2 *nm,f* stutterer, stammerer

tartana *nf Fam (coche viejo)* banger, heap

tártaro,-a *adj* **salsa tártara** tartar sauce

tartera *nf* (**a**) *(fiambrera)* lunch box (**b**) *(cazuela)* baking tin

tarugo *nm* (**a**) *(de madera)* lump of wood (**b**) *Fam (persona)* blockhead

tarumba *adj Fam* crazy, mad; **estar t.** to be bonkers

tasa *nf* (**a**) *(precio)* fee; **tasas académicas** course fees (**b**) *(impuesto)* tax; **tasas de aeropuerto** airport tax (**c**) *(índice)* rate; **t. de natalidad/mortalidad** birth/death rate (**d**) *(valoración)* valuation, appraisal

tasación *nf* valuation

tasador,-a *nm,f* valuer

tasar *vt* (**a**) *(valorar)* to value; **t. una casa en 10 millones de pesetas** to value a house at 10 million pesetas (**b**) *(poner precio)* to set o fix the price of

tasca *nf Fam* bar, pub

tata 1 *nf (niñera)* nanny

2 *nm Am Fam (papá)* dad, daddy, *US* pop

tatarabuelo,-a *nm,f* great-great-grandfather, *f* great-great-grandmother; **tatarabuelos** great-great-grandparents

tataranieto,-a *nm,f* great-great-grandson, *f* great-great-granddaughter; **tataranietos** great-great-grandchildren

tatuaje *nm* tattoo

tatuar [30] *vt* to tattoo

taurino,-a *adj* bullfighting

Tauro *nm* Taurus

tauromaquia *nf* tauromachy, (art of) bullfighting

taxativo,-a *adj* categorical

taxi *nm* taxi

taxímetro *nm* taximeter, clock

taxista *nmf* taxi driver

taza *nf* (**a**) *(recipiente)* cup; **una t. de café** coffee cup; *(contenido)* a cup of coffee (**b**) *(de retrete)* bowl

tazón *nm* bowl

te *pron pers* (**a**) *(complemento directo)* you; *(complemento indirecto)* (to/for) you; **no quiero verte** I don't want to see you; **te compraré uno** I'll buy one for you, I'll buy you one; **te lo dije** I told you so (**b**) *(reflexivo)* yourself; **lávate** wash yourself; *(sin traducción)* **bébetelo todo** drink it up; **no te vayas** don't go

té *nm* (*pl* **tés**) tea; **té con limón** lemon tea

tea *nf* torch

teatral *adj* (**a**) **grupo t.** theatre company; **obra t.** play (**b**) *Fig (teatrero)* theatrical

teatrero,-a *adj* theatrical

teatro *nm* (**a**) theatre; **obra de t.** play; **autor de t.** playwright (**b**) *Lit* drama

tebeo *nm* children's comic

techar *vt* to roof

techo *nm (de habitación)* ceiling; *(tejado)* roof; *Aut* **t. corredizo** sun roof

tecla *nf* key; *Fig* **dar en la t.** to get it right

teclado *nm* keyboard; *Informát* **t. expandido** expanded keyboard

teclear 1 *vt* to key in

2 *vi* to drum with one's fingers

técnica *nf* (**a**) *(tecnología)* technology (**b**) *(método)* technique (**c**) *(habilidad)* skill

técnico,-a 1 *adj* technical

2 *nm,f* technician, technical expert

tecnicolor® *nm* Technicolor®

tecno- *pref* techno-

tecnócrata *nmf* technocrat

tecnología *nf* technology

tecnológico,-a *adj* technological

tecolote *nm CAm, Méx (búho)* owl

tedio *nm* tedium, boredom

tedioso,-a *adj* tedious, boring

teja *nf Constr* tile; *Fam Fig* **a toca t.** on the nail

tejado *nm* roof

tejanos *nmpl* jeans

tejemaneje *nm Fam* (**a**) *(actividad)* bustle, fuss (**b**) *(maquinación)* intrigue, scheming

tejer *vt (en el telar)* to weave; *(hacer punto)* to knit; *(telaraña)* to spin; *Fig (plan)* to plot, to scheme

tejido *nm* (**a**) fabric; **t. de punto** knitted fabric (**b**) *Anat* tissue

tejo *nm Fam* **tirar los tejos** a algn to make a play for sb

tejón *nm* badger

tel. *(abr* **teléfono**) tel.

tela *nf* (**a**) *Tex* material, fabric, cloth; *(de la leche)* skin; **t. de araña** cobweb; **t. metálica** gauze (**b**) *Fam (dinero)* dough (**c**) *Arte* canvas (**d**) *Fig* **poner en t. de juicio** to question; *Fig* **tiene mucha t.** it's not an easy thing

telar *nm Tex* loom

telaraña *nf* cobweb, spider's web

tele *nf Fam* telly, TV

telearrastre *nm* ski lift

telebanca *nf* telephone banking, home banking

telebasura *nf Fam* junkTV

telecabina *nf* cable car

telecomunicaciones *nfpl* telecommunications

telediario *nm TV* television news bulletin

teledirigido,-a *adj* remote-controlled

telefax *nm* telefax, fax

teleférico *nm* cable car/railway

telefilm, telefilme *nm* TV film

telefonazo *nm* **dar un t. (a algn)** to give (sb) a ring

telefonear *vt & vi* to telephone, to phone

telefonía *nf* **t. móvil** mobile phones

telefónica *nf* **Compañía T.** ≃ British Telecom

telefónico,-a *adj* telephone; **llamada telefónica** telephone call

telefonista *nmf* (telephone) operator

teléfono *nm* telephone, phone; **t. portátil** portable telephone; **t. móvil** car phone; **está hablando por t.** she's on the phone; **te llamó por t.** she phoned you

telegrafiar [29] *vt* to telegraph, to wire

telegráfico,-a *adj* telegraphic; **giro t.** giro, money order

telégrafo *nm* (a) telegraph (b) **telégrafos** post office

telegrama *nm* telegram, cable

teleimpresor *nm*, **teleimpresora** *nf* teleprinter

telele *nm Fam* **darle a uno un t.** to have a fit

telemando *nm* remote control (unit)

telenovela *nf* television serial

teleobjetivo *nm* telephoto lens *sing*

telepático,-a *adj* telepathic

telescopio *nm* telescope

teleserie *nf* television series *sing*

telesilla *nm* chair lift

telespectador,-a *nm,f* TV viewer

telesquí *nm* ski lift

teletexto *nm* teletext

teletienda *nf* home shopping programme

teletipo *nm* teleprinter

teletrabajador,-a *nm,f* teleworker

teletrabajo *nm* teleworking

televidente *nmf* TV viewer

televisar *vt* to televise

televisión *nf* (a) *(sistema)* television (b) *Fam (aparato)* television set; **t. en color/en blanco y negro** colour/black-and-white television; **t. digital** digital television;

t. por cable cable television; **ver la t.** to watch television

televisivo,-a *adj* television; **espacio t.** television programme

televisor *nm* television set

télex *nm inv* telex

telón *nm Teatro* curtain; *Pol & Hist* **t. de acero** Iron Curtain; **t. de fondo** *Teatro* backdrop; *Fig* background

telonero,-a *adj* **(grupo) t.** support band

tema *nm* (a) *(asunto)* topic, subject; *(de examen)* subject; **temas de actualidad** current affairs (b) *Mús* theme

temario *nm* *(de examen)* programme

temática *nf* subject matter

temático,-a *adj* thematic

temblar [1] *vi* *(de frío)* to shiver; *(de miedo)* to tremble **(de** with); *(voz)* to quiver; *(pulso)* to shake

tembleque *nm Fam* shaking fit

temblón,-ona *adj Fam* trembling, shaky

temblor *nm* tremor, shudder; **t. de tierra** earth tremor

tembloroso,-a, tembloso,-a *adj* shaking; *(voz)* quivering; *(de frío)* shivering; *(de miedo)* trembling; **manos temblorosas** shaky hands

temer 1 *vt* to fear, to be afraid of; **temo que esté muerto** I fear he's dead; **temo que no podrá recibirte** I'm afraid (that) he won't be able to see you

2 *vi* to be afraid

3 temerse *vpr* to fear, to be afraid; **¡me lo temía!** I was afraid this would happen!

temerario,-a *adj* reckless, rash

temeridad *nf* (a) *(actitud)* temerity, rashness (b) *(acto temerario)* reckless act

temeroso,-a *adj* (a) fearful, timid (b) *(temible)* frightful

temible *adj* fearful, frightful

temor *nm* (a) fear (b) *(recelo)* worry, apprehension

témpano *nm* ice floe

temperamental *adj* temperamental

temperamento *nm* temperament; **tener t.** to have a strong character

temperatura *nf* temperature

tempestad *nf* storm; *Fig* turmoil, uproar

tempestuoso,-a *adj* stormy, tempestuous

templado,-a *adj* (a) *(agua)* lukewarm; *(clima)* mild, temperate (b) *Mús (afinado)* tuned

templanza *nf* moderation, restraint

templar *vt* (a) to moderate (b) *(algo frío)* to warm up; *(algo caliente)* to cool down (c) *Mús (instrumento)* to tune (d) *Téc (metal)* to temper

temple nm (a) (fortaleza) boldness, courage (b) Arte tempera

templete nm bandstand

templo nm temple

temporada nf (a) season; **t. alta** high o peak season; **t. baja** low o off season (b) (período) period, time; **por temporadas** on and off

temporal 1 adj temporary, provisional
2 nm storm

temporario,-a adj Am temporary

temporero,-a nm,f seasonal o temporary worker

tempranero,-a adj (a) (persona) early-rising (b) (cosecha) early

temprano,-a adj & adv early

tenacidad nf (a) (perseverancia) tenacity, perseverance (b) (de metal) tensile strength

tenacillas nfpl (para pelo) curling tongs

tenaz adj tenacious

tenaza nf, **tenazas** nfpl (herramienta) pliers, pincers; (para el fuego) tongs

tendedero nm clothes line, drying place

tendencia nf tendency

tendencioso,-a adj tendentious, biased

tender [3] **1** vt (a) (mantel etc) to spread out; (para secar) to hang out (b) Am (cama) to make; (mesa) to set, to lay (c) (red) to cast; (puente) to build; (vía, cable) to lay; (trampa) to lay, to set (d) (mano) to stretch o hold out (e) (tumbar) to lay
2 vi to tend (a to), to have a tendency (a to)
3 tenderse vpr to lie down, to stretch out

tenderete nm (puesto) market stall

tendero,-a nm,f shopkeeper

tendido nm (a) (de vía, cable) laying; (de puente) construction; **t. eléctrico** electrical installation (b) Taurom (asientos) = front tiers of seats

tendón nm tendon, sinew

tenebroso,-a adj (sombrío) dark, gloomy; (siniestro) sinister, shady

tenedor nm fork

teneduría nf **t. de libros** bookkeeping

tenencia nf Jur **t. ilícita de armas** illegal possession of arms

tener [24] **1** vt (a) to have, to have got; **tenemos un examen** we've got o we have an exam; **va a t. un niño** she's going to have a baby, she's expecting; **¡ahí (lo) tienes!** here you are!
(b) (poseer) to own, to possess
(c) (sostener) to hold; **tenme el bolso un momento** hold my bag a minute; **ten, es para ti** take this o here you are, it's for you
(d) **t. calor/frío** to be hot/cold; **t. cariño**

a algn to be fond of sb; **t. miedo** to be frightened
(e) (edad) to be; **tiene dieciocho (años)** he's eighteen (years old)
(f) Am (llevar) **tengo tres años aquí** I've been here for three years
(g) (medida) **la casa tiene 100 metros cuadrados** the house is 100 square metres
(h) (contener) to hold, to contain
(i) (mantener) to keep; **me tuvo despierto toda la noche** he kept me up all night
(j) **t. por** (considerar) to consider, to think; **me tienen por estúpido** they think I'm a fool; **ten por seguro que lloverá** you can be sure it'll rain
(k) **t. que** to have (got) to; **tengo que irme** I must leave; **tienes/tendrías que verlo** you must/should see it
2 tenerse vpr (a) **t. en pie** to stand (up)
(b) **t. por** (considerarse) to think o consider oneself; **se tiene por muy inteligente** he thinks he's very intelligent

tenga subj pres de tener

tengo indic pres de tener

teniente nm (a) Mil lieutenant (b) **t. (de) alcalde** deputy mayor

tenis nm tennis

tenista nmf tennis player

tenor [1] nm Mús tenor

tenor [2] nm **a t. de** according to

tensar vt (cable etc) to tighten; (arco) to draw

tensión nf (a) tension; **en t.** tense (b) Elec tension, voltage (c) Med **t. arterial** blood pressure; **t. nerviosa** nervous strain (d) Téc stress

tenso,-a adj (a) (cuerda, cable) tense, taut (b) (persona) tense; (relaciones) strained

tentación nf temptation

tentáculo nm tentacle

tentador,-a adj tempting

tentar [1] vt (a) (palpar) to feel, to touch (b) (incitar) to tempt

tentativa nf attempt; Jur **t. de asesinato** attempted murder

tentempié nm Fam (pl **tentempiés**) (a) (comida) snack, bite (b) (juguete) tumbler

tenue adj (a) (luz, sonido) subdued, faint (b) (delgado) thin, light

teñir [6] **1** vt (a) (pelo etc) to dye (b) Fig to tinge with
2 teñirse vpr **t. el pelo** to dye one's hair

teocalli nm Hist = Mexican pyramid

teología nf theology

teorema nm theorem

teoría nf theory; **en t.** theoretically

teórico,-a *adj* theoretical

teorizar [40] *vi* to theorize (**sobre** on)

tepache *nm* = mildly alcoholic Mexican drink made from fermented pineapple peelings and unrefined sugar

tequila *nm* tequila

terapeuta *nmf* therapist

terapia *nf* therapy

tercer *adj* third; **el t. mundo** the third world

tercerización *nf Am Com* outsourcing

tercermundista *adj* third-world

tercero,-a 1 *adj* third

> **Tercer** is used instead of **tercero** before masculine singular nouns (e.g. **el tercer piso** the third floor).

2 *nm,f (de una serie)* third; **a la tercera va la vencida** third time lucky

3 *nm (mediador)* mediator; *Jur* third party

terceto *nm Mús* trio

terciar [43] 1 *vi* (a) *(mediar)* to mediate, to arbitrate (b) *(participar)* to take part, to participate

2 terciarse *vpr* **si se tercia** should the occasion arise

terciario,-a *adj* tertiary

tercio *nm* (a) *(parte)* (one) third (b) *(de cerveza)* = medium-sized bottle of beer (c) *Taurom* stage, part *(of a bullfight)*

terciopelo *nm* velvet

terco,-a *adj* stubborn, obstinate

tereré *nm Arg, Par (mate)* = refreshing drink made from maté in cold water with lemon juice

tergiversar *vt (verdad)* to distort; *(palabras)* to twist

termal *adj* thermal

termas *nfpl (baños)* spa, hot baths *o* springs

térmico,-a *adj* thermal; **central térmica** coal-fired power station

terminación *nf* completion

terminal 1 *adj* terminal

2 *nf* (a) *(de aeropuerto)* terminal; *(de autobús)* terminus (b) *Elec & Informát* terminal

terminante *adj* (a) *(categórico)* categorical, final (b) *(dato, resultado)* conclusive

terminantemente *adv* categorically; **t. prohibido** strictly forbidden

terminar 1 *vt (acabar)* to finish, to complete; *(completamente)* to finish off

2 *vi* (a) *(acabarse)* to finish, to end; **termina en seis** it ends with a six; **no termina de convencerse** he still isn't quite

convinced (b) *(ir a parar)* to end up (**en** in); **terminó por comprarlo** he ended up buying it (c) **t. con** *(eliminar)* to put an end to

3 terminarse *vpr* (a) to finish, to end, to be over (b) *(vino, dinero etc)* to run out

término *nm* (a) *(final)* end, finish (b) *(palabra)* term, word; **en otros términos** in other words; **en términos generales** generally speaking (c) **t. municipal** district (d) **por t. medio** on average (e) *Fig* **en último t.** as a last resort

terminología *nf* terminology

termo *nm* Thermos® (flask), flask

termodinámico,-a *adj* thermodynamic

termómetro *nm* thermometer

termonuclear *adj* thermonuclear

termostato *nm* thermostat

ternera *nf* calf; *(carne)* veal

ternero *nm* calf

terno *nm Andes, Méx (traje)* three-piece suit

ternura *nf* tenderness

terquedad *nf* stubbornness, obstinacy

terracota *nf* terracotta

terraja *adj RP Fam (persona)* flashy; *(cosa)* tacky, kitsch

terrajada *nf RP Fam* tacky thing/act

terral *nm Am (polvareda)* dust cloud

Terranova *n* Newfoundland

terraplén *nm* embankment

terráqueo,-a *adj* **globo t.** *(tierra)* (the) earth; *(esfera)* globe

terrateniente *nmf* landowner

terremoto *nm* earthquake

terrenal *adj* **un paraíso t.** a heaven on earth

terreno *nm* (a) *(tierra)* (piece of) land, ground; *Geol* terrain; *(campo)* field; **ganar/perder t.** to gain/lose ground (b) *Dep* field, ground (c) *Fig* field, sphere

terrestre *adj* (a) *(de la tierra)* terrestrial, earthly (b) *(por tierra)* by land; **por vía t.** by land

terrible *adj* terrible, awful

terrícola *nmf (en ciencia ficción)* earthling

terrier *nm* terrier

territorio *nm* territory

terrón *nm (de azúcar)* lump; *(de tierra)* clod

terror *nm* terror; *Cin* horror

terrorífico,-a *adj* terrifying, frightening

terrorismo *nm* terrorism

terrorista *adj & nmf* terrorist

terroso,-a *adj (color)* earth-coloured

terruño *nm (terreno)* piece of land; *(patria chica)* homeland, native land

terso,-a *adj* smooth

tersura *nf* smoothness

tertulia *nf* get-together; **t. literaria** literary gathering

tesina *nf* first degree dissertation

tesis *nf inv* thesis; *(opinión)* view, theory

tesón *nm* tenacity, firmness

tesorero,-a *nm,f* treasurer

tesoro *nm* (a) treasure (b) *(erario)* exchequer; **T. Público** Treasury

test *nm* test

testaferro *nm* front man

testamentario,-a *Jur* **1** *adj* testamentary **2** *nm,f* executor

testamento *nm* (a) *Jur* will; **hacer** *o* **otorgar t.** to make *o* draw up one's will (b) *Rel* Testament

testar *vi* to make *o* draw up one's will

testarudo,-a *adj* stubborn, obstinate

testear *vt CSur* to test

testículo *nm* testicle

testificar [44] *vt* to testify

testigo 1 *nmf* witness; *Jur* **t. de cargo/descargo** witness for the prosecution/defence; *Jur* **t. ocular/presencial** eyewitness; *Rel* **Testigos de Jehová** Jehovah's Witnesses **2** *nm Dep* baton

testimoniar [43] *vt* (a) *(dar testimonio)* to testify to, to attest to (b) *(mostrar)* to show

testimonio *nm Jur* testimony; *(prueba)* evidence, proof

teta *nf Fam* (a) tit, boob; **niño de t.** breastfeeding baby (b) *(de vaca)* udder

tétanos *nm* tetanus

tetera *nf* teapot

tetero *nm Col, Ven (biberón)* baby's bottle

tetilla *nf* (a) *Anat* man's nipple (b) *(de biberón)* (rubber) teat

tetina *nf* (rubber) teat

tétrico,-a *adj* gloomy, dull

textil *adj & nm* textile

texto *nm* text; **libro de t.** textbook

textual *adj* textual; *(exacto)* literal; **en palabras textuales** literally

textura *nf Tex* texture; *(en minerales)* structure

tez *nf* complexion

ti *pron pers* you; **es para ti** it's for you; **hazlo por ti** do it for your own sake; **piensas demasiado en ti mismo** you think too much about yourself

tía *nf* (a) *(pariente)* aunt (b) *Fam (mujer)* girl, woman

tianguis *nm inv CAm, Méx* open-air market

tibieza *nf* tepidity; *Fig* lack of enthusiasm

tibio,-a *adj* tepid, lukewarm; *Fam* **ponerse t. de cerveza** to get pissed

tiburón *nm* shark

tic *nm* (*pl* **tiques**) tic, twitch; **t. nervioso** nervous tic *o* twitch

ticket *nm* (*pl* **tickets**) *(billete)* ticket; *(recibo)* receipt

tictac *nm* tick-tock, ticking

tiempo *nm* (a) time; **a t. in** time; **a su (debido) t.** in due course; **a un t., al mismo t.** at the same time; **al poco t.** soon afterwards; **antes de t.** (too) early *o* soon; **con el t.** in the course of time, with time; **con t.** in advance; **¿cuánto t.?** how long?; **¿cuánto t. hace?** how long ago?; **demasiado t.** too long; **estar a t. de** to still have time to; **hacer t.** to kill time; **¿nos da t. de llegar?** have we got (enough) time to get there?; **t. libre** free time; *Fig* **dar t. al t.** to let matters take their course

(b) *(meteorológico)* weather; **¿qué t. hace?** what's the weather like?; **hace buen/mal t.** the weather is good/bad

(c) *(edad)* age; **¿cuánto** *o* **qué t. tiene tu niño?** how old is your baby/child?

(d) *Mús* movement

(e) *Dep* half

(f) *Ling* tense

tienda *nf* (a) shop, store; **ir de tiendas** to go shopping (b) **t. (de campaña)** tent

tienta *nf* **a tientas** by touch; **andar a tientas** to feel one's way; **buscar (algo) a tientas** to grope (for sth)

tiento *nm* tact; **con t.** tactfully

tierno,-a *adj* (a) *(blando)* tender, soft (b) *(reciente)* fresh

tierra *nf* (a) *(planeta)* earth (b) *Agr* land, soil (c) *(continente)* land; **t. de nadie** no-man's-land (e) *(suelo)* ground; *Fig* **echar** *o* **tirar por t.** to spoil (f) *Elec* **(toma de) t.** *Br* earth, *US* ground

tierral *nm Am* cloud of dust

tieso,-a *adj (rígido)* stiff, rigid; *(erguido)* upright, erect

tiesto *nm* flowerpot

tifoidea *nf* **(fiebre) t.** typhoid (fever)

tifón *nm* typhoon

tifus *nm inv* typhus (fever)

tigre *nm* tiger; *Am* jaguar

tijeras *nfpl* (pair of) scissors

tijereta *nf* (a) *(insecto)* earwig (b) *Dep* scissors

tila *nf (flor)* lime *o* linden blossom; *(infusión)* lime *o* linden blossom tea

tildar *vt* to call, to brand; **me tildó de ladrón** he called me a thief

tilde *nf* written accent

323   **tilín ▸ tirar**

tilín *nm (sonido)* ting-a-ling; *Fig* **José le hace t.** she fancies José
tilma *nf Méx* woollen blanket
tilo *nm* lime tree
timar *vt* to swindle; **me han timado** they did me
timbal *nm* kettledrum
timbrar *vt (carta)* to stamp; *(documento)* to seal
timbre *nm* (a) *(de la puerta)* bell (b) *(sello)* stamp, seal; *Fin* **fiscal** *o* **revenue stamp** (c) *Mús (sonido)* timbre
timidez *nf* shyness, timidity
tímido,-a *adj* shy, timid; *Fig (mejoría)* light; *(intento)* cautious
timo *nm* swindle, fiddle; **es un t.** it's a rip-off
timón *nm* (a) *Náut & Av* rudder; **golpe de t.** U-turn (b) *Andes Aut* steering wheel
timonel *nm* helmsman
tímpano *nm Anat* eardrum
tina *nf* (a) *(tinaja)* pitcher (b) *(gran cuba)* vat (c) *CAm, Col, Méx (bañera)* bathtub
tinaja *nf* large earthenware jar
tinerfeño,-a 1 *adj* of/from Tenerife
2 *nm,f* person from Tenerife
tinglado *nm* (a) *(intriga)* intrigue (b) *(cobertizo)* shed
tinieblas *nfpl* darkness
tino *nm* (a) *(puntería)* (good) aim; **tener buen t.** to be a good shot (b) *(tacto)* (common) sense, good judgement
tinta *nf* (a) ink; **t. china** Indian ink; **t. simpática** invisible ink (b) *Fig* **medias tintas** ambiguities, half measures
tintar *vt* to dye
tinte *nm* (a) dye (b) *Fig (matiz)* shade, overtone
tintero *nm* inkpot, inkwell; *Fig* **se quedó en el t.** it wasn't said
tintinear *vi (vidrio)* to clink; *(campana)* to jingle, to tinkle
tintineo *nm (de vidrio)* clinking; *(de campana)* jingling
tinto,-a 1 *adj (vino)* red
2 *nm* (a) *(vino)* red wine (b) *Col, Ven (café)* black coffee
tintorería *nf* dry-cleaner's
tintura *nf* (a) *(colorante)* dye (b) *Quím* tincture; **t. de yodo** iodine
tío *nm* (a) *(pariente)* uncle; **mis tíos** my uncle and aunt (b) *Fam* guy, *Br* bloke
tiovivo *nm* roundabout, merry-go-round
tipazo *nm Fam* good figure
tipear *vt & vi Am* to type
típico,-a *adj* (a) typical; **eso es t. de Antonio** that's just like Antonio (b) *(baile, traje)* traditional

tipificar [44] *vt* (a) *(normalizar)* to standardize (b) *(caracterizar)* to typify
tipismo *nm* local colour
tipo *nm* (a) *(clase)* type, kind (b) *Fam (persona)* guy, *Br* bloke; **t. raro** weirdo (c) *Anat (de hombre)* build, physique; *(de mujer)* figure; *Fig* **jugarse el t.** to riskone's neck; **aguantar el t.** to keep one's cool *o* head (d) *Fin* rate; **t. bancario** *o* **de descuento** bank rate; **t. de cambio/interés** rate of exchange/interest (e) **el político t. de la izquierda** the typical left-wing politician
tipografía *nf* typography
tipográfico,-a *adj* typographic; **error t.** printing error
tipógrafo,-a *nm,f* typographer
tiquismiquis *Fam* **1** *nmf inv* fusspot
2 *nmpl* (a) *(escrúpulos)* silly scruples (b) *(rencillas)* bickering
tira *nf* (a) *(banda, cinta)* strip (b) *(de dibujos)* comic strip (c) *Fam* **la t. de gente** a lot *o* loads of people (d) *Méx Fam* **la t.** *(la policía)* the cops (e) **t. y afloja** tug of war
tirabuzón *nm* ringlet
tirachinas *nm inv Br* catapult, *US* slingshot
tirada *nf* (a) *(lanzamiento)* throw (b) *(impresión)* print run
tirado,-a *adj Fam* (a) *(precio)* dirt-cheap (b) *(examen)* dead easy (c) *Fam* **dejar t. (a algn)** to let (sb) down
tirador *nm* (a) *(persona)* marksman (b) *(pomo)* knob, handle; *(cordón)* bell pull (c) *(tirachinas) Br* catapult, *US* slingshot
tiraje *nm Am* print run
tiralíneas *nm inv* tracer, drawing *o* ruling pen
tiranía *nf* tyranny
tiránico,-a *adj* tyrannical
tiranizar [40] *vt* to tyrannize
tirano,-a *nm,f* tyrant
tirante 1 *adj (cable etc)* tight, taut; *(situación, relación)* tense
2 *nm* (a) *(de vestido etc)* strap; **tirantes** *Br* braces, *US* suspenders (b) *Téc* brace, stay
tirar 1 *vt* (a) *(echar)* to throw (b) *(dejar caer)* to drop (c) *(desechar)* to throw away; *Fig (dinero)* to squander (d) *(derribar)* to knock down; **t. la puerta (abajo)** to smash the door in (e) *(foto)* to take (f) *Impr* to print (g) *(beso)* to blow
2 *vi* (a) **t. de** *(cuerda, puerta)* to pull

(**b**) *(chimenea, estufa)* to draw

(**c**) *(funcionar)* to work, to run

(**d**) **ir tirando** to get by

(**e**) **t. a** to tend towards; **tira a rojo** it's reddish

(**f**) **tira a la izquierda** turn left; **¡venga, tira ya!** come on, get going!

(**g**) *(disparar)* to shoot, to fire; *Ftb* **t. a puerta** to shoot at goal

3 tirarse *vpr* (**a**) *(lanzarse)* to throw o hurl oneself; **t. de cabeza al agua** to dive into the water

(**b**) *(tumbarse)* to lie down

(**c**) *Fam (tiempo)* to spend; **me tiré una hora esperando** I waited (for) a good hour

(**d**) *Vulg* **t. a algn** to lay sb

tirita® *nf* Elastoplast®, Band-aid®, plaster

tiritar *vi* to shiver, to shake

tiro *nm* (**a**) *(lanzamiento)* throw (**b**) *(disparo, ruido)* shot; *Ftb* **a gol** shot at goal; **t. al blanco** target shooting; **t. al plato** clay pigeon shooting; **t. con arco** archery (**c**) *(de vestido)* shoulder width (**d**) *(de chimenea)* draught; **animal de t.** draught animal

tirón *nm* pull, tug; *(del bolso)* snatch; *Fam* **de un t.** in one go

tirotear *vt* to shoot at, to snipe at

tiroteo *nm* shooting, firing to and fro

tirria *nf Fam* dislike; **le tengo t.** I dislike him, I can't stand him

tísico,-a *adj* tubercular, consumptive

tisis *nf inv* tuberculosis, consumption

tisú *nm* tissue, paper hankie

títere *nm (marioneta)* puppet; **no dejar t. con cabeza** to spare no one

titilar *vi (luz)* to flicker; *(estrella)* to twinkle

titiritero,-a *nm,f* (**a**) puppeteer (**b**) *(acróbata)* travelling acrobat

titubeante *adj (indeciso)* hesitant; *(al hablar)* stammering

titubear *vi* (**a**) *(dudar)* to hesitate, to waver (**b**) *(al hablar)* to stammer

titubeo *nm* (**a**) *(duda)* hesitation (**b**) *(al hablar)* stammering

titulación *nf* qualifications

titulado,-a *adj (licenciado)* graduate; *(diplomado)* qualified

titular¹ *nmf (persona)* holder

2 *nm Prensa* headline

3 *adj* appointed, official

titular² *vt (poner título)* to call

2 titularse *vpr* (**a**) *(película etc)* to be called; **¿cómo se titula?** what is it called? (**b**) *Educ* to graduate (**en** in)

titularidad *nf Educ* tenure

titulitis **1** *nf* obsession with qualifications

2 *nm Fam* certificate

título *nm* (**a**) title (**b**) *Educ* degree; *(diploma)* diploma (**c**) *Prensa (titular)* headline (**d**) **a t. de ejemplo** by way of example

tiza *nf* chalk; **una t.** a piece of chalk

tiznada *nf Am* **hijo de la t.** son of a bitch

tiznar *vt* to blacken (with soot)

tizne *nm* soot

tizón *nm* half-burnt stick, brand

tlapalería *nf Méx* ironmonger's (shop)

toalla *nf* towel; **tirar la t.** to throw in the towel

toallero *nm* towel *Br* rail o *US* bar

tobera *nf* nozzle

tobillo *nm* ankle

tobogán *nm* slide, chute

toca *nf (sombrero)* headdress; *(de monja)* wimple

tocadiscos *nm inv* record player; **t. digital** o **compacto** CD player

tocado¹ *nm* (**a**) *(peinado)* coiffure, hairdo (**b**) *(prenda)* headdress

tocado²,-a *adj Fam* crazy, touched

tocador *nm* (**a**) *(mueble)* dressing table (**b**) *(habitación)* dressing room; **t. de señoras** powder room

tocante *a loc adv* **en lo t. a ...** with reference to ...

tocar [44] **1** *vt* (**a**) to touch; *Fam Fig* **toca madera** touch wood (**b**) *(instrumento, canción)* to play; *(timbre, campana)* to ring; *(bocina)* to blow (**c**) *(tema, asunto)* to touch on (**d**) *(afectar)* to concern; **por lo que a mí me toca** as far as I am concerned

2 *vi* (**a**) **¿a quién le toca?** *(en juegos)* whose turn is it? (**b**) **me tocó el gordo** *(en rifa)* I won the jackpot (**c**) **t. con** to be next to; *Fig* **t. a su fin** to be coming to an end (**d**) *(llamar)* **t. a la puerta** to knock on the door

3 tocarse *vpr (una cosa con otra)* to touch each other; **¿os tocáis algo?** *(ser parientes)* are you related?

tocarse *vpr (cubrirse)* to cover one's head

tocata 1 *nf Mús* toccata

2 *nm Fam* record player

tocateja: • **a tocateja** *loc adv* **pagar a t.** to pay on the nail

tocayo,-a *nm,f* namesake

tocho *nm Fam (libro grande)* tome

tocino *nm* lard; **t. ahumado** smoked bacon; **t. de cielo** = sweet made with egg yolk

tocólogo,-a *nm,f* obstetrician

tocuyo *nm Am* coarse cotton cloth

todavía *adv* (**a**) *(aún)* still; *(en negativas)* yet; **t. la quiere** he still loves her; **t. no** not yet; **no mires t.** don't look yet (**b**) *(para reforzar)* even, still; **t. más/menos** even more/less

todo,-a 1 *adj* (**a**) all; **t. el pan** all the bread; **t. el mundo** (absolutely) everybody; **t. el día** all day, the whole *o* entire day; *Fam* **t. quisqui** every Tom, Dick and Harry

(**b**) *(cada)* every; **t. ciudadano de más de dieciocho años** every citizen over eighteen years of age

(**c**) *(entero)* complete, thorough; **es toda una mujer** she is every inch a woman

(**d**) **todos,-as** all; *(con expresiones de tiempo)* every; **todos los niños** all the children; **todos los martes** every Tuesday

2 *nm (totalidad)* whole

3 *pron* (**a**) *(sin excluir nada)* all, everything; **ante t.** first of all; **con t.** in spite of everything; **del t.** completely; **después de t.** after all; **eso es t.** that's all, that's it; **estar en t.** to be really with it; **hay de t.** there are all sorts; **lo sé t.** I know all about it; **t. lo contrario** quite the contrary *o* opposite; **t. lo más** at the most

(**b**) *(cualquiera)* anybody; **t. aquél** *o* **el que quiera** anybody who wants (to)

(**c**) *(cada uno)* **todos aprobamos** we all passed; **todos fueron** they all went

4 *adv* completely, totally; **volvió t. sucio** he was all dirty when he got back

todopoderoso,-a *adj* all-powerful, almighty

todoterreno *nm* all-terrain vehicle

toga *nf* (**a**) gown, robe (**b**) *Hist* toga

Tokio *n* Tokyo

toldo *nm* (**a**) *(cubierta)* awning (**b**) *Am (cabaña)* tent, teepee

tolerancia *nf* tolerance

tolerante *adj* tolerant

tolerar *vt* to tolerate; *(situación)* to stand; *(gente)* to put up with

toma *nf* (**a**) *(acción)* taking; *Elec* **t. de corriente** plug, socket (**b**) *Med* dose (**c**) *Mil* capture (**d**) *Cin* take, shot (**e**) **t. de posesión** swearing in (**f**) *Fam Fig* **t. y daca** give and take

tomado,-a *adj* (**a**) *(voz)* hoarse (**b**) *Am (borracho)* drunk (**c**) **tenerla tomada con algn** to have it in for sb

tomadura *nf Fam* **t. de pelo** leg-pull; *(timo)* rip-off

tomar 1 *vt* (**a**) *(coger)* to take; *(autobús, tren)* to take; *(decisión)* to make, to take; **toma** here (you are); **t. el sol** to sunbathe; *Av* **t. tierra** to land; *Fam* **tomarla con algn**

to have it in for sb (**b**) *(comer, beber)* to have (**c**) **t. algo a mal** to take sth badly; **t. en serio/broma** to take seriously/as a joke (**d**) *(confundir)* to take (**por** for) (**e**) *Mil* to take

2 *vi Am (beber alcohol)* to drink

3 tomarse *vpr* (**a**) *(comer)* to eat; *(beber)* to drink (**b**) *Fam* **no te lo tomes así** don't take it like that

tomate *nm* tomato; **salsa de t.** *(de lata)* tomato sauce; *(de botella)* ketchup

tomavistas *nm inv* cine *o* movie camera

tómbola *nf* tombola

tomillo *nm* thyme

tomo *nm* volume; *Fam* **de t. y lomo** utter, out-and-out

ton *nm* **sin t. ni son** without rhyme or reason

tonada *nf* (**a**) *Mús* tune, song (**b**) *Am (acento)* accent

tonalidad *nf* tonality

tonel *nm* barrel, cask

tonelada *nf* ton; **t. métrica** tonne

tonelaje *nm* tonnage

tonelero,-a *nm,f* cooper

tongo *nm* fix

tónico,-a 1 *nm Med* tonic; *(cosmético)* skin tonic

2 *nf* **tónica** (**a**) *(tendencia)* tendency, trend; **tónica general** overall trend (**b**) *(bebida)* tonic (water) (**c**) *Mús* tonic

3 *adj* (**a**) *Ling* tonic, stressed (**b**) *Mús & Med* tonic

tonificante *adj* invigorating

tonificar [44] *vt* to tone up, to invigorate

tono *nm* tone; **a t. con** in tune *o* harmony with; **subir de t.** *o* **el t.** to speak louder; **un t. alto/bajo** a high/low pitch; *Fig* **darse t.** to put on airs; *Fig* **fuera de t.** inappropriate, out of place; **dar el t.** to set the tone

tontear *vi* (**a**) to act the clown, to fool about (**b**) *(galantear)* to flirt

tontería *nf* (**a**) stupidity, silliness (**b**) *(dicho, hecho)* silly *o* stupid thing (**c**) *(insignificancia)* trifle

tonto,-a 1 *adj* silly, dumb

2 *nm,f* fool, idiot; **t. de remate** *o* **de capirote** prize idiot

topacio *nm* topaz

topadora *nf RP* bulldozer

toparse *vpr* **t. con** to bump into; *(dificultades)* to run up against, to encounter; **t. con algo** to come across sth

tope 1 *nm* (**a**) *(límite)* limit, end; *Fam* **a t.** *(al máximo)* flat out; *Fig* **estar hasta los topes** to be full up; **fecha t.** deadline (**b**) *Téc* stop, check (**c**) *Ferroc* buffer

2 *adv Fam* incredibly; **t. difícil** really difficult

tópico,-a 1 *nm* cliché
2 *adj Med & Farm* for external use

> ♪ Observa que la palabra inglesa **topic** es un falso amigo y no es la traducción de la palabra española **tópico**. En inglés, **topic** significa "tema".

topo *nm* mole
topografía *nf* topography
topónimo *nm* place name
toque *nm* (a) touch; *Fam* **dar un t. a algn** *(avisar)* to let sb know; *(advertir)* to warn sb (b) *(de campanas)* peal; *Fig* warning; **t. de queda** curfew
toquetear *vt* to fiddle with, to finger
toquilla *nf* (knitted) shawl
tórax *nm* thorax
torbellino *nm* (a) *(de viento)* whirlwind (b) *Fig (confusión)* whirl, turmoil
torcedura *nf (acción)* twist, twisting; *Med* sprain
torcer [41] 1 *vt* (a) *(metal)* to bend; *(cuerda, hilo)* to twist; *Med* to sprain; *Fig (esquina)* to turn (b) *(inclinar)* to slant
2 *vi* to turn (left o right)
3 torcerse *vpr* (a) *(doblarse)* to twist, to bend (b) *Med* **se me torció el tobillo** I sprained my ankle (c) *(plan)* to fall through (d) *(desviarse)* to go off to the side
torcido,-a *adj* twisted; *(ladeado)* slanted, lopsided; *(corbata)* crooked
tordo,-a 1 *adj* dapple-grey
2 *nm Orn* thrush
torear 1 *vt* to fight; *Fam* **t. a algn** to tease o confuse sb; *Fam* **t. un asunto** to tackle a matter skilfully
2 *vi* to fight
toreo *nm* bullfighting
torero,-a *nm,f* bullfighter
tormenta *nf* storm
tormento *nm (tortura)* torture; *(padecimiento)* torment
tormentoso,-a *adj* stormy
tornado *nm* tornado
tornar *Fml* **1** *vt (convertir)* to transform, to turn (**en** into)
2 *vi (regresar)* to return, to go back; **t. en sí** to regain consciousness
3 tornarse *vpr* to become, to turn
tornasolado,-a *adj* iridescent
torneo *nm* (a) *Dep* tournament (b) *Hist* tourney, joust
tornillo *nm* screw
torniquete *nm* (a) turnstile (b) *Med* tourniquet
torno *nm* (a) *Téc* lathe; *(de alfarero)*

wheel (b) **en t. a** *(alrededor de)* around; *(acerca de)* about
toro *nm* bull; **¿te gustan los toros?** do you like bullfighting?
toronja *nf* grapefruit
torpe *adj* (a) *(sin habilidad)* clumsy (b) *(tonto)* dim, thick (c) *(movimiento)* slow, awkward
torpedear *vt* to torpedo
torpedo *nm* torpedo
torpeza *nf* (a) *(física)* clumsiness; *(mental)* dimness, stupidity (b) *(lentitud)* slowness, heaviness (c) *(error)* blunder
torre *nf* (a) tower (b) *Mil & Náut* turret (c) *(en ajedrez)* rook, castle
torrefacto,-a *adj* roasted; **café t.** high roast coffee
torrencial *adj* torrential
torrente *nm* (a) *(de agua)* torrent (b) *Fig* **t. de voz** strong o powerful voice
torrezno *nm* = rasher of fried bacon
tórrido,-a *adj* torrid
torrija *nf* French toast
torsión *nf* (a) *(torcedura)* twist, twisting (b) *Téc* torsion
torso *nm* (a) *Anat* torso (b) *Arte* bust
torta *nf* (a) *Culin* cake (b) *Fam (golpe)* slap, punch
tortazo *nm Fam* (a) *(bofetada)* slap, punch (b) *(golpe)* whack, thump
tortícolis *nf inv* crick in the neck
tortilla *nf* (a) *(egg)* omelette; **t. francesa/española** (plain)/potato omelette (b) *Am* tortilla
tortillera *nf muy Fam* dyke, lesbian
tórtola *nf* dove
tortuga *nf (de tierra)* tortoise, *US* turtle; *(de mar)* turtle
tortuoso,-a *adj* tortuous
tortura *nf* torture
torturar *vt* to torture
tos *nf* cough; **t. ferina** whooping cough
tosco,-a *adj (basto)* rustic, rough; *(persona)* uncouth
toser *vi* to cough
tosquedad *nf* roughness
tostada *nf* (slice of) toast
tostado,-a *adj* (a) *(pan)* toasted (b) *(moreno)* tanned, brown
tostador *nm* toaster
tostar [2] 1 *vt (pan)* to toast; *(café)* to roast; *(carne, pescado)* to brown; *Fig (la piel)* to tan
tostón *nm* (a) *Culin (pan frito)* crouton (b) *Fam (tabarra)* bore, drag
total 1 *adj (completo)* total
2 *nm* (a) *(todo)* whole; **en t.** in all (b) *Mat* total

3 *adv* so, in short; **¿t. para qué?** what's the point anyhow?; *Fam* **t. que ... so ...; t., tampoco te hará caso** he won't listen to you anyway

totalidad *nf* whole, totality; **la t. de** all of; **en su t.** as a whole

totalitario,-a *adj* totalitarian

totalizar [40] 1 *vt* to total

2 *vi* to amount to

tóxico,-a 1 *adj* toxic, poisonous

2 *nm* poison

toxicología *nf* toxicology

toxicólogo,-a *nm,f* toxicologist

toxicomanía *nf* drug addiction

toxicómano,-a *Med* **1** *adj* addicted to drugs

2 *nm,f* drug addict

tozudo,-a *adj* obstinate, stubborn

traba *nf* (**a**) *(de rueda)* chock; *(enlace)* bond, tie (**b**) *Fig (obstáculo)* hindrance, obstacle

trabajador,-a 1 *nm,f* worker, labourer

2 *adj* hard-working

trabajar 1 *vi* to work; **trabaja mucho** he works hard; **t. de camarera** to work as a waitress

2 *vt* (**a**) to work (on); *(la tierra)* to till (**b**) *(asignatura etc)* to work on (**c**) *Fam (convencer)* to (try to) persuade

trabajo *nm* (**a**) *(ocupación)* work; **t. a destajo** piecework; **t. eventual** casual labour; **trabajos manuales** arts and crafts (**b**) *(empleo)* employment, job (**c**) *(tarea)* task, job (**d**) *Educ (redacción)* report, paper (**e**) *(esfuerzo)* effort; **cuesta t. creerlo** it's hard to believe

trabajoadicto,-a *nm,f* workaholic

trabajoso,-a *adj (laborioso)* hard, laborious; *(difícil)* difficult

trabalenguas *nm inv* tongue twister

trabar 1 *vt* (**a**) *(sujetar)* to lock, to fasten; *(un plan)* to obstruct (**b**) *(conversación, amistad)* to start, to strike up (**c**) *Culin* to thicken

2 trabarse *vpr* (**a**) *(cuerdas)* to get tangled up (**b**) *Fig* **se le trabó la lengua** he got tongue-tied

trabazón *nf (de ideas)* link

trabilla *nf (de pantalón)* belt loop

trabuco *nm* blunderbuss

tracción *nf* traction; *Aut* **t. delantera/ trasera** front-/rear-wheel drive; *Aut* **t. en las cuatro ruedas** four-wheel drive

tractor *nm* tractor

tradición *nf* tradition

tradicional *adj* traditional

traducción *nf* translation; **t. directa/inversa** translation from/into a foreign language

traducir [10] 1 *vt* to translate (**a** into)

2 traducirse *vpr Fig* to result (**en** in)

traductor,-a *nm,f* translator

traer [25] 1 *vt* (**a**) to bring; **trae** give it to me (**b**) *(llevar puesto)* to wear (**c**) *(llevar consigo)* to carry (**d**) *(problemas)* to cause; **traerá como consecuencia ...** it will result in ...

2 traerse *vpr (llevar consigo)* to bring along; *Fig* **¿qué se trae entre manos?** what is he up to?

traficante *nmf (de drogas etc)* trafficker, pusher

traficar [44] *vi (ilegalmente)* to traffic (**con** in)

tráfico *nm* (**a**) *Aut* traffic; **t. rodado** road traffic (**b**) *Com* traffic, trade; **t. de drogas** drug traffic

tragaluz *nm* skylight

tragaperras *nf inv (máquina)* **t.** slot machine

tragar [42] 1 *vt* (**a**) *(ingerir)* to swallow (**b**) *Fam (engullir)* to gobble up, to tuck away (**c**) *Fig (a una persona)* to stand, to stomach (**d**) *Fig (creer)* to believe, to swallow

2 tragarse *vpr* (**a**) *(ingerir)* to swallow (**b**) *Fig (creer)* to believe, to swallow

tragedia *nf* tragedy

trágico,-a *adj* tragic

trago *nm* (**a**) *(bebida)* swig; **de un t.** in one go (**b**) *Fig* **pasar un mal t.** to have a bad time of it

tragón,-ona *nm,f* glutton, big eater

traición *nf* treason, betrayal; **a t.** treacherously; **alta t.** high treason

traicionar *vt* to betray; *(delatar)* to give away, to betray

traicionero,-a *adj* treacherous

traidor,-a 1 *adj* treacherous

2 *nm,f* traitor

traigo *indic pres de* **traer**

tráiler *nm (pl tráilers)* (**a**) *Cin* trailer, *US* preview (**b**) *Aut Br* articulated lorry, *US* semitrailer (**c**) *Méx (casa rodante) Br* caravan, *US* trailer

traje¹ *nm* (**a**) *(de hombre)* suit; **t. de baño** bathing suit o costume, swimsuit; **t. de paisano** civilian clothes; **t. de luces** bullfighter's costume (**b**) *(de mujer)* dress; **t. de chaqueta** two-piece suit; **t. de novia** wedding dress

traje² *pt indef de* **traer**

trajeado,-a *adj Fam* sharp, dapper

trajearse *vpr* to dress up

trajín *nm Fam* comings and goings, hustle and bustle

trajinar *vi* to run o bustle about

trama *nf* (**a**) *Tex* weft, woof (**b**) *Lit* plot

tramar *vt* to plot, to cook up; **¿qué tramas?** what are you up to?

tramitar *vt* (**a**) *(gestionar)* to take the necessary (legal) steps to obtain (**b**) *Fml (despachar)* to convey, to transmit (**c**) *Com, Jur & Fin* to carry out, to process

trámite *nm* *(paso)* step; *(formalidad)* formality; *Com, Jur & Fin* procedures, proceedings

tramo *nm* *(de carretera)* section, stretch; *(de escalera)* flight

tramoya *nf* *(maquinaria)* stage machinery; *(trama)* plot, scheme

trampa *nf* (**a**) *(de caza)* trap, snare (**b**) *(puerta)* trapdoor (**c**) *(engaño)* fiddle; **hacer trampa(s)** to cheat (**d**) *(truco)* trick

> 🖉 Observa que la palabra inglesa **tramp** es un falso amigo y no es la traducción de la palabra española **trampa**. En inglés, **tramp** significa "vagabundo".

trampilla *nf* trapdoor, hatch

trampolín *nm* (**a**) *(de piscina)* diving board (**b**) *(de esquí)* ski jump

> 🖉 Observa que la palabra inglesa **trampoline** es un falso amigo y no es la traducción de la palabra española **trampolín**. En inglés, **trampoline** significa "cama elástica".

tramposo,-a 1 *adj* deceitful

2 *nm,f* cheat; *Naipes* cardsharp

tranca *nf* (**a**) *(garrote)* cudgel; *Fam* **a trancas y barrancas** with great difficulty (**b**) *(en puerta, ventana)* bar

trancar 1 *vt* *(asegurar)* *(con cerrojo)* to bolt; *(con tranca)* to bar

2 trancarse *vpr Am (atorarse)* to get stuck; **la llave se trancó en la cerradura** the key got stuck in the lock

trance *nm* (**a**) *(coyuntura)* (critical) moment; **estar en t. de ...** to be on the point of ... (**b**) *(éxtasis)* trance

tranquilidad *nf* calmness, tranquillity; **con t.** calmly; **pídemelo con toda t.** don't hesitate to ask me

tranquilizante *nm* tranquillizer

tranquilizar [40] **1** *vt* to calm down; **lo dijo para tranquilizarme** he said it to reassure me

2 tranquilizarse *vpr (calmarse)* to calm down

tranquillo *nm Fig* knack; **coger el t. a algo** to get the knack of sth

tranquilo,-a *adj* (**a**) *(persona, lugar)* calm; *(agua)* still; *(conciencia)* clear; *Fam* **tú t.** don't you worry (**b**) *(despreocupado)* placid, easy-going

transacción *nf* transaction, deal

transar *vi Am Fam* (**a**) *(transigir)* to compromise, to give in (**b**) *(negociar)* to negotiate

transatlántico,-a 1 *adj* transatlantic

2 *nm Náut* (ocean) liner

transbordador *nm* (car) ferry; **t. espacial** space shuttle

transbordar 1 *vt* to transfer; *Náut (mercancías)* to tranship

2 *vi Ferroc* to change trains, *US* to transfer

transbordo *nm* (**a**) *Ferroc* change, *US* transfer; **hacer t.** to change, *US* to transfer (**b**) *Náut* transhipment

transcurrir *vi* (**a**) *(tiempo)* to pass, to go by (**b**) *(acontecer)* to take place

transcurso *nm* course o passing (of time); **en el t. de** in the course of, during

transeúnte *nmf* (**a**) *(peatón)* passer-by (**b**) *(residente temporal)* temporary resident

transferencia *nf* transference; *Fin* transfer; **t. bancaria** banker's order

transferible *adj* transferable

transferir [5] *vt* to transfer; *Informát* to download

transformación *nf* transformation

transformador *nm Elec* transformer

transformar 1 *vt* to transform, to change

2 transformarse *vpr* to change, to turn (en into); *(algo plegable)* to convert

tránsfuga *nmf* (**a**) *Mil* deserter (**b**) *Pol* turncoat

transfusión *nf* transfusion

transgénico,-a 1 *adj* transgenic

2 *nmpl* **transgénicos** GM foods

transgredir *vt* defect to transgress, to break

transgresor,-a *nm,f* transgressor, lawbreaker

transición *nf* transition

transido,-a *adj Fml* **t. de angustia** overcome by anxiety; **t. de dolor** racked with pain

transigente *adj* tolerant

transigir [57] *vi* to compromise

transistor *nm* transistor

transitable *adj* passable

transitado,-a *adj (carretera)* busy

transitar *vi* to pass

transitivo,-a *adj* transitive

tránsito *nm* (**a**) *Aut* traffic (**b**) *(movimiento)* movement, passage; **pasajeros en t.** passengers in transit

transitorio,-a *adj* transitory

traslucirse [35] *vpr* = traslucirse

transmisión *nf* (**a**) transmission (**b**) *Téc*

drive; **t. delantera/trasera** front-/rear-wheel drive (**c**) *Rad & TV* transmission, broadcast

transmisor *nm* transmitter

transmitir *vt* (**a**) to transmit, to pass on (**b**) *Rad & TV* to transmit, to broadcast (**c**) *Jur* to transfer, to hand down

transparencia *nf* (**a**) transparency; *Pol* openness (**b**) *Fot* slide

transparentarse *vpr* to be transparent; **esta tela se transparenta** this is see-through material; **se le transparentaban las bragas** you could see her panties

transparente 1 *adj* transparent; *Pol* open **2** *nm* (**a**) (*visillo*) net curtain (**b**) (*pantalla*) shade, blind

transpiración *nf* perspiration

transpirar *vi* to perspire

transplante *nm* transplant; *Med* **t. de corazón/córnea** heart/eye transplant

transponer [**19**] **1** *vt* (*mudar de sitio*) to transpose, to move about
2 transponerse *vpr* (*desmayarse*) to faint

transportar *vt* to transport; (*pasajeros*) to carry; (*mercancías*) to ship

transporte *nm* (**a**) transport (**b**) *Com* freight; **t. de mercancías** freight transport; **t. marítimo** shipment

transportista *nmf* carrier

transvase *nm* (**a**) (*de líquidos*) decanting (**b**) (*de ríos*) transfer

transversal *adj* transverse, cross

tranvía *nm Br* tram, tramcar, *US* streetcar

trapecio *nm* trapeze

trapecista *nmf* trapeze artist

trapero,-a 1 *nm Br* rag-and-bone man, *US* junkman
2 *adj* **puñalada trapera** stab in the back

trapichear *vi* to be up to something

trapicheo *nm* jiggery-pokery

trapo *nm* (**a**) (*viejo, roto*) rag (**b**) (*bayeta*) cloth; **t. de cocina** dishcloth; **t. del polvo** duster; *Fam* **poner (a algn) como un t. (sucio)** to tear (sb) apart

tráquea *nf* trachea, windpipe

traqueteo *nm* rattle, clatter

tras *prep* (**a**) (*después de*) after; **uno t. otro** one after the other (**b**) (*detrás*) behind; **sentados uno t. otro** sitting one behind the other (**c**) **andar/ir t.** to be after; **la policía iba t. ella** the police were after her

trasatlántico,-a *adj & nm* = transatlántico,-a

trasbordador *nm* = transbordador

trasbordar *vt & vi* = transbordar

trasbordo *nm* = transbordo

trascendencia *nf* (**a**) (*importancia*) importance, significance (**b**) (*en filosofía*) transcendence

trascendental, trascendente *adj* (**a**) significant, far-reaching (**b**) (*en filosofía*) transcendental

trascender [**3**] *vi* (**a**) (*noticia*) to become known, to leak out (**b**) (*tener consecuencias*) to have far-reaching consequences (**c**) **t. de** to go beyond

trascurrir *vi* = transcurrir

trascurso *nm* = transcurso

trasero,-a 1 *adj* back, rear; **en la parte trasera** at the back
2 *nm Euf* backside

trasferencia *nf* = transferencia

trasferible *adj* = transferible

trasferir [**5**] *vt* = transferir

trasfondo *nm* background

trasformación *nf* = transformación

trasformador *nm* = transformador

trasformar *vt* = transformar

trásfuga *nmf* = tránsfuga

trasfusión *nf* = transfusión

trasgredir *vt* = transgredir

trasgresor,-a *nm,f* = transgresor,-a

trashumancia *nf* = seasonal movement of livestock

trasiego *nm* comings and goings, hustle and bustle

trasladar 1 *vt* (*cosa*) to move; (*persona*) to move, to transfer
2 trasladarse *vpr* to go, to move

traslado *nm* (*de casa*) move, removal; (*de personal*) transfer; *Educ* **t. de expediente** transfer of student record

traslucirse [**35**] *vpr* to show (through)

trasluz *nm* **mirar algo al t.** to hold sth against the light

trasmano *nm* **a t.** out of reach; **(me) coge a t.** it's out of my way

trasmisión *nf* = transmisión

trasmisor *nm* = transmisor

trasmitir *vt* = transmitir

trasnochado,-a *adj* (*desfasado*) old, hackneyed

trasnochador,-a 1 *adj* given to staying up late
2 *nm,f* night bird, nighthawk

trasnochar *vi* to stay up (very) late

traspapelarse *vpr* to get mislaid o misplaced

trasparencia *nf* = transparencia

trasparentarse *vpr* = transparentarse

trasparente *adj & nm* = transparente

traspasar *vt* (**a**) (*atravesar*) to go through; (*río*) to cross (**b**) (*negocio, local*) to transfer; **se traspasa** (*en letrero*) for sale (**c**) *Fig (exceder)* to exceed, to go beyond

> 🎵 Observa que el verbo inglés **to trespass** es un falso amigo y no es la traducción del verbo español **traspasar**. En inglés, **to trespass** significa "entrar sin autorización".

traspaso *nm* (**a**) *(de propiedad etc)* transfer (**b**) *Com (venta)* sale

traspié *nm* (*pl* **traspiés**) stumble, trip; **dar un t.** to trip; *Fig* to slip up

traspiración *nf* = transpiración

traspirar *vi* = transpirar

trasplante *nm* = transplante

trasponer [19] *vt* = transponer

trasportar *vt* = transportar

trasporte *nm* = transporte

traspuesto,-a *adj* **quedarse t.** to faint

trasquilar *vt (oveja)* to shear; *(pelo)* to crop

trastabillar *vi (tambalearse)* to stagger, to totter

trastada *nf Fam* **hacer trastadas** to be up to mischief

trastazo *nm Fam* wallop, thump

traste¹ *nm Mús* fret

traste² *nm* (**a**) *(trasto)* piece of junk (**b**) *Andes, CAm, Carib, Méx* **trastes** dirty dishes; **fregar los trastes** to wash the dishes, *US* to do the washing-up (**c**) *CSur Fam (trasero)* bottom (**d**) *Fig* **dar al t. con un plan** to spoil a plan; **irse al t.** to fall through

trastear *vi (revolver)* to rummage about

trastero *nm* **(cuarto) t.** junk room

trastienda *nf* back shop

trasto *nm (objeto cualquiera)* thing; *(cosa inservible)* piece of junk

trastocar [44] *vt* = trastornar

trastornado,-a *adj (loco)* mad, unhinged

trastornar 1 *vt* (**a**) *(planes)* to disrupt (**b**) *Fig (persona)* to unhinge

2 trastornarse *vpr (enloquecer)* to go out of one's mind, to go mad

trastorno *nm (molestia)* trouble, inconvenience; **t. mental** mental disorder *o* disturbance

trasvase *nm* = transvase

trasversal *adj* = transversal

trata *nf* slave trade *o* traffic; **t. de blancas** white slave trade

tratable *adj* easy to get along with, congenial

tratado *nm* (**a**) *(pacto)* treaty (**b**) *(estudio)* treatise

tratamiento *nm* (**a**) treatment (**b**) *Téc* processing, treatment (**c**) *Informát*

processing; **t. de textos** word processing

tratar 1 *vt* (**a**) *(atender)* to treat; **t. bien/mal** to treat well/badly (**b**) *Med* to treat (**c**) *(asunto)* to discuss (**d**) *Informát & Téc* to process (**e**) **me trata de tú** he addresses me as "tu"

2 *vi* (**a**) **t. de** *(intentar)* to try (**b**) **t. de** *o* **sobre** *o* **acerca** to be about; **¿de qué trata?** what is it about? (**c**) **t. con** *(tener tratos)* to deal with; *(negociar)* to negotiate with; *(relacionarse)* to move among (**d**) *Com* **t. en** to deal in

3 tratarse *vpr* (**a**) *(relacionarse)* to be on speaking terms (**b**) **se trata de** *(es cuestión de)* it's a question of; **se trata de un caso excepcional** it's an exceptional case

tratativas *nfpl CSur* negotiation

trato *nm* (**a**) *(de personas)* manner; *(contacto)* contact; **malos tratos** ill-treatment (**b**) *(acuerdo)* agreement; **¡t. hecho!** it's a deal! (**c**) *Com* deal

trauma *nm* trauma

traumático,-a *adj* traumatic

traumatizar *vt Med* to traumatize; *Fam* to shock

través 1 *prep* (**a**) **a t. de** *(superficie)* across, over; *(agujero etc)* through; **a t. del río** across the river; **a t. del agujero** through the hole (**b**) *Fig* **a t. de** through; **a t. del periódico** through the newspaper

2 *adv* **de t.** *(transversalmente)* crosswise; *(de lado)* sideways

3 *nm* (*pl* **traveses**) *Fig (desgracia)* misfortune

travesaño *nm Ftb* crossbar

travesía *nf (viaje)* crossing

travesti, travestí *nmf* transvestite

> 🎵 Observa que la palabra inglesa **travesty** es un falso amigo y no es la traducción de la palabra española **travesti**. En inglés, **travesty** significa "parodia burda".

travesura *nf* mischief, childish prank

travieso,-a *adj* mischievous

trayecto *nm* (**a**) *(distancia)* distance; *(recorrido)* route; *(trecho)* stretch (**b**) *(viaje)* journey

trayectoria *nf* (**a**) *(de proyectil, geométrica)* trajectory (**b**) *Fig (orientación)* line, course

traza *nf* (**a**) *(apariencia)* looks, appearance; **no lleva trazas de curarse** it doesn't look as if he's going to get better (**b**) *Arquit* plan, design

trazado *nm* (**a**) *(plano)* layout, plan (**b**) *(de carretera, ferrocarril)* route

trazar [40] *vt (línea)* to draw; *(plano)* to design; *Fig (plan)* to sketch out

trazo *nm* (a) *(línea)* line (b) *(de letra)* stroke

trébol *nm* (a) trefoil (b) *Naipes* club

trece 1 *adj inv* thirteen

　2 *nm inv* thirteen; *Fig* estar o **mantenerse** o **seguir en sus t.** to stick to one's guns

trecho *nm* distance, way; *(tramo)* stretch; **de t. en t.** from time to time

tregua *nf Mil* truce; *Fig* respite

treinta *adj & nm inv* thirty

treintavo,-a *adj & nm* thirtieth

treintena *nf* una t. de *(about)* thirty

tremendista *adj* over the top

tremendo,-a *adj* (a) *(terrible)* terrible, dreadful (b) *(muy grande)* enormous; *Fig* tremendous

trementina *nf* turpentine

trémulo,-a *adj Literario (vacilante)* quivering, tremulous; *(luz)* flickering

tren *nm* (a) train (b) *Av* t. de aterrizaje undercarriage; **t. de lavado** car wash (c) **t. de vida** lifestyle

trenca *nf* duffle coat

trenza *nf (de pelo)* plait, *esp US* braid

trepador,-a *adj* climbing

trepar *vt & vi* to climb

trepidante *adj* vibrating, shaking; *Fig* **lleva un ritmo de vida t.** he leads a hectic o frantic life

trepidar *vi* to vibrate, to shake

tres 1 *adj inv (cardinal)* three; *(ordinal)* third; *Fam* de t. al cuarto cheap, of little value

　2 *nm (pl* treses*)* three; **t. en raya** *Br* noughts and crosses, *US* tick-tack-toe

trescientos,-as *adj & nm* three hundred

tresillo *nm* (a) *(mueble)* (three-piece) suite (b) *Mús* triplet

treta *nf* trick, ruse

triángulo *nm* triangle; *Fig* **t. amoroso** eternal triangle

tribal *adj* tribal

tribu *nf* tribe

tribuna *nf* (a) *(plataforma)* rostrum, dais; **t. de (la) prensa** press box (b) *Dep* stand

tribunal *nm* (a) *Jur* court; **t. de apelación** court of appeal; **T. Supremo** *Br* High Court, *US* Supreme Court; **t. (tutelar) de menores** juvenile court (b) *(de examen)* board of examiners

tributar *vt* to pay

tributario,-a *adj* sistema t. tax system

tributo *nm* (a) *Com* tax (b) **pagar t. a** *(homenaje)* to pay tribute to

triciclo *nm* tricycle

tricornio *nm* three-cornered hat

tridimensional *adj* three-dimensional

trienio *nm* three-year period

trifásico,-a 1 *adj Elec* three-phase

　2 *nm* adapter

trigésimo,-a *adj & nm,f* thirtieth; **t. primero** thirty-first

trigo *nm* wheat

trigueño,-a *adj Am (pelo)* dark brown; *(persona)* olive-skinned

trilla *nf* threshing

trillado,-a *adj Fig* well-worn

trilladora *nf* threshing machine; **t. segadora** combine harvester

trillar *vt* to thresh

trilogía *nf* trilogy

trimestral *adj* quarterly, three-monthly

trimestre *nm* quarter; *Educ* term

trinar *vi* (a) to warble (b) *Fam* to rage, to fume; **Santiago está que trina** Santiago is really fuming

trincar¹ **[44]** *vt Fam (capturar)* to catch

trincar² *vt Fam* to drink

trinchar *vt (carne)* to carve, to slice (up)

trinchera *nf* trench

trineo *nm* sledge, sleigh

Trinidad *nf* **la Santísima T.** the Holy Trinity

trino *nm* (a) warble, trill (b) *Mús* trill

trío *nm* trio

tripa *nf* (a) *(intestino)* gut, intestine; *Fam* tummy; **dolor de t.** stomach ache (b) **tripas** innards

triple *adj & nm* triple

triplicado,-a *adj* triplicate; **por t.** in triplicate

triplicar [44] *vt* to triple, to treble

trípode *nm* tripod

tríptico *nm* (a) *(cuadro)* triptych (b) *(folleto)* leaflet

tripulación *nf* crew

tripulante *nmf* crew member

tripular *vt* to man

triquiñuela *nf Fam* trick, dodge

tris *nm* estar en un t. de to be on the verge of

triste *adj* (a) *(persona, situación)* sad (b) *(lugar)* gloomy

tristeza *nf* sadness

triturar *vt (machacar)* to grind (up)

triunfador,-a 1 *adj* winning

　2 *nm,f* winner

triunfal *adj* triumphant

triunfar *vi* to triumph

triunfo *nm* (a) *(victoria)* triumph, victory; *Dep* win (b) *(éxito)* success

trivial *adj* trivial

trivialidad *nf* triviality

trivializar *vt* to trivialize, to minimize

triza *nf* bit, fragment; **hacer trizas** to tear to shreds

trocar [64] *vt* to barter

trocear *vt* to cut up (into bits o pieces)

trochemoche: •a trochemoche *loc adv Fam* haphazardly

trofeo *nm* trophy

trola *nf Fam* fib

trolebús *nm* trolleybus

tromba *nf* **t. de agua** violent downpour

trombón *nm* trombone

trombosis *nf inv* thrombosis

trompa *nf* (**a**) *Mús* horn (**b**) *(de elefante)* trunk (**c**) *Anat* tube (**d**) *Fam* **estar t.** to be sloshed o plastered

trompazo *nm Fam* bump; **darse** o **pegarse un t.** to have a bump

trompeta *nf* trumpet

trompetista *nmf* trumpet player, trumpeter

trompicón *nm* trip, stumble; **hacer algo a trompicones** to do sth in fits and starts

trompo *nm* spinning top

tronar [2] 1 *vi* to thunder

   2 *vt Méx Fam* (**a**) *(destruir, acabar con)* to destroy; **este remedio es para t. anginas** this remedy will clear up tonsillitis (**b**) *(reprobar)* to fail

tronchar 1 *vt* (*rama, tronco*) to cut down, to fell; *Fig* (*esperanzas etc*) to destroy

   2 **troncharse** *vpr* **t. de risa** to split one's sides with laughter

troncho *nm* stem, stalk

tronco *nm* (**a**) *Anat* trunk, torso (**b**) *Bot* (*de árbol*) trunk; (*leño*) log; *Fam Fig* **dormir como un t.** to sleep like a log

tronera *nf* (**a**) *(de billar)* pocket (**b**) *(ventana)* small window; *(de fortificación)* loophole; *Náut* porthole

trono *nm* throne

tropa *nf* (**a**) squad (**b**) **tropas** troops

tropel *nm* throng, mob; **en t.** in a mad rush

tropezar [1] *vi* (**a**) to trip, to stumble (**con** on) (**b**) **t. con algo** to come across sth; **t. con algn/dificultades** to run into sb/difficulties

tropezón *nm* (**a**) *(traspié)* trip, stumble; **dar un t.** to trip (**b**) *(error)* slip-up, faux pas (**c**) *(de comida)* chunk of meat

tropical *adj* tropical

trópico *nm* tropic

tropiezo 1 *nm* (**a**) *(obstáculo)* trip (**b**) *Fig* (*error*) blunder, faux pas

   2 *indic pres de* **tropezar**

trotamundos *nmf inv* globetrotter

trotar *vi* to trot

trote *nm* (**a**) trot; **al t.** at a trot (**b**) *Fam* **ya no está para esos trotes** he cannot keep up the pace any more

trovador *nm* troubadour

trozar *vt Am* (*carne*) to cut up; *(res, tronco)* to butcher, to cut up

trozo *nm* piece

trucar [44] *vt* to doctor, to alter

trucha *nf* trout

truco *nm* (**a**) *(ardid)* trick; **aquí hay t.** there's something fishy going on here (**b**) **coger el t. (a algo)** to get the knack o hang (of sth)

truculento,-a *adj* horrifying, terrifying

> 🖉 Observa que la palabra inglesa **truculent** es un falso amigo y no es la traducción de la palabra española **truculento**. En inglés, **truculent** significa "agresivo, airado".

trueno *nm* thunder; **un t.** a thunderclap

trueque *nm* barter

trufa *nf* truffle

truhán,-ana *nm,f* rogue, crook

truncar [44] *vt* to truncate; *Fig* (*vida etc*) to cut short; *Fig* (*esperanzas*) to shatter

trusa *nf Méx* (*calzoncillo*) underpants; *(braga)* panties, *Br* knickers

trust *nm* (*pl* **trusts**) trust, cartel

tu *adj pos* your; **tu libro** your book; **tus libros** your books

tú *pron* you; **de tú a tú** on equal terms

> Usually omitted in Spanish except for emphasis or contrast.

tuba *nf* tuba

tubérculo *nm* (**a**) *Bot* tuber (**b**) *Med* tubercle

tuberculosis *nf inv* tuberculosis

tubería *nf* (**a**) *(de agua)* piping, pipes (**b**) *(de gas)* pipeline

tubo *nm* (**a**) tube; **t. de ensayo** test tube (**b**) *(tubería)* pipe; *Aut* **t. de escape** exhaust (pipe)

tucán *nm* toucan

tuerca *nf* nut

tuerto,-a 1 *adj* one-eyed, blind in one eye

   2 *nm,f* one-eyed person

tuerzo *indic pres de* **torcer**

tuétano *nm* marrow; **hasta el t.** to one's fingertips

tufo *nm* foul odour o smell

tugurio *nm* hovel

tul *nm* tulle

tulipa *nf* small tulip

tulipán *nm* tulip

tullido,-a *adj* crippled, disabled

tullir *vt* to cripple

tumba *nf* grave, tomb

tumbar 1 *vt* to knock down o over

   2 **tumbarse** *vpr* (*acostarse*) to lie down, to stretch out

tumbo *nm* **dar tumbos** to reel

tumbona *nf Br* sun-lounger, *US* beach recliner

tumor *nm* tumour

tumulto *nm* tumult, commotion

tumultuoso,-a *adj* tumultuous, riotous

tuna *nf* (a) *(agrupación musical)* = group of student minstrels (b) *Am (higo chumbo)* prickly pear

> ℓ Observa que la palabra inglesa **tuna** es un falso amigo y no es la traducción de la palabra española **tuna**. En inglés, **tuna** significa "atún, bonito".

tunante,-a *nm,f* rogue, crook

túnel *nm* tunnel; **el t. del Canal de la Mancha** the Channel Tunnel

Túnez *n* (a) *(país)* Tunisia (b) *(ciudad)* Tunis

túnica *nf* tunic

tuno,-a 1 *nm,f (bribón)* rogue, crook
  2 *nm* = member of a "tuna"

tuntún: • **al tuntún** *loc adv* haphazardly, any old how

tupé *nm (pl* **tupés)** *(flequillo)* quiff

tupido,-a *adj* thick, dense

turba¹ *nf (combustible)* peat

turba² *nf (muchedumbre)* mob, crowd

turbado,-a *adj* (a) *(alterado)* disturbed (b) *(preocupado)* worried, anxious (c) *(desconcertado)* confused

turbante *nm* turban

turbar 1 *vt* (a) *(alterar)* to unsettle (b) *(preocupar)* to upset o worry (c) *(desconcertar)* to baffle, to put off
  2 turbarse *vpr* (a) *(preocuparse)* to be o become upset (b) *(desconcertarse)* to be o become confused o baffled

turbina *nf* turbine

turbio,-a *adj (agua)* cloudy; *(negocio etc)* shady, dubious

turborreactor *nm* turbojet (engine)

turbulencia *nf* turbulence

turbulento,-a *adj* turbulent

turco,-a 1 *adj* Turkish
  2 *nm,f (persona)* Turk; *Fig* **cabeza de t.** scapegoat
  3 *nm (idioma)* Turkish

turismo *nm* (a) tourism; **ir de t.** to go touring; **t. rural** rural tourism (b) *Aut* car

turista *nmf* tourist

turístico,-a *adj* tourist; **de interés t.** of interest to tourists

turnarse *vpr* to take turns

turno *nm* (a) *(en juegos etc)* turn, go (b) *(de trabajo)* shift; **estar de t.** to be on duty; **t. de día/noche** day/night shift

turquesa *adj inv & nf* turquoise

Turquía *n* Turkey

turrón *nm* nougat

tute *nm Fam* **darse un t. de algo** to go town doing sth

tutear 1 *vt* = to address as "tú"
  2 tutearse *vpr* = to address each other as "tú"

tutela *nf* (a) *Jur* guardianship, tutelage (b) *Fig (protección)* protection, guidance

tuteo *nm* = use of the "tú" form of address

tutor *nm* (a) *Jur* guardian (b) *Educ* tutor

tuve *pt indef de* **tener**

tuyo,-a 1 *adj pos (con personas)* of yours; *(con objetos)* one of your; **¿es amigo t.?** is he a friend of yours?; **unas amigas tuyas** some friends of yours; **un libro t.** one of your books
  2 *pron pos* yours; **éste es t.** this one is yours; *Fam* **los tuyos** *(familiares)* your family

TV *nf (abr* **televisión)** TV

TVE *nf (abr* **Televisión Española)** = Spanish state television network

U, u [u] *nf (la letra)* U, u

u *conj (delante de palabras que empiecen por o o* **ho**) or; **siete u ocho** seven or eight; **ayer u hoy** yesterday or today

ubicación *nf* location, position

ubicar [44] **1** *vt Am (situar)* to locate, to situate
2 ubicarse *vpr* to be situated *o* located

ubicuo,-a *adj* ubiquitous

ubre *nf* udder

Ucrania *n* Ukraine

ucraniano,-a *adj & nm,f* Ukrainian

Ud. (*abr* **usted**) you

Uds. (*abr* **ustedes**) you

UE *nf* (*abr* **Unión Europea**) EU

UEM *nf* (*abr* **unión económica y monetaria**) EMU

ufanarse *vpr* to boast (**de** of)

ufano,-a *adj* conceited

ugetista *adj* = relating to the UGT

UGT *nf* (*abr* **Unión General de los Trabajadores**) = major socialist trade union in Spain

ujier *nm* usher

úlcera *nf* ulcer

ulcerar *vt*, **ulcerarse** *vpr* to ulcerate

ulterior *adj (siguiente)* subsequent

últimamente *adv* lately, recently

ultimar *vt* (**a**) *(terminar)* to finalize (**b**) *Am (matar)* to kill, to finish off

ultimátum *nm* (*pl* **ultimátums**) ultimatum

último,-a **1** *adj* (**a**) *(último)* last; **el ú. día** the last day; **por ú.** finally (**b**) *(más reciente)* latest; **últimas noticias** latest news (**c**) *(más alto)* top; **el ú. piso** the top flat (**d**) *(más bajo)* lowest (**e**) *(más lejano)* back, last; **la última fila** the back row (**f**) *(definitivo)* final
2 *nm,f* **llegar el ú.** to arrive last; **a últimos de mes** at the end of the month; **en las últimas** on one's last legs; *Fam* **a la última** up to the minute; **el ú. de la lista** the lowest in the list

ultra *nmf* extreme right-winger; **los ultras** the extreme right

ultra- *pref* ultra-

ultraderecha *nf Pol* extreme right

ultraderechista *Pol* **1** *adj* extreme right-wing

2 *nmf* extreme right-winger

ultraizquierda *nf* extreme left

ultrajar *vt* to outrage, to offend

ultraje *nm* outrage, offence

ultramar *nm* overseas (countries), abroad; **del** *o* **en u.** overseas

ultramarinos *nmpl* groceries; **tienda de u.** greengrocer's (shop)

ultranza: ● **a ultranza** *loc adv* (**a**) *(a todo trance)* at all costs, at any price; **defender algo a u.** to defend sth to the death (**b**) *(acérrimo)* out-and-out, extreme

ultrasónico,-a *adj* ultrasonic

ultratumba *nf* afterlife

ultravioleta *adj inv* ultraviolet

ulular *vi (viento)* to howl; *(búho)* to hoot

umbral *nm* threshold

umbrío,-a, umbroso,-a *adj* shady

un, una 1 *art indet* (**a**) a; *(antes de vocal)* an; **un coche** a car; **un huevo** an egg; **una flor** a flower (**b**) **unos,-as** some; **unas flores** some flowers
2 *adj (delante de nm sing)* one; **un chico y dos chicas** one boy and two girls; *ver también* **uno,-a**

unánime *adj* unanimous

unanimidad *nf* unanimity; **por u.** unanimously

unción *nf* unction

undécimo,-a *adj* eleventh

UNED *nf* (*abr* **Universidad Nacional de Educación a Distancia**) = Spanish open university

ungir [57] *vt Rel* to anoint

ungüento *nm* ointment

únicamente *adv* only, solely

único,-a *adj* (**a**) *(solo)* only; **es el ú. que tengo** it's the only one I've got; **hijo ú.** only child; **lo ú. que quiero** the only thing I want; **el Mercado Ú.** the Single Market; **el Acta Única** the Single European Act (**b**) *(extraordinario)* unique

unidad *nf* (**a**) unit (**b**) *(cohesión)* unity

unido,-a *adj* united; **están muy unidos** they are very attached to one another; **una familia muy unida** a very close family

unifamiliar *adj* **vivienda u.** detached house

unificación *nf* unification

unificar [44] *vt* to unify

uniformar *vt* (**a**) *(igualar)* to make uniform, to standardize (**b**) *(poner un uniforme a)* to put into uniform, to give a uniform to

uniforme 1 *nm (prenda)* uniform
  2 *adj* (**a**) *(igual)* uniform (**b**) *(superficie)* even

uniformidad *nf* (**a**) *(igualdad)* uniformity (**b**) *(de superficie)* evenness

unilateral *adj* unilateral

unión *nf* union

Unión Soviética *n* Soviet Union

unir 1 *vt* *(juntar)* to unite, to join (together); **esta carretera une las dos comarcas** this road links both districts
  2 unirse *vpr (juntarse)* to unite, to join

unisex *adj inv* unisex

unísono *nm* unison; **al u.** in unison

unitario,-a *adj* unitary; **precio u.** unit price

universal *adj* universal; **historia u.** world history

universidad *nf* university; **u. a distancia** ≃ Open University; **u. laboral** technical college

universitario,-a 1 *adj* university
  2 *nm,f* university student

universo *nm* universe

uno,-a 1 *nm inv* one; **el u.** (number) one; **el u. de mayo** the first of May
  2 *nf* **es la una** *(hora)* it's one o'clock
  3 *adj* **unos,-as** some; **unas cajas** some boxes; **habrá unos** *o* **unas veinte** there must be around twenty
  4 *pron* (**a**) one; **u. (de ellos), una (de ellas)** one of them; **unos cuantos** a few; **se miraron el u. al otro** they looked at each other; **de u. en u.** one by one; **un trás otro** one after the other; **una de dos** one of the two
    (**b**) *(persona)* someone, somebody; **u. que pasaba por allí** some passer-by; **vive con u.** she's living with some man; **unos ... otros** some people ... others
    (**c**) *(impers)* you, one; **u. tiene que ...** you have to ...

untar *vt* to grease, to smear; *(mantequilla)* to spread

untura *nf* ointment

uña *nf* (**a**) nail; **morderse** *o* **comerse las uñas** to bite one's fingernails; *Fig* **ser u. y carne** to be hand in glove (**b**) *Zool (garra)* claw; *(pezuña)* hoof

uperizado,-a *adj* **leche uperizada** UHT milk

Urales *nmpl* **los U.** the Urals

uranio *nm* uranium

Urano *nm* Uranus

urbanidad *nf* urbanity, politeness

urbanismo *nm* town planning

urbanístico,-a *adj* town-planning

urbanización *nf* (**a**) *(barrio)* housing development *o* estate (**b**) *(proceso)* urbanization

urbanizar *vt* to build up

urbano,-a *adj* urban, city; **guardia u.** (traffic) policeman

urbe *nf* large city

urdimbre *nf* (**a**) *Tex* warp (**b**) *(trama)* intrigue

urdir *vt* (**a**) *Tex* to warp (**b**) *(tramar)* to plot, to scheme

urgencia *nf* (**a**) urgency (**b**) *(emergencia)* emergency

urgente *adj* urgent; **correo u.** express mail

urgir [57] *vi* to be urgent *o* pressing; **me urge (tenerlo)** I need it urgently

urinario *nm* urinal

urna *nf* (**a**) *Pol* ballot box (**b**) *(vasija)* urn

urólogo,-a *nm,f Med* urologist

urraca *nf* magpie

URSS *nf Hist* (*abr* **Unión de Repúblicas Socialistas Soviéticas**) USSR

urticaria *nf Med* hives

Uruguay *n* Uruguay

uruguayo,-a *adj & nm,f* Uruguayan

usado,-a *adj (ropa)* second-hand, used

usanza *nf Literario* **a la antigua u.** in the old style

usar 1 *vt* (**a**) to use (**b**) *(prenda)* to wear
  2 usarse *vpr* to be used *o* in fashion

usina *nf Am (central eléctrica)* power station; **u. nuclear** nuclear power station

uso *nm* (**a**) use; *Farm* **u. externo/tópico** external/local application (**b**) *(de poder, privilegio)* exercise (**c**) *(de prenda)* wearing; **haga u. del casco** wear a helmet (**d**) *(costumbre)* usage, custom; **al u.** conventional

usted (*pl* **ustedes**) *pron pers Fml* you; **¿quién es u.?, ¿quiénes son ustedes?** who are you?

> Usually omitted in Spanish except for emphasis or contrast. Although formal in peninsular Spanish, it is not necessarily so in Latin American Spanish.

usual *adj* usual, common

usuario,-a *nm,f* user

usura *nf* usury

usurero,-a *nm,f* usurer

usurpar *vt* to usurp

utensilio *nm* utensil; *(herramienta)* tool

útero *nm* uterus, womb

útil 1 *adj* useful; *(día)* working
  2 *nm (herramienta)* tool, instrument
utilidad *nf* usefulness, utility; *(beneficio)*
 profit
utilitario,-a 1 *nm (coche)* utility vehicle
  2 *adj* utilitarian
utilización *nf* use, utilization

utilizar [40] *vt* to use, to utilize
utopía *nf* utopia
utópico,-a *adj & nm,f* utopian
uva *nf* grape; **u. blanca** green grape
UVI *nf (abr* **unidad de vigilancia intensiva)** ICU
úvula *nf* uvula

V, v ['ue] *nf (la letra)* V, v

V *Elec (abr* **voltio(s))** V

vaca *nf* (a) cow (b) *(carne)* beef

vacaciones *nfpl Br* holidays, *US* vacation; *(viaje)* holiday; **durante las v.** during the holidays; **estar/irse de v.** to be/go on holiday

vacacionista *nmf Am Br* holidaymaker, *US* vacationer

vacante 1 *adj* vacant

2 *nf* vacancy

vaciar [29] **1** *vt* (a) *(recipiente)* to empty; *(contenido)* to empty out (b) *(terreno)* to hollow out (c) *Arte* to cast, to mould

2 vaciarse *upr* to empty

vacilación *nf* hesitation

vacilante *adj* (a) *(persona)* hesitant, irresolute (b) *(voz)* hesitant, faltering (c) *(luz)* flickering

vacilar *vi* (a) *(dudar)* to hesitate; **sin v.** without hesitation (b) *(voz)* to falter (c) *(luz)* to flicker (d) *Fam (jactarse)* to show off

vacilón,-ona *Fam* **1** *adj* (a) *(fanfarrón)* swanky (b) *(bromista)* jokey, teasing (c) *CAm, Méx Fam (juerguista)* fond of partying

2 *nm,f* (a) *(fanfarrón)* show-off (b) *(bromista)* tease

3 *nm Carib (fiesta)* party

vacío,-a 1 *adj* (a) empty; *(hueco)* hollow (b) *(sin ocupar)* vacant, unoccupied

2 *nm* (a) emptiness, void (b) *(hueco)* gap; *(espacio)* (empty) space (c) *Fís* vacuum; **envasado al v.** vacuum-packed

vacuna *nf* vaccine

vacunación *nf* vaccination

vacunar 1 *vt* to vaccinate (**contra** against); *Fig* to inure

2 vacunarse *upr* to get oneself vaccinated

vacuno,-a *adj* bovine; **ganado v.** cattle

vacuo,-a *adj* vacuous, empty

vadear *vt (río)* to ford; *Fig (dificultad)* to overcome

vado *nm* (a) *(de un río)* ford (b) *Aut* **v. permanente** *(en letrero)* keep clear

vagabundear *vi* to wander, to roam

vagabundo,-a 1 *adj (errante)* wandering; *Pey* vagrant; **perro v.** stray dog

2 *nm,f* wanderer; *(sin casa)* tramp, *US* hobo; *Pey* vagrant, tramp

vagancia *nf* idleness, laziness

vagar [42] *vi* to wander about, to roam about

vagido *nm* cry *(of a newborn baby)*

vagina *nf* vagina

vago,-a 1 *adj* (a) *(perezoso)* lazy (b) *(indefinido)* vague

2 *nm,f* (a) *(holgazán)* layabout (b) *Jur* vagrant

vagón *nm (para pasajeros)* carriage, coach, *US* car; *(para mercancías)* truck, wagon, *US* freight car, *US* boxcar

vaguedad *nf* vagueness

vaho *nm (de aliento)* breath; *(vapor)* vapour

vaina 1 *nf* (a) *(de espada)* sheath, scabbard (b) *Bot* pod (c) *Col, Perú, Ven muy Fam (molestia)* bother, pain (in the neck); **¡qué v.!** what a pain!

2 *nmf (persona)* dimwit

vainilla *nf* vanilla

vaivén *nm* (a) *(oscilación)* swinging, to-and-fro movement (b) *(de gente)* coming and going, bustle; *Fig* **vaivenes** ups and downs

vajilla *nf* crockery, dishes; **una v.** a set of dishes, a dinner service

valdré *indic fut de* **valer**

vale¹ *interj* all right!, O.K.!

vale² *nm* (a) *(comprobante)* voucher (b) *(pagaré)* promissory note, IOU (c) *Méx, Ven Fam (amigo)* pal, *Br* mate, *US* buddy

valedero,-a *adj* valid

valenciano,-a *adj* Valencian

valentía *nf* courage, bravery

valentón,-ona *Pey* **1** *adj* bragging, boastful

2 *nm,f* braggart

valer [26] **1** *vt* (a) to be worth; **no vale nada** it is worthless; **vale una fortuna** it is worth a fortune; **no vale la pena (ir)** it's not worth while (going) (b) *(costar)* to cost; **¿cuánto vale?** how much is it? (c) *(proporcionar)* to earn

2 *vi* (a) *(servir)* to be useful, to be of use (b) *(ser válido)* to be valid, to count; **no**

vale hacer trampa cheating isn't on (**c**) **más vale** it is better; **más vale que te vayas ya** you had better leave now

3 valerse *upr* **v. de** to use, to make use of; **v. por sí mismo** to be able to manage on one's own

valeroso,-a *adj* brave, courageous

valgo *indic pres de* **valer**

valía *nf* value, worth

validez *nf* validity

válido,-a *adj* valid

valiente *adj* (**a**) *(valeroso)* brave, courageous (**b**) *Irón* **¡v. amigo eres tú!** a fine friend you are!

valija *nf* (**a**) *(maleta)* case, suitcase; **v. diplomática** diplomatic bag (**b**) *(de correos)* mailbag

valioso,-a *adj* valuable

valla *nf* (**a**) *(cerca)* fence; *(muro)* wall; **v. publicitaria** billboard, *Br* hoarding (**b**) *Dep* hurdle; **los 100 metros vallas** the 100 metres hurdle race

vallado *nm* fence

vallar *vt* to fence (in)

valle *nm* valley

vallisoletano,-a 1 *adj* of/from Valladolid

2 *nm,f* person from Valladolid

valor *nm* (**a**) *(valía)* value, worth; *(precio)* price; **objetos de v.** valuables; **sin v.** worthless; **v. alimenticio** food value (**b**) *(valentía)* courage (**c**) *Fin* **valores** securities, bonds

valoración *nf* valuation

valorar *vt* to value, to calculate the value of

valorización *nf* (**a**) *(tasación)* valuation (**b**) *(revalorización)* appreciation

valorizar [40] *vt* (**a**) *(tasar)* to value (**b**) *(revalorizar)* to raise the value of

vals *nm* waltz; **bailar el v.** to waltz

válvula *nf* valve; **v. de seguridad** safety valve

vampiro *nm* vampire

vanagloriarse [43] *upr* to boast (**de** of)

vandalismo *nm* vandalism

vándalo,-a *nm,f* vandal

vanguardia *nf* (**a**) avant-garde, vanguard; *Fig* **ir a la v. de** to be at the forefront of (**b**) *Mil* vanguard, van

vanguardista 1 *adj* avant-garde

2 *nmf* avant-gardist

vanidad *nf* vanity

vanidoso,-a *adj* vain, conceited

vano,-a *adj* (**a**) *(vanidoso)* vain, conceited (**b**) *(esfuerzo, esperanza)* vain, futile; **en v.** in vain

vapor *nm* (**a**) *(de agua hirviendo)* steam; *Culin* **al v.** steamed (**b**) *(gas)* vapour; **v. de agua** water vapour

vaporizador *nm* vaporizer, spray

vaporizar [40] 1 *vt* to vaporize

2 vaporizarse *upr* to vaporize, to evaporate

vaporoso,-a *adj* vaporous

vapulear *vt* *(físicamente)* to shake; *(con palabras)* to slate

vaqueriza *nf* cowshed

vaquero,-a 1 *nm* cowherd, cowboy

2 *adj* **pantalón v.** jeans, pair of jeans

3 *nmpl* **vaqueros** *(prenda)* jeans, pair of jeans

vara *nf* pole, rod

varar 1 *vt* to beach, to dock

2 *vi* to run aground

variable *adj & nf* variable

variación *nf* variation

variado,-a *adj* varied; **galletas variadas** assorted *Br* biscuits *o US* cookies

variante *nf* variant; *Aut* detour

variar [29] 1 *vt* to vary, to change

2 *vi* to vary, to change; *Irón* **para v.** as usual, just for a change

varice, várice *nf* = **variz**

varicela *nf* chickenpox

variedad *nf* (**a**) *(variety)* (**b**) *Teatro* **variedades** variety show

varilla *nf* *(vara)* rod, stick; *(de abanico, paraguas)* rib

variopinto,-a *adj* diverse, assorted; **un público v.** a varied audience

varios,-as *adj* several

varita *nf* **v. mágica** magic wand

variz *nf* varicose vein

varón *nm* *(hombre)* man; *(chico)* boy; **hijo v.** male child; **sexo v.** male sex

varonil *adj* manly, virile

Varsovia *n* Warsaw

vas *indic pres de* **ir**

vasallo,-a *nm,f Hist* vassal

vasco,-a *adj* Basque; **el País V.** the Basque Country

vascuence *nm* *(idioma)* Basque

vasectomía *nf* vasectomy

vaselina *nf* Vaseline®

vasija *nf* pot

vaso *nm* (**a**) *(para beber)* glass (**b**) *Anat* vessel

> *Observa que la palabra inglesa* **vase** *es un falso amigo y no es la traducción de la palabra española* **vaso**. *En inglés,* **vase** *significa "jarrón".*

vástago *nm* (**a**) *Bot* shoot (**b**) *Fig (hilo)* offspring (**c**) *Téc* rod, stem

vasto,-a *adj* vast

Vaticano *nm* **el V.** the Vatican
vaticinar *vt* to prophesy, to predict
vaticinio *nm* prophecy, prediction
vatio *nm* watt
vaya¹ *interj* ¡v. lío! what a mess!
vaya² *subj pres de* ir
Vd., Vds. (*abr* usted, ustedes) you
ve 1 *imperat de* ir
  2 *indic pres de* ver
vecinal *adj* local
vecindad *nf,* **vecindario** *nm* (**a**) *(área)* neighbourhood, vicinity (**b**) *(vecinos)* community, residents (**c**) *Méx (inquilinato)* tenement house
vecino,-a 1 *nm,f* (**a**) *(persona)* neighbour; **el v. de al lado** the next-door neighbour (**b**) *(residente)* resident
  2 *adj* neighbouring, nearby
veda *nf (de caza)* closed season; **levantar la v.** to open the season
vedado,-a *adj* **coto v. de caza** private hunting ground
vedar *vt* to forbid, to prohibit
vega *nf* fertile plain *o* lowland
vegetación *nf* (**a**) *Bot* vegetation (**b**) *Med* **vegetaciones** adenoids
vegetal *nm* vegetable
vegetar *vi Fig* to vegetate
vegetariano,-a *adj & nm,f* vegetarian
vehemencia *nf* vehemence
vehemente *adj* vehement
vehículo *nm* vehicle
veinte *adj & nm inv* twenty
veintena *nf (veinte)* twenty; **una v. de** about twenty
vejación *nf* humiliation
vejar *vt* to humiliate
vejatorio,-a *adj* humiliating
vejez *nf* old age
vejiga *nf* bladder
vela¹ *nf* (**a**) candle (**b**) *Fam* **quedarse a dos velas** to be in the dark (**c**) **pasar la noche en v.** to have a sleepless night
vela² *nf Náut* sail
velada *nf* evening (party)
velado,-a *adj* (**a**) *(oculto)* veiled, hidden (**b**) *Fot* blurred
velador 1 *nm* (**a**) *(mesa)* table (**b**) *Andes, Méx (mesilla de noche)* bedside table (**c**) *Méx, RP (lámpara)* bedside lamp
  2 *nm Méx (sereno)* nightwatchman
velar¹ *vi* (**a**) **v. por** to watch over (**b**) *(hacer guardia)* to keep watch
velar² *Fot* **1** *vt* to blur
  2 velarse *vpr* to become blurred
velatorio *nm* vigil, wake
veleidad *nf* fickleness
veleidoso,-a *adj* fickle

velero *nm* sailing boat *o* ship
veleta 1 *nf* weather vane, weathercock
  2 *nmf Fam* fickle *o* changeable person
veliz *nf Méx* suitcase, case
vello *nm* hair
vellón *nm* fleece
velloso,-a, velludo,-a *adj* downy
velo *nm* veil
velocidad *nf* (**a**) *(rapidez)* speed; *(de proyectil etc)* velocity; *Aut* **v. máxima** speed limit; *Informát* **v. de transmisión** bit rate; *Informát* **v. operativa** operating speed (**b**) *Aut (marcha)* gear
velocímetro *nm* speedometer
velocista *nmf* sprinter
velódromo *nm* cycle track, velodrome
veloz 1 *adj* swift, rapid
  2 *adv* quickly, fast
vena *nf* vein
venado *nm* deer, stag; *Culin* venison
vencedor,-a 1 *nm,f* winner
  2 *adj* winning
vencejo *nm Orn* swift
vencer [49] 1 *vt* (**a**) *(al enemigo)* to defeat; *(al contrincante)* to beat (**b**) *(dificultad)* to overcome, to surmount
  2 *vi* (**a**) *(pago, deuda)* to fall due, to be payable (**b**) *(plazo)* to expire
  3 vencerse *vpr (torcerse)* to warp
vencido,-a *adj* (**a**) *Mil (derrotado)* defeated; *Dep* beaten; *Fig* **darse por v.** to give up, to accept defeat (**b**) *(pago, deuda)* due, payable (**c**) *(plazo)* expired (**d**) *Fam* **a la tercera va la vencida** third time lucky
vencimiento *nm* (**a**) *Com* maturity (**b**) *(de un plazo)* expiry
venda *nf* bandage
vendaje *nm* dressing
vendar *vt* to bandage; *Fig* **v. los ojos a algn** to blindfold sb
vendaval *nm* gale
vendedor,-a *nm,f* seller; *(hombre)* salesman; *(mujer)* saleswoman
vender 1 *vt* to sell; **v. a plazos/al contado** to sell on credit/for cash; **v. al por mayor/menor** to (sell) wholesale/retail
  2 venderse *vpr* (**a**) to sell; **este disco se vende bien** this record is selling well; **se vende** *(en letrero)* for sale (**b**) *(claudicar)* to sell out
vendimia *nf* grape harvest
vendré *indic fut de* venir
Venecia *n* Venice
veneno *nm* poison; *(de serpiente)* venom
venenoso,-a *adj* poisonous
venerable *adj* venerable
veneración *nf* veneration
venerar *vt* to venerate, to revere

venéreo,-a *adj* venereal

venero *nm* spring

venezolano,-a *adj & nm,f* Venezuelan

Venezuela *n* Venezuela

venga *subj pres de* venir

venganza *nf* vengeance, revenge

vengar [42] 1 *vt* to avenge

  2 vengarse *vpr* to avenge oneself; **v. de algn** to take revenge on sb

vengativo,-a *adj* vengeful, vindictive

vengo *indic pres de* venir

venia *nf* (a) *Fml (permiso)* permission (b) *(perdón)* pardon

venial *adj* venial

venida *nf* coming, arrival

venidero,-a *adj* future, coming

venir [27] 1 *vi* (a) to come; *Fig* **v. a menos** to come down in the world; *Fig* **v. al mundo** to be born; **el año que viene** next year; *Fig* **me viene a la memoria** I remember; *Fam* **¡venga ya!** *(vamos)* come on!; *(expresa incredulidad)* come off it! (b) **v. grande/pequeño** *(ropa)* to be too big/small; **v. mal/bien** to be inconvenient/convenient; **el metro me viene muy bien** I find the *Br* underground o *US* subway very handy (c) *(en pasivas)* **esto vino provocado por ...** this was brought about by ... (d) **esto viene ocurriendo desde hace mucho tiempo** this has been going on for a long time now

  2 venirse *vpr* **v. abajo** to collapse

venta *nf* (a) sale; **en v.** for sale; **a la v.** on sale; **v. a plazos/al contado** credit/cash sale; **v. al por mayor/al por menor** wholesale/retail (b) *(posada)* country inn

ventaja *nf* advantage; **llevar v. a** to have the advantage over; **le sacó 2 m de v.** he beat him by 2 m

ventajoso,-a *adj* advantageous

ventana *nf* (a) window (b) *(de la nariz)* nostril

ventanal *nm* large window

ventanilla *nf* (a) window (b) *(de la nariz)* nostril

ventanuco *nm* small window

ventilación *nf* ventilation; **sin v.** unventilated

ventilador *nm* ventilator; *(de coche)* fan

ventilar 1 *vt* (a) *(habitación)* to ventilate, to air (b) *Fig (opinión)* to air

  2 ventilarse *vpr Fam (terminar)* to finish off

ventisca *nf* blizzard; *(de nieve)* snowstorm

ventosa *nf* sucker; *Med* cupping glass

ventosear *vi* to break wind

ventoso,-a *adj* windy

ventrílocuo,-a *nm,f* ventriloquist

ventura *nf* (a) *(felicidad)* happiness (b) *(suerte)* luck; *(casualidad)* chance

venturoso,-a *adj* lucky, fortunate

Venus *nm* Venus

veo-veo *nm Fam* **el (juego del) v.** I-spy

ver¹ *nm* **de buen v.** good-looking

ver² [28] 1 *vt* (a) to see; *(televisión)* to watch; **a v.** let me see, let's see; **a v. si escribes** I hope you'll write; **(ya) veremos** we'll see; *Fam* **había un jaleo que no veas** you should have seen the fuss that was made; **no veo por qué** I can't see why; **a mi modo de v.** as I see it (b) **no tener nada que v. con** to have nothing to do with

  2 verse *vpr* (a) *(imagen etc)* to be seen (b) *(encontrarse con algn)* to meet, to see each other; **¡nos vemos!** see you later! (c) **no se pueden ni v.** *(soportarse)* they can't stand (the sight of) each other (d) *Am* **te ves divina** you look divine

vera *nf* edge, border; **a la v. de** beside, next to

veracidad *nf* veracity, truthfulness

veraneante *nmf Br* holidaymaker, *US* (summer) vacationer

veranear *vi* to spend one's summer *Br* holiday o *US* vacation

veraneo *nm* summer *Br* holiday o *US* vacation

veraniego,-a *adj* summer

veranillo *nm* Indian summer; **el v. de San Juan** *(en el hemisferio sur)* = warm spell around 24 June; **el v. de San Martín** *(en el hemisferio norte)* = warm spell around 11 November

verano *nm* summer

veras *nfpl* **de v.** really, seriously

veraz *adj* veracious, truthful

verbal *adj* verbal

verbena *nf* street party

verbo *nm* verb

verborrea *nf Fam* verbosity, verbal diarrhoea

verdad *nf* (a) truth; **es v.** it is true; **a decir v.** to tell the truth; **¡de v!** really!, truly!; **un amigo de v.** a real friend (b) *(en frase afirmativa)* **está muy bien, ¿(no es) v.?** it is very good, isn't it?; *(en frase negativa)* **no te gusta, ¿v.?** you don't like it, do you?

verdaderamente *adv* truly, really

verdadero,-a *adj* true, real

verde 1 *adj* (a) green (b) *(fruta)* unripe (c) *Fam (chiste, película)* blue; **viejo v.** dirty old man (d) *Fam Fig* **poner v. a algn** to call sb every name under the sun

  2 *nm* (a) *(color)* green (b) *Pol* **los verdes** the Greens

verdear *vi* to turn green
verdor *nm (color)* greenness; *(de plantas)* verdure
verdoso,-a *adj* greenish
verdugo,-a 1 *nm* executioner
  2 *nm,f Fig* tyrant
verdulería *nf* greengrocer's (shop)
verdulero,-a *nm,f* greengrocer
verdura *nf* vegetables, greens
vereda *nf* (a) *(camino)* path, lane (b) *CSur, Perú (acera) Br* pavement, *US* sidewalk
veredicto *nm* verdict
verga *nf* penis
vergonzoso,-a *adj* (a) *(penoso)* shameful, disgraceful (b) *(tímido)* shy, bashful
vergüenza *nf* (a) shame; **¿no te da v.?** aren't you ashamed?, have you no shame?; **¡es una v.!** it's a disgrace! (b) *(timidez)* shyness, bashfulness; **tener v.** to be shy; **me da v.** I'm too embarrassed
vericueto *nm* winding path; *Fig* **los vericuetos** the ins and outs
verídico,-a *adj* truthful, true
verificar [44] 1 *vt (comprobar)* to check
  2 verificarse *upr* to take place, to occur
verja *nf (reja)* grating; *(cerca)* railing, railings; *(puerta)* iron gate
vermut, vermú *nm (pl vermús)* (a) *(licor)* vermouth (b) *(aperitivo)* aperitif (c) *Andes, RP (en cine)* early evening showing; *(en teatro)* early evening performance
verosímil *adj* probable, likely; *(creíble)* credible
verruga *nf* wart
versado,-a *adj* well-versed (**en** in)
versar *vi* **v. sobre** to be about, to deal with
versátil *adj* (a) versatile (b) *(voluble)* changeable, inconstant
versatilidad *nf* (a) versatility (b) *(volubilidad)* changeableness, inconstancy
versículo *nm* verse
versión *nf* version; **película en v. original** film in the original language
verso *nm* (a) *(poesía)* verse (b) *(línea)* line
vértebra *nf* vertebra
vertebrado,-a *adj & nm* vertebrate
vertedero *nm (de basura) Br* rubbish tip o dump, *US* garbage dump
verter [3] 1 *vt* (a) to pour (out) (b) *(basura)* to dump
  2 *vi (río)* to flow, to run (**a** into)
vertical *adj* vertical
vértice *nm* vertex
vertiente *nf* (a) *(de una montaña, un tejado)* slope; *Fig* aspect (b) *Am (manantial)* spring

vertiginoso,-a *adj* dizzy, giddy; *Fig (velocidad)* breakneck
vértigo *nm* vertigo; **me da v.** it makes me dizzy
vesícula *nf* vesicle; **v. biliar** gall bladder
vespa® *nf* (motor) scooter
vespertino,-a 1 *adj* evening
  2 *nm Prensa* evening newspaper
vespino® *nm* moped
vestíbulo *nm (de casa)* hall; *(de edificio público)* foyer
vestido,-a 1 *nm (ropa)* clothes; *(de mujer)* dress
  2 *adj* dressed; **policía v. de paisano** plain-clothes policeman
vestidura *nf* clothing, clothes
vestigio *nm* vestige, trace
vestimenta *nf* clothes, garments
vestir [6] 1 *vt* (a) *(a algn)* to dress (b) *(llevar puesto)* to wear
  2 *vi* (a) to dress; **ropa de (mucho) v.** formal dress (b) *Fam* **la seda viste mucho** silk always looks very elegant
  3 vestirse *upr* (a) to get dressed, to dress (b) **v. de** to wear, to dress in; *(disfrazarse)* to disguise oneself as, to dress up as
vestuario *nm* (a) *(conjunto de vestidos)* clothes, wardrobe; *Teatro* wardrobe, costumes (b) *(camerino)* dressing room (c) *Dep* changing room
veta *nf Min* vein, seam; *(de carne)* streak
vetar *vt* to veto
veterano,-a *adj & nm,f* veteran
veterinario,-a 1 *nm,f* vet, *Br* veterinary surgeon, *US* veterinarian
  2 *nf* **veterinaria** veterinary medicine o science
veto *nm* veto; **derecho a v.** power o right of veto
vetusto,-a *adj Fml* ancient
vez *nf* (a) time; **una v.** once; **dos veces** twice; **cinco veces** five times; **a** o **algunas veces** sometimes; **cada v.** each o every time; **cada v. más** more and more; **de v. en cuando** now and again, every now and then; **¿le has visto alguna v.?** have you ever seen him?; **otra v.** again; **a la v.** at the same time; **tal v.** perhaps, maybe; **de una v.** in one go; **de una v. para siempre** once and for all; **en v. de** instead of; **érase** o **había una v.** *(en cuentos etc)* once upon a time (b) *(turno)* turn (c) **hacer las veces de** to do duty as
v.g(r). *(abr* **verbigracia)** eg
vía 1 *nf* (a) *Ferroc* track, line (b) *(camino)* road; **v. pública** public thoroughfare; **V. Láctea** Milky Way (c) *Anat* passage, tract; *Farm* **(por) v. oral** to be taken orally (d)

Fig **por v. oficial** through official channels; **por v. aérea/marítima** by air/sea (**e**) **en vías de** in the process of; **países en vías de desarrollo** developing countries
  2 *prep (a través de)* via, through; **v. París** via Paris; **transmisión v. satélite** satellite transmission
viable *adj* viable
viaducto *nm* viaduct
viajante *nmf* commercial traveller, travelling salesman, *f* saleswoman
viajar *vi* to travel
viaje *nm (recorrido)* journey, trip; *(largo, en barco)* voyage; **¡buen v.!** bon voyage!, have a good trip!; **estar de v.** to be away (on a trip); **irse** o **marcharse de v.** to go on a journey o trip; **v. de negocios** business trip; **v. de novios** honeymoon
viajero,-a 1 *nm,f* (**a**) traveller (**b**) *(en transporte público)* passenger
  2 *adj* **cheque v.** traveller's cheque
vianda *nf RP* (**a**) *(tentempié)* packed lunch (**b**) *(fiambrera)* lunchbox
viandante *nmf* passer-by
viario,-a *adj* road, highway; **red viaria** road network
víbora *nf* viper
vibración *nf* vibration
vibrador *nm* vibrator
vibrar *vt & vi* to vibrate
vicario,-a *nm,f* vicar
vicepresidente,-a *nm,f* (**a**) *Pol* vicepresident (**b**) *(de compañía, comité)* vice-chairperson; *(hombre)* vice-chairman; *(mujer)* vice-chairwoman
vicesecretario,-a *nm,f* assistant secretary
viceversa *adv* vice versa
viciado,-a *adj* (**a**) *(corrompido)* corrupt (**b**) *(aire)* foul
viciar [43] 1 *vt* (**a**) *(corromper)* to corrupt (**b**) *(estropear)* to waste
  2 viciarse *vpr* (**a**) *(deformarse)* to go out of shape (**b**) *(corromperse)* to become corrupted
vicio *nm* (**a**) vice (**b**) *(mala costumbre)* bad habit (**c**) *Fam (destreza)* skill
vicioso,-a 1 *adj* (**a**) *(persona)* depraved, perverted (**b**) **círculo v.** vicious circle
  2 *nm,f* depraved person; **v. del trabajo** workaholic
vicisitud *nf (usu pl)* vicissitude
víctima *nf* victim
victimar *vt Am* to kill, to murder
victimario,-a *nm,f Am* killer, murderer
victoria *nf* victory
victorioso,-a *adj* victorious
vicuña *nf* vicuña

vid *nf* vine, grapevine
vida *nf* life; *(período)* lifetime; **de toda la v.** lifelong; **en mi v.** never in my life; **de por v.** for life; **ganarse la v.** to earn one's living; **¿qué es de tu v.?** how's life?; **estar con/sin v.** to be alive/dead
vidente *nmf* clairvoyant
vídeo *nm* video; **grabar en v.** to videotape
videocámara *nf* video camera
videoclub *nm* video club
videoconferencia *nf* videoconferencing; *(sesión)* videoconference
videojuego *nm* video game
vidriera *nf* (**a**) stained-glass window (**b**) *Am (escaparate)* shop window
vidrio *nm* glass
viejo,-a 1 *adj* old; **hacerse v.** to grow old; **un v. amigo** an old friend
  2 *nm,f* (**a**) *(hombre, padre)* old man; *(mujer, madre)* old woman; **los viejos** old people; *Fam* **mis viejos** my parents (**b**) *RP Fam* **¡mi v.!** *(apelativo cariñoso)* young man o fellow!; **¡mi vieja!** *(apelativo cariñoso)* my dear! (**c**) *Chile* **el V. de Pascua** o **Pascuero** Father Christmas
  3 *nf* **vieja** *Col, Méx, Ven Fam (mujer, chica)* chick, *Br* bird, *US* broad
Viena *n* Vienna
vienés,-esa *adj & nm,f* Viennese
viento *nm* wind; **hace** o **sopla mucho v.** it is very windy; *Fam Fig* **¡vete a tomar v.!** get lost!
vientre *nm* (**a**) belly; **hacer de v.** to have a bowel movement (**b**) *(útero)* womb
viernes *nm inv* Friday; **V. Santo** Good Friday
Vietnam *n* Vietnam
vietnamita *adj & nmf* Vietnamese
viga *nf (de madera)* beam; *(de hierro)* girder
vigencia *nf* validity; **entrar en v.** to come into force o effect
vigente *adj* in force
vigésimo,-a *adj & nm,f* twentieth
vigía 1 *nf* watchtower, lookout post
  2 *nmf* lookout; *(hombre)* watchman; *(mujer)* watchwoman
vigilancia *nf* vigilance, watchfulness; *Med* **unidad de v. intensiva** intensive care unit
vigilante *nm* watchman; *(de banco)* guard
vigilar 1 *vt* to watch; *(un lugar)* to guard; **vigila que no entren** make sure they don't get in
  2 *vi (gen)* to keep watch
vigilia *nf* (**a**) vigil (**b**) *(víspera)* eve (**c**) *Rel (abstinencia)* abstinence

vigor nm (a) vigour; (fuerza) strength (b) **en v.** in force

vigoroso,-a adj vigorous

VIH nm (abr **Virus de la Inmunodeficiencia Humana**) HIV

vikingo,-a adj & nm Viking

vil adj Fml vile, base

vileza nf (a) vileness, baseness (b) (acto) vile act, despicable deed

vilipendiar [43] vt Fml to vilify, to revile

villa nf (a) (población) town (b) (casa) villa, country house (c) Arg **v. miseria** shanty town

villancico nm (Christmas) carol

vilo: • **en vilo** loc adv (persona) on tenterhooks; (cosa) up in the air

vinagre nm vinegar

vinagrera nf **vinagreras** oil and vinegar cruets, cruet (stand)

vinagreta nf vinaigrette sauce

vinajeras nfpl cruets

vincha nf Am headband

vinculante adj binding

vincular vt to link, to bind; (relacionar) to relate, to connect

vínculo nm link

vine pt indef de **venir**

vinícola adj wine-producing

vinicultor,-a nm,f wine producer

vinicultura nf wine production o growing

vinilo nm vinyl

vino nm wine; **tomar un v.** to have a glass of wine; **v. blanco/tinto/dulce/seco** white/red/sweet/dry wine; **v. rosado** rosé

viña nf vineyard

viñedo nm vineyard

viñeta nf illustration

viola nf viola

violación nf (a) (de una persona) rape (b) (de ley, derecho) violation, infringement

violador nm rapist

violar vt (a) (persona) to rape (b) (ley, derecho) to violate, to infringe

violencia nf (a) violence; **la no v.** non-violence (b) (incomodidad) embarrassment

violentar vt (a) (forzar) to force, to break open; (sitio) to break into, to enter by force (b) (enojar) to infuriate

violento,-a adj (a) violent (b) (situación) embarrassing, awkward (c) **sentirse v.** (incómodo) to feel embarrassed o awkward

violeta 1 adj & nm (color) violet
2 nf (flor) violet

violín nm violin; Fam fiddle

violinista nmf violinist

violón nm double bass

violoncelista, violonchelista nmf cellist

violoncelo, violonchelo nm violoncello, cello

viraje nm (a) turn (b) Fig about-face, U-turn

virar vi (a) (girar) to turn round (b) Fig to change

virgen 1 adj (a) (persona, selva) virgin (b) (aceite, lana) pure; (cinta) blank
2 nmf virgin; Fam **ser un viva la v.** to be a devil-may-care person

virginidad nf virginity

Virgo nm Virgo

virgo nm hymen

virguería nf Fam gem, marvel; **hacer virguerías** to work wonders, to be a dab hand

virguero,-a adj Fam smart, great; **esta camisa es muy virguera** that shirt is the business

vírico,-a adj viral

viril adj virile, manly; **miembro v.** penis

virilidad nf virility

virtual adj virtual

virtud nf (a) virtue; Fig **en v. de** by virtue of (b) (propiedad) property, quality

virtuoso,-a 1 adj virtuous
2 nm,f (a) virtuous person (b) (músico) virtuoso

viruela nf smallpox; **viruelas** pockmarks

virulé: • **a la virulé** loc adj Fam (a) (torcido) crooked, twisted (b) **un ojo a la v.** a black eye

virulencia nf virulence

virulento,-a adj virulent

virus nm inv virus

visado nm, Am **visa** nf visa

víscera nf (a) internal organ (b) **vísceras** viscera, entrails

visceral adj (a) Anat visceral (b) Fig profound, deep-rooted

viscoso,-a adj viscous

visera nf (de gorra) peak; (de casco) visor

visibilidad nf visibility; **curva con mala v.** blind corner

visible adj visible; (evidente) evident

visillo nm small lace o net curtain

visión nf (a) vision (b) (vista) sight; Fig **v. de conjunto** overall view; **con v. de futuro** forward-looking; (aparición) vision

visionario,-a nm,f visionary; (iluso) person who imagines things

visita nf (a) (acción) visit; **hacer una v.** to pay a visit; **estar de v.** to be visiting (b) (invitado) visitor, guest

visitador,-a *nm,f Farm* pharmaceutical salesman, *f* saleswoman
visitante 1 *nmf* visitor
  2 *adj (equipo)* away
visitar *vt* to visit
vislumbrar *vt* to glimpse
viso *nm* (a) *(reflejo)* sheen (b) *Fig* **tener visos de** to seem, to appear
visón *nm* mink
visor *nm Fot* viewfinder

📙 Observa que la palabra inglesa **visor** es un falso amigo y no es la traducción de la palabra española **visor**. En inglés, **visor** significa "visera".

víspera *nf (día anterior)* day before; *(de festivo)* eve; **en vísperas de** in the period leading up to
vista *nf* (a) sight; **a la v.** visible; **a primera o simple v.** at first sight, on the face of it; **con vistas a** with a view to; **en v. de** in view of, considering; **corto de v.** short-sighted; **conocer a algn de v.** to know sb by sight; **perder de v. a** to lose sight of; **quítalo de mi v.** take it away; *Fig* **tener mucha v. para** to have a good eye for; *Fig* **volver la v. atrás** to look back; *Fam* **¡hasta la v.!** goodbye!, see you!; *Fam* **hacer la v. gorda** to turn a blind eye (b) *(panorama)* view; **con vista(s) al mar** overlooking the sea (c) *Jur* trial, hearing
vistazo *nm* glance; **echar un v. a algo** *(ojear)* to have a (quick) look at sth; *(tener cuidado de)* to keep an eye on sth
visto,-a 1 *adj* (a) **está v. que ...** it is obvious that ...; **por lo v.** evidently, apparently; **v. que** in view of the fact that, seeing o given that (b) **estar bien v.** to be well looked upon, to be considered acceptable; **estar mal v.** to be frowned upon (c) **estar muy v.** to be old hat
  2 *nm* **v. bueno** approval, O.K.
vistoso,-a *adj* eye-catching
visual *adj* visual; **campo v.** field of vision
visualizar [40] *vt* to visualize; *(película)* to view
vital *adj* (a) vital (b) *(persona)* full of vitality
vitalicio,-a *adj* life, for life; **pensión/cargo v.** life pension/permanent post
vitalidad *nf* vitality
vitamina *nf* vitamin
vitamínico,-a *adj* vitamin; **complejo v.** multivitamins
viticultor,-a *nm,f* wine grower
viticultura *nf* wine growing
vitorear *vt* to cheer
vítreo,-a *adj* vitreous

vitrina *nf (aparador)* glass o display cabinet; *(de exposición)* glass case, showcase; *Am (escaparate)* shop window
vituallas *nfpl* provisions
vituperar *vt* to condemn
vituperio *nm* condemnation
viudo,-a *nm,f (hombre)* widower; *(mujer)* widow
viva *interj* **¡v.!** hurrah!
vivacidad *nf* vivacity
vivaracho,-a *adj Fam* lively, sprightly
vivaz *adj* (a) lively, vivacious (b) *(perspicaz)* sharp, quick-witted
vivencias *nfpl* personal experience
víveres *nmpl* provisions, supplies
vivero *nm (de plantas)* nursery; *(de peces)* fish farm o hatchery; *Fig* breeding ground, hotbed
viveza *nf* (a) liveliness, vivacity; *(en los ojos)* sparkle (b) *(agudeza)* sharpness, quick-wittedness
vividor,-a *nm,f Pey* sponger, scrounger
vivienda *nf* (a) housing (b) *(casa)* house; *(piso)* flat
vivir 1 *vi* to live; **vive de sus ahorros** she lives off her savings; **viven de la pesca** they make their living by fishing
  2 *vt* to live through
  3 *nm* life
vivito,-a *adj Fam* **v. y coleando** alive and kicking
vivo,-a 1 *adj* (a) alive; **de viva voz** verbally, by word of mouth; **en v.** *(programa)* live; *Fam* **es el v. retrato o la viva imagen de** she is the spitting image of (b) **al rojo v.** red-hot (c) *(vivaz)* lively, vivacious (d) *(listo)* sharp, clever (e) *(color)* vivid, bright (f) *(descripción)* lively, graphic
  2 *nm,f* **los vivos** the living
Vizcaya *n* **el golfo de V.** the Bay of Biscay
V. B. *(abr visto bueno) (en documento)* approved
vocablo *nm* word, term
vocabulario *nm* vocabulary
vocación *nf* vocation, calling; **con v. europea** with leanings towards Europe
vocacional *adj* vocational
vocal 1 *nf Ling* vowel
  2 *nmf* member
vocalista *nmf Mús* vocalist, singer
vocalizar [40] *vt & vi* to vocalize
voceador,-a *nm,f Am* vendor
vocerío *nm* shouting
vocero,-a *nm,f Am* spokesperson; *(hombre)* spokesman; *(mujer)* spokeswoman
vociferante *adj* vociferous
vociferar *vt & vi* to vociferate
vodka *nm* vodka

vol. (*abr* **volumen**) vol
volado,-a *adj Fam* **estar v.** to have a screw loose
volador,-a *adj* flying
volandas: • **en volandas** *loc adv (por el aire)* in the air, flying through the air
volante 1 *nm* (a) *Aut* steering wheel; **ir al v.** to be driving; **un as del v.** a motor-racing champion (b) *Cost* frill, ruffle (c) *Med* note
  2 *adj* flying; **platillo v.** flying saucer
volantín *nm Am (cometa)* small kite
volar [2] 1 *vi* (a) to fly; *Fig* **lo hizo volando** he did it in a flash (b) *Fam (desaparecer)* to disappear, to vanish
  2 *vt (edificios)* to blow up; *(caja fuerte)* to blow open; *Min* to blast
  3 volarse *vpr (papel etc)* to be blown away
volátil *adj* volatile
volatinero,-a *nm,f* acrobat
volcán *nm* volcano
volcánico,-a *adj* volcanic
volcar [2] 1 *vt* (a) *(cubo etc)* to knock over; *(barco, bote)* to capsize (b) *(vaciar)* to empty out (c) *(tiempo)* to invest
  2 *vi (coche)* to turn over; *(barco)* to capsize
  3 volcarse *vpr* (a) *(vaso, jarra)* to fall over, to tip over; *(coche)* to turn over; *(barco)* to capsize (b) *Fig* **v. con** to do one's utmost for
voleibol *nm* volleyball
voleo *nm Fig* **a(l) v.** at random, haphazardly
voltaje *nm* voltage
voltear 1 *vt* (a) *(dar la vuelta a)* to turn upside down (b) *CSur (derribar)* to knock over (c) *Andes, CAm, Carib, Méx (cabeza)* to turn; **v. la espalda a algn** to turn one's back on sb
  2 *vi* (a) to turn o roll over (b) *Méx (doblar la esquina)* to go round
  3 voltearse *vpr* (a) *Andes, CAm, Carib, Méx (volverse)* to turn around (b) *Méx (vehículo)* to turn over
voltereta *nf* somersault
voltio *nm* volt
voluble *adj* fickle, changeable

> ♪ Observa que la palabra inglesa **voluble** es un falso amigo y no es la traducción de la palabra española **voluble**. En inglés, **voluble** significa "locuaz".

volumen *nm* volume
voluminoso,-a *adj* voluminous; *(enorme)* massive, bulky
voluntad *nf* will; **fuerza de v.** willpower;

tiene mucha v. he is very strong-willed; **v. at will**
voluntario,-a 1 *adj* voluntary
  2 *nm,f* volunteer; **ofrecerse v.** to volunteer
voluntarioso,-a *adj* willing
voluptuoso,-a *adj* voluptuous
volver [4] *(pp* **vuelto)** **1** *vi* (a) to return; *(venir)* to come back; *(ir)* to go back; **v. en sí** to come round, to recover consciousness (b) **v. a hacer algo** to do sth again
  2 *vt* (a) *(convertir)* to turn, to make; **me vas a v. loco** you are driving me mad (b) *(dar vuelta a)* to turn; *(boca abajo)* to turn upside down; *(de fuera adentro)* to turn inside out; *(de atrás adelante)* to turn back to front; *(dar la vuelta a)* to turn over; **volverle la espalda a algn** to turn one's back on sb; *Fig* **v. la vista atrás** to look back; **al v. la esquina** on turning the corner
  3 volverse *vpr* (a) to turn (b) *(regresar) (venir)* to come back; *(ir)* to go back (c) *(convertirse)* to become; **v. loco,-a** to go mad
vomitar 1 *vi* to vomit, to be sick; **tengo ganas de v.** I feel sick, I want to be sick
  2 *vt* to vomit, to bring up
vómito *nm (lo vomitado)* vomit; *(acción)* vomiting
vomitona *nf Fam* vomit
voracidad *nf* voracity, voraciousness
vorágine *nf* whirlpool; *Fig* maelstrom
voraz *adj* voracious; *Fig* raging, fierce
vórtice *nm* vortex
vos *pron pers Am (tú)* you

> The **vos** form is used alongside **tú** in many Latin American countries, and in some countries (Argentina, Paraguay and Uruguay) is the preferred form.

vosotros,-as *pron pers pl* (a) *(sujeto)* you (b) *(con prep)* you; **entre v.** among yourselves; **sin vosotras** without you

> Usually omitted in Spanish except for emphasis or contrast. In Latin America, **vosotros** is not used. Instead, **ustedes** is used as the second person plural in all contexts, without necessarily suggesting formality.

votación *nf* (a) *(voto)* vote, ballot (b) *(acción)* voting
votante *nmf* voter
votar *vi* to vote; **v. a algn** to vote (for) sb
voto *nm* (a) vote; **tener v.** to have the right to vote; **v. secreto** secret ballot (b) *Rel* vow

vox *nf* **esto es v. populi** this is common knowledge

voy *indic pres de* **ir**

voz *nf* (**a**) voice; **en v. alta** aloud; **en v. baja** in a low voice; **a media v.** in a low voice, softly; **de viva v.** verbally (**b**) *(grito)* shout; **a voces** shouting; **dar voces** to shout; *Fig* **estar pidiendo algo a voces** to be crying out for sth; *Fig* **secreto a voces** open secret; **a v. en grito** at the top of one's voice (**c**) **no tener ni v. ni voto** to have no say in the matter; *Fig* **llevar la v. cantante** to rule the roost (**d**) *Gram* **v. pasiva** passive voice

vudú *nm* voodoo

vuelco *nm* upset, tumble; **dar un v.** *(coche)* to overturn; *Fig* **me dio un v. el corazón** my heart missed a beat

vuelo *nm* (**a**) flight; **v. chárter/regular** charter/scheduled flight; **v. sin motor** gliding; *Fig* **cazarlas** *o* **cogerlas al v.** to be quick on the uptake (**b**) *Cost* **una falda de v.** a full skirt

vuelta *nf* (**a**) *(regreso)* return; *(viaje)* return journey; **a v. de** to be back; **estar de v.** to be back; *Dep* **partido de v.** return match (**b**) *(giro)* turn; *(en carreras)* lap; *Dep (ciclista)* tour; **dar media v.** to turn round; *Fig* **la cabeza me da vueltas** my head is spinning; *Fig* **no le des más vueltas** stop worrying about it; **v. de campana** somersault (**c**) *(dinero)* change (**d**) **dar una v.** *(a pie)* to go for a walk *o* stroll; *(en coche)* to go for a drive *o* a spin (in the car) (**e**) *Fig* **no tiene v. de hoja** there's no doubt about it

vuelto,-a **1** *adj* **jersey de cuello v.** rollneck sweater

2 *nm Am* change

vuestro,-a **1** *adj pos (antes del sustantivo)* your; *(después del sustantivo)* of yours; **v. libro** your book; **un amigo v.** a friend of yours

2 *pron pos* yours; **éstos son los vuestros** these are yours; **lo v.** what is yours, what belongs to you

vulgar *adj* (**a**) vulgar (**b**) **el término v.** the everyday term

vulgaridad *nf* vulgarity

vulgarizar [40] *vt (popularizar)* to popularize

vulgarmente *adv* **v. llamado** commonly known as

vulgo *nm* **el v.** the common people; *Pey* the masses

vulnerable *adj* vulnerable

vulnerar *vt (ley, acuerdo)* to violate

vulva *nf* vulva

WXY

W, w [ue'ðole] *nf (la letra)* W, w
W *(abr vatio(s))* W
walkie-talkie *nm* walkie-talkie
walkman® *nm* Walkman®
wáter *nm (pl wáteres) Fam* toilet
waterpolo *nm* water polo
Web, web [web] *Informát* **1** *nf (World Wide Web)* **la W.** the Web
  2 *nm o nf (página web)* web site
whisky *nm (escocés)* whisky; *(irlandés, US)* whiskey
windsurf, windsurfing *nm* windsurfing
windsurfista *nmf* windsurfer

xenofobia *nf* xenophobia
xenófobo,-a 1 *adj* xenophobic
  2 *nm,f* xenophobe

Y, y [iri'ea] *nf (la letra)* Y, y
y *conj* **(a)** and; **una chica alta y morena** a tall, dark-haired girl; **son las tres y cuarto** it's a quarter past three **(b)** *¿y qué?* so what?; *¿y si no llega a tiempo?* what if he doesn't arrive in time?; *¿y tú?* what about you?; *¿y eso?* how come?; **y eso que** although, even though; **¡y tanto!** you bet!, and how!; *ver* **e**
ya 1 *adv* **(a)** already; **ya lo sabía** I already knew; **ya en la Edad Media** as far back as the Middle Ages **(b)** *(ahora mismo)* now; **es preciso actuar ya** it is vital that we act now; **¡hazlo ya!** do it at once!; **ya mismo** right away **(c)** *(en el futuro)* **ya hablaremos luego** we'll talk about it later; **ya nos veremos** see you!; **ya verás** you'll see **(d)** **ya no** no longer; **ya no viene por aquí** he doesn't come round here any more **(e)** *(refuerza el verbo)* **ya era hora** about time too!; **ya lo creo** of course, I should think so; **¡ya voy!** coming!; **¡ya está!** that's it!
  2 *conj* **ya que** since
yacaré *nm* cayman
yacer [61] *vi* to lie, to be lying
yacimiento *nm* bed, deposit; **yacimientos petrolíferos** oilfields
yaguar *nm* jaguar
yanqui *Pey* **1** *adj* Yankee
  2 *nmf* Yankee, Yank
yarará *nf Am* = large poisonous snake

yaraví *nm Am* = Quechuan song
yarda *nf* yard
yate *nm* yacht
yaya *nf Am Bot* lance-wood; *Fam (abuela)* granny
yedra *nf* = hiedra
yegua *nf* mare
yema *nf* **(a)** *(de huevo)* yolk **(b)** *Bot* bud **(c) y. del dedo** fingertip **(d)** *Culin* = sweet made from sugar and egg yolk
Yemen *n* Yemen
yen *nm (moneda)* yen
yendo *ger de* **ir**
yerba *nf* **(a)** = **hierba** **(b)** *RP* maté; **y. mate** yerba maté
yerbatero,-a *Am* **1** *nm,f (curandero)* = witch doctor who uses herbs
  2 *adj* maté
yermo,-a *adj* **(a)** *(baldío)* barren, uncultivated **(b)** *(despoblado)* deserted, uninhabited
yerno *nm* son-in-law
yerro *indic pres de* **errar**
yeso *nm* **(a)** *Geol* gypsum **(b)** *Constr* plaster
Yibuti *n* Djibouti
yiu-yitsu *nm* ju-jitsu
yo *pron pers* I; **entre tú y yo** between you and me; *¿quién es? – soy yo* who is it? – it's me; **yo no** not me; **yo que tú** if I were you; **yo mismo** I myself

> Usually omitted as a personal pronoun in Spanish except for emphasis or contrast.

yodo *nm* iodine
yoga *nm* yoga
yogur *nm* yogurt, yoghurt
yogurtera *nf* yoghurt maker
yonqui *nmf Fam* junkie, drug addict
yoyo, yoyó *nm* yo-yo
yuca *nf* yucca
Yucatán *n* Yucatan
yudo *nm* judo
yudoka *nmf* judoka
yugo *nm* yoke
Yugoslavia *n* Yugoslavia
yugoslavo,-a, yugoeslavo,-a *adj & nm,f* Yugoslav, Yugoslavian
yugular *nf* jugular

yunque *nm* anvil
yunta *nf* yoke *o* team of oxen
yuxtaponer [19] (*pp* **yuxtapuesto**) *vt* to juxtapose

yuxtaposición *nf* juxtaposition
yuyo *nm* (**a**) *CSur (mala hierba)* weed; *(hierba medicinal)* medicinal herb (**b**) *Andes (hierba silvestre)* wild herb

Z, z ['θeta] *nf (la letra)* Z, z
zacate *nm CAm, Méx* fodder
zafarse *vpr (librarse)* to get away (**de** from), to escape (**de** from)
zafio,-a *adj* uncouth
zafiro *nm* sapphire
zaga *nf* **a la z.** behind, at the rear
zaguán *nm* hall, hallway
zaherir *vt* to hurt
zahúrda *nf* pigsty
zaino,-a *adj (caballo)* chestnut; *(toro)* black
Zaire *n* Zaire
zalamería *nf* flattery
zalamero,-a 1 *nm,f* flatterer, fawner
  2 *adj* flattering, fawning
zamarra *nf (prenda)* sheepskin jacket
Zambia *n* Zambia
zambo,-a 1 *adj* (**a**) *(patizambo)* knock-kneed (**b**) *Am (persona)* half Indian and half Negro
  2 *nm,f Am (persona)* = person who is half Indian and half Negro
zambomba *nf* = kind of primitive drum
zambullida *nf* plunge
zambullirse *vpr* to plunge
zamparse *vpr Fam* to gobble down
zanahoria *nf* carrot
zancada *nf* stride
zancadilla *nf* **ponerle la z. a algn** to trip sb up
zanco *nm* stilt
zancudo,-a 1 *adj* (**a**) long-legged (**b**) *Orn* wading; **ave zancuda** wading bird, wader
  2 *nm Am* mosquito
zángano,-a 1 *nm (insecto)* drone
  2 *nm,f Fam (persona)* idler, lazybones *inv*
zanja *nf* ditch, trench
zanjar *vt (asunto)* to settle
zapallito *nm CSur Br* courgette, *US* zucchini
zapallo *nm Andes, RP* sweet pumpkin
zapata *nf* (**a**) *(cuña)* wedge (**b**) *Téc* shoe
zapatear *vi* to tap one's feet
zapatería *nf* shoe shop
zapatero,-a *nm,f (vendedor)* shoe dealer; *(fabricante)* shoemaker, cobbler

zapatilla *nf* slipper; **zapatillas de deporte** trainers
zapato *nm* shoe; **zapatos de tacón** high-heeled shoes
zar *nm* czar, tsar
Zaragoza *n* Saragossa
zaragozano,-a 1 *adj* of/from Saragossa
  2 *nm,f* person from Saragossa
zarandear *vt* to shake
zarandeo *nm* shaking
zarcillo *nm* (**a**) *(pendiente)* earring (**b**) *Bot* tendril
zarina *nf* czarina, tsarina
zarpa *nf* claw
zarpar *vi* to weigh anchor, to set sail
zarpazo *nm* clawing; **dar o pegar un z. a** to claw
zarza *nf* bramble, blackberry bush
zarzal *nm* bramble patch
zarzamora *nf (zarza)* blackberry bush; *(fruto)* blackberry
zarzuela *nf* (**a**) = Spanish operetta (**b**) **la Z.** = royal residence in Madrid (**c**) *Culin* = fish stew
zenit *nm* zenith
zigzag *nm (pl* **zigzags** *o* **zigzagues)** zigzag
zigzaguear *vi* to zigzag
Zimbabwe *n* Zimbabwe
zinc *nm* zinc
zíper *nm CAm, Méx Br* zip, *US* zipper
zócalo *nm* (**a**) *(de pared)* skirting board (**b**) *(pedestal)* plinth
zodiaco, zodíaco *nm* zodiac; **signo del z.** sign of the zodiac
zona *nf* zone; *(región)* region; **z. euro** euro zone; **z. verde** park
zoo *nm* zoo
zoología *nf* zoology
zoológico,-a 1 *adj* zoological; **parque z.** zoo
  2 *nm* zoo
zoom *nm Cin & Fot* zoom
zopenco,-a *nm,f Fam* dope, halfwit
zopilote *nm Am* buzzard
zoquete 1 *nmf Fam* blockhead
  2 *nm CSur (calcetín)* ankle sock
zorra *nf* (**a**) vixen (**b**) *Fam* slut
zorro,-a 1 *nm* fox

2 *adj* **(a)** *(astuto)* cunning, sly **(b)** *muy Fam* **no tengo ni zorra (idea)** I haven't got a *Br* bloody *o US* goddamn clue

zorzal *nm Orn* thrush

zozobrar *vi* to be in danger of going under

zueco *nm* clog

zumbado,-a *adj Fam* crazy, mad

zumbar 1 *vi* to buzz, to hum; **me zumban los oídos** my ears are buzzing; *Fam* **salir zumbando** to zoom off

2 *vt Fam* to thrash

zumbido *nm* buzzing, humming

zumo *nm* juice

zurcir [52] *vt Cost* to darn; *Fam* **¡que te zurzan!** go to hell!

zurda *nf (mano)* left hand

zurdo,-a 1 *nm,f (persona)* left-handed person

2 *adj* left-handed

zurrar *vt (pegar)* to beat, to flog

zutano,-a *nm,f Fam* so-and-so; *(hombre)* what's-his-name; *(mujer)* what's-her-name

Spanish Verbs

Regular Spelling Changes

The rules of spelling in Spanish cause a number of verbs to have regular spelling changes. These are listed below.

Spanish verbs fall into three groups depending on whether their infinitive ends in **-ar, -er** or **-ir**. The stem of the verb is the part which is left when the **-ar, -er** or **-ir** is removed from the infinitive. For example, the stem of **tomar** is **tom**, the stem of **beber** is **beb**, and the stem of **salir** is **sal**.

In the examples given below, the following indicators are used:

- **(1)** = first person singular present indicative
- **(2)** = present subjunctive, all persons
- **(3)** = first person singular preterite

Verbs ending in -ar

Verbs with a stem ending in **c**, for example **buscar**

The **c** changes to **qu** in:

- **(2)** busque, busques, busque, busquemos, busquéis, busquen
- **(3)** busqué

Verbs with a stem ending in **g**, for example **cargar**

The **g** changes to **gu** in:

- **(2)** cargue, cargues, cargue, carguemos, carguéis, carguen
- **(3)** cargué

Verbs with a stem ending in **gu**, for example **averiguar**

The **gu** changes to **gü** in:

- **(2)** averigüe, averigües, averigüe, averigüemos, averigüéis, averigüen
- **(3)** averigüé

Verbs with a stem ending in **z**, for example **realizar**

The **z** changes to **c** in:

- **(2)** realice, realices, realice, realicemos, realicéis, realicen
- **(3)** realicé

Verbs ending in -er *or* -ir

Verbs with a stem ending in **c**, for example **esparcir**

The **c** changes to **z** in:

> (**1**) esparzo
> (**2**) esparza, esparzas, esparza, esparzamos, esparzáis, esparzan

Verbs with a stem ending in **g**, for example **coger**

The **g** changes to **j** in:

> (**1**) cojo
> (**2**) coja, cojas, coja, cojamos, cojáis, cojan

Verbs with a stem ending in **qu**, for example **delinquir**

The **qu** changes to **c** in:

> (**1**) delinco
> (**2**) delinca, delincas, delinca, delincamos, delincáis, delincan

Verbs with a stem ending in **gu**, for example **distinguir**

The **gu** changes to **g** in:

> (**1**) distingo
> (**2**) distinga, distingas, distinga, distingamos, distingáis, distingan

Models for Regular Conjugation

TOMAR to take

INDICATIVE

PRESENT	**FUTURE**	**CONDITIONAL**
1. tomo	tomaré	tomaría
2. tomas	tomarás	tomarías
3. toma	tomará	tomaría
1. tomamos	tomaremos	tomaríamos
2. tomáis	tomaréis	tomarías
3. toman	tomarán	tomarían

IMPERFECT	**PRETERITE**	**PERFECT**
1. tomaba	tomé	he tomado
2. tomabas	tomaste	has tomado
3. tomaba	tomó	ha tomado
1. tomábamos	tomamos	hemos tomado
2. tomabais	tomasteis	habéis tomado
3. tomaban	tomaron	han tomado

FUTURE PERFECT	**CONDITIONAL PERFECT**	**PLUPERFECT**
1. habré tomado	habría tomado	había tomado
2. habrás tomado	habrías tomado	habías tomado
3. habrá tomado	habría tomado	había tomado
1. habremos tomado	habríamos tomado	habíamos tomado
2. habréis tomado	habríais tomado	habíais tomado
3. habrán tomado	habrían tomado	habían tomado

SUBJUNCTIVE

PRESENT	**IMPERFECT**	**PERFECT/PLUPERFECT**
1. tome	tom-ara/ase	haya/hubiera* tomado
2. tomes	tom-aras/ases	hayas/hubieras tomado
3. tome	tom-ara/ase	haya/hubiera tomado
1. tomemos	tom-áramos/ásemos	hayamos/hubiéramos tomado
2. toméis	tom-arais/aseis	hayáis/hubierais tomado
3. tomen	tom-aran/asen	hayan/hubieran tomado

IMPERATIVE   INFINITIVE   PARTICIPLE

IMPERATIVE	INFINITIVE	PARTICIPLE
(tú) toma	**PRESENT**	**PRESENT**
(Vd) tome	tomar	tomando
(nosotros) tomemos		
(vosotros) tomad	**PERFECT**	**PAST**
(Vds) tomen	haber tomado	tomado

* the alternative form 'hubiese' etc is also possible

COMER to eat

INDICATIVE

PRESENT	FUTURE	CONDITIONAL
1. como	comeré	comería
2. comes	comerás	comerías
3. come	comerá	comería
1. comemos	comeremos	comeríamos
2. coméis	comeréis	comeríais
3. comen	comerán	comerían

IMPERFECT	PRETERITE	PERFECT
1. comía	comí	he comido
2. comías	comiste	has comido
3. comía	comió	ha comido
1. comíamos	comimos	hemos comido
2. comíais	comisteis	habéis comido
3. comían	comieron	han comido

FUTURE PERFECT	CONDITIONAL PERFECT	PLUPERFECT
1. habré comido	habría comido	había comido
2. habrás comido	habrías comido	habías comido
3. habrá comido	habría comido	había comido
1. habremos comido	habríamos comido	habíamos comido
2. habréis comido	habríais comido	habías comido
3. habrán comido	habrían comido	habían comido

SUBJUNCTIVE

PRESENT	IMPERFECT	PERFECT/PLUPERFECT
1. coma	com-iera/iese	haya/hubiera* comido
2. comas	com-ieras/ieses	hayas/hubieras comido
3. coma	com-iera/iese	haya/hubiera comido
1. comamos	com-iéramos/iésemos	hayamos/hubiéramos comido
2. comáis	com-ierais/ieseis	hayáis/hubierais comido
3. coman	com-ieran/iesen	hayan/hubieran comido

IMPERATIVE | INFINITIVE | PARTICIPLE

IMPERATIVE	INFINITIVE	PARTICIPLE
(tú) come	**PRESENT**	**PRESENT**
(Vd) coma	comer	comiendo
(nosotros) comamos		
(vosotros) comed	**PERFECT**	**PAST**
(Vds) coman	haber comido	comido

* the alternative form 'hubiese' etc is also possible

PARTIR to leave

INDICATIVE

PRESENT	FUTURE	CONDITIONAL
1. parto	partiré	partiría
2. partes	partirás	partirías
3. parte	partirá	partiría
1. partimos	partiremos	partiríamos
2. partís	partiréis	partiríais
3. parten	partirán	partirían

IMPERFECT	PRETERITE	PERFECT
1. partía	partí	he partido
2. partías	partiste	has partido
3. partía	partió	ha partido
1. partíamos	partimos	hemos partido
2. partíais	partisteis	habéis partido
3. partían	partieron	han partido

FUTURE PERFECT	CONDITIONAL PERFECT	PLUPERFECT
1. habré partido	habría partido	había partido
2. habrás partido	habrías partido	habías partido
3. habrá partido	habría partido	había partido
1. habremos partido	habríamos partido	habíamos partido
2. habréis partido	habríais partido	habíais partido
3. habrán partido	habían partido	habían partido

SUBJUNCTIVE

PRESENT	IMPERFECT	PERFECT/PLUPERFECT
parta	parti-era/ese	haya/hubiera* partido
partas	parti-eras/eses	hayas/hubieras partido
parta	parti-era/ese	haya/hubiera partido
partamos	parti-éramos/ésemos	hayamos/hubiéramos partido
partáis	parti-erais/eseis	hayáis/hubierais partido
partan	parti-eran/esen	hayan/hubieran partido

IMPERATIVE	INFINITIVE	PARTICIPLE
(tú) parte	**PRESENT**	**PRESENT**
(Vd) parta	partir	partiendo
(nosotros) partamos		
(vosotros) partid	**PERFECT**	**PAST**
(Vds) partan	haber partido	partido

* the alternative form 'hubiese' etc is also possible

Models for Irregular Conjugation

[1] **pensar PRES** pienso, piensas, piensa, pensamos, pensáis, piensan; **PRES SUBJ** piense, pienses, piense, pensemos, penséis, piensen; **IMPERAT** piensa, piense, pensemos, pensad, piensen

[2] **contar PRES** cuento, cuentas, cuenta, contamos, contáis, cuentan; **PRES SUBJ** cuente, cuentes, cuente, contemos, contéis, cuenten; **IMPERAT** cuenta, cuente, contemos, contad, cuenten

[3] **perder PRES** pierdo, pierdes, pierde, perdemos, perdéis, pierden; **PRES SUBJ** pierda, pierdas, pierda, perdamos, perdáis, pierdan; **IMPERAT** pierde, pierda, perdamos, perded, pierdan

[4] **morder PRES** muerdo, muerdes, muerde, mordemos, mordéis, muerden; **PRES SUBJ** muerda, muerdas, muerda, mordamos, mordáis, muerdan; **IMPERAT** muerde, muerda, mordamos, morded, muerdan

[5] **sentir PRES** siento, sientes, siente, sentimos, sentís, sienten; **PRES SUBJ** sienta, sientas, sienta, sintamos, sintáis, sientan; **PRES P** sintiendo; **IMPERAT** siente, sienta, sintamos, sentid, sientan

[6] **vestir PRES** visto, vistes, viste, vestimos, vestís, visten; **PRES SUBJ** vista, vistas, vista, vistamos, vistáis, vistan; **PRES P** vistiendo; **IMPERAT** viste, vista, vistamos, vestid, vistan

[7] **dormir PRES** duermo, duermes, duerme, dormimos, dormís, duermen; **PRES SUBJ** duerma, duermas, duerma, durmamos, durmáis, duerman; **PRES P** durmiendo; **IMPERAT** duerme, duerma, durmamos, dormid, duerman

[8] **andar PRET** anduve, anduviste, anduvo, anduvimos, anduvisteis, anduvieron; **IMPERF SUBJ** anduviera/anduviese

[9] **caber PRES** quepo, cabes, cabe, cabemos, cabéis, caben; **PRES SUBJ** quepa, quepas, quepa, quepamos, quepáis, quepan; **FUT** cabré; **COND** cabría; **PRET** cupe, cupiste, cupo, cupimos, cupisteis, cupieron; **IMPERF SUBJ** cupiera/cupiese; **IMPERAT** cabe, quepa, quepamos, cabed, quepan

[10] **conducir PRES** conduzco, conduces, conduce, conducimos, conducís, conducen; **PRES SUBJ** conduzca, conduzcas, conduzca, conduzcamos, conduzcáis, conduzcan; **PRET** conduje, condujiste, condujo, condujimos, condujisteis, condujeron; **IMPERF SUBJ** condujera/condujese; **IMPERAT** conduce, conduzca, conduzcamos, conducid, conduzcan

[11] **dar PRES** doy, das, da, damos, dais, dan; **PRES SUBJ** dé, des, dé, demos, deis, den; **PRET** di, diste, dio, dimos, disteis, dieron; **IMPERF SUBJ** diera/diese; **IMPERAT** da, dé, demos, dad, den

[12] **decir PRES** digo, dices, dice, decimos, decís, dicen; **PRES SUBJ** diga, digas, diga, digamos, digáis, digan; **FUT** diré; **COND** diría; **PRET** dije, dijiste, dijo, dijimos, dijisteis, dijeron; **IMPERF SUBJ** dijera/dijese; **PRES P** diciendo; **PP** dicho; **IMPERAT** di, diga, digamos, decid, digan

[13] **ESTAR** to be

INDICATIVE

PRESENT	FUTURE	CONDITIONAL
1. estoy	estaré	estaría
2. estás	estarás	estarías
3. está	estará	estaría
1. estamos	estaremos	estaríamos
2. estáis	estaréis	estaríais
3. están	estarán	estarían

IMPERFECT	PRETERITE	PERFECT
1. estaba	estuve	he estado
2. estabas	estuviste	has estado
3. estaba	estuvo	ha estado
1. estábamos	estuvimos	hemos estado
2. estabais	estuvisteis	habéis estado
3. estaban	estuvieron	han estado

FUTURE PERFECT	CONDITIONAL PERFECT	PLUPERFECT
1. habré estado	habría estado	había estado
2. habrás estado	habrías estado	habías estado
3. habrá estado	habría estado	había estado
1. habremos estado	habríamos estado	habíamos estado
2. habréis estado	habríais estado	habíais estado
3. habrán estado	habrían estado	habían estado

SUBJUNCTIVE

PRESENT	IMPERFECT	PERFECT/PLUPERFECT
1. esté	estuv-iera/iese	haya/hubiera* estado
2. estés	estuv-ieras/ieses	hayas/hubieras estado
3. esté	estuv-iera/iese	haya/hubiera estado
1. estemos	esuv-iéramos/iésemos	hayamos/hubiéramos estado
2. estéis	estuv-ierais/ieseis	hayáis/hubierais estado
3. estén	estuv-ieran/iesen	hayan/hubieran estado

IMPERATIVE

(tú) está
(Vd) esté
(nosotros) estemos
(vosotros) estad
(Vds) estén

INFINITIVE

PRESENT
estar

PERFECT
haber estado

PARTICIPLE

PRESENT
estando

PAST
estado

* the alternative form 'hubiese' etc is also possible

[14] **HABER** to have (*auxiliary*)

INDICATIVE

PRESENT	FUTURE	CONDITIONAL
1. he	habré	habría
2. has	habrás	habrías
3. ha/hay*	habrá	habría
1. hemos	habremos	habríamos
2. habéis	habréis	habríais
3. han	habrán	habrían

IMPERFECT	PRETERITE	PERFECT
1. había	hube	
2. habías	hubiste	
3. había	hubo	ha habido*
1. habíamos	hubimos	
2. habíais	hubisteis	
3. habían	hubieron	

FUTURE PERFECT	CONDITIONAL PERFECT	PLUPERFECT
1.		
2.		
3. habrá habido*	habría habido*	había habido*
1.		
2.		
3.		

SUBJUNCTIVE

PRESENT	IMPERFECT	PERFECT/PLUPERFECT
1. haya	hub-iera/iese	
2. hayas	hub-ieras/ieses	
3. haya	hub-iera/iese	haya/hubiera** habido*
1. hayamos	hub-iéramos/iésemos	
2. hayáis	hub-ierais/ieseis	
3. hayan	hub-ieran/iesen	

INFINITIVE

PRESENT
haber
PERFECT
haber habido*

PARTICIPLE

PRESENT
habiendo
PAST
habido

* 'haber' is an auxiliary verb used with the participle of another verb to form compound tenses (eg he bebido - I have drunk). 'hay' means 'there is/are' and all third person singular forms in their respective tenses have this meaning. The forms highlighted with an asterisk are used only for this latter construction.

** the alternative form 'hubiese' is also possible.

[15] **hacer PRES** hago, haces, hace, hacemos, hacéis, hacen; **PRES SUBJ** haga, hagas, haga hagamos, hagáis, hagan; **FUT** haré; **COND** haría; **PRET** hice, hiciste, hizo, hicimos, hicisteis, hicieron; **IMPERF SUBJ** hiciera/hiciese; **PP** hecho; **IMPERAT** haz, haga, hagamos, haced, hagan

[16] **ir PRES** voy, vas, va, vamos, vais, van; **PRES SUBJ** vaya, vayas, vaya, vayamos, vayáis, vayan; **IMPERF** iba, ibas, iba, íbamos, ibais, iban; **PRET** fui, fuiste, fue, fuimos, fuisteis, fueron; **IMPERF SUBJ** fuera/fuese; **PRES P** yendo; **IMPERAT** ve, vaya, vamos, id, vayan

[17] **oir PRES** oigo, oyes, oye, oímos, oís, oyen; **PRES SUBJ** oiga, oigas, oiga, oigamos, oigáis, oigan; **PRET** oí, oíste, oyó, oímos, oísteis, oyeron; **IMPERF SUBJ** oyera/oyese; **PRES P** oyendo; **PP** oído; **IMPERAT** oye, oiga, oigamos, oíd, oigan

[18] **poder PRES** puedo, puedes, puede, podemos, podéis, pueden; **PRES SUBJ** pueda, puedas, pueda, podamos, podáis, puedan; **FUT** podré; **COND** podría; **PRET** pude, pudiste, pudo, pudimos, pudisteis, pudieron; **IMPERF SUBJ** pudiera/pudiese; **PRES P** pudiendo; **IMPERAT** puede, pueda, podamos, poded, puedan

[19] **poner PRES** pongo, pones, pone, ponemos, ponéis, ponen; **PRES SUBJ** ponga, pongas, ponga, pongamos, pongáis, pongan; **FUT** pondré; **PRET** puse, pusiste, puso, pusimos, pusisteis, pusieron; **IMPERF SUBJ** pusiera/pusiese; **PP** puesto; **IMPERAT** pon, ponga, pongamos, poned, pongan

[20] **querer PRES** quiero, quieres, quiere, queremos, queréis, quieren; **PRES SUBJ** quiera, quieras, quiera, queramos, queráis, quieran; **FUT** querré; **COND** querría; **PRET** quise, quisiste, quiso, quisimos, quisisteis, quisieron; **IMPERF SUBJ** quisiera/quisiese; **IMPERAT** quiere, quiera, queramos, quered, quieran

[21] **saber PRES** sé, sabes, sabe, sabemos, sabéis, saben; **PRES SUBJ** sepa, sepas, sepa, sepamos, sepáis, sepan; **FUT** sabré; **COND** sabría; **PRET** supe, supiste, supo, supimos, supisteis, supieron; **IMPERF SUBJ** supiera/supiese; **IMPERAT** sabe, sepa, sepamos, sabed, sepan

[22] **salir PRES** salgo, sales, sale, salimos, salís, salen; **PRES SUBJ** salga, salgas, salga, salgamos, salgáis, salgan; **FUT** saldré; **COND** saldría; **IMPERAT** sal, salga salgamos, salid, salgan

[23] **ser PRES** soy, eres, es, somos, sois, son; **PRES SUBJ** sea, seas, sea, seamos, seáis, sean; **IMPERF** era, eras, era, éramos, erais, eran; **PRET** fui, fuiste, fue, fuimos, fuisteis, fueron; **IMPERF SUBJ** fuera/fuese; **IMPERAT** sé, sea, seamos, sed, sean

[24] **tener PRES** tengo, tienes, tiene, tenemos, tenéis, tienen; **PRES SUBJ** tenga, tengas, tenga, tengamos, tengáis, tengan; **FUT** tendré; **COND** tendría; **PRET** tuve, tuviste, tuvo, tuvimos, tuvisteis, tuvieron; **IMPERF SUBJ** tuviera/tuviese; **IMPERAT** ten, tenga, tengamos, tened tengan

[25] **traer PRES** traigo, traes, trae, traemos, traéis, traen; **PRES SUBJ** traiga, traigas, traiga, traigamos, traigáis, traigan; **PRET** traje, trajiste, trajo, trajimos, trajisteis, trajeron; **IMPERF SUBJ** trajera/trajese; **IMPERAT** trae, traiga, traigamos, traed, traigan

[26] **valer** PRES valgo, vales, vale, valemos, valéis, valen; **PRES SUBJ** valga, valgas, valga, valgamos, valgáis, valgan; **FUT** valdré; **COND** valdría; **IMPERAT** vale, valga, valemos, valed, valgan

[27] **venir** PRES vengo, vienes, viene, venimos, venís, vienen; **PRES SUBJ** venga, vengas, venga, vengamos, vengáis, vengan; **FUT** vendré; **COND** vendría; **PRET** vine, viniste, vino, vinimos, vinisteis, vinieron; **IMPERF SUBJ** viniera/viniese; **PRES P** viniendo; **IMPERAT** ven, venga, vengamos, venid, vengan

[28] **ver** PRES veo, ves, ve, vemos, veis, ven; **PRES SUBJ** vea, veas, vea, veamos, veáis, vean; **IMPERF** veía, veías, veía, veíamos, veíais, veían; **PRET** vi, viste, vio, vimos, visteis, vieron; **IMPERF SUBJ** viera/viese; **IMPERAT** ve, vea, veamos, ved, vean

[29] **desviar** PRES desvío, desvías, desvía, desviamos, desviáis, desvían; **PRES SUBJ** desvíe, desvíes, desvíe, desviemos, desviéis, desvíen; **IMPERAT** desvía, desvíe, desviemos, desviéis, desvíen

[30] **continuar** PRES continúo, continúas, continúa, continuamos, continuáis, continúan; **PRES SUBJ** continúe, continúes, continúe, continuemos, continuéis, continúen; **IMPERAT** continúa, continúe, continuemos, continuad, continúen

[31] **adquirir** PRES adquiero, adquieres, adquiere, adquirimos, adquirís, adquieren; **PRES SUBJ** adquiera, adquieras, adquiera, adquiramos, adquiráis, adquieran; **IMPERAT** adquiere, adquiera, adquiramos, adquirid, adquieran

[32] **jugar** PRES juego, juegas, juega, jugamos, jugáis, juegan; **PRES SUBJ** juegue, juegues, juegue, juguemos, juguéis, jueguen; **IMPERAT** juega, juegue, juguemos, jugad, jueguen

[33] **agradecer** PRES agradezco, agradeces, agradece, agradecemos, agradecéis, agradecen; **PRES SUBJ** agradezca, agradezcas, agradezca, agradezcamos, agradezcáis, agradezcan; **IMPERAT** agradece, agradezca, agradezcamos, agradeced, agradezcan

[34] **conocer** PRES conozco, conoces, conoce, conocemos, conocéis, conocen; **PRES SUBJ** conozca, conozcas, conozca, conozcamos, conozcáis, conozcan; **IMPERAT** conoce, conozca, conozcamos, conoced, conozcan

[35] **lucir** PRES luzco, luces, luce, lucimos, lucís, lucen; **PRES SUBJ** luzca, luzcas, luzca, luzcamos, luzcáis, luzcan; **IMPERAT** luce, luzca, luzcamos, lucid, luzcan

[36] **leer** PRET leí, leíste, leyó, leímos, leísteis, leyeron; **IMPERF SUBJ** leyera/leyese; **PRES P** leyendo; **PP** leído; **IMPERAT** lee, lea, leamos, leed, lean

[37] **huir** PRES huyo, huyes, huye, huimos, huís, huyen; **PRES SUBJ** huya, huyas, huya, huyamos, huyáis, huyan; **PRET** huí, huiste, huyó, huimos, huisteis, huyeron; **IMPERF SUBJ** huyera/huyese; **PRES P** huyendo; **PP** huido; **IMPERAT** huye, huya, huyamos, huid, huyan

[38] **roer** PRES roo/roigo/royo, roes, roe, roemos, roéis, roen; **PRES SUBJ** roa/roiga/roya, roas, roa, roamos, roáis, roan; **PRET** roí, roíste, royó, roímos, roísteis, royeron; **IMPERF SUBJ** royera/royese; **PRES P** royendo; **PP** roído; **IMPERAT** roe, roa, roamos, roed, roan

[39] **caer PRES** caigo, caes, cae, caemos, caéis, caen; **PRES SUBJ** caiga, caigas, caiga, caigamos, caigáis, caigan; **PRES P** cayendo; **PP** caído; **IMPERAT** cae, caiga caigamos, caed, caigan

[40] **cazar PRET** cacé, cazaste, cazó, cazamos, cazasteis, cazaron; **PRES SUBJ** cace, caces, cacen, cacemos, cacéis, cacen

[41] **cocer PRES** cuezo, cueces, cuece, cocemos, cocéis, cuecen; **PRES SUBJ** cueza, cuezas, cueza, cozamos, cozáis, cuezan; **IMPERAT** cuece, cueza, cozamos, cozed, cuezan

[42] **llegar PRET** llegué, llegaste, llegó, llegamos, llegasteis, llegaron; **PRES SUBJ** llegue, llegues, llegue, lleguemos, lleguéis, lleguen

[43] **cambiar PRES** cambio, cambias, cambia, cambiamos, cambiáis, cambian; **PRES SUBJ** cambie, cambies, cambie, cambiemos, cambiéis, cambien; **IMPERAT** cambia, cambie, cambiemos, cambiad, cambien

[44] **sacar PRET** saqué, sacaste, sacó, sacamos, sacasteis, sacaron; **PRES SUBJ** saque, saques, saque, saquemos, saquéis, saquen; **IMPERAT** saca, saque, saquemos, sacad, saquen

[45] **averiguar PRET** averigüé, averiguaste, averiguó, averiguamos, averiguasteis, averiguaron; **PRES SUBJ** averigüe, averigües, averigüe, averigüemos, averigüéis, averigüen; **IMPERAT** averigua, averigüe, averigüemos, averiguad, averigüen

[46] **asir PRES** asgo, ases, ase, asimos, asís, asen; **PRES SUBJ** asga, asgas, asga, asgamos, asgáis, asgan; **IMPERAT** ase, asga, asgamos, asid, asgan

[47] **adecuar PRES** adecuo, adecuas, adecua, adecuamos, adecuáis, adecuan; **PRES SUBJ** adecue, adecues, adecue, adecuemos, adecuéis, adecuen; **IMPERAT** adecua, adecuen, adecuemos, adecuad, adecuen

[48] **delinquir PRES** delinco, delinques, delinque, delinquimos, delinquís, delinquen; **PRES SUBJ** delinca, delincas, delinca, delincamos, delincáis, delincan; **IMPERAT** delinque, delinca, delincamos, delinquid, delincan

[49] **mecer PRES** mezo, meces, mece, mecemos, mecéis, mecen; **PRES SUBJ** meza, mezas, meza, mezamos, mezáis, mezan; **IMPERAT** mece, meza, mezamos, meced, mezan

[50] **errar PRES** yerro, yerras, yerra, erramos, erráis, yerran; **PRES SUBJ** yerre, yerres, yerre, erremos, erréis, yerren; **IMPERAT** yerra, yerre, erremos, errad, yerren

[51] **comenzar PRES** comienzo, comienzas, comienza, comenzamos, comenzáis, comienzan; **PRES SUBJ** comience, comiences, comience, comencemos, comencéis, comiencen; **IMPERAT** comienza, comience, comencemos, comenzad, comiencen

[52] **zurcir PRES** zurzo, zurces, zurce, zurcimos, zurcís, zurcen; **PRES SUBJ** zurza, zurzas, zurza, zurzamos, zurzáis, zurzan; **IMPERAT** zurce, zurza, zurzamos, zurcid, zurzan

[53] **proteger PRES** protejo, proteges, protege, protegemos, protegéis, protegen; **PRES SUBJ** proteja, protejas, proteja, protejamos, protejáis, protejan; **IMPERAT** protege, proteja, protejamos, proteged, protejan

[54] **discernir** PRES discierno, disciernes, discierne, discernimos, discernís, disciernen; **PRES SUBJ** discierna, disciernas, discierna, discernamos, discernáis, disciernan; **IMPERAT** discierne, discierna, discernamos, discernid, disciernan

[55] **erguir** PRES irgo/yergo, irgues/yergues, irgue/yergue, erguimos, erguís, irguen/yerguen; **PRET** erguí, erguiste, irguió, erguimos, erguisteis, irguieron; **PRES SUBJ** irga/yerga, irgas/yergas, irga/yerga, irgamos/yergamos, irgáis/yergáis, irgan/yergan; **IMPERF SUBJ** irguiera/irguiese; **IMPERAT** irgue/yergue, irga/yerga, irgamos/yergamos, erguid, irgan/yergan

[56] **reír** PRES río, ríes, ríe, reímos, reís, ríen; **PRET** reí, reíste, rió, reímos, reísteis, rieron; **PRES SUBJ** ría, rías, ría, riamos, riáis, rían; **IMPERF SUBJ** riera/riese; **IMPERAT** ríe, ría, riamos, reíd, rían

[57] **dirigir** PRES dirijo, diriges, dirige, dirigimos, dirigís, dirigen; **PRES SUBJ** dirija, dirijas, dirija, dirijamos, dirijáis, dirijan; **IMPERAT** dirige, dirija, dirijamos, dirigid, dirijan

[58] **regir** PRES rijo, riges, rige, regimos, regís, rigen; **PRES SUBJ** rija, rijas, rija, rijamos, rijáis, rijan; **IMPERAT** rige, rija, rijamos, regid, rijan

[59] **distinguir** PRES distingo, distingues, distingue, distinguimos, distinguís, distinguen; **PRES SUBJ** distinga, distingas, distinga, distingamos, distingáis, distingan; **IMPERAT** distingue, distinga, distingamos, distinguid, distingan

[60] **nacer** PRES nazco, naces, nace, nacemos, nacéis, nacen; **PRES SUBJ** nazca, nazcas, nazca, nazcamos, nazcáis, nazcan; **IMPERAT** nace, nazca, nazcamos, naced, nazcan

[61] **yacer** PRES yazco/yazgo/yago, yaces, yace, yacemos, yacéis, yacen; **PRES SUBJ** yazca/yazga/yaga; **IMPERAT** yace/yaz, yazca/yazga/yaga, yazcamos/yazgamos/yagamos, yaced, yazcan/yazgan/yagan

[62] **argüir** PRES arguyo, arguyes, arguye, argüimos, argüís, arguyen; **PRET** argüí, argüiste, arguyó, argüimos, argüisteis, arguyeron; **PRES SUBJ** arguya, arguyas, arguya, arguyamos, arguyáis, arguyan; **IMPERF SUBJ** arguyera/arguyese; **IMPERAT** arguye, arguya, arguyamos, argüid, arguyan

[63] **avergonzar** PRES avergüenzo, avergüenzas, avergüenza, avergonzamos, avergonzáis, avergüenzan; **PRET** avergoncé, avergonzaste, avergonzó, avergonzamos, avergonzasteis, avergonzaron; **PRES SUBJ** avergüence, avergüences, avergüence, avergoncemos, avergoncéis, avergüencen; **IMPERAT** avergüenza, avergüence, avergoncemos, avergonzad, avergüencen

[64] **trocar** PRES trueco, truecas, trueca, trocamos, trocáis, truecan; **PRET** troqué, trocaste, trocó, trocamos, trocasteis, trocaron; **PRES SUBJ** trueque, trueques, trueque, troquemos, troquéis, truequen; **IMPERAT** trueca, trueque, troquemos, trocad, truequen

[65] **oler** PRES huelo, hueles, huele, olemos, oléis, huelen; **PRES SUBJ** huela, huelas, huela, olamos, oláis, huelan; **IMPERAT** huele, huela, olamos, oled, huelan

Verbos irregulares ingleses

INFINITIVO	PRETÉRITO	PARTICIPIO
arise	arose	arisen
awake	awoke	awoken
awaken	awoke, awakened	awakened, awoken
be	were/was	been
bear	bore	borne
beat	beat	beaten
become	became	become
begin	began	begun
bend	bent	bent
beseech	besought, beseeched	besought, beseeched
bet	bet, betted	bet, betted
bid	bade, bid	bidden, bid
bind	bound	bound
bite	bit	bitten
bleed	bled	bled
blow	blew	blown
break	broke	broken
breed	bred	bred
bring	brought	brought
build	built	built
burn	burnt, burned	burnt, burned
burst	burst	burst
buy	bought	bought
cast	cast	cast
catch	caught	caught
choose	chose	chosen
cling	clung	clung
clothe	clad, clothed	clad, clothed
come	came	come
cost	cost	cost
creep	crept	crept
cut	cut	cut
deal	dealt	dealt
dig	dug	dug
do	did	done
draw	drew	drawn
dream	dreamt, dreamed	dreamt, dreamed
drink	drank	drunk
drive	drove	driven
dwell	dwelt	dwelt
eat	ate	eaten
fall	fell	fallen
feed	fed	fed
feel	felt	felt

INFINITIVO	PRETÉRITO	PARTICIPIO
fight	fought	fought
find	found	found
flee	fled	fled
fling	flung	flung
fly	flew	flown
forget	forgot	forgotten
forgive	forgave	forgiven
forsake	forsook	forsaken
freeze	froze	frozen
get	got	got, *US* gotten
give	gave	given
go	went	gone
grind	ground	ground
grow	grew	grown
hang	hung/hanged	hung/hanged
have	had	had
hear	heard	heard
hide	hid	hidden
hit	hit	hit
hold	held	held
hurt	hurt	hurt
keep	kept	kept
kneel	knelt	knelt
knit	knitted, knit	knitted, knit
know	knew	known
lay	laid	laid
lead	led	led
lean	leant, leaned	leant, leaned
leap	leapt, leaped	leapt, leaped
learn	learnt, learned	learnt, learned
leave	left	left
lend	lent	lent
let	let	let
lie	lay	lain
light	lit	lit
lose	lost	lost
make	made	made
mean	meant	meant
meet	met	met
mow	mowed	mown, mowed
pay	paid	paid
put	put	put
quit	quit	quit
read	read	read
rend	rent	rent
rid	rid	rid
ride	rode	ridden
ring	rang	rung
rise	rose	risen
run	ran	run
saw	sawed	sawn, sawed

INFINITIVO	PRETÉRITO	PARTICIPIO
say	said	said
see	saw	seen
seek	sought	sought
sell	sold	sold
send	sent	sent
set	set	set
sew	sewed	sewn
shake	shook	shaken
shear	sheared	shorn, sheared
shed	shed	shed
shine	shone	shone
shoe	shod	shod
shoot	shot	shot
show	showed	shown
shrink	shrank	shrunk
shut	shut	shut
sing	sang	sung
sink	sank	sunk
sit	sat	sat
slay	slew	slain
sleep	slept	slept
slide	slid	slid
sling	slung	slung
slink	slunk	slunk
slit	slit	slit
smell	smelled, smelt	smelled, smelt
sow	sowed	sown, sowed
speak	spoke	spoken
speed	sped, speeded	sped, speeded
spell	spelt, spelled	spelt, spelled
spend	spent	spent
spill	spilt, spilled	spilt, spilled
spin	span	spun
spit	spat	spat
split	split	split
spoil	spoilt, spoiled	spoilt, spoiled
spread	spread	spread
spring	sprang	sprung
stand	stood	stood
steal	stole	stolen
stick	stuck	stuck
sting	stung	stung
stink	stank, stunk	stunk
strew	strewed	strewed, strewn
stride	strode	stridden
strike	struck	struck
string	strung	strung
strive	strove	striven
swear	swore	sworn
sweep	swept	swept
swell	swelled	swollen

INFINITIVO	PRETÉRITO	PARTICIPIO
swing	swung	swung
swim	swam	swum
take	took	taken
teach	taught	taught
tear	tore	torn
tell	told	told
think	thought	thought
thrive	thrived, throve	thrived, thriven
throw	threw	thrown
thrust	thrust	thrust
tread	trod	trodden
wake	woke	woken
wear	wore	worn
weave	wove	woven
weep	wept	wept
wet	wet	wet
win	won	won
wind	wound	wound
wring	wrung	wrung
write	wrote	written

English – Spanish
Inglés – Español

A, a [eɪ] *n* (**a**) *(the letter)* A, a *f* (**b**) *Mus* **A** la *m* (**c**) *Br* **A road** ≃ carretera *f* nacional

a [eɪ, *unstressed* ə] *indef art* (*before vowel or silent h* **an**) (**a**) un, una; **a man/a woman** un hombre/una mujer; **he has a big nose** tiene la nariz grande (**b**) *(omitted in Spanish)* **half a litre/an hour** medio litro/media hora; **a hundred/thousand people** cien/mil personas; **let's have a drink** vamos a beber algo; **he's a teacher** es profesor; **what a pity** qué pena (**c**) *(each)* **60 pence a kilo** 60 peniques el kilo; **to eat grapes two at a time** comer las uvas de dos en dos; **three times a week** tres veces a la semana (**d**) *(a certain)* un/una tal; **a Mr Rees phoned** llamó un tal Sr. Rees

AA [eɪ'eɪ] *n* (**a**) (*abbr* **Alcoholics Anonymous**) AA, alcohólicos *mpl* anónimos (**b**) (*abbr* **Automobile Association**) ≃ AC

AAA [eɪeɪ'eɪ] *n* (**a**) *Br* (*abbr* **Amateur Athletic Association**) = federación británica de atletismo aficionado (**b**) *US* (*abbr* **American Automobile Association**) ≃ AC

aback [ə'bæk] *adv* **to be taken a.** quedarse de una pieza (**by** por)

abandon [ə'bændən] **1** *n* desenfreno *m*; **with reckless a.** desenfrenadamente

2 *vt* *(child)* abandonar; *(job)* dejar; *(project)* renunciar a

abase [ə'beɪs] *vt* **to a. oneself** humillarse

abashed [ə'bæʃt] *adj* desconcertado(a)

abate [ə'beɪt] *vi* *(anger)* apaciguarse; *(storm)* amainar

abattoir ['æbətwɑː(r)] *n* matadero *m*

abbey ['æbɪ] *n* abadía *f*

abbot ['æbət] *n* abad *m*

abbreviate [ə'briːvɪeɪt] *vt* abreviar

abbreviation [əbriːvɪ'eɪʃən] *n* abreviatura *f*

abdicate ['æbdɪkeɪt] *vt & vi* abdicar

abdication [æbdɪ'keɪʃən] *n* abdicación *f*

abdomen ['æbdəmən] *n* abdomen *m*

abduct [æb'dʌkt] *vt* raptar, secuestrar

aberration [æbə'reɪʃən] *n* aberración *f*

abet [ə'bet] *vt* **to aid and a. sb** ser cómplice de algn

abeyance [ə'beɪəns] *n* **to be in a.** estar en desuso

abhor [əb'hɔː(r)] *vt* aborrecer

abhorrent [əb'hɒrənt] *adj* aborrecible

abide [ə'baɪd] *vt* aguantar; **I can't a. it** no lo aguanto

▸ **abide by** *vt insep* *(promise)* cumplir con; *(rules)* atenerse a

ability [ə'bɪlɪtɪ] *n* *(capability)* capacidad *f*, aptitud *f*; *(talent)* talento *m*

abject ['æbdʒekt] *adj* *(state)* miserable; *(apology)* rastrero(a)

ablaze [ə'bleɪz] *adj & adv* en llamas, ardiendo

able ['eɪbəl] *adj* *(capable)* capaz; **will you be a. to come on Tuesday?** ¿podrás venir el martes?

able-bodied [eɪbəl'bɒdɪd] *adj* sano(a); **a. seaman** marinero *m* de primera

abnormal [æb'nɔːməl] *adj* anormal

abnormally [æb'nɔːməlɪ] *adv* anormalmente; *(large)* extraordinariamente

aboard [ə'bɔːd] **1** *adv* a bordo; **to go a.** *(ship)* embarcarse; *(train)* subir

2 *prep* a bordo de

abode [ə'bəʊd] *n Jur* **of no fixed a.** sin domicilio fijo

abolish [ə'bɒlɪʃ] *vt* abolir

abolition [æbə'lɪʃən] *n* abolición *f*

abominable [ə'bɒmɪnəbəl] *adj* abominable; *(dreadful)* terrible

aborigine [æbə'rɪdʒɪnɪ] *n* aborigen *mf* australiano(a)

abort [ə'bɔːt] **1** *vt Med* hacer abortar; *Fig (plan etc)* archivar

2 *vi Med* abortar

abortion [ə'bɔːʃən] *n Med* aborto *m*; **a. law** ley *f* del aborto; **to have an a.** abortar

abortive [ə'bɔːtɪv] *adj* *(plan)* fracasado(a); *(attempt)* frustrado(a)

abound [ə'baʊnd] *vi* **to a. in** *or* **with** abundar en

about [ə'baʊt] *adv & prep* (**a**) *(concerning)* acerca de, sobre; **a programme a. Paris** un programa sobre París; **to be worried a. sth** estar preocupado(a) por algo; **to speak a. sth** hablar de algo; **what's it all a.?** *(what's happening?)* ¿qué pasa?; *(story etc)* ¿de qué se trata?; *Fam* **how a. a game of tennis?** ¿qué te parece un partido de tenis?

(**b**) *(around)* por todas partes; **don't leave things lying a.** no dejes las cosas por medio; **there's nobody a.** no hay nadie; **to look a.** mirar alrededor; **to rush a.** correr de un lado para otro; **we went for a walk a. the town** dimos una vuelta por el pueblo

(**c**) *(approximately)* más o menos; **it's a. three o'clock** son más o menos las tres; **it's a. time you got up** ya es hora de que te levantes; **it's just a. finished** está casi terminado; **she's a. forty** tiene unos cuarenta años

(**d**) **it's a. to start** está a punto de empezar; **not to be a. to do sth** no estar dispuesto(a) a hacer algo

about-turn [əbaʊtˈtɜːn], *US* **about-face** [əbaʊtˈfeɪs] *n* media vuelta *f*; **to do an a.** dar media vuelta; *Fig* cambiar de idea por completo

above [əˈbʌv] *adv & prep* (**a**) *(higher than)* encima de, sobre, arriba; **100 m a. sea level** 100 m sobre el nivel del mar; **it's a. the door** está encima de la puerta; **the flat a.** el piso de arriba (**b**) *(greater than)* superior a; **amounts a. £10** cantidades superiores a las 10 libras; *Fig* **a policy imposed from a.** una política impuesta desde arriba (**c**) **a. all** sobre todo; **he's not a. stealing** es capaz incluso de robar (**d**) *(in book etc)* más arriba

above-board [əˈbʌvbɔːd] *adj (scheme)* legítimo(a)

above-mentioned [əˈbʌvmenʃənd] *adj* susodicho(a)

abrasive [əˈbreɪsɪv] **1** *adj (substance)* abrasivo(a); *Fig (voice, wit etc)* cáustico(a)

2 *n* abrasivo *m*

abreast [əˈbrest] *adv* **to walk three a.** ir de tres en fondo; *Fig* **to keep a. of things** mantenerse al día

abridged [əˈbrɪdʒd] *adj (book)* abreviado(a)

abroad [əˈbrɔːd] *adv* **to be a.** estar en el extranjero; **to go a.** irse al extranjero

abrupt [əˈbrʌpt] *adj (manner)* brusco(a); *(tone)* áspero(a); *(change)* súbito(a)

abruptly [əˈbrʌptlɪ] *adv (act)* bruscamente; *(speak)* con aspereza; *(change)* repentinamente

abscess [ˈæbses] *n* absceso *m*; *(on gum)* flemón *m*

abscond [əbˈskɒnd] *vi* huir

absence [ˈæbsəns] *n (of person)* ausencia *f*; *(of thing)* falta *f*

absent [ˈæbsənt] *adj* ausente; *Fig* **an a. look** una mirada distraída

absentee [æbsənˈtiː] *n* ausente *mf*

absenteeism [æbsənˈtiːɪzəm] *n* absentismo *m*

absently [ˈæbsəntlɪ] *adv* distraídamente

absent-minded [æbsəntˈmaɪndɪd] *adj* distraído(a)

absolute [ˈæbsəluːt] *adj* absoluto(a); *(failure)* total; *(truth)* puro(a); **it's an a. disgrace** es una auténtica vergüenza

absolutely [æbsəˈluːtlɪ] **1** *adv (completely)* completamente; **a. wrong** totalmente equivocado(a); **a. not** en absoluto; **you're a. right** tienes toda la razón

2 *interj* **a.!** ¡desde luego!

absolve [əbˈzɒlv] *vt* absolver (**from** de)

absorb [əbˈzɔːb] *vt (liquid)* absorber; *(sound, blow)* amortiguar; *Fig* **to be absorbed in sth** estar absorto(a) en algo

absorbing [əbˈzɔːbɪŋ] *adj (book, work)* absorbente

abstain [əbˈsteɪn] *vi* abstenerse (**from** de)

abstemious [əbˈstiːmɪəs] *adj* abstemio(a)

abstention [əbˈstenʃən] *n* abstención *f*

abstinence [ˈæbstɪnəns] *n* abstinencia *f*

abstract [ˈæbstrækt] **1** *adj* abstracto(a)

2 *n (of thesis etc)* resumen *m*

abstruse [əbˈstruːs] *adj* abstruso(a)

absurd [əbˈsɜːd] *adj* absurdo(a)

abundance [əˈbʌndəns] *n* abundancia *f*

abundant [əˈbʌndənt] *adj* abundante, rico(a) (**in** en)

abuse 1 *n* [əˈbjuːs] (**a**) *(ill-treatment)* malos tratos; *(misuse)* abuso *m* (**b**) *(insults)* injurias *fpl*

2 *vt* [əˈbjuːz] (**a**) *(ill-treat)* maltratar; *(misuse)* abusar de (**b**) *(insult)* injuriar

abusive [əbˈjuːsɪv] *adj (insulting)* insultante

abysmal [əˈbɪzməl] *adj (conditions)* extremo(a); *Fam (very bad)* fatal, pésimo(a)

abyss [əˈbɪs] *n* abismo *m*; *Fig* extremo *m*

AC [eɪˈsiː] (*abbr* **alternating current**) CA

academic [ækəˈdemɪk] **1** *adj* académico(a); *(career)* universitario(a); *(discussion)* teórico(a); **a. year** año *m* escolar

2 *n* académico(a) *m,f*

academy [əˈkædəmɪ] *n (society)* academia *f*; *Educ* instituto *m* de enseñanza media; **a. of music** conservatorio *m*

accede [ækˈsiːd] *vi* acceder (**to** a)

accelerate [ækˈseləreɪt] **1** *vt (engine)* acelerar; *(step)* aligerar

2 *vi (car, engine)* acelerar

acceleration [ækseləˈreɪʃən] *n* aceleración *f*

accelerator [æk'seləreɪtə(r)] *n* acelerador *m*

accent ['æksənt] *n* acento *m*

accentuate [æk'sentʃveɪt] *vt* subrayar

accept [ək'sept] *vt & vi* aceptar; *(theory)* admitir; **do you a. that ...?** ¿estás de acuerdo en que ...?

acceptable [ək'septəbəl] *adj (satisfactory)* aceptable; *(tolerable)* admisible

acceptance [ək'septəns] *n (act of accepting)* aceptación *f; (good reception)* aprobación *f*

access ['ækses] *n* acceso *m; Comput* **a. provider** proveedor *m* de acceso (a Internet); **a. road** carretera *f* de acceso; **to have a. to sth** tener libre acceso a algo

accessible [ək'sesəbəl] *adj (place, position)* accesible; *(person)* asequible

accession [ək'seʃən] *n* subida *f* (al trono)

accessory [ək'sesərɪ] *n (a) Jur* cómplice *mf* **(b) accessories** accesorios *mpl; (for outfit)* complementos *mpl*

accident ['æksɪdənt] *n* accidente *m; (coincidence)* casualidad *f;* **it was an a. on my part** lo hice sin querer; **car a.** accidente *m* de carretera; **by a.** por casualidad

accidental [æksɪ'dentəl] *adj* fortuito(a); *(unintended)* imprevisto(a)

accidentally [æksɪ'dentəlɪ] *adv (by chance)* por casualidad; **he did it a.** lo hizo sin querer

accident-prone ['æksɪdəntprəʊn] *adj* propenso(a) a los accidentes

acclaim [ə'kleɪm] **1** *n* aclamación *f* **2** *vt* aclamar

acclimatization [əklaɪmətaɪ'zeɪʃən], *US* **acclimation** [æklɪ'meɪʃən] *n* aclimatación *f*

acclimatize [ə'klaɪmətaɪz], *US* **acclimate** ['æklɪmeɪt] *vt* aclimatar

acclimatized [ə'klaɪmətaɪzd] *adj* aclimatado(a); **to become a.** aclimatarse

accolade ['ækəleɪd] *n* elogio *m*

accommodate [ə'kɒmədeɪt] *vt* **(a)** *(guests)* alojar **(b) to a. sb's wishes** complacer a algn

accommodating [ə'kɒmədeɪtɪŋ] *adj (obliging)* complaciente; *(understanding)* comprensivo(a)

accommodation [əkɒmə'deɪʃən] *n (US also accommodations) (lodgings)* alojamiento *m*

accompany [ə'kʌmpənɪ] *vt* acompañar

accomplice [ə'kʌmplɪs] *n* cómplice *mf*

accomplish [ə'kʌmplɪʃ] *vt (aim)* conseguir; *(task, mission)* llevar a cabo

accomplished [ə'kʌmplɪʃt] *adj* dotado(a), experto(a)

accomplishment [ə'kʌmplɪʃmənt] *n* **(a)** *(of task)* realización *f; (of duty)* cumplimiento *m* **(b) accomplishments** *(talents)* dotes *fpl*

accord [ə'kɔːd] **1** *n (agreement)* acuerdo *m;* **of her/his own a.** espontáneamente **2** *vt (honour etc)* conceder

accordance [ə'kɔːdəns] *n* **in a. with** de acuerdo con

according [ə'kɔːdɪŋ] *prep* **a. to** según; **everything went a. to plan** todo salió conforme a los planes

accordingly [ə'kɔːdɪŋlɪ] *adv* **(a) to act a.** *(appropriately)* obrar según y conforme **(b)** *(therefore)* así pues

accordion [ə'kɔːdɪən] *n* acordeón *m*

account [ə'kaʊnt] *n* **(a)** *(report)* informe *m;* **by all accounts** al decir de todos **(b) I was fearful on her a.** sufría por ella; **it's of no a.** no tiene importancia; **on a. of** a causa de; **on no a.** bajo ningún concepto; **to take a. of, to take into a.** tener en cuenta **(c)** *Com* cuenta *f;* **to keep the accounts** llevar las cuentas; **accounts department** servicio *m* de contabilidad; **to open/close an a.** abrir/cancelar una cuenta; **current a.** cuenta corriente; **a. number** número *m* de cuenta

► **account for** *vt insep (explain)* explicar

accountable [ə'kaʊntəbəl] *adj* **to be a. to sb for sth** ser responsable ante algn de algo

accountancy [ə'kaʊntənsɪ] *n* contabilidad *f*

accountant [ə'kaʊntənt] *n* contable *mf*

accredited [ə'kredɪtɪd] *adj* acreditado(a)

accrue [ə'kruː] *vi (interest)* acumularse

accumulate [ə'kjuːmjʊleɪt] **1** *vt* acumular; *(fortune)* amasar **2** *vi* acumularse

accuracy ['ækjʊrəsɪ] *n (of number etc)* exactitud *f; (of shot, criticism)* certeza *f*

accurate ['ækjʊrət] *adj (number)* exacto(a); *(shot, criticism)* certero(a); *(answer)* correcto(a); *(observation)* acertado(a); *(instrument)* de precisión; *(translation)* fiel

accusation [ækjʊ'zeɪʃən] *n* acusación *f*

accuse [ə'kjuːz] *vt* acusar

accused [ə'kjuːzd] *n* **the a.** el/la acusado(a)

accustom [ə'kʌstəm] *vt* acostumbrar; **to be accustomed to doing sth** estar acostumbrado(a) a hacer algo

ace [eɪs] *n* **(a)** *Cards & Fig* as *m* **(b)** *(in tennis)* ace *m*

acetate ['æsɪteɪt] *n* acetato *m*

acetone ['æsɪtəʊn] *n* acetona *f*

ache [eɪk] **1** *n* dolor *m*; **aches and pains** achaques *mpl*

2 *vi* doler; **my back aches** me duele la espalda

achieve [ə'tʃiːv] *vt (attain)* conseguir, alcanzar; *(accomplish)* llevar a cabo, realizar

achievement [ə'tʃiːvmənt] *n (attainment)* logro *m*; *(completion)* realización *f*; *(feat)* hazaña *f*

acid ['æsɪd] **1** *adj* ácido(a); *(taste)* agrio(a); *(remark)* mordaz; **a. rain** lluvia ácida; *Fig* **a. test** prueba decisiva

2 *n* ácido *m*

acknowledge [ək'nɒlɪdʒ] *vt* (a) *(recognize)* reconocer; *(claim, defeat)* admitir; *(present)* agradecer; *(letter)* acusar recibo de (b) *(greet)* saludar

acknowledgement [ək'nɒlɪdʒmənt] *n* (a) *(recognition)* reconocimiento *m*; *(of letter)* acuse *m* de recibo (b) **acknowledgements** *(in preface)* menciones *fpl*

acne ['ækni] *n* acné *m*

acorn ['eɪkɔːn] *n* bellota *f*

acoustic [ə'kuːstɪk] **1** *adj* acústico(a)

2 *npl* **acoustics** acústica *f*

acquaint [ə'kweɪnt] *vt* **to a. sb with the facts** informar a algn de los detalles; **to be acquainted with the procedure** estar al corriente de como se procede; **to be acquainted with sb** conocer a algn

acquaintance [ə'kweɪntəns] *n* (a) conocimiento *m*; **to make sb's a.** conocer a algn (b) *(person)* conocido(a) *m,f*

acquiesce [ækwɪ'es] *vi* consentir (**in** en)

acquiescent [ækwɪ'esənt] *adj* conforme

acquire [ə'kwaɪə(r)] *vt* adquirir

acquisition [ækwɪ'zɪʃən] *n* adquisición *f*

acquisitive [ə'kwɪzɪtɪv] *adj* codicioso(a)

acquit [ə'kwɪt] *vt* (a) **to a. sb of sth** absolver a algn de algo (b) **to a. oneself well** defenderse bien

acquittal [ə'kwɪtəl] *n* absolución *f*

acre ['eɪkə(r)] *n* acre *m* (= aprox 40,47 áreas)

acrid ['ækrɪd] *adj (smell, taste)* acre

acrimonious [ækrɪ'məʊnɪəs] *adj (remark)* cáustico(a); *(dispute)* enconado(a)

acrobat ['ækrəbæt] *n* acróbata *mf*

across [ə'krɒs] **1** *adv* a través; **the river is 30 m a.** el río mide 30 m de ancho; **to go a.** atravesar; **to run a.** atravesar corriendo

2 *prep* (a) a través de; **they live a. the road** viven enfrente; **to go a. the street** cruzar la calle (b) *(at the other side of)* al otro lado de

acrylic [ə'krɪlɪk] *adj* acrílico(a)

act [ækt] **1** *n* (a) *(action)* acto *m*, acción *f*; **a. of God** caso *m* de fuerza mayor (b) *(in parliament)* ley *f*, decreto *m* (c) *Th* acto *m*; *(turn in show)* número *m*

2 *vt Th (part)* interpretar; *(character)* representar; *Fig* **to a. the fool** hacer el tonto

3 *vi* (a) *Th* hacer teatro; *Cin* hacer cine; *Fig (pretend)* fingir (b) *(behave)* comportarse (c) *(take action)* actuar, obrar; **to a. on sb's advice** seguir el consejo de algn (d) *(work)* funcionar; *(drug etc)* actuar; **to a. as a deterrent** servir de disuasivo (e) **to a. as director** hacer de director

▸ **act out** *vt sep* exteriorizar

▸ **act up** *vi Fam (machine)* funcionar mal; *(child)* dar guerra

acting ['æktɪŋ] **1** *adj* interino(a)

2 *n (profession)* teatro *m*; **he's done some a.** ha hecho algo de teatro

action ['ækʃən] *n* (a) *(deed)* acción *f*; *Mil* acción de combate; **to be out of a.** *(person)* estar fuera de servicio; *(machine)* estar estropeado(a); **to take a.** tomar medidas (b) *Jur* demanda *f* (c) *TV* **a. replay** repetición *f*

activate ['æktɪveɪt] *vt* activar

active ['æktɪv] *adj* activo(a); *(energetic)* vigoroso(a); *(interest)* vivo(a); *Ling* **a. voice** voz activa

activist ['æktɪvɪst] *n* activista *mf*

activity [æk'tɪvɪtɪ] *n (of person)* actividad *f*; *(on street etc)* bullicio *m*

actor ['æktə(r)] *n* actor *m*

actress ['æktrɪs] *n* actriz *f*

actual ['æktʃʊəl] *adj* real, verdadero(a)

> 🖉 Note that the Spanish word **actual** is a false friend and is never a translation for the English word **actual**. In Spanish, **actual** means "current, up-to-date, topical".

actually ['æktʃʊəlɪ] *adv (really)* en efecto, realmente; *(even)* incluso, hasta; *(in fact)* de hecho

> 🖉 Note that the Spanish word **actualmente** is a false friend and is never a translation for the English word **actually**. In Spanish, **actualmente** means "nowadays, at the moment".

acumen ['ækjəmən] *n* perspicacia *f*

acupuncture ['ækjʊpʌŋktʃə(r)] *n* acupuntura *f*

acute [ə'kjuːt] *adj* agudo(a); *(pain)* intenso(a); *(hearing)* muy fino(a); *(shortage)* grave; *(mind)* perspicaz

AD [eɪ'diː] *(abbr* **Anno Domini**) d.J.C., d.C.

ad [æd] *n Fam* anuncio *m*

adamant ['ædəmənt] *adj* firme, inflexible

adapt [ə'dæpt] **1** *vt* adaptar (**to** a); **to a. oneself to sth** adaptarse a algo
2 *vi* adaptarse

adaptable [ə'dæptəbəl] *adj* (*instrument*) ajustable; **he's very a.** se amolda fácilmente a las circunstancias

adaptation [ædəp'teɪʃən] *n* adaptación *f*

adapter, adaptor [ə'dæptə(r)] *n Elec* ladrón *m*

add [æd] **1** *vt* (*numbers*) sumar; (*one thing to another*) añadir
2 *vi* (*count*) sumar
▸ **add to** *vt insep* aumentar
▸ **add up 1** *vt sep* sumar
2 *vi* (*numbers*) sumar; *Fig* **it doesn't a. up** no tiene sentido; **it doesn't a. up to much** no es gran cosa

added ['ædɪd] *adj* adicional

adder ['ædə(r)] *n* víbora *f*

addict ['ædɪkt] *n* adicto(a) *m,f; Fam* **television a.** teleadicto(a) *m,f*

addicted [ə'dɪktɪd] *adj* adicto(a); **to become a. to sth** enviciarse con algo

addiction [ə'dɪkʃən] *n* (*to gambling etc*) vicio *m*; (*to drugs*) adicción *f*

addictive [ə'dɪktɪv] *adj* que crea adicción

addition [ə'dɪʃən] *n Math* adición *f*; (*increase*) aumento *m*; **an a. to the family** un nuevo miembro de la familia; **in a. to** además de

additional [ə'dɪʃənəl] *adj* adicional

additive ['ædɪtɪv] *n* aditivo *m*

address [ə'dres] **1** *n* (**a**) (*on letter*) dirección *f*, señas *fpl* (**b**) (*speech*) discurso *m*
2 *vt* (**a**) (*letter*) dirigir (**b**) (*speak to*) dirigirse (**to** a); **to a. the floor** tomar la palabra (**c**) (*use form of address to*) tratar de

adenoids ['ædɪnɔɪdz] *npl* vegetaciones *fpl* (adenoideas)

adept [ə'dept] **1** *adj* experto(a) (**at** en)
2 *n* experto(a) *m,f*

> 🎵 Note that the Spanish word **adepto** is a false friend and is never a translation for the English word **adept**. In Spanish, **adepto** means "follower, supporter".

adequate ['ædɪkwɪt] *adj* (*enough*) suficiente; (*satisfactory*) adecuado(a)

adhere [əd'hɪə(r)] *vi* (*stick*) pegarse (**to** a)
▸ **adhere to** *vt insep* (*policy*) adherirse a; (*contract*) cumplir con

adherent [əd'hɪərənt] *n* partidario(a) *m,f*

adhesive [əd'hiːsɪv] **1** *adj* adhesivo(a); (*sticky*) pegajoso(a); **a. tape** cinta adhesiva
2 *n* adhesivo *m*

ad hoc [æd'hɒk] *adj* (*remark*) improvisado(a); **an a. committee** un comité especial

ad infinitum [ædɪnfɪ'naɪtəm] *adv* hasta el infinito

adjacent [ə'dʒeɪsənt] *adj* (*building*) contiguo(a); (*land*) colindante; **a. to** contiguo(a) a

adjective ['ædʒɪktɪv] *n* adjetivo *m*

adjoining [ə'dʒɔɪnɪŋ] *adj* contiguo(a); (*land*) colindante; **the a. room** la habitación de al lado

adjourn [ə'dʒɜːn] **1** *vt* (*postpone*) aplazar; (*court*) levantar
2 *vi* aplazarse (**until** hasta)

adjudicate [ə'dʒuːdɪkeɪt] *vt* juzgar

adjudicator [ə'dʒuːdɪkeɪtə(r)] *n* juez(a) *m,f*

adjust [ə'dʒʌst] **1** *vt* (*machine etc*) ajustar; *Fig* (*methods*) variar
2 *vi* (*person*) adaptarse (**to** a)

adjustable [ə'dʒʌstəbəl] *adj* ajustable

adjustment [ə'dʒʌstmənt] *n* (**a**) (*to machine etc*) ajuste *m*; (*by person*) adaptación *f* (**b**) (*change*) modificación *f*

ad lib [æd'lɪb] **1** *adv* (*speak*) sin preparación; (*continue*) a voluntad
2 *adj* (*speech*) improvisado(a)
3 ad-lib *vi* improvisar

administer [əd'mɪnɪstə(r)] *vt* (*country*) gobernar; (*justice*) administrar

administration [ədmɪnɪ'streɪʃən] *n* (*of country*) gobierno *m*; (*of justice*) administración *f*; (*governing body*) dirección *f*

administrative [əd'mɪnɪstrətɪv] *adj* administrativo(a)

admirable [æd'mərəbəl] *adj* admirable

admiral ['ædmərəl] *n* almirante *m*

admiration [ædmə'reɪʃən] *n* admiración *f*

admire [əd'maɪə(r)] *vt* admirar

admirer [əd'maɪərə(r)] *n* admirador(a) *m,f*

admissible [əd'mɪsəbəl] *adj* admisible

admission [əd'mɪʃən] *n* (**a**) (*to school etc*) ingreso *m*; (*price*) entrada *f* (**b**) (*of fact*) reconocimiento *m*; (*confession*) confesión *f*

admit [əd'mɪt] *vt* (**a**) (*person*) dejar entrar; **to be admitted to hospital** ser ingresado(a) en el hospital (**b**) (*acknowledge*) reconocer; (*crime, guilt*) confesar

admittance [əd'mɪtəns] *n* (*entry*) entrada *f*

admittedly [əd'mɪtɪdlɪ] *adv* la verdad es que ...

admonish [əd'mɒnɪʃ] *vt* amonestar

ad nauseam [æd'nɔːzɪæm] *adv* hasta la saciedad

ado [ə'duː] *n* **without further a.** sin más

adolescence [ædə'lesəns] *n* adolescencia *f*

adolescent [ædə'lesənt] *n* adolescente *mf*

adopt [ə'dɒpt] *vt* adoptar; *(suggestion)* aceptar

adopted [ə'dɒptɪd] *adj* **a. child** hijo(a) *m,f* adoptivo(a)

adoption [ə'dɒpʃən] *n* adopción *f;* **country of a.** país adoptivo

adore [ə'dɔː(r)] *vt* adorar

adorn [ə'dɔːn] *vt* adornar

adornment [ə'dɔːnmənt] *n* adorno *m*

adrenalin [ə'drenəlɪn] *n* adrenalina *f*

Adriatic [eɪdrɪ'ætɪk] *adj* **the A. (Sea)** el (mar) Adriático

adrift [ə'drɪft] *adv* **to come a.** *(boat)* irse a la deriva; *(rope)* soltarse; *Fig* **to go a.** *(plans)* ir a la deriva

adult ['ædʌlt] **1** *adj (person)* adulto(a), mayor; *(film, education)* para adultos
2 *n* adulto(a) *m,f*

adulterate [ə'dʌltəreɪt] *vt* adulterar

adulterer [ə'dʌltərə(r)] *n* adúltero *m*

adulteress [ə'dʌltrɪs] *n* adúltera *f*

adultery [ə'dʌltərɪ] *n* adulterio *m*

advance [əd'vɑːns] **1** *n* **(a)** *(movement)* avance *m; Fig (progress)* progreso *m;* **to have sth ready in a.** tener algo preparado de antemano; **to make advances (to)** *(person)* insinuarse (a) **(b)** *(loan)* anticipo *m*
2 *adj (before time)* adelantado(a); *Cin & Th* **a. bookings** reservas *fpl* por adelantado
3 *vt* **(a)** *(troops)* avanzar; *(time, date)* adelantar **(b)** *(idea)* proponer; *(opinion)* dar **(c)** *Fin (sum of money)* anticipar
4 *vi (move forward)* avanzar, adelantarse; *(make progress)* hacer progresos; *(gain promotion)* ascender

advanced [əd'vɑːnst] *adj (developed)* avanzado(a); *(student)* adelantado(a); *(course)* superior; *Educ* **A. level** examen *m* superior de segunda enseñanza, ≃ COU *m*

advancement [əd'vɑːnsmənt] *n (progress)* adelanto *m;* *(promotion)* ascenso *m*

advantage [əd'vɑːntɪdʒ] *n* ventaja *f;* *(in tennis)* **a. Velasco** ventaja para Velasco; **to**

take a. of sb/sth abusar de algn/aprovechar algo

advantageous [ædvən'teɪdʒəs] *adj* ventajoso(a)

advent ['ædvent] *n (arrival)* llegada *f;* *(of Christ)* advenimiento *m;* **A.** Adviento *m*

adventure [əd'ventʃə(r)] *n* aventura *f;* **a. sport** deporte *m* de aventura

adventurous [əd'ventʃərəs] *adj* aventurero(a)

adverb ['ædvɜːb] *n* adverbio *m*

adversary ['ædvəsərɪ] *n* adversario(a) *m,f*

adverse ['ædvɜːs] *adj (effect)* desfavorable, *(conditions)* adverso(a); *(winds)* contrario(a)

adversity [əd'vɜːsɪtɪ] *n* adversidad *f*

advert ['ædvɜːt] *n Fam* anuncio *m*

advertise ['ædvətaɪz] **1** *vt* anunciar
2 *vi* hacer publicidad; *(in newspaper)* poner un anuncio; **to a. for sth/sb** buscar algo/a algn mediante un anuncio

advertisement [əd'vɜːtɪsmənt] *n* anuncio *m;* **advertisements** publicidad *f*

advertiser ['ædvətaɪzə(r)] *n* anunciante *mf*

advertising ['ædvətaɪzɪŋ] **1** *n* publicidad *f,* propaganda *f;* *(in newspaper)* anuncios *mpl*
2 *adj* publicitario(a); **a. agency** agencia *f* de publicidad

advice [əd'vaɪs] *n* consejos *mpl;* **a piece of a.** un consejo; **to take legal a. on a matter** consultar el caso con un abogado; **to take sb's a.** seguir los consejos de algn

advisable [əd'vaɪzəbəl] *adj* aconsejable

advise [əd'vaɪz] *vt* aconsejar; *(on business etc)* asesorar; **I a. you to do it** te aconsejo que lo hagas

adviser [əd'vaɪzə(r)] *n* consejero(a) *m,f;* *(in business etc)* asesor(a) *m,f*

advisory [əd'vaɪzərɪ] *adj* asesor(a)

advocate 1 *n* ['ædvəkɪt] *Scot Jur* abogado(a) *m,f;* *(supporter)* defensor(a) *m,f*
2 *vt* ['ædvəkeɪt] *(reform)* abogar por; *(plan)* apoyar

aerial ['eərɪəl] **1** *adj* aéreo(a)
2 *n* antena *f*

aerobics [eə'rəʊbɪks] *n sing* aerobic *m*

aerodrome ['eərədrəʊm] *n Br* aeródromo *m*

aerodynamics [eərəʊdaɪ'næmɪks] *n sing* aerodinámica *f*

aeroplane ['eərəpleɪn] *n Br* avión *m*

aerosol ['eərəsɒl] *n* aerosol *m*

aerospace ['eərəʊspeɪs] *adj* aeroespacial

aesthetic [iːsˈθetɪk] *adj* estético(a)

afar [əˈfɑː(r)] *adv* lejos; **from a.** desde lejos

affair [əˈfeə(r)] *n* (*matter*) asunto *m*; (*event*) acontecimiento *m*; **that's my a.** eso es asunto mío; **business affairs** negocios *mpl*; **foreign affairs** asuntos exteriores; **love a.** aventura amorosa

affect [əˈfekt] *vt* (*person, health*) afectar; (*prices, future*) influir en; (*touch emotionally*) conmover

affected [əˈfektɪd] *adj* (a) (*unnatural*) afectado(a) (b) (*influenced*) influido(a) (c) (*touched emotionally*) conmovido(a) (d) (*pretended*) fingido(a)

affection [əˈfekʃən] *n* afecto *m*, cariño *m*

affectionate [əˈfekʃənɪt] *adj* cariñoso(a)

affidavit [æfɪˈdeɪvɪt] *n* declaración escrita y jurada

affiliated [əˈfɪlɪeɪtɪd] *adj* afiliado(a); **to be/become a. (to** or **with)** afiliarse (a)

affinity [əˈfɪnɪtɪ] *n* afinidad *f*; (*liking*) simpatía *f*

affirm [əˈfɜːm] *vt* afirmar, sostener

affirmation [æfəˈmeɪʃən] *n* afirmación *f*

affirmative [əˈfɜːmətɪv] **1** *adj* afirmativo(a)
2 *n* **he answered in the a.** contestó que sí

affix [əˈfɪks] *vt* (*stamp*) pegar

afflict [əˈflɪkt] *vt* afligir

affluence [ˈæflʊəns] *n* opulencia *f*

affluent [ˈæflʊənt] *adj* (*society*) opulento(a); (*person*) rico(a)

afford [əˈfɔːd] *vt* (a) (*be able to buy*) permitirse el lujo de; **I can't a. a new car** no puedo pagar un coche nuevo (b) (*be able to do*) permitirse; **you can't a. to miss the opportunity** no puedes perderte la ocasión

affront [əˈfrʌnt] **1** *n* afrenta *f*
2 *vt* afrentar

afield [əˈfiːld] *adv* **far a.** muy lejos

afloat [əˈfləʊt] *adv* **to keep a.** mantenerse a flote

afoot [əˈfʊt] *adv* **there's a plan a.** hay un proyecto en marcha; **there's something strange a.** se está tramando algo

aforementioned [əˈfɔːmenʃənd], **aforesaid** [əˈfɔːsed] *adj* susodicho(a)

afraid [əˈfreɪd] *adj* (a) **to be a.** tener miedo (**of sb** a algn; **of sth** de algo); **I'm a. of it** me da miedo (b) **I'm a. not** me temo que no; **I'm a. so** me temo que sí; **I'm a. you're wrong** me temo que estás equivocado(a)

afresh [əˈfreʃ] *adv* de nuevo

Africa [ˈæfrɪkə] *n* Africa

African [ˈæfrɪkən] *adj & n* africano(a) (*m,f*)

Afro [ˈæfrəʊ] *adj & n Fam* (*hairstyle*) afro (*m*)

aft [ɑːft] *adv* en popa; **to go a.** ir en popa

after [ˈɑːftə(r)] **1** *adv* después; **soon a.** poco después; **the day a.** el día siguiente
2 *prep* (a) (*later*) después de; *US* **it's ten a. five** son las cinco y diez; **soon a. arriving** al poco rato de llegar; **the day a. tomorrow** pasado mañana
(b) (*behind*) detrás de, tras; **a. you!** ¡pase usted!; **they went in one a. the other** entraron uno tras otro; **the police are a. them** la policía anda tras ellos
(c) (*about*) por; **they asked a. you** preguntaron por ti; **what's he a.?** ¿qué pretende?
(d) **he takes a. his uncle** se parece a su tío; **she was named a. her grandmother** le llamaron como su abuela
3 *conj* después (de) que; **a. it happened** después de que ocurriera

after-effect [ˈɑːftərɪfekt] *n* efecto secundario

afterlife [ˈɑːftəlaɪf] *n* vida *f* después de la muerte

aftermath [ˈɑːftəmæθ] *n* secuelas *fpl*

afternoon [ɑːftəˈnuːn] *n* tarde *f*; **good a.!** ¡buenas tardes!; **in the a.** por la tarde

afternoons [ɑːftəˈnuːnz] *adv US* por las tardes

afters [ˈɑːftəz] *npl Fam* postre *m*

after-sales service [ɑːftəseɪlzˈsɜːvɪs] *n Com* servicio *m* posventa

aftershave (lotion) [ˈɑːftəʃeɪv(ˈləʊʃən)] *n* loción *f* para después del afeitado

afterthought [ˈɑːftəθɔːt] *n* ocurrencia *f* tardía

afterwards [ˈɑːftəwədz] *adv* después, más tarde

again [əˈgen] *adv* (a) otra vez, de nuevo; **I tried a. and a.** lo intenté una y otra vez; **to do sth a.** volver a hacer algo; **never a.!** ¡nunca más!; **now and a.** de vez en cuando; **once a.** otra vez (b) (*besides*) además; **then a.** por otra parte

against [əˈgenst] *prep* (a) (*touching*) contra (b) (*opposing*) contra, en contra (de); **a. the grain** a contrapelo; **it's a. the law** es ilegal (c) **as a.** en contraste con, comparado con

age [eɪdʒ] **1** *n* (a) edad *f*; **she's eighteen years of a.** tiene dieciocho años; **to be under a.** ser menor de edad; **to come of a.** llegar a la mayoría de edad; **a. limit** límite *m* de edad; **old a.** vejez *f* (b) (*period*) época *f;* **the Iron A.** la Edad de Hierro (**c**) *Fam (long time)* eternidad *f;* **it's ages since I last saw her** hace siglos que no la veo

2 *vt & vi* envejecer

aged¹ [eɪdʒd] *adj* de *or* a la edad de

aged² ['eɪdʒɪd] *npl* **the a.** los ancianos

agency ['eɪdʒənsɪ] *n* (**a**) *Com* agencia *f* (**b**) **by the a. of** por medio de

agenda [ə'dʒendə] *n* orden *m* del día

agent ['eɪdʒənt] *n* agente *mf; (representative)* representante *mf*

aggravate ['ægrəveɪt] *vt (worsen)* agravar; *(annoy)* molestar

aggregate ['ægrɪgɪt] *n* conjunto *m;* **on a.** en conjunto

aggression [ə'greʃən] *n* agresión *f*

aggressive [ə'gresɪv] *adj (violent)* agresivo(a), violento(a); *(dynamic)* dinámico(a)

aggrieved [ə'griːvd] *adj* apenado(a)

aghast [ə'gɑːst] *adj* espantado(a)

agile ['ædʒaɪl] *adj* ágil

agitate ['ædʒɪteɪt] **1** *vt (shake)* agitar; *Fig (worry)* perturbar

2 *vi Pol* **to a. against sth** hacer campaña en contra de algo

agitator ['ædʒɪteɪtə(r)] *n Pol* agitador(a) *m,f*

AGM [eɪdʒiː'em] *n (abbr* **annual general meeting**) junta *f* general anual

agnostic [æg'nɒstɪk] *n* agnóstico(a) *m,f*

ago [ə'gəʊ] *adv* **a long time a.** hace mucho tiempo; **as long a. as 1910** ya en 1910; **a week a.** hace una semana; **how long a.?** ¿hace cuánto tiempo?

agog [ə'gɒg] *adj* ansioso(a)

agonizing ['ægənaɪzɪŋ] *adj (pain)* atroz; *(decision)* desesperante

agony ['ægənɪ] *n* dolor *m* muy fuerte; *(anguish)* angustia *f;* **he was in a. with his back** tenía un dolor insoportable de espalda

agree [ə'griː] **1** *vi* (**a**) *(be in agreement)* estar de acuerdo; *(reach agreement)* ponerse de acuerdo; *(consent)* consentir; **to a. to do sth** consentir en hacer algo; **to a. with sb** estar de acuerdo con algn (**b**) *(harmonize) (things)* concordar; *(people)* congeniar; **onions don't a. with me** la cebolla no me sienta bien

2 *vt* acordar

agreeable [ə'griːəbl] *adj (pleasant)* agradable; *(person)* simpático(a); *(in agreement)* de acuerdo

agreement [ə'griːmənt] *n (arrangement)* acuerdo *m; Com* contrato *m;* **to reach an a.** llegar a un acuerdo

agricultural [ægrɪ'kʌltʃərəl] *adj* agrícola; *(college)* de agricultura

agriculture ['ægrɪkʌltʃə(r)] *n* agricultura *f*

aground [ə'graʊnd] *adv* **to run a.** encallar, varar

ahead [ə'hed] *adv* delante; *(early)* antes; **go a.!** ¡adelante!; **to be a.** llevar la ventaja; **to go a.** ir adelante; *Fig* **to go a. with sth** llevar algo adelante; *(start)* comenzar algo; **to get a.** triunfar; **to look a.** pensar en el futuro

aid [eɪd] **1** *n* ayuda *f; (rescue)* auxilio *m;* **in a. of** a beneficio de; **to come to the a. of sb** acudir en ayuda de algn; **a. worker** cooperante *mf*

2 *vt* ayudar; **to a. and abet sb** ser cómplice de algn

aide [eɪd] *n* ayudante *mf*

AIDS [eɪdz] *n (abbr* **Acquired Immune Deficiency Syndrome**) sida *m*

ailing ['eɪlɪŋ] *adj* achacoso(a)

ailment ['eɪlmənt] *n* enfermedad *f* (leve), achaque *m*

aim [eɪm] **1** *n (with weapon)* puntería *f; (target)* propósito *m*

2 *vt (gun)* apuntar (**at** *a or hacia); (attack, action)* dirigir (**at** *a or hacia)*

▸ **aim at** *vt insep (target)* tirar para; **to a. at doing sth** tener pensado hacer algo

▸ **aim to** *vt insep* **to a. to do sth** tener la intención de hacer algo

aimless ['eɪmlɪs] *adj* sin objeto, sin propósito

aimlessly ['eɪmlɪslɪ] *adv (wander)* sin rumbo fijo

air [eə(r)] **1** *n* (**a**) aire *m;* **to travel by a.** viajar en avión; **to throw sth up in the a.** lanzar algo al aire; *Fig* **it's still in the a.** todavía queda por resolver; *Aut* **a. bag** airbag *m;* **a. base** base aérea; **a. bed** colchón *m* hinchable; **a. conditioning** aire acondicionado; **A. Force** Fuerzas Aéreas; **a. freshener** ambientador *m;* **a. gun** pistola *f* de aire comprimido; **a. hostess** azafata *f;* **a. letter** carta aérea; **a. pocket** bache *m;* **a. pressure** presión atmosférica; **a. raid** ataque aéreo; **a. terminal** terminal aérea; **a. traffic control** control *m* de tráfico aéreo; **a. traffic controller** controlador(a) *m,f* aéreo(a)

(**b**) *Rad & TV* **to be on the a.** *(programme)* estar emitiendo; *(person)* estar transmitiendo

(**c**) *(appearance)* aspecto *m*

2 *vt (bed, clothes)* airear; *(room)* ventilar; *Fig (grievance)* airear; *(knowledge)* hacer alarde de

airborne ['eəbɔːn] *adj (aircraft)* en vuelo; *(troops)* aerotransportado(a)

air-conditioned ['eəkɒndɪʃənd] *adj* climatizado(a)

aircraft ['eəkrɑːft] *n (pl aircraft)* avión *m*; **a. carrier** portaviones *m inv*

airfield ['eəfiːld] *n* campo *m* de aviación

airlift ['eəlɪft] *n* puente aéreo

airline ['eəlaɪn] *n* línea aérea

airlock ['eəlɒk] *n (in pipe)* bolsa *f* de aire; *(in spacecraft)* esclusa *f* de aire

airmail ['eəmeɪl] *n* correo aéreo; **by a.** por avión

airplane ['eəpleɪn] *n US* avión *m*

airport ['eəpɔːt] *n* aeropuerto *m*; **a. tax** tasas *fpl* de aeropuerto

airsick ['eəsɪk] *adj* **to be a.** marearse en avión

airstrip ['eəstrɪp] *n* pista *f* de aterrizaje

airtight ['eətaɪt] *adj* hermético(a)

airy ['eərɪ] *adj* (**airier, airiest**) *(well-ventilated)* bien ventilado(a); *(vague, carefree)* ligero(a)

aisle [aɪl] *n (in church)* nave *f*; *(in theatre)* pasillo *m*

ajar [ə'dʒɑː(r)] *adj & adv* entreabierto(a)

akin [ə'kɪn] *adj* semejante

alacrity [ə'lækrɪtɪ] *n* with **a.** con presteza

à la mode [ælə'məʊd] *adj US (dessert)* con helado

alarm [ə'lɑːm] **1** *n* (**a**) alarma *f*; **a. clock** despertador *m* (**b**) *(fear)* inquietud *f*; **to cause a.** provocar temor
2 *vt* alarmar

alas [ə'læs] *interj* ¡ay!, ¡ay de mí!

albatross ['ælbətrɒs] *n* albatros *m*

albeit [ɔːl'biːɪt] *conj* aunque, no obstante

album ['ælbəm] *n* álbum *m*

alcohol ['ælkəhɒl] *n* alcohol *m*

alcoholic [ælkə'hɒlɪk] *adj & n* alcohólico(a) *(m,f)*

alcopop ['ælkəʊpɒp] *n Br* refresco *m* con alcohol

alcove ['ælkəʊv] *n* hueco *m*

> 🖉 Note that the Spanish word **alcoba** is a false friend and is never a translation for the English word **alcove**. In Spanish, **alcoba** means "bedroom".

ale [eɪl] *n* cerveza *f*; **brown/pale a.** cerveza negra/rubia

alert [ə'lɜːt] **1** *adj* alerta; *(lively)* despabilado(a)
2 *n* alerta *m*; **to be on the a.** estar alerta
3 *vt* **to a. sb to sth** avisar a algn de algo

A-level ['eɪlevəl] *n Br Educ (abbr Advanced level)* = examen final o diploma en una asignatura de los estudios preuniversitarios

algae ['ældʒiː] *npl* algas *fpl*

algebra ['ældʒɪbrə] *n* álgebra *f*

Algeria [æl'dʒɪərɪə] *n* Argelia

Algerian [æl'dʒɪərɪən] *adj & n* argelino(a) *(m,f)*

Algiers [æl'dʒɪəz] *n* Argel

alias ['eɪlɪəs] **1** *n* alias *m*
2 *adv* alias

alibi ['ælɪbaɪ] *n* coartada *f*

alien ['eɪlɪən] **1** *adj (foreign)* extranjero(a); *(from space)* extraterrestre; **a. to** ajeno(a) a
2 *n (foreigner)* extranjero(a) *m,f*; *(from space)* extraterrestre *mf*

alienate ['eɪlɪəneɪt] *vt* (**a**) **to a. sb** ofender a algn; **to a. oneself from sb** alejarse de algn (**b**) *Jur* enajenar

alight¹ [ə'laɪt] *adj (on fire)* ardiendo(a)

alight² [ə'laɪt] *vi (get off)* apearse (**from** de)

align [ə'laɪn] *vt* alinear

alike [ə'laɪk] **1** *adj (similar)* parecidos(as); *(the same)* iguales
2 *adv (in the same way)* de la misma manera, igualmente; **dressed a.** vestidos(as) iguales

alimony ['ælɪmənɪ] *n Jur* pensión alimenticia

alive [ə'laɪv] *adj* vivo(a); *Fig (teeming)* lleno(a) (**with** de); **to be a.** estar vivo(a)

alkaline ['ælkəlaɪn] *adj* alcalino(a)

all [ɔːl] **1** *adj* todo(a), todos(as); **a. year** *(durante)* todo el año; **a. kinds of things** todo tipo de cosas; **at a. hours** a todas horas; **at a. times** siempre; **she works a. the time** siempre está trabajando; **a. six of us were there** los seis estábamos allí
2 *pron* todo(a), todos(as); **after a.** al fin y al cabo; **a. of his work** toda su obra; **a. of us** todos(as) nosotros(as); **a. who saw it** todos los que lo vieron; **a. you can do is wait** lo único que puedes hacer es esperar; **I don't like it at a.** no me gusta en absoluto; **is that a.?** ¿eso es todo?; **most of** *or* **above a.** sobre todo; **once and for a.** de una vez por todas; **thanks − not at a.** gracias − de nada; **a. in a.** en conjunto; **that's a.** ya está; **the score was one a.** empataron a uno
3 *adv* **a. by myself** completamente solo(a); **a. at once** *(suddenly)* de repente; *(altogether)* de una vez; **a. the better** tanto mejor; **the same** de todos modos; **he knew a. along** lo sabía desde el principio; **if it's a. the same to you** si no te importa; **it's a. but impossible** es casi

imposible; **I'm not a. that tired** no estoy tan cansado(a) como eso

4 *n* **to give one's a.** darse por completo

Allah ['ælə] *n* Alá *m*

allay [ə'leɪ] *vt (fears, doubts)* apaciguar

allegation [ælɪ'geɪʃən] *n* alegato *m*

allege [ə'ledʒ] *vt* sostener, pretender (that que)

allegedly [ə'ledʒɪdlɪ] *adv* supuestamente

allegiance [ə'liːdʒəns] *n* lealtad *f*

allergic [ə'lɜːdʒɪk] *adj* alérgico(a) (**to** a)

allergy ['ælədʒɪ] *n* alergia *f*

alleviate [ə'liːvɪeɪt] *vt (pain)* aliviar

alley ['ælɪ] *n* callejón *m*

alliance [ə'laɪəns] *n* alianza *f*

allied ['ælaɪd] *adj* aliado(a)

alligator ['ælɪgeɪtə(r)] *n* caimán *m*

all-in ['ɔːlɪn] *adj (price)* todo incluido; *Sport* **a. wrestling** lucha *f* libre

alliteration [əlɪtə'reɪʃən] *n* aliteración *f*

all-night ['ɔːlnaɪt] *adj (café etc)* abierto(a) toda la noche; *(vigil)* que dura toda la noche

allocate ['æləkeɪt] *vt* destinar (**to** para)

allocation [ælə'keɪʃən] *n* (**a**) *(distribution)* asignación *f* (**b**) *(amount allocated)* cuota *f*

allot [ə'lɒt] *vt* asignar

allotment [ə'lɒtmənt] *n* (**a**) *(distribution)* asignación *f* (**b**) *(land)* parcela *f*

all-out ['ɔːlaʊt] **1** *adj (effort)* supremo(a); *(attack)* concentrado(a)

2 all out *adv* **to go all out to do sth** emplearse a fondo para hacer algo

allow [ə'laʊ] *vt* (**a**) *(permit)* permitir; *(a request)* acceder a; **to a. sb to do sth** permitir que algn haga algo (**b**) *(allot)* *(time)* dejar; *(money)* destinar

▸ **allow for** *vt insep* tener en cuenta

allowance [ə'laʊəns] *n (payment)* pensión *f*, subvención *f*; *(discount)* descuento *m*; **to make allowances for sb/sth** disculpar a algn/tener algo en cuenta; **tax a.** desgravación *f* fiscal; **travel a.** dietas *fpl* de viaje

alloy ['ælɔɪ] *n* aleación *f*

all right [ɔːl'raɪt] **1** *adj (okay)* bien; **thank you very much – that's a.** muchas gracias – de nada

2 *adv* (**a**) *(well)* bien (**b**) *(definitely)* sin duda (**c**) *(okay)* de acuerdo, vale

all-round ['ɔːlraʊnd] *adj (athlete etc)* completo(a)

all-terrain [ɔːltə'reɪn] *adj* **a. vehicle** todoterreno *m*

all-time ['ɔːltaɪm] *adj* **an a. low** una baja sin antecedentes; **the a. greats** los grandes de siempre

allude [ə'luːd] *vi* **to a. to** aludir a

alluring [ə'ljʊərɪŋ] *adj* atractivo(a)

allusion [ə'luːʒən] *n* alusión *f*

ally ['ælaɪ] **1** *n* aliado(a) *m,f*

2 *vt* **to a. oneself to/with sb** aliarse a/ con algn

almighty [ɔːl'maɪtɪ] **1** *adj (all-powerful)* todopoderoso(a)

2 *n* **the A.** El Todopoderoso

almond ['ɑːmənd] *n* almendra *f*

almost ['ɔːlməʊst] *adv* casi

alms [ɑːmz] *npl* limosna *f*

aloft [ə'lɒft] *adv* arriba

alone [ə'ləʊn] **1** *adj* solo(a); **can I speak to you a.?** ¿puedo hablar contigo a solas?; **let a.** ni mucho menos; **leave it a.!** ¡no lo toques!; **leave me a.** déjame en paz; **to be a.** estar solo(a)

2 *adv* solamente, sólo

along [ə'lɒŋ] **1** *adv* **come a.!** ¡anda, ven!; **he'll be a. in ten minutes** llegará dentro de diez minutos; **a. with** junto con

2 *prep (the length of)* a lo largo de; **to walk a. the street** andar por la calle; **it's just a. the street** está un poco más abajo

alongside [ə'lɒŋsaɪd] **1** *adv Naut* de costado

2 *prep* al lado de

aloof [ə'luːf] **1** *adj (person)* distante

2 *adv* **to keep oneself a. (from)** mantenerse a distancia (de)

aloud [ə'laʊd] *adv* en voz alta

alphabet ['ælfəbet] *n* alfabeto *m*

alphabetical [ælfə'betɪkəl] *adj* alfabético(a)

alphabetically [ælfə'betɪkəlɪ] *adv* por orden alfabético

alpine ['ælpaɪn] *adj* alpino(a)

Alps [ælps] *npl* **the A.** los Alpes

already [ɔːl'redɪ] *adv* ya

alright [ɔːl'raɪt] *adj & adv* = **all right**

Alsatian [æl'seɪʃən] *n* pastor *m* alemán

also ['ɔːlsəʊ] *adv* también, además

also-ran ['ɔːlsəʊræn] *n Fam (person)* segundón(ona) *m,f*

altar ['ɔːltə(r)] *n* altar *m*

alter ['ɔːltə(r)] **1** *vt (plan)* cambiar, retocar; *(project)* modificar; *(clothing)* arreglar; *(timetable)* revisar

2 *vi* cambiar, cambiarse

alteration [ɔːltə'reɪʃən] *n (to plan)* cambio *m*; *(to project)* modificación *f*; *(to clothing)* arreglo *m*; *(to timetable)* revisión *f*; **alterations** *(to building)* reformas *fpl*

alternate 1 *adj* [ɔːl'tɜːnɪt] alterno(a); **on a. days** cada dos días

2 *vt* ['ɔːltəneɪt] alternar

alternately [ɔːl'tɜːnɪtlɪ] *adv* **a. hot and cold** ahora caliente, ahora frío

alternative [ɔːl'tɜːnətɪv] **1** *adj* alternativo(a)

2 *n* alternativa *f*; **I have no a. but to accept** no tengo más remedio que aceptar

alternatively [ɔːl'tɜːnətɪvlɪ] *adv* o bien; **a., you could walk** o bien podrías ir andando

alternator ['ɔːltəneɪtə(r)] *n Aut* alternador *m*

although [ɔːl'ðəʊ] *conj* aunque

altitude ['æltɪtjuːd] *n* altitud *f*

alto ['æltəʊ] *adj & n* (*male singer, instrument*) alto (*m*); (*female singer*) contralto (*f*)

altogether [ɔːltə'geðə(r)] *adv* (*in total*) en conjunto, en total; (*completely*) completamente, del todo

altruism ['æltruːɪzəm] *n* altruismo *m*

aluminium [æljʊ'mɪnɪəm], *US* **aluminum** [ə'luːmɪnəm] *n* aluminio *m*

alumnus [ə'lʌmnəs] *n* (*pl* **alumni** [ə'lʌmnaɪ]) *US* antiguo alumno

always ['ɔːlweɪz] *adv* siempre

AM [eɪ'em] *Rad* (*abbr* **amplitude modulation**) AM

am [æm] *1st person sing pres of* **be**

a.m. [eɪ'em] (*abbr* **ante meridiem**) a.m., de la mañana

amalgamate [ə'mælgəmeɪt] **1** *vt* (*metals*) amalgamar

2 *vi* (*metals*) amalgamarse; (*companies*) fusionarse

amalgamation [əmælgə'meɪʃən] *n* fusión *f*

amass [ə'mæs] *vt* (*money*) amontonar; (*information*) acumular

amateur ['æmətə(r)] **1** *n* amateur *mf*, aficionado(a) *m,f*

2 *adj* aficionado(a); *Pej* (*work etc*) chapucero(a)

amateurish ['æmətərɪʃ] *adj* chapucero(a)

amaze [ə'meɪz] *vt* asombrar, pasmar; **to be amazed at sth** quedarse pasmado(a) de algo

amazement [ə'meɪzmənt] *n* asombro *m*, sorpresa *f*

amazing [ə'meɪzɪŋ] *adj* asombroso(a), increíble

ambassador [æm'bæsədə(r)] *n* embajador(a) *m,f*

amber ['æmbə(r)] **1** *n* ámbar *m*

2 *adj* ambarino(a); (*traffic light*) amarillo(a)

ambiguity [æmbɪ'gjuːɪtɪ] *n* ambigüedad *f*

ambiguous [æm'bɪgjʊəs] *adj* ambiguo(a)

ambition [æm'bɪʃən] *n* ambición *f*

ambitious [æm'bɪʃəs] *adj* ambicioso(a)

ambivalent [æm'bɪvələnt] *adj* ambivalente

amble ['æmbəl] *vi* deambular

ambulance ['æmbjʊləns] *n* ambulancia *f*; **a. man** ambulanciero *m*

ambush ['æmbʊʃ] **1** *n* emboscada *f*

2 *vt* tender una emboscada a; *Fig* atacar por sorpresa

amen [ɑː'men] *interj* amén

amenable [ə'miːnəbəl] *adj* **I'd be quite a. to doing that** no me importaría nada hacer eso; **a. to reason** razonable

amend [ə'mend] *vt* (*law*) enmendar; (*error*) subsanar

amendment [ə'mendmənt] *n* enmienda *f*

amends [ə'mendz] *npl* **to make a. to sb for sth** compensar a algn por algo

amenities [ə'miːnɪtɪz] *npl* comodidades *fpl*

America [ə'merɪkə] *n* (*continent*) América *f*; (*USA*) (los) Estados Unidos; **South A.** América del Sur, Sudamérica *f*

American [ə'merɪkən] *adj & n* americano(a) (*m,f*); (*of USA*) norteamericano(a) (*m,f*), estadounidense (*mf*)

amiable ['eɪmɪəbəl] *adj* amable, afable

amicable ['æmɪkəbəl] *adj* amistoso(a)

amid(st) ['æmɪd(st)] *prep* entre, en medio de

amiss [ə'mɪs] *adj & adv* mal; **there's sth a.** algo anda mal; **to take sth a.** tomar algo a mal

ammonia [ə'məʊnɪə] *n* amoníaco *m*

ammunition [æmjʊ'nɪʃən] *n* municiones *fpl*

amnesia [æm'niːʒə] *n* amnesia *f*

amnesty ['æmnɪstɪ] *n* amnistía *f*

amok [ə'mɒk] *adv Fig* **to run a.** (*child*) desmadrarse; (*inflation etc*) dispararse

among(st) [ə'mʌŋ(st)] *prep* entre

amoral [eɪ'mɒrəl] *adj* amoral

amorous ['æmərəs] *adj* cariñoso(a)

amorphous [ə'mɔːfəs] *adj* amorfo(a)

amount [ə'maʊnt] *n* cantidad *f*; (*of money*) suma *f*; (*of bill*) importe *m*

▸ amount to *vt insep* ascender a; *Fig* equivaler a

amp [æmp], **ampère** ['æmpeə(r)] *n* amperio *m*

amphetamine [æm'fetəmiːn] *n* anfetamina *f*

amphibian [æm'fɪbɪən] *adj & n* anfibio(a) (*m*)

amphibious [æmˈfɪbɪəs] *adj* anfibio(a)
amphitheatre [ˈæmfɪθɪətə(r)] *n* anfiteatro *m*
ample [ˈæmpəl] *adj (enough)* bastante; *(more than enough)* abundante; *(large)* amplio(a)
amplifier [ˈæmplɪfaɪə(r)] *n* amplificador *m*
amputate [ˈæmpjʊteɪt] *vt* amputar
amuck [əˈmʌk] *adv* = amok
amuse [əˈmjuːz] *vt* divertir, entretener
amusement [əˈmjuːzmənt] *n (enjoyment)* diversión *f; (laughter)* risa *f; (pastime)* pasatiempo *m*; **a. arcade** salón *m* de juegos; **a. park** parque *m* de atracciones
amusing [əˈmjuːzɪŋ] *adj* divertido(a)
an [æn, *unstressed* ən] *see* **a**
anabolic steroid [ænəbɒlɪkˈstɪərɔɪd] *n* esteroide *m* anabolizante
anaemia [əˈniːmɪə] *n* anemia *f*
anaemic [əˈniːmɪk] *adj* anémico(a); *Fig (weak)* débil
anaesthetic [ænɪsˈθetɪk] *n* anestesia *f*
anaesthetist [əˈniːsθətɪst] *n* anestesista *mf*
analog(ue) [ˈænəlɒg] *n* análogo *m*; **a. computer** ordenador analógico, *Am* computadora analógica; **a. watch** reloj *m* de agujas
analogy [əˈnælədʒɪ] *n* analogía *f*
analyse [ˈænəlaɪz] *vt* analizar
analysis [əˈnælɪsɪs] *n (pl* **analyses** [əˈnælɪsiːz]*)* análisis *m inv*
analyst [ˈænəlɪst] *n* analista *mf; (psychoanalyst)* psicoanalista *mf*
analytic(al) [ænəˈlɪtɪk(əl)] *adj* analítico(a)
analyze [ˈænəlaɪz] *vt US* = **analyse**
anarchist [ˈænəkɪst] *n* anarquista *mf*
anarchy [ˈænəkɪ] *n* anarquía *f*
anathema [əˈnæθəmə] *n* **the very idea was a. to him** le repugnaba sólo de pensarlo
anatomy [əˈnætəmɪ] *n* anatomía *f*
ancestor [ˈænsestə(r)] *n* antepasado *m*
anchor [ˈæŋkə(r)] **1** *n Naut* ancla *f; Fig* áncora *f*; **to drop a.** echar el ancla; **to weigh a.** zarpar
2 *vt Naut* anclar; *Fig (fix securely)* sujetar
3 *vi* anclar
anchovy [ˈæntʃəvɪ] *n* anchoa *f*
ancient [ˈeɪnʃənt] *adj* antiguo(a)
ancillary [ænˈsɪlərɪ] *adj & n* auxiliar *(mf)*
and [ænd, *unstressed* ənd, ən] *conj* y; *(before i-, hi-)* e; **a hundred a. one** ciento uno; **a. so on** etcétera; **Bill a. Pat** Bill y Pat; **Chinese a. Indian** chino e indio; **come a. see us** ven a vernos; **four a. a half** cuatro y

medio; **she cried a.** cried no paró de llorar; **try a. help me** trata de ayudarme; **wait a. see** espera a ver; **worse a. worse** cada vez peor
Andalusia [ændəˈluːzɪə] *n* Andalucía
Andalusian [ændəˈluːzɪən] *adj* andaluz(a)
Andes [ˈændiːz] *npl* **the A.** los Andes
Andorra [ænˈdɔːrə] *n* Andorra
anecdote [ˈænɪkdəʊt] *n* anécdota *f*
anemia [əˈniːmɪə] *n US* = **anaemia**
anesthetic [ænɪsˈθetɪk] *n US* = **anaesthetic**
angel [ˈeɪndʒəl] *n* ángel *m*
anger [ˈæŋgə(r)] **1** *n* cólera *f*
2 *vt* enojar
angina [ænˈdʒaɪnə] *n* angina *f* (de pecho)
angle [ˈæŋgəl] *n* ángulo *m; Fig* punto *m* de vista
angler [ˈæŋglə(r)] *n* pescador(a) *m,f* de caña
Anglican [ˈæŋglɪkən] *adj & n* anglicano(a) *(m,f)*
Anglo-Saxon [æŋgləʊˈsæksən] *adj & n* anglosajón(ona) *(m,f)*
Angola [æŋˈgəʊlə] *n* Angola
angrily [ˈæŋgrɪlɪ] *adv* furiosamente
angry [ˈæŋgrɪ] *adj (***angrier, angriest***)* *(person etc)* enfadado(a); *(voice)* airado(a); **to get a. with sb about sth** enfadarse con algn por algo
anguish [ˈæŋgwɪʃ] *n* angustia *f*
angular [ˈæŋgjʊlə(r)] *adj (shape)* angular; *(face)* anguloso(a)
animal [ˈænɪməl] **1** *adj* animal
2 *n* animal *m; Fig* bestia *f*
animate 1 *adj* [ˈænɪmɪt] vivo(a)
2 *vt* [ˈænɪmeɪt] animar; *Fig* estimular
animated [ˈænɪmeɪtɪd] *adj (lively)* animado(a)
animosity [ænɪˈmɒsɪtɪ] *n* animosidad *f*
aniseed [ˈænɪsiːd] *n* anís *m*
ankle [ˈæŋkəl] *n* tobillo *m*; **a. boots** botines *mpl;* **a. socks** calcetines cortos
annex [əˈneks] *vt (territory)* anexionar
annexe, *US* **annex** [ˈæneks] *n (building)* (edificio *m)* anexo *m*
annihilate [əˈnaɪəleɪt] *vt* aniquilar
anniversary [ænɪˈvɜːsərɪ] *n* aniversario *m;* **wedding a.** aniversario de bodas
announce [əˈnaʊns] *vt* anunciar; *(news)* comunicar; *(fact)* hacer saber
announcement [əˈnaʊnsmənt] *n* anuncio *m; (news)* comunicación *f; (statement)* declaración *f*
announcer [əˈnaʊnsə(r)] *n TV & Rad* locutor(a) *m,f*
annoy [əˈnɔɪ] *vt* molestar, fastidiar; **to**

get annoyed enfadarse, molestarse

annoyance [ə'nɔɪəns] n (feeling) enojo m; (thing) molestia f, fastidio m

annoying [ə'nɔɪɪŋ] adj molesto(a), fastidioso(a)

annual ['ænjʊəl] 1 adj anual
  2 n (book) anuario m; (plant) anual m

annually ['ænjʊəlɪ] adv anualmente

annul [ə'nʌl] vt anular

annulment [ə'nʌlmənt] n anulación f

anomaly [ə'nɒməlɪ] n anomalía f

anonymity [ænə'nɪmɪtɪ] n anonimato m

anonymous [ə'nɒnɪməs] adj anónimo(a)

anorak ['ænəræk] n anorak m

anorexia [ænə'reksɪə] n anorexia f

another [ə'nʌðə(r)] 1 adj otro(a); **a. one** otro(a); **without a. word** sin más
  2 pron otro(a); **have a.** toma otro(a); **to love one a.** quererse el uno al otro

Ansaphone® ['ɑːnsəfəʊn] n mensáfono m

answer ['ɑːnsə(r)] 1 n (to letter etc) contestación f; (to question) respuesta f; (to problem) solución f; **in a. to your letter** contestando a su carta; **there's no a.** (on telephone) no contestan; (at door) no abren
  2 vt contestar a; (problem) resolver; (door) abrir; (phone) contestar
  3 vi contestar, responder
  ▸ **answer back** vi replicar; **don't a. back!** ¡no seas respondón!
  ▸ **answer for** vt insep responder de; **he's got a lot to a. for** es responsable de muchas cosas
  ▸ **answer to** vt insep (name) responder a; (description) corresponder a

answerable ['ɑːnsərəbəl] adj **to be a. to sb for sth** ser responsable ante algn de algo

answering machine ['ɑːnsərɪŋməʃiːn] n contestador automático

ant [ænt] n hormiga f; **a. hill** hormiguero m

antagonism [æn'tægənɪzəm] n antagonismo m (**between** entre), hostilidad f (**towards** hacia)

antagonize [æn'tægənaɪz] vt enemistar, malquistar

Antarctic [æn'tɑːktɪk] 1 adj antártico(a); **A. Ocean** océano Antártico
  2 n **the A.** la Antártida

Antarctica [æn'tɑːktɪkə] n Antártida

antecedent [æntɪ'siːdənt] n antecedente m

antelope ['æntɪləʊp] n antílope m

antenatal [æntɪ'neɪtəl] adj antenatal; (clinic) prenatal

antenna [æn'tenə] n (a) (pl **antennae** [æn'teniː]) (of animal, insect) antena f (b) (pl **antennas**) TV & Rad antena f

anthem ['ænθəm] n motete m; **national a.** himno m nacional

anthology [æn'θɒlədʒɪ] n antología f

anthracite ['ænθrəsaɪt] n antracita f

anthropology [ænθrə'pɒlədʒɪ] n antropología f

anti-aircraft [æntɪ'eəkrɑːft] adj antiaéreo(a)

antibiotic [æntɪbaɪ'ɒtɪk] n antibiótico m

antibody ['æntɪbɒdɪ] n anticuerpo m

anticipate [æn'tɪsɪpeɪt] vt (**a**) (expect) esperar (**b**) (predict) prever; (get ahead of) anticiparse a, adelantarse a

anticipation [æntɪsɪ'peɪʃən] n (expectation) esperanza f; (expectancy) ilusión f

anticlimax [æntɪ'klaɪmæks] n (disappointment) decepción f

anticlockwise [æntɪ'klɒkwaɪz] adv Br en sentido opuesto al de las agujas del reloj

antics ['æntɪks] npl payasadas fpl; (naughtiness) travesuras fpl

anticyclone [æntɪ'saɪkləʊn] n anticiclón m

antidote ['æntɪdəʊt] n antídoto m

antifreeze ['æntɪfriːz] n anticongelante m

antihistamine [æntɪ'hɪstəmɪn] n antihistamínico m

antinuclear [æntɪ'njuːklɪə(r)] adj antinuclear

antipathy [æn'tɪpəθɪ] n antipatía f (**to** a)

antiquated ['æntɪkweɪtɪd] adj anticuado(a)

antique [æn'tiːk] 1 adj antiguo(a)
  2 n antigüedad f; **a. dealer** anticuario(a) m,f; **a. shop** tienda f de antigüedades

antiquity [æn'tɪkwɪtɪ] n antigüedad f

anti-Semitism [æntɪ'semɪtɪzəm] n antisemitismo m

antiseptic [æntɪ'septɪk] adj & n antiséptico(a) (m)

antisocial [æntɪ'səʊʃəl] adj (delinquent) antisocial; (unsociable) insociable

antithesis [æn'tɪθɪsɪs] n antítesis f

antivirus ['æntɪ'vaɪrəs] adj Comput (program, software) antivirus

antler ['æntlə(r)] n cuerna f; **antlers** cornamenta f

Antwerp ['æntwɜːp] n Amberes

anus ['eɪnəs] n ano m

anvil ['ænvɪl] n yunque m

anxiety [æŋ'zaɪtɪ] n (concern) inquietud f; (worry) preocupación f; (fear) angustia f; (eagerness) ansia f

anxious ['æŋkʃəs] adj (concerned)

inquieto(a); *(worried)* preocupado(a); *(fearful)* angustiado(a); *(eager)* ansioso(a); **to be a. about sth** estar preocupado(a) por algo

any ['enɪ] **1** *adj (in questions, conditionals)* algún(una); *(in negative clauses)* ningún(una); *(no matter which)* cualquier(a); *(every)* todo(a); **a. doctor will say the same** cualquier médico te dirá lo mismo; **are there a. seats left?** ¿quedan plazas?; **at a. moment** en cualquier momento; **have you a. apples?** ¿tienes manzanas?; **have you a. money?** ¿tienes (algo de) dinero?; **I don't have a. time** no tengo tiempo; **in a. case** de todas formas
2 *pron (in questions)* alguno(a); *(in negative clauses)* ninguno(a); *(no matter which)* cualquiera; **do they have a.?** ¿tienen alguno?; **I don't want a.** no quiero ninguno(a); **I need some paper, have you a.?** necesito papel, ¿tienes?; **you can have a. (one)** coge el/la que quieras
3 *adv* **is there a. more?** ¿hay más?; **I used to like it, but not a. more/longer** antes me gustaba pero ya no; **is he a. better?** ¿está mejor?

anybody ['enɪbɒdɪ] *pron (in questions, conditionals)* alguien, alguno(a); *(in negative clauses)* nadie, ninguno(a); *(no matter who)* cualquiera; **a. but me** cualquiera menos yo; **bring a. you like** trae a quien quieras; **do you see a. over there?** ¿ves a alguien allí?; **I can't find a.** no encuentro a nadie

anyhow ['enɪhaʊ] *adv* **(a)** *(in spite of that)* en todo caso, de todas formas; *(changing the subject)* bueno, pues **(b)** *(carelessly)* desordenadamente, de cualquier modo o forma

anyone ['enɪwʌn] *pron* = **anybody**

anyplace ['enɪpleɪs] *adv US* = **anywhere**

anything ['enɪθɪŋ] **1** *pron (in questions, conditionals)* algo, alguna cosa; *(in negative clauses)* nada; *(no matter what)* cualquier cosa; **a. but that** cualquier cosa menos eso; **a. else?** ¿algo más?; **can I do a. for you?** ¿puedo ayudarte en algo?; **hardly a.** casi nada; **if a., I'd buy the big one** de comprar uno compraría el grande; **to run/work like a.** correr/trabajar a más no poder
2 *adv* **is this a. like what you wanted?** ¿viene a ser éste lo que querías?

anyway ['enɪweɪ] *adv* = **anyhow (a)**

anywhere ['enɪweə(r)] *adv* **(a)** *(in questions, conditionals)* (situation) en alguna parte; *(movement)* a alguna parte; **could it be a. else?** ¿podría estar en otro sitio?

(b) *(in negative clauses)* (situation) en ninguna parte; *(movement)* a ninguna parte; *(no matter where)* dondequiera, en cualquier parte; **go a. you like** ve a donde quieras; **we aren't a. near finished** no hemos terminado ni mucho menos

apart [ə'pɑːt] *adv* **(a)** aparte; **to fall a.** deshacerse; **to take sth a.** desmontar algo **(b)** *(distant)* alejado(a); *(separate)* separado(a); **to be poles a.** ser polos opuestos; **you can't tell the twins a.** no se puede distinguir los mellizos el uno del otro **(c) a. from** aparte de

apartheid [ə'pɑːtheɪt] *n* apartheid *m*

apartment [ə'pɑːtmənt] *n (large room)* salón *m*; *US (flat)* piso *m*, apartamento *m*; **a. block** bloque *m* de pisos

apathetic [æpə'θetɪk] *adj* apático(a)

apathy ['æpəθɪ] *n* apatía *f*

ape [eɪp] **1** *n* mono *m*
2 *vt* imitar, copiar

apéritif [ə'perɪtiːf] *n* aperitivo *m*

aperture ['æpətʃə(r)] *n (hole, crack)* resquicio *m*, rendija *f*; *Phot* abertura *f*

apex ['eɪpeks] *n (of triangle)* vértice *m*; *Fig* cumbre *f*

aphrodisiac [æfrə'dɪzɪæk] *n* afrodisíaco *m*

apiece [ə'piːs] *adv* cada uno(a)

aplomb [ə'plɒm] *n* aplomo *m*

apocalypse [ə'pɒkəlɪps] *n* apocalipsis *m inv*

apolitical [eɪpə'lɪtɪkəl] *adj* apolítico(a)

apologetic [əpɒlə'dʒetɪk] *adj (remorseful)* de disculpa; **he was very a.** pidió mil perdones

apologetically [əpɒlə'dʒetɪklɪ] *adv* disculpándose, pidiendo perdón

apologize [ə'pɒlədʒaɪz] *vi (say sorry)* disculparse; **they apologized to us for the delay** se disculparon con nosotros por el retraso

apology [ə'pɒlədʒɪ] *n* disculpa *f*, excusa *f*; *Fam* **what an a. for a meal!** ¡vaya birria de comida!

apoplectic [æpə'plektɪk] *adj Med* apopléctico(a); *Fam* **to be a. with rage** estar furioso(a)

apostle [ə'pɒsəl] *n* apóstol *m*

apostrophe [ə'pɒstrəfɪ] *n* apóstrofo *m*

appal, *US* **appall** [ə'pɔːl] *vt* horrorizar; **to be appalled by sth** quedar horrorizado(a) por algo

appalling [ə'pɔːlɪŋ] *adj (horrifying)* horroroso(a); *Fam (very bad)* pésimo(a), fatal

apparatus [æpə'reɪtəs] *n* aparato *m*; *(equipment)* equipo *m*

apparent [əˈpærənt] *adj (obvious)* evidente; *(seeming)* aparente; **to become a.** ponerse de manifiesto

apparently [əˈpærəntlɪ] *adv (seemingly)* por lo visto

apparition [æpəˈrɪʃən] *n* aparición *f*

appeal [əˈpiːl] **1** *n* (a) *(request)* solicitud *f*; *(plea)* súplica *f* (b) *(attraction)* atractivo *m*; *(interest)* interés *m* (c) *Jur* apelación *f*
   2 *vi* (a) *(plead)* rogar, suplicar (**to** a); **to a. for help** solicitar ayuda (b) *(attract)* atraer; *(interest)* interesar; **it doesn't a. to me** no me dice nada (c) *Jur* apelar

appealing [əˈpiːlɪŋ] *adj (moving)* conmovedor(a); *(attractive)* atractivo(a); *(tempting)* atrayente

appear [əˈpɪə(r)] *vi* (a) *(become visible)* aparecer; *(publicly)* presentarse; *(on stage)* actuar; **to a. before a court** comparecer ante un tribunal; **to a. on television** salir en la televisión (b) *(seem)* parecer; **he appears relaxed** parece relajado; **so it appears** según parece

appearance [əˈpɪərəns] *n* (a) *(becoming visible)* aparición *f*; *(publicly)* presentación *f*; *(on stage)* actuación *f*; *(before court)* comparecencia *f*; *(of book etc)* publicación *f*; **to put in an a.** hacer acto de presencia (b) *(look)* apariencia *f*, aspecto *m*; **to all appearances** al parecer

appease [əˈpiːz] *vt* apaciguar; *(curiosity)* satisfacer

appeasement [əˈpiːzmənt] *n Pol* entreguismo *m*

appendices [əˈpendɪsiːz] *pl of* **appendix**

appendicitis [əpendɪˈsaɪtɪs] *n* apendicitis *f*

appendix [əˈpendɪks] *n (pl* **appendices**) apéndice *m*

appetite [ˈæpɪtaɪt] *n* apetito *m*; *Fig* deseo *m*

appetizer [ˈæpɪtaɪzə(r)] *n (drink)* aperitivo *m*; *(snack)* tapa *f*, pincho *m*

applaud [əˈplɔːd] *vt & vi* aplaudir

applause [əˈplɔːz] *n* aplausos *mpl*

apple [ˈæpəl] *n* manzana *f*; **a. tree** manzano *m*

appliance [əˈplaɪəns] *n* dispositivo *m*

applicable [əˈplɪkəbəl] *adj* aplicable

applicant [ˈæplɪkənt] *n (for post)* candidato(a) *m,f*; *(to court, for tickets)* solicitante *mf*

application [æplɪˈkeɪʃən] *n* (a) *(of cream)* aplicación *f* (b) *(for post etc)* solicitud *f*; **a. form** solicitud; **job a.** solicitud de empleo (c) *(effort)* aplicación *f*; **she lacks a.** no se aplica

applied [əˈplaɪd] *adj* aplicado(a)

apply [əˈplaɪ] **1** *vt* aplicar; *(brake)* echar; *(law)* recurrir a; *(force)* usar; **to a. oneself to** dedicarse a
   2 *vi* (a) *(refer)* aplicarse (**to** a) (b) *(for job)* presentar una solicitud; *(for information, to court)* presentar una petición
   ▸ **apply for** *vt insep (post, information)* solicitar; *(tickets)* pedir

appoint [əˈpɔɪnt] *vt (person)* nombrar; *(time, place etc)* fijar, señalar

appointment [əˈpɔɪntmənt] *n* (a) *(to post)* nombramiento *m*; *(post)* cargo *m* (b) *(meeting)* cita *f*; **to make an a. with** citarse con; *(at doctor's)* pedir hora a

apportion [əˈpɔːʃən] *vt Fig (blame)* echar

appraisal [əˈpreɪzəl] *n* evaluación *f*

appreciable [əˈpriːʃəbəl] *adj (difference)* apreciable; *(sum)* importante

appreciate [əˈpriːʃɪeɪt] **1** *vt* (a) *(be thankful for)* agradecer (b) *(understand)* entender (c) *(value)* apreciar, valorar
   2 *vi (increase in value)* apreciarse

appreciation [əpriːʃɪˈeɪʃən] *n* (a) *(of help, advice)* agradecimiento *m*; *(of difficulty)* comprensión *f*; *(of wine etc)* aprecio *m*; *(appraisal)* evaluación *f* (b) *(increase in value)* apreciación *f*

appreciative [əˈpriːʃɪətɪv] *adj (thankful)* agradecido(a); *(responsive)* apreciativo(a)

apprehend [æprɪˈhend] *vt (arrest)* detener

apprehension [æprɪˈhenʃən] *n* (a) *(arrest)* detención *f* (b) *(fear)* aprensión *f*

apprehensive [æprɪˈhensɪv] *adj (fearful)* aprensivo(a)

apprentice [əˈprentɪs] *n* aprendiz(a) *m,f*

apprenticeship [əˈprentɪsʃɪp] *n* aprendizaje *m*

approach [əˈprəʊtʃ] **1** *n* (a) *(coming near)* acercamiento *m*; *(to town)* acceso *m*; **a. road** vía *f* de acceso (b) *(to problem)* enfoque *m*
   2 *vt (come near to)* acercarse a; *(be similar to)* aproximarse a; *Fig (problem)* abordar; *(person)* dirigirse a; **to a. sb about sth** dirigirse a algn a propósito de algo
   3 *vi* acercarse

approachable [əˈprəʊtʃəbəl] *adj (person)* accesible

appropriate [¹] [əˈprəʊprɪət] *adj (suitable)* apropiado(a), adecuado(a); *(convenient)* oportuno(a)

appropriate [²] [əˈprəʊprɪeɪt] *vt (allocate)* asignar; *(steal)* apropiarse de

approval [əˈpruːvəl] *n* aprobación *f*, visto

bueno; *Com* **to get sth on a.** adquirir algo sin compromiso de compra

approve [ə'pruːv] *vt* aprobar; **approved school** reformatorio *m*
► **approve of** *vt insep* aprobar

approving [ə'pruːvɪŋ] *adj (look etc)* aprobatorio(a)

approx [ə'prɒks] *(abbr* **approximately)** aprox.

approximate 1 *adj* [ə'prɒksɪmɪt] aproximado(a)
2 *vt* [ə'prɒksɪmeɪt] aproximarse a

approximately [ə'prɒksɪmɪtlɪ] *adv* aproximadamente

apricot ['eɪprɪkɒt] *n* albaricoque *m, Am* damasco *m, Méx* chabacano *m*

April ['eɪprəl] *n* abril *m*; **A. Fools' Day** día *m* uno de abril, ≃ día de los Inocentes (28 de diciembre)

apron ['eɪprən] *n* delantal *m; (for workman)* mandil *m*

apt [æpt] *adj* (a) *(suitable)* apropiado(a); *(remark)* acertado(a), oportuno(a); *(name)* justo(a); *(description)* exacto(a) (b) **to be a. to do sth** ser propenso(a) a hacer algo

aptitude ['æptɪtjuːd] *n* capacidad *f*; **a. test** prueba *f* de aptitud

aptly ['æptlɪ] *adv* acertadamente

aqualung ['ækwəlʌŋ] *n* botella *f* de oxígeno

aquamarine [ˌækwəmə'riːn] **1** *n (gem)* aguamarina *f*
2 *adj* de color de aguamarina

aquarium [ə'kweərɪəm] *n* acuario *m*

Aquarius [ə'kweərɪəs] *n* Acuario *m*

aquatic [ə'kwætɪk] *adj* acuático(a)

aqueduct ['ækwɪdʌkt] *n* acueducto *m*

Arab ['ærəb] *adj & n* árabe *(mf)*

Arabian [ə'reɪbɪən] *adj* árabe

Arabic ['ærəbɪk] **1** *adj* árabe, arábigo(a); **A. numerals** numeración arábiga
2 *n (language)* árabe *m*

arable ['ærəbəl] *adj* cultivable

Aragon ['ærəgən] *n* Aragón

arbitrary ['ɑːbɪtrərɪ] *adj* arbitrario(a)

arbitrate ['ɑːbɪtreɪt] *vt & vi* arbitrar

arbitration [ɑːbɪ'treɪʃən] *n* arbitraje *m*

arc [ɑːk] *n* arco *m*; **a. lamp** arco voltaico

arcade [ɑː'keɪd] *n* arcada *f; (passageway)* pasaje *m*; **shopping a.** galerías *fpl* (comerciales)

arch [ɑːtʃ] **1** *n* (a) *Archit* arco *m; (vault)* bóveda *f* (b) *Anat* empeine *m*
2 *vt (back)* arquear

archaeologist [ɑːkɪ'ɒlədʒɪst] *n* arqueólogo(a) *m,f*

archaeology [ɑːkɪ'ɒlədʒɪ] *n* arqueología *f*

archaic [ɑː'keɪɪk] *adj* arcaico(a)

archbishop [ɑːtʃ'bɪʃəp] *n* arzobispo *m*

arched [ɑːtʃt] *adj* arqueado(a)

archeologist [ɑːkɪ'ɒlədʒɪst] *n US* = **archaeologist**

archeology [ɑːkɪ'ɒlədʒɪ] *n US* = **archaeology**

archer ['ɑːtʃə(r)] *n* arquero(a) *m,f*

archery ['ɑːtʃərɪ] *n* tiro *m* con arco

archetypal ['ɑːkɪtaɪpəl] *adj* arquetípico(a)

archipelago [ɑːkɪ'pelɪgəʊ] *n* archipiélago *m*

architect ['ɑːkɪtekt] *n* arquitecto(a) *m,f*

architectural [ɑːkɪ'tektʃərəl] *adj* arquitectónico(a)

architecture ['ɑːkɪtektʃə(r)] *n* arquitectura *f*

archives ['ɑːkaɪvz] *npl* archivos *mpl*

archway ['ɑːtʃweɪ] *n (arch)* arco *m; (vault)* bóveda *f; (in church)* atrio *m; (passage)* pasaje *m*

arctic ['ɑːktɪk] **1** *adj* ártico(a); **A. Circle** círculo *m* polar Ártico
2 *n* **the A.** el Ártico

ardent ['ɑːdənt] *adj (supporter etc)* apasionado(a); *(desire)* ardiente

ardour, *US* **ardor** ['ɑːdə(r)] *n* pasión *f*, ardor *m*

arduous ['ɑːdjʊəs] *adj* arduo(a), penoso(a)

are [ɑː(r)] *2nd person sing pres, 1st, 2nd, 3rd person pl pres of* **be**

area ['eərɪə] *n (surface)* área *f*, superficie *f; (space)* extensión *f; (region)* región *f; (of town)* zona *f; Fig (field)* campo *m; US Tel* **a. code** prefijo *m* local

arena [ə'riːnə] *n (stadium)* estadio *m; (bullring)* plaza *f; (circus)* pista *f; Fig (stage)* campo *m* de batalla

Argentina [ɑːdʒən'tiːnə] *n* Argentina

Argentinian [ɑːdʒən'tɪnɪən] *adj & n* argentino(a) *(m,f)*

arguable ['ɑːgjʊəbəl] *adj* discutible

arguably ['ɑːgjʊəblɪ] *adv* **it's a. the best** hay quienes dicen que es el mejor

argue ['ɑːgjuː] **1** *vt (reason)* discutir; *(point of view)* mantener
2 *vi (quarrel)* discutir; *(reason)* argumentar, razonar; **to a. for** abogar por; **to a. against sth** ponerse en contra de algo

argument ['ɑːgjʊmənt] *n (reason)* argumento *m* (**for** a favor de; **against** en contra de); *(quarrel)* discusión *f*, disputa *f*; **for the sake of a.** por decir algo

argumentative [ɑːgjʊ'mentətɪv] *adj* **she's very a.** le gusta discutir por todo

aria ['ɑːrɪə] *n* aria *f*

arid ['ærɪd] *adj* árido(a)

Aries ['eəriːz] *n* Aries *m*

arise [ə'raɪz] *vi* (*pt* **arose**; *pp* **arisen** [ə'rɪzən]) (*get up*) levantarse; (*happen*) surgir; **should the occasion a.** si se presenta la ocasión

aristocracy [ærɪ'stɒkrəsɪ] *n* aristocracia *f*

aristocrat ['ærɪstəkræt] *n* aristócrata *mf*

arithmetic [ə'rɪθmətɪk] *n* aritmética *f*

ark [ɑːk] *n* arca *f*; **Noah's A.** el arca de Noé

arm [ɑːm] **1** *n* (**a**) brazo *m*; (*of garment*) manga *f*; **to walk a. in a.** ir cogidos(as) del brazo (**b**) *Mil* **arms** armas *fpl*; **arms race** carrera armamentística; **coat of arms** escudo *m*

2 *vt* armar; **to a. oneself against sth** armarse contra algo

armaments ['ɑːməmənts] *npl* armamentos *mpl*

armchair ['ɑːmtʃeə(r)] *n* sillón *m*

armed ['ɑːmd] *adj* armado(a); **a. forces** fuerzas armadas; **a. robbery** robo *m* a mano armada

Armenia [ɑː'miːnɪə] *n* Armenia

armistice [ɑː'mɪstɪs] *n* armisticio *m*

armour, *US* **armor** ['ɑːmə(r)] *n* (*on vehicle*) blindaje *m*; (*suit of*) **a.** armadura *f*

armoured car, *US* **armored car** [ɑːməd'kɑː(r)] *n* coche *m* blindado

armour-plated [ɑːmə'pleɪtɪd] *adj* acorazado(a)

armoury, *US* **armory** ['ɑːmərɪ] *n* arsenal *m*

armpit ['ɑːmpɪt] *n* axila *f*, sobaco *m*

army ['ɑːmɪ] *n* ejército *m*

aroma [ə'rəʊmə] *n* aroma *m*

arose [ə'rəʊz] *pt of* **arise**

around [ə'raʊnd] **1** *adv* alrededor; **all a.** por todos los lados; **are the children a.?** ¿están los niños por aquí?; **he looked a.** miró (a su) alrededor

2 *prep* (**a**) alrededor de; **a. the corner** a la vuelta de la esquina; **a. here** por aquí (**b**) (*approximately*) aproximadamente

arouse [ə'raʊz] *vt* despertar; (*sexually*) excitar

arrange [ə'reɪndʒ] **1** *vt* (**a**) (*order*) ordenar; (*hair, flowers*) arreglar; *Mus* adaptar (**b**) (*plan*) organizar; (*agree on*) quedar en; **to a. a time** fijar una hora; **arranged marriage** boda arreglada

2 *vi* **I shall a. for him to be there** lo arreglaré para que pueda asistir

arrangement [ə'reɪndʒmənt] *n* (**a**) (*display*) colocación *f*; *Mus* adaptación *f* (**b**) (*agreement*) acuerdo *m* (**c**) **arrangements** (*plans*) planes *mpl*; (*preparations*) preparativos *mpl*

array [ə'reɪ] *n* colección *f*; **a great a. of goods** un gran surtido de productos

arrears [ə'rɪəz] *npl* atrasos *mpl*; **to be in a. with the rent** estar atrasado(a) con el alquiler; **to be paid in a.** cobrar con retraso

arrest [ə'rest] **1** *n* detención *f*; **to be under a.** estar detenido(a)

2 *vt* (*criminal*) detener; *Fig* (*progress*) frenar

arresting [ə'restɪŋ] *adj* llamativo(a)

arrival [ə'raɪvəl] *n* llegada *f*; **a new a.** un(a) recién llegado(a)

arrive [ə'raɪv] *vi* llegar (**at/in** a)

arrogance ['ærəgəns] *n* arrogancia *f*

arrogant ['ærəgənt] *adj* arrogante

arrow ['ærəʊ] *n* flecha *f*

arse ['ɑːs] *n Vulg* culo *m*

arsenal ['ɑːsənəl] *n* arsenal *m*

arsenic ['ɑːsənɪk] *n* arsénico *m*

arson ['ɑːsən] *n* incendio *m* provocado

art [ɑːt] *n* (**a**) arte *m*; (*drawing*) dibujo *m*; **the arts** las bellas artes; **arts and crafts** artes *fpl* y oficios *mpl*; **a. gallery** galería *f* de arte (**b**) **arts** (*branch of knowledge*) letras *fpl*

artefact ['ɑːtɪfækt] *n* artefacto *m*; (*in archaeology*) objeto *m* de arte

artery ['ɑːtərɪ] *n* arteria *f*

artful ['ɑːtfəl] *adj* (*cunning*) ladino(a)

arthritis [ɑː'θraɪtɪs] *n* artritis *f*

artichoke ['ɑːtɪtʃəʊk] *n* alcachofa *f*, *RP* alcaucil *m*

article ['ɑːtɪkəl] *n* (**a**) artículo *m*; *Press* artículo; **a. of clothing** prenda *f* de vestir (**b**) *Jur* **articles** contrato *m* de aprendizaje

articulate¹ [ɑː'tɪkjəlɪt] *adj* (*speech*) claro(a); (*person*) que se expresa bien

articulate² [ɑː'tɪkjʊleɪt] *vt & vi* articular; (*words*) pronunciar; *Br* **articulated lorry** camión articulado

artificial [ɑːtɪ'fɪʃəl] *adj* artificial; (*limb*) postizo(a); **a. intelligence** inteligencia *f* artificial

artillery [ɑː'tɪlərɪ] *n* artillería *f*

artisan ['ɑːtɪzæn] *n* artesano(a) *m,f*

artist ['ɑːtɪst] *n* artista *mf*; (*painter*) pintor(a) *m,f*

artistic [ɑː'tɪstɪk] *adj* artístico(a)

artistry ['ɑːtɪstrɪ] *n* arte *m*, talento artístico

as [æz, *unstressed* əz] **1** *adv & conj* (**a**) (*comparison*) **as ... as ...** tan ... como ...; **as far as** hasta; *Fig* **as far as I'm concerned** por lo que a mí respecta; **as many as** tantos(as) como; **as much as** tanto(a) como; **as tall as me** tan alto(a) como yo; **as opposed to** a diferencia de; **as little as**

£5 tan sólos 5 libras ; **as soon as they arrive** en cuanto lleguen; **I'll stay as long as I can** quedaré todo el tiempo que pueda; **just as big** igual de grande; **three times as fast** tres veces más rápido; **the same as** igual que

(**b**) *(manner)* como; **as a rule** por regla general; **as you know** como ya sabéis; **as you like** como quieras; **do as I say** haz lo que yo te digo; **he's working as a doctor** está trabajando de médico; **I thought as much** ya me lo suponía; **it serves as a table** sirve de mesa; **leave it as it is** déjalo tal como está; **he was dressed as a pirate** iba vestido de pirata

(**c**) *(while, when)* mientras (que); **as a child** de niño(a); **as I was eating** mientras comía; **as we were leaving, we saw Pat** al salir vimos a Pat

(**d**) *(though)* aunque; **be that as it may** por mucho que así sea; **young as he is** aunque es joven

(**e**) *(because)* como, ya que

(**f**) *(and so)* igual que; **as do I** igual que yo; **as well** también

(**g**) *(purpose)* para; **so as to do sth** hacer algo

(**h**) **as for my brother** en cuanto a mi hermano

(**i**) **as from, as of** a partir de

(**j**) **to act as if** actuar como si (+ *subj*); **it looks as if the concert is off** parece ser que no habrá concierto

(**k**) **it's late enough as it is** ya es muy tarde; **as it were** por así decirlo

(**l**) **as long as** *(only if)* siempre que, con tal de que

(**m**) **as regards** en cuanto a, por lo que se refiere a; **as usual** como siempre; **as yet** aún, todavía

2 *rel pron* **such as** tal(es) como
asbestos [æz'bestəs] *n* amianto *m*, asbesto *m*
ascend [ə'send] *vi* subir, ascender
ascendancy [ə'sendənsı] *n* dominio *m*, influencia *f*
ascendant [ə'sendənt] *n* **to be in the a.** estar en auge
ascent [ə'sent] *n* subida *f*
ascertain [æsə'teın] *vt* averiguar, enterarse de
ascribe [ə'skraıb] *vt* **to a. sth to sb/sth** imputar algo a alguien/algo
aseptic [ə'septık] *adj* aséptico(a)
ash¹ [æʃ] *n Bot* fresno *m*
ash² [æʃ] *n* ceniza *f*; **a. bin,** *US* **a. can** cubo *m* de la basura; *Rel* **A. Wednesday** miércoles *m inv* de ceniza

ashamed [ə'ʃeımd] *adj* avergonzado(a); **you ought to be a. of yourself!** ¡te debería dar vergüenza!
ashen ['æʃən] *adj (face)* pálido(a)
ashore [ə'ʃɔː(r)] *adv (position)* en tierra; **to go a.** desembarcar; **to swim a.** nadar hacia tierra
ashtray ['æʃtreı] *n* cenicero *m*
Asia ['eıʒə] *n* Asia; **A. Minor** Asia Menor
Asian ['eıʒən] *adj & n* asiático(a) *(m,f)*
aside [ə'saıd] **1** *adv* al lado, aparte; **to cast a.** echar a un lado; **to stand a.** apartarse
2 *prep* **a. from** *(apart from)* aparte de; *(as well as)* además de
3 *n Th* aparte *m*
ask [ɑːsk] **1** *vt* (**a**) preguntar; **to a. sb a question** hacer una pregunta a algn (**b**) *(request)* pedir, solicitar; **she asked me to post it** me pidió que lo echara al buzón (**c**) *(invite)* invitar
2 *vi (inquire)* preguntar; *(request)* pedir
► **ask after** *vt insep* **to a. after sb** preguntar por algn
► **ask for** *vt insep (help)* pedir, solicitar; *(person)* preguntar por algn
► **ask out** *vt sep* **to a. sb out** invitar a algn a salir
askance [ə'skæns] *adv* **to look a. at sb** mirar a algn con recelo
askew [ə'skjuː] **1** *adj* ladeado(a)
2 *adv* de lado
asleep [ə'sliːp] *adj (person)* dormido(a); *(limb)* adormecido(a); **to fall a.** quedarse dormido(a)
asparagus [ə'spærəgəs] *n inv* espárragos *mpl*
aspect ['æspekt] *n* (**a**) *(of question)* aspecto *m* (**b**) *(of building)* orientación *f*
aspersions [ə'spɜːʃənz] *npl* **to cast a. on sb** difamar a algn
asphalt ['æsfælt] *n* asfalto *m*
asphyxiation [æsfıksı'eıʃən] *n* asfixia *f*
aspiration [æspə'reıʃən] *n* aspiración *f*
aspire [ə'spaıə(r)] *vi* **to a.** aspirar a
aspirin ['æsprın] *n* aspirina *f*
ass¹ [æs] *n Zool* asno(a) *m,f*, burro(a) *m,f*; *Fam Fig* burro(a)
ass² [æs] *n US Vulg* culo *m*
assailant [ə'seılənt] *n* agresor(a) *m,f*, atacante *mf*
assassin [ə'sæsın] *n* asesino(a) *m,f*
assassinate [ə'sæsıneıt] *vt* asesinar
assassination [əsæsı'neıʃən] *n* asesinato *m*
assault [ə'sɔːlt] **1** *n Mil* ataque *m* (**on** a); *Jur* agresión *f*
2 *vt Mil* asaltar, atacar; *Jur* agredir; *(sexually)* violar

assemble [ə'sembəl] **1** *vt* (*people*) reunir, juntar; (*furniture*) montar

2 *vi* (*people*) reunirse, juntarse

assembly [ə'semblɪ] *n* reunión *f*, asamblea *f*; *Tech* montaje *m*; *Ind* **a. line** cadena *f* de montaje; *Educ* **morning a.** servicio *m* matinal

assent [ə'sent] **1** *n* (*agreement*) asentimiento *m*; (*consent*) consentimiento *m*; (*approval*) aprobación *f*

2 *vi* asentir, consentir (**to** en)

assert [ə'sɜːt] *vt* afirmar; **to a. oneself** imponerse; **to a. one's rights** hacer valer sus derechos

assertive [ə'sɜːtɪv] *adj* enérgico(a)

assess [ə'ses] *vt* (*estimate value*) valorar; (*damages, price*) calcular; (*tax*) gravar; *Fig* (*effect*) evaluar

assessment [ə'sesmənt] *n* (*of value*) valoración *f*; (*of damages etc*) cálculo *m*; (*of taxes*) gravamen *m*; *Fig* juicio *m*

assessor [ə'sesə(r)] *n* asesor(a) *m,f*

asset ['æset] *n* (**a**) ventaja *f*; **to be an a.** (*person*) ser de gran valor (**b**) *Fin* **assets** bienes *mpl*; **fixed assets** bienes raíces

asshole ['æshəʊl] *n* US Vulg (*unpleasant person*) hijo(a) *m,f* de puta, cabrón(ona) *m,f*

assiduous [ə'sɪdjʊəs] *adj* asiduo(a)

assign [ə'saɪn] *vt* (*task*) asignar; (*property etc*) ceder; **to a. sb to a job** designar a algn para un trabajo

assignment [ə'saɪnmənt] *n* (*allocation*) asignación *f*; (*task*) tarea *f*; (*mission*) misión *f*; (*appointment*) cita *f*

assimilate [ə'sɪmɪleɪt] *vt* asimilar

assist [ə'sɪst] *vt & vi* ayudar

assistance [ə'sɪstəns] *n* ayuda *f*, auxilio *m*

assistant [ə'sɪstənt] *n* ayudante *mf*; **a. manager** subdirector(a) *m,f*; **shop a.** dependiente(a) *m,f*; (**language**) **a.** lector(a) *m,f*

associate¹ [ə'səʊʃɪeɪt] **1** *vt* (*ideas*) relacionar; (*companies*) asociar; **to be associated with sth** estar relacionado(a) con algo

2 *vi* **to a. with** tratar con

associate² [ə'səʊʃɪt] **1** *adj* asociado(a)

2 *n* (*colleague*) colega *mf*; (*partner*) socio(a) *m,f*; (*accomplice*) cómplice *mf*

association [əsəʊsɪ'eɪʃən] *n* asociación *f*; (*company*) sociedad *f*

assorted [ə'sɔːtɪd] *adj* surtido(a), variado(a)

assortment [ə'sɔːtmənt] *n* surtido *m*, variedad *f*

assume [ə'sjuːm] **1** *vt* (*power*) asumir;

(*attitude, name*) adoptar; **an assumed name** un nombre falso

2 *vi* (*suppose*) suponer

assumption [ə'sʌmpʃən] *n* (**a**) (*of power*) toma *f*; **a. of office** toma de posesión (**b**) (*supposition*) suposición *f*

assurance [ə'ʃʊərəns] *n* (**a**) (*guarantee*) garantía *f* (**b**) (*confidence*) confianza *f* (**c**) (*insurance*) seguro *m*

assure [ə'ʃʊə(r)] *vt* asegurar

asterisk ['æstərɪsk] *n* asterisco *m*

astern [ə'stɜːn] *adv* a popa

asthma ['æsmə] *n* asma *f*

astonish [ə'stɒnɪʃ] *vt* asombrar, pasmar; **I was astonished** me quedé pasmado(a)

astonishing [ə'stɒnɪʃɪŋ] *adj* asombroso(a), pasmoso(a)

astonishment [ə'stɒnɪʃmənt] *n* asombro *m*; **to my a.** para gran sorpresa mía

astound [ə'staʊnd] *vt* asombrar, pasmar

astray [ə'streɪ] *adv* **to go a.** extraviarse; *Fig* equivocarse; **to lead sb a.** llevar a algn por mal camino

astride [ə'straɪd] *prep* a horcajadas sobre

astrology [ə'strɒlədʒɪ] *n* astrología *f*

astronaut ['æstrənɔːt] *n* astronauta *mf*

astronomer [ə'strɒnəmə(r)] *n* astrónomo(a) *m,f*

astronomical [æstrə'nɒmɪkəl] *adj* astronómico(a)

astronomy [ə'strɒnəmɪ] *n* astronomía *f*

Asturias [æ'stʊərɪæs] *n* Asturias

astute [ə'stjuːt] *adj* astuto(a)

asylum [ə'saɪləm] *n* (**a**) (*protection*) asilo *m*; **to seek political a.** pedir asilo político (**b**) **mental a.** manicomio *m*

at [æt, *unstressed* ət] *prep* (**a**) (*position*) a, en; **at school/work** en el colegio/trabajo; **at the window** a la ventana; **at the top** en lo alto

(**b**) (*direction*) a; **to be angry at sb/sth** enfadarse con algn/por algo; **to laugh at sb** reírse de algn; **to look at sth/sb** mirar algo/a algn; **to shout at sb** gritarle a algn

(**c**) (*time*) a; **at Easter/Christmas** en Semana Santa/Navidad; **at six o'clock** a las seis; **at first** al principio; **at last** por fin; **at once** enseguida; **at that time** entonces; **at the moment** ahora

(**d**) (*manner*) a, en; **at best/worst** en el mejor/peor de los casos; **at hand** a mano; **at least** por lo menos; **not at all** en absoluto; (*don't mention it*) de nada

(**e**) (*rate*) a; **they retail at 100 pesetas each** se venden a 100 pesetas la unidad; **two at a time** de dos en dos

ate [et, eɪt] *pt of* eat

atheist ['eɪθɪɪst] *n* ateo(a) *m,f*

Athens ['æθɪnz] n Atenas
athlete ['æθliːt] n atleta mf
athletic [æθ'letɪk] 1 adj atlético(a); (sporty) deportista
2 npl **athletics** atletismo m
Atlantic [ət'læntɪk] adj **the A. (Ocean)** el (océano) Atlántico
atlas ['ætləs] n atlas m
atmosphere ['ætməsfɪə(r)] n atmósfera f; Fig (ambience) ambiente m
atmospheric [ætməs'ferɪk] adj atmosférico(a)
atom ['ætəm] n átomo m; **a. bomb** bomba atómica
atomic [ə'tɒmɪk] adj atómico(a)
atone [ə'təʊn] vi **to a. for** expiar
atrocious [ə'trəʊʃəs] adj atroz
attach [ə'tætʃ] vt (stick) pegar; (fasten) sujetar; (document) adjuntar; **to a. importance to sth** dar importancia a algo; Fig **to be attached to** (be fond of) tener cariño a
attaché [ə'tæʃeɪ] n agregado(a) m,f; **a. case** maletín m
attachment [ə'tætʃmənt] n (a) Tech accesorio m; (action) acoplamiento m (b) (fondness) apego m (**to** por) (c) Comput (to e-mail) archivo adjunto, anexo m
attack [ə'tæk] 1 n (a) (assault) ataque m, asalto m; **an a. on sb's life** un atentado contra la vida de algn (b) Med ataque m
2 vt (assault) atacar, asaltar; Fig (problem) abordar; (job) emprender; Fig (criticize) atacar
attacker [ə'tækə(r)] n asaltante mf, agresor(a) m,f
attain [ə'teɪn] vt (aim) lograr; (rank, age) llegar a
attainment [ə'teɪnmənt] n (achievement) logro m; (skill) talento m
attempt [ə'tempt] 1 n intento m, tentativa f; **at the second a.** a la segunda; **an a. on sb's life** un atentado contra la vida de algn
2 vt intentar; **to a. to do sth** tratar de or intentar hacer algo; Jur **attempted murder/rape** intento m de asesinato/violación
attend [ə'tend] 1 vt (be present at) asistir a; (care for, wait on) atender
2 vi (be present) asistir; (pay attention) prestar atención
▸ **attend to** vt insep (business) ocuparse de; (in shop) atender
attendance [ə'tendəns] n asistencia f
attendant [ə'tendənt] n (in cinema etc) acomodador(a) m,f; (in museum) guía mf; (in car park) vigilante(a) m,f

attention [ə'tenʃən] n (a) atención f; **for the a. of Miss Jones** a la atención de la Srta. Jones; **pay a.!** ¡atiende!; **to pay a. to sb/sth** prestar atención a algn/algo (b) Mil **a.!** ¡firmes!; **to stand to a.** estar firmes
attentive [ə'tentɪv] adj (listener) atento(a); (helpful) solícito(a)
attest [ə'test] vi **to a. to** dar testimonio a
attic ['ætɪk] n ático m
attire [ə'taɪə(r)] n Fml traje m
attitude ['ætɪtjuːd] n actitud f; (position of body) postura f; **an a. of mind** un estado de ánimo
attorney [ə'tɜːnɪ] n (a) US (lawyer) abogado(a) m,f; **A. General** ≃ Ministro(a) m,f de Justicia; **district a.** fiscal mf (b) Jur **power of a.** poderes mpl
attract [ə'trækt] vt atraer; **to a. attention** llamar la atención; **to a. a waiter's attention** llamar a un camarero
attraction [ə'trækʃən] n (a) (power) atracción f (b) (attractive thing) atractivo m; (charm) encanto m; (incentive) aliciente m; **the main a.** el número fuerte
attractive [ə'træktɪv] adj atractivo(a); (good-looking) guapo(a); (idea, proposition) atrayente
attribute¹ ['ætrɪbjuːt] n (quality) atributo m
attribute² [ə'trɪbjuːt] vt atribuir
attrition [ə'trɪʃən] n **war of a.** guerra f de desgaste
aubergine ['əʊbəʒiːn] n Br berenjena f
auburn ['ɔːbən] adj castaño rojizo inv
auction ['ɔːkʃən] 1 n subasta f
2 vt subastar
auctioneer [ɔːkʃə'nɪə(r)] n subastador(a) m,f
audacious [ɔː'deɪʃəs] adj (daring) audaz; (bold) atrevido(a); (impudent) descarado(a)
audible ['ɔːdɪbəl] adj audible
audience ['ɔːdɪəns] n (a) (spectators) público m; (at concert, conference) auditorio m; (television) telespectadores mpl (b) (meeting) audiencia f
audio-visual [ɔːdɪəʊ'vɪzjʊəl] adj audiovisual; **a. aids** apoyo m audiovisual
audit ['ɔːdɪt] 1 n revisión f de cuentas
2 vt revisar, intervenir
audition [ɔː'dɪʃən] 1 n prueba f
2 vt **to a. sb for a part** probar a algn para un papel
auditor ['ɔːdɪtə(r)] n revisor(a) m,f de cuentas
auditorium [ɔːdɪ'tɔːrɪəm] n auditorio m
augment [ɔːg'ment] vt aumentar

augur ['ɔːgə(r)] *vi* to a. well ser de buen agüero

August ['ɔːgəst] *n* agosto *m*

aunt [ɑːnt] *n* (*also Fam* **auntie, aunty** ['ɑːntɪ]) tía *f*

au pair [əʊ'peə(r)] *n* a. (girl) au pair *f*

aura ['ɔːrə] *n* aura *f*; *Rel* aureola *f*

aural ['ɔːrəl] *adj* auditivo(a), del oído

auspices ['ɔːspɪsɪz] *npl* under the a. of bajo los auspicios de

auspicious [ɔː'spɪʃəs] *adj* de buen augurio

austere [ɒ'stɪə(r)] *adj* austero(a)

austerity [ɒ'sterɪtɪ] *n* austeridad *f*

Australia [ɒ'streɪlɪə] *n* Australia

Australian [ɒ'streɪlɪən] *adj & n* australiano(a) *(m,f)*

Austria ['ɒstrɪə] *n* Austria

Austrian ['ɒstrɪən] *adj & n* austríaco(a) *(m,f)*

authentic [ɔː'θentɪk] *adj* auténtico(a)

author ['ɔːθə(r)] *n* autor(a) *m,f*

authoritarian [ɔːθɒrɪ'teərɪən] *adj* autoritario(a)

authoritative [ɔː'θɒrɪtətɪv] *adj (reliable)* autorizado(a); *(authoritarian)* autoritario(a)

authority [ɔː'θɒrɪtɪ] *n* autoridad *f*; local a. ayuntamiento *m*

authorize ['ɔːθəraɪz] *vt* autorizar; *(payment etc)* aprobar; to a. sb to do sth autorizar a algn a hacer algo

auto ['ɔːtəʊ] *n US* coche *m, Andes, CAm, Carib, Méx* carro *m*

autobiography [ɔːtəʊbaɪ'ɒgrəfɪ] *n* autobiografía *f*

autograph ['ɔːtəgrɑːf] 1 *n* autógrafo *m*

2 *vt (sign)* firmar; *(book, photo)* dedicar

automata [ɔː'tɒmətə] *pl of* automaton

automatic [ɔːtə'mætɪk] 1 *adj* automático(a)

2 *n (car)* coche automático; *(gun)* pistola automática

automatically [ɔːtə'mætɪklɪ] *adv* automáticamente

automation [ɔːtə'meɪʃən] *n* automatización *f*; office a. ofimática *f*

automaton [ɔː'tɒmətɒn] *n* (*pl* automata) autómata *m*

automobile ['ɔːtəməbiːl] *n US* coche *m,* automóvil *m, Andes, CAm, Carib, Méx* carro *m*

autonomous [ɔː'tɒnəməs] *adj* autónomo(a)

autonomy [ɔː'tɒnəmɪ] *n* autonomía *f*

autopsy ['ɔːtɒpsɪ] *n* autopsia *f*

autumn ['ɔːtəm] *n* otoño *m*

auxiliary [ɔːg'zɪljərɪ] *adj* auxiliar

Av., av. (*abbr* Avenue) Av., Avda.

avail [ə'veɪl] 1 *n* to no a. en vano

2 *vt* to a. oneself of sth aprovecharse de algo

available [ə'veɪləbəl] *adj (thing)* disponible; *(person)* libre

avalanche ['ævəlɑːnʃ] *n* avalancha *f*

avarice ['ævərɪs] *n* avaricia *f*

Ave (*abbr* Avenue) Av., Avda.

avenge [ə'vendʒ] *vt* vengar

avenue ['ævɪnjuː] *n* avenida *f*; *Fig* vía *f*

average ['ævərɪdʒ] 1 *n* promedio *m,* media *f*; on a. por término medio

2 *adj* medio(a); *(condition)* regular

3 *vt* sacar la media de; he averages eight hours' work a day trabaja una media de ocho horas al día

▸ **average out at** *vt insep* salir a una media de

averse [ə'vɜːs] *adj* to be a. to sth ser reacio(a) a algo

aversion [ə'vɜːʃən] *n (feeling)* aversión *f*; *(thing)* bestia negra

avert [ə'vɜːt] *vt (eyes, thoughts)* apartar (from de); *(accident)* impedir; *(danger)* evitar

avid ['ævɪd] *adj (reader)* voraz

avidly ['ævɪdlɪ] *adv* vorazmente

avocado [ævə'kɑːdəʊ] *n* a. (pear) aguacate *m, Andes, RP* palta *f*

avoid [ə'vɔɪd] *vt* evitar; *(question)* eludir

avoidable [ə'vɔɪdəbəl] *adj* evitable

await [ə'weɪt] *vt* esperar, aguardar

awake [ə'weɪk] 1 *adj* despierto(a); to be a. estar despierto(a)

2 *vt (pt* awoke, awaked; *pp* awoken, awaked) despertar

awaken [ə'weɪkən] *vt & vi (pt* awakened; *pp* awoken) = awake 2

awakening [ə'weɪkənɪŋ] *n* despertar *m*

award [ə'wɔːd] 1 *n (prize)* premio *m*; *(medal)* condecoración *f*; *Jur* indemnización *f*; *(grant)* beca *f*

2 *vt (prize)* conceder, otorgar; *(medal)* dar; *(damages)* adjudicar

aware [ə'weə(r)] *adj (informed)* enterado(a); not that I'm a. of que yo sepa no; to be a. of sth ser consciente de algo; to become a. of sth darse cuenta de algo

awareness [ə'weənɪs] *n* conciencia *f* (of de)

awash [ə'wɒʃ] *adj* inundado(a) (with de)

away [ə'weɪ] *adv* far a. lejos; go a.! ¡lárgate!; it's 3 miles a. está a 3 millas (de distancia); keep a. from the fire! ¡no te acerques al fuego!; right a. en seguida; to be a. *(absent)* estar ausente; *(out)* estar fuera; to die a. desvanecerse; to give sth

a. regalar algo; *(secret)* revelar algo; **to go a.** irse; *Sport* **to play a.** jugar fuera; **to turn a.** volver la cara; **to work a.** trabajar

awe [ɔː] *n (fear)* temor *m*; *(amazement)* asombro *m*; **he was in a. of his father** le intimidaba su padre

awe-inspiring [ˈɔːɪnspaɪərɪŋ] *adj* impresionante, imponente

awesome [ˈɔːsəm] *adj* impresionante

awful [ˈɔːfʊl] *adj Fam* espantoso(a); **an a. lot of work** muchísimo trabajo

awfully [ˈɔːfʊlɪ] *adv Fam* terriblemente

awkward [ˈɔːkwəd] *adj (clumsy)* torpe; *(difficult)* pesado(a); *(object)* incómodo(a);

(moment) inoportuno(a); *(situation)* embarazoso(a); *(problem)* difícil

awning [ˈɔːnɪŋ] *n (on ship)* toldo *m*; *(on shop)* marquesina *f*

awoke [əˈwəʊk] *pt of* awake

awoken [əˈwəʊkən] *pp of* awake, awaken

axe, *US* **ax** [æks] **1** *n* hacha *f*
2 *vt Fig (jobs)* eliminar; *(costs)* reducir; *(plan)* cancelar; *(person)* despedir

axis [ˈæksɪs] *n (pl* **axes** [ˈæksiːz]*)* eje *m*

axle [ˈæksəl] *n* eje *m*; *Tech* árbol *m*

ayatollah [aɪəˈtɒlə] *n* ayatolá *m*

Aztec [ˈæztek] *adj & n* azteca *(mf)*

B

B, b [biː] *n* (**a**) *(the letter)* B, b *f; Br Aut* **B road** carretera secundaria (**b**) *Mus* B si *m;* **B flat** si bemol

BA [biːˈeɪ] *n* (*abbr* **Bachelor of Arts**) *(person)* licenciado(a) *m,f* en Filosofía y Letras

babble [ˈbæbəl] *vi (baby)* balbucear; *(brook)* murmurar

babe [beɪb] *n* (**a**) *(baby)* bebé *m* (**b**) *US Fam* **hi, b.!** ¡hola, guapa!

baboon [bəˈbuːn] *n* zambo *m*

baby [ˈbeɪbɪ] *n* (**a**) bebé *m; (young child)* niño(a) *m,f; (young child)* niño(a) *m,f; US* **b. buggy** *or* **carriage** cochecito *m* de niño; **b. face** cara *f* de niño (**b**) *(animal)* cría *f* (**c**) *Fam (darling)* querido(a) *m,f*

baby-sit [ˈbeɪbɪsɪt] *vi* hacer de canguro

baby-sitter [ˈbeɪbɪsɪtə(r)] *n* canguro *mf*

baby-walker [ˈbeɪbɪwɔːkə(r)] *n* tacataca *m*

bachelor [ˈbætʃələ(r)] *n* (**a**) soltero *m* (**b**) *Univ* licenciado(a) *m,f;* **B. of Arts/Science** licenciado(a) *m,f* en Filosofía y Letras/Ciencias

back [bæk] **1** *n* (**a**) *(of person)* espalda *f; (of animal)* lomo *m;* **b. to front** al revés; *Fig* **to get sb's b. up** poner negro a algn; *Fig* **to have one's b. to the wall** estar en un aprieto

(**b**) *(of book)* lomo *m; (of chair)* respaldo *m; (of coin)* reverso *m; (of hand)* dorso *m; (of house, car)* parte *f* de atrás; *Fig* **he knows Leeds like the b. of his hand** se conoce Leeds como la palma de la mano

(**c**) *(of stage, cupboard)* fondo *m; Fam* **at the b. of beyond** en el quinto pino

(**d**) *Ftb* defensa *mf*

(**e**) *US* **in b. (of)** *(behind)* en la parte de atrás (de), detrás (de); *(to the rear of)* al fondo (de)

2 *adj* (**a**) trasero(a), de atrás; **b. door** puerta *f* de atrás; **b. seat** asiento *m* de detrás; *Fig* **to take a b. seat** pasar al segundo plano; *Aut* **b. wheel** rueda trasera

(**b**) **b. rent** alquiler atrasado; **b. pay** atrasos *mpl; Press* **b. number** número *m* atrasado

3 *adv* (**a**) *(to the rear)* atrás; *(towards the rear)* hacia atrás; **b. and forth** de acá para allá

(**b**) **some years b.** hace unos años

4 *vt* (**a**) *(support)* apoyar, respaldar

(**b**) *Fin* financiar

(**c**) *(bet on)* apostar por

(**d**) *(car etc)* dar marcha atrás a

5 *vi* (**a**) *(move backwards)* retroceder

(**b**) *(car etc)* dar marcha atrás

► **back away** *vi* retirarse

► **back down** *vi* echarse atrás

► **back off** *vi* desistir

► **back out** *vi (withdraw)* retractarse, volverse atrás

► **back up 1** *vt sep* (**a**) *(support)* apoyar (**b**) *Comput (file)* hacer una copia de seguridad de

2 *vi Aut* ir marcha atrás

backache [ˈbækeɪk] *n* dolor *m* de espalda

backbencher [bækˈbentʃə(r)] *n* diputado(a) *m,f* que no es ministro

backbiting [ˈbækbaɪtɪŋ] *n* murmuración *f*

backbone [ˈbækbəʊn] *n Anat* columna *f*

backcloth [ˈbæklɒθ] *n* telón *m* de fondo

backdate [bækˈdeɪt] *vt* antedatar

backdated [bækˈdeɪtɪd] *adj* con efecto retroactivo

backdrop [ˈbækdrɒp] *n* telón *m* de fondo

backer [ˈbækə(r)] *n* (**a**) *Fin* promotor(a) *m,f* (**b**) *Pol* partidario(a) *m,f* (**c**) *(person who bets)* apostante *mf*

backfire [bækˈfaɪə(r)] *vi* (**a**) *Aut* petardear (**b**) *Fig* **our plan backfired** nos salió el tiro por la culata

background [ˈbækgraʊnd] *n* (**a**) fondo *m;* **to stay in the b.** quedarse en segundo plano; **b. music** música *f* de fondo (**b**) *(origin)* origen *m; (past)* pasado *m; (education)* formación *f* (**c**) *(circumstances)* antecedentes *mpl* (**d**) *(atmosphere)* ambiente *m*

backhand [ˈbækhænd] *n Sport* revés *m*

backhanded [ˈbækhændɪd] *adj* equívoco(a), ambiguo(a)

backhander [ˈbækhændə(r)] *n Fam (bribe)* soborno *m*

backing [ˈbækɪŋ] *n* (**a**) *(support)* apoyo

m; *Com & Fin* respaldo financiero (**b**) *Mus* acompañamiento *m*

backlash ['bæklæʃ] *n* reacción violenta y repentina

backlog ['bæklɒg] *n* to have a b. of work tener un montón de trabajo atrasado

backpack ['bækpæk] *n* mochila *f*

backpedal [bæk'pedəl] *vi Fam* dar marcha atrás

backside [bæk'saɪd] *n Fam* trasero *m*, culo *m*

backstage [bæk'steɪdʒ] *adv* entre bastidores

backstroke ['bækstrəʊk] *n* espalda *f*

backtrack ['bæktræk] *vi Fig* volverse atrás

backup ['bækʌp] *n* (**a**) *(support)* apoyo *m*, respaldo *m*; *Comput* **b. (file)** fichero *m* de apoyo (**b**) *US (of traffic)* caravana *f*

backward ['bækwəd] **1** *adj* (**a**) *(movement)* hacia atrás (**b**) *(country)* subdesarrollado(a); *(child)* retrasado(a)
2 *adv esp US* hacia atrás

backwards ['bækwədz] *adv* hacia atrás; **to walk b.** andar de espaldas

backyard [bæk'jɑːd] *n* patio trasero; *US* jardín trasero

bacon ['beɪkən] *n* tocino *m*, beicon *m*

bacteria [bæk'tɪərɪə] *npl* bacterias *fpl*

bad [bæd] **1** *adj* (**worse, worst**) (**a**) *(poor)* malo(a); **to go from b. to worse** ir de mal en peor (**b**) *(decayed)* podrido(a); **to go b.** echarse a perder (**c**) **that's too b.!** ¡qué pena! (**d**) *(wicked)* malo(a); **to use b. language** ser mal hablado(a) (**e**) *(accident)* grave; *(headache)* fuerte (**f**) *(ill)* enfermo(a) (**g**) **b. debt** deuda *f* incobrable
2 *n* lo malo

bade [beɪd] *pt of* **bid**

badge [bædʒ] *n* insignia *f*; *(metal disc)* chapa *f*

badger ['bædʒə(r)] **1** *n* tejón *m*
2 *vt* acosar

badly ['bædlɪ] *adv* (**a**) mal; **he did b. in the exam** le salió mal el examen; **to be b. off** andar mal de dinero (**b**) *(seriously)* gravemente (**c**) *(very much)* mucho; **to miss sb b.** echar mucho de menos a algn; **we need it b.** nos hace mucha falta

badminton ['bædmɪntən] *n* bádminton *m*

bad-tempered [bæd'tempəd] *adj* **to be b.** *(temperament)* tener mal genio; *(temporarily)* estar de mal humor

baffle ['bæfəl] **1** *vt* desconcertar
2 *n Tech* pantalla acústica

baffling ['bæflɪŋ] *adj* incomprensible, enigmático(a)

bag [bæg] **1** *n* (**a**) *(large)* bolsa *f*; *(handbag)* bolso *m*, cartera *f*, *Méx* bolsa; *Fam* **bags of** montones de; **travel b.** bolsa de viaje (**b**) *(hunting)* caza *f*; *Fam* **it's in the b.** es cosa hecha (**c**) *Pej* **old b.** *(woman)* bruja *f* (**d**) **bags** *(under eyes)* ojeras *fpl*
2 *vt* (**a**) *(put into sacks)* meter en sacos (**b**) *Fam* coger

baggage ['bægɪdʒ] *n* (**a**) equipaje *m* (**b**) *Mil* bagaje *m*

baggy ['bægɪ] *adj* (**baggier, baggiest**) holgado(a); **b. trousers** pantalones anchos

bagpipes ['bægpaɪps] *npl* gaita *f*

Bahamas [bə'hɑːməz] *npl* **the B.** las Bahamas

bail¹ [beɪl] *n Jur* fianza *f*; **on b.** bajo fianza; **to stand b. for sb** salir fiador por algn
▸ bail out *vt sep Fig (person)* sacar de un apuro

bail² [beɪl] *vi Naut* **to b. (out)** achicar

bailiff ['beɪlɪf] *n* (**a**) *Jur* alguacil *m* (**b**) *(steward)* administrador *m*

bait [beɪt] **1** *n* cebo *m*; **to rise to the b.** tragar el anzuelo, picar
2 *vt* (**a**) *(for fishing)* cebar (**b**) *(torment)* hostigar

baize [beɪz] *n* bayeta *f*; **green b.** tapete *m* verde

bake [beɪk] **1** *vt* (**a**) cocer al horno (**b**) *(harden)* endurecer
2 *vi Fam* hacer mucho calor

baked [beɪkt] *adj* al horno; **b. potato** patata *f* or *Am* papa *f* al horno

baker ['beɪkə(r)] *n* panadero *a m,f*

bakery ['beɪkərɪ] *n* panadería *f*

baking ['beɪkɪŋ] *n* cocción *f*; **b. dish** fuente *f* para horno; **b. powder** levadura *f* en polvo; **b. tin** molde *m*

balaclava [bælə'klɑːvə] *n* pasamontañas *m inv*

balance ['bæləns] **1** *n* (**a**) *(scales)* balanza *f*; *Fig* **to hang in the b.** estar en juego (**b**) *(equilibrium)* equilibrio *m*; *Pol* **b. of power** equilibrio de fuerzas (**c**) *Fin* saldo *m*; **b. of payments** balanza *f* de pagos; **b. sheet** balance *m*; **credit b.** saldo acreedor (**d**) *(remainder)* resto *m*
2 *vt* (**a**) poner en equilibrio (**on** en) (**b**) *(budget)* equilibrar; **to b. the books** hacer el balance (**c**) *(weigh up)* sopesar
3 *vi* guardar el equilibrio
▸ balance out *vi (figures)* corresponderse

balanced ['bælənst] *adj* equilibrado(a)

balcony ['bælkənɪ] *n* balcón *m*; *Th* anfiteatro *m*

bald [bɔːld] *adj* (**a**) *(person)* calvo(a) (**b**)

(tyre) desgastado(a) (**c**) *(style)* escueto(a)

baldness ['bɔːldnɪs] *n* (**a**) *(of person)* calvicie *f* (**b**) *(of tyre)* desgaste *m* (**c**) *(of style)* sencillez *f*

bale¹ [beɪl] **1** *n (of cloth)* fardo *m*
2 *vt* embalar

bale² [beɪl] *vt* = **bail²**
▸ **bale out 1** *vi Av* saltar en paracaídas de un avión
2 *vt sep Fig (person)* sacar de apuros a

Balearic [bælɪ'ærɪk] *adj* **the B. Islands** las Islas Baleares

baleful ['beɪlfʊl] *adj* funesto(a), siniestro(a)

Balkan ['bɔːlkən] *adj* **the Balkans** los Balcanes

ball¹ [bɔːl] *n* (**a**) *(in cricket, tennis etc)* pelota *f*; *Ftb* balón *m*; *(in billiards, golf etc)* bola *f*; *Fig* **the b. is in your court** ahora te toca a ti; *Fig* **to play b. with sb** cooperar con algn; *Fam* **to be on the b.** ser un espabilado; *Tech* **b. bearing** rodamiento *m* de bolas (**b**) *(of paper)* bola *f*; *(of wool)* ovillo *m* (**c**) *US* béisbol *m*; *Fig* **it's a whole new b. game** es otra historia (**d**) *very Fam* **balls** cojones *mpl*

ball² [bɔːl] *n (dance)* baile *m*

ballad ['bæləd] *n* balada *f*

ballast ['bæləst] *n Naut* lastre *m*

ballerina [bælə'riːnə] *n* bailarina *f*

ballet ['bæleɪ] *n* ballet *m*; **b. dancer** bailarín(ina) *m,f*

ballistic [bə'lɪstɪk] *adj* balístico(a)

ballistics [bə'lɪstɪks] *n sing* balística *f*

balloon [bə'luːn] **1** *n* (**a**) *(globo m)* (**b**) *(in cartoon)* bocadillo *m*
2 *vi* hincharse; *Fig* aumentar rápidamente

ballot ['bælət] **1** *n* votación *f*; **b. box** urna *f*; **b. paper** papeleta *f*
2 *vt* someter a votación

ballpoint (pen) ['bɔːlpɔɪnt('pen)] *n* bolígrafo *m*, *CSur* lapicera *f*

ballroom ['bɔːlruːm] *n* salón *m* de baile

ballyhoo [bælɪ'huː] *n Fam (fuss)* jaleo *m*

balm [bɑːm] *n* bálsamo *m*

balmy ['bɑːmɪ] *adj* (**balmier, balmiest**) *(weather)* suave

Baltic ['bɔːltɪk] *adj* báltico(a); **the B. (Sea)** el (mar) Báltico

balustrade ['bæləstreɪd] *n* barandilla *f*

bamboo [bæm'buː] *n* bambú *m*

bamboozle [bæm'buːzəl] *vt Fam* (**a**) *(puzzle)* dejar perplejo (**b**) *(trick)* engañar, embaucar

ban [bæn] **1** *n* prohibición *f*

2 *vt* (**a**) *(prohibit)* prohibir (**b**) *(exclude)* excluir

banal [bə'nɑːl] *adj* banal, trivial

banana [bə'nɑːnə] *n* plátano *m*, banana *f*, *Col* banano *m*, *Ven* cambur *m*; *Fam* **to go bananas** volverse loco(a)

band [bænd] **1** *n* (**a**) *(strip)* tira *f*; *(ribbon)* cinta *f* (**b**) *(stripe)* raya *f* (**c**) *Rad* banda *f* (**d**) *(group)* grupo *m*; *(of youths)* pandilla *f*; *(of thieves)* banda *f* (**e**) *Mus* banda *f*
2 *vi* **to b. together** unirse, juntarse

bandage ['bændɪdʒ] **1** *n* venda *f*
2 *vt* vendar

Band-Aid® ['bændeɪd] *n US* tirita® *f*, *Am* curita *f*

B & B [biːən'biː] *n (abbr bed and breakfast) (hotel)* = hostal familiar en el que el desayuno está incluido en el precio de la habitación

bandit ['bændɪt] *n* bandido *m*

bandstand ['bændstænd] *n* quiosco *m* de música

bandwagon ['bændwægən] *n Fig* **to jump on the b.** subirse al tren

bandy ['bændɪ] **1** *vt (words, ideas)* intercambiar
2 *adj* (**bandier, bandiest**) torcido(a) hacia fuera
▸ **bandy about** *vt sep (ideas)* propagar, difundir

bandy-legged ['bændɪ'leg(ɪ)d] *adj* patizambo(a)

bang [bæŋ] **1** *n* (**a**) *(blow)* golpe *m* (**b**) *(noise)* ruido *m*; *(explosion)* estallido *m*; *(of gun)* estampido *m*; **to shut the door with a b.** dar un portazo
2 *npl US* **bangs** flequillo *m*, *Am* cerquillo *m (corto)*
3 *vt* golpear; **to b. sth shut** cerrar algo de golpe
4 *vi* golpear; **to b. shut** cerrarse de golpe
5 *interj (blow)* ¡zas!; **b., b.!** *(of gun)* ¡pum, pum!
6 *adv Fam* justo

banger ['bæŋə(r)] *n* (**a**) *(firework)* petardo *m* (**b**) *Fam (sausage)* salchicha *f* (**c**) *Fam* **old b.** *(car)* tartana *f*

bangle ['bæŋgəl] *n* brazalete *m*

banish ['bænɪʃ] *vt* desterrar

banister ['bænɪstə(r)] *n* pasamanos *m inv*

bank¹ [bæŋk] **1** *n* (**a**) *Com & Fin* banco *m*; **b. account** cuenta bancaria; **b. card** tarjeta bancaria; **b. clerk** empleado(a) *m,f* de banca; **b. draft** letra bancaria; **b. holiday** fiesta *f* nacional; **b. statement** extracto *m* de cuenta (**b**) *(in gambling)* banca *f* (**c**) *(store)* banco *m*

2 *vt Com & Fin* depositar, ingresar
3 *vi Com & Fin* **to b. with** tener una
cuenta en
▸ **bank on** *vt insep* contar con
bank² [bæŋk] **1** *n* (**a**) *(mound)* loma *f*;
(embankment) terraplén *m* (**b**) *(of river)*
ribera *f*; *(edge)* orilla *f*
2 *vt Av* ladear
3 *vi Av* ladearse
bankbook ['bæŋkbʊk] *n* libreta *f* de
ahorros
banker ['bæŋkə(r)] *n* banquero(a) *m,f*
banking ['bæŋkɪŋ] *n* banca *f*
banknote ['bæŋknəʊt] *n* billete *m* de
banco
bankrupt ['bæŋkrʌpt] **1** *adj* en quiebra;
to go b. quebrar
2 *vt* llevar a la bancarrota
bankruptcy ['bæŋkrʌptsɪ] *n* quiebra *f*,
bancarrota *f*
banner ['bænə(r)] *n* *(in demonstration)*
pancarta *f*; *(flag)* bandera *f*
banns [bænz] *npl* amonestaciones *fpl*
banquet ['bæŋkwɪt] *n* banquete *m*
banter ['bæntə(r)] **1** *n* bromas *fpl*
2 *vi* bromear
bap [bæp] *n* bollo *m*, panecillo *m*
baptism ['bæptɪzəm] *n* bautismo *m*
baptize [bæp'taɪz] *vt* bautizar
bar [bɑː(r)] **1** *n* (**a**) *(of gold)* barra *f*; *(of chocolate)* tableta *f*; *(of soap)* pastilla *f*;
Com **b. code** código *m* de barras (**b**) *(of cage)* barrote *m*; *Fam* **to be behind bars**
estar en la cárcel (**c**) *(obstacle)* obstáculo
m (**d**) *Jur (dock)* banquillo *m*; *(court)*
tribunal *m* (**e**) *Jur* **the B.** *(profession)*
abogacía *f*; *(body of lawyers)* colegio *m*
de abogados (**f**) *(pub)* bar *m*; *(counter)*
barra *f* (**g**) *Mus* compás *o*
2 *vt* (**a**) *(door)* atrancar; *(road)* cortar
(**b**) *(exclude)* excluir (**from** de) (**c**) *(prohibit)* prohibir
3 *prep* salvo; **b. none** sin excepción
barbarian [bɑː'beərɪən] *adj & n* bárbaro(a) *(m,f)*
barbaric [bɑː'bærɪk] *adj* bárbaro(a)
barbecue ['bɑːbɪkjuː] **1** *n* barbacoa *f*
2 *vt* asar a la parrilla
barbed [bɑːbd] *adj* (**a**) **b. wire** alambre *m*
de púas (**b**) *Fig (remark)* mordaz
barber ['bɑːbə(r)] *n* barbero(a) *m,f*; **b.'s**
(shop) barbería *f*
barbiturate [bɑː'bɪtjʊrɪt] *n* barbitúrico *m*
bare [beə(r)] **1** *adj* (**a**) *(naked)* desnudo(a); *(head)*
descubierto(a); *(foot)* descalzo(a);
(room) sin muebles; **to lay b.** poner
al descubierto; **with his b. hands** sólo
con las manos (**b**) *(basic)* mero(a); **the**

b. minimum lo mínimo
2 *vt* desnudar; *(uncover)* descubrir
bareback(ed) ['beə'bæk(t)] *adv* **to ride**
b. montar un caballo a pelo
barefaced ['beəfeɪst] *adj* desvergonzado(a)
barefoot ['beə'fʊt] *adj & adv* descalzo(a)
barely ['beəlɪ] *adv* apenas
bargain ['bɑːgɪn] **1** *n* (**a**) *(agreement)*
pacto *m*; *(deal)* negocio *m*; **into the b.**
por añadidura, además; **to drive a hard**
b. imponer condiciones duras; **to strike a**
b. cerrar un trato (**b**) *(cheap purchase)*
ganga *f*; **b. price** precio *m* de oferta
2 *vi* (**a**) negociar (**b**) *(haggle)* regatear
▸ **bargain for** *vt insep* esperar, contar con
barge [bɑːdʒ] **1** *n* gabarra *f*
2 *vt Fam* **to b. into** *(room)* irrumpir en;
(person) tropezar con
▸ **barge in** *vi Fam* (**a**) *(go in)* entrar sin
permiso (**b**) *(interfere)* entrometerse
baritone ['bærɪtəʊn] *adj & n* barítono *(m)*
bark¹ [bɑːk] **1** *n* ladrido *m*
2 *vi (dog)* ladrar
bark² [bɑːk] *n Bot* corteza *f*
barley ['bɑːlɪ] *n* cebada *f*; **b. sugar** azúcar
m cande
barmaid ['bɑːmeɪd] *n* camarera *f*
barman ['bɑːmən] *n* camarero *m*, barman *m*
barn [bɑːn] *n* granero *m*; **b. dance** baile *m*
popular
barnacle ['bɑːnəkəl] *n* percebe *m*
barometer [bə'rɒmɪtə(r)] *n* barómetro *m*
baron ['bærən] *n* barón *m*
baroness ['bærənɪs] *n* baronesa *f*
baroque [bə'rɒk] *adj* barroco(a)
barrack ['bærək] *vt* abuchear
barracks ['bærəks] *n Mil* cuartel *m*
barrage ['bærɑːdʒ] *n* (**a**) *(dam)* presa *f*
(**b**) *Mil* barrera *f* de fuego (**c**) *Fig (of questions)* lluvia *f*
barrel ['bærəl] *n* (**a**) *(of wine)* tonel *m*; *(of beer, oil)* barril *m* (**b**) *(of firearm)* cañón *m*
barren ['bærən] *adj* estéril; *(land)* yermo(a)
barricade [bærɪ'keɪd] **1** *n* barricada *f*
2 *vt* levantar barricadas; **to b. oneself in**
parapetarse
barrier ['bærɪə(r)] *n* barrera *f*
barrister ['bærɪstə(r)] *n Br* abogado(a)
m,f (capacitado(a) para ejercer ante tribunales superiores)
barrow ['bærəʊ] *n* carretilla *f*
bartender ['bɑːtendə(r)] *n US* camarero
m, barman *m*
barter ['bɑːtə(r)] *vt* trocar (**for** por)
base [beɪs] **1** *n* base *f*; *(foot)* pie *m*; *(of*

column) basa *f*; *Sport (of team)* concentración *f*; **air/naval b.** base *f* aérea/naval
   2 *vt* (**a**) basar, fundar (**on** en) (**b**) *(troops)* estacionar
   3 *adj* (**a**) *(despicable)* bajo(a), despreciable (**b**) *(metals)* común
baseball ['beɪsbɔːl] *n* béisbol *m*
baseline ['beɪslaɪn] *n (in tennis)* línea *f* de saque
basement ['beɪsmənt] *n* sótano *m*
bases ['beɪsiːz] *pl of* basis
bash [bæʃ] **1** *n (heavy blow)* golpetazo *m*; *(dent)* bollo *m*; *Fam (attempt)* intento *m*
   2 *vt* golpear
bashful ['bæʃfʊl] *adj* tímido(a)
basic ['beɪsɪk] **1** *adj* básico(a); **b. pay** sueldo *m* base
   2 *npl* **basics** lo fundamental
basically ['beɪsɪklɪ] *adv* fundamentalmente
basil ['bæzəl] *n* albahaca *f*
basin ['beɪsən] *n* (**a**) *(washbowl)* palangana *f*; *(for washing up)* barreño *m*; *(in bathroom)* lavabo *m*; *(dish)* cuenco *m* (**b**) *(of river)* cuenca *f*
basis ['beɪsɪs] *n (pl* bases*)* base *f*; **on the b. of** en base a
bask [bɑːsk] *vi* tostarse; **to b. in the sun** tomar el sol
basket ['bɑːskɪt] *n* cesta *f*, cesto *m*
basketball ['bɑːskɪtbɔːl] *n* baloncesto *m*
Basque [bæsk, bɑːsk] **1** *adj* vasco(a); **B. Country** País Vasco, Euskadi; **B. flag** ikurriña *f*; **B. nationalist** abertzale *mf*
   2 *n* (**a**) *(person)* vasco(a) *m,f* (**b**) *(language)* vasco *m*, euskera *m*
bass¹ [bæs] *n inv (seawater)* lubina *f*; *(freshwater)* perca *f*
bass² [beɪs] **1** *n* (**a**) *(singer)* bajo *m* (**b**) *(notes)* graves *mpl*; **b. drum** bombo *m*; **b. guitar** bajo *m*
   2 *adj* bajo(a)
bassoon [bə'suːn] *n* fagot *m*
bastard ['bɑːstəd, 'bæstəd] **1** *n* (**a**) bastardo(a) *m,f* (**b**) *Pej* cabrón *m*, hijo *m* de puta; **poor b.!** ¡el pobre!
   2 *adj* bastardo(a)
baste [beɪst] *vt Culin* untar
bastion ['bæstɪən] *n* baluarte *m*, bastión *m*
bat¹ [bæt] **1** *n (in cricket, baseball)* bate *m*; *(in table tennis)* pala *f*; *Fig* **to do sth off one's own b.** hacer algo por cuenta propia
   2 *vi (in cricket, baseball)* batear
bat² [bæt] *n Zool* murciélago *m*
bat³ [bæt] *vt Fam* **without batting an eyelid** sin pestañear

batch [bætʃ] *n (of bread)* hornada *f*; *(of goods)* lote *m*; *Comput* **b. processing** procesamiento *m* por lotes
bated ['beɪtɪd] *adj* **with b. breath** sin respirar
bath [bɑːθ] **1** *n* (**a**) baño *m*; **to have a b.** bañarse; **b. towel** toalla *f* de baño (**b**) *(tub)* bañera *f* (**c**) **baths** piscina *f* municipal
   2 *vt* bañar
bathe [beɪð] **1** *vi* bañarse
   2 *vt* (**a**) *(wound)* lavar (**b**) **he was bathed in sweat** *(covered)* estaba empapado de sudor
bather ['beɪðə(r)] *n* bañista *mf*
bathing ['beɪðɪŋ] *n* baño *m*; **b. cap** gorro *m* de baño; **b. costume** traje *m* de baño; **b. trunks** bañador *m* de hombre
bathrobe ['bɑːθrəʊb] *n* albornoz *m*
bathroom ['bɑːθruːm] *n* cuarto *m* de baño
bathtub ['bɑːθtʌb] *n* bañera *f*
baton ['bætən, 'bætɒn] *n* (**a**) *Mus* batuta *f* (**b**) *(truncheon)* porra *f* (**c**) *Sport* testigo *m*
battalion [bə'tæljən] *n* batallón *m*
batter¹ ['bætə(r)] *vt* aporrear, apalear
batter² ['bætə(r)] *n (in cricket, baseball)* bateador(a) *m,f*
batter³ ['bætə(r)] *Culin* **1** *n* pasta *f* (para rebozar); **fish in b.** pescado rebozado
   2 *vt* rebozar
battered ['bætəd] *adj (car)* abollado(a); *(person)* maltratado(a)
battering ['bætərɪŋ] *n* paliza *f*; **to take a b.** recibir una paliza; *Mil* **b. ram** ariete *m*
battery ['bætərɪ] *n* (**a**) *(for torch, radio)* pila *f*, *Aut* batería *f* (**b**) *Jur* **assault and b.** lesiones *fpl*
battle ['bætəl] **1** *n* batalla *f*; *Fig* lucha *f*; **to do b.** librar batalla; *Fig* **b. cry** lema *m*
   2 *vi* luchar
battlefield ['bætəlfiːld] *n* campo *m* de batalla
battleship ['bætəlʃɪp] *n* acorazado *m*
bauble ['bɔːbəl] *n* chuchería *f*
bawdy ['bɔːdɪ] *adj (joke etc)* verde
bawl [bɔːl] *vi* gritar, chillar
bay¹ [beɪ] *n Geog* bahía *f*; *(large)* golfo *m*; **B. of Biscay** golfo de Vizcaya; **B. of Bengal** golfo de Bengala
bay² [beɪ] *n* (**a**) *(recess)* hueco *m*; **b. window** ventana salediza (**b**) *(in factory)* nave *f*; **cargo b.** bodega *f* de carga
bay³ [beɪ] *n* laurel *m*
bay⁴ [beɪ] **1** *vi (dog)* aullar
   2 *n* ladrido *m*; *Fig* **at b.** acorralado(a); *Fig* **to keep sb at b.** mantener a algn a raya

bayonet [ˈbeɪənɪt] *n* bayoneta *f*

bazaar [bəˈzɑː(r)] *n* (**a**) *(market)* bazar *m* (**b**) *(church)* **b.** *(charity sale)* rastrillo benéfico

BBC [biːbiːˈsiː] *n* *(abbr* **British Broadcasting Corporation***)* BBC *f*

BC [biːˈsiː] *(abbr* **before Christ***)* a.d.C.

be [biː, *unstressed* bɪ]

> En el inglés hablado, y en el escrito en estilo coloquial, el verbo **be** se contrae de forma que **I am** se transforma en **I'm, he/she/it is** se transforman en **he's/she's/it's** y **you/we/they are** se transforman en **you're/we're/they're**. Las formas negativas **is not, are not, was not** y **were not** se transforman en **isn't, aren't, wasn't** y **weren't**.

1 *vi* (*pres 1st person sing* **am**; *3rd person sing* **is**; *2nd person sing & all persons pl* **are**; *pt 1st & 3rd persons sing* **was**; *2nd person sing & all persons pl* **were**; *pp* **been**) (**a**) ser; **he is very tall** es muy alto; **Madrid is the capital** Madrid es la capital; **sugar is sweet** el azúcar es dulce

(**b**) *(nationality, occupation)* ser; **he's Italian** es italiano

(**c**) *(origin, ownership)* ser; **the car is Domingo's** el coche es de Domingo; **this painting is by Goya** este cuadro es de Goya

(**d**) *(price)* costar; *(total)* ser; **a return ticket is £24** un billete de ida y vuelta cuesta £24; **how much is a kilo of cod?** ¿a cuánto está el kilo de bacalao?; **how much is it?** ¿cuánto es?

(**e**) *(temporary state)* estar; **how are you? – I'm very well** ¿cómo estás? – estoy muy bien; **this soup is cold** esta sopa está fría; **to be cold/afraid/hungry** tener frío/miedo/hambre; **to be lucky** tener suerte

(**f**) *(location)* estar; **Aberdeen is in Scotland** Aberdeen está en Escocia; **Birmingham is 200 miles from London** Birmingham está a 200 millas de Londres

(**g**) *(age)* tener; **she is thirty (years old)** tiene treinta años

2 *v aux* (**a**) *(with pres p)* estar; **he is writing a letter** está escribiendo una carta; **she was singing** estaba cantando; **they are leaving next week** se van la semana que viene; **we have been waiting for a long time** hace mucho que estamos esperando; **he is coming** *(emphatic)* es seguro que viene

(**b**) *(passive)* ser; **he was murdered** fue asesinado; **she is allowed to smoke** se le permite fumar

(**c**) *(obligation)* **I am to see him this afternoon** debo verle esta tarde; **you are not to smoke here** no se puede fumar aquí

3 *v impers* (**a**) *(with there)* haber; **there is, there are** hay; **there was, there were** había; **there will be** habrá; **there would be** habría; **there have been a lot of complaints** ha habido muchas quejas; **there were ten of us** éramos diez

(**b**) *(with it)* **it's late** es tarde; **it is said that** se dice que; **who is it? – it's me** ¿quién es? – soy yo; **what is it?** ¿qué pasa?

(**c**) *(weather)* **it's foggy** hay niebla; **it's cold/hot** hace frío/calor

(**d**) *(time)* ser; **it's one o'clock** es la una; **it's four o'clock** son las cuatro

(**e**) *(date)* **it's the 11th/Tuesday today** hoy es 11/martes

(**f**) *(in tag questions)* **it's lovely, isn't it?** es bonito, ¿no?; **you're happy, aren't you?** estás contento, ¿verdad? **he's not very clever, is he?** no es muy listo, ¿verdad?

(**g**) *(unreal conditions)* **if I was/were you ...** yo en tu lugar ...; **if you were a millionaire ...** si fueras millonario ...

(**h**) *pres & past perfect (visit, go)* estar, ir; **I've been to Paris** he estado en París

beach [biːtʃ] **1** *n* playa *f*

2 *vt* varar

beacon [ˈbiːkən] *n* (**a**) *Av & Naut* baliza *f* (**b**) *(lighthouse)* faro *m*

bead [biːd] *n* (**a**) *(of necklace etc)* cuenta *f*; **glass b.** abalorio *m* (**b**) *(of liquid)* gota *f*

beady [ˈbiːdɪ] *adj* (**beadier, beadiest**) *(eyes)* pequeños y brillantes

beagle [ˈbiːgəl] *n* beagle *m*

beak [biːk] *n* (**a**) *(of bird)* pico *m* (**b**) *Fam (nose)* nariz ganchuda

beaker [ˈbiːkə(r)] *n* *(tumbler)* taza alta, jarra *f*

beam [biːm] **1** *n* (**a**) *Archit* viga *f* (**b**) *(of light)* rayo *m*; *Phys* haz *m* (**c**) *(in gymnastics)* barra fija (**d**) *(smile)* sonrisa *f* radiante

2 *vi* (**a**) *(sun)* brillar (**b**) *(smile)* sonreír

3 *vt* (**a**) *(broadcast)* difundir, emitir (**b**) *(transmit)* transmitir

beaming [ˈbiːmɪŋ] *adj (smiling)* radiante

bean [biːn] *n* alubia *f*, judía *f*, *Andes, CAm, Carib, Méx* frijol *m*, *RP* poroto *m*; *Fam* **to spill the beans** descubrir el pastel; **baked beans** = alubias cocidas en salsa de tomate; **broad b.** haba *f*; **butter b.** judía blanca, *Andes, CAm, Carib, Méx* frijol blanco, *RP* poroto de manteca; **coffee b.**

grano *m* de café; **green/runner b.** judía verde, *Bol, RP* chaucha *f*, *CAm* ejote *m*, *Col, Cuba* habichuela *f*, *Chile* poroto verde, *Ven* vainita *f*; **haricot b.** alubia; **kidney b.** frijol

beansprout ['biːnspraʊt] *n* brote *m* de soja

bear¹ [beə(r)] (*pt* **bore**; *pp* **borne**) **1** *vt* (a) (*carry*) llevar
(b) (*support*) sostener
(c) (*endure*) soportar, aguantar; **I can't b. him** no lo soporto
(d) (*fruit*) dar; *Fin (interest)* devengar
(e) **to b. a resemblance to** parecerse a
(f) **to b. a grudge against sb** guardar rencor a algn; **to b. in mind** tener presente
(g) **to b. witness** atestiguar
(h) (*pt* **born** passive only, *not followed by* **by**) (*give birth to*) dar a luz; **he was born in Wakefield** nació en Wakefield
2 *vi* (*turn*) girar, torcer; **to b. left** girar a la izquierda
▸ **bear down** *vi* (*approach*) correr (**on** sobre)
▸ **bear out** *vt sep* (*confirm*) confirmar
▸ **bear up** *vi* (*endure*) resistir
▸ **bear with** *vt insep* tener paciencia con

bear² [beə(r)] *n* (a) oso *m*; **b. cub** osezno *m*; *Astron* **Great B.** Osa *f* Mayor; **Little B.** Osa Menor (b) *Fin* bajista *mf*

beard [bɪəd] *n* barba *f*

bearer ['beərə(r)] *n* portador(a) *m,f*; (*of passport, office*) titular *mf*

bearing ['beərɪŋ] *n* (a) (*posture*) porte *m* (b) (*relevance*) relación *f*; **to have a b. on** estar relacionado(a) con (c)*Tech* cojinete *m* (d) *Naut* **bearings** posición *f*, orientación *f*; **to get one's bearings** orientarse; **to lose one's bearings** desorientarse

beast [biːst] *n* (a) bestia *f*; **b. of burden** bestia de carga (b) *Fig* bestia *f*, bruto *m* (c) **beasts** (*cattle*) reses *fpl*

beastly ['biːstlɪ] *adj* (**beastlier, beastliest**) *Fam* asqueroso(a)

beat [biːt] **1** *vt* (*pt* **beat**; *pp* **beaten** ['biːtən]) (a) (*hit*) pegar, golpear; (*clothes*) sacudir; (*drum*) tocar; **off the beaten track** en un lugar muy apartado; *Fam* **b. it!** ¡lárgate!
(b) *Culin* batir
(c) (*defeat*) batir, vencer; **we b. them 5–2** les ganamos 5 a 2
(d) **to b. a retreat** batirse en retirada
(e) *Mus (time)* marcar
(f) **to b. the traffic** evitar los embotellamientos de tráfico
(g) *Fam (puzzle)* extrañar; **it beats me** no lo entiendo
2 *vi* (a) (*heart*) latir
(b) (*strike*) dar golpes; *Fig* **to b. about the bush** andarse por las ramas
3 *n* (a) (*of heart*) latido *m*
(b) *Mus* ritmo *m*, compás *m*
(c) (*of policeman*) ronda *f*
4 *adj Fam (exhausted)* agotado(a)
▸ **beat down** *vi* (*sun*) apretar
▸ **beat off** *vt sep* rechazar
▸ **beat up** *vt sep Fam* dar una paliza a

beating ['biːtɪŋ] *n* (a) (*thrashing*) paliza *f* (b) (*defeat*) derrota *f* (c) (*of drum*) toque *m* (d) (*of heart*) latido *m*

beautician [bjuːˈtɪʃən] *n* esteticista *mf*

beautiful ['bjuːtɪfəl] *adj* hermoso(a), bello(a); (*delicious*) delicioso(a); **b. people** gente guapa

beauty ['bjuːtɪ] *n* belleza *f*, hermosura *f*; **b. contest** concurso *m* de belleza; **b. queen** miss *f*; **b. salon** salón *m* de belleza; **b. spot** (*on face*) lunar *m*; (*place*) lugar pintoresco

beaver ['biːvə(r)] **1** *n* castor *m*
2 *vi* **to b. away at sth** meterse de lleno en algo

became [bɪˈkeɪm] *pt of* **become**

because [bɪˈkɒz] **1** *conj* porque
2 *prep* **b. of** a causa de, debido a

beckon ['bekən] *vt & vi* llamar (con la mano); **to b. to sb** llamar a algn con señas

become [bɪˈkʌm] **1** *vi* (*pt* **became**; *pp* **become**) (*a teacher, doctor*) hacerse; (*boring, jealous, suspicious*) volverse; (*old, difficult, stronger*) hacerse; (*happy, sad, thin*) ponerse; **to b. angry/interested** enfadarse/interesarse; **what will b. of him?** ¿qué va a ser de él?
2 *vt Fml (of clothes, colour)* sentar bien a

becoming [bɪˈkʌmɪŋ] *adj* (a) (*dress*) favorecedor(a) (b) (*behaviour*) conveniente, apropiado(a)

bed [bed] *n* (a) cama *f*; **to get out of b.** levantarse de la cama; **to go to b.** acostarse; **to make the b.** hacer la cama; *Br* **b. and breakfast** (*service*) cama y desayuno *m*; (*sign*) pensión; **b. linen** ropa *f* de cama (b) (*of river*) lecho *m*; (*of sea*) fondo *m* (c) *Geol* capa *f* (d) (**flower) b.** arriate *m*

bedbug ['bedbʌg] *n* chinche *f*

bedclothes ['bedkləʊðz] *npl*, **bedding** ['bedɪŋ] *n* ropa *f* de cama

bedlam ['bedləm] *n* algarabía *f*, alboroto *m*

bedraggled [bɪˈdrægəld] *adj* (*wet*) mojado(a); (*dirty*) ensuciado(a)

bedridden ['bedrɪdən] *adj* postrado(a) en cama

bedroom ['bedru:m] *n* dormitorio *m*

bedside ['bedsaɪd] *n* **at sb's b.** junto a la cama de algn; **b. table** mesilla *f* de noche

bedsit ['bedsɪt] *n Fam*, **bedsitter** [bed'sɪtə(r)] *n* estudio *m*

bedspread ['bedspred] *n* colcha *f*

bedtime ['bedtaɪm] *n* hora *f* de acostarse

bee [bi:] *n* abeja *f*

beech [bi:tʃ] *n* haya *f*

beef [bi:f] *n* carne *f* de vaca, *Méx* carne de res; **roast b.** rosbif *m*
▶ **beef up** *vt sep Fam* reforzar

beefburger ['bi:fbɜ:gə(r)] *n* hamburguesa *f*

beefsteak ['bi:fsteɪk] *n* bistec *m*

beehive ['bi:haɪv] *n* colmena *f*

beeline ['bi:laɪn] *n Fam* **to make a b. for sth** ir directo hacia algo

been [bi:n, bɪn] *pp of* **be**

beep [bi:p] *n (of apparatus)* pitido *m; (of horn)* pito *m*

beer [bɪə(r)] *n* cerveza *f*; **a glass of b.** una caña

beet [bi:t] *n US* remolacha *f*, *Andes* betarraga *f*, *Méx* betabel *f*; *US* **red b.** remolacha

beetle ['bi:təl] *n* escarabajo *m*

beetroot ['bi:tru:t] *n Br* remolacha *f*, *Andes* betarraga *f*, *Méx* betabel *f*

befit [bɪ'fɪt] *vt* convenir a, corresponder a

before [bɪ'fɔ:(r)] **1** *conj* **(a)** *(earlier than)* antes de que (+ *subj*) antes de (+ *infin*); **b. she goes** antes de que se vaya; **b. leaving** antes de salir **(b)** *(rather than)* antes que (+ *infin*)
2 *prep* **(a)** *(place)* delante de; *(in the presence of)* ante **(b)** *(order, time)* antes de; **b. Christ** antes de Cristo; **b. long** dentro de poco; **b. 1950** antes de 1950; **I saw it b. you** lo vi antes que tú
3 *adv* **(a)** *(time)* antes; **I have met him b.** ya lo conozco; **not long b.** poco antes; **the night b.** la noche anterior **(b)** *(place)* delante, por delante

beforehand [bɪ'fɔ:hænd] *adv* **(a)** *(earlier)* antes **(b)** *(in advance)* de antemano, con anticipación

befriend [bɪ'frend] *vt* trabar amistad con

beg [beg] **1** *vt* **(a)** *(money etc)* pedir **(b)** *(beseech)* rogar, suplicar; **I b. your pardon!** ¡perdone usted!; **I b. your pardon?** ¿cómo ha dicho usted?
2 *vi* **(a)** *(solicit)* mendigar; *(dog)* pedir; **to b. for money** pedir limosna **(b)** **to b.**

for help/mercy *(beseech)* implorar ayuda/compasión

began [bɪ'gæn] *pt of* **begin**

beggar ['begə(r)] *n* **(a)** mendigo(a) *m,f* **(b)** *Fam Euph (chap)* tío *m*

begin [bɪ'gɪn] *vt & vi (pt* **began***; pp* **begun***)* empezar, comenzar; **to b. again** volver a empezar; **to b. at the beginning** empezar por el principio; **to b. doing** or **to do sth** empezar a hacer algo; **to b. with ...** *(initially)* para empezar ...

beginner [bɪ'gɪnə(r)] *n* principiante *mf*

beginning [bɪ'gɪnɪŋ] *n* **(a)** principio *m*, comienzo *m*; **at the b. of May** a principios de mayo; **from the b.** desde el principio; **in the b.** al principio **(b)** *(origin)* origen *m*

begonia [bɪ'gəʊnɪə] *n* begonia *f*

begrudge [bɪ'grʌdʒ] *vt* dar de mala gana; *(envy)* envidiar

beguile [bɪ'gaɪl] *vt (charm)* seducir

begun [bɪ'gʌn] *pp of* **begin**

behalf [bɪ'hɑ:f] *n* **on b. of**, *US* **in b. of** en nombre de, de parte de; **don't worry on my b.** no te preocupes por mí

behave [bɪ'heɪv] *vi* **(a)** *(person)* portarse, comportarse; **b. yourself!** ¡pórtate bien!; **to b. well/badly** portarse bien/mal **(b)** *(machine)* funcionar

behaviour, *US* **behavior** [bɪ'heɪvjə(r)] *n* **(a)** *(of person)* comportamiento *m*, conducta *f* **(b)** *(of machine)* funcionamiento *m*

behead [bɪ'hed] *vt* decapitar

beheld [bɪ'held] *pt & pp of* **behold**

behind [bɪ'haɪnd] **1** *prep* **(a)** detrás de; **b. sb's back** a espaldas de algn; **b. the scenes** entre bastidores; **to be b. sb** apoyar a algn; **what motive was there b. the crime?** ¿cuál fue el móvil del crimen? **(b)** **b. the times** *(less advanced than)* anticuado(a)
2 *adv* **(a)** *(in the rear)* detrás, atrás; **I've left my umbrella b.** se me ha olvidado el paraguas **(b)** **to be b. with one's payments** *(late)* estar atrasado(a) en los pagos
3 *n Fam* trasero *m*

behold [bɪ'həʊld] *vt (pt & pp* **beheld***) Literary* contemplar

beige [beɪʒ] *adj & n* beige *(m)*

being ['bi:ɪŋ] *n* **(a)** ser *m* **(b)** *(existence)* existencia *f*; **to come into b.** nacer

Belarus [belə'ru:s] *n* Bielorrusia

belated [bɪ'leɪtɪd] *adj* tardío(a)

belch [beltʃ] **1** *vi (person)* eructar
2 *vt (smoke, flames)* vomitar, arrojar
3 *n* eructo *m*

beleaguered [bɪ'liːgəd] *adj* asediado(a)

belfry ['belfrɪ] *n* campanario *m*

Belgian ['beldʒən] *adj & n* belga *(mf)*

Belgium ['beldʒəm] *n* Bélgica

Belgrade [bel'greɪd] *n* Belgrado

belie [bɪ'laɪ] *vt* desmentir

belief [bɪ'liːf] *n* (**a**) creencia *f*; **beyond b.** increíble (**b**) *(opinion)* opinión *f* (**c**) *(faith)* fe *f* (**d**) *(confidence)* confianza *f* (in en)

believe [bɪ'liːv] **1** *vi* (**a**) *(have faith)* creer (**b**) **to b. in** *(be in favour of)* ser partidario(a) de (**c**) *(think)* creer; **I b. so** creo que sí
  2 *vt* creer

believer [bɪ'liːvə(r)] *n* (**a**) *Rel* creyente *mf* (**b**) partidario(a) *m,f* (**in** de)

belittle [bɪ'lɪtəl] *vt* *(person)* menospreciar; *(problem)* minimizar

bell [bel] *n* *(of church)* campana *f*; *(small)* campanilla *f*; *(of school, door, bicycle etc)* timbre *m*; *(on cat)* cascabel *m*; *(on cow)* cencerro *m*; *Fig* **that rings a b.** eso me suena; **b. jar** campana; **b. tower** campanario *m*

bell-bottoms ['belbɒtəmz] *npl* pantalones *mpl* de campana

bellboy ['belbɔɪ], *US* **bellhop** ['belhɒp] *n* botones *m inv*

belligerent [bɪ'lɪdʒərənt] *adj* agresivo(a)

bellow ['beləʊ] *vi* *(bull)* bramar; *(person)* rugir

bellows ['beləʊz] *npl* **(pair of) b.** fuelle *m*

belly ['belɪ] *n* (**a**) *(of person)* barriga *f*; **b. flop** panzazo *m* (**b**) *(of animal)* panza *f*

bellyache ['belɪeɪk] *n* *Fam* dolor *m* de vientre

belong [bɪ'lɒŋ] *vi* (**a**) pertenecer (**to** a) (**b**) *(be a member)* ser socio(a) (**to** de); *Pol* **to b. to a party** ser miembro de un partido (**c**) *(have a proper place)* corresponder; **this chair belongs here** esta silla va aquí

belongings [bɪ'lɒŋɪŋz] *npl* efectos *mpl* personales

beloved [bɪ'lʌvɪd, bɪ'lʌvd] **1** *adj* amado(a), querido(a)
  2 *n* amado(a) *m,f*

below [bɪ'ləʊ] **1** *prep* debajo de; **b. average** por debajo de la media; **10 degrees b. zero** 10 grados bajo cero
  2 *adv* abajo; **above and b.** arriba y abajo; **see b.** véase más abajo

belt [belt] **1** *n* (**a**) cinturón *m*; **blow below the b.** golpe bajo (**b**) *Tech* correa *f*, cinta *f* (**c**) *(area)* zona *f*
  2 *vt* *Fam* pegar una paliza a
  ▶ **belt along** *vi* *Fam* ir a todo gas

▶ **belt out** *vt sep* *Fam* *(song)* cantar a voz en grito

▶ **belt up** *vi* *Fam* callarse

beltway ['beltweɪ] *n* *US* carretera *f* de circunvalación

bemused [bɪ'mjuːzd] *adj* perplejo(a)

bench [bentʃ] *n* (**a**) *(seat)* banco *m* (**b**) *(in parliament)* escaño *m* (**c**) *Jur* **the b.** *(judges)* la magistratura (**d**) *Sport* banquillo *m* (**e**) **b. mark** *Geol* cota *f* de referencia; *Fig* punto *m* de referencia

bend [bend] **1** *vt* *(pt & pp* **bent**) doblar; *(back)* encorvar; *(head)* inclinar; *Fam* **to b. the rules** hacer una excepción
  2 *vi* (**a**) doblarse; *(road)* torcerse (**b**) **to b. (over)** inclinarse; *Fam* **he bends over backwards to please her** hace lo imposible por complacerla
  3 *n* *(in river, road)* curva *f*; *(in pipe)* recodo *m*; *Br Fam* **round the b.** loco(a) perdido(a)
  ▶ **bend down** *vi* inclinarse

beneath [bɪ'niːθ] **1** *prep* *(below)* bajo, debajo de; *Fig* **it's b. him** es indigno de él
  2 *adv* debajo

benefactor ['benɪfæktə(r)] *n* bienhechor(a) *m,f*

beneficial [benɪ'fɪʃəl] *adj* (**a**) *(doing good)* benéfico(a) (**b**) *(advantageous)* beneficioso(a)

beneficiary [benɪ'fɪʃərɪ] *n* beneficiario(a) *m,f*

benefit ['benɪfɪt] **1** *vt* beneficiar
  2 *vi* sacar provecho (**from** *or* **by** de)
  3 *n* (**a**) *(advantage)* beneficio *m*, provecho *m*; **for the b. of** en beneficio de; **I did it for your b.** lo hice por tu bien (**b**) *(allowance)* subsidio *m*; **unemployment b.** subsidio de desempleo (**c**) *(event)* función benéfica

benevolent [bɪ'nevələnt] *adj* benévolo(a)

Bengal [beŋ'gɔːl] *n* Bengala

benign [bɪ'naɪn] *adj* benigno(a)

bent [bent] **1** *adj* (**a**) *(curved)* curvado(a) (**b**) **to be b. on doing sth** *(determined)* estar empeñado(a) en hacer algo (**c**) *Fam* *(corrupt)* deshonesto(a) (**d**) *very Fam* *(homosexual)* gay (**e**) *pt & pp of* **bend**
  2 *n* *(inclination)* inclinación *f* (**towards** hacia)

benzine ['benziːn] *n* *Chem* bencina *f*

bequeath [bɪ'kwiːð] *vt* *Jur* legar

bequest [bɪ'kwest] *n* *Jur* legado *m*

bereaved [bɪ'riːvd] *npl* **the b.** los familiares del/de un difunto

bereavement [bɪ'riːvmənt] *n* *(mourning)* duelo *m*

bereft [bɪˈreft] *adj* **b. of** privado(a) de
beret [ˈbereɪ] *n* boina *f*
Berlin [bɜːˈlɪn] *n* Berlín
Bermuda [bəˈmjuːdə] *n* las (Islas) Bermudas; **B. shorts** bermudas *fpl*
Ber ˙ [bɜːn] *n* Berna
ber y [ˈberɪ] *n* baya *f*
berserk [bəˈsɜːk, bəˈzɜːk] *adj* **to go b.** volverse loco(a)
berth [bɜːθ] *Naut* **1** *n* (a) *(mooring)* amarradero *m*; *Fig* **to give sb a wide b.** evitar a algn (b) *(bed)* litera *f*
   2 *vi* atracar
beseech [bɪˈsiːtʃ] *vt* *(pt & pp besought or beseeched)* suplicar, implorar
beset [bɪˈset] *vt* *(pt & pp beset)* acosar; **it is b. with dangers** está plagado de peligros
beside [bɪˈsaɪd] *prep* (a) *(next to)* al lado de, junto a (b) *(compared with)* comparado con (c) **he was b. himself with joy** estaba loco de alegría; **that's b. the point** eso no viene al caso; **to be b. oneself** estar fuera de sí
besides [bɪˈsaɪdz] **1** *prep* (a) *(in addition to)* además de (b) *(except)* excepto, menos; **no one b. me** nadie más que yo
   2 *adv* además
besiege [bɪˈsiːdʒ] *vt* *(city)* sitiar; *Fig* asediar
besought [bɪˈsɔːt] *pt & pp of* **beseech**
best [best] **1** *adj* *(superl of good)* mejor; **b. man** ≃ padrino *m* de boda; **her b. friend** su mejor amiga; **the b. thing would be to phone them** lo mejor sería llamarles; **we had to wait the b. part of a year** tuvimos que esperar casi un año; **with b. wishes from Mary** *(in letter)* con mis mejores deseos, Mary
   2 *adv* *(superl of well)* mejor; **as b. I can** lo mejor que pueda; **I like this one b.** éste es el que más me gusta; **the world's b. dressed man** el hombre mejor vestido del mundo
   3 *n* the b. el/la/lo mejor; **all the b.!** ¡que te vaya bien!; **at b.** a lo más; **to be at one's b.** estar en plena forma; **to do one's b.** hacer todo lo posible; **to make the b. of sth** sacar el mejor partido de algo; **to the b. of my knowledge** que yo sepa
bestiality [bestɪˈælɪtɪ] *n* bestialidad *f*
bestow [bɪˈstəʊ] *vt* *(favour etc)* conceder; *(honours, power)* otorgar (on a); *(title etc)* conferir (on a)
best-seller [bestˈselə(r)] *n* best-seller *m*
best-selling [ˈbestselɪŋ] *adj* **a b. author** un autor de superventas
bet [bet] **1** *n* apuesta *f*

2 *vt* *(pt bet or betted)* ap< star
3 *vi* apostar (on por); *Fam* **you b.!** ¡y tanto!
Bethlehem [ˈbeθlɪhem] *n* Belén
betray [bɪˈtreɪ] *vt* (a) traicionar (b) *(be unfaithful to)* engañar (c) *(reveal)* revelar
betrayal [bɪˈtreɪəl] *n* traición *f*
better [ˈbetə(r)] **1** *adj* (a) *(comp of good)* mejor; **that's b.!** ¡así está mejor!; **the weather is b. than last week** hace mejor tiempo que la semana pasada; **to be no b. than ...** no ser más que ...; **to get b.** mejorar
   (b) *(healthier)* mejor (de salud)
   (c) **b. off** *(better)* mejor; *(richer)* más rico(a); **you'd be b. off going home** lo mejor es que te vayas a casa
   (d) **the b. part of the day** la mayor parte del día
   2 *adv* *(comp of well)* (a) mejor; **all the b., so much the b.** tanto mejor; **b. and b.** cada vez mejor; *Prov* **b. late than never** más vale tarde que nunca
   (b) **we had b. leave** más vale que nos vayamos
   (c) **to think b. of** *(plan)* cambiar de
   3 *n* mejor; **a change for the b.** una mejora; **to get the b. of sb** vencer a algn
   4 *vt* (a) *(improve)* mejorar
   (b) *(surpass)* superar
betting [ˈbetɪŋ] *n* apuestas *fpl*; *Br* **b. shop** quiosco *m* de apuestas
between [bɪˈtwiːn] **1** *prep* entre; **b. you and me** entre nosotros; **closed b. one and two** cerrado de una a dos
   2 *adv* **in b.** *(position)* en medio; *(time)* entretanto, mientras (tanto)
beverage [ˈbevərɪdʒ] *n* bebida *f*
bevy [ˈbevɪ] *n* bandada *f*
beware [bɪˈweə(r)] *vi* tener cuidado (of con); **b.!** ¡cuidado!; **b. of the dog** *(sign)* cuidado con el perro
bewildered [bɪˈwɪldəd] *adj* desconcertado(a)
bewilderment [bɪˈwɪldəmənt] *n* desconcierto *m*
bewitching [bɪˈwɪtʃɪŋ] *adj* fascinador(a)
beyond [bɪˈjɒnd] **1** *prep* más allá de; **b. belief** increíble; **b. doubt** sin lugar a dudas; **it is b. me why ...** no comprendo por qué ...; **it's b. a joke** eso ya no tiene gracia; **she is b. caring** ya no le importa; **this task is b. me** no puedo con esta tarea
   2 *adv* más allá, más lejos
bias [ˈbaɪəs] *n* *(tendency)* tendencia *f* (towards hacia); *(prejudice)* prejuicio *m*
bias(s)ed [ˈbaɪəst] *adj* parcial; **to be b.**

against sth/sb tener prejuicio en contra de algo/algn

bib [bɪb] n (for baby) babero m; (of apron) peto m

Bible ['baɪbəl] n Biblia f; Fam **B. basher, B. thumper** evangelista mf

bibliography [bɪblɪ'ɒɡrəfɪ] n bibliografía f

bicarbonate [baɪ'kɑːbənɪt] n bicarbonato m; **b. of soda** bicarbonato sódico

bicentenary [baɪsen'tiːnərɪ], US **bicentennial** [baɪsen'tenɪəl] n bicentenario m

biceps ['baɪseps] n bíceps m

bicker ['bɪkə(r)] vi reñir

bicycle ['baɪsɪkəl] n bicicleta f; **b. pump** bomba f (de aire); **to go by b.** ir en bicicleta

bid [bɪd] **1** vt (pt bid or bade; pp bid or bidden ['bɪdən]) (a) (say) decir; **to b. sb farewell** despedirse de algn (b) (command) mandar, ordenar; **she bade him be quiet** le mandó que se callase (c) (invite) invitar; **he bade me sit down me** invitó a sentarme (d) (at auction) (pt & pp bid) pujar

2 vi (pt & pp bid) (at auction) pujar (for por)

3 n (a) (offer) oferta f (b) (at auction) puja f (c) (attempt) intento m, tentativa f

bidder ['bɪdə(r)] n **the highest b.** el mejor postor

bidding ['bɪdɪŋ] n (a) (at auction) puja f (b) (order) orden f; **to do sb's b.** cumplir la orden de algn

bide [baɪd] vt (pt bided or bode; pp bided) esperar; **to b. one's time** esperar el momento oportuno

bidet ['biːdeɪ] n bidé m

bifocal [baɪ'fəʊkəl] **1** adj bifocal
2 npl **bifocals** lentes fpl bifocales

big [bɪɡ] **1** adj grande (gran before singular noun); **a b. clock** un reloj grande; **a b. surprise** una gran sorpresa; **my b. brother** mi hermano mayor; Fam Ironic **b. deal!** ¿y qué?; **b. business** los grandes negocios; **b. dipper** montaña rusa; US Astron **B. Dipper** Osa f Mayor; **b. toe** dedo gordo del pie; Fam **b. gun, b. shot** pez gordo; Fam **to make the b. time** tener éxito; Fam **b. top** carpa f

2 adv (a) (on a grand scale) a lo grande (b) (well) de manera excepcional

bigamy ['bɪɡəmɪ] n bigamia f

bighead ['bɪɡhed] n Fam creído(a) m,f, engreído(a) m,f

bigheaded [bɪɡ'hedɪd] adj creído(a), engreído(a)

bigot ['bɪɡət] n intolerante mf

✐ Note that the Spanish word **bigote** is a false friend and is never a translation for the English word **bigot**. In Spanish, **bigote** means "moustache".

bigoted ['bɪɡətɪd] adj intolerante

bigotry ['bɪɡətrɪ] n intolerancia f

bigwig ['bɪɡwɪɡ] n Fam pez gordo

bike [baɪk] n Fam (cycle) bici f, (motorbike) (bicycle) bici f; (motorcycle) moto f; **on your b.!** ¡vete de aquí!

bikini [bɪ'kiːnɪ] n bikini m

bilateral [baɪ'lætərəl] adj bilateral

bile [baɪl] n bilis f

bilingual [baɪ'lɪŋɡwəl] adj bilingüe

Bill [bɪl] n Br Fam **the Old B.** la poli

bill[1] [bɪl] **1** n (a) (for gas etc) factura f, recibo m (b) esp Br (in restaurant) cuenta f (c) Parl proyecto m de ley (d) US (banknote) billete m de banco (e) (poster) cartel m; **on the b.** en cartel; **post no bills** (sign) prohibido fijar carteles; Th **to top the b.** encabezar el reparto; **b. of exchange** letra f de cambio; Pol **B. of Rights** declaración f de derechos

2 vt (a) (send bill to) facturar (b) Th programar

bill[2] [bɪl] n (of bird) pico m

billboard ['bɪlbɔːd] n (hoarding) cartelera f

billet ['bɪlɪt] **1** n alojamiento m
2 vt alojar

billfold ['bɪlfəʊld] n US cartera f, billetero m

billiards ['bɪljədz] n sing billar m

billion ['bɪljən] n US mil millones mpl; Br Old-fashioned billón m

billionaire [bɪljə'neə(r)] n multimillonario(a) m,f

billow ['bɪləʊ] **1** n (of water) ola f; (of smoke) nube f
2 vi (sea) ondear; (sail) hincharse

billy goat ['bɪlɪɡəʊt] n macho cabrío

bin [bɪn] n (for storage) cajón m; **bread b.** panera f; (rubbish) **b.** cubo m de la basura

binary ['baɪnərɪ] adj **b. number** número binario

bind [baɪnd] vt (pt & pp bound) (a) (tie up) atar (b) Med (bandage) vendar (c) (book) encuadernar (d) (require) obligar (e) (join etc) unir
▸ **bind over** vt sep Jur obligar legalmente

binder ['baɪndə(r)] n (file) carpeta f

binding ['baɪndɪŋ] adj (promise) comprometedor(a); (contract) vinculante

binge [bɪndʒ] n Fam borrachera f; **to go on a b.** irse de juerga

bingo ['bɪŋɡəʊ] n bingo m

binoculars [bɪ'nɒkjʊləz] *npl* prismáticos *mpl*, gemelos *mpl*

biochemistry [baɪəʊ'kemɪstrɪ] *n* bioquímica *f*

biodegradable [baɪəʊdɪ'greɪdəbəl] *adj* biodegradable

biography [baɪ'ɒgrəfɪ] *n* biografía *f*

biological [baɪə'lɒdʒɪkəl] *adj* biológico(a); **b. warfare** guerra biológica

biologist [baɪ'ɒlədʒɪst] *n* biólogo(a) *m,f*

biology [baɪ'ɒlədʒɪ] *n* biología *f*

biorhythm ['baɪəʊrɪðəm] *n* biorritmo *m*

biosphere ['baɪəsfɪə(r)] *n* biosfera *f*

birch [bɜːtʃ] **1** *n* (**a**) *Bot* abedul *m* (**b**) *(rod)* vara *f* (de abedul)
2 *vt* azotar

bird [bɜːd] *n* (**a**) pájaro *m*, ave *f*; *Fig* **to kill two birds with one stone** matar dos pájaros de un tiro; **they're birds of a feather** son tal para cual; **b. of prey** ave de rapiña (**b**) *Br Fam (girl)* tía *f*, chica *f*

birdcage ['bɜːdkeɪdʒ] *n* jaula *f*

birdie ['bɜːdɪ] *n (in golf)* birdie *m*

bird's-eye view [bɜːdzaɪ'vjuː] *n* vista *f* de pájaro

bird-watcher ['bɜːdwɒtʃə(r)] *n* ornitólogo(a) *m,f*

Biro® ['baɪrəʊ] *n Fam* boli *m*

birth [bɜːθ] *n* (**a**) nacimiento *m*; *(childbirth)* parto *m*; **by b.** de nacimiento; **to give b. to a child** dar a luz a un niño; **to b. certificate** partida *f* de nacimiento; **b. control** *(family planning)* control *m* de la natalidad; *(contraception)* métodos anticonceptivos; **b. rate** índice *m* de natalidad (**b**) *(parentage)* de noble **b.** *(parentage)* de noble linaje

birthday ['bɜːθdeɪ] *n* cumpleaños *m inv*

birthmark ['bɜːθmɑːk] *n* antojo *m*

birthplace ['bɜːθpleɪs] *n* lugar *m* de nacimiento

Biscay ['bɪskeɪ] *n* Vizcaya *f*; **the Bay of B.** el golfo de Vizcaya

biscuit ['bɪskɪt] *n* (**a**) *Br (sweet, salted)* galleta *f*; *Fam* **that really takes the b.!** ¡eso ya es el colmo! (**b**) *US (savoury)* bollo *m*, bizcocho *m*

bisect [baɪ'sekt] *vt* bisegmentar; *Geom* bisecar

bisexual [baɪ'seksjʊəl] *adj* bisexual

bishop ['bɪʃəp] *n* (**a**) *Rel* obispo *m* (**b**) *(in chess)* alfil *m*

bison ['baɪsən] *n inv* bisonte *m*

bit¹ [bɪt] *n* (**a**) *(small piece)* trozo *m*, pedazo *m*; **to smash sth to bits** hacer añicos algo; *Fig* **thrilled to bits** muy emocionado(a); *Fig* **to do one's b.** poner de su parte (**b**) *(small quantity)* poco *m*; a

b. of sugar un poco de azúcar; **a b. of advice** un consejo; **a b. of news** una noticia; **bits and pieces** trastos *mpl*; **b. by b.** poco a poco (**c**) **a b.** *(slightly)* un poco; **a b. longer** un ratito más; **a b. worried** un poco preocupado (**d**) *(coin)* moneda *f*

bit² [bɪt] *n (of tool)* broca *f*

bit³ [bɪt] *n Comput* bit *m*

bit⁴ [bɪt] *pt of* **bite**

bitch [bɪtʃ] **1** *n* (**a**) *Zool (female)* hembra *f*; *(dog)* perra *f* (**b**) *Fam (spiteful woman)* bruja *f*
2 *vi Fam* **to b. (about)** *(criticize)* criticar

bitchy ['bɪtʃɪ] *adj Fam (spiteful)* maldiciente; *(malicious)* malicioso(a); *(malevolent)* malintencionado(a)

bite [baɪt] **1** *n* (**a**) *(act)* mordisco *m* (**b**) *(wound)* mordedura *f*; **(insect)** b. picadura *f* (**c**) *(mouthful)* bocado *m* (**d**) *Fam (snack)* bocado *m*
2 *vt* (*pt* **bit**; *pp* **bitten**) morder; *(insect)* picar; **to b. one's nails** morderse las uñas; *Fig* **to b. the dust** *(suffer defeat)* morder el polvo; *(die)* palmarla; *Fam* **to b. sb's head off** echarle una bronca a algn
3 *vi* (**a**) morder; *(insect)* picar (**b**) *Fig (take effect)* surtir efecto (**c**) *(fish)* picar

biting ['baɪtɪŋ] *adj (wind)* cortante; *Fig (criticism)* mordaz

bitten ['bɪtən] *pp of* **bite**

bitter ['bɪtə(r)] **1** *adj* (**a**) amargo(a) (**b**) *(weather)* glacial; *(wind)* cortante (**c**) *(person)* amargado(a) (**d**) *(struggle)* enconado(a); *(hatred)* implacable
2 *n* (**a**) *(beer)* cerveza amarga (**b**) **bitters** bíter *m*

bitterly ['bɪtəlɪ] *adv* **she was b. disappointed** sufrió una terrible decepción

bitterness ['bɪtənɪs] *n* (**a**) amargura *f* (**b**) *(of weather)* crudeza *f* (**c**) *(of person)* rencor *m*

bittersweet [bɪtə'swiːt] *adj* agridulce

bitumen ['bɪtjʊmɪn] *n* betún *m*

bizarre [bɪ'zɑː(r)] *adj (odd)* extraño(a); *(eccentric)* estrafalario(a)

blab [blæb] *vi Fam* parlotear; *(let out a secret)* chivarse

black [blæk] **1** *adj* (**a**) *(colour)* negro(a); **a b. and white television** un televisor en blanco y negro; *Fig* **b. and blue** amoratado(a); **to put sth down in b. and white** poner algo por escrito; *Av* **b. box** caja negra; **b. coffee** café solo; **b. eye** ojo morado; **b. hole** agujero negro; **b. humour** humor negro; **b. magic** magia negra; **b. market** mercado negro; *Br* **b. pudding** morcilla *f*; **the B. Sea** el Mar

Negro; *Aut* **b. spot** punto negro; *Br* **the B. Country** = la región de los Midlands; *Fig* **b. sheep** oveja negra

(**b**) *(gloomy)* negro(a); *Fig* **a b. day** un día aciago

2 *n* (**a**) *(colour)* negro *m*

(**b**) *(person)* negro(a) *m,f*

3 *vt* (**a**) *(make black)* ennegrecer

(**b**) *(polish)* lustrar

(**c**) *(boycott)* boicotear

▸ **black out 1** *vt sep* (**a**) *(extinguish lights in)* apagar las luces de (**b**) *(censor)* censurar

2 *vi (faint)* desmayarse

blackberry ['blækbəri] *n* zarzamora *f*

blackbird ['blækbɜːd] *n* mirlo *m*

blackboard ['blækbɔːd] *n* pizarra *f*, encerado *m*

blackcurrant [blæk'kʌrənt] *n* grosella negra

blacken ['blækən] *vt* (**a**) *(make black)* ennegrecer (**b**) *Fig (defame)* manchar

blackhead ['blækhed] *n* espinilla *f*

blackjack ['blækdʒæk] *n Cards* veintiuna *f*

blackleg ['blækleg] *n* esquirol *m*

blacklist ['blæklɪst] *n* lista negra

blackmail ['blækmeɪl] **1** *n* chantaje *m*

2 *vt* chantajear

blackout ['blækaʊt] *n* (**a**) *(of lights)* apagón *m* (**b**) *Rad & TV* censura *f* (**c**) *(fainting)* pérdida *f* de conocimiento

blacksmith ['blæksmɪθ] *n* herrero *m*

bladder ['blædə(r)] *n* vejiga *f*; **gall b.** vesícula *f* biliar

blade [bleɪd] *n* (**a**) *(of grass)* brizna *f* (**b**) *(of knife etc)* hoja *f* (**c**) *(of propeller, oar)* pala *f*

blame [bleɪm] **1** *n* culpa *f*; **to take the b. for sth** asumir la responsabilidad de algo

2 *vt* echar la culpa a; **he is to b.** él tiene la culpa

blameless ['bleɪmlɪs] *adj (person)* inocente; *(conduct)* intachable

blancmange [blə'mɒnʒ] *n* = tipo de budín blanco

bland [blænd] *adj (food)* soso(a)

> 🖉 Note that the Spanish word **blando** is a false friend and is never a translation for the English word **bland**. In Spanish, **blando** means "soft".

blank [blæŋk] **1** *adj* (**a**) *(without writing)* en blanco; *Fin* **b. cheque** cheque *m* en blanco (**b**) *(empty)* vacío(a); **a. b. look** una mirada inexpresiva (**c**) **a b. refusal** *(absolute)* una negativa rotunda

2 *n* (**a**) *(space)* espacio *m* en blanco; **to draw a b.** no tener éxito (**b**) *Mil* cartucho

m de fogueo (**c**) *US (form)* impreso *m*

blanket ['blæŋkɪt] **1** *n* manta *f*, *Am* frazada *f*, cobija *f*; *Fig* capa *f*

2 *adj* general

blare [bleə(r)] *vi* resonar

▸ **blare out** *vt sep* pregonar

blasé ['blɑːzeɪ] *adj* de vuelta (de todo)

blasphemous ['blæsfəməs] *adj* blasfemo(a)

blasphemy ['blæsfəmɪ] *n* blasfemia *f*

blast [blɑːst] **1** *n* (**a**) *(of wind)* ráfaga *f* (**b**) *(of horn etc)* toque *m*; **at full b.** a toda marcha (**c**) *(explosion)* explosión *f*; **b. furnace** alto horno (**d**) *(shock wave)* onda *f* de choque

2 *vt* (**a**) *(blow up)* volar; *Fam* **b. (it)!** ¡maldito sea! (**b**) *Fig (destroy)* arruinar (**c**) *Fig (criticize)* criticar

blasted ['blɑːstɪd] *adj* maldito(a)

blast-off ['blɑːstɒf] *n* despegue *m*

blatant ['bleɪtənt] *adj (very obvious)* evidente; *(shameless)* descarado(a); **a b. lie** una mentira patente

blaze¹ [bleɪz] **1** *n* (**a**) *(burst of flame)* llamarada *f* (**b**) *(fierce fire)* incendio *m* (**c**) *(of sun)* resplandor *m* (**d**) *Fig (of anger)* arranque *m*

2 *vi* (**a**) *(fire)* arder (**b**) *(sun etc)* brillar

blaze² [bleɪz] *vt* **to b. a trail** abrir un camino

blazer ['bleɪzə(r)] *n* chaqueta *f* sport

bleach [bliːtʃ] **1** *n (household)* lejía *f*

2 *vt* (**a**) *(whiten)* blanquear; *(fade)* descolorir (**b**) *(hair)* decolorar

bleachers ['bliːtʃəz] *npl US Sport (seats)* gradas *fpl*

bleak [bliːk] *adj* (**a**) *(countryside)* desolado(a) (**b**) *(weather)* desapacible (**c**) *(future)* poco prometedor(a)

bleary ['blɪərɪ] *adj* (**blearier, bleariest**) *(eyes) (due to tears)* lloroso(a); *(due to tiredness)* cansado(a)

bleary-eyed [blɪərɪ'aɪd] *adj* con los ojos llorosos/cansados

bleat [bliːt] **1** *n* balido *m*

2 *vi (animal)* balar

bleed [bliːd] **1** *vi* (*pt & pp* **bled** [bled]) sangrar

2 *vt Med* sangrar; *Fam* **to b. sb dry** sacarle a algn hasta el último céntimo

bleeding ['bliːdɪŋ] **1** *n (loss of blood)* pérdida *f* de sangre

2 *adj* (**a**) *Med* sangrante (**b**) *Fam Pej* puñetero(a)

bleep [bliːp] **1** *n* bip *m*, pitido *m*

2 *vi* pitar

bleeper ['bliːpə(r)] *n Fam* busca *m*, buscapersonas *m inv*

blemish ['blemɪʃ] *n (flaw)* defecto *m; (on fruit)* maca *f*; *Fig* mancha *f*; *Fig* **without b.** sin tacha

blend [blend] **1** *n* mezcla *f*

2 *vt (mix)* mezclar; *(colours)* armonizar

3 *vi (mix)* mezclarse; *(colours)* armonizar

blender ['blendə(r)] *n* licuadora *f*

bless [bles] *vt (pt & pp* blessed *or* blest) (a) bendecir; *Fam* **b. you!** *(after a sneeze)* ¡Jesús! (b) blessed with good eyesight dotado(a) de buena vista

blessing ['blesɪŋ] *n* bendición *f*; *(advantage)* ventaja *f*; **a mixed b.** una ventaja relativa

blest [blest] *pt & pp of* bless

blew [bluː] *pt of* blow

blight [blaɪt] **1** *n* plaga *f*

2 *vt Fig (spoil)* arruinar; *(frustrate)* frustrar

blimey ['blaɪmɪ] *interj Fam* ¡caramba!, ¡caray!

blind [blaɪnd] **1** *adj* ciego(a); **a b. man** un ciego; **a b. woman** una ciega; *Fig* **b. faith** fe ciega; *Fig* **to turn a b. eye** hacer la vista gorda; **b. alley** callejón *m* sin salida; *Aut* **b. corner** curva *f* sin visibilidad; **b. spot** ángulo muerto; *Fam* **b. date** cita *f* a ciegas

2 *adv* a ciegas; *Fam* **to get b. drunk** agarrar una curda

3 *n* (a) *(on window)* persiana *f* (b) *pl* the **b.** los ciegos

4 *vt* (a) cegar, dejar ciego; *Fig* **blinded by ambition** cegado por la ambición (b) *(dazzle)* deslumbrar

blinders ['blaɪndəz] *npl US* anteojeras *fpl*

blindfold ['blaɪndfəʊld] **1** *n* venda *f*

2 *vt* vendar los ojos a

blinding ['blaɪndɪŋ] *adj* cegador(a), deslumbrante

blindly ['blaɪndlɪ] *adv* a ciegas, ciegamente

blindness ['blaɪndnɪs] *n* ceguera *f*

blink [blɪŋk] *vi (eyes)* pestañear; *(lights)* parpadear

blinkered ['blɪŋkəd] *adj Fig* de miras estrechas

blinkers ['blɪŋkəz] *npl (on horse)* anteojeras *fpl*

bliss [blɪs] *n* felicidad *f*; **it was b.!** ¡fue maravilloso!

blissful ['blɪsfʊl] *adj (happy)* feliz; *(marvellous)* maravilloso(a)

blister ['blɪstə(r)] **1** *n (on skin)* ampolla *f*; *(on paint)* burbuja *f*

2 *vi* ampollarse

blithe [blaɪð] *adj* alegre

blithely ['blaɪðlɪ] *adv* alegremente

blitz [blɪts] **1** *n* bombardeo aéreo

2 *vt* bombardear

blizzard ['blɪzəd] *n* ventisca *f*

bloated ['bləʊtɪd] *adj* hinchado(a)

blob [blɒb] *n (drop)* gota *f*; *(spot)* mancha *f*

bloc [blɒk] *n Pol* bloque *m*

block [blɒk] **1** *n* (a) bloque *m*; *(of wood)* taco *m*; **in b. capitals** en mayúsculas (b) **a b. of flats** un bloque de pisos (c) *(group of buildings)* manzana *f* (d) *(obstruction)* bloqueo *m* (e) *Fin* **a b. of shares** un paquete de acciones (f) *Fam (head)* coco *m*

2 *vt* (a) *(obstruct)* obstruir; *Aut* **road blocked** *(sign)* carretera cortada; **to b. the way** cerrar el paso (b) *Sport (player)* obstaculizar (c) *Fin* bloquear

▶**block up** *vt sep* bloquear, obstruir; **to get blocked up** *(pipe)* obstruirse

blockade [blɒ'keɪd] *n* bloqueo *m*

blockage ['blɒkɪdʒ] *n* bloqueo *m*, obstrucción *f*; *(traffic jam)* atasco *m*

blockbuster ['blɒkbʌstə(r)] *n Fam* exitazo *m*; *Cin & TV* gran éxito *m* de taquilla; *(book)* éxito de ventas

bloke [bləʊk] *n Fam* tío *m*, tipo *m*

blond [blɒnd] *adj & n* rubio *(m)*

blonde [blɒnd] *adj & n* rubia *(f)*

blood [blʌd] *n* (a) sangre *f*; **b. bank** banco *m* de sangre; **b. cell** glóbulo *m*; **b. donor** donante *mf* de sangre; **b. group** grupo sanguíneo; **b. pressure** tensión *f* arterial; *US* **b. sausage** morcilla *f*; **b. test** análisis *m* de sangre; **b. transfusion** transfusión *f* de sangre; **b. vessel** vaso sanguíneo; **blue b.** sangre azul; **high/low b. pressure** hipertensión *f*/hipotensión *f* (b) *(race)* sangre *f*, raza *f*

bloodbath ['blʌdbɑːθ] *n Fig* baño *m* de sangre

bloodhound ['blʌdhaʊnd] *n* sabueso *m*

bloodshed ['blʌdʃed] *n* derramamiento *m* de sangre

bloodshot ['blʌdʃɒt] *adj* inyectado(a) de sangre

bloodstream ['blʌdstriːm] *n* corriente sanguínea

bloodthirsty ['blʌdθɜːstɪ] *adj* sanguinario(a)

bloody ['blʌdɪ] **1** *adj* (bloodier, bloodiest) (a) *(battle)* sangriento(a) (b) *(bloodstained)* manchado(a) de sangre (c) *Br very Fam (damned)* condenado(a), puñetero(a), *Andes* cojudo(a), *Méx* pinche

2 *adv Br very Fam* **it's b. difficult!** ¡joder, qué difícil!; **not b. likely!** ¡ni de coña!

bloody-minded [blʌdɪ'maɪndɪd] *adj Fam* terco(a)

bloom [bluːm] **1** *n* (**a**) *(flower)* flor *f*; **in full b.** en flor (**b**) *(on fruit)* vello *m*

2 *vi (blossom)* florecer

blooming ['bluːmɪŋ] *adj* (**a**) *(blossoming)* floreciente (**b**) *Fam Euph (damned)* maldito(a), condenado(a)

blossom ['blɒsəm] **1** *n (flower)* flor *f*

2 *vi* florecer; *Fig* **to b. out** alcanzar la plenitud

blot [blɒt] **1** *n (of ink)* borrón *m*; *Fig* mancha *f*

2 *vt* (**a**) *(with ink)* emborronar (**b**) *(dry)* secar

3 *vi (ink)* correrse

▸ **blot out** *vt sep (memories)* borrar; *(view)* ocultar

blotchy ['blɒtʃɪ] *adj* (**blotchier, blotchiest**) *(skin etc)* enrojecido(a); *(paint etc)* cubierto(a) de manchas

blotting-paper ['blɒtɪŋpeɪpə(r)] *n* papel *m* secante

blouse [blaʊz] *n* blusa *f*

blow¹ [bləʊ] *n* golpe *m*; **to come to blows** llegar a las manos; **it came as a terrible b.** fue un duro golpe

blow² [bləʊ] **1** *vi* (*pt* **blew**; *pp* **blown**) (**a**) *(wind)* soplar (**b**) *(fuse)* fundirse (**c**) *(tyre)* reventar

2 *vt* (**a**) *(kiss)* mandar (**b**) *(trumpet etc)* tocar; *Fig* **to b. one's own trumpet** darse bombo (**c**) *(one's nose)* sonarse (**d**) *(fuse)* fundir (**e**) *Fam (waste)* despilfarrar (**f**) *Fam (chances)* dar al traste con (**g**) *(explode)* volar; *Fig* **to b. sb's cover** descubrir la tapadera de algn; *Fam* **to b. one's top** salirse de sus casillas

▸ **blow away** *vt sep & vi* = **blow off**

▸ **blow down** *vt sep* derribar

▸ **blow off** **1** *vt sep (by wind)* llevarse

2 *vi (hat)* salir volando

▸ **blow out** **1** *vt sep* apagar

2 *vi* apagarse

▸ **blow over** *vi (storm)* calmarse; *(scandal)* olvidarse

▸ **blow up** **1** *vt sep* (**a**) *(building)* volar (**b**) *(inflate)* inflar (**c**) *Phot* ampliar

2 *vi (explode)* explotar

blowlamp ['bləʊlæmp] *n* soplete *m*

blown [bləʊn] *pp of* **blow**

blowout ['bləʊaʊt] *n Aut* reventón *m*; *Fam (meal)* comilona *f*

blowtorch ['bləʊtɔːtʃ] *n US* soplete *m*

blow-up ['bləʊʌp] *n Phot* ampliación *f*

blubber ['blʌbə(r)] **1** *n* grasa *f* de ballena

2 *vi Fam* llorar a moco tendido

bludgeon ['blʌdʒən] *vt* aporrear; *Fig* **to b. sb into doing sth** forzar a algn a hacer algo

blue [bluː] **1** *adj* (**a**) *(colour)* azul; *Fig* **once in a b. moon** de higos a brevas; *Fam* **to scream b. murder** gritar como un loco; **b. jeans** vaqueros *mpl*, tejanos *mpl* (**b**) *(sad)* triste; **to feel b.** sentirse deprimido (**c**) *(obscene)* verde; **b. joke** chiste *m* verde

2 *n* (**a**) *(colour)* azul *m*; *Fam* **the boys in b.** los maderos (**b**) **out of the b.** *(suddenly)* de repente; *(unexpectedly)* como llovido del cielo

bluebell ['bluːbel] *n* campanilla *f*

blueberry ['bluːbərɪ] *n* arándano *m*

bluebottle ['bluːbɒtəl] *n* moscarda *f*, mosca *f* azul

blue-collar ['bluːkɒlə(r)] *adj* **b. worker** obrero(a) *m,f*

blueprint ['bluːprɪnt] *n* anteproyecto *m*

blues [bluːz] *n* (**a**) *Mus* **the b.** el blues (**b**) *Fam (sadness)* tristeza *f*, melancolía *f*; **to have the b.** sentirse deprimido

bluetit ['bluːtɪt] *n* herrerillo *m* común

bluff [blʌf] **1** *n (trick)* farol *m*; **to call sb's b.** hacer que algn ponga sus cartas encima de la mesa

2 *adj (abrupt)* brusco(a); *(forthright)* francote(a)

3 *vi* tirarse un farol; **to b. one's way through sth** hacer colar algo

blunder ['blʌndə(r)] **1** *n* metedura *f* de pata; *Fam* patinazo *m*

2 *vi* meter la pata, pegar un patinazo

blunt [blʌnt] **1** *adj* (**a**) *(knife)* desafilado(a); *(pencil)* despuntado(a); **b. instrument** instrumento *m* contundente (**b**) *(frank)* directo(a), francote(a); *(statement)* tajante

2 *vt (pencil)* despuntar; *(knife)* desafilar

bluntly ['blʌntlɪ] *adv* francamente

blur [blɜː(r)] **1** *n* aspecto borroso

2 *vt (windows)* empañar; *(shape)* desdibujar; *(memory)* enturbiar

blurb [blɜːb] *n (in book)* resumen *m*

blurred [blɜːd] *adj* borroso(a)

blurt [blɜːt] *vt* **to b. out** dejar escapar

blush [blʌʃ] **1** *n* rubor *m*

2 *vi* ruborizarse

blusher ['blʌʃə(r)] *n* colorete *m*

blustery ['blʌstərɪ] *adj* borrascoso(a)

boar [bɔː(r)] *n* verraco *m*; **wild b.** jabalí *m*

board [bɔːd] **1** *n* (**a**) *(plank)* tabla *f* (**b**) *(work surface)* mesa *f*; *(blackboard)* pizarra *f*; *(for games)* tablero *m* (**c**) *(meals)* pensión *f*; **full b.** pensión completa; **b. and lodging** casa *f* y comida (**d**) *(committee)* junta *f*, consejo *m*; **b. of directors**

consejo de administración; **b. room** sala *f* del consejo (**e**) *Naut* **on b.** a bordo (**f**) *Fig* **above b.** en regla; **across-the-b.** general; **to let sth go by the b.** abandonar algo

2 *vt* (*ship, plane etc*) embarcarse en, subir a

3 *vi* (**a**) (*lodge*) alojarse (**b**) (*at school*) estar interno(a)

▸ **board up** *vt sep* tapar

boarder ['bɔːdə(r)] *n* (**a**) (*in boarding house*) huésped *mf* (**b**) (*at school*) interno(a) *m,f*

boarding ['bɔːdɪŋ] *n* (**a**) (*embarkation*) embarque *m*; **b. card, b. pass** tarjeta *f* de embarque (**b**) (*lodging*) alojamiento *m*, pensión *f*; **b. house** pensión; **b. school** internado *m*

boardwalk ['bɔːdwɔːk] *n US* paseo marítimo entarimado

boast [bəʊst] **1** *n* jactancia *f*, alarde *m*

2 *vi* jactarse, alardear (**about** de)

3 *vt* presumir de, alardear de; **the town boasts an Olympic swimming pool** la ciudad disfruta de una piscina olímpica

boat [bəʊt] *n* barco *m*; (*small*) barca *f*, bote *m*; (*launch*) lancha *f*; (*large*) buque *m*; *Fig* **we're all in the same b.** todos estamos en el mismo barco; **fishing b.** barco de pesca

boater ['bəʊtə(r)] *n* canotié *m*, canotier *m*

boatswain ['bəʊsən] *n* contramaestre *m*

boatyard ['bəʊtjɑːd] *n* astillero *m*

bob [bɒb] **1** *n* (**a**) (*haircut*) pelo *m* a lo chico (**b**) *Fam* (*pl* **bob**) (*shilling*) chelín *m*

2 *vi* **to b. up and down** subir y bajar

bobbin ['bɒbɪn] *n* (*of sewing machine*) canilla *f*; (*for lace-making*) bolillo *m*

bobby ['bɒbɪ] *n Br Fam* (*policeman*) poli *m*

bobby-pin ['bɒbɪpɪn] *n US* (*hairgrip*) horquilla *f*

bobsleigh ['bɒbsleɪ] *n* bobsleigh *m*

bode¹ [bəʊd] *pt of* bide

bode² [bəʊd] *vt & vi* presagiar; **to b. well/ill** ser de buen/mal agüero

bodice ['bɒdɪs] *n* (**a**) (*sleeveless undergarment*) corpiño *m* (**b**) (*of dress*) cuerpo *m*

bodily ['bɒdɪlɪ] **1** *adj* físico(a); **b. harm** daños *mpl* corporales

2 *adv* **to carry sb b.** llevar a algn en brazos

body ['bɒdɪ] *n* (**a**) cuerpo *m*; **b. language** expresión *f* corporal; **b. odour** olor *m* corporal; **b. piercing** perforaciones *fpl* en el cuerpo, piercing *m* (**b**) (*corpse*) cadáver *m* (**c**) (*main part*) parte *f* principal (**d**) *Aut* carrocería *f*; *Naut* casco *m* (**e**)

(*organization*) organismo *m*; (*profession*) cuerpo *m*; **the b. politic** el estado (**f**) (*group of people*) conjunto *m*, grupo *m*

body-blow ['bɒdɪbləʊ] *n Fig* duro golpe

body-builder ['bɒdɪbɪldə(r)] *n* culturista *mf*

body-building ['bɒdɪbɪldɪŋ] *n* culturismo *m*

bodyguard ['bɒdɪgɑːd] *n* guardaespaldas *mf inv*

bodywork ['bɒdɪwɜːk] *n Aut* carrocería *f*

Boer ['bəʊə(r)] *adj* **the B. War** la guerra del Transvaal

bog [bɒg] *n* (**a**) ciénaga *f* (**b**) *Br very Fam* (*lavatory*) meódromo *m*

▸ **bog down** *vt sep* **to get bogged down** atascarse

bogey ['bəʊgɪ] *n* (**a**) (*spectre*) espectro *m*, fantasma *m* (**b**) (*bugbear*) pesadilla *f* (**c**) (*in golf*) bogey *m* (**d**) *Fam* (*mucus*) moco *m*

boggle ['bɒgəl] *vi Fam* **the mind boggles!** ¡es alucinante!

bogus ['bəʊgəs] *adj* falso(a); **b. company** compañía *f* fantasma

boil¹ [bɔɪl] **1** *n* **to come to the b.** empezar a hervir

2 *vt* (*water*) hervir; (*food*) cocer; (*egg*) cocer, pasar por agua

3 *vi* hervir; *Fig* **to b. with rage** estar furioso(a)

▸ **boil down** *vi* reducirse (**to** a)

▸ **boil over** *vi* (*milk*) salirse

boil² [bɔɪl] *n Med* furúnculo *m*

boiled [bɔɪld] *adj* **b. egg** huevo cocido *or* pasado por agua

boiler ['bɔɪlə(r)] *n* caldera *f*; *Br* **b. suit** mono *m*

boiling ['bɔɪlɪŋ] *adj* **b. water** agua hirviendo; **it's b. hot** (*food*) quema; (*weather*) hace un calor agobiante; **b. point** punto *m* de ebullición

boisterous ['bɔɪstərəs] *adj* (**a**) (*person, party*) bullicioso(a) (**b**) (*weather*) borrascoso(a)

bold [bəʊld] *adj* (**a**) (*brave*) valiente (**b**) (*daring*) audaz (**c**) (*features*) marcado(a); *Typ* **b. type** negrita *f* (**d**) (*impudent*) descarado(a)

Bolivia [bə'lɪvɪə] *n* Bolivia

Bolivian [bə'lɪvɪən] *adj & n* boliviano(a) *(m,f)*

bollard ['bɒlɑːd] *n Aut* baliza *f*

bollocks ['bɒləks] *npl Br very Fam* cojones *mpl*; **b.!** (*disagreement*) ¡y un huevo!

Bolshevik ['bɒlʃəvɪk] *adj & n* bolchevique *(mf)*

bolster ['bəʊlstə(r)] **1** n (pillow) cabezal m, travesaño m
2 vt (strengthen) reforzar; (support) apoyar

bolt [bəʊlt] **1** n (a) (on door) cerrojo m; (small) pestillo m (b) Tech perno m, tornillo m (c) (of lightning) rayo m (d) (crossbow) flecha f
2 vt (a) (lock) cerrar con cerrojo (b) Tech sujetar con pernos (c) Fam (food) engullir
3 vi (person) largarse; (horse) desbocarse
4 adv **b. upright** derecho

bomb [bɒm] **1** n bomba f; Br Fam **to cost a b.** costar un ojo de la cara; **b. disposal squad** brigada f de artificieros; **b. scare** amenaza f de bomba; **car b.** cochebomba m; **letter b.** carta-bomba f
2 vt (city etc) bombardear; (by terrorists) volar
3 vi Fam **to b. (along)** (car) ir a toda pastilla

bombard [bɒm'bɑːd] vt bombardear

bombardment [bɒm'bɑːdmənt] n bombardeo m

bombastic [bɒm'bæstɪk] adj rimbombante

bomber ['bɒmə(r)] n (a) Av bombardero m; **b. jacket** cazadora f (b) terrorista mf que coloca bombas

bombshell ['bɒmʃel] n (a) Mil obús m (b) Fig (surprise) bomba f (c) Fam **a blonde b.** una rubia explosiva

bona fide ['bəʊnə'faɪdɪ] adj (a) (genuine) auténtico(a) (b) (in good faith) bienintencionado(a)

bond [bɒnd] **1** n (a) (link) lazo m, vínculo m (b) Fin bono m (c) Jur (bail) fianza f (d) (binding agreement) acuerdo m (e) (warehouse) depósito m; **in b.** en depósito (f) US (guarantee) garantía f (g) **bonds** (shackles) cadenas fpl
2 vt (a) (join) pegar (b) (merchandise) poner en depósito

bondage ['bɒndɪdʒ] n esclavitud f

bone [bəʊn] **1** n (a) hueso m; (in fish) espina f; Fig **b. of contention** manzana f de la discordia; Fig **he made no bones about it** no trató de disimularlo; **b. china** porcelana fina (b) **bones** (remains) restos mpl; **the bare bones** lo esencial
2 vt (meat) deshuesar; (fish) quitar las espinas a
▸ **bone up on** vt insep Fam empollar

bone-dry ['bəʊn'draɪ] adj completamente seco(a)

bone-idle ['bəʊn'aɪdəl] adj gandul(a)

bonfire ['bɒnfaɪə(r)] n hoguera f, fogata f; Br **B. Night** = fiesta del 5 de noviembre en que de noche se hacen hogueras y hay fuegos artificiales

bonkers ['bɒŋkəz] adj Br Fam chalado(a)

bonnet ['bɒnɪt] n (a) (child's) gorra f (b) Br Aut capó m

bonus ['bəʊnəs] n (a) (on wages) prima f (b) Fin (on shares) dividendo m extraordinario (c) Br Ins beneficio m

bony ['bəʊnɪ] adj (**bonier, boniest**) (person) huesudo(a); (fish) lleno(a) de espinas

boo [buː] **1** interj ¡bu!
2 n abucheo m
3 vt abuchear

boob [buːb] n Br Fam (a) (silly mistake) patinazo m (b) **boobs** (breasts) tetas fpl

booby ['buːbɪ] n **b. prize** premio m de consolación; **b. trap** trampa f; Mil trampa explosiva

boogie ['buːgɪ] vi Fam bailar

book [bʊk] **1** n (a) libro m; Fig **in my b.** según mi punto de vista; Fig **by the b.** según las reglas; **b. end** sujetalibros m inv; Br **b. token** vale m para comprar libros; **savings b.** libreta f de ahorros (b) (of stamps) carpeta f; (of matches) cajetilla f (c) Com **books** cuentas fpl; **to keep the books** llevar las cuentas
2 vt (a) (reserve) reservar; (return flight) cerrar (b) (engage) contratar (c) (by police) poner una multa a (d) Ftb amonestar
▸ **book into** vt insep (hotel) reservar una habitación en
▸ **book out** vi (of hotel) marcharse
▸ **book up** vt sep **booked up** (sign) completo

booking ['bʊkɪŋ] n esp Br (reservation) reserva f; **b. office** taquilla f

bookmaker ['bʊkmeɪkə(r)] n corredor(a) m,f de apuestas

bookseller ['bʊkselə(r)] n librero(a) m,f

bookshelf ['bʊkʃelf] n **bookshelves** estantería f

bookshop ['bʊkʃɒp] n librería f

bookstall ['bʊkstɔːl] n quiosco m

bookstore ['bʊkstɔː(r)] n US librería f

bookworm ['bʊkwɜːm] n Fam ratón m de biblioteca

boom¹ [buːm] **1** n (a) (noise) estampido m, trueno m (b) (sudden prosperity) boom m, auge m
2 vi (a) (thunder) retumbar; (cannon) tronar (b) (prosper) estar en auge

boom² [buːm] n (of microphone) jirafa f

boomerang ['buːməræŋ] *n* bumerang *m*, bumerán *m*

booming ['buːmɪŋ] *adj* (**a**) *(voice, thunder)* que retumba (**b**) *(prosperous)* en auge

boon [buːn] *n (blessing)* bendición *f*

boost [buːst] **1** *n* estímulo *m*, empujón *m*
2 *vt* (**a**) *(increase)* aumentar (**b**) **to b. sb's confidence** subirle la moral a algn (**c**) *(tourism, exports)* fomentar (**d**) *(voltage)* elevar

booster ['buːstə(r)] *n* (**a**) *Elec* elevador *m* de voltaje (**b**) *Rad & TV (amplifier)* amplificador *m* (**c**) *Med* **b. (shot)** revacunación *f*

boot¹ [buːt] **1** *n* (**a**) bota *f*; *(short)* botín *m*; *Fig* **he's too big for his boots** es muy creído; *Fam* **to put the b. in** pisotear; *Fam* **she got the b.** la echaron (del trabajo); **b. polish** betún *m* (**b**) *Br Aut* maletero *m*, *CAm, Méx* cajuela *f*, *RP* baúl *m*
2 *vt Fam* (**a**) *Ftb (ball)* chutar (**b**) **to b. (out)** echar a patadas (**c**) *Comput* arrancar
3 *vi Comput* **to b. (up)** arrancar

boot² [buːt] *n* **to b.** además

bootblack ['buːtblæk] *n esp US* limpiabotas *mf inv*

booth [buːð, buːθ] *n* (**a**) *(in language lab etc)* cabina *f*; **telephone b.** cabina telefónica (**b**) *(at fair)* puesto *m*

bootleg ['buːtleg] *adj* de contrabando

bootlegger ['buːtlegə(r)] *n* contrabandista *m*

booty ['buːtɪ] *n* botín *m*

booze [buːz] *Fam* **1** *n* priva *f*
2 *vi* privar

bop [bɒp] **1** *n* (**a**) *Mus* be-bop *m* (**b**) *Fam (dance)* baile *m*
2 *vi Fam (dance)* bailar

Bordeaux [bɔː'dəʊ] *n* (**a**) *(city)* Burdeos (**b**) *(wine)* burdeos *m*

border ['bɔːdə(r)] **1** *n* (**a**) borde *m*, margen *m* (**b**) *Sewing* ribete *m* (**c**) *(frontier)* frontera *f*; **b. town** pueblo fronterizo (**d**) *(flowerbed)* arriate *m*
2 *vt Sewing* ribetear
▶ **border on** *vt insep* (**a**) *Geog* lindar con (**b**) *Fig* rayar en

borderline ['bɔːdəlaɪn] **1** *n* (**a**) *(border)* frontera *f* (**b**) *(dividing line)* línea divisoria
2 *adj* (**a**) *(on the border)* fronterizo(a) (**b**) *Fig (case etc)* dudoso(a)

bore¹ [bɔː(r)] **1** *vt Tech* taladrar, perforar
2 *n* (**a**) *Tech (hole)* taladro *m* (**b**) *(of gun)* calibre *m*

bore² [bɔː(r)] **1** *vt* aburrir

bore³ [bɔː(r)] *pt of* bear

bored [bɔːd] *adj* aburrido(a); **to be b. stiff** *or* **to tears** estar aburrido(a) como una ostra

boredom ['bɔːdəm] *n* aburrimiento *m*

boring ['bɔːrɪŋ] *adj (uninteresting)* aburrido(a); *(tedious)* pesado(a), latoso(a)

born [bɔːn] **1** *pp of* bear; **to be b.** nacer; **I wasn't b. yesterday** no nací ayer
2 *adj (having natural ability)* nato(a); **b. poet** poeta nato

born-again ['bɔːnəgen] *adj Rel* converso(a)

borne [bɔːn] *pp of* bear

borough ['bʌrə] *n* (**a**) *(town)* ciudad *f*; *US (municipality)* municipio *m* (**b**) *esp Br (constituency)* distrito *m* electoral

borrow ['bɒrəʊ] **1** *vt* (**a**) pedir *or* tomar prestado; **can I b. your pen?** ¿me dejas tu bolígrafo? (**b**) *(ideas etc)* apropiarse
2 *vi* pedir *or* tomar prestado

borstal ['bɔːstəl] *n Br Fam* reformatorio *m*

Bosnia ['bɒznɪə] *n* Bosnia

Bosnia-Herzegovina
['bɒznɪəhɜːtsəgəˈviːnə] *n* Bosnia y Hercegóvina

Bosnian ['bɒznɪən] *adj & n* bosnio(a) *(m,f)*

bosom ['bʊzəm] *n* (**a**) *(breast)* pecho *m*; *(breasts)* pechos *mpl*; **b. friend** amigo(a) *m,f* del alma (**b**) *Fig* seno *m*

boss [bɒs] **1** *n* (**a**) *(head)* jefe(a) *m,f*; *(factory owner etc)* patrón(ona) *m,f* (**b**) *esp US Pol* jefe *m*; *Pej* cacique *m*
2 *vt* **to b. sb about** *or* **around** mandar sobre algn

bossy ['bɒsɪ] *adj* (**bossier, bossiest**) *Fam* mandón(ona)

bosun ['bəʊsən] *n* contramaestre *m*

botanic(al) [bə'tænɪk(əl)] *adj* botánico(a); **b. garden** jardín botánico

botany ['bɒtənɪ] *n* botánica *f*

botch [bɒtʃ] **1** *vt* chapucear; **a botched job** una chapuza
2 *n* chapuza *f*

both [bəʊθ] **1** *adj* ambos(as), los dos/las dos; **b. men are teachers** ambos son profesores; **hold it with b. hands** sujétalo con las dos manos
2 *pron* **b. (of them)** ambos(as), los dos/las dos; **b. of you** vosotros dos
3 *conj* a la vez; **b. England and Spain are in Europe** tanto Inglaterra como España están en Europa

bother ['bɒðə(r)] **1** *vt* (**a**) *(disturb)* molestar; *(be a nuisance to)* dar la lata a (**b**) *(worry)* preocupar; *Fam* **I can't be bothered** no tengo ganas

2 *vi* molestarse; **don't b. about me** no te preocupes por mí; **he didn't b. shaving** no se molestó en afeitarse

3 *n* (**a**) *(disturbance)* molestia *f*; *(nuisance)* lata *f* (**b**) *(trouble)* problemas *mpl*

4 *interj Br* ¡maldito sea!

bothersome ['bɒðəsəm] *adj* molesto(a)

bottle ['bɒtəl] **1** *n* (**a**) botella *f*; *(of perfume, ink)* frasco *m*; *Fam* **to hit the b.** darle a la bebida; **baby's b.** biberón *m*; **b. opener** abrebotellas *m inv* (**b**) *Br Fam* **to have a lot of b.** *(nerve)* tener muchas agallas

2 *vt (wine)* embotellar; *(fruit)* enfrascar

▸ **bottle out** *vi Br Fam* encogerse

▸ **bottle up** *vt sep* reprimir

bottle-bank ['bɒtəlbæŋk] *n* contenedor *m* de vidrio

bottled ['bɒtəld] *adj (beer, wine)* en botella, embotellado(a); *(fruit)* envasado(a)

bottle-green ['bɒtəlɡriːn] *adj* verde botella

bottleneck ['bɒtəlnek] *n Aut* embotellamiento *m*, atasco *m*

bottom ['bɒtəm] **1** *adj* (**a**) *(lowest)* más bajo(a); *(drawer, shelf)* de abayo; *Aut* **b. gear** primera *f* (**b**) *(last)* último(a); **b. line** *Fin* saldo *m* final; *Fig* resultado *m* final

2 *n* (**a**) parte *f* inferior; *(of sea, garden, street, box)* fondo *m*; *(of bottle)* culo *m*; *(of page, hill)* pie *m*; *Educ* **to be (at) the b. of the class** ser el último/la última de la clase; **to touch b.** tocar fondo; *Fam* **bottoms up!** ¡salud! (**b**) **to get to the b. of a matter** llegar al meollo de una cuestión; **who is at the b. of all this?** ¿quién está detrás de todo esto? (**c**) *(buttocks)* trasero *m*

▸ **bottom out** *vi Fin* tocar fondo

bottomless ['bɒtəmlɪs] *adj (pit)* sin fondo; *(mystery)* insondable

boudoir ['buːdwɑː(r)] *n* tocador *m*

bough [baʊ] *n* rama *f*

bought [bɔːt] *pt & pp of* **buy**

bouillon ['buːjɒn] *n* caldo *m*

boulder ['bəʊldə(r)] *n* canto rodado

boulevard ['buːlvɑː(r)] *n* bulevar *m*

bounce [baʊns] **1** *vi* (**a**) *(ball)* rebotar (**b**) *(jump)* saltar (**c**) *Fam (cheque)* ser rechazado (por el banco)

2 *vt (ball)* botar

3 *n* (**a**) *(of ball)* bote *m* (**b**) *(jump)* salto *m* (**c**) *(energy)* vitalidad *f*

▸ **bounce back** *vi (recover health)* recuperarse, recobrarse

bouncer ['baʊnsə(r)] *n Fam* gorila *m*

bound¹ [baʊnd] *adj* (**a**) *(tied up)* atado(a) (**b**) *(book)* encuadernado(a) (**c**) *(obliged)* obligado(a) (**d**) **b. (up)** *(linked)* vinculado(a) (**with** a) (**e**) **it's b. to happen** sucederá con toda seguridad; **it was b. to fail** estaba destinado al fracaso

bound² [baʊnd] **1** *vi* saltar

2 *n* salto *m*

bound³ [baʊnd] *pt & pp of* **bind**

bound⁴ [baʊnd] *adj* **b. for** con destino a, rumbo a; **to be b. for** dirigirse a

boundary ['baʊndəri] *n* límite *m*

boundless ['baʊndlɪs] *adj* ilimitado(a), sin límites

bounds [baʊndz] *npl* **beyond the b. of reality** más allá de la realidad; **her ambition knows no b.** su ambición no conoce límites; **the river is out of b.** está prohibido bajar al río

bounty ['baʊntɪ] *n* prima *f*, gratificación *f*

bouquet *n* (**a**) [buːˈkeɪ, bəʊˈkeɪ] *(of flowers)* ramillete *m* (**b**) [buːˈkeɪ] *(of wine)* aroma *m*, buqué *m*

bourbon ['bɜːbən] *n US (whiskey)* whisky americano, bourbon *m*

bourgeois ['bʊəʒwɑː] *adj & n* burgués(esa) *(m,f)*

bourgeoisie [bʊəʒwɑːˈziː] *n* burguesía *f*

bout [baʊt] *n* (**a**) *(of work)* turno *m*; *(of illness)* ataque *m* (**b**) *(in boxing)* combate *m*

boutique [buːˈtiːk] *n* boutique *f*, tienda *f*

bow¹ [baʊ] **1** *vi* (**a**) hacer una reverencia (**b**) *(give in)* ceder

2 *n (with head, body)* reverencia *f*

▸ **bow out** *vi* retirarse (**of** de)

bow² [bəʊ] *n* (**a**) *Sport & Mus* arco *m*; *Fig* **to have more than one string to one's b.** ser una persona de recursos (**b**) *(knot)* lazo *m*; **b. tie** pajarita *f*

bow³ [baʊ] *n esp Naut* proa *f*

bowel ['baʊəl] *n* (**a**) intestino *m* (**b**) **bowels** entrañas *fpl*

bowl¹ [bəʊl] *n* (**a**) *(dish)* cuenco *m*; *(for soup)* tazón *m*; *(for washing hands)* palangana *f*; *(for washing clothes, dishes)* barreño *m*; *(of toilet)* taza *f* (**b**) *Geol* cuenca *f*

bowl² [bəʊl] **1** *n* bola *f*

2 *vt (in cricket)* lanzar

3 *vi* (**a**) *(play bowls)* jugar a los bolos (**b**) *(in cricket)* lanzar la pelota

▸ **bowl along** *vi Fam (car)* ir volando

▸ **bowl out** *vt sep (in cricket)* eliminar

▸ **bowl over** *vt sep* (**a**) *(knock down)* derribar (**b**) *Fig (astonish)* desconcertar

bow-legged ['bəʊleɡ(ɪ)d] *adj* patizambo(a)

bowler¹ ['bəʊlə(r)] *n (in cricket)* lanzador(a) *m,f*

bowler² ['bəʊlə(r)] *n (hat)* bombín *m*

bowling ['bəʊlɪŋ] *n (game)* bolos *mpl;* **b. alley** bolera *f;* **b. ball** bola *f* (de jugar a los bolos)

bowls [bəʊlz] *npl Sport* bolos *mpl*

box¹ [bɒks] **1** *n* (a) *(large)* caja *f; (large)* cajón *m;* *(of matches)* cajetilla *f;* **jewellery b.** joyero *m; Th* **b. office** taquilla *f;* **b. office success** éxito taquillero (b) *Press* recuadro *m* (c) *Th* palco *m* (d) *Br Fam (television)* caja tonta

2 *vt (pack)* embalar

box² [bɒks] *Sport* **1** *vi* boxear

2 *vt (hit)* pegar; **to b. sb's ears** dar un cachete a algn

boxcar ['bɒkskɑ:(r)] *n US* vagón *m* de mercancías, furgón *m* (de mercancías)

boxer ['bɒksə(r)] *n* (a) boxeador *m* (b) *(dog)* bóxer *m*

boxing ['bɒksɪŋ] *n* boxeo *m;* **b. ring** cuadrilátero *m*

Boxing Day ['bɒksɪŋdeɪ] *n Br* = el día de San Esteban *(26 de diciembre)*

boxroom ['bɒksruːm] *n* trastero *m*

boy [bɔɪ] *n* (a) *(child)* niño *m,* chico *m;* *(youth)* joven *m;* **b. band** = grupo musical juvenil compuesto por adolescentes varones; *Fam* **oh b.!** ¡vaya! (b) *(son)* hijo *m*

boycott ['bɔɪkɒt] **1** *n* boicot *m*

2 *vt* boicotear

boyfriend ['bɔɪfrend] *n* novio *m; (live-in)* compañero *m*

boyhood ['bɔɪhʊd] *n* niñez *f,* juventud *f*

boyish ['bɔɪɪʃ] *adj* juvenil, de muchacho

bra [brɑː] *n* sostén *m, Esp* sujetador *m,* Carib, Col, Méx brasier *m, RP* corpiño *m*

brace [breɪs] **1** *n* (a) *(clamp)* abrazadera *f;* *(of drill)* berbiquí *m;* *(for teeth)* aparato *m* (b) *(of wood)* puntal *m* (c) *(pair)* par *m* (d) *Br* **braces** tirantes *mpl*

2 *vt* (a) *(wall)* apuntalar (b) *(strengthen)* reforzar (c) **to b. oneself** prepararse (**for** para)

▸ **brace up** *vi* cobrar ánimo

bracelet ['breɪslɪt] *n* pulsera *f*

bracing ['breɪsɪŋ] *adj (wind)* fresco(a); *(stimulating)* tonificante

bracken ['brækən] *n* helecho *m*

bracket ['brækɪt] **1** *n* (a) *Typ (round)* paréntesis *m; (square)* corchete *m; (curly)* llave *f;* **in brackets** entre paréntesis (b) *(support)* soporte *m; (for lamp)* brazo *m; (shelf)* repisa *f* (c) *(for tax)* sector *m*

2 *vt* (a) *Ling (phrase etc)* poner entre paréntesis (b) *(group together)* agrupar, juntar

brag [bræg] *vi* jactarse (**about** de)

braggart ['brægət] *n* fanfarrón(ona) *m,f*

braid [breɪd] **1** *vt* trenzar

2 *n* (a) *Sewing* galón *m* (b) *esp US (plait)* trenza *f*

Braille [breɪl] *n* braille *m*

brain [breɪn] *n* (a) cerebro *m;* **she's got cars on the b.** está obsesionada por los coches; *Med* **b. death** muerte *f* cerebral; *Fig* **b. drain** fuga *f* de cerebros; **b. wave** idea *f* genial (b) *Fam* **brains** inteligencia *f;* **to have brains** ser inteligente; *Br* **brains** or *US* **b. trust** grupo *m* de expertos (c) *Culin* **brains** sesos *mpl*

brainchild ['breɪntʃaɪld] *n* invento *m,* idea *f* genial

brainpower ['breɪnpaʊə(r)] *n* capacidad *f* intelectual

brainstorm ['breɪnstɔːm] *n* (a) *(outburst)* arranque *m* (b) *(brainwave)* genialidad *f,* lluvia *f* de ideas

brainwash ['breɪnwɒʃ] *vt* lavar el cerebro a

brainy ['breɪnɪ] *adj* (**brainier, brainiest**) *Fam* listo(a)

braise [breɪz] *vt* cocer a fuego lento

brake [breɪk] **1** *n Aut (also pl)* freno *m;* **b. drum** tambor *m* del freno; **b. fluid** líquido *m* de frenos; **b. light** luz *f* de freno

2 *vi* frenar, echar el freno

bramble ['bræmbəl] *n* zarza *f,* zarzamora *f*

bran [bræn] *n* salvado *m*

branch [brɑːntʃ] **1** *n (of tree)* rama *f; (of road)* bifurcación *f; (of science etc)* ramo *m; Com* **b.** *(office)* sucursal *f*

2 *vi (road)* bifurcarse

▸ **branch off** *vi* desviarse

▸ **branch out** *vi* diversificarse

brand [brænd] **1** *n* (a) *Com* marca *f;* **b. name** marca de fábrica (b) *(type)* clase *f* (c) *(on cattle)* hierro *m*

2 *vt* (a) *(animal)* marcar con hierro candente (b) *(label)* tildar

brandish ['brændɪʃ] *vt* blandir

brand-new ['brænd'njuː] *adj* flamante

brandy ['brændɪ] *n* coñac *m,* brandy *m*

brash [bræʃ] *adj* (a) *(impudent)* descarado(a) (b) *(reckless)* temerario(a) (c) *(loud, showy)* chillón(ona)

brass [brɑːs] *n* latón *m; Fam (money)* pasta *f; Mus* instrumentos *mpl* de metal; **b. band** banda *f* de metal

brassiere ['bræzɪə(r)] *n* sostén *m,* sujetador *m*

brat [bræt] *n Fam* mocoso(a) *m,f*

bravado [brə'vɑːdəʊ] *n* bravuconería *f*

brave [breɪv] **1** *adj* valiente, valeroso(a)

2 *n US* **(Indian) b.** guerrero *m* indio
3 *vt* (**a**) *(face)* hacer frente a (**b**) *(defy)* desafiar

bravely ['breɪvlɪ] *adv* valientemente

bravery ['breɪvərɪ] *n* valentía *f*, valor *m*

bravo [brɑː'vəʊ] *interj* ¡bravo!

brawl [brɔːl] **1** *n* reyerta *f*
2 *vi* pelearse

brawn [brɔːn] *n* (**a**) *(strength)* fuerza física (**b**) *Br Culin* queso *m* de cerdo

bray [breɪ] **1** *n* *(of donkey)* rebuzno *m*
2 *vi* rebuznar

brazen ['breɪzən] *adj* descarado(a)

Brazil [brə'zɪl] *n* (el) Brasil

brazil [brə'zɪl] *n* **b. nut** nuez *f* del Brasil

Brazilian [brə'zɪlɪən] *adj & n* brasileño(a) *(m,f)*

breach [briːtʃ] **1** *n* (**a**) *(in wall)* brecha *f* (**b**) *(violation)* incumplimiento *m*; **b. of confidence** abuso *m* de confianza; **b. of contract** incumplimiento de contrato; **b. of the law** violación *f* de la ley; **b. of the peace** alteración *f* del orden público (**c**) *(in relations)* ruptura *f*
2 *vt* violar

bread [bred] *n* (**a**) *(food)* pan *m*; **b. and butter** pan con mantequilla, *Am* pan con manteca; *Fig* **our daily b.** el pan nuestro de cada día (**b**) *Fam (money)* pasta *f*, *Am* plata *f*

breadboard ['bredbɔːd] *n* tabla *f* (para cortar el pan)

breadcrumb ['bredkrʌm] *n* miga *f* de pan; **breadcrumbs** pan rallado

breadline ['bredlaɪn] *n Fam* miseria *f*; **to be on the b.** vivir en la miseria

breadth [bredθ] *n* (**a**) *(width)* anchura *f*; **it is 2 m in b.** tiene 2 m de ancho (**b**) *(extent)* amplitud *f*

breadwinner ['bredwɪnə(r)] *n* cabeza *mf* de familia

break [breɪk] **1** *vt* *(pt* **broke**; *pp* **broken)** (**a**) romper; **to b. a leg** romperse la pierna; **to b. a record** batir un récord; **to b. even** no tener ni ganancias ni pérdidas; *Fig* **to b. one's back** matarse a trabajar; *Fig* **to b. sb's heart** partirle el corazón a algn; *Fig* **to b. the ice** romper el hielo (**b**) *(fail to keep)* faltar a; **to b. a contract** romper un contrato; **to b. the law** violar la ley
(**c**) *(destroy)* destrozar; *Fin* arruinar
(**d**) *(interrupt)* interrumpir
(**e**) *(code)* descifrar
(**f**) *(fall)* amortiguar
(**g**) **she broke the news to him** le comunicó la noticia

2 *vi* (**a**) romperse; *(clouds)* dispersarse; *(waves)* romper
(**b**) *(storm)* estallar
(**c**) *(voice)* cambiar
(**d**) *(health)* resentirse
(**e**) **when day breaks** al rayar el alba
(**f**) *(story)* divulgarse
3 *n* (**a**) *(fracture)* rotura *f*; *(crack)* grieta *f*; *(opening)* abertura *f*
(**b**) *(in relationship)* ruptura *f*
(**c**) *(pause)* pausa *f*, descanso *m*; *(at school)* recreo *m*; **to take a b.** descansar un rato; *(holiday)* tomar unos días libres; **without a b.** sin parar
(**d**) *Fam (chance)* oportunidad *f*; **a lucky b.** un golpe de suerte
▸ **break away** *vi* (**a**) *(become separate)* desprenderse (**from** de) (**b**) *(escape)* escaparse
▸ **break down** **1** *vt sep* (**a**) *(door)* derribar (**b**) *(resistance)* acabar con (**c**) *(costs)* desglosar
2 *vi* (**a**) *Aut* tener una avería (**b**) *(resistance)* ceder (**c**) *(health)* debilitarse (**d**) *(weep)* ponerse a llorar
▸ **break in** *vt sep* acostumbrar; **to b. in a pair of shoes** cogerle la forma a los zapatos
2 *vi* *(burglar)* entrar por la fuerza
▸ **break into** *vt insep* (**a**) *(burgle) (house)* allanar; *(safe)* forzar (**b**) **to b. into song** empezar a cantar
▸ **break off** **1** *vt sep* partir
2 *vi* (**a**) *(become detached)* desprenderse (**b**) *(talks)* interrumpirse (**c**) *(stop)* pararse
▸ **break out** *vi* (**a**) *(prisoners)* escaparse (**b**) *(war etc)* estallar; **she broke out in a rash** le salió un sarpullido
▸ **break through** **1** *vt insep* (**a**) *(crowd)* abrirse paso por; *(cordon)* romper (**b**) *(clouds)* atravesar
2 *vi* (**a**) *(crowd)* abrirse paso (**b**) *(sun)* salir
▸ **break up** **1** *vt sep* *(object)* romper; *(car)* desguazar; *(crowd)* disolver
2 *vi* (**a**) *(object)* romperse (**b**) *(crowd)* disolverse; *(meeting)* levantarse (**c**) *(relationship)* fracasar; *(couple)* separarse (**d**) *Educ* terminar
▸ **break with** *vt insep (past)* romper con

breakable ['breɪkəbəl] *adj* frágil

breakage ['breɪkɪdʒ] *n* *(breaking)* rotura *f*

breakaway ['breɪkəweɪ] *adj* disidente

breakdown ['breɪkdaʊn] *n* (**a**) *Aut* avería *f*; *Br* **b. truck** *or* **van** grúa *f* (**b**) **(nervous) b.** crisis nerviosa (**c**) *(in communications)* ruptura *f* (**d**) *(analysis)* análisis *m*; *Fin* desglose *m*

breaker ['breɪkə(r)] *n* (**a**) *(wave)* ola *f* grande (**b**) *Tech* trituradora *f* (**c**) *(switch)* interruptor automático

breakfast ['brekfəst] **1** *n* desayuno *m*; **to have b.** desayunar
2 *vi* desayunar

break-in ['breɪkɪn] *n* robo *m* *(con allanamiento de morada)*

breaking ['breɪkɪŋ] *n* (**a**) rotura *f*; **b. point** punto *m* de ruptura (**b**) *Jur* **b. and entering** allanamiento *m* de morada

breakthrough ['breɪkθruː] *n* paso *m* adelante, avance *m*

breakwater ['breɪkwɔːtə(r)] *n* rompeolas *m inv*

breast [brest] *n* *(chest)* pecho *m*; *(of woman)* pecho, seno *m*; *(of chicken etc)* pechuga *f*; *Fig* **to make a clean b. of it** dar la cara

breast-feed ['brestfiːd] *vt* dar el pecho a, amamantar a

breaststroke ['breststrəʊk] *n* braza *f*

breath [breθ] *n* (**a**) aliento *m*; *(breathing)* respiración *f*; **in the same b.** al mismo tiempo; **out of b.** sin aliento; **to catch one's b.** recobrar el aliento; **to draw b.** respirar; **under one's b.** en voz baja; *Fig* **to take sb's b. away** dejar pasmado a algn; *Aut* **b. test** alcoholemia *f* (**b**) **to go out for a b. of fresh air** salir a tomar el aire

Breathalyser®, *US* **Breathalyzer**® ['breθəlaɪzə(r)] *n Br* alcoholímetro *m*

breathe [briːð] **1** *vt* respirar; **to b. a sigh of relief** dar un suspiro de alivio
2 *vi* respirar; **to b. in** aspirar; **to b. out** espirar; **to b. heavily** resoplar

breather ['briːðə(r)] *n Fam (rest)* descanso *m*

breathing ['briːðɪŋ] *n* respiración *f*; **b. space** pausa *f*, respiro *m*

breathless ['breθlɪs] *adj* sin aliento, jadeante

breathtaking ['breθteɪkɪŋ] *adj* impresionante

bred [bred] *pt & pp* de **breed**

breeches ['brɪtʃɪz, 'brɪːtʃɪz] *npl* bombachos *mpl*; **knee b., riding b.** pantalones *mpl* de montar

breed [briːd] **1** *n* *(of animal)* raza *f*; *Fig (class)* clase *f*
2 *vt* *(pt & pp* **bred)** *(animals)* criar; *Fig (ideas)* engendrar
3 *vi* *(animals)* reproducirse

breeder ['briːdə(r)] *n* (**a**) *(person)* criador(a) *m,f* (**b**) **(fast) b. reactor** reactor *m* generador

breeding ['briːdɪŋ] *n* (**a**) *(of animals)* cría *f*; *Fig* **b. ground** caldo *m* de cultivo (**b**) *(of person)* educación *f*

breeze [briːz] **1** *n* brisa *f*; *Constr* **b. block** bloque *m* de cemento
2 *vi* **to b. in/out** entrar/salir despreocupadamente

breezy ['briːzɪ] *adj* (**breezier, breeziest**) (**a**) *(weather)* ventoso(a) (**b**) *(person)* despreocupado(a)

brevity ['brevɪtɪ] *n* brevedad *f*

brew [bruː] **1** *vt* *(beer)* elaborar; *(hot drink)* preparar
2 *vi* *(tea)* reposar; *Fig* **a storm is brewing** se prepara una tormenta; *Fam* **something's brewing** algo se está cociendo
3 *n* (**a**) *(of tea)* infusión *f*; *Fam (of beer)* birra *f* (**b**) *(magic potion)* brebaje *m*

brewer ['bruːə(r)] *n* cervecero(a) *m,f*

brewery ['bruːərɪ] *n* cervecería *f*

brewing ['bruːɪŋ] **1** *adj* cervecero(a)
2 *n* *(of beer)* elaboración *f* de la cerveza

briar ['braɪə(r)] *n* brezo *m*

bribe [braɪb] **1** *vt* sobornar
2 *n* soborno *m*

bribery ['braɪbərɪ] *n* soborno *m*

bric-a-brac ['brɪkəbræk] *n* baratijas *fpl*

brick [brɪk] *n* ladrillo *m*; *Fam (reliable person)* persona *f* de confianza

bricklayer ['brɪkleɪə(r)] *n* albañil *m*

brickwork ['brɪkwɜːk] *n* ladrillos *mpl*

bridal ['braɪdəl] *adj* nupcial

bride [braɪd] *n* novia *f*; **the b. and groom** los novios

bridegroom ['braɪdgruːm] *n* novio *m*

bridesmaid ['braɪdzmeɪd] *n* dama *f* de honor

bridge[1] [brɪdʒ] **1** *n* puente *m*; *(of nose)* caballete *m*; *(of ship)* puente de mando
2 *vt* (**a**) *(river)* tender un puente sobre (**b**) *(gap)* llenar; *Fin* **bridging loan** crédito *m* a corto plazo

bridge[2] [brɪdʒ] *n Cards* bridge *m*

bridle ['braɪdəl] **1** *n* brida *f*; *(bit)* freno *m*; **b. path** camino *m* de herradura
2 *vt* *(horse)* embridar

brief [briːf] **1** *adj* (**a**) *(short)* breve (**b**) *(concise)* conciso(a)
2 *n* (**a**) *(report)* informe *m*; **in b.** en resumen; *Jur* expediente *m* (**c**) *Mil* instrucciones *fpl* (**d**) **briefs** *(for men)* calzoncillos *mpl*; *(for women)* bragas *fpl*
3 *vt* (**a**) *(inform)* informar (**b**) *(instruct)* dar instrucciones a

briefcase ['briːfkeɪs] *n* cartera *f*, portafolios *m inv*

briefing ['briːfɪŋ] *n* *(meeting)* reunión informativa

briefly ['briːflɪ] *adv* brevemente; **as b. as possible** con la mayor brevedad (posible)

brigade [brɪ'geɪd] *n* brigada *f*

brigadier [brɪgə'dɪə(r)] *n* general *m* de brigada

bright [braɪt] *adj* (**a**) *(light, sun, eyes)* brillante; *(colour)* vivo(a); *(day)* claro(a); (**b**) *(cheerful)* alegre; **to look on the b. side** mirar el lado bueno (**c**) *(clever)* listo(a), espabilado(a) (**d**) *(promising)* prometedor(a)

brighten ['braɪtən] *vi (prospects)* mejorarse; *(face)* iluminarse
▸ **brighten up 1** *vt sep (room etc)* alegrar
   2 *vi (weather)* despejarse; *(person)* animarse

brightly ['braɪtlɪ] *adv* brillantemente

brightness ['braɪtnɪs] *n* (**a**) *(of sun)* resplandor *m*; *(of day)* claridad *f*; *(of colour)* viveza *f* (**b**) *(cleverness)* inteligencia *f*

brilliance ['brɪljəns] *n* (**a**) *(of light)* brillo *m*; *(of colour)* viveza *f* (**b**) *(of person)* brillantez *f*

brilliant ['brɪljənt] **1** *adj* brillante; *(idea)* genial; *Fam (very good)* estupendo(a)
   2 *n* brillante *m*

brim [brɪm] **1** *n* borde *m*; *(of hat)* ala *f*; **full to the b.** lleno hasta el borde
   2 *vi* rebosar *(with* de)
▸ **brim over** *vi* rebosar

brine [braɪn] *n* salmuera *f*

bring [brɪŋ] *vt (pt & pp* **brought**) (**a**) *(carry, take)* traer; **could you b. that book?** ¿podrías traerme el libro?
   (**b**) *(take to a different position)* llevar; **the war brought hunger to many homes** la guerra llevó el hambre a muchos hogares
   (**c**) *(cause)* provocar; **he brought it upon himself** se lo buscó
   (**d**) *(persuade)* convencer; **how did they b. themselves to do it?** ¿cómo llegaron a hacerlo?
   (**e**) *(lead)* llevar
   (**f**) **to b. an action against** acusar
▸ **bring about** *vt sep* provocar
▸ **bring along** *vt sep* traer
▸ **bring back** *vt sep* (**a**) *(return)* devolver (**b**) *(reintroduce)* volver a introducir (**c**) *(make one remember)* traerle a la memoria
▸ **bring down** *vt sep* (**a**) *(from upstairs)* bajar (**b**) *(government)* derribar; *Th* **to b. the house down** echar el teatro abajo con los aplausos (**c**) *(reduce)* rebajar
▸ **bring forward** *vt sep* (**a**) *(meeting etc)* adelantar (**b**) *(present)* presentar (**c**) *Fin* **brought forward** suma y sigue

▸ **bring in** *vt sep* (**a**) *(yield)* dar (**b**) *(show in)* hacer entrar (**c**) *(law etc)* introducir; *(fashion)* lanzar
▸ **bring off** *vt sep* lograr, conseguir
▸ **bring on** *vt sep* provocar
▸ **bring out** *vt sep* (**a**) *(publish)* publicar (**b**) *(reveal)* recalcar; **he brings out the worst in me** despierta lo peor que hay en mí
▸ **bring round** *vt sep* (**a**) *(revive)* hacer volver en sí (**b**) *(persuade)* convencer
▸ **bring to** *vt sep* reanimar
▸ **bring up** *vt sep* (**a**) *(educate)* criar, educar (**b**) *(subject)* plantear (**c**) *(vomit)* devolver

brink [brɪŋk] *n (edge)* borde *m*; *Fig* **on the b. of ruin** al borde de la ruina; **on the b. of tears** a punto de llorar

brisk [brɪsk] *adj* enérgico(a); *(pace)* rápido(a); *(trade)* activo(a); *(weather)* fresco(a)

bristle ['brɪsəl] **1** *n* cerda *f*
   2 *vi* (**a**) *(a)* erizarse (**b**) *(show anger)* enfurecer *(at* con)
▸ **bristle with** *vt insep (be full of)* estar lleno(a) de

Brit [brɪt] *n Fam* británico(a) *m,f*

Britain ['brɪtən] *n* **(Great) B.** Gran Bretaña

British ['brɪtɪʃ] **1** *adj* británico(a); **the B. Isles** las Islas Británicas
   2 *npl* **the B.** los británicos

brittle ['brɪtəl] *adj* quebradizo(a), frágil

broach [brəʊtʃ] *vt (subject)* abordar

broad [brɔːd] **1** *adj* (**a**) *(wide)* ancho(a); *(large)* extenso(a) (**b**) **a b. hint** *(clear)* una indirecta clara (**c**) *(daylight)* pleno(a) (**d**) *(not detailed)* general (**e**) *(accent)* marcado(a), cerrado(a)
   2 *n US Fam (woman)* tía *f*, chica *f*

broadcast ['brɔːdkɑːst] *Rad & TV* **1** *n* emisión *f*
   2 *vt (pt & pp* **broadcast**) emitir, transmitir

broadcaster ['brɔːdkɑːstə(r)] *n* locutor(a) *m,f*

broadcasting ['brɔːdkɑːstɪŋ] *n Rad* radiodifusión *f*; *TV* transmisión *f*; *Rad* **b. station** emisora *f*

broaden ['brɔːdən] *vt* ensanchar

broadly ['brɔːdlɪ] *adv* en términos generales

broad-minded [brɔːd'maɪndɪd] *adj* liberal, tolerante

broadsheet ['brɔːdʃiːt] *n* folleto *m*

broccoli ['brɒkəlɪ] *n* brécol *m*

brochure ['brəʊʃə(r), 'brəʊʃʊə(r)] *n* folleto *m*

broil [brɔɪl] *vt US* asar a la parrilla

broiler ['brɔɪlə(r)] *n* (**a**) *(chicken)* pollo *m* (tomatero) (**b**) *US (grill)* parrilla *f*

broke [brəʊk] **1** *adj Fam* **to be (flat) b.** estar sin blanca

2 *pt of* **break**

broken ['brəʊkən] **1** *adj* (**a**) roto(a); *(machinery)* averiado(a); *(leg)* fracturado(a) (**b**) *(home)* deshecho(a); *(person)* destrozado(a); *(ground)* accidentado(a); **to speak b. English** chapurrear el inglés

2 *pp of* **break**

broken-hearted [brəʊkən'hɑːtɪd] *adj Fig* con el corazón destrozado

broker ['brəʊkə(r)] *n* corredor *m*, agente *mf* de Bolsa

brolly ['brɒlɪ] *n Fam* paraguas *m inv*

bronchitis [brɒŋ'kaɪtɪs] *n* bronquitis *f*

bronze [brɒnz] **1** *n* bronce *m*

2 *adj (material)* de bronce; *(colour)* bronceado(a)

bronzed [brɒnzd] *adj (suntanned)* bronceado(a)

brooch [brəʊtʃ] *n* broche *m*

brood [bruːd] **1** *n* (birds) cría *f*; *Hum (children)* prole *m*

2 *vi (hen)* empollar; *Fig (ponder)* rumiar; *Fig* **to b. over a problem** darle vueltas a un problema

broody ['bruːdɪ] *adj* (**a**) *Fam (woman)* con ganas de tener hijos (**b**) *(pensive)* pensativo(a) (**c**) *(moody)* melancólico(a)

brook¹ [brʊk] *n* arroyo *m*

brook² [brʊk] *vt (usu in negative)* soportar, aguantar

broom [bruːm] *n* (**a**) escoba *f* (**b**) *Bot* retama *f*

broomstick ['bruːmstɪk] *n* palo *m* de escoba

Bros *Com (abbr* **Brothers**) Hnos

broth [brɒθ] *n* caldo *m*

brothel ['brɒθəl] *n* burdel *m*

brother ['brʌðə(r)] *n* hermano *m*; **brothers and sisters** hermanos

brotherhood ['brʌðəhʊd] *n* hermandad *f*

brother-in-law ['brʌðərɪnlɔː] *n* cuñado *m*

brotherly ['brʌðəlɪ] *adj* fraternal

brought [brɔːt] *pt & pp of* **bring**

brow [braʊ] *n* (**a**) *(forehead)* frente *f* (**b**) *(eyebrow)* ceja *f* (**c**) *(of hill)* cima *f*

brown [braʊn] **1** *adj* (**a**) marrón; *(hair, eyes)* castaño(a); **b. bread** pan *m* integral; **b. paper** papel *m* de estraza; **b. sugar** azúcar moreno (**b**) *(tanned)* moreno(a)

2 *n* marrón *m*

3 *vt Culin* dorar; *(tan)* broncear

Brownie ['braʊnɪ] *n* niña exploradora

brownish ['braʊnɪʃ] *adj* pardusco(a)

browse [braʊz] **1** *vi (in shop)* mirar; *(through book)* hojear

2 *vt Comput* **to b. the Web** navegar por la Web

3 *n* **to have a b. (in)** dar un vistazo (a)

browser ['braʊzə(r)] *n Comput* navegador *m*

bruise [bruːz] **1** *n* morado *m*, cardenal *m*

2 *vt (body)* contusionar; *(fruit)* estropear

3 *vi (body)* magullarse; *(fruit)* estropearse

brunch [brʌntʃ] *n* = combinación de desayuno y almuerzo

brunette [bruː'net] *adj & n* morena *(f)*

brunt [brʌnt] *n* **the b.** lo peor; **to bear the b.** llevar el peso

brush¹ [brʌʃ] **1** *n* (**a**) *(for hair, teeth)* cepillo *m*; *Art* pincel *m*; *(for housepainting)* brocha *f* (**b**) *(with the law)* roce *m*

2 *vt* (**a**) cepillar; **to b. one's hair** cepillarse el pelo; **to b. one's teeth** cepillarse los dientes (**b**) *(touch lightly)* rozar

3 *vi* **to b. against** rozar al pasar

▶ **brush aside** *vt sep* dejar de lado

▶ **brush off** *vt sep* ignorar

▶ **brush up** *vt sep* repasar

brush² [brʌʃ] *n (undergrowth)* broza *f*, maleza *f*

brushwood ['brʌʃwʊd] *n* maleza *f*

brusque [bruːsk, brʊsk] *adj* brusco(a); *(words)* áspero(a)

Brussels ['brʌsəlz] *n* Bruselas

brutal ['bruːtəl] *adj* brutal, cruel

brute [bruːt] **1** *adj* bruto(a); **b. force** fuerza bruta

2 *n (animal)* bruto *m*; *(person)* bestia *f*

BSc [biːes'siː] *n (abbr* **Bachelor of Science**) *(person)* licenciado(a) *m,f* en Ciencias

bubble ['bʌbəl] **1** *n* burbuja *f*; **b. bath** espuma *f* de baño; **b. gum** chicle *m*; **soap b.** pompa *f* de jabón

2 *vi* burbujear; *Culin* borbotear

bubbly ['bʌblɪ] **1** *adj* (**bubblier**, **bubbliest**) efervescente

2 *n Fam* champán *m*, cava *m*

buck¹ [bʌk] **1** *n Zool* macho *m*; *(male deer)* ciervo *m*; *(male goat)* macho cabrío; *Fam* **to pass the b. to sb** echarle el muerto a algn

2 *vi (horse)* corcovear

▶ **buck up 1** *vt sep Fam* **b. your ideas up!** ¡espabílate!

2 *vi (cheer up)* animarse

buck² [bʌk] *n US Fam* dólar *m*

bucket [ˈbʌkɪt] **1** n cubo m; Fam **it rained buckets** llovía a cántaros
2 vi Fam (rain) llover a cántaros
buckle [ˈbʌkəl] **1** n hebilla f
2 vt abrochar con hebilla
3 vi (a) (wall, metal) combarse (b) (knees) doblarse
bud [bʌd] **1** n (shoot) brote m; (flower) capullo m
2 vi brotar; Fig florecer
Buddhism [ˈbʊdɪzəm] n budismo m
budding [ˈbʌdɪŋ] adj en ciernes
buddy [ˈbʌdɪ] n US Fam amigote m, compinche m
budge [bʌdʒ] vi (a) (move) moverse (b) (yield) ceder
budgerigar [ˈbʌdʒərɪgɑː(r)] n periquito m
budget [ˈbʌdʒɪt] **1** n presupuesto m; Br Pol **the B.** ≃ los Presupuestos Generales del Estado
2 vi hacer un presupuesto (**for** para)
budgie [ˈbʌdʒɪ] n Fam = budgerigar
buff¹ [bʌf] **1** adj & n (colour) color (m) de ante
2 vt dar brillo a
buff² [bʌf] n Fam (enthusiast) aficionado(a) m,f
buffalo [ˈbʌfələʊ] n (pl **buffaloes** or **buffalo**) búfalo m
buffer [ˈbʌfə(r)] **1** n (a) (device) amortiguador m; Rail tope m; **b. zone** zona f de seguridad (b) Comput memoria intermedia
2 vt amortiguar
buffet¹ [ˈbʊfeɪ] n (a) (snack bar) bar m; (at railway station) cantina f; Rail **b. car** coche m restaurante (b) (self-service meal) bufet m libre (c) (item of furniture) aparador m
buffet² [ˈbʌfɪt] vt golpear
buffoon [bəˈfuːn] n bufón m, payaso m
bug [bʌg] **1** n (a) (insect) bicho m (b) Fam (microbe) microbio m; **the flu b.** el virus de la gripe (c) (hidden microphone) micrófono oculto (d) Comput error m
2 vt Fam (a) **to b. a room** ocultar micrófonos en una habitación; **to b. a phone** pinchar un teléfono (b) (annoy) fastidiar, molestar
bugger [ˈbʌgə(r)] **1** n (a) sodomita m (b) very Fam Pej (person) gilipollas mf inv; (thing) coñazo m; **poor b.!** ¡el pobre!
2 interj very Fam Pej ¡joder!
3 vt sodomizar
▸ **bugger about** very Fam **1** vi hacer chorradas
2 vt sep **they really buggered him about**

se las hicieron pasar canutas
▸ **bugger off** vi very Fam Pej pirarse; **b. off!** ¡vete a la mierda!
▸ **bugger up** vt sep very Fam jorobar
buggy [ˈbʌgɪ] n (a) Br (baby's pushchair) cochecito m de niño (b) US (pram) cochecito m (de niño)
bugle [ˈbjuːgəl] n bugle m
build [bɪld] **1** vt (pt & pp **built**) construir
2 n (physique) tipo m, físico m
▸ **build up** vt sep (accumulate) acumular; **to b. up a reputation** labrarse una buena reputación
builder [ˈbɪldə(r)] n constructor(a) m,f; (contractor) contratista mf
building [ˈbɪldɪŋ] n edificio m, construcción f; **b. site** obra f; **b. society** sociedad hipotecaria
build-up [ˈbɪldʌp] n (a) (accumulation) aumento m; (of gas) acumulación f (b) (publicity) propaganda f
built [bɪlt] pt & pp of build
built-in [ˈbɪltˈɪn] adj (a) (cupboard) empotrado(a) (b) (incorporated) incorporado(a)
built-up [bɪltˈʌp] adj urbanizado(a)
bulb [bʌlb] n (a) Bot bulbo m (b) (light bulb) bombilla f
Bulgaria [bʌlˈgeərɪə] n Bulgaria
Bulgarian [bʌlˈgeərɪən] **1** adj búlgaro(a)
2 n (a) (person) búlgaro(a) m,f (b) (language) búlgaro m
bulge [bʌldʒ] **1** n protuberancia f; (in pocket) bulto m
2 vi (swell) hincharse; (be full) estar repleto(a)
bulk [bʌlk] n (a) (mass) masa f, volumen m; Com **in b.** a granel; **to buy sth in b.** comprar algo al por mayor (b) (greater part) mayor parte f
bulky [ˈbʌlkɪ] adj (**bulkier**, **bulkiest**) (a) (large) voluminoso(a) (b) **this crate is rather b.** esta caja es un armatoste
bull [bʊl] n (a) toro m; Fig **to take the b. by the horns** coger al toro por los cuernos (b) Fin **b. market** mercado m al alza
bulldog [ˈbʊldɒg] n buldog m
bulldoze [ˈbʊldəʊz] vt (land) nivelar; (building) derribar
bulldozer [ˈbʊldəʊzə(r)] n bulldozer m
bullet [ˈbʊlɪt] n bala f; **b. wound** balazo m
bulletin [ˈbʊlɪtɪn] n boletín m; Rad & TV **news b.** boletín de noticias; US **b. board** tablón m de anuncios
bullet-proof [ˈbʊlɪtpruːf] adj a prueba de balas; **b. vest** chaleco m antibalas
bullfight [ˈbʊlfaɪt] n corrida f de toros
bullfighter [ˈbʊlfaɪtə(r)] n torero(a) m,f

bullfighting ['bʊlfaɪtɪŋ] *n* los toros *mpl*; *(art)* tauromaquia *f*

bullion ['bʊljən] *n (gold, silver)* lingote *m*

bullish ['bʊlɪʃ] *adj Fin (market)* en alza

bullock ['bʊlək] *n* buey *m*

bullring ['bʊlrɪŋ] *n* plaza *f* de toros

bull's-eye ['bʊlzaɪ] *n (of target)* blanco *m*

bully ['bʊlɪ] **1** *n* matón *m*
2 *vt (terrorize)* intimidar; *(bulldoze)* tiranizar
3 *interj Ironic* b. for you! ¡bravo!

bulwark ['bʊlwək] *n* baluarte *m*

bum¹ [bʌm] *n Fam (bottom)* culo *m*

bum² [bʌm] *Fam* **1** *n* (a) *US (tramp)* vagabundo *m* (b) *(idler)* holgazán(ana) *m,f*
2 *vi* gorronear
▶ **bum around** *vi Fam* vaguear

bumblebee ['bʌmbəlbi:] *n* abejorro *m*

bumbling ['bʌmblɪŋ] *adj* torpe

bump [bʌmp] **1** *n* (a) *(swelling)* chichón *m*; *(lump)* abolladura *f*; *(on road)* bache *m* (b) *(blow)* choque *m*, golpe *m* (c) *(jolt)* sacudida *f*
2 *vt* golpear; to b. one's head darse un golpe en la cabeza
3 *vi* chocar (**into** contra)
▶ **bump into** *vt insep (meet)* tropezar con
▶ **bump off** *vt sep Fam* liquidar

bumper ['bʌmpə(r)] **1** *adj* abundante; b. edition edición *f* especial
2 *n Aut* parachoques *m inv*

bumptious ['bʌmpʃəs] *adj* presuntuoso(a), engreído(a)

bumpy ['bʌmpɪ] *adj* (**bumpier, bumpiest**) con muchos baches

bun [bʌn] *n* (a) *(bread)* panecillo *m*; *(sweet)* bollo *m*; *Fig Euph* she's got a b. in the oven está preñada (b) *(of hair)* moño *m*

bunch [bʌntʃ] **1** *n (of keys)* manojo *m*; *(of flowers)* ramo *m*; *(of grapes)* racimo *m*; *(of people)* grupo *m*; *(gang)* pandilla *f*
2 *vi* to b. together juntarse, agruparse

bundle ['bʌndəl] **1** *n (of clothes)* bulto *m*, fardo *m*; *(of papers)* fajo *m*; *(of wood)* haz *m*
2 *vt* (a) *(make a bundle of)* liar, atar (b) *(push)* empujar

bung [bʌŋ] **1** *n* tapón *m*
2 *vt Fam* (a) *(throw)* arrojar (b) *(put)* meter
▶ **bung up** *vt sep Fam* atascar

bungalow ['bʌŋgələʊ] *n* chalé *m*, bungalow *m*

bungle ['bʌŋgəl] *vt* chapucear

bunion ['bʌnjən] *n* juanete *m*

bunk [bʌŋk] *n (bed)* litera *f*

bunker ['bʌŋkə(r)] *n* (a) *(coal)* carbonera *f* (b) *Mil* búnker *m* (c) *(in golf)* búnker *m*

bunny ['bʌnɪ] *n Fam (baby talk)* b. (**rabbit**) conejito *m*

bunting ['bʌntɪŋ] *n (material)* lanilla *f*; *(flags)* banderines *mpl*; *Naut* empavesada *f*

buoy [bɔɪ] *n* boya *f*
▶ **buoy up** *vt sep* (a) *(keep afloat)* mantener a flote (b) *(person, spirits)* alentar, animar

buoyancy ['bɔɪənsɪ] *n* (a) *(of object)* flotabilidad *f* (b) *Fin* tendencia *f* alcista (c) *(optimism)* optimismo *m*

buoyant ['bɔɪənt] *adj* (a) *(object)* flotante (b) *Fin* con tendencia alcista (c) *(optimistic)* optimista

burble ['bɜ:bəl] *vi* (a) *(stream)* murmurar; *(baby)* balbucear (b) *(talk quickly)* farfullar

burden ['bɜ:dən] **1** *n* carga *f*; *Fig* to be a b. to sb ser una carga para algn
2 *vt* cargar (**with** con)

bureau ['bjʊərəʊ] *n (pl* **bureaux**) (a) *(desk)* escritorio *m* (b) *(office)* agencia *f*, oficina *f* (c) *US (chest of drawers)* cómoda *f* (d) *US Pol* departamento *m* del Estado

bureaucracy [bjʊə'rɒkrəsɪ] *n* burocracia *f*

bureaucrat ['bjʊərəkræt] *n* burócrata *mf*

bureaucratic [bjʊərə'krætɪk] *adj* burocrático(a)

burgeon ['bɜ:dʒən] *vi* florecer

burger ['bɜ:gə(r)] *n Fam (hamburger)* hamburguesa *f*

burglar ['bɜ:glə(r)] *n* ladrón(ona) *m,f*; b. alarm alarma *f* antirrobo

burglarize ['bɜ:gləraɪz] *vt US* robar, desvalijar

burglary ['bɜ:glərɪ] *n* robo *m* con allanamiento de morada

burgle ['bɜ:gəl] *vt* robar, desvalijar

burial ['berɪəl] *n* entierro *m*

burly ['bɜ:lɪ] *adj* (**burlier, burliest**) fornido(a), fuerte

Burma ['bɜ:mə] *n* Birmania

Burmese [bɜ:'mi:z] **1** *adj* birmano(a)
2 *n* (a) *(person)* birmano(a) *m,f* (b) *(language)* birmano *m*

burn [bɜ:n] **1** *n* quemadura *f*
2 *vt (pt & pp* **burnt** *or* **burned**) quemar
3 *vi* (a) *(fire)* arder; *(building, food)* quemarse (b) *(lamp)* estar encendido(a) (c) *(sore)* escocer
▶ **burn down 1** *vt sep* incendiar
2 *vi* incendiarse
▶ **burn out** *vi (people)* quemarse

► **burn up** *vt sep (energy, calories)* quemar

burner ['bɜːnə(r)] *n* quemador *m*

burning ['bɜːnɪŋ] *adj* (**a**) *(on fire)* incendiado(a); *(hot)* abrasador(a) (**b**) *(passionate)* ardiente (**c**) **a b. question** una cuestión candente

burnt [bɜːnt] **1** *adj* quemado(a); **b. almonds** almendras tostadas

2 *pt & pp of* **burn**

burp [bɜːp] **1** *n* eructo *m*

2 *vi* eructar

burrow ['bʌrəʊ] **1** *n* madriguera *f; (for rabbits)* conejera *f*

2 *vi* **a**) hacer una madriguera (**b**) *(search)* hurgar

bursar ['bɜːsə(r)] *n* tesorero(a) *m,f*

bursary ['bɜːsərɪ] *n* beca *f*

burst [bɜːst] **1** *n* (**a**) *(explosion)* estallido *m; (of tyre)* reventón *m* (**b**) *(of applause)* arranque *m; (rage)* arrebato *m*; **b. of gunfire** ráfaga *f* de tiros; **b. of laughter** carcajadas *fpl*

2 *vt* (*pt & pp* **burst**) *(balloon)* reventar; *Fig* **the river b. its banks** el río se salió de madre

3 *vi* (**a**) reventarse; *(shell)* estallar (**b**) *(enter suddenly)* irrumpir (**into** en)

► **burst into** *vt insep* **to b. into laughter/tears** echarse a reír/llorar

► **burst open** *vi* abrirse violentamente

► **burst out** *vi* **to b. out laughing** echarse a reír

bursting ['bɜːstɪŋ] *adj* **the bar was b. with people** el bar estaba atestado de gente; *Fam* **to be b. to do sth** reventar por hacer algo

bury ['berɪ] *vt* (**a**) enterrar; **to be buried in thought** estar absorto en pensamientos (**b**) *(hide)* ocultar

bus [bʌs] *n* (*pl* **buses,** *US* **busses**) autobús *m, Andes, CAm, Ven* buseta *f, Arg* colectivo *m, CAm, Méx* camión *m, Chile* micro *m, Cuba* guagua *f, Urug* ómnibus *m*; **b. conductor** revisor *m*; **b. driver** conductor(a) *m,f*; **b. stop** parada *f* de autobús

bush [bʊʃ] *n* (**a**) *(shrub)* arbusto *m* (**b**) *Austral* **the b.** el monte; *Fam* **b. telegraph** radio *f* macuto

bushy ['bʊʃɪ] *adj* espeso(a), tupido(a)

business ['bɪznɪs] *n* (**a**) *(commerce)* negocios *mpl*; **how's b.?** ¿cómo andan los negocios?; **to be away on b.** estar en viaje de negocios; **b. deal** negocio *m*; **b. hours** horas *fpl* de oficina; **b. trip** viaje *m* de negocios (**b**) *(firm)* empresa *f* (**c**) *(matter)* asunto *m*; **I mean b.** estoy hablando en serio; **it's no b. of mine** no es asunto mío; **to make it one's b. to ...**

encargarse de ...; **to get down to b.** ir al grano; **to go about one's b.** ocuparse de sus asuntos

businesslike ['bɪznɪslaɪk] *adj (practical)* eficiente; *(methodical)* metódico(a); *(serious)* serio(a)

businessman ['bɪznɪsmən] *n* hombre *m* de negocios

businesswoman ['bɪznɪswʊmən] *n* mujer *f* de negocios

busker ['bʌskə(r)] *n Fam* músico(a) *m,f* callejero(a)

bust[1] [bʌst] *n* (**a**) *(of woman)* pecho *m* (**b**) *Art* busto *m*

bust[2] [bʌst] *Fam* **1** *vt* (**a**) estropear (**b**) *(person)* trincar; *(place)* hacer una redada en

2 *adj* (**a**) *(damaged)* estropeado(a) (**b**) **to go b.** *(bankrupt)* quebrar

bustle ['bʌsəl] **1** *n (activity, noise)* bullicio *m*

2 *vi* **to b. about** ir y venir

bustling ['bʌslɪŋ] *adj* bullicioso(a)

bust-up ['bʌstʌp] *n Fam* riña *f*, pelea *f*

busy ['bɪzɪ] **1** *adj* (**a**) ocupado(a), atareado(a); *(life)* ajetreado(a); *(street)* concurrido(a) (**b**) *esp US Tel* ocupado(a); **b. signal** señal *f* de comunicando

2 *vt* **to b. oneself doing sth** ocuparse haciendo algo

busybody ['bɪzɪbɒdɪ] *n* entrometido(a) *m,f*

but [bʌt] **1** *conj* (**a**) pero; **b. yet** a pesar de todo (**b**) *(after negative)* sino; **not two b. three** no dos sino tres; **she's not Spanish b. Portuguese** no es española sino portuguesa

2 *adv* **had we b. known** de haberlo sabido; **we can b. try** al menos podemos intentarlo; **b. for her we would have drowned** si no hubiera sido por ella, nos habríamos ahogado

3 *prep* salvo, menos; **everyone b. her** todos menos ella; **he's anything b. handsome** es todo menos guapo

4 *npl* **ifs and buts** pegas *fpl*

butane ['bjuːteɪn] *n* butano *m*; **b. gas** gas butano

butcher ['bʊtʃə(r)] **1** *n* carnicero(a) *m,f*; **b.'s (shop)** carnicería *f*

2 *vt (animals)* matar; *(people)* masacrar

butler ['bʌtlə(r)] *n* mayordomo *m*

butt[1] [bʌt] *n* (**a**) *(end)* extremo *m; (of rifle)* culata *f; (of cigarette)* colilla *f* (**b**) **he was the b. of all the jokes** era el blanco de todas las bromas (**c**) *US Fam (bottom)* culo *m*

butt[2] [bʌt] **1** *n (with head)* cabezazo *m*

2 *vt* (*strike with head*) dar un cabezazo a
► **butt in** *vi* entrar en la conversación
butt³ [bʌt] *n* (*barrel*) tonel *m*
butter ['bʌtə(r)] **1** *n* mantequilla *f*, *Am*
manteca *f*; **b. dish** mantequera *f*
2 *vt* untar con mantequilla *or Am* manteca
buttercup ['bʌtəkʌp] *n* ranúnculo *m*,
botón *m* de oro
butterfingers ['bʌtəfɪŋgəz] *n sing Fam*
manazas *mf inv*
butterfly ['bʌtəflaɪ] *n* mariposa *f*
buttock ['bʌtək] *n* nalga *f*; **buttocks** nalgas *fpl*
button ['bʌtən] **1** *n* (a) (*on clothes, machine*) botón *m* (b) *US* (*badge*) chapa *f*
2 *vt* **to b. (up)** abrochar(se), aboto-
nar(se)
buttonhole ['bʌtənhəʊl] *n* ojal *m*
buttress ['bʌtrɪs] **1** *n* (a) contrafuerte *m*
(b) (*support*) apoyo *m*
2 *vt* apuntalar; *Fig* reforzar, apoyar
buxom ['bʌksəm] *adj* (*woman*) pechu-
gona
buy [baɪ] **1** *n* compra *f*; **a good b.** una
ganga
2 *vt* (*pt & pp* **bought**) (a) comprar; **she
bought that car from a neighbour**
compró ese coche a un vecino (b) *Fam*
(*believe*) tragar
► **buy off** *vt sep* sobornar
► **buy out** *vt sep* adquirir la parte de
► **buy up** *vt sep* comprar en grandes cantidades
buyer ['baɪə(r)] *n* comprador(a) *m,f*
buzz [bʌz] **1** *n* (a) (*of bee*) zumbido *m*; (*of
conversation*) rumor *m* (b) *Fam* (*telephone call*) telefonazo *m*
2 *vi* zumbar
buzzer ['bʌzə(r)] *n* timbre *m*
by [baɪ] **1** *prep* (a) (*indicating agent*) por;
composed by Bach compuesto(a) por
Bach; **a film by Almodóvar** una película
de Almodóvar
(b) (*via*) por; **he left by the back door**
salió por la puerta trasera
(c) (*manner*) por; **by car/train** en coche/
tren; **by credit card** con tarjeta de crédito;
by chance por casualidad; **by oneself**
solo(a); **made by hand** hecho(a) a mano;
**you can obtain a ticket by filling in the
coupon** puede conseguir una entrada
llenando el cupón
(d) (*amount*) por; **little by little** poco a
poco; **they are sold by the dozen** se

venden por docenas; **to be paid by the
hour** cobrar por horas
(e) **by far** con mucho; **he won by a foot**
ganó por un pie
(f) (*beside*) al lado de, junto a; **side by
side** juntos
(g) **to walk by a building** (*pass*) pasar
por delante de un edificio
(h) (*time*) para; **by now** ya; **by then** para
entonces; **we have to be there by nine**
tenemos que estar allí para las nueve; **by
the time we arrive** (para) cuando lleguemos; **by this time next year** el año que
viene por estas fechas
(i) (*during*) de; **by day/night** de día/
noche
(j) (*in an oath*) por; **by God!** ¡por Dios!
(k) *Math* por
(l) (*according to*) según; **is that O.K. by
you?** ¿te viene bien?
(m) **he had two children by his first
wife** tuvo dos hijos con su primera esposa
(n) (*phrases*) **bit by bit** poco a poco; **day
by day** día a día; **what do you mean by
that?** ¿qué quieres decir con eso?; **by the
way** a propósito
2 *adv* (a) **to go by** (*past*) pasar; **she just
walked by** pasó de largo
(b) **by and by** con el tiempo; **by and
large** en conjunto
bye [baɪ] **1** *n* **by the b.** por cierto
2 *interj Fam* ¡hasta luego!
bye-bye ['baɪ'baɪ] *interj Fam* ¡adiós!,
¡hasta luego!
by-election ['baɪɪlekʃən] *n* elección *f*
parcial
bygone ['baɪgɒn] **1** *adj* pasado(a)
2 *npl* **let bygones be bygones** lo pasado
pasado está
by-law ['baɪlɔː] *n* ley *f* municipal
bypass ['baɪpaːs] **1** *n* (a) (*road*) carretera
f de circunvalación (b) *Med* **b. surgery**
cirugía *f* de by-pass
2 *vt* evitar
by-product ['baɪprɒdʌkt] *n Chem & Ind*
derivado *m*, subproducto *m*; *Fig* consecuencia *f*
byroad ['baɪrəʊd] *n* carretera secundaria
bystander ['baɪstændə(r)] *n* testigo *mf*
byte [baɪt] *n Comput* byte *m*, octeto *m*
byword ['baɪwɜːd] *n* **it became a b. for
modernity** se convirtió en sinónimo de
modernidad

C

C, c [si:] *n* (**a**) *(the letter)* C, c *f* (**b**) *Mus* C do *m*

C (**a**) *(abbr* **Celsius**) C (**b**) *(abbr* **centigrade**) C

cab [kæb] *n US* taxi *m*; **c. driver** taxista *mf*

cabaret ['kæbəreɪ] *n* cabaret *m*

cabbage ['kæbɪdʒ] *n* col *f*, berza *f*; **red c.** (col) lombarda *f*

cabin ['kæbɪn] *n* (**a**) *(hut)* choza *f*; **log c.** cabaña *f* (**b**) *Naut* camarote *m* (**c**) *(of lorry, plane)* cabina *f*

cabinet ['kæbɪnɪt] *n* (**a**) *(item of furniture)* armario *m*; *(glass-fronted)* vitrina *f*; **c. maker** ebanista *mf* (**b**) *Pol* gabinete *m*, consejo *m* de ministros

cable ['keɪbəl] **1** *n* cable *m*; **c. car** teleférico *m*; **c. company** cableoperador(a) *m,f*; **c. TV** televisión *f* por cable

2 *vt & vi* cablegrafiar, telegrafiar

caboose [kə'bu:s] *n US (on train)* furgón *m* de cola

cache [kæʃ] *n* (**a**) *(place)* alijo *m* (**b**) *Comput* caché *f*

cackle ['kækəl] *vi* cacarear

cactus ['kæktəs] *n (pl* **cacti** ['kæktaɪ]) cactus *m*

CAD [kæd] *n (abbr* **computer-aided** *or* **-assisted design**) CAD *m*

cad [kæd] *n Br Fam* canalla *m*

caddie ['kædɪ] *n (in golf)* cadi *m*

cadet [kə'det] *n Mil* cadete *m*

cadge [kædʒ] *vt & vi Fam* gorronear

Caesarean [si:'zeərɪən] *n Med* **she had a C.** le hicieron una cesárea; **C. section** operación *f* cesárea

café ['kæfeɪ], **cafeteria** [kæfɪ'tɪərɪə] *n* cafetería *f*

caffeine ['kæfi:n] *n* cafeína *f*

cage [keɪdʒ] **1** *n* jaula *f*

2 *vt* enjaular

cagey ['keɪdʒɪ] *adj* (**cagier**, **cagiest**) *Fam* reservado(a)

cagoule [kə'gu:l] *n (garment)* canguro *m*

Cairo ['kaɪrəʊ] *n* (el) Cairo

cajole [kə'dʒəʊl] *vt* engatusar

cake [keɪk] **1** *n* (**a**) pastel *m*, tarta *f*; *Fam Fig* **it's a piece of c.** está chupado; **birthday c.** pastel de cumpleaños; **c. shop** pastelería *f* (**b**) *(of soap)* pastilla *f*

2 *vi (mud)* endurecerse

3 *vt* **caked with ...** cubierto(a) de ...

calamity [kə'læmɪtɪ] *n* calamidad *f*

calcium ['kælsɪəm] *n* calcio *m*

calculate ['kælkjʊlent] *vt* calcular

calculated ['kælkjʊlentɪd] *adj* intencionado(a)

calculating ['kælkjʊlentɪŋ] *adj* (**a**) **c. machine** calculadora *f* (**b**) *Pej (person)* calculador(a)

calculation [kælkjʊ'leɪʃən] *n* cálculo *m*

calculator ['kælkjʊlentə(r)] *n* calculadora *f*

calendar ['kælɪndə(r)] *n* calendario *m*; **c. year** año *m* civil

calf¹ [kɑ:f] *n (pl* **calves**) *(of cattle)* becerro(a) *m,f*, ternero(a) *m,f*; *(of other animals)* cría *f*

calf² [kɑ:f] *n (pl* **calves**) *Anat* pantorilla *f*

calfskin ['kɑ:fskɪn] *n* piel *f* de becerro

calibre, *US* **caliber** ['kælɪbə(r)] *n* calibre *m*

call [kɔ:l] **1** *vt* (**a**) llamar; **to c. sb names** poner verde a algn; **what's he called?** ¿cómo se llama?

(**b**) *(meeting etc)* convocar; **to c. sth to mind** traer algo a la memoria

2 *vi* (**a**) llamar; *Tel* **who's calling?** ¿de parte de quién?

(**b**) **to c. at sb's (house)** pasar por casa de algn; **to c. for sth/sb** pasar a recoger algo/a algn

(**c**) *(trains)* parar

(**d**) **to c. for** *(require)* exigir; **that wasn't called for** eso no estaba justificado

3 *n* (**a**) llamada *f*, grito *m*

(**b**) *(visit)* visita *f*; **to pay a c. on sb** visitar a algn

(**c**) *Tel (phone)* **c.** llamada *f*, *Am* llamado *m*; **c. box** cabina telefónica; **c. centre** centro *m* de atención telefónica

(**d**) *Med* **to be on c.** estar de guardia

(**e**) **there's no c. for you to worry** no hay motivo para que te preocupes

▸ **call away** *vt sep* **to be called away on business** tener que ausentarse por motivos de trabajo

▸ **call back** *vi (phone again)* llamar otra vez; *(visit again)* volver

▸ **call in 1** vt sep (doctor) llamar

2 vi (**a**) **I'll c. in tomorrow** (visit) mañana me paso (**b**) Naut hacer escala (**at** en)

▸ **call off** vt sep suspender

▸ **call on** vt insep (**a**) visitar (**b**) **to c. on sb for support** recurrir a algn en busca de apoyo

▸ **call out 1** vt sep (**a**) (shout) gritar (**b**) (doctor) hacer venir; (workers) convocar a la huelga

2 vi gritar

▸ **call up** vt sep (**a**) Tel llamar (por teléfono) (**b**) Mil llamar a filas, reclutar

caller ['kɔːlə(r)] n visita mf; Tel persona f que llama

calling ['kɔːlɪŋ] n esp Rel llamada f, vocación f; US **c. card** tarjeta f de visita;

callous ['kæləs] adj insensible, duro(a)

call-up ['kɔːlʌp] n llamamiento m a filas

calm [kɑːm] **1** adj (**a**) (weather, sea) en calma (**b**) (relaxed) tranquilo(a); **keep c.!** ¡tranquilo(a)!

2 n (**a**) (of weather, sea) calma f (**b**) (tranquillity) tranquilidad f

3 vt calmar, tranquilizar

4 vi **to c. (down)** calmarse, tranquilizarse

Calor Gas® ['kæləɡæs] n (gas m) butano m

calorie, calory ['kælərɪ] n caloría f

calve [kɑːv] vi (cow) parir (un becerro)

calves [kɑːvz] pl of **calf¹**, **calf²**

Cambodia [kæm'bəʊdɪə] n Camboya

came [keɪm] pt of **come**

camel ['kæməl] n camello(a) m,f

cameo ['kæmɪəʊ] n camafeo m

camera ['kæmərə] n (**a**) cámara f or máquina f fotográfica; Cin & TV cámara (**b**) Jur **in c.** a puerta cerrada

cameraman ['kæmərəmən] n cámara m

Cameroon [kæmə'ruːn] n Camerún

camomile ['kæməmaɪl] n camomila f; **c. tea** (infusión f de) manzanilla f

camouflage ['kæməflɑːʒ] **1** n camuflaje m

2 vt camuflar

camp¹ [kæmp] **1** n campamento m; **c. bed** cama f plegable; **c. site** camping m

2 vi **to go camping** ir de camping

camp² [kæmp] adj Fam afeminado(a); (affected) amanerado(a)

campaign [kæm'peɪn] **1** n campaña f

2 vi **to c. for/against** hacer campaña a favor de/en contra de

campaigner [kæm'peɪnə(r)] n defensor(a) m,f (**for** de)

camper ['kæmpə(r)] n (**a**) (person) campista mf (**b**) US (vehicle) caravana f

camping ['kæmpɪŋ] n **c. ground**, **c. site** camping m

campus ['kæmpəs] n campus m, ciudad universitaria

can¹ [kæn, unstressed kən] v aux (pt **could**)

El verbo **can** carece de infinitivo, de gerundio y de participio. En infinitivo o en participio, se empleará la forma correspondiente de **be able to**, por ejemplo: **he wanted to be able to speak English; she has always been able to swim.** En el inglés hablado, y en el escrito en estilo coloquial, la forma negativa **cannot** se transforma en **can't** y la forma negativa **could not** se transforma en **couldn't**.

(**a**) (be able to) poder; **he could have come** podría haber venido; **I'll phone you as soon as I c.** te llamaré en cuanto pueda; **she can't do it** no puede hacerlo; **I can't understand why** no entiendo por qué (**b**) (know how to) saber; **c. you ski?** ¿sabes esquiar?; **I can't speak English** no sé hablar inglés (**c**) (be permitted to) poder; **he can't go out tonight** no le dejan salir esta noche (**d**) (be possible) poder; **she could have forgotten** puede (ser) que lo haya olvidado; **they can't be very poor** no deben ser muy pobres; **what c. it be?** ¿qué será?

can² [kæn] **1** n (**a**) (of oil) bidón m (**b**) US (tin) lata f, bote m; **c. opener** abrelatas m inv

2 vt (**a**) (fish, fruit) envasar, enlatar (**b**) US Fam desestimar

Canada ['kænədə] n Canadá

Canadian [kə'neɪdɪən] adj & n canadiense (mf)

canal [kə'næl] n canal m

canary [kə'neərɪ] n canario m

Canary Islands [kə'neərɪaɪləndz] npl (Islas fpl) Canarias fpl

cancel ['kænsəl] vt (train, contract) cancelar; Com anular; (permission) retirar; (decree) revocar

cancellation [kænsɪ'leɪʃən] n cancelación f; Com anulación f

cancer ['kænsə(r)] n (**a**) Med cáncer m; **breast c.** cáncer de mama; **c. research** cancerología f (**b**) **C.** (in astrology) Cáncer m

candelabra [kændɪ'lɑːbrə] n candelabro m

candid ['kændɪd] adj franco(a), sincero(a)

> ℓ Note that the Spanish word **cándido** is a false friend and is never a translation for the English word **candid**. In Spanish, **cándido** means "ingenuous, naïve".

candidate ['kændɪdeɪt, 'kændɪdɪt] n candidato(a) m,f; (in exam) opositor(a) m,f

candle ['kændəl] n vela f; (in church) cirio m

candlelight ['kændəllaɪt] n luz f de vela; **by c.** a la luz de las velas

candlestick ['kændəlstɪk] n candelero m, palmatoria f; (in church) cirial m

candour, US **candor** ['kændə(r)] n sinceridad f, franqueza f

> 🔊 Note that the Spanish word **candor** is a false friend and is never a translation for the English word **candour**. In Spanish, **candor** means "innocence, naïvety".

candy ['kændɪ] n US caramelo m; **c. store** confitería f

candyfloss ['kændɪflɒs] n Br algodón m dulce

cane [keɪn] **1** n (a) Bot caña f; **c. sugar** azúcar m de caña (b) (wicker) mimbre m (c) (walking stick) bastón m; (for punishment) palmeta f

2 vt castigar con la palmeta

canine ['keɪnaɪn] adj Zool canino(a); **tooth** colmillo m

canister ['kænɪstə(r)] n bote m

canned [kænd] adj enlatado(a); **c. foods** conservas fpl

cannelloni [kænə'ləʊnɪ] n canelones mpl

cannibal ['kænɪbəl] adj & n caníbal (mf)

cannon ['kænən] **1** n (a) (pl cannons or cannon) cañón m; Fig **c. fodder** carne f de cañón (b) Br (in billiards, snooker) carambola f

2 vi chocar (into contra)

cannonball ['kænənbɔːl] n bala f de cañón

cannot ['kænɒt, kæ'nɒt] = can not

canoe [kə'nuː] n canoa f; Sport piragua f

canon ['kænən] n Rel canon m

canopy ['kænəpɪ] n (a) (on throne) dosel m (b) (awning) toldo m

can't [kɑːnt] = can not

Cantabria [kæn'tæbrɪə] n Cantabria

cantankerous [kæn'tæŋkərəs] adj intratable

canteen [kæn'tiːn] n (a) (restaurant) cantina f (b) (set of cutlery) juego m de cubiertos (c) (flask) cantimplora f

canter ['kæntə(r)] **1** n medio galope

2 vi ir a medio galope

canvas ['kænvəs] n (a) Tex lona f (b) (painting) lienzo m

canvass ['kænvəs] vi (a) Pol hacer propaganda electoral (b) Com hacer promoción, buscar clientes

canvasser ['kænvəsə(r)] n Pol = persona que hace propaganda electoral de puerta en puerta

canyon ['kænjən] n cañón m; **the Grand C.** el Gran Cañón

canyoning ['kænjənɪŋ] n Sport barranquismo m

cap [kæp] **1** n (a) gorro m; (soldier's) gorra f (b) Br Sport **to win a c. for England** ser seleccionado(a) para el equipo de Inglaterra (c) (of pen) capuchón m; (of bottle) chapa f

2 vt (a) (bottle) poner la chapa a; Fig **to c. it all** para colmo (b) Br Sport seleccionar

capability [keɪpə'bɪlɪtɪ] n habilidad f

capable ['keɪpəbəl] adj (a) (skilful) hábil (b) (able) capaz (**of** de)

capacity [kə'pæsɪtɪ] n (a) capacidad f (b) (position) puesto m; **in her c. as manageress** en calidad de gerente

cape¹ [keɪp] n (garment) capa f

cape² [keɪp] n Geog cabo m, promontorio m; **C. Horn** Cabo de Hornos; **C. Town** Ciudad del Cabo; **C. Verde** Cabo Verde

caper ['keɪpə(r)] n (prank) travesura f

capital ['kæpɪtəl] **1** n (a) (town) capital f (b) Fin capital m; **c. expenditure** inversión f de capital (c) (letter) mayúscula f

2 adj (a) (city) capital (b) **c. punishment** pena f capital (c) (primary) primordial (d) **c. letter** mayúscula f

capitalism ['kæpɪtəlɪzəm] n capitalismo m

capitalist ['kæpɪtəlɪst] adj & n capitalista (mf)

capitalize ['kæpɪtəlaɪz] vi Fin capitalizar; Fig **to c. on sth** sacar provecho or beneficio de algo

capitulate [kə'pɪtjʊleɪt] vi capitular

cappuccino [kæpə'tʃiːnəʊ] n (café m) capuchino m

Capricorn ['kæprɪkɔːn] n Capricornio m

capsicum ['kæpsɪkəm] n pimiento m

capsize [kæp'saɪz] **1** vt hacer zozobrar

2 vi zozobrar

capsule ['kæpsjuːl] n cápsula f

captain ['kæptɪn] **1** n capitán m

2 vt capitanear

caption ['kæpʃən] n (under picture) leyenda f; Cin subtítulo m

captivating ['kæptɪveɪtɪŋ] adj seductor(a)

captive ['kæptɪv] **1** n cautivo(a) m,f

2 adj cautivo(a)

captivity [kæp'tɪvɪtɪ] n cautiverio m

capture ['kæptʃə(r)] **1** vt (a) capturar, apresar; Mil (town) tomar (b) (market) acaparar (**c**) *Fig (mood)* captar

2 *n (of fugitive)* captura *f*; *(of town)* toma *f*

car [kɑː(r)] *n* (**a**) coche *m*, *Andes, CAm, Carib, Méx* carro *m*, *RP* auto *m*; **c. ferry** transbordador *m* para coches; *Br* **c. park** parking *m*, aparcamiento *m*; **c. wash** túnel *m* de lavado (**b**) *US Rail* coche *m*

carafe [kəˈræf, kəˈrɑːf] *n* garrafa *f*

caramel [ˈkærəməl] *n* azúcar *m* quemado; *(sweet)* caramelo *m*

carat [ˈkærət] *n* quilate *m*

caravan [ˈkærəvæn] *n* (**a**) *(vehicle)* remolque *m*, caravana *f* (**b**) *(in desert)* caravana *f*

carbohydrate [kɑːbəʊˈhaɪdreɪt] *n* hidrato *m* de carbono, carbohidrato *m*

carbon [ˈkɑːbən] *n* carbono *m*; **c. copy** copia *f* al papel carbón; *Fig* copia exacta; **c. dioxide** dióxido *m* de carbono; **c. paper** papel *m* carbón

carburettor [kɑːbjʊˈretə(r)], *US* **carburetor** [ˈkɑːbəreɪtə(r)] *n* carburador *m*

carcass [ˈkɑːkəs] *n* res muerta

card [kɑːd] *n* (**a**) *(of cardboard)* cartulina *f*; **birthday/Christmas c.** tarjeta de cumpleaños/de Navidad (**b**) *(in file)* ficha *f*; *(identity)* carnet *m*; **c. index** fichero *m* (**c**) **pack of cards** baraja *f*, cartas *fpl*; **(playing) c.** naipe *m*, carta; *Fig Br* **on** or *US* **in the cards** previsto

cardboard [ˈkɑːdbɔːd] *n* cartón *m*; **c. box** caja *f* de carton; **c. cutout** recortable *m*

cardiac [ˈkɑːdɪæk] *adj* cardíaco(a); **c. arrest** paro cardíaco

cardigan [ˈkɑːdɪɡən] *n* rebeca *f*

cardinal [ˈkɑːdɪnəl] **1** *n Rel* cardenal *m*

2 *adj* cardinal; **c. numbers** números *mpl* cardinales

care [keə(r)] **1** *vi (be concerned)* preocuparse (**about** por); **I don't c.** no me importa; *Fam* **for all I c.** me trae sin cuidado; *Fam* **he couldn't c. less** le importa un bledo

2 *n* (**a**) *(attention, protection)* cuidado *m*, atención *f*; **c. of ...** *(on letter)* al cuidado de ...; **medical c.** asistencia *f* médica; **to take c. of** cuidar; *(business)* ocuparse de (**b**) *(carefulness)* cuidado *m*; **take c.** *(be careful)* ten cuidado; *(as farewell)* ¡cuídate! (**c**) *(worry)* preocupación *f*

▸ **care for** *vt insep* (**a**) *(look after)* cuidar (**b**) *(like)* gustar, interesar; **would you c. for a coffee?** ¿te apetece un café?

career [kəˈrɪə(r)] **1** *n* carrera *f*

2 *vi* correr a toda velocidad

carefree [ˈkeəfriː] *adj* despreocupado(a)

careful [ˈkeəfʊl] *adj* cuidadoso(a); *(cautious)* prudente; **be c.!** ¡ojo!; **to be c.** tener cuidado

carefully [ˈkeəfʊlɪ] *adv (painstakingly)* cuidadosamente; *(cautiously)* con cuidado

careless [ˈkeəlɪs] *adj* descuidado(a); *(about clothes)* desaliñado(a); *(driving)* negligente; **a c. mistake** un descuido

carelessly [ˈkeəlɪslɪ] *adv* descuidadamente, a la ligera

carelessness [ˈkeəlɪsnɪs] *n* descuido *m*

caress [kəˈres] **1** *n* caricia *f*

2 *vt* acariciar

caretaker [ˈkeəteɪkə(r)] *n (in school etc)* bedel *mf*; *(in block of flats)* portero(a) *m,f*

carfare [ˈkɑːfeər] *n US* (precio *m* del) billete *m* or *Am* boleto *m*

cargo [ˈkɑːɡəʊ] *n* (*pl* **cargoes** or **cargos**) carga *f*, cargamento *m*; *Naut* **c. boat** buque *m* de carga, carguero *m*

Caribbean [kærɪˈbɪən, *US* kəˈrɪbɪən] *adj* caribe, caribeño(a); **the C. (Sea)** el (mar) Caribe

caricature [ˈkærɪkətjʊə(r)] *n* caricatura *f*

caring [ˈkeərɪŋ] *adj* solidario(a)

carnage [ˈkɑːnɪdʒ] *n Fig* carnicería *f*

carnal [ˈkɑːnəl] *adj* carnal

carnation [kɑːˈneɪʃən] *n* clavel *m*

carnival [ˈkɑːnɪvəl] *n* carnaval *m*

carnivorous [kɑːˈnɪvərəs] *adj* carnívoro(a)

carol [ˈkærəl] *n* villancico *m*

carom [ˈkærəm] *n US (in billiards, pool)* carambola *f*

carousel [kærəˈsel] *n US* tiovivo *m*

carp¹ [kɑːp] *n (fish)* carpa *f*

carp² [kɑːp] *vi* refunfuñar

carpenter [ˈkɑːpɪntə(r)] *n* carpintero(a) *m,f*

carpentry [ˈkɑːpɪntrɪ] *n* carpintería *f*

carpet [ˈkɑːpɪt] **1** *n* alfombra *f*

2 *vt Fig* **carpeted with** cubierto(a) de

> 📝 Note that the Spanish word **carpeta** is a false friend and is never a translation for the English word **carpet**. In Spanish, **carpeta** means "file, folder".

carriage [ˈkærɪdʒ] *n* (**a**) *(horse-drawn)* carruaje *m*; *Rail* vagón *m*, coche *m*; *(of gun)* cureña *f*; *(of typewriter)* carro *m* (**b**) *(of goods)* porte *m*, transporte *m*

carriageway [ˈkærɪdʒweɪ] *n Br* carril *m*, autovía *f*; **dual c.** autovía *f*

carrier [ˈkærɪə(r)] *n* (**a**) *(company)* transportista *mf*; *Br* **c. bag** bolsa *f* de plástico; **c. pigeon** paloma mensajera (**b**) *Med* portador(a) *m,f*

carrot ['kærət] *n* zanahoria *f*

carry ['kærɪ] **1** *vt* (**a**) llevar; *(goods)* transportar (**b**) *(stock)* tener; *(responsibility, penalty)* conllevar, implicar (**c**) **the motion was carried** se aprobó la moción (**d**) *(disease)* ser portador(a) de

2 *vi (sound)* oírse

▸ **carry away** *vt sep* llevarse; **to get carried away** entusiasmarse

▸ **carry forward** *vt sep* Fin **carried forward** suma y sigue

▸ **carry off** *vt sep (prize)* llevarse; *Fam* **to c. it off** salir airoso(a)

▸ **carry on 1** *vt sep* continuar; *(conversation)* mantener

2 *vi* (**a**) continuar, seguir adelante; **c. on!** ¡adelante! (**b**) *Fam (make a fuss)* hacer una escena; **don't c. on about it!** ¡no te enrolles! (**c**) *Fam* **to c. on with sb** estar liado(a) con algn

▸ **carry out** *vt sep (plan)* llevar a cabo, realizar; *(test)* verificar

carryall ['kærɪɔːl] *n US* bolsa *f (de viaje o de deporte)*

carrycot ['kærɪkɒt] *n Br* cuna *f* portátil

carsick ['kɑːsɪk] *adj* mareado(a) (en el coche)

cart [kɑːt] **1** *n (horse-drawn)* carro *m*; *(handcart)* carretilla *f*; *US (in supermarket)* carrito *m*

2 *vt* carretear

cartel [kɑː'tel] *n* cártel *m*

carton ['kɑːtən] *n (of cream etc)* caja *f*

cartoon [kɑː'tuːn] *n (strip)* tira cómica, historieta *f*; *Art* cartón *m*; *(animated)* dibujos *mpl* animados

cartoonist [kɑː'tuːnɪst] *n* caricaturista *mf*

cartridge ['kɑːtrɪdʒ] *n* (**a**) cartucho *m* (**b**) *(for pen)* recambio *m*; **c. paper** papel guarro

carve [kɑːv] *vt* (**a**) *(wood)* tallar; *(stone, metal)* cincelar, esculpir (**b**) *(meat)* trinchar

cascade [kæ'skeɪd] *n* cascada *f*

case¹ [keɪs] *n* (**a**) caso *m*; **a c. in point** un buen ejemplo; **in any c.** en cualquier caso, de todas formas; **in c. of doubt** en caso de duda; **just in c.** por si acaso (**b**) *Med* caso *m*; **c. history** historial clínico (**c**) *Jur* causa *f*

case² [keɪs] *n* (**a**) *(suitcase)* maleta *f*, *Méx* petaca *f*, *RP* valija *f*, *(small)* estuche *m*; *(soft)* funda *f* (**b**) **a c. of wine** una caja de botellas de vino (**c**) *Typ* **lower c.** minúscula *f*; **upper c.** mayúscula *f*

cash [kæʃ] **1** *n* dinero efectivo; **to pay c.** pagar al contado *or* en efectivo; **c. desk** caja *f*; **c. on delivery** entrega *f* contra reembolso; **c. dispenser** cajero automático; **c. register** caja registradora

2 *vt (cheque)* cobrar

▸ **cash in 1** *vi Fam Fig* **to c. in on sth** sacar provecho de algo

2 *vt sep* hacer efectivo(a)

cash-and-carry [kæʃən'kærɪ] *adj & adv* = de venta al por mayor y pago al contado

cashew ['kæʃuː] *n* **c. (nut)** anacardo *m*

cashier [kæ'ʃɪə(r)] *n* cajero(a) *m,f*

cashmere ['kæʃmɪə(r)] *n* cachemira *f*

casino [kə'siːnəʊ] *n* casino *m*

cask [kɑːsk] *n* tonel *m*, barril *m*

casket ['kɑːskɪt] *n (box)* cofre *m*; *US (coffin)* ataúd *m*

> 🖉 Note that the Spanish word **casquete** is a false friend and is never a translation for the English word **casket**. In Spanish, **casquete** means "shell case".

casserole ['kæsərəʊl] *n* (**a**) *(container)* cacerola *f* (**b**) *Culin* guisado *m*

cassette [kə'set] *n* cassette *f*; **c. recorder** cassette *m*

cast [kɑːst] **1** *vt (pt & pp cast)* (**a**) *(net, fishing line)* echar, arrojar; *(light)* proyectar; *(glance)* lanzar; *(anchor)* echar; *(vote)* emitir; *(skin)* mudar (**b**) *Fig* **to c. doubts on sth** poner algo en duda; **to c. suspicion on sb** levantar sospechas sobre algn (**c**) *(metal)* moldear; **c. iron** hierro fundido (**d**) *Th (play)* hacer el reparto de

2 *n* (**a**) *(mould)* molde *m*; *(product)* pieza *f* (**b**) *Med* **(plaster) c.** escayola *f* (**c**) *Th* reparto *m*

▸ **cast off** *vi Naut* soltar (las) amarras

castanets [kæstə'nets] *npl* castañuelas *fpl*

castaway ['kɑːstəweɪ] *n* náufrago(a) *m,f*

caste [kɑːst] *n* casta *f*

caster ['kɑːstə(r)] *n* **c. sugar** azúcar *m or f* extrafino(a)

Castile [kæ'stiːl] *n* Castilla

Castilian [kæ'stɪlɪən] **1** *adj* castellano(a)

2 *n* **C. (Spanish)** *(language)* castellano *m*

casting ['kɑːstɪŋ] *n* **c. vote** voto *m* de calidad

cast-iron ['kɑːstaɪən] *adj* de hierro fundido

castle ['kɑːsəl] **1** *n* (**a**) castillo *m* (**b**) *(in chess)* torre *f*

2 *vi (in chess)* enrocar

castor¹ ['kɑːstə(r)] *n* **c. oil** aceite *m* de ricino

castor² ['kɑːstə(r)] *n (on furniture)* ruedecilla *f*

castrate [kæ'streɪt] *vt* castrar

casual [ˈkæʒjʊəl] *adj* (**a**) *(meeting etc)* fortuito(a) (**b**) *(worker)* eventual (**c**) *(clothes)* (de) sport (**d**) *(visit)* de paso (**e**) *(person, attitude)* despreocupado(a), informal

casualty [ˈkæʒjʊəltɪ] *n* (**a**) *Mil* baja *f*; **casualties** pérdidas *fpl* (**b**) *(injured)* herido(a) *m,f*

> 🎵 Note that the Spanish word **casualidad** is a false friend and is never a translation for the English word **casualty**. In Spanish, **casualidad** means "chance, coincidence".

cat [kæt] *n* gato(a) *m,f*; *Fig* **to let the c. out of the bag** descubrir el pastel

Catalan [ˈkætələn] **1** *adj* catalán(ana)
2 *n* (**a**) *(person)* catalán(ana) *m,f* (**b**) *(language)* catalán *m*

catalogue, *US* **catalog** [ˈkætəlɒg] **1** *n* catálogo *m*
2 *vt* catalogar

Catalonia [kætəˈləʊnɪə] *n* Cataluña

catalyst [ˈkætəlɪst] *n* catalizador *m*

catapult [ˈkætəpʌlt] *n Br* tirachinas *m inv*

catarrh [kəˈtɑː(r)] *n* catarro *m*

catastrophe [kəˈtæstrəfɪ] *n* catástrofe *f*

catastrophic [kætəˈstrɒfɪk] *adj* catastrófico(a)

catch [kætʃ] **1** *vt* (*pt & pp* **caught**) (**a**) *(ball, thief)* coger; *(fish)* pescar; *(mouse etc)* atrapar; *(train, bus)* coger, *Am* agarrar; **to c. a cold** coger un resfriado; **to c. fire** *(log)* prenderse; *(building)* incendiarse; **to c. hold of** agarrar; **to c. sb's eye** captar la atención de algn; **to c. sight of** entrever
(**b**) *(surprise)* pillar, sorprender
(**c**) *(hear)* entender
(**d**) **to c. one's breath** *(hold)* sostener la respiración; *(recover)* recuperar el aliento
2 *vi* *(sleeve etc)* engancharse (**on** en); *(fire)* encenderse
3 *n* (**a**) *(of ball)* parada *f*; *(of fish)* presa *f* (**b**) *(on door)* pestillo *m* (**c**) *(drawback)* pega *f*; **c. question** pregunta *f* con pega
(**d**) **c. phrase** slogan *m*
► **catch on** *vi Fam* (**a**) *(become popular)* ganar popularidad (**b**) *(understand)* caer en la cuenta
► **catch out** *vt sep Fam* **to c. sb out** pillar a algn cometiendo una falta
► **catch up** *vi* (**a**) **to c. up with sb** *(reach)* alcanzar a algn (**b**) *(with news)* ponerse al corriente (**on** de); **to c. up on sleep** recuperar el sueño perdido; **to c. up with work** ponerse al día de trabajo

catching [ˈkætʃɪŋ] *adj* *(disease)* contagioso(a)

catchment [ˈkætʃmənt] *n* **c. area** zona *f* de captación

catchword [ˈkætʃwɜːd] *n* lema *m*

catchy [ˈkætʃɪ] *adj* (**catchier, catchiest**) *Fam* *(tune)* pegadizo(a)

categoric(al) [kætɪˈgɒrɪk(əl)] *adj* categórico(a)

categorize [ˈkætɪgəraɪz] *vt* clasificar

category [ˈkætɪgərɪ] *n* categoría *f*

cater [ˈkeɪtə(r)] *vi* (**a**) **to c. for** *(wedding etc)* proveer comida para (**b**) **to c. for** *(taste)* atender a

caterer [ˈkeɪtərə(r)] *n* proveedor(a) *m,f*

catering [ˈkeɪtərɪŋ] *n* abastecimiento *m* (de comidas por encargo)

caterpillar [ˈkætəpɪlə(r)] *n* (**a**) oruga *f* (**b**) **c. (tractor)** tractor *m* de oruga

cathedral [kəˈθiːdrəl] *n* catedral *f*

Catholic [ˈkæθəlɪk] *adj & n* católico(a) *(m,f)*

catholic [ˈkæθəlɪk] *adj* católico(a)

Catholicism [kəˈθɒlɪsɪzəm] *n* catolicismo *m*

cat's-eye® [ˈkætsaɪ] *n Br* captafaro *m*, = baliza reflectante en la calzada

cattle [ˈkætəl] *npl* ganado *m* (vacuno)

catty [ˈkætɪ] *adj* (**cattier, cattiest**) *Fam* *(remark)* malintencionado(a); *(person)* malicioso(a)

catwalk [ˈkætwɔːk] *n* pasarela *f*

Caucasian [kɔːˈkeɪzɪən] *adj & n* caucásico(a) *(m,f)*, blanco(a) *(m,f)*

caucus [ˈkɔːkəs] *n* comité *m* central, ejecutiva *f*

caught [kɔːt] *pt & pp* of **catch**

cauliflower [ˈkɒlɪflaʊə(r)] *n* coliflor *f*

cause [kɔːz] **1** *n* (**a**) *(origin)* causa *f* (**b**) *(reason)* motivo *m* (**c**) **for a good c.** por una buena causa
2 *vt* causar; **to c. sb to do sth** hacer que algn haga algo

caustic [ˈkɔːstɪk] *adj* cáustico(a); *Fig* mordaz

caution [ˈkɔːʃən] **1** *n* (**a**) *(care)* cautela *f*, prudencia *f* (**b**) *(warning)* aviso *m*, advertencia *f* (**c**) *Br Jur* represión *f*
2 *vt* advertir, amonestar

cautious [ˈkɔːʃəs] *adj* cauteloso(a), prudente

cavalcade [kævəlˈkeɪd] *n* cabalgata *f*

cavalier [kævəˈlɪə(r)] **1** *adj* arrogante
2 *n* caballero *m*

cavalry [ˈkævəlrɪ] *n* caballería *f*

cave [keɪv] *n* cueva *f*
► **cave in** *vi* *(roof etc)* derrumbarse, hundirse

caveman ['keɪvmæn] n hombre m de las cavernas

cavern ['kævən] n caverna f

caviar(e) ['kævɪɑː(r)] n caviar m

cavity ['kævɪtɪ] n (a) (hole) cavidad f (b) (in tooth) caries f inv

cavort [kə'vɔːt] vi retozar, brincar

CB [siː'biː] (abbr Citizens' Band) banda ciudadana

CBI [siːbiː'aɪ] n Br (abbr Confederation of British Industry) ≃ CEOE f

cc [siː'siː] (abbr cubic centimetre(s)) cc

CD [siː'diː] n (abbr compact disc) CD m; **CD player** (lector m or reproductor m de) CD m

CD-ROM [siːdiː'rɒm] n Comput (abbr compact disc read-only memory) CD-ROM m

cease [siːs] 1 vt cesar; **to c. doing** or **to do sth** dejar de hacer algo
2 vi terminar

cease-fire [siːs'faɪə(r)] n alto m el fuego

ceaseless ['siːslɪs] adj incesante

cedar ['siːdə(r)] n cedro m

cede [siːd] vt ceder

ceiling ['siːlɪŋ] n techo m

celebrate ['selɪbreɪt] 1 vt (occasion) celebrar
2 vi divertirse

celebrated ['selɪbreɪtɪd] adj célebre

celebration [selɪ'breɪʃən] n (a) celebración f (b) **celebrations** festividades fpl

celebrity [sɪ'lebrɪtɪ] n celebridad f

celery ['selərɪ] n apio m

celibate ['selɪbɪt] adj & n célibe (mf)

cell [sel] n (a) (in prison) celda f (b) Biol & Pol célula f (c) Elec pila f

cellar ['selə(r)] n sótano m; (for wine) bodega f

cello ['tʃeləʊ] n violoncelo m

cellophane® ['seləfeɪn] n Br celofán m

celluloid ['seljʊlɔɪd] n celuloide m

cellulose ['seljʊləʊs] n celulosa f

Celsius ['selsɪəs] adj Celsio

Celt [kelt, selt] n celta mf

Celtic ['keltɪk, 'seltɪk] 1 n (language) celta m
2 adj celta

cement [sɪ'ment] 1 n cemento m; **c. mixer** hormigonera f
2 vt Constr unir con cemento; Fig (friendship) cimentar

cemetery ['semɪtrɪ] n cementerio m

censor ['sensə(r)] 1 n censor(a) m,f
2 vt censurar

censorship ['sensəʃɪp] n censura f

censure ['senʃə(r)] 1 n censura f
2 vt censurar

census ['sensəs] n censo m

cent [sent] n (a) centavo m, céntimo m (b) **per c.** por ciento

centenary [sen'tiːnərɪ] n centenario m

center ['sentər] n & vt US = **centre**

centigrade ['sentɪgreɪd] adj centígrado(a)

centilitre, US **centiliter** ['sentɪliːtə(r)] n centilitro m

centimetre, US **centimeter** ['sentɪmiːtə(r)] n centímetro m

centipede ['sentɪpiːd] n ciempiés m inv

central ['sentrəl] adj central; **c. heating** calefacción f central; **C. America** Centroamérica; **C. American** centroamericano(a) m,f; Br **c. reservation** (on motorway) mediana f, Col, Méx camellón m

centralize ['sentrəlaɪz] vt centralizar

centrally ['sentrəlɪ] adv **c. heated** con calefacción central; **c. situated** céntrico(a)

centre ['sentə(r)] 1 n centro m; **town c.** centro de la ciudad; Ftb **c. forward** delantero centro; Ftb **c. half** medio centro; Pol **c. party** partido m centrista; **sports c.** centro deportivo
2 vt (attention etc) centrar (**on** en)

century ['sentʃərɪ] n siglo m; **the nineteenth c.** el siglo diecinueve

ceramic [sɪ'ræmɪk] 1 n cerámica f
2 adj de cerámica

ceramics [sɪ'ræmɪks] n sing cerámica f

cereal ['sɪərɪəl] n cereal m

cerebral ['serɪbrəl, sɪ'riːbrəl] adj cerebral; **c. palsy** parálisis f cerebral

ceremony ['serɪmənɪ] n ceremonia f

certain ['sɜːtən] 1 adj (a) (sure) seguro(a); **to be c.** estar seguro(a); **to make c. of sth** asegurarse de algo (b) **a c. extent** hasta cierto punto (c) (not known) cierto(a); **a c. Miss Ward** una tal señorita Ward (d) (true) cierto(a)
2 adv **for c.** a ciencia cierta

certainly ['sɜːtənlɪ] adv desde luego; **c. not** de ninguna manera

certainty ['sɜːtəntɪ] n certeza f; (assurance) seguridad f

certificate [sə'tɪfɪkɪt] n certificado m; Educ diploma m

certified ['sɜːtɪfaɪd] adj certificado(a); (copy) compulsado(a); US **c. public accountant** censor(a) m,f jurado(a) de cuentas, auditor(a) m,f, Am contador(a) m,f público(a)

certify ['sɜːtɪfaɪ] vt certificar

cervical ['sɜːvɪkəl, sə'vaɪkəl] adj **c. cancer** cáncer m del útero; **c. smear** frotis m cervical

cervix ['sɜːvɪks] *n* (a) *(uterus)* cuello *m* del útero (b) *(neck)* cerviz *f*, cuello *m*

cessation [se'seɪʃən] *n* cese *m*

cesspit ['sespɪt] *n* pozo negro

Ceylon [sɪ'lɒn] *n* Ceilán

cf [siː'ef] *(abbr* **confer, compare)** cf., cfr.

chafe [tʃeɪf] **1** *vt (make sore)* rozar
2 *vi (skin)* irritarse; *(item of clothing)* rozar

chaffinch ['tʃæfɪntʃ] *n* pinzón *m* vulgar

chagrin ['ʃæɡrɪn] *n* disgusto *m*, desilusión *f*

chain [tʃeɪn] **1** *n* cadena *f*; *Fig (of events)* serie *f*; **c. of mountains** cordillera *f*; **c. reaction** reacción *f* en cadena; **c. saw** sierra mecánica
2 *vt* **to c. (up)** encadenar

chain-smoke ['tʃeɪnsməʊk] *vi* fumar un pitillo tras otro

chair [tʃeə(r)] **1** *n* (a) silla *f*; *(with arms)* sillón *m*; **c. lift** telesilla *m* (b) *(position)* presidencia *f*; *Univ* cátedra *f*
2 *vt* presidir

chairman ['tʃeəmən] *n* presidente *m*

chairperson ['tʃeəpɜːsən] *n* presidente(a) *m,f*

chalet ['ʃæleɪ] *n* chalet *m*, chalé *m*

chalk [tʃɔːk] *n (for writing)* tiza *f*
▸ **chalk up** *vt sep Fam (victory etc)* apuntarse

challenge ['tʃælɪndʒ] **1** *vt* (a) retar, desafiar; **to c. sb to do sth** retar a algn a que haga algo (b) *(authority etc)* poner a prueba; *(statement)* poner en duda (c) *Mil* dar el alto a
2 *n* (a) reto *m*, desafío *m* (b) *Mil* quién vive *m*

challenging ['tʃælɪndʒɪŋ] *adj (idea)* desafiante; *(task)* que presenta un desafío

chamber ['tʃeɪmbə(r)] *n* (a) *(hall)* cámara *f*; **C. of Commerce** Cámara de Comercio** (b) *Mus* **c. music** música *f* de cámara (c) *Br Jur* **chambers** gabinete *m*

chambermaid ['tʃeɪmbəmeɪd] *n* camarera *f*

chameleon [kə'miːlɪən] *n* camaleón *m*

champagne [ʃæm'peɪn] *n (French)* champán *m*; *(from Catalonia)* cava *m*

champion ['tʃæmpɪən] *n* campeón(ona) *m,f*; *Fig* **c. of human rights** defensor(a) *m,f* de los derechos humanos

championship ['tʃæmpɪənʃɪp] *n* campeonato *m*

chance [tʃɑːns] **1** *n* (a) *(fortune)* casualidad *f*, azar *m*; **by c.** por casualidad; **to take a c.** arriesgarse; **c. meeting** encuentro *m* casual (b) *(likelihood)* posibilidad *f*; **(the) chances are that ...** lo más posible

es que ... (c) *(opportunity)* oportunidad *f*
2 *vt* arriesgar
▸ **chance upon** *vt insep* encontrar por casualidad

chancellor ['tʃɑːnsələ(r)] *n* (a) *(head of state, in embassy)* canciller *m* (b) *Br Univ* rector(a) *m,f* (c) *Br* **C. of the Exchequer** ≃ ministro(a) *m,f* de Hacienda

chandelier [ʃændɪ'lɪə(r)] *n* araña *f* (de luces)

change [tʃeɪndʒ] **1** *vt* cambiar; **to c. gear** cambiar de marcha; **to c. one's mind/the subject** cambiar de opinión/de tema; **to c. trains** hacer transbordo; **to get changed** cambiarse de ropa; *Fig* **to c. hands** cambiar de dueño/a
2 *vi* cambiar, cambiarse; **to c. for the better/worse** mejorar/empeorar; **to c. into** convertirse en
3 *n* (a) cambio *m*; **for a c.** para variar; **c. of heart** cambio de parecer; **c. of scene** cambio de aires (b) *(money)* cambio *m*; *(after purchase)* vuelta *f*, **small c.** suelto *m*
▸ **change over** *vi* cambiarse

changeable ['tʃeɪndʒəbəl] *adj (weather)* variable; *(person)* inconstante

changeover ['tʃeɪndʒəʊvə(r)] *n* conversión *f*

changing ['tʃeɪndʒɪŋ] **1** *n* (a) **c. room** vestuario *m* (b) *Mil* relevo *m* (de la guardia)
2 *adj* cambiante

channel ['tʃænəl] **1** *n* (a) *Geog* canal *m*; *(of river)* cauce *m*; **the C. Islands** las Islas Anglonormandas; **the English C.** el Canal de la Mancha (b) *(administrative)* vía *f* (c) *TV & Rad* canal *m*, cadena *f*
2 *vt Fig (ideas etc)* canalizar, encauzar

chant [tʃɑːnt] **1** *n* *Rel* cántico *m*; *(of demonstrators)* slogan *m*
2 *vt & vi Rel* cantar; *(demonstrators)* corear

chaos ['keɪɒs] *n* caos *m*

chaotic [keɪ'ɒtɪk] *adj* caótico(a)

chap [tʃæp] *n Fam* chico *m*, tío *m*

chapel ['tʃæpəl] *n* capilla *f*

chaperon(e) ['ʃæpərəʊn] *n* carabina *f*

chaplain ['tʃæplɪn] *n* capellán *m*

chapter ['tʃæptə(r)] *n* (a) capítulo *m* (b) *Rel* cabildo *m*

char [tʃɑː(r)] *vt* chamuscar, carbonizar

character ['kærɪktə(r)] *n* (a) carácter *m* (b) *Fam (person)* tipo *m* (c) *Th* personaje *m*

characteristic [kærɪktə'rɪstɪk] **1** *n* característica *f*
2 *adj* característico(a)

characterize ['kærɪktəraɪz] *vt* caracterizar

charcoal ['tʃɑːkəʊl] *n* carbón *m* vegetal; *Art* **c. drawing** carboncillo *m*; **c. grey** gris marengo *or* oscuro

charge [tʃɑːdʒ] **1** *vt* (**a**) cobrar; **c. it to my account** cárguelo en mi cuenta (**b**) **to c. sb with a crime** acusar a algn de un crimen (**c**) *Mil* cargar contra (**d**) *Elec* cargar
  2 *vi Elec & Mil* cargar; **to c. about** andar a lo loco
  3 *n* (**a**) *(cost)* precio *m*; **bank charges** comisión *f*; **free of c.** gratis; **service c.** servicio *m*; **c. account** cuenta *f* corriente (**b**) **to be in c. of** estar a cargo de; **to take c. of** hacerse cargo de (**c**) *Jur* cargo *m*, acusación *f* (**d**) *(explosive)* carga explosiva (**e**) *Elec* carga *f*

charged [tʃɑːdʒd] *adj Fig* emotivo(a)

charismatic [kærɪz'mætɪk] *adj* carismático(a)

charitable ['tʃærɪtəbəl] *adj (person)* caritativo(a); *(organization)* benéfico(a)

charity ['tʃærɪtɪ] *n* caridad *f*; *(organization)* institución benéfica

charlady ['tʃɑːleɪdɪ] *n Br* mujer *f* de la limpieza

charlatan ['ʃɑːlətən] *n (doctor)* curandero(a) *m,f*

charm [tʃɑːm] **1** *n* (**a**) *(quality)* encanto *m* (**b**) *(spell)* hechizo *m*; **lucky c.** amuleto *m*
  2 *vt* encantar

charming ['tʃɑːmɪŋ] *adj* encantador(a)

chart [tʃɑːt] **1** *n* (**a**) *(giving information)* tabla *f*; *(graph)* gráfico *m* (**b**) *(map)* carta *f* de navegación (**c**) *Mus* **the charts** la lista de éxitos
  2 *vt Av & Naut (on map)* trazar

charter ['tʃɑːtə(r)] **1** *n* (**a**) *(of institution)* estatutos *mpl*; *(of rights)* carta *f* (**b**) **c. flight** vuelo *m* chárter
  2 *vt (plane, boat)* fletar

chartered accountant [tʃɑːtədə'kaʊntənt] *n Br* censor(a) *m,f* jurado(a) de cuentas, *Am* contador(a) *m,f* público(a)

chase [tʃeɪs] **1** *vt* perseguir; *(hunt)* cazar
  2 *n* persecución *f*; *(hunt)* caza *f*

chasm ['kæzəm] *n Geog* sima *f*; *Fig* abismo *m*

chassis ['ʃæsɪ] *n* chasis *m inv*

chastise [tʃæs'taɪz] *vt* castigar

chastity ['tʃæstɪtɪ] *n* castidad *f*

chat [tʃæt] **1** *n* (**a**) *(informal conversation)* charla *f*; *Br* **c. show** coloquio *m* (**b**) *Comput* charla *f*; **c. room** sala *f* de conversación
  2 *vi* (**a**) *(talk informally)* charlar (**b**)

Comput charlar (**to** *or* **with** con)
  ▸ **chat up** *vt sep Br Fam* **to chat sb up** *(intentar)* ligar con algn

chatter ['tʃætə(r)] **1** *vi (person)* parlotear; *(bird)* piar; *(teeth)* castañetear
  2 *n (of person)* parloteo *m*; *(of birds)* gorjeo *m*; *(of teeth)* castañeteo *m*

chatterbox ['tʃætəbɒks] *n Fam* parlanchín(ina) *m,f*

chatty ['tʃætɪ] *adj* (**chattier, chattiest**) hablador(a)

chauffeur ['ʃəʊfə(r), ʃəʊ'fɜː(r)] *n* chófer *m*

chauvinism ['ʃəʊvɪnɪzəm] *n* chovinismo *m*; **male c.** machismo *m*

chauvinist ['ʃəʊvɪnɪst] *adj & n* chovinista *(mf)*; **male c.** machista *m*

cheap [tʃiːp] **1** *adj* barato(a); *(fare)* económico(a); *(joke)* de mal gusto; *(contemptible)* bajo(a); *Fam* **dirt c.** tirado(a)
  2 *n Br Fam* **on the c.** en plan barato
  3 *adv* barato

cheapen ['tʃiːpən] *vt Fig* degradar

cheaply ['tʃiːplɪ] *adv* barato, en plan económico

cheat [tʃiːt] **1** *vt* engañar; **to c. sb out of sth** estafar algo a algn
  2 *vi* (**a**) *(at games)* hacer trampa; *(in exam etc)* copiar(se) (**b**) *Fam (husband, wife)* poner cuernos (**on** a)
  3 *n (trickster)* tramposo(a) *m,f*

check [tʃek] **1** *vt* (**a**) repasar; *(facts)* comprobar; *(tickets)* controlar; *(tyres, oil)* revisar (**b**) *(impulse)* refrenar; *(growth)* retardar (**c**) *(stop)* detener (**d**) *(in chess)* dar jaque a
  2 *vi* comprobar
  3 *n* (**a**) *(of documents etc)* revisión *f*; *(of facts)* comprobación *f* (**b**) *(in chess)* jaque *m* (**c**) *(pattern)* cuadro *m* (**d**) **to keep in c.** *(feelings)* contener; *(enemy)* mantener a raya (**e**) *US* = **cheque**
  ▸ **check in** *vi (at airport)* facturar; *(at hotel)* registrarse (**at** en)
  ▸ **check out 1** *vi (of hotel)* dejar el hotel
  2 *vt sep (facts)* verificar
  ▸ **check up** *vi* **to c. up on sb** hacer averiguaciones sobre algn; **to c. up on sth** comprobar algo

checked [tʃekt] *adj* a cuadros

checker ['tʃekər] *n US (cashier)* cajero(a) *m,f*

checkered ['tʃekərd] *adj US* = **chequered**

checkers ['tʃekərz] *n sing US (game)* damas *fpl*

check-in ['tʃekɪn] *n* **c. desk** *(at airport)* mostrador *m* de facturación

checkmate ['tʃekmeɪt] **1** n jaque mate m
2 vt dar (jaque) mate a; Fig poner en un
callejón sin salida

checkout ['tʃekaʊt] n (counter) caja f

checkpoint ['tʃekpɔɪnt] n control m

checkroom ['tʃekruːm] n US (for coats,
hats) guardarropa m; (for luggage) consigna f

checkup ['tʃekʌp] n Med chequeo m,
examen médico

cheek [tʃiːk] n (a) mejilla f (b) Fam
(nerve) cara f; **what c.!** ¡vaya jeta!

cheekbone ['tʃiːkbəʊn] n pómulo m

cheeky ['tʃiːkɪ] adj (cheekier, cheekiest)
Fam fresco(a), descarado(a)

cheep [tʃiːp] **1** n (of bird) pío m
2 vi piar

cheer [tʃɪə(r)] **1** vi aplaudir, aclamar
2 vt (a) (applaud) vitorear, aclamar (b)
(make hopeful) animar
3 n viva m; **cheers** aplausos mpl; Fam
cheers! (thank you) ¡gracias!; (before
drinking) ¡salud!
▸ **cheer up 1** vi animarse
2 vt sep **to c. sb up** alegrar or animar a
algn

cheerful ['tʃɪəfʊl] adj alegre

cheerio [tʃɪərɪ'əʊ] interj Br Fam ¡hasta
luego!

cheese [tʃiːz] n queso m

cheesecake ['tʃiːzkeɪk] n tarta f de
queso

cheetah ['tʃiːtə] n guepardo m

chef [ʃef] n chef m

chemical ['kemɪkəl] **1** n sustancia química, producto químico
2 adj químico(a)

chemist ['kemɪst] n (a) químico(a) m,f
(b) Br **c.'s (shop)** farmacia f; **(dispensing)
c.** farmacéutico(a) m,f

chemistry ['kemɪstrɪ] n química f

cheque [tʃek] n cheque m; **to pay by c.**
pagar con (un) cheque; **c. book** talonario
m (de cheques); **c. card** tarjeta f de identificación bancaria

chequered ['tʃekəd] adj a cuadros; Fig **a
c. career** una carrera con altibajos

cherish ['tʃerɪʃ] vt (a) (person) tenerle
mucho cariño a (b) Fig (hopes etc) abrigar

cherry ['tʃerɪ] n cereza f

chess [tʃes] n ajedrez m

chessboard ['tʃesbɔːd] n tablero m de
ajedrez

chesspiece ['tʃespiːs] n pieza f de ajedrez

chest [tʃest] n (a) Anat pecho m (b) (for
linen) arca f; (for valuables) cofre m; **c. of
drawers** cómoda f

chestnut ['tʃesnʌt] n (tree, colour) castaño m; (nut) castaña f

chew [tʃuː] vt masticar, mascar

chewing gum ['tʃuːɪŋgʌm] n chicle m

chic [ʃiːk] adj elegante

chick [tʃɪk] n (a) (young chicken) pollito
m (b) Fam (woman) nena f, Arg piba f,
Méx chava f

chicken ['tʃɪkɪn] **1** n (a) pollo m (b) Fam
(coward) gallina mf
2 vi Fam **to c. out** rajarse (por miedo)

chickenpox ['tʃɪkɪnpɒks] n varicela f

chickpea ['tʃɪkpiː] n garbanzo m

chicory ['tʃɪkərɪ] n achicoria f

chief [tʃiːf] **1** n jefe m
2 adj principal

chiefly ['tʃiːflɪ] adv (above all) sobre
todo; (mainly) principalmente

chiffon ['ʃɪfɒn] n gasa f

chilblain ['tʃɪlbleɪn] n sabañón m

child [tʃaɪld] n (pl children) niño(a) m,f;
(son) hijo m; (daughter) hija f; **c. minder** =
persona que cuida niños en su propia
casa

childbirth ['tʃaɪldbɜːθ] n parto m

childhood ['tʃaɪldhʊd] n infancia f, niñez f

childish ['tʃaɪldɪʃ] adj pueril, aniñado(a)

childlike ['tʃaɪldlaɪk] adj infantil

children ['tʃɪldrən] pl of **child**

Chile ['tʃɪlɪ] n Chile

Chilean ['tʃɪlɪən] adj & n chileno(a) (m,f)

chili ['tʃɪlɪ] n = chilli

chill [tʃɪl] **1** n (a) Med resfriado m (b)
(coldness) fresco m
2 adj frío(a)
3 vt (meat) refrigerar; (wine) enfriar

chilli ['tʃɪlɪ] n chile m

chilly ['tʃɪlɪ] adj (chillier, chilliest) frío(a)

chime [tʃaɪm] **1** n (peal) campanada f
2 vt **to c. five o'clock** (of clock) dar las
cinco
3 vi sonar
▸ **chime in** vi Fam intervenir

chimney ['tʃɪmnɪ] n chimenea f; **c.
sweep** deshollinador m

chimpanzee [tʃɪmpæn'ziː] n chimpancé
m

chin [tʃɪn] n barbilla f, mentón m; **double
c.** papada f

China ['tʃaɪnə] n China

china ['tʃaɪnə] n loza f, porcelana f

> ℓ Note that the Spanish word **china** is a
> false friend and is never a translation for
> the English word **china**. In Spanish, **china**
> means "pebble, small stone".

Chinese [tʃaɪ'niːz] **1** adj chino(a)

2 n (**a**) *(person)* chino(a) m,f (**b**) *(language)* chino m

chink¹ [tʃɪŋk] n *(opening)* resquicio m; *(crack)* grieta f

chink² [tʃɪŋk] **1** vi tintinear
2 n tintineo m

chip [tʃɪp] **1** n (**a**) *(of wood)* astilla f; *(of stone)* lasca f; *(in cup)* mella f (**b**) Br Culin **chips** patatas or Am papas fritas; US (**potato**) **chips** *(crisps)* patatas or Am papas fritas *(de bolsa)* (**c**) Comput chip m (**d**) *(in gambling)* ficha f
2 vt *(wood)* astillar; *(stone)* resquebrajar; *(china, glass)* mellar
3 vi *(wood)* astillarse; *(china, glass)* mellarse; *(paint)* desconcharse
▸ **chip in** vi Fam (**a**) meterse (**b**) *(with money)* poner algo (de dinero)

chiropodist [kɪˈrɒpədɪst] n pedicuro(a) m,f

chirp [tʃɜːp] vi *(birds)* gorjear

chisel [ˈtʃɪzəl] n cincel m

chit [tʃɪt] n nota f; *(small invoice)* vale m

chitchat [ˈtʃɪtʃæt] n Fam palique m

chivalry [ˈʃɪvəlrɪ] n caballerosidad f

chives [tʃaɪvz] npl cebolleta f

chlorine [ˈklɔːriːn] n cloro m

chock-a-block [tʃɒkəˈblɒk], **chock-full** [tʃɒkˈfʊl] adj Fam (lleno(a)) hasta los topes

chocolate [ˈtʃɒkəlɪt] **1** n chocolate m; **chocolates** bombones mpl
2 adj de chocolate

choice [tʃɔɪs] **1** n elección f; **a wide c.** un gran surtido; **by c.** por gusto
2 adj selecto(a)

choir [ˈkwaɪə(r)] n coro m, coral f

choirboy [ˈkwaɪəbɔɪ] n niño m de coro

choke [tʃəʊk] **1** vt (**a**) *(person)* ahogar (**b**) *(obstruct)* obstruir
2 vi ahogarse; **to c. on food** atragantarse con la comida
3 n Aut estárter m
▸ **choke back** vt sep *(emotions)* tragarse

cholera [ˈkɒlərə] n cólera m

cholesterol [kəˈlestərɒl] n colesterol m

choose [tʃuːz] **1** vt *(pt chose; pp chosen)* escoger, elegir; *(decide on)* optar por
2 vi escoger, elegir

choos(e)y [ˈtʃuːzɪ] adj (**choosier, choosiest**) Fam exigente

chop [tʃɒp] **1** vt (**a**) *(wood)* cortar; *(tree)* talar (**b**) *(food)* cortar a pedacitos
2 n (**a**) *(blow)* tajo m; *(with axe)* hachazo m (**b**) Culin chuleta f

chopper [ˈtʃɒpə(r)] n Fam helicóptero m

choppy [ˈtʃɒpɪ] adj (**choppier, choppiest**) *(sea)* picado(a)

chopsticks [ˈtʃɒpstɪks] npl palillos mpl

chord [kɔːd] n Mus acorde m; Fig **it strikes a c.** (me) suena

chore [tʃɔː(r)] n quehacer m, tarea f

chortle [ˈtʃɔːtəl] vi reír con ganas

chorus [ˈkɔːrəs] n Mus & Th coro m; *(in a song)* estribillo m; **c. girl** corista f

chose [tʃəʊz] pt of **choose**

chosen [ˈtʃəʊzən] pp of **choose**

Christ [kraɪst] n Cristo m, Jesucristo m

christen [ˈkrɪsən] vt bautizar

christening [ˈkrɪsənɪŋ] n bautizo m

Christian [ˈkrɪstʃən] **1** adj cristiano(a); **c. name** nombre m de pila
2 n cristiano(a) m,f

Christianity [krɪstɪˈænɪtɪ] n cristianismo m

Christmas [ˈkrɪsməs] n Navidad f; **merry C.!** ¡feliz Navidad!; **C. carol** villancico m; **C. Day** día m de Navidad; **C. Eve** Nochebuena f

chrome [krəʊm] n cromo m

chromium [ˈkrəʊmɪəm] n cromo m; **c. plating** cromado m

chromosome [ˈkrəʊməsəʊm] n cromosoma m

chronic [ˈkrɒnɪk] adj crónico(a)

chronicle [ˈkrɒnɪkəl] **1** n crónica f
2 vt hacer la crónica de

chronological [krɒnəˈlɒdʒɪkəl] adj cronológico(a)

chrysanthemum [krɪˈsænθəməm] n crisantemo m

chubby [ˈtʃʌbɪ] adj (**chubbier, chubbiest**) rellenito(a)

chuck [tʃʌk] vt Fam tirar; **to c. one's job in** or **up** dejar el trabajo; **to c. sb out** echar a algn; **to c. sth away** or **out** tirar algo

chuckle [ˈtʃʌkəl] **1** vi reír entre dientes
2 n sonrisita f

chug [tʃʌg] vi traquetear

chum [tʃʌm] n compinche mf, compañero(a) m,f

chunk [tʃʌŋk] n Fam cacho m, pedazo m

church [tʃɜːtʃ] n iglesia f; **to go to c.** ir a misa; **C. of England** Iglesia Anglicana

churchyard [ˈtʃɜːtʃjɑːd] n cementerio m, campo santo

churlish [ˈtʃɜːlɪʃ] adj grosero(a)

churn [tʃɜːn] **1** n *(for butter)* mantequera f; Br *(for milk)* lechera f
2 vt *(butter)* hacer
3 vi revolverse, agitarse
▸ **churn out** vt sep Fam producir en serie

chute [ʃuːt] n *(channel)* conducto m; *(slide)* tobogán m

chutney [ˈtʃʌtnɪ] n conserva f *(de frutas)* picante

CIA [siːaɪˈeɪ] *n US* (*abbr* **Central Intelligence Agency**) CIA *f*

CID [siːaɪˈdiː] *n Br* (*abbr* **Criminal Investigation Department**) = policía judicial británica

cider [ˈsaɪdə(r)] *n* sidra *f*

cigar [sɪˈgɑː(r)] *n* puro *m*

cigarette [sɪgəˈret] *n* cigarrillo *m*; **c. case** pitillera *f*; **c. end** colilla *f*; **c. holder** boquilla *f*; **c. lighter** mechero *m*

Cinderella [sɪndəˈrelə] *n* Cenicienta *f*

cine camera [ˈsɪnɪkæmərə] *n Br* cámara cinematográfica

cinema [ˈsɪnɪmə] *n* (**a**) *Br* (*building*) cine *m* (**b**) (*art*) cine *m*

cinnamon [ˈsɪnəmən] *n* canela *f*

cipher [ˈsaɪfə(r)] *n* (*numeral*) cifra *f*

circle [ˈsɜːkəl] **1** *n* (**a**) círculo *m*; (*of people*) corro *m*; **in business circles** en el mundo de los negocios (**b**) *Th* anfiteatro *m*
  2 *vt* (*surround*) rodear; (*move round*) dar la vuelta a
  3 *vi* dar vueltas

circuit [ˈsɜːkɪt] *n* (**a**) (*journey*) recorrido *m* (**b**) *Elec* circuito *m* (**c**) *Sport* (*events*) liga *f*; *Br* (*track*) circuito *m* (**d**) *Br Jur* **c. judge** juez *mf* de distrito

circular [ˈsɜːkjʊlə(r)] *adj & n* circular (*f*)

circulate [ˈsɜːkjʊleɪt] **1** *vt* (*news*) hacer circular
  2 *vi* circular

circulation [sɜːkjʊˈleɪʃən] *n* (**a**) (*of blood*) circulación *f* (**b**) (*of newspaper*) tirada *f*

circumcise [ˈsɜːkəmsaɪz] *vt* circuncidar

circumference [səˈkʌmfərəns] *n* circunferencia *f*

circumspect [ˈsɜːkəmspekt] *adj* prudente

circumstance [ˈsɜːkəmstəns] *n* (*usu pl*) circunstancia *f*; **under no circumstances** en ningún caso; **economic circumstances** situación económica

circumvent [sɜːkəmˈvent] *vt Fig* burlar

circus [ˈsɜːkəs] *n* circo *m*

cirrhosis [sɪˈrəʊsɪs] *n* cirrosis *f*

CIS [siːaɪˈes] *n* (*abbr* **Commonwealth of Independent States**) CEI *f*

cistern [ˈsɪstən] *n* cisterna *f*

cite [saɪt] *vt* (*quote*) citar

citizen [ˈsɪtɪzən] *n* ciudadano(a) *m,f*

citizenship [ˈsɪtɪzənʃɪp] *n* ciudadanía *f*

citrus [ˈsɪtrəs] *adj* **c. fruits** agrios *mpl*

city [ˈsɪtɪ] *n* (**a**) ciudad *f*; *US* **c. council** ayuntamiento *m*; *US* **c. hall** ayuntamiento *m* (**b**) *Fin* **the C.** = el centro financiero de Londres

civic [ˈsɪvɪk] *adj* cívico(a); *Br* **c. centre** centro cívico; **c. duties** obligaciones cívicas

civil [ˈsɪvəl] *adj* (**a**) civil; **c. defence** defensa *f* civil; **c. rights** derechos *mpl* civiles; **c. servant** funcionario(a) *m,f*; *Pol* **c. service** administración pública (**b**) (*polite*) cortés, educado(a)

civilian [sɪˈvɪljən] *adj & n* civil (*mf*); **c. clothing** traje *m* de paisano

civilization [sɪvɪlaɪˈzeɪʃən] *n* civilización *f*

civilized [ˈsɪvɪlaɪzd] *adj* civilizado(a)

clad [klæd] **1** *adj Literary* vestido(a)
  2 *pt & pp of* **clothe**

claim [kleɪm] **1** *vt* (**a**) (*benefits, rights*) reclamar; *Jur* (*compensation*) exigir (**b**) (*assert*) afirmar
  2 *n* (**a**) (*demand*) reclamación *f*; *Jur* demanda *f*; **to put in a c.** reclamar una indemnización (**b**) (*right*) derecho *m* (**c**) (*assertion*) pretensión *f*

claimant [ˈkleɪmənt] *n Jur* demandante *mf*

clairvoyant [kleəˈvɔɪənt] *n* clarividente *mf*

clam [klæm] *n* almeja *f*
  ► clam up *vi Fam* callarse

clamber [ˈklæmbə(r)] *vi* trepar (**over** por)

clammy [ˈklæmɪ] *adj* (**clammier, clammiest**) (*weather*) bochornoso(a); (*hand*) pegajoso(a)

clamour, *US* **clamor** [ˈklæmə(r)] **1** *n* clamor *m*
  2 *vi* clamar; **to c. for** pedir a gritos

clamp [klæmp] **1** *n* (*for carpentry*) tornillo *m* de banco; *Tech* abrazadera *f*; **wheel c.** cepo *m*
  2 *vt* sujetar con abrazaderas
  ► clamp down on *vt insep* aumentar los esfuerzos contra

clan [klæn] *n* clan *m*

clandestine [klænˈdestɪn] *adj* clandestino(a)

clang [klæŋ] **1** *vi* sonar
  2 *n* sonido metálico

clap [klæp] **1** *vi* aplaudir
  2 *n* (**a**) palmada *f* (**b**) **a c. of thunder** un trueno

clapping [ˈklæpɪŋ] *n* aplausos *mpl*

claret [ˈklærət] *n Br* (*wine*) clarete *m*; (*colour*) burdeos *m*

clarify [ˈklærɪfaɪ] *vt* aclarar

clarinet [klærɪˈnet] *n* clarinete *m*

clarity [ˈklærɪtɪ] *n* claridad *f*

clash [klæʃ] **1** *vi* (**a**) (*cymbals*) sonar; (*swords*) chocar; *Fig* (*disagree*) estar en desacuerdo (**b**) *(colours)* desentonar (**c**) *(dates)* coincidir

2 *n* (**a**) *(sound)* sonido *m* (**b**) *(fight)* choque *m*; *Fig (conflict)* conflicto *m*

clasp [klɑːsp] **1** *n* (**a**) *(on belt)* cierre *m*; *(on necklace)* broche *m* (**b**) *(grasp)* apretón *m*; **c. knife** navaja *f*

2 *vt (object)* agarrar; **to c. hands** juntar las manos

class [klɑːs] **1** *n* clase *f*; **c. struggle** lucha *f* de clases; *US Educ* **c. of '84** promoción *f* de 1984; *Rail* **second c. ticket** billete *m* de segunda (clase)

2 *vt* clasificar

classic ['klæsɪk] **1** *adj* clásico(a)

2 *n* (**a**) *(author)* autor clásico; *(work)* obra clásica (**b**) **the classics** *(literature)* las obras clásicas; **classics** *(languages)* clásicas *fpl*

classical ['klæsɪkəl] *adj* clásico(a)

classified ['klæsɪfaɪd] *adj (information)* secreto(a); **c. advertisements** anuncios *mpl* por palabras

classify ['klæsɪfaɪ] *vt* clasificar

classless ['klɑːslɪs] *adj* sin clases

classmate ['klɑːsmeɪt] *n* compañero(a) *m,f* de clase

classroom ['klɑːsruːm] *n* aula *f*, clase *f*

clatter ['klætə(r)] **1** *vi* hacer ruido; *(things falling)* hacer estrépito

2 *n* ruido *m*, estrépito *m*

clause [klɔːz] *n* (**a**) *Jur* cláusula *f* (**b**) *Ling* oración *f*

claw [klɔː] **1** *n (of bird, lion)* garra *f*; *(of cat)* uña *f*; *(of crab)* pinza *f*

2 *vt* agarrar, arañar; *(tear)* desgarrar

▸ **claw at** *vt insep* agarrar, arañar

clay [kleɪ] *n* arcilla *f*; **c. pigeon shooting** tiro *m* al plato

clean [kliːn] **1** *adj* (**a**) limpio(a) (**b**) *(unmarked, pure)* sin defecto; **a c. copy** una copia en limpio; **to have a c. record** no tener antecedentes (penales) (**c**) *(not obscene)* decente (**d**) *Fig* **to make a c. sweep of it** arrasar

2 *adv* (**a**) **to play c.** jugar limpio; *Fam* **to come c.** confesarlo todo (**b**) *Fam* por completo; **it went c. through the middle** pasó justo por el medio

3 *vt (room)* limpiar; **to c. one's teeth** lavarse los dientes

▸ **clean out** *vt sep (room)* limpiar a fondo

▸ **clean up** *vt sep & vi* limpiar

clean-cut ['kliːn'kʌt] *adj (person)* limpio(a), pulcro(a)

cleaner ['kliːnə(r)] *n* limpiador(a) *m,f*

cleaning ['kliːnɪŋ] *n* limpieza *f*

cleanliness ['klenlɪnɪs] *n* limpieza *f*

cleanse [klenz] *vt* limpiar

cleansing ['klenzɪŋ] *n* **c. lotion** leche limpiadora

clear [klɪə(r)] **1** *adj* (**a**) claro(a); *(road, day)* despejado(a); **c. conscience** conciencia tranquila (**b**) *(obvious)* claro(a); **to make sth c.** aclarar algo (**c**) *(majority)* absoluto(a); *(profit)* neto(a); **three c. days** tres días completos (**d**) *(free)* libre

2 *adv* (**a**) *Fig* **loud and c.** claramente (**b**) **stand c.!** ¡apártese!; **to stay c. of** evitar

3 *vt* (**a**) *(room)* vaciar; *Com* liquidar; **to c. one's throat** aclararse la garganta; **to c. the table** quitar la mesa (**b**) *(authorize)* autorizar (**c**) *(hurdle)* salvar (**d**) **to c. sb of a charge** exculpar a algn de un delito

4 *vi (sky)* despejarse

▸ **clear away** *vt sep* quitar

▸ **clear off** *vi Fam* largarse; **c. off!** ¡largo!

▸ **clear out** *vt sep (room)* limpiar a fondo; *(cupboard)* vaciar

▸ **clear up 1** *vt sep* (**a**) *(tidy)* recoger; *(arrange)* ordenar (**b**) *(mystery)* resolver; *(misunderstanding)* aclarar

2 *vi (weather)* despejarse; *(problem)* desaparecer

clearance ['klɪərəns] *n* (**a**) *(of area)* despeje *m*; *Com* **c. sale** liquidación *f* (de existencias) (**b**) *(space)* espacio *m* libre (**c**) *(authorization)* autorización *f*

clear-cut [klɪə'kʌt] *adj* claro(a)

clearing ['klɪərɪŋ] *n* (**a**) *(in wood)* claro *m* (**b**) *(of rubbish)* limpieza *f* (**c**) *(of cheque)* compensación *f*

clearly ['klɪəlɪ] *adv* (**a**) claramente (**b**) *(at start of sentence)* evidentemente

clearway ['klɪəweɪ] *n Br* = carretera donde está prohibido parar

cleaver ['kliːvə(r)] *n* cuchillo *m* de carnicero

clef [klef] *n* clave *f*; **bass/treble c.** clave de fa/de sol

cleft [kleft] *n* hendidura *f*, grieta *f*

clementine ['kleməntaɪn] *n* clementina *f*

clench [klentʃ] *vt (teeth, fist)* apretar

clergy ['klɜːdʒɪ] *n* clero *m*

clergyman ['klɜːdʒɪmən] *n* clérigo *m*

clerical ['klerɪkəl] *adj* (**a**) *Rel* clerical (**b**) *(staff, work)* de oficina

clerk [klɑːk, *US* klɜːrk] *n* (**a**) *(office worker)* oficinista *mf* (**b**) *(civil servant)* funcionario(a) *m,f* (**b**) *US Com* dependiente(a) *m,f*, vendedor(a) *m,f*

clever ['klevə(r)] *adj* (**a**) *(person)* inteligente, listo(a); **to be c. at sth** tener aptitud para algo; *Fam* **c. Dick** sabiondo(a) *m,f* (**b**) *(argument)* ingenioso(a)

cliché ['kliːʃeɪ] *n* cliché *m*

click [klɪk] **1** *n* (*sound*) clic *m*
  2 *vt* (*tongue*) chasquear
  3 *vi* it didn't c. (*I didn't realize*) no me di cuenta

client ['klaɪənt] *n* cliente *mf*

clientele [kliːɒn'tel] *n* clientela *f*

cliff [klɪf] *n* acantilado *m*

climate ['klaɪmɪt] *n* clima *m*

climax ['klaɪmæks] *n* (**a**) (*peak*) clímax *m*, punto *m* culminante (**b**) (*sexual*) orgasmo *m*

climb [klaɪm] **1** *vt* (*ladder*) subir a; (*mountain*) escalar; (*tree*) trepar a
  2 *vi* (*plants*) trepar; *Av* subir; *Fig* (*socially*) ascender
  3 *n* subida *f*, ascensión *f*
  ► **climb down** *vi* bajar; *Fig* volverse atrás

climber ['klaɪmə(r)] *n* alpinista *mf*, *Am* andinista *mf*

climbing ['klaɪmɪŋ] *n Sport* montañismo *m*, alpinismo *m*, *Am* andinismo *m*

clinch [klɪntʃ] **1** *vt* resolver; (*deal*) cerrar
  2 *n Fam* abrazo apasionado

cling [klɪŋ] *vi* (*pt & pp* **clung**) (*hang on*) agarrarse; (*clothes*) ajustarse; (*smell*) pegarse; **c. together** unirse

clinic ['klɪnɪk] *n* (*in state hospital*) ambulatorio *m*; (*specialized*) clínica *f*

clinical ['klɪnɪkəl] *adj* (**a**) *Med* clínico(a) (**b**) (*detached*) frío(a)

clink [klɪŋk] **1** *vi* tintinear
  2 *n* tintineo *m*

clip¹ [klɪp] **1** *vt* (*cut*) cortar; (*ticket*) picar
  2 *n* (**a**) (*of film*) extracto *m* (**b**) (*with scissors*) tijeretada *f*

clip² [klɪp] **1** *n* (*for hair*) pasador *m*; (*for paper*) clip *m*, sujetapapeles *m inv*; (*brooch*) clip
  2 *vt* sujetar

clippers ['klɪpəz] *npl* (*for hair*) maquinilla *f* para rapar; (*for nails*) cortaúñas *m inv*; (*for hedge*) tijeras *fpl* de podar

clipping ['klɪpɪŋ] *n* recorte *m*

clique [kliːk] *n Pej* camarilla *f*

cloak [kləʊk] **1** *n* (*garment*) capa *f*
  2 *vt* encubrir

cloakroom ['kləʊkruːm] *n* guardarropa *m*; *Euph* (*toilets*) servicios *mpl*

clock [klɒk] **1** *n* reloj *m*
  2 *vt* (*race*) cronometrar
  ► **clock in, clock on** *vi* fichar
  ► **clock off, clock out** *vi* fichar a la salida
  ► **clock up** *vt sep* (*mileage*) hacer

clockwise ['klɒkwaɪz] *adj & adv* en el sentido de las agujas del reloj

clockwork ['klɒkwɜːk] *n* mecanismo *m*; **c. toy** juguete *m* de cuerda

clog [klɒg] **1** *vt* obstruir; (*pipe*) atascar; **to get clogged up** atascarse
  2 *n* (*footwear*) zueco *m*

cloister ['klɔɪstə(r)] *n* claustro *m*

close¹ [kləʊs] **1** *adj* (**a**) (*in space, time*) cercano(a); (*print, weave*) compacto(a); (*encounter*) cara a cara; (*contact*) directo(a); **c. to** cerca de; **c. together** juntos(as); *Fig* **we had a c. shave** nos libramos por los pelos (**b**) (*relationship*) estrecho(a); (*friend*) íntimo(a) (**c**) (*inspection*) detallado(a); (*watch*) atento(a) (**d**) (*contest*) reñido(a); **a c. resemblance** un gran parecido (**e**) (*air*) cargado(a); (*weather*) bochornoso(a) (**f**) (*secretive*) reservado(a) (**g**) **c. season** (*in hunting*) veda *f*
  2 *adv* cerca; **they live c. by** *or* **c. at hand** viven cerca; **to stand c. together** estar apretados(as)

close² [kləʊz] **1** *vt* (**a**) cerrar; **closing time** hora *f* de cierre (**b**) (*end*) concluir, terminar; (*meeting*) levantar
  2 *vi* (**a**) (*shut*) cerrar, cerrarse (**b**) (*end*) concluirse, terminarse
  3 *n* fin *m*, final *m*
  ► **close down** *vi* (*business*) cerrar para siempre; *Rad & TV* cerrar
  ► **close in** *vi* **to c. in on sb** rodear a algn

closed [kləʊzd] *adj* cerrado(a); *Ind* **c. shop** = empresa que emplea solamente a miembros de un sindicato

close-knit [kləʊs'nɪt] *adj Fig* unido(a)

closely ['kləʊslɪ] *adv* (**a**) (*tightly*) estrechamente, muy; **c. contested** muy reñido(a); **they are c. related** (*people*) son parientes próximos (**b**) (*attentively*) con atención; **to follow (events) c.** seguir de cerca (los acontecimientos)

closet ['klɒzɪt] *n US* armario *m*

close-up ['kləʊsʌp] *n* primer plano *m*

closure ['kləʊʒə(r)] *n* cierre *m*

clot [klɒt] **1** *n* (**a**) (*of blood*) coágulo *m*; *Med* **c. on the brain** embolia *f* cerebral (**b**) *Br Fam* tonto(a) *m,f*
  2 *vi* coagularse

cloth [klɒθ] *n* tela *f*, paño *m*; (*rag*) trapo *m*; (*tablecloth*) mantel *m*

clothe [kləʊð] *vt* (*pt & pp* **clothed** *or* **clad**) vestir (*in or* **with** de); *Fig* revestir, cubrir (*in or* **with** de)

clothes [kləʊðz] *npl* ropa *f*, vestidos *mpl*; **c. brush** cepillo *m* de la ropa; **c. hanger** percha *f*; **c. horse** tendedero *m* plegable; **c. line** tendedero *m*; **c. peg** *or US* **pin** pinza *f*

clothing ['kləʊðɪŋ] *n* ropa *f*

cloud [klaʊd] **1** *n* nube *f*

2 *vt* nublar; *Fig* **to c. the issue** complicar el asunto

3 *vi* **to c. over** nublarse

cloudy ['klaʊdɪ] *adj* (**cloudier, cloudiest**) (**a**) *(sky)* nublado(a) (**b**) *(liquid)* turbio(a)

clout [klaʊt] *Fam* **1** *n* (**a**) *(blow)* tortazo *m* (**b**) *(influence)* influencia *f*

2 *vt* dar un tortazo a

clove¹ [kləʊv] *n (spice)* clavo *m*

clove² [kləʊv] *n (of garlic)* diente *m*

clover ['kləʊvə(r)] *n* trébol *m*

clown [klaʊn] **1** *n* payaso *m*

2 *vi* **to c. (about** *or* **around)** hacer el payaso

cloying ['klɔɪɪŋ] *adj* empalagoso(a)

club [klʌb] **1** *n* (**a**) *(society)* club *m*; *sports* **c.** club deportivo (**b**) *(heavy stick)* garrote *m*, porra *f*; *(in golf)* palo *m* (**c**) *Cards* trébol *m* (**d**) *Culin* **c. sandwich** sándwich *m* doble; *US* **c. soda** soda *f*

2 *vt* aporrear

3 *vi* **to c. together** pagar entre varios

clubhouse ['klʌbhaʊs] *n* sede *f* de un club

cluck [klʌk] **1** *n* cloqueo *m*

2 *vi* cloquear

clue [kluː] *n (sign)* indicio *m*; *(to mystery)* pista *f*; *(in crossword)* clave *f*; *Fam* **I haven't a c.** no tengo ni idea

clump [klʌmp] *n (of trees)* grupo *m*; *(of plants)* mata *f*

clumsy ['klʌmzɪ] *adj* (**clumsier, clumsiest**) desmañado(a), torpe; *(awkward)* tosco(a)

clung [klʌŋ] *pt & pp of* **cling**

cluster ['klʌstə(r)] **1** *n* grupo *m*; *(of grapes)* racimo *m*

2 *vi* agruparse

clutch [klʌtʃ] **1** *vt* agarrar

2 *vi* *Fig* **to c. at straws** aferrarse a cualquier cosa

3 *n* (**a**) *Aut* embrague *m* (**b**) *Fig* **to fall into sb's clutches** caer en las garras de algn

clutter ['klʌtə(r)] *vt* **to c. (up)** llenar, atestar

cm *(abbr* **centimetre(s)**) cm

CND [siːen'diː] *n Br* (*abbr* **Campaign for Nuclear Disarmament**) = organización británica en favor del desarme nuclear

Co (**a**) *Com* (*abbr* **Company**) Cía. (**b**) *abbr* **County**

c/o [siːˈəʊ] (*abbr* **care of**) en el domicilio de

coach [kəʊtʃ] **1** *n* (**a**) *Aut* autocar *m*; *(carriage)* carruaje *m*; **c. tour** excursión *f* en autocar (**b**) *Rail* coche *m*, vagón *m* (**c**) *Sport* entrenador(a) *m,f*

2 *vt* *Sport* entrenar; *Educ* dar clases particulares a

coagulate [kəʊˈægjʊleɪt] *vi* coagularse

coal [kəʊl] *n* carbón *m*, hulla *f*; **c. bunker** carbonera *f*; **c. merchant** carbonero *m*; **c. mine** mina *f* de carbón

coalfield ['kəʊlfiːld] *n* yacimiento *m* de carbón

coalition [kəʊəˈlɪʃən] *n* coalición *f*

coarse [kɔːs] *adj (material)* basto(a); *(skin)* áspero(a); *(language)* grosero(a), ordinario(a)

coast [kəʊst] **1** *n* costa *f*, litoral *m*; *Fam Fig* **the c. is clear** no hay moros en la costa

2 *vi* *Aut* ir en punto muerto

coastal ['kəʊstəl] *adj* costero(a)

coaster ['kəʊstə(r)] *n (mat)* salvamanteles *m inv*

coastguard ['kəʊstgɑːd] *n* guardacostas *m inv*

coastline ['kəʊstlaɪn] *n* litoral *m*, costa *f*

coat [kəʊt] **1** *n* (**a**) *(overcoat)* abrigo *m*; *(short)* chaquetón *m*; **c. hanger** percha *f* (**b**) *(of animal)* pelo *m* (**c**) *(of paint)* mano *f*, capa *f* (**d**) **c. of arms** escudo *m* de armas

2 *vt* cubrir (**with** de); *(with liquid)* bañar (**with** en)

coating ['kəʊtɪŋ] *n* capa *f*, baño *m*

coax [kəʊks] *vt* engatusar

cob [kɒb] *n* mazorca *f*

cobble ['kɒbəl] *n* adoquín *m*

cobbler ['kɒblə(r)] *n* zapatero *m*

cobweb ['kɒbweb] *n* telaraña *f*

cocaine [kəˈkeɪn] *n* cocaína *f*

cock [kɒk] **1** *n* (**a**) *Orn* gallo *m*; *(male bird)* macho *m* (**b**) *(on gun)* percutor *m* (**c**) *Vulg (penis)* polla *f*

2 *vt (gun)* amartillar; *(ears)* erguir

► **cock up** *vt sep Br very Fam* chapucear

cocker ['kɒkə(r)] *n* **c. spaniel** cocker *m*

cockerel ['kɒkərəl] *n* gallo *m* joven

cockeyed ['kɒkaɪd] *adj Fam (lopsided)* torcido(a); *(scheme)* disparatado(a)

cockle ['kɒkəl] *n* berberecho *m*

cockney ['kɒknɪ] **1** *adj* = del East End londinense

2 *n* = persona del East End londinense

cockpit ['kɒkpɪt] *n* cabina *f* del piloto

cockroach ['kɒkrəʊtʃ] *n* cucaracha *f*

cocktail ['kɒkteɪl] *n* cóctel *m*; **c. lounge** bar *m*; **c. party** cóctel; **prawn c.** cóctel de gambas; **Molotov c.** cóctel Molotov

cocky ['kɒkɪ] *adj* (**cockier, cockiest**) *Fam* creído(a)

cocoa ['kəʊkəʊ] *n* cacao *m*

coconut ['kəʊkənʌt] *n* coco *m*

cocoon [kəˈkuːn] *n* capullo *m*

COD [siːəʊ'diː] *Br* (*abbr* **cash on delivery**) CAE

cod [kɒd] *n* bacalao *m*; **c. liver oil** aceite *m* de hígado de bacalao

code [kəʊd] **1** *n* código *m*; (*symbol*) clave *f*; *Tel* prefijo *m*
  2 *vt* (*message*) cifrar, poner en clave

co-ed [kəʊ'ed] *Fam* **1** *adj* mixto(a)
  2 *n* colegio mixto

coerce [kəʊ'ɜːs] *vt* coaccionar

coercion [kəʊ'ɜːʃən] *n* coacción *f*

coexist [kəʊɪg'zɪst] *vi* coexistir

coffee [ˈkɒfɪ] *n* café *m*; **c. bar/shop** cafetería *f*; **c. break** descanso *m*; **c. table** mesita *f* de café

coffeepot [ˈkɒfɪpɒt] *n* cafetera *f*

coffer [ˈkɒfə(r)] *n* arca *f*

coffin [ˈkɒfɪn] *n* ataúd *m*

cog [kɒg] *n* diente *m*

cognac [ˈkɒnjæk] *n* coñac *m*

coherent [kəʊ'hɪərənt] *adj* coherente

coil [kɔɪl] **1** *vt* **to c. (up)** enrollar
  2 *vi* enroscarse
  3 *n* (**a**) (*loop*) vuelta *f*; (*of rope*) rollo *m*; (*of hair*) rizo *m* (**b**) (*contraceptive*) espiral *f* (**c**) *Elec* carrete *m*, bobina *f*

coin [kɔɪn] **1** *n* moneda *f*
  2 *vt* (**a**) (*money*) acuñar (**b**) *Fig* **to c. a phrase** por así decirlo

coinage [ˈkɔɪnɪdʒ] *n* moneda *f*, sistema monetario

coincide [kəʊɪn'saɪd] *vi* coincidir (**with** con)

coincidence [kəʊ'ɪnsɪdəns] *n* coincidencia *f*

coincidental [kəʊɪnsɪ'dentəl] *adj* casual

coincidentally [kəʊɪnsɪ'dentəlɪ] *adv* por casualidad *or* coincidencia

Coke® [kəʊk] *n Fam* Coca-Cola® *f*

coke [kəʊk] *n* (*coal*) coque *m*

colander [ˈkɒləndə(r)] *n* colador *m*

cold [kəʊld] **1** *adj* frío(a); **I'm c.** tengo frío; **it's c.** (*weather*) hace frío; (*thing*) está frío(a); *Fig* **to get c. feet** (**about doing sth**) entrarle miedo a algn (de hacer algo); **c. cream** crema *f* hidratante; *Fig* **it leaves me c.** no me dice nada; **c. war** guerra fría
  2 *n* (**a**) frío *m* (**b**) *Med* resfriado *m*; **to catch a c.** resfriarse, acatarrarse; **to have a c.** estar resfriado(a); **c. sore** herpes *m* (en el labio)

cold-blooded [kəʊld'blʌdɪd] *adj* (**a**) (*animal*) de sangre fría (**b**) *Fig* (*person*) frío(a); (*crime*) a sangre fría

coleslaw [ˈkəʊlslɔː] *n* ensalada *f* de col

collaborate [kə'læbəreɪt] *vi* colaborar (**with** con)

collaborator [kə'læbəreɪtə(r)] *n Pol* colaboracionista *mf*

collapse [kə'læps] **1** *vi* (*break down*) derrumbarse; (*cave in*) hundirse; *Fig* (*prices*) caer en picado; *Med* sufrir un colapso
  2 *vt* (*table*) plegar
  3 *n* (*breaking down*) derrumbamiento *m*; (*caving in*) hundimiento *m*; *Med* colapso *m*

collapsible [kə'læpsəbəl] *adj* plegable

collar [ˈkɒlə(r)] **1** *n* (*of garment*) cuello *m*; (*for dog*) collar *m*
  2 *vt Fam* pescar, agarrar

collarbone [ˈkɒləbəʊn] *n* clavícula *f*

collateral [kɒ'lætərəl] **1** *n Fin* garantía subsidiaria
  2 *adj* colateral

colleague [ˈkɒliːg] *n* colega *mf*

collect [kə'lekt] **1** *vt* (**a**) (*gather*) recoger (**b**) (*stamps etc*) coleccionar (**c**) (*taxes*) recaudar
  2 *vi* (**a**) (*people*) reunirse (**b**) (*for charity*) hacer una colecta (**for** para)
  3 *adj US* **c. call** llamada *f* or *Am* llamado *m* a cobro revertido
  4 *adv US Tel* **to call c.** llamar a cobro revertido

collection [kə'lekʃən] *n* (**a**) (*of mail*) recogida *f*; (*of money*) colecta *f* (**b**) (*of stamps*) colección *f* (**c**) (*of taxes*) recaudación *f* (**d**) (*of people*) grupo *m*

collective [kə'lektɪv] **1** *adj* colectivo(a); **c. bargaining** negociación colectiva
  2 *n* colectivo *m*

collector [kə'lektə(r)] *n* (**a**) (*of stamps*) coleccionista *mf* (**b**) **tax c.** recaudador(a) *m,f* (de impuestos)

college [ˈkɒlɪdʒ] *n* colegio *m*; (*of university*) colegio mayor; *US* (*university*) universidad *f*

collide [kə'laɪd] *vi* chocar, colisionar

collie [ˈkɒlɪ] *n* perro *m* pastor escocés

colliery [ˈkɒljərɪ] *n Br* mina *f* de carbón

collision [kə'lɪʒən] *n* choque *m*

colloquial [kə'ləʊkwɪəl] *adj* coloquial

collusion [kə'luːʒən] *n* conspiración *f*

cologne [kə'ləʊn] *n* (agua *f* de) colonia *f*

Colombia [kə'lɒmbɪə] *n* Colombia

Colombian [kə'lɒmbɪən] *adj & n* colombiano(a) (*m,f*)

colon[1] [ˈkəʊlən] *n Typ* dos puntos *mpl*

colon[2] [ˈkəʊlən] *n Anat* colon *m*

colonel [ˈkɜːnəl] *n* coronel *m*

colonial [kə'ləʊnɪəl] *adj* colonial

colonize [ˈkɒlənaɪz] *vt* colonizar

colony [ˈkɒlənɪ] *n* colonia *f*

color [ˈkʌlə(r)] *n, vt & vi US* = **colour**

colossal [kə'lɒsəl] *adj* colosal

colour ['kʌlə(r)] **1** n (a) color m; **what c. is it?** ¿de qué color es?; **c. film/television** película f/televisión f en color; **c. scheme** combinación f de colores (b) *(race)* color m; **c. bar** discriminación f racial (c) **colours** Br Sport colores mpl; Mil *(flag)* bandera f

2 vt colorear

3 vi **to c. (up)** ruborizarse

colour-blind ['kʌləblaɪnd] adj daltónico(a)

Coloured ['kʌləd] adj de color

coloured ['kʌləd] adj *(photograph)* en color

> 🖉 Note that the Spanish word **colorado** is a false friend and is never a translation for the English word **coloured**. In Spanish, **colorado** means "red".

colourful ['kʌləfʊl] adj (a) con muchos colores (b) Fig lleno(a) de color; *(person)* pintoresco(a)

colouring ['kʌlərɪŋ] n *(colour)* colorido m

colourless ['kʌlələs] adj incoloro(a); Fig soso(a)

colt [kəʊlt] n potro m

column ['kɒləm] n columna f

columnist ['kɒləmnɪst] n columnista mf

coma ['kəʊmə] n coma m; **to go into a c.** entrar en coma

comb [kəʊm] **1** n peine m

2 vt peinar; **to c. one's hair** peinarse

combat ['kɒmbæt] **1** n combate m

2 vt *(enemy, disease)* combatir

3 vi combatir *(against contra)*

combination [kɒmbɪ'neɪʃən] n combinación f

combine 1 vt [kəm'baɪn] combinar

2 vi combinarse; *(companies)* asociarse

3 n ['kɒmbaɪn] (a) Com asociación f (b) **c. harvester** cosechadora f

combustion [kəm'bʌstʃən] n combustión f

come [kʌm] vi *(pt* came; *pp* come) (a) venir; *(arrive)* llegar; **coming!** ¡voy!; **to c. and go** ir y venir; Fig **in years to c.** en el futuro

(b) **to c. apart/undone** desatarse/soltarse

(c) *(happen)* suceder; **that's what comes of being too impatient** es lo que pasa por ser demasiado impaciente; Fam **how c.?** ¿y eso?

(d) **I came to believe that ...** llegué a creer que ...

(e) Fig **c. what may** pase lo que pase

(f) very Fam *(have orgasm)* correrse

► **come about** vi ocurrir, suceder

► **come across 1** vt insep *(thing)* encontrar por casualidad; **to c. across sb** tropezar con algn

2 vi Fig **to c. across well** causar buena impresión

► **come along** vi (a) *(arrive)* venir; **c. along!** ¡venga! (b) *(make progress)* progresar

► **come away** vi *(leave)* salir; *(part)* desprenderse (**from** de)

► **come back** vi *(return)* volver

► **come before** vt insep (a) preceder (b) *(court)* comparecer ante

► **come by** vt insep adquirir

► **come down** vi bajar; *(rain)* caer; *(building)* ser derribado(a); **to c. down with the flu** coger la gripe

► **come forward** vi *(advance)* avanzar; *(volunteer)* ofrecerse

► **come in** vi (a) *(enter)* entrar; **c. in!** ¡pase! (b) *(arrive)* *(train)* llegar; *(tide)* subir; Fam Fig **where do I c. in?** y yo ¿qué pinto? (c) **to c. in handy** venir bien (d) **to c. in for** ser objeto de

► **come into** vt insep (a) *(enter)* entrar en (b) *(inherit)* heredar

► **come off 1** vt insep *(fall from)* caerse de; Fam **c. off it!** ¡venga ya!

2 vi (a) *(fall)* caerse; *(stain)* quitarse; *(button)* caerse (b) Fam *(take place)* pasar; *(succeed)* salir bien; **to c. off badly** salir mal

► **come on** vi (a) **c. on!** *(hurry)* ¡venga! (b) *(make progress)* progresar (c) *(rain, illness)* comenzar

► **come out** vi (a) salir (**of** de); *(book)* aparecer; *(product)* estrenarse; *(facts)* revelarse (b) *(stain)* quitarse; *(colour)* desteñir (c) **to c. out against/in favour of sth** declararse en contra/a favor de algo; Br Ind **to c. out (on strike)** declararse en huelga (d) *(turn out)* salir

► **come over 1** vi venir

2 vt insep (a) *(hill)* aparecer en lo alto de (b) Fam **what's c. over you?** ¿qué te pasa?

► **come round 1** vt insep *(corner)* dar la vuelta a

2 vi (a) *(visit)* venir (b) *(regain consciousness)* volver en sí (c) **to c. round to sb's way of thinking** dejarse convencer por algn

► **come through 1** vt insep (a) *(cross)* cruzar (b) *(illness)* recuperarse de; *(accident)* sobrevivir

2 vi *(message)* llegar

► **come to 1** vi *(regain consciousness)* volver en sí

2 *vt insep* (**a**) *Fig* **to c. to one's senses** recobrar la razón (**b**) *(amount to)* costar (**c**) *(arrive at)* llegar a; **to c. to an end** terminar; *Fam* **c. to that** a propósito

▸ **come under** *vt insep Fig* **to c. under fire from sb** ser criticado(a) por algn

▸ **come up** *vi* (**a**) *(rise)* subir; *(approach)* acercarse (**to** a) (**b**) *(difficulty, question)* surgir; **to c. up with a solution** encontrar una solución; **to c. up against problems** encontrarse con problemas (**c**) *(sun)* salir (**d**) **to c. up to** igualar; **to c. up to sb's expectations** satisfacer a algn (**e**) *Fam* **three chips, coming up!** ¡van tres de patatas fritas!

▸ **come upon** *vt insep* = **come across**

comeback ['kʌmbæk] *n Fam* (**a**) *(of person)* reaparición *f*; **to make a c.** reaparecer (**b**) *(answer)* réplica *f*

comedian [kə'miːdɪən] *n* cómico *m*

comedienne [kəmiːdɪ'en] *n* cómica *f*

comedown ['kʌmdaʊn] *n Fam* desilusión *f*, revés *m*

comedy ['kɒmɪdɪ] *n* comedia *f*

comet ['kɒmɪt] *n* cometa *m*

comeuppance [kʌm'ʌpəns] *n Fam* **to get one's c.** llevarse su merecido

comfort ['kʌmfət] **1** *n* (**a**) comodidad *f*; *US* **c. station** servicios *mpl* (**b**) *(consolation)* consuelo *m*; **to take c. in** *or* **from sth** consolarse con algo
2 *vt* consolar

comfortable ['kʌmfətəbəl] *adj (chair, person, margin)* cómodo(a); *(temperature)* agradable

comfortably ['kʌmfətəblɪ] *adv (win)* con facilidad; **to be c. off** vivir cómodamente

comforter ['kʌmfətə(r)] *n* (**a**) *Br (scarf)* bufanda *f* (**b**) *(for baby)* chupete *m* (**c**) *US (quilt)* edredón *m*

comforting ['kʌmfətɪŋ] *adj* consolador(a)

comic ['kɒmɪk] **1** *adj* cómico(a); **c. strip** tira cómica, historieta *f*
2 *n* (**a**) *(person)* cómico(a) *m,f* (**b**) *Press* tebeo *m*, comic *m*

coming ['kʌmɪŋ] **1** *adj (year)* próximo(a); *(generation)* futuro(a)
2 *n* venida *f*, llegada *f*; **comings and goings** idas *fpl* y venidas; *Fig* **c. and going** ajetreo *m*

comma ['kɒmə] *n* coma *f*

command [kə'mɑːnd] **1** *vt* (**a**) mandar (**b**) *(respect)* infundir; *(sympathy)* merecer; *(money)* disponer de
2 *n* (**a**) *(order)* orden *f*; *(authority)* mando *m*; **to be at sb's c.** estar a las órdenes

de algn (**b**) *(of language)* dominio *m* (**c**) *(disposal)* disposición *f* (**d**) *Comput* comando *m*, instrucción *f*

commandeer [kɒmən'dɪə(r)] *vt* requisar

commander [kə'mɑːndə(r)] *n* comandante *m*

commanding [kə'mɑːndɪŋ] *adj* dominante; *Mil* **c. officer** comandante *m*

commandment [kə'mɑːndmənt] *n* mandamiento *m*

commando [kə'mɑːndəʊ] *n* comando *m*

commemorate [kə'meməreɪt] *vt* conmemorar

commence [kə'mens] *vt & vi Fml* comenzar

commend [kə'mend] *vt* (**a**) *(praise)* alabar, elogiar (**b**) *(entrust)* encomendar (**c**) *(recommend)* recomendar

commensurate [kə'menʃərɪt] *adj* proporcional; **c. to** *or* **with** en proporción con

comment ['kɒment] **1** *n* comentario *m*; **no c.** sin comentario
2 *vi* hacer comentarios

commentary ['kɒməntərɪ] *n* comentario *m*

commentator ['kɒmənteɪtə(r)] *n* comentarista *mf*

commerce ['kɒmɜːs] *n* comercio *m*

commercial [kə'mɜːʃəl] **1** *adj* comercial; *TV* **c. break** corte publicitario
2 *n TV* anuncio *m*

commiserate [kə'mɪzəreɪt] *vi* compadecerse (**with** de)

commission [kə'mɪʃən] **1** *n* (**a**) *Mil* despacho *m* (de oficial); **out of c.** fuera de servicio (**b**) *(of inquiry)* comisión *f*; *(job)* encargo *m* (**c**) *(payment)* comisión *f*
2 *vt* (**a**) *Mil* nombrar (**b**) *(order)* encargar (**c**) *Naut* poner en servicio

commissionaire [kəmɪʃə'neə(r)] *n Br* portero *m*

commissioner [kə'mɪʃənə(r)] *n (official)* comisario *m*; **c. of police** comisario de policía

commit [kə'mɪt] *vt* (**a**) *(crime)* cometer; **to c. suicide** suicidarse (**b**) **to c. oneself (to do sth)** comprometerse (a hacer algo) (**c**) **to c. sth to sb's care** confiar algo a algn

commitment [kə'mɪtmənt] *n* compromiso *m*

committee [kə'mɪtɪ] *n* comisión *f*, comité *m*

commode [kə'məʊd] *n (chair)* silla *f* con orinal; *(chest of drawers)* cómoda *f*

commodity [kə'mɒdɪtɪ] *n* producto *m* básico

ℰ Note that the Spanish word **comodidad** is a false friend and is never a translation for the English word **commodity**. In Spanish, **comodidad** means "comfort, convenience".

common [ˈkɒmən] **1** *adj* (a) común; **that's so c.** eso lo sabe todo el mundo; **c. law** derecho consuetudinario; **C. Market** Mercado *m* Común; *Br* **c. room** sala *f* de profesores/de estudiantes (b) *(ordinary)* corriente (c) *(vulgar)* ordinario(a), maleducado(a)
2 *n (land)* campo *m or* terreno *m* comunal
commonplace [ˈkɒmənpleɪs] *adj* corriente
Commons [ˈkɒmənz] *npl Br* **the (House of) C.** (la Cámara de) los Comunes
Commonwealth [ˈkɒmənwelθ] *n Br* **the C.** la Commonwealth; **C. of Independent States** Comunidad *f* de Estados Independientes
commotion [kəˈməʊʃən] *n* alboroto *m*
commune¹ [kəˈmjuːn] *vi (converse)* conversar íntimamente; *(with nature)* estar en comunión (**with** con)
commune² [ˈkɒmjuːn] *n* comuna *f*
communicate [kəˈmjuːnɪkeɪt] **1** *vi* comunicarse (**with** con)
2 *vt* comunicar
communication [kəmjuːnɪˈkeɪʃən] *n* (a) comunicación *f* (b) *Br Rail* **c. cord** timbre *m* de alarma
communion [kəˈmjuːnɪən] *n* comunión *f*; **to take c.** comulgar
communiqué [kəˈmjuːnɪkeɪ] *n* comunicado *m* oficial
communism [ˈkɒmjʊnɪzəm] *n* comunismo *m*
communist [ˈkɒmjʊnɪst] *adj & n* comunista *(mf)*
community [kəˈmjuːnɪtɪ] *n* comunidad *f*; *(people)* colectividad *f*; **c. centre** centro *m* social
commute [kəˈmjuːt] **1** *vi* = viajar diariamente al lugar de trabajo
2 *vt Jur* conmutar
commuter [kəˈmjuːtə(r)] *n* = persona que viaja diariamente al lugar de trabajo
compact¹ 1 *adj* [kəmˈpækt] compacto(a); *(style)* conciso(a)
2 *n* [ˈkɒmpækt] *(for powder)* polvera *f*
compact² [ˈkɒmpækt] *n Pol* pacto *m*
compact disc [ˈkɒmpækˈdɪsk] *n* disco compacto
companion [kəmˈpænjən] *n* compañero(a) *m,f*

companionship [kəmˈpænjənʃɪp] *n* compañerismo *m*
company [ˈkʌmpənɪ] *n* (a) compañía *f*; **to keep sb c.** hacer compañía a algn (b) *Com* empresa *f*, compañía *f*
comparable [ˈkɒmpərəbəl] *adj* comparable (**to** *or* **with** con)
comparative [kəmˈpærətɪv] **1** *adj* comparativo(a); *(relative)* relativo(a)
2 *n Ling* comparativo *m*
comparatively [kəmˈpærətɪvlɪ] *adv* relativamente
compare [kəmˈpeə(r)] **1** *vt* comparar (**to** *or* **with** con); **(as) compared with** en comparación con
2 *vi* compararse
comparison [kəmˈpærɪsən] *n* comparación *f*; **by c.** en comparación; **there's no c.** no se puede comparar
compartment [kəmˈpɑːtmənt] *n (section)* compartimiento *m*; *Rail* departamento *m*
compass [ˈkʌmpəs] *n* (a) brújula *f* (b) **(pair of) compasses** compás *m* (c) *Fig (range)* límites *mpl*
compassion [kəmˈpæʃən] *n* compasión *f*
compassionate [kəmˈpæʃənət] *adj* compasivo(a)
compatible [kəmˈpætəbəl] *adj* compatible
compel [kəmˈpel] *vt* (a) *(oblige)* obligar; **to c. sb to do sth** obligar a algn a hacer algo (b) *(admiration)* despertar
compelling [kəmˈpelɪŋ] *adj* irresistible
compensate [ˈkɒmpənseɪt] **1** *vt* compensar; **to c. sb for sth** indemnizar a algn de algo
2 *vi* compensar
compensation [kɒmpənˈseɪʃən] *n* compensación *f*; *(for loss)* indemnización *f*
compere [ˈkɒmpeə(r)] *n Br* animador(a) *m,f*
compete [kəmˈpiːt] *vi* competir
competence [ˈkɒmpɪtəns] *n* (a) *(ability)* aptitud *f* (b) *(of court etc)* competencia *f*
competent [ˈkɒmpɪtənt] *adj* competente
competition [kɒmpɪˈtɪʃən] *n* (a) *(contest)* concurso *m* (b) *Com* competencia *f*
competitive [kəmˈpetɪtɪv] *adj* competitivo(a)
competitor [kəmˈpetɪtə(r)] *n* competidor(a) *m,f*
compilation [kɒmpɪˈleɪʃən] *n* recopilación *f*
compile [kəmˈpaɪl] *vt* compilar, recopilar
complacency [kəmˈpleɪsənsɪ] *n* autocomplacencia *f*

♪ Note that the Spanish word **complacencia** is a false friend and is never a translation for the English word **complacency**. In Spanish, **complacencia** means "satisfaction, indulgence".

complacent [kəm'pleɪsənt] *adj* autocomplaciente

complain [kəm'pleɪn] *vi* quejarse (**of/about** de)

complaint [kəm'pleɪnt] *n* (**a**) queja *f*; *Com* reclamación *f* (**b**) *Jur* demanda *f* (**c**) *Med* enfermedad *f*

complement ['kɒmplɪmənt] **1** *n* (**a**) complemento *m* (**b**) *Naut* dotación *f*
  2 *vt* complementar

complementary [kɒmplɪ'mentərɪ] *adj* complementario(a)

complete [kəm'pliːt] **1** *adj* (**a**) *(entire)* completo(a) (**b**) *(absolute)* total
  2 *vt* completar; **to c. a form** rellenar un formulario

completely [kəm'pliːtlɪ] *adv* completamente, por completo

completion [kəm'pliːʃən] *n* terminación *f*; **near c.** casi terminado(a); **on c.** en cuanto se termine

complex ['kɒmpleks] **1** *adj* complejo(a)
  2 *n* complejo *m*; **inferiority c.** complejo de inferioridad

complexion [kəm'plekʃən] *n* tez *f*; *Fig* aspecto *m*

♪ Note that the Spanish word **complexión** is a false friend and is never a translation for the English word **complexion**. In Spanish, **complexión** means "build".

compliance [kəm'plaɪəns] *n* conformidad *f*; **in c.** with de acuerdo con

complicate ['kɒmplɪkeɪt] *vt* complicar

complicated ['kɒmplɪkeɪtɪd] *adj* complicado(a)

complication [kɒmplɪ'keɪʃən] *n* complicación *f*

complicity [kəm'plɪsɪtɪ] *n* complicidad *f*

compliment 1 *n* ['kɒmplɪmənt] (**a**) cumplido *m*; **to pay sb a c.** hacerle un cumplido a algn (**b**) **compliments** saludos *mpl*
  2 *vt* ['kɒmplɪment] felicitar; **to c. sb on sth** felicitar a algn por algo

complimentary [kɒmplɪ'mentərɪ] *adj* (**a**) *(praising)* elogioso(a) (**b**) *(free)* gratis

comply [kəm'plaɪ] *vi* obedecer; **to c. with** *(order)* cumplir con; *(request)* acceder a

component [kəm'pəʊnənt] **1** *n* componente *m*
  2 *adj* componente; **c. part** parte *f*

compose [kəm'pəʊz] *vt & vi* (**a**) componer; **to be composed of** componerse de (**b**) **to c. oneself** calmarse

composed [kəm'pəʊzd] *adj (calm)* sereno(a)

composer [kəm'pəʊzə(r)] *n* compositor(a) *m,f*

composite ['kɒmpəzɪt] *adj* compuesto(a)

composition [kɒmpə'zɪʃən] *n* composición *f*; *(essay)* redacción *f*

compost ['kɒmpɒst] *n* abono *m*

composure [kəm'pəʊʒə(r)] *n* calma *f*, serenidad *f*

compound¹ ['kɒmpaʊnd] **1** *n* compuesto *m*
  2 *adj* compuesto(a); *(fracture)* complicado(a)
  3 *vt* [kəm'paʊnd] *(problem)* agravar

compound² ['kɒmpaʊnd] *n* *(enclosure)* recinto *m*

comprehend [kɒmprɪ'hend] *vt* comprender

comprehensible [kɒmprɪ'hensəbəl] *adj* comprensible

comprehension [kɒmprɪ'henʃən] *n* comprensión *f*

comprehensive [kɒmprɪ'hensɪv] *adj* (**a**) *(knowledge)* amplio(a); *(study)* detallado(a) (**b**) *Ins* a todo riesgo (**c**) *Br* **c. school** ≃ instituto *m* de segunda enseñanza

♪ Note that the Spanish word **comprensivo** is a false friend and is never a translation for the English word **comprehensive**. In Spanish, **comprensivo** means "understanding".

compress 1 *vt* [kəm'pres] comprimir
  2 *n* ['kɒmpres] compresa *f*

comprise [kəm'praɪz] *vt* comprender; *(consist of)* constar de

compromise ['kɒmprəmaɪz] **1** *n* solución *f* negociada; **to reach a c.** llegar a un acuerdo
  2 *vi (two people)* llegar a un acuerdo; *(individual)* transigir
  3 *vt (person)* comprometer

♪ Note that the Spanish word **compromiso** is a false friend and is never a translation for the English word **compromise**. In Spanish, **compromiso** means "obligation, commitment, agreement".

compulsion [kəm'pʌlʃən] *n* obligación *f*

compulsive [kəm'pʌlsɪv] *adj* compulsivo(a)

compulsory [kəm'pʌlsərɪ] *adj* obligatorio(a)

computer [kəm'pjuːtə(r)] *n* ordenador *m*, *Am* computadora *f*; **c. programmer** programador(a) *m,f* de ordenadores; **c. science** informática *f*; **personal c.** ordenador personal, *Am* computadora personal

computerize [kəm'pjuːtəraɪz] *vt* informatizar

computing [kəm'pjuːtɪŋ] *n* informática *f*

comrade ['kɒmreɪd] *n* (**a**) *(companion)* compañero(a) *m,f* (**b**) *Pol* camarada *mf*

comradeship ['kɒmreɪdʃɪp] *n* camaradería *f*

con [kɒn] *Fam* **1** *vt* estafar, timar

2 *n* estafa *f*, camelo *m*; **c. man** estafador *m*

concave ['kɒnkeɪv] *adj* cóncavo(a)

conceal [kən'siːl] *vt* ocultar; *(emotions)* disimular

concede [kən'siːd] *vt* conceder

conceit [kən'siːt] *n* presunción *f*, vanidad *f*

conceited [kən'siːtɪd] *adj* presuntuoso(a)

conceivable [kən'siːvəbəl] *adj* concebible

conceive [kən'siːv] *vt & vi* concebir

concentrate ['kɒnsəntreɪt] **1** *vt* concentrar

2 *vi* to c. on sth concentrarse en algo

concentration [kɒnsən'treɪʃən] *n* concentración *f*; **c. camp** campo *m* de concentración

concept ['kɒnsept] *n* concepto *m*

conception [kən'sepʃən] *n Med* concepción *f*; *(understanding)* concepto *m*, idea *f*

concern [kən'sɜːn] **1** *vt* (**a**) concernir, afectar; **as far as I'm concerned** por lo que a mí se refiere (**b**) *(worry)* preocupar

2 *n* (**a**) **it's no c. of mine** no es asunto mío (**b**) *(worry)* preocupación *f* (**c**) *Com* negocio *m*

concerned [kən'sɜːnd] *adj* (**a**) *(affected)* afectado(a) (**b**) *(worried)* preocupado(a) (**about** por)

concerning [kən'sɜːnɪŋ] *prep* con respecto a, en cuanto a

concert ['kɒnsət, 'kɒnsɜːt] *n Mus* concierto *m*; **c. hall** sala *f* de conciertos

concerted [kən'sɜːtɪd] *adj* concertado(a)

concertina [kɒnsə'tiːnə] *n* concertina *f*

concerto [kən'tʃɜːtəʊ] *n* concierto *m*

concession [kən'seʃən] *n* (**a**) concesión *f*; **tax c.** privilegio *m* fiscal (**b**) *Com* reducción *f*

concise [kən'saɪs] *adj* conciso(a)

conclude [kən'kluːd] *vt & vi* concluir

conclusion [kən'kluːʒən] *n* conclusión *f*; **to reach a c.** llegar a una conclusión

conclusive [kən'kluːsɪv] *adj* concluyente

concoct [kən'kɒkt] *vt (dish)* confeccionar; *Fig (plan)* fraguar; *(excuse)* inventar

concoction [kən'kɒkʃən] *n (mixture)* mezcolanza *f*; *Pej (brew)* brebaje *m*

concourse ['kɒŋkɔːs] *n* explanada *f*

> *📏* Note that the Spanish word **concurso** is a false friend and is never a translation for the English word **concourse**. In Spanish, **concurso** means "competition, contest".

concrete ['kɒnkriːt] **1** *n* hormigón *m*; **c. mixer** hormigonera *f*

2 *adj* (**a**) *(definite)* concreto(a) (**b**) *(made of concrete)* de hormigón

concur [kən'kɜː(r)] *vi* (**a**) **to c. with** *(agree)* estar de acuerdo con (**b**) *(coincide)* coincidir

concurrent [kən'kʌrənt] *adj* simultáneo(a)

concussion [kən'kʌʃən] *n* conmoción *f* cerebral

condemn [kən'dem] *vt* condenar

condemnation [kɒndem'neɪʃən] *n* condena *f*

condensation [kɒnden'seɪʃən] *n* condensación *f*

condense [kən'dens] **1** *vt* condensar

2 *vi* condensarse

condensed [kən'denst] *adj* **c. milk** leche condensada

condescending [kɒndɪ'sendɪŋ] *adj* condescendiente

condition [kən'dɪʃən] **1** *n* condición *f*; **to be in good c.** estar en buen estado; **on c. that ...** a condición de que ...; **on one c.** con una condición; **heart c.** enfermedad cardíaca; **conditions** *(circumstances)* circunstancias *fpl*

2 *vt* condicionar

conditional [kən'dɪʃənəl] *adj* condicional

conditioner [kən'dɪʃənə(r)] *n* acondicionador *m*

condolences [kən'dəʊlənsɪz] *npl* pésame *m*; **please accept my c.** le acompaño en el sentimiento

condom ['kɒndəm] *n* preservativo *m*

condominium [kɒndə'mɪnɪəm] *n US (building)* = bloque de apartamentos poseídos por diferentes propietarios; *(apartment)* apartamento *m*, piso *m* *(en propiedad)*

condone [kən'dəʊn] *vt* perdonar, consentir

condor ['kɒndɔː(r)] *n* cóndor *m*

conducive [kən'djuːsɪv] *adj* conducente

conduct 1 *n* ['kɒndʌkt] *(behaviour)*

conducta *f*, comportamiento *m*

2 *vt* [kən'dʌkt] *(lead)* guiar; *(business, orchestra)* dirigir; **conducted tour** visita acompañada; **to c. oneself** comportarse

3 *vi Mus* dirigir

conductor [kən'dʌktə(r)] *n* (**a**) *Br (on bus)* cobrador *m* (**b**) *US Rail* revisor(a) *m,f* (**c**) *Mus* director(a) *m,f* (**d**) *Phys* conductor *m*

conductress [kən'dʌktrɪs] *n (on bus)* cobradora *f*

cone [kəʊn] *n* (**a**) cono *m*; **ice-cream c.** cucurucho *m* (**b**) *Bot* piña *f*

confectioner [kən'fekʃənə(r)] *n* confitero(a) *m,f*; **c.'s (shop)** confitería *f*

confectionery [kən'fekʃənərɪ] *n* dulces *mpl*

confederate [kən'fedərɪt] **1** *adj* confederado(a)

2 *n* confederado(a) *m,f*; *Jur* cómplice *mf*

confer [kən'fɜː(r)] **1** *vt* **to c. a title on sb** conferir un título a algn

2 *vi* consultar

conference ['kɒnfərəns] *n* conferencia *f*

confess [kən'fes] **1** *vi* confesar; *Rel* confesarse

2 *vt* confesar

confession [kən'feʃən] *n* confesión *f*

confessional [kən'feʃənəl] *n* confesionario *m*

confetti [kən'fetɪ] *n* confeti *m*

confide [kən'faɪd] *vi* **to c. in sb** confiar en algn

confidence ['kɒnfɪdəns] *n* (**a**) confianza *f*; **vote of c./no c.** voto *m* de confianza/de censura; **c. trick** camelo *m* (**b**) *(secret)* confidencia *f*; **in c.** en confianza

confident ['kɒnfɪdənt] *adj* seguro(a)

confidential [kɒnfɪ'denʃəl] *adj (secret)* confidencial; *(entrusted)* de confianza

confine [kən'faɪn] *vt* encerrar; *Fig* limitar

confinement [kən'faɪnmənt] *n* (**a**) *(prison)* prisión *f*; **to be in solitary c.** estar incomunicado(a) (**b**) *Med* parto *m*

confirm [kən'fɜːm] *vt* confirmar

confirmation [kɒnfə'meɪʃən] *n* confirmación *f*

confirmed [kən'fɜːmd] *adj* empedernido(a)

confiscate ['kɒnfɪskeɪt] *vt* confiscar

conflict 1 *n* ['kɒnflɪkt] conflicto *m*

2 *vi* [kən'flɪkt] chocar (**with** con)

conflicting [kən'flɪktɪŋ] *adj* contradictorio(a)

conform [kən'fɔːm] *vi* conformarse; **to c. to** *or* **with** *(customs)* amoldarse a; *(rules)* someterse a

confound [kən'faʊnd] *vt* confundir, desconcertar

confront [kən'frʌnt] *vt* hacer frente a

confrontation [kɒnfrʌn'teɪʃən] *n* confrontación *f*

confuse [kən'fjuːz] *vt (person)* despistar; *(thing)* confundir (**with** con); **to get confused** confundirse

confused [kən'fjuːzd] *adj (person)* confundido(a); *(mind, ideas)* confuso(a)

confusing [kən'fjuːzɪŋ] *adj* confuso(a)

confusion [kən'fjuːʒən] *n* confusión *f*

congeal [kən'dʒiːl] *vi* coagularse

congenial [kən'dʒiːnɪəl] *adj* agradable

congenital [kən'dʒenɪtəl] *adj* congénito(a)

congested [kən'dʒestɪd] *adj* (**a**) *(street)* repleto(a) de gente; *(city)* superpoblado(a) (**b**) *Med* congestionado(a)

congestion [kən'dʒestʃən] *n* congestión *f*

conglomeration [kənglɒmə'reɪʃən] *n* conglomeración *f*

congratulate [kən'grætjʊleɪt] *vt* felicitar

congratulations [kəngrætjʊ'leɪʃənz] *npl* felicitaciones *fpl*; **c.!** ¡enhorabuena!

congregate ['kɒŋgrɪgeɪt] *vi* congregarse

congregation [kɒŋgrɪ'geɪʃən] *n (group)* congregación *f*; *Rel* fieles *mpl*

congress ['kɒŋgres] *n* (**a**) *(conference)* congreso *m* (**b**) *US Pol* **C.** el Congreso *(de los Estados Unidos)*

Congressman ['kɒŋgresmən] *n US Pol* congresista *m*, *Am* congresal *m*

Congresswoman ['kɒŋgreswʊmən] *n US Pol* congresista *f*, *Am* congresal *f*

conifer ['kɒnɪfə(r)] *n* conífera *f*

conjecture [kən'dʒektʃə(r)] **1** *n* conjetura *f*

2 *vt* conjeturar

3 *vi* hacer conjeturas

conjugal ['kɒndʒʊgəl] *adj* conyugal

conjugate ['kɒndʒʊgeɪt] *vt* conjugar

conjunction [kən'dʒʌŋkʃən] *n* conjunción *f*; *Fig* **in c. with** conjuntamente con

conjunctivitis [kəndʒʌŋktɪ'vaɪtɪs] *n* conjuntivitis *f*

conjure ['kʌndʒə(r)] **1** *vt* **to c. (up)** *(magician)* hacer aparecer; *(memories)* evocar

2 *vi* hacer juegos de manos

conjurer ['kʌndʒərə(r)] *n* prestidigitador(a) *m,f*

conker ['kɒŋkə(r)] *n Fam* castaña *f*

connect [kə'nekt] **1** *vt* (**a**) *(join)* juntar, unir; *(wires)* empalmar; *Fig* **to be connected by marriage** estar emparentado(a) por matrimonio (**b**) *(install)* instalar; *Elec* conectar (**c**) *Tel (person)* poner (**d**) *Fig (associate)* asociar

2 *vi* unirse; *(rooms)* comunicarse; *(train, flight)* enlazar *or* empalmar (**with** con)

connected [kəˈnektɪd] *adj* unido(a); *(events)* relacionado(a); *Fig* **to be well c.** *(person) (socially)* estar bien relacionado(a)

connection [kəˈnekʃən] *n* (**a**) *(joint)* juntura *f*, unión *f*; *Elec* conexión *f*; *Tel* instalación *f* (**b**) *Rail* correspondencia *f* (**c**) *Fig (of ideas)* relación *f*; **in c. with** *(regarding)* con respecto a (**d**) *(person)* contacto *m*

connive [kəˈnaɪv] *vi* **to c. at** hacer la vista gorda con

connoisseur [kɒnɪˈsɜː(r)] *n* conocedor(a) *m,f*

connotation [kɒnəˈteɪʃən] *n* connotación *f*

conquer [ˈkɒŋkə(r)] *vt (enemy, bad habit)* vencer; *(country)* conquistar

conqueror [ˈkɒŋkərə(r)] *n* conquistador *m*

conquest [ˈkɒŋkwest] *n* conquista *f*

conscience [ˈkɒnʃəns] *n* conciencia *f*; **to have a clear c.** tener la conciencia tranquila; **to have a guilty c.** sentirse culpable

conscientious [kɒnʃɪˈenʃəs] *adj* concienzudo(a); **c. objector** objetor(a) *m,f* de conciencia

conscious [ˈkɒnʃəs] *adj (aware)* consciente; *(choice etc)* deliberado(a)

consciousness [ˈkɒnʃəsnɪs] *n Med* conocimiento *m*; *(awareness)* conciencia *f*

conscript [ˈkɒnskrɪpt] *n* recluta *m*

conscription [kənˈskrɪpʃən] *n* servicio *m* militar obligatorio

consecrate [ˈkɒnsɪkreɪt] *vt* consagrar

consecutive [kənˈsekjʊtɪv] *adj* consecutivo(a)

consensus [kənˈsensəs] *n* consenso *m*

consent [kənˈsent] **1** *n* consentimiento *m*; **by common c.** de común acuerdo

2 *vi* consentir (**to** en)

consequence [ˈkɒnsɪkwəns] *n* consecuencia *f*

consequent [ˈkɒnsɪkwənt] *adj* consiguiente

consequently [ˈkɒnsɪkwəntlɪ] *adv* por consiguiente

conservation [kɒnsəˈveɪʃən] *n* conservación *f*

conservative [kənˈsɜːvətɪv] **1** *adj* cauteloso(a)

2 *adj & n Pol* **C.** conservador(a) *(m,f)*

conservatory [kənˈsɜːvətrɪ] *n* (**a**) *(greenhouse)* invernadero *m* (**b**) *Mus* conservatorio *m*

conserve 1 *vt* [kənˈsɜːv] conservar

2 *n* [ˈkɒnsɜːv] conserva *f*

consider [kənˈsɪdə(r)] *vt* (**a**) *(ponder on, regard)* considerar; **to c. doing sth** pensar hacer algo (**b**) *(keep in mind)* tener en cuenta

considerable [kənˈsɪdərəbəl] *adj* considerable

considerably [kənˈsɪdərəblɪ] *adv* bastante

considerate [kənˈsɪdərɪt] *adj* considerado(a)

consideration [kənsɪdəˈreɪʃən] *n* consideración *f*; **without due c.** sin reflexión

considering [kənˈsɪdərɪŋ] *prep* teniendo en cuenta

consign [kənˈsaɪn] *vt Com* consignar; *Fig* entregar

consignment [kənˈsaɪnmənt] *n* envío *m*

consist [kənˈsɪst] *vi* **to c. of** consistir en

consistency [kənˈsɪstənsɪ] *n* (**a**) *(of actions)* consecuencia *f* (**b**) *(of mixture)* consistencia *f*

consistent [kənˈsɪstənt] *adj* consecuente; **c. with** de acuerdo con

📝 Note that the Spanish word **consistente** *is a false friend and is never a translation for the English word* **consistent**. *In Spanish,* **consistente** *means "firm, solid, sound".*

consolation [kɒnsəˈleɪʃən] *n* consuelo *m*; **c. prize** premio *m* de consolación

console¹ [kənˈsəʊl] *vt* consolar

console² [ˈkɒnsəʊl] *n* consola *f*

consolidate [kənˈsɒlɪdeɪt] **1** *vt* consolidar

2 *vi* consolidarse

consonant [ˈkɒnsənənt] *n* consonante *f*

consortium [kənˈsɔːtɪəm] *n* consorcio *m*

conspicuous [kənˈspɪkjʊəs] *adj (striking)* llamativo(a); *(easily seen)* visible; *(mistake)* evidente

conspiracy [kənˈspɪrəsɪ] *n* conjura *f*

conspire [kənˈspaɪə(r)] *vi* conspirar

constable [ˈkʌnstəbəl] *n* policía *m*, guardia *m*; **chief c.** jefe *m* de policía

constabulary [kənˈstæbjʊlərɪ] *n Br* comisaría *f*

constant [ˈkɒnstənt] **1** *adj* constante; *(continuous)* incesante; *(loyal)* fiel, leal

2 *n* constante *f*

constellation [kɒnstɪˈleɪʃən] *n* constelación *f*

consternation [kɒnstəˈneɪʃən] *n* consternación *f*

constipated [ˈkɒnstɪpeɪtɪd] *adj* **to be c.** estar estreñido(a)

> *ℓ* Note that the Spanish word **constipado** is a false friend and is never a translation for the English word **constipated**. In Spanish, **constipado** means both "cold, chill" and "suffering from a cold".

constipation [kɒnstɪˈpeɪʃən] *n* estreñimiento *m*

constituency [kənˈstɪtjʊənsɪ] *n* circunscripción *f* electoral

constituent [kənˈstɪtjʊənt] **1** *adj (component)* constituyente

2 *n* (**a**) *(part)* componente *m* (**b**) *Pol* votante *mf*

constitute [ˈkɒnstɪtjuːt] *vt* constituir

constitution [kɒnstɪˈtjuːʃən] *n* constitución *f*

constitutional [kɒnstɪˈtjuːʃənəl] *adj* constitucional

constrained [kənˈstreɪnd] *adj* **to feel c. to do sth** sentirse obligado(a) a hacer algo

constraint [kənˈstreɪnt] *n* coacción *f*; **to feel c. in sb's presence** sentirse cohibido(a) ante algn

construct [kənˈstrʌkt] *vt* construir

construction [kənˈstrʌkʃən] *n* construcción *f*

constructive [kənˈstrʌktɪv] *adj* constructivo(a)

construe [kənˈstruː] *vt* interpretar

> *ℓ* Note that the Spanish verb **construir** is a false friend and is never a translation for the English verb **to construe**. In Spanish, **construir** means "to build, to manufacture".

consul [ˈkɒnsəl] *n* cónsul *mf*

consulate [ˈkɒnsjʊlɪt] *n* consulado *m*

consult [kənˈsʌlt] *vt & vi* consultar (**about** sobre)

consultant [kənˈsʌltənt] *n Med* especialista *mf*; *Com & Ind* asesor(a) *m,f*

consultation [kɒnsəlˈteɪʃən] *n* consulta *f*

consulting [kənˈsʌltɪŋ] *adj* **c. room** consulta *f*

consume [kənˈsjuːm] *vt* consumir

consumer [kənˈsjuːmə(r)] *n* consumidor(a) *m,f*; **c. goods** bienes *mpl* de consumo

consummate 1 *vt* [ˈkɒnsəmeɪt] consumar

2 *adj* [ˈkɒnsəmɪt] consumado(a)

consumption [kənˈsʌmpʃən] *n* (**a**) *(of food)* consumo *m*; **fit for c.** apto(a) para el consumo (**b**) *Med* tisis *f*

cont. *(abbr* **continued***)* sigue

contact [ˈkɒntækt] **1** *n* contacto *m*; **c. lenses** lentes *fpl* de contacto

2 *vt* ponerse en contacto con

contagious [kənˈteɪdʒəs] *adj* contagioso(a)

contain [kənˈteɪn] *vt* contener; **to c. oneself** contenerse

container [kənˈteɪnə(r)] *n* (**a**) *(box, package)* recipiente *m*; *(bottle)* envase *m* (**b**) *Naut* contenedor *m*

contaminate [kənˈtæmɪneɪt] *vt* contaminar

contamination [kəntæmɪˈneɪʃən] *n* contaminación *f*

contd. *(abbr* **continued***)* sigue

contemplate [ˈkɒntempleɪt] *vt* (**a**) *(consider)* considerar, pensar en (**b**) *(look at)* contemplar

contemporary [kənˈtemprərɪ] *adj & n* contemporáneo(a) *(m,f)*

contempt [kənˈtempt] *n* desprecio *m*; **to hold in c.** despreciar; **c. of court** desacato *m* a los tribunales

contemptible [kənˈtemptəbəl] *adj* despreciable

contemptuous [kənˈtemptjʊəs] *adj* despectivo(a)

contend [kənˈtend] **1** *vi* competir; *Fig* **there are many problems to c. with** se han planteado muchos problemas

2 *vt* afirmar

contender [kənˈtendə(r)] *n* contendiente *mf*

content¹ [ˈkɒntent] *n* contenido *m*; **table of contents** índice *m* de materias

content² [kənˈtent] **1** *adj* contento(a)

2 *vt* contentar

3 *n* contento *m*; **to one's heart's c.** todo lo que uno quiera

contented [kənˈtentɪd] *adj* contento(a), satisfecho(a)

contention [kənˈtenʃən] *n* (**a**) *(dispute)* controversia *f* (**b**) *(point)* punto *m* de vista

contentment [kənˈtentmənt] *n* contento *m*

contest 1 *n* [ˈkɒntest] concurso *m*; *Sport* prueba *f*

2 *vt* [kənˈtest] (**a**) *(matter)* rebatir; *(verdict)* impugnar; *Fig (will)* disputar (**b**) *Pol (seat)* luchar por

contestant [kənˈtestənt] *n* concursante *mf*

context [ˈkɒntekst] *n* contexto *m*

continent [ˈkɒntɪnənt] *n* continente *m*; **(on) the C.** (en) Europa

continental [kɒntɪˈnentəl] *adj* (**a**) continental; **c. shelf** plataforma *f* continental (**b**) *Br* C. europeo(a); **c. quilt** edredón *m* de pluma

contingency [kən'tındʒənsı] *n* contingencia *f*; **c. plans** planes *mpl* para casos de emergencia

contingent [kən'tındʒənt] *adj & n* contingente *(m)*

continual [kən'tınjʊəl] *adj* continuo(a), constante

continuation [kəntınjʊ'eıʃən] *n (sequel etc)* continuación *f*; *(extension)* prolongación *f*

continue [kən'tınju:] *vt & vi* continuar, seguir; **to c. to do sth** seguir *or* continuar haciendo algo

continuous [kən'tınjʊəs] *adj* continuo(a)

contort [kən'tɔ:t] *vt* retorcer

contortion [kən'tɔ:ʃən] *n* contorsión *f*

contour ['kɒntʊə(r)] *n* contorno *m*; **c. line** línea *f* de nivel

contraband ['kɒntrəbænd] *n* contrabando *m*

contraception [kɒntrə'sepʃən] *n* anticoncepción *f*

contraceptive [kɒntrə'septıv] *adj & n* anticonceptivo *(m)*

contract 1 *vi* [kən'trækt] *Phys* contraerse
  2 *vt* (**a**) contraer (**b**) **to c. to do sth** *(make agreement)* comprometerse por contrato a hacer algo
  3 *n* ['kɒntrækt] contrato *m*; **to enter into a c.** hacer un contrato

contraction [kən'trækʃən] *n* contracción *f*

contractor [kən'træktə(r)] *n* contratista *mf*

contradict [kɒntrə'dıkt] *vt* contradecir

contradiction [kɒntrə'dıkʃən] *n* contradicción *f*; **it's a c. in terms** no tiene lógica

contradictory [kɒntrə'dıktərı] *adj* contradictorio(a)

contraption [kən'træpʃən] *n Fam* cacharro *m*

contrary ['kɒntrərı] **1** *adj* (**a**) *(opposite)* contrario(a) (**b**) [kən'treərı] *(awkward)* terco(a)
  2 *n* **on the c.** todo lo contrario; **unless I tell you to the c.** a menos que te diga lo contrario
  3 *adv* **c. to** en contra de

contrast 1 *vi* [kən'trɑːst] contrastar
  2 *n* ['kɒntrɑːst] contraste *m*

contrasting [kən'trɑːstıŋ] *adj* opuesto(a)

contravene [kɒntrə'viːn] *vt* contravenir

contribute [kən'trıbjuːt] **1** *vt* *(money)* contribuir con; *(ideas, information)* aportar

2 *vi* (**a**) contribuir; *(in discussion)* participar (**b**) *Press* colaborar (**to en**)

contribution [kɒntrı'bjuːʃən] *n* (**a**) *(of money)* contribución *f*; *(of ideas etc)* aportación *f* (**b**) *Press* colaboración *f*

contributor [kən'trıbjʊtə(r)] *n (to newspaper)* colaborador(a) *m,f*

contrive [kən'traıv] *vt* inventar, idear; **to c. to do sth** buscar la forma de hacer algo

contrived [kən'traıvd] *adj* artificial, forzado(a)

control [kən'trəʊl] **1** *vt* controlar; *(person, animal)* dominar; *(vehicle)* manejar; **to c. one's temper** controlarse
  2 *n* (**a**) *(power)* control *m*, dominio *m*; *(authority)* autoridad *f*; **out of c.** fuera de control; **to be in c.** estar al mando; **to be under c.** *(situation)* estar bajo control; **to go out of c.** descontrolarse; **to lose c.** perder los estribos (**b**) *Aut & Av (device)* mando *m*; *Rad & TV* botón *m* de control; **c. panel** tablero *m* de instrumentos; **c. room** sala *f* de control; *Av* **c. tower** torre *f* de control

controversial [kɒntrə'vɜːʃəl] *adj* controvertido(a), polémico(a)

controversy ['kɒntrəvɜːsı, kən'trɒvəsı] *n* polémica *f*

conurbation [kɒnɜː'beıʃən] *n* conurbación *f*

convalesce [kɒnvə'les] *vi* convalecer

convalescence [kɒnvə'lesəns] *n* convalecencia *f*

convalescent [kɒnvə'lesənt] *adj* convaleciente; **c. home** clínica *f* de reposo

convene [kən'viːn] **1** *vt* convocar
  2 *vi* reunirse

convenience [kən'viːnıəns] *n* conveniencia *f*, comodidad *f*; **all modern conveniences** todas las comodidades; **at your c.** cuando le convenga; **c. food** comida precocinada; *Br Euph* **public conveniences** aseos públicos

convenient [kən'viːnıənt] *adj (time, arrangement)* conveniente, oportuno(a); *(place)* bien situado(a)

convent ['kɒnvənt] *n* convento *m*

convention [kən'venʃən] *n* convención *f*

conventional [kən'venʃənəl] *adj* clásico(a); *(behaviour)* convencional

converge [kən'vɜːdʒ] *vi* convergir

conversant [kən'vɜːsənt] *adj Fml* **to be c. with a subject** ser versado(a) en una materia

conversation [kɒnvə'seıʃən] *n* conversación *f*

conversational [kɒnvə'seıʃənəl] *adj* coloquial

converse¹ [kən'vɜːs] *vi* conversar

converse² ['kɒnvɜːs] *n* **the c.** lo opuesto

conversely ['kɒnvɜːslɪ] *adv* a la inversa

conversion [kən'vɜːʃən] *n Math & Rel* conversión *f* (**to** a; **into** en)

convert 1 *vt* [kən'vɜːt] convertir
2 *n* ['kɒnvɜːt] converso(a) *m,f*

convertible [kən'vɜːtəbəl] 1 *adj* convertible
2 *n Aut* descapotable *m*

convex ['kɒnveks, kɒn'veks] *adj* convexo(a)

convey [kən'veɪ] *vt* (**a**) *(carry)* transportar (**b**) *(sound)* transmitir; *(idea)* comunicar

conveyor [kən'veɪə(r)] *n* **c. belt** cinta transportadora

convict 1 *vt* [kən'vɪkt] declarar culpable a, condenar
2 *n* ['kɒnvɪkt] presidiario(a) *m,f*

conviction [kən'vɪkʃən] *n* (**a**) *(belief)* creencia *f*, convicción *f* (**b**) *Jur* condena *f*

convince [kən'vɪns] *vt* convencer

convincing [kən'vɪnsɪŋ] *adj* convincente

convoluted ['kɒnvəluːtɪd] *adj* intrincado(a)

convoy ['kɒnvɔɪ] *n* convoy *m*

convulse [kən'vʌls] *vt* convulsionar; *Fam* **to be convulsed with laughter** troncharse de risa

convulsion [kən'vʌlʃən] *n* convulsión *f*

coo [kuː] *vi (pigeon)* arrullar

cook [kʊk] 1 *vt* cocinar, guisar; *(dinner)* preparar; *Fam* **to c. the books** falsificar las cuentas
2 *vi (person)* cocinar, guisar; *(food)* cocerse
3 *n* cocinero(a) *m,f*

cookbook ['kʊkbʊk] *n US* libro *m* de cocina

cooker ['kʊkə(r)] *n* cocina *f*

cookery ['kʊkərɪ] *n* cocina *f*; **c. book** libro *m* de cocina

cookie ['kʊkɪ] *n US* galleta *f*

cooking ['kʊkɪŋ] *n* cocina *f*

cool [kuːl] 1 *adj* (**a**) *(water)* fresco(a); **it's c.** *(weather)* hace fresquito (**b**) *Fig (calm)* tranquilo(a); *(reserved)* frío(a)
2 *n* (**a**) *(coolness)* fresco *m* (**b**) *Fam* **to lose one's c.** perder la calma
3 *vt (air)* refrescar; *(drink)* enfriar
4 *adv Fam* **to play it c.** hacer como si nada
▸ **cool down, cool off** *vi Fig* calmarse; *(feelings)* enfriarse

coolness ['kuːlnɪs] *n* (**a**) *Fig (calmness)* calma *f*; *(composure)* aplomo *m* (**b**) *Fam (nerve, cheek)* frescura *f*

coop [kuːp] 1 *n* gallinero *m*
2 *vt* **to c. (up)** encerrar

co-operate [kəʊ'ɒpəreɪt] *vi* cooperar

co-operation [kəʊɒpə'reɪʃən] *n* cooperación *f*

co-operative [kəʊ'ɒpərətɪv] 1 *adj (helpful)* cooperador(a)
2 *n* cooperativa *f*

co-ordinate 1 *vt* [kəʊ'ɔːdɪneɪt] coordinar
2 *n* [kəʊ'ɔːdɪnɪt] (**a**) *Math* coordenada *f* (**b**) **co-ordinates** *(clothes)* conjunto *m*

co-ordination [kəʊɔːdɪ'neɪʃən] *n* coordinación *f*

cop [kɒp] *Fam* 1 *n (policeman)* poli *m*
2 *vt* **you'll c. it** te vas a ganar una buena
▸ **cop out** *vi* rajarse

cope [kəʊp] *vi* arreglárselas; **to c. with** *(person, work)* poder con; *(problem)* hacer frente a

Copenhagen [kəʊpən'heɪgən] *n* Copenhague

copious ['kəʊpɪəs] *adj* copioso(a), abundante

copper¹ ['kɒpə(r)] 1 *n (metal)* cobre *m*
2 *adj (colour)* cobrizo(a)

copper² ['kɒpə(r)] *n Fam* poli *mf*

coppice ['kɒpɪs], **copse** [kɒps] *n* arboleda *f*, bosquecillo *m*

copulate ['kɒpjʊleɪt] *vi* copular

copy ['kɒpɪ] 1 *n* (**a**) copia *f* (**b**) *(of book)* ejemplar *m*
2 *vt & vi* copiar

copycat ['kɒpɪkæt] *n Fam* copión(ona) *m,f*

copyright ['kɒpɪraɪt] *n* derechos *mpl* de autor

coral ['kɒrəl] *n* coral *m*; **c. reef** arrecife *m* de coral

cord [kɔːd] *n* (**a**) *(string)* cuerda *f*; *Elec* cordón *m* (**b**) *Tex (corduroy)* pana *f*; **cords** pantalones *mpl* de pana

cordial ['kɔːdɪəl] 1 *adj* cordial
2 *n* licor *m*

cordon ['kɔːdən] 1 *n* cordón *m*
2 *vt* **to c. off a street** acordonar una calle

corduroy ['kɔːdərɔɪ] *n* pana *f*

core [kɔː(r)] 1 *n (of fruit)* corazón *m*; *Elec* núcleo *m*; *Fig* **the hard c.** los incondicionales
2 *vt* quitarle el corazón a

coriander [kɒrɪ'ændə(r)] *n* culantro *m*

cork [kɔːk] *n* corcho *m*; **c. oak** alcornoque *m*

corkscrew ['kɔːkskruː] *n* sacacorchos *m inv*

corn¹ [kɔːn] *n* cereal *m*; *(grain)* granos *mpl*; *(maize)* maíz *m*; **c. on the cob**

mazorca f de maíz or Andes, RP choclo, Méx elote m

corn² [kɔːn] n Med callo m

corncob ['kɔːnkɒb] n mazorca f

cornea ['kɔːnɪə] n córnea f

corner ['kɔːnə(r)] **1** n (**a**) (of street) esquina f; (bend in road) curva f; **round the c.** a la vuelta de la esquina; Ftb **c. kick** córner m; **c. shop** tienda pequeña de barrio (**b**) (of room) rincón m

2 vt (**a**) (enemy) arrinconar (**b**) Com acaparar

3 vi Aut tomar una curva

cornerstone ['kɔːnəstəʊn] n piedra f angular

cornet ['kɔːnɪt] n (**a**) Mus corneta f (**b**) Br (for ice cream) cucurucho m

cornflakes ['kɔːnfleɪks] npl copos mpl de maíz, cornflakes mpl

cornflour ['kɔːnflaʊə(r)], US **cornstarch** ['kɔːnstɑːtʃ] n harina f de maíz

Cornwall ['kɔːnwəl] n Cornualles

corny ['kɔːnɪ] adj (**cornier, corniest**) Fam gastado(a)

corollary [kə'rɒlərɪ] n corolario m

coronary ['kɒrənərɪ] adj coronario(a); **c. thrombosis** trombosis coronaria

coronation [kɒrə'neɪʃən] n coronación f

coroner ['kɒrənə(r)] n juez mf de instrucción

corporal¹ ['kɔːpərəl] adj corporal; **c. punishment** castigo m corporal

corporal² ['kɔːpərəl] n Mil cabo m

corporate ['kɔːpərɪt] adj corporativo(a)

corporation [kɔːpə'reɪʃən] n (**a**) (business) sociedad anónima (**b**) (of city) ayuntamiento m

corps [kɔː(r)] n (pl **corps** [kɔːz]) cuerpo m

corpse [kɔːps] n cadáver m

corpulent ['kɔːpjʊlənt] adj corpulento(a)

corpuscle ['kɔːpʌsəl] n corpúsculo m

corral [kə'rɑːl] n US corral m

correct [kə'rekt] **1** vt (**a**) (mistake) corregir (**b**) (child) reprender

2 adj correcto(a), exacto(a); (behaviour) formal

correction [kə'rekʃən] n corrección f

correlation [kɒrə'leɪʃən] n correlación f

correspond [kɒrɪ'spɒnd] vi (**a**) corresponder; **to c. to** equivaler a (**b**) (by letter) escribirse

correspondence [kɒrɪ'spɒndəns] n correspondencia f; **c. course** curso m por correspondencia

correspondent [kɒrɪ'spɒndənt] n Press corresponsal mf; **special c.** enviado(a) m,f especial

corridor ['kɒrɪdɔː(r)] n pasillo m

corroborate [kə'rɒbəreɪt] vt corroborar

corrode [kə'rəʊd] **1** vt corroer

2 vi corroerse

corrosion [kə'rəʊʒən] n corrosión f

corrugated ['kɒrʊgeɪtɪd] adj **c. iron** hierro ondulado

corrupt [kə'rʌpt] **1** adj (person) corrompido(a), corrupto(a); (actions) deshonesto(a)

2 vt & vi corromper

corruption [kə'rʌpʃən] n corrupción f

corset ['kɔːsɪt] n (garment) faja f

Corsica ['kɔːsɪkə] n Córcega

cortège [kɔː'teɪʒ] n cortejo m, comitiva f

cosh [kɒʃ] n Br porra f

cosmetic [kɒz'metɪk] **1** n cosmético m

2 adj cosmético(a); **c. surgery** cirugía plástica

cosmic [kɒzmɪk] adj cósmico(a)

cosmonaut ['kɒzmənɔːt] n cosmonauta mf

cosmopolitan [kɒzmə'pɒlɪtən] adj cosmopolita

cosset ['kɒsɪt] vt mimar

cost [kɒst] **1** n (price) precio m, coste m; **c. of living** coste de la vida; **to count the c.** considerar las desventajas; **at all costs** a toda costa

2 vt & vi (pt & pp **cost**) costar, valer; **how much does it c.?** ¿cuánto cuesta?; **whatever it costs** cueste lo que cueste

3 vt (pt & pp **costed**) Com & Ind calcular el coste de

co-star ['kəʊstɑː(r)] n Cin & Th coprotagonista mf

Costa Rica [kɒstə'riːkə] n Costa Rica

Costa Rican [kɒstə'riːkən] adj & n costarricense (mf)

cost-effective [kɒstɪ'fektɪv] adj rentable

costly ['kɒstlɪ] adj (**costlier, costliest**) costoso(a)

costume ['kɒstjuːm] n traje m; **swimming c.** bañador m; **c. jewellery** bisutería f

cosy ['kəʊzɪ] adj (**cosier, cosiest**) (atmosphere) acogedor(a); (bed) calentito(a); **it's c. in here** aquí se está bien

cot [kɒt] n (**a**) Br (for child) cuna f (**b**) US (folding bed) catre m, cama f plegable

cottage ['kɒtɪdʒ] n casa f de campo; **c. cheese** queso fresco; **c. industry** industria casera; Br **c. pie** = pastel de carne picada con puré de patatas or Am papas

cotton ['kɒtən] n (**a**) Bot algodonero m; Tex algodón m; Br **c. wool**, US **absorbent c.** algodón hidrófilo (**b**) (thread) hilo m

▸ **cotton on** vi Fam **to c. on to sth** caer en la cuenta de algo

couch [kaʊtʃ] *n* sofá *m*; *(in surgery)* camilla *f*

couchette [kuːˈʃet] *n Rail* litera *f*

cough [kɒf] **1** *vi* toser
   2 *n* tos *f*; **c. drop** pastilla *f* para la tos; **c. mixture** jarabe *m* para la tos
   ▸ **cough up** *vt sep Fam* **to c. up the money** soltar la pasta

could [kʊd] *v aux see* **can¹**

council [ˈkaʊnsəl] *n (body)* consejo *m*; *Br* **c. house** vivienda *f* de protección oficial; **town c.** consejo municipal, ayuntamiento *m*

councillor, *US* **councilor** [ˈkaʊnsələ(r)] *n* concejal *mf*

counsel [ˈkaʊnsəl] **1** *n* (a) *(advice)* consejo *m* (b) *Jur* abogado(a) *m,f*
   2 *vt* aconsejar

counsellor, *US* **counselor** [ˈkaʊnsələ(r)] *n* (a) *(adviser)* asesor(a) *m,f* (b) *US Jur* abogado(a) *m,f*

count¹ [kaʊnt] **1** *vt* (a) contar (b) *Fig* **to c. oneself lucky** considerarse afortunado(a)
   2 *vi* contar; **that doesn't c.** eso no vale; **to c. to ten** contar hasta diez
   3 *n* (a) cuenta *f*; *(total)* recuento *m* (b) *Jur* cargo *m*
   ▸ **count on** *vt insep* contar con

count² [kaʊnt] *n (nobleman)* conde *m*

countdown [ˈkaʊntdaʊn] *n* cuenta *f* atrás

countenance [ˈkaʊntɪnəns] **1** *n* semblante *m*, rostro *m*
   2 *vt* aprobar

counter¹ [ˈkaʊntə(r)] *n* (a) *(in shop)* mostrador *m*; *(in bank)* ventanilla *f* (b) *(in board games)* ficha *f*

counter² [ˈkaʊntə(r)] *n* contador *m*

counter³ [ˈkaʊntə(r)] **1** *adv* **c. to** en contra de
   2 *vt (attack)* contestar a; *(trend)* contrarrestar
   3 *vi* contestar

counteract [kaʊntərˈækt] *vt* contrarrestar

counterattack [ˈkaʊntərətæk] *n* contraataque *m*

counter-clockwise [ˈkaʊntəˈklɒkwaɪz] *adv US* en sentido opuesto al de las agujas del reloj

counterfeit [ˈkaʊntəfɪt] **1** *adj* falsificado(a); **c. coin** moneda falsa
   2 *n* falsificación *f*
   3 *vt* falsificar

counterfoil [ˈkaʊntəfɔɪl] *n Br (of cheque)* matriz *f*

countermand [kaʊntəˈmɑːnd] *vt (command)* revocar; *Com (order)* anular

counterpart [ˈkaʊntəpɑːt] *n* homólogo(a) *m,f*

counterproductive [kaʊntəprəˈdʌktɪv] *adj* contraproducente

countersign [ˈkaʊntəsaɪn] *vt* refrendar

countess [ˈkaʊntɪs] *n* condesa *f*

countless [ˈkaʊntlɪs] *adj* innumerable, incontable

country [ˈkʌntrɪ] *n* (a) *(state)* país *m*; **native c.** patria *f* (b) *(rural area)* campo *m*; **c. dancing** baile *m* popular

countryman [ˈkʌntrɪmən] *n* (a) *(rural)* hombre *m* del campo (b) *(compatriot)* compatriota *m*

countryside [ˈkʌntrɪsaɪd] *n (area)* campo *m*; *(scenery)* paisaje *m*

county [ˈkaʊntɪ] *n* condado *m*

coup [kuː] *n (pl coups [kuːz])* golpe *m*; **c. d'etat** golpe de estado

couple [ˈkʌpəl] **1** *n* (a) *(of people)* pareja *f*; **a married c.** un matrimonio (b) *(of things)* par *m*; *Fam* **a c. of times** un par de veces
   2 *vt (wagons)* enganchar

coupling [ˈkʌplɪŋ] *n Rail* enganche *m*

coupon [ˈkuːpɒn] *n* (a) cupón *m* (b) *Br Ftb* quiniela *f*

courage [ˈkʌrɪdʒ] *n* coraje *m*, valentía *f*

courageous [kəˈreɪdʒəs] *adj* valeroso(a), valiente

courgette [kʊəˈʒet] *n Br* calabacín *m*, *CSur* zapallito *m*

courier [ˈkʊrɪə(r)] *n* (a) *(messenger)* mensajero(a) *m,f* (b) *(guide)* guía *mf* turístico(a)

course [kɔːs] *n* (a) *(of river)* curso *m*; *Naut & Av* rumbo *m* (b) *Fig* desarrollo *m*; **in the c. of construction** en vías de construcción; **in the c. of time** con el tiempo (c) *(series)* ciclo *m*; **a c. of treatment** un tratamiento (d) *Educ* curso *m*; *Univ* asignatura *f* (e) *(for golf)* campo *m*; *(for horseracing)* hipódromo *m* (f) *Culin* plato *m* (g) **of c.** claro, por supuesto; **of c. not!** ¡claro que no!

court [kɔːt] **1** *n* (a) *Jur* tribunal *m*; **c. martial** consejo *m* de guerra; **c. order** orden *f* judicial (b) *(royal)* corte *f* (c) *Sport* pista *f*, cancha *f*
   2 *vt (woman)* hacer la corte a; *Fig* **to c. danger** buscar el peligro; *Fig* **to c. disaster** exponerse al desastre
   3 *vi (couple)* tener relaciones

courteous [ˈkɜːtɪəs] *adj* cortés

courtesy [ˈkɜːtɪsɪ] *n* (a) cortesía *f*, educación *f* (b) **by c. of** por cortesía de

courthouse [ˈkɔːthaʊs] *n US* palacio *m* de justicia

courtier ['kɔːtɪə(r)] *n* cortesano(a) *m,f*
court-martial [kɔːt'mɑːʃəl] *vt* someter a consejo de guerra
courtroom ['kɔːtruːm] *n* sala *f* de justicia
courtyard ['kɔːtjɑːd] *n* patio *m*
cousin ['kʌzən] *n* primo(a) *m,f*; **first c.** primo(a) hermano(a)
cove [kəʊv] *n* cala *f*, ensenada *f*
covenant ['kʌvənənt] *n* convenio *m*, pacto *m*
cover ['kʌvə(r)] **1** *vt* (**a**) cubrir (**with** de); *(furniture)* revestir (**with** de); *(with lid)* tapar
   (**b**) *(hide)* disimular
   (**c**) *(protect)* abrigar
   (**d**) *(distance)* recorrer
   (**e**) *Press* investigar
   (**f**) *(deal with)* abarcar
   (**g**) *(include)* incluir
   (**h**) *Sport* marcar
   2 *vi* **to c. for sb** sustituir a algn
   3 *n* (**a**) cubierta *f*, *(lid)* tapa *f*; *(on bed)* manta *f*, *Am* frazada *f*, cobija *f*; *(of chair etc)* funda *f*
   (**b**) *(of book)* tapa *f*, *(of magazine)* portada *f*; **c. girl** modelo *f* de revista
   (**c**) *(in restaurant)* cubierto *m*
   (**d**) **under separate c.** por separado
   (**e**) *Ins* **full c.** cobertura completa; *Br* **c. note** seguro *m* provisional
   (**f**) *(protection)* abrigo *m*; **to take c.** abrigarse; **under c.** al abrigo; *(indoors)* bajo techo
   ▸ **cover up 1** *vt sep* (**a**) cubrir (**b**) *(crime)* encubrir
   2 *vi* (**a**) *(person)* abrigarse (**b**) **to c. up for sb** encubrir a algn
coverage ['kʌvərɪdʒ] *n* cobertura *f*
coveralls ['kʌvərɔːlz] *npl US* mono *m*
covering ['kʌvərɪŋ] **1** *n* cubierta *f*, envoltura *f*
   2 *adj (letter)* explicatorio(a)
covert ['kʌvət] *adj* disimulado(a), secreto(a)
cover-up ['kʌvərʌp] *n* encubrimiento *m*
covet ['kʌvɪt] *vt* codiciar
cow¹ [kaʊ] *n* vaca *f*; *Pej (woman)* arpía *f*, bruja *f*
cow² [kaʊ] *vt* intimidar
coward ['kaʊəd] *n* cobarde *mf*
cowardice ['kaʊədɪs] *n* cobardía *f*
cowardly ['kaʊədlɪ] *adj* cobarde
cowboy ['kaʊbɔɪ] *n* vaquero *m*
cower ['kaʊə(r)] *vi (with fear)* encogerse
cox [kɒks] *n* timonel *m*
coy [kɔɪ] *adj (shy)* tímido(a); *(demure)* coquetón(ona)
cozy ['kəʊzɪ] *adj US* = **cosy**

crab [kræb] *n* (**a**) cangrejo *m* (**b**) **c. apple** manzana *f* silvestre
crack [kræk] **1** *vt* (**a**) *(cup)* partir; *(bone)* fracturar; *(nut)* cascar; *(safe)* forzar (**b**) *(whip)* hacer restallar (**c**) *Fig (problem)* dar con la solución de; *(joke)* contar
   2 *vi* (**a**) *(glass)* partirse; *(wall)* agrietarse (**b**) *(whip)* restallar (**c**) *Fig* **to get cracking on sth** ponerse a hacer algo
   3 *n* (**a**) *(in cup)* raja *f*, *(in wall, ground)* grieta *f* (**b**) *(of whip)* restallido *m*; *(of gun)* detonación *f* (**c**) *Fam (blow)* golpetazo *m* (**d**) *Fam* **to have a c. at sth** *(attempt)* intentar hacer algo (**e**) *Fam (wisecrack)* réplica aguda (**f**) *Fam (drug)* crack *m*
   4 *adj Fam* de primera
   ▸ **crack down on** *vt insep* atajar con mano dura
   ▸ **crack up** *vi Fam Fig (go mad)* desquiciarse; *(with laughter)* partirse de risa
cracker ['krækə(r)] *n* (**a**) *(biscuit)* galleta salada (**b**) *(firework)* petardo *m*
crackle ['krækəl] *vi* crujir; *(fire)* crepitar
cradle ['kreɪdəl] *n* *(baby's)* cuna *f*
craft [krɑːft] *n* (**a**) *(occupation)* oficio *m*; *(art)* arte *m*; *(skill)* destreza *f* (**b**) *(cunning)* maña *f* (**c**) *Naut* embarcación *f*
craftsman ['krɑːftsmən] *n* artesano *m*
craftsmanship ['krɑːftsmənʃɪp] *n* arte *f*
crafty ['krɑːftɪ] *adj* (**craftier, craftiest**) astuto(a)
crag [kræg] *n* peña *f*, peñasco *m*
cram [kræm] **1** *vt* atiborrar; **crammed with** atestado(a) de
   2 *vi Fam Educ* empollar
cramp¹ [kræmp] *n Med* calambre *m*; **cramps** retortijones *mpl*
cramp² [kræmp] *vt (development etc)* poner trabas a
cramped [kræmpt] *adj* atestado(a); *(writing)* apretado(a)
cranberry ['krænbərɪ] *n* arándano *m*
crane [kreɪn] **1** *n* (**a**) *Zool* grulla *f* común (**b**) *(device)* grúa *f*
   2 *vt* estirar
crank [kræŋk] *n* (**a**) *Tech* manivela *f* (**b**) *Fam (eccentric)* tío raro
crankshaft ['kræŋkʃɑːft] *n* árbol *m* del cigüeñal
cranny ['krænɪ] *n Fig* **in every nook and c.** en todos los rincones
crap [kræp] *n Fam* mierda *f*
crash [kræʃ] **1** *vt* **to c. one's car** tener un accidente con el coche
   2 *vi* (**a**) *(car, plane)* estrellarse; *(collide)* chocar; **to c. into** estrellarse contra (**b**) *Com* quebrar
   3 *n* (**a**) *(noise)* estrépito *m* (**b**) *(collision)*

choque *m*; **car/plane c.** accidente *m* de coche/avión; *Fig* **c. course** curso intensivo; **c. helmet** casco *m* protector (**c**) *Com* quiebra *f*

crash-land [kræʃ'lænd] *vi* hacer un aterrizaje forzoso

crass [kræs] *adj* (*person*) grosero(a); (*error*) garrafal

crate [kreɪt] *n* caja *f*, cajón *m* (*para embalaje*)

crater ['kreɪtə(r)] *n* cráter *m*

cravat [krə'væt] *n* pañuelo *m* (*de hombre*)

crave [kreɪv] *vi* to **c. for sth** ansiar algo

craving ['kreɪvɪŋ] *n* ansia *f*; (*in pregnancy*) antojo *m*

crawfish ['krɔːfɪʃ] *n* langosta *f*

crawl [krɔːl] **1** *vi* (*baby*) gatear; (*vehicle*) avanzar lentamente; *Fig* to **c. to sb** arrastrarse a los pies de algn
2 *n* (*swimming*) crol *m*

crayfish ['kreɪfɪʃ] *n* cangrejo *m* de río

crayon ['kreɪɒn] *n* cera *f*

craze [kreɪz] *n* manía *f*; (*fashion*) moda *f*; **it's the latest c.** es el último grito

crazy ['kreɪzɪ] *adj* (**crazier, craziest**) *Fam* loco(a), chalado(a); *Br* **c. paving** pavimento *m* en mosaico

creak [kriːk] *vi* (*floor*) crujir; (*hinge*) chirriar

cream [kriːm] **1** *n* (**a**) (*of milk*) nata *f*; **c.-coloured** color crema; *Fig* **the c.** la flor y nata; **c. cheese** queso *m* crema (**b**) (*cosmetic*) crema *f*
2 *vt* (**a**) (*milk*) desnatar (**b**) *Culin* batir; **creamed potatoes** puré *m* de patatas *or Am* papas

creamy ['kriːmɪ] *adj* (**creamier, creamiest**) cremoso(a)

crease [kriːs] **1** *n* (*wrinkle*) arruga *f*; (*fold*) pliegue *m*; (*on trousers*) raya *f*
2 *vt* (*clothes*) arrugar
3 *vi* arrugarse

create [kriː'eɪt] *vt* crear

creation [kriː'eɪʃən] *n* creación *f*

creative [kriː'eɪtɪv] *adj* (*person*) creativo(a)

creativity [kriːeɪ'tɪvɪtɪ] *n* creatividad *f*

creator [kriː'eɪtə(r)] *n* creador(a) *m,f*

creature ['kriːtʃə(r)] *n* (*animal*) criatura *f*

crèche [kreɪʃ, kreʃ] *n* guardería *f*

credence ['kriːdəns] *n* to **give c. to** dar crédito a

credentials [krɪ'denʃəlz] *npl* credenciales *fpl*

credible ['kredɪbəl] *adj* creíble

credit ['kredɪt] **1** *n* (**a**) *Com* crédito *m*; **on c.** a crédito; **c. card** tarjeta *f* de crédito (**b**) **to give c. to sb for sth** reconocer algo a

algn (**c**) (*benefit*) honor *m*; **to be a c. to** hacer honor a (**d**) *Cin & TV* **credits** créditos *mpl*
2 *vt* (**a**) *Com* abonar (**b**) (*believe*) creer (**c**) *Fig* atribuir; **he is credited with having** se le atribuye haber

creditor ['kredɪtə(r)] *n* acreedor(a) *m,f*

creed [kriːd] *n* credo *m*

creek [kriːk] *n* (**a**) *Br* cala *f* (**b**) *US & Austral* riachuelo *m*

creep [kriːp] **1** *vi* (*pt & pp* **crept**) andar silenciosamente; (*insect*) arrastrarse; (*plant*) trepar; **to c. up on sb** sorprender a algn
2 *n Fam* (*person*) pelotillero(a) *m,f*

creeper ['kriːpə(r)] *n Bot* trepadora *f*

creepy ['kriːpɪ] *adj* (**creepier, creepiest**) *Fam* espeluznante

cremate [krɪ'meɪt] *vt* incinerar

crematorium [kremə'tɔːrɪəm] *n* crematorio *m*

crêpe [kreɪp] *n* (**a**) *Tex* crepé *m* (**b**) **c. paper** papel *m* crespón

crept [krept] *pt & pp of* **creep**

crescendo [krɪ'ʃendəʊ] *n* crescendo *m*

crescent ['kresənt] **1** *n* (*shape*) medialuna *f*; *Br* (*street*) calle *f* en medialuna
2 *adj* creciente

cress [kres] *n* berro *m*

crest [krest] *n* (**a**) (*of cock, wave*) cresta *f*; (*on helmet*) penacho *m*; (*of hill*) cima *f* (**b**) (*heraldic*) blasón *m*

crestfallen ['krestfɔːlən] *adj* abatido(a)

Crete [kriːt] *n* Creta

cretin ['kretɪn] *n* cretino(a) *m,f*

crevasse [krɪ'væs] *n* grieta *f*, fisura *f*

crevice ['krevɪs] *n* grieta *f*, hendedura *f*

crew [kruː] *n Av & Naut* tripulación *f*; **c. cut** corte *m* al rape; **c.-neck sweater** jersey *m* con cuello redondo

crib [krɪb] **1** *n* (**a**) (*manger*) pesebre *m* (**b**) (*for baby*) cuna *f* (**c**) *Fam* (*in exam*) chuleta *f*, *Arg* machete *m*, *Col, Méx* acordeón *m*
2 *vt Fam* (**a**) (*copy*) copiar (**b**) (*steal*) quitar

crick [krɪk] *n Fam* **a c. in the neck** una tortícolis

cricket¹ ['krɪkɪt] *n* (*insect*) grillo *m*

cricket² ['krɪkɪt] *n Sport* cricket *m*

crikey ['kraɪkɪ] *interj Fam Old-fashioned* ¡caramba!

crime [kraɪm] *n* delincuencia *f*; (*offence*) delito *m*

criminal ['krɪmɪnəl] *adj & n* criminal (*mf*); **c. law** derecho *m* penal; **c. record** antecedentes *mpl* penales

crimson ['krɪmzən] *adj & n* carmesí (*m*)

cringe [krɪndʒ] *vi* abatirse, encogerse

crinkle ['krɪŋkəl] *vt* fruncir, arrugar

cripple ['krɪpəl] **1** *n* lisiado(a) *m,f*, mutilado(a) *m,f*

2 *vt* mutilar, dejar cojo(a); *Fig* paralizar

crisis ['kraɪsɪs] *n* (*pl* **crises** ['kraɪsiːz]) crisis *f inv*

crisp [krɪsp] **1** *adj* crujiente; *(lettuce)* fresco(a); *(banknote)* nuevo(a); *(weather)* frío(a) y seco(a); *Fig (style)* directo(a)

2 *n Br* **(potato) c.** patata *or Am* papa frita

crisscross ['krɪskrɒs] *n* líneas entrecruzadas

criterion [kraɪ'tɪərɪən] *n* (*pl* **criteria** [kraɪ'tɪərɪə]) criterio *m*

critic ['krɪtɪk] *n Art & Th* crítico(a) *m,f*

critical ['krɪtɪkəl] *adj* crítico(a)

critically ['krɪtɪkəlɪ] *adv* críticamente; **c. ill** gravemente enfermo(a)

criticism ['krɪtɪsɪzəm] *n* crítica *f*

criticize ['krɪtɪsaɪz] *vt* criticar

croak [krəʊk] *vi (frog)* croar; *(raven)* graznar; *(person)* hablar con voz ronca

Croat ['krəʊæt] **1** *adj* croata

2 *n* (**a**) *(person)* croata *mf* (**b**) *(language)* croata *m*

Croatia [krəʊ'eɪʃə] *n* Croacia

Croatian [krəʊ'eɪʃən] *adj & n* = **Croat**

crochet ['krəʊʃeɪ] *n* ganchillo *m*

crockery ['krɒkərɪ] *n* loza *f*

crocodile ['krɒkədaɪl] *n* cocodrilo *m*

crocus ['krəʊkəs] *n* azafrán *m*

crony ['krəʊnɪ] *n* compinche *mf*

crook [krʊk] **1** *n* (**a**) *(of shepherd)* cayado *m* (**b**) *Fam* caco *m*

2 *vt (arm)* doblar

crooked ['krʊkɪd] *adj* (**a**) *(stick, picture)* torcido(a); *(path)* tortuoso(a) (**b**) *Fam (dishonest)* deshonesto(a)

crop [krɒp] **1** *n* (**a**) *(cultivo m*; *(harvest)* cosecha *f*; *(of hair)* mata *f* (**b**) *(whip)* fusta *f*

2 *vt (hair)* rapar; *(grass)* cortar

▶ **crop up** *vi Fam* surgir, presentarse

croquet ['krəʊkeɪ] *n* croquet *m*

cross [krɒs] **1** *n* (**a**) cruz *f* (**b**) *(breeds)* cruce *m* (**c**) **c. section** sección *f* transversal

2 *vt* (**a**) cruzar (**b**) *Rel* **to c. oneself** hacer la señal de la cruz; *Fam* **c. my heart!** ¡te lo juro! (**c**) *(thwart)* contrariar

3 *vi* cruzar; *(roads)* cruzarse; **to c. over** cruzar

4 *adj* (**a**) *Fig* **they are at c. purposes** hay un malentendido entre ellos (**b**) *(angry)* enfadado(a)

▶ **cross off, cross out** *vt sep* tachar, rayar

crossbar ['krɒsbɑː(r)] *n* travesaño *m*

cross-country **1** *adj* ['krɒskʌntrɪ] **c. race** cross *m*

2 *adv* [krɒs'kʌntrɪ] campo través

cross-examine [krɒsɪg'zæmɪn] *vt* interrogar

cross-eyed ['krɒsaɪd] *adj* bizco(a)

crossfire ['krɒsfaɪə(r)] *n* fuego cruzado

crossing ['krɒsɪŋ] *n* cruce *m*; **pedestrian c.** paso *m* de peatones; **sea c.** travesía *f*

cross-legged [krɒs'leg(ɪ)d] *adj* con las piernas cruzadas

cross-reference [krɒs'refərəns] *n* remisión *f*

crossroads ['krɒsrəʊdz] *n* cruce *m*; *Fig* encrucijada *f*

crosswalk ['krɒswɔːk] *n US* paso *m* de peatones

crosswind ['krɒswɪnd] *n* viento *m* lateral

crossword ['krɒswɜːd] *n* **c. (puzzle)** crucigrama *m*

crotch [krɒtʃ] *n* entrepierna *f*

crotchet ['krɒtʃɪt] *n Br Mus* negra *f*

crotchety ['krɒtʃɪtɪ] *adj Fam* gruñón(ona)

crouch [kraʊtʃ] *vi* **to c. (down)** agacharse

crow[1] [krəʊ] *n* cuervo *m*; *Fig* **as the c. flies** en línea recta; **c.'s-feet** patas *fpl* de gallo

crow[2] [krəʊ] **1** *vi* (**a**) *(cock)* cantar; *Fig* **c. over sth** jactarse de algo (**b**) *(baby)* balbucir

2 *n (of cock)* canto *m*

crowbar ['krəʊbɑː(r)] *n* palanca *f*

crowd [kraʊd] **1** *n* muchedumbre *f*; *Fam (gang)* pandilla *f*; **the c.** el populacho

2 *vt (streets)* llenar

3 *vi* apiñarse; **to c. in/out** entrar/salir en tropel

crowded ['kraʊdɪd] *adj* atestado(a), lleno(a)

crown [kraʊn] **1** *n* (**a**) corona *f*; *(garland)* guirnalda *f*; **the c. jewels** las joyas de la corona; *Br Jur* **c. court** tribunal *m* superior; **C. Prince** príncipe heredero (**b**) *Anat* coronilla *f*; *(of hat, tree)* copa *f*

2 *vt* coronar; *Fam Fig* **to c. it all** y para más inri

crucial ['kruːʃəl] *adj* decisivo(a)

crucifix ['kruːsɪfɪks] *n* crucifijo *m*

crucifixion [kruːsɪ'fɪkʃən] *n* crucifixión *f*

crucify ['kruːsɪfaɪ] *vt* crucificar

crude [kruːd] *adj* (**a**) *(manners, style)* tosco(a), grosero(a); *(tool)* primitivo(a) (**b**) **c. oil** crudo *m*

cruel [kruːəl] *adj* cruel (**to** con)

cruelty ['kruːəltɪ] *n* crueldad *f* (**to** hacia)

cruet ['kruːɪt] *n* **c. set** vinagreras *fpl*

cruise [kruːz] **1** *vi* (**a**) *Naut* hacer un crucero (**b**) *Aut* viajar a velocidad constante;

Av viajar a velocidad de crucero
   2 *n* (**a**) *Naut* crucero *m* (**b**) **c. missile** misil teledirigido
cruiser ['kruːzə(r)] *n* (barco *m*) crucero *m*
crumb [krʌm] *n* miga *f*, migaja *f*
crumble ['krʌmbəl] **1** *vt* desmigar
   2 *vi* (*wall*) desmoronarse; *Fig* (*hopes*) desvanecerse
crumbly ['krʌmblɪ] *adj* (**crumblier, crumbliest**) que se desmigaja
crumpet ['krʌmpɪt] *n Br* = clase de crepe grueso que se puede tostar
crumple ['krʌmpəl] *vt* arrugar
crunch [krʌntʃ] **1** *vt* (*food*) ronchar; (*with feet*) hacer crujir
   2 *n Fam* **when it comes to the c.** a la hora de la verdad
crunchy ['krʌntʃɪ] *adj* (**crunchier, crunchiest**) crujiente
crusade [kruːˈseɪd] *n* cruzada *f*
crush [krʌʃ] **1** *vt* aplastar; (*wrinkle*) arrugar; (*grind*) moler; (*squeeze*) exprimir
   2 *n* (**a**) (*of people*) gentío *m* (**b**) **orange c.** naranjada *f*
crushing ['krʌʃɪŋ] *adj Fig* (*defeat, reply*) aplastante
crust [krʌst] *n* corteza *f*
crutch [krʌtʃ] *n Med* muleta *f*; *Fig* apoyo *m*
crux [krʌks] *n* **the c. of the matter** el quid de la cuestión
cry [kraɪ] **1** *vi* (*pt & pp* **cried**) (**a**) gritar (**b**) (*weep*) llorar
   2 *vt* gritar; *Fig* **to c. wolf** dar una falsa alarma
   3 *n* (**a**) grito *m* (**b**) (*weep*) llanto *m*
   ► **cry off** *vi Fam* rajarse
   ► **cry out** *vi* gritar; **to c. out for sth** pedir algo a gritos
crying ['kraɪɪŋ] *adj* **it's a c. shame** es una vergüenza
cryptic ['krɪptɪk] *adj* enigmático(a)
crystal ['krɪstəl] *n* cristal *m*
crystal-clear [krɪstəlˈklɪə(r)] *adj* claro(a) como el agua
crystallize ['krɪstəlaɪz] **1** *vt* cristalizar
   2 *vi* cristalizarse
cub [kʌb] *n* (**a**) (*animal*) cachorro *m* (**b**) (*junior scout*) niño *m* explorador
Cuba ['kjuːbə] *n* Cuba
Cuban ['kjuːbən] *adj & n* cubano(a) (*m,f*)
cubbyhole ['kʌbɪhəʊl] *n* cuchitril *m*
cube [kjuːb] **1** *n* cubo *m*; (*of sugar*) terrón *m*; **c. root** raíz cúbica
   2 *vt Math* elevar al cubo
cubic ['kjuːbɪk] *adj* cúbico(a)
cubicle ['kjuːbɪkəl] *n* cubículo *m*; (*at swimming pool*) caseta *f*

cuckoo ['kʊkuː] **1** *n* cuco *m*; **c. clock** reloj *m* de cuco
   2 *adj Fam* lelo(a)
cucumber ['kjuːkʌmbə(r)] *n* pepino *m*
cuddle ['kʌdəl] **1** *vt* abrazar
   2 *vi* abrazarse
cuddly ['kʌdlɪ] *adj* **c. toy** muñeco *m* de peluche
cue¹ [kjuː] *n Th* pie *m*
cue² [kjuː] *n* (*in billiards*) taco *m*; **c. ball** bola blanca
cuff¹ [kʌf] *n* (*of sleeve*) puño *m*; *US* (*of trousers*) dobladillo *m*; *Fig* **to do sth off the c.** improvisar algo
cuff² [kʌf] **1** *vt* abofetear
   2 *n* bofetada *f*
cufflinks ['kʌflɪŋks] *npl* gemelos *mpl*
cul-de-sac ['kʌldəsæk] *n* callejón *m* sin salida
cull [kʌl] *vt* (**a**) (*choose*) escoger (**b**) (*animals*) eliminar
culminate ['kʌlmɪneɪt] *vi* **to c. in** terminar en
culmination [kʌlmɪˈneɪʃən] *n* culminación *f*, punto *m* culminante
culottes [kjuːˈlɒts] *npl* falda-pantalón *f*
culprit ['kʌlprɪt] *n* culpable *mf*
cult [kʌlt] *n* culto *m*; **c. figure** ídolo *m*
cultivate ['kʌltɪveɪt] *vt* cultivar
cultivated ['kʌltɪveɪtɪd] *adj* (*person*) culto(a)
cultivation [kʌltɪˈveɪʃən] *n* cultivo *m* (de la tierra)
cultural ['kʌltʃərəl] *adj* cultural
culture ['kʌltʃə(r)] *n* cultura *f*
cultured ['kʌltʃəd] *adj* = **cultivated**
cumbersome ['kʌmbəsəm] *adj* (*awkward*) incómodo(a); (*bulky*) voluminoso(a)
cum(m)in ['kʌmɪn] *n* comino *m*
cumulative ['kjuːmjʊlətɪv] *adj* acumulativo(a)
cunning ['kʌnɪŋ] **1** *adj* astuto(a)
   2 *n* astucia *f*
cup [kʌp] **1** *n* taza *f*; *Sport* copa *f*; **C. Final** final *f* de copa; **c. tie** partido *m* de copa
   2 *vt* (*hands*) ahuecar
cupboard ['kʌbəd] *n* armario *m*; (*on wall*) alacena *f*
curate ['kjʊərɪt] *n* cura *m* coadjutor
curator [kjʊəˈreɪtə(r)] *n* conservador(a) *m,f*
curb [kɜːb] **1** *n* (**a**) (*limit*) freno *m* (**b**) *US* (*kerb*) bordillo *m*
   2 *vt* (*horse*) refrenar; *Fig* (*public spending*) contener
curd [kɜːd] *n* cuajada *f*
curdle ['kɜːdəl] *vi* cuajarse

cure [kjʊə(r)] **1** vt curar
2 n (remedy) cura f, remedio m

curfew ['kɜːfjuː] n toque m de queda

curiosity [kjʊərɪ'ɒsɪtɪ] n curiosidad f

curious ['kjʊərɪəs] adj (**a**) (inquisitive) curioso(a) (**b**) (odd) extraño(a)

curl [kɜːl] **1** vt (hair) rizar; (lip) fruncir
2 vi rizarse
3 n (of hair) rizo m; (of smoke) espiral f
▸ **curl up** vi enroscarse

curly ['kɜːlɪ] adj (**curlier, curliest**) rizado(a)

currant ['kʌrənt] n pasa f (de Corinto)

currency ['kʌrənsɪ] n (**a**) moneda f; **foreign c.** divisa f (**b**) **to gain c.** cobrar fuerza

current ['kʌrənt] **1** adj (**a**) (opinion) general; (word) en uso; (year) en curso; **c. account** cuenta f corriente; **c. affairs** actualidad f (política); Fin **c. assets** activo m disponible (**b**) **the c. issue** (of magazine, newspaper) el último número
2 n corriente f

currently ['kʌrəntlɪ] adv actualmente

curriculum [kə'rɪkjələm] n (pl **curricula** [kə'rɪkjələ]) plan m de estudios; **c. vitae** curriculum m (vitae)

curry¹ ['kʌrɪ] n curry m; **chicken c.** pollo m al curry

curry² ['kʌrɪ] vt **to c. favour with** congraciarse con

curse [kɜːs] **1** n maldición f; (oath) palabrota f; Fig azote m
2 vt maldecir
3 vi blasfemar

cursor ['kɜːsə(r)] n cursor m

cursory ['kɜːsərɪ] adj rápido(a)

curt [kɜːt] adj brusco(a), seco(a)

curtail [kɜː'teɪl] vt (expenses) reducir; (text) acortar

curtain ['kɜːtən] n cortina f; Th telón m; Fig velo m

curts(e)y ['kɜːtsɪ] **1** n reverencia f
2 vi hacer una reverencia (**to** a)

curve [kɜːv] **1** n curva f
2 vt encorvar
3 vi torcerse, describir una curva

cushion ['kʊʃən] **1** n cojín m; (large) almohadón m; (of billiard table) banda f
2 vt Fig amortiguar; (person) proteger

cushy ['kʊʃɪ] adj (**cushier, cushiest**) Fam cómodo(a)

custard ['kʌstəd] n natillas fpl; **c. powder** polvos mpl para natillas

custodian [kʌ'stəʊdɪən] n conserje mf, guarda mf

custody ['kʌstədɪ] n custodia f; **to take into c.** detener

custom ['kʌstəm] n (**a**) (habit) costumbre f (**b**) Com clientela f

customary ['kʌstəmərɪ] adj habitual

customer ['kʌstəmə(r)] n cliente mf

customize ['kʌstəmaɪz] vt hacer por encargo

custom-made [kʌstəm'meɪd] adj hecho(a) a la medida

customs ['kʌstəmz] n sing or pl aduana f; **c. duty** derechos mpl de aduana; **c. officer** agente mf de aduana

cut [kʌt] **1** vt (pt & pp **cut**) (**a**) cortar; (stone) tallar; (record) grabar; **he's cutting a tooth** le está saliendo un diente; **to c. one's finger** cortarse el dedo; Fig **to c. a long story short** en resumidas cuentas; Fig **to c. corners** recortar presupuestos (**b**) (reduce) reducir (**c**) (divide up) dividir (**into** en)
2 n (**a**) corte m; (in skin) cortadura f; (wound) herida f; (with knife) cuchillada f (**b**) (of meat) clase f de carne (**c**) (reduction) reducción f (**d**) Fig **to be a c. above sb** estar por encima de algn
3 adj cortado(a); (price) reducido(a); Fig **c. and dried** convenido(a) de antemano; **c. glass** cristal tallado
4 vi (**a**) cortar; Fam Fig **to c. loose** romper con todo (**b**) Cin **c.!** ¡corten!
▸ **cut back** vt sep (expenses) reducir; (production) disminuir
▸ **cut down 1** vt sep (tree) talar
2 vt insep **to c. down on** reducir
▸ **cut in** vi (driver) adelantar bruscamente
▸ **cut off** vt sep (water etc) cortar; (place) aislar; (heir) excluir; Tel **I've been c. off** me han cortado (la comunicación)
▸ **cut out 1** vt sep (**a**) (from newspaper) recortar; (person) **to be c. out for sth** estar hecho(a) para algo (**b**) (delete) suprimir
2 vi (engine) calarse
▸ **cut up** vt sep cortar en pedazos

cutback ['kʌtbæk] n reducción f (**in** de)

cute [kjuːt] adj mono(a), lindo(a); US Fam Pej listillo(a)

cuticle ['kjuːtɪkəl] n cutícula f

cutlery ['kʌtlərɪ] n cubiertos mpl

cutlet ['kʌtlɪt] n chuleta f

cut-price [kʌt'praɪs] adj (article) a precio rebajado

cutthroat ['kʌtθrəʊt] **1** n asesino(a) m,f, matón m
2 adj (cruel) cruel; (competition) feroz

cutting ['kʌtɪŋ] **1** n (from newspaper)

recorte *m*; *Rail* tajo *m*
  2 *adj* cortante; *(remark)* mordaz
CV, cv [siːˈviː] *n* (*abbr* **curriculum vitae**)
  CV *m*
cwt. (*abbr* **hundredweight**) *(metric)* 50
  kg; *(imperial) Br* = 50,8 kg; *US* = 45,36 kg
cyanide [ˈsaɪənaɪd] *n* cianuro *m*
cybercafe [ˈsaɪbəkæfeɪ] *n* *Comput* cibercafé *m*
cyberspace [ˈsaɪbəspeɪs] *n* *Comput* ciberespacio *m*
cycle [ˈsaɪkəl] **1** *n* (**a**) ciclo *m* (**b**) *(bicycle)*
  bicicleta *f*; *(motorcycle)* moto *f*
  2 *vi* ir en bicicleta
cycling [ˈsaɪklɪŋ] *n* ciclismo *m*
cyclist [ˈsaɪklɪst] *n* ciclista *mf*
cyclone [ˈsaɪkləʊn] *n* ciclón *m*
cygnet [ˈsɪgnɪt] *n* pollo *m* de cisne
cylinder [ˈsɪlɪndə(r)] *n* (**a**) cilindro *m* (**b**)
  (for gas) bombona *f*
cymbal [ˈsɪmbəl] *n* címbalo *m*, platillo *m*
cynic [ˈsɪnɪk] *n* descreído(a) *m,f*, suspicaz *mf*

> 💡 Note that the Spanish word **cínico** is a
> false friend and is never a translation for
> the English word **cynic**. In Spanish, **cínico**
> means "shameless person".

cynical [ˈsɪnɪkəl] *adj* (**a**) *(sceptical)* des-
  creído(a), suspicaz (**b**) *(unscrupulous)*
  desaprensivo(a), sin escrúpulos

> 💡 Note that the Spanish word **cínico** is a
> false friend and is never a translation for
> the English word **cynical**. In Spanish, **cínico**
> means "shameless".

cynicism [ˈsɪnɪsɪzəm] *n* descreimiento *m*,
  suspicacia *f*

> 💡 Note that the Spanish word **cinismo** is a
> false friend and is never a translation for
> the English word **cynicism**. In Spanish, **cinismo**
> means "shamelessness".

cypress [ˈsaɪprəs] *n* ciprés *m*
Cypriot [ˈsɪprɪət] *adj & n* chipriota (*mf*)
Cyprus [ˈsaɪprəs] *n* Chipre
cyst [sɪst] *n* quiste *m*
cystitis [sɪˈstaɪtɪs] *n* cistitis *f*
czar [zɑː(r)] *n* zar *m*
Czech [tʃek] **1** *adj* checo(a); **the C. Republic** la República Checa
  2 *n* (**a**) *(person)* checo(a) *m,f* (**b**) *(language)* checo *m*
Czechoslovakia [tʃekəʊsləˈvækɪə] *n*
  Checoslovaquia

D

D, d [di:] *n* (**a**) *(the letter)* D, d *f* (**b**) *Mus* D re *m*

D.A. [di:'eɪ] *n US (abbr* **district attorney**) fiscal *mf* (del distrito)

dab [dæb] **1** *n (small quantity)* toque *m*
2 *vt* (**a**) *(apply)* aplicar (**b**) *(touch lightly)* tocar ligeramente

dabble ['dæbəl] *vi* **to d. in politics** meterse en política

dachshund ['dækshʊnd] *n* perro *m* salchicha

dad [dæd], **daddy** ['dædɪ] *n Fam* papá *m*, papi *m*

daddy-longlegs [dædɪ'lɒŋlegz] *n inv Fam* (**a**) *Br (cranefly)* típula *f* (**b**) *US (spider)* segador *m*

daffodil ['dæfədɪl] *n* narciso *m*

daft [dɑːft] *adj Br Fam* chalado(a); *(idea)* tonto(a)

dagger ['dægə(r)] *n* puñal *m*, daga *f*

dahlia ['deɪlɪə] *n* dalia *f*

daily ['deɪlɪ] **1** *adj* diario(a), cotidiano(a)
2 *adv* diariamente; **three times d.** tres veces al día
3 *n* (**a**) *(newspaper)* diario *m* (**b**) *Br Fam (cleaning lady)* asistenta *f*

dainty ['deɪntɪ] *adj* (**daintier, daintiest**) *(flower)* delicado(a); *(child)* precioso(a); *(food)* exquisito(a)

dairy ['deərɪ] *n (on farm)* vaquería *f*; *(shop)* lechería *f*; **d. farming** industria lechera; **d. produce** productos lácteos

dais ['deɪɪs] *n (in hall)* tarima *f*; *(in ceremony)* estrado *m*

daisy ['deɪzɪ] *n* margarita *f*

daisywheel ['deɪzɪwiːl] *n (printer)* margarita *f*

dale [deɪl] *n* valle *m*, hondonada *f*

Dalmatian [dæl'meɪʃən] *n (perro m)* dálmata *m*

dam [dæm] **1** *n (barrier)* dique *m*; *(lake)* presa *f*
2 *vt (water)* represar
▶ **dam up** *vt sep Fig (emotion)* contener

damage ['dæmɪdʒ] **1** *n* (**a**) *(to* daño *m*; *(to health, reputation)* perjuicio *m*; *(to relationship)* deterioro *m* (**b**) *Jur* **damages** daños *mpl* y perjuicios *mpl*
2 *vt (harm)* dañar, hacer daño a; *(spoil)* estropear; *(undermine)* perjudicar

damaging ['dæmɪdʒɪŋ] *adj* perjudicial

damn [dæm] **1** *vt* condenar
2 *interj* **d. (it)!** ¡maldito(a) sea!; **well, I'll be damned!** ¡vaya por Dios!
3 *n Fam* **I don't give a d.** me importa un bledo
4 *adj Fam* maldito(a)
5 *adv Fam* muy, sumamente

damned [dæmd] *adj & adv* = **damn**

damnedest ['dæmdɪst] *n Fam* **to do one's d. to ...** hacer todo lo posible para ...

damning ['dæmɪŋ] *adj (evidence)* irrefutable; *(criticism)* mordaz

damp [dæmp] **1** *adj* húmedo(a); *(wet)* mojado(a)
2 *n* humedad *f*
3 *vt* (**a**) *(for ironing)* humedecer (**b**) **to d. (down)** *(fire)* sofocar; *Fig (violence)* frenar

dampen ['dæmpən] *vt* humedecer; *Fig* frenar

damper ['dæmpə(r)] *n Fig* **to put a d. on sth** poner freno a algo

damsel ['dæmzəl] *n Literary* doncella *f*

damson ['dæmzən] *n* ciruela damascena

dance [dɑːns] **1** *n* baile *m*; *(classical, tribal)* danza *f*; **d. band** orquesta *f* de baile; **d. floor** pista *f* de baile; **d. hall** salón *m* de baile
2 *vi & vt* bailar

dancer ['dɑːnsə(r)] *n (by profession)* bailarín(ina) *m,f*

dandelion ['dændɪlaɪən] *n* diente *m* de león

dandruff ['dændrəf] *n* caspa *f*

Dane [deɪn] *n* danés(esa) *m,f*

danger ['deɪndʒə(r)] *n* (**a**) *(risk)* riesgo *m*; *(of war etc)* amenaza *f* (**b**) *(peril)* peligro *m*; **d.** *(sign)* peligro; **out of d.** fuera de peligro

dangerous ['deɪndʒərəs] *adj* peligroso(a); *(risky)* arriesgado(a); *(harmful)* nocivo(a); *(illness)* grave

dangerously ['deɪndʒərəslɪ] *adv* peligrosamente

dangle ['dæŋgəl] **1** *vi (hang)* colgar; *(swing)* balancearse
2 *vt (legs)* colgar; *(bait)* dejar colgado(a);

(swing) balancear en el aire

Danish ['deɪnɪʃ] **1** *adj* danés(esa); **D. pastry** pastel *m* de hojaldre

2 *n (language)* danés *m*

dapper ['dæpə(r)] *adj* pulcro(a)

dappled ['dæpəld] *adj (shade)* moteado(a)

dare [deə(r)] **1** *vi* atreverse, osar; **he doesn't d. be late** no se atreve a llegar tarde; **how d. you!** ¿cómo te atreves?; *esp Br* **I d. say** quizás; *Ironic* ya (lo creo)

2 *vt (challenge)* desafiar

3 *n* desafío *m*

daredevil ['deədevəl] *adj & n* atrevido(a) *(m,f)*, temerario(a) *(m,f)*

daring ['deərɪŋ] **1** *adj* **(a)** *(bold)* audaz, osado(a) **(b)** *(clothes)* atrevido(a)

2 *n* atrevimiento *m*, osadía *f*

dark [dɑːk] **1** *adj* **(a)** *(room, colour)* oscuro(a); *(hair, complexion)* moreno(a); *(eyes, future)* negro(a) **(b)** *Fig (gloomy)* triste **(c)** *Fig* **to be a d. horse** ser una incógnita; *(discreet)* ser una caja de sorpresas **(d)** *Fig (sinister)* siniestro(a)

2 *n* **(a)** *(darkness)* oscuridad *f*, tinieblas *fpl*; **after d.** después del anochecer **(b)** *Fig* **to be in the d. (about)** estar a oscuras (sobre)

darken ['dɑːkən] **1** *vt (sky)* oscurecer; *(colour)* hacer más oscuro(a)

2 *vi* oscurecerse; *(sky)* nublarse; *Fig (face)* ensombrecerse

darkness ['dɑːknɪs] *n* oscuridad *f*, tinieblas *fpl*

darkroom ['dɑːkruːm] *n* cuarto oscuro

darling ['dɑːlɪŋ] *adj & n* querido(a) *(m,f)*

darn [dɑːn] **1** *vt* zurcir

2 *n* zurcido *m*

dart [dɑːt] **1** *n* **(a)** *(missile)* dardo *m* **(b)** **darts** *sing* dardos *mpl*

2 *vi (fly about)* revolotear; **to d. in/out** entrar/salir corriendo

dartboard ['dɑːtbɔːd] *n* diana *f*

dash [dæʃ] **1** *n* **(a)** *(rush)* carrera *f* **(b)** *esp US (race)* sprint *m* **(c)** *(small amount)* poquito *m*; *(of salt)* pizca *f*; *(of liquid)* gota *f* **(d)** *Typ* guión largo; *(hyphen)* guión **(e)** *(vitality)* brío *m*

2 *vt* **(a)** *(throw)* arrojar **(b)** *(smash)* estrellar; *Fig* **to d. sb's hopes** desvanecer las esperanzas de algn

3 *vi (rush)* correr; **to d. around** correr de un lado a otro; **to d. out** salir corriendo; *Fam* **I must d.!** ¡me voy pitando!

▸**dash off** *vi* salir corriendo

dashboard ['dæʃbɔːd] *n Aut* salpicadero *m*

dashing ['dæʃɪŋ] *adj (appearance)* garboso(a)

data ['deɪtə, 'dɑːtə] *npl* datos *mpl*; **d. bank** *or* **base** banco *m* de datos; **d. processing** *(act)* proceso *m* de datos; *(science)* informática *f*; **d. protection act** ley *f* de informática

date¹ [deɪt] **1** *n* **(a)** *(fecha f;* **what's the d. today?** ¿qué día es hoy?; **out of d.** *(ideas)* anticuado(a); *(expression)* desusado(a); *(invalid)* caducado(a); **to d.** hasta la fecha; *Fig* **to be up to d.** estar al día; **d. of birth** fecha de nacimiento **(b)** *(social event)* compromiso *m*; *Fam (with girl, boy)* cita *f* **(c)** *US Fam (person dated)* ligue *m*

2 *vt (ruins)* datar

3 *vi (ideas)* quedar anticuado(a)

▸**date back to, date from** *vt insep* remontar a, datar de

date² [deɪt] *n (fruit)* dátil *m*; **d. palm** datilera *f*

dated ['deɪtɪd] *adj (idea)* anticuado(a); *(fashion)* pasado(a) de moda; *(expression)* desusado(a)

daub [dɔːb] *vt* embadurnar; *(with oil, grease)* untar

daughter ['dɔːtə(r)] *n* hija *f*

daughter-in-law ['dɔːtərɪnlɔː] *n* nuera *f*, hija política

daunting ['dɔːntɪŋ] *adj* desalentador(a)

dawdle ['dɔːdəl] *vi Fam (walk slowly)* andar despacio; *(waste time)* perder el tiempo

dawn [dɔːn] **1** *n* alba *f*, amanecer *m*

2 *vi* **(a)** *(day)* amanecer **(b)** *Fig (age, hope)* comenzar **(c)** *Fig* **suddenly it dawned on him that ...** de repente cayó en la cuenta de que ...

day [deɪ] *n* **(a)** día *m*; **d. in, d. out** día tras día; **d. by d.** diariamente; **good d.!** ¡buenos días!; **once a d.** una vez al día; **one of these days** un día de éstos; **(on) the next** *or* **following d.** el *or* al día siguiente; **the d. after tomorrow** pasado mañana; **the d. before yesterday** anteayer; **the other d.** el otro día; *Fig* **to live from d. to d.** vivir al día; *Fig* **to win the d.** llevarse la palma; *Fam* **to call it a d.** *(finish)* dar por acabado un trabajo; *(give up)* darse por vencido(a); *Fam* **to make sb's d.** alegrarle a algn el día; *Br Rail* **d. return (ticket)** billete *m* de ida y vuelta para el mismo día; **d. trip** excursión *f* de un día

(b) *(daylight)* día *m*; **by d.** de día; **d. and night** de día y de noche; *Br* **d. shift** turno *m* de día

(c) *(period of work)* jornada *f*; **an eight-hour d.** una jornada de ocho horas; **paid**

by the d. pagado(a) a jornal; **d. off** día de fiesta; **I'll take a d. off tomorrow** mañana me tomaré el día libre

(**d**) *(era)* época *f*; **in those days** en aquellos tiempos; **these days, in this d. and age** hoy (en) día

daybreak ['deɪbreɪk] *n* amanecer *m*

daydream ['deɪdriːm] **1** *n* ensueño *m*; *(vain hope)* fantasía *f*

2 *vi* soñar despierto(a); *(hope vainly)* hacerse ilusiones

daylight ['deɪlaɪt] *n* luz *f* del día; **in broad d.** en pleno día; **to scare the (living) daylights out of sb** pegarle a algn un susto de muerte

daytime ['deɪtaɪm] *n* día *m*; **in the d.** de día

day-to-day ['deɪtədeɪ] *adj* cotidiano(a), diario(a)

daze [deɪz] *n* aturdimiento *m*; **in a d.** aturdido(a)

dazed [deɪzd] *adj* aturdido(a), atontado(a)

dazzle ['dæzəl] *vt* deslumbrar

D-day ['diːdeɪ] *n* día *m* D

deacon ['diːkən] *n* diácono *m*

dead [ded] **1** *adj* (**a**) muerto(a); **he was shot d.** le mataron a tiros; **to be d.** estar muerto(a); *Fam Fig* **over my d. body!** ¡sobre mi cadáver!; **d. man** muerto *m*

(**b**) *(machine)* averiado(a); *(phone)* cortado(a)

(**c**) *(numb)* entumecido(a); *(limb)* adormecido(a); **my leg's gone d.** se me ha dormido la pierna

(**d**) *(silence, secrecy)* total; **d. end** callejón *m* sin salida; *Sport* **d. heat** empate *m*; *Fam* **d. loss** inútil *m*, birria *f*

2 *adv* (**a**) *(exactly)* justo; **d. on time** a la hora en punto

(**b**) **to stop d.** pararse en seco

(**c**) *(very)* muy; *Fam* **d. beat, d. tired** rendido(a); *Fam* **it's d. easy!** ¡está chupado(a)!; *Aut* **d. slow** *(sign)* al paso; *Fam* **you're d. right** tienes toda la razón

3 *n* (**a**) **the d.** *pl* los muertos

(**b**) **at d. of night** a altas horas de la noche

deaden ['dedən] *vt (impact, noise)* amortiguar; *Fig (pain, feeling)* calmar, aliviar

deadline ['dedlaɪn] *n (date)* fecha *f* tope; *(time)* hora *f* tope; **we have to meet the d.** tenemos que hacerlo dentro del plazo

deadlock ['dedlɒk] *n* punto muerto

deadly ['dedlɪ] **1** *adj* (**deadlier, deadliest**) mortal; *(weapon)* mortífero(a); *(aim)* certero(a)

2 *adv (extremely)* terriblemente, sumamente

deadpan ['dedpæn] *adj Fam (face)* sin expresión; *(humour)* guasón(ona)

deaf [def] **1** *adj* sordo(a); *Fig* **to turn a d. ear** hacerse el sordo; **d. mute** sordomudo(a) *m,f*

2 *npl* **the d.** los sordos; **the d. and dumb** los sordomudos

deafen ['defən] *vt* ensordecer

deafening ['defənɪŋ] *adj* ensordecedor(a)

deafness ['defnɪs] *n* sordera *f*

deal [diːl] **1** *n* (**a**) *Com & Pol* trato *m*, pacto *m*; **business d.** negocio *m*, transacción *f*; **to do a d. with sb** *(transaction)* cerrar un trato con algn; *(agreement)* pactar algo con algn; *Fam* **it's a d.!** ¡trato hecho! (**b**) *(amount)* cantidad *f*; **a good d. of criticism** muchas críticas; **a good d. slower** mucho más despacio (**c**) *Cards* reparto *m*

2 *vt (pt & pp* **dealt**) (**a**) *Cards* dar (**to** a) (**b**) **to d. sb a blow** asestarle un golpe a algn

▸ **deal in** *vt insep (goods)* comerciar en, tratar en; *(drugs)* traficar con

▸ **deal out** *vt sep* repartir

▸ **deal with** *vt insep (firm, person)* tratar con; *(subject, problem)* abordar, ocuparse de; *(in book etc)* tratar de

dealer ['diːlə(r)] *n* (**a**) *Com (in goods)* comerciante *mf*; *(in drugs)* traficante *mf* (**b**) *Cards* repartidor(a) *m,f*

dealings ['diːlɪŋz] *npl* (**a**) *(relations)* trato *m* (**b**) *Com* negocios *mpl*

dealt [delt] *pt & pp of* **deal**

dean [diːn] *n* (**a**) *Rel* deán *m* (**b**) *Univ* decano *m*

dear [dɪə(r)] **1** *adj* (**a**) *(loved)* querido(a); **to hold sth/sb d.** apreciar mucho algo/a algn (**b**) *(in letter)* Querido(a); **D. Andrew** Querido Andrew; *Fml* **D. Madam** Estimada señora; *Fml* **D. Sir(s)** Muy señor(es) mío(s) (**c**) **it is very d. to me** *(precious)* le tengo un gran cariño (**d**) *Br (expensive)* caro(a)

2 *n* querido(a) *m,f*; **my d.** mi vida

3 *interj* **oh d.!, d. me!** *(surprise)* ¡caramba!; *(disappointment)* ¡qué pena!

dearly ['dɪəlɪ] *adv* muchísimo; *Fig* **he paid d. for his mistake** su error le costó caro

dearth [dɜːθ] *n Fml* escasez *f*

death [deθ] *n* (**a**) muerte *f*; *Fml* fallecimiento *m*; **to put sb to d.** dar muerte a algn; *Fam* **to be bored to d.** aburrirse como una ostra; *Fam* **to be scared to d.** estar muerto(a) de miedo; *Fam Fig* **to be**

sick to d. of estar hasta la coronilla de; **d. certificate** certificado *m* de defunción; **d. penalty, d. sentence** pena *f* de muerte; **d. rate** índice *m* de mortalidad; **d. squad** escuadrón *m* de la muerte (**b**) *Fig (end)* fin *m*

deathbed ['deθbed] *n* **to be on one's d.** estar en el lecho de muerte

deathly ['deθlɪ] *adj* (**deathlier, deathliest**) *(silence)* sepulcral; **d. pale** pálido(a) como un muerto

debacle [deɪ'bɑːkəl] *n* debacle *f*

debar [dɪ'bɑː(r)] *vt Fml* excluir, prohibir

debase [dɪ'beɪs] *vt Fig* envilecer; **to d. oneself** humillarse

debatable [dɪ'beɪtəbəl] *adj* discutible

debate [dɪ'beɪt] **1** *n* debate *m*; **a heated d.** una discusión acalorada
2 *vt* (**a**) *(discuss)* discutir (**b**) *(wonder about)* dar vueltas a
3 *vi* discutir

debateable dɪ'beɪtəbəl] *adj* = **debatable**

debauchery [dɪ'bɔːtʃərɪ] *n* libertinaje *m*

debilitating [dɪ'bɪlɪteɪtɪŋ] *adj* debilitante; *(heat, climate)* agotador(a)

debit ['debɪt] **1** *n* débito *m*; **d. balance** saldo negativo
2 *vt* **d. Mr Jones with £20** cargar la suma de 20 libras en la cuenta del Sr. Jones

debris ['debriː, 'deɪbriː] *n sing* escombros *mpl*

debt [det] *n* deuda *f*; **to be deeply in d.** estar cargado(a) de deudas; *Fig* **to be in sb's d.** estar en deuda con algn

debtor ['detə(r)] *n* deudor(a) *m,f*

debug [diː'bʌg] *vt Comput* eliminar fallos de

debunk [diː'bʌŋk] *vt Fam* desacreditar, desprestigiar

debut ['debjuː, 'deɪbjuː] *n* debut *m*; **to make one's d.** debutar

debutante ['debjʊtɑːnt] *n* debutante *f*

decade [de'keɪd, 'dekeɪd] *n* decenio *m*, década *f*

decadence ['dekədəns] *n* decadencia *f*

decadent ['dekədənt] *adj* decadente

decaffeinated [diː'kæfɪneɪtɪd] *adj* descafeinado(a)

decanter [dɪ'kæntə(r)] *n* jarra *f*, jarro *m*

decapitate [dɪ'kæpɪteɪt] *vt* decapitar

decay [dɪ'keɪ] **1** *n* (*of food, body*) descomposición *f*; *(of teeth)* caries *f inv*; *(of buildings)* desmoronamiento *m*; *Fig* decadencia *f*
2 *vi* descomponerse; *(teeth)* cariarse; *(building)* deteriorarse; *Fig* corromperse

deceased [dɪ'siːst] *adj Fml* difunto(a), fallecido(a)

deceit [dɪ'siːt] *n* (**a**) *(dishonesty)* falta *f* de honradez, falsedad *f* (**b**) *(trick)* engaño *m*, mentira *f*

deceitful [dɪ'siːtfʊl] *adj* falso(a)

deceive [dɪ'siːv] *vt (mislead)* engañar; *(lie to)* mentir

December [dɪ'sembə(r)] *n* diciembre *m*

decency ['diːsənsɪ] *n* decencia *f*; *(modesty)* pudor *m*; *(morality)* moralidad *f*

decent ['diːsənt] *adj* decente; *(person)* honrado(a); *Fam (kind)* simpático(a)

decentralize [diː'sentrəlaɪz] *vt* descentralizar

deception [dɪ'sepʃən] *n* engaño *m*

> 🖉 Note that the Spanish word **decepción** is a false friend and is never a translation for the English word **deception**. In Spanish, **decepción** means "disappointment".

deceptive [dɪ'septɪv] *adj* engañoso(a)

deceptively [dɪ'septɪvlɪ] *adv* **it looks d. simple** parece engañosamente sencillo(a)

decibel ['desɪbel] *n* decibelio *m*

decide [dɪ'saɪd] **1** *vt* (**a**) *(decide)* decidir; **to d. to do sth** decidir hacer algo (**b**) *(matter, question)* resolver, determinar
2 *vi (reach decision)* decidirse; **to d. against sth** decidirse en contra de algo
▸ **decide on** *vt insep (choose)* optar por

decided [dɪ'saɪdɪd] *adj* (**a**) *(noticeable)* marcado(a) (**b**) *(resolute)* decidido(a); *(views)* categórico(a)

decidedly [dɪ'saɪdɪdlɪ] *adv Fml* (**a**) *(clearly)* indudablemente (**b**) *(resolutely)* decididamente

deciding [dɪ'saɪdɪŋ] *adj* decisivo(a)

deciduous [dɪ'sɪdjʊəs] *adj* de hoja caduca

decimal ['desɪməl] **1** *adj* decimal; **d. point** coma *f* (de fracción decimal)
2 *n* decimal *m*

decimate ['desɪmeɪt] *vt* diezmar

decipher [dɪ'saɪfə(r)] *vt* descifrar

decision [dɪ'sɪʒən] *n* (**a**) decisión *f*; *Jur* fallo *m*; **to come to a d.** llegar a una decisión; **to make a d.** tomar una decisión (**b**) *(resolution)* resolución *f*

decisive [dɪ'saɪsɪv] *adj* (**a**) *(resolute)* decidido(a), resuelto(a) (**b**) *(conclusive)* decisivo(a)

deck [dek] **1** *n* (**a**) *(of ship)* cubierta *f*; **on/below d.** en/bajo cubierta; **d. chair** tumbona *f* (**b**) *(of bus)* piso *m*; **top d.** piso de arriba (**c**) *esp US (of cards)* baraja *f* (**d**) *(of record player)* plato *m*
2 *vt* **to d. out** adornar

declaration [deklə'reɪʃən] *n* declaración *f*

declare [dɪ'kleə(r)] *vt* declarar; *(winner, innocence)* proclamar; *(decision)* manifestar

declared [dɪ'kleəd] *adj (opponent)* declarado(a); *(intention)* manifiesto(a)

decline [dɪ'klaɪn] **1** *n* (**a**) *(decrease)* disminución *f* (**b**) *(deterioration)* deterioro *m*; *(of health)* empeoramiento *m*; **to fall into d.** empezar a decaer

2 *vi* (**a**) *(decrease)* disminuir; *(amount)* bajar; *(business)* decaer (**b**) *(deteriorate)* deteriorarse; *(health)* empeorar (**c**) *(refuse)* negarse

3 *vt* (**a**) *(refuse)* rechazar (**b**) *Ling* declinar

declutch [dɪ'klʌtʃ] *vi* soltar el embrague

decode [di:'kəʊd] *vt* descifrar

decompose [di:kəm'pəʊz] *vi* descomponerse

décor ['deɪkɔː(r)] *n* decoración *f*; *Th* decorado *m*

decorate ['dekəreɪt] *vt* (**a**) *(adorn)* decorar, adornar (**with** con) (**b**) *(paint)* pintar; *(wallpaper)* empapelar (**c**) *(honour)* condecorar

decoration [dekə'reɪʃən] *n* (**a**) *(decor)* decoración *f*; **Christmas decorations** adornos navideños (**b**) *(medal)* condecoración *f*

decorative ['dekərətɪv] *adj* decorativo(a)

decorator ['dekəreɪtə(r)] *n* decorador(a) *m,f*; *(painter)* pintor(a) *m,f*; *(paperhanger)* empapelador(a) *m,f*

decorum [dɪ'kɔːrəm] *n* decoro *m*

decoy ['di:kɔɪ] *n Fig* señuelo *m*

decrease 1 *n* ['di:kri:s] disminución *f*; *(in speed, size, price)* reducción *f*

2 *vi* [dɪ'kri:s] disminuir; *(strength)* menguar; *(price, temperature)* bajar; *(speed, size)* reducir

3 *vt* disminuir, reducir; *(price, temperature)* bajar

decree [dɪ'kri:] **1** *n* (**a**) *Pol & Rel* decreto *m* (**b**) *esp US Jur* sentencia *f*; **d. absolute** sentencia definitiva de divorcio; **d. nisi** sentencia provisional de divorcio

2 *vt Pol & Rel* decretar, pronunciar

decrepit [dɪ'krepɪt] *adj* decrépito(a)

dedicate ['dedɪkeɪt] *vt* consagrar, dedicar

dedicated ['dedɪkeɪtɪd] *adj* ardiente; **d. to** entregado(a) a

dedication [dedɪ'keɪʃən] *n (act)* dedicación *f*; *(commitment)* entrega *f*; *(in book)* dedicatoria *f*

deduce [dɪ'dju:s] *vt* deducir (**from** de)

deduct [dɪ'dʌkt] *vt* descontar (**from** de)

deduction [dɪ'dʌkʃən] *n* (**a**) *(conclusion)* conclusión *f* (**b**) *(subtraction)* descuento *m*

deed [di:d] *n* (**a**) *(act)* acto *m*; *(feat)* hazaña *f* (**b**) *Jur* escritura *f*; **title deeds** título *m* de propiedad

deem [di:m] *vt Fml* estimar

deep [di:p] **1** *adj* (**a**) profundo(a); *(breath, sigh)* hondo(a); **it's 10 m d.** tiene 10 m de profundidad (**b**) *(voice)* grave; *(shame)* grande; *(interest)* vivo(a) (**c**) *(colour)* oscuro(a) (**d**) *(serious)* grave

2 *adv* **to dig d.** cavar hondo; **to be d. in thought** estar absorto(a); **to look d. into sb's eyes** penetrar a algn con la mirada; *Fig* **nine d.** de nueve en fondo

deepen ['di:pən] **1** *vt (well)* profundizar, ahondar; *Fig (knowledge)* aumentar

2 *vi (river etc)* hacerse más hondo *or* profundo; *Fig (knowledge)* aumentar; *(colour, emotion)* intensificarse; *(sound, voice)* hacerse más grave

deep-freeze [di:p'fri:z] **1** *n* congelador *m*

2 *vt* congelar

deep-fry [di:p'fraɪ] *vt* freír en mucho aceite

deeply ['di:plɪ] *adv* profundamente; *(breathe)* hondo; **to be d. in debt** estar cargado(a) de deudas

deep-rooted [di:p'ru:tɪd] *adj Fig* arraigado(a)

deep-seated [di:p'si:tɪd] *adj Fig* arraigado(a)

deep-set [di:p'set] *adj (eyes)* hundido(a)

deer [dɪə(r)] *n inv* ciervo *m*

deface [dɪ'feɪs] *vt (book, poster)* garabatear

de facto [deɪ'fæktəʊ] *adj & adv Fml* de hecho

defamation [defə'meɪʃən] *n* difamación *f*

default [dɪ'fɔːlt] **1** *vi* (**a**) *(not act)* faltar a sus compromisos (**b**) *Jur* estar en rebeldía (**c**) *(not pay)* suspender pagos

2 *n* (**a**) *(failure to act)* omisión *f* (**b**) *(failure to pay)* incumplimiento *m* de pago (**c**) *Jur* rebeldía *f*; **in d. of** a falta de; **to win by d.** ganar por incomparecencia del adversario

defaulter [dɪ'fɔːltə(r)] *n (on loan)* moroso(a) *m,f*; *Jur & Mil* rebelde *mf*

defeat [dɪ'fi:t] **1** *vt* (**a**) derrotar, vencer; *(motion)* rechazar (**b**) *Fig* frustrar

2 *n* (**a**) *(of army, team)* derrota *f*; *(of motion)* rechazo *m* (**b**) *Fig* fracaso *m*

defeatist [dɪˈfiːtɪst] *adj & n* derrotista *(mf)*

defect 1 *n* [ˈdiːfekt] defecto *m*; *(flaw)* desperfecto *m*
2 *vi* [dɪˈfekt] desertar (**from** de); *(from country)* huir

defective [dɪˈfektɪv] *adj (faulty)* defectuoso(a); *(flawed)* con desperfectos; *(lacking)* incompleto(a)

defector [dɪˈfektə(r)] *n Pol* tránsfuga *mf*, tráşfuga *mf*

defence [dɪˈfens] *n* (**a**) defensa *f*; **the Ministry of D.** el Ministerio de Defensa; **to come to sb's d.** salir en defensa de algn (**b**) *usu sing Jur* defensa *f* (**c**) *Sport* [*Br* dɪˈfens, *US* ˈdiːfens] **the d.** la defensa

defenceless [dɪˈfensləs] *adj* indefenso(a)

defend [dɪˈfend] *vt* defender

defendant [dɪˈfendənt] *n Jur* acusado(a) *m,f*

defender [dɪˈfendə(r)] *n* defensor(a) *m,f*; *Sport* defensa *mf*

defending [dɪˈfendɪŋ] *adj Sport* defensor(a); **d. champion** campeón(ona) *m,f* titular

defense [dɪˈfens, ˈdiːfens] *n US* = **defence**

defensive [dɪˈfensɪv] **1** *adj* defensivo(a)
2 *n* **to be on the d.** estar a la defensiva

defer¹ [dɪˈfɜː(r)] *vt* aplazar, retrasar

defer² [dɪˈfɜː(r)] *vi* **to d. to** deferir a

deference [ˈdefərəns] *n Fml* deferencia *f*, respeto *m*; **out of** *or* **in d. to** por respeto *or* por deferencia a

defiance [dɪˈfaɪəns] *n* (**a**) *(challenge)* desafío *m*; **in d. of** a despecho de (**b**) *(resistance)* resistencia *f*

defiant [dɪˈfaɪənt] *adj (challenging)* desafiante; *(bold)* insolente

deficiency [dɪˈfɪʃənsɪ] *n* (**a**) *(lack)* falta *f*, carencia *f* (**b**) *(shortcoming)* defecto *m*

deficient [dɪˈfɪʃənt] *adj* deficiente; **to be d. in sth** carecer de algo

deficit [ˈdefɪsɪt] *n* déficit *m*

defile [dɪˈfaɪl] *vt Fml* (**a**) *(mind)* corromper; *(honour)* manchar; *(woman)* deshonrar (**b**) *(desecrate)* profanar

define [dɪˈfaɪn] *vt* definir; *(duties, powers)* delimitar

definite [ˈdefɪnɪt] *adj* (**a**) *(clear)* claro(a); *(progress)* notable (**b**) *(date, place)* determinado(a); **is it d.?** ¿es seguro?

definitely [ˈdefɪnɪtlɪ] **1** *adv* sin duda; **he was d. drunk** no cabe duda de que estaba borracho
2 *interj* ¡desde luego!

definition [defɪˈnɪʃən] *n* definición *f*; **by d.** por definición

definitive [dɪˈfɪnɪtɪv] *adj* definitivo(a)

deflate [dɪˈfleɪt] *vt* (**a**) *(tyre etc)* desinflar (**b**) *Fig* rebajar; **to d. sb** hacer bajar los humos a algn (**c**) **to d. the economy** tomar medidas deflacionistas

deflationary [dɪˈfleɪʃənərɪ] *adj Econ* deflacionista

deflect [dɪˈflekt] *vt* desviar

deflection [dɪˈflekʃən] *n* desviación *f*

deforestation [diːfɒrɪˈsteɪʃən] *n* deforestación *f*

deformed [dɪˈfɔːmd] *adj* deforme

deformity [dɪˈfɔːmɪtɪ] *n* deformidad *f*

defraud [dɪˈfrɔːd] *vt* estafar

defrost [diːˈfrɒst] *vt* (**a**) *(freezer, food)* descongelar (**b**) *US (windscreen)* desempañar

deft [deft] *adj* hábil, diestro(a)

defunct [dɪˈfʌŋkt] *adj (person)* difunto(a); *(thing)* en desuso

defuse [diːˈfjuːz] *vt (bomb)* desactivar; *Fig* **to d. a situation** reducir la tensión de una situación

defy [dɪˈfaɪ] *vt* (**a**) *(person)* desafiar; *(law, order)* contravenir (**b**) *(challenge)* retar, desafiar

degenerate 1 *vi* [dɪˈdʒenəreɪt] degenerar (**into** en)
2 *adj & n* [dɪˈdʒenərɪt] degenerado(a) *(m,f)*

degrading [dɪˈgreɪdɪŋ] *adj* degradante

degree [dɪˈgriː] *n* (**a**) grado *m*; **to some d.** hasta cierto punto (**b**) *(stage)* etapa *f*; **by degrees** poco a poco (**c**) *(qualification)* título *m*; *(doctorate)* doctorado *m*; **to have a d. in science** ser licenciado(a) en ciencias

dehydrated [diːhaɪˈdreɪtɪd] *adj (person)* deshidratado(a); *(vegetables)* seco(a)

de-ice [diːˈaɪs] *vt* quitar el hielo a, deshelar

de-icer [diːˈaɪsə(r)] *n* anticongelante *m*

deign [deɪn] *vi* dignarse

deity [ˈdeɪtɪ] *n* deidad *f*

dejected [dɪˈdʒektɪd] *adj* desalentado(a), abatido(a)

delay [dɪˈleɪ] **1** *vt* (**a**) *(flight, train)* retrasar; *(person)* entretener; **delayed action** acción retardada (**b**) *(postpone)* aplazar
2 *vi* **don't d.** no lo deje para más tarde
3 *n* retraso *m*

delectable [dɪˈlektəbəl] *adj* delicioso(a)

delegate 1 *n* [ˈdelɪgɪt] delegado(a) *m,f*
2 *vt* [ˈdelɪgeɪt] delegar (**to** en); **to d. sb to do sth** encargar a algn que haga algo

delegation [delɪˈgeɪʃən] *n* delegación *f*

delete [dɪˈliːt] *vt* tachar, suprimir

deliberate 1 *adj* [dɪˈlɪbərɪt] *(intentional)*

deliberado(a), intencionado(a); *(studied)* premeditado(a); *(careful)* prudente; *(unhurried)* pausado(a)
2 *vt* [dɪ'lɪbəreɪt] deliberar
3 *vi* deliberar (**on** *or* **about** sobre)
deliberately [dɪ'lɪbərɪtlɪ] *adv (intentionally)* a propósito; *(unhurriedly)* pausadamente
deliberation [dɪlɪbə'reɪʃən] *n* (**a**) *esp pl (consideration)* deliberación *f* (**b**) *(care)* cuidado *m*; *(unhurriedness)* pausa *f*
delicacy ['delɪkəsɪ] *n* (**a**) delicadeza *f* (**b**) *(food)* manjar *m* (exquisito)
delicate ['delɪkɪt] *adj* delicado(a); *(handiwork)* fino(a); *(instrument)* sensible; *(flavour)* sutil
delicious [dɪ'lɪʃəs] *adj* delicioso(a)
delight [dɪ'laɪt] **1** *n* (**a**) *(pleasure)* placer *m*; **he took d. in it** le encantó (**b**) *(source of pleasure)* encanto *m*, delicia *f*
2 *vt* encantar
delighted [dɪ'laɪtɪd] *adj* encantado(a); *(smile)* de alegría; **I'm d. to see you** me alegro mucho de verte
delightful [dɪ'laɪtfʊl] *adj* encantador(a); *(view, person)* muy agradable; *(meal, weather)* delicioso(a)
delinquency [dɪ'lɪŋkwənsɪ] *n* delincuencia *f*; **juvenile d.** delincuencia juvenil
delinquent [dɪ'lɪŋkwənt] *adj & n* delincuente *(mf)*
delirious [dɪ'lɪrɪəs] *adj* delirante
deliver [dɪ'lɪvə(r)] *vt* (**a**) *(goods)* repartir, entregar; *(message)* dar; *(order)* despachar; *Fig* **to d. the goods** cumplir con la obligación (**b**) *(blow)* asestar; *(speech, verdict)* pronunciar (**c**) *Med* ayudar en el nacimiento de (**d**) *Fml (rescue)* liberar
delivery [dɪ'lɪvərɪ] *n* (**a**) *(of goods)* reparto *m*, entrega *f*; **to take d. of an order** recibir un pedido; *Br* **d. van** furgoneta *f* de reparto (**b**) *(of speech)* declamación *f* (**c**) *(of baby)* parto *m*
delta ['deltə] *n Geog* delta *m*
delude [dɪ'luːd] *vt* engañar; **don't d. yourself** no te hagas ilusiones
deluge ['deljuːdʒ] **1** *n (flood)* inundación *f*; *(rain)* diluvio *m*; *Fig (of letters etc)* avalancha *f*
2 *vt Fml* inundar
delusion [dɪ'luːʒən] *n* (**a**) *(state, act)* engaño *m* (**b**) *(false belief)* ilusión *f* (vana); **delusions of grandeur** delirios *mpl* de grandeza
de luxe [də'lʌks, də'lʊks] *adj* de lujo *inv*
delve [delv] *vi* **to d. into** *(pocket)* hurgar

en; *(subject)* profundizar en
demand [dɪ'mɑːnd] **1** *n* (**a**) solicitud *f*; *(for pay rise, rights)* reclamación *f*; *(need)* necesidad *f*; **on d.** a petición (**b**) *(claim)* exigencia *f*; **to be in d.** ser solicitado(a) (**c**) *Econ* demanda *f*
2 *vt* (**a**) exigir; *(rights)* reclamar; **to d. that ...** insistir en que ... (+ *subj*) (**b**) *(need)* requerir
demanding [dɪ'mɑːndɪŋ] *adj* (**a**) *(person)* exigente (**b**) *(job)* agotador(a)
demean [dɪ'miːn] *vt Fml* **to d. oneself** rebajarse
demeaning [dɪ'miːnɪŋ] *adj Fml* humillante
demeanour, *US* **demeanor** [dɪ'miːnə(r)] *n Fml* (**a**) *(behaviour)* comportamiento *m*, conducta *f* (**b**) *(bearing)* porte *m*
demented [dɪ'mentɪd] *adj Med* demente; *Fam* loco(a)
demise [dɪ'maɪz] *n Fml (death)* fallecimiento *m*; *Fig (of institution)* desaparición *f*; *(of ambition etc)* fracaso *m*
demist [diː'mɪst] *vt Aut* desempañar
demo ['deməʊ] *n Fam* manifestación *f*; **d. tape** maqueta *f*
demobilize [diː'məʊbɪlaɪz] *vt* desmovilizar
democracy [dɪ'mɒkrəsɪ] *n* democracia *f*
democrat ['deməkræt] *n* demócrata *mf*; *Pol* **Christian D.** democratacristiano(a) *m,f*; **Social D.** socialdemócrata *mf*
democratic [demə'krætɪk] *adj* democrático(a); *US Pol* **D. party** partido *m* demócrata
demographic [demə'græfɪk] *adj* demográfico(a)
demolish [dɪ'mɒlɪʃ] *vt (building)* derribar, demoler; *Fig (theory, proposal)* echar por tierra
demolition [demə'lɪʃən] *n* demolición *f*
demon ['diːmən] *n* demonio *m*
demonstrate ['demənstreɪt] **1** *vt* demostrar
2 *vi Pol* manifestarse
demonstration [demən'streɪʃən] *n* (**a**) *(proof)* demostración *f*, prueba *f* (**b**) *(explanation)* explicación *f* (**c**) *Pol* manifestación *f*
demonstrative [dɪ'mɒnstrətɪv] *adj* expresivo(a)
demonstrator ['demənstreɪtə(r)] *n* manifestante *mf*
demoralize [dɪ'mɒrəlaɪz] *vt* desmoralizar
demoralizing [dɪ'mɒrəlaɪzɪŋ] *adj* desmoralizador(a), desmoralizante

demote [dɪ'məʊt] *vt* rebajar de graduación a

demure [dɪ'mjʊə(r)] *adj (person)* recatado(a)

den [den] *n* (a) *(of animal)* guarida *f* (b) *Fam (study)* estudio *m*

denial [dɪ'naɪəl] *n* (a) *(of charge)* desmentido *m* (b) *(of rights)* denegación *f*; *(of request)* negativa *f*

denim ['denɪm] *n* dril *m*; **d. skirt** falda tejana; **denims** tejanos *mpl*, vaqueros *mpl*

Denmark ['denmɑːk] *n* Dinamarca

denomination [dɪnɒmɪ'neɪʃən] *n* (a) *Rel* confesión *f* (b) *Fin (of coins)* valor *m*

denominator [dɪ'nɒmɪneɪtə(r)] *n* denominador *m*

denote [dɪ'nəʊt] *vt (show)* indicar; *(mean)* significar

denounce [dɪ'naʊns] *vt* denunciar; *(criticize)* censurar

dense [dens] *adj* (a) denso(a); *(crowd)* numeroso(a) (b) *Fam (stupid)* torpe

densely ['densli] *adv* densamente

density ['densɪtɪ] *n* densidad *f*

dent [dent] **1** *n* abolladura *f*
2 *vt (car)* abollar

dental ['dentəl] *adj* dental; **d. floss** hilo *m* dental; **d. surgeon** odontólogo(a) *m,f*; **d. surgery** *(place)* clínica *f* dental; *(treatment)* cirugía *f* dental

dentist ['dentɪst] *n* dentista *mf*

dentistry ['dentɪstrɪ] *n* odontología *f*

denture ['dentʃə(r)] *n (usu pl)* dentadura postiza

denunciation [dɪnʌnsɪ'eɪʃən] *n* denuncia *f*, condena *f*

deny [dɪ'naɪ] *vt* (a) *(repudiate)* negar; *(rumour, report)* desmentir; *(charge)* rechazar (b) *(refuse)* negar

deodorant [diː'əʊdərənt] *n* desodorante *m*

depart [dɪ'pɑːt] *vi* marcharse, irse; *Fig (from subject)* desviarse (**from** de)

department [dɪ'pɑːtmənt] *n* sección *f*; *(in university)* departamento *m*; *(in government)* ministerio *m*; **d. store** grandes almacenes *mpl*; *US* **D. of the Interior** Ministerio *m* del Interior

departure [dɪ'pɑːtʃə(r)] *n* partida *f*; *Av & Rail* salida *f*; *Av* **d. lounge** sala *f* de embarque

depend [dɪ'pend] **1** *vi (rely)* fiarse (**on** or **upon** de)
2 *v impers (be determined by)* depender (**on** or **upon** de); **it depends on the weather** según el tiempo que haga; **that depends** según

dependable [dɪ'pendəbəl] *adj (person)* responsable, fiable; *(income)* seguro(a); *(machine)* fiable

dependant, *US* **dependent** [dɪ'pendənt] *n* dependiente *mf*

dependence [dɪ'pendəns] *n* dependencia *f*

dependent [dɪ'pendənt] **1** *adj* dependiente; **to be d. on sth** depender de algo
2 *n US* = **dependant**

depict [dɪ'pɪkt] *vt Art* representar; *Fig* describir

deplete [dɪ'pliːt] *vt* reducir

deplorable [dɪ'plɔːrəbəl] *adj* lamentable

deplore [dɪ'plɔː(r)] *vt* deplorar

deploy [dɪ'plɔɪ] *vt Mil* desplegar; *Fig* utilizar

depopulate [diː'pɒpjʊleɪt] *vt* despoblar

deport [dɪ'pɔːt] *vt* expulsar (**from** de; **to** a)

deportation [diːpɔː'teɪʃən] *n* expulsión *f*

deportment [dɪ'pɔːtmənt] *n Fml* porte *m*

depose [dɪ'pəʊz] *vt* deponer

deposit [dɪ'pɒzɪt] **1** *n* (a) sedimento *m*; *Min* yacimiento *m*; *(in wine)* poso *m* (b) *(in bank)* depósito *m*; **d. account** cuenta *f* de ahorros (**c**) *Com (on purchase)* señal *f*; *(on rented car, flat)* depósito *m*; *(on house)* entrada *f*
2 *vt* depositar; *(into account)* ingresar

deposition [depə'zɪʃən] *n* (a) *(of leader)* destitución *f* (b) *Jur (of witness)* declaración *f*

depositor [dɪ'pɒzɪtə(r)] *n* depositante *mf*

depot ['depəʊ] *n* almacén *m*; *Mil* depósito *m*; *(bus garage)* garaje *m* (de autobuses); *US (bus station)* estación *f* de autobuses

depraved [dɪ'preɪvd] *adj (person)* depravado(a)

deprecate ['deprɪkeɪt] *vt* desaprobar, censurar

depreciate [dɪ'priːʃɪeɪt] *vi* depreciarse

depreciation [dɪpriːʃɪ'eɪʃən] *n* depreciación *f*

depress [dɪ'pres] *vt* (a) *(person)* deprimir (b) *Econ (profits)* reducir; *(trade)* dificultar (c) *Fml (switch, lever etc)* presionar; *(clutch, piano pedal)* pisar

depressed [dɪ'prest] *adj* (a) *(person)* deprimido(a); **to get d.** deprimirse (b) *(market)* en crisis (c) *(surface)* hundido(a)

depressing [dɪ'presɪŋ] *adj* deprimente

depression [dɪ'preʃən] *n* depresión *f*

deprivation [deprɪ'veɪʃən] *n (hardship)* privación *f*; *(loss)* pérdida *f*

deprive [dɪ'praɪv] *vt* privar (**of** de)

deprived [dɪ'praɪvd] *adj* necesitado(a)

dept (*abbr* **department**) dpt, dpto

depth [depθ] *n* (**a**) profundidad *f* (**b**) *Fig (of emotion)* intensidad *f*; *(of thought)* complejidad *f*; **to be in the depths of despair** estar completamente desesperado(a); **in d.** a fondo

deputation [depjʊ'teɪʃən] *n* delegación *f*

deputy ['depjʊtɪ] *n* (**a**) *(substitute)* suplente *mf*; **d. chairman** vicepresidente *m*; **d. head** subdirector(a) *m,f* (**b**) *Pol* diputado(a) *m,f*

derail [dɪ'reɪl] *vt* hacer descarrilar

deranged [dɪ'reɪndʒd] *adj* trastornado(a)

derby *n* (**a**) ['da:bɪ] *Sport* prueba *f* (**b**) ['dɜ:rbɪ] *US* sombrero hongo

derelict ['derɪlɪkt] *adj* abandonado(a), en ruinas

deride [dɪ'raɪd] *vt* ridiculizar, burlarse de

derisive [dɪ'raɪsɪv] *adj* burlón(ona)

derisory [dɪ'raɪsərɪ] *adj* irrisorio(a)

derivative [dɪ'rɪvətɪv] **1** *adj (art, writing)* sin originalidad

2 *n (of word, substance)* derivado *m*

derive [dɪ'raɪv] **1** *vt* sacar

2 *vi (word)* derivarse (**from** de); *(skill)* provenir (**from** de)

derogatory [dɪ'rɒgətərɪ] *adj (remark, article)* despectivo(a); *(meaning)* peyorativo(a)

derrick ['derɪk] *n* torre *f* de perforación

descend [dɪ'send] **1** *vi* descender; **to d. from** *(be related to)* descender de

2 *vt (stairs)* bajar

descendant [dɪ'sendənt] *n* descendiente *mf*

descent [dɪ'sent] *n* (**a**) descenso *m* (**b**) *Fig (into madness, poverty)* caída *f* (**c**) *(slope)* declive *m* (**d**) *(ancestry)* ascendencia *f*

describe [dɪ'skraɪb] *vt* (**a**) describir (**b**) *(circle)* trazar

description [dɪ'skrɪpʃən] *n* (**a**) descripción *f*; **to defy d.** superar la descripción (**b**) *(type)* clase *f*

desecrate ['desɪkreɪt] *vt* profanar

desert¹ ['dezət] *n* desierto *m*

desert² [dɪ'zɜ:t] **1** *vt (place, family)* abandonar

2 *vi Mil* desertar (**from** de)

deserter [dɪ'zɜ:tə(r)] *n* desertor(a) *m,f*

desertion [dɪ'zɜ:ʃən] *n* abandono *m*; *Pol* defección *f*; *Mil* deserción *f*

deserts [dɪ'zɜ:ts] *npl* **to get one's just d.** llevarse su merecido

deserve [dɪ'zɜ:v] *vt (rest, punishment)* merecer; *(prize, praise)* ser digno(a) de

deservedly [dɪ'zɜ:vɪdlɪ] *adv* con (toda) razón

deserving [dɪ'zɜ:vɪŋ] *adj (person)* de valía; *(cause)* meritorio(a)

design [dɪ'zaɪn] **1** *n* (**a**) diseño *m* (**b**) *(drawing, blueprint)* plano *m* (**c**) *(layout)* disposición *f* (**d**) *(pattern)* dibujo *m* (**e**) *Fig (scheme)* intención *f*; **by d.** a propósito; *Fam* **to have designs on** tener puestas las miras en

2 *vt* diseñar

designate 1 *vt* ['dezɪgneɪt] (**a**) *(appoint)* designar, nombrar (**b**) *Fml (boundary)* señalar

2 *adj* ['dezɪgnɪt] designado(a)

designer [dɪ'zaɪnə(r)] *n Art* diseñador(a) *m,f*; **d. jeans** pantalones *mpl* de marca

desirable [dɪ'zaɪərəbəl] *adj* deseable; *(asset, offer)* atractivo(a)

desire [dɪ'zaɪə(r)] **1** *n* deseo *m*; **I haven't the slightest d. to go** no me apetece nada ir

2 *vt* desear

desist [dɪ'zɪst] *vi Fml* desistir (**from** de)

desk [desk] *n (in school)* pupitre *m*; *(in office)* escritorio *m*; *US* **d. clerk** recepcionista *mf*; **d. job** trabajo *m* de oficina; **news d.** redacción *f*; **reception d.** recepción *f*

desktop ['desktɒp] *n Comput* escritorio *m*; **d. computer** ordenador *m* de sobremesa, *Am* computadora *f* de mesa; **d. publishing** autoedición *f*

desolate ['desəlɪt] *adj* (**a**) *(uninhabited)* desierto(a); *(barren)* yermo(a) (**b**) *(person)* desconsolado(a)

desolation [desə'leɪʃən] *n* (**a**) *(of place)* desolación *f*; *(by destruction)* asolamiento *m* (**b**) *(of person)* desconsuelo *m*

despair [dɪ'speə(r)] **1** *n* desesperación *f*; **to drive sb to d.** desesperar a algn

2 *vi* desesperar(se) (**of** de)

despairing [dɪ'speərɪŋ] *adj* desesperado(a)

despatch [dɪ'spætʃ] *n & vt* = **dispatch**

desperate ['despərɪt] *adj* desesperado(a); *(struggle)* encarnizado(a) (**b**) *(need)* apremiante

desperately ['despərɪtlɪ] *adv (recklessly)* desesperadamente; *(struggle)* encarnizadamente; *(ill)* gravemente; *(in love)* locamente; *(difficult)* sumamente

desperation [despə'reɪʃən] *n* desesperación *f*; **in d.** a la desesperada

despicable [dɪ'spɪkəbəl] *adj* despreciable; *(behaviour)* indigno(a)

despise [dɪ'spaɪz] *vt* despreciar, menospreciar

despite [dɪ'spaɪt] *prep Fml* a pesar de

despondent [dɪ'spɒndənt] *adj* abatido(a)

despot ['despɒt] *n* déspota *mf*

dessert [dɪ'zɜːt] *n* postre *m*; **d. wine** vino *m* dulce

dessertspoon [dɪ'zɜːtspuːn] *n* (a) cuchara *f* de postre (b) **dessertspoon(ful)** *(measure)* cucharada *f* de postre

destination [destɪ'neɪʃən] *n* destino *m*

destined ['destɪnd] *adj* (a) **d. to fail** condenado(a) al fracaso (b) *(bound)* con destino (**for** a)

destiny ['destɪnɪ] *n* destino *m*

destitute ['destɪtjuːt] *adj* indigente

destroy [dɪ'strɔɪ] *vt* destruir; *(vehicle, old furniture)* destrozar

destroyer [dɪ'strɔɪə(r)] *n Naut* destructor *m*

destruction [dɪ'strʌkʃən] *n* destrucción *f*, *Fig* ruina *f*

destructive [dɪ'strʌktɪv] *adj (gale etc)* destructor(a); *(tendency, criticism)* destructivo(a)

detach [dɪ'tætʃ] *vt (remove)* separar

detachable [dɪ'tætʃəbəl] *adj* separable (**from** de)

detached [dɪ'tætʃt] *adj* (a) *(separated)* separado(a), **d. house** casa *f* independiente (b) *(impartial)* objetivo(a)

detachment [dɪ'tætʃmənt] *n* (a) *(impartiality)* objetividad *f*, *(aloofness)* desapego *m* (b) *Mil* destacamento *m*

detail ['diːteɪl] **1** *n* (a) detalle *m*, pormenor *m*; **without going into detail(s)** sin entrar en detalles; **details** *(information)* información *f* (b) *Mil* destacamento *m*
2 *vt* (a) *(list)* detallar, enumerar (b) *Mil (appoint)* destacar

detailed ['diːteɪld] *adj* detallado(a), minucioso(a)

detain [dɪ'teɪn] *vt* (a) *Jur* detener (b) *(delay)* retener

detainee [diːteɪ'niː] *n Pol* preso(a) *m,f*

detect [dɪ'tekt] *vt* (a) *(error, movement)* advertir; *(difference)* notar; *(smell, sound)* percibir (b) *(discover)* descubrir; *(enemy ship)* detectar; *(position)* localizar

detection [dɪ'tekʃən] *n* (a) *(discovery)* descubrimiento *m*; *(of smell, sound)* percepción *f* (b) *(discovery) (of enemy ship)* detección *f*

detective [dɪ'tektɪv] *n* detective *mf*; **d. story** novela policíaca

detector [dɪ'tektə(r)] *n* aparato *m* detector

detention [dɪ'tenʃən] *n (of suspect etc)* detención *f*, arresto *m*; *Educ* **to get d.** quedarse castigado(a)

deter [dɪ'tɜː(r)] *vt (dissuade)* disuadir (**from** de); *(stop)* impedir

detergent [dɪ'tɜːdʒənt] *n* detergente *m*

deteriorate [dɪ'tɪərɪəreɪt] *vi* deteriorarse

deterioration [dɪtɪərɪə'reɪʃən] *n* empeoramiento *m*; *(of substance, friendship)* deterioro *m*

determination [dɪtɜːmɪ'neɪʃən] *n (resolution)* resolución *f*

determine [dɪ'tɜːmɪn] *vt* determinar

determined [dɪ'tɜːmɪnd] *adj (person)* decidido(a); *(effort)* enérgico(a)

deterrent [dɪ'terənt] **1** *adj* disuasivo(a)
2 *n* fuerza disuasoria

detest [dɪ'test] *vt* detestar, odiar

detonate ['detəneɪt] *vt & vi* detonar

detonation [detə'neɪʃən] *n* detonación *f*

detour ['diːtʊə(r)] *n* desvío *m*

detract [dɪ'trækt] *vi* quitar mérito (**from** a)

detractor [dɪ'træktə(r)] *n* detractor(a) *m,f*

detriment ['detrɪmənt] *n* perjuicio *m* (**to** de)

detrimental [detrɪ'mentəl] *adj* perjudicial (**to** para)

deuce [djuːs] *n (in tennis)* cuarenta iguales *mpl*

devaluation [diːvæljuː'eɪʃən] *n* devaluación *f*

devastate ['devəsteɪt] *vt (city, area)* asolar; *Fig (person)* desolar

devastating ['devəsteɪtɪŋ] *adj (fire)* devastador(a); *(wind, flood)* arrollador(a)

devastation [devə'steɪʃən] *n* asolación *f*

develop [dɪ'veləp] **1** *vt* (a) *(trade)* desarrollar; *(trade)* fomentar; *(skill)* perfeccionar; *(plan)* elaborar; *(habit)* contraer; *(interest)* mostrar (b) *(natural resources)* aprovechar; *Constr (site)* urbanizar (c) *Phot* revelar
2 *vi* (a) *(body, industry)* desarrollarse; *(system)* perfeccionarse; *(interest)* crecer (b) *(appear)* crearse; *(evolve)* evolucionar

developer [dɪ'veləpə(r)] *n* **(property) d.** inmobiliaria *f*

development [dɪ'veləpmənt] *n* (a) desarrollo *m*; *(of trade)* fomento *m*; *(of skill)* perfección *f*; *(of character)* formación *f*; **d. aid** ayuda *f* al desarrollo (b) *(advance)* avance *m* (c) **there are no new developments** no hay ninguna novedad (d) *(exploitation)* explotación *f* (e) *Constr* urbanización *f*

deviate ['diːvɪeɪt] *vi* desviarse (**from** de)

deviation [diːvɪ'eɪʃən] *n (from norm, route)* desviación *f* (**from** de); *(from truth)* alejamiento *m*

device [dɪ'vaɪs] *n* (**a**) aparato *m*; *(mechanism)* mecanismo *m* (**b**) *(trick, scheme)* ardid *m*

devil ['devəl] *n* diablo *m*, demonio *m*; **d.'s advocate** abogado(a) *m,f* del diablo; *Fam* **where the h. did you put it?** ¿dónde demonios lo pusiste?; **you lucky d.!** ¡vaya suerte que tienes!

devious ['diːvɪəs] *adj* (**a**) *(winding)* tortuoso(a) (**b**) *esp Pej (person)* taimado(a)

devise [dɪ'vaɪz] *vt* idear, concebir

devoid [dɪ'vɔɪd] *adj* desprovisto(a) (**of** de)

devolution [diːvə'luːʃən] *n Pol* = transmisión de poderes a las regiones

devote [dɪ'vəʊt] *vt* dedicar; **she devoted her life to helping the poor** consagró su vida a la ayuda de los pobres

devoted [dɪ'vəʊtɪd] *adj* fiel, leal (**to** a)

devotee [devə'tiː] *n (of religion)* devoto(a) *m,f*; *(of theatre, sport)* aficionado(a) *m,f*; *Pol* partidario(a) *m,f*

devotion [dɪ'vəʊʃən] *n* devoción *f*; *(to cause)* dedicación *f*

devour [dɪ'vaʊə(r)] *vt* devorar

devout [dɪ'vaʊt] *adj* devoto(a)

dew [djuː] *n* rocío *m*

dexterity [dek'sterɪtɪ] *n* destreza *f*

dext(e)rous ['dekstrəs] *adj* diestro(a)

diabetes [daɪə'biːtiːz, daɪə'biːtɪs] *n* diabetes *f*

diabetic [daɪə'betɪk] *adj & n* diabético(a) (*m,f*)

diabolical [daɪə'bɒlɪkəl] *adj* (**a**) *(evil)* diabólico(a) (**b**) *Fam (unbearable)* espantoso(a)

diagnose ['daɪəgnəʊz] *vt* diagnosticar

diagnosis [daɪəg'nəʊsɪs] *n (pl* **diagnoses** [daɪəg'nəʊsiːz]) diagnóstico *m*

diagonal [daɪ'ægənəl] *adj & n* diagonal (*f*)

diagonally [daɪ'ægənəlɪ] *adv* en diagonal, diagonalmente

diagram ['daɪəgræm] *n* diagrama *m*; *(of process, system)* esquema *m*; *(of workings)* gráfico *m*

dial ['daɪəl, daɪl] **1** *n (of clock)* esfera *f*; *(of radio)* cuadrante *m*; *(of telephone)* disco *m*; *(of machine)* botón *m* selector

2 *vt & vi Tel* marcar; *Br* **dialling** *or US* **d. code** prefijo *m*; *Br* **dialling** *or US* **d. tone** señal *f* de marcar

dialect ['daɪəlekt] *n* dialecto *m*

dialogue, *US* **dialog** ['daɪəlɒg] *n* diálogo *m*

diameter [daɪ'æmɪtə(r)] *n* diámetro *m*

diametrically [daɪə'metrɪkəlɪ] *adv* diametralmente

diamond ['daɪəmənd] *n* (**a**) diamante *m* (**b**) *(shape)* rombo *m*

diaphragm ['daɪəfræm] *n* diafragma *m*

diarrhoea, *US* **diarrhea** [daɪə'rɪə] *n* diarrea *f*

diary ['daɪərɪ] *n* (**a**) diario *m*; **to keep a d.** llevar un diario (**b**) *Br (for appointments)* agenda *f*

dice [daɪs] **1** *n (pl* **dice**) dado *m*

2 *vt Culin* cortar en cuadritos

dichotomy [daɪ'kɒtəmɪ] *n* dicotomía *f*

dictate 1 *vt* [dɪk'teɪt] *(letter, order)* dictar

2 *vi* **to d. to sb** dar órdenes a algn

3 *n* ['dɪkteɪt] *Fig* **the dictates of conscience** los dictados de la conciencia

dictation [dɪk'teɪʃən] *n* dictado *m*

dictator [dɪk'teɪtə(r)] *n* dictador(a) *m,f*

dictatorship [dɪk'teɪtəʃɪp] *n* dictadura *f*

diction ['dɪkʃən] *n* dicción *f*

dictionary ['dɪkʃənərɪ] *n* diccionario *m*

did [dɪd] *pt of* **do**

die [daɪ] *vi* (**a**) morir, morirse; *Fam Fig* **to be dying for sth/to do sth** morirse por algo/de ganas de hacer algo (**b**) *Fig (flame)* extinguirse; *Fig* **to d. hard** *(habit)* tardar en desaparecer (**c**) *(engine)* calarse; *(battery)* agotarse

▸ **die away** *vi* desvanecerse

▸ **die down** *vi (fire)* extinguirse; *(wind)* amainar; *(noise, excitement)* disminuir

▸ **die off** *vi* morir uno por uno

▸ **die out** *vi* extinguirse

die-hard ['daɪhɑːd] *n* reaccionario(a) *m,f*

diesel ['diːzəl] *n* (**a**) *(oil)* gasoil *m*; **d. engine** motor *m* diesel (**b**) *Fam (vehicle)* vehículo *m* diesel

diet ['daɪət] **1** *n (normal food)* dieta *f*; *(selected food)* régimen *m*; **to be on a d.** estar a régimen

2 *vi* estar a régimen

dietician [daɪə'tɪʃən] *n* especialista *mf* en dietética

differ ['dɪfə(r)] *vi (be unlike)* ser distinto(a); *(disagree)* discrepar

difference ['dɪfərəns] *n* (**a**) *(dissimilarity)* diferencia *f*; **it makes no d. (to me)** (me) da igual; **what d. does it make?** ¿qué más da? (**b**) *(disagreement)* desacuerdo *m*

different ['dɪfərənt] *adj* diferente, distinto(a); **you look d.** pareces otro(a)

differentiate [dɪfə'renʃɪeɪt] **1** *vt* distinguir, diferenciar (**from** de)

2 *vi* distinguir (**between** entre)

differently ['dɪfərəntlɪ] *adv* de otra manera

difficult ['dɪfɪkəlt] *adj* difícil

difficulty ['dɪfɪkəltɪ] n dificultad f; *(problem)* problema m; **to be in difficulties** estar en un apuro

diffident ['dɪfɪdənt] adj tímido(a)

diffuse 1 adj [dɪ'fju:s] *(light)* difuso(a); *Fig* ʌgo(a)
2 t [dɪ'fju:z] difundir; *(heat)* desprender

dig [dɪg] **1** n (a) *(poke)* codazo m (b) *Fam (gibe)* pulla f (c) *(archaeological)* excavación f (d) *Br* **digs** *(lodgings)* alojamiento m; *(room)* habitación f alquilada
2 vt *(pt & pp* **dug)** (a) *(earth)* cavar; *(tunnel)* excavar (b) *Fam Fig* **to d. one's heels in** mantenerse en sus trece
3 vi *(person)* cavar; *(animal)* escarbar; *(excavate)* excavar
▸ **dig in** vi *Mil* atrincherarse
▸ **dig out** vt sep *Fig (old suit)* sacar; *(information)* descubrir
▸ **dig up** vt sep *(weeds)* arrancar; *(buried object)* desenterrar; *(road)* levantar; *Fig* sacar a relucir

digest 1 n ['daɪdʒest] *(summary)* resumen m
2 vt [dɪ'dʒest] *(food)* digerir; *Fig (facts)* asimilar

digestion [dɪ'dʒestʃən] n digestión f

digestive [dɪ'dʒestɪv] adj digestivo(a); *Br* **d. biscuit** galleta f integral

digger ['dɪgə(r)] n excavadora f

digit ['dɪdʒɪt] n (a) *Math* dígito m (b) *Fml Anat* dedo m

digital ['dɪdʒɪtəl] adj digital; **d. television** televisión f digital

dignified ['dɪgnɪfaɪd] adj *(manner)* solemne, serio(a); *(appearance)* majestuoso(a)

dignitary ['dɪgnɪtərɪ] n dignatario m

dignity ['dɪgnɪtɪ] n dignidad f

digress [daɪ'gres] vi apartarse del tema

dike [daɪk] n *US* = **dyke**

dilapidated [dɪ'læpɪdeɪtɪd] adj en mal estado

dilemma [dɪ'lemə, daɪ'lemə] n dilema m

diligent ['dɪlɪdʒənt] adj *(worker)* diligente; *(inquiries, search)* esmerado(a)

dilute [daɪ'lu:t] **1** vt diluir; *(wine, milk)* aguar; *Fig (effect, influence)* atenuar
2 vi diluirse

dim [dɪm] **1** adj (**dimmer, dimmest**) (a) *(light)* débil, tenue; *(room)* oscuro(a); *(outline)* borroso(a); *(eyesight)* defectuoso(a); *Fig (memory)* vago(a); *Fig (future)* sombrío(a) (b) *Fam (stupid)* torpe
2 vt *(light)* bajar
3 vi *(light)* bajarse; *(sight)* nublarse; *Fig (joy)* extinguirse

dime [daɪm] n *US* monedɑ f de 10 centavos

dimension [daɪ'menʃən] n dimensión f

diminish [dɪ'mɪnɪʃ] vt & vi disminuir

diminutive [dɪ'mɪnjʊtɪv] **1** adj diminuto(a)
2 n *Ling* diminutivo m

dimly ['dɪmlɪ] adv vagamente

dimmer ['dɪmə(r)] n **d. (switch)** regulador m de voltaje

dimple ['dɪmpəl] n hoyuelo m

din [dɪn] n *(of crowd)* alborotɔ m; *(of machinery)* estruendo m

dine [daɪn] vi *Fml* cenar; **to d. out** cenar fuera

diner ['daɪnə(r)] n (a) *(person)* comensal mf (b) *US (restaurant)* restaurante barato

dinghy ['dɪŋɪ] n bote m; **(rubber) d.** bote neumático

dingy ['dɪndʒɪ] adj (**dingier, dingiest**) (a) *(dark)* oscuro(a) (b) *(dirty)* sucio(a) (c) *(colour)* desteñido(a)

dining car ['daɪnɪŋkɑ:(r)] n vagón m restaurante

dining room ['daɪnɪŋru:m] n comedor m

dinner ['dɪnə(r)] n *(at midday)* comida f; *(in evening)* cena f; **d. jacket** smoking m; **d. service** vajilla f; **d. table** mesa f de comedor

dinosaur ['daɪnəsɔ:(r)] n dinosaurio m

dint [dɪnt] n **by d. of** a fuerza de

diocese ['daɪəsɪs] n diócesis f inv

dioxide [daɪ'ɒksaɪd] n bióxido m

dip [dɪp] **1** n (a) *Fam (bathe)* chapuzón m (b) *(of road)* pendiente f; *(in ground)* depresión f (c) *Culin* salsa f
2 vt (a) bañar; *(spoon, hand)* meter (b) *Br Aut* **to d. one's lights** poner luces de cruce
3 vi *(road)* bajar
▸ **dip into** vt insep (a) *(savings)* echar mano de (b) *(book)* hojear

diphthong ['dɪfθɒŋ] n dip'ongo m

diploma [dɪ'pləʊmə] n diploma m

diplomacy [dɪ'pləʊːməsɪ] n diplomacia f

diplomat ['dɪpləmæt] n diplomático(a) m,f

diplomatic [dɪplə'mætɪk] adj diplomático(a)

dipstick ['dɪpstɪk] n indicador m de nivel del aceite

dire ['daɪə(r)] adj *(urgent)* extremo(a); *(serious)* grave

direct [dɪ'rekt, 'daɪrekt] **1** adj (a) directo(a); **d. current** corriente continua (b) **the d. opposite** todo lo contrario
2 adv directamente
3 vt (a) dirigir; **can you d. me to a bank?**

¿me puede indicar dónde hay un banco? (**b**) *Fml (order)* mandar

direction [dɪˈrekʃən, daɪˈrekʃən] *n* (**a**) dirección *f*; **sense of d.** sentido *m* de la orientación (**b**) **directions** *(to place)* señas *fpl*; **directions for use** modo *m* de empleo (**c**) *Th* puesta *f* en escena

directive [dɪˈrektɪv, daɪˈrektɪv] *n* directiva *f*

directly [dɪˈrektlɪ, daɪˈrektlɪ] **1** *adv* (**a**) *(above etc)* exactamente, justo (**b**) *(speak)* francamente (**c**) *(descend)* directamente (**d**) *(come)* en seguida
2 *conj Fam* en cuanto

director [dɪˈrektə(r), daɪˈrektə(r)] *n* director(a) *m,f*

directory [dɪˈrektərɪ, daɪˈrektərɪ] *n Tel* guía telefónica; **d. enquiries** (servicio *m* de) información *f*

dirt [dɜːt] *n* suciedad *f*

dirt-cheap [dɜːtˈtʃiːp] *adv & adj Fam* tirado(a)

dirty [ˈdɜːtɪ] **1** *adj* (dirtier, dirtiest) (**a**) sucio(a) (**b**) **to give sb a d. look** fulminar a algn con la mirada (**c**) *(joke)* verde; *(mind)* pervertido(a) (**c**) **d. word** palabrota *f*; **d. old man** viejo *m* verde
2 *vt* ensuciar

disability [dɪsəˈbɪlɪtɪ] *n* incapacidad *f*, discapacidad *f*; **d. pension** pensión *f* por invalidez

disabled [dɪˈseɪbəld] **1** *adj* minusválido(a)
2 *npl* **the d.** los minusválidos

disadvantage [dɪsədˈvɑːntɪdʒ] *n* desventaja *f*; *(obstacle)* inconveniente *m*

disaffection [dɪsəˈfekʃən] *n* descontento *m*

disagree [dɪsəˈgriː] *vi* (**a**) *(differ)* no estar de acuerdo (**with** con); **to d. on** *or* **over sth** reñir por algo (**b**) *(not match)* discrepar (**with** de *or* con) (**c**) **garlic disagrees with me** el ajo no me sienta bien

disagreeable [dɪsəˈgriːəbəl] *adj* desagradable

disagreement [dɪsəˈgriːmənt] *n* (**a**) desacuerdo *m*; *(argument)* riña *f* (**b**) *(non-correspondence)* discrepancia *f*

disallow [dɪsəˈlaʊ] *vt (goal)* anular; *(objection)* rechazar

disappear [dɪsəˈpɪə(r)] *vi* desaparecer

disappearance [dɪsəˈpɪərəns] *n* desaparición *f*

disappoint [dɪsəˈpɔɪnt] *vt (person)* decepcionar, defraudar; *(hope, ambition)* frustrar

disappointed [dɪsəˈpɔɪntɪd] *adj* decepcionado(a)

disappointing [dɪsəˈpɔɪntɪŋ] *adj* decepcionante

disappointment [dɪsəˈpɔɪntmənt] *n* decepción *f*

disapproval [dɪsəˈpruːvəl] *n* desaprobación *f*

disapprove [dɪsəˈpruːv] *vi* **to d. of** desaprobar

disarm [dɪsˈɑːm] **1** *vt* desarmar
2 *vi* desarmarse

disarmament [dɪsˈɑːməmənt] *n* desarme *m*

disarray [dɪsəˈreɪ] *n Fml* **in d.** *(room, papers)* en desorden; *(hair)* desarreglado(a); *(thoughts)* confuso(a)

disaster [dɪˈzɑːstə(r)] *n* desastre *m*

disastrous [dɪˈzɑːstrəs] *adj* desastroso(a)

disband [dɪsˈbænd] **1** *vt* disolver
2 *vi* disolverse

disbelief [dɪsbɪˈliːf] *n* incredulidad *f*

disc [dɪsk] *n* disco *m*; *Comput* disquete *m*; **d. jockey** disc-jockey *mf*, pinchadiscos *mf inv*

discard [dɪsˈkɑːd] *vt (old things)* deshacerse de; *(plan)* descartar

discern [dɪˈsɜːn] *vt (shape, difference)* percibir; *(truth)* darse cuenta de

discerning [dɪˈsɜːnɪŋ] *adj (person)* perspicaz; *(taste)* refinado(a)

discharge *Fml* **1** *vt* [dɪsˈtʃɑːdʒ] (**a**) *(smoke)* emitir; *(liquid)* echar; *(cargo)* descargar (**b**) *(prisoner)* soltar; *(patient)* dar de alta a; *(soldier)* licenciar; *(employee)* despedir (**c**) *(debt)* saldar (**d**) *(fulfil)* cumplir
2 *n* [ˈdɪstʃɑːdʒ] (**a**) *(of current, load)* descarga *f*; *(of gases)* escape *m* (**b**) *(of prisoner)* liberación *f*; *(of patient)* alta *f*; *(of soldier)* licencia *f* (**c**) *(of debt)* descargo *m* (**d**) *(of duty)* cumplimiento *m*

disciple [dɪˈsaɪpəl] *n* discípulo(a) *m,f*

discipline [ˈdɪsɪplɪn] **1** *n* disciplina *f*
2 *vt (child)* castigar; *(worker)* sancionar; *(official)* expedientar

disclaim [dɪsˈkleɪm] *vt Fml* negar tener

disclose [dɪsˈkləʊz] *vt* revelar

disclosure [dɪsˈkləʊʒə(r)] *n* revelación *f*

disco [ˈdɪskəʊ] *n Fam (abbr* **discotheque**) disco *f*

discolour, *US* **discolor** [dɪsˈkʌlə(r)] *vt* descolorir

discomfort [dɪsˈkʌmfət] *n* (**a**) *(lack of comfort)* incomodidad *f* (**b**) *(pain)* malestar *m* (**c**) *(unease)* inquietud *f*

disconcert [dɪskənˈsɜːt] *vt* desconcertar

disconcerting [dɪskənˈsɜːtɪŋ] *adj* desconcertante

disconnect [dɪskə'nekt] *vt* desconectar (**from** de); *(gas, electricity)* cortar

disconnected [dɪskə'nektɪd] *adj* inconexo(a)

disconsolate [dɪs'kɒnsəlɪt] *adj* desconsolado(a)

discontent [dɪskən'tent] *n* descontento *m*

discontented [dɪskən'tentɪd] *adj* descontento(a)

discontinue [dɪskən'tɪnjuː] *vt Fml* abandonar; *(work)* interrumpir

discord ['dɪskɔːd] *n* (a) *Fml* discordia *f* (b) *Mus* disonancia *f*

discordant [dɪs'kɔːdənt] *adj* discordante

discotheque ['dɪskətek] *n* discoteca *f*

discount 1 *n* ['dɪskaʊnt] descuento *m*
   2 *vt* [dɪs'kaʊnt] (a) *(price)* rebajar (b) *(view, suggestion)* descartar

discourage [dɪs'kʌrɪdʒ] *vt (dishearten)* desanimar; *(advances)* rechazar

discouraging [dɪs'kʌrɪdʒɪŋ] *adj* desalentador(a)

discover [dɪ'skʌvə(r)] *vt* descubrir; *(missing person, object)* encontrar

discovery [dɪ'skʌvərɪ] *n* descubrimiento *m*

discredit [dɪs'kredɪt] 1 *n* descrédito *m*
   2 *vt (person, régime)* desacreditar; *(theory)* poner en duda

discreet [dɪ'skriːt] *adj* discreto(a); *(distance, silence)* prudente; *(hat, house)* modesto(a)

discrepancy [dɪ'skrepənsɪ] *n* diferencia *f*

discretion [dɪ'skreʃən] *n* discreción *f*; *(prudence)* prudencia *f*; **at the d. of** ... a juicio de ...

discriminate [dɪ'skrɪmɪneɪt] *vi* discriminar (**between** entre); **to d. against** sth/sb discriminar algo/a algn

discriminating [dɪ'skrɪmɪneɪtɪŋ] *adj (person)* entendido(a); *(taste)* refinado(a)

discrimination [dɪskrɪmɪ'neɪʃən] *n* (a) *(bias)* discriminación *f* (b) *(distinction)* diferenciación *f*

discuss [dɪ'skʌs] *vt* discutir; *(in writing)* tratar de

discussion [dɪ'skʌʃən] *n* discusión *f*

disdain [dɪs'deɪn] *Fml* 1 *n* desdén *m*
   2 *vt* desdeñar

disdainful [dɪs'deɪnfʊl] *adj Fml* desdeñoso(a)

disease [dɪ'ziːz] *n* enfermedad *f*; *Fig* mal *m*

disembark [dɪsɪm'bɑːk] *vt & vi* desembarcar

disenchanted [dɪsɪn'tʃɑːntɪd] *adj* desencantado(a), desilusionado(a)

disengage [dɪsɪn'geɪdʒ] *vt* soltar; *Aut* **to d. the clutch** soltar el embrague, desembragar

disentangle [dɪsɪn'tæŋgəl] *vt* desenredar

disfigure [dɪs'fɪgə(r)] *vt* desfigurar

disgrace [dɪs'greɪs] 1 *n* (a) *(disfavour)* desgracia *f*; **to be in d.** estar desacreditado(a); **to fall into d.** caer en desgracia (b) *(shame)* vergüenza *f*, escándalo *m*
   2 *vt* deshonrar, desacreditar

disgraceful [dɪs'greɪsfʊl] *adj* vergonzoso(a)

disgruntled [dɪs'grʌntəld] *adj* contrariado(a), disgustado(a)

disguise [dɪs'gaɪz] 1 *n* disfraz *m*; **in d.** disfrazado(a)
   2 *vt* (a) *(person)* disfrazar (**as** de) (b) *(feelings)* disimular

disgust [dɪs'gʌst] 1 *n* (a) *(loathing)* repugnancia *f*, asco *m* (b) *(strong disapproval)* indignación *f*
   2 *vt (revolt)* repugnar, dar asco a (b) *(offend)* indignar

> 🖉 Note that the Spanish words **disgusto** and **disgustar** are false friends and are never a translation for the English word **disgust**. In Spanish, **disgusto** means "annoyance, trouble", and **disgustar** means "to upset".

disgusting [dɪs'gʌstɪŋ] *adj* asqueroso(a), repugnante; *(behaviour, state of affairs)* intolerable

dish [dɪʃ] *n (for serving)* fuente *f*; *(course)* plato *m*; **to wash** *or* **do the dishes** fregar los platos
   ▸ **dish out** *vt sep Fam (food)* servir; *(books, advice)* repartir; **to d. it out (to sb)** *(criticize)* criticar (a algn)
   ▸ **dish up** *vt sep (meal)* servir

dishcloth ['dɪʃklɒθ] *n* trapo *m* de fregar

dishearten [dɪs'hɑːtən] *vt* desanimar

dishevelled, *US* **disheveled** [dɪ'ʃevəld] *adj (hair)* despeinado(a); *(appearance)* desaliñado(a)

dishonest [dɪs'ɒnɪst] *adj (person)* poco honrado(a); *(means)* fraudulento(a)

dishonesty [dɪs'ɒnɪstɪ] *n (of person)* falta *f* de honradez

dishonour, *US* **dishonor** [dɪs'ɒnə(r)] 1 *n Fml* deshonra *f*
   2 *vt (name)* deshonrar

dishonourable, *US* **dishonorable** [dɪs'ɒnərəbəl] *adj* deshonroso(a)

dishtowel ['dɪʃtaʊəl] *n US* trapo *m* de cocina

dishwasher ['dɪʃwɒʃə(r)] *n* lavaplatos *m*

inv; *(person)* lavaplatos *mf inv*
disillusion [dɪsɪ'luːʒən] *vt* desilusionar
disincentive [dɪsɪn'sentɪv] *n* freno *m*
disinfect [dɪsɪn'fekt] *vt* desinfectar
disinfectant [dɪsɪn'fektənt] *n* desinfectante *m*
disinherit [dɪsɪn'herɪt] *vt* desheredar
disintegrate [dɪs'ɪntɪgreɪt] *vi* desintegrarse
disintegration [dɪsɪntɪ'greɪʃən] *n* desintegración *f*
disinterested [dɪs'ɪntrɪstɪd] *adj* desinteresado(a)
disjointed [dɪs'dʒɔɪntɪd] *adj* inconexo(a)
disk [dɪsk] *n US* disco *m*; *Comput* disquete *m*; **on d.** en disco; **d. drive** disquetera *f*, disketera *f*
diskette [dɪs'ket] *n Comput* disquete *m*
dislike [dɪs'laɪk] **1** *n* antipatía *f*, aversión *f* (**of** a *or* hacia)
2 *vt* tener antipatía *or* aversión a *or* hacia
dislocate ['dɪsləkeɪt] *vt* (*joint*) dislocar
dislodge [dɪs'lɒdʒ] *vt* sacar
disloyal [dɪs'lɔɪəl] *adj* desleal
dismal ['dɪzməl] *adj* (**a**) *(prospect)* sombrío(a); *(place, weather)* deprimente; *(person)* triste (**b**) *(failure)* lamentable
dismantle [dɪs'mæntəl] *vt* desmontar
dismay [dɪs'meɪ] **1** *n* consternación *f*
2 *vt* consternar
dismiss [dɪs'mɪs] *vt* (**a**) *(idea)* descartar (**b**) *(employee)* despedir; *(official)* destituir (**c**) **to d. sb** *(from room, presence)* dar permiso a algn para retirarse (**d**) *(reject)* rechazar; *Jur* desestimar; *(case)* sobreseer
dismissal [dɪs'mɪsəl] *n* (**a**) *(of employee)* despido *m*; *(of official)* destitución *f* (**b**) *(of claim)* rechazo *m*; *Jur* desestimación *f*
dismount [dɪs'maʊnt] *vi Fml* apearse (**from** de)
disobedience [dɪsə'biːdɪəns] *n* desobediencia *f*
disobedient [dɪsə'biːdɪənt] *adj* desobediente
disobey [dɪsə'beɪ] *vt & vi* desobedecer; *(law)* violar
disorder [dɪs'ɔːdə(r)] *n* (**a**) *(untidiness)* desorden *m* (**b**) *(riot)* disturbio *m* (**c**) *(of organ, mind)* trastorno *m*; *(of speech)* defecto *m*
disorderly [dɪs'ɔːdəlɪ] *adj* (**a**) *(untidy)* desordenado(a) (**b**) *(meeting)* alborotado(a); *(conduct)* escandaloso(a)
disorganized [dɪs'ɔːgənaɪzd] *adj* desorganizado(a)

disorient [dɪs'ɔːrɪənt], **disorientate** [dɪs'ɔːrɪenteɪt] *vt* desorientar
disown [dɪs'əʊn] *vt* desconocer
disparaging [dɪ'spærɪdʒɪŋ] *adj* despectivo(a)
disparity [dɪ'spærɪtɪ] *n Fml* disparidad *f*
dispassionate [dɪs'pæʃənɪt] *adj* desapasionado(a)
dispatch [dɪ'spætʃ] **1** *n* (**a**) *(official message)* despacho *m*; *(journalist's report)* reportaje *m*; *(military message)* parte *m* (**b**) *(of mail)* envío *m*; *(of goods)* consignación *f*
2 *vt* (**a**) *(mail)* enviar; *(goods)* expedir (**b**) *Fam (food)* zamparse; *(job)* despachar
dispel [dɪ'spel] *vt* disipar
dispensary [dɪ'spensərɪ] *n* dispensario *m*
dispense [dɪ'spens] *vt (supplies)* repartir; *(justice)* administrar
▸**dispense with** *vt insep (do without)* prescindir de
dispenser [dɪ'spensə(r)] *n* máquina expendedora; **cash d.** cajero automático; **soap d.** dosificador *m* de jabón
dispensing chemist [dɪspensɪŋ'kemɪst] *n Br* farmacéutico(a) *m,f*
dispersal [dɪ'spɜːsəl] *n* dispersión *f*
disperse [dɪ'spɜːs] *vt* dispersar
2 *vi* dispersarse; *(fog)* disiparse
dispirited [dɪ'spɪrɪtɪd] *adj* abatido(a)
displace [dɪs'pleɪs] *vt* (**a**) desplazar; **displaced person** desterrado(a) *m,f* (**b**) *(supplant)* sustituir
display [dɪ'spleɪ] **1** *n* *(exhibition)* exposición *f*; *Comput* visualización *f*; *(of feelings, skills)* demostración *f*; *(of force)* despliegue *m*; **d. window** escaparate *m*; **military d.** desfile *m* militar
2 *vt* (**a**) mostrar; *(goods)* exponer; *Comput* visualizar (**b**) *(feelings)* manifestar
displease [dɪs'pliːz] *vt* disgustar; *(offend)* ofender
displeasure [dɪs'pleʒə(r)] *n* disgusto *m*
disposable [dɪ'spəʊzəbəl] *adj* (**a**) *(throwaway)* desechable (**b**) *(available)* disponible
disposal [dɪ'spəʊzəl] *n* (**a**) *(removal)* eliminación *f* (**b**) *(availability)* disponibilidad *f*; **at my d.** a mi disposición (**c**) *Fml (arrangement)* disposición *f* (**d**) *(sale)* venta *f*; *(of property)* traspaso *m*
dispose [dɪ'spəʊz] **1** *vi* **to d. of** *(remove)* eliminar; *(rubbish)* tirar; *(unwanted object)* deshacerse de; *(matter)* resolver; *(sell)* vender; *(property)* traspasar
2 *vt Fml (arrange)* disponer

disposed [dɪˈspəʊzd] *adj (inclined)* dispuesto(a)

disposition [dɪspəˈzɪʃən] *n* (**a**) *(temperament)* genio *m* (**b**) *Fml (arrangement)* disposición *f*

disproportionate [dɪsprəˈpɔːʃənɪt] *adj* desproporcionado(a) (**to** a)

disprove [dɪsˈpruːv] *vt* refutar

dispute 1 *n* [ˈdɪspjuːt] *(disagreement)* discusión *f; (quarrel)* disputa *f*; **industrial d.** conflicto *m* laboral

2 *vt* [dɪˈspjuːt] *(claim)* refutar; *(territory)* disputar; *(matter)* discutir

3 *vi* discutir (**about** *or* **over** de *o* sobre)

disqualify [dɪsˈkwɒlɪfaɪ] *vt* (**a**) *Sport* descalificar (**b**) *(make ineligible)* incapacitar

disquiet [dɪsˈkwaɪət] *n* preocupación *f*, inquietud *f*

disregard [dɪsrɪˈgɑːd] 1 *n* indiferencia *f; (for safety)* despreocupación *f*

2 *vt* descuidar; *(ignore)* ignorar

disrepair [dɪsrɪˈpeə(r)] *n* mal estado *m*; **in (a state of) d.** en mal estado; **to fall into d.** deteriorarse

disreputable [dɪsˈrepjʊtəbəl] *adj (person, area)* de mala fama; *(behaviour)* vergonzoso(a)

disrepute [dɪsrɪˈpjuːt] *n* mala fama, oprobio *m*

disrespectful [dɪsrɪˈspektfʊl] *adj* irrespetuoso(a)

disrupt [dɪsˈrʌpt] *vt (meeting, traffic)* interrumpir; *(schedule etc)* desbaratar

disruption [dɪsˈrʌpʃən] *n (of meeting, traffic)* interrupción *f; (of schedule etc)* desbaratamiento *m*

dissatisfaction [dɪssætɪsˈfækʃən] *n* descontento *m*, insatisfacción *f*

dissatisfied [dɪsˈsætɪsfaɪd] *adj* descontento(a)

dissect [dɪˈsekt, daɪˈsekt] *vt* disecar

disseminate [dɪˈsemɪneɪt] *vt Fml* diseminar, difundir

dissent [dɪˈsent] 1 *n* disentimiento *m*

2 *vi* disentir

dissertation [dɪsəˈteɪʃən] *n* disertación *f; Univ* tesina *f* (**on** sobre)

disservice [dɪsˈsɜːvɪs] *n* perjuicio *m*; **to do sth/sb a d.** perjudicar algo/a algn

dissident [ˈdɪsɪdənt] *adj & n* disidente (*mf*)

dissimilar [dɪˈsɪmɪlə(r)] *adj* distinto(a)

dissipate [ˈdɪsɪpeɪt] 1 *vt* (**a**) disipar (**b**) *(waste)* derrochar

2 *vi* disiparse

dissociate [dɪˈsəʊʃɪeɪt] *vt* **to d. oneself** distanciarse

dissolute [ˈdɪsəluːt] *adj* disoluto(a)

dissolution [dɪsəˈluːʃən] *n* disolución *f; (of agreement)* rescisión *f*

dissolve [dɪˈzɒlv] 1 *vt* disolver

2 *vi* disolverse

dissuade [dɪˈsweɪd] *vt* disuadir (**from** de)

distance [ˈdɪstəns] 1 *n* distancia *f*; **in the d.** a lo lejos; *Fam* **to stay the d.** completar la prueba

2 *vt* **to d. oneself (from)** distanciarse (de)

distant [ˈdɪstənt] *adj* (**a**) *(place, time)* lejano(a); *(look)* distraído(a) (**b**) *(aloof)* distante, frío(a)

distaste [dɪsˈteɪst] *n* aversión *f*

distasteful [dɪsˈteɪstfʊl] *adj* desagradable

distend [dɪˈstend] *Fml* 1 *vt* dilatar

2 *vi* dilatarse

distil, *US* **distill** [dɪˈstɪl] *vt* destilar

distillery [dɪˈstɪlərɪ] *n* destilería *f*

distinct [dɪˈstɪŋkt] *adj* (**a**) *(different)* diferente; **as d. from** a diferencia de (**b**) *(smell, change)* marcado(a); *(idea, intention)* claro(a)

distinction [dɪˈstɪŋkʃən] *n* (**a**) *(difference)* diferencia *f* (**b**) *(excellence)* distinción *f* (**c**) *Educ* sobresaliente *m*

distinctive [dɪˈstɪŋktɪv] *adj* distintivo(a)

distinguish [dɪˈstɪŋgwɪʃ] *vt* distinguir

distinguished [dɪˈstɪŋgwɪʃt] *adj* distinguido(a)

distinguishing [dɪˈstɪŋgwɪʃɪŋ] *adj* distintivo(a), característico(a)

distort [dɪˈstɔːt] *vt (misrepresent)* deformar; *(words)* tergiversar

distortion [dɪˈstɔːʃən] *n* deformación *f; (of sound, image)* distorsión *f*

distract [dɪˈstrækt] *vt* distraer

distracted [dɪˈstræktɪd] *adj* distraído(a)

distraction [dɪˈstrækʃən] *n (interruption)* distracción *f; (confusion)* confusión *f*; **to drive sb to d.** sacar a algn de quicio

distraught [dɪˈstrɔːt] *adj (anguished)* afligido(a)

distress [dɪˈstres] 1 *n (mental)* angustia *f; (physical)* dolor *m*; **d. signal** señal *f* de socorro

2 *vt (upset)* apenar

distressing [dɪˈstresɪŋ] *adj* penoso(a)

distribute [dɪˈstrɪbjuːt] *vt* distribuir, repartir

distribution [dɪstrɪˈbjuːʃən] *n* distribución *f*

distributor [dɪˈstrɪbjʊtə(r)] *n* (**a**) *Com* distribuidor(a) *m,f* (**b**) *Aut* delco *m*

district [ˈdɪstrɪkt] *n (of country)* región *f*;

(of town) barrio *m*; *US* **d. attorney** fiscal *m*; **d. council** corporación *f* local; **d. nurse** practicante *mf*

distrust [dɪs'trʌst] **1** *n* recelo *m*
2 *vt* desconfiar de

disturb [dɪ'stɜːb] *vt* **(a)** *(inconvenience)* molestar **(b)** *(silence)* romper; *(sleep)* interrumpir **(c)** *(worry)* perturbar **(d)** *(papers)* desordenar

disturbance [dɪ'stɜːbəns] *n* **(a)** *(of routine)* alteración *f* **(b)** *(commotion)* disturbio *m*, alboroto *m*

disturbed [dɪ'stɜːbd] *adj (mentally)* inestable

disturbing [dɪ'stɜːbɪŋ] *adj* inquietante

disuse [dɪs'juːs] *n* desuso *m*

disused [dɪs'juːzd] *adj* abandonado(a)

ditch [dɪtʃ] **1** *n* zanja *f*; *(at roadside)* cuneta *f*; *(for irrigation)* acequia *f*
2 *vt Fam (plan, friend)* abandonar

dither ['dɪðə(r)] *vi Br Fam* vacilar, titubear

ditto ['dɪtəʊ] *adv* ídem, lo mismo

dive [daɪv] **1** *n* **(a)** *(into water)* salto *m* de cabeza; *(of submarine)* inmersión *f*; *(of plane)* picado *m*; *Sport* salto **(b)** *Fam (bar)* antro *m*
2 *vi* **(a)** *(from poolside, diving board)* tirarse de cabeza; *(submarine)* sumergirse; *(plane)* bajar en picado; *Sport* saltar **(b)** *(move quickly)* **he dived for the phone** se precipitó hacia el teléfono

diver ['daɪvə(r)] *n (person)* buceador(a) *m,f*; *(professional)* buzo *m*; *Sport* saltador(a) *m,f*

diverge [daɪ'vɜːdʒ] *vi* divergir

diverse [daɪ'vɜːs] *adj (varied)* diverso(a), variado(a); *(different)* distinto(a), diferente

diversion [daɪ'vɜːʃən] *n* **(a)** *(distraction)* distracción *f* **(b)** *Br (detour)* desvío *m*

divert [daɪ'vɜːt] *vt* desviar

divide [dɪ'vaɪd] **1** *vt* dividir
2 *vi (road, stream)* bifurcarse
3 *n* división *f*, diferencia *f*

dividend ['dɪvɪdend] *n Com* dividendo *m*; *Fig* beneficio *m*

divine [dɪ'vaɪn] *adj* divino(a)

diving board ['daɪvɪŋbɔːd] *n* trampolín *m*

divinity [dɪ'vɪnɪtɪ] *n* **(a)** divinidad *f* **(b)** *(subject)* teología *f*

division [dɪ'vɪʒən] *n* **(a)** división *f* **(b)** *(sharing)* reparto *m* **(c)** *(of organization)* sección *f*

divorce [dɪ'vɔːs] **1** *n* divorcio *m*
2 *vt* **she divorced him** se divorció de él
3 *vi* divorciarse

divorcé [dɪ'vɔːseɪ], **divorcée** [dɪvɔː'siː] *n* divorciado(a) *m,f*

divulge [daɪ'vʌldʒ] *vt Fml* divulgar, revelar

DIY [diːaɪ'waɪ] *n Br (abbr* **do-it-yourself)** bricolaje *m*

dizziness ['dɪzɪnɪs] *n* vértigo *m*

dizzy ['dɪzɪ] *adj* **(dizzier, dizziest)** **(a)** *(person) (unwell)* mareado(a) **(b)** *(height, pace)* vertiginoso(a)

DJ ['diːdʒeɪ] *n Fam (abbr* **disc jockey)** pinchadiscos *mf inv*, disc-jockey *mf*

DNA [diːen'eɪ] *n (abbr* **deoxyribonucleic acid)** ADN *m*

do [duː, *unstressed* dʊ, də] **1** *v aux*

En el inglés hablado, y en el escrito en estilo coloquial, las formas negativas **do not**, **does not** y **did not** se transforman en **don't**, **doesn't** y **didn't**.

(3rd person sing pres **does**; *pt* **did**; *pp* **done)** **(a)** *(in negatives and questions) (not translated in Spanish)* **do you want some coffee?** ¿quieres café?; **do you drive?** ¿tienes carnet de conducir?; **don't you want to come?** ¿no quieres venir?; **he doesn't smoke** no fuma

(b) *(emphatic) (not translated in Spanish)* **do come with us!** ¡ánimo, vente con nosotros!; **I do like your bag** me encanta tu bolso

(c) *(substituting main verb in sentence) (not translated in Spanish)* **I don't believe him – neither do I** no le creo – yo tampoco; **I'll go if you do** si vas tú, voy yo; **I think it's dear, but he doesn't** a mí me parece caro pero a él no; **who went? – I did** ¿quién asistió? – yo

(d) *(in question tags)* **he refused, didn't he?** dijo que no, ¿verdad?; **I don't like it, do you?** a mí no me gusta, ¿y a ti?

2 *vt* **(a)** hacer; *(task)* realizar; *(duty)* cumplir con; **to do one's best** hacer todo lo posible; **to do sth again** volver a hacer algo; **to do sth for sb** hacer algo por algn; **to do the cooking/cleaning** cocinar/limpiar; **to do the dishes** lavar los platos; **what can I do for you?** ¿en qué puedo servirle?; **what do you do (for a living)?** ¿a qué te dedicas?; **what's to be done?** ¿qué se puede hacer?; *Fam* **he's done it!** ¡lo ha conseguido!

(b) **do you do sportswear?** *(make, offer)* ¿(aquí) tienen ropa de deporte?

(c) *(distance) (speed)* **we were doing 80** íbamos a 80; **this car can do 120** este coche puede alcanzar los 120

Do, unido a muchos nombres, expresa actividades, como **to do the gardening, to do the ironing**, etc. En este diccionario, estas estructuras se encuentran bajo los nombres respectivos.

3 *vi* (a) *(act)* hacer; **do as I tell you** haz lo que te digo; **you did right** hiciste bien (b) **he did badly in the exams** los exámenes le salieron mal; **how are you doing?** ¿qué tal?; **how do you do?** *(greeting)* ¿cómo está usted?; *(answer)* mucho gusto; **to do well** *(person)* tener éxito; *(business)* ir bien (c) **£5 will do** *(suffice)* con 5 libras será suficiente; *Fam* **that will do!** ¡basta ya! (d) **this cushion will do as a pillow** *(be suitable)* este cojín servirá de almohada; **this won't do** esto no puede ser

4 *n Fam* (a) *Br (party)* fiesta *f*; *(event)* ceremonia *f* (b) **do's and don'ts** reglas *fpl* de conducta

▸**do away with** *vt insep* (a) *(abolish)* abolir; *(discard)* deshacerse de (b) *(kill)* asesinar

▸**do down** *vt sep Fam (humiliate)* hacer quedar mal

▸**do for** *vt insep Fam (destroy, ruin)* arruinar; *Fig* **I'm done for if I don't finish this** estoy perdido(a) si no acabo esto

▸**do in** *vt sep Fam* (a) *(kill)* cargarse (b) **I'm done in** *(exhausted)* estoy hecho(a) polvo

▸**do over** *vt sep Fam* (a) *US (repeat)* repetir (b) *Br (thrash)* dar una paliza a

▸**do up** *vt sep* (a) *(wrap)* envolver (b) *(belt etc)* abrochar; *(laces)* atar (c) *(dress up)* arreglar (d) *Fam (redecorate)* renovar

▸**do with** *vt insep* (a) **I could do with a rest** *(need)* un descanso no me vendría nada mal (b) **to have** *or* **be to do with** *(concern)* tener que ver con

▸**do without** *vt insep* pasar sin, prescindir de

docile ['dəʊsaɪl] *adj* dócil; *(animal)* manso(a)

dock¹ [dɒk] **1** *n Naut* **the docks** el muelle **2** *vi* (a) *(ship)* atracar (b) *(spacecraft)* acoplarse

dock² [dɒk] *vt (reduce)* descontar

dock³ [dɒk] *n Jur* banquillo *m* (de los acusados)

docker ['dɒkə(r)] *n* estibador *m*

dockland ['dɒklænd] *n* zona *f* del puerto

dockyard ['dɒkjɑːd] *n* astillero *m*

doctor ['dɒktə(r)] **1** *n* (a) *Med* médico(a) *m,f* (b) *Univ* doctor(a) *m,f*; **D. of Law** doctor en derecho

2 *vt Pej (figures)* falsificar; *(text)* arreglar; *(drink etc)* adulterar

doctorate ['dɒktərɪt] *n* doctorado *m*

doctrine ['dɒktrɪn] *n* doctrina *f*

document ['dɒkjʊmənt] **1** *n* documento *m*; **documents** documentación *f*
2 *vt* documentar

documentary [dɒkjʊ'mentərɪ] *adj & n* documental *(m)*

dodge [dɒdʒ] **1** *vt* (a) *(blow)* esquivar; *(pursuer)* despistar; *Fig* eludir (b) *Fam* **to d. one's taxes** engañar a Hacienda
2 *vi (move aside)* echarse a un lado
3 *n* (a) *(movement)* regate *m* (b) *Fam (trick)* truco *m*

Dodgem® ['dɒdʒəm] *n Br* **D. (car)** coche *m* de choque

dodgy ['dɒdʒɪ] *adj* **(dodgier, dodgiest)** *Br Fam (risky)* arriesgado(a); *(tricky)* difícil; *(dishonest, not working properly)* chungo(a)

doe [dəʊ] *n (of deer)* gama *f*; *(of rabbit)* coneja *f*

does [dʌz] *3rd person sing pres of* **do**

doesn't ['dʌzənt] = **does not**

dog [dɒg] **1** *n* (a) *(animal)* perro(a) *m,f*; *Fam Fig* **a d.'s life** una vida de perros; **d. collar** *(of dog)* collar *m* de perro; *Fam Rel* alzacuello *m* (b) *(male canine)* macho *m*; *(fox)* zorro *m*; *(wolf)* lobo *m* (c) *Fam* **dirty d.** canalla *m* (d) *US Fam (disappointment)* desastre *m*
2 *vt* acosar; **to d. sb's footsteps** seguir los pasos de algn; *Fig* **dogged by bad luck** perseguido(a) por la mala suerte

dog-eared ['dɒgɪəd] *adj (book)* con los bordes de las páginas doblados; *(shabby)* sobado(a)

dogged ['dɒgɪd] *adj* obstinado(a), tenaz

doghouse ['dɒghaʊs] *n US Fam* perrera *f*; *Fig* **to be in the d.** estar castigado(a)

dogma ['dɒgmə] *n* dogma *m*

dogmatic [dɒg'mætɪk] *adj* dogmático(a)

dogsbody ['dɒgzbɒdɪ] *n Br Fam (drudge)* burro *m* de carga

doh [dəʊ] *n Mus* do *m*

doing ['duːɪŋ] *n* (a) *(action)* obra *f*; **it was none of my d.** yo no tuve nada que ver; *Fig* **it took some d.** costó trabajo hacerlo (b) **doings** *(activities)* actividades *fpl*

do-it-yourself [duːɪtjə'self] *n* bricolaje *m*

doldrums ['dɒldrəmz] *npl Fam Fig* **to be in the d.** *(person)* estar abatido(a); *(trade)* estar estancado(a)

dole [dəʊl] *Fam* **1** *n Br* **the d.** el paro; **to be on the d.** cobrar el paro; **to go on the d.**

apuntarse al paro; *Fig* **d. queue** los parados

  2 *vt* **to d. (out)** repartir

doleful ['dəʊlfʊl] *adj* triste, afligido(a)

doll [dɒl] **1** *n* (**a**) *(toy)* muñeca *f* (**b**) *US Fam (girl)* muñeca *f*

  2 *vt Fam* **to d. oneself up** ponerse guapa

dollar ['dɒlə(r)] *n* dólar *m*

dolphin ['dɒlfɪn] *n* delfín *m*

domain [də'meɪn] *n* (**a**) *(sphere)* campo *m*, esfera *f*; **that's not my d.** no es de mi competencia (**b**) *(territory)* dominio *m* (**c**) *Comput* dominio *m*; **d. name** nombre *m* de dominio

dome [dəʊm] *n (roof)* cúpula *f*; *(ceiling)* bóveda *f*

domestic [də'mestɪk] *adj* (**a**) *(appliance, pet)* doméstico(a); **d. science** economía doméstica (**b**) *(home-loving)* casero(a) (**c**) *(flight, news)* nacional; *(trade, policy)* interior

domesticate [də'mestɪkeɪt] *vt (make home-loving)* volver hogareño(a) *or* casero(a)

domicile ['dɒmɪsaɪl] *n* domicilio *m*

dominant ['dɒmɪnənt] *adj* dominante

dominate ['dɒmɪneɪt] *vt & vi* dominar

domineering [dɒmɪ'nɪərɪŋ] *adj* dominante

Dominican [də'mɪnɪkən] *adj & n (of Dominica)* dominicano(a) *(m,f)*; **D. Republic** República Dominicana

dominion [də'mɪnjən] *n* dominio *m*

domino ['dɒmɪnəʊ] *n (pl* **dominoes***) (piece)* ficha *f* de dominó; **dominoes** *(game)* dominó *m*

don [dɒn] *n Br Univ* catedrático(a) *m,f*

donate [dəʊ'neɪt] *vt* donar

donation [dəʊ'neɪʃən] *n* donativo *m*

done [dʌn] **1** *adj* (**a**) *(finished)* terminado(a); **it's over and d. with** se acabó (**b**) *Fam (tired)* rendido(a) (**c**) *(meat)* hecho(a); *(vegetables)* cocido(a)

  2 *pp* of **do**

donkey ['dɒŋkɪ] *n* burro(a) *m,f*

donor ['dəʊnə(r)] *n* donante *m*

don't [dəʊnt] = **do not**

donut ['dəʊnʌt] *n US* dónut® *m*

doodle ['duːdəl] *vi Fam (write)* garabatear; *(draw)* hacer dibujos

doom [duːm] **1** *n (fate)* destino *m (funesto)*; *(ruin)* perdición *f*; *(death)* muerte *f*

  2 *vt usu pass (destine)* destinar; **doomed to failure** condenado(a) al fracaso

doomsday ['duːmzdeɪ] *n* día *m* del juicio final

door [dɔː(r)] *n* puerta *f*; **front/back d.** puerta principal/trasera; *Fig* **behind**

---

closed doors a puerta cerrada; **d. handle** manilla *f* (de la puerta); **d. knocker** picaporte *m*; **next d. (to)** (en) la casa de al lado (de)

doorbell ['dɔːbel] *n* timbre *m* (de la puerta)

doorknob ['dɔːnɒb] *n* pomo *m*

doorman ['dɔːmən] *n* portero *m*

doormat ['dɔːmæt] *n* felpudo *m*, esterilla *f*; *Fam Fig (person)* trapo *m*

doorstep ['dɔːstep] *n* peldaño *m*; *Fig* **on one's d.** a la vuelta de la esquina

door-to-door ['dɔːtə'dɔː(r)] *adj* a domicilio

doorway ['dɔːweɪ] *n* portal *m*, entrada *f*

dope [dəʊp] **1** *n* (**a**) *Fam (drug)* chocolate *m* (**b**) *Fam (person)* imbécil *mf*

  2 *vt (food, drink)* adulterar con drogas; *Sport* dopar

dop(e)y ['dəʊpɪ] *adj* (**dopier, dopiest**) *Fam* (**a**) *(sleepy)* medio dormido(a); *(fuddled)* atontado(a) (**b**) *Fam (silly)* torpe

dork [dɔːk] *n US Fam* petardo(a) *m,f*

dormant ['dɔːmənt] *adj* inactivo(a); *Fig (rivalry)* latente

dormitory ['dɔːmɪtərɪ] *n* (**a**) *(in school)* dormitorio *m* (**b**) *US (in university)* colegio *m* mayor

dosage ['dəʊsɪdʒ] *n Fml (amount)* dosis *f inv*

dose [dəʊs] **1** *n* dosis *f inv*

  2 *vt (patient)* medicar

doss [dɒs] *vi Br Fam* sobar

dosshouse ['dɒshaʊs] *n Br Fam* pensión *f* de mala muerte

dossier ['dɒsɪeɪ] *n* expediente *m*

dot [dɒt] **1** *n* punto *m*; **on the d.** en punto; *Comput* **d. matrix printer** impresora *f* matricial *or* de agujas

  2 *vt* (**a**) *Fam* **to d. one's i's and cross one's t's** poner los puntos sobre las íes (**b**) *(scatter)* esparcir, salpicar

dote [dəʊt] *vi* **to d. on sb** chochear con algn

double ['dʌbəl] **1** *adj* doble; **it's d. the price** cuesta dos veces más; **d. bass** contrabajo *m*; **d. bed** cama *f* de matrimonio; **d. bill** programa *m* doble; *Br* **d. cream** nata *f* para montar; **d. glazing** ventana *f* doble

  2 *adv* doble; **folded d.** doblado(a) por la mitad

  3 *n* (**a**) vivo retrato *m*; *Cin & Th* doble *m* (**b**) *to earn* el doble; *Fam* **at** *or* **on the d.** corriendo (**c**) **doubles** *(in chess)* *(partido m de)* dobles *mpl*

  4 *vt* doblar; *Fig (efforts)* redoblar

5 *vi* (**a**) *(increase)* doblarse (**b**) **to d. as** *(serve)* hacer las veces de
▸ **double back** *vi* **to d. back on one's tracks** volver sobre sus pasos
▸ **double up 1** *vt sep (bend)* doblar
2 *vi* (**a**) *(bend)* doblarse (**b**) *(share room)* compartir la habitación (**with** con)

double-barrelled [ˈdʌbəlbærəld] *adj* (**a**) *(gun)* de dos cañones (**b**) *Br (surname)* compuesto(a)

double-breasted [ˈdʌbəlbrestɪd] *adj* cruzado(a)

double-check [dʌbəlˈtʃek] *vt & vi* repasar dos veces

double-cross [dʌbəlˈkrɒs] *Fam* **1** *vt* engañar, traicionar
2 *n* engaño *m*, traición *f*

double-decker [dʌbəlˈdekə(r)] *n Br* **d.** **(bus)** autobús *m* de dos pisos

double-edged [ˈdʌbəledʒd] *adj* de doble filo

doubt [daʊt] **1** *n* duda *f*; **beyond (all) d.** sin duda alguna; **no d.** sin duda; **there's no d. about it** no cabe la menor duda; **to be in d. about sth** dudar algo; **to be open to d.** *(fact)* ser dudoso(a); *(outcome)* ser incierto(a)
2 *vt* (**a**) *(distrust)* desconfiar de (**b**) *(not be sure of)* dudar; **I d. if** *or* **whether he'll come** dudo que venga

doubtful [ˈdaʊtfʊl] *adj* (**a**) *(future)* dudoso(a), *(look)* dubitativo(a); **I'm a bit d. about it** no me convence del todo; **it's d. whether ...** no se sabe seguro si ... (**b**) *(questionable)* sospechoso(a)

doubtless [ˈdaʊtlɪs] *adv* sin duda, seguramente

dough [dəʊ] *n* (**a**) *(for bread)* masa *f*; *(for pastries)* pasta *f* (**b**) *Fam (money)* pasta *f*

doughnut [ˈdəʊnʌt] *n* rosquilla *f*, dónut® *m*

douse [daʊs] *vt* (**a**) *(soak)* mojar (**b**) *(extinguish)* apagar

dove [dʌv] *n* paloma *f*

dovetail [ˈdʌvteɪl] *vt Fig (plans)* sincronizar

dowdy [ˈdaʊdɪ] *adj* (**dowdier, dowdiest**) poco elegante

down¹ [daʊn] **1** *prep* (**a**) *(to or at a lower level)* **d. the river** río abajo; **to go d. the road** bajar la calle
(**b**) *(along)* por
2 *adv* (**a**) *(to lower level)* (hacia) abajo; *(to floor)* al suelo; *(to ground)* a tierra; **to fall d.** caerse; **to go d.** *(price, person)* bajar; *(sun)* ponerse
(**b**) *(at lower level)* abajo; **d. there** allí abajo; **face d.** boca abajo; *Fig* **to be d.**

with a cold estar resfriado(a); *Fam Fig* **to feel d.** estar deprimido(a); *Fam Fig* **d. under** en/a Australia y Nueva Zelanda
(**c**) **I'm d. to my last stamp** no me queda más que un solo sello; **sales are d. by 5 percent** las ventas han bajado un 5 por ciento
(**d**) **to take sth d.** *(in writing)* apuntar algo
(**e**) **d. through the ages** a través de los siglos
3 *adj (payment)* al contado; *(on property)* de entrada
4 *vt Fam (drink)* tomarse de un trago; *(food)* zamparse
5 *n* **ups and downs** altibajos *mpl*
6 *interj* **d. with taxes!** ¡abajo los impuestos!

down² [daʊn] *n* (**a**) *(on bird)* plumón *m* (**b**) *(on cheek, peach)* pelusa *f*; *(on body)* vello *m*

down-and-out [ˈdaʊnənˈaʊt] **1** *adj* en las últimas
2 *n* vagabundo(a) *m,f*

downbeat [ˈdaʊnbiːt] *adj Fam (gloomy)* deprimido(a)

downcast [ˈdaʊnkɑːst] *adj* abatido(a)

downfall [ˈdaʊnfɔːl] *n (of regime)* caída *f*; *(of person)* perdición *f*

downgrade [ˈdaʊngreɪd] *vt* degradar

downhearted [daʊnˈhɑːtɪd] *adj* desalentado(a)

downhill [daʊnˈhɪl] **1** *adj (skiing)* de descenso; *Fam* **after his first exam, the rest were all d.** después del primer examen, los demás le fueron sobre ruedas
2 *adv* **to go d.** ir cuesta abajo; *Fig (standards)* deteriorarse

download [ˈdaʊnˈləʊd] *vt Comput* bajar, descargar

down-market [daʊnˈmɑːkɪt] **1** *adj* barato(a)
2 *adv* **to move d.** *(of company)* producir artículos más asequibles

downpour [ˈdaʊnpɔː(r)] *n* chaparrón *m*

downright [ˈdaʊnraɪt] *Fam* **1** *adj (blunt)* tajante; *(categorical)* categórico(a); **it's a d. lie** es una mentira y gorda
2 *adv (totally)* completamente

downsizing [ˈdaʊnsaɪzɪŋ] *n Com* reajuste *m* de plantillas

downstairs 1 *adv* [daʊnˈsteəz] abajo; *(to ground floor)* a la planta baja; **to go d.** bajar la escalera
2 *adj* [ˈdaʊnsteəz] *(on ground floor)* de la planta baja

downstream [daʊnˈstriːm] *adv* río abajo

down-to-earth [daʊntʊˈɜːθ] *adj* realista

downtown [daʊnˈtaʊn] *adv US* en el centro (de la ciudad)

downturn [ˈdaʊntɜːn] *n* baja *f*

downward [ˈdaʊnwəd] **1** *adj (slope)* descendente; *(look)* hacia abajo; *Fin (tendency)* a la baja
  2 *adv* = **downwards**

downwards [ˈdaʊnwədz] *adv* hacia abajo

dowry [ˈdaʊərɪ] *n* dote *f*

doz (*abbr* **dozen**) docena *f*

doze [dəʊz] **1** *vi* dormitar
  2 *n* cabezada *f*; **to have a d.** echar una cabezada
  ▸ **doze off** *vi* quedarse dormido(a)

dozen [ˈdʌzən] *n* docena *f*; **half a d./a d. eggs** media docena/una docena de huevos; *Fam* **dozens of** un montón de

Dr (*abbr* **Doctor**) Dr., Dra.

drab [dræb] *adj* (**drabber, drabbest**) (**a**) *(ugly)* feo(a); *(dreary)* monótono(a), gris (**b**) *(colour)* pardo(a)

draft [drɑːft] **1** *n* (**a**) borrador *m* (**b**) *(bill of exchange)* giro *m* (**c**) *US* servicio militar obligatorio (**d**) *US* = **draught**
  2 *vt* (**a**) hacer un borrador de (**b**) *US Mil* reclutar

draftsman [ˈdrɑːftsmən] *n US* = **draughtsman**

drag [dræg] **1** *vt* (**a**) *(pull)* arrastrar; *Fig* **to d. one's heels (over sth)** dar largas a algo) (**b**) *(lake)* rastrear
  2 *vi* (**a**) *(trail)* arrastrarse (**b**) *(person)* rezagarse
  3 *n* (**a**) *Tech* resistencia *f* (aerodinámica) (**b**) *Fam (nuisance)* lata *f* (**c**) *Fam (on cigarette)* calada *f* (**d**) *Fam* **to be in d.** ir vestido de mujer (**e**) *US Fam* **the main d.** la calle mayor *or* principal
  ▸ **drag off** *vt sep* llevarse arrastrando
  ▸ **drag on** *vi (war, strike)* hacerse interminable
  ▸ **drag out** *vt sep (speech etc)* alargar

dragon [ˈdrægən] *n* dragón *m*

dragonfly [ˈdrægənflaɪ] *n* libélula *f*

drain [dreɪn] **1** *n* (**a**) *(for water)* desagüe *m*; *(for sewage)* alcantarilla *f* (**b**) *(grating)* sumidero *m* (**c**) *Fig* **the boys are a d. on her strength** los niños la dejan agotada
  2 *vt* (**a**) *(marsh etc)* avenar; *(reservoir)* desecar (**b**) *(crockery)* escurrir (**c**) *(empty) (glass)* apurar; *Fig (capital etc)* agotar
  3 *vi* (**a**) *(crockery)* escurrirse (**b**) **to d. (away)** *(liquid)* irse

drainage [ˈdreɪnɪdʒ] *n (of marsh)* drenaje *m*; *(of reservoir, building)* desagüe *m*; *(of town)* alcantarillado *m*

drainpipe [ˈdreɪnpaɪp] *n* tubo *m* de desagüe

dram [dræm] *n Fam* trago *m (de whisky)*

drama [ˈdrɑːmə] *n* (**a**) *(play)* obra *f* de teatro; *Fig* drama *m* (**b**) *(subject)* teatro *m*

dramatic [drəˈmætɪk] *adj* (**a**) *(change)* impresionante; *(moment)* emocionante (**b**) *Th* dramático(a), teatral

dramatist [ˈdræmətɪst] *n* dramaturgo(a) *m,f*

dramatization [dræmətaɪˈzeɪʃən] *n* adaptación teatral

dramatize [ˈdræmətaɪz] *vt* (**a**) *(adapt)* hacer una adaptación teatral de (**b**) *(exaggerate)* dramatizar

drank [dræŋk] *pt of* **drink**

drape [dreɪp] **1** *vt* **to d. sth over sth** colgar algo sobre algo; **draped with** cubierto(a) de
  2 *n* (**a**) *(of fabric)* caída *f* (**b**) *US* cortina *f*

draper [ˈdreɪpə(r)] *n Br* pañero(a) *m,f*

drastic [ˈdræstɪk] *adj* (**a**) *(measures)* drástico(a), severo(a) (**b**) *(change)* radical

draught [drɑːft] **1** *n* (**a**) *(of cold air)* corriente *f* (de aire) (**b**) *(of liquid)* trago *m* (**c**) **d. (beer)** cerveza *f* de barril (**d**) *Br* **draughts** *(game)* damas *fpl* (**e**) *Naut* calado *m*
  2 *adj (animal)* de tiro

draughtboard [ˈdrɑːftbɔːd] *n Br* tablero *m* de damas

draughtsman [ˈdrɑːftsmən] *n* delineante *mf*

draw [drɔː] **1** *vt* (*pt* **drew**; *pp* **drawn**) (**a**) *(picture)* dibujar; *(line)* trazar
  (**b**) *(pull)* tirar de; *(train, carriage)* arrastrar; *(curtains) (open)* descorrer; *(close)* correr; *(blinds)* bajar
  (**c**) *(remove)* sacar; *(salary)* cobrar; *(cheque)* librar
  (**d**) *(attract)* atraer; *(attention)* llamar
  (**e**) *Fig (strength)* sacar
  (**f**) **to d. breath** respirar
  (**g**) **to d. lots** echar a suertes
  (**h**) *(comparison)* hacer; *(conclusion)* sacar
  2 *vi* (**a**) *(sketch)* dibujar
  (**b**) *(move)* **the train drew into/out of the station** el tren entró en/salió de la estación; **to d. apart (from)** separarse (de); **to d. to an end** acabarse
  (**c**) *Sport* **they drew two all** empataron a dos
  3 *n* (**a**) *(raffle)* sorteo *m*
  (**b**) *Sport* empate *m*
  (**c**) *Fig (attraction)* atracción *f*
  ▸ **draw in** *vi (days)* acortarse

▸**draw on** vt insep (savings) recurrir a; (experience) aprovecharse de

▸**draw out** vt sep (a) (make long) alargar (b) (encourage to speak) desatar la lengua a (c) (from pocket, drawer etc) sacar

▸**draw up** vt sep (contract) preparar; (plan) esbozar

drawback ['drɔːbæk] n desventaja f, inconveniente m

drawbridge ['drɔːbrɪdʒ] n puente levadizo

drawer ['drɔːə(r)] n cajón m

drawing ['drɔːɪŋ] n dibujo m; Fam Fig to go back to the d. board volver a empezar; Br d. pin chincheta f; Fml d. room sala f de estar

drawl [drɔːl] 1 vi hablar arrastrando las palabras
2 n voz cansina; US a Southern d. un acento sureño

drawn [drɔːn] 1 adj (tired) ojeroso(a)
2 pp of draw

dread [dred] 1 vt temer a, tener pavor a
2 n temor m

dreadful ['dredfʊl] adj (a) (shocking) espantoso(a) (b) Fam (awful) fatal; how d.! ¡qué horror!

dreadfully ['dredfʊlɪ] adv Fam (horribly) terriblemente; (very) muy, sumamente

dream [driːm] 1 n (a) sueño m (b) (daydream) ensueño m (c) Fam (marvel) maravilla f
2 vt (pt & pp dreamed or dreamt) soñar
3 vi soñar (of or about con)

dreamer ['driːmə(r)] n soñador(a) m,f

dreamt [dremt] pt & pp of dream

dreamy ['driːmɪ] adj (dreamier, dreamiest) (absent-minded) distraído(a); (wonderful) de ensueño

dreary ['drɪərɪ] adj (drearier, dreariest) (a) (gloomy) triste (b) Fam (boring) aburrido(a), pesado(a)

dredge [dredʒ] vt & vi dragar, rastrear

▸**dredge up** vt sep (a) (body) sacar del agua (b) Fam Fig sacar a relucir

dregs [dregz] npl poso m

drench [drentʃ] vt empapar

dress [dres] 1 n (a) (frock) vestido m (b) (clothing) ropa f; d. rehearsal ensayo m general; d. shirt camisa f de etiqueta
2 vt (a) (person) vestir; he was dressed in a grey suit llevaba (puesto) un traje gris (b) (salad) aliñar (c) (wound) vendar
3 vi vestirse

▸**dress up** 1 vi (a) (in disguise) disfrazarse (as de) (b) (in best clothes) vestirse elegante
2 vt sep Fig disfrazar

dresser ['dresə(r)] n (a) Br (in kitchen) aparador m (b) US (in bedroom) tocador m (c) Th ayudante mf de camerino

dressing ['dresɪŋ] n (a) (bandage) vendaje m (b) (salad) d. aliño m (c) d. gown bata f; d. room Th camerino m; Sport vestuario m; d. table tocador m

dressmaker ['dresmeɪkə(r)] n modista mf

dressy ['dresɪ] adj (dressier, dressiest) vistoso(a)

drew [druː] pt of draw

dribble ['drɪbəl] 1 vi (a) (baby) babear (b) (liquid) gotear
2 vt Sport (ball) driblar
3 n (saliva) saliva f; (of water, blood) gotas fpl

dried [draɪd] adj (fruit) seco(a); (milk) en polvo

drier ['draɪə(r)] n = dryer

drift [drɪft] 1 vi (a) (boat) ir a la deriva; Fig (person) ir sin rumbo, vagar; they drifted away se marcharon poco a poco (b) (snow) amontonarse
2 n (a) (flow) flujo m (b) (of snow) ventisquero m; (of sand) montón m (c) Fig (meaning) idea f

driftwood ['drɪftwʊd] n madera f flotante

drill [drɪl] 1 n (a) (hand tool) taladro m; Min barrena f; dentist's d. fresa f; pneumatic d. martillo neumático (b) esp Mil instrucción f
2 vt (a) (wood etc) taladrar (b) (soldiers, children) instruir
3 vi (by hand) taladrar; (for oil, coal) perforar, sondar

drink [drɪŋk] 1 vt (pt drank; pp drunk) beber
2 vi beber; to have sth to d. tomarse algo; to d. to sth/sb brindar por algo/algn
3 n bebida f; (alcoholic) copa f

drinker ['drɪŋkə(r)] n bebedor(a) m,f

drinking ['drɪŋkɪŋ] n d. water agua f potable

drip [drɪp] 1 n (a) (goteo m (b) Med gota a gota m inv (c) Fam (person) necio(a) m,f
2 vi gotear; he was dripping with sweat el sudor le caía a gotas

drip-dry ['drɪp'draɪ] adj que no necesita planchado

dripping ['drɪpɪŋ] n Culin pringue f

drive [draɪv] 1 vt (pt drove; pp driven) (a) (vehicle) conducir, Am manejar; (person) llevar
(b) (power) impulsar

(**c**) *(enemy)* acosar; *(ball)* mandar
(**d**) *(stake)* hincar; *(nail)* clavar
(**e**) *(compel)* forzar, obligar; **to d. sb mad** volver loco(a) a algn
(**f**) **to d. (off)** rechazar
2 *vi Aut* conducir, *Am* manejar
3 *n* (**a**) *(trip)* paseo *m* en coche; **to go for a d.** dar una vuelta en coche
(**b**) *(to house)* camino *m* de entrada
(**c**) *(transmission)* transmisión *f*; *Aut* tracción *f*; *Aut* **left-hand d.** conducción *f* por la izquierda
(**d**) *(in golf)* golpe *m* inicial
(**e**) *(campaign)* campaña *f*
(**f**) *(need)* necesidad *f*; *(energy)* energía *f*, vigor *m*; **sex d.** instinto *m* sexual
(**g**) *Comput* unidad *f* de disco

drive-in ['draɪvɪn] *n US (cinema)* autocine *m*

driven ['drɪvən] *pp of* **drive**

driver ['draɪvə(r)] *n (of car, bus)* conductor(a) *m,f*; *(of train)* maquinista *mf*; *(of lorry)* camionero(a) *m,f*; *(of racing car)* piloto *mf*; *US* **d.'s license** carnet *m* de conducir

driveway ['draɪvweɪ] *n (to house)* camino *m* de entrada

driving ['draɪvɪŋ] **1** *n Br* **d. licence** carnet *m* de conducir; **d. school** autoescuela *f*; **d. test** examen *m* de conducir
2 *adj* (**a**) *(rain)* intenso(a) (**b**) **d. force** fuerza *f* motriz

drizzle ['drɪzəl] **1** *n* llovizna *f*
2 *vi* lloviznar

droll [drəʊl] *adj* gracioso(a)

dromedary ['drɒmədərɪ] *n* dromedario *m*

drone [drəʊn] *vi (bee etc)* zumbar

droop [druːp] *vi (flower)* marchitarse; *(eyelids)* caerse

drop [drɒp] **1** *n* (**a**) *(of liquid)* gota *f*; **eye drops** colirio *m*
(**b**) *(sweet)* pastilla *f*
(**c**) *(descent)* desnivel *m*
(**d**) *(in price)* bajada *f*; *(in temperature)* descenso *m*
2 *vt* (**a**) *(let fall)* dejar caer; *(lower)* bajar; *(reduce)* disminuir; **to d. a hint** soltar una indirecta
(**b**) *(abandon) (subject, charge etc)* abandonar, dejar; *Sport* **he was dropped from the team** lo echaron del equipo
(**c**) *(omit) (spoken syllable)* comerse
3 *vi (object)* caerse; *(person)* tirarse; *(voice, price, temperature)* bajar; *(wind)* amainar; *(speed)* disminuir
▸ **drop by, drop in** *vi Fam (visit)* pasarse (**at** por)

▸ **drop off 1** *vi Fam (fall asleep)* quedarse dormido(a)
2 *vt sep (deliver)* dejar
▸ **drop out** *vi (from college)* dejar los estudios; *(from society)* marginarse; *(from competition)* retirarse
▸ **drop round** *vi Fam* = **drop by**

dropout ['drɒpaʊt] *n Fam Pej* automarginado(a) *m,f*

dropper ['drɒpə(r)] *n* cuentagotas *m inv*

droppings ['drɒpɪŋz] *npl* excrementos *mpl*

drought [draʊt] *n* sequía *f*

drove [drəʊv] **1** *n (of cattle)* manada *f*
2 *pt of* **drive**

drown [draʊn] **1** *vt* (**a**) ahogar (**b**) *(place)* inundar
2 *vi* ahogarse; **he (was) drowned** murió ahogado

drowsy ['draʊzɪ] *adj* (**drowsier, drowsiest**) soñoliento(a); **to feel d.** tener sueño

drudgery ['drʌdʒərɪ] *n* trabajo duro y pesado

drug [drʌg] **1** *n* (**a**) *(medicine)* medicamento *m* (**b**) *(narcotic)* droga *f*, estupefaciente *m*; **to be on drugs** drogarse; **d. addict** drogadicto(a) *m,f*; **d. addiction** drogadicción *f*; **d. squad** brigada *f* antidroga
2 *vt (person)* drogar; *(food, drink)* adulterar con drogas

druggist ['drʌgɪst] *n US* farmacéutico(a) *m,f*

drugstore ['drʌgstɔːr] *n US* = establecimiento donde se compran medicamentos, periódicos, etc.

drum [drʌm] **1** *n* (**a**) tambor *m*; **to play the drums** tocar la batería (**b**) *(container)* bidón *m*
2 *vi Fig (with fingers)* tabalear
3 *vt Fig* **to d. sth into sb** enseñar algo a algn a machamartillo
▸ **drum up** *vt sep Fam* solicitar

drummer ['drʌmə(r)] *n (in band)* tambor *mf*; *(in pop group)* batería *mf*

drumstick ['drʌmstɪk] *n* (**a**) *Mus* baqueta *f* (**b**) *(chicken leg)* muslo *m*

drunk [drʌŋk] **1** *adj* borracho(a); **to get d.** emborracharse
2 *n* borracho(a) *m,f*
3 *pp of* **drink**

drunkard ['drʌŋkəd] *n* borracho(a) *m,f*

dry [draɪ] **1** *adj* (**drier, driest** *or* **dryer, dryest**) (**a**) seco(a); *US* **d. goods store** mercería *f*, tienda *f* de confección (**b**) *(wry)* socarrón(ona)
2 *vt (pt & pp dried)* secar

3 *vi* **to d. (off)** secarse

dry-clean [draɪˈkliːn] *vt* limpiar *or* lavar en seco

dryer [ˈdraɪə(r)] *n* secadora *f*

dub¹ [dʌb] *vt* (*subtitle*) doblar (**into** a)

dub² [dʌb] *vt* (**a**) (*give nickname to*) apodar (**b**) (*knight*) armar

dubious [ˈdjuːbɪəs] *adj* (**a**) (*morals etc*) dudoso(a); (*compliment*) equívoco(a) (**b**) (*doubting*) indeciso(a)

Dublin [ˈdʌblɪn] *n* Dublín

duchess [ˈdʌtʃɪs] *n* duquesa *f*

duck¹ [dʌk] *n* pato(a) *m,f*; *Culin* pato *m*

duck² [dʌk] **1** *vt* (**a**) (*submerge*) dar una ahogadilla a (**b**) (*evade*) esquivar

2 *vi* (**a**) (*evade blow*) esquivar (**b**) *Fam* **to d. (out)** rajarse

duckling [ˈdʌklɪŋ] *n* patito *m*

duct [dʌkt] *n* (*for fuel etc*) conducto *m*; *Anat* canal *m*

dud [dʌd] *Fam* **1** *adj* (**a**) (*useless*) inútil; (*defective*) estropeado(a) (**b**) (*banknote*) falso(a); (*cheque*) sin fondos

2 *n* (*useless thing*) engañifa *f*; (*person*) desastre *m*

dude [duːd] *n US Fam* (*man*) tipo *m*, tío *m*

due [djuː] **1** *adj* (**a**) (*expected*) esperado(a); **the train is d. (to arrive) at ten** el tren debe llegar a las diez (**b**) *Fml* (*proper*) debido(a); **in d. course** a su debido tiempo (**c**) (*owing*) pagadero(a); **how much are you d.?** (*owed*) ¿cuánto te deben? (**d**) **to be d. to** (*caused by*) deberse a; **d. to** (*because of*) debido de

2 *adv* (*north etc*) derecho hacia

3 *n* (**a**) **to give sb their d.** dar a algn su merecido (**b**) **dues** (*fee*) cuota *f*

duel [ˈdjuːəl] *n* duelo *m*

duet [djuːˈet] *n* dúo *m*

duffel [ˈdʌfəl] *n* **d. bag** petate *m*; **d. coat** trenca *f*

dug [dʌg] *pt & pp of* **dig**

duke [djuːk] *n* duque *m*

dull [dʌl] **1** *adj* (**a**) (*boring*) pesado(a); (*place*) sin interés (**b**) (*light*) apagado(a); (*weather*) gris (**c**) (*sound, ache*) sordo(a) (**d**) *Fig* (*slow-witted*) torpe

2 *vt* (**a**) (*pain*) aliviar (**b**) *Fig* (*faculty*) embotar

duly [ˈdjuːlɪ] *adv Fml* (*properly*) debidamente; (*as expected*) como era de esperar; (*in due course*) a su debido tiempo

dumb [dʌm] **1** *adj* (**a**) *Med* mudo(a) (**b**) *Fam* (*stupid*) tonto(a)

2 *npl* **the d.** los mudos

dumbbell [ˈdʌmbel] *n Sport* pesa *f*

dumbfounded [dʌmˈfaʊndɪd], **dumbstruck** [ˈdʌmstrʌk] *adj* pasmado(a)

dummy [ˈdʌmɪ] *n* (**a**) (*sham*) imitación *f* (**b**) (*in shop window*) maniquí *m*; (*of ventriloquist*) muñeco *m* (**c**) *Br* (*for baby*) chupete *m*

dump [dʌmp] **1** *n* (**a**) (*tip*) vertedero *m*; (*for old cars*) cementerio *m* (de coches) (**b**) *Fam Pej* (*place*) estercolero *m*; (*town*) poblacho *m*; (*dwelling*) tugurio *m* (**c**) *Mil* depósito *m*

2 *vt* (**a**) (*rubbish*) verter; (*truck contents*) descargar (**b**) (*person*) dejar; *Com* inundar el mercado con (**c**) *Comput* (*transfer*) copiar de memoria interna

dumping [ˈdʌmpɪŋ] *n* vertido *m*

dumpling [ˈdʌmplɪŋ] *n Culin* = bola de masa hervida

dumpy [ˈdʌmpɪ] *adj* (**dumpier, dumpiest**) *Fam* rechoncho(a)

dunce [dʌns] *n Fam* tonto(a) *m,f*

dune [djuːn] *n* (**sand**) **d.** duna *f*

dung [dʌŋ] *n* estiércol *m*

dungarees [dʌŋgəˈriːz] *npl* mono *m*

dungeon [ˈdʌndʒən] *n* calabozo *m*, mazmorra *f*

duo [ˈdjuːəʊ] *n Mus* dúo *m*; *Fam* pareja *f*

dupe [djuːp] **1** *vt* engañar

2 *n* ingenuo(a) *m,f*

duplex [ˈdjuːpleks] *n US* (*house*) casa adosada; **d. apartment** dúplex *m inv*

duplicate 1 *vt* [ˈdjuːplɪkeɪt] (**a**) (*copy*) duplicar; (*film, tape*) reproducir (**b**) (*repeat*) repetir

2 *n* [ˈdjuːplɪkɪt] duplicado *m*; **in d.** por duplicado

durable [ˈdjʊərəbəl] *adj* duradero(a)

duration [djʊˈreɪʃən] *n Fml* duración *f*

duress [djʊˈres] *n Fml* coacción *f*

🔎 Note that the Spanish word **dureza** is a false friend and is never a translation for the English word **duress**. In Spanish, **dureza** means "hardness, harshness".

during [ˈdjʊərɪŋ] *prep* durante

dusk [dʌsk] *n Fml* crepúsculo *m*; **at d.** al anochecer

dust [dʌst] **1** *n* polvo *m*; **d. cloud** polvareda *f*; **d. jacket** sobrecubierta *f*

2 *vt* (**a**) (*furniture*) quitar el polvo a (**b**) (*cake*) espolvorear

dustbin [ˈdʌstbɪn] *n Br* cubo *m* de la basura

dustcart [ˈdʌstkɑːt] *n Br* camión *m* de la basura

duster [ˈdʌstə(r)] *n* (*for housework*) trapo *m or* paño *m* (del polvo); **feather d.** plumero *m*

dustman [ˈdʌstmən] *n Br* basurero *m*

dustpan [ˈdʌstpæn] *n* recogedor *m*

dusty ['dʌstɪ] *adj* (**dustier, dustiest**) polvoriento(a)

Dutch [dʌtʃ] **1** *adj* holandés(esa); *Fig* **D. cap** diafragma *m*

  2 *n* (**a**) *pl* **the D.** los holandeses (**b**) *(language)* holandés *m*; **it's double D. to me** me suena a chino

  3 *adv Fig* **to go D.** pagar cada uno lo suyo

Dutchman ['dʌtʃmən] *n* holandés *m*

Dutchwoman ['dʌtʃwʊmən] *n* holandesa *f*

duty ['djuːtɪ] *n* (**a**) deber *m*; **to do one's d.** cumplir con su deber (**b**) *(task)* función *f* (**c**) **to be on d.** estar de servicio; *Med & Mil* estar de guardia; **d. chemist** farmacia *f* de guardia (**d**) *(tax)* impuesto *m*; **customs d.** derechos *mpl* de aduana

duty-free [djuːtɪ'friː] **1** *adj* libre de impuestos

  2 *adv* sin pagar impuestos

  3 *n* duty-free *m*

duvet ['duːveɪ] *n* edredón *m*

DVD [diːviː'diː] *n Comput* (*abbr* **Digital Versatile Disk, Digital Video Disk**) DVD *m*

dwarf [dwɔːf] **1** *n* (*pl* **dwarves** [dwɔːvz]) *(person)* enano(a) *m,f*

  2 *vt* hacer parecer pequeño(a) a

dwell [dwel] *vi* (*pt & pp* **dwelt**) *Fml* morar

 ▸ **dwell on** *vt insep* hablar extensamente de; **let's not d. on it** olvidémoslo

dwelling ['dwelɪŋ] *n Fml & Hum* morada *f*, vivienda *f*

dwelt [dwelt] *pt & pp of* **dwell**

dwindle ['dwɪndəl] *vi* menguar, disminuir

dye [daɪ] **1** *n* tinte *m*

  2 *vt* (*pres p* **dyeing**; *pt & pp* **dyed**) teñir; **to d. one's hair black** teñirse el pelo de negro

dying ['daɪɪŋ] *adj* *(person)* moribundo(a), agonizante; *Fig (custom)* en vías de desaparición

dyke [daɪk] *n* (**a**) *(bank)* dique *m*; *(causeway)* terraplén *m* (**b**) *very Fam Pej* tortillera *f*

dynamic [daɪ'næmɪk] *adj* dinámico(a)

dynamics [daɪ'næmɪks] *n sing* dinámica *f*

dynamism ['daɪnəmɪzəm] *n* dinamismo *m*

dynamite ['daɪnəmaɪt] *n* dinamita *f*

dynamo ['daɪnəməʊ] *n* dínamo *f*

dynasty ['dɪnəstɪ] *n* dinastía *f*

dysentery ['dɪsəntrɪ] *n* disentería *f*

dyslexia [dɪs'leksɪə] *n* dislexia *f*

E

E, e [i:] *n* (**a**) *(the letter)* E, e *f* (**b**) *Mus* E mi *m*
E [i:] *n* (**a**) *(abbr* **East)** E (**b**) *Fam (abbr*
ecstasy) *(drug)* éxtasis *m inv*
each [i:tʃ] **1** *adj* cada; **e. day/month** todos
los días/meses; **e. person** cada cual; **e.
time I see him** cada vez que lo veo
 2 *pron* (**a**) cada uno(a); **£2 e.** 2 libras
cada uno; **we bought one e.** nos compra-
mos uno cada uno (**b**) **e. other** el uno al
otro; **they hate e. other** se odian
eager ['i:gə(r)] *adj (anxious)* impaciente;
(desirous) deseoso(a); **e. to begin** impaciente por empezar; **to be e. for success**
codiciar el éxito
eagerly ['i:gəlɪ] *adv (anxiously)* con impaciencia; *(keenly)* con ilusión
eagle ['i:gəl] *n* águila *f*
ear [ɪə(r)] *n* (**a**) oreja *f*, *(sense of hearing)*
oído *m* (**b**) *(of corn etc)* espiga *f*
earache ['ɪəreɪk] *n* dolor *m* de oídos
eardrum ['ɪədrʌm] *n* tímpano *m*
earl [ɜ:l] *n* conde *m*
earlobe ['ɪələʊb] *n* lóbulo *m*
early ['ɜ:lɪ] *(earlier, earliest)* **1** *adj* (**a**)
(before the usual time) temprano(a); **to
have an e. night** acostarse pronto; **you're
e.!** ¡qué pronto has venido!
 (**b**) *(at first stage, period)* **at an e. age**
siendo joven; **in e. July** a principios de
julio; **e. work** obra de juventud; **in her e.
forties** a los cuarenta y pocos; **it's still e.
days** aún es pronto
 (**c**) *(in the near future)* **an e. reply** una
respuesta pronta; **at the earliest** cuanto
antes
 2 *adv* (**a**) *(before the expected time)*
temprano, pronto; **earlier on** antes; **five
minutes e.** con cinco minutos de adelanto; **to leave e.** irse pronto
 (**b**) *(near the beginning)* **as e. as 1914** ya
en 1914; **as e. as possible** tan pronto como
sea posible; **to book e.** reservar con
tiempo; **e. on** temprano
earmark ['ɪəmɑːk] *vt* destinar (**for** para
or a)
earn [ɜ:n] *vt* (**a**) *(money)* ganar; **to e. one's
living** ganarse la vida (**b**) *(reputation)*
ganarse (**c**) **to e. interest** cobrar interés
or intereses

earnest ['ɜ:nɪst] **1** *adj* serio(a), formal
 2 *n* **in e.** de veras, en serio
earnings ['ɜ:nɪŋz] *npl* ingresos *mpl*
earring ['ɪərɪŋ] *n* pendiente *m*
earshot ['ɪəʃɒt] *n* **out of e.** fuera del
alcance del oído; **within e.** al alcance
del oído
earth [ɜ:θ] **1** *n* (**a**) tierra *f*, *Fig* **to be down
to e.** ser práctico; *Fam* **where/why on e.
...?** ¿pero dónde/por qué demonios ...?
(**b**) *Br Elec* toma *f* de tierra
 2 *vt Br Elec* conectar a tierra
earthenware ['ɜ:θənweə(r)] **1** *n* loza *f*
 2 *adj* de barro
earthquake ['ɜ:θkweɪk] *n* terremoto *m*
earthshattering ['ɜ:θʃætərɪŋ] *adj* trascendental; **e. news** noticia bomba
earthworm ['ɜ:θwɜ:m] *n* lombriz *f* de
tierra
earthy ['ɜ:θɪ] *adj* (**earthier, earthiest)**
(**a**) *(taste)* terroso(a) (**b**) *(bawdy)* tos-
co(a)
earwig ['ɪəwɪg] *n* tijereta *f*
ease [i:z] **1** *n* (**a**) *(freedom from discomfort)* tranquilidad *f*, *Mil* posición *f* de
descanso; **at e.** relajado(a) (**b**) *(lack of
difficulty)* facilidad *f* (**c**) *(affluence)*
comodidad *f* (**d**) **e. of manner** naturalidad *f*
 2 *vt* (**a**) *(pain)* aliviar (**b**) *(move gently)*
deslizar con cuidado
 ► **ease off, ease up** *vi* (**a**) *(decrease)* disminuir (**b**) *(slow down)* ir más despacio
easel ['i:zəl] *n* caballete *m*
easily ['i:zɪlɪ] *adv* fácilmente; **e. the best**
con mucho el mejor
east [i:st] **1** *n* este *m*; **the Middle E.** el
Oriente Medio
 2 *adj* del este, oriental; **E. Germany**
Alemania Oriental
 3 *adv* al *or* hacia el este
Easter ['i:stə(r)] *n* Semana Santa, Pascua
f; **E. egg** huevo *m* de Pascua; **E. Sunday**
Domingo *m* de Resurrección
easterly ['i:stəlɪ] *adj (from the east)* del
este; *(to the east)* hacia al este
eastern ['i:stən] *adj* oriental, del este
eastward(s) ['i:stwəd(z)] *adv* hacia el
este

easy ['iːzɪ] (**easier, easiest**) 1 *adj* (a) *(simple)* fácil, sencillo(a) (b) *(unworried, comfortable)* cómodo(a), tranquilo(a); *Fam* **I'm e.!** ¡me da lo mismo!; **e. chair** butacón *m*

2 *adv* **go e. on the wine** no te pases con el vino; *Fam* **to take things e.** tomarse las cosas con calma; *Fam* **take it e.!** ¡tranquilo!

easy-going [iːzɪ'gəʊɪŋ] *adj (calm)* tranquilo(a); *(lax)* despreocupado(a); *(undemanding)* poco exigente

eat [iːt] *vt (pt* **ate** [et, eɪt]; *pp* **eaten**) comer
▸ **eat away** *vt sep* desgastar; *(metal)* corroer
▸ **eat into** *vt insep* (a) *(wood)* roer (b) *Fig (savings)* consumir
▸ **eat out** *vi* comer fuera
▸ **eat up** *vt sep* (a) *(meal)* terminar (b) *Fig (petrol)* consumir; *(miles)* recorrer rápidamente

eatable ['iːtəbəl] *adj* comestible

eaten ['iːtən] *pp of* **eat**

eau de Cologne [əʊdəkə'ləʊn] *n* colonia *f*

eaves [iːvz] *npl* alero *m*

eavesdrop ['iːvzdrɒp] *vi* escuchar disimuladamente

ebb [eb] 1 *n* reflujo *m*; **e. and flow** flujo y reflujo; *Fig* **to be at a low e.** estar decaído
2 *vi* (a) *(tide)* bajar; **to e. and flow** subir y bajar (b) *Fig* **to e. away** decaer

ebony ['ebənɪ] 1 *n* ébano *m*
2 *adj* de ébano

eccentric [ɪk'sentrɪk] *adj & n* excéntrico(a) *(m,f)*

ecclesiastic [ɪkliːzɪ'æstɪk] *adj & n* eclesiástico(a) *(m,f)*

echelon ['eʃəlɒn] *n* escalafón *m*

echo ['ekəʊ] 1 *n (pl* **echoes**) eco *m*
2 *vt (repeat)* repetir
3 *vi* resonar, hacer eco

eclectic [ɪ'klektɪk] *adj* ecléctico(a)

eclipse [ɪ'klɪps] 1 *n* eclipse *m*
2 *vt* eclipsar

ecological [iːkə'lɒdʒɪkəl] *adj* ecológico(a)

ecology [ɪ'kɒlədʒɪ] *n* ecología *f*

e-commerce [iː'kɒmɜːs] *n* comercio electrónico

economic [iːkə'nɒmɪk] *adj* económico(a); *(profitable)* rentable

economical [iːkə'nɒmɪkəl] *adj* económico(a)

economics [iːkə'nɒmɪks] *n sing (science)* economía *f*, *Educ* (ciencias *fpl*) económicas *fpl*

economist [ɪ'kɒnəmɪst] *n* economista *mf*

economize [ɪ'kɒnəmaɪz] *vi* economizar

economy [ɪ'kɒnəmɪ] *n* (a) *Pol* **the e.** la economía (b) *(saving)* ahorro *m*; **e. class** clase *f* turista

ecosystem ['iːkəʊsɪstəm] *n* ecosistema *m*

ecotax ['iːkəʊtæks] *n* ecotasa *f*

ecotourism ['iːkəʊtɔːrɪzəm] *n* ecoturismo *m*

ecstasy ['ekstəsɪ] *n* éxtasis *m*

ecstatic [ek'stætɪk] *adj* extático(a)

Ecuador ['ekwədɔː(r)] *n* Ecuador *m*

eczema ['eksɪmə] *n* eczema *m*

eddy ['edɪ] 1 *n* remolino *m*
2 *vi* arremolinarse

edge [edʒ] 1 *n* borde *m*; *(of knife)* filo *m*; *(of coin)* canto *m*; *(of water)* orilla *f*; **on the e. of town** en las afueras de la ciudad; **to have the e. on sb** llevar ventaja a algn; *Fig* **to be on e.** tener los nervios de punta
2 *vt Sewing* ribetear
3 *vi* **to e. closer** acercarse lentamente; **to e. forward** avanzar poco a poco

edgeways ['edʒweɪz], **edgewise** ['edʒwaɪz] *adv* de lado; *Fig* **I couldn't get a word in e.** no pude decir ni pío

edging ['edʒɪŋ] *n* borde *m*; *Sewing* ribete *m*

edgy ['edʒɪ] *adj* (**edgier, edgiest**) nervioso(a)

edible ['edɪbəl] *adj* comestible

edict ['iːdɪkt] *n Hist* edicto *m*; *Jur* decreto *m*

Edinburgh ['edɪnbrə] *n* Edimburgo

edit ['edɪt] *vt* (a) *(prepare for printing)* preparar para la imprenta (b) *(rewrite)* corregir; **to e. sth out** suprimir algo (c) *Press* ser redactor(a) de (d) *Cin, Rad & TV* montar; *(cut)* cortar

edition [ɪ'dɪʃən] *n* edición *f*

editor ['edɪtə(r)] *n (of book)* editor(a) *m,f*; *Press* redactor(a) *m,f*; *Cin & TV* montador(a) *m,f*

editorial [edɪ'tɔːrɪəl] 1 *adj* editorial; **e. staff** redacción *f*
2 *n* editorial *m*

educate ['edjʊkeɪt] *vt* educar

educated ['edjʊkeɪtɪd] *adj* culto(a)

education [edjʊ'keɪʃən] *n* (a) *(schooling)* enseñanza *f*; **adult e.** educación *f* de adultos; **Ministry of E.** Ministerio *m* de Educación (b) *(training)* formación *f* (c) *(studies)* estudios *mpl* (d) *(culture)* cultura *f*

educational [edjʊ'keɪʃənəl] *adj* educativo(a), educacional

eel [iːl] *n* anguila *f*

eerie ['ɪərɪ] *adj* (**eerier, eeriest**) siniestro(a)

efface [ɪ'feɪs] *vt* borrar

effect [ɪ'fekt] **1** *n* (**a**) efecto *m*; **in e.** efectivamente; **to come into e.** entrar en vigor; **to have an e. on** afectar a; **to no e.** sin resultado alguno; **to take e.** *(drug)* surtir efecto; *(law)* entrar en vigor (**b**) *(impression)* impresión *f* (**c**) **effects** *(possessions)* efectos *mpl*
2 *vt Fml* provocar

effective [ɪ'fektɪv] *adj* (**a**) *(successful)* eficaz (**b**) *(real)* efectivo(a) (**c**) *(impressive)* impresionante

effectively [ɪ'fektɪvlɪ] *adv* (**a**) *(successfully)* eficazmente (**b**) *(in fact)* en efecto

effeminate [ɪ'femɪnɪt] *adj* afeminado(a)

effervescent [efə'vesənt] *adj* efervescente

efficiency [ɪ'fɪʃənsɪ] *n* *(of person)* eficacia *f*; *(of machine)* rendimiento *m*

efficient [ɪ'fɪʃənt] *adj* eficaz, eficiente; *(machine)* de buen rendimiento

effigy ['efɪdʒɪ] *n* efigie *f*

effluent ['eflʊənt] *n* vertidos *mpl*

effort ['efət] *n* (**a**) esfuerzo *m*; **to make an e.** hacer un esfuerzo, esforzarse (**b**) *(attempt)* intento *m*

effortless ['efətlɪs] *adj* sin esfuerzo

effrontery [ɪ'frʌntərɪ] *n* desfachatez *f*

effusive [ɪ'fjuːsɪv] *adj* efusivo(a)

eg [iː'dʒiː] *(abbr* **exempli gratia**) p. ej.

egalitarian [ɪgælɪ'teərɪən] *adj* igualitario(a)

egg [eg] **1** *n* huevo *m*; *Fam Fig* **to put all one's eggs in one basket** jugárselo todo a una carta; **e. cup** huevera *f*; **e. timer** reloj *m* de arena; **e. white** clara *f* de huevo
2 *vt* **to e. sb on (to do sth)** empujar a algn (a hacer algo)

eggplant ['egplɑːnt] *n US* berenjena *f*

eggshell ['egʃel] *n* cáscara *f* de huevo

ego ['iːgəʊ,'egəʊ] *n* (**a**) ego *m*; *Fam* **e. trip** autobombo *m* (**b**) *Fam* amor propio

egocentric(al) [iːgəʊ'sentrɪk(əl)] *adj* egocéntrico(a)

egoism ['iːgəʊɪzəm] *n* egoísmo *m*

egoist ['iːgəʊɪst] *n* egoísta *mf*

egotistic(al) [iːgəʊ'tɪstɪk(əl)] *adj* egotista

Egypt ['iːdʒɪpt] *n* Egipto

Egyptian [ɪ'dʒɪpʃən] *adj & n* egipcio(a) *(m,f)*

eiderdown ['aɪdədaʊn] *n* edredón *m*

eight [eɪt] *adj & n* ocho *(m inv)*

eighteen [eɪ'tiːn] *adj & n* dieciocho *(m inv)*

eighteenth [eɪ'tiːnθ] **1** *adj & n* decimoctavo *(m,f)*
2 *n* *(fraction)* decimoctavo *m*

eighth [eɪtθ] **1** *adj & n* octavo(a) *(m,f)*
2 *n* *(fraction)* octavo *m*

eighty ['eɪtɪ] *adj & n* ochenta *(m inv)*

Eire ['eərə] *n* Eire

either ['aɪðə(r), 'iːðə(r)] **1** *pron* (**a**) *(affirmative)* cualquiera; **e. of them** cualquiera de los dos; **e. of us** cualquiera de nosotros dos (**b**) *(negative)* ninguno/ninguna, ni el uno ni el otro/ni la una ni la otra; **I don't want e. of them** no quiero ninguno de los dos
2 *adj* *(both)* cada, los dos/las dos; **on e. side** en ambos lados; **in e. case** en cualquier de los dos casos
3 *conj* o; **e. ... or ...** o ... o ...; **e. Friday or Saturday** o (bien) el viernes o el sábado
4 *adv* *(after negative)* tampoco; **I don't want to do it e.** yo tampoco quiero hacerlo

ejaculate [ɪ'dʒækjʊleɪt] *vi* *(man)* eyacular

eject [ɪ'dʒekt] **1** *vt* expulsar
2 *vi Av* eyectarse

eke [iːk] *vt* **to e. out a living** ganarse la vida a duras penas

elaborate *vt* [ɪ'læbəreɪt] (**a**) *(devise)* elaborar (**b**) *(explain)* explicar detalladamente
2 *vi* explicarse; **to e. on sth** explicar algo con más detalles
3 *adj* [ɪ'læbərɪt] (**a**) *(complicated)* complicado(a) (**b**) *(detailed)* detallado(a); *(style)* esmerado(a)

elapse [ɪ'læps] *vi* transcurrir, pasar

elastic [ɪ'læstɪk] **1** *adj* elástico(a); *Fig* flexible; **e. band** goma elástica
2 *n* elástico *m*

Elastoplast® [ɪ'lɑːstəplɑːst] *n* tirita *f*, *Am* curita *f*

elated [ɪ'leɪtɪd] *adj* eufórico(a)

elation [ɪ'leɪʃən] *n* regocijo *m*

elbow ['elbəʊ] **1** *n* (**a**) codo *m*; *Fig* **e. room** espacio *m* (**b**) *(bend)* recodo *m*
2 *vt* **to e. sb** dar un codazo a algn

elder¹ ['eldə(r)] **1** *adj* mayor
2 *n* **the elders** los ancianos

elder² ['eldə(r)] *n Bot* saúco *m*

elderly ['eldəlɪ] **1** *adj* anciano(a)
2 *npl* **the e.** los ancianos

eldest ['eldɪst] **1** *adj* mayor
2 *n* **the e.** el/la mayor

elect [ɪ'lekt] **1** *vt* (**a**) *Pol* elegir (**b**) **to e. to do sth** *(choose)* decidir hacer algo
2 *adj* **the president e.** el presidente electo

election [ɪˈlekʃən] **1** n elección f; **general e.** elecciones fpl generales
2 adj electoral

electioneering [ɪlekʃəˈnɪərɪŋ] n electoralismo m

elector [ɪˈlektə(r)] n elector(a) m,f

electoral [ɪˈlektərəl] adj electoral

electorate [ɪˈlektərɪt] n electorado m

electric [ɪˈlektrɪk] adj (**a**) eléctrico(a); **e. blanket** manta eléctrica, Am frazada eléctrica; **e. chair** silla eléctrica; **e. shock** electrochoque m (**b**) Fig electrizante

electrical [ɪˈlektrɪkəl] adj eléctrico(a)

electrician [ɪlekˈtrɪʃən] n electricista mf

electricity [ɪlekˈtrɪsɪtɪ] n electricidad f; **e. bill** recibo m de la luz

electrify [ɪˈlektrɪfaɪ] vt (**a**) (railway line) electrificar (**b**) Fig (excite) electrizar

electrocute [ɪˈlektrəkjuːt] vt electrocutar

electron [ɪˈlektrɒn] n electrón m

electronic [ɪlekˈtrɒnɪk] adj electrónico(a); **e. banking** banca electrónica, telebanca f

electronics [ɪlekˈtrɒnɪks] **1** n sing (science) electrónica f
2 npl (of machine) componentes mpl electrónicos

elegant [ˈelɪɡənt] adj elegante

element [ˈelɪmənt] n (**a**) elemento m (**b**) (part) parte f (**c**) (electrical) resistencia f (**d**) Fam Fig **to be in one's e.** estar en su salsa

elementary [elɪˈmentərɪ] adj (basic) elemental; (not developed) rudimentario(a); (easy) fácil; US **e. school** escuela primaria

elephant [ˈelɪfənt] n elefante m

elevate [ˈelɪveɪt] vt elevar; (in rank) ascender

elevation [elɪˈveɪʃən] n (**a**) elevación f (**b**) Archit alzado m (**c**) (above sea level) altitud f

elevator [ˈelɪveɪtər] n US ascensor m

eleven [ɪˈlevən] adj & n once (m inv)

elevenses [ɪˈlevənzɪz] npl Fam bocadillo m de las once

eleventh [ɪˈlevənθ] **1** adj & n undécimo(a) (m,f)
2 n (fraction) undécimo m

elicit [ɪˈlɪsɪt] vt obtener

eligible [ˈelɪdʒəbəl] adj apto(a); **he isn't e. to vote** no tiene derecho al voto

eliminate [ɪˈlɪmɪneɪt] vt eliminar

elite [ɪˈliːt] n elite f

elitist [ɪˈliːtɪst] adj elitista

elm [elm] n olmo m

elocution [eləˈkjuːʃən] n elocución f

elongate [ˈiːlɒŋɡeɪt] vt alargar

elope [ɪˈləʊp] vi fugarse para casarse

eloquent [ˈeləkwənt] adj elocuente

else [els] adv (**a**) **anyone e.** alguien más; **anything e.?** ¿algo más?; **everything e.** todo lo demás; **no one e.** nadie más; **someone e.** otro(a); **something e.** otra cosa, algo más; **somewhere e.** en otra parte; **what e.?** ¿qué más?; **where e.?** ¿en qué otro sitio? (**b**) **or e.** (otherwise) si no

elsewhere [elsˈweə(r)] adv en otra parte

elucidate [ɪˈluːsɪdeɪt] vt aclarar

elude [ɪˈluːd] vt (**a**) (escape) eludir; **his name eludes me** no consigo acordarme de su nombre (**b**) (avoid) esquivar

elusive [ɪˈluːsɪv] adj esquivo(a); (evasive) evasivo(a)

emaciated [ɪˈmeɪsɪeɪtɪd] adj demacrado(a)

e-mail [ˈiːmeɪl] Comput **1** n (system) correo m electrónico; (message) (mensaje m por) correo m electrónico; **e. address** dirección f de correo electrónico
2 vt (person) enviar un correo electrónico a; (file) enviar por correo electrónico

emanate [ˈeməneɪt] vi provenir (**from** de)

emancipate [ɪˈmænsɪpeɪt] vt emancipar

emancipation [ɪmænsɪˈpeɪʃən] n emancipación f

embankment [ɪmˈbæŋkmənt] n (**a**) (made of earth) terraplén m (**b**) (of river) dique m

embargo [emˈbɑːɡəʊ] n (pl **embargoes**) embargo m

embark [emˈbɑːk] **1** vt (merchandise) embarcar
2 vi embarcar, embarcarse; Fig **to e. upon** emprender; (sth difficult) embarcarse en

embarkation [embɑːˈkeɪʃən] n embarque m

embarrass [ɪmˈbærəs] vt avergonzar, Andes, CAm, Carib, Méx apenar

embarrassed [ɪmˈbærəst] adj avergonzado(a), Andes, CAm, Carib, Méx apenado(a)

> ⚠ Note that the Spanish word **embarazado** is a false friend and is never a translation for the English word **embarrassed**. In Spanish, **embarazado** means "pregnant".

embarrassing [ɪmˈbærəsɪŋ] adj embarazoso(a), Andes, CAm, Carib, Méx penoso(a)

embarrassment [ɪmˈbærəsmənt] n vergüenza f, Andes, CAm, Carib, Méx pena f

embassy [ˈembəsɪ] n embajada f

embed [ɪmˈbed] *vt (jewels)* incrustar; *Fig* grabar

embellish [ɪmˈbelɪʃ] *vt* embellecer; *(story)* exagerar

ember [ˈembə(r)] *n* ascua *f*, rescoldo *m*

embezzle [ɪmˈbezəl] *vt* desfalcar, malversar

embezzlement [ɪmˈbezəlmənt] *n* malversación *f*

embitter [ɪmˈbɪtə(r)] *vt* amargar

embittered [ɪmˈbɪtəd] *adj* amargado(a), resentido(a)

emblem [ˈembləm] *n* emblema *m*

embody [ɪmˈbɒdɪ] *vt* (a) *(include)* abarcar (b) *(personify)* encarnar

embossed [ɪmˈbɒst] *adj* en relieve

embrace [ɪmˈbreɪs] **1** *vt* (a) abrazar (b) *(accept)* adoptar (c) *(include)* abarcar
2 *vi* abrazarse
3 *n* abrazo *m*

embroider [ɪmˈbrɔɪdə(r)] *vt* (a) *Sewing* bordar (b) *Fig (story, truth)* adornar, embellecer

embroidery [ɪmˈbrɔɪdərɪ] *n* bordado *m*

embryo [ˈembrɪəʊ] *n* embrión *m*

emerald [ˈemərəld] *n* esmeralda *f*

emerge [ɪˈmɜːdʒ] *vi* salir; *(problem)* surgir; **it emerged that ...** resultó que ...

emergence [ɪˈmɜːdʒəns] *n* aparición *f*

emergency [ɪˈmɜːdʒənsɪ] *n* emergencia *f*; *Med* urgencia *f*; **in an e.** en caso de emergencia; **e. exit** salida *f* de emergencia; **e. landing** aterrizaje forzoso; **e. measures** medidas *fpl* de urgencia; *US* **e. room** sala *f* de urgencias; *Aut* **e. stop** frenazo *m* en seco; *Pol* **state of e.** estado *m* de excepción

emery [ˈemərɪ] *n* **e. board** lima *f* de uñas

emigrant [ˈemɪgrənt] *n* emigrante *mf*

emigrate [ˈemɪgreɪt] *vi* emigrar

emigration [emɪˈgreɪʃən] *n* emigración *f*

eminent [ˈemɪnənt] *adj* eminente

emission [ɪˈmɪʃən] *n* emisión *f*

emit [ɪˈmɪt] *vt (signals)* emitir; *(smells)* despedir; *(sound)* producir

emotion [ɪˈməʊʃən] *n* emoción *f*

emotional [ɪˈməʊʃənəl] *adj* (a) emocional (b) *(moving)* conmovedor(a)

emotive [ɪˈməʊtɪv] *adj* emotivo(a)

emperor [ˈempərə(r)] *n* emperador *m*

emphasis [ˈemfəsɪs] *n* (pl **emphases** [ˈemfəsiːz]) énfasis *m*; **to place e. on sth** hacer hincapié en algo

emphasize [ˈemfəsaɪz] *vt* subrayar, hacer hincapié en; *(insist)* insistir; *(highlight)* hacer resaltar

emphatic [emˈfætɪk] *adj (forceful)* enfático(a); *(convinced)* categórico(a)

emphatically [emˈfætɪklɪ] *adv* categóricamente

empire [ˈempaɪə(r)] *n* imperio *m*

employ [ɪmˈplɔɪ] *vt* emplear; *(time)* ocupar

employee [emˈplɔɪiː, emplɔɪˈiː] *n* empleado(a) *m,f*

employer [ɪmˈplɔɪə(r)] *n* patrón(ona) *m,f*

employment [ɪmˈplɔɪmənt] *n* empleo *m*; **e. agency** agencia *f* de colocaciones; **full e.** pleno empleo

empower [ɪmˈpaʊə(r)] *vt* autorizar

empress [ˈemprɪs] *n* emperatriz *f*

emptiness [ˈemptɪnɪs] *n* vacío *m*

empty [ˈemptɪ] **1** *adj* (**emptier, emptiest**) vacío(a); **an e. house** una casa deshabitada; **e. promises** promesas *fpl* vanas
2 *vt* vaciar
3 *vi* (a) vaciarse (b) *(river)* desembocar (**into** en)
4 *npl* **empties** envases vacíos

empty-handed [emptɪˈhændɪd] *adj* con las manos vacías

EMU [iːemˈjuː] *n Fin (abbr* **Economic and Monetary Union**) UEM *f*

emulate [ˈemjʊleɪt] *vt* emular

emulsion [ɪˈmʌlʃən] *n* emulsión *f*; **e. paint** pintura *f* mate

enable [ɪˈneɪbəl] *vt* permitir

enact [ɪˈnækt] *vt (play)* representar; *(law)* promulgar

enamel [ɪˈnæməl] *n* esmalte *m*

enamoured, *US* **enamored** [ɪˈnæməd] *adj* **to be e. of** estar enamorado(a) de; **I'm not greatly e. of the idea** no me entusiasma la idea

encase [ɪnˈkeɪs] *vt* **encased in** revestido de

enchant [ɪnˈtʃɑːnt] *vt* encantar

enchanting [ɪnˈtʃɑːntɪŋ] *adj* encantador(a)

encircle [ɪnˈsɜːkəl] *vt* rodear

enclave [ˈenkleɪv] *n* enclave *m*

enclose [ɪnˈkləʊz] *vt* (a) *(surround)* rodear (b) *(fence in)* cercar (c) *(in envelope)* adjuntar; **please find enclosed** le enviamos adjunto

enclosure [ɪnˈkləʊʒə(r)] *n* (a) *(fenced area)* cercado *m* (b) *(in envelope)* documento adjunto (c) *(of racecourse)* recinto *m*

encompass [ɪnˈkʌmpəs] *vt* abarcar

encore [ˈɒŋkɔː(r)] **1** *interj* ¡otra!, ¡bis!
2 *n* repetición *f*, bis *m*

encounter [ɪnˈkaʊntə(r)] **1** *n (meeting)* encuentro *m*
2 *vt* encontrar, encontrarse con; *(problems)* tropezar con

encourage [ɪnˈkʌrɪdʒ] *vt* (**a**) *(person)* animar (**b**) *(tourism, trade)* fomentar

encouragement [ɪnˈkʌrɪdʒmənt] *n* estímulo *m*

encroach [ɪnˈkrəʊtʃ] *vi* **to e. on** *(territory)* invadir; *(rights)* usurpar; *(time, freedom)* quitar

encrusted [ɪnˈkrʌstɪd] *adj* incrustado(a) (**with** de)

encumber [ɪnˈkʌmbə(r)] *vt* estorbar; *(with debts)* gravar

encyclop(a)edia [ensaɪkləˈpiːdɪə] *n* enciclopedia *f*

end [end] **1** *n* (**a**) *(of stick)* punta *f*; *(of street)* final *m*; *(of table)* extremo *m*; *Fig* **to make ends meet** llegar a final de mes; *Fig* **it makes my hair stand on e.** me pone el pelo de punta (**b**) *(conclusion)* fin *m*, final *m*; **in the e.** al final; **for hours on e.** hora tras hora; **no e. of** un sinfín de; **to bring an e. to sth** poner fin a algo; **to put an e. to** acabar con (**c**) *(aim)* objetivo *m*, fin *m*; **to no e.** en vano
    2 *vt* acabar, terminar
    3 *vi* acabarse, terminarse
  ▸ **end up** *vi* terminar; **it ended up in the dustbin** fue a parar al cubo de la basura; **to e. up doing sth** terminar por hacer algo

endanger [ɪnˈdeɪndʒə(r)] *vt* poner en peligro

endangered [ɪnˈdeɪndʒəd] *adj* en peligro

endearing [ɪnˈdɪərɪŋ] *adj* simpático(a)

endeavour, *US* **endeavor** [ɪnˈdevə(r)] **1** *n* esfuerzo *m*
    2 *vt* intentar, procurar

ending [ˈendɪŋ] *n* final *m*

endive [ˈendaɪv] *n Bot* (**a**) *(curly)* escarola *f* (**b**) *esp US (chicory)* endibia *f*

endless [ˈendlɪs] *adj* interminable

endorse [ɪnˈdɔːs] *vt* (**a**) *Fin* endosar (**b**) *(approve)* aprobar; *(support)* apoyar

endorsement [ɪnˈdɔːsmənt] *n* (**a**) *Fin* endoso *m* (**b**) *Aut* nota *f* de sanción (**c**) *(approval)* aprobación *f*

endow [ɪnˈdaʊ] *vt* dotar; **to be endowed with** estar dotado(a) de

endurance [ɪnˈdjʊərəns] *n* resistencia *f*

endure [ɪnˈdjʊə(r)] **1** *vt* *(bear)* aguantar, soportar
    2 *vi* perdurar

enemy [ˈenəmɪ] *adj & n* enemigo(a) *(m,f)*

energetic [enəˈdʒetɪk] *adj* enérgico(a)

energy [ˈenədʒɪ] *n* energía *f*

enforce [ɪnˈfɔːs] *vt* *(law)* hacer cumplir

enforcement [ɪnˈfɔːsmənt] *n* aplicación *f*

engage [ɪnˈɡeɪdʒ] *vt* (**a**) *(hire)* contratar (**b**) *(attention)* llamar (**c**) *(in conversation)* entablar (**d**) *Tech* engranar; *Aut* **to e. the clutch** pisar el embrague

engaged [ɪnˈɡeɪdʒd] *adj* (**a**) *(betrothed)* prometido(a); **to get e.** prometerse (**b**) *(busy)* ocupado(a); *Br Tel* **it's e.** está comunicando

engagement [ɪnˈɡeɪdʒmənt] *n* (**a**) *(betrothal)* petición *f* de mano; *(period)* noviazgo *m*; **e. ring** anillo *m* de compromiso (**b**) *(appointment)* cita *f* (**c**) *Mil* combate *m*

engaging [ɪnˈɡeɪdʒɪŋ] *adj* simpático(a), agradable

engender [ɪnˈdʒendə(r)] *vt* engendrar

engine [ˈendʒɪn] *n* motor *m*; *Rail* locomotora *f*; **e. room** sala *f* de máquinas; **e. driver** maquinista *mf*

engineer [endʒɪˈnɪə(r)] **1** *n* (**a**) ingeniero(a) *m,f*; **civil e.** ingeniero de caminos (**b**) *US Rail* maquinista *mf*
    2 *vt Fig (contrive)* maquinar

engineering [endʒɪˈnɪərɪŋ] *n* ingeniería *f*; **electrical e.** electrotecnia *f*; **civil e.** ingeniería civil

England [ˈɪŋɡlənd] *n* Inglaterra

English [ˈɪŋɡlɪʃ] **1** *adj* inglés(esa)
    2 *n* (**a**) *(language)* inglés *m* (**b**) *pl* **the E.** los ingleses

Englishman [ˈɪŋɡlɪʃmən] *n* inglés *m*

English-speaking [ˈɪŋɡlɪʃspiːkɪŋ] *adj* de habla inglesa

Englishwoman [ˈɪŋɡlɪʃwʊmən] *n* inglesa *f*

engraving [ɪnˈɡreɪvɪŋ] *n* grabado *m*

engrossed [ɪnˈɡrəʊst] *adj* absorto(a) (**in** en)

engulf [ɪnˈɡʌlf] *vt* tragarse

enhance [ɪnˈhɑːns] *vt* *(beauty)* realzar; *(power, chances)* aumentar

enigma [ɪˈnɪɡmə] *n* enigma *m*

enjoy [ɪnˈdʒɔɪ] *vt* (**a**) disfrutar de; **to e. oneself** pasarlo bien (**b**) *(benefit from)* gozar de

enjoyable [ɪnˈdʒɔɪəbəl] *adj* agradable; *(amusing)* divertido(a)

enjoyment [ɪnˈdʒɔɪmənt] *n* placer *m*, gusto *m*

enlarge [ɪnˈlɑːdʒ] **1** *vt* extender, ampliar; *Phot* ampliar
    2 *vi* **to e. upon a subject** extenderse sobre un tema

enlargement [ɪnˈlɑːdʒmənt] *n Phot* ampliación *f*

enlighten [ɪnˈlaɪtən] *vt* iluminar

enlightened [ɪnˈlaɪtənd] *adj* (**a**) *(learned)* culto(a); *(informed)* bien informado(a) (**b**) *Hist* ilustrado(a)

enlightenment [ɪnˈlaɪtənmənt] *n* the Age of E. el Siglo de las Luces

enlist [ɪnˈlɪst] **1** *vt Mil* reclutar; **to e. sb's help** conseguir ayuda de algn
2 *vi Mil* alistarse

enmity [ˈenmɪtɪ] *n* enemistad *f*, hostilidad *f*

enormous [ɪˈnɔːməs] *adj* enorme
enormously [ɪˈnɔːməslɪ] *adv* enormemente; **I enjoyed myself e.** lo pasé genial

enough [ɪˈnʌf] **1** *adj* bastante, suficiente; **e. books** bastantes libros; **e. money** bastante dinero; **have we got e. petrol?** ¿tenemos suficiente gasolina?
2 *adv* bastante; **oddly e. ...** lo curioso es que ...; **sure e.** en efecto
3 *pron* lo bastante, lo suficiente; **e. to live on** lo suficiente para vivir; **it isn't e.** no basta; **more than e.** más que suficiente; *Fam* **e. is e.!** ¡ya está!; *Fam* **I've had e.!** ¡estoy harto!

enquire [ɪnˈkwaɪə(r)] *vi* preguntar
enquiry [ɪnˈkwaɪərɪ] *n* (**a**) *(question)* pregunta *f*; **to make an e.** preguntar; **enquiries** información *f* (**b**) *(investigation)* investigación *f*

enrage [ɪnˈreɪdʒ] *vt* enfurecer

enrich [ɪnˈrɪtʃ] *vt* enriquecer

enrol, *US* **enroll** [ɪnˈrəʊl] **1** *vt* matricular, inscribir
2 *vi* matricularse, inscribirse

> *Note that the Spanish verb **enrollar** is a false friend and is never a translation for the English verb **to enrol**. In Spanish, **enrollar** means "to roll up".*

enrolment [ɪnˈrəʊlmənt] *n* matrícula *f*
en route [ɒnˈruːt] *adv* en *or* por el camino

ensign [ˈensaɪn] *n* (**a**) *(flag)* bandera *f*; *Naut* pabellón *m* (**b**) *US (naval officer)* alférez *m* de fragata

enslave [ɪnˈsleɪv] *vt* esclavizar

ensue [ɪnˈsjuː] *vi* (**a**) *(follow)* seguir (**b**) *(result)* resultar (**from** de)

ensure [ɪnˈʃʊə(r)] *vt* asegurar

entail [ɪnˈteɪl] *vt (involve)* suponer

entangle [ɪnˈtæŋɡəl] *vt* enredar

enter [ˈentə(r)] **1** *vt* (**a**) *(go into)* entrar en; *Fig (join)* ingresar en (**b**) *(write down)* apuntar, anotar (**c**) **to e. one's name for a course** *(register)* matricularse en un curso (**d**) *Comput* dar entrada a
2 *vi* entrar
▸ **enter into** *vt insep* (**a**) *(agreement)* firmar; *(negotiations)* iniciar; *(bargain)* cerrar (**b**) *(relations)* establecer; *(conversation)* entablar

enterprise [ˈentəpraɪz] *n* empresa *f*; **free e.** libre empresa; **private e.** iniciativa privada; *(as a whole)* el sector privado; **public e.** el sector público

enterprising [ˈentəpraɪzɪŋ] *adj* emprendedor(a)

entertain [entəˈteɪn] **1** *vt* (**a**) *(amuse)* divertir (**b**) *(consider)* considerar; **to e. an idea** abrigar una idea
2 *vi* tener invitados

entertainer [entəˈteɪnə(r)] *n* artista *mf*

entertaining [entəˈteɪnɪŋ] *adj* divertido(a)

entertainment [entəˈteɪnmənt] *n* (**a**) diversión *f* (**b**) *Th* espectáculo *m*

enthralling [ɪnˈθrɔːlɪŋ] *adj* fascinante

enthuse [ɪnˈθjuːz] *vi* entusiasmarse (**over** por)

enthusiasm [ɪnˈθjuːzɪæzəm] *n* entusiasmo *m*

enthusiast [ɪnˈθjuːzɪæst] *n* entusiasta *mf*

enthusiastic [ɪnθjuːzɪˈæstɪk] *adj* entusiasta; *(praise)* caluroso(a); **to be e. about sth** entusiasmarse por algo

entice [ɪnˈtaɪs] *vt* seducir, atraer

enticing [ɪnˈtaɪsɪŋ] *adj* atractivo(a), tentador(a)

entire [ɪnˈtaɪə(r)] *adj* entero(a), todo(a)

entirely [ɪnˈtaɪəlɪ] *adv* (**a**) *(completely)* totalmente (**b**) *(solely)* exclusivamente

entirety [ɪnˈtaɪərɪtɪ] *n* **in its e.** en su totalidad

entitle [ɪnˈtaɪtəl] *vt* (**a**) dar derecho a; **to be entitled to** tener derecho a (**b**) *(book etc)* titular

entity [ˈentɪtɪ] *n* entidad *f*

entourage [ɒntʊˈrɑːʒ] *n* séquito *m*

entrails [ˈentreɪlz] *npl* tripas *fpl*; *Fig* entrañas *fpl*

entrance[1] [ˈentrəns] *n* (**a**) entrada *f*; **e. fee** *(to museum etc)* entrada; *(to organization)* cuota *f* (**b**) *(admission)* ingreso *m*; **e. examination** examen *m* de ingreso

entrance[2] [ɪnˈtrɑːns] *vt* encantar

entrant [ˈentrənt] *n* *(in competition)* participante *mf*; *(applicant)* aspirante *mf*

entreat [ɪnˈtriːt] *vt Fml* suplicar, rogar

entrée [ˈɒntreɪ] *n Br (first course)* entrada *f*, primer plato *m*; *US (main course)* plato principal

entrenched [ɪnˈtrentʃt] *adj* firmemente enraizado(a)

entrepreneur [ɒntrəprəˈnɜː(r)] *n* empresario(a) *m,f*

entrust [ɪnˈtrʌst] *vt* encargar (**with** de); **to e. sth to sb** dejar algo al cuidado de algn

entry [ˈentrɪ] *n* (**a**) *(entrance)* entrada *f*;

no e. *(sign)* dirección prohibida (**b**) *(in competition)* participante *mf*

enumerate [ɪ'njuːməreɪt] *vt* enumerar

enunciate [ɪ'nʌnsɪeɪt] *vt (words)* articular; *(ideas)* formular

envelop [ɪn'veləp] *vt* envolver

envelope ['envələʊp] *n* sobre *m*

envious ['envɪəs] *adj* envidioso(a); **to feel e.** tener envidia

environment [ɪn'vaɪərənmənt] *n* medio *m* ambiente

environmental [ɪnvaɪərən'mentəl] *adj* medioambiental

environmentally [ɪnvaɪərən'mentəlɪ] *adv* ecológicamente; **e. friendly** ecológico(a), que no daña el medio ambiente

envisage [ɪn'vɪzɪdʒ] *vt (imagine)* imaginarse; *(foresee)* prever

envoy ['envɔɪ] *n* enviado(a) *m,f*

envy ['envɪ] **1** *n* envidia *f*
2 *vt* envidiar, tener envidia de

enzyme ['enzaɪm] *n* enzima *m*

ephemeral [ɪ'femərəl] *adj* efímero(a)

epic ['epɪk] **1** *n* epopeya *f*
2 *adj* épico(a)

epidemic [epɪ'demɪk] *n* epidemia *f*; *Fig (of crime etc)* ola *f*

epilepsy ['epɪlepsɪ] *n* epilepsia *f*

epilogue, *US* **epilog** ['epɪlɒg] *n* epílogo *m*

episode ['epɪsəʊd] *n* episodio *m*

epistle [ɪ'pɪsəl] *n* epístola *f*

epitaph ['epɪtɑːf] *n* epitafio *m*

epitome [ɪ'pɪtəmɪ] *n Fml* personificación *f*

epitomize [ɪ'pɪtəmaɪz] *vt Fml* personificar

epoch ['iːpɒk] *n* época *f*

equable ['ekwəbəl] *adj* (**a**) *(person)* ecuánime (**b**) *(climate)* uniforme

equal ['iːkwəl] **1** *adj* igual; **to be e. to the occasion** estar a la altura de las circunstancias; **e. pay** igualdad *f* de salarios
2 *n* igual *mf*; **to treat sb as an e.** tratar a algn de igual a igual
3 *vt* (**a**) *Math* equivaler (**b**) *(match)* igualar

equality [iː'kwɒlɪtɪ] *n* igualdad *f*

equalize ['iːkwəlaɪz] **1** *vi Ftb* empatar
2 *vt* igualar

equalizer ['iːkwəlaɪzə(r)] *n Ftb* gol *m* del empate; *(of sound)* ecualizador *m*

equally ['iːkwəlɪ] *adv* igualmente; **e. pretty** igual de bonito; **to share sth e.** dividir algo en partes iguales

equanimity [ekwə'nɪmɪtɪ] *n* ecuanimidad *f*

equate [ɪ'kweɪt] *vt* equiparar, comparar (**to** con)

equation [ɪ'kweɪʒən, ɪ'kweɪʃən] *n Math* ecuación *f*

equator [ɪ'kweɪtə(r)] *n* ecuador *m*

equatorial [ekwə'tɔːrɪəl] *adj* ecuatorial

equestrian [ɪ'kwestrɪən] *adj* ecuestre

equilibrium [iːkwɪ'lɪbrɪəm] *n* equilibrio *m*

equinox ['iːkwɪnɒks] *n* equinoccio *m*

equip [ɪ'kwɪp] *vt (with tools, machines)* equipar; *(with food)* proveer

equipment [ɪ'kwɪpmənt] *n (materials)* equipo *m*; **office e.** material *m* de oficina

equipped [ɪ'kwɪpt] *adj (with tools, machines)* equipado(a); *(with skills)* dotado(a)

equitable ['ekwɪtəbəl] *adj* equitativo(a)

equities ['ekwɪtɪz] *npl* acciones ordinarias

equivalent [ɪ'kwɪvələnt] *adj & n* equivalente *(m)*; **to be e. to** equivaler a, ser equivalente a

equivocal [ɪ'kwɪvəkəl] *adj* equívoco(a)

era ['ɪərə] *n* era *f*

eradicate [ɪ'rædɪkeɪt] *vt* erradicar

erase [ɪ'reɪz] *vt* borrar

eraser [*Br* ɪ'reɪzə(r), *US* ɪ'reɪsər] *n* goma *f* de borrar

erect [ɪ'rekt] **1** *adj* (**a**) *(upright)* erguido(a) (**b**) *(penis)* erecto(a)
2 *vt (monument)* levantar, eregir

erection [ɪ'rekʃən] *n* (**a**) *(of building)* construcción *f* (**b**) *(penis)* erección *f*

ermine ['ɜːmɪn] *n* armiño *m*

erode [ɪ'rəʊd] *vt* (**a**) *(rock, soil)* erosionar (**b**) *(metal)* corroer, desgastar; *Fig (power, confidence)* hacer perder

erosion [ɪ'rəʊʒən] *n Geol* erosión *f*

erotic [ɪ'rɒtɪk] *adj* erótico(a)

err [ɜː(r)] *vi* errar; **to e. on the side of caution** pecar de prudente

errand ['erənd] *n* recado *m*; **e. boy** recadero *m*

erratic [ɪ'rætɪk] *adj (performance, behaviour)* irregular; *(weather)* muy variable; *(person)* caprichoso(a)

erroneous [ɪ'rəʊnɪəs] *adj* erróneo(a)

error ['erə(r)] *n* error *m*, equivocación *f*

erupt [ɪ'rʌpt] *vi* (**a**) *(volcano)* entrar en erupción; *(violence)* estallar (**b**) **his skin erupted in a rash** le salió una erupción

eruption [ɪ'rʌpʃən] *n* erupción *f*

escalate ['eskəleɪt] *vi (war)* intensificarse; *(prices)* aumentar; *(change)* convertirse (**into** en)

escalation [eskə'leɪʃən] *n (of war)* intensificación *f*, escalada *f*; *(of prices)* subida *f*

escalator ['eskəleɪtə(r)] *n* escalera mecánica

🖋 Note that the Spanish word **escalador** is a false friend and is never a translation for the English word **escalator**. In Spanish, **escalador** means "climber, mountaineer".

escalope ['eskələp] n escalope m
escapade ['eskəpeɪd] n aventura f

🖋 Note that the Spanish word **escapada** is a false friend and is never a translation for the English word **escapade**. In Spanish, **escapada** means both "escape" and "quick trip".

escape [ɪ'skeɪp] **1** n huída f, fuga f; (of gas) escape m; **e. route** vía f de escape
   2 vi escaparse
   3 vt (**a**) (avoid) evitar, huir de; **to e. punishment** librarse del castigo (**b**) Fig **his name escapes me** no recuerdo su nombre
escapism [ɪ'skeɪpɪzəm] n evasión f
escort 1 n ['eskɔːt] (**a**) (companion) acompañante mf (**b**) Mil escolta f
   2 vt [ɪ'skɔːt] (**a**) (accompany) acompañar (**b**) (protect) escoltar
Eskimo ['eskɪməʊ] adj & n esquimal (mf)
esoteric [esəʊ'terɪk] adj esotérico(a)
especial [ɪ'speʃəl] adj especial
especially [ɪ'speʃəlɪ] adv especialmente, sobre todo
espionage ['espɪənɑːʒ] n espionaje m
esplanade [esplə'neɪd] n paseo marítimo
espouse [ɪ'spaʊz] vt Fml (cause) abrazar, adoptar
espresso [e'spresəʊ] n **e. (coffee)** café m exprés
esquire [ɪ'skwaɪə(r)] n Br señor m; **Timothy Whiteman E.** Sr. Don Timothy Whiteman
essay ['eseɪ] n Educ redacción f
essence ['esəns] n esencia f; **in e.** esencialmente
essential [ɪ'senʃəl] **1** adj esencial, imprescindible
   2 n necesidad básica; **the essentials** lo fundamental
essentially [ɪ'senʃəlɪ] adv esencialmente
establish [ɪ'stæblɪʃ] vt (**a**) (found) establecer; (business) montar (**b**) Jur **to e. a fact** probar un hecho; **to e. the truth** demostrar la verdad
established [ɪ'stæblɪʃt] adj (person) establecido(a); (fact) conocido(a)
establishment [ɪ'stæblɪʃmənt] n establecimiento m; **the E.** el sistema
estate [ɪ'steɪt] n (**a**) (land) finca f; Br **e.**

agent agente mf inmobiliario(a); Br **e. car** coche m modelo familiar (**b**) **(housing) e.** zona urbanizada (**c**) (property) bienes mpl (**d**) (inheritance) herencia f
esteem [ɪ'stiːm] **1** n **to hold sb in great e.** apreciar mucho a algn
   2 vt estimar
esthetic [es'θetɪk] adj US estético(a)
estimate 1 n ['estɪmɪt] (calculation) cálculo m; (likely cost of work) presupuesto m; **rough e.** cálculo aproximado
   2 vt ['estɪmeɪt] calcular; Fig pensar, creer
estimation [estɪ'meɪʃən] n (**a**) (opinion) juicio m, opinión f (**b**) (esteem) estima f
Estonia [e'stəʊnɪə] n Estonia
Estonian [e'stəʊnɪən] **1** adj estonio(a)
   2 n (**a**) (person) estonio(a) m,f (**b**) (language) estonio m
estrange [ɪ'streɪndʒ] vt **to become estranged (from)** alejarse (de)
Estremadura [estreɪmə'dʊrə] n Extremadura
estuary ['estjʊərɪ] n estuario m
etching ['etʃɪŋ] n aguafuerte m
eternal [ɪ'tɜːnəl] adj eterno(a), incesante; **e. triangle** triángulo amoroso
eternity [ɪ'tɜːnɪtɪ] n eternidad f
ether ['iːθə(r)] n éter m
ethereal [ɪ'θɪərɪəl] adj etéreo(a)
ethical ['eθɪkəl] adj ético(a)
ethics ['eθɪks] n ética f
Ethiopia [iːθɪ'əʊpɪə] n Etiopía
ethnic ['eθnɪk] adj étnico(a)
ethos ['iːθɒs] n carácter distintivo
etiquette ['etɪket] n protocolo m, etiqueta f
etymology [etɪ'mɒlədʒɪ] n etimología f
EU [iː'juː] n (abbr **European Union**) UE f
eucalyptus [juːkə'lɪptəs] n eucalipto m
euphemism ['juːfɪmɪzəm] n eufemismo m
euphoria [juː'fɔːrɪə] n euforia f
euro ['jʊərəʊ] n (pl **euros**) (European currency) euro m
Eurocheque ['jʊərəʊtʃek] n eurocheque m
Eurocrat ['jʊərəʊkræt] n eurócrata mf
Euro-MP ['jʊərəʊempiː] n eurodiputado(a) m,f
Europe ['jʊərəp] n Europa
European [jʊərə'piːən] adj & n europeo(a) (m,f); **E. Economic Community** Comunidad Económica Europea
Eurosceptic ['jʊərəʊskeptɪk] n Br euroescéptico(a) m,f
euthanasia [juːθə'neɪzɪə] n eutanasia f
evacuate [ɪ'vækjʊeɪt] vt evacuar

evacuation [ɪvækjʊ'eɪʃən] n evacuación f

evade [ɪ'veɪd] vt evadir

evaluate [ɪ'væljʊeɪt] vt evaluar

evaluation [ɪvæljʊ'eɪʃən] n evaluación f

evangelical [iːvæn'dʒelɪkəl] adj evangélico(a)

evangelist [ɪ'vændʒɪlɪst] n evangelista mf

evaporate [ɪ'væpəreɪt] **1** vt evaporar; **evaporated milk** leche condensada sin endulzar
2 vi evaporarse; Fig desvanecerse

evasion [ɪ'veɪʒən] n (**a**) evasión f (**b**) (evasive answer) evasiva f

evasive [ɪ'veɪsɪv] adj evasivo(a)

eve [iːv] n víspera f; **on the e. of** en vísperas de

even ['iːvən] **1** adj (**a**) (smooth) liso(a); (level) llano(a)
(**b**) (regular) uniforme
(**c**) (equally balanced) igual; Sport **to be e.** ir empatados(as); **to get e. with sb** desquitarse con algn
(**d**) (number) par
(**e**) (at the same level) a nivel
(**f**) (quantity) exacto(a)
2 adv (**a**) incluso, hasta, aun; **e. now** incluso ahora; **e. so** aun así; **e. the children knew** hasta los niños lo sabían
(**b**) (negative) ni siquiera; **she can't e. write her name** ni siquiera sabe escribir su nombre; **without e. speaking** sin hablar siquiera
(**c**) (before comparative) aun, todavía; **e. worse** aun peor
(**d**) **e. as** mientras; **e. if** incluso si; **e. though** aunque
3 vt igualar

evening ['iːvnɪŋ] n (**a**) (early) tarde f; (late) noche f; **in the e.** por la tarde; **tomorrow e.** mañana por la tarde; **e. class** clase nocturna; **e. dress** (for man) traje m de etiqueta; (for woman) traje de noche; **e. paper** periódico vespertino (**b**) (greeting) **good e.!** (early) ¡buenas tardes!; (late) ¡buenas noches!

event [ɪ'vent] n (**a**) (happening) suceso m, acontecimiento m (**b**) (case) caso m; **at all events** en todo caso; **in the e. of fire** en caso de incendio (**c**) Sport prueba f

eventful [ɪ'ventfʊl] adj **an e. day** (busy) un día agitado; (memorable) un día memorable

eventual [ɪ'ventʃʊəl] adj (ultimate) final; (resulting) consiguiente

> *ℰ* Note that the Spanish word **eventual** is a false friend and is never a translation for the English word **eventual**. In Spanish, **eventual** means both "possible" and "temporary".

eventuality [ɪventʃʊ'ælɪtɪ] n eventualidad f

eventually [ɪ'ventʃʊəlɪ] adv finalmente

> *ℰ* Note that the Spanish word **eventualmente** is a false friend and is never a translation for the English word **eventually**. In Spanish, **eventualmente** means both "by chance" and "possibly".

ever ['evə(r)] adv (**a**) nunca, jamás; **stronger than e.** más fuerte que nunca (**b**) (interrogative) alguna vez; **have you e. been there?** ¿has estado allí alguna vez? (**c**) (always) siempre; **for e.** para siempre; **for e. and e.** para siempre jamás (**d**) (emphasis) **how e. did you manage it?** ¿cómo diablos lo conseguiste?; **why e. not?** ¿por qué no?; Fam **e. so expensive** tan carísimo; **e. such a lot of money** tantísimo dinero; **thank you e. so much** muchísimas gracias

evergreen ['evəgriːn] **1** adj de hoja perenne
2 n árbol m/planta f de hoja perenne

everlasting [evə'lɑːstɪŋ] adj eterno(a)

evermore [evə'mɔː(r)] adv **for e.** para siempre jamás

every ['evrɪ] adj (**a**) (each) cada; **e. now and then** de vez en cuando; **e. day** todos los días; **e. other day** cada dos días; **e. one of you** todos(as) vosotros(as); **e. citizen** todo ciudadano (**b**) **you had e. right to be angry** tenías toda la razón para estar enfadado

everybody ['evrɪbɒdɪ] pron todo el mundo, todos(as)

everyday ['evrɪdeɪ] adj diario(a), de todos los días; **an e. occurrence** un suceso cotidiano

everyone ['evrɪwʌn] pron todo el mundo, todos(as)

everyplace ['evrɪpleɪs] adv US = everywhere

everything ['evrɪθɪŋ] pron todo; **he eats e.** come de todo; **she means e. to me** ella lo es todo para mí

everywhere ['evrɪweə(r)] adv en todas partes, por todas partes

evict [ɪ'vɪkt] vt desahuciar

evidence ['evɪdəns] n (**a**) (proof) evidencia f (**b**) Jur testimonio m; **to give e.** prestar declaración (**c**) (sign) indicio m, señal f; **to be in e.** dejarse notar

evident ['evɪdənt] *adj* evidente, manifiesto(a)

evidently ['evɪdəntlɪ] *adv* evidentemente, al parecer

evil ['iːvəl] **1** *adj (wicked)* malo(a), malvado(a); *(harmful)* nocivo(a); *(unfortunate)* aciago(a)
2 *n* mal *m*

evocative [ɪ'vɒkətɪv] *adj* evocador(a)

evoke [ɪ'vəʊk] *vt* evocar

evolution [iːvə'luːʃən] *n* evolución f; *Biol* desarrollo *m*

evolve [ɪ'vɒlv] **1** *vi (species)* evolucionar; *(ideas)* desarrollarse
2 *vt* desarrollar

ewe [juː] *n* oveja f

ex [eks] *n* **her ex** su ex marido; **his ex** su ex mujer

ex- [eks] *pref* ex, antiguo(a); **ex-minister** ex ministro *m*

exacerbate [ɪg'zæsəbeɪt] *vt* exacerbar

exact [ɪg'zækt] **1** *adj (accurate)* exacto(a); *(definition)* preciso(a); **this e. spot** ese mismo lugar
2 *vt* exigir

exacting [ɪg'zæktɪŋ] *adj* exigente

exactly [ɪg'zæktlɪ] *adv* exactamente; precisamente; **e.!** ¡exacto!

exaggerate [ɪg'zædʒəreɪt] *vi & vt* exagerar

exaggeration [ɪgzædʒə'reɪʃən] *n* exageración f

exalt [ɪg'zɔːlt] *vt Fml* exaltar

exam [ɪg'zæm] *n Fam* examen *m*

examination [ɪgzæmɪ'neɪʃən] *n* (**a**) *Educ* examen *m*; **to sit an e.** hacer un examen (**b**) *Med* reconocimiento *m* (**c**) *Jur* interrogatorio *m*

examine [ɪg'zæmɪn] *vt Educ* examinar; *(customs)* registrar; *Med* hacer un reconocimiento médico a; *Jur* interrogar

examiner [ɪg'zæmɪnə(r)] *n* examinador(a) *m,f*

example [ɪg'zɑːmpəl] *n* ejemplo *m*; *(specimen)* ejemplar *m*; **for e.** por ejemplo

exasperate [ɪg'zɑːspəreɪt] *vt* exasperar

exasperation [ɪgzɑːspə'reɪʃən] *n* exasperación f

excavate ['ekskəveɪt] *vt* excavar

excavation [ekskə'veɪʃən] *n* excavación f

exceed [ek'siːd] *vt* exceder, sobrepasar

exceedingly [ek'siːdɪŋlɪ] *adv* extremadamente, sumamente

excel [ɪk'sel] **1** *vi* sobresalir
2 *vt* superar

excellency ['eksələnsɪ] *n* **His E.** Su Excelencia

excellent ['eksələnt] *adj* excelente

except [ɪk'sept] **1** *prep* excepto, salvo; **e. for the little ones** excepto los pequeños; **e. that ...** salvo que ...
2 *vt* exceptuar

exception [ɪk'sepʃən] *n* (**a**) excepción f; **with the e. of** a excepción de; **without e.** sin excepción (**b**) *(objection)* objeción f; **to take e. to sth** ofenderse por algo

exceptional [ɪk'sepʃənəl] *adj* excepcional

excerpt ['eksɜːpt] *n* extracto *m*

excess **1** *n* [ɪk'ses] exceso *m*
2 *adj* ['ekses] excedente; **e. baggage** exceso *m* de equipaje; **e. fare** suplemento *m*

excessive [ɪk'sesɪv] *adj* excesivo(a)

excessively [ɪk'sesɪvlɪ] *adv* excesivamente, en exceso

exchange [ɪks'tʃeɪndʒ] **1** *n* (**a**) cambio *m*; **e. of ideas** intercambio *m* de ideas; **in e. for** a cambio de (**b**) *Fin* **e. rate** tipo *m* de cambio (**c**) **(telephone) e.** central telefónica
2 *vt* (**a**) intercambiar; **to e. blows** golpearse (**b**) *(prisoners)* canjear

exchequer [ɪks'tʃekə(r)] *n Br* **the E.** Hacienda f; **Chancellor of the E.** Ministro *m* de Hacienda

excise ['eksaɪz] *n* impuesto *m* sobre el consumo; **e. duty** derechos *mpl* de aduana

excitable [ɪk'saɪtəbəl] *adj* excitable

excite [ɪk'saɪt] *vt (stimulate)* excitar; *(move)* emocionar; *(enthuse)* entusiasmar; *(arouse)* provocar

excitement [ɪk'saɪtmənt] *n (stimulation)* excitación f; *(emotion)* emoción f; *(commotion)* agitación f

exciting [ɪk'saɪtɪŋ] *adj* apasionante, emocionante

exclaim [ɪk'skleɪm] **1** *vi* exclamar
2 *vt* gritar

exclamation [eksklə'meɪʃən] *n* exclamación f; **e.** *Br* **mark** *or US* **point** signo *m* de admiración

exclude [ɪk'skluːd] *vt* excluir; *(from club)* no admitir

excluding [ɪk'skluːdɪŋ] *prep* excepto

exclusion [ɪk'skluːʒən] *n* exclusión f

exclusive [ɪk'skluːsɪv] **1** *adj* exclusivo(a); *(neighbourhood)* selecto(a); *(club)* cerrado(a)
2 *n Press* exclusiva f

exclusively [ɪk'skluːsɪvlɪ] *adv* exclusivamente

excommunicate [ekskə'mjuːnɪkeɪt] *vt* excomulgar

excrement ['ekskrɪmənt] *n* excremento *m*

excruciating [ɪk'skruːʃɪeɪtɪŋ] *adj* insoportable

excruciatingly [ɪk'skruːʃɪeɪtɪŋlɪ] *adv* horriblemente

excursion [ɪk'skɜːʃən] *n* excursión *f*

excusable [ɪk'skjuːzəbəl] *adj* perdonable

excuse 1 *vt* [ɪk'skjuːz] (**a**) perdonar, disculpar; **e. me!** *(to attract attention)* ¡perdón!, ¡oiga (por favor)!; *(when trying to get past)* con permiso; **may I be excused for a moment?** ¿puedo salir un momento? (**b**) *(exempt)* dispensar (**c**) *(justify)* justificar
2 *n* [ɪk'skjuːs] excusa *f*; **to make an e.** dar excusas

ex-directory [eksdɪ'rektərɪ] *adj Br Tel* = que no se encuentra en la guía telefónica

execute ['eksɪkjuːt] *vt* (**a**) *(order)* cumplir; *(task)* realizar (**b**) *Jur* cumplir (**c**) *(person)* ejecutar

execution [eksɪ'kjuːʃən] *n* (**a**) *(of order)* cumplimiento *m*; *(of task)* realización *f* (**b**) *Jur* cumplimiento *m* (**c**) *(of person)* ejecución *f*

executioner [eksɪ'kjuːʃənə(r)] *n* verdugo *m*

executive [ɪg'zekjʊtɪv] **1** *adj* ejecutivo(a)
2 *n* ejecutivo(a) *m,f*

executor [ɪg'zekjʊtə(r)] *n* albacea *m*

exemplary [ɪg'zemplərɪ] *adj* ejemplar

exemplify [ɪg'zemplɪfaɪ] *vt* ejemplificar

exempt [ɪg'zempt] **1** *vt* eximir (**from** de)
2 *adj* exento(a); **e. from tax** libre de impuesto

exemption [ɪg'zempʃən] *n* exención *f*

exercise ['eksəsaɪz] **1** *n* ejercicio *m*; **e. book** cuaderno *m*
2 *vt* (**a**) *(rights, duties)* ejercer (**b**) *(dog)* sacar de paseo
3 *vi* hacer ejercicio

exert [ɪg'zɜːt] *vt* *(influence)* ejercer; **to e. oneself** esforzarse

exertion [ɪg'zɜːʃən] *n* esfuerzo *m*

exhale [eks'heɪl] **1** *vt* *(breathe)* exhalar
2 *vi* espirar

exhaust [ɪg'zɔːst] **1** *vt* agotar
2 *n* *(gas)* gases *mpl* de combustión; **e. pipe** tubo *m* de escape

exhausted [ɪg'zɔːstɪd] *adj* agotado(a)

exhaustion [ɪg'zɔːstʃən] *n* agotamiento *m*

exhaustive [ɪg'zɔːstɪv] *adj* exhaustivo(a)

exhibit [ɪg'zɪbɪt] **1** *n* *Art* objeto expuesto; *Jur* prueba *f* instrumental
2 *vt Art* exponer; *(surprise etc)* mostrar

exhibition [eksɪ'bɪʃən] *n* exposición *f*

exhibitionist [eksɪ'bɪʃənɪst] *adj & n* exhibicionista *(mf)*

exhilarating [ɪg'zɪləreɪtɪŋ] *adj* estimulante

exhilaration [ɪgzɪlə'reɪʃən] *n* regocijo *m*

exhume [eks'hjuːm] *vt* exhumar

exile ['eksaɪl] **1** *n* (**a**) *(banishment)* exilio *m* (**b**) *(person)* exiliado(a) *m,f*
2 *vt* exiliar

exist [ɪg'zɪst] *vi* existir; *(have little money)* malvivir

existence [ɪg'zɪstəns] *n* existencia *f*

existing [ɪg'zɪstɪŋ] *adj* existente, actual

exit ['eksɪt] **1** *n* (**a**) salida *f* (**b**) *Th* mutis *m*
2 *vi Th* hacer mutis

> ✎ Note that the Spanish word **éxito** is a false friend and is never a translation for the English word **exit**. In Spanish, **éxito** means "success".

exodus ['eksədəs] *n* éxodo *m*

exonerate [ɪg'zɒnəreɪt] *vt Fml* exonerar (**from** de)

exorbitant [ɪg'zɔːbɪtənt] *adj* exorbitante, desorbitado(a)

exotic [ɪg'zɒtɪk] *adj* exótico(a)

expand [ɪk'spænd] **1** *vt (enlarge)* ampliar; *(gas, metal)* dilatar
2 *vi (grow)* ampliarse; *(metal)* dilatarse; *(become more friendly)* abrirse
▸ **expand on** *vt insep* ampliar

expanse [ɪk'spæns] *n* extensión *f*

expansion [ɪk'spænʃən] *n (in size)* expansión *f*; *(of gas, metal)* dilatación *f*

expatriate 1 *adj & n* [eks'pætrɪɪt] expatriado(a) *(m,f)*
2 *vt* [eks'pætrɪeɪt] expatriar

expect [ɪk'spekt] **1** *vt* (**a**) *(anticipate)* esperar; **I half-expected that to happen** suponía que iba a ocurrir (**b**) *(demand)* contar con (**c**) *(suppose)* suponer
2 *vi Fam* **to be expecting** estar embarazada

expectancy [ɪk'spektənsɪ] *n* expectación *f*

expectant [ɪk'spektənt] *adj* ilusionado(a); **e. mother** mujer embarazada

expectation [ekspek'teɪʃən] *n* esperanza *f*; **contrary to e.** contrariamente a lo que se esperaba

expedient [ɪk'spiːdɪənt] **1** *adj* conveniente, oportuno(a)
2 *n* expediente *m*, recurso *m*

expedition [ekspɪ'dɪʃən] *n* expedición *f*

expel [ɪk'spel] *vt* expulsar

expend [ɪk'spend] *vt* gastar

expendable [ɪk'spendəbəl] *adj* prescindible

expenditure [ɪk'spendɪtʃə(r)] *n* desembolso *m*

expense [ɪk'spens] *n* gasto *m*; **all expenses paid** con todos los gastos pagados; **to spare no e.** no escatimar gastos; *Fig* **at the e. of** a costa de; **e. account** cuenta *f* de gastos de representación

expensive [ɪk'spensɪv] *adj* caro(a), costoso(a)

experience [ɪk'spɪərɪəns] **1** *n* experiencia *f*

2 *vt* (*sensation*) experimentar; (*difficulty, loss*) sufrir

experienced [ɪk'spɪərɪənst] *adj* experimentado(a)

experiment [ɪk'sperɪmənt] **1** *n* experimento *m*

2 *vi* experimentar, hacer experimentos (**on** *or* **with** con)

experimental [ɪkˌsperɪ'mentəl] *adj* experimental

expert ['ekspɜːt] **1** *adj* experto(a)

2 *n* experto(a) *m,f*, especialista *mf*

expertise [ekspɜː'tiːz] *n* pericia *f*

expire [ɪk'spaɪə(r)] *vi* (a) (*die*) expirar; (*mandate*) terminar (b) *Com & Ins* vencer; (*ticket*) caducar

expiry [ɪk'spaɪərɪ] *n* vencimiento *m*; **e. date** fecha *f* de caducidad

explain [ɪk'spleɪn] **1** *vt* explicar; (*clarify*) aclarar; **to e. oneself** justificarse

2 *vi* explicarse

explanation [eksplə'neɪʃən] *n* explicación *f*; (*clarification*) aclaración *f*

explanatory [ɪk'splænətərɪ] *adj* explicativo(a), aclaratorio(a)

explicit [ɪk'splɪsɪt] *adj* explícito(a)

explode [ɪk'spləʊd] **1** *vt* (a) (*bomb*) hacer explotar (b) *Fig* (*theory*) echar por tierra

2 *vi* (*bomb*) estallar, explotar; *Fig* **to e. with** *or* **in anger** montar en cólera

exploit 1 *n* ['eksplɔɪt] proeza *f*, hazaña *f*

2 *vt* [ek'splɔɪt] explotar

exploitation [eksplɔɪ'teɪʃən] *n* explotación *f*

exploratory [ek'splɒrətərɪ] *adj* exploratorio(a)

explore [ɪk'splɔː(r)] *vt* explorar

explorer [ɪk'splɔːrə(r)] *n* explorador(a) *m,f*

explosion [ɪk'spləʊʒən] *n* explosión *f*

explosive [ɪk'spləʊsɪv] **1** *adj* explosivo(a); **e. issue** asunto delicado

2 *n* explosivo *m*

exponent [ɪk'spəʊnənt] *n* exponente *m*; (*supporter*) defensor(a) *m,f*

export 1 *vt* [ɪk'spɔːt] exportar

2 *n* ['ekspɔːt] (a) (*trade*) exportación *f*

(b) (*commodity*) artículo *m* de exportación

exporter [ek'spɔːtə(r)] *n* exportador(a) *m,f*

expose [ɪk'spəʊz] *vt* (*uncover*) exponer; (*secret*) revelar; (*plot*) descubrir; **to e. oneself** exhibirse desnudo

exposed [ɪk'spəʊzd] *adj* expuesto(a)

exposure [ɪk'spəʊʒə(r)] *n* (a) (*to light, cold, heat*) exposición *f*; **to die of e.** morir de frío (b) *Phot* fotografía *f*; **e. meter** fotómetro *m* (c) (*of criminal*) descubrimiento *m*

expound [ɪk'spaʊnd] *vt* exponer

express [ɪk'spres] **1** *adj* (a) (*explicit*) expreso(a) (b) *Br* (*letter*) urgente; **e. train** expreso *m*

2 *n* *Rail* expreso *m*

3 *vt* expresar

4 *adv* **send it e.** mándalo urgente

expression [ɪk'spreʃən] *n* expresión *f*

expressly [ɪk'spreslɪ] *adv* *Fml* expresamente

expressway [ɪk'spresweɪ] *n* *US* autopista *f*

expulsion [ɪk'spʌlʃən] *n* expulsión *f*

exquisite [ɪk'skwɪzɪt] *adj* exquisito(a)

extend [ɪk'stend] **1** *vt* (a) (*enlarge*) ampliar; (*lengthen*) alargar; (*increase*) aumentar; *Fig* **the prohibition was extended to cover cigarettes** extendieron la prohibición a los cigarrillos (b) (*give*) rendir, dar; **to e. a welcome to sb** recibir a algn (c) (*prolong*) prolongar

2 *vi* (a) (*stretch*) extenderse (b) (*last*) prolongarse

extension [ɪk'stenʃən] *n* (a) extensión *f*; (*of time*) prórroga *f* (b) *Constr* anexo *m*

extensive [ɪk'stensɪv] *adj* extenso(a)

extent [ɪk'stent] *n* (a) (*area*) extensión *f* (b) **to some e.** hasta cierto punto; **to a large e.** en gran parte; **to a lesser e.** en menor grado; **to such an e.** hasta tal punto

extenuating [ɪk'stenjʊeɪtɪŋ] *adj* atenuante

exterior [ɪk'stɪərɪə(r)] **1** *adj* exterior, externo(a)

2 *n* exterior *m*

exterminate [ɪk'stɜːmɪneɪt] *vt* exterminar

extermination [ɪkstɜːmɪ'neɪʃən] *n* exterminación *f*, exterminio *m*

external [ɪk'stɜːnəl] *adj* externo(a), exterior

extinct [ɪk'stɪŋkt] *adj* extinguido(a)

extinction [ɪk'stɪŋkʃən] *n* extinción *f*

extinguish [ɪk'stɪŋgwɪʃ] *vt* extinguir, apagar

extinguisher [ɪkˈstɪŋgwɪʃə(r)] *n* extintor *m*

extol, *US* **extoll** [ɪkˈstəʊl] *vt* ensalzar, alabar

extort [ɪkˈstɔːt] *vt* arrancar; *(money)* sacar

extortion [ɪkˈstɔːʃən] *n* extorsión *f*

extortionate [ɪkˈstɔːʃənɪt] *adj* desorbitado(a)

extra [ˈekstrə] **1** *adj* extra; *(spare)* de sobra; **e. time** *(in soccer match)* prórroga *f*
  2 *adv* extra; **e. fine** extra fino
  3 *n* *(additional charge)* suplemento *m*; *Cin* extra *mf*; *(newspaper)* edición *f* especial

extract 1 *n* [ˈekstrækt] extracto *m*
  2 *vt* [ɪkˈstrækt] *(tooth, information)* extraer; *(confession)* arrancar

extraction [ɪkˈstrækʃən] *n* extracción *f*

extracurricular [ekstrəkəˈrɪkjʊlə(r)] *adj* extracurricular

extradite [ˈekstrədaɪt] *vt* extraditar

extramarital [ekstrəˈmærɪtəl] *adj* extramatrimonial

extramural [ekstrəˈmjʊərəl] *adj* **e. course** = curso para estudiantes libres

extraordinary [ɪkˈstrɔːdənərɪ] *adj* *(meeting)* extraordinario(a); *(behaviour etc)* extraño(a)

extravagance [ɪkˈstrævəgəns] *n* *(with money)* derroche *m*; *(of behaviour)* extravagancia *f*

extravagant [ɪkˈstrævəgənt] *adj* *(wasteful)* derrochador(a); *(excessive)* exagerado(a); *(luxurious)* lujoso(a)

extreme [ɪkˈstriːm] **1** *adj* extremo(a); **an e. case** un caso excepcional; **to hold e. views** tener opiniones radicales
  2 *n* extremo *m*; **in the e.** en sumo grado

extremely [ɪkˈstriːmlɪ] *adv* extremadamente; **I'm e. sorry** lo siento de veras

extremist [ɪkˈstriːmɪst] *n* extremista *mf*

extremity [ɪkˈstremɪtɪ] *n* extremidad *f*

extricate [ˈekstrɪkeɪt] *vt* sacar; **to e. oneself (from)** lograr salir (de)

extrovert [ˈekstrəvɜːt] *adj & n* extrovertido(a) *(m,f)*

exuberant [ɪgˈzjuːbərənt] *adj* exuberante

exude [ɪgˈzjuːd] *vt & vi* *(moisture, sap)* exudar; *Fig* rebosar

exultant [ɪgˈzʌltənt] *adj* jubiloso(a)

eye [aɪ] **1** *n* ojo *m*; *Fig* **I couldn't believe my eyes** no podía creerlo; *Fig* **in the eyes of** según; *Fig* **not to take one's eyes off sb/sth** no quitar la vista de encima a algn/algo; *Fig* **to catch sb's e.** llamar la atención a algn; *Fig* **to have an e. for** tener buen ojo para; *Fig* **to make eyes at sb** echar miraditas a algn; *Fig* **to see e. to e. with sb** estar de acuerdo con algn; *Fig* **to turn a blind e. (to)** hacer la vista gorda (a); *Fig* **with an e. to** con miras a; **to keep an e. on sb/sth** vigilar a algn/algo; **to keep an e. out for** estar pendiente de; **black e.** ojo morado; *US* **e. doctor** óptico(a) *m,f*
  2 *vt* observar

eyeball [ˈaɪbɔːl] *n* globo *m* ocular

eyebrow [ˈaɪbraʊ] *n* ceja *f*

eyecatching [ˈaɪkætʃɪŋ] *adj* llamativo(a)

eye-drops [ˈaɪdrɒps] *npl* *(medicine)* colirio *m*

eyeglasses [ˈaɪglɑːsɪz] *npl* *US* *(spectacles)* gafas *fpl*, *Am* lentes *mpl*, anteojos *mpl*

eyelash [ˈaɪlæʃ] *n* pestaña *f*

eyelid [ˈaɪlɪd] *n* párpado *m*

eyeliner [ˈaɪlaɪnə(r)] *n* lápiz *m* de ojos

eye-opener [ˈaɪəʊpənə(r)] *n* revelación *f*, gran sorpresa *f*

eyeshadow [ˈaɪʃædəʊ] *n* sombra *f* de ojos

eyesight [ˈaɪsaɪt] *n* vista *f*

eyesore [ˈaɪsɔː(r)] *n* monstruosidad *f*

eyestrain [ˈaɪstreɪn] *n* vista cansada

eyewash [ˈaɪwɒʃ] *n* colirio *m*; *Fig* **it's all e.** eso son disparates

eyewitness [ˈaɪwɪtnɪs] *n* testigo *mf* ocular

F

F, f [ef] *n* (**a**) *(the letter)* F, f *f* (**b**) *Mus* F fa *m*
F [ef] *(abbr* **Fahrenheit**) F
fable ['feɪbəl] *n* fábula *f*
fabric ['fæbrɪk] *n* (**a**) *Tex* tejido *m* (**b**) *Constr* estructura *f*

> 🔎 Note that the Spanish word **fábrica** is a false friend and is never a translation for the English word **fabric**. In Spanish, **fábrica** means "factory".

fabricate ['fæbrɪkeɪt] *vt* fabricar
fabrication [fæbrɪ'keɪʃən] *n* *Fig* fabricación *f*
fabulous ['fæbjʊləs] *adj* fabuloso(a)
façade [fə'sɑːd, fæ'sɑːd] *n* fachada *f*
face [feɪs] **1** *n* (**a**) cara *f*, rostro *m*; **f. to f.** cara a cara; **I told him to his f.** se lo dije en la cara; **she slammed the door in my f.** me dió con la puerta en las narices; **to look sb in the f.** mirarle a algn a la cara; **f. cloth** paño *m*; **f. cream** crema *f* facial; **f. pack** mascarilla *f* facial
(**b**) *(expression)* cara *f*, expresión *f*; **to pull a long f.** poner cara larga; **to pull faces** hacer muecas
(**c**) *(surface)* superficie *f*; *(of card, coin)* cara *f*; *(of watch)* esfera *f*; **f. down/up** boca abajo/arriba; *Fig* **in the f. of danger** ante el peligro; **f. value** valor *m* nominal; **to take sth at f. value** entender algo sólo en su sentido literal
(**d**) *(appearance)* aspecto *m*; **on the f. of it** a primera vista; **to lose f.** desprestigiarse; **to save f.** salvar las apariencias
2 *vt* (**a**) *(look on to)* dar a; *(be opposite)* estar enfrente de
(**b**) **to f. the wall/window** *(of person)* estar de cara a la pared/ventana
(**c**) *(confront)* hacer frente a; **let's f. it** hay que reconocerlo; **to f. up to** hacer cara a
(**d**) *(tolerate)* soportar, aguantar
3 *vi* **to f. on to** dar a; **to f. towards** mirar hacia; **f. this way** vuélvase de este lado
facelift ['feɪslɪft] *n* *Med* lifting *m*; *Fig* renovación *f*
facet ['fæsɪt] *n* faceta *f*
facetious [fə'siːʃəs] *adj* bromista

facial ['feɪʃəl] *adj* facial
facile ['fæsaɪl] *adj* superficial
facilitate [fə'sɪlɪteɪt] *vt* facilitar
facility [fə'sɪlɪtɪ] *n* (**a**) *(ease)* facilidad *f* (**b**) **facilities** *(means)* facilidades *fpl*; **credit facilities** facilidades de crédito (**c**) **facilities** *(rooms, equipment)* instalaciones *fpl*; **cooking facilities** derecho *m* a cocina
facing ['feɪsɪŋ] *adj* de enfrente
facsimile [fæk'sɪmɪlɪ] *n* (**a**) *(copy)* facsímil *m* (**b**) *(message)* telefax *m* (**c**) *(machine)* facsímil *m*
fact [fækt] *n* hecho *m*; **as a matter of f.** de hecho; **the f. that he confessed** el hecho de que confesara; **in f.** en realidad
fact-finding ['fæktfaɪndɪŋ] *adj* investigador(a)
faction ['fækʃən] *n* *(group)* facción *f*
factor ['fæktə(r)] *n* factor *m*
factory ['fæktərɪ] *n* fábrica *f*
factual ['fæktʃʊəl] *adj* **a f. error** un error de hecho
faculty ['fækəltɪ] *n* (**a**) facultad *f* (**b**) *US Univ* profesorado *m*, cuerpo *m* docente
fad [fæd] *n* *Fam* *(craze)* moda pasajera; *(whim)* capricho *m*
fade [feɪd] *vi* *(colour)* desteñirse; *(flower)* marchitarse; *(light)* apagarse
▸ **fade away** *vi* desvanecerse
▸ **fade in, fade out** *vt sep* *Cin & TV* fundir
faded ['feɪdɪd] *adj* *(colour)* desteñido(a); *(flower)* marchito(a)
fag [fæg] *n* (**a**) *Br Fam* *(cigarette)* pitillo *m* (**b**) *US very Fam* *(homosexual)* marica *m*
faggot ['fægət] *n* (**a**) *Br* *(meatball)* albóndiga *f* (**b**) *US very Fam* *(homosexual)* maricón *m*
fail [feɪl] **1** *n* (**a**) *Educ* suspenso *m* (**b**) **without f.** sin falta
2 *vt* (**a**) **don't f. me** no me falles; **words f. me** no encuentro palabras (**b**) *(exam)* suspender (**c**) *(to be unable)* no lograr; **he failed to score** no logró marcar (**d**) *(neglect)* dejar de; **don't f. to come** no deje de venir
3 *vi* (**a**) *(show, film)* fracasar; *(brakes)* fallar (**b**) *(business)* quebrar; *Educ* suspender (**c**) *(of health)* deteriorarse

failing ['feɪlɪŋ] **1** n (**a**) *(shortcoming)* defecto m (**b**) *(weakness)* punto m débil
2 prep a falta de
failure ['feɪljə(r)] n (**a**) fracaso m (**b**) *Com* quiebra f (**c**) *Educ* suspenso m (**d**) *(person)* fracasado(a) m,f (**e**) *(breakdown)* avería f; **brake f.** fallo m de los frenos; **power f.** apagón m; *Med* **heart f.** paro cardíaco (**f**) **her f. to answer** *(neglect)* el hecho de que no contestara
faint [feɪnt] **1** adj (**a**) *(sound)* débil; *(colour)* pálido(a); *(outline)* borroso(a); *(recollection)* vago(a); **I haven't the faintest idea** no tengo la más mínima idea (**b**) *(giddy)* mareado(a)
2 n desmayo m
3 vi desmayarse
faint-hearted [feɪnt'hɑːtɪd] adj temeroso(a)
fair [feə(r)] **1** adj (**a**) *(impartial)* imparcial; *(just)* justo(a); **it's not f.** no hay derecho; *Fam* **f. enough!** ¡vale!; **f. trade** comercio justo (**b**) *(hair)* rubio(a) (**c**) *(weather)* bueno(a) (**d**) *(beautiful)* bello(a) (**e**) **a f. number** un buen número; **he has a f. chance** tiene bastantes probabilidades
2 adv **to play f.** jugar limpio
fair [feə(r)] n feria f; **trade f.** feria de muestras
fairground ['feəgraʊnd] n real m de la feria
fairly ['feəlɪ] adv (**a**) *(justly)* justamente (**b**) *(moderately)* bastante
fairness ['feənɪs] n justicia f, equidad f; **in all f.** para ser justo(a)
fairy ['feərɪ] n (**a**) hada f; **f. godmother** hada madrina; **f. tale** cuento m de hadas (**b**) *Fam Pej* marica m
fait accompli [feɪtə'kɒmpliː] n *Fml* hecho consumado
faith [feɪθ] n (**a**) *Rel* fe f (**b**) *(trust)* confianza f; **in good f.** de buena fe
faithful ['feɪθfʊl] **1** adj fiel
2 npl **the f.** los fieles
faithfully ['feɪθfʊlɪ] adv fielmente; **yours f.** *(in letter)* le saluda atentamente
fake [feɪk] **1** adj falso(a)
2 n (**a**) *(object)* falsificación f (**b**) *(person)* impostor(a) m,f
3 vt (**a**) *(forge)* falsificar (**b**) *(feign)* fingir
4 vi *(pretend)* fingir
falcon ['fɔːlkən] n halcón m
Falklands ['fɔːklændz] npl **the F.** las (Islas) Malvinas
fall [fɔːl] **1** n (**a**) caída f (**b**) *(of rock)* desprendimiento m; **f. of snow** nevada f (**c**) *(decrease)* baja f (**d**) *US* otoño m (**e**)

(usu pl) cascada f; **Niagara Falls** las cataratas del Niágara
2 vi *(pt fell; pp fallen)* (**a**) caer, caerse; **they f. into two categories** se dividen en dos categorías; *Fig* **night was falling** anochecía; *Fig* **to f. into line** aceptar las reglas; *Fig* **to f. short (of)** no alcanzar (**b**) *(in battle)* caer (**c**) *(temperature, prices)* bajar (**d**) **to f. asleep** dormirse; **to f. ill** caer enfermo(a); **to f. in love** enamorarse
▸ **fall back** vi replegarse
▸ **fall back on** vt insep echar mano a, recurrir a
▸ **fall behind** vi *(in race)* quedarse atrás; **to f. behind with one's work** retrasarse en el trabajo
▸ **fall down** vi (**a**) *(picture etc)* caerse (**b**) *(building)* derrumbarse (**c**) *(argument)* fallar
▸ **fall for** vt insep (**a**) *(person)* enamorarse de (**b**) *(trick)* dejarse engañar por
▸ **fall in** vi (**a**) *(roof)* desplomarse (**b**) *Mil* formar filas
▸ **fall off 1** vi (**a**) *(drop off)* caerse (**b**) *(part)* desprenderse (**c**) *(diminish)* disminuir
2 vt insep **to f. off sth** caerse de algo
▸ **fall out** vi (**a**) *(hair)* caerse (**b**) *Mil* romper filas (**c**) *(quarrel)* pelearse
▸ **fall over** vi caerse
▸ **fall through** vi *(plan)* fracasar
fallacy ['fæləsɪ] n falacia f
fallen ['fɔːlən] pp of **fall**
fallible ['fælɪbəl] adj falible
fall-out ['fɔːlaʊt] n *(radioactive)* **f.** lluvia radioactiva; **f. shelter** refugio antiatómico
fallow ['fæləʊ] adj *Agr* en barbecho
false [fɔːls] adj falso(a); **f. step** paso m en falso; **f. start** salida nula; **f. teeth** dentadura postiza; **f. alarm** falsa alarma
falsehood ['fɔːlshʊd] n falsedad f
falsify ['fɔːlsɪfaɪ] vt *(records, accounts)* falsificar; *(story)* falsear
falter ['fɔːltə(r)] vi vacilar; *(voice)* fallar
faltering ['fɔːltərɪŋ] adj vacilante
fame [feɪm] n fama f
familiar [fə'mɪlɪə(r)] adj (**a**) *(common)* familiar, conocido(a); **his face is f.** su cara me suena (**b**) *(aware, knowledgeable)* enterado(a), al corriente (**with** de) (**c**) **to be on f. terms with sb** *(know well)* tener confianza con algn
familiarity [fəmɪlɪ'ærɪtɪ] n (**a**) *(awareness, knowledge)* familiaridad f (**with** con) (**b**) *(intimacy)* confianza f
familiarize [fə'mɪlɪəraɪz] vt (**a**) *(become acquainted)* familiarizar (**with** con); **to f.**

oneself with sth familiarizarse con algo (b) *(make widely known)* popularizar

family ['fæmɪlɪ] *n* familia *f*; **f. allowance** subsidio *m* familiar; **f. doctor** médico *m* de cabecera; **f. man** hombre hogareño; **f. planning** planificación *f* familiar; **f. tree** árbol genealógico

famine ['fæmɪn] *n* hambre *f*, escasez *f* de alimentos

famished ['fæmɪʃt] *adj Fam* muerto(a) de hambre

famous ['feɪməs] *adj* célebre, famoso(a) (**for** por)

famously ['feɪməslɪ] *adv Fam* estupendamente

fan [fæn] **1** *n* (a) abanico *m*; *Elec* ventilador *m* (b) *(person)* aficionado(a) *m,f*; *(of pop star etc)* fan *mf*; **f. club** club *m* de fans; **football f.** hincha *mf*
2 *vt* (a) abanicar (b) *(fire, passions)* avivar
▸ **fan out** *vi (troops)* desplegarse en abanico

fanatic [fə'nætɪk] *adj & n* fanático(a) *(m,f)*

fanatical [fə'nætɪkəl] *adj* fanático(a)

fanciful ['fænsɪfʊl] *adj* (a) *(person)* caprichoso(a) (b) *(idea)* fantástico(a)

fancy ['fænsɪ] **1** *adj* (**fancier, fanciest**) de fantasía; **f. dress** disfraz *m*; **f. dress ball** baile *m* de disfraces; **f. prices** precios *mpl* exorbitantes
2 *n* (a) *(imagination)* fantasía *f* (b) *(whim)* capricho *m*, antojo *m*; **to take a f. to sb** cogerle cariño a algn; **to take a f. to sth** encapricharse con algo; **what takes your f.?** ¿qué se le antoja?
3 *vt* (a) *(imagine)* imaginarse; *Fam* **f. that!** ¡fíjate!; *Fam* **f. seeing you here!** ¡qué casualidad verte por aquí! (b) *(like, want)* apetecer; **do you f. a drink?** ¿te apetece una copa?; *Fam* **I f. her** ella me gusta; *Fam* **to f. oneself** ser creído(a) or presumido(a)

fanfare ['fænfeə(r)] *n* fanfarria *f*

fang [fæŋ] *n* colmillo *m*

fanny ['fænɪ] *n* (a) *US Fam (buttocks)* culo *m*, *Am* cola *f* (b) *Br Vulg (vagina)* coño *m*, *Andes, RP* concha *f*

fantasize ['fæntəsaɪz] *vi* fantasear

fantastic [fæn'tæstɪk] *adj* fantástico(a)

fantasy ['fæntəsɪ] *n* fantasía *f*

far [fɑː(r)] (**farther** or **further, farthest** or **furthest**) **1** *adj* (a) *(distant)* lejano(a); **the F. East** el Lejano Oriente (b) **at the f. end** en el otro extremo (c) **the f. left** la extrema izquierda
2 *adv* (a) *(distant)* lejos; **f. and wide** por

todas partes; **f. off** a lo lejos; **farther back** más atrás; **farther north** más al norte; **how f. is it to Cardiff?** ¿cuánto hay de aquí a Cardiff?; *Fig* **as f. as I can** en lo que puedo; **as f. as I know** que yo sepa; **as f. as possible** en lo posible; *Fig* **f. from complaining, he seemed pleased** lejos de quejarse, parecía contento; *Fig* **he went so f. as to swear** llegó a jurar; *Fig* **I'm f. from satisfied** no estoy satisfecho(a) ni mucho menos; *Fig* **in so f. as ...** en la medida en que usted ...; *Fam* **to go too f.** pasarse de la raya
(b) *(in time)* **as f. back as the fifties** ya en los años cincuenta; **f. into the night** hasta muy entrada la noche; **so f.** hasta ahora
(c) *(much)* mucho; **by f.** con mucho; **f. cleverer** mucho más listo(a); **f. too much** demasiado; **you're not f. wrong** casi aciertas

faraway ['fɑːrəweɪ] *adj* lejano(a), remoto(a)

farce [fɑːs] *n* farsa *f*

farcical ['fɑːsɪkəl] *adj* absurdo(a)

fare [feə(r)] **1** *n* (a) *(ticket price)* tarifa *f*, precio *m* del billete; *(for boat)* pasaje *m*; **half f.** media tarifa (b) *(passenger)* pasajero(a) *m,f* (c) *(food)* comida *f*
2 *vi* **how did you f.?** ¿qué tal te fue?

farewell [feə'wel] **1** *interj Literary* ¡adiós!
2 *n* despedida *f*

far-fetched [fɑː'fetʃt] *adj* rebuscado(a)

farm [fɑːm] **1** *n* granja *f*, *Am* hacienda *f*
2 *vt* cultivar, labrar
▸ **farm out** *vt sep* encargar fuera

farmer ['fɑːmə(r)] *n* granjero(a) *m,f*, *Am* hacendado(a) *m,f*

farmhand ['fɑːmhænd] *n* peón *m*, labriego(a) *m,f*

farmhouse ['fɑːmhaʊs] *n* granja *f*, *Am* hacienda *f*

farming ['fɑːmɪŋ] **1** *n* (a) *(agriculture)* agricultura *f* (b) *(of land)* cultivo *m*, labranza *f*
2 *adj* agrícola

farmyard ['fɑːmjɑːd] *n* corral *m*

far-reaching [fɑː'riːtʃɪŋ] *adj* de gran alcance

far-sighted [fɑː'saɪtɪd] *adj* (a) *(person)* con visión de futuro (b) *(plan)* con miras al futuro

fart [fɑːt] *Fam* **1** *n* pedo *m*
2 *vi* echarse un pedo

farther ['fɑːðə(r)] *adj & adv comp of* **far**

farthest ['fɑːðɪst] *adj & adv superl of* **far**

fascinate ['fæsɪneɪt] *vt* fascinar

fascinating ['fæsɪneɪtɪŋ] *adj* fascinante

fascination [fæsɪ'neɪʃən] n fascinación f

fascism ['fæʃɪzəm] n fascismo m

fascist ['fæʃɪst] adj & n fascista (mf)

fashion ['fæʃən] **1** n (a) (manner) manera f, modo m; **after a f.** más o menos f; (latest style) moda f; **to go/be out of f.** pasar/no estar de moda; **f. designer** diseñador(a) m,f de modas; **f. parade** desfile m de modelos
2 vt (metal) labrar; (clay) formar

fashionable ['fæʃənəbəl] adj (a) de moda (b) (area, hotel) elegante

fast¹ [fɑːst] **1** adj (a) (quick) rápido(a) (b) hard and f. rules reglas estrictas (c) (clock) adelantado(a)
2 adv (a) rápidamente, deprisa; **how f.?** ¿a qué velocidad? (b) (securely) firmemente; **f. asleep** profundamente dormido(a)

fast² [fɑːst] **1** n ayuno m
2 vi ayunar

fasten ['fɑːsən] **1** vt (a) (attach) sujetar; (fix) fijar (b) (belt) abrochar; (bag) asegurar; (shoelaces) atar
2 vi (dress) abrocharse

fastener ['fɑːsənə(r)] n cierre m

fastidious [fæ'stɪdɪəs] adj quisquilloso(a)

fat [fæt] **1** adj (fatter, fattest) (a) gordo(a) (b) (book, file) grueso(a) (c) (meat) que tiene mucha grasa
2 n grasa f; **cooking f.** manteca f de cerdo

fatal ['feɪtəl] adj (a) (accident, illness) mortal (b) (ill-fated) fatal, funesto(a) (c) (fateful) fatídico(a)

fatalistic [feɪtə'lɪstɪk] adj fatalista

fatality [fə'tælɪtɪ] n víctima f mortal

> ♪ Note that the Spanish word **fatalidad** is a false friend and is never a translation for the English word **fatality**. In Spanish, **fatalidad** means both "fate" and "misfortune".

fatally ['feɪtəlɪ] adv **f. wounded** mortalmente herido(a)

fate [feɪt] n destino m, suerte f

fateful ['feɪtfʊl] adj fatídico(a), aciago(a)

father ['fɑːðə(r)] n (a) padre m; **my f. and mother** mis padres; **F. Christmas** Papá m Noel (b) Rel padre m

father-in-law ['fɑːðərɪnlɔː] n suegro m

fatherland ['fɑːðəlænd] n patria f

fatherly ['fɑːðəlɪ] adj paternal

fathom ['fæðəm] **1** n Naut braza f
2 vt comprender
▶ **fathom out** vt sep comprobar; **I can't f. it out** no me lo explico

fatigue [fə'tiːg] n (a) (tiredness) fatiga f (b) Mil faena f; **f. dress** traje m de faena

fatten ['fætən] vt engordar

fattening ['fætənɪŋ] adj que engorda

fatty ['fætɪ] **1** adj (food) graso(a); Anat (tissue) adiposo(a)
2 n Fam (person) gordinflón(ona) m,f

fatuous ['fætjʊəs] adj necio(a)

faucet ['fɔːsɪt] n US grifo m, Chile, Méx llave f, RP canilla f

fault [fɔːlt] **1** n (a) (defect) defecto m (b) (in merchandise) desperfecto m; **to find f. with** poner reparos a (c) (blame) culpa f; **to be at f.** tener la culpa (d) (mistake) error m (e) Geol falla f (f) (in tennis) falta f
2 vt criticar

faultless ['fɔːltlɪs] adj intachable

faulty ['fɔːltɪ] adj defectuoso(a)

fauna ['fɔːnə] n fauna f

faux pas [fəʊ'pɑː] n (pl faux pas) Fml (mistake) paso m en falso; (blunder) metedura f de pata

favour, US favor ['feɪvə(r)] **1** n (a) favor m; **in f. of a favor de**; **to be in f. with sb** gozar del favor de algn; **to ask sb a f.** pedirle un favor a algn (b) **1–0 in our f.** (advantage) 1-0 a favor nuestro
2 vt (a) (person) favorecer a (b) (approve) estar a favor de

favourable ['feɪvərəbəl] adj favorable

favourite ['feɪvərɪt] adj & n favorito(a) (m,f)

favouritism ['feɪvərɪtɪzəm] n favoritismo m

fawn¹ [fɔːn] **1** adj (de) color café claro
2 n (a) Zool cervato m (b) color m café claro

fawn² [fɔːn] vi adular (on a)

fax [fæks] **1** n (machine, message) fax m; **f. modem** modem m fax
2 vt mandar por fax

fear [fɪə(r)] **1** n miedo m, temor m; **for f. of** por temor a; Fam **no f.!** ¡ni pensarlo!
2 vt temer; **I f. it's too late** me temo que ya es tarde
3 vi temer (for por)

fearful ['fɪəfʊl] adj (a) (person) temeroso(a) (b) (frightening) espantoso(a)

fearless ['fɪəlɪs] adj intrépido(a)

feasibility [fiːzə'bɪlɪtɪ] n viabilidad f

feasible ['fiːzəbəl] adj (practicable) factible; (possible) viable

feast [fiːst] n (a) banquete m; Fam comilona f (b) Rel f. day fiesta f de guardar

feat [fiːt] n hazaña f

feather ['feðə(r)] **1** n pluma f; **f. duster** plumero m
2 vt Fam **to f. one's nest** hacer su agosto

feature [ˈfiːtʃə(r)] **1** n (a) (of face) rasgo m, facción f (b) (characteristic) característica f (c) **f. film** largometraje m (d) Press crónica f especial

2 vt (a) poner de relieve (b) Cin tener como protagonista a

3 vi figurar

February [ˈfebrʊərɪ] n febrero m

fed [fed] **1** adj Fam **f. up (with)** harto(a) (de)

2 pt & pp of **feed**

federal [ˈfedərəl] adj federal

federation [fedəˈreɪʃən] n federación f

fee [fiː] n (of lawyer, doctor) honorarios mpl; Ftb **transfer f.** prima f de traslado; Univ **tuition fees** derechos mpl de matrícula

feeble [ˈfiːbəl] adj débil

feed [fiːd] **1** vt (pt & pp **fed**) (a) (give food to) dar de comer a; Fig (fire) alimentar; **to f. a baby** (breast-feed) amamantar a un bebé; (with bottle) dar el biberón a un bebé (b) Elec alimentar (c) (insert) introducir

2 vi (cows, sheep) pacer; **to f. on sth** (person) comer algo

3 n (a) (food) comida f; **cattle f.** pienso m (b) Tech alimentación f

▸ **feed up** vt sep cebar

feedback [ˈfiːdbæk] n (a) Tech feedback m (b) Fig reacción f

feeder [ˈfiːdə(r)] n Tech alimentador m

feeding [ˈfiːdɪŋ] n **f. bottle** biberón m

feel [fiːl] **1** vi (pt & pp **felt**) (a) (emotion, sensation) sentir; **how do you f.?** ¿qué tal te encuentras?; **I f. bad about it** me da pena; **I f. (sorry) for him** le compadezco; **to f. happy/uncomfortable** sentirse feliz/incómodo; **to f. cold/sleepy** tener frío/sueño; Fam **to f. up to (doing) sth** sentirse con ánimos para hacer algo

(b) (seem) **your hand feels cold** tienes la mano fría; **it feels like summer** parece verano

(c) (opinion) opinar; **I f. sure that ...** estoy seguro(a) de que ...

(d) **I f. like an ice cream** me apetece un helado; **to f. like doing sth** tener ganas de hacer algo

2 vt (a) (touch) tocar

(b) **she feels a failure** se siente inútil

(c) (notice, be aware of) notar

3 n (a) (touch, sensation) tacto m; Fig **to get the f. for sth** cogerle el truco a algo

(b) (atmosphere) ambiente m

▸ **feel for** vt insep (a) (search for) buscar (b) (have sympathy for) compadecer

feeler [ˈfiːlə(r)] n (of insect) antena f; Fig

to put one's feelers out tantear el terreno

feeling [ˈfiːlɪŋ] **1** n (a) (emotion) sentimiento m; **ill f.** rencor m (b) (compassion) compasión f (c) **I had the f. that ...** (impression) tuve la impresión de que ... (d) (sensitivity) sensibilidad f (e) (opinion) opinión f; **to express one's feelings** expresar sus opiniones

2 adj sensible, compasivo(a)

feet [fiːt] pl of **foot**

feign [feɪn] vt fingir

feint [feɪnt] Sport **1** n finta f

2 vi fintar

fell¹ [fel] pt of **fall**

fell² [fel] vt (trees) talar; Fig (enemy) derribar

fellow [ˈfeləʊ] n (a) (companion) compañero(a) m,f; **f. citizen** conciudadano(a) m,f; **f. countryman/countrywoman** compatriota mf; **f. men** prójimos mpl; **f. passenger/student** compañero(a) m,f de viaje/estudios (b) Fam (chap) tipo m, tío m (c) (of society) socio(a) m,f

fellowship [ˈfeləʊʃɪp] n (a) (comradeship) camaradería f (b) Univ beca f de investigación

felony [ˈfelənɪ] n crimen m, delito m mayor

felt¹ [felt] pt & pp of **feel**

felt² [felt] n Tex fieltro m

felt-tip(ped) [ˈfelttɪp(t)] adj **f. pen** rotulador m

female [ˈfiːmeɪl] **1** adj (a) Zool hembra (b) femenino(a)

2 n (a) Zool hembra f (b) (woman) mujer f; (girl) chica f

feminine [ˈfemɪnɪn] adj femenino(a)

feminism [ˈfemɪnɪzəm] n feminismo m

feminist [ˈfemɪnɪst] adj & n feminista (mf)

fence [fens] **1** n cerca f, valla f; Fig **to sit on the f.** ver los toros desde la barrera

2 vi Sport practicar la esgrima

▸ **fence in** vt sep meter en un cercado

fencing [ˈfensɪŋ] n Sport esgrima f

fend [fend] vi **to f. for oneself** valerse por sí mismo

▸ **fend off** vt sep (blow) parar; (question) rehuir; (attack) rechazar

fender [ˈfendə(r)] n (a) (fireplace) pantalla f (b) US Aut guardabarros mpl (c) Naut defensa f

ferment 1 n [ˈfɜːment] Fig **in a state of f.** agitado(a)

2 vt & vi [fəˈment] fermentar

fern [fɜːn] n helecho m

ferocious [fəˈrəʊʃəs] adj feroz

ferocity [fəˈrɒsɪtɪ] n ferocidad f

ferret ['ferɪt] **1** n hurón m
  2 vi huronear, husmear
  ▸ **ferret out** vt sep descubrir
ferry ['ferɪ] **1** n (a) (small) barca f de pasaje (b) (large, for cars) transbordador m, ferry m
  2 vt transportar
fertile ['fɜːtaɪl] adj fértil
fertility [fə'tɪlɪtɪ] n (of soil) fertilidad f
fertilize ['fɜːtɪlaɪz] vt (a) (soil) abonar (b) (egg) fecundar
fertilizer ['fɜːtɪlaɪzə(r)] n abono m
fervent ['fɜːvənt] adj ferviente
fervour, US **fervor** ['fɜːvə(r)] n fervor m
fester ['festə(r)] vi supurar
festival ['festɪvəl] n (event) festival m; (celebration) fiesta f
festive ['festɪv] adj festivo(a); **the f. season** las fiestas de Navidad
festivity [fe'stɪvɪtɪ] n **the festivities** las fiestas
festoon [fe'stuːn] vt adornar
fetch [fetʃ] vt (a) (go for) ir a buscar (b) (bring) traer (c) **how much did it f.?** (sell for) ¿por cuánto se vendió?
fetching ['fetʃɪŋ] adj atractivo(a)
fete [feɪt] **1** n fiesta f
  2 vt festejar
fetish ['fetɪʃ, 'fiːtɪʃ] n fetiche m
fetus ['fiːtəs] n US = **foetus**
feud [fjuːd] **1** n enemistad duradera
  2 vi pelear
feudal ['fjuːdəl] adj feudal
fever ['fiːvə(r)] n fiebre f
feverish ['fiːvərɪʃ] adj febril
few [fjuː] **1** adj (a) (not many) pocos(as); **as f. as** solamente (b) (some) algunos(as), unos(as) cuantos(as); **a f. books** unos or algunos libros; **she has fewer books than I thought** tiene menos libros de lo que pensaba; **for the past f. years** durante estos últimos años; **in the next f. days** dentro de unos días; **quite a f.** bastantes
  2 pron (a) (not many) pocos(as); **there are too f.** no hay suficientes; **the fewer the better** cuantos menos mejor (b) **a f.** (some) algunos(as), unos(as) cuantos(as); **the chosen f.** los elegidos; **who has the fewest?** ¿quién tiene menos?
fiancé [fɪ'ɒnseɪ] n prometido m
fiancée [fɪ'ɒnseɪ] n prometida f
fiasco [fɪ'æskəʊ] n fiasco m
fib [fɪb] Fam **1** n trola f
  2 vi contar trolas
fibre, US **fiber** ['faɪbə(r)] n fibra f
fibreglass, US **fiberglass** ['faɪbəɡlɑːs] n fibra f de vidrio

fickle ['fɪkəl] adj inconstante, voluble
fiction ['fɪkʃən] n ficción f
fictional ['fɪkʃənəl] adj (a) Lit novelesco(a) (b) (imaginative) ficticio(a)
fictitious [fɪk'tɪʃəs] adj ficticio(a)
fiddle ['fɪdəl] Fam **1** n (a) Mus violín m (b) (shady deal) trampa f
  2 vt estafar; (accounts) falsificar
  3 vi juguetear (with con)
  ▸ **fiddle about** vi perder tiempo
fiddly ['fɪdlɪ] adj Fam laborioso(a)
fidelity [fɪ'delətɪ] n fidelidad f
fidget ['fɪdʒɪt] vi (a) moverse; **stop fidgeting!** ¡estáte quieto! (b) jugar (with con)
field [fiːld] **1** n (a) campo m; **f. glasses** gemelos mpl; **f. marshal** mariscal m de campo (b) Geol & Min yacimiento m (c) **f. trip** viaje m de estudios; **f. work** trabajo m de campo
  2 vt Sport (a) (ball) parar y devolver (b) (team) presentar
fiend [fiːnd] n demonio m; Fam (fanatic) fanático(a) m,f
fiendish ['fiːndɪʃ] adj Fam diabólico(a)
fierce [fɪəs] adj (animal) feroz; (argument) acalorado(a); (heat, competition) intenso(a); (wind) violento(a)
fiery ['faɪərɪ] adj (temper) fogoso(a); (speech) acalorado(a); (colour) encendido(a)
fifteen [fɪf'tiːn] adj & n quince (m inv)
fifteenth [fɪf'tiːnθ] **1** adj & n decimoquinto(a) (m,f)
  2 n (fraction) quinzavo m
fifth [fɪfθ] **1** adj & n quinto(a) (m,f)
  2 n (fraction) quinto m
fifty ['fɪftɪ] adj & n cincuenta (m inv)
fifty-fifty ['fɪftɪ'fɪftɪ] Fam **1** adj **a f. chance** una probabilidad del cincuenta por ciento
  2 adv **to go f.** ir a medias
fig¹ [fɪɡ] n (fruit) higo m
fig² [fɪɡ] (abbr **figure**) fig
fight [faɪt] **1** vt (pt & pp **fought**) (a) pelear(se) con, luchar con; (of boxer) enfrentarse a, luchar con; (of bullfighter) lidiar; Fig (corruption) combatir (b) (battle) librar; (war) hacer (c) (decision) recurrir contra
  2 vi (a) pelear(se), luchar (b) (quarrel) reñir; **to f. over sth** disputarse la posesión de algo (c) Fig (struggle) luchar (**for**/**against** por/contra)
  3 n (a) pelea f, lucha f; (in boxing) combate m (b) (quarrel) riña f (c) Fig (struggle) lucha f (d) (spirit) combatividad f

▸ **fight back 1** *vt sep (tears)* contener
  2 *vi* contraatacar
▸ **fight off** *vt sep* (**a**) *(attack)* rechazar (**b**) *(illness)* cortar
▸ **fight out** *vt sep* discutir
fighter ['faɪtə(r)] *n* (**a**) *(person)* combatiente *mf; (in boxing)* púgil *m* (**b**) *Fig* luchador(a) *m,f;* **f. (plane)** *(avión m* de) caza *m;* **f. bomber** cazabombardero *m*
fighting ['faɪtɪŋ] **1** *adj* **he's got a f. chance** tiene verdaderas posibilidades
  2 *n* lucha *f*
figment ['fɪgmənt] *n* **it's a f. of your imagination** es un producto de tu imaginación
figurative ['fɪgərətɪv] *adj* figurado(a)
figure ['fɪgə(r), *US* 'fɪgjər] **1** *n* (**a**) *(form, outline)* forma *f*, silueta *f* (**b**) *(shape, statue, character)* figura *f;* **she has a good f.** tiene buen tipo; *Br* **f. of eight,** *US* **f. eight** ocho *m* (**c**) *(in book)* dibujo *m* (**d**) **f. of speech** figura retórica (**e**) *Math* cifra *f*
  2 *vt US Fam* imaginarse
  3 *vi* (**a**) *(appear)* figurar (**b**) *US Fam* **that figures** eso tiene sentido
▸ **figure out** *vt sep Fam* comprender; **I can't f. it out** no me lo explico
figurehead ['fɪgəhed] *n Fig* figura decorativa
filament ['fɪləmənt] *n* filamento *m*
filch [fɪltʃ] *vt Fam* mangar, birlar
file [faɪl] **1** *n* (**a**) *(tool)* lima *f* (**b**) *(folder)* carpeta *f* (**c**) *(archive, of computer)* archivo *m;* **on f.** archivado(a) (**d**) *(line)* fila *f;* **in single f.** en fila india
  2 *vt* (**a**) *(smooth)* limar (**b**) *(put away)* archivar
  3 *vi* **to f. past** desfilar
filing ['faɪlɪŋ] *n* clasificación *f;* **f. cabinet** archivador *m; (for cards)* fichero *m*
Filipino [fɪlɪ'piːnəʊ] *n* filipino(a) *m,f*
fill [fɪl] **1** *vt* (**a**) *(space, time)* llenar (**with** de) (**b**) *(post, requirements)* cubrir (**c**) *Culin* rellenar
  2 *vi* llenarse (**with** de)
  3 *n* **to eat one's f.** comer hasta hartarse
▸ **fill in 1** *vt sep* (**a**) *(space, form)* rellenar (**b**) *Fam (inform)* poner al corriente (**on** de); (**c**) *(time)* pasar
  2 *vi* **to f. in for sb** sustituir a algn
▸ **fill out 1** *vt sep US (form)* llenar
  2 *vi Fam* engordar
▸ **fill up 1** *vt sep* llenar hasta arriba; *Fam Aut* **f. her up!** ¡llénelo!
  2 *vi* llenarse
fillet ['fɪlɪt] *n* filete *m;* **f. steak** filete
filling ['fɪlɪŋ] **1** *adj* que llena mucho
  2 *n* (**a**) *(stuffing)* relleno *m* (**b**) *(in tooth)*

empaste *m* (**c**) *Br* **f. station** gasolinera *f*, estación *f* de servicio, *Andes, Ven* bomba *f*, *Méx* gasolinería *f*, *Perú* grifo *m*
fillip ['fɪlɪp] *n Fam* estímulo *m*
film [fɪlm] **1** *n* (**a**) *Cin & Phot* película *f;* **f. star** estrella *f* de cine (**b**) *(layer)* capa *f*
  2 *vt Cin* filmar
  3 *vi Cin* rodar
film-strip ['fɪlmstrɪp] *n* cortometraje *m*
filter ['fɪltə(r)] **1** *n* filtro *m; Aut* **f. lane** carril *m* de acceso
  2 *vt* filtrar
  3 *vi Aut* **to f. to the right** girar a la derecha
▸ **filter through** *vi Fig* filtrarse (**to** a)
filter-tip ['fɪltətɪp] *n (cigarette)* cigarrillo *m* con filtro
filth [fɪlθ] *n (dirt)* porquería *f; Fig* porquerías *fpl*
filthy ['fɪlθɪ] *adj* (**filthier, filthiest**) (**a**) *(dirty)* asqueroso(a) (**b**) *(obscene)* obsceno(a)
fin [fɪn] *n Zool & Av* aleta *f*
final ['faɪnəl] **1** *adj* (**a**) *(last)* último(a), final (**b**) *(definitive)* definitivo(a)
  2 *n* (**a**) *Sport* final *f* (**b**) *Univ* **finals** exámenes *mpl* de fin de carrera
finale [fɪ'nɑːlɪ] *n* final *m*
finalist ['faɪnəlɪst] *n* finalista *mf*
finalize ['faɪnəlaɪz] *vt* ultimar; *(date)* fijar
finally ['faɪnəlɪ] *adv (lastly)* por último; *(at last)* por fin
finance ['faɪnæns, fɪ'næns] **1** *n* (**a**) *(finanzas fpl* (**b**) **finances** fondos *mpl*
  2 *vt* financiar
financial [faɪ'nænʃəl, fɪ'nænʃəl] *adj* financiero(a); **f. crisis** crisis económica; **f. year** año económico
financier [faɪ'nænsɪə(r), fɪ'nænsɪə(r)] *n* financiero(a) *m,f*
finch [fɪntʃ] *n* pinzón *m*
find [faɪnd] **1** *vt (pt & pp* **found**) (**a**) *(locate)* encontrar (**b**) *(think)* encontrar (**c**) **this found its way into my bag** esto vino a parar a mi bolso (**d**) *(discover)* descubrir; **it has been found that ...** se ha comprobado que ... (**e**) *Jur* **to f. sb guilty/not guilty** declarar culpable/inocente a algn (**f**) **I can't f. the courage to tell him** no tengo valor para decírselo; **I found it impossible to get away** me resultó imposible irme
  2 *n* hallazgo *m*
▸ **find out 1** *vt sep* (**a**) *(inquire)* averiguar (**b**) *(discover)* descubrir
  2 *vi* (**a**) **to f. out about sth** informarse sobre algo (**b**) *(discover)* enterarse
findings ['faɪndɪŋz] *npl* conclusiones *fpl*

fine¹ [faɪn] **1** *n* multa *f*
2 *vt* multar

fine² [faɪn] **1** *adj* (**a**) *(delicate etc)* fino(a) (**b**) *(subtle)* sutil (**c**) *(excellent)* excelente (**d**) *(weather)* bueno(a); **it was f.** hacía buen tiempo (**e**) **the f.** arts las bellas artes (**f**) *(all right)* bien
2 *adv* *Fam* muy bien
3 *interj* ¡vale!

finely ['faɪnlɪ] *adv* (**a**) finamente; **f. chopped** picado fino (**b**) **f. tuned** a punto

finery ['faɪnərɪ] *n* galas *fpl*

finesse [fɪ'nes] *n* *(delicacy)* finura *f*; *(cunning)* astucia *f*; *(tact)* sutileza *f*

finger ['fɪŋɡə(r)] **1** *n* dedo *m* (de la mano); *Fam* **to keep one's fingers crossed** esperar que todo salga bien; *Fam* **you've put your f. on it** has dado en el clavo; **middle f.** dedo corazón
2 *vt* tocar; *Pej* manosear

fingernail ['fɪŋɡəneɪl] *n* uña *f*

fingerprint ['fɪŋɡəprɪnt] *n* huella *f* dactilar

fingertip ['fɪŋɡətɪp] *n* punta *f* *or* yema *f* del dedo

finicky ['fɪnɪkɪ] *adj* *(person)* quisquilloso(a)

finish ['fɪnɪʃ] **1** *n* (**a**) fin *m*; *(of race)* llegada *f* (**b**) *(surface)* acabado *m*
2 *vt* (**a**) *(complete)* acabar, terminar; **to f. doing sth** terminar de hacer algo (**b**) *(use up)* agotar
3 *vi* acabar, terminar; **to f. second** quedar el segundo
▶ **finish off** *vt sep* (**a**) *(complete)* terminar completamente (**b**) *Fam (kill)* rematar
▶ **finish up** **1** *vt sep* acabar, agotar
2 *vi* **to f. up in jail** ir a parar a la cárcel

finished ['fɪnɪʃt] *adj* (**a**) *(product)* acabado(a) (**b**) *Fam (exhausted)* rendido(a)

finishing ['fɪnɪʃɪŋ] *adj* **to put the f. touch(es) to sth** darle los últimos toques a algo; **f. line** (línea *f* de) meta *f*; **f. school** = escuela privada de modales para señoritas

finite ['faɪnaɪt] *adj* finito(a); *(verb)* conjugable

Finland ['fɪnlənd] *n* Finlandia

Finn [fɪn] *n* finlandés(esa) *m,f*

Finnish ['fɪnɪʃ] **1** *adj* finlandés(esa)
2 *n* *(language)* finlandés *m*

fir [fɜ:(r)] *n* abeto *m*

fire ['faɪə(r)] **1** *n* (**a**) fuego *m* (**b**) *(accident etc)* incendio *m*; **to be on f.** estar en llamas; **to catch f.** incendiarse; **f. alarm** alarma *f* de incendios; *Br* **f. brigade,** *US* **f. department** (cuerpo *m* de) bomberos

mpl; **f. engine** coche *m* de bomberos; **f. escape** escalera *f* de incendios; **f. exit** salida *f* de emergencia; **f. extinguisher** extintor *m*; **f. fighting** extinción *f* de incendios; **f. station** parque *m* de bomberos (**c**) *(heater)* estufa *f* (**d**) *Mil* fuego *m*; **to open f.** abrir fuego; *Fig* **to come under f.** ser el blanco de las críticas
2 *vt* (**a**) *(gun)* disparar (**at** a); *(rocket)* lanzar; *Fig* **to f. questions at sb** bombardear a algn a preguntas (**b**) *Fam (dismiss)* despedir
3 *vi* *(shoot)* disparar (**at** sobre)

firearm ['faɪərɑ:m] *n* arma *f* de fuego

fire-fighter ['faɪəfaɪtə(r)] *n* *US* bombero *m*

fireman ['faɪəmən] *n* bombero *m*

fireplace ['faɪəpleɪs] *n* chimenea *f*; *(hearth)* hogar *m*

fireside ['faɪəsaɪd] *n* hogar *m*; **by the f.** al calor de la lumbre

firewood ['faɪəwʊd] *n* leña *f*

fireworks ['faɪəwɜ:ks] *npl* fuegos *mpl* artificiales

firing ['faɪərɪŋ] *n* *Mil* tiroteo *m*; **f. line** línea *f* de fuego; **f. squad** pelotón *m* de fusilamiento

firm [fɜ:m] **1** *adj* firme; **to be f. with sb** *(strict)* tratar a algn con firmeza
2 *n* *Com* empresa *f*, firma *f*

firmly ['fɜ:mlɪ] *adv* firmemente

firmness ['fɜ:mnɪs] *n* firmeza *f*

first [fɜ:st] **1** *adj* primero(a); *(before masculine singular noun)* primer; **Charles the F.** Carlos Primero; **for the f. time** por primera vez; **in the f. place** en primer lugar; **f. aid** primeros auxilios; **f. aid box** botiquín *m*; **f. floor** primer piso, *US* planta baja; **f. name** nombre *m* de pila
2 *adv* *(before anything else)* primero; **f. and foremost** ante todo; **f. of all** en primer lugar
3 *n* (**a**) **the f.** el primero/la primera; **the f. of April** el uno *or* el primero de abril (**b**) **at f.** al principio; **from the (very) f.** desde el principio (**c**) *Aut* primera *f* (**d**) *Univ* **to get a f.** sacar un sobresaliente

first-class ['fɜ:st'klɑ:s] **1** *adj* de primera clase
2 *adv* **to travel f.** viajar en primera

first-hand ['fɜ:st'hænd] *adv & adj* de primera mano

firstly ['fɜ:stlɪ] *adv* en primer lugar

first-rate ['fɜ:streɪt] *adj* de primera

fiscal ['fɪskəl] *adj* fiscal

fish [fɪʃ] **1** *n* (*pl* **fish**) (**a**) pez *m*; **f. shop** pescadería *f* (**b**) *Culin* pescado *m*; **f. and chips** = pescado frito con patatas *or* *Am* papas fritas; **f.** *Br* **finger** *or US* **stick** palito *m* de pescado

2 *vi* pescar; *Fig* **to f. in one's pocket for sth** buscar algo en el bolsillo

fishbone ['fɪʃbəʊn] *n* espina *f*, raspa *f*

fisherman ['fɪʃəmən] *n* pescador *m*

fishfinger [fɪʃ'fɪŋgə(r)] *n* palito *m* de pescado

fishing ['fɪʃɪŋ] *n* pesca *f*; **to go f.** ir de pesca; **f. net** red *f* de pesca; **f. rod** caña *f* de pescar; **f. tackle** aparejo *m* de pescar

fishmonger ['fɪʃmʌŋgə(r)] *n Br* pescadero(a) *m,f*, **fishmonger's (shop)** pescadería *f*

fishy ['fɪʃɪ] *adj* (**fishier, fishiest**) de pescado; *Fam Fig* **there's something f. going on** aquí hay gato encerrado

fist [fɪst] *n* puño *m*

fit[1] [fɪt] **1** *vt* (**a**) ir bien a; **that suit doesn't f. you** ese traje no te entalla

(**b**) *Sewing* probar

(**c**) **the key doesn't f. the lock** la llave no es de esta cerradura

(**d**) *(install)* colocar; **a car fitted with a radio** un coche provisto de radio

(**e**) *Fig* **she doesn't f. the description** no responde a la descripción

2 *vi* (**a**) *(be of right size)* caber

(**b**) *(facts etc)* cuadrar

3 *adj* (**a**) *(suitable)* apto(a), adecuado(a) *(for* para*)*; **are you f. to drive?** ¿estás en condiciones de conducir?

(**b**) *(healthy)* en (plena) forma; **to keep f.** mantenerse en forma

4 *n* ajuste *m*; *Sewing* corte *m*; **to be a good f.** encajar bien

▸ **fit in 1** *vi* (**a**) **he didn't f. in with his colleagues** no encajó con sus compañeros de trabajo (**b**) *(tally)* cuadrar (**with** con)

2 *vt sep (find time for)* encontrar un hueco para

▸ **fit out** *vt sep* equipar

fit[2] [fɪt] *n* (**a**) *Med* ataque *m* (**b**) *Fig* arrebato *m*; **f. of anger** arranque *m* de cólera; *Fig* **by fits and starts** a trompicones

fitful ['fɪtfʊl] *adj* discontinuo(a)

fitness ['fɪtnɪs] *n* (**a**) *(aptitude)* aptitud *f*, capacidad *f* (**b**) *(health)* (buen) estado físico

fitted ['fɪtɪd] *adj* empotrado(a); **f. carpet** moqueta *f*; **f. cupboard** armario empotrado

fitter ['fɪtə(r)] *n* ajustador(a) *m,f*

fitting ['fɪtɪŋ] **1** *adj* apropiado(a)

2 *n* (**a**) *(of dress)* prueba *f*; **f. room** probador *m* (**b**) *(usu pl)* accesorio *m*;

light fittings apliques eléctricos

five [faɪv] *adj & n* cinco *(m inv)*

fiver ['faɪvə(r)] *n Fam* billete *m* de 5 libras/dólares

fix [fɪks] **1** *n* (**a**) *Fam* **to be in a f.** estar en un apuro (**b**) *Fam (drugs)* chute *m*

2 *vt* (**a**) *(fasten)* fijar, asegurar (**b**) *(date, price)* fijar; *(limit)* señalar (**c**) **he'll f. it with the boss** *(arrange)* se las arreglará con el jefe (**d**) *(repair)* arreglar (**e**) *US (food, drink)* preparar

▸ **fix up** *vt sep (arrange)* arreglar; **to f. sb up with sth** proveer a algn de algo

fixation [fɪk'seɪʃən] *n* idea fija

fixed [fɪkst] *adj* (**a**) fijo(a) (**b**) *Fam (match etc)* amañado(a)

fixture ['fɪkstʃə(r)] *n* (**a**) *Sport* encuentro *m* (**b**) **fixtures** *(in building)* accesorios *mpl*

fizz [fɪz] **1** *n* burbujeo *m*

2 *vi* burbujear

▸ **fizzle out** ['fɪzəl] *vi* quedar en nada

fizzy ['fɪzɪ] *adj* (**fizzier, fizziest**) *(water)* con gas

flabbergasted ['flæbəgɑːstɪd] *adj* pasmado(a)

flabby ['flæbɪ] *adj* (**flabbier, flabbiest**) fofo(a)

flag [flæg] **1** *n* bandera *f*; *Naut* pabellón *m*

2 *vt Fig* **to f. down a car** hacer señales a un coche para que pare

3 *vi (interest)* decaer; *(conversation)* languidecer

flagpole ['flægpəʊl] *n* asta *f* de bandera

flagrant ['fleɪgrənt] *adj* flagrante

flagship ['flægʃɪp] *n* buque *m* insignia

flagstone ['flægstəʊn] *n* losa *f*

flair [fleə(r)] *n* facilidad *f*

flak [flæk] *n* (**a**) *Mil* fuego antiaéreo (**b**) *Fam* críticas *fpl*

flake [fleɪk] **1** *n (of snow)* copo *m*; *(of skin, soap)* escama *f*; *(of paint)* desconchón *m*

2 *vi (skin)* descamarse; *(paint)* desconcharse

flamboyant [flæm'bɔɪənt] *adj* extravagante

flame [fleɪm] *n* (**a**) *(of fire)* llama *f*; **to go up in flames** incendiarse (**b**) *Comput* llamarada *f*, = mensaje ofensivo

flameproof ['fleɪmpruːf] *adj* ininflamable

flamingo [flə'mɪŋgəʊ] *n* flamenco *m*

flammable ['flæməbəl] *adj* inflamable

flan [flæn] *n* tarta *f*; **fruit f.** tarta de fruta

> *Note that the Spanish word* **flan** *is a false friend and is never a translation for the English word* **flan**. *In Spanish,* **flan** *means "crème caramel".*

flank [flæŋk] **1** n (a) (of animal) ijada f (b) Mil flanco m
2 vt flanquear
flannel ['flænəl] n (a) Tex franela f (b) Br (face cloth) toallita f
flap [flæp] **1** vt (wings, arms) batir
2 vi (wings) aletear; (flag) ondear
3 n (a) (of envelope, pocket) solapa f; (of tent) faldón m (b) (of wing) aletazo m (c) Fam **to get into a f.** ponerse nervioso(a)
flare [fleə(r)] **1** n (a) (flame) llamarada f (b) Mil & Naut bengala f
2 vi **to f. (up)** (fire) llamear; Fig (person) encolerizarse; (trouble) estallar
flared [fleəd] adj (trousers etc) acampanado(a)
flash [flæʃ] **1** n (a) (of light) destello m; (of lightning) relámpago m; Fig **in a f.** en un santiamén; Fig **a f. in the pan** un éxito fugaz (b) **news f.** noticia f de última hora (c) Phot flash m
2 adj Fam chulo(a)
3 vt (a) (torch) dirigir (b) Rad & TV transmitir (c) **he flashed his card** enseñó rápidamente su carnet
4 vi (a) (light) destellar (b) **a car flashed past** un coche pasó como un rayo
flashback ['flæʃbæk] n flashback m
flashcube ['flæʃkjuːb] n cubo m flash
flashlight ['flæʃlaɪt] n US linterna f
flashy ['flæʃɪ] adj (flashier, flashiest) Fam chillón(ona)
flask [flɑːsk, flæsk] n frasco m; **(Thermos®) f.** termo m
flat [flæt] **1** adj (flatter, flattest) (a) (surface) llano(a) (b) (beer) sin gas (c) (battery) descargado(a); (tyre) desinflado(a) (d) (rate) fijo(a) (e) (categorical) rotundo(a) (f) (dull) soso(a) (g) Mus **B f.** si m bemol
2 adv (a) **to fall f. on one's face** caerse de bruces (b) **in ten seconds f.** en diez segundos justos (c) Fam **to go f. out** ir a todo gas
3 n (a) (apartment) piso m (b) US Aut pinchazo m (c) **mud flats** marismas fpl
flatly ['flætlɪ] adv rotundamente
flatmate ['flætmeɪt] n Br compañero(a) m,f de piso
flatten ['flætən] vt (a) (make level) allanar (b) (crush) aplastar
flatter ['flætə(r)] vt (a) adular, halagar (b) (clothes, portrait) favorecer (c) **to f. oneself** hacerse ilusiones
flattering ['flætərɪŋ] adj (a) (words) halagador(a) (b) (dress, portrait) favorecedor(a)
flattery ['flætərɪ] n adulación f, halago m

flaunt [flɔːnt] vt hacer alarde de
flavour, US **flavor** ['fleɪvə(r)] **1** n sabor m
2 vt Culin sazonar (**with** con)
flavoured, US **flavored** ['fleɪvəd] adj **strawberry f.** con sabor a fresa, Bol, CSur, Ecuad frutilla
flavouring, US **flavoring** ['fleɪvərɪŋ] n condimento m; **artificial f.** aroma m artificial
flaw [flɔː] n (failing) defecto m; (fault) desperfecto m
flawless ['flɔːlɪs] adj perfecto(a)
flax [flæks] n lino m
flaxen ['flæksən] adj (hair) rubio pajizo
flea [fliː] n pulga f; **f. market** rastro m
fleck [flek] n (speck) mota f, punto m
fled [fled] pt & pp of **flee**
fledg(e)ling ['fledʒlɪŋ] adj Fig novato(a)
flee [fliː] **1** vt (pt & pp fled) huir de
2 vi huir (**from** de)
fleece [fliːs] **1** n (a) (sheep's coat) lana f (b) (sheared) vellón m
2 vt Fam (cheat) sangrar
fleet [fliːt] n flota f
fleeting ['fliːtɪŋ] adj fugaz
Flemish ['flemɪʃ] **1** adj flamenco(a)
2 n (language) flamenco m
flesh [fleʃ] n (a) carne f; Fig **in the f.** en persona; Fig **to be of f. and blood** ser de carne y hueso; **f. wound** herida f superficial (b) (of fruit) pulpa f
flew [fluː] pt of **fly**
flex [fleks] **1** n Br Elec cable m
2 vt (muscles) flexionar
flexibility [fleksɪ'bɪlɪtɪ] n flexibilidad f
flexible ['fleksɪbəl] adj flexible
flick [flɪk] **1** n movimiento rápido; (of finger) capirotazo m
2 vt (with finger) dar un capirotazo a
▸ **flick through** vt insep (book) hojear
flicker ['flɪkə(r)] **1** n (a) parpadeo m; (of light) titileo m (b) Fig **a f. of hope** un destello de esperanza
2 vi (eyes) parpadear; (flame) vacilar
flier ['flaɪə(r)] n aviador(a) m,f
flight [flaɪt] n (a) vuelo m; **f. path** trayectoria f de vuelo; **f. recorder** registrador m de vuelo (b) (of ball) trayectoria f (c) (escape) huida f, fuga f; **to take f.** darse a la fuga (d) (of stairs) tramo m
flight-deck ['flaɪtdek] n (cockpit) cabina f del piloto
flimsy ['flɪmzɪ] adj (flimsier, flimsiest) (cloth) ligero(a); (paper) fino(a); (structure) poco sólido(a); (excuse) poco convincente
flinch [flɪntʃ] vi (wince) estremecerse
fling [flɪŋ] **1** vt (pt & pp flung) arrojar

2 n *Fam* **to have a f.** echar una cana al aire

flint [flɪnt] n (a) *(stone)* pedernal m (b) *(in lighter)* piedra f de mechero

flip [flɪp] 1 n *(flick)* capirotazo m; **f. chart** flip chart m, pizarra f de conferencia *(con bloc)*

2 vt *(toss)* tirar (al aire); **to f. a coin** echar a cara o cruz

flip-flop ['flɪpflɒp] n (a) *Comput* báscula f biestable (b) *Br (footwear)* chancla f

flippant ['flɪpənt] adj frívolo(a)

flipper ['flɪpə(r)] n aleta f

flirt [flɜːt] 1 n coqueto(a) m,f

2 vi flirtear, coquetear; **to f. with death** jugar con la muerte

flirtation [flɜː'teɪʃən] n flirteo m, coqueteo m

flit [flɪt] vi revolotear

float [fləʊt] 1 n (a) flotador m (b) *(money)* cambio m (c) *(in procession)* carroza f

2 vt (a) poner a flote (b) *(shares)* emitir; *(currency, business)* hacer flotar

3 vi flotar

floating ['fləʊtɪŋ] adj flotante; *(voter)* indeciso(a)

flock [flɒk] 1 n *Zool* rebaño m; *Orn* bandada f; *Rel* grey f; *(crowd)* multitud f

2 vi acudir en masa

flog [flɒg] vt (a) azotar; *Fam Fig* **flogged to death** *(idea)* trillado(a) (b) *Fam (sell)* vender

flood [flʌd] 1 n inundación f; *(of river)* riada f; *Fig* torrente m

2 vt inundar

3 vi *(river)* desbordarse; *Fig* **to f. in** entrar a raudales

flooding ['flʌdɪŋ] n inundaciones fpl

floodlight ['flʌdlaɪt] n foco m

floor [flɔː(r)] 1 n (a) *(of room)* suelo m; **dance f.** pista f de baile (b) *(of ocean, forest)* fondo m (c) *(storey)* piso m; **first f.** *Br* primer piso, *US* planta baja; *Br* **ground f.** planta baja

2 vt *Fig* dejar perplejo(a)

floorboard ['flɔːbɔːd] n tabla f (del suelo)

flop [flɒp] 1 n *Fam* fracaso m

2 vi (a) **to f. down on the bed** tumbarse en la cama (b) *Fam* fracasar

floppy ['flɒpɪ] adj (floppier, floppiest) flojo(a); *Comput* **f. disk** disco m flexible

flora ['flɔːrə] n flora f

florid ['flɒrɪd] adj *(style)* florido(a)

florist ['flɒrɪst] n florista mf; **f.'s shop** floristería f

flounce¹ [flaʊns] vi **to f. in/out** entrar/salir airadamente

flounce² [flaʊns] n *Sewing* volante m

flounder¹ ['flaʊndə(r)] n *(fish)* platija f

flounder² ['flaʊndə(r)] vi (a) *(struggle)* forcejear; *Fig* enredarse (b) *(be at a loss)* no saber que decir or hacer

flour ['flaʊə(r)] n harina f

flourish ['flʌrɪʃ] 1 n (a) *(gesture)* ademán m (teatral) (b) *(under signature)* rúbrica f

2 vt *(brandish)* agitar

3 vi *(thrive)* florecer; *(plant)* crecer

flourishing ['flʌrɪʃɪŋ] adj floreciente

flout [flaʊt] vt *Jur* desacatar

flow [fləʊ] 1 n flujo m; *(of river)* corriente f; *(of traffic)* circulación f; *(of capital)* movimiento m; *(of people, goods)* afluencia f; **f. chart** diagrama m de flujo; *Comput* organigrama m

2 vi *(blood, river)* fluir; *(sea)* subir; *(traffic)* circular

flower ['flaʊə(r)] 1 n flor f; **f. bed** arriate m

2 vi florecer

flowerpot ['flaʊəpɒt] n maceta f

flowery ['flaʊərɪ] adj *Fig* florido(a)

flowing ['fləʊɪŋ] adj *(hair)* suelto(a); *(dress)* de mucho vuelo; *(style)* fluido(a); *(shape, movement)* natural

flown [fləʊn] pp of **fly**

flu [fluː] n *(abbr* **influenza)** gripe f

fluctuate ['flʌktjʊeɪt] vi fluctuar

fluctuation [flʌktjʊ'eɪʃən] n fluctuación f

flue [fluː] n conducto m de humos; *(chimney)* cañón m

fluent ['fluːənt] adj (a) **he speaks f. German** habla el alemán con soltura (b) *(eloquent)* fluido(a)

fluff [flʌf] 1 n *(down)* pelusa f

2 vt *Fam* **to f. sth** hacer algo mal

fluffy ['flʌfɪ] adj (fluffier, fluffiest) *(pillow)* mullido(a); *(toy)* de peluche; *(cake)* esponjoso(a)

fluid ['fluːɪd] 1 adj *(movement)* natural; *(style, prose)* fluido(a); *(situation)* incierto(a)

2 n fluido m, líquido m

fluke [fluːk] n *Fam* chiripa f; **by a f.** por chiripa

flummox ['flʌməks] vt *Fam* desconcertar

flung [flʌŋ] pt & pp of **fling**

flunk [flʌŋk] vt & vi *US Fam* catear

fluorescent [flʊə'resənt] adj fluorescente

fluoride ['flʊəraɪd] n fluoruro m

flurry ['flʌrɪ] n (a) *(of wind)* ráfaga f; *(of snow)* nevasca f (b) *Fig (bustle)* agitación f

flush [flʌʃ] 1 adj **f. with** *(level)* a ras de

2 n *(blush)* rubor m

3 *vt* **to f. the lavatory** tirar de la cadena
4 *vi* (a) **the loo won't f.** la cisterna del wáter no funciona (b) (blush) ruborizarse

flushed [flʌʃt] *adj* (cheeks) rojo(a), encendido(a); *Fig* **f. with success** emocionado(a) ante el éxito

fluster ['flʌstə(r)] *vt* **to get flustered** ponerse nervioso(a)

flute [fluːt] *n* flauta f

flutist ['fluːtɪst] *n US Mus* flautista mf

flutter ['flʌtə(r)] **1** *vi* (leaves, birds) revolotear; (flag) ondear
2 *n Fam* (bet, gambling) apuesta pequeña

flux [flʌks] *n* (flow) flujo m; (instability) inestabilidad f; *Fig* **to be in a state of f.** estar cambiando constantemente

fly¹ [flaɪ] **1** *vt* (pt flew; pp flown) (a) Av pilotar (b) (merchandise, troops) transportar (c) (distance) recorrer (d) (kite) hacer volar
2 *vi* (a) (bird, plane) volar (b) (go by plane) ir en avión (c) (flag) ondear (d) **to f. into a rage** montar en cólera (e) **the train flew past** el tren pasó volando (f) *Fam* **to go flying** (fall) caerse
3 *npl* **flies** bragueta f

fly² [flaɪ] *n* (insect) mosca f; **f. spray** spray m matamoscas

flying ['flaɪɪŋ] **1** *adj* volador(a); (rapid) rápido(a); **a f. visit** una visita relámpago; *Fig* **to come out of an affair with f. colours** salir airoso(a) de un asunto; *Fig* **to get off to a f. start** empezar con buen pie; **f. picket** piquete m (informativo); **f. saucer** platillo m volante
2 *n* (a) (action) vuelo m (b) (aviation) aviación f

flyleaf ['flaɪliːf] *n* (of book) guarda f

flyover ['flaɪəʊvə(r)] *n Br* paso elevado

flypast ['flaɪpɑːst] *n Br Av* desfile aéreo

flyweight ['flaɪweɪt] *n* (in boxing) peso m mosca

foal [fəʊl] *n* potro(a) m,f

foam [fəʊm] **1** *n* espuma f; **f. bath** espuma de baño; **f. rubber** goma espuma
2 *vi* hacer espuma

fob [fɒb] *n* (chain) cadena f (de reloj)
► **fob off** *vt sep Fam* **he fobbed off his old radio on a stranger** le colocó su radio vieja a un desconocido; **to f. sb off with excuses** darle largas a algn

focus ['fəʊkəs] **1** *vt* centrarse (on en)
2 *vi* enfocar; **to f. on sth** *Phot* enfocar algo; *Fig* centrarse en algo
3 *n* (pl focuses) foco m; **to be in f./out of f.** estar enfocado(a)/desenfocado(a);

Com & Pol **f. group** grupo m muestra

fodder ['fɒdə(r)] *n* pienso m

foe [fəʊ] *n Fml* enemigo(a) m,f

foetus ['fiːtəs] *n* feto m

fog [fɒg] *n* niebla f; (at sea) bruma f

fogey ['fəʊgɪ] *n Fam* **old f.** cascarrabias mf inv

foggy ['fɒgɪ] *adj* (foggier, foggiest) **it is f.** hay niebla; *Fam* **I haven't the foggiest (idea)** no tengo la más mínima idea

foghorn ['fɒghɔːn] *n* sirena f (de niebla)

foglamp ['fɒglæmp], *US* **foglight** ['fɒglaɪt] *n* faro m antiniebla

foil [fɔɪl] **1** *n* (a) **aluminium f.** papel m de aluminio (b) (in fencing) florete m
2 *vt* (plot) desbaratar

fold [fəʊld] **1** *n* (crease) pliegue m
2 *vt* plegar, doblar; **to f. one's arms** cruzar los brazos
3 *vi* **to f. (up)** (chair etc) plegarse; *Com* quebrar

folder ['fəʊldə(r)] *n* carpeta f

folding ['fəʊldɪŋ] *adj* (chair etc) plegable

foliage ['fəʊlɪdʒ] *n* follaje m

folk [fəʊk] **1** *npl* (a) (people) gente f (b) *Fam* **folks** (family) padres mpl; **one's folks** la familia
2 *adj* popular; **f. music** música f folk; **f. song** canción f popular

folklore ['fəʊklɔː(r)] *n* folklore m

follow ['fɒləʊ] **1** *vt* seguir; (pursue) perseguir; (understand) comprender; (way of life) llevar
2 *vi* (a) (come after) seguir; **as follows** como sigue (b) (result) resultar; **that doesn't f.** eso no es lógico (c) (understand) entender
► **follow through, follow up** *vt sep* (idea) llevar a cabo; (clue) investigar

follower ['fɒləʊə(r)] *n* seguidor(a) m,f

following ['fɒləʊɪŋ] **1** *adj* siguiente
2 *n* seguidores mpl

folly ['fɒlɪ] *n* locura f, desatino m

fond [fɒnd] *adj* (loving) cariñoso(a); **to be f. of sb** tenerle mucho cariño a algn; **to be f. of doing sth** ser aficionado(a) a hacer algo

fondle ['fɒndəl] *vt* acariciar

fondness ['fɒndnɪs] *n* (love) cariño m (for a); (liking) afición f (for a)

font [fɒnt] *n Rel* pila f

food [fuːd] *n* comida f; **f. chain** cadena trófica; **f. poisoning** intoxicación alimenticia

foodstuffs ['fuːdstʌfs] *npl* productos alimenticios

fool [fuːl] **1** *n* (a) tonto(a) m,f, imbécil mf; **to make a f. of sb** poner a algn en ridículo; **to play the f.** hacer el tonto (**b**) *Culin* ≃ mousse *f* de fruta

2 *vt (deceive)* engañar

3 *vi (joke)* bromear; **to f. about** *or* **around** hacer el tonto

foolhardy ['fu:lhɑ:dɪ] *adj* (**foolhardier, foolhardiest**) temerario(a); *(person)* intrépido(a)

foolish ['fu:lɪʃ] *adj* estúpido(a)

foolproof ['fu:lpru:f] *adj* infalible

foot [fʊt] **1** *n (pl* **feet**) pie *m*; *Zool* pata *f*; **on f.** a pie, andando; *Fam Fig* **to find one's feet** acostumbrarse; *Fam Fig* **to put one's f. down** *(control)* imponerse; *(in car)* pisar a fondo; *Fam Fig* **to put one's f. in it** meter la pata; *Fam Fig* **to put one's feet up** descansar

2 *vt* **to f. the bill** *(pay)* pagar la cuenta

footage ['fʊtɪdʒ] *n Cin* metraje *m*

football ['fʊtbɔ:l] *n* (**a**) *(soccer)* fútbol *m*; **bar f.** futbolín *m*; **f. ground** campo *m* de fútbol; **f. match** partido *m* de fútbol; **f. pools** quinielas *fpl* (**b**) *(ball)* balón *m*

footballer ['fʊtbɔ:lə(r)] *n* futbolista *mf*

footbridge ['fʊtbrɪdʒ] *n* puente *m* para peatones

foothills ['fʊthɪlz] *npl* estribaciones *fpl*

foothold ['fʊthəʊld] *n Fig* **to gain a f.** afianzarse en una posición

footing ['fʊtɪŋ] *n* **to lose one's f.** perder el equilibrio; **on a friendly f.** en plan amistoso; **on an equal f.** en pie de igualdad

footlights ['fʊtlaɪts] *npl* candilejas *fpl*

footman ['fʊtmən] *n* lacayo *m*

footnote ['fʊtnəʊt] *n* nota *f* a pie de página

footpath ['fʊtpɑ:θ] *n (track)* sendero *m*

footprint ['fʊtprɪnt] *n* pisada *f*

footsore ['fʊtsɔ:(r)] *adj* con los pies doloridos

footstep ['fʊtstep] *n* paso *m*

footwear ['fʊtweə(r)] *n* calzado *m*

for [fɔ:(r), *unstressed* fə(r)] **1** *prep* (**a**) *(intended)* para; **curtains f. the bedroom** cortinas para el dormitorio; **f. sale** en venta; **it's time f. bed** es hora de acostarse

(**b**) *(representing)* por; **a cheque f. £10** un cheque de 10 libras; **J f. John** J de Juan; **what's the Spanish f. "rivet"?** ¿cómo se dice "rivet" en español?

(**c**) *(purpose)* para; **it's good f. the digestion** es bueno para la digestión; **what's this f.?** ¿para qué sirve esto?

(**d**) *(because of)* por; **famous f. its cuisine** famoso(a) por su cocina; **to jump f. joy** saltar de alegría

(**e**) *(on behalf of)* por; **the campaign f.**

peace la campaña por la paz; **will you do it f. me?** ¿lo harás por mí?

(**f**) *(during)* por, durante; **I lent it to her f. a year** se lo presté por un año; **I shall stay f. two weeks** me quedaré dos semanas; **I was ill f. a month** estuve enfermo(a) durante un mes; **I've been here f. three months** hace tres meses que estoy aquí

(**g**) *(distance)* **I walked f. 10 km** caminé 10 km

(**h**) *(at a point in time)* para; **I can do it f. next Monday** puedo hacerlo para el lunes que viene; **f. the last time** por última vez

(**i**) *(destination)* para

(**j**) *(amount of money)* por; **I got the car f. £500** conseguí el coche por 500 libras

(**k**) *(in favour of)* a favor de; **are you f. or against?** ¿estás a favor o en contra?; **to vote f. sb** votar a algn

(**l**) *(to obtain)* para; **to run f. the bus** correr para coger al autobús; **to send sb f. water** mandar a algn a por agua

(**m**) *(with respect to)* en cuanto a; **as f. him** en cuanto a él; **f. all I care** por mí; **f. all I know** que yo sepa; **f. one thing** para empezar

(**n**) *(despite)* a pesar de; **f. all that** aún así; **he's tall f. his age** está muy alto para su edad

(**o**) *(instead of)* por; **can you go f. me?** ¿puede ir por mí?

(**p**) *(towards)* hacia, por; **affection f. sb** cariño hacia algn; **his love f. you** su amor por ti

(**q**) *(as)* por; **to leave sb f. dead** dar a algn por muerto(a); **what do you use f. fuel?** ¿qué utilizan como combustible?

(**r**) *(in exchange)* por; **to exchange one thing f. another** cambiar una cosa por otra; **how much did you sell it f.?** ¿por cuánto lo vendiste?

(**s**) *(+ object + infin)* **there's no reason f. us to quarrel** no hay motivo para que riñamos; **it's time f. you to go** es hora de que os marchéis; **it's easy f. him to say that** le es fácil decir eso

2 *conj (since, as)* ya que, puesto que

forage ['fɒrɪdʒ] **1** *n* forraje *m*

2 *vi* hurgar

foray ['fɒreɪ] *n* incursión *f*

forbade [fə'beɪd] *pt of* **forbid**

forbearance [fɔ:'beərəns] *n* paciencia *f*

forbid [fə'bɪd] *vt (pt* **forbade** [fə'beɪd]; *pp* **forbidden** [fə'bɪdən]) prohibir; **to f. sb to do sth** prohibirle a algn hacer algo

forbidding [fə'bɪdɪŋ] *adj (stern)* severo(a); *(bleak)* inhóspito(a)

force [fɔːs] **1** n (**a**) fuerza f; **by f.** por la fuerza; **to come into f.** entrar en vigor (**b**) Mil cuerpo m; **the (armed) forces** las fuerzas armadas; **the police f.** la policía
2 vt forzar; **to f. sb to do sth** forzar a algn a hacer algo
forced [fɔːst] adj forzado(a); **f. landing** aterrizaje forzoso
force-feed ['fɔːsfiːd] vt alimentar a la fuerza
forceful ['fɔːsfʊl] adj (**a**) (person) enérgico(a) (**b**) (argument) convincente
forceps ['fɔːseps] npl fórceps m
forcible ['fɔːsəbəl] adj **f. entry** allanamiento m de morada
forcibly ['fɔːsəblɪ] adv a or por la fuerza
ford [fɔːd] **1** n vado m
2 vt vadear
fore [fɔː(r)] n Fig **to come to the f.** empezar a destacar
forearm ['fɔːrɑːm] n antebrazo m
foreboding [fɔː'bəʊdɪŋ] n presentimiento m
forecast ['fɔːkɑːst] **1** n pronóstico m
2 vt (pt & pp **forecast** or **forecasted**) pronosticar
forecourt ['fɔːkɔːt] n (of garage) área f de servicio
forefathers ['fɔːfɑːðəz] npl antepasados mpl
forefinger ['fɔːfrʌnt] n **in the f.** a la vanguardia
forego [fɔː'gəʊ] vt (pt **forewent**; pp **foregone** [fɔː'gɒn]) Fml sacrificar
foregone ['fɔːgɒn] adj **a f. conclusion** un resultado inevitable
foreground ['fɔːgraʊnd] n primer plano m
forehead ['fɒrɪd, 'fɔːhed] n frente f
foreign ['fɒrɪn] adj extranjero(a); (trade, policy) exterior; **f. exchange** divisas fpl; **the F. Office** el Ministerio de Asuntos Exteriores; **f. body** cuerpo extraño
foreigner ['fɒrɪnə(r)] n extranjero(a) m,f
foreman ['fɔːmən] n (**a**) Ind capataz m (**b**) Jur presidente m del jurado
foremost ['fɔːməʊst] adj principal; **first and f.** ante todo
forename ['fɔːneɪm] n nombre m de pila
forensic [fə'rensɪk] adj forense
forerunner ['fɔːrʌnə(r)] n precursor/a m,f
foresee [fɔː'siː] vt (pt **foresaw** [fɔː'sɔː]; pp **foreseen**) prever
foreseeable [fɔː'siːəbəl] adj previsible; **in the f. future** en un futuro próximo
foreseen [fɔː'siːn] pp of **foresee**
foreshadow [fɔː'ʃædəʊ] vt presagiar
foresight ['fɔːsaɪt] n previsión f

forest ['fɒrɪst] n bosque m
forestall [fɔː'stɔːl] vt (plan) anticiparse a; (danger) prevenir
forestry ['fɒrɪstrɪ] n silvicultura f
foretaste ['fɔːteɪst] n anticipo m (**of** de)
foretell [fɔː'tel] vt (pt & pp **foretold** [fɔː'təʊld]) presagiar
forever [fə'revə(r)] adv (**a**) (eternally) siempre (**b**) (for good) para siempre (**c**) Fam (ages) siglos mpl
forewent [fɔː'went] pt of **forego**
foreword ['fɔːwɜːd] n prefacio m
forfeit ['fɔːfɪt] **1** n (penalty) pena f; (in games) prenda f
2 vt perder
forgave [fə'geɪv] pt of **forgive**
forge [fɔːdʒ] **1** n (**a**) (furnace) fragua f (**b**) (blacksmith's) herrería f
2 vt (**a**) (counterfeit) falsificar (**b**) (metal) forjar
3 vi **to f. ahead** hacer grandes progresos
forger ['fɔːdʒə(r)] n falsificador(a) m,f
forgery ['fɔːdʒərɪ] n falsificación f
forget [fə'get] **1** vt (pt **forgot**; pp **forgotten**) olvidar, olvidarse de; **I forgot to close the window** se me olvidó cerrar or me olvidé de cerrar la ventana; **I've forgotten my key** he olvidado la llave
2 vi olvidarse
forgetful [fə'getfʊl] adj olvidadizo(a)
forget-me-not [fə'getmɪnɒt] n nomeolvides f inv
forgive [fə'gɪv] vt (pt **forgave**; pp **forgiven** [fə'gɪvən]) perdonar; **to f. sb for sth** perdonarle algo a algn
forgiveness [fə'gɪvnɪs] n perdón m
forgo [fɔː'gəʊ] vt Fml = **forego**
forgot [fə'gɒt] pt of **forget**
forgotten [fə'gɒtən] pp of **forget**
fork [fɔːk] **1** n (**a**) Agr horca f (**b**) (cutlery) tenedor m (**c**) (in road) bifurcación f
2 vi (roads) bifurcarse
▸ **fork out** vt sep Fam (money) soltar
fork-lift truck [fɔːklɪft'trʌk] n carretilla f elevadora de horquilla
forlorn [fə'lɔːn] adj (forsaken) abandonado(a); (desolate) triste; (without hope) desesperado(a)
form [fɔːm] **1** n (**a**) (shape) forma f (**b**) (type) clase f (**c**) **for f.'s sake** para guardar las formas (**d**) (document) formulario m (**e**) **on/on top/off f.** en/en plena/en baja forma (**f**) Br Educ clase f; **the first f.** el primer curso
2 vt formar; **to f. an impression** formarse una impresión
3 vi formarse
formal ['fɔːməl] adj (**a**) (official) oficial;

a f. application una solicitud en forma (**b**) *(party, dress)* de etiqueta (**c**) *(ordered)* formal (**d**) *(person)* formalista

formality [fɔːˈmælɪtɪ] *n* formalidad *f*

formally [ˈfɔːməlɪ] *adv* oficialmente

format [ˈfɔːmæt] **1** *n* formato *m*
2 *vt Comput* formatear

formation [fɔːˈmeɪʃən] *n* formación *f*

formative [ˈfɔːmətɪv] *adj* formativo(a)

former [ˈfɔːmə(r)] *adj* (**a**) *(time)* anterior (**b**) *(one-time)* antiguo(a); *(person)* ex; **the f. champion** el excampeón (**c**) *(first)* aquél/aquélla; **Peter and Lisa came, the f. wearing a hat** vinieron Peter y Lisa, aquél llevaba sombrero

formerly [ˈfɔːməlɪ] *adv* antiguamente

formidable [ˈfɔːmɪdəbəl] *adj (prodigious)* formidable; *(daunting)* terrible

formula [ˈfɔːmjʊlə] *n* fórmula *f*

forsake [fəˈseɪk] *vt (pt* **forsook** [fəˈsʊk]; *pp* **forsaken** [fəˈseɪkən]) *Literary* (**a**) *(abandon, desert)* abandonar (**b**) *(give up)* renunciar a

fort [fɔːt] *n* fortaleza *f*

forte [ˈfɔːteɪ] *n* fuerte *m*

forth [fɔːθ] *adv Fml* **and so f.** y así sucesivamente; **to go back and f.** ir de acá para allá

forthcoming [fɔːθˈkʌmɪŋ] *adj* (**a**) *(event)* próximo(a) (**b**) **no money was f.** no hubo oferta de dinero (**c**) *(communicative)* comunicativo(a)

forthright [ˈfɔːθraɪt] *adj* franco(a)

fortify [ˈfɔːtɪfaɪ] *vt* fortificar

fortitude [ˈfɔːtɪtjuːd] *n* fortaleza *f*, fuerza *f*

fortnight [ˈfɔːtnaɪt] *n Br* quincena *f*

fortnightly [ˈfɔːtnaɪtlɪ] *Br* **1** *adj* quincenal
2 *adv* cada quince días

fortress [ˈfɔːtrɪs] *n* fortaleza *f*

fortunate [ˈfɔːtʃənɪt] *adj* afortunado(a); **it was f. that he came** fue una suerte que viniera

fortunately [ˈfɔːtʃənɪtlɪ] *adv* afortunadamente

fortune [ˈfɔːtʃən] *n* (**a**) *(luck, fate)* suerte *f*; **to tell sb's f.** echar la buenaventura a algn (**b**) *(money)* fortuna *f*

fortune-teller [ˈfɔːtʃəntelə(r)] *n* adivino(a) *m,f*

forty [ˈfɔːtɪ] *adj & n* cuarenta *(m inv)*

forum [ˈfɔːrəm] *n* foro *m*

forward [ˈfɔːwəd] **1** *adv* (**a**) *(also forwards) (direction and movement)* hacia adelante (**b**) *Fig* **to come f.** ofrecerse (**c**) **from this day f.** de ahora en adelante
2 *adj* (**a**) *(movement)* hacia adelante;

(position) delantero(a) (**b**) *(person)* fresco(a)
3 *n Sport* delantero(a) *m,f*
4 *vt* (**a**) *(send on)* remitir (**b**) *Fml (send goods)* expedir (**c**) *Fml (further)* fomentar

fossil [ˈfɒsəl] *n* fósil *m*; **f. fuel** combustible *m* fósil

foster [ˈfɒstə(r)] **1** *vt* (**a**) *(child)* criar (**b**) *Fml (hopes)* abrigar; *(relations)* fomentar
2 *adj* **f. child** hijo(a) adoptivo(a); **f. father** padre adoptivo; **f. mother** madre adoptiva; **f. parents** padres adoptivos

fought [fɔːt] *pt & pp of* **fight**

foul [faʊl] **1** *adj* (**a**) *(smell)* fétido(a); *(taste)* asqueroso(a) (**b**) *(deed)* atroz; *(weather)* de perros (**c**) *(language)* grosero(a) (**d**) **to fall f. of** tener problemas con; *Sport* **f. play** juego sucio; *Jur* **f. play is suspected** se sospecha que se haya cometido un acto criminal
2 *n Sport* falta *f*
3 *vt* (**a**) *(dirty)* ensuciar; *(air)* contaminar (**b**) *Sport* cometer una falta contra

found¹ [faʊnd] *pt & pp of* **find**

found² [faʊnd] *vt (establish)* fundar

foundation [faʊnˈdeɪʃən] *n* (**a**) *(establishment)* fundación *f* (**b**) *(basis)* fundamento *m* (**c**) **f. (cream)** maquillaje *m* de fondo (**d**) *Constr* **foundations** cimientos *mpl*

founder¹ [ˈfaʊndə(r)] *n* fundador(a) *m,f*

founder² [ˈfaʊndə(r)] *vi* (**a**) *Fml (sink)* hundirse (**b**) *Fig (plan, hopes)* fracasar

foundry [ˈfaʊndrɪ] *n* fundición *f*

fountain [ˈfaʊntɪn] *n (structure)* fuente *f*; *(jet)* surtidor *m*; **f. pen** pluma estilográfica, *CSur* lapicera *f* fuente, *Perú* lapicero *m*

four [fɔː(r)] *adj & n* cuatro *(m inv)*; **on all fours** a gatas

four-door [ˈfɔːdɔː(r)] *adj Aut* de cuatro puertas

four-poster [fɔːˈpəʊstə(r)] *adj & n* **f. (bed)** cama *f* con dosel

foursome [ˈfɔːsəm] *n* grupo *m* de cuatro personas

fourteen [fɔːˈtiːn] *adj & n* catorce *(m inv)*

fourteenth [fɔːˈtiːnθ] **1** *adj & n* decimocuarto(a) *(m,f)*
2 *n (fraction)* catorceavo *m*

fourth [fɔːθ] **1** *adj & n* cuarto(a) *(m,f)*
2 *n (fraction)* cuarto *m* (**b**) *Aut* cuarta *f* (velocidad)

fowl [faʊl] *n (pl* **fowl**) ave *f* de corral

fox [fɒks] **1** *n* zorro(a) *m,f*
2 *vt* (**a**) *(perplex)* dejar perplejo(a) (**b**) *(deceive)* engañar

foyer [ˈfɔɪeɪ, ˈfɔɪə(r)] *n* vestíbulo *m*

fracas ['fræka:] *n* gresca *f*, refriega *f*

> 🖉 Note that the Spanish word **fracaso** is a false friend and is never a translation for the English word **fracas**. In Spanish, **fracaso** means "failure".

fraction ['frækʃən] *n* fracción *f*
fracture ['fræktʃə(r)] **1** *n* fractura *f*
   2 *vt* fracturar
fragile ['frædʒaɪl] *adj* frágil
fragment ['frægmənt] *n* fragmento *m*
fragrance ['freɪgrəns] *n* fragancia *f*, perfume *m*
fragrant ['freɪgrənt] *adj* fragante, aromático(a)
frail [freɪl] *adj* frágil, delicado(a)
frame [freɪm] **1** *n* (**a**) *(of window, door, picture)* marco *m*; *(of machine)* armazón *m*; *(of bicycle)* cuadro *m*; *(of spectacles)* montura *f*, *Fig* **f. of mind** estado *m* de ánimo (**b**) *Cin & TV* fotograma *m*
   2 *vt* (**a**) *(picture)* enmarcar (**b**) *(question)* formular (**c**) *Fam (innocent person)* incriminar
framework ['freɪmwɜːk] *n Fig* **within the f. of ...** dentro del marco de ...
franc [fræŋk] *n* franco *m*
France [frɑːns] *n* Francia
franchise ['fræntʃaɪz] *n* (**a**) *Pol* derecho *m* al voto (**b**) *Com* concesión *f*, licencia *f*
frank [fræŋk] **1** *adj* franco(a)
   2 *vt (mail)* franquear
frankly ['fræŋklɪ] *adv* francamente
frankness ['fræŋknɪs] *n* franqueza *f*
frantic ['fræntɪk] *adj (anxious)* desesperado(a); *(hectic)* frenético(a)
fraternal [frə'tɜːnəl] *adj* fraterno(a)
fraternity [frə'tɜːnɪtɪ] *n (society)* asociación *f*, *Rel* cofradía *f*, *US Univ* club *m* de estudiantes
fraud [frɔːd] *n* (**a**) fraude *m* (**b**) *(person)* impostor(a) *m,f*
fraught [frɔːt] *adj* (**a**) *(full)* cargado(a) (**with** de) (**b**) *(tense)* nervioso(a)
fray¹ [freɪ] *vi* (**a**) *(cloth)* deshilacharse (**b**) *(nerves)* crisparse; **his temper frequently frayed** se irritaba a menudo
fray² [freɪ] *n* combate *m*
freak [friːk] **1** *n* (**a**) *(monster)* monstruo *m* (**b**) *Fam (eccentric)* estrafalario(a) *m,f* (**c**) *Fam (fan)* fanático(a) *m,f*
   2 *adj* (**a**) *(unexpected)* inesperado(a) (**b**) *(unusual)* insólito(a)
freckle ['frekəl] *n* peca *f*
free [friː] **1** *adj* (**a**) libre; **to set sb f.** poner en libertad a algn; **f. kick** tiro *m* libre; **f. speech** libertad *f* de expresión; **f. will** libre albedrío *m*; **f. trade** libre cambio *m*;

f. time tiempo *m* libre (**b**) **f. (of charge)** *(gratis)* gratuito(a); **f. gift** obsequio *m* (**c**) *(generous)* generoso(a)
   2 *adv* (**a**) **(for) f.** gratis (**b**) *(loose)* suelto(a)
   3 *vt* (**a**) *(liberate)* poner en libertad (**b**) *(let loose, work loose)* soltar (**c**) *(untie)* desatar (**d**) *(exempt)* eximir (**from** de)
freedom ['friːdəm] *n* (**a**) *(liberty)* libertad *f*; **f. of the press** libertad de prensa (**b**) *(exemption)* exención *f*
free-for-all ['friːfərɔːl] *n* pelea *f*
freehold ['friːhəʊld] *adj* en propiedad absoluta
freelance ['friːlɑːns] *adj* independiente
freely ['friːlɪ] *adv* (**a**) libremente (**b**) *(openly)* abiertamente
freemason ['friːmeɪsən] *n* francmasón *m*
free-range ['friːreɪndʒ] *adj Br* de granja
free-style ['friːstaɪl] *n* estilo *m* libre
freeway ['friːweɪ] *n US* autopista *f*
freewheel [friː'wiːl] *vi* ir en punto muerto
freeze [friːz] **1** *vt (pt* **froze***; pp* **frozen**) congelar
   2 *n Met* helada *f*; **price f.** congelación *f* de precios; *TV & Cin* **f. frame** imagen congelada
   3 *vi (liquid)* helarse; *(food)* congelarse
freeze-dried ['friːzdraɪd] *adj* liofilizado(a)
freezer ['friːzə(r)] *n* congelador *m*
freezing ['friːzɪŋ] *adj* (**a**) glacial (**b**) **f. point** punto *m* de congelación; **above/ below f. point** sobre/bajo cero
freight [freɪt] *n* (**a**) *(transport)* transporte *m* (**b**) *(goods, price)* flete *m*; *US* **f. car** vagón *m*; *US* **f. elevator** montacargas *m inv*; **f. train** tren *m* de mercancías
French [frentʃ] **1** *adj* francés(esa); **F. bean** judía *f* verde, *Bol, RP* chaucha *f*, *CAm* ejote *m*, *Col, Cuba* habichuela *f*, *Chile* poroto *m* verde, *Ven* vainita *f*; **F. dressing** vinagreta *f*; *US* **F. fries** patatas *fpl or Am* papas *fpl* fritas; **F. window** puerta *f* vidriera
   2 *n* (**a**) *(language)* francés *m* (**b**) *pl* **the F.** los franceses
Frenchman ['frentʃmən] *n* francés *m*
Frenchwoman ['frentʃwʊmən] *n* francesa *f*
frenetic [frɪ'netɪk] *adj* frenético(a)
frenzy ['frenzɪ] *n* frenesí *m*
frequency ['friːkwənsɪ] *n* frecuencia *f*
frequent 1 *adj* ['friːkwənt] frecuente
   2 *vt* [frɪ'kwent] frecuentar
frequently ['friːkwəntlɪ] *adv* frecuentemente, a menudo

fresh [freʃ] *adj* (**a**) fresco(a); **f. water** agua *f* dulce; **f. bread** pan del día (**b**) *(new)* nuevo(a); **open a f. packet** abre otro paquete (**c**) *(air)* puro(a); **in the f. air** al aire libre (**d**) *US Fam (cheeky)* fresco(a)

freshen ['freʃən] *vi (wind)* refrescar
▸ **freshen up** *vi* asearse

fresher ['freʃə(r)] *n Univ* estudiante *mf* de primer año, novato(a) *m,f*

freshly ['freʃlɪ] *adv* recién, recientemente

freshman ['freʃmən] *n US* = fresher

freshness ['freʃnɪs] *n* frescura *f*

freshwater ['freʃwɔːtə(r)] *adj* de agua dulce

fret [fret] *vi* preocuparse (**about** por)

FRG [efɑː'dʒiː] *n Hist (abbr Federal Republic of Germany)* RFA *f*

friar ['fraɪə(r)] *n* fraile *m*

friction ['frɪkʃən] *n* fricción *f*

Friday ['fraɪdɪ] *n* viernes *m*

fridge [frɪdʒ] *n* nevera *f*, frigorífico *m*, *Andes* frigider *m*, *RP* heladera *f*

friend [frend] *n* amigo(a) *m,f*; **a f. of mine** un(a) amigo(a) mío(a); **to make friends with sb** hacerse amigo(a) de algn; **to make friends again** hacer las paces

friendliness ['frendlɪnɪs] *n* amabilidad *f*, simpatía *f*

friendly ['frendlɪ] *adj (friendlier, friendliest) (person)* simpático(a); *(atmosphere)* acogedor(a); **f. advice** consejo *m* de amigo; **f. nation** nación amiga

friendship ['frendʃɪp] *n* amistad *f*

frieze [friːz] *n* friso *m*

frigate ['frɪgɪt] *n* fragata *f*

fright [fraɪt] *n* (**a**) *(fear)* miedo *m*; **to take f.** asustarse (**b**) *(shock)* susto *m*; **to get a f.** pegarse un susto

frighten ['fraɪtən] *vt* asustar
▸ **frighten away, frighten off** *vt sep* ahuyentar

frightened ['fraɪtənd] *adj* asustado(a); **to be f. of sb** tenerle miedo a algn

frightening ['fraɪtənɪŋ] *adj* espantoso(a)

frightful ['fraɪtfʊl] *adj* espantoso(a), horroroso(a)

frightfully ['fraɪtfʊlɪ] *adv* tremendamente, terriblemente

frigid ['frɪdʒɪd] *adj* frígido(a)

frill [frɪl] *n (on dress)* volante *m*; *Fig* **frills** *(decorations)* adornos *mpl*

fringe [frɪndʒ] *n* (**a**) *Br (of hair)* flequillo *m*, *Am* cerquillo *m* (**b**) *(edge)* borde *m*; *Fig* **on the f. of society** al margen de la sociedad; **f. theatre** teatro *m* experimental; **f. benefits** extras *mpl*

Frisbee® ['frɪzbɪ] *n* platillo *m*

frisk [frɪsk] *vt Fam (search)* registrar

frisky ['frɪskɪ] *adj (friskier, friskiest)* (**a**) *(children, animals)* juguetón(ona) (**b**) *(adult)* vivo(a)

fritter ['frɪtə(r)] *n* buñuelo *m*
▸ **fritter away** *vt sep* malgastar

frivolous ['frɪvələs] *adj* frívolo(a)

frizzy ['frɪzɪ] *adj (frizzier, frizziest)* crespo(a)

frock [frɒk] *n* vestido *m*; **f. coat** levita *f*

frog [frɒg] *n* rana *f*; **frogs' legs** ancas *fpl* de rana; *Fig* **to have a f. in one's throat** tener carraspera

frogman ['frɒgmən] *n* hombre *m* rana

frolic ['frɒlɪk] *vi* retozar, juguetear

from [frɒm, *unstressed* frəm] *prep* (**a**) *(time)* desde, a partir de; **f. now on** a partir de ahora; **f. Monday to Friday** de lunes a viernes; **f. the 8th to the 17th** desde el 8 hasta el 17; **f. time to time** de vez en cuando

(**b**) *(price, number)* desde, de; **dresses f. £5** vestidos desde 5 libras; **a number f. one to ten** un número del uno al diez

(**c**) *(origin)* de; **a letter f. her father** una carta de su padre; **f. English into Spanish** del inglés al español; **he's f. Malaga** es de Málaga; **the train f. Bilbao** el tren procedente de Bilbao; **to go f. door to door** ir de puerta en puerta; **her eyes were red f. crying** tenía los ojos rojos de llorar

(**d**) *(distance)* de; **the town is 4 miles f. the coast** el pueblo está a 4 millas de la costa

(**e**) *(out of)* de; **bread is made f. flour** el pan se hace con harina

(**f**) *(remove, subtract)* a; **he took the book f. the child** le quitó el libro al niño; **take three f. five** restar tres a cinco

(**g**) *(according to)* según, por; **f. what the author said** según lo que dijo el autor; **speaking f. my own experience** hablando por experiencia propia

(**h**) *(position)* desde, de; **f. here** desde aquí

(**i**) **can you tell margarine f. butter?** ¿puedes distinguir entre la margarina y la mantequilla?

front [frʌnt] **1** *n* (**a**) parte delantera; **in f. (of)** delante (de) (**b**) *(of building)* fachada *f* (**c**) *Mil, Pol & Met* frente *m* (**d**) *(seaside)* paseo marítimo (**e**) *Fig* **she put on a brave f.** hizo de tripas corazón

2 *adj* delantero(a), de delante; *Pol* **f. bench** = primera fila de escaños donde se sientan los ministros del Gobierno o de la Oposición; **f. door** puerta *f* principal; **f. room** salón *m*; **f. seat** asiento *m* de delante

frontier ['frʌntɪə(r)] *n* frontera *f*

front-page ['frʌntpeɪdʒ] *adj* de primera página

frost [frɒst] **1** *n* (**a**) *(covering)* escarcha *f* (**b**) *(freezing)* helada *f*
2 *vt US Culin* recubrir con azúcar glas
▸ **frost over** *vi* escarchar

frostbite ['frɒstbaɪt] *n* congelación *f*

frosted ['frɒstɪd] *adj* (**a**) *(glass)* esmerilado(a) (**b**) *US Culin* recubierto(a) de azúcar glas

frosty ['frɒstɪ] *adj* (**frostier, frostiest**) (**a**) **it will be a f. night tonight** esta noche habrá helada (**b**) *Fig* glacial

froth [frɒθ] **1** *n* espuma *f*; *(from mouth)* espumarajos *mpl*
2 *vi* espumar

frothy ['frɒθɪ] *adj* (**frothier, frothiest**) espumoso(a)

frown [fraʊn] *vi* fruncir el ceño
▸ **frown upon** *vt insep* desaprobar

froze [frəʊz] *pt of* **freeze**

frozen ['frəʊzən] **1** *adj (liquid, feet etc)* helado(a); *(food)* congelado(a)
2 *pp of* **freeze**

frugal ['fruːgəl] *adj* frugal

fruit [fruːt] *n* (**a**) *Bot* fruto *m* (**b**) *(apple, orange etc)* fruta *f*; **f. cake** pastel *m* con fruto seco; **f. machine** máquina *f* tragaperras; **f. salad** macedonia *f* de frutas (**c**) **fruits** *(rewards)* frutos *mpl*

fruitful ['fruːtfʊl] *adj Fig* provechoso(a)

fruition [fruːˈɪʃən] *n Fml* **to come to f.** realizarse

frustrate [frʌˈstreɪt] *vt* frustrar

frustrated [frʌˈstreɪtɪd] *adj* frustrado(a)

frustration [frʌˈstreɪʃən] *n* frustración *f*

fry¹ [fraɪ] **1** *vt (pt & pp* **fried**) freír
2 *vi Fig* asarse

fry² [fraɪ] *npl* **small f.** gente *f* de poca monta

frying pan ['fraɪɪŋpæn], *US* **fry-pan** ['fraɪpæn] *n* sartén *f*

ft (*abbr* **foot**) pie *m*; (*abbr* **feet**) pies *mpl*

fuck [fʌk] *vt & vi Vulg* joder; **f. (it)!** ¡joder!
▸ **fuck off** *vi Vulg* **f. off!** ¡vete a la mierda!
▸ **fuck up** *vt sep Vulg* joder

fucking ['fʌkɪŋ] *Vulg* **1** *adj* **f. idiot!** ¡gilipollas!; **where are my f. keys?** ¿dónde coño están las llaves?
2 *adv* **a f. good film** una película de puta madre

fuddy-duddy ['fʌdɪdʌdɪ] *n Fam* **an old f.** un carcamal *or Am* carcamán

fudge [fʌdʒ] **1** *n Culin* = dulce hecho con azúcar, leche y mantequilla
2 *vt (figures)* amañar

fuel ['fjʊəl] **1** *n* combustible *m*; *(for engines)* carburante *m*; **f. tank** depósito *m* de combustible
2 *vt Fig (ambition)* estimular; *(difficult situation)* empeorar

fugitive ['fjuːdʒɪtɪv] *n Fml* fugitivo(a) *m,f*

fulfil, *US* **fulfill** [fʊlˈfɪl] *vt* (**a**) *(task, ambition)* realizar; *(promise)* cumplir; *(role)* desempeñar (**b**) *(wishes)* satisfacer

fulfilment, *US* **fulfillment** [fʊlˈfɪlmənt] *n* (**a**) *(of ambition)* realización *f* (**b**) *(of duty, promise)* cumplimiento *m*

full [fʊl] **1** *adj* (**a**) lleno(a); **f. of** lleno(a) de; **I'm f. (up)** no puedo más (**b**) *(complete)* completo(a); **at f. speed** a toda velocidad; **f. text** texto íntegro; *Fam* **in f. swing** en plena marcha; **f. board** pensión completa; **f. employment** pleno empleo; **f. house** lleno total; **f. moon** luna llena; **f. stop** punto *m*
2 *n* **in f.** en su totalidad; **name in f.** nombre y apellidos completos
3 *adv* **f. well** perfectamente

full-blown ['fʊlbləʊn] *adj* auténtico(a)

full-fledged ['fʊlfledʒd] *adj US* = **fully-fledged**

fullness ['fʊlnɪs] *n* **in the f. of time** con el tiempo

full-scale ['fʊlskeɪl] *adj* (**a**) *(model)* de tamaño natural (**b**) **f. search** registro *m* a fondo; **f. war** guerra generalizada *or* total

full-time ['fʊl'taɪm] **1** *adj* de jornada completa
2 *adv* **to work f.** trabajar a tiempo completo

fully ['fʊlɪ] *adv* completamente

fully-fledged ['fʊlɪfledʒd] *adj* hecho(a) y derecho(a)

fulsome ['fʊlsəm] *adj* excesivo(a), exagerado(a)

fumble ['fʌmbəl] *vi* hurgar; **to f. for sth** buscar algo a tientas; **to f. with sth** manejar algo con torpeza

fume [fjuːm] **1** *n (usu pl)* humo *m*
2 *vi* despedir humo

📖 Note that the Spanish verb **fumar** is a false friend and is never a translation for the English verb **to fume**. In Spanish, **fumar** means "to smoke".

fun [fʌn] **1** *n (amusement)* diversión *f*; **in** or **for f.** en broma; **to have f.** divertirse, pasarlo bien; **to make f. of sb** reírse de algn
2 *adj* divertido(a)

function ['fʌŋkʃən] **1** n (**a**) función f (**b**) (ceremony) acto m; (party) recepción f
2 vi funcionar

functional ['fʌŋkʃənəl] adj funcional

fund [fʌnd] **1** n (**a**) Com fondo m (**b**) **funds** fondos mpl
2 vt (finance) financiar

📎 Note that the Spanish verb **fundar** is a false friend and is never a translation for the English verb **to fund**. In Spanish, **fundar** means "to found".

fundamental [fʌndə'mentəl] **1** adj fundamental
2 npl **fundamentals** los fundamentos

funeral ['fju:nərəl] n funeral m; US **f. home** funeraria f; **f. march** marcha f fúnebre; Br **f. parlour** funeraria; **f. service** misa f de cuerpo presente

funfair ['fʌnfeə(r)] n Br parque m de atracciones

fungus ['fʌŋgəs] n (pl **fungi** ['fʌŋgaɪ]) (**a**) Bot hongo m (**b**) Med fungo m

funnel ['fʌnəl] **1** n (**a**) (for liquids) embudo m (**b**) Naut chimenea f
2 vt Fig (funds, energy) encauzar

funnily ['fʌnɪlɪ] adv Fam **f. enough** aunque parezca extraño

funny ['fʌnɪ] adj (**funnier, funniest**) (**a**) (peculiar) raro(a), extraño(a); **that's f.!** ¡qué raro! (**b**) (amusing) divertido(a), gracioso(a); **I found it very f.** me hizo mucha gracia (**c**) Fam (ill) mal (**d**) Fam (dishonest) dudoso(a)

fur [fɜː(r)] **1** n (**a**) (of living animal) pelo m (**b**) (of dead animal) piel f (**c**) (in kettle, on tongue) sarro m
2 adj de piel; **f. coat** abrigo m de pieles

furious ['fjʊərɪəs] adj (**a**) (angry) furioso(a) (**b**) (vigorous) violento(a)

furlong ['fɜːlɒŋ] n (measurement) = aprox 201 m

furnace ['fɜːnɪs] n horno m

furnish ['fɜːnɪʃ] vt (**a**) (house) amueblar (**b**) Fml (food) suministrar; (details) facilitar

furnishings ['fɜːnɪʃɪŋz] npl (**a**) muebles mpl (**b**) (fittings) accesorios mpl

furniture ['fɜːnɪtʃə(r)] n muebles mpl; **a piece of f.** un mueble

furrow ['fʌrəʊ] n Agr surco m; (on forehead) arruga f

furry ['fɜːrɪ] adj (**furrier, furriest**) (**a**) (hairy) peludo(a) (**b**) (tongue, kettle) sarroso(a)

further ['fɜːðə(r)] **1** adj (comp of **far**) (**a**) (new) nuevo(a); **until f. notice** hasta nuevo aviso (**b**) (additional) otro(a), adicional (**c**) (later) posterior; **f. education** estudios mpl superiores
2 adv (**a**) (more) más; **f. back** más atrás; **f. along** más adelante; **she heard nothing f.** no volvió a saber nada más (**b**) Fml **f. to your letter of the 9th** con referencia a su carta del 9 del corriente (**c**) Fml (besides) además
3 vt fomentar

furthermore [fɜːðə'mɔː(r)] adv Fml además

furthest ['fɜːðɪst] adj (superl of **far**) más lejano(a)

furtive ['fɜːtɪv] adj furtivo(a)

fury ['fjʊərɪ] n furia f, furor m

fuse [fju:z] **1** n (**a**) Elec fusible m; **f. box** caja f de fusibles (**b**) (of bomb) mecha f
2 vi (**a**) Elec **the lights fused** se fundieron los plomos (**b**) Fig (merge) fusionarse (**c**) (melt) fundirse
3 vt (**a**) Elec fundir los plomos de (**b**) Fig (merge) fusionar (**c**) (melt) fundir

fuselage ['fju:zɪlɑːʒ] n fuselaje m

fuss [fʌs] **1** n (commotion) jaleo m; **to kick up a f.** armar un escándalo; **stop making a f.** (complaining) deja ya de quejarte; **to make a f. of** (pay attention to) mimar a
2 vi preocuparse (about por)

fussy ['fʌsɪ] adj (**fussier, fussiest**) exigente; (nitpicking) quisquilloso(a)

futile ['fju:taɪl] adj inútil, vano(a)

futility [fju:'tɪlɪtɪ] n inutilidad f

future ['fju:tʃə(r)] **1** n futuro m, porvenir m; **in the near f.** en un futuro próximo; **in f.** de aquí en adelante
2 adj futuro(a)

futuristic [fju:tʃə'rɪstɪk] adj futurista

fuze [fju:z] n, vi & vt US = **fuse**

fuzzy ['fʌzɪ] adj (**fuzzier, fuzziest**) (**a**) (hair) muy rizado(a) (**b**) (blurred) borroso(a)

G, g [dʒiː] *n* (**a**) *(the letter)* G, g *f* (**b**) *Mus* **G** sol *m*

G [dʒiː] *adj US Cin* ≃ (apta) para todos los públicos

g *(abbr* **gramme**) g

gabble ['gæbəl] **1** *n* chapurreo *m*
2 *vi* hablar atropelladamente

gable ['geɪbəl] *n* aguilón *m*

gadget ['gædʒɪt] *n* artilugio *m*, aparato *m*

Gaelic ['geɪlɪk] **1** *adj* gaélico(a)
2 *n (language)* gaélico *m*

gaffe [gæf] *n* metedura *f* de pata, desliz *m*; **to make a g.** meter la pata, patinar

> 🖉 Note that the Spanish word **gafe** is a false friend and is never a translation for the English word **gaffe**. In Spanish, **gafe** means "jinxed person".

gag [gæg] **1** *n* (**a**) mordaza *f* (**b**) *Fam (joke)* chiste *m*
2 *vt* amordazar

gage [geɪdʒ] *n & vt US* = **gauge**

gaiety ['geɪətɪ] *n* regocijo *m*

gaily ['geɪlɪ] *adv* alegremente

gain [geɪn] **1** *n* ganancia *f*, beneficio *m*; *(increase)* aumento *m*
2 *vt* ganar; *Fig* **to g. ground** ganar terreno; **to g. speed** ganar velocidad, acelerar; **to g. weight** aumentar de peso

gait [geɪt] *n* (manera *f* de) andar *m*

gal *(pl* **gal** *or* **gals**) *(abbr* **gallon**) galón *m*

gala ['gɑːlə, 'geɪlə] *n* gala *f*, fiesta *f*

galaxy ['gæləksɪ] *n* galaxia *f*

gale [geɪl] *n* vendaval *m*

Galicia [gə'lɪʃə] *n* Galicia

Galician [gə'lɪʃɪən, gə'lɪʃən] **1** *adj* gallego(a)
2 *n* (**a**) *(person)* gallego(a) *m,f* (**b**) *(language)* gallego *m*

gall [gɔːl] **1** *n Fam* descaro *m*
2 *vt* molestar, irritar

gallant ['gælənt] *adj (brave)* valiente; *(also* [gə'lænt]) *(chivalrous)* galante

gallantry ['gæləntrɪ] *n (bravery)* gallardía *f*, *(politeness)* galantería *f*

galleon ['gælɪən] *n* galeón *m*

gallery ['gælərɪ] *n* (**a**) galería *f* (**b**) *Th*

gallinero *m* (**c**) *(court)* tribuna *f*

galley ['gælɪ] *n* (**a**) *(ship)* galera *f*; **g. slave** galeote *m* (**b**) *(kitchen)* cocina *f*

Gallicism ['gælɪsɪzəm] *n* galicismo *m*

gallivant ['gælɪvænt] *vi Fam* callejear

gallon ['gælən] *n* galón *m (Br* = 4,55 l; *US* = 3,79 l)

gallop ['gæləp] **1** *n* galope *m*
2 *vi* galopar

gallows ['gæləʊz] *n sing* horca *f*, patíbulo *m*

gallstone ['gɔːlstəʊn] *n* cálculo *m* biliar

galore [gə'lɔː(r)] *adv Fam* en cantidad, en abundancia

galvanize ['gælvənaɪz] *vt (metal)* galvanizar; *Fig* **to g. sb into action** galvanizar a algn

galvanized ['gælvənaɪzd] *adj* galvanizado(a)

gambit ['gæmbɪt] *n (in chess)* gambito *m*; *Fig* táctica *f*

gamble ['gæmbəl] **1** *n (risk)* riesgo *m*; *(risky undertaking)* empresa arriesgada; *(bet)* apuesta *f*
2 *vi (bet)* jugar; *(take a risk)* arriesgarse

gambler ['gæmblə(r)] *n* jugador(a) *m,f*

gambling ['gæmblɪŋ] *n* juego *m*

gambol ['gæmbəl] *vi* brincar

game [geɪm] **1** *n* (**a**) juego *m*; **g. of chance** juego de azar (**b**) *(match)* partido *m*; *(of bridge)* partida *f* (**c**) **games** *Sport* juegos *mpl*; *Br Educ* educación física (**d**) *(hunting)* caza *f*; *Fig* presa *f*; **g. reserve** coto *m* de caza
2 *adj* **g. for anything** dispuesto(a) a todo

gamekeeper ['geɪmkiːpə(r)] *n* guardabosque *mf*

gamely ['geɪmlɪ] *adv* resueltamente

gammon ['gæmən] *n Br* jamón ahumado *or* curado

gamut ['gæmət] *n* gama *f*; **to run the g. of ...** experimentar todas las posibilidades de ...

gang [gæŋ] *n (of criminals)* banda *f*, *(of youths)* pandilla *f*, *(of workers)* cuadrilla *f*
▸ **gang up** *vi Fam* confabularse (**on** contra)

gangplank ['gæŋplæŋk] *n* plancha *f*

gangrene ['gæŋɡriːn] *n* gangrena *f*

gangster ['gæŋstə(r)] n gángster m

gangway ['gæŋweɪ] n Naut pasarela f; Th pasillo m

gantry ['gæntrɪ] n puente m transversal

gaol [dʒeɪl] n & vt Br = **jail**

gap [gæp] n (**a**) abertura f, hueco m; (blank space) blanco m; (in traffic) claro m; **to bridge a g.** rellenar un hueco (**b**) (in time) intervalo m; (emptiness) vacío m (**c**) (gulf) diferencia f (**d**) (deficiency) laguna f

gape [geɪp] vi (person) quedarse boquiabierto(a), mirar boquiabierto(a); (thing) estar abierto(a)

gaping ['geɪpɪŋ] adj Fig profundo(a)

garage ['gærɑːʒ, 'gærɪdʒ] n garaje m; (for repairs) taller mecánico; (filling station) gasolinera f, estación f de servicio, Andes, Ven bomba f, Méx gasolinería f, Perú grifo m

garbage ['gɑːbɪdʒ] n US basura f, Fig tonterías fpl; **g. can** cubo m de la basura; **g. dump** vertedero m; **g. man** basurero m; **g. truck** camión m de la basura

garbled ['gɑːbəld] adj embrollado(a); **g. account** relato confuso

garden ['gɑːdən] n jardín m; **g. centre** centro m de jardinería; **g. party** recepción f al aire libre

gardener ['gɑːdənə(r)] n jardinero(a) m,f

gardenia [gɑːˈdiːnɪə] n gardenia f

gardening ['gɑːdənɪŋ] n jardinería f; **his mother does the g.** su madre es la que cuida el jardín

gargle ['gɑːgəl] vi hacer gárgaras

gargoyle ['gɑːgɔɪl] n gárgola f

garish ['geərɪʃ] adj chillón(ona)

garland ['gɑːlənd] n guirnalda f

garlic ['gɑːlɪk] n ajo m

garment ['gɑːmənt] n prenda f

garnish ['gɑːnɪʃ] vt guarnecer

garrison ['gærɪsən] n guarnición f

garrulous ['gærələs] adj locuaz

garter ['gɑːtə(r)] n liga f

gas [gæs] **1** n (**a**) gas m; **g. chamber** cámara f de gas; **g. cooker** cocina f de gas; **g. fire** estufa f de gas; **g. mask** careta f antigás; **g. ring** hornillo m de gas (**b**) US gasolina f, RP nafta f; **g. pump** surtidor m de gasolina; **g. station** gasolinera f, estación f de servicio, Andes, Ven bomba f, Méx gasolinería f, Perú grifo m; **g. tank** depósito m de la gasolina

2 vt (asphyxiate) asfixiar con gas

3 vi Fam (talk) charlotear

gash [gæʃ] **1** n herida profunda

2 vt hacer un corte en; **he gashed his forehead** se hizo una herida en la frente

gasket ['gæskɪt] n junta f

gasoline ['gæsəliːn] n US gasolina f

gasp [gɑːsp] **1** n (cry) grito sordo; (breath) bocanada f; Fig **to be at one's last g.** estar en las últimas

2 vi (in surprise) quedar boquiabierto(a); (breathe) jadear

gassy ['gæsɪ] adj (**gassier, gassiest**) gaseoso(a)

gastric ['gæstrɪk] adj gástrico(a)

gastronomic [gæstrə'nɒmɪk] adj gastronómico(a)

gate [geɪt] n (**a**) puerta f (**b**) (at football ground) entrada f; **g. (money)** taquilla f (**c**) (attendance) entrada f

gateau ['gætəʊ] n (pl gateaux ['gætəʊz]) pastel m con nata

gatecrash ['geɪtkræʃ] **1** vt colarse en

2 vi colarse

gateway ['geɪtweɪ] n puerta f; Fig pasaporte m

gather ['gæðə(r)] **1** vt (**a**) (collect) juntar; (pick) coger; (pick up) recoger (**b**) (bring together) reunir (**c**) (harvest) cosechar (**d**) **to g. speed** ir ganando velocidad; **to g. strength** cobrar fuerzas (**e**) (understand) suponer; **I g. that ...** tengo entendido que ... (**f**) Sewing fruncir

2 vi (**a**) (come together) reunirse (**b**) (form) formarse

▸ **gather round** vi agruparse

gathering ['gæðərɪŋ] **1** adj creciente

2 n reunión f

gauche [gəʊʃ] adj (clumsy) torpe; (tactless) sin tacto

gaudy ['gɔːdɪ] adj (**gaudier, gaudiest**) chillón(ona)

gauge [geɪdʒ] **1** n (**a**) medida f estándar; (of gun, wire) calibre m (**b**) Rail ancho m de vía (**c**) (calibrator) indicador m (**d**) Fig (indication) indicación f

2 vt (**a**) (measure) medir, calibrar (**b**) Fig (judge) juzgar

gaunt [gɔːnt] adj (lean) demacrado(a); (desolate) lúgubre

gauntlet ['gɔːntlɪt] n guantelete m; Fig **to run the g. of ...** estar sometido(a) a ...; Fig **to throw down the g.** arrojar el guante

gauze [gɔːz] n gasa f

gave [geɪv] pt of **give**

gawky ['gɔːkɪ] adj (**gawkier, gawkiest**) desgarbado(a)

gay [geɪ] adj (**a**) (homosexual) gay (**b**) (happy) alegre

gaze [geɪz] **1** n mirada fija

2 vi mirar fijamente

gazelle [gə'zel] n gacela f

gazette [gə'zet] n gaceta f, US periódico m

gazump [gə'zʌmp] vi Br Fam = romper

un compromiso de venta para vender a un precio más alto

GB [dʒiː'biː] (*abbr* **Great Britain**) GB

GCE [dʒiːsiː'iː] *n Br Formerly* (*abbr* **General Certificate of Education (A-Level)**) = certificado de enseñanza secundaria

GCSE [dʒiːsiːes'iː] *n Br* (*abbr* **General Certificate of Secondary Education**) = certificado de enseñanza secundaria

GDP [dʒiːdiː'piː] *n* (*abbr* **gross domestic product**) PIB *m*

GDR [dʒiːdiː'ɑː(r)] *n Hist* (*abbr* **German Democratic Republic**) RDA *f*

gear [gɪə(r)] **1** *n* (**a**) (*equipment*) equipo *m* (**b**) *Fam* (*belongings*) bártulos *mpl* (**c**) *Fam* (*clothing*) ropa *f* (**d**) *Tech* engranaje *m* (**e**) *Aut* velocidad *f*, marcha *f*; **first g.** primera *f* (velocidad *f*); **g. lever** *or US* **shift** palanca *f* de cambio
    2 *vt* ajustar, adaptar

gearbox ['gɪəbɒks] *n* caja *f* de cambios

gearstick ['gɪəstɪk], *US* **gearshift** ['gɪəʃɪft] *n* palanca *f* de cambio

gee [dʒiː] *interj US* ¡caramba!

geese [giːs] *pl of* **goose**

gel [dʒel] **1** *n* gel *m*; (*for hair*) gomina *f*
    2 *vi Fig* (*ideas etc*) cuajar
    3 *vt* (*hair*) engominar

gelatin ['dʒelətɪn] *n* gelatina *f*

gelignite ['dʒelɪgnaɪt] *n* gelignita *f*

gem [dʒem] *n* piedra preciosa; *Fig* (*person*) joya *f*

Gemini ['dʒemɪnaɪ] *n* Géminis *m*

gen [dʒen] *n Fam* **to get the g. on sth** informarse sobre algo

gender ['dʒendə(r)] *n* género *m*

gene [dʒiːn] *n* gene *m*, gen *m*

general ['dʒenərəl] **1** *adj* general; **g. knowledge** conocimientos *mpl* generales; **in g.** en general; **the g. public** el público; **g. practitioner** médico *m* de cabecera
    2 *n Mil* general *m*; *US* **g. of the army** mariscal *m* de campo

generalization [dʒenərəlaɪ'zeɪʃən] *n* generalización *f*

generalize ['dʒenərəlaɪz] *vt & vi* generalizar

generally ['dʒenərəlɪ] *adv* generalmente, en general

generate ['dʒenəreɪt] *vt* generar

generation [dʒenə'reɪʃən] *n* generación *f*; **g. gap** abismo *m* or conflicto *m* generacional

generator ['dʒenəreɪtə(r)] *n* generador *m*

generosity [dʒenə'rɒsɪtɪ] *n* generosidad *f*

generous ['dʒenərəs] *adj* generoso(a); (*plentiful*) copioso(a)

genetic [dʒɪ'netɪk] *adj* genético(a); **g. engineering** ingeniería genética

genetically [dʒɪ'netɪklɪ] *adv* genéticamente; (*plant, food*) modificado(a) genéticamente

genetics [dʒɪ'netɪks] *n sing* genética *f*

Geneva [dʒɪ'niːvə] *n* Ginebra

genial ['dʒiːnɪəl, 'dʒiːnjəl] *adj* cordial, amable

🖉 Note that the Spanish word **genial** is a false friend and is never a translation for the English word **genial**. In Spanish, **genial** means both "brilliant" and "terrific".

genie ['dʒiːnɪ] *n* duende *m*, genio *m*

genitals ['dʒenɪtəlz] *npl* órganos *mpl* genitales

genius ['dʒiːnjəs, 'dʒiːnɪəs] *n* (**a**) (*person*) genio *m* (**b**) (*gift*) don *m*

genre ['ʒɑːnrə] *n* género *m*

gent [dʒent] *n Fam* (*abbr* **gentleman**) señor *m*, caballero *m*; **the gents** los servicios (de caballeros)

genteel [dʒen'tiːl] *adj* fino(a), distinguido(a)

🖉 Note that the Spanish word **gentil** is a false friend and is never a translation for the English word **genteel**. In Spanish, **gentil** means "kind" and "pagan".

gentle ['dʒentəl] *adj* dulce, tierno(a); (*breeze*) suave

gentleman ['dʒentəlmən] *n* caballero ;b*m*; **g.'s agreement** pacto *m* de caballeros

gently ['dʒentlɪ] *adv* con cuidado

gentry ['dʒentrɪ] *n* pequeña nobleza, alta burguesía

genuine ['dʒenjʊɪn] *adj* auténtico(a), genuino(a); (*sincere*) sincero(a)

genuinely ['dʒenjʊɪnlɪ] *adv* auténticamente

geographic(al) [dʒɪə'græfɪk(əl)] *adj* geográfico(a)

geography [dʒɪ'ɒgrəfɪ, 'dʒɒgrəfɪ] *n* geografía *f*

geologic(al) [dʒɪə'lɒdʒɪk(əl)] *adj* geológico(a)

geology [dʒɪ'ɒlədʒɪ] *n* geología *f*

geometric(al) [dʒɪə'metrɪk(əl)] *adj* geométrico(a)

geometry [dʒɪ'ɒmɪtrɪ] *n* geometría *f*

geopolitical [dʒiːəʊpə'lɪtɪkəl] *adj* geopolítico(a)

geranium [dʒɪ'reɪnɪəm] *n* geranio *m*

geriatric [dʒerɪ'ætrɪk] *adj* geriátrico(a)

germ [dʒɜːm] *n* (**a**) *Biol & Fig* germen *m*
(**b**) *Med* microbio *m*

German ['dʒɜːmən] **1** *adj* alemán(ana);
G. measles rubeola *f*
2 *n* (**a**) alemán(ana) *m,f* (**b**) *(language)*
alemán *m*

Germany ['dʒɜːmənɪ] *n* Alemania

germinate ['dʒɜːmɪneɪt] *vi* germinar

gestation [dʒe'steɪʃən] *n* gestación *f*

gesticulate [dʒe'stɪkjʊleɪt] *vi* gesticular

gesture ['dʒestʃə(r)] **1** *n* gesto *m*, ademán *m*; **it's an empty g.** es pura formalidad
2 *vi* gesticular, hacer gestos

get [get] **1** *vt* (*pt & pp* got; *pp US also* gotten) (**a**) *(obtain)* obtener, conseguir;
to g. one's own way salirse con la suya
(**b**) *(earn)* ganar
(**c**) *(fetch) (something)* traer; *(somebody)* ir a por; **g. the police!** ¡llama a la policía!;
Tel **g. me Mr Brown** póngame con el Sr. Brown
(**d**) *(receive)* recibir; *Fam* **he got the sack** le despidieron
(**e**) *(bus, train, thief etc)* coger; *Am* agarrar
(**f**) *(prepare)* preparar; **can I g. you something to eat?** ¿quieres comer algo?
(**g**) *(ask)* pedir; **g. him to call me** dile que me llame
(**h**) **to g. sb to agree to sth** conseguir que algn acepte algo
(**i**) **when did you g. the house painted?** ¿cuándo os pintaron la casa?; **to g. one's hair cut** cortarse el pelo
(**j**) **they got him in the chest** le dieron en el pecho
(**k**) **have got, have got to** *see* have
(**l**) *Fam (understand)* entender
(**m**) *(record) (in writing)* apuntar; *(on tape)* grabar
2 *vi* (**a**) *(become)* ponerse; **to g. dark** anochecer; **to g. dressed** vestirse; **to g. drunk** emborracharse; **to g. late** hacerse tarde; **to g. married** casarse; **to g. used to doing sth** acostumbrarse a hacer algo; **to g. paid** cobrar
(**b**) *Fig* **we are not getting anywhere** así no vamos a ninguna parte
(**c**) *(arrive)* llegar
(**d**) **to g. to** *(come to)* llegar a; **to g. to know sb** llegar a conocer a algn
▸ **get about** *vi (person)* salir; *(news)* difundirse
▸ **get across** *vt sep (idea etc)* hacer comprender
▸ **get ahead** *vi* progresar
▸ **get along** *vi* (**a**) *(leave)* marcharse (**b**)

(manage) arreglárselas (**c**) *(two people)* llevarse bien
▸ **get around** *vi (person)* salir; *(travel)* viajar; *(news)* difundirse
▸ **get at** *vt insep* (**a**) *(reach)* alcanzar (**b**) *(ascertain)* descubrir (**c**) *(insinuate)* insinuar; **what are you getting at?** ¿a dónde quieres llegar? (**d**) *(criticize)* criticar
▸ **get away** *vi* escaparse
▸ **get away with** *vt insep* salir impune de
▸ **get back 1** *vi* (**a**) *(return)* regresar, volver (**b**) **g. back!** *(move backwards)* ¡atrás!
2 *vt sep (recover)* recuperar; *Fam* **to g. one's own back on sb** vengarse de algn
▸ **get by** *vi* (**a**) *(manage)* arreglárselas; **she can g. by in French** sabe defenderse en francés (**b**) *(pass)* pasar
▸ **get down 1** *vt sep (depress)* deprimir
2 *vi (descend)* bajar
▸ **get down to** *vt insep* ponerse a; **to g. down to the facts** ir al grano
▸ **get in 1** *vi* (**a**) *(arrive)* llegar (**b**) *Pol* ser elegido(a)
2 *vt sep* (**a**) *(buy)* comprar (**b**) *(collect)* recoger; *Fam* **he couldn't g. a word in edgeways** no pudo decir ni pío
▸ **get into** *vt insep Fig* **to g. into bad habits** adquirir malas costumbres; **to g. into trouble** meterse en un lío
▸ **get off 1** *vt insep (bus etc)* bajarse de
2 *vt sep (remove)* quitarse
3 *vi* (**a**) bajarse; *Fam* **g. off!** ¡fuera! (**b**) **to g. off to a good start** *(begin)* empezar bien (**c**) *(escape)* escaparse; **to g. off lightly** salir bien librado(a)
▸ **get off with** *vt insep Fam* ligar
▸ **get on 1** *vt insep (board)* subir a
2 *vi* (**a**) *(board)* subirse (**b**) *(make progress)* hacer progresos; **how are you getting on?** ¿cómo te van las cosas? (**c**) **to g. on (well) (with sb)** llevarse bien (con algn) (**d**) *(continue)* seguir; **to g. on with one's work** seguir trabajando (**e**) **it's getting on for eleven** son casi las once; **time's getting on** se está haciendo tarde
▸ **get on to** *vt insep* (**a**) *(find a person)* localizar; *(find out)* descubrir (**b**) *(continue)* pasar a
▸ **get out 1** *vt sep (object)* sacar
2 *vi* (**a**) *(room etc)* salir (**of** de); *(train)* bajar (**of** de) (**b**) *(escape)* escaparse (**of** de); **to g. out of an obligation** librarse de un compromiso (**c**) *(news)* difundirse; *(secret)* hacerse público
▸ **get over 1** *vt insep* (**a**) *(illness)* recuperarse de; **I can't g. over him** no le puedo olvidar (**b**) *(difficulty)* vencer

2 *vt sep (convey)* hacer comprender

▶ **get round** *vt insep* (**a**) *(problem)* salvar; *(difficulty)* vencer (**b**) *(rule)* soslayar (**c**) *(win over)* persuadir

▶ **get round to** *vt insep* **if I g. round to it si tengo tiempo**

▶ **get through 1** *vi* (**a**) *(message)* llegar (**b**) *Educ* aprobar (**c**) *Tel* **to g. through to sb** conseguir comunicar con algn

2 *vt insep* (**a**) **to g. through a lot of work** trabajar mucho (**b**) *(consume)* consumir (**c**) *Educ* aprobar

▶ **get together 1** *vi (people)* juntarse, reunirse

2 *vt sep (people)* juntar, reunir

▶ **get up 1** *vi (rise)* levantarse

2 *vt sep* (**a**) *(wake)* despertar (**b**) *(disguise)* **to g. oneself up as …** disfrazarse de …

▶ **get up to** *vt insep* hacer; **to g. up to mischief** hacer de las suyas

getaway ['getəweɪ] *n* fuga *f*; **to make one's g.** fugarse

get-together ['gettəgeðə(r)] *n* reunión *f*

geyser ['giːzə(r), *US* 'gaɪzər] *n* (**a**) *Geog* géiser *m* (**b**) *(water heater)* calentador *m* de agua

ghastly ['gɑːstlɪ] *adj* (**ghastlier, ghastliest**) horrible, espantoso(a)

gherkin ['gɜːkɪn] *n* pepinillo *m*

ghetto ['getəʊ] *n* gueto *m*

ghost [gəʊst] *n* fantasma *m*; **g. story** cuento *m* de fantasmas; **g. town** pueblo *m* fantasma

ghost-writer ['gəʊstraɪtə(r)] *n* negro(a) *m,f*

ghoulish ['guːlɪʃ] *adj* macabro(a)

giant ['dʒaɪənt] *adj & n* gigante *(m)*

gibberish ['dʒɪbərɪʃ] *n* galimatías *m inv*

gibe [dʒaɪb] **1** *n* mofa *f*

2 *vi* mofarse (**at** de)

giblets ['dʒɪblɪts] *npl* menudillos *mpl*

Gibraltar [dʒɪˈbrɔːltə(r)] *n* Gibraltar

Gibraltarian [dʒɪbrɔːlˈteərɪən] *adj & n* gibraltareño(a) *(m,f)*

giddiness ['gɪdɪnɪs] *n* mareo *m*; *(vertigo)* vértigo *m*

giddy ['gɪdɪ] *adj* (**giddier, giddiest**) mareado(a); **it makes me g.** me da vértigo; **to feel g.** sentirse mareado(a)

gift [gɪft] *n* (**a**) *(present)* regalo *m*; *Com* obsequio *m*; **g. token** vale *m* (**b**) *(talent)* don *m*; **to have a g. for music** estar muy dotado(a) para la música

gifted ['gɪftɪd] *adj* dotado(a)

gig [gɪg] *n Fam Mus* actuación *f*

gigantic [dʒaɪˈgæntɪk] *adj* gigantesco(a)

giggle ['gɪgəl] **1** *n* (**a**) risita *f* (**b**) *(lark)* broma *f*, diversión *f*

2 *vi* reírse tontamente

gild [gɪld] *vt* dorar

gill[1] [dʒɪl] *n (liquid measure)* = 0,142 l

gill[2] [gɪl] *n (of fish)* branquia *f*, agalla *f*

gilt [gɪlt] **1** *adj* dorado(a)

2 *n (colour)* dorado *m*

gilt-edged ['gɪltedʒd] *adj* **g. securities** valores *mpl* de máxima garantía

gimmick ['gɪmɪk] *n* truco *m*; *(in advertising)* reclamo *m*

gin [dʒɪn] *n* ginebra *f*; **g. and tonic** gin tonic *m*

ginger ['dʒɪndʒə(r)] **1** *n* jengibre *m*; **g. ale** ginger ale *m*

2 *adj* (**a**) *(de jengibre)* de jengibre (**b**) *(hair)* pelirrojo(a)

gingerbread ['dʒɪndʒəbred] *n* pan *m* de jengibre

gingerly ['dʒɪndʒəlɪ] *adv* cautelosamente

gipsy ['dʒɪpsɪ] *adj & n* gitano(a) *(m,f)*

giraffe [dʒɪˈrɑːf] *n* jirafa *f*

girder ['gɜːdə(r)] *n* viga *f*

girdle ['gɜːdəl] *n* faja *f*

girl [gɜːl] *n* (**a**) chica *f*, joven *f*; *(child)* niña *f*; **g. guide**, *US* **g. scout** exploradora *f* (**b**) *(daughter)* hija *f* (**c**) *(sweetheart)* novia *f*

girlfriend ['gɜːlfrend] *n* (**a**) *(lover)* novia *f* (**b**) *(female friend)* amiga *f*

girlhood ['gɜːlhʊd] *n* niñez *f*

girlish ['gɜːlɪʃ] *adj* (**a**) de niña (**b**) *(effeminate)* afeminado(a)

giro ['dʒaɪrəʊ] *n Br* giro *m* (postal); **g. (cheque)** cheque *m* de giros postales

gist [dʒɪst] *n* esencia *f*; **did you get the g. of what he was saying?** ¿cogiste la idea de lo que decía?

give [gɪv] **1** *n (elasticity)* elasticidad *f*

2 *vt (pt gave; pp given)* (**a**) dar; **to g. sth to sb** dar algo a algn; **to g. a start** pegar un salto; **to g. sb a present** regalar algo a algn

(**b**) *(provide)* suministrar; **to g. sb sth to eat** dar de comer a algn

(**c**) *(pay)* pagar

(**d**) *(concert)* dar; *(speech)* pronunciar

(**e**) *(dedicate)* dedicar

(**f**) *(grant)* otorgar; **to g. sb one's attention** prestar atención a algn

(**g**) **to g. sb to understand that …** dar a entender a algn que …

(**h**) *(yield)* ceder; **to g. way** *Aut* ceder el paso; *Fig* ceder; *(of legs)* flaquear

3 *vi* (**a**) **to g. as good as one gets** devolver golpe por golpe

(**b**) *(yield)* ceder; *(fabric)* dar de sí

▸**give away** *vt sep* (**a**) repartir; *(present)* regalar (**b**) *(disclose)* revelar; **to g. the game away** descubrir el pastel (**c**) *(betray)* traicionar

▸**give back** *vt sep* devolver

▸**give in 1** *vi* (**a**) *(admit defeat)* darse por vencido(a); *(surrender)* rendirse (**b**) **to g. in to** ceder ante

2 *vt sep (hand in)* entregar

▸**give off** *vt sep (smell etc)* despedir

▸**give out** *vt sep* distribuir, repartir

▸**give over 1** *vt sep (hand over)* entregar; *(devote)* dedicar

2 *vi Fam* **g. over!** ¡basta ya!

▸**give up 1** *vt sep* (**a**) *(idea)* abandonar; **to g. up smoking** dejar de fumar (**b**) *(betray)* traicionar (**c**) *(hand over)* entregar; **to g. oneself up** entregarse

2 *vi (admit defeat)* darse por vencido(a), rendirse

▸**give up on** *vt insep* darse por vencido con

given ['gɪvən] **1** *adj* (**a**) *(particular)* dado(a); **at a g. time** en un momento dado (**b**) **g. to** dado(a) a

2 *conj* (**a**) *(considering)* dado(a) (**b**) *(if)* si

3 *pp of* **give**

glacial ['gleɪsɪəl] *adj* (**a**) *Geol* glaciar (**b**) *(icy)* glacial; *Fig* **g. look** mirada *f* glacial

glacier ['glæsɪə(r)] *n* glaciar *m*

glad [glæd] *adj* (**gladder, gladdest**) contento(a); *(happy)* alegre; **he'll be only too g. to help you** tendrá mucho gusto en ayudarle; **to be g.** alegrarse

gladiator ['glædɪeɪtə(r)] *n Hist* gladiador *m*

gladly ['glædlɪ] *adv* con mucho gusto

glamor ['glæmər] *n US* = **glamour**

glamorous ['glæmərəs] *adj* atractivo(a), encantador(a)

glamour ['glæmə(r)] *n* atractivo *m*; *(charm)* encanto *m*; **a g. girl** una belleza

glance [glɑːns] **1** *n* mirada *f*, vistazo *m*; **at a g.** de un vistazo; **at first g.** a primera vista

2 *vi* echar un vistazo (**at** a)

▸**glance off** *vt insep (of ball etc)* rebotar de

glancing ['glɑːnsɪŋ] *adj (blow)* oblicuo(a)

gland [glænd] *n* glándula *f*

glandular ['glændjʊlə(r)] *adj* glandular; **g. fever** mononucleosis infecciosa

glare [gleə(r)] **1** *n (light)* luz *f* deslumbrante; *(dazzle)* deslumbramiento *m*; *(look)* mirada *f* feroz

2 *vi (dazzle)* deslumbrar; *(look)* lanzar

una mirada furiosa (**at** a)

glaring ['gleərɪŋ] *adj (light)* deslumbrante; *(colour)* chillón(ona); *(obvious)* evidente

glass [glɑːs] *n* (**a**) *(material)* vidrio *m*; **pane of g.** cristal *m* (**b**) *(drinking vessel)* vaso *m*; **wine g.** copa *f* (para vino) (**c**) **glasses** gafas *fpl, Am* lentes *mpl*, anteojos *mpl*; **to wear glasses** llevar gafas *or Am* lentes *or* anteojos

glasshouse ['glɑːshaʊs] *n* invernadero *m*

glassware ['glɑːsweə(r)] *n* cristalería *f*

glassy ['glɑːsɪ] *adj* (**glassier, glassiest**) *(water)* cristalino(a); *(eyes)* vidrioso(a)

glaze [gleɪz] **1** *n (varnish)* barniz *m*; *(for pottery)* vidriado *m*

2 *vt* (**a**) *(windows)* acristalar; (**b**) *(varnish)* barnizar; *(ceramics)* vidriar (**c**) *Culin* glasear

glazed [gleɪzd] *adj (eyes)* de mirada ausente

glazier ['gleɪzɪə(r)] *n* vidriero(a) *m,f*

gleam [gliːm] **1** *n* (**a**) destello *m* (**b**) *Fig (glimmer)* rayo *m*

2 *vi* brillar, relucir

gleaming ['gliːmɪŋ] *adj* brillante, reluciente

glean [gliːn] *vt Fig* recoger, cosechar

glee [gliː] *n* gozo *m*

gleeful ['gliːfʊl] *adj* gozoso(a)

glen [glen] *n* cañada *f*

glib [glɪb] *adj* (**glibber, glibbest**) *Pej* de mucha labia

glide [glaɪd] *vi* (**a**) *(slip, slide)* deslizarse (**b**) *Av* planear

glider ['glaɪdə(r)] *n* planeador *m*

gliding ['glaɪdɪŋ] *n* vuelo *m* sin motor

glimmer ['glɪmə(r)] *n* (**a**) *(light)* luz *f* tenue (**b**) *Fig (trace)* destello *m*

glimpse [glɪmps] **1** *n* atisbo *m*

2 *vt* atisbar

glint [glɪnt] **1** *n* destello *m*, centelleo *m*; **he had a g. in his eye** le brillaban los ojos

2 *vi* destellar, centellear

glisten ['glɪsən] *vi* relucir, brillar

glitter ['glɪtə(r)] **1** *n* brillo *m*

2 *vi* relucir

gloat [gləʊt] *vi* jactarse; **to g. over another's misfortune** recrearse con la desgracia de otro

global ['gləʊbəl] *adj* (**a**) *(of the world)* mundial (**b**) *(overall)* global

globe [gləʊb] *n* globo *m*, esfera *f*

gloom [gluːm] *n (obscurity)* penumbra *f*; *(melancholy)* melancolía *f*; *(despair)* desolación *f*

gloomy ['gluːmɪ] *adj* (**gloomier, gloomiest**) *(dark)* oscuro(a); *(weather)* gris;

(dismal) deprimente; *(despairing)* pesimista; *(sad)* triste

glorify ['glɔːrɪfaɪ] *vt* glorificar

glorious ['glɔːrɪəs] *adj (momentous)* glorioso(a); *(splendid)* magnífico(a), espléndido(a)

glory ['glɔːrɪ] *n* gloria *f; Fig (splendour)* esplendor *m; Fig (triumph)* triunfo *m*

gloss [glɒs] **1** *n* (**a**) *(explanation)* glosa *f* (**b**) *(sheen)* brillo *m*; **g. (paint)** pintura *f* brillante
  2 *vi* glosar
  ▶ **gloss over** *vt insep Fig* encubrir

glossary ['glɒsərɪ] *n* glosario *m*

glossy ['glɒsɪ] *adj* (**glossier, glossiest**) lustroso(a); **g. magazine** revista *f* de lujo

glove [glʌv] *n* guante *m; Aut* **g. compartment** guantera *f*

glow [gləʊ] **1** *n* brillo *m*; *(of fire)* incandescencia *f*; *(of sun)* arrebol *m*; *(heat)* calor *m*; *(light)* luz *f*; *(in cheeks)* rubor *m*
  2 *vi* brillar; *(fire)* arder; *Fig* rebosar de

glower ['glaʊə(r)] *vi* poner cara de enfadado(a)

glowing ['gləʊɪŋ] *adj* (**a**) *(fire)* incandescente; *(colour)* vivo(a); *(light)* brillante (**b**) *(cheeks)* encendido(a) (**c**) *Fig (report)* entusiasta

glucose ['gluːkəʊz] *n* glucosa *f*

glue [gluː] **1** *n* pegamento *m*, cola *f*
  2 *vt* pegar (**to** a)

glum [glʌm] *adj* (**glummer, glummest**) alicaído(a)

glut [glʌt] *n* superabundancia *f*, exceso *m*

glutton ['glʌtən] *n* glotón(ona) *m,f; Fam Fig* you're a g. for punishment eres masoquista

GM [dʒiː'em] *adj* (*abbr* **genetically modified**) transgénico(a), modificado(a) genéticamente; **GM food** (alimentos) transgénicos

GMO [dʒiːem'əʊ] *n* (*abbr* **genetically modified organism**) OMG *m*

GMT [dʒiːem'tiː] *n* (*abbr* **Greenwich Mean Time**) hora *f* del meridiano de Greenwich

gnarled [nɑːld] *adj* nudoso(a)

gnash [næʃ] *vt* rechinar

gnat [næt] *n* mosquito *m*

gnaw [nɔː] *vt & vi (chew)* roer

gnome [nəʊm] *n* gnomo *m*

GNP [dʒiːen'piː] *n* (*abbr* **gross national product**) PNB *m*

go [gəʊ] **1** *vi* (3rd person sing pres **goes**; *pt* **went**; *pp* **gone**) (**a**) ir; **to go by car/on foot** ir en coche/a pie; **to go for a walk** (ir a) dar un paseo; **to g. on a journey** ir de viaje; **to go shopping** ir de compras; *Fig* **to go too far** pasarse (de la raya)

(**b**) *(depart)* irse, marcharse; *(bus)* salir
(**c**) *(disappear)* desaparecer
(**d**) *(function)* funcionar; *Fig* **to get things going** poner las cosas en marcha
(**e**) *(sell)* venderse; **shoes going cheap** zapatos a precios de rebaja
(**f**) *(become)* quedarse, volverse; **to go blind** quedarse ciego(a); **to go mad** volverse loco(a)
(**g**) *(progress)* ir, marchar; **everything went well** todo salió bien; **how's it going?** ¿qué tal (te van las cosas)?
(**h**) **to be going to** *(in the future)* ir a; *(on the point of)* estar a punto de
(**i**) *(fit)* caber
(**j**) *(be kept)* guardarse
(**k**) *(be available)* quedar; **I'll take whatever's going** me conformo con lo que hay
(**l**) *(be acceptable)* valer; **anything goes** todo vale
(**m**) *(break)* romperse; *(yield)* ceder
(**n**) **how does that song go?** ¿cómo es aquella canción?
(**o**) *(time)* pasar; **there are only two weeks to go** sólo quedan dos semanas
(**p**) *(be inherited)* pasar (**to** a)
(**q**) *(say)* decir; **as the saying goes** según el dicho
(**r**) **to let sth go** soltar algo
  2 *vt* (**a**) *(travel)* hacer, recorrer
  (**b**) **to go it alone** apañárselas solo
  3 *n* (**a**) *(energy)* energía *f*, dinamismo *m*
  (**b**) *(try)* intento *m*; **to have a go at sth** probar suerte con algo
  (**c**) *(turn)* turno *m*; **it's your go** te toca a ti
  (**d**) **to make a go of sth** tener éxito en algo
  (**e**) **I knew from the word go** lo sabía desde el principio
  (**f**) **to have a go at sb** criticar a algn
  ▶ **go about 1** *vt insep* (**a**) *(task)* emprender; **how do you go about it?** ¿cómo hay que hacerlo? (**b**) **to go about one's business** ocuparse de sus asuntos
  2 *vi (rumour)* correr
  ▶ **go after** *vt insep (pursue)* andar tras
  ▶ **go against** *vt insep (oppose)* ir en contra de; *(verdict)* ser desfavorable a
  ▶ **go ahead** *vi* (**a**) *(proceed)* proceder (**b**) **we'll go on ahead** iremos delante
  ▶ **go along 1** *vt insep (street)* pasar por
  2 *vi (progress)* progresar
  ▶ **go along with** *vt insep* (**a**) *(agree with)* estar de acuerdo con (**b**) *(accompany)* acompañar
  ▶ **go around** *vi* (**a**) *(rumour)* correr (**b**) **there's enough to go around** hay para todos

▸ **go away** *vi* marcharse

▸ **go back** *vi* (**a**) *(return)* volver, regresar (**b**) *Fig* **to go back to** *(date from)* datar de

▸ **go back on** *vt insep* **to go back on one's word** faltar a su palabra

▸ **go back to** *vt insep* volver a

▸ **go by** *vi* pasar; **as time goes by** con el tiempo

▸ **go down** *vi* (**a**) *(descend)* bajar; *(sun)* ponerse; *(ship)* hundirse (**b**) *(diminish)* disminuir; *(temperature)* bajar (**c**) *(be received)* ser acogido(a)

▸ **go down with** *vt insep (contract)* coger

▸ **go for** *vt insep* (**a**) *(attack)* lanzarse sobre; *Fam Fig* **go for it!** ¡a por ello! (**b**) *(fetch)* ir por (**c**) *Fam (like)* gustar

▸ **go in** *vi* entrar

▸ **go in for** *vt insep (exam)* presentarse a; *(hobby)* dedicarse a

▸ **go into** *vt insep* (**a**) *(enter)* entrar en; **to go into journalism** dedicarse al periodismo (**b**) *(study)* examinar; *(matter)* investigar (**c**) *(energy, money)* invertir en

▸ **go off 1** *vi* (**a**) *(leave)* irse, marcharse (**b**) *(bomb)* explotar; *(gun)* dispararse; *(alarm)* sonar (**c**) *(food)* pasarse (**d**) *(event)* resultar

2 *vt insep Fam* **to go off sth** perder el gusto *or* el interés por algo

▸ **go on** *vi* (**a**) *(continue)* seguir, continuar; **to go on talking** seguir hablando; *Fam* **to go on and on about sth** no parar de hablar sobre algo; *(complain)* quejarse constantemente de algo (**b**) *(happen)* pasar, ocurrir (**c**) *(time)* transcurrir, pasar (**d**) *(light)* encenderse

▸ **go out** *vi* (**a**) *(leave)* salir; **to go out for a meal** comer *or* cenar fuera (**b**) *(boy and girl)* salir juntos (**c**) *(fire, light)* apagarse (**d**) *(tide)* bajar (**e**) *TV & Rad* transmitirse (**f**) **to go (all) out** ir a por todas (**g**) *(in competition)* perder la eliminatoria

▸ **go over** *vt insep (revise)* repasar

▸ **go over to** *vt insep* (**a**) acercarse a; **to go over to the enemy** pasarse al enemigo (**b**) *(switch to)* pasar a

▸ **go round** *vi* (**a**) *(revolve)* dar vueltas (**b**) **to go round to sb's house** pasar por casa de algn

▸ **go through 1** *vi (bill)* ser aprobado(a)

2 *vt insep* (**a**) *(examine)* examinar; *(search)* registrar (**b**) *(rehearse)* ensayar (**c**) *(spend)* gastar (**d**) *(list etc)* explicar (**e**) *(endure)* sufrir

▸ **go through with** *vt insep* llevar a cabo

▸ **go under** *vi* (**a**) *(ship)* hundirse (**b**) *(business)* fracasar

▸ **go up** *vi* (**a**) *(price etc)* subir (**b**) **to go up**

to sb acercarse a algn (**c**) *(in a lift)* subir (**d**) **to go up in flames** quemarse (**e**) *Sport (be promoted)* subir

▸ **go with** *vt insep* (**a**) *(accompany)* ir con (**b**) *(colours)* hacer juego con

▸ **go without 1** *vt insep* (**a**) pasarse sin, prescindir de (**b**) *Fam* **that goes without saying** eso es evidente

2 *vi (not have)* aguantarse sin nada

goad [gəʊd] *vt* aguijonear

go-ahead ['gəʊəhed] *n Fam* **to give sb the g.** dar luz verde a algn

goal [gəʊl] *n* (**a**) *Sport* gol *m*; **g. kick** saque *m* de puerta; **g. post** poste *m*; **g. scorer** goleador(a) *m,f* (**b**) *(aim, objective)* meta *f*, objetivo *m*

goalkeeper ['gəʊlkiːpə(r)] *n* portero(a) *m,f*

goat [gəʊt] *n (female)* cabra *f*; *(male)* macho cabrío

gob [gɒb] *n Br Fam* boca *f*

gobble ['gɒbəl] *vt* engullir

go-between ['gəʊbɪtwiːn] *n* intermediario(a) *m,f*

goblet ['gɒblɪt] *n* copa *f*

god [gɒd] *n* dios *m*; **for G.'s sake!** ¡por Dios!; **G.** Dios; **(my) G.!** ¡Dios mío!; **G. forbid!** ¡Dios no lo quiera!; **G. only knows** sabe Dios

godchild ['gɒdtʃaɪld] *n* ahijado(a) *m,f*

goddam(n) ['gɒdæm] *US Fam* **1** *adj* maldito(a), dichoso(a), *Méx* pinche

2 *adv* **that was g. stupid!** ¡eso fue una auténtica estupidez!

goddaughter ['gɒddɔːtə(r)] *n* ahijada *f*

goddess ['gɒdɪs] *n* diosa *f*

godfather ['gɒdfɑːðə(r)] *n* padrino *m*

godforsaken ['gɒdfəseɪkən] *adj (place)* remoto(a)

godmother ['gɒdmʌðə(r)] *n* madrina *f*

godparents ['gɒdpeərənts] *npl* padrinos *mpl*

godsend ['gɒdsend] *n* regalo inesperado

godson ['gɒdsʌn] *n* ahijado *m*

goggles ['gɒgəlz] *npl* gafas *fpl* protectoras, *CSur* antiparras *fpl*

going ['gəʊɪŋ] **1** *adj* (**a**) *(price)* corriente; **the g. rate** el precio medio (**b**) **a g. concern** un negocio que marcha bien (**c**) **to get** *or* **be g.** marcharse (**d**) **to keep g.** resistir

2 *n* (**a**) **that was good g.!** ¡qué rápido! (**b**) *Fig* **to get out while the g. is good** retirarse antes que sea demasiado tarde

goings-on [gəʊɪŋz'ɒn] *npl Fam* tejemanejes *mpl*

go-kart ['gəʊkɑːt] *n Sport* kart *m*

gold [gəʊld] **1** *n* oro *m*; **g. leaf** pan *m* de

oro; **g. medal** medalla f de oro; **g. mine** mina f de oro

2 adj de oro; (colour) oro, dorado(a)

golden ['gəʊldən] adj de oro; (colour) dorado(a); Fig **a g. opportunity** una excelente oportunidad; Orn **g. eagle** águila f real; Fig **g. handshake** indemnización f por despido; **g. wedding** bodas fpl de oro

goldfish ['gəʊldfɪʃ] n pez m de colores

gold-plated [gəʊld'pleɪtɪd] adj chapado(a) en oro

goldsmith ['gəʊldsmɪθ] n orfebre m

golf [gɒlf] n golf m; **g. ball** pelota f de golf; **g. club** (stick) palo m de golf; (place) club m de golf; **g. course** campo m de golf

golfer ['gɒlfə(r)] n golfista mf

golly ['gɒlɪ] interj ¡vaya!

gone [gɒn] **1** adj desaparecido(a)

2 pp of **go**

gong [gɒŋ] n gong m

good [gʊd] **1** adj (**better, best**) (**a**) (before noun) buen(a); (after noun) bueno(a); **a g. book** un buen libro; **g. afternoon/evening** buenas tardes; **g. morning** buenos días; **g. night** buenas noches; **it looks g.** tiene buena pinta; **to be as g. as new** estar como nuevo(a); **to feel g.** sentirse bien; **to have a g. time** pasarlo bien; **to smell g.** oler bien; **G. Friday** Viernes m Santo

(**b**) (kind) amable; (generous) generoso(a)

(**c**) (healthy) sano(a)

(**d**) (morally correct) correcto(a); **be g.!** ¡pórtate bien!

(**e**) **he's g. at languages** tiene facilidad para los idiomas

(**f**) (attractive) bonito(a); **red looks g. on you** el rojo te favorece mucho; **g. looks** atractivo m, belleza f

(**g**) **it's as g. as an offer** equivale a una oferta; **it's as g. a way as any** es una manera como otra cualquiera

(**h**) (at least) como mínimo

(**i**) (sufficient) bastante

(**j**) **to make g.** (injustice) reparar; (loss) compensar; (succeed in life) triunfar

(**k**) (reliable) de confianza

(**l**) (propitious) propicio(a)

(**m**) **she comes from a g. family** es de buena familia

(**n**) (character) agradable; **he's in a g. mood** está de buen humor

2 n (**a**) bien m; **g. and evil** el bien y el mal; **to do g.** hacer el bien

(**b**) (advantage) bien m, provecho m; **for your own g.** para tu propio bien; **it's no g. waiting** no sirve de nada esperar; **it** **will do you g.** te hará bien

(**c**) **goods** (possessions) bienes mpl

(**d**) Com **goods** artículos mpl, géneros mpl; **goods train** tren m de mercancías

3 adv **she's gone for g.** se ha ido para siempre

4 interj ¡muy bien!

goodbye [gʊd'baɪ] **1** interj ¡adiós!

2 n adiós m, despedida f; **to say g. to sb** despedirse de algn

good-for-nothing ['gʊdfənʌθɪŋ] adj & n inútil (mf)

good-hearted [gʊd'hɑːtɪd] adj de buen corazón

good-looking [gʊd'lʊkɪŋ] adj guapo(a)

good-natured [gʊd'neɪtʃəd] adj amable, bondadoso(a)

goodness ['gʊdnɪs] n bondad f; **my g.!** ¡Dios mío!; **thank g.!** ¡gracias a Dios!; **for g. sake!** ¡por Dios!

good-tempered [gʊd'tempəd] adj apacible

goodwill [gʊd'wɪl] n (**a**) buena voluntad f (**b**) Com (reputation) buen nombre m

goof [guːf] US Fam **1** n metedura f or Am metida f de pata

2 vi meter la pata

goose [guːs] n (pl **geese**) ganso m, oca f

gooseberry ['gʊzbərɪ, 'guːsbərɪ] n uva espina, grosella espinosa; Fam **to play g.** hacer de carabina

gooseflesh ['guːsfleʃ] n, **goosepimples** ['guːspɪmpəlz] npl carne f de gallina

goose-step ['guːsstep] vi ir a paso de la oca

gore[1] [gɔː(r)] n sangre derramada

gore[2] [gɔː(r)] vt (of bull) cornear, dar cornadas a

gorge [gɔːdʒ] **1** n desfiladero m

2 vt & vi **to g. (oneself) (on)** atiborrarse (de)

gorgeous ['gɔːdʒəs] adj magnífico(a), estupendo(a); (person) atractivo(a), guapo(a)

gorilla [gə'rɪlə] n gorila m

gorse [gɔːs] n aulaga f

gory ['gɔːrɪ] adj (**gorier, goriest**) sangriento(a)

gosh [gɒʃ] interj Fam ¡cielos!, ¡caray!

go-slow [gəʊ'sləʊ] n huelga f de celo

gospel ['gɒspəl] n **the G.** el Evangelio; Fam **it's the g. truth** es la pura verdad

gossip ['gɒsɪp] **1** n (**a**) (rumour) cotilleo m; **g. column** ecos mpl de sociedad (**b**) (person) chismoso(a) m,f, cotilla mf

2 vi (natter) cotillear, chismorrear

got [gɒt] pt & pp of **get**

Gothic ['gɒθɪk] adj gótico(a)

gotten ['gɒtən] US pp of **get**

gourmet ['gʊəmeɪ] n gourmet mf

gout [gaʊt] n gota f

govern ['gʌvən] vt (a) gobernar (b) (determine) determinar

governess ['gʌvənɪs] n institutriz f

governing ['gʌvənɪŋ] adj gobernante; **g. body** consejo m de administración

government ['gʌvənmənt] n gobierno m

governmental [gʌvən'mentəl] adj gubernamental

governor ['gʌvənə(r)] n (ruler) gobernador(a) m,f; (of prison) director(a) m,f; (of school) administrador(a) m,f

gown [gaʊn] n (dress) vestido largo; Jur & Univ toga f

GP [dʒiː'piː] n (abbr **general practitioner**) médico(a) m,f de familia or de cabecera

GPO [dʒiːpiː'əʊ] n Br Formerly (abbr **General Post Office**) ≃ (Administración f Central de) Correos mpl

grab [græb] **1** n agarrón m; Fam **to be up for grabs** estar disponible

2 vt (a) agarrar; **to g. hold of sb** agarrarse a algn (b) Fig **g. a bottle of wine** píllate una botella de vino (c) Fig **how does that g. you?** ¿qué te parece?

grace [greɪs] **1** n (a) gracia f; Fig **to fall from g.** caer en desgracia (b) **to say g.** bendecir la mesa (c) **to do sth with good g.** hacer algo de buena gana (d) **five days' g.** (reprieve) un plazo de cinco días (e) (elegance) elegancia f (f) **Your G.** (Su) Excelencia

2 vt (a) (adorn) adornar (b) (honour) honrar

graceful ['greɪsfʊl] adj elegante; (movement) garboso(a)

gracefully ['greɪsfʊlɪ] adv (a) (beautifully) con gracia, con elegancia (b) (accept) con cortesía

gracious ['greɪʃəs] **1** adj (a) (elegant) elegante (b) (courteous) cortés (c) (kind) amable

2 interj **good g. (me)!, goodness g.!** ¡santo cielo!

grade [greɪd] **1** n (a) (quality) grado m; (rank) categoría f, Mil rango m (b) US Educ (mark) nota f (c) US Educ (class) clase f; **g. school** escuela primaria (d) (level) nivel m; **to make the g.** llegar al nivel deseado (e) US (slope) pendiente f (f) US **g. crossing** paso m a nivel

2 vt clasificar

gradient ['greɪdɪənt] n (graph) declive m; (hill) cuesta f, pendiente f

gradual ['grædjʊəl] adj gradual, progresivo(a)

gradually ['grædjʊəlɪ] adv poco a poco

graduate 1 n ['grædjʊɪt] Educ titulado(a) m,f; Univ licenciado(a) m,f; US **g. school** escuela f para graduados

2 vi ['grædjʊeɪt] (a) Educ sacarse el título; Univ licenciarse (**in** en) (b) **to g. to** pasar a (c) US (from high school) ≃ sacar el bachillerato

graduation [grædjʊ'eɪʃən] n graduación f; Univ **g. ceremony** ceremonia f de entrega de los títulos

graffiti [grə'fiːtiː] npl grafiti mpl

graft [grɑːft] **1** n (a) Med injerto m (b) Fam (work) trabajo m (c) US (bribery) soborno m

2 vt Med injertar (**on to** en)

3 vi Fam trabajar duro

grain [greɪn] n (a) (cereals) cereales mpl (b) (particle) grano m; Fig **there's not a g. of truth in it** no tiene ni pizca de verdad (c) (in wood) fibra f; (in stone) veta f; (in leather) flor f; Fig **to go against the g.** ir a contrapelo

gram [græm] n gramo m

grammar ['græmə(r)] n gramática f; **g. (book)** libro m de gramática; Br **g. school** = instituto estatal de segunda enseñanza al que se ingresa por examen selectivo

grammatical [grə'mætɪkəl] adj gramatical

gramme [græm] n gramo m

gramophone ['græməfəʊn] n gramófono m

granary ['grænərɪ] n granero m

grand [grænd] **1** adj (a) grande; (before singular noun) gran; **g. piano** piano m de cola; **G. Prix** Gran Premio m (b) (splendid) grandioso(a), magnífico(a); (impressive) impresionante (c) **g. total** total m (d) Fam (wonderful) estupendo(a)

2 n Fam mil libras fpl; US mil dólares mpl

grandchild ['græntʃaɪld] n nieto(a) m,f

granddad ['grændæd] n Fam abuelo m

granddaughter ['grændɔːtə(r)] n nieta f

grandeur ['grændʒə(r)] n grandeza f, grandiosidad f

grandfather ['grænfɑːðə(r)] n abuelo m; **g. clock** reloj m de caja

grandiose ['grændɪəʊs] adj grandioso(a)

grandma ['grænmɑː] n Fam abuelita f

grandmother ['grænmʌðə(r)] n abuela f

grandpa ['grænpɑː] n Fam abuelito m

grandparents ['grænpeərənts] npl abuelos mpl

grandson ['grænsʌn] n nieto m

grandstand ['grænstænd] n tribuna f

granite ['grænɪt] n granito m

granny ['grænɪ] n Fam abuelita f

grant [grɑːnt] **1** vt (**a**) (allow) conceder, otorgar (**b**) (admit) admitir; **to take sb for granted** no apreciar a algn en lo que vale; **to take sth for granted** dar algo por sentado
2 n Educ beca f; (subsidy) subvención f

granulated ['grænjʊleɪtɪd] adj granulado(a)

granule ['grænjuːl] n gránulo m

grape [greɪp] n uva f; **g. juice** mosto m

grapefruit ['greɪpfruːt] n pomelo m

grapevine ['greɪpvaɪn] n Bot vid f; (against wall) parra f; Fam **I heard it on** or **through the g.** me enteré por ahí

graph [grɑːf, græf] n gráfica f

graphic ['græfɪk] adj gráfico(a); **g. arts** artes gráficas; **g. designer** grafista mf

graphics ['græfɪks] n (**a**) (study) grafismo m (**b**) pl Comput gráficas fpl

grapple ['græpəl] **1** vi (struggle) luchar cuerpo a cuerpo (**with** con); Fig **to g. with a problem** intentar resolver un problema
2 n (hook) garfio m

grasp [grɑːsp] **1** vt (**a**) agarrar (**b**) (understand) comprender
2 n (**a**) (grip) agarrón m (**b**) (understanding) comprensión f; **within sb's g.** al alcance de algn

grasping ['grɑːspɪŋ] adj avaro(a)

grass [grɑːs] **1** n (**a**) hierba f; (lawn) césped m; (pasture) pasto m; **keep off the g.** (sign) prohibido pisar el césped; **g. court** pista f de hierba; **g. roots** base f; **g. snake** culebra f (**b**) Fam (drug) hierba f (**c**) Br Fam (informer) soplón(ona) m,f, chivato(a) m,f
2 vi Br Fam chivarse (**on** a)
▸ **grass over** vi cubrirse de hierba

grasshopper ['grɑːshɒpə(r)] n saltamontes m inv

grassland ['grɑːslænd] n pradera f

grass-roots ['grɑːsruːts] adj de base; **at g. level** a nivel popular

grassy ['grɑːsɪ] adj (grassier, grassiest) cubierto(a) de hierba

grate¹ [greɪt] **1** vt Culin rallar
2 vi chirriar

grate² [greɪt] n (**a**) (in fireplace) rejilla f (**b**) (fireplace) chimenea f (**c**) Constr rejilla f, reja f

grateful ['greɪtfʊl] adj agradecido(a); **to be g. for** agradecer

grater ['greɪtə(r)] n Culin rallador m

gratification [grætɪfɪ'keɪʃən] n (pleasure) placer m, satisfacción f

gratify ['grætɪfaɪ] vt (**a**) (please) complacer (**b**) (yield to) sucumbir a

gratifying ['grætɪfaɪɪŋ] adj grato(a)

grating¹ ['greɪtɪŋ] n rejilla f, reja f

grating² ['greɪtɪŋ] adj chirriante; (tone) áspero(a)

gratis ['greɪtɪs, 'grætɪs] adv gratis

gratitude ['grætɪtjuːd] n agradecimiento m

gratuitous [grə'tjuːɪtəs] adj gratuito(a)

gratuity [grə'tjuːɪtɪ] n gratificación f

grave¹ [greɪv] n sepultura f, tumba f

grave² [greɪv] adj (look etc) serio(a); (situation) grave

gravel ['grævəl] n grava f, gravilla f

gravestone ['greɪvstəʊn] n lápida f sepulcral

graveyard ['greɪvjɑːd] n cementerio m

gravity ['grævɪtɪ] n gravedad f

gravy ['greɪvɪ] n salsa f, jugo m (de la carne)

gray [greɪ] adj & n US = **grey**

graze¹ [greɪz] vi pacer, pastar

graze² [greɪz] **1** vt (scratch) rasguñar; (brush against) rozar
2 n rasguño m

grease [griːs, griːz] **1** n grasa f
2 vt engrasar

greaseproof ['griːspruːf] adj **g. paper** papel graso

greasy ['griːsɪ, 'griːzɪ] adj (greasier, greasiest) (**a**) (oily) grasiento(a); (hair, food) graso(a) (**b**) (slippery) resbaladizo(a) (**c**) Fam (ingratiating) pelotillero(a)

great [greɪt] **1** adj (**a**) grande; (before singular noun) gran; (pain, heat) fuerte; **a g. many** muchos(as); **G. Britain** Gran Bretaña; Br **G. Bear** Osa f Mayor (**b**) Fam (excellent) estupendo(a), magnífico(a); **to have a g. time** pasarlo en grande
2 adv Fam muy bien, estupendamente

great-aunt [greɪt'ɑːnt] n tía abuela

great-grandchild [greɪt'græntʃaɪld] n bisnieto(a) m,f

great-grandfather [greɪt'grænfɑːðə(r)] n bisabuelo m

great-grandmother [greɪt'grænmʌðə(r)] n bisabuela f

greatly ['greɪtlɪ] adv muy, mucho

greatness ['greɪtnɪs] n grandeza f

great-uncle [greɪt'ʌŋkəl] n tío abuelo

Greece [griːs] n Grecia

greed [griːd], **greediness** ['griːdɪnɪs] n (for food) gula f; (for money) codicia f, avaricia f

greedy ['griːdɪ] adj (greedier, greediest) (for food) glotón(ona); (for money) codicioso(a) (**for** de)

Greek [griːk] **1** *adj* griego(a)
2 *n* (**a**) *(person)* griego(a) *m,f* (**b**) *(language)* griego *m*

green [griːn] **1** *n* (**a**) *(colour)* verde *m* (**b**) *(in golf)* campo *m*; **village g.** plaza *f* (del pueblo) (**c**) **greens** verdura *f*, verduras *fpl*
2 *adj* (**a**) verde; **g. bean** judía *f* verde, *Bol, RP* chaucha *f*, *CAm* ejote *m*, *Col, Cuba* habichuela *f*, *Chile* poroto *m* verde, *Ven* vainita *f*; **g. belt** zona *f* verde; *US* **g. card** *(work permit)* permiso *m* de trabajo; **g. pepper** pimiento *m* verde; **she was g. with envy** se la comía la envidia (**b**) *(inexperienced)* verde, novato(a); *(gullible)* crédulo(a) (**c**) *Pol* **G. Party** Partido *m* Verde

greenery ['griːnəri] *n* follaje *m*
greenfly ['griːnflaɪ] *n* pulgón *m*
greengage ['griːngeɪdʒ] *n* ciruela claudia
greengrocer ['griːngrəʊsə(r)] *n* *Br* verdulero(a) *m,f*
greenhouse ['griːnhaʊs] *n* invernadero *m*; **g. effect** efecto invernadero
greenish ['griːnɪʃ] *adj* verdoso(a)
Greenland ['griːnlənd] *n* Groenlandia
greet [griːt] *vt (wave at)* saludar; *(receive)* recibir; *(welcome)* dar la bienvenida a
greeting ['griːtɪŋ] *n* (**a**) saludo *m*; **greetings card** tarjeta *f* de felicitación (**b**) *(reception)* recibimiento *m*; *(welcome)* bienvenida *f*
gregarious [grɪ'geərɪəs] *adj* gregario(a), sociable
Grenada [grɪ'neɪdə] *n* Granada
grenade [grɪ'neɪd] *n* granada *f*
grew [gruː] *pt of* **grow**
grey [greɪ] **1** *adj (colour)* gris; *(hair)* cano(a); *(sky)* nublado(a); **g. matter** materia *f* gris
2 *n* (**a**) *(colour)* gris *m* (**b**) *(horse)* caballo tordo
grey-haired ['greɪheəd] *adj* canoso(a)
greyhound ['greɪhaʊnd] *n* galgo *m*
greyish ['greɪɪʃ] *adj* grisáceo(a)
grid [grɪd] *n* (**a**) *(on map)* cuadrícula *f* (**b**) *(of electricity etc)* red *f* nacional (**c**) = **gridiron**
gridiron ['grɪdaɪən] *n* *Culin* parrilla *f*
grief [griːf] *n* dolor *m*, pena *f*; *Fam* **to come to g.** *(car, driver)* sufrir un accidente; *(plans)* irse al traste
grievance ['griːvəns] *n* *(wrong)* agravio *m*; *(resentment)* queja *f*
grieve [griːv] **1** *vt* apenar, dar pena a
2 *vi* apenarse, afligirse; **to g. for sb** llorar la muerte de algn
grievous ['griːvəs] *adj (offence)* grave; **g.**

bodily harm lesiones *fpl* corporales graves
grill [grɪl] **1** *vt* (**a**) *Culin* asar a la parrilla (**b**) *Fam (interrogate)* interrogar duramente
2 *n* parrilla *f*; *(dish)* parrillada *f*
grill(e) [grɪl] *n (grating)* reja *f*
grim [grɪm] *adj* (**grimmer, grimmest**) (**a**) *(sinister)* macabro(a); *(landscape)* lúgubre; *(smile)* sardónico(a) (**b**) *(manner)* severo(a); *(person)* ceñudo(a) (**c**) *(resolute)* inexorable (**d**) *Fam (unpleasant)* desagradable; **g. reality** la dura realidad
grimace [grɪ'meɪs] **1** *n* mueca *f*
2 *vi* hacer una mueca
grimy ['graɪmɪ] *adj* (**grimier, grimiest**) mugriento(a)
grin [grɪn] **1** *vi* sonreír abiertamente
2 *n* sonrisa abierta
grind [graɪnd] **1** *vt* (*pt & pp* **ground**) *(mill)* moler; *(crush)* triturar; *(sharpen)* afilar; *US (meat)* picar; **to g. one's teeth** hacer rechinar los dientes
2 *vi* (**a**) rechinar; *Fig* **to g. to a halt** *(vehicle)* pararse lentamente; *(production etc)* pararse poco a poco (**b**) *US Fam* empollar
3 *n* (**a**) *Fam* **the daily g.** la rutina cotidiana; **what a g.!** ¡qué rollo! (**b**) *US Fam (studious pupil)* empollón(ona) *m,f*
▸ **grind down** *vt sep Fig* **to g. down the opposition** acabar con la oposición
grip [grɪp] **1** *n* (**a**) *(hold)* agarrón *m*; *(handshake)* apretón *m*; *(of tyre)* adherencia *f*; **get a g. on yourself!** ¡tranquilízate!; **to get to grips with a problem** superar un problema (**b**) *(handle)* asidero *m* (**c**) *(travel bag)* maletín *m* (**d**) *(hairgrip)* pasador *m*
2 *vt* (**a**) agarrar, asir; *(hand)* apretar (**b**) *Fig (of film, story)* captar la atención de; **to be gripped by fear** ser presa del miedo
gripe [graɪp] **1** *vi* *Fam (complain)* quejarse
2 *n* (**a**) *Med (pain)* retortijón *m* (**b**) *Fam (complaint)* queja *f*
gripping ['grɪpɪŋ] *adj (film, story)* apasionante
grisly ['grɪzlɪ] *adj* (**grislier, grisliest**) espeluznante
gristle ['grɪsəl] *n* cartílago *m*, ternilla *f*
grit [grɪt] **1** *n* (**a**) *(gravel)* grava *f* (**b**) *Fam (courage)* valor *m*
2 *vt* *Fig* **to g. one's teeth** apretar los dientes
gritty ['grɪtɪ] *adj* (**grittier, grittiest**) valiente
grizzly ['grɪzlɪ] *adj* **g. bear** oso pardo

groan [grəʊn] **1** *n* (**a**) *(of pain)* gemido *m* (**b**) *Fam (of disapproval)* gruñido *m*

2 *vi* (**a**) *(in pain)* gemir (**b**) *Fam (complain)* quejarse (**about** de)

grocer ['grəʊsə(r)] *n* tendero(a) *m,f*; **g.'s (shop)** tienda *f* de comestibles, *CSur* almacén *m*, *Andes, CAm, Méx* tienda *f* de abarrotes

groceries ['grəʊsərɪz] *npl* comestibles *mpl*

grocery ['grəʊsərɪ] *n (shop)* tienda *f* de ultramarinos; *US* **g. store** supermercado *m*

groggy ['grɒgɪ] *adj* (**groggier, groggiest**) *Fam (boxer)* grogui; *Fig (unsteady)* atontado(a); *(weak)* débil

groin [grɔɪn] *n* ingle *f*

groom [gruːm] **1** *n* (**a**) *(of horse)* mozo *m* de cuadra (**b**) *(bridegroom)* novio *m*

2 *vt (horse)* almohazar; *(clothes, appearance)* cuidar

groove [gruːv] *n (furrow etc)* ranura *f*; *(of record)* surco *m*

grope [grəʊp] *vi* (**a**) *(search about)* andar a tientas; **to g. for sth** buscar algo a tientas (**b**) *Fam (fondle)* meter mano

gross [grəʊs] **1** *adj* (**a**) grosero(a); *(joke)* verde (**b**) *(fat)* obeso(a) (**c**) *(flagrant)* flagrante; *(ignorance)* craso(a) (**d**) *Com & Econ* bruto(a); **g. national product** producto nacional bruto

2 *vt Com* recaudar (en bruto)

grossly ['grəʊslɪ] *adv* enormemente

grotesque [grəʊ'tesk] *adj* grotesco(a)

grotto ['grɒtəʊ] *n* gruta *f*

ground¹ [graʊnd] **1** *n* (**a**) *(earth)* suelo *m*, tierra *f*; **at g. level** al nivel del suelo; *Av* **to get off the g.** despegar; *Av* **g. control** control *m* de tierra; **g. floor** planta baja; *Av* **g. staff** personal *m* de tierra; *Fig* **g. swell** marejada *f* (**b**) *(terrain)* terreno *m*; **to gain/lose g.** ganar/perder terreno; *Fig* **to stand one's g.** mantenerse firme; **football g.** campo *m* de fútbol (**c**) *US Elec* toma *f* de tierra (**d**) **grounds** *(gardens)* jardines *mpl* (**e**) **grounds** *(reason)* motivo *m* (**f**) **grounds** *(sediment)* poso *m*

2 *vt* (**a**) *Av* obligar a quedarse en tierra; *Naut* varar (**b**) *US Elec* conectar con tierra

ground² [graʊnd] **1** *adj (coffee)* molido(a); *US (meat)* picado(a)

2 *pt & pp of* **grind**

grounding ['graʊndɪŋ] *n* base *f*; **to have a good g. in** tener buenos conocimientos de

groundless ['graʊndlɪs] *adj* infundado(a)

groundsheet ['graʊndʃiːt] *n* tela *f* impermeable

groundsman ['graʊndzmən] *n* encargado *m* de campo

groundwork ['graʊndwɜːk] *n* trabajo preparatorio

group [gruːp] **1** *n* grupo *m*, conjunto *m*

2 *vt* agrupar, juntar (**into** en)

3 *vi* **to g. (together)** agruparse, juntarse

grouse¹ [graʊs] *n Orn* urogallo *m*

grouse² [graʊs] *Fam* **1** *vi* quejarse (**about** de)

2 *n* queja *f*

grove [grəʊv] *n* arboleda *f*

grovel ['grɒvəl] *vi* humillarse (**to** ante); *(crawl)* arrastrarse (**to** ante)

grow [grəʊ] **1** *vt (pt* **grew***; pp* **grown***) (cultivate)* cultivar; **to g. a beard** dejarse (crecer) la barba

2 *vi* (**a**) crecer; *(increase)* aumentar (**b**) *(become)* hacerse, volverse; **to g. accustomed to** acostumbrarse a; **to g. dark** oscurecer; **to g. old** envejecer

▶ **grow out of** *vt insep* (**a**) **he's grown out of his shirt** se le ha quedado pequeña la camisa (**b**) *Fig (phase etc)* superar

▶ **grow up** *vi* crecer, hacerse mayor

grower ['grəʊə(r)] *n* cultivador(a) *m,f*

growing ['grəʊɪŋ] *adj (child)* que crece; *(problem etc)* creciente; **he's a g. boy** está dando el estirón

growl [graʊl] **1** *vi* gruñir

2 *n* gruñido *m*

grown [grəʊn] **1** *adj* crecido(a), adulto(a)

2 *pp of* **grow**

grown-up ['grəʊnʌp] *adj & n* adulto(a) *(m,f)*; **the grown-ups** los mayores

growth [grəʊθ] *n* (**a**) crecimiento *m*; *(increase)* aumento *m*; *(development)* desarrollo *m* (**b**) *Med* bulto *m*

grub [grʌb] *n* (**a**) *(larva)* gusano *m* (**b**) *Fam (food)* papeo *m*

grubby ['grʌbɪ] *adj* (**grubbier, grubbiest**) sucio(a)

grudge [grʌdʒ] **1** *n* rencor *m*; **to bear sb a g.** guardar rencor a algn

2 *vt (give unwillingly)* dar a regañadientes; **he grudges me my success** me envidia el éxito

grudgingly ['grʌdʒɪŋlɪ] *adv* a regañadientes

gruelling, *US* **grueling** ['gruːəlɪŋ] *adj* penoso(a)

gruesome ['gruːsəm] *adj* espantoso(a), horrible

gruff [grʌf] *adj (manner)* brusco(a); *(voice)* áspero(a)

grumble ['grʌmbəl] **1** *vi* refunfuñar

2 *n* queja *f*

grumpy ['grʌmpɪ] *adj* (**grumpier, grumpiest**) gruñón(ona)

grunt [grʌnt] **1** *vi* gruñir
2 *n* gruñido *m*

guarantee [gærən'tiː] **1** *n* garantía *f*; *(certificate)* certificado *m* de garantía
2 *vt* garantizar; *(assure)* asegurar

guard [gɑːd] **1** *vt* (**a**) *(protect)* defender, proteger; *(keep watch over)* vigilar (**b**) *(control)* guardar
2 *vi* protegerse (**against** de *or* contra)
3 *n* (**a**) **to be on one's g.** estar en guardia; **to catch sb off his g.** coger desprevenido a algn (**b**) *(sentry)* guardia *mf*; **g. of honour** guardia de honor; **to stand g.** montar la guardia; **g. dog** perro *m* guardián (**c**) *Br Rail* jefe *m* de tren; **g.'s van** furgón *m* de cola (**d**) *(on machine)* dispositivo *m* de seguridad; **fire g.** pantalla *f*

guarded ['gɑːdɪd] *adj* cauteloso(a), precavido(a)

guardhouse ['gɑːdhaʊs] *n Mil* (**a**) *(headquarters)* cuerpo *m* de guardia (**b**) *(prison)* prisión *f* militar

guardian ['gɑːdɪən] *n* (**a**) guardián(ana) *m,f*; **g. angel** ángel *m* de la guarda (**b**) *Jur* *(of minor)* tutor(a) *m,f*

Guatemala [gwɑːtə'mɑːlə] *n* Guatemala

Guatemalan [gwɑːtə'mɑːlən] *adj & n* guatemalteco(a) *(m,f)*

guava ['gwɑːvə] *n Bot* guayaba *f*; **g. tree** guayabo *m*

guer(r)illa [gə'rɪlə] *n* guerrillero(a) *m,f*; **g. warfare** guerra *f* de guerrillas

guess [ges] **1** *vt & vi* (**a**) adivinar; **I guessed as much** me lo imaginaba; **to g. right/wrong** acertar/no acertar (**b**) *US Fam* pensar, suponer; **I g. so** supongo que sí
2 *n* conjetura *f*; *(estimate)* cálculo *m*; **at a rough g.** a ojo de buen cubero; **to have** *or* **make a g.** intentar adivinar

guesswork ['geswɜːk] *n* conjetura *f*

guest [gest] *n* *(at home)* invitado(a) *m,f*; *(in hotel)* cliente(a) *m,f*, huésped(a) *m,f*; **g. artist** artista *mf* invitado(a); **g. room** cuarto *m* de los invitados

guesthouse ['gesthaʊs] *n* casa *f* de huéspedes

guffaw [gʌ'fɔː] *vi* reírse a carcajadas

guidance ['gaɪdəns] *n* orientación *f*, consejos *mpl*; **for your g.** a título de información

guide [gaɪd] **1** *vt* guiar, dirigir
2 *n* (**a**) *(person)* guía *mf*; *Br* **girl g.** exploradora *f*; **g. dog** perro lazarillo (**b**) *(guidebook)* guía *f*

guidebook ['gaɪdbʊk] *n* guía *f*

guided ['gaɪdɪd] *adj* dirigido(a); **g. tour** visita con guía; **g. missile** misil teledirigido

guideline ['gaɪdlaɪn] *n* pauta *f*

guild [gɪld] *n* gremio *m*

guile [gaɪl] *n* astucia *f*

guillotine ['gɪlətiːn] *n* guillotina *f*

guilt [gɪlt] *n* (**a**) culpa *f* (**b**) *Jur* culpabilidad *f*

guilty ['gɪltɪ] *adj* (**guiltier, guiltiest**) culpable (**of** de); **to have a g. conscience** remorderle a uno la conciencia

guinea¹ ['gɪnɪ] *n* **g. pig** conejillo *m* de Indias, cobayo *m*; *Fig* **to act as a g. pig** servir de conejillo de Indias

guinea² ['gɪnɪ] *n* *(coin)* guinea *f* (*= 21 chelines*)

guise [gaɪz] *n* **under the g. of** so pretexto de

guitar [gɪ'tɑː(r)] *n* guitarra *f*

guitarist [gɪ'tɑːrɪst] *n* guitarrista *mf*

gulf [gʌlf] *n* (**a**) golfo *m*; **G. of Mexico** Golfo de Méjico; **G. Stream** corriente *f* del Golfo de Méjico; **the G. War** la guerra del Golfo (**b**) *Fig* abismo *m*

gull [gʌl] *n* gaviota *f*

gulley ['gʌlɪ] *n* = **gully**

gullible ['gʌləbəl] *adj* crédulo(a)

gully ['gʌlɪ] *n* barranco *m*, hondonada *f*

gulp [gʌlp] **1** *n* trago *m*
2 *vt* tragar; **to g. sth down** *(drink)* tomarse algo de un trago; *(food)* engullir algo
3 *vi* (**a**) *(swallow air)* tragar aire (**b**) *Fig (with fear)* tragar saliva

gum¹ [gʌm] **1** *n* goma *f*
2 *vt* pegar con goma

gum² [gʌm] *n Anat* encía *f*

gumboots ['gʌmbuːts] *npl* botas *fpl* de agua

gun [gʌn] *n* arma *f* de fuego; *(handgun)* pistola *f*, revólver *m*; *(rifle)* fusil *m*, escopeta *f*; *(cannon)* cañón *m*; *Fam* **the big guns** los peces gordos
▶ **gun down** *vt sep* matar a tiros

gunboat ['gʌnbəʊt] *n* cañonero *m*

gunfire ['gʌnfaɪə(r)] *n* tiros *mpl*

gunman ['gʌnmən] *n* pistolero *m*, gángster *m*

gunpoint ['gʌnpɔɪnt] *n* **at g.** a punta de pistola

gunpowder ['gʌnpaʊdə(r)] *n* pólvora *f*

gunrunner ['gʌnrʌnə(r)] *n* traficante *mf* de armas

gunshot ['gʌnʃɒt] *n* disparo *m*, tiro *m*

gunsmith ['gʌnsmɪθ] *n* armero *m*

gurgle ['gɜːgəl] *vi* *(baby)* gorjear; *(liquid)* gorgotear; *(stream)* murmurar

guru ['gʊruː, 'guːruː] *n* gurú *m*

gush [gʌʃ] **1** *vi* (**a**) brotar (**b**) *Fig* **to g. over sb** enjabonar a algn

2 *n* (*of water*) chorro *m*; (*of words*) torrente *m*

gushing ['gʌʃɪŋ] *adj Fig* (*person*) efusivo(a)

gusset ['gʌsɪt] *n* escudete *m*

gust [gʌst] *n* (*of wind*) ráfaga *f*, racha *f*

gusto ['gʌstəʊ] *n* entusiasmo *m*

gut [gʌt] **1** *n* (**a**) *Anat* intestino *m* (**b**) (*catgut*) cuerda *f* de tripa (**c**) **guts** (*entrails*) tripas *fpl*; *Fam* **to have guts** tener agallas

2 *vt* (**a**) (*fish*) destripar (**b**) (*destroy*) destruir por dentro

3 *adj Fam* **g. reaction** reacción *f* visceral

gutter ['gʌtə(r)] *n* (*in street*) arroyo *m*; (*on roof*) canalón *m*; *Fig* **g. press** prensa amarilla

guttural ['gʌtərəl] *adj* gutural

guy¹ [gaɪ] *n Fam* tipo *m*, tío *m*

guy² [gaɪ] *n* (*rope*) viento *m*, cuerda *f*

guzzle ['gʌzəl] *vt & vi Fam* (*food etc*) zamparse; (*car*) tragar mucho

gym [dʒɪm] *Fam* (**a**) (*gymnasium*) gimnasio *m* (**b**) (*gymnastics*) gimnasia *f*; **g. shoes** zapatillas *fpl* de deporte

gymnasium [dʒɪm'neɪzɪəm] *n* gimnasio *m*

gymnast ['dʒɪmnæst] *n* gimnasta *mf*

gymnastics [dʒɪm'næstɪks] *n sing* gimnasia *f*

gynaecologist, *US* **gynecologist** [gaɪnɪ'kɒlədʒɪst] *n* ginecólogo(a) *m,f*

gypsy ['dʒɪpsɪ] *adj & n* gitano(a) (*m,f*)

gyrate [dʒaɪ'reɪt] *vi* girar

H

H, h [eɪtʃ] *n (the letter)* H, h *f*

haberdashery [hæbə'dæʃərɪ] *n* **(a)** *Br* artículos *mpl* de mercería **(b)** *US* ropa masculina

habit ['hæbɪt] *n* **(a)** costumbre *f* **(b)** *(garment)* hábito *m*

habitable ['hæbɪtəbəl] *adj* habitable

habitat ['hæbɪtæt] *n* hábitat *m*

habitual [hə'bɪtjʊəl] *adj* habitual; *(drinker, liar)* empedernido(a)

habitually [hə'bɪtjʊəlɪ] *adv* por costumbre

hack¹ [hæk] **1** *n (cut)* corte *m*; *(with an axe)* hachazo *m*
   2 *vt (with knife, axe)* cortar; *(kick)* dar un puntapié a

hack² [hæk] *n Fam (writer)* escritorzuelo(a) *m,f*; *(journalist)* gacetillero(a) *m,f*

hackneyed ['hæknɪd] *adj* trillado(a)

hacksaw ['hæksɔ:] *n* sierra *f* para metales

had [hæd] *pt & pp of* **have**

haddock ['hædək] *n* abadejo *m*

haemophilia [hi:mə'fɪlɪə] *n* hemofilia *f*

haemophiliac [hi:mə'fɪlɪæk] *adj & n* hemofílico(a) *(m,f)*

haemorrhage ['hemərɪdʒ] *n* hemorragia *f*

haemorrhoids ['hemərɔɪdz] *npl* hemorroides *fpl*

hag [hæg] *n Pej* bruja *f*, arpía *f*

haggard ['hægəd] *adj* ojeroso(a)

haggle ['hægəl] *vi* regatear

Hague [heɪg] *n* **The H.** La Haya

hail¹ [heɪl] **1** *n* granizo *m*; *Fig* **a h. of bullets/insults** una lluvia de balas/insultos
   2 *vi* granizar

hail² [heɪl] **1** *vt* **(a)** *(taxi etc)* parar **(b)** *(acclaim)* aclamar
   2 *vi* **to h. from** *(originate)* ser nativo(a) de

hailstone ['heɪlstəʊn] *n* granizo *m*

hailstorm ['heɪlstɔ:m] *n* granizada *f*

hair [heə(r)] *n (strand)* pelo *m*, cabello *m*; *(mass)* pelo, cabellos *mpl*; *(on arm, leg)* vello *m*; **to have long h.** tener el pelo largo

hairbrush ['heəbrʌʃ] *n* cepillo *m* (para el pelo)

haircut ['heəkʌt] *n* corte *m* de pelo; **to have a h.** cortarse el pelo

hairdo ['heədu:] *n Fam* peinado *m*

hairdresser ['heədresə(r)] *n* peluquero(a) *m,f*; **h.'s (shop)** peluquería *f*

hairdryer, hairdrier ['heədraɪə(r)] *n* secador *m* (de pelo)

hairgrip ['heəgrɪp] *n Br* horquilla *f*

hairline ['heəlaɪn] **1** *adj* muy fino(a)
   2 *n* nacimiento *m* del pelo; **receding h.** entradas *fpl*

hairnet ['heənet] *n* redecilla *f*

hairpiece ['heəpi:s] *n* postizo *m*

hairpin ['heəpɪn] *n* horquilla *f*; **h. bend** curva muy cerrada

hair-raising ['heəreɪzɪŋ] *adj* espeluznante

hair-remover ['heərɪmu:və(r)] *n* depilatorio *m*

hairspray ['heəspreɪ] *n* laca *f* (para el pelo)

hairstyle ['heəstaɪl] *n* peinado *m*, corte *m* de pelo

hairy ['heərɪ] *adj* **(hairier, hairiest)** **(a)** *(with hair)* peludo(a) **(b)** *Fig (frightening)* enervante, espantoso(a)

hake [heɪk] *n* merluza *f*; *(young)* pescadilla *f*

half [hɑ:f] **1** *n (pl* **halves)** mitad *f*; *Sport (period)* tiempo *m*; **he's four and a h.** tiene cuatro años y medio; **to cut in h.** cortar por la mitad
   2 *adj* medio(a); **h. a dozen/an hour** media docena/hora; **h. board** media pensión; **h. fare** media tarifa; **h. term** medio trimestre; **h. year** semestre *m*
   3 *adv* medio, a medias; **h. asleep** medio dormido(a)

half-caste ['hɑ:fkɑ:st] *adj & n* mestizo(a) *(m,f)*

half-day [hɑ:f'deɪ] *n* media jornada

half-hearted [hɑ:f'hɑ:tɪd] *adj* poco entusiasta

half-hour [hɑ:f'aʊə(r)] *n* media hora

half-life ['hɑ:flaɪf] *n* media vida

half-mast [hɑ:f'mɑ:st] *n* **at h.** a media asta

half-price [hɑ:f'praɪs] *adv* a mitad de precio

half-time ['hɑːf 'taɪm] n descanso m
half-way ['hɑːfweɪ] **1** adj intermedio(a)
  2 halfway [hɑːf'weɪ] adv a medio camino, a mitad de camino
half-yearly ['hɑːfjɪəlɪ] adj semestral
halibut ['hælɪbət] n mero m
hall [hɔːl] n (a) (lobby) vestíbulo m (b) (building) sala f; Univ **h. of residence** colegio m mayor
hallmark ['hɔːlmɑːk] n (a) (on gold, silver) contraste m (b) Fig sello m
hallo [həˈləʊ] interj ¡hola!
hallowed ['hæləʊd] adj santificado(a)
Hallowe(')en [hæləʊ'iːn] n víspera f de Todos los Santos
hallucinate [həˈluːsɪneɪt] vi alucinar
hallucination [həluːsɪˈneɪʃən] n alucinación f
hallucinogenic [həluːsɪnəʊˈdʒenɪk] adj alucinógeno(a)
hallway ['hɔːlweɪ] n vestíbulo m
halo ['heɪləʊ] n (a) Rel aureola f (b) Astron halo m
halt [hɔːlt] **1** n (stop) alto m, parada f; **to call a h. to sth** poner fin a algo
  2 vt parar
  3 vi pararse
halting ['hɔːltɪŋ] adj vacilante
halve [hɑːv] vt (a) partir por la mitad; (reduce by half) reducir a la mitad (b) (share) compartir
halves [hɑːvz] pl of half
ham [hæm] n jamón m; **boiled h.** jamón de York; **Parma** or **cured h.** jamón serrano
hamburger ['hæmbɜːgə(r)] n hamburguesa f
hamlet ['hæmlɪt] n aldea f
hammer ['hæmə(r)] **1** n (a) martillo m; **the h. and sickle** la hoz y el martillo (b) (of gun) percursor m (c) Sport lanzamiento m de martillo
  2 vt (a) martillar; (nail) clavar; Fig **to h. home** insistir sobre (b) Fam (defeat) dar una paliza a
  3 vi martillar, dar golpes
hammering ['hæmərɪŋ] n Fam paliza f
hammock ['hæmək] n hamaca f; Naut coy m
hamper¹ ['hæmpə(r)] n cesta f
hamper² ['hæmpə(r)] vt estorbar, dificultar
hamster ['hæmstə(r)] n hámster m
hamstring ['hæmstrɪŋ] n tendón m de la corva
hand [hænd] **1** n (a) mano f; **by h.** a mano; **(close) at h.** a mano; **hands up!** ¡manos arriba!; **on the one/other h.** por una/otra parte; Fig **to get out of h.** descontrolarse;

Fig **to be on h.** estar a mano; Fig **to have a h. in** intervenir en; Fig **to have time in h.** sobrarle a uno tiempo; Fig **to wash one's hands of sth** lavarse las manos de algo; Fig **to give sb a h.** echarle una mano a algn; **h. grenade** granada f de mano
  (b) (worker) trabajador(a) m,f; Naut tripulante m
  (c) (of clock) aguja f
  (d) **to give sb a big h.** (applause) dedicar a algn una gran ovación
  (e) (handwriting) letra f
  2 vt (give) dar, entregar; Fam Fig **I have to h. it to you** tengo que reconocerlo
▸ **hand back** vt sep devolver
▸ **hand down** vt sep dejar en herencia
▸ **hand in** vt sep (homework) entregar; (resignation) presentar
▸ **hand out** vt sep repartir
▸ **hand over** vt sep entregar
▸ **hand round** vt sep repartir
handbag ['hændbæg] n Br bolso m, cartera f, Méx bolsa f
handball ['hændbɔːl] n Sport balonmano m
handbook ['hændbʊk] n manual m
handbrake ['hændbreɪk] n freno m de mano
handcuff ['hændkʌf] **1** vt esposar
  2 npl **handcuffs** esposas fpl
handful ['hændfʊl] n puñado m
handicap ['hændɪkæp] **1** n (a) Med minusvalía f (b) Sport hándicap m, desventaja f
  2 vt impedir
handicapped ['hændɪkæpt] adj (a) (physically) minusválido(a); (mentally) retrasado(a) (b) Sport en desventaja (c) Fig desfavorecido(a)
handicraft ['hændɪkrɑːft] n artesanía f
handiwork ['hændɪwɜːk] n (work) obra f; (craft) artesanía f
handkerchief ['hæŋkətʃiːf] n pañuelo m
handle ['hændəl] **1** n (of knife) mango m; (of cup) asa f; (of door) pomo m; (of lever) palanca f; (of drawer) tirador m
  2 vt (a) manejar; **h. with care** (sign) frágil (b) (problem) encargarse de; (people) tratar; Fam (put up with) soportar
  3 vi (car) comportarse
handlebar ['hændəlbɑː(r)] n manillar m
handmade [hænd'meɪd] adj hecho(a) a mano
hand-out ['hændaʊt] n (a) (leaflet) folleto m; Press nota f de prensa (b) (charity) limosna f
hand-picked [hænd'pɪkt] adj selecto(a)
handrail ['hændreɪl] n pasamanos m inv

handshake ['hændʃeɪk] n apretón m de manos

handsome ['hænsəm] adj (a) (person) guapo(a) (b) (substantial) considerable

handwriting ['hændraɪtɪŋ] n letra f

han·dy ['hændɪ] adj (handier, handiest) (a) (useful) útil, práctico(a); (nearby) a mano (b) (dextrous) diestro(a)

hang [hæŋ] 1 vt (pt & pp hung) (a) colgar (b) (head) bajar (c) (pt hanged) ahorcar
2 vi (a) colgar (from de); (in air) flotar (b) (criminal) ser ahorcado(a); **to h. one-self** ahorcarse
▸ **hang about** vi Fam (a) perder el tiempo (b) (wait) esperar
▸ **hang around** vi Fam (a) esperar (b) frecuentar; **where does he h. around?** ¿a que lugares suele ir?
▸ **hang on** vi (a) agarrarse (b) (wait) esperar
▸ **hang out 1** vt sep (washing) tender
2 vi Fam (frequent) frecuentar
▸ **hang round** vi Fam = hang about
▸ **hang together** vi (ideas) ser coherente
▸ **hang up** vt sep (picture, telephone) colgar

hangar ['hæŋə(r)] n hangar m

hanger ['hæŋə(r)] n percha f

hang-glider ['hæŋglaɪdə(r)] n ala delta

hang-gliding ['hæŋglaɪdɪŋ] n vuelo m libre

hangman ['hæŋmən] n verdugo m

hangover ['hæŋəʊvə(r)] n resaca f

hang-up ['hæŋʌp] n Fam (complex) complejo m

hanker ['hæŋkə(r)] vi **to h. after sth** anhelar algo

hankie, hanky ['hæŋkɪ] n Fam pañuelo m

haphazard [hæp'hæzəd] adj caótico(a), desordenado(a)

happen ['hæpən] vi suceder, ocurrir; **it so happens that** lo que pasa es que; **if you h. to see my friend** si por casualidad ves a mi amigo

happening ['hæpənɪŋ] n acontecimiento m

happily ['hæpɪlɪ] adv (with pleasure) felizmente; (fortunately) afortunadamente

happiness ['hæpɪnɪs] n felicidad f

happy ['hæpɪ] adj (happier, happiest) (cheerful) feliz, contento(a); (fortunate) afortunado(a); **h. birthday!** ¡feliz cumpleaños!

happy-go-lucky [hæpɪgəʊ'lʌkɪ] adj despreocupado(a); **a h. fellow** un viva la virgen

harangue [hə'ræŋ] 1 vt arengar
2 n arenga f

harass ['hærəs] vt acosar

harassment ['hærəsmənt, hə'ræsmənt] n hostigamiento m, acoso m

harbour, US harbor ['hɑːbə(r)] 1 n puerto m
2 vt (a) (criminal) encubrir (b) (doubts) abrigar

hard [hɑːd] 1 adj (a) duro(a); (solid) sólido(a); **h. court** pista (de tenis) rápida; Comput **h. disk** disco duro; Br Aut **h. shoulder** arcén m, Andes berma f, Méx acotamiento m, RP banquina f, Ven hombrillo m
(b) (difficult) difícil; **h. of hearing** duro(a) de oído; Fam Fig **to be h. up** estar sin blanca
(c) (harsh) severo(a); (strict) estricto(a); **to take a h. line** tomar medidas severas; **h. drugs** droga dura; Pol **h. left** extrema izquierda; **h. porn** pornografía dura; **h. sell** promoción f de venta agresiva
(d) **a h. drinker** un bebedor inveterado; **a h. worker** un trabajador concienzudo
(e) **h. luck!** ¡mala suerte!
(f) **h. evidence** pruebas definitivas; Com **h. cash** dinero m en metálico; **h. currency** divisa f fuerte
2 adv (a) (hit) fuerte
(b) (work) mucho, concienzudamente; Fig **to be h. on sb's heels** pisar los talones a algn
(c) **to be h. done by** ser tratado(a) injustamente

hardback ['hɑːdbæk] n edición f de tapas duras

hard-boiled ['hɑːdbɔɪld] adj duro(a)

hard-core ['hɑːdkɔ:(r)] adj irreductible

harden ['hɑːdən] 1 vt endurecer
2 vi endurecerse

hardened ['hɑːdənd] adj Fig habitual

hard-headed [hɑːd'hedɪd] adj realista

hard-hearted [hɑːd'hɑːtɪd] adj insensible

hardliner [hɑːd'laɪnə(r)] n duro(a) m,f

hardly ['hɑːdlɪ] adv apenas; **h. anyone/ever** casi nadie/nunca; **he had h. begun when ...** apenas había comenzado cuando ...; **I can h. believe it** apenas lo puedo creer

hardship ['hɑːdʃɪp] n privación f, apuro m

hardware ['hɑːdweə(r)] n (a) (goods) ferretería f; **h. shop** ferretería (b) Comput hardware m

hardwearing [hɑːd'weərɪŋ] adj duradero(a)

hardworking ['hɑːdwɜːkɪŋ] adj muy trabajador(a)

hardy ['hɑːdɪ] *adj* (**hardier, hardiest**) *(person)* robusto(a), fuerte; *(plant)* resistente

hare [heə(r)] **1** *n* liebre *f*
　2 *vi* correr muy de prisa

haricot ['hærɪkəʊ] *n* **h. (bean)** alubia *f*

harm [hɑːm] **1** *n* daño *m*, perjuicio *m*; **to be out of h.'s way** estar a salvo
　2 *vt* hacer daño a, perjudicar

harmful ['hɑːmfʊl] *adj* perjudicial (**to** para)

harmless ['hɑːmlɪs] *adj* inofensivo(a)

harmonica [hɑːˈmɒnɪkə] *n* armónica *f*

harmonize ['hɑːmənaɪz] *vt & vi* armonizar

harmony ['hɑːmənɪ] *n* armonía *f*

harness ['hɑːnɪs] **1** *n* (for horse) arreos *mpl*
　2 *vt* (**a**) *(horse)* enjaezar (**b**) *Fig (resources etc)* aprovechar

harp [hɑːp] *n* arpa *f*
　▸ **harp on** *vi Fam* hablar sin parar

harpoon [hɑːˈpuːn] **1** *n* arpón *m*
　2 *vt* arponear

harrowing ['hærəʊɪŋ] *adj* angustioso(a)

harsh [hɑːʃ] *adj* severo(a); *(voice)* áspero(a); *(sound)* discordante

harvest ['hɑːvɪst] **1** *n* cosecha *f*; *(of grapes)* vendimia *f*
　2 *vt* cosechar, recoger

harvester ['hɑːvɪstə(r)] *n* (**a**) *(person)* segador(a) *m,f* (**b**) *(machine)* cosechadora *f*

has [hæz] *3rd person sing pres of* **have**

hash¹ [hæʃ] *n Culin* sofrito *m* de carne; *Fam Fig* **to make a h. of sth** estropear algo

hash² [hæʃ] *n Fam* hachís *m*

hashish ['hæʃiːʃ] *n* hachís *m*

hassle ['hæsəl] *Fam* **1** *n* (**a**) *(nuisance)* rollo *m* (**b**) *(problem)* lío *m* (**c**) *(wrangle)* bronca *f*
　2 *vt* fastidiar

haste [heɪst] *n Fml* prisa *f*; **to make h.** darse prisa

hasten ['heɪsən] *vi* apresurarse

hastily ['heɪstɪlɪ] *adv (quickly)* de prisa

hasty ['heɪstɪ] *adj* (**hastier, hastiest**) apresurado(a); *(rash)* precipitado(a)

hat [hæt] *n* sombrero *m*

hatch¹ [hætʃ] *n* escotilla *f*; **serving h.** ventanilla *f*

hatch² [hætʃ] *vt* (**a**) *(eggs)* empollar (**b**) *Fig (plan)* tramar
　▸ **hatch out** *vi* salirse del huevo

hatchback ['hætʃbæk] *n* coche *m* de 3/5 puertas

hatchet ['hætʃɪt] *n* hacha *f*; *Fam* **h. man** matón *m*

hate [heɪt] **1** *n* odio *m*
　2 *vt* odiar

hateful ['heɪtfʊl] *adj* odioso(a)

hatred ['heɪtrɪd] *n* odio *m*

haughty ['hɔːtɪ] *adj* (**haughtier, haughtiest**) altanero(a), arrogante

haul [hɔːl] **1** *n* (**a**) *(journey)* trayecto *m* (**b**) *(of fish)* redada *f* (**c**) *(loot)* botín *m*
　2 *vt* (**a**) tirar; *(drag)* arrastrar (**b**) *(transport)* acarrear
　▸ **haul up** *vt sep Fam (to court)* llevar

haulage ['hɔːlɪdʒ] *n* transporte *m*

haulier ['hɔːljə(r)] *n* transportista *mf*

haunch [hɔːntʃ] *n* cadera *f*; *Culin* pernil *m*

haunt [hɔːnt] **1** *n* guarida *f*
　2 *vt* (**a**) *(of ghost)* aparecerse en (**b**) *Fig* atormentar (**c**) *(frequent)* frecuentar

haunted ['hɔːntɪd] *adj* encantado(a), embrujado(a)

Havana [həˈvænə] *n* La Habana; **H. cigar** habano *m*

have [hæv]

En el inglés hablado, y en el escrito en estilo coloquial, el verbo auxiliar **have** se contrae de forma que **I have** se transforma en **I've**, **he/she/it has** se transforman en **he's/she's/it's** y **you've/we've/they have** se transforman en **you've/we've/they've**. Las formas de pasado **I/you/he** *etc* **had** se transforman en **I'd, you'd, he'd** *etc*. Las formas negativas **has not, have not** y **had not** se transforman en **hasn't, haven't** y **hadn't**.

1 *vt* (*3rd person sing pres* **has**; *pt & pp* **had**)
　(**a**) *(possess)* tener; **h. you got a car?** ¿tienes coche?
　(**b**) *(get, experience, suffer)* tener; **to h. a holiday** tomarse unas vacaciones
　(**c**) *(partake of)* tomar; **to h. a cigarette** fumarse un cigarrillo; **to h. breakfast/lunch/tea/dinner** desayunar/comer/merendar/cenar
　(**d**) **to h. a bath/shave** bañarse/afeitarse; **to h. a nap** echar la siesta
　(**e**) **to h. to** *(obligation)* tener que, deber
　(**f**) *(make happen)* hacer que; **I'll h. someone come round** haré que venga alguien
　(**g**) *(receive)* recibir; **to h. people round** invitar a gente
　(**h**) **can I h. your pen a moment?** *(borrow)* ¿me dejas tu bolígrafo un momento?
　(**i**) *(party, meeting)* hacer, celebrar
　(**j**) **to h. a baby** tener un niño

(**k**) **we won't h. it** (allow) no lo consentiremos

(**l**) (hold) tener; Fig **to h. sth against sb** tener algo en contra de algn

(**m**) **legend has it that ...** según la leyenda ...

(**n**) Fam (deceive) engañar

(**o**) **you'd better stay** más vale que te quedes

2 v aux (**a**) (compound) haber; **I had been waiting for half an hour** hacía media hora que esperaba; **he hasn't eaten yet** no ha comido aún; **she had broken the window** había roto el cristal; **we h. lived here for ten years** hace diez años que vivimos aquí; **so I h.!** (emphatic) ¡ay, sí!, es verdad; **yes I h.!** ¡que sí!

(**b**) (tag questions) **you haven't seen my book, h. you?** no has visto mi libro, ¿verdad?; **he's been to France, hasn't he?** ha estado en Francia, ¿verdad? or ¿no?

(**c**) (have + just) acabar de

▸ **have on** vt sep (**a**) (wear) vestir (**b**) Fam **to h. sb on** tomarle el pelo a algn

▸ **have out** vt sep Fam **to h. it out with sb** ajustar cuentas con algn

▸ **have over** vt sep (invite) recibir

haven ['heɪvən] n puerto m; Fig refugio m

haversack ['hævəsæk] n mochila f

havoc ['hævək] n **to play h. with** hacer estragos en

hawk [hɔːk] n Orn & Pol halcón m

hawker ['hɔːkə(r)] n vendedor(a) m,f ambulante

hawthorn ['hɔːθɔːn] n espino m albar

hay [heɪ] n heno m; **h. fever** fiebre f del heno

haystack ['heɪstæk] n almiar m

haywire ['heɪwaɪə(r)] adj Fam en desorden; **to go h.** (machine etc) estropearse; (person) volverse loco(a)

hazard ['hæzəd] **1** n peligro m, riesgo m; (in golf) obstáculo m
2 vt Fml arriesgar; **to h. a guess** intentar adivinar

hazardous ['hæzədəs] adj arriesgado(a), peligroso(a)

haze [heɪz] n (mist) neblina f; Fig (blur) confusión f

hazel ['heɪzəl] adj (de color) avellana

hazelnut ['heɪzəlnʌt] n avellana f

hazy ['heɪzɪ] adj (hazier, haziest) nebuloso(a)

he [hiː] pers pron él (usually omitted in Spanish, except for contrast); **he did it** ha sido él; **he who** el que

head [hed] **1** n (**a**) cabeza f; (mind) mente f; Fig **£3 a h.** 3 libras por cabeza; Fig **to be**

h. over heels in love estar locamente enamorado(a); Fig **to keep one's h.** mantener la calma; Fig **to lose one's h.** perder la cabeza; **success went to his h.** se le subió el éxito a cabeza; **h. start** ventaja f

(**b**) (of nail) cabeza f; (of beer) espuma f; (of tape recorder) cabezal m; (of steam) presión f; Fig **to come to a h.** llegar a un momento decisivo

(**c**) (boss) cabeza m; (of company) director(a) m,f; **h. teacher** director(a) m,f

(**d**) (of coin) cara f; **heads or tails** cara o cruz

2 adj principal; **h. office** oficina f central

3 vt (**a**) (list etc) encabezar

(**b**) Ftb cabecear

▸ **head for** vt insep dirigirse hacia

▸ **head off 1** vi irse
2 vt sep (avert) evitar

headache ['hedeɪk] n dolor m de cabeza; Fig quebradero m de cabeza

headcheese ['hedtʃiːz] n US queso m de cerdo

header ['hedə(r)] n Ftb cabezazo m

head-first [hed'fɜːst] adv de cabeza

head-hunter ['hedhʌntə(r)] n Fig cazatalentos mf inv

heading ['hedɪŋ] n título m; (of letter) membrete m

headlamp ['hedlæmp] n faro m

headland ['hedlənd] n punta f, cabo m

headlight ['hedlaɪt] n faro m

headline ['hedlaɪn] n titular m; **the headlines** (on radio, TV) los titulares

headlong ['hedlɒŋ] adj & adv de cabeza; **to rush h. into sth** lanzarse a hacer algo sin pensar

headmaster [hed'mɑːstə(r)] n director m

headmistress [hed'mɪstrɪs] n directora f

head-on ['hedɒn] adj **a h. collision** un choque frontal

headphones ['hedfəʊnz] npl auriculares mpl

headquarters ['hedkwɔːtəz] npl (**a**) oficina f central, sede f (**b**) Mil cuartel m general

headrest ['hedrest] n Aut apoyacabezas m

headroom ['hedruːm] n altura f libre

headscarf ['hedskɑːf] n pañuelo m

headstrong ['hedstrɒŋ] adj testarudo(a)

headway ['hedweɪ] n **to make h.** avanzar, progresar

headwind ['hedwɪnd] n viento m de proa

heady ['hedɪ] adj (headier, headiest) embriagador(a)

heal [hiːl] **1** vi cicatrizar
2 vt (wound) curar

health [helθ] *n* salud *f*; *Fig* prosperidad *f*; **to be in good/bad h.** estar bien/mal de salud; **your good h.!** ¡salud!; **h. foods** alimentos *mpl* naturales; **h. food shop** tienda *f* de alimentos naturales; *Br* **H. Service** ≃ Insalud *m*

healthy [ˈhelθɪ] *adj* (**healthier, healthiest**) sano(a); (*good for health*) saludable; (*thriving*) próspero(a)

heap [hiːp] **1** *n* montón *m*

 2 *vt* amontonar; *Fig* **to h. praise on sb** colmar a algn de alabanzas; **a heaped spoonful** una cucharada colmada

hear [hɪə(r)] **1** *vt* (*pt & pp* **heard** [hɜːd]) (**a**) oír (**b**) (*listen to*) escuchar (**c**) **I won't h. of it!** ¡ni hablar! (**d**) (*find out*) enterarse (**e**) *Jur* ver; (*evidence*) oír

 2 *vi* **to h. from sb** tener noticias de algn

hearing [ˈhɪərɪŋ] *n* (**a**) oído *m*; **h. aid** audífono *m* (**b**) *Jur* audiencia *f*; *Fig* **to give sb a fair h.** escuchar a algn

hearsay [ˈhɪəseɪ] *n* rumores *mpl*

hearse [hɜːs] *n* coche *m* fúnebre

heart [hɑːt] *n* (**a**) corazón *m*; **h. attack** infarto *m* de miocardio; **h. transplant** trasplante *m* de corazón; **a broken h.** un corazón roto; **at h.** en el fondo; **to take sth to h.** tomarse algo a pecho; **to have a good h.** (*be kind*) tener buen corazón (**b**) (*courage*) valor *m*; **his h. wasn't in it** no ponía interés en ello; **to lose h.** desanimarse (**c**) (*core*) meollo *m*; (*of lettuce*) cogollo *m*

heartbeat [ˈhɑːtbiːt] *n* latido *m* del corazón

heart-breaking [ˈhɑːtbreɪkɪŋ] *adj* desgarrador(a)

heart-broken [ˈhɑːtbrəʊkən] *adj* hundido(a); **he's h.** tiene el corazón destrozado

heartburn [ˈhɑːtbɜːn] *n* acedía *f*

heartening [ˈhɑːtənɪŋ] *adj* alentador(a)

heartfelt [ˈhɑːtfelt] *adj* sincero(a)

hearth [hɑːθ] *n* (**a**) (*fireplace*) chimenea *f* (**b**) *Fml* (*home*) hogar *m*

heartless [ˈhɑːtlɪs] *adj* cruel, insensible

heart-throb [ˈhɑːtθrɒb] *n* ídolo *m*

hearty [ˈhɑːtɪ] *adj* (**heartier, heartiest**) (*person*) francote; (*meal*) abundante; (*welcome*) cordial; **to have a h. appetite** ser de buen comer

heat [hiːt] **1** *n* (**a**) calor *m* (**b**) *Sport* eliminatoria *f* (**c**) *Zool* **on h.** en celo

 2 *vt* calentar

 ▸ **heat up** *vi* (**a**) (*warm up*) calentarse (**b**) (*increase excitement*) acalorarse

heated [ˈhiːtɪd] *adj Fig* (*argument*) acalorado(a)

heater [ˈhiːtə(r)] *n* calentador *m*

heath [hiːθ] *n* (*land*) brezal *m*

heathen [ˈhiːðən] *adj & n* pagano(a) (*m,f*)

heather [ˈheðə(r)] *n* brezo *m*

heating [ˈhiːtɪŋ] *n* calefacción *f*

heatwave [ˈhiːtweɪv] *n* ola *f* de calor

heave [hiːv] **1** *n* (*pull*) tirón *m*; (*push*) empujón *m*

 2 *vt* (**a**) (*lift*) levantar; (*haul*) tirar; (*push*) empujar (**b**) (*throw*) arrojar

 3 *vi* subir y bajar

heaven [ˈhevən] **1** *n* (**a**) cielo *m*; **for h.'s sake!** ¡por Dios!; **h. on earth** un paraíso en la tierra (**b**) **heavens** cielo *m*

 2 *interj* **good heavens!** ¡por Dios!

heavenly [ˈhevənlɪ] *adj* celestial

heavily [ˈhevɪlɪ] *adv* **it rained h.** llovió mucho; **to sleep h.** dormir profundamente

heavy [ˈhevɪ] **1** *adj* (**heavier, heaviest**) pesado(a); (*rain, meal*) fuerte; (*traffic*) denso(a); (*loss*) grande; **is it h.?** ¿pesa mucho?; **a h. drinker/smoker** un(a) bebedor(a)/fumador(a) empedernido(a); *Mus* **h. metal** heavy metal *m*

 2 *n Fam* gorila *m*

heavyweight [ˈhevɪweɪt] *n* peso pesado

Hebrew [ˈhiːbruː] **1** *adj* hebreo(a)

 2 *n* (*language*) hebreo *m*

Hebrides [ˈhebrɪdiːz] *npl* **the H.** las (Islas) Hébridas

heckle [ˈhekəl] *vt* interrumpir

heckler [ˈheklə(r)] *n* altercador(a) *m,f*

hectare [ˈhektɑː(r)] *n* hectárea *f*

hectic [ˈhektɪk] *adj* agitado(a)

hedge [hedʒ] **1** *n* seto *m*

 2 *vt* cercar con un seto; *Fig* **to h. one's bets** cubrirse

hedgehog [ˈhedʒhɒg] *n* erizo *m*

hedgerow [ˈhedʒrəʊ] *n* seto vivo

heed [hiːd] *n* **to take h. of** hacer caso de

heedless [ˈhiːdlɪs] *adj* desatento(a)

heel [hiːl] *n* (*of foot*) talón *m*; (*of shoe*) tacón *m*; (*of palm*) pulpejo *m*; *Fig* **to be on sb's heels** pisarle los talones a algn; **high heels** zapatos *mpl* de tacón alto

heeled [hiːld] *adj Fam Fig* **well-h.** adinerado(a)

hefty [ˈheftɪ] *adj* (**heftier, heftiest**) (**a**) (*person*) fornido(a); (*package*) pesado(a) (**b**) (*large*) grande

height [haɪt] *n* (**a**) altura *f*; (*of person*) estatura *f*; *Av* **to gain/lose h.** subir/bajar; **what h. are you?** ¿cuánto mides?; *Fig* **the h. of ignorance** el colmo de la ignorancia (**b**) *Geog* cumbre *f*

heighten [ˈhaɪtən] *vt* (*intensify*) realzar; (*increase*) aumentar

heir [eə(r)] *n* heredero *m*

heiress ['eərɪs] *n* heredera *f*

heirloom ['eəlu:m] *n* reliquia *f*/joya *f* de familia

held [held] *pt & pp of* **hold**

helicopter ['helɪkɒptə(r)] *n* helicóptero *m*

helium ['hi:lɪəm] *n* helio *m*

hell [hel] *n* infierno *m*; *Fam* **what the h. are you doing?** ¿qué diablos estás haciendo?; *Fam Pej* **go to h.!** ¡vete a hacer puñetas!; *Fam* **a h. of a party** una fiesta estupenda; *Fam* **she's had a h. of a day** ha tenido un día fatal

hellish ['helɪʃ] *adj Fam* infernal

hello [hə'ləʊ, he'ləʊ] *interj* ¡hola!; *Tel* ¡diga!; *(showing surprise)* ¡hala!

helm [helm] *n* timón *m*; **to be at the h.** llevar el timón

helmet ['helmɪt] *n* casco *m*

help [help] **1** *n* (a) ayuda *f*; **h.!** ¡socorro! (b) *(daily)* **h.** asistenta *f*
2 *vt* (a) ayudar; **can I h. you?** *(in shop)* ¿qué desea? (b) *(alleviate)* aliviar (c) **h. yourself!** *(to food etc)* ¡sírvete! (d) *(avoid)* evitar; **I can't h. it** no lo puedo remediar
▸ **help out** *vt sep* **to h. sb out** echarle una mano a algn

helper ['helpə(r)] *n* ayudante(a) *m,f*

helpful ['helpfʊl] *adj (person)* amable; *(thing)* útil

helping ['helpɪŋ] *n* ración *f*; **who wants a second h.?** ¿quién quiere repetir?

helpless ['helplɪs] *adj (defenceless)* desamparado(a); *(powerless)* incapaz

helplessly ['helplɪslɪ] *adv* inútilmente, en vano

helter-skelter [heltə'skeltə(r)] **1** *n* tobogán *m*
2 *adj* atropellado(a)
3 *adv* atropelladamente

hem [hem] **1** *n Sewing* dobladillo *m*
2 *vt Sewing* hacer un dobladillo a
▸ **hem in** *vt sep* cercar, rodear

hemisphere ['hemɪsfɪə(r)] *n* hemisferio *m*

hemophilia [hi:məʊ'fɪlɪə] *n US =* **haemophilia**

hemophiliac [hi:məʊ'fɪlɪæk] *adj & n =* **haemophiliac**

hemorrhage ['hemərɪdʒ] *n US =* **haemorrhage**

hen [hen] *n* gallina *f*; *Fam* **h. party** reunión *f* de mujeres

hence [hens] *adv Fml* (a) **six months h.** *(from now)* de aquí a seis meses (b) *(consequently)* por lo tanto

henceforth [hens'fɔ:θ] *adv Fml* de ahora en adelante

henchman ['hentʃmən] *n Pej* secuaz *m*

henna ['henə] *n Bot* alheña *f*; *(dye)* henna *f*

henpecked ['henpekt] *adj Fam* **a h. husband** un calzonazos

hepatitis [hepə'taɪtɪs] *n* hepatitis *f*

her [hɜ:(r), *unstressed* hə(r)] **1** *poss adj (one thing)* su; *(more than one)* sus; *(to distinguish)* de ella; **are they h. books or his?** ¿los libros son de ella o de él?; **she has cut h. finger** se ha cortado el dedo
2 *pron* (a) *(direct object)* la; **I saw h. recently** la vi hace poco (b) *(indirect object)* le; *(with other third person pronouns)* se; **he gave h. money** le dio dinero; **they handed it to h.** se lo entregaron (c) *(after prep)* ella; **for h.** para ella (d) *(as subject) Fam* ella; **look, it's h.!** ¡mira, es ella!

herald ['herəld] **1** *n* heraldo *m*
2 *vt* anunciar

heraldry ['herəldrɪ] *n* heráldica *f*

herb [hɜːb, *US* ɜːrb] *n* hierba *f*; **h. tea** infusión *f*

herbal ['hɜːbəl] *adj* herbario(a); **h. remedies** curas *fpl* de hierbas

herd [hɜːd] *n (of cattle)* manada *f*; *(of goats)* rebaño *m*; *Fig (large group)* multitud *f*

here [hɪə(r)] **1** *adv* aquí; **come h.** ven aquí; **h.!** ¡presente!; **h. goes!** ¡vamos a ver!; **here's to success!** ¡brindemos por el éxito!; **h. you are!** ¡toma!
2 *interj* **look h., you can't do that!** ¡oiga, que no se permite hacer eso!

hereafter [hɪər'ɑ:ftə(r)] *Fml* **1** *adv* de ahora en adelante
2 *n* **the h.** la otra vida, el más allá

hereby [hɪə'baɪ] *adv Fml* por la presente

hereditary [hɪ'redɪtərɪ] *adj* hereditario(a)

heresy ['herəsɪ] *n* herejía *f*

heretic ['herətɪk] *n* hereje *mf*

heritage ['herɪtɪdʒ] *n* patrimonio *m*; *Jur* herencia *f*

hermetically [hɜː'metɪklɪ] *adv* **h. sealed** herméticamente cerrado(a)

hermit ['hɜːmɪt] *n* ermitaño(a) *m,f*

> 🖉 Note that the Spanish word **ermita** is a false friend and is never a translation for the English word **hermit**. In Spanish, **ermita** means "hermitage".

hermitage ['hɜːmɪtɪdʒ] *n* ermita *f*

hernia ['hɜːnɪə] *n* hernia *f*

hero ['hɪərəʊ] *n (pl heroes)* héroe *m*; *(in*

novel) protagonista *m*; **h. worship** idolatría *f*

heroic [hɪ'rəʊɪk] *adj* heroico(a)

heroin ['herəʊɪn] *n* heroína *f*

heroine ['herəʊɪn] *n* heroína *f*; *(in novel)* protagonista *f*

heron ['herən] *n* garza *f*

herring ['herɪŋ] *n* arenque *m*

hers [hɜːz] *poss pron* (**a**) *(attribute) (one thing)* suyo(a); *(more than one)* suyos(as); *(to distinguish)* de ella; **they are h., not his** son de ella, no de él (**b**) *(noun reference) (one thing)* el suyo/la suya; *(more than one)* los suyos/las suyas; **my car is blue and h. is red** mi coche es azul y el suyo es rojo

herself [hɜː'self] *pers pron* (**a**) *(reflexive)* se; **she dressed h.** se vistió (**b**) *(alone)* ella misma; **she was by h.** estaba sola (**c**) *(emphatic)* **she told me so h.** eso dijo ella

hesitant ['hezɪtənt] *adj* vacilante

hesitate ['hezɪteɪt] *vi* vacilar

hesitation [hezɪ'teɪʃən] *n* indecisión *f*

heterogeneous [hetərəʊ'dʒiːnɪəs] *adj* heterogéneo(a)

heterosexual [hetərəʊ'seksjʊəl] *adj & n* heterosexual *(mf)*

hey [heɪ] *interj* ¡oye!, ¡oiga!

heyday ['heɪdeɪ] *n* auge *m*, apogeo *m*

HGV [eɪtʃdʒiː'viː] *n Br (abbr* **heavy goods vehicle**) vehículo *m* de carga pesada

hi [haɪ] *interj Fam* ¡hola!

hiatus [haɪ'eɪtəs] *n Fml* laguna *f*

hibernate ['haɪbəneɪt] *vi* hibernar

hibernation [haɪbə'neɪʃən] *n* hibernación *f*

hibiscus [haɪ'bɪskəs] *n* hibisco *m*

hiccup, hiccough ['hɪkʌp] *n* hipo *m*; *Fam (minor problem)* problemilla *m*; **to have hiccups** tener hipo

hide¹ [haɪd] **1** *vt (pt* **hid** [hɪd]; *pp* **hidden** ['hɪdən]) *(conceal)* esconder; *(obscure)* ocultar

    2 *vi* esconderse, ocultarse

    3 *n* puesto *m*

hide² [haɪd] *n (of animal)* piel *f*

hide-and-seek [haɪdən'siːk] *n* escondite *m*

hideous ['hɪdɪəs] *adj (horrific)* horroroso(a); *(extremely ugly)* espantoso(a)

hide-out ['haɪdaʊt] *n* escondrijo *m*, guarida *f*

hiding¹ ['haɪdɪŋ] *n* **to go into h.** esconderse

hiding² ['haɪdɪŋ] *n Fam* paliza *f*

hierarchy ['haɪərɑːkɪ] *n* jerarquía *f*

hi-fi ['haɪfaɪ] *n* hifi *m*; **h. equipment** equipo *m* de alta fidelidad

high [haɪ] **1** *adj* (**a**) alto(a); **how h. is that wall?** ¿qué altura tiene esa pared?; **it's 3 feet h.** tiene 3 pies de alto; **h. chair** silla alta para niños; **h. jump** salto *m* de altura

  (**b**) *(elevated)* elevado(a); **h. blood pressure** tensión alta; **h. prices** precios elevados; **to be in h. spirits** estar de buen humor

  (**c**) *(important)* importante; **h. wind** viento *m* fuerte; **to have a h. opinion of sb** tener muy buena opinión de algn; **H. Court** Tribunal Supremo; **h. fidelity** alta fidelidad; **h. road** carretera *f* principal; **h. school** instituto *m* de enseñanza media; **the H. Street** la Calle Mayor

  (**d**) *Fam (drugged)* colocado(a)

  2 *adv* alto; **to fly h.** volar a gran altura

  3 *n (high point)* punto máximo

highbrow ['haɪbraʊ] *adj & n* intelectual *(mf)*

high-class ['haɪklɑːs] *adj* de alta categoría

higher ['haɪə(r)] **1** *adj* superior; **h. education** enseñanza *f* superior

  2 *n Scot Educ* **H.** = examen final de los estudios preuniversitarios

high-five ['haɪ'faɪv] *n US Fam* palmada *f* en el aire *(saludo entre dos)*

high-flier, high-flyer [haɪ'flaɪə(r)] *n Fig* = persona dotada y ambiciosa

high-handed [haɪ'hændɪd] *adj* despótico(a)

high-heeled ['haɪhiːld] *adj* de tacón alto

highlands ['haɪləndz] *npl* tierras altas

highlight ['haɪlaɪt] **1** *n* (**a**) *(in hair)* reflejo *m* (**b**) *(of event)* atracción *f* principal

  2 *vt* (**a**) hacer resaltar (**b**) *(text)* marcar con un rotulador fosforescente

highly ['haɪlɪ] *adv (very)* sumamente; **to speak h. of sb** hablar muy bien de algn

highly-strung [haɪlɪ'strʌŋ] *adj* muy nervioso(a)

Highness ['haɪnɪs] *n* alteza *mf*; **Your H.** Su Alteza

high-pitched ['haɪpɪtʃt] *adj* estridente

high-powered ['haɪpaʊəd] *adj (person)* dinámico(a)

high-ranking ['haɪræŋkɪŋ] *adj* **h. official** alto funcionario

high-rise ['haɪraɪz] *adj* **h. building** rascacielos *m inv*

high-speed ['haɪspiːd] *adj* **h. lens** objetivo ultrarrápido; **h. train** tren *m* de alta velocidad

highway ['haɪweɪ] *n US* carretera *f*, autopista *f*; *Br* **H. Code** código *m* de la circulación

highwayman ['haɪweɪmən] *n* salteador *m* de caminos

hijack ['haɪdʒæk] **1** *vt* secuestrar
2 *n* secuestro *m*

hijacker ['haɪdʒækə(r)] *n* secuestrador(a) *m,f*; *(of planes)* pirata *mf* del aire

hike [haɪk] **1** *n* (**a**) *(walk)* excursión *f* (**b**) **price h.** aumento *m* de precio
2 *vi* ir de excursión

hiker ['haɪkə(r)] *n* excursionista *mf*

hilarious [hɪ'leərɪəs] *adj* graciosísimo(a)

hill [hɪl] *n* colina *f*; *(slope)* cuesta *f*

hillside ['hɪlsaɪd] *n* ladera *f*

hilltop ['hɪltɒp] *n* cima *f* de una colina

hilly ['hɪlɪ] *adj* (**hillier, hilliest**) accidentado(a)

hilt [hɪlt] *n* puño *m*, empuñadura *f*; **I'll support you up to the h.** te daré mi apoyo total

him [hɪm] *pron* (**a**) *(direct object)* lo, le; **hit h.!** ¡pégale!; **she loves h.** lo quiere (**b**) *(indirect object)* le; *(with other third person pronouns)* se; **give h. the money** dale el dinero; **give it to h.** dáselo (**c**) *(after prep)* él; **it's not like h. to say that** no es propio de él decir eso (**d**) *Fam (as subject)* él; **it's h.** es él

himself [hɪm'self] *pers pron* (**a**) *(reflexive)* se; **he hurt h.** se hizo daño (**b**) *(alone)* solo, por sí mismo; **by h.** solo (**c**) *(emphatic)* él mismo

hind¹ [haɪnd] *adj* trasero(a); **h. legs** patas traseras

hind² [haɪnd] *n Zool* cierva *f*

hinder ['hɪndə(r)] *vt* dificultar, estorbar; **to h. sb from doing sth** impedir a algn hacer algo

hindrance ['hɪndrəns] *n* estorbo *m*

hindsight ['haɪndsaɪt] *n* retrospectiva *f*

Hindu [hɪn'duː, 'hɪnduː] *adj & n* hindú (*mf*)

Hinduism ['hɪnduːɪzəm] *n* hinduismo *m*

hinge [hɪndʒ] **1** *n* bisagra *f*; *Fig* eje *m*
2 *vt* engoznar
► **hinge on** *vt insep* depender de

hint [hɪnt] **1** *n* (**a**) indirecta *f*; **to take the h.** coger la indirecta (**b**) *(clue)* pista *f* (**c**) *(trace)* pizca *f* (**d**) *(advice)* consejo *m*
2 *vi* (**a**) lanzar indirectas (**b**) *(imply)* insinuar algo

hip¹ [hɪp] *n* cadera *f*; **h. flask** petaca *f*

hip² [hɪp] *adj Fam* en la onda

hippie ['hɪpɪ] *adj & n Fam* hippy (*mf*)

hippopotamus [hɪpə'pɒtəməs] *n* hipopótamo *m*

hire ['haɪə(r)] **1** *n* alquiler *m*; **bicycles for h.** se alquilan bicicletas; **taxi for h.** taxi *m* libre; **h. purchase** compra *f* a plazos
2 *vt* (**a**) *(rent)* alquilar, *Méx* rentar (**b**) *(employ)* contratar

► **hire out** *vt sep (car)* alquilar, *Méx* rentar; *(people)* contratar

his [hɪz] **1** *poss adj (one thing)* su; *(more than one)* sus; *(to distinguish)* de él; **he washed h. face** se lavó la cara; **is it h. dog or hers?** ¿el perro es de él o de ella?
2 *poss pron* (**a**) *(attribute) (one thing)* suyo(a); *(more than one)* suyos(as); *(to distinguish)* de él (**b**) *(noun reference) (one thing)* el suyo/la suya; *(more than one)* los suyos/las suyas; **my car is blue and h. is red** mi coche es azul y el suyo es rojo

Hispanic [hɪ'spænɪk] **1** *adj* hispánico(a)
2 *n US* hispano(a) *m,f*, latino(a) *m,f*

hiss [hɪs] **1** *n* siseo *m*; *Th* silbido *m*
2 *vt & vi* silbar

historian [hɪ'stɔːrɪən] *n* historiador(a) *m,f*

historic [hɪ'stɒrɪk] *adj* histórico(a)

historical [hɪ'stɒrɪkəl] *adj* histórico(a); **h. novel** novela histórica

history ['hɪstərɪ] *n* historia *f*

hit [hɪt] **1** *n* (**a**) *(blow)* golpe *m*; **direct h.** impacto directo; *Fam* **h. list** lista negra; *Fam* **h. man** asesino *m* a sueldo (**b**) *(success)* éxito *m*; **h. parade** lista *f* de éxitos (**c**) *Comput (visit to web site)* acceso *m*, visita *f*
2 *vt* (*pt & pp* **hit**) (**a**) *(strike)* golpear, pegar; **he was h. in the leg** le dieron en la pierna; **the car h. the kerb** el coche chocó contra el bordillo; *Fam Fig* **to h. the roof** poner el grito en el cielo (**b**) *(affect)* afectar (**c**) **to h. the headlines** ser noticia
► **hit back** *vi (reply to criticism)* replicar
► **hit on** *vt insep* dar con; **we h. on the idea of ...** se nos ocurrió la idea de ...
► **hit out** *vi* **to h. out at sb** atacar a algn
► **hit upon** *vt insep* = **hit on**

hit-and-run [hɪtən'rʌn] *adj* **h. driver** = conductor que atropella a algn y no para

hitch [hɪtʃ] **1** *n* dificultad *f*
2 *vt (fasten)* atar
3 *vi Fam (hitch-hike)* hacer autostop
► **hitch up** *vt sep* remangarse

hitch-hike ['hɪtʃhaɪk] *vi* hacer autostop *or* dedo

hitch-hiker ['hɪtʃhaɪkə(r)] *n* autostopista *mf*

hitherto [hɪðə'tuː] *adv Fml* hasta la fecha

HIV [eɪtʃaɪ'viː] *n (abbr* **human immunodeficiency virus)** VIH *m*; **to be diagnosed HIV positive/negative** dar seropositivo(a)/seronegativo(a) en la prueba del SIDA

hive [haɪv] *n* colmena *f*; *Fig* lugar muy activo

HM (*abbr* **His/Her Majesty**) SM

hoard [hɔːd] **1** *n* (*provisions*) reservas *fpl*; (*money etc*) tesoro *m*

   2 *vt* (*objects*) acumular; (*money*) atesorar

hoarding ['hɔːdɪŋ] *n* (*temporary fence*) valla *f*; *Br* (*billboard*) valla publicitaria

hoarfrost ['hɔːfrɒst] *n* escarcha *f*

hoarse [hɔːs] *adj* ronco(a); **to be h.** tener la voz ronca

hoax [hɒʊks] *n* (*joke*) broma pesada; (*trick*) engaño *m*

hob [hɒb] *n* (*of cooker*) encimera *f*

hobble ['hɒbəl] *vi* cojear

hobby ['hɒbɪ] *n* pasatiempo *m*, afición *f*

hobbyhorse ['hɒbɪhɔːs] *n* (*toy*) caballito *m* de juguete; *Fig* (*fixed idea*) idea fija, manía *f*

hobo ['hɒʊbɒʊ] *n US* vagabundo(a) *m,f*

hockey ['hɒkɪ] *n* hockey *m*

hog [hɒg] **1** *n* cerdo *m*, puerco *m*; *Fam* **to go the whole h.** liarse la manta a la cabeza

   2 *vt Fam* acaparar

hoist [hɔɪst] **1** *n* (*crane*) grúa *f*; (*lift*) montacargas *m inv*

   2 *vt* levantar, subir; **to h. the flag** izar la bandera

hold [hɒʊld] **1** *vt* (*pt & pp* held) (a) (*keep in hand*) aguantar, tener (en la mano); (*grip*) agarrar; (*support*) (*weight*) soportar; (*opinion*) sostener; **to h. sb** abrazar a algn; **to h. sb's hand** cogerle la mano a algn; *Fig* **she can h. her own in French** se defiende en francés

   (b) (*contain*) dar cabida a; **the jug holds a litre** en la jarra cabe un litro

   (c) (*meeting*) celebrar; (*conversation*) mantener

   (d) (*reserve*) guardar

   (e) **to h. office** ocupar un puesto

   (f) (*consider*) considerar

   (g) **he was held for two hours at the police station** estuvo detenido durante dos horas en la comisaría; **to h. one's breath** contener la respiración; **to h. sb hostage** retener a algn como rehén

   (h) *Tel* **to h. the line** no colgar

   2 *vi* (a) (*rope*) aguantar

   (b) *Fig* (*offer*) ser válido(a)

   3 *n* (a) **to get h. of** (*grip*) coger, agarrar; *Fig* localizar; **can you get h. of a newspaper?** ¿puedes conseguir un periódico?

   (b) (*control*) control *m*

   (c) *Naut* bodega *f*

   (d) (*in wrestling*) llave *f*

▸**hold back 1** *vt sep* (*crowd*) contener; (*feelings*) reprimir; (*truth*) ocultar; **I don't**

want to h. you back (*delay*) no quiero entretenerte

   2 *vi* (*hesitate*) vacilar

▸**hold down** *vt sep* (a) (*control*) dominar (b) *Fam* (*job*) desempeñar

▸**hold off** *vt sep* mantener a distancia

▸**hold on** *vi* (a) (*keep a firm grasp*) agarrarse bien (b) (*wait*) esperar; *Tel* **h. on!** ¡no cuelgue!

▸**hold out 1** *vt sep* (*hand*) tender

   2 *vi* (a) (*last*) (*things*) durar; (*person*) resistir (b) **to h. out for** insistir en

▸**hold up** *vt sep* (a) (*rob*) (*train*) asaltar; (*bank*) atracar (b) (*delay*) retrasar; **we were held up for half an hour** sufrimos media hora de retraso (c) (*raise*) levantar (d) (*support*) apuntalar

holdall ['hɒʊldɔːl] *n Br* bolsa *f* de viaje

holder ['hɒʊldə(r)] *n* (a) (*receptacle*) recipiente *m* (b) (*owner*) poseedor(a) *m,f*; (*bearer*) portador(a) *m,f*; (*of passport*) titular *mf*; **record h.** plusmarquista *mf*

holding ['hɒʊldɪŋ] *n* (a) (*property*) propiedad *f* (b) *Fin* valor *m* en cartera; **h. company** holding *m*

hold-up ['hɒʊldʌp] *n* (a) (*robbery*) atraco *m* (b) (*delay*) retraso *m*; (*in traffic*) atasco *m*

hole [hɒʊl] *n* (a) agujero *m*; (*large*) hoyo *m*; (*in the road*) bache *m* (b) (*in golf*) hoyo *m* (c) *Fam* (*of place*) antro *m*

holiday ['hɒlɪdeɪ] **1** *n* (*one day*) día *m* de fiesta; *Br* (*several days*) vacaciones *fpl*; **to be/go on h.** estar/ir de vacaciones; **h. resort** lugar turístico

   2 *vi Br* pasar las vacaciones; (*in summer*) veranear

holiday-maker ['hɒlɪdeɪmeɪkə(r)] *n Br* turista *mf*; (*in summer*) veraneante *mf*

holiness ['hɒʊlɪnɪs] *n* santidad *f*

Holland ['hɒlənd] *n* Holanda

hollow ['hɒləʊ] **1** *adj* (a) hueco(a) (b) (*cheeks, eyes*) hundido(a) (c) *Fig* (*insincere*) falso(a); (*empty*) vacío(a)

   2 *n* hueco *m*; *Geog* hondonada *f*

   3 *vt* **to h. (out)** hacer un hueco en

holly ['hɒlɪ] *n* acebo *m*

holocaust ['hɒləkɔːst] *n* holocausto *m*

holster ['hɒʊlstə(r)] *n* pistolera *f*

holy ['hɒʊlɪ] *adj* sagrado(a), santo(a); (*blessed*) bendito(a); **H. Ghost** Espíritu Santo; **H. Land** Tierra Santa; **H. See** Santa Sede

homage ['hɒmɪdʒ] *n* homenaje *m*; **to pay h. to sb** rendir homenaje a algn

home [hɒʊm] **1** *n* (a) casa *f*, hogar *m*; **at h.** en casa; *Fig* **make yourself at h.!** ¡estás en tu casa!; *Fig* **to feel at h.** estar a gusto;

h. banking telebanco *m*; *Comput* **h. page** *(initial page)* portada *f*, página *f* inicial *or* de inicio; *(personal page)* página personal; **h. shopping** telecompra *f*, **h. shopping channel** teletienda *f*
(**b**) *(institution)* asilo *m*; **old people's h.** asilo de ancianos
(**c**) *(country)* patria *f*
(**d**) *Sport* **to play at h.** jugar en casa; *US* **h. base** *(in baseball)* base *f* del bateador; **h. run** carrera completa
2 *adj* (**a**) *(domestic)* del hogar; *Br* **h. help** asistenta *f*
(**b**) *Pol* interior; **h. affairs** asuntos *mpl* interiores; *Br* **H. Office** Ministerio *m* del Interior; *Br* **H. Secretary** Ministro(a) *m,f* del Interior
(**c**) *(native)* natal
3 *adv* en casa; **to go h.** irse a casa; **to leave h.** irse de casa

homeland ['həʊmlænd] *n* patria *f*; *(birthplace)* tierra *f* natal

homeless ['həʊmlɪs] **1** *adj* sin techo
2 *npl* **the h.** los sin techo

homely ['həʊmlɪ] *adj* (**homelier, homeliest**) (**a**) *Br (person)* casero(a); *(atmosphere)* familiar (**b**) *US (unattractive)* sin atractivo

home-made ['həʊmmeɪd] *adj* casero(a)

homeopathy [həʊmɪ'ɒpəθɪ] *n US* = **homoeopathy**

homesick ['həʊmsɪk] *adj* **to be h.** tener morriña

homeward(s) ['həʊmwəd(z)] *adv* hacia casa

homework ['həʊmwɜːk] *n* deberes *mpl*

homey ['həʊmɪ] *adj US Fam* hogareño(a)

homicide ['hɒmɪsaɪd] *n* homicidio *m*

homing ['həʊmɪŋ] *adj* (**a**) **h. device** cabeza buscadora (**b**) **h. pigeon** paloma mensajera

homoeopathy [həʊmɪ'ɒpəθɪ] *n* homeopatía *f*

homogeneous [hɒmə'dʒiːnɪəs] *adj* homogéneo(a)

homosexual [hɒməʊ'seksjʊəl] *adj & n* homosexual *(mf)*

Honduran [hɒn'dʒʊərən] *adj & n* hondureño(a) *(m,f)*

Honduras [hɒn'dʒʊərəs] *n* Honduras

honest ['ɒnɪst] *adj* honrado(a); *(sincere)* sincero(a), franco(a); *(fair)* justo(a); **the h. truth** la pura verdad

honestly ['ɒnɪstlɪ] *adv* honradamente; *(question)* ¿de verdad?; *(exclamation)* ¡hay que ver!; **h., it doesn't matter** de verdad, no tiene importancia

honesty ['ɒnɪstɪ] *n* honradez *f*

honey ['hʌnɪ] *n* miel *f*; *US Fam (endearment)* cariño *m*

honeycomb ['hʌnɪkəʊm] *n* panal *m*

honeymoon ['hʌnɪmuːn] *n* luna *f* de miel

honeysuckle ['hʌnɪsʌkəl] *n* madreselva *f*

honk [hɒŋk] *vi Aut* tocar la bocina

honor ['ɒnər] *n & vt US* = **honour**

honorary ['ɒnərərɪ] *adj (member)* honorario(a); *(duties)* honorífico(a)

honour ['ɒnər] **1** *n* (**a**) honor *m* (**b**) *US Jur* **Her H./His H./Your H.** Su Señoría *f* (**c**) *Mil* **honours** honores *mpl* (**d**) **Honours degree** licenciatura *f* superior
2 *vt* (**a**) *(respect)* honrar (**b**) *(obligation)* cumplir con

honourable ['ɒnərəbəl] *adj (person)* honrado(a); *(action)* honroso(a)

hood [hʊd] *n* (**a**) *(of garment)* capucha *f* (**b**) *(of car)* capota *f*; *US (bonnet)* capó *m* (**c**) *US Fam (gangster)* matón(ona) *m,f*

hoodlum ['huːdləm] *n* matón *m*

hoodwink ['hʊdwɪŋk] *vt* engañar

hoof [huːf] *n (pl* **hoofs** *or* **hooves**) *(of horse)* casco *m*; *(of cow, sheep)* pezuña *f*

hook [hʊk] **1** *n* (**a**) gancho *m*; *(in fishing)* anzuelo *m*; *Sewing* **hooks and eyes** corchetes *mpl*; **to take the phone off the h.** descolgar el teléfono (**b**) *(in boxing)* gancho *m*
2 *vt* enganchar
▸ **hook up** *vt sep & vi Rad, TV & Comput* conectar (**with** con)

hooked [hʊkt] *adj* (**a**) *(nose)* aguileño(a) (**b**) *Fam (addicted)* enganchado(a) (**on** a); **to get h.** engancharse

hooker ['hʊkər] *n US Fam (prostitute)* fulana *f*, puta *f*

hookey ['hʊkɪ] *n US Fam* **to play h.** hacer novillos

hook-up ['hʊkʌp] *n* (**a**) *Comput* conexión *f* (**b**) *Rad & TV* emisión *f* múltiple

hooky ['hʊkɪ] *n US Fam* = **hookey**

hooligan ['huːlɪgən] *n Fam* gamberro(a) *m,f*

hoop [huːp] *n* aro *m*; *(of barrel)* fleje *m*

hooray [huː'reɪ] *interj* ¡hurra!

hoot [huːt] **1** *n* (**a**) ululato *m*; *Fam* **hoots of laughter** carcajadas *fpl*; *Fam* **I don't care a h.** me importa un pepino (**b**) *(of car horn)* bocinazo *m*
2 *vi* (**a**) *(owl)* ulular (**b**) *(car)* dar un bocinazo; *(train)* silbar; *(siren)* pitar

hooter ['huːtə(r)] *n esp Br (of car)* bocina *f*; *(siren)* sirena *f*

Hoover® ['huːvə(r)] *Br* **1** *n* aspiradora *f*
2 *vt* **to h.** pasar la aspiradora por

hooves [huːvz] *pl of* **hoof**

hop¹ [hɒp] **1** *vi* saltar; **to h. on one leg** andar a la pata coja
2 *n (small jump)* brinco *m*

hop² [hɒp] *n Bot* lúpulo *m*

hope [həʊp] **1** *n* esperanza *f; (false)* ilusión *f;* **to have little h. of doing sth** tener pocas posibilidades de hacer algo
2 *vt & vi* esperar; **I h. so/not** espero que sí/no; **we h. you're well** esperamos que estés bien

hopeful ['həʊpfʊl] *adj (confident)* optimista; *(promising)* prometedor(a)

hopefully ['həʊpfʊlɪ] *adv* **(a)** *(confidently)* con optimismo **(b) h. the weather will be fine** *(it is hoped)* esperemos que haga buen tiempo

hopeless ['həʊplɪs] *adj* desesperado(a); *Fam* **to be h. at sports** ser negado(a) para los deportes

hopelessly ['həʊplɪslɪ] *adv* desesperadamente; **h. lost** completamente perdido(a)

horde [hɔːd] *n* multitud *f*

horizon [hə'raɪzən] *n* horizonte *m*

horizontal [hɒrɪ'zɒntəl] *adj* horizontal

hormone ['hɔːməʊn] *n* hormona *f*

horn [hɔːn] *n* **(a)** cuerno *m* **(b)** *Fam Mus* trompeta *f;* **French h.** trompa *f;* **hunting h.** cuerno *m* de caza **(c)** *Aut* bocina *f*

hornet ['hɔːnɪt] *n* avispón *m*

horny ['hɔːnɪ] *adj (hornier, horniest)* **(a)** *(hands)* calloso(a) **(b)** *very Fam (sexually aroused)* caliente, cachondo(a)

horoscope ['hɒrəskəʊp] *n* horóscopo *m*

horrendous [hɒ'rendəs] *adj* horrendo(a)

horrible ['hɒrəbəl] *adj* horrible

horrid ['hɒrɪd] *adj* horrible

horrific [hə'rɪfɪk] *adj* horrendo(a)

horrify ['hɒrɪfaɪ] *vt* horrorizar

horror ['hɒrə(r)] *n* horror *m; Fam* **a little h.** un diablillo; **h. film** película *f* de miedo *or* de terror

hors d'oeuvre [ɔː'dɜːvr] *n (pl* **hors d'oeuvres)** entremés *m*

horse [hɔːs] *n* **(a)** caballo *m;* **h. race** carrera *f* de caballos **(b)** *(in gymnastics)* potro *m* **(c)** *Tech* caballete *m* **(d) h. chestnut** *(tree)* castaño *m* de Indias

horseback ['hɔːsbæk] *n* **on h.** a caballo; *US* **h. riding** equitación *f*

horseman ['hɔːsmən] *n* jinete *m*

horseplay ['hɔːspleɪ] *n* payasadas *fpl*

horsepower ['hɔːspaʊə(r)] *n* caballo *m* (de vapor)

horseradish ['hɔːsrædɪʃ] *n* rábano rusticano

horseshoe ['hɔːsʃuː] *n* herradura *f*

horsewoman ['hɔːswʊmən] *n* amazona *f*

horticulture ['hɔːtɪkʌltʃə(r)] *n* horticultura *f*

hose [həʊz] *n (pipe)* manguera *f*

hosiery ['həʊzɪərɪ] *n* medias *fpl* y calcetines *mpl*

hospice ['hɒspɪs] *n* residencia *f* para enfermos terminales

hospitable ['hɒspɪtəbəl, hɒ'spɪtəbəl] *adj* hospitalario(a); **h. atmosphere** ambiente acogedor

hospital ['hɒspɪtəl] *n* hospital *m*

hospitality [hɒspɪ'tælɪtɪ] *n* hospitalidad *f*

Host [həʊst] *n Rel* hostia *f*

host¹ [həʊst] **1** *n* **(a)** *(at home)* anfitrión *m* **(b)** *Th & TV* presentador *m* **(c)** *Biol* huésped *m*
2 *vt Th & TV* presentar

host² [həʊst] *n (large number)* montón *m*

hostage ['hɒstɪdʒ] *n* rehén *m*

hostel ['hɒstəl] *n* hostal *m*

hostess ['həʊstɪs] *n* **(a)** *(at home etc)* anfitriona *f* **(b)** *Th & TV* presentadora *f* **(c) (air) h.** azafata *f*

hostile ['hɒstaɪl] *adj* hostil

hostility [hɒ'stɪlɪtɪ] *n* hostilidad *f*

hot [hɒt] *adj (hotter, hottest)* **(a)** caliente; *Fig* **h. line** teléfono rojo; **h. spot** *(nightclub)* club nocturno **(b)** *(weather)* caluroso(a); **it's very h.** hace mucho calor; **to feel h.** tener calor **(c)** *(spicy)* picante; **h. dog** perrito *m* caliente **(d)** *(temper)* fuerte **(e)** *Fam (fresh)* de última hora **(f)** *Fam (good)* bueno(a); **it's not so h.** no es nada del otro mundo **(g)** *(popular)* popular **(h)** *(dangerous)* peligroso(a); *Fig* **to get oneself into h. water** meterse en un lío; *Fam* **h. seat** primera fila
▸ **hot up** *vi Fam* **things are hotting up** la cosa se está poniendo al rojo vivo

hotbed ['hɒtbed] *n Fig* hervidero *m*

hotel [həʊ'tel] *n* hotel *m*

hotelier [həʊ'teljeɪ] *n* hotelero(a) *m,f*

hot-headed [hɒt'hedɪd] *adj* impetuoso(a)

hothouse ['hɒthaʊs] *n* invernadero *m*

hotplate ['hɒtpleɪt] *n (cooker)* placa *f* de cocina; *(to keep food warm)* calientaplatos *m inv*

hotshot ['hɒtʃɒt] *n Fam* as *m*

hot-water [hɒt'wɔːtə(r)] *adj* **h. bottle** bolsa *f* de agua caliente

hound [haʊnd] **1** *n* perro *m* de caza
2 *vt* acosar

hour ['aʊə(r)] *n* hora *f;* **60 miles an h.** 60 millas por hora; **by the h.** por horas; **h. hand** manecilla *f*

hourly [ˈaʊəlɪ] **1** *adj* cada hora
2 *adv* por horas
house 1 *n* [haʊs] (**a**) casa *f*; **at my h.** en mi casa; *Fig* **on the h.** cortesía de la casa; (**h. arrest** arresto domiciliario; **h. plant** planta *f* de interior (**b**) *Pol* **H. of Commons** Cámara *f* de los Comunes; **H. of Lords** Cámara de los Lores; *US* **H. of Representatives** Cámara de Representantes; **Houses of Parliament** Parlamento *m* (**c**) *(company)* empresa *f*; **publishing h.** editorial *f* (**d**) *Th* sala *f*
2 *vt* [haʊz] alojar; *(store)* guardar
houseboat [ˈhaʊsbəʊt] *n* casa *f* flotante
housebreaking [ˈhaʊsbreɪkɪŋ] *n* allanamiento *m* de morada
housebroken [ˈhaʊsbrəʊkən] *adj US (pet)* = que ya ha aprendido a no hacer sus necesidades en casa
housecoat [ˈhaʊskəʊt] *n* bata *f*
household [ˈhaʊshəʊld] *n* hogar *m*; **h. products** productos domésticos
housekeeper [ˈhaʊskiːpə(r)] *n* ama *f* de llaves
housekeeping [ˈhaʊskiːpɪŋ] *n* administración doméstica; **h. money** dinero *m* para los gastos domésticos
house-train [ˈhaʊstreɪn] *vt (pet)* educar
house-warming [ˈhaʊswɔːmɪŋ] *n* **h. (party)** = fiesta que se da al estrenar casa
housewife [ˈhaʊswaɪf] *n* ama *f* de casa
housework [ˈhaʊswɜːk] *n* trabajo doméstico
housing [ˈhaʊzɪŋ] *n* vivienda *f*; **h. estate** urbanización *f*
hovel [ˈhɒvəl, ˈhʌvəl] *n* casucha *f*
hover [ˈhɒvə(r)] *vi (bird)* cernerse; *(aircraft)* permanecer inmóvil (en el aire)
hovercraft [ˈhɒvəkrɑːft] *n* aerodeslizador *m*
how [haʊ] *adv* (**a**) *(direct question)* ¿cómo?; **h. are you?** ¿cómo estás?; *Fam* **h. come?** ¿por qué? (**b**) *(indirect question)* cómo; **I don't know h. to tell you** no sé cómo decírtelo (**c**) *(very)* qué; **h. funny!** ¡qué divertido! (**d**) *(suggestion)* **h. about going to the cinema?** ¿te apetece ir al cine?; **h. about a stroll?** ¿qué te parece un paseo? (**e**) *(quantity)* cuánto; **h. old is she?** ¿cuántos años tiene?; **h. tall are you?** ¿cuánto mides? (**f**) **h. many?** ¿cuántos(as)?; **h. much?** ¿cuánto(a)?; **I don't know h. many people there were** no sé cuánta gente había
however [haʊˈevə(r)] *adv* (**a**) *(nevertheless)* no obstante, sin embargo (**b**) *(with adjective)* **h. difficult it may be** por difícil que sea; **h. much** por mucho que (+ *subj*)

howl [haʊl] **1** *n* aullido *m*
2 *vi* aullar
howler [ˈhaʊlə(r)] *n Fam* despiste *m*
HP, hp [eɪtʃˈpiː] *n* (**a**) *Br (abbr* **hire purchase)** compra *f* a plazos (**b**) *(abbr* **horsepower)** cv *mpl*
HQ [eɪtʃˈkjuː] *n (abbr* **headquarters)** sede *f*, central *f*
hub [hʌb] *n Aut* cubo *m*; *Fig* eje *m*
hubbub [ˈhʌbʌb] *n* alboroto *m*
hubcap [ˈhʌbkæp] *n Aut* tapacubos *m inv*
huddle [ˈhʌdəl] **1** *n* grupo *m*
2 *vi* **to h. (up** or **together)** acurrucarse
hue¹ [hjuː] *n (colour)* tinte *m*; *(shade)* matiz *m*
hue² [hjuː] *n* **h. and cry** fuerte protesta *f*
huff [hʌf] *n* **to be in a h.** estar de mala uva
hug [hʌɡ] **1** *vt* abrazar
2 *n* abrazo *m*
huge [hjuːdʒ] *adj* enorme
hugely [ˈhjuːdʒlɪ] *adv* enormemente
hulk [hʌlk] *n* (**a**) *Naut* casco *m* (**b**) *(thing, person)* armatoste *m*
hull [hʌl] *n Naut* casco *m*
hullabal(l)oo [hʌləbəˈluː] *n Fam* follón *m*
hullo [hʌˈləʊ] *interj Br* ¡hola!
hum [hʌm] **1** *vt (tune)* tararear
2 *vi (bees, engine)* zumbar; *(sing)* tararear
3 *n (of bees)* zumbido *m*
human [ˈhjuːmən] **1** *adj* humano(a); **h. race** raza humana; **h. being** ser humano
2 *n* ser humano
humane [hjuːˈmeɪn] *adj* humano(a)
humanitarian [hjuːmænɪˈteərɪən] *adj* humanitario(a)
humanity [hjuːˈmænɪtɪ] *n* (**a**) humanidad *f* (**b**) *Univ* **the humanities** las humanidades
humble [ˈhʌmbəl] **1** *adj* humilde
2 *vt* humillar
humbug [ˈhʌmbʌɡ] *n* (**a**) *Fam* tonterías *fpl* (**b**) *Br (mint)* **h.** caramelo *m* de menta
humdrum [ˈhʌmdrʌm] *adj* monótono(a), aburrido(a)
humid [ˈhjuːmɪd] *adj* húmedo(a)
humidity [hjuːˈmɪdɪtɪ] *n* humedad *f*
humiliate [hjuːˈmɪlɪeɪt] *vt* humillar
humiliation [hjuːmɪlɪˈeɪʃən] *n* humillación *f*
humility [hjuːˈmɪlɪtɪ] *n* humildad *f*
humor [ˈhjuːmə(r)] *n US* = **humour**
humorous [ˈhjuːmərəs] *adj (writer)* humorístico(a); *(person, story)* gracioso(a), divertido(a)
humour [ˈhjuːmə(r)] **1** *n* humor *m*
2 *vt* seguir la corriente a
hump [hʌmp] **1** *n* (**a**) *(on back)* joroba *f*

(**b**) *(small hill)* montículo *m*

2 *vt Br Fam (carry)* cargar (a la espalda)

humus ['hjuːməs] *n* mantillo *m*, humus *m*

hunch [hʌntʃ] *n Fam* corazonada *f*

hunchback ['hʌntʃbæk] *n* jorobado(a) *m,f*

hundred ['hʌndrəd] **1** *n* cien *m*, ciento *m*; *(rough number)* centenar *m*; **a h. and twenty-five** ciento veinticinco; **five h.** quinientos

2 *adj* cien; **a h. people** cien personas; **a h. percent** cien por cien; **two h. chairs** doscientas sillas

hundredth ['hʌndrədθ] *adj & n* centésimo(a) *(m,f)*

hundredweight ['hʌndrədweɪt] *n Br* = 50,8 kg; *US* = 45,36 kg

hung [hʌŋ] **1** *adj Fam* (**a**) **h. over** con resaca (**b**) **h. up** acomplejado(a)

2 *pt & pp of* hang

Hungarian [hʌŋ'geərɪən] *adj & n* húngaro(a) *(m,f)*

Hungary ['hʌŋgərɪ] *n* Hungría

hunger ['hʌŋgə(r)] **1** *n* hambre *f*; **h. strike** huelga *f* de hambre

2 *vi Fig* tener hambre (**for** de)

hungry ['hʌŋgrɪ] *adj* (**hungrier, hungriest**) hambriento(a); **to be h.** tener hambre; **to go h.** pasar hambre

hunk [hʌŋk] *n* (**a**) *(piece)* buen pedazo *m* (**b**) *Fam (man)* machote *m*

hunt [hʌnt] **1** *vt* cazar

2 *vi (for game)* cazar; *(search)* buscar

3 *n* caza *f*; *(search)* búsqueda *f*

▶ **hunt down** *vt sep* perseguir

hunter ['hʌntə(r)] *n* cazador(a) *m,f*

hunting ['hʌntɪŋ] *n* caza *f*; *(expedition)* cacería *f*

hurdle ['hɜːdəl] *n Sport* valla *f*; *Fig* obstáculo *m*

hurl [hɜːl] *vt* arrojar, lanzar

hurrah [hʊ'rɑː], **hurray** [hʊ'reɪ] *interj* ¡hurra!; **h. for John!** ¡viva John!

hurricane ['hʌrɪkən, 'hʌrɪkeɪn] *n* huracán *m*

hurried ['hʌrɪd] *adj* apresurado(a); *(action etc)* hecho(a) de prisa

hurriedly ['hʌrɪdlɪ] *adv* deprisa, apresuradamente

hurry ['hʌrɪ] **1** *vi* darse prisa

2 *vt* meter prisa a

3 *n* **to be in a h.** tener prisa

hurt [hɜːt] **1** *vt* (*pt & pp* hurt) hacer daño a; *(wound)* herir; *(feelings)* ofender

2 *vi* doler; **my arm hurts** me duele el brazo; *Fam* **it doesn't h. to go out once in a while** no viene mal salir de vez en cuando

3 *adj (physically)* herido(a); *(mentally)* dolido(a)

hurtful ['hɜːtfʊl] *adj* hiriente

hurtle ['hɜːtəl] *vi* lanzarse; **to h. down** desplomarse

husband ['hʌzbənd] *n* marido *m*, esposo *m*

hush [hʌʃ] **1** *vt* callar; **to h. sth up** echar tierra a un asunto

2 *n* silencio *m*

3 *interj* ¡silencio!

hush-hush [hʌʃ'hʌʃ] *adj Fam* confidencial

husky¹ ['hʌskɪ] *adj* (**huskier, huskiest**) ronco(a)

husky² ['hʌskɪ] *n (dog)* perro *m* esquimal

hustings ['hʌstɪŋz] *npl Pol* (**a**) *(platform)* tribuna *f* electoral (**b**) *(election)* elecciones *fpl*

hustle ['hʌsəl] **1** *vt* (**a**) *(jostle)* empujar (**b**) *Fam* meter prisa a

2 *n* bullicio *m*; **h. and bustle** ajetreo *m*

hut [hʌt] *n* cabaña *f*; *(shed)* cobertizo *m*; *Mil* barraca *f*

hutch [hʌtʃ] *n* jaula *f*; **rabbit h.** conejera *f*

hyacinth ['haɪəsɪnθ] *n* jacinto *m*

hybrid ['haɪbrɪd] *adj & n* híbrido(a) *(m,f)*

hydrant ['haɪdrənt] *n* **fire h.** boca *f* de incendio

hydraulic [haɪ'drɒlɪk] *adj* hidráulico(a)

hydrocarbon [haɪdrəʊ'kɑːbən] *n* hidrocarburo *m*

hydrochloric [haɪdrəʊ'klɒrɪk] *adj* **h. acid** ácido clorhídrico

hydroelectric [haɪdrəʊɪ'lektrɪk] *adj* hidroeléctrico(a)

hydrofoil ['haɪdrəfɔɪl] *n* hidroala *f*

hydrogen ['haɪdrədʒən] *n* hidrógeno *m*

hydroplane ['haɪdrəpleɪn] *n US (seaplane)* hidroavión *m*

hyena [haɪ'iːnə] *n* hiena *f*

hygiene ['haɪdʒiːn] *n* higiene *f*

hygienic [haɪ'dʒiːnɪk] *adj* higiénico(a)

hymn [hɪm] *n* himno *m*; **h. book** cantoral *m*

hype [haɪp] *n Fam* campaña publicitaria, movida *f*

hyper- ['haɪpə(r)] *pref* hiper-; **hyperactive** hiperactivo(a)

hypermarket ['haɪpəmɑːkɪt] *n Br* hipermercado *m*

hypersensitive [haɪpə'sensɪtɪv] *adj* hipersensible

hyphen ['haɪfən] *n* guión *m*

hypnosis [hɪp'nəʊsɪs] *n* hipnosis *f*

hypnotist ['hɪpnətɪst] *n* hipnotizador(a) *m,f*

hypnotize [ˈhɪpnətaɪz] *vt* hipnotizar
hypochondriac [haɪpəˈkɒndrɪæk] *adj &*
n hipocondríaco(a) *(m,f)*
hypocrisy [hɪˈpɒkrəsɪ] *n* hipocresía *f*
hypocrite [ˈhɪpəkrɪt] *n* hipócrita *mf*
hypocritical [hɪpəˈkrɪtɪkəl] *adj* hipócrita
hypodermic [haɪpəˈdɜːmɪk] *adj Med* hi-
podérmico(a); **h. needle** aguja hipodér-
mica

hypothesis [haɪˈpɒθɪsɪs] *n (pl* **hypo-
theses** [haɪˈpɒθɪsiːz]) hipótesis *f*
hypothetic(al) [haɪpəˈθetɪk(əl)] *adj* hi-
potético(a)
hysteria [hɪˈstɪərɪə] *n* histeria *f*
hysterical [hɪˈsterɪkəl] *adj* histérico(a)
hysterics [hɪˈsterɪks] *npl* (**a**) ataque *m* de
histeria (**b**) *Fam (of laughter)* ataque *m* de
risa

I, i [aɪ] *n (the letter)* I, i *f*

I [aɪ] *pers pron* yo *(usually omitted in Spanish, except for contrast)*; **I know her** (yo) la conozco

ICBM [aɪsiːbiːˈem] *n (abbr* **intercontinental ballistic missile**) misil *m* balístico intercontinental

ice [aɪs] **1** *n* hielo *m*; **i. axe** pico *m* (de alpinista); **i. cream** helado *m*; **i. cube** cubito *m* de hielo; **i. hockey** hockey *m* sobre hielo; *Br* **i. lolly** polo *m*; **i. rink** pista *f* de patinaje; **i. skate** patín *m* de cuchilla
2 *vt (cake)* alcorzar
▸ **ice over, ice up** *vi (pond etc)* helarse; *(windscreen, plane wings)* cubrirse de hielo

iceberg [ˈaɪsbɜːg] *n* iceberg *m*

icebox [ˈaɪsbɒks] *n* **(a)** *(compartment of fridge)* congelador *m* **(b)** *US (fridge)* nevera *f*, frigorífico *m*, *Andes* frigider *m*, *RP* heladera *f*

icecap [ˈaɪskæp] *n* casquete *m* glaciar

Iceland [ˈaɪslənd] *n* Islandia

ice-skating [ˈaɪsskeɪtɪŋ] *n* patinaje *m* sobre hielo

icicle [ˈaɪsɪkəl] *n* carámbano *m*

icing [ˈaɪsɪŋ] *n* alcorza *f*; **i. sugar** azúcar *m* glas

icon [ˈaɪkɒn] *n* icono *m*

icy [ˈaɪsɪ] *adj* (**icier, iciest**) *(road etc)* helado(a); *Fig (smile)* glacial

ID [aɪˈdiː] *n US* documentación *f*; **ID card** DNI *m*

I'd [aɪd] = **I would; I had**

idea [aɪˈdɪə] *n* **(a)** idea *f* **(b)** *(aim)* intención *f* **(c)** *(impression)* impresión *f*

ideal [aɪˈdɪəl] *adj & n* ideal *(m)*

idealist [aɪˈdɪəlɪst] *n* idealista *mf*

idealistic [aɪdɪəˈlɪstɪk] *adj* idealista

idealize [aɪˈdɪəlaɪz] *vt* idealizar

ideally [aɪˈdɪəlɪ] *adv* **(a)** *(perfectly)* perfectamente **(b)** *(in the best conditions)* de ser posible

identical [aɪˈdentɪkəl] *adj* idéntico(a)

identification [aɪdentɪfɪˈkeɪʃən] *n* **(a)** identificación *f* **(b)** *(papers)* documentación *f*

identify [aɪˈdentɪfaɪ] **1** *vt (body)* identificar; *(cause)* descubrir
2 *vi* identificarse (**with** con)

Identikit® [aɪˈdentɪkɪt] *n* **I. picture** retrato *m* robot

identity [aɪˈdentɪtɪ] *n* identidad *f*; **i. card** carné *m* de identidad; **proof of i.** prueba *f* de identidad

ideological [aɪdɪəˈlɒdʒɪkəl] *adj* ideológico(a)

ideology [aɪdɪˈɒlədʒɪ] *n* ideología *f*

idiom [ˈɪdɪəm] *n* modismo *m*; *Fig (style)* lenguaje *m*

idiomatic [ɪdɪəˈmætɪk] *adj* idiomático(a)

idiosyncrasy [ɪdɪəʊˈsɪŋkrəsɪ] *n* idiosincrasia *f*

idiot [ˈɪdɪət] *n* idiota *mf*, tonto(a) *m,f*

idiotic [ɪdɪˈɒtɪk] *adj (behaviour)* idiota, tonto(a); *(joke, plan)* estúpido(a)

idle [ˈaɪdəl] **1** *adj* holgazán(ana); *(not working) (person)* desempleado(a); *(machinery)* parado(a); *(gossip)* frívolo(a); *(threat)* vano(a)
2 *vi (engine)* funcionar en vacío
▸ **idle away** *vt sep (time)* desperdiciar

idleness [ˈaɪdəlnɪs] *n (laziness)* holgazanería *f*; *(unemployment)* desempleo *m*; *(stoppage)* paro *m*

idol [ˈaɪdəl] *n* ídolo *m*

idolize [ˈaɪdəlaɪz] *vt* idolatrar

idyllic [ɪˈdɪlɪk] *adj* idílico(a)

i.e. *(abbr* **id est**) i.e.

if [ɪf] *conj* **1 (a)** si; **if at all** si acaso; **rarely, if ever** raras veces; **if I were rich** si fuera rico(a); **if necessary** (en) caso de que sea necesario; **if not** si no; **if so** de ser así; **if I were you** yo en tu lugar **(b)** *(whenever)* si; **if you need help, ask** siempre que necesites ayuda, pídela **(c)** *(although)* aunque, si bien **(d)** *(exclamations)* **if only I'd known!** ¡de haberlo sabido!; **if only she were here!** ¡ojalá estuviera aquí!
2 *n* **ifs and buts** pegas *fpl*

igloo [ˈɪgluː] *n* iglú *m*

ignite [ɪgˈnaɪt] **1** *vt* encender
2 *vi* encenderse

ignition [ɪgˈnɪʃən] *n* ignición *f*; *Aut* encendido *m*; **i. key** llave *f* de contacto

ignorance [ˈɪgnərəns] *n* ignorancia *f*

ignorant [ˈɪgnərənt] *adj* ignorante (**of** de); **to be i. of the facts** ignorar *or* desconocer los hechos

ignore [ɪgˈnɔː(r)] *vt (warning, remark)* no hacer caso de; *(behaviour, fact)* pasar por alto

ill [ɪl] **1** *adj* (**a**) enfermo(a); **to be taken i.** caer enfermo(a); **to feel i.** encontrarse mal (**b**) *(bad)* malo(a); **i. feeling** resentimiento *m*; **i. will** mala voluntad
2 *n* mal *m*
3 *adv* difícilmente

I'll [aɪl] = **I shall; I will**

ill-advised [ɪləd'vaɪzd] *adj (person)* imprudente; *(act)* desatinado(a); **you'd be i. to go** harías mal en ir

ill-disposed [ɪldɪ'spəʊzd] *adj* poco dispuesto(a)

illegal [ɪ'liːgəl] *adj* ilegal

illegible [ɪ'ledʒɪbəl] *adj* ilegible

illegitimate [ɪlɪ'dʒɪtɪmɪt] *adj* ilegítimo(a)

ill-fated [ɪl'feɪtɪd] *adj* abocado(a) al fracaso

ill-founded [ɪl'faʊndɪd] *adj* infundado(a)

illicit [ɪ'lɪsɪt] *adj* ilícito(a)

illiteracy [ɪ'lɪtərəsɪ] *n* analfabetismo *m*

illiterate [ɪ'lɪtərɪt] *adj (person)* analfabeto(a); *Fam (uneducated)* inculto(a)

illness ['ɪlnɪs] *n* enfermedad *f*

illogical [ɪ'lɒdʒɪkəl] *adj* ilógico(a)

ill-treat [ɪl'triːt] *vt* maltratar

illuminate [ɪ'luːmɪneɪt] *vt* (**a**) *(light up)* iluminar, alumbrar; *Fig (clarify)* aclarar (**b**) *(manuscript)* iluminar

illuminating [ɪ'luːmɪneɪtɪŋ] *adj (experience, book)* instructivo(a); *(remark)* revelador(a)

illumination [ɪluːmɪ'neɪʃən] *n* (**a**) iluminación *f*, *Fig (clarification)* aclaración *f* (**b**) *Br* **illuminations** iluminación *f*

illusion [ɪ'luːʒən] *n* ilusión *f*; **to be under the i. that ...** engañarse pensando que ...

illusory [ɪ'luːsərɪ] *adj* ilusorio(a)

illustrate ['ɪləstreɪt] *vt* ilustrar

illustration [ɪlə'streɪʃən] *n* ilustración *f*; *(example)* ejemplo *m*

illustrious [ɪ'lʌstrɪəs] *adj* ilustre

I'm [aɪm] = **I am**

image ['ɪmɪdʒ] *n* imagen *f*

imagery ['ɪmɪdʒərɪ] *n Lit* imágenes *fpl*

imaginary [ɪ'mædʒɪnərɪ] *adj* imaginario(a)

imagination [ɪmædʒɪ'neɪʃən] *n* imaginación *f*; *(inventiveness)* inventiva *f*

imaginative [ɪ'mædʒɪnətɪv] *adj* imaginativo(a)

imagine [ɪ'mædʒɪn] *vt (visualize)* imaginar; *(think)* suponer, imaginarse; **just i.!** ¡imagínate!

imbalance [ɪm'bæləns] *n* desequilibrio *m*

imbecile ['ɪmbɪsiːl] *n* imbécil *mf*

imitate ['ɪmɪteɪt] *vt* imitar

imitation [ɪmɪ'teɪʃən] **1** *n* imitación *f*, copia *f*, *Pej* remedo *m*
2 *adj* de imitación

immaculate [ɪ'mækjʊlɪt] *adj (clean)* inmaculado(a); *(tidy)* perfectamente ordenado(a); *(clothes)* impecable; *(work)* perfecto(a); **the I. Conception** la Inmaculada Concepción

immaterial [ɪmə'tɪərɪəl] *adj* irrelevante; **it's i. to me whether ...** me trae sin cuidado si ...

immature [ɪmə'tjʊə(r)] *adj* inmaduro(a)

immediate [ɪ'miːdɪət] *adj* (**a**) inmediato(a); *(urgent)* urgente (**b**) *(close)* cercano(a); *(danger)* inminente (**c**) *(cause)* primero(a)

immediately [ɪ'miːdɪətlɪ] **1** *adv* (**a**) inmediatamente (**b**) *(directly)* directamente
2 *conj* en cuanto

immense [ɪ'mens] *adj* inmenso(a), enorme

immensely [ɪ'menslɪ] *adv (rich)* enormemente; *(interesting, difficult)* sumamente

immerse [ɪ'mɜːs] *vt* sumergir (**in** en); *Fig* **to be immersed in sth** estar absorto(a) en algo

immersion [ɪ'mɜːʃən] *n* inmersión *f*; *Br* **i. heater** calentador *m* de inmersión; **i. course** cursillo intensivo

immigrant ['ɪmɪgrənt] *adj & n* inmigrante *(mf)*

immigration [ɪmɪ'greɪʃən] *n* inmigración *f*

imminent ['ɪmɪnənt] *adj* inminente

immobile [ɪ'məʊbaɪl] *adj* inmóvil

immobilize [ɪ'məʊbɪlaɪz] *vt* inmovilizar

immodest [ɪ'mɒdɪst] *adj* indecente

immoral [ɪ'mɒrəl] *adj* inmoral

immortal [ɪ'mɔːtəl] *adj* inmortal

immortality [ɪmɔː'tælɪtɪ] *n* inmortalidad *f*

immortalize [ɪ'mɔːtəlaɪz] *vt* inmortalizar

immune [ɪ'mjuːn] *adj* inmune; *(exempt)* exento(a)

immunity [ɪ'mjuːnɪtɪ] *n* inmunidad *f*

immunize ['ɪmjʊnaɪz] *vt* inmunizar (**against** contra)

impact ['ɪmpækt] *n* impacto *m*; *(crash)* choque *m*

impair [ɪm'peə(r)] *vt* perjudicar; *(sight etc)* dañar

impart [ɪm'pɑːt] *vt Fml (news)* comunicar; *(knowledge)* transmitir

impartial [ɪm'pɑːʃəl] *adj* imparcial

impassable [ɪm'pɑːsəbəl] *adj (road, ground)* intransitable; *(barrier)* infranqueable

impasse [æm'pɑːs] *n* punto muerto

impassive [ɪm'pæsɪv] *adj* impasible

impatience [ɪm'peɪʃəns] *n* impaciencia *f*

impatient [ɪm'peɪʃənt] *adj* impaciente; *(fretful)* irritable; **to get i.** perder la paciencia

impeccable [ɪm'pekəbəl] *adj* impecable

impede [ɪm'piːd] *vt (prevent)* impedir; *(hinder)* estorbar; *(obstruct)* poner trabas a

impediment [ɪm'pedɪmənt] *n* impedimento *m*; *(obstacle)* estorbo *m*; **speech i.** defecto *m* del habla

impending [ɪm'pendɪŋ] *adj Fml* inminente

impenetrable [ɪm'penɪtrəbəl] *adj* impenetrable; *Fig (mystery, thoughts)* insondable

imperative [ɪm'perətɪv] **1** *adj Fml* imperativo(a); *(tone)* imperioso(a); *(urgent)* urgente

2 *n Ling* imperativo *m*

imperceptible [ɪmpə'septəbəl] *adj* imperceptible

imperfect [ɪm'pɜːfɪkt] **1** *adj* imperfecto(a); *(goods)* defectuoso(a)

2 *n Ling* imperfecto *m*

imperfection [ɪmpə'fekʃən] *n* defecto *m*

imperial [ɪm'pɪərɪəl] *adj* **(a)** imperial **(b)** *(measure)* **i. gallon** galón británico *(aprox 4,546 l)*

imperialism [ɪm'pɪərɪəlɪzəm] *n* imperialismo *m*

imperialist [ɪm'pɪərɪəlɪst] *adj & n* imperialista *(mf)*

imperious [ɪm'pɪərɪəs] *adj* imperioso(a)

impersonal [ɪm'pɜːsənəl] *adj* impersonal

impersonate [ɪm'pɜːsəneɪt] *vt* hacerse pasar por; *(famous people)* imitar

impersonation [ɪmpɜːsə'neɪʃən] *n* imitación *f*

impertinent [ɪm'pɜːtɪnənt] *adj* impertinente

impervious [ɪm'pɜːvɪəs] *adj (rock)* impermeable; *Fig* **to be i. to reason** no atender a razones

impetuous [ɪm'petjʊəs] *adj* impetuoso(a)

impetus ['ɪmpɪtəs] *n* ímpetu *m*; *Fig* impulso *m*

impinge [ɪm'pɪndʒ] *vi Fml* afectar (**on** a)

implant *Med* **1** *vt* [ɪm'plɑːnt] implantar

2 *n* ['ɪmplɑːnt] implantación *f*

implement 1 *n* ['ɪmplɪmənt] *(tool)* herramienta *f*; *(instrument)* instrumento *m*; **farm implements** aperos *mpl* de labranza

2 *vt* ['ɪmplɪment] *(decision, plan)* llevar a cabo; *(law, policy)* aplicar

implicate ['ɪmplɪkeɪt] *vt* implicar (**in** en)

implication [ɪmplɪ'keɪʃən] *n* implicación *f*; *(consequence)* consecuencia *f*

implicit [ɪm'plɪsɪt] *adj (implied)* implícito(a); *(trust)* absoluto(a); *(faith)* incondicional

implore [ɪm'plɔː(r)] *vt* implorar, suplicar

imply [ɪm'plaɪ] *vt* **(a)** *(involve)* implicar **(b)** *(hint)* dar a entender; *(mean)* significar

impolite [ɪmpə'laɪt] *adj* maleducado(a)

import 1 *n* ['ɪmpɔːt] **(a)** *Com (usu pl)* importación *f*; **i. duty** derechos *mpl* de importación **(b)** *Fml (meaning)* sentido *m*

2 *vt* [ɪm'pɔːt] *Com* importar

importance [ɪm'pɔːtəns] *n* importancia *f*; *(standing)* envergadura *f*; **of little i.** de poca monta

important [ɪm'pɔːtənt] *adj* importante; **it's not i.** no importa

importer [ɪm'pɔːtə(r)] *n Com* importador(a) *m,f*

impose [ɪm'pəʊz] **1** *vt* imponer (**on** or **upon** a)

2 *vi* **to i. on** or **upon** *(take advantage of)* abusar de

imposing [ɪm'pəʊzɪŋ] *adj* imponente, impresionante

imposition [ɪmpə'zɪʃən] *n (of tax etc)* imposición *f*; *(unfair demand)* abuso *m*; **would it be an i. if …?** ¿le molestaría si …?

impossibility [ɪmpɒsə'bɪlɪtɪ] *n* imposibilidad *f*

impossible [ɪm'pɒsəbəl] **1** *adj* imposible; *(person)* insoportable

2 *n* **to do the i.** hacer lo imposible

impossibly [ɪm'pɒsəblɪ] *adv* de manera insoportable; **i. difficult** de una dificultad insuperable

impostor [ɪm'pɒstə(r)] *n* impostor(a) *m,f*

impotent ['ɪmpətənt] *adj* impotente

impound [ɪm'paʊnd] *vt* incautarse de

impoverished [ɪm'pɒvərɪʃt] *adj (person, country)* empobrecido(a); *(soil)* agotado(a)

impracticable [ɪm'præktɪkəbəl] *adj* impracticable, irrealizable

impractical [ɪm'præktɪkəl] *adj (person)* poco práctico(a); *(project, solution etc)* poco viable

imprecise [ɪmprɪ'saɪs] *adj* impreciso(a)

impregnable [ɪmˈpregnəbəl] *adj* inexpugnable

impregnate [ˈɪmpregneɪt] *vt* (**a**) *(soak)* impregnar (**with** de) (**b**) *Fml (fertilize)* fecundar

impress [ɪmˈpres] *vt* (**a**) impresionar; **to i. sb favourably/unfavourably** dar a algn buena/mala impresión (**b**) *(mark)* imprimir (**on** en); *(pattern)* estampar (**on** en); *Fig* **to i. sth on sb** convencer a algn de la importancia de algo

impression [ɪmˈpreʃən] *n* (**a**) impresión *f*; **to be under the i. that ...** tener la impresión de que ...; **to give the i. of ...** dar la impresión de ... (**b**) *(imprint)* marca *f*; *(in snow)* huella *f* (**c**) *(imitation)* imitación *f*

impressionist [ɪmˈpreʃənɪst] *adj & n* impresionista *(mf)*

impressive [ɪmˈpresɪv] *adj* impresionante

imprint 1 *vt* [ɪmˈprɪnt] *(mark)* dejar huella (**on** en)
2 *n* [ˈɪmprɪnt] (**a**) *(mark)* marca *f*; *(left by foot etc)* huella *f* (**b**) *(publisher's name)* pie *m* de imprenta

imprison [ɪmˈprɪzən] *vt* encarcelar

imprisonment [ɪmˈprɪzənmənt] *n* encarcelamiento *m*

improbable [ɪmˈprɒbəbəl] *adj (event)* improbable; *(story)* inverosímil

impromptu [ɪmˈprɒmptjuː] **1** *adj (speech)* improvisado(a); *(visit)* imprevisto(a)
2 *adv* de improviso

improper [ɪmˈprɒpə(r)] *adj* (**a**) impropio(a); *(method)* inadecuado(a) (**b**) *(indecent)* indecente; *(behaviour)* deshonesto(a) (**c**) *(wrong)* incorrecto(a)

improve [ɪmˈpruːv] **1** *vt* mejorar; *(knowledge)* perfeccionar; *(mind)* cultivar; *(increase)* aumentar
2 *vi* mejorarse; *(increase)* aumentar
▸ **improve on** *vt insep* superar; *(offer, bid)* sobrepujar

improvement [ɪmˈpruːvmənt] *n* mejora *f*; *(in skill)* perfeccionamiento *m*; *(increase)* aumento *m*

improvise [ˈɪmprəvaɪz] *vt & vi* improvisar

imprudent [ɪmˈpruːdənt] *adj* imprudente

impudence [ˈɪmpjʊdəns] *n* insolencia *f*

impudent [ˈɪmpjʊdənt] *adj* insolente

impulse [ˈɪmpʌls] *n* impulso *m*; **to act on (an) i.** dejarse llevar por un impulso

impulsive [ɪmˈpʌlsɪv] *adj* irreflexivo(a)

impunity [ɪmˈpjuːnɪtɪ] *n* impunidad *f*

impure [ɪmˈpjʊə(r)] *adj* (**a**) *(act)* impuro(a); *(thought)* impúdico(a) (**b**) *(air)* contaminado(a)

impurity [ɪmˈpjʊərɪtɪ] *n* (**a**) *(of act)* deshonestidad *f* (**b**) *(usu pl) (in air, substance)* impureza *f*

in [ɪn] **1** *prep* (**a**) *(place)* en; *(within)* dentro de; **in bed** en la cama; **in England/Brazil/China** en Inglaterra/Brasil/China; **in prison** en la cárcel; **in the distance** a lo lejos
(**b**) *(motion)* en; **I threw it in the fire** lo eché al fuego; **she arrived in Paris** llegó a París
(**c**) *(time) (during)* en, durante; **I haven't seen her in years** hace años que no la veo; **in May/1945** en mayo/1945; **in spring** en primavera; **in the daytime** durante el día; **in the morning** por la mañana; **at ten in the morning** a las diez de la mañana
(**d**) *(time) (within)* dentro de; **I arrived in time** llegué a tiempo
(**e**) *(time) (after)* al cabo de
(**f**) *(manner)* en; **in alphabetical order** en orden alfabético; **in a loud/quiet voice** en voz alta/baja; **in fashion** de moda; **in French** en francés; **in an odd way** de una manera rara; **in writing** por escrito; **write in pencil** escribe con lápiz
(**g**) *(wearing)* en; **dressed in blue** vestido(a) de azul; **in uniform** de uniforme
(**h**) *(weather etc)* a, en; **in the rain** bajo la lluvia; **in the sun** al sol; **in darkness** en la oscuridad; **in daylight** a la luz del día; **in the shade** a la sombra
(**i**) *(state, emotion)* en; **carved in wood** tallado(a) en madera; **in bloom/danger/public/silence** en flor/peligro/público/silencio; **in love** enamorado(a); **in tears** llorando
(**j**) *(ratio, numbers)* de; **cut in half** cortado(a) por la mitad; **in threes** de tres en tres; **one in six** uno de cada seis; **2 m in length** 2 m de largo
(**k**) *(profession)* en; **to be in insurance** trabajar en seguros
(**l**) *(person)* en; **he has it in him to win** es capaz de ganar
(**m**) *(after superlative)* de; **the smallest car in the world** el coche más pequeño del mundo
(**n**) *(before present participle)* **in behaving this way** con su comportamiento; **in so doing** con ello
(**o**) *(phrases)* **in all** en total; **in itself/himself/herself** en sí; **in that ...** dado que ...

2 *adv* **in here/there** aquí/allí dentro; **let's go in** vamos adentro; **to be in** *(at home)* estar (en casa); *(at work)* estar; *(tide)* estar alta; *Fam (in fashion)* estar de moda; **the bus is in** el autobús ha llegado; **to invite sb in** invitar a algn a entrar; *Fam* **to be in on sth** estar enterado(a) de algo; *Fam* **we're in for a storm** vamos a tener tormenta

3 *adj Fam* (**a**) *(fashionable) (place)* de moda; *(clothes)* del último grito

(**b**) **an in joke** una broma privada

4 *n Fam* **ins and outs** detalles *mpl*

inability [ɪnəˈbɪlɪtɪ] *n* incapacidad *f*

inaccessible [ɪnækˈsesəbəl] *adj* inaccesible

inaccurate [ɪnˈækjʊrɪt] *adj* inexacto(a); *(statement)* erróneo(a); *(figures, total)* incorrecto(a)

inactivity [ɪnækˈtɪvɪtɪ] *n* inactividad *f*

inadequate [ɪnˈædɪkwɪt] *adj* (**a**) *(lacking)* insuficiente (**b**) *(not capable)* incapaz; *(unsuitable)* inadecuado(a) (**c**) *(defective)* defectuoso(a)

inadvertent [ɪnədˈvɜːtənt] *adj* involuntario(a)

inadvertently [ɪnədˈvɜːtəntlɪ] *adv* involuntariamente

inadvisable [ɪnədˈvaɪzəbəl] *adj* imprudente

inane [ɪˈneɪn] *adj* necio(a), fatuo(a)

inanimate [ɪnˈænɪmɪt] *adj* inanimado(a)

inappropriate [ɪnəˈprəʊprɪɪt] *adj* inoportuno(a); *(behaviour)* poco apropiado(a)

inarticulate [ɪnɑːˈtɪkjʊlɪt] *adj* *(cry, sound)* inarticulado(a); *(words)* mal pronunciado(a)

inasmuch as [ɪnəzˈmʌtʃəz] *conj Fml* (**a**) *(since)* puesto que, ya que (**b**) *(in so far as)* en la medida en que

inattentive [ɪnəˈtentɪv] *adj* desatento(a)

inaudible [ɪnˈɔːdəbəl] *adj* inaudible

inaugural [ɪnˈɔːgjʊrəl] *adj* inaugural

inaugurate [ɪnˈɔːgjʊreɪt] *vt* *(building)* inaugurar; *(president)* investir

inauguration [ɪnɔːgjʊˈreɪʃən] *n* *(of building)* inauguración *f*; *(of president)* investidura *f*

inauspicious [ɪnɔːˈspɪʃəs] *adj* *(start)* poco prometedor(a); *(circumstances)* desfavorable

inborn [ˈɪnbɔːn] *adj* innato(a)

inbred [ˈɪnbred] *adj* (**a**) *(quality)* innato(a) (**b**) *(family)* endogámico(a)

Inc, inc *US Com (abbr* **Incorporated**) ≃ S.A.

incalculable [ɪnˈkælkjʊləbəl] *adj* incalculable

incapable [ɪnˈkeɪpəbəl] *adj* incapaz

incapacitate [ɪnkəˈpæsɪteɪt] *vt Fml* incapacitar

incapacity [ɪnkəˈpæsɪtɪ] *n* incapacidad *f*

incarcerate [ɪnˈkɑːsəreɪt] *vt Fml* encarcelar

incarnation [ɪnkɑːˈneɪʃən] *n* encarnación *f*

incendiary [ɪnˈsendɪərɪ] **1** *adj* incendiario(a)

2 *n* bomba incendiaria

incense¹ [ˈɪnsens] *n* incienso *m*

incense² [ɪnˈsens] *vt* enfurecer, sacar de quicio

incentive [ɪnˈsentɪv] *n* incentivo *m*

incessant [ɪnˈsesənt] *adj* incesante; *(demands)* constante

incessantly [ɪnˈsesəntlɪ] *adv* sin cesar

incest [ˈɪnsest] *n* incesto *m*

inch [ɪntʃ] *n* pulgada *f* *(aprox 2,54 cm)*; *Fig* **i. by i.** poco a poco; *Fig* **she wouldn't give an i.** no quería ceder ni un ápice
▸ **inch forward** *vt sep & vi* avanzar poco a poco

incidence [ˈɪnsɪdəns] *n* frecuencia *f*

incident [ˈɪnsɪdənt] *n* incidente *m*

incidental [ɪnsɪˈdentəl] *adj* *(accessory)* incidental, accesorio(a); *(risk)* inherente (**to** a); **i. music** música *f* de fondo

incidentally [ɪnsɪˈdentəlɪ] *adv* a propósito

incinerator [ɪnˈsɪnəreɪtə(r)] *n* incinerador *m*

incipient [ɪnˈsɪpɪənt] *adj Fml* incipiente

incision [ɪnˈsɪʒən] *n* incisión *f*

incisive [ɪnˈsaɪsɪv] *adj* *(comment)* incisivo(a); *(reply)* tajante; *(mind)* penetrante

incite [ɪnˈsaɪt] *vt* incitar; **to i. sb to do sth** incitar a algn a hacer algo

inclination [ɪnklɪˈneɪʃən] *n* inclinación *f*; **my i. is to stay** yo prefiero quedarme

incline [ɪnˈklaɪn] **1** *vt* (**a**) **I'm inclined to believe him** me inclino a creerlo; **if you feel so inclined** si quieres; **she's inclined to be aggressive** tiende a ser agresiva (**b**) *(head etc)* inclinar

2 *vi* *(slope)* inclinarse

3 *n* [ˈɪnklam] *(slope)* pendiente *f*; **steep i.** cuesta empinada

include [ɪnˈkluːd] *vt* incluir (**in** en); *(in price)* comprender (**in** en); *(in list)* figurar (**in** en)

including [ɪnˈkluːdɪŋ] *prep* incluso, inclusive

inclusion [ɪnˈkluːʒən] *n* inclusión *f*

inclusive [ɪnˈkluːsɪv] *adj* inclusivo(a); **pages 6 to 10 i.** de la página 6 a la 10, ambas inclusive; **the rent is i. of bills** el alquiler incluye las facturas

incognito [ɪnkɒgˈniːtəʊ] *adv* de incógnito

incoherent [ɪnkəʊˈhɪərənt] *adj* incoherente

income [ˈɪnkʌm] *n* ingresos *mpl*; *(from investment)* réditos *mpl*; **i. tax** impuesto *m* sobre la renta; **i. tax return** declaración *f* de la renta

incoming [ˈɪnkʌmɪŋ] *adj (flight, train)* de llegada; *(tide)* ascendente; *(mail, message, call)* recibido(a)

incomparable [ɪnˈkɒmpərəbəl] *adj* incomparable, sin par

incompatible [ɪnkəmˈpætəbəl] *adj* incompatible (**with** con)

incompetence [ɪnˈkɒmpɪtəns] *n* incompetencia *f*

incompetent [ɪnˈkɒmpɪtənt] *adj* incompetente

incomplete [ɪnkəmˈpliːt] *adj* incompleto(a)

incomprehensible [ɪnkɒmprɪˈhensəbəl] *adj* incomprensible

inconceivable [ɪnkənˈsiːvəbəl] *adj* inconcebible

inconclusive [ɪnkənˈkluːsɪv] *adj (vote)* no decisivo(a); *(proof)* no concluyente

incongruous [ɪnˈkɒŋɡrʊəs] *adj* incongruente

inconsiderate [ɪnkənˈsɪdərɪt] *adj* desconsiderado(a); **how i. of you!** ¡qué falta de consideración por tu parte!

inconsistency [ɪnkənˈsɪstənsɪ] *n* inconsecuencia *f*; *(contradiction)* contradicción *f*

inconsistent [ɪnkənˈsɪstənt] *adj* inconsecuente; *(contradictory)* contradictorio(a); **your evidence is i. with the facts** su testimonio no concuerda con los hechos

inconspicuous [ɪnkənˈspɪkjʊəs] *adj* que pasa desapercibido(a); *(discreet)* discreto(a)

incontrovertible [ɪnkɒntrəˈvɜːtəbəl] *adj Fml* incontrovertible

inconvenience [ɪnkənˈviːnɪəns] **1** *n* inconveniente *f*; *(annoyance)* molestia *f*
2 *vt (annoy)* molestar; *(cause difficulty to)* incomodar

inconvenient [ɪnkənˈviːnɪənt] *adj* molesto(a); *(time)* inoportuno(a); *(design)* poco práctico(a)

incorporate [ɪnˈkɔːpəreɪt] *vt* incorporar (**in** o **into** a); *(include)* incluir; *(contain)* contener

incorporated [ɪnˈkɔːpəreɪtɪd] *adj US Com* **i. company** sociedad anónima

incorrect [ɪnkəˈrekt] *adj* incorrecto(a)

incorrigible [ɪnˈkɒrɪdʒəbəl] *adj* incorregible

increase 1 *n* [ˈɪnkriːs] aumento *m*; *(in number)* incremento *m*; *(in price etc)* subida *f*
2 *vt* [ɪnˈkriːs] aumentar; *(price etc)* subir
3 *vi* aumentar

increasing [ɪnˈkriːsɪŋ] *adj* creciente

increasingly [ɪnˈkriːsɪŋlɪ] *adv* cada vez más

incredible [ɪnˈkredəbəl] *adj* increíble

incredulous [ɪnˈkredjʊləs] *adj* incrédulo(a)

increment [ˈɪnkrɪmənt] *n* incremento *m*

incriminate [ɪnˈkrɪmɪneɪt] *vt* incriminar

incriminating [ɪnˈkrɪmɪneɪtɪŋ] *adj* incriminatorio(a)

incubation [ɪnkjʊˈbeɪʃən] *n* incubación *f*

incubator [ˈɪnkjʊbeɪtə(r)] *n* incubadora *f*

incumbent [ɪnˈkʌmbənt] **1** *n* titular *mf*
2 *adj Fml* **to be i. on sb to do sth** ser la obligación de algn hacer algo

incur [ɪnˈkɜː(r)] *vt (blame)* incurrir en; *(risk)* correr; *(debt)* contraer; *(loss)* sufrir

incurable [ɪnˈkjʊərəbəl] *adj* incurable

indebted [ɪnˈdetɪd] *adj* endeudado(a); *Fig (grateful)* agradecido(a); *Fig* **to be i. to sb** estar en deuda con algn

indecent [ɪnˈdiːsənt] *adj* indecente; **i. assault** atentado *m* contra el pudor; **i. exposure** exhibicionismo *m*

indecision [ɪndɪˈsɪʒən] *n* indecisión *f*

indecisive [ɪndɪˈsaɪsɪv] *adj (person)* indeciso(a); *(evidence)* poco concluyente; *(victory)* no decisivo(a)

indeed [ɪnˈdiːd] *adv* **(a)** *Fml (in fact)* efectivamente, en realidad **(b) I'm very sorry i.** lo siento de veras; **it's very hard i.** es verdaderamente difícil; **thank you very much i.** muchísimas gracias

indefinite [ɪnˈdefɪnɪt] *adj* indefinido(a)

indelible [ɪnˈdeləbəl] *adj* indeleble

indemnify [ɪnˈdemnɪfaɪ] *vt* indemnizar (**for** por)

indemnity [ɪnˈdemnɪtɪ] *n* **(a)** *(insurance)* indemnidad *f* **(b)** *(compensation)* indemnización *f*

indentation [ɪndenˈteɪʃən] *n* **(a)** *Typ* sangría *f* **(b)** *(of edge)* muesca *f*; *(of surface)* depresión *f*

independence [ɪndɪˈpendəns] *n* independencia *f*; *US* **I. Day** día *m* de la Independencia *(4 julio)*

independent [ɪndɪˈpendənt] *adj* independiente; *Br* **i. school** = colegio no subvencionado por el estado; **to become i.** independizarse

in-depth ['ɪndepθ] *adj* minucioso(a), exhaustivo(a)

indestructible [ɪndɪ'strʌktəbəl] *adj* indestructible

indeterminate [ɪndɪ'tɜːmɪnɪt] *adj* indeterminado(a)

index ['ɪndeks] **1** *n* (*pl* **indexes** *or* **indices**) (**a**) (*in book*) índice *m*; (*in library*) catálogo *m*; **i. card** ficha *f* (**b**) *Math* exponente *m*; *Econ* índice *m* (**c**) **i. finger** dedo *m* índice
2 *vt* catalogar

index-linked ['ɪndekslɪŋkt] *adj* sujeto(a) al aumento de la inflación

India ['ɪndɪə] *n* (la) India

Indian ['ɪndɪən] *adj* & *n* (*of America*) indio(a) (*m,f*); (*of India*) hindú (*mf*); **I. Ocean** Océano ndico; **I. Summer** veranillo *m* de San Martín

indicate ['ɪndɪkeɪt] **1** *vt* indicar
2 *vi Aut* poner el intermitente

indication [ɪndɪ'keɪʃən] *n* indicio *m*

indicative [ɪn'dɪkətɪv] **1** *adj* indicativo(a)
2 *n Ling* indicativo *m*

indicator ['ɪndɪkeɪtə(r)] *n* indicador *m*; *Br Aut* intermitente *m*

indices ['ɪndɪsiːz] *pl of* **index**

indict [ɪn'daɪt] *vt* acusar (**for** de)

indictment [ɪn'daɪtmənt] *n Jur* acusación *f*; *Fig* **a damning i. of his books** una crítica feroz de sus libros

indifference [ɪn'dɪfərəns] *n* indiferencia *f*

indifferent [ɪn'dɪfərənt] *adj* (**a**) (*uninterested*) indiferente (**b**) (*mediocre*) regular

indigenous [ɪn'dɪdʒɪnəs] *adj* indígena

indigestion [ɪndɪ'dʒestʃən] *n* indigestión *f*; **to suffer from i.** tener un empacho

indignant [ɪn'dɪgnənt] *adj* indignado(a); (*look*) de indignación; **to get i. about sth** indignarse por algo

indignity [ɪn'dɪgnɪtɪ] *n* indignidad *f*

indigo ['ɪndɪgəʊ] **1** *n* añil *m*
2 *adj* (de color) añil

indirect [ɪndɪ'rekt, ɪndaɪ'rekt] *adj* indirecto(a)

indiscreet [ɪndɪ'skriːt] *adj* indiscreto(a)

indiscretion [ɪndɪ'skreʃən] *n* indiscreción *f*

indiscriminate [ɪndɪ'skrɪmɪnɪt] *adj* (*punishment, shooting*) indiscriminado(a); (*praise, reading*) sin criterio

indispensable [ɪndɪ'spensəbəl] *adj* indispensable, imprescindible

indisposed [ɪndɪ'spəʊzd] *adj Fml* indispuesto(a)

indisputable [ɪndɪ'spjuːtəbəl] *adj* indiscutible, incontestable

indistinct [ɪndɪ'stɪŋkt] *adj* indistinto(a); (*memory*) confuso(a), vago(a); (*shape etc*) borroso(a)

indistinguishable [ɪndɪ'stɪŋgwɪʃəbəl] *adj* indistinguible

individual [ɪndɪ'vɪdjʊəl] **1** *adj* (**a**) (*separate*) individual; (*for one*) particular; (*personal*) personal (**b**) (*characteristic*) particular; (*original*) original
2 *n* (*person*) individuo *m*; **private i.** particular *m*

individualist [ɪndɪ'vɪdjʊəlɪst] *n* individualista *mf*

indoctrinate [ɪn'dɒktrɪneɪt] *vt* adoctrinar

indoctrination [ɪndɒktrɪ'neɪʃən] *n* adoctrinamiento *m*

indolent ['ɪndələnt] *adj Fml* indolente

Indonesia [ɪndəʊ'niːzɪə] *n* Indonesia

Indonesian [ɪndəʊ'niːzɪən] **1** *adj* indonesio(a)
2 *n* (**a**) (*person*) indonesio(a) *m,f* (**b**) (*language*) indonesio *m*

indoor ['ɪndɔː(r)] *adj* (*plant*) de interior; **i. football** fútbol *m* sala; **i. pool** piscina cubierta

indoors [ɪn'dɔːz] *adv* (*inside*) dentro (de casa); (*at home*) en casa; **let's go i.** vamos adentro

induce [ɪn'djuːs] *vt* (**a**) (*persuade*) inducir, persuadir (**b**) (*cause*) producir; *Med* (*labour*) provocar

inducement [ɪn'djuːsmənt] *n* incentivo *m*, aliciente *m*

induction [ɪn'dʌkʃən] *n* (**a**) *Med* (*of labour*) provocación *f* (**b**) *Elec* inducción *f* (**c**) *Educ* introducción *f*

indulge [ɪn'dʌldʒ] **1** *vt* (**a**) (*child*) consentir; (*person*) complacer; **to i. oneself** darse gusto (**b**) (*whim*) ceder a, satisfacer
2 *vi* darse el gusto (**in** de)

indulgence [ɪn'dʌldʒəns] *n* (**a**) (*of child*) mimo *m*; (*of attitude*) indulgencia *f* (**b**) (*of whim*) satisfacción *f*

indulgent [ɪn'dʌldʒənt] *adj* indulgente

industrial [ɪn'dʌstrɪəl] *adj* industrial; (*accident*) laboral; (*disease*) profesional; *Br* **to take i. action** declararse en huelga; *Br* **i. dispute** conflicto *m* laboral; **i.** *Br* **estate** *or US* **park** polígono *m* industrial; **i. relations** relaciones *fpl* laborales

industrialist [ɪn'dʌstrɪəlɪst] *n* industrial *mf*

industrialize [ɪn'dʌstrɪəlaɪz] *vt* industrializar; **to become industrialized** industrializarse

industrious [ɪn'dʌstrɪəs] *adj* trabajador(a)

industry ▸ informal

industry ['ɪndəstrɪ] n (**a**) industria f (**b**) *(diligence)* aplicación f

inebriated [ɪn'iːbrɪeɪtɪd] adj embriagado(a)

inedible [ɪn'edəbəl] adj incomible

ineffective [ɪnɪ'fektɪv] adj ineficaz

ineffectual [ɪnɪ'fektʃʊəl] adj (aim, protest) ineficaz; (person) incompetente

inefficiency [ɪnɪ'fɪʃənsɪ] n ineficacia f; (of person) incompetencia f

inefficient [ɪnɪ'fɪʃənt] adj ineficaz; (person) inepto(a)

ineligible [ɪn'elɪdʒəbəl] adj no apto(a) (**for** para)

inept [ɪn'ept] adj (person) inepto(a); (remark) estúpido(a)

inequality [ɪnɪ'kwɒlɪtɪ] n desigualdad f

inert [ɪn'ɜːt] adj inerte

inertia [ɪn'ɜːʃə] n inercia f

inescapable [ɪnɪ'skeɪpəbəl] adj ineludible

inevitability [ɪnevɪtə'bɪlɪtɪ] n inevitabilidad f

inevitable [ɪn'evɪtəbəl] adj inevitable

inexcusable [ɪnɪk'skjuːzəbəl] adj inexcusable, imperdonable

inexhaustible [ɪnɪg'zɔːstəbəl] adj inagotable

inexorable [ɪn'eksərəbəl] adj Fml inexorable

inexpensive [ɪnɪk'spensɪv] adj económico(a)

inexperience [ɪnɪk'spɪərɪəns] n inexperiencia f

inexperienced [ɪnɪk'spɪərɪənst] adj inexperto(a)

inexplicable [ɪnɪk'splɪkəbəl] adj inexplicable

infallible [ɪn'fæləbəl] adj infalible

infamous ['ɪnfəməs] adj infame

infancy ['ɪnfənsɪ] n infancia f

infant ['ɪnfənt] n niño(a) m,f; Br **i. school** parvulario m

infantile ['ɪnfəntaɪl] adj infantil

infantry ['ɪnfəntrɪ] n infantería f

infatuated [ɪn'fætjʊeɪtɪd] adj encaprichado(a)

infatuation [ɪnfætjʊ'eɪʃən] n encaprichamiento m

infect [ɪn'fekt] vt (cut) infectar; (water) contaminar; (person) contagiar

infection [ɪn'fekʃən] n (of cut) infección f; (of water) contaminación f; (with illness) contagio m

infectious [ɪn'fekʃəs] adj (disease) infeccioso(a); Fig contagioso(a)

infer [ɪn'fɜː(r)] vt inferir (**from** de)

inference ['ɪnfərəns] n inferencia f

inferior [ɪn'fɪərɪə(r)] **1** adj inferior (**to** a) **2** n Pej inferior mf

inferiority [ɪnfɪərɪ'ɒrɪtɪ] n inferioridad f

inferno [ɪn'fɜːnəʊ] n Literary infierno m; Fig **the house was a raging i.** la casa ardía en llamas

infertile [ɪn'fɜːtaɪl] adj estéril

infertility [ɪnfə'tɪlɪtɪ] n esterilidad f

infest [ɪn'fest] vt infestar, plagar (**with** de)

infighting ['ɪnfaɪtɪŋ] n Fig luchas fpl internas

infiltrate ['ɪnfɪltreɪt] vt infiltrarse (**into** en)

infinite ['ɪnfɪnɪt] adj infinito(a)

infinitive [ɪn'fɪnɪtɪv] n infinitivo m

infinity [ɪn'fɪnɪtɪ] n infinidad f; Math infinito m

infirm [ɪn'fɜːm] **1** adj (ailing) enfermizo(a); (weak) débil **2** npl **the i.** los inválidos

infirmary [ɪn'fɜːmərɪ] n hospital m

infirmity [ɪn'fɜːmɪtɪ] n Fml (ailment) enfermedad f; (weakness) debilidad f

inflame [ɪn'fleɪm] vt (passion) encender; (curiosity) avivar; (crowd) excitar; **to be inflamed with rage** rabiar

inflamed [ɪn'fleɪmd] adj inflamado(a); **to become i.** inflamarse

inflammable [ɪn'flæməbəl] adj (material) inflamable; Fig (situation) explosivo(a)

inflammation [ɪnflə'meɪʃən] n inflamación f

inflatable [ɪn'fleɪtəbəl] adj inflable

inflate [ɪn'fleɪt] **1** vt inflar **2** vi inflarse

inflated [ɪn'fleɪtɪd] adj (**a**) Fig (prices) inflacionista (**b**) Pej (view, idea) exagerado(a)

inflation [ɪn'fleɪʃən] n inflación f

inflexible [ɪn'fleksəbəl] adj inflexible

inflict [ɪn'flɪkt] vt (blow) asestar (**on** a); (damage) causar (**on** a); (defeat) infligir (**on** a)

in-flight ['ɪnflaɪt] adj durante el vuelo

influence ['ɪnflʊəns] **1** n influencia f; Fam **to be under the i.** llevar una copa de más **2** vt influir en

influential [ɪnflʊ'enʃəl] adj influyente

influenza [ɪnflʊ'enzə] n gripe f

influx ['ɪnflʌks] n afluencia f

inform [ɪn'fɔːm] **1** vt informar (**of** or **about** de or sobre); (police) avisar (**of** or **about** de) **2** vi **to i. against** or **on** denunciar

informal [ɪn'fɔːməl] adj (**a**) (occasion, behaviour) informal; (language, treatment) familiar (**b**) *(unofficial)* no oficial

informality [ɪnfɔː'mælɪtɪ] *n (of occasion, behaviour)* sencillez *f*; *(of treatment)* familiaridad *f*

informant [ɪn'fɔːmənt] *n* informante *mf*

information [ɪnfə'meɪʃən] *n* información *f*; *(details)* detalles *mpl*; *(facts)* datos *mpl*; *(knowledge)* conocimientos *mpl*; *(news)* noticias *fpl*; **a piece of i.** un dato; **i. bureau** centro *m* de información; **i. (super)highway** autopista *f* de la información; **i. technology** informática *f*

informative [ɪn'fɔːmətɪv] *adj* informativo(a)

informed [ɪn'fɔːmd] *adj* enterado(a); **keep me i.** téngame al corriente

informer [ɪn'fɔːmə(r)] *n* delator(a) *m,f*; *(to the police)* soplón(ona) *m,f*

infrared [ɪnfrə'red] *adj* infrarrojo(a)

infrastructure ['ɪnfrəstrʌktʃə(r)] *n* infraestructura *f*

infringe [ɪn'frɪndʒ] **1** *vt (law, rule)* infringir; *(copyright)* no respetar

   2 *vi* **to i. on** or **upon** *(rights)* violar; *(privacy)* invadir

infringement [ɪn'frɪndʒmənt] *n (of law, rule)* infracción *f*; *(of rights)* violación *f*

infuriate [ɪn'fjʊərɪeɪt] *vt* poner furioso(a)

infuriating [ɪn'fjʊərɪeɪtɪŋ] *adj* exasperante

infusion [ɪn'fjuːʒən] *n* infusión *f*

ingenious [ɪn'dʒiːnɪəs] *adj* ingenioso(a)

ingenuity [ɪndʒɪ'njuːɪtɪ] *n* ingenio *m*

ingenuous [ɪn'dʒenjʊəs] *adj* ingenuo(a)

ingot ['ɪŋɡət] *n* lingote *m*

ingrained [ɪn'ɡreɪnd] *adj Fig* arraigado(a)

ingratiate [ɪn'ɡreɪʃɪeɪt] *vt Pej* **to i. oneself with sb** congraciarse con algn

ingratiating [ɪn'ɡreɪʃɪeɪtɪŋ] *adj* zalamero(a)

ingratitude [ɪn'ɡrætɪtjuːd] *n* ingratitud *f*

ingredient [ɪn'ɡriːdɪənt] *n* ingrediente *m*

inhabit [ɪn'hæbɪt] *vt* vivir en, ocupar

inhabitable [ɪn'hæbɪtəbəl] *adj* habitable

> 🔎 Note that the Spanish word **inhabitable** is a false friend and is never a translation for the English word **inhabitable**. In Spanish, **inhabitable** means "uninhabitable".

inhabitant [ɪn'hæbɪtənt] *n* habitante *mf*

inhale [ɪn'heɪl] **1** *vt (gas)* inhalar; *(air)* aspirar

   2 *vi* aspirar; *(smoker)* tragar el humo

inherent [ɪn'hɪərənt] *adj* inherente

inherit [ɪn'herɪt] *vt* heredar (**from** de)

inheritance [ɪn'herɪtəns] *n* herencia *f*

inhibit [ɪn'hɪbɪt] *vt (freedom)* limitar;

(person) cohibir; **to i. sb from doing sth** impedir a algn hacer algo

inhibited [ɪn'hɪbɪtɪd] *adj* cohibido(a)

inhibition [ɪnhɪ'bɪʃən] *n* cohibición *f*

inhospitable [ɪnhɒ'spɪtəbəl] *adj* inhospitalario(a); *(climate, place)* inhóspito(a)

inhuman [ɪn'hjuːmən] *adj* inhumano(a)

iniquity [ɪ'nɪkwɪtɪ] *n Fml* iniquidad *f*

initial [ɪ'nɪʃəl] **1** *adj* inicial, primero(a)

   2 *n* (**a**) inicial *f* (**b**) **initials** *(of name)* iniciales *fpl*; *(of abbreviation)* siglas *fpl*

   3 *vt* firmar con las iniciales

initially [ɪ'nɪʃəlɪ] *adv* al principio

initiate [ɪ'nɪʃɪeɪt] *vt* (**a**) iniciar; *(reform)* promover; *(lawsuit)* entablar (**b**) *(into society)* admitir (**into** en); *(into knowledge)* iniciar (**into** en)

initiation [ɪnɪʃɪ'eɪʃən] *n* (**a**) *(start)* principio *m* (**b**) *(admission)* iniciación *f*

initiative [ɪ'nɪʃɪətɪv] *n* iniciativa *f*

inject [ɪn'dʒekt] *vt* (**a**) *(drug etc)* inyectar (**b**) *Fig (capital)* invertir; *(life, hope)* infundir

injection [ɪn'dʒekʃən] *n* (**a**) inyección *f* (**b**) *Fig (capital)* inversión *f*

injunction [ɪn'dʒʌŋkʃən] *n* interdicto *m*

injure ['ɪndʒə(r)] *vt* herir; **to i. oneself** hacerse daño; *Fig (health, reputation)* perjudicar

injured ['ɪndʒəd] **1** *adj* herido(a); *Fig (look, tone)* ofendido(a)

   2 *npl* **the i.** los heridos

injury ['ɪndʒərɪ] *n (hurt)* herida *f*; *Fig (harm)* daño *m*; *Sport* **i. time** (tiempo *m* de) descuento *m*

injustice [ɪn'dʒʌstɪs] *n* injusticia *f*

ink [ɪŋk] *n* tinta *f*; **invisible i.** tinta simpática

inkjet printer ['ɪŋkdʒet'prɪntə(r)] *n Comput* impresora *f* de chorro de tinta

inkling ['ɪŋklɪŋ] *n (idea)* idea *f*; *(suspicion)* sospecha *f*; *(sign)* señal *f*

inkwell ['ɪŋkwel] *n* tintero *m*

inlaid [ɪn'leɪd] *adj (wood)* taraceado(a); *(ivory, gems)* incrustado(a)

inland 1 *adj* ['ɪnlənd] *(del)* interior; *Br* **I. Revenue** Hacienda *f*

   2 *adv* [ɪn'lænd] *(travel)* tierra adentro

in-laws ['ɪnlɔːz] *npl Fam* familia *f* política

inlet ['ɪnlet] *n* (**a**) *(in coastline)* ensenada *f*, cala *f* (**b**) *(in pipe, machine)* entrada *f*, admisión *f*

inline ['ɪnlaɪn] *adj* **i. skates** patines *mpl* en línea

inmate ['ɪnmeɪt] *n (of prison)* preso(a) *m,f*; *(of hospital)* enfermo(a) *m,f*; *(of asylum, camp)* internado(a) *m,f*

inn [ɪn] *n* *(with lodging)* posada *f*, mesón *m*

innate [ɪ'neɪt] *adj* innato(a)

inner ['ɪnə(r)] *adj* **(a)** *(region)* interior; *(structure)* interno(a); **i. city** zona urbana desfavorecida; **i. tube** cámara *f* de aire **(b)** *Fig (thoughts)* íntimo(a); *(peace etc)* interior

innermost ['ɪnəməʊst] *adj* *(room)* más interior; *Fig (thoughts)* más íntimo(a)

innings ['ɪnɪŋz] *npl (in cricket)* entrada *f*, turno *m*

innocence ['ɪnəsəns] *n* inocencia *f*

innocent ['ɪnəsənt] *adj & n* inocente *(mf)*

innocuous [ɪ'nɒkjʊəs] *adj* inocuo(a)

innovation [ɪnə'veɪʃən] *n* novedad *f*

innuendo [ɪnjʊ'endəʊ] *n* indirecta *f*

inoculate [ɪ'nɒkjʊleɪt] *vt* inocular

inoculation [ɪnɒkjʊ'leɪʃən] *n* inoculación *f*

inoffensive [ɪnə'fensɪv] *adj* inofensivo(a)

inopportune [ɪn'ɒpətjuːn, ɪnɒpə'tjuːn] *adj* inoportuno(a)

inordinate [ɪ'nɔːdɪnɪt] *adj* desmesurado(a)

inpatient ['ɪnpeɪʃənt] *n* interno(a) *m,f*

input ['ɪnpʊt] *n (of resources)* inversión *f*; *(of power)* entrada *f*; *Comput (of data)* input *m*, entrada

inquest ['ɪnkwest] *n* investigación *f* judicial

inquire [ɪn'kwaɪə(r)] **1** *vt* preguntar; *(find out)* averiguar

2 *vi* preguntar (**about** por); *(find out)* informarse (**about** de)

▸ **inquire after** *vt insep* preguntar por

▸ **inquire into** *vt insep* investigar, indagar

inquiry [ɪn'kwaɪərɪ] *n* **(a)** pregunta *f*; **inquiries** *(sign)* información **(b)** *(investigation)* investigación *f*

inquisitive [ɪn'kwɪzɪtɪv] *adj (curious)* curioso(a); *(questioning)* preguntón(ona)

inroads ['ɪnrəʊdz] *npl* **the firm is making i. into the market** la empresa está ganando terreno en el mercado; **to make i. into one's capital** reducir su capital

insane [ɪn'seɪn] *adj* loco(a); *(act)* insensato(a); *Fig* **to drive sb i.** volver loco(a) a algn

insanity [ɪn'sænɪtɪ] *n* demencia *f*, locura *f*

insatiable [ɪn'seɪʃəbəl] *adj* insaciable

inscribe [ɪn'skraɪb] *vt* *Fml* inscribir; *(book)* dedicar

inscription [ɪn'skrɪpʃən] *n* *(on stone, coin)* inscripción *f*; *(in book, on photo)* dedicatoria *f*

inscrutable [ɪn'skruːtəbəl] *adj* inescrutable, insondable

insect ['ɪnsekt] *n* insecto *m*; **i. bite** picadura *f*

insecticide [ɪn'sektɪsaɪd] *n* insecticida *m*

insecure [ɪnsɪ'kjʊə(r)] *adj* inseguro(a)

insecurity [ɪnsɪ'kjʊərɪtɪ] *n* inseguridad *f*

insemination [ɪnsemɪ'neɪʃən] *n* inseminación *f*

insensible [ɪn'sensəbəl] *adj* *Fml* inconsciente

insensitive [ɪn'sensɪtɪv] *adj* insensible

inseparable [ɪn'sepərəbəl] *adj* inseparable

insert 1 *n* ['ɪnsɜːt] encarte *m*

2 *vt* [ɪn'sɜːt] introducir

insertion [ɪn'sɜːʃən] *n* introducción *f*; *(of clause, text)* inserción *f*

inshore 1 *adj* ['ɪnʃɔː(r)] *(fishing)* de bajura

2 *adv* [ɪn'ʃɔː(r)] cerca de la costa

inside [ɪn'saɪd] **1** *n* **(a)** interior *m*; **on the i.** por dentro; **to turn sth i. out** volver algo al revés **(b)** *Fam* **insides** tripas *fpl*

2 ['ɪnsaɪd] *adj* interior; *Sport* **i. forward** interior *mf*; *Aut* **i. lane** carril *m* interior

3 *adv* **(a)** *(be)* dentro, adentro; *(run etc)* (hacia) adentro; **to come i.** entrar; *Br Fam* **he spent a year i.** pasó un año en chirona

4 *prep* **(a)** *(place)* dentro de **(b)** *Fam* **i. (of)** *(time)* en menos de

insider [ɪn'saɪdə(r)] *n* **i. dealing** = uso indebido de información privilegiada y confidencial para operaciones comerciales

insidious [ɪn'sɪdɪəs] *adj* insidioso(a)

insight ['ɪnsaɪt] *n* perspicacia *f*

insignia [ɪn'sɪgnɪə] *n inv* insignia *f*

insignificant [ɪnsɪg'nɪfɪkənt] *adj* insignificante

insincere [ɪnsɪn'sɪə(r)] *adj* poco sincero(a)

insinuate [ɪn'sɪnjʊeɪt] *vt* insinuar

insipid [ɪn'sɪpɪd] *adj* soso(a), insulso(a)

insist [ɪn'sɪst] **1** *vi* insistir (**on** en); *(argue)* obstinarse (**on** en)

2 *vt* **to i. that ...** insistir en que ...

insistence [ɪn'sɪstəns] *n* insistencia *f*

insistent [ɪn'sɪstənt] *adj* insistente

in so far as [ɪnsəʊ'fɑːrəz] *adv* en tanto que

insole ['ɪnsəʊl] *n (of shoe)* plantilla *f*

insolent ['ɪnsələnt] *adj* insolente

insoluble [ɪn'sɒljʊbəl] *adj* insoluble

insomnia [ɪn'sɒmnɪə] *n* insomnio *m*

insomniac [ɪn'sɒmnɪæk] *n* insomne *mf*

inspect [ɪn'spekt] *vt* inspeccionar, examinar; *(troops)* pasar revista a

inspection [ɪnˈspekʃən] *n* inspección *f*; *(of troops)* revista *f*

inspector [ɪnˈspektə(r)] *n* inspector(a) *m,f*; *(on bus, train)* revisor(a) *m,f*

inspiration [ɪnspɪˈreɪʃən] *n* inspiración *f*; **to get i. from sb/sth** inspirarse en algn/algo

inspire [ɪnˈspaɪə(r)] *vt* (a) inspirar; **to i. respect in sb** infundir respeto a algn (b) **to i. sb to do sth** animar a algn a hacer algo

inspired [ɪnˈspaɪəd] *adj* inspirado(a)

instability [ɪnstəˈbɪlɪtɪ] *n* inestabilidad *f*

install, *US* **instal** [ɪnˈstɔːl] *vt* instalar

installation [ɪnstəˈleɪʃən] *n* instalación *f*

instalment, *US* **installment** [ɪnˈstɔːlmənt] *n* (a) *(of payment)* plazo *m*; **to pay by instalments** pagar a plazos; *US* **i. plan** venta *f*/compra *f* a plazos (b) *(of novel, programme)* entrega *f*; *(of journal)* fascículo *m*

instance [ˈɪnstəns] *n* caso *m*, ejemplo *m*; **for i.** por ejemplo; **in the first i.** en primer lugar

> 🔎 Note that the Spanish word **instancia** is a false friend and is never a translation for the English word **instance**. In Spanish, **instancia** means "request".

instant [ˈɪnstənt] **1** *n (moment)* instante *m*, momento *m*; **in an i.** en un instante

2 *adj* inmediato(a); *(coffee, meal)* instantáneo(a)

instantly [ˈɪnstəntlɪ] *adv* inmediatamente

instead [ɪnˈsted] **1** *adv* en cambio

2 *prep* **i. of** en vez de, en lugar de

instep [ˈɪnstep] *n* empeine *m*

instigation [ɪnstɪˈgeɪʃən] *n* instigación *f*

instil, *US* **instill** [ɪnˈstɪl] *vt (idea, habit)* inculcar (**in** a *or* en); *(courage, respect)* infundir (**in** a)

instinct [ˈɪnstɪŋkt] *n* instinto *m*

instinctive [ɪnˈstɪŋktɪv] *adj* instintivo(a)

institute [ˈɪnstɪtjuːt] **1** *n* instituto *m*; *(centre)* centro *m*; *(professional body)* colegio *m*

2 *vt Fml* (a) *(system)* establecer (b) *(start)* iniciar; *(proceedings)* entablar

institution [ɪnstɪˈtjuːʃən] *n* (a) institución *f* (b) *(home)* asilo *m*; *(asylum)* manicomio *m*

instruct [ɪnˈstrʌkt] *vt* instruir; *(order)* mandar; **I am instructed to say that ...** me han encargado decir que ...

instruction [ɪnˈstrʌkʃən] *n* (a) instrucción *f* (b) **instructions** instrucciones *fpl*; **instructions for use** modo de empleo

instructive [ɪnˈstrʌktɪv] *adj* instructivo(a)

instructor [ɪnˈstrʌktə(r)] *n* instructor(a) *m,f*; *(of driving)* profesor(a) *m,f*

instrument [ˈɪnstrəmənt] *n* instrumento *m*; **i. panel** tablero *m* de mandos

instrumental [ɪnstrəˈmentəl] *adj* (a) *Mus* instrumental (b) **to be i. in sth** contribuir decisivamente a algo

insubordinate [ɪnsəˈbɔːdɪnɪt] *adj* insubordinado(a)

insubstantial [ɪnsəbˈstænʃəl] *adj* insubstancial; *(structure)* poco sólido(a)

insufferable [ɪnˈsʌfərəbəl] *adj* insoportable

insufficient [ɪnsəˈfɪʃənt] *adj* insuficiente

insular [ˈɪnsjʊlə(r)] *adj* (a) *Geog* insular (b) *Fig Pej* estrecho(a) de miras

insulate [ˈɪnsjʊleɪt] *vt* aislar (**against** *or* **from** de)

insulating tape [ˈɪnsjʊleɪtɪŋteɪp] *n* cinta *f* aislante

insulation [ɪnsjʊˈleɪʃən] *n* aislamiento *m*

insulin [ˈɪnsjʊlɪn] *n* insulina *f*

insult 1 [ˈɪnsʌlt] *(words)* insulto *m*; *(action)* afrenta *f*, ofensa *f*

2 *vt* [ɪnˈsʌlt] insultar, ofender

insulting [ɪnˈsʌltɪŋ] *adj* insultante, ofensivo(a)

insuperable [ɪnˈsuːpərəbəl] *adj* insuperable

insurance [ɪnˈʃʊərəns] *n* seguro *m*; **fire i.** seguro contra incendios; **i. broker** agente *mf* de seguros; **i. company** compañía *f* de seguros; **i. policy** póliza *f* (de seguros); **private health i.** seguro médico privado

insure [ɪnˈʃʊə(r)] *vt* asegurar (**against** contra)

insurgent [ɪnˈsɜːdʒənt] *adj & n* insurrecto(a) *(m,f)*

insurmountable [ɪnsəˈmaʊntəbəl] *adj (problem etc)* insuperable; *(barrier)* infranqueable

intact [ɪnˈtækt] *adj* intacto(a)

intake [ˈɪnteɪk] *n* (a) *(of air, water)* entrada *f*; *(of electricity etc)* toma *f* (b) *(of food, calories)* consumo *m* (c) *(of students, recruits)* número *m* de admitidos

integral [ˈɪntɪgrəl] **1** *adj* (a) *(intrinsic)* integrante (b) *(whole)* íntegro(a) (c) *Math* integral

2 *n Math* integral *f*

integrate [ˈɪntɪgreɪt] **1** *vt* integrar

2 *vi* integrarse

integration [ɪntɪˈgreɪʃən] *n* integración *f*

integrity [ɪnˈtegrɪtɪ] *n* integridad *f*, honradez *f*

intellect [ˈɪntɪlekt] *n* intelecto *m*

intellectual [ɪntɪ'lektʃʊəl] *adj & n* intelectual *(mf)*

intelligence [ɪn'telɪdʒəns] *n* (a) inteligencia *f* (b) *(information)* información *f*

intelligent [ɪn'telɪdʒənt] *adj* inteligente

intelligentsia [ɪntelɪ'dʒentsɪə] *n* intelectualidad *f*

intelligible [ɪn'telɪdʒəbəl] *adj* inteligible

intend [ɪn'tend] *vt* (a) *(mean)* tener la intención de (b) **to i.** sth for sb destinar algo a algn

intended [ɪn'tendɪd] *adj (planned)* previsto(a)

intense [ɪn'tens] *adj* intenso(a); *(person)* muy serio(a)

intensely [ɪn'tenslɪ] *adv (extremely)* enormemente, sumamente

intensify [ɪn'tensɪfaɪ] *vt (search)* intensificar; *(effort)* redoblar; *(production, pollution)* aumentar

intensity [ɪn'tensɪtɪ] *n* intensidad *f*

intensive [ɪn'tensɪv] *adj* intensivo(a); *Med* **i. care unit** unidad *f* de vigilancia intensiva

intent [ɪn'tent] **1** *adj (absorbed)* absorto(a); *(gaze etc)* atento(a); **to be i. on doing sth** estar resuelto(a) a hacer algo
2 *n Fml* intención *f*, propósito *m*; **to all intents and purposes** a todos los efectos

intention [ɪn'tenʃən] *n* intención *f*

intentional [ɪn'tenʃənəl] *adj* deliberado(a)

intentionally [ɪn'tenʃənəlɪ] *adv* a propósito

interact [ɪntər'ækt] *vi (people)* interrelacionarse

interaction [ɪntər'ækʃən] *n* interacción *f*

interactive [ɪntər'æktɪv] *adj* interactivo(a)

intercede [ɪntə'siːd] *vi* interceder (**with** ante)

intercept [ɪntə'sept] *vt* interceptar

interchange 1 *n* ['ɪntətʃeɪndʒ] (a) *(exchange)* intercambio *m* (b) *(on motorway)* cruce *m*
2 *vt* [ɪntə'tʃeɪndʒ] intercambiar (**with** con)

interchangeable [ɪntə'tʃeɪndʒəbəl] *adj* intercambiable

intercity [ɪntə'sɪtɪ] *adj Rail* de largo recorrido

intercom ['ɪntəkɒm] *n* portero automático

intercontinental [ɪntəkɒntɪ'nentəl] *adj* **i. ballistic missile** misil balístico intercontinental

intercourse ['ɪntəkɔːs] *n* (a) *(dealings)* trato *m* (b) *(sexual)* relaciones *fpl* sexuales

interest ['ɪntrɪst] **1** *n* (a) interés *m* (b) *(advantage)* provecho *m*; **in the i. of** en pro de (c) *Com (share)* participación *f* (d) *Fin* interés *m*; **i. rate** tipo *m* de interés
2 *vt* interesar; **he's interested in politics** le interesa la política

interesting ['ɪntrɪstɪŋ] *adj* interesante

interface ['ɪntəfeɪs] *n* interface *f*

interfere [ɪntə'fɪə(r)] *vi* (a) *(meddle)* entrometerse (**in** en); **to i. with** *(hinder)* dificultar; *(spoil)* estropear; *(prevent)* impedir (b) *Rad & TV* interferir (**with** con)

interference [ɪntə'fɪərəns] *n (meddling)* intromisión *f*; *(hindrance)* estorbo *m*; *Rad & TV* interferencia *f*

interim ['ɪntərɪm] **1** *n Fml* **in the i.** en el ínterin
2 *adj* interino(a), provisional

interior [ɪn'tɪərɪə(r)] **1** *adj* interior
2 *n* interior *m*; **i. design** diseño *m* de interiores

interlock [ɪntə'lɒk] *vi* encajarse; *(fingers)* entrelazarse; *(cogs)* engranarse

interloper ['ɪntələʊpə(r)] *n* intruso(a) *m,f*

interlude ['ɪntəluːd] *n (break)* intervalo *m*; *Cin & Th* intermedio *m*; *Mus* interludio *m*

intermediary [ɪntə'miːdɪərɪ] *n* intermediario(a) *m,f*

intermediate [ɪntə'miːdɪɪt] *adj* intermedio(a)

interminable [ɪn'tɜːmɪnəbəl] *adj* interminable

intermission [ɪntə'mɪʃən] *n Cin & Th* intermedio *m*

intermittent [ɪntə'mɪtənt] *adj* intermitente

intern 1 *vt* [ɪn'tɜːn] internar
2 *n* ['ɪntɜːn] *US Med* interno(a) *m,f*

internal [ɪn'tɜːnəl] *adj* interior; *(dispute, injury)* interno(a); *US* **I. Revenue Service** ≃ Hacienda *f*

internally [ɪn'tɜːnəlɪ] *adv* interiormente; **not to be taken i.** *(on medicine)* uso externo

international [ɪntə'næʃənəl] **1** *adj* internacional
2 *n Sport (player)* internacional *mf*; *(match)* partido *m* internacional

Internet ['ɪntənet] *n Comput* **the I.** Internet; **it's on the I.** está en Internet; **I. access provider** proveedor *m* de acceso a Internet; **I. service provider** proveedor *m* de (acceso a) Internet

interplay ['ɪntəpleɪ] *n* interacción *f*

interpret [ɪn'tɜːprɪt] **1** *vt* interpretar
2 *vi* actuar de intérprete

interpretation [ɪntɜːprɪˈteɪʃən] *n* interpretación *f*

interpreter [ɪnˈtɜːprɪtə(r)] *n* intérprete *mf*

interrelated [ɪntərɪˈleɪtɪd] *adj* estrechamente relacionado(a)

interrogate [ɪnˈterəgeɪt] *vt* interrogar

interrogation [ɪnterəˈgeɪʃən] *n* interrogatorio *m*

interrogative [ɪntəˈrɒgətɪv] *Ling* **1** *adj* interrogativo(a)
2 *n (word)* palabra interrogativa

interrupt [ɪntəˈrʌpt] *vt & vi* interrumpir

interruption [ɪntəˈrʌpʃən] *n* interrupción *f*

intersect [ɪntəˈsekt] **1** *vt* cruzar
2 *vi* cruzarse

intersection [ɪntəˈsekʃən] *n* (**a**) *(crossroads)* cruce *m* (**b**) *(of two lines)* intersección *f*

intersperse [ɪntəˈspɜːs] *vt* esparcir

intertwine [ɪntəˈtwaɪn] **1** *vt* entrelazar (**with** con)
2 *vi* entrelazarse (**with** con)

interval [ˈɪntəvəl] *n* (**a**) *(of time, space)* intervalo *m*; **at intervals** *(time, space)* a intervalos; *(time)* de vez en cuando (**b**) *Br Cin & Th* intermedio *m*

intervene [ɪntəˈviːn] *vi* (**a**) *(person)* intervenir (**in** en) (**b**) *(event)* sobrevenir (**c**) *(time)* transcurrir

intervention [ɪntəˈvenʃən] *n* intervención *f*

interview [ˈɪntəvjuː] **1** *n* entrevista *f*; **to give an i.** conceder una entrevista
2 *vt* entrevistar

interviewer [ˈɪntəvjuːə(r)] *n* entrevistador(a) *m,f*

intestine [ɪnˈtestɪn] *n (usu pl)* intestino *m*; **large/small i.** intestino grueso/delgado

intimacy [ˈɪntɪməsɪ] *n (closeness)* intimidad *f*; *Euph (sex)* relación íntima; **intimacies** intimidades *fpl*

intimate¹ [ˈɪntɪmɪt] *adj* íntimo(a); *(knowledge)* profundo(a)

intimate² [ˈɪntɪmeɪt] *vt Fml* dar a entender

intimidate [ɪnˈtɪmɪdeɪt] *vt* intimidar

intimidating [ɪnˈtɪmɪdeɪtɪŋ] *adj* atemorizante

into [ˈɪntuː, *unstressed* ˈɪntə] *prep* (**a**) *(motion)* en, a, con; **he fell i. the water** se cayó al agua; **I bumped i. a friend** me topé con un amigo; **to get i. a car** subir a un coche; **to go i. a house** entrar en una casa (**b**) *(state)* en, a; **he grew i. a man** se hizo un hombre; **to burst i. tears** echarse

a llorar; **to change pounds i. pesetas** cambiar libras en *or* por pesetas; **to translate sth i. French** traducir algo al francés (**c**) **to work i. the night** trabajar hasta muy avanzada la noche (**d**) **to divide sth i. three** dividir algo en tres (**e**) *Fam* **to be i. sth** ser aficionado(a) a algo

intolerable [ɪnˈtɒlərəbəl] *adj* intolerable

intolerant [ɪnˈtɒlərənt] *adj* intolerante

intonation [ɪntəˈneɪʃən] *n* entonación *f*

intoxicated [ɪnˈtɒksɪkeɪtɪd] *adj* borracho(a)

> 🖉 Note that the Spanish word **intoxicado** is a false friend and is never a translation for the English word **intoxicated**. In Spanish, **intoxicado** means "poisoned".

intoxicating [ɪnˈtɒksɪkeɪtɪŋ] *adj* embriagador(a); **i. liquor** bebida alcohólica

intoxication [ɪntɒksɪˈkeɪʃən] *n* embriaguez *f*

> 🖉 Note that the Spanish word **intoxicación** is a false friend and is never a translation for the English word **intoxication**. In Spanish, **intoxicación** means "poisoning".

intractable [ɪnˈtræktəbəl] *adj Fml (person)* intratable; *(problem)* insoluble

intranet [ˈɪntrənet] *n Comput* intranet *f*

intransigent [ɪnˈtrænsɪdʒənt] *adj Fml* intransigente, intolerante

intransitive [ɪnˈtrænsɪtɪv] *adj* intransitivo(a)

intravenous [ɪntrəˈviːnəs] *adj* intravenoso(a)

in-tray [ˈɪntreɪ] *n* bandeja *f* de asuntos pendientes

intrepid [ɪnˈtrepɪd] *adj* intrépido(a), audaz

intricate [ˈɪntrɪkɪt] *adj* intrincado(a)

intrigue 1 *n* [ɪnˈtriːg, ˈɪntriːg] intriga *f*
2 *vt* [ɪnˈtriːg] intrigar
3 *vi* intrigar, conspirar

intriguing [ɪnˈtriːgɪŋ] *adj* intrigante

intrinsic [ɪnˈtrɪnsɪk] *adj Fml* intrínseco(a)

introduce [ɪntrəˈdjuːs] *vt* (**a**) *(person, programme)* presentar (**to** a) (**b**) *(bring in)* introducir (**into** *or* **to** en); *Com* lanzar (**into** *or* **to** a); *(topic)* proponer

introduction [ɪntrəˈdʌkʃən] *n* (**a**) *(of person, programme)* presentación *f*; *(in book)* introducción *f* (**b**) *(bringing in)* introducción *f*; *Com (of product)* lanzamiento *m*

introductory [ɪntrəˈdʌktərɪ] *adj* introductorio(a); *(remarks)* preliminar; *Com* de lanzamiento

introspective [ɪntrəˈspektɪv] *adj* introspectivo(a)

introvert [ˈɪntrəvɜːt] *n* introvertido(a) *m,f*

intrude [ɪnˈtruːd] *vi* entrometerse (**into** *or* **on** en); *(disturb)* molestar

intruder [ɪnˈtruːdə(r)] *n* intruso(a) *m,f*

intrusion [ɪnˈtruːʒən] *n* incursión *f*

intuition [ɪntjʊˈɪʃən] *n* intuición *f*

inundate [ˈɪnʌndeɪt] *vt* inundar (**with** de)

invade [ɪnˈveɪd] *vt* invadir

invader [ɪnˈveɪdə(r)] *n* invasor(a) *m,f*

invalid¹ [ˈɪnvəlɪd] *n (disabled person)* minusválido(a) *m,f*; *(sick person)* enfermo(a) *m,f*

invalid² [ɪnˈvælɪd] *adj* inválido(a), nulo(a)

invalidate [ɪnˈvælɪdeɪt] *vt* invalidar

invaluable [ɪnˈvæljʊəbəl] *adj* inestimable

invariable [ɪnˈveərɪəbəl] *adj* invariable

invasion [ɪnˈveɪʒən] *n* invasión *f*

invent [ɪnˈvent] *vt* inventar

invention [ɪnˈvenʃən] *n* invento *m; (creativity)* inventiva *f; (lie)* mentira *f*

inventive [ɪnˈventɪv] *adj* inventivo(a)

inventor [ɪnˈventə(r)] *n* inventor(a) *m,f*

inventory [ˈɪnvəntərɪ] *n* inventario *m*

invert [ɪnˈvɜːt] *vt* invertir

invertebrate [ɪnˈvɜːtɪbrɪt] **1** *adj* invertebrado(a)
2 *n* invertebrado *m*

inverted [ɪnˈvɜːtɪd] *adj* **(in) i. commas** (entre) comillas *fpl*

invest [ɪnˈvest] **1** *vt* invertir (**in** en); **to i. sb with sth** conferir algo a algn
2 *vi* invertir (**in** en)

investigate [ɪnˈvestɪgeɪt] *vt (crime, subject)* investigar; *(cause, possibility)* estudiar

investigation [ɪnvestɪˈgeɪʃən] *n (of crime)* investigación *f; (of cause)* examen *m*

investigator [ɪnˈvestɪgeɪtə(r)] *n* investigador(a) *m,f*; **private i.** detective privado

investment [ɪnˈvestmənt] *n* inversión *f*

investor [ɪnˈvestə(r)] *n* inversor(a) *m,f*

inveterate [ɪnˈvetərɪt] *adj* empedernido(a)

invidious [ɪnˈvɪdɪəs] *adj (task)* ingrato(a); *(comparison)* injusto(a)

> 🖉 Note that the Spanish word **envidioso** is a false friend and is never a translation for the English word **invidious**. In Spanish, **envidioso** means "envious".

invigilator [ɪnˈvɪdʒɪleɪtə(r)] *n Br* vigilante *mf*

invigorating [ɪnˈvɪgəreɪtɪŋ] *adj* vigorizante

invincible [ɪnˈvɪnsəbəl] *adj* invencible

invisible [ɪnˈvɪzəbəl] *adj* invisible

invitation [ɪnvɪˈteɪʃən] *n* invitación *f*

invite [ɪnˈvaɪt] *vt* **(a)** invitar (**to** a) **(b)** *(comments etc)* solicitar; *(criticism)* provocar; **to i. trouble** buscarse problemas

inviting [ɪnˈvaɪtɪŋ] *adj (attractive)* atractivo(a); *(food)* apetitoso(a)

invoice [ˈɪnvɔɪs] **1** *n* factura *f*
2 *vt* facturar

invoke [ɪnˈvəʊk] *vt Fml* invocar

involuntary [ɪnˈvɒləntərɪ] *adj* involuntario(a)

involve [ɪnˈvɒlv] *vt* **(a)** *(concern)* implicar (**in** en); **the issues involved** las cuestiones en juego; **to be involved in an accident** sufrir un accidente **(b)** *(entail)* suponer, implicar; *(trouble, risk)* acarrear

involved [ɪnˈvɒlvd] *adj (complicated)* complicado(a); *Fam (romantically attached)* enredado(a), liado(a)

involvement [ɪnˈvɒlvmənt] *n (participation)* participación *f; (in crime)* implicación *f*

inward [ˈɪnwəd] **1** *adj* interior
2 *adv* = **inwards**

inwardly [ˈɪnwədlɪ] *adv* interiormente, por dentro

inwards [ˈɪnwədz] *adv* hacia dentro

in-your-face [ˈɪnjəˈfeɪs] *adj Fam (style)* descarado(a); *(movie, advert)* impactante, fuerte

iodine [ˈaɪədiːn] *n* yodo *m*

iota [aɪˈəʊtə] *n* pizca *f*, ápice *m*

IOU [aɪəʊˈjuː] *n (abbr* **I owe you***)* pagaré *m*

IQ [aɪˈkjuː] *n (abbr* **intelligence quotient***)* CI *m*

IRA [aɪɑːˈreɪ] *n (abbr* **Irish Republican Army***)* IRA *m*

Iran [ɪˈrɑːn] *n* Irán *m*

Iranian [ɪˈreɪnɪən] *adj & n* iraní *(mf)*

Iraq [ɪˈrɑːk] *n* Irak *m*

Iraqi [ɪˈrɑːkɪ] *adj & n* iraquí *(mf)*

irascible [ɪˈræsɪbəl] *adj Fml* irascible

irate [aɪˈreɪt] *adj* airado(a), furioso(a)

Ireland [ˈaɪələnd] *n* Irlanda; **Republic of I.** República de Irlanda

iris [ˈaɪərɪs] *n* **(a)** *Anat* iris *m inv* **(b)** *Bot* lirio *m*

Irish [ˈaɪrɪʃ] **1** *adj* irlandés(esa); **I. coffee** café *m* irlandés; **I. Sea** Mar *m* de Irlanda
2 *n* **(a)** *(language)* irlandés *m* **(b)** *pl* **the I.** los irlandeses

Irishman [ˈaɪrɪʃmən] *n* irlandés *m*

Irishwoman [ˈaɪrɪʃwʊmən] *n* irlandesa *f*

irksome [ˈɜːksəm] *adj* fastidioso(a)

iron ['aɪən] **1** *n* (**a**) hierro *m*; **the i. and steel industry** la industria siderúrgica; **I. Curtain** Telón *m* de Acero; **i. ore** mineral *m* de hierro (**b**) *(for clothes)* plancha *f* (**c**) *(for golf)* hierro *m* (**d**) **irons** *(chains)* grillos *mpl*

  2 *vt (clothes)* planchar

  ▸ **iron out** *vt sep* (**a**) *(crease)* planchar (**b**) *Fam Fig (problem)* resolver

ironic(al) [aɪ'rɒnɪk(əl)] *adj* irónico(a)

ironing ['aɪənɪŋ] *n* (**a**) **to do the i.** planchar; **i. board** mesa *f* de la plancha (**b**) *(clothes to be ironed)* ropa *f* para planchar; *(clothes ironed)* ropa planchada

ironmonger ['aɪənmʌŋgə(r)] *n Br* ferretero(a) *m,f*; **i.'s (shop)** ferretería *f*

irony ['aɪrənɪ] *n* ironía *f*

irrational [ɪ'ræʃənəl] *adj* irracional

irreconcilable [ɪrekən'saɪləbəl] *adj* irreconciliable

irrefutable [ɪrɪ'fjuːtəbəl] *adj Fml* irrefutable

irregular [ɪ'regjʊlə(r)] *adj* (**a**) irregular; *(abnormal)* anormal (**b**) *(uneven)* desigual

irrelevant [ɪ'reləvənt] *adj* no pertinente

irreparable [ɪ'repərəbəl] *adj* irreparable

irreplaceable [ɪrɪ'pleɪsəbəl] *adj* irremplazable

irrepressible [ɪrɪ'presəbəl] *adj* incontenible

irresistible [ɪrɪ'zɪstəbəl] *adj* irresistible

irresolute [ɪ'rezəluːt] *adj Fml* indeciso(a)

irrespective [ɪrɪ'spektɪv] *adj* **i. of** sin tener en cuenta

irresponsible [ɪrɪ'spɒnsəbəl] *adj* irresponsable

irreverent [ɪ'revərənt] *adj* irreverente

irrevocable [ɪ'revəkəbəl] *adj* irrevocable

irrigate ['ɪrɪgeɪt] *vt* regar

irrigation [ɪrɪ'geɪʃən] *n* riego *m*; **i. channel** acequia *f*; **i. system** sistema *m* de regadío

irritable ['ɪrɪtəbəl] *adj* irritable

irritate ['ɪrɪteɪt] *vt (annoy)* fastidiar; *Med* irritar

irritating ['ɪrɪteɪtɪŋ] *adj* irritante

irritation [ɪrɪ'teɪʃən] *n* (**a**) *(annoyance)* fastidio *m*; *(ill humour)* mal humor *m* (**b**) *Med* irritación *f*

is [ɪz] *3rd person sing pres of* **be**

Islam ['ɪzlɑːm] *n* Islam *m*

Islamic [ɪz'læmɪk] *adj* islámico(a)

island ['aɪlənd] *n* isla *f*; (**traffic**) **i.** isleta *f*

islander ['aɪləndə(r)] *n* isleño(a) *m,f*

isle [aɪl] *n* isla *f*

isn't ['ɪzənt] = **is not**

isolate ['aɪsəleɪt] *vt* aislar (**from** de)

isolated ['aɪsəleɪtɪd] *adj* aislado(a)

isolation [aɪsə'leɪʃən] *n* aislamiento *m*

ISP [aɪes'piː] *n Comput (abbr* **Internet Service Provider)** PSI *m*

Israel ['ɪzreɪəl] *n* Israel

Israeli [ɪz'reɪlɪ] *adj & n* israelí *(mf)*

issue ['ɪʃuː] **1** *n* (**a**) *(matter)* cuestión *f*; **to take i. with sb (over sth)** manifestar su desacuerdo con algn (en algo) (**b**) *(of banknotes etc)* emisión *f*; *(of passport)* expedición *f* (**c**) *(of journal etc)* ejemplar *m* (**d**) *(of supplies)* reparto *m* (**e**) *Fml (outcome)* resultado *m* (**f**) *Jur (offspring)* descendencia *f*

  2 *vt* (**a**) *(book)* publicar; *(banknotes etc)* emitir; *(passport)* expedir (**b**) *(supplies)* repartir (**c**) *(order, instructions)* dar; *(warrant)* dictar

  3 *vi Fml (blood)* brotar (**from** de); *(smoke)* salir (**from** de)

isthmus ['ɪsməs] *n* istmo *m*

it [ɪt] *pers pron* (**a**) *(subject)* él/ella/ello *(usually omitted in Spanish, except for contrast)*; **it's here** está aquí

  (**b**) *(direct object)* lo/la; **I don't believe it** no me lo creo; **I liked the house and bought it** me gustó la casa y la compré

  (**c**) *(indirect object)* le; **give it a kick** dale una patada

  (**d**) *(after prep)* él/ella/ello; **I saw the beach and ran towards it** vi la playa y fui corriendo hacia ella; **we'll talk about it later** ya hablaremos de ello

  (**e**) *(abstract)* ello; **let's get down to it!** ¡vamos a ello!

  (**f**) *(impersonal)* **it's late** es tarde; **it's me** soy yo; **it's raining** está lloviendo; **it's said that ...** se dice que ...; **it's 2 miles to town** hay 2 millas de aquí al pueblo; **that's it!** *(agreeing)* ¡precisamente!; *(finishing)* ¡se acabó!; **this is it!** ¡ha llegado la hora!; **who is it?** ¿quién es?

Italian [ɪ'tæljən] **1** *adj* italiano(a)

  2 *n* (**a**) *(person)* italiano(a) *m,f* (**b**) *(language)* italiano *m*

italic [ɪ'tælɪk] *n* cursiva *f*

Italy ['ɪtəlɪ] *n* Italia

itch [ɪtʃ] **1** *n* picor *m*; *Fig* **an i. to travel** unas ganas locas de viajar

  2 *vi* (**a**) *(skin)* picar (**b**) *Fig* anhelar; *Fam* **to be itching to do sth** tener muchas ganas de hacer algo

itchy ['ɪtʃɪ] *adj* (**itchier, itchiest**) que pica

item ['aɪtəm] *n* (**a**) *(in list)* artículo *m*; *(in collection)* pieza *f*; **i. of clothing** prenda *f* de vestir (**b**) *(on agenda)* asunto *m*; *(in show)* número *m*; **news i.** noticia *f*

itemize ['aɪtəmaɪz] *vt* detallar

itinerant [ɪˈtɪnərənt] *adj Fml* itinerante
itinerary [aɪˈtɪnərərɪ] *n* itinerario *m*
it'll [ˈɪtəl] = **it will**
its [ɪts] *poss adj (one thing)* su; *(more than one)* sus
itself [ɪtˈself] *pers pron* (**a**) *(reflexive)* se; **the cat scratched i.** el gato se arañó (**b**) *(emphatic)* él mismo/ella misma/ello mismo; *(after prep)* sí (mismo(a)); **in i.** en sí

ITV [aɪtiːˈviː] *n Br (abbr* **Independent Television**) = canal privado de televisión británico
IUD [aɪjuːˈdiː] *n (abbr* **intrauterine (contraceptive) device**) DIU *m*
IVF [aɪviːˈef] *n Med (abbr* **in vitro fertilization**) fertilización *f* in vitro
ivory [ˈaɪvərɪ] *n* marfil *m*
ivy [ˈaɪvɪ] *n* hiedra *f*

J

J, j [dʒeɪ] *n (the letter)* J, j *f*

jab [dʒæb] **1** *n* pinchazo *m; (poke)* golpe seco

2 *vt* pinchar; *(with fist)* dar un puñetazo a

jabber ['dʒæbə(r)] *vi Fam (chatter)* charlotear; *(speak quickly)* hablar atropelladamente

jack [dʒæk] *n* **(a)** *Aut* gato *m* **(b)** *Cards* sota *f* **(c)** *(bowls)* boliche *m*
▸ **jack in** *vt sep Br Fam* dejar
▸ **jack up** *vt sep Aut* levantar (con el gato); *Fig (prices)* aumentar

jackal ['dʒækɔːl] *n* chacal *m*

jackdaw ['dʒækdɔː] *n Orn* grajilla *f*

jacket ['dʒækɪt] *n* **(a)** chaqueta *f; (of suit)* americana *f; (bomber jacket)* cazadora *f* **(b)** *(of book)* sobrecubierta *f;* US *(of record)* funda *f* **(c)** **j. potatoes** patatas *fpl* or *Am* papas *fpl* al horno

jack-knife ['dʒæknaɪf] **1** *n* navaja *f*
2 *vi* colear

jack-of-all-trades [dʒækəv'ɔːltreɪdz] *n* persona *f* mañosa or de muchos oficios

jackpot ['dʒækpɒt] *n (premio m)* gordo *m*

Jacuzzi® [dʒə'kuːzɪ] *n* jacuzzi® *m*

jade [dʒeɪd] *n* jade *m*

jaded ['dʒeɪdɪd] *adj (tired)* agotado(a); *(palate)* hastiado(a)

jagged ['dʒægɪd] *adj* dentado(a)

jaguar ['dʒægjʊə(r)] *n* jaguar *m*

jail [dʒeɪl] **1** *n* cárcel *f,* prisión *f*
2 *vt* encarcelar

jailbreak ['dʒeɪlbreɪk] *n* fuga *f,* evasión *f*

jailer ['dʒeɪlə(r)] *n* carcelero(a) *m,f*

jam¹ [dʒæm] *n Culin* mermelada *f*

jam² [dʒæm] **1** *n* **(a)** *(blockage)* atasco *m; Fam (fix)* apuro *m* **(b)** *Mus* improvisación *f*
2 *vt* **(a)** *(cram)* meter a la fuerza **(b)** *(block)* atascar; *Rad* interferir
3 *vi (door)* atrancarse; *(brakes)* agarrotarse

Jamaica [dʒə'meɪkə] *n* Jamaica *f*

jam-packed [dʒæm'pækt] *adj Fam (with people)* atestado(a); *(with things)* atiborrado(a)

jangle ['dʒæŋgəl] *vi* tintinear

janitor ['dʒænɪtə(r)] *n* portero *m,* conserje *m*

January ['dʒænjʊərɪ] *n* enero *m*

Japan [dʒə'pæn] *n* (el) Japón

Japanese [dʒæpə'niːz] **1** *adj* japonés(esa)
2 *n (person)* japonés(esa) *m,f; (language)* japonés *m*

jar¹ [dʒɑː(r)] *n (glass)* tarro *m; (earthenware)* tinaja *f; (jug)* jarra *f; Br Fam* **to have a j.** tomar una copa

jar² [dʒɑː(r)] *vi (sounds)* chirriar; *(appearance)* chocar; *(colours)* desentonar; *Fig* **to j. on one's nerves** ponerle a uno los nervios de punta

jargon ['dʒɑːgən] *n* jerga *f,* argot *m*

jasmin(e) ['dʒæzmɪn] *n* jazmín *m*

jaundice ['dʒɔːndɪs] *n* ictericia *f*

jaundiced ['dʒɔːndɪst] *adj Med* ictérico(a); *Fig (bitter)* amargado(a)

jaunt [dʒɔːnt] *n (walk)* paseo *m; (trip)* excursión *f*

jaunty ['dʒɔːntɪ] *adj* **(jauntier, jauntiest)** *(sprightly)* garboso(a); *(lively)* vivaz

javelin ['dʒævəlɪn] *n* jabalina *f*

jaw [dʒɔː] **1** *n* mandíbula *f*
2 *vi Fam* estar de palique

jay [dʒeɪ] *n Orn* arrendajo *m* (común)

jaywalker ['dʒeɪwɔːkə(r)] *n* peatón *m* imprudente

jazz [dʒæz] *n* jazz *m*
▸ **jazz up** *vt sep* alegrar; *(premises)* arreglar

jazzy ['dʒæzɪ] *adj* **(jazzier, jazziest)** *Fam (showy)* llamativo(a); *(brightly coloured)* de colores chillones

jealous ['dʒeləs] *adj* celoso(a); *(envious)* envidioso(a); **to be j. of ...** tener celos de ...

jealousy ['dʒeləsɪ] *n* celos *mpl; (envy)* envidia *f*

jeans [dʒiːnz] *npl* vaqueros *mpl,* tejanos *mpl*

Jeep® [dʒiːp] *n* jeep *m,* todo terreno *m inv*

jeer [dʒɪə(r)] **1** *n (boo)* abucheo *m; (mocking)* mofa *f*
2 *vi (boo)* abuchear; *(mock)* burlarse

jeering ['dʒɪərɪŋ] *adj* burlón(ona)

Jehovah [dʒɪ'həʊvə] *n* **J.'s Witness** testigo *mf* de Jehová

Jell-O®, jello ['dʒeləʊ] *n* US gelatina *f*

jelly ['dʒelɪ] n gelatina f

jellyfish ['dʒelɪfɪʃ] n medusa f

jeopardize ['dʒepədaɪz] vt poner en peligro; (agreement etc) comprometer

jeopardy ['dʒepədɪ] n riesgo m, peligro m

jerk [dʒɜːk] 1 n (a) (jolt) sacudida f; (pull) tirón m (b) Pej (idiot) imbécil mf
2 vt (shake) sacudir; (pull) dar un tirón a
3 vi (move suddenly) dar una sacudida; **the car jerked forward** el coche avanzaba a tirones

jerkin ['dʒɜːkɪn] n chaleco m

jersey ['dʒɜːzɪ] n jersey m, suéter m, pulóver m, Andes chompa f, Urug buzo m

jest [dʒest] 1 n broma f
2 vi bromear

Jesuit ['dʒezjʊɪt] adj & n jesuita (m)

Jesus ['dʒiːzəs] n Jesús m; **J. Christ** Jesucristo m

jet¹ [dʒet] 1 n (a) (stream of water) chorro m (b) (spout) surtidor m (c) Av reactor m; **j. engine** reactor m; **j. lag** = cansancio debido al desfase horario; **j. ski** moto náutica or acuática
2 vi Fam volar

jet² [dʒet] n **j. black** negro(a) como el azabache

jet-set ['dʒetset] n **the j.** la alta sociedad, la jet

jettison ['dʒetɪsən] vt echar al mar; Fig deshacerse de; (project etc) abandonar

jetty ['dʒetɪ] n muelle m, malecón m

Jew [dʒuː] n judío(a) m,f

jewel ['dʒuːəl] n joya f; (stone) piedra preciosa; (in watch) rubí m; Fig (person) joya

jeweller, jeweler ['dʒuːələ(r)] n joyero(a) m,f; **j.'s (shop)** joyería f

jewellery, jewelry ['dʒuːəlrɪ] n joyas fpl, alhajas fpl

Jewess ['dʒuːɪs] n judía f

Jewish ['dʒuːɪʃ] adj judío(a)

jibe [dʒaɪb] n & vi = **gibe**

jiffy ['dʒɪfɪ] n Fam momento m; **in a j.** en un santiamén; **just a j.!** ¡un momento!

jig [dʒɪg] n Mus giga f

jigsaw ['dʒɪgsɔː] n (puzzle) rompecabezas m inv

jilt [dʒɪlt] vt Fam dejar plantado(a)

jingle ['dʒɪŋgəl] 1 n Rad & TV = canción que acompaña un anuncio
2 vi tintinear

jingoistic [dʒɪŋgəʊ'ɪstɪk] adj patriotero(a)

jinx [dʒɪŋks] 1 n (person) gafe mf
2 vt gafar

jitters ['dʒɪtəz] npl Fam **to get the j.** tener canguelo

jive [dʒaɪv] 1 n swing m
2 vi bailar el swing

job [dʒɒb] n (a) trabajo m; (task) tarea f; **to give sth up as a bad j.** darse por vencido(a); Fam **just the j.!** ¡me viene de perlas! (b) (occupation) (puesto m de) trabajo m, empleo m; (trade) oficio m; Br Fam **jobs for the boys** enchufismo m; US **j. office** oficina f de empleo; **j. hunting** búsqueda f de empleo; **j. sharing** trabajo compartido a tiempo parcial (c) Fam **we had a j. to ...** nos costó (trabajo) ... (d) (duty) deber m (e) Fam **it's a good j. that ...** menos mal que ...

Jobcentre ['dʒɒbsentə(r)] n Br oficina f de empleo

jobless ['dʒɒblɪs] adj parado(a)

jockey ['dʒɒkɪ] 1 n jinete m, jockey m
2 vi **to j. for position** luchar para conseguir una posición aventajada

jocular ['dʒɒkjʊlə(r)] adj jocoso(a)

jog [dʒɒg] 1 n trote m
2 vt empujar; Fig (memory) refrescar
3 vi Sport hacer footing; Fig **to j. along** (progress slowly) avanzar poco a poco; (manage) ir tirando

jogging ['dʒɒgɪŋ] n footing m

john [dʒɒn] n US Fam **the j.** (lavatory) el váter

join [dʒɔɪn] 1 vt (a) juntar; **to j. forces with sb** unir fuerzas con algn (b) (road) empalmar con; (river) desembocar en (c) (meet) reunirse con (d) (group) unirse a; (institution) entrar; (army) alistarse a (e) (party) afiliarse a; (club) hacerse socio(a) de
2 vi (a) unirse (b) (roads) empalmar; (rivers) confluir (c) (become member of political party) afiliarse; (become member of club) hacerse socio(a)
3 n juntura f
▸ **join in** vi participar, tomar parte en; (debate) intervenir
2 vt insep participar en, tomar parte en
▸ **join up** 1 vt sep juntar
2 vi (of roads) unirse; Mil alistarse

joiner ['dʒɔɪnə(r)] n Br carpintero(a) m,f

joinery ['dʒɔɪnərɪ] n carpintería f

joint [dʒɔɪnt] 1 n (a) juntura f, unión f; Tech & Anat articulación f; **out of j.** dislocado(a) (b) Culin = corte de carne para asar; (once roasted) asado m (c) Fam (nightclub etc) garito m (d) Fam (drug) porro m
2 adj colectivo(a); **j. (bank) account** cuenta conjunta; **j. venture** empresa conjunta

jointly ['dʒɔɪntlɪ] adv conjuntamente, en común

joist [dʒɔɪst] n vigueta f

joke [dʒəʊk] **1** n (**a**) chiste m; (prank) broma f; **to play a j. on sb** gastarle una broma a algn; **to tell a j.** contar un chiste (**b**) Fam (person) hazmerreír m, payaso(a) m,f; **to be a j.** (of thing) ser de chiste **2** vi estar de broma; **you must be joking!** ¡no hablarás en serio!

joker ['dʒəʊkə(r)] n (**a**) bromista mf (**b**) Cards comodín m

jolly ['dʒɒlɪ] **1** adj (**jollier, jolliest**) alegre **2** adv Fam (very) muy; **she played j. well** jugó muy bien

jolt [dʒəʊlt] **1** n (**a**) sacudida f; (pull) tirón m (**b**) Fig (fright) susto m **2** vi moverse a sacudidas **3** vt sacudir

Jordan ['dʒɔːdən] n (**a**) (river) Jordán m (**b**) (country) Jordania

joss-stick ['dʒɒsstɪk] n varita f de incienso

jostle ['dʒɒsəl] **1** vi dar empujones **2** vt dar empujones a

jot [dʒɒt] n jota f, pizca f; **not a j.** ni jota ▶ **jot down** vt sep apuntar

jotter ['dʒɒtə(r)] n Br bloc m

journal ['dʒɜːnəl] n (**a**) revista f (**b**) (diary) diario m (**c**) (newspaper) periódico m

> 🖉 Note that the Spanish word **jornal** is a false friend and is never a translation for the English word **journal**. In Spanish, **jornal** means "day's wage".

journalism ['dʒɜːnəlɪzəm] n periodismo m

journalist ['dʒɜːnəlɪst] n periodista mf

journey ['dʒɜːnɪ] **1** n viaje m; (distance) trayecto m **2** vi Fml viajar

jovial ['dʒəʊvɪəl] adj jovial

jowl [dʒaʊl] n quijada f

joy [dʒɔɪ] n alegría f; (pleasure) placer m

joyful ['dʒɔɪfʊl] adj alegre, contento(a)

joyous ['dʒɔɪəs] adj Literary alegre

joyride ['dʒɔɪraɪd] n Fam = paseo en un coche robado

joystick ['dʒɔɪstɪk] n Av palanca f de mando; (of video game) joystick m

JP [dʒeɪ'piː] n Br Law (abbr **Justice of the Peace**) juez mf de paz

Jr (abbr **Junior**) Neil Smith, Jr Neil Smith, hijo

jubilant ['dʒuːbɪlənt] adj jubiloso(a)

jubilation [dʒuːbɪ'leɪʃən] n júbilo m

jubilee ['dʒuːbɪliː] n festejos mpl; **golden j.** quincuagésimo aniversario

judge [dʒʌdʒ] **1** n juez mf, jueza f; (in competition) jurado m **2** vt (**a**) Jur juzgar (**b**) (estimate) considerar (**c**) (competition) actuar de juez de (**d**) (assess) juzgar **3** vi juzgar; **judging from what you say** a juzgar por lo que dices

judg(e)ment ['dʒʌdʒmənt] n (**a**) Jur sentencia f, fallo m; **to pass j.** dictar sentencia (**b**) (opinion) juicio m; **to pass j. (on)** opinar (sobre); **to reserve j. (on)** no opinar (sobre) (**c**) (ability) buen juicio m (**d**) (trial) juicio m

judicial [dʒuː'dɪʃəl] adj judicial

judiciary [dʒuː'dɪʃərɪ] n magistratura f

judicious [dʒuː'dɪʃəs] adj Fml juicioso(a)

judo ['dʒuːdəʊ] n judo m

jug [dʒʌg] n Br jarra f; **milk j.** jarra de leche

juggernaut ['dʒʌgənɔːt] n Br camión pesado

juggle ['dʒʌgəl] vi (perform) hacer juegos malabares (**with** con); Fig (responsibilities) ajustar

juggler ['dʒʌglə(r)] n malabarista mf

juice [dʒuːs] n jugo m; (of citrus fruits) zumo m

juicy ['dʒuːsɪ] adj (**juicier, juiciest**) (**a**) jugoso(a) (**b**) Fam Fig picante

jukebox ['dʒuːkbɒks] n rocola f

July [dʒuː'laɪ, dʒʊ'laɪ] n julio m

jumble ['dʒʌmbəl] **1** n revoltijo m; **j. sale** mercadillo m de caridad **2** vt revolver

jumbo ['dʒʌmbəʊ] n **j.** (jet) jumbo m

jump [dʒʌmp] **1** n salto m; (sudden increase) subida repentina; **j. leads** cables mpl de emergencia; **j. suit** mono m **2** vi (**a**) saltar, dar un salto; Fig **to j. to conclusions** sacar conclusiones precipitadas (**b**) Fig (start) sobresaltarse (**c**) (increase) aumentar de golpe **3** vt saltar; Fam Fig **to j. the gun** precipitarse; **to j. the lights** saltarse el semáforo; Br **to j. the queue** colarse; US **to j. rope** saltar a la comba ▶ **jump at** vt insep aceptar sin pensarlo

jumper ['dʒʌmpə(r)] n (**a**) Br (sweater) jersey m, suéter m, pulóver m, Andes chompa f, Urug buzo m (**b**) US (dress) pichi m, falda f con peto (**c**) US Aut **j. cables** cables mpl de emergencia

jumpy ['dʒʌmpɪ] adj (**jumpier, jumpiest**) Fam nervioso(a)

junction ['dʒʌŋkʃən] n (of roads) cruce m; Rail & Elec empalme m

juncture ['dʒʌŋktʃə(r)] n Fml **at this j.** en esta coyuntura

June [dʒuːn] *n* junio *m*

jungle ['dʒʌŋgəl] *n* jungla *f*, selva *f*; *Fig* laberinto *m*; **the concrete j.** la jungla de asfalto

junior ['dʒuːnjə(r)] **1** *adj* (**a**) *(son of)* hijo; **David Hughes J.** David Hughes hijo (**b**) *US* **j. high (school)** *(between 11 and 15)* escuela secundaria; *Br* **j. school** *(between 7 and 11)* escuela primaria; **j. team** equipo *m* juvenil (**c**) *(lower in rank)* subalterno(a)

2 *n* (**a**) *(person of lower rank)* subalterno(a) *m,f* (**b**) *(younger person)* menor *mf*

junk [dʒʌŋk] *n* (**a**) *Fam* trastos *mpl*; **j. food** comida basura; **j. mail** propaganda *f* (por correo); **j. shop** tienda *f* de segunda mano (**b**) *(boat)* junco *m*

junkie ['dʒʌŋkɪ] *n Fam* yonqui *mf*

junkman ['dʒʌŋkmæn] *n US* trapero(a) *m,f*

junta ['dʒʌntə, *US* 'hʊntə] *n* junta *f* militar

jurisdiction [dʒʊərɪs'dɪkʃən] *n Fml* jurisdicción *f*

juror ['dʒʊərə(r)] *n* jurado(a) *m,f*

jury ['dʒʊərɪ] *n* jurado *m*

just [dʒʌst] **1** *adj (fair)* justo(a); *Fml (well-founded)* justificado(a)

2 *adv* (**a**) **he had j. arrived** acababa de llegar

(**b**) *(at this very moment)* ahora mismo, en este momento; **he was j. leaving when Rosa arrived** estaba a punto de salir cuando llegó Rosa; **I'm j. coming!** ¡ya voy!; **j. as ...** cuando ..., justo al ...; **j. as I**

thought me lo figuraba

(**c**) *(only)* solamente; **j. in case** por si acaso; **j. a minute!** ¡un momento!

(**d**) *(barely)* por poco; **I only j. caught the bus** cogí el autobús por los pelos; **j. about** casi; **j. enough** justo lo suficiente

(**e**) *(emphatic)* **it's j. fantastic!** ¡es sencillamente fantástico!; **you'll j. have to wait** tendrás que esperar

(**f**) *(exactly)* exactamente, justo; **that's j. it!** ¡precisamente!

(**g**) *(equally)* **j. as fast as** tan rápido como

justice ['dʒʌstɪs] *n* (**a**) justicia *f*; **he was brought to j.** lo llevaron ante los tribunales; **you didn't do yourself j.** no diste lo mejor de ti (**b**) *US (judge)* juez *mf*; *Br* **J. of the Peace** juez de paz

justifiable ['dʒʌstɪfaɪəbəl] *adj* justificable

justification [dʒʌstɪfɪ'keɪʃən] *n* justificación *f*

justified ['dʒʌstɪfaɪd] *adj* **to be j. in doing sth** tener razón en hacer algo

justify ['dʒʌstɪfaɪ] *vt* justificar

jut [dʒʌt] *vi* sobresalir; **to j. out over** proyectarse sobre

juvenile ['dʒuːvənaɪl] **1** *adj* (**a**) juvenil; **j. court** tribunal *m* de menores; **j. delinquent** delincuente *mf* juvenil (**b**) *(immature)* infantil

2 *n* menor *mf*, joven *mf*

juxtapose [dʒʌkstə'pəʊz] *vt* yuxtaponer

K

K, k [keɪ] *n* (*the letter*) K, k *f*

kaleidoscope [kə'laɪdəskəʊp] *n* caleidoscopio *m*

Kampuchea [kæmpʊ'tʃɪə] *n* Kampuchea

kangaroo [kæŋgə'ruː] *n* canguro *m*

karat ['kærət] *n US* quilate *m*

karate [kə'rɑːtɪ] *n* kárate *m*

kebab [kə'bæb] *n Culin* pincho moruno, brocheta *f*

keel [kiːl] *n* quilla *f*; *Fig* **to be on an even k.** estar en calma
  ▸ **keel over** *vi Fam* desmayarse

keen [kiːn] *adj* (**a**) (*eager*) entusiasta (**b**) (*intense*) profundo(a) (**c**) (*mind, senses*) agudo(a); (*look*) penetrante; (*blade*) afilado(a); (*competition*) fuerte

keep [kiːp] **1** *n* (**a**) **to earn one's k.** ganarse el pan
  (**b**) (*tower*) torreón *m*
  (**c**) *Fam* **for keeps** para siempre
2 *vt* (*pt & pp* **kept**) (**a**) guardar; **to k. one's room tidy** mantener su cuarto limpio; **to k. sb informed** tener a algn al corriente; **to k. sth in mind** tener algo en cuenta
  (**b**) (*not give back*) quedarse con
  (**c**) (*detain*) detener; **to k. sb waiting** hacer esperar a algn
  (**d**) (*maintain*) mantener; (*animals*) criar
  (**e**) (*the law*) observar; (*a promise*) cumplir
  (**f**) (*a secret*) guardar
  (**g**) (*diary, accounts*) llevar
  (**h**) (*prevent*) **to k. sb from doing sth** impedir a algn hacer algo
  (**i**) (*own, manage*) tener; (*shop, hotel*) llevar
  (**j**) (*stock*) tener
3 *vi* (**a**) (*remain*) seguir; **k. still!** ¡estáte quieto/a!; **to k. fit** mantenerse en forma; **to k. going** seguir adelante; **to k. in touch** no perder el contacto
  (**b**) (*do frequently*) no dejar de; **she keeps forgetting her keys** siempre se olvida las llaves
  (**c**) (*food*) conservarse
  ▸ **keep at** *vt insep* perseverar en
  ▸ **keep away 1** *vt sep* mantener a distancia
  2 *vi* mantenerse a distancia
  ▸ **keep back** *vt sep* (*information*) ocultar, callar; (*money etc*) retener
  ▸ **keep down** *vt sep* **to k. prices down** mantener los precios bajos
  ▸ **keep off** *vt insep* **k. off the grass** (*sign*) prohibido pisar la hierba
  ▸ **keep on 1** *vt sep* (**a**) (*clothes etc*) no quitarse; **to k. an eye on sth/sb** vigilar algo/a algn (**b**) (*continue to employ*) no despedir a
  2 *vi* (*continue to do*) seguir
  ▸ **keep out 1** *vt sep* no dejar pasar
  2 *vi* no entrar; **k. out!** (*sign*) ¡prohibida la entrada!
  ▸ **keep to** *vt insep* (*subject*) limitarse a; **to k. to one's room** quedarse en el cuarto; **k. to the point!** ¡cíñete a la cuestión!; **to k. to the left** circular por la izquierda
  ▸ **keep up** *vt sep* (**a**) mantener; **to k. up appearances** guardar las apariencias (**b**) **k. it up!** ¡sigue así! (**c**) (*prevent from sleeping*) mantener despierto(a)
  ▸ **keep up with** *vt insep* **to k. up with the times** estar al día

keeper ['kiːpə(r)] *n* (*in zoo*) guarda *mf*; (*in record office*) archivero(a) *m,f*; (*in museum*) conservador(a) *m,f*

keeping ['kiːpɪŋ] *n* (**a**) (*care*) cuidado *m* (**b**) **in k. with** en armonía con; **out of k. with** en desacuerdo con

keepsake ['kiːpseɪk] *n* recuerdo *m*

keg [keg] *n* barril *m*

kennel ['kenəl] *n* caseta *f* para perros; **kennels** hotel *m* de perros

Kenya ['kenjə, 'kiːnjə] *n* Kenia

Kenyan ['kenjən, 'kiːnjən] *adj & n* keniano(a) *(m,f)*

kept [kept] *pt & pp of* **keep**

kerb [kɜːb] *n Br* bordillo *m*

kernel ['kɜːnəl] *n* (*of fruit, nut*) pepita *f*; (*of wheat*) grano *m*; *Fig* meollo *m*

kerosene, kerosine ['kerəsiːn] *n US* queroseno *m*

ketchup ['ketʃəp] *n* ketchup *m*, salsa *f* de tomate

kettle ['ketəl] *n* hervidor *m*; **that's a different k. of fish** eso es harina de otro costal

key [kiː] **1** *n* (**a**) *(for lock)* llave *f*; **k. ring** llavero *m* (**b**) *(to code)* clave *f* (**c**) *(of piano, typewriter)* tecla *f* (**d**) *Mus* tono *m*
2 *adj* clave; *Br Educ* **k. stage** etapa educativa
3 *vt Comput* teclear
▶ **key in** *vt sep Comput* introducir
keyboard ['kiːbɔːd] *n* teclado *m*
keyed up [kiːd'ʌp] *adj* nervioso(a)
keyhole ['kiːhəʊl] *n* ojo *m* de la cerradura
keynote ['kiːnəʊt] *n Mus* tónica *f*; *Fig* nota *f* dominante
kg *(abbr* **kilogram(s))** kg
khaki ['kɑːkɪ] *adj & n* caqui *(m)*
kick [kɪk] **1** *n* (**a**) *(from person)* patada *f*, puntapié *m*; *(from horse etc)* coz *f*; *(from gun)* culatazo *m* (**b**) *Fam* **I get a k. out of it** eso me encanta; **to do sth for kicks** hacer algo por gusto
2 *vi (animal)* cocear; *(person)* dar patadas; *(gun)* dar un culatazo
3 *vt* dar un puntapié a
▶ **kick off** *vi Fam* empezar; *Ftb* sacar
▶ **kick out** *vt sep* echar a patadas
▶ **kick up** *vt insep Fam (fuss)* armar
kick-off ['kɪkɒf] *n Ftb* saque *m* inicial
kid¹ [kɪd] *n* (**a**) *Zool* cabrito *m*; *Fig* **to handle sb with k. gloves** tratar a algn con guante blanco (**b**) *Fam* niño(a) *m,f*, chiquillo(a) *m,f*; **the kids** los críos
kid² [kɪd] **1** *vi Fam* tomar el pelo; **no kidding!** ¡va en serio!
2 *vt* tomar el pelo a; **to k. oneself** *(fool)* hacerse ilusiones
kidnap ['kɪdnæp] *vt* secuestrar
kidnapper ['kɪdnæpə(r)] *n* secuestrador(a) *m,f*
kidnapping ['kɪdnæpɪŋ] *n* secuestro *m*
kidney ['kɪdnɪ] *n* riñón *m*
kill [kɪl] *vt* matar; *Fig* **to k. time** pasar el rato; *Fam* **my feet are killing me!** ¡cómo me duelen los pies!
▶ **kill off** *vt sep* exterminar
killer ['kɪlə(r)] *n* asesino(a) *m,f*; **k. whale** orca *f*
killing ['kɪlɪŋ] *n* asesinato *m*; *Fig* **to make a k.** forrarse de dinero
killjoy ['kɪldʒɔɪ] *n* aguafiestas *mf inv*
kiln [kɪln] *n* horno *m*
kilo ['kiːləʊ] *n* kilo *m*
kilogram(me) ['kɪləʊgræm] *n* kilogramo *m*
kilometre, *US* **kilometer** [kɪ'lɒmɪtə(r)] *n* kilómetro *m*
kilowatt ['kɪləʊwɒt] *n* kilovatio *m*
kilt [kɪlt] *n* falda escocesa, kilt *m*
kin [kɪn] *n* familiares *mpl*, parientes *mpl*

kind¹ [kaɪnd] **1** *n* tipo *m*, clase *f*; **they are two of a k.** son tal para cual; **in k.** *(payment)* en especie; *(treatment)* con la misma moneda
2 *adv Fam* **k. of** en cierta manera
kind² ['kaɪnd] *adj* amable, simpático(a); *Fml* **would you be so k. as to ...?** ¿me haría usted el favor de ...?
kindergarten ['kɪndəgɑːtən] *n* jardín *m* de infancia
kind-hearted [kaɪnd'hɑːtɪd] *adj* bondadoso(a)
kindle ['kɪndəl] *vt* encender
kindly ['kaɪndlɪ] **1** *adj* (**kindlier, kindliest**) amable, bondadoso(a)
2 *adv Fml (please)* por favor; **k. remit a cheque** sírvase enviar cheque; **to look k. on** aprobar
kindness ['kaɪndnɪs] *n* bondad *f*, amabilidad *f*
kindred ['kɪndrɪd] *adj* **k. spirits** almas gemelas
kinetic [kɪ'netɪk] *adj* cinético(a)
king [kɪŋ] *n* rey *m*; *(draughts)* dama *f*
kingdom ['kɪŋdəm] *n* reino *m*
kingfisher ['kɪŋfɪʃə(r)] *n Orn* martín *m* pescador
king-size ['kɪŋsaɪz] *adj* extralargo(a)
kink [kɪŋk] *n (in rope)* coca *f*; *(in hair)* rizo *m*
kinky ['kɪŋkɪ] *adj* (**kinkier, kinkiest**) *Fam* raro(a); *(sexually)* pervertido(a)
kiosk ['kiːɒsk] *n* quiosco *m*
kiss [kɪs] **1** *n* beso *m*
2 *vt* besar
3 *vi* besarse
kit [kɪt] *n* (**a**) *(gear)* equipo *m*; *Mil* avíos *mpl* (**b**) *(clothing)* ropa *f* (**c**) *(toy model)* maqueta *f*
▶ **kit out** *vt sep* equipar
kitchen ['kɪtʃɪn] *n* cocina *f*; **k. sink** fregadero *m*
kite [kaɪt] *n* (**a**) *(toy)* cometa *f* (**b**) *Orn* milano *m*
kitten ['kɪtən] *n* gatito(a) *m,f*
kitty ['kɪtɪ] *n* (**a**) *(money)* fondo *m* común; *Cards* bote *m*
kiwi ['kiːwiː] *n Bot & Orn* kiwi *m*
km *(pl* **km** *or* **kms)** *(abbr* **kilometre(s))** km
knack [næk] *n* **to get the k. of doing sth** cogerle el truquillo a algo
knapsack ['næpsæk] *n* mochila *f*
knead [niːd] *vt* dar masaje a; *(bread etc)* amasar
knee [niː] **1** *n* rodilla *f*
2 *vt* dar un rodillazo a
kneecap ['niːkæp] **1** *n* rótula *f*
2 *vt* romper la rótula a

kneel [niːl] *vi* (*pt & pp* **knelt**) **to k. (down)** arrodillarse

knell [nel] *n Literary* toque *m* de difuntos

knelt [nelt] *pt & pp of* **kneel**

knew [njuː] *pt of* **know**

knickers ['nɪkəz] *npl Br* bragas *fpl*

knife [naɪf] **1** *n* (*pl* **knives**) cuchillo *m*
2 *vt* apuñalar, dar una puñalada a

knight [naɪt] **1** *n Hist* caballero *m*; (*in chess*) caballo *m*
2 *vt* armar caballero

knighthood ['naɪthʊd] *n* (*rank*) título *m* de caballero

knit [nɪt] **1** *vt* (*pt & pp* **knitted** *or* **knit**) (a) tejer (**b**) **to k. (together)** (*join*) juntar; *Fig* **to k. one's brow** fruncir el ceño
2 *vi* (**a**) tejer, hacer punto (**b**) (*bone*) soldarse

knitting ['nɪtɪŋ] *n* punto *m*; **k. machine** máquina *f* de tejer; **k. needle** aguja *f* de tejer

knitwear ['nɪtweə(r)] *n* géneros *mpl* de punto

knives [naɪvz] *pl of* **knife**

knob [nɒb] *n* (**a**) (*of stick*) puño *m*; (*of drawer*) tirador *m*; (*button*) botón *m* (**b**) (*small portion*) trozo *m*

knock [nɒk] **1** *n* golpe *m*; *Fig* revés *m*
2 *vt* (**a**) golpear (**b**) *Fam* (*criticize*) criticar
3 *vi* chocar (**against** *or* **into** contra); (*at door*) llamar (**at** a)
▸ **knock down** *vt sep* (**a**) (*demolish*) derribar (**b**) *Aut* atropellar (**c**) (*price*) rebajar
▸ **knock off 1** *vt sep* (**a**) tirar (**b**) *Fam* (*steal*) birlar (**c**) *Fam* (*kill*) liquidar
2 *vi Fam* **they k. off at five** se piran a las cinco
▸ **knock out** *vt sep* (**a**) (*make unconscious*) dejar sin conocimiento; (*in boxing*) poner fuera de combate, derrotar por K.O. (**b**) (*surprise*) dejar pasmado(a)
▸ **knock over** *vt sep* (*cup*) volcar; (*with car*) atropellar

knocker ['nɒkə(r)] *n* (*on door*) aldaba *f*

knock-kneed [nɒk'niːd] *adj* patizambo(a)

knockout ['nɒkaʊt] *n* (**a**) (*in boxing*) K.O. *m*, knock-out *m* (**b**) *Fam* maravilla *f*

knot [nɒt] **1** *n* nudo *m*; (*group*) grupo *m*
2 *vt* anudar

knotty ['nɒtɪ] *adj* (**knottier**, **knottiest**) nudoso(a); *Fig* **a k. problem** un problema espinoso

know [nəʊ] *vt & vi* (*pt* **knew**; *pp* **known**) (**a**) saber; **as far as I k.** que yo sepa; **she knows how to ski** sabe esquiar; **to get to k. sth** enterarse de algo; **to let sb k.** avisar al algn (**b**) (*be acquainted with*) conocer; **we got to k. each other at the party** nos conocimos en la fiesta

know-all ['nəʊɔːl] *n Fam* sabelotodo *mf*

know-how ['nəʊhaʊ] *n Fam* conocimiento práctico

knowing ['nəʊɪŋ] *adj* (*deliberate*) deliberado(a); **a k. smile** una sonrisa de complicidad

knowingly ['nəʊɪŋlɪ] *adv* (*shrewdly*) a sabiendas; (*deliberately*) deliberadamente

knowledge ['nɒlɪdʒ] *n* (**a**) conocimiento *m*; **without my k.** sin saberlo yo (**b**) (*learning*) conocimientos *mpl*

knowledgeable ['nɒlɪdʒəbəl] *adj* erudito(a); **k. about** muy entendido(a) en

known [nəʊn] **1** *adj* conocido(a)
2 *pp of* **know**

knuckle ['nʌkəl] *n Anat* nudillo *m*; *Culin* hueso *m*
▸ **knuckle down** *vi Fam* ponerse a trabajar en serio

KO [keɪ'əʊ] *n Fam* (*abbr* **knockout**) K.O. *m*

Koran [kɔː'rɑːn] *n* Corán *m*

Korea [kə'riːə] *n* Corea

Korean [kə'riːən] *adj & n* coreano(a) (*m,f*)

Kurd [kɜːd] *n* curdo(a) *m,f*

Kuwait [kʊ'weɪt] *n* Kuwait

L

L, l [el] *n (the letter)* L, l *f*

lab [læb] *n Fam (abbr* **laboratory***)* laboratorio *m*

label ['leɪbəl] **1** *n* etiqueta *f*; **record l.** ≃ casa discográfica

2 *vt* poner etiqueta a

labor ['leɪbər] *n, adj, vt & vi US =* **labour**

laboratory [ləˈbɒrətərɪ, *US* ˈlæbrətɔːrɪ] *n* laboratorio *m*

laborious [ləˈbɔːrɪəs] *adj* penoso(a)

labour ['leɪbə(r)] **1** *n* **(a)** *(work)* trabajo *m; (task)* tarea *f* **(b)** *(workforce)* mano *f* de obra **(c)** **labours** esfuerzos *mpl* **(d)** **the L. Party** el Partido Laborista **(e)** *(childbirth)* parto *m;* **to be in l.** estar de parto

2 *adj* laboral

3 *vt (stress, linger on)* machacar; *(a point)* insistir en

4 *vi* **(a)** *(work)* trabajar (duro) **(b)** *(move with difficulty)* avanzar penosamente

laboured ['leɪbəd] *adj (breathing)* fatigoso(a); *(style)* forzado(a)

labourer ['leɪbərə(r)] *n* peón *m;* **farm l.** peón *m* agrícola

labour-saving ['leɪbəseɪvɪŋ] *adj* **l. devices** electrodomésticos *mpl*

labyrinth ['læbərɪnθ] *n* laberinto *m*

lace [leɪs] **1** *n* **(a)** *(fabric)* encaje *m* **(b)** **laces** cordones *mpl*

2 *vt* **(a)** *(shoes)* atar (los cordones de) **(b)** *(add spirits to)* echar licor a

▸ **lace up** *vt sep* atar con cordones

lacerate ['læsəreɪt] *vt* lacerar

lack [læk] **1** *n* falta *f*, escasez *f;* **for l. of** por falta de

2 *vt* carecer de

3 *vi* carecer (**in** de)

lackadaisical [lækəˈdeɪzɪkəl] *adj (lazy)* perezoso(a); *(indifferent)* indiferente

lacklustre, *US* **lackluster** ['læklʌstə(r)] *adj (eyes)* apagado(a); *(performance)* anodino(a)

laconic [ləˈkɒnɪk] *adj* lacónico(a)

lacquer ['lækə(r)] **1** *n* laca *f*

2 *vt (hair)* poner laca en

lad [læd] *n Fam* chaval *m*, muchacho *m; Fam* **the lads** los amigotes; **(stable) l.** mozo *m* de cuadra

ladder ['lædə(r)] **1** *n* **(a)** escalera *f* (de mano); *Fig* escala *f* **(b)** *(in stocking)* carrera *f*

2 *vt* **I've laddered my stocking** me he hecho una carrera en las medias

laden ['leɪdən] *adj* cargado(a) (**with** de)

ladle ['leɪdəl] *n* cucharón *m*

lady ['leɪdɪ] *n* señora *f; Pol* **First L.** primera dama; **Ladies** *(sign on WC)* Señoras; **ladies and gentlemen!** ¡señoras y señores!; **L. Brown** Lady Brown

ladybird ['leɪdɪbɜːd], *US* **ladybug** ['leɪdɪbʌg] *n* mariquita *f*

lady-in-waiting [leɪdɪɪnˈweɪtɪŋ] *n* dama *f* de honor

ladylike ['leɪdɪlaɪk] *adj* elegante

ladyship ['leɪdɪʃɪp] *n* **her l./your l.** su señoría

lag [læg] **1** *n* **time l.** demora *f*

2 *vi* **to l. (behind)** quedarse atrás, retrasarse

3 *vt Tech* revestir

lager ['lɑːgə(r)] *n* cerveza rubia

lagoon [ləˈguːn] *n* laguna *f*

laid [leɪd] *pt & pp of* **lay**

laid-back [leɪdˈbæk] *adj Fam* tranquilo(a)

lain [leɪn] *pp of* **lie²**

lair [leə(r)] *n* guarida *f*

lake [leɪk] *n* lago *m*

lamb [læm] *n* cordero *m; (meat)* carne *f* de cordero; **l. chop** chuleta *f* de cordero; **l.'s wool** lana *f* de cordero

lame [leɪm] *adj* **(a)** cojo(a) **(b)** *Fig (excuse)* poco convincente; *(argument)* flojo(a)

lament [ləˈment] **1** *n Mus* elegia *f*

2 *vt (death)* llorar, lamentar

3 *vi* llorar (**for** a), lamentarse (**over** de)

lamentable ['læməntəbəl] *adj* lamentable

laminated ['læmɪneɪtɪd] *adj (metal)* laminado(a); *(glass)* inastillable; *(paper)* plastificado(a)

lamp [læmp] *n* lámpara *f; Aut* faro *m*

lampoon [læmˈpuːn] **1** *n* sátira *f*

2 *vt* satirizar

lamp-post ['læmppəʊst] *n* farola *f*

lampshade ['læmpʃeɪd] *n* pantalla *f*

lance [lɑːns] **1** *n* lanza *f; Br Mil* **l. corporal**

cabo interino; *Med* lanceta *f*
  2 *vt Med* abrir con lanceta

> 🖉 Note that the Spanish word **lance** is a false friend and is never a translation for the English word **lance**. In Spanish, **lance** means "event, incident".

land [lænd] **1** *n* (**a**) *(plane)* tierra *f*; *(soil)* suelo *m*; **by l.** por tierra; **farm l.** tierras *fpl* de cultivo (**b**) *(country)* país *m* (**c**) *(property)* tierras *fpl*; *(estate)* finca *f*; **piece of l.** terreno *m*
  2 *vt* (**a**) *(plane)* hacer aterrizar (**b**) *(disembark)* desembarcar (**c**) *(fish)* pescar (**d**) *Fam (obtain)* conseguir; *(contract)* ganar (**e**) *Fam* **she got landed with the responsibility** tuvo que cargar con la responsabilidad (**f**) *Fam (blow)* asestar
  3 *vi* (**a**) *(plane)* aterrizar (**b**) *(disembark)* desembarcar (**c**) *(after falling)* caer (**in** sobre)
  ▸ **land up** *vi Fam* ir a parar

landing ['lændɪŋ] *n* (**a**) *(of staircase)* rellano *m* (**b**) *(of plane)* aterrizaje *m*; **l. strip** pista *f* de aterrizaje (**c**) *(of passengers)* desembarco *m*; **l. stage** desembarcadero *m*

landlady ['lændleɪdɪ] *n (of flat)* dueña *f*, propietaria *f*; *(of boarding house)* patrona *f*; *(of pub)* dueña

landlord ['lændlɔːd] *n (of flat)* dueño *m*, propietario *m*; *(of pub)* patrón *m*, dueño

landmark ['lændmɑːk] *n* (**a**) señal *f*, marca *f*; *(well-known place)* lugar muy conocido (**b**) *Fig* hito *m*

landowner ['lændəʊnə(r)] *n* terrateniente *mf*

landscape ['lændskeɪp] **1** *n* paisaje *m*
  2 *vt* ajardinar

landslide ['lændslaɪd] *n* desprendimiento *m* de tierras; **l. victory** victoria arrolladora

lane [leɪn] *n (in country)* camino *m*; *(in town)* callejón *m*; *(of motorway)* carril *m*; *Sport* calle *f*; *Naut* ruta *f*

language ['læŋgwɪdʒ] *n* (**a**) lenguaje *m*; **bad l.** palabrotas *fpl* (**b**) *(of a country)* idioma *m*, lengua *f*; **l. laboratory** laboratorio *m* de idiomas; **l. school** academia *f* de idiomas

languid ['læŋgwɪd] *adj* lánguido(a)

languish ['læŋgwɪʃ] *vi* languidecer; *(project, plan etc)* quedar abandonado(a); *(in prison)* pudrirse

lank [læŋk] *adj (hair)* lacio(a)

lanky ['læŋkɪ] *adj* (**lankier, lankiest**) larguirucho(a)

lantern ['læntən] *n* farol *m*

lap¹ [læp] *n Anat* regazo *m*

lap² [læp] **1** *n (circuit)* vuelta *f*; *Fig* etapa *f*
  2 *vt (overtake)* doblar

lap³ [læp] **1** *vt (pt & pp lapped) (of cat)* beber a lengüetadas
  2 *vi (waves)* lamer, besar
  ▸ **lap up** *vt sep* (**a**) *(of cat)* beber a lengüetadas (**b**) *Fig (wallow in)* disfrutar con; *(flattery)* recibir con estusiasmo (**c**) *Fig (believe)* tragar

lapel [lə'pel] *n* solapa *f*

Lapland ['læplænd] *n* Laponia

lapse [læps] **1** *n* (**a**) *(of time)* lapso *m* (**b**) *(error)* error *m*, desliz *m*; *(of memory)* fallo *m*
  2 *vi* (**a**) *(time)* pasar, transcurrir (**b**) *(expire)* caducar (**c**) *(err)* cometer un error; *(fall back)* caer (**into** en) (**d**) *Rel* perder la fe

larceny ['lɑːsənɪ] *n Br* latrocinio *m*; *US* hurto *m*

larch [lɑːtʃ] *n* alerce *m*

lard [lɑːd] *n* manteca *f* de cerdo

larder ['lɑːdə(r)] *n* despensa *f*

large [lɑːdʒ] **1** *adj* grande; *(amount)* importante; *(extensive)* amplio(a); **by and l.** por lo general
  2 *n* **to be at l.** andar suelto(a); **the public at l.** el público en general

> 🖉 Note that the Spanish word **largo** is a false friend and is never a translation for the English word **large**. In Spanish, **largo** means "long".

largely ['lɑːdʒlɪ] *adv (mainly)* en gran parte; *(chiefly)* principalmente

large-scale ['lɑːdʒskeɪl] *adj (project, problem etc)* de gran envergadura; *(map)* a gran escala

lark¹ [lɑːk] *n Orn* alondra *f*

lark² [lɑːk] *n Fam (joke)* broma *f*; **what a l.!** ¡qué risa!
  ▸ **lark about, lark around** *vi Fam* hacer el tonto

larva ['lɑːvə] *n* larva *f*

laryngitis [lærɪn'dʒaɪtɪs] *n* laringitis *f*

larynx ['lærɪŋks] *n Anat* laringe *f*

laser ['leɪzə(r)] *n* láser *m*; **l. printer** impresora *f* láser

lash [læʃ] **1** *n* (**a**) *(eyelash)* pestaña *f* (**b**) *(blow with whip)* latigazo *m*
  2 *vt* (**a**) *(beat)* azotar (**b**) *(rain)* azotar (**c**) *(tie)* atar
  ▸ **lash out** *vi* (**a**) *(with fists)* repartir golpes a diestro y siniestro; *(verbally)* criticar (**at** a) (**b**) *Fam (spend money)* tirar la casa por la ventana

lass [læs] *n Fam* chavala *f*, muchacha *f*

lasso [læ'su:] **1** n lazo m
  2 vt coger con el lazo

last [lɑːst] **1** adj (**a**) (final) último(a), final;
Fam **the l. straw** el colmo (**b**) (most recent) último(a) (**c**) (past) pasado(a); (previous) anterior; **l. but one** penúltimo(a); **l.
month** el mes pasado; **l. night** anoche;
the night before l. anteanoche
  2 adv (**a**) **when l l. saw her** la última vez
que la vi (**b**) (at the end) en último lugar;
(in race etc) último; **at (long) l.** por fin; **l.
but not least** el último en orden pero no
en importancia
  3 n **the l.** el último/la última
  4 vi (**a**) (time) durar; (hold out) aguantar
(**b**) (be enough for) llegar, alcanzar

last-ditch ['lɑːstdɪtʃ] adj (effort, attempt)
último(a) y desesperado(a)

lasting ['lɑːstɪŋ] adj duradero(a)

lastly ['lɑːstlɪ] adv por último, finalmente

last-minute ['lɑːstmɪnɪt] adj de última
hora

latch [lætʃ] n picaporte m, pestillo m

late [leɪt] **1** adj (**a**) (not on time) tardío(a);
(hour) avanzado(a); **to be five minutes l.**
llegar con cinco minutos de retraso (**b**)
(far on in time) tarde; **in l. autumn** a
finales del otoño; **in the l. afternoon** a
última hora de la tarde; **she's in her l.
twenties** ronda los treinta (**c**) (dead)
difunto(a)
  2 adv (**a**) (not on time) tarde; **to arrive l.**
llegar tarde (**b**) (far on in time) tarde; **l. at
night** a altas horas de la noche; **l. in life**
una edad avanzada (**c**) **as l. as 1950**
todavía en 1950; **of l.** últimamente

latecomer ['leɪtkʌmə(r)] n tardón(ona)
m,f

lately ['leɪtlɪ] adv últimamente, recientemente

latent ['leɪtənt] adj (**a**) latente (**b**) (desire) oculto(a)

later ['leɪtə(r)] **1** adj (**a**) (subsequent) más
tarde; **in her l. novels** en sus novelas
posteriores (**b**) (more recent) más reciente
  2 adv más tarde, después; **l. on** más
adelante, más tarde

lateral ['lætərəl] adj lateral

latest ['leɪtɪst] **1** adj (superl of **late**) (most
recent) último(a), más reciente
  2 n **the l.** lo último; **have you heard the
l.?** ¿te enteraste de lo último?; **Friday at
the l.** el viernes a más tardar

lathe [leɪð] n Tech torno m

lather ['lɑːðə(r)] **1** n (of soap) espuma f;
(horse's sweat) sudor m
  2 vt (with soap) enjabonar

Latin ['lætɪn] **1** adj & n latino(a) (m,f); **L.
America** América Latina, Latinoamérica;
L. American latinoamericano(a) (m,f)
  2 n (language) latín m

latitude ['lætɪtjuːd] n latitud f

latrine [lə'triːn] n letrina f

latter ['lætə(r)] **1** adj (**a**) (last) último(a)
(**b**) (second of two) segundo(a)
  2 pron éste(a); **the former … the l.** aquél
… éste/aquélla … ésta

lattice ['lætɪs] n enrejado m, rejilla f

laudable ['lɔːdəbəl] adj loable

laugh [lɑːf] **1** n risa f; (guffaw) carcajada f;
for a l. para divertirse
  2 vi reír, reírse
  ▶ **laugh at** vt insep **to l. at sb/sth** reírse de
algn/algo
  ▶ **laugh about** vt insep **to l. about sb/sth**
reírse de algn/algo
  ▶ **laugh off** vt sep tomar a risa

laughable ['lɑːfəbəl] adj (situation, suggestion) ridículo(a); (amount, offer) irrisorio(a)

laughing-stock ['lɑːfɪŋstɒk] n hazmerreír m inv

laughter ['lɑːftə(r)] n risa f

launch [lɔːntʃ] **1** n (**a**) (vessel) lancha f
(**b**) = **launching**
  2 vt (**a**) (attack, rocket, new product)
lanzar (**b**) (ship) botar (**c**) (film, play)
estrenar (**d**) (company) fundar (**e**) Fig
(scheme) iniciar

launching ['lɔːntʃɪŋ] n (**a**) (of rocket, new
product) lanzamiento m (**b**) (of ship) botadura f (**c**) (of film, play) estreno m (**d**)
(of new company) fundación f

launchpad ['lɔːntʃpæd] n plataforma f de
lanzamiento

launder ['lɔːndə(r)] vt lavar y planchar;
Fig (money) blanquear

launderette [lɔːndə'ret], US **Laundromat**® ['lɔːndrəmæt] n lavandería automática

laundry ['lɔːndrɪ] n (**a**) (place) lavandería f (**b**) (dirty clothes) ropa sucia; **to do
the l.** lavar la ropa

laurel ['lɒrəl] n laurel m; Fam Fig **to rest
on one's laurels** dormirse en los laureles

lava ['lɑːvə] n lava f

lavatory ['lævətərɪ] n (**a**) excusado m,
retrete m (**b**) (room) baño m; **public l.**
servicios mpl, aseos mpl

lavender ['lævəndə(r)] n lavanda f

lavish ['lævɪʃ] **1** adj (**a**) (generous) pródigo(a) (**b**) (abundant) abundante (**c**)
(luxurious) lujoso(a)
  2 vt **to l. praise on sb** colmar de alabanzas a alguien; **to l. attention on sb**

prodigarse en atenciones con alguien

law [lɔː] n (a) ley f; **by l.** según la ley; **l. and order** el orden público; **to lay down the l.** dictar la ley (b) (as subject) derecho m; **l. court** tribunal m de justicia (c) Fam **the l.** los maderos

law-abiding ['lɔːəbaɪdɪŋ] adj respetuoso(a) de la ley

lawful ['lɔːfʊl] adj legal; (permitted by law) lícito(a); (legitimate) legítimo(a)

lawn [lɔːn] n césped m; **l. tennis** tenis m sobre hierba

lawnmower ['lɔːnməʊə(r)] n cortacésped m

lawsuit ['lɔːsjuːt] n pleito m

lawyer ['lɔːjə(r)] n abogado(a) m,f; **l.'s office** bufete m de abogados

lax [læks] adj (not strict) relajado(a); (not demanding) poco exigente; (careless) descuidado(a)

laxative ['læksətɪv] adj & n laxante (m)

laxity ['læksɪtɪ] n relajamiento m; (carelessness) descuido m; (negligence) negligencia f

lay¹ [leɪ] adj (a) Rel laico(a) (b) (non-specialist) lego(a)

lay² [leɪ] vt (pt & pp laid) (a) (place) poner, colocar; (cable, trap) tender; (foundations) echar (b) (fire) preparar; (table) poner (c) (leave) dejar (d) (eggs) poner (e) very Fam (have sex with) follar (f) (set down) asentar; (blame) echar
▸ **lay aside** vt sep dejar a un lado
▸ **lay by** vt sep (save) guardar; (money) ahorrar
▸ **lay down** vt sep (a) (put down) poner; (let go) dejar; **to l. down one's arms** rendir las armas (b) (plan) formular (c) (establish) fijar, imponer; (principles) sentar
▸ **lay into** vt insep Fam (physically) dar una paliza a; (verbally) arremeter contra
▸ **lay off 1** vt sep (dismiss) despedir
2 vt insep Fam dejar en paz
3 vi **l. off!** ¡para ya!
▸ **lay on** vt sep (a) (provide) proveer de; (food) preparar (b) (spread) aplicar; Fam **to l. it on (thick)** cargar las tintas
▸ **lay out** vt sep (a) (open out) extender (b) (arrange) disponer (c) (ideas) exponer (d) (plan) trazar (e) Fam (spend) gastar (f) Fam (knock out) derribar
▸ **lay up** vt sep (a) (store) guardar (b) (accumulate) almacenar (c) Fam **to be laid up** tener que guardar cama

lay³ [leɪ] pt of **lie²**

layabout ['leɪəbaʊt] n Fam vago(a) m,f

lay-by ['leɪbaɪ] n área f de descanso

layer ['leɪə(r)] n capa f

layman ['leɪmən] n lego(a) m,f

layout ['leɪaʊt] n (arrangement) disposición f; (presentation) presentación f; Typ composición f; (plan) diseño m, trazado m

laze [leɪz] vi holgazanear, gandulear

laziness ['leɪzɪnɪs] n pereza f, holgazanería f

lazy ['leɪzɪ] adj (lazier, laziest) perezoso(a), holgazán(ana); **at a l. pace** a paso lento

lb (abbr **pound**) libra f

lead¹ [led] n (a) (metal) plomo m (b) (in pencil) mina f

lead² [liːd] **1** n (a) (front position) delantera f; (advantage) ventaja f; **to take the l.** (in race) tomar la delantera; (score) adelantarse
(b) (clue) pista f
(c) Th primer papel m; **l. singer** cantante mf principal
(d) (leash) correa f
(e) Elec cable m
2 vt (pt & pp led) (a) (conduct) llevar, conducir
(b) (be the leader of) dirigir, encabezar
(c) (influence) llevar a; **this leads me to believe that** esto me lleva a creer que; **she's easily led** se deja llevar fácilmente
(d) (life) llevar
3 vi (a) (road) llevar, conducir (**to** a)
(b) (go first) ir delante; (in race) llevar la delantera
(c) **to l. to** llevar a
▸ **lead away** vt sep llevar
▸ **lead on 1** vi (go ahead) ir adelante
2 vt sep (deceive) engañar, timar
▸ **lead up to** vt insep llevar a

leaden ['ledən] adj (sky) plomizo(a); (food) pesado(a)

leader ['liːdə(r)] n (a) jefe(a) m,f, líder mf; (in race) líder (b) Press editorial m, artículo m de fondo

leadership ['liːdəʃɪp] n (a) (command) dirección f, mando m; Pol liderazgo m (b) (leaders) dirigentes mpl, cúpula f

lead-free ['ledfriː] adj sin plomo

leading ['liːdɪŋ] adj (a) (main) principal (b) (outstanding) destacado(a)

leaf [liːf] n (pl leaves) hoja f; **to turn over a new l.** hacer borrón y cuenta nueva
▸ **leaf through** vt insep hojear

leaflet ['liːflɪt] n folleto m

league [liːg] n (a) (alliance) alianza f; (association) sociedad f; Fam **to be in l. with sb** estar conchabado(a) con algn (b) Sport liga f

leak [liːk] **1** n (a) (hole) agujero m; (in

roof) gotera f (**b**) *(of gas, liquid)* fuga f, escape m; *(of information)* filtración f

2 vi (**a**) *(container)* tener un agujero; *(pipe)* tener un escape; *(roof)* gotear; *(boat)* hacer agua (**b**) *(gas, liquid)* escaparse; *(information)* filtrarse; *(news)* trascender

3 vt *(information)* filtrar (**to** a)

leaky ['li:kɪ] adj (**leakier, leakiest**) *(container)* agujereado(a); *(roof)* que tiene goteras; *(ship)* que hace agua

lean¹ [li:n] adj *(meat)* magro(a); *(person)* flaco(a); *(harvest)* escaso(a)

lean² [li:n] **1** vi (pt & pp **leaned** or **leant**) (**a**) inclinarse (**b**) to **l. on/against** apoyarse en/contra; Fig to **l. on sb** *(pressurize)* presionar a algn; *(depend)* depender de algn

2 vt apoyar (**on** en)
▸ **lean back** vi reclinarse
▸ **lean forward** vi inclinarse hacia delante
▸ **lean out** vi asomarse
▸ **lean over** vi inclinarse

leaning ['li:nɪŋ] **1** adj inclinado(a)

2 n Fig *(tendency)* inclinación f, tendencia f

leant [lent] pt & pp of **lean**

lean-to ['li:ntu:] n *(hut)* cobertizo m

leap [li:p] **1** n *(jump)* salto m; Fig paso m; **l. year** año bisiesto

2 vi (pt & pp **leaped** or **leapt**) saltar; Fig **her heart leapt** su corazón dio un vuelco
▸ **leap at** vt insep Fig *(chance)* no dejar escapar

leapfrog ['li:pfrɒg] n pídola f

leapt [lept] pt & pp of **leap**

learn [lɜ:n] **1** vt (pt & pp **learned** or **learnt**) (**a**) aprender; to **l. (how) to ski** aprender a esquiar (**b**) to **l. that** enterarse de que

2 vi (**a**) aprender (**b**) to **l. about** or **of** *(find out)* enterarse de

learned ['lɜ:nɪd] adj erudito(a)

learner ['lɜ:nə(r)] n *(beginner)* principiante mf; **l. driver** aprendiz(a) m,f de conductor

learning ['lɜ:nɪŋ] n *(knowledge)* conocimientos mpl; *(erudition)* saber m

learnt [lɜ:nt] pt & pp of **learn**

lease [li:s] **1** n contrato m de arrendamiento; Fig to **give sb a new l.** Br of or US **on life** dar nueva vida a algn

2 vt arrendar

leasehold ['li:shəʊld] **1** n derechos mpl de arrendamiento

2 adj *(property)* arrendado(a)

leash [li:ʃ] n correa f

least [li:st] *(superl of little)* **1** adj menor,

mínimo(a); **he has the l. time** él es quien menos tiempo tiene

2 adv menos; **l. of all him** él menos que nadie

3 n **the l.** lo menos; **at l.** por lo menos, al menos; **not in the l.!** ¡en absoluto!; **to say the l.** por no decir más

leather ['leðə(r)] **1** n piel f, cuero m

2 adj de piel

leave¹ [li:v] **1** vt (pt & pp **left**) (**a**) dejar; *(go away from)* abandonar; *(go out of)* salir de (**b**) **l. him alone!** ¡déjale en paz!; Fam **l. it to me** yo me encargo (**c**) *(bequeath)* legar (**d**) *(forget)* dejarse, olvidarse (**e**) **I have two biscuits left** me quedan dos galletas (**f**) **to be left over** sobrar

2 vi *(go away)* irse, marcharse; *(go out)* salir; **the train leaves in five minutes** el tren sale dentro de cinco minutos
▸ **leave behind** vt sep (**a**) dejar atrás (**b**) *(forget)* olvidarse
▸ **leave on** vt sep (**a**) *(clothes)* dejar puesto(a) (**b**) *(lights, radio)* dejar encendido(a)
▸ **leave out** vt sep *(omit)* omitir; Fig **to feel left out** sentirse excluido(a)

leave² [li:v] n (**a**) *(permission)* permiso m (**b**) *(time off)* vacaciones fpl; Mil on **l.** de permiso; **l. of absence** excedencia f (**c**) to **take one's l. of sb** despedirse de algn

leaves [li:vz] pl of **leaf**

Lebanon ['lebənən] n (**the**) **L.** (el) Líbano

lecherous ['letʃərəs] adj lascivo(a)

lecture ['lektʃə(r)] **1** n (**a**) conferencia f; Univ clase f; **to give a l. (on)** dar una conferencia (sobre); **l. hall, l. room, l. theatre** sala f de conferencias; Univ aula f (**b**) *(rebuke)* sermón m

2 vi dar una conferencia; Univ dar clases

3 vt *(reproach)* sermonear

lecturer ['lektʃərə(r)] n conferenciante mf; Univ profesor(a) m,f

led [led] pt & pp of **lead**

ledge [ledʒ] n (**a**) *(shelf)* repisa f; *(of window)* alféizar m (**b**) *(on mountain)* saliente m

ledger ['ledʒə(r)] n libro m mayor

lee [li:] n (**a**) Naut sotavento m (**b**) Fig abrigo m

leech [li:tʃ] n sanguijuela f

leek [li:k] n puerro m

leer [lɪə(r)] n vi mirar con lascivia

leeway ['li:weɪ] n libertad f; **this gives me a certain amount of l.** esto me da cierto margen de libertad

left¹ [left] **1** adj izquierdo(a); Pol **l. wing** izquierda f

2 adv a la izquierda

3 *n* (**a**) izquierda *f*; **on the l.** a mano izquierda (**b**) *Pol* **to be on the l.** ser de izquierdas

left² [left] *pt & pp of* **leave**

left-hand ['lefthænd] *adj* **l. drive** con el volante a la izquierda; **on the l. side** a mano izquierda

left-handed [left'hændɪd] *adj* zurdo(a)

left-luggage [left'lʌgɪdʒ] *n Br* **l. office** consigna *f*

leftovers ['leftəʊvəz] *npl* sobras *fpl*

left-wing ['leftwɪŋ] *adj* de izquierdas, izquierdista

leg [leg] *n* (**a**) *(of person)* pierna *f*; *(of animal, table)* pata *f*; *Culin (of lamb)* pierna; *(of trousers)* pernera *f* (**b**) *(stage)* etapa *f*

legacy ['legəsɪ] *n* herencia *f*, legado *m*

legal ['liːgəl] *adj* (**a**) legal; *(permitted by law)* lícito(a); **l. tender** moneda *f* de curso legal (**b**) *(relating to the law)* jurídico(a); **l. aid** asesoramiento jurídico gratuito; **l. dispute** contencioso *m*; *US* **l. holiday** fiesta *f* nacional

legalize ['liːgəlaɪz] *vt* legalizar

legally ['liːgəlɪ] *adv* legalmente

legend ['ledʒənd] *n* leyenda *f*

legendary ['ledʒəndərɪ] *adj* legendario(a)

leggings ['legɪŋz] *npl* polainas *fpl*

legible ['ledʒəbəl] *adj* legible

legion ['liːdʒən] *n* legión *f*

legislation [ledʒɪs'leɪʃən] *n* legislación *f*

legislative ['ledʒɪslətɪv] *adj* legislativo(a)

legislator ['ledʒɪsleɪtə(r)] *n* legislador(a) *m,f*

legislature ['ledʒɪsleɪtʃə(r)] *n* asamblea legislativa

legitimate [lɪ'dʒɪtɪmɪt] *adj* legítimo(a)

legroom ['legruːm] *n* espacio *m* para las piernas

leisure ['leʒə(r), *US* 'liːʒər] *n* ocio *m*, tiempo *m* libre; **at l.** con calma; **do it at your l.** hazlo cuando tengas tiempo; **l. activities** pasatiempos *mpl*; **l. centre** centro recreativo

leisurely ['leʒəlɪ, *US* 'liːʒərlɪ] *adj (unhurried)* tranquilo(a); *(slow)* lento(a)

lemon ['lemən] *n* limón *m*; **l. curd** crema *f* de limón; **l. juice** zumo *m* de limón; **l. tea** té *m* con limón

lemonade [lemə'neɪd] *n* limonada *f*

lend [lend] *vt (pt & pp* **lent**) prestar; **to l. oneself/itself to sth** prestarse a *or* para algo

lending ['lendɪŋ] *n* **l. library** biblioteca pública

length [leŋθ, leŋθ] *n* (**a**) longitud *f*, largo *m*; **it is 5 m l.** tiene 5 m de largo (**b**) *(duration)* duración *f* (**c**) *(of string)* trozo *m*; *(of cloth)* retal *m* (**d**) *(of swimming pool)* largo *m*; *Fig* **to go to any lengths to achieve sth** hacer lo que sea para conseguir algo (**e**) **at l.** *(finally)* finalmente; *(in depth)* a fondo

lengthen ['leŋθən, 'leŋθən] **1** *vt* alargar; *(lifetime)* prolongar

2 *vi* alargarse; *(lifetime)* prolongarse

lengthways ['leŋθweɪz] *adv* a lo largo

lengthy ['leŋθɪ, 'leŋθɪ] *adj* (**lengthier, lengthiest**) largo(a); *(film, illness)* de larga duración; *(meeting, discussion)* prolongado(a)

lenient ['liːnɪənt] *adj* indulgente

lens [lenz] *n* *(of eye)* cristalino *m*; *(of spectacles)* lente *f*; *Phot* objetivo *m*

Lent [lent] *n* Cuaresma *f*

lent [lent] *pt & pp of* **lend**

lentil ['lentɪl] *n* lenteja *f*

Leo ['liːəʊ] *n* Leo *m*

leopard ['lepəd] *n* leopardo *m*

leotard ['liːətɑːd] *n* leotardo *m*

leper ['lepə(r)] *n* leproso(a) *m,f*

leprosy ['leprəsɪ] *n* lepra *f*

lesbian ['lezbɪən] *adj & n* lesbiana (*f*)

less [les] **1** *adj (comp of* **little**) menos

2 *pron* menos; **the l. said about it, the better** cuanto menos se hable de eso mejor

3 *adv* menos; **l. and l.** cada vez menos; **still l.** menos aún

4 *prep* menos; **a year l. two days** un año menos dos días

lessen ['lesən] *vt & vi* disminuir

lesser ['lesə(r)] *adj* menor; **to a l. extent** en menor grado

lesson ['lesən] *n* (**a**) clase *f*; *(in book)* lección *f*; **Spanish lessons** clases de español (**b**) *Rel* lectura *f*

lest [lest] *conj Fml* (**a**) para (que) no; **l. we forget** para que no lo olvidemos (**b**) *(for fear that)* por miedo a que

let [let] **1** *vt (pt & pp* **let**) (**a**) dejar, permitir; **to l. go of sth** soltar algo; **to l. sb know** avisar a algn; *Fig* **to l. oneself go** dejarse ir (**b**) *(rent out)* alquilar, *Méx* rentar; **to l.** *(sign)* se alquila (**c**) **l. alone** ni mucho menos

2 *v aux* **l. him wait** que espere; **l. me go!** ¡suéltame!; **l.'s go!** ¡vamos!, ¡vámonos!; **l.'s see** a ver

▸ **let down** *vt sep* (**a**) *(lower)* bajar; *(lengthen)* alargar; *Fam Fig* **to l. one's hair down** desmelenarse (**b**) *(deflate)* desinflar (**c**) *(fail)* fallar, defraudar

▸ **let in** *vt sep* (**a**) *(admit)* dejar entrar (**b**) **to l. oneself in for** meterse en

▸ **let off** *vt sep* (**a**) *(bomb)* hacer explotar; *(fireworks)* hacer estallar (**b**) *(liquid, air)* soltar (**c**) *Fam* **to l. sb off** *(pardon)* perdonar

▸ **let on** *vi Fam* **don't l. on** *(reveal information)* no se lo digas

▸ **let out** *vt sep* (**a**) *(release)* soltar; *(news)* divulgar; *(secret)* revelar (**b**) *(air, water)* dejar salir (**c**) *(cry)* soltar (**d**) *Sewing* ensanchar

▸ **let up** *vi* cesar, parar

letdown ['letdaʊn] *n* decepción *f*

lethal ['liːθəl] *adj* letal

lethargic [lɪ'θɑːdʒɪk] *adj* aletargado(a)

letter ['letə(r)] *n* (**a**) *(of alphabet)* letra *f*; *Fig* **to the l.** al pie de la letra (**b**) *(written message)* carta *f*; *Br* **l. box** buzón *m*; *Com* **l. of credit** carta de crédito

letterhead ['letəhed] *n* membrete *m*

lettering ['letərɪŋ] *n* rótulo *m*

lettuce ['letɪs] *n* lechuga *f*

let-up ['letʌp] *n Fam* descanso *m*, respiro *m*

leukaemia, *US* **leukemia** [luː'kiːmɪə] *n* leucemia *f*

level ['levəl] **1** *adj* (**a**) *(flat)* llano(a); *(even)* nivelado(a); *(equal)* igual, parejo(a); **a l. spoonful of** una cucharada rasa de; **to be l. with** estar a nivel de; *Br* **l. crossing** paso *m* a nivel (**b**) *(steady)* estable; *(tone)* uniforme

2 *vt* (**a**) nivelar, allanar (**b**) *(building)* arrasar (**c**) *(stare, criticism)* dirigir

3 *n* nivel *m*; **to be on a l. with** estar al mismo nivel que; *Fam* **to be on the l.** *(be honest)* ser de fiar; *(be truthful)* decir la verdad

▸ **level off, level out** *vi* estabilizarse

▸ **level with** *vt insep Fam* ser franco(a) con

level-headed [levəl'hedɪd] *adj* sensato(a)

lever ['liːvə(r)] **1** *n* palanca *f*

2 *vt* apalancar; **to l. sth out** sacar algo con palanca

leverage ['liːvərɪdʒ] *n Fig* influencia *f*

levy ['levɪ] **1** *vt (tax)* recaudar; *(fine)* imponer

2 *n (of tax)* recaudación *f*; *(of fine)* imposición *f*

lewd [luːd] *adj (person)* lascivo(a); *(story)* obsceno(a)

liability [laɪə'bɪlɪtɪ] *n* (**a**) *Jur* responsabilidad *f* (**b**) *(handicap)* estorbo *m* (**c**) *Fin* **liabilities** pasivo *m*

liable ['laɪəbəl] *adj* (**a**) *Jur* responsable; *(susceptible)* sujeto(a); **to be l. for** ser responsable de (**b**) **to be l. to do sth** ser propenso(a) a hacer algo; **it's l. to happen** es muy probable que (así) suceda

liaise [liː'eɪz] *vi* comunicarse (**with** con)

liaison [liː'eɪzɒn] *n* (**a**) enlace *m*; **l. officer** oficial *mf* de enlace (**b**) *(love affair)* amorío *m*

liar ['laɪə(r)] *n* mentiroso(a) *m,f*, embustero(a) *m,f*

libel ['laɪbəl] **1** *n* libelo *m*

2 *vt* difamar, calumniar

liberal ['lɪbərəl] **1** *adj* (**a**) liberal; **L. Party** Partido *m* Liberal (**b**) *(abundant)* abundante

2 *n Pol* **L.** liberal *mf*

liberate ['lɪbəreɪt] *vt* liberar; *(prisoner etc)* poner en libertad; **liberated woman** mujer liberada

liberation [lɪbə'reɪʃən] *n* liberación *f*

liberty ['lɪbətɪ] *n* libertad *f*; **to be at l. to say sth** ser libre de decir algo; **to take liberties** tomarse libertades

Libra ['liːbrə] *n* Libra *f*

librarian [laɪ'breərɪən] *n* bibliotecario(a) *m,f*

> 🖉 Note that the Spanish word **librero** is a false friend and is never a translation for the English word **librarian**. In Spanish, **librero** means "bookseller".

library ['laɪbrərɪ] *n* biblioteca *f*

> 🖉 Note that the Spanish word **librería** is a false friend and is never a translation for the English word **library**. In Spanish, **librería** means "bookshop".

Libya ['lɪbɪə] *n* Libia

Libyan ['lɪbɪən] *adj & n* libio(a) *(m,f)*

lice [laɪs] *pl of* **louse**

licence ['laɪsəns] *n* (**a**) *(permit)* licencia *f*, permiso *m*; *Aut* **l. number** matrícula *f*; *US* **l. plate** (placa *f* de la) matrícula (**b**) *(freedom)* libertad *f*, *(excessive freedom)* libertinaje *m*

license ['laɪsəns] **1** *vt* dar licencia a, autorizar

2 *n US* = **licence**

licensed ['laɪsənst] *adj* autorizado(a); **l. premises** = local autorizado para la venta de bebidas alcohólicas

licentious [laɪ'senʃəs] *adj* licencioso(a)

lichen ['laɪkən, 'lɪtʃən] *n* liquen *m*

lick [lɪk] **1** *vt* lamer; **to l. one's lips** relamerse

2 *n* lamedura *f*; *Fam* **a l. of paint** una mano de pintura

licorice ['lɪkərɪs, 'lɪkərɪʃ] *n US* = **liquorice**

lid [lɪd] n (**a**) *(cover)* tapa f (**b**) *(of eye)* párpado m

lie¹ [laɪ] **1** vi mentir
2 n mentira f

lie² [laɪ] **1** vi *(pt lay; pp lain)* (**a**) *(act)* echarse, acostarse; *(state)* estar echado(a), estar acostado(a); *(be buried)* yacer (**b**) *(be situated)* encontrarse, hallarse; **the valley lay before us** el valle se extendía ante nosotros (**c**) *(remain)* quedarse
2 n *(position)* situación f; *(direction)* orientación f
▸ **lie about, lie around** vi *(person)* estar tumbado(a); *(things)* estar tirado(a)
▸ **lie down** vi acostarse, echarse

lie-in ['laɪɪn] n Fam **to have a l.** levantarse tarde

lieu [ljuː, luː] n **in l. of** en lugar de

lieutenant [lef'tenənt, US luː'tenənt] n (**a**) Mil teniente m (**b**) *(non-military)* lugarteniente m

life [laɪf] n *(pl lives)* (**a**) vida f; **to come to l.** cobrar vida; **to take one's own l.** suicidarse; Fam **how's l.?** ¿qué tal?; **l. belt** cinturón m salvavidas; **l. imprisonment** cadena perpetua; **l. insurance** seguro m de vida; **l. jacket** chaleco m salvavidas; **l. style** estilo m de vida; **l. story** biografía f (**b**) *(liveliness)* vitalidad f; Fam Fig **to be the l. and soul of the party** ser el alma de la fiesta

lifeboat ['laɪfbəʊt] n *(on ship)* bote m salvavidas; *(on shore)* lancha f de socorro

lifeguard ['laɪfɡɑːd] n socorrista mf

lifeless ['laɪflɪs] adj sin vida

lifelike ['laɪflaɪk] adj natural; *(portrait)* fiel

lifeline ['laɪflaɪn] n Fig cordón m umbilical

lifelong ['laɪflɒŋ] adj de toda la vida

life-size(d) ['laɪfsaɪz(d)] adj *(de)* tamaño natural

lifetime ['laɪftaɪm] n vida f; **in his l.** durante su vida; **it's the chance of a l.** es una ocasión única

lift [lɪft] **1** vt (**a**) levantar; *(head etc)* alzar; *(pick up)* coger (**b**) *(troops)* transportar (**c**) Fam *(steal)* birlar; *(plagiarize)* plagiar
2 vi *(clouds, mist)* disiparse
3 n (**a**) Br *(elevator)* ascensor m (**b**) **to give sb a l.** llevar a algn en coche (**c**) Fig *(boost)* estímulo m
▸ **lift up** vt sep levantar, alzar

lift-off ['lɪftɒf] n despegue m

light¹ [laɪt] **1** n (**a**) luz f; Fig **in the l. of** en vista de; Fig **to bring sth to l.** sacar algo a la luz; Fig **to come to l.** salir a la luz; **l.**

bulb bombilla f; **l. meter** fotómetro m; **l. pen** lápiz óptico; **l. switch** interruptor m de la luz; **l. year** año m luz (**b**) *(lamp)* luz f, lámpara f; *(traffic light)* semáforo m; *(headlight)* faro m (**c**) *(flame)* lumbre f; **to set l. to sth** prender fuego a algo; Fam **have you got a l.?** ¿tiene fuego?
2 vt *(pt & pp lighted or lit)* (**a**) *(illuminate)* iluminar, alumbrar (**b**) *(ignite)* encender
3 adj claro(a); *(hair)* rubio(a)
▸ **light up 1** vt sep iluminar, alumbrar
2 vi (**a**) iluminarse (**b**) Fam encender un cigarrillo

light² [laɪt] **1** adj ligero(a); *(rain)* fino(a); *(breeze)* suave; Fig *(sentence etc)* leve; Fig **to make l. of sth** dar poca importancia a algo
2 adv **to travel l.** ir ligero(a) de equipaje

lighten¹ ['laɪtən] **1** vt (**a**) *(colour)* aclarar (**b**) *(illuminate)* iluminar
2 vi aclararse

lighten² ['laɪtən] vt (**a**) *(weight)* aligerar (**b**) Fig *(mitigate)* aliviar; *(heart)* alegrar

lighter¹ ['laɪtə(r)] n **(cigarette) l.** encendedor m, mechero m

light-headed [laɪt'hedɪd] adj (**a**) *(dizzy)* mareado(a) (**b**) *(frivolous)* frívolo(a)

light-hearted ['laɪthɑːtɪd] adj alegre

lighthouse ['laɪthaʊs] n faro m

lighting ['laɪtɪŋ] n (**a**) *(act)* iluminación f (**b**) *(system)* alumbrado m

lightly ['laɪtlɪ] adv (**a**) ligeramente (**b**) **to get off l.** salir casi indemne

lightness¹ ['laɪtnɪs] n luminosidad f, claridad f

lightness² ['laɪtnɪs] n *(of weight)* ligereza f

lightning ['laɪtnɪŋ] n *(flash)* relámpago m; *(stroke)* rayo m; **l. conductor** or **rod** pararrayos m inv; **l. strike** huelga f relámpago

lightweight ['laɪtweɪt] adj *(suit etc)* ligero(a); *(boxer)* de peso ligero; Fig *(person)* light

like¹ [laɪk] **1** adj (**a**) parecido(a), semejante (**b**) *(equal)* igual
2 adv **(as) l. as not** a lo mejor
3 prep (**a**) *(similar to)* como, parecido(a) a; *(the same as)* igual que; **it's not l. her to do that** no es propio de ella hacer eso; **I've never seen anything l. it** nunca he visto cosa igual; **l. that** así; **people l. that** ese tipo de gente; **what's he l.?** ¿cómo es?; Fam **that's more l. it!** ¡así se hace! (**b**) **to feel l.** *(want)* tener ganas de; **I feel l. a change** me apetece un cambio
4 n **brushes, combs and the l.** cepillos,

peines y cosas por el estilo

like² [laɪk] **1** vt (**a**) **do you l. chocolate?** ¿te gusta el chocolate?; **he likes dancing** le gusta bailar; **she likes children** le gustan los niños (**b**) (want) querer; **whether you l. it or not** quieras o no (quieras); **would you l. a drink?** ¿te apetece tomar algo?

2 vi querer, gustar; **as you l.** como quieras; **whenever you l.** cuando quieras

3 n gusto m

likeable ['laɪkəbəl] adj simpático(a)

likelihood ['laɪklɪhʊd] n probabilidad f

likely ['laɪklɪ] **1** adj (**likelier, likeliest**) probable; **he's l. to cause trouble** es probable que cause problemas; **where are you l. to be this afternoon?** ¿dónde piensas estar esta tarde?

2 adv probablemente; **not l.!** ¡ni hablar!

likeness ['laɪknɪs] n (**a**) semejanza f, parecido m (**b**) (portrait) retrato m

likewise ['laɪkwaɪz] adv (**a**) (also) también, asimismo (**b**) (the same) lo mismo, igual

liking ['laɪkɪŋ] n (for thing) afición f; (for person) simpatía f; (for friend) cariño m; **to take a l. to sth** cogerle el gusto a algo; **to take a l. to sb** coger cariño a algn

lilac ['laɪlək] **1** n (**a**) Bot lila f (**b**) (colour) lila m

2 adj lila, de color lila

lilt [lɪlt] n melodía f

lily ['lɪlɪ] n lirio m, azucena f; **l. of the valley** lirio de los valles

limb [lɪm] n miembro m; Fig **to be out on a l.** (in danger) estar en peligro; Br (isolated) estar aislado(a)

▸ **limber up** ['lɪmbə(r)] vi Sport entrar en calor; Fig prepararse (**for** para)

limbo ['lɪmbəʊ] n limbo m; Fig olvido m; **to be in l.** caer en el olvido

lime¹ [laɪm] n Chem cal f

lime² [laɪm] n (fruit) lima f; (tree) limero m

limelight ['laɪmlaɪt] n Fig **to be in the l.** estar en el candelero

limerick ['lɪmərɪk] n quintilla humorística

limestone ['laɪmstəʊn] n piedra caliza

limit ['lɪmɪt] **1** n límite m; (maximum) máximo m; (minimum) mínimo m

2 vt (restrict) limitar

limitation [lɪmɪ'teɪʃən] n limitación f

limited ['lɪmɪtɪd] adj limitado(a); **l. edition** edición limitada; Br **l. (liability) company** sociedad anónima

limitless ['lɪmɪtlɪs] adj ilimitado(a)

limousine ['lɪməziːn, lɪmə'ziːn] n limusina f

limp¹ [lɪmp] **1** vi cojear

2 n cojera f

limp² [lɪmp] adj (**a**) (floppy) flojo(a) (**b**) (weak) débil

limpet ['lɪmpɪt] n lapa f

linchpin ['lɪntʃpɪn] n Tech pezonera f; Fig eje m

line¹ [laɪn] n (**a**) línea f; (straight) raya f; **to be on the right lines** ir por buen camino; US State **l.** límite m de un Estado

(**b**) (of writing) renglón m; (of poetry) verso m; Th **to learn one's lines** aprenderse el papel

(**c**) (row) fila f; (of trees) hilera f; US (queue) cola f; Mil **l. of fire** línea f de fuego; Mil **to be in the front l.** estar en primera línea; Fig **to be in l. (with)** coincidir (con); Fam **to bring sb into l.** pararle los pies a algn; US **to stand in l.** (queue) hacer cola; Fam **to step out of l.** salirse de las reglas; Fig **to go along these lines** algo por el estilo; **l. dancing** = baile al ritmo de música country en el que los participantes se colocan en hileras y se mueven todos al mismo tiempo dando los mismos pasos

(**d**) (rope) cuerda f; (wire) cable m; **fishing l.** sedal m

(**e**) Tel línea f; **hold the l.!** ¡no cuelgue!

(**f**) Br Rail vía f

(**g**) (range of goods) surtido m; **a new l.** una nueva línea

(**h**) (of descent) linaje m

line² [laɪn] vt (pipe etc) revestir; Sewing forrar; Fam **to l. one's pockets** forrarse

▸ **line up 1** vt sep (**a**) (arrange in rows) poner en fila (**b**) **he has something lined up for this evening** tiene algo organizado para esta noche

2 vi (people) ponerse en fila; (troops) formar; (in queue) hacer cola

linear ['lɪnɪə(r)] adj lineal

lined [laɪnd] adj (**a**) (paper) rayado(a); (face) arrugado(a) (**b**) (garment) forrado(a)

linen ['lɪnɪn] n (**a**) (cloth) lino m (**b**) (clothes) ropa f; (sheets etc) ropa blanca

liner ['laɪnə(r)] n transatlántico m

linesman ['laɪnzmən] n Sport juez m de línea

line-up ['laɪnʌp] n Sport alineación f

linger ['lɪŋgə(r)] vi tardar; (dawdle) rezagarse; (smell, doubt) persistir; Fig (memory) perdurar

lingerie ['lænʒəriː] n Fml ropa f interior (de mujer)

lingering ['lɪŋgərɪŋ] adj (doubt) persistente; (look) fijo(a)

lingo ['lɪŋgəʊ] n (pl **lingoes**) Fam (a) (language) lengua f, idioma m (b) (jargon) jerga f

linguist ['lɪŋgwɪst] n lingüista mf; **he's a good l.** se le dan bien los idiomas

linguistic [lɪŋ'gwɪstɪk] adj lingüístico(a)

linguistics [lɪŋ'gwɪstɪks] n sing lingüística f

lining ['laɪnɪŋ] n forro m

link [lɪŋk] **1** n (a) (of chain) eslabón m (b) (connection) conexión f; Fig vínculo m; **rail l.** enlace ferroviario (c) **links** campo m de golf

2 vt unir

► **link up** vi unirse; (meet) encontrarse; (spaceships) acoplarse

link-up ['lɪŋkʌp] n Tel & TV conexión f; (meeting) encuentro m; (of spaceships) acoplamiento m

lino ['laɪnəʊ] n Fam linóleo m

linoleum [lɪ'nəʊlɪəm] n linóleo m, linóleum m

lion ['laɪən] n león m

lioness ['laɪənɪs] n leona f

lip [lɪp] n (a) labio m (b) (of jug) pico m

lip-read ['lɪpriːd] vt & vi leer en los labios

lip-service ['lɪpsɜːvɪs] n palabrería f

lipstick ['lɪpstɪk] n lápiz m de labios

liqueur [lɪ'kjʊə(r)] n licor m

liquid ['lɪkwɪd] adj & n líquido(a) (m)

liquidate ['lɪkwɪdeɪt] vt liquidar

liquidation [lɪkwɪ'deɪʃən] n liquidación f; **to go into l.** entrar en liquidación

liquidize ['lɪkwɪdaɪz] vt licuar

liquidizer ['lɪkwɪdaɪzə(r)] n licuadora f

liquor ['lɪkər] n US alcohol m, bebidas alcohólicas; **l. store** tienda f de bebidas alcohólicas

liquorice ['lɪkərɪs, 'lɪkərɪʃ] n regaliz m

Lisbon ['lɪzbən] n Lisboa

lisp [lɪsp] **1** n ceceo m

2 vi cecear

list¹ [lɪst] **1** n lista f; (catalogue) catálogo m

2 vt (make a list of) hacer una lista de; (put on a list) poner en una lista; **it is not listed** no figura en la lista

list² [lɪst] Naut **1** n escora f

2 vi escorar

listen ['lɪsən] vi escuchar; (pay attention) prestar atención

► **listen out for** vt insep estar atento(a) a

listener ['lɪsənə(r)] n oyente mf

listless ['lɪstlɪs] adj apático(a)

lit [lɪt] pt & pp of **light**

liter ['liːtər] n US = **litre**

literacy ['lɪtərəsɪ] n alfabetización f

literal ['lɪtərəl] adj literal

literally ['lɪtərəlɪ] adv literalmente

literary ['lɪtərərɪ] adj literario(a)

literate ['lɪtərɪt] adj alfabetizado(a)

⚠ Note that the Spanish word **literato** is a false friend and is never a translation for the English word **literate**. In Spanish, **literato** means "writer, author."

---

literature ['lɪtərətʃə(r)] n (a) literatura f (b) Fam (documentation) folleto informativo

lithe [laɪð] adj Fml ágil

Lithuania [lɪθjʊ'eɪnɪə] n Lituania

Lithuanian [lɪθjʊ'eɪnɪən] **1** adj lituano(a)

2 n (person) lituano(a) m,f; (language) lituano m

litigation [lɪtɪ'geɪʃən] n litigio m

litmus ['lɪtməs] n Fig **l. test** prueba f contundente

litre ['liːtə(r)] n litro m

litter ['lɪtə(r)] **1** n (a) (rubbish) basura f; (papers) papeles mpl; **l. bin** papelera f (b) (offspring) camada f

2 vt ensuciar

littered ['lɪtəd] adj cubierto(a) (**with** de)

little ['lɪtəl] **1** adj (a) pequeño(a); **a l. dog** un perrito; **a l. house** una casita; **l. finger** dedo m meñique; **L.** Br **Bear** or US **Dipper** Osa f Menor (b) (not much) poco(a); **a l. cheese** un poco de queso

2 pron poco m; **save me a l.** guárdame un poco

3 adv poco; **l. by l.** poco a poco; **as l. as possible** lo menos posible; **they were a l. surprised** se quedaron algo sorprendidos

live¹ [lɪv] **1** vi vivir; **long l. the King!** ¡viva el Rey!

2 vt vivir; **to l. an interesting life** vivir una vida interesante

► **live down** vt sep conseguir que se olvide

► **live for** vt insep vivir para

► **live off** vt insep vivir de

► **live on 1** vt insep (food, money) vivir de

2 vi (memory) persistir

► **live through** vt insep vivir durante

► **live together** vi vivir juntos

► **live up** vt sep Fam **to l. it up** pegarse la gran vida

► **live up to** vt insep (promises) cumplir con; **it didn't l. up to expectations** no fue lo que se esperaba

► **live with** vt insep (a) vivir con (b) Fig (accept) aceptar

live² [laɪv] adj (a) (living) vivo(a) (b) TV & Rad en directo, en vivo (c) (ammunition) real; (bomb) sin explotar; Elec con corriente; Fam **he's a real l. wire!** ¡éste sí que nunca!

livelihood ['laɪvlɪhʊd] *n* sustento *m*
lively ['laɪvlɪ] *adj* (**livelier, liveliest**) *(person)* vivo(a); *(place)* animado(a); *Fig (interest)* entusiástico(a)
liven ['laɪvən] *vt* **to l. (up)** animar
liver ['lɪvə(r)] *n* hígado *m*
livery ['lɪvərɪ] *n* librea *f*
lives [laɪvz] *pl of* **life**
livestock ['laɪvstɒk] *n* ganado *m*
livid ['lɪvɪd] *adj* lívido(a); *Fam (angry)* furioso(a)
living ['lɪvɪŋ] **1** *adj* vivo(a)
 2 *n* vida *f*; **l. conditions** condiciones *fpl* de vida; **l. expenses** dietas *fpl*; **to earn or make one's l.** ganarse la vida; **l. room** sala *f* de estar; **l. standards** nivel *m* de vida; **l. wage** sueldo mínimo
lizard ['lɪzəd] *n (large)* lagarto *m*; *(small)* lagartija *f*
llama ['lɑːmə] *n* llama *f*
load [ləʊd] **1** *n (cargo)* carga *f*; *(weight)* peso *m*; *Elec & Tech* carga; *Fam* **loads (of)** montones de; *Fam* **that's a l. of rubbish!** ¡no son más que tonterías!
 2 *vt* cargar
 ▶ **load up** *vi & vt sep* cargar
loaded ['ləʊdɪd] *adj* (**a**) cargado(a) (**with** de); *Fig* **a l. question** una pregunta intencionada (**b**) *Fam* **to be l.** *(rich)* estar forrado(a) (**c**) *(dice)* trucado(a)
loading ['ləʊdɪŋ] *n* carga *f*; **l. bay** cargadero *m*
loaf¹ [ləʊf] *n (pl* **loaves**) pan *m*; *(French stick)* barra *f* de pan; *(sliced)* pan de molde
loaf² [ləʊf] *vi* **to l. (about or around)** holgazanear
loan [ləʊn] **1** *n* préstamo *m*; *Fin* empréstito *m*; **on l.** prestado(a); *(footballer)* cedido(a)
 2 *vt* prestar
loath [ləʊθ] *adj* **to be l. to do sth** ser reacio(a) a hacer algo
loathe [ləʊð] *vt* aborrecer, odiar
loathing ['ləʊðɪŋ] *n* aborrecimiento *m*, odio *m*
loathsome ['ləʊðsəm] *adj* odioso(a), repugnante
loaves [ləʊvz] *pl of* **loaf**
lobby ['lɒbɪ] **1** *n* (**a**) *(hall)* vestíbulo *m* (**b**) *(pressure group)* grupo *m* de presión, lobby *m*
 2 *vt* presionar
 3 *vi* ejercer presiones
lobe [ləʊb] *n* lóbulo *m*
lobster ['lɒbstə(r)] *n* langosta *f*
local ['ləʊkəl] **1** *adj* local; *(person)* del pueblo; *Med* **l. anaesthetic** anestesia *f*

local; *Tel* **l. call** llamada urbana; **l. government** gobierno *m* municipal
 2 *n Fam* (**a**) **the locals** los vecinos (**b**) *Br (pub)* bar *m* del barrio
locality [ləʊˈkælɪtɪ] *n* localidad *f*
locally ['ləʊkəlɪ] *adv* en *or* de la localidad
locate [ləʊˈkeɪt] *vt (situate)* situar, ubicar; *(find)* localizar
location [ləʊˈkeɪʃən] *n* (**a**) lugar *m*, situación *f* (**b**) *Cin* **l. shots** exteriores *mpl*; **they're on l. in Australia** están rodando en Australia
loch [lɒx, lɒk] *n Scot* lago *m*
lock¹ [lɒk] **1** *n* (**a**) *(on door etc)* cerradura *f*; *(bolt)* cerrojo *m*; *(padlock)* candado *m* (**b**) *(on canal)* esclusa *f*
 2 *vt* cerrar con llave/cerrojo/candado
 3 *vi (door etc)* cerrarse; *(wheels)* trabarse
 ▶ **lock up** *vt sep (house)* cerrar; *(jail)* meter en la cárcel
lock² [lɒk] *n Literary (of hair)* mechón *m*
locker ['lɒkə(r)] *n (cupboard)* armario ropero; *US* **l. room** vestuario *m* con armarios roperos
locket ['lɒkɪt] *n* medallón *m*
lockout ['lɒkaʊt] *n* cierre *m* patronal
locksmith ['lɒksmɪθ] *n* cerrajero *m*
lockup ['lɒkʌp] *n (garage)* garaje alejado de la casa; *US (prison)* cárcel *f*
loco ['ləʊkəʊ] *adj US Fam* pirado(a)
locomotive [ləʊkəˈməʊtɪv] *n* locomotora *f*
locust ['ləʊkəst] *n* langosta *f*
lodge [lɒdʒ] **1** *n (gamekeeper's)* casa *f* del guarda; *(porter's)* portería *f*; *(hunter's)* refugio *m* (**b**) *(masonic)* logia *f* (**c**) *(beaver's den)* madriguera *f*
 2 *vt* (**a**) *(accommodate)* alojar (**b**) *(complaint)* presentar
 3 *vi* (**a**) *(live)* alojarse (**b**) *(get stuck)* meterse (**in** en)
lodger ['lɒdʒə(r)] *n* huésped(a) *m,f*
lodging ['lɒdʒɪŋ] *n* alojamiento *m*; **l. house** casa *f* de huéspedes
loft [lɒft] *n* desván *m*
lofty ['lɒftɪ] *adj* (**loftier, loftiest**) *Literary (high)* alto(a); *Pej (haughty)* altivo(a)
log [lɒg] **1** *n* (**a**) tronco *m*; *(for fuel)* leño *m*; **l. cabin** cabaña *f* de troncos (**b**) *Naut* diario *m* de a bordo
 2 *vt (record)* registrar
 ▶ **log in, log on** *vi Comput* entrar (en sistema)
 ▶ **log out, log off** *vi Comput* salir (del sistema)
logarithm ['lɒgərɪðəm] *n* logaritmo *m*
log-book ['lɒgbʊk] *n Naut* diario *m* de a

bordo; *Av* diario de vuelo; *Aut* documentación *f* (del coche)

loggerheads ['lɒgəhedz] *npl* **to be at l. with sb** estar a mal con algn

logic ['lɒdʒɪk] *n* lógica *f*

logical ['lɒdʒɪkəl] *adj* lógico(a)

logistics [lə'dʒɪstɪks] *npl* logística *f*

logo ['ləʊgəʊ] *n* logotipo *m*

loin [lɔɪn] *n* (*of animal*) ijada *f*; *Culin* (*of pork*) lomo *m*; (*of beef*) solomillo *m*

loiter ['lɔɪtə(r)] *vi* (*hang about*) holgazanear; (*lag behind*) rezagarse; (*prowl*) merodear

loll [lɒl] *vi* (*tongue, head*) colgar
▸ **loll about, loll around** *vi* repantigarse

lollipop ['lɒlɪpɒp] *n* piruli *m*, chupachup® *m*; **ice(d) l.** polo *m*; *Br Fam* **l. lady/ man** = guardia que para el tráfico para que crucen los colegiales

lolly ['lɒlɪ] *n Fam* (a) (*sweet*) piruli *m*, chupachup® *m*; **ice(d) l.** polo *m* (b) *Fam* (*money*) pasta *f*

London ['lʌndən] *n* Londres

Londoner ['lʌndənə(r)] *n* londinense *mf*

lone [ləʊn] *adj* (*solitary*) solitario(a); (*single*) solo(a)

loneliness ['ləʊnlɪnɪs] *n* soledad *f*

lonely ['ləʊnlɪ] *adj* (**lonelier, loneliest**) solo(a), solitario(a)

long¹ [lɒŋ] **1** *adj* (a) (*size*) largo(a); **how l. is the table?** ¿cuánto tiene de largo la mesa?; **it's 3 m l.** tiene 3 m de largo; **l. jump** salto *m* de longitud (b) (*time*) mucho(a); **at l. last** por fin; **how l. is the film?** ¿cuánto tiempo dura la película?
   2 *adv* mucho, mucho tiempo; **all day l.** todo el día; **as l. as the exhibition lasts** mientras dure la exposición; **as l. as** so **l. as you don't mind** con tal de que no te importe; **before l.** dentro de poco; **how l. have you been here?** ¿cuánto tiempo llevas aquí?

long² [lɒŋ] *vi* añorar; **to l. for** anhelar

long-distance ['lɒŋdɪstəns] *adj* de larga distancia; **l. call** conferencia interurbana; **l. runner** corredor(a) *m,f* de fondo

longhand ['lɒŋhænd] *n* escritura *f* a mano

longing ['lɒŋɪŋ] *n* (*desire*) anhelo *m*; (*nostalgia*) nostalgia *f*

longitude ['lɒndʒɪtjuːd] *n* longitud *f*

long-playing ['lɒŋpleɪɪŋ] *adj* de larga duración; **l. record** elepé *m*

long-range ['lɒŋreɪndʒ] *adj* (*missile etc*) de largo alcance; (*weather forecast*) de largo plazo

long-sighted [lɒŋ'saɪtɪd] *adj* (a) *Med* présbita (b) *Fig* previsor(a)

long-standing ['lɒŋstændɪŋ] *adj* antiguo(a), de mucho tiempo

long-suffering ['lɒŋsʌfərɪŋ] *adj* sufrido(a)

long-term ['lɒŋtɜːm] *adj* a largo plazo

long-winded [lɒŋ'wɪndɪd] *adj* prolijo(a)

loo [luː] *n Br Fam* váter *m*

look [lʊk] **1** *n* (a) (*glance*) mirada *f*; **to take a l. at** (*peep*) echar un vistazo a; (*examine*) examinar (b) (*appearance*) aspecto *m*, apariencia *f*; **I don't like the l. of it** me da mala espina (c) (*fashion*) moda *f* (d) (**good**) **looks** belleza *f*
   2 *vi* (a) mirar (b) (*seem*) parecer; **he looks well** tiene buena cara; **it looks delicious** tiene un aspecto buenísimo; **she looks like her father** (*resembles*) se parece a su padre
   3 *vt* mirar
▸ **look after** *vt insep* cuidar a, ocuparse de
▸ **look at** *vt insep* mirar; *Fig* **whichever way you l. at it** desde cualquier punto de vista
▸ **look away** *vi* apartar la mirada
▸ **look back** *vi* (a) mirar hacia atrás; *Fig* **since then he has never looked back** desde entonces ha ido prosperando (b) (*remember*) recordar
▸ **look down** *vi Fig* **to l. down on sth/sb** despreciar algo/a algn
▸ **look for** *vt insep* buscar
▸ **look forward to** *vt insep* esperar con ansia; **I l. forward to hearing from you** (*in letter*) espero noticias suyas
▸ **look into** *vt insep* examinar, investigar
▸ **look on 1** *vt insep* (*consider*) considerar
   2 *vi* quedarse mirando
▸ **look onto** *vt insep* dar a
▸ **look out** *vi* (a) **the bedroom looks out onto the garden** el dormitorio da al jardín (b) **l. out!** (*take care*) ¡cuidado!, ¡ojo!
▸ **look over** *vt sep* (*examine*) revisar; (*place*) inspeccionar
▸ **look round 1** *vi* mirar alrededor; (*turn head*) volver la cabeza
   2 *vt insep* (*house, shop*) ver
▸ **look through** *vt insep* (a) (*window*) mirar por (b) (*leaf through*) hojear; (*examine*) revisar; (*check*) registrar
▸ **look to** *vt insep* (a) (*take care of*) velar por (b) (*turn to*) recurrir a
▸ **look up 1** *vi* (a) (*glance upwards*) alzar la vista (b) *Fam* (*improve*) mejorar
   2 *vt sep* (a) (*look for*) buscar (b) (*visit*) ir a visitar
▸ **look upon** *vt insep* considerar
▸ **look up to** *vt insep* (*person*) respetar

lookout ['lʊkaʊt] *n (person)* centinela *mf*; *(place)* mirador *m*; **to be on the l. for** estar al acecho de; *Fam* **that's his l.!** ¡eso es asunto suyo!

loom¹ [lu:m] *n* telar *m*

loom² [lu:m] *vi* alzarse; *Fig (threaten)* amenazar

loony ['lu:nɪ] *adj* (**loonier, looniest**) *Fam* loco(a)

loop [lu:p] **1** *n* (**a**) lazo *m* (**b**) *Comput* bucle *m*
   2 *vt* (**a**) encordar (**b**) *Av* **to l. the loop** rizar el rizo

loophole ['lu:phəʊl] *n Fig* escapatoria *f*

loose [lu:s] *adj* (**a**) *(not secure)* flojo(a); *(papers, hair, clothes)* suelto(a); *(tongue)* desatado(a); *(baggy)* holgado(a); **to set sb l.** soltar a algn; *Fam* **to be at a l. end** no saber qué hacer (**b**) *(not packaged)* a granel; **l. tobacco** tabaco *m* en hebras; **l. change** suelto *m* (**c**) *(not exact)* vago(a); *(translation)* libre (**d**) *(lax)* relajado(a); **a l. woman** una mujer fácil

loosely ['lu:slɪ] *adv* (**a**) *(approximately)* aproximadamente (**b**) *(vaguely)* vagamente

loosen ['lu:sən] **1** *vt* aflojar; *(belt)* desabrochar; *Fig (restrictions)* flexibilizar
   2 *vi (slacken)* aflojarse

loot [lu:t] **1** *n* botín *m*
   2 *vt* saquear

lop [lɒp] *vt* podar
   ▸ **lop off** *vt sep* cortar

lope [ləʊp] *vi* andar a zancadas

lopsided [lɒp'saɪdɪd] *adj* ladeado(a)

lord [lɔːd] *n* (**a**) señor *m*; *(British peer)* lord *m*; **the House of Lords** la Cámara de los Lores; **the L. Mayor** el señor alcalde (**b**) *Rel* **the L.** El Señor; **good L.!** ¡Dios mío!; **the L.'s Prayer** el Padrenuestro (**c**) *(judge)* señoría *mf*

lordship ['lɔːdʃɪp] *n Br* **his l./your l.** su señoría

lorry ['lɒrɪ] *n Br* camión *m*; **l. driver** camionero(a) *m,f*; **l. load** carga *f*

lose [lu:z] **1** *vt (pt & pp lost)* perder; **to l. time** *(of clock)* atrasarse
   2 *vi* perder; **to l. to sb** perder contra algn; **to l. out** salir perdiendo

loser ['lu:zə(r)] *n* perdedor(a) *m,f*

loss [lɒs] *n* pérdida *f*; **to make a l.** perder; *Fig* **to be at a l. for words** quedarse una pieza; **to be at a l. what to do** no saber qué hacer

lost [lɒst] **1** *adj* (**a**) perdido(a); **to get l.** perderse; *Fam* **get l.!** ¡vete a la porra!; **l. property office,** *US* **l. and found department** oficina *f* de objetos perdidos (**b**)

(disoriented) desorientado(a); *(distracted)* distraído(a); **l. in thought** ensimismado(a)
   2 *pt & pp of* **lose**

lot [lɒt] *n* (**a**) *(fate)* suerte *f* (**b**) **to cast lots for sth** echar algo a suertes (**c**) *US (plot of land)* parcela *f* (**d**) *(in an auction)* lote *m* (**e**) *(everything)* todo *m*; **he ate the l.** se lo comió todo (**f**) **a l. of** *(much)* mucho(a); *(many)* muchos(as); **he feels a l. better** se encuentra mucho mejor; **she reads a l.** lee mucho; *Fam* **lots of** montones de, cantidad de

lotion ['ləʊʃən] *n* loción *f*

lottery ['lɒtərɪ] *n* lotería *f*; **l. ticket** ≃ décimo *m* de lotería

loud [laʊd] **1** *adj* (**a**) *(voice)* alto(a); *(noise)* fuerte; *(laugh)* estrepitoso(a); *(applause)* clamoroso(a); *(protests, party)* ruidoso(a) (**b**) *(flashy)* chillón(ona) (**c**) *(vulgar)* hortera
   2 *adv* **to read/think out l.** leer/pensar en voz alta

loud-hailer [laʊd'heɪlə(r)] *n* megáfono *m*

loudspeaker [laʊd'spi:kə(r)] *n* altavoz *m*

lounge [laʊndʒ] **1** *n Br* salón *m*, sala *f* de estar
   2 *vi* hacer el vago

louse [laʊs] *n (pl* **lice**) piojo *m*

lousy ['laʊzɪ] *adj* (**lousier, lousiest**) *Fam* fatal; **a l. trick** una cochinada

lout [laʊt] *n* gamberro *m*

lovable ['lʌvəbəl] *adj* adorable

love [lʌv] **1** *n* (**a**) amor *m* (**for** por); *(passion)* pasión *f* (**for** por); **to be in l. with sb** estar enamorado(a) de algn; **to fall in l.** enamorarse; **to make l.** hacer el amor; **(with) l. (from) Mary** *(in letter)* un abrazo, Mary; **l. affair** amorío *m*; **l. letter/story** carta *f*/historia *f* de amor; **l. life** vida *f* sentimental (**b**) *(person)* amor *m*, cariño *m*; *Fam* **chato(a)** *m,f*; **my l.** mi amor (**c**) *(in tennis)* **forty l.** cuarenta a cero
   2 *vt (person)* querer a, amar a; **he loves cooking/football** le encanta cocinar/el fútbol

lovely ['lʌvlɪ] *adj* (**lovelier, loveliest**) *(charming)* encantador(a); *(beautiful)* hermoso(a), precioso(a); *(delicious)* riquísimo(a)

lover ['lʌvə(r)] *n* (**a**) *(sexual partner)* amante *mf* (**b**) *(enthusiast)* aficionado(a) *m,f*, amigo(a) *m,f*

loving ['lʌvɪŋ] *adj* cariñoso(a)

low¹ [ləʊ] **1** *adj* (**a**) bajo(a); *(neckline)* escotado(a); **the L. Countries** los Países Bajos (**b**) *(in quantity)* bajo(a) (**c**) *(poor)* pobre (**d**) *(battery)* gastado(a); **l. frequency** baja frecuencia (**e**) **to feel l.** sentirse deprimido(a) (**f**) *(reprehensible)* malo(a)

  2 *adv* bajo

  3 *n* (**a**) *Met* área *f* de baja presión (**b**) *(low point)* punto más bajo; **to reach an all-time l.** tocar fondo

low² [ləʊ] *vi (cow)* mugir

lowdown ['ləʊdaʊn] *n Fam* pormenores *mpl*

lower ['ləʊə(r)] **1** *adj (comp of* **low**) inferior; *Typ* **l. case** minúscula *f*; **l. class** clase baja

  2 *adv comp of* **low**

  3 *vt* bajar; *(flag)* arriar; *(reduce)* reducir; *(price)* rebajar

lower-class ['ləʊəklɑːs] *adj* de clase baja

lowest ['ləʊɪst] **1** *adj (superl of* **low**) más bajo(a); *(price, speed)* mínimo(a)

  2 *n* **at the l.** como mínimo

low-key [ləʊ'kiː] *adj* sin ceremonia

lowlands ['ləʊləndz] *npl* tierras bajas

lowly ['ləʊlɪ] *adj (lowlier, lowliest)* humilde

low-necked ['ləʊnekt] *adj* escotado(a)

loyal ['lɔɪəl] *adj* leal, fiel

loyalty ['lɔɪəltɪ] *n* lealtad *f*, fidelidad *f*

lozenge ['lɒzɪndʒ] *n* pastilla *f*

LP [el'piː] *n (abbr* **long-playing record**) LP *m*

L-plate ['elpleɪt] *n Br* placa *f* de la "L"

LSD [eles'diː] *n (abbr* **lysergic acid diethylamide**) LSD *m*

Ltd *Br Com (abbr* **Limited (Liability)**) ≃ S.A.

lubricant ['luːbrɪkənt] *n* lubricante *m*

lubricate ['luːbrɪkeɪt] *vt* lubricar; *(engine)* engrasar

lubrication [luːbrɪ'keɪʃən] *n* engrase *m*

lucid ['luːsɪd] *adj* lúcido(a)

luck [lʌk] *n* suerte *f*; **bad l.!** ¡mala suerte!; **good l.!** ¡(buena) suerte!; **to be in l.** estar de suerte; **to be out of l.** no tener suerte; *Fig* **to push one's l.** tentar la suerte; *Fig* **to try one's l.** probar fortuna

luckily ['lʌkɪlɪ] *adv* por suerte, afortunadamente

lucky ['lʌkɪ] *adj (luckier, luckiest) (person)* afortunado(a); *(day)* de suerte; *(move)* oportuno(a); *(charm)* de la suerte; **a l. break** una oportunidad

lucrative ['luːkrətɪv] *adj* lucrativo(a)

ludicrous ['luːdɪkrəs] *adj* absurdo(a), ridículo(a)

lug [lʌɡ] *vt Fam* arrastrar

luggage ['lʌɡɪdʒ] *n* equipaje *m*; **l. rack**

Aut baca *f*; *Rail* portaequipajes *m inv*

lukewarm ['luːkwɔːm] *adj (water etc)* tibio(a); *Fig (reception etc)* poco entusiasta

lull [lʌl] **1** *n (in storm)* calma chicha; *(in fighting)* tregua *f*

  2 *vt (cause to sleep)* adormecer; **to l. sb into a false sense of security** infundir una falsa seguridad a algn

lullaby ['lʌləbaɪ] *n* canción *f* de cuna, nana *f*

lumbago [lʌm'beɪɡəʊ] *n* lumbago *m*

lumber ['lʌmbə(r)] **1** *n* (**a**) *Br (junk)* trastos viejos (**b**) *US (timber)* maderos *mpl*

  2 *vt Fam* cargar (**with** de)

lumberjack ['lʌmbədʒæk] *n* leñador *m*

luminous ['luːmɪnəs] *adj* luminoso(a)

lump [lʌmp] **1** *n (of coal etc)* trozo *m*; *(of sugar, earth)* terrón *m*; *(in sauce)* grumo *m*; *(swelling)* bulto *m*; *Fam Fig (in throat)* nudo *m*; **l. sum** cantidad *f* global

  2 *vt Fam (endure)* aguantar

  ▸ **lump together** *vt sep* apelotonar

lumpy ['lʌmpɪ] *adj (lumpier, lumpiest) (bed)* lleno(a) de bultos; *(sauce)* grumoso(a)

lunacy ['luːnəsɪ] *n* locura *f*

lunar ['luːnə(r)] *adj* lunar

lunatic ['luːnətɪk] *adj & n* loco(a) *(m,f)*; **l. asylum** manicomio *m*

lunch [lʌntʃ] **1** *n* comida *f*, almuerzo *m*; **l. hour** hora *f* de comer

  2 *vi* comer, almorzar

luncheon ['lʌntʃən] *n Old-fashioned Fml* almuerzo *m*; **l. voucher** vale *m* de comida; **(pork) l. meat** carne *f* de cerdo troceada, chopped *m*

lunchtime ['lʌntʃtaɪm] *n* hora *f* de comer

lung [lʌŋ] *n* pulmón *m*

lunge [lʌndʒ] **1** *n* arremetida *f*

  2 *vi* **to l. (forward)** arremeter; **to l. (out) at sb** arremeter contra algn

lurch [lɜːtʃ] **1** *n* (**a**) *(of vehicle)* sacudida *f*; *(of person)* tambaleo *m* (**b**) *Fam* **to leave sb in the l.** dejar a algn en la cuneta

  2 *vi (vehicle)* dar sacudidas; *(person)* tambalearse

lure [lʊə(r)] **1** *n (decoy)* señuelo *m*; *(bait)* cebo *m*; *Fig (charm)* aliciente *m*

  2 *vt* atraer con engaños

lurid ['lʊərɪd] *adj* (**a**) *(gruesome)* espeluznante; *(sensational)* sensacionalista (**b**) *(gaudy)* chillón(ona)

lurk [lɜːk] *vi (lie in wait)* estar al acecho; *(hide)* esconderse

luscious ['lʌʃəs] *adj (food)* delicioso(a)

lush [lʌʃ] *adj (vegetation)* exuberante

lust [lʌst] **1** n (sexual desire) lujuria f; (craving) ansia f; (greed) codicia f
  2 vi **to l. after sth/sb** codiciar algo/desear a algn
lustre, US **luster** ['lʌstə(r)] n lustre m
lusty ['lʌstɪ] adj (**lustier, lustiest**) robusto(a)
lute [luːt] n laúd m
Luxembourg ['lʌksəmbɜːg] n Luxemburgo
luxuriant [lʌg'zjʊərɪənt] adj (plants) exuberante; (hair etc) abundante
luxurious [lʌg'zjʊərɪəs] adj lujoso(a)
luxury ['lʌkʃərɪ] n lujo m; **l. flat** piso m de lujo

> ✎ Note that the Spanish word **lujuria** is a false friend and is never a translation for the English word **luxury**. In Spanish, **lujuria** means "lust".

lychee ['laɪtʃiː] n lichi m
lying ['laɪɪŋ] **1** adj mentiroso(a)
  2 n mentiras fpl
lynch [lɪntʃ] vt linchar
lyre [laɪə(r)] n Mus lira f
lyric ['lɪrɪk] **1** adj lírico(a)
  2 n (**a**) (poem) poema lírico (**b**) **lyrics** (words of song) letra f
lyrical ['lɪrɪkəl] adj lírico(a)

M

M, m [em] *n (the letter)* M, m *f*
m (**a**) *(abbr* **metre(s))** m (**b**) *(abbr* **million(s))** m
mac [mæk] *n Br Fam (raincoat)* impermeable *m*, gabardina *f*
macabre [mə'kɑːbrə] *adj* macabro(a)
mac(c)aroni [mækə'rəʊnɪ] *n* macarrones *mpl*
mace¹ [meɪs] *n (club, ceremonial staff)* maza *f*
mace² [meɪs] *n (spice)* macis *f inv*
machine [mə'ʃiːn] **1** *n* máquina *f*; **m. gun** ametralladora *f*; **m. language** lenguaje *m* máquina
   2 *vt* trabajar a máquina
machine-gun [mə'ʃiːngʌn] *vt* ametrallar
machine-readable [mə'ʃiːn'riːdəbəl] *adj Comput* para ser leído(a) por ordenador *or Am* computadora
machinery [mə'ʃiːnərɪ] *n (machines)* maquinaria *f*; *(workings of machine)* mecanismo *m*; *Fig* **the bureaucratic m.** la maquinaria burocrática
macintosh 'mækɪntɒʃ] *n* = **mackintosh**
mackerel ['mækrəl] *n (pl* **mackerel)** caballa *f*
mackintosh ['mækɪntɒʃ] *n* impermeable *m*
macroeconomics [mækrəʊiːkə'nɒmɪks] *n sing* macroeconomía *f*
mad [mæd] *adj* (**madder, maddest**) (**a**) loco(a); *(animal)* furioso(a); *(dog)* rabioso(a); **to be m.** estar loco(a); **to drive sb m.** volver loco(a) a algn; **to go m.** volverse loco(a); **you must be m.!** ¡estás loco?; *Fam* **m. cow disease** el mal de las vacas locas (**b**) *(idea, plan)* disparatado(a) (**c**) *Fam* **to be m. about sth/sb** estar loco(a) por algo/algn (**d**) *esp US Fam* **to be m. at sb** estar enfadado(a) con algn (**e**) *(gallop, race etc)* desenfrenado(a)
madam ['mædəm] *n* (**a**) señora *f*; **Dear M.** *(in letter)* Muy señora mía, Estimada señora (**b**) *(of brothel)* madam *f*
madden ['mædən] *vt* volver loco(a)
maddening ['mædənɪŋ] *adj* exasperante
made [meɪd] *pt & pp of* **make**

Madeira [mə'dɪərə] *n* (**a**) *(island)* Madeira (**b**) *(wine)* madeira *m*; **M. cake** bizcocho *m*
made-to-measure ['meɪdtə'meʒə(r)] *adj* hecho(a) a (la) medida
made-up ['meɪdʌp] *adj* (**a**) *(face, person)* maquillado(a); *(eyes, lips)* pintado(a) (**b**) *(story, excuse)* inventado(a)
madly ['mædlɪ] *adv Fam (extremely)* terriblemente; **to be m. in love with sb** estar locamente enamorado(a) de algn
madman ['mædmən] *n* loco *m*
madness ['mædnɪs] *n* locura *f*
Madrid [mə'drɪd] *n* Madrid
Mafia ['mæfɪə] *n* mafia *f*
magazine [mægə'ziːn] *n* (**a**) *(periodical)* revista *f* (**b**) *(in rifle)* recámara *f* (**c**) *Mil (storehouse)* almacén *m*; *(for explosives)* polvorín *m*
maggot ['mægət] *n* larva *f*, gusano *m*
magic ['mædʒɪk] **1** *n* magia *f*
   2 *adj* (**a**) mágico(a); **m. wand** varita mágica (**b**) *Fam (wonderful)* estupendo(a)
magical ['mædʒɪkəl] *adj* mágico(a)
magician [mə'dʒɪʃən] *n* (**a**) *(wizard)* mago(a) *m,f* (**b**) *(conjurer)* prestidigitador(a) *m,f*
magistrate ['mædʒɪstreɪt] *n* juez *mf* de primera instancia; **magistrates' court** juzgado *m* de primera instancia
magnanimous [mæg'nænɪməs] *adj* magnánimo(a)
magnet ['mægnɪt] *n* imán *m*
magnetic [mæg'netɪk] *adj* magnético(a); *Fig (personality)* carismático(a); **m. tape** cinta magnetofónica
magnetism ['mægnɪtɪzəm] *n* magnetismo *m*
magnificence [mæg'nɪfɪsəns] *n* magnificencia *f*
magnificent [mæg'nɪfɪsənt] *adj* magnífico(a)
magnify ['mægnɪfaɪ] *vt* (**a**) *(enlarge)* aumentar (**b**) *Fig (exaggerate)* exagerar
magnifying glass ['mægnɪfaɪŋglɑːs] *n* lupa *f*
magnitude ['mægnɪtjuːd] *n* magnitud *f*
magpie ['mægpaɪ] *n* urraca *f*

mahogany [mə'hɒgənɪ] **1** n caoba f
2 adj de caoba

maid [meɪd] n (**a**) criada f, Andes, RP
mucama f (**b**) Pej old m. solterona f

maiden ['meɪdən] **1** n Literary doncella f
2 adj (**a**) (unmarried) soltera; **m. aunt** tía
soltera; **m. name** apellido m de soltera
(**b**) (voyage, flight) inaugural

mail [meɪl] **1** n correo m; **by m.** por correo;
m. order venta f por correo; **m. train** tren
m correo
2 vt (post) echar al buzón; (send) enviar
por correo

mailbox ['meɪlbɒks] n US buzón m

mailing list ['meɪlɪŋlɪst] n lista f de direcciones

mailman ['meɪlmæn] n US cartero m

maim [meɪm] vt lisiar

main [meɪn] **1** adj (problem, door etc)
principal; (square, mast, sail) mayor; (office) central; **the m. thing is to keep calm**
lo esencial es mantener la calma; Culin
m. course plato m principal; **m. road**
carretera f principal; US **M. Street** la
Calle Mayor
2 n (**a**) (pipe, wire) conducto m principal; **the mains** (water or gas system) la
cañería maestra; Elec la red eléctrica; **a
radio that works on battery or mains** una
radio que funciona con pilas o con corriente (**b**) **in the m.** por regla general

mainframe ['meɪnfreɪm] n **m. computer**
computer or Am ordenadora f central

mainland ['meɪnlənd] n continente m

mainly ['meɪnlɪ] adv principalmente, sobre todo; (for the most part) en su mayoría

mainstay ['meɪnsteɪ] n Fig sustento m,
sostén m

mainstream ['meɪnstriːm] n corriente f
principal

maintain [meɪn'teɪn] vt mantener;
(conversation) sostener; (silence, appearances) guardar; (road, machine) conservar en buen estado

maintenance ['meɪntənəns] n (**a**) mantenimiento m (**b**) (divorce allowance)
pensión f

maisonette [meɪzə'net] n Br dúplex m

maître d' ['meɪtrə'diː] n US maître mf

maize [meɪz] n maíz m

majestic [mə'dʒestɪk] adj majestuoso(a)

majesty ['mædʒɪstɪ] n majestad f

major ['meɪdʒə(r)] **1** adj (**a**) principal,
mayor; (contribution, operation) importante (**b**) Mus mayor
2 n (**a**) Mil comandante m (**b**) US Univ
especialidad f

3 vi US Univ **to m. in** especializarse en

Majorca [mə'jɔːkə] n Mallorca

Majorcan [mə'jɔːkən] adj & n mallor-
quín(ina) (m,f)

majority [mə'dʒɒrɪtɪ] n mayoría f; **to be
in the m.** ser (la) mayoría

make [meɪk] (pt & pp **made**) **1** vt (**a**)
hacer; (manufacture) fabricar; (create)
crear; (clothes, curtains) confeccionar;
(meal) preparar; (payment) efectuar;
(speech) pronunciar; (decision) tomar;
(mistake) cometer; **to be made of** ser de;
to m. a noise hacer ruido
(**b**) (render) poner, volver; (convert)
convertir (**into** en); (appoint) nombrar;
he made it clear that ... dejó claro que ...
(**c**) (force, compel) obligar; (cause) causar; **to m. do with sth** arreglárselas con
algo
(**d**) (earn) ganar; **to m. a living** ganarse
la vida; **to m. a name for oneself** hacerse
famoso(a); Fig **to m. the best of sth** sacar
partido de algo
(**e**) **7 and 5 m. 12** 7 y 5 son 12
(**f**) (calculate, reckon) calcular; **what
time do you m. it?** ¿qué hora tienes?
(**g**) (think) opinar; **I don't know what to
m. of it** no sé qué pensar de eso; **it
doesn't m. sense** no tiene sentido
(**h**) (achieve) alcanzar, conseguir
(**i**) **it will m. or break her** será su consagración o su ruina
(**j**) **to m. a fresh start** volver a empezar
2 vi (**a**) hacer; **to m. sure of sth** asegurarse de algo
(**b**) **she made as if to leave** hizo como si
quisiera marcharse
3 n (**a**) (brand) marca f
(**b**) Fam **to be on the m.** andar tras el
dinero
▸ **make for** vt insep (**a**) (move towards)
dirigirse hacia; (attack) atacar a (**b**) **this
makes for less work** esto ahorra trabajo
▸ **make out 1** vt sep (**a**) (list, receipt)
hacer; (cheque) extender (**b**) (perceive)
distinguir; (writing) descifrar (**c**) (understand) entender (**d**) (claim) pretender (**e**)
to m. out a case for doing sth exponer los
argumentos para hacer algo
2 vi **how did you m. out?** ¿qué tal te
fue?
▸ **make up 1** vt sep (**a**) (parcel, list) hacer;
(prescription) preparar; (assemble) montar (**b**) (story) inventar (**c**) (apply
cosmetics to) maquillar; (one's face) maquillarse (**d**) (loss) compensar; (lost
time) recuperar (**e**) (constitute) componer (**f**) **to m. it up (with sb)** hacer las

paces (con algn) **(g)** to **m. up one's mind** decidirse

2 *vi* maquillarse

▸ **make up to 1** *vt insep Br Fam* to **m. up to sb** congraciarse con algn

2 *vt sep* to **m. it up to sb for sth** compensar a algn por algo

make-believe ['meɪkbɪliːv] *n (fantasy)* fantasía *f*; *(pretence)* fingimiento *m*; **to live in a world of m.** vivir en un mundo de ensueño

maker ['meɪkə(r)] *n* fabricante *mf*

makeshift ['meɪkʃɪft] *adj (improvised)* improvisado(a); *(temporary)* provisional

make-up ['meɪkʌp] *n* **(a)** *(cosmetics)* maquillaje *m*; **m. remover** desmaquillador *m* **(b)** *(composition)* composición *f*; *(character)* carácter *m*

making ['meɪkɪŋ] *n* **(a)** *(manufacture)* fabricación *f*; *(preparation)* preparación *f* **(b)** **he has the makings of a politician** tiene madera de político

malaise [mæ'leɪz] *n* malestar *m*

malaria [mə'leərɪə] *n* malaria *f*

Malay [mə'leɪ] **1** *adj* malayo(a)

2 *n* **(a)** *(person)* malayo(a) *m,f* **(b)** *(language)* malayo *m*

Malaysia [mə'leɪzɪə] *n* Malasia

male [meɪl] **1** *adj (animal, plant)* macho; *(person)* varón; *(sex)* masculino; *Pej* **m. chauvinism** machismo *m*

2 *n (person)* varón *m*; *(animal, plant)* macho *m*

malevolent [mə'levələnt] *adj* malévolo(a)

malfunction [mæl'fʌŋkʃən] **1** *n* mal funcionamiento *m*

2 *vi* funcionar mal

malice ['mælɪs] *n* malicia *f*; *Jur* **with m. aforethought** con premeditación

malicious [mə'lɪʃəs] *adj* malévolo(a)

malign [mə'laɪn] **1** *adj* maligno(a); *(influence)* perjudicial

2 *vt* calumniar, difamar

malignant [mə'lɪɡnənt] *adj* **(a)** *(person)* malvado(a) **(b)** *Med* maligno(a)

mall [mɔːl] *n US* centro *m* comercial

malleable ['mælɪəbəl] *adj* maleable

mallet ['mælɪt] *n* mazo *m*

malnutrition [mælnjuː'trɪʃən] *n* desnutrición *f*

malpractice [mæl'præktɪs] *n* procedimiento *m* ilegal; *Med* negligencia *f*

malt [mɔːlt] *n* malta *f*

Malta ['mɔːltə] *n* Malta

mammal ['mæməl] *n* mamífero *m*

mammary ['mæmərɪ] *adj* **m. gland** mama *f*

mammoth ['mæməθ] **1** *n Zool* mamut *m*

2 *adj* gigantesco(a)

man [mæn] **1** *n (pl* **men)** **(a)** hombre *m*; **old m.** viejo *m*; **young m.** joven *m*; *Fig* **he's a m. of his word** es hombre de palabra; *Fig* **the m. in the street** el hombre de la calle; **m. Friday** factótum *m*; *Fam* **dirty old m.** viejo verde **(b)** *(humanity)* el hombre **(c)** *(husband)* marido *m*; *(partner)* pareja *f* **(d)** **our m. in Madrid** nuestro representante en Madrid **(e)** *(in chess)* pieza *f*

2 *vt (boat, plane)* tripular; *(post)* servir; **manned flight** vuelo tripulado

manage ['mænɪdʒ] **1** *vt* **(a)** *(company, household)* llevar; *(money, affairs, person)* manejar **(b)** *(succeed)* conseguir; **to m. to do sth** lograr hacer algo

2 *vi (cope physically)* poder; *(esp financially)* arreglárselas; **we're managing** vamos tirando

manageable ['mænɪdʒəbəl] *adj* manejable

management ['mænɪdʒmənt] *n* dirección *f*

manager ['mænɪdʒə(r)] *n* **(a)** *(of company, bank)* director(a) *m,f*; *(head of department)* jefe(a) *m,f* **(b)** *(of pop group etc)* mánager *m* **(c)** *Sport* entrenador *m*

manageress [mænɪdʒə'res] *n (of shop, restaurant)* encargada *f*; *(of company)* directora *f*

managerial [mænɪ'dʒɪərɪəl] *adj* directivo(a)

managing ['mænɪdʒɪŋ] *adj* directivo(a); **m. director** director(a) *m,f* gerente

mandarin ['mændərɪn] *n* **m. (orange)** mandarina *f*

mandate ['mændeɪt] *n* mandato *m*

mandatory ['mændətərɪ] *adj Fml* obligatorio(a)

mane [meɪn] *n (of horse)* crin *f*; *(of lion)* melena *f*

maneuver [mə'nuːvər] *n, vt & vi US* = **manoeuvre**

manfully ['mænfʊlɪ] *adv* valientemente

manger ['meɪndʒə(r)] *n* pesebre *m*

mangle¹ ['mæŋɡəl] *n (for wringing)* rodillo *m*

mangle² ['mæŋɡəl] *vt (crush)* aplastar; *(destroy by cutting)* despedazar

mango ['mæŋɡəʊ] *n (pl* **mangoes)** mango *m*

mangy ['meɪndʒɪ] *adj* **(mangier, mangiest)** *(animal)* sarnoso(a); *Fam (carpet)* raído(a)

manhandle ['mænhændəl] *vt* maltratar

manhole ['mænhəʊl] *n* boca *f* de acceso

manhood ['mænhʊd] *n* **(a)** *(age)* mayoría

f de edad; **to reach m.** llegar a la edad viril
(**b**) *(manly qualities)* virilidad *f*

mania ['meɪnɪə] *n* manía *f*

maniac ['meɪnɪæk] *n* maníaco(a) *m,f*;
Fam loco(a) *m,f*

manic ['mænɪk] *adj* maníaco(a)

manic-depressive ['mænɪkdɪ'presɪv]
adj & n maníaco(a) *(m,f)* depresivo(a) *f*

manicure ['mænɪkjʊə(r)] **1** *n* manicura *f*
2 *vt* **to m. one's nails** hacerse la manicura

manifest ['mænɪfest] *Fml* **1** *adj* manifies-
to(a)
2 *vt* manifestar

manifesto [mænɪ'festəʊ] *n* programa *m*
electoral

manifold ['mænɪfəʊld] *adj Fml (many)*
múltiples; *(varied)* diversos(as)

manipulate [mə'nɪpjʊleɪt] *vt* (**a**) manipular (**b**) *Fig (accounts etc)* falsificar

mankind [mæn'kaɪnd] *n* la humanidad,
el género humano

manly ['mænlɪ] *adj* (**manlier, manliest**)
varonil, viril

man-made ['mænmeɪd] *adj (lake)* artificial; *(fibres, fabric)* sintético(a)

manner ['mænə(r)] *n* (**a**) *(way, method)*
manera *f*, modo *m*; **in this m.** de esta
manera (**b**) *(way of behaving)* forma *f* de
ser (**c**) *Fml (type, class)* clase *f* (**d**) *(etiquette)* **(good) manners** buenos modales;
bad manners falta *f* de educación

mannerism ['mænərɪzəm] *n (gesture)*
gesto *m*; *(affectation)* amaneramiento *m*

manoeuvre [mə'nuːvə(r)] **1** *n* maniobra *f*
2 *vt* maniobrar; *(person)* manejar
3 *vi* maniobrar

manor ['mænə(r)] *n* **m. house** casa solariega

manpower ['mænpaʊə(r)] *n* mano *f* de
obra

mansion ['mænʃən] *n* casa *f* grande; *(in
country)* casa solariega

manslaughter ['mænslɔːtə(r)] *n* homicidio involuntario

mantelpiece ['mæntəlpiːs] *n (shelf)* repisa *f* de chimenea; *(fireplace)* chimenea *f*

mantle ['mæntəl] *n Fig (of snow)* manto
m, capa *f*

⚓ Note that the Spanish word **mantel** is a
false friend and is never a translation for the
English word **mantle**. In Spanish, **mantel**
means "tablecloth".

manual ['mænjʊəl] *adj & n* manual *(m)*

manufacture [mænjʊ'fæktʃə(r)] **1** *vt* fabricar
2 *n* fabricación *f*

manufacturer [mænjʊ'fæktʃərə(r)] *n* fabricante *mf*

manure [mə'njʊə(r)] *n* abono *m*, estiércol *m*

manuscript ['mænjʊskrɪpt] *n* manuscrito *m*

many ['menɪ] **1** *adj* (**more, most**) mu-
cho(a)/muchos(as); **a great m.** muchísi-
mos(as); **as m. ... as ...** tantos(as) ... como
...; **how m. days?** ¿cuántos días?; **m. a
time** muchas veces; **so m. flowers!**
¡cuántas flores!; **too m.** demasiados(as)
2 *pron* muchos(as)

map [mæp] **1** *n (of country)* mapa *m*; *(of
town, bus route)* plano *m* de
2 *vt* trazar un mapa de
▸ **map out** *vt sep (route)* trazar en un
mapa; *Fig (future etc)* planear

maple ['meɪpəl] *n* arce *m*

mar [mɑː(r)] *vt* estropear; **to m. sb's enjoyment** aguarle la fiesta a algn

marathon ['mærəθən] *n* maratón *m*

marble ['mɑːbəl] **1** *n* (**a**) *(stone)* mármol
m (**b**) *(glass ball)* canica *f*
2 *adj* de mármol

March [mɑːtʃ] *n* marzo *m*

march [mɑːtʃ] **1** *n* (**a**) *Mil* marcha *f*; *Fig* **to
steal a m. on sb** tomar la delantera a algn;
m. past desfile *m* (**b**) *(demonstration)*
manifestación *f*
2 *vi* (**a**) marchar (**b**) *(demonstrate)* manifestarse
3 *vt Mil* hacer marchar

mare [meə(r)] *n* yegua *f*

margarine [mɑːdʒə'riːn] *n* margarina *f*

margin ['mɑːdʒɪn] *n* margen *m*; *Fig* **to
win by a narrow m.** ganar por escaso
margen; **m. of error** *(in statistics)* margen
de error

marginal ['mɑːdʒɪnəl] *adj* marginal; *Pol*
m. seat escaño *m* pendiente

marginally ['mɑːdʒɪnəlɪ] *adv* ligeramente

marigold ['mærɪɡəʊld] *n* caléndula *f*

marijuana, marihuana [mærɪ'hwɑːnə]
n marihuana *f*, mariguana *f*

marinate ['mærɪneɪt] *vt* adobar

marine [mə'riːn] **1** *adj* marino(a)
2 *n* soldado *m* de infantería de marina;
Br **the Marines,** *US* **the M. Corps** la infantería de marina

marital ['mærɪtəl] *adj* matrimonial; **m.
status** estado *m* civil

maritime ['mærɪtaɪm] *adj* marítimo(a)

marjoram ['mɑːdʒərəm] *n* mejorana *f*

mark¹ [mɑːk] **1** *n* (**a**) *(left by blow etc)*
señal *f*; *(stain)* mancha *f*; *Fig* **to make
one's m.** distinguirse (**b**) *(sign, token)*

señal *f; (indication)* indicio *m* (**c**) *Br (in exam etc)* nota *f;* **to get high marks** sacar buenas notas (**d**) *Fig* **to hit the m.** dar en el clavo; *Fig* **to be wide of the m.** estar lejos de la verdad

2 *vt* (**a**) *(stain)* manchar (**b**) *(with tick, cross)* señalar (**c**) *(exam)* corregir; *(student)* dar notas a (**d**) **10 percent off marked price** *(sign)* descuento del 10 por ciento sobre el precio indicado (**e**) **m. my words** fíjate en lo que te digo (**f**) *Sport* marcar (**g**) **to m. time** *Mil* marcar el paso; *Fig* hacer tiempo

▸ **mark out** *vt sep* (**a**) *(area)* delimitar (**b**) **to m. sb out for** destinar a algn a

mark² [mɑːk] *n (unit of currency)* marco *m*

marked [mɑːkt] *adj (noticeable)* marcado(a), acusado(a)

marker ['mɑːkə(r)] *n* (**a**) *(bookmark)* registro *m* (**b**) *Sport* marcador(a) *m,f* (**c**) *(pen)* rotulador *m* fluorescente

market ['mɑːkɪt] **1** *n* mercado *m;* **on the m.** en venta; **m. forces** tendencias *fpl* del mercado; *Br* **m. garden** *(small)* huerto *m;* *(large)* huerta *f; Br* **m. gardener** hortelano(a) *m,f;* **m. price** precio *m* de mercado; **m. research** estudio *m* de mercado

2 *vt (sell)* poner en venta; *(promote)* promocionar

marketable ['mɑːkɪtəbəl] *adj* comerciable

marketing ['mɑːkɪtɪŋ] *n* marketing *m,* mercadotecnia *f*

marketplace ['mɑːkɪtpleɪs] *n* mercado *m*

marksman ['mɑːksmən] *n* tirador *m*

marmalade ['mɑːməleɪd] *n* mermelada *f (de cítricos)*

maroon [mə'ruːn] *adj (de color)* granate

marooned [mə'ruːnd] *adj* bloqueado(a)

marquee [mɑː'kiː] *n* (**a**) *Br (tent)* carpa *f* (**b**) *US (of building)* marquesina *f*

marquess, marquis ['mɑːkwɪs] *n* marqués *m*

marriage ['mærɪdʒ] *n (state)* matrimonio *m; (wedding)* boda *f;* **m. bureau** agencia *f* matrimonial; **m. certificate** certificado *m* de matrimonio

married ['mærɪd] *adj* casado(a); **m. life** vida *f* conyugal

marrow ['mærəʊ] *n* (**a**) *(bone)* **m.** médula *f* (**b**) **(vegetable) m.** calabacín *m*

marry ['mærɪ] *vt (take in marriage)* casarse con; *(give in marriage)* casar (**to** con); *(unite in marriage)* casar; **to get married** casarse

Mars [mɑːz] *n* Marte *m*

marsh [mɑːʃ] *n* pantano *m;* **salt m.** marisma *f*

marshal ['mɑːʃəl] **1** *n* (**a**) *Mil* mariscal *m* (**b**) *Br (at sports event etc)* oficial *mf* (**c**) *US (sheriff)* alguacil *m* (**d**) *US (of police or fire department)* jefe *m*

2 *vt* (**a**) *Mil* formar (**b**) *(facts etc)* ordenar

marshy ['mɑːʃɪ] *adj* (**marshier, marshiest**) pantanoso(a)

martial ['mɑːʃəl] *adj* marcial; **m. arts** artes *fpl* marciales; **m. law** ley *f* marcial

Martian ['mɑːʃən] *adj & n* marciano(a) *(m,f)*

martyr ['mɑːtə(r)] **1** *n* mártir *mf*

2 *vt* martirizar

martyrdom ['mɑːtədəm] *n* martirio *m*

marvel ['mɑːvəl] **1** *n* maravilla *f*

2 *vi* **to m. at** maravillarse de

marvellous, *US* **marvelous** ['mɑːvələs] *adj* maravilloso(a)

Marxism ['mɑːksɪzəm] *n* marxismo *m*

Marxist ['mɑːksɪst] *adj & n* marxista *(mf)*

marzipan ['mɑːzɪpæn] *n* mazapán *m*

mascara [mæ'skɑːrə] *n* rímel *m*

> 🖉 Note that the Spanish word **máscara** is a false friend and is never a translation for the English word **mascara**. In Spanish, **máscara** means "mask".

mascot ['mæskət] *n* mascota *f*

masculine ['mæskjʊlɪn] *adj* masculino(a); *(woman)* hombruna

mash [mæʃ] **1** *n (for animals)* afrecho *m*

2 *vt* **to m. (up)** machacar; **mashed potatoes** puré *m* de patatas *or Am* papas

mask [mɑːsk] **1** *n* máscara *f; (of doctor, dentist etc)* mascarilla *f*

2 *vt* enmascarar; *Fig (conceal)* ocultar (**from** de)

masochist ['mæsəkɪst] *adj & n* masoquista *(mf)*

mason ['meɪsən] *n* (**a**) *(builder)* albañil *m* (**b**) *(freemason)* masón *m,* francmasón *m*

masonic [mə'sɒnɪk] *adj* masónico(a)

masonry ['meɪsənrɪ] *n (stonework)* albañilería *f*

masquerade [mæskə'reɪd] **1** *n (pretence)* farsa *f*

2 *vi* **to m. as** hacerse pasar por

mass¹ [mæs] *n Rel* misa *f;* **to say m.** decir misa

mass² [mæs] **1** *n* (**a**) masa *f* (**b**) *(large quantity)* montón *m; (of people)* multitud *f* (**c**) **the masses** las masas

2 *adj* masivo(a); **m. media** medios *mpl* de comunicación (*de masas*); **m. production** fabricación *f* en serie

3 *vi (people)* congregarse; *Mil* concentrarse

massacre ['mæsəkə(r)] **1** *n* masacre *f*
2 *vt* masacrar
massage ['mæsɑːʒ, məˈsɑːdʒ] **1** *n* masaje
m
2 *vt* (**a**) dar masajes a (**b**) *Fig (figures)*
amañar
masseur [mæˈsɜː(r)] *n* masajista *m*
masseuse [mæˈsɜːz] *n* masajista *f*
massive ['mæsɪv] *adj* enorme; *(heart attack)* grave
mast [mɑːst] *n* (**a**) *Naut* mástil *m* (**b**) *Rad & TV* torre *f*
master ['mɑːstə(r)] **1** *n* (**a**) *(of dog, servant)* amo *m*; *(of household)* señor *m* (**b**) *Br (teacher)* profesor *m* (**c**) *Univ* **m.'s degree** ≃ máster *m* (**d**) *(expert)* maestro *m* (**e**) *(boy)* **M. James Brown** el señor James Brown
2 *adj* (**a**) **m. copy** original *m*; **m. key** llave *f* maestra (**b**) *(expert)* maestro(a)
3 *vt* (**a**) *(person, situation)* dominar (**b**) *(subject, skill)* llegar a dominar
masterful ['mɑːstəfʊl] *adj* autoritario(a); *(imperious)* imperioso(a); *(personality)* dominante
masterly ['mɑːstəlɪ] *adj* magistral
mastermind ['mɑːstəmaɪnd] **1** *n (person)* cerebro *m*
2 *vt* ser el cerebro de
masterpiece ['mɑːstəpiːs] *n* obra *f* maestra
mastery ['mɑːstərɪ] *n* (**a**) *(control)* dominio *m* (**of** de) (**b**) *(skill, expertise)* maestría *f*
masturbate ['mæstəbeɪt] *vi* masturbarse
mat¹ [mæt] *n (rug)* alfombrilla *f*; *(doormat)* felpudo *m*; *(rush mat)* estera *f*; *Sport* colchoneta *f*
mat² [mæt] *adj* mate
match¹ [mætʃ] *n* cerilla *f*, fósforo *m*
match² [mætʃ] **1** *n* (**a**) *Sport* partido *m*; *(in boxing)* combate *m* (**b**) *Fig* **to meet one's m.** *(equal)* encontrar uno la horma de su zapato
2 *vt* (**a**) *(equal, be the equal of)* igualar (**b**) *(be in harmony with)* armonizar; **they are well matched** *(teams)* van iguales; *(couple)* hacen buena pareja (**c**) *(colours, clothes)* hacer juego con; *(pair of socks, gloves)* ser el compañero de
3 *vi (harmonize)* hacer juego
matchbox ['mætʃbɒks] *n* caja *f* de cerillas
matching ['mætʃɪŋ] *adj* que hace juego
mate [meɪt] **1** *n* (**a**) *(at school, work)* compañero(a) *m,f*, colega *mf*; *Br Fam (friend)* amigo(a) *m,f* (**b**) *Zool (male)* macho *m*; *(female)* hembra *f* (**c**) *(assistant)*

ayudante *mf* (**d**) *Naut* **first/second m.** primer/segundo oficial
2 *vt Zool* aparear
3 *vi Zool* aparearse
material [məˈtɪərɪəl] **1** *n* (**a**) *(substance)* materia *f* (**b**) *(cloth)* tejido *m*, tela *f* (**c**) *(information)* material *m* (**d**) **materials** *(ingredients, equipment)* materiales *mpl*
2 *adj* (**a**) *(substancial* (**b**) *(not spiritual)* material
materialistic [mətɪərɪəˈlɪstɪk] *adj* materialista
materialize [məˈtɪərɪəlaɪz] *vi* (**a**) *(hopes)* realizarse; *(plan, idea)* concretarse (**b**) *(show up)* presentarse
maternal [məˈtɜːnəl] *adj* maternal; *(uncle etc)* materno(a)
maternity [məˈtɜːnɪtɪ] *n* maternidad *f*; **m. dress** vestido *m* premamá; **m. hospital** maternidad
math [mæθ] *n US* = **maths**
mathematical [mæθəˈmætɪkəl] *adj* matemático(a)
mathematician [mæθəməˈtɪʃən] *n* matemático(a) *m,f*
mathematics [mæθəˈmætɪks] *n sing* matemáticas *fpl*
maths [mæθs] *n sing Fam* matemáticas *fpl*
matinée ['mætɪneɪ] *n Cin* sesión *f* de tarde; *Th* función *f* de tarde
mating ['meɪtɪŋ] *n* apareamiento *m*; **m. call** reclamo *m*; **m. season** época *f* de celo
matrices ['meɪtrɪsiːz] *pl of* **matrix**
matriculation [mətrɪkjʊˈleɪʃən] *n Univ* matriculación *f*
matrimonial [mætrɪˈməʊnɪəl] *adj* matrimonial
matrimony ['mætrɪmənɪ] *n* matrimonio *m*; *(married life)* vida *f* conyugal
matrix ['meɪtrɪks] *n (pl* **matrices)** matriz *f*
matron ['meɪtrən] *n (in hospital)* enfermera *f* jefe
matronly ['meɪtrənlɪ] *adj* madura y recia
matt [mæt] *adj* mate
matted ['mætɪd] *adj* enmarañado(a)
matter ['mætə(r)] **1** *n* (**a**) *(affair, question)* asunto *m*; **as a m. of course** por rutina; **as a m. of fact** en realidad; **that's another m.** eso es otra cosa (**b**) *(problem)* **what's the m.?** ¿qué pasa? (**c**) **no m. what he does** haga lo que haga; **no m. when** no importa cuando; **no m. where you go** dondequiera que vayas; **no m. how clever he is** por muy inteligente que sea; **no m. how** como sea (**d**) *(substance)* materia *f*, sustancia *f* (**e**) *(content)* contenido *m*;

(subject) tema *m* (**f**) *Med (pus)* pus *m*

2 *vi* importar; **it doesn't m.** no importa, da igual

matter-of-fact ['mætərəv'fækt] *adj* *(person)* práctico(a); *(account)* realista; *(style)* prosaico(a)

mattress ['mætrıs] *n* colchón *f*

mature [mə'tʃʊə(r)] **1** *adj* maduro(a); *Fin* vencido(a)

2 *vi* madurar; *Fin* vencer

3 *vt* madurar

maturity [mə'tʃʊərıtı] *n* madurez *f*

maul [mɔːl] *vt* (**a**) *(wound)* agredir (**b**) *(handle roughly)* maltratar (**c**) *(touch in unpleasant way)* sobar

mauve [məʊv] *adj & n* malva *(m)*

max [mæks] *n (abbr maximum)* máx

maxim ['mæksım] *n* máxima *f*

maxima ['mæksımə] *pl of* **maximum**

maximize ['mæksımaız] *vt* maximizar

maximum ['mæksıməm] **1** *n (pl* **maxima**) máximo *m*

2 *adj* máximo(a)

May [meı] *n* mayo *m*; **M. Day** el Primero *or* el Uno de Mayo

may [meı] *v aux (pt* **might**)

> En el inglés hablado, y en el escrito en estilo coloquial, la forma negativa **might not** se transforma en **mightn't**. La forma **might have** se transforma en **might've**.

(**a**) *(expressing possibility)* poder, ser posible; **be that as it m.** sea como sea; **come what m.** pase lo que pase; **he m.** *or* **might come** puede que venga; **you m.** *or* **might as well stay** más vale que te quedes (**b**) *(permission)* poder; **m. I?** ¿me permite?; **you m. smoke** pueden fumar (**c**) *(wish)* ojalá *(+ subj)*; **m. you always be happy!** ¡ojalá seas siempre feliz!

maybe ['meıbı] *adv* quizá(s), tal vez

mayhem ['meıhem] *n (disturbance)* alboroto *m*; *(havoc)* estragos *mpl*

mayonnaise [meıə'neız] *n* mayonesa *f*, mahonesa *f*

mayor [meə(r)] *n (man)* alcalde *m*; *(woman)* alcaldesa *f*

mayoress ['meəres] *n* alcaldesa *f*

maze [meız] *n* laberinto *m*

MD [em'diː] *n* (**a**) *(abbr* **Doctor of Medicine**) Dr. en Medicina (**b**) *Fam (abbr* **Managing Director**) director(a) *m,f* gerente

me [miː, *unstressed* mı] *pron* (**a**) *(as object)* me; **he gave it to me** me lo dio; **listen to me** escúchame; **she knows me** me conoce (**b**) *(after prep)* mí; **it's for me** es para mí; **with me** conmigo (**c**) *(emphatic)* yo; **it's me** soy yo; **what about me?** ¿y yo, qué?

meadow ['medəʊ] *n* prado *m*, pradera *f*

meagre, *US* **meager** ['miːgə(r)] *adj* exiguo(a)

meal¹ [miːl] *n (flour)* harina *f*

meal² [miːl] *n (food)* comida *f*

mealtime ['miːltaım] *n* hora *f* de comer

mean¹ [miːn] *vt (pt & pp* **meant**) (**a**) *(signify)* significar, querer decir; **what do you m. by that?** ¿qué quieres decir con eso? (**b**) *(intend)* pensar, tener la intención de; **I m. it** (te) lo digo en serio; **she was meant to arrive on the 7th** tenía que *or* debía llegar el día 7; **they m. well** tienen buenas intenciones; **she didn't m. to do it** lo hizo sin querer (**c**) *(entail)* suponer (**d**) *(refer to)* referirse a (**e**) *(destine)* destinar (**for** a *or* para)

mean² [miːn] *adj* (**meaner, meanest**) (**a**) *(miserly)* tacaño(a) (**b**) *(unkind)* malo(a); *(petty)* mezquino(a); *US (bad-tempered)* malhumorado(a); **to be m. to sb** tratar mal a algn (**c**) *(inferior)* mediocre; *(origins)* humilde (**d**) **it was no m. feat** fue toda una hazaña

mean³ [miːn] **1** *adj (average)* medio(a)

2 *n (average)* promedio *m*; *Math* media *f*

meander [mı'ændə(r)] *vi (river)* serpentear; *(person)* vagar; *Fig (digress)* divagar

meaning ['miːnıŋ] *n* sentido *m*, significado *m*

meaningful ['miːnıŋfʊl] *adj* significativo(a)

meaningless ['miːnıŋlıs] *adj* sin sentido

meanness ['miːnnıs] *n* (**a**) *(miserliness)* tacañería *f* (**b**) *(nastiness)* maldad *f*

means [miːnz] *n* (**a**) *sing or pl (method)* medio *m*, manera *f*; **by m. of** por medio de, mediante (**b**) *pl (resources, wealth)* medios *mpl* (de vida), recursos *mpl* (económicos); **to live beyond one's m.** vivir por encima de sus posibilidades (**c**) **by all m.!** ¡por supuesto!; **by no m.** de ninguna manera

meant [ment] *pt & pp of* **mean**

meantime ['miːntaım] **1** *adv* mientras tanto

2 *n* **in the m.** mientras tanto

meanwhile ['miːnwaıl] *adv* mientras tanto

measles ['miːzəlz] *n sing* sarampión *m*

measure ['meʒə(r)] **1** *n* (**a**) *(action, step)* medida *f* (**b**) *(ruler)* regla *f* (**c**) **in some m.** hasta cierto punto (**d**) *Mus* compás *m*

2 *vt (object, area)* medir; *(person)* tomar las medidas de

ℐ Note that the Spanish word **mesura** is a false friend and is never a translation for the English word **measure**. In Spanish, **mesura** means "moderation, restraint".

▸ **measure up** *vi* **to m. up (to sth)** estar a la altura (de algo)
measurement ['meʒəmənt] *n* medida *f*
meat [mi:t] *n* carne *f*; *Culin* **m. pie** empanada *f* de carne
meatball ['mi:tbɔ:l] *n* albóndiga *f*
meaty ['mi:tɪ] *adj* (**meatier, meatiest**) (a) carnoso(a) (b) *Fig* (*story*) jugoso(a)
Mecca ['mekə] *n* la Meca
mechanic [mɪ'kænɪk] *n* (*person*) mecánico(a) *m,f*
mechanical [mɪ'kænɪkəl] *adj* mecánico(a)
mechanics [mɪ'kænɪks] **1** *n sing* (*science*) mecánica *f*
  2 *npl* (*technical aspects*) mecanismo *m*
mechanism ['mekənɪzəm] *n* mecanismo *m*
medal ['medəl] *n* medalla *f*
medallion [mɪ'dæljən] *n* medallón *m*
medallist, *US* **medalist** ['medəlɪst] *n* medalla *f*
meddle ['medəl] *vi* entrometerse (**in** en); **to m. with sth** manosear algo
media ['mi:dɪə] *npl* medios *mpl* de comunicación; **m. coverage** cobertura periodística

ℐ Note that the Spanish word **media** is a false friend and is never a translation for the English word **media**. In Spanish, **media** means both "stocking, sock" and "average".

median ['mi:dɪən] **1** *adj* mediano(a); *US Aut* **m. (strip)** mediana *f*, *Col, Méx* camellón *m*
  2 *n Geom* mediana *f*; *Math* valor mediano
mediate ['mi:dɪeɪt] *vi* mediar
mediator ['mi:dɪeɪtə(r)] *n* mediador(a) *m,f*
Medicaid ['medɪkeɪd] *n* (*in US*) = seguro médico estatal para personas con renta baja
medical ['medɪkəl] **1** *adj* (*treatment*) médico(a); (*book*) de medicina
  2 *n Fam* reconocimiento médico
Medicare ['medɪkeə(r)] *n* (*in US*) = seguro médico para ancianos y algunos discapacitados
medicated ['medɪkeɪtɪd] *adj* medicinal
medicine ['medsɪn] *n* (*science*) medicina *f*; (*drugs etc*) medicamento *m*
medieval [medɪ'i:vəl] *adj* medieval

mediocre [mi:dɪ'əʊkə(r)] *adj* mediocre
meditate ['medɪteɪt] *vi* meditar (**on** sobre)
meditation [medɪ'teɪʃən] *n* meditación *f*
Mediterranean [medɪtə'reɪnɪən] **1** *adj* mediterráneo(a)
  2 *n* **the M.** el Mediterráneo
medium ['mi:dɪəm] **1** *adj* (*average*) mediano(a); *Rad* **m. wave** onda media
  2 *n* (a) (*pl* **media**) (*means*) medio *m* (b) (*pl* **mediums**) (*spiritualist*) médium *mf*
medley ['medlɪ] *n* (*mixture*) mezcla *f*; *Mus* popurrí *m*
meek [mi:k] *adj* manso(a), sumiso(a); (*humble*) humilde
meet [mi:t] **1** *vt* (*pt & pp* **met**) (a) (*by chance*) encontrar, encontrarse con; (*by arrangement*) reunirse con; (*in formal meeting*) entrevistarse con
  (b) (*get to know*) conocer; **I'd like you to m. my mother** quiero presentarte a mi madre; **the first time I met him** cuando lo conocí; **pleased to m. you!** ¡mucho gusto!
  (c) (*await arrival of*) esperar; (*collect*) ir a buscar
  (d) (*danger*) encontrar; (*opponent*) enfrentarse con
  (e) (*satisfy*) satisfacer; (*obligations*) cumplir con; (*expenses*) hacer frente a
  2 *vi* (*by chance*) encontrarse; (*by arrangement*) reunirse; (*formal meeting*) entrevistarse; (*get to know each other*) conocerse; *Sport* enfrentarse; (*join*) unirse; (*rivers*) confluir; **their eyes met** cruzaron las miradas
  3 *n* (*sports event*) encuentro *m*; (*in athletics*) reunión *f* atlética
  ▸ **meet with** *vt insep* (*difficulty*) tropezar con; (*loss*) sufrir; (*success*) tener; *esp US* (*person*) reunirse con
meeting ['mi:tɪŋ] *n* (*chance encounter*) encuentro *m*; (*prearranged*) cita *f*; (*formal*) entrevista *f*; (*of committee etc*) reunión *f*; (*of assembly*) sesión *f*; (*of shareholders*) junta *f*, (*rally*) mitin *m*; *Sport* encuentro *m*; (*of rivers*) confluencia *f*
mega ['megə] *adj Fam* (*excellent*) genial, guay, *Andes, CAm, Carib, Méx* chévere, *RP* bárbaro
megabyte ['megəbaɪt] *n Comput* megabyte *m*
megaphone ['megəfəʊn] *n* megáfono *m*
melancholy ['melənkəlɪ] **1** *n* melancolía *f*
  2 *adj* melancólico(a)
Melilla [me'li:jə] *n* Melilla
mellow ['meləʊ] **1** *adj* maduro(a); (*wine*)

añejo(a); *(colour, voice)* suave; *(person)* apacible

2 *vi (fruit)* madurar; *(colour, voice)* suavizarse

melodramatic [melǝdrǝ'mætɪk] *adj* melodramático(a)

melody ['melǝdɪ] *n* melodía *f*

melon ['melǝn] *n* melón *m*

melt [melt] **1** *vt (metal)* fundir; *Fig (sb's heart)* ablandar

2 *vi (snow)* derretirse; *(metal)* fundirse; *Fig* ablandarse

▸ **melt away** *vi (snow)* derretirse; *Fig (money)* desaparecer; *Fig (confidence)* desvanecerse

▸ **melt down** *vt sep (metal)* fundir

melting ['meltɪŋ] *n* fundición *f*; **m. point** punto *m* de fusión; **m. pot** crisol *m*

member ['membǝ(r)] *n* miembro *mf*; *(of a society)* socio(a) *m,f*; *(of party, union)* afiliado(a) *m,f*; *US* **M. of Congress** congresista *mf*; *Br* **M. of Parliament** diputado(a) *m,f*

membership ['membǝʃɪp] *n (state)* calidad *f* de socio; *(entry)* ingreso *m*; *Pol* afiliación *f*; *(number of members)* número *m* de socios; **m. card** carnet *m* de socio

memento [mǝ'mentǝʊ] *n* recuerdo *m*

memo ['memǝʊ] *n (official note)* memorándum *m*; *(personal note)* nota *f*, apunte *m*

memoirs ['memwɑːz] *npl* memorias *fpl*

memorable ['memǝrǝbǝl] *adj* memorable

memorandum [memǝ'rændǝm] *n (pl* **memoranda**) *(official note)* memorándum *m*; *(personal note)* nota *f*, apunte *m*

memorial [mɪ'mɔːrɪǝl] **1** *adj (plaque etc)* conmemorativo(a)

2 *n* monumento conmemorativo

memorize ['memǝraɪz] *vt* memorizar, aprender de memoria

memory ['memǝrɪ] *n* memoria *f*, *(recollection)* recuerdo *m*

men [men] *pl of* **man**

menace ['menɪs] **1** *n (threat)* amenaza *f*; *(danger)* peligro *m*; *Fam (person)* pesado(a) *m,f*

2 *vt* amenazar

menacing ['menɪsɪŋ] *adj* amenazador(a)

menagerie [mɪ'nædʒǝrɪ] *n* casa *f* de fieras

mend [mend] **1** *vt* reparar, arreglar; *(clothes)* remendar; *(socks etc)* zurcir

2 *vi (ill person)* reponerse

3 *n (patch)* remiendo *m*; *(darn)* zurcido *m*; *Fig* **to be on the m.** ir mejorando

mending ['mendɪŋ] *n (repair)* reparación

f, *(darning)* zurcido *m*; *(clothes for mending)* ropa *f* para remendar

menial ['miːnɪǝl] *adj (task)* servil, bajo(a)

menopause ['menǝpɔːz] *n* menopausia *f*

menstrual ['menstrʊǝl] *adj* menstrual

menstruation [menstrʊ'eɪʃǝn] *n* menstruación *f*

mental ['mentǝl] *adj* (**a**) mental; **m. home, m. hospital** hospital psiquiátrico; **m. illness** enfermedad *f* mental (**b**) *Fam (crazy)* chalado(a)

mentality [men'tælɪtɪ] *n* mentalidad *f*

mentally ['mentǝlɪ] *adv* **m. ill** enfermo(a) mental; **to be m. handicapped** ser un(a) disminuido(a) psíquico(a)

mention ['menʃǝn] **1** *n* mención *f*

2 *vt* mencionar; **don't m. it!** ¡de nada!

mentor ['mentɔː(r)] *n* mentor *m*

menu ['menjuː] *n* (**a**) *(card)* carta *f*; *(fixed meal)* menú *m*; **today's m.** menú del día (**b**) *Comput* menú *m*

MEP [emiː'piː] *n (abbr* **Member of the European Parliament**) eurodiputado(a) *m,f*

mercenary ['mɜːsɪnǝrɪ] *adj & n* mercenario(a) *(m,f)*

merchandise ['mɜːtʃǝndaɪz] *n* mercancías *fpl*, géneros *mpl*

merchant ['mɜːtʃǝnt] *n Com & Fin* comerciante *mf*; *(retailer)* detallista *mf*; **m. bank** banco *m* comercial; **m. navy** marina *f* mercante

merciful ['mɜːsɪfʊl] *adj* clemente, compasivo(a) (**towards** con)

merciless ['mɜːsɪlɪs] *adj* despiadado(a)

Mercury ['mɜːkjʊrɪ] *n* Mercurio *m*

mercury ['mɜːkjʊrɪ] *n* mercurio *m*

mercy ['mɜːsɪ] *n* misericordia *f*, compasión *f*; **at the m. of** a la merced de; **to have m. on** tener compasión de

mere [mɪǝ(r)] *adj* mero(a), simple

merely ['mɪǝlɪ] *adv* simplemente

merge [mɜːdʒ] **1** *vt (blend)* unir (**with** con); *Com* fusionar

2 *vi* unirse; *(roads)* empalmar; *Com* fusionarse

merger ['mɜːdʒǝ(r)] *n Com* fusión *f*

meringue [mǝ'ræŋ] *n* merengue *m*

merit ['merɪt] **1** *n (of person)* mérito *m*; *(of plan etc)* ventaja *f*

2 *vt* merecer

mermaid ['mɜːmeɪd] *n* sirena *f*

merry ['merɪ] *adj* (**merrier, merriest**) alegre; *Fam (tipsy)* achispado(a); **m. Christmas!** ¡felices Navidades!

merry-go-round ['merɪgǝʊraʊnd] *n* tiovivo *m*

mesh [meʃ] **1** *n Tex* malla *f*; *Tech* engranaje *m*; *Fig* red *f*

2 *vt Tech* engranar

mesmerize ['mezməraɪz] *vt* hipnotizar

mess [mes] **1** *n* (**a**) *(confusion)* confusión *f*; *(disorder)* desorden *m*; **to be in a m.** *(of room etc)* estar desordenado(a) (**b**) *(in life, affairs)* lío *m*; **to get into a m.** meterse en un lío (**c**) *(dirt)* suciedad *f* (**d**) *Mil (food)* rancho *m* (**e**) *Mil (room)* comedor *m*

▸ **mess about, mess around** *Fam* **1** *vt sep* fastidiar

2 *vi* (**a**) *(act the fool)* hacer el primo; *(idle)* gandulear; *(kill time)* pasar el rato

▸ **mess about with** *vt insep Fam (fiddle with)* manosear; **to m. about with sb** tener un lío con algn

▸ **mess up** *vt sep Fam (make untidy)* desordenar; *(dirty)* ensuciar; *(spoil)* estropear

message ['mesɪdʒ] *n (communication)* recado *m*; *(of story etc)* mensaje *m*; *Fam* **to get the m.** comprender

messenger ['mesɪndʒə(r)] *n* mensajero(a) *m,f*

Messrs ['mesəz] *npl (abbr* **Messieurs**) Sres.

messy ['mesɪ] *adj* (**messier, messiest**) *(untidy)* desordenado(a); *(confused)* enredado(a); *(dirty)* sucio(a)

met [met] *pt & pp of* **meet**

metabolism [me'tæbəlɪzəm] *n* metabolismo *m*

metal ['metəl] **1** *n* metal *m*

2 *adj* metálico(a)

metallic [mɪ'tælɪk] *adj* metálico(a); **m. blue** azul metalizado

metallurgy [me'tælədʒɪ] *n* metalurgia *f*

metalwork ['metəlwɜːk] *n (craft)* metalistería *f*; *(objects)* objetos *mpl* de metal

metaphor ['metəfə(r)] *n* metáfora *f*

mete [miːt] *vt* **to m. out** imponer

meteor ['miːtɪə(r)] *n* bólido *m*

meteoric [miːtɪ'ɒrɪk] *adj* meteórico(a)

meteorite ['miːtɪəraɪt] *n* meteorito *m*

meteorology [miːtɪə'rɒlədʒɪ] *n* meteorología *f*

meter¹ ['miːtə(r)] *n* contador *m*

meter² ['miːtər] *n US =* **metre**

method ['meθəd] *n* método *m*

methodical [mɪ'θɒdɪkəl] *adj* metódico(a)

Methodist ['meθədɪst] *adj & n* metodista *(mf)*

meths [meθs] *n sing Br Fam* alcohol *m* de quemar

methylated spirits ['meθɪleɪtɪd'spɪrɪts]

n alcohol metilado *or* desnaturalizado

meticulous [mə'tɪkjʊləs] *adj* meticuloso(a)

metre ['miːtə(r)] *n* metro *m*

metric ['metrɪk] *adj* métrico(a)

metropolis [mɪ'trɒpəlɪs] *n* metrópoli *f*

metropolitan [metrə'pɒlɪtən] *adj* metropolitano(a)

mettle ['metəl] *n* valor *m*

mew [mjuː] *vi (cat)* maullar

mews [mjuːz] *n sing (street)* callejuela *f*; **m. flat** = apartamento de lujo en unas caballerizas reconvertidas

Mexican ['meksɪkən] *adj & n* mejicano(a) *(m,f)*, mexicano(a) *(m,f)*

Mexico ['meksɪkəʊ] *n* Méjico, México

miaow [miː'aʊ] **1** *vi* maullar

2 *n* maullido *m*

mice [maɪs] *pl of* **mouse**

mickey ['mɪkɪ] *n Fam* **to take the m. (out of sb)** tomar el pelo (a algn)

microbe ['maɪkrəʊb] *n* microbio *m*

microchip ['maɪkrəʊtʃɪp] *n* microplaqueta *f*, microchip *m*

microcomputer ['maɪkrəʊkəm'pjuːtə(r)] *n* microordenador *m*

microcosm ['maɪkrəʊkɒzəm] *n* microcosmo *m*

microfilm ['maɪkrəʊfɪlm] *n* microfilm *m*

microphone ['maɪkrəfəʊn] *n* micrófono *m*

microprocessor [maɪkrəʊ'prəʊsesə(r)] *n* microprocesador *m*

microscope ['maɪkrəskəʊp] *n* microscopio *m*

microwave ['maɪkrəʊweɪv] *n* microonda *f*; **m. (oven)** (horno *m*) microondas *m inv*

mid [mɪd] *adj* (**in**) **m. afternoon** a media tarde; (**in**) **m. April** a mediados de abril; **to be in one's m. thirties** tener unos treinta y cinco años

midair 1 *adj* ['mɪdeə(r)] *(collision, explosion)* en el aire

2 *n* [mɪd'eə(r)] *Fig* **to leave sth in m.** dejar algo en el aire

midday 1 *n* [mɪd'deɪ] mediodía *m*

2 *adj* ['mɪddeɪ] de mediodía

middle ['mɪdəl] **1** *adj* de en medio; **m. age** mediana edad; **the M. Ages** la Edad Media; **the m. class** la clase media

2 *n* (**a**) *(centre)* centro *m*, medio *m*; **in the m. of** en medio de; **in the m. of winter** en pleno invierno; *Fam* **in the m. of nowhere** en el quinto pino (**b**) *Fam (waist)* cintura *f*

middle-aged [mɪdəl'eɪdʒd] *adj* de mediana edad

middle-class [mɪdəl'klɑːs] *adj* de clase media

middleman ['mɪdəlmæn] *n* intermediario *m*

middleweight ['mɪdəlweɪt] *n* peso medio

middling ['mɪdlɪŋ] *adj* mediano(a)

midfielder [mɪd'fiːldə(r)] *n Sport* centrocampista *mf*

midge [mɪdʒ] *n* mosca enana

midget ['mɪdʒɪt] *n* enano(a) *m,f*

Midlands ['mɪdləndz] *npl* **the M.** = la región central de Inglaterra

midnight ['mɪdnaɪt] *n* medianoche *f*

midst [mɪdst] *n* **in the m. of** en medio de

midsummer [mɪd'sʌmə(r)] *n* pleno verano; **M.'s Day** Día *m* de San Juan *(24 de junio)*

midway ['mɪdweɪ] *adv* a medio camino

midweek 1 *adv* [mɪd'wiːk] entre semana
2 *adj* ['mɪdwiːk] de entre semana

midwife ['mɪdwaɪf] *n* comadrona *f*, partera *f*

midwifery ['mɪdwɪfərɪ] *n* obstetricia *f*

midwinter [mɪd'wɪntə(r)] *n* pleno invierno *m*

might¹ [maɪt] *v aux see* **may**

might² [maɪt] *n Fml* fuerza *f*, poder *m*

mighty ['maɪtɪ] **1** *adj* (**mightier, mightiest**) *(strong)* fuerte; *(powerful)* poderoso(a); *(great)* enorme
2 *adv US Fam* cantidad de, muy

migraine ['miːɡreɪn, 'maɪɡreɪn] *n* jaqueca *f*

migrant ['maɪɡrənt] **1** *adj* migratorio(a)
2 *n (person)* emigrante *mf*; *(bird)* ave migratoria

migrate [maɪ'ɡreɪt] *vi* emigrar

migration [maɪ'ɡreɪʃən] *n* migración *f*

mike [maɪk] *n Fam* micro *m*

mild [maɪld] *adj (person, character)* apacible; *(climate)* templado(a); *(punishment)* leve; *(tobacco, taste)* suave

mildew ['mɪldjuː] *n* moho *m*; *(on plants)* añublo *m*

mildly ['maɪldlɪ] *adv (softly, gently)* suavemente; *(slightly)* ligeramente; **and that's putting it m.** y esto es decir poco

mildness ['maɪldnɪs] *n (of character)* apacibilidad *f*; *(of climate, taste)* suavidad *f*; *(of punishment)* levedad *f*

mile [maɪl] *n* milla *f*; *Fam* **miles better** muchísimo mejor

mileage ['maɪlɪdʒ] *n* kilometraje *m*

milestone ['maɪlstəʊn] *n* hito *m*

milieu ['miːljɜː] *n* medio *m* ambiente

militant ['mɪlɪtənt] *adj & n* militante *(mf)*

military ['mɪlɪtərɪ] *adj* militar; **to do one's m. service** hacer el servicio militar

militia [mɪ'lɪʃə] *n* milicia *f*

milk [mɪlk] **1** *n* leche *f*; **m. chocolate** chocolate *m* con leche; **m. shake** batido *m*
2 *vt* (**a**) *(cow, goat)* ordeñar (**b**) *Fam* **they milked him of all his money** le sangraron hasta la última peseta

milkman ['mɪlkmən] *n* lechero *m*

milky ['mɪlkɪ] *adj* (**milkier, milkiest**) lechoso(a); *(colour)* pálido(a); **M. Way** Vía Láctea

mill [mɪl] **1** *n (grinder)* molino *m*; *(for coffee)* molinillo *m*; *(factory)* fábrica *f*; **cotton m.** hilandería *f*
2 *vt* moler
▸**mill about, mill around** *vi* arremolinarse

millennium [mɪ'lenɪəm] *n (pl* **millenniums** *or* **millennia** [mɪ'lenɪə]*)* milenio *m*

miller ['mɪlə(r)] *n* molinero(a) *m,f*

millet ['mɪlɪt] *n* mijo *m*

milligram(me) ['mɪlɪɡræm] *n* miligramo *m*

millilitre, *US* **milliliter** ['mɪlɪliːtə(r)] *n* mililitro *m*

millimetre, *US* **millimeter** ['mɪlɪmiːtə(r)] *n* milímetro *m*

milliner ['mɪlɪnə(r)] *n* sombrerero(a) *m,f*

millinery ['mɪlɪnərɪ] *n* sombreros *mpl* de señora

million ['mɪljən] *n* millón *m*

millionaire [mɪljə'neə(r)] *n* millonario(a) *m,f*

millstone ['mɪlstəʊn] *n* muela *f*; *Fig* carga *f*

mime [maɪm] **1** *n (art)* mímica *f*; *(play)* pantomima *f*
2 *vt* representar con gestos

> 🖉 Note that the Spanish verb **mimar** is a false friend and is never a translation for the English verb **to mime**. In Spanish, **mimar** means "to spoil, to pamper".

mimic ['mɪmɪk] **1** *adj & n* mímico(a) *(m,f)*
2 *vt* imitar

mimicry ['mɪmɪkrɪ] *n* imitación *f*

minaret ['mɪnəret] *n* alminar *m*, minarete *m*

mince [mɪns] **1** *n Br (meat)* carne picada; **m. pie** *(containing meat)* = especie de empanada de carne picada; *(containing fruit)* pastel *m* de picadillo de fruta
2 *vt* picar; *Fig* **he doesn't m. his words** no tiene pelos en la lengua
3 *vi (walk)* **to m. (along)** andar con pasos menuditos

mincemeat ['mɪnsmiːt] *n (dried fruit)* conserva *f* de picadillo de fruta; *(meat)* carne picada

mincer ['mɪnsə(r)] *n* picadora *f* de carne

mind [maɪnd] **1** n (a) (intellect) mente f; (brain) cabeza f; **what kind of car do you have in m.?** ¿en qué clase de coche estás pensando?; **to lose one's m.** perder el juicio; **it slipped my m.** lo olvidé por completo; **to call sth to m.** recordar algo
(b) (opinion) **to be in two minds (about sth)** estar indeciso(a) (acerca de algo); **to my m.** a mi parecer
2 vt (a) (child) cuidar; (house) vigilar; (be careful of) tener cuidado con; **m. the step!** ¡ojo con el escalón!; **m. your own business!** ¡no te metas donde no te llaman!
(b) (object to) tener inconveniente en; **I wouldn't m. a cup of coffee** me vendría bien un café; **never m.** no importa
3 vi (a) **m. you, he is fifty** ten en cuenta que tiene cincuenta años
(b) (object) importar; **do you m. if I open the window?** ¿le importa que abra la ventana?

minder ['maɪndə(r)] n Fam (bodyguard) guardaespaldas m inv; (for child) niñera f; (babysitter) canguro mf

mindful ['maɪndfʊl] adj consciente

mindless ['maɪndlɪs] adj (task) de autómata; (violence) injustificable

mine¹ [maɪn] poss pron (el) mío/(la) mía/(los) míos, (las) mías, lo mío; **a friend of m.** un amigo mío; **these gloves are m.** estos guantes son míos; **which is m.?** ¿cuál es el mío?

mine² [maɪn] **1** n mina f; Fig **a m. of information** un pozo de información
2 vt (coal etc) extraer; Mil minar

minefield ['maɪnfiːld] n campo m de minas

miner ['maɪnə(r)] n minero(a) m,f

mineral ['mɪnərəl] **1** adj mineral; **m. water** agua f mineral
2 n mineral m

minesweeper ['maɪnswiːpə(r)] n dragaminas m inv

mingle ['mɪŋgəl] vi mezclarse

miniature ['mɪnɪtʃə(r)] **1** n miniatura f
2 adj (railway) en miniatura; (camera, garden) diminuto(a)

minibus ['mɪnɪbʌs] n microbús m

minim ['mɪnɪm] n Mus blanca f

minimal ['mɪnɪməl] adj mínimo(a)

minimum ['mɪnɪməm] **1** adj mínimo(a); **m. wage** salario mínimo
2 n mínimo m

mining ['maɪnɪŋ] **1** n minería f, explotación f de minas; Mil & Naut minado m
2 adj minero(a)

miniskirt ['mɪnɪskɜːt] n minifalda f

minister ['mɪnɪstə(r)] **1** n ministro(a) m,f; Rel pastor(a) m,f
2 vi **to m. to sb** atender a algn

ministerial [mɪnɪ'stɪərɪəl] adj Pol ministerial

ministry ['mɪnɪstrɪ] n Pol ministerio m; Rel sacerdocio m

mink [mɪŋk] n visón m; **m. coat** abrigo m de visón

minnow ['mɪnəʊ] n piscardo m

minor ['maɪnə(r)] **1** adj (lesser) menor; (unimportant) sin importancia; (role) secundario(a); Mus menor
2 n Jur menor mf de edad

Minorca [mɪ'nɔːkə] n Menorca

minority [maɪ'nɒrɪtɪ] n minoría f; **to be in the m.** ser (la) minoría; Pol **m. party** partido minoritario

mint¹ [mɪnt] **1** n Fin **the M.** la Casa de la Moneda; **in m. condition** en perfecto estado
2 vt (coin, words) acuñar

mint² [mɪnt] n Bot menta f; (sweet) pastilla f de menta

minus ['maɪnəs] **1** prep **5 m. 3** 5 menos 3; **m. 10 degrees** 10 grados bajo cero
2 adj negativo(a)
3 n **m. (sign)** signo m (de) menos

minute¹ ['mɪnɪt] n (a) minuto m; **at the last m.** a última hora; **just a m.** (espera) un momento; **this very m.** ahora mismo
(b) minutes (notes) n el acta

minute² [maɪ'njuːt] adj (tiny) diminuto(a); (examination) minucioso(a)

miracle ['mɪrəkəl] n milagro m

miraculous [mɪ'rækjʊləs] adj milagroso(a)

mirage [mɪ'rɑːʒ] n espejismo m

mire [maɪə(r)] n fango m, lodo m; (muddy place) lodazal m

mirror ['mɪrə(r)] **1** n espejo m; Fig reflejo m; **rear-view m.** retrovisor m; **m. image** réplica f
2 vt reflejar

mirth [mɜːθ] n alegría f, (laughter) risas fpl

misadventure [mɪsəd'ventʃə(r)] n desgracia f; **death by m.** muerte f accidental

misanthropist [mɪ'zænθrəpɪst] n misántropo(a) m,f

misapprehension [mɪsæprɪ'henʃən] n malentendido m

misbehave [mɪsbɪ'heɪv] vi portarse mal

miscalculate [mɪs'kælkjʊleɪt] vt & vi calcular mal

miscarriage ['mɪskærɪdʒ] n Med aborto m (espontáneo); **m. of justice** error m judicial

miscellaneous [mɪsɪ'leɪnɪəs] *adj* variado(a); **m. expenses** gastos diversos

mischief ['mɪstʃɪf] *n (naughtiness)* travesura *f; Fml (evil)* malicia *f; Fam (harm)* daño *m;* **to get up to m.** hacer travesuras

mischievous ['mɪstʃɪvəs] *adj (naughty)* travieso(a); *(playful)* juguetón(ona); *Fml (wicked)* malicioso(a)

misconception [mɪskən'sepʃən] *n* concepto erróneo

misconduct [mɪs'kɒndʌkt] *n* mala conducta; **professional m.** error *m* profesional

misconstrue [mɪskən'stru:] *vt* interpretar mal

miscount [mɪs'kaʊnt] *vt (votes etc)* contar mal

misdeed [mɪs'di:d] *n* fechoría *f*

misdemeanour, *US* **misdemeanor** [mɪsdɪ'mi:nə(r)] *n (misdeed)* fechoría *f; Jur* delito *m* menor

miser ['maɪzə(r)] *n* avaro(a) *m,f*

miserable ['mɪzərəbəl] *adj (sad)* triste; *(unfortunate)* desgraciado(a); *(wretched)* miserable

miserly ['maɪzəlɪ] *adj* avaro(a), tacaño(a)

misery ['mɪzərɪ] *n (sadness)* tristeza *f; (wretchedness)* desgracia *f; (suffering)* sufrimiento *m; (poverty)* miseria *f; Fam (person)* aguafiestas *mf*

misfire [mɪs'faɪə(r)] *vi (engine, plan etc)* fallar

misfit ['mɪsfɪt] *n (person)* inadaptado(a) *m,f*

misfortune [mɪs'fɔːtʃən] *n* desgracia *f*

misgiving [mɪs'gɪvɪŋ] *n (doubt)* recelo *m; (fear)* temor *m*

misguided [mɪs'gaɪdɪd] *adj* equivocado(a)

mishandle [mɪs'hændəl] *vt* llevar *or* manejar mal

mishap ['mɪshæp] *n* contratiempo *m*

misinform [mɪsɪn'fɔːm] *vt* informar mal

misinterpret [mɪsɪn'tɜːprɪt] *vt* interpretar mal

misjudge [mɪs'dʒʌdʒ] *vt* juzgar mal

mislay [mɪs'leɪ] *vt* extraviar

mislead [mɪs'li:d] *vt* despistar; *(deliberately)* engañar

misleading [mɪs'li:dɪŋ] *adj (erroneous)* erróneo(a); *(deliberately)* engañoso(a)

mismanagement [mɪs'mænɪdʒmənt] *n* mala administración *f*

misnomer [mɪs'nəʊmə(r)] *n* nombre equivocado

misogynist [mɪ'sɒdʒɪnɪst] *n* misógino(a) *m,f*

misplace [mɪs'pleɪs] *vt (trust)* encauzar mal; *(book, spectacles etc)* extraviar

misprint ['mɪsprɪnt] *n* errata *f,* error *m* de imprenta

misrepresent [mɪsreprɪ'zent] *vt (facts)* desvirtuar; *(words)* tergiversar

miss¹ [mɪs] *n* señorita *f*

miss² [mɪs] **1** *n (throw etc)* fallo *m; Fam* **to give sth a m.** pasar de algo

2 *vt* **(a)** *(when throwing)* fallar; *(when shooting)* errar **(b)** *(train etc)* perder; *(opportunity)* dejar pasar; **you have missed the point** no has captado la idea; *Fig* **to m. the boat** perder el tren **(c)** *(omit)* saltarse **(d)** **I m. you** te echo de menos

3 *vi (when throwing)* fallar; *(when shooting)* errar; **is anything missing?** ¿falta algo?

▸ miss out 1 *vt sep (omit)* saltarse; *(on purpose)* pasar por alto

2 *vt insep* **to m. out on** perderse

misshapen [mɪs'ʃeɪpən] *adj* deforme

missile ['mɪsaɪl, *US* 'mɪsəl] *n Mil* misil *m; (object thrown)* proyectil *m*

missing ['mɪsɪŋ] *adj (object)* perdido(a); *(person)* desaparecido(a); *(from meeting etc)* ausente; **m. person** desaparecido(a) *m,f;* **three cups are m.** faltan tres tazas

mission ['mɪʃən] *n* misión *f*

missionary ['mɪʃənərɪ] *n* misionero(a) *m,f*

misspent ['mɪsspent] *adj (youth)* malgastado(a)

mist [mɪst] **1** *n* neblina *f; (thick)* niebla *f; (at sea)* bruma *f*

2 *vi* **to m. over** *or* **up** *(countryside)* cubrirse de neblina; *(window etc)* empañarse

mistake [mɪ'steɪk] **1** *n* error *m;* **by m.** por equivocación; **I hurt him by m.** le golpeé sin querer; **to make a m.** equivocarse, cometer un error

2 *vt (pt* **mistook;** *pp* **mistaken)** *(meaning)* malentender; **to m. Jack for Bill** confundir a Jack con Bill

mistaken [mɪ'steɪkən] *adj* equivocado(a), erróneo(a); **you are m.** estás equivocado(a)

mister ['mɪstə(r)] *n* señor *m*

mistletoe ['mɪsəltəʊ] *n* muérdago *m*

mistook [mɪ'stʊk] *pt of* **mistake**

mistreat [mɪs'tri:t] *vt* tratar mal

mistress ['mɪstrɪs] *n (of house)* señora *f,* ama *f; (lover)* amante *f; Educ (primary school)* maestra *f; (secondary school)* profesora *f*

mistrust [mɪs'trʌst] **1** *n* recelo *m*

2 *vt* desconfiar de

misty ['mɪstɪ] *adj* (**mistier, mistiest**) *(day)* de niebla; *(window etc)* empañado(a)

misunderstand [mɪsʌndə'stænd] *vt & vi* malentender

misunderstanding [mɪsʌndə'stændɪŋ] *n* r alentendido *m*; *(disagreement)* desave encia *f*

misuse 1 *n* [mɪs'juːs] mal uso *m*; *(of funds)* malversación *f*; *(of power)* abuso *m*
2 *vt* [mɪs'juːz] emplear mal; *(funds)* malversar; *(power)* abusar de

miter ['maɪtər] *n US* = mitre

mitigate ['mɪtɪgeɪt] *vt* atenuar

mitigating ['mɪtɪgeɪtɪŋ] *adj* **m. circumstances** circunstancias *fpl* atenuantes

mitre ['maɪtə(r)] *n* mitra *f*

mitten ['mɪtən] *n* manopla *f*; *(fingerless)* mitón *m*

mix [mɪks] 1 *n* mezcla *f*
2 *vt* mezclar
3 *vi* (*blend*) mezclarse (**with** con); *(go well together)* ir bien juntos
▸ **mix up** *vt sep* (*confuse*) confundir (**with** con); *(papers)* revolver; **to be mixed up in sth** estar involucrado(a) en algo

mixed [mɪkst] *adj* (*assorted*) surtido(a); *(varied)* variado(a); *(school)* mixto(a); *(feelings)* contradictorio(a)

mixed-up [mɪkst'ʌp] *adj* (*objects, papers etc*) revuelto(a); *(person)* confuso(a)

mixer ['mɪksə(r)] *n* (**a**) *Culin* batidora *f* (**b**) **to be a good m.** (*person*) tener don de gentes

mixture ['mɪkstʃə(r)] *n* mezcla *f*

mix-up ['mɪksʌp] *n Fam* confusión *f*, lío *m*

mm (*abbr* **millimetre(s)**) mm

moan [məʊn] 1 *n* (*groan*) gemido *m*, quejido *m*
2 *vi* (*groan*) gemir; *(complain)* quejarse (**about** de)

moat [məʊt] *n* foso *m*

mob [mɒb] 1 *n* multitud *f*; *(riff-raff)* gentuza *f*; **the m.** el populacho
2 *vt* acosar

mobile ['məʊbaɪl, *US* 'məʊbəl] 1 *adj* móvil; **m. home** caravana *f*; **m. phone** teléfono *m* móvil, *Am* teléfono *m* celular
2 *n* (**a**) (*hanging ornament*) móvil *m* (**b**) *Fam* (*mobile phone*) móvil *m*, *Am* celular *m*

mobility [məʊ'bɪlɪtɪ] *n* movilidad *f*

mobilize ['məʊbɪlaɪz] *vt* movilizar

mock [mɒk] 1 *adj* (*sympathy etc*) fingido(a); *(objects)* de imitación
2 *vt* (*make fun of*) burlarse de
3 *vi* burlarse (**at** de)

mockery ['mɒkərɪ] *n* burla *f*

mode [məʊd] *n* (*manner*) modo *m*, estilo *m*; *(fashion)* moda *f*

model ['mɒdəl] 1 *n* modelo *m*; *(fashion model)* modelo *mf*; **(scale) m.** maqueta *f*
2 *adj* (*railway*) en miniatura; *(pupil)* ejemplar; *(school)* modelo
3 *vt* (*clay etc*) modelar; *(clothes)* presentar
4 *vi* (*make models*) modelar; *(work as model)* trabajar de modelo

modem ['məʊdem] *n Comput* modem *m*

moderate¹ ['mɒdərɪt] 1 *adj* moderado(a); *(reasonable)* razonable; *(average)* regular; *(ability)* mediocre
2 *n Pol* moderado(a) *m,f*

moderate² ['mɒdəreɪt] 1 *vt* moderar
2 *vi* moderarse; *(wind)* calmarse; *(in debate)* arbitrar

moderately ['mɒdərɪtlɪ] *adv* medianamente

moderation [mɒdə'reɪʃən] *n* moderación *f*; **in m.** con moderación

modern ['mɒdən] *adj* moderno(a); *(history)* contemporáneo(a); **m. languages** lenguas modernas

modernize ['mɒdənaɪz] *vt* modernizar

modest ['mɒdɪst] *adj* modesto(a); *(chaste)* púdico(a); *(price)* módico(a); *(success)* discreto(a)

modesty ['mɒdɪstɪ] *n* (*humility*) modestia *f*; *(chastity)* pudor *m*

modification [mɒdɪfɪ'keɪʃən] *n* modificación *f*

modify ['mɒdɪfaɪ] *vt* modificar

module ['mɒdjuːl] *n* módulo *m*

mogul ['məʊgʌl] *n* magnate *m*

mohair ['məʊheə(r)] 1 *n* mohair *m*
2 *adj* de mohair

moist [mɔɪst] *adj* húmedo(a)

moisten ['mɔɪsən] *vt* humedecer

moisture ['mɔɪstʃə(r)] *n* humedad *f*

moisturizer ['mɔɪstʃəraɪzə(r)] *n* crema *f* *or* leche *f* hidratante

molar ['məʊlə(r)] *n* muela *f*

molasses [mə'læsɪz] *n sing* melaza *f*

mold¹ [məʊld] *n US* = **mould¹**

mold² [məʊld] *n & vt US* = **mould²**

molder ['məʊldər] *vi US* = **moulder**

molding ['məʊldɪŋ] *n US* = **moulding**

moldy ['məʊldɪ] *adj US* = **mouldy**

mole¹ [məʊl] *n* (*beauty spot*) lunar *m*

mole² [məʊl] *n* (*animal*) topo *m*

molecule ['mɒlɪkjuːl] *n* molécula *f*

molest [mə'lest] *vt* importunar; *(sexually assault)* acosar (sexualmente)

mollycoddle ['mɒlɪkɒdəl] *vt Fam* mimar, consentir

molt [məʊlt] *vi US* = **moult**

molten ['məʊltən] *adj* fundido(a); *(lava)* líquido(a)

mom [mɒm] *n US Fam* mamá *f*

moment ['məʊmənt] *n* momento *m*; **at the m.** en este momento; **for the m.** de momento; **in a m.** dentro de un momento; **at any m.** de un momento a otro

momentarily ['məʊməntərɪlɪ] *adv* momentáneamente; *US (soon)* dentro de poco

momentary ['məʊməntərɪ] *adj* momentáneo(a)

momentous [məʊ'mentəs] *adj* trascendental

momentum [məʊ'mentəm] *n Phys* momento *m*; *(speed)* velocidad *f*; *Fig* **to gather m.** cobrar velocidad

mommy ['mɒmɪ] *n US Fam* mamá *f*

Monaco ['mɒnəkəʊ] *n* Mónaco

monarch ['mɒnək] *n* monarca *m*

monarchy ['mɒnəkɪ] *n* monarquía *f*

monastery ['mɒnəstərɪ] *n* monasterio *m*

Monday ['mʌndɪ] *n* lunes *m*

monetarism ['mʌnɪtərɪzəm] *n* monetarismo *m*

monetary ['mʌnɪtərɪ] *adj* monetario(a)

money ['mʌnɪ] *n* dinero *m*; *(currency)* moneda *f*; **to make m.** ganar dinero; **to put m.** on apostar por

moneylender ['mʌnɪlendə(r)] *n* prestamista *mf*

money-spinner ['mʌnɪspɪnə(r)] *n Fam* negocio *m* rentable

Mongolia [mɒŋ'gəʊlɪə] *n* Mongolia

mongolism ['mɒŋgəlɪzəm] *n* mongolismo *m*

mongrel ['mʌŋgrəl] *n* perro mestizo

monitor ['mɒnɪtə(r)] **1** *n (screen)* monitor *m*; *Educ* delegado(a) *m,f*
2 *vt (check)* controlar; *(progress, events)* seguir de cerca

monk [mʌŋk] *n* monje *m*

monkey ['mʌŋkɪ] *n* mono *m*; **m. nut** cacahuete *m*, maní *m*, *Méx* cacahuate *m*; **m. wrench** llave inglesa

monochrome ['mɒnəkrəʊm] *adj* monocromo(a); *(television, photo)* en blanco y negro

monocle ['mɒnəkəl] *n* monóculo *m*

monologue, *US* **monolog** ['mɒnəlɒg] *n* monólogo *m*

monopolize [mə'nɒpəlaɪz] *vt Fin* monopolizar; *(attention etc)* acaparar

monopoly [mə'nɒpəlɪ] *n* monopolio *m*

monotone ['mɒnətəʊn] *n* **in a m.** con una voz monótona

monotonous [mə'nɒtənəs] *adj* monótono(a)

monotony [mə'nɒtənɪ] *n* monotonía *f*

monsoon [mɒn'su:n] *n* monzón *m*

monster ['mɒnstə(r)] *n* monstruo *m*

monstrosity [mɒn'strɒsɪtɪ] *n* monstruosidad *f*

monstrous ['mɒnstrəs] *adj (huge)* enorme; *(hideous)* monstruoso(a); *(outrageous)* escandaloso(a)

montage ['mɒntɑ:ʒ] *n* montaje *m*

month [mʌnθ] *n* mes *m*

monthly ['mʌnθlɪ] **1** *adj* mensual; **m. instalment** mensualidad *f*
2 *n (periodical)* revista *f* mensual
3 *adv* mensualmente, cada mes

monument ['mɒnjʊmənt] *n* monumento *m*

monumental [mɒnjʊ'mentəl] *adj* monumental; *Fam (huge)* enorme

moo [mu:] **1** *n* mugido *m*
2 *vi* mugir

mooch [mu:tʃ] *Fam* **1** *vi* **to m. around** vagar, dar vueltas
2 *vt* **to m. sth off sb** *(cadge)* gorronearle algo a algn

mood [mu:d] *n* humor *m*; **to be in a good/bad m.** estar de buen/mal humor; **to be in the m. for (doing) sth** estar de humor para (hacer) algo

moody ['mu:dɪ] *adj (moodier, moodiest)* *(changeable)* de humor variable; *(bad-tempered)* malhumorado(a)

moon [mu:n] *n* luna *f*; *Fam* **over the m.** en el séptimo cielo

moonlight ['mu:nlaɪt] *n* luz *f* de la luna

moonlighting ['mu:nlaɪtɪŋ] *n Fam* pluriempleo *m*

moonlit ['mu:nlɪt] *adj (night)* de luna

Moor [mʊə(r)] *n* moro(a) *m,f*

moor¹ [mʊə(r)] *n (heath)* páramo *m*

moor² [mʊə(r)] *vt Naut* amarrar

Moorish ['mʊərɪʃ] *adj* moro(a)

moorland ['mʊələnd] *n* páramo *m*

moose [mu:s] *n (pl moose)* alce *m*

moot [mu:t] *adj* **it's a m. point** es discutible

mop [mɒp] **1** *n (for floor)* fregona *f*; *Fam* **m. of hair** melena *f*
2 *vt* fregar
▸ **mop up** *vt sep (liquids)* enjugar; *(enemy forces)* acabar con

mope [məʊp] *vi* estar alicaído(a)
▸ **mope about, mope around** *vi* andar abatido(a)

moped ['məʊped] *n* ciclomotor *m*, vespa *f*

moral ['mɒrəl] **1** *adj* moral
2 *n* moraleja *f*; **morals** moral *f*, moralidad *f*

morale [mə'rɑːl] n moral f, estado m de ánimo

morality [mə'rælɪtɪ] n moralidad f

morass [mə'ræs] n pantano m; Fig lío m

moratorium [mɒrə'tɔːrɪəm] n moratoria f (**on** en)

morbid ['mɔːbɪd] adj Med mórbido(a); (mind) morboso(a)

more [mɔː(r)] **1** adj más; **is there any m. tea?** ¿queda más té?; **I've no m. money** no me queda más dinero; **m. tourists** más turistas

2 pron más; **how many m.?** ¿cuántos más?; **I need some m.** necesito más; **it's m. than enough** es más que suficiente; **many/much m.** muchos(as)/mucho más; **m. than a hundred** más de cien; **the m. he has, the m. he wants** cuanto más tiene más quiere; **and what is m.** y lo que es más

3 adv más; **I won't do it any m.** no lo volveré a hacer; **she doesn't live here any m.** ya no vive aquí; **m. and m. difficult** cada vez más difícil; **m. or less** más o menos; **once m.** una vez más

moreover [mɔː'rəʊvə(r)] adv además

morgue [mɔːg] n depósito m de cadáveres

morning ['mɔːnɪŋ] **1** n mañana f; (before dawn) madrugada f; **in the m.** por la mañana; **on Monday mornings** los lunes por la mañana; **tomorrow m.** mañana por la mañana

2 adj matutino(a)

Moroccan [mə'rɒkən] adj & n marroquí (mf)

Morocco [mə'rɒkəʊ] n Marruecos

moron ['mɔːrɒn] n Fam imbécil mf

morose [mə'rəʊs] adj hosco(a), huraño(a)

> 🔎 Note that the Spanish word **moroso** is a false friend and is never a translation for the English word **morose**. In Spanish, **moroso** means "bad debtor".

morphine ['mɔːfiːn] n morfina f

Morse [mɔːs] n **M. (code)** (alfabeto m) Morse m

morsel ['mɔːsəl] n (of food) bocado m; Fig trozo m

mortal ['mɔːtəl] **1** adj mortal

2 n mortal mf

mortality [mɔː'tælɪtɪ] n mortalidad f

mortally ['mɔːtəlɪ] adv mortalmente; **m. wounded** herido(a) de muerte

mortar ['mɔːtə(r)] n mortero m

mortgage ['mɔːgɪdʒ] **1** n hipoteca f

2 vt hipotecar

mortician [mɔː'tɪʃən] n US (undertaker) encargado(a) m,f de funeraria

mortify ['mɔːtɪfaɪ] vt mortificar; Fam **I was mortified** me sentí avergonzado(a)

mortuary ['mɔːtʃʊərɪ] n depósito m de cadáveres

mosaic [mə'zeɪɪk] n mosaico m

Moscow ['mɒskəʊ, US 'mɒskaʊ] n Moscú

Moslem ['mɒzləm] adj & n musulmán(ana) (m,f)

mosque [mɒsk] n mezquita f

mosquito [mɒs'kiːtəʊ] n (pl mosquitoes) mosquito m; **m. net** mosquitero m

moss [mɒs] n musgo m

most [məʊst] **1** adj (superl of **much, many**) (a) (greatest in quantity etc) más; **this house suffered (the) m. damage** esta casa fue la más afectada; **who made (the) m. mistakes?** ¿quién cometió más errores?

(b) (the majority of) la mayoría de, la mayor parte de; **for the m. part** por lo general; **m. of the time** la mayor parte del tiempo; **m. people** la mayoría de la gente

2 pron (greatest part) la mayor parte; (greatest number) lo máximo, lo más; (the majority of people) la mayoría; **at the (very) m.** como máximo; **to make the m. of sth** aprovechar algo al máximo

3 adv (superl of **much**) (a˜ más; **the m. intelligent student** el estudiante más inteligente; **what I like m.** lo que más me gusta

(b) (very) muy; **m. likely** muy probablemente; **m. of all** sobre todo

mostly ['məʊstlɪ] adv (chiefly) en su mayor parte; (generally) generalmente; (usually) normalmente

MOT [eməʊ'tiː] n Br (abbr Ministry of Transport) **M. test** inspección técnica de vehículos, ≃ ITV

motel [məʊ'tel] n motel m

moth [mɒθ] n mariposa nocturna; **clothes m.** polilla f

mother ['mʌðə(r)] **1** n madre f; **unmarried m.** madre soltera; **M.'s Day** Día m de la Madre; **m. tongue** lengua materna

2 vt cuidar maternalmente

motherhood ['mʌðəhʊd] n maternidad f

mother-in-law ['mʌðərɪnlɔː] n suegra f

motherly ['mʌðəlɪ] adj maternal

mother-of-pearl [mʌðərəv'pɜːl] n madreperla f, nácar m

mother-to-be [mʌðətə'biː] n futura madre

motif [məʊ'tiːf] n Art & Mus motivo m; (embroidered etc) adorno m; Fig (main subject) tema m

motion ['məʊʃən] **1** *n (movement)* movimiento *m*; *(gesture)* ademán *m*; *(proposal)* moción *f*

2 *vt & vi* hacer señas; **to m. (to) sb to do sth** hacer señas a algn para que haga algo

motionless ['məʊʃənlıs] *adj* inmóvil

motivate ['məʊtıveıt] *vt* motivar

motivation [məʊtı'veıʃən] *n* motivación *f*

motive ['məʊtıv] **1** *adj (force)* motriz

2 *n (reason)* motivo *m*; *Jur* móvil *m*; **with the best of motives** con la mejor intención

motley ['mɒtlı] *adj* (**motlier, motliest**) *(multicoloured)* abigarrado(a); *(varied)* variado(a)

motor ['məʊtə(r)] *n (engine)* motor *m*; *Fam (car)* máquina *f*; **m. racing** carreras *fpl* de coches

motorbike ['məʊtəbaık] *n Fam* motocicleta *f*, moto *f*

motorboat ['məʊtəbəʊt] *n* (lancha) motora *f*

motorcar ['məʊtəkɑː(r)] *n* coche *m*, automóvil *m*

motorcycle ['məʊtəsaıkəl] *n* motocicleta *f*

motorcyclist ['məʊtəsaıklıst] *n* motociclista *mf*

motoring ['məʊtərıŋ] *n* automovilismo *m*

motorist ['məʊtərıst] *n* automovilista *mf*

motorway ['məʊtəweı] *n Br* autopista *f*

mottled ['mɒtəld] *adj (skin, animal)* con manchas; *(surface)* moteado(a)

motto ['mɒtəʊ] *n* lema *m*

mould[1] [məʊld] *n (fungus)* moho *m*

mould[2] [məʊld] **1** *n* molde *m*

2 *vt* moldear; *(clay)* modelar

moulder ['məʊldə(r)] *vi* **to m. (away)** desmoronarse

moulding ['məʊldıŋ] *n* moldura *f*

mouldy ['məʊldı] *adj* (**mouldier, mouldiest**) mohoso(a); **to go m.** enmohecerse

moult [məʊlt] *vi* mudar

mound [maʊnd] *n* montón *m*; *(small hill)* montículo *m*

mount[1] [maʊnt] *n* monte *m*; **M. Everest** (Monte) Everest *m*

mount[2] [maʊnt] **1** *n (horse)* montura *f*; *(support)* soporte *m*, base *f*; *(for photograph)* marco *m*; *(for jewel)* engaste *m*

2 *vt (horse)* subirse *or* montar a; *(campaign)* organizar; *(photograph)* enmarcar; *(jewel)* engastar

3 *vi (go up)* subir; *(get on horse, bike)* montar; *(increase)* subir

▸ **mount up** *vi (accumulate)* acumularse

mountain ['maʊntın] **1** *n* montaña *f*; *Fig (pile)* montón *m*

2 *adj* de montaña, montañés(esa); **m. bike** bicicleta *f* de montaña; **m. range** sierra *f*, cordillera *f*

mountaineer [maʊntı'nıə(r)] *n* alpinista *mf*, *Am* andinista *mf*

mountaineering [maʊntı'nıərıŋ] *n* alpinismo *m*, *Am* andinismo *m*

mountainous ['maʊntınəs] *adj* montañoso(a)

mourn [mɔːn] *vt & vi* **to m. (for) sb** llorar la muerte de algn

mourner ['mɔːnə(r)] *n* doliente *mf*

mournful ['mɔːnfʊl] *adj* triste; *(voice)* lúgubre

mourning ['mɔːnıŋ] *n* luto *m*; **in m.** de luto

mouse [maʊs] *n (pl* **mice**) *also Comput* ratón *m*

mousetrap ['maʊstræp] *n* ratonera *f*

mousse [muːs] *n Culin* mousse *f*; *(for hair)* **(styling) m.** espuma *f* (moldeadora)

moustache [mə'stɑːʃ] *n* bigote *m*

mousy ['maʊsı] *adj* (**mousier, mousiest**) *(colour)* pardusco(a); *(hair)* castaño claro; *(shy)* tímido(a)

mouth [maʊθ] **1** *n (pl* **mouths** [maʊðz]) (**a**) boca *f*; *Fam* **down in the m.** deprimido(a) (**b**) *(of cave etc)* entrada *f*; *(of river)* desembocadura *f*

2 *vt* [maʊð] pronunciar; *(insults)* proferir

mouthful ['maʊθfʊl] *n (of food)* bocado *m*; *(of drink)* sorbo *m*; **to be a bit of a m.** ser difícil de pronunciar

mouth organ ['maʊθɔːgən] *n* armónica *f*

mouthpiece ['maʊθpiːs] *n Mus* boquilla *f*; *(of telephone)* micrófono *m*; *Fig (spokesman)* portavoz *m*

mouthwash ['maʊθwɒʃ] *n* elixir *m*, enjuague *m* bucal

mouthwatering ['maʊθwɔːtərıŋ] *adj* muy apetitoso(a), que le hace a uno la boca agua

movable ['muːvəbəl] *adj* movible, móvil

move [muːv] **1** *n* (**a**) *(movement)* movimiento *m*; **to be on the m.** estar en marcha; **we must make a m.** debemos irnos ya; *Fam* **get a m. on!** ¡date prisa!

(**b**) *(in game)* jugada *f*; *(turn)* turno *m*

(**c**) *(course of action)* medida *f*; **to make the first m.** dar el primer paso

(**d**) *(to new home)* mudanza *f*, *(to new job)* traslado *m*

2 *vt* (**a**) mover; *(furniture etc)* cambiar de

sitio; *(transfer)* trasladar; **to m. house** mudarse (de casa)

(**b**) *(in game)* mover

(**c**) *(motivate)* inducir; *(persuade)* persuadir; **I won't be moved** no me harán cambiar de parecer

(**d**) *(affect emotionally)* conmover

(**e**) *(resolution etc)* proponer

3 *vi* (**a**) *(change position)* moverse, desplazarse; *(change house)* mudarse (de casa); *(change post)* trasladarse; **m. out of the way!** ¡quítate de en medio!

(**b**) *(train etc)* estar en marcha; **to start moving** ponerse en marcha

(**c**) *(travel)* ir

(**d**) *(leave)* irse, marcharse

(**e**) *(in game)* hacer una jugada

(**f**) *(take action)* tomar medidas

► **move about** *vt sep* cambiar de sitio

2 *vi (be restless)* ir y venir; *(travel)* viajar de un lugar a otro

► **move along 1** *vt sep (move forward)* hacer avanzar; *(keep moving)* hacer circular

2 *vi (move forward)* avanzar; *(keep moving)* circular; **m. along!** *(to person on bench)* ¡haz sitio!

► **move around** *vt sep & vi* = **move about**

► **move away 1** *vt sep* alejar, apartar (**from** de)

2 *vi (move aside)* alejarse, apartarse; *(leave)* irse; *(change house)* mudarse (de casa)

► **move back 1** *vt sep (to original place)* volver

2 *vi (withdraw)* retirarse; *(to original place)* volver

► **move forward 1** *vt sep* avanzar; *(clock)* adelantar

2 *vi* avanzar, adelantarse

► **move in** *vi (into new home)* instalarse

► **move off** *vi (go away)* irse, marcharse; *(train)* salir

► **move on** *vi (keep moving)* circular; *(go forward)* avanzar; *(time)* transcurrir

► **move out** *vi (leave)* irse, marcharse; *(leave house)* mudarse

► **move over** *vi* correrse

► **move up** *vi (go up)* subir; *Fig (be promoted)* ser ascendido(a), ascender; *(move along)* correrse, hacer sitio

movement ['muːvmənt] *n* (**a**) movimiento *m*; *(gesture)* gesto *m*, ademán *m* (**b**) *(of goods)* transporte *m*; *(of employees)* traslado *m* (**c**) *(trend)* corriente *f* (**d**) *(of machine)* mecanismo *m* (**e**) *(of goods, capital)* circulación *f*

movie ['muːvɪ] *n* película *f*; **to go to the**

movies ir al cine; **m. star** estrella *f* de cine; *US* **m. theater** cine *m*

moving ['muːvɪŋ] *adj (that moves)* móvil; *(car etc)* en marcha; *Fig (touching)* conmovedor(a)

mow [məʊ] *vt (pt* mowed; *pp* mown *or* mowed) *(lawn)* cortar; *(corn, wheat)* segar; *Fig* **to m. down** segar

mower ['məʊə(r)] *n* cortacésped *m*

mown [məʊn] *pp of* mow

MP [em'piː] *n Br Pol (abbr* **Member of Parliament**) diputado(a) *m,f*

mph [empiː'eɪtʃ] *(abbr* **miles per hour**) millas *fpl* por hora

MPhil [em'fɪl] *n (abbr* **Master of Philosophy**) = curso de posgrado de dos años de duración, superior a un máster e inferior a un doctorado

Mr ['mɪstə(r)] *(abbr* **Mister**) Sr

Mrs ['mɪsɪz] *(abbr* **Missus**) Sra

Ms [məz] *n* Sra/Srta

Ms es el equivalente femenino de **Mr**, y se utiliza para dirigirse a una mujer sin precisar su estado civil.

MSc [emes'siː] *n (abbr* **Master of Science**) máster *m* en Ciencias

much [mʌtʃ] **1** *adj* mucho(a); **as m. ... as** tanto(a) ... como; **how m. chocolate?** ¿cuánto chocolate?; **m. admiration** mucha admiración; **so m.** tanto(a)

2 *adv* mucho; **as m. as** tanto como; **as m. as possible** todo lo posible; **how m.?** ¿cuánto?; **how m. is it?** ¿cuánto es?, ¿cuánto vale?; **m. better** mucho mejor; **m. more** mucho más; **so m. the better!** ¡tanto mejor!; **thank you very m.** muchísimas gracias; **they are m. the same** son más o menos iguales; **too m.** demasiado; **without so m. as** sin siquiera

3 *pron* mucho; **I thought as m.** lo suponía; **m. of the town was destroyed** gran parte de la ciudad quedó destruida; **m. remains to be done** queda mucho por hacer

muck [mʌk] *n (dirt)* suciedad *f*; *(mud)* lodo *m*; *Fig* porquería *f*

► **muck about, muck around** *Fam* **1** *vi (idle)* perder el tiempo; *(play the fool)* hacer el tonto

2 *vt sep* **to m. sb about** fastidiar a algn

► **muck up** *vt sep (dirty)* ensuciar; *Fig (spoil)* echar a perder

mucky ['mʌkɪ] *adj* (**muckier, muckiest**) sucio(a)

mucus ['mjuːkəs] *n* moco *m*, mucosidad *f*

mud [mʌd] *n* lodo *m*, barro *m*; *(thick)* fango *m*; *Fig* **to sling m. at sb** poner a algn por los suelos; **m. flat** marisma *f*

muddle ['mʌdəl] **1** *n* desorden *m; Fig (mix-up)* embrollo *m,* lío *m;* **to get into a m.** hacerse un lío

2 *vt* confundir

▸ **muddle through** *vi* arreglárselas, ingeniárselas

▸ **muddle up** *vt sep* confundir

muddy ['mʌdɪ] *adj* (**muddier, muddiest**) *(lane)* fangoso(a); *(hands)* cubierto(a) de lodo; *(liquid)* turbio(a)

mudguard ['mʌdgɑːd] *n Br* guardabarros *m inv*

muff¹ [mʌf] *n* manguito *m;* **ear muffs** orejeras *fpl*

muff² [mʌf] *vt Fam* pifiar; **to m. it (up)** estropearlo

muffin ['mʌfɪn] *n* panecillo *m*

muffle ['mʌfəl] *vt (sound)* amortiguar; **to m. (up)** *(person)* abrigar

muffler ['mʌflə(r)] *n US Aut* silenciador *m*

mug¹ [mʌg] *n (large cup)* tazón *m; (beer tankard)* jarra *f*

mug² [mʌg] **1** *n Fam (fool)* tonto(a) *m,f; (face)* jeta *f*

2 *vt* atracar, asaltar

mugging ['mʌgɪŋ] *n* asalto *m*

muggy ['mʌgɪ] *adj* (**muggier, muggiest**) bochornoso(a)

mule [mjuːl] *n* mulo(a) *m,f*

mull [mʌl] *vt* mulled wine = vino caliente con especias

▸ **mull over** *vt sep* **to m. over sth** reflexionar sobre algo

multicoloured, *US* **multicolored** ['mʌltɪkʌləd] *adj* multicolor

multinational [mʌltɪ'næʃənəl] *adj & n* multinacional *(f)*

multiple ['mʌltɪpəl] **1** *adj* múltiple; **m. sclerosis** esclerosis *f* múltiple

2 *n* múltiplo *m*

multiplication [mʌltɪplɪ'keɪʃən] *n* multiplicación *f;* **m. sign** signo *m* de multiplicar

multiply ['mʌltɪplaɪ] **1** *vt* multiplicar (**by** por)

2 *vi* multiplicarse

multipurpose [mʌltɪ'pɜːpəs] *adj* multiuso *inv*

multistorey [mʌltɪ'stɔːrɪ] *adj (building)* de varios pisos; **m. car park** parking *m* de varias plantas

multitude ['mʌltɪtjuːd] *n* multitud *f,* muchedumbre *f*

mum¹ [mʌm] *n Fam* mamá *f*

mum² [mʌm] *adj* **to keep m.** no decir ni pío

mumble ['mʌmbəl] **1** *vi* hablar entre dientes

2 *vt* decir entre dientes

mumbo-jumbo ['mʌmbəʊ'dʒʌmbəʊ] *n (nonsense)* palabrería *f,* monsergas *fpl*

mummy¹ ['mʌmɪ] *n Fam (mother)* mamá *f,* mami *f*

mummy² ['mʌmɪ] *n (body)* momia *f*

mumps [mʌmps] *n sing* paperas *fpl*

munch [mʌntʃ] *vt & vi* mascar

mundane [mʌn'deɪn] *adj Pej (ordinary)* prosaico(a); *(job, life)* rutinario(a)

> 🔎 Note that the Spanish word **mundano** is a false friend and is never a translation for the English word **mundane**. In Spanish, **mundano** means "worldly".

municipal [mjuː'nɪsɪpəl] *adj* municipal

municipality [mjuːnɪsɪ'pælɪtɪ] *n* municipio *m*

mural ['mjʊərəl] *adj & n* mural *(m)*

Murcia [muː'siːə] *n* Murcia

murder ['mɜːdə(r)] **1** *n* asesinato *m,* homicidio *m*

2 *vt* asesinar

murderer ['mɜːdərə(r)] *n* asesino(a) *m,f*

murderess ['mɜːdərɪs] *n* asesina *f*

murderous ['mɜːdərəs] *adj* homicida

murky ['mɜːkɪ] *adj* (**murkier, murkiest**) oscuro(a); *(water)* turbio(a)

murmur ['mɜːmə(r)] **1** *n* murmullo *m; (of traffic)* ruido *m; (complaint)* queja *f*

2 *vt & vi* murmurar

muscle ['mʌsəl] **1** *n* músculo *m*

2 *vi Fam* **to m. in on sth** entrometerse en asuntos ajenos

muscular ['mʌskjʊlə(r)] *adj (pain, tissue)* muscular; *(person)* musculoso(a)

Muse [mjuːz] *n (in mythology)* musa *f*

muse [mjuːz] *vi* **to m. on** *or* **about sth** meditar algo

museum [mjuː'zɪəm] *n* museo *m*

mushroom ['mʌʃruːm] **1** *n* seta *f,* hongo *m; Culin* champiñón *m*

2 *vi Fig* crecer de la noche a la mañana

music ['mjuːzɪk] *n* música *f;* **m. hall** teatro *m* de variedades; **m. library** fonoteca *f; Psy* **m. therapy** musicoterapia *f*

musical ['mjuːzɪkəl] **1** *adj* musical; **to be m.** estar dotado(a) para la música

2 *n* musical *m*

musician [mjuː'zɪʃən] *n* músico(a) *m,f*

Muslim ['mʊzlɪm] *adj & n* musulmán(a-na) *(m,f)*

muslin ['mʌzlɪn] *n* muselina *f*

mussel ['mʌsəl] *n* mejillón *m*

must [mʌst] **1** *v aux* **(a)** *(obligation)* deber, tener que; **you m. arrive on time**

tienes que *or* debes llegar a la hora (**b**) *(probability)* deber de; **he m. be ill** debe de estar enfermo

2 *n Fam* **to be a m.** ser imprescindible

mustache ['mʌstæʃ] *n US* bigote *m*

mustard ['mʌstəd] *n* mostaza *f*

muster ['mʌstə(r)] **1** *vt Fig* **to m. (up) courage** cobrar fuerzas

2 *vi* reunirse, juntarse

mustn't ['mʌsənt] = **must not**

musty ['mʌstɪ] *adj* (**mustier, mustiest**) que huele a cerrado *or* a humedad

mute ['mjuːt] **1** *adj* mudo(a)

2 *n (person)* mudo(a) *m,f; Mus* sordina *f*

muted ['mjuːtɪd] *adj (sound)* sordo(a); *(colour)* suave

mutilate ['mjuːtɪleɪt] *vt* mutilar

mutiny ['mjuːtɪnɪ] **1** *n* motín *m*

2 *vi* amotinarse

mutter ['mʌtə(r)] **1** *n (mumble)* murmullo *m*

2 *vt* murmurar, decir entre dientes

3 *vi (angrily)* refunfuñar

mutton ['mʌtən] *n* (carne *f* de) cordero *m*

mutual ['mjuːtʃʊəl] *adj* mutuo(a); *(shared)* común

Muzak® ['mjuːzæk] *n* música *f* de supermercado

muzzle ['mʌzəl] **1** *n (snout)* hocico *m*; *(for dog)* bozal *m*; *(of gun)* boca *f*

2 *vt (dog)* abozalar; *Fig* amordazar

my [maɪ] *poss adj* mi; **my cousins** mis primos; **my father** mi padre; **one of my friends** un amigo mío; **I washed my hair** me lavé el pelo; **I twisted my ankle** me torcí el tobillo

myriad ['mɪrɪəd] *n Literary* miríada *f*

myself [maɪ'self] *pers pron* (**a**) *(emphatic)* yo mismo(a); **my husband and m.** mi marido y yo (**b**) *(reflexive)* me; **I hurt m.** me hice daño (**c**) *(after prep)* mí (mismo(a))

mysterious [mɪ'stɪərɪəs] *adj* misterioso(a)

mystery ['mɪstərɪ] *n* misterio *m*

mystical ['mɪstɪkəl] *adj* místico(a)

mystify ['mɪstɪfaɪ] *vt* dejar perplejo(a)

mystique [mɪ'stiːk] *n* mística *f*

myth [mɪθ] *n* mito *m*; **it's a complete m.** es pura fantasía

mythology [mɪ'θɒlədʒɪ] *n* mitología *f*

N, n [en] *n (the letter)* N, n *f*
N *(abbr* **North)** N
nab [næb] *vt Fam* pillar
naff [næf] *adj Br Fam* **(a)** *(tasteless)* hortera, cutre **(b)** *(for emphasis)* **n. all** nada de nada
NAFTA ['næftə] *n (abbr* **North American Free Trade Agreement)** NAFTA *f*, TLC *m*
nag [næg] **1** *vt* dar la tabarra a; **to n. sb to do sth** dar la tabarra a algn para que haga algo
 2 *vi* quejarse
nagging ['nægɪŋ] *adj (persistent)* continuo(a)
nail [neɪl] **1** *n* **(a)** *(of finger, toe)* uña *f*; **n. clippers** cortaúñas *m inv*; **n. polish** *or* **varnish** esmalte *m or* laca *f* de uñas **(b)** *(metal)* clavo *m*; *Fig* **to hit the n. on the head** dar en el clavo
 2 *vt* **(a)** *(clavar* **(b)** *Fam (catch, trap)* pillar, coger
nailbrush ['neɪlbrʌʃ] *n* cepillo *m* de uñas
nailfile ['neɪlfaɪl] *n* lima *f* de uñas
nail-scissors ['neɪlsɪzəz] *npl* tijeras *fpl* de uñas
naïve [naɪ'iːv] *adj* ingenuo(a)
naked ['neɪkɪd] *adj* desnudo(a); *(flame)* sin protección; **the n. truth** la pura verdad
name [neɪm] **1** *n* **(a)** nombre *m*; *(surname)* apellido *m*; **what's your n.?** ¿cómo te llamas?; **to call sb names** poner verde a algn **(b)** *(reputation)* reputación *f*; **to have a bad/good n.** tener mala/buena reputación; **to make a n. for oneself** hacerse famoso(a)
 2 *vt* **(a)** llamar; **to n. sb after** *or US* **for sb** poner a algn el nombre de algn **(b)** *(appoint)* nombrar **(c)** *(refer to)* mencionar
nameless ['neɪmlɪs] *adj* anónimo(a); **to remain n.** permanecer en el anonimato
namely ['neɪmlɪ] *adv* a saber
namesake ['neɪmseɪk] *n* tocayo(a) *m,f*
nanny ['nænɪ] *n* niñera *f*
nap [næp] **1** *n (sleep)* siesta *f*; **to have a n.** echar la *or* una siesta
 2 *vi Fig* **to catch sb napping** coger a algn desprevenido(a)

napalm ['neɪpɑːm] *n* napalm *m*
nape [neɪp] *n* nuca *f*, cogote *m*
napkin ['næpkɪn] *n* **(table)** n. servilleta *f*
Naples ['neɪpəlz] *n* Nápoles
nappy ['næpɪ] *n Br* pañal *m*
narcissus [nɑː'sɪsəs] *n Bot* narciso *m*
narcotic [nɑː'kɒtɪk] **1** *adj* narcótico(a)
 2 *n (usu pl)* narcótico *m*, estupefaciente *m*
narrate [nə'reɪt] *vt* narrar, relatar
narration [nə'reɪʃən] *n* narración *f*, relato *m*
narrative ['nærətɪv] **1** *n Lit* narrativa *f*; *(story)* narración *f*
 2 *adj* narrativo(a)
narrator [nə'reɪtə(r)] *n* narrador(a) *m,f*
narrow ['nærəʊ] **1** *adj* **(a)** *(passage, road etc)* estrecho(a), angosto(a) **(b)** *(restricted)* reducido(a); *(sense)* estricto(a); **to have a n. escape** librarse por los pelos
 2 *vi* estrecharse
narrowly ['nærəʊlɪ] *adv* **(a)** *(closely)* de cerca **(b)** *(by a small margin)* por poco
 ▸**narrow down 1** *vt sep* reducir, limitar
 2 *vi* **to n. down to** reducirse a
narrow-minded ['nærəʊ'maɪndɪd] *adj* de miras estrechas
nasal ['neɪzəl] *adj* nasal; *(voice)* gangoso(a)
nastiness ['nɑːstɪnɪs] *n* **(a)** *(unpleasantness)* carácter *m* desagradable **(b)** *(maliciousness)* mala intención
nasty ['nɑːstɪ] *adj* **(nastier, nastiest)** **(a)** *(person)* desagradable; **a n. business** un asunto feo; **a n. trick** una mala jugada *or* pasada; **cheap and n.** hortera; **to turn n.** *(of weather, situation)* ponerse feo(a) **(b)** *(unfriendly)* antipático(a); *(malicious)* mal intencionado(a); *Fam* **he's a n. piece of work** es un asco de tío **(c)** *(dirty)* sucio(a), asqueroso(a) **(d)** *(illness, accident)* grave
nation ['neɪʃən] *n* nación *f*
national ['næʃnəl] **1** *adj* nacional; **n. anthem** himno *m* nacional; **n. insurance** seguridad *f* social; *Br Mil* **n. service** servicio *m* militar
 2 *n* súbdito(a) *m,f*
nationalism ['næʃnəlɪzəm] *n* nacionalismo *m*

nationalist ['næʃnəlɪst] *adj & n* nacionalista *(mf)*

nationality [næʃə'nælɪtɪ] *n* nacionalidad *f*

nationalization [næʃnəlaɪ'zeɪʃən] *n* na-
cionalización *f*

nationalize ['næʃnəlaɪz] *vt* nacionalizar

nationwide ['neɪʃənwaɪd] *adj* de ámbito
nacional

native ['neɪtɪv] **1** *adj* (**a**) *(place)* natal; **n.
land** patria *f*; **n. language** lengua materna
(**b**) *(innate)* innato(a) (**c**) *(plant, animal)*
originario(a) (**to** de)
2 *n* nativo(a) *m,f*, natural *mf*; *(original
inhabitant)* indígena *mf*

NATO, Nato ['neɪtəʊ] *n* (*abbr* **North
Atlantic Treaty Organization**) OTAN *f*

natter ['nætə(r)] *Fam* **1** *vi* charlar
2 *n* charla *f*

natural ['nætʃərəl] **1** *adj* (**a**) natural (**b**)
(normal) normal; **it's only n. that ...** es
lógico que ... (**c**) *(born)* nato(a)
2 *n* (**a**) **she's a n. for the job** es la
persona ideal para el trabajo (**b**) *Mus*
becuadro *m*

naturalize ['nætʃərəlaɪz] *vt* **to become
naturalized** naturalizarse

naturally ['nætʃərəlɪ] *adv* (**a**) *(of course)*
naturalmente (**b**) *(by nature)* por naturaleza (**c**) *(in a relaxed manner)* con naturalidad

nature ['neɪtʃə(r)] *n* (**a**) naturaleza *f* (**b**)
(character) naturaleza *f*, carácter *m*; **by n.**
por naturaleza; **human n.** la naturaleza
humana (**c**) *(sort, kind)* índole *f*, clase *f*

naught [nɔːt] *n Literary* nada *f*; **to come
to n.** fracasar

naughtily ['nɔːtɪlɪ] *adv* **to behave n.** portarse mal

naughty ['nɔːtɪ] *adj* (**naughtier, naugh-
tiest**) (**a**) *(child)* travieso(a) (**b**) *(joke,
story)* atrevido(a), picante

nausea ['nɔːzɪə] *n Med (sickness)* náusea
f

nauseate ['nɔːzɪeɪt] *vt (disgust)* dar asco
a

nauseating ['nɔːzɪeɪtɪŋ] *adj* nauseabun-
do(a)

nautical ['nɔːtɪkəl] *adj* náutico(a); **n. mile**
milla marítima

naval ['neɪvəl] *adj* naval; **n. officer** oficial
mf de marina; **n. power** potencia marítima *or* naval

Navarre [nə'vɑː(r)] *n* Navarra

nave [neɪv] *n Archit* nave *f*

navel ['neɪvəl] *n Anat* ombligo *m*

navigate ['nævɪgeɪt] **1** *vt (river)* navegar
por; *Naut (ship)* gobernar

2 *vi* navegar; *(in driving)* indicar la dirección

navigation [nævɪ'geɪʃən] *n Naut* navegación *f*

navigator ['nævɪgeɪtə(r)] *n* (**a**) *Naut* na-
vegante *mf*, oficial *mf* de derrota (**b**) *Aut
& Av* copiloto *mf*

navvy ['nævɪ] *n Br Fam* peón *m*

navy ['neɪvɪ] *n* marina *f*; **n. blue** azul
marino

Nazi ['nɑːtsɪ] *adj & n* nazi *(mf)*

Nazism ['nɑːtsɪzəm] *n* nazismo *m*

NB, nb [en'biː] (*abbr* **nota bene**) N.B.

neap [niːp] *n* **n. (tide)** marea muerta

near [nɪə(r)] **1** *adj (in space)* cercano(a);
(in time) próximo(a); **in the n. future** en
un futuro próximo; **it was a n. thing** poco
faltó
2 *adv (in space)* cerca; **n. and far** por
todas partes; **that's n. enough** (ya) vale,
está bien
3 *prep* cerca de; **n. the end of the film**
hacia el final de la película
4 *vt* acercarse a

nearby [nɪə'baɪ] **1** *adj* cercano(a)
2 *adv* cerca

nearly ['nɪəlɪ] *adv* casi; **very n.** casi, casi;
we haven't n. enough no alcanza ni con
mucho

nearside ['nɪəsaɪd] *n Aut (with left-hand
drive)* lado izquierdo; *(with right-hand
drive)* lado derecho

near-sighted [nɪə'saɪtɪd] *adj* miope

neat [niːt] *adj* (**a**) *(room, habits etc)* orde-
nado(a); *(handwriting)* claro(a); *(appearance)* pulcro(a) (**b**) *(idea)* ingenioso(a)
(**c**) *(whisky etc)* solo(a) (**d**) *US Fam (fine)*
chulísimo(a)

neatly ['niːtlɪ] *adv* (**a**) *(carefully)* cuidadosamente (**b**) *(cleverly)* hábilmente

necessarily [nesɪ'serɪlɪ] *adv* necesaria-
mente, por fuerza

necessary ['nesɪsərɪ] **1** *adj* (**a**) *(essential)*
necesario(a); **to do what is n.** hacer lo
que haga falta; **if n.** si es preciso (**b**)
(unavoidable) inevitable
2 *n* **the n.** lo necesario

necessitate [nɪ'sesɪteɪt] *vt* necesitar, exigir

necessity [nɪ'sesɪtɪ] *n* (**a**) necesidad *f*;
out of n. por necesidad (**b**) *(article)* requisito *m* indispensable; **necessities** artículos *mpl* de primera necesidad

neck [nek] **1** *n* cuello *m*; *(of animal)*
pescuezo *m*; **to be n. and n.** ir parejos;
to be up to one's n. in debt estar hasta el
cuello de deudas; **to risk one's n.** jugarse
el tipo; **to stick one's n. out** arriesgarse; **to**

win/lose by a n. *(in horse racing)* ganar/perder por una cabeza; **low n.** escote bajo

2 *vi Fam* magrearse

necklace ['neklɪs] *n* collar *m*

neckline ['neklaɪn] *n (of dress)* escote *m*

necktie ['nektaɪ] *n US* corbata *f*

nectar ['nektə(r)] *n* néctar *m*

nectarine ['nektəriːn] *n* nectarina *f*

née [neɪ] *adj* **n.** Brown de soltera Brown

need [niːd] **1** *n* **(a)** necesidad *f*; **if n. be** si fuera necesario; **there's no n. for you to do that** no hace falta que hagas eso **(b)** *(poverty)* indigencia *f*; **to be in n.** estar necesitado; **to help a friend in n.** sacar a un amigo de un apuro

2 *vt* **(a)** necesitar; **I n. to see him** tengo que verle; *Ironic* **that's all I n.** sólo me faltaba eso **(b)** *(action, solution etc)* requerir, exigir

3 *v aux* tener que, deber; **n. he go?** ¿tiene que ir?; **you needn't wait** no hace falta que esperes

---

Cuando se emplea como verbo modal sólo existe una forma, y los auxiliares **do/does** no se usan: **he need only worry about himself; need she go?; it needn't matter.**

---

needle ['niːdəl] **1** *n* **(a)** *(for sewing, knitting)* aguja *f* **(b)** *Bot* hoja *f* **(c)** *Br Fam* **to get the n.** picarse

2 *vt Fam* pinchar

needless ['niːdlɪs] *adj* innecesario(a); **n. to say** huelga decir

needlessly ['niːdlɪslɪ] *adv* innecesariamente

needlework ['niːdəlwɜːk] *n (sewing)* costura *f*; *(embroidery)* bordado *m*

needy ['niːdɪ] *adj* **(needier, neediest)** necesitado(a)

negate [nɪ'geɪt] *vt* **(a)** *(deny)* negar **(b)** *(nullify)* anular

negative ['negətɪv] **1** *adj* negativo(a)

2 *n* **(a)** *Ling* negación *f* **(b)** *Phot* negativo *m*

neglect [nɪ'glekt] **1** *vt* **(a)** *(child, duty etc)* descuidar, desatender **(b)** **to n. to do sth** *(omit to do)* no hacer algo

2 *n* dejadez *f*; **n. of duty** incumplimiento *m* del deber

neglectful [nɪ'glektfʊl] *adj* descuidado(a), negligente

negligée ['neglɪʒeɪ] *n* salto *m* de cama

negligence ['neglɪdʒəns] *n* negligencia *f*, descuido *m*

negligent ['neglɪdʒənt] *adj* negligente, descuidado(a)

negligible ['neglɪdʒɪbəl] *adj* insignificante

negotiate [nɪ'gəʊʃɪeɪt] **1** *vt* **(a)** *(contract)* negociar **(b)** *Fig (obstacle)* salvar, franquear

2 *vi* negociar

negotiation [nɪgəʊʃɪ'eɪʃən] *n* negociación *f*

negro ['niːgrəʊ] *n (pl* **negroes)** negro(a) *m,f*

neigh [neɪ] **1** *n* relincho *m*

2 *vi* relinchar

neighbour, *US* **neighbor** ['neɪbə(r)] *n* vecino(a) *m,f*; *Rel* prójimo *m*

neighbourhood, *US* **neighborhood** ['neɪbəhʊd] *n (district)* vecindad *f*, barrio *m*; *(people)* vecindario *m*

neighbouring, *US* **neighboring** ['neɪbərɪŋ] *adj* vecino(a)

neither ['naɪðə(r), 'niːðə(r)] **1** *adj & pron* ninguno de los dos/ninguna de las dos

2 *adv & conj* **(a)** ni; **n. ... nor** ni ... ni; *Fig* **it's n. here nor there** no viene al caso **(b)** tampoco; **she was not there and n. was her sister** ella no estaba, ni su hermana tampoco

neon ['niːɒn] *n* neón *m*; **n. light** luz *f* de neón

nephew ['nefjuː] *n* sobrino *m*

nerd [nɜːd] *n Fam* **(a)** *(boring person)* petardo(a) *m,f*, plasta *mf*, *Méx* sangrón(ona) *m,f*, *RP* nerd *mf* **(b)** *(as insult)* bobo(a) *m,f*, memo(a) *m,f*

nerve [nɜːv] *n* **(a)** *Anat* nervio *m*; **to get on sb's nerves** poner los nervios de punta a algn; **n. gas** gas nervioso **(b)** *(courage)* valor *m* **(c)** *Fam (cheek)* cara *f*, descaro *m*; **what a n.!** ¡qué cara!

nerve-racking ['nɜːvrækɪŋ] *adj* crispante, exasperante

nervous ['nɜːvəs] *adj* **(a)** nervioso(a); **n. breakdown** depresión nerviosa **(b)** *(afraid)* miedoso(a) **(c)** *(timid)* tímido(a)

nest [nest] **1** *n Orn* nido *m*; *(hen's)* nidal *m*; *(animal's)* madriguera *f*; *Fig* **n. egg** ahorros *mpl*

2 *vi (birds)* anidar

nestle ['nesəl] **1** *vt* recostar

2 *vi (settle comfortably)* acomodarse

Net [net] *n Fam Comput* **the N.** *(Internet)* la Red; **N. user** internauta *mf*

net¹ [net] *n* red *f*; *Br* **n. curtains** visillos *mpl*

net² [net] **1** *adj* neto(a); **n. weight** peso neto

2 *vt (earn)* ganar neto

netball ['netbɔːl] *n Sport* baloncesto femenino

Netherlands ['neðələndz] *npl* **the N.** los Países Bajos

netting ['netɪŋ] *n* redes *fpl*, malla *f*

nettle ['netəl] **1** *n Bot* ortiga *f*
2 *vt Fam* irritar

network ['netwɜːk] **1** *n* red *f*
2 *vi (establish contacts)* establecer contactos

neurosis [njʊ'rəʊsɪs] *n* neurosis *f*

neurotic [njʊ'rɒtɪk] *adj & n* neurótico(a) *(m,f)*

neuter ['njuːtə(r)] **1** *adj* neutro(a)
2 *n Ling* neutro *m*
3 *vt (geld)* castrar

neutral ['njuːtrəl] **1** *adj* neutro(a); *Pol* **to remain n.** permanecer neutral
2 *n Aut* punto muerto

neutrality [njuː'trælɪtɪ] *n* neutralidad *f*

neutralize ['njuːtrəlaɪz] *vt* neutralizar

neutron ['njuːtrɒn] *n Phys* neutrón *m*; **n. bomb** bomba *f* de neutrones

never ['nevə(r)] *adv* nunca, jamás; **he n. complains** nunca se queja, no se queja nunca; **n. again** nunca (ja)más; **n. in all my life** jamás en la vida; *Fam* **n. mind** da igual, no importa; *Fam* **well, I n. (did)!** ¡no me digas!

never-ending ['nevər'endɪŋ] *adj* sin fin, interminable

nevertheless [nevəðə'les] *adv* sin embargo, no obstante

new [njuː] *adj* nuevo(a); **as good as n.** como nuevo; **n. baby** recién nacido *m*; **n. moon** luna nueva; **N. Year** Año nuevo; **N. Year's Eve** Nochevieja *f*; **N. York** Nueva York; **N. Zealand** Nueva Zelanda

newborn ['njuːbɔːn] *adj* recién nacido(a)

newcomer ['njuːkʌmə(r)] *n* recién llegado(a) *m,f*; *(to job etc)* nuevo(a) *m,f*

newfangled ['njuːfæŋgəld] *adj* novedoso(a)

newly ['njuːlɪ] *adv* recién, recientemente

newlywed ['njuːlɪwed] *n* recién casado(a) *m,f*

news [njuːz] *n sing* noticias *fpl*; **a piece of n.** una noticia; *Fam* **it's n. to me** ahora me entero; **n. agency** agencia *f* de información; *US* **n. in brief** avance informativo; **n. bulletin** boletín informativo; **n. clipping** recorte *m* de periódico; **n. summary** avance informativo

newsagent ['njuːzeɪdʒənt] *n* vendedor(a) *m,f* de periódicos

newsflash ['njuːzflæʃ] *n* noticia *f* de última hora

newsgroup ['njuːzgruːp] *n Comput* grupo *m* de noticias

newsletter ['njuːzletə(r)] *n* hoja informativa

newspaper ['njuːzpeɪpə(r)] *n* periódico *m*, diario *m*

newsprint ['njuːzprɪnt] *n* papel *m* de periódico

newsreader ['njuːzriːdə(r)] *n TV & Rad* presentador(a) *m,f* de los informativos

newsreel ['njuːzriːl] *n* noticiario *m*

news-stand ['njuːzstænd] *n* quiosco *m* de periódicos

newt [njuːt] *n Zool* tritón *m*

next [nekst] **1** *adj* (**a**) *(in place)* de al lado (**b**) *(in time)* próximo(a); **the n. day** el día siguiente; **n. Friday** el viernes que viene; **n. time** la próxima vez; **the week after n.** dentro de dos semanas (**c**) *(in order)* siguiente, próximo(a); **n. of kin** pariente *m* más cercano
2 *adv* después, luego; **what shall we do n.?** ¿qué hacemos ahora?
3 *prep* **n.** to al lado de, junto a; **n. to nothing** casi nada

next-door 1 *adj* ['neksdɔː(r)] de al lado; **our n. neighbour** el vecino/la vecina de al lado
2 *adv* [neks'dɔː(r)] al lado

NHS [eneɪtʃ'es] *n Br (abbr* **National Health Service**) Seguridad *f* Social

nib [nɪb] *n* plumilla *f*

nibble ['nɪbəl] *vt & vi* mordisquear

nice [naɪs] *adj* (**a**) *(person)* simpático(a); *(thing)* agradable; **n. and cool** fresquito(a); **to smell/taste n.** oler/saber bien (**b**) *(nice-looking)* bonito(a), *Am* lindo(a) (**c**) *Ironic* menudo(a); **a n. mess you've made!** ¡menudo lío has hecho! (**d**) *Fml (subtle)* sutil

nicely ['naɪslɪ] *adv* muy bien

niche [niːʃ] *n* (**a**) hornacina *f*, nicho *m* (**b**) *Fig* hueco *m*

nick [nɪk] **1** *n* (**a**) *(notch)* muesca *f*; *(cut)* herida pequeña; *Fam* **in the n. of time** en el momento preciso (**b**) *Br Fam* **the n. (prison)** chirona *f*
2 *vt Br Fam* (**a**) *(steal)* birlar (**b**) *(arrest)* pillar

nickel ['nɪkəl] *n* (**a**) níquel *m*; **n. silver** alpaca *f* (**b**) *US* moneda *f* de 5 centavos

nickname ['nɪkneɪm] **1** *n* apodo *m*
2 *vt* apodar

nicotine ['nɪkətiːn] *n* nicotina *f*

niece [niːs] *n* sobrina *f*

nifty ['nɪftɪ] *adj* (**niftier, niftiest**) (**a**) *(quick)* rápido(a); *(agile)* ágil (**b**) *(ingenious)* ingenioso(a)

Nigeria [naɪ'dʒɪərɪə] *n* Nigeria

nigger ['nɪgə(r)] *n Fam Pej* negro(a) *m,f*

niggling ['nɪgəlɪŋ] *adj (trifling)* insignificante; *(irritating)* molesto(a)

night [naɪt] *n* noche *f*; **at n.** de noche; **at twelve o'clock at n.** a las doce de la noche; **last n.** anoche; **to have a n. out** salir por la noche; **n. life** vida nocturna; *Fam* **n. owl** trasnochador(a) *m,f*; **n. school** escuela nocturna; **n. shift** turno *m* de noche

nightclub ['naɪtklʌb] *n* sala *f* de fiestas; *(disco)* discoteca *f*

nightdress ['naɪtdres] *n* camisón *m*

nightfall ['naɪtfɔːl] *n* anochecer *m*

nightgown ['naɪtgaʊn] *n* camisón *m*

nightingale ['naɪtɪŋgeɪl] *n* ruiseñor *m*

nightly ['naɪtlɪ] **1** *adj* de cada noche
2 *adv* todas las noches

nightmare ['naɪtmeə(r)] *n* pesadilla *f*

nightshade ['naɪtʃeɪd] *n Bot* **deadly n.** belladona *f*

night-time ['naɪttaɪm] *n* noche *f*; **at n.** por la noche

nil [nɪl] *n* nada *f*; *Sport* cero *m*; **two n.** dos a cero

Nile [naɪl] *n* **the N.** el Nilo

nimble ['nɪmbəl] *adj* ágil, rápido(a)

nine [naɪn] *adj & n* nueve *(m inv)*; *Fam* **dressed up to the nines** de punta en blanco

nineteen [naɪn'tiːn] *adj & n* diecinueve *(m inv)*

nineteenth [naɪn'tiːnθ] *adj* decimonoveno(a)

ninety ['naɪntɪ] *adj & n* noventa *(m inv)*

ninth [naɪnθ] **1** *adj & n* noveno(a) *(m,f)*
2 *n (fraction)* noveno *m*

nip [nɪp] **1** *vt* **(a)** *(pinch)* pellizcar **(b)** *(bite)* morder; **to n. sth in the bud** cortar algo de raíz
2 *n* **(a)** *(pinch)* pellizco *m* **(b)** *(bite)* mordisco *m*

nipple ['nɪpəl] *n* **(a)** *Anat (female)* pezón *m*; *(male)* tetilla *f* **(b)** *US (on baby's bottle)* tetilla *f*, tetina *f*

nippy ['nɪpɪ] *adj* **(nippier, nippiest)** *Fam* **(a)** *Br (quick)* rápido(a) **(b)** *(cold)* fresquito(a)

nit [nɪt] *n* liendre *f*

nitrogen ['naɪtrədʒən] *n Chem* nitrógeno *m*

nitroglycerin(e) [naɪtrəʊ'glɪsəriːn] *n Chem* nitroglicerina *f*

nitty-gritty [nɪtɪ'grɪtɪ] *n Fam* **to get down to the n.** ir al grano

nitwit ['nɪtwɪt] *n Fam* imbécil *mf*

no [nəʊ] **1** *adv* no; **come here! – no!** ¡ven aquí! – ¡no!; **no longer** ya no; **no less than** no menos de

2 *adj* ninguno(a); **she has no children** no tiene hijos; **I have no idea** no tengo (ni) idea; **it's no good** *or* **use** no vale la pena; *Aut* **no parking** *(sign)* prohibido aparcar; **no sensible person** ninguna persona razonable; *Fam* **no way!** ¡ni hablar!

3 *n* no *m*; **she won't take no for an answer** no para hacia salirse con la suya; **to say no** decir que no

no. *(pl* **nos.)** *(abbr* **number)** n, núm.

nobility [nəʊ'bɪlɪtɪ] *n* nobleza *f*

noble ['nəʊbəl] *adj* noble

nobleman ['nəʊbəlmən] *n* noble *m*

noblewoman ['nəʊbəlwʊmən] *n* noble *f*

nobody ['nəʊbədɪ] **1** *pron* nadie; **there was n. there** no había nadie; **n. else** nadie más

2 *n* nadie *m*; **he's a n.** es un don nadie

nocturnal [nɒk'tɜːnəl] *adj* nocturno(a)

nod [nɒd] **1** *n (of greeting)* saludo *m (con la cabeza)*; *(of agreement)* señal *f* de asentimiento

2 *vi (greet)* saludar con la cabeza; *(agree)* asentir con la cabeza

3 *vt* **to n. one's head** inclinar la cabeza
▸ **nod off** *vi* dormirse

no-go ['nəʊ'gəʊ] *adj* **n. area** zona prohibida

noise [nɔɪz] *n* ruido *m*; **to make a n.** hacer ruido

noiseless ['nɔɪzlɪs] *adj* silencioso(a), sin ruido

noisy ['nɔɪzɪ] *adj* **(noisier, noisiest)** ruidoso(a)

nomad ['nəʊmæd] *n* nómada *mf*

no-man's-land ['nəʊmænzlænd] *n* tierra *f* de nadie

nominal ['nɒmɪnəl] *adj* nominal; *(payment, rent)* simbólico(a)

nominate ['nɒmɪneɪt] *vt* **(a)** *(propose)* designar, proponer **(b)** *(appoint)* nombrar

nomination [nɒmɪ'neɪʃən] *n* **(a)** *(proposal)* propuesta *f* **(b)** *(appointment)* nombramiento *m*

nominative ['nɒmɪnətɪv] *n* nominativo *m*

nominee [nɒmɪ'niː] *n* persona propuesta

non- [nɒn] *pref* no

non-aggression [nɒnə'greʃən] *n Pol* no agresión *f*; **n. pact** pacto *m* de no agresión

non-alcoholic [nɒnælkə'hɒlɪk] *adj* sin alcohol

non-aligned [nɒnə'laɪnd] *adj Pol* no alineado(a)

nonchalant ['nɒnʃələnt] *adj (indifferent)*

indiferente; *(calm)* imperturbable, impasible

noncommittal ['nɒnkəmɪtəl] *adj (person)* evasivo(a); *(answer)* que no compromete (a nada)

nonconformist [nɒnkən'fɔːmɪst] *n* inconformista *mf*

nondescript ['nɒndɪskrɪpt] *adj* indescriptible; *(uninteresting)* soso(a)

none [nʌn] **1** *pron* ninguno(a); **I know n. of them** no conozco a ninguno de ellos; **n. at all** nada en absoluto; **n. other than ...** nada menos que ...

2 *adv* de ningún modo; **she's n. the worse for it** no se ha visto afectada *or* perjudicada por ello; **n. too soon** a buena hora

nonentity [nɒ'nentɪtɪ] *n (person)* cero *m* a la izquierda

nonetheless [nʌnðə'les] *adv* no obstante, sin embargo

nonevent [nɒnɪ'vent] *n* fracaso *m*

nonexistent [nɒnɪg'zɪstənt] *adj* inexistente

nonfiction [nɒn'fɪkʃən] *n* no ficción *f*

no-nonsense ['nəʊ'nɒnsəns] *adj (person)* recto(a), serio(a)

nonplussed [nɒn'plʌst] *adj* perplejo(a)

non-profit(-making) [nɒn'prɒfɪt(meɪkɪŋ)] *adj* sin fin lucrativo

nonreturnable [nɒnrɪ'tɜːnəbəl] *adj* no retornable

nonsense ['nɒnsəns] *n* tonterías *fpl*, disparates *mpl*; **that's n.** eso es absurdo

nonsmoker [nɒn'sməʊkə(r)] *n* no fumador(a) *m,f*, persona *f* que no fuma

nonstarter [nɒn'stɑːtə(r)] *n Fig* **to be a n.** *(person)* estar destinado a fracasar; *(plan)* ser irrealizable

nonstick [nɒn'stɪk] *adj* antiadherente

nonstop [nɒn'stɒp] **1** *adj* sin parar; *(train)* directo(a)

2 *adv* sin parar

noodles ['nuːdəlz] *npl Culin* fideos *mpl*

nook [nʊk] *n* recoveco *m*, rincón *m*

noon [nuːn] *n* mediodía *m*; **at n.** a mediodía

no one ['nəʊwʌn] *pron* nadie; **n. came** no vino nadie

noose [nuːs] *n* lazo *m*; *(hangman's)* soga *f*

nor [nɔː(r)] *conj* ni, ni tampoco; **neither ... n. ni ... ni; neither you n.** I ni tú ni yo; **n. do I** (ni) yo tampoco

norm [nɔːm] *n* norma *f*

normal ['nɔːməl] *adj* normal

normality [nɔː'mælɪtɪ] *n* normalidad *f*

normally ['nɔːməlɪ] *adv* normalmente

Normandy ['nɔːməndɪ] *n* Normandía

north [nɔːθ] **1** *n* norte *m*; **the N.** el norte; **N. America** América del Norte, Norteamérica; **N. Korea** Corea del Norte; **N. Pole** Polo *m* Norte; **N. Sea** Mar *m* del Norte

2 *adv* hacia el norte, al norte

3 *adj* del norte; **n. wind** viento *m* del norte

northeast [nɔː'θiːst] *n* nor(d)este *m*

northerly ['nɔːðəlɪ] *adj* del norte

northern ['nɔːðən] *adj* del norte, septentrional; **n. hemisphere** hemisferio *m* norte; **N. Ireland** Irlanda del Norte

northerner ['nɔːðənə(r)] *n* norteño(a) *m,f*

northward ['nɔːθwəd] *adj & adv* hacia el norte

northwest [nɔː'θ'west] *n* noroeste *m*

Norway ['nɔːweɪ] *n* Noruega

Norwegian [nɔː'wiːdʒən] **1** *adj* noruego(a)

2 *n* **(a)** *(person)* noruego(a) *m,f* **(b)** *(language)* noruego *m*

nose [nəʊz] *n* **(a)** nariz *f*; *Fig* **(right) under sb's n.** delante de las propias narices de algn; *Br Fam* **to get up sb's n.** hincharle a algn las narices **(b)** *(sense of smell)* olfato *m* **(c)** *(of car, plane)* morro *m*

▸ **nose about, nose around** *vi* curiosear

nosebleed ['nəʊzbliːd] *n* hemorragia *f* nasal

nosedive ['nəʊzdaɪv] *Av* **1** *n* picado *m*

2 *vi* descender en picado

nostalgia [nɒ'stældʒɪə] *n* nostalgia *f*

nostalgic [nɒ'stældʒɪk] *adj* nostálgico(a)

nostril ['nɒstrɪl] *n Anat* orificio *m* nasal

nosy ['nəʊzɪ] *adj* **(nosier, nosiest)** *Fam* entrometido(a)

not [nɒt] *adv* no; **he's n. in today** hoy no está; **I'm n. sorry to leave** no siento nada irme; **n. at all** en absoluto; **thank you – n. at all** gracias – no hay de qué; **n. one (of them)** thanked me nadie me dio las gracias; **n. that I don't want to come** no es que no quiera ir; **n. too well** bastante mal; **n. without reason** no sin razón; *Fam* **n. likely!** ¡ni hablar!

En el inglés hablado, y en el escrito en estilo coloquial, **not** se contrae después de verbos modales y auxiliares.

notable ['nəʊtəbəl] *adj* notable

notably ['nəʊtəblɪ] *adv* notablemente

notary ['nəʊtərɪ] *n* notario *m*

notch [nɒtʃ] *n* muesca *f*; *(cut)* corte *m*

▸ **notch up** *vt sep Fig* **to n. up a victory** apuntarse una victoria

note [nəʊt] **1** *n* **(a)** *Mus* nota *f*; *Fig* **to strike**

the right n. acertar (**b**) *(on paper)* nota *f* (**c**) **to take n. of** *(notice)* prestar atención a (**d**) *(banknote)* billete *m* (de banco) (**e**) **notes** apuntes *mpl*; **to take n.** tomar apuntes

2 *vt* (**a**) *(write down)* apuntar, anotar (**b**) *(notice)* notar, fijarse en

notebook ['nəʊtbʊk] *n* cuaderno *m*, libreta *f*

noted ['nəʊtɪd] *adj* notable, célebre

notepad ['nəʊtpæd] *n* bloc *m* de notas

notepaper ['nəʊtpeɪpə(r)] *n* papel *m* de carta

noteworthy ['nəʊtwɜːðɪ] *adj* digno(a) de mención

nothing ['nʌθɪŋ] **1** *n* nada; **I saw n.** no vi nada; **for n.** *(free of charge)* gratis; **it's n.** no es nada; **it's n. to do with you** no tiene nada que ver contigo; **n. else** nada más; **there's n. in it** no es cierto; *Fam* **n. much** poca cosa; *Fam* **there's n. to it** es facilísimo

2 *adv* **she looks n. like her sister** no se parece en nada a su hermana

notice ['nəʊtɪs] **1** *n* (**a**) *(warning)* aviso *m*; **he gave a month's n.** presentó la dimisión con un mes de antelación; **at short n.** con poca antelación; **until further n.** hasta nuevo aviso; **without n.** sin previo aviso (**b**) *(attention)* atención *f*; **to take no n. of sth** no hacer caso de algo; **to take n. of sth** prestar atención a algo; **it escaped my n.** se me escapó; **to come to one's n.** llegar al conocimiento de uno (**c**) *(in newspaper etc)* anuncio *m* (**d**) *(sign)* letrero *m*, aviso *m*

2 *vt* darse cuenta de, notar

> *♪* Note that the Spanish word **noticia** is a false friend and is never a translation for the English word **notice**. In Spanish, **noticia** means "(piece of) news".

noticeable ['nəʊtɪsəbəl] *adj* que se nota, evidente

noticeboard ['nəʊtɪsbɔːd] *n Br* tablón *m* de anuncios

notification [nəʊtɪfɪ'keɪʃən] *n* aviso *m*

notify ['nəʊtɪfaɪ] *vt* avisar

notion ['nəʊʃən] *n* (**a**) idea *f*, concepto *m* (**b**) *(whim)* capricho *m* (**c**) *US Sewing* **notions** artículos *mpl* de mercería

notorious [nəʊ'tɔːrɪəs] *adj Pej* tristemente célebre

> *♪* Note that the Spanish word **notorio** is a false friend and is never a translation for the English word **notorious**. In Spanish, **notorio** means both "obvious" and "famous, well-known".

notwithstanding [nɒtwɪθ'stændɪŋ] **1** *prep* a pesar de

2 *adv* sin embargo, no obstante

nougat ['nuːgɑː] *n* turrón blando

nought [nɔːt] *n* cero *m*; *Br* **noughts and crosses** *(game)* tres en raya *m*

noun [naʊn] *n* nombre *m*, sustantivo *m*

nourish ['nʌrɪʃ] *vt* nutrir; *Fig (hopes)* abrigar

nourishing ['nʌrɪʃɪŋ] *adj* nutritivo(a)

nourishment ['nʌrɪʃmənt] *n* alimentación *f*, nutrición *f*

novel¹ ['nɒvəl] *n* novela *f*

novel² ['nɒvəl] *adj* original, novedoso(a)

novelist ['nɒvəlɪst] *n* novelista *mf*

novelty ['nɒvəltɪ] *n* novedad *f*

November [nəʊ'vembə(r)] *n* noviembre *m*

novice ['nɒvɪs] *n* (**a**) *(beginner)* novato(a) *m,f*, principiante *mf* (**b**) *Rel* novicio(a) *m,f*

now [naʊ] **1** *adv* (**a**) *(at this moment)* ahora; **just n., right n.** ahora mismo; **from n. on** de ahora en adelante; **n. and then, n. and again** de vez en cuando (**b**) *(for events in past)* entonces (**c**) *(at present, these days)* actualmente, hoy (en) día (**d**) *(not related to time)* ahora bien; **n., n.!** ¡vamos!, ¡ya está bien!

2 *conj* **n. (that)** ahora que, ya que

3 *n* **until n.** hasta ahora; **he'll be home by n.** ya habrá llegado a casa

nowadays ['naʊədeɪz] *adv* hoy (en) día, actualmente

nowhere ['nəʊweə(r)] *adv* en ninguna parte; **that will get you n.** eso no te servirá de nada; **it's n. near ready** no está preparado, ni mucho menos

noxious ['nɒkʃəs] *adj* nocivo(a)

nozzle ['nɒzəl] *n* boca *f*, boquilla *f*

nuance ['njuːɑːns] *n* matiz *m*

nub [nʌb] *n* **the n. of the matter** el quid de la cuestión

nuclear ['njuːklɪə(r)] *adj* nuclear; **n. arms** armas *fpl* nucleares; **n. disarmament** desarme *m* nuclear; **n. power** energía *f* nuclear; **n. power station** central *f* nuclear

nucleus ['njuːklɪəs] *n* núcleo *m*

nude [njuːd] **1** *adj* desnudo(a)

2 *n Art & Phot* desnudo *m*; **in the n.** al desnudo

nudge [nʌdʒ] **1** *vt* dar un codazo a

2 *n* codazo *m*

nudist ['njuːdɪst] *adj & n* nudista *(mf)*

nudity ['njuːdɪtɪ] *n* desnudez *f*

nugget ['nʌgɪt] *n Min* pepita *f*; **gold n.** pepita de oro

nuisance ['njuːsəns] *n* (**a**) molestia *f*,

pesadez *f*; **what a n.!** ¡qué lata! (**b**) (*person*) pesado(a) *m,f*

nuke [njuːk] *Fam* **1** *n* (*bomb*) bomba *f* nuclear *or* atómica

2 *vt* atacar con armas nucleares

null [nʌl] *adj* nulo(a); **n. and void** nulo y sin valor

nullify ['nʌlɪfaɪ] *vt* anular

numb [nʌm] **1** *adj* (*without feeling*) entumecido(a); *Fig* paralizado(a); **n. with fear** paralizado de miedo

2 *vt* (*with cold*) entumecer (de frío); (*with anaesthetic*) adormecer

number ['nʌmbə(r)] **1** *n* (**a**) número *m*; *Tel* **have you got my n.?** ¿tienes mi (número de) teléfono?; *Fam* **to look after n. one** barrer para adentro (**b**) (*quantity*) **a n. of people** varias personas (**c**) *Br* (*of car*) matrícula *f*; **n. plate** (placa *f* de la) matrícula *f*

2 *vt* (**a**) (*put a number on*) numerar (**b**) (*count*) contar; **his days are numbered** tiene los días contados

numeral ['njuːmərəl] *n* número *m*, cifra *f*

numerate ['njuːmərət] *adj* **to be n.** tener un conocimiento básico de matemáticas

numerical [njuːˈmerɪkəl] *adj* numérico(a)

numerically [njuːˈmerɪkəlɪ] *adv* numéricamente

numerous ['njuːmərəs] *adj* numeroso(a)

numismatics [njuːmɪzˈmætɪks] *n sing* numismática *f*

nun [nʌn] *n* monja *f*

nuptial ['nʌpʃəl] *adj* nupcial

nurse [nɜːs] **1** *n* enfermera *f*; (*male*) enfermero *m*

2 *vt* (**a**) (*look after*) cuidar, atender (**b**) (*baby*) acunar (**c**) (*suckle*) amamantar (**d**) *Fig* (*grudge etc*) guardar

nursery ['nɜːsərɪ] *n* (**a**) (*institution*) guardería *f*; **n. school** jardín *m* de infancia (**b**) (*in house*) cuarto *m* de los niños; **n. rhyme** poema *m* infantil (**c**) (*garden centre*) vivero *m*

nursing ['nɜːsɪŋ] *n* **n. home** clínica *f*

nurture ['nɜːtʃə(r)] *vt* (*animal*) alimentar; (*feelings*) abrigar

nut [nʌt] *n* (**a**) (*fruit*) fruto seco; *Fig* **a tough n. to crack** un hueso duro de roer (**b**) *Fam* (*head*) coco *m* (**c**) *Fam* (*mad person*) loco(a) *m,f* (**d**) *Tech* tuerca *f*

nutcracker ['nʌtkrækə(r)] *n* cascanueces *m inv*

nutmeg ['nʌtmeg] *n* nuez moscada

nutrition [njuːˈtrɪʃən] *n* nutrición *f*

nutritious [njuːˈtrɪʃəs] *adj* nutritivo(a), alimenticio(a)

nuts [nʌts] *adj Fam* chalado(a); **to go n.** volverse loco; **he's n. about motorbikes** las motos le chiflan

nutshell ['nʌtʃel] *n* cáscara *f*; *Fig* **in a n.** en pocas palabras

nylon ['naɪlɒn] **1** *n* (**a**) nilón *m*, nailon *m* (**b**) **nylons** medias *fpl* de nilón

2 *adj* de nilón

nymph [nɪmf] *n* ninfa *f*

nymphomaniac [nɪmfəˈmeɪnɪæk] *n* ninfómana *f*

O, o [əʊ] *n* (**a**) *(the letter)* O, o *f* (**b**) *Math & Tel* cero *m*

oak [əʊk] *n* roble *m*

OAP [əʊeɪ'piː] *n Br (abbr* **old-age pensioner**) pensionista *mf*, jubilado(a) *m,f*

oar [ɔː(r)] *n* remo *m*

oarsman ['ɔːzmən] *n* remero *m*

oasis [əʊ'eɪsɪs] *n (pl* **oases** [əʊ'eɪsiːz]) oasis *m inv*

oat [əʊt] *n* avena *f*; **rolled oats** copos *mpl* de avena

oath [əʊθ] *n (pl* **oaths** [əʊðz]) (**a**) *Jur* juramento *m*; **to take an o.** prestar juramento; *Fam* **on my o.** palabra de honor (**b**) *(swearword)* palabrota *f*

oatmeal ['əʊtmiːl] *n* harina *f* de avena

obedience [ə'biːdɪəns] *n* obediencia *f*

obedient [ə'biːdɪənt] *adj* obediente

obese [əʊ'biːs] *adj* obeso(a)

obey [ə'beɪ] *vt* obedecer; *(law)* cumplir con

obituary [ə'bɪtjʊərɪ] *n* necrología *f*

object¹ ['ɒbdʒekt] *n* (**a**) *(thing)* objeto *m* (**b**) *(aim, purpose)* fin *m*, objetivo *m* (**c**) **the o. of criticism** el blanco de las críticas (**d**) *(obstacle)* inconveniente *m* (**e**) *Ling* complemento *m*

object² [əb'dʒekt] *vi* oponerse (**to** a); **do you o. to my smoking?** ¿le molesta que fume?

objection [əb'dʒekʃən] *n* (**a**) objeción *f* (**b**) *(drawback)* inconveniente *m*; **provided there's no o.** si no hay inconveniente

objectionable [əb'dʒekʃənəbəl] *adj (unacceptable)* inaceptable; *(unpleasant)* ofensivo(a)

objective [əb'dʒektɪv] **1** *adj* objetivo(a) **2** *n* objetivo *m*

objector [əb'dʒektə(r)] *n* objetor(a) *m,f*

obligation [ɒblɪ'geɪʃən] *n* obligación *f*; **to be under an o. to sb** estarle muy agradecido(a) a algn

obligatory [ɒ'blɪgətərɪ] *adj* obligatorio(a)

oblige [ə'blaɪdʒ] *vt* (**a**) *(compel)* obligar; **I'm obliged to do it** me veo obligado(a) a hacerlo (**b**) *(do a favour for)* hacer un favor a (**c**) **to be obliged** *(grateful)* estar agradecido(a)

obliging [ə'blaɪdʒɪŋ] *adj* solícito(a)

oblique [ə'bliːk] *adj* oblicuo(a), inclinado(a); *Fig* **an o. reference** una alusión indirecta

obliterate [ə'blɪtəreɪt] *vt* (**a**) *(memory)* borrar (**b**) *(species, race)* eliminar; *(village)* arrasar

oblivion [ə'blɪvɪən] *n* olvido *m*; **to sink into o.** caer en el olvido

oblivious [ə'blɪvɪəs] *adj* inconsciente

oblong ['ɒblɒŋ] **1** *adj* oblongo(a) **2** *n* rectángulo *m*

obnoxious [əb'nɒkʃəs] *adj* repugnante

oboe ['əʊbəʊ] *n* oboe *m*

obscene [əb'siːn] *adj* obsceno(a)

obscure [əb'skjʊə(r)] **1** *adj* (**a**) oscuro(a); *(vague)* vago(a) (**b**) *(author, poet etc)* desconocido(a) **2** *vt (truth)* ocultar

obsequious [əb'siːkwɪəs] *adj* servil

observance [əb'zɜːvəns] *n* (**a**) observancia *f* (**b**) *Rel* **observances** prácticas religiosas

observant [əb'zɜːvənt] *adj* observador(a)

observation [ɒbzə'veɪʃən] *n* observación *f*; *(surveillance)* vigilancia *f*

observatory [əb'zɜːvətərɪ] *n* observatorio *m*

observe [əb'zɜːv] *vt* (**a**) observar; *(in surveillance)* vigilar (**b**) *(remark)* advertir (**c**) *(obey)* respetar

observer [əb'zɜːvə(r)] *n* observador(a) *m,f*

obsess [əb'ses] *vt* obsesionar; **to be obsessed (with** or **by)** estar obsesionado(a) (con)

obsession [əb'seʃən] *n* obsesión *f*

obsessive [əb'sesɪv] *adj* obsesivo(a)

obsolete ['ɒbsəliːt, ɒbsə'liːt] *adj* obsoleto(a)

obstacle ['ɒbstəkəl] *n* obstáculo *m*; *Fig* impedimento *m*; **o. race** carrera *f* de obstáculos

obstinate ['ɒbstɪnɪt] *adj* (**a**) *(person)* obstinado(a), terco(a) (**b**) *(pain)* persistente

obstruct [əb'strʌkt] *vt* (**a**) obstruir; *(pipe etc)* atascar; *(view)* tapar (**b**) *(hinder)* estorbar; *(progress)* dificultar

obstruction [əb'strʌkʃən] *n* (**a**) obstrucción *f* (**b**) *(hindrance)* obstáculo *m*

obtain [əb'teɪn] *vt* obtener, conseguir

obtainable [əb'teɪnəbəl] *adj* obtenible

obtrusive [əb'truːsɪv] *adj* (**a**) *(interfering)* entrometido(a) (**b**) *(noticeable)* llamativo(a)

obtuse [əb'tjuːs] *adj* obtuso(a)

obviate ['ɒbvɪeɪt] *vt Fml* obviar

obvious ['ɒbvɪəs] *adj* obvio(a), evidente

obviously ['ɒbvɪəslɪ] *adv* evidentemente; **o.!** ¡claro!, ¡por supuesto!

occasion [ə'keɪʒən] **1** *n* (**a**) ocasión *f*; **on o. de** vez en cuando; **on the o. of** con motivo de (**b**) *(event)* acontecimiento *m* (**c**) *(cause)* motivo *m*
2 *vt Fml* ocasionar

occasional [ə'keɪʒənəl] *adj* esporádico(a), eventual

occasionally [ə'keɪʒənəlɪ] *adv* de vez en cuando

occupant ['ɒkjʊpənt] *n* ocupante *mf*; *(tenant)* inquilino(a) *m,f*

occupation [ɒkjʊ'peɪʃən] *n* (**a**) *(job, profession)* profesión *f*, ocupación *f* (**b**) *(pastime)* pasatiempo *m* (**c**) *(of building, house, country)* ocupación *f*

occupational [ɒkjʊ'peɪʃənəl] *adj* profesional, laboral; **o. hazards** gajes *mpl* del oficio

occupied ['ɒkjʊpaɪd] *adj* ocupado(a)

occupier ['ɒkjʊpaɪə(r)] *n Br* ocupante *mf*; *(tenant)* inquilino(a) *m,f*

occupy ['ɒkjʊpaɪ] *vt* (**a**) *(live in)* ocupar, habitar (**b**) *(time)* pasar; **to o. one's time in doing sth** dedicar su tiempo a hacer algo (**c**) *(building, factory etc in protest)* tomar posesión de

occur [ə'kɜː(r)] *vi* (**a**) *(event)* suceder, acaecer; *(change)* producirse (**b**) *(be found)* encontrarse (**c**) **it occurred to me that ...** se me ocurrió que ...

occurrence [ə'kʌrəns] *n* suceso *m*, incidencia *f*

> 📖 Note that the Spanish word **ocurrencia** is a false friend and is never a translation for the English word **occurrence**. In Spanish, **ocurrencia** means "witty remark" and "bright idea".

ocean ['əʊʃən] *n* océano *m*

ocean-going ['əʊʃəngəʊɪŋ] *adj* de alta mar

ochre, *US* **ocher** ['əʊkə(r)] **1** *n* ocre *m*; **red o.** almagre *m*; **yellow o.** ocre amarillo
2 *adj* (de color) ocre

o'clock [ə'klɒk] *adv* **(it's) one o.** (es) la una; **(it's) two o.** (son) las dos

octave ['ɒktɪv] *n* octava *f*

October [ɒk'təʊbə(r)] *n* octubre *m*

octogenarian [ɒktəʊdʒɪ'neərɪən] *adj & n* octogenario(a) *m,f*

octopus ['ɒktəpəs] *n* pulpo *m*

OD [əʊ'diː] (*pt & pp* **OD'd** *or* **OD'ed**) *vi Fam* meterse una sobredosis

odd [ɒd] **1** *adj* (**a**) *(strange)* raro(a), extraño(a) (**b**) *(occasional)* esporádico(a); **at o. times** de vez en cuando; **the o. customer** algún que otro cliente; **o. job** trabajillo *m* (**c**) **an o. number** *(not even)* un impar (**d**) *(unpaired)* desparejado(a); **an o. sock** un calcetín suelto; *Fig* **to be the o. man out** estar de más
2 *adv* y pico; **twenty o. people** veinte y pico *or* y tantas personas

oddity ['ɒdɪtɪ] *n* (**a**) *(thing)* curiosidad *f*; *(person)* estrafalario(a) *m,f* (**b**) *(quality)* rareza *f*

oddly ['ɒdlɪ] *adv* extrañamente; **o. enough** por extraño que parezca

odds [ɒdz] *npl* (**a**) *(chances)* probabilidades *fpl*; **he's fighting against the o.** lleva las de perder; **the o. are that ...** lo más probable es que ... (+ *subj*) (**b**) *(in betting)* puntos *mpl* de ventaja; **the o. are five to one** las apuestas están cinco a uno (**c**) *Br* **it makes no o.** da lo mismo; *Fig* **at o. with sb** reñido(a) con algn (**d**) **o. and ends** *(small things)* cositas *fpl*; *(trinkets)* chucherías *fpl*

odds-on ['ɒdzɒn] *adj* seguro(a); **o. favourite** *(horse)* caballo favorito

ode [əʊd] *n* oda *f*

odious ['əʊdɪəs] *adj* repugnante

odour, *US* **odor** ['əʊdə(r)] *n* olor *m*; *(fragrance)* perfume *m*

OECD [əʊiːsiː'diː] *n* (*abbr* **Organization for Economic Co-operation and Development**) OCDE *f*

of [ɒv, *unstressed* əv] *prep* (**a**) *(belonging to, part of)* de; **a friend of mine** un amigo mío; **the end of the novel** el final de la novela
(**b**) *(containing)* de; **a bottle of wine** una botella de vino
(**c**) *(origin)* de; **of good family** de buena familia
(**d**) *(by)* de, por; **beloved of all** amado(a) por todos
(**e**) *(quantity)* de; **there are four of us** somos cuatro; **two of them** dos de ellos
(**f**) *(from)* de; **free of** libre de; **south of** al sur de
(**g**) *(material)* de; **a dress (made) of silk** un vestido de seda

(**h**) *(apposition)* de; **the city of Lisbon** la ciudad de Lisboa

(**i**) *(characteristic)* de; **that's typical of her** es muy propio de ella; **that's very kind of you** es usted muy amable

(**j**) *(with adj)* de; **hard of hearing** duro(a) de oído

(**k**) *(after superlative)* de; **the thing she wanted most of all** lo que más quería

(**l**) *(cause)* por, de; **because of** a causa de; **of necessity** por necesidad

(**m**) *(concerning, about)* de, sobre; **to dream of sth/sb** soñar con algo/algn; **to think of sb** pensar en algn

(**n**) *(with dates)* de; **the 7th of November** el 7 de noviembre

off [ɒf] **1** *prep* (**a**) *(movement)* de; **she fell o. her horse** se cayó del caballo

(**b**) *(removal)* de; **I'll take sth o. the price for you** se lo rebajaré un poco

(**c**) *(distance, situation)* de; **a few kilometres o. the coast** a unos kilómetros de la costa; **a house o. the road** una casa apartada de la carretera

(**d**) **the ship went o. course** el barco se desvió; **to be o. form** no estar en forma

(**e**) **I'm o. wine** he perdido el gusto al vino

2 *adv* (**a**) **he turned o. the radio** apagó la radio

(**b**) *(absent)* fuera; **I have a day o.** tengo un día libre; **to be o. sick** estar de baja por enfermedad

(**c**) *(completely)* **this will kill o. any germs** esto rematará cualquier germen

(**d**) **his arrival is three days o.** faltan tres días para su llegada; **6 miles o.** a 6 millas

(**e**) **I'm o. to London** me voy a Londres; **she ran o.** se fue corriendo

(**f**) **10 percent o.** un descuento del 10 por ciento; **to take one's shoes o.** quitarse los zapatos

(**g**) **o. and on** de vez en cuando

3 *adj* (**a**) *(gas etc)* apagado(a); *(water)* cortado(a)

(**b**) *(cancelled)* cancelado(a)

(**c**) *(low)* bajo(a); *(unsatisfactory)* malo(a); **on the o. chance** por si acaso; **the o. season** la temporada baja

(**d**) **you're better o. like that** así estás mejor

(**e**) *(gone bad)* *(meat, fish)* malo(a), pasado(a); *(milk)* agrio(a)

offal ['ɒfəl] *n (of chicken etc)* menudillos *mpl*; *(of cattle, pigs)* asaduras *fpl*

off-colour, US **off-color** ['ɒf'kʌlə(r)] *adj* (**a**) *Br (ill)* indispuesto(a) (**b**) *(joke, story)* indecente

offence [ə'fens] *n* (**a**) *Jur* delito *m* (**b**) *(insult)* ofensa *f*; **to give o.** ofender; **to take o. at sth** ofenderse por algo (**c**) *Mil (attack)* ofensiva *f*

offend [ə'fend] *vt* ofender

offender [ə'fendə(r)] *n (criminal)* delincuente *mf*

offense [ə'fens] *n US* = **offence**

offensive [ə'fensɪv] **1** *adj* (**a**) *(insulting)* ofensivo(a) (**b**) *(repulsive)* repugnante

2 *n Mil* ofensiva *f*; **to be on the o.** estar a la ofensiva

offer ['ɒfə(r)] **1** *vt* (**a**) ofrecer; **to o. to do a job** ofrecerse para hacer un trabajo (**b**) *(propose)* proponer

2 *n* (**a**) oferta *f*; *(proposal)* propuesta *f*; **o. of marriage** proposición *f* de matrimonio (**b**) *Com* **on o.** de oferta

offering ['ɒfərɪŋ] *n* (**a**) ofrecimiento *m* (**b**) *Rel* ofrenda *f*

offhand 1 *adj* ['ɒfhænd] *(abrupt)* brusco(a); *(inconsiderate)* descortés

2 *adv* [ɒf'hænd] **I don't know o.** así sin pensarlo, no lo sé

office ['ɒfɪs] *n* (**a**) *(room)* despacho *m*; *(building)* oficina *f*; *(of lawyer)* despacho, bufete *m*; *US (of doctor, dentist)* consulta *f*; **o. hours** horas *fpl* de oficina (**b**) *Br Pol* ministerio *m* (**c**) *US (federal agency)* agencia *f* gubernamental (**d**) *(position)* cargo *m*; **to hold o.** ocupar un cargo (**e**) *Pol* **to be in o.** estar en el poder

officer ['ɒfɪsə(r)] *n* (**a**) *Mil* oficial *mf* (**b**) **(police) o.** agente *mf* de policía (**c**) *(government official)* funcionario(a) *m,f* (**d**) *(of company, society)* director(a) *m,f*

official [ə'fɪʃəl] **1** *adj* oficial

2 *n* funcionario(a) *m,f*

officiate [ə'fɪʃɪeɪt] *vi* ejercer; **to o. as** ejercer de (**b**) *Rel* oficiar

officious [ə'fɪʃəs] *adj Pej* excesivamente celoso(a) *or* diligente

> ♪ Note that the Spanish word **oficioso** is a false friend and is never a translation for the English word **officious**. In Spanish, **oficioso** means "unofficial".

off-licence ['ɒflaɪsəns] *n Br* tienda *f* de bebidas alcohólicas

off-line ['ɒflaɪn] *adj Comput* desconectado(a)

off-peak [ɒf'pi:k] *adj (flight)* de temporada baja; *(rate)* de fuera de las horas punta

off-putting ['ɒfpʊtɪŋ] *adj Br Fam* desconcertante

offset ['ɒf'set] *vt (pt & pp offset) (balance out)* compensar

offshoot ['ɒfʃuːt] n (a) Bot renuevo m (b) Fig (of organization) ramificación f

offshore ['ɒf'ʃɔː(r)] adj (a) (breeze etc) terral (b) (oil rig) costa afuera (c) (overseas) en el extranjero; **o. investment** inversión f en el extranjero

offside 1 adv [ɒf'saɪd] Ftb fuera de juego **2** n ['ɒfsaɪd] Aut (with left-hand drive) lado derecho; (with right-hand drive) lado izquierdo

offspring ['ɒfsprɪŋ] n (pl **offspring**) (child) vástago m; (children) progenitura f

offstage [ɒf'steɪdʒ] adj & adv entre bastidores

often ['ɒfən,'ɒftən] adv a menudo, con frecuencia; **every so o.** de vez en cuando

ogle ['əʊgəl] vt & vi **to o. (at) sb** comerse a algn con los ojos

oh [əʊ] interj ¡oh!, ¡ay!; **oh, my God!** ¡Dios mío!

oil [ɔɪl] **1** n (a) aceite m; **o. lamp** lámpara f de aceite, quinqué m; **o. slick** mancha f de aceite; **olive o.** aceite de oliva (b) (petroleum) petróleo m; **o. rig** plataforma petrolera; **o. tanker** petrolero m (c) (painting) pintura f al óleo; **o. paint** óleo m
2 vt engrasar

oilcan ['ɔɪlkæn] n aceitera f

oilfield ['ɔɪlfiːld] n yacimiento petrolífero

oilskin ['ɔɪlskɪn] n (a) hule m (b) **oilskins** chubasquero m, impermeable m de hule

oily ['ɔɪlɪ] adj (**oilier, oiliest**) aceitoso(a), grasiento(a); (hair, skin) graso(a)

ointment ['ɔɪntmənt] n ungüento m, pomada f

O.K., okay [əʊ'keɪ] Fam **1** interj ¡vale!, ¡de acuerdo!
2 adj bien; **is it O.K. if ...?** ¿está bien si ...?
3 vt dar el visto bueno a

old [əʊld] **1** adj (a) viejo(a); **an o. man** un anciano; **o. age** vejez f; **o.-age pensioner** pensionista mf; Br **o. boy** antiguo alumno; **o. hand** veterano(a) m,f; **good o. John!** ¡el bueno de John! (b) **how o. are you?** ¿cuántos años tienes?; **she's five years o.** tiene cinco años (c) (previous) antiguo(a)
2 n **of o.** de antaño

old-fashioned [əʊld'fæʃənd] adj (outdated) a la antigua; (unfashionable) anticuado(a), pasado(a) de moda

olive ['ɒlɪv] n (a) (tree) olivo m; **o. grove** olivar m (b) (fruit) aceituna f, oliva f (c) (wood) olivo m (d) **o. (green)** (colour) verde m oliva

Olympic [ə'lɪmpɪk] **1** adj olímpico(a); **O.**

Games Juegos Olímpicos
2 npl **the Olympics** las Olimpiadas

omelette, US omelet ['ɒmlɪt] n tortilla f; **Spanish o.** tortilla española or de patatas or Am papas

omen ['əʊmen] n presagio m

ominous ['ɒmɪnəs] adj de mal agüero

omission [əʊ'mɪʃən] n omisión f; Fig olvido m

omit [əʊ'mɪt] vt omitir; (accidentally) pasar por alto; (forget) olvidarse (**to** de)

omnipotent [ɒm'nɪpətənt] **1** adj omnipotente
2 n **the O.** el Todopoderoso

on [ɒn] **1** prep (a) (location) sobre, encima de, en; **I hit him on the head** le di un golpe en la cabeza; **it's on the desk** está encima de or sobre el escritorio; **hanging on the wall** colgado de la pared; **on page 4** en la página 4; **have you got any money on you?** ¿llevas dinero?; **the drinks are on me/the house** invito yo/invita la casa (b) (alongside) en; **a town on the coast** un pueblo en la costa (c) (direction) en, a; **on the right** a la derecha; **on the way** en el camino (d) (time) **on 3 April** el 3 de abril; **on a sunny day** un día de sol; **on Monday** el lunes; **on Mondays** los lunes; **on that occasion** en aquella ocasión; **on the following day** al día siguiente; **on time** a tiempo (e) en; **on TV/the radio** en la tele/radio; **to play sth on the piano** tocar algo al piano; **on the phone** al teléfono (f) (at the time of) a; **on his arrival** a su llegada; **on second thoughts** pensándolo bien; **on learning of this** al conocer esto (g) **she lives on bread** vive de pan; **to depend on** depender de (h) (transport) en/a; **on foot** a pie; **on the train/plane/bus** en el tren/avión/autobús; (travel by) en tren/avión/autobús (i) (state, process) en/de; **on holiday** de vacaciones; **she is here on business** está aquí de negocios (j) (regarding) sobre; **a lecture on numismatics** una conferencia sobre numismática; **they congratulated him on his success** le felicitaron por su éxito (k) **on condition that** (subject to) bajo la condición de que (l) (against) contra; **an attack on** un ataque contra (m) **he's on the Times** (working for) trabaja para el Times
2 adv (a) (covering) encima, puesto; **she had a coat on** llevaba puesto un abrigo

(b) *Fam* **have you anything on tonight?** ¿tienes algún plan para esta noche?

(c) **and so on** y así sucesivamente; **go on!** ¡sigue!; **he talks on and on** habla sin parar; **to work on** seguir trabajando

(d) **from that day on** a partir de aquel día; **later on** más tarde

3 *adj Fam* (a) **to be on** *(TV, radio, light)* estar encendido(a); *(engine)* estar en marcha; *(film, play)* estar en cartelera; **that film was on last week** pusieron esa película la semana pasada

(b) *Th & TV* **you're on!** ¡a escena!

(c) *(definitely planned)* previsto(a); **you're on!** ¡trato hecho!

(d) **that isn't on** eso no vale

once [wʌns] **1** *adv* (a) *(one time)* una vez; **o. a week** una vez por semana; **o. in a while** de vez en cuando; **o. more** una vez más; **o. or twice** un par de veces; *Fig* **o. and for all** de una vez por todas (b) *(formerly)* en otro tiempo; **o. (upon a time) there was ...** érase una vez ... (c) **at o.** en seguida, inmediatamente; **don't all speak at o.** no habléis todos a la vez

2 *conj* una vez que (+ *subj*), en cuanto (+ *subj*)

oncoming ['ɒnkʌmɪŋ] *adj (car, traffic)* que viene en dirección contraria

one [wʌn] **1** *adj* (a) *(in number)* un/una; **for o. thing** primero; **you're the o. person who knows** tú eres el único que lo sabe; **the o. and only** el único/la única; **o. and the same** el mismo/la misma

(b) *(indefinite)* un/una; **he'll come back o. day** un día volverá

2 *dem pron* **any o.** cualquiera; **that o.** ése/ésa; **this o.** éste/ésta; *(distant)* aquél/aquélla; **the blue ones** los azules/ las azules; **the o. on the table** el/la que está encima de la mesa; **the ones that, the ones who** los/las que

3 *indef pron* (a) uno(a) *m,f*; **I, for o., am against it** yo, por lo menos, estoy en contra; **I'm not o. to complain** no soy de los que se quejan; **o. at a time** de uno en uno; **o. by o.** uno tras otro; *Fig* **o. and all** todo el mundo

(b) *(indefinite person)* uno(a) *m,f*; **o. has to fight** hay que luchar; **o. hopes that will never happen** esperemos que no ocurra; **to break o.'s leg/arm** romperse la pierna/ el brazo

(c) *(one another)* el uno al otro; **they love o. another** se aman

4 *n (digit)* uno *m*; **o. hundred/thousand** cien/mil

one-armed ['wʌnɑːmd] *adj Fig* **o.**

bandit máquina *f* tragaperras

one-man ['wʌnmæn] *adj* **a o. show** un espectáculo con un solo artista

one-man band [wʌnmæn'bænd] *n* hombre *m* orquesta

one-off ['wʌnɒf] *adj Br Fam* único(a), fuera de serie

oneself [wʌn'self] *pron* (a) *(reflexive)* uno(a) mismo(a) *m,f*, sí mismo(a) *m,f*; **to talk to o.** hablar para sí (b) *(alone)*uno(a) mismo(a) *m,f*; **by o.** solo(a) (c) *(one's usual self)* el/la de siempre

one-sided [wʌn'saɪdɪd] *adj (bargain)* desigual; *(judgement)* parcial; *(decision)* unilateral

one-to-one ['wʌntə'wʌn] *adj* **o. tuition** clase *f* individual

one-way ['wʌnweɪ] *adj* (a) *US (ticket)* de ida (b) *(street)* de dirección única

ongoing ['ɒngəʊɪŋ] *adj* (a) *(in progress)* en curso, actual (b) *(developing)* en desarrollo

onion ['ʌnjən] *n* cebolla *f*

on-line ['ɒnlaɪn] *adj Comput* conecta-do(a)

onlooker ['ɒnlʊkə(r)] *n* espectador(a) *m,f*

only ['əʊnlɪ] **1** *adj* único(a); **o. son** hijo único

2 *adv* (a) solamente, sólo; **staff o.** *(sign)* reservado al personal (b) *(not earlier than)* apenas; **he has o. just left** acaba de marcharse hace un momento; **o. yesterday** ayer mismo (c) **o. too glad!** ¡con mucho gusto!

3 *conj* pero

onset ['ɒnset] *n (start)* comienzo *m*

onslaught ['ɒnslɔːt] *n* embestida *f*

onto ['ɒntʊ, *unstressed* 'ɒntə] *prep* = **on to**

onus ['əʊnəs] *n* responsabilidad *f*

onward ['ɒnwəd] *adj* hacia adelante

onward(s) ['ɒnwəd(z)] *adv* a partir de, en adelante; **from this time o.** de ahora en adelante

ooze [uːz] **1** *vi* rezumar

2 *vt* rebosar

opaque [əʊ'peɪk] *adj* opaco(a)

OPEC ['əʊpek] *n (abbr* **Organization of Petroleum-Exporting Countries)** OPEP *f*

open ['əʊpən] **1** *adj* (a) abierto(a); **half o.** entreabierto; **wide o.** abierto de par en par; **in the o. air** al aire libre; **to be o. with sb** ser sincero(a) con algn; *Fig* **with o. arms** con los brazos abiertos; **to keep an o. mind** no tener prejuicios; **I am o. to suggestions** acepto cualquier sugerencia; **o. to criticism** susceptible a la crítica;

o. admiration franca admiración; *US* **o. house** fiesta *f* de inauguración de residencia; **an o. question** una cuestión sin resolver; **o. season** *(in hunting)* temporada *f* de caza; *Av & Rail* **o. ticket** billete abierto; *Br* **O. University** Universidad *f* a Distancia; **o. verdict** veredicto inconcluso

(**b**) *(car etc)* descubierto(a)

(**c**) *(opposition)* manifiesto(a)

2 *vt* (**a**) abrir; **to o. fire** abrir fuego; *Fig* **to o. one's heart to sb** sincerarse con algn

(**b**) *(exhibition etc)* inaugurar; *(negotiations, conversation)* entablar

3 *vi* (**a**) abrir, abrirse; **to o. onto** *(of door, window)* dar a

(**b**) *(start)* empezar; *Th & Cin* estrenarse

4 *n* (**a**) **in the o.** al aire libre; *Fig* **to bring into the o.** hacer público

(**b**) *Sport* open *m*

▸ **open out 1** *vt sep* abrir, desplegar

2 *vi (flowers)* abrirse; *(view)* extenderse

▸ **open up 1** *vt sep (market etc)* abrir; *(possibilities)* crear

2 *vi* (**a**) abrirse; *Fam* **o. up!** ¡abre la puerta! (**b**) *(start)* empezar

opener ['əʊpənə(r)] *n* tin or *US* can **o.** abrelatas *m inv*

opening ['əʊpənɪŋ] *n* (**a**) *(act)* apertura *f*; **o. night** noche *f* de estreno; *Br* **o. time** hora *f* de apertura de los bares (**b**) *(beginning)* comienzo *m* (**c**) *(aperture)* abertura *f*; *(gap)* brecha *f* (**d**) *Com* oportunidad *f* (**e**) *(vacancy)* vacante *f*

openly ['əʊpənlɪ] *adv* abiertamente

open-minded [əʊpən'maɪndɪd] *adj* sin prejuicios

openness ['əʊpənnɪs] *n* franqueza *f*

open-plan ['əʊpənplæn] *adj (office)* abierto(a)

opera ['ɒpərə] *n* ópera *f*; **o. house** ópera, teatro *m* de la ópera

operate ['ɒpəreɪt] **1** *vi* (**a**) *(function)* funcionar (**b**) *Med* operar; **to o. on sb for appendicitis** operar a algn de apendicitis

2 *vt* (**a**) *(control)* manejar (**b**) *(business)* dirigir

operatic [ɒpə'rætɪk] *adj* de ópera

operating ['ɒpəreɪtɪŋ] *n* (**a**) **o. costs** gastos *mpl* de funcionamiento (**b**) *Med* **o. table** mesa *f* de operaciones; **o. theatre** or *US* **room** quirófano *m*

operation [ɒpə'reɪʃən] *n* (**a**) *(of machine)* funcionamiento *m*; *(by person)* manejo *m* (**b**) *Mil* maniobra *f* (**c**) *Med* operación *f*, intervención quirúrgica; **to undergo an o. for** ser operado(a) de

operational [ɒpə'reɪʃənəl] *adj* (**a**) *(ready for use)* operativo(a) (**b**) *Mil* operacional

operative ['ɒpərətɪv] *adj* (**a**) *Jur (in force)* vigente; **to become o.** entrar en vigor (**b**) *(significant)* clave, significativo(a); **the o. word** la palabra clave

operator ['ɒpəreɪtə(r)] *n* (**a**) *Ind* operario(a) *m,f* (**b**) *Tel* operador(a) *m,f* (**c**) *(dealer)* negociante *mf*, agente *mf*; **tour o.** agente de viajes

opinion [ə'pɪnjən] *n* opinión *f*; **in my o.** en mi opinión, a mi juicio; **it's a matter of o.** es cuestión de opiniones; **to have a high o. of sb** tener buen concepto de algn; **o. poll** encuesta *f*, sondeo *m*

opinionated [ə'pɪnjəneɪtɪd] *adj* dogmático(a)

opium ['əʊpɪəm] *n* opio *m*

opponent [ə'pəʊnənt] *n* adversario(a) *m,f*

opportune ['ɒpətjuːn] *adj* oportuno(a)

opportunist [ɒpə'tjuːnɪst] *adj & n* oportunista *(mf)*

opportunity [ɒpə'tjuːnɪtɪ] *n* (**a**) oportunidad *f*, ocasión *f* (**b**) *(prospect)* perspectiva *f*

oppose [ə'pəʊz] *vt* oponerse a

opposed [ə'pəʊzd] *adj* opuesto(a); **to be o. to sth** estar en contra de algo; **as o. to** comparado(a) con

opposing [ə'pəʊzɪŋ] *adj* adversario(a)

opposite ['ɒpəzɪt] **1** *adj* (**a**) *(facing)* de enfrente; *(page)* contiguo(a) (**b**) *(contrary)* opuesto(a), contrario(a); **in the o. direction** en dirección contraria

2 *n* **the o.** lo contrario; **quite the o.!** ¡al contrario!

3 *prep* enfrente de, frente a

4 *adv* enfrente

opposition [ɒpə'zɪʃən] *n* (**a**) oposición *f*; **in o. to** en contra de (**b**) *Pol* **the o.** la oposición

oppress [ə'pres] *vt* oprimir

oppression [ə'preʃən] *n* opresión *f*

oppressive [ə'presɪv] *adj* opresivo(a); *(atmosphere)* agobiante; *(heat)* sofocante

opt [ɒpt] *vi* optar; **to o. for** optar por; **to o. to do sth** optar por hacer algo

▸ **opt out** *vi* retirarse; **to o. out of doing sth** decidir no hacer algo

optical ['ɒptɪkəl] *adj* óptico(a)

optician [ɒp'tɪʃən] *n* óptico(a) *m,f*

optics ['ɒptɪks] *n sing* óptica *f*

optimist ['ɒptɪmɪst] *n* optimista *mf*

optimistic [ɒptɪ'mɪstɪk] *adj* optimista

optimistically [ɒptɪ'mɪstɪkəlɪ] *adv* con optimismo

optimum ['ɒptɪməm] **1** *n* grado óptimo

2 *adj* óptimo(a)

option ['ɒpʃən] *n* opción *f*; **I have no o.** no tengo más remedio; **to keep one's options open** no comprometerse; **with the o. of** con opción a

optional ['ɒpʃənəl] *adj* optativo(a), facultativo(a); *Educ* **o. subject** (asignatura *f*) optativa *f*

opulence ['ɒpjʊləns] *n* opulencia *f*

or [ɔː(r), *unstressed* ə(r)] *conj* (**a**) o; *(before a word beginning with* **o** *or* **ho**) u; **or else** si no, o bien; **whether you like it or not** tanto si te gusta como si no; **either a bun or a piece of cake** (o) una magdalena o un trozo de pastel (**b**) *(with negative)* ni; **he can't read or write** no sabe leer ni escribir; *see* **nor**

oral ['ɔːrəl, 'ɒrəl] **1** *adj* oral
2 *n* examen *m* oral

orally ['ɔːrəlɪ, 'ɒrəlɪ] *adv* **to be taken o.** *(on medicine)* por vía oral

orange ['ɒrɪndʒ] **1** *n* naranja *f*; **o. juice** zumo *m* or *Am* jugo *m* de naranja
2 *adj* de color naranja

orator ['ɒrətə(r)] *n* orador(a) *m,f*

oratory ['ɒrətərɪ] *n* oratoria *f*

orbit ['ɔːbɪt] **1** *n* *Astron* órbita *f*
2 *vt* girar alrededor de
3 *vi* girar

orchard ['ɔːtʃəd] *n* huerto *m*

orchestra ['ɔːkɪstrə] *n* orquesta *f*; *US (in theatre)* platea *f*

orchestral [ɔː'kestrəl] *adj* orquestal

orchid ['ɔːkɪd] *n* orquídea *f*

ordain [ɔː'deɪn] *vt* (**a**) *Rel* ordenar; **to be ordained** ordenarse (**b**) *(decree)* decretar

ordeal [ɔː'diːl] *n* mala experiencia

order ['ɔːdə(r)] **1** *n* (**a**) *(sequence)* orden *m*; **in alphabetical o.** por orden alfabético; **to put in o.** ordenar
(**b**) *(condition)* estado *m*; **is your passport in o.?** ¿tienes el pasaporte en regla?; **out of o.** *(sign)* averiado(a)
(**c**) *(peace)* orden *m*; **to restore o.** reestablecer el orden publico
(**d**) *(command)* orden *f*
(**e**) *Com* pedido *m*, encargo *m*; **to be on o.** estar pedido; **to o.** a la medida; **o. form** hoja *f* de pedido
(**f**) *Rel* orden *f*
(**g**) **of the highest o.** *(quality)* de primera calidad
(**h**) *(kind)* índole *f*, tipo *m*; *Biol* orden *m*
(**i**) **in the o. of** del orden de
(**j**) **in o. that** para que (+ *subj*), a fin de que (+ *subj*); **in o. to** (+ *infin*) para (+ *infin*), a fin de (+ *infin*)
2 *vt* (**a**) *(command)* ordenar, mandar; **to o. sb to do sth** mandar a algn hacer algo

(**b**) *Com* pedir, encargar; **to o. a dish** pedir un plato

orderly ['ɔːdəlɪ] **1** *adj* (tidy etc) ordenado(a)
2 *n* (**a**) *Med* enfermero *m* (**b**) *Mil* ordenanza *m*

ordinary ['ɔːdənrɪ] **1** *adj* usual, normal; *(average)* corriente, común; **the o. citizen** el ciudadano de a pie
2 *n* **the o.** lo corriente, lo normal; **out of the o.** fuera de lo común

ordnance ['ɔːdnəns] *n* *Br* **O. Survey** = instituto británico de cartografía

ore [ɔː(r)] *n* mineral *m*

organ ['ɔːgən] *n* *Mus & Anat etc* órgano *m*

organic [ɔː'gænɪk] *adj* orgánico(a); *(farming, food)* biológico(a), ecológico(a)

organism ['ɔːgənɪzəm] *n* organismo *m*

organization [ɔːgənaɪ'zeɪʃən] *n* organización *f*

organize ['ɔːgənaɪz] *vt* organizar

organizer ['ɔːgənaɪzə(r)] *n* organizador(a) *m,f*

orgasm ['ɔːgæzəm] *n* orgasmo *m*

orgy ['ɔːdʒɪ] *n* orgía *f*

Orient ['ɔːrɪənt] *n* **the O.** el Oriente

Oriental [ɔːrɪ'entəl] *adj & n* oriental *(mf)*

origin ['ɒrɪdʒɪn] *n* origen *m*; **country of o.** país *m* natal *or* de origen

original [ə'rɪdʒɪnəl] **1** *adj* (**a**) original; *(first)* primero(a) (**b**) *(imaginative)* original
2 *n* original *m*

originality [ərɪdʒɪ'nælɪtɪ] *n* originalidad *f*

originally [ə'rɪdʒɪnəlɪ] *adv* (**a**) *(at first)* en un principio (**b**) *(with imagination)* con originalidad

originate [ə'rɪdʒɪneɪt] **1** *vt* originar
2 *vi* **to o. from** *or* **in** tener su origen en

Orkneys ['ɔːknɪz] *npl* **the O.** las (Islas) Orcadas

ornament ['ɔːnəmənt] *n* ornamento *m*, adorno *m*

ornamental [ɔːnə'mentəl] *adj* decorativo(a)

ornate [ɔː'neɪt] *adj* vistoso(a)

ornithology [ɔːnɪ'θɒlədʒɪ] *n* ornitología *f*

orphan ['ɔːfən] **1** *n* huérfano(a) *m,f*
2 *vt* **she was orphaned** quedó huérfana

orphanage ['ɔːfənɪdʒ] *n* orfanato *m*

orthodox ['ɔːθədɒks] *adj* ortodoxo(a)

orthodoxy ['ɔːθədɒksɪ] *n* ortodoxia *f*

orthopaedic, *US* **orthopedic** [ɔːθəʊ-'piːdɪk] *adj* ortopédico(a)

Oscar ['ɒskə(r)] *n* Óscar *m*

oscillate [ˈɒsɪleɪt] *vi* oscilar
ostensible [ɒˈstensɪbəl] *adj* (a) *(apparent)* ostensible (b) *(pretended)* aparente
ostentatious [ɒstenˈteɪʃəs] *adj* ostentoso(a)
osteopath [ˈɒstɪəpæθ] *n* osteópata *mf*
ostracize [ˈɒstrəsaɪz] *vt (from society)* condenar al ostracismo; *(from group)* aislar, excluir
ostrich [ˈɒstrɪtʃ] *n* avestruz *f*
other [ˈʌðə(r)] **1** *adj* (a) otro(a); **every o. day** cada dos días; **on the o. hand** por otra parte; **o. people have seen it** otros lo han visto; **the o. four** los otros cuatro; **the o. one** el otro/la otra; **the o. thing** lo otro (b) **he must be somewhere or o.** debe de estar en alguna parte
2 *pron* otro(a) *m,f*; **many others** otros muchtos; **the others** los otros, los demás; **we see each o. quite often** nos vemos con bastante frecuencia
otherwise [ˈʌðəwaɪz] **1** *adv* (a) *(if not)* si no (b) *(differently)* de otra manera (c) *(in other respects)* por lo demás
2 *adj* distinto(a)
OTT [əʊtiːˈtiː] *adj Br Fam (abbr* **over the top)** exagerado(a)
otter [ˈɒtə(r)] *n* nutria *f*
ought [ɔːt] *v aux*

> En el inglés hablado, y en el escrito en estilo coloquial, la forma negativa **ought not** se transforma en **oughtn't**.

(a) *(obligation)* deber; **I thought I o. to tell you** creí que debía decírtelo; **she o. to do it** debería hacerlo (b) *(vague desirability)* tener que, deber; **you o. to see the exhibition** deberías ver la exposición (c) *(expectation)* **he o. to pass the exam** seguramente aprobará el examen; **that o. to do** con eso bastará
ounce [aʊns] *n* onza *f*
our [aʊə(r)] *poss adj* nuestro(a)
ours [aʊəz] *poss pron* (a) (el) nuestro/(la) nuestra (b) o. nuestro(a); **a friend of o.** un amigo nuestro
ourselves [aʊəˈselvz] *pers pron pl* (a) *(reflexive)* nos (b) *(emphatic)* nosotros mismos/nosotras mismas (c) **by o.** a solas
oust [aʊst] *vt* (a) *(from a post)* desbancar (b) *(from property etc)* desalojar
out [aʊt] **1** *adv* (a) *(outside, away)* fuera; **o. there** ahí fuera; **to go o.** salir (b) **I told him straight o.** se lo dije muy claramente; **o. loud** en voz alta
  (c) **hear me o.** escúchame hasta el final
  (d) **o. of** *(place)* fuera de; **move o. of the**

way! ¡quítate de en medio!; **o. of danger** fuera de peligro; **to go o. of the room** salir de la habitación; **o. of control** fuera de control; **o. of date** *(expired)* caducado(a); *(old-fashioned)* pasado(a) de moda
  (e) **o. of** *(cause, motive)* por
  (f) **o. of** *(made from)* de
  (g) **o. of** *(short of, without)* sin; **I'm o. of money** se me ha acabado el dinero; **o. of breath** sin aliento
  (h) **o. of** *(among)* entre; **forty o. of fifty** cuarenta de cada cincuenta; *(in exam etc)* cuarenta sobre cincuenta
2 *adj* (a) **the sun is o.** ha salido el sol
  (b) *(unfashionable)* pasado(a) de moda
  (c) *(fire)* apagado(a)
  (d) *(not working)* estropeado(a)
  (e) **she's o.** *(not in)* ha salido, no está
  (f) **to be o. for sth** buscar algo; **to be o. to do sth** pretender hacer algo
  (g) **the book is just o.** el libro acaba de salir
  (h) *(inaccurate)* equivocado(a); **to be o. in one's calculations** equivocarse en los cálculos
  (i) **before the week is o.** antes de que acabe la semana
3 *prep (out of)* por; **he jumped o. of the window** saltó por la ventana
out-and-out [ˈaʊtənaʊt] *adj* redomado(a)
outboard [ˈaʊtbɔːd] *adj* **o. motor** fueraborda *m*
outbreak [ˈaʊtbreɪk] *n (of war)* comienzo *m*; *(of spots)* erupción *f*; *(of disease)* brote *m*; *(of violence)* ola *f*; *(of anger)* arrebato *m*; **at the o. of war** cuando estalló la guerra
outbuilding [ˈaʊtbɪldɪŋ] *n* dependencia *f*
outburst [ˈaʊtbɜːst] *n (of anger)* arrebato *m*; *(of generosity)* arranque *m*
outcast [ˈaʊtkɑːst] *n* marginado(a) *m,f*
outcome [ˈaʊtkʌm] *n* resultado *m*
outcrop [ˈaʊtkrɒp] *n Geol* afloramiento *m*
outcry [ˈaʊtkraɪ] *n* **there was an o.** hubo fuertes protestas
outdated [aʊtˈdeɪtɪd] *adj* anticuado(a), obsoleto(a)
outdo [aʊtˈduː] *vt (pt* **outdid** [aʊtˈdɪd]; *pp* **outdone** [aʊtˈdʌn]) **to o. sb** superar a algn
outdoor [ˈaʊtdɔː(r)] *adj* (a) al aire libre (b) *(clothes)* de calle
outdoors [aʊtˈdɔːz] *adv* fuera, al aire libre

outer ['aʊtə(r)] *adj* exterior, externo(a)

outfit ['aʊtfɪt] *n* (a) *(kit, equipment)* equipo *m* (b) *(set of clothes)* conjunto *m* (c) *Fam (group)* grupo *m*

outgoing ['aʊtgəʊɪŋ] **1** *adj* (a) *(departing)* saliente (b) *(sociable)* extrovertido(a)
   2 *npl* **outgoings** gastos *mpl*

outgrow [aʊt'grəʊ] *vt* (*pt* **outgrew** [aʊt'gruː]; *pp* **outgrown** [aʊt'grəʊn]) **he's outgrowing all his clothes** toda la ropa se le está quedando pequeña; **she'll o. it** se le pasará con la edad

outhouse ['aʊthaʊs] *n* = **outbuilding**

outing ['aʊtɪŋ] *n* excursión *f*

outlandish [aʊt'lændɪʃ] *adj* estrafalario(a)

outlast [aʊt'lɑːst] *vt* durar más que

outlaw ['aʊtlɔː] **1** *n* proscrito(a) *m,f*
   2 *vt* prohibir

outlet ['aʊtlet] *n* (a) *(opening)* salida *f* (b) *(for emotions)* válvula *f* de escape (c) *Com* mercado *m* (d) *(for water)* desagüe *m*

outline ['aʊtlaɪn] **1** *n* (a) *(draft)* bosquejo *m* (b) *(outer line)* contorno *m*; *(silhouette)* perfil *m*
   2 *vt* (a) *(draw lines of)* perfilar (b) *(summarize)* resumir (c) *(describe roughly)* trazar las líneas generales de

outlive [aʊt'lɪv] *vt* sobrevivir a

outlook ['aʊtlʊk] *n* (a) *(point of view)* punto *m* de vista (b) *(prospect)* perspectiva *f*; *Met* previsión *f*

outlying ['aʊtlaɪɪŋ] *adj (remote)* aislado(a)

outmoded [aʊt'məʊdɪd] *adj* anticuado(a)

outnumber [aʊt'nʌmbə(r)] *vt* exceder en número

out-of-the-way ['aʊtəvðə'weɪ] *adj* (a) *(distant)* apartado(a), aislado(a) (b) *(uncommon)* poco corriente

outpatient ['aʊtpeɪʃənt] *n* paciente externo(a); **outpatients' department** clínica ambulatoria

outpost ['aʊtpəʊst] *n* avanzada *f*

output ['aʊtpʊt] *n* (a) *(production)* producción *f*; *(of machine)* rendimiento *m* (b) *Elec* potencia *f* (c) *Comput* salida *f*

outrage ['aʊtreɪdʒ] **1** *n* ultraje *m*; **it's an o.!** ¡es un escándalo!
   2 *vt* **to be outraged by sth** indignarse por algo

outrageous [aʊt'reɪdʒəs] *adj (behaviour)* escandaloso(a); *(clothes)* extravagante; *(price)* exorbitante

outright 1 *adj* ['aʊtraɪt] *(absolute)* absoluto(a)

   2 *adv* [aʊt'raɪt] (a) *(completely)* por completo (b) *(directly)* directamente, sin reserva (c) *(immediately)* en el acto

outset ['aʊtset] *n* comienzo *m*, principio *m*

outside 1 *prep* [aʊt'saɪd, 'aʊtsaɪd] (a) fuera de (b) *(beyond)* más allá de (c) *(other than)* aparte de
   2 *adj* ['aʊtsaɪd] (a) *(exterior)* exterior, externo(a) (b) *(remote)* remoto(a)
   3 *adv* [aʊt'saɪd] fuera, afuera
   4 *n* [aʊt'saɪd, 'aʊtsaɪd] exterior *m*; **on the o.** por fuera; *Fam* **at the o.** como mucho

outsider [aʊt'saɪdə(r)] *n* (a) *(stranger)* extraño(a) *m,f*, forastero(a) *m,f* (b) *Pol* = candidato(a) con pocas posibilidades de ganar

outsize(d) ['aʊtsaɪz(d)] *adj (clothes)* de talla muy grande

outskirts ['aʊtskɜːts] *npl* afueras *fpl*

outsourcing ['aʊtsɔːsɪŋ] *n Com* externalización *f*, subcontratación *f*, *Am* tercerización *f*

outspoken [aʊt'spəʊkən] *adj* directo(a), abierto(a)

outstanding [aʊt'stændɪŋ] *adj* (a) *(exceptional)* destacado(a) (b) *(unpaid, unresolved)* pendiente

outstretched [aʊt'stretʃt] *adj* extendido(a)

outward ['aʊtwəd] **1** *adj* (a) *(external)* exterior, externo(a) (b) **the o. journey** el viaje de ida
   2 *adv* = **outwards**

outwardly ['aʊtwədlɪ] *adv* aparentemente

outwards ['aʊtwədz] *adv* hacia (a)fuera

outweigh [aʊt'weɪ] *vt* (a) *(prevail over)* prevalecer sobre (b) *(weigh more than)* pesar más que

oval ['əʊvəl] **1** *adj* oval, ovalado(a)
   2 *n* óvalo *m*

ovary ['əʊvərɪ] *n* ovario *m*

ovation [əʊ'veɪʃən] *n* ovación *f*

oven ['ʌvən] *n* horno *m*

ovenproof ['ʌvənpruːf] *adj* refractario(a)

over ['əʊvə(r)] **1** *prep* (a) *(above)* encima de
   (b) *(on top of)* sobre, encima de
   (c) *(across)* al otro lado de; **the bridge o. the river** el puente que cruza el río
   (d) *(during)* durante
   (e) *(throughout)* por
   (f) **all o.** por todo(a); **famous all o. the world** famoso en el mundo entero
   (g) *(by the agency of)* por; **o. the phone** por teléfono

(**h**) *(more than)* más de; **men o. twenty-five** hombres mayores de veinticinco años; **o. and above** además de

(**i**) *(recovered from)* recuperado(a) de

2 *adv* (**a**) **o. there** allá; **why don't you come o. tomorrow?** ¿por qué no vienes a casa mañana?

(**b**) *(throughout)* por; **all o.** por todas partes

(**c**) *(more)* más

(**d**) *(again)* otra vez; **o. and o. (again)** una y otra vez; **twice o.** dos veces seguidas

(**e**) *(in excess)* de más

3 *adj (finished)* acabado(a); **it's (all) o.** se acabó; **the danger is o.** ha pasado el peligro

overall ['əʊvərɔːl] **1** *adj* total, global

2 *n* (**a**) *Br* guardapolvo *m* (**b**) **overalls** mono *m*

3 *adv* [əʊvər'ɔːl] *(on the whole)* por lo general, en conjunto

overawe [əʊvər'ɔː] *vt* **to be overawed** sobrecogerse

overbearing [əʊvə'beərɪŋ] *adj (domineering)* dominante; *(important)* significativo(a)

overboard ['əʊvəbɔːd] *adv* por la borda; **man o.!** ¡hombre al agua!; *Fam* **to go o.** pasarse

overcast ['əʊvəkɑːst] *adj* nublado(a)

overcharge [əʊvə'tʃɑːdʒ] *vt* (**a**) *(charge too much)* cobrar demasiado (**b**) *(overload)* sobrecargar

overcoat ['əʊvəkəʊt] *n* abrigo *m*

overcome [əʊvə'kʌm] *vt* (**a**) *(conquer)* vencer; **o. by grief** deshecho por el dolor (**b**) *(obstacle)* superar

overconfident [əʊvə'kɒnfɪdənt] *adj* presumido(a), creído(a)

overcrowded [əʊvə'kraʊdɪd] *adj (room)* atestado(a) *(de gente)*; *(country)* superpoblado(a)

overcrowding [əʊvə'kraʊdɪŋ] *n (of prisons etc)* hacinamiento *m*; *(of country)* superpoblación *f*

overdo [əʊvə'duː] *vt (pt* **overdid** [əʊvə'dɪd]; *pp* **overdone** [əʊvə'dʌn]) (**a**) *(carry too far)* exagerar; **don't o. it** no te pases (**b**) *Culin* cocer *or* asar demasiado

overdose ['əʊvədəʊs] *n* sobredosis *f*

overdraft ['əʊvədrɑːft] *n* giro *m* en descubierto; *(amount)* saldo *m* deudor

overdraw [əʊvə'drɔː] *vt* **to be overdrawn** tener la cuenta en descubierto

overdue [əʊvə'djuː] *adj (rent, train etc)* atrasado(a); *(reform)* largamente esperado(a)

overestimate [əʊvər'estɪmeɪt] *vt* sobreestimar

overflow 1 *vi* [əʊvə'fləʊ] *(river)* desbordarse; *(cup etc)* derramarse

2 *n* ['əʊvəfləʊ] *(of river etc)* desbordamiento *m*; **o. pipe** cañería *f* de desagüe

overgrown [əʊvə'grəʊn] *adj* (**a**) *(with grass)* cubierto(a) (de hierba) (**b**) *(in size)* demasiado grande

overhaul 1 *vt* [əʊvə'hɔːl] revisar

2 *n* ['əʊvəhɔːl] revisión *f* y reparación *f*

overhead 1 *adj* ['əʊvəhed] *(por)* encima de la cabeza; **o. cable** cable aéreo

2 *adv* [əʊvə'hed] arriba, por encima de la cabeza

3 *n* ['əʊvəhed] *US* = **overheads**

overheads ['əʊvəhedz] *npl Br* gastos *mpl* generales

overhear [əʊvə'hɪə(r)] *vt (pt & pp* **overheard** [əʊvə'hɜːd]) oír por casualidad

overheat [əʊvə'hiːt] *vi* recalentarse

overjoyed [əʊvə'dʒɔɪd] *adj* rebosante de alegría

overlap [əʊvə'læp] *vi* superponerse; *Fig* **our plans o.** nuestros planes coinciden parcialmente

overleaf [əʊvə'liːf] *adv* al dorso

overload 1 *vt* [əʊvə'ləʊd] sobrecargar

2 *n* ['əʊvələʊd] sobrecarga *f*

overlook [əʊvə'lʊk] *vt* (**a**) *(fail to notice)* saltarse (**b**) *(ignore)* no hacer caso de; **we'll o. it this time** esta vez haremos la vista gorda (**c**) *(have a view of)* dar a, tener vista a

overmanning [əʊvə'mænɪŋ] *n Ind* exceso *m* de empleados

overnight 1 *adv* [əʊvə'naɪt] (**a**) *(during the night)* por la noche; **we stayed there o.** pasamos la noche allí (**b**) *(suddenly)* de la noche a la mañana

2 *adj* ['əʊvənaɪt] *(sudden)* repentino(a)

overpass ['əʊvəpɑːs] *n Br* paso *m* elevado

overpay [əʊvə'peɪ] *vt (pt & pp* **overpaid** [əʊvə'peɪd]) pagar demasiado

overpower [əʊvə'paʊə(r)] *vt* (**a**) *(subdue)* dominar (**b**) *(affect strongly)* abrumar

overrate [əʊvə'reɪt] *vt* sobreestimar, supervalorar

override [əʊvə'raɪd] *vt (pt* **overrode**; *pp* **overridden** [əʊvə'rɪdən] (**a**) *(disregard)* hacer caso omiso de (**b**) *(annul, cancel out)* anular (**c**) *(be more important than)* contar más que

overriding [əʊvə'raɪdɪŋ] *adj* principal; *(importance)* primordial; *(need)* imperioso(a)

overrode [əʊvə'rəʊd] *pt of* **override**

overrule [əʊvə'ruːl] *vt* invalidar; *Jur* denegar

overrun [əʊvə'rʌn] *vt* (**a**) *(country)* invadir (**b**) *(allotted time)* excederse de

oversaw [əʊvə'sɔː] *pt of* **oversee**

overseas 1 *adv* [əʊvə'siːz] en ultramar; **to live o.** vivir en el extranjero

2 *adj* ['əʊvəsiːz] de ultramar; *(person)* extranjero(a); *(trade)* exterior

oversee [əʊvə'siː] *vt* (*pt* **oversaw**; *pp* **overseen** [əʊvə'siːn]) supervisar

overseer ['əʊvəsiːə(r)] *n* supervisor(a) *m,f*; *(foreman)* capataz *m*

overshadow [əʊvə'ʃædəʊ] *vt Fig* eclipsar

overshoot [əʊvə'ʃuːt] *vt* (*pt & pp* **overshot** [əʊvə'ʃɒt]) **to o. a turning** pasarse un cruce; *Fig* **to o. the mark** pasarse de la raya

oversight ['əʊvəsaɪt] *n* descuido *m*

oversleep [əʊvə'sliːp] *vi* (*pt & pp* **overslept** [əʊvə'slept]) quedarse dormido(a)

overspill ['əʊvəspɪl] *n* exceso *m* de población

overstate [əʊvə'steɪt] *vt* exagerar

overstep [əʊvə'step] *vt Fig* **to o. the mark** pasarse de la raya

overt [əʊ'vɜːt] *adj* patente

overtake [əʊvə'teɪk] *vt* (*pt* **overtook**; *pp* **overtaken** [əʊvə'teɪkən]) (**a**) *Br Aut* adelantar (**b**) *(surpass)* superar a (**c**) *(of night)* sorprender

overthrow [əʊvə'θrəʊ] *vt* (*pt* **overthrew** [əʊvə'θruː]; *pp* **overthrown** [əʊvə'θrəʊn]) *(government)* derribar

overtime ['əʊvətaɪm] *n* (**a**) *(work)* horas *fpl* extra (**b**) *US* prórroga *f*

overtone ['əʊvətəʊn] *n* matiz *m*

overtook [əʊvə'tʊk] *pt of* **overtake**

overture ['əʊvətjʊə(r)] *n* (**a**) *Mus* obertura *f*; *Fig (introduction)* introducción *f* (**b**) *(proposal)* propuesta *f*

overturn [əʊvə'tɜːn] *vt & vi* volcar

overweight [əʊvə'weɪt] *adj* demasiado pesado(a)

overwhelm [əʊvə'welm] *vt* (**a**) *(defeat)* aplastar; *(overpower)* abrumar; **I'm overwhelmed** estoy abrumado (**b**) *(with letters, work etc)* inundar

overwhelming [əʊvə'welmɪŋ] *adj* *(defeat)* aplastante; *(desire etc)* irresistible

overwork [əʊvə'wɜːk] **1** *vi* trabajar demasiado

2 *vt (person)* forzar; *(excuse etc)* abusar de

overwrought [əʊvə'rɔːt] *adj* (**a**) *(tense)* muy nervioso(a) (**b**) *Literary (too elaborate)* forzado(a)

owe [əʊ] *vt* deber

owing ['əʊɪŋ] *adj* **o. to** debido a, a causa de

owl [aʊl] *n* lechuza *f*, búho *m*

own [əʊn] **1** *adj* propio(a); **it's his o. fault** es culpa suya

2 *pron* (**a**) **my o./your o./his o.***etc* lo mío/lo tuyo/lo suyo*/etc*; **to be on one's o.** realizarse; *Fam* **to get one's o. back** tomarse la revancha (**b**) **on one's o.** *(without help)* uno(a) mismo(a); *(alone)* solo(a)

3 *vt* poseer, ser dueño(a) de

▶**own up** *vi* **to o. up (to sth)** confesar (algo)

owner ['əʊnə(r)] *n* propietario(a) *m,f*, dueño(a) *m,f*

ownership ['əʊnəʃɪp] *n* propiedad *f*, posesión *f*

ox [ɒks] *n* (*pl* **oxen** ['ɒksən]) buey *m*

oxide ['ɒksaɪd] *n Chem* óxido *m*

oxtail ['ɒksteɪl] *n* rabo *m* de buey

oxygen ['ɒksɪdʒən] *n* oxígeno *m*; **o. mask** máscara *f* de oxígeno

oyster ['ɔɪstə(r)] *n* ostra *f*

ozone ['əʊzəʊn] *n* ozono *m*; **o. layer** capa *f* de ozono

P

P, p [piː] *n (the letter)* P, p *f*

p (a) (*pl* **pp**) (*abbr* **page**) pág., p (b) [piː] *Br Fam* (*abbr* **penny, pence**) penique(s) *m(pl)*

PA [piːˈeɪ] *n Fam* (a) (*abbr* **personal assistant**) ayudante *mf* personal (b) (*abbr* **public-address (system)**) megafonía *f*

p.a. (*abbr* **per annum**) al año

pace [peɪs] **1** *n (step)* paso *m; (speed)* ritmo *m;* **to keep p. with** seguir a; *Fig* avanzar al mismo ritmo que; **to set the p.** marcar el paso; *Fig* marcar la pauta
2 *vi* **to p. up and down** ir de un lado a otro

pacemaker [ˈpeɪsmeɪkə(r)] *n Sport* liebre *f; Med* marcapasos *m inv*

Pacific [pəˈsɪfɪk] *adj* **the P. (Ocean)** el (océano) Pacífico

pacifier [ˈpæsɪfaɪə(r)] *n US (for baby)* chupete *m*

pacifist [ˈpæsɪfɪst] *adj & n* pacifista (*mf*)

pacify [ˈpæsɪfaɪ] *vt (person)* calmar; *(country)* pacificar

pack¹ [pæk] **1** *n (parcel)* paquete *m; (bundle)* bulto *m; US (of cigarettes)* paquete; *Br (of cards)* baraja *f; (of hounds)* jauría *f*
2 *vt* (a) *(goods)* embalar, envasar; *(in suitcase)* poner; **to p. one's bags** hacer las maletas; *Fig* marcharse (b) *(fill)* atestar (c) *(press down) (snow)* apretar
3 *vi* (a) hacer las maletas; *Fam* **to send sb packing** mandar a paseo a algn (b) *(of people)* apiñarse (**into** en)
► **pack in** *vt sep Br Fam (give up)* dejar
► **pack off** *vt sep Fam* mandar
► **pack up** *Fam* **1** *vt sep (give up)* dejar
2 *vi (stop working)* terminar; *(machine etc)* estropearse

pack² [pæk] *vt (meeting)* llenar de partidarios

package [ˈpækɪdʒ] **1** *n* (a) *(parcel)* paquete *m; (bundle)* bulto *m* (b) *(of proposals etc)* paquete *m; (agreement)* acuerdo *m;* **p. deal** convenio *m* general; **p. tour** viaje *m* todo incluido
2 *vt (goods)* envasar, embalar

packet [ˈpækɪt] *n* paquete *m; Fam (fortune)* dineral *m*

packing [ˈpækɪŋ] *n* embalaje *m;* **p. case** caja *f* de embalar; **to do one's p.** hacer las maletas

pact [pækt] *n* pacto *m*

pad¹ [pæd] **1** *n* (a) almohadilla *f; (of paper)* bloc *m,* taco *m* (b) **launch p.** plataforma *f* de lanzamiento (c) *Fam (flat)* piso *m*
2 *vt (chair)* acolchar
► **pad out** *vt sep Fig* meter paja en

pad² [pæd] *vi* **to p. about** *or* **around** andar silenciosamente

padding [ˈpædɪŋ] *n (material)* relleno *m; Fig (in speech etc)* paja *f*

paddle¹ [ˈpædəl] **1** *n* (a) *(oar)* pala *f;* **p. boat** *or* **steamer** vapor *m* de ruedas (b) *US (for table tennis)* pala *f*
2 *vt (boat)* remar con pala en
3 *vi (in boat)* remar con pala

paddle² [ˈpædəl] *vi* chapotear

paddling pool [ˈpædlɪŋpuːl] *n Br* piscina *f* para niños

paddock [ˈpædək] *n* potrero *m; (in race course)* paddock *m*

paddy [ˈpædɪ] *n* arrozal *m*

padlock [ˈpædlɒk] **1** *n* candado *m*
2 *vt* cerrar con candado

paediatrician [piːdɪəˈtrɪʃən] *n* pediatra *mf*

pagan [ˈpeɪɡən] *adj & n* pagano(a) *(m,f)*

page¹ [peɪdʒ] *n* página *f*

page² [peɪdʒ] **1** *n (servant)* paje *m; (of knight)* escudero *m; (at club)* botones *m inv*
2 *vt (call)* llamar por altavoz

pageant [ˈpædʒənt] *n (show)* espectáculo *m; (procession)* desfile *m; (on horses)* cabalgata *f*

pageantry [ˈpædʒəntrɪ] *n* pompa *f,* boato *m*

paid [peɪd] **1** *adj* pagado(a); *Fig* **to put p. to sth** acabar con algo
2 *pt & pp of* **pay**

pail [peɪl] *n* cubo *m; (child's)* cubito *m*

pain [peɪn] **1** *n* (a) dolor *m; (grief)* sufrimiento *m; Fam* **he's a p. (in the neck)** es un pelmazo; **on p. of death** so pena de muerte (b) **to take pains over sth** esmerarse en algo

2 *vt (grieve)* dar pena a

pained [peɪnd] *adj* de reproche

painful ['peɪnfʊl] *adj* doloroso(a); *Fam (very bad)* malísimo(a)

painfully ['peɪnfʊlɪ] *adv* (**a**) **p. shy** lastimosamente tímido(a) (**b**) *Fam* terriblemente

painkiller ['peɪnkɪlə(r)] *n* analgésico *m*

painless ['peɪnlɪs] *adj* sin dolor; *Fig* sin dificultades

painstaking ['peɪnzteɪkɪŋ] *adj (person)* concienzudo(a); *(care, research)* esmerado(a)

paint [peɪnt] **1** *n* pintura *f*
2 *vt* pintar; **to p. sth white** pintar algo de blanco
3 *vi* pintar

paintbrush ['peɪntbrʌʃ] *n Art* pincel *m*; *(for walls)* brocha *f*

painter ['peɪntə(r)] *n* pintor(a) *m,f*

painting ['peɪntɪŋ] *n* cuadro *m*; *(activity)* pintura *f*

paintwork ['peɪntwɜːk] *n* pintura *f*

pair [peə(r)] *n (of gloves, shoes)* par *m*; *(of people, cards)* pareja *f*; **a p. of scissors** unas tijeras; **a p. of trousers** un pantalón, unos pantalones

pajamas [pə'dʒæməz] *npl US* = **pyjamas**

Pakistan [pɑːkɪ'stɑːn] *n* Paquistán

Pakistani [pɑːkɪ'stɑːnɪ] *adj & n* paquistaní *(mf)*

pal [pæl] *n Fam* amigo(a) *m,f*, colega *mf*

palace ['pælɪs] *n* palacio *m*

palatable ['pælətəbəl] *adj (tasty)* sabroso(a); *Fig* aceptable

palate ['pælɪt] *n* paladar *m*

palatial [pə'leɪʃəl] *adj* suntuoso(a), señorial

palaver [pə'lɑːvə(r)] *n Fam* lío *m*, follón *m*

pale¹ [peɪl] **1** *adj (skin)* pálido(a); *(colour)* claro(a); *(light)* tenue; **to turn p.** palidecer
2 *vi* palidecer

pale² [peɪl] *n Fig* **to be beyond the p.** ser inaceptable

Palestine ['pælɪstaɪn] *n* Palestina

Palestinian [pælɪ'stɪnɪən] *adj & n* palestino(a) *(m,f)*

palette ['pælɪt] *n* paleta *f*; **p. knife** espátula *f*

paling ['peɪlɪŋ] *n* valla *f*

palisade [pælɪ'seɪd] *n* palizada *f*, estacada *f*

pall¹ [pɔːl] *n Fig* manto *m*; *(of smoke)* cortina *f*

pall² [pɔːl] *vi* aburrir; **it never palls** nunca cansa

pallet ['pælɪt] *n* plataforma *f* de carga

pallid ['pælɪd] *adj* pálido(a)

pallor ['pælə(r)] *n* palidez *f*

palm¹ [pɑːm] *n (tree)* palmera *f*; *(leaf)* palma *f*; **date p.** palma datilera; **P. Sunday** domingo *m* de Ramos

palm² [pɑːm] *n Anat* palma *f*
▸ **palm off** *vt sep* **to p. sth off on sb** colocar *or* endosar algo a algn

palmistry ['pɑːmɪstrɪ] *n* quiromancia *f*

palpable ['pælpəbəl] *adj* palpable

palpitate ['pælpɪteɪt] *vi* palpitar

palpitation [pælpɪ'teɪʃən] *n* palpitación *f*

paltry ['pɔːltrɪ] *adj* (**paltrier, paltriest**) insignificante

pamper ['pæmpə(r)] *vt* mimar, consentir

pamphlet ['pæmflɪt] *n* folleto *m*

pan¹ [pæn] **1** *n* (**a**) *(saucepan)* cazuela *f*, cacerola *f* (**b**) *(of scales)* platillo *m* (**c**) *(of lavatory)* taza *f*
2 *vt Fam (criticize)* dejar por los suelos

pan² [pæn] *vi Cin* tomar vistas panorámicas

panacea [pænə'sɪə] *n* panacea *f*

panache [pə'næʃ] *n* garbo *m*, salero *m*

Panama ['pænəmɑː] *n* Panamá; **P. Canal** Canal *m* de Panamá

pancake ['pænkeɪk] *n* crepe *f*

panda ['pændə] *n* panda *m*; *Br* **p. car** coche *m* patrulla

pandemonium [pændɪ'məʊnɪəm] *n* alboroto *m*

pander ['pændə(r)] *vi* **to p. to** *(person)* complacer a; *(wishes)* acceder a

pane [peɪn] *n* cristal *m*, vidrio *m*

panel ['pænəl] *n* (**a**) *(of wall)* panel *m*; *(flat surface)* tabla *f*; *(of instruments)* tablero *m*; *(of ceiling)* artesón *m* (**b**) *(jury)* jurado *m*; *Rad & TV* concursantes *mpl*

panelling, *US* **paneling** ['pænəlɪŋ] *n* paneles *mpl*

pang [pæŋ] *n (of pain, hunger)* punzada *f*; *(of childbirth)* dolores *mpl*; *Fig (of conscience)* remordimiento *m*

panic ['pænɪk] **1** *n* pánico *m*; **to get into a p.** ponerse histérico(a)
2 *vi* aterrarse

panicky ['pænɪkɪ] *adj* asustadizo(a)

panic-stricken ['pænɪkstrɪkən] *adj* aterrado(a)

panorama [pænə'rɑːmə] *n* panorama *m*

pansy ['pænzɪ] *n Bot* pensamiento *m*; *Fam Pej* mariquita *m*

pant [pænt] **1** *n* jadeo *m*
2 *vi* jadear

panther ['pænθə(r)] *n* pantera *f*

panties ['pæntɪz] *npl* bragas *fpl*

🖉 Note that the Spanish word **panty** is a false friend and is never a translation for the English word **panties**. In Spanish, **panty** means "(pair of) tights".

---

pantomime ['pæntəmaɪm] n Th (play) función f musical navideña; (mime) pantomima f

pantry ['pæntrɪ] n despensa f

pants [pænts] npl Br (underpants) (ladies') bragas fpl; (men's) calzoncillos mpl; US (trousers) pantalones mpl, pantalón m

pantyhose ['pæntɪhəʊz] n US medias fpl, pantis mpl

papal ['peɪpəl] adj papal

paper ['peɪpə(r)] 1 n (a) papel m; Fig on p. en teoría; **p. money** papel moneda; **writing p.** papel de escribir (b) (exam) examen m; (essay) trabajo m (escrito) (c) Pol libro m (d) (newspaper) periódico m; **the papers** la prensa (e) **papers** (documents) documentos mpl
2 vt empapelar

paperback ['peɪpəbæk] n libro m en rústica

paperclip ['peɪpəklɪp] n clip m, sujetapapeles m inv

paperweight ['peɪpəweɪt] n pisapapeles m inv

paperwork ['peɪpəwɜːk] n papeleo m

papier-mâché [pæpjeɪ'mæʃeɪ] n cartón m piedra

paprika ['pæprɪkə] n pimentón molido

par [pɑː(r)] n (parity) igualdad f; (in golf) par m; Fig **it's p. for the course** es lo normal en estos casos; Fig **to feel below p.** estar en baja forma

parable ['pærəbəl] n parábola f

paracetamol [pærə'siːtəmɒl] n paracetamol m

parachute ['pærəʃuːt] 1 n paracaídas m inv
2 vi **to p. (down)** saltar or lanzarse en paracaídas

parade [pə'reɪd] 1 n desfile m; Mil **to be on p.** pasar revista
2 vt Mil hacer desfilar; Fig (flaunt) hacer alarde de
3 vi (troops) pasar revista; (procession) desfilar

paradise ['pærədaɪs] n paraíso m

paradox ['pærədɒks] n paradoja f

paradoxical [pærə'dɒksɪkəl] adj paradójico(a)

paraffin ['pærəfɪn] n parafina f; **liquid p.** aceite m de parafina; **p. lamp** lámpara f de petróleo

paragliding ['pærəglaɪdɪŋ] n parapente m

paragon ['pærəgən] n modelo m

paragraph ['pærəgrɑːf] n párrafo m

Paraguay ['pærəgwaɪ] n Paraguay

Paraguayan [pærə'gwaɪən] adj & n paraguayo(a) (m,f)

parallel ['pærəlel] 1 adj paralelo(a) (**to** or **with** a); Fig comparable (**to** or **with** a)
2 n Geog paralelo m; Geom paralela f; Fig paralelo
3 vt Fig ser paralelo(a) a

paralyse ['pærəlaɪz] vt paralizar

paralysis [pə'rælɪsɪs] n parálisis f

paralyze ['pærəlaɪz] vt US = **paralyse**

paramedic [pærə'medɪk] n auxiliar mf sanitario(a)

parameter [pə'ræmɪtə(r)] n parámetro m

paramilitary [pærə'mɪlɪtərɪ] adj paramilitar

paramount ['pærəmaʊnt] adj **of p. importance** de suma importancia

paranoid ['pærənɔɪd] adj & n paranoico(a) (m,f)

paraphernalia [pærəfə'neɪlɪə] n parafernalia f

paraphrase ['pærəfreɪz] vt parafrasear

parasite ['pærəsaɪt] n parásito m

parasol ['pærəsɒl] n sombrilla f

paratrooper ['pærətruːpə(r)] n paracaidista m

parcel ['pɑːsəl] 1 n paquete m; **p. bomb** paquete bomba
2 vt **to p. up** envolver, empaquetar

parched [pɑːtʃt] adj (land) reseco(a); (lips, mouth) seco(a); Fig **to be p.** estar muerto(a) de sed

parchment ['pɑːtʃmənt] n pergamino m

pardon ['pɑːdən] 1 n perdón m; Jur indulto m; **I beg your p.** (Usted) perdone; (**I beg your) p.?** ¿cómo (dice)?
2 vt perdonar; Jur indultar; **p. me!** ¡Usted perdone!

parent ['peərənt] n **parents** padres mpl

🖉 Note that the Spanish word **pariente** is a false friend and is never a translation for the English word **parent**. In Spanish, **pariente** means "relative, relation".

---

parental [pə'rentəl] adj paternal; **p. guidance** consejos mpl paternales

parenthesis [pə'renθɪsɪs] n (pl **parentheses** [pə'renθɪsiːz]) paréntesis m inv; **in p.** entre paréntesis

pariah [pə'raɪə] n paria mf

Paris ['pærɪs] n París

parish ['pærɪʃ] n parroquia f

Parisian [pə'rɪzɪən] *adj & n* parisino(a) *(m,f)*

parity ['pærɪtɪ] *n* igualdad *f*; *(of shares)* paridad *f*

park [pɑːk] **1** *n* parque *m*

2 *vt (car)* aparcar, *Carib, Col, Pan* parquear

parking ['pɑːkɪŋ] *n* aparcamiento *m*, estacionamiento *m*; **no p.** *(sign)* prohibido aparcar; *US* **p. lot** parking *m*, aparcamiento *m*; **p. meter** parquímetro *m*; **p. space** aparcamiento

parliament ['pɑːləmənt] *n* parlamento *m*

parliamentary [pɑːlə'mentərɪ] *adj* parlamentario(a)

parlour, *US* **parlor** ['pɑːlə(r)] *n* salón *m*

parochial [pə'rəʊkɪəl] *adj* parroquial; *Pej (narrow-minded)* de miras estrechas

parody ['pærədɪ] *n* parodia *f*

parole [pə'rəʊl] *n Jur* libertad *f* condicional; **on p.** en libertad bajo palabra

parquet ['pɑːkeɪ] *n* **p. floor** suelo *m* de parqué

parrot ['pærət] *n* loro *m*, papagayo *m*

parry ['pærɪ] *vt* parar

parsimonious [pɑːsɪ'məʊnɪəs] *adj* tacaño(a)

parsley ['pɑːslɪ] *n* perejil *m*

parsnip ['pɑːsnɪp] *n* chirivía *f*

parson ['pɑːsən] *n* cura *m*

part [pɑːt] **1** *n* (**a**) parte *f*; *(piece)* trozo *m*; *(episode)* capítulo *m*; *Tech* pieza *f*; **for the most p.** en la mayor parte (**b**) *Cin & Th* papel *m*; **to play a p. in sth** desempeñar un papel en algo; **to take p. in sth** participar en algo (**c**) *(place)* lugar *m*; **in these parts** por estos lugares (**d**) **for my p.** por mi parte; **to take sb's p.** tomar partido por algn; **to take sth in good p.** tomarse bien algo (**e**) *US (in hair)* raya *f*

2 *adj (partial)* parcial; **in p. exchange** como parte del pago

3 *adv (partly)* en parte

4 *vt (separate)* separar; **to p. company with sb** separarse de algn; **to p. one's hair** hacerse la raya (en el pelo)

5 *vi* separarse; *(say goodbye)* despedirse

▸ **part with** *vt insep* separarse de

partial ['pɑːʃəl] *adj* parcial; **to be p. to sth** ser aficionado(a) a algo

participant [pɑː'tɪsɪpənt] *n* participante *mf*; *(in competition)* concursante *mf*

participate [pɑː'tɪsɪpeɪt] *vi* participar (**in** en)

participation [pɑːtɪsɪ'peɪʃən] *n* participación *f*

participle ['pɑːtɪsɪpəl] *n* participio *m*

particle ['pɑːtɪkəl] *n* partícula *f*

particular [pə'tɪkjʊlə(r)] **1** *adj* (**a**) *(special)* particular, especial; **in this p. case** en este caso concreto; **that p. person** esa persona en particular (**b**) *(fussy)* exigente

2 *npl* **particulars** pormenores *mpl*; **to take down sb's particulars** anotar los datos personales de algn

particularly [pə'tɪkjʊləlɪ] *adv* particularmente, especialmente

parting ['pɑːtɪŋ] **1** *n (separation)* separación *f*; *(farewell)* despedida *f*; *Br (in hair)* raya *f*

2 *adj* de despedida

partisan [pɑːtɪ'zæn, 'pɑːtɪzæn] **1** *n Mil* guerrillero(a) *m,f*; *(supporter)* partidario(a) *m,f*

2 *adj (supporter)* a ultranza; *(of party)* partidista

partition [pɑː'tɪʃən] **1** *n (wall)* tabique *m*; *(of country)* partición *f*

2 *vt* dividir

partly ['pɑːtlɪ] *adv* en parte

partner ['pɑːtnə(r)] **1** *n* compañero(a) *m,f*; *(in dancing, tennis)* pareja *f*; *(husband)* marido *m*; *(wife)* mujer *f*; *Com* socio(a) *m,f*

2 *vt* acompañar

partnership ['pɑːtnəʃɪp] *n (relationship)* vida *f* en común; *Com* sociedad *f*

partridge ['pɑːtrɪdʒ] *n* perdiz pardilla

part-time ['pɑːt'taɪm] **1** *adj (work etc)* de tiempo parcial

2 *adv* a tiempo parcial

party ['pɑːtɪ] **1** *n* (**a**) *(celebration)* fiesta *f* (**b**) *(group)* grupo *m* (**c**) *Pol* partido *m*; **p. political broadcast** espacio *m* electoral (**d**) *Jur* parte *f*

2 *adj* de fiesta; *Tel* **p. line** línea compartida

pass [pɑːs] **1** *n* (**a**) *(of mountain)* desfiladero *m*

(**b**) *(permit)* permiso *m*; **bus p.** abono *m* de autobús

(**c**) *Sport* pase *m*

(**d**) *Fam* **to make a p. at sb** intentar ligar con algn

2 *vt* (**a**) pasar; *(overtake)* adelantar

(**b**) *(exam, law)* aprobar; *Jur* **to p. sentence** dictar sentencia

3 *vi* (**a**) pasar; *(procession)* desfilar; *(car)* adelantar; *(people)* cruzarse; *Sport* hacer un pase; **we passed on the stairs** nos cruzamos en la escalera

(**b**) *(pain)* remitir; *(opportunity)* perderse; *(time)* pasar

(**c**) *(happen)* ocurrir, pasar

(d) *(in exam)* aprobar
▸ **pass away** *vi Euph* pasar a mejor vida
▸ **pass by 1** *vt sep* pasar de largo
 2 *vi* pasar
▸ **pass for** *vt insep* pasar por
▸ **pass off 1** *vt sep* hacer pasar; **to p. oneself off as sth** hacerse pasar por algo
 2 *vi (happen)* transcurrir
▸ **pass on 1** *vt sep (hand on)* transmitir
 2 *vi Euph* pasar a mejor vida
▸ **pass out** *vi (faint)* desmayarse; *Mil* graduarse
▸ **pass over** *vt insep* (a) *(aircraft)* volar por (b) *(disregard)* pasar por alto
▸ **pass up** *vt sep Fam (opportunity)* renunciar; *(offer)* rechazar

passable ['pɑːsəbəl] *adj (road)* transitable; *(acceptable)* pasable

passage ['pæsɪdʒ] *n* (a) *(alleyway)* callejón *m*; *(hallway)* pasillo *m* (b) *(movement)* tránsito *m*; *Naut* travesía *f* (c) *Mus & Lit* pasaje *m*

passageway ['pæsɪdʒweɪ] *n (interior)* pasillo *m*; *(exterior)* pasaje *m*

passbook ['pɑːsbʊk] *n* libreta *f* de banco

passenger ['pæsɪndʒə(r)] *n* pasajero(a) *m,f*

passer-by [pɑːsə'baɪ] *n* transeúnte *mf*

passing ['pɑːsɪŋ] **1** *n* (a) *(of time)* transcurso *m*; **in p.** de pasada (b) *(of law)* aprobación *f*
 2 *adj* que pasa; *(glance)* rápido(a); *(thought)* pasajero(a)

passion ['pæʃən] *n* pasión *f*; **p. fruit** granadilla *f*

passionate ['pæʃənɪt] *adj* apasionado(a)

passive ['pæsɪv] *adj* pasivo(a)

Passover ['pɑːsəʊvə(r)] *n* Pascua *f* de los judíos

passport ['pɑːspɔːt] *n* pasaporte *m*

password ['pɑːswɜːd] *n* contraseña *f*

past [pɑːst] **1** *n* pasado *m*; **in the p.** en el pasado; **to have a p.** tener antecedentes
 2 *adj* pasado(a); *(former)* anterior; **in the p. weeks** en las últimas semanas
 3 *adv* por delante; **to run p.** pasar corriendo
 4 *prep (beyond)* más allá de; *(more than)* más de; **he's p. forty** pasa de los cuarenta (años); **it's five p. ten** son las diez y cinco; *Fam* **to be p. it** estar muy carroza

pasta ['pæstə] *n* pasta *f*, pastas *fpl*

paste [peɪst] **1** *n* pasta *f*; *(glue)* engrudo *m*
 2 *vt (stick)* pegar; *(put paste on)* engomar

pastel ['pæstəl] *adj & n* pastel *(m)*

pasteurized ['pæstjəraɪzd] *adj* pasteurizado(a)

pastille ['pæstɪl] *n* pastilla *f*

pastime ['pɑːstaɪm] *n* pasatiempo *m*

pastor ['pɑːstə(r)] *n* pastor *m*

pastoral ['pɑːstərəl] *adj* pastoral

pastry ['peɪstrɪ] *n (dough)* pasta *f*; *(cake)* pastel *m*

pasture ['pɑːstʃə(r)] *n* pasto *m*

pasty¹ ['pæstɪ] *n Culin* empanada *f*, pastel *m* de carne

pasty² ['peɪstɪ] *adj* (**pastier, pastiest**) *(complexion)* pálido(a)

pat [pæt] **1** *n (caress)* caricia *f*; *(tap)* palmadita *f*; *Fig* **to give sb a p. on the back** felicitar a algn
 2 *vt* acariciar; **to p. sb on the back** dar a algn una palmadita en la espalda

patch [pætʃ] *n (of material)* parche *m*; *(of land)* terreno *m*; *(of colour)* mancha *f*; *Fig* **to go through a bad p.** pasar por una mala racha
▸ **patch up** *vt sep (garment)* poner un parche en; **to p. things up** *(after argument)* limar asperezas

patchwork ['pætʃwɜːk] **1** *n* labor *f* de retales
 2 *adj (quilt etc)* hecho(a) con retales distintos

patchy ['pætʃɪ] *adj* (**patchier, patchiest**) *(colour, performance)* desigual; *(knowledge)* incompleto(a)

pâté ['pæteɪ] *n* paté *m*

patent¹ ['peɪtənt] **1** *n Com* patente *f*
 2 *adj (obvious)* patente, evidente; **p. medicine** específico *m*
 3 *vt Com* patentar

patent² ['peɪtənt] *n* **p. (leather)** charol *m*

patently ['peɪtəntlɪ] *adv* **it is p. obvious** está clarísimo

paternal [pə'tɜːnəl] *adj* paternal; *(grandmother etc)* paterno(a)

paternity [pə'tɜːnɪtɪ] *n* paternidad *f*

path [pɑːθ] *n* camino *m*, sendero *m*; *(route)* ruta *f*; *(of missile)* trayectoria *f*

pathetic [pə'θetɪk] *adj (pitiful)* patético(a); *Fam (hopeless)* malísimo(a); **she was a p. sight** daba lástima verla

pathological [pæθə'lɒdʒɪkəl] *adj* patológico(a)

pathologist [pə'θɒlədʒɪst] *n* patólogo(a) *m,f*

pathology [pə'θɒlədʒɪ] *n* patología *f*

pathos ['peɪθɒs] *n* patetismo *m*

pathway ['pɑːθweɪ] *n* camino *m*, sendero *m*

patience ['peɪʃəns] *n* (a) paciencia *f*; **to lose one's p. with sb** perder la paciencia con algn (b) *Br Cards* solitario *m*

patient ['peɪʃənt] **1** *adj* paciente; **to be p.**

with sb tener paciencia con algn
   2 *n Med* paciente *mf*
patio ['pætɪəʊ] *n* patio *m*
patriotic [pætrɪ'ɒtɪk] *adj (person)* patriota; *(speech, act)* patriótico(a)
patrol [pə'trəʊl] **1** *n* patrulla *f*; **p. car** coche *m* patrulla
   2 *vt* patrullar por
patrolman [pə'trəʊlmən] *n US* policía *m*
patron ['peɪtrən] *n* **(a)** *(of charity)* patrocinador(a) *m,f*; *(of arts)* mecenas *m inv*; **p. saint** (santo(a) *m,f*) patrón(ona) *m,f* **(b)** *(customer)* cliente(a) *m,f* habitual
patronize ['pætrənaɪz] *vt* **(a)** *(arts)* fomentar; *(shop)* ser cliente(a) *m,f* habitual de; *(club etc)* frecuentar **(b)** *Pej (person)* tratar con condescendencia
patronizing ['pætrənaɪzɪŋ] *adj Pej* condescendiente
patter¹ ['pætə(r)] **1** *n (of rain)* repiqueteo *m*; *(of feet)* pasito *m*
   2 *vi (rain)* repiquetear; *(feet)* hacer ruido sordo
patter² ['pætə(r)] *n Fam* labia *f*; *(of salesman)* discursillo preparado
pattern ['pætən] *n Sewing* patrón *m*; *(design)* dibujo *m*; *(on material)* estampado *m*; *Fig (of behaviour)* modelo *m*
paunch [pɔːntʃ] *n* panza *f*
pauper ['pɔːpə(r)] *n* pobre *mf*
pause [pɔːz] **1** *n* pausa *f*; *(silence)* silencio *m*
   2 *vi* hacer una pausa; *(be silent)* callarse
pave [peɪv] *vt* pavimentar; *(with stones)* empedrar; *Fig* **to p. the way for sb/sth** preparar el terreno para algn/algo
pavement ['peɪvmənt] *n* **(a)** *Br (beside road)* acera *f*, *CSur, Perú* vereda *f*, *CAm, Méx* banqueta *f* **(b)** *US (roadway)* calzada *f*, pavimento *m*
pavilion [pə'vɪljən] *n* pabellón *m*; *Br Sport (changing rooms)* vestuarios *mpl*
paving ['peɪvɪŋ] *n (on road)* pavimento *m*; *(on floor)* enlosado *m*; *(with stones)* empedrado *m*; **p. stone** losa *f*
paw [pɔː] **1** *n (foot)* pata *f*; *(of cat)* garra *f*; *(of lion)* zarpa *f*
   2 *vt (of lion)* dar zarpazos a; *Pej (of person)* manosear, sobar
pawn¹ [pɔːn] *n (in chess)* peón *m*; *Fig* **to be sb's p.** ser el juguete de algn
pawn² [pɔːn] *vt* empeñar
pawnbroker ['pɔːnbrəʊkə(r)] *n* prestamista *mf*
pawnshop ['pɔːnʃɒp] *n* casa *f* de empeños
pay [peɪ] **1** *n (wages)* paga *f*, sueldo *m*; **p.**

Br **packet** *or US* **envelope** sobre *m* de la paga; **p. rise** aumento *m* del sueldo; **p. slip** nómina *f*
   2 *vt (pt & pp paid)* **(a)** pagar; **to be** *or* **get paid** cobrar **(b)** *(attention)* prestar; *(homage)* rendir; *(visit)* hacer; **to p. sb a compliment** halagar a algn **(c)** *(be profitable for)* compensar
   3 *vi* **(a)** pagar; **to p. for sth** pagar (por) algo **(b)** *(be profitable)* ser rentable
   ▶ **pay back** *vt sep* reembolsar; *Fig* **to p. sb back** vengarse de algn
   ▶ **pay in** *vt sep (money)* ingresar
   ▶ **pay off 1** *vt sep (debt)* liquidar; *(mortgage)* cancelar
      2 *vi (be successful)* dar resultado
   ▶ **pay out** *vt sep (spend)* gastar (**on** en)
   ▶ **pay up** *vi* pagar
payable ['peɪəbəl] *adj* pagadero(a)
payday ['peɪdeɪ] *n* día *m* de pago
payee [peɪ'iː] *n* portador(a) *m,f*
payment ['peɪmənt] *n* pago *m*; *(of cheque)* cobro *m*; **advance p.** anticipo *m*; **down p.** entrada *f*; **monthly p.** mensualidad *f*
payoff ['peɪɒf] *n (reward)* recompensa *f*; *Fam (bribe)* soborno *m*
pay-per-view ['peɪpə'vjuː] *n* pago *m* por visión
payroll ['peɪrəʊl] *n* nómina *f*
PC ['piː'siː] **1** *n* **(a)** *Br (abbr* **Police Constable)** agente *mf* de policía **(b)** *(abbr* **personal computer)** PC *m*
   2 *adj (abbr* **politically correct)** políticamente correcto(a)
pc *(abbr* **per cent)** p.c.
PE ['piː'iː] *n Sch (abbr* **physical education)** educación *f* física
pea [piː] *n* guisante *m*, *Andes, Carib, RP* arveja *f*, *CAm, Méx* chícharo *m*
peace [piːs] *n* paz *f*; *(calm)* tranquilidad *f*; **at** *or* **in p.** en paz; **p. and quiet** tranquilidad; **to make p.** hacer las paces; *(of countries)* firmar la paz
peaceable ['piːsəbəl] *adj* pacífico(a)
peaceful ['piːsfʊl] *adj (demonstration)* pacífico(a); *(place)* tranquilo(a)
peace-keeping ['piːskiːpɪŋ] *adj* pacificador(a); **p. forces** fuerzas *fpl* de pacificación
peach [piːtʃ] *n* melocotón *m*, *Am* durazno *m*
peacock ['piːkɒk] *n* pavo *m* real
peak [piːk] *n (of cap)* visera *f*; *(of mountain)* pico *m*; *(summit)* cima *f*; *Fig* cumbre *f*; **p. hours** horas *fpl* punta; **p. period** horas de mayor consumo; **p. season** temporada alta

peal [piːl] *n (of bells)* repique *m*; **p. of thunder** trueno *m*; **peals of laughter** carcajadas *fpl*

peanut [ˈpiːnʌt] *n* cacahuete *m*, maní *m*, *Méx* cacahuate *m*; **p. butter** mantequilla *f* or manteca *f* de cacahuete, maní, *Méx* cacahuate

pear [peə(r)] *n* pera *f*

pearl [pɜːl] *n* perla *f*

peasant [ˈpezənt] *adj & n* campesino(a) *(m,f)*

peat [piːt] *n* turba *f*; **p. bog** turbera *f*

pebble [ˈpebəl] *n* guijarro *m*; *(small)* china *f*

pecan [pɪˈkæn] *n (nut)* pacana *f*

peck [pek] **1** *n (of bird)* picotazo *m*; *Fam (kiss)* besito *m*
2 *vt (bird)* picotear; *Fam (kiss)* dar un besito a
3 *vi* **to p. at one's food** picar la comida

pecking order [ˈpekɪŋɔːdə(r)] *n Fig* jerarquía *f*

peckish [ˈpekɪʃ] *adj Fam* **to feel p.** empezar a tener hambre

peculiar [pɪˈkjuːlɪə(r)] *adj (odd)* extraño(a); *(particular)* característico(a)

peculiarity [pɪkjuːlɪˈærɪtɪ] *n (oddity)* rareza *f*; *(characteristic)* característica *f*, peculiaridad *f*

pedal [ˈpedəl] **1** *n* pedal *m*
2 *vi* pedalear

pedantic [pɪˈdæntɪk] *adj* pedante

peddle [ˈpedəl] *vt & vi Com* vender de puerta en puerta; **to p. drugs** traficar con drogas

peddler [ˈpedlə(r)] *n (of drugs)* traficante *mf*

pedestal [ˈpedɪstəl] *n* pedestal *m*; *Fig* **to put sb on a p.** poner a algn sobre un pedestal

pedestrian [pɪˈdestrɪən] **1** *n* peatón(ona) *m,f*; **p. crossing** paso *m* de peatones
2 *adj Pej* prosaico(a)

pediatrician [piːdɪəˈtrɪʃən] *n US* = paediatrician

pedigree [ˈpedɪɡriː] **1** *n* linaje *m*; *(family tree)* árbol genealógico; *(of animal)* pedigrí *m*
2 *adj (animal)* de raza

pee [piː] *Fam* **1** *n* pis *m*
2 *vi* hacer pis

peek [piːk] **1** *n* ojeada *f*
2 *vi* **to p. at sth** mirar algo a hurtadillas

peel [piːl] **1** *n* piel *f*; *(of orange, lemon)* cáscara *f*
2 *vt (fruit)* pelar
3 *vi (paint)* desconcharse; *(wallpaper)* despegarse; *(skin)* pelarse

peeler [ˈpiːlə(r)] *n* **potato p.** pelapatatas *m inv*

peelings [ˈpiːlɪŋz] *npl* peladuras *fpl*, mondaduras *fpl*

peep¹ [piːp] *n (sound)* pío *m*

peep² [piːp] **1** *n (glance)* ojeada *f*; *(furtive look)* mirada furtiva
2 *vi* **to p. at sth** echar una ojeada a algo; **to p. out from behind sth** dejarse ver detrás de algo

peephole [ˈpiːphəʊl] *n* mirilla *f*

peer¹ [pɪə(r)] *n (noble)* par *m*; *(equal)* igual *mf*; **p. group** grupo parejo

peer² [pɪə(r)] *vi* mirar detenidamente; *(shortsightedly)* mirar con ojos de miope

peerage [ˈpɪərɪdʒ] *n* título *m* de nobleza

peeved [piːvd] *adj Fam* fastidiado(a), de mal humor

peevish [ˈpiːvɪʃ] *adj* malhumorado(a)

peg [peɡ] **1** *n* clavija *f*; *(for coat, hat)* percha *f*
2 *vt (clothes)* tender; *(prices)* fijar

pejorative [pɪˈdʒɒrətɪv] *adj* peyorativo(a)

Pekinese [piːkəˈniːz] *adj & n* pequinés(esa) *(m,f)*

Peking [piːˈkɪŋ] *n* Pekín

pelican [ˈpelɪkən] *n* pelícano *m*; *Br* **p. crossing** paso *m* de peatones

pellet [ˈpelɪt] *n* bolita *f*; *(for gun)* perdigón *m*

pelt¹ [pelt] *n (skin)* pellejo *m*

pelt² [pelt] **1** *vt* **to p. sb with sth** tirar algo a algn
2 *vi Fam* **(a) it's pelting (down)** *(raining)* llueve a cántaros **(b) to p. along** *(rush)* correr a toda prisa

pelvis [ˈpelvɪs] *n* pelvis *f*

pen¹ [pen] **1** *n* pluma *f*, *RP* birome *f*
2 *vt* escribir

pen² [pen] **1** *n (enclosure)* corral *m*; *(for sheep)* redil *m*; *(for children)* corralito *m*
2 *vt* **to p. in** acorralar

penal [ˈpiːnəl] *adj* penal

penalize [ˈpiːnəlaɪz] *vt* castigar; *Sport* penalizar

penalty [ˈpenəltɪ] *n (punishment)* pena *f*; *Sport* castigo *m*; *Ftb* penalti *m*; **to pay the p. for sth** cargar con las consecuencias de algo; **p. area** área *f* de castigo

penance [ˈpenəns] *n* penitencia *f*

pence [pens] *pl of* **penny**

pencil [ˈpensəl] *n* lápiz *m*; **p. case** estuche *m* de lápices; **p. sharpener** sacapuntas *m inv*

pendant [ˈpendənt] *n* colgante *m*

pending [ˈpendɪŋ] **1** *adj* pendiente
2 *prep* a la espera de; **p. a decision** *(until)*

hasta que se tome una decisión

pendulum ['pendjʊləm] *n* péndulo *m*

penetrate ['penɪtreɪt] **1** *vt* penetrar; *Fig* adentrarse en

2 *vi* atravesar; *(get inside)* penetrar

penetrating ['penɪtreɪtɪŋ] *adj (look)* penetrante; *(mind)* perspicaz; *(sound)* agudo(a)

penfriend ['penfrend] *n* amigo(a) *m,f* por carta

penguin ['peŋgwɪn] *n* pingüino *m*

penicillin [penɪ'sɪlɪn] *n* penicilina *f*

peninsula [pɪ'nɪnsjʊlə] *n* península *f*

penis ['piːnɪs] *n* pene *m*

penitent ['penɪtənt] *adj Rel* penitente; *(repentant)* arrepentido(a)

penitentiary [penɪ'tenʃərɪ] *n US* cárcel *f*, penal *m*

penknife ['pennaɪf] *n* navaja *f*, cortaplumas *m inv*

penniless ['penɪlɪs] *adj* sin dinero

penny ['penɪ] *n (pl* **pennies, pence)** *Br* penique *m*; *US* centavo *m*

penpal ['penpæl] *n US* = penfriend

pension ['penʃən] *n* pensión *f*; **retirement p.** jubilación *f*

pensioner ['penʃənə(r)] *n* jubilado(a) *m,f*

pensive ['pensɪv] *adj* pensativo(a)

pentagon ['pentəgɒn] *n US Pol* **the P.** el Pentágono

Pentecost ['pentɪkɒst] *n* Pentecostés *m*

penthouse ['penthaʊs] *n* ático *m*

pent-up ['pentʌp] *adj* reprimido(a)

penultimate [pɪ'nʌltɪmɪt] *adj* penúltimo(a)

people ['piːpəl] *npl* **(a)** gente *f*; *(individuals)* personas *fpl*; **many p.** mucha gente; **old p.'s home** asilo *m* de ancianos; **p. say that ...** se dice que ...; **some p.** algunas personas **(b)** *(citizens)* ciudadanos *mpl*; *(inhabitants)* habitantes *mpl*; **the p.** el pueblo **(c)** *(nation)* pueblo *m*, nación *f*

pep [pep] *n Fam* ánimo *m*, energía *f*; **p. talk** discurso *m* enardecedor

▸ **pep up** *vt sep Fam* animar

pepper ['pepə(r)] **1** *n (spice)* pimienta *f*; *(fruit)* pimiento *m*; **black p.** pimienta negra; **p. pot** pimentero *m*; **red/green p.** pimiento rojo/verde; **p. mill** molinillo *m* de pimienta

2 *vt Fig* **peppered with** salpicado(a) de

peppermint ['pepəmɪnt] *n* menta *f*; *(sweet)* pastilla *f* de menta

per [pɜː(r)] *prep* por; **five times p. week** cinco veces a la semana; **p. cent** por

ciento; **p. day/annum** al *or* por día/año; **p. capita** per cápita

perceive [pə'siːv] *vt (see)* percibir

percentage [pə'sentɪdʒ] *n* porcentaje *m*

perceptible [pə'septəbəl] *adj (visible)* perceptible; *(sound)* audible; *(improvement)* sensible

perception [pə'sepʃən] *n* percepción *f*

perceptive [pə'septɪv] *adj* perspicaz

perch¹ [pɜːtʃ] *n (fish)* perca *f*

perch² [pɜːtʃ] **1** *n (for bird)* percha *f*

2 *vi (bird)* posarse **(on** en)

percolate ['pɜːkəleɪt] **1** *vt* filtrar; **percolated coffee** café *m* de cafetera

2 *vi* filtrarse

percolator ['pɜːkəleɪtə(r)] *n* cafetera *f*

percussion [pə'kʌʃən] *n* percusión *f*

perennial [pə'renɪəl] *adj Bot* perenne

perfect 1 *adj* ['pɜːfɪkt] perfecto(a); **he's a p. stranger to us** nos es totalmente desconocido; **p. tense** tiempo perfecto

2 *vt* [pə'fekt] perfeccionar

perfection [pə'fekʃən] *n* perfección *f*

perfectly ['pɜːfɪktlɪ] *adv* perfectamente; *(absolutely)* completamente

perforate ['pɜːfəreɪt] *vt* perforar

perforation [pɜːfə'reɪʃən] *n* perforación *f*, *(on stamps etc)* perforado *m*

perform [pə'fɔːm] **1** *vt (task)* ejecutar, realizar; *(piece of music)* interpretar; *Th* representar

2 *vi (machine)* funcionar; *Mus* interpretar; *Th* actuar

performance [pə'fɔːməns] *n (of task)* ejecución *f*, realización *f*; *Mus* interpretación *f*; *Th* representación *f*; *Sport* actuación *f*; *(of machine etc)* rendimiento *m*

performer [pə'fɔːmə(r)] *n Mus* intérprete *mf*; *Th* actor *m*, actriz *f*

perfume ['pɜːfjuːm] *n* perfume *m*

perfunctory [pə'fʌŋktərɪ] *adj* superficial

perhaps [pə'hæps, præps] *adv* tal vez, quizá(s)

peril ['perɪl] *n (risk)* riesgo *m*; *(danger)* peligro *m*

perilous ['perɪləs] *adj (risky)* arriesgado(a); *(dangerous)* peligroso(a)

perilously ['perɪləslɪ] *adv* peligrosamente

perimeter [pə'rɪmɪtə(r)] *n* perímetro *m*

period ['pɪərɪəd] **1** *n* **(a)** período *m*; *(stage)* etapa *f* **(b)** *Educ* clase *f* **(c)** *US (full stop)* punto *m* **(d)** *(menstruation)* regla *f*

2 *adj (dress, furniture)* de época

periodic [pɪərɪ'ɒdɪk] *adj* periódico(a)

periodical [pɪərɪ'ɒdɪkəl] **1** *adj* periódico(a)

2 *n* revista *f*

periodically [pɪərɪ'ɒdɪklɪ] *adv* de vez en cuando

peripheral [pə'rɪfərəl] **1** *adj* periférico(a) **2** *n Comput* unidad periférica

perish ['perɪʃ] *vi* perecer; *(material)* echarse a perder

perishable ['perɪʃəbəl] *adj* perecedero(a)

perjury ['pɜːdʒərɪ] *n* perjurio *m*

perk [pɜːk] *n Fam* extra *m*
▸**perk up** *vi (person)* animarse; *(after illness)* reponerse

perky ['pɜːkɪ] *adj* (**perkier, perkiest**) animado(a), alegre

perm [pɜːm] **1** *n* permanente *f*
2 *vt* **to have one's hair permed** hacerse la permanente

permanent ['pɜːmənənt] *adj* permanente; *(address, job)* fijo(a)

permeate ['pɜːmɪeɪt] *vt & vi* penetrar; *Fig* extenderse por

permissible [pə'mɪsəbəl] *adj* admisible

permission [pə'mɪʃən] *n* permiso *m*

permissive [pə'mɪsɪv] *adj* permisivo(a)

permit 1 *n* ['pɜːmɪt] permiso *m*; *Com* licencia *f*
2 *vt* [pə'mɪt] **to p. sb to do sth** permitir a algn hacer algo

pernicious [pə'nɪʃəs] *adj* pernicioso(a)

perpendicular [pɜːpən'dɪkjʊlə(r)] **1** *adj* perpendicular; *(cliff)* vertical
2 *n* perpendicular *f*

perpetrate ['pɜːpɪtreɪt] *vt* cometer

perpetual [pə'petʃʊəl] *adj (noise)* continuo(a); *(arguing)* interminable; *(snow)* perpetuo(a)

perplex [pə'pleks] *vt* dejar perplejo(a)

perplexing [pə'pleksɪŋ] *adj* desconcertante

persecute ['pɜːsɪkjuːt] *vt* perseguir; *(harass)* acosar

persecution [pɜːsɪ'kjuːʃən] *n* persecución *f*; *(harassment)* acoso *m*

perseverance [pɜːsɪ'vɪərəns] *n* perseverancia *f*

persevere [pɜːsɪ'vɪə(r)] *vi* perseverar

Persian ['pɜːʒən] *adj* persa; **P. Gulf** golfo Pérsico

persist [pə'sɪst] *vi* empeñarse (**in** en)

persistence [pə'sɪstəns] *n* empeño *m*

persistent [pə'sɪstənt] *adj (person)* perseverante; *(smell etc)* persistente; *(continual)* constante

person ['pɜːsən] *n (pl* **people)** persona *f*; *(individual)* individuo *m*; **in p.** en persona

personable ['pɜːsənəbəl] *adj (handsome)* bien parecido(a); *(pleasant)* amable

personal ['pɜːsənəl] **(a)** *adj (private)* personal; *(friend)* íntimo(a); **p. computer** ordenador *m* personal, *Am* computadora *f* personal; **p. column** anuncios *mpl* personales; **p. pronoun** pronombre *m* personal **(b)** *(in person)* en persona; **he will make a p. appearance** estará aquí en persona **(c)** *Pej (comment etc)* indiscreto(a)

personality [pɜːsə'nælɪtɪ] *n* personalidad *f*

personally ['pɜːsənəlɪ] *adv (for my part)* personalmente; *(in person)* en persona

personify [pɜː'sɒnɪfaɪ] *vt* personificar, encarnar

personnel [pɜːsə'nel] *n* personal *m*

perspective [pə'spektɪv] *n* perspectiva *f*

Perspex® ['pɜːspeks] *n* plexiglás® *m*

perspiration [pɜːspə'reɪʃən] *n* transpiración *f*

perspire [pə'spaɪə(r)] *vi* transpirar

persuade [pə'sweɪd] *vt* persuadir; **to p. sb to do sth** persuadir a algn para que haga algo

persuasion [pə'sweɪʒən] *n* persuasión *f*; *(opinion, belief)* credo *m*

persuasive [pə'sweɪsɪv] *adj* persuasivo(a)

pert [pɜːt] *adj* pizpireta, coqueto(a)

pertain [pə'teɪn] *vi* estar relacionado(a) (**to** con)

pertinent ['pɜːtɪnənt] *adj (relevant)* pertinente; **p. to** relacionado(a) con, a propósito de

perturbing [pə'tɜːbɪŋ] *adj* inquietante

Peru [pə'ruː] *n* Perú *m*

peruse [pə'ruːz] *vt Fml* leer

Peruvian [pə'ruːvɪən] *adj & n* peruano(a) *(m,f)*

pervade [pɜː'veɪd] *vt (of smell)* penetrar; *(of light)* difundirse por; *Fig (of influence)* extenderse por

pervasive [pɜː'veɪsɪv] *adj (smell)* penetrante; *(influence)* extendido(a)

perverse [pə'vɜːs] *adj (wicked)* perverso(a); *(contrary)* contrario(a) a todo

perversion [pə'vɜːʃən] *n Med & Psy* perversión *f*; *(of justice, truth)* desvirtuación *f*

pervert 1 *n* ['pɜːvɜːt] *Med* pervertido(a) *m,f* (sexual)
2 *vt* [pə'vɜːt] pervertir; *(justice, truth)* desvirtuar

pessimist ['pesɪmɪst] *n* pesimista *mf*

pessimistic [pesɪ'mɪstɪk] *adj* pesimista

pest [pest] *n* **(a)** *Zool* animal nocivo; *Bot* planta nociva **(b)** *Fam (person)* pelma *mf*; *(thing)* lata *f*

pester ['pestə(r)] *vt* molestar, fastidiar

pet [pet] **1** *n* (**a**) animal doméstico (**b**) *(favourite)* preferido(a) *m,f*; *Fam* cariño *m*

  2 *adj (favourite)* preferido(a)

  3 *vt* acariciar

  4 *vi (sexually)* besuquearse

petal ['petəl] *n* pétalo *m*

peter ['piːtə(r)] *vi* **to p. out** agotarse

petite [pə'tiːt] *adj* menuda, chiquita

petition [pɪ'tɪʃən] *n* petición *f*

petrify ['petrɪfaɪ] *vt Literary* petrificar; *Fig* **they were petrified** se quedaron de piedra

petrol ['petrəl] *n Br* gasolina *f*, *RP* nafta *f*; **p. can** bidón *m* de gasolina; **p. pump** surtidor *m* de gasolina; **p. station** gasolinera *f*, estación *f* de servicio, *Andes, Ven* bomba *f*, *Méx* gasolinería *f*, *Perú* grifo *m*; **p. tank** depósito *m* de gasolina

> 🖉 Note that the Spanish word **petróleo** is a false friend and is never a translation for the English word **petrol**. In Spanish, **petróleo** means "oil, petroleum".

petroleum [pə'trəʊliəm] *n* petróleo *m*

petticoat ['petɪkəʊt] *n* enaguas *fpl*

petty ['petɪ] *adj* (**pettier, pettiest**) *(trivial)* insignificante; *(small-minded)* mezquino(a); **p. cash** dinero *m* para gastos pequeños; *Naut* **p. officer** sargento *m* de marina

petulant ['petjʊlənt] *adj* malhumorado(a)

> 🖉 Note that the Spanish word **petulante** is a false friend and is never a translation for the English word **petulant**. In Spanish, **petulante** means "opinionated, arrogant".

pew [pjuː] *n* banco *m* de iglesia; *Fam* **take a p.!** ¡siéntate!

pewter ['pjuːtə(r)] *n* peltre *m*

phantom ['fæntəm] *adj & n* fantasma *(m)*

pharmaceutical [fɑːmə'sjuːtɪkəl] *adj* farmacéutico(a)

pharmacist ['fɑːməsɪst] *n* farmacéutico(a) *m,f*

pharmacy ['fɑːməsɪ] *n* farmacia *f*

phase [feɪz] **1** *n* fase *f*

  2 *vt* **to p. sth in/out** introducir/retirar algo progresivamente

PhD [piːeɪtʃ'diː] *n* (*abbr* **Doctor of Philosophy**) *(person)* Doctor(a) *m,f* en Filosofía

pheasant ['fezənt] *n* faisán *m* (vulgar)

phenomena [fɪ'nɒmɪnə] *pl of* **phenomenon**

phenomenal [fɪ'nɒmɪnəl] *adj* fenomenal

phenomenon [fɪ'nɒmɪnən] *n* (*pl* **phenomena**) fenómeno *m*

phial [faɪəl] *n* frasco *m*

philanthropist [fɪ'lænθrəpɪst] *n* filántropo(a) *m,f*

philately [fɪ'lætəlɪ] *n* filatelia *f*

Philippines ['fɪlɪpiːnz] *npl* **the P.** las (Islas) Filipinas

philosopher [fɪ'lɒsəfə(r)] *n* filósofo(a) *m,f*

philosophical [fɪlə'sɒfɪkəl] *adj* filosófico(a)

philosophy [fɪ'lɒsəfɪ] *n* filosofía *f*

phlegm [flem] *n* flema *f*

phlegmatic [fleg'mætɪk] *adj* flemático(a)

phobia ['fəʊbɪə] *n* fobia *f*

phone [fəʊn] *n* = **telephone**

phone-in ['fəʊnɪn] *n Fam* = programa de radio o televisión con línea telefónica abierta

phonetic [fə'netɪk] **1** *adj* fonético(a)

  2 *n* **phonetics** fonética *f*

phoney ['fəʊnɪ] **1** *adj* (**phonier, phoniest**) *(thing)* falso(a); *(person)* farsante

  2 *n* *(person)* farsante *mf*

phonograph ['fəʊnəgrɑːf] *n US* tocadiscos *m inv*

phosphate ['fɒsfeɪt] *n* fosfato *m*

photo ['fəʊtəʊ] *n* foto *f*

photocopier ['fəʊtəʊkɒpɪə(r)] *n* fotocopiadora *f*

photocopy ['fəʊtəʊkɒpɪ] **1** *n* fotocopia *f*

  2 *vt* fotocopiar

photogenic [fəʊtəʊ'dʒenɪk] *adj* fotogénico(a)

photograph ['fəʊtəgræf, 'fəʊtəgrɑːf] **1** *n* fotografía *f*; **black and white/colour p.** fotografía en blanco y negro/en color

  2 *vt* fotografiar

photographer [fə'tɒgrəfə(r)] *n* fotógrafo(a) *m,f*

photography [fə'tɒgrəfɪ] *n* fotografía *f*

phrase [freɪz] **1** *n* frase *f*; **p. book** libro *m* de frases

  2 *vt* expresar

physical ['fɪzɪkəl] *adj* físico(a); **p. education** educación física

physically ['fɪzɪkəlɪ] *adv* físicamente; **p. handicapped** minusválido(a); **to be p. fit** estar en forma

physician [fɪ'zɪʃən] *n* médico(a) *m,f*

physicist ['fɪzɪsɪst] *n* físico(a) *m,f*

physics ['fɪzɪks] *n sing* física *f*

physiological [fɪzɪə'lɒdʒɪkəl] *adj* fisiológico(a)

physiotherapist [fɪzɪəʊ'θerəpɪst] *n* fisioterapeuta *mf*

physique [fɪˈziːk] n físico m
pianist [ˈpɪənɪst] n pianista mf
piano [pɪˈænəʊ] n piano m
piccolo [ˈpɪkələʊ] n flautín m
pick [pɪk] **1** n (a) (tool) pico m, piqueta f (b) **take your p.** (choice) elige el que quieras
  2 vt (a) (choose) escoger; (team) seleccionar (b) (flowers, fruit) coger, recoger (c) (scratch) hurgar; **to p. one's nose** hurgarse la nariz; **to p. one's teeth** mondarse los dientes (d) **to p. sb's pocket** robar algo del bolsillo de algn (e) (lock) forzar
  3 vi **to p. at one's food** comer sin ganas
  ▸ **pick off** vt sep (a) (remove) quitar (b) (shoot) matar uno a uno
  ▸ **pick on** vt insep (persecute) meterse con
  ▸ **pick out** vt sep (choose) elegir; (distinguish) distinguir; (identify) identificar
  ▸ **pick up 1** vt sep (a) (object on floor) recoger; (telephone) descolgar; **to p. oneself up** levantarse; Fig reponerse (b) (collect) recoger; (shopping, person) buscar; **to p. up speed** ganar velocidad (c) (acquire) conseguir; (learn) aprender
  2 vi (improve) mejorarse, ir mejorando; (prices) subir
pickaxe, US **pickax** [ˈpɪkæks] n piqueta f
picket [ˈpɪkɪt] **1** n piquete m; **p. line** piquete
  2 vt piquetear
  3 vi hacer piquete
pickle [ˈpɪkəl] **1** n (a) Br Culin salsa f picante (b) Fam (mess) lío m, apuro m
  2 vt Culin conservar en adobo or escabeche; **pickled onions** cebollas fpl en vinagre
pick-me-up [ˈpɪkmɪʌp] n Fam reconstituyente m, tónico m
pickpocket [ˈpɪkpɒkɪt] n carterista mf
pick-up [ˈpɪkʌp] n **p. (arm)** (on record player) brazo m; **p. (truck)** furgoneta f
picnic [ˈpɪknɪk] **1** n comida f de campo, picnic m
  2 vi hacer una comida de campo
pictorial [pɪkˈtɔːrɪəl] adj ilustrado(a)
picture [ˈpɪktʃə(r)] **1** n (a) (painting) cuadro m; (drawing) dibujo m; (portrait) retrato m; (photo) foto f; (illustration) ilustración f; **p. book** libro ilustrado; **p. postcard** tarjeta f postal TV imagen f; Cin película f; **to go to the pictures** ir al cine
  2 vt (imagine) imaginarse
picturesque [pɪktʃəˈresk] adj pintoresco(a)
pie [paɪ] n (of fruit) tarta f, pastel m; (of

meat etc) pastel, empanada f; (pasty) empanadilla f
piece [piːs] n (a) (of food) pedazo m, trozo m; (of paper) trozo; (part) pieza f; **a p. of advice** un consejo; **a p. of furniture** un mueble; **a p. of land** una parcela; **a p. of news** una noticia; **to break sth into pieces** hacer algo pedazos; Fig **to go to pieces** perder el control (de sí mismo) (b) Lit & Mus obra f, pieza f (c) (coin) moneda f (d) (in chess) pieza f; (in draughts) ficha f
  ▸ **piece together** vt sep (facts) reconstruir; (jigsaw) hacer
piecemeal [ˈpiːsmiːl] adv (by degrees) poco a poco, a etapas; (unsystematically) desordenadamente
piecework [ˈpiːswɜːk] n trabajo m a destajo; **to be on p.** trabajar a destajo
pier [pɪə(r)] n embarcadero m, muelle m; (promenade) = paseo de madera que entra en el mar
pierce [pɪəs] vt perforar; (penetrate) penetrar en
piercing [ˈpɪəsɪŋ] adj (sound etc) penetrante
piety [ˈpaɪɪtɪ] n piedad f
pig [pɪg] n (a) cerdo m (b) Fam (person) cochino m; (glutton) tragón(ona) m,f (c) Fam Pej (policeman) madero m
pigeon [ˈpɪdʒɪn] n paloma f; Culin & Sport pichón m
pigeonhole [ˈpɪdʒɪnhəʊl] n casilla f
piggy [ˈpɪgɪ] n **p. bank** = hucha en forma de cerdito
pigheaded [pɪgˈhedɪd] adj terco(a), cabezota
piglet [ˈpɪglɪt] n cerdito m, lechón m
pigment [ˈpɪgmənt] n pigmento m
pigskin [ˈpɪgskɪn] n piel f de cerdo
pigsty [ˈpɪgstaɪ] n pocilga f
pigtail [ˈpɪgteɪl] n trenza f; (bullfighter's) coleta f
pike [paɪk] n (fish) lucio m
pilchard [ˈpɪltʃəd] n sardina f
pile¹ [paɪl] **1** n montón m
  2 vt amontonar
  3 vi **to p. into** apiñarse en; **to p. on/off a bus** subir a/bajar de un autobús en tropel
  ▸ **pile up 1** vt sep (things) amontonar; (riches, debts) acumular
  2 vi amontonarse
pile² [paɪl] n (on carpet) pelo m; **thick p.** pelo largo
piles [paɪlz] npl Med almorranas fpl, hemorroides fpl
pile-up [ˈpaɪlʌp] n Aut choque m en cadena
pilfer [ˈpɪlfə(r)] vt & vi hurtar

pilgrim ['pɪlgrɪm] *n* peregrino(a) *m,f*
pilgrimage ['pɪlgrɪmɪdʒ] *n* peregrinación *f*
pill [pɪl] *n* píldora *f*, pastilla *f*; **to be on the p.** estar tomando la píldora (anticonceptiva)
pillage ['pɪlɪdʒ] *vt & vi* pillar, saquear
pillar ['pɪlə(r)] *n* pilar *m*, columna *f*; *Br* **p. box** buzón *m*
pillion ['pɪljən] *n* asiento trasero *(de una moto)*
pillow ['pɪləʊ] *n* almohada *f*
pillowcase ['pɪləʊkeɪs] *n* funda *f* de almohada
pilot ['paɪlət] **1** *n* piloto *m*
2 *adj (trial)* piloto *inv*; **p. light** piloto *m*; **p. scheme** proyecto piloto
3 *vt* pilotar
pimp [pɪmp] *n* chulo *m*
pimple ['pɪmpəl] *n* grano *m*, espinilla *f*
PIN [pɪn] *n (abbr* **personal identification number) P. (number)** PIN *m*
pin [pɪn] **1** *n* alfiler *m*; *Tech* clavija *f*; *(wooden)* espiga *f*; *(in plug)* polo *m*; *(in bowling)* bolo *m*; *US (brooch)* broche *m*; **pins and needles** hormigueo *m*
2 *vt (on board)* clavar con chinchetas; *(garment etc)* sujetar con alfileres; **to p. sb against a wall** tener a algn contra una pared; *Fig* **to p. one's hopes on sth** poner sus esperanzas en algo; *Fam* **to p. a crime on sb** endosar un delito a algn
▸ **pin down** *vt sep Fig* **to p. sb down** hacer que algn se comprometa
pinafore ['pɪnəfɔː(r)] *n (apron)* delantal *m*; **p. dress** pichi *m*
pinball ['pɪnbɔːl] *n* flipper *m*, máquina *f* de petacos
pincers ['pɪnsəz] *npl (on crab)* pinzas *fpl*; *(tool)* tenazas *fpl*
pinch [pɪntʃ] **1** *n (nip)* pellizco *m*; *Fig Br* **at** *or US* **in a p.** en caso de apuro; **a p. of salt** una pizca de sal
2 *vt* pellizcar; *Fam (steal)* birlar
3 *vi (shoes)* apretar

> 🖉 Note that the Spanish verb **pinchar** is a false friend and is never a translation for the English verb **to pinch**. In Spanish, **pinchar** means "to prick, to puncture".

pincushion ['pɪnkʊʃən] *n* acerico *m*
pine¹ [paɪn] *n (tree)* pino *m*; **p. cone** piña *f*
pine² [paɪn] *vi* **to p. (away)** consumirse, morirse de pena; **to p. for sth/sb** añorar algo/a algn
pineapple ['paɪnæpəl] *n* piña *f*
ping [pɪŋ] *n* sonido metálico; *(of bullet)* silbido *m*

Ping-Pong® ['pɪŋpɒŋ] *n* ping-pong® *m*
pink [pɪŋk] **1** *n (colour)* rosa *m*; *Bot* clavel *m*
2 *adj (colour)* rosa *inv*; *Pol Fam* rojillo(a)
pinnacle ['pɪnəkəl] *n (of building)* pináculo *m*; *(of mountain)* cima *f*, pico *m*; *Fig (of success)* cumbre *f*
pinpoint ['pɪnpɔɪnt] *vt* señalar
pinstripe ['pɪnstraɪp] *adj* a rayas
pint [paɪnt] *n* pinta *f*; *Br Fam* **a p. (of beer)** una pinta (de cerveza)
pioneer [paɪə'nɪə(r)] **1** *n (settler)* pionero(a) *m,f*; *(forerunner)* precursor(a) *m,f*
2 *vt* ser pionero(a) en
pious ['paɪəs] *adj* piadoso(a), devoto(a); *Pej* beato(a)
pip¹ [pɪp] *n (seed)* pepita *f*
pip² [pɪp] *n (sound)* señal *f* (corta); *(on dice)* punto *m*
pipe [paɪp] **1** *n* **(a)** conducto *m*, tubería *f*; *(of organ)* caramillo *m*; *Fam* **the pipes** *(bagpipes)* la gaita **(b)** *(for smoking)* pipa *f*; **p. cleaner** limpiapipas *m inv*; *Fig* **p. dream** sueño *m* imposible
2 *vt (water)* llevar por tubería; *(oil)* transportar por oleoducto; **piped music** hilo *m* musical
▸ **pipe down** *vi Fam* callarse
▸ **pipe up** *vi Fam* hacerse oír
pipeline ['paɪplaɪn] *n* tubería *f*, cañería *f*; *(for gas)* gasoducto *m*; *(for oil)* oleoducto *m*
piper ['paɪpə(r)] *n* gaitero(a) *m,f*
piping ['paɪpɪŋ] **1** *n (for water, gas etc)* tubería *f*, cañería *f*
2 *adj* **p. hot** bien caliente
piquant ['piːkənt] *adj* picante; *(fig)* intrigante
pique [piːk] **1** *n* enojo *m*
2 *vt* herir
pirate ['paɪrɪt] *n* pirata *m*; **p. edition** edición *f* pirata; **p. radio** emisora *f* pirata; **p. ship** barco *m* pirata
pirouette [pɪru'et] **1** *n* pirueta *f*
2 *vi* hacer piruetas
Pisces ['paɪsiːz] *n* Piscis *m*
piss [pɪs] *very Fam* **1** *vi* mear
2 *n* meada *f*
pissed [pɪst] *adj very Fam* **(a)** *Br (drunk)* borracho(a) **(b)** *US (angry)* cabreado(a)
pistachio [pɪs'tɑːʃɪəʊ] *n (nut)* pistacho *m*
pistol ['pɪstəl] *n* pistola *f*
piston ['pɪstən] *n* pistón *m*
pit¹ [pɪt] **1** *n* hoyo *m*; *(large)* hoya *f*; *(coal mine)* mina *f* de carbón; *Th* platea *f*; *(in motor racing)* foso *m*, box *m*
2 *vt* **to p. one's wits against sb** medirse con algn

pit² [pɪt] *n (of cherry)* hueso *m*, pipo *m*; *US (of peach, plum)* hueso

pitch¹ [pɪtʃ] **1** *vt* (**a**) *Mus (sound)* entonar (**b**) *(throw)* lanzar, arrojar (**c**) *(tent)* armar

2 *vi (ship)* cabecear; **to p. forward** caerse hacia adelante

3 *n* (**a**) *Mus (of sound)* tono *m* (**b**) *Sport* campo *m*, cancha *f* (**c**) *(in market etc)* puesto *m* (**d**) *(throw)* lanzamiento *m*

pitch² [pɪtʃ] *n (tar)* brea *f*, pez *f*

pitch-black [pɪtʃˈblæk], **pitch-dark** [pɪtʃˈdɑːk] *adj* negro(a) como la boca del lobo

pitched [pɪtʃt] *adj* **p. battle** batalla *f* campal

pitcher [ˈpɪtʃə(r)] *n (container)* cántaro *m*, jarro *m*

pitchfork [ˈpɪtʃfɔːk] *n* horca *f*

piteous [ˈpɪtɪəs] *adj* lastimoso(a)

pitfall [ˈpɪtfɔːl] *n* dificultad *f*, obstáculo *m*

pith [pɪθ] *n (of orange)* piel blanca; *Fig* meollo *m*

pithy [ˈpɪθɪ] *adj* (**pithier, pithiest**) *Fig* contundente

pitiful [ˈpɪtɪfʊl] *adj (producing pity)* lastimoso(a), *(terrible)* lamentable

pitiless [ˈpɪtɪlɪs] *adj* despiadado(a), implacable

pittance [ˈpɪtəns] *n* miseria *f*

pity [ˈpɪtɪ] **1** *n* (**a**) *(compassion)* compasión *f*, piedad *f*; **to take p. on sb** compadecerse de algn (**b**) *(shame)* lástima *f*, pena *f*; **what a p.!** ¡qué pena!, ¡qué lástima!

2 *vt* compadecerse de; **I p. them** me dan pena

pivot [ˈpɪvət] **1** *n* pivote *m*

2 *vi* girar sobre su eje

pizza [ˈpiːtsə] *n* pizza *f*; **p. parlour** pizzería *f*

placard [ˈplækɑːd] *n* pancarta *f*

placate [pləˈkeɪt] *vt* aplacar, apaciguar

place [pleɪs] **1** *n* (**a**) *(site)* sitio *m*, lugar *m*; **to be in/out of p.** estar en/fuera de su sitio; **to take p.** tener lugar

(**b**) *(seat)* sitio *m*; *(on bus)* asiento *m*; *(at university)* plaza *f*; **to change places with sb** intercambiar el sitio con algn; **to feel out of p.** encontrarse fuera de lugar; **to take sb's p.** sustituir a algn

(**c**) *(position on scale)* posición *f*; *(social position)* rango *m*; **in the first p.** en primer lugar; **to take first p.** ganar el primer lugar

(**d**) *(house)* casa *f*; *(building)* lugar *m*; **we're going to his p.** vamos a su casa

2 *vt* (**a**) poner, colocar; **to p. a bet** hacer

una apuesta; **to p. an order with sb** hacer un pedido a algn

(**b**) *(face, person)* recordar; *(in job)* colocar en un empleo

placid [ˈplæsɪd] *adj* apacible

plagiarize [ˈpleɪdʒəraɪz] *vt* plagiar

plague [pleɪg] **1** *n (of insects)* plaga *f*; *Med* peste *f*

2 *vt* **to p. sb with requests** acosar a algn a peticiones

plaice [pleɪs] *n (pl plaice) (fish)* platija *f*

plaid [plæd, pleɪd] *n (cloth)* tejido *m* escocés

plain [pleɪn] **1** *adj* (**a**) *(clear)* claro(a), evidente; *Fig* **he likes p. speaking** le gusta hablar con franqueza (**b**) *(simple)* sencillo(a); *(chocolate)* amargo(a); *(flour)* sin levadura; **in p. clothes** vestido(a) de paisano; **the p. truth** la verdad lisa y llana (**c**) *(unattractive)* poco atractivo(a)

2 *n Geog* llanura *f*, llano *m*

plainly [ˈpleɪnlɪ] *adv* claramente; *(simply)* sencillamente; **to speak p.** hablar con franqueza

plaintiff [ˈpleɪntɪf] *n* demandante *mf*

plaintive [ˈpleɪntɪv] *adj* lastimero(a)

plait [plæt] **1** *n* trenza *f*

2 *vt* trenzar

plan [plæn] **1** *n (scheme)* plan *m*, proyecto *m*; *(drawing)* plano *m*

2 *vt* (**a**) *(for future)* planear, proyectar; *(economy)* planificar (**b**) *(intend)* pensar, tener la intención de; **it wasn't planned** no estaba previsto

3 *vi* hacer planes; **to p. on doing sth** tener la intención de hacer algo

plane¹ [pleɪn] **1** *n* (**a**) *Math* plano *m*; *Fig* nivel *m* (**b**) *Fam Av* avión *m*

2 *adj Geom* plano(a)

3 *vi (glide)* planear

plane² [pleɪn] **1** *n (tool)* cepillo *m*

2 *vt* cepillar

plane³ [pleɪn] *n Bot* **p. (tree)** plátano *m*

planet [ˈplænɪt] *n* planeta *m*

plank [plæŋk] *n* tabla *f*, tablón *m*

planner [ˈplænə(r)] *n* planificador(a) *m,f*

planning [ˈplænɪŋ] *n* planificación *f*; **family p.** planificación familiar; **p. permission** permiso *m* de obras

plant¹ [plɑːnt] **1** *n* planta *f*

2 *vt (flowers)* plantar; *(seeds)* sembrar; *(bomb)* colocar

plant² [plɑːnt] *n (factory)* planta *f*, fábrica *f*; *(machinery)* maquinaria *f*

plantation [plænˈteɪʃən] *n* plantación *f*

plaque [plæk] *n* placa *f*, *(on teeth)* sarro *m*

plaster [ˈplɑːstə(r)] **1** *n Constr* yeso *m*;

Med escayola *f; Br* **sticking p.** esparadrapo *m*, tirita® *f, Am* curita *f;* **p. of Paris** yeso mate

2 *vt Constr* enyesar; *Fig (cover)* cubrir (**with** de)

plastered ['plɑːstəd] *adj Fam* borracho(a), trompa

plasterer ['plɑːstərə(r)] *n* yesero(a) *m,f*

plastic ['plæstɪk] **1** *n* plástico *m*

2 *adj (cup, bag)* de plástico; **p. surgery** cirugía plástica

Plasticine® ['plæstɪsiːn] *n* plastilina® *f*

plate [pleɪt] **1** *n* (**a**) plato *m* (**b**) *(sheet)* placa *f;* **gold p.** chapa *f* de oro; **p. glass** vidrio cilindrado (**c**) *(in book)* grabado *m*, lámina *f*

2 *vt* chapar

plateau ['plætəʊ] *n* meseta *f*

platform ['plætfɔːm] *n* (**a**) plataforma *f;* *(stage)* estrado *m; (at meeting)* tribuna *f* (**b**) *Rail* andén *m;* **p. ticket** billete *m* de andén (**c**) *Pol (programme)* programa *m*

platinum ['plætɪnəm] *n* platino *m*

platitude ['plætɪtjuːd] *n* lugar *m* común, tópico *m*

platoon [plə'tuːn] *n Mil* pelotón *m*

platter ['plætə(r)] *n* fuente *f*

plausible ['plɔːzəbəl] *adj* plausible

play [pleɪ] **1** *vt* (**a**) *(game)* jugar a (**b**) *Sport (position)* jugar de; *(team)* jugar contra; **to p. a shot** *(in golf, tennis)* golpear

(**c**) *(instrument, tune)* tocar; **to p. a record** poner un disco

(**d**) *Th (part)* hacer (el papel) de; *(play)* representar; *Fig* **to p. a part in sth** participar en algo; *Fig* **to p. the fool** hacer el tonto

2 *vi* (**a**) *(children)* jugar (**with** con); *(animals)* juguetear

(**b**) *Sport* jugar; **to p. fair** jugar limpio; *Fig* **to p. for time** tratar de ganar tiempo

(**c**) *(joke)* bromear

(**d**) *Mus* tocar; *(instrument)* sonar

3 *n* (**a**) *Th* obra *f* de teatro

(**b**) *Sport* juego *m;* **fair/foul p.** juego limpio/sucio

(**c**) *Tech & Fig (movement)* juego *m; Fig* **to bring sth into p.** poner algo en juego; **a p. on words** un juego de palabras

▸ **play around** *vi (waste time)* gandulear; *(be unfaithful)* tener líos

▸ **play down** *vt sep* minimizar, quitar importancia a

▸ **play on** *vt insep (take advantage of)* aprovecharse de; *(nerves etc)* exacerbar

▸ **play up 1** *vt sep (annoy)* dar la lata a, fastidiar

2 *vi (child etc)* dar guerra

playboy ['pleɪbɔɪ] *n* playboy *m*

player ['pleɪə(r)] *n Sport* jugador(a) *m,f; Mus* músico(a) *m,f; Th (man)* actor *m; (woman)* actriz *f*

playful ['pleɪfʊl] *adj* juguetón(ona)

playground ['pleɪɡraʊnd] *n* patio *m* de recreo

playgroup ['pleɪɡruːp] *n* jardín *m* de infancia

playing ['pleɪɪŋ] *n* juego *m;* **p. card** carta *f*, naipe *m;* **p. field** campo *m* de deportes

playmate ['pleɪmeɪt] *n* compañero(a) *m,f* de juego

play-off ['pleɪɒf] *n Sport* partido *m* de desempate

playpen ['pleɪpen] *n* corralito *m or* parque *m* (de niños)

playschool ['pleɪskuːl] *n* jardín *m* de infancia

plaything ['pleɪθɪŋ] *n* juguete *m*

playwright ['pleɪraɪt] *n* dramaturgo(a) *m,f*

PLC, plc [piːel'siː] *n Br (abbr* **public limited company)** ≃ S.A.

plea [pliː] *n* (**a**) *(request)* petición *f,* súplica *f; (excuse)* pretexto *m,* disculpa *f* (**b**) *Jur* alegato *m*

plead [pliːd] **1** *vt* (**a**) *Jur & Fig* **to p. sb's cause** defender la causa de algn (**b**) **to p. ignorance** *(give as excuse)* alegar ignorancia

2 *vi* (**a**) *(beg)* rogar, suplicar; **to p. with sb to do sth** suplicar a algn que haga algo (**b**) *Jur* **to p. guilty/not guilty** declararse culpable/inocente

pleasant ['plezənt] *adj* agradable

pleasantry ['plezəntrɪ] *n* cumplido *m*

please [pliːz] **1** *vt (give pleasure to)* agradar, complacer; *(satisfy)* satisfacer; *Fam* **p. yourself** como quieras

2 *vi* complacer; *(give satisfaction)* satisfacer; **easy/hard to p.** poco/muy exigente

3 *adv* por favor; **may I? – p. do** ¿me permite? – desde luego; **p. do not smoke** *(sign)* se ruega no fumar; **yes, p.** sí, por favor

pleased [pliːzd] *adj (happy)* contento(a); *(satisfied)* satisfecho(a); **p. to meet you!** ¡encantado(a)!, ¡mucho gusto!; **to be p. about sth** alegrarse de algo

pleasing ['pliːzɪŋ] *adj (pleasant)* agradable, grato(a); *(satisfactory)* satisfactorio(a)

pleasure ['pleʒə(r)] *n* placer *m;* **it's a p. to talk to him** da gusto hablar con él; **to take great p. in doing sth** disfrutar mucho haciendo algo; **with p.** con mucho gusto

pleat [pliːt] **1** n pliegue m
2 vt hacer pliegues en

pledge [pledʒ] **1** n promesa f; (token of love etc) señal f; (guarantee) prenda f
2 vt (promise) prometer; (pawn) empeñar

plentiful [ˈplentɪfʊl] adj abundante

plenty [ˈplentɪ] n abundancia f; **p. of books** muchos libros; **p. of time** tiempo de sobra; **we've got p.** tenemos de sobra

Plexiglas® [ˈpleksɪglɑːs] n US plexiglás® m

pliable [ˈplaɪəbəl] adj flexible

pliers [ˈplaɪəz] npl alicates mpl, tenazas fpl

plight [plaɪt] n situación f grave

plimsolls [ˈplɪmsəlz] npl Br zapatos mpl de tenis

plinth [plɪnθ] n plinto m

plod [plɒd] vi andar con paso pesado; Fig **to p. on** perseverar; Fig **to p. through a report** estudiar laboriosamente un informe

plodder [ˈplɒdə(r)] n trabajador(a) m,f/ estudiante mf tenaz

plonk¹ [plɒŋk] vt Fam dejar caer

plonk² [plɒŋk] n Br Fam (wine) vinazo m

plot¹ [plɒt] **1** n (a) (conspiracy) complot m (b) Th & Lit (story) argumento m, trama f
2 vt (a) (course, route) trazar (b) (scheme) fraguar
3 vi conspirar, tramar

plot² [plɒt] n Agr terreno m; (for building) solar m; **vegetable p.** campo m de hortalizas

plough [plaʊ] **1** n arado m
2 vt arar
3 vi Fig **the car ploughed through the fencing** el coche atravesó la valla; **to p. into sth** chocar contra algo; Fig **to p. through a book** leer un libro con dificultad
▶ **plough back** vt sep (profits) reinvertir

plow [plaʊ] n, vt & vi US = **plough**

ploy [plɔɪ] n estratagema f

pluck [plʌk] **1** vt (a) arrancar (**out of** de) (b) (flowers) coger (c) (chicken) desplumar (d) (guitar) puntear
2 n (courage) valor m, ánimo m
▶ **pluck up** vt sep **to p. up courage** armarse de valor

plucky [ˈplʌkɪ] adj (**pluckier, pluckiest**) valiente

plug [plʌg] **1** n (a) (in bath etc) tapón m (b) Elec enchufe m, clavija f; **two-/three-pin p.** clavija bipolar/tripolar

2 vt (a) (hole) tapar (b) Fam (publicize) dar publicidad a; (idea etc) hacer hincapié en
▶ **plug in** vt sep & vi enchufar

plum [plʌm] n (fruit) ciruela f; Fig **a p. job** un chollo

plumage [ˈpluːmɪdʒ] n plumaje m

plumb [plʌm] **1** n plomo m; **p. line** plomada f
2 adj vertical
3 adv Fam **p. in the middle** justo en medio; US **he's p. crazy** está completamente loco
4 vt Fig **to p. the depths** tocar fondo

plumber [ˈplʌmə(r)] n fontanero(a) m,f

plumbing [ˈplʌmɪŋ] n (occupation) fontanería f; (system) tuberías fpl, cañerías fpl

plume [pluːm] n penacho m

plummet [ˈplʌmɪt] vi (bird, plane) caer en picado; Fig (prices) bajar vertiginosamente; (morale) caer a plomo

plump¹ [plʌmp] adj (person) relleno(a); (baby) rechoncho(a)

plump² [plʌmp] vi **to p. for sth** optar por algo
▶ **plump down** vt sep dejar caer
▶ **plump up** vt sep (cushions) ahuecar

plunder [ˈplʌndə(r)] **1** vt saquear
2 n (action) saqueo m, pillaje m; (loot) botín m

plunge [plʌndʒ] **1** vt (immerse) sumergir; (thrust) arrojar
2 vi (dive) lanzarse, zambullirse; Fig (fall) caer, hundirse; (prices) desplomarse
3 n (dive) zambullida f; Fig (fall) desplome m; **to take the p.** dar el paso decisivo

plunger [ˈplʌndʒə(r)] n Tech émbolo m; (for pipes) desatascador m

pluperfect [pluːˈpɜːfɪkt] n pluscuamperfecto m

plural [ˈplʊərəl] adj & n plural (m)

plus [plʌs] **1** prep más; **three p. four makes seven** tres más cuatro hacen siete
2 n Math signo m más; Fig (advantage) ventaja f

plush [plʌʃ] **1** n felpa f
2 adj Fam lujoso(a)

plutonium [pluːˈtəʊnɪəm] n plutonio m

ply [plaɪ] **1** vt **to p. one's trade** ejercer su oficio; **to p. sb with drinks** no parar de ofrecer copas a algn
2 vi (ship) ir y venir; **to p. for hire** ir en busca de clientes

plywood [ˈplaɪwʊd] n madera contrachapada

PM [piː'em] *n Br* (*abbr* **Prime Minister**) primer(a) ministro(a) *m,f*

p.m. [piː'em] (*abbr* **post meridiem**) después del mediodía; **at 2 p.m.** a las dos de la tarde

PMT [piːem'tiː] *n* (*abbr* **premenstrual tension**) tensión *f* premenstrual

pneumatic [njʊ'mætɪk] *adj* neumático(a)

pneumonia [njuː'məʊnɪə] *n* pulmonía *f*

PO [piː'əʊ] *n* (*abbr* **Post Office**) oficina *f* de correos; **PO Box** apartado *m* de correos, *CAm, Carib, Méx* casilla *f* postal, *Andes, RP* casilla de correos

poach¹ [pəʊtʃ] *vt* (**a**) **to p. fish/game** pescar/cazar furtivamente (**b**) *Fam Fig* (*steal*) birlar

poach² [pəʊtʃ] *vt Culin* (*egg*) escalfar; (*fish*) hervir

poacher ['pəʊtʃə(r)] *n* pescador/cazador furtivo

pocket ['pɒkɪt] **1** *n* (**a**) bolsillo *m*; *Fig* **to be £10 in/out of p.** salir ganando/perdiendo 10 libras; **p. money** dinero *m* de bolsillo (**b**) (*of air*) bolsa *f* (**c**) (*of resistance*) foco *m*

2 *vt* (*money*) embolsar

pocketbook ['pɒkɪtbʊk] *n US* bolso *m*

pocketknife ['pɒkɪtnaɪf] *n* navaja *f*

pod [pɒd] *n* vaina *f*

podgy ['pɒdʒɪ] *adj* (**podgier, podgiest**) gordinflón(ona), regordete

podiatrist [pə'daɪətrɪst] *n US* pedicuro(a) *m,f*

podium ['pəʊdɪəm] *n* podio *m*

poem ['pəʊɪm] *n* poema *m*

poet ['pəʊɪt] *n* poeta *mf*

poetic [pəʊ'etɪk] *adj* poético(a)

poetry ['pəʊɪtrɪ] *n* poesía *f*

poignant ['pɔɪnjənt] *adj* conmovedor(a)

point [pɔɪnt] **1** *n* (**a**) (*sharp end*) punta *f*

(**b**) (*place*) punto *m*; *Fig* **p. of no return** punto sin retorno

(**c**) (*quality*) **good/bad p.** cualidad buena/mala; **weak/strong p.** punto débil/fuerte

(**d**) (*moment*) **at that p.** en aquel momento; **from that p. onwards** desde entonces; **to be on the p. of doing sth** estar a punto de hacer algo

(**e**) (*score*) punto *m*, tanto *m*; **to win on points** ganar por puntos; **match p.** (*in tennis*) pelota *f* de match

(**f**) (*in argument*) punto *m*; **to make one's p.** insistir en el argumento; **I take your p.** entiendo lo que quieres decir

(**g**) (*purpose*) propósito *m*; **I don't see the p.** no veo el sentido; **that isn't the p.,**

it's **beside the p.** eso no viene al caso; **there's no p. in going** no merece la pena ir; **to come to the p.** llegar al meollo de la cuestión

(**h**) (*on scale*) punto *m*; (*in share index*) entero *m*; **six p. three** seis coma tres; *Fig* **up to a p.** hasta cierto punto

(**i**) *Geog* punta *f*

(**j**) **power p.** toma *f* de corriente

(**k**) **points** *Aut* platinos *mpl*; *Rail* agujas *fpl*

2 *vt* (*way etc*) señalar, indicar; **to p. a gun at sb** apuntar a algn con una pistola

3 *vi* señalar, indicar; **to p. at sth/sb** señalar algo/a algn con el dedo

▶ **point out** *vt sep* indicar, señalar; (*mention*) hacer resaltar

point-blank ['pɔɪnt'blæŋk] **1** *adj* a quemarropa; (*refusal*) rotundo(a)

2 *adv* (*shoot*) a quemarropa; (*refuse*) rotundamente

pointed ['pɔɪntɪd] *adj* (*sharp*) puntiagudo(a); *Fig* (*comment*) intencionado(a); (*cutting*) mordaz

pointedly ['pɔɪntɪdlɪ] *adv Fig* (*significantly*) con intención; (*cuttingly*) con mordacidad

pointer ['pɔɪntə(r)] *n* (**a**) (*indicator*) indicador *m*, aguja *f*; (*for map*) puntero *m* (**b**) (*dog*) perro *m* de muestra

pointless ['pɔɪntlɪs] *adj* sin sentido

poise [pɔɪz] **1** *n* (*bearing*) porte *m*; (*self-assurance*) aplomo *m*

2 *vt Fig* **to be poised to do sth** estar listo(a) para hacer algo

poison ['pɔɪzən] **1** *n* veneno *m*

2 *vt* envenenar

poisoning ['pɔɪzənɪŋ] *n* envenenamiento *m*; (*by food etc*) intoxicación *f*

poisonous ['pɔɪzənəs] *adj* (*plant, snake*) venenoso(a); (*gas*) tóxico(a); *Fig* (*rumour*) pernicioso(a)

poke [pəʊk] *vt* (*with finger or stick*) dar con la punta del dedo/del bastón a; **to p. one's head out** asomar la cabeza; **to p. the fire** atizar el fuego

▶ **poke about, poke around** *vi* fisgonear, hurgar

▶ **poke out** *vt sep* (*eye*) sacar

poker¹ ['pəʊkə(r)] *n* (*for fire*) atizador *m*

poker² ['pəʊkə(r)] *n Cards* póquer *m*

poker-faced ['pəʊkəfeɪst] *adj Fam* de cara impasible

poky ['pəʊkɪ] *adj* (**pokier, pokiest**) *Fam Pej* minúsculo(a); **a p. little room** un cuartucho

Poland ['pəʊlənd] *n* Polonia

polar ['pəʊlə(r)] *adj* polar; **p. bear** oso *m* polar

Pole [pəʊl] *n* polaco(a) *m,f*

pole¹ [pəʊl] *n* palo *m*; **p. vault** salto *m* con pértiga

pole² [pəʊl] *n Geog* polo *m*; *Fig* **to be poles apart** ser polos opuestos

police [pə'liːs] **1** *npl* policía *f*; **p. car** coche *m* patrulla; **p. constable** policía *m*; **p. force** cuerpo *m* de policía; **p. record** antecedentes *mpl* penales; **p. state** estado *m* policial; **p. station** comisaría *f*
2 *vt* vigilar

policeman [pə'liːsmən] *n* policía *m*

policewoman [pə'liːswʊmən] *n* (mujer *f*) policía *f*

policy ['pɒlɪsɪ] *n Pol* política *f*; *(of company)* norma *f*, principio *m*; *Ins* póliza *f* (de seguros)

polio ['pəʊlɪəʊ] *n* poliomielitis *f*

Polish ['pəʊlɪʃ] **1** *adj* polaco(a)
2 *n* **(a) the P.** los polacos **(b)** *(language)* polaco *m*

polish ['pɒlɪʃ] **1** *vt* pulir; *(furniture)* encerar; *(shoes)* limpiar; *(silver)* sacar brillo a
2 *n* **(a)** *(for furniture)* cera *f*; *(for shoes)* betún *m*; *(for nails)* esmalte *m* **(b)** *(shine)* brillo *m*; *Fig (refinement)* refinamiento *m*
▸ **polish off** *vt sep Fam (work)* despachar; *(food)* zamparse
▸ **polish up** *vt sep Fig* perfeccionar

polished ['pɒlɪʃt] *adj Fig (manners)* refinado(a); *(style)* pulido(a); *(performance)* impecable

polite [pə'laɪt] *adj* educado(a)

politeness [pə'laɪtnɪs] *n* educación *f*

politic ['pɒlɪtɪk] *adj* prudente

political [pə'lɪtɪkəl] *adj* político(a)

politically [pə'lɪtɪklɪ] *adv* políticamente; **p. correct** políticamente correcto(a)

politician [pɒlɪ'tɪʃən] *n* político(a) *m,f*

politics ['pɒlɪtɪks] *n sing* política *f*

polka ['pɒlkə] *n (dance)* polca *f*; **p. dot** lunar *m*

poll [pəʊl] **1** *n* **(a)** votación *f*; **the polls** las elecciones; **to go to the polls** acudir a las urnas **(b)** *(survey)* encuesta *f*
2 *vt (votes)* obtener

pollen ['pɒlən] *n* polen *m*

polling ['pəʊlɪŋ] *n* votación *f*; **p. booth** cabina *f* electoral; **p. station** colegio *m* electoral

pollute [pə'luːt] *vt* contaminar

pollution [pə'luːʃən] *n* contaminación *f*, polución *f*; **environmental p.** contaminación ambiental

polo ['pəʊləʊ] *n Sport* polo *m*; **p. neck (sweater)** jersey *m* de cuello vuelto

polyester [pɒlɪ'estə(r)] *n* poliéster *m*

polyethylene [pɒlɪ'eθɪliːn] *n US* polietileno *m*

polymer ['pɒlɪmə(r)] *n Chem* polímero *m*

Polynesia [pɒlɪ'niːʒɪə] *n* Polinesia

polystyrene [pɒlɪ'staɪriːn] *n* poliestireno *m*

polytechnic [pɒlɪ'teknɪk] *n* escuela politécnica, politécnico *m*

polythene ['pɒlɪθiːn] *n Br* polietileno *m*

pomegranate ['pɒmɪɡrænɪt] *n* granada *f*

pomp [pɒmp] *n* pompa *f*

pompom ['pɒmpɒm], **pompon** ['pɒmpɒn] *n* borla *f*, pompón *m*

pompous ['pɒmpəs] *adj (person)* presumido(a); *(speech)* rimbombante

pond [pɒnd] *n* estanque *m*

ponder ['pɒndə(r)] **1** *vt* considerar
2 *vi* **to p. over sth** meditar sobre algo

ponderous ['pɒndərəs] *adj* pesado(a)

pong [pɒŋ] *n Br Fam* hedor *m*

pontoon¹ [pɒn'tuːn] *n Constr* pontón *m*

pontoon² [pɒn'tuːn] *n Cards* veintiuna *f*

pony ['pəʊnɪ] *n* poney *m*

ponytail ['pəʊnɪteɪl] *n* cola *f* de caballo

poodle ['puːdəl] *n* caniche *m*

poof [pʊf] *n Br Fam Pej* marica *m*

pool¹ [puːl] *n (of water, oil etc)* charco *m*; *(pond)* estanque *m*; *(in river)* pozo *m*; **swimming p.** piscina *f*

pool² [puːl] **1** *n* **(a)** *(common fund)* fondo *m* común **(b)** **typing p.** servicio *m* de mecanografía **(c)** *US (snooker)* billar americano **(d)** *Br* **football pools** quinielas *fpl*
2 *vt (funds)* reunir; *(ideas, resources)* juntar

poor [pʊə(r)] **1** *adj* pobre; *(quality)* malo(a); *Fam* **you p. thing!** ¡pobrecito!
2 *npl* **the p.** los pobres

poorly ['pʊəlɪ] **1** *adv (badly)* mal
2 *adj (poorlier, poorliest) (ill)* mal, malo(a)

pop [pɒp] **1** *vt (burst)* hacer reventar; *(cork)* hacer saltar
2 *vi (burst)* reventar; *(cork)* saltar; *Fam* **I'm just popping over to Ian's** voy un momento a casa de Ian
3 *n* **(a)** *(noise)* pequeña explosión **(b)** *Fam (drink)* gaseosa *f* **(c)** *US Fam (father)* papá *m* **(d)** *Fam Mus* música *f* pop; **p. singer** cantante *mf* pop
▸ **pop in** *vi Fam* entrar un momento, pasar

popcorn ['pɒpkɔːn] *n* palomitas *fpl*

Pope [pəʊp] *n* **the P.** el Papa

poplar ['pɒplə(r)] *n* álamo *m*

poppy ['pɒpɪ] *n* amapola *f*

Popsicle® ['pɒpsɪkəl] *n US* polo *m*

populace ['pɒpjʊləs] *n (people)* pueblo *m*

popular ['pɒpjʊlə(r)] *adj* popular; *(fashionable)* de moda; *(common)* corriente

popularity [pɒpjʊ'lærɪtɪ] *n* popularidad *f*

popularize ['pɒpjʊləraɪz] *vt* popularizar

populate ['pɒpjʊleɪt] *vt* poblar

population [pɒpjʊ'leɪʃən] *n* población *f*; **the p. explosion** la explosión demográfica

porcelain ['pɔːsəlɪn] *n* porcelana *f*

porch [pɔːtʃ] *n (of church)* pórtico *m*; *(of house)* porche *m*, entrada *f*; *US (veranda)* terraza *f*

porcupine ['pɔːkjʊpaɪn] *n* puerco *m* espín

pore¹ [pɔː(r)] *vi* **to p. over sth** leer *or* estudiar algo detenidamente

pore² [pɔː(r)] *n Anat* poro *m*

pork [pɔːk] *n* carne *f* de cerdo

pornography [pɔː'nɒgrəfɪ] *n* pornografía *f*

porous ['pɔːrəs] *adj* poroso(a)

porpoise ['pɔːpəs] *n* marsopa *f*

porridge ['pɒrɪdʒ] *n* gachas *fpl* de avena

port¹ [pɔːt] *n (harbour)* puerto *m*; **p. of call** puerto de escala

port² [pɔːt] *n Naut & Av* babor *m*

port³ [pɔːt] *n (wine)* vino *m* de Oporto, oporto *m*

portable ['pɔːtəbəl] *adj* portátil

portal ['pɔːtəl] *n Comput (web page)* portal *m*

portent ['pɔːtent] *n Fml* augurio *m*

porter ['pɔːtə(r)] *n (in hotel etc)* portero(a) *m,f*; *Rail* mozo *m* de estación; *US* mozo de los coches-cama

portfolio [pɔːt'fəʊlɪəʊ] *n (file)* carpeta *f*; *(of artist, politician)* cartera *f*

porthole ['pɔːthəʊl] *n* portilla *f*

portion ['pɔːʃən] *n (part, piece)* parte *f*, porción *f*; *(of food)* ración *f*
▸ **portion out** *vt sep* repartir

portly ['pɔːtlɪ] *adj* (**portlier, portliest**) corpulento(a)

portrait ['pɔːtreɪt] *n* retrato *m*

portray [pɔː'treɪ] *vt (paint portrait of)* retratar; *(describe)* describir; *Th* representar

Portugal ['pɔːtjʊgəl] *n* Portugal

Portuguese [pɔːtjʊ'giːz] **1** *adj* portugués(esa)
2 *n (person)* portugués(esa) *m,f*; *(language)* portugués *m*

pose [pəʊz] **1** *vt (problem)* plantear; *(threat)* representar
2 *vi (for painting)* posar; *Pej (behave affectedly)* hacer pose; **to p. as** hacerse pasar por
3 *n (stance)* postura *f*; *Pej (affectation)* pose *f*

posh [pɒʃ] *adj Br Fam* elegante, de lujo; *(person)* presumido(a); *(accent)* de clase alta

position [pə'zɪʃən] **1** *n* (**a**) *(place)* posición *f*; *(location)* situación *f*; *(rank)* rango *m*; **to be in a p. to do sth** estar en condiciones de hacer algo (**b**) *(opinion)* postura *f* (**c**) *(job)* puesto *m*
2 *vt* colocar

positive ['pɒzɪtɪv] *adj* positivo(a); *(sign)* favorable; *(proof)* incontrovertible; *(sure)* seguro(a); *Fam (absolute)* auténtico(a)

possess [pə'zes] *vt* poseer; *(of fear)* apoderarse de

possessed [pə'zest] *adj* poseído(a)

possession [pə'zeʃən] *n* posesión *f*; **possessions** bienes *mpl*

possessive [pə'zesɪv] *adj* posesivo(a)

possibility [pɒsɪ'bɪlɪtɪ] *n* posibilidad *f*; **possibilities** *(potential)* potencial *m*

possible ['pɒsɪbəl] *adj* posible; **as much as p.** todo lo posible; **as often as p.** cuanto más mejor; **as soon as p.** cuanto antes

possibly ['pɒsɪblɪ] *adv* posiblemente; *(perhaps)* tal vez, quizás; **I can't p. come** no puedo venir de ninguna manera

post¹ [pəʊst] **1** *n (of wood)* poste *m*
2 *vt (fix)* fijar

post² [pəʊst] **1** *n (job)* puesto *m*; *US* **trading p.** factoría *f*
2 *vt* enviar

post³ [pəʊst] *Br* **1** *n (mail)* correo *m*; **by p.** por correo; **p. office** oficina *f* de correos; **P. Office Box** apartado *m* de correos
2 *vt (letter)* echar al correo; **to p. sth to sb** mandar algo por correo a algn

postage ['pəʊstɪdʒ] *n* franqueo *m*

postal ['pəʊstəl] *adj* postal, de correos; *Br* **p. code** código *m* postal **p. order** giro *m* postal; **p. vote** voto *m* por correo

postbox ['pəʊstbɒks] *n Br* buzón *m*

postcard ['pəʊstkɑːd] *n* (tarjeta *f*) postal *f*

postcode ['pəʊstkəʊd] *n Br* código *m* postal

postdate [pəʊst'deɪt] *vt (cheque)* extender con fecha posterior

poster ['pəʊstə(r)] *n* póster *m*; *(advertising)* cartel *m*

posterior [pɒ'stɪərɪə(r)] **1** *n Hum* trasero *m*, pompis *m*
2 *adj* posterior

posterity [pɒ'sterɪtɪ] *n* posteridad *f*

postgraduate [pəʊst'grædjʊɪt] **1** *n* posgraduado(a) *m,f*
2 *adj* de posgraduado
posthumous ['pɒstjʊməs] *adj* póstumo(a)
postman ['pəʊstmən] *n Br* cartero *m*
postmark ['pəʊstmɑːk] *n* matasellos *m inv*
postmaster ['pəʊstmɑːstə(r)] *n* administrador *m* de correos; **p. general** director *m* general de correos
postmortem [pəʊst'mɔːtəm] *n* autopsia *f*
postpone [pəs'pəʊn] *vt* aplazar
postscript ['pəʊsskrɪpt] *n* posdata *f*
posture ['pɒstʃə(r)] **1** *n* postura *f*; *(affected)* pose *f*
2 *vi* adoptar una pose
postwar ['pəʊstwɔː(r)] *adj* de la posguerra
posy ['pəʊzɪ] *n* ramillete *m*
pot [pɒt] **1** *n (container)* tarro *m*, pote *m*; *(for cooking)* olla *f*; *(for flowers)* maceta *f*; *Fam* **to go to p.** irse al traste; **p. shot** tiro *m* al azar
2 *vt (plant)* poner en una maceta
potassium [pə'tæsɪəm] *n* potasio *m*
potato [pə'teɪtəʊ] *n (pl* **potatoes***)* patata *f*, *Am* papa *f*
potent ['pəʊtənt] *adj* potente
potential [pə'tenʃəl] **1** *adj* potencial, posible
2 *n* potencial *m*
potentially [pə'tenʃəlɪ] *adv* en potencia
pothole ['pɒthəʊl] *n Geol* cueva *f*; *(in road)* bache *m*
potholing ['pɒthəʊlɪŋ] *n Br* espeleología *f*
potion ['pəʊʃən] *n* poción *f*, pócima *f*
potluck [pɒt'lʌk] *n Fam* **to take p.** conformarse con lo que haya
potted ['pɒtɪd] *adj (food)* en conserva; *(plant)* en maceta *or* tiesto
potter[1] ['pɒtə(r)] *n* alfarero(a) *m,f*
potter[2] ['pɒtə(r)] *vi Br* **to p. about** *or* **around** entretenerse
pottery ['pɒtərɪ] *n (craft, place)* alfarería *f*; *(objects)* cerámica *f*
potty[1] ['pɒtɪ] *adj* (**pottier, pottiest**) *Br Fam* chiflado(a)
potty[2] ['pɒtɪ] *n Fam* orinal *m*
pouch [paʊtʃ] *n* (**a**) bolsa pequeña; *(for ammunition)* morral *m*; *(for tobacco)* petaca *f* (**b**) *Zool* bolsa *f* abdominal
poultry ['pəʊltrɪ] *n (live)* aves *fpl* de corral; *(food)* pollos *mpl*
pounce [paʊns] *vi* **to p. on** abalanzarse encima de

pound[1] [paʊnd] **1** *vt (strike)* aporrear
2 *vi (heart)* palpitar; *(walk heavily)* andar con paso pesado
pound[2] [paʊnd] *n (money, weight)* libra *f*
pound[3] [paʊnd] *n (for dogs)* perrera *f*; *(for cars)* depósito *m* de coches
pour [pɔː(r)] **1** *vt* echar, verter; **to p. sb a drink** servirle una copa a algn
2 *vi* correr, fluir; **it's pouring with rain** está lloviendo a cántaros
▶ **pour out** *vt sep* echar, verter; *Fig* **to p. one's heart out to sb** desahogarse con algn
pouring ['pɔːrɪŋ] *adj (rain)* torrencial
pout [paʊt] **1** *vi* hacer pucheros
2 *n* puchero *m*
poverty ['pɒvətɪ] *n* pobreza *f*
poverty-stricken ['pɒvətɪstrɪkən] *adj* necesitado(a); **to be p.** vivir en la miseria
powder ['paʊdə(r)] **1** *n* polvo *m*; **p. compact** polvera *f*, **p. keg** polvorín *m*; **p. puff** borla *f*, **p. room** servicios *mpl* de señoras
2 *vt* **to p. one's nose** ponerse polvos en la cara; *Euph* ir a los servicios *or* al tocador
powdered ['paʊdəd] *adj (milk)* en polvo
power ['paʊə(r)] **1** *n* (**a**) fuerza *f*; *(energy)* energía *f*; *Elec* **to cut off the p.** cortar la corriente; **p. point** enchufe *m*; **p. station** central eléctrica (**b**) *(ability)* poder *m* (**c**) *(authority)* poder *m*; *(nation)* potencia *f*; *(influence)* influencia *f*; **to be in p.** estar en el poder; *Pol* **to come into p.** subir al poder; **the p. of veto** el derecho de veto (**d**) *Tech* potencia *f*; *(output)* rendimiento *m*
2 *vt* propulsar, impulsar
powerboat ['paʊəbəʊt] *n* lancha *f* (motora)
powerful ['paʊəfʊl] *adj (strong)* fuerte; *(influential)* poderoso(a); *(remedy)* eficaz; *(engine, machine)* potente; *(emotion)* fuerte; *(speech)* conmovedor(a)
powerless ['paʊəlɪs] *adj* impotente, ineficaz
pp *(abbr* **pages***)* págs., pp
PR [piː'ɑː(r)] *(abbr* **public relations***)* relaciones *fpl* públicas
practicable ['præktɪkəbəl] *adj* factible
practical ['præktɪkəl] *adj* práctico(a); *(useful)* útil; *(sensible)* adecuado(a)
practicality [præktɪ'kælɪtɪ] *n (of suggestion, plan)* factibilidad *f*; **practicalities** detalles prácticos
practically ['præktɪkəlɪ] *adv (almost)* casi
practice ['præktɪs] **1** *n* (**a**) *(habit)* costumbre *f* (**b**) *(exercise)* práctica *f*; *Sport*

entrenamiento *m*; *Mus* ensayo *m*; **to be out of p.** no estar en forma (**c**) *(way of doing sth)* práctica *f*; **in p.** en la práctica; **to put sth into p.** poner algo en práctica (**d**) *(of profession)* ejercicio *m* (**e**) *(place) (of doctors)* consultorio *m*; *(of lawyers)* bufete *m* (**f**) *(clients) (of doctors)* pacientes *mpl*; *(of lawyers)* clientela *f*

2 *vt & vi US* = **practise**

practicing ['præktısıŋ] *adj US* = **practising**

practise ['præktıs] **1** *vt* practicar; *(method)* seguir; *(principle)* poner en práctica; *Mus* ensayar; *(profession)* ejercer

2 *vi* practicar; *Sport* entrenar; *Mus* ensayar; *(doctor)* practicar; *(lawyer)* ejercer

practising ['præktısıŋ] *adj (doctor etc)* en ejercicio; *(Christian etc)* practicante

practitioner [præk'tıʃənə(r)] *n Br Med* **general p.** médico(a) *m,f* de cabecera; **medical p.** médico(a) *m,f*

pragmatic [præg'mætık] *adj* pragmático(a)

prairie ['preərı] *n* pradera *f*; *US* llanura *f*

praise [preız] **1** *n* alabanza *f*

2 *vt* alabar, elogiar

praiseworthy ['preızwɜːðı] *adj* loable

pram [præm] *n Br* cochecito *m* de niño

prance [prɑːns] *vi (horse)* encabritarse; **to p. about** *(person)* pegar brincos

prank [præŋk] *n* broma *f*; *(of child)* travesura *f*

prat [præt] *n Br Fam* soplagaitas *mf inv*, *Am* pendejo(a) *m,f*

prawn [prɔːn] *n* gamba *f*

pray [preı] *vi* rezar, orar

prayer [preə(r)] *n* rezo *m*, oración *f*; *(entreaty)* súplica *f*; **p. book** misal *m*

preach [priːtʃ] *vi* predicar

preacher ['priːtʃə(r)] *n* predicador(a) *m,f*

precarious [prı'keərıəs] *adj* precario(a)

precaution [prı'kɔːʃən] *n* precaución *f*

precede [prı'siːd] *vt* preceder

precedence ['presıdəns] *n* preferencia *f*, prioridad *f*; **to take p. over sth/sb** tener prioridad sobre algo/algn

precedent ['presıdənt] *n* precedente *m*

preceding [prı'siːdıŋ] *adj* precedente

precinct ['priːsıŋkt] *n* (**a**) *(area)* recinto *m*; **pedestrian/shopping p.** zona *f* peatonal/comercial (**b**) *US (administrative, police division)* distrito *m*; *(police station)* comisaría *f* (de policía)

> 📖 Note that the Spanish word **precinto** is a false friend and is never a translation for the English word **precinct**. In Spanish, **precinto** means "seal".

precious ['preʃəs] **1** *adj* precioso(a); **p. stones** piedras preciosas

2 *adv Fam* **p. little/few** muy poco/pocos

precipice ['presıpıs] *n* precipicio *m*

precipitate 1 *vt* [prı'sıpıteıt] precipitar; *Fig* arrojar

2 *adj* [prı'sıpıtət] precipitado(a)

precise [prı'saıs] *adj* preciso(a), exacto(a); *(meticulous)* meticuloso(a)

precisely [prı'saıslı] *adv (exactly)* precisamente, exactamente; **p.!** ¡eso es!, ¡exacto!

precision [prı'sıʒən] *n* precisión *f*

preclude [prı'kluːd] *vt* excluir; *(misunderstanding)* evitar

precocious [prı'kəʊʃəs] *adj* precoz

preconceived [priːkən'siːvd] *adj* preconcebido(a)

precondition [priːkən'dıʃən] *n* condición previa

precursor [prı'kɜːsə(r)] *n* precursor(a) *m,f*

predator ['predətə(r)] *n* depredador *m*

predecessor ['priːdısesə(r)] *n* antecesor(a) *m,f*

predetermine [priːdı'tɜːmın] *vt* predeterminar

predicament [prı'dıkəmənt] *n* apuro *m*, aprieto *m*

predict [prı'dıkt] *vt* predecir, pronosticar

predictable [prı'dıktəbəl] *adj* previsible

prediction [prı'dıkʃən] *n* pronóstico *m*

predispose [priːdı'spəʊz] *vt* **to be predisposed to doing sth** estar predispuesto(a) a hacer algo

predominant [prı'dɒmınənt] *adj* predominante

predominantly [prı'dɒmınəntlı] *adv* en su mayoría

predominate [prı'dɒmıneıt] *vi* predominar

pre-empt [prı'empt] *vt* adelantarse a

preen [priːn] *vt* **to p. oneself** *(of bird)* arreglarse las plumas; *Fig (of person)* pavonearse

prefab ['priːfæb] *n Br Fam (house)* casa prefabricada

prefabricated [priː'fæbrıkeıtıd] *adj* prefabricado(a)

preface ['prefıs] **1** *n* prefacio *m*

2 *vt* prologar

prefect ['priːfekt] *n Br Educ* monitor(a) *m,f*

prefer [prı'fɜː(r)] *vt* preferir; **I p. coffee to tea** prefiero el café al té

preferable ['prefərəbəl] *adj* preferible (**to** a)

preferably ['prefərəblɪ] *adv* preferentemente

preference ['prefərəns] *n* preferencia *f*; *(priority)* prioridad *f*; **to give p. to sth** dar prioridad a algo

preferential [prefə'renʃəl] *adj* preferente

prefix ['priːfɪks] *n* prefijo *m*

pregnancy ['pregnənsɪ] *n* embarazo *m*

pregnant ['pregnənt] *adj (woman)* embarazada; *(animal)* preñada; *Fig* **a p. pause** una pausa cargada de significado

prehistoric(al) [priːhɪ'stɒrɪk(əl)] *adj* prehistórico(a)

prejudice ['predʒʊdɪs] **1** *n (bias)* prejuicio *m*; *(harm)* perjuicio *m*
2 *vt (bias)* predisponer; *(harm)* perjudicar

prejudiced ['predʒʊdɪst] *adj* parcial; **to be p. against/in favour of** estar predispuesto(a) en contra/a favor de

preliminary [prɪ'lɪmɪnərɪ] **1** *adj* preliminar; *Sport (round)* eliminatorio(a)
2 *n* **preliminaries** preliminares *mpl*

prelude ['preljuːd] *n* preludio *m*

premarital [priː'mærɪtəl] *adj* prematrimonial

premature [premə'tjʊə(r), 'premətjʊə(r)] *adj* prematuro(a)

prematurely [premə'tjʊəlɪ, 'premətjʊəlɪ] *adv* antes de tiempo

premeditate [prɪ'medɪteɪt] *vt (crime)* premeditar

premenstrual [priː'menstrʊəl] *adj* **p. tension** tensión *f* premenstrual

premier ['premjə(r)] **1** *n Pol* primer(a) ministro(a) *m,f*
2 *adj* primer, primero(a)

premiere ['premɪeə(r)] *n Cin* estreno *m*

premise ['premɪs] *n* premisa *f*

premises ['premɪsɪz] *npl* local *m*; **on the p.** en el local

premium ['priːmɪəm] *n Com, Fin & Ind* prima *f*; **to be at a p.** tener sobreprecio; *Fig* estar muy solicitado(a); *Br* **p. bonds** = bonos numerados emitidos por el Gobierno británico, cuyo comprador entra en un sorteo mensual de premios en metálico

premonition [premə'nɪʃən] *n* presentimiento *m*

preoccupied [priː'ɒkjʊpaɪd] *adj* preocupado(a); **to be p. with sth** preocuparse por algo

prep [prep] *n Br Fam* deberes *mpl*; **p. school** = colegio privado para alumnos de entre 7 y 13 años

prepacked [priː'pækt] *adj* empaquetado(a)

prepaid [priː'peɪd] *adj* con el porte pagado

preparation [prepə'reɪʃən] *n* preparación *f*; *(plan)* preparativo *m*

preparatory [prɪ'pærətərɪ] *adj* preparatorio(a), preliminar; **p. school** *Br* = colegio privado para alumnos de entre 7 y 13 años; *US* = escuela secundaria privada

prepare [prɪ'peə(r)] **1** *vt* preparar; **to p. to do sth** prepararse para hacer algo
2 *vi* prepararse **(for** para)

prepared [prɪ'peəd] *adj (ready)* preparado(a); **to be p. to do sth** *(willing)* estar dispuesto(a) a hacer algo

preponderance [prɪ'pɒndərəns] *n* preponderancia *f*

preposition [prepə'zɪʃən] *n* preposición *f*

preposterous [prɪ'pɒstərəs] *adj* absurdo(a), ridículo(a)

prerequisite [priː'rekwɪzɪt] *n* condición *f* previa

prerogative [prɪ'rɒgətɪv] *n* prerrogativa *f*

preschool [priː'skuːl] *adj* preescolar

prescribe [prɪ'skraɪb] *vt (set down)* prescribir; *Med* recetar; *Fig (recommend)* recomendar

prescription [prɪ'skrɪpʃən] *n Med* receta *f*

presence ['prezəns] *n* presencia *f*; *(attendance)* asistencia *f*; *Fig* **p. of mind** presencia de ánimo

present¹ ['prezənt] **1** *adj* **(a)** *(in attendance)* presente; *Ling* **p. tense** (tiempo *m*) presente *m*; **to be p. at** estar presente en **(b)** *(current)* actual
2 *n (time)* presente *m*, actualidad *f*; **at p.** actualmente; **for the p.** de momento; **up to the p.** hasta ahora

present² **1** *vt* [prɪ'zent] **(a)** *(give as gift)* regalar; *(medals, prizes etc)* entregar; **to p. sb with sth** obsequiar a algn con algo **(b)** *(report etc)* presentar; *(opportunity)* ofrecer; *(problems)* plantear **(c)** *(introduce)* *(person, programme)* presentar
2 *n* ['prezənt] *(gift)* regalo *m*; *(formal)* obsequio *m*

presentable [prɪ'zentəbəl] *adj* presentable; **to make oneself p.** arreglarse

presentation [prezən'teɪʃən] *n* **(a)** presentación *f*; **p. ceremony** ceremonia *f* de entrega **(b)** *Rad & TV* representación *f*

present-day ['prezəntdeɪ] *adj* actual, de hoy en día

presenter [prɪ'zentə(r)] *n Rad* locutor(a) *m,f*; *TV* presentador(a) *m,f*

presently ['prezəntlɪ] *adv (soon)* dentro de poco; *US (now)* ahora

preservation [prezə'veɪʃən] *n* conservación *f*

preservative [prɪ'zɜːvətɪv] *n* conservante *m*

preserve [prɪ'zɜːv] **1** *vt* (**a**) *(keep)* mantener (**b**) *Culin* conservar

2 *n* (**a**) *(hunting)* coto *m* (**b**) *Culin* conserva *f*

preside [prɪ'zaɪd] *vi* presidir

president ['prezɪdənt] *n Pol* presidente(a) *m,f*; *US Com* director(a) *m,f*, gerente *mf*

presidential [prezɪ'denʃəl] *adj* presidencial

press [pres] **1** *vt* (**a**) apretar; *(button)* pulsar; *(grapes)* pisar; *(trousers etc)* planchar

(**b**) *(urge)* presionar; **to p. sb to do sth** acosar a algn para que haga algo

2 *vi* (**a**) *(push)* apretar; **to p. against sb/ sth** apretarse contra algn/algo; **to p. (down) on sth** hacer presión sobre algo

(**b**) *(urge)* apremiar; **time presses** el tiempo apremia

3 *n* (**a**) **p. stud** botón *m* de presión

(**b**) *(machine)* prensa *f*; **to go to p.** *(of newspaper)* entrar en prensa

(**c**) *Press* prensa *f*; **the p.** la prensa; **to get a good/bad p.** tener buena/mala prensa; **p. agency** agencia *f* de prensa; **p. conference** rueda *f* de prensa; **p. cutting** recorte *m* de prensa

▸ **press on** *vi* seguir adelante

pressed [prest] *adj* **to be (hard) p. for** andar escaso(a) de; **I'd be hard p. to do it** me costaría mucho hacerlo

pressing ['presɪŋ] *adj* apremiante, urgente

press-up ['presʌp] *n Br* flexión *f* (de brazos)

pressure ['preʃə(r)] *n* presión *f*; *Med & Met* **high/low p.** altas/bajas presiones; **p. cooker** olla *f* a presión; **p. gauge** manómetro *m*; *Fig* **to bring p. (to bear) on sb** ejercer presión sobre algn

pressurize ['preʃəraɪz] *vt Fig* presionar; **pressurized cabin** cabina presurizada

prestige [pre'stiːʒ] *n* prestigio *m*

presumably [prɪ'zjuːməblɪ] *adv* es de suponer que

presume [prɪ'zjuːm] **1** *vt* suponer, presumir

2 *vi* *(suppose)* suponer; **we p. so/not** suponemos que sí/no

presumption [prɪ'zʌmpʃən] *n* (**a**) *(supposition)* suposición *f* (**b**) *(boldness)* osadía *f*; *(conceit)* presunción *f*

presumptuous [prɪ'zʌmptjʊəs] *adj* impertinente

🖉 Note that the Spanish word **presuntuoso** is a false friend and is never a translation for the English word **presumptuous**. In Spanish, **presuntuoso** means "vain" and "pretentious".

presuppose [priːsə'pəʊz] *vt* presuponer

pretence [prɪ'tens] *n* (**a**) *(deception)* fingimiento *m*; **false pretences** estafa *f*; **under the p. of** so pretexto de (**b**) *(claim)* pretensión *f*

pretend [prɪ'tend] **1** *vt (feign)* fingir, aparentar; *(claim)* pretender

2 *vi (feign)* fingir

pretense [prɪ'tens] *n US* = pretence

pretention [prɪ'tenʃən] *n* pretensión *f*

pretentious [prɪ'tenʃəs] *adj* presuntuoso(a), pretencioso(a)

pretext ['priːtekst] *n* pretexto *m*; **on the p. of** so pretexto de

pretty ['prɪtɪ] **1** *adj* (**prettier**, **prettiest**) bonito(a), guapo(a)

2 *adv Fam* bastante; **p. much the same** más o menos lo mismo

prevail [prɪ'veɪl] *vi* (**a**) predominar (**b**) *(win through)* prevalecer (**c**) **to p. upon** or **on sb to do sth** *(persuade)* persuadir or convencer a algn para que haga algo

prevailing [prɪ'veɪlɪŋ] *adj (wind)* predominante; *(opinion)* general; *(condition, fashion)* actual

prevalent ['prevələnt] *adj* predominante; *(illness)* extendido(a)

prevaricate [prɪ'værɪkeɪt] *vi* andar con ambages

prevent [prɪ'vent] *vt* impedir; *(accident)* evitar; *(illness)* prevenir; **to p. sb from doing sth** impedir a algn hacer algo; **to p. sth from happening** evitar que pase algo

prevention [prɪ'venʃən] *n* prevención *f*

preventive [prɪ'ventɪv] *adj* preventivo(a)

preview ['priːvjuː] *n (of film etc)* preestreno *m*

previous ['priːvɪəs] **1** *adj* anterior, previo(a); **p. conviction** antecedente *m* penal

2 *adv* **p. to going** antes de ir

previously ['priːvɪəslɪ] *adv* anteriormente, previamente

prewar ['priːwɔː(r)] *adj* de antes de la guerra

prey [preɪ] **1** *n* presa *f*; *Fig* víctima *f*

2 *vi* **to p. on** alimentarse de

price [praɪs] **1** *n* precio *m*; **what p. is that**

coat? ¿cuánto cuesta el abrigo?; **p. list** lista *f* de precios; **p. tag** etiqueta *f*

2 *vt (put price on)* poner un precio a; *(value)* valorar

priceless ['praɪslɪs] *adj* que no tiene precio

prick [prɪk] **1** *vt* picar; **to p. one's finger** pincharse el dedo; *Fig* **to p. up one's ears** aguzar el oído

2 *n* **(a)** *(with pin)* pinchazo *m* **(b)** *very Fam (penis)* polla *f* **(c)** *very Fam Pej (person)* gilipollas *mf inv*

prickle ['prɪkəl] **1** *n* espina *f*; *(spike)* pincho *m*; *(sensation)* picor *m*

2 *vt & vi* pinchar, picar

prickly ['prɪklɪ] *adj* (**pricklier, prickliest**) espinoso(a); *Fig (touchy)* enojadizo(a); **p. heat** = sarpullido por causa del calor; **p. pear** higo chumbo

pride [praɪd] **1** *n* orgullo *m*; *(arrogance)* soberbia *f*; **to take p. in sth** enorgullecerse de algo

2 *vt* **to p. oneself on** enorgullecerse de algo

priest [priːst] *n* sacerdote *m*, cura *m*

priestess ['priːstɪs] *n* sacerdotisa *f*

priesthood ['priːsthʊd] *n (clergy)* clero *m*; *(office)* sacerdocio *m*

prig [prɪg] *n* gazmoño(a) *m,f*, mojigato(a) *m,f*

prim [prɪm] *adj* (**primmer, primmest**) **p. (and proper)** remilgado(a)

primaeval [praɪ'miːvəl] *adj* primitivo(a)

primarily ['praɪmərɪlɪ] *adv* ante todo

primary ['praɪmərɪ] **1** *adj* fundamental, principal; **of p. importance** primordial; **p. colour** color primario; **p. education/school** enseñanza/escuela primaria

2 *n US Pol* (elección *f*) primaria *f*

primate¹ ['praɪmeɪt] *n Rel* primado *m*

primate² ['praɪmeɪt] *n Zool* primate *m*

prime [praɪm] **1** *adj* **(a)** principal; *(major)* primordial; **P. Minister** primer(a) ministro(a) *m,f* **(b)** *(first-rate)* de primera; **p. number** número primo

2 *n* **in the p. of life** en la flor de la vida

3 *vt (pump, engine)* cebar; *(surface)* imprimar; *Fig (prepare)* preparar

primer¹ ['praɪmə(r)] *n (textbook)* cartilla *f*

primer² ['praɪmə(r)] *n (paint)* imprimación *f*

primeval [praɪ'miːvəl] *adj* = **primaeval**

primitive ['prɪmɪtɪv] *adj* primitivo(a); *(method, tool)* rudimentario(a)

primrose ['prɪmrəʊz] *n* primavera *f*

Primus® ['praɪməs] *n* hornillo *m* de camping

prince [prɪns] *n* príncipe *m*; **P. Charming** Príncipe Azul

princess [prɪn'ses] *n* princesa *f*

principal ['prɪnsɪpəl] **1** *adj* principal

2 *n Educ* director(a) *m,f*; *Th (in play)* protagonista *mf* principal

principle ['prɪnsɪpəl] *n* principio *m*; **in p.** en principio; **on p.** por principio

print [prɪnt] **1** *vt* **(a)** imprimir; *(publish)* publicar; *Fig* grabar; **printed matter** impresos *mpl* **(b)** *(write)* escribir con letra de imprenta

2 *n* **(a)** *(of hand, foot)* huella *f* **(b)** *(written text)* letra *f*; **out of p.** agotado(a) **(c)** *Tex* estampado *m*; **p. skirt** falda estampada **(d)** *Art* grabado *m*; *Phot* copia *f*
▸ **print out** *vt sep Comput* imprimir

printer ['prɪntə(r)] *n (person)* impresor(a) *m,f*; *(machine)* impresora *f*

printing ['prɪntɪŋ] *n (industry)* imprenta *f*; *(process)* impresión *f*; *(print run)* tirada *f*; **p. press** prensa *f*

print-out ['prɪntaʊt] *n Comput* impresión *f*; *(copy)* copia impresa

prior ['praɪə(r)] *adj* previo(a), anterior; **p. to leaving** antes de salir

priority [praɪ'ɒrɪtɪ] *n* prioridad *f*

prise [praɪz] *vt* **to p. sth open** abrir algo con palanca; **to p. sth off** arrancar algo

prism ['prɪzəm] *n* prisma *f*

prison ['prɪzən] *n* cárcel *f*, prisión *f*

prisoner ['prɪzənə(r)] *n* preso(a) *m,f*; **to hold sb p.** detener a algn; **p. of war** prisionero(a) *m,f* de guerra

privacy ['praɪvəsɪ, 'prɪvəsɪ] *n* intimidad *f*

private ['praɪvɪt] **1** *adj* privado(a); *(secretary)* particular; *(matter)* personal; *(letter)* confidencial; **one's p. life** la vida privada de uno; **p.** *(notice)* *(on road)* carretera privada; *(on gate)* propiedad privada; *(on envelope)* confidencial; **p. detective, Fam p. eye** detective *mf* privado(a); **p. school** escuela privada

2 *n Mil* soldado raso

privately ['praɪvɪtlɪ] *adv* en privado; *(personally)* personalmente

privet ['prɪvɪt] *n* alheña *f*

privilege ['prɪvɪlɪdʒ] *n* privilegio *m*

privileged ['prɪvɪlɪdʒd] *adj* privilegiado(a)

privy ['prɪvɪ] **1** *adj Br* **P. Council** Consejo Privado; **to be p. to sth** estar enterado(a) de algo

2 *n (lavatory)* retrete *m*

prize [praɪz] **1** *n* premio *m*

2 *adj (first-class)* de primera (categoría or clase)

3 *vt (value)* apreciar, valorar

prize-giving ['praɪzgɪvɪŋ] *n* distribución *f* de premios

prizewinner ['praɪzwɪnə(r)] *n* premiado(a) *m,f*

pro¹ [prəʊ] *n* pro *m*; **the pros and cons of an issue** los pros y los contras de una cuestión

pro² [prəʊ] *n Fam* profesional *mf*

pro- [prəʊ] *pref (in favour of)* pro-

probability [prɒbə'bɪlɪtɪ] *n* probabilidad *f*

probable ['prɒbəbəl] *adj* probable

probably ['prɒbəblɪ] *adv* probablemente

probation [prə'beɪʃən] *n Jur* **to be on p.** estar en libertad condicional; **to be on two months' p.** *(at work)* trabajar dos meses de prueba

probe [prəʊb] **1** *n Med & (in outer space)* sonda *f*; *(investigation)* sondeo *m*
2 *vt Med* sondar; *(investigate)* investigar
▸ **probe into** *vt insep* investigar

problem ['prɒbləm] *n* problema *m*

problematic(al) [prɒblə'mætɪk(əl)] *adj* problemático(a); **it's p.** tiene sus problemas

procedure [prə'siːdʒə(r)] *n* procedimiento *m*; *(legal, business)* gestión *f*, trámite *m*

proceed [prə'siːd] *vi* seguir, proceder; **to p. to do sth** ponerse a hacer algo; **to p. to the next matter** pasar a la siguiente cuestión

proceedings [prə'siːdɪŋz] *npl (of meeting)* actas *fpl*; *(measures)* medidas *fpl*; *Jur* proceso *m*

proceeds ['prəʊsiːdz] *npl* ganancias *fpl*

process ['prəʊses] **1** *n* proceso *m*; *(method)* método *m*, sistema *m*; **in the p. of** en vías de
2 *vt (information)* tramitar; *(food)* tratar; *Comput* procesar

processing ['prəʊsesɪŋ] *n (of information)* evaluación *f*; *Comput* tratamiento *m*

procession [prə'seʃən] *n* desfile *m*; *Rel* procesión *f*

proclaim [prə'kleɪm] *vt* proclamar, declarar

proclamation [prɒklə'meɪʃən] *n* proclamación *f*

procrastinate [prəʊ'kræstɪneɪt] *vi* dejar las cosas para después

procure [prə'kjʊə(r)] *vt* conseguir, procurarse

prod [prɒd] *vt (with stick etc)* golpear; *(push)* empujar

prodigal ['prɒdɪgəl] *adj* pródigo(a)

prodigious [prə'dɪdʒəs] *adj* prodigioso(a)

prodigy ['prɒdɪdʒɪ] *n* prodigio *m*

produce 1 *vt* [prə'djuːs] *(a)* producir; *Ind* fabricar *(b)Th* dirigir; *Rad & TV* realizar; *Cin* producir *(c) (give birth to)* dar a luz a *(d) (document)* enseñar; *(bring out)* sacar
2 *n* ['prɒdjuːs] productos *mpl*; **p. of Spain** producto *m* de España

producer [prə'djuːsə(r)] *n* *(a)* productor(a) *m,f*; *Ind* fabricante *mf* *(b)Th* director(a) *m,f* de escena; *Rad & TV* realizador(a) *m,f*; *Cin* productor(a) *m,f*

product ['prɒdʌkt] *n* producto *m*

production [prə'dʌkʃən] *n* *(a)* producción *f*; *Ind* fabricación *f* *(b)Th* representación *f*; *Rad & TV* realización *f*; *Cin* producción *f*; **p. line** cadena *f* de montaje

productive [prə'dʌktɪv] *adj* productivo(a)

productivity [prɒdʌk'tɪvɪtɪ] *n* productividad *f*

profane [prə'feɪn] *adj (secular)* profano(a); *(language)* blasfemo(a)

profess [prə'fes] *vt (faith)* profesar; *(opinion)* expresar; *(claim)* pretender

profession [prə'feʃən] *n* profesión *f*

professional [prə'feʃənəl] **1** *adj* profesional; *(soldier)* de profesión; *(polished)* de gran calidad
2 *n* profesional *mf*

professor [prə'fesə(r)] *n Univ Br* catedrático(a) *m,f*; *US* profesor(a) *m,f*

proficiency [prə'fɪʃənsɪ] *n (in language)* capacidad *f*; *(in skill)* pericia *f*

proficient [prə'fɪʃənt] *adj (in language)* experto(a); *(in skill)* hábil

profile ['prəʊfaɪl] *n* perfil *m*; **in p.** de perfil

profit ['prɒfɪt] **1** *n* *(a)* beneficio *m*, ganancia *f*; **to make a p. on** sacar beneficios de *(b) Fml (benefit)* provecho *m*
2 *vi Fig* sacar provecho; **to p. from** aprovecharse de

profitability [prɒfɪtə'bɪlɪtɪ] *n* rentabilidad *f*

profitable ['prɒfɪtəbəl] *adj Com* rentable; *Fig (worthwhile)* provechoso(a)

profiteer [prɒfɪ'tɪə(r)] **1** *n* especulador(a) *m,f*
2 *vi* obtener beneficios excesivos

profound [prə'faʊnd] *adj* profundo(a)

profuse [prə'fjuːs] *adj* profuso(a), abundante

profusely [prə'fjuːslɪ] *adv* con profusión; **to sweat p.** sudar mucho

profusion [prə'fjuːʒən] *n* profusión *f*, abundancia *f*

prognosis [prɒg'nəʊsɪs] *n Med* pronóstico *m*; *Fig (prediction)* augurio *m*

program ['prəʊgræm] *Comput* **1** *n* programa *m*
  2 *vi & vt* programar
  3 *US* = **programme**

programmer ['prəʊgræmər] *n US* = **programmer**

programme ['prəʊgræm] **1** *n* programa *m*; *(plan)* plan *m*
  2 *vt* **(a)** *(plan)* planear, planificar **(b)** *(computer)* programar

programmer ['prəʊgræmə(r)] *n* programador(a) *m,f*

progress 1 *n* ['prəʊgres] progreso *m*; *(development)* desarrollo *m*; *Med* mejora *f*; **to make p.** hacer progresos; **in p.** en curso
  2 *vi* [prəʊ'gres] avanzar; *(develop)* desarrollar; *(improve)* hacer progresos; *Med* mejorar

progressive [prə'gresɪv] *adj (increasing)* progresivo(a); *Pol* progresista

progressively [prə'gresɪvlɪ] *adv* progresivamente

prohibit [prə'hɪbɪt] *vt* prohibir; **to p. sb from doing sth** prohibir a algn hacer algo

prohibitive [prə'hɪbɪtɪv] *adj* prohibitivo(a)

project 1 *n* ['prɒdʒekt] proyecto *m*; *(plan)* plan *m*; *Educ* trabajo *m*; *US* **(housing) p.** = urbanización con viviendas de protección oficial
  2 *vt* [prə'dʒekt] proyectar, planear
  3 *vi (stick out)* sobresalir

projectile [prə'dʒektaɪl] *n Fml* proyectil *m*

projection [prə'dʒekʃən] *n* **(a)** *(overhang)* saliente *m* **(b)** *Cin* proyección *f* **(c)** *(forecast)* proyección *f*

projector [prə'dʒektə(r)] *n Cin* proyector *m*

proletariat [prəʊlɪ'eərɪət] *n* proletariado *m*

prolific [prə'lɪfɪk] *adj* prolífico(a)

prologue ['prəʊlɒg] *n* prólogo *m*

prolong [prə'lɒŋ] *vt* prolongar

prom [prɒm] *n Br Fam (seafront)* paseo marítimo; *Br (concert)* = concierto sinfónico en que parte del público está de pie; *US (school dance)* = baile de fin de curso

promenade [prɒmə'nɑːd] **1** *n (at seaside)* paseo marítimo
  2 *vi* pasearse

prominence ['prɒmɪnəns] *n* prominencia *f*; *Fig (importance)* importancia *f*

prominent ['prɒmɪnənt] *adj (standing out)* saliente; *Fig (important)* importante; *(famous)* eminente

promiscuous [prə'mɪskjʊəs] *adj* promiscuo(a)

promise ['prɒmɪs] **1** *n* promesa *f*; **to show p.** ser prometedor(a)
  2 *vt & vi* prometer

promising ['prɒmɪsɪŋ] *adj* prometedor(a)

promontory ['prɒməntərɪ] *n* promontorio *m*

promote [prə'məʊt] *vt* ascender; *(product)* promocionar; *(ideas)* fomentar; *Ftb* **they've been promoted** han subido

promoter [prə'məʊtə(r)] *n* promotor(a) *m,f*

promotion [prə'məʊʃən] *n (in rank)* promoción *f*, ascenso *m*; *(of product)* promoción; *(of arts etc)* fomento *m*

prompt ['prɒmpt] **1** *adj (quick)* rápido(a); *(punctual)* puntual
  2 *adv* **at two o'clock p.** a las dos en punto
  3 *vt* **(a)** *(motivate)* incitar; **to p. sb to do sth** instar a algn a hacer algo **(b)** *(actor)* apuntar

promptly [prɒmptlɪ] *adv (quickly)* rápidamente; *(punctually)* puntualmente

prone [prəʊn] *adj* **(a) to be p. to do sth** ser propenso(a) a hacer algo **(b)** *Fml (face down)* boca abajo

prong [prɒŋ] *n* punta *f*, diente *m*

pronoun ['prəʊnaʊn] *n* pronombre *m*

pronounce [prə'naʊns] **1** *vt* pronunciar; *Fml (declare)* declarar
  2 *vi Fml* **to p. on sth** opinar sobre algo

pronounced [prə'naʊnst] *adj* pronunciado(a)

pronouncement [prə'naʊnsmənt] *n Fml* declaración *f*

pronunciation [prənʌnsɪ'eɪʃən] *n* pronunciación *f*

proof [pruːf] **1** *n* prueba *f*
  2 *adj* **(a)** *(secure)* a prueba de **(b) this rum is 70 percent p.** este ron tiene 70 grados
  3 *vt* impermeabilizar

prop¹ [prɒp] **1** *n (support)* puntal *m*; *Fig* sostén *m*
  2 *vt (support)* apoyar; *Fig* sostener
  ▶ **prop up** *vt sep* apoyar

prop² [prɒp] *n FamTh* accesorio *m*

propaganda [prɒpə'gændə] *n* propaganda *f*

propel [prə'pel] *vt* propulsar

propeller [prə'pelə(r)] *n* hélice *f*

propelling pencil [prə'pelɪŋ'pensəl] *n* portaminas *m inv*

propensity [prə'pensɪtɪ] *n Fml* propensión *f*

proper ['prɒpə(r)] *adj* **(a)** adecuado(a),

correcto(a); **the p. time** el momento oportuno (**b**) *(real)* real, auténtico(a); *(actual, exact)* propiamente dicho(a) (**c**) *(characteristic)* propio(a); *Ling* **p. noun** nombre propio

properly ['prɒpəlɪ] *adv (suitably, correctly, decently)* correctamente; **it wasn't p. closed** no estaba bien cerrado(a); **she refused, quite p.** se negó, y con razón

property ['prɒpətɪ] *n* (**a**) *(quality)* propiedad *f* (**b**) *(possession)* propiedad *f*, posesión *f*; **personal p.** bienes *mpl*; **public p.** dominio público (**c**) *(estate)* finca *f*

prophecy ['prɒfɪsɪ] *n* profecía *f*

prophesy ['prɒfɪsaɪ] *vt (predict)* predecir; *Rel* profetizar

prophet ['prɒfɪt] *n* profeta *mf*

proportion [prə'pɔːʃən] *n* proporción *f*; *(part, quantity)* parte *f*; **in p. to** *or* **with** en proporción a

proportional [prə'pɔːʃənəl] *adj* proporcional (**to** a); *Pol* **p. representation** representación *f* proporcional

proportionate [prə'pɔːʃənɪt] *adj* proporcional

proposal [prə'pəʊzəl] *n* propuesta *f*; *(suggestion)* sugerencia *f*; **p. of marriage** propuesta de matrimonio

propose [prə'pəʊz] **1** *vt* proponer; *(suggest)* sugerir; *Fml (intend)* tener la intención de
2 *vi* declararse

proposition [prɒpə'zɪʃən] *n* propuesta *f*; *Math* proposición *f*

proprietor [prə'praɪətə(r)] *n* propietario(a) *m,f*

propriety [prə'praɪətɪ] *n (decency)* decoro *m*

propulsion [prə'pʌlʃən] *n* propulsión *f*

prosaic [prəʊ'zeɪɪk] *adj* prosaico(a)

prose [prəʊz] *n Lit* prosa *f*; *Educ* texto *m* para traducir

prosecute ['prɒsɪkjuːt] *vt* procesar

prosecution [prɒsɪ'kjuːʃən] *n (action)* proceso *m*, juicio *m*; **the p.** la acusación

prosecutor ['prɒsɪkjuːtə(r)] *n* acusador(a) *m,f*

prospect 1 *n* ['prɒspekt] *(outlook)* perspectiva *f*; *(hope)* esperanza *f*; **the job has prospects** es un trabajo con porvenir
2 *vt* [prə'spekt] explorar
3 *vi* **to p. for gold/oil** buscar oro/petróleo

prospective [prə'spektɪv] *adj (future)* futuro(a); *(possible)* eventual, probable

prospector [prə'spektə(r)] *n* **gold p.** buscador(a) *m,f* del oro

prospectus [prə'spektəs] *n* prospecto *m*

prosper ['prɒspə(r)] *vi* prosperar

prosperity [prɒ'sperɪtɪ] *n* prosperidad *f*

prosperous ['prɒspərəs] *adj* próspero(a)

prostitute ['prɒstɪtjuːt] *n* prostituta *f*

prostitution [prɒstɪ'tjuːʃən] *n* prostitución *f*

prostrate ['prɒstreɪt] *adj (face down)* boca abajo; **p. with grief** deshecho(a) de dolor

protagonist [prəʊ'tægənɪst] *n* protagonista *mf*

protect [prə'tekt] *vt* proteger; *(interests etc)* salvaguardar; **to p. sb from sth** proteger a algn de algo

protection [prə'tekʃən] *n* protección *f*

protective [prə'tektɪv] *adj* protector(a)

protégé ['prɒtəʒeɪ] *n* protegido *m*

protégée ['prɒtəʒeɪ] *n* protegida *f*

protein ['prəʊtiːn] *n* proteína *f*

protest 1 *n* ['prəʊtest] protesta *f*; *(complaint)* queja *f*
2 *vt* [prə'test] *US* protestar en contra de
3 *vi Br* protestar

Protestant ['prɒtɪstənt] *adj & n* protestante *(mf)*

protester [prə'testə(r)] *n* manifestante *mf*

protocol ['prəʊtəkɒl] *n* protocolo *m*

prototype ['prəʊtətaɪp] *n* prototipo *m*

protracted [prə'træktɪd] *adj* prolongado(a)

protrude [prə'truːd] *vi Fml* sobresalir

protuberance [prə'tjuːbərəns] *n Fml* protuberancia *f*

proud [praʊd] *adj* orgulloso(a); *(arrogant)* soberbio(a)

prove [pruːv] *vt* (**a**) probar, demostrar; *Math* comprobar; **to p. oneself** dar pruebas de valor (**b**) **it proved to be disastrous** *(turned out)* resultó ser desastroso(a)

proverb ['prɒvɜːb] *n* refrán *m*, proverbio *m*

provide [prə'vaɪd] **1** *vt* proporcionar; *(supplies)* suministrar, proveer
2 *vi* proveer; **to p. for sb** mantener a algn

provided [prə'vaɪdɪd] *conj* **p. (that)** con tal de que

providing [prə'vaɪdɪŋ] *conj* = **provided**

province ['prɒvɪns] *n* provincia *f*; *Fig (field of knowledge)* campo *m*

provincial [prə'vɪnʃəl] **1** *adj* provincial; *Pej* provinciano(a)
2 *n Pej (person)* provinciano(a) *m,f*

provision [prə'vɪʒən] *n* provisión *f*; *(supply)* suministro *m*; **provisions** *(food)* provisiones *fpl*, víveres *mpl*

provisional [prə'vɪʒənəl] *adj* provisional

proviso [prə'vaɪzəʊ] *n* with the p. that a condición de que

provocation [prɒvə'keɪʃən] *n* provocación *f*

provocative [prə'vɒkətɪv] *adj* provocador(a); *(flirtatious)* provocativo(a)

provoke [prə'vəʊk] *vt* provocar

prow [praʊ] *n* proa *f*

prowess ['praʊɪs] *n* destreza *f*

prowl [praʊl] **1** *n* merodeo *m*; **to be on the p.** merodear, rondar
  2 *vi* merodear; *Fam* **to p. about** *or* **around** rondar

prowler ['praʊlə(r)] *n Fam* merodeador *m*

proximity [prɒk'sɪmɪtɪ] *n* proximidad *f*; **in p. to, in the p. of** cerca de

proxy ['prɒksɪ] *n Jur (power)* poderes *mpl*; *(person)* apoderado(a) *m,f*; **by p.** por poderes

prudence ['pruːdəns] *n* prudencia *f*

prudent ['pruːdənt] *adj* prudente

prudish ['pruːdɪʃ] *adj* remilgado(a)

prune¹ [pruːn] *n* ciruela pasa

prune² [pruːn] *vt (roses etc)* podar; *Fig* acortar

pry [praɪ] *vi* curiosear, husmear; **to p. into sb's affairs** meterse en asuntos ajenos

PS, ps [piː'es] *(abbr* **postscript**) P.S., P.D.

psalm [sɑːm] *n* salmo *m*

pseudo- ['sjuːdəʊ] *pref* pseudo-, seudo-

pseudonym ['sjuːdənɪm] *n* (p)seudónimo *m*

psyche ['saɪkɪ] *n* psique *f*

psychiatric [saɪkɪ'ætrɪk] *adj* psiquiátrico(a)

psychiatrist [saɪ'kaɪətrɪst] *n* psiquiatra *mf*

psychiatry [saɪ'kaɪətrɪ] *n* psiquiatría *f*

psychic ['saɪkɪk] **1** *adj* psíquico(a)
  2 *n* médium *mf*

psychoanalysis [saɪkəʊə'nælɪsɪs] *n* psicoanálisis *f*

psychoanalyst [saɪkəʊ'ænəlɪst] *n* psicoanalista *mf*

psychological [saɪkə'lɒdʒɪkəl] *adj* psicológico(a)

psychologist [saɪ'kɒlədʒɪst] *n* psicólogo(a) *m,f*

psychology [saɪ'kɒlədʒɪ] *n* psicología *f*

psychopath ['saɪkəʊpæθ] *n* psicópata *mf*

psychotherapist ['saɪkəʊ'θerəpɪst] *n* psicoterapeuta *mf*

psychotherapy ['saɪkəʊ'θerəpɪ] *n* psicoterapia *f*

psychotic [saɪ'kɒtɪk] *adj & n* psicótico(a) *(m,f)*

PT [piː'tiː] *n (abbr* **physical training**) educación *f* física

PTA [piːtiː'eɪ] *n (abbr* **Parent-Teacher Association**) = asociación de padres de alumnos y profesores, ≃ APA *f*

PTO, pto [piːtiː'əʊ] *(abbr* **please turn over)** sigue

pub [pʌb] *n Br Fam* bar *m*, pub *m*

puberty ['pjuːbətɪ] *n* pubertad *f*

pubic ['pjuːbɪk] *adj* púbico(a)

public ['pʌblɪk] **1** *adj* público(a); **to make sth p.** hacer público algo; *Com* **to go p.** *(of company)* pasar a cotizar en Bolsa; **p. company** empresa pública; **p. convenience** servicios *mpl*, aseos *mpl*; **p. holiday** fiesta *f* nacional; *Br* **p. house** pub *m*, taberna *f*; *Br* **p. limited company** sociedad anónima; **p. opinion** opinión pública; *Br* **p. prosecutor** fiscal *m*; **p. relations** relaciones públicas; **p. school** *Br* colegio privado; *US* colegio público; **p. transport** transporte público
  2 *n* **the p.** el público; **in p.** en público

public-address system ['pʌblɪkə'dresɪstəm] *n* megafonía *f*

publican ['pʌblɪkən] *n* tabernero(a) *m,f*

publication [pʌblɪ'keɪʃən] *n* publicación *f*

publicity [pʌ'blɪsɪtɪ] *n* publicidad *f*

publicize ['pʌblɪsaɪz] *vt (make public)* hacer público(a); *(advertise)* hacer publicidad a

public-spirited [pʌblɪk'spɪrɪtɪd] *adj* de espíritu cívico

publish ['pʌblɪʃ] *vt* publicar, editar

publisher ['pʌblɪʃə(r)] *n (person)* editor(a) *m,f*; *(firm)* (casa *f*) editorial *f*

publishing ['pʌblɪʃɪŋ] *n (business)* industria *f* editorial; **p. company** *or* **house** casa *f* editorial

pucker ['pʌkə(r)] *vt (lips, brow)* fruncir, arrugar

pudding ['pʊdɪŋ] *n Culin* pudín *m*; *(dessert)* postre *m*; **Christmas p.** = pudín a base de frutos secos típico de Navidad; **p. basin** cuenco *m*; **steamed p.** budín *m*

puddle ['pʌdəl] *n* charco *m*

Puerto Rican ['pweətəʊ'riːkən] *adj & n* portorriqueño(a) *(m,f)*, puertorriqueño(a) *(m,f)*

Puerto Rico ['pweətəʊ'riːkəʊ] *n* Puerto Rico

puff [pʌf] **1** *n (of wind)* racha *f*; *(of smoke)* bocanada *f*; **p. pastry** pasta *f* de hojaldre
  2 *vi (person)* jadear, resoplar; *(train)* echar humo; **to p. on one's pipe** chupar la pipa

3 *vt (cigarette)* dar una calada a
▸ **puff up** *vi* hincharse
puffy ['pʌfɪ] *adj* (**puffier, puffiest**) hinchado(a)
pugnacious [pʌg'neɪʃəs] *adj* belicoso(a)
pull [pʊl] **1** *n* (**a**) **to give sth a p.** *(tug)* dar un tirón a algo (**b**) *(of engine)* tracción *f*; *Fig (attraction)* atracción *f*; *(influence)* enchufe *m*
2 *vt* (**a**) *(tug)* dar un tirón a; **to p. a muscle** sufrir un tirón en un músculo; **to p. the trigger** apretar el gatillo; **to p. to pieces** hacer pedazos; *Fig* poner algo por los suelos; *Fig* **to p. sb's leg** tomar el pelo a algn (**b**) *(draw)* tirar, arrastrar; *Fig* **to p. one's weight** hacer su parte del trabajo (**c**) *(draw out)* sacar (**d**) *Fam (people)* atraer
3 *vi (drag)* tirar; **to p. alongside sb** acercarse a algn
▸ **pull apart** *vt sep* desmontar; *Fig (criticize)* poner por los suelos
▸ **pull down** *vt sep (building)* derribar
▸ **pull in 1** *vt sep (crowds)* atraer
2 *vi (train)* entrar en la estación; *(stop)* parar
▸ **pull off 1** *vt sep Fam (carry out)* llevar a cabo
2 *vi (vehicle)* arrancar
▸ **pull out 1** *vt sep (withdraw)* retirar
2 *vi Aut* **to p. out to overtake** salir para adelantar
▸ **pull over** *vi* hacerse a un lado
▸ **pull through** *vi* reponerse, restablecerse
▸ **pull together** *vt sep* **to p. oneself together** calmarse
▸ **pull up 1** *vt sep* (**a**) *(uproot)* desarraigar; **to p. up one's socks** subirse los calcetines; *Fig* espabilarse (**b**) *(chair)* acercar
2 *vi (stop)* pararse
pulley ['pʊlɪ] *n* polea *f*
pullover ['pʊləʊvə(r)] *n* jersey *m*, suéter *m*, pulóver *m*, *Andes* chompa *f*, *Urug* buzo *m*
pulp [pʌlp] **1** *n* (*of paper, wood*) pasta *f*; *(of fruit)* pulpa *f*; *Fam Fig (book etc)* basura *f*
2 *vt* reducir a pulpa
pulpit ['pʊlpɪt] *n* púlpito *m*
pulsate [pʌl'seɪt] *vi* vibrar, palpitar
pulse¹ [pʌls] *n Anat* pulso *m*
pulse² [pʌls] *n Bot & Culin* legumbre *f*
pumice ['pʌmɪs] *n* **p. (stone)** piedra *f* pómez
pummel ['pʌməl] *vt* aporrear
pump¹ [pʌmp] **1** *n* bomba *f*
2 *vt* bombear; **to p. sth in/out** meter/

sacar algo con una bomba; *Fam Fig* **to p. sb for information** sonsacar información a algn
▸ **pump out** *vt sep (empty)* vaciar
▸ **pump up** *vt sep (tyre)* inflar
pump² [pʌmp] *n (shoe)* zapatilla *f*
pumpkin ['pʌmpkɪn] *n* calabaza *f*
pun [pʌn] *n* juego *m* de palabras
punch¹ [pʌntʃ] **1** *n (for making holes)* perforadora *f*; *(for tickets)* taladradora *f*; *(for leather etc)* punzón *m*
2 *vt (make hole in)* perforar; *(ticket)* picar; *(leather)* punzar
punch² [pʌntʃ] **1** *n (blow)* puñetazo *m*; *(in boxing)* pegada *f*; *Fig* **it lacks p.** le falta fuerza; **p. line** remate *m (de un chiste)*
2 *vt (with fist)* dar un puñetazo a
punch³ [pʌntʃ] *n (drink)* ponche *m*
punch-up ['pʌntʃʌp] *n Fam* pelea *f*
punctual ['pʌŋktjʊəl] *adj* puntual
punctuate ['pʌŋktjʊeɪt] *vt* puntuar; *Fig* salpicar
punctuation [pʌŋktjʊ'eɪʃən] *n* puntuación *f*
puncture ['pʌŋktʃə(r)] **1** *n* pinchazo *m*
2 *vt (tyre)* pinchar
pundit ['pʌndɪt] *n Fam* experto(a) *m,f*
pungent ['pʌndʒənt] *adj (smell)* acre; *(taste)* fuerte
punish ['pʌnɪʃ] *vt* castigar
punishable ['pʌnɪʃəbəl] *adj* castigable, punible
punishment ['pʌnɪʃmənt] *n* castigo *m*
punk [pʌŋk] *n Fam* (**a**) *punk mf*; **p. music** música *f* punk (**b**) *US* mamón *m*
punt [pʌnt] **1** *n (boat)* batea *f*
2 *vi* ir en batea
punter ['pʌntə(r)] *n Br (gambler)* jugador(a) *m,f*; *(customer)* cliente(a) *m,f*
puny ['pjuːnɪ] *adj* (**punier, puniest**) enclenque, endeble
pup [pʌp] *n* cachorro(a) *m,f*
pupil¹ ['pjuːpəl] *n Educ* alumno(a) *m,f*
pupil² ['pjuːpəl] *n Anat* pupila *f*
puppet ['pʌpɪt] *n* títere *m*
puppy ['pʌpɪ] *n* cachorro(a) *m,f*, perrito *m*
purchase ['pɜːtʃɪs] **1** *n* compra *f*
2 *vt* comprar; **purchasing power** poder adquisitivo
purchaser ['pɜːtʃɪsə(r)] *n* comprador(a) *m,f*
pure [pjʊə(r)] *adj* puro(a)
purée ['pjʊəreɪ] *n* puré *m*
purely ['pjʊəlɪ] *adv* simplemente
purge [pɜːdʒ] **1** *n* purga *f*
2 *vt* purgar
purify ['pjʊərɪfaɪ] *vt* purificar

purl [pɜːl] *vt (in knitting)* hacer punto del revés

purple ['pɜːpəl] *adj* morado(a), purpúreo(a); **to go p. (in the face)** ponerse morado(a)

purport [pɜː'pɔːt] *vi Fml* pretender; **to p. to be sth** pretender ser algo

purpose ['pɜːpəs] *n* (**a**) propósito *m*, intención *f*; **on p.** a propósito (**b**) *(use)* utilidad *f*

purposeful ['pɜːpəsfʊl] *adj (resolute)* decidido(a), resoluto(a)

purr [pɜː(r)] *vi (cat)* ronronear; *(engine)* zumbar

purse [pɜːs] **1** *n Br* monedero *m*; *US (bag)* bolso *m*, cartera *f*, *Méx* bolsa *f*; *(prize money)* premio *m* en metálico
2 *vt* **to p. one's lips** apretarse los labios

purser ['pɜːsə(r)] *n* contador(a) *m,f*

pursue [pə'sjuː] *vt (criminal)* perseguir; *(person)* seguir; *(pleasure)* buscar; *(career)* ejercer

pursuer [pə'sjuːə(r)] *n Fml* perseguidor(a) *m,f*

pursuit [pə'sjuːt] *n (of criminal)* persecución *f*, *(of animal)* caza *f*, *(of pleasure)* búsqueda *f*; *(pastime)* pasatiempo *m*

purveyor [pə'veɪə(r)] *n Fml* proveedor(a) *m,f*

pus [pʌs] *n* pus *m*

push [pʊʃ] **1** *n* empujón *m*; *Fig (drive)* brío *m*, dinamismo *m*
2 *vt* (**a**) empujar; *(button)* pulsar, apretar; **to p. one's finger into a hole** meter el dedo en un agujero (**b**) *Fig (pressurize)* instar; *(harass)* acosar; *Fam* **to be (hard) pushed for time** andar justo(a) de tiempo (**c**) *Fam (product)* promover; **to p. drugs** pasar droga
3 *vi* empujar

▶ **push aside** *vt sep (object)* apartar

▶ **push in** *vi* colarse

▶ **push off** *vi (in boat)* desatracar; *Fam* **p. off!** ¡lárgate!

▶ **push on** *vi (continue)* seguir adelante

▶ **push through** *vt sep* abrirse paso entre

pushchair ['pʊʃtʃeə(r)] *n Br* sillita *f* (de ruedas)

pusher ['pʊʃə(r)] *n Fam (of drugs)* camello *m*

pushover ['pʊʃəʊvə(r)] *n Fam* **it's a p.** está chupado; **she's a p.** es un ligue fácil

push-up ['pʊʃʌp] *n* flexión *f* (de brazos)

pushy ['pʊʃɪ] *adj* (**pushier, pushiest**) *Fam* agresivo(a)

puss [pʊs], **pussy** ['pʊsɪ] *n Fam* minino *m*

put [pʊt] **1** *vt* (*pt & pp* **put**) (**a**) poner; *(place)* colocar; *(insert)* meter; **to p. to**

bed acostar a; **to p. a picture up on the wall** colgar un cuadro en la pared; **to p. a stop to sth** poner término a algo; *Fig* **to p. one's foot in it** meter la pata
(**b**) *(present)* presentar, exponer; **to p. a question to sb** hacer una pregunta a algn
(**c**) *(express)* expresar, decir; **to p. it mildly** y me quedo corto; **to p. sth simply** explicar algo de manera sencilla
(**d**) *(estimate)* calcular
(**e**) *(money)* ingresar; *(invest)* invertir
2 *vi Naut* **to p. to sea** zarpar
3 *adv* **to stay p.** quedarse quieto(a)

▶ **put about** *vt sep (rumour)* hacer correr

▶ **put across** *vt sep (idea etc)* comunicar

▶ **put aside** *vt sep (money)* ahorrar; *(time)* reservar

▶ **put away** *vt sep (tidy away)* recoger; *Fam (eat)* zamparse; *(save money)* ahorrar

▶ **put back** *vt sep (postpone)* aplazar; **to p. the clock back** retrasar la hora

▶ **put by** *vt sep (money)* ahorrar

▶ **put down** *vt sep (set down)* dejar; *(suppress)* sofocar; *(humiliate)* humillar; *(criticize)* criticar; *(animal)* provocar la muerte de; *(write down)* apuntar

▶ **put down to** *vt sep* achacar a

▶ **put forward** *vt sep (theory)* exponer; *(proposal)* hacer; **to p. one's name forward for sth** presentarse como candidato(a) para algo

▶ **put in 1** *vt sep (install)* instalar; *(complaint, request)* presentar; *(time)* pasar
2 *vi Naut* hacer escala (**at** en)

▶ **put off** *vt sep (postpone)* aplazar; **to p. sb off (doing) sth** *(dissuade)* disuadir a algn de (hacer) algo

▶ **put on** *vt sep (clothes)* poner, ponerse; *(show)* montar; *(concert)* dar; *(switch on) (radio)* poner; *(light)* encender; *(water, gas)* abrir; **to p. on weight** aumentar de peso; **to p. on the brakes** frenar; *Fig* **to p. on a straight face** poner cara de serio(a)

▶ **put out** *vt sep (light, fire)* apagar; *(place outside)* sacar; *(extend) (arm)* extender; *(tongue)* sacar; *(hand)* tender; *(spread) (rumour)* hacer correr; *(annoy)* molestar; *(inconvenience)* incordiar; *(anger)* **to be p. out by sth** enojarse por algo

▶ **put through** *vt sep Tel* **p. me through to Pat, please** póngame con Pat, por favor

▶ **put together** *vt sep (join)* unir, reunir; *(assemble)* armar, montar

▶ **put up** *vt sep (raise)* levantar, subir; *(picture)* colocar; *(curtains)* colgar; *(building)* construir; *(tent)* armar; *(prices)*

subir, aumentar; *(accommodate)* alojar, hospedar; **to p. up a fight** ofrecer resistencia

▸ **put up to** *vt sep* **to p. sb up to sth** incitar a algn a hacer algo

▸ **put up with** *vt insep* aguantar, soportar

putrid ['pjuːtrɪd] *adj Fml* putrefacto(a)

putt [pʌt] **1** *n* tiro *m* al hoyo

2 *vt & vi* tirar al hoyo

putting ['pʌtɪŋ] *n* **p. green** minigolf *m*

putty ['pʌtɪ] *n* masilla *f*

puzzle ['pʌzəl] **1** *n* rompecabezas *m inv*; *(crossword)* crucigrama *m*; *Fig (mystery)* misterio *m*

2 *vt* dejar perplejo(a); **to be puzzled about sth** no entender algo

▸ **puzzle over** *vt insep* **to p. over sth** dar vueltas a algo (en la cabeza)

puzzling ['pʌzlɪŋ] *adj* extraño(a), curioso(a)

PVC [piːviːˈsiː] *n (abbr* **polyvinyl chloride)** PVC *m*

pygmy ['pɪgmɪ] *n* pigmeo(a) *m,f; Fig* enano(a) *m,f*

pyjamas [pəˈdʒɑːməz] *npl* pijama *m*

pylon ['paɪlən] *n* torre *f* (de conducción eléctrica)

pyramid ['pɪrəmɪd] *n* pirámide *f*

Pyrenees [pɪrəˈniːz] *npl* **the P.** los Pirineos

Pyrex® ['paɪreks] *n* pírex® *m*

python ['paɪθən] *n* pitón *m*

Q

Q, q [kjuː] *n (the letter)* Q, q *f*

quack [kwæk] **1** *n* (**a**) *(of duck)* graznido *m* (**b**) *Fam (doctor)* curandero(a) *m,f*
2 *vi* graznar

quad [kwɒd] *n Fam* (**a**) *Br (of school, university)* patio *m* interior (**b**) *(quadruplet)* cuatrillizo(a) *m,f*

quadrangle ['kwɒdræŋɡəl] *n* (**a**) *Geom* cuadrángulo *m* (**b**) *(courtyard)* patio *m* interior

quadruple ['kwɒdrʊpəl, kwɒ'druːpəl] **1** *n* cuádruplo *m*
2 *adj* cuádruple
3 *vt* cuadruplicar
4 *vi* cuadruplicarse

quadruplet ['kwɒdrʊplɪt, kwɒ'druːplɪt] *n* cuatrillizo(a) *m,f*

quagmire ['kwæɡmaɪə(r), 'kwɒɡmaɪə(r)] *n (land)* cenagal *m*

quail¹ [kweɪl] *n Orn* codorniz *f*

quail² [kweɪl] *vi Fig* encogerse

quaint [kweɪnt] *adj (picturesque)* pintoresco(a); *(original)* singular

quake [kweɪk] **1** *vi* temblar
2 *n Fam* temblor *m* de tierra

Quaker ['kweɪkə(r)] *n* cuáquero(a) *m,f*

qualification [kwɒlɪfɪ'keɪʃən] *n* (**a**) *(ability)* aptitud *f* (**b**) *(requirement)* requisito *m* (**c**) *(diploma etc)* título *m* (**d**) *(reservation)* reserva *f*

qualified ['kwɒlɪfaɪd] *adj* (**a**) capacitado(a); **q. teacher** profesor titulado (**b**) **q. approval** *(modified)* aprobación *f* condicional

qualify ['kwɒlɪfaɪ] **1** *vt* (**a**) *(entitle)* capacitar (**b**) *(modify)* modificar; *(statement)* matizar; *Ling* calificar
2 *vi* (**a**) **to q. as** *(doctor etc)* sacar el título de; **when did you q.?** ¿cúando terminaste la carrera? (**b**) *(in competition)* quedar clasificado(a)

qualifying ['kwɒlɪfaɪɪŋ] *adj (round, exam)* eliminatorio(a)

quality ['kwɒlɪtɪ] *n* (**a**) *(excellence)* calidad *f*; **q. control** control *m* de calidad; *Br* **q. newspapers** prensa *f* no sensacionalista (**b**) *(attribute)* cualidad *f*

qualm [kwɑːm] *n* (**a**) *(scruple)* escrúpulo *m* (**b**) *(doubt)* duda *f*

quandary ['kwɒndərɪ, 'kwɒndrɪ] *n* **to be in a q.** estar en un dilema

quango ['kwæŋɡəʊ] *n* = organización semi-autónoma paralela

quantity ['kwɒntɪtɪ] *n* cantidad *f*

quarantine ['kwɒrəntiːn] *n* cuarentena *f*

quarrel ['kwɒrəl] **1** *n (argument)* riña *f*, pelea *f*; *(disagreement)* desacuerdo *m*
2 *vi (argue)* pelearse, reñir; **to q. with sth** discrepar de algo

quarrelsome ['kwɒrəlsəm] *adj* camorrista

quarry¹ ['kwɒrɪ] *Min* **1** *n* cantera *f*
2 *vt* extraer

quarry² ['kwɒrɪ] *n* presa *f*

quart [kwɔːt] *n (measurement)* = cuarto de galón (*Br = 1,13 l; US = 0,94 l*)

quarter ['kwɔːtə(r)] **1** *n* (**a**) cuarto *m*, cuarta parte; **a q. of an hour** un cuarto de hora; **a q. of a cake** la cuarta parte de un pastel
(**b**) **it's a q.** *Br* **to** *or US* **of three** son las tres menos cuarto; **it's a q.** *Br* **past** *or US* **after six** son las seis y cuarto
(**c**) *(three months)* trimestre *m*
(**d**) *Br (weight)* cuarto *m* de libra
(**e**) *US (coin)* cuarto *m* (de dólar)
(**f**) *(district)* barrio *m*
(**g**) **there was criticism from all quarters** *(areas, people)* todos lo criticaron
(**h**) *(of moon)* cuarto *m*
(**i**) **quarters** *(lodgings)* alojamiento *m*; *Mil* **officers' quarters** residencia *f* de oficiales; **at close quarters** muy cerca
(**j**) *US Mus* **q. note** negra *f*
2 *vt* (**a**) *(cut into quarters)* dividir en cuartos
(**b**) *(accommodate)* alojar

quarterfinal ['kwɔːtəfaɪnəl] *n Sport* cuarto *m* de final

quarterly ['kwɔːtəlɪ] **1** *adj* trimestral
2 *n* publicación *f* trimestral
3 *adv* trimestralmente

quartermaster ['kwɔːtəmɑːstə(r)] *n* (**a**) *Mil* oficial *m* de intendencia (**b**) *Naut* cabo *m* de la Marina

quartet(te) [kwɔː'tet] *n* cuarteto *m*

quartz [kwɔːts] *n* cuarzo *m*; **q. watch** reloj *m* de cuarzo

quash [kwɒʃ] *vt Jur* anular; *(uprising)* aplastar

quasi ['kwɑːzɪ, 'kweɪzaɪ, 'kweɪsaɪ] *pref* cuasi

quaver ['kweɪvə(r)] **1** *n* (a) *Mus* corchea *f* (b) *(in voice)* temblor *m*
2 *vi (voice)* temblar

quay(side) ['kiː(saɪd)] *n* muelle *m*

queasy ['kwiːzɪ] *adj* (**queasier, queasiest**) **to feel q.** *(ill)* tener náuseas

queen [kwiːn] *n* (a) reina *f* (b) *Fam Pej* loca *f*, marica *m*

queer [kwɪə(r)] **1** *adj* (a) *(strange)* extraño(a), raro(a) (b) *Fam (mad)* loco(a) (c) *Fam (unwell)* mareado(a) (d) *Fam Pej* maricón
2 *n Fam Pej* marica *m*, maricón *m*

quell [kwel] *vt* reprimir

quench [kwentʃ] *vt* apagar

querulous ['kwerʊləs, 'kwerjʊləs] *adj Fml* quejumbroso(a)

query ['kwɪərɪ] **1** *n (question)* pregunta *f*
2 *vt (ask questions about)* preguntar acerca de; *(have doubts about)* poner en duda

quest [kwest] *n Literary* búsqueda *f*, busca *f*

question ['kwestʃən] **1** *n* (a) *(interrogative)* pregunta *f*; **to ask sb a q.** hacer una pregunta a algn; **he did it without q.** lo hizo sin rechistar; **q. mark** signo *m* de interrogación; *Fig* interrogante *m* (b) *(problem, issue)* asunto *m*, cuestión *f*; **it's a q. of two hours** es cuestión de dos horas (c) *(doubt)* duda *f*; **beyond q.** fuera de duda; **in q.** en duda; **to call sth into q.** poner algo en duda (d) **out of the q.** imposible; **that's out of the q.!** ¡ni hablar! (e) *Educ* problema *m*
2 *vt (ask questions of)* hacer preguntas a; *(interrogate)* interrogar; *(query)* poner en duda

questionable ['kwestʃənəbəl] *adj (doubtful)* dudoso(a); *(debatable)* discutible

questionnaire [kwestʃə'neə(r)] *n* cuestionario *m*

queue [kjuː] *Br* **1** *n* cola *f*
2 *vi* **to q. (up)** hacer cola

quibble ['kwɪbəl] **1** *n* pega *f*
2 *vi* poner pegas (**with** a); *Fam* buscarle tres pies al gato

quiche [kiːʃ] *n* quiche *m* or *f*

quick [kwɪk] *adj* (a) *(fast)* rápido(a); **a q. look** un vistazo; **a q. snack** un bocado; **be q.!** ¡date prisa! (b) *(clever)* espabilado(a);

(wit) agudo(a) (c) **she has a q. temper** se enfada con nada

quicken ['kwɪkən] **1** *vt* acelerar; **to q. one's pace** acelerar el paso
2 *vi (speed up)* acelerarse

quickly ['kwɪklɪ] *adv* rápidamente, de prisa

quickness ['kwɪknɪs] *n* (a) *(speed)* rapidez *f* (b) *(of wit)* agudeza *f*, viveza *f*

quicksand ['kwɪksænd] *n* arenas movedizas

quicksilver ['kwɪksɪlvə(r)] *n* mercurio *m*

quick-witted [kwɪk'wɪtɪd] *adj* agudo(a)

quid [kwɪd] *n* (*pl* **quid**) *Br Fam* libra *f* (esterlina)

quiet ['kwaɪət] **1** *n* (a) *(silence)* silencio *m* (b) *(calm)* tranquilidad *f*
2 *adj* (a) *(silent)* silencioso(a); *(street)* tranquilo(a); **a q. voice** una voz suave; **keep q.!** ¡silencio! (b) *(calm)* tranquilo(a) (c) *Com & Fin* **business is q. today** hoy hay poco negocio (d) *(person)* reservado(a) (e) *(secret)* confidencial (f) *(not showy) (clothes)* sobrio(a); *(colours)* apagado(a) (g) *(ceremony, dinner)* íntimo(a)
2 *vt US* calmar
3 *vi US* calmarse

quieten ['kwaɪətən] **1** *vt (silence)* callar; *(calm)* calmar
2 *vi (silence)* callarse; *(calm)* calmarse
▶ **quieten down** *Br* **1** *vt sep* calmar
2 *vi* calmarse

quietly ['kwaɪətlɪ] *adv* (a) *(silently)* silenciosamente; **he spoke q.** habló en voz baja (b) *(calmly)* tranquilamente (c) *(discreetly)* discretamente

quietness ['kwaɪətnɪs] *n* (a) *(silence)* silencio *m* (b) *(calm)* tranquilidad *f*

quill [kwɪl] *n (feather, pen)* pluma *f*; *(of porcupine)* púa *f*

quilt [kwɪlt] **1** *n* edredón *m*
2 *vt* acolchar

quin [kwɪn] *n Fam* quintillizo(a) *m,f*

quinine ['kwɪniːn, *US* 'kwaɪnaɪn] *n* quinina *f*

quint [kwɪnt] *n Fam US* = **quin**

quintessential [kwɪntɪ'senʃəl] *adj* fundamental

quintet(te) [kwɪn'tet] *n* quinteto *m*

quintuple ['kwɪntjʊpəl, kwɪn'tjuːpəl] **1** *adj* quíntuplo(a)
2 *n* quíntuplo *m*
3 *vt* quintuplicar

quintuplet ['kwɪntjʊplɪt, kwɪn'tjuːplɪt] *n* quintillizo(a) *m,f*

quip [kwɪp] **1** *n* salida *f*; *(joke)* chiste *m*
2 *vi* bromear

quirk [kwɜːk] *n* (a) *(peculiarity)* manía *f*

(**b**) *(of fate)* arbitrariedad *f*

quit [kwɪt] **1** *vt* (*pt & pp* **quitted** or **quit**) (**a**) *(leave)* dejar, abandonar (**b**) **q. making that noise!** ¡deja de hacer ese ruido!

2 *vi* (**a**) *(go)* irse; *(give up)* dimitir (**b**) *(cease)* dejar de hacer algo

3 *adj* **let's call it quits** dejémoslo estar

ℓ Note that the Spanish verb **quitar** is a false friend and is never a translation for the English verb **to quit**. In Spanish, **quitar** means both "to remove" and "to take away".

---

quite [kwaɪt] *adv* (**a**) *(entirely)* totalmente; **she's q. right** tiene toda la razón (**b**) *(rather)* bastante; **q. a few** bastantes; **q. a while** un buen rato; **q. often** con bastante frecuencia; **that's q. enough!** ¡ya está bien! (**c**) **he's q. a character** es un tipo original; **it's q. something** es increíble (**d**) *(exactly)* exactamente; **q.**

(**so**)! ¡en efecto!, ¡exacto!

quiver¹ ['kwɪvə(r)] *vi* temblar

quiver² ['kwɪvə(r)] *n* *(for arrows)* aljaba *f*, carcaj *m*

quiz [kwɪz] **1** *n* *Rad & TV* **q. show** concurso *m*

2 *vt* hacer preguntas a

quizzical ['kwɪzɪkəl] *adj* (**a**) *(bemused)* burlón(ona) (**b**) *(enquiring)* curioso(a)

quota ['kwəʊtə] *n* (**a**) *(proportional share)* cuota *f*, parte *f* (**b**) *(prescribed amount, number)* cupo *m*

quotation [kwəʊ'teɪʃən] *n* (**a**) *Lit* cita *f*; **q. marks** comillas *fpl* (**b**) *Fin* cotización *f*

quote [kwəʊt] **1** *vt* (**a**) *(cite)* citar (**b**) *Com* **to q. a price** dar un presupuesto (**c**) *Fin* cotizar

2 *n* (**a**) *Lit* cita *f* (**b**) *Com* presupuesto *m*

quotient ['kwəʊʃənt] *n* cociente *m*

R, r [ɑː(r)] *n (the letter)* R, r *f*
rabbi ['ræbaɪ] *n* rabí *m*, rabino *m*
rabbit ['ræbɪt] **1** *n* conejo(a) *m,f*; **r. hutch** conejera *f*
 2 *vi Fam* **to r. (on)** enrollarse
rabble ['ræbəl] *n Pej* **the r.** el populacho
rabies ['reɪbiːz] *n* rabia *f*
RAC [ɑːreɪ'siː] *n Br (abbr Royal Automobile Club)* = organización británica de ayuda al automovilista, ≃ RACE *m*
race¹ [reɪs] **1** *n* (**a**) *Sport* carrera *f* (**b**) *Br* **the races** las carreras (de caballos)
 2 *vt* (**a**) **I'll r. you!** ¡te echo una carrera! (**b**) *(car, horse)* hacer correr (**c**) *(engine)* acelerar
 3 *vi (go quickly)* correr; *(pulse)* acelerarse
race² [reɪs] *n (people)* raza *f*
racecourse ['reɪskɔːs] *n Br* hipódromo *m*
racehorse ['reɪshɔːs] *n* caballo *m* de carreras
racer ['reɪsə(r)] *n Sport* (**a**) *(person)* corredor(a) *m,f* (**b**) *(bicycle)* bicicleta *f* de carreras; *(car)* coche *m* de carreras
racetrack ['reɪstræk] *n (for cars, people, bikes)* pista *f*; *US (for horses)* hipódromo *m*
racial ['reɪʃəl] *adj* racial
racing ['reɪsɪŋ] **1** *n* carreras *fpl*
 2 *adj* de carreras; **r. car/bike** coche *m*/moto *f* de carreras
racism ['reɪsɪzəm] *n* racismo *m*
racist ['reɪsɪst] *adj & n* racista *(mf)*
rack [ræk] **1** *n* (**a**) *(shelf)* estante *m*; *(for clothes)* percha *f*; **luggage r.** portaequipajes *m inv*; **roof r.** baca *f* (**b**) *(for torture)* potro *m*
 2 *vt Literary (torment)* atormentar; *Fam Fig* **to r. one's brains** devanarse los sesos
racket¹ ['rækɪt] *n* (**a**) *(din)* ruido *m*, jaleo *m* (**b**) *(swindle)* timo *m*; *(shady business)* chanchullo *m*
racket² ['rækɪt] *n Sport* raqueta *f*
racquet ['rækɪt] *n* = **racket²**
racy ['reɪsɪ] *adj* (**racier, raciest**) *(lively)* vivo(a); *(risqué)* atrevido(a)
radar ['reɪdɑː(r)] *n* radar *m*
radiance ['reɪdɪəns] *n* resplandor *m*

radiant ['reɪdɪənt] *adj* radiante, resplandeciente
radiate ['reɪdɪeɪt] *vt* irradiar; *Fig* **she radiated happiness** rebosaba de alegría
radiation [reɪdɪ'eɪʃən] *n* radiación *f*
radiator ['reɪdɪeɪtə(r)] *n* radiador *m*
radical ['rædɪkəl] *adj* radical
radio ['reɪdɪəʊ] *n* radio *f*; **on the r.** en *or* por la radio; **r. station** emisora *f* (de radio)
radioactive [reɪdɪəʊ'æktɪv] *adj* radiactivo(a)
radio-controlled [reɪdɪəʊkən'trəʊld] *adj* teledirigido(a)
radiography [reɪdɪ'ɒɡrəfɪ] *n* radiografía *f*
radiology [reɪdɪ'ɒlədʒɪ] *n* radiología *f*
radiotherapy [reɪdɪəʊ'θerəpɪ] *n* radioterapia *f*
radish ['rædɪʃ] *n* rábano *m*
radius ['reɪdɪəs] *n* radio *m*; **within a r. of** en un radio de
RAF [ɑːreɪ'ef] *n Br (abbr Royal Air Force)* = fuerzas aéreas británicas
raffle ['ræfəl] **1** *n* rifa *f*
 2 *vt* rifar
raft [rɑːft] *n* balsa *f*
rafter ['rɑːftə(r)] *n* viga *f* de madera
rag¹ [ræɡ] *n* (**a**) *(torn piece)* harapo *m*; **r. doll** muñeca *f* de trapo (**b**) *(for cleaning)* trapo *m* (**c**) *Fam* **rags** *(clothes)* trapos *mpl* (**d**) *Pej Press* periodicucho *m*
rag² [ræɡ] **1** *n Br Univ* función benéfica
 2 *vt* gastar bromas a
rag-and-bone ['ræɡən'bəʊn] *adj Br* **r. man** trapero *m*
rage [reɪdʒ] **1** *n* (**a**) *(fury)* cólera *f* (**b**) *Fam* **it's all the r.** hace furor
 2 *vi* (**a**) *(person)* rabiar, estar furioso(a) (**b**) *Fig (storm, sea)* rugir; *(wind)* bramar
ragged ['ræɡɪd] *adj* (**a**) *(clothes)* hecho(a) jirones (**b**) *(person)* harapiento(a) (**c**) *(edge)* mellado(a) (**d**) *Fig (uneven)* desigual
raging ['reɪdʒɪŋ] *adj* (**a**) *(angry)* furioso(a) (**b**) *Fig (sea)* embravecido(a) (**c**) *(intense)* feroz; *(storm)* violento(a)
raid [reɪd] **1** *n Mil* incursión *f*; *(by police)* redada *f*; *(robbery etc)* atraco *m*
 2 *vt Mil* hacer una incursión en; *(police)*

hacer una redada en; *(rob)* asaltar; *Fam* **to r. the larder** vaciar la despensa

raider ['reɪdə(r)] *n (invader)* invasor(a) *m,f*

rail [reɪl] *n* (a) barra *f* (b) *(railing)* barandilla *f* (c) *Rail* carril *f*; **by r.** *(send sth)* por ferrocarril; *(travel)* en tren

railcard ['reɪlkɑːd] *n Br* abono *m*

railing ['reɪlɪŋ] *n (usu pl)* verja *f*

railroad ['reɪlrəʊd] *n US* ferrocarril *m*

railway ['reɪlweɪ] *n Br* ferrocarril *m*; **r. line, r. track** vía férrea; **r. station** estación *f* de ferrocarril

railwayman ['reɪlweɪmən] *n Br* ferroviario *m*

rain [reɪn] **1** *n* lluvia *f*; **in the r.** bajo la lluvia

2 *vi* llover; **it's raining** llueve

rainbow ['reɪnbəʊ] *n* arco *m* iris

raincoat ['reɪnkəʊt] *n* impermeable *m*

raindrop ['reɪndrɒp] *n* gota *f* de lluvia

rainfall ['reɪnfɔːl] *n (falling of rain)* precipitación *f*; *(amount)* pluviosidad *f*

rainforest ['reɪnfɒrɪst] *n* selva *f* tropical

rainy ['reɪnɪ] *adj* (**rainier, rainiest**) lluvioso(a)

raise [reɪz] **1** *n US* aumento *m* (de sueldo)

2 *vt* (a) levantar; *(glass)* brindar; *(voice)* subir; *(building)* erigir (b) *(prices)* aumentar (c) *(money, help)* reunir (d) *(issue)* plantear (e) *(crops, children)* criar (f) *Rad* comunicar con (g) *(standards)* mejorar (h) *(laugh)* provocar

raisin ['reɪzən] *n* pasa *f*

rake¹ [reɪk] **1** *n (garden tool)* rastrillo *m*; *(for fire)* hurgón *m*

2 *vt (leaves)* rastrillar; *(fire)* hurgar; *(with machine gun)* barrer

rake² [reɪk] *n (dissolute man)* calavera *m*, libertino *m*

rally ['rælɪ] **1** *n* (a) *(gathering)* reunión *f*; *Pol* mitin *m* (b) *Aut* rallye *m* (c) *(in tennis)* jugada *f*

2 *vt (support)* reunir

3 *vi* recuperarse

▶ **rally round** *vi* formar una piña

RAM [ræm] *n Comput (abbr* **random access memory)** RAM *f*

ram [ræm] **1** *n* (a) *Zool* carnero *m* (b) *Tech* maza *f*

2 *vt* (a) *(drive into place)* hincar; *(cram)* embutir; *Fam* **to r. sth home** hacer algo patente (b) *(crash into)* chocar con

ramble ['ræmbəl] **1** *n (walk)* caminata *f*

2 *vi* (a) *(walk)* hacer una excursión a pie (b) *Fig (digress)* divagar

rambler ['ræmblə(r)] *n* (a) *(person)* excursionista *mf* (b) *Bot* rosal *m* trepador

rambling ['ræmblɪŋ] *adj* (a) *(incoherent)* incoherente (b) *(house)* laberíntico(a) (c) *Bot* trepador(a)

ramp [ræmp] *n* (a) rampa *f* (b) *Av (movable stairway)* escalerilla *f*

rampage 1 *n* ['ræmpeɪdʒ] **to be on the r.** desmandarse

2 *vi* [ræm'peɪdʒ] **to r. about** comportarse como un loco

rampant ['ræmpənt] *adj* incontrolado(a); **corruption is r.** la corrupción está muy extendida

rampart ['ræmpɑːt] *n* muralla *f*

ramshackle ['ræmʃækəl] *adj* destartalado(a)

ran [ræn] *pt of* **run**

ranch [rɑːntʃ] *n US* rancho *m*, hacienda *f*

rancher ['rɑːntʃə(r)] *n US* ranchero(a) *m,f*

rancid ['rænsɪd] *adj* rancio(a)

rancour, *US* **rancor** ['ræŋkə(r)] *n Fml* rencor *m*

R & D [ɑːrən'diː] *n (abbr* **Research and Development)** I+D

random ['rændəm] **1** *n* **at r.** al azar

2 *adj* fortuito(a); **r. selection** selección hecha al azar

randy ['rændɪ] *adj* (**randier, randiest**) *Br Fam* cachondo(a), caliente

rang [ræŋ] *pt of* **ring**

range [reɪndʒ] **1** *n* (a) *(of mountains)* cordillera *f*, sierra *f* (b) *(of open land)* pradera *f* (c) *(choice)* surtido *m*; *(of products)* gama *f* (d) *Mus* registro *m* (e) **firing r.** campo *m* de tiro (f) *(of missile)* alcance *m*; **at close r.** de cerca; **long-/short-r. missiles** misiles *mpl* de largo/corto alcance (g) *Culin* cocina *f* de carbón

2 *vi (extend)* extenderse (**to** hasta); **prices r. from £5 to £20 pounds** los precios oscilan entre 5 y 20 libras

3 *vt Literary (wander)* vagar por

ranger ['reɪndʒə(r)] *n* (a) **(forest) r.** guardabosques *mf inv* (b) *US (mounted policeman)* policía montado

rank¹ [ræŋk] **1** *n* (a) *Mil (row)* fila *f*; **the ranks** los soldados rasos; **the r. and file** la base (b) *(position in army)* graduación *f*; *(in society)* rango *m* (c) *(taxi)* **r.** parada *f* de taxis

2 *vt (classify)* clasificar

3 *vi (figure)* figurar; **to r. above/below sb** figurar por encima/debajo de algn; **to r. with** estar al mismo nivel que

rank² [ræŋk] *adj Fml* (a) *(vegetation)* exuberante (b) *(foul-smelling)* fétido(a) (c) *(thorough)* total, absoluto(a)

ransack ['rænsæk] *vt (plunder)* saquear; *(rummage in)* registrar

ransom ['rænsəm] *n* rescate *m*; **to hold sb to r.** pedir rescate por algn; *Fig* poner a algn entre la espada y la pared

rant [rænt] *vi* vociferar; *Fam* **to r. and rave** pegar gritos

rap [ræp] **1** *n* (a) *(blow)* golpe *m* seco; *(on door)* golpecito *m* (b) *Mus* rap *m*
2 *vt & vi (knock)* golpear

rape¹ [reɪp] *Jur* **1** *n* violación *f*
2 *vt* violar

rape² [reɪp] *n Bot* colza *f*

rapeseed ['reɪpsiːd] *n* **r. oil** aceite *m* de colza

rapid ['ræpɪd] **1** *adj* rápido(a)
2 *n* **rapids** *(in river)* rápidos *mpl*

rapidity [rə'pɪdɪtɪ] *n* rapidez *f*

rapist ['reɪpɪst] *n* violador(a) *m,f*

rapport [ræ'pɔː(r)] *n* compenetración *f*

rapture ['ræptʃə(r)] *n* éxtasis *m*

rapturous ['ræptʃərəs] *adj* muy entusiasta

rare¹ [reə(r)] *adj* raro(a), poco común

rare² [reə(r)] *adj (steak)* poco hecho(a)

rarefied ['reərɪfaɪd] *adj* enrarecido(a)

rarely ['reəlɪ] *adv* raras veces

raring ['reərɪŋ] *adj Fam* **to be r. to do sth** morirse de ganas de hacer algo

rarity ['reərɪtɪ] *n* rareza *f*

rascal ['rɑːskəl] *n* granuja *mf*

rash¹ [ræʃ] *n* (a) *Med* erupción *f*, sarpullido *m* (b) *Fig (of robberies etc)* racha *f*

rash² [ræʃ] *adj (reckless)* impetuoso(a); *(words, actions)* precipitado(a), imprudente

rasher ['ræʃə(r)] *n* loncha *f*

raspberry ['rɑːzbərɪ] *n* frambuesa *f*

rasping ['rɑːspɪŋ] *adj* áspero(a)

rat [ræt] *n* (a) *(animal)* rata *f*; **r. poison** raticida *m* (b) *US Fam (informer)* soplón(ona) *m,f*, chivato(a) *m,f*

rate [reɪt] **1** *n* (a) *(ratio)* índice *m*, tasa *f*; **at any r.** *(at least)* al menos; *(anyway)* en cualquier caso (b) *(cost)* precio *m*; *Fin (of interest, exchange)* tipo *m* (c) **at the r. of** *(speed)* a la velocidad de; *(quantity)* a razón de (d) **first r.** de primera categoría (e) *Br* **rates** impuestos *mpl* municipales
2 *vt* (a) *(estimate)* estimar (b) *(evaluate)* tasar (c) *(consider)* considerar

rateable ['reɪtəbəl] *adj Br* **r. value** valor *m* catastral

ratepayer ['reɪtpeɪə(r)] *n Br* contribuyente *mf*

rather ['rɑːðə(r)] *adv* (a) *(quite)* más bien, bastante; *(very much so)* muy (b) *(more accurately)* mejor dicho; **r. than** *(instead of)* en vez de; *(more than)* más que (c) **she would r. stay here** *(prefer to)* prefiere quedarse aquí

ratify ['rætɪfaɪ] *vt* ratificar

rating ['reɪtɪŋ] *n* (a) *(valuation)* tasación *f*; *(score)* valoración *f* (b) *TV* **(programme) ratings** índice *m* de audiencia (c) *Naut* marinero *m* sin graduación

ratio ['reɪʃɪəʊ] *n* razón *f*; **in the r. of** a razón de

ration ['ræʃən] **1** *n* (a) *(allowance)* ración *f* (b) **rations** víveres *mpl*
2 *vt* racionar

rational ['ræʃənəl] *adj* racional

rationale [ræʃə'nɑːl] *n* base *f*

rationalize ['ræʃənəlaɪz] *vt* racionalizar

rattle ['rætəl] **1** *n* (a) *(of train, cart)* traqueteo *m*; *(of metal)* repiqueteo *m*; *(of glass)* tintineo *m* (b) *(toy)* sonajero *m*; *(instrument)* carraca *f*
2 *vt* (a) *(keys etc)* hacer sonar (b) *Fam (unsettle)* poner nervioso(a)
3 *vi* sonar; *(metal)* repiquetear; *(glass)* tintinear

rattlesnake ['rætəlsneɪk] *n* serpiente *f* de cascabel

raucous ['rɔːkəs] *adj* estridente

ravage ['rævɪdʒ] *Fml* **1** *n (usu pl)* estragos *mpl*
2 *vt* asolar, devastar

rave [reɪv] **1** *vi* (a) *(be delirious)* delirar (b) *(be angry)* enfurecerse (**at** con) (c) *Fam (show enthusiasm)* entusiasmarse (**about** por)
2 *n Fam* **r. review** crítica *f* muy favorable

raven ['reɪvən] *n* cuervo *m*

ravenous ['rævənəs] *adj* **I'm r.** tengo un hambre que no veo

ravine [rə'viːn] *n* barranco *m*

raving ['reɪvɪŋ] *n Fam* **r. mad** loco(a) de atar

ravishing ['rævɪʃɪŋ] *adj (person)* encantador(a)

raw [rɔː] *adj* (a) *(uncooked)* crudo(a) (b) *(not processed)* bruto(a); *(alcohol)* puro(a); **r. material** materia prima (c) *(emotion)* instintivo(a) (d) *(weather)* crudo(a) (e) **r. deal** trato injusto (f) *(wound)* abierto(a); **r. flesh** carne viva (g) *US (inexperienced)* novato(a) (h) *(frank)* franco(a)

ray¹ [reɪ] *n* rayo *m*; *Fig* **r. of hope** rayo de esperanza

ray² [reɪ] *n (fish)* raya *f*

rayon ['reɪɒn] *n* rayón *m*

raze [reɪz] *vt* arrasar

razor ['reɪzə(r)] *n (for shaving)* maquinilla *f* de afeitar; **r. blade** hoja *f* de afeitar

Rd *(abbr Road)* calle *f*, c/

re [riː] *prep* respecto a, con referencia a

reach [riːtʃ] **1** *vt* (a) *(arrive at)* llegar a (b) *(contact)* localizar
2 *vi* alcanzar; **to r. for sth** intentar coger algo; **to r. out** extender la mano
3 *n* (a) *(range)* alcance *m*; **out of r.** fuera del alcance; **within r.** al alcance (b) *(in boxing)* extensión *f* del brazo (c) **reaches** *(on a river)* recta *f*

react [rɪˈækt] *vi* reaccionar

reaction [rɪˈækʃən] *n* reacción *f*

reactor [rɪˈæktə(r)] *n* reactor *m*

read [riːd] **1** *vt* (*pt & pp* **read** [red]) (a) leer (b) *(decipher)* descifrar (c) *(understand)* entender; *(interpret)* interpretar (d) *Univ* estudiar (e) *(of dial)* marcar (f) *(of signpost, text)* decir
2 *vi* leer
► read out *vt sep* leer en voz alta

readable [ˈriːdəbəl] *adj* (a) *(interesting)* interesante (b) *(legible)* legible

reader [ˈriːdə(r)] *n* (a) lector(a) *m,f* (b) *(book)* libro *m* de lectura (c) *Br Univ* profesor(a) *m,f* adjunto(a)

readership [ˈriːdəʃɪp] *n Press* lectores *mpl*

readily [ˈredɪlɪ] *adv* (a) *(easily)* fácilmente; **r. available** disponible en el acto (b) *(willingly)* de buena gana

readiness [ˈredɪnɪs] *n* (a) *(preparedness)* preparación *f* (b) *(willingness)* buena disposición

reading [ˈriːdɪŋ] *n* (a) lectura *f* (b) *Fig* interpretación *f* (c) *(of laws, bill)* presentación *f*

readjust [riːəˈdʒʌst] **1** *vt* reajustar
2 *vi (adapt oneself)* adaptarse

ready [ˈredɪ] *adj* (a) *(prepared)* listo(a), preparado(a); **r., steady, go!** ¡preparados, listos, ya! (b) **r. to** *(about to)* a punto de (c) *(to hand)* a mano; **r. cash** dinero *m* en efectivo (d) *(willing)* dispuesto(a)

ready-cooked [ˈredɪˈkʊkt] *adj* precocinado(a)

ready-made [ˈredɪˈmeɪd] *adj* confeccionado(a); *(food)* preparado(a)

real [rɪəl] *adj* (a) real, verdadero(a); *Fam* **for r.** de veras (b) *(genuine)* auténtico(a); **r. leather** piel legítima (c) *US Com* **r. estate** bienes *mpl* inmuebles; **r. estate agent** agente inmobiliario

realism [ˈrɪəlɪzəm] *n* realismo *m*

realistic [rɪəlɪstɪk] *adj* realista

reality [rɪˈælɪtɪ] *n* realidad *f*; **in r.** en realidad

realization [rɪəlaɪˈzeɪʃən] *n* (a) *(understanding)* comprensión *f* (b) *(of plan, assets)* realización *f*

realize [ˈrɪəlaɪz] *vt* (a) *(become aware of)* darse cuenta de (b) *(assets, plan)* realizar

really [ˈrɪəlɪ] *adv* verdaderamente, realmente; **I r. don't know** no lo sé de verdad; **r.?** ¿de veras?

realm [relm] *n* *(kingdom)* reino *m*; *Fig (field)* terreno *m*

realtor [ˈrɪəltə(r)] *n US* agente *mf* inmobiliario(a)

ream [riːm] *n (of paper)* resma *f*

reap [riːp] *vt Agr* cosechar; *Fig* **to r. the benefits** llevarse los beneficios

reappear [riːəˈpɪə(r)] *vi* reaparecer

reappraisal [riːəˈpreɪzəl] *n* revaluación *f*

rear¹ [rɪə(r)] **1** *n* (a) *(back part)* parte *f* de atrás (b) *Fam (buttocks)* trasero *m*
2 *adj* trasero(a); **r. entrance** puerta *f* de atrás

rear² [rɪə(r)] **1** *vt* (a) *(breed, raise)* criar (b) *(lift up)* levantar
2 *vi* **to r. up** *(horse)* encabritarse

rearguard [ˈrɪəɡɑːd] *n* retaguardia *f*

rearmament [riːˈɑːməmənt] *n* rearme *m*

rearrange [riːəˈreɪndʒ] *vt* (a) *(furniture)* colocar de otra manera (b) *(appointment)* fijar otra fecha para

rear-view [ˈrɪəvjuː] *adj* **r. mirror** (espejo *m*) retrovisor *m*

reason [ˈriːzən] **1** *n* (a) motivo *m*, razón *f*; **for no r.** sin razón; **for some r.** por algún motivo (b) *(good sense)* razón *f*; **it stands to r.** es lógico; **to listen to r.** atender a razones
2 *vi* (a) **to r. with sb** convencer a algn (b) *(argue, work out)* razonar

reasonable [ˈriːzənəbəl] *adj* (a) *(fair)* razonable (b) *(sensible)* sensato(a) (c) *(average)* regular

reasonably [ˈriːzənəblɪ] *adv (fairly)* bastante

reasoning [ˈriːzənɪŋ] *n* razonamiento *m*

reassurance [riːəˈʃʊərəns] *n* consuelo *m*

reassure [riːəˈʃʊə(r)] *vt* (a) *(comfort)* tranquilizar (b) *(restore confidence)* dar confianza a

reassuring [riːəˈʃʊərɪŋ] *adj* consolador(a)

rebate [ˈriːbeɪt] *n* devolución *f*; **tax r.** devolución fiscal

> *Note that the Spanish verb **rebatir** is a false friend and is never a translation for the English verb **to rebate**. In Spanish, **rebatir** means "to refute".*

rebel 1 *adj & n* [ˈrebəl] rebelde *(mf)*
2 *vi* [rɪˈbel] rebelarse, sublevarse *(against* contra*)*

rebellion [rɪˈbeljən] *n* rebelión *f*

rebellious [rɪ'beljəs] *adj* rebelde

rebound 1 *n* ['riːbaʊnd] *(of ball)* rebote *m*; *Fig* **on the r.** de rebote
  2 *vi* [rɪ'baʊnd] *(ball)* rebotar

rebuff [rɪ'bʌf] **1** *n* desaire *m*
  2 *vt* desairar

rebuild [riː'bɪld] *vt* reconstruir

rebuke [rɪ'bjuːk] **1** *n* reproche *m*
  2 *vt* reprochar

rebut [rɪ'bʌt] *vt* refutar

recalcitrant [rɪ'kælsɪtrənt] *adj Fml* recalcitrante

recall [rɪ'kɔːl] *vt* **(a)** *(soldiers, products)* hacer volver; *(ambassador)* retirar **(b)** *(remember)* recordar

recant [rɪ'kænt] *vi Fml* retractarse

recap **1** *vt & vi* [riː'kæp] resumir; **to r.** en resumen
  2 *n* ['riːkæp] recapitulación *f*

recapitulate [riːkə'pɪtjʊleɪt] *vt & vi Fml* recapitular

recapture [riː'kæptʃə(r)] *vt Fig* recuperar

recd *Com (abbr* **received***)* recibido(a)

recede [rɪ'siːd] *vi* retroceder; *(fade)* desvanecerse

receipt [rɪ'siːt] *n* **(a)** *(act)* recepción *f*; **to acknowledge r. of sth** acusar recibo de algo **(b)** *Com (paper)* recibo *m* **(c)** **receipts** *(takings)* recaudación *f*

receive [rɪ'siːv] *vt* **(a)** recibir **(b)** *Jur (stolen goods)* ocultar **(c)** *(welcome)* acoger **(d)** *TV & Rad* captar

receiver [rɪ'siːvə(r)] *n* **(a)** *(person)* receptor(a) *m,f* **(b)** *Jur (of stolen goods)* perista *mf* **(c)** *Br Jur* **official r.** síndico *m* **(d)** *Tel* auricular *m* **(e)** *Rad* receptor *m*

recent ['riːsənt] *adj* reciente; **in r. years** en los últimos años

recently ['riːsəntlɪ] *adv* hace poco, recientemente

receptacle [rɪ'septəkəl] *n* receptáculo *m*

reception [rɪ'sepʃən] *n* **(a)** *(welcome)* acogida *f* **(b)** *(party)* recepción *f*; **wedding r.** banquete *m* de bodas **(c)** **r. (desk)** recepción *f* **(d)** *Rad & TV* recepción *f*

receptionist [rɪ'sepʃənɪst] *n* recepcionista *mf*

recess ['riːses, rɪ'ses] *n* **(a)** *(in a wall)* hueco *m* **(b)** *(secret place)* escondrijo *m* **(c)** *US Educ* recreo *m*; *Pol* período *m* de vacaciones

recession [rɪ'seʃən] *n* recesión *f*

recharge [riː'tʃɑːdʒ] *vt (battery)* recargar

rechargeable [riː'tʃɑːdʒəbəl] *adj* recargable

recipe ['resɪpɪ] *n Culin* receta *f*; *Fig* fórmula *f*

recipient [rɪ'sɪpɪənt] *n* receptor(a) *m,f*; *(of letter)* destinatario(a) *m,f*

> 🖉 Note that the Spanish word **recipiente** is a false friend and is never a translation for the English word **recipient**. In Spanish, **recipiente** means "receptacle, container".

reciprocate [rɪ'sɪprəkeɪt] **1** *vt (favour etc)* devolver
  2 *vi* hacer lo mismo

recital [rɪ'saɪtəl] *n* recital *m*

recite [rɪ'saɪt] *vt & vi* recitar

reckless ['reklɪs] *adj (unwise)* imprudente; *(fearless)* temerario(a)

reckon ['rekən] *vt & vi* **(a)** *(calculate)* calcular; *(count)* contar **(b)** *Fam (think)* creer; *(consider)* considerar
  ▸ **reckon on** *vt insep* contar con

reckoner ['rekənə(r)] *n* **ready r.** tabla *f* de cálculo

reckoning ['rekənɪŋ] *n* cálculo *m*; **by my r. ...** según mis cálculos ...; *Fig* **day of r.** día *m* del juicio final

reclaim [rɪ'kleɪm] *vt* **(a)** *(recover)* recuperar; *(demand back)* reclamar **(b)** *(marshland etc)* convertir

recline [rɪ'klaɪn] *vi* recostarse, reclinarse

reclining [rɪ'klaɪnɪŋ] *adj* recostado(a); **r. seat** asiento *m* abatible

recluse [rɪ'kluːs] *n* solitario(a) *m,f*

> 🖉 Note that the Spanish word **recluso** is a false friend and is never a translation for the English word **recluse**. In Spanish, **recluso** means "prisoner".

recognition [rekəg'nɪʃən] *n* reconocimiento *m*; *(appreciation)* apreciación *f*; **changed beyond all r.** irreconocible

recognizable [rekəg'naɪzəbəl] *adj* reconocible

recognize ['rekəgnaɪz] *vt* reconocer

recoil **1** *n* ['riːkɔɪl] *(of gun)* culatazo *m*; *(of spring)* aflojamiento *m*
  2 *vi* [rɪ'kɔɪl] **(a)** *(gun)* dar un culatazo; *(spring)* aflojarse **(b)** *(in fear)* espantarse

recollect [rekə'lekt] *vt* recordar

recollection [rekə'lekʃən] *n* recuerdo *m*

> 🖉 Note that the Spanish word **recolección** is a false friend and is never a translation for the English word **recollection**. In Spanish, **recolección** means "harvest, collection".

recommend [rekə'mend] *vt* recomendar

recommendation [rekəmen'deɪʃən] *n* recomendación *f*

recompense ['rekəmpens] **1** *n* recompensa *f*; *Jur* indemnización *f*
  2 *vt* recompensar; *Jur* indemnizar

reconcile ['rekənsaɪl] *vt (two people)* reconciliar; *(two ideas)* conciliar; **to r. oneself** to resignarse a

recondition [riːkən'dɪʃən] *vt (engine)* revisar

reconnaissance [rɪ'kɒnɪsəns] *n Mil* reconocimiento *m*

reconnoitre, *US* **reconnoiter** [rekə'nɔɪtə(r)] *vt Mil* reconocer

reconsider [riːkən'sɪdə(r)] *vt* reconsiderar

reconstruct [riːkən'strʌkt] *vt* reconstruir

reconstruction [riːkən'strʌkʃən] *n* reconstrucción *f*

record 1 *n* ['rekɔːd] (a) *(account)* relación *f*; *(of meeting)* actas *fpl*; **off the r.** confidencialmente (b) *(document)* documento *m*; **r. of attendance** registro *m* de asistencia; **public records** archivos *mpl* (c) *Med* historial médico (d) *Mus* disco *m*; **r. player** tocadiscos *m inv* (e) *Sport* récord *m*

2 *vt* [rɪ'kɔːd] (a) *(relate)* hacer constar; *(note down)* apuntar (b) *(record, voice)* grabar (c) *(of thermometer etc)* marcar

recorded [rɪ'kɔːdɪd] *adj* **r. delivery** correo certificado; **r. message** mensaje grabado

recorder [rɪ'kɔːdə(r)] *n* (a) *(person)* registrador(a) *m,f; Jur* magistrado(a) *m,f* (b) *Mus* flauta *f*

recording [rɪ'kɔːdɪŋ] *n (registering)* registro *m*; *(recorded music, message etc)* grabación *f*

recount [rɪ'kaʊnt] *vt (tell)* contar

re-count 1 *vi* [riː'kaʊnt] *Pol* hacer un recuento

2 *n* ['riːkaʊnt] *Pol* recuento *m*

recoup [rɪ'kuːp] *vt (losses etc)* recuperar

recourse [rɪ'kɔːs] *n* **to have r. to** recurrir a

recover [rɪ'kʌvə(r)] **1** *vt (items, lost time)* recuperar; *(consciousness)* recobrar

2 *vi (from illness etc)* reponerse

recovery [rɪ'kʌvərɪ] *n* (a) *(retrieval)* recuperación *f* (b) *(from illness)* restablecimiento *m*

recreation [rekrɪ'eɪʃən] *n* (a) diversión *f* (b) *Educ (playtime)* recreo *m*; **r. ground** terreno *m* de juegos

recreational [rekrɪ'eɪʃənəl] *adj* recreativo(a)

recrimination [rɪkrɪmɪ'neɪʃən] *n* reproche *m*

recruit [rɪ'kruːt] **1** *n* recluta *m*

2 *vt (soldiers)* reclutar; *(workers)* contratar

recruitment [rɪ'kruːtmənt] *n (of soldiers)* reclutamiento *m*; *(of employees)* contratación *f*

rectangle ['rektæŋgəl] *n* rectángulo *m*

rectangular [rek'tæŋgjʊlə(r)] *adj* rectangular

rectify ['rektɪfaɪ] *vt* rectificar

rector ['rektə(r)] *n* (a) *Rel* párroco *m* (b) *Scot Educ* director(a) *m,f*

recuperate [rɪ'kuːpəreɪt] *vi* reponerse

recur [rɪ'kɜː(r)] *vi* repetirse

> Note that the Spanish verb **recurrir** is a false friend and is never a translation for the English verb **to recur**. In Spanish, **recurrir** means "to appeal, to resort".

recurrence [rɪ'kʌrəns] *n* repetición *f*, reaparición *f*

recurrent [rɪ'kʌrənt] *adj* constante; *Med* recurrente

recycle [riː'saɪkəl] *vt* reciclar

recycling [riː'saɪklɪŋ] *n* reciclaje *m*

red [red] **1** *adj* **(redder, reddest)** rojo(a); **r. light** semáforo *m* en rojo; **r. wine** vino tinto; **to go r.** ponerse colorado(a); **to have r. hair** ser pelirrojo(a); *Fig* **r. herring** truco *m* para despistar; *Fam* **to roll out the r. carpet for sb** recibir a algn con todos los honores; **R. Cross** Cruz Roja; **R. Indian** piel roja *mf*; **R. Riding Hood** Caperucita Roja; **R. Sea** Mar Rojo; **r. tape** papeleo *m*

2 *n* (a) *(colour)* rojo *m* (b) *Fin* **to be in the r.** estar en números rojos

redcurrant ['redkʌrənt] *n* grosella roja

redden ['redən] **1** *vi (blush)* enrojecerse, ponerse colorado(a)

2 *vt (make red)* teñir de rojo

reddish ['redɪʃ] *adj* rojizo(a)

redeem [rɪ'diːm] *vt* (a) *(regain)* recobrar; *(from pawn)* desempeñar; *(voucher)* canjear (b) *(debt)* amortizar (c) *(film, novel etc)* salvar (d) *Rel* redimir; *Fig* **to r. oneself** redimirse

redeeming [rɪ'diːmɪŋ] *adj* compensatorio(a); **his only r. feature** lo único que le salva

redemption [rɪ'dempʃən] *n Fml* (a) *(of debt)* amortización *f* (b) *Rel* redención *f*; **beyond r.** sin remedio

redeploy [riːdɪ'plɔɪ] *vt* redistribuir

red-handed [red'hændɪd] *adj* **to catch sb r.** coger a algn con las manos en la masa

redhead ['redhed] *n* pelirrojo(a) *m,f*

red-hot [red'hɒt] *adj* (a) *(metal)* candente; **r. news** noticia(s) *f(pl)* de última hora (b) *Fam (passionate)* ardiente

redial [riː'daɪəl] *n Tel (facility)* rellamada *f*

redirect [riːdɪ'rekt] *vt* (a) *(funds)* redistribuir (b) *(letter)* remitir a la nueva dirección

red-light [red'laɪt] *adj Fam* **r. district** barrio chino

redouble [riːˈdʌbəl] *vt* redoblar

redress [rɪˈdres] *Fml* **1** *n* reparación *f*
  2 *vt* reparar

redskin [ˈredskɪn] *n* piel roja *mf*

reduce [rɪˈdjuːs] *vt* (a) reducir (b) *(in rank)* degradar (c) *Culin (sauce)* espesar (d) *Med* recomponer

reduction [rɪˈdʌkʃən] *n* reducción *f*; *Com (in purchase price)* descuento *m*, rebaja *f*

redundancy [rɪˈdʌndənsɪ] *n* despido *m*

redundant [rɪˈdʌndənt] *adj* (a) *(superfluous)* redundante (b) *Ind* **to be made r.** perder el empleo; **to make sb r.** despedir a algn

reed [riːd] *n* (a) *Bot* caña *f* (b) *Mus* caramillo *m*

reef [riːf] *n* arrecife *m*

reek [riːk] **1** *n* tufo *m*
  2 *vi* apestar

reel [riːl] **1** *n* (a) *(spool)* bobina *f*, carrete *m* (b) *Scot Mus* danza *f* tradicional
  2 *vi (stagger)* tambalearse

re-elect [riːɪˈlekt] *vt* reelegir

ref [ref] *n* (a) *Fam Sport* árbitro *m* (b) *Com (abbr* **reference***)* ref

refectory [rɪˈfektərɪ] *n* refectorio *m*

refer [rɪˈfɜː(r)] **1** *vt* mandar, enviar; **to r. a matter to a tribunal** remitir un asunto a un tribunal
  2 *vi* (a) *(allude)* referirse, aludir (**to** a) (b) **to r. to** *(consult)* consultar

referee [refəˈriː] **1** *n* (a) *Sport* árbitro(a) *m,f* (b) *(for job application)* garante *mf*
  2 *vt Sport* arbitrar

reference [ˈrefərəns] *n* (a) referencia *f*; **with r. to** referente a, con referencia a; **r. book** libro *m* de consulta; **r. library** biblioteca *f* de consulta (b) *(character report)* informe *m*, referencia *f*

referendum [refəˈrendəm] *n* referéndum *m*

refill 1 *n* [ˈriːfɪl] (a) *(replacement)* recambio *m*, carga *f* (b) *Fam (drink)* otra copa
  2 *vt* [riːˈfɪl] rellenar

refine [rɪˈfaɪn] *vt* refinar

refined [rɪˈfaɪnd] *adj* refinado(a)

refinement [rɪˈfaɪnmənt] *n* refinamiento *m*

refinery [rɪˈfaɪnərɪ] *n* refinería *f*

reflect [rɪˈflekt] **1** *vt (light, attitude)* reflejar
  2 *vi (think)* reflexionar; **to r. on sth** meditar sobre algo

reflection [rɪˈflekʃən] *n* (a) *(indication, mirror image)* reflejo *m* (b) *(thought)*

reflexión *f*; **on r.** pensándolo bien (**c**) *(criticism)* crítica *f*

reflector [rɪˈflektə(r)] *n (of vehicle)* cataḟaro *m*

reflex [ˈriːfleks] *n* reflejo *m*

reflexive [rɪˈfleksɪv] *adj* reflexivo(a)

reform [rɪˈfɔːm] **1** *n* reforma *f*; **r. school** reformatorio *m*
  2 *vt* reformar

reformation [refəˈmeɪʃən] *n* reforma *f*

reformatory [rɪˈfɔːmətərɪ] *n* reformatorio *m*

reformer [rɪˈfɔːmə(r)] *n* reformador(a) *m,f*

refrain [rɪˈfreɪn] **1** *n Mus* estribillo *m*; *Fig* lema *m*
  2 *vi* abstenerse (**from** de)

refresh [rɪˈfreʃ] *vt* refrescar

refresher [rɪˈfreʃə(r)] *n* **r. course** cursillo *m* de reciclaje

refreshing [rɪˈfreʃɪŋ] *adj* refrescante; **a r. change** un cambio muy agradable

refreshment [rɪˈfreʃmənt] *n* refresco *m*

refrigerator [rɪˈfrɪdʒəreɪtə(r)] *n* nevera *f*, frigorífico *m*, *Andes* frigider *m*, *RP* heladera *f*

refuel [riːˈfjuːəl] *vi* repostar combustible

refuge [ˈrefjuːdʒ] *n* refugio *m*, cobijo *m*; **to take r.** refugiarse

refugee [refjuˈdʒiː] *n* refugiado(a) *m,f*

refund 1 *n* [ˈriːfʌnd] reembolso *m*
  2 *vt* [rɪˈfʌnd] reembolsar, devolver

refurbish [riːˈfɜːbɪʃ] *vt* redecorar

refusal [rɪˈfjuːzəl] *n* negativa *f*; **to have first r. on sth** tener la primera opción en algo

refuse¹ [rɪˈfjuːz] **1** *vt* rechazar; **to r. sb sth** negar algo a algn
  2 *vi* negarse

refuse² [ˈrefjuːs] *n* basura *f*; **r. collector** basurero *m*

refute [rɪˈfjuːt] *vt* refutar, rebatir

regain [rɪˈgeɪn] *vt* recuperar; *(consciousness)* recobrar

regal [ˈriːgəl] *adj* regio(a)

regard [rɪˈgɑːd] **1** *n* (a) *(concern)* consideración *f*, respeto *m*; **with r. to** respecto a (b) *(esteem)* estima *f* (c) **regards** *(good wishes)* recuerdos *mpl*; **give him my regards** dale recuerdos de mi parte
  2 *vt* (a) *(consider)* considerar (b) **as regards** *(regarding)* respecto a

regarding [rɪˈgɑːdɪŋ] *prep* respecto a

regardless [rɪˈgɑːdlɪs] **1** *prep* **r. of** sin tener en cuenta; **r. of the outcome** pase lo que pase
  2 *adv* a toda costa

regime [reɪˈʒiːm] *n* régimen *m*

regiment ['redʒɪmənt] **1** n regimiento m
2 vt regimentar

regimental [redʒɪ'mentəl] adj del regimiento

region ['riːdʒən] n (**a**) región f (**b**) **in the r. of** aproximadamente

regional ['riːdʒənəl] adj regional

regionalism ['riːdʒənəlɪzəm] n regionalismo m

register ['redʒɪstə(r)] **1** n registro m
2 vt (**a**) (record) registrar (**b**) (letter) certificar (**c**) (show) mostrar; **his face registered fear** en su rostro se reflejaba el miedo
3 vi (for course) inscribirse; Univ matricularse

registered ['redʒɪstəd] adj certificado(a); **r. letter** carta certificada; **r. trademark** marca registrada

registrar [redʒɪ'strɑː(r), 'redʒɪstrɑː(r)] n (**a**) (record keeper) registrador(a) m,f (**b**) Br Med interno(a) m,f (**c**) Univ secretario(a) m,f general

registration [redʒɪ'streɪʃən] n inscripción f; Univ matrícula f; Br Aut **r. number** matrícula f

registry ['redʒɪstrɪ] n registro m; **to get married in a r. office** casarse por lo civil; **r. office** registro civil

regret [rɪ'gret] **1** n (remorse) remordimiento m; (sadness) pesar m; **regrets** (excuses) excusas fpl; **to have no regrets** no arrepentirse de nada
2 vt arrepentirse de, lamentar

regretful [rɪ'gretfʊl] adj arrepentido(a)

regrettable [rɪ'gretəbəl] adj lamentable

regroup [riː'gruːp] **1** vt reagrupar
2 vi reagruparse

regular ['regjʊlə(r)] **1** adj (**a**) regular (**b**) (usual) normal (**c**) (staff) permanente (**d**) (frequent) frecuente (**e**) **r. army** tropas fpl regulares (**f**) US Fam **a r. guy** un tío legal, Am un tipo derecho
2 n (**a**) (customer) cliente mf habitual (**b**) Mil militar m de carrera

regularity [regjʊ'lærɪtɪ] n regularidad f

regularly ['regjʊləlɪ] adv con regularidad

regulate ['regjʊleɪt] vt regular

regulation [regjʊ'leɪʃən] **1** n (**a**) (control) regulación f (**b**) (rule) regla f
2 adj reglamentario(a)

rehabilitation [riːəbɪlɪ'teɪʃən] n rehabilitación f; **r. centre** centro m de reinserción

rehearsal [rɪ'hɜːsəl] n ensayo m

rehearse [rɪ'hɜːs] vt & vi ensayar

reign [reɪn] **1** n reinado m
2 vi reinar

reigning ['reɪnɪŋ] adj **r. champion** campeón m actual

reimburse [riːɪm'bɜːs] vt reembolsar

rein [reɪn] n (for horse) rienda f; Fig **he gave free r. to his emotions** dio rienda suelta a sus emociones

reindeer ['reɪndɪə(r)] n reno m

reinforce [riːɪn'fɔːs] vt (strengthen) reforzar; (support) apoyar; **reinforced concrete** hormigón armado

reinforcement [riːɪn'fɔːsmənt] n (**a**) refuerzo m; Constr armazón m (**b**) Mil **reinforcements** refuerzos mpl

reinstate [riːɪn'steɪt] vt (to job) reincorporar

reiterate [riː'ɪtəreɪt] vt & vi reiterar

reject 1 n ['riːdʒekt] (**a**) desecho m (**b**) Com **rejects** artículos defectuosos
2 vt [rɪ'dʒekt] rechazar

rejection [rɪ'dʒekʃən] n rechazo m

rejoice [rɪ'dʒɔɪs] vi regocijarse (**at** or **over** de)

rejuvenate [rɪ'dʒuːvɪneɪt] vt rejuvenecer; Fig revitalizar

relapse [rɪ'læps] **1** n (**a**) Med recaída f; **to have a r.** sufrir una recaída (**b**) (into crime, alcoholism) reincidencia f
2 vi recaer

relate [rɪ'leɪt] **1** vt (**a**) (connect) relacionar (**b**) (tell) relatar
2 vi relacionarse

related [rɪ'leɪtɪd] adj (**a**) (linked) relacionado(a) (**to** con) (**b**) **to be r. to sb** ser pariente de algn

relation [rɪ'leɪʃən] n (**a**) (link) relación f; **in** or **with r. to** respecto a; **it bears no r. to what we said** no tiene nada que ver con lo que dijimos (**b**) (member of family) pariente(a) m,f

relationship [rɪ'leɪʃənʃɪp] n (**a**) (link) relación f (**b**) (between people) relaciones fpl; **to have a good/bad r. with sb** llevarse bien/mal con algn

relative ['relətɪv] **1** n pariente mf
2 adj relativo(a)

relatively ['relətɪvlɪ] adv relativamente

relax [rɪ'læks] **1** vt (muscles, rules) relajar
2 vi relajarse

relaxation [riːlæk'seɪʃən] n (**a**) (rest) descanso m, relajación f (**b**) (of rules) relajación f (**c**) (pastime) distracción f

relaxed [rɪ'lækst] adj relajado(a); (peaceful) tranquilo(a)

relaxing [rɪ'læksɪŋ] adj relajante

relay 1 n [rɪ'leɪ] (**a**) relevo m; **r. (race)** carrera f de relevos (**b**) Rad & TV retransmisión f

2 *vt* [rɪ'leɪ] (**a**) *(pass on)* difundir (**b**) *Rad & TV* retransmitir

release [rɪ'liːs] **1** *n* (**a**) *(of prisoner)* liberación *f*, puesta *f* en libertad; *(of gas)* escape *m* (**b**) *Com* puesta *f* en venta (**c**) *Cin* estreno *m* (**d**) *(record)* disco *m* (**e**) *Press* comunicado *m*
2 *vt* (**a**) *(let go)* soltar; *(prisoner)* poner en libertad; *(gas)* despedir (**b**) *Com* poner en venta (**c**) *Cin* estrenar (**d**) *(record)* editar (**e**) *(publish)* publicar

relegate ['relɪgeɪt] *vt* (**a**) relegar (**b**) *Ftb* **to be relegated** bajar a una división inferior

relent [rɪ'lent] *vi* ceder; *(storm)* aplacarse

relentless [rɪ'lentlɪs] *adj* implacable

relevant ['reləvənt] *adj* pertinente (**to** a); **it is not r.** no viene al caso

ℓ Note that the Spanish word **relevante** is a false friend and is never a translation for the English word **relevant**. In Spanish, **relevante** means "outstanding, important".

reliability [rɪlaɪə'bɪlɪtɪ] *n* (**a**) *(of person)* formalidad *f* (**b**) *(of car, machine)* fiabilidad *f*

reliable [rɪ'laɪəbəl] *adj (person)* de fiar; **a r. car** un coche seguro; **a r. source** una fuente fidedigna

reliably [rɪ'laɪəblɪ] *adv* **to be r. informed that** saber de buena tinta que

reliant [rɪ'laɪənt] *adj* **to be r. on** depender de

relic ['relɪk] *n* (**a**) *Rel* reliquia *f* (**b**) *(reminder of past)* vestigio *m*

relief [rɪ'liːf] *n* (**a**) alivio *m* (**b**) *(help)* auxilio *m*, ayuda *f*; *US* **to be on r.** cobrar un subsidio (**c**) *Art & Geog* relieve *m*

relieve [rɪ'liːv] *vt* (**a**) aliviar; *(monotony)* romper (**b**) *(take over from)* relevar (**c**) *Euph* **to r. oneself** hacer sus necesidades (**d**) **to r. sb of sth** coger algo a algn

relieved [rɪ'liːvd] *adj* aliviado(a), tranquilizado(a)

religion [rɪ'lɪdʒən] *n* religión *f*

religious [rɪ'lɪdʒəs] *adj* religioso(a)

relinquish [rɪ'lɪŋkwɪʃ] *vt* renunciar a; **to r. one's hold on sth** soltar algo

relish ['relɪʃ] **1** *n* (**a**) *(enjoyment)* deleite *m* (**b**) *Culin* condimento *m*
2 *vt* agradar

relocate [riːləʊ'keɪt] *vt* trasladar

reluctance [rɪ'lʌktəns] *n* desgana *f*

reluctant [rɪ'lʌktənt] *adj* reacio(a); **to be r. to do sth** estar poco dispuesto(a) a hacer algo

reluctantly [rɪ'lʌktəntlɪ] *adv* de mala gana, a regañadientes

rely [rɪ'laɪ] *vi* contar (**on** con), confiar (**on** en)

remain [rɪ'meɪn] **1** *vi* (**a**) *(stay)* permanecer, quedarse (**b**) *(be left)* quedar; **it remains to be seen** está por ver
2 *npl* **remains** restos *mpl*

remainder [rɪ'meɪndə(r)] *n* resto *m*

remaining [rɪ'meɪnɪŋ] *adj* restante

remand [rɪ'mɑːnd] *Jur* **1** *vt* remitir; **remanded in custody** en prevención
2 *n* detención *f*; **on r.** detenido(a)

remark [rɪ'mɑːk] **1** *n* comentario *m*
2 *vt* comentar, observar

ℓ Note that the Spanish verb **remarcar** is a false friend and is never a translation for the English verb **to remark**. In Spanish, **remarcar** means "to stress, to underline".

remarkable [rɪ'mɑːkəbəl] *adj* extraordinario(a); *(strange)* curioso(a)

remedial [rɪ'miːdɪəl] *adj* reparador(a); **r. classes** clases *fpl* para niños atrasados en los estudios

remedy ['remɪdɪ] **1** *n* remedio *m*
2 *vt* remediar

remember [rɪ'membə(r)] **1** *vt* (**a**) acordarse de, recordar (**b**) **r. me to your mother** dale recuerdos a tu madre
2 *vi* acordarse, recordar; **I don't r.** no me acuerdo

remembrance [rɪ'membrəns] *n* **in r. of** en recuerdo de; *Br* **R. Day** *or* **Sunday** = día en que se conmemora el armisticio de 1918

remind [rɪ'maɪnd] *vt* recordar; **r. me to do it** recuérdame que lo haga; **she reminds me of your sister** me recuerda a tu hermana; **that reminds me** ahora que me acuerdo

reminder [rɪ'maɪndə(r)] *n* recordatorio *m*, aviso *m*

reminisce [remɪ'nɪs] *vi* rememorar

reminiscent [remɪ'nɪsənt] *adj Fml* nostálgico(a); **to be r. of** recordar

remiss [rɪ'mɪs] *adj (negligent)* descuidado(a)

remission [rɪ'mɪʃən] *n* (**a**) *Med* remisión *f* (**b**) *Jur* perdón *m*

remit [rɪ'mɪt] *vt* (**a**) *(send)* remitir (**b**) *Jur* referir a otro tribunal

remittance [rɪ'mɪtəns] *n* (**a**) *(sending)* envío *m* (**b**) *(payment)* giro *m*, pago *m*

remnant ['remnənt] *n* resto *m*; **remnants** *(of cloth)* retales *mpl*

remold ['riːməʊld] *n US* = **remould**

remorse [rɪ'mɔːs] *n* remordimiento *m*

remorseful [rɪ'mɔːsfʌl] *adj* lleno(a) de remordimiento

remorseless [rɪ'mɔːslɪs] *adj* despiadado(a)

remote [rɪ'məʊt] *adj* (**a**) *(far away)* remoto(a); **r. control** mando *m* a distancia (**b**) *(isolated)* aislado(a) (**c**) *(possibility)* remoto(a); **I haven't the remotest idea** no tengo la más mínima idea

remote-controlled [rɪ'məʊtkən'trəʊld] *adj* teledirigido(a)

remotely [rɪ'məʊtlɪ] *adv* (**a**) *(vaguely)* vagamente (**b**) *(distantly)* en lugar aislado

remould ['riːməʊld] *n Aut* neumático recauchutado

removable [rɪ'muːvəbəl] *adj* *(detachable)* que se puede quitar

removal [rɪ'muːvəl] *n* (**a**) *(moving house)* mudanza *f*; **r. van** camión *m* de mudanzas (**b**) *(of stain etc)* eliminación *f*

remove [rɪ'muːv] *vt* (**a**) *(move)* quitar; **to r. one's make-up** desmaquillarse; **to r. one's name from a list** tachar su nombre de una lista (**b**) *(from office)* despedir

> ⚠ Note that the Spanish verb **remover** is a false friend and is never a translation for the English verb **to remove**. In Spanish, **remover** means "to move over, to turn over, to stir".

removed [rɪ'muːvd] *adj* **far r. from** muy diferente de

remover [rɪ'muːvə(r)] *n* **make-up r.** desmaquillador *m*; **nail varnish r.** quitaesmalte *m*; **stain r.** quitamanchas *m inv*

remuneration [rɪmjuːnə'reɪʃən] *n Fml* remuneración *f*

renaissance [rə'neɪsəns] **1** *n* renacimiento *m*; **the R.** el Renacimiento
2 *adj* renacentista

rend [rend] *vt (pt & pp* **rent**) *Fml* rasgar

render ['rendə(r)] *vt Fml* (**a**) *(give)* dar (**b**) *(make)* hacer (**c**) *Com* presentar (**d**) *(translate)* traducir

rendering ['rendərɪŋ] *n* (**a**) *(of song, piece of music)* interpretación *f* (**b**) *(translation)* traducción *f*

rendezvous ['rɒndɪvuː] **1** *n* (**a**) *(meeting)* cita *f* (**b**) *(place)* lugar *m* de reunión
2 *vi* reunirse

renegade ['renɪgeɪd] *n* renegado(a) *m,f*

renew [rɪ'njuː] *vt (contract etc)* renovar; *(talks etc)* reanudar; **with renewed vigour** con renovadas fuerzas

renewal [rɪ'njuːəl] *n (of contract etc)* renovación *f*; *(of talks etc)* reanudación *f*

renounce [rɪ'naʊns] *vt Fml* renunciar

renovate ['renəveɪt] *vt* renovar, hacer reformas en

renown [rɪ'naʊn] *n* renombre *m*

renowned [rɪ'naʊnd] *adj* renombrado(a)

rent [rent] **1** *n* (**a**) *(for building, car, TV)* alquiler *m* (**b**) *(for land)* arriendo *m*
2 *vt* (**a**) *(building, car, TV)* alquilar, *Méx* rentar (**b**) *(land)* arrendar
3 *pt & pp of* **rend**

rental ['rentəl] *n (of house etc)* alquiler *m*

renunciation [rɪnʌnsɪ'eɪʃən] *n Fml* renuncia *f*

reorganize [riː'ɔːgənaɪz] *vt* reorganizar

rep [rep] *n Fam* (**a**) *Com* representante *mf* (**b**) *Th* teatro *m* de repertorio

repaid [riː'peɪd] *pt & pp of* **repay**

repair [rɪ'peə(r)] **1** *n* reparación *f*, arreglo *m*; **in good/bad r.** en buen/mal estado
2 *vt* (**a**) *(car)* arreglar; *(car)* reparar; *(clothes)* remendar (**b**) *(make amends for)* reparar

repartee [repɑː'tiː] *n* réplica aguda

repatriate [riː'pætrɪeɪt] *vt* repatriar

repay [riː'peɪ] *vt (pt & pp* **repaid**) devolver; **to r. a debt** liquidar una deuda; **to r. a kindness** devolver un favor

repayment [riː'peɪmənt] *n* pago *m*

repeal [rɪ'piːl] *Jur* **1** *n* revocación *f*
2 *vt* revocar

repeat [rɪ'piːt] **1** *vt* repetir; **to r. oneself** repetirse
2 *n (repetition)* repetición *f*; *TV* reposición *f*

repeated [rɪ'piːtɪd] *adj* repetido(a)

repeatedly [rɪ'piːtɪdlɪ] *adv* repetidas veces

repel [rɪ'pel] *vt* (**a**) *(fight off)* repeler (**b**) *(disgust)* repugnar

repellent [rɪ'pelənt] **1** *adj* repelente; **water-r.** impermeable
2 *n* **(insect) r.** loción *f* or spray *m* antiinsectos

repent [rɪ'pent] *vt & vi* arrepentirse (de)

repentance [rɪ'pentəns] *n* arrepentimiento *m*

repercussion [riːpə'kʌʃən] *n (usu pl)* repercusión *f*

repertoire ['repətwɑː(r)] *n* repertorio *m*

repertory ['repətərɪ] *n Th* teatro *m* de repertorio

repetition [repɪ'tɪʃən] *n* repetición *f*

repetitive [rɪ'petɪtɪv] *adj* repetitivo(a)

replace [rɪ'pleɪs] *vt* (**a**) *(put back)* volver a poner en su sitio (**b**) *(substitute for)* sustituir, reemplazar

replacement [rɪ'pleɪsmənt] *n* (**a**) *(returning)* reemplazo *m* (**b**) *(person)* sustituto(a) *m,f* (**c**) *(part)* pieza *f* de recambio

replay ['riːpleɪ] *n* repetición *f*

replenish [rɪ'plenɪʃ] *vt* (**a**) *(fill up)* rellenar (**b**) **to r. stocks** reponer las existencias

replete [rɪ'pliːt] *adj Fml* repleto(a)
replica ['replɪkə] *n* réplica *f*
reply [rɪ'plaɪ] **1** *n* respuesta *f*, contestación *f*
   2 *vi* responder, contestar
report [rɪ'pɔːt] **1** *n* (**a**) informe *m*; **medical r.** parte médico; *Br* **school r.** informe escolar (**b**) *(piece of news)* noticia *f* (**c**) *Press, Rad & TV* reportaje *m* (**d**) *(rumour)* rumor *m* (**e**) *Fml (of gun)* estampido *m*
   2 *vt* (**a**) **it is reported that ...** se dice que ... (**b**) *(tell authorities about)* denunciar (**c**) *Press* hacer un reportaje sobre
   3 *vi* (**a**) *(of committee member etc)* hacer un informe (**b**) *Press* hacer un reportaje (**c**) *(for duty etc)* presentarse; *Mil* **to r. sick** coger la baja por enfermedad
reported [rɪ'pɔːtɪd] *adj* **r. speech** estilo indirecto
reportedly [rɪ'pɔːtɪdlɪ] *adv Fml* según se dice
reporter [rɪ'pɔːtə(r)] *n* periodista *mf*
repose [rɪ'pəʊz] *Fml* **1** *n* reposo *m*
   2 *vt & vi* reposar
repossess [riːpə'zes] *vt* **our house has been repossessed** el banco ha ejecutado la hipoteca de nuestra casa
reprehensible [reprɪ'hensəbəl] *adj* reprensible, censurable
represent [reprɪ'zent] *vt* representar
representation [reprɪzen'teɪʃən] *n* (**a**) representación *f* (**b**) *Fml* **representations** queja *f*
representative [reprɪ'zentətɪv] **1** *adj* representativo(a)
   2 *n* (**a**) representante *mf* (**b**) *US Pol* diputado(a) *m,f*
repress [rɪ'pres] *vt* reprimir, contener
repressed [rɪ'prest] *adj* **to be r.** estar reprimido(a)
repression [rɪ'preʃən] *n* represión *f*
repressive [rɪ'presɪv] *adj* represivo(a)
reprieve [rɪ'priːv] **1** *n* (**a**) *Jur* indulto *m* (**b**) *Fig* alivio *m*
   2 *vt Jur* indultar
reprimand ['reprɪmɑːnd] **1** *n* reprimenda *f*
   2 *vt* reprender
reprisal [rɪ'praɪzəl] *n* represalia *f*
reproach [rɪ'prəʊtʃ] **1** *n* reproche *m*; **beyond r.** intachable
   2 *vt* reprochar
reproachful [rɪ'prəʊtʃfʊl] *adj* reprobador(a)
reproduce [riːprə'djuːs] **1** *vt* reproducir
   2 *vi* reproducirse
reproduction [riːprə'dʌkʃən] *n* reproducción *f*

reproof [rɪ'pruːf] *n Fml* reprobación *f*, censura *f*
reprove [rɪ'pruːv] *vt Fml* reprobar, censurar
reptile ['reptaɪl] *n* reptil *m*
republic [rɪ'pʌblɪk] *n* república *f*
republican [rɪ'pʌblɪkən] *adj & n* republicano(a) *(m,f)*; *US Pol* **R. Party** Partido Republicano
repudiate [rɪ'pjuːdɪeɪt] *vt Fml* (**a**) *(reject)* rechazar (**b**) *(not acknowledge)* negarse a reconocer
repugnant [rɪ'pʌgnənt] *adj* repugnante
repulse [rɪ'pʌls] *vt* rechazar
repulsive [rɪ'pʌlsɪv] *adj* repulsivo(a)
reputable ['repjʊtəbəl] *adj (company etc)* acreditado(a); *(person, products)* de toda confianza
reputation [repjʊ'teɪʃən] *n* reputación *f*
repute [rɪ'pjuːt] *n Fml* reputación *f*
reputed [rɪ'pjuːtɪd] *adj* supuesto(a); **to be r. to be** ser considerado(a) como
reputedly [rɪ'pjuːtɪdlɪ] *adv* según se dice
request [rɪ'kwest] **1** *n* petición *f*, solicitud *f*; **available on r.** disponible a petición de los interesados; *Br* **r. stop** *(for bus)* parada *f* discrecional
   2 *vt* pedir, solicitar
require [rɪ'kwaɪə(r)] *vt* (**a**) *(need)* necesitar, requerir (**b**) *(demand)* exigir
requirement [rɪ'kwaɪəmənt] *n* (**a**) *(need)* necesidad *f* (**b**) *(demand)* requisito *m*

> 🔎 Note that the Spanish word **requerimiento** is a false friend and is never a translation for the English word **requirement**. In Spanish, **requerimiento** means both "entreaty" and "writ, injunction".

requisite ['rekwɪzɪt] *Fml* **1** *adj* requerido(a)
   2 *n* requisito *m*
requisition [rekwɪ'zɪʃən] **1** *n* requisición *f*
   2 *vt* requisar
rescind [rɪ'sɪnd] *vt Fml (contract)* rescindir; *(law)* abrogar
rescue ['reskjuː] **1** *n* rescate *m*; **r. team** equipo *m* de rescate
   2 *vt* rescatar
rescuer ['reskjʊə(r)] *n* rescatador(a) *m,f*
research [rɪ'sɜːtʃ] **1** *n* investigación *f*; **R. and Development** Investigación más Desarrollo
   2 *vt & vi* investigar
researcher [rɪ'sɜːtʃə(r)] *n* investigador(a) *m,f*
resemblance [rɪ'zembləns] *n* semejanza *f*

resemble [rɪ'zembəl] *vt* parecerse a

resent [rɪ'zent] *vt* ofenderse por

resentful [rɪ'zentfʊl] *adj* ofendido(a)

resentment [rɪ'zentmənt] *n* resentimiento *m*

reservation [rezə'veɪʃən] *n* reserva *f*

reserve [rɪ'zɜːv] **1** *n* (a) reserva *f*; **to keep sth in r.** guardar algo de reserva (b) *Sport* suplente *mf* (c) *Mil* **reserves** reservas *fpl*
2 *vt* reservar

reserved [rɪ'zɜːvd] *adj* reservado(a)

reservoir [rezəvwɑː(r)] *n* embalse *m*, pantano *m*; *Fig* reserva *f*

reshape [riː'ʃeɪp] *vt* rehacer; *Fig* reorganizar

reshuffle [riː'ʃʌfəl] *n Pol* remodelación *f*

reside [rɪ'zaɪd] *vi Fml* residir

residence ['rezɪdəns] *n Fml (home)* residencia *f; (address)* domicilio *m; (period of time)* permanencia *f*

resident ['rezɪdənt] *adj & n* residente *(mf); US Med* = médico que ha cumplido la residencia y prosigue con su especialización; **to be r. in** estar domiciliado(a) en

residential [rezɪ'denʃəl] *adj* residencial

residual [rɪ'zɪdjʊəl] *adj* residual

residue ['rezɪdjuː] *n* residuo *m*

resign [rɪ'zaɪn] **1** *vt* (a) *(give up)* dimitir (b) **to r. oneself to sth** resignarse a algo
2 *vi (from job)* dimitir

resignation [rezɪg'neɪʃən] *n* (a) *(from a job)* dimisión *f* (b) *(acceptance)* resignación *f*

resigned [rɪ'zaɪnd] *adj* resignado(a)

resilience [rɪ'zɪlɪəns] *n* resistencia *f*

resilient [rɪ'zɪlɪənt] *adj (strong)* resistente

resin ['rezɪn] *n* resina *f*

resist [rɪ'zɪst] **1** *vt* (a) *(not yield to)* resistir (b) *(oppose)* oponerse a
2 *vi* resistir

resistance [rɪ'zɪstəns] *n* resistencia *f*

resit [riː'sɪt] *vt (exam)* volver a presentarse a

resolute ['rezəluːt] *adj* resuelto(a), decidido(a)

resolution [rezə'luːʃən] *n* resolución *f*

resolve [rɪ'zɒlv] **1** *n* resolución *f*
2 *vt* resolver; **to r. to do** resolverse a hacer
3 *vi* resolverse

resonant ['rezənənt] *adj* resonante

resort [rɪ'zɔːt] **1** *n* (a) *(place)* lugar *m* de vacaciones; **tourist r.** centro turístico (b) *(recourse)* recurso *m*; **as a last r.** como último recurso
2 *vi* recurrir (**to** a)

𝒪 Note that the Spanish word **resorte** is a false friend and is never a translation for the English word **resort**. In Spanish, **resorte** means both "spring" and "means".

resound [rɪ'zaʊnd] *vi* resonar; *Fig* tener resonancia

resounding [rɪ'zaʊndɪŋ] *adj* **a r. failure** un fracaso total; **a r. success** un éxito rotundo

resource [rɪ'sɔːs] *n* recurso *m*

resourceful [rɪ'sɔːsfʊl] *adj* ingenioso(a)

respect [rɪ'spekt] **1** *n* (a) *(deference)* respeto *m*; **to pay one's respects to sb** presentar sus respetos a algn (b) *(relation, reference)* respecto *m*; **in that r.** a ese respecto; **with r. to** con referencia a
2 *vt* respetar

respectable [rɪ'spektəbəl] *adj* respetable; *(clothes)* decente

respectful [rɪ'spektfʊl] *adj* respetuoso(a)

respective [rɪ'spektɪv] *adj* respectivo(a)

respectively [rɪ'spektɪvlɪ] *adv* respectivamente

respite ['respaɪt] *n Fml* respiro *m*

resplendent [rɪ'splendənt] *adj* resplandeciente

respond [rɪ'spɒnd] *vi* responder

response [rɪ'spɒns] *n* (a) *(reply)* respuesta *f* (b) *(reaction)* reacción *f*

responsibility [rɪspɒnsə'bɪlɪtɪ] *n* responsabilidad *f*

responsible [rɪ'spɒnsəbəl] *adj* responsable (**for** de); **to be r. to sb** tener que dar cuentas a algn

responsive [rɪ'spɒnsɪv] *adj* sensible

rest¹ [rest] **1** *n* (a) *(break)* descanso *m*; **r. cure** cura *f* de reposo; *US* **r. room** aseos *mpl* (b) *(peace)* tranquilidad *f*; **at r.** *(object)* inmóbil (c) *(support)* apoyo *m* (d) *Mus* pausa *f*
2 *vt* (a) descansar (b) *(lean)* apoyar; **to r. a ladder against a wall** apoyar una escalera contra una pared
3 *vi* (a) descansar (b) *(be calm)* quedarse tranquilo(a) (c) **it doesn't r. with me** no depende de mí; **we'll let the matter r.** dejémoslo estar

rest² [rest] *n* **the r.** *(remainder)* el resto, lo demás; **the r. of the day** el resto del día; **the r. of the girls** las demás chicas; **the r. of us** los demás

restaurant ['restərɒnt] *n* restaurante *m*; *Rail* **r. car** coche *m* restaurante

restful ['restfʊl] *adj* relajante

restitution [restɪ'tjuːʃən] *n Fml* restitución *f*; **to make r.** restituir

restive ['restɪv] *adj* inquieto(a), nervioso(a)

restless ['restlɪs] *adj* agitado(a), inquieto(a)

restoration [restə'reɪʃən] *n* (a) *(giving back)* devolución *f* (b) *Br Hist* **the R.** la Restauración (c) *(of building, piece of furniture)* restauración *f*

restore [rɪ'stɔ:(r)] *vt* (a) *(give back)* devolver (b) *(re-establish)* restablecer (c) *(building etc)* restaurar

restrain [rɪ'streɪn] *vt* contener; **to r. one's anger** reprimir la cólera; **to r. oneself** contenerse

restrained [rɪ'streɪnd] *adj (person)* moderado(a); *(emotion)* contenido(a)

restraint [rɪ'streɪnt] *n* (a) *(restriction)* restricción *f*, *(hindrance)* traba *f* (b) *(moderation)* moderación *f*

restrict [rɪ'strɪkt] *vt* restringir, limitar

restriction [rɪ'strɪkʃən] *n* restricción *f*, limitación *f*

restrictive [rɪ'strɪktɪv] *adj* restrictivo(a)

result [rɪ'zʌlt] 1 *n* (a) resultado *m* (b) *(consequence)* consecuencia *f*; **as a r. of** como consecuencia de
2 *vi* (a) resultar; **to r. from** resultar de (b) **to r. in** causar

resume [rɪ'zju:m] 1 *vt* *(journey, work, conversation)* reanudar; *(control)* reasumir
2 *vi* recomenzar

> 🖉 Note that the Spanish verb **resumir** is a false friend and is never a translation for the English verb **to resume**. In Spanish, **resumir** means "to sum up, to summarize".

résumé ['rezjʊmeɪ] *n* (a) *(summary)* resumen *m* (b) *US (curriculum vitae)* currículum (vitae) *m*

resumption [rɪ'zʌmpʃən] *n* *(of journey, work, conversation)* reanudación *f*

resurface [ri:'sɜ:fɪs] 1 *vt (road)* rehacer el firme de
2 *vi Fig* resurgir

resurgence [rɪ'sɜ:dʒəns] *n* resurgimiento *m*

resurrection [rezə'rekʃən] *n* resurrección *f*

resuscitate [rɪ'sʌsɪteɪt] *vt Med* reanimar

retail ['ri:teɪl] 1 *n* venta *f* al por menor; **r. outlet** punto *m* de venta; **r. price** precio *m* de venta al público; **R. Price Index** Índice *m* de Precios al Consumo
2 *vt* vender al por menor
3 *vi* venderse al por menor
4 *adv* al por menor

retailer ['ri:teɪlə(r)] *n* detallista *mf*

retain [rɪ'teɪn] *vt* (a) *(heat)* conservar; *(personal effects)* guardar (b) *(water)* retener (c) *(facts, information)* recordar (d) **to r. the services of a lawyer** contratar a un abogado

retainer [rɪ'teɪnə(r)] *n* (a) *(payment)* anticipo *m* sobre los honorarios (b) *(servant)* criado(a) *m,f*

retaliate [rɪ'tælɪeɪt] *vi* tomar represalias (**against** contra)

retaliation [rɪtælɪ'eɪʃən] *n* represalias *fpl*; **in r.** en represalia

retarded [rɪ'tɑ:dɪd] *adj* retrasado(a)

retch [retʃ] *vi* tener náuseas

retentive [rɪ'tentɪv] *adj* retentivo(a)

rethink ['ri:θɪŋk] *n Fam* **to have a r. about sth** volver a reflexionar sobre algo

reticent ['retɪsənt] *adj* reticente

retina ['retɪnə] *n* retina *f*

retinue ['retɪnju:] *n* séquito *m*

retire [rɪ'taɪə(r)] 1 *vt* jubilar
2 *vi* (a) *(stop working)* jubilarse (b) *(from race)* retirarse; **to r. for the night** irse a la cama, acostarse

retired [rɪ'taɪəd] *adj* jubilado(a)

retiree [rɪtaɪə'ri:] *n US* retirado(a) *m,f*

retirement [rɪ'taɪəmənt] *n* jubilación *f*

retiring [rɪ'taɪərɪŋ] *adj* (a) *(reserved)* reservado(a) (b) *(official)* saliente

retort [rɪ'tɔ:t] 1 *n* réplica *f*
2 *vi* replicar

retrace [ri:'treɪs] *vt (recall)* reconstruir; **to r. one's steps** volver sobre sus pasos

retract [rɪ'trækt] 1 *vt* (a) *(claws)* retraer; *(landing gear)* replegar (b) *(statement)* retirar
2 *vi* (a) *(claws)* retraerse; *(landing gear)* replegarse (b) *Fml* retractarse

retread ['ri:tred] *n Aut* neumático recauchutado

retreat [rɪ'tri:t] 1 *n* (a) *Mil* retirada *f* (b) *(shelter)* refugio *m* (c) *Rel* retiro *m*
2 *vi* retirarse (**from** de)

retrial ['ri:traɪəl] *n Jur* nuevo juicio

retribution [retrɪ'bju:ʃən] *n* represalias *fpl*

> 🖉 Note that the Spanish word **retribución** is a false friend and is never a translation for the English word **retribution**. In Spanish, **retribución** means "payment, reward".

retrieval [rɪ'tri:vəl] *n* recuperación *f*; *Comput* **information r. system** sistema *m* de recuperación de datos

retrieve [rɪ'tri:v] *vt* (a) *(recover)* recuperar; *(of dog)* cobrar; *Comput* recoger (b) *(rescue)* salvar

retriever [rɪ'tri:və(r)] *n* perro *m* cazador

retrograde ['retrəʊgreɪd] *adj* retrógrado(a)

retrospect ['retrəʊspekt] *n* **in r.** retrospectivamente

retrospective [retrəʊ'spektɪv] **1** *adj* retrospectivo(a)

2 *n Art* (exposición *f*) retrospectiva *f*

return [rɪ'tɜːn] **1** *n* (*of person*) regreso *m*, vuelta *f*; **by r. of post** a vuelta de correo; **in r. for** a cambio de; **many happy returns!** ¡felicidades!; **r. match** partido *m* de vuelta; *Br* **r. (ticket)** billete *m* de ida y vuelta **(b)** (*of sth borrowed, stolen*) devolución *f* **(c)** (*profit*) beneficio *m*, ganancia *f* **(d)** (*interest*) interés *m*

2 *vt* (a) (*give back*) devolver; **r. to sender** (*on envelope*) devuélvase al remitente; **to r. a favour/sb's love** corresponder a un favor/al amor de algn **(b)** *Br Pol* elegir **(c)** *Jur* (*verdict*) pronunciar

3 *vi* (a) (*come or go back*) volver, regresar **(b)** (*reappear*) reaparecer

returnable [rɪ'tɜːnəbəl] *adj* (*bottle*) retornable

reunion [riː'juːnjən] *n* reunión *f*

reunite [riːjuː'naɪt] *vt* **to be reunited with** (*after separation*) reunirse con

rev [rev] *Fam Aut* **1** *n* revolución *f*

2 *vi* **to r. (up)** acelerar el motor

revamp [riː'væmp] *vt Fam* modernizar, renovar

reveal [rɪ'viːl] *vt* (*make known*) revelar; (*show*) dejar ver

revealing [rɪ'viːlɪŋ] *adj* revelador(a)

reveille [rɪ'vælɪ] *n* diana *f*

revel ['revəl] *vi* disfrutar (**in** con); **to r. in doing sth** gozar muchísimo haciendo algo

revelation [revə'leɪʃən] *n* revelación *f*

revelry ['revəlrɪ] *n* jarana *f*, juerga *f*

revenge [rɪ'vendʒ] *n* venganza *f*; **to take r. on sb for sth** vengarse de algo en algn

revenue ['revɪnjuː] *n* renta *f*

reverberate [rɪ'vɜːbəreɪt] *vi* (a) (*sound*) reverberar **(b)** (*ideas, news*) resonar

reverberation [rɪvɜːbə'reɪʃən] *n* resonancia *f*

revere [rɪ'vɪə(r)] *vt* reverenciar

reverence ['revərəns] *n* reverencia *f*

reverend ['revərənd] *Rel* **1** *adj* reverendo(a); **R. Mother** reverenda madre

2 *n* (*Protestant*) pastor *m*; (*Catholic*) padre *m*

reverie ['revərɪ] *n* ensueño *m*

reversal [rɪ'vɜːsəl] *n* (a) (*of order*) inversión *f* **(b)** (*of attitude, policy*) cambio *m* total **(c)** *Jur* revocación *f*

reverse [rɪ'vɜːs] **1** *adj* inverso(a); *Br*

r.-charge call llamada *f or Am* llamado *m* a cobro revertido

2 *n* (a) **quite the r.** todo lo contrario **(b)** (*other side*) (*of cloth*) revés *m*; (*of coin*) cruz *f*; (*of page*) dorso *m* **(c)** *Aut* **r. gear** marcha *f* atrás

3 *vt* (a) (*order*) invertir **(b)** (*turn round*) volver del revés **(c)** (*change*) cambiar totalmente **(d)** *Jur* revocar **(e)** *Br Tel* **to r. the charges** poner una conferencia a cobro revertido

4 *vi Aut* dar marcha atrás

revert [rɪ'vɜːt] *vi* volver (**to** a)

review [rɪ'vjuː] **1** *n* (a) (*examination*) examen *m* **(b)** *Mil* revista *f* **(c)** *Press* crítica *f*, reseña *f* **(d)** (*magazine*) revista *f*

2 *vt* (a) (*examine*) examinar **(b)** *Mil* **to r. the troops** pasar revista a las tropas **(c)** (*book etc*) hacer una crítica de

reviewer [rɪ'vjuːə(r)] *n* crítico(a) *m,f*

revile [rɪ'vaɪl] *vt Fml* injuriar

revise [rɪ'vaɪz] *vt* (a) (*look over*) revisar; (*at school*) repasar **(b)** (*change*) modificar **(c)** (*proofs*) corregir

revision [rɪ'vɪʒən] *n* (a) revisión *f*; (*at school*) repaso *m* **(b)** (*change*) modificación *f* **(c)** (*of proofs*) corrección *f*

revitalize [riː'vaɪtəlaɪz] *vt* revivificar

revival [rɪ'vaɪvəl] *n* (a) (*of interest*) renacimiento *m*; (*of economy, industry*) reactivación *f*; (*of fashion*) resurgimiento *m* **(b)** *Th* reestreno *m* **(c)** *Med* reanimación *f*

revive [rɪ'vaɪv] **1** *vt* (a) (*interest*) renovar; (*a law*) restablecer; (*economy, industry*) reactivar; (*hopes*) despertar **(b)** *Th* reestrenar **(c)** *Med* reanimar

2 *vi* (a) (*interest, hopes*) renacer **(b)** *Med* volver en sí

revoke [rɪ'vəʊk] *vt* revocar; (*permission*) suspender

revolt [rɪ'vəʊlt] **1** *n* rebelión *f*, sublevación *f*

2 *vi* rebelarse, sublevarse

3 *vt* repugnar, dar asco a

revolting [rɪ'vəʊltɪŋ] *adj* repugnante

revolution [revə'luːʃən] *n* revolución *f*

revolutionary [revə'luːʃənərɪ] *adj & n* revolucionario(a) *(m,f)*

revolve [rɪ'vɒlv] **1** *vi* girar; *Fig* **to r. around** girar en torno a

2 *vt* hacer girar

> ⚲ Note that the Spanish verb **revolver** is a false friend and is never a translation for the English verb **to revolve**. In Spanish, **revolver** means "to stir, to mix" and "to mess up".

revolver [rɪ'vɒlvə(r)] *n* revólver *m*

revolving [rɪ'vɒlvɪŋ] *adj* giratorio(a)

revue [rɪ'vjuː] n revista f

revulsion [rɪ'vʌlʃən] n repulsión f

reward [rɪ'wɔːd] **1** n recompensa f
2 vt recompensar

rewarding [rɪ'wɔːdɪŋ] adj provechoso(a)

rewire [riː'waɪə(r)] vt Elec **to r. a house**
poner nueva instalación eléctrica a una
casa

reword [riː'wɜːd] vt expresar con otras
palabras

rewrite [riː'raɪt] vt (pt **rewrote** [riː'rəʊt];
pp **rewritten** [riː'rɪtən]) escribir de nuevo

rhapsody ['ræpsədɪ] n Mus rapsodia f

rhetoric ['retərɪk] n retórica f

rhetorical [rɪ'tɒrɪkəl] adj retórico(a)

rheumatism ['ruːmətɪzəm] n reuma m

rheumatoid ['ruːmətɔɪd] adj **r. arthritis**
reuma m articular

Rhine [raɪn] n **the R.** el Rin

rhinoceros [raɪ'nɒsərəs] n rinoceronte m

rhododendron [rəʊdə'dendrən] n rododendro m

Rhone [rəʊn] n **the R.** el Ródano

rhubarb ['ruːbɑːb] n ruibarbo m

rhyme [raɪm] **1** n rima f; (poem) poema m
2 vi rimar

rhythm ['rɪðəm] n ritmo m

rib¹ [rɪb] n (a) Anat costilla f; **r. cage** caja
torácica (b) (in knitting) canalé m (c) (of
umbrella) varilla f (d) Bot (of leaf) nervio
m

rib² [rɪb] vt Fam burlarse de

ribald ['rɪbəld] adj (humour) verde

ribbon ['rɪbən] n cinta f; (in hair etc) lazo
m; **torn to ribbons** hecho(a) jirones

rice [raɪs] n arroz m; **brown r.** arroz integral; **r. paper** papel de arroz; **r. pudding**
arroz con leche

rich [rɪtʃ] **1** adj (person, food) rico(a);
(soil) fértil; (voice) sonoro(a); (colour)
vivo(a)
2 npl **the r.** los ricos

riches ['rɪtʃɪz] npl riquezas fpl

richly ['rɪtʃlɪ] adv ricamente; **r. deserved**
bien merecido(a)

richness ['rɪtʃnɪs] n riqueza f; (of soil)
fertilidad f; (of voice) sonoridad f; (of
colour) viveza f

rickets ['rɪkɪts] n sing Med raquitismo m

rickety ['rɪkətɪ] adj (chair etc) cojo(a);
(car) desvencijado(a)

ricochet ['rɪkəʃeɪ, 'rɪkəʃet] **1** n rebote m
2 vi rebotar

rid [rɪd] vt (pt & pp rid) librar; **to get r. of
sth** deshacerse de algo; **to r. oneself of**
librarse de

riddance ['rɪdəns] n Fam **good r.!** ¡ya era
hora!

ridden ['rɪdən] pp of **ride**

riddle¹ ['rɪdəl] n (a) (puzzle) acertijo m,
adivinanza f (b) (mystery) enigma m

riddle² ['rɪdəl] vt (with bullets) acribillar

ride [raɪd] **1** n paseo m, vuelta f; **a short
bus r.** un corto trayecto en autobús; Fam
to take sb for a r. tomar el pelo a algn;
horse r. paseo a caballo
2 vt (pt **rode**; pp **ridden**) (bicycle, horse)
montar en; **can you r. a bike?** ¿sabes
montar en bici?
3 vi (a) (on horse) montar a caballo (b)
(travel) (in bus, train etc) viajar (c) Naut **to
r. at anchor** estar anclado(a)
▸ **ride out** vt sep sobrevivir; **to r. out the
storm** capear el temporal

rider ['raɪdə(r)] n (of horse) (man) jinete
m; (woman) amazona f; (of bicycle) ciclista mf; (of motorbike) motociclista mf

ridge [rɪdʒ] n (crest of a hill) cresta f;
(hillock) loma f; (of roof) caballete m;
Met área m

ridicule ['rɪdɪkjuːl] **1** n burla f
2 vt burlarse de

ridiculous [rɪ'dɪkjʊləs] adj ridículo(a)

riding ['raɪdɪŋ] n equitación f; **r. breeches**
pantalones mpl de montar; **r. school** escuela hípica

rife [raɪf] adj abundante; **rumour is r. that
...** corre la voz de que ...; **to be r. with**
abundar en

riffraff ['rɪfræf] n Fam chusma f, gentuza
f

rifle¹ ['raɪfəl] n fusil m, rifle m; **r. range**
campo m de tiro

rifle² ['raɪfəl] vt desvalijar

rift [rɪft] n (a) Geol falla f (b) Fig (in
friendship) ruptura f; Pol (in party) escisión f; (quarrel) desavenencia f

rig [rɪg] **1** n (a) Naut aparejo m (b) (oil) **r.**
(onshore) torre f de perforación; (off-
shore) plataforma petrolífera
2 vt Pej amañar
▸ **rig out** vt sep Fam ataviar
▸ **rig up** vt sep improvisar

rigging ['rɪgɪŋ] n aparejo m, jarcia f

right [raɪt] **1** adj (a) (not left) derecho(a);
the r. hand la mano derecha
(b) (correct) correcto(a); (time) exac-
to(a); **to be r.** tener razón; **all r.** de acuerdo; **r.?** ¿vale?; **that's r.** eso es; **the r. word**
la palabra justa
(c) (true) cierto(a)
(d) (suitable) adecuado(a); **the r. time** el
momento oportuno
(e) (proper) apropiado(a)
(f) Fam (healthy) bien
(g) Fam (complete) auténtico(a)

(**h**) *(in order)* en orden

(**i**) **r. angle** ángulo recto

2 *n* (**a**) *(right side)* derecha *f*

(**b**) *(right hand)* mano derecha

(**c**) *Pol* **the R.** la derecha

(**d**) *(lawful claim)* derecho *m*; **in one's own r.** por derecho propio; **r. of way** *(across land)* derecho de paso; *(on roads)* prioridad *f*; **civil rights** derechos civiles

(**e**) **r. and wrong** el bien y el mal

3 *adv* (**a**) *(correctly)* bien; **it's just r.** es justo lo que hace falta

(**b**) **r. away** *(immediately)* en seguida

(**c**) *(to the right)* a la derecha; **r. and left** a diestro y siniestro; **to turn r.** girar a la derecha

(**d**) *(directly)* directamente; **go r. on** sigue recto; **r. at the top** en todo lo alto; **r. in the middle** justo en medio; **r. to the end** hasta el final

4 *vt* (**a**) *(correct)* corregir

(**b**) *(put straight)* enderezar

righteous [ˈraɪtʃəs] *adj (upright)* recto(a)

rightful [ˈraɪtfʊl] *adj* legítimo(a)

right-hand [raɪtˈhænd] *adj* derecho(a); **r. drive** conducción *f* por la derecha; **r. side** lado derecho; *Fam* **r. man** brazo derecho

right-handed [raɪtˈhændɪd] *adj (person)* que usa la mano derecha; *(tool)* para la mano derecha

rightly [ˈraɪtlɪ] *adv* debidamente; **and r. so** y con razón

right-wing [ˈraɪtwɪŋ] *adj* de derechas, derechista

right-winger [raɪtˈwɪŋə(r)] *n* derechista *mf*

rigid [ˈrɪdʒɪd] *adj* rígido(a), inflexible

rigidity [rɪˈdʒɪdɪtɪ] *n* rigidez *f*, inflexibilidad *f*

rigmarole [ˈrɪgmərəʊl] *n Fam* galimatías *m inv*

rigor [ˈrɪgər] *n US* = **rigour**

rigorous [ˈrɪgərəs] *adj* riguroso(a)

rigour [ˈrɪgə(r)] *n* rigor *m*, severidad *f*

rile [raɪl] *vt Fam* irritar, sacar de quicio

rim [rɪm] *n (edge)* borde *m*; *(of wheel)* llanta *f*; *(of spectacles)* montura *f*

rind [raɪnd] *n (of fruit, cheese)* corteza *f*

ring¹ [rɪŋ] **1** *n* (**a**) *(sound of bell)* toque *m*; *(of doorbell, alarm clock)* timbre *m* (**b**) *Tel* llamada *f*

2 *vt (pt* **rang**; *pp* **rung)** (**a**) *(bell)* tocar; *Fig* **it rings a bell** me suena (**b**) *Br Tel* llamar por teléfono

3 *vi* (**a**) *(bell, phone etc)* sonar (**b**) **my ears are ringing** tengo un pitido en los oídos (**c**) *Tel* llamar

▸ **ring back** *vt sep Br Tel* volver a llamar

▸ **ring off** *vi Br Tel* colgar

▸ **ring out** *vi* resonar

▸ **ring up** *vt sep Br Tel* llamar por teléfono a

ring² [rɪŋ] **1** *n* (**a**) *(metal hoop)* aro *m*; **curtain r.** anilla *f*; **r. binder** carpeta *f* de anillas (**b**) *(for finger)* anillo *m*, sortija *f*; **r. finger** dedo *m* anular (**c**) *(circle)* círculo *m*; *Br* **r. road** carretera *f* de circunvalación (**d**) **rings** *(in gymnastics)* anillas *fpl* (**e**) *(group of people)* corro *m*; *(of spies)* red *f*; *(of thieves)* banda *f* (**f**) *(arena)* pista *f*; *(for boxing)* cuadrilátero *m*; *(for bullfights)* ruedo *m*; **circus r.** pista de circo

2 *vt* (**a**) *(bird, animal)* anillar (**b**) *(surround)* rodear

ringing [ˈrɪŋɪŋ] *n (of bell)* toque *m*, repique *m*; *(in ears)* pitido *m*

ringleader [ˈrɪŋliːdə(r)] *n* cabecilla *mf*

ringlet [ˈrɪŋlɪt] *n* tirabuzón *m*

rink [rɪŋk] *n* pista *f*; **ice r.** pista de hielo

rinse [rɪns] **1** *n* (**a**) *(of clothes, hair)* aclarado *m*, enjuague *m*; *(of dishes)* enjuagado *m* (**b**) *(tint for hair)* reflejo *m*

2 *vt* (**a**) aclarar; *(the dishes)* enjuagar (**b**) **to r. one's hair** *(tint)* darse reflejos en el pelo

riot [ˈraɪət] **1** *n* (**a**) disturbio *m*, motín *m*; **to run r.** desmandarse; **r. police** policía *f* antidisturbios (**b**) *Fig (of colour)* profusión *f*

2 *vi* amotinarse

rioter [ˈraɪətə(r)] *n* amotinado(a) *m,f*

riotous [ˈraɪətəs] *adj* (**a**) amotinado(a) (**b**) *(noisy)* bullicioso(a) (**c**) *(unrestrained)* desenfrenado(a)

rip [rɪp] **1** *n (tear)* rasgón *m*

2 *vt* rasgar, rajar; **to r. one's trousers** rajarse los pantalones

3 *vi* rasgarse, rajarse

▸ **rip off** *vt sep Fam* **to r. sb off** timar a algn

▸ **rip up** *vt sep* hacer pedacitos

ripcord [ˈrɪpkɔːd] *n* cuerda *f* de apertura

ripe [raɪp] *adj* (**a**) maduro(a) (**b**) *(ready)* listo(a); **the time is r.** es el momento oportuno

ripen [ˈraɪpən] *vt & vi* madurar

rip-off [ˈrɪpɒf] *n Fam* timo *m*

ripple [ˈrɪpəl] **1** *n* (**a**) *(on water, fabric)* onda *f* (**b**) *(sound)* murmullo *m*

2 *vt (water)* ondular

3 *vi* (**a**) *(water)* ondularse (**b**) *(applause)* extenderse

rise [raɪz] **1** *n* (**a**) *(of slope, hill)* cuesta *f*

(**b**) *(of waters)* crecida *f*

(**c**) *(in status)* ascenso *m*

(**d**) *(in prices, temperature)* subida *f; (in wages)* aumento *m*
(**e**) *(in sound)* aumento *m*
(**f**) **to give r. to** ocasionar
2 *vi (pt* rose; *pp* risen ['rɪzən]) (**a**) *(land etc)* elevarse
(**b**) *(waters)* crecer; *(river)* nacer; *(tide)* subir; *(wind)* levantarse
(**c**) *(sun, moon)* salir
(**d**) *(voice)* alzarse
(**e**) *(in rank)* ascender
(**f**) *(prices, temperature)* subir; *(wages)* aumentar
(**g**) *(curtain)* subir
(**h**) *(from bed)* levantarse
(**i**) *(stand up)* levantarse; *Fig (city, building)* erguirse
(**j**) **to r. to a challenge** aceptar un reto; **to r. to the occasion** ponerse a la altura de las circunstancias
▸ **rise above** *vt insep* estar por encima de
▸ **rise up** *vi (rebel)* sublevarse

rising ['raɪzɪŋ] **1** *adj (sun)* naciente; *(tide)* creciente; *(prices)* en aumento; **r. damp** humedad *f*
2 *n* (**a**) *(of sun)* salida *f* (**b**) *(rebellion)* levantamiento *m*

risk [rɪsk] **1** *n* riesgo *m*; **at r.** en peligro; **at your own r.** por su cuenta y riesgo; **to take risks** arriesgarse
2 *vt* arriesgar; **I'll r. it** correré el riesgo

risky ['rɪskɪ] *adj* (**riskier, riskiest**) arriesgado(a)

risqué ['riːskeɪ] *adj* atrevido(a); *(joke)* picante

rite [raɪt] *n* rito *m*; **the last rites** la extremaunción

ritual ['rɪtjʊəl] *adj & n* ritual *(m)*

rival ['raɪvəl] **1** *adj & n* rival *(mf)*
2 *vt* rivalizar con

rivalry ['raɪvəlrɪ] *n* rivalidad *f*

river ['rɪvə(r)] *n* río *m*; **down/up r.** río abajo/arriba

river-bank ['rɪvəbæŋk] *n* orilla *f*, ribera *f*

river-bed ['rɪvəbed] *n* lecho *m*

rivet ['rɪvɪt] **1** *n Tech* remache *m*, roblón *f*
2 *vt Tech* remachar; *Fig* cautivar

riveting ['rɪvɪtɪŋ] *adj Fig* fascinante

roach [rəʊtʃ] *n US Fam (cockroach)* cucaracha *f*

road [rəʊd] *n* (**a**) carretera *f; Br* **A/B r.** carretera nacional/secundaria; **main r.** carretera principal; **r. accident** accidente *m* de tráfico; **r. safety** seguridad *f* vial; **r. sign** señal *f* de tráfico; **r.** *Br* **works** *or US* **work** obras *fpl* (**b**) *(street)* calle *f* (**c**) *(way)* camino *m*

roadblock ['rəʊdblɒk] *n* control *m* policial

roadhog ['rəʊdhɒg] *n Fam* loco(a) *m,f* del volante, dominguero(a) *m,f*

roadside ['rəʊdsaɪd] *n* borde *m* de la carretera; **r. restaurant/café** restaurante *m*/cafetería *f* de carretera

roadway ['rəʊdweɪ] *n* calzada *f*

roadworthy ['rəʊdwɜːðɪ] *adj (vehicle)* en buen estado

roam [rəʊm] **1** *vt* vagar por, rondar
2 *vi* vagar

roar [rɔː(r)] **1** *n (of lion)* rugido *m; (of bull, sea, wind)* bramido *m; (of crowd)* clamor *m*
2 *vi (lion, crowd)* rugir; *(bull, sea, wind)* bramar; *(crowd)* clamar; *Fig* **to r. with laughter** reírse a carcajadas

roaring ['rɔːrɪŋ] *adj Fam Fig* un éxito clamoroso; **to do a r. trade** hacer un negocio redondo

roast [rəʊst] **1** *adj (meat)* asado(a); **r. beef** rosbif *m*
2 *n Culin* asado *m*
3 *vt (meat)* asar; *(coffee, nuts)* tostar
4 *vi* asarse; *Fam Fig* **I'm roasting** me aso de calor

rob [rɒb] *vt* robar; *(bank)* atracar

robber ['rɒbə(r)] *n* ladrón(ona) *m,f;* **bank r.** atracador(a) *m,f*

robbery ['rɒbərɪ] *n* robo *m*

robe [rəʊb] *n (ceremonial)* toga *f; (dressing gown)* bata *f*

robin ['rɒbɪn] *n* petirrojo *m*

robot ['rəʊbɒt] *n* robot *m*

robust [rəʊˈbʌst] *adj (sturdy)* robusto(a)

rock [rɒk] **1** *n* (**a**) roca *f; Fig* **to be on the rocks** *(of marriage)* estar a punto de fracasar; *Fig* **whisky on the rocks** whisky *m* con hielo (**b**) *US (stone)* piedra *f* (**c**) *Br (sweet)* **stick of r.** barra *f* de caramelo (**d**) *Mus* música *f* rock; **r. and roll** rock and roll *m*
2 *vt* (**a**) *(chair)* mecer; *(baby)* acunar (**b**) *(shake)* hacer temblar; *Fig (shock)* conmover
3 *vi* (**a**) *(move to and fro)* mecerse (**b**) *(shake)* vibrar

rock-bottom ['rɒkˈbɒtəm] *adj* bajísimo(a); **r. prices** precios regalados

rockery ['rɒkərɪ] *n* jardín *m* de rocas

rocket ['rɒkɪt] **1** *n* cohete *m*; **r. launcher** lanzacohetes *m inv*
2 *vi Fam (prices)* dispararse

rocking-chair ['rɒkɪŋtʃeə(r)] *n* mecedora *f*

rocking-horse ['rɒkɪŋhɔːs] *n* caballito *m* de balancín

rocky ['rɒkɪ] *adj* (**rockier, rockiest**) rocoso(a); *Fam Fig* (*unsteady*) inseguro(a); **the R. Mountains** las Montañas Rocosas

rod [rɒd] *n* (*of metal*) barra *f*; (*stick*) vara *f*; **fishing r.** caña *f* de pescar

rode [rəʊd] *pt of* **ride**

rodent ['rəʊdənt] *n* roedor *m*

roe¹ [rəʊ] *n Zool* **r.** (**deer**) corzo(a) *m,f*

roe² [rəʊ] *n* (*fish eggs*) hueva *f*

rogue [rəʊg] *n* granuja *m*

role, rôle [rəʊl] *n* papel *m*; **to play a r.** desempeñar un papel

roll [rəʊl] **1** *n* (**a**) rollo *m*; **r. of banknotes** fajo *m* de billetes; *Fam Fig* **rolls of fat** michelines *mpl* (**b**) (**bread**) **r.** bollo *m* (**c**) (*list of names*) lista *f*, nómina *f*; **to call the r.** pasar lista (**d**) (*movement of ship*) balanceo *m* (**e**) (*of drum*) redoble *m*; (*of thunder*) fragor *m*
  2 *vt* (**a**) (*ball*) hacer rodar (**b**) (*cigarette*) liar (**c**) (*move*) mover (**d**) (*push*) empujar (**e**) (*lawn, road*) allanar
  3 *vi* (**a**) (*ball*) rodar; *Fam* **to be rolling in money** estar forrado(a) (**b**) (*animal*) revolcarse (**c**) (*ship*) balancearse (**d**) (*drum*) redoblar; (*thunder*) retumbar
  ▶ **roll about, roll around** *vi* rodar (de acá para allá)
  ▶ **roll by** *vi* (*years*) pasar
  ▶ **roll in** *vi Fam* (**a**) (*arrive*) llegar (**b**) (*money*) llegar a raudales
  ▶ **roll over** *vi* dar una vuelta
  ▶ **roll up 1** *vt sep* enrollar; (*blinds*) subir; **to r. up one's sleeves** (ar)remangarse
  2 *vi Fam* (*arrive*) llegar

roll-call ['rəʊlkɔːl] *n* **to have a r.** pasar lista

roller ['rəʊlə(r)] *n* (**a**) *Tech* rodillo *m*; **r. blades** patines *mpl* en línea; **r. coaster** montaña rusa; **r. skates** patines *mpl* (de ruedas) (**b**) (*large wave*) ola *f* grande (**c**) (*for hair*) rulo *m*

rolling ['rəʊlɪŋ] **1** *adj* (**a**) *Rail* **r. stock** material *m* rodante (**b**) (*countryside*) ondulado(a)
  2 *n* rodamiento *m*; (*of ground*) apisonamiento *m*; **r. pin** rodillo *m* (de cocina)

ROM [rɒm] *n Comput* (*abbr* **read-only memory**) ROM *f*

Roman ['rəʊmən] *adj & n* romano(a) (*m,f*); **R. Catholic** católico(a) *m,f* (romano(a)); **R. law** derecho romano; **R. numerals** números romanos

Romance [rəʊˈmæns] *adj Ling* románico(a), romance; **R. languages** lenguas románicas

romance [rəʊˈmæns] **1** *n* (**a**) (*tale*) novela romántica (**b**) (*love affair*) aventura

amorosa (**c**) (*romantic quality*) lo romántico
  2 *vi* fantasear

Romania [rəˈmeɪnɪə] *n* Rumanía

Romanian [rəˈmeɪnɪən] **1** *adj* rumano(a)
  2 *n* (*person*) rumano(a) *m,f*; (*language*) rumano *m*

romantic [rəʊˈmæntɪk] *adj & n* romántico(a) (*m,f*)

Rome [rəʊm] *n* Roma

romp [rɒmp] **1** *n* jugueteo *m*
  2 *vi* juguetear

rompers ['rɒmpəz] *npl* pelele *m*

roof [ruːf] **1** *n* (*pl* **roofs** [ruːfs, ruːvz]) (**a**) tejado *m*; *Fam Fig* **to go through the r.** (*of prices*) estar por las nubes; (*with anger*) subirse por las paredes (**b**) *Aut* techo *m*; **r. rack** baca *f* (**c**) (*of mouth*) cielo *m*
  2 *vt* techar

roofing ['ruːfɪŋ] *n* materiales *mpl* usados para techar

rook [rʊk] *n* (**a**) *Orn* grajo *m* (**b**) (*in chess*) torre *f*

rookie ['rʊkɪ] *n US Fam* (*novice*) novato(a) *m,f*

room [ruːm] *n* (**a**) habitación *f*, cuarto *m*; **single r.** habitación individual; **r. service** servicio *m* de habitación (**b**) (*space*) sitio *m*, espacio *m*; **make r. for me** hazme sitio

rooming-house ['ruːmɪŋhaʊs] *n US* pensión *f*

roommate ['ruːmmeɪt] *n* compañero(a) *m,f* de habitación

roomy ['ruːmɪ] *adj* (**roomier, roomiest**) amplio(a)

roost [ruːst] **1** *n* palo *m*, percha *f*; (**hen**) gallinero *m*; *Fig* **to rule the r.** llevar la batuta
  2 *vi* posarse

rooster ['ruːstə(r)] *n esp US* gallo *m*

root¹ [ruːt] **1** *n* raíz *f*; **to take r.** echar raíces
  2 *vt* arraigar
  3 *vi* arraigar
  ▶ **root out, root up** *vt sep* arrancar de raíz

root² [ruːt] *vi* (*search*) buscar; **to r. about** *or* **around for sth** hurgar en busca de algo

root³ [ruːt] *vi Fam* **to r. for a team** animar a un equipo

rope [rəʊp] **1** *n* (**a**) (*thin*) cuerda *f*; (*thick*) soga *f*, *Naut* cabo *m* (**b**) *Fig* **to have sb on the ropes** tener a algn contra las cuerdas; *Fam Fig* **to know the ropes** estar al tanto
  2 *vt* (*package*) atar; (*climbers*) encordar

───────────────

𝓵 Note that the Spanish word **ropa** is a false friend and is never a translation for the English word **rope**. In Spanish, **ropa** means "clothes".

▸ **rope in** *vt sep Fam* enganchar

▸ **rope off** *vt sep* acordonar

rop(e)y ['rəʊpɪ] *adj* (**ropier, ropiest**) *Br Fam* chungo(a)

rosary ['rəʊzərɪ] *n* rosario *m*

rose¹ [rəʊz] *pt of* **rise**

rose² [rəʊz] *n* (**a**) *Bot* rosa *f*; **r. bed** rosaleda *f*; **r. bush** rosal *m* (**b**) *(colour)* rosa *m* (**c**) *(of watering can)* alcachofa *f*

rosé ['rəʊzeɪ] *n* (vino *m*) rosado *m*

rosebud ['rəʊzbʌd] *n* capullo *m* de rosa

rosemary ['rəʊzmərɪ] *n* romero *m*

rosette [rəʊ'zet] *n* (*of ribbons*) escarapela *f*

roster ['rɒstə(r)] *n* lista *f*

rostrum ['rɒstrəm] *n* estrado *m*

> 🖉 Note that the Spanish word **rostro** is a false friend and is never a translation for the English word **rostrum**. In Spanish, **rostro** means "face".

rosy ['rəʊzɪ] *adj* (**rosier, rosiest**) (**a**) *(complexion)* sonrosado(a) (**b**) *Fig (future)* prometedor(a)

rot [rɒt] **1** *n* (**a**) *(decay)* putrefacción *f*; **dry r.** putrefacción de la madera (**b**) *Fam (nonsense)* tonterías *fpl*

2 *vt* pudrir

▸ **rot away** *vi* pudrirse

rota ['rəʊtə] *n esp Br* lista *f*

rotary ['rəʊtərɪ] **1** *n US (for traffic)* rotonda *f*

2 *adj* rotatorio(a), giratorio(a)

rotate [rəʊ'teɪt] **1** *vt* (**a**) *(revolve)* hacer girar (**b**) *(jobs, crops)* alternar

2 *vi (revolve)* girar

rotating [rəʊ'teɪtɪŋ] *adj* rotativo(a)

rotation [rəʊ'teɪʃən] *n* rotación *f*

rote [rəʊt] *n* **by r.** de memoria

rotten ['rɒtən] *adj* (**a**) *(decayed)* podrido(a); *(tooth)* picado(a) (**b**) *Fam (very bad)* malísimo(a); *Fam* **I feel r.** me encuentro fatal

rouble ['ruːbəl] *n* rublo *m*

rouge [ruːʒ] **1** *n* colorete *m*

2 *vt* poner colorete a

rough [rʌf] **1** *adj* (**a**) *(surface, skin)* áspero(a); *(terrain)* accidentado(a); *(road)* desigual; *(sea)* agitado(a); *(weather)* tempestuoso(a)

(**b**) *(rude)* grosero(a); *(violent)* violento(a)

(**c**) *(voice)* bronco(a)

(**d**) *(wine)* áspero(a)

(**e**) *(bad)* malo(a); *Fam* **to feel r.** encontrarse fatal

(**f**) *(approximate)* aproximado(a)

(**g**) *(plan etc)* preliminar; **r. draft** borrador *m*; **r. sketch** esbozo *m*

(**h**) *(harsh)* severo(a)

2 *adv* duramente; *Fam Fig* **to sleep r.** dormir a la intemperie

3 *n* (**a**) *Fam (person)* matón *m*

(**b**) **the r.** *(in golf)* la hierba alta

4 *vt Fam* **to r. it** vivir sin comodidades

roughage ['rʌfɪdʒ] *n (substance)* fibra *f*

rough-and-ready ['rʌfən'redɪ] *adj* improvisado(a)

roughen ['rʌfən] *vt* poner áspero

roughly ['rʌflɪ] *adv* (**a**) *(crudely)* toscamente (**b**) *(clumsily)* torpemente (**c**) *(not gently)* bruscamente (**d**) *(approximately)* aproximadamente

roulette [ruː'let] *n* ruleta *f*

Roumania [ruː'meɪnɪə] *n* = **Romania**

round [raʊnd] **1** *adj* redondo(a); **in r. figures** en números redondos; **r. table** mesa redonda; **r. trip** viaje *m* de ida y vuelta

2 *n* (**a**) *(circle)* círculo *m*

(**b**) *(series)* serie *f*; **r. of talks** ronda *f* de negociaciones

(**c**) *(of ammunition)* cartucho *m*; *(salvo)* salva *f*

(**d**) **a r. of toast** una tostada

(**e**) *(of drinks)* ronda *f*

(**f**) **the daily r.** *(routine)* la rutina diaria

(**g**) *(in golf)* partido *m*; *Cards* partida *f*

(**h**) *(in boxing)* round *m*

(**i**) *(in a competition)* eliminatoria *f*

(**j**) **rounds** *(doctor's)* visita *f*; *(of salesman)* recorrido *m*

3 *adv* **all year r.** durante todo el año; **to invite sb r.** invitar a algn a casa

4 *prep* alrededor de; **r. here** por aquí; **r. the clock** día y noche; **r. the corner** a la vuelta de la esquina

5 *vt (turn)* dar la vuelta a

▸ **round off** *vt sep* acabar, concluir

▸ **round on** *vt insep (attack)* atacar

▸ **round up** *vt sep (cattle)* acorralar, rodear; *(people)* reunir

roundabout ['raʊndəbaʊt] **1** *n* (**a**) *(merry-go-round)* tiovivo *m* (**b**) *Br Aut* rotonda *f*

2 *adj* indirecto(a)

rounders ['raʊndəz] *n Br* = juego parecido al béisbol

roundly ['raʊndlɪ] *adv* completamente, totalmente

round-shouldered ['raʊnd'ʃəʊldəd] *adj* cargado(a) de espaldas

round-trip ['raʊnd'trɪp] *US* **1** *n* billete *m* de ida y vuelta

2 *adj (ticket)* de ida y vuelta

round-up ['raʊndʌp] *n* (**a**) *(of cattle)*

rodeo *m*; *(of suspects)* redada *f* (**b**) *(summary)* resumen *m*

rouse [raʊz] *vt* despertar; *(stir up)* suscitar

rousing ['raʊzɪŋ] *adj (cheer)* entusiasta; *(applause)* caluroso(a); *(speech, song)* conmovedor(a)

rout [raʊt] **1** *n* aniquilación *f*
   2 *vt* aniquilar

route [ruːt] **1** *n* (**a**) *(way)* ruta *f*; *(of bus)* línea *f*; *Naut* derrota *f*; *Fig* camino *m*; **r. map** mapa *m* de carreteras (**b**) *US* **R.** ≃ carretera *f* nacional
   2 *vt* encaminar

routine [ruːˈtiːn] **1** *n* (**a**) rutina *f* (**b**) *Th* número *m*
   2 *adj* rutinario(a)

roving ['rəʊvɪŋ] *adj* errante; **r. reporter** enviado(a) *m,f* especial

row ¹ [rəʊ] *n* fila *f*, hilera *f*; *Fig* **three times in a r.** tres veces seguidas

row ² [rəʊ] *vt & vi (in a boat)* remar

row ³ [raʊ] **1** *n* (**a**) *(quarrel)* pelea *f*, bronca *f* (**b**) *(noise)* jaleo *m*; *(protest)* escándalo *m*
   2 *vi* pelearse

rowboat ['rəʊbəʊt] *n US* bote *m* de remos

rowdy ['raʊdɪ] **1** *adj* (**rowdier, rowdiest**) (**a**) *(noisy)* ruidoso(a); *(disorderly)* alborotador(a) (**b**) *(quarrelsome)* camorrista
   2 *n* camorrista *mf*

rowing ['rəʊɪŋ] *n* remo *m*; **r. boat** bote *m* de remos

royal ['rɔɪəl] **1** *adj* real; **r. blue** azul marino; **the R. Family** la Familia Real
   2 *npl* **the Royals** los miembros de la Familia Real

royally ['rɔɪəlɪ] *adv Fig* magníficamente

royalty ['rɔɪəltɪ] *n* (**a**) *(royal persons)* miembro(s) *m(pl)* de la Familia Real (**b**) **royalties** derechos *mpl* de autor

RPI [ɑːpiːˈaɪ] *n* (*abbr* **Retail Price Index**) IPC *m*

rpm [ɑːpiːˈem] *n* (*abbr* **revolutions per minute**) r.p.m.

RSPCA [ɑːrespiːsiːˈeɪ] *n Br* (*abbr* **Royal Society for the Prevention of Cruelty to Animals**) ≃ Sociedad *f* Protectora de Animales

RSVP [ɑːresviːˈpiː] (*abbr* **répondez s'il vous plaît**) se ruega contestación, S.R.C.

Rt Hon *Br Pol* (*abbr* **(the) Right Honourable**) su Señoría

rub [rʌb] **1** *n* **to give sth a r.** frotar algo
   2 *vt* frotar; *(hard)* restregar; *(massage)* friccionar
   3 *vi* rozar (**against** contra)

▸ **rub down** *vt sep* rotar; *(horse)* almohazar; *(surface)* raspar

▸ **rub in** *vt sep* (**a**) *(cream etc)* frotar con (**b**) *Fam* **don't r. it in** no me lo refriegues

▸ **rub off** *vt sep (erase)* borrar
   2 *vi Fig* **to r. off on sb** influir en algn

▸ **rub out** *vt sep* borrar

▸ **rub up** *vt sep Fam Fig* **to r. sb up the wrong way** fastidiar a algn

rubber ¹ ['rʌbə(r)] *n* (**a**) *(substance)* caucho *m*, goma *f*; **r. band** goma; **r. plant** gomero *m*; **r. stamp** tampón *m* (**b**) *Br (eraser)* goma *f* (de borrar) (**c**) *Fam (condom)* goma *f*

rubber ² ['rʌbə(r)] *n (in bridge)* rubber *m*

rubbery ['rʌbərɪ] *adj (elastic)* elástico(a)

rubbish ['rʌbɪʃ] *n* (**a**) *Br (refuse)* basura *f*; **r. bin** cubo *m* de la basura; **r. dump** *or* **tip** vertedero *m* (**b**) *Fam (worthless thing)* birria *f* (**c**) *Fam (nonsense)* tonterías *fpl*

rubble ['rʌbəl] *n* escombros *mpl*

rubric ['ruːbrɪk] *n* rúbrica *f*

ruby ['ruːbɪ] *n* rubí *m*

rucksack ['rʌksæk] *n* mochila *f*

ructions ['rʌkʃənz] *npl Fam* jaleo *m*

rudder ['rʌdə(r)] *n* timón *m*

ruddy ['rʌdɪ] *adj* (**ruddier, ruddiest**) (**a**) *(complexion)* rojizo(a), colorado(a) (**b**) *Br Fam (damned)* maldito(a)

rude [ruːd] *adj* (**a**) *(impolite)* maleducado(a); *(foul-mouthed)* grosero(a); **don't be r. to your mother** no le faltes al respeto a tu madre (**b**) *(abrupt)* **a r. awakening** un despertar repentino

rudimentary [ruːdɪˈmentərɪ] *adj* rudimentario(a)

rudiments ['ruːdɪmənts] *npl* rudimentos *mpl*

rue [ruː] *vt* arrepentirse de

rueful ['ruːfʊl] *adj (regretful)* arrepentido(a); *(sad)* triste

ruff [rʌf] *n (collar)* gorguera *f*

ruffian ['rʌfɪən] *n* canalla *m*

ruffle ['rʌfəl] *vt* (**a**) *(water)* agitar (**b**) *(feathers)* encrespar; *(hair)* despeinar (**c**) *Fig (annoy)* hacer perder la calma a

ruffled ['rʌfəld] *adj* (**a**) *(hair)* alborotado(a); *(clothes)* en desorden (**b**) *(perturbed)* perturbado(a)

rug [rʌg] *n* alfombra *f*, alfombrilla *f*

rugby ['rʌgbɪ] *n* rugby *m*; **r. league** rugby a trece; **r. union** rugby a quince

rugged ['rʌgɪd] *adj* (**a**) *(terrain)* accidentado(a) (**b**) *(features)* marcado(a) (**c**) *(character)* vigoroso(a)

rugger ['rʌgə(r)] *n Fam* rugby *m*

ruin ['ruːɪn] **1** *n* (**a**) ruina *f* (**b**) **ruins** ruinas *fpl*, restos *mpl*; **in ruins** en ruinas
   2 *vt* arruinar; *(spoil)* estropear

rule [ruːl] **1** *n* (**a**) regla *f*, norma *f*; **to work**

to r. hacer una huelga de celo; **as a r.** por regla general (**b**) *(government)* dominio *m*; *(of monarch)* reinado *m*; **r. of law** imperio *m* de la ley

2 *vt & vi* (**a**) *(govern)* gobernar; *(of monarch)* reinar (**b**) *(decide)* decidir; *(decree)* decretar (**c**) *(draw)* tirar

▸ **rule out** *vt sep* descartar

ruled [ruːld] *adj* rayado(a)

ruler ['ruːlə(r)] *n* (**a**) dirigente *mf*; *(monarch)* soberano(a) *m,f* (**b**) *(for measuring)* regla *f*

ruling ['ruːlɪŋ] **1** *adj (in charge)* dirigente; *Fig (predominant)* predominante; **the r. party** el partido en el poder

2 *n Jur* fallo *m*

rum [rʌm] *n* ron *m*

Rumania [ruːˈmeɪnɪə] *n* = Romania

Rumanian [ruːˈmeɪnɪən] *adj & n* = Romanian

rumble ['rʌmbəl] **1** *n* (**a**) ruido sordo; *(of thunder)* estruendo *m* (**b**) *(of stomach)* ruido *m*

2 *vi* (**a**) hacer un ruido sordo; *(thunder)* retumbar (**b**) *(stomach etc)* hacer ruidos

ruminate ['ruːmɪneɪt] *vi (chew, ponder)* rumiar

rummage ['rʌmɪdʒ] *vi* revolver (**through** en); *US* **r. sale** *(in store)* = venta de productos discontinuados o sin salida en un almacén; *(for charity)* rastrillo benéfico

rumour, *US* **rumor** ['ruːmə(r)] **1** *n* rumor *m*; **r. has it that ...** se dice que ...

2 *vt* **it is rumoured that** se rumorea que

rump [rʌmp] *n (of animal)* ancas *fpl; Fam Hum (of person)* trasero *m*; **r. steak** filete *m* de lomo

rumpus ['rʌmpəs] *n Fam* jaleo *m*

run [rʌn] **1** *n* (**a**) carrera *f*; **on the r.** fugado(a); **to go for a r.** hacer footing; *Fig* **in the long r.** a largo plazo

(**b**) *(trip)* paseo *m*, vuelta *f*

(**c**) *(sequence)* serie *f*

(**d**) **ski r.** pista *f* de esquí

(**e**) *(demand)* gran demanda *f*; **a r. on** una gran demanda de

(**f**) **to give sb the r. of a house** poner una casa a disposición de algn

(**g**) *(print run)* tirada *f*

(**h**) *(in stocking)* carrera *f*

2 *vt (pt* **ran**; *pp* **run**) (**a**) correr; **to r. a race** correr en una carrera; **to r. errands** hacer recados

(**b**) *(drive)* llevar

(**c**) *(house, business)* llevar; *(company)* dirigir; *(organize)* organizar

(**d**) *(fingers)* pasar

(**e**) **it's a cheap car to r.** *(operate)* es un coche económico; *Comput* **to r. a program** pasar un programa

(**f**) *Press* publicar

3 *vi* (**a**) correr

(**b**) *(colour)* desteñirse

(**c**) *(water, river)* correr; **to leave the tap running** dejar el grifo abierto; *Fam* **your nose is running** se te caen los mocos

(**d**) *(operate) (machine)* funcionar (**on** con); **trains r. every two hours** hay trenes cada dos horas

(**e**) *Naut* **to r. aground** encallar

(**f**) *Pol* **to r. for president** presentarse como candidato a la presidencia

(**g**) **so the story runs** según lo que se dice

(**h**) *(range)* oscilar (**between** entre)

(**i**) **we're running low on milk** nos queda poca leche

(**j**) **shyness runs in the family** la timidez le viene de familia

(**k**) *Cin & Th* estar en cartel

(**l**) *(last)* durar

(**m**) *(stocking)* tener una carrera

▸ **run about** *vi* corretear

▸ **run across** *vt insep (meet)* tropezar con

▸ **run away** *vi* fugarse; *(horse)* desbocarse

▸ **run down 1** *vt insep (stairs)* bajar corriendo

2 *vt sep* (**a**) *(in car)* atropellar (**b**) *(criticize)* criticar

3 *vi (battery)* agotarse; *(clock)* pararse

▸ **run in** *vt sep Aut* rodar

▸ **run into** *vt insep* (**a**) *(room)* entrar corriendo en (**b**) *(people, problems)* tropezar con (**c**) *(crash into)* chocar contra

▸ **run off 1** *vt sep (print)* tirar

2 *vi* escaparse

▸ **run on 1** *vt sep Typ* enlazar

2 *vi (meeting)* continuar

▸ **run out** *vi* (**a**) *(exit)* salir corriendo (**b**) *(come to an end)* agotarse; *(of contract)* vencer; **to r. out of** quedarse sin

▸ **run over 1** *vt sep (in car)* atropellar

2 *vt insep (rehearse)* ensayar

3 *vi (overflow)* rebosar

▸ **run through** *vt insep* (**a**) *(of river)* pasar por (**b**) *(read quickly)* echar un vistazo a (**c**) *(rehearse)* ensayar

▸ **run up** *vt sep* (**a**) *(flag)* izar (**b**) *(debts)* acumular

▸ **run up against** *vt insep* tropezar con

runaway ['rʌnəweɪ] **1** *n* fugitivo(a) *m,f*

2 *adj (person)* huido(a); *(horse)* desbocado(a); *(vehicle)* incontrolado(a); *(inflation)* galopante; *(success)* clamoroso(a)

rundown ['rʌndaʊn] *n Fam* **to give sb a r.** poner a algn al corriente

run-down [rʌn'daʊn] *adj* (**a**) *(exhausted)* agotado(a) (**b**) *(dilapidated)* ruinoso(a)

rung¹ [rʌŋ] *pp of* **ring**

rung² [rʌŋ] *n (of ladder)* escalón *m*, peldaño *m*

runner ['rʌnə(r)] *n* (**a**) *(person)* corredor(a) *m,f* (**b**) *(horse)* caballo *m* de carreras (**c**) *(of skate)* cuchilla *f* (**d**) *(on table)* tapete *m* (**e**) **r. bean** judía escarlata

runner-up [rʌnər'ʌp] *n* subcampeón(ona) *m,f*

running ['rʌnɪŋ] **1** *n* (**a**) **he likes r.** le gusta correr; *Fig* **to be in the r. for sth** tener posibilidades de conseguir algo (**b**) *(of company)* dirección *f* (**c**) *(of machine)* funcionamiento *m*

2 *adj* (**a**) **r. commentary** comentario *m* en directo; **r. costs** gastos *mpl* de mantenimiento; *Pol* **r. mate** candidato *m* a la vicepresidencia; **r. water** agua *f* corriente (**b**) **three weeks r.** tres semanas seguidas

runny ['rʌnɪ] *adj* (**runnier, runniest**) blando(a); *(egg)* crudo(a); *(butter)* derretido(a); *(nose)* que moquea

run-of-the-mill ['rʌnəvðə'mɪl] *adj* corriente y moliente

runt [rʌnt] *n Fam* enano(a) *m,f*

run-up ['rʌnʌp] *n (to elections)* preliminares *mpl*

runway ['rʌnweɪ] *n Av* pista *f* (de aterrizaje y despegue)

rupee [ruː'piː] *n* rupia *f*

rupture ['rʌptʃə(r)] **1** *n* (**a**) *Med* hernia *f* (**b**) *Fig* ruptura *f*

2 *vt* (**a**) **to r. oneself** herniarse (**b**) *(break)* romper

rural ['rʊərəl] *adj* rural

ruse [ruːz] *n* ardid *m*, astucia *f*

rush¹ [rʌʃ] *n Bot* junco *m*

rush² [rʌʃ] **1** *n* (**a**) *(hurry)* prisa *f*; *(hustle and bustle)* ajetreo *m*; **there's no r.** no corre prisa; **r. hour** hora punta (**b**) *(demand)* demanda *f* (**c**) *(of wind)* ráfaga *f* (**d**) *(of water)* torrente *m* (**e**) *Mil* ataque *m*

2 *vt* (**a**) *(task)* hacer de prisa; *(person)* meter prisa a; **to r. sb to hospital** llevar a algn urgentemente al hospital (**b**) *(attack)* abalanzarse sobre; *Mil* tomar por asalto

3 *vi (go quickly)* precipitarse

▸ **rush about** *vi* correr de un lado a otro

▸ **rush into** *vt insep Fig* **to r. into sth** hacer algo sin pensarlo bien

▸ **rush off** *vi* irse corriendo

rusk [rʌsk] *n* = galleta dura para niños

Russia ['rʌʃə] *n* Rusia

Russian ['rʌʃən] **1** *adj* ruso(a)

2 *n* (**a**) *(person)* ruso(a) *m,f* (**b**) *(language)* ruso *m*

rust [rʌst] **1** *n* (**a**) *(substance)* herrumbre *f* (**b**) *(colour)* pardo rojizo

2 *vt* oxidar

3 *vi* oxidarse

rustic ['rʌstɪk] *adj* rústico(a)

rustle ['rʌsəl] **1** *n* crujido *m*

2 *vt (papers etc)* hacer crujir

3 *vi (steal cattle)* robar ganado

rustproof ['rʌstpruːf] *adj* inoxidable

rusty ['rʌstɪ] *adj* (**rustier, rustiest**) oxidado(a); *Fam Fig* **my French is a bit r.** tengo el francés un poco oxidado

rut [rʌt] *n* (**a**) *(furrow)* surco *m*; *(groove)* ranura *f* (**b**) *Fig* **to be in a r.** ser esclavo de la rutina (**c**) *Zool* celo *m*

ruthless ['ruːθlɪs] *adj* despiadado(a)

rye [raɪ] *n* centeno *m*; **r. bread** pan *m* de centeno; **r. grass** ballica *f*; *US* **r. (whiskey)** whisky *m* de centeno

S, s [es] *n (the letter)* S, s *f*
Sabbath ['sæbəθ] *n (Jewish)* sábado *m*; *(Christian)* domingo *m*
sabbatical [sə'bætɪkəl] *adj* sabático(a)
sabotage ['sæbətɑːʒ] **1** *n* sabotaje *m*
2 *vt* sabotear
saccharin ['sækərɪn] *n* sacarina *f*
sachet ['sæʃeɪ] *n* bolsita *f*, sobrecito *m*
sack [sæk] **1** *n* (a) *(bag)* saco *m* (b) *Br Fam* **to get the s.** ser despedido(a); *Fam* **to give sb the s.** despedir a algn
2 *vt* (a) *Br Fam* despedir (b) *Mil* saquear
sacking ['sækɪŋ] *n Tex* arpillera *f*
sacrament ['sækrəmənt] *n* sacramento *m*
sacred ['seɪkrɪd] *adj* sagrado(a)
sacrifice ['sækrɪfaɪs] **1** *n* sacrificio *m*
2 *vt* sacrificar
sacrificial [sækrɪ'fɪʃəl] *adj* **s. lamb** chivo expiatorio
sacrilege ['sækrɪlɪdʒ] *n* sacrilegio *m*
sacrosanct ['sækrəʊsæŋkt] *adj* sacrosanto(a)
sad [sæd] *adj* (**sadder, saddest**) triste; **how s.!** ¡qué pena!
sadden ['sædən] *vt* entristecer
saddle ['sædəl] **1** *n (for horse)* silla *f* (de montar); *(of bicycle etc)* sillín *m*
2 *vt (horse)* ensillar; *Fam* **to s. sb with sth** cargarle a algn con algo
saddlebag ['sædəlbæg] *n* alforja *f*
sadist ['seɪdɪst] *n* sádico(a) *m,f*
sadistic [sə'dɪstɪk] *adj* sádico(a)
sadness ['sædnɪs] *n* tristeza *f*
sadomasochism [seɪdəʊ'mæsəkɪzəm] *n* sadomasoquismo *m*
sae [eseɪ'iː] *n Br (abbr* **stamped addressed envelope**) = sobre franqueado con la dirección del remitente
safari [sə'fɑːrɪ] *n* safari *m*; **s. park** reserva *f*
safe [seɪf] **1** *adj* (a) *(unharmed)* ileso(a); *(out of danger)* a salvo; **s. and sound** sano(a) y salvo(a) (b) *(not dangerous)* inocuo(a) (c) *(secure, sure)* seguro(a); **to be on the s. side** para mayor seguridad; **s. house** *(for spies etc)* piso franco (d) *(driver)* prudente
2 *n (for money etc)* caja *f* fuerte

safe-conduct [seɪf'kɒndʌkt] *n* salvoconducto *m*
safe-deposit [seɪfdɪ'pɒzɪt] *n* **s. (box)** cámara blindada
safeguard ['seɪfgɑːd] **1** *n (protection)* salvaguarda *f*; *(guarantee)* garantía *f*
2 *vt* proteger, salvaguardar
safekeeping [seɪf'kiːpɪŋ] *n* custodia *f*
safely ['seɪflɪ] *adv* (a) con toda seguridad (b) **to arrive s.** llegar sin incidentes
safety ['seɪftɪ] *n* seguridad *f*; **s. first!** ¡la seguridad ante todo!; **s. belt** cinturón *m* de seguridad; **s. net** red *f* de protección; **s. pin** imperdible *m*
saffron ['sæfrən] *n* azafrán *m*
sag [sæg] *vi* (a) *(roof)* hundirse; *(wall)* pandear; *(wood, iron)* combarse; *(flesh)* colgar (b) *Fig (spirits)* flaquear
sage¹ [seɪdʒ] **1** *adj (wise)* sabio(a)
2 *n (person)* sabio(a) *m,f*
sage² [seɪdʒ] *n* salvia *f*
Sagittarius [sædʒɪ'teərɪəs] *n* Sagitario *m*
Sahara [sə'hɑːrə] *n* **the S.** el Sahara
Saharan [sə'hɑːrən] *adj* saharaui, sahariano(a)
said [sed] **1** *adj* dicho(a)
2 *pt & pp of* **say**
sail [seɪl] **1** *n* (a) *(canvas)* vela *f*; **to set s.** zarpar (b) *(trip)* paseo *m* en barco
2 *vt (ship)* gobernar; *Literary* navegar
3 *vi* (a) ir en barco (b) *(set sail)* zarpar
▸ **sail through** *vt insep Fam* **he sailed through university** en la universidad todo le fue sobre ruedas
sailboat ['seɪlbəʊt] *n US* velero *m*
sailing ['seɪlɪŋ] *n* navegación *f*; *(yachting)* vela *f*; *Fam* **it's all plain s.** es todo coser y cantar; *Br* **s. boat** *or* **ship** velero *m*, barco *m* de vela
sailor ['seɪlə(r)] *n* marinero *m*
saint [seɪnt] *n* santo *m,f*; *(before all masculine names except those beginning* **Do** *or* **To**) San; *(before feminine names)* Santa; **S. Dominic** Santo Domingo; **S. Helen** Santa Elena; **S. John** San Juan; **All Saints' Day** Día *m* de Todos los Santos
saintly ['seɪntlɪ] *adj* (**saintlier, saintliest**) santo(a)
sake [seɪk] *n* **for the s. of** por (el bien de);

for your own s. por tu propio bien

salad ['sæləd] n ensalada f; **potato s.** ensalada de patatas or Am papas; **s. bowl** ensaladera f; **s. cream** salsa f tipo mahonesa; **s. dressing** vinagreta f, aliño m

salami [sə'lɑːmɪ] n salchichón m, salami m

salary ['sælərɪ] n salario m, sueldo m

sale [seɪl] n (a) venta f; **for** or **on s.** en venta; **sales department** departamento m comercial; **sales manager** jefe(a) m,f de ventas (b) (at low prices) rebajas fpl

salesclerk ['seɪlzklɑːk] n US dependiente(a) m,f

salesman ['seɪlzmən] n (a) vendedor m; (in shop) dependiente m (b) (commercial traveller) representante m

salesroom ['seɪlzruːm] n sala f de subastas

saleswoman ['seɪlzwʊmən] n (a) vendedora f; (in shop) dependienta f (b) (commercial traveller) representante f

salient ['seɪlɪənt] adj Fig sobresaliente

saliva [sə'laɪvə] n saliva f

sallow ['sæləʊ] adj cetrino(a)

salmon ['sæmən] 1 n salmón m
2 adj (de color) salmón

salmonella [sælmə'nelə] n Biol & Med (bacteria) salmonela f; (food poisoning) salmonelosis f

salon ['sælɒn] n salón m

saloon [sə'luːn] n (a) (on ship) cámara f (b) US (bar) taberna f, bar m; Br **s. (bar)** bar de lujo (c) (car) turismo m

salt [sɔːlt] 1 n sal f; Fig **to take sth with a pinch of s.** creer algo con reservas; **bath salts** sales de baño; **smelling salts** sales aromáticas
2 adj salado(a)
3 vt (a) (cure) salar (b) (add salt to) echar sal a

saltcellar ['sɔːltselə(r)] n salero m

saltwater ['sɔːltwɔːtə(r)] adj de agua salada

salty ['sɔːltɪ] adj (**saltier, saltiest**) salado(a)

salubrious [sə'luːbrɪəs] adj salubre, sano(a)

salutary ['sæljʊtərɪ] adj (experience) beneficioso(a); (warning) útil

salute [sə'luːt] 1 n (greeting) saludo m
2 vt (a) Mil saludar (b) Fig (achievement etc) aplaudir
3 vi Mil saludar

salvage ['sælvɪdʒ] 1 n (a) (of ship etc) salvamento m, rescate m (b) (objects recovered) objetos recuperados (c) Jur derecho m de salvamento

2 vt (from ship etc) rescatar

salvation [sæl'veɪʃən] n salvación f; **S. Army** Ejército m de Salvación

Samaritan [sə'mærɪtən] n samaritano(a) m,f; **the Samaritans** ≃ el teléfono de la Esperanza

same [seɪm] 1 adj mismo(a); **at that very s. moment** en ese mismísimo momento; **at the s. time** (simultaneously) al mismo tiempo; (however) sin embargo; **in the s. way** del mismo modo; **the two cars are the s.** los dos coches son iguales
2 pron **the s.** el mismo/la misma/lo mismo; Fam **the s. here** lo mismo digo yo; Fam **the s. to you!** ¡igualmente!
3 adv del mismo modo, igual; **all the s., just the s.** sin embargo, aun así; **it's all the s. to me** (a mí) me da igual or lo mismo

sample ['sɑːmpəl] 1 n muestra f
2 vt (wines) catar; (dish) probar

sanatorium [sænə'tɔːrɪəm] n sanatorio m

sanctimonious [sæŋktɪ'məʊnɪəs] adj beato(a)

sanction ['sæŋkʃən] 1 n (a) (authorization) permiso m (b) (penalty) sanción f (c) Pol **sanctions** sanciones fpl
2 vt sancionar

sanctity ['sæŋktɪtɪ] n (sacredness) santidad f; (of marriage) indisolubilidad f

sanctuary ['sæŋktjʊərɪ] n (a) Rel santuario m (b) Pol asilo m (c) (for birds, animals) reserva f

sand [sænd] 1 n arena f; **s. castle** castillo m de arena; **s. dune** duna f
2 vt **to s. (down)** lijar

sandal ['sændəl] n sandalia f

sandalwood ['sændəlwʊd] n sándalo m

sandbag ['sændbæg] n saco terrero

sandbox ['sændbɒks] n US arenal m

sandpaper ['sændpeɪpə(r)] n papel m de lija

sandpit ['sændpɪt] n Br (in playground etc) arenal m

sandshoe ['sændʃuː] n Br playera f

sandstone ['sændstəʊn] n arenisca f

sandwich ['sænwɪdʒ, 'sænwɪtʃ] 1 n (bread roll) bocadillo m; (sliced bread) sándwich m; Educ **s. course** curso teórico-práctico
2 vt intercalar; **it was sandwiched between two lorries** quedó encajonado entre dos camiones

sandy ['sændɪ] adj (**sandier, sandiest**) (a) (earth, beach) arenoso(a) (b) (hair) rubio rojizo

sane [seɪn] *adj (not mad)* cuerdo(a); *(sensible)* sensato(a)

> 🖉 Note that the Spanish word **sano** is a false friend and is never a translation for the English word **sane**. In Spanish, **sano** means "healthy".

sang [sæŋ] *pt of* **sing**

sanitarium [sænɪ'teərɪəm] *n US* sanatorio *m*

sanitary ['sænɪtərɪ] *adj* sanitario(a); *(hygienic)* higiénico(a); **s.** *Br* **towel** *or US* **napkin** compresa *f*

sanitation [sænɪ'teɪʃən] *n* sanidad *f* (pública); *(plumbing)* sistema *m* de saneamiento

sanity ['sænɪtɪ] *n* cordura *f*, juicio *m*; *(good sense)* sensatez *f*

> 🖉 Note that the Spanish word **sanidad** is a false friend and is never a translation for the English word **sanity**. In Spanish, **sanidad** means "health".

sank [sæŋk] *pt of* **sink**

Santa Claus ['sæntə'klɔːz] *n* Papá Noel *m*, San Nicolás *m*

sap¹ [sæp] *n Bot* savia *f*

sap² [sæp] *vt (undermine)* minar; *Fig* agotar

sapling ['sæplɪŋ] *n Bot* árbol *m* joven

sapphire ['sæfaɪə(r)] *n* zafiro *m*

sarcasm ['sɑːkæzəm] *n* sarcasmo *m*

sarcastic [sɑː'kæstɪk] *adj* sarcástico(a)

sardine [sɑː'diːn] *n* sardina *f*

Sardinia [sɑː'dɪnɪə] *n* Cerdeña

sardonic [sɑː'dɒnɪk] *adj* sardónico(a)

SASE [eseɪes'iː] *n US (abbr* **self-addressed stamped envelope)** = sobre franqueado con la dirección del remitente

sash¹ [sæʃ] *n* faja *f*

sash² [sæʃ] *n* **s. window** ventana *f* de guillotina

sat [sæt] *pt & pp of* **sit**

Satan ['seɪtən] *n* Satán *m*, Satanás *m*

satanic [sə'tænɪk] *adj* satánico(a)

satchel ['sætʃəl] *n* cartera *f* de colegial

satellite ['sætəlaɪt] *n* satélite *m*; **s. dish (aerial)** antena parabólica

satin ['sætɪn] *n* satén *m*; **s. finish** (acabado *m*) satinado *m*

satire ['sætaɪə(r)] *n* sátira *f*

satirical [sə'tɪrɪkəl] *adj* satírico(a)

satisfaction [sætɪs'fækʃən] *n* satisfacción *f*

satisfactory [sætɪs'fæktərɪ] *adj* satisfactorio(a)

satisfied ['sætɪsfaɪd] *adj* satisfecho(a)

satisfy ['sætɪsfaɪ] *vt* **(a)** satisfacer **(b)**

(fulfil) cumplir con **(c)** *(convince)* convencer

satisfying ['sætɪsfaɪɪŋ] *adj* satisfactorio(a); *(pleasing)* agradable; *(meal)* que llena

saturate ['sætʃəreɪt] *vt* saturar (**with** de)

Saturday ['sætədɪ] *n* sábado *m*

sauce [sɔːs] *n* **(a)** salsa *f* **(b)** *Fam (impudence)* descaro *m*

saucepan ['sɔːspən] *n* cacerola *f*, *(large)* olla *f*

saucer ['sɔːsə(r)] *n* platillo *m*

saucy ['sɔːsɪ] *adj* **(saucier, sauciest)** *Fam* fresco(a)

Saudi Arabia ['saʊdɪə'reɪbɪə] *n* Arabia *f* Saudita *or* Saudí

Saudi Arabian ['saʊdɪə'reɪbɪən] *adj & n* saudita *(mf)*, saudí *(mf)*

sauna ['sɔːnə] *n* sauna *f*

saunter ['sɔːntə(r)] **1** *n* paseo *m*
2 *vi* pasearse

sausage ['sɒsɪdʒ] *n (raw)* salchicha *f*; *(cured)* salchichón *m*; *(spicy)* chorizo *m*; *Fam* **s. dog** perro *m* salchicha; *Br* **s. roll** empanada *f* de carne

sauté ['səʊteɪ] **1** *adj* salteado(a)
2 *vt* saltear

savage ['sævɪdʒ] **1** *adj* **(a)** *(ferocious)* feroz; *(cruel)* cruel; *(violent)* salvaje **(b)** *(primitive)* salvaje
2 *n* salvaje *mf*
3 *vt (attack)* embestir; *Fig (criticize)* criticar despiadadamente

save [seɪv] **1** *vt* **(a)** *(rescue)* salvar, rescatar; *Fig* **to s. face** salvar las apariencias **(b)** *(put by)* guardar; *(money, energy, time)* ahorrar; *(food)* almacenar; **it saved him a lot of trouble** le evitó muchos problemas
2 *vi* **(a)** **to s. (up)** ahorrar **(b)** **to s. on paper** *(economize)* ahorrar papel
3 *n Ftb* parada *f*
4 *prep Literary* salvo, excepto

saving ['seɪvɪŋ] **1** *n* **(a)** *(of time, money)* ahorro *m* **(b)** **savings** ahorros *mpl*; **savings account** cuenta *f* de ahorros; **savings bank** caja *f* de ahorros
2 *adj* **it's his only s. grace** es el único mérito que tiene

saviour, *US* **savior** ['seɪvjə(r)] *n* salvador(a) *m,f*

savour, *US* **savor** ['seɪvə(r)] **1** *n* sabor *m*, gusto *m*
2 *vi* saborear

savoury, *US* **savory** ['seɪvərɪ] *adj (tasty)* sabroso(a); *(salted)* salado(a); *(spicy)* picante

saw¹ [sɔː] **1** *n (tool)* sierra *f*

2 *vt & vi* (*pt* sawed; *pp* sawed *or* sawn)
serrar

▸ **saw up** *vt sep* serrar (**into** en)

saw² [sɔː] *pt of* see

sawdust ['sɔːdʌst] *n* (a)serrín *m*

sawmill ['sɔːmɪl] *n* aserradero *m*, serre-
ría *f*

sawn [sɔːn] *pp of* saw

sawn-off ['sɔːnɒf], *US* **sawed-off** ['sɔːd-
ɒf] *adj* recortado(a); **s. shotgun** escopeta
f de cañones recortados

saxophone ['sæksəfəʊn] *n* saxofón *m*

say [seɪ] **1** *vt* (*pt & pp* said) (a) decir; **it
goes without saying that ...** huelga decir
que ...; **it is said that ...** se dice que ...; **not
to s. ...** por no decir ...; **that is to s.** es
decir; **to s. yes/no** decir que sí/no; *Fam* **I
s.!** ¡oiga!; **what does the sign s.?** ¿qué
pone en el letrero? (b) *(think)* pensar (c)
shall we s. Friday then? ¿quedamos el
viernes, pues?

2 *n* **I have no s. in the matter** no tengo ni
voz ni voto en el asunto; **to have one's s.**
dar su opinión

saying ['seɪɪŋ] *n* refrán *m*, dicho *m*

scab [skæb] *n* (a) *Med* costra *f* (b) *Fam Pej*
esquirol *mf*

scaffold ['skæfəld] *n* (*for execution*) patíbulo *m*

scaffolding ['skæfəldɪŋ] *n Constr* andamio *n*

scald [skɔːld] **1** *n* escaldadura *f*
2 *vt* escaldar

scale¹ [skeɪl] *n* (*of fish, on skin*) escama *f*;
(*in boiler*) incrustaciones *fpl*

scale² [skeɪl] **1** *n* (a) escala *f*; **on a large s.**
a gran escala; **to s.** a escala; **s. model**
maqueta *f* (b) *(extent)* alcance *m* (c) *Mus*
escala *f*
2 *vt (climb)* escalar

▸ **scale down** *vt sep* *(drawing)* reducir a
escala; *(production)* reducir

scales [skeɪlz] *npl* (**pair of**) **s.** *(shop, kitchen)* balanza *f*; *(bathroom)* báscula *f*

scallop ['skɒləp] *n* (a) *(mollusc)* vieira *f*
(b) *(shell)* venera *f*

scalp [skælp] **1** *n* cuero cabelludo
2 *vt* arrancar el cuero cabelludo a

scalpel ['skælpəl] *n* bisturí *m*

scamper ['skæmpə(r)] *vi* corretear

scampi ['skæmpɪ] *n* gambas empana-
das

scan [skæn] **1** *vt* (a) *(scrutinize)* escrutar;
(horizon) otear (b) *(glance at)* ojear (c)
(of radar) explorar
2 *n Med* exploración ultrasónica; *(in
gynaecology etc)* ecografía *f*

scandal ['skændəl] *n* (a) escándalo *m*;

what a s.! ¡qué vergüenza! (b) *(gossip)*
chismes *mpl*

Scandinavia [skændɪ'neɪvɪə] *n* Escandinavia

Scandinavian [skændɪ'neɪvɪən] *adj & n*
escandinavo(a) *(m,f)*

scanner ['skænə(r)] *n Med & Comput*
escáner *m*

scant [skænt] *adj* escaso(a)

scanty ['skæntɪ] *adj* (**scantier, scantiest**)
escaso(a); *(meal)* insuficiente; *(clothes)*
ligero(a)

scapegoat ['skeɪpgəʊt] *n* chivo expiatorio

scar [skɑː(r)] *n* cicatriz *f*

scarce [skeəs] *adj* escaso(a); *Fig* **to make
oneself s.** largarse

scarcely ['skeəslɪ] *adv* apenas

scarcity ['skeəsɪtɪ] *n* escasez *f*, *(rarity)*
rareza *f*

scare [skeə(r)] **1** *n (fright)* susto *m*; *(widespread alarm)* pánico *m*; **bomb s.** amenaza *f* de bomba
2 *vt* asustar, espantar; *Fam* **to be scared
stiff** estar muerto(a) de miedo

▸ **scare away, scare off** *vt sep* ahuyentar

scarecrow ['skeəkrəʊ] *n* espantapájaros
m inv

scarf [skɑːf] *n* (*pl* scarfs *or* scarves) *(long,
woollen)* bufanda *f*; *(square)* pañuelo *m*;
(silk) fular *m*

scarlet ['skɑːlɪt] **1** *adj* escarlata
2 *n* escarlata *f*; **s. fever** escarlatina *f*

scarves [skɑːvz] *pl of* scarf

scathing ['skeɪðɪŋ] *adj* mordaz, cáusti-
co(a)

scatter ['skætə(r)] **1** *vt* (a) *(papers etc)*
esparcir, desparramar (b) *(crowd)* dispersar
2 *vi* dispersarse

scatterbrained ['skætəbreɪnd] *adj Fam*
ligero(a) de cascos; *(forgetful)* despista-
do(a)

scattered ['skætəd] *adj* **s. showers** chu-
bascos aislados

scavenger ['skævɪndʒə(r)] *n* (a) *(person)*
rebuscador(a) *m,f*, trapero *m* (b) *(animal)* (animal *m*) carroñero(a) *mf*

scenario [sɪ'nɑːrɪəʊ] *n* (a) *Cin* guión *m*
(b) *(situation)* situación *f* hipotética

scene [siːn] *n* (a) *Th, Cin & TV* escena *f*;
behind the scenes entre bastidores (b)
(place) lugar *m*, escenario *m*; **a change of
s.** un cambio de aires (c) *(view)* panorama *m* (d) **to make a s.** *(fuss)* montar un
espectáculo

scenery ['siːnərɪ] *n* (a) *(landscape)* paisaje *m* (b) *Th* decorado *m*

scenic ['si:nɪk] *adj (picturesque)* pintoresco(a)

scent [sent] **1** *n* (**a**) *(smell)* olor *m*; *(of food)* aroma *m* (**b**) *(perfume)* perfume *m* (**c**) *(in hunting)* pista *f*
2 *vt (add perfume to)* perfumar; *(smell)* olfatear; *Fig* presentir

septic ['skeptɪk] *n* escéptico(a) *m,f*

sceptical ['skeptɪkəl] *adj* escéptico(a)

scepticism ['skeptɪsɪzəm] *n* escepticismo *m*

sceptre ['septə(r)] *n* cetro *m*

schedule ['ʃedju:l, *US* 'skedʒʊəl] **1** *n* (**a**) *(plan, agenda)* programa *m*; *(timetable)* horario *m*; **on s.** a la hora (prevista); **to be behind s.** llevar retraso (**b**) *(list)* lista *f*; *(inventory)* inventario *m*
2 *vt (plan)* programar, fijar

scheduled ['ʃedju:ld, *US* 'skedʒʊəld] *adj* previsto(a), fijo(a); **s. flight** vuelo regular

scheme [ski:m] **1** *n* (**a**) *(plan)* plan *m*; *(project)* proyecto *m*; *(idea)* idea *f*; **colour s.** combinación *f* de colores (**b**) *(plot)* intriga *f*; *(trick)* ardid *m*
2 *vi (plot)* tramar, intrigar

scheming ['ski:mɪŋ] *adj* intrigante, maquinador(a)

schism ['sɪzəm] *n* cisma *m*

schizophrenic [skɪtsəʊ'frenɪk] *adj & n* esquizofrénico(a) *(m,f)*

scholar ['skɒlə(r)] *n (learned person)* erudito(a) *m,f*, *(pupil)* alumno(a) *m,f*

scholarship ['skɒləʃɪp] *n* (**a**) *(learning)* erudición *f* (**b**) *(grant)* beca *f*; **s. holder** becario(a) *m,f*

school [sku:l] **1** *n* (**a**) escuela *f*, colegio *m*; **drama s.** academia *f* de arte dramático; **of s. age** en edad escolar; **s. year** año *m* escolar (**b**) *US (university)* universidad *f* (**c**) *(university department)* facultad *f* (**d**) *(group of artists)* escuela *f*; **s. of thought** corriente *f* de opinión
2 *vt (teach)* enseñar; *(train)* formar

schoolbook ['sku:lbʊk] *n* libro *m* de texto

schoolboy ['sku:lbɔɪ] *n* alumno *m*

schoolchild ['sku:ltʃaɪld] *n* alumno(a) *m,f*

schooldays ['sku:ldeɪz] *npl* años *mpl* de colegio

schoolgirl ['sku:lgɜ:l] *n* alumna *f*

schooling ['sku:lɪŋ] *n* educación *f*, estudios *mpl*

schoolmaster ['sku:lmɑ:stə(r)] *n* profesor *m*; *(primary school)* maestro *m*

schoolmistress ['sku:lmɪstrɪs] *n* profesora *f*; *(primary school)* maestra *f*

schoolteacher ['sku:lti:tʃə(r)] *n* profesor(a) *m,f*; *(primary school)* maestro(a) *m,f*

schooner ['sku:nə(r)] *n Naut* goleta *f*

sciatica [saɪ'ætɪkə] *n* ciática *f*

science ['saɪəns] *n* ciencia *f*; *(school subject)* ciencias; **s. fiction** ciencia-ficción *f*

scientific [saɪən'tɪfɪk] *adj* científico(a)

scientist ['saɪəntɪst] *n* científico(a) *m,f*

scintillating ['sɪntɪleɪtɪŋ] *adj* brillante

scissors ['sɪzəz] *npl* tijeras *fpl*; **a pair of s.** unas tijeras

scoff¹ [skɒf] *vi (mock)* mofarse (**at** de)

scoff² [skɒf] *vt Fam (eat)* zamparse

scold [skəʊld] *vt* regañar, reñir

scone [skəʊn, skɒn] *n* bollo *m*, pastelito *m*

scoop [sku:p] *n* (**a**) *(for flour)* pala *f*; *(for ice cream)* cucharón *m*; *(amount)* palada *f*, cucharada *f* (**b**) *Press* exclusiva *f*
▸ **scoop out** *vt sep (flour etc)* sacar con pala; *(water) (from boat)* achicar
▸ **scoop up** *vt sep* recoger

scooter ['sku:tə(r)] *n (child's)* patinete *m*; *(adult's)* Vespa® *f*

scope [skəʊp] *n* (**a**) *(range)* alcance *m*; *(of undertaking)* ámbito *m* (**b**) *(freedom)* libertad *f*

scorch [skɔ:tʃ] *vt (singe)* chamuscar

scorching ['skɔ:tʃɪŋ] *adj Fam* abrasador(a)

score [skɔ:(r)] **1** *n* (**a**) *Sport* tanteo *m*; *Cards & (in golf)* puntuación *f*; *(result)* resultado *m*
(**b**) *(notch)* muesca *f*
(**c**) **I have a s. to settle with you** tengo que ajustar las cuentas contigo
(**d**) **on that s.** a ese respecto
(**e**) *(twenty)* veintena *f*
(**f**) *Mus (of opera)* partitura *f*; *(of film)* música *f*
2 *vt* (**a**) *(goal)* marcar; *(points)* conseguir
(**b**) *(wood)* hacer una muesca en; *(paper)* rayar
3 *vi* (**a**) *Sport* marcar un tanto; *Ftb* marcar un gol; *(keep the score)* llevar el marcador
(**b**) *(have success)* tener éxito (**with** con); *Fam* ligar (**with** con)
▸ **score out** *vt sep (word etc)* tachar

scoreboard ['skɔ:bɔ:d] *n* marcador *m*

scorer ['skɔ:rə(r)] *n* (**a**) *(goal striker)* goleador *m* (**b**) *(scorekeeper)* encargado(a) *m,f* del marcador

scorn [skɔ:n] **1** *n* desprecio *m*
2 *vt* despreciar

scornful ['skɔ:nfʊl] *adj* desdeñoso(a)

Scorpio ['skɔːpɪəʊ] n Escorpión m

scorpion ['skɔːpɪən] n alacrán m, escorpión m

Scot [skɒt] n escocés(esa) m,f

Scotch [skɒtʃ] 1 adj escocés(esa); US **S. tape®** cinta adhesiva, celo® m
2 n (whisky) whisky m escocés

scotch [skɒtʃ] vt (plot) frustrar; (rumour) negar, desmentir

scot-free ['skɒt'friː] adj impune

Scotland ['skɒtlənd] n Escocia

Scots [skɒts] 1 adj escocés(esa)
2 n (dialecto m) escocés m

Scotsman ['skɒtsmən] n escocés m

Scotswoman ['skɒtswʊmən] n escocesa f

Scottish ['skɒtɪʃ] adj escocés(esa)

scoundrel ['skaʊndrəl] n sinvergüenza mf, canalla m

scour¹ [skaʊə(r)] vt (clean) fregar, restregar

scour² [skaʊə(r)] vt (search) (countryside) rastrear; (building) registrar

scourge [skɜːdʒ] n Fig azote m

scout [skaʊt] 1 n Mil explorador(a) m,f; Sport & Cin cazatalentos m inv; **boy s.** boy m scout
2 vi Mil reconocer el terreno; **to s. around for sth** andar en busca de algo

scowl [skaʊl] 1 vi fruncir el ceño; **to s. at sb** mirar a algn con ceño
2 n ceño m

scrabble ['skræbəl] vi escarbar; Fig **to s. around for sth** revolver todo para encontrar algo

scraggy ['skrægɪ] adj (scraggier, scraggiest) delgado(a), flacucho(a)

scramble ['skræmbəl] 1 vi trepar; **to s. for** pelearse por; **to s. up a tree** trepar a un árbol
2 vt (a) Culin **scrambled eggs** huevos revueltos (b) Rad & Tel (message) codificar; (broadcast) interferir
3 n (climb) subida f; Fig **it's going to be a s.** (rush) va a ser muy apresurado

scrap¹ [skræp] 1 n (a) (small piece) pedazo m; **there isn't a s. of truth in it** no tiene ni un ápice de verdad; **s. (metal)** chatarra f, **s. dealer** or **merchant** chatarrero(a) m,f; **s. paper** papel m de borrador; **s. yard** (for cars) cementerio m de coches (b) **scraps** restos mpl; (of food) sobras fpl
2 vt (discard) desechar; Fig (idea) descartar

scrap² [skræp] Fam 1 n (fight) pelea f
2 vi pelearse (**with** con)

scrapbook ['skræpbʊk] n álbum m de recortes

scrape [skreɪp] 1 vt (paint, wood) raspar; (knee) arañarse, hacerse un rasguño en
2 vi (make noise) chirriar; (rub) rozar
3 n Fam (trouble) lío m
▸ **scrape through** vi Fam (exam) aprobar por los pelos
▸ **scrape together** vt sep reunir a duras penas

scraper ['skreɪpə(r)] n rasqueta f

scrapheap ['skræphiːp] n (dump) vertedero m

scratch [skrætʃ] 1 n (a) (on skin, paintwork) arañazo m; (on record) raya f (b) (noise) chirrido m (c) Fig **to be up to s.** dar la talla; Fig **to start from s.** partir de cero
2 adj **s. team** equipo improvisado
3 vt (a) (with nail, claw) arañar, rasguñar; (paintwork) rayar (b) (to relieve itching) rascarse

scrawl [skrɔːl] 1 n garabatos mpl
2 vt (message etc) garabatear
3 vi hacer garabatos

scrawny ['skrɔːnɪ] adj (**scrawnier, scrawniest**) delgado(a), flaco(a)

scream [skriːm] 1 n chillido m; **screams of laughter** carcajadas fpl
2 vt (insults etc) gritar
3 vi chillar; **to s. at sb** chillar a algn

scree [skriː] n pedregal m

screech [skriːtʃ] 1 n (of person) chillido m; (of tyres, brakes) chirrido m
2 vi (person) chillar; (tyres) chirriar

screen [skriːn] 1 n (a) (movable partition) biombo m (b) Fig cortina f (c) Cin, TV & Comput pantalla f; **s. test** casting m
2 vt (a) (protect) proteger; (conceal) tapar (b) (sieve) (coal etc) tamizar; Fig (candidates) seleccionar (c) (show) (film) proyectar; (for first time) estrenar (d) Med examinar

screening ['skriːnɪŋ] n (a) (of film) proyección f; (for first time) estreno m (b) Med exploración f

screenplay ['skriːnpleɪ] n guión m

screw [skruː] 1 n (a) tornillo m (b) (propeller) hélice f
2 vt (a) atornillar; **to s. sth down** or in or on fijar algo con tornillos (b) Vulg joder
▸ **screw up** vt sep (a) (piece of paper) arrugar; (one's face) torcer (b) very Fam (ruin) joder

screwdriver ['skruːdraɪvə(r)] n destornillador m

scribble ['skrɪbəl] 1 n garabatos mpl
2 vt (message etc) garabatear
3 vi hacer garabatos

script [skrɪpt] n (a) (writing) escritura f; (handwriting) letra f; Typ letra cursiva (b) *(in exam)* escrito *m* (**c**) *Cin* guión *m*

Scripture ['skrɪptʃə(r)] *n* **Holy S.** Sagrada Escritura

scroll [skrəʊl] *n* rollo *m* de pergamino

scrounge [skraʊndʒ] *Fam* **1** *vi* gorronear; **to s. (around) for** buscar; **to s. off sb** vivir a costa de algn
2 *vt* gorronear

scrounger ['skraʊndʒə(r)] *n Fam* gorrón(ona) *m,f*

scrub¹ [skrʌb] *n (undergrowth)* maleza *f*

scrub² [skrʌb] **1** *vt* (**a**) frotar (**b**) *Fam (cancel)* borrar
2 *n (cleaning)* fregado *m*

scruff [skrʌf] *n* pescuezo *m*, cogote *m*

scruffy ['skrʌfɪ] *adj* (**scruffier, scruffiest**) *Fam* desaliñado(a)

scrum [skrʌm] *n* melée *f*; **s. half** medio *m* melée

scruple ['skruːpəl] *n* escrúpulo *m*

scrupulous ['skruːpjʊləs] *adj* escrupuloso(a)

scrupulously ['skruːpjʊləslɪ] *adv* **s. honest** sumamente honrado(a)

scrutinize ['skruːtɪnaɪz] *vt* escudriñar

scrutiny ['skruːtɪnɪ] *n* escrutinio *m*

scuff [skʌf] *vt (the floor)* rayar; *(one's feet)* arrastrar

scuffle ['skʌfəl] **1** *n* pelea *f*
2 *vi* pelearse (**with** con)

scullery ['skʌlərɪ] *n* cuarto *m* de pila

sculptor ['skʌlptə(r)] *n* escultor(a) *m,f*

sculpture ['skʌlptʃə(r)] *n* escultura *f*

scum [skʌm] *n* (**a**) *(on liquid)* espuma *f* (**b**) *Fig* escoria *f*

scupper ['skʌpə(r)] *vt Br Fam (plan etc)* desbaratar

scurrilous ['skʌrɪləs] *adj (abusive)* difamatorio(a)

scurry ['skʌrɪ] *vi (run)* corretear; *(hurry)* apresurarse; **to s. away** *or* **off** escabullirse

scuttle¹ ['skʌtəl] *n* cubo *m*; **coal s.** cubo del carbón

scuttle² ['skʌtəl] *vt (ship)* barrenar

scuttle³ ['skʌtəl] *vi* **to s. away** *or* **off** escabullirse

scythe [saɪð] **1** *n* guadaña *f*
2 *vt* guadañar

SDI [esdiː'aɪ] *n (abbr* **Strategic Defence Initiative)** Iniciativa *f* para la Defensa Estratégica

sea [siː] *n* mar *m* or *f*; **by the s.** a orillas del mar; **out at s.** en alta mar; **to go by s.** ir en barco; **to put to s.** zarpar; *Fig* **to be all at s.** estar desorientado(a); **s. breeze** brisa marina; *Fig* **s. change** metamorfosis *f*; **s. level** nivel *m* del mar; **s. lion** león marino; **s. water** agua *f* de mar

seabed ['siːbed] *n* fondo *m* del mar

seaboard ['siːbɔːd] *n US* costa *f*, litoral *m*

seafood ['siːfuːd] *n* mariscos *mpl*

seafront ['siːfrʌnt] *n* paseo marítimo

seagull ['siːgʌl] *n* gaviota *f*

seal¹ [siːl] *n Zool* foca *f*

seal² [siːl] **1** *n* (**a**) *(official stamp)* sello *m* (**b**) *(airtight closure)* cierre hermético; *(on bottle)* precinto *m*
2 *vt* (**a**) *(with official stamp)* sellar; *(with wax)* lacrar (**b**) *(close)* cerrar; *(make airtight)* cerrar herméticamente (**c**) *(determine)* **this sealed his fate** esto decidió su destino
▸ **seal off** *vt sep (pipe etc)* cerrar; *(area)* acordonar

seam [siːm] *n* (**a**) *Sewing* costura *f*; *Tech* juntura *f*; *Fam* **to be bursting at the seams** *(room)* rebosar de gente (**b**) *Geol & Min* veta *f*, filón *m*

seaman ['siːmən] *n* marinero *m*

seamy ['siːmɪ] *adj* (**seamier, seamiest**) *Fig* sórdido(a)

séance ['seɪɑːns] *n* sesión *f* de espiritismo

seaplane ['siːpleɪn] *n* hidroavión *m*

seaport ['siːpɔːt] *n* puerto marítimo

search [sɜːtʃ] **1** *vt (files etc)* buscar en; *(building, suitcase)* registrar; *(person)* cachear; *(one's conscience)* examinar
2 *vi* buscar; **to s. through** registrar
3 *n* búsqueda *f*; *(of building etc)* registro *m*; *(of person)* cacheo *m*; **in s. of** en busca de; *Comput* **s. engine** motor *m* de búsqueda; **s. party** equipo *m* de salvamento; **s. warrant** orden *f* de registro

searching ['sɜːtʃɪŋ] *adj (look)* penetrante; *(question)* indagatorio(a)

searchlight ['sɜːtʃlaɪt] *n* reflector *m*

seashell ['siːʃel] *n* concha marina

seashore ['siːʃɔː(r)] *n (beach)* playa *f*

seasick ['siːsɪk] *adj* mareado(a); **to get s.** marearse

seaside ['siːsaɪd] *n* playa *f*, costa *f*; **s. resort** lugar turístico de veraneo; **s. town** pueblo costero

season¹ ['siːzən] *n* época *f*; *(of year)* estación *f*; *(for sport etc)* temporada *f*; **the busy s.** la temporada alta; **the rainy s.** la estación de lluvias; **in s.** *(fruit)* en sazón; *(animal)* en celo; *Br* **s. ticket** abono *m*

season² ['siːzən] *vt Culin* sazonar

seasonal ['siːzənəl] *adj* estacional

seasoned ['siːzənd] *adj* (**a**) *Culin* sazonado(a) (**b**) *Fig (campaigner)* curtido(a), avezado(a)

seasoning ['siːzənɪŋ] *n* condimento *m*, aderezo *m*

seat [siːt] **1** n (**a**) asiento m; *(place)* plaza f; *Cin & Th* localidad f; **to take a s.** sentarse; *Aut* **s. belt** cinturón m de seguridad (**b**) *(of cycle)* sillín m; *Fam (buttocks)* trasero m (**c**) *(of power, learning)* centro m, sede f (**d**) *Parl* escaño m

2 vt (**a**) *(guests etc)* sentar (**b**) *(accommodate)* tener cabida para

seating [ˈsiːtɪŋ] n asientos mpl; **s. capacity** cabida f, aforo m

seaweed [ˈsiːwiːd] n alga f *(marina)*

seaworthy [ˈsiːwɜːðɪ] adj en condiciones de navegar

sec [sek] n *Fam (abbr* **second)** segundo m

secede [sɪˈsiːd] vi separarse (**from** de)

secluded [sɪˈkluːdɪd] adj retirado(a), apartado(a)

second¹ [ˈsekənd] **1** adj segundo(a); **every s. day** cada dos días; **it's the s. highest mountain** es la segunda montaña más alta; **on s. thought(s) ...** pensándolo bien ...; **to have s. thoughts about sth** dudar de algo; **to settle for s. best** conformarse con lo que hay

2 n (**a**) *(in series)* segundo(a) m,f; **Charles the S.** Carlos Segundo; **the s. of October** el dos de octubre (**b**) *Aut (gear)* segunda f (**c**) *Com* **seconds** artículos defectuosos

3 vt *(motion)* apoyar

4 adv **to come s.** terminar en segundo lugar

second² [ˈsekənd] n *(time)* segundo m; *Fam* **in a s.** enseguida; *Fam* **just a s.!** ¡un momentito!; **s. hand** *(of watch, clock)* segundero m

secondary [ˈsekəndərɪ] adj secundario(a); *Br* **s. school** escuela secundaria

second-class [ˈsekəndˈklɑːs] **1** adj de segunda clase

2 adv **to travel s.** viajar en segunda

second-hand [ˈsekəndˈhænd] adj & adv de segunda mano

secondly [ˈsekəndlɪ] adv en segundo lugar

secondment [sɪˈkɒndmənt] n *Br* traslado m temporal

second-rate [ˈsekəndˈreɪt] adj de segunda categoría

secrecy [ˈsiːkrəsɪ] n secreto m; **in s.** en secreto

secret [ˈsiːkrɪt] **1** adj secreto(a); **to keep sth s.** mantener algo en secreto; **s. ballot** votación secreta

2 n secreto m; *Fig* clave f; **in s.** en secreto; **to keep a s.** guardar un secreto

secretarial [sekrɪˈteərɪəl] adj de secretario(a)

secretary [ˈsekrətrɪ] n secretario(a) m,f; **S. of State** *Br* ministro(a) m,f con cartera; *US* ministro(a) m,f de Asuntos Exteriores

secretion [sɪˈkriːʃən] n secreción f

secretive [ˈsiːkrɪtɪv] adj reservado(a)

secretly [ˈsiːkrɪtlɪ] adv en secreto

sect [sekt] n secta f

sectarian [sekˈteərɪən] adj & n sectario(a) *(m,f)*

section [ˈsekʃən] n (**a**) *(part)* sección f, parte f; *(of law)* artículo m; *(of community)* sector m; *(of orchestra, department)* sección (**b**) *(cut)* corte m

sector [ˈsektə(r)] n sector m

secular [ˈsekjʊlə(r)] adj *(school, teaching)* laico(a); *(music, art)* profano(a); *(priest)* seglar, secular

secure [sɪˈkjʊə(r)] **1** adj seguro(a); *(window, door)* bien cerrado(a); *(ladder etc)* firme

2 vt (**a**) *(make safe)* asegurar (**b**) *(fix) (rope, knot)* sujetar, fijar; *(object to floor)* afianzar; *(window, door)* cerrar bien (**c**) *(obtain)* conseguir, obtener (**d**) *Fin (guarantee)* avalar

security [sɪˈkjʊərɪtɪ] n (**a**) seguridad f; **national s.** seguridad nacional; **S. Council** *(of United Nations)* Consejo m de Seguridad (**b**) *Fin (guarantee)* fianza f; *(guarantor)* fiador(a) m,f (**c**) *Fin* **securities** valores mpl

sedan [sɪˈdæn] n (**a**) *Hist* **s. chair** silla f de manos (**b**) *US Aut* turismo m

sedate [sɪˈdeɪt] **1** adj sosegado(a)

2 vt sedar

sedation [sɪˈdeɪʃən] n sedación f

sedative [ˈsedətɪv] adj & n sedante *(m)*

sediment [ˈsedɪmənt] n sedimento m; *(of wine)* poso m

seduce [sɪˈdjuːs] vt seducir

seduction [sɪˈdʌkʃən] n seducción f

seductive [sɪˈdʌktɪv] adj seductor(a)

see¹ [siː] vt & vi *(pt* **saw**; *pp* **seen)** (**a**) ver; **I'll s. what can be done** veré lo que se puede hacer; **let's s.** a ver; **that remains to be seen** eso queda por ver; **s. page 10** véase la página 10; **s. you (later)/soon!** ¡hasta luego/pronto!

(**b**) *(meet with)* ver, tener cita con; **they are seeing each other** *(of couple)* salen juntos

(**c**) *(visit)* ver; **to s. the world** recorrer el mundo

(**d**) *(understand)* entender; **as far as I can s.** por lo visto; **I s.** ya veo; **you s., he hasn't got a car** es que no tiene coche, ¿sabes?

(e) he sees himself as a second Caruso se cree otro Caruso

(f) *(ensure)* asegurarse de (g) to s. sb home acompañar a algn a casa

▸ see about *vt insep (deal with)* ocuparse de

▸ see off *vt sep (say goodbye to)* despedirse de

▸ see out *vt sep* (a) *(show out)* acompañar hasta la puerta (b) *(survive)* sobrevivir

▸ see through 1 *vt insep Fam* to s. through sb verle el plumero a algn

2 *vt sep* (a) I'll s. you through puedes contar con mi ayuda; £20 should s. me through con 20 libras me las apaño (b) to s. sth through *(carry out)* llevar algo a cabo

▸ see to *vt insep (deal with)* ocuparse de

see² [si:] *n Rel* sede *f*; the Holy S. la Santa Sede

seed [si:d] 1 *n* (a) *Bot* semilla *f*; *(of fruit)* pepita *f*; to go to s. *(of plant)* granar; *Fig (of person)* descuidarse (b) *(in tennis) (player)* cabeza *mf* de serie

2 *vt* (a) *(sow with seed)* sembrar (b) *(grapes)* despepitar (c) *(in tennis)* preseleccionar

seedling ['si:dlɪŋ] *n* plantón *m*

seedy ['si:dɪ] *adj* (seedier, seediest) *Fam (bar etc)* sórdido(a); *(clothes)* raído(a); *(appearance)* desaseado(a)

seeing ['si:ɪŋ] *conj* s. that visto que, dado que

seeing-eye dog ['si:ŋaɪ'dɒg] *n US* perro *m* lazarillo

seek [si:k] 1 *vt (pt & pp sought)* (a) *(look for)* buscar (b) *(advice, help)* solicitar

2 *vt* buscar; to s. to do sth procurar hacer algo

▸ seek after *vt insep* buscar; much sought after *(person)* muy solicitado(a); *(thing)* muy cotizado(a)

seem [si:m] *vi* parecer; I s. to remember his name was Colin creo recordar que su nombre era Colin; it seems to me that me parece que; so it seems eso parece

seeming ['si:mɪŋ] *adj* aparente

seemingly ['si:mɪŋlɪ] *adv* aparentemente, según parece

seen [si:n] *pp of* see

seep [si:p] *vi* to s. through/into/out filtrarse por/en/de

seesaw ['si:sɔ:] 1 *n* balancín *m*, subibaja *m*

2 *vi* (a) columpiarse, balancearse (b) *Fig* vacilar, oscilar

seethe [si:ð] *vi* bullir, hervir; *Fig* to s.

with anger rabiar; to s. with people rebosar de gente

see-through ['si:θru:] *adj* transparente

segment ['segmənt] *n* segmento *m*; *(of orange)* gajo *m*

segregate ['segrɪgeɪt] *vt* segregar (from de)

segregation [segrɪ'geɪʃən] *n* segregación *f*

seize [si:z] *vt (grab)* agarrar, asir; *Jur (property, drugs)* incautar; *(assets)* secuestrar; *(territory)* tomar; *(arrest)* detener; to s. an opportunity aprovechar una ocasión; to s. power hacerse con el poder

▸ seize on *vt insep (chance)* agarrar; *(idea)* aferrarse a

▸ seize up *vi* agarrotarse

seizure ['si:ʒə(r)] *n* (a) *Jur (of property, drugs)* incautación *f*; *(of newspaper)* secuestro *m*; *(arrest)* detención *f* (b) *Med* ataque *m* (de apoplejía)

seldom ['seldəm] *adv* rara vez, raramente

select [sɪ'lekt] 1 *vt (thing)* escoger, elegir; *(team)* seleccionar

2 *adj* selecto(a)

selected [sɪ'lektɪd] *adj* selecto(a), escogido(a); *(team, player)* seleccionado(a); *Lit* s. works obras escogidas

selection [sɪ'lekʃən] *n (choosing)* elección *f*; *(people or things chosen)* selección *f*; *(range)* surtido *m*

selective [sɪ'lektɪv] *adj* selectivo(a)

self [self] *n (pl* selves) uno(a) mismo(a), sí mismo(a); *Psy* the s. el yo

self- [self] *pref* auto-

self-adhesive [selfəd'hi:sɪv] *adj* autoadhesivo(a)

self-assured [selfə'ʃʊəd] *adj* seguro(a) de sí mismo(a)

self-catering [self'keɪtərɪŋ] *adj* sin servicio de comida

self-centred, *US* self-centered [self'sentəd] *adj* egocéntrico(a)

self-confessed [selfkən'fest] *adj* confeso(a)

self-confidence [self'kɒnfɪdəns] *n* confianza *f* en sí mismo(a)

self-confident [self'kɒnfɪdənt] *adj* seguro(a) de sí mismo(a)

self-conscious [self'kɒnʃəs] *adj* cohibido(a)

self-contained [selfkən'teɪnd] *adj (flat)* con entrada propia; *(person)* independiente

self-control [selfkən'trəʊl] *n* autocontrol *m*

self-defence, *US* **self-defense** [self-dɪ'fens] *n* autodefensa *f*

self-discipline [self'dɪsɪplɪn] *n* autodisciplina *f*

self-employed [selfɪm'plɔɪd] *adj (worker)* autónomo(a)

self-esteem [selfɪ'stiːm] *n* amor propio, autoestima *f*

self-evident [self'evɪdənt] *adj* evidente, patente

self-governing [self'gʌvənɪŋ] *adj* autónomo(a)

self-important [selfɪm'pɔːtənt] *adj* engreído(a), presumido(a)

self-indulgent [selfɪn'dʌldʒənt] *adj* inmoderado(a)

self-interest [self'ɪntrɪst] *n* egoísmo *m*

selfish ['selfɪʃ] *adj* egoísta

selfishness ['selfɪʃnɪs] *n* egoísmo *m*

selfless ['selflɪs] *adj* desinteresado(a)

self-made ['selfmeɪd] *adj* **s. man** hombre *m* que se ha hecho a sí mismo

self-pity [self'pɪtɪ] *n* autocompasión *f*

self-portrait [self'pɔːtreɪt] *n* autorretrato *m*

self-possessed [selfpə'zest] *adj* sereno(a), dueño(a) de sí mismo(a)

self-preservation [selfprezə'veɪʃən] *n* **(instinct of) s.** instinto *m* de conservación

self-raising ['selfreɪzɪŋ] *adj* **s. flour** harina *f* con levadura

self-reliant [selfrɪ'laɪənt] *adj* autosuficiente

self-respect [selfrɪ'spekt] *n* amor propio, dignidad *f*

self-righteous [self'raɪtʃəs] *adj* santurrón(ona)

self-rising ['selfraɪzɪŋ] *adj US =* **self-raising**

self-satisfied [self'sætɪsfaɪd] *adj* satisfecho(a) de sí mismo(a)

self-service [self'sɜːvɪs] **1** *n (in shop etc)* autoservicio *m*

2 *adj* de autoservicio

self-sufficient [selfsə'fɪʃənt] *adj* autosuficiente

self-taught [self'tɔːt] *adj* autodidacta

sell [sel] **1** *vt (pt & pp* **sold)** vender

2 *vi* venderse; **this record is selling well** este disco se vende bien

3 *n* **hard/soft s.** *(in advertising)* publicidad agresiva/discreta

▸ **sell off** *vt sep* vender; *(goods)* liquidar

▸ **sell out 1** *vi* **to s. out to the enemy** claudicar ante el enemigo

2 *vt sep Com* **we're sold out of sugar** se nos ha agotado el azúcar; *Th* **sold out**

(sign) agotadas las localidades

seller ['selə(r)] *n* vendedor(a) *m,f*

selling ['selɪŋ] *n* venta *f*; **s. point** atractivo *m* comercial; **s. price** precio *m* de venta

Sellotape® ['seləteɪp] **1** *n* celo® *m*, cinta adhesiva

2 *vt* pegar *or* fijar con celo®

sell-out ['selaʊt] *n* **(a)** *Th* éxito *m* de taquilla **(b)** *(act of disloyalty)* claudicación *f*

selves [selvz] *pl of* **self**

semaphore ['seməfɔː(r)] *n* semáforo *m*

semblance ['sembləns] *n* apariencia *f*; **there was some s. of truth in it** había algo de verdad en ello

semen ['siːmen] *n* semen *m*

semester [sɪ'mestə(r)] *n* semestre *m*

semi- ['semɪ] *pref* semi-

semicircle ['semɪsɜːkəl] *n* semicírculo *m*

semicolon [semɪ'kəʊlən] *n* punto y coma *m*

semiconductor ['semɪkən'dʌktə(r)] *n* semiconductor *m*

semidetached [semɪdɪ'tætʃt] *Br* **1** *adj* adosado(a)

2 *n* chalé adosado, casa adosada

semifinal [semɪ'faɪnəl] *n* semifinal *f*

seminar ['semɪnɑː(r)] *n* seminario *m*

seminary ['semɪnərɪ] *n* seminario *m*

semitrailer ['semɪtreɪlə(r)] *n US* camión articulado

semolina [semə'liːnə] *n* sémola *f*

senate ['senɪt] *n* **(a)** *Pol* senado *m* **(b)** *Univ* claustro *m*

senator ['senətə(r)] *n* senador(a) *m,f*

send [send] **1** *vt (pt & pp* **sent) (a)** *(letter)* enviar, mandar; *(radio signal)* transmitir; *(rocket, ball)* lanzar; **he was sent to prison** lo mandaron a la cárcel; **to s. sth flying** tirar algo **(b) to s. sb mad** *(cause to become)* volver loco(a) a algn

2 *vi* **to s. for sb** mandar llamar a algn; **to s. for sth** encargar algo

▸ **send away 1** *vt sep (dismiss)* despedir

2 *vi* **to s. away for sth** escribir pidiendo algo

▸ **send back** *vt sep (goods etc)* devolver; *(person)* hacer volver

▸ **send in** *vt sep (application etc)* mandar; *(troops)* enviar

▸ **send off** *vt sep* **(a)** *(letter etc)* enviar; *(goods)* despachar **(b)** *Ftb (player)* expulsar

▸ **send on** *vt sep (luggage) (ahead)* facturar; *(later)* mandar (más tarde)

▸ **send out** *vt sep* **(a)** *(person)* echar **(b)** *(invitations)* enviar **(c)** *(emit)* emitir

▸ **send up** *vt sep* **(a)** hacer subir; *(rocket)*

lanzar; *(smoke)* echar (**b**) *Br Fam (make fun of) (person)* burlarse de; *(book etc)* satirizar

sender [ˈsendə(r)] *n* remitente *mf*

sendoff [ˈsendɒf] *n Fam* despedida *f*

senile [ˈsiːnaɪl] *adj* senil

senior [ˈsiːnjə(r)] **1** *adj* (**a**) *(in age)* mayor; **William Armstrong S.** William Armstrong padre; **s. citizen** jubilado(a) *m,f* (**b**) *(in rank)* superior; *(with longer service)* más antiguo(a); *Mil* **s. officer** oficial *mf* de alta graduación

2 *n* (**a**) **she's three years my s.** *(in age)* me lleva tres años (**b**) *US Educ* estudiante *mf* del último curso

seniority [siːnɪˈɒrɪtɪ] *n* antigüedad *f*

sensation [senˈseɪʃən] *n* sensación *f*; **to be a s.** ser un éxito; **to cause a s.** causar sensación

sensational [senˈseɪʃənəl] *adj (marvellous)* sensacional; *(exaggerated)* sensacionalista

sense [sens] **1** *n* (**a**) *(faculty)* sentido *m*; *(feeling)* sensación *f*; **s. of direction/humour** sentido *m* de la orientación/del humor (**b**) *(wisdom)* sentido *m* común, juicio *m*; **common s.** sentido común (**c**) *(meaning)* sentido *m*; *(of word)* significado *m*; **in a s.** en cierto sentido; **it doesn't make s.** no tiene sentido (**d**) **to come to one's senses** recobrar el juicio

2 *vt* sentir, percatarse de

senseless [ˈsenslɪs] *adj* (**a**) *(absurd)* insensato(a), absurdo(a) (**b**) *(unconscious)* sin conocimiento

sensibility [sensɪˈbɪlɪtɪ] *n* (**a**) *(sensitivity)* sensibilidad *f* (**b**) **sensibilities** susceptibilidad *f*

sensible [ˈsensɪbəl] *adj* (**a**) *(wise)* sensato(a) (**b**) *(choice)* acertado(a) (**c**) *(clothes, shoes)* práctico(a), cómodo(a)

> 🖉 Note that the Spanish word **sensible** is a false friend and is never a translation for the English word **sensible**. In Spanish, **sensible** means both "sensitive" and "perceptible".

sensitive [ˈsensɪtɪv] *adj* (**a**) *(person)* sensible; *(touchy)* susceptible (**b**) *(skin)* delicado(a); *(document)* confidencial

sensor [ˈsensə(r)] *n* sensor *m*

sensual [ˈsensjʊəl] *adj* sensual

sensuous [ˈsensjʊəs] *adj* sensual

sent [sent] *pt & pp of* **send**

sentence [ˈsentəns] **1** *n* (**a**) *(in speech)* frase *f*; *Ling* oración *f* (**b**) *Jur* sentencia *f*; **to pass s. on sb** imponer una pena a algn; **life s.** cadena perpetua

2 *vt Jur* condenar

sentiment [ˈsentɪmənt] *n* (**a**) *(sentimentality)* sensiblería *f* (**b**) *(feeling)* sentimiento *m* (**c**) *(opinion)* opinión *f*

sentimental [sentɪˈmentəl] *adj* sentimental

sentry [ˈsentrɪ] *n* centinela *m*

separate 1 *vt* [ˈsepəreɪt] separar (**from** de); *(divide)* dividir (**into** en); *(distinguish)* distinguir

2 *vi* separarse

3 *adj* [ˈsepərɪt] separado(a); *(different)* distinto(a); *(entrance)* particular

4 *npl* **separates** [ˈsepərɪts] *(clothes)* piezas *fpl*

separately [ˈsepərətlɪ] *adv* por separado

separation [sepəˈreɪʃən] *n* separación *f*

separatist [ˈsepərətɪst] *n* separatista *mf*

September [sepˈtembə(r)] *n* se(p)tiembre *m*

septic [ˈseptɪk] *adj* séptico(a); **to become s.** *(of wound)* infectarse; **s. tank** fosa séptica

sequel [ˈsiːkwəl] *n* secuela *f*; *(of film etc)* continuación *f*

sequence [ˈsiːkwəns] *n* (**a**) *(order)* secuencia *f*, orden *m* (**b**) *(series)* serie *f*, sucesión *f*; *Cin* **film s.** secuencia *f*

serenade [serɪˈneɪd] *n* serenata *f*

serene [sɪˈriːn] *adj* sereno(a), tranquilo(a)

sergeant [ˈsɑːdʒənt] *n Mil* sargento *mf*; *(of police)* ≃ oficial *mf* de policía; **s. major** sargento *mf* mayor

serial [ˈsɪərɪəl] *n* (**a**) *Rad & TV* serial *m*; *(soap opera)* radionovela *f*, telenovela *f* (**b**) **s. number** número *m* de serie

series [ˈsɪəriːz] *n* (*pl* **series**) serie *f*; *(of books)* colección *f*; *(of concerts, lectures)* ciclo *m*

serious [ˈsɪərɪəs] *adj* (**a**) *(solemn, earnest)* serio(a); **I am s.** hablo en serio (**b**) *(causing concern)* grave

seriously [ˈsɪərɪəslɪ] *adv* (**a**) *(in earnest)* en serio (**b**) *(dangerously, severely)* gravemente

seriousness [ˈsɪərɪəsnɪs] *n* gravedad *f*, seriedad *f*; **in all s.** hablando en serio

sermon [ˈsɜːmən] *n* sermón *m*

serpent [ˈsɜːpənt] *n* serpiente *f*

serrated [sɪˈreɪtɪd] *adj* dentado(a)

serum [ˈsɪərəm] *n* suero *m*

servant [ˈsɜːvənt] *n (domestic)* criado(a) *m,f*; *Fig* servidor(a) *m,f*

serve [sɜːv] **1** *vt* (**a**) servir (**b**) *(customer)* atender a (**c**) *(in tennis)* servir (**d**) **if my memory serves me right** si mal no recuerdo; **it serves him right** bien merecido lo tiene (**e**) *Fam* **to s. time** cumplir una condena; **to s. one's apprenticeship** hacer el aprendizaje

2 *vi* (**a**) servir; **to s. on a committee** ser miembro de una comisión (**b**) *(in tennis)* servir (**c**) *(be useful)* servir (**as** de)

3 *n (in tennis)* servicio *m*

▸ **serve out, serve up** *vt sep* servir

service ['sɜːvɪs] **1** *n* (**a**) servicio *m*; **at your s.!** ¡a sus órdenes!; **how can I be of s. to you?** ¿en qué puedo servirle?; **s. (charge) included** servicio incluido; **s. area** área *m* de servicio; **s. industry** sector *m* de servicios; *Br* **s. lift** montacargas *m inv*; **s. station** estación *f* de servicio (**b**) **medical s.** servicios médicos; *Mil* **the Services** las Fuerzas Armadas; **the train s. to Bristol** la línea de trenes a Bristol (**c**) *(maintenance)* revisión *f* (**d**) *Rel* oficio *m*; *(mass)* misa *f* (**e**) *(in tennis)* servicio *m*; **s. line** línea *f* de saque (**f**) *(set of dishes)* juego *m*

2 *vt (car, machine)* revisar

serviceable ['sɜːvɪsəbəl] *adj* (**a**) *(fit for use)* útil, servible (**b**) *(practical)* práctico(a)

serviceman ['sɜːvɪsmən] *n* militar *m*

serviette [sɜːvɪ'et] *n Br* servilleta *f*

sesame ['sesəmɪ] *n* sésamo *m*

session ['seʃən] *n* (**a**) sesión *f*; **to be in s.** estar reunido(a); *(of Parliament, court)* celebrar una sesión (**b**) *Educ (academic year)* año académico

set¹ [set] **1** *vt (pt & pp set)* (**a**) *(put, place)* poner, colocar; *(trap)* poner (**for** para); **the novel is s. in Moscow** la novela se desarrolla en Moscú; **to s. fire to sth** prender fuego a algo

(**b**) *(time, price)* fijar; *(record)* establecer; *(trend)* imponer

(**c**) *(mechanism etc)* ajustar; *(bone)* encajar; **to s. one's watch** poner el reloj en hora

(**d**) *(arrange)* arreglar; **he s. the words to music** puso música a la letra; **to s. the table** poner la mesa

(**e**) *(exam, homework)* poner; *(example)* dar; *(precedent)* sentar

(**f**) **to s. sail** zarpar; **to s. sb free** poner en libertad a algn; **to s. sth going** poner algo en marcha

(**g**) *(pearl, diamond etc)* engastar

(**h**) *Typ* componer

2 *vi* (**a**) *(sun, moon)* ponerse

(**b**) *(jelly, jam)* cuajar; *(cement)* fraguar; *(bone)* encajarse

(**c**) **to s. to** *(begin)* ponerse a

3 *n* (**a**) **shampoo and s.** lavar y marcar

(**b**) *(stage) Cin* plató *m*; *Th* escenario

m; (scenery) decorado *m*

4 *adj* (**a**) *(task, idea)* fijo(a); *(date, time)* señalado(a); *(opinion)* inflexible; *(smile)* rígido(a); *(gaze)* fijo(a); **s. phrase** frase hecha; **to be s. on doing sth** estar empeñado(a) en hacer algo; **s. square** cartabón *m*

(**b**) *(ready)* listo(a)

▸ **set about** *vt insep* (**a**) *(begin)* empezar (**b**) *(attack)* agredir

▸ **set aside** *vt sep (time, money)* reservar; *(differences)* dejar de lado

▸ **set back** *vt sep* (**a**) *(delay)* retrasar; *(hinder)* entorpecer (**b**) *Fam (cost)* costar

▸ **set down** *vt sep (luggage etc)* dejar (en el suelo); *Br (passengers)* dejar

▸ **set in** *vi (winter, rain)* comenzar; **panic s. in** cundió el pánico

▸ **set off 1** *vi (depart)* salir

2 *vt sep* (**a**) *(bomb)* hacer estallar; *(burglar alarm)* hacer sonar; *(reaction)* desencadenar (**b**) *(enhance)* hacer resaltar

▸ **set out 1** *vi* (**a**) *(depart)* salir; **to s. out for ...** partir hacia ... (**b**) **to s. out to do sth** proponerse hacer algo

2 *vt sep (arrange)* disponer; *(present)* presentar

▸ **set up 1** *vt sep* (**a**) *(position)* colocar; *(statue, camp)* levantar; *(tent, stall)* montar (**b**) *(business etc)* establecer; *Fam* montar; *(committee)* constituir; *Fam* **you've been s. up!** ¡te han timado!

2 *vi* establecerse

set² [set] *n* (**a**) *(series)* serie *f*; *(of golf clubs etc)* juego *m*; *(of tools)* estuche *m*; *(of turbines etc)* equipo *m*; *(of books, poems)* colección *f*; *(of teeth)* dentadura *f*; **chess s.** juego de ajedrez; **s. of cutlery** cubertería *f*; **s. of kitchen utensils** batería *f* de cocina (**b**) *(of people)* grupo *m*; *Pej (clique)* camarilla *f* (**c**) *Math* conjunto *m* (**d**) *(in tennis)* set *m* (**e**) *TV* **s.** televisor *m*

setback ['setbæk] *n* revés *m*, contratiempo *m*

settee [se'tiː] *n* sofá *m*

setting ['setɪŋ] *n* (**a**) *(background)* marco *m; (of novel, film)* escenario *m* (**b**) *(of jewel)* engaste *m*

settle ['setəl] **1** *vt* (**a**) *(put in position)* colocar

(**b**) *(decide on)* acordar; *(date, price)* fijar; *(problem)* resolver; *(differences)* arreglar

(**c**) *(debt)* pagar; *(account)* saldar

(**d**) *(nerves)* calmar; *(stomach)* asentar

(**e**) *Fam (put an end to)* acabar con

(**f**) *(establish) (person)* instalar

(**g**) *(colonize)* asentarse en

2 *vi* (**a**) *(bird, insect)* posarse; *(dust)* depositarse; *(snow)* cuajar; *(sediment)* precipitarse; *(liquid)* asentarse; **to s. into an armchair** acomodarse en un sillón (**b**) *(put down roots)* afincarse; *(in a colony)* asentarse (**c**) *(weather)* serenarse (**d**) *(child, nerves)* calmarse (**e**) *(pay)* pagar; **to s. out of court** llegar a un acuerdo amistoso

▸**settle down** *vi* (**a**) *(put down roots)* instalarse; *(marry)* casarse (**b**) **to s. down to work** ponerse a trabajar (**c**) *(child)* calmarse; *(situation)* normalizarse

▸**settle for** *vt insep* conformarse con

▸**settle in** *vi (move in)* instalarse; *(become adapted)* adaptarse

▸**settle with** *vt sep (pay debt to)* ajustar cuentas con

settlement ['setəlmənt] *n* (**a**) *(agreement)* acuerdo *m* (**b**) *(of debt)* pago *m*; *(of account)* liquidación *f* (**c**) *(dowry)* dote *m* (**d**) *(colonization)* colonización *f* (**e**) *(colony)* asentamiento *m*; *(village)* poblado *m*

settler ['setlə(r)] *n* colono *m*

setup ['setʌp] *n (system)* sistema *m*; *(situation)* situación *f*; *Fam* montaje *m*

seven ['sevən] *adj & n* siete *(m inv)*

seventeen [sevən'tiːn] *adj & n* diecisiete *(m inv)*, diez y siete *(m inv)*

seventeenth [sevən'tiːnθ] **1** *adj & n* decimoséptimo(a) *(m,f)*
2 *n (fraction)* decimoséptima parte

seventh ['sevənθ] **1** *adj & n* séptimo(a) *(m,f)*
2 *n* séptimo *m*

seventy ['sevəntɪ] *adj & n* setenta *(m inv)*

sever ['sevə(r)] *vt (cut)* cortar; *Fig (relations)* romper

several ['sevərəl] **1** *adj* (**a**) *(more than a few)* varios(as) (**b**) *(different)* distintos(as)
2 *pron* algunos(as)

severance ['sevərəns] *n (of relations etc)* ruptura *f*; **s. pay** indemnización *f* por despido

severe [sɪ'vɪə(r)] *adj* severo(a); *(climate, blow)* duro(a); *(illness, loss)* grave; *(pain)* intenso(a)

severity [sɪ'verɪtɪ] *n (of person, criticism, punishment)* severidad *f*; *(of climate)* rigor *m*; *(of illness)* gravedad *f*; *(of pain)* intensidad *f*; *(of style)* austeridad *f*

Seville [sə'vɪl] *n* Sevilla

sew [səʊ] *vt & vi (pt sewed; pp sewed or sewn)* coser

▸**sew up** *vt sep (stitch together)* coser; *(mend)* remendar

sewage ['suːɪdʒ] *n* aguas *fpl* residuales

sewer ['suːə(r)] *n* alcantarilla *f*, cloaca *f*

sewerage ['suːərɪdʒ] *n* alcantarillado *m*

sewing ['səʊɪŋ] *n* costura *f*; **s. machine** máquina *f* de coser

sewn [səʊn] *pp of* **sew**

sex [seks] *n* sexo *m*; **s. education** educación *f* sexual; **to have s. with sb** tener relaciones sexuales con algn; **s. appeal** sex-appeal *m*

sexist ['seksɪst] *adj & n* sexista *(mf)*

sexual ['seksjʊəl] *adj* sexual

sexuality [seksjʊ'ælɪtɪ] *n* sexualidad *f*

sexy ['seksɪ] *adj (sexier, sexiest) Fam* sexi, erótico(a)

shabby ['ʃæbɪ] *adj (shabbier, shabbiest)* (**a**) *(garment)* raído(a); *(house)* desvencijado(a); *(person) (in rags)* harapiento(a); *(unkempt)* desaseado(a) (**b**) *(treatment)* mezquino(a)

shack [ʃæk] *n* choza *f*

shackles ['ʃækəlz] *npl* grilletes *mpl*, grillos *mpl*; *Fig* trabas *fpl*

shade [ʃeɪd] **1** *n* (**a**) *(shadow)* sombra *f*; **in the s.** a la sombra (**b**) *(eyeshade)* visera *f*; *(lampshade)* pantalla *f*; *US (blind)* persiana *f* (**c**) *(of colour)* tono *m*, matiz *m*; *Fig (of meaning)* matiz *m* (**d**) *(small amount)* poquito *m* (**e**) *Fam* **shades** gafas *fpl* or *Am* anteojos *mpl* de sol
2 *vt (from sun)* proteger contra el sol

shadow ['ʃædəʊ] **1** *n* (**a**) *(shade)* sombra *f*; *(darkness)* oscuridad *f*; *Fig* **without a s. of a doubt** sin lugar a dudas (**b**) *Br* **the S. Cabinet** el gabinete de la oposición
2 *vt Fig* seguir la pista a

shadowy ['ʃædəʊɪ] *adj (dark)* oscuro(a); *(hazy)* vago(a)

shady ['ʃeɪdɪ] *adj (shadier, shadiest) (place)* a la sombra; *(suspicious) (person)* sospechoso(a); *(deal)* turbio(a)

shaft [ʃɑːft] *n* (**a**) *(of tool, golf club)* mango *m*; *(of lance)* asta *f*; *(of arrow)* astil *m* (**b**) *Tech* eje *m* (**c**) *(of mine)* pozo *m*; *(of lift, elevator)* hueco *m* (**d**) *(beam of light)* rayo *m*

shaggy ['ʃægɪ] *adj (shaggier, shaggiest) (hairy)* peludo(a); *(long-haired)* melenudo(a); *(beard)* desgreñado(a)

shake [ʃeɪk] **1** *n* sacudida *f*
2 *vt (pt shook; pp shaken* ['ʃeɪkən]*) (carpet etc)* sacudir; *(bottle)* agitar; *(dice)* mover; *(building)* hacer temblar; **the news shook him** la noticia le conmocionó; **to s. hands with sb** estrechar la mano a algn; **to s. one's head** negar con la cabeza

3 *vi (person, building)* temblar; **to s. with cold** tiritar de frío

▸ **shake off** *vt sep* (**a**) *(dust etc)* sacudirse (**b**) *Fig (bad habit)* librarse de; *(cough, cold)* quitarse de encima; *(pursuer)* dar esquinazo a

▸ **shake up** *vt sep Fig (shock)* trastornar; *(reorganize)* reorganizar

shake-up ['ʃeɪkʌp] *n Fig* reorganización *f*

shaky ['ʃeɪkɪ] *adj* (**shakier, shakiest**) *(hand, voice)* tembloroso(a); *(step)* inseguro(a); *(handwriting)* temblón(ona)

shall [ʃæl, *unstressed* ʃəl] *v aux*

> En el inglés hablado, y en el escrito en estilo coloquial, el verbo **shall** se contrae de manera que **I/you/he** *etc* **shall** se transforman en **I'll/you'll/he'll** *etc*. La forma negativa **shall not** se transforma en **shan't**.

(**a**) *(used to form future tense) (first person only)* **I s.** *or* **I'll buy it** lo compraré; **I s. not** *or* **I shan't say anything** no diré nada (**b**) *(used to form questions) (usu first person)* **s. I close the door?** ¿cierro la puerta?; **s. I mend it for you?** ¿quieres que te lo repare?; **s. we go?** ¿nos vamos? (**c**) *(emphatic, command, threat) (all persons)* **we s. overcome** venceremos; **you s. leave immediately** te irás enseguida

shallow ['ʃæləʊ] *adj* poco profundo(a); *Fig* superficial

sham [ʃæm] **1** *adj* falso(a); *(illness etc)* fingido(a)
2 *n* (**a**) *(pretence)* engaño *m*, farsa *f* (**b**) *(person)* fantoche *m*
3 *vt* fingir, simular
4 *vi* fingir

shambles ['ʃæmbəlz] *n sing* confusión *f*; **the performance was a s.** la función fue un desastre

shame [ʃeɪm] **1** *n* (**a**) *(guilt)* vergüenza *f*, *Andes, CAm, Carib, Méx* pena *f*; **to put to s.** *(far outdo)* eclipsar, sobrepasar (**b**) *(pity)* pena *f*, lástima *f*; **what a s.!** ¡qué pena!, ¡qué lástima!
2 *vt* avergonzar, *Andes, CAm, Carib, Méx* apenar; *(disgrace)* deshonrar

shamefaced ['ʃeɪmfeɪst] *adj* avergonzado(a), *Andes, CAm, Carib, Méx* apenado(a)

shameful ['ʃeɪmfʊl] *adj* vergonzoso(a)

shameless ['ʃeɪmlɪs] *adj* descarado(a)

shampoo [ʃæm'puː] **1** *n* champú *m*
2 *vt* lavar con champú; **to s. one's hair** lavarse el pelo

shamrock ['ʃæmrɒk] *n* trébol *m*

shandy ['ʃændɪ] *n Br* clara *f*, cerveza *f* con gaseosa

shantytown ['ʃæntɪtaʊn] *n* barrio *m* de chabolas, *Arg* villa *f* miseria, *Chile* población *f* callampa, *Méx* ciudad *f* perdida, *Urug* cantegril *m*, *Ven* rancho *m*

shape [ʃeɪp] **1** *n* (**a**) *(form)* forma *f*; *(shadow)* silueta *m*; **to take s.** tomar forma (**b**) **in good/bad s.** *(condition)* en buen/mal estado; **to be in good s.** *(health)* estar en forma
2 *vt* dar forma a; *(clay)* modelar; *(stone)* tallar; *(character)* formar; *(destiny)* determinar; **star-shaped** con forma de estrella
3 *vi* (*also* **s. up**) tomar forma; **to s. up well** *(events)* tomar buen cariz; *(person)* hacer progresos

shapeless ['ʃeɪplɪs] *adj* amorfo(a), informe

shapely ['ʃeɪplɪ] *adj* (**shapelier, shapeliest**) escultural

share ['ʃeə(r)] **1** *n* (**a**) *(portion)* parte *f* (**b**) *Fin* acción *f*; **s. index** índice *m* de la Bolsa; **s. prices** cotizaciones *fpl*
2 *vt* (**a**) *(divide)* dividir (**b**) *(have in common)* compartir
3 *vi* compartir

▸ **share out** *vt sep* repartir

shareholder ['ʃeəhəʊldə(r)] *n* accionista *mf*

shark [ʃɑːk] *n* (**a**) *(fish)* tiburón *m* (**b**) *Fam (swindler)* estafador(a) *m,f*; **loan s.** usurero(a) *m,f*

sharp [ʃɑːp] **1** *adj* (**a**) *(razor, knife)* afilado(a); *(needle, pencil)* puntiagudo(a)
(**b**) *(angle)* agudo(a); *(features)* anguloso(a); *(bend)* cerrado(a)
(**c**) *(outline)* definido(a); *(contrast)* marcado(a)
(**d**) *(observant)* perspicaz; *(clever)* listo(a); *(quick-witted)* avispado(a); *(cunning)* astuto(a)
(**e**) *(sudden)* brusco(a)
(**f**) *(pain, cry)* agudo(a); *(wind)* penetrante
(**g**) *(sour)* acre
(**h**) *(criticism)* mordaz; *(temper)* arisco(a); *(tone)* seco(a)
(**i**) *Mus* sostenido(a); *(out of tune)* desafinado(a)
2 *adv* **at two o'clock s.** *(exactly)* a las dos en punto
3 *n Mus* sostenido *m*

sharpen ['ʃɑːpən] *vt* (**a**) *(knife)* afilar; *(pencil)* sacar punta a (**b**) *Fig (desire, intelligence)* agudizar

sharpener ['ʃɑːpənə(r)] *n (for knife)* afilador *m*; *(for pencil)* sacapuntas *m inv*

sharp-eyed ['ʃɑːpaɪd] *adj* con ojos de lince

sharply ['ʃɑːplɪ] *adv* (a) *(abruptly)* bruscamente (b) *(clearly)* marcadamente

shatter ['ʃætə(r)] **1** *vt* hacer añicos; *(nerves)* destrozar; *(hopes)* frustrar
  2 *vi* hacerse añicos

shave [ʃeɪv] **1** *n* afeitado *m*; **to have a s.** afeitarse/Fig **to have a close s.** escaparse por los pelos
  2 *vt* (*pt* **shaved**; *pp* **shaved** *or* **shaven** ['ʃeɪvən]) *(person)* afeitar; *(wood)* cepillar
  3 *vi* afeitarse

shaver ['ʃeɪvə(r)] *n* (electric) s. máquina *f* de afeitar

shaving ['ʃeɪvɪŋ] *n* (a) *(of wood)* viruta *f* (b) **s. brush** brocha *f* de afeitar; **s. cream** crema *f* de afeitar; **s. foam** espuma *f* de afeitar

shawl [ʃɔːl] *n* chal *m*

she [ʃiː] *pers pron* ella *(usually omitted in Spanish, except for contrast)*

she- [ʃiː] *pref* *(of animal)* hembra; **s.-cat** gata *f*

sheaf [ʃiːf] *n* (*pl* **sheaves**) *Agr* gavilla *f*; *(of arrows)* haz *m*; *(of papers, banknotes)* fajo *m*

shear [ʃɪə(r)] **1** *vt* (*pt* **sheared**; *pp* **shorn** *or* **sheared**) *(sheep)* esquilar; **to s. off** cortar
  2 *vi* esquilar ovejas

shears [ʃɪəz] *npl* tijeras *fpl* (grandes)

sheath [ʃiːθ] *n* (a) *(for sword)* vaina *f*; *(for knife, scissors)* funda *f* (b) *(contraceptive)* preservativo *m*

sheaves [ʃiːvz] *pl of* **sheaf**

shed¹ [ʃed] *n* *(in garden)* cobertizo *m*; *(workmen's hut)* barraca *f*; *(for cattle)* establo *m*; *(in factory)* nave *f*

shed² [ʃed] *vt* (*pt & pp* **shed**) (a) *(clothes)* despojarse de; *(unwanted thing)* deshacerse de; **the snake s. its skin** la serpiente mudó de piel (b) *(blood, tears)* derramar

sheen [ʃiːn] *n* brillo *m*

sheep [ʃiːp] *n* (*pl* **sheep**) oveja *f*

sheepdog ['ʃiːpdɒg] *n* perro *m* pastor

sheepish ['ʃiːpɪʃ] *adj* avergonzado(a)

sheepskin ['ʃiːpskɪn] *n* piel *f* de carnero

sheer [ʃɪə(r)] *adj* (a) *(utter)* total, puro(a) (b) *(cliff)* escarpado(a); *(drop)* vertical (c) *(stockings, cloth)* fino(a)

sheet [ʃiːt] *n* (a) *(on bed)* sábana *f* (b) *(of paper)* hoja *f*; *(of tin, glass, plastic)* lámina *f*; *(of ice)* capa *f*

sheik(h) [ʃeɪk] *n* jeque *m*

shelf [ʃelf] *n* (*pl* **shelves**) *(on bookcase)* estante *m*; *(in cupboard)* tabla *f*; **shelves** estantería *f*

shell [ʃel] **1** *n* (a) *(of egg, nut)* cáscara *f*; *(of pea)* vaina *f*; *(of tortoise etc)* caparazón *m*; *(of snail etc)* concha *f* (b) *(of building)* armazón *m* (c) *(mortar etc)* obús *m*, proyectil *m*; *(cartridge)* cartucho *m*; **s. shock** neurosis *f* de guerra
  2 *vt* (a) *(peas)* desvainar; *(nuts)* pelar (b) *Mil* bombardear

shellfish ['ʃelfɪʃ] *n* (*pl* **shellfish**) marisco *m*, mariscos *mpl*

shelter ['ʃeltə(r)] **1** *n* (a) *(protection)* abrigo *m*, amparo *m*; **to take s. (from)** refugiarse (de) (b) *(place)* refugio *m*; *(for homeless)* asilo *m*; **bus s.** marquesina *f*
  2 *vt* (a) *(protect)* abrigar, proteger (b) *(take into one's home)* ocultar
  3 *vi* refugiarse

sheltered ['ʃeltəd] *adj* *(place)* abrigado(a); **to lead a s. life** vivir apartado(a) del mundo

shelve [ʃelv] *vt* Fig *(postpone)* dar carpetazo a

shelves [ʃelvz] *pl of* **shelf**

shepherd ['ʃepəd] **1** *n* pastor *m*; **s.'s pie** = pastel de carne picada con puré de patatas *or* Am papas
  2 *vt* Fig **to s. sb in** hacer entrar a algn

sheriff ['ʃerɪf] *n* *Br* gobernador *m* civil; *Scot* juez *m* presidente; *US* sheriff *m*

sherry ['ʃerɪ] *n* jerez *m*

Shetland ['ʃetlənd] *n* **the S. Isles, S.** las Islas Shetland; **S. wool** lana *f* Shetland

shield [ʃiːld] **1** *n* (a) *(of policeman)* placa *f* (b) *(on machinery)* blindaje *m*
  2 *vt* proteger (**from** de)

shift [ʃɪft] **1** *n* (a) *(change)* cambio *m*; *US Aut* (gear) s. cambio de velocidades (b) *(period of work, group of workers)* turno *m*; **to be on the day s.** hacer el turno de día
  2 *vt* *(change)* cambiar; *(move)* cambiar de sitio, trasladar
  3 *vi* *(move)* moverse; *(change place)* cambiar de sitio; *(opinion)* cambiar; *(wind)* cambiar de dirección

shiftless ['ʃɪftlɪs] *n* perezoso(a), vago(a)

shiftwork ['ʃɪftwɜːk] *n* trabajo *m* por turnos

shifty ['ʃɪftɪ] *adj* (**shiftier, shiftiest**) *(look)* furtivo(a); *(person)* sospechoso(a)

shilling ['ʃɪlɪŋ] *n* chelín *m*

shimmer ['ʃɪmə(r)] **1** *vi* relucir; *(shine)* brillar
  2 *n* luz trémula, reflejo trémulo; *(shining)* brillo *m*

shin [ʃɪn] *n* espinilla *f*; **s. pad** espinillera *f*

shine [ʃaɪn] **1** *vi* (*pt & pp* **shone**) (a) *(light)*

brillar; *(metal)* relucir (**b**) *Fig (excel)* sobresalir (**at** en)

  2 *vt* (**a**) *(lamp)* dirigir (**b**) *(pt & pp* **shined**)
(polish) sacar brillo a; *(shoes)* limpiar

  3 *n* brillo *m*, lustre *m*

shingle ['ʃɪŋgəl] *n* (**a**) *(pebbles)* guijarros
mpl (**b**) *(roof tile)* tablilla *f*

shingles ['ʃɪŋgəlz] *n sing Med* herpes *m*

shining ['ʃaɪnɪŋ] *adj Fig (outstanding)*
ilustre

shiny ['ʃaɪnɪ] *adj* (**shinier, shiniest**) brillante

ship [ʃɪp] **1** *n* barco *m*, buque *m*

  2 *vt* (**a**) *(take on board)* embarcar (**b**)
(transport) transportar (en barco); *(send)*
enviar, mandar

shipbuilding ['ʃɪpbɪldɪŋ] *n* construcción *f* naval

shipment ['ʃɪpmənt] *n* (**a**) *(act)* transporte *m* (**b**) *(load)* consignación *f*, envío
m

shipper ['ʃɪpə(r)] *n (person)* cargador(a)
m,f

shipping ['ʃɪpɪŋ] *n* (**a**) *(ships)* barcos
mpl; **s. lane** vía *f* de navegación (**b**)
(loading) embarque *m*; *(transporting)*
transporte *m* (en barco); **s. company**
compañía naviera

shipshape ['ʃɪpʃeɪp] *adj & adv* en perfecto orden

shipwreck ['ʃɪprek] **1** *n* naufragio *m*

  2 *vt* **to be shipwrecked** naufragar

shipyard ['ʃɪpjɑːd] *n* astillero *m*

shire [ʃaɪə(r)] *n Br* condado *m*

shirk [ʃɜːk] **1** *vt (duty)* faltar a; *(problem)*
eludir

  2 *vi* gandulear

shirt [ʃɜːt] *n* camisa *f*; **in s. sleeves** en
mangas de camisa; *Fam* **keep your s. on!**
¡no te sulfures!

shit [ʃɪt] *Vulg* **1** *n* mierda *f*; **in the s.**
jodido(a)

  2 *interj* ¡mierda!

  3 *vi* cagar

shiver ['ʃɪvə(r)] **1** *vi (with cold)* tiritar;
(with fear) temblar, estremecerse

  2 *n (with cold, fear)* escalofrío *m*

shoal [ʃəʊl] *n (of fish)* banco *m*

shock [ʃɒk] **1** *n* (**a**) *(jolt)* choque *m*; **s.
absorber** amortiguador *m*; **s. wave** onda
expansiva (**b**) *(upset)* conmoción *f*;
(scare) susto *m* (**c**) *Med* shock *m*

  2 *vt (upset)* conmover; *(startle)* sobresaltar; *(scandalize)* escandalizar

shocking ['ʃɒkɪŋ] *adj* (**a**) *(causing horror)* espantoso(a); *Fam (very bad)* horro-
roso(a) (**b**) *(disgraceful)* escandaloso(a)
(**c**) **s. pink** rosa chillón

shod [ʃɒd] *pt & pp of* **shoe**

shoddy ['ʃɒdɪ] *adj* (**shoddier, shoddiest**)
(goods) de mala calidad; *(work)* chapu-
cero(a)

shoe [ʃuː] **1** *n* (**a**) zapato *m*; *(for horse)*
herradura *f*; **brake s.** zapata *f*; **s. polish**
betún *m*; **s. repair (shop)** remiendo *m* de
zapatos; **s. shop,** *US* **s. store** zapatería *f*
(**b**) **shoes** calzado *m*

  2 *vt (pt & pp* **shod**) *(horse)* herrar

shoebrush ['ʃuːbrʌʃ] *n* cepillo *m* para los
zapatos

shoehorn ['ʃuːhɔːn] *n* calzador *m*

shoelace ['ʃuːleɪs] *n* cordón *m* (de zapatos)

shoestring ['ʃuːstrɪŋ] *n Fig* **to do sth on a
s.** hacer algo con poquísimo dinero

shone [ʃɒn, *US* ʃəʊn] *pt & pp of* **shine**

shoo [ʃuː] **1** *interj* ¡fuera!

  2 *vt* **to s. (away)** espantar

shook [ʃʊk] *pt of* **shake**

shoot [ʃuːt] **1** *n Bot* retoño *m*; *(of vine)*
sarmiento *m*

  2 *vt (pt & pp* **shot**) (**a**) pegar un tiro a;
(kill) matar; *(execute)* fusilar; *(hunt)* cazar; **to s. dead** matar a tiros (**b**) *(missile,
glance)* lanzar; *(bullet, ball)* disparar (**c**)
(film) rodar, filmar; *Phot* fotografiar

  3 *vi (with gun)* disparar (**at sb** a
algn); **to s. at a target** tirar al blanco; *Ftb*
to s. at the goal chutar a puerta (**b**) **to s.
past** *or* **by** pasar flechado(a)

  ▸ **shoot down** *vt sep (aircraft)* derribar

  ▸ **shoot out** *vi (person)* salir disparado(a);
(water) brotar; *(flames)* salir

  ▸ **shoot up** *vi* (**a**) *(flames)* salir; *(water)*
brotar; *(prices)* dispararse (**b**) *Fam (inject
drugs)* chutarse

shooting ['ʃuːtɪŋ] **1** *n* (**a**) *(shots)* tiros *mpl*;
(murder) asesinato *m*; *(hunting)* caza *f*; **s.
star** estrella *f* fugaz (**b**) *(of film)* rodaje *m*

  2 *adj (pain)* punzante

shoot-out ['ʃuːtaʊt] *n* tiroteo *m*

shop [ʃɒp] **1** *n* (**a**) tienda *f*; *(large store)*
almacén *m*; **s. assistant** dependiente(a)
m,f; **s. window** escaparate *m* (**b**) *(workshop)* taller *m*; **s. floor** *(place)* planta *f*;
(workers) obreros *mpl*; **s. steward** enlace
mf sindical

  2 *vi* hacer compras; **to go shopping** ir de
compras

shopkeeper ['ʃɒpkiːpə(r)] *n* tendero(a)
m,f

shoplifter ['ʃɒplɪftə(r)] *n* ladrón(ona)
m,f (de tiendas)

shopper ['ʃɒpə(r)] *n* comprador(a) *m,f*

shopping ['ʃɒpɪŋ] *n (purchases)* compras *fpl*; **s. bag/basket** bolsa *f*/cesta *f* de

la compra; **s. centre** *or* **precinct** centro *m* comercial

shopsoiled ['ʃɒpsɔɪld], *US* **shopworn** ['ʃɒpwɔːn] *adj* deteriorado(a)

shore [ʃɔː(r)] *n (of sea, lake)* orilla *f*; *US (beach)* playa *f*; *(coast)* costa *f*; **to go on s.** desembarcar
▸ **shore up** *vt sep* apuntalar

shorn [ʃɔːn] *pp of* **shear**

short [ʃɔːt] **1** *adj* **(a)** corto(a); *(not tall)* bajo(a); **in a s. while** dentro de un rato; **in the s. term** a corto plazo; **s. circuit** cortocircuito *m*; **s. cut** atajo *m*; *Br* **s. list** lista *f* de seleccionados; **s. story** relato corto, cuento *m*; **s. wave** onda corta
    (b) *(brief)* corto(a), breve; **"Bob" is s. for "Robert"** "Bob" es el diminutivo de "Robert"; **for s.** para abreviar; **in s.** en pocas palabras
    (c) to be s. of breath faltarle a uno la respiración; **to be s. of food** andar escaso(a) de comida
    (d) *(curt)* brusco(a), seco(a)
  2 *adv* **(a) to pull up s.** pararse en seco
    (b) to cut s. *(holiday)* interrumpir; *(meeting)* suspender; **we're running s. of coffee** se nos está acabando el café
    (c) s. of *(except)* excepto, menos
  3 *n* **(a)** *Cin* cortometraje *m*
    (b) *Fam (drink)* copa *f*
  4 *vi* **to s. (out)** tener un cortocircuito

shortage ['ʃɔːtɪdʒ] *n* escasez *f*

shortbread ['ʃɔːtbred] *n* mantecado *m*

short-change [ʃɔːt'tʃeɪndʒ] *vt* **to s. sb** no devolver el cambio completo a algn; *Fig* timar a algn

short-circuit [ʃɔːt'sɜːkɪt] **1** *vt* provocar un cortocircuito en
  2 *vi* tener un cortocircuito

shortcomings ['ʃɔːtkʌmɪŋz] *npl* defectos *mpl*

shortcrust ['ʃɔːtkrʌst] *n* **s. pastry** pasta brisa

shorten ['ʃɔːtən] *vt (skirt, visit)* acortar; *(word)* abreviar; *(text)* resumir

shortfall ['ʃɔːtfɔːl] *n* déficit *m*

shorthand ['ʃɔːthænd] *n* taquigrafía *f*; *Br* **s. typist** taquimecanógrafo(a) *m,f*

short-list ['ʃɔːtlɪst] *vt* poner en la lista de seleccionados

short-lived [ʃɔːt'lɪvd] *adj* efímero(a)

shortly ['ʃɔːtlɪ] *adv (soon)* dentro de poco; **s. after** poco después

short-range ['ʃɔːtreɪndʒ] *adj* de corto alcance

shorts [ʃɔːts] *npl* **(a)** pantalones *mpl* cortos; **a pair of s.** un pantalón corto **(b)** *US (underpants)* calzoncillos *mpl*

short-sighted [ʃɔːt'saɪtɪd] *adj (person)* miope; *Fig (plan etc)* sin visión de futuro

short-staffed [ʃɔːt'stɑːft] *adj* escaso(a) de personal

short-tempered [ʃɔːt'tempəd] *adj* de mal genio

short-term ['ʃɔːtɜːm] *adj* a corto plazo

shot¹ [ʃɒt] *n* **(a)** *(act, sound)* tiro *m*, disparo *m* **(b)** *(projectile)* bala *f*; *(pellets)* perdigones *mpl*; *Fig* **he was off like a s.** salió disparado; *Sport* **s. put** lanzamiento *m* de peso **(c)** *(person)* tirador(a) *m,f* **(d)** *Ftb (kick)* tiro *m* (a puerta); *(in billiards, cricket, golf)* golpe *m* **(e)** *(attempt)* tentativa *f*; **to have a s. at sth** intentar hacer algo **(f)** *(injection)* inyección *f*; *Fam* pinchazo *m* **(g)** *(drink)* trago *m* **(h)** *Phot* foto *f*; *Cin* toma *f*

shot² [ʃɒt] *pt & pp of* **shoot**

shotgun ['ʃɒtgʌn] *n* escopeta *f*

should [ʃʊd, *unstressed* ʃəd] *v aux* **(a)** *(duty)* deber; **all employees s. wear helmets** todos los empleados deben llevar casco; **he s. have been an architect** debería haber sido arquitecto **(b)** *(probability)* deber de; **he s. have finished by now** ya debe de haber acabado; **this s. be interesting** esto promete ser interesante **(c)** *(conditional use)* **if anything strange s. happen** si pasara algo raro **(d)** **I s. like to ask a question** quisiera hacer una pregunta

La forma negativa **should not** se transforma en **shouldn't**.

shoulder ['ʃəʊldə(r)] **1** *n* **(a)** hombro *m*; **s. blade** omóplato *m*; **s. strap** *(of garment)* tirante *m*; *(of bag)* correa *f*; *Br Aut* **hard s.** arcén *m*, *Andes* berma *f*, *Méx* acotamiento *m*, *RP* banquina *f*, *Ven* hombrillo *m* **(b)** *Culin* paletilla *f* **(c)** *US Aut* arcén *m*, *Andes* berma *f*, *Méx* acotamiento *m*, *RP* banquina *f*, *Ven* hombrillo *m*
  2 *vt Fig (responsibilities)* cargar con

shout [ʃaʊt] **1** *n* grito *m*
  2 *vt* gritar
  3 *vi* gritar; **to s. at sb** gritar a algn
▸ **shout down** *vt sep* abuchear

shouting ['ʃaʊtɪŋ] *n* gritos *mpl*, vocerío *m*

shove [ʃʌv] **1** *n Fam* empujón *m*
  2 *vt* empujar; **to s. sth into one's pocket** meterse algo en el bolsillo a empellones
  3 *vi* empujar; *(jostle)* dar empellones
▸ **shove off** *vi Fam* largarse
▸ **shove up** *vi Fam (move along)* correrse

shovel ['ʃʌvəl] **1** *n* pala *f*; **mechanical s.** excavadora *f*

2 *vt* mover con pala *or* a paladas

show [ʃəʊ] **1** *vt* (*pt* **showed**; *pp* **shown** *or* **showed**) (**a**) (*ticket etc*) mostrar; (*painting etc*) exponer; (*film*) poner; (*latest plans etc*) presentar

(**b**) (*display*) demostrar; **to s. oneself to be** comportarse como

(**c**) (*teach*) enseñar; (*explain*) explicar

(**d**) (*temperature, way etc*) indicar; (*profit etc*) registrar

(**e**) (*prove*) demostrar

(**f**) (*conduct*) llevar; **to s. sb in** hacer pasar a algn; **to s. sb to the door** acompañar a algn hasta la puerta

2 *vi* (**a**) (*be visible*) notarse

(**b**) *Fam* (*turn up*) aparecer

(**c**) *Cin* **what's showing?** ¿qué ponen?

3 *n* (**a**) (*display*) demostración *f*

(**b**) (*outward appearance*) apariencia *f*

(**c**) (*exhibition*) exposición *f*; **on s.** expuesto(a); **boat s.** salón náutico; **motor s.** salón del automóvil

(**d**) *Th* (*entertainment*) espectáculo *m*; (*performance*) función *f*; *Rad & TV* programa *m*; **s. business** *or Fam* **biz** el mundo del espectáculo

▸ **show off 1** *vt sep* (**a**) (*highlight*) hacer resaltar (**b**) *Fam* (*flaunt*) hacer alarde de

2 *vi Fam* farolear

▸ **show up 1** *vt sep* (**a**) (*reveal*) sacar a luz; (*highlight*) hacer resaltar (**b**) *Fam* (*embarrass*) dejar en evidencia

2 *vi* (**a**) (*stand out*) destacarse (**b**) *Fam* (*arrive*) aparecer

showdown [ˈʃəʊdaʊn] *n* enfrentamiento *m*

shower [ˈʃaʊə(r)] **1** *n* (**a**) (*rain*) chubasco *m*, chaparrón *m* (**b**) *Fig* (*of stones, blows etc*) lluvia *f* (**c**) (*bath*) ducha *f*, *Col, Méx, Ven* regadera *f*; **to have a s.** ducharse

2 *vt* (**a**) (*spray*) rociar (**b**) *Fig* **to s. gifts/praise on sb** colmar a algn de regalos/elogios

3 *vi* ducharse

showerproof [ˈʃaʊəpruːf] *adj* impermeable

showing [ˈʃəʊɪŋ] *n* (*of film*) proyección *f*

showjumping [ˈʃəʊdʒʌmpɪŋ] *n* hípica *f*

shown [ʃəʊn] *pp of* **show**

show-off [ˈʃəʊɒf] *n Fam* farolero(a) *m,f*

showpiece [ˈʃəʊpiːs] *n* (*in exhibition etc*) obra maestra; *Fig* (*at school etc*) modelo *m*

showroom [ˈʃəʊruːm] *n Com* exposición *f*; *Art* galería *f*

shrank [ʃræŋk] *pt of* **shrink**

shrapnel [ˈʃræpnəl] *n* metralla *f*

shred [ʃred] **1** *n* triza *f*; (*of cloth*) jirón *m*; (*of paper*) tira *f*

2 *vt* (*paper*) hacer trizas; (*vegetables*) rallar

shredder [ˈʃredə(r)] *n* (*for waste paper*) trituradora *f*; (*for vegetables*) rallador *m*

shrew [ʃruː] *n* (**a**) *Zool* musaraña *f* (**b**) *Fig* (*woman*) arpía *f*

shrewd [ʃruːd] *adj* astuto(a); (*clearsighted*) perspicaz; (*wise*) sabio(a); (*decision*) acertado(a)

shriek [ʃriːk] **1** *n* chillido *m*; **shrieks of laughter** carcajadas *fpl*

2 *vi* chillar

shrill [ʃrɪl] *adj* agudo(a), estridente

shrimp [ʃrɪmp] **1** *n* camarón *m*

2 *vi* pescar camarones

shrine [ʃraɪn] *n* (*tomb*) sepulcro *m*; (*chapel*) capilla *f*; (*holy place*) lugar sagrado

shrink [ʃrɪŋk] **1** *vt* (*pt* **shrank**; *pp* **shrunk**) encoger

2 *vi* (**a**) (*clothes*) encoger(se) (**b**) (*savings*) disminuir (**c**) **to s. (back)** echarse atrás; **to s. from doing sth** no tener valor para hacer algo

2 *n Fam* (*psychiatrist*) psiquiatra *mf*

shrinkage [ˈʃrɪŋkɪdʒ] *n* (**a**) (*of cloth*) encogimiento *m*; (*of metal*) contracción *f* (**b**) (*of savings etc*) disminución *f*

shrink-wrapped [ˈʃrɪŋkræpt] *adj* envuelto(a) en plástico

shrivel [ˈʃrɪvəl] **1** *vt* **to s. (up)** encoger; (*plant*) secar; (*skin*) arrugar

2 *vi* encogerse; (*plant*) secarse; (*skin*) arrugarse

shroud [ʃraʊd] **1** *n Rel* sudario *m*

2 *vt Fig* envolver

Shrove Tuesday [ˈʃrəʊvˈtjuːzdɪ] *n* martes *m* de carnaval

shrub [ʃrʌb] *n* arbusto *m*

shrubbery [ˈʃrʌbərɪ] *n* arbustos *mpl*

shrug [ʃrʌg] **1** *vt* **to s. one's shoulders** encogerse de hombros

2 *vi* encogerse de hombros

3 *n* encogimiento *m* de hombros

▸ **shrug off** *vt sep* no dejarse desanimar por

shrunk [ʃrʌŋk] *pp of* **shrink**

shudder [ˈʃʌdə(r)] **1** *n* (**a**) escalofrío *m*, estremecimiento *m* (**b**) (*of machinery*) sacudida *f*

2 *vi* (**a**) (*person*) estremecerse (**b**) (*machinery*) dar sacudidas

shuffle [ˈʃʌfəl] **1** *vt* (*feet*) arrastrar (**b**) (*papers etc*) revolver; (*cards*) barajar

2 *vi* (*walk*) andar arrastrando los pies (**b**) *Cards* barajar

shun [ʃʌn] *vt* (*person*) esquivar; (*responsibility*) rehuir

shunt [ʃʌnt] *vt Rail* cambiar de vía; *Elec* derivar

shut [ʃʌt] **1** *vt* (*pt & pp* **shut**) cerrar

2 *vi* cerrarse

3 *adj* cerrado(a)

▸ **shut down 1** *vt sep* (*factory*) cerrar

2 *vi* (*factory*) cerrar

▸ **shut off** *vt sep* (*gas, water etc*) cortar

▸ **shut out** *vt sep* (**a**) (*lock out*) dejar fuera a (**b**) (*exclude*) excluir

▸ **shut up 1** *vt sep* (**a**) (*close*) cerrar (**b**) (*imprison*) encerrar (**c**) *Fam* (*silence*) callar

2 *vi Fam* (*keep quiet*) callarse

shutdown ['ʃʌtdaʊn] *n* cierre *m*

shutter ['ʃʌtə(r)] *n* (**a**) (*on window*) contraventana *f*, postigo *m* (**b**) *Phot* obturador *m*

shuttle ['ʃʌtəl] **1** *n* (**a**) (*in weaving*) lanzadera *f* (**b**) *Av* puente aéreo; (**space**) **s.** transbordador *m* espacial

2 *vi* ir y venir

shuttlecock ['ʃʌtəlkɒk] *n* volante *m*

shy [ʃaɪ] **1** *adj* (**shyer, shyest** *or* **shier, shiest**) (*timid*) tímido(a), *Andes, CAm, Carib, Méx* penoso(a); (*reserved*) reservado(a)

2 *vi* (*horse*) espantarse (**at** de); *Fig* **to s. away from doing sth** negarse a hacer algo

shyness ['ʃaɪnɪs] *n* timidez *f*

Siberia [saɪ'bɪərɪə] *n* Siberia

sibling ['sɪblɪŋ] *n Fml* (*brother*) hermano *m*; (*sister*) hermana *f*; **siblings** hermanos

Sicily ['sɪsɪlɪ] *n* Sicilia

sick [sɪk] *adj* (**a**) (*ill*) enfermo(a); **s. leave** baja *f* por enfermedad; **s. pay** subsidio *m* de enfermedad (**b**) **to feel s.** (*about to vomit*) tener ganas de devolver; **to be s.** devolver (**c**) *Fam* (*fed up*) harto(a) (**d**) *Fam* (*mind, joke*) morboso(a); **s. humour** humor negro

sickbay ['sɪkbeɪ] *n* enfermería *f*

sicken ['sɪkən] **1** *vt* (*make ill*) poner enfermo; (*revolt*) dar asco a

2 *vi* (*fall ill*) enfermar

sickening ['sɪkənɪŋ] *adj* nauseabundo(a); (*revolting*) repugnante; (*horrifying*) escalofriante

sickle ['sɪkəl] *n* hoz *f*

sickly ['sɪklɪ] *adj* (**sicklier, sickliest**) (**a**) (*person*) enfermizo(a) (**b**) (*taste*) empalagoso(a) (**c**) (*smile*) forzado(a)

sickness ['sɪknɪs] *n* (**a**) (*illness*) enfermedad *f* (**b**) (*nausea*) náuseas *fpl*

side [saɪd] **1** *n* (**a**) lado *m*; (*of coin etc*) cara *f*, (*of hill*) ladera *f*; **by the s. of** junto a (**b**) (*of body*) costado *m*; (*of animal*) ijar

m; **a s. of bacon** una pieza de tocino; **by my s.** a mi lado; **s. by s.** juntos

(**c**) (*edge*) borde *m*; (*of lake, river*) orilla *f* (**d**) *Fig* (*aspect*) aspecto *m*

(**e**) (*team*) equipo *m*; *Pol* partido *m*; **she's on our s.** está de nuestro lado; **to take sides with sb** ponerse de parte de algn; **s. dish** plato *m* de guarnición; **s. effect** efecto secundario; **s. entrance** entrada *f* lateral; **s. street** calle *f* lateral

2 *vi* **to s. with sb** ponerse de parte de algn

sideboard ['saɪdbɔːd] *n* aparador *m*

sideboards ['saɪdbɔːdz], **sideburns** ['saɪdbɜːnz] *npl* patillas *fpl*

sidelight ['saɪdlaɪt] *n Aut* luz *f* lateral, piloto *m*

sideline ['saɪdlaɪn] *n* (**a**) *Sport* línea *f* de banda (**b**) *Com* (*product*) línea suplementaria; (*job*) empleo suplementario

sidelong ['saɪdlɒŋ] *adj* de reojo

side-saddle ['saɪdsædəl] **1** *n* silla *f* de amazona

2 *adv* **to ride s.** montar a la inglesa

sideshow ['saɪdʃəʊ] *n* atracción secundaria

sidestep ['saɪdstep] *vt* (*issue*) esquivar

sidetrack ['saɪdtræk] *vt Fig* (*person*) despistar

sidewalk ['saɪdwɔːk] *n US* acera *f*, *CSur, Perú* vereda *f*, *CAm, Méx* banqueta *f*

sideways ['saɪdweɪz] **1** *adj* (*movement*) lateral; (*look*) de reojo

2 *adv* de lado

siding ['saɪdɪŋ] *n Rail* apartadero *m*, vía muerta

sidle ['saɪdəl] *vi* **to s. up to sb** acercarse furtivamente a algn

siege [siːdʒ] *n* sitio *m*, cerco *m*; **to lay s. to** sitiar

sieve [sɪv] **1** *n* (*fine*) tamiz *m*; (*coarse*) criba *f*

2 *vt* (*fine*) tamizar; (*coarse*) cribar

sift [sɪft] *vt* (*sieve*) tamizar; *Fig* **to s. through** examinar cuidadosamente

sigh [saɪ] **1** *vi* suspirar

2 *n* suspiro *m*

sight [saɪt] **1** *n* (**a**) (*faculty*) vista *f*; **at first s.** a primera vista; **to catch s. of** divisar; **to know by s.** conocer de vista; **to lose s. of sth/sb** perder algo/a algn de vista (**b**) (*range of vision*) vista *f*; **within s.** a la vista; **to come into s.** aparecer (**c**) (*spectacle*) espectáculo *m* (**d**) (*on gun*) mira *f*; *Fig* **to set one's sights on** tener la mira puesta en (**e**) **sights** monumentos *mpl*

2 *vt* ver; (*land*) divisar

sightseeing ['saɪtsiːɪŋ] *n* turismo *m*; **to go s.** hacer turismo

sign [saɪn] **1** n (**a**) (symbol) signo m (**b**) (gesture) gesto m, seña f; (signal) señal f (**c**) (indication) señal f; (trace) rastro m, huella f; **as a s. of** como muestra de (**d**) (notice) anuncio m; (board) letrero m
2 vt (**a**) (letter etc) firmar (**b**) Ftb fichar
3 vi firmar
▸ **sign on 1** vt sep (worker) contratar
2 vi (worker) firmar un contrato; Br Fam apuntarse al paro; (regularly) firmar el paro
▸ **sign up 1** vt sep (soldier) reclutar; (worker) contratar
2 vi (soldier) alistarse; (worker) firmar un contrato

signal ['sɪgnəl] **1** n señal f; Rad & TV sintonía f; Rail **s. box** garita f de señales
2 vt (a) (message) transmitir por señales (b) (direction etc) indicar
3 vi (with hands) hacer señales; (in car) señalar

signalman ['sɪgnəlmən] n guardavía m

signature ['sɪgnɪtʃə(r)] n (name) firma f; Rad & TV **s. tune** sintonía f

signet ['sɪgnɪt] n **s. ring** (anillo m de) sello m

significance [sɪg'nɪfɪkəns] n (meaning) significado m; (importance) importancia f

significant [sɪg'nɪfɪkənt] adj (meaningful) significativo(a); (important) importante

significantly [sɪg'nɪfɪkəntlɪ] adv (markedly) sensiblemente

signify ['sɪgnɪfaɪ] vt (a) (mean) significar (b) (show, make known) indicar

signpost ['saɪnpəʊst] n poste m indicador

silence ['saɪləns] **1** n silencio m
2 vt acallar; (engine) silenciar

silencer ['saɪlənsə(r)] n (a) (on gun) silenciador m (b) Br (on car) silenciador m

silent ['saɪlənt] adj silencioso(a); (not talkative) callado(a); (film) mudo(a); **be s.!** ¡cállate!; **to remain s.** guardar silencio

silently ['saɪləntlɪ] adv silenciosamente

silhouette [sɪluː'et] n silueta f

silicon ['sɪlɪkən] n silicio m; **s. chip** chip m (de silicio)

silk [sɪlk] **1** n seda f
2 adj de seda

silky ['sɪlkɪ] adj (silkier, silkiest) (cloth) sedoso(a); (voice etc) aterciopelado(a)

sill [sɪl] n (of window) alféizar m

silly ['sɪlɪ] adj (sillier, silliest) tonto(a)

silo ['saɪləʊ] n silo m

silt [sɪlt] n cieno m
▸ **silt up** vi obstruirse con cieno

silver ['sɪlvə(r)] **1** n (a) (metal) plata f (b) (coins) monedas fpl (de plata) (c) (tableware) vajilla f de plata
2 adj de plata; **s. foil** (tinfoil) papel m de aluminio; **s. paper** papel de plata; **s. wedding** bodas fpl de plata

silver-plated [sɪlvə'pleɪtɪd] adj plateado(a)

silversmith ['sɪlvəsmɪθ] n platero(a) m,f

silverware ['sɪlvəweə(r)] n vajilla f de plata

silvery ['sɪlvərɪ] adj plateado(a)

similar ['sɪmɪlə(r)] adj parecido(a), semejante (**to** a); **to be s.** parecerse

similarity [sɪmɪ'lærɪtɪ] n semejanza f

similarly ['sɪmɪləlɪ] adv (a) (as well) igualmente (b) (likewise) del mismo modo, asimismo

simile ['sɪmɪlɪ] n símil m

simmer ['sɪmə(r)] **1** vt cocer a fuego lento
2 vi cocerse a fuego lento
▸ **simmer down** vi Fam calmarse

simpering ['sɪmpərɪŋ] adj melindroso(a)

simple ['sɪmpəl] adj (a) sencillo(a); **s. interest** interés m simple (b) (natural) natural (c) (foolish) simple; (naïve) ingenuo(a); (dim) de pocas luces

simplicity [sɪm'plɪsɪtɪ] n (a) sencillez f (b) (naïveté) ingenuidad f

simplify ['sɪmplɪfaɪ] vt simplificar

simply ['sɪmplɪ] adv (a) (plainly) sencillamente (b) (only) simplemente, sólo

simulate ['sɪmjʊleɪt] vt simular

simulator ['sɪmjʊleɪtə(r)] n **flight s.** simulador de vuelo

simultaneous [sɪməl'teɪnɪəs] adj simultáneo(a)

simultaneously [sɪməl'teɪnɪəslɪ] adv simultáneamente

sin [sɪn] **1** n pecado m
2 vi pecar

since [sɪns] **1** adv (ever) **s.** desde entonces; **long s.** hace mucho tiempo; **it has s. come out that ...** desde entonces se ha sabido que ...
2 prep desde; **she has been living here s. 1975** vive aquí desde 1975
3 conj (a) (time) desde que; **how long is it s. you last saw him?** ¿cuánto tiempo hace que lo viste por última vez? (b) (because, as) ya que, puesto que

sincere [sɪn'sɪə(r)] adj sincero(a)

sincerely [sɪn'sɪəlɪ] adv sinceramente; **Yours s.** (in letter) (le saluda) atentamente

sincerity [sɪn'serɪtɪ] n sinceridad f

sinew ['sɪnjuː] n (tendon) tendón m; (in meat) nervio m

sinful ['sɪnfʊl] *adj (person)* pecador(a); *(act, thought)* pecaminoso(a); *Fig (waste etc)* escandaloso(a)

sing [sɪŋ] **1** *vt (pt* **sang**; *pp* **sung**) cantar
2 *vi (person, bird)* cantar; *(kettle, bullets)* silbar

singe [sɪndʒ] *vt* chamuscar

singer ['sɪŋə(r)] *n* cantante *mf*

singing ['sɪŋɪŋ] *n (art)* canto *m*; *(songs)* canciones *fpl*; *(of kettle)* silbido *m*

single ['sɪŋgəl] **1** *adj* (a) *(solitary)* solo(a) (b) *(only one)* único(a) (c) *(not double)* sencillo(a); **s. bed/room** cama *f*/habitación *f* individual (d) *(unmarried)* soltero(a)
2 *n* (a) *Br Rail* billete *m* or *Am* boleto *m* or *Am* pasaje *m* sencillo *or* de ida (b) *(record)* single *m* (c) *Sport* **singles** individuales *mpl*
▸ **single out** *vt sep (choose)* escoger; *(distinguish)* distinguir

single-breasted ['sɪŋgəl'brestɪd] *adj (suit, jacket)* recto(a)

single-handed ['sɪŋgəl'hændɪd] *adj & adv* sin ayuda

single-minded ['sɪŋgəl'maɪndɪd] *adj* resuelto(a)

singlet ['sɪŋglɪt] *n Br* camiseta *f*

singly ['sɪŋglɪ] *adv (individually)* por separado; *(one by one)* uno por uno

singular ['sɪŋgjʊlə(r)] **1** *adj* (a) *Ling* singular (b) *Fml (outstanding)* excepcional (c) *Fml (unique)* único(a)
2 *n Ling* singular *m*

singularly ['sɪŋgjʊləlɪ] *adv* excepcionalmente

sinister ['sɪnɪstə(r)] *adj* siniestro(a)

sink¹ [sɪŋk] *n (in kitchen)* fregadero *m*

sink² [sɪŋk] **1** *vt (pt* **sank**; *pp* **sunk**) (a) *(ship)* hundir, echar a pique; *Fig (hopes)* acabar con (b) *(hole, well)* cavar; *(post, knife, teeth)* hincar
2 *vi* (a) *(ship)* hundirse (b) *Fig* **my heart sank** se me cayó el alma a los pies (c) *(sun)* ponerse (d) **to s. to one's knees** hincarse de rodillas
▸ **sink in** *vi (penetrate)* penetrar; *Fig* **it hasn't sunk in yet** todavía no me he/se ha/*etc* hecho a la idea

sinner ['sɪnə(r)] *n* pecador(a) *m,f*

sinus ['saɪnəs] *n* seno *m* (nasal)

sip [sɪp] **1** *n* sorbo *m*
2 *vt* sorber, beber a sorbos

siphon ['saɪfən] *n* sifón *m*
▸ **siphon off** *vt sep (liquid)* sacar con sifón; *Fig (funds, traffic)* desviar

sir [sɜː(r)] *n Fml* (a) señor *m*; **yes, s.** sí, señor (b) *(title)* sir; **S. Walter Raleigh** Sir Walter Raleigh

siren ['saɪrən] *n* sirena *f*

sirloin ['sɜːlɔɪn] *n* solomillo *m*

sissy ['sɪsɪ] *n Fam (coward)* miedica *mf*

sister ['sɪstə(r)] *n* (a) *(relation)* hermana *f* (b) *Br Med* enfermera *f* jefe (c) *Rel* hermana *f*; *(before name)* sor

sister-in-law ['sɪstərɪnlɔː] *n* cuñada *f*

sit [sɪt] **1** *vt (pt & pp* **sat**) (a) *(child etc)* sentar (**in/on** en) (b) *Br (exam)* presentarse a
2 *vi* (a) *(action)* sentarse (b) *(be seated)* estar sentado(a) (c) *(object)* estar; *(be situated)* hallarse; *(person)* quedarse (d) *(assembly)* reunirse
▸ **sit back** *vi* recostarse
▸ **sit down** *vi* sentarse
▸ **sit in on** *vt insep* asistir sin participar a
▸ **sit out** *vt sep* aguantar hasta el final
▸ **sit through** *vt insep* aguantar
▸ **sit up** *vi* (a) incorporarse (b) *(stay up late)* quedarse levantado(a)

site [saɪt] **1** *n* (a) *(area)* lugar *m*; **building s.** solar *m*; *(under construction)* obra *f* (b) *(location)* situación *f*; **nuclear testing s.** zona *f* de pruebas nucleares
2 *vt* situar

sit-in ['sɪtɪn] *n Fam (demonstration)* sentada *f*; *(strike)* huelga *f* de brazos caídos

sitting ['sɪtɪŋ] **1** *n (of committee)* sesión *f*; *(in canteen)* turno *m*
2 *adj* **s. room** sala *f* de estar

situated ['sɪtjʊeɪtɪd] *adj* situado(a), ubicado(a)

situation [sɪtjʊ'eɪʃən] *n* (a) situación *f* (b) *(job)* puesto *m*; *Br* **situations vacant** *(in newspaper)* ofertas de trabajo

six [sɪks] *adj & n* seis *(m inv)*

sixteen [sɪks'tiːn] *adj & n* dieciséis *(m inv)*, diez y seis *(m inv)*

sixteenth [sɪks'tiːnθ] **1** *adj & n* decimosexto(a) *(m,f)*
2 *n (fraction)* dieciseisavo *m*

sixth [sɪksθ] **1** *adj* sexto(a); *Br Educ* **s. form** ≃ COU; **s. former** ≃ estudiante de COU
2 *n* (a) *(in series)* sexto(a) *m,f* (b) *(fraction)* sexto *m*, sexta parte

sixty ['sɪkstɪ] *adj & n* sesenta *(m inv)*

sizable ['saɪzəbəl] *adj* = **sizeable**

size [saɪz] *n* tamaño *m*; *(of garment)* talla *f*; *(of shoes)* número *m*; *(of person)* estatura *f*; *(scope)* alcance *m*; **what s. do you take?** *(garment)* ¿qué talla tienes?; *(shoes)* ¿qué número calzas?
▸ **size up** *vt sep (person)* juzgar; *(situation, problem)* evaluar

sizeable ['saɪzəbəl] *adj (building etc)*

(bastante) grande; *(sum)* considerable; *(problem)* importante

sizzle ['sɪzəl] *vi* chisporrotear

skate¹ [skeɪt] **1** *n* patín *m*
2 *vi* patinar

skate² [skeɪt] *n (fish)* raya *f*

skateboard ['skeɪtbɔːd] *n* monopatín *m*

skater ['skeɪtə(r)] *n* patinador(a) *m,f*

skating ['skeɪtɪŋ] *n* patinaje *m*; **s. rink** pista *f* de patinaje

skeleton ['skelɪtən] **1** *n* (**a**) esqueleto *m* (**b**) *(of building)* armazón *m* (**c**) *(outline)* esquema *m*
2 *adj (staff, service)* reducido(a); **s. key** llave maestra

skeptic ['skeptɪk] *n US* = **sceptic**

sketch [sketʃ] **1** *n* (**a**) *(preliminary drawing)* bosquejo *m*, esbozo *m*; *(drawing)* dibujo *m*; *(outline)* esquema *m*; *(rough draft)* boceto *m* (**b**) *Th & TV* sketch *m*
2 *vt* (draw) dibujar; *(preliminary drawing)* bosquejar, esbozar

sketch-book ['sketʃbʊk], **sketch-pad** ['sketʃpæd] *n* bloc *m* de dibujo

sketchy ['sketʃɪ] *adj* (**sketchier, sketchiest**) *(incomplete)* incompleto(a); *(not detailed)* vago(a)

skewer ['skjʊə(r)] *n* pincho *m*, broqueta *f*

ski [skiː] **1** *n* esquí *m*
2 *adj* de esquí; **s. boots** botas *fpl* de esquiar; **s. jump** *(action)* salto *m* con esquís; **s. lift** telesquí *m*; *(with seats)* telesilla *f*; **s. pants** pantalón *m* de esquiar; **s. resort** estación *f* de esquí; **s. stick** *or* **pole** bastón *m* de esquiar
3 *vi* esquiar; **to go skiing** ir a esquiar

skid [skɪd] **1** *n* patinazo *m*
2 *vi* patinar

skier ['skiːə(r)] *n* esquiador(a) *m,f*

skiing ['skiːɪŋ] *n* esquí *m*

skilful ['skɪlfʊl] *adj* hábil, diestro(a)

skill [skɪl] *n* (**a**) *(ability)* habilidad *f*, destreza *f*; *(talent)* don *m* (**b**) *(technique)* técnica *f*

skilled [skɪld] *adj* (**a**) *(dextrous)* hábil, diestro(a); *(expert)* experto(a) (**b**) *(worker)* cualificado(a)

skillet ['skɪlɪt] *n US* sartén *f*

skillful ['skɪlfʊl] *adj US* = **skilful**

skim [skɪm] **1** *vt* (**a**) *(milk)* desnatar; **skimmed milk** leche desnatada (**b**) *(brush against)* rozar; **to s. the ground** *(bird, plane)* volar a ras de suelo
2 *vi Fig* **to s. through a book** hojear un libro

skimp [skɪmp] *vt & vi (food, material)* escatimar; *(work)* chapucear

skimpy ['skɪmpɪ] *adj* (**skimpier,**

skimpiest) *(shorts)* muy corto(a); *(meal)* escaso(a)

skin [skɪn] **1** *n* (**a**) piel *f*; *(of face)* cutis *m*; *(complexion)* tez *f*; **s. cream** crema *f* de belleza (**b**) *(of fruit)* piel *f*; *(of lemon)* cáscara *f*; *(peeling)* mondadura *f* (**c**) *(of sausage)* pellejo *m* (**d**) *(on milk etc)* nata *f*
2 *vt* (**a**) *(animal)* despellejar (**b**) *(graze)* arañar

skin-deep ['skɪn'diːp] *adj* superficial

skin-diving ['skɪndaɪvɪŋ] *n* buceo *m*, submarinismo *m*

skinhead ['skɪnhed] *n Fam* cabeza *mf* rapada

skinny ['skɪnɪ] *adj* (**skinnier, skinniest**) *Fam* flaco(a)

skin-tight ['skɪntaɪt] *adj (clothing)* muy ajustado(a)

skip¹ [skɪp] **1** *n (jump)* salto *m*, brinco *m*
2 *vi (jump)* saltar, brincar; *(with rope)* saltar a la comba; *Fig* **to s. over sth** saltarse algo
3 *vt Fig* saltarse

skip² [skɪp] *n Br (for rubbish)* contenedor *m*

skipper ['skɪpə(r)] *n Naut & Sport Fam* capitán(ana) *m,f*

skipping ['skɪpɪŋ] *n* comba *f*; **s. rope** comba

skirmish ['skɜːmɪʃ] *n* escaramuza *f*

skirt [skɜːt] **1** *n* falda *f*
2 *vt (town etc)* rodear; *(coast)* bordear; *Fig (problem)* esquivar

skirting ['skɜːtɪŋ] *n Br* **s. (board)** zócalo *m*

skit [skɪt] *n* sátira *f*, parodia *f*

skittle ['skɪtəl] *n* (**a**) *(pin)* bolo *m* (**b**) **skittles** *(game)* (juego *m* de los) bolos *mpl*, boliche *m*

skive [skaɪv] *vi Br Fam* escaquearse

skulk [skʌlk] *vi (hide)* esconderse; *(prowl)* merodear; *(lie in wait)* estar al acecho

skull [skʌl] *n Anat* cráneo *m*; *Fam* calavera *f*

skunk [skʌŋk] *n* mofeta *f*

sky [skaɪ] *n* cielo *m*; **s. blue** azul *m* celeste

skylight ['skaɪlaɪt] *n* tragaluz *m*, claraboya *f*

skyline ['skaɪlaɪn] *n (of city)* perfil *m*

skyscraper ['skaɪskreɪpə(r)] *n* rascacielos *m inv*

slab [slæb] *n (of stone)* losa *f*; *(of chocolate)* tableta *f*; *(of cake)* trozo *m*

slack [slæk] **1** *adj* (**a**) *(not taut)* flojo(a) (**b**) *(lax)* descuidado(a); *(lazy)* vago(a) (**c**) *(market)* flojo(a); **business is s.** hay poco negocio
2 *n (in rope)* parte floja

slacken ['slækən] **1** vt (a) (rope) aflojar (b) (speed) reducir

2 vi (a) (rope) aflojarse; (wind) amainar (b) (trade) aflojar

▸ **slacken off** vi disminuirse

slacks [slæks] npl pantalones mpl ajustados

slag [slæg] n (a) Min escoria f; **s. heap** escorial m (b) Br very Fam (woman) puta f

▸ **slag off** vt sep Br poner verde a

slain [sleɪn] **1** npl **the s.** los caídos

2 pp of **slay**

slam [slæm] **1** n (of door) portazo m

2 vt (bang) cerrar de golpe; **to s. sth down on the table** soltar algo sobre la mesa de un palmetazo; **to s. the door** dar un portazo; **to s. on the brakes** dar un frenazo

3 vi (door) cerrarse de golpe

slander ['slɑːndə(r)] **1** n difamación f, calumnia f

2 vt difamar, calumniar

slang [slæŋ] n argot m, jerga f

slant [slɑːnt] **1** n (a) inclinación f; (slope) pendiente f (b) Fig (point of view) punto m de vista

2 vt Fig (problem etc) enfocar subjetivamente

3 vi inclinarse

slanting ['slɑːntɪŋ] adj inclinado(a)

slap [slæp] **1** n palmada f; (in face) bofetada f

2 adv Fam **he ran s. into the fence** se dio de lleno contra la valla; **s. in the middle of ...** justo en medio de ...

3 vt pegar con la mano; (hit in face) dar una bofetada a; **to s. sb on the back** dar a algn una palmada en la espalda

slapdash ['slæp'dæʃ] adj Fam descuidado(a); (work) chapucero(a)

slapstick ['slæpstɪk] n bufonadas fpl, payasadas fpl

slap-up ['slæpʌp] adj Fam **s. meal** comilona f

slash [slæʃ] **1** n Fam Typ barra oblicua

2 vt (a) (with knife) acuchillar; (with sword) dar un tajo a (b) Fig (prices) rebajar

slat [slæt] n tablilla f, listón m

slate [sleɪt] **1** n pizarra f; Fig **to wipe the s. clean** hacer borrón y cuenta nueva

2 vt Br Fam criticar duramente

slaughter ['slɔːtə(r)] **1** n (of animals) matanza f; (of people) carnicería f

2 vt (animals) matar; (people) matar brutalmente; (in large numbers) masacrar

slaughterhouse ['slɔːtəhaʊs] n matadero m

Slav [slɑːv] adj & n eslavo(a) (m,f)

slave [sleɪv] **1** n esclavo(a) m,f; **s. trade** trata f de esclavos

2 vi **to s. (away)** dar el callo

slavery ['sleɪvərɪ] n esclavitud f

Slavonic [slə'vɒnɪk] adj eslavo(a)

slay [sleɪ] vt (pt slew; pp slain) matar

sleazy ['sliːzɪ] adj (sleazier, sleaziest) sórdido(a)

sled [sled] **1** n US trineo m

2 vi ir en trineo

sledge [sledʒ] n Br trineo m

sledgehammer ['sledʒhæmə(r)] n almádena f

sleek [sliːk] adj (hair) lustroso(a); (appearance) impecable

sleep [sliːp] **1** n sueño m

2 vi (pt & pp slept) (a) dormir; **to go to s.** dormirse; Fig **to send to s.** (hacer) dormir; Fam **to s. like a log** dormir como un lirón (b) **my foot has gone to s.** se me ha dormido el pie

▸ **sleep in** vi Br (oversleep) quedarse dormido(a); (have a lie-in) quedarse en la cama

▸ **sleep with** vt insep Fam **to s. with sb** acostarse con algn

sleeper ['sliːpə(r)] n (a) (person) durmiente mf; **to be a heavy s.** tener el sueño pesado (b) Br Rail (on track) traviesa f (c) Rail (coach) coche-cama m; (berth) litera f

sleeping ['sliːpɪŋ] adj **s. bag** saco m de dormir; **S. Beauty** la Bella durmiente; **s. car** coche-cama m; Br Com **s. partner** socio(a) m,f comanditario(a); **s. pill** somnífero m

sleepless ['sliːplɪs] adj **to have a s. night** pasar la noche en blanco

sleepwalker ['sliːpwɔːkə(r)] n sonámbulo(a) m,f

sleepy ['sliːpɪ] adj (sleepier, sleepiest) soñoliento(a); **to be** or **feel s.** tener sueño

sleet [sliːt] **1** n aguanieve f

2 vi **it's sleeting** cae aguanieve

sleeve [sliːv] n (of garment) manga f; (of record) funda f

sleigh [sleɪ] n trineo m; **s. bell** cascabel m

sleight [slaɪt] n **s. of hand** juego m de manos

slender ['slendə(r)] adj (a) (thin) delgado(a) (b) Fig (hope, chance) remoto(a)

slept [slept] pt & pp of **sleep**

slew [sluː] pt of **slay**

slice [slaɪs] **1** n (a) (of bread) rebanada f; (of ham) loncha f; (of beef etc) tajada f; (of *lemon etc)* rodaja *f*; *(of cake)* trozo *m* (**b**) *(utensil)* pala *f*

2 *vt (food)* cortar a rebanadas/tajos/rodajas; *(divide)* partir

slick [slɪk] **1** *adj* (**a**) *(programme, show)* logrado(a) (**b**) *(skilful)* hábil, mañoso(a)

2 *n* (oil) **s.** marea negra

slide [slaɪd] **1** *n* (**a**) *(act)* resbalón *m* (**b**) *(in prices etc)* baja *f* (**c**) *(in playground)* tobogán *m* (**d**) *Phot* diapositiva *f*; **s. projector** proyector *m* de diapositivas (**e**) **s. rule** regla *f* de cálculo (**f**) *Br (for hair)* pasador *m*

2 *vt (pt & pp* **slid** [slɪd]) deslizar; *(furniture)* correr

3 *vi (on purpose)* deslizarse; *(slip)* resbalar

sliding ['slaɪdɪŋ] *adj (door, window)* corredizo(a); *Fin* **s. scale** escala *f* móvil

slight [slaɪt] **1** *adj* (**a**) *(small)* pequeño(a); **not in the slightest** en absoluto (**b**) *(build)* menudo(a); *(slim)* delgado(a); *(frail)* delicado(a) (**c**) *(trivial)* leve

2 *n (affront)* desaire *m*

3 *vt* (**a**) *(scorn)* despreciar (**b**) *(snub)* desairar

slightly ['slaɪtlɪ] *adv (a little)* ligeramente, algo

slim [slɪm] **1** *adj* (**slimmer, slimmest**) (**a**) *(person)* delgado(a) (**b**) *Fig (resources)* escaso(a); *(hope, chance)* remoto(a)

2 *vi* adelgazar

slime [slaɪm] *n (mud)* lodo *m*, cieno *m*; *(of snail)* baba *f*

slimming ['slɪmɪŋ] **1** *adj (diet, pills)* para adelgazar; *(food)* que no engorda

2 *n (process)* adelgazamiento *m*

slimy ['slaɪmɪ] *adj (slimier, slimiest)* (**a**) *(muddy)* lodoso(a); *(snail)* baboso(a) (**b**) *Fig (person)* zalamero(a)

sling [slɪŋ] **1** *n* (**a**) *(catapult)* honda *f*; *(child's)* tirador *m* (**b**) *Med* cabestrillo *m*

2 *vt (pt & pp* **slung**) *(throw)* tirar

slingshot ['slɪŋʃɒt] *n US* tirachinas *m inv*

slink [slɪŋk] *vi (pt & pp* **slunk**) **to s. off** escabullirse

slip [slɪp] **1** *n* (**a**) *(slide)* resbalón *m*; *Fam Fig* **to give sb the s.** dar esquinazo a algn (**b**) *(mistake)* error *m*; *(moral)* desliz *m*; **a s. of the tongue** un lapsus linguae (**c**) *(underskirt)* combinación *f* (**d**) *(of paper)* trocito *m*

2 *vi* (**a**) *(slide)* resbalar (**b**) *Med* dislocarse; **slipped disc** vértebra dislocada (**c**) *(move quickly)* ir de prisa (**d**) *(standards etc)* deteriorarse

3 *vt* (**a**) *(slide)* dar a escondidas (**b**) **it slipped my memory** se me fue de la cabeza

▸ **slip away** *vi (person)* escabullirse

▸ **slip off** *vt sep (clothes)* quitarse rápidamente

▸ **slip on** *vt sep (clothes)* ponerse rápidamente

▸ **slip out** *vi* (**a**) *(leave)* salir (**b**) *Fig* **the secret slipped out** se le escapó el secreto

▸ **slip up** *vi Fam (blunder)* cometer un desliz

slipper ['slɪpə(r)] *n* zapatilla *f*

slippery ['slɪpərɪ] *adj* resbaladizo(a)

slip-road ['slɪprəʊd] *n Br* vía *f* de acceso

slipshod ['slɪpʃɒd] *adj* descuidado(a); *(work)* chapucero(a)

slip-up ['slɪpʌp] *n Fam (blunder)* desliz *m*

slipway ['slɪpweɪ] *n* grada *f*

slit [slɪt] **1** *n (opening)* hendidura *f*; *(cut)* corte *m*, raja *f*

2 *vt (pt & pp* **slit**) cortar, rajar

slither ['slɪðə(r)] *vi* deslizarse

sliver ['slɪvə(r)] *n (of wood, glass)* astilla *f*; *(of ham)* loncha *f*

slob [slɒb] *n Fam* dejado(a) *m,f*

slog [slɒg] **1** *n Fam* **it was a hard s.** costó un montón

2 *vi* (**a**) *Fam* **to s. away** sudar tinta (**b**) *(walk)* caminar trabajosamente

3 *vt (hit)* golpear fuerte

slogan ['sləʊgən] *n* (e)slogan *m*, lema *m*

slop [slɒp] **1** *vi* **to s. (over)** derramarse; **to s. about** chapotear

2 *vt* derramar

slope [sləʊp] **1** *n (incline)* cuesta *f*, pendiente *f*; *(up)* subida *f*; *(down)* bajada *f*; *(of mountain)* ladera *f*; *(of roof)* vertiente *f*

2 *vi* inclinarse; **to s. up/down** subir/bajar en pendiente

▸ **slope off** *vi Fam* largarse

sloping ['sləʊpɪŋ] *adj* inclinado(a)

sloppy ['slɒpɪ] *adj* (**sloppier, sloppiest**) *Fam* descuidado(a); *(work)* chapucero(a); *(appearance)* desaliñado(a)

slot [slɒt] **1** *n* (**a**) *(for coin)* ranura *f*; *(opening)* rendija *f*; **s. machine** *(for gambling)* (máquina *f*) tragaperras *f inv*; *(vending machine)* distribuidor automático (**b**) *Rad & TV* espacio *m*

2 *vt (place)* meter; *(put in)* introducir

3 *vi* **to s. in** *or* **together** encajar

sloth [sləʊθ] *n Fml (laziness)* pereza *f*

slouch [slaʊtʃ] *vi* andar *or* sentarse con los hombros caídos

Slovakia [sləʊ'vækɪə] *n* Eslovaquia

Slovakian [sləʊ'vækɪən] *adj & n* eslovaco(a) *(m,f)*

Slovene ['sləʊviːn] **1** *n* (**a**) *(person)* esloveno(a) *m,f* (**b**) *(language)* esloveno *m*

2 *adj* esloveno(a)

Slovenia [sləʊˈviːnɪə] *n* Eslovenia

slovenly [ˈslʌvənlɪ] *adj* descuidado(a); *(appearance)* desaliñado(a); *(work)* chapucero(a)

slow [sləʊ] **1** *adj* (**a**) lento(a); **in s. motion** a cámara lenta; **to be s. to do sth** tardar en hacer algo (**b**) *(clock)* atrasado(a) (**c**) *(stupid)* lento(a), torpe

2 *adv* despacio, lentamente

3 *vt (car)* reducir la marcha de; *(progress)* retrasar

4 *vi* **to s. down** *or* **up** ir más despacio; *(in car)* reducir la velocidad

slowly [ˈsləʊlɪ] *adv* despacio, lentamente

sludge [slʌdʒ] *n (mud)* fango *m*, lodo *m*

slug [slʌg] **1** *n* (**a**) *Zool* babosa *f* (**b**) *US Fam (bullet)* posta *f* (**c**) *Fam (blow)* porrazo *m*

2 *vt Fam (hit)* aporrear

sluggish [ˈslʌgɪʃ] *adj* (**a**) *(river, engine)* lento(a); *Com* flojo(a) (**b**) *(lazy)* perezoso(a)

sluice [sluːs] *n (waterway)* canal *m*

sluicegate [ˈsluːsgeɪt] *n* esclusa *f*

slumber [ˈslʌmbə(r)] *Fml* **1** *n (sleep)* sueño *m*

2 *vi* dormir

slump [slʌmp] **1** *n* (**a**) *(drop in sales etc)* bajón *m* (**b**) *(economic depression)* crisis económica

2 *vi* (**a**) *(sales etc)* caer de repente; *(prices)* desplomarse; *(the economy)* hundirse; *Fig (morale)* hundirse (**b**) *(fall)* caer

slums [slʌmz] *npl* barrios bajos

slung [slʌŋ] *pt & pp of* **sling**

slunk [slʌŋk] *pt & pp of* **slink**

slur [slɜː(r)] **1** *n (stigma)* mancha *f; (slanderous remark)* calumnia *f*

2 *vt (word)* tragarse

slush [slʌʃ] *n* (**a**) *(melting snow)* nieve medio fundida (**b**) *Fam* sentimentalismo *m* (**c**) *US Fam* **s. fund** fondos *mpl* para sobornos

slut [slʌt] *n very Fam Pej* (**a**) *(untidy woman)* marrana *f* (**b**) *(whore)* fulana *f*

sly [slaɪ] *adj* (**slyer, slyest** *or* **slier, sliest**) (**a**) *(cunning)* astuto(a) (**b**) *(secretive)* furtivo(a) (**c**) *(mischievous)* travieso(a) (**d**) *(underhand)* malicioso(a)

smack¹ [smæk] **1** *n* (**a**) *(slap)* bofetada *f* (**b**) *(sharp sound)* ruido sonoro

2 *vt* (**a**) *(slap)* dar una bofetada a (**b**) *(hit)* golpear; *Fig* **to s. one's lips** relamerse

smack² [smæk] *vi Fig* **to s. of** oler a

small [smɔːl] **1** *adj* (**a**) pequeño(a); **a s.**

table una mesita; **in s. letters** en minúsculas; **in the s. hours** a altas horas de la noche; **s. ads** anuncios *mpl* por palabras; *Fig* **s. print** letra pequeña (**b**) *(in height)* bajo(a) (**c**) *(scant)* escaso(a); **s. change** cambio *m*, suelto *m* (**d**) *(minor)* insignificante; **s. businessmen** pequeños comerciantes; **s. talk** charloteo *m* (**e**) *(increase)* ligero(a)

2 *n* (**a**) **s. of the back** región *f* lumbar (**b**) *Br Fam* **smalls** *(underwear)* paños *mpl* menores

smallholder [ˈsmɔːlhəʊldə(r)] *n* minifundista *mf*

smallpox [ˈsmɔːlpɒks] *n* viruela *f*

smarmy [ˈsmɑːmɪ] *adj* (**smarmier, smarmiest**) *Fam* cobista, zalamero(a)

smart [smɑːt] **1** *adj* (**a**) *(elegant)* elegante (**b**) *(clever)* listo(a), inteligente; *Fam* **s. alec(k)** listillo (**c**) *(quick)* rápido(a); *(pace)* ligero(a)

2 *vi* (**a**) *(sting)* picar, escocer (**b**) *Fig* sufrir

smarten [ˈsmɑːtən] **1** *vt* **to s. (up)** arreglar

2 *vi* **to s. (oneself) up** arreglarse

smash [smæʃ] **1** *n* (**a**) *(loud noise)* estrépito *m; (collision)* choque violento (**b**) *(in tennis)* smash *m*

2 *vt* (**a**) *(break)* romper; *(shatter)* hacer pedazos; *(crush)* aplastar (**b**) *(destroy)* destrozar; *(defeat)* aplastar (**c**) *(record)* fulminar

3 *vi (break)* romperse; *(shatter)* hacerse pedazos; *(crash)* estrellarse; *(in tennis)* hacer un mate

▸ **smash up** *vt sep Fam (car)* hacer pedazos; *(place)* destrozar

smashing [ˈsmæʃɪŋ] *adj Br Fam* estupendo(a)

smattering [ˈsmætərɪŋ] *n* **he had a s. of French** hablaba un poquito de francés

smear [smɪə(r)] **1** *n* (**a**) *(smudge)* mancha *f;* **s. (test)** citología *f* (**b**) *Fig (defamation)* calumnia *f*

2 *vt* (**a**) *(butter etc)* untar; *(grease)* embadurnar (**b**) *(make dirty)* manchar (**c**) *Fig (defame)* calumniar, difamar

smell [smel] **1** *n* (**a**) *(sense)* olfato *m* (**b**) *(odour)* olor *m*

2 *vt (pt & pp* **smelled** *or* **smelt**) oler; *Fig* olfatear

3 *vi* oler (**of** a); **it smells good/like lavender** huele bien/a lavanda; **he smelt of whisky** olía a whisky

smelly [ˈsmelɪ] *adj* (**smellier, smelliest**) *Fam* maloliente, apestoso(a)

smelt¹ [smelt] *vt (ore)* fundir

smelt² [smelt] *pt & pp of* **smell**

smidgen ['smɪdʒən] n Fam pizca f

smile [smaɪl] 1 n sonrisa f

2 vi sonreír; **to s. at sb** sonreír a algn; **to s. at sth** reírse de algo

smiling ['smaɪlɪŋ] adj sonriente, risueño(a)

smirk [smɜːk] 1 n (conceited) sonrisa satisfecha; (foolish) sonrisa boba

2 vi (conceitedly) sonreír con satisfacción; (foolishly) sonreír bobamente

smith [smɪθ] n herrero m

smithereens [smɪðə'riːnz] npl **to smash/blow sth to s.** hacer algo añicos

smithy ['smɪðɪ] n herrería f

smitten ['smɪtən] adj Fam **to be s. with sb** estar enamorado(a) de algn

smock [smɒk] n (blouse) blusón m; (worn in pregnancy) blusón de premamá; (overall) bata f

smog [smɒg] n niebla tóxica, smog m

smoke [sməʊk] 1 n humo m; **s. bomb** bomba f de humo; **s. screen** cortina f de humo

2 vi fumar; (chimney etc) echar humo

3 vt (a) (tobacco) fumar; **to s. a pipe** fumar en pipa (b) (fish, meat) ahumar

smoked [sməʊkt] adj ahumado(a)

smokeless ['sməʊklɪs] adj **s. fuel** combustible sin humo; **s. zone** zona libre de humos

smoker ['sməʊkə(r)] n (a) (person) fumador(a) m,f (b) Rail vagón m de fumadores

smoking ['sməʊkɪŋ] n **no s.** (sign) prohibido fumar

smoky ['sməʊkɪ] adj (smokier, smokiest) (a) (chimney) humeante; (room) lleno(a) de humo; (atmosphere) cargado(a) de humo; (taste) ahumado(a) (b) (colour) ahumado(a)

smolder ['sməʊldə(r)] vi US = smoulder

smooth [smuːð] 1 adj (a) (surface) liso(a); (skin) suave; (road) llano(a); (sea) tranquilo(a) (b) (beer, wine) suave (c) (flowing) fluido(a) (d) (flight) tranquilo(a); (transition) sin problemas (e) Pej (slick) zalamero(a)

2 vt (a) (hair etc) alisar (b) (plane down) limar

▸ **smooth out** vt sep (creases) alisar; Fig (difficulties) allanar; (problems) resolver

▸ **smooth over** vt sep Fig **to s. things over** limar asperezas

smoothly ['smuːðlɪ] adv sobre ruedas

smother ['smʌðə(r)] vt (a) (asphyxiate) asfixiar; (suffocate) sofocar (b) Fig (cover) cubrir (**with** de)

smoulder ['sməʊldə(r)] vi (fire) arder sin llama; Fig (passions) arder; **smouldering hatred** odio latente

smudge [smʌdʒ] 1 n (stain) mancha f; (of ink) borrón m

2 vt manchar; (piece of writing) emborronar

smug [smʌg] adj (smugger, smuggest) engreído(a)

smuggle ['smʌgəl] vt pasar de contrabando

smuggler ['smʌglə(r)] n contrabandista mf

smuggling ['smʌglɪŋ] n contrabando m

smutty ['smʌtɪ] adj (smuttier, smuttiest) Fam obsceno(a); (joke) verde; (book, film etc) pornográfico(a)

snack [snæk] n bocado m; **s. bar** cafetería f

snag [snæg] 1 n (difficulty) pega f, problemilla m

2 vt (clothing) enganchar

snail [sneɪl] n caracol m

snake [sneɪk] n (big) serpiente f; (small) culebra f

snap [snæp] 1 n (a) (noise) ruido seco; (of branch, fingers) chasquido m (b) (bite) mordisco m (c) Phot (foto f) instantánea f

2 adj (sudden) repentino(a)

3 vt (a) (branch etc) partir (en dos) (b) (make noise) **to s. one's fingers** chasquear los dedos; **to s. sth shut** cerrar algo de golpe (c) Phot sacar una foto de

4 vi (a) (break) romperse (b) (make noise) hacer un ruido seco (c) (whip) chasquear; **to s. shut** cerrarse de golpe (d) **to s. at sb** (dog) intentar morder a algn; Fam (person) regañar a algn

▸ **snap off** vt sep (branch etc) arrancar

2 vi (branch etc) separarse

▸ **snap up** vt sep Fam **to s. up a bargain** llevarse una ganga

snappy ['snæpɪ] adj (snappier, snappiest) Fam (a) (quick) rápido(a); **look s.!, make it s.!** ¡date prisa! (b) (stylish) elegante (c) (short-tempered) irritable

snapshot ['snæpʃɒt] n (foto f) instantánea f

snare [sneə(r)] 1 n trampa f

2 vt (animal) cazar con trampa; Fig (person) hacer caer en la trampa

snarl¹ [snɑːl] 1 n gruñido m

2 vi gruñir

snarl² [snɑːl] 1 n (in wool) maraña f

2 vt **to s. (up)** (wool) enmarañar; (traffic) atascar; (plans) enredar

snatch [snætʃ] 1 n (a) Fam (theft) robo m; **bag s.** tirón m (b) (fragment) fragmentos mpl

2 vt (**a**) (grab) arrebatar (**b**) Fam (steal) robar; (kidnap) secuestrar

3 vi **to s. at sth** intentar agarrar algo

sneak [sniːk] **1** n Fam chivato(a) m,f

2 (pt & pp **sneaked** or US **snuck**) vt **to s. sth out of a place** sacar algo de un lugar a escondidas

3 vi (**a**) **to s. off** escabullirse; **to s. in/out** entrar/salir a hurtadillas (**b**) Fam **to s. on sb** (tell tales) chivarse de algn

sneaker ['sniːkə(r)] n US playera f

sneaky ['sniːkɪ] adj (**sneakier, sneakiest**) solapado(a)

sneer [snɪə(r)] vi **to s. at** hacer un gesto de desprecio a

sneeze [sniːz] **1** n estornudo m

2 vi estornudar

sniff [snɪf] **1** n (by person) aspiración f; (by dog) husmeo m

2 vt (flower etc) oler; (suspiciously) husmear; (snuff etc) aspirar; (glue) esnifar

3 vi aspirar por la nariz

snigger ['snɪgə(r)] **1** n risa disimulada

2 vi reír disimuladamente; **to s. at sth** burlarse de algo

snip [snɪp] **1** n (**a**) (cut) tijeretada f; (small piece) recorte m (**b**) Br Fam (bargain) ganga f

2 vt cortar a tijeretazos

sniper ['snaɪpə(r)] n francotirador(a) m,f

snippet ['snɪpɪt] n (of cloth, paper) recorte m; (of conversation) fragmento m

snivel ['snɪvəl] vi lloriquear

snivelling ['snɪvəlɪŋ] adj llorón(ona)

snob [snɒb] n (e)snob m

snobbery ['snɒbərɪ] n (e)snobismo m

snobbish ['snɒbɪʃ] adj (e)snob

snooker ['snuːkə(r)] n snooker m, billar ruso

snoop [snuːp] vi fisgar, fisgonear

snooty ['snuːtɪ] adj (**snootier, snootiest**) Fam (e)snob

snooze [snuːz] Fam **1** n cabezada f

2 vi echar una cabezada

snore [snɔː(r)] **1** n ronquido m

2 vi roncar

snoring ['snɔːrɪŋ] n ronquidos mpl

snorkel ['snɔːkəl] n (of swimmer) tubo m de respiración; (of submarine) esnórquel m

snort [snɔːt] **1** n resoplido m

2 vi resoplar

snout [snaʊt] n (of animal, gun etc) morro m

snow [snəʊ] **1** n nieve f; **s. shower** nevada f

2 vi nevar; **it's snowing** está nevando

3 vt Fig **to be snowed under with work** estar agobiado(a) de trabajo

snowball ['snəʊbɔːl] **1** n bola f de nieve

2 vi Fig aumentar rápidamente

snowbound ['snəʊbaʊnd] adj aislado(a) por la nieve

snowdrift ['snəʊdrɪft] n ventisquero m

snowdrop ['snəʊdrɒp] n campanilla f de invierno

snowfall ['snəʊfɔːl] n nevada f

snowflake ['snəʊfleɪk] n copo m de nieve

snowman ['snəʊmæn] n hombre m de nieve

snowplough, US **snowplow** ['snəʊplaʊ] n quitanieves m inv

snowshoe ['snəʊʃuː] n raqueta f (de nieve)

snowstorm ['snəʊstɔːm] n nevasca f

snowy ['snəʊɪ] adj (**snowier, snowiest**) (mountain) nevado(a); (climate) nevoso(a); (day) de nieve

Snr (abbr **Senior**) **Neil Smith S.** Neil Smith Snr

snub [snʌb] **1** n (of person) desaire m; (of offer) rechazo m

2 vt (person) desairar; (offer) rechazar

snub-nosed ['snʌbnəʊzd] adj de nariz respingona

snuck [snʌk] US pt & pp of **sneak**

snuff [snʌf] n rapé m

snug [snʌg] adj (**snugger, snuggest**) (**a**) (cosy) cómodo(a) (**b**) (tightfitting) ajustado(a)

snuggle ['snʌgəl] vi **to s. down in bed** acurrucarse en la cama; **to s. up to sb** arrimarse a algn

snugly ['snʌglɪ] adv **to fit s.** (clothes) quedar ajustado(a); (object in box etc) encajar

so [səʊ] **1** adv (**a**) (to such an extent) tanto; **he was so tired that ...** estaba tan cansado que ...; **it's so long since ...** hace tanto tiempo que ...; **he isn't so nice as his sister** no es tan agradable como su hermana; Fam **so long!** ¡hasta luego!

(**b**) (degree) tanto; **a week or so** una semana más o menos; **twenty or so** una veintena; **we loved her so (much)** la queríamos tanto; **so many books** tantos libros; Fam **he's ever so handsome!** ¡es tan guapo!; Ironic **so much for that** ¿qué le vamos a hacer?

(**c**) (thus, in this way) así, de esta manera; **and so on, and so forth** y así sucesivamente; **if so** en este caso; **I think/hope so** creo/espero que sí; **I told you so** ya te lo dije; **it so happens that ...** da la casualidad de que ...; **so be it!** ¡así sea!; **so far** hasta ahora or allí; **so it seems** eso parece; **so they say** eso dicen; **you're late!** – **so I am!** ¡llegas tarde! – ¡tienes razón!

　(**d**) *(also)* **I'm going to Spain – so am I** voy a España – yo también

　2 *conj* (**a**) *(expresses result)* así que; **so you like England, do you?** ¿así que te gusta Inglaterra, pues?; *Fam* **so what?** ¿y qué?

　(**b**) *(expresses purpose)* para que; **I'll put the key here so (that) everyone can see it** pongo la llave aquí para que todos la vean

soak [səʊk] **1** *vt (washing, food)* remojar; *(cotton, wool)* empapar (**in** en)

　2 *vi (washing, food)* estar en remojo

　▸ **soak in** *vi* penetrar

　▸ **soak up** *vt sep* absorber

soaking ['səʊkɪŋ] *adj (object)* empapado(a); *(person)* calado(a) hasta los huesos

so-and-so ['səʊənsəʊ] *n Fam* **Mr So-and-so** Don Fulano (de tal); *Pej* **an old so-and-so** un viejo imbécil

soap [səʊp] **1** *n* (**a**) jabón *m*; **s. flakes** jabón en escamas; **s. powder** jabón en polvo (**b**) *TV* **s. opera** culebrón *m*

　2 *vt* enjabonar

soapy ['səʊpɪ] *adj* (**soapier, soapiest**) jabonoso(a); *(hands)* cubierto(a) de jabón

soar [sɔː(r)] *vi (bird, plane)* remontar el vuelo; *Fig (skyscraper)* elevarse; *(hopes, prices)* aumentar

sob [sɒb] **1** *n* sollozo *m*

　2 *vi* sollozar

sober ['səʊbə(r)] *adj (not drunk, moderate)* sobrio(a); *(sensible)* sensato(a); *(serious)* serio(a); *(colour)* discreto(a)

　▸ **sober up** *vi* **he sobered up** se le pasó la borrachera

so-called ['səʊkɔːld] *adj* supuesto(a), llamado(a)

soccer ['sɒkə(r)] *n* fútbol *m*

sociable ['səʊʃəbəl] *adj (gregarious)* sociable; *(friendly)* amistoso(a)

social ['səʊʃəl] *adj* social; **s. class** clase *f* social; **s. climber** arribista *mf*; **S. Democratic** socialdemócrata; *US* **s. insurance** seguro *m* social; **s. security** seguridad *f* social; **the s. services** los servicios sociales; **s. work** asistencia *f* social; **s. worker** asistente(a) *m,f* social

socialist ['səʊʃəlɪst] *adj & n* socialista *(mf)*

socialite ['səʊʃəlaɪt] *n* vividor(a) *m,f*

socialize ['səʊʃəlaɪz] **1** *vi* alternar, mezclarse con la gente

　2 *vt* socializar

socially ['səʊʃəlɪ] *adv* socialmente

society [sə'saɪətɪ] **1** *n* (**a**) sociedad *f*; **the consumer s.** la sociedad de consumo; **(high) s.** la alta sociedad (**b**) *(club)* asociación *f* (**c**) *(companionship)* compañía *f*

　2 *adj* de sociedad; **s. column** ecos *mpl* de sociedad

sociologist [səʊsɪ'ɒlədʒɪst] *n* sociólogo(a) *m,f*

sociology [səʊsɪ'ɒlədʒɪ] *n* sociología *f*

sock [sɒk] *n* calcetín *m, CSur* zoquete *m*

socket ['sɒkɪt] *n* (**a**) *(of eye)* cuenca *f* (**b**) *Elec* enchufe *m*

sod[1] [sɒd] *n Fml (piece of turf)* terrón *m*

sod[2] [sɒd] *very Fam* **1** *n* (**a**) *Pej (bastard)* cabrón(ona) *m,f*; **the lazy s.!** ¡qué tío más vago! (**b**) *(wretch)* desgraciado(a) *m,f*; **the poor s.** el pobrecito (**c**) **I've done s. all today** hoy no he pegado ni golpe

　2 *vt* **s. it!** ¡maldita sea!

soda ['səʊdə] *n* (**a**) *Chem* sosa *f*; **baking s.** bicarbonato sódico (**b**) **s. water** soda *f* (**c**) *US (fizzy drink)* gaseosa *f*

sodden ['sɒdən] *adj* empapado(a)

sodium ['səʊdɪəm] *n* sodio *m*

sofa ['səʊfə] *n* sofá *m*; **s. bed** sofá cama *m*

soft [sɒft] *adj* (**a**) *(not hard)* blando(a); **s. toy** muñeco *m* de peluche (**b**) *(skin, colour, hair, light, music)* suave; *(breeze, steps)* ligero(a) (**c**) *(lenient)* permisivo(a) (**d**) *(voice)* bajo(a) (**e**) *(foolish)* lelo(a); **to be a s. touch** ser fácil de engañar (**f**) **to have a s. spot for sb** tener debilidad por algn (**g**) *(easy)* fácil; **s. job** chollo *m* (**h**) *(drink)* no alcohólico(a); **s. drinks** refrescos *mpl* (**i**) **s. drugs** drogas blandas; **s. porn** pornografía blanda

soften ['sɒfən] **1** *vt (leather, heart)* ablandar; *(skin)* suavizar; *Fig (blow)* amortiguar

　2 *vi (leather, heart)* ablandarse; *(skin)* suavizarse

softly ['sɒftlɪ] *adv (gently)* suavemente; *(quietly)* silenciosamente

softness ['sɒftnɪs] *n* (**a**) blandura *f* (**b**) *(of hair, skin)* suavidad *f* (**c**) *(foolishness)* estupidez *f*

software ['sɒftweə(r)] *n Comput* software *m*; **s. package** paquete *m*

soggy ['sɒgɪ] *adj* (**soggier, soggiest**) empapado(a); *(bread)* pastoso(a)

soil [sɔɪl] **1** *n (earth)* tierra *f*

　2 *vt (dirty)* ensuciar; *Fig (reputation)* manchar

soiled [sɔɪld] *adj* sucio(a)

solace ['sɒlɪs] *n Fml* consuelo *m*

solar ['səʊlə(r)] *adj* solar

sold [səʊld] *pt & pp of* sell

solder ['sɒldə(r)] **1** *n* soldadura *f*
  2 *vt* soldar
soldier ['səʊldʒə(r)] *n* soldado *m; (officer)* militar *m;* **toy s.** soldadito *m* de plomo
  ▸ **soldier on** *vi Fig* continuar contra viento y marea
sole¹ [səʊl] *n (of foot)* planta *f; (of shoe, sock)* suela *f*
sole² [səʊl] *n (fish)* lenguado *m*
sole³ [səʊl] *adj (only)* único(a)
solemn ['sɒləm] *adj* solemne
solicit [sə'lɪsɪt] **1** *vt (request)* solicitar
  2 *vi (prostitute)* abordar a los clientes
solicitor [sə'lɪsɪtə(r)] *n* abogado(a) *m,f; (for wills)* notario(a) *m,f*
solid ['sɒlɪd] **1** *adj* **(a)** *(not liquid)* sólido(a); *(firm)* firme **(b)** *(not hollow, pure) (metal)* macizo(a) **(c)** *(fog etc)* espeso(a); *(of strong material)* resistente; **a man of s. build** un hombre fornido **(d)** *(reliable)* formal **(e)** *(unanimous)* unánime
  2 *n* sólido *m*
solidarity [sɒlɪ'dærɪtɪ] *n* solidaridad *f*
solidify [sə'lɪdɪfaɪ] *vi* solidificarse
solidly ['sɒlɪdlɪ] *adv* sólidamente; **s. built** *(house etc)* de construcción sólida; **to work s.** trabajar sin descanso
soliloquy [sə'lɪləkwɪ] *n* soliloquio *m*
solitaire [sɒlɪteə(r)] *n* solitario *m*
solitary ['sɒlɪtərɪ] *adj* **(a)** *(alone)* solitario(a); *(secluded)* apartado(a) **(b)** *(only)* solo(a)
solitude ['sɒlɪtjuːd] *n* soledad *f*
solo ['səʊləʊ] *n* solo *m*
soloist ['səʊləʊɪst] *n* solista *mf*
solstice ['sɒlstɪs] *n* solsticio *m*
solution [sə'luːʃən] *n* solución *f*
solve [sɒlv] *vt* resolver, solucionar
solvent ['sɒlvənt] *adj & n* solvente *(m)*
sombre, *US* **somber** ['sɒmbə(r)] *adj (dark)* sombrío(a); *(gloomy)* lúgubre; *(pessimistic)* pesimista
some [sʌm] **1** *adj* **(a)** *(with plural nouns)* unos(as), algunos(as); *(several)* varios(as); *(a few)* unos(as) cuantos(as); **did she bring s. flowers?** ¿trajo flores?; **there were s. roses** había unas rosas; **s. more peas** más guisantes
  (b) *(with singular nouns)* algún/alguna; *(a little)* un poco de; **if you need s. help** si necesitas ayuda; **there's s. wine left** queda un poco de vino; **would you like s. coffee?** ¿quiere café?
  (c) *(certain)* cierto(a), alguno(a); **in s. ways** en cierto modo; **to s. extent** hasta cierto punto; **s. people say that ...** algunas personas dicen que ...
  (d) *(unspecified)* algún/alguna; **for s.**

reason or other por una razón o por otra; **in s. book or other** en algún libro que otro; **s. day** algún día; **s. other time** otro día
  (e) *(quite a lot of)* bastante; **it's s. distance away** queda bastante lejos; **s. years ago** hace algunos años
  2 *pron* **(a)** *(people)* algunos(as), unos(as); **s. go by bus and s. by train** unos van en autobús y otros en tren
  (b) *(objects)* algunos(as); *(a few)* unos(as) cuantos(as); *(a little)* algo, un poco; *(certain ones)* algunos(as)
  3 *adv* **s. thirty cars** unos treinta coches
somebody ['sʌmbədɪ] *pron* alguien; **s. else** otro(a)
somehow ['sʌmhaʊ] *adv* **(a)** *(in some way)* de alguna forma **(b)** *(for some reason)* por alguna razón
someone ['sʌmwʌn] *pron* = **somebody**
someplace ['sʌmpleɪs] *adv US* = **somewhere**
somersault ['sʌməsɔːlt] **1** *n* voltereta *f; (by acrobat etc)* salto *m* mortal; *(by car)* vuelta *f* de campana
  2 *vi* dar volteretas; *(acrobat etc)* dar un salto mortal; *(car)* dar una vuelta de campana
something ['sʌmθɪŋ] *pron & n* algo; **s. to eat/drink** algo de comer/beber; **are you drunk or s.?** ¿estás borracho o qué?; **s. must be done** hay que hacer algo; **she has a certain s.** tiene un no sé qué; **is s. the matter?** ¿le pasa algo?; **s. else** otra cosa; **s. of the kind** algo por el estilo
sometime ['sʌmtaɪm] *adv* algún día; **s. last week** un día de la semana pasada; **s. next year** durante el año que viene
sometimes ['sʌmtaɪmz] *adv* a veces, de vez en cuando
somewhat ['sʌmwɒt] *adv Fml* algo, un tanto
somewhere ['sʌmweə(r)] *adv* **(a)** *(in some place)* en alguna parte; *(to some place)* a alguna parte; **s. else** *(in some other place)* en otra parte; *(to some other place)* a otra parte; **s. or other** no sé dónde; **s. in the region of** *(approximately)* más o menos
son [sʌn] *n* hijo *m;* **eldest/youngest s.** hijo mayor/menor
song [sɒŋ] *n* canción *f; (of bird)* canto *m*
songwriter ['sɒŋraɪtə(r)] *n* compositor(a) *m,f* (de canciones)
sonic ['sɒnɪk] *adj* sónico(a)
son-in-law ['sʌnɪnlɔː] *n* yerno *m*
sonnet ['sɒnɪt] *n* soneto *m*
sonny ['sʌnɪ] *n Fam* hijo *m,* hijito *m*

soon [su:n] *adv* (**a**) *(within a short time)* pronto, dentro de poco; *(quickly)* rápidamente; **see you s.!** ¡hasta pronto!; **s. after midnight** poco después de medianoche; **s. afterwards** poco después

(**b**) **as s. as I arrived** en cuanto llegué; **as s. as possible** cuanto antes

(**c**) *(early)* pronto; *Fig* **don't speak too s.** no cantes victoria

(**d**) *(preference)* **I would just as s. stay at home** prefiero quedarme en casa

(**e**) *(indifference)* **I would (just) as s. read as watch TV** tanto me da leer como ver la tele

sooner ['su:nə(r)] *adv* (**a**) *(earlier)* más temprano; **s. or later** tarde o temprano; **the s. the better** cuanto antes mejor (**b**) **no s. had he finished than he fainted** *(immediately after)* nada más acabar se desmayó (**c**) **I would s. do it alone** *(rather)* prefiero hacerlo yo solo

soot [sʊt] *n* hollín *m*

soothe [su:ð] *vt* *(calm)* tranquilizar; *(pain)* aliviar

sop [sɒp] *n* *(concession)* favor *m*; *(bribe)* soborno *m*
▸ **sop up** *vt sep* empapar

sophisticated [sə'fɪstɪkeɪtɪd] *adj* sofisticado(a)

sophomore ['sɒfəmɔ:(r)] *n US Univ* = estudiante de segundo curso

soporific [sɒpə'rɪfɪk] *adj* soporífero(a)

sopping ['sɒpɪŋ] *adj Fam* **s. (wet)** como una sopa

soppy ['sɒpɪ] *adj* (**soppier, soppiest**) *Fam* sentimentaloide

soprano [sə'prɑ:nəʊ] *n* soprano *mf*

sorcerer ['sɔ:sərə(r)] *n* brujo *m*

sorceress ['sɔ:sərɪs] *n* bruja *f*

sordid ['sɔ:dɪd] *adj* sórdido(a)

sore [sɔ:(r)] **1** *adj* (**a**) dolorido(a); **to have a s. throat** tener dolor de garganta (**b**) *Fam (angry)* enfadado(a); **to feel s. about sth** estar resentido(a) por algo
2 *n* llaga *f*

sorely ['sɔ:lɪ] *adv* *(very)* muy; *(a lot)* mucho; *(deeply)* profundamente

sorrow ['sɒrəʊ] *n* pena *f*, dolor *m*

sorrowful ['sɒrəʊfʊl] *adj* afligido(a)

sorry ['sɒrɪ] **1** *adj* (**sorrier, sorriest**) (**a**) **I feel very s. for her** me da mucha pena (**b**) *(pitiful)* triste (**c**) **to be s. (about sth)** sentir (algo); **I'm s. I'm late** siento llegar tarde
2 *interj* (**a**) *(apology)* ¡perdón! (**b**) *Br (for repetition)* ¿cómo?

sort [sɔ:t] **1** *n* (**a**) *(kind)* clase *f*, tipo *m*; *(brand)* marca *f*; **it's a s. of teapot** es una

especie de tetera (**b**) **he is a musician of sorts** tiene algo de músico; **there's an office of sorts** hay una especie de despacho (**c**) **s. of** en cierto modo
2 *vt (classify)* clasificar
▸ **sort out** *vt sep* (**a**) *(classify)* clasificar; *(put in order)* ordenar (**b**) *(problem)* arreglar, solucionar

sorting ['sɔ:tɪŋ] *n* **s. office** sala *f* de batalla

SOS [esəʊ'es] *n* (*abbr* **save our souls**) S.O.S. *m*

so-so ['səʊsəʊ] *adv Fam* así así, regular

soufflé ['su:fleɪ] *n* soufflé *m*, suflé *m*

sought [sɔ:t] *pt & pp of* **seek**

soul [səʊl] *n* (**a**) alma *f* (**b**) **he's a good s.** *(person)* es muy buena persona (**c**) *Mus* *(música f)* soul *m*

soul-destroying ['səʊldɪstrɔɪŋ] *adj* *(boring)* monótono(a); *(demoralizing)* desmoralizador(a)

soulful ['səʊlfʊl] *adj* conmovedor(a)

sound¹ [saʊnd] **1** *n* sonido *m*; *(noise)* ruido *m*; *Fig* **I don't like the s. of it** no me gusta nada la idea; **s. barrier** barrera *f* del sonido; **s. effects** efectos sonoros
2 *vt (bell, trumpet)* tocar; **to s. the alarm** dar la señal de alarma
3 *vi* (**a**) *(trumpet, bell, alarm)* sonar (**b**) *(give an impression)* parecer; **how does it s. to you?** ¿qué te parece?; **it sounds interesting** parece interesante

sound² [saʊnd] **1** *adj* (**a**) *(healthy)* sano(a); *(in good condition)* en buen estado (**b**) *(safe, dependable)* seguro(a); *(correct)* acertado(a); *(logical)* lógico(a) (**c**) *(basis etc)* sólido(a) (**d**) *(defeat etc)* rotundo(a) (**e**) *(sleep)* profundo(a)
2 *adv* **to be s. asleep** estar profundamente dormido(a)

sound³ [saʊnd] *vt Naut & Med* sondar
▸ **sound out** *vt sep* sondear

sound⁴ [saʊnd] *n Geog* estrecho *m*

sounding ['saʊndɪŋ] *n Naut* sondeo *m*

soundproof ['saʊndpru:f] *adj* insonorizado(a)

soundtrack ['saʊndtræk] *n* banda sonora

soup [su:p] *n* sopa *f*; *(thin, clear)* caldo *m*; *Fam* **in the s.** en un apuro; **s. dish** plato hondo; **s. spoon** cuchara *f* sopera

sour [saʊə(r)] *adj* (**a**) *(fruit, wine)* agrio(a); *(milk)* cortado(a); **to go s.** *(milk)* cortarse; *(wine)* agriarse; *Fig (situation)* empeorar (**b**) *Fig (person)* amargado(a)

source [sɔ:s] *n* fuente *f*; *(of infection)* foco *m*

south [saʊθ] **1** *n* sur *m*; **in the s. of England** en el sur de Inglaterra; **to the s. of York** al sur de York

2 *adj* del sur; **S. Africa** Sudáfrica; **S. African** sudafricano(a) *(m,f)*; **S. Korea** Corea del Sur; **S. Pole** Polo *m* Sur

3 *adv (location)* al sur; *(direction)* hacia el sur

southeast [saʊθ'iːst] **1** *n* sudeste *m*

2 *adv (location)* al sudeste; *(direction)* hacia el sudeste

southeasterly [saʊθ'iːstəlɪ] *adj* del sudeste

southerly ['sʌðəlɪ] *adj (direction)* hacia el sur; *(point)* al sur; *(wind)* del sur

southern ['sʌðən] *adj* del sur, meridional; **S. Europe** Europa del Sur; **the s. hemisphere** el hemisferio sur

southerner ['sʌðənə(r)] *n* sureño(a) *m,f*

southward ['saʊθwəd] *adj & adv* hacia el sur

southwest [saʊθ'west] **1** *n* suroeste *m*

2 *adj* suroeste

3 *adv (location)* al suroeste; *(direction)* hacia el suroeste

souvenir [suːvə'nɪə(r)] *n* recuerdo *m*, souvenir *m*

sovereign ['sɒvrɪn] **1** *n* **(a)** *(monarch)* soberano(a) *m,f* **(b)** *Hist (coin)* soberano *m*

2 *adj* soberano(a)

soviet ['səʊvɪət] **1** *n* **(a)** *(council)* soviet *m* **(b) the Soviets** los soviéticos

2 *adj* soviético(a); *Hist* **S. Union** Unión Soviética

sow¹ [səʊ] *vt (pt sowed; pp sowed or sown)* sembrar

sow² [saʊ] *n Zool* cerda *f*

sown [səʊn] *pp of* **sow**

soy [sɔɪ] *n* soja *f*; **s. sauce** salsa *f* de soja

soya ['sɔɪə] *n* soja *f*; **s. bean** semilla *f* de soja

spa [spɑː] *n* balneario *m*

space [speɪs] **1** *n* **(a)** espacio *m*; **s. age** era *f* espacial; **s. shuttle** transbordador *m* espacial; **s. station** estación *f* espacial **(b)** *(room)* sitio *m*; **in a confined s.** en un espacio reducido

2 *vt (also s. out)* espaciar, separar

spacecraft ['speɪskrɑːft] *n (pl* spacecraft*)* nave *f* espacial

spaceman ['speɪsmən] *n* astronauta *m*, cosmonauta *m*

spacing ['speɪsɪŋ] *n* **double s.** doble espacio

spacious ['speɪʃəs] *adj* espacioso(a), amplio(a)

spade¹ [speɪd] *n (for digging)* pala *f*

> 🎵 Note that the Spanish word **espada** is a false friend and is never a translation for the English word **spade**. In Spanish, **espada** means "sword".

spade² [speɪd] *n Cards* pica *f*

spaghetti [spə'getɪ] *n* espaguetis *mpl*

Spain [speɪn] *n* España

span [spæn] **1** *n* **(a)** *(of wing)* envergadura *f*; *(of hand)* palmo *m*; *(of arch)* luz *f*; *(of road)* tramo *m*; *(of time)* lapso *m*; **life s.** vida *f*

2 *vt (river etc)* extenderse sobre, atravesar; *(period of time etc)* abarcar

3 *pt of* **spin**

Spaniard ['spænjəd] *n* español(a) *m,f*

spaniel ['spænjəl] *n* perro *m* de aguas

Spanish ['spænɪʃ] **1** *adj* español(a)

2 *n* **(a) the S.** los españoles **(b)** *(language)* español *m*, castellano *m*

Spanish-speaking ['spænɪʃspiːkɪŋ] *adj* de habla española, hispanohablante

spank [spæŋk] *vt* zurrar

spanner ['spænə(r)] *n* llave *f* (para tuercas); *Br Fam* **to throw a s. in the works** estropear los planes

spar¹ [spɑː(r)] *n Naut* palo *m*, verga *f*

spar² [spɑː(r)] *vi* **(a)** *(boxers)* entrenarse **(b)** *(argue)* discutir

spare [speə(r)] **1** *vt* **(a)** *(do without)* prescindir de; **can you s. me ten?** ¿me puedes dejar diez?; **I can't s. the time** no tengo tiempo; **there's none to s.** no sobra nada **(b)** *(begrudge)* escatimar **(c)** *(show mercy to)* perdonar **(d) s. me the details** ahórrate los detalles

2 *adj* **(a)** *(left over)* sobrante; *(surplus)* de sobra, de más; **a s. moment** un momento libre; **s. part** (pieza *f* de) recambio *m*; **s. room** cuarto *m* de los invitados; **s. tyre** *Aut* neumático *m* de recambio; *Br Fam (on body)* michelines *mpl*; **s. wheel** rueda *f* de recambio **(b)** *(thin)* enjuto(a)

3 *n Aut* (pieza *f* de) recambio *m*

sparing ['speərɪŋ] *adj* **to be s. with praise** escatimar elogios; **to be s. with words** ser parco(a) en palabras

sparingly ['speərɪŋlɪ] *adv* en poca cantidad

spark [spɑːk] **1** *n* chispa *f*; *Aut* **s. plug** bujía *f*

2 *vi* echar chispas

▸ **spark off** *vt sep* desatar

sparking ['spɑːkɪŋ] *adj* **s. plug** bujía *f*

sparkle ['spɑːkəl] **1** *vi (diamond, glass)* centellear, destellar; *(eyes)* brillar

2 *n (of diamond, glass)* centelleo *m*,

destello *m*; (*of eyes*) brillo *m*

sparkling ['spɑːklɪŋ] *adj* (**a**) (*diamond, glass*) centelleante; (*eyes*) brillante; **s. wine** vino espumoso (**b**) *Fig* (*person, conversation*) vivaz

sparrow ['spærəʊ] *n* gorrión *m*

sparse [spɑːs] *adj* (*thin*) escaso(a); (*scattered*) esparcido(a); (*hair*) ralo(a)

Spartan ['spɑːtən] *adj & n* espartano(a) (*m,f*)

spasm ['spæzəm] *n* (**a**) *Med* espasmo *m*; (*of coughing*) acceso *m* (**b**) (*of anger, activity*) arrebato *m*

spasmodic [spæz'mɒdɪk] *adj* (**a**) *Med* espasmódico(a) (**b**) (*irregular*) irregular

spastic ['spæstɪk] *adj & n Med* espástico(a) (*m,f*)

spat [spæt] *pt & pp of* spit

spate [speɪt] *n* (**a**) (*of letters*) avalancha *f*; (*of words*) torrente *m*; (*of accidents*) racha *f* (**b**) *Br* (*river*) desbordamiento *m*; **to be in full s.** estar crecido(a)

spatter ['spætə(r)] *vt* salpicar (**with** de)

spatula ['spætjʊlə] *n* espátula *f*

spawn [spɔːn] **1** *n* (*of fish, frogs*) huevas *fpl*

2 *vi* (*fish, frogs*) frezar

3 *vt Fig Pej* generar

speak [spiːk] **1** *vt* (*pt* **spoke**; *pp* **spoken**) (**a**) (*utter*) decir; **to s. the truth** decir la verdad

(**b**) (*language*) hablar

2 *vi* (*gen*) hablar; **roughly speaking** a grandes rasgos; **so to s.** por así decirlo; **speaking of ...** a propósito de ...; **to s. to sb** hablar con algn

(**b**) (*make a speech*) pronunciar un discurso; (*take the floor*) tomar la palabra

(**c**)*Tel* hablar; **speaking!** ¡al habla!; **who's speaking, please?** ¿de parte de quién?

▶ **speak for** *vt insep* (*person, group*) hablar en nombre de; **it speaks for itself** es evidente

▶ **speak out** *vi* **to s. out against sth** denunciar algo

▶ **speak up** *vi* hablar más fuerte; *Fig* **to s. up for sb** intervenir a favor de algn

speaker ['spiːkə(r)] *n* (**a**) (*in dialogue*) interlocutor(a) *m,f*; (*lecturer*) conferenciante *mf*; (**public**) **s.** orador(a) *m,f* (**b**) (*of language*) hablante *mf* (**c**) *Br Pol* **the S.** el Presidente de la Cámara de los Comunes; *US* **the S. of the House** el Presidente de la Cámara de los Representantes (**d**) (*loudspeaker*) altavoz *m*

spear [spɪə(r)] *n* lanza *f*; (*javelin*) jabalina *f*; (*harpoon*) arpón *m*

spearhead ['spɪəhed] *vt* encabezar

spec [spek] *n Fam* **on s.** sin garantías

special ['speʃəl] **1** *adj* especial; (*specific*) específico(a); (*exceptional*) extraordinario(a); **s. delivery** (*letter*) exprés; (*parcel*) de entrega inmediata; **s. edition** número *m* especial; **s. effects** efectos *mpl* especiales

2 *n Rad & TV* programa *m* especial

specialist ['speʃəlɪst] *n* especialista *mf*

speciality [speʃɪ'ælɪtɪ] *n esp Br* especialidad *f*

specialize ['speʃəlaɪz] *vi* especializarse (**in** en)

specially ['speʃəlɪ] *adv* (*specifically*) especialmente; (*on purpose*) a propósito

specialty ['speʃəltɪ] *n US* = **speciality**

species ['spiːʃiːz] *n* (*pl* **species**) especie *f*

specific [spɪ'sɪfɪk] *adj* específico(a); (*definite*) concreto(a); (*precise*) preciso(a); **to be s.** concretar

specifically [spɪ'sɪfɪklɪ] *adv* (*exactly*) específicamente; (*expressly*) expresamente; (*namely*) en concreto

specifications [spesɪfɪ'keɪʃənz] *npl* datos específicos

specify ['spesɪfaɪ] *vt* especificar, precisar

specimen ['spesɪmɪn] *n* (*sample*) muestra *f*; (*example*) ejemplar *m*; **urine/tissue s.** espécimen de orina/tejido

speck [spek] *n* (*of dust*) mota *f*; (*stain*) manchita *f*; (*small trace*) pizca *f*

speckled ['spekəld] *adj* moteado(a)

specs [speks] *npl Fam* (*spectacles*) gafas *fpl*

spectacle ['spektəkəl] *n* (**a**) (*display*) espectáculo *m* (**b**) **spectacles** (*glasses*) gafas *fpl, Am* lentes *mpl*, anteojos *mpl*

spectacular [spek'tækjʊlə(r)] **1** *adj* espectacular, impresionante

2 *n Cin & TV* (gran) espectáculo *m*

spectator [spek'teɪtə(r)] *n* espectador(a) *m,f*

spectre, *US* **specter** ['spektə(r)] *n* espectro *m*, fantasma *m*

spectrum ['spektrəm] *n* espectro *m*

speculate ['spekjʊleɪt] *vi* especular

speculation [spekjʊ'leɪʃən] *n* especulación *f*

sped [sped] *pt & pp of* speed

speech [spiːtʃ] *n* (**a**) (*faculty*) habla *f*; (*pronunciation*) pronunciación *f*; **freedom of s.** libertad *f* de expresión (**b**) (*address*) discurso *m*; **to give a s.** pronunciar un discurso (**c**) *Ling* **part of s.** parte *f* de la oración

speechless ['spiːtʃlɪs] *adj* mudo(a), boquiabierto(a)

speed [spiːd] **1** *n* velocidad *f*; (*rapidity*)

rapidez *f*; **at top s.** a toda velocidad; **s. limit** límite *m* de velocidad

  2 *vi* (**a**) (*pt & pp* **sped**) (*go fast*) ir corriendo; (*hurry*) apresurarse; **to s. along** (*car etc*) ir a toda velocidad; **to s. past** (*exceed speed limit*) conducir con exceso de velocidad

▸ **speed up 1** *vt sep* acelerar; (*person*) meter prisa a

  2 *vi* (*person*) darse prisa

speedboat ['spiːdbəʊt] *n* lancha rápida

speeding ['spiːdɪŋ] *n* exceso *m* de velocidad

speedometer [spɪˈdɒmɪtə(r)] *n* velocímetro *m*

speedway ['spiːdweɪ] *n* (**a**) (*racing*) carreras *fpl* de motos (**b**) (*track*) pista *f* de carreras

speedy ['spiːdɪ] *adj* (**speedier, speediest**) veloz, rápido(a)

spell¹ [spel] **1** *vt* (*pt & pp* **spelt** *or* **spelled**) (*letter by letter*) deletrear; *Fig* (*denote*) significar; **how do you s. your name?** ¿cómo se escribe su nombre?

  2 *vi* **she can't s.** comete faltas de ortografía

▸ **spell out** *vt sep Fig* explicar con detalle

spell² [spel] *n* (*magical*) hechizo *m*, encanto *m*

spell³ [spel] *n* (**a**) (*period*) período *m*; (*short period*) rato *m*; *Met* **cold s.** ola *f* de frío (**b**) (*shift*) turno *m*

spellbound ['spelbaʊnd] *adj* hechizado(a), embelesado(a)

spelling ['spelɪŋ] *n* ortografía *f*

spelt [spelt] *pt & pp of* **spell**

spend [spend] *vt* (*pt & pp* **spent**) (**a**) (*money*) gastar (**on** en) (**b**) (*time*) pasar; **to s. time on sth** dedicar tiempo a algo

spending ['spendɪŋ] *n* -gastos *mpl*; **s. money** dinero *m* de bolsillo; **s. power** poder adquisitivo

spendthrift ['spendθrɪft] *adj & n* derrochador(a) (*m,f*)

spent [spent] **1** *adj* gastado(a)

  2 *pt & pp of* **spend**

sperm [spɜːm] *n* esperma *m*; **s. bank** banco *m* de esperma; **s. whale** cachalote *m*

spew [spjuː] *vt* **to s. (up)** vomitar

sphere [sfɪə(r)] *n* esfera *f*

spice [spaɪs] **1** *n* (**a**) especia *f* (**b**) *Fig* sal *f*

  2 *vt* (**a**) *Culin* sazonar (**b**) **to s. (up)** (*story etc*) salpimentar

spick-and-span [spɪkənˈspæn] *adj* (*very clean*) limpísimo(a); (*well-groomed*) acicalado(a)

spicy ['spaɪsɪ] *adj* (**spicier, spiciest**) (**a**) *Culin* sazonado(a); (*hot*) picante (**b**) *Fig* (*story etc*) picante

spider ['spaɪdə(r)] *n* araña *f*; **s.'s web** telaraña *f*

spike¹ [spaɪk] *n* (*sharp point*) punta *f*; (*metal rod*) pincho *m*; (*on railing*) barrote *m*; *Sport* (*on shoes*) clavo *m*

spike² [spaɪk] *n Bot* espiga *f*

spiky ['spaɪkɪ] *adj* (**spikier, spikiest**) puntiagudo(a); (*hairstyle*) de punta

spill [spɪl] **1** *vt* (*pt & pp* **spilled** *or* **spilt** [spɪlt]) derramar

  2 *vi* (*liquid*) derramarse

▸ **spill over** *vi* desbordarse

spin [spɪn] **1** *vt* (*pt* **span** *or* **spun**; *pp* **spun**) (**a**) (*wheel etc*) hacer girar; (*washing*) centrifugar (**b**) (*cotton, wool*) hilar; (*spider's web*) tejer

  2 *vi* (*wheel etc*) girar; *Av* caer en barrena; *Aut* patinar

  3 *n* (**a**) (*turn*) vuelta *f*, giro *m* (**b**) *Sport* efecto *m* (**c**) *Av* barrena *f*; *Aut* patinazo *m* (**d**) *Br* **to go for a s.** (*ride*) dar una vuelta (**e**) *Pol* (*on news story*) sesgo *m*; **s. doctor** asesor(a) *m,f* político(a) (*para dar buena prensa a un partido o político*)

spinach ['spɪnɪtʃ] *n* espinacas *fpl*

spinal ['spaɪnəl] *adj* espinal, vertebral; **s. column** columna *f* vertebral; **s. cord** médula *f* espinal

spindly ['spɪndlɪ] *adj* (**spindlier, spindliest**) *Fam* (*long-bodied*) larguirucho(a); (*long-legged*) zanquilargo(a)

spin-dryer [spɪnˈdraɪə(r)] *n* secador centrífugo

spine [spaɪn] *n* (**a**) *Anat* columna *f* vertebral, espinazo *m*; (*of book*) lomo *m* (**b**) *Zool* púa *f*; *Bot* espina *f*

spineless ['spaɪnlɪs] *adj Fig* (*weak*) sin carácter

spinning ['spɪnɪŋ] *n* (**a**) (*of cotton etc*) (*act*) hilado *m*; (*art*) hilandería *f*; **s. wheel** rueca *f* (**b**) **s. top** peonza *f*

spin-off ['spɪnɒf] *n* (*by-product*) derivado *m*; *Fig* efecto secundario

spinster ['spɪnstə(r)] *n* soltera *f*

spiral ['spaɪərəl] **1** *n* espiral *f*

  2 *adj* en espiral; **s. staircase** escalera *f* de caracol

spirit¹ ['spɪrɪt] *n* (**a**) (*soul*) espíritu *m*, alma *f*; (*ghost*) fantasma *m* (**b**) (*attitude*) espíritu *m*; (*mood*) humor *m*; **to take sth in the right s.** tomar algo a bien; **community s.** civismo *m* (**c**) (*courage*) valor *m*; (*liveliness*) ánimo *m*; (*vitality*) vigor *m*; **to break sb's s.** quebrar la voluntad de algn (**d**) **spirits** (*mood*) humor *m*; **to be in**

good spirits estar de buen humor; **to be in high/low spirits** estar muy animado/ desanimado

spirit² ['spɪrɪt] n (a) Chem alcohol m; **s. level** nivel m de aire (b) **spirits** (alcoholic drinks) licores mpl

spirited ['spɪrɪtɪd] adj (person, attempt) valiente; (horse) fogoso(a); (attack) enérgico(a)

spiritual ['spɪrɪtjʊəl] adj espiritual

spit¹ [spɪt] **1** vt (pt & pp **spat**) escupir
2 vi escupir; Fam **he's the spitting image of his father** es el vivo retrato de su padre
3 n (saliva) saliva f

spit² [spɪt] n Culin asador m

spite [spaɪt] **1** n (a) (ill will) rencor m, ojeriza f (b) **in s. of** a pesar de, pese a; **in s. of the fact that** a pesar de que, pese a que
2 vt (annoy) fastidiar

spiteful ['spaɪtfʊl] adj (person) rencoroso(a); (remark) malévolo(a); (tongue) viperino(a)

spittle ['spɪtəl] n saliva f

spittoon [spɪ'tuːn] n escupidera f

splash [splæʃ] **1** vt salpicar
2 vi (a) **to s. (about)** (in water) chapotear (b) (water etc) salpicar
3 n (a) (noise) chapoteo m (b) (spray) salpicadura f; Fig (of colour) mancha f
▶ **splash out** vi Fam tirar la casa por la ventana

spleen [spliːn] n Anat bazo m

splendid ['splendɪd] adj espléndido(a)

splendour, US **splendor** ['splendə(r)] n esplendor m

splint [splɪnt] n tablilla f

splinter ['splɪntə(r)] **1** n (wood) astilla f; (bone, stone) esquirla f; (glass) fragmento m; **s. group** grupo m disidente
2 vi (a) (wood etc) astillarse (b) Pol escindirse

split [splɪt] **1** n (a) (crack) grieta f, hendidura f; (tear) desgarrón m; Fig (division) cisma m; Pol escisión f (b) **to do the splits** abrir las piernas en cruz
2 adj partido(a); **in a s. second** en una fracción de segundo; **s. personality** desdoblamiento m de personalidad
3 vt (pt & pp **split**) (a) (crack) agrietar; (cut) partir; (tear) rajar; (atom) desintegrar; Fig **to s. hairs** buscarle tres pies al gato (b) (divide) dividir (c) (share out) repartir (d) Pol escindir
4 vi (a) (crack) agrietarse; (into two parts) partirse; (garment) rajarse (b) (divide) dividirse (c) Pol escindirse
▶ **split up 1** vt sep (break up) partir; (divide

up) dividir; (share out) repartir
2 vi (couple) separarse

splutter ['splʌtə(r)] vi (person) balbucear; (candle, fat) chisporrotear; (engine) petardear

spoil [spɔɪl] **1** vt (pt & pp **spoiled** or **spoilt**) (a) (ruin) estropear, echar a perder (b) (child) mimar a; **to be spoilt for choice** tener demasiadas cosas para elegir
2 vi (food) estropearse

spoilsport ['spɔɪlspɔːt] n Fam aguafiestas mf inv

spoilt [spɔɪlt] **1** adj (a) (food, merchandise) estropeado(a) (b) (child) mimado(a)
2 pt & pp of **spoil**

spoke¹ [spəʊk] pt of **speak**

spoke² [spəʊk] n (of wheel) radio m, rayo m

spoken ['spəʊkən] pp of **speak**

spokesman ['spəʊksmən] n portavoz m

spokeswoman ['spəʊkswʊmən] n portavoz f

sponge [spʌndʒ] **1** n esponja f; Fig **to throw in the s.** arrojar la toalla; Br **s. cake** bizcocho m
2 vt (wash) lavar con esponja
3 vi Fam vivir de gorra
▶ **sponge off, sponge on** vt insep vivir a costa de

spongy ['spʌndʒɪ] adj (**spongier, spongiest**) esponjoso(a)

sponsor ['spɒnsə(r)] **1** vt patrocinar; Fin avalar; (support) respaldar
2 n patrocinador(a) m,f; Fin avalador(a) m,f

sponsorship ['spɒnsəʃɪp] n patrocinio m; Fin aval m; (support) respaldo m

spontaneous [spɒn'teɪnɪəs] adj espontáneo(a)

spoof [spuːf] n Fam (a) (parody) burla f (b) (hoax) engaño m

spooky ['spuːkɪ] adj (**spookier, spookiest**) Fam espeluznante

spool [spuːl] n bobina f, carrete m

spoon [spuːn] **1** n cuchara f; (small) cucharita f
2 vt sacar con cuchara; (serve) servir con cuchara

spoon-feed ['spuːnfiːd] vt (baby) dar de comer con cuchara a; Fig (spoil) mimar

spoonful ['spuːnfʊl] n cucharada f

sporadic [spə'rædɪk] adj esporádico(a)

sport [spɔːt] **1** n (a) deporte m (b) Fam **he's a good s.** es buena persona; **be a s.!** ¡sé amable!
2 vt (display) lucir

sporting ['spɔːtɪŋ] adj deportivo(a)

sports [spɔːts] **1** *npl* deportes *mpl*, deporte *m*
2 *adj* **s. car** coche deportivo; **s. jacket** chaqueta *f* (de) sport

sportsman [ˈspɔːtsmən] *n* deportista *m*

sportsmanlike [ˈspɔːtsmənlaɪk] *adj* deportivo(a)

sportsmanship [ˈspɔːtsmənʃɪp] *n* deportividad *f*

sportswear [ˈspɔːtsweə(r)] *n* (for sport) ropa *f* de deporte; (casual clothes) ropa (de) sport

sportswoman [ˈspɔːtswʊmən] *n* deportista *f*

sporty [ˈspɔːtɪ] *adj* (**sportier, sportiest**) *Fam* deportivo(a)

spot [spɒt] **1** *n* (a) (dot) punto *m*; (on fabric) lunar *m*
(b) (stain) mancha *f*
(c) (pimple) grano *m*
(d) (place) sitio *m*, lugar *m*; **on the s.** (person) allí, presente; **to decide sth on the s.** decidir algo en el acto; **s. check** chequeo rápido; *Fig* **weak s.** punto débil; **to be in a tight s.** estar en un apuro; **to put sb on the s.** poner a algn en un aprieto
(e) *Fam (small amount)* poquito *m*; **a s. of bother** unos problemillas
(f) *Rad, TV & Th (in show)* espacio *m*; (advertisement) spot *m*, anuncio *m*
2 *vt* (notice) darse cuenta de, notar; (see) ver

spotless [ˈspɒtlɪs] *adj (very clean)* impecable; *Fig (reputation etc)* intachable

spotlight [ˈspɒtlaɪt] *n* foco *m*; *Aut* faro *m* auxiliar; *Fig* **to be in the s.** ser objeto de la atención pública

spot-on [spɒtˈɒn] *adj Fam* exacto(a)

spotted [ˈspɒtɪd] *adj (with dots)* con puntos; (fabric) con lunares; (speckled) moteado(a)

spotty [ˈspɒtɪ] *adj* (**spottier, spottiest**) *Pej* con granos

spouse [spaʊs] *n* cónyuge *mf*

spout [spaʊt] **1** *n* (of jug) pico *m*; (of teapot) pitorro *m*
2 *vt Fam (nonsense)* soltar
3 *vi* **to s. out/up** (liquid) brotar

sprain [spreɪn] **1** *n* esguince *m*
2 *vt* torcer; **to s. one's ankle** torcerse el tobillo

sprang [spræŋ] *pt of* spring

sprawl [sprɔːl] **1** *vi* (a) (sit, lie) tumbarse
(b) (city, plant) extenderse
2 *n* (of city) extensión *f*

spray¹ [spreɪ] **1** *n* (a) (of water) rociada *f*, (from sea) espuma *f*, (from aerosol) pulverización *f* (b) (aerosol) spray *m*; (for plants) pulverizador *m*; **s. can** aerosol *m*
2 *vt* (water) rociar; (insecticide, perfume) pulverizar

spray² [spreɪ] *n* (of flowers) ramita *f*

spread [spred] **1** *n* (a) extensión *f*; (of ideas) difusión *f*; (of disease, fire) propagación *f*; (of terrorism) generalización *f*
(b) (range) gama *f*
(c) (of wings) envergadura *f*
(d) (for bread) pasta *f*; **cheese s.** queso *m* para untar
(e) *Fam (large meal)* banquetazo *m*
(f) *Press* **full-page s.** plana entera; **two-page s.** doble página *f*
2 *vt* (pt & pp **spread**) (a) (unfold) desplegar; (lay out) extender; *Fig* **to s. one's wings** desplegar las alas
(b) (butter etc) untar
(c) (news) difundir; (rumour) hacer correr; (disease, fire) propagar; (panic) sembrar
3 *vi* (a) (stretch out) extenderse; (unfold) desplegarse
(b) (news) difundirse; (rumour) correr; (disease) propagarse

spread-eagled [spredˈiːɡəld] *adj* despatarrado(a)

spreadsheet [ˈspredʃiːt] *n Comput* hoja *f* de cálculo

spree [spriː] *n* juerga *f*; **to go on a s.** ir de juerga

sprig [sprɪɡ] *n* ramita *f*

sprightly [ˈspraɪtlɪ] *adj* (**sprightlier, sprightliest**) (nimble) ágil; (energetic) enérgico(a); (lively) animado(a)

spring¹ [sprɪŋ] **1** *n* (season) primavera *f*
2 *adj* primaveral; **s. onion** cebolleta *f*; **s. roll** rollo *m* de primavera

spring² [sprɪŋ] **1** *n* (a) (of water) manantial *m*, fuente *f* (b) (of watch etc) resorte *m*; (of mattress) muelle *m*; *Aut* ballesta *f*
2 *vi* (pt **sprang**; pp **sprung**) (a) (jump) saltar; **the lid sprang open** la tapa se abrió de golpe (b) (appear) aparecer (de repente)
3 *vt* (a) **to s. a leak** hacer agua (b) *Fig (news, surprise)* dar de golpe
▸**spring up** *vi* aparecer; (plants) brotar; (buildings) elevarse; (problems) surgir

springboard [ˈsprɪŋbɔːd] *n* trampolín *m*

spring-clean [sprɪŋˈkliːn] *vt* limpiar a fondo

springtime [ˈsprɪŋtaɪm] *n* primavera *f*

springy [ˈsprɪŋɪ] *adj* (**springier, springiest**) (bouncy) elástico(a); *Fig (step)* saltarín

sprinkle [ˈsprɪŋkəl] *vt (with water)* rociar

(**with** de); *(with sugar)* espolvorear (**with** de)

sprint [sprɪnt] **1** *n* esprint *m*
 2 *vi* esprintar

sprinter ['sprɪntə(r)] *n* esprínter *mf*, velocista *mf*

sprout [spraʊt] **1** *vi (bud)* brotar; *Fig* crecer rápidamente
 2 *n* (**Brussels**) **sprouts** coles *fpl* de Bruselas

spruce¹ [spruːs] *n Bot* picea *f*

spruce² [spruːs] *adj (neat)* pulcro(a); *(smart)* apuesto(a)
 ▶ **spruce up** *vt sep* acicalar

sprung [sprʌŋ] *pp of* **spring**

spry [spraɪ] *adj* (**sprier**, **spriest**) *(nimble)* ágil; *(active)* activo(a); *(lively)* vivaz

spun [spʌn] *pt & pp of* **spin**

spur [spɜː(r)] **1** *n* (**a**) *(stimulus)* acicate *m*; **on the s. of the moment** sin pensarlo
 2 *vt* (**a**) *(horse)* espolear (**b**) *Fig* incitar

spurious ['spjʊərɪəs] *adj* falso(a), espurio(a)

spurn [spɜːn] *vt Fml* desdeñar, rechazar

spurt [spɜːt] **1** *n* (**a**) *(of liquid)* chorro *m* (**b**) *Fig (of activity etc)* racha *f*; *(effort)* esfuerzo *m*
 2 *vi* (**a**) *(liquid)* chorrear (**b**) *(make an effort)* hacer un último esfuerzo; *(accelerate)* acelerar

spy [spaɪ] **1** *n* espía *mf*
 2 *vt Fml (see)* divisar
 3 *vi* espiar (**on** a)

spyhole ['spaɪhəʊl] *n* mirilla *f*

spying ['spaɪɪŋ] *n* espionaje *m*

squabble ['skwɒbəl] **1** *n* riña *f*, pelea *f*
 2 *vi* reñir, pelearse (**over** *or* **about** por)

squad [skwɒd] *n Mil* pelotón *m*; *(of police)* brigada *f*; *Sport* equipo *m*; **drugs s.** brigada antidroga

squadron ['skwɒdrən] *n Mil* escuadrón *m*; *Av* escuadrilla *f*; *Naut* escuadra *f*

squalid ['skwɒlɪd] *adj (very dirty)* asqueroso(a); *(poor)* miserable; *(motive)* vil

squall¹ [skwɔːl] *n (wind)* ráfaga *f*

squall² [skwɔːl] *vi* chillar, berrear

squalor ['skwɒlə(r)] *n (dirtiness)* mugre *f*; *(poverty)* miseria *f*

squander ['skwɒndə(r)] *vt (money)* derrochar, despilfarrar; *(time)* desperdiciar

square [skweə(r)] **1** *n* (**a**) *(shape)* cuadro *m*; *(on chessboard, crossword)* casilla *f*; *Fig* **we're back to s. one!** ¡volvemos a partir desde cero!
 (**b**) *(in town)* plaza *f*
 (**c**) *Math* cuadrado *m*
 2 *adj* (**a**) *(in shape)* cuadrado(a)

(**b**) *Math* cuadrado(a); **s. metre** metro cuadrado; **s. root** raíz cuadrada
 (**c**) *Fam (fair)* justo(a); **to be s. with sb** *(honest)* ser franco(a) con algn
 (**d**) **a s. meal** una buena comida
 (**e**) *(old-fashioned)* carroza; *(conservative)* carca
 3 *vt* (**a**) *(make square)* cuadrar; **to s. one's shoulders** sacar el pecho
 (**b**) *Math* elevar al cuadrado
 (**c**) *(settle)* arreglar
 4 *vi (agree)* cuadrar (**with** con)

squarely ['skweəlɪ] *adv (directly)* directamente, de lleno

squash¹ [skwɒʃ] **1** *n Br (drink)* concentrado *m*
 2 *vt* (**a**) *(crush)* aplastar (**b**) *Fig (objection)* echar por tierra
 3 *vi (crush)* aplastarse

squash² [skwɒʃ] *n Sport* squash *m*

squash³ [skwɒʃ] *n US (vegetable)* calabacín *m*

squat [skwɒt] **1** *adj (person)* rechoncho(a)
 2 *vi* (**a**) *(crouch)* agacharse, sentarse en cuclillas (**b**) *(in building)* ocupar ilegalmente
 3 *n (building)* edificio *m* ocupado ilegalmente

squatter ['skwɒtə(r)] *n* ocupante *mf* ilegal, okupa *mf*

squawk [skwɔːk] **1** *n* graznido *m*
 2 *vi* graznar

squeak [skwiːk] **1** *n (of mouse)* chillido *m*; *(of hinge, wheel)* chirrido *m*; *(of shoes)* crujido *m*
 2 *vi (mouse)* chillar; *(hinge, wheel)* chirriar, rechinar; *(shoes)* crujir

squeaky ['skwiːkɪ] *adj* (**squeakier**, **squeakiest**) *(hinge)* chirriante; *(voice)* chillón(ona); *(shoes)* que crujen

squeal [skwiːl] **1** *n (of animal, person)* chillido *m*
 2 *vi* (**a**) *(animal, person)* chillar (**b**) *Fam (inform)* chivarse

squeamish ['skwiːmɪʃ] *adj* muy sensible

squeeze [skwiːz] **1** *vt* apretar; *(lemon etc)* exprimir; *(sponge)* estrujar; **to s. paste out of a tube** sacar pasta de un tubo apretando
 2 *vi* **to s. in** apretujarse
 3 *n* (**a**) *(pressure)* estrujón *m*; **a s. of lemon** unas gotas de limón (**b**) *(of hand)* apretón *m*; *(hug)* abrazo *m*; *(crush)* apiñamiento *m*; **credit s.** reducción *f* de créditos

squelch [skweltʃ] *vi* chapotear

squid [skwɪd] *n* calamar *m*; *(small)* chipirón *m*

squiggle [ˈskwɪɡəl] *n* garabato *m*

squint [skwɪnt] **1** *n* (a) bizquera *f*; **to have a s.** ser bizco(a) (b) *Fig (quick look)* vistazo *m*

2 *vi* (a) ser bizco(a) (b) **to s. at sth** *(glance)* echar un vistazo a algo; *(with eyes half-closed)* mirar algo con los ojos entrecerrados

squirm [skwɜːm] *vi* retorcerse; *Fig (feel embarrassed)* sentirse incómodo(a)

squirrel [ˈskwɪrəl] *n* ardilla *f*

squirt [skwɜːt] **1** *n (of liquid)* chorro *m*

2 *vt* lanzar a chorro

3 *vi* **to s. out** salir a chorros

Sr *(abbr Senior)* Thomas Smith, Sr Thomas Smith, padre

Sri Lanka [sriːˈlæŋkə] *n* Sri Lanka

St (a) *(abbr Saint)* S./Sto./Sta. (b) *(abbr Street)* c/

st *Br (abbr stone)* = peso que equivale a 6,348 kg

stab [stæb] **1** *n (with knife)* puñalada *f*; *(of pain)* punzada *f*; *Fam Fig* **to have a s. at doing sth** intentar hacer algo

2 *vt* apuñalar

stabbing [ˈstæbɪŋ] *adj (pain)* punzante

stability [stəˈbɪlɪtɪ] *n* estabilidad *f*

stable¹ [ˈsteɪbəl] *adj* estable

stable² [ˈsteɪbəl] *n* cuadra *f*, caballeriza *f*

stack [stæk] **1** *n (pile)* montón *m*; *Fam* **he's got stacks of money** está forrado

2 *vt (pile up)* amontonar, apilar; *Fig* **the odds are stacked against us** todo está en contra nuestra

stadium [ˈsteɪdɪəm] *n* estadio *m*

staff [stɑːf] **1** *n* (a) *(personnel)* personal *m*; *Mil* estado *m* mayor; **s. meeting** claustro *m*; *Br* **s. nurse** enfermera cualificada (b) *(stick)* bastón *m*; *(of shepherd)* cayado *m*

2 *vt* proveer de personal

staffroom [ˈstɑːfruːm] *n* sala *f* de profesores

stag [stæg] *n* ciervo *m*, venado *m*; *Fam* **s. party** despedida *f* de soltero

stage [steɪdʒ] **1** *n* (a) *(platform)* plataforma *f* (b) *(in theatre)* escenario *m*; **s. door** entrada *f* de artistas; **s. fright** miedo escénico; **s. manager** director(a) *m,f* de escena (c) *(phase) (of development, journey, rocket)* etapa *f*; *(of road, pipeline)* tramo *m*; **at this s. of the negotiations** a estas alturas de las negociaciones; **in stages** por etapas

2 *vt* (a) *(play)* poner en escena, montar (b) *(arrange)* organizar; *(carry out)* llevar a cabo

stagecoach [ˈsteɪdʒkəʊtʃ] *n* diligencia *f*

stagger [ˈstæɡə(r)] **1** *vi* tambalearse

2 *vt* (a) *(amaze)* asombrar (b) *(hours, work)* escalonar

staggering [ˈstæɡərɪŋ] *adj* asombroso(a)

stagnant [ˈstæɡnənt] *adj* estancado(a)

stagnate [stæɡˈneɪt] *vi* estancarse

staid [steɪd] *adj (person)* conservador(a); *(manner, clothes)* serio(a), formal

stain [steɪn] **1** *n* (a) mancha *f*; **s. remover** quitamanchas *m inv* (b) *(dye)* tinte *m*

2 *vt* (a) manchar (b) *(dye)* teñir

3 *vi* mancharse

stained [steɪnd] *adj* **s. glass window** vidriera *f* de colores

stainless [ˈsteɪnlɪs] *adj (steel)* inoxidable

stair [steə(r)] *n* escalón *m*, peldaño *m*; **stairs** escalera *f*

staircase [ˈsteəkeɪs] *n* escalera *f*

stake¹ [steɪk] **1** *n (stick)* estaca *f*; *(for plant)* rodrigón *m*; *(post)* poste *m*

2 *vt* **to s. (out)** cercar con estacas

stake² [steɪk] **1** *n* (a) *(bet)* apuesta *f*; **the issue is at s.** el tema en cuestión; **to be at s.** *(at risk)* estar en juego (b) *(investment)* interés *m*

2 *vt (bet)* apostar; *(invest)* invertir; **to s. a claim to sth** reivindicar algo

stale [steɪl] *adj (food)* pasado(a); *(bread)* duro(a)

stalemate [ˈsteɪlmeɪt] *n (in chess)* tablas *fpl*; *Fig* **to reach s.** llegar a un punto muerto

stalk¹ [stɔːk] *n (of plant)* tallo *m*; *(of fruit)* rabo *m*

stalk² [stɔːk] **1** *vt (of hunter)* cazar al acecho; *(of animal)* acechar

2 *vi* **he stalked out** salió airado

stall¹ [stɔːl] **1** *n* (a) *(in market)* puesto *m*; *(at fair)* caseta *f* (b) *(stable)* establo *m*; *(stable compartment)* casilla *f* de establo (c) *Br Th* **stalls** platea *f*

2 *vt Aut* calar

3 *vi Aut* calarse; *Av* perder velocidad

stall² [stɔːl] *vi* **to s. (for time)** intentar ganar tiempo

stallion [ˈstæljən] *n* semental *m*

stalwart [ˈstɔːlwət] *n* incondicional *mf*

stamina [ˈstæmɪnə] *n* resistencia *f*

stammer [ˈstæmə(r)] **1** *n* tartamudeo *m*

2 *vi* tartamudear

stamp [stæmp] **1** *n* (a) *(postage stamp)* sello *m*; **s. album** álbum *m* de sellos; **s. collector** filatelista *mf*; *Br* **s. duty** póliza *f* (b) *(rubber stamp)* tampón *m*; *(for metals)* cuño *m* (c) *(with foot)* patada *f*

2 *vt* (a) *(with postage stamp)* poner el sello a; *Br* **stamped addressed envelope,**

US **self-addressed stamped envelope** sobre franqueado con la dirección del remitente (**b**) *(with rubber stamp)* sellar (**c**) **to s. one's feet** patear; *(in dancing)* zapatear

3 *vi* patear

🖉 Note that the Spanish word **estampa** is a false friend and is never a translation for the English word **stamp**. In Spanish, **estampa** means "print, image".

▸ **stamp out** *vt sep Fig (racism etc)* acabar con; *(rebellion)* sofocar

stampede [stæm'pi:d] **1** *n* estampida *f*; *Fig (rush)* desbandada *f*

2 *vi* desbandarse; *Fig (rush)* precipitarse

stance [stæns] *n* postura *f*

stand [stænd] **1** *n* (**a**) *(position)* posición *f*, postura *f*; **to make a s.** resistir

(**b**) *(of lamp, sculpture)* pie *m*

(**c**) *(market stall)* puesto *m*; *(at fair)* caseta *f*; *(at exhibition)* stand *m*; **newspaper s.** quiosco *m*

(**d**) *(platform)* plataforma *f*; *(in stadium)* tribuna *f*; *US (witness box)* estrado *m*

2 *vt (pt & pp stood)* (**a**) *(place)* poner, colocar

(**b**) *(tolerate)* aguantar, soportar

(**c**) **to s. one's ground** mantenerse firme

3 *vi* (**a**) *(be upright)* estar de pie; *(get up)* levantarse; *(remain upright)* quedarse de pie; **s. still!** ¡estáte quieto(a)!

(**b**) *(measure)* medir

(**c**) *(be situated)* estar, encontrarse

(**d**) *(remain unchanged)* permanecer

(**e**) *(remain valid)* seguir vigente

(**f**) **as things s.** tal como están las cosas

(**g**) *Pol* presentarse

▸ **stand back** *vi (allow sb to pass)* abrir paso

▸ **stand by 1** *vi* (**a**) *(do nothing)* quedarse sin hacer nada (**b**) *(be ready)* estar listo(a)

2 *vt insep (person)* apoyar a; *(promise)* cumplir con; *(decision)* atenerse a

▸ **stand down** *vi Fig* retirarse

▸ **stand for** *vt insep* (**a**) *(mean)* significar (**b**) *(represent)* representar (**c**) *(tolerate)* aguantar

▸ **stand in** *vi* sustituir

▸ **stand in for** *vt insep* sustituir

▸ **stand out** *vi (mountain etc)* destacarse (**against** contra); *Fig (person)* destacar

▸ **stand up** *vi (get up)* ponerse de pie; *(be standing)* estar de pie; *Fig* **it will s. up to wear and tear** es muy resistente; *Fig* **to s. up for sb** defender a algn; *Fig* **to s. up to sb** hacer frente a algn

standard ['stændəd] **1** *n* (**a**) *(level)* nivel *m*; **s. of living** nivel de vida (**b**) *(criterion)* criterio *m* (**c**) *(norm)* norma *f*, estándar *m* (**d**) *(flag)* estandarte *m*

2 *adj* normal, estándar; **s. lamp** lámpara *f* de pie

standardize ['stændədaɪz] *vt* normalizar

standby ['stændbaɪ] *n* (**a**) *(thing)* recurso *m* (**b**) *(person)* suplente *mf*; **to be on s.** *Mil* estar de retén; *Av* estar en la lista de espera; **s. ticket** billete *m* sin reserva

stand-in ['stændɪn] *n* suplente *mf*; *Cin* doble *mf*

standing ['stændɪŋ] **1** *adj* (**a**) *(not sitting)* de pie; *(upright)* recto(a); **to give sb a s. ovation** ovacionar a algn de pie; **there was s. room only** no quedaban asientos (**b**) *(committee)* permanente; *(invitation)* permanente; *Br* **s. order** pago fijo

2 *n* (**a**) *(social position)* rango *m* (**b**) *(duration)* duración *f*; *(in job)* antigüedad *f*

stand-offish [stænd'ɒfɪʃ] *adj Fam* distante

standpoint ['stændpɔɪnt] *n* punto *m* de vista

standstill ['stændstɪl] *n* **at a s.** *(car, traffic)* parado(a); *(industry)* paralizado(a); **to come to a s.** *(car, traffic)* pararse; *(industry)* paralizarse

stand-up ['stændʌp] *adj* **s. comic** *or* **comedian** = humorista que basa su actuación en contar chistes al público solo desde el escenario

stank [stæŋk] *pt of* **stink**

staple¹ ['steɪpəl] **1** *n (fastener)* grapa *f*

2 *vt* grapar

staple² ['steɪpəl] **1** *adj (food)* básico(a); *(product)* de primera necesidad

2 *n (food)* alimento básico

stapler ['steɪpələ(r)] *n* grapadora *f*

star [stɑː(r)] **1** *n* estrella *f*

2 *adj* estelar

3 *vt Cin* tener como protagonista a

4 *vi Cin* **to s. in a film** protagonizar una película

starboard ['stɑːbəd] *n* estribor *m*

starch [stɑːtʃ] **1** *n* almidón *m*

2 *vt* almidonar

stardom ['stɑːdəm] *n* estrellato *m*

stare [steə(r)] **1** *n* mirada fija

2 *vi* mirar fijamente

starfish ['stɑːfɪʃ] *n* estrella *f* de mar

stark [stɑːk] *adj (landscape)* desolado(a); *(décor)* austero(a); **the s. truth** la dura realidad; **s. poverty** la miseria

stark-naked ['stɑːkneɪkɪd] *adj Fam* en cueros

starling ['stɑːlɪŋ] *n* estornino *m*

starry ['stɑːrɪ] *adj* (**starrier, starriest**) estrellado(a)

starry-eyed [stɑːrɪ'aɪd] *adj* (*idealistic*) idealista; (*in love*) enamorado(a)

start [stɑːt] **1** *n* (**a**) (*beginning*) principio *m*, comienzo *m*; (*of race*) salida *f*; **at the s.** al principio; **for a s.** para empezar; **from the s.** desde el principio; **to make a fresh s.** volver a empezar

(**b**) (*advantage*) ventaja *f*

(**c**) (*jump*) sobresalto *m*

2 *vt* (**a**) (*begin*) empezar, comenzar; **to s. doing sth** empezar a hacer algo

(**b**) (*cause*) causar, provocar

(**c**) (*found*) fundar; **to s. a business** montar un negocio

(**d**) (*set in motion*) arrancar

3 *vi* (**a**) (*begin*) empezar, comenzar; (*engine*) arrancar; **starting from Monday** a partir del lunes

(**b**) (*take fright*) asustarse, sobresaltarse

▸ **start off** *vi* (**a**) (*begin*) empezar, comenzar; **to s. off by/with** empezar por/con

(**b**) (*leave*) salir, ponerse en camino

▸ **start up 1** *vt sep* (*engine*) arrancar

2 *vi* empezar; (*car*) arrancar

starter ['stɑːtə(r)] *n* (**a**) *Sport* (*official*) juez *mf* de salida; (*competitor*) competidor(a) *m,f* (**b**) *Aut* motor *m* de arranque (**c**) *Culin* entrada *f*

starting ['stɑːtɪŋ] *n* **s. block** taco *m* de salida; **s. point** punto *m* de partida; **s. post** línea *f* de salida

startle ['stɑːtəl] *vt* asustar

startling ['stɑːtlɪŋ] *adj* (**a**) (*frightening*) alarmante (**b**) (*news etc*) asombroso(a); (*coincidence*) extraordinario(a)

starvation [stɑː'veɪʃən] *n* hambre *f*

starve [stɑːv] **1** *vt* privar de comida; *Fig* **he was starved of affection** fue privado de cariño

2 *vi* pasar hambre; **to s. to death** morirse de hambre

starving ['stɑːvɪŋ] *adj* hambriento(a); *Fam* **I'm s.!** ¡estoy muerto(a) de hambre!

state [steɪt] **1** *n* (**a**) estado *m*; **s. of emergency** estado de emergencia; **s. of mind** estado de ánimo; **to be in no fit s. to do sth** no estar en condiciones de hacer algo

(**b**) **the States** los Estados Unidos; *US* **s. highway** ≃ carretera *f* nacional; *US* **the S. Department** el Ministerio de Asuntos Exteriores

2 *adj* (**a**) *Pol* estatal; **s. education** enseñanza pública; **s. ownership** propiedad *f* del Estado (**b**) (*ceremonial*) de gala; **s. visit** visita *f* oficial

3 *vt* declarar, afirmar; (*case*) exponer; (*problem*) plantear

stated ['steɪtɪd] *adj* indicado(a)

stately ['steɪtlɪ] *adj* (**statelier, stateliest**) majestuoso(a); **s. home** casa solariega

statement ['steɪtmənt] *n* (**a**) declaración *f*; **official s.** comunicado *m* oficial; *Jur* **to make a s.** prestar declaración (**b**) *Fin* estado *m* de cuenta; **monthly s.** balance *m* mensual

statesman ['steɪtsmən] *n* estadista *m*

static ['stætɪk] **1** *adj* estático(a)

2 *n Rad* ruido *m*

station ['steɪʃən] **1** *n* (**a**) estación *f*; *US* **s. wagon** camioneta *f* (**b**) (*position*) puesto *m* (**c**) (*social standing*) rango *m*

2 *vt* (*place*) colocar; *Mil* apostar

stationary ['steɪʃənərɪ] *adj* (*not moving*) inmóvil; (*unchanging*) estacionario(a)

stationer ['steɪʃənə(r)] *n* papelero(a) *m,f*; **s.'s (shop)** papelería *f*

stationery ['steɪʃənərɪ] *n* (*paper*) papel *m* de escribir; (*pens, ink etc*) artículos *mpl* de escritorio

stationmaster ['steɪʃənmɑːstə(r)] *n* jefe *m* de estación

statistic [stə'tɪstɪk] *n* estadística *f*

statistical [stə'tɪstɪkəl] *adj* estadístico(a)

statistics [stə'tɪstɪks] **1** *n sing* (*science*) estadística *f*

2 *npl* (*data*) estadísticas *fpl*

statue ['stætjuː] *n* estatua *f*

status ['steɪtəs] *n* estado *m*; **social s.** estatus *m*; **s. symbol** signo *m* de prestigio; **s. quo** status quo *m*

statute ['stætjuːt] *n* estatuto *m*

statutory ['stætjʊtərɪ] *adj* reglamentario(a); (*offence*) contemplado(a) por la ley; (*right*) legal; (*holiday*) oficial

staunch [stɔːntʃ] *adj* incondicional, acérrimo

stave [steɪv] *n Mus* pentagrama *m*

▸ **stave off** *vt sep* (*repel*) rechazar; (*avoid*) evitar; (*delay*) aplazar

stay¹ [steɪ] **1** *n* estancia *f*

2 *vi* (**a**) (*remain*) quedarse, permanecer (**b**) (*reside temporarily*) alojarse; **she's staying with us for a few days** ha venido a pasar unos días con nosotros

3 *vt Fig* **to s. the course** aguantar hasta el final; **staying power** resistencia *f*

▸ **stay in** *vi* quedarse en casa

▸ **stay on** *vi* quedarse

▸ **stay out** *vi* **to s. out all night** no volver a casa en toda la noche

▸ **stay up** *vi* no acostarse

stay² [steɪ] *n* (*rope*) estay *m*, viento *m*

stead [sted] *n* **in sb's s.** en lugar de algn; **to**

stand sb in good s. resultar muy útil a algn

steadfast ['stedfəst, 'stedfɑːst] *adj* firme

steadily ['stedɪlɪ] *adv (improve)* constantemente; *(walk)* con paso seguro; *(gaze)* fijamente; *(rain, work)* sin parar

steady ['stedɪ] **1** *adj* (**steadier, steadiest**) firme, seguro(a); *(gaze)* fijo(a); *(prices)* estable; *(demand, speed)* constante; *(pace)* regular; *(worker)* aplicado(a); **s. job** empleo fijo

2 *vt (table etc)* estabilizar; *(nerves)* calmar

3 *vi (market)* estabilizarse

steak [steɪk] *n* bistec *m*

steal [stiːl] (*pt* **stole**; *pp* **stolen**) **1** *vt* robar; **to s. a glance at sth** echar una mirada furtiva a algo; **to s. the show** llevarse todos los aplausos

2 *vi* (**a**) *(rob)* robar (**b**) *(move quietly)* moverse con sigilo; **to s. away** escabullirse

stealth [stelθ] *n* sigilo *m*

stealthily ['stelθɪlɪ] *adv* a hurtadillas

stealthy ['stelθɪ] *adj* (**stealthier, stealthiest**) sigiloso(a), furtivo(a)

steam [stiːm] **1** *n* vapor *m*; *Fam* **to let off s.** desahogarse; **s. engine** máquina *f* de vapor

2 *vt Culin* cocer al vapor

3 *vi (give off steam)* echar vapor; *(bowl of soup etc)* humear

▸ **steam up** *vi (window etc)* empañarse

steamer ['stiːmə(r)] *n Naut* vapor *m*

steamroller ['stiːmrəʊlə(r)] *n* apisonadora *f*

steamship ['stiːmʃɪp] *n* vapor *m*

steamy ['stiːmɪ] *adj* (**steamier, steamiest**) lleno(a) de vapor

steel [stiːl] **1** *n* acero *m*; **s. industry** industria siderúrgica

2 *vt Fig* **to s. oneself to do sth** armarse de valor para hacer algo

steelworks ['stiːlwɜːks] *npl* acería *f*

steep¹ [stiːp] *adj (hill etc)* empinado(a); *Fig (price, increase)* excesivo(a)

steep² [stiːp] *vt (washing)* remojar; *(food)* poner en remojo

steeple ['stiːpəl] *n* aguja *f*

steeplechase ['stiːpəltʃeɪs] *n* carrera *f* de obstáculos

steer [stɪə(r)] **1** *vt* dirigir; *(car)* conducir; *(ship)* gobernar

2 *vi (car)* conducirse; *Fig* **to s. clear of sth** evitar algo

steering ['stɪərɪŋ] *n* dirección *f*; **assisted s.** dirección asistida; **s. wheel** volante *m*

stem [stem] **1** *n* (**a**) *(of plant)* tallo *m*; *(of glass)* pie *m*; *(of pipe)* tubo *m* (**b**) *(of word)* raíz *f*

2 *vi* **to s. from** derivarse de

3 *vt (blood)* restañar; *(flood, attack)* contener

stench [stentʃ] *n* hedor *m*

stencil ['stensəl] *n* (**a**) *(for artwork etc)* plantilla *f* (**b**) *(for typing)* cliché *m*

step [step] **1** *n* (**a**) paso *m*; *(sound)* paso, pisada *f*; **s. by s.** poco a poco (**b**) *(measure)* medida *f*; **a s. in the right direction** un paso acertado (**c**) *(stair)* peldaño *m*, escalón *m* (**d**) **steps** escalera *f*

2 *vi* dar un paso; **s. this way, please** haga el favor de pasar por aquí; **to s. aside** apartarse

▸ **step down** *vi* dimitir

▸ **step forward** *vi (volunteer)* ofrecerse

▸ **step in** *vi* intervenir

▸ **step up** *vt sep* aumentar

stepbrother ['stepbrʌðə(r)] *n* hermanastro *m*

stepchild ['steptʃaɪld] *n* hijastro(a) *m,f*

stepdaughter ['stepdɔːtə(r)] *n* hijastra *f*

stepfather ['stepfɑːðə(r)] *n* padrastro *m*

stepladder ['steplædə(r)] *n* escalera *f* de tijera

stepmother ['stepmʌðə(r)] *n* madrastra *f*

stepping-stone ['stepɪŋstəʊn] *n* pasadera *f*; *Fig* trampolín *m*

stepsister ['stepsɪstə(r)] *n* hermanastra *f*

stepson ['stepsʌn] *n* hijastro *m*

stereo ['sterɪəʊ] **1** *n* estéreo *m*

2 *adj* estereo(fónico(a))

stereotype ['sterɪətaɪp] *n* estereotipo *m*

sterile ['steraɪl] *adj (barren)* estéril

sterilize ['sterɪlaɪz] *vt* esterilizar

sterling ['stɜːlɪŋ] **1** *n* libras *fpl* esterlinas; **s. silver** plata *f* de ley; **the pound s.** la libra esterlina

2 *adj (person, quality)* excelente

stern¹ [stɜːn] *adj (severe)* severo(a)

stern² [stɜːn] *n Naut* popa *f*

steroid ['sterɔɪd] *n* esteroide *m*

stethoscope ['steθəskəʊp] *n* estetoscopio *m*

stew [stjuː] **1** *n* estofado *m*, cocido *m*

2 *vt (meat)* guisar, estofar; *(fruit)* cocer

steward ['stjʊəd] *n (on estate)* administrador *m*; *(on ship)* camarero *m*; *(on plane)* auxiliar *m* de vuelo

stewardess ['stjʊədɪs] *n (on ship)* camarera *f*; *(on plane)* azafata *f*

stick¹ [stɪk] *n* (**a**) palo *m*; *(walking stick)* bastón *m*; *(of dynamite)* cartucho *m*; *Fam* **to give sb s.** dar caña a algn (**b**) *Fam* **to live in the sticks** vivir en el quinto pino

stick² [stɪk] **1** vt (pt & pp **stuck**) (**a**) (push) meter; (knife) clavar; **he stuck his head out of the window** asomó la cabeza por la ventana (**b**) Fam (put) meter (**c**) (with glue etc) pegar (**d**) Fam (tolerate) soportar, aguantar

2 vi (**a**) (become attached) pegarse (**b**) (window, drawer) atrancarse; (machine part) encasquillarse

▸ **stick at** vt insep perseverar en

▸ **stick by** vt insep (friend) ser fiel a; (promise) cumplir con

▸ **stick out 1** vi (project) sobresalir; (be noticeable) resaltar

2 vt sep (tongue) sacar; Fig **to s. one's neck out** jugarse el tipo

▸ **stick to** vt insep (principles) atenerse a

▸ **stick up 1** vi (project) sobresalir; (hair) ponerse de punta

2 vt sep (**a**) (poster) fijar (**b**) (hand etc) levantar

▸ **stick up for** vt insep defender

sticker ['stɪkə(r)] n (label) etiqueta adhesiva; (with slogan) pegatina f

sticking-plaster ['stɪkɪŋ'plɑːstə(r)] n Br tirita® f, Am curita f

stickler ['stɪklə(r)] n meticuloso(a) m,f; **to be a s. for detail** ser muy detallista

stick-up ['stɪkʌp] n US Fam atraco m, asalto m

sticky ['stɪkɪ] adj (**stickier**, **stickiest**) pegajoso(a); (label) engomado(a); (weather) bochornoso(a); Fam (situation) difícil

stiff [stɪf] **1** adj (**a**) rígido(a), tieso(a); (collar, lock) duro(a); (joint) entumecido(a); (machine part) atascado(a); **to have a s. neck** tener tortícolis (**b**) Fig (test) difícil; (punishment) severo(a); (price) excesivo(a); (drink) fuerte; (person) (unnatural) estirado(a)

2 n Fam (corpse) fiambre m

stiffen ['stɪfən] **1** vt (fabric) reforzar; (collar) almidonar; Fig (resistance) fortalecer

2 vi (person) ponerse tieso(a); (joints) entumecerse; Fig (resistance) fortalecerse

stiffness ['stɪfnɪs] n rigidez f

stifle ['staɪfəl] **1** vt sofocar; (yawn) reprimir

2 vi ahogarse, sofocarse

stifling ['staɪflɪŋ] adj sofocante, agobiante

stigma ['stɪgmə] n estigma m

stile [staɪl] n = escalones para pasar por encima de una valla

stiletto [stɪ'letəʊ] n zapato m con tacón de aguja

still¹ [stɪl] **1** adv (**a**) (up to this time) todavía, aún

(**b**) (with comp adj & adv) (even) aún; **s. colder** aún más frío

(**c**) (nonetheless) no obstante, con todo

(**d**) (however) sin embargo

(**e**) (motionless) quieto; **to stand s.** no moverse

2 adj (calm) tranquilo(a); (peaceful) sosegado(a); (silent) silencioso(a); (motionless) inmóvil

3 n Cin fotograma m; Art **s. life** naturaleza muerta

4 vt Fml (fears etc) calmar

still² [stɪl] n (apparatus) alambique m

stillborn ['stɪlbɔːn] adj nacido(a) muerto(a)

stillness ['stɪlnɪs] n calma f; (silence) silencio m

stilt [stɪlt] n zanco m

stilted ['stɪltɪd] adj afectado(a)

stimulant ['stɪmjʊlənt] n estimulante m

stimulate ['stɪmjʊleɪt] vt estimular

stimulating ['stɪmjʊleɪtɪŋ] adj estimulante

stimulus ['stɪmjʊləs] n (pl **stimuli** ['stɪmjʊlaɪ]) estímulo m; Fig incentivo m

sting [stɪŋ] **1** n (part of bee, wasp) aguijón m; (wound) picadura f; (burning) escozor m; Fig (of remorse) punzada f; Fig (of remark) sarcasmo m

2 vt (pt & pp **stung**) picar; Fig (conscience) remorder; Fig (remark) herir en lo vivo

3 vi picar

stingy ['stɪndʒɪ] adj (**stingier**, **stingiest**) Fam (person) tacaño(a); (amount) escaso(a); **to be s. with** escatimar

stink [stɪŋk] **1** n peste m, hedor m

2 vi (pt **stank** or **stunk**; pp **stunk**) apestar, heder (**of** a)

stinking ['stɪŋkɪŋ] **1** adj (smelly) apestoso(a); Fam **to have a s. cold** tener un catarro bestial

2 adv Fam **he's s. rich** está podrido de dinero

stint [stɪnt] **1** n (period) período m, temporada f; (shift) turno m; **he did a two-year s. in the navy** sirvió durante dos años en la Marina

2 vt escatimar

stipulate ['stɪpjʊleɪt] vt estipular

stipulation [stɪpjʊ'leɪʃən] n estipulación f

stir [stɜː(r)] **1** n Fig revuelo m

2 vt (**a**) (liquid) remover (**b**) (move) agitar (**c**) Fig (curiosity, interest) despertar; (anger) provocar

3 vi (move) rebullirse

▶**stir up** *vt sep Fig* (*memories, curiosity*) despertar; (*passions*) excitar; (*anger*) provocar; (*revolt*) fomentar

stirring ['stɜːrɪŋ] *adj* conmovedor(a)

stirrup ['stɪrəp] *n* estribo *m*

stitch [stɪtʃ] **1** *n* (a) *Sewing* puntada *f*; (*in knitting*) punto *m*; *Med* punto (de sutura); *Fam* **we were in stitches** nos tronchábamos de risa (b) (*pain*) punzada *f*
  2 *vt Sewing* coser; *Med* suturar, dar puntos a

stoat [stəʊt] *n* armiño *m*

stock [stɒk] **1** *n* (a) (*supply*) reserva *f*; *Com* (*goods*) existencias *fpl*, stock *m*; (*selection*) surtido *m*; **out of s.** agotado(a); **to have sth in s.** tener existencias de algo; *Fig* **to take s. of** evaluar
  (b) *Fin* capital *m*; **stocks and shares** acciones *fpl*, valores *mpl*; **S. Exchange** Bolsa *f* (de valores); **s. market** bolsa
  (c) *Agr* ganado *m*; **s. farming** ganadería *f*
  (d) *Culin* caldo *m*; **s. cube** cubito *m* de caldo
  (e) (*descent*) estirpe *f*
  2 *adj* (a) (*goods*) corriente
  (b) (*excuse, response*) de siempre; (*phrase*) gastado(a)
  3 *vt* (a) (*have in stock*) tener existencias de
  (b) (*provide*) abastecer, surtir (**with** de); (*cupboard*) llenar (**with** de)
▶**stock up** *vi* abastecerse (**on** *or* **with** de)

stockbroker ['stɒkbrəʊkə(r)] *n* corredor(a) *m,f* de Bolsa

stockholder ['stɒkhəʊldə(r)] *n US* accionista *mf*

stocking ['stɒkɪŋ] *n* media *f*; **a pair of stockings** unas medias

stockist ['stɒkɪst] *n* distribuidor(a) *m,f*

stockpile ['stɒkpaɪl] **1** *n* reservas *fpl*
  2 *vt* almacenar; (*accumulate*) acumular

stocks [stɒks] *npl Hist* cepo *m*

stocktaking ['stɒkteɪkɪŋ] *n Com* inventario *m*

stocky ['stɒkɪ] *adj* (**stockier, stockiest**) (*squat*) rechoncho(a); (*heavily built*) fornido(a)

stodgy ['stɒdʒɪ] *adj* (**stodgier, stodgiest**) (*food*) indigesto(a); *Fig* (*book, person*) pesado(a)

stoical ['stəʊɪkəl] *adj* estoico(a)

stoke [stəʊk] *vt* (*poke*) atizar; **to s. (up)** (*feed*) alimentar

stole¹ [stəʊl] *pt of* **steal**

stole² [stəʊl] *n* estola *f*

stolen ['stəʊlən] *pp of* **steal**

stolid ['stɒlɪd] *adj* impasible

stomach ['stʌmək] **1** *n* estómago *m*; **s. ache** dolor *m* de estómago; **s. upset** trastorno gástrico
  2 *vt Fig* aguantar

stone [stəʊn] **1** *n* (a) (*supply*) piedra *f*; (*on grave*) lápida *f*; *Fig* **at a s.'s throw** a tiro de piedra (b) *Med* cálculo *m* (c) (*of fruit*) hueso *m* (d) (*weight*) = 6,348 kg
  2 *adj* de piedra; **the S. Age** la Edad de Piedra
  3 *vt* (*kill*) lapidar

stone-cold [stəʊn'kəʊld] *adj* helado(a)

stoned [stəʊnd] *adj Fam* (*drugged*) colocado(a); (*drunk*) como una cuba

stone-deaf [stəʊn'def] *adj* sordo(a) como una tapia

stonework ['stəʊnwɜːk] *n* mampostería *f*

stony ['stəʊnɪ] *adj* (**stonier, stoniest**) (*ground*) pedregoso(a); *Fig* (*look, silence*) glacial

stood [stʊd] *pt & pp of* **stand**

stool [stuːl] *n* (a) (*seat*) taburete *m* (b) *Med* heces *fpl*

stoop [stuːp] *vi* (a) (*have a stoop*) andar encorvado(a) (b) (*bend*) **to s. down** inclinarse, agacharse (c) *Fig* **to s. to** rebajarse a; **he wouldn't s. so low** no se rebajaría tanto

stop [stɒp] **1** *n* (a) (*halt*) parada *f*, alto *m*; **to come to a s.** pararse; **to put a s. to sth** poner fin a algo
  (b) (*break*) pausa *f*; (*for refuelling etc*) escala *f*
  (c) (*for bus, tram*) parada *f*
  (d) (*punctuation mark*) punto *m*
  2 *vt* (a) parar; (*conversation*) interrumpir; (*pain, abuse etc*) poner fin a
  (b) (*payments*) suspender; (*cheque*) anular
  (c) **to s. doing sth** dejar de hacer algo; **s. singing** deja de cantar; **s. it!** ¡basta ya!
  (d) (*prevent*) evitar; **to s. sb from doing sth** impedir a algn hacer algo
  (e) (*hole*) tapar; (*gap*) rellenar
  3 *vi* (a) (*person, moving vehicle*) pararse, detenerse; **my watch has stopped** se me ha parado el reloj; **to s. dead** pararse en seco
  (b) (*cease*) acabarse, terminar
  (c) *Fam* (*stay*) pararse
▶**stop by** *vi Fam* visitar
▶**stop off** *vi* pararse un rato
▶**stop over** *vi* (*spend the night*) pasar la noche; (*for refuelling etc*) hacer escala
▶**stop up** *vt sep* (*hole*) tapar

stopgap ['stɒpgæp] *n* (*thing*) medida *f* provisional; (*person*) sustituto(a) *m,f*

stopover ['stɒpəʊvə(r)] *n* parada *f*; *Av* escala *f*

stoppage ['stɒpɪdʒ] *n* (a) *(of game, payments)* suspensión *f*; *(of work)* paro *m*; *(strike)* huelga *f*; *(deduction)* deducción *f* (b) *(blockage)* obstrucción *f*

stopper ['stɒpə(r)] *n* tapón *m*

stop-press [stɒp'pres] *n* noticias *fpl* de última hora

stopwatch ['stɒpwɒtʃ] *n* cronómetro *m*

storage ['stɔːrɪdʒ] *n* almacenaje *m*, almacenamiento *m*; **s. battery** acumulador *m*; **s. heater** placa acumuladora

store [stɔː(r)] **1** *n* (a) *(stock)* provisión *f*; *Fig (of wisdom)* reserva *f* (b) **stores** víveres *mpl* (c) *(warehouse)* almacén *m* (d) *esp US (shop)* tienda *f*; **department s.** gran almacén *m*
  2 *vt* (a) *(furniture, computer data)* almacenar; *(keep)* guardar (b) **to s. (up)** acumular

storekeeper ['stɔːkiːpə(r)] *n US* tendero(a) *m,f*

storeroom ['stɔːruːm] *n* despensa *f*

storey ['stɔːrɪ] *n* piso *m*

stork [stɔːk] *n* cigüeña *f*

storm [stɔːm] **1** *n* tormenta *f*; *(with wind)* vendaval *m*; *Fig (uproar)* revuelo *m*; *Fig* **she has taken New York by s.** ha cautivado a todo Nueva York
  2 *vt* tomar por asalto
  3 *vi (with rage)* echar pestes

stormy ['stɔːmɪ] *adj* (**stormier, stormiest**) *(weather)* tormentoso(a); *Fig (discussion)* acalorado(a); *(relationship)* tempestuoso(a)

story¹ ['stɔːrɪ] *n* historia *f*; *(tale, account)* relato *m*; *(article)* artículo *m*; *(plot)* trama *f*; *(joke)* chiste *m*; *(rumour)* rumor *m*; **it's a long s.** sería largo de contar; **tall s.** cuento chino

story² ['stɔːrɪ] *n US* = **storey**

storybook ['stɔːrɪbʊk] *n* libro *m* de cuentos

storyteller ['stɔːrɪtelə(r)] *n* cuentista *mf*

stout [staʊt] **1** *adj* (a) *(fat)* gordo(a), corpulento(a) (b) *(strong)* fuerte (c) *(brave)* valiente; *(determined)* firme
  2 *n (beer)* cerveza negra

stoutly ['staʊtlɪ] *adv* resueltamente

stove [stəʊv] *n* (a) *(for heating)* estufa *f* (b) *(cooker)* cocina *f*

stow [stəʊ] *vt* (a) *(cargo)* estibar (b) *(put away)* guardar
  ▸ **stow away** *vi (on ship, plane)* viajar de polizón

stowaway ['stəʊəweɪ] *n* polizón *mf*

straddle ['strædəl] *vt* (a) *(horse etc)* sentarse a horcajadas sobre (b) *Fig (embrace)* abarcar

straggle ['strægəl] *vi* (a) *(lag behind)* rezagarse (b) *(spread untidily)* desparramarse

straggler ['stræglə(r)] *n* rezagado(a) *m,f*

straight [streɪt] **1** *adj* (a) *(not bent)* recto(a), derecho(a); *(hair)* liso(a); **to keep a s. face** contener la risa
  (b) **I work eight hours s.** trabajo ocho horas seguidas
  (c) *(honest)* honrado(a); *(answer)* sincero(a); *(refusal)* rotundo(a); **let's get things s.** pongamos las cosas claras
  (d) *(drink)* solo(a), sin mezcla
  2 *adv* (a) *(in a straight line)* en línea recta
  (b) *(directly)* directamente, derecho; **keep s. ahead** sigue todo recto; **she walked s. in** entró sin llamar
  (c) **s. away** en seguida; **s. off** en el acto
  (d) *(frankly)* francamente
  3 *n Br Sport* **the home s.** la recta final

straighten ['streɪtən] *vt (sth bent)* enderezar, poner derecho(a); *(tie, picture)* poner bien; *(hair)* alisar
  ▸ **straighten out** *vt sep (problem)* resolver

straight-faced ['streɪt'feɪst] *adj* con la cara seria

straightforward [streɪt'fɔːwəd] *adj* (a) *(honest)* honrado(a); *(sincere)* franco(a) (b) *Br (simple)* sencillo(a)

strain¹ [streɪn] **1** *vt* (a) *(rope etc)* estirar; *Fig* crear tensiones en (b) *Med* torcer(se); *(eyes, voice)* forzar; *(heart)* cansar (c) *(liquid)* filtrar; *(vegetables, tea)* colar
  2 *vi (pull)* tirar (**at** de); *Fig* **to s. to do sth** esforzarse por hacer algo
  3 *n* (a) *(tension) f (effort)* esfuerzo *m* (b) *(exhaustion)* agotamiento *m* (c) *Med* torcedura *f* (d) *Mus* **strains** son *m*

strain² [streɪn] *n* (a) *(breed)* raza *f* (b) *(streak)* vena *f*

strained ['streɪnd] *adj* (a) *(muscle)* torcido(a); *(eyes)* cansado(a); *(voice)* forzado(a) (b) *(atmosphere)* tenso(a)

strainer ['streɪnə(r)] *n* colador *m*

strait [streɪt] *n* (a) *Geog* estrecho *m* (b) *(usu pl) (difficulty)* aprieto *m*; **in dire straits** en un gran aprieto

straitjacket ['streɪtdʒækɪt] *n* camisa *f* de fuerza

strait-laced [streɪt'leɪst] *adj* remilgado(a)

strand¹ [strænd] *vt Fig (person)* abandonar; **to leave stranded** dejar plantado(a)

strand² [strænd] *n (of thread)* hebra *f*; *(of hair)* pelo *m*

strange [streɪndʒ] *adj* (**a**) *(unknown)* desconocido(a); *(unfamiliar)* nuevo(a) (**b**) *(odd)* raro(a), extraño(a)

stranger ['streɪndʒə(r)] *n (unknown person)* desconocido(a) *m,f*, *(outsider)* forastero(a) *m,f*

strangle ['stræŋɡəl] *vt* estrangular

stranglehold ['stræŋɡəlhəʊld] *n* **to have a s. on sb** tener a algn agarrado(a) por el cuello

strangulation [stræŋɡjʊ'leɪʃən] *n* estrangulación *f*

strap [stræp] **1** *n (of leather)* correa *f*, *(on bag)* bandolera *f*, *(on dress)* tirante *m*
2 *vt* atar con correa

strapping ['stræpɪŋ] *adj Fam* fornido(a), robusto(a)

strata ['strɑːtə] *pl of* **stratum**

strategic [strə'tiːdʒɪk] *adj* estratégico(a)

strategy ['strætɪdʒɪ] *n* estrategia *f*

stratosphere ['strætəsfɪə(r)] *n* estratosfera *f*

stratum ['strɑːtəm] *n (pl* **strata**) estrato *m*

straw [strɔː] *n* (**a**) paja *f*, *Fig* **to clutch at straws** agarrarse a un clavo ardiente; *Fam* **that's the last s.!** ¡eso ya es el colmo! (**b**) *(for drinking)* pajita *f*

strawberry ['strɔːbərɪ] *n* fresa *f*, *Bol, CSur, Ecuad* frutilla *f*, *(large)* fresón *m*

stray [streɪ] **1** *vi (from path)* desviarse; *(get lost)* extraviarse
2 *n* animal extraviado
3 *adj (bullet)* perdido(a); *(animal)* callejero(a)

streak [striːk] **1** *n* (**a**) *(line)* raya *f*, **s. of lightning** rayo *m* (**b**) *(in hair)* reflejo *m* (**c**) *Fig (of genius etc)* vena *f*, *Fig (of luck)* racha *f*
2 *vt* rayar (**with** de)
3 *vi* **to s. past** pasar como un rayo

stream [striːm] **1** *n* (**a**) *(brook)* arroyo *m*, riachuelo *m* (**b**) *(current)* corriente *f* (**c**) *(of water, air)* flujo *m*; *(of tears)* torrente *m*; *(of blood)* chorro *m*; *(of light)* raudal *m* (**d**) *Fig (of abuse)* sarta *f*, *(of people)* oleada *f* (**e**) *Br Educ* clase *f*
2 *vt Br Educ* poner en grupos
3 *vi* (**a**) *(liquid)* correr (**b**) *Fig* **to s. in/out/past** *(people etc)* entrar/salir/pasar en tropel (**c**) *(hair, banner)* ondear

streamer ['striːmə(r)] *n (paper ribbon)* serpentina *f*

streamlined ['striːmlaɪnd] *adj* (**a**) *(car)* aerodinámico(a) (**b**) *(system, method)* racionalizado(a)

street [striːt] *n* calle *f*, **the man in the s.** el hombre de la calle; **s. map, s. plan** (plano *m*) callejero *m*

streetcar ['striːtkɑː(r)] *n US* tranvía *m*

streetlamp ['striːtlæmp] *n* farol *m*

streetwise ['striːtwaɪz] *adj* espabilado(a)

strength [streŋθ] *n* (**a**) fuerza *f*, *(of rope etc)* resistencia *f*, *(of emotion, colour)* intensidad *f*, *(of alcohol)* graduación *f* (**b**) *(power)* poder *m*; **on the s. of** a base de (**c**) *(ability)* punto *m* fuerte (**d**) **to be at full s./below s.** tener/no tener completo el cupo

strengthen ['streŋθən] **1** *vt* (**a**) reforzar; *(character)* fortalecer (**b**) *(intensify)* intensificar
2 *vi* (**a**) *(gen)* reforzarse (**b**) *(intensify)* intensificarse

strenuous ['strenjʊəs] *adj* (**a**) *(denial)* enérgico(a); *(effort, life)* intenso(a) (**b**) *(exhausting)* fatigoso(a), cansado(a)

stress [stres] **1** *n* (**a**) *Tech* tensión *f* (**b**) *Med* estrés *m* (**c**) *(emphasis)* hincapié *m*; *(on word)* acento *m*
2 *vt (emphasize)* subrayar; *(word)* acentuar

stretch [stretʃ] **1** *vt (elastic)* estirar; *(wings)* desplegar
2 *vi (elastic)* estirarse; *Fig* **my money won't s. to it** mi dinero no me llegará para eso
3 *n* (**a**) *(length)* trecho *m*, tramo *m* (**b**) *(of land)* extensión *f*, *(of time)* intervalo *m*

> 🔊 Note that the Spanish verb **estrechar** is a false friend and is never a translation for the English verb **to stretch**. In Spanish, **estrechar** means "to make narrow, to tighten".

▸ **stretch out 1** *vt sep (arm, hand)* alargar; *(legs)* estirar
2 *vi* (**a**) *(person)* estirarse (**b**) *(countryside, years etc)* extenderse

stretcher ['stretʃə(r)] *n* camilla *f*

strew [struː] *vt (pt* strewed; *pp* strewed or strewn [struːn]) esparcir

stricken ['strɪkən] *adj (with grief)* afligido(a); *(with illness)* aquejado(a); *(by disaster etc)* afectado(a); *(damaged)* dañado(a)

strict [strɪkt] *adj* (**a**) estricto(a) (**b**) *(absolute)* absoluto(a)

strictly ['strɪktlɪ] *adv* (**a**) *(categorically)* terminantemente (**b**) *(precisely)* estrictamente; **s. speaking** en sentido estricto

stride [straɪd] **1** *n* zancada *f*, tranco *m*; *Fig (progress)* progresos *mpl*
2 *vi (pt* strode; *pp* stridden ['strɪdən]) **to s. (along)** andar a zancadas

strident ['straɪdənt] *adj (voice, sound)*

estridente; *(protest etc)* enérgico(a)

strife [straɪf] *n* conflictos *mpl*

strike [straɪk] **1** *vt* (*pt & pp* **struck**) **(a)** *(hit)* pegar, golpear

(b) *(collide with)* chocar contra; *(of bullet, lightning)* alcanzar

(c) *(match)* encender

(d) *(pose)* adoptar

(e) *(bargain)* cerrar; *(balance)* encontrar

(f) the clock struck three el reloj dio las tres

(g) *(oil, gold)* descubrir; *Fam* **to s. it lucky/rich** tener suerte/hacerse rico(a)

(h) *(impress)* impresionar; **it strikes me ... me parece ...**

2 *vi* **(a)** *(attack)* atacar; *(disaster)* sobrevenir

(b) *(clock)* dar la hora

(c) *(workers)* declararse en huelga

3 *n* **(a)** *(by workers)* huelga *f*; **on s.** en huelga; **to call a s.** convocar una huelga

(b) *(of oil, gold)* descubrimiento *m*

(c) *(blow)* golpe *m*

(d) *Mil* ataque *m*

▸ **strike back** *vi* devolver el golpe

▸ **strike down** *vt sep* fulminar, abatir

▸ **strike out 1** *vt sep* *(cross out)* tachar

2 *vi* **to s. out at sb** arremeter contra algn

▸ **strike up** *vt insep* **(a)** *(friendship)* trabar; *(conversation)* entablar **(b)** *(tune)* empezar a tocar

striker ['straɪkə(r)] *n* **(a)** *(worker)* huelguista *mf* **(b)** *Fam Ftb* marcador(a) *m,f*

striking ['straɪkɪŋ] *adj (eye-catching)* llamativo(a); *(noticeable)* notable; *(impressive)* impresionante

string [strɪŋ] **1** *n* **(a)** *(cord)* cuerda *f*; *Fig* **to pull strings for sb** enchufar a algn; **s. bean** judía *f* verde, *Bol, RP* chaucha *f*, *CAm* ejote *m*, *Col, Cuba* habichuela *f*, *Chile* poroto *m* verde, *Ven* vainita *f* **(b)** *(of events)* cadena *f*; *(of lies)* sarta *f* **(c)** *(of racket, guitar)* cuerda *f*; *Mus* **the strings** los instrumentos de cuerda

2 *vt* (*pt & pp* **strung**) **(a)** *(beads)* ensartar **(b)** *(racket etc)* encordar **(c)** *(beans)* quitar la hebra a

stringent ['strɪndʒənt] *adj* severo(a), estricto(a)

strip¹ [strɪp] **1** *vt* **(a)** *(person)* desnudar; *(bed)* quitar la ropa de; *(paint)* quitar **(b)** *Tech* **to s. (down)** desmontar

2 *vi* *(undress)* desnudarse; *(perform striptease)* hacer un striptease

▸ **strip off 1** *vt sep* quitar

2 *vi* *(undress)* desnudarse

strip² [strɪp] *n* tira *f*; *(of land)* franja *f*; *(of*

metal) fleje *m*; **s. cartoon** historieta *f*; **s. lighting** alumbrado *m* fluorescente; **to tear sb off a s.** echar una bronca a algn

stripe [straɪp] *n* raya *f*; *Mil* galón *m*

striped [straɪpt] *adj* rayado(a), a rayas

stripper ['strɪpə(r)] *n* artista *mf* de striptease

strive [straɪv] *vi* (*pt* **strove**; *pp* **striven** ['strɪvən]) **to s. to do sth** esforzarse por hacer algo

strobe [strəʊb] *n* **s. lighting** luces estroboscópicas

strode [strəʊd] *pt of* **stride**

stroke [strəʊk] **1** *n* **(a)** **a s. of luck** un golpe de suerte **(b)** *(in golf, cricket)* golpe *m*; *(in rowing)* remada *f*; *(in swimming)* brazada *f* **(c)** *(of pen)* trazo *m*; *(of brush)* pincelada *f* **(d)** *(caress)* caricia *f* **(e)** *Med* apoplejía *f*

2 *vt* acariciar

stroll [strəʊl] **1** *vi* dar un paseo

2 *n* paseo *m*

stroller ['strəʊlə(r)] *n US (for baby)* cochecito *m*

strong [strɒŋ] **1** *adj* **(a)** fuerte **(b)** *(durable)* sólido(a) **(c)** *(firm, resolute)* firme **(d)** *(colour)* intenso(a); *(light)* brillante **(e)** *(incontestable)* convincente **(f) to be twenty s.** contar con veinte miembros

2 *adv* fuerte; **to be going s.** *(business)* ir fuerte; *(elderly person)* conservarse bien

strongbox ['strɒŋbɒks] *n* caja *f* fuerte

stronghold ['strɒŋhəʊld] *n Mil* fortaleza *f*; *Fig* baluarte *m*

strongly ['strɒŋlɪ] *adv* fuertemente

strongroom ['strɒŋruːm] *n* cámara acorazada

stroppy ['strɒpɪ] *adj* (**stroppier, stroppiest**) *Br Fam* de mala uva

strove [strəʊv] *pt of* **strive**

struck [strʌk] *pt & pp of* **strike**

structural ['strʌktʃərəl] *adj* estructural

structure ['strʌktʃə(r)] *n* estructura *f*; *(constructed thing)* construcción *f*; *(building)* edificio *m*

struggle ['strʌgəl] **1** *vi* luchar

2 *n* lucha *f*; *(physical fight)* pelea *f*

strum [strʌm] *vt (guitar)* rasguear

strung [strʌŋ] *pt & pp of* **string**

strut [strʌt] *vi* pavonearse

stub [stʌb] **1** *n* *(of cigarette)* colilla *f*; *(of pencil)* cabo *m*; *(of cheque)* matriz *f*

2 *vt* **(a)** *(strike)* golpear **(b) to s. (out)** apagar

stubble ['stʌbəl] *n (in field)* rastrojo *m*; *(on chin)* barba *f* de tres días

stubborn ['stʌbən] *adj* **(a)** terco(a),

testarudo(a) **(b)** (stain) difícil **(c)** (refusal) rotundo(a)

stucco ['stʌkəʊ] n estuco m

stuck [stʌk] pt & pp of **stick**

stuck-up [stʌk'ʌp] adj Fam creído(a)

stud¹ [stʌd] **1** n (on clothing) tachón m; (on football boots) taco m; (on shirt) botonadura f

2 vt (decorate) tachonar (**with** de); Fig (dot, cover) salpicar (**with** de)

stud² [stʌd] n (horse) semental m

student ['stju:dənt] n estudiante mf; **s. teacher** profesor(a) m,f en prácticas

studio ['stju:dɪəʊ] n TV & Cin estudio m; (artist's) taller m; **s. (apartment** or Br **flat)** estudio

studious ['stju:dɪəs] adj estudioso(a)

studiously ['stju:dɪəslɪ] adv cuidadosamente

study ['stʌdɪ] **1** vt estudiar; (facts etc) examinar, investigar; (behaviour) observar

2 vi estudiar; **to be a doctor** estudiar para médico

3 n **(a)** estudio m; **s. group** grupo m de trabajo **(b)** (room) despacho m, estudio m

stuff [stʌf] **1** vt **(a)** (container) llenar (**with** de); Culin rellenar (**with** con or de); (animal) disecar **(b)** (cram) atiborrar (**with** de)

2 n Fam **(a)** (substance) cosa f **(b)** (things) cosas fpl

stuffing ['stʌfɪŋ] n Culin relleno m

stuffy ['stʌfɪ] adj (stuffier, stuffiest) **(a)** (room) mal ventilado(a); (atmosphere) cargado(a) **(b)** (pompous) estirado(a); (narrow-minded) de miras estrechas

stumble ['stʌmbəl] vi tropezar, dar un traspié; Fig **to s. across** or **on** or **upon** tropezar or dar con

stumbling ['stʌmblɪŋ] n **s. block** escollo m

stump [stʌmp] **1** n **(a)** (of pencil) cabo m; (of tree) tocón m; (of arm, leg) muñón m **(b)** (in cricket) estaca f

2 vt (puzzle) confundir; **to be stumped** estar perplejo(a)

stun [stʌn] vt (of blow) aturdir; Fig (of news etc) sorprender

stung [stʌŋ] pt & pp of **sting**

stunk [stʌŋk] pt & pp of **stink**

stunning ['stʌnɪŋ] adj (blow) duro(a); (news) sorprendente; Fam (woman, outfit) fenomenal

stunt¹ [stʌnt] vt (growth) atrofiar

stunt² [stʌnt] n **(a)** Av acrobacia f **(b)** **publicity s.** truco publicitario **(c)** Cin

escena peligrosa; **s. man** doble m

stunted ['stʌntɪd] adj enano(a), mal desarrollado(a)

stupefy ['stju:pɪfaɪ] vt (alcohol, drugs) aturdir; Fig (news etc) dejar pasmado(a)

stupendous [stju:'pendəs] adj (wonderful) estupendo(a)

stupid ['stju:pɪd] adj estúpido(a), imbécil

stupidity [stju:'pɪdɪtɪ] n estupidez f

stupor ['stju:pə(r)] n estupor m

sturdy ['stɜ:dɪ] adj (sturdier, sturdiest) robusto(a), fuerte; (resistance) enérgico(a)

stutter ['stʌtə(r)] **1** vi tartamudear

2 n tartamudeo m

sty [staɪ] n (pen) pocilga f

sty(e) [staɪ] n Med orzuelo m

style [staɪl] **1** n **(a)** estilo m; (of dress) modelo m **(b)** (fashion) moda f **(c)** **to live in s.** (elegance) vivir a lo grande

2 vt (hair) marcar

stylish ['staɪlɪʃ] adj con estilo

stylist ['staɪlɪst] n (hairdresser) peluquero(a) mf

stylus ['staɪləs] n (of record player) aguja f

suave [swɑ:v] adj amable, afable; Pej zalamero(a)

> 📝 Note that the Spanish word **suave** is a false friend and is never a translation for the English word **suave**. In Spanish, **suave** means both "smooth" and "soft".

sub [sʌb] n Fam **(a)** (to magazine) suscripción f; (to club) cuota f **(b)** (substitute) suplente mf

sub- [sʌb] pref sub-

subconscious [sʌb'kɒnʃəs] **1** adj subconsciente

2 n the s. el subconsciente

subcontract [sʌbkən'trækt] vt subcontratar

subcontractor [sʌbkən'træktə(r)] n subcontratista mf

subdivide [sʌbdɪ'vaɪd] vt subdividir (**in-**to en)

subdue [səb'dju:] vt **(a)** (nation, people) sojuzgar **(b)** (feelings) dominar **(c)** (colour, light) atenuar

subdued [səb'dju:d] adj **(a)** (person, emotion) callado(a) **(b)** (voice, tone) bajo(a) **(c)** (light) tenue; (colour) apagado(a)

subject ['sʌbdʒɪkt] **1** n **(a)** (citizen) súbdito m **(b)** (topic) tema m; **s. matter** materia f; (contents) contenido m **(c)** Educ asignatura f **(d)** Ling sujeto m

2 adj **s. to** (law, tax) sujeto(a) a; (charge)

expuesto(a) a; *(changes, delays)* susceptible de; *(illness)* propenso(a) a; *(conditional upon)* previo(a)
   3 *vt* [səb'dʒekt] someter
subjective [səb'dʒektɪv] *adj* subjetivo(a)
subjunctive [səb'dʒʌŋktɪv] **1** *adj* subjun-
tivo(a)
   2 *n* subjuntivo *m*
sublet [ˌsʌb'let] *vt & vi* subarrendar
sublime [sə'blaɪm] *adj* sublime
submachine-gun [ˌsʌbmə'ʃiːngʌn] *n*
metralleta *f*
submarine ['sʌbməriːn] *n* submarino *m*
submerge [səb'mɜːdʒ] *vt* sumergir;
(flood) inundar; *Fig* **submerged in ...**
sumido(a) en ...
submission [səb'mɪʃən] *n* **(a)** *(yielding)*
sumisión *f* **(b)** *(of documents)* presentación *f* **(c)** *(report)* informe *m*
submissive [səb'mɪsɪv] *adj* sumiso(a)
submit [səb'mɪt] **1** *vt* **(a)** *(present)* presentar **(b)** *(subject)* someter (**to** a)
   2 *vi (surrender)* rendirse
subnormal [ˌsʌb'nɔːməl] *adj* subnormal
subordinate [sə'bɔːdɪnɪt] *adj & n* subor-
dinado(a) *(m,f)*
subpoena [səb'piːnə] *Jur* **1** *n* citación *f*
   2 *vt* citar
subscribe [səb'skraɪb] *vi (magazine)*
suscribirse (**to** a); *(opinion, theory)* adherirse (**to** a)
subscriber [səb'skraɪbə(r)] *n* abona-
do(a) *m,f*
subscription [səb'skrɪpʃən] *n (to magazine)* suscripción *f*; *(to club)* cuota *f*
subsequent ['sʌbsɪkwənt] *adj* subsi-
guiente
subsequently ['sʌbsɪkwəntlɪ] *adv* posteriormente
subside [səb'saɪd] *vi (land)* hundirse;
(floodwater) bajar; *(wind, anger)* amainar
subsidence [səb'saɪdəns] *n (of land)*
hundimiento *m*; *(of floodwater)* bajada *f*;
(of wind) amaine *m*
subsidiary [sʌb'sɪdɪərɪ] **1** *adj (role)* se-
cundario(a)
   2 *n Com* sucursal *f*, filial *f*
subsidize ['sʌbsɪdaɪz] *vt* subvencionar
subsidy ['sʌbsɪdɪ] *n* subvención *f*
subsistence [səb'sɪstəns] *n* subsistencia
f
substance ['sʌbstəns] *n* **(a)** sustancia *f*
(b) *(essence)* esencia *f* **(c)** **a woman of s.**
(wealth) una mujer acaudalada
substantial [səb'stænʃəl] *adj* **(a)** *(solid)*
sólido(a) **(b)** *(sum, loss)* importante; *(difference, improvement)* notable; *(meal)*
abundante

substantiate [səb'stænʃɪeɪt] *vt* respaldar
substitute ['sʌbstɪtjuːt] **1** *vt* sustituir; **to
s. X for Y** sustituir X por Y
   2 *n (person)* suplente *mf*; *(thing)* sucedáneo *m*
subtitle ['sʌbtaɪtəl] *n* subtítulo *m*
subtle ['sʌtəl] *adj* sutil; *(taste)* delica-
do(a); *(remark)* ingenioso(a); *(irony)* fi-
no(a)
subtlety ['sʌtəltɪ] *n* sutileza *f*; *(of remark)*
ingeniosidad *f*; *(of irony, joke)* finura *f*
subtract [səb'trækt] *vt* restar
subtraction [səb'trækʃən] *n* resta *f*
suburb ['sʌbɜːb] *n* barrio periférico; **the
suburbs** las afueras
suburban [sə'bɜːbən] *adj* suburbano(a)
suburbia [sə'bɜːbɪə] *n* barrios residen-
ciales periféricos
subversive [səb'vɜːsɪv] *adj & n* subversi-
vo(a) *(m,f)*
subway ['sʌbweɪ] *n* **(a)** *Br (underpass)*
paso subterráneo **(b)** *US (underground
railway)* metro *m*
succeed [sək'siːd] **1** *vi* **(a)** *(person)* tener
éxito; *(plan)* salir bien; **to s. in doing sth**
conseguir hacer algo **(b)** *(follow after)*
suceder; **to s. to** *(throne)* suceder a
   2 *vt (monarch)* suceder a
succeeding [sək'siːdɪŋ] *adj* sucesivo(a)
success [sək'ses] *n* éxito *m*

> 🔎 Note that the Spanish word **suceso** is a
> false friend and is never a translation for the
> English word **success**. In Spanish, **suceso**
> means both "event" and "incident".

successful [sək'sesfʊl] *adj* de éxito, exi-
toso(a); *(business)* próspero(a); *(marriage)* feliz; **to be s. in doing sth** lograr
hacer algo
successfully [sək'sesfʊlɪ] *adv* con éxito
succession [sək'seʃən] *n* sucesión *f*, serie *f*; **in s.** sucesivamente
successive [sək'sesɪv] *adj* sucesivo(a),
consecutivo(a)
successor [sək'sesə(r)] *n* sucesor(a) *m,f*
succinct [sək'sɪŋkt] *adj* sucinto(a)
succumb [sə'kʌm] *vi* sucumbir (**to** a)
such [sʌtʃ] **1** *adj* **(a)** *(of that sort)* tal,
semejante; **artists s. as Monet** artistas
como Monet; **at s. and s. a time** a tal hora;
in s. a way that de tal manera que **(b)** *(so
much, so great)* tanto(a); **he's always in s.
a hurry** siempre anda con tanta prisa;
she was in s. pain sufría tanto
   2 *adv (so very)* tan; **it's s. a long time ago**
hace tanto tiempo; **she's s. a clever wo-
man** es una mujer tan inteligente; **s. a lot
of books** tantos libros; **we had s. good**

weather hizo un tiempo tan bueno
suchlike [ˈsʌtʃlaɪk] **1** *adj* tal
  2 *pron (things)* cosas *fpl* por el estilo; *(people)* gente *f* por el estilo
suck [sʌk] **1** *vt (by pump)* aspirar; *(liquid)* sor¹ er; *(lollipop, blood)* chupar
  2 *ι (person)* chupar; *(baby)* mamar
  ▸ **su k in** *vt sep (of whirlpool)* tragar
sucker [ˈsʌkə(r)] *n* (a) *Fam* primo(a) *m,f*, bobo(a) *m,f* (b) *Zool* ventosa *f*; *Bot* chupón *m*
suckle [ˈsʌkəl] *vt (mother)* amamantar
suction [ˈsʌkʃən] *n* succión *f*
sudden [ˈsʌdən] *adj* (a) *(hurried)* súbito(a), repentino(a) (b) *(unexpected)* imprevisto(a) (c) *(abrupt)* brusco(a); **all of a s.** de repente
suddenly [ˈsʌdənlɪ] *adv* de repente
suds [sʌdz] *npl* espuma *f* de jabón, jabonaduras *fpl*
sue [suː, sjuː] *Jur* **1** *vt* demandar
  2 *vi* presentar una demanda; **to s. for divorce** solicitar el divorcio
suede [sweɪd] *n* ante *m*, gamuza *f*; *(for gloves)* cabritilla *f*
suet [ˈsuːɪt] *n* sebo *m*
suffer [ˈsʌfə(r)] **1** *vt* (a) sufrir (b) *(tolerate)* aguantar, soportar
  2 *vi* sufrir; **to s. from** sufrir de
sufferer [ˈsʌfərə(r)] *n Med* enfermo(a) *m,f*
suffering [ˈsʌfərɪŋ] *n (affliction)* sufrimiento *m*; *(pain, torment)* dolor *m*
suffice [səˈfaɪs] *vi Fml* bastar, ser suficiente
sufficient [səˈfɪʃənt] *adj* suficiente, bastante
sufficiently [səˈfɪʃəntlɪ] *adv* suficientemente, bastante
suffocate [ˈsʌfəkeɪt] **1** *vt* asfixiar
  2 *vi* asfixiarse
suffocating [ˈsʌfəkeɪtɪŋ] *adj (heat)* agobiante, sofocante
suffrage [ˈsʌfrɪdʒ] *n* sufragio *m*
suffuse [səˈfjuːz] *vt Literary* bañar, cubrir (with de)
sugar [ˈʃʊɡə(r)] **1** *n* azúcar *m* or *f*; **s. beet** remolacha *f* (azucarera); **s. bowl** azucarero *m*; **s. cane** caña *f* de azúcar
  2 *vt* azucarar, echar azúcar a
sugary [ˈʃʊɡərɪ] *adj* (a) *(like sugar)* azucarado(a) (b) *Fig (insincere)* zalamero(a); *(over-sentimental)* sentimentaloide
suggest [səˈdʒest] *vt* (a) *(propose)* sugerir (b) *(advise)* aconsejar (c) *(indicate, imply)* indicar
suggestion [səˈdʒestʃən] *n* (a) *(proposal)* sugerencia *f* (b) *(trace)* sombra *f*; *(small amount)* toque *m*
suggestive [səˈdʒestɪv] *aaⱼ* (a) *(reminiscent, thought-provoking)* sugerente (b) *(remark)* insinuante
suicidal [sjuːɪˈsaɪdəl] *adj* suicida
suicide [ˈsjuːɪsaɪd] *n* suicidio *m*
suit [suːt, sjuːt] **1** *n* (a) *(clothes)* traje *m* de chaqueta (b) *Jur* pleito *m* (c) *Cards* palo *m*; *Fig* **to follow s.** seguir el ejemplo
  2 *vt* (a) *(be convenient to)* convenir a, venir bien a (b) *(be right, appropriate for)* ir bien a; **red really suits you** el rojo te favorece mucho; **they are wel¹ suited** están hechos el uno para el otro (c) *(adapt)* adaptar a (d) *(please)* **s. yourself!** ¡como quieras!
suitable [ˈsjuːtəbəl] *adj (convenient)* conveniente; *(appropriate)* adecuado(a); **the most s. woman for the job** la mujer más indicada para el puesto
suitably [ˈsjuːtəblɪ] *adv (correctly)* correctamente; *(properly)* adecuadamente
suitcase [ˈsuːtkeɪs] *n* maleta *f*, *Méx* petaca *f*, *RP* valija *f*
suite [swiːt] *n* (a) *(of furniture)* juego *m* (b) *(of hotel rooms, music)* suite *f*
suitor [ˈsjuːtə(r)] *n Literary (wooer)* pretendiente *m*
sulfur [ˈsʌlfə(r)] *n US* = **sulphur**
sulk [sʌlk] *vi* enfurruñarse
sulky [ˈsʌlkɪ] *adj* **(sulkier, sulkiest)** malhumorado(a), enfurruñado(a)
sullen [ˈsʌlən] *adj (sky)* hosco(a); *(sky)* plomizo(a)
sulphur [ˈsʌlfər] *n* azufre *m*
sulphuric [sʌlˈfjʊərɪk] *adj* sulfúrico(a)
sultan [ˈsʌltən] *n* sultán *m*
sultana [sʌlˈtɑːnə] *n (raisin)* pasa *f* de Esmirna
sultry [ˈsʌltrɪ] *adj* **(sultrier, sultriest)** (a) *(muggy)* bochornoso(a) (b) *(seductive)* sensual
sum [sʌm] *n* (a) *(arithmetic problem, amount)* suma *f* (b) *(total amount)* total *m*; *(of money)* importe *m*
  ▸ **sum up 1** *vt sep* resumir
  2 *vi* resumir; **to s. up ...** en resumidas cuentas ...
summarize [ˈsʌmərnaɪz] *vt & vi* resumir
summary [ˈsʌmərɪ] **1** *n* resumen *m*
  2 *adj* sumario(a)
summer [ˈsʌmə(r)] **1** *n* verano *m*
  2 *adj (holiday etc)* de verano; *(weather)* veraniego(a); *(resort)* de veraneo
summerhouse [ˈsʌməhaʊs] *n* cenador *m*, glorieta *f*
summertime [ˈsʌmətaɪm] *n* verano *m*
summit [ˈsʌmɪt] *n* (a) *(of mountain)* cima

f, cumbre *f* (**b**) *Pol* **s. (meeting)** cumbre *f*

summon ['sʌmən] *vt* (**a**) *(meeting, person)* convocar (**b**) *(aid)* pedir (**c**) *Jur* citar

  ► **summon up** *vt sep (resources)* reunir; **to s. up one's courage** armarse de valor

summons ['sʌmənz] **1** *n sing* (**a**) *(call)* llamada *f*, llamamiento *m* (**b**) *Jur* citación *f* judicial

  2 *vt Jur* citar

sumptuous ['sʌmptjʊəs] *adj* suntuoso(a)

sun [sʌn] **1** *n* sol *m*

  2 *vt* **to s. oneself** tomar el sol

sunbathe ['sʌnbeɪð] *vi* tomar el sol

sunbed ['sʌnbed] *n (in garden)* tumbona *f*; *(with sunlamp)* solario *m*

sunburn ['sʌnbɜːn] *n (burn)* quemadura *f* de sol

sunburnt ['sʌnbɜːnt] *adj (burnt)* quemado(a) por el sol; *(tanned)* bronceado(a)

Sunday ['sʌndeɪ] *n* domingo *m inv*; **S. newspaper** periódico *m* del domingo; **S. school** catequesis *f*

sundial ['sʌndaɪəl] *n* reloj *m* de sol

sundown ['sʌndaʊn] *n US* anochecer *m*

sundry ['sʌndrɪ] **1** *adj* diversos(as), varios(as); *Fam* **all and s.** todos sin excepción

  2 *npl Com* **sundries** artículos *mpl* diversos; *(expenses)* gastos diversos

sunflower ['sʌnflaʊə(r)] *n* girasol *m*

sung [sʌŋ] *pp of* **sing**

sunglasses ['sʌnɡlɑːsɪz] *npl* gafas *fpl* de sol, *Am* lentes *mpl* de sol, anteojos *mpl* de sol

sunk [sʌŋk] *pp of* **sink**

sunlamp ['sʌnlæmp] *n* lámpara *f* solar

sunlight ['sʌnlaɪt] *n* sol *m*, luz *f* del sol

sunlit ['sʌnlɪt] *adj* iluminado(a) por el sol

sunny ['sʌnɪ] *adj* (**sunnier, sunniest**) (**a**) *(day)* de sol; *(place)* soleado(a); **it is s.** hace sol (**b**) *Fig (smile, disposition)* alegre; *(future)* prometedor(a)

sunrise ['sʌnraɪz] *n* salida *f* del sol

sunroof ['sʌnruːf] *n Aut* techo corredizo

sunset ['sʌnset] *n* puesta *f* del sol

sunshade ['sʌnʃeɪd] *n* sombrilla *f*

sunshine ['sʌnʃaɪn] *n* sol *m*, luz *f* del sol

sunstroke ['sʌnstrəʊk] *n* insolación *f*

suntan ['sʌntæn] *n* bronceado *m*; **s. oil** crema protectora; **s. lotion** (aceite *m*) bronceador *m*

super ['suːpə(r)] *adj Fam* fenomenal

super- ['suːpə(r)] *pref* super-, sobre-

superannuation [suːpərænjʊ'eɪʃən] *n Br* jubilación *f*, pensión *f*

superb [sʊ'pɜːb] *adj* espléndido(a)

supercilious [suːpə'sɪlɪəs] *adj (condescending)* altanero(a); *(disdainful)* desdeñoso(a)

superficial [suːpə'fɪʃəl] *adj* superficial

superfluous [suː'pɜːflʊəs] *adj* sobrante, superfluo(a); **to be s.** sobrar

superglue ['suːpəɡluː] *n* pegamento rápido

superhuman [suːpə'hjuːmən] *adj* sobrehumano(a)

superimpose [suːpərɪm'pəʊz] *vt* sobreponer

superintendent [suːpərɪn'tendənt] *n* director(a) *m,f*; **police s.** subjefe(a) *m,f* de policía

superior [suː'pɪərɪə(r)] **1** *adj* (**a**) superior (**b**) *(haughty)* altivo(a)

  2 *n* superior(a) *m,f*

superiority [suːpɪərɪ'ɒrɪtɪ] *n* superioridad *f*

superlative [suː'pɜːlətɪv] **1** *adj* superlativo(a)

  2 *n Ling* superlativo *m*

superman ['suːpəmæn] *n* superhombre *m*, supermán *m*

supermarket ['suːpəmɑːkɪt] *n* supermercado *m*

supernatural [suːpə'nætʃərəl] **1** *adj* sobrenatural

  2 *n* **the s.** lo sobrenatural

superpower ['suːpəpaʊə(r)] *n Pol* superpotencia *f*

supersede [suːpə'siːd] *vt Fml* suplantar

supersonic [suːpə'sɒnɪk] *adj* supersónico(a)

superstitious [suːpə'stɪʃəs] *adj* supersticioso(a)

supertanker ['suːpətæŋkə(r)] *n* superpetrolero *m*

supervise ['suːpəvaɪz] *vt* supervisar; *(watch over)* vigilar

supervision [suːpə'vɪʒən] *n* supervisión *f*

supervisor ['suːpəvaɪzə(r)] *n* supervisor(a) *m,f*

supper ['sʌpə(r)] *n* cena *f*; **to have s.** cenar

supplant [sə'plɑːnt] *vt* suplantar

supple ['sʌpəl] *adj* flexible

supplement 1 *n* ['sʌplɪmənt] suplemento *m*

  2 *vt* ['sʌplɪment] complementar

supplementary [sʌplɪ'mentərɪ] *adj* adicional

supplier [sə'plaɪə(r)] *n* suministrador(a) *m,f*; *Com* proveedor(a) *m,f*

supply [sə'plaɪ] **1** *n* (**a**) suministro *m*; *Com* provisión *f*; *(stock)* surtido *m*; **s. and**

demand oferta *f* y demanda (**b**) **supplies** (*food*) víveres *mpl*; *Mil* pertrechos *mpl*; **office supplies** material *m* para oficina

2 *vt* (**a**) (*provide*) suministrar (**b**) (*with provisions*) aprovisionar (**c**) (*information*) facilitar (**d**) *Com* surtir

support [sə'pɔːt] **1** *n* (**a**) (*moral*) apoyo *m* (**b**) (*funding*) ayuda económica

2 *vt* (**a**) (*weight etc*) sostener (**b**) *Fig* (*back*) apoyar; (*substantiate*) respaldar (**c**) *Sport* ser (hincha) de (**d**) (*sustain*) mantener; (*feed*) alimentar

supporter [sə'pɔːtə(r)] *n* *Pol* partidario(a) *m,f*; *Sport* hincha *mf*

suppose [sə'pəʊz] *vt* suponer; (*presume*) creer; **I s. not/so** supongo que no/sí; **you're not supposed to smoke in here** no está permitido fumar aquí dentro; **you're supposed to be in bed** deberías estar acostado(a) ya

supposed [sə'pəʊzd] *adj* supuesto(a)

supposedly [sə'pəʊzdlɪ] *adv* teóricamente

suppress [sə'pres] *vt* suprimir; (*feelings, laugh etc*) contener; (*news, truth*) callar; (*revolt*) sofocar

supremacy [sʊ'preməsɪ] *n* supremacía *f*

supreme [sʊ'priːm] *adj* supremo(a); **with s. indifference** con total indiferencia; *US Law* **S. Court** Tribunal *m* Supremo, *Am* Corte *f* Suprema

supremely [sʊ'priːmlɪ] *adv* sumamente

surcharge ['sɜːtʃɑːdʒ] *n* recargo *m*

sure [ʃʊə(r)] **1** *adj* (**a**) seguro(a); **I'm s. (that) ...** estoy seguro(a) de que ...; **make s. that it's ready** asegúrate de que esté listo; **s. of oneself** seguro(a) de sí mismo(a) (**b**) *Fam* **s. thing!** ¡claro!; *US* **it s. is cold** qué frío que hace

2 *adv* (**a**) (*of course*) claro (**b**) (*certainly*) seguro (**c**) **s. enough** efectivamente

surely ['ʃʊəlɪ] *adv* (*without a doubt*) sin duda; **s. not!** ¡no puede ser!

surety ['ʃʊərɪtɪ] *n* (**a**) (*sum*) fianza *f* (**b**) (*person*) fiador(a) *m,f*; **to stand s. for sb** ser fiador de algn

surf [sɜːf] **1** *n* (*waves*) oleaje *m*; (*foam*) espuma *f*

2 *vt* *Comput* **to s. the Net** navegar por Internet

3 *vi* *Sport* hacer surf

surface ['sɜːfɪs] **1** *n* superficie *f*; (*of road*) firme *m*

2 *adj* superficial; **s. area** área *f* de la superficie; **by s. mail** por vía terrestre *or* marítima

3 *vt* (*road*) revestir

4 *vi* (*submarine etc*) salir a la superficie;

Fam (*wake up*) levantarse

surface-to-air ['sɜːfɪstʊ'eə(r)] *adj* **s. missile** misil *m* tierra-aire

surfboard ['sɜːfbɔːd] *n* tabla *f* de surf

surfeit ['sɜːfɪt] *n* *Fml* exceso *m*

surfer ['sɜːfə(r)] *n* surfista *mf*

surfing ['sɜːfɪŋ] *n* surf *m*, surfing *m*

surge [sɜːdʒ] **1** *n* (**a**) (*growth*) alza *f* (**b**) (*of sea, sympathy*) oleada *f*; *Fig* (*of anger, energy*) arranque *m*

2 *vi* **to s. forward** (*people*) avanzar en tropel

surgeon ['sɜːdʒən] *n* cirujano(a) *m,f*

surgery ['sɜːdʒərɪ] *n* (**a**) (*operation*) cirugía *f* (**b**) *Br* (*consulting room*) consultorio *m*; **s. hours** horas *fpl* de consulta

surgical ['sɜːdʒɪkəl] *adj* quirúrgico(a); **s. spirit** alcohol *m* de 90°

surly ['sɜːlɪ] *adj* (**surlier, surliest**) (*bad-tempered*) hosco(a), malhumorado(a); (*rude*) maleducado(a)

surmount [sɜː'maʊnt] *vt* superar, vencer

surname ['sɜːneɪm] *n* apellido *m*

surpass [sɜː'pɑːs] *vt* superar

surplus ['sɜːpləs] **1** *n* (*of goods*) excedente *m*; (*of budget*) superávit *m*

2 *adj* excedente

surprise [sə'praɪz] **1** *n* sorpresa *f*; **to take sb by s.** coger desprevenido(a) a algn

2 *adj* (*visit*) inesperado(a); **s. attack** ataque *m* sorpresa

3 *vt* sorprender

surprising [sə'praɪzɪŋ] *adj* sorprendente

surprisingly [sə'praɪzɪŋlɪ] *adv* sorprendentemente, de modo sorprendente

surrealist [sə'rɪəlɪst] *adj & n* surrealista (*mf*)

surrender [sə'rendə(r)] **1** *n* *Mil* rendición *f*; (*of weapons*) entrega *f*; *Ins* rescate *m*

2 *vt* *Mil* rendir; (*right*) renunciar a

3 *vi* (*give in*) rendirse

surreptitious [sʌrəp'tɪʃəs] *adj* subrepticio(a)

surrogate ['sʌrəgɪt] *n* *Fml* sustituto(a) *m,f*; **s. mother** madre *f* de alquiler

surround [sə'raʊnd] **1** *n* marco *m*, borde *m*

2 *vt* rodear

surrounding [sə'raʊndɪŋ] **1** *adj* circundante

2 *npl* **surroundings** (*of place*) alrededores *mpl*, cercanías *fpl*

surveillance [sɜː'veɪləns] *n* vigilancia *f*

survey 1 *n* ['sɜːveɪ] (**a**) (*of building*) inspección *f*; (*of land*) reconocimiento *m* (**b**) (*of trends etc*) encuesta *f* (**c**) (*overall view*) panorama *m*

2 *vt* [sə'veɪ] (**a**) (*building*) inspeccionar;

(land) medir (**b**) *(trends etc)* hacer una encuesta sobre (**c**) *(look at)* contemplar

surveyor [sə'veɪə(r)] *n* agrimensor(a) *m,f*; **quantity s.** aparejador(a) *m,f*

survival [sə'vaɪvəl] *n* supervivencia *f*

survive [sə'vaɪv] **1** *vi* sobrevivir; *(remain)* perdurar

   2 *vt* sobrevivir a

survivor [sə'vaɪvə(r)] *n* superviviente *mf*

susceptible [sə'septəbəl] *adj (to attack)* susceptible (**to** a); *(to illness)* propenso(a) (**to** a)

suspect 1 ['sʌspekt] **1** *adj (dubious)* sospechoso(a)

   2 *n* sospechoso(a) *m,f*

   3 *vt* [sə'spekt] (**a**) *(person)* sospechar (**of** de); *(plot, motives)* recelar de (**b**) *(think likely)* imaginar, creer

suspend [sə'spend] *vt* suspender; *(pupil)* expulsar por un tiempo

suspended [sə'spendɪd] *adj* (**a**) suspendido(a); *Jur* **s. sentence** condena *f* condicional (**b**) *Sport* sancionado(a)

suspender [sə'spendə(r)] *n* (**a**) *Br (for stocking)* liga *f*; **s. belt** liguero *m* (**b**) *US* **suspenders** tirantes *mpl*

suspense [sə'spens] *n* incertidumbre *f*; *Cin & Th* suspense *m*; **to keep sb in s.** mantener a algn en la incertidumbre

suspension [sə'spenʃən] *n* (**a**) suspensión *f* (**b**) *Sport* sanción *f* (**c**) *(of pupil, employee)* expulsión *f* temporal (**d**) **s. bridge** puente *m* colgante

suspicion [sə'spɪʃən] *n* (**a**) sospecha *f*; *(mistrust)* recelo *m*; *(doubt)* duda *f* (**b**) *(trace)* pizca *f*

suspicious [sə'spɪʃəs] *adj* (**a**) *(arousing suspicion)* sospechoso(a) (**b**) *(distrustful)* receloso(a); **to be s. of sb** desconfiar de algn

▸ **suss out** [sʌs] *vt sep Br Fam (person)* calar; *(system)* coger *or Am* agarrar el truco a; **I haven't sussed out how it works yet** todavía no me he enterado de cómo funciona

sustain [sə'steɪn] *vt* (**a**) sostener (**b**) *(nourish)* sustentar (**c**) *Jur (objection)* admitir (**d**) *(injury etc)* sufrir

sustained [sə'steɪnd] *adj* sostenido(a)

sustenance ['sʌstənəns] *n* sustento *m*

swab [swɒb] **1** *n (cotton wool)* algodón *m*; *(for specimen)* frotis *m*

   2 *vt (wound)* limpiar

swagger ['swægə(r)] **1** *n* pavoneo *m*

   2 *vi* pavonearse

swallow¹ ['swɒləʊ] **1** *n (of drink, food)* trago *m*

   2 *vt* (**a**) *(drink, food)* tragar (**b**) *Fig (believe)* tragarse

   3 *vi* tragar

▸ **swallow up** *vt sep Fig* (**a**) *(engulf)* tragar (**b**) *(eat up)* consumir

swallow² ['swɒləʊ] *n Orn* golondrina *f*

swam [swæm] *pt of* **swim**

swamp [swɒmp] **1** *n* ciénaga *f*

   2 *vt* (**a**) *(boat)* hundir (**b**) *Fig* inundar (**with** *or* **by** de)

swan [swɒn] **1** *n* cisne *m*

   2 *vi Fam* **to s. around** pavonearse; **to s. around doing nothing** hacer el vago

swap [swɒp] **1** *n Fam* intercambio *m*

   2 *vt* cambiar

▸ **swap round, swap over** *vt sep (switch)* cambiar

swarm [swɔːm] **1** *n* enjambre *m*

   2 *vi (bees)* enjambrar; *Fig* **Neath was swarming with tourists** Neath estaba lleno de turistas

swarthy ['swɔːðɪ] *adj* (**swarthier, swarthiest**) moreno(a)

swastika ['swɒstɪkə] *n* esvástica *f*, cruz gamada

swat [swɒt] *vt* aplastar

swathe [sweɪð] *vt (bind up)* envolver

sway [sweɪ] **1** *n* (**a**) *(movement)* balanceo *m* (**b**) **to hold s. over sb** dominar a algn

   2 *vi* (**a**) *(swing)* balancearse, mecerse (**b**) *(totter)* tambalearse

   3 *vt Fig (persuade)* convencer

swear [sweə(r)] **1** *vt (pt swore; pp sworn)* *(vow)* jurar; **to s. an oath** prestar juramento

   2 *vi* (**a**) *(formally)* jurar, prestar juramento (**b**) *(curse)* soltar tacos, decir palabrotas; *(blaspheme)* jurar; **to s. at sb** echar pestes contra algn

swear-word ['sweəwɜːd] *n* palabrota *f*

sweat [swet] **1** *n (perspiration)* sudor *m*; *Fam (hard work)* trabajo duro

   2 *vi (perspire)* sudar; *Fig (work hard)* sudar la gota gorda

   3 *vt Fam* **to s. it out** aguantar

sweater ['swetə(r)] *n* suéter *m*

sweatshirt ['swetʃɜːt] *n* sudadera *f*

sweaty ['swetɪ] *adj* (**sweatier, sweatiest**) sudoroso(a)

Swede [swiːd] *n (person)* sueco(a) *m,f*

swede [swiːd] *n Bot* nabo sueco

Sweden ['swiːdən] *n* Suecia

Swedish ['swiːdɪʃ] **1** *adj* sueco(a)

   2 *n* (**a**) *(language)* sueco *m* (**b**) **the S.** los suecos

sweep [swiːp] **1** *n* (**a**) *(with broom)* barrido *m*; *Fig* **to make a clean s. of things** hacer tabla rasa (**b**) *(of arm)* gesto amplio

(c) *(of river, road)* curva *f* (d) **(chimney)** s. deshollinador(a) *m,f*

2 *vt (pt & pp swept)* (a) *(floor etc)* barrer (b) *(of searchlight)* recorrer; *(minefield)* rastrear (c) *(spread throughout)* extenderse por

3 *vi* (a) *(with broom)* barrer (b) **to s. in/out/past** entrar/salir/pasar rápidamente

▸ **sweep aside** *vt sep* apartar bruscamente; *Fig (objections)* rechazar

▸ **sweep away** *vt sep* (a) *(dust)* barrer (b) *(of storm)* arrastrar

▸ **sweep up** *vi* barrer

sweeper ['swiːpə(r)] *n* (a) *(machine)* barredora *f* (b) *Ftb* líbero *m*

sweeping ['swiːpɪŋ] *adj* (a) *(broad)* amplio(a); **a s. statement** una declaración demasiado general (b) *(victory)* aplastante (c) *(reforms, changes etc)* radical

sweet [swiːt] **1** *adj* (a) dulce; *(sugary)* azucarado(a); **to have a s. tooth** ser goloso(a); **s. pea** guisante *m* de olor; **s. shop** confitería *f* (b) *(pleasant)* agradable; *(smell)* fragante; *(sound)* melodioso(a) (c) *(person, animal)* encantador(a)

2 *n* (a) *Br (chocolate)* bombón *m*; **(boiled)** s. caramelo *m* (b) *(dessert)* postre *m*

sweet-and-sour ['swiːtən'saʊə(r)] *adj* agridulce

sweetcorn ['swiːtkɔːn] *n* maíz tierno

sweeten ['swiːtən] *vt* (a) *(tea etc)* azucarar (b) *Fig (temper)* aplacar; **to s. the pill** suavizar el golpe

sweetener ['swiːtənə(r)] *n (for tea, coffee)* edulcorante *m*

sweetheart ['swiːthɑːt] *n* (a) *(boyfriend)* novio *m*; *(girlfriend)* novia *f* (b) *(dear, love)* cariño *m*, amor *m*

sweetness ['swiːtnɪs] *n* dulzura *f*; *(of smell)* fragancia *f*; *(of sound)* suavidad *f*

swell [swel] **1** *n (of sea)* marejada *f*, oleaje *m*

2 *adj US Fam* fenomenal

3 *vi (pt swelled; pp swollen)* (part of body) hincharse; *(river)* subir

▸ **swell up** *vi* hincharse

swelling ['swelɪŋ] *n* hinchazón *f*; *Med* tumefacción *f*

sweltering ['sweltərɪŋ] *adj* agobiante

swept [swept] *pt & pp of* **sweep**

swerve [swɜːv] **1** *n* (a) *(by car)* viraje *m* (b) *Sport (by player)* regate *m*

2 *vi* (a) *(car)* dar un viraje brusco (b) *Sport (player)* dar un regate

swift [swɪft] **1** *adj* rápido(a), veloz

2 *n Orn* vencejo *m* (común)

swiftly ['swɪftlɪ] *adv* rápidamente

swig [swɪg] *Fam* **1** *n* trago *m*

2 *vt* beber a tragos

swill [swɪl] **1** *n* (a) bazofia *f* (b) *(rinse)* enjuague *m*

2 *vt* (a) *(rinse)* enjuagar (b) *Fam (drink)* beber a grandes tragos

▸ **swill out** *vt sep* enjuagar

swim [swɪm] **1** *vi (pt swam; pp swum)* nadar; **to go swimming** ir a nadar; *Fam* **my head is swimming** la cabeza me da vueltas

2 *vt (the Channel)* pasar a nado

3 *n* baño *m*; **to go for a s.** ir a nadar *or* bañarse

swimmer ['swɪmə(r)] *n* nadador(a) *m,f*

swimming ['swɪmɪŋ] *n* natación *f*; **s. cap** gorro *m* de baño; **s. costume** traje *m* de baño, bañador *m*; **s. pool** piscina *f*; **s. trunks** bañador *m*

swimsuit ['swɪmsuːt] *n* traje *m* de baño, bañador *m*

swindle ['swɪndəl] **1** *n* estafa *f*

2 *vt* estafar

swindler ['swɪndlə(r)] *n* estafador(a) *m,f*

swine [swaɪn] *n* (a) *(pl swine) (pig)* cerdo *m*, puerco *m* (b) *(pl swines) Fam (person)* canalla *mf*, cochino(a) *m,f*

swing [swɪŋ] **1** *n* (a) balanceo *m*, vaivén *m*; *Fig (in votes etc)* viraje *m*; **s. bridge** puente giratorio; **s. door** puerta giratoria (b) *(in golf)* swing *m* (c) *(plaything)* columpio *m* (d) *(rhythm)* ritmo *m*; *(jazz style)* swing *m*; **in full s.** en plena marcha

2 *vi (pt & pp swung)* (a) *(move to and fro)* balancearse; *(arms, legs)* menearse; *(on swing)* columpiarse; **to s. open/shut** abrirse/cerrarse de golpe

(b) *(turn)* girar; **he swung round** dio media vuelta

3 *vt* (a) *(cause to move to and fro)* balancear; *(arms, legs)* menear; *(on swing)* columpiar

(b) *(turn)* hacer girar; **she swung the sack onto her back** se echó el saco a los hombros

swingeing ['swɪndʒɪŋ] *adj* drástico(a)

swipe [swaɪp] **1** *n* golpe *m*

2 *vt* (a) *(hit)* dar un tortazo a (b) *Fam (steal)* birlar

swirl [swɜːl] **1** *n* remolino *m*; *(of cream, smoke)* voluta *f*

2 *vi* arremolinarse

swish [swɪʃ] **1** *adj Fam (smart)* elegante

2 *vt (tail)* menear

3 *vi (whip)* dar un chasquido; *(skirt)* crujir

Swiss [swɪs] **1** *adj* suizo(a)
  2 *n* (*pl* **Swiss**) (*person*) suizo(a) *m,f*; **the S.** los suizos

switch [swɪtʃ] **1** *n* (**a**) *Elec* interruptor *m* (**b**) (*changeover*) cambio repentino; (*exchange*) intercambio *m* (**c**) (*stick*) vara *f*; (*riding whip*) fusta *f* (**d**) *US Rail* agujas *fpl*
  2 *vt* (**a**) (*jobs, direction*) cambiar de (**b**) (*allegiance*) cambiar (**to** por); (*attention*) desviar (**to** hacia)
 ▶ **switch off** *vt sep* apagar
 ▶ **switch on** *vt sep* encender
 ▶ **switch over** *vi* cambiar (**to** a)

switchboard ['swɪtʃbɔːd] *n* centralita *f*

Switzerland ['swɪtsələnd] *n* Suiza

swivel ['swɪvəl] **1** *n* **s. chair** silla giratoria
  2 *vt & vi* girar

swollen ['swəʊlən] **1** *adj* (*ankle, face*) hinchado(a); (*river, lake*) crecido(a)
  2 *pp of* **swell**

swoon [swuːn] **1** *n* desmayo *m*
  2 *vi* desmayarse

swoop [swuːp] **1** *n* (**a**) (*of bird*) calada *f*; (*of plane*) descenso *m* en picado (**b**) (*by police*) redada *f*
  2 *vi* (**a**) **to s. down** (*bird*) abalanzarse (**on** sobre); (*plane*) bajar en picado (**b**) (*police*) hacer una redada

swop [swɒp] *n & vt* = **swap**

sword [sɔːd] *n* espada *f*

swordfish ['sɔːdfɪʃ] *n* pez *m* espada

swore [swɔː(r)] *pt of* **swear**

sworn [swɔːn] **1** *adj* jurado(a)
  2 *pp of* **swear**

swot [swɒt] *vi Br Fam* empollar

swum [swʌm] *pp of* **swim**

swung [swʌŋ] *pt & pp of* **swing**

sycamore ['sɪkəmɔː(r)] *n* (**a**) *Br* sicomoro *m* (**b**) *US* (*plane tree*) plátano *m*

syllable ['sɪləbəl] *n* sílaba *f*

syllabus ['sɪləbəs] *n* programa *m* de estudios

symbol ['sɪmbəl] *n* símbolo *m*

symbolic [sɪm'bɒlɪk] *adj* simbólico(a)

symbolize ['sɪmbəlaɪz] *vt* simbolizar

symmetry ['sɪmɪtrɪ] *n* simetría *f*

sympathetic [sɪmpə'θetɪk] *adj* (**a**) (*showing pity*) compasivo(a) (**b**) (*understanding*) comprensivo(a); (*kind*) amable

---

  📖 Note that the Spanish word **simpático** is a false friend and is never a translation for the English word **sympathetic**. In Spanish, **simpático** means "nice, likeable".

---

sympathize ['sɪmpəθaɪz] *vi* (**a**) (*show pity*) compadecerse (**with** de) (**b**) (*understand*) comprender

sympathizer ['sɪmpəθaɪzə(r)] *n* simpatizante *mf*

sympathy ['sɪmpəθɪ] *n* (**a**) (*pity*) compasión *f* (**b**) (*condolences*) pésame *m*; **letter of s.** pésame; **to express one's s.** dar el pésame (**c**) (*understanding*) comprensión *f*

  📖 Note that the Spanish word **simpatía** is a false friend and is never a translation for the English word **sympathy**. In Spanish, **simpatía** means "liking, affection".

---

symphony ['sɪmfənɪ] *n* sinfonía *f*

symposium [sɪm'pəʊzɪəm] *n* simposio *m*

symptom ['sɪmptəm] *n* síntoma *m*

symptomatic [sɪmptə'mætɪk] *adj* sintomático(a)

synagogue ['sɪnəgɒg] *n* sinagoga *f*

synchronize ['sɪŋkrənaɪz] *vt* sincronizar

syndicate ['sɪndɪkɪt] *n* corporación *f*; **newspaper s.** sindicato periodístico

syndrome ['sɪndrəʊm] *n* síndrome *m*

synonym ['sɪnənɪm] *n* sinónimo *m*

synopsis [sɪ'nɒpsɪs] *n* sinopsis *f inv*

syntax ['sɪntæks] *n* sintaxis *f inv*

synthesis ['sɪnθɪsɪs] *n* (*pl* **syntheses** ['sɪnθɪsiːz]) síntesis *f inv*

synthesizer ['sɪnθɪsaɪzə(r)] *n* sintetizador *m*

synthetic [sɪn'θetɪk] *adj* sintético(a)

syphilis ['sɪfɪlɪs] *n* sífilis *f*

syphon ['saɪfən] *n* = **siphon**

Syria ['sɪrɪə] *n* Siria

Syrian ['sɪrɪən] *adj & n* sirio(a) (*m,f*)

syringe [sɪ'rɪndʒ] *n* jeringa *f*, jeringuilla *f*

syrup ['sɪrəp] *n* jarabe *m*, almíbar *m*

system ['sɪstəm] *n* sistema *m*; *Fam* **the s.** el orden establecido; *Comput* **systems analyst** analista *mf* de sistemas

systematic [sɪstɪ'mætɪk] *adj* sistemático(a)

T

T, t [tiː] *n (the letter)* T, t *f*

t *(abbr* **ton(s))** tonelada(s) *f(pl)*

ta [tɑː] *interj Br Fam* gracias

tab [tæb] *n* **(a)** *(flap)* lengüeta *f; (label)* etiqueta *f; Fam* **to keep tabs on sb** vigilar a algn **(b)** *US Fam (bill)* cuenta *f*

tabby [ˈtæbɪ] *n* **t. (cat)** gato(a) *m,f* romano(a)

table [ˈteɪbəl] **1** *n* **(a)** mesa *f;* **to lay** *or* **set the t.** poner la mesa; **t. lamp** lámpara *f* de mesa; **t. mat** salvamanteles *m inv;* **t. tennis** ping-pong® *m,* tenis *m* de mesa; **t. wine** vino *m* de mesa **(b)** *(of figures)* tabla *f,* cuadro *m;* **t. of contents** índice *m* de materias

2 *vt (motion, proposal) Br* presentar; *US* posponer

tablecloth [ˈteɪbəlklɒθ] *n* mantel *m*

tablespoon [ˈteɪbəlspuːn] *n* cucharón *m*

tablespoonful [ˈteɪbəlspuːnfʊl] *n* cucharada *f* grande

tablet [ˈtæblɪt] *n* **(a)** *Med* pastilla *f* **(b)** *(of stone)* lápida *f* **(c)** *(of soap)* pastilla *f, (of chocolate)* tableta *f* **(d)** *US (of writing paper)* bloc *m*

tableware [ˈteɪbəlweə(r)] *n* vajilla *f*

tabloid [ˈtæblɔɪd] *n* periódico *m* de pequeño formato; **t. press** prensa sensacionalista

taboo [təˈbuː] *adj & n* tabú *(m)*

tabulate [ˈtæbjʊleɪt] *vt* disponer en listas

tacit [ˈtæsɪt] *adj* tácito(a)

taciturn [ˈtæsɪtɜːn] *adj* taciturno(a)

tack [tæk] **1** *n* **(a)** *(small nail)* tachuela *f* **(b)** *Sewing* hilván *m* **(c)** *Naut* amura *f; (distance)* bordada *f; Fig* **to change t.** cambiar de rumbo

2 *vt* **(a) to t. sth down** clavar algo con tachuelas **(b)** *Sewing* hilvanar

3 *vi Naut* virar de bordo

▸ **tack on** *vt sep (add)* añadir

tackle [ˈtækəl] **1** *n* **(a)** *(equipment)* aparejos *mpl; fishing* **t.** aparejos de pescar **(b)** *Sport* placaje *m; Ftb* entrada *f*

2 *vt* agarrar; *(task)* emprender; *(problem)* abordar; *Sport* placar; *Ftb* entrar a

tacky¹ [ˈtækɪ] *adj* **(tackier, tackiest)** pegajoso(a)

tacky² [ˈtækɪ] *adj Fam (shoddy)* cutre

tact [tækt] *n* tacto *m,* diplomacia *f*

tactful [ˈtæktfʊl] *adj* diplomático(a)

tactic [ˈtæktɪk] *n* táctica *f;* **tactics** táctica *f*

tactical [ˈtæktɪkəl] *adj* táctico(a)

tactless [ˈtæktlɪs] *adj (person)* poco diplomático(a); *(question)* indiscreto(a)

tadpole [ˈtædpəʊl] *n* renacuajo *m*

taffy [ˈtæfɪ] *n US* caramelo *m* de melaza

tag [tæg] *n* **(a)** *(label)* etiqueta *f* **(b)** *(saying)* coletilla *f*

▸ **tag along** *vi Fam* pegarse

▸ **tag on** *vt sep (add to end)* añadir

tail [teɪl] *n* **(a)** *(of animal)* cola *f;* **t. end** cola *f; (of shirt)* faldón *m;* **to wear tails** ir de frac; **t. coat** frac *m* **(c)** **tails** *(of coin)* cruz *f*

2 *vt Fam (follow)* seguir de cerca

▸ **tail away, tail off** *vi* desvanecerse

tailback [ˈteɪlbæk] *n Br* caravana *f*

tail-gate [ˈteɪlgeɪt] **1** *n Aut* puerta trasera

2 *vt US* conducir *or Am* manejar pegado a, pisar los talones a

tailor [ˈteɪlə(r)] **1** *n* sastre *m;* **t.'s (shop)** sastrería *f*

2 *vt (suit)* confeccionar; *Fig* adaptar

tailor-made [teɪləˈmeɪd] *adj* hecho(a) a la medida

tailwind [ˈteɪlwɪnd] *n* viento *m* de cola

taint [teɪnt] *vt* contaminar; *Fig* corromper

tainted [ˈteɪntɪd] *adj* contaminado(a); *(reputation)* manchado(a)

take [teɪk] **1** *vt (pt* **took;** *pp* **taken) (a)** tomar, coger; **to t. an opportunity** aprovechar una oportunidad; **to t. hold of sth** agarrar algo; **to t. sth from one's pocket** sacarse algo del bolsillo; **t. your time!** ¡tómate el tiempo que quieras!; **to t. a bath** bañarse; **to t. care (of oneself)** cuidarse; **his car takes six people** caben seis personas en su coche; **is this seat taken?** ¿está ocupado este asiento?; **to t. a decision** tomar una decisión; **to t. a liking/dislike to sb** tomar cariño/antipatía a algn; **to t. a photograph** sacar una fotografía; **t. the first road on the left** coja la primera a la izquierda; **to t. the train** coger el tren

(b) *(accept)* aceptar; *(earn)* **to t. so much per week** recaudar tanto por semana

(c) *(win)* ganar; *(prize)* llevarse

(d) *(eat, drink)* tomar; **to t. drugs** drogarse

(e) **she's taking (a degree in)** law estudia derecho; **to t. an exam (in ...)** examinarse (de ...)

(f) *(person to a place)* llevar

(g) *(endure)* aguantar

(h) *(consider)* considerar

(i) **I t. it that ...** supongo que ...; **what do you t. me for?** ¿por quién me tomas?

(j) *(require)* requerir; **it takes an hour to get there** se tarda una hora en llegar hasta allí

(k) **to be taken ill** enfermar

2 *n Cin* toma *f*

▸ **take after** *vt insep* parecerse a

▸ **take apart** *vt sep (machine)* desmontar

▸ **take away** *vt sep* (a) *(carry off)* llevarse (b) **to t. sth away from sb** quitarle algo a algn (c) *Math* restar

▸ **take back** *vt sep* (a) *(give back)* devolver; *(receive back)* recuperar (b) *(withdraw)* retractarse

▸ **take down** *vt sep* (a) *(lower)* bajar (b) *(demolish)* derribar (c) *(write)* apuntar

▸ **take in** *vt sep* (a) *(shelter, lodge)* alojar, acoger (b) *Sewing* meter (c) *(include)* abarcar (d) *(understand)* entender (e) *(deceive)* engañar

▸ **take off** *vt sep* (a) *(quitar;* **he took off his jacket** se quitó la chaqueta (b) *(lead or carry away)* llevarse (c) *(deduct)* descontar (d) *(imitate)* imitar burlonamente

2 *vi Av* despegar

▸ **take on** *vt sep* (a) *(undertake)* encargarse de (b) *(acquire)* tomar (c) *(employ)* contratar (d) *(compete with)* competir con

▸ **take out** *vt sep* sacar, quitar; **he's taking me out to dinner** me ha invitado a cenar fuera

▸ **take over 1** *vt sep Com & Pol* tomar posesión de; **the rebels took over the country** los rebeldes se apoderaron del país

2 *vi* **to t. over from sb** relevar a algn

▸ **take to** *vt insep (become fond of)* coger cariño a; **to t. to drink** darse a la bebida

▸ **take up** *vt sep* (a) *Sewing* acortar (b) *(accept)* aceptar; *(adopt)* adoptar (c) **I've taken up the piano/French** he empezado a tocar el piano/a aprender francés (d) *(occupy)* ocupar

takeaway ['teɪkəweɪ] *Br* **1** *n (food)* comida *f* para llevar; *(restaurant)* restaurante *m* que vende comida para llevar

2 *adj (food)* para llevar

take-home pay ['teɪkhəʊm'peɪ] *n* sueldo neto

taken ['teɪkən] *pp of* take

takeoff ['teɪkɒf] *n* (a) *Av* despegue *m* (b) *(imitation)* imitación burlona

takeout ['teɪkaʊt] *US* **1** *n (food)* comida *f* para llevar

2 *adj (food)* para llevar

takeover ['teɪkəʊvə(r)] *n Com* absorción *f*; **military t.** golpe *m* de estado; **t. bid** oferta pública de adquisición, OPA *f*

takings ['teɪkɪŋz] *npl Com* recaudación *f*

talc [tælk] *n* talco *m*

talcum powder ['tælkəmpaʊdə(r)] *n* (polvos *mpl* de) talco *m*

tale [teɪl] *n* cuento *m*; **to tell tales** contar chismes

talent ['tælənt] *n* talento *m*

talented ['tæləntɪd] *adj* dotado(a)

talk [tɔːk] **1** *vi* hablar; *(chat)* charlar; *(gossip)* chismorrear; *Fam* **now you're talking!** ¡eso sí que me interesa!

2 *vt* **to t. nonsense** decir tonterías; **to t. sense** hablar con sentido común; **to t. shop** hablar del trabajo

3 *n* (a) *(conversation)* conversación *f* (b) *(words)* palabras *fpl*; **he's all t.** no hace más que hablar (c) *(rumour)* rumor *m*; *(gossip)* chismes *mpl* (d) *(lecture)* charla *f*

▸ **talk into** *vt sep* **to t. sb into sth** convencer a algn para que haga algo

▸ **talk out of** *vt sep* **to t. sb out of sth** disuadir a algn de que haga algo

▸ **talk over** *vt sep* discutir

talkative ['tɔːkətɪv] *adj* hablador(a)

talking ['tɔːkɪŋ] *n* **no t. please!** ¡silencio, por favor!; **t. point** tema *m* de conversación

talking-to ['tɔːkɪŋtuː] *n Fam* bronca *f*

tall [tɔːl] *adj* alto(a); **a tree 10 m t.** un árbol de 10 m (de alto); **how t. are you?** ¿cuánto mides?; *Fig* **that's a t. order** eso es mucho pedir

tally ['tælɪ] **1** *vi* **to t. with sth** corresponderse con algo

2 *n Com* apunte *m*; **to keep a t. of** llevar la cuenta de

talon ['tælən] *n* garra *f*

> 🖉 Note that the Spanish word **talón** is a false friend and is never a translation for the English word **talon**. In Spanish, **talón** means both "heel" and "cheque".

tambourine [tæmbə'riːn] *n* pandereta *f*

tame [teɪm] **1** *adj* (a) *(animal)* domado(a); *(by nature)* manso(a); *(person)* dócil (b) *(style)* soso(a)

2 *vt* domar

tamper ['tæmpə(r)] *vi* **to t. with** *(text)* adulterar; *(records, an entry)* falsificar; *(lock)* intentar forzar

tampon ['tæmpon] *n* tampón *m*

tan [tæn] **1** *n* (**a**) *(colour)* marrón rojizo (**b**) *(of skin)* bronceado *m*
  2 *adj (colour)* marrón rojizo
  3 *vt* (**a**) *(leather)* curtir (**b**) *(skin)* broncear
  4 *vi* ponerse moreno(a)

tang [tæŋ] *n* sabor *m* fuerte

tangent ['tændʒənt] *n* tangente *f*; *Fig* **to go off at a t.** salirse por la tangente

tangerine [tændʒə'ri:n] *n* clementina *f*

tangible ['tændʒəbəl] *adj* tangible

tangle ['tæŋgəl] *n (of thread)* maraña *f*; *Fig* lío *m*; *Fig* **to get into a t.** hacerse un lío

tank [tæŋk] *n* (**a**) *(container)* depósito *m* (**b**) *Mil* tanque *m*

tanker ['tæŋkə(r)] *n Naut* tanque *m*; *(for oil)* petrolero *m*; *Aut* camión *m* cisterna

Tannoy® ['tænɔɪ] *n* sistema *m* de megafonía

tantalize ['tæntəlaɪz] *vt* atormentar

tantalizing ['tæntəlaɪzɪŋ] *adj* atormentador(a)

tantamount ['tæntəmaʊnt] *adj* **t. to** equivalente a

tantrum ['tæntrəm] *n* rabieta *f*

tap[1] [tæp] **1** *vt* golpear suavemente; *(with hand)* dar una palmadita a
  2 *vi* **to t. at the door** llamar suavemente a la puerta
  3 *n* golpecito *m*; **t. dancing** claqué *m*

tap[2] [tæp] **1** *n Br (for water)* grifo *m*, *Chile*, *Méx* llave *f*, *RP* canilla *f*; *Fig* **funds on t.** fondos *mpl* disponibles
  2 *vt* (**a**) *(tree)* sangrar; *Fig* **to t. new markets** explotar nuevos mercados (**b**) *(phone)* pinchar

tape [teɪp] **1** *n* (**a**) *(tape)* cinta *f*; **sticky t.** cinta adhesiva; **t. measure** cinta métrica (**b**) *(for recording)* cinta *f* (magnetofónica); **t. recorder** magnetófono *m*, cassette *m*; **t. recording** grabación *f*
  2 *vt* (**a**) pegar (con cinta adhesiva) (**b**) *(record)* grabar (en cinta)

taper ['teɪpə(r)] **1** *vi* estrecharse; *(to a point)* afilarse
  2 *n (candle)* vela *f*
  ▶ **taper off** *vi* ir disminuyendo

tapestry ['tæpɪstrɪ] *n* tapiz *m*

tapping ['tæpɪŋ] *n* (**a**) *(of tree)* sangría *f*; *(of resources)* explotación *f* (**b**) *Tel* intervención *f* ilegal de un teléfono

tar [tɑ:(r)] *n* alquitrán *m*

target ['tɑ:gɪt] *n* (**a**) *(object aimed at)* blanco *m*; **t. practice** tiro *m* al blanco (**b**) *(purpose)* meta *f*

tariff ['tærɪf] *n* tarifa *f*, arancel *m*

tarmac® ['tɑ:mæk] **1** *n* (**a**) *(substance)* alquitrán *m* (**b**) *Av* pista *f* de aterrizaje
  2 *vt* alquitranar

tarnish ['tɑ:nɪʃ] *vt* deslustrar

tarpaulin [tɑ:'pɔ:lɪn] *n* lona *f*

tart[1] [tɑ:t] *n Br Culin* tarta *f*

tart[2] [tɑ:t] *adj (taste)* ácido(a), agrio(a)

tart[3] [tɑ:t] *Fam* **1** *n* puta *f*
  2 *vt Br* **to t. oneself up** emperifollarse

tartan ['tɑ:tən] *n* tartán *m*

tartar ['tɑ:tə(r)] *n* (**a**) *Chem* tártaro *m* (**b**) *Culin* **t. sauce** salsa tártara

task [tɑ:sk] *n* tarea *f*; **to take sb to t.** reprender a algn; *Mil* **t. force** destacamento *m* (de fuerzas)

tassel ['tæsəl] *n* borla *f*

taste [teɪst] **1** *n* (**a**) *(sense)* gusto *m*; *(flavour)* sabor *m*; **it has a burnt t.** sabe a quemado (**b**) *(sample) (of food)* bocado *m*; *(of drink)* trago *m*; **to give sb a t. of his own medicine** pagar a algn con la misma moneda (**c**) *(liking)* afición *f*; **to have a t. for sth** gustarle a uno algo (**d**) **in bad t.** de mal gusto; **to have (good) t.** tener (buen) gusto
  2 *vt (sample)* probar
  3 *vi* **to t. of sth** saber a algo

tasteful ['teɪstfʊl] *adj* de buen gusto

tasteless ['teɪstlɪs] *adj* (**a**) *(food)* soso(a) (**b**) *(in bad taste)* de mal gusto

tasty ['teɪstɪ] *adj* (**tastier, tastiest**) sabroso(a)

tattered ['tætəd] *adj* hecho(a) jirones

tatters ['tætəz] *npl* **in t.** hecho(a) jirones

tattoo[1] [tæ'tu:] *n Mil* retreta *f*

tattoo[2] [tæ'tu:] **1** *vt* tatuar
  2 *n (mark)* tatuaje *m*

tatty ['tætɪ] *adj* (**tattier, tattiest**) *Br* en mal estado; *(material, clothing)* raído(a); *(décor)* deslustrado(a)

taught [tɔ:t] *pt & pp of* **teach**

taunt [tɔ:nt] **1** *vt* **to t. sb with sth** echar algo en cara a algn
  2 *n* pulla *f*

Taurus ['tɔ:rəs] *n* Tauro *m*

taut [tɔ:t] *adj* tenso(a), tirante

tavern ['tævən] *n* taberna *f*

tawdry ['tɔ:drɪ] *adj* (**tawdrier, tawdriest**) hortera

tawn(e)y ['tɔ:nɪ] *adj* leonado(a), rojizo(a)

tax [tæks] **1** *n* impuesto *m*; **t. free** exento(a) de impuestos; **t. collector** recaudador(a) *m,f* (de impuestos); **t. evasion** evasión *f* fiscal; **t. return** declaración *f* de renta

2 *vt* (**a**) gravar (**b**) *(patience etc)* poner a prueba

taxable ['tæksəbəl] *adj* imponible

taxation [tæk'seɪʃən] *n* impuestos *mpl*

taxi ['tæksɪ] **1** *n* taxi *m*; **t. driver** taxista *mf*; **t.** *Br* **rank** *or US* **stand** parada *f* de taxis

2 *vi (aircraft)* rodar por la pista

taxidermy ['tæksɪdɜːmɪ] *n* taxidermia *f*

taxing ['tæksɪŋ] *adj* exigente

taxpayer ['tækspeɪə(r)] *n* contribuyente *mf*

TB [tiː'biː] *n (tuberculosis)* tuberculosis *f inv*

tea [tiː] *n* (**a**) té *m*; **t. bag** bolsita *f* de té; **t. break** descanso *m*; **t. cosy** cubretetera *f*; **t. leaf** hoja *f* de té; **t. service** *or* **set** juego *m* de té; **t. towel** paño *m* (de cocina) (**b**) *(snack)* merienda *f*; **(high) t.** merienda-cena *f*

teach [tiːtʃ] **1** *vt (pt & pp taught)* enseñar; *(subject)* dar clases de; **to t. sb (how) to do sth** enseñar a algn a hacer algo; *US* **to t. school** ser profesor(a)

2 *vi* dar clases, ser profesor(a)

teacher ['tiːtʃə(r)] *n* profesor(a) *m,f*; *(in primary school)* maestro(a) *m,f*

teaching ['tiːtʃɪŋ] *n* enseñanza *f*

teacup ['tiːkʌp] *n* taza *f* de té

teak [tiːk] *n* teca *f*

team [tiːm] *n* equipo *m*; *(of oxen)* yunta *f*

team-mate ['tiːmmeɪt] *n* compañero(a) *m,f* de equipo

teamwork ['tiːmwɜːk] *n* trabajo *m* en equipo

teapot ['tiːpɒt] *n* tetera *f*

tear[1] [tɪə(r)] *n* lágrima *f*; **to be in tears** estar llorando; **t. gas** gas lacrimógeno

tear[2] [teə(r)] **1** *vt (pt tore; pp torn)* (**a**) rajar, desgarrar (**b**) **to t. sth out of sb's hands** arrancarle algo de las manos a algn

2 *vi* (**a**) *(cloth)* rajarse (**b**) **to t. along** ir a toda velocidad

3 *n* desgarrón *m*; *(in clothes)* rasgón *m*

▶ **tear down** *vt sep* derribar

▶ **tear off** *vt sep* arrancar

▶ **tear out** *vt sep* arrancar

▶ **tear up** *vt sep* (**a**) romper, hacer peda-zos (**b**) *(uproot)* arrancar de raiz

tearful ['tɪəfʊl] *adj* lloroso(a)

tearoom ['tiːruːm] *n Br* = teashop

tease [tiːz] **1** *vt* tomar el pelo a

2 *n* bromista *mf*

teashop ['tiːʃɒp] *n Br* salón *m* de té

teaspoon ['tiːspuːn] *n* cucharilla *f*

teaspoonful ['tiːspuːnfʊl] *n* cucharadita *f*

teat [tiːt] *n (of animal)* teta *f*; *(of bottle)* tetina *f*

teatime ['tiːtaɪm] *n* hora *f* del té

technical ['teknɪkəl] *adj* técnico(a); **t. college** instituto *m* de formación profe-sional

technicality [teknɪ'kælɪtɪ] *n* detalle téc-nico

technically ['teknɪkəlɪ] *adv (theoretic-ally)* en teoría

technician [tek'nɪʃən] *n* técnico(a) *m,f*

technique [tek'niːk] *n* técnica *f*

technological [teknə'lɒdʒɪkəl] *adj* tec-nológico(a)

technology [tek'nɒlədʒɪ] *n* tecnología *f*

teddy bear ['tedɪbeə(r)] *n* oso *m* de felpa

tedious ['tiːdɪəs] *adj* tedioso(a), aburri-do(a)

tee [tiː] *n (in golf)* tee *m*

teem [tiːm] *vi* **to t. with** rebosar de; *Fam* **it was teeming down** llovía a cántaros

teenage ['tiːneɪdʒ] *adj* adolescente

teenager ['tiːneɪdʒə(r)] *n* adolescente *mf*

teens [tiːnz] *npl* adolescencia *f*

tee-shirt ['tiːʃɜːt] *n* camiseta *f*

teeter ['tiːtə(r)] *vi* balancearse

teeth [tiːθ] *pl of* **tooth**

teethe [tiːð] *vi* echar los dientes

teething ['tiːðɪŋ] *n* **t. ring** chupador *m*; *Fig* **t. troubles** dificultades *fpl* iniciales

teetotaller [tiː'təʊtələ(r)] *n* abstemio(a) *m,f*

telecommunications ['telɪkəmjuːnɪ-'keɪʃənz] *n sing* telecomunicaciones *fpl*

telegram ['telɪgræm] *n* telegrama *m*

telegraph ['telɪgrɑːf] **1** *n* telégrafo *m*; **t. pole** poste telegráfico

2 *vt & vi* telegrafiar

telepathy [tɪ'lepəθɪ] *n* telepatía *f*

telephone ['telɪfəʊn] **1** *n* teléfono *m*; **t. banking** telebanca *f*; *Br* **t. booth** *or* **box** cabina *f* (telefónica); **t. call** llamada tele-fónica; **t. directory** guía telefónica; **t. number** número *m* de teléfono

2 *vt* telefonear, llamar por teléfono

telephonist [tɪ'lefənɪst] *n Br* telefonista *mf*

telephoto ['telɪfəʊtəʊ] *adj* **t. lens** teleob-jetivo *m*

teleprinter ['telɪprɪntə(r)] *n* teletipo *m*

telescope ['telɪskəʊp] **1** *n* telescopio *m*

2 *vi* plegarse (como un catalejo)

3 *vt* plegar

telescopic [telɪ'skɒpɪk] *adj (umbrella)* plegable

televise ['telɪvaɪz] *vt* televisar

television ['telɪvɪʒən] *n* televisión *f*; **t. programme** programa *m* de televisión; **t. (set)** televisor *m*

teleworker ['telɪwɜːkə(r)] *n* teletrabajador(a) *m,f*

teleworking ['telɪwɜːkɪŋ] *n* teletrabajo *m*

telex ['teleks] **1** *n* télex *m*
2 *vt* enviar por télex

tell [tel] **1** *vt* (*pt & pp* **told**) (**a**) (*say*) decir; (*relate*) contar; (*inform*) comunicar; **to t. lies** mentir; **to t. sb about sth** contarle algo a algn; **you're telling me!** ¡a mí me lo vas a contar! (**b**) (*order*) mandar; **to t. sb to do sth** decir a algn que haga algo (**c**) (*distinguish*) distinguir; **to know how to t. the time** saber decir la hora (**d**) **all told** en total
2 *vi* (**a**) (*reveal*) reflejar (**b**) **who can t.?** (*know*) ¿quién sabe? (**c**) (*have effect*) notarse; **the pressure is telling on her** está acusando la presión
▶ **tell off** *vt sep Fam* regañar, reñir

teller ['telə(r)] *n* (*in bank etc*) cajero(a) *m,f*

telling ['telɪŋ] *adj* (*action*) eficaz; (*blow, argument*) contundente

telltale ['telteɪl] *n* chivato(a) *m,f*; **t. signs** señales reveladoras

telly ['telɪ] *n Br Fam* **the t.** la tele

temp [temp] *n Fam* trabajador(a) *m,f* temporal

temper ['tempə(r)] **1** *n* (**a**) (*mood*) humor *m*; **to keep one's t.** no perder la calma; **to lose one's t.** perder los estribos (**b**) (*temperament*) **to have a bad t.** tener (mal) genio
2 *vt* (*in metallurgy*) templar; *Fig* suavizar

temperament ['tempərəmənt] *n* temperamento *m*

temperamental [tempərəmentəl] *adj* temperamental

temperate ['tempərɪt] *adj* (**a**) (*mesurado*(a)) (**b**) (*climate*) templado(a)

temperature ['temprɪtʃə(r)] *n* temperatura *f*; **to have a t.** tener fiebre

tempest ['tempɪst] *n* tempestad *f*

temple¹ ['tempəl] *n Archit* templo *m*

temple² ['tempəl] *n Anat* sien *f*

tempo ['tempəʊ] *n* tempo *m*

temporary ['tempərərɪ] *adj* provisional; (*setback, improvement*) momentáneo(a); (*staff*) temporal

tempt [tempt] *vt* tentar; **to t. providence** tentar la suerte; **to t. sb to do sth** incitar a algn a hacer algo

temptation [temp'teɪʃən] *n* tentación *f*

tempting ['temptɪŋ] *adj* tentador(a)

ten [ten] *adj & n* diez (*m inv*)

tenable ['tenəbəl] *adj* (*opinion*) sostenible

tenacious [tɪ'neɪʃəs] *adj* tenaz

tenancy ['tenənsɪ] *n* (*of house*) alquiler *m*; (*of land*) arrendamiento *m*

tenant ['tenənt] *n* (*of house*) inquilino(a) *m,f*; (*of farm*) arrendatario(a) *m,f*

tend¹ [tend] *vi* (*be inclined*) tender, tener tendencia (**to** a)

tend² [tend] *vt* (*care for*) cuidar

tendency ['tendənsɪ] *n* tendencia *f*

tender¹ ['tendə(r)] *adj* (*affectionate*) cariñoso(a); (*compassionate*) compasivo(a); (*meat*) tierno(a)

tender² ['tendə(r)] **1** *vt* ofrecer; **to t. one's resignation** presentar la dimisión
2 *vi Com* **to t. for** sacar a concurso
3 *n* (**a**) *Com* oferta *f* (**b**) **legal t.** moneda *f* de curso legal

tenderness ['tendənɪs] *n* ternura *f*

tendon ['tendən] *n* tendón *m*

tenement ['tenɪmənt] *n* casa *f* de vecindad

tenet ['tenɪt] *n* principio *m*

tennis ['tenɪs] *n* tenis *m*; **t. ball** pelota *f* de tenis; **t. court** pista *f* de tenis; **t. player** tenista *mf*; **t. racket** raqueta *f* de tenis; **t. shoe** zapatilla *f* de tenis

tenor ['tenə(r)] *n Mus* tenor *m*

tense¹ [tens] *adj* tenso(a)

tense² [tens] *n Gram* tiempo *m*

tension ['tenʃən] *n* tensión *f*

tent [tent] *n* tienda *f* de campaña; **t. peg** estaca *f*

tentacle ['tentəkəl] *n* tentáculo *m*

tentative ['tentətɪv] *adj* (**a**) (*not definite*) de prueba (**b**) (*hesitant*) indeciso(a)

tenterhooks ['tentəhʊks] *npl Fig* **on t.** sobre ascuas

tenth [tenθ] **1** *adj & n* décimo(a) (*m,f*)
2 *n* (*fraction*) décimo *m*

tenuous ['tenjʊəs] *adj* (**a**) tenue (**b**) (*argument*) flojo(a)

tenure ['tenjʊə(r)] *n* (**a**) (*of office*) ocupación *f* (**b**) (*of property*) arrendamiento *m*

tepid ['tepɪd] *adj* tibio(a)

term [tɜːm] **1** *n* (**a**) (*period*) período *m*; *Educ* trimestre *m*; **t. of office** mandato *m*, legislatura *f*; **in the long/short t.** a largo/corto plazo (**b**) (*word*) término *m*; *Fig* **in terms of money** en cuanto al dinero (**c**) **terms** (*conditions*) condiciones *fpl*; **to come to terms with** hacerse a la idea de (**d**) **to be on good/bad terms with sb** tener buenas/malas relaciones con algn
2 *vt* calificar de

terminal ['tɜːmɪnəl] **1** *adj* terminal; **t. cancer** cáncer incurable
2 *n* terminal *f*

terminate ['tɜːmɪneɪt] **1** *vt* terminar; **to t. a pregnancy** abortar
2 *vi* terminarse

termini ['tɜːmɪnaɪ] *pl of* **terminus**

terminology [tɜːmɪ'nɒlədʒɪ] *n* terminología *f*

terminus ['tɜːmɪnəs] *n (pl* **termini**) terminal *m*

terrace ['terəs] *n* (**a**) *Agr* bancal *m* (**b**) *Br (of houses)* hilera *f* de casas (**c**) *(patio)* terraza *f* (**d**) *Ftb* **the terraces** las gradas

terraced ['terəst] *adj Br* **t. houses** casas *fpl* (de estilo uniforme) en hilera

terrain [tə'reɪn] *n* terreno *m*

terrible ['terəbəl] *adj* terrible; *Fig* **I feel t.** *(ill)* me encuentro fatal

terribly ['terəblɪ] *adv* terriblemente

terrier ['terɪə(r)] *n* terrier *m*

terrific [tə'rɪfɪk] *adj* (**a**) *Fam (excellent)* fenomenal (**b**) *(extreme)* tremendo(a)

terrify ['terɪfaɪ] *vt* aterrorizar

terrifying ['terɪfaɪɪŋ] *adj* aterrador(a)

territory ['terɪtərɪ] *n* territorio *m*

terror ['terə(r)] *n* terror *m*

terrorism ['terərɪzəm] *n* terrorismo *m*

terrorist ['terərɪst] *adj & n* terrorista *(mf)*

terrorize ['terəraɪz] *vt* aterrorizar

terry ['terɪ] *n* **t. towel** toalla *f* de rizo

terse [tɜːs] *adj (curt)* lacónico(a)

test [test] **1** *vt* probar, someter a una prueba; *(analyse)* analizar; *Med* hacer un análisis de
2 *n* prueba *f*, examen *m*; **to put to the t.** poner a prueba; **to stand the t.** pasar la prueba; **t. match** partido *m* internacional; **t. pilot** piloto *m* de pruebas; **t. tube** probeta *f*; **t.-tube baby** niño *m* probeta

testament ['testəmənt] *n* testamento *m*; **Old/ New T.** Antiguo/Nuevo Testamento *m*

testicle ['testɪkəl] *n* testículo *m*

testify ['testɪfaɪ] **1** *vt* declarar
2 *vi Fig* **to t. to sth** atestiguar algo

testimonial [testɪ'məʊnɪəl] *n* recomendación *f*

testimony ['testɪmənɪ] *n* testimonio *m*, declaración *f*

tetanus ['tetənəs] *n* tétano(s) *m inv*

tether ['teðə(r)] **1** *n* ronzal *m*; *Fig* **to be at the end of one's t.** estar hasta la coronilla
2 *vt (animal)* atar

Texas ['teksəs] *n* Tejas

text [tekst] *n* texto *m*

textbook ['tekstbʊk] *n* libro *m* de texto

textile ['tekstaɪl] **1** *n* tejido *m*
2 *adj* textil

texture ['tekstʃə(r)] *n* textura *f*

Thai [taɪ] *adj & n* tailandés(esa) *(m,f)*

Thailand ['taɪlænd] *n* Tailandia

Thames [temz] *n* **the T.** el Támesis

than [ðæn, *unstressed* ðən] *conj* que; *(with numbers)* de; **he's older t. me** es mayor que yo; **I have more/less t. you** tengo más/menos que tú; **more interesting t. we thought** más interesante de lo que creíamos; **more t. once** más de una vez; **more t. ten people** más de diez personas

thank [θæŋk] *vt* agradecer a; **t. you** gracias

thankful ['θæŋkfʊl] *adj* agradecido(a)

thankless ['θæŋklɪs] *adj (task)* ingrato(a)

thanks [θæŋks] *npl* gracias *fpl*; **no t.** no gracias; **many t.** muchas gracias; **t. for phoning** gracias por llamar; **t. to** gracias a

thanksgiving [θæŋks'gɪvɪŋ] *n US* **T. Day** Día *m* de Acción de Gracias

that [ðæt, *unstressed* ðət] **1** *dem pron (pl* **those**) (**a**) ése *m*, ésa *f*; *(further away)* aquél *m*, aquélla *f*; **this one is new but t. is old** éste es nuevo pero ése es viejo
(**b**) *(indefinite)* eso; *(remote)* aquello; **after t.** después de eso; **like t.** así; **t.'s right** eso es; **t.'s where I live** allí vivo yo; **what's t.?** ¿qué es eso?; **who's t.?** ¿quién es?
(**c**) *(with relative)* el/la; **all those I saw** todos los que vi
2 *dem adj (pl* **those**) *(masculine)* ese; *(feminine)* esa; *(further away) (masculine)* aquel; *(feminine)* aquella; **at t. time** en aquella época; **t. book** ese/aquel libro; **t. one** ése/aquél
3 *rel pron* (**a**) *(subject, direct object)* que; **all (t.) you said** todo lo que dijiste; **the letter (t.) I sent you** la carta que te envié
(**b**) *(governed by preposition)* que, el/la que, los/las que, el/la cual, los/las cuales; **the car (t.) they came in** el coche en el que vinieron
(**c**) *(when)* que, en que; **the moment (t.) you arrived** el momento en que llegaste

El pronombre relativo **that** puede omitirse salvo cuando es sujeto de la oración subordinada.

4 *conj* que; **come here so (t.) I can see you** ven aquí (para) que te vea; **he said (t.) he would come** dijo que vendría

La conjunción **that** se puede omitir cuando introduce una oración subordinada.

5 *adv* así de, tanto, tan; **cut off t. much** córteme un trozo así de grande; **I don't think it can be t. old** no creo que sea tan viejo; **we haven't got t. much money**

no tenemos tanto dinero

thatched [θætʃt] *adj* cubierto(a) con paja; **t. cottage** casita *f* con techo de paja; **t. roof** techo *m* de paja

thaw [θɔː] **1** *vt (snow)* derretir; *(food, freezer)* descongelar

  2 *vi* descongelarse; *(snow)* derretirse

  3 *n* deshielo *m*

the [ðə, *before vowel sound* ðı, *emphatic* ðiː] **1** *def art* (**a**) el/la; *pl* los/las; **at/to t.** al/a la; *pl* a los/a las; **of** *or* **from t.** del/de la; *pl* de los/de las; **t. Alps** los Alpes; **t. right time** la hora exacta; **t. voice of t. people** la voz del pueblo

   (**b**) *(omitted)* **George t. Sixth** Jorge Sexto

   (**c**) **by t. day** al día; **by t. dozen** a docenas

   (**d**) *(with adjectives used as nouns)* **t. elderly** los ancianos

   (**e**) *(indicating kind)* **he's not t. person to do that** no es de los que hacen tales cosas

   (**f**) *(enough)* **he hasn't t. patience to wait** no tiene suficiente paciencia para esperar

  2 *adv* **t. more t. merrier** cuantos más mejor; **t. sooner t. better** cuanto antes mejor

theatre, *US* **theater** [θıətə(r)] *n* teatro *m*

theatre-goer, *US* **theater-goer** [θıətə-ɡəʊə(r)] *n* aficionado(a) *m,f* al teatro

theatrical [θı'ætrıkəl] *adj* teatral

theft [θeft] *n* robo *m*; **petty t.** hurto *m*

their [ðeə(r)] *poss adj (one thing)* su; *(various things)* sus

theirs [ðeəz] *poss pron* (el) suyo/(la) suya; *pl* (los) suyos/(las) suyas

them [ðem, *unstressed* ðəm] *pers pron pl* (**a**) *(direct object)* los/las; *(indirect object)* les; **I know t.** los/las conozco; **I shall tell t. so** se lo diré (a ellos/ellas); **it's t.!** ¡son ellos!; **speak to t.** hábleles (**b**) *(with preposition)* ellos/ellas; **walk in front of t.** camine delante de ellos; **they took the keys away with t.** se llevaron las llaves; **both of t., the two of t.** los dos; **neither of t.** ninguno de los dos; **none of t.** ninguno de ellos

theme [θiːm] *n* tema *m*; **t. tune** sintonía *f*

themselves [ðəm'selvz] *pers pron pl (as subject)* ellos mismos/ellas mismas; *(as direct or indirect object)* se; *(after a preposition)* sí mismos/sí mismas; **they did it by t.** lo hicieron ellos solos

then [ðen] **1** *adv* (**a**) *(at that time)* entonces; **since t.** desde entonces; **there and t.** en el acto; **till t.** hasta entonces (**b**) *(next, afterwards)* luego (**c**) *(anyway)* de todas

formas (**d**) *(in that case)* entonces; **go t.** pues vete

  2 *conj* entonces

  3 *adj* **the t. president** el entonces presidente

theology [θı'ɒlədʒı] *n* teología *f*

theoretic(al) [θıə'retık(əl)] *adj* teórico(a)

theoretically [θıə'retıklı)] *adv* teóricamente

theory ['θıərı] *n* teoría *f*

therapist ['θerəpıst] *n* terapeuta *mf*

therapy ['θerəpı] *n* terapia *f*

there [ðeə(r), *unstressed* ðə(r)] **1** *adv* (**a**) *(indicating place)* allí, allá; *(nearer speaker)* ahí; **here and t.** acá y allá; **in t.** ahí dentro; **is Peter t.?** ¿está Peter? (**b**) *(emphatic)* **that man t.** aquel hombre (**c**) *(unstressed)* **t. is .../t. are ...** hay...; **t. were many cars** había muchos coches; **t. were six of us** éramos seis (**d**) *(in respect)* **t.'s the difficulty** ahí está la dificultad

  2 *interj* **so t.!** ¡ea!; **t., t.** bien, bien

thereabouts ['ðeərəbaʊts], *US* **thereabout** ['ðeərəbaʊt] *adv* **in Cambridge or t.** en Cambridge o por allí cerca; **at four o'clock or t.** a las cuatro o así

thereafter [ðeər'ɑːftə(r)] *adv* a partir de entonces

thereby ['ðeəbaı] *adv* por eso *or* ello

therefore ['ðeəfɔː(r)] *adv* por lo tanto, por eso

thermal ['θɜːməl] **1** *adj (spring)* termal; *Phys* térmico(a)

  2 *n Met* corriente térmica

thermometer [θə'mɒmıtə(r)] *n* termómetro *m*

Thermos® ['θɜːməs] *n* **T. (flask)** termo *m*

thermostat ['θɜːməstæt] *n* termostato *m*

thesaurus [θı'sɔːrəs] *n* diccionario *m* de sinónimos

these [ðiːz] **1** *dem adj pl* estos(as)

  2 *dem pron pl* éstos(as); *see* **this**

thesis ['θiːsıs] *n (pl* **theses** ['θiːsiːz]) tesis *f inv*

they [ðeı] *pron pl* (**a**) ellos/ellas *(usually omitted in Spanish, except for contrast)*; **t. are dancing** están bailando; **t. are rich** son ricos (**b**) *(stressed)* **t. alone** ellos solos; **t. themselves told me** me lo dijeron ellos mismos (**c**) *(with relative)* los/las (**d**) *(indefinite)* **that's what t. say** eso es lo que se dice; **t. say that ...** se dice que ...

thick [θık] **1** *adj* (**a**) *(book etc)* grueso(a); **a wall 2 m t.** un muro de 2 m de espesor (**b**) *(dense)* espeso(a) (**c**) *Fam (stupid)* tonto(a)

  2 *adv* densamente

3 *n* **to be in the t. of it** estar metido(a) de lleno

thicken ['θɪkən] **1** *vt* espesar

2 *vi* espesarse; *Fig (plot)* complicarse

thickness ['θɪknɪs] *n (of wall etc)* espesor *m*; *(of wire, lips)* grueso *m*; *(of liquid, woodland)* espesura *f*

thickset [θɪk'set] *adj (person)* rechoncho(a)

thick-skinned [θɪk'skɪnd] *adj Fig* poco sensible

thief [θiːf] *n (pl* **thieves** [θiːvz]) ladrón(ona) *m,f*

thigh [θaɪ] *n* muslo *m*

thimble ['θɪmbəl] *n* dedal *m*

thin [θɪn] **1** *adj* (**thinner, thinnest**) (**a**) delgado(a); **a t. slice** una loncha fina (**b**) *(hair, vegetation)* ralo(a); *(liquid)* claro(a); *(population)* escaso(a) (**c**) *Fig (voice)* débil; **a t. excuse** un pobre pretexto

2 *vt* **to t. (down)** *(paint)* diluir

thing [θɪŋ] *n* (**a**) cosa *f*; **my things** *(clothing)* mi ropa *f*; *(possessions)* mis cosas *fpl*; **for one t.** en primer lugar; **the t. is ...** resulta que ...; **what with one t. and another** entre unas cosas y otras; **as things are** tal como están las cosas (**b**) **poor little t.!** ¡pobrecito(a)!

think [θɪŋk] **1** *vt (pt & pp* **thought**) (**a**) *(believe)* pensar, creer; **I t. so/not** creo que sí/no (**b**) **I thought as much** yo me lo imaginaba

2 *vi* (**a**) pensar (**of** *or* **about** en); **give me time to t.** dame tiempo para reflexionar; **to t. ahead** prevenir (**b**) *(have as opinion)* opinar, pensar; **to t. highly of sb** apreciar a algn; **what do you t.?** ¿a ti qué te parece? (**c**) **just t.!** ¡imagínate!

▶ **think out** *vt sep* meditar; **a carefully thought-out answer** una respuesta razonada

▶ **think over** *vt sep* reflexionar; **we'll have to t. it over** lo tendremos que pensar

▶ **think up** *vt sep* imaginar, idear

thinking ['θɪŋkɪŋ] *adj* racional

think-tank ['θɪŋktæŋk] *n Fam* grupo *m* de expertos

thinly ['θɪnlɪ] *adv* poco, ligeramente

third [θɜːd] **1** *adj* tercero(a); *(before masculine singular noun)* tercer; **(on) the t. of March** el tres de marzo; **the T. World** el Tercer Mundo; **t. party insurance** seguro *m* a terceros

2 *n* (**a**) *(in series)* tercero(a) *m,f* (**b**) *(fraction)* tercio *m*, tercera parte

thirdly ['θɜːdlɪ] *adv* en tercer lugar

third-rate ['θɜːdreɪt] *adj* de calidad inferior

thirst [θɜːst] *n* sed *f*

thirsty ['θɜːstɪ] *adj* (**thirstier, thirstiest**) sediento(a); **to be t.** tener sed

thirteen [θɜː'tiːn] *adj & n* trece (*m inv*)

thirteenth [θɜː'tiːnθ] **1** *adj & n* decimotercero(a) *(m,f)*

2 *n (fraction)* decimotercera parte

thirtieth ['θɜːtɪθ] **1** *adj & n* trigésimo(a) *(m,f)*

2 *n (fraction)* trigésima parte

thirty ['θɜːtɪ] *adj & n* treinta (*m inv*)

this [ðɪs] **1** *dem adj (pl* **these**) *(masculine)* este; *(feminine)* esta; **t. book/these books** este libro/estos libros; **t. one** éste/ésta

2 *dem pron (pl* **these**) (**a**) *(indefinite)* esto; **it was like t.** fue así (**b**) *(place)* **t. is where we met** fue aquí donde nos conocimos (**c**) *(time)* **it should have come before t.** debería haber llegado ya (**d**) *(specific person or thing)* éste *m*, ésta *f*; **I prefer these to those** me gustan más éstos que aquéllos; *(introduction)* **t. is Mr Álvarez** le presento al Sr. Álvarez; *Tel* **t. is Julia (speaking)** soy Julia

3 *adv* **he got t. far** llegó hasta aquí; **t. small/big** así de pequeño/grande

thistle ['θɪsəl] *n* cardo *m*

thong [θɒŋ] *n* (**a**) *(for fastening)* correa *f* (**b**) *US & Austral (sandal)* chancla *f*

thorax ['θɔːræks] *n* tórax *m*

thorn [θɔːn] *n* espina *f*

thorough ['θʌrə] *adj (careful)* minucioso(a); *(work)* concienzudo(a); *(knowledge)* profundo(a); **to carry out a t. enquiry into a matter** investigar a fondo un asunto

thoroughbred ['θʌrəbred] **1** *adj (horse)* de pura sangre

2 *n (horse)* pura sangre *mf*

thoroughfare ['θʌrəfeə(r)] *n (road)* carretera *f*; *(street)* calle *f*

thoroughly ['θʌrəlɪ] *adv (carefully)* a fondo; *(wholly)* completamente

those [ðəʊz] **1** *dem pron pl* ésos(as); *(remote)* aquéllos(as); **t. who** los que/las que

2 *dem adj pl* esos(as); *(remote)* aquellos(as); *see* **that**

though [ðəʊ] **1** *conj* (**a**) aunque; **strange t. it may seem** por (muy) extraño que parezca (**b**) **as t.** como si; **it looks as t. he's gone** parece que se ha ido

2 *adv* sin embargo

thought [θɔːt] **1** *n* (**a**) *(act of thinking)* pensamiento *m*; **what a tempting t.!** ¡qué

idea más tentadora! **(b)** *(reflection)* reflexión *f* **(c)** *(intention)* lo que cuenta es la intención
  2 *pt & pp of* **think**

thoughtful ['θɔːtfʊl] *adj (pensive)* pensativo(a); *(considerate)* atento(a)

thoughtless ['θɔːtlɪs] *adj (person)* desconsiderado(a); *(action)* irreflexivo(a)

thousand ['θaʊzənd] *adj & n* mil *(m inv)*; **thousands of people** miles de personas

thousandth ['θaʊzənθ] **1** *adj* milésimo(a)
  2 *n* **(a)** *(in series)* milésimo(a) *m,f* **(b)** *(fraction)* milésima parte

thrash [θræʃ] **1** *vt* dar una paliza a
  2 *vi* **to t. about** *or* **around** agitarse
  ▸ **thrash out** *vt sep* discutir a fondo

thread [θred] **1** *n* **(a)** hilo *m*; **length of t.** hebra *f* **(b)** *(of screw)* rosca *f*
  2 *vt* **(a)** *(needle)* enhebrar **(b)** **to t. one's way (through)** colarse (por)

threadbare ['θredbeə(r)] *adj* raído(a)

threat [θret] *n* amenaza *f*

threaten ['θretən] *vt* amenazar; **to t. to do sth** amenazar con hacer algo

threatening ['θretənɪŋ] *adj* amenazador(a)

threateningly ['θretənɪŋlɪ] *adv* de modo amenazador

three [θriː] *adj & n* tres *(m inv)*

three-dimensional ['θriːdɪ'menʃənəl] *adj* tridimensional

threefold ['θriːfəʊld] **1** *adj* triple
  2 *adv* tres veces; **to increase t.** triplicarse

three-piece ['θriːpiːs] *adj* **t. suit** traje *m* de tres piezas; **t. suite** tresillo *m*

three-ply ['θriːplaɪ] *adj* de tres hebras

three-wheeler [θriː'wiːlə(r)] *n Aut* coche *m* de tres ruedas; *(tricycle)* triciclo *m*

thresh [θreʃ] *vt* trillar

threshold ['θreʃəʊld] *n* umbral *m*; *Fig* **to be on the t. of** estar a las puertas *or* en los umbrales de

threw [θruː] *pt of* **throw**

thrifty ['θrɪftɪ] *adj* **(thriftier, thriftiest)** económico(a), ahorrador(a)

thrill [θrɪl] **1** *n* **(a)** *(excitement)* emoción *f* **(b)** *(quiver)* estremecimiento *m*
  2 *vt (excite)* emocionar; *(audience)* entusiasmar

thriller ['θrɪlə(r)] *n* novela *f*/película *f* de suspense

thrilling ['θrɪlɪŋ] *adj* emocionante

thrive [θraɪv] *vi (pt* **thrived** *or* **throve***; pp* **thrived** *or* **thriven** ['θrɪvən]) **(a)** *(person)* rebosar de salud **(b)** *Fig (business)* prosperar; **he thrives on it** le viene de maravilla

thriving ['θraɪvɪŋ] *adj Fig* próspero(a)

throat [θrəʊt] *n* garganta *f*

throb [θrɒb] **1** *n* *(of heart)* latido *m*; *(of machine)* zumbido *m*
  2 *vi (heart)* latir; *(machine)* zumbar; **my head is throbbing** me va a estallar la cabeza

throes [θrəʊz] *npl* **to be in one's death t.** estar agonizando; *Fig* **in the t. of ...** en pleno(a)...

thrombosis [θrɒm'bəʊsɪs] *n Med* trombosis *f inv*

throne [θrəʊn] *n* trono *m*

throng [θrɒŋ] **1** *n* multitud *f*, gentío *m*
  2 *vi* apiñarse
  3 *vt* atestar

throttle ['θrɒtəl] **1** *n* **t. (valve)** *(of engine)* válvula reguladora
  2 *vt (person)* estrangular
  ▸ **throttle back** *vt sep (engine)* desacelerar

through [θruː] **1** *prep* **(a)** *(place)* a través de, por; **to look t. the window** mirar por la ventana
  (b) *(time)* a lo largo de; **all t. his life** durante toda su vida; *US* **Tuesday t. Thursday** desde el martes hasta el jueves inclusive
  (c) *(by means of)* por, mediante; **I learnt of it t.** Jack me enteré por Jack
  (d) *(because of)* a *or* por causa de; **t. ignorance** por ignorancia
  2 *adj* **a t. train** un tren directo; **t. traffic** tránsito *m*
  3 *adv* **(a)** *(from one side to the other)* de un lado a otro; **to let sb t.** dejar pasar a algn; *Fig* **socialist/French t. and t.** socialista/francés por los cuatro costados
  (b) **I'm t. with him** he terminado con él
  (c) *Tel* **to get t. to sb** comunicar con algn; **you're t.** ¡hablen!

throughout [θruː'aʊt] **1** *prep* por todo(a); **t. the year** durante todo el año
  2 *adv (place)* en todas partes; *(time)* todo el tiempo

throve [θrəʊv] *pt of* **thrive**

throw [θrəʊ] **1** *vt (pt* **threw***; pp* **thrown**) **(a)** tirar, arrojar; *(to the ground)* derribar; *(rider)* desmontar; *Fig* **he threw a fit** le dio un ataque; *Fig* **to t. a party** dar una fiesta **(b)** *(disconcert)* desconcertar
  2 *n* tiro *m*, lanzamiento *m*; *(in wrestling)* derribo *m*
  ▸ **throw away** *vt sep (rubbish)* tirar; *(money)* malgastar; *(opportunity)* perder
  ▸ **throw in** *vt sep (a)* tirar; *Sport* sacar de banda; *Fig* **to t. in the towel** arrojar la toalla **(b)** *(include)* añadir; *(in deal)* incluir (gratis)

► **throw off** *vt sep (person, thing)* deshacerse de; *(clothes)* quitarse

► **throw out** *vt sep (rubbish)* tirar; *(person)* echar

► **throw up 1** *vt sep* (a) lanzar al aire (b) *Constr* construir rápidamente

2 *vi Fam* vomitar, devolver

throwaway ['θrəʊəweɪ] *adj* desechable

throw-in ['θrəʊɪn] *n Sport* saque *m* de banda

thrown [θrəʊn] *pp of* **throw**

thru [θruː] *prep, adj & adv US Fam* = **through**

thrush [θrʌʃ] *n Orn* tordo *m*, zorzal *m*

thrust [θrʌst] **1** *vt (pt & pp* thrust) empujar con fuerza; **he t. a letter into my hand** me puso una carta violentamente en la mano

2 *n (push)* empujón *m; Av & Phys* empuje *m*

thud [θʌd] *n* ruido sordo

thug [θʌg] *n (lout)* gamberro *m; (criminal)* criminal *m*

thumb [θʌm] **1** *n* pulgar *m*

2 *vt* (a) manosear (b) **to t. a lift** hacer autostop

► **thumb through** *vt insep (book)* hojear

thumbtack ['θʌmtæk] *n US* chincheta *f*

thump [θʌmp] **1** *n* (a) *(sound)* ruido sordo (b) *(blow)* golpazo *m; Fam* torta *f*

2 *vt* golpear

3 *vi* (a) **to t. on the table** golpear la mesa (b) *(heart)* latir ruidosamente

thunder ['θʌndə(r)] **1** *n* trueno *m;* **t. of applause** estruendo *m* de aplausos

2 *vi* tronar

thunderbolt ['θʌndəbəʊlt] *n (lighting)* rayo *m; Fig (news)* bomba *f*

thunderclap ['θʌndəklæp] *n* trueno *m*

thunderous ['θʌndərəs] *adj Fig* ensordecedor(a)

thunderstorm ['θʌndəstɔːm] *n* tormenta *f*

thundery ['θʌndərɪ] *adj (weather)* tormentoso(a)

Thursday ['θɜːzdɪ] *n* jueves *m*

thus [ðʌs] *adv* así, de esta manera; **and t. ... así que ...**

thwart [θwɔːt] *vt* frustrar, desbaratar

thyme [taɪm] *n* tomillo *m*

thyroid ['θaɪrɔɪd] *n* tiroides *f inv*

tiara [tɪ'ɑːrə] *n* diadema *f; Rel* tiara *f*

tic [tɪk] *n* tic *m*

tick¹ [tɪk] **1** *n* (a) *(sound)* tic-tac *m* (b) *Br Fam* **I'll do it in a t.** ahora mismo lo hago (c) *(mark)* marca *f* de visto bueno

2 *vi* hacer tic-tac

3 *vt* marcar

► **tick off** *vt sep* (a) *(mark)* marcar (b) *Br Fam (reprimand)* regañar

► **tick over** *vi Aut* funcionar al ralentí

tick² [tɪk] *n (insect)* garrapata *f*

ticket ['tɪkɪt] *n* (a) *(for bus etc)* billete *m, Am* boleto *m; (for theatre, cinema)* entrada *f, Méx* boleto; *(for lottery)* décimo *m, Am* boleto; **t. collector** revisor(a) *m,f;* **t. office** taquilla *f;* **t.** *Br* **tout** *or US* **scalper** revendedor *m* de entradas (b) *(receipt)* recibo *m* (c) *(label)* etiqueta *f* (d) *Aut* multa *f*

tickle ['tɪkəl] **1** *vt* hacer cosquillas a

2 *vi* hacer cosquillas

3 *n* cosquillas *fpl*

ticklish ['tɪklɪʃ] *adj* **to be t.** tener cosquillas

tick-tack-toe ['tɪktæk'təʊ] *n US* tres en raya *m*

tidal ['taɪdəl] *adj* de la marea; **t. wave** ola *f* gigante

tidbit ['tɪdbɪt] *n US* = **titbit**

tiddlywinks ['tɪdlɪwɪŋks] *n sing (game)* pulga *f*

tide [taɪd] *n* (a) marea *f;* **high/low t.** marea alta/baja (b) *Fig (of events)* curso *m;* **the t. has turned** han cambiado las cosas; **to go against the t.** ir contra corriente

tidings ['taɪdɪŋz] *npl Fml* noticias *fpl*

tidy ['taɪdɪ] **1** *adj* (**tidier, tidiest**) (a) *(room, habits)* ordenado(a) (b) *(appearance)* arreglado(a)

2 *vt* arreglar; **to t. away** poner en su sitio

3 *vi* **to t. (up)** ordenar las cosas

tie [taɪ] **1** *vt (shoelaces etc)* atar; **to t. a knot** hacer un nudo

2 *vi Sport* empatar (**with** con)

3 *n* (a) *(bond)* lazo *m*, vínculo *m* (b) *Fig (hindrance)* atadura *f* (c) *(clothing)* corbata *f* (d) *Sport (match)* partido *m; (draw)* empate *m*

► **tie down** *vt sep* sujetar; *Fig* **to be tied down** estar atado(a); *Fig* **to t. sb down to a promise** obligar a algn a cumplir una promesa

► **tie up** *vt sep* (a) *(parcel, dog)* atar (b) *(deal)* concluir (c) *(capital)* inmovilizar; *Fig* **I'm tied up just now** de momento estoy muy ocupado(a)

tiebreaker ['taɪbreɪkə(r)] *n* tie-break *m*

tiepin ['taɪpɪn] *n* alfiler *m* de corbata

tier [tɪə(r)] *n (of seats)* fila *f; (in stadium)* grada *f;* **four-t. cake** pastel *m* de cuatro pisos

tiger ['taɪgə(r)] *n* tigre *m*

tight [taɪt] **1** *adj* (a) apretado(a); *(clothing)* ajustado(a); *(seal)* hermético(a);

my shoes are too t. me aprietan los zapatos; *Fig* **to be in a t. corner** estar en un apuro **(b)** *(scarce)* escaso(a); **money's a bit t.** estamos escasos de dinero **(c)** *(mean)* agarrado(a) **(d)** *Fam (drunk)* borracho(a)

2 *adv* estrechamente; *(seal)* herméticamente; **hold t.** agárrate fuerte; **shut t.** bien cerrado(a); **to sit t.** no moverse de su sitio

tighten ['taɪtən] **1** *vt (screw)* apretar, *(rope)* tensar; *Fig* **to t. (up) restrictions** intensificar las restricciones

2 *vi* apretarse; *(cable)* tensarse

tightfisted [taɪt'fɪstɪd] *adj* tacaño(a)

tightrope ['taɪtrəʊp] *n* cuerda floja; **t. walker** funámbulo(a) *m,f*

tights [taɪts] *npl (thick)* leotardos *mpl*; *(of dancer)* mallas *fpl*; *Br (thin)* medias *fpl*, pantis *mpl*

tile [taɪl] **1** *n (of roof)* teja *f*; *(glazed)* azulejo *m*; *(for floor)* baldosa *f*

2 *vt (roof)* tejar; *(wall)* azulejar; *(floor)* embaldosar

tiled [taɪld] *adj (roof)* de *or* con tejas; *(wall)* revestido(a) de azulejos; *(floor)* embaldosado(a)

till¹ [tɪl] *n (for cash)* caja *f*

till² [tɪl] *vt (field)* labrar, cultivar

till³ [tɪl] **1** *prep* hasta; **from morning t. night** de la mañana a la noche; **t. then** hasta entonces

2 *conj* hasta que

tiller ['tɪlə(r)] *n Naut* caña *f* del timón

tilt [tɪlt] **1** *n* **(a)** *(angle)* inclinación *f* **(b) (at) full t.** *(speed)* a toda velocidad

2 *vi* **to t. over** volcarse; **to t. (up)** inclinarse

3 *vt* inclinar

timber ['tɪmbə(r)] *n (wood)* madera *f* (de construcción); *(trees)* árboles *mpl*; **(piece of) t.** viga *f*

time [taɪm] **1** *n* **(a)** tiempo *m*; **all the t.** todo el tiempo; **for some t. (past)** desde hace algún tiempo; **I haven't seen him for a long t.** hace mucho (tiempo) que no lo veo; **in a short t.** en poco tiempo; **in no t.** en un abrir y cerrar de ojos; **in t.** a tiempo; **in three weeks' t.** dentro de tres semanas; **to take one's t. over sth** hacer algo con calma; *Fam* **to do t.** cumplir una condena; **t. bomb** bomba *f* de relojería; **t. limit** límite *m* de tiempo; *(for payment etc)* plazo *m*; **t. switch** interruptor *m* electrónico automático; **t. zone** huso horario

(b) *(era)* época *f*, tiempos *mpl*; **a sign of the times** un signo de los tiempos; **to be**

behind the times tener ideas anticuadas

(c) *(point in time)* momento *m*; **(at) any t. (you like)** cuando quiera; **at no t.** en ningún momento; **at that t.** (en aquel) entonces; **at the same t.** al mismo tiempo; **at times** a veces; **from t. to t.** de vez en cuando; **he may turn up at any t.** puede llegar en cualquier momento

(d) *(time of day)* hora *f*; **and about t. too!** ¡ya era hora!; **in good t.** con anticipación; **on t.** puntualmente; **what's the t.?** ¿qué hora es?

(e) **t. of year** época *f* del año

(f) **to have a good/bad t.** pasarlo bien/mal

(g) *(occasion)* vez *f*; **four at a t.** cuatro a la vez; **next t.** la próxima vez; **several times over** varias veces; **three times running** tres veces seguidas; **t. after t.** una y otra vez

(h) *(in multiplication)* **three times four** tres (multiplicado) por cuatro; **four times as big** cuatro veces más grande

(i) *Mus* compás *m*; **in t.** al compás

2 *vt* **(a)** *(speech)* calcular la duración de; *Sport (race)* cronometrar

(b) *(choose the time of)* escoger el momento oportuno para

time-consuming ['taɪmkənsjuːmɪŋ] *adj* que ocupa mucho tiempo

time-lag ['taɪmlæg] *n* intervalo *m*

timeless ['taɪmlɪs] *adj* eterno(a)

timely ['taɪmlɪ] *adj* (**timelier, timeliest**) oportuno(a)

timer ['taɪmə(r)] *n (device)* temporizador *m*

timetable ['taɪmteɪbəl] *n* horario *m*

timid ['tɪmɪd] *adj* tímido(a)

timing ['taɪmɪŋ] *n* **(a)** *(timeliness)* oportunidad *f*, *(coordination)* coordinación *f*; **your t. was wrong** no calculaste bien **(b)** *Sport* cronometraje *m*

tin [tɪn] **1** *n* **(a)** *(metal)* estaño *m*; **t. plate** hojalata *f* **(b)** *(container)* lata *f*

2 *vt (tins)* enlatar; **tinned food** conservas *fpl*

tinfoil ['tɪnfɔɪl] *n* papel *m* de estaño

tinge [tɪndʒ] **1** *n* tinte *m*, matiz *m*

2 *vt* teñir

tingle ['tɪŋɡəl] *vi* **my feet are tingling** siento un hormigueo en los pies

tinker ['tɪŋkə(r)] **1** *n Pej* calderero(a) *mf*

2 *vi* **stop tinkering with the radio** deja de toquetear la radio

tinkle ['tɪŋkəl] *vi* tintinear

tin-opener ['tɪnəʊpənə(r)] *n* abrelatas *m inv*

tinsel ['tɪnsəl] *n* oropel *m*

tint [tɪnt] **1** *n* tinte *m*, matiz *m*
2 *vt* teñir; **to t. one's hair** teñirse el pelo
tiny ['taɪnɪ] *adj* (**tinier, tiniest**) pequeñito(a); **a t. bit** un poquitín
tip¹ [tɪp] **1** *n* (*end*) punta *f; (of cigarette)* colilla *f;* **it's on the t. of my tongue** lo tengo en la punta de la lengua
2 *vt* poner cantera a; **tipped with steel** con punta de acero
tip² [tɪp] **1** *n* (**a**) (*gratuity*) propina *f* (**b**) (*advice*) consejo *m* (**c**) *Sport (racing)* pronóstico *m*
2 *vt* (**a**) dar una propina a (**b**) *Sport* pronosticar
▸ **tip off** *vt sep (police)* dar el chivatazo a
tip³ [tɪp] **1** *n Br* **rubbish t.** vertedero *m*
2 *vt* inclinar; *Br (rubbish)* verter
3 *vi* **to t. (up)** ladearse; *(cart)* bascular
▸ **tip over 1** *vt sep* volcar
2 *vi* volcarse
tipple ['tɪpəl] *Fam* **1** *vi* empinar el codo
2 *n* bebida alcohólica; **what's your t.?** ¿qué te gusta beber?
tipsy ['tɪpsɪ] *adj* (**tipsier, tipsiest**) contentillo(a)
tiptoe ['tɪptəʊ] **1** *vi* andar de puntillas; **to t. in/out** entrar/salir de puntillas
2 *n* **on t.** de puntillas
tiptop ['tɪptɒp] *adj Fam* de primera
tire¹ [taɪə(r)] *n US* = tyre
tire² [taɪə(r)] **1** *vt* cansar; **to t. sb out** agotar a algn
2 *vi* cansarse; **to t. of doing sth** cansarse de hacer algo
tired ['taɪəd] *adj* cansado(a); **t. out** rendido(a); **to be t.** estar cansado(a); **to be t. of sth** estar harto(a) de algo
tireless ['taɪəlɪs] *adj* incansable
tiresome ['taɪəsəm] *adj* pesado(a)
tiring ['taɪərɪŋ] *adj* agotador(a)
tissue ['tɪʃuː, 'tɪsjuː] *n* (**a**) *Biol* tejido *m* (**b**) *Tex* tisú *m;* **t. paper** papel *m* de seda (**c**) *(handkerchief)* pañuelo *m* de papel, kleenex® *m*
tit¹ [tɪt] *n* **to give t. for tat** devolver la pelota
tit² [tɪt] *n very Fam (breast)* teta *f*
titbit ['tɪtbɪt] *n* golosina *f*
titillate ['tɪtɪleɪt] *vt* excitar
title ['taɪtl] *n* (**a**) título *m; Cin* **credit titles** ficha técnica; **t. page** portada *f;* **t. role** papel *m* principal (**b**) *Jur* título *m*
titter ['tɪtə(r)] **1** *vi* reírse nerviosamente; *(foolishly)* reírse tontamente
2 *n* risa ahogada; *(foolish)* risilla tonta
titular ['tɪtjʊlə(r)] *adj* titular
TM *n* (*abbr* **trademark**) marca registrada
to [tuː, *unstressed before vowels* tʊ, *before*

consonants tə] **1** *prep* (**a**) (*with place*) a; *(expressing direction)* hacia; **from town to town** de ciudad en ciudad; **he went to France/Japan** fue a Francia/Japón; **I'm going to Mary's** voy a casa de Mary; **it is 30 miles to London** Londres está a 30 millas; **the train to Madrid** el tren de Madrid; **to the east** hacia el este; **to the right** a la derecha; **what school do you go to?** ¿a qué escuela vas?
(**b**) (*time*) a; **from day to day** de día en día; **from two to four** de dos a cuatro; **ten (minutes) to six** las seis menos diez
(**c**) (*as far as*) hasta; **accurate to a millimetre** exacto(a) hasta el milímetro
(**d**) (*with indirect object*) **he gave it to his cousin** se lo dio a su primo; **what's that to you?** ¿qué te importa a ti?
(**e**) *(towards a person)* **he was very kind to me** se portó muy bien conmigo
(**f**) (*of*) de; **heir to an estate** heredero *m* de una propiedad; **adviser to the president** consejero *m* del presidente
(**g**) **to come to sb's assistance** acudir en ayuda de algn; **to everyone's surprise** para sorpresa de todos; **to this end** con este fin
(**h**) **to the best of my knowledge** que yo sepa
(**i**) (*compared to*) **that's nothing to what I've seen** eso no es nada en comparación con lo que he visto yo
(**j**) (*in proportion*) **one house to the square kilometre** una casa por kilómetro cuadrado; **six votes to four** seis votos contra cuatro
(**k**) (*about*) **what did he say to my suggestion?** ¿qué contestó a mi sugerencia?
2 *n infin* (**a**) *with simple infinitives* **to** *is not translated but is shown by the verb endings;* **to buy** comprar; **to come** venir
(**b**) (*in order to*) para; *(with words of motion or purpose)* a, por; **he did it to help me** lo hizo para ayudarme; **he stopped to talk** se detuvo a hablar; **he fought to convince them** luchó por convencerlos
(**c**) *various verbs followed by dependent infinitives take particular prepositions* (a, de, en, por, con, para *etc*) *and others take no preposition; see the entry of the verb in question*
(**d**) (*with adj and infin*) a, de; **difficult to do** difícil de hacer; **ready to listen** dispuesto(a) a escuchar; **too hot to drink** demasiado caliente para bebérselo
(**e**) (*with noun and infin*) **the first to complain** el primero en quejarse; **this is**

the time to do it éste es el momento de hacerlo; **to have a great deal to do** tener mucho que hacer

(f) *(expressing following action)* **he awoke to find the light still on** al despertarse encontró la lámpara todavía encendida

(g) *(with verbs of ordering, wishing etc)* **he asked me to do it** me pidió que lo hiciera

(h) *(expressing obligation)* **fifty employees are to go** cincuenta empleados deben ser despedidos; **to have to do sth** tener que hacer algo

(i) *(replacing infin)* **go if you want to** váyase si quiere

3 *adv* **to go to and fro** ir y venir; **to push the door to** encajar la puerta

toad [təʊd] *n* sapo *m*

toadstool ['təʊdstuːl] *n* hongo *m* (venenoso)

toast¹ [təʊst] *Culin* **1** *n* pan tostado; **a slice of t.** una tostada

2 *vt* tostar

toast² [təʊst] **1** *n (drink)* brindis *m inv*; **to drink a t.** to brindar por

2 *vt* brindar por

toaster ['təʊstə(r)] *n* tostador *m* (de pan)

tobacco [tə'bækəʊ] *n* tabaco *m*

tobacconist [tə'bækənɪst] *n Br* estanquero(a) *m,f*; *Br* **t.'s (shop)** estanco *m*

toboggan [tə'bɒgən] *n* tobogán *m*

today [tə'deɪ] **1** *n* hoy *m*

2 *adv* hoy; *(nowadays)* hoy en día; **a week t.** justo dentro de una semana

toddler ['tɒdlə(r)] *n* niño(a) *m,f* que empieza a andar; **the toddlers** los pequeñitos

toddy ['tɒdɪ] *n (drink)* ponche *m*

to-do [tə'duː] *n* lío *m*, jaleo *m*

toe [təʊ] **1** *n* dedo *m* del pie; **big t.** dedo gordo

2 *vt* **to t. the line** conformarse

toenail ['təʊneɪl] *n* uña *f* del dedo del pie

toffee ['tɒfɪ] *n* caramelo *m*

together [tə'geðə(r)] *adv* junto, juntos(as); **all t.** todos juntos; **t. with** junto con; **to bring t.** reunir

toil [tɔɪl] **1** *n* trabajo duro

2 *vi* afanarse, trabajar (duro); **to t. up a hill** subir penosamente una cuesta

toilet ['tɔɪlɪt] *n (a)* wáter *m*, retrete *m*; *(for public)* servicios *mpl*; **t. paper** *or* **tissue** papel higiénico; **t. roll** rollo *m* de papel higiénico *(b) (washing etc)* aseo *m* (personal); **t. bag** neceser *m*; **t. soap** jabón *m* de tocador

toiletries ['tɔɪlɪtrɪz] *npl* artículos *mpl* de aseo

token ['təʊkən] **1** *n (a) (sign)* señal *f*; **as a t. of respect** en señal de respeto *(b) Com* vale *m*; **book t.** vale para comprar libros

2 *adj* simbólico(a)

told [təʊld] *pt & pp of* **tell**

tolerable ['tɒlərəbl] *adj* tolerable

tolerance ['tɒlərəns] *n* tolerancia *f*

tolerant ['tɒlərənt] *adj* tolerante

tolerate ['tɒləreɪt] *vt* tolerar

toll¹ [təʊl] **1** *vt* tocar

2 *vi* doblar

toll² [təʊl] *n (a) Aut* peaje *m (b) (loss)* pérdidas *fpl*; **the death t.** el número de víctimas mortales

toll-free [təʊl'friː] *US* **1** *adj* **t. number** (número *m* de) teléfono *m* gratuito

2 *adv (call)* gratuitamente

tomato [tə'mɑːtəʊ, *US* tə'meɪtəʊ] *n (pl* **tomatoes)** tomate *m*; **t. sauce** salsa *f* de tomate

tomb [tuːm] *n* tumba *f*, sepulcro *m*

tomboy ['tɒmbɔɪ] *n* marimacho *f*

tombstone ['tuːmstəʊn] *n* lápida *f* sepulcral

tomcat ['tɒmkæt] *n* gato *m* (macho)

tomorrow [tə'mɒrəʊ] **1** *n* mañana *m*; **the day after t.** pasado mañana; **t. night** mañana por la noche

2 *adv* mañana; **see you t.!** ¡hasta mañana!; **t. week** dentro de ocho días a partir de mañana

ton [tʌn] *n* tonelada *f*; *Fam* **tons of** montones de

tone [təʊn] **1** *n* tono *m*

2 *vi* **to t. (in) with sth** armonizar con algo

► tone down *vt sep* atenuar

tone-deaf ['təʊn'def] *adj* **to be t.** no tener oído

tongs [tɒŋz] *npl (for sugar, hair)* tenacillas *fpl*; **(fire) t.** tenazas *fpl*

tongue [tʌŋ] *n (a)* lengua *f*; *Fig* **to say sth t. in cheek** decir algo con la boca pequeña; *Fig* **t. twister** trabalenguas *m inv (b) (of shoe)* lengüeta *f*; *(of bell)* badajo *m*

tongue-tied ['tʌŋtaɪd] *adj* mudo(a) *(por la timidez)*

tonic ['tɒnɪk] **1** *n (a) Med* tónico *m (b) (drink)* tónica *f*

2 *adj* tónico(a)

tonight [tə'naɪt] *adv & n* esta noche

tonnage ['tʌnɪdʒ] *n (of ship)* tonelaje *m*

tonne [tʌn] *n* = **ton**

tonsil ['tɒnsəl] *n* amígdala *f*; **to have one's tonsils out** ser operado(a) de las amígdalas

tonsillitis [tɒnsɪ'laɪtɪs] *n* amigdalitis *f*

too [tuː] *adv (a) (besides)* además *(b)*

(also) también (**c**) *(excessively)* demasiado; **t. much money** demasiado dinero; **£10 t. much** 10 libras de más; **t. frequently** con demasiada frecuencia; **t. old** demasiado viejo

took [tʊk] *pt of* **take**

tool [tuːl] *n (utensil)* herramienta *f*

toolbox ['tuːlbɒks] *n* caja *f* de herramientas

toot [tuːt] *Aut* **1** *vt* tocar
2 *vi* tocar la bocina

tooth [tuːθ] *n (pl teeth)* (**a**) diente *m*; *(molar)* muela *f*; *Fig* **to fight t. and nail** luchar a brazo partido (**b**) *(of saw)* diente *m*; *(of comb)* púa *f*

toothache ['tuːθeɪk] *n* dolor *m* de muelas

toothbrush ['tuːθbrʌʃ] *n* cepillo *m* de dientes

toothpaste ['tuːθpeɪst] *n* pasta dentífrica

toothpick ['tuːθpɪk] *n* mondadientes *m inv*

top¹ [tɒp] **1** *n* (**a**) *(upper part)* parte *f* de arriba; *(of hill)* cumbre *f*, cima *f*; *(of tree)* copa *f*; **from t. to bottom** de arriba a abajo; **on t. of** encima de; *Fig* **on t. of it all ...** para colmo ...; **t. hat** sombrero *m* de copa
(**b**) *(surface)* superficie *f*
(**c**) *(of list etc)* cabeza *f*
(**d**) *(of bottle etc)* tapa *f*, tapón *m*
(**e**) *(garment)* camiseta *f*
(**f**) *(best)* lo mejor
(**g**) *Fig* **at the t. of one's voice** a voz en grito
2 *adj* (**a**) *(part)* superior, de arriba; **the t. floor** el último piso; **t. coat** *(of paint)* última mano
(**b**) *(highest)* más alto(a); *Aut* **t. gear** directa *f*
(**c**) *(best)* mejor
3 *vt* (**a**) *(place on top of)* coronar
(**b**) *Th* **to t. the bill** encabezar el reparto
▸ **top up** *vt sep* llenar hasta el tope; **to t. up the petrol tank** llenar el depósito; *Fig* **and to t. it all** y para colmo

top² [tɒp] *n (toy)* peonza *f*

topic ['tɒpɪk] *n* tema *m*

📝 Note that the Spanish word **tópico** is a false friend and is never a translation for the English word **topic**. In Spanish, **tópico** means "cliché".

topical ['tɒpɪkəl] *adj* de actualidad

top-level ['tɒpˌlevəl] *adj* de alto nivel

topmost ['tɒpməʊst] *adj* (el) más alto/(la) más alta

topple ['tɒpəl] **1** *vi (building)* venirse

abajo; **to t. (over)** volcarse
2 *vt* volcar; *Fig (government)* derrocar

top-secret ['tɒp'siːkrɪt] *adj* de alto secreto

topsy-turvy ['tɒpsɪ'tɜːvɪ] *adj & adv* al revés; *(in confusion)* en desorden, patas arriba

torch [tɔːtʃ] *n (electric)* linterna *f*

tore [tɔː(r)] *pt of* **tear**

torment 1 *vt* [tɔː'ment] atormentar
2 *n* ['tɔːment] tormento *m*, suplicio *m*

torn [tɔːn] *pp of* **tear**

tornado [tɔː'neɪdəʊ] *n* tornado *m*

torpedo [tɔː'piːdəʊ] *n* torpedo *m*

torrent ['tɒrənt] *n* torrente *m*

torrential [tə'renʃəl] *adj* torrencial

torrid ['tɒrɪd] *adj* tórrido(a)

torso ['tɔːsəʊ] *n* torso *m*

tortoise ['tɔːtəs] *n* tortuga *f* (de tierra)

tortoiseshell ['tɔːtəsʃel] *adj* de carey

torture ['tɔːtʃə(r)] **1** *vt* torturar; *Fig* atormentar
2 *n* tortura *f*; *Fig* tormento *m*

Tory ['tɔːrɪ] *adj & n Br Pol* conservador(a) *(m,f)*

toss [tɒs] **1** *vt* (**a**) *(ball)* tirar; **to t. a coin** echar a cara o cruz (**b**) *(throw about)* sacudir
2 *vi* (**a**) **to t. about** agitarse; **to t. and turn** dar vueltas en la cama (**b**) *Sport* **to t. (up)** sortear
3 *n* (**a**) *(of ball)* lanzamiento *m*; *(of coin)* sorteo *m* (a cara o cruz) (**b**) *(of head)* sacudida *f*

tot¹ [tɒt] *n* (**a**) *(tiny)* **t.** *(child)* nene(a) *m,f*
(**b**) *(of whisky etc)* trago *m*

tot² [tɒt] *vt Br* **to t. up** sumar

total ['təʊtəl] **1** *n* total *m*; *(in bill)* importe *m*; **grand t.** suma *f* total
2 *adj* total
3 *vt* sumar
4 *vi* **to t. up** ascender a

totalitarian [təʊtælɪ'teərɪən] *adj* totalitario(a)

totally ['təʊtəlɪ] *adv* totalmente

tote [təʊt] *n Fam Sport* totalizador *m*

tote bag ['təʊtbæg] *n US* petate *m*

totem ['təʊtəm] *n* tótem *m*

totter ['tɒtə(r)] *vi* tambalearse

touch [tʌtʃ] **1** *vt* (**a**) tocar; *Fig* **to t. on a subject** tocar un tema
(**b**) *(equal)* igualar
(**c**) *(move)* conmover
2 *vi* tocarse; *Fig* **it was t. and go whether we caught the train** estuvimos a punto de perder el tren
3 *n* (**a**) toque *m*
(**b**) *(sense of touch)* tacto *m*

(c) **it was a nice t. of his** fue un detalle de su parte; **to put the finishing touches to sth** dar los últimos toques a algo
(d) *(ability)* habilidad f
(e) *(contact)* contacto m; **to be/get/ keep in t. with sb** estar/ponerse/mantenerse en contacto con algn; **to be out of t. with sth** no estar al tanto de algo
(f) *(small amount)* pizca f
(g) *Sport* **in t.** fuera de banda
▸ **touch down** vi *(plane)* aterrizar
▸ **touch off** vt sep desencadenar
▸ **touch up** vt sep *(picture)* retocar
touchdown ['tʌtʃdaʊn] n (a) *(of plane)* aterrizaje m; *(of space capsule)* amerizaje m (b) *(in American football)* ensayo m
touched [tʌtʃt] adj (a) *(moved)* emocionado(a) (b) *Fam (crazy)* tocado(a)
touching ['tʌtʃɪŋ] adj conmovedor(a)
touchline ['tʌtʃlaɪn] n línea f de banda
touchy ['tʌtʃɪ] adj (**touchier, touchiest**) *Fam (person)* susceptible; *(subject)* delicado(a)
tough [tʌf] **1** adj *(material, competitor etc)* fuerte, resistente; *(test, criminal, meat)* duro(a); *(punishment)* severo(a); *(problem)* difícil
2 n *(person)* matón m
toughen ['tʌfən] vt endurecer
toupee ['tuːpeɪ] n tupé m
tour [tʊə(r)] **1** n (a) *(journey)* viaje m; **package t.** viaje organizado (b) *(of monument etc)* visita f; *(of city)* recorrido turístico (c) *Sport & Th* gira f; **on t.** de gira
2 vt (a) *(country)* viajar por (b) *(building)* visitar (c) *Th* estar de gira en
3 vi estar de viaje
tourism ['tʊərɪzəm] n turismo m
tourist ['tʊərɪst] n turista mf; **t. centre** centro m de información turística; *Av* **t. class** clase f turista
tournament ['tʊənəmənt] n torneo m
tousled ['taʊzəld] adj *(hair)* despeinado(a)
tout [taʊt] **1** vt *Com* tratar de vender; *(tickets)* revender
2 vi = salir a la caza y captura de compradores
3 n *Com* gancho m
tow [təʊ] **1** n **to take a car in t.** remolcar un coche; *US* **t. truck** grúa f
2 vt remolcar
towards [tə'wɔːdz, tɔːdz] prep (a) *(direction, time)* hacia (b) *(with regard to)* hacia, (para) con; **our duty t. others** nuestro deber para con los demás; **what is your attitude t. religion?** ¿cuál es su actitud respecto a la religión?

towel ['taʊəl] **1** n toalla f; **hand t.** toallita f; **t.** *Br* **rail** or *US* **bar** toallero m
2 vt **to t. dry** secar con una toalla
towelling ['taʊəlɪŋ] n felpa f
tower ['taʊə(r)] **1** n torre f
2 vi **to t. over** or **above sth** dominar algo
towering ['taʊərɪŋ] adj impresionante, enorme
town [taʊn] n ciudad f; *(small)* pueblo m; **to go into t.** ir al centro; *Fam* **to go to t.** tirar la casa por la ventana; **t. council** ayuntamiento m; **t. councillor** concejal(a) m,f; **t. hall** ayuntamiento m; **t. planning** urbanismo m
townspeople ['taʊnzpiːpəl] npl ciudadanos mpl
towpath ['taʊpɑːθ] n sendero m a lo largo de un canal
towrope ['taʊrəʊp] n cable m de remolque
toxic ['tɒksɪk] adj tóxico(a)
toy [tɔɪ] **1** n juguete m
2 vi **to t. with an idea** acariciar una idea; **to t. with one's food** comer sin gana
toyshop ['tɔɪʃɒp] n juguetería f
trace [treɪs] **1** n (a) *(sign)* indicio m, vestigio m (b) *(tracks)* huella(s) f(pl)
2 vt (a) *(drawing)* calcar (b) *(plan)* bosquejar (c) *(locate)* seguir la pista de
tracing ['treɪsɪŋ] n **t. paper** papel m de calco
track [træk] **1** n (a) *(trail)* huellas fpl, pista f; **to keep/lose t. of sb** no perder/perder de vista a algn
(b) *(pathway)* camino m; **to be on the right/wrong t.** ir por el buen/mal camino
(c) *Sport* pista f; *(for motor racing)* circuito m; *Fig* **t. record** historial m
(d) *Rail* vía f; *Fig* **he has a one-t. mind** tiene una única obsesión
(e) *(on record, CD)* canción f
(f) *US Educ* = cada una de las divisiones del alumnado en grupos por niveles de aptitud
2 vt seguir la pista de; *(with radar)* seguir la trayectoria de
▸ **track down** vt sep *(locate)* localizar
tracksuit ['træksuːt] n chándal m, *Arg* buzo m, *Méx* pants m, *Urug* jogging m, *Ven* mono m
tract¹ [trækt] n *(expanse)* extensión f
tract² [trækt] n *(treatise)* tratado m; *(pamphlet)* folleto m
traction ['trækʃən] n tracción f
tractor ['træktə(r)] n tractor m
trade [treɪd] **1** n (a) *(profession)* oficio m; **by t.** de oficio (b) *Com* comercio m; **it's good for t.** es bueno para los negocios;

the building t. (la industria de) la construcción; **t. name** nombre *m* comercial; **t. union** sindicato *m*; **t. unionist** sindicalista *mf*

2 *vi* comerciar (**in** en)

3 *vt* **to t. sth for sth** trocar algo por algo

▸ **trade in** *vt sep* dar como entrada

trademark ['treidmɑːk] *n* marca *f* (de fábrica); **registered t.** marca registrada

trader ['treidə(r)] *n* comerciante *mf*

tradesman ['treidzmən] *n (shopkeeper)* tendero *m*

trading ['treidɪŋ] *n* comercio *m*; *Br* **t. estate** polígono *m* industrial

tradition [trə'dɪʃən] *n* tradición *f*

traditional [trə'dɪʃənəl] *adj* tradicional

traffic ['træfɪk] **1** *n* (**a**) tráfico *m*, circulación *f*; *US* **t. circle** rotonda *f*; **t. island** isleta *f*; **t. jam** atasco *m*; **t. lights** semáforo *m*; *Br* **t. warden** ≃ guardia *mf* urbano(a) (**b**) *(trade)* tráfico *m*

2 *vi (pt & pp* **trafficked)** **to t. in drugs** traficar con droga

trafficker ['træfɪkə(r)] *n* traficante *mf*

tragedy ['trædʒɪdɪ] *n* tragedia *f*

tragic ['trædʒɪk] *adj* trágico(a)

trail [treɪl] **1** *vt* (**a**) *(drag)* arrastrar (**b**) *(follow)* rastrear

2 *vi* (**a**) *(drag)* arrastrarse (**b**) **to t. behind** rezagarse

3 *n* (**a**) *(track)* pista *f*, rastro *m* (**b**) *(path)* senda *f*, camino *m* (**c**) *(of smoke)* estela *f*

trailer ['treɪlə(r)] *n* (**a**) *Aut* remolque *m* (**b**) *US Aut (caravan)* caravana *f* (**c**) *Cin* trailer *m*, avance *m*

train [treɪn] **1** *n* (**a**) *Rail* tren *m* (**b**) *(of vehicles)* convoy *m*; *(of followers)* séquito *m*; *(of events)* serie *f* (**c**) *(of dress)* cola *f*

2 *vt* (**a**) *(teach)* formar; *Sport* entrenar; *(animal)* amaestrar; *(voice etc)* educar (**b**) *(gun)* apuntar (**on** a); *(camera)* enfocar (**on** a)

3 *vi* prepararse; *Sport* entrenarse

trainee [treɪ'niː] *n* aprendiz(a) *m,f*

trainer ['treɪnə(r)] *n* (**a**) *Sport* entrenador(a) *m,f*; *(of dogs)* amaestrador(a) *m,f*; *(of lions)* domador(a) *m,f* (**b**) **trainers** *(shoes)* zapatillas *fpl* de deporte

training ['treɪnɪŋ] *n (instruction)* formación *f*; *Sport* entrenamiento *m*; *(of animals)* amaestramiento *m*; *(of lions)* doma *f*; **to go into t.** empezar el entrenamiento; **vocational t.** formación profesional

traipse [treɪps] *vi Fam* vagar

trait [treɪt] *n* rasgo *m*

traitor ['treɪtə(r)] *n* traidor(a) *m,f*

trajectory [trə'dʒektərɪ] *n* trayectoria *f*

tram [træm], **tramcar** ['træmkɑː(r)] *n Br* tranvía *m*

tramp [træmp] **1** *vi* (**a**) *(travel on foot)* caminar (**b**) *(walk heavily)* andar con pasos pesados

2 *n (person)* vagabundo(a) *m,f*; *Pej* **she's a t.** es una fulana

> ℘ Note that the Spanish word **trampa** is a false friend and is never a translation for the English word **tramp**. In Spanish, **trampa** means both "trap" and "trick".

trample ['træmpəl] *vt* **to t. down the grass** pisotear la hierba; **to t. sth underfoot** pisotear algo

trampoline ['træmpəliːn] *n* cama elástica

> ℘ Note that the Spanish word **trampolín** is a false friend and is never a translation for the English word **trampoline**. In Spanish, **trampolín** means both "diving board" and "ski jump".

trance [trɑːns] *n* trance *m*

tranquil ['træŋkwɪl] *adj* tranquilo(a)

tranquillity [træŋ'kwɪlɪtɪ] *n* tranquilidad *f*

tranquillizer ['træŋkwɪlaɪzə(r)] *n* tranquilizante *m*

transact [træn'zækt] *vt* negociar

transaction [træn'zækʃən] *n (procedure)* tramitación *f*; *(deal)* transacción *f*

transatlantic [trænzət'læntɪk] *adj* transatlántico(a)

transcend [træn'send] *vt* trascender

transcribe [træn'skraɪb] *vt* transcribir

transcript ['trænskrɪpt] *n* transcripción *f*

transcription [træn'skrɪpʃən] *n* transcripción *f*

transfer 1 *vt* [træns'fɜː(r)] trasladar; *(funds)* trasferir; *Jur* ceder; *Ftb* traspasar; *US Rail* hacer transbordo

2 *n* ['trænsfɜː(r)] (**a**) traslado *m*; *(of funds)* transferencia *f*; *Jur* cesión *f*; *Ftb* traspaso *m* (**b**) *(picture, design)* calcomanía *f* (**c**) *US Rail* transbordo *m*

transform [træns'fɔːm] *vt* trasformar

transformation [trænsfə'meɪʃən] *n* trasformación *f*

transfusion [træns'fjuːʒən] *n Med* transfusión *f* (de sangre)

transgenic [trænz'dʒiːnɪk] *adj* transgénico(a)

transgress [trænz'gres] *vi Fml* transgredir

transient ['trænzɪənt] *adj* transitorio(a)

transistor [træn'zɪstə(r)] *n* transistor *m*

transit ['trænzɪt] *n* tránsito *m*; **in t.** de tránsito

transition [træn'zɪʃən] *n* transición *f*

transitive ['trænzɪtɪv] *adj* transitivo(a)

transitory ['trænzɪtərɪ] *adj* transitorio(a)

translate [træns'leɪt] *vt* traducir

translation [træns'leɪʃən] *n* traducción *f*

translator [træns'leɪtə(r)] *n* traductor(a) *m,f*

translucent [trænz'luːsənt] *adj* translúcido(a)

transmission [trænz'mɪʃən] *n* transmisión *f*

transmit [trænz'mɪt] *vt* transmitir

transmitter [trænz'mɪtə(r)] *n Rad (set)* transmisor *m; Rad & TV (station)* emisora *f*

transparency [træns'pærənsɪ] *n Phot* diapositiva *f*

transparent [træns'pærənt] *adj* transparente

transpire [træn'spaɪə(r)] *vi (happen)* ocurrir; **it transpired that ...** ocurrió que ...

transplant 1 *vt* [træns'plɑːnt] trasplantar
2 *n* ['trænsplɑːnt] trasplante *m*

transport 1 *vt* [træns'pɔːt] transportar
2 *n* ['trænspɔːt] transporte *m*; **t. aircraft/ ship** avión *m*/buque *m* de transporte; *Br* **t. café** bar *m* de carretera

transportation [trænspɔː'teɪʃən] *n* transporte *m*

transvestite [trænz'vestaɪt] *n Fam* travestí *mf*

trap [træp] **1** *n* trampa *f*; **t. door** trampilla *f*; *Th* escotillón *m*
2 *vt* atrapar

trapeze [trə'piːz] *n* trapecio *m*

trappings ['træpɪŋz] *npl* parafernalia *f*

trash [træʃ] *n (inferior goods)* bazofia *f*; *US (rubbish)* basura *f*; *Fig* **to talk a lot of t.** decir tonterías; *US* **t. can** cubo *m* de la basura

trashy ['træʃɪ] *adj* (**trashier, trashiest**) de ínfima calidad

trauma ['trɔːmə] *n* trauma *m*

traumatic [trɔː'mætɪk] *adj* traumático(a)

travel ['trævəl] **1** *vi* (**a**) viajar; **to t. through** recorrer (**b**) *(vehicle, electric current)* ir; *Fig (news)* propagarse
2 *vt* recorrer
3 *n* viajar *m*; **t. agency** agencia *f* de viajes

traveller, *US* **traveler** ['trævələ(r)] *n* viajero(a) *m,f*; **t.'s** *Br* **cheque** *or US* **check** cheque *m* de viaje

travelling, *US* **traveling** ['trævəlɪŋ] **1** *adj (salesman)* ambulante
2 *n* viajes *mpl*, (el) viajar *m*; **I'm fond of t.** me gusta viajar; **t. expenses** gastos *mpl* de viaje

travel-sick ['trævəlsɪk] *adj* **to be t.** estar mareado(a)

travesty ['trævɪstɪ] *n* parodia *f* burda

> *✏️* Note that the Spanish word **travesti** is a false friend and is never a translation for the English word **travesty**. In Spanish, **travesti** means "transvestite".

trawler ['trɔːlə(r)] *n* barco *m* de arrastre

tray [treɪ] *n (for food)* bandeja *f*; *(for letters)* cesta *f (para la correspondencia)*

treacherous ['tretʃərəs] *adj* (**a**) *(person)* traidor(a); *(action)* traicionero(a) (**b**) *(dangerous)* peligroso(a)

treachery ['tretʃərɪ] *n* traición *f*

treacle ['triːkəl] *n Br* melaza *f*

tread [tred] **1** *vi* (*pt* **trod**; *pp* **trod** *or* **trodden**) pisar; **to t. on** pisar
2 *vt* (**a**) *(step on)* pisar (**b**) **to t. water** mantenerse a flote verticalmente
3 *n* (**a**) *(step)* paso *m*; *(sound)* ruido *m* de pasos (**b**) *(of tyre)* banda *f* de rodadura

treadmill ['tredmɪl] *n Fig* rutina *f*

treason ['triːzən] *n* traición *f*

treasure ['treʒə(r)] **1** *n* tesoro *m*
2 *vt (keep)* guardar como oro en paño; *(value)* apreciar muchísimo

treasurer ['treʒərə(r)] *n* tesorero(a) *m,f*

treasury ['treʒərɪ] *n Pol Br* **the T.,** *US* **the Department of the T.** ≃ el Ministerio de Hacienda; **T. bill** bono *m* del Tesoro

treat [triːt] **1** *n* (**a**) *(present)* regalo *m* (**b**) *(pleasure)* placer *m*
2 *vt* (**a**) tratar; **to t. badly** maltratar (**b**) *(regard)* considerar (**c**) **he treated them to dinner** les invitó a cenar

treatise ['triːtɪz] *n* tratado *m*

treatment ['triːtmənt] *n* (**a**) *(of person)* trato *m* (**b**) *(of subject, of patient)* tratamiento *m*

treaty ['triːtɪ] *n* tratado *m*

treble ['trebəl] **1** *adj* (**a**) *(triple)* triple (**b**) *Mus* **t. clef** clave *f* de sol; **t. voice** voz *f* tiple
2 *vt* triplicar
3 *vi* triplicarse

tree [triː] *n* árbol *m*; **apple/cherry t.** manzano *m*/cerezo *m*

treetop ['triːtɒp] *n* copa *f*

trek [trek] **1** *n (journey)* viaje *m* (largo y difícil); *Fam (walk)* caminata *f*
2 *vi* (*pt & pp* **trekked**) hacer un viaje largo y difícil; *Fam (walk)* ir caminando

trellis ['trelɪs] *n* enrejado *m*

tremble ['trembəl] *vi* temblar, estremecerse

trembling ['tremblɪŋ] *adj* tembloroso(a)

tremendous [trɪ'mendəs] *adj (huge)* enorme; *(success)* arrollador(a); *(shock* *etc)* tremendo(a); *Fam (marvellous)* estupendo(a)

tremor ['tremə(r)] *n* temblor *m*

trench [trentʃ] *n* (**a**) *(ditch)* zanja *f*; *Mil* trinchera *f* (**b**) **t. coat** trinchera *f*

trend [trend] **1** *n (tendency)* tendencia *f*; *(fashion)* moda *f*

  2 *vi* tender (**to** *or* **towards**) hacia)

trendy ['trendɪ] *adj* (**trendier, trendiest**) *Fam (person)* moderno(a); *(clothes)* a la última

trepidation [trepɪ'deɪʃən] *n* turbación *f*

trespass ['trespəs] *vi* entrar sin autorización

> 🖋 Note that the Spanish verb **traspasar** is a false friend and is never a translation for the English verb **to trespass**. In Spanish, **traspasar** means "to go through, to cross, to transfer" and "to exceed".

trespasser ['trespəsə(r)] *n* intruso(a) *m,f*

trestle ['tresəl] *n* caballete *m*

trial ['traɪəl] *n* (**a**) *Jur* proceso *m*, juicio *m* (**b**) *(test)* prueba *f*; **on t.** a prueba; **by t. and error** a fuerza de equivocarse (**c**) *trials (competition)* concurso *m* (**d**) *trials (suffering)* sufrimiento *m*; **trials and tribulations** tribulaciones *fpl*

triangle ['traɪæŋgəl] *n* triángulo *m*

tribe [traɪb] *n* tribu *f*

tribunal [traɪ'bjuːnəl] *n* tribunal *m*

tributary ['trɪbjʊtərɪ] *n (river)* afluente *m*

tribute ['trɪbjuːt] *n* (**a**) *(payment)* tributo *m* (**b**) *(mark of respect)* homenaje *m*; **to pay t.** to rendir homenaje a

trice [traɪs] *n Fam* **in a t.** en un abrir y cerrar de ojos

trick [trɪk] **1** *n* (**a**) *(ruse)* ardid *m*; *(dishonest)* engaño *m*; *(in question)* trampa *f* (**b**) *(practical joke)* broma *f*; **to play a t. on sb** gastarle una broma a algn; *(malicious)* jugar una mala pasada a algn (**c**) *(of magic, knack)* truco *m*; **that'll do the t.!** ¡eso es exactamente lo que hace falta! (**d**) *Cards* baza *f*

  2 *vt* engañar; **to t. sb out of sth** estafar algo a algn

trickery ['trɪkərɪ] *n* engaños *mpl*, trampas *fpl*

trickle ['trɪkəl] **1** *vi* discurrir; *(water)* gotear

  2 *n* hilo *m*

tricky ['trɪkɪ] *adj* (**trickier, trickiest**) *(person)* astuto(a); *(situation, mechanism)* delicado(a)

tricycle ['traɪsɪkəl] *n* triciclo *m*

tried [traɪd] *pt & pp of* **try**

trifle ['traɪfəl] **1** *n* (**a**) *(insignificant thing)*

bagatela *f*; **he's a t. optimistic** es ligeramente optimista (**b**) *Br Culin* = postre de bizcocho, gelatina, frutas y nata

  2 *vi* **to t. with** tomar a la ligera

trifling ['traɪflɪŋ] *adj* insignificante, trivial

trigger ['trɪgə(r)] **1** *n (of gun)* gatillo *m*; *(of mechanism)* disparador *m*

  2 *vt* **to t. (off)** desencadenar

trill [trɪl] *n (of music, bird)* trino *m*; *Ling* vibración *f*

trilogy ['trɪlədʒɪ] *n* trilogía *f*

trim [trɪm] **1** *adj* (**trimmer, trimmest**) *(neat)* aseado(a); **to have a t. figure** tener buen tipo

  2 *vt* (**a**) *(cut)* recortar; *Fig (expenses)* disminuir (**b**) *(decorate)* adornar

  3 *n* (**a**) *(condition)* estado *m*; *Naut* asiento *m* (**b**) *(cut)* recorte *m*

trimming ['trɪmɪŋ] *n* (**a**) *(cut)* recorte *m* (**b**) *(on clothes)* adorno *m* (**c**) *Culin* **trimmings** guarnición *f*

trinket ['trɪŋkɪt] *n* baratija *f*

trio ['triːəʊ] *n* trío *m*

trip [trɪp] **1** *n* (**a**) *(journey)* viaje *m*; *(excursion)* excursión *f*; **to go on a t.** ir de excursión (**b**) *Fam* **to be on a t.** *(on drugs)* estar colocado(a)

  2 *vi* (**a**) **to t. (up)** *(stumble)* tropezar (**over** con); *Fig (err)* equivocarse (**b**) **to t. along** ir con paso ligero

  3 *vt* **to t. sb (up)** poner la zancadilla a algn; *Fig* coger *or* pillar a algn

tripe [traɪp] *n* (**a**) *Culin* callos *mpl* (**b**) *Fam* bobadas *fpl*

triple ['trɪpəl] **1** *adj* triple

  2 *vt* triplicar

  3 *vi* triplicarse

triplet ['trɪplɪt] *n* trillizo(a) *m,f*

triplicate ['trɪplɪkɪt] *adj* **in t.** por triplicado

tripod ['traɪpɒd] *n* trípode *m*

trite [traɪt] *adj (sentiment)* banal; *(subject)* trillado(a)

triumph ['traɪəmf] **1** *n* triunfo *m*

  2 *vi* triunfar

triumphant [traɪ'ʌmfənt] *adj* triunfante

trivia ['trɪvɪə] *npl* trivialidades *fpl*

trivial ['trɪvɪəl] *adj* trivial, banal

trod [trɒd] *pt & pp of* **tread**

trodden ['trɒdən] *pp of* **tread**

trolley ['trɒlɪ] *n Br* carro *m*

trombone [trɒm'bəʊn] *n* trombón *m*

troop [truːp] **1** *n* (**a**) *(of people)* grupo *m* (**b**) *Mil* **troops** tropas *fpl*

  2 *vi* **to t. in/out/off** entrar/salir/marcharse en tropel

trooper ['truːpə(r)] *n* (**a**) *(soldier)* soldado

m de caballería (**b**) *US (policeman)* policía *mf*

trooping ['tru:pɪŋ] *n Br* **t. the colour** = ceremonia de homenaje a la bandera de un regimiento

trophy ['trəʊfɪ] *n* trofeo *m*

tropic ['trɒpɪk] *n* trópico *m*

tropical ['trɒpɪkəl] *adj* tropical

trot [trɒt] **1** *n* trote *m*; **to go at a t.** ir al trote; *Fam* **on the t.** *(in succession)* seguidos(as)
2 *n* trote *m*; **to go at a t.** ir al trote; *Fam* **on the t.** *(in succession)* seguidos(as)

trouble ['trʌbəl] **1** *n* (**a**) *(misfortune)* desgracia *f*
(**b**) *(problems)* problemas *mpl*; **to be in t.** estar en un lío; **to cause sb t.** ocasionar problemas a algn; **to get sb out of t.** sacar a algn de un apuro; **the t. is that ...** lo que pasa es que ...
(**c**) *(effort)* esfuerzo *m*; **it's no t.** no es ninguna molestia; **it's not worth the t.** no merece la pena; **to take the t. to do sth** molestarse en hacer algo
(**d**) *(conflict)* conflicto *m*
(**e**) *Med* enfermedad *f*; **to have liver t.** tener problemas de hígado
2 *vt* (**a**) *(affect)* afligir; *(worry)* preocupar; **that doesn't t. him at all** eso le tiene sin cuidado
(**b**) *(bother)* molestar
3 *vi* molestarse

troubled ['trʌbəld] *adj* agitado(a)

troublemaker ['trʌbəlmeɪkə(r)] *n* alborotador(a) *m,f*

troubleshooter ['trʌbəlʃu:tə(r)] *n Ind* = persona encargada de solucionar problemas

troublesome ['trʌbəlsəm] *adj* molesto(a)

trough [trɒf] *n* (**a**) **(drinking)** t. abrevadero *m*; **(feeding)** t. pesebre *m* (**b**) *(of wave)* seno *m* (**c**) *Geog & Met* depresión *f*

trounce [traʊns] *vt* dar una paliza a

troupe [tru:p] *n Th* compañía *f*

trousers ['traʊzəz] *npl* pantalón *m*, pantalones *mpl*

trousseau ['tru:səʊ] *n* ajuar *m*

trout [traʊt] *n* trucha *f*

trowel ['traʊəl] *n* (**a**) *(builder's)* palustre *m* (**b**) *(for gardening)* desplantador *m*

truant ['tru:ənt] *n Br* **to play t.** hacer novillos

truce [tru:s] *n* tregua *f*

truck¹ [trʌk] *n* (**a**) *Br Rail* vagón *m* (**b**) *Aut* camión *m*; **t. driver** camionero(a) *m,f*; *US* **t. farm** huerta *f*; *US* **t. farmer** hortelano(a) *m,f*

truck² [trʌk] *n* (**a**) **to have no t. with** no

estar dispuesto a tolerar (**b**) *US* verduras *fpl*; **t. farm** huerta *f*; **t. farming** cultivo *m* de hortalizas

truculent ['trʌkjʊlənt] *adj* agresivo(a), airado(a)

> 🖉 Note that the Spanish word **truculento** is a false friend and is never a translation for the English word **truculent**. In Spanish, **truculento** means "horrifying, terrifying".

trudge [trʌdʒ] *vi* caminar con dificultad

true [tru:] *adj* (**truer, truest**) (**a**) *(real)* verdadero(a); **it's t. that ...** es verdad que ...; **to come t.** cumplirse, hacerse realidad (**b**) *(faithful)* fiel (**c**) *(aim)* acertado(a)

truffle ['trʌfəl] *n* trufa *f*

truly ['tru:lɪ] *adv* (**a**) de verdad; **really and t.?** ¿de veras? (**b**) *(faithfully)* fielmente; **yours t.** atentamente

trump [trʌmp] *Cards* **1** *n* triunfo *m*
2 *vt* fallar

trumped-up ['trʌmptʌp] *adj* inventado(a)

trumpet ['trʌmpɪt] *n* trompeta *f*

trumpeting ['trʌmpɪtɪŋ] *n (of elephant)* berrido *m*

truncheon ['trʌntʃən] *n Br* porra *f (de policía)*

trundle ['trʌndəl] *vi* rodar

trunk [trʌŋk] *n* (**a**) *(of tree, body)* tronco *m* (**b**) *(of elephant)* trompa *f* (**c**) *(luggage)* baúl *m* (**d**) *Br Tel* **t. call** conferencia interurbana; *Br* **t. road** carretera *f* principal (**e**) *US (of car)* maletero *m*, *CAm, Méx* cajuela *f*, *RP* baúl *m*

trunks [trʌŋks] *npl* **(bathing)** t. bañador *m*

truss [trʌs] **1** *vt (tie)* atar
2 *n* (**a**) *Constr* cuchillo *m* de armadura (**b**) *Med* braguero *m*

trust [trʌst] **1** *n* (**a**) confianza *f*; **breach of t.** abuso *m* de confianza (**b**) *Jur* fideicomiso *m* (**c**) *Fin* trust *m*
2 *vt* (**a**) *(hope)* esperar (**b**) *(rely upon)* fiarse de; **to t. sb with sth** confiar algo a algn
3 *vi* confiar (**in** en)

trusted ['trʌstɪd] *adj* de fiar

trustee [trʌs'ti:] *n Jur* fideicomisario(a) *m,f*; *(in bankruptcy)* síndico *m*

trustful ['trʌstfʊl], **trusting** ['trʌstɪŋ] *adj* confiado(a)

trustworthy ['trʌstwɜ:ðɪ] *adj (person)* de confianza; *(information)* fidedigno(a)

trusty ['trʌstɪ] *adj* (**trustier, trustiest**) fiel, leal

truth [tru:θ] *n* verdad *f*; **to tell the t.** decir la verdad

truthful ['truːθful] *adj (person)* veraz, sincero(a); *(testimony)* verídico(a)

truthfully ['truːθfʊlɪ] *adv* sinceramente

try [traɪ] **1** *vt (pt & pp* **tried**) (**a**) *(attempt)* intentar; **to t. to do sth** tratar de *or* intentar hacer algo (**b**) *(test)* probar, ensayar; **to t. sb's patience** poner a prueba la paciencia de algn (**c**)*Jur* juzgar

    2 *vi* intentar

    3 *n* (**a**) *(attempt)* tentativa *f*, intento *m* (**b**) *Sport* ensayo *m*

  ▸ **try on** *vt sep (dress)* probarse

  ▸ **try out** *vt sep* probar

trying ['traɪɪŋ] *adj (person)* molesto(a), pesado(a); **to have a t. time** pasar un mal rato

tsar [zɑː(r)] *n* zar *m*

T-shirt ['tiːʃɜːt] *n* camiseta *f*

tub [tʌb] *n* (**a**) *(container)* tina *f*, cuba *f* (**b**) *(bath)* bañera *f*

tuba ['tjuːbə] *n* tuba *f*

tubby ['tʌbɪ] *adj* (**tubbier, tubbiest**) rechoncho(a)

tube [tjuːb] *n* (**a**) *(container)* tubo *m*; *Anat* conducto *m*; *(of bicycle)* cámara *f* (de aire) (**b**) *Br Fam* **the t.** *(underground)* el metro

tuberculosis [tjʊbɜːkjʊ'ləʊsɪs] *n* tuberculosis *f*

tubing ['tjuːbɪŋ] *n* tubería *f*; **(piece of) t.** (trozo *m* de) tubo *m*

tubular ['tjuːbjʊlə(r)] *adj* tubular

tuck [tʌk] **1** *vt* **to t. in the bedclothes** remeter la ropa de la cama; **to t. sb in** arropar a algn; **to t. one's shirt into one's trousers** meterse la camisa por dentro (de los pantalones)

    2 *n Sewing* pliegue *m*

  ▸ **tuck in** *vi Fam* devorar

Tuesday ['tjuːzdɪ] *n* martes *m*

tuft [tʌft] *n (of hair)* mechón *m*

tug [tʌg] **1** *vt (pull at)* tirar de; *(haul along)* arrastrar; *Naut* remolcar

    2 *n* (**a**) *(pull)* tirón *m*; **t. of war** *(game)* lucha *f* de la cuerda; *Fig* lucha encarnizada (**b**) *Naut* remolcador *m*

tugboat ['tʌgbəʊt] *n* remolcador *m*

tuition [tjuː'ɪʃən] *n* instrucción *f*; **private t.** clases *fpl* particulares; **t. fees** honorarios *mpl*

tulip ['tjuːlɪp] *n* tulipán *m*

tumble ['tʌmbəl] **1** *vi (person)* caerse; *(acrobat)* dar volteretas; *(building)* venirse abajo

    2 *vt* volcar

    3 *n* (**a**) caída *f* (**b**) **t. dryer** secadora *f*

tumbledown ['tʌmbəldaʊn] *adj* en ruinas

tumbler ['tʌmblə(r)] *n* vaso *m*

tummy ['tʌmɪ] *n Fam* estómago *m*, barriga *f*

tumour, *US* **tumor** ['tjuːmə(r)] *n* tumor *m*

tumult ['tjuːmʌlt] *n* tumulto *m*

tuna ['tjuːnə] *n* atún *m*, bonito *m*

  ⎙ Note that the Spanish word **tuna** is a false friend and is never a translation for the English word **tuna**. In Spanish, **tuna** means "group of student minstrels".

tune [tjuːn] **1** *n* (**a**) *(melody)* melodía *f*; *Fig* **to change one's t.** cambiar de tono (**b**) *Mus* tono *m*; **in/out of t.** afinado/desafinado; **to sing out of t.** desafinar

    2 *vt Mus* afinar

    3 *vi Rad & TV* **to t. in to a station** sintonizar una emisora

  ▸ **tune up** *vi* afinar los instrumentos

tuneful ['tjuːnfʊl] *adj* melodioso(a)

tuner ['tjuːnə(r)] (**a**) *(of pianos)* afinador(a) *m,f* (**b**) *Rad & TV (knob)* sintonizador *m*

tunic ['tjuːnɪk] *n* túnica *f*

tuning ['tjuːnɪŋ] *n* (**a**) *Mus* afinación *f*; **t. fork** diapasón *m* (**b**) *Rad & TV* **t. in** sintonización *f*

Tunisia [tjuː'nɪzɪə] *n* Túnez *m*

Tunisian [tjuː'nɪzɪən] *adj & n* tunecino(a) *(m,f)*

tunnel ['tʌnəl] **1** *n* túnel *m*; *Min* galería *f*

    2 *vt* **to t. through** abrir un túnel a través de

turban ['tɜːbən] *n* turbante *m*

turbine ['tɜːbaɪn] *n* turbina *f*

turbulent ['tɜːbjʊlənt] *adj* turbulento(a)

tureen [tə'riːn] *n* sopera *f*

turf [tɜːf] *n* (**a**) *(grass)* césped *m*; *(peat)* turba *f* (**b**) *Br* **t. accountant** *(in horse racing)* corredor(a) *m,f* de apuestas

  ▸ **turf out** *vt sep Br Fam* **to t. sb out** poner a algn de patitas en la calle

Turk [tɜːk] *n* turco(a) *m,f*

Turkey ['tɜːkɪ] *n* Turquía *f*

turkey ['tɜːkɪ] *n* pavo *m*

Turkish ['tɜːkɪʃ] **1** *adj* turco(a)

    2 *n (language)* turco *m*

turmoil ['tɜːmɔɪl] *n* confusión *f*

turn [tɜːn] **1** *vt* (**a**) volver; *(rotate)* girar, hacer girar; **to t. sth inside out** volver algo del revés; **to t. a page** volver una hoja; **to t. one's head/gaze** volver la cabeza/mirada (**towards** hacia); **to t. the corner** doblar la esquina; *Fig* **he's turned forty** ha cumplido los cuarenta (**b**) *(change)* transformar (**into** en) (**c**) *(on lathe)* tornear

    2 *vi* (**a**) *(rotate)* girar

(b) (turn round) volverse, dar la vuelta; **to t.** te toca a ti; **to take it in turns to do sth** turnarse para hacer algo

(f) Th número m

(g) **t. of phrase** giro m

▸ **turn aside 1** vt sep desviar

2 vi desviarse

▸ **turn away 1** vt sep (person) rechazar

2 vi volver la cabeza

▸ **turn back 1** vt sep (person) hacer retroceder; (clock) retrasar

2 vi volverse

▸ **turn down** vt sep (a) (gas, radio etc) bajar (b) (reject) rechazar (c) (fold) doblar

▸ **turn in** Fam **1** vt sep (person) entregar a la policía

2 vi acostarse

▸ **turn off 1** vt sep (electricity) desconectar; (gas, light) apagar; (water) cerrar

2 vi desviarse

▸ **turn on** vt sep (electricity) encender; (tap, gas) abrir; (machine) poner en marcha; Fam **it turns me on** me encanta

▸ **turn out 1** vt sep (a) (extinguish) apagar (b) (eject) echar; (empty) vaciar (c) (produce) producir

2 vi (a) (attend) asistir (b) **it turns out that ...** resulta que ...; **things have turned out well** las cosas han salido bien

▸ **turn over 1** vt sep (turn upside down) poner al revés; (page) dar la vuelta a

2 vi volverse

▸ **turn round 1** vt sep volver

2 vi (rotate) girar, dar vueltas

▸ **turn up 1** vt sep (a) (collar) levantar; **to t. up one's shirt sleeves** arremangarse; **turned-up nose** nariz respingona (b) Rad & TV subir

2 vi (a) Fig **something is sure to t. up** algo saldrá (b) (arrive) llegar, presentarse;

nobody turned up nadie se presentó

(c) (attend) asistir

turning ['tɜːnɪŋ] n (a) Fig **t. point** punto decisivo (b) (in road) salida f

turnip ['tɜːnɪp] n nabo m

turnout ['tɜːnaʊt] n asistencia f

turnover ['tɜːnəʊvə(r)] n Com (sales) facturación f; (of goods) movimiento m

turnpike ['tɜːnpaɪk] n US autopista f de peaje

turnstile ['tɜːnstaɪl] n torniquete m

turntable ['tɜːnteɪbəl] n (for record) plato m (giratorio)

turn-up ['tɜːnʌp] n Br (a) (of trousers) vuelta f (b) Fam Fig **what a t. for the books!** ¡vaya sorpresa!

turpentine ['tɜːpəntaɪn] n (esencia f de) trementina f

turquoise ['tɜːkwɔɪz] **1** n (colour, stone) turquesa f

2 adj **t. (blue)** azul turquesa

turret ['tʌrɪt] n torrecilla f

turtle ['tɜːtəl] n tortuga f; US (tortoise) tortuga f

turtledove ['tɜːtəldʌv] n tórtola f

turtleneck ['tɜːtəlnek] n a **t. (sweater)** un jersey de cuello alto

tusk [tʌsk] n colmillo m

tussle ['tʌsəl] n pelea f, lucha f

tutor ['tjuːtə(r)] n Univ tutor(a) m,f; **private t.** profesor(a) m,f particular

tutorial [tjuː'tɔːrɪəl] n Univ tutoría f, seminario m

tuxedo [tʌk'siːdəʊ] n US smoking m

TV [tiː'viː] n (abbr **television**) televisión f

twang [twæŋ] **1** n (a) (of instrument) sonido m vibrante (b) **nasal t.** gangueo m

2 vt puntear

3 vi (string) vibrar

tweak [twiːk] vt pellizcar

tweed [twiːd] n cheviot m

tweezers ['twiːzəz] npl pinzas fpl

twelfth [twelfθ] **1** adj & n duodécimo(a) (m,f)

2 n (fraction) duodécimo m

twelve [twelv] adj & n doce (m inv)

twentieth ['twentɪθ] **1** adj & n vigésimo(a) (m,f)

2 n (fraction) vigésimo m

twenty ['twentɪ] adj & n veinte (m inv)

twice [twaɪs] adv dos veces; **he's t. as old as I am** tiene el doble de años que yo

twiddle ['twɪdəl] **1** vt dar vueltas a; **to t. one's moustache** mesarse el bigote; **to t. one's thumbs** estar mano sobre mano

2 vi **to t. with sth** juguetear con algo

twig¹ [twɪg] n ramilla f

twig² [twɪg] vi Br Fam caer en la cuenta

twilight ['twaɪlaɪt] n crepúsculo m

twin [twɪn] **1** n mellizo(a) m,f; **identical twins** gemelos (idénticos); **t. brother/ sister** hermano gemelo/hermana geme-la; **t. beds** camas fpl gemelas
  2 vt hermanar

twine [twaɪn] **1** n bramante m
  2 vt entretejer
  3 vi **to t. round sth** enroscarse alrededor de algo

twinge [twɪndʒ] n (of pain) punzada f; Fig **t. of conscience** remordimiento m

twinkle ['twɪŋkəl] vi (stars) centellear; (eyes) brillar

twinkling ['twɪŋklɪŋ] n (of stars) cente-lleo m; Fig **in the t. of an eye** en un abrir y cerrar de ojos

twirl [twɜːl] **1** vt girar rápidamente
  2 vi (spin) girar rápidamente; (dancer) piruetear
  3 n (movement) giro rápido; (of dancer) pirueta f

twist [twɪst] **1** vt torcer; (sense) tergiver-sar; **to t. one's ankle** torcerse el tobillo
  2 vi (smoke) formar volutas; (path) ser-pentear
  3 n (a) (of yarn) torzal m (b) (movement) torsión f; Med torcedura f; Fig **to give a new t. to sth** dar un nuevo enfoque a algo (c) (in road) vuelta f (d) (dance) twist m

twit [twɪt] n Br Fam memo(a) m,f

twitch [twɪtʃ] **1** vt dar un tirón a
  2 vi crisparse; **his face twitches** tiene un tic en la cara

twitter ['twɪtə(r)] **1** vi gorjear
  2 n gorjeo m

two [tuː] **1** adj dos inv; Fig **to be in** or **of t. minds about sth** estar indeciso(a) res-pecto a algo
  2 n dos m inv; Fig **to put t. and t. together** atar cabos

two-faced ['tuːˈfeɪst] adj hipócrita

two-party ['tuːpɑːtɪ] adj **t. system** bipar-tidismo m

twopence ['tʌpəns] n Br dos peniques

two-piece ['tuːˈpiːs] **1** adj de dos piezas
  2 n (suit) traje m de dos piezas

two-seater ['tuːˈsiːtə(r)] adj & n biplaza (f)

twosome ['tuːsəm] n pareja f

two-time ['tuːtaɪm] vt Fam poner los cuernos a

two-way ['tuːweɪ] adj (a) (street) de dos direcciones (b) **t. radio** aparato m emisor y receptor

tycoon [taɪˈkuːn] n magnate m

type [taɪp] **1** n (a) (kind) tipo m, clase f; (brand) marca f; (of car) modelo m (b) Typ carácter m; (print) caracteres mpl
  2 vt & vi escribir a máquina

typecast ['taɪpkɑːst] vt encasillar

typescript ['taɪpskrɪpt] n texto m escrito a máquina

typeset ['taɪpset] vt componer

typesetter ['taɪpsetə(r)] n (a) (person) cajista mf (b) (machine) máquina f para componer tipos

typewriter ['taɪpraɪtə(r)] n máquina f de escribir

typewritten ['taɪprɪtən] adj escrito(a) a máquina

typhoid ['taɪfɔɪd] n **t. (fever)** fiebre tifoi-dea

typhoon [taɪˈfuːn] n tifón m

typical ['tɪpɪkəl] adj típico(a)

typify ['tɪpɪfaɪ] vt tipificar

typing ['taɪpɪŋ] n mecanografía f

typist ['taɪpɪst] n mecanógrafo(a) m,f

tyrannical [tɪˈrænɪkəl] adj tiránico(a)

tyrannize ['tɪrənaɪz] vt tiranizar

tyranny ['tɪrənɪ] n tiranía f

tyrant ['taɪrənt] n tirano(a) m,f

tyre [taɪə(r)] n neumático m; **t. pressure** presión f de los neumáticos

U

U, u [ju:] *n (the letter)* U, u *f*
U [ju:] *adj (film)* ≃ (apta) para todos los públicos
ubiquity [ju:'bɪkwɪtɪ] *n* ubicuidad *f*
udder ['ʌdə(r)] *n* ubre *f*
UFO, ufo ['ju:ef'əʊ, 'ju:fəʊ] *n (abbr unidentified flying object)* OVNI *m*
ugh [ʌx] *interj* ¡uf!, ¡puf!
ugly ['ʌglɪ] *adj (uglier, ugliest)* feo(a); *(situation)* desagradable; *Fig* **u. duckling** patito feo
UK [ju:'keɪ] *n (abbr United Kingdom)* R.U. *m*
Ukraine [ju:'kreɪn] *n* **the U.** Ucrania
ulcer ['ʌlsə(r)] *n (sore)* llaga *f*; *(internal)* úlcera *f*
ulterior [ʌl'tɪərɪə(r)] *adj (motive)* oculto(a)
ultimate ['ʌltɪmɪt] *adj* **(a)** *(final)* último(a); *(aim)* final **(b)** *(basic)* esencial
ultimately ['ʌltɪmɪtlɪ] *adv* **(a)** *(finally)* finalmente **(b)** *(basically)* en el fondo
ultimatum [ʌltɪ'meɪtəm] *n* ultimátum *m*
ultrasound ['ʌltrəsaʊnd] *n* ultrasonido *m*
ultraviolet [ʌltrə'vaɪəlɪt] *adj* ultravioleta
umbilical [ʌm'bɪlɪkəl] *adj* **u. cord** cordón *m* umbilical
umbrella [ʌm'brelə] *n* paraguas *m inv*
umpire ['ʌmpaɪə(r)] **1** *n* árbitro *m*
2 *vt* arbitrar
umpteen [ʌmp'ti:n] *adj Fam* muchísimos(as), la tira de
umpteenth [ʌmp'ti:nθ] *adj* enésimo(a)
UN [ju:'en] *n (abbr United Nations (Organization))* ONU *f*
unabashed [ʌnə'bæʃt] *adj* **(a)** *(unperturbed)* inmutable, imperturbable **(b)** *(shameless)* desvergonzado(a), descarado(a)
unable [ʌn'eɪbəl] *adj* incapaz; **to be u. to do sth/anything** no poder hacer algo/nada
unacceptable [ʌnək'septəbəl] *adj* inaceptable
unaccompanied [ʌnə'kʌmpənɪd] *adj* solo(a)
unaccountable [ʌnə'kaʊntəbəl] *adj* inexplicable

unaccounted-for [ʌnə'kaʊntɪdfɔː(r)] *adj* **to be u.** faltar
unaccustomed [ʌnə'kʌstəmd] *adj* **he's u. to this climate** no está muy acostumbrado a este clima
unaffected [ʌnə'fektɪd] *adj* **(a)** no afectado(a) **(by** por) **(b)** *(indifferent)* indiferente **(by** a) **(c)** *(natural) (person)* natural; *(style)* llano(a)
unaided [ʌn'eɪdɪd] *adj* sin ayuda, solo(a)
unanimous [ju:'nænɪməs] *adj* unánime
unannounced [ʌnə'naʊnst] *adj* sin avisar
unanswered [ʌn'ɑːnsəd] *adj* sin contestar
unapproachable [ʌnə'prəʊtʃəbəl] *adj* inabordable, inaccesible
unarmed [ʌn'ɑːmd] *adj* desarmado(a)
unashamed [ʌnə'ʃeɪmd] *adj* desvergonzado(a)
unasked [ʌn'ɑːskt] *adv* **u. (for)** *(unrequested)* no solicitado(a); *(spontaneous)* espontáneo(a)
unassuming [ʌnə'sju:mɪŋ] *adj* sin pretensiones
unattached [ʌnə'tætʃt] *adj* **(a)** *(independent)* libre; *(loose)* suelto(a) **(b)** *(person)* soltero(a) y sin compromiso
unattended [ʌnə'tendɪd] *adj (counter etc)* desatendido(a); **to leave a child u.** dejar a un niño solo
unauthorized [ʌn'ɔːθəraɪzd] *adj* **(a)** *(person)* no autorizado(a) **(b)** *(trade etc)* ilícito(a), ilegal
unavoidable [ʌnə'vɔɪdəbəl] *adj* inevitable; *(accident)* imprevisible
unaware [ʌnə'weə(r)] *adj* **to be u. of sth** ignorar algo
unawares [ʌnə'weəz] *adv* **(a)** *(unexpectedly)* desprevenido(a) **(b)** *(without knowing)* inconscientemente
unbalanced [ʌn'bælənst] *adj* desequilibrado(a)
unbearable [ʌn'beərəbəl] *adj* insoportable
unbeatable [ʌn'bi:təbəl] *adj (team)* invencible; *(price, quality)* inmejorable
unbelievable [ʌnbɪ'li:vəbəl] *adj* increíble

unbend [ʌn'bend] *vi Fam Fig* relajarse

unbia(s)sed [ʌn'baɪəst] *adj* imparcial

unborn [ʌn'bɔːn] *adj* sin nacer, nona-to(a)

unbreakable [ʌn'breɪkəbəl] *adj* irrompible; *Fig* inquebrantable

unbroken [ʌn'brəʊkən] *adj* (a) *(whole)* intacto(a) (b) *(uninterrupted)* continuo(a) (c) *(record)* imbatido(a)

unbutton [ʌn'bʌtən] *vt* desabrochar

uncalled-for [ʌn'kɔːldfɔː(r)] *adj* (inappropriate) insensato(a); *(unjustified)* inmerecido(a)

uncanny [ʌn'kænɪ] *adj* misterioso(a), extraño(a)

unceasing [ʌn'siːsɪŋ] *adj* incesante

uncertain [ʌn'sɜːtən] *adj* (a) *(not certain)* incierto(a); *(doubtful)* dudoso(a); **in no u. terms** claramente (b) *(hesitant)* indeciso(a)

uncertainty [ʌn'sɜːtəntɪ] *n* incertidumbre *f*

unchanged [ʌn'tʃeɪndʒd] *adj* igual

unchecked [ʌn'tʃekt] *adj* (a) *(unrestrained)* desenfrenado(a) (b) *(not examined)* no comprobado(a)

uncivilized [ʌn'sɪvɪlaɪzd] *adj* (tribe) incivilizado(a), salvaje; *(not cultured)* inculto(a)

uncle ['ʌŋkəl] *n* tío *m*

uncomfortable [ʌn'kʌmftəbəl] *adj* incómodo(a); **to make things u. for** complicarle la vida a

uncommon [ʌn'kɒmən] *adj* (a) *(rare)* poco común; *(unusual)* extraordinario(a) (b) *(excessive)* excesivo(a)

uncommonly [ʌn'kɒmənlɪ] *adv* **not u.** con cierta frecuencia

uncompromising [ʌn'kɒmprəmaɪzɪŋ] *adj* intransigente; **u. honesty** sinceridad absoluta

unconcerned [ʌnkən'sɜːnd] *adj* indiferente (**about** a)

unconditional [ʌnkən'dɪʃənəl] *adj* incondicional; **u. refusal** negativa rotunda

unconnected [ʌnkə'nektɪd] *adj* no relacionado(a)

unconscious [ʌn'kɒnʃəs] **1** *adj* (a) inconsciente (**of** de) (b) *(unintentional)* involuntario(a)
2 *n* **the u.** el inconsciente

unconsciousness [ʌn'kɒnʃəsnɪs] *n Med* pérdida *f* del conocimiento

uncontested [ʌnkən'testɪd] *adj Pol* **u. seat** escaño *m* ganado sin oposición

uncontrollable [ʌnkən'trəʊləbəl] *adj* incontrolable; *(desire)* irresistible

unconventional [ʌnkən'venʃənəl] *adj* poco convencional, original

uncooperative [ʌnkəʊ'ɒpərətɪv] *adj* poco cooperativo(a)

uncouth [ʌn'kuːθ] *adj* (rude) grosero(a)

uncover [ʌn'kʌvə(r)] *vt* destapar; *Fig* descubrir

undamaged [ʌn'dæmɪdʒd] *adj* (article etc) sin desperfectos; *(person)* indemne; *(reputation)* intacto(a)

undaunted [ʌn'dɔːntɪd] *adj* firme, impávido(a)

undecided [ʌndɪ'saɪdɪd] *adj* (a) *(person)* indeciso(a) (b) *(issue)* pendiente; **it's still u.** está aún por decidir

undefeated [ʌndɪ'fiːtɪd] *adj* invicto(a)

undefined [ʌndɪ'faɪnd] *adj* indeterminado(a)

undeniable [ʌndɪ'naɪəbəl] *adj* innegable

under ['ʌndə(r)] **1** *prep* (a) debajo de; **u. the sun** bajo el sol (b) *(less than)* menos de; **incomes u. £1,000** ingresos inferiores a 1.000 libras; **u. age** menor de edad (c) *(of rank)* de rango inferior a (d) **u. Caesar** bajo César (e) *(subject to)* bajo; **u. arrest** detenido(a); **u. cover** a cubierto; **u. obligation to** en la obligación de; **u. the circumstances** dadas las circunstancias; *Fig* **I was u. the impression that ...** tenía la impresión de que ... (f) *(according to)* según, conforme a
2 *adv* abajo, debajo

under- ['ʌndə(r)] *pref (below)* sub-, infra-; *(insufficiently)* insuficientemente

underarm ['ʌndərɑːm] **1** *adj* **u. deodorant** desodorante *m* para las axilas
2 *adv Sport* por debajo del hombro

undercarriage ['ʌndəkærɪdʒ] *n* tren *m* de aterrizaje

undercharge [ʌndə'tʃɑːdʒ] *vt* cobrar menos de lo debido

underclothes ['ʌndəkləʊðz] *npl* ropa *f* interior

undercoat ['ʌndəkəʊt] *n (of paint)* primera mano

undercover [ʌndə'kʌvə(r)] *adj* secreto(a)

undercurrent ['ʌndəkʌrənt] *n* (a) *(in sea)* corriente submarina (b) *Fig* sentimiento *m* latente

undercut [ʌndə'kʌt] *vt* (*pt & pp* **undercut**) *Com* vender más barato que

underdeveloped [ʌndədɪ'veləpt] *adj* subdesarrollado(a)

underdog ['ʌndədɒg] *n* desvalido(a) *m,f*

underestimate [ʌndər'estɪmeɪt] *vt* infravalorar

underexposure [ʌndərɪk'spəʊʒə(r)] *n Phot* subexposición *f*

underfed [ʌndə'fed] *adj* subalimentado(a)

underfoot [ʌndə'fʊt] *adv* en el suelo

undergo [ʌndə'gəʊ] *vt* (*pt* **underwent**; *pp* **undergone** [ʌndə'gɒn]) experimentar; *(change)* sufrir; *(test etc)* pasar por

undergraduate [ʌndə'grædjʊɪt] *n* estudiante *mf* universitario(a)

underground ['ʌndəgraʊnd] **1** *adj* subterráneo(a); *Fig* clandestino(a)
2 *n* (a) *Pol* movimiento clandestino (b) *Br* the u. *(train)* el metro
3 *adv* [ʌndə'graʊnd] *Fig* to go u. pasar a la clandestinidad

undergrowth ['ʌndəgrəʊθ] *n* maleza *f*

underhand 1 *adj* ['ʌndəhænd] *(method)* ilícito(a); *(person)* solapado(a)
2 *adv* [ʌndə'hænd] bajo cuerda

underline [ʌndə'laɪn] *vt* subrayar

underling ['ʌndəlɪŋ] *n Pej* mandado(a) *m,f*

underlying [ʌndə'laɪɪŋ] *adj (basic)* fundamental

undermine [ʌndə'maɪn] *vt* socavar, minar

underneath [ʌndə'niːθ] **1** *prep* debajo de, bajo
2 *adv* abajo, debajo
3 *adj* de abajo
4 *n* parte *f* inferior

undernourished [ʌndə'nʌrɪʃt] *adj* desnutrido(a)

underpaid [ʌndə'peɪd] *adj* mal pagado(a)

underpass ['ʌndəpɑːs] *n* paso subterráneo

underprivileged [ʌndə'prɪvɪlɪdʒd] **1** *adj* desfavorecido(a)
2 *npl* the u. los menos favorecidos

under-secretary [ʌndə'sekrətərɪ] *n* subsecretario(a) *m,f*

undershirt ['ʌndəʃɜːt] *n US* camiseta *f*

underskirt ['ʌndəskɜːt] *n* combinación *f*

understand [ʌndə'stænd] *vt & vi* (*pt & pp* **understood**) (a) *(comprehend)* entender, comprender; **do I make myself understood?** ¿me explico? (b) *(assume, believe)* entender; **she gave me to u. that ...** me dio a entender que ... (c) *(hear)* tener entendido (d) **to u. one another** entenderse

understandable [ʌndə'stændəbəl] *adj* comprensible

understanding [ʌndə'stændɪŋ] **1** *n* (a) *(intellectual grasp)* entendimiento *m*, comprensión *f* (b) *(interpretation)* interpretación *f* (c) *(agreement)* acuerdo *m*

(d) **on the u. that ...** a condición de que ...
2 *adj* comprensivo(a)

understatement [ʌndə'steɪtmənt] *n* **to make an u.** minimizar, subestimar; **to say that the boy is rather clever is an u.** decir que el chico es bastante listo es quedarse corto

understood [ʌndə'stʊd] **1** *adj* (a) **I wish it to be u. that ...** que conste que ... (b) *(agreed on)* convenido(a) (c) *(implied)* sobreentendido(a)
2 *pt & pp of* **understand**

understudy ['ʌndəstʌdɪ] *n* suplente *mf*

undertake [ʌndə'teɪk] *vt* (*pt* **undertook**; *pp* **undertaken** [ʌndə'teɪkən]) (a) *(responsibility)* asumir; *(task, job)* encargarse de (b) *(promise)* comprometerse a

undertaker ['ʌndəteɪkə(r)] *n* empresario(a) *m,f* de pompas fúnebres; **u.'s** funeraria *f*

undertaking [ʌndə'teɪkɪŋ] *n* (a) *(task)* empresa *f* (b) *(promise)* compromiso *m*

undertone ['ʌndətəʊn] *n* **in an u.** en voz baja

undertook [ʌndə'tʊk] *pt of* **undertake**

underwater [ʌndə'wɔːtə(r)] **1** *adj* submarino(a)
2 *adv* bajo el agua

underwear ['ʌndəweə(r)] *n* ropa *f* interior

underwent [ʌndə'went] *pt of* **undergo**

underworld ['ʌndəwɜːld] *n (criminals)* hampa *f*, bajos fondos

underwrite [ʌndə'raɪt] *vt* (*pt* **underwrote**; *pp* **underwritten**) (a) *(guarantee)* garantizar, avalar (b) *(insure)* asegurar

underwriter ['ʌndəraɪtə(r)] *n* (a) *Fin* suscriptor(a) *m,f* (b) *(insurer)* asegurador(a) *m,f*

underwritten [ʌndə'rɪtən] *pp of* **underwrite**

underwrote [ʌndə'rəʊt] *pt of* **underwrite**

undesirable [ʌndɪ'zaɪrəbəl] *adj & n* indeseable *(mf)*

undeterred [ʌndɪ'tɜːd] *adj* sin inmutarse; **u. by** sin arredrarse ante

undid [ʌn'dɪd] *pt of* **undo**

undies ['ʌndɪz] *npl Fam* bragas *fpl*

undignified [ʌn'dɪgnɪfaɪd] *adj (attitude etc)* indecoroso(a)

undisciplined [ʌn'dɪsɪplɪnd] *adj* indisciplinado(a)

undisclosed [ʌndɪs'kləʊzd] *adj* sin revelar

undiscovered [ʌndɪ'skʌvəd] *adj* sin descubrir

undisguised [ʌndɪs'gaɪzd] *adj Fig* no disimulado(a)

undisputed [ʌndɪ'spjuːtɪd] *adj (unchallenged)* incontestable; *(unquestionable)* indiscutible

undivided [ʌndɪ'vaɪdɪd] *adj* **to giveone's u. attention** prestar toda la atención

undo [ʌn'duː] *vt (pt* **undid**; *pp* **undone)** **(a)** deshacer; *(button)* desabrochar **(b)** *(put right)* enmendar

undone¹ [ʌn'dʌn] *adj (unfinished)* inacabado(a)

undone² [ʌn'dʌn] **1** *adj (knot etc)* deshecho(a); **to come u.** *(shoelace)* desatarse; *(button, blouse)* desabrocharse; *(necklace etc)* soltarse
2 *pp of* **undo**

undoubted [ʌn'daʊtɪd] *adj* indudable

undress [ʌn'dres] **1** *vt* desnudar
2 *vi* desnudarse

undressed [ʌn'drest] *adj (naked)* desnudo(a)

undue [ʌn'djuː] **(a)** *adj (excessive)* excesivo(a) **(b)** *(improper)* indebido(a)

undulate ['ʌndjʊleɪt] *vi* ondular, ondear

unearth [ʌn'ɜːθ] *vt* desenterrar

unearthly [ʌn'ɜːθlɪ] *adj* **(a)** *(being)* sobrenatural **(b)** *Fam (din)* espantoso(a); **at an u. hour** a una hora intempestiva

uneasy [ʌn'iːzɪ] *adj* **(a)** *(worried)* preocupado(a); *(disturbing)* inquietante **(b)** *(uncomfortable)* incómodo(a)

uneconomic(al) [ʌniːkə'nɒmɪk(əl)] *adj* poco económico(a)

uneducated [ʌn'edjʊkeɪtɪd] *adj* inculto(a)

unemployed [ʌnɪm'plɔɪd] **1** *adj* en paro, parado(a) **to be u.** estar en paro
2 *npl* **the u.** los parados

unemployment [ʌnɪm'plɔɪmənt] *n* paro *m*, desempleo *m*; **u. benefit,** *US* **u. compensation** subsidio *m* de desempleo

unending [ʌn'endɪŋ] *adj* interminable

unenviable [ʌn'envɪəbəl] *adj* poco envidiable

unequal [ʌn'iːkwəl] *adj* desigual

unequivocal [ʌnɪ'kwɪvəkəl] *adj* inequívoco(a)

uneven [ʌn'iːvən] *adj* **(a)** *(not level)* desigual; *(bumpy)* accidentado(a) **(b)** *(variable)* irregular

uneventful [ʌnɪ'ventfʊl] *adj* sin acontecimientos

unexceptional [ʌnɪk'sepʃənəl] *adj* ordinario(a)

unexpected [ʌnɪk'spektɪd] *adj (unhoped for)* inesperado(a); *(event)* imprevisto(a)

unfailing [ʌn'feɪlɪŋ] *adj* indefectible; *(incessant)* constante; *(patience)* inagotable

unfair [ʌn'feə(r)] *adj* injusto(a); *Sport* sucio(a)

unfaithful [ʌn'feɪθfʊl] *adj (friend)* desleal; *(husband, wife)* infiel

unfamiliar [ʌnfə'mɪljə(r)] *adj (unknown)* desconocido(a); *(not conversant)* no familiarizado(a) *(with* con)

unfashionable [ʌn'fæʃənəbəl] *adj* pasado(a) de moda; *(ideas etc)* poco popular

unfasten [ʌn'fɑːsən] *vt (knot)* desatar; *(clothing, belt)* desabrochar

unfavourable, *US* **unfavorable** [ʌn'feɪvərəbəl] *adj* desfavorable; *(criticism)* adverso(a); *(winds)* contrario(a)

unfeeling [ʌn'fiːlɪŋ] *adj* insensible

unfinished [ʌn'fɪnɪʃt] *adj* inacabado(a); **u. business** un asunto pendiente

unfit [ʌn'fɪt] *adj* **(a)** *(thing)* inadecuado(a); *(person)* no apto(a) *(for* para) **(b)** *(incompetent)* incompetente **(c)** *(physically)* incapacitado(a); **to be u.** no estar en forma

unflinching [ʌn'flɪntʃɪŋ] *adj* **(a)** *(determined)* resuelto(a) **(b)** *(fearless)* impávido(a)

unfold [ʌn'fəʊld] **1** *vt* **(a)** *(sheet)* desdoblar; *(newspaper)* abrir **(b)** *(plan, secret)* revelar
2 *vi* **(a)** *(open up)* abrirse; *(landscape)* extenderse **(b)** *(plot)* desarrollarse **(c)** *(secret)* descubrirse

unforeseen [ʌnfɔː'siːn] *adj* imprevisto(a)

unforgettable [ʌnfə'getəbəl] *adj* inolvidable

unforgivable [ʌnfə'gɪvəbəl] *adj* imperdonable

unfortunate [ʌn'fɔːtʃənɪt] *adj (person, event)* desgraciado(a); *(remark)* desafortunado(a); **how u.!** ¡qué mala suerte!

unfortunately [ʌn'fɔːtʃənɪtlɪ] *adv* desgraciadamente, por desgracia

unfounded [ʌn'faʊndɪd] *adj* infundado(a)

unfriendly [ʌn'frendlɪ] *adj* **(unfriendlier, unfriendliest)** antipático(a), poco amistoso(a)

unfurl [ʌn'fɜːl] *vi* desplegarse

unfurnished [ʌn'fɜːnɪʃt] *adj* sin amueblar

ungainly [ʌn'geɪnlɪ] *adj (gait)* desgarbado(a)

ungodly [ʌn'gɒdlɪ] *adj* **(ungodlier, ungodliest)** *(behaviour)* impío(a); *Fam Fig* **at an u. hour** a una hora intempestiva

ungrateful [ʌn'greɪtfʊl] *adj (person)* desagradecido(a); *(task)* ingrato(a)

unguarded [ʌnˈgɑːdɪd] *adj* (**a**) *(unprotected)* desatendido(a); *(imprudent)* desprevenido(a) (**b**) *(frank)* franco(a)

unhappiness [ʌnˈhæpɪnɪs] *n* (**a**) *(sadness)* tristeza *f* (**b**) *(wretchedness)* desdicha *f*

unhappy [ʌnˈhæpɪ] *adj* (**unhappier, unhappiest**) (**a**) *(sad)* triste (**b**) *(wretched)* desgraciado(a), infeliz; *(unfortunate)* desafortunado(a)

unharmed [ʌnˈhɑːmd] *adj* ileso(a), indemne

unhealthy [ʌnˈhelθɪ] *adj* (**unhealthier, unhealthiest**) (**a**) *(ill)* enfermizo(a) (**b**) *(unwholesome)* malsano(a)

unheard [ʌnˈhɜːd] *adj* (**a**) **her request went u.** su petición no fue atendida (**b**) **u. of** *(outrageous)* inaudito(a); *(without precedent)* sin precedente

unhesitating [ʌnˈhezɪteɪtɪŋ] *adj* resuelto(a)

unhook [ʌnˈhʊk] *vt (from hook)* descolgar; *(clothing)* desabrochar

unhurt [ʌnˈhɜːt] *adj* ileso(a), indemne

unhygienic [ʌnhaɪˈdʒiːnɪk] *adj* antihigiénico(a)

unidentified [ʌnaɪˈdentɪfaɪd] *adj* **u. flying object** objeto volador no identificado, ovni *m*

unification [juːnɪfɪˈkeɪʃən] *n* unificación *f*

uniform [ˈjuːnɪfɔːm] *adj & n* uniforme *(m)*

uniformity [juːnɪˈfɔːmɪtɪ] *n* uniformidad *f*

unify [ˈjuːnɪfaɪ] *vt* unificar

unilateral [juːnɪˈlætərəl] *adj* unilateral

unimportant [ʌnɪmˈpɔːtənt] *adj* poco importante

uninformed [ʌnɪnˈfɔːmd] *adj (opinion)* sin fundamento

uninhabited [ʌnɪnˈhæbɪtɪd] *adj* despoblado(a)

uninhibited [ʌnɪnˈhɪbɪtɪd] *adj* sin inhibición

uninspired [ʌnɪnˈspaɪəd] *adj (person)* falto(a) de inspiración; *(performance)* insulso(a)

uninspiring [ʌnɪnˈspaɪərɪŋ] *adj* que no inspira

unintelligible [ʌnɪnˈtelɪdʒəbəl] *adj* ininteligible, incomprensible

unintentional [ʌnɪnˈtenʃənəl] *adj* involuntario(a)

unintentionally [ʌnɪnˈtenʃənəlɪ] *adv* sin querer

uninteresting [ʌnˈɪntrɪstɪŋ] *adj* poco interesante

uninterrupted [ʌnɪntəˈrʌptɪd] *adj* ininterrumpido(a)

union [ˈjuːnjən] **1** *n* (**a**) unión *f* (**b**) *(organization)* sindicato *m* (**c**) *US* **the U.** los Estados Unidos; *Br* **U. Jack** bandera *f* del Reino Unido
2 *adj* sindical

unique [juːˈniːk] *adj* único(a)

unison [ˈjuːnɪsən] *n Mus* unisonancia *f*; *Fig (harmony)* armonía *f*; **in u.** al unísono

unit [ˈjuːnɪt] *n* (**a**) unidad *f*; **monetary u.** unidad monetaria; *Br Fin* **u. trust** sociedad *f* de inversiones (**b**) *(piece of furniture)* módulo *m*; **kitchen u.** mueble *m* de cocina (**c**) *Tech* grupo *m*; *Comput* **central processing u.** procesador *m* central; **visual display u.** monitor *m* (**d**) *(department)* servicio *m* (**e**) *(team)* equipo *m*

unite [juːˈnaɪt] **1** *vt* unir
2 *vi* unirse

united [juːˈnaɪtɪd] *adj* unido(a); **U. Kingdom** Reino Unido; **U. States (of America)** Estados Unidos (de América); **U. Nations** Naciones Unidas

unity [ˈjuːnɪtɪ] *n* unidad *f*; *(harmony)* armonía *f*

universal [juːnɪˈvɜːsəl] *adj* universal

universe [ˈjuːnɪvɜːs] *n* universo *m*

university [juːnɪˈvɜːsɪtɪ] **1** *n* universidad *f*
2 *adj* universitario(a)

unjust [ʌnˈdʒʌst] *adj* injusto(a)

unkempt [ʌnˈkempt] *adj* descuidado(a); *(hair)* despeinado(a); *(appearance)* desaliñado(a)

unkind [ʌnˈkaɪnd] *adj (not nice)* poco amable; *(cruel)* despiadado(a)

unknown [ʌnˈnəʊn] **1** *adj* desconocido(a); **u. quantity** incógnita *f*
2 *n* **the u.** lo desconocido

unlawful [ʌnˈlɔːfʊl] *adj (not legal)* ilegal

unleash [ʌnˈliːʃ] *vt* (**a**) *(dog)* soltar (**b**) *Fig (release)* liberar; *(provoke)* desencadenar

unless [ʌnˈles] *conj* a menos que, a no ser que

unlike [ʌnˈlaɪk] **1** *adj* diferente, distinto(a)
2 *prep* a diferencia de

unlikely [ʌnˈlaɪklɪ] *adj* (**a**) *(improbable)* poco probable (**b**) *(unusual)* raro(a)

unlimited [ʌnˈlɪmɪtɪd] *adj* ilimitado(a)

unlisted [ʌnˈlɪstɪd] *adj US Tel* que no se encuentra en la guía telefónica

unload [ʌnˈləʊd] *vt & vi* descargar

unlock [ʌnˈlɒk] *vt* abrir (con llave)

unluckily [ʌnˈlʌkɪlɪ] *adv* desafortunadamente, por desgracia

unlucky [ʌnˈlʌkɪ] *adj* (**unluckier, unluckiest**) *(unfortunate)* desgraciado(a); **to be**

u. *(person)* tener mala suerte; *(thing)* traer mala suerte

unmanageable [ʌnˈmænɪdʒəbəl] *adj (people)* ingobernable; *(child, hair)* incontrolable

unmanned [ʌnˈmænd] *adj (spacecraft etc)* no tripulado(a)

unmarried [ʌnˈmærɪd] *adj* soltero(a)

unmask [ʌnˈmɑːsk] *vt Fig (plot)* descubrir

unmistak(e)able [ʌnmɪsˈteɪkəbəl] *adj* inconfundible

unmistak(e)ably [ʌnmɪsˈteɪkəblɪ] *adv* sin lugar a dudas

unmitigated [ʌnˈmɪtɪɡeɪtɪd] *adj* (**a**) *(absolute)* absoluto(a); *(liar)* rematado(a) (**b**) *(grief)* profundo(a)

unnamed [ʌnˈneɪmd] *adj (anonymous)* anónimo(a)

unnatural [ʌnˈnætʃərəl] *adj* (**a**) *(against nature)* antinatural; *(abnormal)* anormal (**b**) *(affected)* afectado(a)

unnecessary [ʌnˈnesɪsərɪ] *adj* innecesario(a), inútil; **it's u. to add that ...** sobra añadir que ...

unnoticed [ʌnˈnəʊtɪst] *adj* desapercibido(a); **to let sth pass u.** pasar algo por alto

unobserved [ʌnɒbˈzɜːvd] *adj* inadvertido(a)

unobtainable [ʌnəbˈteɪnəbəl] *adj* inasequible, inalcanzable

unobtrusive [ʌnəbˈtruːsɪv] *adj* discreto(a)

unoccupied [ʌnˈɒkjʊpaɪd] *adj (house)* desocupado(a); *(seat)* libre

unofficial [ʌnəˈfɪʃəl] *adj* no oficial; *Ind* **u. strike** huelga *f* no apoyada por los sindicatos

unorthodox [ʌnˈɔːθədɒks] *adj* (**a**) *(behaviour etc)* poco ortodoxo(a) (**b**) *Rel* heterodoxo(a)

unpack [ʌnˈpæk] **1** *vt (boxes)* desembalar; *(suitcase)* deshacer **2** *vi* deshacer la(s) maleta(s)

unpalatable [ʌnˈpælətəbəl] *adj* desagradable

unparalleled [ʌnˈpærəleld] *adj* (**a**) *(in quality)* incomparable (**b**) *(without precedent)* sin precedente

unpardonable [ʌnˈpɑːdənəbəl] *adj* imperdonable

unperturbed [ʌnpəˈtɜːbd] *adj* impasible

unpleasant [ʌnˈplezənt] *adj* desagradable (**to** con)

unpleasantness [ʌnˈplezəntnɪs] *n* disgusto *m*

unplug [ʌnˈplʌɡ] *vt* desenchufar

unpopular [ʌnˈpɒpjʊlə(r)] *adj* impopular; **to make oneself u.** ganarse la antipatía de todos

unprecedented [ʌnˈpresɪdentɪd] *adj* sin precedente

unpredictable [ʌnprɪˈdɪktəbəl] *adj* imprevisible

unprepared [ʌnprɪˈpeəd] *adj (speech etc)* improvisado(a); *(person)* desprevenido(a)

unprincipled [ʌnˈprɪnsɪpəld] *adj* sin escrúpulos

unprintable [ʌnˈprɪntəbəl] *adj (word, comment)* malsonante

unproductive [ʌnprəˈdʌktɪv] *adj (inefficient)* improductivo(a); *(fruitless)* infructuoso(a)

unprofessional [ʌnprəˈfeʃənəl] *adj (unethical)* poco profesional; *(substandard)* de aficionado(a)

unprotected [ʌnprəˈtektɪd] *adj* indefenso(a)

unprovoked [ʌnprəˈvəʊkt] *adj* gratuito(a)

unpunished [ʌnˈpʌnɪʃt] *adj* impune

unqualified [ʌnˈkwɒlɪfaɪd] *adj* (**a**) *(without qualification)* sin título; *(incompetent)* incompetente (**b**) *(unconditional)* incondicional; *(denial)* rotundo(a); *(endorsement)* sin reserva; *(success)* total

unquestionable [ʌnˈkwestʃənəbəl] *adj* indiscutible

unquestioning [ʌnˈkwestʃənɪŋ] *adj* incondicional; *(obedience)* ciego(a)

unravel [ʌnˈrævəl] **1** *vt* desenmarañar **2** *vi* desenmarañarse

unreadable [ʌnˈriːdəbəl] *adj* (**a**) *(handwriting)* ilegible (**b**) *(book)* imposible de leer

unreal [ʌnˈrɪəl] *adj* irreal

unrealistic [ʌnrɪəˈlɪstɪk] *adj* poco realista

unreasonable [ʌnˈriːzənəbəl] *adj* poco razonable; *(demands)* desmedido(a); *(prices)* exorbitante; *(hour)* inoportuno(a)

unrefined [ʌnrɪˈfaɪnd] *adj* (**a**) *(sugar, oil etc)* sin refinar (**b**) *(person)* tosco(a), basto(a)

unrelated [ʌnrɪˈleɪtɪd] *adj (not connected)* no relacionado(a)

unrelenting [ʌnrɪˈlentɪŋ] *adj (behaviour)* implacable; *(struggle)* encarnizado(a)

unreliable [ʌnrɪˈlaɪəbəl] *adj* (**a**) *(person)* de poca confianza (**b**) *(information)* que no es de fiar; *(machine)* poco fiable

unrelieved [ʌnrɪˈliːvd] *adj (boredom)* total

unremitting [ʌnrɪˈmɪtɪŋ] *adj* (**a**) *(efforts etc)* (**b**) *(person)* incansable

unrepentant [ʌnrɪˈpentənt] *adj* impenitente

unreserved [ʌnrɪˈzɜːvd] *adj (praise, support)* sin reserva

unreservedly [ʌnrɪˈzɜːvɪdlɪ] *adv* sin reserva

unrest [ʌnˈrest] *n (social etc)* malestar *m*; **political u.** agitación política

unrivalled, *US* **unrivaled** [ʌnˈraɪvəld] *adj* sin par, sin rival

unroll [ʌnˈrəʊl] *vt* desenrollar

unruffled [ʌnˈrʌfəld] *adj* *Fig* tranquilo(a)

unruly [ʌnˈruːlɪ] *adj* (**unrulier, unruliest**) (**a**) *(child)* revoltoso(a) (**b**) *(hair)* rebelde

unsafe [ʌnˈseɪf] *adj (dangerous)* peligroso(a); *(risky)* inseguro(a); **to feel u.** sentirse expuesto(a)

unsaid [ʌnˈsed] *adj* **it's better left u.** más vale no decir nada; **much was left u.** quedó mucho por decir

unsatisfactory [ʌnsætɪsˈfæktərɪ] *adj* insatisfactorio(a); **it's most u.** deja mucho que desear

unsavoury, *US* **unsavory** [ʌnˈseɪvərɪ] *adj* desagradable

unscathed [ʌnˈskeɪðd] *adj* ileso(a), indemne

unscrew [ʌnˈskruː] *vt* destornillar

unscrupulous [ʌnˈskruːpjʊləs] *adj* sin escrúpulos

unseemly [ʌnˈsiːmlɪ] *adj* impropio(a)

unseen [ʌnˈsiːn] **1** *adj* invisible; *(unnoticed)* inadvertido(a)
2 *n Br Educ* = texto no trabajado en clase

unselfish [ʌnˈselfɪʃ] *adj* desinteresado(a)

unsettle [ʌnˈsetəl] *vt* perturbar

unsettled [ʌnˈsetəld] *adj* (**a**) *(person)* nervioso(a); *(situation)* inestable (**b**) *(weather)* inestable (**c**) *(matter, debt)* pendiente (**d**) *(land)* sin colonizar

unshaven [ʌnˈʃeɪvən] *adj* sin afeitar

unsightly [ʌnˈsaɪtlɪ] *adj* feo(a), desagradable

unskilled [ʌnˈskɪld] *adj (worker)* no cualificado(a); *(work)* no especializado(a)

unsociable [ʌnˈsəʊʃəbəl] *adj* insociable, huraño(a)

unsophisticated [ʌnsəˈfɪstɪkeɪtɪd] *adj* (**a**) *(naïve)* ingenuo(a) (**b**) *(simple)* poco sofisticado(a)

unsound [ʌnˈsaʊnd] *adj* (**a**) *(unstable)* inestable; **of u. mind** demente (**b**) *(fallacious)* falso(a)

unspeakable [ʌnˈspiːkəbəl] *adj* (**a**) indecible (**b**) *Fig (evil)* atroz

unspoken [ʌnˈspəʊkən] *adj* (**a**) *(tacit)* tácito(a) (**b**) *(feeling)* interior, secreto(a)

unstable [ʌnˈsteɪbəl] *adj* inestable

unsteady [ʌnˈstedɪ] *adj (not firm)* inestable; *(table, chair)* cojo(a); *(hand, voice)* tembloroso(a)

unstinting [ʌnˈstɪntɪŋ] *adj* pródigo(a) (**in** en)

unstuck [ʌnˈstʌk] *adj* **to come u.** despegarse; *Fig* venirse abajo

unsuccessful [ʌnsəkˈsesfʊl] *adj* (**a**) *(fruitless)* fracasado(a); *(useless)* vano(a) (**b**) *(businessman etc)* fracasado(a); *(candidate)* derrotado(a); **to be u. at sth** no tener éxito con algo

unsuccessfully [ʌnsəkˈsesfʊlɪ] *adv* sin éxito, en vano

unsuitable [ʌnˈsuːtəbəl] *adj* (**a**) *(person)* no apto(a) (**b**) *(thing)* inadecuado(a); *(remark)* inoportuno(a); *(time)* inconveniente

unsuited [ʌnˈsuːtɪd] *adj* (**a**) *(person)* no apto(a); *(thing)* impropio(a) (**to** para) (**b**) *(incompatible)* incompatible

unsure [ʌnˈʃʊə(r)] *adj* poco seguro(a)

unsuspecting [ʌnsəˈspektɪŋ] *adj* confiado(a); **he went in u.** entró sin sospechar nada

unswerving [ʌnˈswɜːvɪŋ] *adj* firme

unsympathetic [ʌnsɪmpəˈθetɪk] *adj (unfeeling)* impasible; *(not understanding)* poco comprensivo(a)

untapped [ʌnˈtæpt] *adj (resource)* sin explotar

untarnished [ʌnˈtɑːnɪʃt] *adj* *Fig* sin mancha

untenable [ʌnˈtenəbəl] *adj* insostenible

unthinkable [ʌnˈθɪŋkəbəl] *adj* impensable, inconcebible

untidy [ʌnˈtaɪdɪ] *adj* (**untidier, untidiest**) *(room, person)* desordenado(a); *(hair)* despeinado(a); *(appearance)* desaseado(a)

untie [ʌnˈtaɪ] *vt* desatar; *(free)* soltar

until [ʌnˈtɪl] **1** *conj* hasta que; **she worked u. she collapsed** trabajó hasta desfallecer; **u. she gets back** hasta que vuelva
2 *prep* hasta; **u. now** hasta ahora; **u. ten o'clock** hasta las diez; **not u. Monday** hasta el lunes no

untimely [ʌnˈtaɪmlɪ] *adj* (**a**) *(premature)* prematuro(a) (**b**) *(inopportune)* inoportuno(a); *(hour)* intempestivo(a)

untold [ʌnˈtəʊld] *adj* (**a**) *(indescribable)* indecible (**b**) *Fig (loss, wealth)* incalculable (**c**) *(not told)* sin contar

untouchable [ʌn'tʌtʃəbəl] *adj & n* intocable *(mf)*

untoward [ʌntə'wɔːd] *adj* (a) *(unfortunate)* desafortunado(a) (b) *(adverse)* adverso(a)

untrained [ʌn'treɪnd] *adj* (a) *(unskilled)* sin preparación profesional (b) *(inexpert)* inexperto(a)

untrue [ʌn'truː] *adj* (a) *(false)* falso(a) (b) *(unfaithful)* infiel (c) *(inexact)* inexacto(a)

untrustworthy [ʌn'trʌstwɜːðɪ] *adj* (a) *(person)* de poca confianza (b) *(source)* no fidedigno(a)

unused [ʌn'juːzd] *adj* (a) *(car)* sin usar; *(flat etc)* sin estrenar; *(stamp)* sin matar (b) *(not in use)* que ya no se utiliza (c) [ʌn'juːst] *(unaccustomed)* desacostumbrado(a) (**to** a)

unusual [ʌn'juːʒʊəl] *adj (rare)* insólito(a), poco común; *(original)* original; *(exceptional)* excepcional

unusually [ʌn'juːʒʊəlɪ] *adv* excepcionalmente

unveil [ʌn'veɪl] *vt* descubrir

unwarranted [ʌn'wɒrəntɪd] *adj* injustificado(a); *(remark)* gratuito(a)

unwavering [ʌn'weɪvərɪŋ] *adj (loyalty)* constante, firme; *(courage)* inquebrantable

unwelcome [ʌn'welkəm] *adj (visitor)* molesto(a); *(visit)* inoportuno(a); *Fig (news etc)* desagradable

unwell [ʌn'wel] *adj* malo(a), indispuesto(a)

unwieldy [ʌn'wiːldɪ] *adj (difficult to handle)* poco manejable; *(clumsy)* torpe

unwilling [ʌn'wɪlɪŋ] *adj* **to be u. to do sth** no estar dispuesto a hacer algo

unwillingly [ʌn'wɪlɪŋlɪ] *adv* de mala gana

unwind [ʌn'waɪnd] **1** *vt (pt & pp unwound)* desenrollar
2 *vi* (a) desenrollarse (b) *(relax)* relajarse

unwise [ʌn'waɪz] *adj* imprudente, desaconsejable

unwitting [ʌn'wɪtɪŋ] *adj* involuntario(a)

unworkable [ʌn'wɜːkəbəl] *adj (not feasible)* impracticable; *(suggestion)* irrealizable

unworthy [ʌn'wɜːðɪ] *adj* indigno(a)

unwound [ʌn'waʊnd] *pt & pp of* unwind

unwrap [ʌn'ræp] *vt (gift)* desenvolver; *(package)* deshacer

unwritten [ʌn'rɪtən] *adj* no escrito(a); *(agreement)* verbal

unyielding [ʌn'jiːldɪŋ] *adj* inflexible

up [ʌp] **1** *prep* (a) *(movement)* **to climb up the mountain** escalar la montaña; **to walk up the street** ir calle arriba
(b) *(position)* en lo alto de; **further up the street** más adelante (en la misma calle); **halfway up the ladder** a mitad de la escalera

2 *adv* (a) *(upwards)* arriba, hacia arriba; *(position)* arriba; **from £10 up** de 10 libras para arriba; **halfway up** a medio camino; **right up (to the top)** hasta arriba (del todo); **to go/come up** subir; **this side up** *(sign)* este lado hacia arriba
(b) **the moon is up** ha salido la luna
(c) *(towards)* hacia; **to come** *or* **go up to sb** acercarse a algn; **to walk up and down** ir de un lado a otro
(d) *(in, to)* **he's up in Yorkshire** está en Yorkshire
(e) *(increased)* **bread is up** el pan ha subido
(f) **it's up for discussion** se está discutiendo; **up for sale** en venta
(g) *Fam* **something's up** pasa algo; **what's up (with you)?** ¿qué pasa (contigo)?
(h) **to be up against sth** enfrentarse con algo
(i) **up to** *(as far as, until)* hasta; **I can spend up to £5** puedo gastar un máximo de 5 libras; **up to here** hasta aquí; **up to now** hasta ahora
(j) **to be up to** *(depend on)* depender de; *(be capable of)* estar a la altura de; **I don't feel up to doing it today** hoy no me encuentro con fuerzas para hacerlo; **it's not up to much** no vale gran cosa
(k) **he's up to sth** está tramando algo

3 *adj* (a) *(out of bed)* levantado(a)
(b) *(finished)* terminado(a); **time's up** (ya) es la hora

4 *vt Fam* aumentar

5 *n Fig* **ups and downs** altibajos *mpl*

up-and-coming ['ʌpən'kʌmɪŋ] *adj* prometedor(a)

upbringing ['ʌpbrɪŋɪŋ] *n* educación *f*

update [ʌp'deɪt] *vt* actualizar, poner al día

upgrade 1 *vt* [ʌp'greɪd] (a) *(promote)* ascender (b) *(improve)* mejorar la calidad de (c) *Comput (software, hardware)* actualizar
2 *n* ['ʌpgreɪd] *Comput* actualización *f*

upheaval [ʌp'hiːvəl] *n* trastorno *m*

upheld [ʌp'held] *pt & pp of* uphold

uphill 1 *adj* ['ʌphɪl] ascendente; *Fig* arduo(a)
2 *adv* [ʌp'hɪl] cuesta arriba

uphold [ʌp'həʊld] *vt* (*pt & pp* **upheld**) sostener

upholstery [ʌp'həʊlstərɪ] *n* tapizado *m*, tapicería *f*

upkeep ['ʌpkiːp] *n* mantenimiento *m*

up-market ['ʌpmɑːkɪt] *adj* de categoría

upon [ə'pɒn] *prep Fml* en, sobre; **once u. a time ...** érase una vez ...; **u. my word** (mi) palabra de honor

upper ['ʌpə(r)] **1** *adj* (**a**) (*position*) superior; **u. storey** piso de arriba; *Fig* **to have the u. hand** llevar la delantera (**b**) (*in rank*) alto(a); **the u. class** la clase alta; **the U. House** la Cámara Alta

2 *n* (*of shoe*) pala *f*

upper-class ['ʌpə'klæs] *adj* de la clase alta

uppermost ['ʌpəməʊst] *adj* más alto(a); *Fig* **it was u. in my mind** era lo que me preocupaba más

upright ['ʌpraɪt] **1** *adj* (**a**) (*vertical*) vertical (**b**) (*honest*) honrado(a)

2 *adv* derecho

3 *n Ftb* (*post*) poste *m*

uprising ['ʌpraɪzɪŋ] *n* sublevación *f*

uproar ['ʌprɔː(r)] *n* tumulto *m*, alboroto *m*

uproot [ʌp'ruːt] *vt* (*plant*) arrancar de raíz

upset [ʌp'set] **1** *vt* (*pt & pp* **upset**) (**a**) (*overturn*) volcar; (*spill*) derramar (**b**) (*shock*) trastornar; (*worry*) preocupar; (*displease*) disgustar (**c**) (*spoil*) desbaratar (**d**) (*make ill*) sentar mal a

2 *adj* (*shocked*) alterado(a); (*displeased*) disgustado(a); **to have an u. stomach** sentirse mal del estómago

3 *n* ['ʌpset] (**a**) (*reversal*) revés *m* (**b**) *Sport* resultado inesperado

upshot ['ʌpʃɒt] *n* resultado *m*

upside ['ʌpsaɪd] *n* **u. down** al revés

upstage [ʌp'steɪdʒ] *vt Fam* eclipsar

upstairs [ʌp'steəz] **1** *adv* al piso de arriba; **she lives u.** vive en el piso de arriba

2 *n* piso *m* de arriba

upstart ['ʌpstɑːt] *n* advenedizo *m,f*

upstream [ʌp'striːm] *adv* río arriba

uptake ['ʌpteɪk] *n Fam* **to be quick on the u.** cogerlas al vuelo

uptight [ʌp'taɪt] *adj Fam* nervioso(a)

up-to-date [ʌptə'deɪt] *adj* (**a**) (*current*) al día (**b**) (*modern*) moderno(a)

upturn ['ʌptɜːn] *n* mejora *f*

upward ['ʌpwəd] *adj* ascendente

upward(s) ['ʌpwəd(z)] *adv* hacia arriba; **from ten (years) u.** a partir de los diez años; *Fam* **u. of** algo más de

uranium [jʊ'reɪnɪəm] *n* uranio *m*

urban ['ɜːbən] *adj* urbano(a)

urbane [ɜː'beɪn] *adj* urbano(a), cortés

urchin ['ɜːtʃɪn] *n* (**a**) (*child*) pilluelo(a) *m,f* (**b**) **sea u.** erizo *m* de mar

urge [ɜːdʒ] **1** *vt* (**a**) (*plead*) exhortar (**b**) (*advocate*) preconizar; **to u. that sth should be done** insistir en que se haga algo

2 *n* impulso *m*

▸ **urge on** *vt sep* animar a

urgency ['ɜːdʒənsɪ] *n* urgencia *f*

urgent ['ɜːdʒənt] *adj* urgente; (*need, tone*) apremiante

urinal [jʊ'raɪnəl] *n* (*toilet*) urinario *m*; (*bowl*) orinal *m*

urinate ['jʊərɪneɪt] *vi* orinar

urine ['jʊərɪn] *n* orina *f*

URL [juːɑː'rel] *n Comput* (*abbr* **uniform resource locator**) URL *m*

urn [ɜːn] *n* (**a**) urna *f* (**b**) **tea u.** tetera *f* grande

Uruguay ['jʊərəgwaɪ] *n* Uruguay

Uruguayan [jʊərə'gwaɪən] *adj & n* uruguayo(a) (*m,f*)

US [juː'es] *n* (*abbr* **United States**) EE.UU. *mpl*

us [ʌs, *unstressed* əs] *pers pron* (**a**) (*as object*) nos; **let's forget it** olvidémoslo (**b**) (*after prep*) nosotros(as); **both of us** nosotros dos; **he's one of us** es de los nuestros (**c**) (*after v* **to be**) nosotros(as); **she wouldn't believe it was us** no creía que fuéramos nosotros (**d**) *Fam* me; **give us a kiss!** ¡dame un beso!

USA [juːes'eɪ] *n* (*abbr* **United States of America**) EE.UU. *mpl*

usage ['juːsɪdʒ] *n* (**a**) (*habit, custom*) costumbre *f* (**b**) *Ling* uso *m*

use [juːz] **1** *vt* (**a**) emplear, utilizar; **what is it used for?** ¿para qué sirve?; **to u. force** hacer uso de la fuerza

(**b**) (*consume*) consumir, gastar

(**c**) (*take unfair advantage of*) aprovecharse de

(**d**) *Fam* **I could u. a drink** no me vendría mal un trago

2 *v aux* **used to** ['juːstə] soler, acostumbrar; **where did you u. to live?** ¿dónde vivías (antes)?

> Como verbo auxiliar, aparece siempre en la forma **used to**. Se traduce al español por el verbo principal en pretérito imperfecto, o por el pretérito imperfecto de **soler** más infinitivo.

3 *n* [juːs] (**a**) uso *m*, empleo *m*; (*handling*) manejo *m*; **directions for u.** modo de empleo; **in u.** en uso; **not in u.** (*on* *lift)* no funciona; **ready for u.** listo para usar; **to make (good) u. of sth** aprovechar algo; **to put to good u.** sacar partido de

(**b**) *(application)* aplicación *f*

(**c**) *(usefulness)* utilidad *f*; **it's no u.** es inútil; **what's the u.?** ¿para qué?; *Fam* **it's no u. crying** no sirve de nada llorar; **of u.** útil; **to be of u.** servir

▸ **use up** *vt sep* acabar

used *adj* (**a**) [juːzd] *(second-hand)* usado(a) (**b**) [juːst] **to be u. to** estar acostumbrado(a) a

useful ['juːsfʊl] *adj* útil; *(practical)* práctico(a); **to come in u.** venir bien

usefulness ['juːsfʊlnɪs] *n* utilidad *f*

useless ['juːslɪs] *adj* inútil

user ['juːzə(r)] *n* (**a**) usuario(a) *m,f* (**b**) *Fam (of drugs)* drogadicto(a) *m,f*

usher ['ʌʃə(r)] **1** *n* (**a**) *Cin & Th* acomodador(a) *m,f* (**b**) *(in court etc)* ujier *m*

2 *vt* **to u.** *in Cin & Th* acomodar; *(at home)* hacer pasar; **to u. out** acompañar hasta la puerta

USSR [juːɛsɛs'ɑː(r)] *n Hist (abbr* **Union of Soviet Socialist Republics)** URSS *f*

usual ['juːʒʊəl] **1** *adj* corriente, normal; **as u.** como siempre; **at the u. hour** a la hora habitual; **earlier than u.** más pronto que de costumbre; **the u. problems** los problemas de siempre

2 *n* lo habitual; **out of the u.** fuera de lo común

usually ['juːʒʊəlɪ] *adv* normalmente

usurp [juːˈzɜːp] *vt* usurpar

utensil [juːˈtensəl] *n* utensilio *m*; **kitchen utensils** batería *f* de cocina

uterus ['juːtərəs] *n* útero *m*

utilitarian [juːtɪlɪˈteərɪən] *adj* (**a**) *(in philosophy)* utilitarista (**b**) *(useful)* utilitario(a)

utility [juːˈtɪlɪtɪ] *n* (**a**) utilidad *f*; **u. room** cuarto *m* de planchar; *(for storage)* trascocina *f* (**b**) **(public) u.** empresa *f* de servicio público

utilize ['juːtɪlaɪz] *vt* utilizar

utmost ['ʌtməʊst] **1** *adj* sumo(a); **of the u. importance** de suma importancia

2 *n* máximo *m*; **to do** *or* **try one's u.** hacer todo lo posible; **to the u.** al máximo, a más no poder

utopian [juːˈtəʊpɪən] *adj* utópico(a)

utter ¹ ['ʌtə(r)] *vt (words)* pronunciar; *(sigh)* dar; *(cry, threat)* lanzar

utter ² ['ʌtə(r)] *adj* total, completo(a)

utterance ['ʌtərəns] *n* declaración *f*

U-turn ['juːtɜːn] *n* cambio *m* de sentido; *Pol* giro *m* de 180 grados

V, v [viː] *n (the letter)* V, v *f*

V *(abbr* **volt(s)**) V

v (a) *(abbr* **verse)** v **(b)** *(also* **vs**) *(abbr* **versus)** contra

vacancy ['veɪkənsɪ] *n* **(a)** *(job)* vacante *f* **(b)** *(room)* habitación *f* libre; **no vacancies** *(sign)* completo

vacant ['veɪkənt] *adj* **(a)** *(empty)* vacío(a) **(b)** *(job)* vacante; *Br* **situations v.** *(in newspaper)* ofertas de trabajo **(c)** *(free, not in use)* libre

vacate [və'keɪt] *vt (flat)* desalojar

vacation [və'keɪʃən] *US* **1** *n* vacaciones *fpl*; **on v.** de vacaciones
2 *vi* pasar las vacaciones (**in/at** en)

vacationer [və'keɪʃənə(r)], **vacationist** [və'keɪʃənɪst] *n US* **summer v.** veraneante *mf*

vaccinate ['væksɪneɪt] *vt* vacunar

vaccine ['væksiːn] *n* vacuna *f*

vacuum ['vækjʊəm] **1** *n* vacío *m*; **v. cleaner** aspiradora *f*; **v. flask** termo *m*
2 *vt (carpet, room)* pasar la aspiradora por

vacuum-packed ['vækjʊəm'pækt] *adj* envasado(a) al vacío

vagina [və'dʒaɪnə] *n* vagina *f*

vagrant ['veɪɡrənt] *adj & n* vagabundo(a) *(m,f)*

vague [veɪɡ] *adj (imprecise)* vago(a), impreciso(a); *(indistinct)* borroso(a)

vain [veɪn] *adj* **(a)** *(proud)* vanidoso(a), presumido(a) **(b)** *(hopeless)* vano(a); **in v.** en vano

valentine ['væləntaɪn] *n* **(a)** *(card)* = tarjeta que se manda el Día de los Enamorados **(b)** *(sweetheart)* novio(a) *m,f*

valet ['vælɪt, 'væleɪ] *n* ayuda *m* de cámara

valiant ['væljənt] *adj* valiente

valid ['vælɪd] *adj* válido(a); **no longer v.** caducado(a)

valley ['vælɪ] *n* valle *m*

valour, *US* **valor** ['vælə(r)] *n* valor *m*, valentía *f*

valuable ['væljʊəbəl] **1** *adj* valioso(a), de valor
2 *npl* **valuables** objetos *mpl* de valor

valuation [væljʊ'eɪʃən] *n* **(a)** *(act)* valoración *f* **(b)** *(price)* valor *m*

value ['væljuː] **1** *n* valor *m*; **50 pence is good v.** 50 peniques es un buen precio; **to get good v. for money** sacarle jugo al dinero; **v.-added tax** impuesto *m* sobre el valor añadido
2 *vt* valorar

valve [vælv] *n* **(a)** *Anat & Tech* válvula *f* **(b)** *Rad* lámpara *f*

vampire ['væmpaɪə(r)] *n* vampiro *m*

van [væn] *n Br* **(a)** *Aut* furgoneta *f* **(b)** *Rail* furgón *m*

vandal ['vændəl] *n* vándalo(a) *m,f*

vandalism ['vændəlɪzəm] *n* vandalismo *m*

vandalize ['vændəlaɪz] *vt* destruir, destrozar

vanguard ['væŋɡɑːd] *n* vanguardia *f*

vanilla [və'nɪlə] *n* vainilla *f*

vanish ['vænɪʃ] *vi* desaparecer

vanity ['vænɪtɪ] *n* vanidad *f*; **v. bag** *or* **case** neceser *m*

vantage ['vɑːntɪdʒ] *n* ventaja *f*; **v. point** posición estratégica

vapor ['veɪpər] *n US* = **vapour**

vaporizer ['veɪpəraɪzə(r)] *n (device)* vaporizador *m*; *(spray)* pulverizador *m*

vapour ['veɪpə(r)] *n* vapor *m*; *(on windowpane)* vaho *m*; **v. trail** estela *f* de humo

variable ['veərɪəbəl] *adj & n* variable *(f)*

variance ['veərɪəns] *n Fml* **to be at v.** no concordar; **to be at v. with sb** estar en desacuerdo con algn

variation [veərɪ'eɪʃən] *n* variación *f*

varicose ['værɪkəʊs] *adj* **v. veins** varices *fpl*

varied ['veərɪd] *adj* variado(a), diverso(a)

variety [və'raɪətɪ] *n* **(a)** *(diversity)* variedad *f*; *(assortment)* surtido *m*; **for a v. of reasons** por razones diversas **(b)** **v. show** espectáculo *m* de variedades

various ['veərɪəs] *adj* diversos(as), varios(as)

varnish ['vɑːnɪʃ] **1** *n* barniz *m*; *Br* **nail v.** esmalte *m* de uñas
2 *vt* barnizar; *(nails)* esmaltar

vary ['veərɪ] *vi* variar; **prices v. from £2 to**

£4 los precios oscilan entre 2 y 4 libras; **to v. in size** variar de tamaño

varying ['veərɪŋ] *adj* **with v. degrees of success** con más o menos éxito

vase [*Br* vɑːz, *US* veɪs] *n* jarrón *m*

> Note that the Spanish word **vaso** is a false friend and is never a translation for the English word **vase**. In Spanish, **vaso** means both "glass" and "vessel".

vasectomy [vəˈsektəmɪ] *n Med* vasectomía *f*

Vaseline® ['væsɪliːn] *n* vaselina *f*

vast [vɑːst] *adj* vasto(a); *(majority)* inmenso(a)

VAT [viːeɪˈtiː, væt] *n (abbr* **value-added tax)** IVA *m*

vat [væt] *n* cuba *f*, tina *f*

Vatican ['vætɪkən] *n* **the V.** el Vaticano

vault¹ [vɔːlt] *n* bóveda *f*; *(for wine)* bodega *f*; *(tomb)* cripta *f*; *(of bank)* cámara acorazada

vault² [vɔːlt] **1** *vt & vi* saltar
2 *n* salto *m*

vaunt [vɔːnt] *vt Fml* jactarse de, hacer alarde de

VCR [viːsiːˈɑː(r)] *n (abbr* **video cassette recorder)** (aparato *m* de) vídeo *m*

VD [viːˈdiː] *n (abbr* **venereal disease)** enfermedad venérea

VDU [viːdiːˈjuː] *n (abbr* **visual display unit)** monitor *m*

veal [viːl] *n* ternera *f*

veer [vɪə(r)] *vi (ship)* virar; *(car)* girar

vegan ['viːɡən] *n* vegetaliano(a) *m,f,* = vegetariano estricto que no come ningún producto de origen animal

vegeburger ['vedʒɪbɜːɡə(r)] *n* hamburguesa vegetariana

vegetable ['vedʒtəbəl] *n (food)* verdura *f*, hortaliza *f*; **v. garden** huerta *f*, huerto *m*

vegetarian [vedʒɪˈteərɪən] *adj & n* vegetariano(a) *(m,f)*

vegetation [vedʒɪˈteɪʃən] *n* vegetación *f*

vehement ['viːmənt] *adj* vehemente

vehicle ['viːkəl] *n* vehículo *m*

veil [veɪl] **1** *n* velo *m*
2 *vt* velar

vein [veɪn] *n* vena *f*

velocity [vɪˈlɒsɪtɪ] *n* velocidad *f*

velvet ['velvɪt] *n* terciopelo *m*

velvety ['velvɪtɪ] *adj* aterciopelado(a)

vendetta [venˈdetə] *n* vendetta *f*

vending ['vendɪŋ] *n* **v. machine** máquina expendedora

vendor ['vendɔː(r)] *n* vendedor(a) *m,f*

veneer [vɪˈnɪə(r)] *n (a) (covering)* chapa *f*
(b) Fig apariencia *f*

venerable ['venərəbəl] *adj* venerable

venereal [vɪˈnɪərɪəl] *adj* venéreo(a)

Venetian [vɪˈniːʃən] *adj & n* veneciano(a) *(m,f)*; **v. blind** persiana *f* graduable

Venezuela [venɪˈzweɪlə] *n* Venezuela

Venezuelan [venɪˈzweɪlən] *adj & n* venezolano(a) *(m,f)*

vengeance ['vendʒəns] *n* venganza *f*; *Fam* **it was raining with a v.** llovía con ganas

Venice ['venɪs] *n* Venecia

venison ['venɪsən] *n* carne *f* de venado

venom ['venəm] *n* veneno *m*

venomous ['venəməs] *adj* venenoso(a); *Fig* **v. tongue** lengua viperina

vent [vent] **1** *n* **(a)** *(opening)* abertura *f*, orificio *m*; *(grille)* rejilla *f* de ventilación; **air v.** respiradero *m* **(b)** *(of volcano)* chimenea *f*
2 *vt Fig (feelings)* descargar

ventilate ['ventɪleɪt] *vt* ventilar

ventilation [ventɪˈleɪʃən] *n* ventilación *f*

ventilator ['ventɪleɪtə(r)] *n* ventilador *m*

ventriloquist [venˈtrɪləkwɪst] *n* ventrílocuo(a) *m,f*

venture ['ventʃə(r)] **1** *vt* arriesgar, aventurar; **he didn't v. to ask** no se atrevió a preguntarlo
2 *vi* arriesgarse; **to v. out of doors** atreverse a salir
3 *n* empresa arriesgada, aventura *f; Com* **business/joint v.** empresa comercial/colectiva

venue ['venjuː] *n* **(a)** *(meeting place)* lugar *m* de reunión **(b)** *(for concert etc)* local *m*

Venus ['viːnəs] *n (goddess)* Venus *f*; *(planet)* Venus *m*

veranda(h) [vəˈrændə] *n* porche *m*, terraza *f*

verb [vɜːb] *n* verbo *m*

verbal ['vɜːbəl] *adj* verbal

verbatim [vəˈbeɪtɪm] **1** *adj* textual
2 *adv* textualmente

verbose [vɜːˈbəʊs] *adj* prodigo(a) en palabras

verdict ['vɜːdɪkt] *n* **(a)** *Jur* veredicto *m*, fallo *m* **(b)** *(opinion)* opinión *f*, juicio *m*

verge [vɜːdʒ] **1** *n* **(a)** *(margin)* borde *m*; *Fig* **on the v. of** al borde de; *Fig* **to be on the v. of doing sth** estar a punto de hacer algo **(b)** *Br (of road)* arcén *m*, *Andes* berma *f*, *Méx* acotamiento *m*, *RP* banquina *f*, *Ven* hombrillo *m*
2 *vi* rayar **(on** en)

verification [verɪfɪˈkeɪʃən] *n* verificación *f*, comprobación *f*

verify ['verɪfaɪ] *vt* verificar, comprobar

veritable ['verɪtəbəl] *adj* auténtico(a)

vermicelli [vɜːmɪ'tʃelɪ] *n* fideos *mpl*

vermin ['vɜːmɪn] *npl* (a) *(animals)* bichos *mpl*, sabandijas *fpl* (b) *Fig* gentuza *f*

vermouth ['vɜːməθ] *n* vermú *m*, vermut *m*

verruca [və'ruːkə] *n* verruga *f*

versatile ['vɜːsətaɪl] *adj (person)* polifacético(a); *(object)* versátil

verse [vɜːs] *n* (a) *(stanza)* estrofa *f* (b) *(poetry)* versos *mpl*, poesía *f* (c) *(of song)* copla *f* (d) *(of Bible)* versículo *m*

versed [vɜːst] *adj* **to be (well) v. in** ser (muy) versado en

version ['vɜːʃən, 'vɜːʒən] *n* (a) versión *f*; **stage v.** adaptación *f* teatral (b) *Aut* modelo *m*

versus ['vɜːsəs] *prep* contra

vertebra ['vɜːtɪbrə] *n (pl* **vertebras** *or* **vertebrae** ['vɜːtɪbriː]) vértebra *f*

vertical ['vɜːtɪkəl] *adj & n* vertical *(f)*

vertigo ['vɜːtɪɡəʊ] *n* vértigo *m*

verve [vɜːv] *n* vigor *m*, brío *m*

very ['verɪ] **1** *adv* (a) *(extremely)* muy; **to be v. hungry** tener mucha hambre; **v. much** muchísimo; **v. well** muy bien (b) *(emphatic)* **at the v. latest** como máximo; **at the v. least** como mínimo; **the v. best** el mejor de todos; **the v. first/last** el primero/último de todos; **the v. same day** el mismo día

2 *adj* (a) **at the v. end/beginning** al final/principio de todo (b) *(precise)* **at this v. moment** en este mismo momento; **her v. words** sus palabras exactas; **in the v. middle** justo en medio (c) *(mere)* **the v. thought of it!** ¡sólo con pensarlo!

vespers ['vespəz] *npl* vísperas *fpl*

vessel ['vesəl] *n* (a) *(container)* vasija *f* (b) *Naut* buque *m*, nave *f* (c) *Anat & Bot* vaso *m*

vest [vest] **1** *n* (a) *Br (undershirt)* camiseta *f* de tirantes (b) *US* chaleco *m*

2 *vt Jur* **by the power vested in me ...** por los poderes que se me han conferido ...

vested ['vestɪd] *adj Jur & Fin* **v. interests** derechos adquiridos; *Fig* intereses *mpl* personales

vestibule ['vestɪbjuːl] *n* vestíbulo *m*

vestige ['vestɪdʒ] *n* vestigio *m*

vestry ['vestrɪ] *n* sacristía *f*

vet [vet] **1** *n* veterinario(a) *m,f*

2 *vt Br* someter a investigación, examinar

veteran ['vetərən] *n* (a) veterano(a) *m,f* (b) *US (war)* **v.** ex combatiente *mf*

veterinarian [vetərɪ'neərɪən] *n US* veterinario(a) *m,f*

veterinary ['vetərɪnərɪ] *adj* veterinario(a); **v. medicine** veterinaria *f*; *Br* **v. surgeon** veterinario(a) *m,f*

veto ['viːtəʊ] **1** *n (pl* **vetoes)** veto *m*

2 *vt Pol* vetar; *(suggestion etc)* descartar

vexed [vekst] *adj* (a) *(annoyed)* disgustado(a) (b) *(debated)* controvertido(a)

VHF [viːeɪtʃ'ef] *(abbr* **very high frequency)** VHF

via ['vaɪə] *prep* por, vía

viable ['vaɪəbəl] *adj* viable, factible

viaduct ['vaɪədʌkt] *n* viaducto *m*

vibrant ['vaɪbrənt] *adj* (a) *(sound)* vibrante (b) *Fig (personality)* vital; *(city)* animado(a)

vibrate [vaɪ'breɪt] *vi* vibrar (**with** de)

vibration [vaɪ'breɪʃən] *n* vibración *f*

vicar ['vɪkə(r)] *n* párroco *m*

vicarage ['vɪkərɪdʒ] *n* casa *f* del párroco

vicarious [vɪ'keərɪəs] *adj* experimentado(a) por otro; *(punishment)* sufrido(a) por otro

vice¹ [vaɪs] *n* vicio *m*

vice² [vaɪs] *n Br (tool)* torno *m* de banco

vice- [vaɪs] *pref* vice-; **v.-chancellor** rector(a) *m,f*; **v.-president** vicepresidente(a) *m,f*

vice-chairman [vaɪs'tʃeəmən] *n* vicepresidente *m*

vice versa [vaɪsɪ'vɜːsə] *adv* viceversa

vicinity [vɪ'sɪnɪtɪ] *n (area)* vecindad *f*; **in the v. of** *(geographic location)* cerca de, en las inmediaciones de; *(amount)* alrededor de

vicious ['vɪʃəs] *adj (violent)* violento(a); *(malicious)* malintencionado(a); *(cruel)* cruel; **v. circle** círculo vicioso

victim ['vɪktɪm] *n* víctima *f*

victimize ['vɪktɪmaɪz] *vt* perseguir, tratar injustamente

victor ['vɪktə(r)] *n* vencedor(a) *m,f*

victorious [vɪk'tɔːrɪəs] *adj* victorioso(a)

victory ['vɪktərɪ] *n* victoria *f*

video ['vɪdɪəʊ] *n* vídeo *m*; **v. camera** videocámara *f*; **v. cassette** videocasete *m*; **v. club** videoclub *m*; **v. game** videojuego *m*; **v. (cassette) recorder** vídeo *m*; **v. tape** cinta *f* de vídeo

video-tape ['vɪdɪəʊteɪp] *vt* grabar (en vídeo)

vie [vaɪ] *vi* competir (**against** *or* **with** con)

Vienna [vɪ'enə] *n* Viena

Viennese [vɪə'niːz] *adj & n* vienés(esa) *(m,f)*

Vietnam [vjet'næm] *n* Vietnam

view [vjuː] **1** *n* (a) *(sight)* vista *f*, panorama *m*; **in full v.** completamente visible; **on v.** a la vista; **to come into v.** aparecer;

Fig in **v. of** the fact that ... dado que ... (**b**) *(opinion)* opinión *f*; **point of v.** punto *m* de vista; **to take a dim v. of** ver con malos ojos (**c**) *(aim)* fin *m*; **with a v. to** con la intención de

2 *vt* (**a**) *(look at)* mirar; *(house etc)* visitar (**b**) *(consider)* contemplar; *(topic, problem)* enfocar

viewer ['vjuːə(r)] *n* (**a**) *TV* televidente *mf* (**b**) *Phot* visionador *m*

viewfinder ['vjuːfaɪndə(r)] *n* visor *m*

viewpoint ['vjuːpɔɪnt] *n* punto *m* de vista

vigil ['vɪdʒɪl] *n* vigilia *f*

vigilante [vɪdʒɪ'læntɪ] *n* **v. group** patrulla ciudadana

vigorous ['vɪgərəs] *adj* vigoroso(a), enérgico(a)

vigour, *US* **vigor** ['vɪgə(r)] *n* vigor *m*

vile [vaɪl] *adj* (**a**) *(evil)* vil, infame (**b**) *(disgusting)* repugnante (**c**) *Fam (awful)* horrible

vilify ['vɪlɪfaɪ] *vt* denigrar

villa ['vɪlə] *n* (**a**) *(in country)* casa *f* de campo (**b**) *Br* chalet *m*

village ['vɪlɪdʒ] *n (small)* aldea *f*; *(larger)* pueblo *m*

villager ['vɪlɪdʒə(r)] *n* aldeano(a) *m,f*

villain ['vɪlən] *n* villano(a) *m,f*; *Cin & Th* malo(a) *m,f*

vinaigrette [vɪneɪ'gret] *n* vinagreta *f*

vindicate ['vɪndɪkeɪt] *vt* justificar, vindicar

vindictive [vɪn'dɪktɪv] *adj* vengativo(a)

vine [vaɪn] *n* vid *f*; *(climbing)* parra *f*

vinegar ['vɪnɪgə(r)] *n* vinagre *m*

vineyard ['vɪnjəd] *n* viña *f*, viñedo *m*

vintage ['vɪntɪdʒ] **1** *n* (**a**) *(crop, year)* cosecha *f* (**b**) *(season)* vendimia *f* (**c**) *(era)* era *f*

2 *adj* (**a**) *(wine)* añejo(a) (**b**) *(classic)* clásico(a); **v. car** coche *m* de época

vinyl ['vaɪnɪl] *n* vinilo *m*

viola [vɪ'əʊlə] *n* viola *f*

violate ['vaɪəleɪt] *vt* violar

violence ['vaɪələns] *n* violencia *f*

violent ['vaɪələnt] *adj* (**a**) violento(a) (**b**) *(intense)* intenso(a)

violet ['vaɪəlɪt] **1** *n* (**a**) *Bot* violeta *f* (**b**) *(colour)* violeta *m*

2 *adj* violeta

violin [vaɪə'lɪn] *n* violín *m*

violinist [vaɪə'lɪnɪst] *n* violinista *mf*

VIP [viːaɪ'piː] *n Fam (abbr* **very important person)** personaje *m* muy importante

viper ['vaɪpə(r)] *n* víbora *f*

virgin ['vɜːdʒɪn] **1** *n* virgen *f*; **the V. Mary** la Virgen María; **to be a v.** ser virgen

2 *adj* virgen

virginity [və'dʒɪnɪtɪ] *n* virginidad *f*

Virgo ['vɜːgəʊ] *n* Virgo *m*

virile ['vɪraɪl] *adj* viril

virtual ['vɜːtjʊəl] *adj* virtual; *Comput* **v. reality** realidad *f* virtual

virtually ['vɜːtjʊəlɪ] *adv (almost)* prácticamente

virtue ['vɜːtjuː] *n* virtud *f*; **by v. of** en virtud de

virtuous ['vɜːtjʊəs] *adj* virtuoso(a)

virulent ['vɪrʊlənt] *adj* virulento(a)

virus ['vaɪrəs] *n* virus *m inv*; *Comput* **v. check** detección *m* de virus

visa ['viːzə] *n* visado *m*, *Am* visa *f*

vis-à-vis [viːzaː'viː] *prep* (**a**) *(regarding)* respecto a (**b**) *(opposite)* frente a

viscose ['vɪskəʊs] *n* viscosa *f*

viscount ['vaɪkaʊnt] *n* vizconde *m*

vise [vaɪs] *n US (tool)* torno *m* de banco

visibility [vɪzɪ'bɪlɪtɪ] *n* visibilidad *f*

visible ['vɪzɪbəl] *adj* visible

vision ['vɪʒən] *n* (**a**) visión *f* (**b**) *(eyesight)* vista *f*

visit ['vɪzɪt] **1** *vt* (**a**) *(person)* visitar, hacer una visita a (**b**) *(place)* visitar, ir a

2 *n* visita *f*; **to pay sb a v.** hacerle una visita a algn

visiting ['vɪzɪtɪŋ] *adj* **v. card** tarjeta *f* de visita; *Med* **v. hours** horas *fpl* de visita; *Sport* **v. team** equipo *m* visitante

visitor ['vɪzɪtə(r)] *n* (**a**) *(guest)* invitado(a) *m,f*; **we've got visitors** tenemos visita (**b**) *(in hotel)* cliente(a) *m,f* (**c**) *(tourist)* turista *mf*

visor ['vaɪzə(r)] *n* visera *f*

> Note that the Spanish word **visor** is a false friend and is never a translation for the English word **visor**. In Spanish, **visor** means "viewfinder".

vista ['vɪstə] *n* vista *f*, panorama *m*

visual ['vɪʒʊəl] *adj* visual; **v. aids** medios *mpl* visuales

visualize ['vɪʒʊəlaɪz] *vt* (**a**) *(imagine)* imaginar(se) (**b**) *(foresee)* prever

vital ['vaɪtəl] *adj* (**a**) *(lively)* enérgico(a) (**b**) *(essential)* fundamental (**c**) *(decisive)* decisivo(a); *Fam* **v. statistics** medidas *fpl* del cuerpo de la mujer (**d**) *Med (function, sign)* vital

vitality [vaɪ'tælɪtɪ] *n* vitalidad *f*

vitally ['vaɪtəlɪ] *adv* **it's v. important** es de vital importancia

vitamin ['vɪtəmɪn, *US* 'vaɪtəmɪn] *n* vitamina *f*

viva ['vaɪvə] *n Br* examen *m* oral

vivacious [vɪ'veɪʃəs] *adj* vivaz

vivacity [vɪ'væsɪtɪ] *n* viveza *f*, vivacidad *f*

vivid ['vɪvɪd] adj (a) (bright, lively) vivo(a), intenso(a) (b) (graphic) gráfico(a)

vixen ['vɪksən] n zorra f

V-neck(ed) ['viːnek(t)] adj con el cuello en pico

vocabulary [və'kæbjʊlərɪ] n vocabulario m

vocal ['vəʊkəl] adj vocal; **v. cords** cuerdas fpl vocales

vocalist ['vəʊkəlɪst] n cantante mf

vocation [vəʊ'keɪʃən] n vocación f

vocational [vəʊ'keɪʃənəl] adj profesional; **v. training** formación f profesional

vociferous [vəʊ'sɪfərəs] adj (a) (protest) enérgico(a) (b) (noisy) clamoroso(a)

vodka ['vɒdkə] n vodka m

vogue [vəʊg] n boga f, moda f; **in v.** de moda

voice [vɔɪs] **1** n voz f; **to lose one's v.** quedarse afónico; Fig **at the top of one's v.** a voz en grito; Comput **v. mail** buzon m de voz
    2 vt (a) (express) manifestar (b) Ling sonorizar

void [vɔɪd] **1** adj (a) **v. of** sin (b) Jur nulo(a), inválido(a)
    2 n vacío m

volatile ['vɒlətaɪl] adj volátil

volcanic [vɒl'kænɪk] adj volcánico(a)

volcano [vɒl'keɪnəʊ] n (pl **volcanoes**) volcán m

volition [və'lɪʃən] n Fml **of one's own v.** por voluntad propia

volley ['vɒlɪ] **1** n (a) (of shots) descarga f (b) Fig (of stones, insults) lluvia f (c) (in tennis, football) volea f
    2 vt (in tennis, football) volear

volleyball ['vɒlɪbɔːl] n voleibol m

volt [vəʊlt] n voltio m.

voltage ['vəʊltɪdʒ] n voltaje m

voluble ['vɒljʊbəl] adj locuaz

> *ℓ* Note that the Spanish word **voluble** is a false friend and is never a translation for the English word **voluble**. In Spanish, **voluble** means "fickle, changeable".

volume ['vɒljuːm] n (a) volumen m (b) (book) volumen m, tomo m; Fig **to speak volumes** decirlo todo

voluntary ['vɒləntərɪ] adj voluntario(a); **v. organization** organización benéfica

volunteer [vɒlən'tɪə(r)] **1** n voluntario(a) m,f
    2 vt (help etc) ofrecer
    3 vi (a) ofrecerse (**for** para) (b) Mil alistarse como voluntario

voluptuous [və'lʌptjʊəs] adj voluptuoso(a)

vomit ['vɒmɪt] **1** vt & vi vomitar
    2 n vómito m

voracious [vɒ'reɪʃəs] adj voraz

vortex ['vɔːteks] n (pl **vortices** ['vɔːtɪsiːz]) vórtice m; Fig vorágine f

vote [vəʊt] **1** n voto m; (voting) votación f; **v. of confidence** voto de confianza; **to take a v. on sth** someter algo a votacíon; **to have the v.** tener derecho al voto
    2 vt (a) votar (b) (elect) elegir (c) Fam proponer
    3 vi votar; **to v. for sb** votar a algn

voter ['vəʊtə(r)] n votante mf

voting ['vəʊtɪŋ] n votación f

vouch [vaʊtʃ] vi **to v. for sth/sb** responder de algo/por algn

voucher ['vaʊtʃə(r)] n Br vale m

vow [vaʊ] **1** n voto m
    2 vt jurar

vowel ['vaʊəl] n vocal f

voyage ['vɔɪɪdʒ] n viaje m; (crossing) travesía f; **to go on a v.** hacer un viaje (en barco)

vulgar ['vʌlgə(r)] adj (coarse) vulgar, ordinario(a); (in poor taste) de mal gusto

vulgarity [vʌl'gærɪtɪ] n (coarseness) vulgaridad f, ordinariez f; (poor taste) mal gusto m

vulnerable ['vʌlnərəbəl] adj vulnerable

vulture ['vʌltʃə(r)] n buitre m

vulva ['vʌlvə] n vulva f

W, w [ˈdʌbəljuː] n (the letter) W, w f
W (**a**) (abbr **West**) O (**b**) (abbr **Watt(s)**) W
wad [wɒd] n (of paper) taco m; (of cotton wool) bolita f; (of banknotes) fajo m
waddle [ˈwɒdəl] vi andar como los patos
wade [weɪd] vi caminar por el agua; **to w. across a river** vadear un río
▸ **wade through** vt insep hacer con dificultad; **I'm wading through the book** me cuesta mucho terminar el libro
wading pool [ˈweɪdɪŋpuːl] n US piscina f para niños
wafer [ˈweɪfə(r)] n barquillo m; Rel hostia f
waffle¹ [ˈwɒfəl] n Culin = tipo de barquillo
waffle² [ˈwɒfəl] Br Fam **1** vi meter mucha paja; **to w. on** parlotear
2 n paja f
waft [wɑːft, wɒft] **1** vt llevar por el aire
2 vi flotar (por or en el aire)
wag [wæg] **1** vt menear
2 vi (tail) menearse
wage [weɪdʒ] **1** n (also **wages**) salario m, sueldo m; **w. earner** asalariado(a) m,f; **w. freeze** congelación f salarial
2 vt (campaign) realizar (**against** contra); **to w. war (on)** hacer la guerra (a)
wage-packet [ˈweɪdʒpækɪt] n sueldo m
wager [ˈweɪdʒə(r)] **1** n apuesta f
2 vt apostar
waggle [ˈwægəl] **1** vt menear
2 vi menearse
wa(g)gon [ˈwægən] n (horse-drawn) carro m; Br Rail vagón m
wail [weɪl] **1** n lamento m, gemido m
2 vi (person) lamentar, gemir
waist [weɪst] n Anat cintura f; Sewing talle m
waistcoat [ˈweɪstkəʊt] n Br chaleco m
waistline [ˈweɪstlaɪn] n Anat cintura f; Sewing talle m
wait [weɪt] **1** n espera f; (delay) demora f; **to lie in w.** estar al acecho
2 vi (**a**) esperar, aguardar; **I can't w. to see her** me muero de ganas de verla; **while you w.** en el acto; **to keep sb waiting** hacer esperar a algn (**b**) **to w. at table** servir la mesa

▸ **wait about, wait around** vi esperar
▸ **wait on** vt insep servir
waiter [ˈweɪtə(r)] n camarero m, CAm, Col, Méx mesero m, Chile, Ven mesonero m, Perú, RP mozo m
waiting [ˈweɪtɪŋ] n **no w.** (sign) prohibido aparcar; **w. list** lista f de espera; **w. room** sala f de espera
waitress [ˈweɪtrɪs] n camarera f, CAm, Col, Méx mesera f, Chile, Ven mesonera f, Perú, RP moza f
waive [weɪv] vt Fml (rule) no aplicar
wake¹ [weɪk] **1** vt (pt **woke**; pp **woken**) **to w. sb (up)** despertar a algn
2 vi **to w. (up)** despertar(se)
3 n (for dead) velatorio m
wake² [weɪk] n (in water) estela f; Fig **in the w. of** tras
waken [ˈweɪkən] vt Literary despertar
Wales [weɪlz] n (el país de) Gales
walk [wɔːk] **1** n (**a**) (long) caminata m; (short) paseo m; **it's an hour's w.** está a una hora de camino; **to go for a w.** dar un paseo; **to take the dog for a w.** sacar a pasear al perro (**b**) (gait) modo m de andar (**c**) **people from all walks of life** gente f de toda condición
2 vt (**a**) **we walked her home** la acompañamos a casa (**b**) (dog) pasear
3 vi (**a**) andar (**b**) (go on foot) ir andando
▸ **walk away** vi alejarse; Fig **to w. away with a prize** llevarse un premio
▸ **walk into** vt insep (**a**) (place) entrar en; Fig (trap) caer en (**b**) (bump into) chocarse contra
▸ **walk out** vi salir; Ind declararse en huelga; **to w. out on sb** abandonar a algn
▸ **walk up** vi **to w. up to sb** abordar a algn
walkabout [ˈwɔːkəbaʊt] n (by Queen etc) = paseo informal entre la gente
walker [ˈwɔːkə(r)] n paseante mf; Sport marchador(a) m,f
walkie-talkie [wɔːkɪˈtɔːkɪ] n walkie-talkie m
walking [ˈwɔːkɪŋ] **1** n andar m; (hiking) excursionismo m
2 adj **at w. pace** a paso de marcha; **w. shoes** zapatos mpl de andar; **w. stick** bastón m

Walkman® ['wɔːkmən] n (pl **Walkmans**) walkman® m

walkout ['wɔːkaʊt] n Ind huelga f

walkover ['wɔːkəʊvə(r)] n **it was a w.** fue pan comido

walkway ['wɔːkweɪ] n paso m de peatones

wall [wɔːl] n (a) (freestanding, exterior) muro m; Fig **to have one's back to the w.** estar entre la espada y la pared; **city w.** muralla f; **garden w.** tapia f (b) (interior) pared f; **w. map** mapa m mural (c) Ftb barrera f
▸ **wall up** vt sep (door, fireplace) tabicar

walled [wɔːld] adj (city) amurallado(a); (garden) cercado(a) con tapia

wallet ['wɒlɪt] n cartera f

wallflower ['wɔːlflaʊə(r)] n (a) Bot alhelí m (b) Fam **to be a w.** ser un convidado de piedra

wallop ['wɒləp] Fam **1** n golpazo m
2 vt (a) (hit) pegar fuerte (b) (defeat) dar una paliza a

wallow ['wɒləʊ] vi revolcarse (en in); Fig **to w. in self-pity** sumirse en la autocompasión

wallpaper ['wɔːlpeɪpə(r)] **1** n papel pintado
2 vt empapelar

wally ['wɒlɪ] n Fam idiota mf

walnut ['wɔːlnʌt] n nuez f; (tree, wood) nogal m

walrus ['wɔːlrəs] n morsa f

waltz [wɔːls] **1** n vals m
2 vi bailar un vals

wan [wɒn] adj (wanner, wannest) pálido(a); (look, smile) apagado(a)

wand [wɒnd] n (magic) **w.** varita f (mágica)

wander ['wɒndə(r)] **1** vt **to w. the streets** vagar por las calles
2 vi (a) (aimlessly) vagar, errar; **to w. about** deambular; **to w. in/out** entrar/salir sin prisas (b) (stray) desviarse; (mind) divagar; **his glance wandered round the room** recorrió el cuarto con la mirada

wandering ['wɒndərɪŋ] adj errante; (tribe) nómada; (speech) divagador(a)

wane [weɪn] vi menguar; (interest) decaer

wangle ['wæŋgəl] vt Fam agenciarse

wank [wæŋk] Br Vulg **1** n paja f
2 vi hacerse una paja

wanker ['wæŋkə(r)] n Br Vulg mamón(ona) m,f

want [wɒnt] **1** n (a) (lack) falta f; **for w. of** por falta de (b) (poverty) miseria f

2 vt (a) (desire) querer, desear; **to w. to do sth** querer hacer algo (b) Fam (need) necesitar; **the grass wants cutting** hace falta cortar el césped (c) (seek) buscar; **you're wanted on the phone** te llaman al teléfono
▸ **want for** vt insep carecer de; **to w. for nothing** tenerlo todo

wanting ['wɒntɪŋ] adj (a) **she is w. in tact** le falta tacto (b) **he was found w.** no daba la talla

wanton ['wɒntən] adj (a) (motiveless) sin motivo; **w. cruelty** crueldad gratuita (b) (unrestrained) desenfrenado(a); (licentious) lascivo(a)

war [wɔː(r)] n guerra f; **to be at w. (with)** estar en guerra (con); Fig **to declare/wage w. on** declarar/hacer la guerra a; **w. crime** crimen m de guerra

warble ['wɔːbəl] vi gorjear

ward [wɔːd] n (a) (of hospital) sala f (b) Jur pupilo(a) m,f, **w. of court** pupilo(a) bajo tutela judicial (c) Br Pol distrito m electoral
▸ **ward off** vt sep (blow) parar, desviar; (attack) rechazar; (danger) evitar; (illness) prevenir

warden ['wɔːdən] n (of residence) guardián(ana) m,f; **game w.** guardia m de coto

warder ['wɔːdə(r)] n Br carcelero(a) m,f

wardrobe ['wɔːdrəʊb] n (a) armario m, ropero m (b) (clothes) guardarropa m (c) Th vestuario m

warehouse ['weəhaʊs] n almacén m

wares [weəz] npl mercancías fpl

warfare ['wɔːfeə(r)] n guerra f

warhead ['wɔːhed] n (nuclear) **w.** ojiva f nuclear

warm [wɔːm] **1** adj (a) (water) tibio(a); (hands) caliente; (climate) cálido(a); **a w. day** un día de calor; **I am w.** tengo calor; **it is (very) w. today** hoy hace (mucho) calor; **w. clothing** ropa f de abrigo (b) (welcome, applause) cálido(a)
2 vt calentar; Fig alegrar
3 vi calentarse; **to w. to sb** cogerle simpatía a algn
▸ **warm up** **1** vt sep (a) calentar; (soup) (re)calentar (b) (audience) animar
2 vi (a) calentarse; (food) (re)calentarse; (person) entrar en calor (b) (athlete) hacer ejercicios de calentamiento (c) Fig (audience, party) animarse

warm-blooded [wɔːm'blʌdɪd] adj de sangre caliente

warm-hearted [wɔːm'hɑːtɪd] adj afectuoso(a)

warmly ['wɔːmlɪ] *adv Fig* calurosamente; *(thank)* con efusión

warmth [wɔːmθ] *n (heat)* calor *m*; *Fig* cordialidad *f*

warn [wɔːn] *vt* avisar (**of** de), advertir (**about/against** sobre/contra); **he warned me not to go** me advirtió que no fuera; **to w. sb that** advertir a algn que

warning ['wɔːnɪŋ] **1** *adj* **w. light** piloto *m*; **w. sign** señal *f* de aviso
 2 *n* (**a**) *(of danger)* advertencia *f*, aviso *m* (**b**) *(replacing punishment)* amonestación *f* (**c**) *(notice)* aviso *m*; **without w.** sin previo aviso

warp [wɔːp] **1** *vt* (**a**) *(wood)* alabear, combar (**b**) *Fig (mind)* pervertir
 2 *vi* alabearse, combarse

warrant ['wɒrənt] **1** *n* (**a**) *Jur* orden *f* judicial; **death w.** sentencia *f* de muerte (**b**) *(authorization note)* cédula *f*, *Com* bono *m*
 2 *vt* (**a**) *(justify)* justificar (**b**) *(guarantee)* garantizar

warranty ['wɒrəntɪ] *n Com* garantía *f*

warren ['wɒrən] *n* conejera *f*; *Fig* laberinto *m*

warrior ['wɒrɪə(r)] *n* guerrero(a) *m,f*

Warsaw ['wɔːsɔː] *n* Varsovia

warship ['wɔːʃɪp] *n* buque *m* or barco *m* de guerra

wart [wɔːt] *n* verruga *f*

wartime ['wɔːtaɪm] *n* tiempos *mpl* de guerra

wary ['weərɪ] *adj* (**warier, wariest**) cauteloso(a); **to be w. of doing sth** dudar en hacer algo; **to be w. of sb/sth** recelar de algn/algo

was [wɒz] *pt of* **be**

wash [wɒʃ] **1** *n* (**a**) lavado *m*; **to have a w.** lavarse (**b**) *(of ship)* estela *f*; *(sound)* chapoteo *m*
 2 *vt* (**a**) lavar; *(dishes)* fregar; **to w. one's hair** lavarse el pelo (**b**) *(of sea, river)* arrastrar
 3 *vi* (**a**) *(person)* lavarse; *(do the laundry)* hacer la colada (**b**) *(lap)* batir
 ▸ **wash away** *vt sep (of sea)* llevarse; *(traces)* borrar
 ▸ **wash off** *vi* quitarse lavando
 ▸ **wash out 1** *vt sep* (**a**) *(stain)* quitar lavando (**b**) *(bottle)* enjuagar
 2 *vi* quitarse lavando
 ▸ **wash up 1** *vt sep Br (dishes)* fregar
 2 *vi* (**a**) *Br* fregar los platos (**b**) *US* lavarse rápidamente

washable ['wɒʃəbəl] *adj* lavable

washbasin ['wɒʃbeɪsən], *US* **washbowl** ['wɒʃbəʊl] *n* palangana *f*

washcloth ['wɒʃklɒθ] *n US* manopla *f*

washer ['wɒʃə(r)] *n (on tap)* junta *f*

washing ['wɒʃɪŋ] *n (action)* lavado *m*; *(of clothes)* colada *f*; **(dirty) w.** ropa sucia; **to do the w.** hacer la colada; **w. line** tendero *m*; **w. machine** lavadora *f*; **w. powder** detergente *m*

washing-up [wɒʃɪŋˈʌp] *n Br* (**a**) *(action)* fregado *m*; **w. bowl** barreño *m*; **w. liquid** (detergente *m*) lavavajillas (**b**) *(dishes)* platos *mpl* (para fregar)

washout ['wɒʃaʊt] *n Fam* fracaso *m*

washroom ['wɒʃruːm] *n US* servicios *mpl*

wasp [wɒsp] *n* avispa *f*

wastage ['weɪstɪdʒ] *n* pérdidas *fpl*

waste [weɪst] **1** *adj* (**a**) *(unwanted)* desechado(a); **w. food** restos *mpl* de comida; **w. products** productos *mpl* de desecho (**b**) *(ground)* baldío(a)
 2 *n* (**a**) *(unnecessary use)* desperdicio *m*; *(of resources, effort, money)* derroche *m*; *(of time)* pérdida *f*; **to go to w.** echarse a perder (**b**) *(leftovers)* desperdicios *mpl*; *(rubbish)* basura *f*; **radioactive w.** desechos radioactivos; **w. disposal unit** trituradora *f* (de desperdicios); **w. pipe** tubo *m* de desagüe
 3 *vt (squander)* desperdiciar, malgastar; *(resources)* derrochar; *(money)* despilfarrar; *(time)* perder
 ▸ **waste away** *vi* consumirse

wasteful ['weɪstfʊl] *adj* derrochador(a)

wasteland ['weɪstlænd] *n* baldío *m*

wastepaper [weɪstˈpeɪpə(r)] *n* papeles usados; **w. basket** papelera *f*

watch [wɒtʃ] **1** *n* (**a**) *(look-out)* vigilancia *f*; **to keep a close w. on sth/sb** vigilar algo/a algn muy atentamente (**b**) *Mil (body)* guardia *f*; *(individual)* centinela *m*; **to be on w.** estar de guardia (**c**) *(timepiece)* reloj *m*
 2 *vt* (**a**) *(observe)* mirar, observar (**b**) *(keep an eye on)* vigilar; *(with suspicion)* acechar (**c**) *(be careful of)* tener cuidado con; *Fig* **to w. one's step** ir con pies de plomo
 3 *vi (look)* mirar, observar; **w. out!** ¡cuidado!
 ▸ **watch out for** *vt insep (be careful of)* tener cuidado con

watchband ['wɒtʃbænd] *n US* = **watch-strap**

watchdog ['wɒtʃdɒg] *n* perro *m* guardián; *Fig* guardián(ana) *m,f*

watchful ['wɒtʃfʊl] *adj* vigilante

watchmaker ['wɒtʃmeɪkə(r)] *n* relojero(a) *m,f*

watchman ['wɒtʃmən] n vigilante m;
night w. (of site) vigilante nocturno
watchstrap ['wɒtʃstræp] n correa f (de
reloj)
watchtower ['wɒtʃtaʊə(r)] n atalaya f
water ['wɔːtə(r)] 1 n (a) agua f; **w. bottle**
cantimplora f; **w. lily** nenúfar m; **w. main**
conducción f de aguas; **w. polo** water
polo m; **w. sports** deportes acuáticos;
w. tank depósito m de agua; **territorial
waters** aguas jurisdiccionales; Fig **it's all
w. under the bridge** ha llovido mucho
desde entonces (b) **to pass w.** orinar
   2 vt (plants) regar
   3 vi **my eyes are watering** me lloran los
ojos; **my mouth watered** se me hizo la
boca agua
▸ **water down** vt sep (drink) aguar
watercolour, US **watercolor** ['wɔːtə-
kʌlə(r)] n acuarela f
watercress ['wɔːtəkres] n berro m
waterfall ['wɔːtəfɔːl] n cascada f; (very
big) catarata f
waterfront ['wɔːtəfrʌnt] n (shore) orilla f
del agua; (harbour) puerto m
watering ['wɔːtərɪŋ] n (of plants) riego m;
w. can regadera f; **w. place** abrevadero m
waterline ['wɔːtəlaɪn] n línea f de flota-
ción
waterlogged ['wɔːtəlɒgd] adj anega-
do(a)
watermark ['wɔːtəmɑːk] n filigrana f
watermelon ['wɔːtəmelən] n sandía f
waterproof ['wɔːtəpruːf] 1 adj (material)
impermeable; (watch) sumergible
   2 n (coat) impermeable m
watershed ['wɔːtəʃed] n Geog línea divisoria de aguas; Fig punto decisivo
water-skiing ['wɔːtəskiːɪŋ] n esquí
acuático
watertight ['wɔːtətaɪt] adj hermético(a)
waterway ['wɔːtəweɪ] n vía f fluvial
waterworks ['wɔːtəwɜːks] npl central f
de abastecimiento de agua; Fig **to turn
on the w.** empezar a llorar
watery ['wɔːtərɪ] adj (a) (soup) agua-
do(a); (coffee) flojo(a) (b) (eyes) lacrimo-
so(a) (c) (pale) pálido(a)
watt [wɒt] n vatio m
wave [weɪv] 1 n (a) (at sea) ola f (b) (in
hair) & Rad onda f (c) Fig (of anger, strikes
etc) oleada f (d) (gesture) saludo m con la
mano
   2 vt (a) agitar; (brandish) blandir (b)
(hair) ondular
   3 vi (a) agitar el brazo; **she waved (to
me)** (greeting) me saludó con la mano;
(goodbye) se despidió (de mí) con la

mano; (signal) me hizo señas con la
mano (b) (flag) ondear; (corn) ondular
wavelength ['weɪvleŋθ] n longitud f de
onda
waver ['weɪvə(r)] vi (hesitate) vacilar
(**between** entre); (voice) temblar; (courage) flaquear
wavy ['weɪvɪ] adj (**wavier, waviest**) on-
dulado(a)
wax¹ [wæks] 1 n cera f
   2 vt encerar
wax² [wæks] vi (a) (moon) crecer (b) **to
w. lyrical** exaltarse
waxworks ['wæks:wɜːks] n sing museo m
de cera
way [weɪ] 1 n (a) (route) camino m; (road)
vía f, camino; **a letter is on the w.** una
carta está en camino; **on the w.** en el
camino; **on the w. here** de camino para
aquí; **out of the w.** apartado(a); **to ask
the w.** preguntar el camino; **to go the
wrong w.** ir por el camino equivocado; **to
lose one's w.** perderse; **to make one's w.
through the crowd** abrirse camino entre
la multitud; **which is the w. to the station?** ¿por dónde se va a la estación?; Fig
she went out of her w. to help se des-
vivió por ayudar; **w. in** entrada f; **w. out**
salida f; Fig **the easy w. out** la solución
fácil; **I can't find my w. out** no encuentro
la salida; **on the w. back** en el viaje de
regreso; **on the w. up/down** en la subida/
bajada; **there's no w. through** el paso
está cerrado; **you're in the w.** estás es-
torbando; (**get**) **out of the w.!** ¡quítate de
en medio!; Fig **to get sb out of the w.**
desembarazarse de algn/algo; **I kept out
of the w.** me mantuve a distancia; Aut
right of w. prioridad f; **there's a wall in
the w.** hay un muro en medio; **to give w.**
ceder; Aut ceder el paso
   (b) (direction) dirección f; **come this w.**
venga por aquí; **which w. did he go?** ¿por
dónde se fue?; **that w.** por allá; **the other
w. round** al revés
   (c) (distance) distancia f; **a long w. off**
lejos; Fig **he'll go a long w.** llegará lejos;
Fig **we've come a long w.** hemos hecho
grandes progresos
   (d) **to get under w.** (travellers, work)
ponerse en marcha; (meeting, match)
empezar
   (e) (means, method) método m, manera
f; **do it any w. you like** hazlo como
quieras; **I'll do it my w.** lo haré a mi
manera
   (f) (manner) modo m, manera f; **in a
friendly w.** de modo amistoso; **one w. or**

another de un modo o de otro; **the French w. of life** el estilo de vida francés; **the w. things are going** tal como van las cosas; **to my w. of thinking** a mi modo de ver; *Fam* **no w.!** ¡ni hablar!; **she has a w. with children** tiene un don para los niños; **by w. of** a modo de; **either w.** en cualquier caso; **in a w.** en cierto sentido; **in many ways** desde muchos puntos de vista; **in some ways** en algunos aspectos; **in no w.** de ninguna manera

(**g**) *(custom)* hábito *m*, costumbre *f*; **to be set in one's ways** tener costumbres arraigadas

(**h**) *(state)* estado *m*; **leave it the w. it is** déjalo tal como está; **he is in a bad w.** está bastante mal

(**i**) **by the w.** a propósito; **in the w. of business** en el curso de los negocios

2 *adv Fam* mucho, muy; **it was w. off target** cayó muy desviado del blanco; **w. back in 1940** allá en 1940

waylay [weɪ'leɪ] *vt* (*pt & pp* **waylaid** [weɪ'leɪd]) (**a**) *(attack)* atacar por sorpresa (**b**) *Fig (intercept)* abordar, detener

wayside ['weɪsaɪd] *n Fig* **to fall by the w.** quedarse en el camino

wayward ['weɪwəd] *adj* rebelde; *(capricious)* caprichoso(a)

WC [dʌblju:'si:] *n* (*abbr* **water closet**) wáter *m*, WC *m*

we [wi:] *pers pron* nosotros(as) *(usually omitted in Spanish, except for contrast)*

weak [wi:k] *adj* débil; *(argument, excuse)* pobre; *(team, piece of work, tea)* flojo(a)

weaken ['wi:kən] **1** *vt* debilitar; *(argument)* quitar fuerza a

2 *vi* (**a**) debilitarse (**b**) *(concede ground)* ceder

weakling ['wi:klɪŋ] *n* enclenque *mf*

weakness ['wi:knɪs] *n* debilidad *f*; *(character flaw)* punto flaco

wealth [welθ] *n* riqueza *f*; *Fig* abundancia *f*

wealthy ['welθɪ] *adj* (**wealthier, wealthiest**) rico(a)

wean [wi:n] *vt (child)* destetar; *Fig* **to w. sb from a habit** desacostumbrar (gradualmente) a algn de un hábito

weapon ['wepən] *n* arma *f*

wear [weə(r)] **1** *vt* (*pt* **wore**; *pp* **worn**) (**a**) *(clothes)* llevar puesto, vestir; *(shoes)* llevar puestos, calzar; **he wears glasses** lleva gafas; **to w. black** vestirse de negro (**b**) *(erode)* desgastar

2 *vi* **to w. (thin/smooth)** desgastarse (con el roce); *Fig* **my patience is wearing thin** se me está acabando la paciencia

3 *n* (**a**) ropa *f*; **leisure w.** ropa de sport (**b**) *(use) (clothes)* uso *m* (**c**) *(deterioration)* desgaste *m*; **normal w. and tear** desgaste natural

▸ **wear away 1** *vt sep* erosionar

2 *vi (stone etc)* erosionarse; *(inscription)* borrarse

▸ **wear down 1** *vt sep (heels)* desgastar; *Fig* **to w. sb down** vencer la resistencia de algn

2 *vi* desgastarse

▸ **wear off** *vi (effect, pain)* pasar, desaparecer

▸ **wear out 1** *vt sep* gastar; *Fig* agotar

2 *vi* gastarse

wearily ['wɪərɪlɪ] *adv* con cansancio

wearisome ['wɪərɪsəm] *adj* fatigoso(a)

weary ['wɪərɪ] **1** *adj* (**wearier, weariest**) (**a**) *(tired)* cansado(a) (**b**) *(fed up)* harto(a)

2 *vt* cansar

3 *vi* cansarse (**of** de)

weasel ['wi:zəl] *n* comadreja *f*

weather ['weðə(r)] **1** *n* tiempo *m*; **the w. is fine** hace buen tiempo; *Fig* **to feel under the w.** no encontrarse bien; **w. chart** mapa meteorológico; **w. forecast** parte meteorológico; **w. vane** veleta *f*

2 *vt Fig (crisis)* aguantar; *Fig* **to w. the storm** capear el temporal

weather-beaten ['weðəbi:tən] *adj* curtido(a)

weathercock ['weðəkɒk] *n* veleta *f*

weatherman ['weðəmæn] *n* hombre *m* del tiempo

weave [wi:v] **1** *n* tejido *m*

2 *vt* (*pt* **wove**; *pp* **woven**) (**a**) *Tex* tejer (**b**) *(intertwine)* entretejer (**c**) *(intrigues)* tramar

3 *vi (person, road)* zigzaguear

weaver ['wi:və(r)] *n* tejedor(a) *m,f*

web [web] *n* (**a**) *(of spider)* telaraña *f* (**b**) *(of lies)* sarta *f* (**c**) *Comput* **the W.** la Web; **w. page** página *f* web; **w. site** sitio *m* web

webbed [webd] *adj Orn* palmeado(a)

wed [wed] *vt Literary* (*pt & pp* **wed** *or* **wedded**) casarse con

wedding ['wedɪŋ] *n* boda *f*, casamiento *m*; **w. cake** tarta *f* nupcial; **w. day** día *m* de la boda; **w. dress** traje *m* de novia; **w. present** regalo *m* de boda; **w. ring** alianza *f*

wedge [wedʒ] **1** *n* (**a**) cuña *f*; *(for table leg)* calce *m* (**b**) *(of cake, cheese)* trozo *m* grande

2 *vt* calzar; **to be wedged tight** *(object)* estar completamente atrancado(a)

Wednesday ['wenzdɪ] *n* miércoles *m*

wee¹ [wiː] *adj esp Scot* pequeñito(a)

wee² [wiː] *Fam* **1** *n* pipí *m*

2 *vi* hacer pipí

weed [wiːd] **1** *n Bot* mala hierba

2 *vt* (**a**) *(garden)* escardar (**b**) *Fig* **to w. out** eliminar

3 *vi* escardar

weedkiller ['wiːdkɪlə(r)] *n* herbicida *m*

weedy ['wiːdɪ] *adj* (**weedier, weediest**) *Pej* debilucho(a)

week [wiːk] *n* semana *f*; **a w. (ago) to-day/yesterday** hoy hace/ayer hizo una semana; **a w. today** justo dentro de una semana; **last/next w.** la semana pasada/que viene; **once a w.** una vez por semana; **w. in, w. out** semana tras semana

weekday ['wiːkdeɪ] *n* día *m* laborable

weekend [wiːk'end] *n* fin *m* de semana

weekly ['wiːklɪ] **1** *adj* semanal

2 *adv* semanalmente; **twice w.** dos veces por semana

3 *n Press* semanario *m*

weep [wiːp] *vi* (*pt & pp* **wept**) llorar; **to w. for sb** llorar la muerte de algn

2 *vt (tears)* derramar

weeping ['wiːpɪŋ] *adj* **w. willow** sauce *m* llorón

weigh [weɪ] **1** *vt* (**a**) pesar (**b**) *Fig (consider)* ponderar (**c**) **to w. anchor** levar anclas

2 *vi* (**a**) pesar (**b**) *Fig (influence)* influir

▸ weigh down *vt sep* sobrecargar

▸ weigh in *vi* (**a**) *Sport* pesarse (**b**) *Fam (join in)* intervenir

▸ weigh up *vt sep (matter)* evaluar; *(person)* formar una opinión sobre; **to w. up the pros and cons** sopesar los pros y los contras

weight [weɪt] *n* (**a**) peso *m*; **to lose w.** adelgazar; **to put on w.** subir de peso; *Fam Fig* **to pull one's w.** poner de su parte (**b**) *(of clock, scales)* pesa *f* (**c**) *Fig* **that's a w. off my mind** eso me quita un peso de encima

weighting ['weɪtɪŋ] *n Br (on salary)* suplemento *m* de salario

weightlifter ['weɪtlɪftə(r)] *n* halterófilo(a) *m,f*

weighty ['weɪtɪ] *adj* (**weightier, weightiest**) pesado(a); *Fig (problem, matter)* importante, grave; *(argument)* de peso

weir [wɪə(r)] *n* presa *f*

weird [wɪəd] *adj* raro(a), extraño(a)

welcome ['welkəm] **1** *adj (person)* bienvenido(a); *(news)* grato(a); *(change)* oportuno(a); **to make sb w.** acoger a algn calurosamente; **you're w.!** ¡no hay de qué!

2 *n (greeting)* bienvenida *f*

3 *vt* acoger; *(more formally)* darle la bienvenida a; *(news)* acoger con agrado; *(decision)* aplaudir

welcoming ['welkəmɪŋ] *adj (person)* acogedor(a); *(smile)* de bienvenida

weld [weld] *vt* soldar

welfare ['welfeə(r)] *n* (**a**) *(well-being)* bienestar *m*; **animal/child w.** protección *f* de animales/de menores; **w. work** asistencia *f* social; **w. worker** asistente *mf* social (**b**) *US (social security)* seguridad *f* social

well¹ [wel] *n* (**a**) pozo *m* (**b**) *(of staircase, lift)* hueco *m* (**c**) *(of court, hall)* hemiciclo *m*

▸ well up *vi* brotar

well² [wel] **1** *adj* (**a**) *(healthy)* bien; **are you keeping w.?** ¿estás bien de salud?; **to get w.** reponerse (**b**) *(satisfactory)* **to get w.** reponerse (**b**) *(satisfactory)* **all is w.** todo va bien; **it's just as w.** menos mal (**c**) **it is as w. to remember that** conviene recordar que

2 *adv* (**better, best**) (**a**) *(properly)* bien; **he has done w. (for himself)** ha prosperado; **the business is doing w.** el negocio marcha bien; **she did w. in the exam** el examen le fue bien; **w. done!** ¡muy bien!; **he took it w.** lo tomó a bien (**b**) *(thoroughly)* bien; **I know it only too w.** lo sé de sobra; *Culin* **w. done** muy hecho(a) (**c**) **he's w. over thirty** tiene treinta años bien cumplidos; **w. after six o'clock** mucho después de las seis (**d**) *(easily, with good reason)* **he couldn't very w. say no** difícilmente podía decir que no; **I may w. do that** puede que haga eso (**e**) **as w.** también; **as w. as** así como; **children as w. as adults** tanto niños como adultos

3 *interj* (**a**) *(surprise)* ¡bueno!, ¡vaya!; **w. I never!** ¡no me digas! (**b**) *(agreement, interrogation, resignation)* bueno; **very w.** bueno; **w.?** ¿y bien? (**c**) *(doubt)* pues; **w., I don't know** pues no sé (**d**) *(resumption)* **w., as I was saying** pues (bien), como iba diciendo

well-behaved ['welbɪheɪvd] *adj (child)* formal, educado(a)

well-being ['welbiːɪŋ] *n* bienestar *m*

well-built ['welbɪlt] *adj (building etc)* de construcción sólida; *(person)* fornido(a)

well-earned ['welɜːnd] *adj* merecido(a)

well-educated [wel'edʊkeɪtd] *adj* culto(a)

well-heeled ['welhiːld] *adj Fam* adinerado(a)

well-informed ['welɪnfɔːmd] *adj* bien informado(a)

wellingtons ['welɪŋtənz] *npl* botas *fpl* de goma

well-known ['welnəʊn] *adj* (bien) conocido(a)

well-mannered ['welmænəd] *adj* educado(a)

well-meaning [wel'miːnɪŋ] *adj* bien intencionado(a)

well-off [wel'ɒf] *adj (rich)* acomodado(a)

well-read [wel'red] *adj* culto(a)

well-spoken [wel'spəʊkən] *adj* con acento culto

well-to-do [weltə'duː] *adj* acomodado(a)

well-wisher ['welwɪʃə(r)] *n* admirador(a) *m,f*

Welsh [welʃ] **1** *adj* galés(esa); **W. rarebit** = tostada con queso fundido
2 *n* (**a**) *(language)* galés *m* (**b**) **the W.** los galeses

Welshman ['welʃmən] *n* galés *m*

Welshwoman ['welʃwʊmən] *n* galesa *f*

welterweight ['welterweɪt] *n* (peso *m*) wélter *m*

wench [wentʃ] *n Old-fashioned* moza *f*

went [went] *pt of* **go**

wept [wept] *pt & pp of* **weep**

were [wɜː(r), *unstressed* wə(r)] *pt of* **be**

west [west] **1** *n* oeste *m*, occidente *m*; **in/to the w.** al oeste; *Pol* **the W.** los países occidentales
2 *adj* del oeste, occidental; **the W. Indies** las Antillas; **W. Indian** antillano(a)
3 *adv* al oeste, hacia el oeste

westerly ['westəlɪ] *adj (wind)* del oeste

western ['westən] **1** *adj* del oeste, occidental; **W. Europe** Europa Occidental
2 *n Cin* western *m*, película *f* del oeste

westward ['westwəd] *adj* **in a w. direction** hacia el oeste

westwards ['westwədz] *adv* hacia el oeste

wet [wet] **1** *adj* (**wetter, wettest**) (**a**) mojado(a); *(slightly)* húmedo(a); **w. paint** *(sign)* recién pintado; **w. through** *(person)* calado(a) hasta los huesos; *(thing)* empapado(a); **w. suit** traje isotérmico (**b**) *(rainy)* lluvioso(a) (**c**) *Fam (person)* soso(a); **w. blanket** aguafiestas *mf inv*
2 *n Fam* apocado(a) *m,f*
3 *vt (pt & pp* **wet**) mojar; **to w. oneself** orinarse

whack [wæk] **1** *vt (hit hard)* golpear fuertemente
2 *n* (**a**) *(blow)* porrazo *m* (**b**) *Fam (share)* parte *f*, porción *f*

whale [weɪl] *n* ballena *f*

wharf [wɔːf] *n* (*pl* **wharves** [wɔːvz]) muelle *m*

what [wɒt, *unstressed* wət] **1** *adj* (**a**) *(direct question)* qué; **w. (sort of) bird is that?** ¿qué tipo de ave es ésa?; **w. good is that?** ¿para qué sirve eso?
(**b**) *(indirect question)* qué; **ask her w. colour she likes** pregúntale qué color le gusta
2 *pron* (**a**) *(direct question)* qué; **w. are you talking about?** ¿de qué estás hablando?; **w. about your father?** ¿y tu padre (qué)?; **w. about going tomorrow?** ¿qué te parece si vamos mañana?; **w. can I do for you?** ¿en qué puedo servirle?; **w. did it cost?** ¿cuánto costó?; **w. did you do that for?** ¿por qué hiciste eso?; **w. (did you say)?** ¿cómo?; **w. does it sound like?** ¿cómo suena?; **w. is happening?** ¿qué pasa?; **w. is it?** *(definition)* ¿qué es?; *(what's the matter)* ¿qué pasa?; **w.'s it called?** ¿cómo se llama?; **w.'s this for?** ¿para qué sirve esto?
(**b**) *(indirect question)* qué, lo que; **he asked me w. I thought** me preguntó lo que pensaba; **I didn't know w. to say** no sabía qué decir
(**c**) *(and)* **w.'s more** y además; **come w. may** pase lo que pase; **guess w.!** ¿sabes qué?; **it's just w. I need** es exactamente lo que necesito
(**d**) *(in exclamations)* **w. a goal!** ¡qué *or* vaya golazo!; **w. a lovely picture!** ¡qué cuadro más bonito!
3 *interj (surprise, indignation)* ¡cómo!; **w., no dessert?** ¿cómo, no hay postre?

whatever [wɒt'evə(r), *unstressed* wət-'evə(r)] **1** *adj* (**a**) *(any)* cualquiera que; **at w. time you like** a la hora que quieras; **of w. colour** no importa de qué color (**b**) *(with negative)* **nothing w.** nada en absoluto; **with no interest w.** sin interés alguno
2 *pron* (**a**) *(what)* **w. happened?** ¿qué pasó? (**b**) *(anything, all that)* (todo) lo que; **do w. you like** haz lo que quieras (**c**) *(no matter what)* **don't tell him, w. you do** no se lo ocurra decírselo; **w. (else) you find** cualquier (otra) cosa que encuentres; **he goes out w. the weather** sale haga el tiempo que haga

whatsoever [wɒtsəʊ'evə(r)] *adj* **anything w.** cualquier cosa; **nothing w.** nada en absoluto

wheat [wiːt] *n* trigo *m*; **w. germ** germen *m* de trigo

wheedle ['wiːdəl] *vt* **to w. sb into doing sth** engatusar a algn para que haga algo;

to w. sth out of sb sonsacar algo a algn halagándole

wheel [wiːl] **1** *n* rueda *f*

2 *vt (bicycle)* empujar

3 *vi* (a) *(bird)* revolotear (b) **to w. round** girar sobre los talones

wheelbarrow ['wiːlbærəʊ] *n* carretilla *f*

wheelchair ['wiːltʃeə(r)] *n* silla *f* de ruedas

wheeze [wiːz] *vi* respirar con dificultad, resollar

when [wen] **1** *adv* (a) *(direct question)* cuándo; **since w.?** ¿desde cuándo?; **w. did he arrive?** ¿cuándo llegó? (b) *(indirect question)* cuándo; **tell me w. to go** dime cuándo debo irme (c) *(on which)* cuando, en que; **the days w. I work** los días en que trabajo

2 *conj* (a) cuando; **I'll tell you w. she comes** se lo diré cuando llegue; **w. he was a boy ...** de niño ... (b) *(whenever)* cuando (c) *(given that, if)* si (d) *(although)* aunque

whence [wens] *adv Fml Literary (from where)* de dónde

whenever [wen'evə(r)] **1** *conj (when)* cuando; *(every time)* siempre que

2 *adv* **w. that might be** sea cuando sea

where [weə(r)] *adv* (a) *(direct question)* dónde; *(direction)* adónde; **w. are you going?** ¿adónde vas?; **w. did we go wrong?** ¿en qué nos equivocamos?; **w. do you come from?** ¿de dónde es usted? (b) *(indirect question)* dónde; *(direction)* adónde; **tell me w. you went** dime adónde fuiste (c) *(at, in which)* donde; *(direction)* adonde, a donde (d) *(when)* cuando

whereabouts 1 *adv* [weərə'baʊts] **w. do you live?** ¿por dónde vives?

2 *n* ['weərəbaʊts] paradero *m*

whereas [weər'æz] *conj* (a) *(but, while)* mientras que (b) *Jur* considerando que

whereby [weə'baɪ] *adv* por el/la/lo cual

whereupon [weərə'pɒn] *conj Fml* después de lo cual

wherever [weər'evə(r)] **1** *conj* dondequiera que; **I'll find him w. he is** le encontraré dondequiera que esté; **sit w. you like** siéntate donde quieras

2 *adv (direct question)* adónde

wherewithal ['weəwɪðɔːl] *n Fam* pelas *fpl*

whet [wet] *vt* **to w. sb's appetite** abrir el apetito a algn

whether ['weðə(r)] *conj* (a) *(if)* si; **I don't know w. it is true** no sé si es verdad; **I doubt w. he'll win** dudo que gane (b) **w.**

he comes or not venga o no

which [wɪtʃ] **1** *adj* (a) *(direct question)* qué; **w. colour do you prefer?** ¿qué color prefieres?; **w. one?** ¿cuál?; **w. way?** ¿por dónde?

(b) *(indirect question)* qué; **tell me w. dress you like** dime qué vestido te gusta

(c) **by w. time** y para entonces; **in w. case** en cuyo caso

2 *pron* (a) *(direct question)* cuál/cuáles; **w. of you did it?** ¿quién de vosotros lo hizo?

(b) *(indirect question)* cuál/cuáles; **I don't know w. I'd rather have** no sé cuál prefiero

(c) *(defining relative)* que; *(after preposition)* que, el/la cual, los/las cuales, el/la que, los/las que; **here are the books (w.) I have read** aquí están los libros que he leído; **the accident (w.) I told you about** el accidente del que te hablé; **the car in w. he was travelling** el coche en (el) que viajaba; **this is the one (w.) I like** éste es el que me gusta

(d) *(non-defining relative)* el/la cual, los/las cuales; **I played three sets, all of w. I lost** jugué tres sets, todos los cuales perdí

(e) *(referring to a clause)* lo cual, lo que; **he won, w. made me very happy** ganó, lo cual *or* lo que me alegró mucho

whichever [wɪtʃ'evə(r)] **1** *adj* el/la que, cualquiera que; **I'll take w. books you don't want** tomaré los libros que no quieras; **w. system you choose** cualquiera que sea el sistema que elijas

2 *pron* el/la que

whiff [wɪf] *n* (a) *(quick smell)* ráfaga *f*; *(of air, smoke)* bocanada *f* (b) *Fam (bad smell)* tufo *m*

while [waɪl] **1** *n* (a) *(length of time)* rato *m*, tiempo *m*; **in a little w.** dentro de poco; **once in a w.** de vez en cuando (b) **it's not worth your w. staying** no merece la pena que te quedes

2 *conj* (a) *(time)* mientras; **he fell asleep w. driving** se durmió mientras conducía (b) *(although)* aunque (c) *(whereas)* mientras que

▸ **while away** *vt sep* **to w. away the time** pasar el rato

whilst [waɪlst] *conj* = **while**

whim [wɪm] *n* capricho *m*, antojo *m*

whimper ['wɪmpə(r)] **1** *n* quejido *m*

2 *vi* lloriquear

whine [waɪn] *vi* (a) *(child)* lloriquear; *(with pain)* dar quejidos (b) *(complain)* quejarse (c) *(engine)* chirriar

whip [wɪp] **1** *n* (**a**) *(for punishment)* látigo *m*; *(for riding)* fusta *f* (**b**) *Br Pol* = oficial encargado(a) de la disciplina de un partido

2 *vt* (**a**) *(as punishment)* azotar; *(horse)* fustigar (**b**) *Culin* batir; **whipped cream** nata montada (**c**) *Fam (steal)* mangar

▸ **whip away** *vi sep* arrebatar

▸ **whip up** *vt sep (passions, enthusiasm)* avivar; *(support)* incrementar

whipping ['wɪpɪŋ] *n Fig* **w. boy** cabeza *f* de turco

whip-round ['wɪpraʊnd] *n Fam* colecta *f*

whir [wɜː(r)] *vi* = **whirr**

whirl [wɜːl] **1** *n* giro *m*; *Fig* torbellino *m*

2 *vt* **to w. sth round** dar vueltas a o hacer girar algo

3 *vi* **to w. round** girar con rapidez; *(leaves etc)* arremolinarse; **my head's whirling** me está dando vueltas la cabeza

whirlpool ['wɜːlpuːl] *n* remolino *m*

whirlwind ['wɜːlwɪnd] *n* torbellino *m*

whirr [wɜː(r)] *vi* zumbar, runrunear

whisk [wɪsk] **1** *n Culin* batidor *m*; *(electric)* batidora *f*

2 *vt Culin* batir

▸ **whisk away, whisk off** *vt sep* quitar bruscamente, llevarse de repente

whisker ['wɪskə(r)] *n* **whiskers** *(of person)* patillas *fpl*; *(of cat)* bigotes *mpl*

whisky, *US* **whiskey** ['wɪskɪ] *n* whisky *m*

whisper ['wɪspə(r)] **1** *n* (**a**) *(sound)* susurro *m* (**b**) *(rumour)* rumor *m*

2 *vt* decir en voz baja

3 *vi* susurrar

whistle ['wɪsəl] **1** *n* (**a**) *(instrument)* pito *m* (**b**) *(sound)* silbido *m*, pitido *m*

2 *vt (tune)* silbar

3 *vi (person, kettle, wind)* silbar; *(train)* pitar

white [waɪt] **1** *adj* blanco(a); **to go w.** *(face)* palidecer; *(hair)* encanecer; **w. coffee** café *m* con leche; **w. hair** pelo cano; **a w. Christmas** una Navidad con nieve; *Fig* **a w. lie** una mentira piadosa; *US* **the W. House** la Casa Blanca; *Pol* **w. paper** libro blanco; **w. sauce** bechamel *f*

2 *n* (**a**) *(colour, person, of eye)* blanco *m* (**b**) *(of egg)* clara *f* (**c**) **whites** ropa *f* blanca

white-collar ['waɪtkɒlə(r)] *adj* **w. worker** empleado *m* de oficina

whiteness ['waɪtnɪs] *n* blancura *f*

whitewash ['waɪtwɒʃ] **1** *n* (**a**) *(wall)* cal *f* (**b**) *Fig (cover-up)* encubrimiento *m* (**c**) *Fig (defeat)* paliza *f*

2 *vt* (**a**) *(wall)* enjalbegar, blanquear (**b**) *Fig* encubrir

whiting ['waɪtɪŋ] *n* (*pl* **whiting**) *(fish)* pescadilla *f*

Whitsun(tide) ['wɪtsən(taɪd)] *n* pentecostés *m*

whittle ['wɪtəl] *vt* cortar en pedazos; **to w. away at** roer; *Fig* **to w. down** reducir poco a poco

whiz(z) [wɪz] *vi* (**a**) *(sound)* silbar (**b**) **to w. past** pasar volando; *Fam* **w. kid** joven *mf* dinámico(a) y emprendedor(a)

who [huː] *pron* (**a**) *(direct question)* quién/quiénes; **w. are they?** ¿quiénes son?; **w. is it?** ¿quién es? (**b**) *(indirect question)* quién; **I don't know w. did it** no sé quién lo hizo (**c**) *rel (defining)* que; **those w. don't know** los que no saben (**d**) *rel (nondefining)* quien/quienes, el/la cual, los/las cuales; **Elena's mother, w. is very rich ...** la madre de Elena, la cual es muy rica ...

whodun(n)it [huːˈdʌnɪt] *n Fam* novela *f*/ obra *f* de teatro/película *f* de suspense

whoever [huːˈevə(r)] *pron* (**a**) quienquiera que; **give it to w. you like** dáselo a quien quieras; **w. said that is a fool** el que dijo eso es un tonto; **w. you are** quienquiera que seas (**b**) *(direct question)* **w. told you that?** ¿quién te dijo eso?

whole [həʊl] **1** *adj* (**a**) *(entire)* entero(a), íntegro(a); **a w. week** una semana entera; **he took the w. lot** se los llevó todos (**b**) *(in one piece)* intacto(a)

2 *n* (**a**) *(single unit)* todo *m*, conjunto *m*; **as a w.** en su totalidad (**b**) *(all)* totalidad *f*; **the w. of London** todo Londres (**c**) **on the w.** en general

wholefood ['həʊlfuːd] *n* alimentos *mpl* integrales

wholehearted [həʊlˈhɑːtɪd] *adj (enthusiastic)* entusiasta; *(sincere)* sincero(a); *(unreserved)* incondicional

wholemeal ['həʊlmiːl] *adj Br* integral

wholesale ['həʊlseɪl] *Com* **1** *n* venta *f* al por mayor

2 *adj* al por mayor; *Fig* total

3 *adv* al por mayor; *Fig* en su totalidad

wholesaler ['həʊlseɪlə(r)] *n* mayorista *mf*

wholesome ['həʊlsəm] *adj* sano(a)

wholly ['həʊllɪ] *adv* enteramente, completamente

whom [huːm] *pron Fml* (**a**) *(direct question) (accusative)* a quién; **w. did you talk to?** ¿con quién hablaste?; *(after preposition) (accusative)* **who are you referring to w.?** ¿de quién?; **to w. are you referring?** ¿a quién te refieres? (**b**) *rel (accusative)* que, a quien/a quienes; **those w. I have seen** aquéllos a quien he

visto (**c**) *rel (after preposition)* quien/
quienes, el/la cual, los/las cuales; **my
brothers, both of w. are miners** mis hermanos, que son mineros los dos

> En la actualidad, sólo aparece en contextos
> formales. **Whom** se puede sustituir por
> **who** en todos los casos salvo cuando va
> después de preposición.

whooping cough ['hu:pɪŋkɒf] *n* tos ferina

whopping ['wɒpɪŋ] *adj Fam* enorme

whore [hɔː(r)] *n very Fam Pej* puta *f*

whose [hu:z] **1** *pron* (**a**) *(direct question)*
de quién/de quiénes; **w. are these gloves?**
¿de quién son estos guantes?; **w. is this?**
¿de quién es esto? (**b**) *(indirect question)*
de quién/de quiénes; **I don't know w.
these coats are** no sé de quién son estos
abrigos (**c**) *rel* cuyo(s)/cuya(s); **the man
w. children we saw** el hombre a cuyos
hijos vimos
2 *adj* **w. car/house is this?** ¿de quién es
este coche/esta casa?

why [waɪ] **1** *adv* por qué; *(for what purpose)* para qué; **w. did you do that?** ¿por
qué hiciste eso?; **w. not go to bed?** ¿por
qué no te acuestas?; **I don't know w. he
did it** no sé por qué lo hizo; **that is w. I
didn't come** por eso no vine; **there's no
reason w. you shouldn't go** no hay motivo para que no vayas
2 *interj* (**a**) *(fancy that!)* ¡toma!, ¡vaya!;
w., it's David! ¡sí es David! (**b**) *(protest,
assertion)* sí, vamos

wick [wɪk] *n* mecha *f*

wicked ['wɪkɪd] *adj* (**a**) malvado(a) (**b**)
Fam malísimo(a); *(temper)* de perros

wicker ['wɪkə(r)] **1** *n* mimbre *m*
2 *adj* de mimbre

wickerwork ['wɪkəwɜːk] *n* *(material)*
mimbre *m*; *(articles)* artículos *mpl* de
mimbre

wicket ['wɪkɪt] *n* *(in cricket) (stumps)*
palos *mpl*

wide [waɪd] **1** *adj* (**a**) *(road, trousers)*
ancho(a); *(gap, interval)* grande; **it is 10
m w.** tiene 10 m de ancho (**b**) *(area,
knowledge, support, range)* amplio(a); **w.
interests** intereses muy diversos (**c**) *(off
target)* desviado(a)
2 *adv* **from far and w.** de todas partes; **to
open one's eyes w.** abrir los ojos de par en
par; **w. apart** muy separados(as); **w.
awake** completamente despierto(a); **w.
open** abierto(a) de par en par; **with
mouth w. open** boquiabierto(a)

wide-angle ['waɪdæŋgəl] *adj Phot* **w.**

lens objetivo *m* gran angular

widely ['waɪdlɪ] *adv (travel etc)* extensamente; *(believed)* generalmente; **he is w.
known** es muy conocido

widen ['waɪdən] **1** *vt* ensanchar; *(interests)* ampliar
2 *vi* ensanchar

wide-ranging ['waɪd'reɪndʒɪŋ] *adj (interests)* muy diversos(as); *(discussion)*
amplio(a); *(study)* de gran alcance

widespread ['waɪdspred] *adj (unrest, belief)* general; *(damage)* extenso(a); **to
become w.** generalizarse

widow ['wɪdəʊ] *n* viuda *f*

widowed ['wɪdəʊd] *adj* enviudado(a)

widower ['wɪdəʊə(r)] *n* viudo *m*

width [wɪdθ] *n* (**a**) anchura *f* (**b**) *(of
material, swimming pool)* ancho *m*

wield [wiːld] *vt (weapon)* blandir; *Fig
(power)* ejercer

wife [waɪf] *n (pl* **wives**) mujer *f*, esposa *f*

wig [wɪg] *n* peluca *f*

wiggle ['wɪgəl] **1** *vt (finger etc)* menear;
to w. one's hips contonearse
2 *vi* menearse

Wight [waɪt] *n* Isle of W. Isla *f* de Wight

wild [waɪld] **1** *adj* (**a**) *(animal, tribe)* salvaje; **w. beast** fiera *f*; *Fig* **w. goose chase**
búsqueda *f* inútil
(**b**) *(plant)* silvestre
(**c**) *(landscape)* agreste; **the W. West** el
Salvaje Oeste
(**d**) *(temperament, behaviour)* aloca-
do(a); *(appearance)* desordenado(a);
(passions etc) desenfrenado(a); *(laughter, thoughts)* loco(a); *(applause)* fervoro-
so(a); **to make a w. guess** adivinar al
azar; *Fam Fig* **she is w. about him/about
tennis** está loca por él/por el tenis
(**e**) *Br Fam Fig (angry)* furioso(a)
2 *adv Fig* **to run w.** *(children)* desmandarse
3 *n* **in the w.** en el estado salvaje; *Fig* **to
live out in the wilds** vivir en el quinto pino

wildcat ['waɪldkæt] *n* **w. strike** huelga *f*
salvaje

wilderness ['wɪldənɪs] *n* desierto *m*

wildfire ['waɪldfaɪə(r)] *n* **to spread like
w.** correr como la pólvora

wildlife ['waɪldlaɪf] *n* fauna *f*; **w. park**
parque *m* natural

wildly ['waɪldlɪ] *adv* (**a**) *(rush round etc)*
como un(a) loco(a); *(shoot)* sin apuntar;
(hit out) a tontas y a locas (**b**) **w. enthusiastic** loco(a) de entusiasmo; **w. inaccurate** totalmente erróneo(a)

wilful, *US* **wilfull** ['wɪlfʊl] *adj* (**a**) *(stubborn)* terco(a) (**b**) *Jur* premeditado(a)

will¹ [wɪl] **1** n (a) voluntad f; **good/ill w.** buena/mala voluntad; **of my own free w.** por mi propia voluntad (b) Jur (testament) testamento m; **to make one's w.** hacer testamento

2 vt **fate willed that ...** el destino quiso que ...

will² [wɪl] v aux (pt **would**)

> En el inglés hablado, y en el escrito en estilo coloquial, el verbo **will** se contrae de manera que **I/you/he** etc **will** se transforman en **I'll, you'll, he'll** etc y el verbo **would** se contrae de manera que **I/you/he** etc **would** se transforman en **I'd, you'd, he'd** etc. Las formas negativas **will not** y **would not** se transforman en **won't** y **wouldn't**.

(a) (future) (esp 2nd & 3rd person) **they'll come** vendrán; **w. he be there? – yes, he w.** ¿estará allí? – sí(, estará); **you'll tell him, won't you?** se lo dirás, ¿verdad?; **don't forget, w. you!** ¡que no se te olvide, vale!; **she won't do it** no lo hará

(b) (command) **you w. be here at eleven!** ¡debes estar aquí a las once!

(c) (future perfect) **they'll have finished by tomorrow** habrán terminado para mañana

(d) (willingness) **be quiet, w. you! – no, I won't!** ¿quiere callarse? – no quiero; **I won't have it!** ¡no lo permito!; **w. you have a drink? – yes, I w.** ¿quiere tomar algo? – sí, por favor; **won't you sit down?** ¿quiere sentarse?

(e) (custom) **accidents w. happen** siempre habrá accidentes

(f) (persistence) **if you w. go out without a coat ...** si te empeñas en salir sin abrigo ...

(g) (probability) **he'll be on holiday now** ahora estará de vacaciones

(h) (ability) **the lift w. hold ten people** en el ascensor caben diez personas

willing ['wɪlɪŋ] adj (obliging) complaciente; **I'm quite w. to do it** lo haré con mucho gusto; **to be w. to do sth** estar dispuesto(a) a hacer algo

willingly ['wɪlɪŋlɪ] adv de buena gana

willingness ['wɪlɪŋnɪs] n buena voluntad

willow ['wɪləʊ] n **w. (tree)** sauce m

willpower ['wɪlpaʊə(r)] n (fuerza f de) voluntad f

willy-nilly ['wɪlɪ'nɪlɪ] adv por gusto o por fuerza

wilt [wɪlt] vi marchitarse

wily ['waɪlɪ] adj (**wilier, wiliest**) astuto(a)

wimp [wɪmp] n Fam (physically) debilucho(a) m,f; (lacking character) blandengue mf

win [wɪn] **1** n victoria f

2 vt (pt & pp **won**) (a) ganar; (prize) llevarse; (victory) conseguir (b) Fig (sympathy, friendship) ganarse; (praise) cosechar; **to w. sb's love** conquistar a algn

3 vi ganar

▸ **win back** vt sep recuperar

▸ **win over** vt sep (to cause, idea) atraer (**to** a); (voters, support) ganarse

▸ **win through** vi conseguir triunfar

wince [wɪns] vi tener un rictus de dolor

winch [wɪntʃ] n cigüeña f, torno m

wind¹ [wɪnd] **1** n (a) viento m; Fig **to get w. of sth** olerse algo; **w. farm** parque eólico; **w. tunnel** túnel aerodinámico (b) (breath) aliento m; **to get one's second w.** recobrar el aliento (c) Med flato m, gases mpl (d) **w. instrument** instrumento m de viento

2 vt **to be winded** quedarse sin aliento

wind² [waɪnd] **1** vt (pt & pp **wound**) (a) (on to a reel) enrollar; **to w. a bandage round one's finger** vendarse el dedo (b) **to w. on/back** (film, tape) avanzar/rebobinar (c) (clock) dar cuerda a

2 vi (road, river) serpentear

▸ **wind down 1** vt sep (window) bajar

2 vi Fam (person) relajarse

▸ **wind up 1** vt sep (a) (roll up) enrollar (b) (business etc) cerrar; (debate) clausurar (c) (clock) dar cuerda a

2 vi (meeting) terminar

windfall ['wɪndfɔːl] n Fig ganancia inesperada

winding ['waɪndɪŋ] adj (road, river) sinuoso(a); (staircase) de caracol

windmill ['wɪndmɪl] n molino m (de viento)

window ['wɪndəʊ] n ventana f; (of vehicle, ticket office etc) ventanilla f; (shop) **w.** escaparate m; **to clean the windows** limpiar los cristales; **w. box** jardinera f; **w. cleaner** limpiacristales mf inv

windowpane ['wɪndəʊpeɪn] n cristal m

window-shopping ['wɪndəʊʃɒpɪŋ] n **to go w.** ir a mirar escaparates

windowsill ['wɪndəʊsɪl] n alféizar m

windpipe ['wɪndpaɪp] n tráquea f

windscreen ['wɪndskriːn], US **windshield** ['wɪndfiːld] n parabrisas m inv; **w. washer** lavaparabrisas m inv; **w. wiper** limpiaparabrisas m inv

windswept ['wɪndswept] adj (landscape) expuesto(a) a los vientos; (person, hair) despeinado(a) (por el viento)

windy ['wɪndɪ] *adj* (**windier, windiest**) *(weather)* ventoso(a); *(place)* desprotegido(a) del viento; **it is very w. today** hoy hace mucho viento

wine [waɪn] *n* vino *m*; **w. cellar** bodega *f*; **w. list** lista *f* de vinos; **w. merchant** vinatero(a) *m,f*; **w. tasting** cata *f* de vinos; **w. vinegar** vinagre *m* de vino

wineglass ['waɪnglɑːs] *n* copa *f* (para vino)

wing [wɪŋ] *n* (**a**) *Orn & Av* ala *f* (**b**) *(of building)* ala *f* (**c**) *Aut* aleta *f*; **w. mirror** retrovisor *m* externo (**d**) *Th* (**in the**) **wings** (entre) bastidores *mpl* (**e**) *Ftb* banda *f* (**f**) *Pol* ala *f*; **the left w.** la izquierda

winger ['wɪŋə(r)] *n Ftb* extremo *m*

wink [wɪŋk] **1** *n* guiño *m*; *Fam Fig* **I didn't get a w. (of sleep)** no pegué ojo
2 *vi* (**a**) *(person)* guiñar (el ojo) (**b**) *(light)* parpadear

winner ['wɪnə(r)] *n* ganador(a) *m,f*

winning ['wɪnɪŋ] *adj* (*person, team*) ganador(a); *(number)* premiado(a); *(goal)* decisivo(a); **w. post** meta *f*

winnings ['wɪnɪŋz] *npl* ganancias *fpl*

winter ['wɪntə(r)] **1** *n* invierno *m*
2 *adj* de invierno; **w. sports** deportes *mpl* de invierno
3 *vi* invernar

wintry ['wɪntrɪ] *adj* (**wintrier, wintriest**) invernal

wipe [waɪp] *vt* limpiar; **to w. one's brow** enjugarse la frente; **to w. one's feet/nose** limpiarse los pies/las narices
▸ **wipe away** *vt sep (tear)* enjugar
▸ **wipe off** *vt sep* quitar frotando; **to w. sth off the blackboard/the tape** borrar algo de la pizarra/de la cinta
▸ **wipe out** *vt sep* (**a**) *(erase)* borrar (**b**) *(army)* aniquilar; *(species etc)* exterminar
▸ **wipe up** *vt sep* limpiar

wire [waɪə(r)] **1** *n* (**a**) alambre *m*; *Elec* cable *m*; *Tel* hilo; **w. cutters** cizalla *f* (**b**) *(telegram)* telegrama *m*
2 *vt* (**a**) **to w. (up) a house** poner la instalación eléctrica de una casa; **to w. (up) an appliance to the mains** conectar un aparato a la toma eléctrica (**b**) *(information)* enviar por telegrama

wireless ['waɪəlɪs] *n* radio *f*

wiring ['waɪərɪŋ] *n (network)* cableado *m*; *(action)* instalación *f* del cableado

wiry ['waɪərɪ] *adj* (**wirier, wiriest**) *(hair)* estropajoso(a); *(person)* nervudo(a)

wisdom ['wɪzdəm] *n* (**a**) *(learning)* sabiduría *f*, saber *m* (**b**) *(good sense) (of person)* cordura *f*; *(of action)* sensatez *f* (**c**) **w. tooth** muela *f* del juicio

wise [waɪz] *adj* (**a**) sabio(a); **a w. man** un sabio; **the Three W. Men** los Reyes Magos (**b**) *(remark)* juicioso(a); *(decision)* acertado(a); **it would be w. to keep quiet** sería prudente callarse

wisecrack ['waɪzkræk] *n Fam* salida *f*, ocurrencia *f*

wisely ['waɪzlɪ] *adv (with prudence)* prudentemente

wish [wɪʃ] **1** *n* (**a**) *(desire)* deseo *m* (**for** de); **to make a w.** pedir un deseo
(**b**) **best wishes** felicitaciones *fpl*; **give your mother my best wishes** salude a su madre de mi parte; **with best wishes, Peter** *(at end of letter)* saludos cordiales, Peter
2 *vt* (**a**) *(want)* querer, desear; **I w. I could stay longer** me gustaría poder quedarme más tiempo; **I w. you had told me!** ¡ojalá me lo hubieras dicho!; **to w. to do sth** querer hacer algo
(**b**) **to w. sb goodnight** darle las buenas noches a algn; **to w. sb well** desearle a algn mucha suerte
3 *vi* *(want)* desear; **as you w.** como quieras; **do as you w.** haga lo que quiera; **to w. for sth** desear algo

wishful ['wɪʃfʊl] *adj* **it's w. thinking** es hacerse ilusiones

wishy-washy ['wɪʃɪ'wɒʃɪ] *adj Fam (person)* soso(a); *(ideas)* poco definido(a)

wisp [wɪsp] *n (of wool, hair)* mechón *m*; *(of smoke)* voluta *f*

wistful ['wɪstfʊl] *adj* melancólico(a)

wit [wɪt] *n* (**a**) *(intelligence)* (often pl) inteligencia *f*; *Fig* **to be at one's wits' end** estar para volverse loco(a); *Fam Fig* **to have one's wits about one** ser despabilado(a) (**b**) *(humour)* ingenio *m* (**c**) *(person)* ingenioso(a) *m,f*

witch [wɪtʃ] *n* bruja *f*; *Fig* **w. hunt** caza *f* de brujas

witchcraft ['wɪtʃkrɑːft] *n* brujería *f*

with [wɪð, wɪθ] *prep* con; **a room w. a bath** un cuarto con baño; **do you have any money w. you?** ¿traes dinero?; **the man w. the glasses** el hombre de las gafas; **he went w. me/you** fue conmigo/contigo; *Fam* **w. (sugar) or without (sugar)?** ¿con o sin azúcar?; **I have six w. this one** con éste tengo seis; **w. all his faults, I admire him** le admiro con todos sus defectos; **w. your permission** con su permiso; **we're all w. you** *(support)* todos estamos contigo; **you're not w. me, are you?** *(understand)* no me entiendes, ¿verdad?; **he's w. Lloyds** trabaja para Lloyds; **she is popular w. her colleagues**

todos sus colegas la estiman mucho; **to fill a vase w. water** llenar un jarrón de agua; **it is made w. butter** está hecho con mantequilla; **she put on weight w. so much eating** engordó de tanto comer; **to be paralysed w. fear** estar paralizado(a) de miedo; **w. experience** con la experiencia

withdraw [wɪð'drɔː] **1** *vt* (*pt* **withdrew**; *pp* **withdrawn**) (**a**) retirar, sacar; **to w. money from the bank** sacar dinero del banco (**b**) (*go back on*) retirar; (*statement*) retractarse de; (*plan, claim*) renunciar a

2 *vi* (**a**) retirarse (**b**) (*drop out*) renunciar

withdrawal [wɪð'drɔːəl] *n* retirada *f*; (*of statement*) retractación *f*; (*of complaint, plan*) renuncia *f*; **w. symptoms** síndrome *m* de abstinencia

withdrawn [wɪð'drɔːn] **1** *adj* (*person*) introvertido(a)

2 *pp of* **withdraw**

withdrew [wɪð'druː] *pt of* **withdraw**

wither ['wɪðə(r)] *vi* marchitarse

withering ['wɪðərɪŋ] *adj* (*look*) fulminante; (*criticism*) mordaz

withhold [wɪð'həʊld] *vt* (*pt & pp* **withheld** [wɪð'held]) (*money*) retener; (*decision*) aplazar; (*consent*) negar; (*information*) ocultar

within [wɪ'ðɪn] **1** *prep* (**a**) (*inside*) dentro de (**b**) (*range*) **the house is w. walking distance** se puede ir andando a la casa; **situated w. 5 km of the town** situado(a) a menos de 5 km de la ciudad; **w. sight of the sea** con vistas al mar; *Fig* **w. an inch of death** a dos dedos de la muerte (**c**) (*time*) **they arrived w. a few days of each other** llegaron con pocos días de diferencia; **w. the hour** dentro de una hora; **w. the next five years** durante los cinco próximos años

2 *adv* dentro; **from w.** desde dentro

with-it ['wɪðɪt] *adj Fam* **she is very w.** tiene ideas muy modernas; **to get w.** ponerse de moda

without [wɪ'ðaʊt] *prep* sin; **he did it w. my knowing** lo hizo sin que lo supiera yo; *Fig* **to do** *or* **go w. sth** (*voluntarily*) prescindir de algo; (*forcibly*) pasar(se) sin algo

withstand [wɪð'stænd] *vt* (*pt & pp* **withstood** [wɪð'stʊd]) resistir a; (*pain*) aguantar

witness ['wɪtnɪs] **1** *n* (**a**) (*person*) testigo *mf*; **w. box**, *US* **w. stand** barra *f* de los testigos (**b**) (*evidence*) **to bear w. to sth** dar fe de algo

2 *vt* (**a**) (*see*) presenciar, ser testigo de (**b**) *Fig* (*notice*) notar (**c**) *Jur* **to w. a document** firmar un documento como testigo

witticism ['wɪtɪsɪzəm] *n* ocurrencia *f*, salida *f*

witty ['wɪtɪ] *adj* (**wittier**, **wittiest**) ingenioso(a), agudo(a)

wives [waɪvz] *pl of* **wife**

wizard ['wɪzəd] *n* hechicero *m*, mago *m*

wizened ['wɪzənd] *adj* (*face*) arrugado(a)

wobble ['wɒbəl] *vi* (*table, ladder etc*) tambalearse; (*jelly*) temblar

woe [wəʊ] *n Literary* infortunio *m*; **w. betide you if I catch you!** ¡ay de ti si te cojo!

woeful ['wəʊfʊl] *adj* (**a**) (*person*) afligido(a) (**b**) (*sight*) penoso(a); **w. ignorance** una ignorancia lamentable

woke [wəʊk] *pt of* **wake**

woken ['wəʊkən] *pp of* **wake**

wolf [wʊlf] *n* (*pl* **wolves** [wʊlvz]) lobo *m*; *Fig* **a w. in sheep**'s clothing un lobo con piel de cordero

woman ['wʊmən] *n* (*pl* **women**) mujer *f*; **old w.** vieja *f*; *Fam* **women's libber** feminista *mf*; *Fam* **women's lib** movimiento *m* feminista; **women's rights** derechos *mpl* de la mujer

womanhood ['wʊmənhʊd] *n* (*adult*) edad adulta de la mujer

womanizer ['wʊmənaɪzə(r)] *n* mujeriego *m*

womanly ['wʊmənlɪ] *adj* femenino(a)

womb [wuːm] *n* matriz *f*, útero *m*

women ['wɪmɪn] *pl of* **woman**

won [wʌn] *pt & pp of* **win**

wonder ['wʌndə(r)] **1** *n* (**a**) (*miracle*) milagro *m*; **no w. he hasn't come** no es de extrañar que no haya venido (**b**) (*amazement*) admiración *f*, asombro *m*

2 *vt* (**a**) (*be surprised*) sorprenderse (**b**) (*ask oneself*) preguntarse; **I w. why** ¿por qué será?

3 *vi* (**a**) (*marvel*) maravillarse; **to w. at sth** admirarse de algo (**b**) **it makes you w.** (*reflect*) te da que pensar

wonderful ['wʌndəfʊl] *adj* maravilloso(a)

wonderfully ['wʌndəfʊlɪ] *adv* maravillosamente

wont [wəʊnt] *Fml* **1** *adj* **to be w. to** soler

2 *n* costumbre *f*; **it is his w. to ...** tiene la costumbre de ...

woo [wuː] *vt Literary* (*court*) cortejar; *Fig* intentar congraciarse con

wood [wʊd] *n* (**a**) (*forest*) bosque *m* (**b**)

(material) madera *f*; *(for fire)* leña *f*; *Fam Fig* **touch w.!** ¡toca madera! **(c)** *(in golf)* palo *m* de madera **(d)** *(bowling)* bola *f*

woodcarving ['wʊdkɑːvɪŋ] *n* **(a)** *(craft)* tallado *m* en madera **(b)** *(object)* talla *f* en madera

woodcutter ['wʊdkʌtə(r)] *n* leñador(a) *m,f*

wooded ['wʊdɪd] *adj* arbolado(a)

wooden ['wʊdən] *adj* **(a)** de madera; **w. spoon/leg** cuchara *f*/pata *f* de palo **(b)** *Fig* rígido(a); *(acting)* sin expresión

woodlouse ['wʊdlaʊs] *n* cochinilla *f*

woodpecker ['wʊdpekə(r)] *n* pájaro carpintero

woodwind ['wʊdwɪnd] *n* **w. (instruments)** instrumentos *mpl* de viento de madera

woodwork ['wʊdwɜːk] *n* **(a)** *(craft)* carpintería *f* **(b)** *(of building)* maderaje *m*

woodworm ['wʊdwɜːm] *n* carcoma *f*

wool [wʊl] *n* **1** lana *f*; *Fig* **to pull the w. over sb's eyes** dar gato por liebre a algn **2** *adj* de lana

woollen, *US* **woolen** ['wʊlən] **1** *adj* **(a)** de lana **(b)** *(industry)* lanero(a)
2 *npl* **woollens** géneros *mpl* de lana *or* de punto

woolly, *US* **wooly** ['wʊlɪ] *adj* (**woollier, woolliest,** *US* **woolier, wooliest**) **(a)** *(made of wool)* de lana **(b)** *Fig (unclear)* confuso(a)

word [wɜːd] *n* **1** *(a)** *(spoken, written)* palabra *f*; **in other words ...** es decir ..., o sea ...; **words failed me** me quedé sin habla; **I'd like a w. of advice** un consejo; *Fig* **I'd like a w. with you** quiero hablar contigo un momento; *Fig* **she didn't say it in so many words** no lo dijo de modo tan explícito; **in the words of the poet ...** como dice el poeta ...; *Fig* **w. for w.** palabra por palabra; **w. processing** tratamiento *m* de textos; **w. processor** procesador *m* de textos
(b) *Fig (message)* mensaje *m*; **by w. of mouth** de palabra; **is there any w. from him?** ¿hay noticias de él?; **to send w.** mandar recado
(c) *Fig (rumour)* voz *f*, rumor *m*
(d) *Fig (promise)* palabra *f*; **he's a man of his w.** es hombre de palabra
2 *vt (express)* formular; **a badly worded letter** una carta mal redactada

wording ['wɜːdɪŋ] *n* expresión *f*; **I changed the w. slightly** cambié algunas palabras

word-perfect [wɜːd'pɜːfekt] *adj* **to be w.** saberse el papel perfectamente

wore [wɔː(r)] *pt of* **wear**

work [wɜːk] **1** *n* **(a)** trabajo *m*; **his w. in the field of physics** su labor en el campo de la física; **it's hard w.** cuesta trabajo
(b) *(employment)* trabajo *m*, empleo *m*; **out of w.** parado(a)
(c) *(action)* obra *f*, acción *f*; **keep up the good w.!** ¡que siga así!
(d) **a piece of w.** un trabajo; **a w. of art** una obra de arte
(e) **works** obras *fpl*; **public works** obras (públicas)
(f) **works** *(machinery)* mecanismo *m*
(g) *Br* **works** *(factory)* fábrica *f*
2 *vt* **(a)** *(drive)* hacer trabajar; **to w. one's way up/down** subir/bajar a duras penas; *Fig* **to w. one's way up in a firm** trabajarse el ascenso en una empresa
(b) *(machine)* manejar; *(mechanism)* accionar
(c) *(miracles, changes)* operar, hacer
(d) *(land)* cultivar; *(mine)* explotar
(e) *(wood, metal etc)* trabajar
3 *vi* **(a)** trabajar (**on** *or* **at** en); **to w. as a gardener** trabajar de jardinero
(b) *(machine)* funcionar; **it works on gas** funciona con gas
(c) *(drug)* surtir efecto; *(system)* funcionar bien; *(plan, trick)* salir bien
(d) *(operate)* obrar; **to w. loose** soltarse; **we have no data to w. on** no tenemos datos en que basarnos
▸ **work off** *vt sep (fat)* eliminar trabajando; *(anger)* desahogar
▸ **work out 1** *vt sep* **(a)** *(plan)* idear; *(itinerary)* planear; *(details)* desarrollar
(b) *(problem)* solucionar; *(solution)* encontrar; *(amount)* calcular; **I can't w. out how he did it** no me explico cómo lo hizo
2 *vi* **(a)** **things didn't w. out for her** las cosas no le salieron bien **(b)** **it works out at five each** sale a cinco cada uno **(c)** *Sport* hacer ejercicio
▸ **work through** *vi* penetrar (**to** hasta)
▸ **work up** *vt sep (excite)* acalorar; **to get worked up** excitarse; **to w. up enthusiasm (for)** entusiasmarse (con)

workable ['wɜːkəbəl] *adj* factible

workaholic [wɜːkə'hɒlɪk] *n Fam* trabajoadicto(a) *m,f*

workbench ['wɜːkbentʃ] *n* obrador *m*

worker ['wɜːkə(r)] *n* trabajador(a) *m,f*; *(manual)* obrero(a) *m,f*

workforce ['wɜːkfɔːs] *n* mano *f* de obra

working ['wɜːkɪŋ] **1** *adj* **(a)** *(population, capital)* activo(a); **w. class** clase obrera; **w. man** obrero *m* **(b)** *(clothes, conditions, hours)* de trabajo; **w. day** día *m* laborable;

(number of hours) jornada *f* laboral (**c**) **it is in w. order** funciona (**d**) *(majority)* suficiente; **w. knowledge** conocimientos básicos

2 *n* **workings** *(mechanics)* funcionamiento *m*; *Min* explotación *f*

workman ['wɜːkmən] *n (manual)* obrero *m*

workmanship ['wɜːkmənʃɪp] *n (appearance)* acabado *m; (skill)* habilidad *f*, arte *m*; **a fine piece of w.** un trabajo excelente

workmate ['wɜːkmeɪt] *n* compañero(a) *m,f* de trabajo

work-out ['wɜːkaʊt] *n* entrenamiento *m*

worksheet ['wɜːkʃiːt] *n* plan *m* de trabajo

workshop ['wɜːkʃɒp] *n* taller *m*

worktop ['wɜːktɒp] *n* encimera *f*

work-to-rule ['wɜːktə'ruːl] *n* huelga *f* de celo

world [wɜːld] *n* mundo *m*; **all over the w.** en todo el mundo; **the best in the w.** el mejor del mundo; *Fig* **there is a w. of difference between A and B** hay un mundo de diferencia entre A y B; *Fig* **to feel on top of the w.** sentirse fenomenal; *Fig* **to think the w. of sb** adorar a algn; *Fam Fig* **it is out of this w.** es una maravilla; **the W. Bank** el Banco Mundial; *Ftb* **the W. Cup** los Mundiales; **w. record** récord *m* mundial; **w. war** guerra *f* mundial

world-class ['wɜːld'klɑːs] *adj* de categoría mundial

world-famous ['wɜːld'feɪməs] *adj* de fama mundial

worldly ['wɜːldlɪ] *adj* mundano(a)

worldwide ['wɜːldwaɪd] *adj* mundial

worm [wɜːm] **1** *n* (**a**) gusano *m*; *(earth)* **w.** lombriz *f* (**b**) *Med* **worms** lombrices *fpl*

2 *vt* **to w. a secret out of sb** sonsacarle un secreto a algn

worn [wɔːn] **1** *adj* gastado(a), usado(a)

2 *pp* of **wear**

worn-out ['wɔːnaʊt] *adj (thing)* gastado(a); *(person)* rendido(a), agotado(a)

worried ['wʌrɪd] *adj* inquieto(a), preocupado(a)

worry ['wʌrɪ] **1** *vt* (**a**) preocupar, inquietar; **it doesn't w. me** me trae sin cuidado (**b**) *(pester)* molestar

2 *vi* preocuparse (**about** por); **don't w.** no te preocupes

3 *n (state)* inquietud *f; (cause)* preocupación *f*

worrying ['wʌrɪɪŋ] *adj* inquietante, preocupante

worse [wɜːs] **1** *adj (comp of* **bad**) peor; **he** gets **w. and w.** va de mal en peor; **to get w.** empeorar; *Fam* **w. luck!** ¡mala suerte!

2 *n* **a change for the w.** un empeoramiento; *Fig* **to take a turn for the w.** empeorar

3 *adv (comp of* **badly**) peor; **w. than ever** peor que nunca

worship ['wɜːʃɪp] **1** *vt* adorar

2 *n* (**a**) adoración *f* (**b**) *(ceremony)* culto *m* (**c**) *Br* **his W. the Mayor** el señor alcalde; *Jur* **your W.** señoría

worshipper ['wɜːʃɪpə(r)] *n* devoto(a) *m,f*

worst [wɜːst] **1** *adj (superl of* **bad**) peor; **the w. part about it is that ...** lo peor es que ...

2 *n* (**a**) *(person)* el/la peor, los/las peores (**b**) **the w. of the storm is over** ya ha pasado lo peor de la tormenta

3 *adv (superl of* **badly**) peor; *Fig* **to come off w.** salir perdiendo

worth [wɜːθ] **1** *adj* (**a**) **to be w. £3** valer 3 libras; **a house w. £50,000** una casa que vale 50.000 libras (**b**) *(deserving of)* merecedor(a) de; **a book w. reading** un libro que merece la pena leer; **for what it's w.** por si sirve de algo; **it's w. your while, it's w.** it vale *or* merece la pena; **it's w. mentioning** es digno de mención

2 *n* (**a**) *(in money)* valor *m*; **£5 w. of petrol** gasolina por valor de 5 libras (**b**) *(of person)* valía *f*

worthless ['wɜːθlɪs] *adj* sin valor; *(person)* despreciable

worthwhile ['wɜːθ'waɪl] *adj* valioso(a), que vale la pena

worthy ['wɜːðɪ] *adj* (**worthier, worthiest**) (**a**) *(deserving)* digno(a) (**of** de); *(winner, cause)* justo(a) (**b**) *(citizen)* respetable; *(effort, motives, action)* loable

would [wʊd, *unstressed* wəd] *v aux* (**a**) *(conditional)* **I w. go if I had time** iría si tuviera tiempo; **he w. have won but for that** habría ganado si no hubiera sido por eso; **we w. if we could** lo haríamos si pudiéramos; **you w. have to choose me!** ¡tenías que elegirme precisamente a mí!

(**b**) *(reported speech)* **he said that he w. come** dijo que vendría

(**c**) *(willingness)* **the car wouldn't start** el coche no arrancaba; **they asked him to come but he wouldn't** le invitaron a venir pero no quiso; **w. you do me a favour?** ¿quiere hacerme un favor?

(**d**) *(wishing)* **he w. like to know why** quisiera saber por qué; **I'd rather go home** preferiría ir a casa; **w. you like a cigarette?** ¿quiere un cigarrillo?

(e) *(custom)* **we w. go for walks** solíamos dar un paseo

(f) **try as I w.** por mucho que lo intentara

(g) *(conjecture)* **it w. have been about three weeks ago** debe haber sido hace unas tres semanas; **w. this be your cousin?** ¿será éste tu primo?

(h) *(expectation)* **so it w. appear** según parece

would-be ['wʊdbiː] *adj* en potencia; **a w. politician** un aspirante a político; *Pej* **a w. poet** un supuesto poeta

wound¹ [waʊnd] *pt & pp of* **wind²**

wound² [wuːnd] **1** *n* herida *f*

2 *vt* herir

wove [wəʊv] *pt of* **weave**

woven ['wəʊvən] *pp of* **weave**

wow [waʊ] *Fam* **1** *vt* encandilar

2 *interj* ¡caramba!

WP *n* (a) *(abbr* **word processor***)* procesador *m* de textos (b) *(abbr* **word processing***)* tratamiento *m* de textos

wrangle ['ræŋɡəl] **1** *n* disputa *f*

2 *vi* disputar (**over** por)

wrap [ræp] **1** *vt* **to w. (up)** envolver; **he wrapped his arms around her** la estrechó entre sus brazos; *Fam* **we wrapped up the deal** concluimos el negocio

2 *vi Fam* **w. up well** abrígate

3 *n* (shawl) chal *m*; (cape) capa *f*

wrapper ['ræpə(r)] *n* (of sweet) envoltorio *m*; (of book) sobrecubierta *f*

wrapping ['ræpɪŋ] *n* **w. paper** papel *m* de envolver

wreath [riːθ] *n* (pl **wreaths** [riːðz, riːθs]) (of flowers) corona *f*; **laurel w.** corona de laurel

wreck [rek] **1** *n* (a) *Naut* naufragio *m*; (ship) barco naufragado (b) (of car, plane) restos *mpl*; (of building) ruinas *fpl* (c) *Fig* (person) ruina *f*

2 *vt* (a) (ship) hacer naufragar (b) (car, machine) destrozar (c) *Fig* (health, life) arruinar; (plans, hopes) desbaratar; (chances) echar a perder

wreckage ['rekɪdʒ] *n* (of ship, car, plane) restos *mpl*; (of building) ruinas *fpl*

wren [ren] *n* chochín *m*

wrench [rentʃ] **1** *n* (a) (pull) tirón *m* (b) *Med* torcedura *f* (c) (tool) *Br* llave inglesa; *US* llave

2 *vt* **to w. oneself free** soltarse de un tirón; **to w. sth off sb** arrebatarle algo a algn; **to w. sth off/open** quitar/abrir algo de un tirón

wrestle ['resəl] *vi* luchar

wrestler ['reslə(r)] *n* luchador(a) *m,f*

wrestling ['reslɪŋ] *n* lucha *f*

wretch [retʃ] *n* (poor) **w.** desgraciado(a) *m,f*

wretched ['retʃɪd] *adj* (a) desdichado(a); (conditions) deplorable; *Fam* (bad, poor) horrible (b) **I feel w.** (ill) me siento fatal (c) (contemptible) despreciable (d) *Fam* (damned) maldito(a), condenado(a)

wriggle ['rɪɡəl] **1** *vt* menear

2 *vi* **to w. (about)** (worm) serpentear; (restless child) moverse nerviosamente; **to w. free** escapar deslizándose

wring [rɪŋ] *vt* (pt & pp **wrung**) (a) (clothes) escurrir; (hands) retorcer (b) *Fig* (extract) arrancar, sacar

wringing ['rɪŋɪŋ] *adj* **to be w. wet** estar empapado(a)

wrinkle ['rɪŋkəl] **1** *n* arruga *f*

2 *vt* arrugar

3 *vi* arrugarse

wrist [rɪst] *n* muñeca *f*

wristwatch ['rɪstwɒtʃ] *n* reloj *m* de pulsera

writ [rɪt] *n* orden *f* judicial

write [raɪt] **1** *vt* (pt **wrote**; pp **written**) escribir; (article) redactar; (cheque) extender

2 *vi* escribir (**about** sobre); **to w. for a paper** colaborar en un periódico

▸ **write back** *vi* contestar

▸ **write down** *vt sep* poner por escrito; (note) apuntar

▸ **write in** *vi* escribir

▸ **write off 1** *vt sep* (debt) condonar; (car) destrozar

2 *vi* **to w. off for sth** pedir algo por escrito

▸ **write out** *vt sep* (cheque, recipe) extender

▸ **write up** *vt sep* (notes) redactar; (diary, journal) poner al día

write-off ['raɪtɒf] *n* **the car's a w.** el coche está hecho una ruina

writer ['raɪtə(r)] *n* (by profession) escritor(a) *m,f*; (of book, letter) autor(a) *m,f*

writhe [raɪð] *vi* retorcerse

writing ['raɪtɪŋ] *n* (a) (script) escritura *f*; (handwriting) letra *f*; **in w.** por escrito (b) **writings** escritos *mpl* (c) (action) escritura *f*; **w. desk** escritorio *m*

written ['rɪtən] *pp of* **write**

wrong [rɒŋ] **1** *adj* (a) (person) equivocado(a); **I was w. about that boy** me equivoqué con ese chico; **to be w.** no tener razón; **you're w. in thinking that ...** te equivocas si piensas que ...

(b) (answer, way) incorrecto(a), equivocado(a); **my watch is w.** mi reloj anda

mal; **to drive on the w. side of the road**
conducir por el lado contrario de la carretera; **to go the w. way** equivocarse de
camino; *Tel* **I've got the w. number** me he
confundido de número
  (**c**) *(unsuitable)* impropio(a), inadecua-
do(a); *(time)* inoportuno(a); **to say the w.
thing** decir algo inoportuno
  (**d**) *(immoral etc)* malo(a); **there's nothing w. in that** no hay nada malo en ello;
what's w. with smoking? ¿qué tiene de
malo fumar?
  (**e**) **is anything w.?** ¿pasa algo?; **something's w.** hay algo que no está bien;
what's w.? ¿qué pasa?; **what's w. with
you?** ¿qué te pasa?
  2 *adv* mal, incorrectamente; **to get it w.**
equivocarse; *Fam* **to go w.** *(plan)* fallar,
salir mal

  3 *n* (**a**) *(evil, bad action)* mal *m*; **you did
w. to hit him** hiciste mal en pegarle
  (**b**) *(injustice)* injusticia *f*; *(offence)* agravio *m*; **the rights and wrongs of a matter**
lo justo y lo injusto de un asunto
  (**c**) **to be in the w.** *(be to blame)* tener la
culpa
  4 *vt (treat unfairly)* ser injusto(a) con;
(offend) agraviar

wrongdoing ['rɒŋduːɪŋ] *n* maldad *f*

wrongful ['rɒŋfʊl] *adj* injusto(a)

wrongly ['rɒŋlɪ] *adv* (**a**) *(incorrectly)* incorrectamente (**b**) *(mistakenly)* equivo-
cadamente (**c**) *(unjustly)* injustamente

wrote [rəʊt] *pt of* write

wrung [rʌŋ] *pt & pp of* wring

wry [raɪ] *adj* (**wrier, wriest** or **wryer,
wryest**) sardónico(a)

XYZ

xenophobia [zenə'fəʊbɪə] n xenofobia f

Xerox® ['zɪərɒks] **1** n fotocopia f, xerocopia f
2 vt fotocopiar

Xmas ['krɪsməs, 'eksməs] n (abbr **Christmas**) Navidad f

X-ray ['eksreɪ] **1** n (radiation) rayo m X; (picture) radiografía f; **to have an X.** hacerse una radiografía
2 vt radiografiar

Y, y [waɪ] n (the letter) Y, y f

yacht [jɒt] n yate m; **y. club** club náutico

yachting ['jɒtɪŋ] n Sport navegación f a vela; (competition) regatas fpl

yachtsman ['jɒtsmən] n balandrista m

yachtswoman ['jɒtswʊmən] n balandrista f

yam [jæm] n (**a**) ñame m (**b**) US (sweet potato) boniato m, batata f, Andes, CAm, Carib, Méx camote m

Yank [jæŋk] n Br Pej yanqui mf

yank [jæŋk] vt Fam tirar; (tooth) arrancar

Yankee ['jæŋkɪ] adj & n Pej yanqui (mf)

yap [jæp] vi (dog) aullar; Fam (person) darle al pico

yard¹ [jɑːd] n (measure) yarda f (aprox 0,914 m)

yard² [jɑːd] n patio m; US jardín m

yardstick ['jɑːdstɪk] n Fig criterio m, norma f

yarn [jɑːn] n (**a**) Sewing hilo m (**b**) (story) historia f, cuento m; **to spin a y.** (lie) inventarse una historia

yawn [jɔːn] **1** vi bostezar
2 n bostezo m

yawning ['jɔːnɪŋ] adj (gap) profundo(a)

yd (pl **yds**) (abbr **yard**) yarda f

yeah [jeə] adv Fam sí

year [jɪə(r)] n (**a**) año m; **all y. round** durante todo el año; **last y.** el año pasado; **next y.** el año que viene; **y. in, y. out** año tras año; **I'm ten years old** tengo diez años (**b**) Educ curso m; **first-y. student** estudiante mf de primero

yearly ['jɪəlɪ] **1** adj anual
2 adv anualmente, cada año

yearn [jɜːn] vi **to y. for sth** anhelar algo

yearning ['jɜːnɪŋ] n anhelo m (**for** de)

yeast [jiːst] n levadura f

yell [jel] **1** vi gritar
2 n grito m, alarido m

yellow ['jeləʊ] **1** adj amarillo(a); Fam Fig (cowardly) cobarde; Tel **Y. Pages®** páginas amarillas
2 n amarillo m

yelp [jelp] **1** vi aullar
2 n aullido m

yen [jen] n (**a**) (currency) yen m (**b**) **to have a y. for sth** tener ganas de algo

yeoman ['jəʊmən] n Br **Y. of the Guard** = alabardero de la Casa Real británica

yes [jes] **1** adv sí; **you said y.** dijiste que sí
2 n sí m

yesterday ['jestədeɪ] adv & n ayer m; **the day before y.** anteayer; **y. morning** ayer por la mañana

yet [jet] **1** adv (**a**) **not y.** aún no, todavía no; **as y.** hasta ahora; **I haven't eaten y.** no he comido todavía (**b**) (in questions) ya; **has he arrived y.?** ¿ha venido ya? (**c**) (even) más; **y. again** otra vez; **y. more** todavía más (**d**) (eventually) todavía, aún; **he'll win y.** todavía puede ganar
2 conj sin embargo

yew [juː] n tejo m

yield [jiːld] **1** n (**a**) rendimiento m (**b**) Agr cosecha f (**c**) Fin beneficio m
2 vt producir; Agr dar; (money) producir
3 vi (**a**) (surrender, break) ceder (**b**) US Aut ceder el paso

YMCA [waɪemsiː'eɪ] n (abbr **Young Men's Christian Association**) ACJ f, Asociación f Cristiana de Jóvenes (que regenta hostales económicos)

yob(bo) ['jɒb(əʊ)] n Fam gamberro(a) m,f

yoga ['jəʊgə] n yoga m

yog(h)urt ['jɒgət] n yogur m

yoke [jəʊk] **1** n yugo m
2 vt (oxen) uncir; Fig unir

yokel ['jəʊkəl] n Pej paleto(a) m,f

yolk [jəʊk] n yema f

yonder ['jɒndə(r)] adv más allá

you [juː, unstressed jʊ] pers pron (**a**) (subject) (usually omitted in Spanish, except for contrast) (familiar use) (singular) tú; (pl) vosotros(as); **how are y.?** ¿cómo estás?, ¿cómo estáis?

(**b**) *(subject) (polite use) (singular)* usted; *(pl)* ustedes; **how are y.?** ¿cómo está?, ¿cómo están?

(**c**) *(subject) (impers use)* **y. never know** nunca se sabe

(**d**) *(object) (familiar use) (singular) (before verb)* te; *(after preposition)* ti; *(pl) (before verb)* os; *(after preposition)* vosotros(as); **I saw y.** te vi/os vi; **it's for y.** es para ti/es para vosotros(as); **with y.** contigo/con vosotros(as)

(**e**) *(object) (polite use) (singular) (before verb)* le; *(after preposition)* usted; *(pl) (before verb)* les; *(after preposition)* ustedes; **I saw y.** le vi/les vi; **it's for y.** es para usted/es para ustedes; **with y.** con usted/ con ustedes

(**f**) *(object) (impers use)* **alcohol makes y. drunk** el alcohol emborracha

---

In Spanish, the formal form **usted** takes a third person singular verb, and **ustedes** takes a third person plural verb. In many Latin American countries, **ustedes** is the standard form of the second person plural (**vosotros**) and is not considered formal. Note also that in some of these countries **usted** is used in the second person singular (**tú**), and is likewise not considered formal.

---

young [jʌŋ] **1** *adj (age)* joven; *(brother etc)* pequeño(a); **y. lady** señorita *f*; **y. man** joven *m*

2 *npl* (**a**) *(people)* **the y.** los jóvenes, la juventud (**b**) *(animals)* crías *fpl*

youngster ['jʌŋstə(r)] *n* muchacho(a) *m,f*

your [jɔː(r), *unstressed* jə(r)] *poss adj* (**a**) *(familiar use) (singular)* tu/tus; *(pl)* vuestro(a)/vuestros(as) (**b**) *(polite use)* su/sus (**c**) *(impers use)* **the house is on y. right** la casa queda a la derecha; **they clean y. shoes for you** te limpian los zapatos (**d**) *(formal address)* Su; **Y. Majesty** Su Majestad

yours [jɔːz] *poss pron* (**a**) *(familiar use) (singular)* el tuyo/la tuya/los tuyos/las tuyas; *(pl)* el vuestro/la vuestra/los vuestros/las vuestras; **the house is y.** la casa es tuya (**b**) *(polite use) (singular)* el suyo/la suya; *(pl)* los suyos/las suyas; **the house is y.** la casa es suya (**c**) *(in letters)* **y. faithfully** le(s) saluda atentamente; **y. sincerely** reciba un cordial saludo de

---

In Spanish, the forms **tuyo(a)**, **suyo(a)** and **vuestro(a)** require a definite article in the singular and in the plural when they are the subject of the phrase.

---

yourself [jɔːˈself, *unstressed* jəˈself] *(pl* **yourselves** [jɔːˈselvz]) **1** *pers pron* (**a**) *(familiar use) (singular)* tú mismo(a); *(pl)* vosotros(as) mismos(as); **by y.** (tú) solo; **by yourselves** vosotros(as) solos(as) (**b**) *(polite use) (singular)* usted mismo(a); *(pl)* ustedes mismos(as); **by y.** (usted) solo(a); **by yourselves** (ustedes) solos(as)

2 *reflexive pron* (**a**) *(familiar use) (singular)* te; *(pl) (familiar use)* os; **enjoy y.!** ¡diviértete!; **enjoy yourselves!** ¡divertíos! (**b**) *(polite use)* se; **enjoy y.!** ¡diviértase!; **enjoy yourselves!** ¡diviértanse!

In many Latin American countries, **se/ustedes** is the standard form of the second person plural and is not considered formal.

---

youth [juːθ] *n* (**a**) juventud *f* (**b**) *(young man)* joven *m*; **y. club** club *m* juvenil; **y. hostel** albergue *m* juvenil

youthful ['juːθfʊl] *adj* juvenil, joven

Yugoslav ['juːɡəʊslɑːv] *adj & n* yugoslavo(a) *(m,f)*

Yugoslavia [juːɡəʊˈslɑːvɪə] *n* Yugoslavia

Yugoslavian [juːɡəʊˈslɑːvɪən] *adj & n* yugoslavo(a) *(m,f)*

YWCA ['waɪdʌbəljuːsiːˈeɪ] *n (abbr* **Young Women's Christian Association**) ACJ *f*, Asociación *f* Cristiana de Jóvenes *(que regenta hostales económicos)*

Z, z [zed, *US* ziː] *n (the letter)* Z, z *f*

zany ['zeɪnɪ] *adj* (**zanier, zaniest**) *Fam* (**a**) *(mad)* chiflado(a) (**b**) *(eccentric)* estrafalario(a)

zap [zæp] **1** *interj* ¡zas!

2 *vt Fam* (**a**) *(hit)* pegar (**b**) *(kill)* cargarse a

3 *vi TV* hacer zapping

zeal [ziːl] *n (enthusiasm)* entusiasmo *m*

zealous ['zeləs] *adj (enthusiastic)* entusiasta

zebra ['ziːbrə, 'zebrə] *n* cebra *f*; *Br* **z. crossing** paso *m* de cebra

zenith ['zenɪθ] *n Astron* cenit *m*; *Fig* apogeo *m*

zero ['zɪərəʊ] *n* cero *m*; **z. hour** hora *f* cero

zest [zest] *n (eagerness)* entusiasmo *m*

zigzag ['zɪɡzæɡ] **1** *n* zigzag *m*

2 *vi* zigzaguear

Zimbabwe [zɪmˈbɑːbweɪ] *n* Zimbabue

zinc [zɪŋk] *n* cinc *m*, zinc *m*

zip [zɪp] **1** *n* (**a**) *Br* **z. (fastener)** cremallera *f* (**b**) *Fam* brío *m*; *US* **z. code** código *m* postal

2 *vi* cerrarse con cremallera

▸ **zip by** *vi* pasar como un rayo

▸ **zip up** *vt sep* cerrar con cremallera; **to z. sb up** cerrar la cremallera a algn
zipper ['zɪpə(r)] *n US* cremallera *f*
zodiac ['zəʊdɪæk] *n* zodiaco *m*, zodíaco *m*
zombie ['zɒmbɪ] *n* zombie *mf*
zone [zəʊn] **1** *n* zona *f*
  2 *vt* dividir en zonas
zoo [zuː] *n* zoo *m*
zoological [zuːə'lɒdʒɪkəl] *adj* zoológico(a)

zoologist [zuː'ɒlədʒɪst] *n* zoólogo(a) *m,f*
zoology [zuː'ɒlədʒɪ] *n* zoología *f*
zoom [zuːm] **1** *n* (**a**) *(buzz)* zumbido *m* (**b**) **z. lens** zoom *m*, teleobjetivo *m*
  2 *vi* (**a**) *(buzz)* zumbar (**b**) **to z. past** pasar volando
▸ **zoom in** *vi (camera)* acercarse rápidamente
zucchini [zuː'kiːnɪ] *n US* calabacín *m*, *CSur* zapallito *m*
Zulu ['zuːluː] *adj & n* zulú *(mf)*